13/12/17

Stoke-on-Trent Libraries

Please return or renew by last date shown

NOT TO BE TAKEN AWAY

WITHDRAWN AND SOLD BY STOKE-ON-TRENT LIBRARIES

REFERENCE COPY PLEASE DO NOT TAKE AWAY

Please return or renew this item by the date shown above or as shown on your self service receipt. Books may be renewed in the library, over the phone or online at stoke.gov.uk/libraries.

DTPC1178

Stoke-on-Trent Libraries

3 8080 20038 431 9

The EUROPEAN UNION ENCYCLOPEDIA and DIRECTORY 2018

The EUROPEAN UNION ENCYCLOPEDIA and DIRECTORY 2018

Routledge
Taylor & Francis Group

LONDON AND NEW YORK

18th edition published 2017
by Routledge
2 Park Square, Milton Park, Abingdon, Oxon, OX14 4RN

and by Routledge
711 Third Avenue, New York, NY 10017

Routledge is an imprint of the Taylor & Francis Group, an informa business

© 2017 Routledge

The right of the editor to be identified as the author of the editorial material, and of the authors for their individual chapters, has been asserted in accordance with sections 77 and 78 of the Copyright, Designs and Patents Act 1988.

All rights reserved. No part of this publication may be photocopied, recorded, or otherwise reproduced, stored in a retrieval system or transmitted in any form or by any electronic or mechanical means without the prior permission of the copyright owner.

Trademark notice: Product or corporate names may be trademarks, and are used only for identification and explanation without intention to infringe.

First published 1995

ISBN: 978-1-85743-913-7

ISSN 1363-7045

Editor Imogen Gladman

Senior Editor, Directory Iain Frame

Editorial Assistant Eleanor Catchpole-Simmons

Directory Editorial Researchers Arijit Khasnobis (Team Manager), C. Sandhya (Team Leader), Gurkiran Shahi

Publisher Juliet Love

Typeset in Times New Roman
by Taylor & Francis Books

FOREWORD

The eighteenth edition of the EUROPEAN UNION ENCYCLOPEDIA AND DIRECTORY (previously the EUROPEAN COMMUNITIES ENCYCLOPEDIA AND DIRECTORY) aims to provide a comprehensive guide to the European Union (EU), both as it operates today and in an historical perspective. Information usually only available from many separate sources has been brought together in a single volume to give the reader a wide range of facts, data and background knowledge on the EU.

The thoroughly cross-referenced **A–Z of the European Union** provides concise and factual information on the institutions of the EU and their operation, the EU's activities, member states, people who have played an important role in the development of the Union, and countries and international organizations of relevance to the Union, including those countries that have applied for membership. The A–Z section also explains a large number of widely used acronyms and terms.

The seven **Essays on the European Union** complement the A–Z section in providing extended information on the EU's legal and social frameworks, foreign and security policy, migration and asylum policy, environmental policy and the future of the EU. All essays have been extensively revised in order to provide the most up-to-date information. This edition also includes a new essay on the issue of Euroscepticism.

The **Directory of the European Union** consists of sections on each institution of the Union, giving, where appropriate, addresses, telephone and fax numbers, e-mail and internet addresses, and detailed information on principal officers and their areas of work. It also contains summaries of treaties of major importance in the formation of the Union, and details of EU-level trade and professional associations.

The book concludes with an extensive **Statistical Survey of the European Union**, which includes sections providing demographic, agricultural, industrial, trade and financial figures, as well as several others. Data are provided for individual member states, enabling comparisons to be made between countries, and for the EU as a whole.

October 2017

ACKNOWLEDGEMENTS

The editors would like to acknowledge the interest, co-operation and enthusiasm of all the contributors to this volume.

We are particularly grateful to the Publications Office of the European Union for allowing us to reproduce, in the Statistical Survey of the European Union, statistics from the website of the Statistical Office of the European Union (Eurostat).

THE CONTRIBUTORS

A–Z OF THE EUROPEAN UNION

Toni Haastrup. Deputy Director, Global Europe Centre, and Lecturer in International Security, School of Politics and International Relations, Rutherford College, University of Kent, United Kingdom.

Lee McGowan. Professor of Comparative European Politics and Jean Monnet Chair in European Integration at the School of History, Anthropology, Philosophy and Politics, Queen's University Belfast, United Kingdom.

David Phinnemore. Professor of European Politics, Jean Monnet Chair in European Political Science and Dean of Education in the School of History, Anthropology, Philosophy and Politics, Queen's University Belfast, United Kingdom.

ESSAYS

Susan Baker. Professor at the Cardiff School of Social Sciences, Cardiff University, United Kingdom.

Rose M. D'Sa. (LLB (Hons), PhD, Barrister-at-Law), Member of the European Economic and Social Committee, Brussels; Consultant in European Union Law; former Professor of European Law and Jean Monnet Chair, University of Glamorgan, United Kingdom.

Andrew Geddes. Chair in Migration Studies and Director of the Migration Policy Centre, European University Institute, Florence, Italy.

Ana E. Juncos. Reader in European Politics, University of Bristol, United Kingdom.

Emil J. Kirchner. Emeritus Professor and Jean Monnet Chair in European Political Integration, University of Essex, United Kingdom, and Associate Editor of the *Journal of European Integration*.

Juliet Lodge. Emeritus Professor of European Studies, School of Media and Communication, University of Leeds, United Kingdom.

Sofia Vasilopoulou. Senior Lecturer in Politics, University of York, United Kingdom.

CONTENTS

Abbreviations	page x
Member States of the European Union	xii
International Telephone Codes	xiii
Select chronology of the European Union	xiv

A–Z OF THE EUROPEAN UNION

Toni Haastrup, Lee McGowan and David Phinnemore — 3

ESSAYS ON THE EUROPEAN UNION

The Legal Framework of the European Union Rose M. D'Sa	211
The Future of the European Union Juliet Lodge	245
Foreign and Security Policy in the 21st Century: Challenges and Opportunities Ana E. Juncos	260
Euroscepticism in Times of Crisis Sofia Vasilopoulou	265
The Social Framework of the European Union Emil J. Kirchner	270
European Union Environmental Policy Susan Baker	278
Migration and Asylum Policy Andrew Geddes	288

DIRECTORY OF THE EUROPEAN UNION

Council of the European Union	297
Presidency	297
Members of the Council of the European Union	297
EU Member States' Permanent Representations	317
Administrative Units	321
The Council's Committees and Working Parties	328
ACP—EC Council	330
European Council	331
President of the European Council	331
European Commission	332
The Commissioners	332
Secretariat-General of the Commission	332
Legal Service	333
DG COMM—Directorate-General for Communication	333
European Political Strategy Centre (EPSC)	335
TF 50—Article 50 Task Force	335
DG ECFIN—Directorate-General for Economic and Financial Affairs	335
DG GROW—Directorate-General for Internal Market, Industry, Entrepreneurship and SMEs	337
DG COMP—Directorate-General for Competition	338
DG EMPL—Directorate-General for Employment, Social Affairs and Inclusion	340
DG AGRI—Directorate-General for Agriculture and Rural Development	341
DG ENER—Directorate-General for Energy	343
DG MOVE—Directorate-General for Mobility and Transport	343
DG CLIMA—Directorate-General for Climate Action	344
DG ENV—Directorate-General for Environment	345
DG RTD—Directorate-General for Research and Innovation	346
Joint Research Centre	348
DG CNECT—Directorate-General for Communications Networks, Content and Technology	350
DG MARE—Directorate-General for Maritime Affairs and Fisheries	352
DG FISMA—Directorate-General for Financial Stability, Financial Services and Capital Markets Union	353
DG REGIO—Directorate-General for Regional and Urban Policy	353
DG TAXUD—Directorate-General for Taxation and Customs Union	354
DG EAC—Directorate-General for Education, Youth, Sport and Culture	355
DG SANTE—Directorate-General for Health and Food Safety	356
DG HOME—Directorate-General for Migration and Home Affairs	357
DG JUST—Directorate-General for Justice and Consumers	358
Service for Foreign Policy Instruments	359
DG TRADE—Directorate-General for Trade	359
DG NEAR— Directorate-General for Neighbourhood and Enlargement Negotiations	360
DG DEVCO—Directorate-General for International Co-operation and Development	361
DG ECHO—Directorate-General for European Civil Protection and Humanitarian Aid Operations	362
Eurostat	363
DG HR—Directorate-General for Human Resources and Security	364
DG DIGIT—Directorate-General for Informatics	366
DG BUDG—Directorate-General for Budget	366
DG IAS—Internal Audit Service	367
OLAF—European Anti-Fraud Office	368
DG SCIC—Directorate-General for Interpretation	368
DG DGT—Directorate-General for Translation	370
Publications Office	372
Office for Infrastructure and Logistics—Brussels (OIB)	373
Office for Administration and Payment of Individual Entitlements (PMO)	373
Office for Infrastructure and Logistics—Luxembourg (OIL)	374
European Personnel Selection Office (EPSO)	374
Diplomatic Corps Accredited to the European Union	374
European External Action Service (EEAS)	380
Secretariat-General	380
External Delegations to Non-Member States	381
European Parliament	387
Bureau	387
Members of the European Parliament	387
Committees and Delegations	399
Political Groups' Secretariats	402
National Parties and Lists Represented in the European Parliament	403
Member Parties of Political Groups	413
Administrative Units	416
Court of Justice and General Court	432
Court of Justice	432
General Court	432

CONTENTS

European Court of Auditors	434
European Economic and Social Committee	438
Committee of the Regions	444
European Investment Bank (EIB)	451
European Central Bank (ECB)	459
European System of Central Banks (ESCB)	462
European Ombudsman	464
EU Agencies	465
Agency for the Co-operation of Energy Regulators (ACER)	465
Body of European Regulators for Electronic Communications (BEREC)	465
Community Plant Variety Office (CPVO)	465
European Agency for the Operational Management of Large-scale IT Systems in the Area of Freedom, Security and Justice (EU-LISA)	465
European Agency for Safety and Health at Work (EU-OSHA)	465
European Asylum Support Office (EASO)	465
European Aviation Safety Agency (EASA)	466
European Bank Authority (EBA)	466
European Border and Coast Guard Agency (FRONTEX)	466
European Centre for the Development of Vocational Training (Cedefop)	466
European Centre for Disease Prevention and Control (ECDC)	467
European Chemicals Agency (ECHA)	467
European Defence Agency (EDA)	467
European Environment Agency (EEA)	468
European Fisheries Control Agency (EFCA)	468
European Food Safety Authority (EFSA)	468
European Foundation for the Improvement of Living and Working Conditions (Eurofound)	469
European Global Navigations Satellite Systems (GNSS) Agency (GSA)	469
European Institute for Gender Equality (EIGE)	469
European Insurance and Occupational Pensions Authority (EIOPA)	470
European Judicial Co-operation Unit (Eurojust)	470
European Maritime Safety Agency (EMSA)	470
European Medicines Agency (EMA)	470
European Monitoring Centre for Drugs and Drug Addiction (EMCDDA)	471
European Securities and Markets Authority (ESMA)	472
European Training Foundation (ETF)	472
European Union Agency for Fundamental Rights (FRA)	472
European Union Agency for Law Enforcement Co-operation (Europol)	472
European Union Agency for Law Enforcement Training (CEPOL)	473
European Union Agency for Network and Information Security (ENISA)	473
European Union Agency for Railways (ERA)	473
European Union Institute for Security Studies (EUISS)	473
European Union Intellectual Property Office (EUIPO)	473
European Union Satellite Centre (EU SatCen)	474
Single Resolution Board	475
Translation Centre for the Bodies of the European Union (CdT)	475
EU Executive Agencies	475
Consumers, Health and Food Executive Agency (Chafea)	475
European Research Council Executive Agency (ERCEA)	476
Innovation and Networks Executive Agency (INEA)	476
Education, Audiovisual and Culture Executive Agency (EACEA)	476
Executive Agency for Small and Medium-sized Enterprises (EASME)	477
Research Executive Agency (REA)	477
Euratom Agencies	478
Euroatom Supply Agency	478
European Joint Undertaking for ITER and the Development of Fusion Energy	478
Treaties	479
Summary of the Treaty of Paris establishing the European Coal and Steel Community (ECSC)	479
Summary of the Treaty of Rome establishing the European Atomic Energy Community (Euratom)	482
Summary of the Treaty of Rome establishing the European Economic Community (EEC)	485
The Single European Act (SEA)	494
Summary of the Treaty on European Union (Maastricht Treaty)	494
Summary of the Treaty of Amsterdam	497
Summary of the Treaty of Nice	498
Principal Elements of the Treaty of Lisbon	502
Other Treaties	502
EU-Level Trade and Professional Associations	504
Index of Keywords relating to the list of EU-Level Trade and Professional Associations	533

STATISTICAL SURVEY OF THE EUROPEAN UNION

Population	539
Total Population	539
Population Change	541
Marriage and Divorce	545
Labour	547
Labour Force	547
Employment	548
Unemployment	557
Health and Welfare	559
Health Personnel	559
Health Facilities	560
Financing of Social Protection	561
Childcare	564
Agriculture, Forestry and Fishing	566
Land Use	566
Crop Production	567
Production of Fruits and Vegetables	571
Livestock Population	579
Production of Meat	581
Milk and Dairy Products	583
Production of Wine	585
Forestry	585
Fishing	587
Aquaculture	588
Energy	590
Mining of Energy Materials	590
Energy Supply and Consumption	591
Nuclear Energy	594
Electrical Energy	595
Renewable Energies	597
Industry	599
Industrial Enterprises	599

CONTENTS

Industrial Employment	600
Industrial Production	601
Indices of Industrial Production	603
The Environment	605
Resource Productivity	605
Environmental Protection Expenditure	605
Finance	607
Exchange Rates	607
Public Finance	607
Official Reserves	611
Consumer Prices	613
National Accounts	618
European Union Totals (EU-28)	618
Distribution by Country	619
Individual Countries	622
Balance of Payments	632
European Union Totals	632
Statistics by Country	632
External Trade	636
Summary Statistics	636
Trade by Commodity Groups	637
Transport	641
Railways	641
Road Transport	645
Inland Waterways	649
Oil and Gas Pipelines	650
Maritime Transport	650
Aviation	651
Communications	653
Telecommunications	653
Information Technology	654
Tourism	657
Accommodation	657
Occupancy	658
Tourist Arrivals by Country	661
Education	667
Enrolment	667
Personnel	670

ABBREVIATIONS

Acad	Academician; Academy
ACP	African, Caribbean and Pacific States
Admin	Administration; Administrator
AG	Aktiengesellschaft (Joint Stock Company)
a.i.	ad interim
AIDS	Acquired Immunodeficiency Syndrome
Alt	Alternate
Apdo	Apartado (Post Box)
Apt	Apartment
ASEAN	Association of South East Asian Nations
asscn	association
assoc	associate
Asst	Assistant
Aug.	August
Av, Avda	Avenida (Avenue)
Ave	Avenue
Bd	Board
Bldg	Building
Blvd	Boulevard
BP	Boîte Postale (Post Box)
bte	boîte (box)
bul	bulvar (boulevard)
c	*circa*
Cad	Caddesi (Street)
CAP	Common Agricultural Policy
CARICOM	Caribbean Community
CDE	Centre de Documentation Européenne (European Documentation Centre)
CE	Communauté Européenne (European Community)
CEE	Communauté Economique Européenne (European Economic Community)
Cen	Central
CET	Common External Tariff
Chair	Chairman/woman
CMEA	Council for Mutual Economic Assistance
COAFR	Working group of the Council on Africa
COASI	Working group of the Council on Asia and Oceania
COEST	Working group of the Council on Eastern Europe and Central Asia
COMEP	Working group of the Council on the Middle East peace process
Coll	College
Confed	Confederation
cnr	corner
Co	Company
Commdr	Commander
COREPER	Committee of Permanent Representatives
COWEB	Consultations on the Western Balkans
CP	Caixa Postal; Case Postale; Casella Postale; Casilla Postal (Post Box)
Cres	Crescent
Crta	Carretera
Cttee	Committee
cu	cubic
DC	District of Columbia; Distrito Central
Dec.	December; Decision
Del	Delegate
Dem	Democratic
Dep	Deputy
Dept	Department
devt	development
DG	Directorate-General
Dir	Director; Directive
Div	Division
Dr	Doctor; Drive
E	East; Eastern
EAGGF	European Agricultural Guidance and Guarantee Fund
EC	European Communities; European Community
ECB	European Central Bank
Econ	Economist; Economics
ECOSOC	Economic and Social Committee
ECU	European Currency Unit
ECSC	European Coal and Steel Community
Ed	Editor
EDA	European Defence Agency
EDC	European Documentation Centre
EEAS	European External Action Service
EEC	European Economic Community
EDF	European Development Fund
Edif	Edificio (building)
EFTA	European Free Trade Association
EG	Europäische Gemeinschaft (European Community)
e.g.	exempli gratia (for example)
EIB	European Investment Bank
EMEA	Euro-Mediterranean Economic Area
EMS	European Monetary System
EMU	Economic and Monetary Union
ENP	European Neighbourhood Policy
EP	European Parliament
EPC	European Political Co-operation
ERDF	European Regional Development Fund
ERM	Exchange Rate Mechanism
ESA	European System of Integrated Economic Accounts
ESC	Economic and Social Committee
ESF	European Social Fund
ESM	European Stability Mechanism
esq	esquina (corner)
etc	et cetera
EU	European Union
EUROMED	Euro-Mediterranean Partnership
EUR-OP	Office for Official Publications of the European Communities
Euratom	European Atomic Energy Community
Eurostat	Statistical Office of the European Union
eV	eingetragener Verein
EWG	Europäische Wirtschaftsgemeinschaft (European Economic Community)
f.	founded
fax	facsimile
Feb.	February
Fed	Federal
FEOGA	Fonds Européen d'Orientation et de Garantie Agricole (European Agricultural Guidance and Guarantee Fund)
fob	free on board
GDP	gross domestic product
Gen	General
GmbH	Gesellschaft mit beschränkter Haftung (Limited Liability Company)
GNI	Gross National Income

ABBREVIATIONS

GNP	Gross National Product	PMB	Private Mail Bag
Gov	Governor	PMG	Politico-Military Group
Govt	Government	POB	Post Office Box
grt	gross registered tons	pp	pages
GSP	Generalized System of Preferences	Pres	President
GVA	Gross Value Added	Prof	Professor, professional
GWh	gigawatt hours	Prin	Principal
		Publ	Publication; published
ha	hectares	Pvt	Private
HICP	harmonized indices of consumer prices		
hl	hectolitre(s)	q.v.	quod vide (to which refer)
HM	Her/His Majesty		
Hon	Honorary; Honourable	Rd	Road
		Rec	Recommendation
ibid	ibidem (in the same place)	Reg	Regulation
i.e.	id est (that is to say)	Regd	Registered
Inc	Incorporated	rep	representative
Ind	Independent	Repub	Republic
Insp	Inspector	Rev	Reverend
Inst	Institute	Rm	Room
Int	International	Rt	Right
Jan.	January	S	South
Jr	Junior	SA	Sociedade Anónima, Société Anonyme (Limited Company); South Australia
JRC	Joint Research Centre		
Jt	Joint	SAD	Single Administrative Document
		SARL	Sociedade Anônima de Responsibilidade Limitada (Joint Stock Company of Limited Liability)
kg	kilogram(s)		
kJ	kilojoule		
km	kilometre	SEA	Single European Act
kv	kvartal (apartment block)	Sec	Secretary
kWh	kilowatt hours	Secr	Secretariat
		Sen	Senior; Senator
Ltd	Limited	Sept.	September
		SITC	Standard International Trade Classification
Man	Manager; managing	SME	Small and Medium-Sized Enterprise(s)
m	metre(s)	s/n	sin número (without number)
m.	million	Soc	Society
mbH	mit beschränkter Haftung (with limited liability)	SpA	Società per Azioni (Joint Stock Company)
Mem	Member	Sq	Square
MEP	Member of the European Parliament	Srl	Società a Responsabilità Limitata (Limited Company)
Mgr	Monseigneur; Monsignor		
		St	Saint; street
N	North; Northern	Ste	Sainte
n/a	not available	Str	Strasse (street)
nám	náměstí (square)		
NACE	General Industrial Classification of Economic Activities within the European Communities	tel	telephone
		TEU	Treaty on European Union
		TJ	terajoule
Nat	National	Treas	Treasurer
NATO	North Atlantic Treaty Organization		
NGO	Non-Governmental Organization	u	utca (street)
NNI	Net National Income	UAE	United Arab Emirates
no	number; numero	UE	Union Européenne (European Union)
Nov.	November	UK	United Kingdom
nr	near	ul	ulitsa (street)
NV	Naamloze Vennootschap (Limited Company)	UN	United Nations
NW	North West	Univ	University
		USA	United States of America
Oct.	October	USSR	Union of Soviet Socialist Republics
OCTs	Overseas Countries and Territories		
OJ	*Official Journal*	v	versus
OPEC	Organization of Petroleum Exporting Countries	VAT	Value Added Tax
opp	opposite	Vn	Veien (street)
Org	Organization	Vol	Volume
p	page	W	West, Western
Parl	Parliament(ary)	WC	Water-closet
perm	permanent		
pl	place; platz; ploshchad (square)	yr	Year
PLC	Public Limited Company		

Note: Please also see A–Z of the European Union.

MEMBER STATES OF THE EUROPEAN UNION

	Capital city	Currency
Austria	Vienna	euro
Belgium	Brussels	euro
Bulgaria	Sofia	lev
Croatia	Zagreb	kuna
Cyprus*	Nicosia	euro
Czech Republic	Prague	Czech koruna
Denmark	Copenhagen	krone
Estonia	Tallinn	euro
Finland	Helsinki	euro
France	Paris	euro
Germany	Berlin	euro
Greece	Athens	euro
Hungary	Budapest	forint
Ireland	Dublin	euro
Italy	Rome	euro
Latvia	Rīga	euro
Lithuania	Vilnius	euro
Luxembourg	Luxembourg	euro
Malta	Valletta	euro
Netherlands	Amsterdam	euro
Poland	Warsaw	złoty
Portugal	Lisbon	euro
Romania	Bucharest	leu
Slovakia	Bratislava	euro
Slovenia	Ljubljana	euro
Spain	Madrid	euro
Sweden	Stockholm	krona
United Kingdom	London	pound sterling

* Government-controlled area only.

INTERNATIONAL TELEPHONE CODES

The code and number must be preceded by the International Dialling Code of the country from which you are calling.

Country	Code	Country	Code
Austria	43	Italy	39
Belgium	32	Latvia	371
Bulgaria	359	Lithuania	370
Croatia	385	Luxembourg	352
Cyprus	357	Malta	356
Czech Republic	420	Netherlands	31
Denmark	45	Poland	48
Estonia	372	Portugal	351
Finland	358	Romania	40
France	33	Slovakia	421
Germany	49	Slovenia	386
Greece	30	Spain	34
Hungary	36	Sweden	46
Ireland	353	United Kingdom	44

SELECT CHRONOLOGY OF THE EUROPEAN UNION

1947: The Treaty of Dunkirk, a defensive alliance, was signed by France and the United Kingdom.

1948: The Organisation for European Economic Co-operation (OEC) was established.

1 Jan. 1948: A customs union was established between Belgium, Luxembourg and the Netherlands.

17 March 1948: The Treaty of Brussels alliance was signed between Belgium, France, Luxembourg, the Netherlands and the UK.

7–11 May 1948: The Congress of Europe was held in The Hague, the Netherlands. Delegates expressed their support for the political and economic integration of the countries of Europe and for the adoption of a human rights charter and a European Court of Justice.

1948: The European Movement was founded following the Congress of Europe.

4 April 1949: The North Atlantic Treaty, setting up the North Atlantic Treaty Organization (NATO), was signed between the USA, Canada, Belgium, Denmark, France, Iceland, Italy, Luxembourg, the Netherlands, Norway, Portugal and the UK.

5 May 1949: The Statute of the Council of Europe was signed in London, UK. The Council comprised an intergovernmental Committee of Ministers and a Consultative Assembly.

3 Aug. 1949: The Statute of the Council of Europe entered into force.

10 Aug. 1949: The first session of the Consultative Assembly opened in Strasbourg, France.

1949: The Council for Mutual Economic Assistance (CMEA) was established by the USSR as an organ for economic co-operation in Eastern Europe.

9 May 1950: Robert Schuman, the French Minister for Foreign Affairs, put forward a plan to pool the production and consumption of coal and steel under a European organization ('Schuman Declaration').

3 June 1950: Belgium, France, Federal Republic of Germany (FRG—West Germany), Italy, Luxembourg and the Netherlands—later referred to as 'the Six'—subscribed to the Schuman Declaration.

4 Nov. 1950: The European Convention on Human Rights, which established the European Commission of Human Rights and the European Court of Human Rights, was signed in Rome, Italy.

18 April 1951: The Treaty of Paris set up the European Coal and Steel Community (ECSC), comprising a High Authority and a Common Assembly. Member states were the Six. The Treaty came into force on 25 July 1952.

27 May 1952: The European Defence Community (EDC) was established by the Six.

1952: A European Political Community was subsequently proposed by the Six to incorporate the EDC and the ECSC. A treaty on Political Community was drafted but the proposal ultimately collapsed in 1954 when France refused to ratify the EDC treaty.

23 July 1952: The Treaty of Paris entered into force. Paul-Henri Spaak was appointed President of the Common Assembly.

10 Aug. 1952: The ECSC High Authority began functioning, with Jean Monnet as President.

1952: The Nordic Council was established by Denmark, Iceland, Norway and Sweden; Finland joined in 1955.

1952: Greece and Turkey joined NATO.

1 Jan. 1953: An ECSC levy—the first European tax—came into force.

10 Feb. 1953: The Six abolished customs duties and quantitative restrictions on coal and iron ore. A common market for scrap iron was established on 15 March.

12 Aug. 1953: The ECSC signed a Co-operation Agreement with the International Labour Organization (ILO).

1953: The European Convention on Human Rights came into effect and the European Commission of Human Rights began operating in Strasbourg.

11 May 1954: Alcide de Gasperi was elected President of the Common Assembly.

30 Aug. 1954: The French National Assembly rejected the EDC Treaty. Monnet subsequently resigned (10 Nov.).

21 Dec. 1954: The ECSC Court of Justice delivered its first ruling.

1–2 June 1955: At the Messina Conference, Italy, ministers responsible for foreign affairs of the Six met to discuss greater European unity. An intergovernmental committee was set up under Paul-Henri Spaak to investigate the prospects for closer unity in general and nuclear energy terms. René Mayer was elected President of the ECSC High Authority.

1955: Western European Union (WEU) was established—the Treaty of Brussels countries plus the FRG and Italy. Portugal and Spain joined in 1988.

1955: The FRG joined NATO.

19 May 1956: The Spaak Report, initiated at the Messina Conference, was approved by ministers responsible for foreign affairs of the Six. The Six and other European countries were invited to start intergovernmental negotiations on new Treaties.

26 June 1956: Negotiations for drafting of new treaties opened in Brussels.

25 March 1957: The Treaties of Rome establishing the European Economic Community (EEC) and the European Atomic Energy Community (EAEC or Euratom) were signed by the Six. The treaties were effective from 1 Jan. 1958. These two bodies, together with the ECSC, comprised the European Communities (EC).

27 Nov. 1957: Hans Furler was elected President of the Common Assembly.

7 Jan. 1958: Walter Hallstein was appointed President of the Commission of the EC, Louis Armand was appointed President of Euratom and Paul Finet was elected President of the ECSC High Authority.

19 March 1958: A session establishing the European Parliamentary Assembly was held in Strasbourg, at which Robert Schuman was elected President.

7 July 1958: A formal Liaison and Collaboration Agreement was signed between the EC and the ILO.

7 Oct. 1958: The European Court of Justice was established in Luxembourg.

1958: The Overseas Development Fund (ODF) was established to clarify details of the relationship between the EC and its Overseas Countries and Territories (OCTs); the ODF was superseded by the Yaoundé Convention in 1963.

SELECT CHRONOLOGY OF THE EUROPEAN UNION

1958: The European Social Fund (ESF) was established to promote employment, training and mobility of workers within the EC.

2 Feb. 1959: Etienne Hirsch was elected President of Euratom.

Feb. 1959: The Benelux states (Belgium, Luxembourg and the Netherlands) signed a new treaty of economic union, establishing the Benelux Economic Union.

8 June 1959: Greece applied to the EC to become an associated state. Negotiations began on 10 Sept.

20–21 July 1959: Seven countries of the OEC (Austria, Denmark, Norway, Portugal, Sweden, Switzerland and the UK) agreed to establish the European Free Trade Association (EFTA).

31 July 1959: Turkey applied to the EC for association status. Negotiations began on 27 Sept.

11 Sep. 1959: Piero Malvestiti was elected President of the ECSC High Authority.

Jan. 1960: The Benelux Economic Union formally came into operation.

4 Jan. 1960: The EFTA Convention was signed in Stockholm, Sweden.

3 May 1960: The Stockholm Convention establishing EFTA came into force.

14 Dec. 1960: The OEC became the Organisation for Economic Co-operation and Development (OECD).

9 July 1961: An Association Agreement was signed between the EC and Greece, coming into effect on 1 Nov. 1962.

1961: Ireland, on 31 July, Denmark, on 9 Aug., and the UK, on 10 Aug., applied to join the EC.

1 Sept. 1961: The first regulation came into effect regarding free movement of workers from Members States within the EC.

2 Nov. 1961: The Fouchet Plan draft treaty for political union was published; it was rejected by all of the Six except France.

14 Jan. 1962: The principle of a Common Agricultural Policy (CAP) was accepted by member states, and the European Agricultural Guidance and Guarantee Fund (EAGGF or FEOGA) was set up; the Fund began operating on 1 July 1964.

29 Jan. 1962: Negotiations between the EC and the UK were broken off after a French veto on British entry. (The French President, Charles de Gaulle, believed that British and US influence in Europe would be too great if the UK were accepted.)

1962: Spain, on 9 Feb., and Portugal, on 18 May, began negotiations for association with EC.

March 1962: The Parliamentary Assembly voted to change its name to the European Parliament (EP); Gaetano Martino was elected as its President.

30 April 1962: Norway applied to join the EC.

30 July 1962: Regulations creating the CAP entered into force.

22 Jan. 1963: The Treaty of Friendship (Elysée Treaty) was signed between France and the FRG.

20 July 1963: The Yaoundé Convention was signed, a Trade and Development Agreement uniting the EC with 18 countries, known as the Associated African States and Madagascar (AASM).

12 Sep. 1963: An Association Agreement was signed by the EC and Turkey.

8 Oct. 1963: Dino del Bo was elected President of the ECSC High Authority.

20 March 1964: Jean Duvieusart was elected President of the European Parliament.

1 June 1964: The Yaoundé Convention entered into force.

1 Dec. 1964: The Association Agreement with Turkey entered into force.

1964: The common agricultural market was established. Uniform prices were adopted for cereals on 15 Dec. 1964, coming into effect in 1967.

1964: The Committee of Governors of the Central Banks of Member States was established.

2 March 1965: Victor Leemans was elected President of the European Parliament.

8 April 1965: The Merger Treaty, establishing a single Council of Ministers and a single Commission, was signed in Brussels, integrating executives of the ECSE, EC, and Euratom. Effective from 1 July 1967.

30 June 1965: The empty chair crisis; French representatives boycotted all meetings of the Council of Ministers for seven months, in protest at the EC timetable for the increased use of qualified majority voting and other issues.

28 Jan. 1966: The Luxembourg Compromise resolved the empty chair crisis by extending to member states the right to use a veto in the Council of Ministers if they believed their national interests were being compromised.

7 March 1966: Alain Poher was elected President of the European Parliament.

1966: France withdrew from NATO's integrated military structure.

1967: An Association Agreement with Greece was suspended following a military coup d'état in that country.

10 May 1967: The UK reapplied to join the EC, followed by Ireland, Denmark and later Norway; France refused to begin negotiations owing to President Charles de Gaulle's reluctance to allow British accession.

30 June 1967: The Kennedy Round of General Agreement on Tariffs and Trade (GATT) ended with a reduction in customs tariffs by major trading countries; agreements were signed by member states and the Commission.

1967: Walter Hallstein resigned as President of the Commission; Jean Rey was appointed as the new President of the single Commission, which assumed office on 6 July.

3 July 1967: The EC Council of Ministers held its first session.

1 July 1968: The customs union was completed, removing all customs duties in trade between the Six.

26 July 1968: An Association Agreement was signed in Arusha, Tanzania, between the EC and Kenya, Uganda and Tanzania; it was renewed on 24 Sept 1969.

18 Dec. 1968: The Mansholt Plan of price guarantees, restructuring and modernization for agriculture was proposed as a framework for the CAP.

29 July 1969: The second Yaoundé Convention was signed.

19–22 Dec. 1969: The Council of Ministers agreed to increase the European Parliament's budgetary powers and to provide the EC with financial autonomy.

10 March 1970: Mario Scelba was elected President of the European Parliament.

22 April 1970: The Treaty of Luxembourg, an amendment to the Treaty of Rome, was signed by the member states.

30 June 1970: The UK, Ireland, Denmark and Norway began negotiations to join the EC.

1 July 1970: Franco Maria Malfatti was appointed President of the Commission.

27 Oct. 1970: The Davignon Report was approved by the member states, initiating European Political Co-operation (EPC).

Oct. 1970: The Werner Report presented governments of member states with a blueprint for full Economic and Monetary Union (EMU).

1970: An Association Agreement was signed between the EC and Malta, and a preferential Trade Agreement was arranged in Spain.

1 Jan. 1971: The second Yaoundé Convention and Arusha Agreement entered into force.

22 March 1971: The Werner Plan was adopted by the Council of Ministers, which obliged member states to reduce the margins of fluctuation between currencies and to bring their budgetary policies into line with one another.

May 1971: The EC issued their first joint foreign policy declaration on the Middle East.

22 Jan. 1972: The treaties of accession were signed and ratified by the UK, Ireland and Denmark; on 25 Sept. Norway rejected its accession treaty in a referendum.

22 March 1972: Sicco Mansholt was appointed President of the Commission.

24 April 1972: A system was established, known as the Snake, which set maximum margins for the fluctuation of exchange rates at 2.5% between the currencies of member states, including UK, Ireland and Denmark; the Snake was not successful and was succeeded by the European Monetary System (EMS) in 1979.

24–25 April 1972: The Council of Ministers approved an Association Agreement admitting Mauritius to the Yaoundé Convention.

22 July 1972: Austria, Portugal, Iceland, Sweden and Switzerland signed Special Relations Agreements with the EC.

18 Dec. 1972: Trade Agreements were signed with Egypt and Lebanon.

19 Dec. 1972: An Association Agreement was signed between the EC and Cyprus, coming into effect on 1 June 1973.

1 Jan. 1973: The UK, Ireland and Denmark became official members of the new Community of Nine. Free Trade Agreements with Austria, Portugal, Sweden and Switzerland came into force.

6 Jan. 1973: François-Xavier Ortoli was appointed President of the Commission.

13 March 1973: Cornelis Berkhouwer was elected President of the European Pariament.

1 April 1973: A Free Trade Agreement with Iceland came into force.

2 April 1973: A Trade Agreement was signed between the EC and Uruguay.

14 May 1973: A Free Trade Agreement was signed between the EC and Norway, which came into force on 1 July.

July 1973: Negotiations began with Yaoundé Convention countries and with 27 other developing countries in Africa, the Caribbean and the Pacific.

3–7 July 1973: The Conference on Security and Co-operation in Europe (CSCE) began in Helsinki, Finland.

5 Oct. 1973: A Free Trade Agreement was signed with Finland, which entered into force on 1 Jan. 1974.

Oct. 1973: The energy crisis provoked by the Yom Kippur war between Israel and Egypt had an adverse effect on the EC economy.

5 Nov. 1973: Member states issued a joint statement on the Middle East situation, stipulating conditions for a peaceful settlement of the conflict.

14–15 Dec. 1973: Prompted by the energy crisis, member states agreed at a summit conference held in Copenhagen, Denmark, to introduce a common energy policy.

Dec. 1973: A Trade Agreement was signed with Brazil and India.

1973: A second Davignon Report on political co-operation was published.

21 Jan. 1974: The Social Action Programme was introduced by the Council of Ministers.

April 1974: After the Labour Party had defeated the Conservative Party in the British elections in Feb., it sought to renegotiate the country's terms of accession to the EC.

July 1974: Turkey took control of the northern third of Cyprus, complicating negotiations for full customs union with Cyprus.

30 Nov. 1974: Agreements between the ECSC and Finland and Norway were ratified by the member states. They came into force on 1 Jan. 1975.

9–10 Dec. 1974: A summit of Heads of State or Government in Paris agreed on the allocation of resources from the EC to a European Regional Development Fund (ERDF) and discussed the election of the European Parliament by direct universal suffrage; the summit agreed that Heads of State or Government should meet more frequently to discuss important matters; thus the European Council was established.

28 Feb. 1975: The Lomé Convention (Lomé I) was signed by the EC and 46 African, Caribbean and Pacific (ACP) States, replacing the 1963 and 1969 Yaoundé Conventions and the Arusha Agreement. It came into force on 1 April 1976.

11 March 1975: Georges Spénale was elected President of the European Parliament.

18 March 1975: The ERDF was established.

11 May 1975: The EC signed a Trade Agreement with Israel.

12 June 1975: Greece applied to join the EC.

2 July 1975: The Court of Auditors of the EC was set up by the Treaty of Brussels; the treaty came into force on 1 July 1977.

15 July 1975: A Trade Agreement was signed between the EC and Mexico.

16 Sept. 1975: Official relations were established between the EC and the People's Republic of China.

1–2 Dec. 1975: The European Council, meeting in Rome, decided on the election of the European Parliament by direct universal suffrage.

29 Dec. 1975: The Tindemans Report on political co-operation, called for at the Paris Summit of 1974, was presented to member state Governments. It was published on 7 Jan. 1976.

1975: The European Foundation for the Improvement of Living and Working Conditions was established.

1975: The Council of Ministers adopted an Anti-Poverty Programme and a directive to pursue a policy of equal treatment for male and female workers.

1975: The EC and Sri Lanka signed a commercial Co-operation Agreement.

16 Feb. 1976: The CMEA sought negotiations with the EC, but discussions proved inconclusive.

25–27 April 1976: The EC signed collective bilateral trade and aid agreements with the Maghreb States (Algeria, Morocco and Tunisia).

1 June 1976: The EC and Pakistan signed a trade Co-operation Agreement.

6 July 1976: A framework document for a commercial and economic agreement was signed between the EC and Canada.

27 Aug. 1976: Negotiations opened on the accession of Greece to the EC.

3 Nov. 1976: The beginnings of a common fisheries policy were established with the decision by the Council of Ministers that member states should extend fishing limits to 200 miles off their North Sea and North Atlantic coasts, with effect from 1 Jan. 1977.

SELECT CHRONOLOGY OF THE EUROPEAN UNION

1976: The EC signed a Co-operation Agreement with Bangladesh.

6 Jan. 1977: A new Commission assumed office, with Roy Jenkins as President.

18 Jan. 1977: The EC signed collective bilateral trade and aid agreements with the Mashreq States (Egypt, Jordan and Syria).

9 March 1977: The European Centre for the Development of Vocational Trading (CEDEFOP) was set up in Berlin.

28 March 1977: Portugal submitted a formal application to join the EC. São Tomé and Príncipe, Cape Verde and Papua New Guinea signed agreements for accession to the Lomé Convention.

3 May 1977: The EC signed a Trade Agreement with Lebanon.

1 July 1977: The Court of Auditors came into operation, holding its inaugural meeting on 25 Oct.; a common customs tariff extended to the three newest member states (Denmark, Ireland and the UK).

28 July 1977: Spain applied to join the EC.

9 Nov. 1977: Michael Murphy was elected President of the Court of Auditors.

1977: The MacDougall Report on EMU was published.

3 April 1978: The EC signed a Trade Agreement with the People's Republic of China, which came into force on 1 June.

6 June 1978: Accession negotiations opened with Portugal.

6–7 July 1978: At a meeting in Bremen, Germany, the Council of Ministers agreed upon the establishment of the EMS.

1 Jan. 1979: The European Currency Unit (ECU) was devised, as a replacement for the European Unit of Account (EUA).

5 Feb. 1979: Spanish accession negotiations began.

20 Feb. 1979: The *Cassis de Dijon* ruling was made by the Court of Justice, declaring that a member state could not prohibit import and sale of a product legally manufactured and on sale in another member state.

9 March 1979: The EMS was brought into operation by the European Council in Paris, aiming to create closer monetary co-operation through the Exchange Rate Mechanism (ERM); not all member states participated fully in the EMS.

18 May 1979: Greece signed a treaty of accession, and became the 10th member of the EC from 1 Jan. 1981.

7–10 June 1979: Citizens of the nine member states voted in the first direct elections to the European Parliament.

31 Oct. 1979: The second Lomé Convention (Lomé II) was signed by member states and 58 ACP countries.

20 Nov. 1979: The Council of Ministers endorsed the results of the Tokyo Round of GATT negotiations, which further reduced customs duties. The Tokyo Round agreements were signed by the EC on 17 Dec.

7–8 March 1980: The EC signed a Co-operation Agreement with the Association of South East Asian Nations (ASEAN)—Brunei, Indonesia, Malaysia, the Philippines, Singapore and Thailand—which came into force on 1 Oct.

2 April 1980: A Co-operation Agreement was signed with Yugoslavia.

30 May 1980: The Council of Ministers reached a compromise agreement on the British budgetary contribution, which was reduced for 1980 and 1981; for subsequent years, the Commission was invited to prepare a package of reforms styled 'the mandate of 30 May 1980'.

1980: A worldwide steel crisis prompted the Commission to declare a state of manifest crisis, laying down production quotas for steel firms in the EC; short-term financial aid was granted as steel firms were restructured and manpower reduced.

1980: The Crocodile Group was established by a group of Members of the European Parliament (MEPs) to develop plans for radical reform of the EC.

1980: An agreement was signed with Romania; a draft Co-operation Agreement was signed with Brazil, which entered into force on 1 Oct 1982.

1 Jan. 1981: Greece became the 10th member of EC. The ECU replaced the EUA in the EC general budget.

20 Jan. 1981: Gaston Thorn was appointed President of the new Commission.

23 June 1981: A commercial and economic agreement was signed between the EC and India.

18 Oct. 1981: During legislative elections Greece elected its MEPs.

7 Nov. 1981: The Genscher-Colombo Plan for political union was presented by France and the FRG in the form of a draft European Act.

19 Jan. 1982: Pieter Dankert was elected President of the European Parliament.

23 Feb. 1982: Greenland, which joined as part of Denmark, voted to leave the EC.

30 May 1982: Spain joined NATO.

1982: The Council of Ministers adopted a Community Action Programme on the Promotion of Equal Opportunities for Women.

25 Jan. 1983: The Council of Ministers established the Common Fisheries Policy (CFP).

17–19 June 1983: The Heads of State or Government and ministers responsible for foreign affairs signed the Solemn Declaration on European Union.

17 Dec. 1983: The Andean Pact or Acuerdo de Cartagena countries (Bolivia, Ecuador, Peru and Venezuela) signed an agreement with the EC on bilateral trade and aid.

1983: The Albert-Ball Report was published by the European Parliament, promoting efforts to secure a single internal market.

14 Feb. 1984: The European Parliament adopted a Draft Treaty on European Union, presented by its Committee on Institutional Affairs.

30 March 1984: The Council of Ministers adopted measures to reform the CAP.

14–17 June 1984: The second elections by direct universal suffrage to the European Parliament took place.

25 June 1984: The European Council granted compensation to the UK in order to reduce its budget contribution.

June 1984: The Committee for a People's Europe was established by the European Council; the Dooge Committee was set up to examine the possibilities of institutional reform of the EC.

24 July 1984: Pierre Pflimlin was elected President of the European Parliament.

9 Oct. 1984: The EC signed a non-preferential Co-operation Agreement with Yemen Arab Republic.

18 Oct. 1984: Marcel Mart was elected President of the Court of Auditors.

8 Dec. 1984: The third Lomé Convention (Lomé III) was signed by the 10 member states and 65 ACP States. It came into force on 1 May 1985.

1 Jan. 1985: European passports began to be introduced in member states.

7 Jan. 1985: A new Commission took office with Jacques Delors as President.

1 Feb. 1985: Greenland officially left the EC.

29–30 March 1985: Integrated Mediterranean Programmes (IMPs) were adopted, which were designed to help the EC southern regions.

12 June 1985: Spain and Portugal signed a treaty of accession and became full members of the EC on 1 Jan. 1986.

SELECT CHRONOLOGY OF THE EUROPEAN UNION

14 June 1985: The Commission presented the Council of Ministers with the White Paper on the completion of the internal market, setting out a timetable for completion. The Schengen Agreement was signed by Belgium, France, the FRG, Luxembourg and the Netherlands, creating a border-free zone among themselves; Italy signed the Agreement in Nov. 1990.

1 Jan. 1986: Spain and Portugal became the 11th and 12th members of the EC.

17 Feb. 1986: The Single European Act (SEA) was signed in Luxembourg by Belgium, France, the FRG, Ireland, Luxembourg, the Netherlands, Portugal, Spain and the UK.

28 Feb. 1986: The SEA was signed in The Hague by Denmark, Greece and Italy.

29 May 1986: The European flag, adopted by EC institutions, was displayed for the first time.

20 Jan. 1987: Lord Henry Plumb was elected President of the European Parliament.

Feb. 1987: Delors I was proposed by the Commission to rectify the EC budgetary situation; it was accepted in Feb. 1988.

14 April 1987: Turkey applied to join EC.

13 May 1987: Spain signed an agreement to join the EMS.

10 June 1987: Spain held its first elections to the European Parliament.

1 July 1987: The SEA came into force.

8 July 1987: Morocco applied to join the EC.

19 July 1987: European elections were held in Portugal for the first time.

10 Nov. 1987: Portugal agreed to join the EMS.

Nov. 1987: The Nyborg Agreements were made by EC finance ministers.

1987: A Customs Union Agreement was concluded between the EC and Cyprus.

Jan. 1988: The Single Administrative Document came into operation, replacing the various transit documents hitherto required by drivers of commercial vehicles in order to cross borders within the EU.

Feb. 1988: The Council of Ministers agreed upon budgetary reforms, including a legally enforceable upper limit on agricultural expenditure.

Feb. 1988: The Balladur Memorandum summarized reforms to the EMS necessary for the completion of the internal market.

29 March 1988: The Cecchini Report was published as 'The European Challenge 1992—The Benefits of a Single Community'.

15 June 1988: The EC signed a Co-operation Agreement with members of the Co-operation Council for Arab States of the Gulf.

25 June 1988: A joint declaration, establishing official relations, was signed between the EC and the CMEA.

26 Sept. 1988: The EC signed a trade, commercial and economic Co-operation Agreement with Hungary.

24 Oct. 1988: The Council of Ministers adopted a decision establishing the Court of First Instance of the EC.

1988: The Combined Nomenclature was created to replace the common external tariff (CET) nomenclature and Nomenclature of Goods for the External Trade Statistics of the Community and Statistics of Trade between member states.

1988: Spain and Portugal joined WEU.

12 April 1989: The European Parliament adopted the Declaration of Fundamental Rights and Freedoms.

June 1989: The Delors Plan was presented to Heads of Government, setting Stage One of EMU for 1 July 1990 and trying to involve all member states in the ERM.

15–18 June 1989: The third election by direct universal suffrage to the European Parliament.

19 June 1989: The Spanish currency entered the EMS.

17 July 1989: Austria applied to join the EC.

July 1989: The Poland and Hungary Assistance for Economic Restructuring programme (Operation Phare) was established; it was extended in 1990 to include other Central and Eastern European states.

19 Sept. 1989: An agreement on trade and economic co-operation was concluded between the EC and Poland.

15 Dec. 1989: The fourth Lomé Convention (Lomé IV) was signed with 69 ACP States.

18 Dec. 1989: An agreement on trade, economic and commercial co-operation was concluded between the EC and the USSR.

21 Dec. 1989: The Council of Ministers adopted a Commission proposal concerning the control of mergers and acquisitions.

1989: The Delors Plan proposals for EMU were accepted by the European Council.

9 Jan. 1990: Aldo Angioi was elected President of the Court of Auditors.

5 Feb. 1990: The Council of Ministers defined the Action Programme for development of relations between the EC and countries of Central and Eastern Europe.

March 1990: The Oslo Declaration was issued by Heads of Government of EFTA States, confirming their desire to strengthen their association with the EC.

2 April 1990: The EC signed a framework agreement on commercial and economic co-operation with Argentina.

28 April 1990: In Dublin, Ireland, an extraordinary European Council agreed on a united approach to German reunification and to relations with the countries of Central and Eastern Europe.

April 1990: The German Chancellor, Helmut Kohl, and the French President François Mitterrand, issued a joint appeal for European union.

7 May 1990: Negotiations for a Trade and Co-operation Agreement between the EC and Romania began; diplomatic relations had been suspended between 20 Dec. 1989 and March 1990.

8 May 1990: The EC signed trade, commercial and economic Co-operation Agreements with Czechoslovakia, Bulgaria and the German Democratic Republic (GDR—East Germany), the last of which was never ratified because of the reunification of the two Germanies.

29 May 1990: An agreement establishing the European Bank for Reconstruction and Development (EBRD) was signed in Paris.

29 June 1990: The Council of Ministers issued negotiating directives for an agreement with EFTA countries on the establishment of a European Economic Space (EES).

1 July 1990: Stage One of EMU began.

4 July 1990: Cyprus applied for membership of the EC.

16 July 1990: Malta applied for membership of the EC.

Oct 1990: A trade and economic Co-operation Agreement was concluded between the EC and Romania.

3 Oct. 1990: German reunification took place; the former GDR automatically attained membership of the EC.

5 Oct. 1990: The UK allowed sterling to become a full member of the ERM.

27–28 Oct. 1990: EC Heads of Government in Rome set a starting date for Stage Two of EMU, involving the establishment of a European Central Bank (ECB), at Jan. 1994.

SELECT CHRONOLOGY OF THE EUROPEAN UNION

7 Nov. 1990: The Commission proposed directives to the Council of Ministers authorizing it to negotiate Association or Europe Agreements with Czechoslovakia, Hungary and Poland.

19–21 Nov. 1990: The Heads of State or Government of 34 countries met in Paris for a Conference on Security and Co-operation in Europe (CSCE); the Charter of Paris for a New Europe (Charter of Paris) was signed and has often been regarded as marking the formal end of the Cold War.

23 Nov. 1990: The Transatlantic Declaration on EC-US relations was released.

Nov. 1990: Hungary joined the Council of Europe.

Nov. 1990: Italy signed the Schengen Agreement.

15 Dec. 1990: Intergovernmental Conferences on Political Union and EMU opened.

Dec. 1990: Sweden's Parliament voted in favour of applying to join the EC.

Dec. 1990: The Uruguay Round of GATT talks broke down owing to disagreements over the EC Common Agricultural Policy (CAP). Talks recommenced, on a technical level, in Geneva, Switzerland, on 20 Feb. 1991.

1990: EC ministers responsible for the environment agreed to establish a European environment agency.

Jan. 1991: EFTA and the EC agreed to prepare a treaty by July laying down terms for the creation of the EES by 1993.

4–5 Feb. 1991: EC ministers responsible for agriculture rejected an ambitious package of agricultural policy reforms proposed by the Commission.

21 Feb. 1991: Czechoslovakia joined the Council of Europe.

Feb. 1991: The Commission began negotiations to conclude Association or Europe Agreements with Czechoslovakia, Poland and Hungary.

8 April 1991: An emergency summit of Heads of State or Government took place to define a common position on Middle East problems following the Gulf War.

15 April 1991: The EBRD was inaugurated in London.

1 July 1991: Sweden applied for EC membership.

Nov. 1991: Negotiations were completed on the establishment of the European Economic Area (EEA), as the EES had become known.

Nov. 1991: Poland joined the Council of Europe.

Dec. 1991: The Maastricht Summit, the European Council meeting in Maastricht, the Netherlands took place; agreement was reached on the text of the Treaty on European Union (TEU), which included substantial revision of the Treaties of Rome.

14 Jan. 1992: Egon Klepsch was elected President of the European Parliament.

Jan. 1992: The EC rejected the draft final act of the Uruguay Round of GATT negotiations on the grounds that it would adversely affect the CAP if implemented.

7 Feb. 1992: The TEU was signed by representatives of the 12 member states. The Treaty was effective from 1 Nov. 1993.

Feb. 1992: Delors II, a set of budgetary measures, was proposed by the Commission.

18 March 1992: Finland applied for EC membership.

April 1992: Portugal joined the ERM.

26 May 1992: Switzerland applied for EC membership.

May 1992: Bulgaria joined the Council of Europe.

June 1992: Denmark narrowly rejected ratification of the TEU in a referendum.

Sept. 1992: The Italian and Spanish currencies were devalued within the ERM, by 7% and 5% respectively; Italy and the UK left the ERM.

Nov. 1992: Denmark and Ireland gained observer status within WEU.

Nov. 1992: The Portuguese and Spanish currencies were both devalued by 6% within the ERM.

Nov. 1992: Negotiators representing the USA and the Commission agreed upon a significant reduction of the EC's production of oil-seeds and of the volume and value of its subsidized exports of farm produce; these accords were strongly opposed by the French Government but formed the basis for the conclusion of the Uruguay Round of GATT negotiations in Dec. 1993.

25 Nov. 1992: Norway applied for EC membership.

6 Dec. 1992: Switzerland rejected ratification of the EEA Agreement in a referendum.

Dec. 1992: At the European Council meeting in Edinburgh, UK, Denmark was granted exemption from certain provisions of the TEU. A revised version of Delors II was approved.

1 Jan. 1993: The internal market was completed.

May 1993: The Portuguese and Spanish currencies were further devalued within the ERM, by 6.5% and 8% respectively.

May 1993: Slovenia joined the Council of Europe.

June 1993: The Copenhagen summit set requirements for countries wishing to be considered for EC membership.

July 1993: The ERM virtually collapsed as a result of currency speculation on the European financial markets.

2 Aug. 1993: Permitted ERM fluctuation margins were widened to 15% for all currencies except those of Germany and the Netherlands.

Oct. 1993: Heads of State or Government reaffirmed their commitment to achieving monetary union by the end of the century.

1 Nov. 1993: The TEU entered into force. Member states and their territories were subsequently known as the European Union (EU). The composition of ECU baskets of currencies was 'frozen'.

Dec. 1993: A bilateral agreement between the USA and the EU was followed by the conclusion of the Uruguay Round of GATT negotiations.

1 Jan. 1994: Stage Two of EMU began; the European Monetary Institute (EMI) was established.

1 Jan. 1994: The agreement establishing the EEA entered into force.

1 Feb. 1994: Europe agreements with Poland and Hungary entered into force.

9–10 Feb. 1994: The inaugural session of the Committee of the Regions was held.

30 March 1994: Negotiations on the accession to the EU of Austria, Finland, Norway and Sweden concluded in Brussels.

31 March 1994: Hungary applied for EU membership.

5 April 1994: Poland applied for EU membership.

25 May 1994: The European Investment Fund was established by the Board of Governors of the European Investment Bank.

9–12 June 1994: Direct elections to the European Parliament were held.

12 June 1994: A referendum in Austria endorsed that country's terms of entry to the EU.

24–25 June 1994: The European Council meeting was held in Corfu, Greece; the Treaty concerning the accession of Austria, Finland, Norway and Sweden to the EU was signed; the British Government vetoed the candidacy of Jean-Luc Dehaene, the Prime Minister of Belgium, as the next President of the Commission.

15 July 1994: An extraordinary meeting of the European Council was held in Brussels; Jacques Santer, then Prime Minister of Luxembourg, was designated to succeed Jacques Delors as President of the Commission.

19–26 July 1994: Klaus Hänsch was elected President of the new European Parliament; Jacques Santer was formally appointed President of the Commission.

19 Aug. 1994: The Council of Ministers (officially known as the Council of the European Union from Nov. 1993) extended the Generalized System of Preferences (GSP) to South Africa.

16 Oct. 1994: A referendum in Finland approved that country's accession to the EU.

31 Oct. 1994: The Council of Ministers designated the 20 members of the new, enlarged Commission.

13 Nov. 1994: A referendum in Sweden approved that country's accession to the EU.

27–28 Nov. 1994: A referendum in Norway rejected accession to the EU.

Jan. 1995: The European Training Foundation (ETF) began operations in Turin, Italy.

1 Jan. 1995: Austria, Finland and Sweden became the 13th, 14th and 15th member states of the EU. Austria joined the EMS.

24 Jan. 1995: The new Commission formally took office, under the presidency of Jacques Santer.

1 Feb. 1995: Europe Agreements with Bulgaria, the Czech Republic, Romania and Slovakia entered into force.

March 1995: The Spanish and Portuguese currencies were devalued within the ERM, by 7% and 3.5% respectively.

26 March 1995: The date was agreed by Belgium, France, Germany, Luxembourg, Netherlands, Portugal and Spain for the opening of their common borders in accordance with the Schengen Agreement; France did not at first fully implement the accord.

2 June 1995: EU ministers responsible for foreign affairs met in Messina, Italy, on the 40th anniversary of the original Messina Conference, to discuss the agenda of the Intergovernmental Conference (IGC), which was scheduled to begin in 1996. The Reflection Group, the body responsible for preparing the IGC agenda, also attended the meeting and held its own inaugural session the following day.

12 June 1995: Europe Agreements were signed with Estonia, Latvia and Lithuania.

12 July 1995: The EU's first Ombudsman, Jacob Magnus Söderman, was elected by the European Parliament.

26 July 1995: The Europol Convention, an agreement to establish a European Police Office, was signed in Brussels. It entered into force on 1 Oct.

17 Sept. 1995: The first direct elections of Swedish MEPs took place.

26 Sept. 1995: The European Monitoring Centre for Drugs and Drug Addiction, based in Lisbon, became operational.

Oct. 1995: Latvia applied for EU membership.

Nov. 1995: The Maghreb and Mashreq agreement countries, Cyprus, Israel, Malta and Turkey and the EU finalized an agreement on the establishment of a Euro-Mediterranean Economic Area (EMEA).

Dec. 1995: The European Council confirmed that Stage Three of EMU was planned to begin on 1 Jan. 1999; the proposed single currency would be officially known as the euro. An accord was signed by the EU creating two self-governing entities within Bosnia and Herzegovina, with 51% of territory allocated to the Muslim-Croat Federation, and 49% to the Bosnian Serbs.

17 Jan. 1996: The Czech Republic applied to join the EU.

18 Jan. 1996: Bernhard Friedmann was elected President of the Court of Auditors.

26 Feb. 1996: A Euro-Mediterranean Association Agreement was signed with Morocco.

March 1996: The first Asia-Europe meeting (ASEM) was held in Bangkok, Thailand, between representatives of EU member states and 10 East Asian countries; the EU-Korea framework agreement was initialled.

29 March 1996: The European Council opened the IGC in Turin, Italy, on revision of the TEU; issues discussed included unemployment, justice and home affairs.

22 April 1996: Partnership and Co-operation Agreements were signed with Armenia, Azerbaijan and Georgia.

June 1996: A Europe Agreement was signed with Slovenia; ministers responsible for energy from the EU member states and 12 Mediterranean countries met in Trieste, Italy, to discuss the development of a Euro-Mediterranean gas and electricity network.

10 June 1996: Slovenia applied for EU membership.

21 June 1996: Co-operation Agreements were signed with Chile and Uzbekistan.

13 Oct. 1996: The first elections in Austria to the European Parliament took place.

14 Oct. 1996: Finland joined the EMS.

28 Oct. 1996: A Co-operation Agreement was signed with the Republic of Korea.

Nov. 1996: Malta announced its intention to freeze its application for EU membership. Non-preferential Co-operation Agreements were signed with Cambodia and Laos.

25 Nov. 1996: The Italian currency was readmitted to the ERM.

13–14 Dec. 1996: The European Council meeting in Dublin, Ireland, agreed a stability and growth pact for EMU; the designs for euro bank notes were presented.

14 Jan. 1997: José-María Gil-Robles Gil Delgado was elected President of the European Parliament.

May 1997: The British Government approved the Social Charter which was to be incorporated into the Treaty of Amsterdam (see below).

13 May 1997: The first Euro-Mediterranean Energy Forum opened in Brussels.

16–17 June 1997: The Treaty of Amsterdam, amending and updating the TEU agreed at Maastricht in 1991, was drawn up at the IGC in Amsterdam, the Netherlands.

July 1997: An Economic partnership, political co-ordination and Co-operation Agreement and an interim Trade Agreement were signed with Mexico.

15 July 1997: Agenda 2000 was published by the Commission, including proposals for the strengthening and enlargement of the EU.

2 Oct. 1997: The Treaty of Amsterdam was signed by EU ministers responsible for foreign affairs.

14 Oct. 1997: The Commission reported that Greece alone would fail to fulfil the conditions required to join the single currency.

1 Feb. 1998: Europe Agreements with Estonia, Latvia and Lithuania entered into force.

1 March 1998: A Partnership and Co-operation Agreement with Ukraine came into force, as did the Euro-Mediterranean Association Agreement with Tunisia.

12 March 1998: The European Conference in London took place to discuss the enlargement of the EU. Participants were the Heads of State or Government of EU Member States and those of the 10 applicant countries of Central and Eastern Europe and Cyprus.

16 March 1998: The Greek currency was admitted to the ERM.

25 March 1998: The Commission recommended that 11 member states (namely Austria, Belgium, Finland, France, Germany, Ireland, Italy, Luxembourg, the Netherlands, Portugal and Spain) participate in the EMU from 1 Jan. 1999. Denmark and the UK confirmed that they would not participate in the EMU and Greece and Sweden failed to meet the necessary conditions. Accession Partnerships were approved for the 10 applicant countries of Central and Eastern Europe (Bulgaria, the Czech Republic, Estonia, Hungary, Latvia, Lithuania, Poland, Romania, Slovakia and Slovenia).

30 March 1998: Accession negotiations began with Cyprus, the Czech Republic, Estonia, Hungary, Poland and Slovenia. Accession process began with Bulgaria, Latvia, Lithuania, Romania and Slovakia.

3–4 April 1998: The second Asia-Europe Meeting (ASEM) was held in London; it was agreed that the ASEM Trust Fund was to be established to assist Asia during its financial crisis.

May 1998: The EU-US Transatlantic Economic Partnership was launched at EU-US summit meeting.

3 May 1998: Member states to participate in EMU were formally selected.

26 May 1998: The Council of Ministers agreed on the appointment of Wim Duisenberg as the first President of the ECB.

1 June 1998: The ECB began operating in Frankfurt, Germany.

July 1998: A Partnership and Co-operation Agreement with Moldova and a Co-operation Agreement with Yemen came into force.

31 Dec. 1998: Conversion rates between the euro and the currencies of the 11 member states participating in the EMU were irrevocably fixed.

1 Jan. 1999: The euro came into existence for the member states participating in EMU, replacing the ECU.

14 Jan. 1999: The European Parliament held a vote of censure on the dismissal of the Commission following accusations of fraudulent behaviour. The vote was defeated but the Committee of Independent Experts was established to investigate the Commission's policy towards fraud.

17 Feb. 1999: The Commission recommended that accession negotiations with Malta begin, following Malta's renewed application after a change of government in 1998.

15 March 1999: The Commission collectively resigned, following allegations in a report by the Committee of Independent Experts of fraud, mismanagement and nepotism.

24 March 1999: The Council of Ministers nominated Romano Prodi as the new President of the Commission.

1 May 1999: The Treaty of Amsterdam entered into force.

5 May 1999: The European Parliament approved Prodi's nomination.

10–13 June 1999: Elections to the European Parliament were held.

28–29 June 1999: At the first summit between the EU's Heads of State or Government and the countries of South America, Central America and the Caribbean the Rio Declaration was adopted, which stressed the need for a strategic partnership between the two regions.

20 July 1999: Nicole Fontaine was elected President of the European Parliament.

15 Sept. 1999: The European Parliament approved a new Commission.

19 Oct. 1999: The first Annual Report on Human Rights was published by the Council of Ministers.

10–11 Dec. 1999: The European Council, meeting in Helsinki, Finland, agreed to open accession negotiations with Bulgaria, Latvia, Lithuania, Malta, Romania and Slovakia; Turkey was approved as an applicant country.

15 Jan. 2000: Accession negotiations between representatives of the EU and Bulgaria, Latvia, Lithuania, Malta, Romania and Slovakia began in Brussels.

3 May 2000: The Commission recommended that Greece become the 12th member state to participate in the single European currency.

19–20 June 2000: In Santa Maria de Feira, Portugal, the European Council approved Greece's entry into the eurozone.

June 2000: The Cotonou Agreement, which succeeded Lomé IV, was signed.

28 June 2000: The first EU-India summit was held in Lisbon, Portugal.

22 Sept. 2000: The ECB, the US Federal Reserve and the Bank of Japan jointly intervened in support of the euro.

28 Sept. 2000: In a referendum in Denmark a majority of the population voted against EMU.

7 Dec. 2000: The Charter of Fundamental Rights was jointly proclaimed by the Presidents of the European Council, the Commission and the European Parliament at the European Council meeting in Nice, France.

2 Jan. 2001: Greece became a member of the eurozone.

26 Feb. 2001: the Treaty of Nice was signed, following the European Council meeting of Dec. 2000, which amended the TEU and earlier treaties establishing the EC.

7 June 2001: A majority of the population of Ireland rejected the Treaty of Nice in a referendum.

21 Sept. 2001: In Brussels an extraordinary European Council assessed the effects of the terrorist attacks on the USA of 11 Sept and set guidelines for the EU's response to the attacks.

14 Dec. 2001: In advance of the official changeover to the single European currency, euro coins were made available in the 12 participating member states.

14–15 Dec. 2001: At a meeting of the European Council in Laeken, Belgium, it was agreed to conclude negotiations with the countries ready for accession by the end of Dec. 2002 in order to allow those states to participate in elections to the European Parliament scheduled for 2004.

1 Jan. 2002: Euro bank notes and coins entered into circulation in the 12 countries of the eurozone.

15 Jan. 2002: Pat Cox was elected President of the European Parliament.

28 Feb. 2002: The European Convention met for the first time. Presided over by Valéry Giscard d'Estaing, it was charged with proposing reforms of the EU in order primarily to bring it closer to its citizens and to ensure that it could function with an enlarged membership.

28 Feb. 2002: The period of dual circulation of national currencies and the euro ended.

22 April 2002: An Association Agreement was signed with Algeria.

23 July 2002: After 50 years in force, the Treaty of Paris expired and the ECSC was disbanded.

19 Oct. 2002: In a second referendum, the Treaty of Nice was accepted by a majority of the population of Ireland.

18 Nov. 2002: An Association Agreement was signed with Chile.

12–13 Dec. 2002: Accession negotiations with 10 candidate countries were concluded at the Copenhagen European Council.

15 Jan. 2003: The first EU police mission was inaugurated in Bosnia and Herzegovina.

SELECT CHRONOLOGY OF THE EUROPEAN UNION

1 Feb. 2003: The Treaty of Nice entered into force.

21 Feb. 2003: Croatia applied for membership of the EU.

8 March 2003: In a referendum on accession, a majority of the population of Malta voted in favour of joining the EU.

14 March 2003: The Security Pact was signed with NATO in Athens, Greece, which delineated the areas in Europe where NATO was not active and in which EU forces might thus be deployed.

23 March 2003: A majority of the population of Slovenia voted in a referendum to accede to the EU.

31 March 2003: In the EU's first ever military operation, Operation Concordia, a force of 300 lightly armed peacekeepers was deployed in the former Yugoslav republic of Macedonia (FYRM).

9 April 2003: The European Parliament voted in favour of the 10 applicant countries becoming members of the EU in 2004.

12 April 2003: In both Hungary and Malta a majority of the population voted in favour of joining the EU.

16 April 2003: In Athens a treaty of accession was signed between the EU and the 10 applicant countries.

24 April 2003: Greek Cypriots rejected a United Nations-brokered plan to reunify the divided island. As a consequence, only the southern part of the island joined the EU on 1 May 2004.

8 May 2003: The Polish population voted overwhelmingly in a referendum in favour of joining the EU.

11 May 2003: A majority of Lithuanians voted in favour of EU membership.

16 May 2003: It was disclosed that French prosecutors would be investigating Eurostat, EU's statistical office in Luxembourg, following allegations of false accounting.

18 May 2003: Despite a low turnout, a majority of Slovakians voted in a referendum to join the EU.

19 May 2003: The EU ministers responsible for defence declared that a new 60,000-strong 'rapid-reaction force' was ready for peacekeeping operations.

11 June 2003: Talks to discuss radical reform of the CAP opened in Brussels.

13 June 2003: The European Convention adopted a Draft Treaty Establishing a Constitution for Europe.

13–14 June 2003: A majority of participants in a referendum in the Czech Republic voted in favour of joining the EU.

20 June 2003: Valéry Giscard d'Estaing presented Parts I and II of the European Convention's Draft Treaty Establishing a Constitution for Europe to EU leaders at the Thessaloniki European Council. EU leaders agreed that the document would form the basis of negotiations in an IGC to be opened in the autumn.

26 June 2003: EU agricultural ministers agreed to reduce substantially subsidies granted to farmers under the CAP.

9 July 2003: The European Commission opened disciplinary proceedings against the former Director-General of Eurostat, Yves Franchet; Eurostat appointed Michel van den Abeele as its new head.

18 July 2003: The final text of the Draft Treaty Establishing a Constitution for Europe was forwarded to the European Council.

14 Sept. 2003: A referendum on joining the euro took place in Sweden, where a clear majority rejected membership.

20 Sept. 2003: A referendum on joining the EU was held in Latvia and a large majority voted in favour of membership.

4 Oct. 2003: An IGC opened in Rome. It had the task of drawing up the final version of a Treaty Establishing a Constitution for Europe.

1 Nov. 2003: Jean-Claude Trichet succeeded Dr Wilhelm Duisenberg as President of the ECB.

12–13 Dec. 2003: The European Council met in Brussels but the national leaders were unable to reach agreement on a Treaty Establishing a Constitution for Europe, owing to strong opposition from both Poland and Spain to the proposed new voting procedures in the Council.

22 March 2004: The FYRM applied for membership of the EU.

1 May 2004: The EU enlarged for the fifth time when it admitted 10 new states (Cyprus, Czech Republic, Estonia, Hungary, Latvia, Lithuania, Malta, Poland, Slovakia and Slovenia).

1 May 2004: Procedures for the formulation of EU competition policy (specifically restrictive practices and mergers) were overhauled.

5 May 2004: The European Parliament formally approved the new Commissioners from the 10 new member states.

10–13 June 2004: Elections were held for the sixth time across the EU, for the 732-seat European Parliament.

14 June 2004: Bulgaria completed accession negotiations with the EU.

17–18 June 2004: The European Council met in Brussels and finally agreed a Treaty Establishing a Constitution for Europe, but failed to find general consensus on a candidate for President of the European Commission. It also agreed to open accession negotiations with Croatia.

29 June 2004: José Manuel Durão Barroso was nominated as President designate of the Commission and Javier Solana was re-appointed as Secretary-General of the Council and High Representative for CFSP. The European Council also agreed that Solana would be appointed as EU Minister for Foreign Affairs on the day that the Constitution for Europe came into force.

20 July 2004: The recently elected European Parliament voted for Josep Borrell Fontelles as its President.

22 July 2004: The European Parliament approved the appointment of José Manuel Barroso as the new President of the European Commission.

12 Aug. 2004: José Manuel Barroso, the President-designate of the European Commission, presented the policy portfolios of the 24 nominee Commissioners who were due to commence duties on 1 Nov. 2004.

26 Oct. 2004: President-designate Barroso withdrew his proposal for the team of European Commissioners, following criticism and concerns in the European Parliament about three of his team. Two (one from Italy and one from Latvia) were withdrawn in favour of two new candidates from those member states, and the portfolio of a third was changed.

29 Oct. 2004: The Heads of State and Government and the EU Foreign Ministers signed the Treaty establishing a Constitution for Europe in Rome.

18 Nov. 2004: The European Parliament approved the new Barroso Commission. There were 449 votes in favour to 149 votes against, and 82 abstentions.

14 Dec. 2004: Romania completed accession negotiations with the EU.

26 Jan. 2005: The European Commission published its Strategic Objectives for 2005–09.

1 Feb. 2005: An Association Agreement between the EU and Croatia came into force.

20 Feb. 2005: A referendum on the Treaty establishing a Constitution for Europe took place in Spain. The vote approved the so-called constitutional treaty.

13 April 2005: The European Parliament endorsed the entry of Romania and Bulgaria into the EU. Actual accessions were scheduled to begin from 2007.

SELECT CHRONOLOGY OF THE EUROPEAN UNION

29 May 2005: A referendum on the Treaty establishing a Constitution for Europe was held in France and a majority of the voters (nearly 55%) rejected the treaty.

1 June 2005: A referendum on the Treaty establishing a Constitution for Europe was held in the Netherlands and a majority of the voters (nearly 63%) rejected the treaty.

17 June 2005: The European Council met in Luxembourg to discuss the way ahead following the referendum results in France and the Netherlands, but the summit meeting quickly became embroiled in controversy over the future funding of the EU and specifically the issue of the UK budget rebate.

3 Oct. 2005: Accession negotiations were launched with Turkey and Croatia.

16 Dec. 2005: The European Council reached agreement on the financing of the EU for the period 2007–13.

16 Feb. 2006: The European Parliament adopted a first-reading report on the Services Directive (the so-called Bolkestein Directive) that sought to open up the single market for services.

16 June 2006: In the absence of agreement on what to do with the Treaty Establishing a Constitution for Europe, the European Council agreed to extend the 'period of reflection' on the future of the EU.

15 Dec. 2006: The European Council decided to partially suspend accession negotiations with Turkey.

1 Jan. 2007: The EU enlarged for a sixth time when it admitted Bulgaria and Romania as member states. On the same day Slovenia joined the eurozone.

16 Jan. 2007: Hans-Gert Pöttering was elected as the new President of the European Parliament.

24–25 March 2007: EU leaders adopted the Berlin Declaration on the occasion of the 50th anniversary of the signature of the Treaties of Rome. The Declaration outlined some of the EU's key objectives.

21–22 June 2007: The European Council met in Brussels and adopted a mandate for an intergovernmental conference (IGC) to draw up a new reform treaty to replace the Treaty establishing a Constitution for Europe before the end of 2007. It also agreed that Cyprus and Malta should join the eurozone and adopt the euro on 1 Jan. 2008.

23 July 2007: The IGC opened in Brussels to consider the text for the draft reform treaty.

18–19 Oct. 2007: At a Summit in Lisbon, the final text was agreed for the reform treaty, the Treaty of Lisbon.

12 Dec. 2007: The Presidents of the European Commission, the European Parliament and the Council of the European Union signed the Charter of Fundamental Rights of the European Union. The Charter gives European citizens various rights that are legally binding on the institutions and bodies of the EU and on the member states when they are implementing EU law.

13 Dec. 2007: The Treaty of Lisbon was signed in Lisbon by the Heads of State or Government of the EU's member states. It was scheduled to come into force on 1 Jan. 2009, providing it had been ratified by all 27 member states.

21 Dec. 2007: The Czech Republic, Estonia, Hungary, Latvia, Lithuania, Malta, Poland, Slovakia and Slovenia were incorporated in the Schengen area.

1 Jan. 2008: Cyprus and Malta joined the eurozone.

30 March 2008: The EU-US Air Transport Agreement (also known as the Open Skies agreement) took effect, allowing European and US airlines to fly without restriction to any points in Europe and the USA.

12 June 2008: The Irish electorate rejected the Treaty of Lisbon in a referendum.

18–19 June 2008: The European Council decided to continue the ratification process for the Treaty of Lisbon.

12 Dec. 2008: At a summit meeting in Brussels, agreement was reached on action to deal with both climate change and the deteriorating global economic and financial situation, and the Irish Government promised to hold a further referendum on the Lisbon Treaty if enough concessions were offered to make acceptance by Irish voters likely. On the same day Switzerland was incorporated in the Schengen area.

1 Jan. 2009: Slovakia joined the eurozone.

4–7 June 2009: Elections were held across the EU to the European Parliament.

18–19 June 2009: At an EU summit in Brussels, the Irish government was given guarantees that the Lisbon Treaty would not affect Irish policy on military neutrality, taxes and abortion, and so agreed to move forward with a second Lisbon Treaty referendum in Ireland on 2 Oct. 2009.

14 July 2009: Polish MEP Jerzy Buzek was elected President of the European Parliament.

16 July 2009: Iceland applied for membership of the EU.

16 Sept. 2009: The European Parliament approved the appointment of José Manuel Barroso for a second five-year term as President of the European Commission.

3 Oct. 2009: Voters in Ireland approved the Treaty of Lisbon in a second referendum.

20 Nov. 2009: The European Council appointed Herman van Rompuy as its first permanent President, and Catherine Ashton as the first High Representative of the Union for Foreign Affairs and Security Policy.

1 Dec. 2009: The Treaty of Lisbon entered into force.

22 Dec. 2009: Serbia applied for membership of the EU.

9 Feb. 2010: The European Parliament voted to approve the second Barroso Commission.

11 Feb. 2010: At an informal meeting in Brussels, heads of state and government agreed to support the Greek Government in its attempts to meet the Stability Programme targets for 2010. President of the European Commission, José Manuel Barroso, presented his priorities for the Europe 2020 strategy, including the creation of a new economic model.

26 March 2010: Europe 2020 targets were approved at a meeting of the European Council and the eurozone countries agreed to help Greece deal with its financial deficit.

7 May 2010: Heads of state and government within the eurozone agreed a policy of greater fiscal consolidation, stronger economic co-ordination and budgetary surveillance in order to help protect the euro.

7 June 2010: EU Ministers of Finance approved a €4,400m. European Financial Stability Facility (EFSF) to provide rapid assistance to eurozone members.

17 June 2010: The 10-year Europe 2020 strategy, seeking economic revival and growth, was approved at a meeting of the European Council. A decision was also taken to open accession negotiations with Iceland.

21 June 2010: EU institutions reached agreement on the structure of the European External Action Service (EEAS), and how it would function.

1 Dec. 2010: The EEAS was formally established, under the authority of the High Representative of the Union for Foreign Affairs and Security Policy, Catherine Ashton.

17 Dec. 2010: Montenegro was formally awarded the status of a candidate country for EU membership.

1 Jan. 2011: Estonia became a member of the eurozone.

30 June 2011: Accession negotiations with Croatia were closed.

2 July 2011: Four days after the Greek Vouli (Parliament) approved a programme of austerity measures, deemed necessary by the EU and the IMF in order to mitigate the deepening financial crisis, EU Ministers of Finance approved the disbursement of further lending to Greece, temporarily alleviating the threat of default.

2 Oct. 2011: The Greek Government indicated that it would not satisfy budget deficit targets agreed with the EU and the IMF, and as part of its draft 2012 budget agreed further harsh austerity measures.

11 Oct. 2011: The Slovakian legislature failed to support EU plans to enhance the powers of the EFSF. The Government of Iveta Radičová subsequently collapsed, owing to opposition to the plans by coalition partner the Freedom and Solidarity Party. The expanded EFSF was finally ratified by Slovakia two days later, after Radičová secured the support of opposition party Direction-Social Democracy, by agreeing to call early legislative elections.

26–27 Oct. 2011: EU leaders, meeting in Brussels, reached agreement on emergency measures designed to resolve the eurozone debt crisis. The agreement aimed to recapitalize private banks; provide for losses of one-half of their holdings of Greek debt; and increase the financial strength of the EFSF.

9 Dec. 2011: The majority of EU member states reached agreement in principle on new fiscal arrangements, designed to increase fiscal discipline and convergence in the eurozone. The so-called fiscal compact required member states to maintain a balanced budget (or a deficit of no more than 0.5% of nominal GDP). Agreement was reached on increased co-operation on economic policy, and an acceleration of arrangements for the introduction of the European Stability Mechanism (ESM).

17 Jan. 2012: Martin Schulz was elected President of the European Parliament.

21 Feb. 2012: Eurozone Ministers of Finance formally approved a €130,000m. rescue plan for Greece, agreed in Oct., with a number of additional pre-conditions, including an undertaking by Greece to reduce its debt from 160% to 120.5% of GDP within eight years, and to accept a permanent EU economic monitoring mission.

1 March 2012: Herman Van Rompuy was re-elected as President of the European Council. On the same day Serbia was awarded the status of a candidate country for accession to the EU.

2 March 2012: The Treaty on Stability, Co-ordination and Governance in the Economic Union (TSCG or Fiscal Compact) was signed at a European Council meeting in Brussels (without the participation of the Czech Republic and the UK).

17 June 2012: Repeat legislative elections in Greece (following inconclusive elections in the previous month), resulted in the conservative New Democracy winning 29.7% of the votes cast and 129 seats in the Vouli, and were widely interpreted as indicating an endorsement of continued Greek membership of the eurozone.

25 June 2012: Cyprus became the latest member state (after Greece, Ireland, Portugal and Spain) to request financial assistance from the EFSF/ESM.

28–29 June 2012: The European Council met in Brussels, and a parallel summit of the member nations of the eurozone took place to discuss the sovereign debt crisis; the German Chancellor, Angela Merkel, notably abandoned her objections to the use of EU funds for the recapitalization of banks. A Compact for Growth and Jobs was also adopted. On 29 June membership negotiations with Montenegro commenced.

8 Oct. 2012: The ESM was inaugurated. The ESM had been established by a treaty signed on 2 Feb. by representatives of the 17 eurozone member countries, meeting in Brussels, Belgium, and replacing a treaty signed in July 2011. The ESM superseded the EFSF and the European Financial Stability Mechanism (EFSM), which remained responsible for lending approved prior to the establishment of the ESM.

12 Oct. 2012: It was announced that the Nobel Peace Prize was to be awarded to the EU.

7 Nov. 2012: The Greek Vouli (Parliament) approved fresh austerity measures, in an effort to secure further international lending. The approval of the measures (with 153 votes cast in favour, and 128 against), took place amid violent protests by anti-austerity demonstrators.

8 Nov. 2012: Following the certification by the World Trade Organization (WTO) of reduced banana tariffs, which had been agreed under the Geneva Agreement in Dec. 2009, the EU and the 10 main banana-producing countries signed a Mutually Agreed Solution, ending eight pending banana dispute settlement proceedings at the WTO.

1 Jan. 2013: The Fiscal Compact entered into effect.

11 March 2013: An EU-wide ban on the sale of cosmetics developed through the use of animal testing outside the EU member states came into effect.

25 March 2013: Following the approval by eurozone ministers of finance, in mid-March, of lending to Cyprus, contingent on that country's imposition of a levy on bank deposits, an agreement was finally reached between Cyprus and the EU, when EU ministers of finance approved the terms required for the disbursement of lending: deposits under €100,000 were to be exempt from any losses, but larger deposits in the country's two largest banks, the Bank of Cyprus and the Cyprus Popular Bank (Laiki Bank), were to be frozen and subject to deductions of up to 40%; some of Laiki Bank's assets were to be merged into the Bank of Cyprus, and the institution closed.

9 April 2013: The new Schengen Information System (SIS II) commenced operations, with the aim of improving security and facilitating free movement within the Schengen area.

14 April 2013: Croatia, in advance of its accession to the EU, held elections to the European Parliament to elect 12 representatives to serve until 2014.

30 May 2013: Agreement was reached by the Council of Ministers and the European Parliament on reform of the CFP.

13 June 2013: Iceland withdrew its application for EU membership.

26 June 2013: Political agreement on the reform of the CAP was reached.

28 June 2013: The Council endorsed the initiation of accession negotiations with Serbia; these were expected to commence by Jan. 2014.

1 July 2013: Croatia became the 28th member of the EU.

3 July 2013: The European Parliament endorsed the conclusions of negotiations with the Council on the Multi-annual Financial Framework (MFF) for 2014–20. Also on 3 July Emily O'Reilly was elected as the new European Ombudsman.

8 July 2013: Negotiations between the EU and the USA commenced, with the aim of creating a transatlantic free trade zone.

15 Oct. 2013: The Economic and Financial Affairs Council of Ministers (ECOFIN) adopted regulations providing for the creation of a single supervisory mechanism (SSM) to oversee financial institutions. The SSM became operational in 2014, and was to co-operate closely with national regulatory authorities, with the aim of safeguarding financial stability.

2 Dec. 2013: Following approval by the Parliament (on 19 Nov.) of the MFF for 2014–20, it was adopted by the Council.

1 Jan. 2014: Latvia became the 18th member of the eurozone.

21 Jan. 2014: Accession negotiations with Serbia commenced.

20 Feb. 2014: EU ministers responsible for foreign affairs voted in favour of the imposition of sanctions against senior

Ukrainian officials, after more than 75 people were reportedly shot and killed by security forces during action to remove demonstrators from central Kyiv on 19–20 Feb. The protests had been prompted by the failure of the Ukrainian President, Viktor Yanukovych, to sign an Association Agreement and accompanying agreement on free trade with the EU.

22–25 May 2014: Elections to the eighth European Parliament took place, with an overall rate of participation by the electorate of the EU-28 of 42.5%.

4 June 2014: The European Commission recommended that Lithuania be admitted to the eurozone from 1 Jan. 2015. On 16 July 2014 the European Parliament approved Lithuania's admission to the eurozone, following the Council's approval on 27 June.

24 June 2014: The European Commission announced that Albania was to be granted candidate status, which was confirmed at the European Council of 26–27 June.

26–27 June 2014: The European Council adopted the decision (after a formal vote by qualified majority), to propose Jean-Claude Juncker (a former Prime Minister of Luxembourg) as its candidate for President of the European Commission in 2014–19.

27 June 2014: Association Agreements were signed with Georgia, Moldova and Ukraine, each of which made provision for a Deep and Comprehensive Free Trade Area (DCFTA). (The political provisions of the Association Agreement with Ukraine had been signed in March, following the removal of Yanukovych.)

25 July 2014: A Stabilization and Association Agreement (SAA) was initialled with Kosovo; it was adopted by the European Commission in April 2015.

30–31 Aug. 2014: A special Council meeting agreed to the appointment of Donald Tusk as President of the European Council and Federica Mogherini as High Representative.

26 Sept. 2014: Negotiations were concluded on a Comprehensive Economic and Trade Agreement (CETA) between the EU and Canada.

1 Nov. 2014: The new European Commission, led by Jean-Claude Juncker, took office. On the same day Mogherini formally became High Representative of the Union for Foreign Affairs and Security Policy.

4 Nov. 2014: The ECB-led SSM commenced operations.

1 Dec. 2014: Donald Tusk officially took office as President of the European Council.

1 Jan. 2015: Lithuania formally adopted the the euro as its national currency, becoming the 19th member of the eurozone.

9 March 2015: A programme of quantitive easing began, known as the Public Sector Purchase Programme.

6 May 2015: The Commission published plans for a new, three-pillar Digital Single Market.

9 May 2015: Amid a severe migration crisis, precipitated by unrest in the Middle East and North Africa, the Commission published a European Agenda on Migration, which proposed the compulsory relocation within the EU of up to 20,000 refugees from the region, and the redistribution up to 40,000 asylum seekers from Greece and Italy (the countries most affected by unauthorized border crossings and asylum applications) to other member states, over a two-year period.

1 June 2015: An SAA with Bosnia and Herzegovina entered into force, following its approval by the Council in March.

26 June 2015: At a summit meeting of the European Council, recently re-elected British Prime Minister David Cameron set out the Government's plans for a referendum to be held in the UK by the end of 2017 to decide whether the country should remain part of the EU.

1 July 2015: Jeppe Tranholm-Mikkelsen, who had been named on 21 April as Secretary-General of the Council of the European Union, formally took office, succeeding Uwe Corsepius.

30 June 2015: Agreement was reached to abandon so-called roaming charges for mobile phone use throughout the EU from 2017 as a part of a major overhaul of telecommunications legislation.

19 Aug. 2015: The Commission signed an agreement with Greece, following approval by the Board of Governors of the ESM of new lending, worth up to €86,000m. over a period of three years. A Memorandum of Understanding committed Greece to further widespread economic reforms. The agreement followed months of uncertainty and new fears that Greece might be compelled to exit the eurozone.

9 Sept. 2015: With the publication of the Second Implementation Package for the European Agenda on Migration, the Commission sought to introduce additional emergency measures to provide for the relocation of some 120,000 migrants from Greece and Italy over a three-year period.

2 Dec. 2015: Negotiations with Viet Nam, on the terms of a free trade agreement, were concluded.

1 Jan. 2016: The DCFTA with Ukraine, forming part of the Association Agreement reached with that country in 2014, entered into effect. (However, on 6 April a referendum held in the Netherlands failed to support ratification of the Association Agreement.) Also on 1 Jan. the Single Resolution Mechanism become operational, implementing the EU's Bank Recovery and Resolution Directive for the countries of the eurozone.

25 Jan. 2016: A European Counter Terrorism Centre was established, under Europol, and based in the Hague.

15 Feb. 2016: Bosnia and Herzegovina formally applied for membership of the EU.

11 March 2016: Negotiations on a Political Dialogue and Co-operation Agreement (PDCA) between Cuba and the EU were concluded.

18 March 2016: EU heads of state and of government reached an agreement with Turkey, which aimed to stop 'irregular migration' to the EU, primarily via Greece. The accord provided for the return of migrants crossing into Greek territory and considered not to be in immediate need of international protection; the EU pledged to accept a Syrian refugee from inside Turkey for each migrant returned to that country, and to provide up to €6,000m. in assistance by the end of 2018, together with the acceleration of visa liberalization for Turkish citizens.

1 April 2016: The SAA with Kosovo entered into force.

23 June 2016: The UK held a referendum on its continuing membership of the EU. Voters were asked whether they wished the UK to remain a member of the Union, or to leave the organization: 51.9% supported an exit from the EU (widely referred to as Brexit), while 48.1% backed remaining. The results highlighted deep divisions within the UK, as 62.0% of voters in Scotland, 55.8% of voters in Northern Ireland and 95.9% of voters in Gibraltar voted to remain in the EU, as did many of those in some of the major cities in England, including Liverpool, Manchester and London. Turnout was registered at 72.2%. British Prime Minister Cameron announced his resignation on 24 June.

28 June 2016: Federica Mogherini presented a new Global Strategy on Foreign and Security Policy at a meeting of EU leaders in Brussels.

1 July 2016: Association Agreements with Georgia and Moldova entered into effect. On the same day the European Police College (CEPOL) changed its name to the European Union Agency for Law Enforcement Training, retaining the same acronym.

2 Oct. 2016: A popular referendum was held in Hungary, in opposition to EU plans for the compulsory resettlement of refugees, according to a quota system. Although 98.4% of the votes cast supported the Government's view that the EU should not be able to impose mandatory quotas for the settlement of non-Hungarians, in the absence of approval by the national legislature, a low rate of participation, of 44.0%, meant that the referendum was invalid.

6 Oct. 2016: A new European Border and Coast Guard was launched.

30 Nov. 2016: Plans for a new European Defence Fund were announced by the Commission. The Fund, which sought to provide funding for research and development in the fields of defence technology and equipment, was officially launched on 7 June 2017.

17 Jan. 2017: Antonio Tajani took office as President of the European Parliament, succeeding Martin Schulz.

9 March 2017: Donald Tusk was re-elected to a second term as President of the European Council, with effect from 1 June; Poland (Tusk's country of origin) was the only member state to object to his re-election.

29 March 2017: The British Prime Minister, Theresa May, officially informed European Council President Tusk of the UK's intention to leave both the EU and Euratom, thereby formally invoking Article 50.

29 April 2017: The European Council agreed guidelines for the conduct of Brexit negotiation with the UK Government, which were, in the first instance, to focus on the areas of citizens' rights; the agreement of financial terms (the so-called divorce settlement); and border issues, including the maintenance of the Good Friday Agreement.

1 May 2017: A new regulation on Europol, adopted in May 2016, entered into force, changing the name of the agency to the European Union Agency for Law Enforcement Co-operation, and facilitating the intensification of efforts to combat terrorism, cybercrime and other areas of organized crime.

19 June 2017: Brexit negotiations between the EU and the UK commenced.

7 July 2017: Mariya Gabriel took office as the new Bulgarian Commissioner, with responsibility for Digital Economy and Society, following the departure of Kristalina Georgieva in January (upon her appointment as Chief Executive Officer at the World Bank).

12 July 2017: Karl-Heinz Lambertz took office as President of the Committee of the Regions.

27 July 2017: Werner Hoyer was re-appointed as President of the European Investment Bank.

1 Sept. 2017: The EU-Ukraine Association Agreement was finally fully implemented, following ratification by the Netherlands in May, and approval by the Council in July.

21 Sept. 2017: The CETA reached between the EU and Canada entered into force, on a provisional basis.

A–Z OF THE EUROPEAN UNION

Toni Haastrup, Lee McGowan and David Phinnemore

Note: Words printed in bold type indicate that an entry on the subject so marked is to be found elsewhere in the A–Z of the European Union

A

À LA CARTE EUROPE is a term related to concepts of differentiated integration. Effectively, it suggests that European Union (EU) member states could select the programmes and policies that they wish to adopt and participate in. Opponents of the concept argue that such a development would lead to disarray and confusion, undermine solidarity and make the EU unmanageable. Nevertheless, the idea is not infrequently espoused by some member states as a means of showing their opposition towards certain priorities. After the **United Kingdom** referendum vote in June 2016 in favour of a withdrawal from the EU, the UK was warned that it should not expect to have 'à la carte' access to the **single market** and other benefits of EU membership.

ABATEMENT is the term used to describe the annually calculated 'rebate' received by the **United Kingdom** from the European Communities' **budget** following an agreement reached in 1984 at the **Fontainebleau summit** of the **European Council**. The UK came under increasing pressure to accept a reduction in the rebate. A deal was reached at a meeting of the European Council in December 2005 whereby the UK agreed to a reduction in the rebate, of £1,000m. per year, to invest in the future prosperity of Eastern Europe. The UK subsequently came under further pressure to accept an additional reduction in the rebate. During negotiation of the Multi-annual Financial Framework (MFF) for 2014–20 the UK insisted that there be no further amendment of the abatement. The June 2013 summit of the European Council confirmed that the means of calculating the abatement for the UK would remain unchanged. Following the creation of the rebate, several other member states argued that their EU budgetary burden was excessive, and requested reductions in their contributions, including to the financing of the UK's rebate. This led to a complex system of ad hoc permanent and temporary corrections. For 2014–20 member states other than the UK benefiting from rebates from the EU budget are **Austria**, **Denmark**, **Germany**, the **Netherlands** and **Sweden**.

ABSTENTION: See **Constructive Abstention**

ACCESSION CRITERIA, also referred to as the **Copenhagen criteria**, were adopted at the **Copenhagen summit** of the **European Council** in June 1993, when the European Community committed itself to admitting the countries of **Central and Eastern Europe** (CEE). Accession was, however, to depend on the **candidate countries** meeting the following criteria: having stable institutions guaranteeing democracy, the rule of law, **human rights** and protection of minorities; possessing a functioning market economy and the capacity to cope with the competitive pressures of the **internal market**; and having the ability to take on the obligations of membership, including adherence to the aims of the European Union (EU), notably political, economic and monetary union. In 1995 a **summit meeting** of the European Council held in Madrid, **Spain**, added a further criterion: that the countries seeking membership should possess the administrative capacity to implement the *acquis communautaire*. Formally, countries in the **Western Balkans** also have to pursue regional co-operation before they can be admitted to the EU. In addition, states are required to have made every effort to resolve any outstanding border disputes and other related issues. This was agreed in 1999, with a particular view to the division of Cyprus being resolved before **Turkey** could join the EU. Since the **enlargements** of the EU in 2004 and 2007 there has been a noticeable tightening of the criteria. The EU has also placed increased emphasis on its own **integration capacity**. This has led to justifiable claims that accession to the EU is becoming more difficult, and indeed the **European Commission** that took office in 2014 effectively stated that there would be no further accessions to the EU during its five-year term.

ACCESSION NEGOTIATIONS need to be completed before **applicant countries** can join the European Union (EU). They are conducted on a bilateral basis, with the **European Commission** co-ordinating the position of the EU's member states. Recent decades have seen the EU engaged in an unprecedented number of accession negotiations, beginning with Cyprus and five Central and Eastern European countries (the **Czech Republic**, **Estonia**, **Hungary**, **Poland** and **Slovenia**—the 'Luxembourg group') in 1998. In 2000 accession negotiations were opened with **Bulgaria**, **Latvia**, **Lithuania**, **Malta**, **Romania** and **Slovakia**. Negotiations with those applicant countries meeting the **accession criteria**—the Luxembourg group plus Latvia, Lithuania, Malta and Slovakia—were concluded at the **Copenhagen summit** of the **European Council** held on 12–13 December 2002. The **Treaty of Accession** was signed on 16 April 2003. Following **ratification** of the Treaty of Accession, the 10 countries joined the EU on 1 May 2004. The following month, Bulgaria concluded its accession negotiations with the EU. Romania followed suit in December 2004, and a Treaty of Accession was signed on 25 April 2005. Bulgaria and Romania joined the EU on 1 January 2007. Accession negotiations with **Croatia** and **Turkey** were opened on 4 October 2005. Progress in the negotiations with Turkey proved to be particularly slow, partly because the EU insisted on certain benchmarks being met before negotiations were opened and partly owing to political opposition, notably from **France**, to the prospect of Turkish membership. Negotiations with Croatia were completed in 2011, and the Treaty of Accession was signed on 9 December. Croatia became a member of the EU in July 2013. Of the current applicants, the EU opened accession negotiations with **Montenegro** on 29 June 2012 and with **Serbia** on 21 January 2014. The three other candidate states are the **former Yugoslav republic of Macedonia**, **Turkey** and **Albania**. Most recently, Albania was granted candidate status by the European Council of 26–27 June 2014, which was held in **Brussels**, **Belgium**.

ACCESSION PARTNERSHIPS were first adopted by the European Union (EU) for **applicant countries** from **Central and Eastern Europe** in 1998 and were designed to assist them in meeting the **accession criteria** and preparing themselves for membership of the EU. They list priority areas for legal adaptation and administrative reform in the countries concerned and for EU financial assistance through the former **instrument for structural policies for pre-accession** (ISPA), **PHARE** and

SAPARD programmes (which were replaced in January 2007 by the **instrument for pre-accession assistance**). Accession partnerships have since been adopted for **Turkey** and the **former Yugoslav republic of Macedonia**. Similar in purpose and content, and precursors to accession partnerships, **European partnerships** have been developed for other countries of the **Western Balkans** seeking membership of the EU.

ACCESSION TREATY: see **Treaty of Accession**

ACCOUNTABILITY has often been raised as a major issue within the construct of the European Union (EU), as the EU's institutions have been widely perceived to be increasingly remote from the people. Although the EU has a democratically elected **European Parliament**, which has become a co-legislator in many areas, issues about an enduring **democratic deficit** still abound. The issue is presented as one where the citizens are far removed from unaccountable decision makers in **Brussels**. The issue, however, may have been overplayed, as the institutions are accountable to each other and to the public. Indeed, the institutions of the EU have been seeking to promote greater **transparency** and **openness** since the 1990s. The **European Commission** has placed more emphasis on engaging with civil society and on seeking views on its policy ideas through **Green Papers** and wider consultations. It has also sought to ensure tighter financial control over the **budget**. The Council also pledged to make more of its business open to media and public scrutiny.

ACP STATES is the collective title of those African, Caribbean and Pacific developing countries that entered into an **association agreement** with the European Communities (EC) under Articles 182–188 of the **Treaty of Rome** (now Articles 198–204 of the **Treaty on the Functioning of the European Union**) 'to further the interests and prosperity of the inhabitants of these countries and territories in order to lead them to the economic, social and cultural development to which they aspire'. The provisions were originally directed towards the colonies and ex-colonies of the **Six**, and were finalized in the **Yaoundé Conventions** of 1963 and 1969. With the successive rounds of **enlargement**, ex-colonies of new member states have joined the arrangement, which from 1975 was regulated by the **Lomé Convention** (Lomé I-IV). The **Cotonou Agreement** replaced the Conventions in 2000. In parallel and since 2002 the bilateral **economic partnership agreements** (EPAs) were being negotiated to take over the trade dimensions of the ACP-EU relationship. The original 18 participants were known collectively as the Associated African States and Madagascar. The present title was adopted in 1975, and 79 states signed the Cotonou Agreement. ACP states have traditionally been allowed duty-free entry to the European Union market for most of their products on a non-reciprocal basis, and are also eligible to receive both grants from the **European Development Fund** and low-interest loans from the **European Investment Bank**. Preferential treatment for ACP states caused friction between the EC and members of the **World Trade Organization** (WTO), especially the **USA**, which long objected to the preferential treatment given to **banana** producers in Caribbean states. Indeed, the EPAs were a response to a WTO ruling that the Cotonou Agreement was not WTO-compatible. (See also **Development Aid** and **Overseas Countries and Territories**). At 2017 the EU and ACP countries were seeking to negotiate a successor to the Cotonou Agreement in 2020 to align with the Sustainable Development Goals. Negotiations were expected to start in 2018.

ACQUIS COMMUNAUTAIRE is a phrase that collectively describes all the secondary **legislation** of the European Union (EU) passed under the provisions of the **founding treaties** and their subsequent amendments. It covers all the **directives**, **decisions** and **regulations** adopted by the EU. States that apply for EU membership have to accept the *acquis communautaire*.

ACQUIS POLITIQUE is a phrase describing all the **decisions** and **resolutions** adopted by the member states of the European Union (EU) in the field of foreign policy. It is also used in a broader sense to describe the principles and goals underpinning the activities of the EU.

ADDITIONALITY is a principle first applied to the allocation of money from the **European Regional Development Fund** (ERDF) in 1989. It means that ERDF funding is additional to that provided by local and national authorities. The principle is designed to ensure that member states contribute to the financing of infrastructural projects.

ADONNINO REPORTS: See **Committee for a People's Europe**

ADVISORY COMMITTEE FOR THE CO-ORDINATION OF FRAUD PREVENTION (Cocolaf) has responsibility for co-ordinating action by the member states and the **European Commission** to combat fraud affecting the financial interests of the European Union.

ADVISORY COMMITTEES are bodies that advise the **European Commission** on problems and issues in specific areas. They are part of the world of **comitology**. More than 200 such committees exist and include advisory committees on food, consumer products, health and environmental risks, and equal opportunities. The membership of each committee is drawn from experts and professionals in the relevant area.

ADVOCATES-GENERAL: See **Court of Justice**

The *AETR* **JUDGMENT**, sometimes referred to by its English equivalent—the *ERTA* Judgment—was a 1971 ruling by the **Court of Justice**, which established the important principle that, where the European Communities (EC) had an explicit internal competence, they also had a parallel external competence. Its implication was that in such areas of competence, member states could not act independently of the EC. Where a member state entered into an international agreement that conflicted with EC law, the latter took precedence over any obligation arising from the agreement.

AFRICAN, CARIBBEAN AND PACIFIC STATES: See **ACP States**

The **AFRICAN UNION** (AU) is a regional organization that was established on 26 May 2001 in Addis Ababa, Ethiopia as the successor organization to the Organization of African Unity (OAU). It launched the following year in Durban, South Africa. The idea of forming such a body was conceived by the former leader of Libya, Col Muammar al-Qaddafi, and in the Sirte Declaration the AU aspired to 'an integrated, prosperous and peaceful Africa, driven by its own citizens and representing a dynamic force in the global arena'. The AU has some institutions that are similar to the EU's including an Assembly, an Executive Council, a Commission, a Pan-African Parliament (established in March 2004) and an African Court of Justice. The AU comprises 55 African states. **Morocco** became the AU's 55th member in January 2017. The AU's broad aims are: to accelerate the political and socioeconomic integration of the African continent; to promote and defend common positions on key issues that are vital to the states in Africa; to pursue peace and security in Africa; and to work towards the creation and development of democratic institutions, good governance systems and **human rights** across the continent. In accordance with these goals, a number of member states have been suspended from the AU. The AU's secretariat is based in Addis Ababa. Similar to the EU, the AU aims to create an African Economic Community and to introduce a single African currency by 2023. However, the Union recognizes the need to resolve conflicts on the continent and the majority of the AU's activities are to support peace there. The African Peace and Security Architecture (APSA) established by the 2002 Protocol Establishing the Peace and Security Council of the AU seeks to prevent, manage and resolve conflict and crises on the African continent. The EU maintains close relations with the AU through the EU delegation to the organization in Addis Ababa.

AGENDA 2000 was an **enlargement** strategy developed by the **European Commission** in 1997 following a request from the **European Council**. Its objectives were to strengthen growth, **competitiveness** and **employment**; to reform agriculture and structural policies; and to expand the membership of the European Union (EU) eastwards, to include 10 countries from **Central and Eastern Europe** (CEE). The report comprised three sections: the first covered measures to strengthen and reform policies, in particular the **common agricultural policy** and economic and social cohesion (see **cohesion policy**); the second contained recommendations for preparing the EU for enlargement; and the third proposed a new financial framework, covering 2000–06. Also published as part of Agenda 2000 were the Commission's *avis* on the membership applications from the 10 CEE countries. In these, the Commission assessed the extent to which the applicants had met the **accession criteria**. A report on the status of Cyprus was also included.

AGGREGATE MEASURE OF SUPPORT: See **AMS**

AGRICULTURAL POLICY: See **Common Agricultural Policy**

AIR TRANSPORT POLICY was slow to develop towards a level that met the **competition policy** requirements of the European Communities (EC). The airline industry has been dominated by an international **cartel**, the International Air Transport Association (IATA), and by a series of intergovernmental agreements. The emphasis of these was upon the mutual protection by governments of state-owned airlines, their pricing arrangements and access to scheduled routes. The result was an absence of competition, and some of the highest air fares in the world, in terms of cost per kilometre. Before 1986, **European Commission** initiatives were restricted to technical matters relating to, for example, co-operation on accident procedures and noise emissions. Challenges to the government-supported IATA structure were largely left to small, independent airlines.

In April 1986 the **Court of Justice** ruled in the *Nouvelles Frontières* case that EC competition policy also applied to air transport. The European Commission immediately threatened legal action against 10 European airlines unless they substantially modified their price-fixing arrangements. Simultaneously, it sought to persuade the member states to opt for more liberal policies. In April 1987 the airlines indicated that they would comply with the Commission's demands. Subsequently, progress was positive, but slow. In anticipation of the introduction of the **internal market**, and partly because many state-owned airlines were substantial money-losers, governments began to accept a greater degree of private ownership and capital, and also to urge the consolidation of their national companies as a way of warding off foreign competition in a more competitive market. Matters were complicated by the fact that the major carriers, to meet the conditions of the internal market and global developments in air transport, began to seek closer and more formal collaboration, which, in turn, threatened the survival of smaller, independent airlines. However, airline agreements and co-operative arrangements were subject to Commission approval and the EC's **merger policy**. The acceptance of liberalization also varied from one country to another. Full liberalization of the market took place in 1997, when restrictions on European airlines within the European Union (EU) were removed, with the result that airlines were able to operate domestic air services in EU countries other than their own. In 2002 the European Commission adopted proposals for the creation of a **European Aviation Safety Agency** (EASA), as an independent organization within the EC; the EASA began operating in September 2003. In October 2001 the Commission adopted proposals for a Single European Sky (SES), which aimed to establish a single legislative framework for aviation in the EU. Accordingly, a first legislative package, SES I, was adopted by the **European Parliament** and the **European Council** in March 2004. Revised SES regulations, incorporating improvements aimed at addressing environmental challenges and fuel cost efficiency, were adopted in June 2008 as the Single European Sky second package, SES II. In 2013 the European Commission presented its so-called SES II+ package of measures, which aim to challenge the system of state-owned monopolies responsible for providing air navigation services.

AIRBUS is one of the successes of European industrial co-operation. Founded in 1967 as a consortium of European aircraft manufacturers, Airbus aimed to design and build large passenger aircraft that could compete with Boeing, the large US corporation. From 1992, Airbus's share of the large civil aircraft market grew steadily, from over 30% to more than one-half by 2004, and its future success seemed assured with the launch of the new double-decker-style aircraft (Airbus A380) in 2005. This new plane was specifically designed to carry 525–853 passengers (depending on the aircraft's class configuration) and has been marketed to fly to a series of hub international airports. However, Boeing met the challenge by building a smaller plane, able to land in smaller airports.

Airbus currently comprises four partners: British Aerospace, Construcciones Aeronáuticas SA (CASA) of **Spain**, Daimler-Benz Aerospace of **Germany** and Aérospatiale of **France**. Each of the four partners specializes in producing different parts of the aircraft. (Airbus has its European final assembly lines in Toulouse, France; Hamburg, Germany; and Seville, Spain; Airbus opened assembly lines for its A320 model in Tianjin in the People's Republic of China in 2008, and in Mobile, Alabama, **USA**, in July 2015.) Boeing, however, complained about the massive government **subsidies** channelled into Airbus in order to make it viable, and labelled such activity as constituting unfair competition. Tension was particularly acute in the 1980s, until a bilateral agreement on civil aircraft, which capped government support for new aircraft, was reached in June 1992. Nevertheless, relations remained tense, as was evident in the opposition of the European Union (EU) to the planned merger between Boeing and McDonnell Douglas in 1997. This merger aimed to create the world's largest aerospace and defence company. The USA saw EU **competition policy** as another unfair means to protect Airbus, and the issue was only resolved when the **European Commission** sanctioned a merger, providing that many of the clauses that would have tied Boeing customers to the new company for 20 years were removed. In an effort to make Airbus more competitive and more efficient, it was transformed in 1999 into a limited company; it became a single integrated operating company in 2001. Tensions between Airbus and Boeing over the degree of subsidies supporting the activities of both companies became a frequent feature of EU/US trade discussions. In October 2004 both companies launched the largest trade dispute in the short history of the **World Trade Organization** (WTO). However, aware of the economic repercussions of any damaging ruling against them, both parties agreed in January 2005 to resume negotiations in an effort to consider how to cut subsidies. A renewed bitter dispute erupted between both companies in May 2005 centred on the failure of both Airbus and Boeing to agree on the level of subsidies, which led both sides to revive their charges before the WTO.

The ongoing competition between the two international giants continued to intensify, with the launch of a newly designed A350 in July 2006. The new long-haul, mid-sized plane was to compete directly with the Boeing 787 Dreamliner. The A350 has been designed to be more fuel-efficient and is built with carbon composites. The new A350 commenced services in January 2015. By 2016 some 810 A350 planes had been ordered (fewer than the 900 early orders for Boeing's Dreamliner), although only 30 were in operation by that time.

There have been other issues for Airbus. Doubts, for example, were raised at the beginning of 2010 over whether any further progress could be made in the production of Airbus's A400M Atlas military transport aircraft—which was already over budget—without a significant financial contribution from European governments. The member states themselves were divided over the issue; but they could not risk abandoning the venture, as it would open the way for an alternative aircraft, the C-17, from Boeing. The plans for the A400M were launched in 2003 to meet demands from seven European nations (**Belgium**, **France**, **Germany**, **Luxembourg**, **Spain**, **Turkey** and the **United Kingdom**) for a new 'state of the art' plane, which was better equipped to engage in tactical and logistical missions. After the A400M was put through successful flight testing in May 2012 the plane received its European Aviation Safety certification in March 2013 and Airbus delivered the first of the new military aircraft in August. In September 2014 Airbus initiated collaboration with US company Aerion to design a supersonic private business aircraft, with the aim of entering into operation in 2021.

ALBANIA concluded a trade and co-operation agreement with the **European Community** in 1992 that held out the prospect of negotiating an **association agreement**. Progress towards such a goal was hampered in the 1990s by domestic political and economic instability. In 1999, however, the country became part of the **Stabilization and Association Process** that the European Union (EU) launched in the aftermath of the **Kosovo** crisis. This led to assistance under the former **CARDS** programme, and the possibility of opening negotiations on a **stabilization and association agreement** (SAA). Albania is keen to become a member of the EU, a point recognized at a **summit meeting** of the **European Council**, held in Feira, **Portugal** in 2000, when Albania, along with other countries in the **Western Balkans**, was confirmed as a **potential candidate state**. In 2003 EU membership clearly remained a priority for the Albanian Government. Although negotiations on an SAA were opened in February of that year, effectively representing Albania's first step towards eventual EU membership, the then Commission President, Romano Prodi, asserted that substantial problems remained, which required serious consideration by the Albanian authorities before any real progress could be made towards the acquisition of full EU membership. These included suppressing criminal activities and showing evidence of solid economic progress. A **European partnership** was adopted in 2004, however, and negotiations on the SAA were eventually concluded in February 2006. Albania also began to receive pre-accession financial assistance under the new **instrument for pre-accession assistance**, with €213m. allocated for the period 2007–09. A new European partnership was adopted in 2008, the same year that an EU-Albania agreement on visa facilitation, signed in 2007, entered into force. This was followed by the entry into force of the SAA on 1 April 2009, the same day that the country joined the **North Atlantic Treaty Organization**, and Albania's integration with the EU entered a new phase. Further confirmation of this came with the submission of an application for EU membership on 28 April 2009. The Commission's **opinion** in November 2010 was critical of the political situation in the country and of the Government's faltering record on reform; the Commission reached a similar conclusion a year later. In October 2012 the Commission recommended that the European Council give Albania **candidate status**, provided that further reform of the judiciary and public administration were undertaken in advance of legislative elections in June 2013. The EU provided Albania with some €95m. in 2013 to assist with its transitional reforms. On 27 June 2014 the **European Council** granted Albania candidate status. The EU welcomed the adoption of legislation regulating holders of public office in December 2015. The opening of EU accession negotiations remained contingent on the adoption of planned reforms of the judicial system, in accordance with stipulations of the **European Commission**. Membership of the EU is not expected before 2020, at the earliest.

ALDE: See **Group of the Alliance of Liberals and Democrats for Europe**

ALE: See **European Free Alliance**

ALGERIA: See **Maghreb States**

ALLIANCE OF LIBERALS AND DEMOCRATS FOR EUROPE: See **Group of the Alliance of Liberals and Democrats for Europe**

ALTENER stands for Alternative Energy, an initiative relating to the development of new and renewable energy resources (RES) (see **electricity**). It was established in 1993 and its objectives were to make such resources competitive, to eliminate barriers to their marketability, and to develop public awareness about their availability and virtues. The 1997 **White Paper** laid down a clear strategy of doubling the proportion of RES in the European Union's gross domestic energy consumption from 6% in 1997 to 12% in 2010. The Altener II programme was launched in 1998. In September 2001 a directive was adopted on the production of electricity and RES, which aimed to increase reliance on RES by advocating greater use of 'green' electricity. Altener III was incorporated into the Intelligent Energy-Europe programme from 2007. In April 2009 the **European Council** and the **European Parliament** adopted a new directive on the promotion of the use of energy from renewable sources, which superseded earlier legislation.

ALTERNATIVE FÜR DEUTSCHLAND (AfD—Alternative for Germany) is one of **Germany**'s newest political parties. The AfD was established in February 2013, initially as a centre-right conservative party, but has since gained the reputation of being a right-wing populist party. It is widely considered to be Germany's first **Eurosceptic** party, with a majority of male supporters. Many of its supporters formerly belonged to **Angela Merkel**'s Christlich-Demokratische Union Deutschlands (CDU—Christian Democratic Union). The party has attracted considerable attention and interest both in Germany and abroad, and narrowly missed securing representation in the Federal Assembly (Bundestag) following the September 2013 elections, falling just short of the required 5% threshold. Such thresholds have since been deemed unconstitutional and seven AfD **Members of the European Parliament** (MEPs) were elected at the elections to the **European Parliament** (EP) in May 2014. In late 2014 the AfD secured its first representation in the three regional parliaments of Brandenburg, Saxony and Thuringia, and it gained representation in Bremen and Hamburg in the first half of 2015. However, in mid-2015 the AfD experienced internal divisions, and a number of members left the party, forming a new centre-right party, the Allianz für Fortschritt und Aufbruch (Alliance for Progress and Renewal). The AfD's electoral gains continued, none the less: in March 2016 the party finished second in regional elections in Saxony-Anhalt, and third in Rhineland-Palatinate and Baden-Württemburg. In regional elections in Mecklenburg-Vorpommern in September, the AfD finished second, ahead of the CDU, amid popular opposition to Merkel's liberal policy on accepting refugees. The party performed strongly in the federal elections of September 2017.

In the EP, the AfD was initially part of the **European Conservatives and Reformists** (ECR) group. The AfD was expelled following an alliance with the **far-right** Freedom Party of **Austria** and controversial comments by its leadership, calling for the shooting of immigrants. One AfD MEP was subsequently admitted to the **Europe of Freedom and Direct Democracy group** (EFDD), and the other became a member of the **Europe of Nations and Freedom** (ENF). The AfD, like the Government, is highly critical of the case for Turkish membership of the EU. However, unlike the Government, the AfD staunchly opposes the country's membership of the euro and the earlier decisions to bail out ailing economies such as **Greece**. The AfD is known for its anti-immigration stance and opposition to Islam, and has been accused of **Islamophobia**. The party has advocated the complete exclusion of asylum applicants to Germany and a willingness to revoke the German citizenship of those born to non-German parents. At the party conference in 2016, the AfD adopted a manifesto banning Islamic symbols, including burqas, minarets and the call to prayer.

AMS is the acronym for Aggregate Measure of Support, the calculation of the costs to taxpayers and consumers of both the domestic farm support and the export subsidies provided by the **common agricultural policy** (CAP).

AMSTERDAM TREATY: See **Treaty of Amsterdam**

The **ANDEAN COMMUNITY OF NATIONS** (**Comunidad Andina**—CAN), formerly the Andean Pact, comprises four South American countries: Bolivia, Colombia, Ecuador, and Peru. The community is based on a **customs union**, and formal ties with the **European Community** date back to agreements on bilateral trade and aid signed in 1983 and 1986. Since then, co-operation has developed both on a European Union (EU)-Andean Community basis and within the context of the EU's developing relations with **South and Central America**. Following a series of declarations in 1996, a new institutional framework for relations was developed, with dialogue focusing particularly on drugs. A political dialogue and co-operation agreement with the Andean Community and its member states was signed in December 2003. In mid-2007 the EU and the Andean Community initiated negotiations on an Association Agreement, which were, however, suspended in mid-2008. On 1 March 2010 an agreement on trade was concluded between the EU and Colombia and Peru. The trade agreement was signed in June 2012 and was provisionally applied from 2013. A draft text for a proposed free trade agreement between the EU and Ecuador was published in February 2015. In November 2016 the EU and its member states, together with Ecuador, Colombia and Peru, signed the accession protocol of Ecuador to the trade agreement. Ecuador joined the trade agreement on 1 January 2017.

VYTENIS ANDRIUKAITIS (1951–) was nominated in 2014 as the Lithuanian Commissioner to the new 28-member **European Commission** led by President-elect **Jean-Claude Juncker**. In September 2014 Juncker named Andriukaitis as Commissioner-designate for Health and Food Safety, subject to approval by the **European Parliament** (EP). Prior to his nomination to the Commission, Andriukaitis held a number of senior professional and political roles in **Lithuania**, including that of cardiovascular surgeon, and most recently Minister of Health and Vice-President of the World Health Assembly. Andriukaitis graduated with a medical degree from Kaunas Institute of Medicine in 1975. He also holds a Master's degree in history from Vilnius University. Following the approval of Juncker's Commission by the EP and the **European Council** in late October 2014, Andriukaitis took up office on 1 November.

ANIMAL WELFARE aims to address issues surrounding the keeping of millions of animals for economic purposes (for example, farming) across Europe. The **European Commission** regards animals as sentient beings and seeks to ensure that they do not encounter avoidable pain or suffering. The Commission seeks to ensure minimum welfare requirements for all those who keep animals (including pet owners). The Commission adopted its first animal welfare strategy in 2006: an Action Plan on the Protection and Welfare of Animals (2006–10). A new, four-year, improved strategy was adopted in January 2012 and was to run until the end of 2015. (In November 2015 the **European Parliament** urged the Commission to implement a new animal welfare strategy to run from 2016 to 2020.) The **Treaty on the Functioning of the European Union** reaffirms a number of fundamental principles regarding animal welfare (first introduced under the **Treaty of Amsterdam**) that should be respected. Article 13 states that 'in formulating and implementing the Union's agriculture, fisheries, transport, **internal market**, **research and technological development** and space policies, the Union and the Member States shall ... pay full regard to the welfare requirements of animals, while respecting the legislative or administrative customs of the Member States'.

The **ANNUAL REPORT** is a general report on the activities of the European Union (EU) and the member states. It is published annually in all EU languages and is submitted to the **European Parliament**.

ANDRUS ANSIP (1956–) was named as the Estonian representative to the **European Commission** for 2014–19. He was appointed Mayor of Tartu in 1998, and entered the Estonian Parliament in 2004, becoming first Minister of Economic Affairs, and subsequently Prime Minister of **Estonia** between 2005 and 2014, and Chairman of the liberal Estonian Reform Party in 2004–14. In September 2014 the then President-elect of the Commission, **Jean-Claude Juncker**, nominated Ansip as Vice-President of the Commission, with responsibility for the Digital Single Market. Following the approval of the Juncker Commission by the European Parliament, and with the endorsement of the **European Council**, Ansip took up his post on 1 November 2014.

ANTICI GROUP is named after its Italian founder, Paolo M. Antici. The Antici Group comprises the personal assistants of the Permanent Representatives (see **Permanent Representation**) in **Brussels**, Belgium, a member of the private office of the head of the secretariat of the Council of Ministers and a member of the Council's legal service. It has no formal status, but functions as an integral and important part of the structure of the **Committee of Permanent Representatives**, and is consulted by the presidency on work programmes and procedures.

ANTI-DUMPING: See **Dumping**

ANTI-TRUST: See **Competition Policy**

APPLE INC. is a multinational information technology company, which was originally founded in 1976 by Steve Jobs, Steve Wozniak and Ronald Wayne, to produce and distribute personal computers. The company is based in the USA's so-called Silicon Valley, in Cupertino, CA, and now designs, develops and sells electronics, including mobile telecommunications and tablet computer devices (such as iPads and iPhones), consumer software (including the OS X and iOS operating systems) and online services. At 2016 Apple Inc. was reportedly the largest publicly traded corporation worldwide, in terms of market capitalization. At the end of August the European Union's Commissioner, responsible for Competition, Margrethe Vestager, concluded that Apple had been in receipt of illegal **state aid** from **Ireland**, and had been directing much of its sales and profits outside the USA through Apple International in Ireland, an artificial corporate structure without premises or personnel. Apple was ordered to pay unpaid taxes amounting to as much as €13,000m., in addition to interest. The ruling was the result of a three-year investigation into claims that Ireland had violated EU legislation in offering Apple tax advantages not available to other companies, amid increased efforts to combat tax avoidance, following the financial crisis. The EU has pursued these efforts through the EU's state aid policy, which gives the **European Commission** the authority to monitor the state support offered to companies to guarantee competition. Apple's Chief Executive Tim Cook responded by accusing the Commission of making politically motivated charges.

The **APPLICANT COUNTRIES**, in order of application for membership of the European Union (EU), are: **Turkey** (14 April 1987), the **former Yugoslav republic of Macedonia**—FYRM (22 March 2004), **Montenegro** (15 December 2008), **Albania** (28 April 2009), **Iceland** (16 July 2009—withdrawn in June 2013), **Serbia** (22 December 2009) and **Bosnia and Herzegovina** (15 February 2016). Other countries have also signalled their intention to apply for EU membership in the future. These include **Moldova** and **Ukraine**. **Switzerland** has applied for membership, but the Swiss Government froze its application following popular rejection of Swiss participation in the **European Economic Area** in 1992.

Of the current applicant countries, Albania, the FYRM, Montenegro, Serbia and Turkey are formally **candidate countries**, Albania having had the status conferred on it most recently, in June 2014. Of the candidates, Turkey opened **accession negotiations** in October 2005, Iceland in July 2010 (later suspended), Montenegro in June 2012 and Serbia in January 2014. The FYRM and Albania are awaiting the opening of accession negotiations.

APPROXIMATION is a term used to describe the process of removing undesired or unwarranted differences in national **legislation** within the context of the **internal market**. Proposals for approximation come from the **European Commission**, but must be approved by the **Council of the European Union**. Approximation can involve not only member states, but also non-member countries.

'ARAB SPRING' is the term coined to describe the popular uprisings that took place across the Middle East and North Africa from December 2010. A series of large-scale demonstrations in Tunisia followed the self-immolation of a young Tunisian man in protest at state restrictions in mid-December 2010, and led President Zine al-Abidine Ben Ali to flee the country in mid-January 2011. A number of governments in the region were subsequently overthrown with significant political effects in Egypt, Iraq, Libya and Yemen, and civil conflict in **Syria** is ongoing. Additionally, there were sustained protests in Algeria, Bahrain, Iran, Jordan, Kuwait, Lebanon, Oman and Sudan. In February 2011, at a Senior Officials' meeting to discuss the unrest in the Middle East, the **High Representative of the Union for Foreign Affairs and Security Policy** and Vice-President of the **European Commission**, Catherine Ashton, identified the need for the European Union (EU) to respond in three ways: by helping to develop 'deep democracy', through a process of political reform, democratic elections, institution building, measures to combat corruption, and support for the independent judiciary and civil society; through economic development; and by facilitating the movement of people and of communications, while avoiding mass migration. In March a joint partnership for democracy and shared prosperity with the Southern Mediterranean was published. In June Ashton established a new Task Force for the Southern Mediterranean, which aimed to combine expertise from the **European External Action Service**, the Commission, the **European Investment Bank**, the **European Bank for Reconstruction and Development** and other international financial institutions to act as a focal point for assistance to countries in North Africa experiencing political transformation. The Council appointed an EU Special Representative for the Southern Mediterranean in July, who was to strengthen the EU's political role in North Africa and the Middle East, to ensure the coherence of EU actions in relation to the region and to support the transition to democracy in the EU's southern neighbourhood. In September the Commission agreed to new economic support for the Middle East. The Support for Partnership Reform and Inclusive Growth (SPRING) programme was allocated a budget of €350m. in additional funds for 2011–12, to provide support on a so-called more-for-more basis to those countries that demonstrated progress in implementing democratic reforms. The Civil Society Facility was established, with a budget of €26.4m., with the objective of strengthening the capacity of civil society to promote reform and increase public accountability. In November 2013 the Commission announced that the SPRING programme had been allocated €150m. for 2013.

Creating an **AREA OF FREEDOM, SECURITY AND JUSTICE** was a goal inserted into the **Treaty of Rome** by the **Treaty of Amsterdam**, involving co-operation in many of the areas previously dealt with under pillar III of the European Union (EU), the third **pillar** covering **justice and home affairs** (JHA). The Treaty of Amsterdam transferred the issues of asylum, immigration and judicial co-operation in civil matters from this third pillar into the European Community pillar, leaving the more sensitive issues of police and judicial co-operation in criminal matters in a newly renamed pillar III, **Police and Judicial Cooperation in Criminal Matters** (PJCCM). Hence, an emphasis on assuring the **freedom of movement** of persons is accompanied by measures governing external border controls, asylum, immigration and the prevention and combating of crime. How to realize the area of freedom, security and justice was the principal focus of the **Tampere summit** in 1999, which produced a five-year action programme focused on progress towards a common EU asylum and migration policy, mutual recognition of judicial decisions, and enhanced cross-border co-operation against crime, including with non-member states. Subsequently, a second action plan—the Hague Action Plan—was adopted in 2004. The **Stockholm Programme** followed in December 2009. The **Treaty of Lisbon** abolished the pillar structure and brought all JHA and PJCCM issues back together under the Area of Freedom, Security and Justice. It also enabled the **European Parliament** and the **European Court of Justice** to wield greater influence regarding these issues.

ARIANE is the name of a series of European civilian rockets that have been taking satellites into space since the late 1970s. The Ariane project, originally conceived as a French-designed rocket-launcher, became Western Europe's second attempt successfully to design commercial rockets to compete with their US and Soviet counterparts. The Ariane project was partly funded by loans from the **European Investment Bank**. In 1980 the **European Space Agency** (ESA) established the Ariane space company (Arianespace) to market the launcher commercially. Its facilities were made available to all, and Arianespace has shareholders from 10 European states, with **France** the largest by far. There are over 300 employees working in the company's headquarters in Évry, France, and in French Guiana, as well as in local offices in the USA, Singapore and Japan. The company has been involved in a regular programme of launches, putting satellites in space since 1979. Over time the rockets have been adapted and re-designed to allow for greater efficiency and capacity. The latest version is the Ariane 5.

MIGUEL ARIAS CAÑETE (1950–) was nominated in 2014 as the Spanish Commissioner-designate to the new 28-member **European Commission** led by President-elect **Jean-Claude Juncker**. In September 2014 Juncker had named Arias Cañete as Commissioner-designate for Climate Action and Energy, subject to approval by the **European Parliament** (EP). When the EP and the **European Council** approved the Juncker Commission, Arias Cañete took up his position as a European Commissioner on 1 November. He studied law at the Complutense University of Madrid and worked as a civil servant after graduation as well as a law lecturer (1979–82), before entering politics as a member of the Andalusian assembly. In June 2014 immediately prior to his appointment to the Commission, Arias Cañete was elected to the EP. He had previously been a member of the EP from 1986 to 1999, but prior to his current appointment spent 15 years involved in national politics, where he held the role of Spanish Minister of Agriculture, Food and the Environment on two occasions.

An **ARTICLE** is the basic clause or unit of a European treaty. It may be subdivided into paragraphs.

ARTICLE 36 COMMITTEE, formerly the K.4 Committee, and also known as CATS, was established by the **Treaty on European Union**. Its role is primarily to co-ordinate European Union **police and judicial co-operation in criminal matters**. In addition, the Committee is expected to provide the **Council of the European Union** with opinions and assist in the preparation of the Council's discussions, along with the **Committee of Permanent Representatives**.

ARTICLE 50 of the **Treaty of Lisbon** allows any member state of the European Union (EU) to decide to withdraw from the Union, 'in accordance with its own constitutional requirements'. Should a member state decide to leave the Union, it is obliged to notify the **European Council** of its intention, thereby formally invoking Article 50. In accordance with guidelines provided by the European Council, upon being informed of a member state's intention to withdraw, the Union begins negotiations with that state, with the aim of concluding an agreement to establish arrangements for the country's withdrawal, while taking into account the framework for the country's future relations with the rest of the Union. Any such agreement must be concluded on behalf of the Union by the European Council, acting by means of a qualified majority (see **Qualified Majority Voting**), and with the consent of the **European Parliament** (EP). The treaties of the EU cease to apply to the withdrawing member state upon the entry into force of the withdrawal agreement or, alternatively, two years after the government of the withdrawing state has invoked Article 50 (unless the European Council, in agreement with the relevant member state, unanimously decides to an extension of this period). Members of the European Council or of the **Council of the European Union** representing the withdrawing member state are not permitted to take part in discussions in those bodies or in decisions concerning it; however, members of the EP from the withdrawing member state retain the right to vote in discussions pertaining to its withdrawal. The eventual withdrawal agreement is not considered to be primary law, as it will not amend EU treaties. If the withdrawing member state wished to apply in future to rejoin the

EU as a full member, it would be considered as a third country (under Article 49 of the Treaty of Lisbon). The resulting **association agreement** could take, should the applicant state wish, an entirely new, unique format, not comparable with existing agreements for associate members of the bloc. The **United Kingdom** became the first member state to invoke Article 50, under Prime Minister **Theresa May**, after voters decided in a national referendum in June 2016 to leave the Union (see **Brexit**). On 29 March 2017 the Prime Minister formally informed European Council President **Donald Tusk** of the UK's intention to leave the Union, thereby invoking Article 50.

ARTICLE 352 (formerly Article 308) allows the European Union, in the absence of any explicit powers and acting by **unanimity**, to take 'appropriate measures' to achieve a particular treaty objective.

ASEAN: See **Association of Southeast Asian Nations**

ASIA has not been the subject of a co-ordinated **regional policy** by the European Union (EU), although most Asian countries participate in the EU Generalized System of Preferences, and the EU has developed links with the **Association of Southeast Asian Nations** (ASEAN). In addition, there are **co-operation agreements** and **strategic partnerships** with several Asian countries, including the People's Republic of China, India and Japan, while others have been the subjects of separate economic and development accords. India is the largest single recipient of EU aid among developing countries. In 2012 the EU acceded to the Treaty of Amity and Cooperation in South East Asia.

ASIA-PACIFIC ECONOMIC CO-OPERATION (APEC): See **Association of Southeast Asian Nations**

ASSIZES (or Conferences of the Parliaments) are consultative meetings of representatives of **national parliaments** designed to improve awareness of and support for the integration process.

ASSOCIATION AGREEMENTS were concluded with numerous countries both within Europe and beyond. Agreements concluded with the latter include the **Lomé Conventions** and the **Cotonou Agreement**. Within Europe, association agreements were initially drawn up only with countries aspiring to but as yet insufficiently developed economically for membership. Hence, those with **Greece** (1961) and **Turkey** (1963) envisaged the creation of a **customs union** with the EC as well as co-operation in a wide variety of areas. Later agreements with **Malta** (1971) and **Cyprus** (1972) were, by contrast, far less ambitious, restricting themselves to little more than the creation of a free trade area, although they too involved the establishment of a series of bodies (e.g. an Association Council and an Association Committee) to oversee the operation of the Association. Since the early 1990s an increasing number of association agreements have been concluded with European countries. These include the formation of a **European Economic Area** with the member states of the **European Free Trade Association** (EFTA), **Europe agreements** with the countries of **Central and Eastern Europe**, and the **stabilization and association agreements** with countries in the **Western Balkans**. Association agreements were subsequently envisaged for the Eastern European countries covered by the EU's Eastern partnership. In June 2014 association agreements were signed with Georgia and **Moldova** (both of which entered into force in 2016), and the process of signature (which had commenced in March) was completed with **Ukraine**. An association agreement with **Kosovo** was signed in October 2015 and entered into force in April 2016.

The **ASSOCIATION OF SOUTHEAST ASIAN NATIONS** (ASEAN) is a regional organization. When formed in 1967, it comprised Indonesia, Malaysia, the Philippines, Singapore and Thailand. Brunei and Viet Nam joined in 1984 and 1995 respectively, with Myanmar and Laos joining in 1997. Cambodia became a member of ASEAN in 1999. The Association's main current purpose is to promote free trade between its member states and other members of the Asia-Pacific Economic Co-operation (APEC) organization, which includes Australia, **Japan**, the **Russian Federation** and the People's Republic of China among its 21 members. Relations with the European Union (EU) date back to the early 1970s and include a **co-operation agreement** signed in 1980, although at times development of relations has been hampered by concerns over alleged **human rights** abuses in certain ASEAN countries, notably Indonesia. In 1997 a 'new dynamic' to EU-ASEAN relations was launched with a view to increasing co-operation and encouraging greater collaboration in business and trade. In 2007 the first EU-ASEAN summit took place in Singapore. This endorsed a Plan of Action to implement an Enhanced Partnership covering political and security co-operation, as well as co-operation on economic, energy, environmental and sociocultural issues. A second EU-ASEAN summit was held in Brunei in April 2012. The EU is ASEAN's third largest trading partner, after the People's Republic of China and Japan. In May 2015 the High Representative of the Union for Foreign Affairs and Security Policy and the European Commission adopted a joint communication entitled 'The EU and ASEAN: A Partnership with a Strategic Purpose', and in September the first ASEAN-EU Policy Dialogue on Human Rights took place, with a focus on women's rights, child protection and the safety of migrant workers.

ASYLUM, MIGRATION AND INTEGRATION FUND (AMIF): See **Migration and Asylum Policy**

ATLANTIC ALLIANCE is a popular alternative name for the **North Atlantic Treaty Organization** (NATO).

The **ATLANTIC ARC COMMISSION** (ARC) is an intergovernmental association of regional authorities from those regions of the European Union (EU) that border the Atlantic, including islands located in this ocean and any other regions with close economic and cultural ties with areas bordering the Atlantic. The five states covered are: **France**, **Ireland**, **Portugal**, **Spain** and the **United Kingdom**. The ARC was founded in 1989 and has as its main objective securing EU funding for infrastructural developments for the poorer, more peripheral areas of the EU that border the Atlantic Ocean. In 2016–18 the presidency was held by Juan José Sota Verdión of the Cantabria region of Spain.

ATMOSPHERIC POLLUTION was a central element of initiatives in the field of **environmental policy** from the mid-1980s. Regulations governing automobile emissions were introduced in 1985 and 1987, though the extent of improvement was hindered by disagreements between the member states. There was also a series of **directives** on industrial pollution, especially the discharge of sulphur dioxide and chlorofluorocarbons

(CFCs) into the atmosphere, which provided for CFCs to be totally banned by 1997. The European Union (EU) agreed in 1997 to curb emissions of six greenhouse gases by 8%, in comparison to 1990 levels, by 2008–12. The Clean Air for Europe (CAFE) programme began in 2001, aiming to co-ordinate the collection of scientific and technical data necessary for policy-making in this area. As part of the EU's Sixth Environmental Action Plan, adopted in 2002, the EU aimed to bring about, *inter alia*, by 2020: a 47% reduction in the erosion of life expectancy owing to exposure to particulate matter and a 10% reduction in acute mortality resulting from ozone exposure. An **Emissions Trading Scheme** (ETS) was launched in January 2005, which obliges companies that exceed their agreed carbon dioxide emissions to buy extra allowances from more efficient companies or incur considerable fines. In April 2008 a new air quality directive was approved by the Council, which merged five existing pieces of legislation into a single directive, and imposed limits on fine particle emissions (PM2.5) from vehicles, agriculture and small-scale industry. Emissions of PM2.5 in urban areas were to be reduced by 20% by 2020, compared with 2010 levels. The Commission estimated that some 370,000 EU citizens died each year from conditions linked to air pollution. A review of legislation on air pollution commenced in 2011, which concluded in December 2013 with the adoption by the Commission of a new CAFE, specifying objectives for air quality until 2030. An amended National Emissions Ceilings Directive was also adopted, which introduced more restrictive maximum levels for national emissions of the six principal pollutants. The **European Environment Agency** is the body that monitors atmospheric pollution and air quality, and supports the implementation of related EU legislation.

AUDIOVISUAL POLICY dates from the 1980s and activity in the audiovisual sector comprises two broad aspects. The first focuses mainly on industry sector considerations that centre on efforts to ensure the standardization of the systems used in the member states to broadcast programmes by satellite and cable. The first **directive** on this specific issue was approved in 1986. In 1989 objectives were defined for the development of high-definition television (HDTV). In 1991 a single standard for high-definition television production and financial support for a programme of co-operation between the businesses concerned were introduced. There is also a legal dimension to audiovisual policy and this centred on the Television without Frontiers directive, which was adopted in 1989 and amended in 1997. This directive sought to provide a harmonized framework in order to promote the free movement, production and distribution of European television programmes. To this end, common rules were agreed on advertising, sponsorship, the protection of minors and the right of reply. This directive also introduced distribution quotas, thus requiring TV channels to reserve, whenever possible, more than one-half of their transmission time for European productions. An updated Television without Frontiers directive, renamed the Audiovisual Media Services without Frontiers directive, was adopted by the **European Parliament** in November 2007. In March 2010 the European Parliament and the Council adopted a directive on Audiovisual Media Services, with the aim of implementing a cross-border framework for audiovisual media services, thereby strengthening the EU's market for both production and distribution, and ensuring fair competition. In May 2016 new amendments were made to the Audiovisual Media Services Directive to reform and update the directive for the 21st century, as part of the EU's **Media Policy**.

The European audiovisual market faces a series of hurdles: continuing language barriers which prevent the free movement of programmes; an unwieldy decision making process which generally requires **unanimity**; and the need to make considerable investment to anticipate technological developments, which requires international alliances and/or mergers. It is important to stress that the development of European Union (EU) audiovisual policy must respect certain interests and priorities, such as competition rules (especially regarding state aid—see **subsidies**), the rules on intellectual property and the principles of public service.

From 1991 the MEDIA programme (measures to promote the development of the audiovisual industry) supported the European audiovisual industry by encouraging the development and distribution of European works and financing schemes to improve the training of professionals in the sector. The **MEDIA 2007** Programme (2007–13), which followed on from MEDIA II (1996–2000) and Media Plus (2000–05), had a budget of €755m. The **European Commission**'s MEDIA programme was incorporated into the **Creative Europe** Programme (2014–20). This new programme was to receive some €1,460m., and aims to stimulate employment in the cultural and creative industries.

AUSTRIA for many years felt unable to consider European Communities (EC) membership because of its neutral status and the terms of the Austrian State Treaty of 1955, which ended the Allied military occupation of the country. It did, however, become a founder member of the **European Free Trade Association** (EFTA) in 1960, despite the disapproval of the **USSR**, which had been a party to the 1955 Treaty. Austria requested a special arrangement with the EC, and exploratory talks began in 1964. The Italian Government vetoed subsequent negotiations in 1967. Hence, it was not until **enlargement** was included on the agenda of the EC that Austria concluded a **free trade agreement** with the EC, in 1972. Given its large volume of trade with the EC, especially with the Federal Republic of **Germany**, in the late 1980s Austria began to fear that its economy would suffer from the establishment of the **internal market**, unless it was party to the process. It supported the attempt by EFTA to reach a general agreement with the EC, but soon broke ranks with its EFTA partners to apply formally for EC membership in July 1989, arguing that membership was not, in fact, precluded by the 1955 State Treaty. Although the EC indicated that action on the application was unlikely until after 1992, the collapse of communism in **Central and Eastern Europe**, the successful completion of the **European Economic Area** talks and the decision by most of the other EFTA states to seek EC membership led to early progress being made. Negotiations on terms of entry began in 1993 and the terms were endorsed by a popular referendum in June 1994. Austria's membership of the European Union (EU) was effective from 1 January 1995 (**Finland** and **Sweden** also joined on the same date). Adapting to membership was a relatively smooth process, although Austria endured a period of diplomatic isolation in 2000 when the **far-right** Freedom Party led by Jörg Haider entered briefly into coalition government. The Austrian Government found itself isolated in 2005 when it strongly resisted the opening of accession negotiations with **Turkey**. Austria eventually agreed to remove all obstacles to the opening of talks with Turkey, provided that accession negotiations could commence with **Croatia**. However, Austrian attitudes towards Turkish accession to the EU remain somewhat mixed, and in May 2011 the Austrian Vice-Chancellor and Federal Minister of European and International Affairs expressed a preference for a special relationship with Turkey over Turkish membership of the EU. Austria held presidential elections in June 2016, in which the Eurosceptic candidate of the Freedom Party, Norbert Hofer, was narrowly defeated. Upon an appeal to the Constitutional Court by the party's supporters, the result was overturned in July, after it was demonstrated that absentee votes had been mishandled; fresh elections took place in December, in which Hofer was defeated by Alexander Van der Bellen, the former leader of the Greens, who stood as an independent.

AVIS is the term applied to the opinion issued by the **European Commission** on the acceptability of a country's formal application for membership of the European Union.

DIMITRIS AVRAMOPOULOS (1953–) was nominated in 2014 as the Greek Commissioner to the new 28-member **European Commission** led by President **Jean-Claude Juncker**. In September 2014 Juncker named Avramopoulos as Commissioner-designate for Migration, Home Affairs and Citizenship, subject to approval by the **European Parliament** (EP). Avramopoulos graduated with a BA degree in Public Law and Political Science from Athens University in 1975. After his military service he entered the Greek diplomatic service (1980–93), working in the cabinet office of the Greek Prime Minister and serving as Mayor of Athens (1995–2002), as well as becoming a Vice-President of the **Committee of the Regions** (1997–2002). Prior to his appointment to the Commission Avramopoulos held a number of senior political roles in **Greece**, most recently that of Minister of National Defence from June 2013, but earlier roles included Minister of Foreign Affairs (2012–13), Minister of National Defence (2011–12) and Minister of Health (2006–09). Avramopoulos took up his current post on 1 November 2014.

B

BALKANS: See **Western Balkans**

BALTIC STATES: See **Estonia**; **Latvia**; **Lithuania**

BANANAS were the cause of a trade dispute between the European Union (EU) and the **USA** throughout the 1990s. The EU's banana regime had always been strongly contested as it granted preferential access to British and French markets to banana producers in their former colonies among the **ACP** (African, Caribbean and Pacific) **States**. The EU banana trade regime (BTR) antagonized the Government of the USA as it restricted access for US producers. With the support of several Central American producers, an appeal was made by the USA to the **World Trade Organization** (WTO) disputes settlement panel against this apparent discrimination. The WTO backed the US complaint and forced the EU to reconsider its BTR. Although a majority of EU member states wanted to abolish the BTR, a minority, including **France** and the **United Kingdom**, wished to defend it. Efforts to enlarge the quota for Central American producers were rejected by the USA in 1999 and heralded the imposition of substantial tariffs on a range of British and French goods entering the US market. This trade war was resolved in April 2001 when a resolution was reached between the EU and the USA, which agreed a transition to a tariff-only system by 2006. Despite this, in June 2007 the USA again raised allegations at the WTO that EU treatment of Latin American banana producers was unfair, citing the continued existence of a 'discriminatory' tariff quota. In December 2009 the EU-Latin American Bananas Agreement (the Geneva Agreement) finally sought to end the 20-year dispute between the EU and Latin America over the former's preferential treatment of the ACP states. In the agreement, the EU opted to reduce its tariffs and the Latin American states pledged to abandon all disputes over bananas before the WTO. It was hoped that the agreement would bring greater stability to the banana market and form the basis of a more significant agreement. In November 2012, after much deliberation, a new agreement between the EU and 11 Latin American states (Brazil, Colombia, Costa Rica, Ecuador, Guatemala, Honduras, Mexico, Nicaragua, Panama, Peru and Venezuela) brought to an end one of the longest trade disputes in the EU's history. Pascal Lamy, the then Director-General of the WTO, described the agreement as 'truly historic'. The agreement pledged the signatories to start moving towards a new set of maximum tariffs.

The **BANK FOR INTERNATIONAL SETTLEMENTS** (BIS) is a joint venture, originally of European national central banks, established in 1930 as an aid to the resolution of the problem of German reparations. After 1945 it extended its activities and membership to include, among others, Canada, **Japan** and the **USA**. Based in Basel, **Switzerland**, it has served as the headquarters of the **Committee of the Governors of the Central Banks**, and has acted on behalf of the European Communities as their agent for the **European Monetary Co-operation Fund** (EMCF). By working closely with the IMF, BIS provides a forum for the co-ordination of international monetary policy and holds deposits for international financial institutions and central banks worldwide.

The **BANKING UNION** refers specifically to the countries of the **eurozone**. Its origins evolved as a response by the **European Commission** to the financial crisis that commenced in 2008. The Commission sought to pursue a series of initiatives to create a much safer and sounder financial sector for the **single market**. At the heart of its plans the Commission sought to ensure greater prudential requirements for banks, to ensure that banks provided increased protection to depositors, and to agree rules for managing failing banks across the **European Union** (EU). These initiatives were brought together within a **single rulebook** for all financial sectors and for all 28 member states. This rulebook comprises a series of legislative texts that all banks (some 8,300) within the EU must adhere to. However, as the debt crisis within the eurozone deepened, it became ever clearer that the countries that shared the single currency required a more interdependent and deeper form of banking integration. The Banking Union is the product of these initiatives and necessitated the creation of a **Single Supervisory Mechanism** and a **Single Resolution Mechanism**. It is intended that these mechanisms will prevent a recurrence of the crises that erupted in a number of countries, notably **Greece** and **Ireland**, and which necessitated substantive bailouts from public funds. Although the Banking Union applies to eurozone member countries, countries outside the euro area can also opt to participate. **Sweden** and the **United Kingdom** are the only member states not to participate in the Single Resolution Mechanism, which entered into force in 2015.

BARBER PROTOCOL is the name given informally to a **protocol** introduced by the **Treaty on European Union** intended to clarify the remuneration criteria contained within Article 141 of the **Treaty of Rome** (now Article 157 of the **Treaty on the Functioning of the European Union**) regarding **equal pay** for equal work by men and women. It restricts the definition of remuneration by largely excluding benefits under occupational social security schemes, and has been interpreted as meaning that the **Court of Justice** has a more limited ability to clarify its own judgments. The protocol results from political pressures and financial expediency.

The **BARCELONA DECLARATION** of November 1995 launched the **Euro-Mediterranean partnership** and, in doing so, committed the signatories to the establishment of a **Euro-Mediterranean Economic Area** (EMEA). The signatories were the European Union and the so-called MED-12 states: Algeria, **Cyprus**, Egypt, Israel, Jordan, Lebanon, **Malta**, Morocco, the Palestinian Authority (now Palestinian Territories), **Syria**, Tunisia and **Turkey**. (See also **Barcelona Process** and **Union for the Mediterranean**.)

The **BARCELONA PROCESS**, initiated in 1995, was designed to promote closer ties between the European Union (EU) and the so-called MED-12 states of the Mediterranean (Algeria, **Cyprus**, Egypt, Israel, Jordan, Lebanon, **Malta**, Morocco, the Palestinian Authority—now Palestinian Territories, **Syria**, Tunisia and **Turkey**). Forming the central element of the EU's **Mediterranean Policy**, it was initiated by the **Barcelona Declaration** of 1995, and subsequently came to form part of the **European Neighbourhood Policy**. In July 2008 a new, but rather vague, multilateral partnership, the **Union for the Mediterranean**, was created; the Union comprises the 28 EU member states and 16 Mediterranean partner countries from North Africa, the Middle East and the Balkans.

MICHEL BARNIER (1951–) is the European Union's (EU) chief negotiator for the **United Kingdom**'s exit from the EU, and a former French Commissioner to the **European Commission**. Barnier graduated from ESPC Europe in 1972 and then worked for a number of centre-right Gaullist ministers in successive French governments, before being elected to the National Assembly in 1979, in which he served as a deputy until 1993, when he joined the Government of Prime Minister Jacques Chirac, as Minister for the Environment. In 1995 Chirac appointed him Secretary of State for European Affairs, in which post he served until 1997. In 1999 he was appointed the French Commissioner to the European Commission as Commissioner for Regional Policy, until 2004. He then re-entered the domestic French political arena as Minister of Foreign Affairs until 2005, when he resigned after the French electorate rejected the **Treaty establishing a Constitution for Europe**, in a national referendum in June. In March 2006 Barnier was elected Vice-President of the **European People's Party** for a three-year term, during which time he served as an adviser to Commission President José Manuel Durão Barroso, and participated in a panel of senior European politicians who redrafted the Treaty establishing a Constitution for Europe into what eventually became the **Treaty of Lisbon**. Under Nicolas Sarkozy's presidency he re-joined the French Cabinet as Minister of Agriculture in 2007, serving until 2009 when he was elected as a **Member of the European Parliament**. He resigned from that position in February 2010 when he was appointed as France's Commissioner for the Internal Market and Services, in which role he served until May 2014 (he was succeeded by Elżbieta Bieńkowska), overseeing significant new legislation on financial regulation, **Banking Union** and the single European digital market. From 2015 he was a special adviser to European Commission President **Jean-Claude Juncker** on defence policy, until he was appointed in July 2016 as the Commission's chief negotiator for the UK's exit (**Brexit**) from the EU and director of the so-called Brexit task force.

The **BARRE PLAN** was one of the alternative strategies for **economic and monetary union** that was advanced after the 1969 **Hague summit**. Prepared by Raymond Barre, who was the French Minister of Economy and Finance in 1976–78, and written at the request of the **European Commission**, it was supported by **Belgium** as well as **France**. It favoured a monetarist approach to union with the immediate introduction of fixed exchange rates. This tactic, it argued, would enforce a **convergence** and **harmonization** of the economic policies of the member states. The alternative argument, an economic approach, was expounded in the Schiller Plan. (See also **Optimum Currency Area**; **Werner Report**.)

BASIC PRICE: See **Target Price**

BATTLEGROUPS have been created as part of the EU's commitment, following the development of the **European Rapid Reaction Force**, to equip itself with the military capacity to fulfil the Petersberg tasks set out in the **Treaty on European Union** and pursue its **European security and defence policy** (notably the **European security strategy**). The battlegroups, usually drawing on personnel from a coalition of member states and often with niche capabilities, each consist of up to 1,500 personnel deployable within five–10 days.

BELGIUM is a constitutional monarchy and dates its origins to 1830. It emerged as one of the pioneers of European integration after 1945. It is part of the **Benelux** Economic Union, and a founder member of the European Communities (EC). Belgian governments have been consistent supporters of the European Union (EU) integration process and all have regarded economic integration as only a step towards a political union. In the 1960s Belgium was strongly in favour of **enlargement**, especially the admission of the **United Kingdom**. After the mid-1980s it believed that neither the **Single European Act** nor the **Treaty on European Union** (TEU) had been sufficiently far-reaching, and was critical of states such as the UK and **Denmark** that were reluctant to accept fully the political implications of integration. However, it has at times been wary of a too forceful Franco-German leadership in the EC; this was a further reason for it to favour a strengthening of the EC's supranational institutions. Belgium was one of the first member states to ratify the TEU. It has, overall, been a net beneficiary of EC membership, not least perhaps in terms of the employment possibilities that membership has created in **Brussels**: the fact that the city is the institutional heart of the EU means that Belgium has developed almost a proprietorial interest in the organization. However, the formal decentralization of the state on linguistic lines, which was concluded in 1993, along with an expensive social security system, imposed heavy public sector costs and raised initial doubts as to whether the country could meet the **convergence criteria** set by the TEU for **economic and monetary union** (EMU). In the end, the criteria were relaxed sufficiently for Belgium to be declared eligible for EMU membership, and the country entered as one of the first wave of 11 states in January 1999.

Belgium remains one of the EU's most enthusiastic members and maintains that a flexible approach to EU integration should be adopted so as to enable a central core of states to integrate faster than others, if they so desire. In contrast, Belgium's internal political scene is much more complex and divides along linguistic lines that see two main communities within the state, each with its own political parties, newspapers and television networks. An inconclusive general election in June 2007 prevented agreement on the formation of a new federal government as divisions intensified between the two main communities within Belgium, the French-speaking Walloons and the Flemish-speaking population. After six months without a government, an emergency coalition Government was established in December under the temporary leadership of (outgoing) **Guy Verhofstadt**. Yves Leterme became the new Belgian Prime Minister in March 2008 ending some nine months of political impasse. Leterme was replaced by a fellow Christian Democrat, Herman Van Rompuy, in December 2008, but became Prime Minister for a second time when Van Rompuy was appointed President of the European Council in December 2009. Ongoing tensions, primarily over language issues and rights within Belgium between the Flemish and the Walloons, led to the collapse of the Government and Leterme's resignation as Prime Minister in April 2010. The domestic difficulties were not resolved in the subsequent legislative elections (of 9 June) and were the backdrop to Belgium assuming responsibility for the EU's six-month rotating presidency in July. In the absence of an agreement on the formation of a new government, Leterme continued to serve as the head of what was widely viewed as an ineffective administration. A new Government, headed by the francophone socialist Elio Di Rupo, took office on 6 December 2011. On 25 May 2014 a general election was held concurrently with elections to the **European Parliament**. Prime Minister Di Rupo tendered his resignation, and negotiations commenced on the formation of a new governing coalition. Di Rupo carried on as caretaker Prime Minister until the appointment of Charles Michel on 11 October 2014. Michel, the leader of the Reformist Movement since 2011, became, at the age of 39, the youngest Prime Minister in Belgium's history, and his selection also marked the first occasion on which one francophone Prime Minister had been succeeded by another. Belgium became associated with Islamist terrorist attacks in the EU from late 2015, when it emerged that a number of the assailants in a series of co-ordinated terrorist attacks in Paris, **France** in November, which killed 130 people, originated from Brussels. The assailants, who claimed allegiance to **Islamic State** (previously known as Islamic State in Iraq and the Levant), and some of whom had fought in the ongoing civil conflict in **Syria**, had apparently evaded adequate surveillance from the Belgian security agencies. In March 2016 suicide bombers linked to Islamic State killed 35 people in attacks at Brussels international airport, and on an underground train in the city centre, in what appeared to be a symbolic assault against Brussels as representative of the heart of the EU (Belgium was not involved in any military action in Islamic nations at that time, having suspended air strikes against Islamic State in Syria in 2015 on grounds of cost, although it rejoined the US-led coalition against Islamic State in Syria in July 2016). The apparent lack of co-ordination in Belgium between different levels of government, and between police and security agencies at federal, regional, community and municipal levels attracted severe criticism. One of the principal tasks of the new **European Counter Terrorism Centre**, established in January 2016 under **Europol**, would be to address the issue of violent Islamism apparently being fomented in Belgium.

The **BELGO-LUXEMBOURG ECONOMIC UNION** (BLEU) is primarily a **customs union**, but in many ways a complete economic union, between **Belgium** and **Luxembourg**. The BLEU agreement dates from 1921 and led to the removal of frontier controls between the two states from May 1922. Although originally scheduled to last for some 50 years, the agreement has been renewed every 10 years since 1971. In 1944 the customs union element was extended with the creation of **Benelux**, although BLEU still exists within Benelux. As a result of the BLEU agreement, both countries hold their gold and foreign exchange reserves in common, while many financial, trade and other statistics for Belgium and Luxembourg are recorded together.

BENCHMARKING is an increasingly familiar part of European Union (EU) vocabulary. It involves the use of comparison (from the perspective of a member state or an EU institution) with other states or organizations (for example, with regard to issues such as pension reform or employment practices) with the aim of improving one's own performance by learning from the experience of others.

BENELUX is the commonly used shortened name of the Benelux Economic Union, an economic grouping of **Belgium**, the **Netherlands** and **Luxembourg** within the broader economic structure of the European Union (EU). The exiled Governments of the three states formed the Benelux in 1944, and a Customs Union was formally established in January 1948. Ten years later a new treaty of economic union was signed in The Hague and came into operation in January 1960. As this treaty was due to expire in 2010, a new legal framework (known as the Treaty revising the Treaty establishing the Benelux Economic Union) was signed on 17 June 2008. The most recent treaty has no fixed expiry date, and the name of the Benelux Economic Union was changed to the Benelux Union, to reflect the wide scope of the union. Benelux survives within the EU because the **Treaty of Rome** permits the existence of internal regional groupings of states, as long as these conform to its own stipulated goals. (See also **Belgo-Luxembourg Economic Union—BLEU**.)

BEP: See **Biotech**

BERLAYMONT is the name of the large 13-storey building in **Brussels** that was purpose-built in 1969 to house the **European Commission** and its administrative personnel, although not all Commission employees based in the city work in the building, with others housed in the Charlemagne building. Berlaymont became a shorthand term often used to describe the Commission and the administrative structures of the European Communities, and has sometimes been employed in a derogatory sense to refer to bureaucratization. In 1991 the building had to be evacuated for substantial renovations because large quantities of asbestos had been used in the original construction. The staff was relocated to a number of adjacent buildings, with the Commissioners moving initially into the Breydel building. The renovation and futuristic makeover of this vast star-shaped building, measuring 230,000 sq m (which critics dubbed the 'Berlaymonster'), took 13 years to complete. The building opened again in November 2004. In 2002 the Commission opted to buy the building from the Belgian state for €553m. by means of a 27-year annuity. Structural problems remained, and the building was damaged in a major fire in May 2009.

The **BERLIN DECLARATION** was adopted at an informal gathering of the **European Council** on the 50th anniversary of the signing of the **Treaties of Rome**, on 25 March 2007. It offered a formal statement on the achievements and purposes of the European Union and paved the way for negotiations on a mandate for an **intergovernmental conference**, which resulted in the **Treaty of Lisbon.**

BICS: See **Business and Innovation Centres**

ELŻBIETA BIEŃKOWSKA (1964–) was nominated as the Polish Commissioner to the new 28-member **European Commission** led by President-elect **Jean-Claude Juncker**. In September 2014 Juncker named Bieńkowska as Commissioner-designate for the **Internal Market**, Industry, Entrepreneurship and Small and Medium-sized Enterprises (replacing **Michel Barnier**). Bieńkowska graduated from Jagellonian University in 1989 with an MA in Oriental Philology and successfully undertook an MBA at the Warsaw School of Economics before taking up a senior post in the Silesian Regional Development Office. She joined Civic Platform, was elected to the Polish Parliament and served as Minister of Regional Development in the Government of **Donald Tusk** in 2007–13. She took up her post as Commissioner on 1 November 2014.

BIOTECH (Biotechnology) is an area in which the **European Union** has been promoting research and development policy since the mid-1980s. In 1985 the Biotechnology Action Programme (BAP) was established as part of the new emphasis on the importance of **research and technological development (RTD) policy**. BAP succeeded the 1982–86 Biomolecular Engineering Programme (BEP), sponsoring collaborative research and training between industry and research institutions across the whole field of biotechnology. The original programme was concluded in 1989, but its work and objectives were incorporated into the subsequent Bridge programme of 1990, which also later changed its name to Biotech. This was superseded by the **quality of life and management of living resources programme** in 1999. A Life Patent directive on biotechnology was adopted in 1997 in an attempt to harmonize rules on gene patenting. In the context of the Lisbon strategy (see **Lisbon agenda**), in February 2002 the Commission presented a communication setting out a strategic vision for life sciences and biotechnology up to 2010, and proposing how to address ethical issues, following a broad public consultation. In 2007 the Commission carried out a mid-term review of the progress made since 2002, and examining the economic, social and environmental impact of biotechnology, in order to enable it to draw up proposed revisions to its strategy for Europe on life sciences and biotechnology. Europe had some 1,836 dedicated biotechnology companies in 2009, compared with the USA's 1,754. However, European companies are smaller, employ fewer people, are much less well capitalized, and have far fewer biotechnology products in development.

BLEU: See **Belgo-Luxembourg Economic Union**

BLOCK EXEMPTIONS refers to those categories of agreements under **European Union** (EU) **competition policy** between the EU member states and other states that, as stipulated by the **European Commission**, are exempted from the general prohibition of restrictive trade agreements. Under these, specific economic sectors are exempted from the general provisions relating to competition policy for a period of up to 10 years, after which time they need to be renewed or they lapse. Although such exemptions were initially designed as a means to allow the EU competition authorities greater time to investigate more pressing cases, the Commission is rather cautious about allowing too many block exemptions, and they are granted only rarely. The first, covering exclusive dealing agreements, came into force in 1967 and the second in 1972. They have been applied, for example, to patent licences, specialization agreements, research and development agreements, and motor vehicle distribution and servicing agreements. Block exemptions provide some legal certainty for firms and have benefited **small and medium-sized enterprises** (SMEs) in particular. There is even evidence that company lawyers draft their agreements using the block exemption regulations as a starting point in order to ensure that they satisfy the Commission guidelines. As both policy statements and enforcement tools, they exclude the application of competition law for certain types of agreement (such as liner shipping agreements) and provide delineation between law-abiding and illegal practice. There remain less well-defined areas where the competition rules *might* apply, but the regulations also take these into consideration and make allowances for agreements that are not clear-cut. However, if there is any doubt, firms are wise to pursue the more conventional individual exemption route. This applies when firms draft or alter their agreements to include provisions that are not covered by the block exemption. Block exemption regulations are frequently renewed and updated to incorporate the latest data. A General Block Exemption regulation was adopted in August 2008 and in May 2014 the Commission adopted a revised regulation.

The **BLUE FLAG** is a voluntary eco-label that is awarded annually to bathing beaches and marinas in 47 countries around the world that meet strict standards of water quality and environmental management. The idea of the Blue Flag originated in **France** and the scheme was presented to the **European Commission** by the Foundation for Environmental Education in Europe (FEEE) in 1987 as part of the 'European Year of the Environment'. The programme is run by the non-governmental organization, which was renamed the Foundation for Environmental Education (FEE) in 2000 to reflect the global nature of the scheme. The Blue Flag concept is a core aspect of the **environmental policy** of the European Union, and specifically its water framework **directive**. More than 4,400 beaches and marinas in 46 countries have been awarded a Blue Flag. Information on the recipients of the award is published annually.

The **BOLKESTEIN DIRECTIVE** or, officially, the Directive on Services in the Internal Market, prompted a great deal of debate and controversy in various European Union (EU) countries, and especially **Belgium**, **France**, **Germany** and **Italy**, in the first half of 2005. The directive was put together by Frits Bolkestein, the former Commissioner for the **internal market**, and aimed to establish a single market for services within the EU. Services are a rapidly growing sector and account for around 70% of EU economic activity. The directive contained changes to the EU services market, which can be summarized via two fundamental principles. The first principle focused on the 'freedom of establishment' and sought to ensure that any company or individual who provided a service in one EU member state should be allowed to provide it in all EU member states. The second was the 'country of origin' principle. This sought to establish that if goods were produced in one EU member state, then it was legitimate and acceptable to sell such goods in other EU member states. In short, the Services Directive sought to remove the administrative and legal barriers that prevented firms from offering their services in other countries. The directive presented a radical vision and certainly could have had a wide-reaching impact in the EU services sector. Services that were covered included, for example, car hire, estate agencies, advice from architects, social care and environmental services. Trade unions argued that such changes would culminate in **social dumping** practices, as rules in Eastern European countries were often less rigid than in Western Europe. The Commission maintained that the directive would create 600,000 jobs, stimulate economic growth and provide greater choice for consumers. Critics feared, however, that the directive would unleash unwelcome competition between workers in different parts of the EU, reduce income levels and lower standards of social and environmental protection. These fears, combined with concerns about the dangers of companies opting to relocate to low-cost economies, led to a series of mass protests, which culminated in a 100,000-strong march through **Brussels**, **Belgium**, in opposition to this directive in March 2005.

The pressure of public opinion led the **European Council** effectively to postpone the directive in late March 2005 by demanding amendments. There can be little doubt that this example of liberalization fed into the discussions on the **Treaty establishing a Constitution for Europe** in France. The **European Parliament** (EP) approved the Services Directive at its first reading in February 2006. However, the directive excluded a number of services such as broadcasting, postal services, gambling and audiovisual services. The **European Commission** pledged to take the EP's views into account before producing an amended proposal in April 2006, which would serve as a basis for a second reading in the EP. After substantial amendments (including for example the exclusion of public and private health care and social services), the directive was finally adopted in December 2006 by the EP and European Council, and came into force in December 2009.

BOSNIA AND HERZEGOVINA declared its independence from **Yugoslavia** in 1992 only to become the focus of a civil war, which lasted until 1995, when the Dayton Peace Accords, marking an agreement to end the war, were signed. Subsequently, the government of the country has been overseen by the Office of the High Representative of the International Community (which was created under the agreement) and by the Special Representative of the European Union (between 2002 and 2011 these two positions were held concurrently by the same person), with initially a **North Atlantic Treaty Organization**-led force (IFOR) and, since December 2004, a European Union (EU) peacekeeping force (EUFOR), seeking to maintain peace and stability. Since 1999 relations with the EU have developed, albeit slowly, in the context of the **Stabilization and Association Process** (SAP). A road map initially detailed a catalogue of essential measures that would have to be adopted in the country before the feasibility of concluding a **stabilization and association agreement** (SAA) could be explored. Appropriate measures were eventually taken, with negotiations on an SAA opening on 25 January 2006. These were closed in December 2007 and the agreement was eventually signed in June 2008, following the implementation of further reform of the police, public broadcasting and public administration and an improvement in the country's co-operation with the International Criminal Tribunal for the former Yugoslavia.

Along with the other countries in the **Western Balkans**, Bosnia and Herzegovina was granted the status of **potential candidate state** in 2000. The country also has a **European partnership** arrangement with the EU. This was first adopted in 2004 and has subsequently been revised, with a new European partnership being adopted in February 2008. This followed a **European Commission** progress report on Bosnia and Herzegovina, which noted the deceleration of political reforms, limited progress with economic reforms, that state institutions continued to be compromised by ethnic division and that the country had yet to assume full ownership of its own governance. The report, however, recorded the EU's continued commitment to supporting reform, noting that pre-accession financial assistance to the country was being provided under the **instrument for pre-accession assistance**. Subsequent reports have raised similar concerns. Although Bosnia and Herzegovina had planned to submit an application for EU membership by the end of 2010, and the EU had then provided the Bosnian Government with a road map in 2012 for submitting such an application, no application has been submitted. Under an initiative by the British and German Governments, in late 2014 a new EU action plan was proposed, under which financial assistance would be released in exchange for commitments by all main political parties to significant reforms. In February 2015 both houses of the Parliamentary Assembly of Bosnia and Herzegovina approved a statement committing the country to reforms, and the SAA with the EU entered into effect on 1 June. Following the further adoption of a Reform Agenda by the authorities in July, Bosnia and Herzegovina submitted a formal application for membership of the EU in February 2016. EU officials welcomed the initiative; however, they indicated that further significant reforms were necessary before it could be considered. Although the main state and Federation parties in Bosnia and Herzegovina declared support for EU membership, those in the Republika Srpska entity expressed strong reservations.

BOVINE SPONGIFORM ENCEPHALOPATHY (BSE) or, as it is more widely known, 'mad cow disease', became an issue for the European Union (EU) in early 1996 following a public announcement made by the British Government about the possible connection between BSE and a new variant of Creutzfeldt-Jakob disease (a degenerative and ultimately deadly brain disease) in humans. Several British scientists had long believed that there was a link between the two diseases that originated in feeding offal (the remains of sheep and cattle) to cattle, and that the disease was being passed to humans following their consumption of BSE-infected beef. The British Government's recognition of that possibility prompted public alarm about the safety of eating diseased beef, and the fact that John Major's Government had not consulted its EU partners prior to its announcement only made matters worse. The **European Commission** responded by banning the import of all British beef into the EU, as did the Governments of both the **USA** and

Australia. The British agricultural community suddenly lost its export markets and sales of beef in the **United Kingdom** fell dramatically. Major responded by introducing a 'no co-operation agreement' with the EU that effectively meant blocking all proposals (even those supported by the British Government) that were subject to unanimity in the **Council of the European Union**. At the same time many cattle herds were slaughtered on suspicion of infection. In June 1996 the **European Council** approved a plan to have the ban on British beef gradually lifted once each sector was given the all-clear by the Commission's Scientific Veterinary Committee. The episode was investigated by the **European Parliament**, which in a 1997 report was critical of the Commission's handling of the crisis, accusing it of placing farmers' interests above those of consumers. Despite the lifting of the ban on British beef, some states, notably **France**, continued to refuse to import British beef, which led to legal action against the French Government before the European Courts. Exports of British beef to France resumed in 2002.

ALENKA BRATUŠEK (1970–) nominated herself as the Slovenian Commissioner to the new 28-member **European Commission** led by President-elect **Jean-Claude Juncker**, (which took office on 1 November 2014). In September Juncker named Bratušek as a Vice-President of the European Commission, subject to approval by the **European Parliament** (EP) and the **European Council**. After graduating from the University of Ljubljana and before entering politics, Bratušek worked in the Slovenian civil service. Bratušek enjoyed a rapid rise in Slovenian politics. She was elected to Kranj city council in 2006 and 2010. In 2011 she was elected to the Slovenian parliament and held a number of senior political roles in **Slovenia**, most importantly serving as Slovenia's first female Prime Minister from March 2013 until her resignation in May 2014. Her nomination to the Commission was made while she was heading a caretaker administration in Slovenia, and was subject to an investigation by an ethics commission. Bratušek's candidacy was rejected by the EP following a confirmation hearing in October 2014. She withdrew her candidacy and the Slovenian Prime Minister put forward a new candidate for the post of European Commissioner, **Violeta Bulc**.

BRETTON WOODS in New Hampshire, **USA**, was the location and name of an agreement, made in 1944 by several Western countries, on the introduction of a new international monetary system based upon fixed exchange rates, and backed by two reserve currencies, the US dollar and British pound sterling. The intention was to make currencies convertible on current account, so facilitating multilateral trade and reducing the need for disruptive devaluations. The system experienced a number of problems in the late 1940s, and did not become fully operational until 1958. In the 1960s the fixed exchange-rate system, especially the two reserve currencies, came under increasing pressure. The agreement effectively disintegrated in 1971, when the USA unilaterally suspended dollar convertibility against gold. The Smithsonian Agreement and the European **Snake** were efforts to salvage some advantage from the failure of the Bretton Woods agreement since, despite the benefits that floating currencies may have held for governments, the consequent currency fluctuations adversely affected international monetary stability. The **European Monetary System** (EMS) of 1979 was an attempt by the European Communities to stabilize currency fluctuations by introducing a modified exchange-rate system that would replicate what were believed to have been the virtues of Bretton Woods.

BREXIT is a term that has been coined to refer to the eventual departure of the **United Kingdom** from the **European Union** (EU), following that country's decision to hold an 'in/out' referendum in June 2016, at which the British electorate voted by a margin of 51.9% to 48.1% to leave the EU. (The term **Brexit** evolved from the increasingly widespread use of the popular term **Grexit**, to describe a possible Greek exit from the EU, from 2012.) The decision of the British electorate, which few opinion polls, political observers, financial markets or even, indeed, leaders of the 'Leave' campaign (then Secretary of State for Justice Michael Gove, former Conservative Mayor of London Boris Johnson, and leader of the **UK Independence Party** Nigel Farage) had predicted, caused immediate and significant shockwaves throughout the bloc and beyond, both politically and economically. Equity markets immediately sustained heavy losses, and the British pound sterling lost around one-10th of its value against other major currencies within 24 hours, notably falling to US $1.30 = GBP on the morning of 24 June, from $1.50 = GBP on the previous day, its lowest point since 1984. Immediately following the announcement of the result, British Prime Minister **David Cameron** (who had made a manifesto pledge in 2015 to hold a referendum on EU membership, and subsequently urged British voters to choose continued membership of the EU, having negotiated concessions on British membership of the bloc in early 2016) announced his intention to resign as premier, pending the appointment of his successor as leader of the Conservative Party. Cameron was succeeded by **Theresa May** in July 2016. Upon forming a new administration, May appointed David Davis as Secretary of State for Exiting the European Union. Uncertainty prevailed about the exact nature of the UK's future relationship with the EU, upon formally exiting the bloc. In March 2017 the British Government invoked **Article 50** of the Treaty of Lisbon, initiating formal proceedings for an eventual (and unprecedented) departure from the bloc. The UK was duly scheduled to leave the EU by 29 March 2019. Formal negotiations commenced between the EU and the UK on 19 June 2017, with the aim of concluding an agreement establishing arrangements for the country's departure from the Union, while seeking to develop a framework for the country's future relations with the EU. However, by September little progress had been made, with the fourth negotiating round in late September ending in deadlock, and terms still to be agreed over, *inter alia*, any financial settlement between the two sides.

Some observers suggested that leaving the EU without an agreement could be economically catastrophic for the UK, as the immediate effect would be the non-application of the European treaties and EU law without any agreed replacement, which would mean that the UK would, in terms of international trade in services at least, be subject to trading by **World Trade Organization** rules, which would not give Britain any special privileges in trading with the EU, as WTO rules generally prevent members from discriminating in favour of a trading partner. At the time of the vote in favour of Brexit, the EU had 22 separate free trade agreements with individual countries, and five multilateral agreements covering multiple countries or trading blocs (comprising 30 countries). Therefore, the UK would effectively have to renegotiate, separately, 52 trade agreements to retain a preferential trading relationship with these countries.

Other than a complete rupture with the EU and all its institutions and treaties (which initially appeared to be the route favoured by Theresa May), alternative proposals among observers for future relations with the EU had included a model based on the relationship between the EU and **Norway**, according to which the UK would be included within the **European Free Trade Association** and the **European Economic Area** and enjoy the attendant benefits. Proposals also included a tailor-made agreement, as the EU has with **Switzerland**, **Canada** and **Turkey**. A final deal would come about only after the questions of any transition arrangements, the UK's financial commitments, **citizens' rights** and Northern Ireland, as well as trade, had been resolved to the satisfaction of the EU and British negotiators. Observers noted the inherent risk to the EU of so-called political and economic contagion from Brexit: the UK was the second largest country in the bloc, in terms of both population and economic output. The UK still had an important role to play in Europe, and a delicate balance had to be struck to maintain a good relationship with the EU in terms of trade and diplomatic relations, without agreeing such lenient terms that other EU member states with a significant proportion of Eurosceptic voters were encouraged to demand that their governments hold a similar referendum on membership. Although parties with a Eurosceptic inclination were widespread throughout EU member states, **Austria**, **Denmark**, **Sweden** and France were the most notable examples. In July 2016 former European Commissioner **Michel Barnier** of France was appointed as the EU's chief negotiator with the UK over its planned exit from the bloc, and subsequently director at the **European Commission** of a so-called Brexit Task Force, and in September former Belgian premier and senior **MEP Guy Verhofstadt** was appointed as the representative of the European Parliament. The deputy chief negotiator of the Commission task force, from October of that year, was Sabine Weyand of Germany, hitherto a deputy director-general at the European Commission's Directorate-General for Trade. President of the Commission **Jean-Claude Juncker**, in a State of the Union speech to the European Parliament in mid-September, warned the British Government that it should not expect '**à la carte** access to the benefits of the EU', without assuming responsibilities to member states (such as **freedom of movement**). This view was reiterated by Michel Barnier in August 2017, following the largely inconclusive third round of Brexit negotiations, when he stated that 'The UK wants to take back control but also wants (its regulatory) standards recognized automatically in the EU … this is simply impossible. You cannot be outside the single market and shape its legal order'. It remained to be seen how significant the impact of the UK's departure from the EU would be on schemes that have facilitated co-operation in, variously: combating cross-border criminality, such as **Europol**; managing the security of the EU's borders, such as **FRONTEX**; and education, such as the **Erasmus+** scheme, which allow students in any EU member state to study at universities throughout the Union.

BRITAIN: See **United Kingdom**

BROADCASTING: See **Cultural Policy**; **European Broadcasting Union**; **Media Policy**

BRUSSELS is the capital city of **Belgium**, with a population of some 1m people. Brussels is also home to the executive and administrative branches of the European Union (EU). In addition to being the location of the **European Commission** and the Secretariat of the **Council of the European Union**, it houses the offices of both the **Committee of the Regions** and the **European Economic and Social Committee**. The **European Parliament** has much of its staff in this city and the majority of its committee meetings take place in its new Brussels headquarters. In addition, all the national representations of the member states reside in Brussels, as do representations of many regions (e.g. the German *Länder*) and sub-national authorities (e.g. the **Northern Ireland Executive Office** in Brussels and **Scotland Europa**), which currently have premises near the EU institutions. Moreover, Brussels has attracted the attention of a variety of public, private and voluntary organizations that either own or rent offices in the city in the hope of being able to influence policy development and EU **decision making**. Finally, Brussels has also been the home of the **North Atlantic Treaty Organization** (NATO) since 1967. The concentration of EU institutions in the city has meant that the name 'Brussels' has often been used as a term to describe the EU and its decision making bodies. Suggestions have been made that Brussels, as it functions in many ways as a capital-elect of the EU, should be given a special status similar to that accorded to Canberra (Australian Capital Territory) or Washington, DC (**USA**).

BRUSSELS, TREATY OF: See **Treaty of Brussels**

'**BRUSSELSIZATION**' is a term that is associated with the evolution of the European Union's (EU) **common foreign and security policy** established under Pillar II of the **Treaty on European Union** in 1993. Although the EU's supranational powers are highly marginalized in this policy area, there is a growing sense that this policy's development is being determined to a greater extent than ever in **Brussels** by a number of Pillar II working groups. Since the days of **European political co-operation** in the 1970s and the 1980s, working groups have played an instrumental role in EU foreign policy business. There are an estimated 20 in existence and they exchange information on issues ranging from landmines to the **Organization for Security and Co-operation in Europe** (OSCE). Foreign policy may remain firmly under the control of the national governments, but since the **Maastricht summit** it has become increasingly apparent that more authority and expertise on Pillar II questions has shifted from member states to their national delegations (**Permanent Representations**) in Brussels, which collaborate with the working groups. In other words, the process of 'Brusselsization' ensures that a substantial amount of information on foreign policy is exchanged between the national delegations, and more so than between any other sovereign states in any other international organization.

BSE: See **Bovine Spongiform Encephalopathy**

The **BUDGET** has always proved to be a source of controversy, first for the European Communities (EC) and then for the European Union (EU). When the **European Economic Community** was established in 1957, it was agreed that its budget would be financed by national contributions from the member states, the contribution of each state to be determined by its gross national product (GNP). This was the standard means for financing international organizations such as the **United Nations**. The **European Commission** regarded the EC as being a different type of organization, however, and since the mid-1960s has sought access to its own revenue sources. In 1970 the original **six** member states in the **Treaty of Luxembourg** decided that national contributions would be progressively phased out by 1975, to be replaced by a system of EC **own resources**, that is, funds that originate in the member states but are the property of the EC. In other words, the amount of money that is available to the EU is determined by an agreement among the member states. It was generally assumed at the outset that the contributions and the receipts would more or less balance. This has not been the case, and the budget has been a politically sensitive issue. However, the European Commission states that the financial contributions made by EU countries to the EU budget are distributed equitably, so that each country contributes a percentage of its **value-added tax** (VAT), together with 1% of its gross national income.

Revenue comes from two main additional sources, as the EU receives levies on imports of sugar, and **customs duties** from outside the EU. In addition, fines imposed by the Commission for infringements of EC **competition policy** were added to the budget, and in recent years accounted for approximately 1% to 2% of the entire budget. The now defunct **European Coal and Steel Community** (ECSC) retained its own budget, which was financed by a direct levy upon coal and steel enterprises within the EU. The **Treaty on European Union** formally recognized that the EC have their own sources of revenue, stipulating that there must be sufficient own resources to cover all agreed expenditure.

The annual spending plans of the EU are determined after lengthy negotiations between the Council and the **European Parliament** (EP). The budget process consists of five stages. The Commission prepares a preliminary draft budget for presentation to the **Council of the European Union** no later than 1 September of the year before the one during which the budget is to be implemented. The Council can then accept or amend the draft: it has tended invariably to reduce the total amount of proposed expenditure. By 5 October the Council must have agreed, by a qualified majority (see **Qualified Majority Voting**), upon a draft budget and have sent it to the EP. The EP enjoys 'power of the purse' with regard to the budget and has 45 days in which to consider the draft. Prior to the entry into force of the **Treaty of Lisbon**, on those items that represented compulsory expenditure, the EP was only able to suggest modifications to the Council's proposals; the EP has since gained co-decision over the entire budget. On **non-compulsory expenditure**, it is free to amend the draft budget, albeit only within a general limit previously defined by the Council. Once its deliberations are complete, the revised budget returns to the Council, which may reject the EP's changes. When the proposed modifications to compulsory expenditure do not entail an overall increase in expenditure, a qualified majority vote is needed in the Council; when an increase is involved, a positive majority in the Council is required for rejection.

In cases where the Council decides to reject EP amendments to non-compulsory expenditure, the two institutions are obliged to enter into a conciliation procedure to seek a compromise. The final revised document is then returned to the EP for adoption. For the budget to be rejected by the EP a two-thirds' majority of the recorded votes must be against adoption, and this qualified majority must also constitute an overall majority of the total EP membership. If the EP votes against adoption, the net effect is that the EU does not have a budget for the new calendar year, and expenditure is restricted each month to one-12th of the budget approved for the previous year. This restriction remains in force until a new budget can be approved. The EP rejected the budget in 1979 and 1984, but each time it ultimately accepted a version that was only marginally different from the one it had refused to adopt. Since 1993 the budget has been the subject of an inter-institutional agreement that seeks to inject greater budgetary discipline and to improve budgetary procedures between the Council, the Commission and the EP. This 1993 agreement was judged a success and was renewed in 1998.

Fraud remains a significant problem and it is estimated that between 2% and 10% of the budget becomes subject to fraudulent financial claims, primarily from the operation of the **Common Agricultural Policy** (CAP). The **Treaty of Amsterdam** introduced measures to protect against fraud and misuse of EU finances. It also provided for greater scrutiny of agricultural expenditure. The **European Court of Auditors** was to have an enhanced role in ensuring that the budget was not being misspent.

Discussions for the financial perspective running from 2007 to 2013 began in earnest at the end of 2004 and proved to be contentious. The difficulties centred on the overall level of spending and the breakdown between the various headings of expenditure. The Commission, with the support of some of the smaller EU states, had been keen to maintain the existing level of 1.24% of GNP to determine the overall size of the budget. However, the net contributors to the budget (**Germany**, **Sweden**, the **Netherlands** and the **United Kingdom**) wanted to limit spending to 1% of GNP. The final agreement was to be determined by the member state governments and was capped at 1.05%. In the 2000s the issue of EU financing became more controversial than at any time since the early 1980s. For example, discussions between the EU member states stalled in June 2005 at a meeting of the **European Council**, as the UK refused to compromise on its rebate unless the French Government showed willingness to engage in serious CAP reform. The ramifications of this meeting endured for the remainder of 2005, with the French and British Governments in conflict over how best to finance the 2004 **enlargement** to the advantage of the new entrants. The UK came under increasing pressure from the other member states to reach an agreement on the budget and to recognize that the UK was no longer in a position to need the maintenance of the rebate. EU leaders finally secured an agreement for the new financial perspective (2007–13) of €862,400m. As part of the overall agreement, the UK agreed to relinquish approximately €10,500m. over this period in return for serious consideration of a farm subsidy reduction in 2008. The leaders of the states from **Central and Eastern Europe** expressed their satisfaction at the outcome, particularly the Polish Prime Minister, Kazimierz Marcinkiewicz, who secured an additional €4,000m. in aid. Overall aid to the new member states was capped at €157,000m. Farm and rural development remained the most significant area of expenditure, accounting for €292,000m.

In June 2011 the European Commission, in the course of preparations for the 2014–20 Multi-annual Financial Framework (MFF), proposed to increase the **transparency** and fairness of the system for financing the EU budget by introducing a new financial transaction tax (FTT). In late September the Commission presented a directive on the proposed FTT, which would be levied on all transactions between financial institutions, provided that at least one of those institutions was located in the EU; it was proposed that the exchange of shares and bonds be taxed at a rate of 0.1%, and derivatives at a rate of 0.01%. Two-thirds of revenue from the FTT was to be directed to the EU budget, thereby reducing the gross national income (GNI)-based contributions of member states, while the remaining one-third would be retained by individual member states. In February 2013 the Commission tabled its proposal on the FTT. The 11 member states involved with this area (including **France** and Germany) agreed to adopt the new FTT.

The budget for 2014 was adopted after intense interinstitutional discussions in November 2013. It totalled some €142,640.5m. in commitments and €135,504.6m. in payments. The UK, the Netherlands, **Denmark** and **Finland** reportedly voted against this agreement in the Council as they hoped for a further reduction to the EU budget. However, qualified majority and not unanimity determine voting and it was duly approved. Combating unemployment was a principal aim for 2014. The budget adopted by the Commission for 2015 retained the focus on helping Europe to recover from the economic crisis and paid close attention to **employment** and **competitiveness**. It envisaged commitments totalling some €145,300m. and payments of some €141,200m. The budget for 2016 was adopted in November 2015. It totalled €155,004.2m. in commitments and €143,890.0m. in payments. This left a margin of €2,300m. under the expenditure ceiling of the MFF, allowing the EU to finance unforeseen requirements and challenges, if necessary. The budget made available more than €4,000m. in commitments for helping member states and third countries to address the **European migration crisis**, while increasing resources for the fight against crime and protection against terrorist attacks, which had increased markedly in France in 2015, with jihadist networks operating elsewhere, notably **Belgium**. The internal security fund for 2016 increased by 64.0% in commitments and by 46.7% in payments compared with the 2015 budget. The fund is designed to help to implement the EU's internal security strategy, law enforcement co-operation and the management of the EU's external borders. Meanwhile, €698m. in extraordinary additional funding for farmers was granted to alleviate the effects of the embargo that was imposed in 2014 by the Russian Government on certain agricultural products from the EU, and to the dairy and pig meat sectors. The budget for 2016 also included a commitment from the EP to reduce the number of posts by 197 employees by 2019 (the Council of the EU, the EP and the Commission had agreed in December 2013 to reduce their staff by 5% between 2013 and 2017). The EU budget for 2017 was adopted on 1 December 2016, and set the total level of commitments at €157,858m. and payments at €134,490m. The budget made available almost €6,000m. in commitments to help to strengthen borders and to address the ongoing European migration crisis; it also provided for some €200m. to fund an instrument for the provision of **humanitarian assistance** within the EU.

The political sensitivities behind the drawing up and objective setting of the EU budget, and over identifying the net beneficiaries and net contributors, have become a routine aspect of EU affairs. The tensions were displayed once again as EU member state governments entered into the final stage negotiations for a new financial perspective for 2014–20. Although the European Council agreed on the terms and size of the 2014–20 budget in February 2013, the **European Parliament** raised concerns about some of the budget lines and especially the cuts in expenditure. The financial perspective took over two-and-a-half years to be negotiated. In November 2013 the EP endorsed the EU's MFF for 2014–20. The **European Council** approved the MFF deal in December 2013. The new framework enables the EU to invest some €960,000m. (or 1% of EU GNI) in commitments and €908,400m. in payments. Jobs and **competitiveness** are at the heart of the MFF. Broken down into specific fields, some 6% will go towards funding the administration of the EU; 6% will be directed towards Global Europe; 1% to the operation of the **Common Fisheries Policy**; 2% to security and citizenship; and 9% will be directed towards the rural development objectives within the CAP. Most will go to three core EU areas: some 29% will be allocated to market-related expenditure and direct payments under the CAP; some 13% has been set aside for competitiveness, growth and jobs; and 34% is to be targeted towards economic and social cohesion. The new MFF introduced programmes that seek to enhance Europe's political priorities. Some of the most high profile of these centre on issues such as research and innovation (**Horizon 2020**), education (**Erasmus+**) and the competitiveness of businesses (COSME). (Agreement on the new MFF enabled the final realization of the 2014 EU budget.)

VIOLETA BULC (1964–) was nominated in October 2014 as Slovenia's representative in **Jean-Claude Juncker**'s **European Commission** after the initial candidate, **Alenka Bratušek**, failed to win the confidence of **Members of the European Parliament** (MEPs) at the Commission hearings. Bulc did win the support of MEPs and the **European Parliament** and the **European Council** approved Juncker's Commission. Bulc took up her position as the Commissioner for Transport in November. Bulc studied for a degree in Computer Science and Informatics at the University of Ljubljana before successfully undertaking a postgraduate degree in the USA and returning to Slovenia to undertake an MBA. Immediately prior to her appointment to the Commission, Bulc had served as a minister without portfolio in the Slovenian Government.

BULGARIA is one of the 10 Central and Eastern European countries that applied for European Union (EU) membership in the 1990s, submitting its formal application in 1995. Prior to this it had signed a **Europe agreement** with the European Communities in 1993, which entered into force in 1995. The **European Commission**'s report on the **applicant countries** of July 1997, entitled **Agenda 2000**, proposed that **accession negotiations** with Bulgaria should be deferred, owing to the limited measures undertaken with regard to economic reform and the degree of political instability experienced in the early to mid-1990s. Although the country had almost fulfilled the political criteria for membership, the report stated that investment was still needed in the areas of environment, transport, energy, home affairs, justice and agriculture. Bulgaria was thus not a participant in the first round of accession negotiations that began in March 1998. However, greater political stability helped Bulgaria's image, and the country was included in the second round of negotiations that commenced in 2000. The country continued to make steady progress, although difficulties persisted over specific economic targets and the EU's demands for the early closure of the obsolete reactors at the controversial Kozloduy nuclear plant. The Bulgarian Government closed two of the reactors in December 2002 and announced its intention to shut down a further two by the end of 2006. The final negotiating chapters were closed in June 2004 and in April 2005 a **Treaty of Accession** was signed. This was ratified by the Bulgarian parliament on 11 May 2005, with 230 MPs voting in favour and two against. Bulgaria joined the EU on 1 January 2007 alongside **Romania**. From 26 September 2005 to 31 December 2006, Bulgaria had 18 observers in the European Parliament (EP), who were appointed from government and opposition parties, as agreed by the Bulgarian National Assembly. Following accession on 1 January 2007 the observers became MEPs, who then contested the EP elections, which were held in June 2009. Upon Bulgaria's accession to the EU in 2007, many existing EU member states imposed extensive labour market restrictions; only nine countries guaranteed unlimited access to migrant workers from Bulgaria and Romania; however, all transitional migration restrictions were lifted from 1 January 2014. As with Romania, Bulgaria has been subjected to post-accession monitoring by the Commission of progress in compliance with judicial reform and anti-corruption measures. The Commission suspended nearly €500m. in development aid to Bulgaria in July 2008, after releasing a report that strongly criticized the country's continued failure to reduce levels of organized crime and corruption. After taking office in July 2009, the administration of Prime Minister Boyko Borisov introduced measures aimed at improving the management of EU funds. In September it was announced that the Commission was to resume farm subsidy payments and other agricultural aid to Bulgaria. In December 2015 the National Assembly adopted a reform intended to strengthen the independence of the Bulgarian judiciary (in accordance with EU requirements). However, most parties opposed curbs on the powers of the Prosecutor-General and voted in favour of an amended version of the legislation. In a report issued in January 2017, a decade after Bulgaria's accession to the EU, the Commission noted that although Bulgaria had made progress in implementing judicial reforms, significant efforts to combat corruption were still required. It would be necessary for the third Borisov Government, appointed in May, to accelerate the country's anti-corruption efforts.

The **BUNDESBANK** is the central bank of the Federal Republic of **Germany**, and was established in 1957. Because of the importance of the German economy and the strength of its currency, the Bank has had a substantial influence upon Western European economic policy and activity, and was the core of the **European Monetary System**. The Bundesbank's central policy concern was to fight inflation in West Germany. However, this obsession with price stability as the core policy objective in turn affected other European economies, which experienced rising unemployment and weaker economic growth. This was particularly the case in **France** by the late 1980s, and was a prime motivating factor behind the French Prime Minister Edouard Balladur's pursuit of **economic and monetary union** (EMU). By the early 1990s the heavy financial strains of the German reunification process only fortified the Bundesbank's priorities of controlling domestic inflation and maintaining high interest rates, and led to further political controversy in 1992–93, when these domestic objectives took precedence over policies that other member states believed the Bank should have adopted in order to preserve the **exchange-rate mechanism** (ERM). The problem with the Bundesbank's policy was external, in that other countries, with weaker currencies, had to match the level of German interest rates if they wished to stay in the ERM. This adversely affected their own economies, while exposing them to market speculation on the grounds that their currency values were artificially high. The Bundesbank and a majority of the German electorate remained unenthusiastic about the notion of EMU and feared that any new currency would be less stable than the Deutsche Mark. The decision for Germany to embark on the EMU project was, however, politically driven and decided. With the establishment of the **euro** and the **European Central Bank** (ECB), the direct influence of the Bundesbank over European finance policy inevitably declined.

The **BUREAU** or Executive Committee is an essential part of the organization of the **European Parliament**. The Bureau comprises the President, Vice-Presidents, Quaestors and potentially others, and focuses its activities on both political and administrative matters.

BUSINESS AND INNOVATION CENTRES (BICs) were launched by the **European Commission** in 1984 to encourage diversification of activity by small enterprises, and to help establish new small companies in innovative areas of activity and production. Their role today is very much to promote regional development. By 2016 there were more than 160 BICs (full members) in the 28 member states. (See also **European Business and Innovation Centre Network**.)

BUSINESSEUROPE was until January 2007 known as the **Union of Industrial and Employers' Confederations of Europe** (UNICE), a transnational federation of employers' associations. It is one of the earliest (founded in 1958) and most influential of the pressure groups (see **Interest groups**; **Lobbying**) operating in **Brussels**. BUSINESSEUROPE represents the interests of industry as a whole, and comprises a confederation of national federations of major business associations from across Europe. For example, it includes the Confederation of British Industry and the Irish Business and Employers' Confederation, as well as groups from the largest states such as the German Confederation for Industry (Bundesverband der Deutschen Industrie) and the smallest states such as the **Malta** Confederation of Industry. In 2017 there were 39 members from 34 countries, including the European Union countries, the **European Economic Area** countries, and some Central and Eastern European countries. BUSINESSEUROPE plays both an informal and a formal role in European public affairs. On an informal level, its representatives meet **European Commission** officials on an almost daily basis, and on a more formal level it is frequently asked for its views on policy initiatives. Its priorities centre on market **liberalization** and **deregulation**. It remains much more unenthusiastic, however, about initiatives in the area of **social policy**. BUSINESSEUROPE has as one of its objectives the promotion and elaboration 'of an industrial policy in a European spirit', which is qualified by the statement that it 'should mainly consist in taking into consideration the industrial imperatives in the various policies of the European Communities and not become an instrument of intervention'. BUSINESSEUROPE has therefore tended to oppose measures such as the proposed **Company Law Statute**, which threatened to place restraints upon its members, although on occasion its impact on the European Communities was weakened by differences of interest among both its economic and its national components. BUSINESSEUROPE operates as one of the Commission's **social partners** alongside the **European Trade Union Confederation**. The organization's activities can be grouped under six principal headings. These strive to release entrepreneurial energy; to promote innovation; to liberate the **internal market**; to improve the functioning of the labour market; to make **environmental policy** more effective and efficient; and to foster international trade and investment.

C

CABINET is the name given to the group of personal advisers and aides attached to each Commissioner within the **European Commission**. Its purpose is to provide the Commissioner with political and policy advice, as well as liaising with other groups within the European Union and speaking for the Commissioner in meetings of officials.

CABOTAGE is the system whereby transport providers may offer services in the domestic market of another member state. As part of the European Communities' (EC) **road transport** policy, the Council of Ministers (see **Council of the European Union**) agreed in 1993 on measures including a common tax system for heavy goods vehicles using EC roads, which led to full liberalization of road *cabotage* by 1998. Since then efforts have focused on promoting *cabotage* on the rail network and within shipping.

DAVID CAMERON (1966–) was Prime Minister of the **United Kingdom** between May 2010 and July 2016, when he resigned following a national referendum on British membership of the European Union, in which voters chose by a narrow majority to exit the bloc (see **Brexit**—Cameron had supported remaining a member of the EU). Cameron was elected as the leader of the Conservative Party of the UK in December 2005, in which role he served until July 2016, when he was succeeded as both Prime Minister and party leader by **Theresa May**. In March 2007 Cameron identified three main areas for future EU concern and development, namely **globalization**, global warming and global poverty. Opposed to the **Treaty of Lisbon** and committed to a British referendum on it, Cameron was swift to urge the abandonment of **ratification** following the Irish 'no' to the treaty in June 2008. Following the outcome of the 2009 **European Parliament** (EP) elections, in June Cameron unveiled his new European alliance—the **European Conservatives and Reformists Group**. Following the 2014 elections to the EP, this group comprised 19 British Conservative **Members of the European Parliament** (MEPs) and one Ulster Unionist, meaning that the British Conservative Party accounted for over 25% of the group's then total membership of 70.

Cameron's pledge to hold a referendum in the UK on the Treaty of Lisbon was dropped once the treaty had been ratified and came into force in December 2009. Nevertheless, Cameron recognized that the 'Europe issue' remained contentious within parts of the Conservative Party and pledged to renegotiate a number of aspects of the EU treaties (especially social and employment issues) if the Conservatives won the 2010 British general election. Cameron won a majority of the votes at the 2010 general election, but the Conservative Party did not win enough to secure a majority of the seats within the House of Commons (producing the first 'hung parliament' since 1974). To resolve the political impasse, Cameron opted to enter into a coalition government with the Liberal Democrats. Although the coalition with the pro-EU Liberal Democrats had been expected to dilute the more abrasive tone towards the EU that many Conservative supporters may have wanted, in November the Cameron-led Government introduced an 'EU Bill', which required increased parliamentary and, in several cases, popular approval of further treaty amendments and decisions concerning the UK's position within the EU (for example, with regard to **euro** membership). The bill received royal assent in July 2011. In an attempt to dampen dissent among his backbench colleagues and to dent the growing popularity of the **UK Independence Party** (UKIP) in marginal parliamentary seats, Cameron expressed his view in June 2012 that a referendum on the UK's relationship with the EU should take place. In January 2013 Cameron made a major speech (the so-called Bloomberg speech) on the EU, pledging, on the assumption that the Conservatives won the 2015 general election, to hold an 'in/out' referendum by the end of 2017 on the UK's membership of the EU. In June 2013 Cameron argued that **Eurosceptics** who advocated the UK's departure from the EU were in denial, and that any such move would not serve the national interest. Cameron's efforts to appease his internal critics on the issue of EU membership did not work and he increasingly found himself at odds with many of his Conservative party backbenchers, especially after the emergence of UKIP as the largest British party at the 2014 EP elections and his own inability to prevent the European Council's selection of **Jean-Claude Juncker** as its choice for the post of **European Commission** President in June 2014. In the general election held in May 2015 the Conservatives secured a majority and subsequently formed a single-party administration, again led by Cameron. In January 2016 Cameron negotiated a series of concessions from the EU at a meeting of the **European Council** in Brussels. The promised in/out referendum on EU membership was subsequently scheduled for 23 June, with voters offered the option of continuing membership of the EU (on terms that would take into account the recently negotiated concessions), or leaving the bloc altogether. Amid an often fractious and divisive contest, in which Cameron was a strong advocate of the 'Remain' (pro-EU) camp, he and his Chancellor of the Exchequer, George Osborne, attracted criticism for an important pillar of their campaign, which opponents in the 'Leave' camp called 'Project Fear'. The Leave camp suggested that Cameron and Osborne were making deliberately and excessively pessimistic economic forecasts in the event of an eventual British exit from the EU, in an attempt to persuade voters that anything other than a vote to remain in the EU would be catastrophic. As it transpired, Cameron was unable to persuade a majority of the British electorate to vote to remain in the EU, and within hours of the result being announced (with 51.9% of the 72.2% of the electorate who participated voting to leave the EU), on 24 June Cameron announced his intention to resign, pending a leadership election in the Conservative Party, in order to choose his successor. Theresa May was appointed leader of the party in July, and Prime Minister, ahead of the leadership contest schedule, after her remaining rival, Andrea Leadsom, withdrew from the campaign. Cameron would be remembered, in the short term at least, as the figure that effectively facilitated the UK's exit from the EU—not intentionally, but as the result of political miscalculation. In September 2016 Cameron also announced his resignation as a member of parliament.

CANDIDATE COUNTRIES was the term adopted by the Helsinki **summit meeting** of the **European Council** in December

1999 to refer to those countries involved in **accession negotiations** launched in February 2000. At the time, the term covered the 10 **applicant countries** from **Central and Eastern Europe**, **Cyprus**, **Malta** and **Turkey**. With the recent **enlargements** of the European Union (EU) on 1 May 2004, on 1 January 2007 and on 1 July 2013, the number now stands at five: **Albania**, **Serbia**, **Montenegro**, Turkey and the **former Yugoslav republic of Macedonia**. In addition to adopting the term 'candidate countries', the European Council in 2000 introduced the term **potential candidate state** to describe other countries in the **Western Balkans** that aspire to membership. These are **Bosnia and Herzegovina** (which made a formal application for membership of the EU in February 2016) and **Kosovo**.

CAP: See **Common Agricultural Policy**

CARBON TAX is a tax imposed on the carbon content of fuels and is a form of carbon pricing. The idea of a carbon tax at the EU level first arose in the form of a proposed energy tax presented by the **European Commission** in the early 1990s. The idea constituted part of the campaign to reduce **atmospheric pollution**. It emerged as a principal element of the European Commission's efforts to develop an **energy policy** that would be closely linked to EU **environmental policy**. The tax would involve a levy on petroleum produced within the European Union (EU) as well as upon the fuel and carbon content of all non-renewable fuel. The tax was seen as part of the EU's acceptance of the agreement at the **United Nations** Framework Convention on Climate Change, held in Rio de Janeiro, Brazil, in 1992, to stabilize carbon dioxide emissions at 1990 levels by the end of the century. The proposal found support among the traditional 'leader' member states on environmental policy (the **Netherlands**, **Germany** and **Denmark**), which sought EU-wide measures to match taxes already in place at the national level, but it provoked strong opposition from the poorer member states, as well as from energy-intensive industries. Concerns are often expressed that the imposition of a carbon tax may lead some firms to relocate to other countries where no such taxes exist, having a negative impact on employment. An **Emissions Trading Scheme** (ETS) was launched in January 2005, which obliges companies that exceed agreed carbon dioxide emissions to buy extra allowances from more efficient companies or incur considerable fines. The ETS is currently in its third phase, which runs between 2013 and 2020. In 2009 a significant revision was approved, strengthening and harmonizing the system.

CARDS (Community Assistance for Reconstruction, Development and Stabilization) was the financial assistance programme dedicated to the **Western Balkans** as part of the **Stabilization and Association Process** launched in 1999. It replaced the OBNOVA programme and involved total funding to the region of €4,560m. in 2000–06. From 1 January 2007 CARDS was replaced by the **instrument for pre-accession assistance**.

CARTELS: See: **Competition Policy**; **Transport Policy**

CARTOON is another name for the European Association of Animation Film. It is based in **Brussels** and is linked to the MEDIA programme (see **Media Policy**).

CASE LAW: See **Court of Justice**; **Law**; **Legislation**

CASSIS DE DIJON is the popular name of an important ruling (Rewe-Zentral AG v Bundesmonopolverwaltung für Branntwein) by the **Court of Justice**. The Court ruled in 1979 that, where a product is manufactured and legally on sale in one member state, another member state cannot prohibit its import and sale, except on grounds of its constituting a risk to public health. The product in question was a French fruit liqueur, whose importer into the Federal Republic of **Germany** (West Germany) had appealed to the Court of Justice against a decision by the German courts to ban its import. The West German case rested on the argument that, under the national spirits monopoly, potable spirits had to contain at least 25% by volume of wine spirits to be marketable in the country: the product in question, *Cassis de Dijon*, had less than 20% by volume of wine spirits. In rejecting the West German argument, the Court delivered a decisive legal precedent for the European Communities (EC) in its affirmation of the unconstitutionality of national legislation and technical regulations in relation to intra-EC trade. It enabled the **European Commission** to develop the principle of **mutual recognition** as an important instrument of **harmonization** and the development of the **internal market**. The ruling was subsequently applied to a wide range of products, and its essence was formally incorporated into the **Treaty of Rome**.

CCP: See **Common Commercial Policy**

CCT: See **Common External Tariff**

CDP: See **Common Defence Policy**

The **CECCHINI REPORT** of 1988 gave the **European Commission** powerful ammunition in its quest to introduce a range of practical measures that would ensure the effective operation of the **internal market** by 1992. Requested by the Commission, the report was compiled by a committee of experts under the chairmanship of Paolo Cecchini, and published in 16 large volumes, with a summary presentation also published as *The European Challenge 1992—The Benefits of a Single Community*. The committee consulted both economic and financial data collections and analyses, as well as other official and academic studies. It also interviewed some 11,000 companies across the European Communities (EC). The result was an extensive listing and costing of the obstacles—national practices, regulations and standards—that prevented the realization of the objective of **freedom of movement** contained in the **Treaty of Rome**. The report concluded that the cost of these obstacles was about €200,000m., or some 5% of the EC gross domestic product. Although it was accepted by the EC, not all authorities agreed with its findings.

CEDEFOP: See **European Centre for the Development of Vocational Training**

CEE: See **Central and Eastern Europe**

CEFTA: See **Central European Free Trade Area**

CELAD: See **European Committee to Combat Drugs**

CELEX stands for Communitatis Europae Lex, an inter-institutional database for European Union (EU) law, compiled by the **Legal Service** of the **European Commission**. Established in

1971, it contains details of, and provides an information service on, treaties, legal agreements resulting from the external relationships of the EU, all secondary **legislation**, case-law and **Court of Justice** rulings, and questions and answers in the **European Parliament**.

CEN is the acronym of the European Committee for Standardization (Comité Européen de Normalisation), a body of experts based in **Brussels** that was established in 1961 to assist in the advancement of the **industrial policy** and research and development policy of the European Communities. Funded by the **European Commission**, it was given a general remit to prepare European standards across a whole range of products, processes and appliances, as well as in the field of information technology. The variety of systems of national standards employed by the member states was believed to be a barrier to the effective **implementation** of the **internal market**. A number of the smaller states were concerned that **France**, **Germany** and the **United Kingdom** would dominate the process of integrating the national standards, which collectively produced some 85% of the national standards. Around 2,000 subjects have been covered by CEN. The field of electrotechnical standardization is the brief of a parallel committee, the European Committee for Electrotechnical Standardization (**CENELEC**).

CENELEC, the European Committee for Electrotechnical Standardization (Comité Européen de Normalisation Electrotechnique), is an expert body based in **Brussels** and funded by the **European Commission**, the role of which is to prepare European technical standards across a range of products and appliances as well as in the field of information technology. Its work is regarded as important for both the research and development policy and the **industrial policy** of the European Union. Its work is similar to that of the European Committee for Standardization (**CEN**).

CENTRAL AMERICA: See **South and Central America**

CENTRAL AND EASTERN EUROPE (CEE), as far as the European Union is concerned, comprises 11 countries: **Bulgaria**, **Croatia**, the **Czech Republic**, **Estonia**, **Hungary**, **Latvia**, **Lithuania**, **Poland**, **Romania**, **Slovakia** and **Slovenia**.

The **CENTRAL EUROPEAN FREE TRADE AREA** (CEFTA) agreement entered into force in 1993, agreed on by the so-called **Visegrad group** of countries (Czechoslovakia—now the **Czech Republic** and **Slovakia**—along with **Hungary** and **Poland**), with **Slovenia** and **Romania** joining them in 1996 and 1997, respectively. **Bulgaria** joined the association in 1999, followed by **Croatia** in 2003 and the **former Yugoslav republic of Macedonia** (FYRM) in 2006. The agreement led to the establishment of free trade in industrial goods between the nine countries. Although free trade is an important goal in itself, the main purpose behind CEFTA has always been to facilitate integration with the **European Union** (EU) and enhance the prospects of the participant countries obtaining EU membership. Indeed, five of CEFTA's members joined the EU on 1 May 2004, and two more on 1 January 2007, thus reducing the membership of CEFTA to just two countries, Croatia and the FYRM. In December 2006 CEFTA was therefore extended to include **Albania**, **Bosnia and Herzegovina**, **Moldova**, **Montenegro**, **Serbia** and the United Nations Interim Administration Mission in Kosovo (UNMIK) on behalf of **Kosovo**. Croatia left CEFTA when it became the 28th member of the EU in July 2013.

CERIF stands for Common European Research Information Format. It is a facility established in 1991 to enable the member states to exchange information on research projects as a prelude to a planned network of European research databases.

CERN is the acronym of the European Organization for Nuclear Research, a transnational research institution founded in 1954 and based in Geneva, **Switzerland**. CERN is a pure, as opposed to an applied, research institute, focusing upon the theoretical basis of nuclear and particle physics. Twenty-two nations, including 19 member states of the European Union (the other two being **Norway** and **Switzerland**), as well as Israel, are members, and the **European Commission** acts as an observer. CERN maintains links with the **European Atomic Energy Community**.

CET: See **Common External Tariff**

CFP: See **Common Fisheries Policy**

CFR: See **Charter of Fundamental Rights**

CFSP: See **Common Foreign and Security Policy**

CHAPTER is the term denoting a subdivision of a **Title** in a European Treaty. A Chapter may in turn be subdivided into **Sections**.

CHARTER FOR A NEW EUROPE: See **Charter of Paris for a New Europe**

The **CHARTER OF FUNDAMENTAL RIGHTS** (CFR) was proclaimed by the Presidents of the **European Commission**, the **Council of the European Union** and the **European Parliament** at the Nice **summit meeting** of the **European Council** in December 2000. Since then it has been included as Part II of the **Treaty establishing a Constitution for Europe**. It should not be confused with either the **European Convention on Human Rights** (ECHR) adopted by the **Council of Europe** in 1950 or the **Charter of Fundamental Social Rights of Workers**, otherwise known as the Social Charter, adopted in 1989. These two documents did, however, inspire some of the content of the CFR. Its existence owes much to the increased awareness of fundamental rights within the European Union (EU) and the desire of the EU to promote such, whether internally through, for example, **citizenship**, or externally through the **common foreign and security policy**.

The text of the CFR comprises seven chapters covering Dignity, Freedoms, Equality, Solidarity, Citizen's Rights, Justice and General Provisions. These contain a total of 54 **articles** setting out individual rights such as those to life, liberty and freedom, education, non-discrimination, good administration, and a fair trial. As such, therefore, it presents in a single document the existing rights and freedoms enjoyed by EU citizens whether through the **European treaties** or through the ECHR or the Social Charter. Indeed, no new rights were created. All the same, the member states were not willing at the time to make the CFR a legally binding document. However, they accepted the proposal of the **European Convention** to include it in the Treaty establishing a Constitution for Europe. This was only possible, however, after a number of additional clauses had been inserted clarifying the interpretation and application of the rights contained in the CFR. Further clarifications and a partial **opt-out** for the **United Kingdom** were negotiated as part of the **intergovernmental conference** of 2007 that led to agreement on the **Treaty of Lisbon** which, upon **ratification**, made the CFR legally binding on the member states and the EU's institutions when implementing EU law. As part of this process, the CFR was duly signed and proclaimed again by the Presidents of the European Commission, the Council of the European Union and the European Parliament on 12 December 2007. The Charter became legally binding on member states upon the entry into force of the Treaty of Lisbon in December 2009.

CHARTER OF FUNDAMENTAL SOCIAL RIGHTS OF WORKERS is the official title of the original document that later became known as the Social Charter. It originated in the review of progress towards the target of completing the **internal market** by the end of 1992, in which the **European Council** referred to the equal importance of developing the social aspects of the single market. The **European Commission** subsequently drew up a set of proposals for the introduction of a European Communities (EC) charter of fundamental social rights. The European Council at its **Strasbourg** summit approved a modified version of these proposals in December 1989, although British opposition meant that only 11 of the 12 member states signed the document. Thereafter, the Social Charter figured prominently in the discussions leading up to the **Treaty on European Union**, but persistent British opposition prevented it from being included in the treaty. Instead a Social Chapter, complete with an **opt-out** arrangement for the **United Kingdom**, was agreed allowing the 11 to proceed with measures, notably on **health and safety** and worker consultation, to implement the Charter. The Labour Government elected to power in the UK in May 1997 agreed to sign the Charter shortly after taking office. Following this, the **Treaty of Amsterdam** removed the opt-out clause and incorporated the Social Chapter in the revised **Treaty of Rome**.

The Charter set out to codify in general terms what the EC had already begun to do in the social sector, as well as introducing some new proposals. In emphasizing that the single internal market must benefit workers as well as employers, the Charter set out a code of practice that dealt with living and working conditions, **freedom of movement** of labour, collective bargaining, training, equal opportunities, gender equality, measures to protect underprivileged groups, and safety and health protection. Much of this was already the subject of EC **directives** and **regulations**. The Commission wanted a further **harmonization** of practices that would bring them to the level of the best national practices currently in existence, and stressed the appropriateness of EC action where the desired goals could be more easily achieved at the EC, rather than the national, level. Since the Charter's adoption, many of the rights of workers contained in it have been incorporated into the **Charter of Fundamental Rights** proclaimed in 2000.

The **CHARTER OF PARIS FOR A NEW EUROPE**, often referred to simply as the Charter of Paris, was a document signed at the meeting of the Conference on Security and Co-operation in Europe (see **Organization for Security and Co-operation in Europe**) in Paris in November 1990. The signatories, including the European Communities' member states, declared that 'the era of confrontation and division in Europe has ended', and committed themselves to the promotion and defence of democracy, **human rights** and a free market economy. The Charter has often been held to mark the formal end of the **Cold War**.

CHASSE GARDÉE is a phrase ('protected competition') that has been employed within the European Union (EU) by opponents of too great a movement towards free trade. It refers to a belief that the EU's ability to survive economically in the context of international competition depends upon the provision of a protected domestic market for EU companies.

CHRISTIAN DEMOCRATIC GROUP: See **Group of the European People's Party (Christian Democrats)**

CIS: See **Commonwealth of Independent States**

The **CITIZENS' INITIATIVE** was introduced as a new means of public participation in European Union (EU) policymaking as part of the **Treaty of Lisbon**. It enables EU citizens to bring forward ideas for the **European Commission** to consider as policy proposals when 1m people have signed a petition.

CITIZENS' RIGHTS are determined and guaranteed by the provisions of the **Treaty of Rome** and others of the **European treaties**. However, the treaties only deal with rights in terms of general principles and in specific, mainly economic, areas. A second source of citizens' rights, again only in specific areas, has been the rulings of the **Court of Justice** in the context of its interpretation of the treaties. These cases have been concerned primarily with the principle of equality between citizens within a single member state, especially for minority groups. In the 1980s the European Communities (EC) began to emphasize citizens' rights as part of their promotion of awareness of, and loyalty to, the EC at the level of the individual. This was one of the objectives of the 1984 **Committee for a People's Europe**, but **implementation** of its proposals was slow. The **Treaty on European Union** attempted to expand the rights already enjoyed by individuals into a broader notion of **citizenship**. The **Treaty of Amsterdam** continued to build on this idea, and focused further attention on the citizen's rights. A new **Article** permits the **Council of the European Union** to take action, by unanimity, in cases of **discrimination** based on sex, race, ethnic origin, religion or belief, disability, age or sexual orientation. Member states signing the treaty also agreed to eliminate inequalities between men and women; to protect citizens against misuse of data held by EC institutions; and to maintain and establish co-operation in areas of public health, the environment and sustainability, and development and consumer protection. The Treaty of Amsterdam, moreover, incorporated the **protocol** on social policy (see **Charter of Fundamental Social Rights of Workers**) into the revised Treaty of Rome. At Nice, in December 2000, the rights of citizens were once again on the agenda with the proclamation of the **Charter of Fundamental Rights**, which contains a section dedicated to citizens' rights.

CITIZENSHIP is a concept that remained undeveloped within the European Communities (EC) until the **intergovernmental conferences** of 1991 that preceded the **Maastricht summit**. While certain individual rights were provided by the **Treaty of Rome**, they were based essentially upon the economic objectives set by the treaty. While these rights were strengthened by rulings of the **Court of Justice**, they were limited in number and scope, and did not in any way provide a condition of citizenship. This lacuna in EC thinking was directly addressed by the **Treaty on European Union** (TEU), which attempted to formalize and develop the concept of citizenship beyond the economic rights of workers. The aim of introducing and defining European Union (EU) citizenship was part of the ambition to make the EU more democratic and to instil identity with, and commitment to, the EU in its inhabitants. However, it was not totally clear what citizenship was or what it involved. There were no references to the duties of citizens and, since the EU did not at the time have **legal personality**, citizenship appeared to lie within the EC **pillar**, which was the only part of the EU in which the Court of Justice, as the guarantor of rights, had jurisdiction. With the **Treaty of Lisbon** the situation changed and the EU gained legal personality. In addition, the TEU reaffirmed that **sovereignty** rested with the member states, thus accepting that questions of nationality and citizenship should be decided at the national level. Even though EU citizenship is therefore indirect, its establishment was not accepted unanimously. There were fears, particularly among **Eurosceptics**, that European institutions would use the introduction of a formalized citizenship to reduce further the freedom of the states, with the long-term aim of EU citizenship superseding national citizenship. Under the 2006 **budget**, citizenship emerged as a new, albeit very small, category of expenditure. Initiatives under this heading included efforts to combat health threats from animal diseases such as bird flu, **Bovine Spongiform Encephalopathy** (BSE) and foot and mouth disease. Under the provisions of the **Treaty on the Functioning of the European Union** (TFEU) citizens have the right to move to and freely live in other EU states; have the right to vote in, and stand as candidates to, the **European Parliament** (EP) and local elections; are protected by the diplomatic and consular authorities of other EU states; and have the right to petition the EP and to complain to the European **Ombudsman**. Other rights bestowed on EU citizens include: the right to contact and receive a response from any EU institution in any one of the 24 official languages; the right to access documents from the EU institutions (under certain conditions) and the right of equal access to the Commission. The Treaty of Lisbon introduced a new form of public participation for EU citizens in the form of the **Citizens' Initiative**. The **European Commission** adopted its second Citizenship Report in 2013. The report is the product of wide-ranging consultations and considers ways further to reinforce citizenship, but also identifies obstacles to be overcome to enhance the principle of EU citizenship. A third Citizenship Report was commissioned in 2016, and published in January 2017.

CIVIL PROTECTION is a new area of European Union (EU) competence, contained in the **Treaty of Lisbon**. It envisages the EU encouraging co-operation between member states to improve the effectiveness of systems for preventing and protecting against natural or man-made disasters within the EU.

CMEA: See **Council for Mutual Economic Assistance**

CN: See **Combined Nomenclature**

COAL: See **European Coal and Steel Community**

COCOLAF: See **Advisory Committee for the Co-ordination of Fraud Prevention**

CO-DECISION PROCEDURE: See **Ordinary Legislative Procedure**

The **COHESION FUND** was established by the **Treaty on European Union** (TEU) in 1993 as part of the European Communities' cohesion policy. It is a financial instrument available to finance transport infrastructure and environmental programmes in member states with a gross national product (GNP) per head of less than 90% of the European Union (EU) average. The Fund was not designated as a structural fund, but was linked directly to the move towards **economic and monetary union** (EMU) and was designed to ease the fiscal problems experienced by the poorer member states as they tried to meet the excessive deficit criteria for EMU membership. Originally, only the four poorest countries in the EU-15—**Spain**, **Greece**, **Portugal** and **Ireland**—were eligible for support from the Fund. Member state governments agreed to support this fund with annual commitment appropriations amounting to €2,615m. for each of the first four years, €2,515m. for 2004 and 2005, and, finally, €2,510m. for 2006. If a member state became ineligible it was always intended that the available resources would be reduced accordingly. Exactly how the overall resources of the Fund are allocated among the member states is determined by a series of criteria that takes into account member state population and area, overall GNP per head and socio-economic factors. The original financial allocation provided Spain with 61%–63.5% of the fund; Greece with 16%–18%; Ireland with 2%–6%; and Portugal with 16%–18%. It should be noted that the total amount that member states can receive from the Cohesion Fund each year (including any monies under structural funds) should not exceed 4% of their gross domestic product (GDP). In 2006 the Cohesion Fund was substantially increased to provide €6,000m. for some 200 environment and transport projects to assist the regions in the less prosperous member states to meet and comply with environmental standards. In 2014–20 the Cohesion Fund was to provide funding of some €63,400m., with the level of support and the national contribution adjusted according to the level of development: less developed regions were defined as those with levels of GDP amounting to less than 75% of the EU average; transition regions were those with GDP of between 75% and 90% of the EU average; and more developed regions had GDP of more than 90% of the EU average. The Cohesion Fund for 2014–20 is targeted at specific objectives and these include trans-European networks and environmental issues relating to renewable energies, energy efficiency, developing rail networks and strengthening public transport. Monies under the Cohesion Fund are available to the following states: **Bulgaria**, **Croatia**, **Cyprus**, **the Czech Republic**, **Estonia**, Greece, **Hungary**, **Latvia**, **Lithuania**, **Malta**, **Poland**, Portugal, **Romania**, **Slovakia** and **Slovenia**. The financial assistance of the Cohesion Fund can be suspended by a decision of the Council of the EU (taken by **qualified majority voting**) if a member state records an excessive budget deficit (commonly above 3% of GDP, as stipulated by the **Stability and Growth Pact**), and if it has not resolved the situation or has not taken the appropriate action eventually to do so.

COHESION POLICY: See **Structural and Cohesion Funds**

COLD WAR is a term that was first used in the late 1940s to describe the competition and tension that arose soon after the end of the Second World War, especially in Europe, between the **USSR** and its East European satellites on the one side and the

USA and its Western associates on the other. Relations between the two sides were definitively frozen by 1948, as illustrated by the Berlin Airlift (1948–49), with the imposition of Soviet hegemony over Eastern Europe being matched by a series of US commitments to Western Europe through the Truman Doctrine, the **Marshall Plan** and the **North Atlantic Treaty Organization** (NATO). The Cold War made impossible the pan-European alliance envisaged by some in the immediate aftermath of the Second World War, and ensured that any movement towards integration would be confined to Western Europe. It further strengthened US support for European integration. The fear of Soviet intentions also gave a powerful impetus within Western Europe to efforts at collaboration and integration for the sake of self-preservation, and to the feeling that the Federal Republic of **Germany** (West Germany), itself a product of the Cold War, must be thoroughly integrated with the rest of Western Europe. The US military protection guaranteed by NATO allowed the European Communities (EC) to develop without having to be overly concerned with political and defence requirements. However, the EC's later attempts, in the 1970s, to develop **European political co-operation** (EPC) were in part a response to the bipolarity engendered by the Cold War and the result of a desire to secure a distinctive Western European voice within it. While the necessity of preserving the US commitment limited the extent of EPC to the political and economic aspects of security, the end of the Cold War (as marked by the signing of the **Charter of Paris for a New Europe** in 1990) meant that the EC could feel less reliant upon US views, and less obliged to take account of them, and begin to consider developing their own **common foreign and security policy**. The Cold War between the 'superpowers' shaped and provided the backdrop to European political and security developments for over 40 years, and on occasions it seemed that the rivalries, as seen during the Cuban Missile Crisis in 1962, the Soviet invasion of Afghanistan in 1979 and the deployment of US cruise missiles in West Germany in the early 1980s, would lead to war. Ultimately the economic and political costs of the Cold War led both the Americans under Ronald Reagan and the Soviets under Mikhail Gorbachev to re-evaluate their positions. It caused the latter to commence his policies of *perestroika* (reform) and *glasnost* (openness), which gave rise to the 'revolutions' in Eastern Europe in the second half of 1989, the breaching of the Berlin Wall and the fall from power of Eastern Europe's communist systems. The USSR was not immune to these processes and began to fragment in 1991. Its collapse signalled the end of the Cold War.

COLUMBUS is the **European Space Agency**'s research laboratory that forms part of the international space station. Originally linked to the Hermes space shuttle project, the project to produce Columbus began in 1988. Columbus launched on 7 February 2008 and had an anticipated 10-year lifespan.

COM DOCUMENTS are part of the official working documents of the **European Commission**. They are documents prepared by the **Directorates-General** and submitted to the **Secretariat-General** for placement on the agenda of Commission meetings. They consist of proposals for **legislation**, policy discussion papers, and reports on the implementation of policies.

COMBINED NOMENCLATURE (CN) is the goods nomenclature created by the European Communities. Established in 1988, it replaced two previous systems: the **common external tariff** (CET) nomenclature and the Nomenclature of Goods for the External Trade Statistics of the Community and Statistics of Trade between member states (NIMEXE). The CN is published in the *Official Journal of the European Union* (OJ), and is updated annually.

COMECON: See **Council for Mutual Economic Assistance**

COMENIUS formed part of the European Union (EU)'s **Lifelong Learning Programme** (2007–13) and was a **European Commission**-sponsored support initiative that sought to foster greater contacts between schools (from pre-school, through primary school and up to secondary school level) across the EU. With a budget of almost €7,000m., the scheme was designed to help young people and their teachers better to appreciate and understand European cultures, languages and values, as well as providing some important life skills for personal development and future employment. The programme was also open to local authorities, parents' associations, **non-governmental organizations** and teacher-training institutes. Comenius aimed to enhance the quality of teaching and strengthen its European dimension by facilitating both pupil and teacher mobility between schools throughout the EU. As part of its ethos, Comenius also emphasized issues such as multi-cultural education, support for disadvantaged groups, countering under-achievement at school and preventing exclusion. The ideas behind Comenius were carried forward to the 2014–20 financial period under a new programme for education, training, youth and sport 'Erasmus for all' or 'Yes Europe'. This programme involved the creation of a more integrated system under the banner of **Erasmus+**. It also aimed to increase by almost two-fold the number of people (up to 5m.) who were eligible to complete part of their education abroad. (See also **Socrates**.)

COMEXT is a databank of external trade statistics produced by the Statistical Office of the European Union (**Eurostat**).

COMITOLOGY: See **Committee Procedure**

COMMISSION: See **European Commission**

COMMISSION OF THE EUROPEAN UNION is the official title of the **European Commission**.

COMMISSION PRESIDENT: See **European Commission**

COMMISSIONER: See **European Commission**

COMMITTEE FOR A PEOPLE'S EUROPE is the name of a committee established by the **European Council** at the June 1984 **Fontainebleau summit**. Its aim was to create an entry point for engagement with the **European Union** at individual level and to improve the image of the European Community to citizens. The Committee was composed of personal representatives of the heads of government, and was chaired by Pietro Adonnino, a **Member of the European Parliament** (MEP) for **Italy**. The Committee produced two reports, often referred to as the Adonnino Reports. Both contained a series of recommendations based on the Committee's brief, as well as proposals for measures to improve the rights and freedoms of European Communities (EC) citizens, and both were approved in principle by the European Council.

The first report was submitted in March 1985. It recommended the immediate **implementation** of a number of specific measures relating to the simplification of border crossing formalities, duty-free allowances, tax exemption for books and magazines, the taxation of trans-frontier workers, rights of residence, and the reciprocal recognition of equivalent diplomas and other forms of professional qualifications. Several of these proposals were incorporated into the longer second report presented in June 1985. This report listed longer-term targets relating to **citizens' rights, cultural policy**, youth exchange schemes and education policy, **sport** and strengthening the image of Europe. It urged, for example, greater use to be made of the **European anthem, European flag** and **European passport**, as well as the introduction of special postage stamps. The European Commission drafted legislative proposals on most of the Committee's recommendations in 1986 and 1987. Some of the proposals with direct relevance to the **internal market** were incorporated into the **Single European Act**, which also referred to social justice. The more political and general rights were eventually to be incorporated into those provisions of the **Treaty on European Union** that related to **citizenship**; others were the theme of specific EC programmes. People's Europe was not so much a programme as a set of unco-ordinated initiatives. The fact that over one-half of European Union (EU) citizens surveyed claimed never to have considered themselves European indicates that in some ways the People's Europe concept has had little effect on national identity. The **Treaty of Amsterdam** further emphasized the desire of the EU to move closer to the people by introducing new social measures. These included measures to combat unemployment, to extend **citizens' rights**, to expand the role of the **European Parliament**, and to encourage greater involvement of **national parliaments**; measures that emphasize the principle of **subsidiarity**; and measures making public access to information relating to the European institutions easier, with a view to ensuring greater **openness** and **accountability** within the EU.

COMMITTEE OF THE GOVERNORS OF THE CENTRAL BANKS was a body established in 1964. It was essentially a consultative body, charged with overseeing and commenting on monetary developments. However, because it consisted of the heads of the central banks of the member states, its opinions had considerable influence. It provided technical and managerial advice and assistance for the operation of the **European Monetary System**, and was central to the planning and institutional development of **economic and monetary union** (EMU) from January 1999. The Committee elected its own President on an annual basis, without any principle of rotation by state. It met on a monthly basis at the headquarters of the **Bank for International Settlements** in Basel, **Switzerland**. The Committee ceased to exist on the establishment of the **European Monetary Institute** in January 1994 (the start of stage two of EMU), although the governors of the central banks of the member states were to play an important role in the Governing Council of the **European Central Bank** and in the **European System of Central Banks**.

The **COMMITTEE OF PERMANENT REPRESENTATIVES** (COREPER) consists formally of the heads of the delegation, or **Permanent Representation**, which each member state maintains in **Brussels**, but the term COREPER is also used to refer to the totality of the delegations and their various committees and subcommittees. The members of COREPER, the Permanent Representatives, have senior ambassadorial status. COREPER's task, which expanded enormously as the European Communities (EC) extended the range and volume of their activities, acts as both service agent and 'gatekeeper' for the **Council of the European Union**. Supported by diplomatic and bureaucratic personnel, it prepares the agenda for Council meetings. If the members of COREPER, who receive their instructions from their own national capitals, are able to reach unanimous agreement on a particular issue, the proposal is given an 'A' category on the Council agenda. This means that the Council approves the proposal without discussion. Where COREPER finds it impossible to reach a consensus, the issue is referred back for discussion and possible resolution. More generally, COREPER holds frequent meetings to review and consider the details of all proposals for EC **legislation**, in order to seek a common position acceptable to all national governments, upon which it could make recommendations to the Council of the European Union.

The workload of COREPER has increased to the extent that the Permanent Representatives do not always attend its meetings. Deputies, who meet as COREPER I, handle much of the agenda evaluation, while the ambassadors' committee is known as COREPER II. By tradition, COREPER does not discuss agricultural questions: these are the province of the **Special Committee on Agriculture**. The centrality of COREPER to the decision making process of the EC has been the subject of much criticism, notably from the **European Parliament**, particularly on the grounds that it both reinforces the role of national governments and lacks **accountability** within the EC institutional framework. However, its existence was given formal recognition in the **Treaty on European Union**: previously, its authority was based only on the Rules of Procedure of the Council of the European Union.

The **COMMITTEE OF PROFESSIONAL AGRICULTURAL ORGANIZATIONS** (COPA) is based in **Brussels** and is a transnational federation of farming unions and associations, which supplements the activities of the national agricultural unions by lobbying in the various institutions of the European Union (EU) for farming interests. COPA was created in 1958 and established its secretariat in Brussels a year later. In 1962 COPA merged with European Agricultural Cooperatives (COGECA). COPA comprises 60 organizations from across the EU and 36 partner organizations from other states such as **Iceland, Norway, Switzerland** and **Turkey**. It represents some 13m farmers and 38,000 co-operatives. COPA pulls together representatives from the various agricultural production sectors and the EU institutions to discuss matters concerning the agricultural sector. COPA leaders maintain a regular contact with the Directorate-General and, especially, the Commissioner for Agriculture and Rural Development. Its influence has been far in excess of the importance of farmers in European society and to the economy. COPA concerns itself primarily with the operations of the **common agricultural policy** (CAP), discussions on reforming the CAP and wider agricultural trade issues. COPA lobbies the **European Commission**, the national governments and, increasingly, the **European Parliament**.

The **COMMITTEE OF THE REGIONS** (CoR) was established by the **Treaty on European Union** (TEU), thereby formalizing a grouping that had emerged in the late 1980s. It was recognition of the fact that many regional political authorities in the European Communities (EC) had established their own liaison offices in **Brussels**. It was intended, in keeping with the principle of **subsidiarity**, to involve representatives of elected local and regional authorities in EC decision making in an advisory capacity. After the European Union (EU) was enlarged to 28 member states on 1 July 2013, the Committee was expanded to comprise 353 members appointed by the Council for terms of five years on the proposals of member state governments and an equal number of alternates; it elects its own officers. It was reduced to 350 members in January 2015, according to the stipulations of the **Treaty of Lisbon**. The current President is Markku Markkula of Espoo City Council, in Finland. The Bureau is the ruling body of the CoR and comprises some 60 members—the President, the First Vice-President, the 28 Vice-Presidents (i.e. one member from each member state), the presidents of the four CoR political groups and 28 other members. In general, the Bureau meets on seven occasions throughout the year and is responsible for drawing up the Committee's annual work programme.

The **European Commission**, the **Council of the European Union** and the **European Parliament** must consult the CoR as directed by the treaties or when they believe an opinion from it would be useful. The areas upon which the Committee must, according to the Treaty on European Union, be consulted are: economic and social cohesion; **Trans-European Networks** in the areas of transport, telecommunications and energy; public health; education and youth; and culture. It was also given the right to issue opinions on matters that have been referred to the **European Economic and Social Committee** (ECOSOC), where it feels regional issues are involved. The regions represented by the Committee's members do not correspond rigidly to any single level of **Nomenclature of Territorial Units for Statistics** (NUTS) regions.

Under the terms of the **Treaty of Amsterdam**, the range of areas on which the Committee must be consulted was extended to include aspects of employment policy, **social policy**, **environmental policy** and vocational training. None the less, the CoR's impact has been relatively modest. It has proved difficult to maintain a common purpose in a committee with such a disparate membership (ranging in depth and significance from local councillors in the **United Kingdom** to the premiers of the German *Länder*). Instead, many regions have opted to utilize the CoR as simply another avenue to pursue their particular interests and gain access to the European Communities' decision makers. The **Treaty of Nice** in February 2001 established an overall ceiling of 350 for CoR membership. Significantly, the Treaty of Nice linked membership of the CoR to holding a regional or local authority mandate, with membership of the CoR lapsing simultaneously with the ending of an elected mandate. The final declaration of a Committee conference convened in Salamanca, **Spain**, in September 2001 included a proposal that the Committee be given the status of an institution in its own right, with the power to bring cases of alleged infringement of subsidiarity before the **Court of Justice**. With the entry into force of the Treaty of Lisbon on 1 December 2009 the role of the CoR was further strengthened. The treaty obliged the Commission to consult with local and regional authorities across the EU and also with the CoR. This ensures that both local and regional representatives are actively involved at a very early stage of policy proposals and pre-legislation activities. The Treaty of Lisbon also added other policy areas to the CoR's remit. These included: **civil protection**, climate change, energy and services of general interest. For the first time, the Treaty of Lisbon stipulates that the European Parliament must consult the CoR.

COMMITTEE OF THREE WISE MEN is the popular title of a body established in 1978 by the **European Council**, following a proposal by President Valéry Giscard d'Estaing of **France** that the Council should launch a further review of the operation of the institutional machinery of the European Communities (EC), even though the Council had not discussed the **Tindemans Report** of 1976, which covered the same theme. The committee consisted of three senior politicians: Barend Biesheuvel of the Netherlands, Edmund Dell of the **United Kingdom** and Robert Marjolin of **France**, whose task it was to investigate the EC institutions with a view to suggesting amendments to augment their effectiveness, and to consider progress towards European union. The group reported back to the European Council in 1979, commenting adversely on the negative role of the Council of Ministers (see **Council of the European Union**), concluding that the **European Commission** should be reorganized and endowed with more authority, and that **qualified majority voting** should be more widely applied in the Council of Ministers. Although the European Council welcomed the report, no action was taken on its recommendations.

COMMITTEE PROCEDURE or 'comitology', is a name given to the process of decision making and its scrutiny within committees of the **European Commission**. It describes a process whereby the Commission consults with a series of specialist advisory and other committees when seeking to draft and implement European Union (EU) law. Under Article 291 of the **Treaty on the Functioning of the European Union**, it is the task of the Commission to implement **legislation**. The nature of the committees, which are made up of national bureaucrats, technical experts and representatives of interest groups, varies: some are management committees, with executive powers, whereas others are only advisory. The latter do, however, allow access to decision making and can be highly influential.

There were previously three types of committee. These were the **advisory committees**, the management committees and the regulatory committees. A fourth, the regulatory and scrutiny committee, was created in 2006. All have different powers when it comes to decision making. All are chaired by the Commission and enable the Commission to establish a dialogue with national administrations before adopting implementation measures. The Commission ensures that they reflect as far as possible the situation in each country in question.

Procedures that govern relations between the Commission and the committees are based on models set out in a Council Decision (Comitology Decision) of 13 July 1987. However, this initial decision was modernized by the Council Decision of 28 June 1999, to take into account treaty changes and the enhanced powers of the **European Parliament** (EP) under co-decision, and also to respond to increasing criticism that the system was too complicated.

The 1999 Decision ensured that the EP could watch over the implementation of legislative instruments adopted under the **co-decision procedure**. In cases where legislation came under this procedure, the EP could express its disapproval of measures proposed by the Commission or, where appropriate, by the Council, which, in the EP's opinion, go beyond the implementing powers provided for in the legislation.

Lastly, several innovations in the latest council decision enhance the **transparency** of the committee system to the benefit of the EP and the general public: committee documents were to be more readily accessible to the citizen (the arrangements are the same as those applying to Commission documents); committee documents were also to be recorded in a public register; and, since 2000, the Commission has published an annual report giving a summary of committee activities during the previous year.

In 2006 (following years of complaint from the EP) the committee procedure underwent significant reform, when it placed the EP and the Council on an equal footing. This decision was the outcome of an initiative of the EP's Constitutional Affairs Committee and was agreed under the Austrian presidency (of 2006). The EP was given the right to block individual Commission comitology decisions where the original legislation was adopted by both the EP and the Council under the co-decision procedure. This newer Regulatory Procedure with Scrutiny was another major development for the EP, but it occurred only under co-decision and when powers had been conferred upon the Commission to implement measures, and was subject to a strict timetable.

Pressure for reform of the comitology procedure intensified as critics argued that it was too complicated. Following the terms of Article 290 of the **Treaty of Lisbon**, new rules were introduced from 1 March 2010 (and agreed by the **Council of the European Union** in February 2011) to change how this procedure worked and effectively further enhanced the role of both the Commission and the EP. Under the previous system, member state governments were able to block a Commission proposal by a simple majority. The new procedure only allows member state governments to do so if they can reach a qualified majority. The new regulation also confers a right of scrutiny on both the EP and the Council. These institutions can now inform the Commission at any time if they believe the Commission has exceeded its powers. The Commission is then obliged to review the draft act and decide whether to maintain it, amend it or withdraw it. In short, the Commission is obliged to respond to objections, although these are not commonplace.

The **COMMON AGRICULTURAL POLICY** (CAP) is one of the obligations imposed on the European Communities (EC) by the **Treaty of Rome**. It represents one of the oldest and most established European Union (EU) policy responsibilities. Agriculture has long been deemed a special area of economic activity. Rural areas make up over 90% of the EU's territory and account for approximately 50% of its population. **Enlargement** from the **Twenty-Five** brought an extra 4m farmers into the EU, increasing the total farming population to some 7m. The enlargement process also added a further 38m. ha of land to the 130m. ha that existed in the **Fifteen**. Agriculture and forestry are the main land users and play a fundamental role in the management of natural resources in rural areas and in determining the rural landscape. The Commission argues that agriculture makes an important contribution to the EU's overall prosperity and estimates that the agri-food sector (including beverages) accounts for some 14% of total EU manufacturing output. None the less, the CAP remains an issue of controversy and its future is one that clearly divides the member states. It is important to stress that the CAP has changed fundamentally from the mid-1980s, as old subsidies were replaced by a new rhetoric, advancing a more market-driven solution.

The original **Six** members of the EC agreed, in January 1962, on the principles of a common market for agriculture based upon five objectives set down in Article 33 of the Treaty of Rome (now Article 39 of the **Treaty on the Functioning of the European Union**): an increase in agricultural productivity; a fair standard of living for the agricultural community; stabilized markets; guaranteed regular supplies of agricultural products; and a guarantee of reasonable prices to consumers. The 1962 agreement was an interim arrangement due to expire at the end of 1965, and the need for the EC to finalize the financial arrangements concerning the reform of agriculture in the various member states was one factor contributing to the **empty chair crisis**. In 1968 the framework for the CAP was described in detail in the **Mansholt Plan**. However, only a diluted version of the Plan was finally adopted by the Council of Ministers (see **Council of the European Union**) in 1972.

The CAP was established with three main components: a single market for agricultural products, with common prices; community preference with a **common external tariff** (CET) and levies on agricultural imports from outside the EC; and common financial solidarity or responsibility. A further element, the development of which remained at a very basic stage, was the restructuring of European agriculture.

Common prices for agricultural products were introduced between 1962 and 1967. The increasing volatility of exchange rates in the late 1960s that heralded the breakdown of the **Bretton Woods** agreement made it increasingly difficult to maintain a common price structure, except by artificial means. The solution was the adoption of artificial green currencies, with the difference in value between green rates (the original common prices) and real rates prevailing on the money markets being covered by monetary compensatory amounts (MCAs). In the 1980s the **European Commission** came to favour the abolition of green currencies, but continued resistance by several member states preserved them until 1993.

In addition to protecting farmers within the EU, the CAP helps European agriculture to compete on world markets. It guarantees the payment of export subsidies or **restitutions**, whereby exporters of EU agricultural produce receive refunds to cover the difference between the lower prices at which they must sell on the world markets and the high EU prices at which they must purchase produce. During the 1970s and the 1980s, higher agricultural prices, as determined by the Council of the European Union, encouraged over-production and moves to more intensive farming, which had a negative impact on the environment, failed to improve the incomes of the smallest farmers and consumed ever more of the **European Economic Community**'s limited **budget**. The highest levels of over-production occurred in dairy farming, which, although producing only one-fifth of EC total agricultural produce, had by 1980 come to absorb some two-fifths of CAP financial support. Cereal and sugar cultivators were other major over-producers.

The core of the CAP has been the guaranteed price system, administered through the **European Agricultural Guarantee Fund** (EAGF), which replaced the European Agricultural Guidance and Guarantee Fund in 2007. Prices are determined each year by the EU agricultural ministers. Two basic prices are set each year. The first is a **target price** for each product covered by the price support mechanism; the other, set at a slightly lower level, is the **intervention price** below which the market price is not allowed to fall. Prices fixed under the CAP have invariably been higher than those prevailing on world markets. The price support mechanism operates in four different ways, which together cover almost the whole of the EU agricultural output. The majority of produce has enjoyed full CAP protection, with guaranteed support and sale prices, and with intervention buying if market prices fall below the levels fixed in the annual review. Some 25% of production, including eggs, poultry, pork, quality wines and some minor cereals, fruit and vegetables, has been protected only against lower-priced imports. Most remaining products have enjoyed direct **subsidies** to strike a balance between consumer prices and adequate income for the affected EU farmers. In the case of oilseed, where variable import duties apply, the CAP has operated a system of **deficiency payments** to cover the difference between the guaranteed price for the EU producer and the world price. Finally, a very small amount of produce, mainly cottonseed, flax, hemp and hops, has been covered by a flat rate of aid based upon the quantity produced or the number of hectares planted.

The domination of the guaranteed price system meant that, of the original aims of the Treaty of Rome, the CAP greatly improved agricultural production, self-sufficiency and prosperity. This, however, came at the expense of the fifth aim. The fact that the farm support prices of the CAP have invariably been higher than world market prices has led to greater costs for the consumer, not only directly through higher prices, but also indirectly, because of the demands made by the CAP on the EU budget. The CAP has consumed almost one-half of the annual budget, and of this amount some 95% has been taken up by the guarantee system.

The CAP has been unpopular with non-EU countries. The **USA** and other efficient and traditional exporters of food were critical of its protectionist nature, as well as of the practice of **dumping** its stored surplus produce at reduced prices, which, they argued, distorted world trade. There is also a widespread opinion among developing countries that EU agricultural policy has been detrimental to an effective development of their own agriculture. Internal criticism of the CAP has been less marked, except in the **United Kingdom**, where the costs of the CAP were seen as being directly related to the level of its own net budget contribution; this was a consequence in part of its own agricultural structure and its policy of importing large quantities of food from outside the EU. Moreover, the CAP appears to contravene the broader EU **development aid** support, since the subsidies attached to it undercut agriculture in many developing countries which rely on the sale of agricultural produce.

By the early 1980s the European Commission had accepted the need for restraints on agricultural expenditure, first because it was rising at a much faster rate than the **own resources** of the EC could bear, and second because its financial appetite effectively prevented the development of other EC policies. It was agreed at the 1984 **Fontainebleau summit** that CAP expenditure should increase at a lower rate than that of the budget as a whole. International currency instability over the next few years frustrated this objective, although **guarantee thresholds** and **quota restrictions** were introduced for some products in 1984 and 1986, and in 1988 it was agreed to introduce **stabilizers** for most products. It was also agreed in 1988 that the future annual growth of agricultural expenditure should not exceed 74% of the increase in total gross national product of the EC member states. These measures contributed to a reduction in the share of the budget consumed by the CAP, but in the early 1990s the problem intensified again with the re-emergence of surpluses and because CAP protectionism had become a major issue which threatened to prevent a satisfactory conclusion to the **Uruguay Round** negotiations on international trade. In June 1992 the Commission agreed on a new programme of reforms, which involved a further reduction of guaranteed prices for some products, a shift from subsidies for production to income support for producers, a considerable extension of **set-aside schemes**, the encouragement of less intensive and more environmentally friendly farming methods, and opportunities for early retirement.

In March 1999 the **European Council**, in Berlin, Germany, agreed upon reforms to the CAP. Certain intervention prices (for example, for cereals and beef) were to be reduced in stages, although intervention prices for dairy produce were not to be lowered until 2005. The aim of the reforms was to limit spending on the CAP while supporting farmers with direct income support. However, the accord reached did not go as far as the pro-reform member states (which included **Denmark**, **Sweden** and the UK) wished, and exceeded budgetary stabilization limits. Moreover, the source of the problem remained to be tackled—and would entail a radical overhaul of agricultural policy and a changed political climate. This was especially necessary by the end of the 1990s, as the eastward expansion of the EU from 2004 incorporated states with large agricultural sectors by Western European standards, which were generally inefficient.

The **Agenda 2000** programme aimed to reshape the CAP and prepare the rural sectors of the EU for enlargement and integration. Greater emphasis was to be placed on the integration of agricultural policy within the broader socio-economic context of rural areas, and the development of a coherent rural policy. From the late 1990s, multifunctionality emerged as one of the principal concepts in the operations of the CAP.

In 2002 the European Commission tabled a mid-term review of the CAP, which expressed the opinion that public expenditure for the farming sector must be better justified. The review aimed to free farmers from excessive bureaucracy, encouraging them to produce at high standards for the highest market return rather than for the sake of the maximum possible subsidy. To achieve these objectives the Commission proposed: to cut the link between production and direct payments; to make those payments conditional on the appliance and maintenance of environmental, food safety, **animal welfare** and occupational safety standards; to increase EU support for rural development; to introduce a new farming audit system; and to adopt new rural development measures to improve quality production, food safety and animal welfare and to cover the cost of the farming audit.

As for the market policy that remained an essential pillar of the CAP, the Commission proposed to bring to a close the process of cereal reforms, notably with a 5% reduction in the intervention price and a new border protection system. Like all previous reforms of the CAP (e.g. the Mansholt Plan in 1968 and the MacSharry Plan in 1991), these radical proposals had to be approved by the member states. At a meeting of EU ministers of agriculture in Luxembourg in June 2003, agreement was reached on what amounted to a fundamental reform of the CAP, and spending levels were determined for 2007 to 2013. The Council and the accession states ratified the compromise agreement in September. Production-linked subsidies were to be replaced by a Single Farm Payment, and linked to environmental, food safety and animal welfare standards. Obligatory decoupling was only partial for beef, cereal and mutton, with production still accounting for as much as 25% of payments for cereals and as much as 40% for beef. Overall, however, 90% of payments would no longer be linked to production. The agreement contained a commitment to reduce all payments above €5,000 a year by 3% in 2005, by 4% in 2006 and by 5% in 2007. Increased resources were to be directed towards rural development projects, protecting the environment and improvements to food quality; organic farmers and those offering high-quality produce with special guarantees were to receive grants of up to €3,000 a year for five years. Under the principle of 'modulation', an increasing percentage of direct farm subsidies was retained by individual member states to finance rural development measures. The equivalent of at least 80% of the funds gathered in each member state (90% in **Germany**) was to be spent in that country. Implementation of the CAP reforms agreed in June 2003 commenced on 1 January 2005.

Meanwhile, in April 2004 the EU Council of Ministers of Agriculture reached agreement for CAP reform of the olive oil, cotton, hops and tobacco sectors. The principle of decoupling aid from production was to be extended to these commodities. A significant share of the existing production-linked payments was to be transferred to the Single Farm Payment (which was provided independently of production), although production-linked subsidies were permitted of up to 60% for tobacco, 40% for olive oil, 35% for cotton and 25% for hops. Moreover, full decoupling in the tobacco sector was to be introduced progressively over the four years to 2010 and rural development aid was to finance conversion to other crops in tobacco-producing areas. The remaining production aid for olive oil was to be directed at maintaining olive groves with environmental or social value.

In September 2006 the **European Court of Justice** annulled the CAP provisions on cotton, proposing a slightly revised reform of the support scheme in November 2007. The new proposal maintained the support arrangements agreed in 2004 (i.e. production-linked subsidies of up to 35%), but provided for additional funding for support measures in cotton-producing regions and the creation of a 'label of origin' to enhance the promotion of EU cotton.

The EU finally agreed on reforms to the sugar industry in November 2005, following a **World Trade Organization** (WTO) ruling earlier in the year (after an action brought by Brazil, Australia and Thailand) that the current level of subsidy breached legal limits. In 2005 the EU sugar sector was still characterized by large subsidies, high internal prices, and imports by **ACP** (African, Caribbean and Pacific) **states** on favourable terms under quotas. The EU produced large surpluses of sugar, which were disposed of on the world market to the detriment of more competitive producers, notably developing countries. The reforms, implemented from July 2006, included the gradual reduction of the internal EU market price (which was three times the international price for the commodity in 2005) by 36% by 2009, and direct aid payments of €6,300m. over the four years of the phased introduction of the reforms to EU sugar producers as compensation. The proposals were criticized by **non-governmental organizations** (NGOs), as they would not help create a sustainable international sugar market, and by ACP countries, which claimed the measures would adversely affect their economies. A fundamental element in the reform of the EU sugar sector was the establishment of a restructuring fund, financed by sugar producers, to ease the transition to greater **competitiveness**. The objective was to remove a total of some 6m. metric tons of sugar quota during the four-year reform period. Amendments to the sugar-restructuring scheme were adopted in October 2007 in an attempt to encourage greater participation, and, by the conclusion of the reform period, in early 2009, some 5.8m. tons of sugar quota had been renounced.

At the Doha round of the WTO in Hong Kong in December 2005, agreement was reached on the elimination of export subsidies on farm goods by the end of 2013, three years later than the date sought by the USA and developing countries. A new regulation laying down specific rules concerning the fruit and vegetables sector was adopted in September 2007 and entered into force in January 2008. Notable reforms included: the integration of the sector into the Single Farm Payment scheme; the requirement that producer organizations allocate at least 10% of their annual expenditure to environmental concerns; an increase in EU funding for the promotion of fruit and vegetable consumption and for organic production; and the abolition of export subsidies for fruit and vegetables. In April 2008 agriculture ministers adopted a new regulation on the reform of the wine sector. The regulation provided, *inter alia*, for the inclusion of the sector in the Single Farm Payment scheme, while distillation subsidies were to be gradually withdrawn by 2012, releasing funds for measures such as wine promotion in third countries and the modernization of vineyards and cellars. In addition, the regulation provided for the introduction of a voluntary scheme, under which wine producers were to receive subsidies over a three-year period, with the aim of removing surplus and uncompetitive wine from the market.

In May 2008 the European Commission proposed a number of **regulations** to reform and simplify the CAP further in 2009–13, including additional reductions in production-linked payments and increased funding for rural development. In November 2008 the European Council reached agreement on the proposed reforms, which: raised the rate of decoupling in those countries that maintained the link between subsidy and production; provided for reform of the dairy sector; abolished the **set-aside scheme** from 2009; and provided for payments to farms qualifying for subsidies of at least €5,000 a year to be reduced gradually, so that by 2012 10% of funds (compared with the existing 5%) would be transferred to the rural development budget (large-scale farms would be required to transfer a greater proportion of funds). Milk quotas were to be increased by 1% per year in 2009–13, before their eventual expiry in 2015.

As a result of a severe decline in dairy prices from 2008, in June 2009 the Commissioner for Agriculture and Rural Development established a High Level Experts' Group on Milk (HLG), comprising representatives of the then 27 EU member states, and chaired by the Director-General for Agriculture and Rural Development. The HLG sought to identify medium- and long-term measures for stabilizing the market and incomes, and increasing **transparency**, given the expiry of milk quotas from 1 April 2015. The HLG identified significant problems in the supply chain, and in September 2010 its proposals for addressing these were endorsed by the Council's presidency. The Dairy Package was formally approved by the **European Parliament** in February 2012 and was to remain in effect until mid-2020.

In November 2010 the European Commission launched the consultation process on further reform of the CAP, based on the results of large-scale public debate on the issue of CAP reform, which had been summarized at a conference held in **Brussels** in July. The two existing pillars of the CAP, comprising direct annual payments and market measures, on the one hand, and flexible rural development measures, on the other, were to be retained. The existing, two-tier system of direct payments was to be reviewed, removing the CAP's reliance on outdated reference criteria, calculated on production volumes in 2000–02, prior to the expansion of the EU. In October 2011 the Commission presented its full set of legal proposals that were designed not only to make the CAP a more competitive and sustainable economic system but also to assist the continued vibrancy of rural areas. The proposals were passed to the European Parliament and the Council for consideration. CAP reform remained under negotiation throughout the first half of 2013, and political agreement on the future reform of the CAP was reached between the European Commission, the Council and the European Parliament in late June 2013 (with the new arrangements coming into force from 1 January 2014 following their formal adoption by the European Parliament and the Council). In December 2013, following approval by the Parliament in the previous month, the Council formally adopted four basic regulations for the reformed CAP, and the transition arrangements for its implementation from 2014 (although some elements did not come into operation until 2015). The regulations provided for the administration of the CAP to be simplified, and transparency increased. The budget for agricultural research and innovation was to be increased two-fold, supported by the creation of a new European Innovation Partnership. Direct payments were to be distributed more equitably: by 2019 no single member state was to receive less than 75% of the EU average; only practising farmers would be eligible for income support, and incentives were to be introduced for younger farmers to enter the sector (some 65% of farmers were at least 55 years of age). Sugar quotas were to be removed by the end of 2017. Improved tools for managing economic crises were to be introduced: the Commission would be able to intervene temporarily to manage the volume of agricultural products in the market; a 'crisis reserve' was to be established; and farmers were to be encouraged to take part in risk-prevention schemes. A 'greening' component was to be introduced, to reward environmental competitiveness by directing up to 30% of the value of direct payments towards encouraging better use of natural resources, through crop diversification; the preservation of grassland; and the conservation of 5% (potentially rising to 7%) of areas of ecological interest from 2018 (or the introduction of measures deemed to be of equivalent environmental worth). By 2014 spending on agriculture still accounted for some 41% of the EU budget. The two largest headings are the **European Agricultural Guarantee Fund** (EAGF) and the **European Agriculture Fund for Rural Development** (EAFRD). The Commissioner with responsibility for Agriculture and Rural Development from November 2014, **Phil Hogan**, seeks further to simplify the CAP. In October 2016 the Commission published a draft Omnibus Regulation, as part of the review process for the Multi-annual Financial Framework for 2014–20, predominantly comprising technical proposals to facilitate CAP policy, in an effort to improve the means of targeting funds and increasing competitiveness. The proposals aimed to benefit, in particular, younger farmers, by facilitating access to investment capital. It was envisaged that the proposals would enter into force at the beginning of 2018.

COMMON CARRIER LEGISLATION refers to European Union **legislation** that requires transmission systems to carry energy between any third-party supplier and the consumer at a reasonable tariff.

The **COMMON COMMERCIAL POLICY** (CCP) (often referred to as the EU Trade Policy) is at the core of European Union (EU) external relations and has been in place since the **customs union** of the European Communities (EC) was established in the late 1960s. It is the aim of the CCP under Article 206 of the **Treaty on the Functioning of the European Union** (**TFEU**) to contribute to the harmonious development of world trade, to work for the progressive abolition of restrictions in international trade and on foreign direct investment and to secure the lowering of customs duties. The CCP results from EU competence to regulate non-member state access to the single European market. The CCP therefore confers on the EC, via Article 133 of the Treaty of Rome (now Article 207 of the TFEU), so-called 'treaty making powers'. This means that tariff and trade agreements are no longer conducted by the member states, but by the EU. Agreements are negotiated by the **European Commission** under the supervision of the Article 207 Committee (formerly 133 Committee) and formally adopted by the Council of Ministers (see **Council of the European Union**), by a **qualified majority** and by the **European Parliament** (EP). Indeed, it is the European Commission that represents the EU and its member states in both bilateral and multilateral trade negotiations, such as those conducted within the framework of the former **General Agreement on Tariffs and Trade** (GATT) and the **World Trade Organization**. Responsibility for conducting multilateral trade negotiations rests with the Commission and specifically its Directorate-General for Trade. The principal objectives behind EU trade policy centre on the goals of securing and maintaining a competitive global trading system as well as opening up new markets through trade agreements.

Member states have a presence at these meetings but the Commission is the body that is heavily involved in discussions. It conducts its negotiations in consultation with the Article 207 Committee, the members of which are determined by the Council. The Commission must report at regular intervals to this Committee and to the EP on the progress of negotiations. In those policy areas where the EU holds exclusive responsibility (e.g. agriculture and fisheries) the Commission negotiates directly on behalf of the Council. External trade policy is identified as one of the EU's exclusive competences under the **Treaty of Lisbon**. The Lisbon Treaty is also significant because under its terms (Article 207 of the TFEU) both the European Parliament and the Council using the **ordinary legislative procedure** now adopt the measures defining the framework for implementing the CCP. Most agreements involve granting non-member states preferential access to the customs union and **internal market** through an increase in or abolition of quotas, or a lowering of the **common external tariff**. However, GATT rules dictated that most agreements must involve the creation of a free trade area or a customs union within a reasonable period of time and cover substantially all goods. This is true of various **free trade agreements** concluded on the basis of Article 207 (formerly 133) and trade arrangements contained in **association agreements**. Traditionally, the CCP has covered mainly trade in goods, although the EU has tended to be highly protective of its own agricultural markets and therefore access here has been less liberal. With the **Treaty of Nice**, the coverage of the CCP was extended to include trade in services. In this area and the commercial aspects of intellectual property, the Council acts (under Article 207) by **unanimity**. It also acts unanimously in relation to trade in cultural and audiovisual services, in the area of social, educational and health services, and in relation to transport agreements.

COMMON CUSTOMS TARIFF (CCT): See **Common External Tariff**

COMMON DEFENCE, perhaps in the form of a common European army, is a long-term aspiration of the European

Union and is asserted in the **Treaty on European Union** as the extension of a **common defence policy**.

A **COMMON DEFENCE POLICY** (CDP) has been the goal of the European Union (EU) since the **Treaty on European Union** was signed in 1992. Originally, it was to be pursued as an extension of the **common foreign and security policy** and in co-operation with **Western European Union**, although the gradual transfer of this organization's functions to the EU since the late 1990s has meant that the CDP is being developed very much within the framework of the EU, notably as part of the **Common Security and Defence Policy**.

The **COMMON EXTERNAL TARIFF** (CET), also known as the common customs tariff (CCT), is a term that refers to an essential element of any **customs union**, and an integral part of the **Treaty of Rome**. A common external tariff, imposed on goods entering any member state from outside the European Union (EU), was first introduced in the early 1960s, based on an average of the customs levies previously exacted by the member states, although with some downward adjustment. Since then the CET has been further lowered from around 10% to less than 5%, in accordance with the EU's acceptance of decisions on tariff barriers and international trade as part of the former **General Agreement on Tariffs and Trade**. Certain exceptions are permitted. The **Council of the European Union** may reduce or waive the CET for a member state where domestic production of the goods being imported cannot meet demand. The **European Commission** may do the same where there is a general shortage of that product within the EU.

The **COMMON FISHERIES POLICY** (CFP) was provided for by the **Treaty of Rome**. The first proposals for a CFP were not, however, made until 1966, and it was not until 1970 that the **Six** committed themselves to such a policy. The Council of Ministers (see **Council of the European Union**) adopted a limited scheme according to the principle of free access for all European Union (EU) fishermen within EU waters. The scheme, modelled on the principles of the **common agricultural policy** (CAP), envisaged price support mechanisms and protection for the **European Communities** (EC) market, with measures to ensure equal competition within the market, modernization of the industry, and **harmonization**, if necessary by intervention, of national policies.

These proposals were adopted by the Six at the same time that they were negotiating terms of entry to the EC with **Denmark**, **Ireland**, **Norway** and the **United Kingdom**. All the applicant states had important fishing interests, and the EC plan was, to some extent, perceived and resented by those states as a stratagem to rush through a common policy that, while it might benefit the Six, did not necessarily take into account their own interests. The fisheries issue is widely believed to have been a factor in the Norwegian rejection of membership, at the referendum of 1972. The EC eventually negotiated a compromise agreement with the other three applicant states, whereby each member state could, as an interim measure until 1982, restrict entry within a zone of six nautical miles (11.1 km) around its shores, or 12 miles in certain areas, to fishing vessels that had traditionally operated within those limits.

The scheme never worked satisfactorily, either in terms of national interests or in encouraging the preservation of fishing stocks. A major disruptive factor was the extension in the 1970s by many countries bordering the Atlantic Ocean, but particularly by **Iceland**, of an exclusive fishing zone to 200 nautical miles, an action that was subsequently endorsed by the **United Nations** Convention on the Law of the Sea. Deep-sea vessels from the EC were excluded from many of their traditional fishing grounds. They were obliged, if they were not to be forced out of business, to concentrate in EC waters. While the EC also adopted a 200-mile limit in 1977, this did little to obviate the fierce competition within the zone between national fleets, and the inevitable overfishing that followed.

After much disagreement, a common fisheries policy was adopted in 1983. Its two central elements related to access to stocks and their preservation. As far as access was concerned, it endorsed the principle of all waters being open to all EC fishermen within a 200-mile limit of EC shores (which is inevitably less in the Baltic and Mediterranean Seas). However, individual member states were permitted to retain an exclusion zone of up to 12 miles, within which fishing rights were restricted to their own fleets, and to vessels from other member states that hitherto had possessed traditional rights of access.

The central concept of conservation is the **total allowable catch** (TAC). Each year the Council of the European Union agrees on TACs for different species. The TAC is the total amount of that species permitted to be caught in EU waters, and each member state is allotted a quota within each TAC, often only after long and acrimonious bargaining. The operation of the TAC system through the surveillance and inspection policies and practices of the member states is monitored by a body of inspectors answerable to the **European Commission**. However, problems of verification and enforcement have persisted. Other conservation measures not only relate to the extent of fishing in certain areas, governed by the system of EC licences, but also regulate the size of fish that may be caught, and the type and size of mesh that may be used. Any member state may introduce further conservation measures within its own zone, as long as these do not discriminate against other vessels from the EU.

Other CFP provisions are modelled on the CAP. The **Council of the European Union** sets guide prices for all categories of fish on an annual basis. The EC provides compensation for catches that have to be withdrawn from the market, setting a withdrawal price of between 70% and 90% of the guide price. If both guide and withdrawal prices are higher than world prices, a system of refunds to exporters applies, along the lines of CAP **restitutions**, to maintain the income of the fishing industry. By contrast, when catches in the EU are insufficient to meet market demands, customs duties on imports can be suspended. By the early 1990s quota controls and limited stocks had fallen below demand, with the shortfall being made up by imports. The volume of cheaper imports deflated price levels, obliging the EU to introduce a system of minimum prices in 1993.

The European Commission has also set common marketing standards and principles on, for example, the size, weight, quality and packaging of fish. The **implementation** of these standards is the responsibility of the member states, but the Commission monitors them regularly. The CFP was also charged with providing some limited financial assistance to the industry to help with the modernization and restructuring of fishing fleets, but the funds available to it have been very modest, rather less than 1% of the EC **budget**. The basic problem faced by the CFP is that the objective of reducing overfishing and preserving fish stocks has tended to increase the relative capacity of the fishing fleet, and reductions in capacity have been strenuously resisted by member states. In 1991 the

Council of Ministers introduced the first of a series of measures intended to address this problem, and in late 1992 it agreed to establish a **Financial Instrument for Fisheries Guidance** (FIFG) as part of the **structural and cohesion funds**. The **European Fisheries Fund** (EFF) replaced the FIFG in January 2007. In 1994 EU fisheries ministers agreed on a revision of the CFP, allowing for the integration of **Spain** and **Portugal** into the CFP by 1 January 1996. A compromise accord was reached on Spanish access to waters around **Ireland** and South-West Great Britain (the 'Irish Box'); this was strongly opposed by Irish and British fishermen. In 1996, following some controversy over the Commission's proposals to reduce the number of fishing vessels, and the British Government's objection to 'quota-hopping' (in which boats registered in one member state are bought by operators in other EU countries, which are thus able to gain part of the former member state's fishing quotas), quotas were set for 1997. These fixed catch reductions at 30% for species most at risk, and at 20% for other overfished species. Moreover, the Council in 1998 agreed a ban on fishing using drift nets from January 2002. However, the issues of equal access, capacity and overfishing persisted and remained as politically sensitive as ever.

In December 2002 the EU fisheries ministers met in **Brussels** to decide on the much-needed reform of the CFP. Agreement was reached at the end of a five-day consideration of the Commission's proposals on CFP reform. Ministers agreed on three major issues: the need to reform the CFP; the adoption of urgent recovery measures for some cod stocks that were in imminent danger of collapse; and the establishment of TACs and quotas for 2003, including substantial reductions for a number of threatened stocks. In general, the objectives of the CFP were reviewed to focus more on the sustainable exploitation of living aquatic resources—based on sound scientific advice and on the precautionary approach to fisheries management—on the one hand, and on sustainable aquaculture on the other.

According to the Commission, the decisions taken in December 2002 would make fisheries management more effective and better able to ensure the long-term viability of the fisheries sector through sustainable exploitation of resources. The Council accepted the necessity of a more long-term approach to fisheries management, involving the setting of multi-annual recovery plans for stocks outside safe biological limits and of multi-annual management plans for other stocks. It also endorsed a simpler system for limiting the fishing capacity of the EU fleet in order to reach a better match with available resources. To this end, it was to replace the former system of Multi-annual Guidance Programmes (MAGPs), generally regarded as ineffective, with a new system which was designed to give more responsibility to the member states to achieve a better balance between the fishing capacity of their fleets and the available resources.

Many EU fishermen did not welcome the plans. To compensate for the continuing decline of the EU fishing fleet, the EU has instigated a series of socioeconomic measures. These include the provision of aid from member states to fishermen and vessel owners who have temporarily to stop their fishing activity. Aid was also increased to support the retraining of fishermen to help them convert to professional activities outside the fisheries sector, while allowing them to continue fishing on a part-time basis. The new measures entered into force on 1 January 2003. They replaced the basic rules governing the CFP since 1993 and substantially amended the Regulation on structural assistance in the fisheries sector through the FIFG. A new Regulation establishing an emergency fund to encourage the decommissioning of vessels (the so-called 'Scrapping Fund') was also adopted.

In view of the high risk of collapse of a number of cod stocks and the difficulty of controlling compliance with low catch limits, scientists from the International Council for the Exploration for the Sea (ICES) and the Scientific, Technical, Economic Committee on Fisheries (STECF) recommended in 2003 a moratorium on the fisheries involved in overfishing. Aware of the potential economic and social impact of such measures on fishing communities, the Commission proposed, rather than a moratorium, substantially reduced fishing possibilities for a number of stocks (primarily cod), as well as improved measures to ensure their proper implementation. Accordingly, the TAC reductions were less severe than had been initially proposed. For example, the TACs for Celtic Sea cod stocks and stocks associated with recovery stocks in this area were reduced by 15% (instead of by 47% as initially proposed) for cod in the Celtic Sea, west of Ireland and the English Channel, by 15% (instead of 55.5%) for whiting and by 15% (instead of 33%) for sole. The Council's request that Commission proposals be presented for incorporation within existing recovery plans for stocks newly identified as being below safe biological limits also permitted less stringent measures in 2004.

The Council decided in December 2003 to extend the scope of the interim measures restricting fishing effort adopted by the Council in December 2002 to protect certain cod stocks. The measures, which had been applied in the Skagerrak, the Kattegat, the North Sea and west of Scotland since 1 February 2003 were extended to the eastern Channel and the Irish Sea. Reinforced inspection and control measures were also adopted, applicable from 1 February 2004.

As a corollary to the CFP, the EC signed reciprocal agreements with other European and Atlantic states that permit some limited access to one another's zones and markets. Nevertheless, in early 1995 Spanish vessels fishing in the North Atlantic were the subject of an acrimonious dispute between Canada and Spain, and the EC played a significant role in subsequent negotiations. In 1996, following the publication of a report warning that herring stocks were in danger of being completely eradicated, the EU and Norway agreed an emergency measure to reduce by 50% catches in the North Sea and the waters around **Denmark**. Further afield, agreements have been signed with some African and Indian Ocean countries which allow EU vessels access to their waters in return for the provision of technical and financial aid.

Poland is the main fishing nation among the 10 EU member states that acceded in 2004. The fishing fleet is involved with three main types of fishing: coastal fleet, cutter fleet and high-seas fleet. The small fishing vessels operate in the territorial waters and in the Vistula and Szczecin lagoons and catch cod, herring and flatfish. The cutter fleet operates in the Baltic Sea and to a lesser extent in the North-east Atlantic, and is fishing mainly for cod, herring and salmon. The Polish high-seas fleet traverses the North Atlantic in search of shrimp, Antarctic krill and poutassou. Fishing proved a particularly sensitive issue for **Croatia** in its efforts to join the EU. There were a number of disagreements between the Commission and the Croatian Government over the latter's attempt to protect a part of the Adriatic. The Polish Government also expressed its concerns over the EU's cod fishing quotas, and there were numerous impasses between Poland and the Commission, and Poland took the issue before the **Court of First Instance**.

In December 2007 the Council agreed further to reduce cod quotas, by between 9% and 18%, and to reduce the number of days that could be spent at sea by fishermen. The deal was a compromise and a smaller reduction in quotas than the Commission had wanted (25%). Ministers also agreed to make quota cuts for other fish, such as blue whiting, herring and plaice. Environmentalists were highly critical of the agreement, as were fishermen's associations. Around 200 environmental activists had used barriers and concrete blocks to seal off the entrance to the Council building to express their anger at overfishing in European waters.

Confronted with growing opposition from both the fishing industry and the wider public, in May 2009 the Council opted to initiate measures radically to overhaul the operation of the CFP. The moves towards a new approach to fishing were endorsed by all 27 member states and welcomed by the industry in general. The Commission published its draft proposals for the reform of the CFP in July 2011. The proposals provided for returning fish stocks to sustainable levels by 2015, using an ecosystem approach based on scientific advice. The proposals also aimed to provide consumers with a stable, secure and healthy food supply while ending the dependence on subsidies and creating new employment opportunities in coastal areas; to eliminate 'discards' (unwanted fish or other marine organisms that are dumped overboard, having been caught unintentionally); and to provide for the establishment of clear targets and timetables to prevent overfishing. The Commission's new framework for fisheries policy formed the basis for discussions between the Council (led by the Irish presidency in the first half of 2013) and the **European Parliament** (EP). The Commission acted as a facilitator throughout these discussions and welcomed the agreement reached between the Council and the EP in May 2013. The agreement was later validated at the second reading, and the new CFP entered into operation on 1 January 2014. The reform was designed to bring fish stocks above sustainable levels; banned the unpopular policy of discards; sought better management of fishing fleet capacity; aimed to ensure greater international responsibility in terms of conservation measures and illegal fishing; and provided more support for small-scale fisheries. This last point was welcomed by many fishing communities as, from 2022, it would enable member state governments to extend exclusive fishing rights for their own fleets within 12 nautical miles of the coastline. The European Commission adopted regulations in September 2016 that facilitated the implementation of two directives: the Marine Strategy Framework applies to the North Sea, where new fishing bans will apply to a marine protected area in Swedish waters and to some Natura 2000 sites in Danish waters; while the Habitats and Birds Directives applies to Danish Natura 2000 sites in the Baltic Sea and replaces Regulation (EU) 2015/1778. The new measures aim to protect reefs, sea-pens and burrowing fauna. The protection measures also prohibit fishing with bottom-trawling gears, and in some cases, all types of fishing.

In December 2011 the Commission also proposed a new fund, the **European Maritime and Fisheries Fund** (EMFF), for 2014–20. This new fund, replacing the EFF, was primarily designed to deliver the ambitious goals of the proposed CFP reforms, but it was also aimed at ensuring that fishermen accepted the need for sustainable fishing and providing fishing communities with greater opportunities to diversify into other economic areas and secure more jobs. The EMFF proved rather contentious, but political agreement between the EP, the Commission and the Council was finally agreed in January 2014. The EMFF provides for a budget of €6,500m. (approximately 1% of the overall EU budget) for 2014–20. The EMFF is designed to provide financial support to fishermen, fish farmers and coastal communities. There are three thematic objectives over this period: promoting employment and labour mobility; enhancing the **competitiveness** of fisheries and aquaculture; and protecting the environment and securing greater resource efficiency. The largest beneficiaries of the EMFF for 2014–20 are Spain (€1,160m.), France (€588m.) and Italy (€537m.).

After British voters elected to leave the EU in a national referendum in June 2016 (see **Brexit**), it remained to be seen how the CFP would be affected by the eventual exit of the UK from the bloc, and the provisions of EU fishing policy. Members of the fishing industry in the UK suggested that local fishing communities would eventually thrive, once the UK reasserted control over its 200-mile exclusive economic zone, and guaranteed itself a greater share of local catching grounds than it was entitled to under the CFP.

The **COMMON FOREIGN AND SECURITY POLICY** (CFSP) was one of the three **pillars** that form the European Union (EU) created by the **Treaty on European Union** (TEU). The **intergovernmental conference** of 1990 that prepared drafts on political union for the **Maastricht summit** had as one of its briefs the task of considering collective action by the member states in the post-**Cold War** era. In part, this came from a desire that the European Communities (EC) should develop an international role more commensurate with their economic standing. It was felt that **European political co-operation** (EPC) was no longer adequate, a view underlined by the different national positions in relation to the Gulf War in 1991. The CFSP became the successor to EPC. Not being part of the EC, the CFSP was not subject to normal EC **decision making** procedures: direction was given by the **European Council**, not the **European Commission**. With the **Treaty of Amsterdam**, the Secretary-General of the Council acted also as the **High Representative for the Common Foreign and Security Policy**, and in this capacity assisted the presidency of the EU and was responsible for policy planning and monitoring international developments. The actions of the CFSP were also not subject to scrutiny by the **Court of Justice**. With the entry into force of the **Treaty of Lisbon**, some aspects of the CFSP changed. However, despite abandonment of the EU's pillar structure, the CFSP remains essentially intergovernmental in character.

The objectives of the CFSP are to safeguard the common values, interests and security of the EU, to preserve peace and strengthen international security, and to promote international co-operation, democracy, the rule of law and respect for **human rights**. While the European Council is free to define how the CFSP is to be implemented, the TEU defines the member states' duty, first to pursue a practice of 'systematic co-operation' through information, consultation and policy co-ordination, and second to adopt 'common positions' and 'joint action' when dealing with CFSP matters. The CFSP also includes 'the eventual framing of a **common defence policy**, which might in time lead to a common defence'. Originally, it was accepted that, until such a position could be reached, **Western European Union** (WEU) would act for the EU where defence implications arose, and those EU states not members of WEU were invited to join the organization, at least as observers. However, the EU subsequently took a more prominent role in military matters, as seen in the development of a **European security and defence policy** (ESDP) and the creation of a **European rapid reaction** force. This has not been without its problems, given concerns over the impact that such developments might have on the role of the **North Atlantic Treaty Organization** (NATO) and consequently on the effectiveness of that body. Moreover, conflicts in the former **Yugoslavia** illustrated the extreme difficulty of achieving a co-ordinated policy among the member states, even when there was a predisposition to work together.

That there were difficulties in implementing a CFSP was recognized in the Treaty of Amsterdam, which encouraged the adoption of **common strategies**, facilitated decision making through the introduction of **constructive abstention** and encouraged closer co-operation with WEU. Thereafter, the **Treaty of Nice** downplayed relations with WEU and removed the requirement for all the member states to co-operate on CFSP matters, through the introduction of a modified definition of **enhanced co-operation**. This was followed in 2003 by the adoption of a **European security strategy**. Various reforms were subsequently agreed as part of the **Treaty establishing a Constitution for Europe**. These included the creation of a **Union Minister for Foreign Affairs** and a **President of the European Council**, the establishment of a **European External Action Service** (EEAS), greater use of **qualified majority voting** and **permanent structured co-operation** in defence matters. The non-**ratification** of the Treaty establishing a Constitution for Europe threatened these, although most were subsequently carried forward into the Treaty of Lisbon. Moreover, work began as early as 2005 on the creation of the EEAS. This, alongside the development of the ESDP, emphasizes the commitment that exists among the member states to ensure that the CFSP continues to develop. In July 2016 the **High Representative of the Union for Foreign Affairs and Security Policy**, **Federica Mogherini**, launched a new EU Global Strategy on Foreign and Security Policy.

COMMON MARKET is a popular alternative name for the **European Economic Community** and, later, for the European Communities (EC) and the European Union (EU). It summarizes the primary economic objectives of the **Treaty of Rome**, a goal that originally was to be achieved by 1970. In the 1960s it was a relatively neutral term, but it later acquired some political connotations, often being used in preference to the term European Communities by those who rejected any notion of political integration, insisting that the common market should be the only ambition of the EC.

The **COMMON SECURITY AND DEFENCE POLICY** (CSDP), succeeded the European Security and Defence Policy (ESDP), emerging from the **common foreign and security policy** (CFSP) and European Union (EU) efforts to assume a greater role in military and defence matters since the late 1990s. It thus represents progress towards establishing a **common defence policy** and ultimately a **common defence** for the EU. As part of the ESDP, the EU assumed greater responsibility for the so-called **Petersberg tasks**—humanitarian and rescue operations, peacekeeping activities and combat-force tasks in crisis management, including peacemaking—and established a **European rapid reaction force** of 60,000 persons, as well as **battlegroups**, to carry out the full range of them at short notice. In addition, institutional structures have been put in place, notably the **European Union Military Committee** and the European Union Military Staff. These provide military expertise and support to the ESDP, including the conduct of EU-led military crisis management operations. Closer links have also been developed with the **North Atlantic Treaty Organization** (NATO), but the conflict in Iraq in early 2003 clearly laid bare the differences and disagreements among the members of both the EU and NATO on security issues. In an attempt to give greater strategic direction to the ESDP, the **High Representative for the Common Foreign and Security Policy**, Javier Solana, subsequently devised a **European security strategy** (ESS) for the EU. The **European Council** formally adopted the ESS in December 2003. Further initiatives designed to promote the development of the ESDP were agreed as part of the **Treaty establishing a Constitution for Europe** and subsequently included in the **Treaty of Lisbon**. These include **permanent structured co-operation**, further development of the **European Defence Agency**, and the introduction of a mutual assistance clause in the event of a member state being the victim of armed aggression on its territory. The Treaty of Lisbon also renamed the ESDP as the CSDP. In a speech in September 2016 **European Commission** President **Jean-Claude Juncker** called for the creation of a joint command centre for EU military missions in an effort eventually to create a single European military force, and urged closer co-operation between national armed forces of member states. He claimed that no single member state army could effectively deal with the security challenges facing Europe, ranging from Islamist militia operating near the EU's southern borders, in Libya or Syria, to a resurgent and more assertive **Russian Federation**. Juncker envisaged a force to complement the **North Atlantic Treaty Organization**, although Eastern European countries interpreted such a command as undermining co-operation with NATO. In March 2017 EU member states agreed to establish a Brussels-based command centre, with an initial intended focus on operations in Africa.

COMMON STRATEGIES are an instrument for implementing the **common foreign and security policy** (CFSP), which were introduced by the 1997 **Treaty of Amsterdam**. Article 21 of the **Treaty on European Union** lays down the principles and general guidelines for the CFSP, which are decided by the European Council. The same body also determines whether to introduce common strategies in areas where the member states share important interests in common. A common strategy defines aims, objectives and timetables involved and, more importantly, outlines the means to be made available by the European Union and the member states in order to realize them. Common strategies are then implemented by the Council, through the adoption of joint actions and common positions and the recommendation of common strategies to the European Council.

The **COMMONWEALTH OF INDEPENDENT STATES** (CIS) is a loose association of most of the former constituent republics of the **USSR**. It was established in December 1991 and in September 1993 agreed a framework that would serve as the basis of an economic union. The CIS was the focus of much attention from the European Union in terms of political co-operation and economic aid and agreements.

COMMUNITARIZATION is a term used to describe the transfer of competences to the European Communities **pillar** of the European Union.

COMMUNITY ASSISTANCE FOR RECONSTRUCTION, DEVELOPMENT AND STABILIZATION: See **CARDS**

COMMUNITY METHOD was a term used to describe policymaking procedures undertaken through community institutions, as opposed to those carried out through inter-governmental structures and mechanisms. The **Treaty of Lisbon** abolished the previous 'pillar' structure, creating the European Union (EU), with decisions primarily to be taken in accordance with the so-called **ordinary legislative procedure**.

The **COMMUNITY PLANT VARIETY OFFICE** (CPVO) was established in April 1995 and has been located in Angers, **France**, since 1996. The CPVO is a decentralized agency of the European Union (EU), and implements and applies an EU scheme to allow intellectual property rights to be granted for plant varieties. These rights are valid throughout the EU.

COMMUNITY PREFERENCE is a term that refers to the situation within the **common agricultural policy** when the price of domestic agricultural products falls below that of imported products.

COMMUNITY SUPPORT FRAMEWORKS: See **Structural and Cohesion Funds**

The **COMPANY LAW STATUTE** has long been a contentious issue among European Union (EU) member states. The original **European Commission** proposal dates back to 1975 and was an attempt to facilitate the establishment of new multinational companies across the European Communities (EC). The proposal encountered immediate opposition, largely as a result of its focus on **workers' rights**, and was promptly abandoned. A second proposal in 1989, which suggested that companies might choose to adopt a company statute in return for certain tax incentives, proved equally contentious. All issues relating to the rights and interests of the labour force can only be decided upon by unanimity in the **Council of the European Union**. These proposals were particularly unacceptable to the German Government, which insisted that a European company law statute must contain a requirement for workers' representatives to sit on supervisory boards and to be consulted on all aspects of work-force-related decision making, in keeping with the German national model.

However, pressure for a European company law statute intensified following the European Council's Nice declaration in favour of harmonizing company law across the EU. Nevertheless, the Council still needed to address concerns among the member states and some doubts expressed by the **European Parliament**. The latter was anxious to ensure that **legislation** in the area of workers' rights should be subject to the **co-decision procedure** and continued to press the case for greater protection of workers' rights within any European company statute.

Finally, however, after some 30 years of debate, on 8 October 2001 the Council Regulation (EC) No. 2157/2001 on the Statute for a European Company (or Societas Europaea, SE) was adopted. Member states had to adopt the laws, **regulations** and administrative provisions necessary to comply with the Directive by 8 October 2004 (the date on which the European Company Statute, or ECS, Regulation, which is directly applicable in the member states, came into force), or ensure by then that management and labour introduced the required provisions by agreement.

The ECS Regulation gives companies the option of forming a European Company (SE), which can operate on a Europe-wide basis and be governed by EU law directly applicable in all member states (rather than national law). The Directive lays down the employee involvement provisions to apply to SEs, providing for negotiations between management and employees' representatives in each SE on the arrangements to apply, with a set of back-up statutory 'standard rules' where no agreement is reached. Involvement constitutes the information and consultation of employees and, in some cases, board-level participation. The adoption of the ECS was a highly significant development in both EU company law and social policy.

COMPETENCE is a term that described the authority of the European Communities to undertake specific activities. The authority was usually based upon an **Article** of one of the **Founding Treaties**.

COMPETITION POLICY is crucial to the creation of a successful **internal market**. It would have been counter-productive to dismantle trade barriers between the member states if private industry had been free and able to engage in **cartel**-like restrictions on competition and undermine the advantages of opening up the markets in the first place. Moreover, from an economic viewpoint, the force of competition is to be welcomed as it unleashes dynamic effects that can be transformed into greater efficiencies, innovation and, ultimately, lower prices for the consumer. Overall, competition policy describes the objective of striking a balance between the imposition, by **legislation**, of necessary restrictions upon unbridled economic competition, and the elimination of harmful restrictive practices that prevent a coherent integration of markets. As such, it formed an essential part of both the **Treaty of Paris** and the **Treaty of Rome**. The original competition rules were contained in Articles 85–94, but these were renumbered under the **Treaty of Amsterdam** in 1999 to run from Article 81 to Article 90. The **Treaty of Lisbon** renumbered the articles again, and they now run from 101 to 110 of the **Treaty on the Functioning of the European Union**.

The European Union (EU) competition rules extend over five substantial policy areas. The first of these addresses the endemic cartels and restrictive practices (such as price-fixing and market-sharing agreements). Cartel policy has emerged as the core activity in terms of staff, time and resources and is the most developed aspect of policy. The malignant threat posed by cartels to both the business environment and the consumer was recognized under Article 101, which prohibits all agreements 'which may affect trade between member states and which have as their object, the prevention, restriction or distortion of competition within the common market'. Framed in very general terms, it is designed to catch and prohibit (paragraph 2) all agreements that restrict the spirit of free competition. Some types of anti-competitive agreement are entitled to exemptions if they improve the production or distribution of goods, promote technical and economic progress or ensure that consumers reap considerable benefits. The second policy area centres on merger control and the Commission's power to prohibit mergers. **Merger policy** (originally omitted in the Treaty of Rome) was added as a belated weapon to the Commission's arsenal in 1990 after the member states bowed to the wishes of the Commission and demands from the business community for a level playing field and a single point of entry for assessing EU mergers. In effect, this regulation bestowed a Community dimension on the Commission's responsibility for all mergers that exceeded specified thresholds. The Commission's handling of mergers has drawn almost universal praise from industry as the European competition regulator has been able to process merger notifications speedily.

The third and fourth principal aspects of EU competition policy focus, respectively, on monopolies that are abusing their dominant position in the market place (under Article 102) and on efforts to inject greater competition into the public utility sectors such as telecommunications and energy (under Article 106).

All these four areas bring the Commission into direct dealings with the business world, but uniquely the fifth area, which centres on the granting of state subsidies (under Articles 8108–9110), involves direct contact with member state governments and has proven the most contentious aspect of the EU competition brief. State aid (see **subsidies**) has featured as an aspect of government–industry relations to varying degrees across Western Europe since 1945. It has often been justified as an essential aspect of government-driven industrial policy and has been designed to secure employment, particularly in peripheral and economically depressed regions, to respond to issues of national prestige, or to create European champions.

The **European Commission** (and particularly the **Directorate-General**—DG—for Competition) is entrusted with the task of ensuring that the member states and companies conform to the provisions of the treaty. In this policy field the Commission operates as an autonomous and quasi-judicial policymaking institution, largely free from interference from either the **Council of Ministers** or the **European Parliament** in day-to-day decision making. The member states simply delegated responsibility for all competition issues to the Commission, and competition policy became one of the few exclusive competences (see Treaty of Lisbon) of European governance.

The Commission's decisions on competition policy are subject to review only by the European courts. While the Commission's powers were first established in 1962 (under Regulation 17), before the mid-1980s, competition policy was a relatively low priority. Since then, as a result of a shift in economic philosophy (towards neoliberalism), the accumulation of case law and the involvement of a succession of dynamic and forceful personalities, there has been enormous growth in the role and prominence of competition policy. This policy area represents one of the best examples of supranational regulation. The competition regime in relation to Articles 101 and 102 was 'modernized' through the adoption of Regulation 1/2003, which replaced the original procedural 'bible' encapsulated by Regulation 17.

The Commission has the authority to act, either on its own initiative, or upon receipt of complaints from member states, companies or individuals, without reference to the **Council of the European Union**, concerning possible infringements of EU rules. Its powers to investigate alleged breaches of competition policy are very wide. In the first stage of investigation, its inspectors are entitled to visit companies without prior warning, to see any documents they wish, and to retain photographic evidence. The national authorities are contacted in advance for assistance. The Commission is also allowed, under Regulation 1/2003, to conduct home searches. The second stage of the process is a series of hearings with the company concerned and other competitors. On the basis of the evidence and depositions, the Commission then issues its verdict. If it finds against the company, it has the right to demand a change of policy, impose a fine or combine both courses of action. The level of fines can be substantial in order to deter anti-competitive practices (for example, **Apple Inc.** was found liable to a substantial fine in 2016), reflecting the Commission's growing determination to tackle anti-competitive activities. Cartels also became a principal focus of anti-trust regulators worldwide. Companies that have been found guilty by the Commission of infringing the EU competition rules have the right of appeal to the **General Court** and then to the **Court of Justice**. The decision of the latter is final, in appeals against either the verdict or the size of the financial penalty. The Commission usually investigates several hundred cases of alleged infringements each year. Through the multitude of appeals against Commission decisions that have come before them, the European Courts have built up a substantial body of case law.

Competition policy rules apply to both private and publicly owned companies, and to nationalized industries. Companies that are negotiating or contemplating an agreement that may not satisfy the treaty provisions are obliged to inform the European Commission of their intentions. In addition, companies have the right to apply to the Commission for either a 'negative clearance', which recognizes that there is no threat to competition policy, or an 'exemption', which may be granted if the company or companies can demonstrate that, competition rules notwithstanding, a restrictive agreement should nevertheless be permitted on the grounds that it will provide substantial public benefits. With the **internal market** programme, which did not specifically deal with competition policy, the Commission also devoted considerably more attention to **public procurement**.

The European Commission may use its discretion to grant exemptions on the grounds mentioned above, or where the effect on free competition would be minimal. In particular, it has sought to balance a strict application of competition policy with its concern for the viability of small companies. Because it has wished to encourage co-operation between small companies, the Commission has outlined several categories of agreement that it may be prepared to exempt from a general ban: small-scale agreements in cases where turnover is less than €200m. and the market share less than 5%; agreements in various areas such as research and development and the exchange of information; and those that are essentially franchising or sub-contractual. The Commission is also prepared to be flexible where companies are confronted with adverse economic conditions and a sustained decline in demand. In such circumstances, companies may be permitted to collaborate in co-ordinating an orderly reduction in the resulting over-capacity.

The European Commission also monitors government activity. This has been a difficult task, because of the tendency of governments to shield their own companies from competition through a variety of techniques and mechanisms, which may or may not amount to state aid. The Commission is, however, willing to accept exceptions to the general ban on state subsidies that might distort competition. Member states wishing to provide aid to companies are expected to inform the Commission of their intentions. If the Commission rejects the plan, and if the latter goes ahead, it has the authority to demand the repayment of unauthorized subsidies, and even to impose fines on recalcitrant member states. Categories of state aid that have been exempted from the general rules include grants to areas afflicted by a natural disaster and aid to economically depressed regions that is designed to assist the development of new forms of economic activity. The Commission has also issued guidelines governing state aid to industries severely affected by recession, but has insisted that such aid must have a specific purpose and fixed duration, and be regarded as totally exceptional. The Court of Justice may, in the last resort, resolve disputes with member states about state aid. Competition policy does not necessarily apply to goods imported into the EU, where several bilateral or international agreements exist, and where some products have been affected by voluntary export restraints.

An International Competition Network (ICN) was established in October 2001 as an informal forum for competition authorities from around the world to discuss the function of competition policy and its enforcement. Progress has been more pronounced in respect of merger investigations than in cartel cases.

COMPETITIVENESS was the focus of the **European Commission's** 1994 **White Paper** on Growth, Competitiveness and **Employment**. This paper presented guidelines for pursuing a policy of global competitiveness. The policy comprised four objectives: provision for assistance to those European firms seeking to adapt to the new globalized economy; the ability for firms to exploit the competitive advantages associated with the rapid move to a knowledge-based economy; the ability to foster and promote sustainable industrial development; and the need to reduce the time differential between the pace of change in supply and the corresponding adjustments in demand. The White Paper's recommendations informed negotiations on the new title on employment introduced by the 1997 **Treaty of Amsterdam**. Competitiveness has emerged as a highly salient theme in both the Commission and the **Council of the European Union**. Its significance was illustrated in the **Lisbon agenda** and in a new heading of priorities in the annual **budget**. The theme remains a core aspect of planning and features regularly as a goal in EU communications. The EU budget for 2016 devoted some 12.2% of its spending to competitiveness for growth and jobs.

COMPULSORY EXPENDITURE is related to the budgetary decision making procedure of the European Union (EU). Prior to the **Treaty of Lisbon**, during the negotiations surrounding the annual budgetary process, a distinction was made between compulsory and **non-compulsory expenditure**. This mattered because the distinction determined the ability of the **European Parliament** (EP) to influence outcomes. The EP had a decision making role in relation to non-compulsory expenditure, while the **Council of the European Union** had a similar role in relation to compulsory expenditure. The distinction between the two types of expenditure has led to tensions between the Council and the EP. According to the old Article 272 (prior to the Treaty of Lisbon amendments), compulsory expenditure referred to spending on those policies arising directly out of the **founding treaties** and their amendments. The major item of cost has traditionally been the **common agricultural policy** (CAP). In reviewing the annual draft budget submitted to it by the Council of the European Union, the EP had been allowed to modify only the proposals on non-compulsory expenditure. It should be noted that, in a major shift of policy, the Treaty of Lisbon introduced significant changes regarding the financial and budgetary procedures of the EU. It shortened the annual budgetary policymaking procedure, confirmed existing practices of working within the Multi-annual Financial Framework (MFF) and abolished the distinction between compulsory and non-compulsory expenditure, and provided for practically full parity between the EP and the Council over EU expenditure items. This enabled, for example, the EP to be involved fully in discussions and decisions over the running of the CAP.

The **CONCILIATION COMMITTEE** is composed of 28 members of the **Council of the European Union**, or their representatives, and an equal number of representatives of the **European Parliament** (EP). The rules are laid down in Article 294 of the **Treaty on the Functioning of the European Union**. It meets as part of the **co-decision procedure** when the EP fails to adopt the common position of the Council. The **European Commission** participates in the Committee's proceedings, initiating proposals to overcome any impasse between the Council and the EP's representatives. Indeed, the most meaningful negotiations occur in the so-called trialogue between all three institutions. The aim of the Conciliation Committee is to approve a joint text that is acceptable to all sides and may subsequently be adopted by the Council and by a plenary session of the EP.

CONDITIONALITY is widely used in the context of European Union (EU) external relations and **enlargement**. It entails the EU making closer ties or **development aid** conditional on non-member states meeting certain political, if not economic, conditions. The conditionality underpinning enlargement is based on **applicant countries** meeting the so-called **Copenhagen criteria** adopted in 1993. Once a country is a member of the EU, conditionality is still relevant. Since the **Treaty of Amsterdam**, member states that do not respect principles of liberty, democracy, respect for **human rights** and fundamental freedoms and the rule of law may have certain of their rights under the **European treaties** suspended. Conditionality tied to aid requires recipient countries of EU development aid to spend in very specific ways as agreed by, and in accordance with, EU norms and rules.

CONECCS: See **Interest Groups**; **Lobbying**

The **CONFEDERAL GROUP OF THE EUROPEAN UNITED LEFT/NORDIC GREEN LEFT** (GUE/NGL) is one of the **party groups** in the **European Parliament** (EP). Prior to the 1994 elections it was known as the Group for the European Unitarian Left (GUE) and was one of the two communist groups that emerged in 1989 following a division of the original Communists and Allies group. Originally dominated by the Italian communists, GUE had a more Eurocommunist profile than the former French-dominated Left Unity group. When the **Members of the European Parliament** (MEPs) from **Denmark**, **Finland** and **Sweden** joined it in 1995, the group changed its name again. The two largest national delegations represented within the GUE/NGL group in the 2009–14 Parliament came from **Germany** and the **Czech Republic**. The group, which is still opposed to neoliberalism and highly critical of business and capital, has experienced a growth in support. At the 2014 EP elections the group secured 52 seats (compared with 35 in 2009). The group re-elected Gabriele Zimmer (from the German Die Linke party) as its President in June 2014. The 2014 EP elections brought new members into the GUE, including Podemos (**Spain**), L'Altra Europe con Tsirpas (**Italy**), and two animal rights parties in both Germany and the **Netherlands** as well as a new independent from **Ireland** (Luke 'Ming' Flanagan), while SYRIZA (**Greece**) increased its representation from one to six deputies, behind only Die Linke, with seven. The parliamentary group supports the construction of a new vision of European co-operation and is particularly keen to tackle the **democratic deficit** and promote ecology. GUE is best described as a **Eurosceptic** party although its members display various levels of Euroscepticism. Given the political background and leanings of GUE members, the group is opposed to the **North Atlantic**

Treaty Organization (NATO) and seeks greater development of the **Organization for Security and Co-operation in Europe** (OSCE). The group also campaigns for better job and educational opportunities and places considerable emphasis on social solidarity, securing peace and pursuing sustainable economic development.

CONFERENCE ON SECURITY AND CO-OPERATION IN EUROPE (CSCE): See **Organization for Security and Co-operation in Europe**

CONFERENCES OF THE PARLIAMENTS: See **Assizes**

CONGRESS OF EUROPE was the name of the first post-war European gathering, held in The Hague in May 1948. It was organized by the **International Committee of the Movements for European Unity** and was attended by several hundred delegates from 16 countries, as well as by observers from the **USA** and Canada. Most political groupings, except those at the extremes, were represented, and many leading political figures attended. The major absentee was a strong delegation from the British Labour Party, in power at the time in the **United Kingdom**, which had dismissed the Congress as a body of 'unrepresentative interests'. The Congress sought the establishment of a European assembly, a charter of **human rights** and a European court. It demanded that the European states 'transfer and merge some portion of their sovereign rights so as to secure common political and economic action for the integration and proper development of their common resources'. Few practical measures were adopted, but it did agree to the formation of a **European Movement**. The latter, responding to a request from Paul-Henri Spaak, the Prime Minister of **Belgium**, produced a memorandum that contained the first draft for what would become the **Council of Europe**.

The European Union (EU) has no formal **CONSTITUTION**, although the **European treaties** are regarded as providing the constitutional framework of the EU, and the **Court of Justice** has referred to the **Treaty of Rome** as being the 'Constitutional Charter' of the European Communities. However, the issue of whether the EU should have a constitution was placed on the agenda of the **European Convention** launched in February 2002. This produced a **draft Treaty establishing a Constitution for Europe**, which subsequently formed the focus of negotiations in an **intergovernmental conference,** convened in October 2003 and resulted in the **Treaty establishing a Constitution for Europe**. Although this was formally abandoned as a text, much of its content found its way into the **Treaty of Lisbon**, leading to claims that this was the 'EU Constitution' in all but name.

CONSTITUTIONAL TREATY is the term often used to describe the outcome of the **intergovernmental conference** launched in October 2003. (See **Treaty establishing a Constitution for Europe**.)

CONSTITUTIVE TREATIES: See **Founding Treaties**

CONSTRUCTIVE ABSTENTION is employed during consideration of matters of **common foreign and security policy** and allows decisions requiring unanimity within the **Council of the European Union** to be taken without the express support of all member states. Abstentions do not count as votes in opposition to a proposal.

The **CONSULTATION PROCEDURE** is the oldest and simplest of all decision making procedures in the European Communities: the **Council of the European Union** has only to consult the **European Parliament** when adopting **legislation** proposed by the **European Commission**. Although the consultation procedure is still used for legislation adopted as part of the **common agricultural policy**, for example, most **decisions** within the European Union are now adopted under the **Ordinary Legislative Procedure**. (See also **Co-operation Procedure**.)

The **CONSULTATIVE COMMITTEE OF THE EUROPEAN COAL AND STEEL COMMUNITY** was established in 1951 as a part of the now defunct **European Coal and Steel Community** (ECSC). It was charged with advising the High Authority, the executive of the ECSC, on all aspects of the operation of the ECSC and of the national coal and steel industries. The Committee assumed a similar role in relation to the **European Commission** following the merger of the executives of the European Communities in 1967. Composed of representatives of producers, employees and consumers, it had a purely advisory and consultative role, with no decision making authority.

The **CONSULTATIVE COUNCIL OF SOCIAL AND REGIONAL AUTHORITIES** was an advisory body attached to the **European Commission**, and was consulted on issues of regional development. Its role was taken over by the **Committee of the Regions**.

The **CONSUMER COMMITTEE**: See **European Consumer Consultative Group**

CONSUMER CONSULTATIVE COUNCIL: See **European Consumer Consultative Group**

CONSUMER POLICY was not mentioned in the **Treaty of Rome**. Although consumer interests and the **European Parliament** pressed for a consumer policy for several years, action was not taken until the Paris summit of the heads of government in 1972. Agreement was reached on the establishment within the **European Commission** of a section, later upgraded to a **Directorate-General** (DG), DG-XI, for consumer and environmental protection, a Consumer Consultative Committee (later the Consumer Consultative Council, or CCC, then the **Consumer Committee**, and subsequently as the **European Consumer Consultative Group**, or ECCG) and a Consumer Policy Service (which later became DG-XXIV, for consumer policy and health protection). In April 1975 the Council of Ministers (see **Council of the European Union**) launched a consumer information and protection programme which established five fundamental consumer rights: safeguards against risks to health and safety; economic justice; redress for damages; consultation; and information and education. These rights were to be the basis of specific measures of consumer protection. Although consumer policy was strengthened in 1983, when the national ministers responsible for consumer affairs began to meet regularly within the Council of Ministers, the bulk of consumer protection **legislation** was not adopted until after the launch of the Third Consumer Programme of 1986. The action was part of the effort to prepare for the **internal market**, and the **Single European Act** incorporated consumer policy within the treaty framework. A firm legal basis for consumer policy was created via the **Treaty on European Union**.

The Commission adopted a Consumer Policy Strategy (2007–13) in March 2007. In terms of priorities, the Commission aimed to increase consumer confidence in the internal market (by establishing a uniform regulatory environment); to strengthen the individual consumer's position and rights in the marketplace; and to seek to ensure that consumers' concerns were incorporated into all European Union policies. A European Commission Directorate-General for Justice and Consumers was created in 2010. The Consumer Policy Strategy was succeeded by a new European Consumer Agenda (drawn up and agreed in 2012), which sought to build directly on the former and began to enter into force in 2014. The Agenda aims to maximize consumer participation and trust in the marketplace. It contains four main objectives: reinforcing consumer safety; enhancing knowledge; stepping up enforcement and securing redress; and aligning consumers. Essentially, EU consumer policy aims to value the consumer, and seeks to guarantee that consumers are provided with certain rights as buyers and entitles them to a high level of protection and support.

CONVENTION ON THE FUTURE OF EUROPE: See **European Convention**

CONVERGENCE is a term used to describe the objective of encouraging the economies of the member states to develop in the same way, especially with regard to inflation, deficits and interest rates. It emerged during the arguments in the 1980s for an **internal market**, and later was applied to the declared objective of **economic and monetary union** by 1999. In a wider context, it has also been used to explain why a number of other policy areas, such as **competition policy**, have been aligned at both the national and European Union levels.

CONVERGENCE CRITERIA for progression to stage three of **economic and monetary union** (EMU) were established by the **Treaty on European Union**. The four criteria were: an avoidance of excessive government deficits (i.e. an annual deficit of no more than 3% of gross domestic product—GDP, and no more than 60% of GDP for stock of government debt); a rate of inflation no more than 1.5 percentage points above the average of that of the three best-performing member states; exchange rate stability within the **European Monetary System** over the two previous years, without devaluation; and long-term interest rates to be within two percentage points of the average in the three member states with the lowest inflation rates in the European Union. However, economic difficulties were such that few states met the convergence criteria. Consequently, a less strict interpretation of the criteria was applied, and in 1998 it was declared that, of those member states wishing to participate in EMU, only **Greece** had failed to meet the convergence criteria.

CO-OPERATION refers more specifically to intergovernmental co-operation, a process of collaboration by the member states, with the intention of securing agreement on objectives and strategies without the involvement of supranational institutions. It is the opposite of the **community method**.

CO-OPERATION AGREEMENTS are similar to (but less comprehensive than) **association agreements**, which aim to promote intensive economic co-operation. Co-operation agreements have been concluded since the mid-1970s by the European Communities with many countries outside Europe, as well as being, before 1991, the favoured form of relationship with Eastern European countries. After 1989 many Central and Eastern European countries preferred to seek **Europe agreements**, the new form of association agreement being offered to them. Successor states to the **USSR** were offered **partnership and co-operation agreements**.

The **CO-OPERATION PROCEDURE** was introduced by the **Single European Act** in 1987 as a means of enhancing the role of the **European Parliament** in EC decision making. With the subsequent emergence of and increased recourse to the **co-decision procedure**, its use was soon limited to certain **decisions** in the area of **economic and monetary union**. It was eventually abandoned entirely with the **Treaty of Lisbon**.

COPA: See **Committee of Professional Agricultural Organizations**

The **COPENHAGEN CRITERIA**, sometimes referred to as the **accession criteria**, are the conditions that countries of **Central and Eastern Europe** must meet if they are to be admitted to the European Union (EU). They were adopted at the **Copenhagen summit** of the **European Council** in June 1993, and require those countries seeking to join the EU to possess stable institutions which guarantee democracy; to respect the rule of law and human and minority rights; to possess a functioning market economy able to cope with competitive pressure and market forces; and to be capable of meeting the obligations of membership (i.e. adherence to the *acquis communautaire* as well as the *finalité politique* of the EU).

Two **COPENHAGEN SUMMITS** of the **European Council** met specifically to discuss the eastward **enlargement** of the European Union (EU). The first met in 1993 and established the **Copenhagen criteria** for EU membership, while the second, convened in December 2002, formally approved the accession of the first 10 **candidate countries** to the EU. The states were: **Cyprus**, the **Czech Republic**, **Estonia**, **Hungary**, **Latvia**, **Lithuania**, **Malta**, **Poland**, **Slovakia** and **Slovenia**. Following the successful outcome of the second Copenhagen summit, the **Treaty of Accession** was signed, and the 10 states joined the EU on 1 May 2004.

COR: See **Committee of the Regions**

CORDIS stands for Community Research and Development Information Service. It provides a database and summary information on all current research projects within the European Union.

CORE EUROPE refers to the notion that a group of states within the European Union would opt to forge closer economic, political and military links between themselves, if some of the other states showed a degree of reluctance to pursue the policy agenda of a core group. The concept of core Europe is usually understood to mean **France**, **Germany** and the **Benelux** states, that is, all the original members of the **European Coal and Steel Community** except **Italy**.

COREPER: See **Committee of Permanent Representatives**

CO-RESPONSIBILITY LEVIES were introduced in 1986 and, along with the later **stabilizers**, were seen as a means of attempting to halt the open-ended **subsidies** on production and the huge surpluses that the guaranteed price support system had imposed upon the **common agricultural policy**. The levies were set to come into operation whenever predetermined production quantities for a product were exceeded, making them, in effect, a tax on excess output. Many people argued that the levies had been set at too low a level to be properly effective.

COREU (Correspondance Européenne) is a secure communications system that connects all the foreign ministries of the European Union (EU) member states. The objective of this link is to improve and foster co-operation in the development of the EU's **common foreign and security policy**.

COSAC is the acronym for Conférence des Organes Spécialisés dans les Affaires Communautaires, the gathering, every six months, of **Members of the European Parliament** and members of the European Union affairs committees of **national parliaments**.

COSI is the acronym for the Standing Committee on Operational Cooperation on Internal Security, created by the **Council** under the terms of the **Treaty on the functioning of the European Union** to facilitate co-operation on internal security within the European Union (EU). The rationale for this committee stems from Article 71 of the TFEU. COSI comprises high-level representatives from each EU member country's Ministry of the Interior and/or Justice, as well as officials from the **European Commission** and the **European External Action Service**. Delegates from **Europol**, **EUROJUST**, **FRONTEX**, the European Union Agency for Law Enforcement Training (CEPOL) and other associated agencies may also, on occasion, attend meetings as observers. COSI co-ordinates activities relating to, *inter alia*, policy and customs co-operation, external border protection and judicial co-operation in criminal matters. COSI is also responsible for informing the Council, the **European Parliament** and **national parliaments** about its activities. COSI is mandated to help the Council in accordance with the so-called 'Solidarity Clause' contained within Article 222 of the TFEU, which pledges that the EU will use all the tools at its disposal to assist a member state that becomes the target of a terrorist attack or suffers a disaster, whether natural or manmade. Responsibility for preparing legislative acts pertaining to any of the above issues remains with the **Committee of Permanent Representatives** (COREPER) rather than COSI.

COST is an intergovernmental framework for European Co-operation in Science and Technology, which is designed to co-ordinate nationally funded research at the European level. COST was established in 1970 with a membership of 19 countries, which increased to 25 countries in 1994, including all the member states of the European Union (EU). By 2007 it had 35 members. It is a framework for the preparation and implementation of European projects relating to applied scientific research. It plays a vital role in building a European Research Area (ERA) and seeks to complement the activities of the **Research Framework Programmes** and to facilitate the mobility of researchers across Europe. COST aims to establish scientific excellence in nine areas that include: biomedicine and molecular biosciences; food and agriculture; forests, their products and services; materials, physics and nanosciences; and transport and urban development. The COST Secretariat is attached to the **Council of the European Union** and the European Commission has handled the technical management of projects. Each project, however, has been individually negotiated by those states that wish to participate in it. Several collaborative projects have been pursued in 10 areas: information technology, **telecommunications**, transport, oceanography, metallurgy and materials science, meteorology, agriculture, food technology, environmental protection and medical research and health. (See also **EUREKA**.)

COSTA V ENEL the name of an important case in which the **Court of Justice**, in 1964, established the **primacy of European Community law** and confirmed that it could not be overruled.

The **COTONOU AGREEMENT** was signed in June 2000 by the European Union (EU) and the **ACP** (African, Caribbean and Pacific) **states** (all ACP members signed except Cuba) and superseded the fourth **Lomé Convention** (1990–2000). It provided longer-term (20-year) support for the ACP-EU relationship, which was to be developed on the basis of five interdependent pillars: comprehensive political dialogue; the enhanced participation of civil society in partnership affairs; a strengthened focus on poverty reduction; a new framework for economic and trade co-operation; and a reform of financial co-operation. The new Agreement therefore placed greater emphasis on establishing and maintaining good governance in the ACP states. It also envisaged the establishment of an ACP-EU free trade area by 2020, and committed €13,500m. in aid for the first five years of the Agreement. These funds were directed at poverty reduction and at encouraging non-state sectors to participate in the development process. The new Agreement was also notable for its insistence that respect for **human rights**, democratic principles and the rule of law should form the core criteria for aid policy decisions. From a practical perspective, the Agreement can be revisited every five years, as can the aid **protocols**, which are bound to a similar timetable. Progress is reviewed on an annual basis. Negotiations to revise the Cotonou Agreement were initiated in May 2004 and concluded in February 2005. The political dimension of the Agreement was broadly strengthened and a reference to co-operation in counter-terrorism and the prevention of the proliferation of weapons of mass destruction was included. The revised Cotonou Agreement was signed on 24 June. The second revised Cotonou Agreement was formally signed in Ouagadougou, Burkina Faso, in June 2010, and entered into effect, on a provisional basis, on 1 November. This revised Agreement placed an emphasis on the importance of regional integration among ACP states (fostering co-operation, peace and security, and promoting growth) and on the relevance of the **African Union** as a partner in ACP-EU relations. It also sought to promote conflict resolution and, for the first time, recognized the global challenge of climate change and the need for the ACP states to address some of the concerns surrounding this pressing issue. The revised Agreement also took into account other urgent problems and realities for the ACP states (including HIV/AIDS and food security). From its perspective, the EU displayed a strong interest in developing contacts and relations with a broad range of actors in the ACP states—national and local parliaments, civil society and the private sector. Negotiations are scheduled to begin in 2018 on a successor to the Cotonou Agreement.

The **COUNCIL FOR MUTUAL ECONOMIC ASSISTANCE** (CMEA), also known as Comecon, was established in 1949 by the **USSR** and subsequently developed into an organ for economic co-operation and co-ordination in the Communist bloc. At first, the European Communities (EC) expressed little interest in an arrangement with the CMEA. Any agreement would have been difficult because of the non-convertibility of CMEA currencies and its operation of a centralized planning and production system, whereby trade was based on an exchange or barter system rather than money transfers. These problems were compounded by Soviet hostility towards the EC. Talks between the EC and the CMEA began only in 1976. They had not produced any results by 1980, when discussions were broken off as a result of the Soviet invasion of Afghanistan. They were not resumed until 1986, after Mikhail Gorbachev's accession to power in the USSR, and a mutual recognition agreement was signed in June 1988. Among other things, it permitted the establishment of diplomatic relations between the EC and individual Eastern European countries: several, including the USSR, established diplomatic posts in **Brussels** with accreditation to the EC. Prior to the 1988 agreement, the EC had signed only limited sectoral agreements with Eastern European countries. The German Democratic Republic (GDR—East **Germany**) had been in a different position since the 1972 **Ostpolitik** agreement with the Federal Republic of Germany (FRG—West Germany), which had given its products access to the EC.

The relationship with the CMEA was confused and disrupted by the events of 1989, which removed the communist parties from power or forced them to share it. In October 1990 the former GDR automatically became part of the EC when it was subsumed into the FRG by German reunification. At a CMEA meeting in 1990 the new governments of the other Eastern European states expressed strong dissatisfaction with the past performance of the CMEA and its current condition: several declared an interest in EC membership in the medium term. In 1991 it was agreed to replace the CMEA by a two-year interim organization based upon market economy principles, to be called the Organization for International Economic Co-operation. However, with the disintegration of the USSR at the end of 1991, all semblance of continuing collaboration ceased, and the CMEA effectively disappeared.

The **COUNCIL OF THE BARS AND LAW SOCIETIES OF THE EUROPEAN UNION** (CCBE) is the officially recognized representative organization for the legal profession in the European Union and the **European Economic Area**.

The **COUNCIL OF EUROPE**, which should not be confused with either the **Council of the European Union** or the **European Council**, was formed in 1949 as Western Europe's first post-war political organization. Its Statute was signed as the Treaty of Westminster by 10 states, and permanent offices were provided for the organization in **Strasbourg, France**. The Council has established other offices with specific functions and responsibilities in cities across Europe. For example, the Europe Development Bank is located in Paris and the Centre for Modern Languages is situated in Graz in **Austria**. In addition, the Council has placed heavy emphasis on youth and operates a European Youth Centre from Budapest. As an organization the Council of Europe is well resourced and maintains offices in Paris and in other European capital cities. The Council's declared objective was to achieve 'a greater unity between its members for the purpose of safeguarding and realizing the ideals and principles which are their common heritage and facilitating their economic and social progress'. These objectives were to be secured through 'discussions of questions of common concern and by agreements and common action in economic, social, scientific, legal and administrative matters and in the maintenance and further realization of **human rights** and fundamental freedoms'. Its membership grew until, by the 1980s, it incorporated all the non-communist states of Europe.

The Council consists of two main bodies: a Committee of Ministers and an Assembly. With each state having one vote and a veto, the Committee of Ministers is essentially an intergovernmental conference of foreign ministers from all 47 member states, meeting twice yearly. Chairmanships of the Committee of Ministers are held for six months, in alphabetical order, and the current running order is as follows: the **Czech Republic** (May–November 2017), **Denmark** (November 2017–May 2018), **Croatia** (May–November 2018), **Finland** (November 2018–May 2019) and **France** (May–November 2019). Since 1952 the practice of deputies (usually diplomats) representing the ministers has been normal for all but the most symbolic meetings. In relaying decisions to the member states, the Committee is allowed only to make recommendations. States are not obliged to accept decisions of the Council of Europe.

Similarly, the Assembly, renamed the Parliamentary Assembly (PACE) in 1974, is essentially a discussion chamber, with hardly any substantive powers (and it should not be confused with the **European Parliament**). It comprises national parliamentarians from all 47 member states, who elect a President for a three-year term (which is renewable). The Assembly appoints members as *rapporteurs*, with the mandate to prepare parliamentary reports on specific subjects, which cover a multitude of areas and most recently, rendition flights, the abolition of the death penalty in Europe and, of course, regular reports on the **human rights** situation across Europe. Ever since its first session in 1949, the majority of the delegates, who are appointed by their national parliaments, have been strong supporters of European integration. The fact that it has shared a common home in **Strasbourg** with the European Parliament has helped this commitment. However, the Assembly can only put recommendations forward to the Committee of Ministers, which can, and often does, ignore or reject them.

The Council of Europe has produced about 200 conventions and agreements, most of which have been accepted by almost all the member states. Its greatest achievement, perhaps, was to secure agreement on a **European Convention on Human Rights** in 1950, with a concomitant **European Commission of Human Rights** and a **European Court of Human Rights**, both of which operate under the aegis of the Council. Much of the Council of Europe's success has been in the less politically contentious cultural field. It sponsored, for example, the European Cultural Convention in 1954 and a European Social Charter in 1961. In 1960 it was handed the social and cultural responsibilities that **Western European Union** had been granted by the **Treaty of Brussels**.

In the 1950s it also sought to achieve some form of policy co-ordination in agriculture, civil aviation and transport. However, by itself the Council could not advance European integration much beyond such symbolic actions as seating the Assembly delegates in alphabetical order rather than by nationality. The **United Kingdom** and the Scandinavian states were firmly opposed to it becoming anything more than an inter-governmental deliberative body. After the early 1950s it was overtaken by the developments that led to the establishment of the European Communities (EC). Although its major historical significance was that it was the first European organization of a political nature, its later importance was two-fold. It was the European organization with the broadest membership, albeit limited to democracies, a claim that was later challenged by the formation of the **Conference on Security and Co-operation in Europe**. Also, because of its broad membership, it remained important as a forum where a wide range of ideas and views could be expressed, and as a central clearing-house for co-operation and co-ordination, receiving and discussing annual reports from a wide range of European and other international organizations and agencies, including the EC. The ending of the **Cold War** offered the Council an opportunity of expanding its membership, and in the early 1990s most of the Central and Eastern European countries and the western republics of the former **USSR** (for example, the **Russian Federation**) either joined the Council or at least applied for membership. At 2017 the Council's 47 members included all 28 member states of the EU.

Relations between the Council of Europe and the European Union (EU) are drawing ever closer. It is expected (under the **Treaty of Lisbon**) that the EU will join the European Convention on Human Rights in the near future as all 47 governments are keen to ensure consistent human rights protection across Europe and, above all, to avoid any inconsistency in the developing case law between the EU Courts and the European Court of Human Rights.

The **COUNCIL OF THE EUROPEAN UNION** is frequently referred to as the Council of Ministers, and prior to 1993 its full official title was the Council of Ministers of the European Communities (EC). It should not be confused with either the **Council of Europe** or the **European Council**, although it is closely related to the latter. The Council of the European Union shares executive responsibility in the European Union (EU) with the **European Commission**. Whereas the Commission represents and defends general European and EC interests, the Council essentially represents the interests of the individual member states. It began life with the **Treaty of Rome**, as the main decision making institution, although, in later treaties, it has become a co-legislator with the **European Parliament** in most policy areas. The membership of the Council consists of ministerial representatives of the member states. Its meetings are serviced by officials from its own secretariat, the existence of which was formally acknowledged only in the **Treaty on European Union** (TEU), and one or more Commissioners, depending on the topics listed on its agenda for the day, may also attend them. The Council's headquarters are in the **Justus Lipsius** building in **Brussels**, but on three occasions each year (in April, June and October) the Council meets in **Luxembourg**. This is a legacy of the merger of the executives of the EC in 1967: the executive High Authority of the **European Coal and Steel Community** had been based in Luxembourg. Council meetings are normally held in private, although there have been some sessions where elements of the proceedings have been televised. Moreover, spokespersons for each of the member governments hold extensive and detailed press briefings after each Council session.

The Council of the European Union has no fixed membership other than permitting one representative from each member state. In purely legal terms there is only one Council, but its actual composition changes depending on the policy area in question. There are, in effect, a range of different Council formats, some of which can even meet simultaneously in parallel sessions. Some meet more often than others, and this reflects the greater salience of some policy areas. The composition of each Council is determined by a particular policy agenda: if, for example, the topic to be discussed is agriculture, the Council consists of the national ministers with responsibility for agriculture; if the agenda is to deal with **consumer policy**, it will be the national ministers responsible for consumer affairs who are in attendance, and so on. When the EU **budget** is to be discussed, the national finance ministers form the Council. The four most important formats of the Council, which meet monthly, are those dealing with General Affairs (covering a range of policy issues, such as negotiations on EU enlargement, and budgetary and administrative issues), Foreign Affairs, Economic and Financial Affairs, and Agriculture and Fisheries. The other formats cover: co-operation in the fields of Justice and Home Affairs; Employment, Social Policy, Health and Consumer Affairs; Competitiveness; Transport, Telecommunications and Energy; Environment; and finally, Education, Youth, Culture and Sport.

The Council of the European Union is a core legislative element of the EU. While the **right of initiative** for most **legislation** lies with the European Commission, it is only the Council that, after some involvement of the European Parliament (EP) and consultation with one or more **advisory committees** and agencies, is empowered to adopt proposals and so legislate for the EU. Other responsibilities include the obligation, in conjunction with the EP, to adopt the EU budget, and the power of appointment to other EU institutions, including the Commission.

To aid it in its tasks, the Council has its own secretariat in Brussels. Central to this are the delegations or **Permanent Representations** that each member state maintains in Brussels. The **Committee of Permanent Representatives** (COREPER) has the task of ensuring that issues awaiting a decision by the Council have been thoroughly discussed and analysed by Council staff. When COREPER reaches agreement on proposals, the Council normally adopts these without discussion. On all other issues the Council reaches its decision by voting. The Treaty of Rome and its amendments define the way in which the Council votes on issues. Depending upon the issue under discussion, a proposal may be adopted by **majority voting**, by **qualified majority voting**, or unanimously. The incidence and importance of decision making by simple majority is negligible, and it is used only for a few minor questions, usually of a procedural nature.

The Treaty of Rome anticipated that, after an initial transitional period, qualified majority voting would become more usual, with **unanimity** restricted to a few issues of major importance. The **empty chair crisis** of 1965 and the **Luxembourg Compromise** of 1966 disrupted this plan. The use of qualified majorities remained limited, with the Council preferring not to jeopardize unanimity by pushing issues to a vote. This made for slow progress. Almost all the reviews of EC practices conducted after the mid-1970s commented adversely on the slowness of decision making, and recommended a greater use of majority voting; this was finally introduced by the **Single European Act**. The creation of the EU and its potentially extensive **enlargement** in the early years of the 21st century forced further re-examination of the decision making process. In fact, the TEU, the **Treaty of Amsterdam**, the **Treaty of Nice** and the **Treaty of Lisbon** all extended the use of qualified majority voting to new areas of policy. The Treaty of Lisbon also provided for the eventual switch to a form of **double majority voting**.

The task of directing the Council in its various functions falls to its President. Member states hold the **Council presidency** in rotation, the position shifting from state to state every six months. The member state currently holding the presidency is responsible during those six months for organizing the business of the Council, in conjunction with the secretariat. With the Treaty of Lisbon, the situation has changed somewhat (see below). Although each member state holding the presidency will hope to advance its own priority issues, by convention, the President is expected to be a neutral arbiter, securing, by compromise and bargaining, Council agreement on as many issues as possible.

As a result of measures introduced by the Treaty of Amsterdam, the Council plays a more active role in **employment** affairs by encouraging member states to exchange information and best practice in this field. Its role in protecting **citizens' rights** was also expanded, a new **Article** permitting the Council to take action, by **unanimity**, in cases of **discrimination**. However, the Treaty of Amsterdam also increased the powers of the EP at the expense of the Council, by strengthening the **co-decision procedure**, granting the EP full co-legislative powers in a number of policy areas. The Treaty of Amsterdam, the Treaty of Nice and the Treaty of Lisbon have extended the areas in which the Council can take decisions using qualified majority voting, although unanimity is still required in core areas such as taxation and in constitutional matters. Attempts to speed up the EU's reaction in times of international crisis have also been introduced as part of reforms to the **common foreign and security policy** (CFSP). In situations in which member states have common foreign policy interests, the Council of the European Union is to decide by consensus the principles and strategies to be employed in joint actions. If the Council of the European Union cannot reach agreement, the final decision on EU foreign policy actions is to be taken by the European Council. For member states not opposed to proposed actions but not prepared to participate directly, there is the '**constructive abstention**' option. The Treaty of Lisbon has sought to enable the EU to speak with a single voice on foreign policy issues through the enhanced role of the **High Representative of the Union for Foreign Affairs and Security Policy**. According to the Treaty of Lisbon the role of High Representative combines three different functions: she is the Council's representative on foreign policy issues, she is President of the Foreign Affairs Council, and she serves as a Vice-President of the Commission. In terms of fulfilling her duties, she is supported by a policy planning and early warning unit and by the **European External Action Service**. Reflecting developments within the CFSP, a **European Union Military Committee** has also been established within the Council.

COUNCIL OF MINISTERS: See **Council of the European Union**

The **COUNCIL PRESIDENCY** rotates in a predetermined sequence (until 1995 it was arranged alphabetically) among the members of the European Union (EU). Each member state holds the presidency for a period of six months and can influence the focus of its presidency and attempt to steer policy agendas accordingly. However, it is extremely difficult to carry through specific **legislation** in this short period. Moreover, there are concerns that this mode of organization will not be productive in an enlarged EU. Hence, the **Treaty establishing a Constitution for Europe** envisaged three changes: team presidencies comprising three member states and lasting 18 months; a **President of the European Council** in office for two and a half years; and a **Union Minister for Foreign Affairs** chairing Council meetings dealing with foreign affairs. These changes have since been carried forward into the **Treaty of Lisbon**, although the term of Union Minister for Foreign Affairs has been dropped in favour of **High Representative of the Union for Foreign Affairs and Security Policy**. **Malta** held the presidency in January–June 2017, and **Estonia** in July–December. **Bulgaria** assumes it in January–June 2018, and **Austria** in the second half of that year. **Romania** was to hold the presidency in the first half of 2019. The **United Kingdom** had been due to hold the Presidency for the six-month period from July 2017, but incoming Prime Minister **Theresa May** announced in July 2016 that the UK was to relinquish the role, following the British vote to leave the EU in a referendum held in the previous month (see **Brexit**).

The **COUNCIL SECRETARIAT** (officially the General Secretariat of the Council of the European Union) is a professional civil service that forms part of the Eurocracy residing in Brussels. The Council Secretariat is considerably smaller than the **European Commission** and currently comprises approximately 3,000 staff from all 28 EU member states. The purpose of the Council Secretariat is essentially to draft the six-month legislative programme for each **Council presidency**, providing legal service, briefing government ministers on salient EU issues, preparing the agenda for Council meetings and drafting Council meetings minutes. In terms of structure, the Council Secretariat mirrors the Commission in so far as it is divided into **Directorates-General**, although along very different lines. The Council Secretariat comprises seven Directorates-General, together with a legal service and a private office for the Secretary-General. The Directorates-General handle administration in the following areas: agriculture, fisheries, social affairs and health; foreign affairs, enlargement and **civil protection**; justice and home affairs; environment, education, transport and energy; communication and information; and economic affairs and competitiveness. The legal service exists to represent the Council before the courts. The **Treaty of Amsterdam** provided for the Council Secretary-General becoming **High Representative for the Common Foreign and Security Policy** and a Deputy Secretary-General assuming responsibility for the Secretariat. This development meant that the role of the Secretary-General changed from civil servant to high-ranking politician. The **Treaty of Lisbon** has reversed this situation. The current Secretary-General of the Council Secretariat is **Jeppe Tranholm-Mikkelsen**. It should be noted that the respective Secretariats of **Western European Union** and the **Schengen Agreement** were merged into the Council Secretariat. The Council Secretariat has become an active participant in the design of policy formulation, especially in the realm of the **common foreign and security policy** and the **Common Security and Defence Policy**. Many people are engaged on foreign policy issues within the Secretariat's Directorates, and the Secretariat also hosts the European Union Military Staff. Since January 2007 the Council Secretariat has functioned with its own independent Operations Centre.

COUNCIL TRADE POLICY COMMITTEE, as the Article 133 Committee (formerly the Article 113 Committee) became known under the **Treaty of Lisbon**, consists of representatives of European Union member states. It assists the **European Commission** in trade negotiations with non-member states and within the **World Trade Organization**.

COURT OF AUDITORS: See **European Court of Auditors**

COURT OF FIRST INSTANCE: See **General Court**

The **COURT OF JUSTICE** of the European Union, based in Luxembourg, was, until the establishment of the Court of First Instance (now the **General Court**), the only court of the former European Communities (EC). The Court of Justice is charged with ensuring that the operation of the European Union (EU) concurs with the provisions of the **founding treaties** and their amendments. It has no hierarchical links with the courts of the different legal systems of the member states, and has no jurisdiction over the application and interpretation of purely national laws by the national courts, except insofar as those laws conflict with EU law, which takes precedence over them. Within its area of competence, the Court is supreme: there is no appeal against its rulings.

The **pillar** structure that was introduced under the **Treaty on European Union** (TEU) was abolished by the **Treaty of Lisbon**. Under the Treaty of Lisbon the entire court system of the EU is now known as the Court of Justice of the European Union, and it comprises the Court of Justice and the **General Court** (in September 2016 the Civil Service Tribunal merged with the General Court, and its seven judges became part of the merged institution). The Court of Justice is concerned primarily with EU law. Although the pillar structure has been abolished, the **common foreign and security policy** (CFSP) remains subject to special rules and specific procedures and, thus, the Court's rulemaking powers in this area are curtailed.

The Court is composed of one judge from each member state, so that all of the EU's national legal systems are represented. Even after the EU's **enlargement** to 28 member states in July 2013, there was still one judge per member state. For the sake of efficiency, however, the Court may sit as a 'Grand Chamber' of just 13 judges or in Chambers of three or four judges instead of in a plenary session attended by all the judges. There are also 11 **Advocates-General**. These have similar privileges to judges, but act more as consultants and advisers than as referees. Members of the Court have to be individuals 'whose independence is beyond doubt and who possess the qualifications required for appointment to the highest judicial offices in their respective countries or who are jurisconsults of recognized competence'. Although it is the member governments who formally submit nominations to the Court, appointment is made by the Council of Ministers (see **Council of the European Union**). Judges and Advocates-General are appointed for renewable six-year terms of office, with one-half of the Court being renewed every three years. The judges elect the President of the Court from among their own members, for a renewable three-year term.

The Court meets both in plenary sessions and in smaller subdivisions called Chambers. The latter enable the Court to carry a larger case load at any one time. Important cases, including virtually all those brought by an EU institution or by a member state, are heard in plenary session, where eight judges constitute a quorum. Other cases are referred to a Chamber, of which there are six. Any Chamber is free to request that a case currently before it should be transferred to the full Court when it considers that the case merits the fullest possible hearing.

In its various guises, the Court hears three different types of case: opinions, referrals and disputes. The least contentious are opinions, which refer to opinions given by the Court on international agreements to which the EU is party. Referrals describe preliminary rulings by the Court on cases brought before it from national court systems. When a point of EU law is raised in a case before a national court, the point at issue is referred to the Court of Justice for a preliminary ruling, because EU law takes precedence over national law. The national court must take this into account in hearing the case before it. Referrals have been an important way in which the Court has been able to ensure that EU law is applied uniformly across all the member states.

Under the Treaty of Lisbon the preliminary ruling procedure has been extended to acts of EU bodies, offices or agencies. It also introduces a provision that requires the Court of Justice to act with the minimum of delay when dealing with preliminary rulings. The Court of Justice can also review acts of the **European Council**. Most cases involve disputes, and the Court is largely reactive. There are four main types of dispute: those between the EU and member states; between member states; between EU institutions; and between individuals or corporate bodies (including EU employees) and the EU. Any of these categories can initiate Court proceedings. In the case of an individual, they must be able to demonstrate a direct personal interest in the case and its outcome. Under the terms of the TEU, disputes between individuals and the EU were made the responsibility of the Court of First Instance, which now has jurisdiction in this fourth area of disputes.

When the Court first receives a written complaint, it has to establish whether the charge falls within its remit and within the time limits stipulated by the treaties. If it decides in the affirmative, the written charge is sent to the defendant, who has one month in which to make a rebuttal. The plaintiff is then granted an additional month in which a response may be made to the defendant's statement. Finally, the defendant has a further month in which to prepare an additional response. Once this process is completed, the case, if not settled out of court, moves to the stage of a formal hearing. The responsibility for a case belongs to a judge rapporteur, who is appointed by the President of the Court. The judge rapporteur, after studying all the documents, sends a preliminary report to the Court, which must then decide whether to hold a preliminary inquiry, which could involve a request for further documentation and/or the need for the two sides in the case to give oral testimony before the Court. It is at this point that the Court decides whether to hear the case in plenary session or to refer it to one of the Chambers. The President of the Court sets a date for the public hearing. The conduct of the public hearing follows normal legal convention: plaintiff and defendant present their arguments and call witnesses; the judges and the Advocate-General appointed to the case carry out cross-questioning. The Advocate-General acts as a public prosecutor of the kind found in many European legal systems. The Court does not give its verdict immediately upon the conclusion of the public hearing. A further hearing is held some weeks later at which the Advocate-General reviews the oral and written evidence and proposes a verdict. The opinion of the Advocate-General is not final, but in the majority of cases it is a good indication of the likely decision of the Court. If, during their consideration of the evidence, the judges feel they need more information or explanation, they may extend the hearing. Finally, the Court delivers its verdict at a public hearing. Unanimity is not required, and judgments are reached by majority vote. Normally, the case will be heard by an uneven number of judges: where this is not the case and there is no majority, a decision is reached by eliminating the vote of the most junior judge. Judgments are nevertheless collective, to emphasize the independence of the Court from both other EU institutions and national governments. Voting is secret, and the voting record of any individual judge is not known. At September 2016 the Court had a total of 935 cases pending. In 2015 a total of 604 new cases were lodged, and 571 were closed.

Apart from EU employees, the largest number of cases have related to agriculture and the **common agricultural policy**, followed by those concerning the **customs union**, **freedom of movement**, **competition policy** and **workers' rights**. Individuals and companies, mostly protesting against EC regulations, have brought the majority of actions, although a significant number have been directed against member states. The **European Commission** has been the most vigorous plaintiff, as well as being the most common defendant. Cases brought by one EC institution against another have been comparatively rare, but the Council of Ministers and the **European Parliament** (EP) have, on occasion, brought each other before the Court. The TEU increased the ability of the EP to bring cases before the Court. Member states have initiated actions less frequently. They have often, however, been the subject of actions brought by the Commission, when the latter alleged failure to carry out their obligations. The country most involved in legal action has been **Italy**, most notably as a defendant, owing mainly to its tardiness in implementing EU **legislation**, but also as the state that has initiated the most actions. The TEU remedied a previous deficiency by giving the Court powers of enforcement (usually fines) against member states that do not conform to its judgments.

The Court has become one of the most important EC institutions, playing a vital role in consolidating and harmonizing the EU. In the cases brought before it both by the Commission and by individuals, it has made a significant contribution towards ensuring that member states and their governments acknowledge the superiority of EU law and honour their EU obligations.

CREATIVE EUROPE entered into effect in January 2014, as the successor to the Culture and **MEDIA** programmes. Creative Europe has a budget of some €1,460m. for 2014–20 (representing a 9% increase in spending, in real terms, compared with 2007–13), and aims to stimulate employment in the cultural and creative industries. Creative Europe includes two sub-programmes: first a programme on culture that aims to support culture sector initiatives (such as cross-border co-operation and networking) and a second MEDIA section that focuses on audiovisual initiatives. In terms of **audiovisual policy** and **media policy**, the MEDIA strand is designed to support the worldwide distribution of European films as well as to make it easier for those involved in the sector to enhance cross-border activities. The Commission plans to allocate some €900m. to the cinema and audiovisual sector by 2020, with increased support for European culture, cinema, music, literature, performing arts and heritage and related activities. A number of events and activities (such as the **European Capital of Culture** and heritage days) as well as a series of European prizes (such as the prize for contemporary architecture and the EU prize for literature) will receive support from Creative Europe.

CREEPING COMPETENCE is a phrase that has been used, mainly by critics of further integration, to refer to the extension of the role and powers of the supranational institutions at the expense of the member states, usually through a more expansive interpretation of the treaties and their amendments.

CREST: See **Scientific and Technical Research Committee**

CORINA CREȚU (1967–) was born in Bucharest, **Romania**. She was nominated in 2014 as the Romanian Commissioner to the new 28-member **European Commission** led by **Jean-Claude Juncker**. In September Juncker named Crețu as the Commissioner responsible for Regional Policy, subject to approval by the **European Parliament** (EP). Prior to her appointment to the Commission Crețu had been a **Member of the European Parliament** (MEP) since 2007, and prior to that had notably served as spokesperson for Romanian President Ion Iliescu. She graduated from the Academy of Economic Studies in Bucharest in 1989 and was elected to the Romanian Parliament in 2000. Following the endorsement of the Juncker Commission by both the EP and the European Council, Crețu took up her post as Commissioner on 1 November 2014.

CROATIA, a country of some 4.5m people, emerged as an independent European state following its secession from the **Yugoslav** federation in 1991. This successful move to independence was due in large amount to **Germany**'s unilateral decision to recognize the new state, even though Croatia's action aroused Belgrade's animosity and led to a short and bitter war with the Serbian minority in Croatia from 1991 to 1994, which included the bombardment of the historic city of Dubrovnik. Initially, Croatia was beset by severe problems, which were epitomized by economic stagnation and a high rate of unemployment (which had soared to 20% by 2000) and by the stubbornness and style of authoritarian nationalism created under the President, Franjo Tudjman, who died in 1999. In 2000 the new Government was determined to bring Croatia into the European mainstream, and signalled its intention to reform the economy and to apply for membership of the European Union (EU). In October 2001 it signed a **stabilization and association agreement** with the EU, which subsequently entered into force on 1 February 2005. By early 2003 it had made sufficient economic and political progress to apply formally for EU membership, becoming the second former Yugoslav republic, after **Slovenia**, to do so. In June 2004, following a positive *avis* from the **European Commission**, the **European Council** conferred candidate country status on Croatia and announced that **accession negotiations** would be opened in 2005. Croatia's failure to co-operate fully with the International Criminal Tribunal for the Former Yugoslavia (ICTY) or to hand over General Ante Gotovina, who had been accused of ordering the killing of more than 100 ethnic Serbs and expelling 150,000 in 1995, meant that the planned opening of negotiations in early 2005 was postponed. Only following confirmation from the ICTY chief prosecutor, Carla del Ponte, that Croatia was now fully co-operating with the ICTY did the EU's member states agree to open negotiations in early October 2005. The decision was somewhat controversial and was widely seen as part of a deal that allowed **Austria** to abandon its opposition to the opening of accession negotiations with **Turkey**.

With Gotovina finally captured and handed over to the ICTY in December 2005, the EU opened substantive negotiations. It also adopted a revised **accession partnership** and allocated Croatia €140m. pre-accession financial assistance for the year. A further €141m. was allocated for 2007 under the **instrument for pre-accession assistance**. By the end of February 2010 30 out of 35 negotiating chapters had been opened and 17 closed. Progress could have been quicker had Slovenia not vetoed negotiations for much of 2009 over a bilateral dispute concerning territorial waters. In June 2011 the EU confirmed that Croatia had complied with the requirements of the final outstanding negotiating chapters of the *acquis communautaire*, thereby allowing the country's accession to the Union. The Croatian Government officially signed the EU **Treaty of Accession** in December 2011. Croatia's membership of the EU was submitted for approval at a national referendum in January 2012 when it was endorsed by some 66.3% of the votes cast (with a participation rate of only about 44%). Croatia became the 28th member state of the EU on 1 July 2013. Croatia had already joined the **North Atlantic Treaty Organization** (in April 2009). Unlike **Bulgaria** and **Romania**, which sent appointed observers to the **European Parliament** (EP) from the time of their accession in January 2007 until the EP elections of June 2009, Croatia held elections to the EP in April 2013 to elect its 12 deputies (the number of which was reduced to 11 upon the restructuring of the EP at the elections in May 2014).

An escalation in refugee arrivals during 2015, caused by flight, in particular, from the ongoing civil conflict in **Syria**, precipitated a regional crisis in Central and South-Eastern Europe. In mid-September the Hungarian Government sealed its border with **Serbia**, causing migrants, often seeking asylum in Western Europe, to divert their route via Croatia. In response to the mass influx, on 17 September the Croatian authorities closed seven of its eight border crossings with Serbia; following EU pressure (and counter-measures by Serbia), Croatia reopened two main border crossings on 25 September. In mid-October **Hungary** also closed its border with Croatia. Slovenia's erection of a razor wire fence on its border with western Croatia in late December, which was intended to control refugee flows, prompted criticism from within both countries, and prompted the Croatian Government to submit a complaint to the **European Commission** on the grounds that the fence endangered wildlife. In December the Commission launched legal action against Croatia (and four other countries) for failing to register migrants adequately (estimating that 340,000 people had arrived in the country since mid-September, but only 575 had been documented fully).

CROCODILE GROUP is the name of an action group founded in July 1980 by Altiero Spinelli and other **Members of the European Parliament** (MEPs) who wished to persuade the new, directly elected **European Parliament** (EP) to develop a plan for a radical reform of the European Communities and a grand strategy for an all-embracing European union. The name derived from the restaurant in **Strasbourg** where the Group first met. The Group met at frequent intervals to plan strategy and formulate proposals, and circulated newsletters to all MEPs. Its principal argument was that the EP had a duty to consider constitutional reforms and to compile a draft that would be transmitted to the proper constitutional authorities in the member states for **ratification**. By 1981 it had won the support of a substantial number of MEPs, and the EP voted to establish an Institutional Committee to deliberate on the topic. This process resulted in the **draft Treaty establishing the European Union**.

CSCE: See **Organization for Security and Co-operation in Europe**

CSDP: See **Common Security and Defence Policy**

CSF (Community Support Frameworks): See **Structural and Cohesion Funds**

CULTURAL POLICY was for a long time a relatively undeveloped aspect of the European Union's (EU) policy remit. The EU had supported the initiatives of the **Council of Europe**, which had always been active in seeking to protect and develop the European cultural heritage. It was the rapid advance of technological developments in the 1980s that pushed the EU into greater activity, and the **European Commission** began to define the outlines of a cultural policy. Most of its efforts have been concentrated upon film and television (see **Media Policy**). It has also focused upon free trade in cultural goods, improving the working conditions and prospects of artists, encouraging a wider audience for cultural activities, and preserving the architectural heritage of the EU. It has emphasized the **freedom of movement** of both artists and their products throughout the EU, although it is agreed that 'national art treasures' should be excluded from these general provisions. Such treasures, however, have to be strictly defined. The EU has attempted to seek greater **harmonization** in various areas, including national copyright laws, public subsidies, resale rights and royalties. Several activities have been sponsored: the EU Youth and Baroque Orchestras; the translation of contemporary literature, especially from the minority languages of the EU; a European Film Festival (held in a different city each year); and the European Theatre in Milan, **Italy**, and Paris, **France**. The most widely known initiative, perhaps, is the designation each year, beginning with Athens, **Greece**, in 1985, of a different city as European City of Culture, where the EU also sponsors several events. One of the more contentious policy initiatives was the 1991 Television without Frontiers Directive (see Media Policy), which attempted to protect EU television producers against non-European programmes. Since 1982 grants, as well as loans from the **European Investment Bank**, have been advanced for architectural preservation and restoration, and have benefited more than 30 sites that are deemed to be of significance for the EU as a whole or that are located in poorer and undeveloped regions of the EU. A more concerted effort linking these activities was launched in a four-year Action Programme in 1988, and in 1991 the **Treaty on European Union** made specific references to cultural policy. A Culture 2000 framework programme was proposed in 1998 to cover the period 2000–04. This operated in three main areas: **legislation** favourable to culture, the cultural dimension of existing policies, and culture and external relations. It superseded the Kaleidoscope, **ARIANE** and **Raphael** programmes. In January 2005 the Commission adopted Decision 2005/56/EC setting up a new **Education, Audiovisual and Culture Executive Agency** (EACEA). This Agency, which began operations in January 2006 took over responsibility for the management of certain parts of the EU's programmes in the education, culture and audiovisual fields. Two subsequent programmes succeeded the Culture 2000 programme. Its main aim was to promote a 'common cultural area' inclusive of cultural diversity and common cultural heritage, with a view to encouraging the emergence of European citizenship. The new **Creative Europe** programme entered into effect in January 2014 as the successor to the Culture and MEDIA programmes. (See also **Audiovisual Policy**.)

CULTURE 2000: See **Cultural Policy**.

The **CUSTOMS 2020 Programme** is a customs co-operation programme running from 1 January 2014 until 2020. It succeeds the Customs 2013 programme (2008–13), and has a larger budget, of some €547m. The programme aims to support co-operation between customs authorities within the European Union, with the aim of securing improved efficiency and avoiding mismatches that hinder the functioning of the customs union. It also aims to facilitate networking between the national authorities and to provide training for customs personnel.

CUSTOMS DUTIES are those taxes levied by states at their border upon imports into their territory. The **Treaty of Rome** committed the member states to 'the elimination, as between member states, of customs duties and of quantitative restrictions on the import and export of goods, and of all other measures having equivalent effect'. The removal of internal duties and restrictions, and the imposition of a **common external tariff** (CET), constitutes a **customs union**. Customs duties on goods imported from outside the European Union (EU) are collected by the member states in accordance with the CET, but they are regarded as part of EU **own resources** and are a source of **revenue** for the EU **budget**.

CUSTOMS UNION is the name of an economic structure whereby a group of states agree to belong to a single tariff area, where there are no **customs duties** on goods circulating within the union, but where there is a **common external tariff** (CET) levied on all imports into the union. The **Treaty of Rome** created a precise timetable for the establishment of a customs union, which was largely completed by July 1968. New members of the European Communities (EC) were granted a short transitional period of adjustment in which to comply with the full requirements of a customs union. The CET was introduced in the 1960s, but its level was determined by the terms of the several accords with the now superseded GATT (**General Agreement on Tariffs and Trade**), to which the European Union (EU) member states individually and collectively were party. It was generally accepted that a customs union would not be sufficient to bring about the original EC goal of a **common market**, but it was not until the late 1980s that the EC began to consider seriously the problem of non-customs obstacles to the establishment of a common **internal market**. Certain non-member states—for example, **Turkey**—signed agreements with the EU whereby they were incorporated into the customs union.

CYPRUS became a member of the European Union (EU) on 1 May 2004. Prior to this, it concluded an **association agreement** with the former European Community (EC) in 1972. The intention was that the agreement would prepare the way for a full **customs union** between Cyprus and the EC. Developments proved to be much slower than originally anticipated, and were complicated by the de facto partition of the island after the invasion of northern Cyprus by **Turkey** in 1974. The EC refused to deal with the administration of the Turkish-controlled sector of the island. In 1987 Cyprus concluded a customs union agreement with the EC, which included arrangements concerning agriculture. The customs union was to come into force in stages over a 10-year period. In 1990, however, Cyprus applied for full membership of the EC. Given the wish of Turkey also to become a member, this created a dilemma for the EC. The **European Commission** published its *avis* in 1993, and indicated that, if partition was not ended, the EC would consider negotiating only with the Greek Cypriot Government. Following this *avis*, in 1995 the **European Council** decided that negotiations with Cyprus would begin six months after the end of the **intergovernmental conference** which was held in 1996–97. Formal negotiations began in March 1998 and were concluded in December 2002. Although some member states still had reservations about admitting a divided island into the European Union (EU), the signing of the **Treaty of Accession** in April 2003 committed the EU to admitting Cyprus irrespective of the political situation on the island. Nevertheless, the prospect of membership did lead to improved relations between the two parts of the island, notably in 2003 when travel restrictions were substantially eased. Subsequently, and despite the breakdown of earlier UN-brokered talks, efforts were made during the months leading up to membership on 1 May 2004 to secure agreement on the reunification of the island so that it could join the EU as a single political entity. Although an agreement was reached, it failed to gain the approval of Greek Cypriots in a referendum in April 2004. As a result, only the southern half of the island became part of the EU the following month.

Cyprus ratified the **Treaty establishing a Constitution for Europe** in June 2005, but efforts, including those originating from the **United Nations**, to end the division of the island have stalled. At elections in 2006 a majority of Greek Cypriot voters backed the ruling coalition's opposition to reunification, which angered Turkey. Relations between Cyprus and Turkey remained strained. The Turkish Government stated in June 2006 that it was not prepared to open its ports and airports to Cyprus so long as the Turkish Cypriots in the north of the island remained isolated. In response, Cyprus vowed to block the EU's ongoing talks with Turkey until the ports and airports were opened. In practice the blockage was not total. It nevertheless showed how much influence a small state could wield within the EU. Frustration within the EU with Cyprus's attempts to block negotiations with Turkey did not prevent agreement being reached in 2007 on Cyprus joining the **eurozone** and adopting the **euro** from 1 January 2008. In March 2013 eurozone Ministers of Finance approved lending of some €10,000m. to Cyprus, contingent on the country's imposition of a levy on selected bank deposits.

Meanwhile, Demetris Christofias won the presidential election in 2008 and pledged to recommence negotiations regarding reunification of the island. Although contact was quickly re-established with the then leader of Northern Cyprus, Mehmet Ali Talat, progress was very slow. The President elected in February 2013, Nikos Anastasiades, pledged to continue reunification talks, which accelerated after the election of Mustafa Akıncı as President of the 'Turkish Republic of Northern Cyprus' in April 2015. The new Turkish Cypriot leader was known to be in favour of intensifying bilateral efforts to reach a permanent settlement and achieve a peaceful, unified Cyprus; Turkish recognition of Cyprus was a key issue in need of resolution before Turkey could hope to accede to full membership of the EU. In January 2017 Anastasiades and Akıncı held UN-sponsored direct discussions in Geneva, **Switzerland**. These discussions were followed in the same month by an international conference on Cyprus. The President of the European Commission, **Jean-Claude Juncker**, at the head of an EU delegation attending the conference in an observer capacity, described the talks as 'the very last chance' for Cypriot leaders to end the island's partition.

The **CZECH REPUBLIC** signed a **Europe agreement** with the European Community (EC) in 1993, whereby the EC accepted in principle the possibility of membership. This accord superseded the earlier Europe agreement signed between the EC and the former Czech and Slovak Federative Republic (Czechoslovakia) in 1991. The first agreement had become obsolete in January 1993 with the creation of two separate states, the Czech Republic and Slovakia. There existed a strong body of opinion that the Czech Republic's application could not be considered until the European Union (EU) had been consolidated, and the **European Free Trade Association** states admitted. In 1997 the Czech Republic's 1996 application to join the EU was considered favourably, and **accession negotiations** began in March 1998. The country was deemed to have completed the necessary economic and institutional reforms. The application was considered by the **European Commission** to be integral to its **Agenda 2000** 'for a stronger and wider Europe' initiative, although it noted that investment would be needed to transpose EC rules on agriculture, the environment and energy, and that administrative reforms would be required to 'provide the country with the structures it needs for effective application and enforcement of the full body of Community law.' Although the Czech Republic had long been considered among the best placed of the **candidate countries** to join the EU, this did not prevent the Commission from criticizing its preparations for membership. However, the Czech Republic completed accession negotiations with the EU in December 2002. Following its signing in April 2003, the **Treaty of Accession** was approved in a national referendum held in June 2003. The rate of participation by the electorate was 55.2%, 77.3% of whom favoured membership. The Czech Republic joined the EU on 1 May 2004. Relations between the Czech Government and the EU were on occasions tense given the **Eurosceptic** views of the then Czech President, Václav Klaus.

The Czech Republic became part of the EU's **Schengen Area** in December 2007 and assumed the presidency of the **Council of the European Union** in January 2009. At the outset, the Czech Republic was keen to develop closer EU-US relations and also to establish ever better links with the countries of the **Western Balkans**. Both houses of parliament ratified the Treaty of Lisbon easily, but the process of final **ratification** required presidential assent. Klaus had long expressed his opposition to the Treaty of Lisbon and resisted giving his approval for as long as possible, but he eventually signed once the Irish Government had successfully carried out its second referendum on the treaty, after the German courts had not found it to be in conflict with the German Constitution, and after the Polish President had signed it. The Czech Republic was the last EU member state to ratify the Treaty of Lisbon, in November 2009. A subsequent example of Czech Euroscepticism and the Czech authorities' strong resistance to any moves that deepen EU integration was provided by the Czech Government's refusal to sign the Treaty on Stability, Co-ordination and Governance in the Economic and Monetary Union **(Fiscal Compact)** in March 2012. Miloš Zeman was elected President in early 2013. Pre-term legislative elections took place in late 2013, and a new Government was formed under Bohuslav Sobotka of the Czech Social Democrat Party. Subsequently, in a reversal of previous policy, in March 2014 the Czech Government agreed to accede to the Fiscal Compact (subject to legislative approval). The Czech Republic opposed the proposals by the EU in September 2015 for quotas for the mandatory relocation of refugees, to manage the inflow of asylum seekers entering the bloc (see **Migration and Asylum Policy**). President Zeman publicly criticized the quota scheme, stating that the ultimate decision on who to allow into the Czech Republic should rest with the Czech Government, amid protests in that country against hosting migrants from Muslim countries. In mid-2017 the EU announced that it was to commence legal action against the Czech Republic and two other countries, in response to their refusal to implement the quota scheme.

D

DANGEROUS SUBSTANCES were the subject of several European Communities (EC) **directives** regulating the classification, use, labelling and marketing of many products deemed to be potentially dangerous. These directives covered, *inter alia*, asbestos, glues, paints, pesticides and solvents. EC directives also controlled the production and distribution of pharmaceuticals. The **European Atomic Energy Community** (EAEC) and the **Joint Research Centre** have handled nuclear-related matters. In 1981 the EC adopted a scheme for the rapid exchange of information between the appropriate national authorities about accidents and risks to **health and safety** that arise from the use of potentially dangerous products, and a system of monitoring accidents caused by consumer goods was subsequently introduced. (See also **Consumer Policy**.)

DAPHNE was a programme, originally launched in 1997 but extended under Daphne II to cover the years 2000–04, that supported projects by **non-governmental organizations** to combat violence against women, young people and children, especially in the areas of trafficking in women and the sexual exploitation of children. Daphne III ran from 2007 until 2013, with a budget of €116.9m. In November 2011 the **European Commission** adopted a proposal for the establishment of a new Rights, Equality and Citizenship programme for 2014–20, which superseded the Fundamental Rights and Justice programme, Daphne III and the parts of the PROGRESS programme dedicated to non-discrimination and diversity and gender equality. The programme was duly adopted with a budget for 2014–20 of €439m.

DAVIGNON REPORT is the name usually given to a document that was a product of the **Hague summit** held in the Netherlands in December 1969, when the heads of government agreed to return to the theme of political integration. The summit charged the foreign ministers with the responsibility of studying 'the best way of achieving progress in the matter of political unification, within the context of **enlargement**'. Mindful perhaps of the arguments that this had caused in the past, the leaders did not try to be specific as to which route such political progress might follow. The foreign ministers opted for a compromise solution in order to achieve agreement. The conclusions were presented in a report compiled by Etienne Davignon (1932–), political director in the Ministry of Foreign Affairs of **Belgium**. The Davignon Report of 1970 accepted that political integration should ideally begin in a policy sphere where the member states, both current and projected, already possessed an identifiable common interest, and recommended that it should be in the co-ordination of foreign policy 'that the first concrete efforts should be made to show the world that Europe has a political vocation'. The Report included several specific recommendations: a regular consultation process of meetings of the foreign ministers, backed by a support group, a Political Committee, formed by the political directors of the national foreign ministries; ongoing liaison between the then European

Communities (EC) ambassadors in foreign capitals; and the issuing, by the EC states, of common instructions on certain matters to their ambassadors abroad. The Report was widely welcomed, and its main recommendations were put into effect more or less immediately. The first ministerial meeting under the new regime was held in Munich, **Germany**, in November 1970, and the EC made their first joint policy declaration, on the Middle East, the following May. The process was judged a success, and a second Davignon Report in 1973 recommended its continuation. This second report stressed the non-binding aspects of political co-operation: its aims were 'to ensure a better mutual understanding of the major problems of international politics through regular information and consultation; to promote the **harmonization** of views and the co-ordination of positions; to attempt to achieve a common approach to specific cases'. The Davignon Reports were the basis of what came to be known as **European political co-operation**.

DE: See **Group of the European People's Party (Christian Democrats)**

DECISION MAKING in the European Union is often considered complex, malleable and incomprehensible. In a 1995 report the **European Commission** itself identified 29 different decision making procedures. The key to understanding the decision making processes lies within the **founding treaties** and subsequent **regulations**. The **decisions** can be classified loosely into different category headings: constitutional decisions (concern the **European Council**); legislative decisions (concern the Commission, the **Council of the European Union** and the **European Parliament** (EP) and are subject to either **consultation, co-decision** or consent procedures); **trade** policy decisions (Council and Commission); **competition policy** decisions (Commission and courts); **common foreign and security policy** (concerns primarily the member states, as did **justice and home affairs** issues falling under the former pillar III); and finally, decisions relating to the **budget** (which fall to the EP and the Council). Recent treaty changes have sought to simplify procedures and create more effective and efficient decision making. The **Treaty of Lisbon** created a new **double majority voting** system in the Council and made co-decision, which is now rebranded as the '**ordinary legislative procedure**', the default decision making procedure.

DECISIONS are one of three different types of **legal instrument** that the **European Commission** and the **Council of the European Union** are empowered to issue. Decisions by either the Commission or the Council are binding upon the member states; they may be addressed to named individuals or enterprises. Decisions can be made by the European Union (EU) executives on the basis of the direct authority they possess under the terms of the **Treaty of Rome** and its amendments, or on the basis of earlier **regulations** or **directives**. (See also **Law**; **Opinions**; **Recommendations**; **Resolutions**.)

A **DECLARATION**, as far as the **European treaties** are concerned, is a political statement issued by one or more member states or the **intergovernmental conference** clarifying provisions of a treaty or outcomes of the negotiations. Of lesser status than a **protocol**, it has limited judicial force; its main purpose is to express the intention of the signatories. Declarations are also often issued following meetings of the **European Council**. The deliberations are usually produced in the form of 'conclusions of the presidency' and supplemented by declarations containing more detailed information on certain points of substance.

A **DEEP AND COMPREHENSIVE FREE TRADE AREA** (DCFTA) has been the goal of negotiations between the European Union (EU) and various countries involved in the **European Neighbourhood Policy**, notably **Ukraine** and **Moldova**. A DCFTA differs from a free trade area in that it involves not only the removal of tariff barriers and quotas, but also the adoption by the EU's partner of EU laws and standards. They include provisions on the facilitation of customs procedures, measures to prevent fraud and tools for trade defence. Such rules seek to ensure that trade is liberalized as fully as possible, but also include precautions so that preferential treatment only applies to certain goods. A bilateral dispute settlement procedure aims to ensure that any issues of contention are resolved quickly and easily.

DEEPENING refers to the process of European integration. From its early incarnation as a **customs union** and through its steady evolution to a **common market** and now the **eurozone**, the European Union (EU) has aspired to 'ever closer union' among the peoples of Europe. Since the **Treaty of Paris** the EU's competence, policy remit and powers have steadily increased. The debate on deepening usually occurs alongside that of widening (**enlargement**) and there is a generally held view that the enlargements (in 2004, 2007 and 2013) to 28 member states, coupled with the prospect of further enlargement, necessitated further deepening, or the EU would become a weaker entity, as it would be increasingly difficult to reach agreement on important **decisions**. Such thinking was part of the rationale behind the **Laeken Declaration** on the Future of the European Union, the establishment of the **European Convention** and the convening of a further **intergovernmental conference** in 2003, which led to the adoption of the **Treaty establishing a Constitution for Europe** in June 2004 and the subsequent adoption of its replacement, the **Treaty of Lisbon**.

DEFENCE: See **Common Defence Policy**; **Common Security and Defence Policy**

DEFICIENCY PAYMENTS are a means of ensuring producers a fair price for their products and labour when the costs of the latter are higher than the prices for produce obtainable on the free market. When market prices are too low to cover the costs of production, compensation is given to the producer in the form of **subsidies**. Deficiency payments have been employed in the **common agricultural policy** as an integral part of the price guarantee system.

DELORS I is a name (after the President of the European Commission in 1985–95, Jacques Delors) that was given to a set of ambitious budgetary measures put forward in February 1987 by the **European Commission**, as a response to the continued difficulties in funding European Communities (EC) operations (see **budget**). The collection of reforms was intended to enable the EC to realize the aim of implementing an **internal market** by the end of 1992. It outlined four objectives: an increase in EC **revenue**; firmer budgetary discipline; reforms and stricter control of the **common agricultural policy** in order to release more funds for other initiatives, especially in the field of **research and technological development (RTD) policy**; and increased resources for the **structural and cohesion funds** and the policy of **cohesion**. The proposed measures proved controversial among the 12 member states. Three meetings of the **European Council** were necessary before agreement on the reforms could be reached at a special European Council meeting in **Brussels** in February 1988 under the German presidency. The 1988 deal established the first of the multi-annual **financial perspectives**, which ran from 1988 to 1992, and saw an effective doubling of the money devoted to the structural funds for **Greece**, **Ireland**, **Portugal** and **Spain**. With the agreement secure, the Commission felt able to turn its attention to the issue of **economic and monetary union**.

DELORS II is the popular name of a set of budgetary measures proposed by the **European Commission** in February 1992 (and named after the French President of the European Commission in 1985–95, Jacques Delors). It sought a one-third increase in European Communities (EC) **revenue** in order to cover the additional costs imposed by the **Treaty on European Union**, in particular those incurred by the objectives of **cohesion**, improving the **competitiveness** of EC industry, and greater foreign policy obligations, while still maintaining budgetary discipline and reflecting the ability and willingness of member states to pay. The proposals' progress was hindered by the difficulties surrounding **ratification** of the treaty, and final agreement upon a revised version was not reached until late 1992 at the meeting of the **European Council** in Edinburgh, the **United Kingdom**, in December.

The **DELORS PLAN** is the popular name (after the President of the European Commission in 1985–95, Jacques Delors) of a report on **economic and monetary union** (EMU) published in April 1989. The official title is the Report of the Committee for the Study of Economic and Monetary Union. The report was the work of a committee appointed by the **European Council**. Mainly composed of the central bank governors, it was chaired by Jacques Delors and outlined a sequence of three stages, with full EMU to be achieved by the end of the 20th century. The first stage involved consolidating the achievement of free movement of capital, and closer monetary and macroeconomic co-operation between the member states and their central banks. The second stage comprised a new system of European central banks, before the **implementation** of full EMU. The European Council, despite British objections, agreed in December 1989 that an **intergovernmental conference** would consider the treaty changes necessary for implementation of the Plan. The conclusions were presented at the **Maastricht summit**, and the relevant provisions in the **Treaty on European Union** on EMU largely followed the structure of the Delors Plan.

DEMANDEUR is the French term often used to refer to a state requesting something (e.g. increased **structural and cohesion fund** receipts) from the European Union.

DEMOCRATIC DEFICIT is a term that has frequently been applied to procedures and structures relating to the European Union (EU) over the past three decades. It refers to the belief that there is a lack of proper democratic and parliamentary supervision and **accountability** in the EU's decision making procedures. The lack arose from the diminution of national **sovereignty** and the relative inability of national legislatures, owing to legal restraints and pressure of time, to monitor both the **European Commission** and the **Council of the European Union**, and because the **European Parliament** (EP) had insufficient authority to fill the gap.

As European integration has progressed, the question of democratic legitimacy has become increasingly sensitive. The more recent treaties (Maastricht, Amsterdam, Nice and Lisbon) have triggered the inclusion of the principle of democratic legitimacy within the institutional system by reinforcing the powers of Parliament with regard to the appointment and control of the Commission and successively extending the scope of the **co-decision procedure**.

The **Treaty of Amsterdam**, for example, sought to address this problem by expanding the areas in which the EP participates under the co-decision procedure. Members of member state **national parliaments** may also be able to play a greater role in EU decision making, since the treaty includes a **protocol** stipulating that, in the area of **justice and home affairs**, there must be a six-week interval between the tabling of a legislative proposal and its appearance on the Council's agenda. This should permit national members of parliament to participate more directly in EU **decisions**. The Conference of European Affairs Committees of national parliaments of the member states is also encouraged to provide its views on **subsidiarity**, justice and security, and fundamental rights and freedoms. In addition, the EU institutions have been opened to public scrutiny, with easier access to the documents of the European Commission, and to the voting results of the Council of the European Union, where decisions have legal effect. Institutional design and inter-institutional relationships formed a core rationale behind the **Treaty of Nice**, which was agreed in December 2000 and came into force on 1 February 2003. It re-examined such issues as the use of **qualified majority voting** in the Council, allocation of seats in the EP and the extension of the co-decision procedure in an effort to inject greater accountability and **transparency** in the **decision making** processes. More innovative measures for reducing the democratic deficit were contained in the **Treaty of Lisbon**. Indeed, measures to enhance democratic equality and improve both representative and participatory democracy include stronger powers for the EP through the extension of co-decision to almost all policy areas (especially agriculture and the **budget**), a stronger role for national parliaments in scrutinizing EU **legislation** (and provision for a 'yellow card' in respect of Commission proposals), the creation of a President for the European Council, the opening up of Council meetings to the public and the possibility of a citizens' petition. How far such issues can really reduce notions of a democratic deficit is debatable, and some have urged increased direct participation of the electorate, for example, in the election of the Commission President.

DENMARK is a constitutional monarchy, currently under Queen Margrethe II. Denmark has had a particularly difficult relationship with the European Communities (EC) over the past two decades, as its citizens have twice (in 1992 and 2000) voted against participation in further stages of European integration, namely **ratification** of the **Treaty on European Union** (TEU) and adoption of the single European currency (**euro**). This reflects a tradition of rather marked Euroscepticism encouraged by a history of notable maritime achievement and long-standing trading links with the **USA**. Originally Denmark declined in the 1940s and 1950s to participate in any integrative venture that went beyond intergovernmental co-operation. In 1960 it became a founder member of the **European Free Trade Association**. However, it reversed its position as a consequence of the British decision to apply for EC membership, and submitted its own application in 1961, and a re-application in 1967. Denmark was not willing, primarily on economic grounds, to join the EC without the **United Kingdom**, although it was informed that it was not affected by the veto on British membership. Discussions on accession were resumed in 1970, and the Danish Folketing (parliament) passed the Enabling Act ratifying the **Treaty of Accession** in September 1972. Because the parliamentary majority was slightly less than the five-sixths' majority constitutionally required to approve any delegation of national sovereignty, a referendum had to be held. In October the referendum resulted in a vote of 63.3% in favour of EC entry. Denmark formally acceded to the EC on 1 January 1973.

One of the wealthiest member states, Denmark has been a net beneficiary of the **common agricultural policy** and has benefited from the **internal market**. It has strongly supported a more comprehensive and rigorous **environmental policy** and **workers' rights**, but has remained outside moves towards a single currency and **economic and monetary union**, and expressed doubts about a **common defence policy**. With the exception of the UK, Denmark was the least enthusiastic member on the issue of closer political integration. Its policy within and towards the EC has been generally based upon a strict constructionist interpretation of the **founding treaties** and their amendments. Because, from the 1970s, relatively weak minority coalition governments governed the country, the Danish Folketing acquired a decisive voice in European affairs. The Folketing initially rejected the **Single European Act** (SEA); the Prime Minister attempted to bypass the opposition by scheduling a referendum for February 1986 before which he made it clear that Denmark's continuing membership of the EC was at stake. Even so, the referendum resulted in only a small majority (56.2%) in favour of ratifying the SEA. Denmark's doubts returned in the aftermath of the **Maastricht summit**. While the Government endorsed the TEU, ratification was rejected by a small majority in a referendum held in 1992, a result which threw the EC into disarray. The result was significant because it was the first of several popular expressions of discontent within the EC over the pace of integration, indicating that there were limits to how far governments could proceed without paying attention to their electorates. More specifically, crisis meetings had to be held to maintain the momentum of integration and resolve the Danish problem. At the **Edinburgh summit** of 1992 Denmark was granted a number of exemptions, or **opt-outs**, from provisions of the TEU. A small majority, in a further referendum, subsequently approved the new conditions in 1993. In 1998 a referendum narrowly endorsed the **Treaty of Amsterdam**, which contains **protocols** relating to Denmark and its decision to opt out of certain provisions of the treaty. The Danish Government decided not to hold a referendum on the **Treaty of Lisbon**, and the Folketing ratified the treaty in 2008. The current Prime Minister is the Liberal Lars Løkke Rasmussen, who replaced Helle Thorning-Schmidt following a general election in June 2015. Against a background of unprecedented levels of immigration into the EU (almost 70,000 foreign nationals arrived in Denmark in the 12 months to the end of June 2015), and under pressure from the far-right Dansk Folkeparti, Rasmussen's administration enacted legislation in September in an attempt to dissuade refugees and migrants from travelling to Denmark, by reducing the welfare benefits made available to new arrivals by as much as 50%. In October the Government tightened the eligibility criteria for Danish citizenship. At a national referendum in December voters rejected, by 53.1% to 46.9%, a proposal to convert Denmark's existing full opt-out on home and justice affairs directives of the **European Commission**, into an opt-out with a case-by-case opt-in, similar to that held by **Ireland** and the **United Kingdom**. Denmark's exemption made it increasingly difficult for the country to participate fully in the EU's law enforcement agency, **Europol**. Controversial legislation to confiscate money from refugees arriving with more than 10,000 kroner, and certain valuable items, was approved by the legislature in January 2016. In the same month the Government was accused by the European Commission of violating the terms of the **Schengen Agreement**, when it introduced temporary controls along its border with **Germany**. Rasmussen claimed that Denmark had been compelled to adopt these measures following **Sweden's** imposition of border controls at the Øresund bridge (connecting the two Scandinavian countries) in an attempt to limit the flow of unauthorized asylum seekers. Popular support for Denmark's continuing membership of the EU increased sharply in the wake of the UK's referendum vote to leave in June 2016, countering fears that Denmark might be tempted to hold a similar referendum.

DEP is the acronym for a European Depository Library, where holdings of European Union documents are less complete than those in a **European Documentation Centre** (EDC). A DEP is intended primarily for use by the general public.

DEREGULATION has a specific meaning within the European Union. It refers not just to the ending of unnecessary rules inhibiting the working of the economy or to the reduction of government interference, but also more directly to all those measures intended to remove restrictions to **trade** as part of the implementation of the **internal market**.

DEROGATION is a term that refers to a decision by the European Union (EU) to exempt one or more member states from the provisions of a **directive**; it may apply to the whole or part of a directive or **regulation**. Member states that feel that their situation constitutes special circumstances may apply to the **European Commission** for a derogation, subject to agreement by the **European Council**. In principle, derogations are meant to be temporary, to permit a member state time in which to adapt itself to EU requirements more gradually. For example, **Greece**, **Ireland**, **Luxembourg**, **Spain** and **Portugal** all received five-year derogations from the planned start of a single market in **telecommunications** (the liberalization of voice telephony and network operation that began in 1998). In practice, derogations sometimes continue indefinitely. Derogations are most widely granted to new member states for periods of five or 10 years under the terms of the relevant **treaty of accession**.

DÉTENTE is a term first used in the mid-1950s to describe a lessening of the tensions between East and West during the **Cold War**. The term is a highly subjective one: while the hostility of the late 1940s and early 1950s may not have been repeated, the two sides never ceased entirely their competition and rivalry. The importance of détente, for European integration, lies less in its questionable reality than in the perception by Europe of a lessening of international tension. This perception allowed Western Europe to rely less heavily upon the **USA** and perhaps permitted the member states of the European Communities (EC) to concentrate more upon their own plans and development. The changes in **Central and Eastern Europe** after 1989 may have, in a way, created a new sense of détente, but they also persuaded many that the EC should develop their own **common foreign and security policy**.

DEVELOPMENT AID comes from the **budget** of the European Union (EU), the **European Development Fund** (EDF), and the **European Investment Bank** (EIB) and falls into several different categories. Firstly, there is the aid provided to the **African, Caribbean and Pacific** (ACP) **States** (79 countries) under the terms of the **Cotonou Agreement** and previously the **Lomé Conventions**. Over time the EU has also concluded agreements with a number of countries in **Asia** and **South and Central America**, which incorporate provisions for development aid. Similar help has been given to the **Maghreb states** and to the **Mashreq states**, as well as to Israel, under **protocols** in the agreements signed between these countries and the EU. A further element of aid is food and emergency provision forwarded to countries requesting EU assistance in coping with severe food shortages or the aftermath of natural disasters. This form of assistance has mainly been given to African and Asian countries, but in July 1989 the then European Communities agriculture ministers agreed to provide food aid to **Poland** as part of what became known as operation **PHARE**. In 1992 the **European Commission** created the European Community Humanitarian Office (ECHO) to help provide emergency relief to the former **Yugoslavia**. The amount of development aid provided by the EU has been substantial as a proportion of gross national product. The EU is the world's largest donor of humanitarian aid. Collectively, the **ACP States** have consumed the largest amount of aid, although, because of their number, the funds have been distributed rather thinly among them. The largest element of aid to ACP states consists of grants from the EDF and low-interest loans from the EIB, together comprising just over two-thirds of EU assistance in this area. EU development aid policy has not been entirely disinterested. Food aid has been a means of reducing EU surpluses, while the aid programmes have benefited EU companies and enterprises, which have won most of the contracts awarded under the programmes. For 2008–13, some €22,700m. was made available for EDF-backed projects that seek to reform education, modernize health and transport systems, support debt relief and balance of payments difficulties and further institutional development. The EU identified its Agenda for Change as the theme of its new development aid policy under the current financial perspective for 2014–20. It forms part of the section on Global Europe. The amount of aid made available through the EDF has been increased to €27,000m. for 2014–20. The European Commission's Directorate-General for International Co-operation and Development (DEVCO) holds responsibility for administering and developing EU policies in this area.

DEVELOPMENT POLICY in the European Union (EU) seeks to reduce and ultimately to eradicate poverty in the developing countries and to promote sustainable development, peace and security as well as a stable and democratic political environment in the EU's partner countries. This particular theme has grown in importance as a priority for the **European Commission** and has been developed considerably since 2000.

The central EU institution in this policy area remains the Commission, and specifically the **Directorate-General** (DG) for International Co-operation and Development (DEVCO). DG DEVCO was charged with the role of initiating and formulating the EU's development co-operation policy for all developing countries as defined in Title XX of the **Treaty establishing the European Community**, and with co-ordinating relations with the sub-Saharan **African, Caribbean and Pacific** (ACP) **States** and the **Overseas Countries and Territories** (OCTs). The **Cotonou Agreement** provides the framework for a 20-year partnership for **development aid** to the 79 ACP countries, funded mainly by the **European Development Fund**. Support for DG DEVCO also came through specified budget lines in terms of the EU **budget**; it prepared strategies for co-operation with ACP countries and OCTs, and also monitored their **implementation**.

In fulfilling its role, DG DEVCO (previously DG Development) has worked in close collaboration and interaction with other services of the European Commission, in particular the EuropeAid Co-operation Office, the European Community Humanitarian Office (ECHO), and the Directorates-General for External Relations, Trade, Economic and Financial Affairs, Fisheries, Agriculture, Environment, Transport, Energy and Justice and Home Affairs. It has been committed to strong co-ordination and complementarity between the Commission, the EU member states and organizations such as the World Bank, regional development banks, the **Organisation for Economic Co-operation and Development** and the **United Nations**. The DG worked in partnership with government, civil society, and the economic and social spheres, including the private sector in ACP countries and other developing countries.

The European Commission published a European Consensus on Development in 2005. This document identified a number of shared values, goals and commitments that the EU and its member states are tasked with implementing. These come under the headings of reducing poverty, promoting development based on Europe's democratic values (i.e. **human rights**, democracy, rule of law, good governance and social justice) and assisting the countries of the developing world in designing their own national strategies. In the 2010s EU aid accounted for over 50% of all development aid worldwide of which more than one-half went to Africa.

In October 2011 the Commission presented its Agenda for Change, which aims to produce a more strategic EU approach to reducing poverty. EU assistance is to be focused on two main themes: first, human rights, democracy and good governance, and, second, inclusive and sustainable growth for human development. The new DG Development and Co-operation—EuropeAid (an amalgamation of DG Development and DG EuropeAid, and currently known as the DG for International Co-operation and Development—DEVCO) was created in January 2011 with responsibility for designing EU development policies and delivering aid through a number of programmes worldwide. It was hoped that having one DG would provide greater coherence to EU development strategy by providing a single contact point. The remit of the DG is considerable and includes promoting good governance, human and economic development, fighting hunger and preserving natural resources.

DG: See **Directorates-General**

DIFFERENTIATED INTEGRATION: See **À La Carte Europe**

The **DIGITAL AGENDA FOR EUROPE** was established as one of seven principal initiatives of the **European Commission**'s **Europe 2020** strategy in March 2010. It sought to exploit the economic and social potential of Information and Communications Technology (ICT), in particular the internet, to promote innovation and economic growth, through the creation of a Digital Single Market. The Commission identified seven principal objectives: the creation of a new single, online market; improved standards and interoperability; enhanced trust and security for internet users; improved access to fast internet speeds; research and innovation; digital literacy; and using ICT to address issues of importance to society, e.g. mitigating rising health costs and digitizing the EU's cultural heritage. The Connecting Europe Facility provides investment funding of €1,000m. for 2014–20. In March 2015 the Commission agreed priorities for the new Digital Single Market, comprising 16 initiatives, based on three themes: improved access to digital goods and services, for both consumers and commercial enterprises; the development of an infrastructure conducive to the evolution of digital networks and innovative services; and stimulating potential for growth in the digital economy and society. It was envisaged that the successful implementation of the Digital Single Market could add €415,000m. per year to the EU economy, and lead to the creation of employment and improved public services.

JEROEN DIJSSELBLOEM is the head of the **eurozone's** 'Eurogroup' of Ministers of Finance since January 2013, and Minister of Finance of the **Netherlands** since November 2012. He became President of the Board of Governors of the **European Stability Mechanism** in February 2013, and was elected to the Dutch House of Representatives in March 2017 (having previously been a member in both 2000–02 and 2002–12). Dijsselbloem studied at Wageningen University in 1985–91, and subsequently spent a period in the 1990s as a member of Wageningen's municipal council.

DIPLOMATIC REPRESENTATION abroad was not initially formally maintained by the European Union (EU), although the **European Commission** had External Delegations in most countries and to international organizations. Collaboration between ambassadors of the EU states was developed as part of **European political co-operation**, and member states began to agree to share embassies and missions. The EU also had its own non-diplomatic representation in several international economic forums, such as the **World Trade Organization** (formerly the **General Agreement on Tariffs and Trade**). Many states have diplomatic representatives accredited to the EU, giving the latter a partial diplomatic status. These are often the countries' ambassadors to **Belgium**. (See also **Permanent mission**; **Permanent representation**.) With the entry into force of the **Treaty of Lisbon**, the EU's external representation was increased with the creation of a **European External Action Service**.

DIRECT EFFECT, together with primacy, is one of the fundamental legal principles underpinning European Communities (EC) **law**. Essentially, by interpreting the **Treaty of Rome** as having established individual rights that had to be protected at member state level, the **Court of Justice** established the doctrine of direct effect. As a result, a mechanism was created for individuals and institutions to challenge the compatibility of national law with EC law. Thenceforth the Court of Justice could be invoked in national policy debates and, more importantly, any national laws that were deemed to run contrary to EC law had to be set aside.

DIRECT ELECTIONS to the **European Parliament** (EP) were provided for by the **Treaty of Rome**. The Council of Ministers (see **Council of the European Union**) declined for some time to initiate the legislation for direct elections, despite considerable agitation by the EP, which even threatened to take the Council to the **Court of Justice** for failing to honour its treaty obligations. The first direct elections were eventually held in June 1979, and since then they have been held regularly at five-year intervals. Despite a widespread belief that there should be electoral **harmonization** across the member states, it has proved impossible to reach an agreement on either a single day for the election or a common electoral system, although all now use varying systems of proportional representation. The elections are spread over several days because states insist on holding them on the day traditionally used for national elections (Sunday in most countries, Thursday in the others). Counting of votes does not begin until polls have closed in all member states. Each member state has also been free to decide upon its own electoral system: this is usually the same as, or is based upon, that used for the election of the national legislature. The **United Kingdom** initially retained its traditional single member, simple majority constituency system, also known as the first-past-the-post system, except in Northern Ireland, where since 1979 three seats have always been determined by the single transferable vote (STV) method of proportional representation. (The national Boundary Commission determines constituencies in the UK, which are essentially amalgamations of those for national elections.) The British Government, however, introduced a method of proportional representation, using a regional party list system, for the first time in the European elections held in June 1999. All the other member states employ proportional representation and, with the exception of **Ireland**, which uses the STV method, they all employ a party list system. The lists of candidates submitted by the competing political parties are national lists in most countries, including **Austria**, where direct elections to the EP were held for the first time in late 1996. However, in **Belgium**, **Germany**, **Italy** and **Spain**—as well as **Finland**, where the first elections were held in 1996—regional party lists are employed, so that the region becomes, in effect, a kind of constituency. (See also **Party groups**.) Those of June 2004 were the first European elections to involve the new member states from **Central and Eastern Europe** and the Mediterranean. The overall rate of voter participation across the European Union (EU) was some 45%. At the 2009 poll, turnout fell to some 43%. The elections to the eighth EP in May 2014 recorded a turnout of 42.5%.

DIRECTIVES are one of three different types of **legal instrument** that the **European Commission** and the **Council of the European Union** are empowered to issue for the adoption of **legislation**. A directive is the most common form of European Union legislation. Directives are binding upon all member states, but take the form of general instructions on the goal to be achieved, while leaving the way in which it will be attained to the discretion of each member state. The conditions of a directive are normally met by the member states introducing national legislation in conformity with EU stipulations. (See also **Decisions**; **Law**; **Opinions**; **Recommendations**; **Regulations**; **Resolutions**.)

The **DIRECTORATE-GENERAL FOR EUROPEAN CIVIL PROTECTION AND HUMANITARIAN AID OPERATIONS (ECHO)** is a division of the **European Commission**. This office, originally established in 1992, is based in **Brussels** and aims to provide emergency **humanitarian assistance** and food aid to many parts of the world, including the countries of the former **Yugoslavia**, the **African, Caribbean and Pacific (ACP) states**, the Near and Middle East, the **Commonwealth of Independent States** and the Far East. ECHO aims to meet the immediate needs of victims of mostly manmade disasters worldwide, in such areas as assisting displaced persons, and health, sanitary and mine-clearance programmes. In 2015 ECHO committed funds totalling €1,587m. to humanitarian assistance.

DIRECTORATES-GENERAL (DGs) are the principal bureaucratic 'ministries' or departments of the **European Commission**, to which they are responsible. The General Secretariat of the **Council of the European Union** and the **Secretariat-General** of the **European Parliament** also have DGs, but these are fewer in number, have fewer powers and are generally less well known. The duty of the DGs of the European Commission is to carry out, or to ensure that the member states carry out, European Union (EU) policy, and to administer allocations from the **budget** to different policy areas and the **structural and cohesion funds**. They are, in turn, divided into Directorates and Units. Each DG is expected to serve and advise the Commission through the Commissioner or Commissioners who hold the portfolios for its areas of responsibility. Appointment of staff to the DGs is by competition and merit, although the allocation of posts has to ensure a fair distribution between nationals of the member states. In addition, as far as possible, it is usual for the Director-General in charge of a given DG and any relevant Commissioners not to be of the same nationality.

The European Commission is currently divided into some 33 DGs, 11 service departments and numerous decentralized agencies and bodies. The number of DGs has altered over the years as new ones have been created and others have been merged. Until the late 1990s they were usually identified by number (e.g. DG IV), but, since reorganization in 2000, they are now identified by their policy area (e.g. DG for Competition). The titles of the DGs are susceptible to tweaks and changes, but they are currently named as follows: Agriculture and Rural Development (AGRI); Budget (BUDG); Climate Action (CLIMA); Communication (COMM); Communications Networks, Content and Technology (CNECT); Competition (COMP); International Co-operation and Development (DEVCO); Economic and Financial Affairs (ECFIN); Education and Culture (EAC); Employment, Social Affairs and Inclusion (EMPL); Energy (ENER); Environment (ENV); Eurostat (ESTAT); Financial Stability, Financial Services and Capital Markets Union (FISMA); Health and Food Safety (SANTE); Migration and Home Affairs (HOME); European Civil Protection and Humanitarian Aid (ECHO); Human Resources and Security (HR); Informatics (DIGIT); Internal Market, Industry, Entrepreneurship and SMEs (GROW); Interpretation (SCIC); Joint Research Centre (JRC); Justice and Consumers (JUST); Maritime Affairs and Fisheries (MARE); Mobility and Transport (MOVE); Neighbourhood and Enlargement Negotiations (NEAR); Regional and Urban Policy (REGIO); Research and Innovation (RTD); Secretariat-General (SG); Service for Foreign Policy Instruments (FPI); Taxation and Customs Union (TAXUD); Trade (TRADE); and Translation (DGT). Given the uneven degree of EC development in different policy areas, DGs have been far from equal in size. Groups of Directors-General meet at intervals to discuss the linkages and overlaps between their areas of responsibility, of which there are many. In particular, the DG responsible for the **budget** attempts to keep an overview of EC **expenditure**—and hence that of all the other DGs—though with less success and authority than national finance ministries.

The DGs are complemented by European Commission Service departments and agencies, which carry out specialized functions. These include the **Legal Service**, the Internal Audit Service, the **European Anti-Fraud Office** (OLAF) and the **Publications Office**. A few other agencies of the Commission are based in centres throughout the EU. The new Commission took office on 1 November 2014.

The European Union's **DISABILITY POLICY** has three main areas of focus: co-operation between the **European Commission** and the member states; the full participation of people with disabilities; and ensuring disability issues are fully recognized in policy formulation (particularly with regard to **employment**). Ongoing EU activities relating to disability include dialogue with the European Disability Forum and a European Day of Disabled People, which takes place in December each year. A disability action plan for 2004–10 aimed to enhance the economic and social integration of people with disabilities. In November 2010 the Commission launched the EU Disability Strategy 2010–20. The strategy sought, *inter alia*, to improve accessibility to goods and services for people with disabilities, and to consider a European Accessibility Act; help disabled people to exercise their right to vote; use the European Platform Against Poverty to reduce the risk of poverty; ensure that the European Social Fund offered ongoing support to disability-related projects; carry out data collection with the aim of improving opportunities for the employment of disabled people; develop policies to ensure inclusive education; facilitate the mutual recognition of disability cards and related entitlements throughout Europe; and promote the rights of people with disabilities through the EU's external activities.

DISCRIMINATION can refer to the application of restrictive **trade** practices by one member state at the expense of goods and companies from other member states. Equally, it has long been used within the European Communities (EC) to refer to inequitable treatment between individuals based on nationality and, with regard to pay, sex. The **Treaty of Amsterdam** demanded that the EC take measures to combat discrimination on the basis of racial or ethnic origin, religion or belief, disability, age or sexual orientation.

The **DOHA ROUND** is the latest round in a series of ongoing trade negotiations that commenced in the late 1940s. These rounds were designed to work towards a system of more liberalized trade rules and, in more recent times, ones that were fairer to developing countries. This latest trade round was agreed after arduous negotiations during 9–13 November 2001 in Qatar. It resulted in some far-reaching decisions on the future development of the **World Trade Organization** (WTO); these included the launch of a new round of trade negotiations—the Doha Development Agenda (DDA)—comprising both further trade liberalization and new rulemaking, underpinned by commitments substantially to strengthen assistance to developing countries. It also sought to assist developing countries to implement the existing WTO agreements. In addition, the meeting approved the long-awaited waiver from WTO rules of the **Cotonou Agreement** between the European Union (EU) and **African, Caribbean and Pacific states**.

Each trade round is not a new set of rules, principles or procedures for global trade, but rather a catch-all term for the intense discussions that aim to result in such rules. The last successful attempt, the **Uruguay Round**, ran from 1986 to 1993, before the WTO itself was formed in 1995. Attempts to set up a Seattle Round foundered under the weight of international protests and economic tension in 1999. The initial deal in Doha merely helps to set the agenda for a new set of trade talks, which commenced in 2002. The fact that 142 countries were able to conclude a trade deal in Doha was greeted as a triumph by governments and commentators around the world. The result was a clear success, given that the gulfs separating various trade blocs were alarmingly wide. However, Doha is a preliminary to a deal, rather than a deal in itself. The main issues dealt with at

Doha included the liberalization of agricultural trade; the opening up of the financial services market; the general reduction of tariff barriers; rules on subsidies for steel and textiles; the dispute settlement system; new 'greener' rules for trade; the labelling of and copyright protection for drinks; and the relaxation of control of drug manufacturing. It quickly became evident that reaching a deal was going to be extremely difficult.

In September 2003, in Cancún, Mexico, a summit took place that sought to make progress on agreement on the Doha Round, and concentrated on four main areas: agriculture, industrial goods, trade in services, and a new customs code. However, these talks failed; a new alliance of developing nations emerged that refused to sign a proposed agreement which they felt favoured the richer WTO members. A deal was finally reached, however, in Geneva, **Switzerland**, in August 2004. This deal opened the way for full negotiations to start. However, the next WTO ministerial meeting in Hong Kong in December 2005 broke up without any agreements being reached. The WTO operates through consensus, and the entire experience of the Doha Round illustrated how difficult it was to attain. The Doha Round was characterized by the more active participation (than in earlier Rounds) of the developing countries, but their involvement further complicated negotiations. Agriculture proved to be the substantial point of contention. Discussions on agriculture had centred on three main aspects—market access, levels of domestic support and export competition policies—but clear division between the players prevented any chance of a deal. It should be noted that the EU had agreed in 2005 to eradicate all agricultural export **subsidies** by 2013. The most problematic point of the discussions centred on the support that the richer nations give to their farmers. Other issues included the USA's unwillingness to reduce its domestic subsidies to agriculture, concerns about the openness of the EU agricultural markets and a reticence from emerging economies such as Brazil and India to allow better access to their own markets. Within the EU, **France** remained one of the most vocal opponents of plans to reduce tariffs. Further unsuccessful rounds of negotiations took place in Potsdam, **Germany**, in 2007, and in Geneva, in 2008. In December 2013 the so-called Bali Ministerial Declaration was adopted, which addressed bureaucratic matters relating to commerce, but the future of the Doha Round appeared uncertain. Some argue that the collapse of the Doha Round and multilateral negotiations might reinforce the growing trend towards regionalism.

VALDIS DOMBROVSKIS (1971–) was nominated in 2014 as the Latvian Commissioner to the new 28-member **European Commission** led by **Jean-Claude Juncker**. In September Juncker named Dombrovskis as Vice-President of the Commission for the Euro and Social Dialogue, subject to approval by the **European Parliament**. Dombrovskis took his first degree in Physics at the University of Latvia before taking another at Rīga Technical University. He also holds two Masters' degrees in Physics and Customs and Tax Administration, respectively. On completing his studies he joined the Bank of Latvia in 2001. Prior to this appointment, Dombrovskis had served as Minister of Finance (2002–04), and subsequently served as a Member of the European Parliament, before becoming Prime Minister (2009–14). He resigned as Prime Minister after a supermarket building collapsed in the Latvian capital, killing more than 50 people. He founded the political party Vienotība (Unity) in 2011, which is affiliated to the **Group of the European People's Party (Christian Democrats)**. Following endorsement of the Juncker Commission by the EP and the European Council, Dombrovskis took up his post as Commissioner on 1 November 2014. Dombrovskis assumed additional responsibility for Financial Stability, Financial Services and Capital Markets Union, following the resignation of British Commissioner Jonathan Hill in June 2016, in the wake of the **United Kingdom**'s referendum vote in favour of a departure from the EU.

DOMINANT FIRM ABUSE is dealt with under Article 102 of the **Treaty on the Functioning of the European Union** on **competition policy** and refers to companies that enjoy a hegemonic market position for particular products. It is not monopolies in themselves that are problematic or the focus of attention, but rather those holding a monopoly that use it to try to undermine competition by attempting to eject competitors from the market through the imposition of unfair pricing regimes or by deliberately imposing restrictions on the distributors of their own goods. Article 102 has been more severely limited in operation than the more widely used Article 101, which targets **cartels**, but the **European Commission** has upheld the tenets of the treaty, and its charges, when cases have proceeded to such an advanced stage, have usually been supported by the **Court of Justice** and the **Court of First Instance**.

DOOGE COMMITTEE, also known as the Committee on Institutions, is the name of an ad hoc group of 'personal representatives' of the heads of government, which the **European Council** agreed to establish at its **Fontainebleau summit** in June 1984. The task of the group was to examine the possibility of institutional reform of the European Communities (EC) in the light of the **draft Treaty establishing the European Union** issued by the **European Parliament** (EP). Chaired by James Dooge of **Ireland**, the Committee was intended to conduct a preliminary exploration of the positions of the heads of government in order to determine the extent to which there existed common ground for further integration. It issued a preliminary report in December 1984, and its final report was presented for discussion at the **Milan summit** of the Council in June 1985. The Committee stated that its overall aim was to turn the EC into a 'true political entity with the power to take **decisions** in the name of all citizens by a democratic process'. It outlined the following themes of institutional reform: strengthening both the **European Commission** and the EP—the former to be made more independent and streamlined, with only one Commissioner per country, the latter to be given joint decision making authority with the Council of Ministers (see **Council of the European Union**); simplifying decision making in the Council of Ministers by restricting the requirement of unanimity to proposals for new areas of EC action and to applications for EC membership; and allotting a strategic role to the European Council, which, meeting twice instead of three times each year, should concern itself with diplomatic and external affairs, and not the daily routine of the EC.

There were several disagreements over the report at the Milan summit, with the non-founding member states all expressing reservations about some sections of the report. In general, however, its major recommendations were not rejected outright. The Committee had also suggested that a special **intergovernmental conference** be established to consider its ideas and construct a reform package from all the reports and initiatives delivered over the previous few years. This proposal was also accepted at the Milan summit, although **Denmark**, **Greece** and the **United Kingdom** voted against it. The intergovernmental conference prepared the way for the **Single European Act**.

DOUBLE MAJORITY VOTING is a system of voting that, under the **Treaty of Lisbon**, replaced **qualified majority voting** (QMV) in the **Council of the European Union** from 1 November 2014. Originally envisaged in the **Treaty establishing a Constitution for Europe**, the double majority voting system allows decisions to be taken provided they have the support of 55% of member states representing 65% of the population of the European Union (EU). The measure being adopted also has to command the support of at least 15 member states. In certain areas of **justice and home affairs**, the **common foreign and security policy** and economic and monetary policy, where the Council does not act on the basis of a proposal from the Commission, a measure requires the support of 72% of member states representing 65% of the EU's population. A blocking minority needs to include at least four member states. Owing to the uncompromising position adopted by **Poland** in the 2007 **intergovernmental conference**, until 31 March 2017 member states retained the right to request that a decision be adopted using the existing QMV system. At Poland's insistence, a modified version of the **Ioannina Compromise** was also available during this period and after. It is anticipated that the double majority voting system will facilitate decision making and make the process easier to understand.

The **DRAFT TREATY ESTABLISHING A CONSTITUTION FOR EUROPE** was drawn up by the **European Convention** under the chairpersonship of Valéry Giscard d'Estaing. It brought together the existing **Treaty on European Union** and the **Treaty of Rome** to create a 'constitution' for the European Union (EU). In addition, the draft contained a variety of policy and institutional innovations and reforms. All this was brought together via four parts. The first, *inter alia*, set out the objectives of the EU, established EU **citizens' rights**, defined the EU's **competences**, presented the EU's **institutions**, determined how the EU should exercise its competences, established mechanisms for **enhanced co-operation**, outlined the EU's **budget**, and determined the mechanisms for accession. The second part incorporated the **Charter of Fundamental Rights**. The third part then outlined in much greater detail the policies (e.g. **economic and monetary union**, **social policy**) and functioning (e.g. **decision making**) of the EU. The fourth part contained 'general and final provisions' and was followed by a number of **protocols** and **declarations**.

Following its adoption on the basis of 'consensus' by the European Convention in June and July 2003, the draft Treaty establishing a Constitution for Europe was submitted to the **European Council**, which welcomed it as 'a good basis' for starting negotiations on a **'Constitutional Treaty'**. These negotiations began with the launch of an **intergovernmental conference** (IGC) in October 2003, which was scheduled to complete its work prior to the **enlargement** of the EU on 1 May 2004. Although broad agreement existed on adopting the structure of the European Convention's draft Treaty as the basis for the 'Constitutional Treaty', some of its provisions proved unacceptable to certain member states, as was evident at the **Brussels** European Council in 2003 when **Spain** and **Poland** rejected replacement of the existing system of **qualified majority voting** in the Council with a system based on dual majority of member states and population. This meant that the timetable for the IGC was somewhat disrupted, with negotiations continuing until June 2004 when agreement on the **Treaty establishing a Constitution for Europe** was finally reached.

DRAFT TREATY ESTABLISHING THE EUROPEAN UNION is the name of a document prepared by the **European Parliament** (EP) under the direction of Altiero Spinelli. An EP Institutional Committee began drafting the document in 1981. The Draft Treaty originated in the work of the **Crocodile Group** (a group of **Members of the European Parliament**—MEPs—who first met in the *Crocodile* restaurant in **Strasbourg**) and sought to revive the European project. Spinelli believed that following the first **direct elections** to the EP in 1979 the MEPs were now in a position (in terms of legitimacy) to re-examine the original three treaties establishing the European Communities (EC) in the 1950s. Moreover, it was generally felt that a new treaty was needed to reorder the European institutions and to expand the policy remit. This document proposed greater powers for the **European Commission** and EP, and a severe reduction of the member states' right of veto on proposed policies. The Commission, which would supervise the implementation of the new treaty establishing a European union, would become the sole EC executive, accountable to the EP and a weakened Council of Ministers (see **Council of the European Union**). The EP would have an independent revenue-raising responsibility and share budgetary powers with the downgraded Council, which was to be only a legislative body, renamed the Council of the Union. The EP approved the Draft Treaty in February 1984 but no action was taken on it directly by either the Council of Ministers or the **European Council**, owing to the sensitivity of many of its suggestions. However, several of its ideas were taken up by the **Dooge Committee** on institutional reform, and subsequently influenced the new integration initiatives of the late 1980s and 1990s.

MARIO DRAGHI (1947–) is an Italian banker, who was appointed Governor of the central bank of **Italy** in January 2006 and succeeded Jean-Claude Trichet as the third President of the **European Central Bank** (ECB) in November 2011. In July Draghi, while announcing a new bond-buying scheme to assist the Spanish and Italian positions in the markets, stated that his office would do everything possible to protect the euro in its existing form. In September Draghi announced that the governing council of the ECB had approved a new plan for the introduction of outright monetary transactions (OMT). The OMT would allow the ECB to purchase, in unlimited quantities, the short-term bonds of member countries of the eurozone seeking financial assistance from the European Union's emergency funding mechanisms, and thereby protect the long-term future of the euro. In September 2014 Draghi announced that the ECB was to cut its main rate of interest to 0.05%, and announced that the ECB was to introduce asset-buying measures. The news was widely welcomed by investors, although the ECB reportedly remained divided internally. In January 2015 Draghi announced a new programme of stimulus measures, including an asset-purchasing programme, which was to run for at least 18 months. In March 2016 he increased the value of the ECB's asset-purchasing scheme from some €60,000m. a month to €80,000m., and announced that the scheme would be extended until 2017, while reducing the main interest rate from 0.05% to zero, although he announced that no further cuts were planned.

DUAL MANDATE refers to those politicians who were members both of the **European Parliament** (EP) and of a **national parliament**. Before **direct elections** to the EP were introduced in 1979 the double mandate was the norm, as **Members of the European Parliament** (MEPs) were selected from within the ranks of their own national parliaments. From 1979, however, double mandates became less common, as parties tended to discourage, and in some cases refuse to allow, their members to sit in both the EP and their national parliament simultaneously.

However, many still existed. Indeed, it was also possible to speak of a triple mandate as some individuals sat in the EP, their national parliament and a regional assembly. The major concern surrounding double (and triple) mandates centred on the degree to which such members could adequately master their individual briefs and represent the electorate at both (or all three) levels. This situation caused general dissatisfaction. A proposal by European Union member state governments to abolish dual membership of the EP and **national parliaments** was approved by MEPs in 2003 (399 votes in favour of this motion, 111 against with 25 abstentions). The proposal formed part of a number of changes to the 1976 Act on the election of members of the EP. The abolition of the dual mandate took effect at the 2004 elections to the EP, although the **United Kingdom** negotiated an exemption until the June 2009 EP elections.

DUBLIN FOUNDATION: See **European Foundation for the Improvement of Living and Working Conditions**

The **DUBLIN REGULATION** was adopted in 2013, and entered into force in January 2014, replacing the Dublin II Regulation of 2003. The Dublin II Regulation had replaced the Dublin Convention on Asylum, a document outlining common formal arrangements relating to asylum throughout the European Union. It was initially conceived in response to worries that the **internal market** and the **freedom of movement** it entailed would attract large numbers of economic asylum seekers, especially from Eastern Europe. The Convention was signed by member states in June 1990 (with the exception of **Denmark**, which signed a year later), but the slow pace of the **ratification** process in many member states delayed its introduction. In 2016, in response to what became commonly known as the **European migration crisis**, the European Commission proposed reforming the Dublin Regulation. The Dublin Regulation had been intended to prevent the same individual from making multiple asylum claims, by asserting that asylum applications were to be the responsibility of the state in which a claim for asylum was first made, and by establishing that refugees should claim asylum in the first EU member state reached. The Regulation stipulates that should an individual be refused asylum in one member state, they may not then seek asylum in another signatory state. However, following the unprecedented upsurge in the number of migrants reaching countries such as **Greece**, **Italy** and **Hungary** in 2015, the countries of arrival struggled to register all of the migrants passing through their borders. In August **Germany**, under Chancellor **Angela Merkel**, offered voluntarily to assume responsibility for processing asylum applications from individuals fleeing the civil conflict in **Syria**. Although the measure was intended to alleviate the crisis, it led to chaotic scenes throughout Europe, with, for example, the largest railway station in the Hungarian capital, Budapest, becoming overwhelmed with refugees trying to reach Germany. In July 2017 the **European Court of Justice** upheld the terms of the Dublin Regulation, in a case brought by Austria and Slovenia, declaring its terms remained valid despite the difficulties experienced during the European migration crisis from 2015, and effectively confirming the right of EU member states to deport migrants to their initial point of entry within the EU. (See also **Migration and Asylum Policy**; **Immigration Policy**.)

DUMPING is the selling of produce at greatly reduced, below-cost prices, and such practices by any member state within the European Union (EU) are banned. The **European Commission** has the authority to permit the affected member states to take appropriate protective measures if the offending country does not heed its recommendations and warnings. One difficulty is that national perceptions of what constitutes dumping can vary, because of different rates and costs of production, and on occasion this has led to disputes between member states. The Commission can also act by imposing anti-dumping duties where it believes that other countries are engaged in dumping within the EU. By contrast, the policy of disposing of surplus agricultural produce (accumulated under the intervention element of the **common agricultural policy**) at greatly reduced prices abroad was often claimed by other countries with a major agricultural export industry to constitute a dumping practice.

DUNKIRK TREATY: See **Treaty of Dunkirk**

E

eEUROPE: See **Information Society**

E-NUMBERS are pan-European code numbers identifying a range of food additives. Their use is demanded by various **directives**.

EACEA (Education, Audiovisual and Culture Executive Agency): See **MEDIA 2007**

EAEC: See **European Atomic Energy Community**

EAGGF: See **European Agricultural Guidance and Guarantee Fund**

EaP: See **Eastern Partnership**

EAP: See **Environmental Action Programme**

EASA (European Aviation Safety Agency): See **Air Transport Policy**

EAST GERMANY: See **Germany**

The **EASTERN PARTNERSHIP** (EaP) between the European Union (EU) and its eastern neighbours—Armenia, Azerbaijan, Belarus, Georgia, **Moldova** and **Ukraine**—was launched at a dedicated summit in Prague, the **Czech Republic**, in May 2009 as part of EU efforts to respond to the wish of most of these countries for closer ties. The EaP is part of the **European Neighbourhood Policy** and is aimed at strengthening relations through increased bilateral co-operation, new **association agreements**, **deep and comprehensive free trade areas**, visa facilitation and liberalization, and co-operation on energy security matters, notably security of supply to the EU. Multilateral co-operation is also envisaged, and heads of government and state were expected to meet every two years.

EBA: See **European Banking Authority**

EBN: See **European Business and Innovation Centre Network**

EBRD: See **European Bank for Reconstruction and Development**

EBU: See **European Broadcasting Union**

EC: See **European Communities; European Community**, but note that, in a streamlining and simplification exercise under the **Treaty of Lisbon**, this term has been replaced by the term **European Union**.

ECA: See **European Court of Auditors**

ECB: See **European Central Bank**

ECCG: See **Consumer Committee**

ECDIN: See **Environmental Chemicals Data Information Network**

ECE: See **Economic Commission for Europe**

ECHO: See **Directorate-General for European Civil Protection and Humanitarian Aid Operations**

ECISS: See **European Committee for Iron and Steel Standards**

ECLAS was established as the **European Commission**'s automated online library system; from December 2017 it was to be replaced by the search instrument Find-er.

ECOFIN: See **Economic and Financial Affairs Council of Ministers**

ECOIN is the acronym of the European Core Inventory of Chemicals.

ECOLABEL has been designed as a means of promoting products with a reduced environmental impact and of providing consumers with accurate information about the product. Regulation No. 1980/2000 replaced the earlier 1992 regulation on a European Communities Ecolabel award scheme. Certain categories are excluded from the Regulation's scope, including **foodstuffs**, beverages and pharmaceutical products.

The **ECO-MANAGEMENT AND AUDIT SCHEME** (EMAS) of the European Communities is a 1993 initiative to promote responsible environmental management in industry. (An existing regulation—No. 1836/93—was replaced by Regulation No. 761/2001). Participation in the scheme is voluntary. The objective of EMAS is to promote continuous improvement in the environmental achievements of all European organizations, while providing the public and interested parties with any relevant information.

The **ECONOMIC AND FINANCIAL AFFAIRS COUNCIL OF MINISTERS** (Ecofin) is one of the most important formats of the **Council of the European Union** (alongside the General Council, the Foreign Affairs Council and the Special Council for Agriculture) through which specific policy areas are addressed. Ecofin is the name given to the regular meetings of the economic and finance ministers of the member states, which are held, on average, once a month. The ministers, who also meet in the **Economic and Financial Committee**, discuss both broad and more detailed issues of economic management. The informal **Eurogroup** group of ministers of finance of the member states participating in the eurozone discuss issues pertaining to **economic and monetary union**.

ECONOMIC AND FINANCIAL COMMITTEE is the name of an institution created by the **Treaty on European Union** as part of the development of **economic and monetary union** (EMU). It was first instituted at the start of the third and final stage of EMU on 1 January 1999 as a replacement for the **Monetary Committee**, although it was not charged with reviewing the monetary situation in the European Communities. The committee comprises senior individuals from member state finance ministries and representatives from the **European Central Bank**. The Treaty charged it with monitoring the economic situation in the European Union and reporting to and advising the **European Commission** and the **Council of the European Union**. Despite its largely advisory function, the Committee is highly influential, given its policy remit over EMU.

ECONOMIC AND FINANCIAL POLICY is mentioned in the **Treaty of Rome**, which obligates the member states to co-operate with each other in planning their economic policies. Since the establishment of the European Communities (EC), the member states have broadly followed similar economic policies, but this has owed less to co-ordination of effort and more to common reactions to worldwide problems and trends in the international economy. The **European Commission** has issued annual economic reports, which have included recommendations, but its advice and suggestions have not been binding upon the member states. Broad questions of economic policy have been discussed by the **European Council** and have been a concern of what is now the **Economic and Financial Affairs Council of Ministers**. Further co-operation was achieved through the regular meetings of the consultative **Committee of the Governors of the Central Banks**. These consultation exercises together constituted a reasonable level of co-operation, but they fell short of the level of co-ordination anticipated by the Treaty of Rome. Only in two areas was the EC able to wield a significant influence upon economic policy. The first is the raising of loans on behalf of member states through a variety of instruments: the **European Investment Bank**, the **European Coal and Steel Community**, the **European Atomic Energy Community** and the New Community Instrument. The other, prior to **economic and monetary union** (EMU), was the ability to limit exchange-rate fluctuations through the **exchange-rate mechanism** of the **European Monetary System**. More generally, however, EC authority and the EC **budget** were too limited to have any kind of decisive impact upon macroeconomic policy analogous to that wielded by national governments. These deficiencies explain the interest in EMU. The details and timetable for EMU set down by the **Treaty on European Union** were intended to provide the EC with a common economic and financial policy by 1999. Eleven member states were ready to participate as planned by this date, but the reality of four member states (**Greece**, **Denmark**, **Sweden** and the **United Kingdom**) not taking part in EMU imposed some limitations on that objective. Greece entered EMU in 2001, but the decision for the other three states was to be determined by **referenda**. Two have taken place: in Denmark and Sweden. In both instances the respective electorates voted against participation, and the UK's decision in June 2016 to leave the EU (see **Brexit**) made redundant the need for a specific British referendum on EMU. By 2017 19 states were participating in EMU. The EU's policy on economic governance seeks to identify, prevent and resolve economic trends considered to present a risk to growth and to individual member state economies.

ECONOMIC AND MONETARY UNION (EMU) was on the European Communities (EC) agenda from 1969, when the **Six** agreed to the principle at the **Hague summit** in the **Netherlands** and set 1980 as the completion date for full EMU. The **Werner Report** of 1970 established a timetable for the programme. The plans for EMU were effectively destroyed by the severe decline and general turmoil in the international economic climate of the 1970s. The member states became more introspective in their economic policies, and the idea of EMU by the end of the decade was abandoned. All that survived was the **European Monetary Co-operation Fund**. The **European Monetary System**, launched in 1979, was not a replacement for EMU, though it did constitute a step in that direction. The next step towards EMU was precipitated by the plans for a single market that comprised the substance of the **Single European Act**. Although this treaty did not describe EMU as an immediate objective it did refer to the idea in the preamble to the treaty, which Jacques Delors pushed forward and presented to the Hanover meeting of the **European Council** in June 1988. Despite the objections of the **United Kingdom**, the European Council agreed to establish a committee to examine the idea and benefits of realizing EMU; Delors was asked to chair this committee.

EMU was revived formally in June 1989, when the European Council accepted the proposals of the **Delors Plan**, which envisaged a three-stage movement towards the goal, with the first stage, the involvement of all member states in the **exchange-rate mechanism** (ERM), to begin in July 1990. In Rome in October 1990 the Council endorsed January 1994 as the beginning of the second stage of a more intensive economic and monetary co-ordination in anticipation of the creation of a **European Central Bank** (ECB) and single currency. An **intergovernmental conference** of EC finance ministers began in December 1990. Its deliberations were synchronous with those on closer political integration, and EMU became therefore a major theme of the **Maastricht summit** and the consequent **Treaty on European Union**. The Treaty provisions relating to EMU broadly followed the outline of the Delors Plan, confirming January 1994 as the date for commencement of closer co-ordination, and preparing for the establishment of a **European Monetary Institute**, which would assume some responsibility from the **Council of the European Union** for monitoring how national policies and budget deficits were conforming to guidelines. The final stage of EMU was set for January 1999. It would entail a **European System of Central Banks** along with the ECB, with the **European Currency Unit** (ecu) becoming the single currency of the European Union (EU—however, it was decided in 1995 that the new single currency would be the **euro**, which would replace the ecu on a one-for-one basis).

Participation in the third stage would depend upon individual member states meeting the following **convergence criteria**: a high degree of price stability measured by an inflation rate no higher than 1.5% above the average of that of the three best performing member states; a budget deficit no greater than 3% of gross domestic product (GDP) and a governmental debt no greater than 60% of GDP; staying within the permissible fluctuation limits of the ERM for at least two years without any realignment or devaluation; and interest rates no more than 2% higher than the three best-performing member states in terms of price stability. However, it was agreed that EMU would begin in 1999 regardless of how many states had met the criteria. The schedule and deadlines were immediately questioned, not least because **Denmark** and the UK were later given exemptions, or **opt-outs**, from the final stage. There was also considerable popular opposition in **Germany** to a single currency. Economic and monetary conditions in the 1990s threatened the achievement of EMU. Turmoil and speculation on the money markets in 1992 and 1993 put the ERM under extreme pressure, revealing that the EMU plans and the ERM took little account of the real strength of national currencies.

The UK and **Italy** were forced to leave the ERM, and many other countries' currencies were devalued. The ERM survived only by extending the permissible fluctuation limits to such an extent that what resulted was almost a system of floating currencies. Equally important was the recession in Western Europe. The economic difficulties were such that by 1994 very few states met the convergence criteria. However, a much less strict interpretation of the criteria was eventually applied, and in 1998 it was declared that, of those member states that wished to be part of EMU, only **Greece** had failed to meet the criteria. **Denmark**, Sweden and the UK had already decided not to join in the venture, which was launched in January 1999 after the inauguration of the ECB and the launch of the euro. Greece joined the initial 11 member states in 2001, leaving only Denmark, **Sweden** and the UK outside the **eurozone**; their entry would depend on the outcome of a referendum that would be held in each state if and when their governments decided they were ready to join. The Danish people rejected membership of the euro in a referendum in September 2000. Full EMU for participating states occurred in 2002, when national notes and coins were replaced by the euro. **Ireland** was the first EU member state successfully to replace its former national currency, in early February 2002. In a referendum in Sweden in September 2003 a majority of voters opted to reject membership of the eurozone. As regards the states that joined the EU on 1 May 2004, it was considered unlikely that any would adopt the euro until at least two years after accession. **Slovenia**'s application was successful and the country became the 13th to adopt the euro, on 1 January 2007. **Malta** and **Cyprus** both adopted the euro on 1 January 2008. **Slovakia** joined the eurozone on 1 January 2009 and **Estonia** became the eurozone's 17th member, adopting the euro on 1 January 2011. **Latvia** adopted the euro in January 2014, and **Lithuania** became the 19th EU member state to adopt the euro in January 2015.

The 10th anniversary of the launch of EMU in 2009 seemed an occasion for modest self-congratulation on the part of the EU. The euro had been introduced, the ECB had established its credibility as a force for monetary stability, and EMU was attracting new members. However, the concurrent economic and financial crisis laid bare a number of important structural weaknesses, notably the absence of EU-level tools for effective economic governance, and the presence in the eurozone of some member states running excessive deficits. The euro constituted only a monetary union and not an economic union. The euro had functioned well in the boom years, but deteriorating economic circumstances tested its stability and durability in 2010. Greece became the focal point. As the economic situation in Greece worsened in early 2010, the Greek Government introduced an austerity programme, which was greeted with public opposition. The German Government sought to maintain the stability of the euro by co-ordinating substantial loans to Greece, but did not dispel the doubts of its critics about the longer-term prospects for the euro and particularly the future of certain states within the eurozone. Ensuing problems in **Ireland**,

Portugal and Spain, by early 2012, intensified criticism of the euro regarding its suitability and desirability for all current participant states. A banking crisis in Cyprus in early 2013 once again raised issues about the euro, but disaster was averted when European leaders, the International Monetary Fund and the ECB agreed to grant the country bailout funding of €10,000m. to help ease its difficulties. Overall, however, stability subsequently increased within the euro system. Nevertheless, the election of a new, far-left Government in Greece in early 2015 led to new fears of instability, and negotiations on the terms of Greece's bailout programme with the EU took place throughout the first half of the year, culminating in August in political agreement on new lending arrangements. Meanwhile, in an effort to prevent further instability in the European banking sector and to avoid any repetition of events and future public bailouts, in recent years the European Commission has moved towards a **banking union** within the eurozone. The main components of this banking union are the **single rulebook**, the **single supervisory mechanism** and the **single resolution mechanism**. These mechanisms, designed to strengthen EMU, were approved, and in late 2014 the ECB became responsible for the supervision of Europe's largest banks.

ECONOMIC AND SOCIAL COMMITTEE: See **European Economic and Social Committee**

The **ECONOMIC COMMISSION FOR EUROPE** (ECE) is a regional agency of the **United Nations** established in 1947. Until the formation of the **Conference on Security and Co-operation in Europe**, it was the only European body that allowed the states of both Eastern and Western Europe an opportunity to meet on a regular basis. It concerned itself primarily with the exchange of information and development of ideas in non-contentious areas, especially relating to environmental problems.

ECONOMIC PARTNERSHIP AGREEMENTS (EPAs) have been concluded by the European Union (EU) with a number of **African, Caribbean and Pacific** (ACP) countries and regions. This followed the **World Trade Organization**'s (WTO) ruling that the 2000 **Cotonou Agreement** contravened its rules. The bilateral agreements, the first of which were concluded in 2007, provide for the liberalization of trade and are designed to support regional integration among ACP countries and foster their 'smooth and gradual integration … into the world economy, particularly by helping create larger ACP regional markets, thereby contributing to sustainable development and poverty reduction'. EPAs are expected to be extended to cover service sector liberalization and rules governing foreign direct investment. Critics of EPAs contend that the requirement for reciprocal trade liberalization damages the economic development of the ACP countries and that, in its haste to conclude the agreements by the WTO deadline of 31 January 2007, the EU did little to ensure that they promote regional integration, particularly in Africa.

ECOSOC: See **European Economic and Social Committee**

ECSAS: See **European Community Studies Associations**

ECSC: See **European Coal and Steel Community**

ECTC: See **European Counter Terrorism Centre**

ECTS stands for the European Communities course credit transfer system, established as part of the European Community action scheme for the mobility of university students (**Erasmus**).

ECU is the acronym used to refer to the European Currency Unit. The ecu was introduced in 1979 as a central element of the **European Monetary System** (EMS), as a common artificial currency unit supporting the **exchange-rate mechanism** (ERM) of the EMS. It replaced the **European Unit of Account** (EUA). Although not all the member states participated in the ERM, all subscribed to the ecu. Its value was based upon a weighted 'basket' of currencies. Each currency received a different weighting in the basket, with the allocation of weights being subject to regular review. The weights (in percentages) for each national currency were frozen as follows in November 1993 under the terms of the **Treaty on European Union** (TEU): **Germany** 32.0; **France** 20.4; the **United Kingdom** 11.2; the **Netherlands** 10.0; **Italy** 8.5; **Belgium** 8.2; **Spain** 4.5; **Denmark** 2.7; **Ireland** 1.1; **Portugal** 0.7; **Greece** 0.5; **Luxembourg** 0.3. (The currencies of **Austria**, **Finland** and **Sweden** were not represented.) The US dollar was used as a reference point. The specified amounts of the national currencies were converted into dollars, and added together to give the value of the ecu, which could then be translated back into national currencies and used for transactions. The central rate of the ecu was used to calculate bilateral central rates for each pair of European Union (EU) currencies. The **European Monetary Co-operation Fund** (EMCF) supported the ecu. The EMCF was established as a reserve fund into which the countries participating in the basket had to place 20% of both their gold and dollar reserves. It established itself as an accepted currency in international money markets, widely used in international Eurobond issues, as well as in commercial transactions, loans, bank deposits and cheques. Internally, it became a book-keeping device. It was also originally conceived to evolve into the single currency of the EU once full **economic and monetary union** (EMU) was established. This was confirmed by the TEU, which set completion of the third and final stage of EMU for 1997–99, at which point the ecu would replace the national currencies of participating member states. However, at a **European Council** meeting in Dublin, Ireland, in 1995, it was decided that the ecu would be replaced by the **euro** on 1 January 1999 on a one-for-one basis. The euro became the new currency unit within the newly established **eurozone**, and replaced the national currencies of the 11 member states participating in EMU at that stage. In January 2017 French far-right presidential candidate Marine Le Pen appeared to advocate France's withdrawal from the eurozone and the revival of the ECU.

ED: European Democratic Group. See **Group of the European People's Party**

EDA: See **European Defence Agency**

EDC: See **European Defence Community**

EDCs: See **European Documentation Centres**

EDD: See **Group for a Europe of Democracies and Diversities**

EDF: See **European Development Fund**

EDINBURGH SUMMIT

The **EDINBURGH SUMMIT** of the **European Council** in 1992 took place in the Scottish city of Edinburgh, the **United Kingdom**, in the aftermath of the Danish electorate's rejection of the **Treaty on European Union**. It saw the **European Council** agree on a number of exemptions, or **opt-outs**, for **Denmark** as well as issuing a statement that sought to clarify the principle of **subsidiarity** and emphasize the European Union's commitment to **transparency** and greater **openness**.

The **EDUCATION, AUDIOVISUAL AND CULTURE EXECUTIVE AGENCY** (EACEA) was established in January 2006. It is based in **Brussels** and seeks to co-ordinate and implement existing EU-funded programmes in the areas of education and training, citizenship and youth policy, as well as schemes that focus on audiovisual and cultural themes. Although it possesses its own legal identity, the EACEA reports directly to the **European Commission**. The EACEA is particularly charged with managing funding opportunities and networks in the fields of education and training.

EDUCATION INFORMATION NETWORK IN THE EUROPEAN UNION: See **EURYDICE**

EDUCATION, VOCATIONAL TRAINING AND YOUTH POLICY was originally largely excluded from the **Treaty of Rome**, other than in a reference to the reciprocal recognition by the member states of diplomas, professional qualifications and vocational training. The European Communities long accepted that national traditions and practices in education are both important and too complex or sensitive to be easily standardized. Initiatives to foster member state co-operation on educational matters began to materialize only in the 1970s in a series of non-binding **resolutions**. The **Single European Act** emphasized the need for a European dimension in this area. This manifested itself in a 1988 resolution urging all member states to integrate the European dimension into the school curriculum. Education was first recognized as a policy competence when Articles 149 and 150 were inserted into the Treaty of Rome by the **Treaty on European Union**. These—now Articles 165–166 of the **Treaty on the Functioning of the European Union**—spoke of 'the development of quality education by encouraging co-operation … with a view to developing the European dimension in education' and envisaged, for example, the teaching of member state **languages** in other European Union (EU) states, plans to encourage greater mobility of students and teachers, and efforts to develop educational exchanges and establish distance-learning programmes.

The **Treaty of Amsterdam** altered nothing substantial, but did determine that measures relating to education and vocational training were to be adopted under **co-decision procedures**. The 2007 Treaty of Lisbon did not change the provisions on the role of the EU in education and training at all. Education policy in the EU continues to confine itself to stressing the need for closer collaboration and mutual understanding, and continues to take the form of **recommendations** to member states, rather than binding **legislation**. States have been urged to improve training opportunities for, and the cultural integration of, migrant workers; to co-operate in higher education; and to improve the quality and extent of the teaching of EU languages. The few **directives** that have been issued relate to **freedom of movement** in jobs and professions. Three main education and vocational training programmes were introduced in 1985: **Socrates**, to encourage student mobility; **Leonardo** (da Vinci), to promote access to vocational training and lifelong learning, training exchanges and cross-border projects, and to foster innovation and entrepreneurship, improve the quality of training and make it easier to obtain and use vocational training and skills in other European countries; and Youth for Europe, which aimed to facilitate the mobility of young people from disadvantaged backgrounds. In addition, the **Tempus** programme, launched in 1990, encouraged exchanges in higher education between the EU and the states of **Central and Eastern Europe**. The Tempus programme was extended in 2004 to enable students from around the world (the so-called Tempus Mundus) to study in the EU. These programmes were open to people of all ages because lifelong learning and building a Europe of knowledge know no age barriers. In addition, under the Socrates programme, more than 10,000 schools benefited each year from **Lingua**, to promote the learning of languages, particularly lesser-used languages, and **Minerva**, to apply new technologies in education.

The oldest and probably the best known sub-programme established under the Socrates umbrella was **Erasmus**. It devoted more than €100m. annually to grants for students and teachers to spend time at higher education establishments in other European countries. Some 4,000 institutions in 33 countries were involved in the programme. By 2007, more than 2.2m. students had been able to study in another country. From 2007 Erasmus and Leonardo were incorporated into the new **Lifelong Learning Programme** 2007–13, which replaced the Socrates and eLearning programmes (which expired at the end of 2006). (See also **European Centre for the Development of Vocational Training**; **European schools**; **European University Institute**.) Other sub-programmes within the Lifelong Learning Programme included **Grundtvig**, for adult learners and their teachers, to develop European teaching materials and networks and short teaching exchanges, the **Jean Monnet** Programme, which supported institutions and actions in favour of European integration, and **Comenius**, for schools and their teachers. The Lifelong Learning Programme remained the flagship policy in the education field and offered opportunities for a wide range of educational programmes for people from early childhood until old age. It provided €7,000m. in funding over its duration. From 2014 the **European Commission**'s priorities within the field of education and vocational training were encapsulated in the new **Erasmus+** programme, which runs until 2020. The overall programme has a budget of €14,774m. for 2014–20 and aims to enable some 5m. EU citizens to experience training, youth educational schemes and educational provision in other states.

The Commission's activities in education and training are designed to improve the quality of learning systems across the EU and to provide greater opportunities for people. The Commission co-operates with member state authorities to improve policies and exchange best practices and continues to fund a range of education-based programmes. Co-operation between the Commission and the national authorities in the education and training arena intensified following the European Council's adoption of the **Lisbon agenda** in 2000. Indeed, as part of this strategy the Commission launched the 'Education and Training 2010' programme in 2002. This programme led to a number of initiatives to support lifelong learning and included the European Qualifications Framework (EQF), which is essentially a framework of main competences that every EU citizen should possess in today's knowledge society.

The Education and Training 2010 programme also supported the Bologna Process and greater co-operation and coherence in the provision of university education and the creation of a European Higher Education Area. Even more importantly, the European Institute of Innovation and Technology was established in an effort to foster greater cross-European research and education. It is seen as a European counterpart to the world-renowned Massachusetts Institute of Technology. The successor programme to Education and Training 2010 was formally approved in 2009, as the framework structure 'Education and Training 2020', with the primary objectives of providing lifelong learning, better-quality education and the provision of basic skills such as literacy and numeracy, and improving the appeal of mathematics, science and technology; fostering social cohesion, active citizenship, and the development of job-specific skills throughout citizens' lifetimes; and supporting creativity, innovation, digital competence and entrepreneurship.

EEA: See **European Economic Area**

EEA: See **European Environment Agency**

EEAS: See **European External Action Service**

EEC: See **European Economic Community**

EEIG: See **European Economic Interest Grouping**

EESC: See **European Economic and Social Committee**

EFA: See **European Free Alliance**

EFDA: See **European Fusion Development Agreement**

EFDD: See **Europe of Freedom and Direct Democracy Group**

EFDO: See **European Film Distribution Office**

EFSF: See **European Financial Stability Facility**

EFSM: See **European Financial Stabilization Mechanism**

EFTA: See **European Free Trade Association**

The **EHIC**, or European health insurance card, replaced the E111 form from January 2006, and entitles its holders to reduced-cost, or sometimes free, medical treatment should it become necessary when they are staying in another EU member state, a member of the **European Economic Area** (EEA—**Iceland**, **Liechtenstein** and **Norway**) or **Switzerland**. The EHIC is normally valid for three to five years. The card provides access to state-provided medical treatment only, and specifically does not cover those who are intent on travelling to one of the states listed above solely for the purpose of receiving medical treatment.

EIB: See **European Investment Bank**

EIF: See **European Investment Fund**

EIGE: See **European Institute for Gender Equality**

EINECS: See **European Inventory of Existing Chemical Substances**

EIS: See **Schengen Information System**

EJN: See **European Judicial Network in Criminal Matters**

ELDR: See **Group of the European Liberal Democratic and Reform Party**

ELECTIONS: See **Direct Elections**

ELECTRICITY has been considered by the European Union (EU) in the context of its overall **energy policy**. The first programme concerning electricity was drawn up by the Council of Ministers (see **Council of the European Union**) in 1974, and updated in 1980 and 1986. The 1986 review defined objectives for the period up to 1995. It urged continuation of the policy of reducing the reliance of electricity generation on petroleum, which was to constitute less than 15% of total electricity generation by 1995. It further suggested that by 1995 some 40% of electricity generation should be nuclear-based, rising to 50% by 2000. Owing to subsequent concerns about the safety and costs of nuclear energy, these projections have become less realistic.

Electricity policy forms a core element of the EU's pursuit of an **internal market** for energy. In the case of electricity, its objective is to ensure the free movement of electricity while improving security of supply and the **competitiveness** of this particular sector. In 1997 a **directive** (96/92/EC) concerning common rules for the internal market in electricity came into force. In June 2002 the European Council confirmed amended target dates for the complete two-stage liberalization of the markets: opening up by July 2004 for non-domestic users and by July 2007 for domestic users. The European Regulators Group for electricity and gas (ERGEG) was established in November 2003 to act as an advisory group of independent national regulatory authorities to assist the **European Commission** in consolidating the internal market for electricity and gas. In early 2006 the ERGEG launched a regional initiative, which created three gas and seven electricity zones within the EU. The initiative focused on removing barriers to market integration at a regional level, in order to facilitate the creation of a single competitive market. In 2011 ERGEG was superseded by the Agency for the Co-operation of Energy Regulators (ACER), based in Ljubljana, **Slovenia**.

In October 2005 the EU signed a treaty establishing an Energy Community, which entered into force in July 2006 and extended the EU's internal energy market to South-Eastern Europe and further afield (contracting parties to the treaty comprise **Albania**, **Bosnia and Herzegovina**, **Kosovo**, the **former Yugoslav republic of Macedonia**, **Moldova**, **Montenegro**, **Serbia** and **Ukraine**). Armenia, Georgia, **Norway** and **Turkey** have been admitted as observers. The treaty, which aimed to facilitate the creation of an integrated pan-European market for electricity and gas, required the signatories to adopt EU energy regulations. The treaty provided for the liberalization of electricity and gas markets within participating countries by 2008 for non-domestic users, and by 2015 for domestic users. The World Bank estimated that this planned extension of the single European market for electricity and gas would lead to investment of €21,000m. in energy infrastructure in South-Eastern Europe over 15 years.

In June 2009 the Council formally adopted a new liberalization agreement for the EU's gas and electricity markets, the Third Energy Package (the Second Energy Package had been agreed in 2003), which entered into force in March 2011 and which established common rules for the internal markets in gas and electricity; included regulations on conditions for access to natural gas transmission networks and the network for cross-border exchanges in electricity; and provided for the establishment of ACER.

In February 2015 the Commission adopted a strategy paper on the so-called Energy Union, which included plans to overhaul the electricity market, and to this end a Consultation was launched in July. By late 2017 the implementation of its proposals, which included democratization of the ownership of electricity infrastructure, community-based energy projects, and diversification to local and renewable forms of energy, away from reliance on sources in the **Russian Federation**, Central Asia and the Middle East, had not yet taken place.

ÉLYSÉE TREATY: See **Treaty of Friendship**

EMA: See **European Medicines Agency**

EMAS: See **Eco-Management and Audit Scheme**

EMCDDA: See **European Monitoring Centre for Drugs and Drug Addiction**

EMCF: See **European Monetary Co-operation Fund**

EMEA: See **Euro-Mediterranean Economic Area**

EMEP is the acronym of a co-operative programme set up in 1986 to monitor and evaluate the transmission of air pollutants over long distances.

EMFTA: See **Euro-Mediterranean Free Trade Area**

EMI: See **European Monetary Institute**

The **EMISSIONS TRADING SCHEME** or (ETS) was the first, and remains the largest, emissions trading scheme worldwide. The ETS commenced in 2005 and formed an integral aspect of European Union (EU) environmental and climate change policy. It covers more than 11,000 factories and power stations across all 28 EU member states (and also **Iceland**, **Liechtenstein** and **Norway**). The installations that are regulated by the ETS are together responsible for some 40% of the EU's total emissions of carbon dioxide and greenhouse gases. The ETS has been organized into distinct time phases. The first ran from 2005–07, and the second (2008–12) coincided with the commitments agreed at Kyoto (Japan). The third trading period started in January 2013 and will continue until 2020. During this period the EU sought to achieve a 21% reduction in greenhouse gases. Efforts were made to extend the scheme to the airline industry in 2012 (see **carbon tax**), but it was suspended following opposition from some non-EU states—the EU is seeking to secure wider international consensus on a global emissions trading system. In July 2015 the **European Commission** presented a proposal to review the ETS and to identify and formalize the role that it should play in facilitating the achievement of the EU's greenhouse gas emissions targets for 2030.

EMP: See **Euro-Mediterranean Partnership**

EMPLOYMENT is the focus of a **title** inserted into the **Treaty of Rome** (Articles 125–130—now Articles 145–150 of the **Treaty on the Functioning of the European Union**) by the **Treaty of Amsterdam**. The promotion of employment ranks as one of the European Union's objectives and as a matter of common concern. Member states are encouraged to co-ordinate their employment strategies in moves to combat high unemployment, although there are no plans for a common employment policy. Under the terms of the Treaty, the **European Council** is to conduct an annual review of the state of employment, and the **Council of the European Union** must play a more active role in employment affairs by encouraging the exchange of information in this field between member states. This objective was reinforced at the **Luxembourg** jobs summit, an extraordinary European Council meeting convened in November 1997 where it was decided to develop a **European Employment Strategy** built on thematic priorities and described in employment guidelines adopted by the Essen summit meeting of the European Council. Every year these guidelines have to be translated by member states into national action plans for employment, which are later assessed by the Council of the European Union and the **European Commission** prior to the publication of a joint employment report. An **Employment Committee** was established to oversee the co-ordination of the employment strategies of the member states.

The European Commission has its own specific **Directorate-General** (DG) for Employment, Social Affairs and Inclusion that seeks to stimulate more and better jobs, secure better working conditions and promote social inclusion and non-discrimination and equality between men and women. This DG works closely with national authorities, social partners and other relevant actors, and addresses the challenges that confront the working environment, such as the impact of recession and an ageing population. (See also **Disability Policy**; **Social Policy**.)

The **EMPLOYMENT COMMITTEE** (EMCO) was established in 2000 by a decision of the **Council of the European Union**, under Article 150 of the **Treaty of Lisbon**. The EMCO functions as the main advisory committee for ministers responsible for employment and social affairs, and works within the policy framework of the European Employment Strategy. It comprises two sub-groups: the policy analysis group, which provides evidence-based advice to strengthen the EMCO's work and discussions, and the indicators group, which undertakes technical work relating to the indicators used to monitor EU strategy on employment.

EMPTY CHAIR CRISIS refers to the period of seven months after June 1965, when **France** boycotted meetings of the Council of Ministers (see **Council of the European Union**) and the **Committee of Permanent Representatives** (COREPER), although it continued to send junior representatives to some sessions in order for minor routine business to be carried out. This French ploy effectively paralysed the European Communities (EC). The French protest was over the EC timetable for the increased use of **qualified majority voting** in the Council of Ministers after January 1966 and over a collection of proposals from the **European Commission**. These included the finalization of the financial regulations for the **common agricultural policy** (of which France was in favour), as well as more powers for the **European Parliament**—especially in relation to the **budget**—and an independent source of **revenue** for the Commission (both of which proposals France opposed). The crisis was resolved by a compromise, which was largely to France's advantage. The most important element of the resolution was the **Luxembourg Compromise**, which, although maintaining the principle of majority voting, extended to member states the right to use a veto in the

Council of Ministers if they believed that their national interests were being compromised. This agreement among the **Six** undermined the prestige of the Commission and impaired the EC's political development for nearly 20 years, until the **Single European Act**.

EMS: See **European Monetary System**

EMSA: See **European Maritime Safety Agency**

EMU: See **Economic and Monetary Union**

ENERGY POLICY has been a rather problematic area for the European Communities (EC), as it touches on sensitive national concerns. Two of the initial Communities (the **European Coal and Steel Community** and the **European Atomic Energy Community**) dealt with energy. A first attempt at co-ordinating member states' energy policy (to secure fair competition, low process and freedom of choice for the consumer) occurred in a **protocol** on Energy in 1964, but progress was limited. A further, unsuccessful effort was made in 1968. The difficulties were revealed by the different national responses to the petroleum crisis of 1973. In 1974 a **European Commission** energy programme was accepted by the Council of Ministers (see **Council of the European Union**) and it has since served as the basis for discussions on energy policy. It was revised in 1980, and again in 1986. The original priority was to reduce dependence on petroleum, especially on supplies from politically volatile regions. Within 10 years, petroleum imports had been reduced by one-half, owing to increased efficiency, the successful exploitation of North Sea petroleum and a diversification of energy sources.

The 1986 revision of energy policy set priority targets until 1995. As far as the supply and use of energy were concerned, it urged that petroleum imports be held at a level below one-third of total EC energy consumption, with greater reliance upon **coal** and nuclear energy, the latter to supply 40% of EC needs by 1995. All developments were to take place within the context of greater efficiency, and a further improvement in energy saving of at least 20% was to be secured by 1995. More financial assistance was to be made available for the exploration of alternative energy sources such as solar, wave and wind energy, in the hope that these would provide up to 5% of EC needs by 2000. The programme also set several further objectives. It recommended more internal trade in natural gas and **electricity** (accepting that little more could be done for trade in petroleum and coal), and a common pricing system across all energy sectors. It confirmed the importance of maintaining a contingency supply of fuel reserves equal to 30 days' consumption at power stations (and 90 days' consumption in the case of petroleum stocks), and of increased flexibility and co-operation between the member states.

There were potential conflicts between energy needs and environmental protection, and a growing objection to nuclear power. In the 1990s there were three major aspects to energy policy. First, as a consequence of the **internal market**, there was a new emphasis upon a single energy market. This would entail liberalization of gas and electricity markets by removing the dominance of state monopolies by 2000. The European Commission issued several **directives**: on price **transparency**, the transit of energy, and the development of energy infrastructures. The EC also took the lead in the establishment in 1991 of a **European Energy Charter** linking Western with Eastern Europe.

Later, in 1996, the Commission would establish as part of its **Mediterranean policy** a Euro-Mediterranean Energy Forum to assist in the development of co-operation projects. Finally, the Commission linked the development of energy more closely with **environmental policy**. The major symbol of this commitment was the proposal for a **carbon tax**.

Much of the proposed energy programme was contentious, since the energy requirements of the European Union (EU) were likely to continue to grow. Given its potential importance, it is surprising that only limited reference was made to energy in the **Treaty on European Union** (TEU): it referred only to the existence of EC powers in the area of energy and the need for the development of European energy infrastructures. Moreover, although it was agreed that the possibility of incorporating energy into the treaty basis of the EU would be reviewed by an **intergovernmental conference** at the end of 1996 considering possible revisions of the Treaty, the **Treaty of Amsterdam** went no further than the TEU. In 1995 the European Commission published a **White Paper** on energy policy, prioritizing security of supply and improved **competitiveness** of European businesses, and emphasizing environmental constraints. Following this, in 1997 the Commission proposed a framework programme for the energy sector, which, following approval by the Council of the European Union in December 1998, covered the period 1998–2002. The objective of this programme was to guarantee the coherence and efficiency of EC energy policy by bringing together all ongoing energy actions and programmes across all EC policies. Objectives for this five-year period included: the strengthening of international co-operation; the promotion of renewable energy sources; the encouragement of an efficient use of energy sources; an improvement of safety in the use of nuclear energy; and increased industrial co-operation with the **Russian Federation**. The Commission was charged with reviewing the **implementation** of this framework on an annual basis. In November 2000 the Commission launched a **Green Paper** on the security of energy supply. This aimed to ensure a supply of energy to consumers at reasonable prices while maintaining the competitiveness of the sector and respecting both the environment and sustainable development. It resulted in the Intelligent Energy—Europe initiative.

Money was allocated for energy research in the EU's Sixth Framework Programme for Research and Technological Development (2002–06). In addition, the EU planned to spend €200m. from its Intelligent Energy for Europe programme between 2003 and 2006 to support research into energy saving, energy efficiency, renewable energies and the energy-related aspects of transport. The Lisbon **summit meeting** of the **European Council** in March 2000 urged the creation of a genuine single market for energy, and in March 2001 the Commission responded by adopting a series of measures to open up the gas and **electricity** markets completely by the end of 2005. In the past, national gas and electricity markets were separate 'islands' within the EU, where supply and distribution were controlled by monopolies. Now, consumers not only have the right to choose their supplier, but they also have a right to gas and electricity supply at reasonable prices. Problems persisted as a result of limited progress in cross-border trade and differing stages of implementation across member states. Further progress needed to be made, particularly with regard to the pricing of cross-border trade and the rules for the allocation and management of scarce resources. To facilitate further developments the Commission established two new consultative bodies: the Electricity Regulatory Forum of Florence and the Gas Regulatory

Forum of Madrid. In September 2002 the Commission, increasingly aware of the EU's heavy reliance and dependence on external supplies of petroleum and gas, adopted two directive proposals that were designed to maintain the security of EU energy sources at affordable prices. By 2004 all businesses were free to choose their own suppliers of gas and electricity, and consumers followed suit by 2007. For their part, all suppliers have guarantees under single energy market rules that they can have access to the distribution grid and pipeline networks of other EU countries and that they will pay a fair price for access. Consideration of energy policy has always provoked controversy at the EU level. Nevertheless, the dependence of many EU states on foreign-owned energy sources is undeniable. The dangers of such dependency were apparent when Russia threatened to suspend all gas supplies to **Ukraine** in January 2006 and thereby disrupt gas supplies to Western Europe via Ukraine.

The **Twenty-Five** relied on imports for 50.5% of their energy needs. The figures relating to oil and gas requirements were higher, at 80.2% and 54.5%, respectively. The European Council recognized the rather grim realities of the situation when it settled on an action plan for energy policy in March 2007. This programme ran from 2007 and sought to improve energy efficiency and save up to 20% of energy consumption by 2020. It simultaneously wanted to increase the amount of renewable energy and raise the share of biofuels.

In November 2010 the Commission adopted the communication 'Energy 2020: a strategy for competitive, sustainable and secure energy'. This strategy seeks to define the energy challenges for Europe over the current decade and how best to meet these challenges. This communication was followed by the first ever special European Council summit on energy, which took place in February 2011. Agreement was reached on a number of strategic energy-related areas. In particular, the summit concluded that work should be undertaken to develop a transparent, rule-governed relationship with Russia. The summit also made clear its intention to promote investment in renewable energy, and sustainable low-carbon technologies; to accelerate the full liberalization of energy markets, in order to bring them into accordance with EU law; to improve adherence to the 2020 energy-efficiency target of 20% (which aimed to reduce the use of greenhouse gases by 20%, to increase the proportion of renewable energy used to 20%, and to improve overall energy efficiency by 20% by 2020); and to investigate the potential extraction and use of unconventional fossil fuel sources, such as shale gas and oil shale, favoured, in particular, by **Poland**.

In March 2013 the European Commission adopted a Green Paper on a '2030 framework for climate and energy policies'. This framework aims to build on earlier programmes and aspires to a competitive, low-carbon economy by 2050. The new framework raised a number of issues, such as the type, nature and level of climate and energy targets; and how energy systems can facilitate EU competitiveness. In October 2014 EU member states agreed on the final '2030 Framework for climate and energy', which included EU-wide targets and policy objectives for the period 2020–30, in order to help the EU to achieve a more competitive, secure and sustainable energy system, and to meet its long-term greenhouse gas reductions target for 2050. A principal pillar of this was 'decarbonization'—the shift from tradition fuel sources such as coal, oil and gas, toward low-carbon technologies. Targets for the EU for 2030 include a 40% cut in greenhouse gas emissions compared with 1990 levels; renewable energy consumption to increase to at least 27% of total energy consumption by 2030; and energy savings of at least 27% by 2030, compared with the level of usage recorded in 2014. Policies for 2030 proposed by the Commission include a reformed **emissions trading scheme**; new indicators for the competitiveness and security of the energy system, such as price differences with major trading partners; diversification of supply; and increased interconnection capacity between EU member states.

The crisis in Ukraine from early 2014 again focused attention on Europe's overdependence on Russian energy supplies. In May the Commission announced a new Energy Security Strategy, and in February 2015 the Commission adopted a strategy paper on the so-called Energy Union. The Energy Union seeks to reduce dependence on single suppliers and, through increased transparency, facilitate agreements with non-EU countries. It also aims to promote an environmentally sustainable, low-carbon economy; and to improve competitiveness and energy efficiency, with increased liberalization. By late 2017 the Energy Union had not yet been formalized by the European Commission.

ENERGY TAX: See **Carbon Tax**

ENGRENAGE is a term that comes from a French expression meaning 'getting caught up in the gears'. It relates closely to the '**Monnet method**' of integration, whereby individuals, governments, interest groups and European Union institutions, having embarked on a particular course of action, find themselves compelled to take additional measures that deepen European integration.

ENHANCED CO-OPERATION was substantially overhauled at the **intergovernmental conference** convened in Nice in December 2000, specifically by listing in a single provision the 10 conditions necessary to establish enhanced co-operation. Although the essential characteristics of this instrument (whereby enhanced co-operation should only be taken as a measure of last resort) were not changed significantly, there were some notable alterations. For example, the minimum number of member states required to establish enhanced co-operation was designated as eight, rather than a majority, thus facilitating use of enhanced co-operation on the **enlargement** of the European Union (EU).

In pillar I (the European Communities) and in pillar III (**police and judicial co-operation in criminal matters**) the possibility of opposing enhanced co-operation (by employing a veto) was removed. With regard to pillar II on the **common foreign and security policy** (CFSP), the deliberations in Nice made it possible to establish enhanced co-operation for the implementation of joint action or a common position, except for matters pertaining to defence. Authorization for enhanced co-operation rests with the **Council of the European Union**, and the Council is to decide by **qualified majority voting** (QMV). Member states are entitled to ask the Council to adopt a decision by unanimity if they are convinced that an issue is of particular importance. When enhanced co-operation concerns an area determined by the **co-decision procedure**, the consent of the **European Parliament** is required. With the **ratification** of the **Treaty of Lisbon** there have been a number of significant changes concerning enhanced co-operation (that were originally contained in the **Treaty establishing a Constitution for Europe**). First, the minimum number of states needed for enhanced co-operation has changed, from eight to one-third of the total membership. Second, the launching of enhanced co-operation no longer requires unanimity, but QMV. The exception here is in relation to the CFSP, where unanimity is still necessary. And third, in those policy areas where the Council acts by unanimity, member states participating in enhanced co-operation are now able to use QMV and to introduce co-decision when adopting measures other than those that have either military or defence implications. Finally, the Treaty of Lisbon, like the Treaty establishing a Constitution for Europe before it, provided for a further form of enhanced co-operation—**permanent structured co-operation**—under the **Common Security and Defence Policy**.

Enhanced co-operation has proven exceptionally difficult to establish. Member states supportive of a particular measure have generally been unwilling to isolate member states that are opposed. However, two enhanced co-operation measures have been launched, relating to cross-border divorce (2010) and the adoption of an **EU Patent** (2011).

ENLARGEMENT is a general term used to describe the process of admission of new states into the European Union (EU). The procedures for enlargement are contained in Article 49 of the **Treaty on European Union**. All applicants for membership must possess a democratic form of government, respect the principles on which the EU is based (i.e. liberty, democracy, respect for **human rights** and fundamental freedoms, and the rule of law), and be prepared to accept not only the provisions of the **European treaties**, but also the *acquis communautaire*, the accumulated **legislation** of the EU. Because of the last-mentioned requirement and the desire of both member states and applicants to protect their own interests as much as possible, negotiations tend to be complex and protracted. The **European Commission** undertakes an analysis of each country's application, focusing on both the economic situation and the political stability of each state. Thereafter, the Commission presents its *avis* to the **Council of the European Union**, where a decision on the applicant will be made. If negotiations are successful and an **accession treaty** is signed, this must be ratified by the **national parliaments** of the acceding states, by all the member states and, since the **Single European Act**, also by the **European Parliament** (EP).

The first round of enlargement included applications in 1961–62, and again in 1967. Applications were from **Denmark**, **Ireland**, **Norway** and the **United Kingdom**. On each occasion, **France** vetoed the British application, and the other three applicants chose not to pursue the matter further without the UK. The applications were renewed in 1970, leading to the signing of Treaties of Accession in 1972. As a result of a national referendum, Norway declined to join. The other three states became full members of the European Communities (EC) on 1 January 1973. The second and third rounds involved **Greece**, **Portugal** and **Spain**, all of which applied for membership after establishing a democratic form of government in the mid-1970s. Greece formally became a member on 1 January 1981, followed by Portugal and Spain on 1 January 1986.

The EC decision to create an **internal market** was a matter of concern to the **European Free Trade Association** states, most of which between 1989 and 1992 eventually submitted formal applications for membership. Negotiations with **Austria**, **Finland**, Norway and **Sweden** were concluded in 1994, with membership offered subject to **ratification**. Following another national referendum, Norway again declined membership, but the other three states joined the EU on 1 January 1995.

After the collapse of communism in Eastern Europe in 1989, most of the newly democratized states indicated an interest in seeking membership in the medium term. The EC's response was that this would be limited in the first instance to members of the **Visegrad Group**, namely **Hungary**, **Poland** and the former Czechoslovakia (see the **Czech Republic** and **Slovakia**). Other applicant states have been **Turkey** in 1987, and **Cyprus** and **Malta** in 1990. These applications initially met with considerable resistance within the EU even though the countries had all signed **association agreements**. However, in 1996 the **European Council** decided that **accession negotiations** with Cyprus would begin six months after the conclusion of the 1996 **intergovernmental conference**.

By this time the EU had also received applications for membership from the 10 Central and Eastern European countries with which **Europe agreements** had already been signed: Hungary, Poland, **Romania**, Slovakia, **Latvia**, **Estonia**, **Lithuania**, **Bulgaria**, the Czech Republic and **Slovenia**. This block of applications constituted the largest enlargement of the EU to date and also the most difficult, given the economic challenges facing the countries of **Central and Eastern Europe**. As a result, the EU progressed with the applications cautiously. In 1997, as part of **Agenda 2000**, the European Commission, using the **accession criteria** established in 1993 at the **Copenhagen summit**, assessed each country's ability to fulfil membership obligations, and recommended that accession negotiations begin with Hungary, Poland, Estonia, the Czech Republic and Slovenia. Negotiations with these five countries (plus Cyprus) began in March 1998. Meanwhile, the other applicants were included in an 'inclusive and evaluative' accession process, and would have to wait until late 1999 before they, along with Malta—which had renewed its application for membership in 1998—were recommended for negotiations. Following the recommendation, the European Council, meeting in Helsinki, Finland, in December 1999, decided to open negotiations in 2000. Moreover, it conferred on all the applicant states, including Turkey, the status of **candidate country**.

The completion of accession negotiations currently requires the closure of 35 chapters, most of which deal with particular areas of the *acquis communautaire* (e.g. **competition policy**, the **common agricultural policy**, **telecommunications** policy, and **energy policy**). In the case of 10 candidate countries—Cyprus, the Czech Republic, Estonia, Hungary, Latvia, Lithuania, Malta, Poland, Slovakia and Slovenia—the then 31 chapters were finally closed in December 2002. This paved the way for the EU to enlarge to 25 member states on 1 May 2004. As a consequence, the EU underwent its greatest enlargement to become a union covering another third of the European continent and comprising nearly 500m people.

Prior to the 2004 enlargement, each of the candidate countries, as well as the member states, had to ratify the **Treaty of Accession** signed on 16 April 2003. Nine candidate countries— the exception being Cyprus—successfully held **referenda** on EU membership between March and September 2003. At the same time, negotiations with Bulgaria and Romania continued, with the EU committing itself to realizing the two countries' goal of membership in 2007. This it did, although consideration was given to delaying accession by one year, owing to concerns over judicial reform and corruption. Turkey, meanwhile, continues to present a more problematic case, although negotiations on membership opened in October 2005. The prospects for Turkish accession, however, remain uncertain.

Enlargement has not been straightforward, since the process has budgetary implications and threatens to result in institutional paralysis unless there is institutional reform. Thus, from the mid-1990s the EU sought to reform its most significant areas of expenditure—the **common agricultural policy** (CAP) and the **structural and cohesion funds**—as well as its **institutions**. Prior to the 2004 enlargement the EU provided pre-accession assistance to the candidate countries. This included €1,500m. annually under the **PHARE** programme; €1,000m. annually under the **instrument for structural policies for pre-accession**; and €540m. annually under the Special Accession Programme for Agriculture and Regional Development. Less progress was initially made on institutional reform. Measures introduced by the **Treaty of Amsterdam** prepared the EU only marginally for future enlargement, by avoiding any significant changes to the institutions so as to enable them to cope with the extra demands that would be placed on them. However, the following reforms were introduced as a result: a limit was placed on the size of the EP; the European Commission was to undergo a review process; the **co-decision procedure** was simplified; and agreement was reached on greater use of **qualified majority voting** (QMV) in the Council of the European Union, to ensure that decision making was not slowed down unduly. In **protocol**s attached to the Treaty of Amsterdam references were made to the fact that each member state would have only one Commissioner after enlargement: the larger member states were previously entitled to have two Commissioners each. The Treaty also promised that a further review of the institutions was to take place if the EU grew to more than 20 member states. The whole array of institutional issues relating to enlargement was tackled more fully by the **Treaty of Nice**, agreed by the Governments of the 15 existing member states in December 2000. This reformed the Commission, the **Court of Justice** and the Court of First Instance (now **General Court**); extended QMV; re-allocated votes in the Council of the European Union; and agreed the distribution of votes and seats in an enlarged EU of 27 members. Yet concerns that the reforms were insufficient to ensure that a substantially enlarged EU could function smoothly persisted. The result was the **European Convention**'s reform proposals contained in the **draft Treaty establishing a Constitution for Europe**. Many of these survived the intergovernmental conference launched in October 2003 and appeared in the Treaty establishing a Constitution for Europe, and subsequently its replacement, the **Treaty of Lisbon**.

With Bulgaria and Romania joining the EU on 1 January 2007 the fifth enlargement was completed. **Croatia** became a member of the EU in July 2013. A range of countries still aspire to EU membership. In 2004 the **former Yugoslav republic of Macedonia** applied for membership, as did **Montenegro** in 2008 and **Albania**, **Iceland** and **Serbia** in 2009. Iceland opened negotiations in July 2010 (although they were suspended in mid-2013); Montenegro commenced talks in June 2012. In June 2013 the Council officially endorsed the opening of talks on accession with Serbia, and these commenced in January 2014. In June the European Council granted Albania candidate status; membership of the EU is not expected before 2020. Meanwhile, membership bids from other countries in Europe cannot be ruled out. **Norway** may apply again, and **Switzerland** may reactivate its 1992 application. **Moldova** and **Ukraine** have also expressed interest in future EU membership. Increasingly concerns are being expressed that the EU does not have sufficient '**integration capacity**' to admit more states, although the entry into force of the Treaty of Lisbon assuaged immediate concerns over admitting a small number. The EU is certainly supporting, through the **Stabilization and Association Process**, the **European partnerships**, the **accession partnerships** and the **instrument for pre-accession assistance**, the efforts of countries wishing to join. However, popular support within the EU for further enlargement is far from universal. The Turkish accession bid is controversial. Accession negotiations were opened, but progress was slower, and in November 2016 the European Parliament approved a non-binding resolution supporting the suspension of accession negotiations with Turkey, owing to concerns over human rights and the rule of law following the suppression of an attempted coup in July. In mid-December the European Council confirmed that negotiations would not be launched in any new policy areas while the ongoing political situation in Turkey prevailed. Meanwhile, **Bosnia and Herzegovina** submitted a formal application for membership of the EU in February 2016. EU officials welcomed the initiative. They, nevertheless, indicated that significant reforms were necessary, of the police and public administration, and an improvement in the country's co-operation with the International Criminal Tribunal for the former Yugoslavia, before membership could be considered. The prospects for the accession of other countries from the **Western Balkans** will depend very much on their own domestic reform efforts, especially with regard to the establishment of the rule of law and the eradication of corruption.

ENTERPRISE POLICY aims to ensure that the European Union (EU) helps to stimulate a climate in which enterprise, industry and innovation flourish. Enterprise is crucial to the EU's economic growth and the EU hopes to foster and encourage innovative business practices that will create jobs and promote growth. Enterprise policy was designed at European Communities (EC) level to meet the requirements of the entire business community (whether large or small businesses) and its environment. Article 157 of the **Treaty of Rome** (now Article 173 of the **Treaty on the Functioning of the European Union**) provides the legal basis for enterprise policy. Historically, work on enterprise policy has consisted of three key areas: **small and medium-sized enterprises** (SMEs), innovation and **competitiveness**, and making the most of opportunities and benefits arising from the single market. The level of EC interest in all three aspects was evident from the number of action programmes and **Green** and **White Papers** dedicated to these matters over the last two decades.

Support for SMEs dates back to 1983 and the adoption of the first EC action programme to assist their development. The business community currently places considerable emphasis on the notion of promoting innovation. In 1995 the **European Commission** produced a Green Paper on this subject, and this led in 1996 to the first action programme for innovation in Europe. In April 2000 the Commission produced a communication on the challenges ahead for enterprise policy, which envisaged an 'Enterprise Europe'. More recently, in 2012 the EU renewed its programme on industrial policy, 'A stronger European industry for growth and economic recovery', with a focus on SMEs and entrepreneurship. In April 2016 the Commission adopted a new communication on 'Digitising European Industry', as part of the strategy for the creation of a Digital Single Market, which was initiated in 2015. The Start-up and Scale-up Initiative, proposed by the Commission in November 2016, seeks to encourage the creation of industrial start-ups in the EU (as opposed to so-called third countries) through simplified taxation measures, improved access to financing and proposed amendments to legislation on insolvency, to facilitate restructuring.

The first **ENVIRONMENTAL ACTION PROGRAMME** (EAP) of the European Communities (EC) was introduced in 1973. The sixth EAP was proposed by the **European Commission** in January 2001 and adopted by the **European Parliament** (EP) and the **European Council** in July 2002. The programme covered the period 2002–12 and was an integral element of EC **environmental policy**. The sixth EAP expired on 30 June 2012 and a seventh EAP was agreed in June 2013.

The **ENVIRONMENTAL CHEMICALS DATA INFORMATION NETWORK** (ECDIN) is a database that also contains the **European Inventory of Existing Chemical Substances** (EINECS).

ENVIRONMENTAL POLICY was not specifically mentioned or provided for in the **Treaty of Rome**. The **Single European Act** gave the European Communities (EC) competence, and this was extended into a policy remit by the **Treaty on European Union** (TEU). The objectives are those that the EC has pursued for some time. The aim of EC environmental policy is to preserve, protect and improve the quality of the environment and to protect people's health. The TEU added another dimension: the promotion of measures for dealing with global environmental problems. The concept of sustainable development was enshrined in the **Treaty of Amsterdam** as one of the EC's objectives. Moreover, environmental protection requirements were given greater emphasis in other EC policies, and especially in relation to the single market. Significantly, the treaty also simplified decision making by allowing **co-decision procedure** to replace **co-operation procedure** where the latter had applied to certain parts of environmental policymaking.

EC activity in the area of environment policy first commenced in the early 1970s, when specific environmental problems were incorporated into a series of five-year programmes for dealing with generalized issues of environmental enhancement and protection. The main policy principles were defined in the first **Environmental Action Programme** (EAP): the polluter must pay the costs of repair to the environment; prevention of environmental damage is preferable to remedial measures; and all EC initiatives in all policy areas must take their likely effect upon the environment into account. The TEU further stressed the precautionary principle and the need for environment policy to take into account the regional economic diversity of the EU.

Environmental policy has become increasingly significant for the EU. More than 300 **directives** or **regulations** on the environment had been adopted by the mid-1990s. Since then there has been a noticeable decline in the number of regulations and directives, reflecting the sensitivity and controversy surrounding environmental policy or, more accurately, the costs of implementing tougher environmental regimes that impact either on central and local government or on the business community. Nevertheless, activity has concentrated on six broad problem areas: **water**; **atmospheric pollution**; **noise**; chemical products; waste disposal; and the preservation and restoration of natural habitats and the conservation of wildlife. Several directives deal with the pollution of all forms of water and with relevant quality standards, and the EC have participated in international conventions dealing with the reduction of pollution in international waterways and rivers. Other directives cover the discharge of pollutants into the atmosphere from industrial plants, and exhaust emissions from motor vehicles. Maximum noise levels have been established for a range of machinery and household equipment. Chemical products have been subject to regulation since 1967. Control of chemicals became more urgent after the Seveso incident in **Italy** in 1976, leading to a range of further directives on their manufacture and usage, and on safety precautions. A **European Inventory of Existing Chemical Substances** (EINECS) was established in 1986. The EC committed themselves to reducing chlorofluorocarbons (CFCs) by 85% by 2000, and in 1993 the **European Commission** proposed the elimination of hydrochlorofluorocarbons by 2014. To protect natural habitats and conserve wildlife, a number of directives relate to the preservation of species and to scientific experiments on animals. Funds have been provided for the preservation of natural habitats, and the EC signed several international conventions on the conservation of wildlife. EC **legislation** also covers the dangers posed by radiation. Following the accident at the Chernobyl nuclear power station in the former **USSR** in 1986, maximum levels of radiation contamination in **foodstuffs** were set.

As part of the EC's efforts to promote awareness of environmental issues and encourage companies to do likewise, an **eco-management and audit scheme** (EMAS) was set up in 1995. Participation is voluntary and involves industrial companies undergoing an independent audit of their environmental performance. In the area of transport, harmful emissions from road vehicles were to be reduced by 60%–70% by 2010, and measures were agreed to lower the allowable limits for certain chemical substances in petrol and diesel fuel by 2000. Leaded petrol was to be phased out, for most vehicles, by 2000. There has also been legislation concerning the protection of groundwater resources, waste disposal in landfill sites, genetically engineered foods, and trade in endangered species.

The fourth EAP (1987–92) increased EC activity, conferring stronger powers on the European Commission, including the right to take member states to the **Court of Justice** for non-compliance with environmental legislation. As part of the task of raising public awareness, 1987 was designated as the European Year of the Environment (EYE), and the Network for Environmental Technology Transfer (NETT) was established to aid the realization of its activities. The pursuit of these objectives was potentially strengthened by the 1990 decision to set up a **European Environment Agency** (EEA) and a special environment fund, **LIFE**. The EC also agreed, in principle, to introduce a **carbon tax**. The importance of these measures and programmes was reiterated in the fifth EAP (1993–2000), which also stressed that EC activity must be more anticipatory, less devoted to problem-solving, and focus more on the causes of environmental problems as part of a commitment to 'sustainable development'. The sixth EAP (2002–12) was guided by the fifth programme, and defined the priorities and aims of EC environmental policy to 2012. Four areas were given particular emphasis: climate change, nature and biodiversity, environment and health, management of natural resources and waste. It also identified explicitly the measures needed to implement successfully the EU's sustainable development strategy, which had been given much wider prominence following the adoption of the EU Sustainable Development Strategy in 2001.

An initiative launched in January 2004, deriving from the priorities of the sixth EAP, envisaged a 'Thematic Strategy on the Urban Environment'. This communication from the Commission seeks to identify the problems and challenges experienced by urban areas. Environmental problems are a global concern, and there have been high-profile conferences at the international level (Rio de Janeiro, 1992; Kyoto, 1997; and The Hague, 2000) to address the issues of ozone depletion and global warming. The **Fifteen** (EU15), at the time of the ratification of the Kyoto **Protocol**, agreed to reduce their emissions to 8% below the base year's level (usually 1990) by 2012. According to the Commission, the **Twenty-Five** (EU25) succeeded in bringing about a 7.3% reduction in emissions between 1990 and 2004. Interestingly, US emissions rose by 15.8% for the same reporting period.

In June 2013 agreement was reached between the European Commission, the **Council of the European Union** and the **European Parliament** on the seventh EAP for 2014–20, 'Living well, within the limits of our planet'. The new EAP entered into force in January 2014, and focuses on three principal thematic goals: the protection of nature and improvements in ecological resilience; increased sustainable, resource-efficient, low-carbon growth; and addressing environmental health risks. Four principal measures were to facilitate implementation of these objectives: increasing implementation of legislation; improving information, by developing the knowledge base; better-targeted investment for environment and climate policy; and the integration of environmental issues into other policy areas. The programme also sought to improve the sustainability of EU cities, and to help the EU to address more effectively international environmental and climate challenges. In December 2011 the European Commission published proposals for a new LIFE programme, for the period until 2020. The revised LIFE programme, which entered into effect in January 2014, had a budget of some €3,400m.

The Kyoto Protocol entered into force in early 2005. By September 2011 a total of 191 countries had signed and ratified the protocol, although certain emerging economies, such as the People's Republic of China and India, were exempt (at least temporarily) from the obligations to reduce emissions. In December 2011 Canada formally withdrew from the Protocol. The **USA** was the only major country not to agree to the terms of Kyoto. However, it should be noted that some US federal states moved towards the adoption of Kyoto's emission standards. This international dimension has enabled the EU to establish a global presence in the field of environmental policy, a position that has led it into dispute with the USA. More positively, the German European Council presidency in the first half of 2007 laid particular emphasis on the need to tackle climate change, and it was agreed by the EU25 to cut emissions by 20% from 1990 levels by 2020. More recently, the Council (of environment ministers) agreed to impose emissions quotas on airlines (which are estimated to account for 3% of carbon emissions) in an effort to confront climate change. Under this agreement, the EU would set the limits, but the decision encountered severe opposition from the USA. In mid-December 2016 the European Parliament and the Council signed into law a new National Emissions Directive, which strengthened limits on five principal pollutants, with effect from 31 December. The new Directive sought to reduce pollution-related ill health by almost 50% by 2030.

In 2007 the **G-8** committed themselves to agreeing a successor to Kyoto by the end of 2012. In December 2007 delegates at a **United Nations** (UN) conference in Bali finally agreed on a new deal to tackle climate change. The final text did not quantify the percentage cuts, but it explicitly acknowledged the need for them. It is important to stress that the USA agreed to participate, despite some reservations, along with both Canada and **Japan**. All three states opposed EU demands for cuts of 25%–40% by 2020. Nevertheless, the so-called 'Bali Roadmap' provides evidence of greater international recognition of the problem and a determination to do something.

In recent years the EU has been instrumental in advancing the climate change agenda and some member states have been keen to initiate substantive cuts in emissions. A special UN-sponsored conference on climate change took place in Copenhagen, **Denmark**, in December 2009. The **Copenhagen Summit** was attended by 119 world leaders and attracted considerable media attention. However, divisions were apparent among the delegates at Copenhagen. There was disagreement and resistance on the depth of such cuts from many countries in the developing world and from other key states such as Brazil, China and **South Africa**. Although a deal was reached to reduce emissions and to raise finance to assist developing countries to reduce emissions, many commentators argued that the summit had produced limited results, especially as the agreement was not legally binding.

A UN Climate Change Conference was held in Paris, **France**, in November–December 2015, at which 195 countries adopted the first-ever universal, legally binding global climate agreement. The adopted plan aimed to avoid significant climate change by limiting global warming to well below 2°C above pre-industrial levels. The agreement also recognized the need for global emissions to peak as soon as possible, acknowledging that this would take longer for developing countries, but urging such nations to undertake rapid reductions thereafter, in accordance with the latest available technology. The agreement was due to enter into force in 2020, after 55 countries, accounting for at least 55% of global emissions, had deposited their instruments of ratification.

Before and during the Paris conference, countries and trading blocs submitted comprehensive national climate action plans to the UN, detailing their intended nationally determined contributions (INDC). The EU was one of the leaders of international efforts toward securing a global climate deal. Following the limited efficacy of the Kyoto Protocol and the lack of agreement at the Copenhagen Summit in 2009, the EU had built a broad coalition of developed and developing countries in favour of adopting ambitious targets, which shaped the outcome of the Paris conference. In March 2015 the EU was the first major economy to submit its INDC to the new agreement. It was already taking steps to implement its new target of reducing emissions by at least 40% by 2030, compared with their 1990 level. Notably, however, in mid-2017 US President Donald Trump (who took office in January) announced his intention to withdraw the USA from the Paris agreement.

EP: See **European Parliament**

EPAs: See **Economic Partnership Agreements**

EPC: See **European Political Co-operation**

EPP: See **Group of the European People's Party (Christian Democrats)**

EPPO: See **European Public Prosecutor's Office**

EPU: See **European Payments Union**

EQUAL PAY policy was laid down in Article 141 of the **Treaty of Rome**. It now appears in Article 157 of the **Treaty on the Functioning of the European Union**. While it refers specifically to gender discrimination, obliging the member states to 'ensure and subsequently maintain the application of the principle that men and women should receive equal pay for equal work', the Article has been taken to refer to equality in general. A series of **directives** between 1975 and 1986 extended the meaning of equal pay for equal work, as well as enabling those who consider themselves to be discriminated against to take their case, without fear of dismissal or reprisal, to a national tribunal. Where there is a difference of opinion over the meaning of EU **law**, the question may be referred to the **Court of Justice**, the rulings of which are binding on all national bodies.

ERAC: See **European Research Area Committee**

ERASMUS: See **ERASMUS+**

ERASMUS+ succeeds Erasmus, which stood for European Community Action Scheme for the Mobility of University Students, a programme established in 1987 with the purpose of encouraging students to spend an integral part of their studies at a university in another country of the European Communities (EC). This programme of student mobility was widened to include **European Free Trade Association** (EFTA) countries in 1991 and countries from **Central and Eastern Europe** as well as **Cyprus** in 1998. The students' home universities recognized the periods of study abroad by means of a course credit transfer scheme. The original goal was that some 10% of the EC student population would be participants in the scheme by 1992. Despite the problems created by linguistic diversity and different national systems of higher education, Erasmus proved a success. Its popularity increased the costs of the programme at a time when EC expenditure came under closer scrutiny, leading to pressure for the target figure to be reduced to 5% of the student population. Erasmus encompassed more than just student mobility, and contains chapters on: teacher exchanges; joint preparation of courses, where at least three establishments from different countries pool their resources to create a programme of study, a module, a curriculum or a Master's programme; intensive programmes (such as summer schools); and thematic networks on a subject area or a specific platform for analysis and discussion of a European theme. The Thematic Network in Public Administration (based at Leiden University), for example, is an initiative whereby academics meet on an annual basis to discuss the **Europeanization** of public administration and to seek co-operation and teaching links across Europe. Erasmus became part of the **Socrates** programme in 1995. In 2007 the **Lifelong Learning Programme** (LLP) 2007–13 replaced the Socrates, **Leonardo** da Vinci, and eLearning programmes, which expired at the end of 2006. Erasmus was one of the six sub-programmes supported under the Lifelong Learning Programme. The LLP has been replaced by a new Erasmus Charter for Higher Education, as part of the European Union's (EU) programme for education, training, youth and sports (under the Erasmus+ programme), and once again stresses the importance of an international agenda.

The purpose of the Erasmus+ scheme was to create a single integrated programme that brings together the LLP, **Grundtvig**, Leonardo, **Comenius**, Erasmus, **Erasmus Mundus**, **Tempus** and **Youth in Action** programmes within a more streamlined architecture to supply greater focus, effectiveness and simplification of the various schemes and objectives. Some €14,774m. were allocated for Erasmus+ in 2014–20, representing 40% more in funds compared with 2007–13. This new programme has set itself ambitious targets and aspires to engage the participation of some 2m. university students and 650,000 vocational learners in exchanges, to get an additional 600,000 young people participating in youth exchanges and some 800,000 teachers, education staff and youth workers establishing and engaging with exchange programmes. It also aims to secure greater mobility by opening the scheme beyond EU/**European Economic Area** member states, and is developing an international dimension. Overall, the programme is designed to support some 4m. people by giving them support to study, train, work or volunteer abroad.

ERASMUS MUNDUS was designed as a co-operation and mobility programme in the field of higher education. It aimed to promote the European Union (EU) as a centre of excellence in learning around the world. It supported European high-quality Masters' Courses and Doctorates and enhanced the visibility and attractiveness of European higher education in third countries. It also provided EU-funded scholarships for third country nationals participating in these Masters' Courses and Doctorates, as well as scholarships for EU nationals studying in third countries. From 2014 Erasmus Mundus was incorporated into the EU's **ERASMUS+** programme.

ERDF: See **European Regional Development Fund**

ERM: See **Exchange-Rate Mechanism**

ERTA **JUDGMENT**: See *AETR* **Judgment**

ESA: See **European Space Agency**

ESA: See **European System of Integrated Economic Accounts**

ESC: See **European Economic and Social Committee**

ESCB: See **European System of Central Banks**

ESF: See **European Social Fund**

ESFS: See **European System of Financial Supervision**

ESM: See **European Stability Mechanism**

ESPRIT: See **European Strategic Programme for Research and Development in Information Technology**

ESRO: See **European Space Research Organization**

ESTI is the European Solar Test Installation at Ispra, the **Joint Research Centre** (JRC) establishment in **Italy**.

ESTONIA joined the European Union (EU) on 1 May 2004. It is one of the smallest member states, with a population of some 1.3m. Following the collapse of the **USSR** in the early 1990s, the Baltic states of **Estonia**, Latvia and **Lithuania** immediately began to develop closer links with Western Europe and particularly the EU. The EU responded by providing technical (see **PHARE**) and financial assistance to Estonia. Relations with Estonia progressed swiftly from a **free trade agreement** to a **Europe agreement**, and then to preparations for eventual EU membership. Estonia applied for membership in November 1995 and participated in the first phase of **accession negotiations**, which began in March 1998. Negotiations were completed in December 2002, the outcome being approved by popular referendum nine months later. With a rate of participation by the electorate of just over 64%, two-thirds (66.8%) of voters supported accession. Estonia opted to approve the **Treaty establishing a Constitution for Europe** through the normal parliamentary process rather than holding a referendum, and the Government was determined to press on with **ratification**, even after events in **France** and the **Netherlands**. Estonia duly became the 15th country in the EU to complete the parliamentary stage of ratifying the draft European Constitution in May 2006. The text was approved by 73 votes in favour, with one vote against in the 101-seat parliament. Estonia became part of the EU's **Schengen Area** in December 2007. The Commission approved Estonia's application to join the **euro** after it judged that the country easily fulfilled the target criteria, and Estonia became a member of the **eurozone** from 1 January 2011.

ETF: See **European Training Foundation**

ETS: See **Emissions Trading Scheme EU**

ETSI is the European Telecommunications Standards Institute, set up in 1987 to harmonize European technological specifications and standards in the field of **telecommunications**. ETSI aims to harmonize standards in the European Union through the development of mandatory norms known as 'common technical regulations'. The Institute is based at the Sophia Antipolis technology park near Nice, **France**. In 2015 ETSI's budget exceeded €23m.

ETUC: See **European Trade Union Confederation**

EU: See **European Union**

EU FRAMEWORK PROGRAMMES: See **Research Framework Programme**

EU PATENT: See **Unitary Patent Convention**

EU WHOISWHO is the official directory of managers and services in the various European Union (EU) institutions, bodies and agencies, accessible online and in e-book and paper form.

EUA: See **European Unit of Account**

EUI: See **European University Institute**

EUMC: See **European Monitoring Centre on Racism and Xenophobia**

EUMETSAT is the European Operational Satellite Agency for Monitoring Weather, Climate and the Environment. It was established in 1986 and operates a system of meteorological satellites that monitor the atmosphere and ocean and land surfaces throughout the year. EUMETSAT formalized the co-operation between the national meteorological institutions, which began with the launch of the first European meteorological satellite in 1977, and took over the operational programme agreed upon in 1981. The information collected on the climate is passed to the National Meteorological services of the organization's members and affiliated members. Twenty-six of the European Union (EU) member states belong to EUMETSAT, which does not have formal links with the EU. Funded by the national authorities, EUMETSAT works in conjunction with the **European Space Agency** (ESA).

EURATEX is the European Apparel and Textile Confederation. It represents the European textiles and clothing industry on matters of common interest—that is 186,000 mainly small and medium-sized companies across the European Union (EU), employing some 1.8m. workers. Its main objective is to promote the interests of its members while taking into account the institutional framework of the EU and its international obligations. It resulted from the merger of various textiles and clothing organizations, including the Co-ordinating Committee for the Textile Industries in the EEC (Comitextil) in 1994. The EU is the world's second largest exporter of textiles and third largest for clothing, and the industry employs some 2.4m. people across Europe. Euratex is based in **Brussels**, close to the principal EU institutions and seeks to engage with the **European Commission**, the **Council of the European Union** and the **European Parliament** in all matters relating to the textiles industry. It has interests in various parts of the Commission's work and organization including trade, the environment, education, training, research and development, innovation and industry.

EURATOM: See **European Atomic Energy Community**

EUREKA is the acronym of the European Research Co-ordination Agency, a body established in 1985 in **Brussels**. It originated in an initiative by President François Mitterrand of **France** to establish a programme of non-military **research and technological development** that would keep the European Communities (EC) at the forefront in these fields. EUREKA was intended to be responsible for a European Programme for High Technology Research and Development agreed to by several European countries, including non-EC states. EUREKA is not an EU programme but an intergovernmental initiative of which the EU is a member. In 2017 EUREKA had 41 members (including all the EU member states), and others, including Monaco, **Montenegro**, **Norway**, the **Russian Federation**, **Serbia**, **Turkey** and **Ukraine**. EUREKA is more a sponsor of projects than a programme, and in that sense it overlaps with the activities of the European Co-operation in the field of Scientific and Technical Research (**COST**) programme. It has launched well over 100 separate transnational collaborative projects in a diverse number of fields, including factory automation, ceramic turbines, computers, lasers and robotics. It raises most of its funding from private sources or on the capital markets, since the EU and the member states of the Union make only relatively small contributions to its budget. To complement the activities of EUREKA the **European Commission** has created its own **research framework programmes** to foster research, and in 2000 it established the European Research Area (ERA) as a means of encouraging industry to invest more in research.

EURISTOTE is an online directory of university theses and studies on the theme of European integration.

EUR-Lex is a European Union (EU) database containing the contents of the *Official Journal of the European Union* (OJ) 'L' and 'C' series. It was to be extended to include all **legislation** in force, along with the treaties, proposals for legislation, and recent judgments of the **Court of Justice**. EUR-Lex is available online (in all the official languages of the EU), and is updated daily.

The **EURO** (€) was adopted in 1995 as the name of the common currency of the European Union (EU), and was to replace the **European Currency Unit** on a one-for-one basis at the start of **economic and monetary union** (EMU). By 1998, however, only 11 member states (the Euro-11) had agreed to proceed with EMU and adopt the euro on 1 January 1999. (**Greece** did not meet the **convergence criteria** at that time, although it joined in 2001, while **Denmark, Sweden** and the **United Kingdom** decided not to join.) On 1 January 1999 the conversion rates of the national currencies of the participating member states against the euro were fixed, and a single monetary policy implemented by the new **European Central Bank** (ECB) and the **European System of Central Banks** (ESCB).

The movement towards EMU and a single currency in the EU was slow. However, pressure from business and financial sectors within the EU forced governments to co-operate and to harmonize their approach to introducing a common currency. **Belgium** was the first member state to announce that its government departments would change to the euro. In all participant member states there was a transition period between 1999 and 2002 (by which time euro banknotes and coins were to have been introduced), during which national budgets were drawn up in national currencies, but payments by government departments were made in euros. From 1999 businesses were able to make social security contributions and pay taxes in euros. They were also able to establish capital in euros. Moreover, in participating member states, with the exception of **Germany**, tax returns were accepted in euros, and in most participating states people were also able to pay their taxes, including income tax, in euros. Financial markets were also to use the euro.

The three member states remaining outside the **eurozone** were to continue to work towards EMU. In 1998 Denmark retained the position it held during the **Treaty on European Union** (TEU) debate in 1992, remaining firmly opposed to the idea and the practice of the single currency. Despite broad support from government and business circles, the people of Denmark voted against Danish adoption of the euro by a narrow margin in 2000. Sweden held a referendum in September 2003, as a result of which it, too, elected not to join the eurozone. The British Government, although realizing that British business would participate in the eurozone to an extent, remained cautious about full participation and, combined with considerable public opposition to the euro, postponed indefinitely any plans for a referendum on the issue. **Slovenia** adopted the euro in January 2007 followed by **Cyprus** and **Malta** in January 2008. Following a positive recommendation from the **European Commission**, **Slovakia** joined the eurozone in January 2009. **Estonia** and **Latvia** adopted the euro in January 2011 and January 2014, respectively. **Lithuania** acceded to the eurozone in January 2015, bringing the number of EU member states using the euro to 19. The euro is also the sole currency in a number of small non-EU states, such as Andorra, **Kosovo**, Monaco, **Montenegro**, San Marino and Vatican City.

The euro entered its most turbulent phase from early 2010 when the financial difficulties and levels of debt in some states led several eurozone counties (most notably Greece, **Ireland**, **Portugal** and **Spain**) to introduce severe austerity programmes, which in turn led speculators to gamble on the stability of the euro and to test the determination of other eurozone states (most notably Germany) to come to the defence of these states. Among the emergency measures adopted were the **European Financial Stabilization Mechanism** and a **European Financial Stability Facility**. Subsequently plans were agreed for a more substantial **European Stability Mechanism** (ESM). For the first time in the euro's short history, serious doubts were raised about the durability of the euro in the context of a lack of a genuine economic policy across the EU and demands for some countries to be decoupled from the eurozone, notably Greece. Subsequent bailouts awarded to both Ireland and Portugal, and more specifically the crisis surrounding Greece's state finances, amid growing fears from 2011 about the country's ability to avoid default on its mounting debts, underlined the major challenges confronting the eurozone in maintaining a single currency for the participating member states. Cyprus received a bailout in 2013, and a new programme of lending was agreed with Greece in 2015. In August the Board of Governors of the ESM approved new lending to Greece, worth €86,000m. over a period of three years, to be disbursed in several tranches, according to Greece's fulfilment of promised reforms. A Memorandum of Understanding with Greece was also adopted, according to which the Greek Government agreed to implement further widespread economic reforms.

The **EURO-ATLANTIC PARTNERSHIP COUNCIL** (EAPC) is the forum in which members of the **North Atlantic Treaty Organization** (NATO) meet on a regular basis with representatives of its 28 partner countries to discuss political and security-related issues and develop co-operation in a wide range of areas. It replaced the **North Atlantic Co-operation Council** in 1997.

EUROBAROMETER is the name of a series of public opinion polls carried out and published on a biannual basis throughout all the member states of the European Union (EU) since 1973. The operation is the responsibility of **Eurostat**. A diverse range of topics is covered by the questionnaires used for polling purposes. These include questions on knowledge of the EU institutions, questions on the availability of information on the EU and questions on a range of EU policies. As well as providing profiles of the European population, the **European Commission** and its agencies use the Eurobarometers for planning purposes.

EUROBONDS were controversially proposed by the **European Commission** in November 2011 as a means of combating the European sovereign debt crisis. Government bonds are issued in euros by the states comprising the **eurozone**. The use of eurobonds would enable funds to be lent to the eurozone as a bloc, which would then have the facility to release funds to individual indebted governments, which would, thereby, secure access to lending with improved repayment terms, as they would benefit from the credit ratings of other, financially stronger, member states. However, the issue is a highly sensitive one and the German Government under **Angela Merkel** remained resolutely opposed to the issuing of Eurobonds.

EUROCODES are common codes for the European construction industry, which are intended to standardize and replace the different national specifications for materials, skills and personnel.

EUROCONTROL: See **European Organisation for the Safety of Air Navigation**

EURO COOP: See **European Consumer Consultative Group**

EUROCORPS is the name given to an integrated transnational military unit formally inaugurated in November 1992 following agreement at the 59th Franco-German summit in La Rochelle,

France, in May 1992. Its origins lay in a joint Franco-German brigade formed in 1987. Its supporters have argued that it could become the nucleus of a European army at the centre of a reconstructed **Western European Union** (WEU), and therefore a central element of security in the European Union (EU). In July 1993 **Belgium** indicated that it would join the Eurocorps. **Spain** agreed to contribute troops to the force in December 1993 and Luxembourg joined in May 1996. Based in **Strasbourg**, the Eurocorps became operational in November 1995. From May 1995 two new WEU bodies complemented it: Euroforce (based in Florence, **Italy**) and Euromarforce (a maritime force serving the Mediterranean), constituted by France, Italy, **Portugal** and Spain. Since Eurocorps' establishment, the EU has gradually taken over many of the roles of WEU as part of the development of a **European security and defence policy** (ESDP). Hence, in June 1999, at the Cologne meeting of the **European Council**, it was announced that Eurocorps would be put at the disposal of the EU for crisis response operations. It was subsequently decided that Eurocorps would become part of the **European Rapid Reaction Force**, a process that began in June 2001. Six countries participate in Eurocorps: Belgium, France, **Germany**, Luxembourg and Spain. There are currently five associated states: **Greece**, Italy, **Poland**, **Romania** and **Turkey**. The **Treaty of Lisbon** gave legality to Eurocorps and formally identified it as part of the EU's **Common Security and Defence Policy**.

EUROCRAT is a colloquial term used to describe a bureaucrat or administrator employed by the European Union.

EUROFER: See **European Confederation of Iron and Steel Industries**

The **EUROGROUP** is the informal council of ministers of finance and of the economy of the 19 member states participating in **economic and monetary union**. It held its first meeting in Luxembourg in June 1998. The group, sometimes also referred to as euro-X or Euro-12 group (before the addition of **Slovenia**, **Cyprus**, **Malta**, **Slovakia**, **Estonia**, **Latvia** and **Lithuania**), was conceived as a forum for policy co-ordination rather than **decision making**, which would continue under the aegis of what is now the **Economic and Financial Affairs Council of Ministers**, the monthly meetings of the finance ministers of the 28 full member states of the European Union.

EUROIZATION refers to the process whereby non-participants in **economic and monetary union** link their national currencies to the **euro** (€). Examples include **Montenegro** and **Bosnia and Herzegovina**.

EUROJUST is a European Union body charged with promoting co-operation among authorities in the member states dealing with the investigation and prosecution of serious cross-border and organized crimes. Established in 2002, it comprises a representative from each of the member states. (See also **police and judicial co-operation in criminal matters**.)

EUROKOM was set up as a teleconference and e-mail facility that would contain details of organizations and enterprises seeking partners in other member states for participation in projects of the **European strategic programme for research and development in information technology** (ESPRIT) and the European Research Co-ordination Agency (**EUREKA**).

EUROLAND, generally referred to as the **eurozone**, is an informal way of referring to those European Union member states (numbering 19 in 2015: **Austria**, **Belgium**, **Cyprus**, **Estonia**, **Finland**, **France**, **Germany**, **Greece**, **Ireland**, **Italy**, **Latvia**, **Lithuania**, **Luxembourg**, **Malta**, the **Netherlands**, **Portugal**, **Slovakia**, **Slovenia** and **Spain**) participating in full **economic and monetary union**, having replaced their national currencies with the **euro**. These states are also subject to the new rules established under the **banking union**.

The **EURO-MEDITERRANEAN ECONOMIC AREA** (EMEA) now generally referred to as the Euro-Mediterranean Free Trade Area, is the medium-term goal of the **Euro-Mediterranean partnership**. Based on the idea of the **European Economic Area**, this is a key element of the European Union's **Mediterranean policy**.

EURO-MEDITERRANEAN FREE TRADE AREA: See **Euro-Mediterranean Economic Area**

The **EURO-MEDITERRANEAN PARTNERSHIP** (EUROMED) lies at the heart of the **Mediterranean policy** of the European Union (EU). Often referred to as the **Barcelona Process**, EUROMED was launched in 1995 and involves the 28 member states of the EU and 15 non-member states in the Mediterranean region: **Albania**, Algeria, **Bosnia and Herzegovina**, Egypt, Israel, Jordan, Lebanon, Mauritania, Monaco, **Montenegro**, **Morocco**, the Palestinian Authority (now Palestinian Territories), **Syria**, Tunisia and **Turkey**. The three main components of the partnership are: political and security partnership; economic and financial partnership; and partnership in social, cultural and human affairs. Agreements have been concluded in a range of specific policy areas such as energy, the environment, media and migration. They are supported through finance from the **MEDA** programme. EUROMED was effectively re-launched in 2008 with the establishment of a **Union for the Mediterranean**.

EURONORMS or ENs, were originally standards produced by the **European Coal and Steel Community** covering the quality, dimensions, tolerances and methods of testing of steel, as well as providing a glossary of terms. The term was later also used for more general European standards set by **CEN** and **Cenelec**.

EUR-OP: See **Publications Office of the European Union**

EUROPA is the name of the main **European Commission** internet information site (europa.eu), which provides information on the institutions and activities of the European Union.

The **EUROPE 2020** strategy was launched by the **European Commission** in March 2010. The 10-year strategy was designed to help steer the **European Union** (EU) economy through and out of the economic crisis, encouraging growth and fostering innovation. It seeks to achieve more sustainable growth and a low-carbon economy. It set a number of specific targets, with aims that include seeing 75% of the population (people aged between 20 and 64 years) in work, getting 3% of EU gross domestic product put into research and development, and removing 20m more people from the risk of poverty. To this end, the strategy envisages a series of initiatives that include a new agenda for skills and jobs, the pursuit of a digital agenda (i.e. access to the internet for all), greater student and young professional mobility across Europe, and an EU platform against poverty. The **European Council** approved the Commission's strategy in March 2010.

EUROPE AGREEMENTS are types of **association agreement** and were concluded by the European Communities with countries in **Central and Eastern Europe** (CEE) subsequent to the latter's democratization after 1989. The first such agreements were signed in December 1991, and by mid-1995 agreements existed with nine countries (**Bulgaria**, the **Czech Republic**, **Estonia**, **Hungary**, **Latvia**, **Lithuania**, **Poland**, **Romania** and **Slovakia**). A further agreement was signed with **Slovenia** in June 1996, which came into effect in early 1999. Each agreement provided for free trade in industrial goods, political dialogue, wide-ranging co-operation and legislative **harmonization**. Bilateral institutions were also established to manage the association created. After concluding Europe agreements, each of the CEE countries went on to apply for membership of the European Union (EU). All except Bulgaria and Romania joined the EU on 1 May 2004; those two countries joined on 1 January 2007. When devising **stabilization and association agreements** for the countries of the **Western Balkans**, the **European Commission** drew heavily on the structure and content of the Europe agreements.

EUROPE BY SATELLITE (EbS) is the TV news agency of the European Union (EU). It was launched in 1995 and provides EU-related information for professionals working in television and radio and for other European institutions. EbS transmits via satellite a 'free to air' signal. It can be received in the EU, as well as the Mediterranean region and **Central and Eastern Europe**. For the rest of the world (**Asia**, Africa, Latin America, southern regions of the **USA** and north Australia), EbS provides an hour-long selection from its daily transmissions in collaboration with Canal France International. EbS is also available via the internet. The **European Commission** has long wanted to make much more of this resource, and sees it as a valuable tool in its communications strategy.

EUROPE DAY refers to 9 May 1950, the day when Robert Schuman, the French Foreign Minister, presented **Jean Monnet**'s proposal for the creation of a new European institution that became the **European Coal and Steel Community**. This date marks the birth of what is now known as the European Union (EU), and 9 May is observed as Europe Day. The day is marked at EU level by activities and festivities that are aimed to enhance the relationship between the EU and its citizens. Nevertheless, the date goes largely unnoticed. (See also **Schuman Plan**.)

The **EUROPE DIRECT INFORMATION NETWORK** was launched in May 2005 to provide a new means for the European Union (EU) to communicate with ordinary citizens. The information centres provide, among other things, brochures on how the EU works and takes **decisions** and also about EC laws, institutions and policies. The network is open to all member states and it has a presence, comprising a total of some 500 information centres, in every country in the EU. It also includes documentation centres at European universities and research centres.

EUROPE OF DEMOCRACIES AND DIVERSITIES was a group comprising a number of anti-European Union parties in the **European Parliament**. Formally known as the Europe of Nations group after the 1994 elections, it regrouped and renamed itself the Europe of Democracies and Diversities Group after the 1999 elections. Some 16 **Members of the European Parliament** belonged to the group. In 2004 the group was re-formed as the **Independence and Democracy Group** (ID).

THE EUROPE OF FREEDOM AND DIRECT DEMOCRACY GROUP (EFDD) is one of the newer **party groups** within the **European Parliament** (EP). The EFDD was originally established as the Europe of Freedom and Democracy (EFD) in 2009, but amended its name in mid-2014. The EFDD effectively replaced the **Independence and Democracy Group**, which collapsed when it failed to return enough **Members of the European Parliament** (MEPs) at the 2009 elections. Due to this loss it was not allowed to form a party group within the EP. Under existing EP rules, 25 MEPs are required from at least seven member states to form a party group. Membership of the EFD was a little fluid at the outset, but by March 2012 the group comprised 34 MEPs. After the 2014 EP elections the EFDD group emerged as the sixth-largest force in the parliament. In September 2016 the group had 46 members from eight member states. The two largest national parties within the EFDD are the **UK Independence Party** (UKIP—22 members) and the Five Star Movement from Italy (17). It also includes two independent representatives, as well as members from the Swedish Democrats (Sverigedemokraterna), and represents smaller **Eurosceptic** movements from the **Czech Republic** and **Lithuania**. The group also comprises one member each from **France** (from the Front National, who left the **Europe of Nations and Freedom**) and **Germany** (with one representative from the **Alternative für Deutschland**, formerly a member of the **European Conservatives and Reformists** Group). Initially, the EFDD also included a Latvian MEP, Iveta Grigule from the Latvian Farmers' Party, but she resigned from the group in October 2014. Her departure caused immediate difficulties for the EFDD, as it left it with representation from only six member states, when seven were required for it to be formally recognized as an EP party group. This crisis was short-lived, with a Polish MEP, Robert Iwaszkieswic, joining the EFDD four days later. The President of the EFDD is former UKIP leader Nigel Farage. The EFDD group contains some colourful personalities and has appeared to be adopting a more nationalist approach towards politics. It is set on placing stronger emphasis on anti-immigration as a core policy tenet of its activities than did its predecessor group. According to its political platform, the EFDD is committed to the principles of democracy, freedom and co-operation among nation states and welcomes co-operation among sovereign states, but opposes any further European integration and argues that any new treaty should be subject to approval by referendum across the entire European Union.

The **EUROPE OF NATIONS AND FREEDOM** (ENF) is the newest party group in the European Parliament (EP). Established in June 2015 and led by the Front National leader Marine Le Pen (of France) and the Dutch politician Marcel de Graaff, the ENF is a far-right, nationalist grouping. In mid-2017 Marine Le Pen left the EP, following her election as a member of the French parliament. At 2017 it comprised 39 members from **Austria**, **Belgium**, **France**, **Germany**, **Italy**, the **Netherlands**, **Poland**, **Romania** and the **United Kingdom**. The group seeks increased sovereignty for EU member states and opposes mass immigration.

EUROPE OF THE REGIONS is a phrase that came into common usage in the late 1980s. Those who wished local and regional authorities to have a greater input into the European Communities used this phrase. Many of them already maintained liaison offices in **Brussels, Belgium**. The establishment of the **Committee of the Regions** under the **Treaty on European Union** acknowledged its importance.

The **EUROPEAN AGENCY FOR SAFETY AND HEALTH AT WORK** (EU-OSHA) is a decentralized European Union agency, established in 1996 to promote the exchange of information and co-operation on measures dealing with **health and safety** at work. It is located in Bilbao, **Spain**. EU-OSHA played a central role in the EU's strategy for health and safety at work, and aims to reduce the number of work-related injuries and to work with governments, employers and workers to promote a risk-prevention culture, to collect and analyse new scientific statistics on risks at work, to share information and disseminate examples of good practice. EU-OSHA strongly supports smoke-free workplaces and many EU member states have implemented strong anti-smoking legislation.

EUROPEAN AGENDA ON MIGRATION: See **Migration and Asylum Policy**; **European migration crisis**; **Immigration Policy**

A new **EUROPEAN AGENDA ON SECURITY** was adopted by the **European Commission** in late April 2015 which outlined the principal actions required to ensure an effective response by the European Union (EU) to threats of terrorism and risks to security in 2015–20, as part of a reformed Internal Security Strategy, which was subsequently adopted by the **Council of the European Union** in mid-June 2015. In December action plans on firearms and explosives were adopted, followed in February 2016 by an action plan on strengthening efforts to combat the financing of terrorist operations. In April two communications were adopted, on information systems for border security and on combating terrorism and creating an effective Security Union. The ninth report on progress towards the creation of the Security Union was published in July 2017.

The **EUROPEAN AGRICULTURAL FUND FOR RURAL DEVELOPMENT** (EAFRD): See the **European Agricultural Guarantee Fund** (EAGF). The category of sustainable development and growth; natural resources accounted for 41.6% of the total 2014 budget of the European Union. Within this section some €13,991m. (23.6% of overall spending in this category) was directed towards the EAFRD.

The **EUROPEAN AGRICULTURAL GUARANTEE FUND** (EAGF), together with the **European Agricultural Fund for Rural Development** (EAFRD), replaced the **European Agricultural Guidance and Guarantee Fund** (EAGFF) on 1 January 2007. The EAGF forms the largest part of the European Union's budget heading within the category of sustainable development and growth; natural resources. The entire category accounted for 41.6% of the total 2014 budget. Within this section some €43,778m. (73.9% of overall spending in this category) was directed towards the EAGF.

The **EUROPEAN AGRICULTURAL GUIDANCE AND GUARANTEE FUND** (EAGGF): See the **European Agricultural Guarantee Fund** (EAGF)

The **EUROPEAN ANTHEM** adopted by both the European Union in 1986 and the **Council of Europe** in 1972 for use on ceremonial occasions, consists of the words of Schiller's *Ode to Joy* as set to music in the final movement of Beethoven's Ninth Symphony. The **Treaty establishing a Constitution for Europe** had been due to give it formal status, but the idea was abandoned during the negotiations that led to the **Treaty of Lisbon**.

The **EUROPEAN ANTI-FRAUD OFFICE** (OLAF), an independent office within the **European Commission**, has, since June 1999, been responsible for combating fraud against the European Union (EU) **budget**, corruption and serious misconduct within the EU institutions, as well as transnational organized crime and any fraud or illegal activity prejudicial to the budget. OLAF was established in April 1999 and replaced UCLAF (the Task Force for the Co-ordination of Fraud Prevention), created in 1988. In contrast to its predecessor, OLAF is empowered to examine the management and the financing of all of the EU's institutions (not just the European Commission). It also supports the EU institutions in the development and implementation of anti-fraud legislation. OLAF falls under the responsibility of the Commissioner in charge of Budget and Human Resources, **Günther Oettinger**. A Director-General of OLAF is appointed by agreement between the **European Parliament**, the Commission and the **Council of the European Union**. The current Director-General, appointed in 2011, is **Giovanni Kessler**. OLAF has completed almost 4,000 case investigations since 1999, which have enabled the retrieval of a total of around €1,300m. for the EU budget. In 2016 OLAF opened 219 new cases, closed 272, and recovered some €631m.

EUROPEAN ARMAMENTS, RESEARCH AND MILITARY CAPABILITIES AGENCY: See **European Defence Agency**

The **EUROPEAN ARREST WARRANT** (EAW) allows a person to be transferred from one member state to another without the judiciary having to go through a formal extradition procedure, where a person is wanted for criminal prosecution or for a custodial sentence. The Council Framework decision on a European Arrest Warrant was agreed on 13 June 2002 and came into force in January 2004. This law has been modified since, but has been judged a success. Since it became operational, there has been a notable rise in the number of requests from some 3,000 in 2004 to 15,800 by 2009. The issue of the EAW was more problematically received in the **United Kingdom**, and in 2012 the Government of **David Cameron** suggested withdrawing from 133 European Union police and criminal justice measures. In July 2013 the Government expressed a desire to apply only 35 of the measures under the EAW. However, in practice the UK was required to withdraw from all 133 measures, and then opt back in to its 35 preferred areas. Proponents of the EAW questioned this move as the EAW was deemed an essential tool (under the **Schengen Information System**—SIS II) to help counter cross-border crime as the members of the EAW share information.

The **EUROPEAN ATOMIC ENERGY COMMUNITY** (EAEC) is also known by its acronym Euratom. One of several sectoral organizations conceived by **Jean Monnet**, the EAEC was established in 1957 at the same time as the **European Economic Community**. With the entry into force of the **Treaty of Lisbon**, it is the only remaining 'community'. The aims of the EAEC are defined as promoting research and disseminating technical information; establishing uniform safety standards; facilitating investment and the establishment of the necessary basic installations for the development of nuclear energy; ensuring a regular and equitable supply of ores and nuclear fuels; preventing the improper use of fissile materials; exercising the right of ownership over fissile materials (mainly uranium and plutonium); developing wide commercial outlets; and working for progress in the peaceful uses of nuclear energy. The EAEC has experienced many problems, being from the outset somewhat overshadowed by other developments in the emerging European Union (EU). Technical problems, costs and worries about nuclear safety have hindered its work, and the EAEC has found it difficult to control and direct national developments.

However, EU **energy policy** has placed considerable emphasis on nuclear energy. In seeking to facilitate nuclear research, the **European Commission** has the right to insist that national programmes are co-ordinated in order to avoid unnecessary duplication of effort. It also undertakes regular reviews of nuclear research and indicates areas of possible future research. It was under the aegis of the EAEC that the **Joint Research Centres** and the **Joint European Torus** were established. Beyond research, the EAEC may also help states to acquire nuclear ores and materials: supply policy is administered through the EAEC Supply Agency. While bound by the obligations of professional secrecy, the Commission is entitled to receive details of all relevant patents sought or obtained in the member states. In certain circumstances, it may seek licences to use them through a compulsory purchase order, although this would probably be impossible to implement without the consent of the member state concerned. There have also been several initiatives on **health and safety** standards for workers in the industry. The Commission may also demand the imposition of extra precautions where particularly dangerous experiments are being conducted, especially if these may affect other member states. The task of the routine monitoring of nuclear installations is, however, the responsibility of the member states.

From its inception the EAEC was considered the least significant of the founding communities, and its identity and sense of autonomy essentially disappeared following its merger with the European Communities executives in 1967 (see **Merger Treaty**). Concerns about the safety of nuclear installations and doubts about their economic viability may well have been expected to reduce the significance of nuclear energy and the role of the EAEC, but nuclear energy has been resurfacing.

EUROPEAN AVIATION SAFETY AGENCY (EASA): See **Air Transport Policy**

The **EUROPEAN BANK FOR RECONSTRUCTION AND DEVELOPMENT** (EBRD) was established as a body, the purpose of which was initially to provide aid for countries in **Central and Eastern Europe** that had adopted a democratic form of government and had managed the transition towards stable market economies. A proposal from the French President, François Mitterrand, for the creation of such a body to assist these regions was accepted in December 1989 by the **European Council in Strasbourg**, which also agreed to the participation of other Western countries (something that had not been part of the original French proposal). The EBRD was sited in London, the United Kingdom and its first President was Jacques Attali, a close associate of Mitterrand. The bank began operations in March 1991 with a membership of European and other countries belonging to the International Monetary Fund (IMF), as well as the **European Communities** (EC, now the European Union, EU) and the **European Investment Bank** (EIB). The EC took a 51% stake in the enterprise, which set out to help eligible countries with market transition, privatization programmes, direct investment and environmental rehabilitation. In 1992 participation was extended to the successor states of the **USSR**. It was affected by scandal in 1993 when it was disclosed that it had spent more on furnishing its headquarters in London and on expense accounts than it had advanced in loans. In addition, there was a strong view that its establishment had been primarily a political gesture, since it could not provide anything the IMF and the International Bank for Reconstruction and Development (IBRD—World Bank) did not already make available. The scandal toppled Attali, who was replaced by Jacques de Larosière (1993–98). It was under the latter's tenure that the EBRD secured international credibility and began to see returns from its investments in Central and Eastern Europe. The EBRD has a subscribed capital totalling some €20,000m. and a triple-A credit rating. The EBRD has played a significant role in the redevelopment of some 30 countries, mostly the former Soviet states and countries of Central and Eastern Europe, but also countries in North Africa. Today the EBRD provides financing for banks, industries and businesses. As well as boosting economic transformation, the EBRD has promoted political change, with loans conditional on guarantees that countries apply the principles of multi-party democracy and are openly pluralist. By 2016 a total of 65 countries (as well as the EU and the EIB) had placed capital subscriptions with the EBRD and the EBRD was working in 29 countries in Europe and Central Asia. In 2006 the EBRD signalled that from 2010 it intended to shift funding away from the countries of the Baltic region and Central Europe and instead towards Armenia, Kazakhstan, the **Russian Federation**, **Ukraine** and Uzbekistan. Suma Chakrabarti became President of the EBRD in 2012, and was re-elected for a second four-year term in 2016.

The **EUROPEAN BANKING AUTHORITY** (EBA) was established in January 2011 as part of the **European System of Financial Supervision** (ESFS). It has been designed to exist as an independent European Union (EU) authority that is tasked with maintaining financial stability in the EU and to this end ensuring effective and constant prudential regulation across the entire European banking sector. The EBA took over all the former responsibilities and tasks of the Committee of European Banking Supervisors. Its main task was to help establish a European **Single Rulebook** for the banking industry, as well as to identify the potential risks and vulnerabilities in the EU banking sector. The first Chair of the EBA is Andrea Enria. He took up his post in March and is tasked with representing the EBA externally, and responsibility for chairing the EBA's meetings and preparing the work of its board of advisers. He is assisted by Adam Farkas, who became the EBA's first Executive Director in March, and is responsible for implementing the EBA's annual work programme and preparing the work of the management board.

EUROPEAN BORDER AND COAST GUARD: See **FRONTEX**

The **EUROPEAN BROADCASTING UNION** (EBU) is an international federation of broadcasting organizations formed in 1950 and based in Geneva, **Switzerland**. It has 73 active members in 56 countries, including all the member states of the

European Union. The EBU has encouraged collaboration and development within European broadcasting, especially in terms of increasing the European content of programming, but it has no authority over national broadcasting networks. It has collaborated with the **European Commission** on several initiatives. Its most recognizable broadcast, outside the sporting arena, remains the annual Eurovision Song Contest.

The **EUROPEAN BUSINESS AND INNOVATION CENTRE NETWORK** (EBN) is a **European Commission** initiative to encourage **small and medium-sized enterprises** (SMEs), and to ensure that they are able to benefit from European Union **competition policy** and the **internal market**. It is essentially an advisory body that disseminates information on innovations and ideas to companies. (See also **European Private Equity and Venture Capital Association**; **SME Task Force**; and **Business and Innovation Centres**.)

The **EUROPEAN CAPITAL OF CULTURE**, which was known as the European City of Culture until 1999, is one of the best-known examples of the fledgling cultural policy of the European Communities (EC). The programme dates from 1985 and is now funded as part of the EC **cultural policy**. It has subsequently become one of most keenly sought-after titles among cities across Europe. Cities and were formerly chosen by member states are given a subsidy by the **European Commission**. A new procedure was adopted in 2005 for selecting the capitals for the period 2005–19, in order to enable the new member states to participate. Recent Capitals of Culture include Umeå, **Sweden**, and Rīga, **Latvia** (2014); Mons, **Belgium**, and Plzeň, **Czech Republic** (2015); San Sebastián, **Spain**, and Wrocław, **Poland** (2016); and Aarhus, **Denmark**, and Pafos, **Cyprus** (2017). Upcoming Capitals of Culture were Leeuwarden, the **Netherlands**, and Valletta, **Malta**, in 2018; Plovdiv, **Bulgaria**, and Matera, **Italy**, in 2019; and Rijeka, **Croatia**, and Galway, **Ireland**, in 2020.

The **EUROPEAN CENTRAL BANK** (ECB) has long been held to be essential to **economic and monetary union** (EMU) as a body with powers to issue the European single currency (the **euro**) and control monetary policy for the 19 members of the **eurozone**. At its core the ECB is tasked with managing the euro and safeguarding price stability. Its origins lie in the **Treaty on European Union**, which confirmed that the ECB would come into operation at the beginning of the third stage of EMU, between 1997 and 1999. A **European Monetary Institute** (EMI) preceded the ECB. In 1993 it was agreed that the ECB would be located in Frankfurt am Main, **Germany**, and it was formally established in June 1998. The first President, appointed for a period of eight years, was Wim Duisenberg. He was replaced in July 2003 by Jean-Claude Trichet, formerly Governor of the Banque de France, who was, in turn, succeeded by **Mario Draghi**, the erstwhile Governor of the Bank of Italy, in November 2011.

Prior to the launching of stage three of EMU in January 1999 the ECB's capital was just under €4,000m. The national central banks of the member states are the only subscribers to and holders of the ECB's capital. The ECB Governing Council initially set the percentage shares of the national central banks of the member states in the ECB's capital in June 1998 (based on the member states' respective shares in the gross domestic product and population of the European Communities). They were subsequently revised, with effect from 1 January 2004 and were revised again following the 2004, 2007 and 2013 **enlargements** of the European Union (EU). According to the ECB, at 1 January 2015 the contributions of the national central banks of eurozone member states to the ECB's capital were as follows: **Austria** 1.9631; **Belgium** 2.4778; **Cyprus** 0.1513; **Estonia** 0.1928; **Finland** 1.2564; **France** 14.1792; **Germany** 17.9973; **Greece** 2.0332; **Ireland** 1.1607; **Italy** 12.3108; **Latvia** 0.2821; **Luxembourg** 0.2030; **Malta** 0.0648; the **Netherlands** 4.0035; **Portugal** 1.7434; **Slovakia** 0.7725; **Slovenia** 0.3455; **Spain** 8.8409; and **Lithuania** 0.4132.

The Governing Council of the ECB is the main **decision making** body of the Eurosystem. It comprises 25 individuals: all the members of the Executive Board of the ECB, as well as the governors and/or presidents of all the national central banks where the euro has been adopted. The Governing Council takes the most important and strategically significant decisions for the Eurosystem. When taking decisions on monetary policy and on other tasks of the Eurosystem, the members of the Governing Council are expected to act with mind to the overall economy in a fully independent capacity.

The Governing Council meets twice a month, usually on the first and third Thursday. Interest rate decisions are normally discussed at the first meeting of the month only. The President of the EU Council/**Eurogroup** and a member of the **European Commission** are entitled to attend these meetings but they do not have a vote. A simple majority determines votes and where a tie occurs, the President has the casting vote. Although the proceedings of the meetings are confidential, the Governing Council makes the outcome of its deliberations public, primarily those about setting the key interest rates. The number of staff of the ECB totals around 2,650 (in 2016) and it is truly European. It is worth noting that its members come from all 28 countries of the EU. In the early days, the EMI and the ECB recruited many staff from the national central banks of the EU member states, but now the ECB also attracts staff members from other sectors. Under the terms of the **Treaty of Lisbon** (Article 13) the ECB was upgraded to the status of an EU institution. A new, purpose-built headquarters in Frankfurt was completed in late 2014, and opened in March 2015. From November 2014 the ECB assumed a central role in supervising banks within the eurozone under the new rules of the **banking union**, as part of the **Single Supervisory Mechanism**.

The **EUROPEAN CENTRE FOR THE DEVELOPMENT OF VOCATIONAL TRAINING** (Cedefop) is a service agency of the **European Commission**, established in 1975. Originally located in Berlin, Cedefop relocated to Thessaloníki, **Greece**, in 1995. It is charged with the task of encouraging the development of vocational and in-service training for adults, and of standardizing national qualifications. It assists the Commission in the preparation of European Union training programmes. Much of its recent work has focused upon the **employment** problems of women, especially those who wish to return to work after a long absence. A council, consisting of representatives from the national governments, employers, trade unions and the Commission, directs its work. Cedefop is closely involved with the **European Training Foundation**, with **Eurostat** and with the **Lifelong Learning Programme**.

EUROPEAN CITY OF CULTURE: See **European Capital of Culture**

The **EUROPEAN COAL AND STEEL COMMUNITY** (ECSC) was the body that emerged from the **Schuman Plan**. It was established by the **Treaty of Paris** of 18 April 1951, which was effective from 23 July 1952 until 23 July 2002 when the ECSC was disbanded. One of the greatest difficulties during the negotiations between **France** and West **Germany** centred on the scope and content of the **competition policy** provisions and, specifically, French demands for further German decartelization, but agreement was finally reached. Formed by the **Six** European states (**Belgium**, **France**, the Federal Republic of Germany, **Italy**, **Luxembourg** and the **Netherlands**) that later went on to create the **European Economic Community** (EEC) and the **European Atomic Energy Community** (EAEC or Euratom), the ECSC had as its general objective the fostering of 'economic expansion, growth of employment and a rising standard of living' in the member states through the development of a common market in coal and steel. The common market would commence after a transitional period of five years.

The ECSC's historic importance lies in the fact that it was the first European organization to embrace **supranationalism**. This was represented by the executive High Authority, which was complemented as an executive by a Council of Ministers. Its indirectly elected Assembly, though possessing only advisory powers, was the first European assembly with a legally guaranteed basis. The other institutions of the ECSC were a **Court of Justice** as a final arbiter of the Treaty of Paris, and a Consultative Committee of representatives of national interest groups. This institutional framework was the model used later for the EEC.

The ECSC enjoyed some success in the 1950s, presiding over a large expansion in output, although this was as much the result of world economic conditions as of ECSC. However, it failed to cope satisfactorily with a major crisis in the coal industry in 1959 and to overcome the many barriers to the establishment of a common market. Moreover, it did not by itself make much progress towards political integration. One of its major problems was that it was difficult to achieve co-ordination and integration in only one economic sector; it was difficult, if not impossible, to isolate coal and steel from the national economies in general. This was a major reason for the switch by the Six from **sectoral integration** to the broader EEC.

With the establishment of the EEC and Euratom, the ECSC lost all its independent institutions except for its two executive bodies. In 1967 these were merged with those of the other two European Communities (EC). The ECSC continued, however, to have a semi-independent existence, with its own source of **revenue**, derived from a direct levy upon coal and steel producers, and its own **budget** out of which it financed development and restructuring plans for the industries. It also set prices and supervised production levels in the coal and steel industries. Much of its activity had to be devoted to helping remedy the severe social and economic consequences of the reduction in the workforces of both industries through early retirement schemes, retraining and redeployment, especially in those regions where these industries had traditionally dominated the local economy. The **European Commission** inherited the powers of the old High Authority over the coal and steel industries, powers which were much more substantial than in most policy areas of the EC, and used them to the extent of seeking the declaration of a state of manifest crisis, which gave the Commission even greater powers of direction and punishment. A state of manifest crisis was declared in the steel industry between 1980 and 1988.

The **EUROPEAN COMMISSION**, officially known as the Commission of the European Union (after the **Treaty of Lisbon**), was established as one of the two executive institutions of the European Communities (EC). As opposed to the then Council of Ministers (see **Council of the European Union**), which represents the member states, the Commission has been regarded as both the European, or supranational, and the administrative arm of the European Union (EU) executive. The term refers to the collectivity of, first, the College of Commissioners (currently 28 in number, including the executive head of this institution), and second, the administrative apparatus that serves them. The Commission employed a workforce of some 33,000 people in 2017. These were mainly based in **Brussels**, but some were in **Luxembourg**, in EU offices in member states, or in delegations to non-member countries. Others, primarily engaged in scientific projects, are located in centres throughout the EU.

Under the treaty base, the Commission was charged with bringing policy proposals forward and it holds the monopoly on policy initiation. It is also charged with operating as the 'guardian of the treaties'. In terms of supervision, the Commission was given a general responsibility to ensure that other EU institutions and the member states fulfilled those tasks and provisions assigned to them under the **founding treaties**. It had a duty to ensure that **decisions** taken by the Council and, increasingly the norm after 2009, by the Council and the **European Parliament** (EP) under the **co-decision procedure**, are carried out, or adhered to, by the member states. Most EU **legislation** is implemented, not at the EU level, but at the national level, and the Commission has a duty to see that legislation is implemented correctly and on time. If implementation does not occur, the Commission is empowered to bring the recalcitrant states before the judges of the **Court of Justice**, where fines can be levied against the states in question. In addition to these general areas of constitutional obligation, the Commission came to enjoy further and significant autonomous authority in the operation of the **common agricultural policy** (CAP) and **competition policy**. A further area of autonomy lay, after the 1967 **Merger Treaty**, in its inheritance of the substantial decision making powers of the previous High Authority of the **European Coal and Steel Community**, which gave it the right to act without regard to the Council of Ministers.

These 'constitutional' powers do not give a complete picture of the overall role acquired by the European Commission since 1957. The extent of its activities, along with its unelected nature, has made it the most controversial of the EU institutions. While during the **empty chair crisis** President Charles de Gaulle of **France** obstructed the original activism under the leadership of Walter Hallstein, events internal and external to the EU after the early 1980s contributed to a new dynamism on the part of the Commission, especially under the first half of the presidency of Jacques Delors (1985–95). The **Treaty on European Union** (TEU) made few constitutional changes to the Commission's role. Some of those changes recognized an extension of its competence, while others perhaps indicated a reduction in its independence (see below) as the powers of the EP were extended and the **European Council** became more of an agenda setter. Moreover, the **Treaty of Amsterdam** stipulated that the **European Parliament** must formally approve the President of the Commission. The Treaty also enhanced the authority of the President as the Commission prepared to review its organization and procedures prior to **enlargement**.

The Commission is also responsible for the financial management of the EU. It prepares the preliminary draft annual **budget** that must be submitted to both the Council of the European Union and the EP for approval and adoption. It is further responsible for the administration of the budget and the allocation of money from the budget to the **structural and cohesion funds**, other programmes and salaries. The TEU imposed more stringent controls and **accountability** on the Commission. A further responsibility is the representation of the EU abroad. It is the Commission that negotiates international agreements on behalf of the EU, and that maintains and staffs EU offices in other countries. Finally, because of its multifarious roles, the Commission has one further task. It has become widely regarded as the body that deals with the problems and issues that other EU institutions cannot or will not tackle. An activist Commission can seek to utilize this role to maintain the momentum of integration as has occurred in the past, for example, in relation to both the **single market** and the **single currency** initiatives.

The 28 Commissioners meet formally, as the College of Commissioners, once a week to discuss an agenda that has been prepared in advance. Additional and sometimes more informal meetings can be held to discuss general questions of European development, or more specific problems. If a majority of Commissioners are present, a meeting is considered to be quorate and a simple majority takes decisions. Once the Commission has taken a decision, however, its members are expected to abide by the principle of collective responsibility.

On assuming office, each Commissioner has to take an oath of loyalty to the EU, swearing that they will serve EU interests exclusively, and will not seek or take instructions from any national government or other body. Commissioners are appointed for a five-year term, which is renewable. The fact that about one-half are not reappointed for a further term suggests that Commissioners who act more independently than their governments might wish do not receive a further nomination. Most Commissioners have previously been national politicians, and normally belong to the party, or one of the parties, making up the government that submits their nomination. A few have previously been university academics, bureaucrats, industrialists or trade union leaders. There is no means of dismissal other than by a collective vote of censure in the EP. Since 1995 terms of office for Commissioners have begun after the election of the EP and coincided with the duration of the Parliament. Since 2004 each member state has been entitled to nominate just one Commissioner. In other words, **France**, **Germany**, **Italy**, **Spain** and the **United Kingdom** each lost a Commissioner. Membership grew to 28 following the accession of both **Bulgaria** and **Romania** in January 2007, and **Croatia** in July 2013.

Each Commissioner has a portfolio, which usually consists of several areas of policy responsibility, and which may not correspond exactly to the fields of activity of the **Directorates-General** (DGs) and the special services that together constitute the administrative arm of the EU. While the relevant sections of the bureaucracy report directly to the appropriate Commissioners, the latter have adopted the French practice of employing **Cabinets**, a group of personally appointed advisers and aides answerable solely to their Commissioner, providing him or her with assistance and liaising with other Commissioners and the various parts of the administration.

The EP can dismiss the Commission en bloc through a vote of censure. In January 1999 the EP's Socialist group (see **Group of the Party of European Socialists**) presented a censure motion, in order to ensure the Commission's accountability in the face of allegations of fraud, financial mismanagement and nepotism. Although a compromise deal ensured that the motion was defeated, concessions won by the EP during the dispute were widely felt to mark a significant reduction in the extent of the Commission's perceived autonomy. This was reinforced two months later, when an independent report into the allegations found considerable evidence of incompetence and corruption and, while detailing charges against several Commissioners, also judged the Commission to be collectively responsible for a 'dysfunctional' political environment, marked by a culture of evasion and an absence of leadership. On 16 March 1999 for the first time in its history, the Commission resigned en masse. The Commissioners retained their positions and exercised limited duties until a new Commission was appointed. The Treaty of Nice made a further significant alteration to rules pertaining to the **nomination procedure** for the Commission. Under its terms, the nomination of the President became a matter for the European Council acting by **qualified majority**, rather than unanimity. The Treaty of Nice increased the Commission President's powers to allow him or her to decide on how the Commission is structured internally; to enable him or her to allocate portfolios, and if necessary to reassign policy portfolios; and to enable him or her to demand the resignation of an individual Commissioner.

From 2014, under the terms of the Treaty of Lisbon, the heads of state and of government of the EU member states have nominated an individual for the post of Commission President. The EP must then elect the nominee by majority vote; if the Parliament fails to elect the nominated candidate, a new candidate must be nominated within a period of one month. The governments of member states then nominate the other members of the Commission, who must be approved by the European Parliament. In the performance of their duties, the members of the Commission are forbidden to seek or accept instructions from any government or other body, or to engage in any other paid or unpaid professional activity. Each member state is entitled to put forward one candidate as its prospective Commissioner. The Commissioners are nominated by the national governments but, since the **Treaty of Nice**, only after intensive consultation with the Commission President, who is chosen first and who will determine the policy portfolio for each Commissioner. Formally, governments submit nominations for approval by the Council of the European Union, but in practice each Commissioner-designate has to appear before the EP to answer questions about his or her aims and objectives over the next five years. The EP must take a vote to approve all 28 Commissioners. Strong opposition within the EP in respect of the competence of some individuals is increasingly sufficient to compel a Commissioner-designate to stand aside.

Before the TEU, the President of the European Commission was appointed by the Council of Ministers for a two-year term, but in practice this was automatically extended to four years, with Walter Hallstein and Jacques Delors serving even longer. Former Presidents of the Commission and the years of their appointment are as follows: Walter Hallstein 1958; Jean Rey 1967; Franco Maria Malfatti 1970; Sicco Mansholt (see **Mansholt Plan**) 1972; François-Xavier Ortoli 1973; Roy Jenkins 1977; Gaston Thorn 1981; Jacques Delors 1985; Jacques Santer 1995; Romano Prodi 1999. The **European Council** appointed José Manuel Durão Barroso President in 2004 and again in 2009, and the EP subsequently approved this appointment.

As mentioned above, the EP had been given the right to elect the Commission president and the EP signalled its selection of **Jean-Claude Juncker**, a former Prime Minister of Luxembourg, as its choice for the new Commission President (2014–19), following the success of the **European People's Party** at the 2014 EP elections. The EP's support for Juncker presented a new and seemingly unforeseen challenge to the **European Council**'s traditional role of choosing the Commission president. The European Council subsequently endorsed the EP's candidate in June 2014; 26 member states agreed to the selection of Juncker, with only the Prime Ministers of **Hungary** (Viktor Orbán) and the UK (**David Cameron**) voting against him. The EP formally approved Juncker in July. The European Parliament and the European Council endorsed the Commission selected by Juncker in late October, and the Juncker Commission took office on 1 November. Juncker has added some innovation in terms of structure to his Commission by allocating the Commissioners to clusters of activities and responsibilities. Thus, new 'Project Teams' were created, each headed by a Vice-President, and falling under the headings of: a connected digital single market; a deeper and fairer economic and monetary union; a new boost for jobs, growth and investment; a resilient energy union with a forward-looking climate change policy; and a stronger global actor.

The **EUROPEAN COMMISSION OF HUMAN RIGHTS** is a body established in 1953, which operates under the aegis of the **Council of Europe** in **Strasbourg**. Although it has no formal connection with the European Union, the latter accepts the principles that govern the operation of the Commission and acknowledges its role in the field of **human rights**, including the right to investigate alleged infringements of the **European Convention on Human Rights** by and within the member states. These can be brought before the **European Court of Human Rights**.

EUROPEAN COMMITTEE FOR ELECTROTECHNICAL STANDARDIZATION: See **CENELEC**

The **EUROPEAN COMMITTEE FOR IRON AND STEEL STANDARDS** (ECISS) is a body established in 1986 that replaced an Iron and Steel Nomenclature and Co-ordinating Committee. Its purpose was to replace national iron and steel standards with common European standards.

EUROPEAN COMMITTEE FOR STANDARDIZATION: See **CEN**

The **EUROPEAN COMMITTEE TO COMBAT DRUGS** (CELAD) is a group within the **TREVI** framework established in December 1989. The idea originated with French President François Mitterrand, who wanted to tackle the growing drugs problem in Europe. It was intended to follow up work carried out since 1971 by the so-called Pompidou Group of the **Council of Europe** on the promotion of collaborative measures within the European Communities (EC) and between the EC and other states and international organizations on drugs-related problems and issues, especially the illegal traffic in drugs, the monitoring of drugs that have a potential for being misused, and the prevention of the laundering of money gained from drugs trafficking. The Pompidou initiative had been purely intergovernmental, and outside the EC framework. Mitterrand's idea envisaged a specific EC angle, greater political co-ordination among the member states and a role for the Commission. Mitterrand's proposal led to the creation of the ad hoc European Committee to Combat Drugs group (CELAD) as a first step in this direction. Agreement on the **Treaty on European Union** (1991) provided the first references to drugs in the European Union (EU) treaty base and led to the creation of the **European Monitoring Centre for Drugs and Drug Addiction** (EMCDDA) in 1994.

EUROPEAN COMMUNITIES (EC) is a term that described the unified body that resulted from the merger in 1967 of the administrative networks of the **European Economic Community** (EEC), the **European Coal and Steel Community** (ECSC) and the **European Atomic Energy Community** (EAEC or Euratom). The term was also formerly used to describe collectively the signatories of the three Communities' **founding treaties** and their territories. The singular of the term (European Community) was widely used as an alternative for both meanings.

The main institutions of the EC were the **European Commission**, the **Council of the European Union** (known as the Council of Ministers until November 1993), the **European Parliament** and the **Court of Justice**. Under the **Treaty on European Union** (TEU), signed in 1992, the EC institutions became one of the then three **pillars** of the broader European Union (EU). Although European Union was subsequently the preferred term for the collective member states, it nevertheless remained correct to refer to the relevant institutions as the EC and to the law made by the Court of Justice as EC law.

Following the first **enlargement** beyond the original **Six** member states, the EC expanded progressively, and by January 2007 the EU had **Twenty-Seven** member states (**Twenty-Eight** upon the accession of **Croatia** in 2013). The **Treaty of Lisbon** replaced all references to the European Communities in favour of the term European Union. The EC as such ceased to exist, although Euratom continued to operate as the last remaining 'community'.

EUROPEAN COMMUNITY (EC) was the often-used singular of the term **European Communities**. Following **ratification** of the **Treaty on European Union** (TEU), it also became the official title of the **European Economic Community** (EEC). The **Treaty of Lisbon** replaced all references to the EC in favour of the term **European Union**. With the Treaty of Lisbon's entry into force, the EC ceased to exist.

EUROPEAN COMMUNITY ACTION SCHEME FOR THE MOBILITY OF UNIVERSITY STUDENTS: See **ERASMUS**

EUROPEAN COMMUNITY OF CONSUMER CO-OPERATIVES: See **European Consumer Consultative Group**

EUROPEAN COMMUNITY STUDIES ASSOCIATIONS (ECSAs) are nationally based academic organizations (from some 52 countries and with a membership of around 9,000) that support research on all aspects of the European integration process. The activities of the European associations are co-ordinated through ECSA-Europe, an umbrella organization largely funded by the **European Commission**. ECSA-Europe seeks to promote teaching and university research on European integration; to develop co-operation among its members; to encourage and manage transnational programmes of research and technical assistance; to foster networks of academic co-operation; and to disseminate information on university activities, especially through use of the internet. The representative organization in the **United Kingdom** is the University Association for Contemporary European Studies (UACES). The representative organization in the **USA** is the European Union Studies Association (EUSA).

EUROPEAN COMMUNITY TRADE MARKS OFFICE: See **Office for Harmonization in the Internal Market**

EUROPEAN COMPANY STATUTE: See **Company Law Statute**

The **EUROPEAN CONFEDERATION OF IRON AND STEEL INDUSTRIES** (Eurofer) brings together all the steel companies and national steel federations from across Europe to promote the interests of stainless steel. It represents more than 500 steel production sites in 24 European Union (EU) member states. The steel industry still represents a sizeable sector for the European economy and as a world leader employs about 330,000 people across the EU, producing an average 197m. metric tonnes of steel each year. It had an annual revenue of some €170,000m. Eurofer was created in 1976 and is based in **Brussels**. The initiative was taken by the **European Commission**, which hoped that such a body would be able to deal more decisively with a continuing crisis caused by decreasing demand for steel, poor productivity, an under-utilization of capacity, and the reluctance of national governments to accept mass redundancies. Eurofer was meant to work for a rationalization of the industry, assisted by the Commission, through reductions in output, to bring productivity and capacity more in line with demand. It had some limited success, but its voluntary nature could not persuade national governments always to follow its guidelines, nor could it prevent individual companies from taking unilateral action. Today, Eurofer continues to promote co-operation among national federations and companies in all matters concerning the development of the European steel industry. It organizes conferences and seeks to influence EU developments. It also represents the common interests of its members vis-à-vis third parties, notably the EU institutions and other international organizations.

The **EUROPEAN CONSERVATIVES AND REFORMISTS GROUP** (ECR) was established as a political group within the **European Parliament** (EP) on 22 June 2009. It is considered a moderately **Eurosceptic** party. The group owes its origins primarily to the British Conservative Party under **David Cameron**, who carried out his earlier promise to withdraw his **Members of the European Parliament** (MEPs) from what he considered the more 'Eurofederalist' stance of the **Group of the European People's Party**. As of September 2017 the ECR comprises 73 MEPs from 16 European Union (EU) member states and forms the third largest force within the EP. Of its members, 20 come from the British Conservative Party, together with 19 members from the Polish Law and Justice Party. The ECR believes that the creation of a non-federalist centre/centre-right group in the EP enhances European democracy. The leaders of the ECR group are Syed Kamall and Ryszard Legutko.

The **EUROPEAN CONSORTIUM FOR THE DEVELOPMENT OF FUSION ENERGY** (EUROfusion) was established by the **European Commission** in October 2014, superseding the **European Fusion Development Agreement**. Twenty-nine research organizations and universities from 26 EU member states, plus Switzerland, signed the EUROfusion consortium agreement in that year, with the objective of realizing fusion electricity by 2050.

EUROPEAN CONSTITUTION: See **Treaty Establishing a Constitution for Europe**

The **EUROPEAN CONSUMER CONSULTATIVE GROUP** (ECCG) was established, as the Consumer Committee, in 1995 as a successor to the Consumers' Consultative Council (CCC), a body that had been established as the Consumer Consultative Committee in 1973. The CCC had been active in forwarding opinions and proposals for action to the Commission. However, by 1995 it had 48 members, which meant that it found it difficult to co-ordinate the views of its disparate membership. A Consumer Committee, appointed by the **European Commission**, and consisting of 20 members, therefore replaced it. The Consumer Committee was rebranded the European Consumer Consultative Group (ECCG) in October 2003 and is the Commission's preferred forum for engaging with consumer organizations. It meets in **Brussels** four times per year. Membership is made up of one member from each of the European Consumers' Organization (BEUC), the European Association for the Co-ordination of Consumer Representation in Standardisation (ANEC), the Confederation of Family Organizations in the European Union (COFACE), the European Community of Consumer Co-operatives (Euro Coop), the **European Trade Union Confederation** (ETUC) and the Institut Européen Interrégional de la Consommation (IEIC—a grouping of regional bodies concerned with consumer affairs), together with two observers from **Iceland** and **Norway**, and representatives from member states. A senior official from the **Directorate-General** (DG) in charge of consumer policy chairs meetings. The Commission consults the ECCG, an advisory body, on proposed initiatives that may have a bearing on consumer interests.

EUROPEAN CONSUMERS' ORGANIZATION (BEUC): See **European Consumer Consultative Group**

The **EUROPEAN CONVENTION**, formally the **Convention on the Future of Europe**, and not to be confused with the **European Convention on Human Rights**, was launched on 28 February 2002 under the leadership of the former French President Valéry Giscard d'Estaing. It brought together representatives of the heads of governments and of the parliaments of the member states and the **candidate countries**, and representatives from the **European Commission** and the **European Parliament**, as well as a number of observers. In total there were 207 participants (including alternates) whose task was to debate the issues raised by the **Laeken Declaration** and formulate an agenda for the **intergovernmental conference** (IGC) that began work in October 2003.

The Convention was modelled on that which successfully drafted the **Charter of Fundamental Rights** in 2000, and was a response to growing concerns about popular perceptions of the remoteness of IGCs. Supporters of the Convention believed that it was more likely than an IGC to reach decisions on the future of the European Union (EU) that would accurately reflect the concerns and wishes of EU citizens. While this may have been a key assumption behind the launching of the Convention, the deliberations of the 207 participants failed to generate much popular interest. The same was generally true of the Convention's output, the **draft Treaty establishing a Constitution for Europe**, which was adopted 'by consensus' in June and July 2003 and forwarded to the **European Council**.

The **EUROPEAN CONVENTION ON HUMAN RIGHTS**, the full title of which is the European Convention for the Protection of Human Rights and Fundamental Freedoms, is a document sponsored in 1950 by the **Council of Europe**. It represents an unprecedented system of international protection for **human rights** and enables individuals to apply to the courts for the enforcement of their rights. It came into operation in 1953. All the member states of the European Union (EU) are signatories to the Convention and, in accepting it, the EU has also accepted the role and predominance in this area of both the associated **European Commission of Human Rights** and the **European Court of Human Rights**. The EU is not yet a signatory to the Convention, although concerns about its democratic credentials and the meaning of **citizens' rights** led to some pressure to accede. The EU drew up its own **Charter of Fundamental Rights**, which was proclaimed in 2000. Moreover, the **Treaty of Lisbon**, like the abandoned **Treaty establishing a Constitution for Europe**, contains a provision committing the EU to accede to the Convention.

EUROPEAN CO-OPERATION IN THE FIELD OF SCIENTIFIC AND TECHNICAL RESEARCH: See **COST**

EUROPEAN COUNCIL is the name used to describe meetings of the heads of state or government of European Union (EU) member states, their foreign ministers, and senior officials of the **European Commission**. It should not be confused with the **Council of Europe**, which is an entirely unrelated body, nor should it be identified too closely with the **Council of the European Union**. The **Treaty of Rome** made no provision for the existence of the European Council, and this created some lack of clarity about its constitutional position in, and relationship to, the European Communities (EC). The Treaty had stipulated the Council of Ministers (see Council of the European Union) as the only executive body in the EC representing the national governments. No provision was made for meetings of the heads of state or government, and the latter at first seemingly paid little attention to EC affairs, meeting on only three occasions during the first decade. The problems of the 1960s and the **Luxembourg Compromise** suggested that if the member states were serious about membership of the EC, then the heads of government, who ultimately controlled the Council of Ministers, should become more directly involved, particularly in order to give a strategic purpose to the EC on a range of issues where the normal institutional framework could not proceed without the consent of the national governments.

Four ad hoc **summit meetings** were held between 1969 and 1974. At the fourth, in Paris, the government leaders accepted 'the need for an overall approach to the internal problems in achieving European unity and the external problems facing Europe'; they agreed to a proposal from President Valéry Giscard d'Estaing of **France** that they should meet on a regular basis under the rubric of the European Council. The meetings would take place three times a year (amended in December 1985 to twice yearly) 'to ensure progress and overall consistency in the activities of the Communities and in the work on political co-operation'. The presidency of the Council would rotate between the member states, changing every six months, with the meetings being held in the capital of the country currently occupying the presidency, and the third meeting each year (until 1985) being held in **Brussels**. Further extraordinary sessions could be arranged, should circumstances demand it. The first meeting was held in Dublin, **Ireland**, in March 1975.

The principle of rotation emphasizes that all member states are equal. Despite the heavy workload that the presidency involves, it is particularly important for the smaller states since it offers them the opportunity to become a centre of European, and even world, diplomacy once every few years. All states treat the presidency seriously, and most have attempted to use their presidency to promote numerous potentially important initiatives. **Enlargement** of the EU since 2004, however, prompted consideration of moving away from existing practice and establishing a **President of the European Council** who would hold office for two-and-a-half years.

Before the **ratification** of the **Single European Act** (SEA), the European Council had no legal recognition within the EC. This suited the interests of the member states, since the more informal atmosphere gave them freedom to discuss broad questions of politics and policy without the pressure of having to come to a decision. The European Council became the only EC institution where such broad-ranging discussions could occur. Each meeting normally lasts for two days. Their informality is indicated by the fact that most meetings are not attended by large numbers of national officials and advisers. Only the foreign ministers accompany their leaders. The only other participants are the President of the European Commission, one of the Vice-Presidents and, since 1983, the Secretary-General. The European Council gatherings also provide an opportunity for informal discussion of more sensitive topics outside the scheduled plenary sessions.

The European Council has become central to the EU. Its emergence confirmed that nothing could be achieved unless the member states were in agreement, and virtually all the major advances since the mid-1980s have occurred because of European Council agreement on their desirability. However, its presence has sometimes hindered effective decision making at lower EU levels. Because ultimate authority rests with the government leaders, they have often been expected to resolve relatively minor issues, which other agencies were competent, but either unwilling or unable, to deal with.

The position of the European Council within the EC was acknowledged and regularized by the SEA. It is another version of the Council of the European Union, albeit the most senior. When the European Council takes policy **decisions** that conform to the constitutional requirements of the **founding treaties**, they have the force of EU **legislation**. More generally, European Council agreements are framed as general principles or a broad consensus on future action, which are then passed on to the European Commission and the Council of the European Union for further research, discussion and possible adoption. The **Treaty on European Union** (TEU) strengthened the role of the European Council further. It was directly responsible for the two new **pillars** of the EU: the **common foreign and security policy** (CFSP) and **justice and home affairs** (JHA). It is also the body to which changes in **economic and monetary union** (EMU) are reported and which puts forward further guidelines for EMU. The European Council's decisions have normally been taken on the basis of **unanimity**, although on a few occasions a vote has been employed to overcome the resistance of one or two member states. In 2002 new rules governing the organization and proceedings of the European Council were adopted to ensure its effective functioning in the new EU of **Twenty-Seven**. These effectively limit the duration of the meetings to two days, enhance the preparatory role of the General Affairs and External Relations Council, limit the size of each meeting and, as with formations of the Council of the European Union, strengthen the role of the presidency as chair.

Further change has also been introduced as a consequence of a declaration annexed to the **Treaty of Nice**. This stipulated that, as from 2002, one European Council meeting per presidency would be held in Brussels, and went on to declare that once the EU comprised 18 member states, all European Councils would be held in Brussels. In practice, formal meetings of the European Council have all been held in Brussels since the Italian presidency in the second half of 2003. The **Treaty establishing a Constitution for Europe** provided for the election by **qualified majority** of a **President of the European Council** to give greater coherence and direction to EU initiatives. This post was scheduled to last for a period of two-and-a-half years with the possibility of one further term. The same post and job description was written into the **Treaty of Lisbon**. Under this latest treaty, which came into force in December 2009, the European Council became a fully fledged EU institution in its own right. It did not gain any new powers, but was headed by the **European Council President**, Herman Van Rompuy (in office in 2009–14). On 1 December 2014 **Donald Tusk** replaced Van Rompuy as President; Tusk was re-elected in March 2017.

EUROPEAN COUNCIL PRESIDENT: see **President of the European Council**

The **EUROPEAN COUNTER TERRORISM CENTRE** (ECTC) was established as a department within **Europol** in January 2016 based in The Hague, the **Netherlands**. After lethal terrorist attacks in Paris, **France** in 2015 (which remained a target for acts of terrorism in 2016–17, together with **Belgium**, **Germany**, **Spain**, **Sweden** and the **United Kingdom**), in November 2015 EU justice and home affairs ministers urged the **European Commission** to augment its counter-terrorism capability. The ECTC is intended to become an enhanced centralized source of information for member states, to facilitate improved information-sharing and operational co-ordination between national law enforcement agencies, in combating terrorism. The ECTC is to have a focus on identifying and halting sources of terrorist financing, online terrorist propaganda and extremist material, and illegal arms trafficking, and prosecuting individuals considered liable to carry out terrorist attacks. The director of the ECTC is Manuel Navarrete Paniagua, a senior Spanish Guardia Civil officer, who has accumulated substantial counter-terrorism experience during his time at Europol.

The **EUROPEAN COURT OF AUDITORS** (ECA) was established in 1977, under the 1975 Treaty of **Brussels**. The European Court of Auditors scrutinizes the accounts of European Union (EU) institutions and any agencies handling EU funds in order to verify that they possess satisfactory financial management, with all revenue having been legally received and all expenditure properly accounted for. The Court is based in Luxembourg and publishes an annual report providing details of its activities and findings, which is presented to the **European Parliament** (EP) and the **Council of the European Union**. The EP analyses this annual report and needs to decide whether or not to approve the way in which the **European Commission** has handled the budget. Cases of fraud and other financial irregularities are passed to OLAF (the **European Anti-Fraud Office**).

The Court may, either on its own initiative or at the request of another EU institution, prepare other, more specific reports. The Court has in the past drawn attention to the existence of wasteful expenditure in several policy areas, and on a few occasions has found evidence of financial mismanagement. Its role has been important in forcing the EU institutions to improve their procedures and introduce more effective financial regimes. The **Treaty on European Union** elevated the Court to the status of an EU institution, with the consequent implications on legality and **decision making** authority. Its status was further enhanced by the **Treaty of Amsterdam**, which aimed to ensure better financial management of EU monies by introducing measures to curtail fraud, by extending the ECA's auditing powers to the then second and third **pillars**, and by giving it an additional right to refer cases to the **Court of Justice**. The ECA provides and audits all of the EU's revenue and expenditure. It examines accounts and produces a sound annual financial management plan. It also provides the EP and the Council of the European Union with a statement of assurance.

The membership of the Court consists of one individual from each member state, and the ECA had a total staff of around 1,000 in 2017. Prior to a **European Council summit meeting** in Nice, **France**, in December 2000 the Commission suggested capping the membership of the Court rather than allowing it to expand with each new accession. This view did not prevail at Nice where agreement was reached by the member states to maintain the current practice of requiring the Court of Auditors to consist of one member from each member state. It was generally assumed that having a national member would facilitate co-operation with the national audit offices. Appointments to the Court are made by the Council of the European Union for renewable six-year terms and, since Nice, by **qualified majority voting** on the basis of a list drawn up in accordance with proposals made by each member state. In practice, however, the Council simply endorses the candidates put forward by the member states. In making the appointments, the Council must normally select individuals who belong to, or have had experience of, the external audit departments of their own national administration. Exceptionally, individuals with other special qualifications may also be eligible for appointment. The Court elects its President from among its own members, for a renewable term of three years. In 2016 Klaus-Heiner Lehne succeeded Vítor Manuel da Silva Caldeira as President.

The **EUROPEAN COURT OF HUMAN RIGHTS**, which is based in **Strasbourg**, operates under the aegis of the **Council of Europe**. It hears cases concerning individuals and practices in those states that are party to the **European Convention on Human Rights**. Individuals or the **European Commission of Human Rights** may bring cases to the Court. All the member states of the European Union (EU) have ratified the Convention, and the EU has accepted the jurisdiction of this court in the sphere of **human rights**.

EUROPEAN COURT OF JUSTICE: See **Court of Justice**

EUROPEAN CURRENCY UNIT: See **Ecu**

The **EUROPEAN DEFENCE AGENCY** (EDA) was established in July 2004 to support member states' efforts to improve European defence capabilities in the field of crisis management and to sustain and improve the **Common Security and Defence Policy**. The EDA's principal functions relate to defence capabilities development; armaments co-operation; the European defence technological and industrial base and defence equipment market; and research and technology. It also provides a forum for defence ministers to meet. All the EU member states, with the exception of **Denmark**, participate in the EDA.

The **EUROPEAN DEFENCE COMMUNITY** (EDC) was an initiative based on the 1950 Pleven Plan (named after a former French premier, René Pleven). It was established by a treaty signed in Paris, in May 1952, by representatives of the **Six** states that had formed the **European Coal and Steel Community** (ECSC). Attempts to persuade other European countries, especially the **United Kingdom**, to join the venture failed. The origins of the EDC lay in the evaluation by the **USA**, as a result of the Korean War, of its global commitments, and in US demands for greater European support for the **North Atlantic Treaty Organization** (NATO), either by increased expenditure or through the rearmament of the Federal Republic of **Germany** (FRG—West Germany). However, no state was willing to consider increased expenditure, and none, apart from the FRG, really desired West German rearmament. The EDC was a device to permit rearmament without a separate and independent West German military contingent under national command. It also served a European purpose, being viewed as a further sectoral advance towards integration, with an institutional framework modelled upon that of the ECSC. Unlike the ECSC, however, it was not to be a partnership of equals: more restrictions would be placed upon the FRG.

The proposal provoked a great deal of opposition throughout the Six, but especially in **France**. No French government, fearing defeat, dared for some time to submit the treaty to a parliamentary vote. The French legislature finally defeated it on a technicality in August 1954, and the EDC project was abandoned. West German rearmament nevertheless took place on a national basis within NATO, supervised, at least implicitly, by the newly created but virtually non-existent **Western European Union** (WEU). At the same time, the collapse of the EDC was widely regarded as a major reverse for European integration. (See also **European Political Community**.)

EUROPEAN DEMOCRATIC ALLIANCE: See **Group of the European Democratic Alliance**

The **EUROPEAN DEMOCRATS** (DE) sit with the Group of the European People's Party in the **European Parliament**. (See **Group of the European People's Party (Christian Democrats)**.

EUROPEAN DEPOSITORY LIBRARIES: See **DEP**

The **EUROPEAN DEVELOPMENT FUND** (EDF) was established under the terms of the First **Yaoundé Convention** of 1963, and was retained in the subsequent **Lomé Convention** between the European Communities (EC) and the **African, Caribbean and Pacific** (ACP) **States**. It was set up to provide grants to the ACP States for development programmes, focusing after 1984 on rural and agricultural projects, and on broad integrated development programmes. As the member states were signatories of the 1963 Convention in their own right, and as they are eager to control spending in this area, the EDF is not included in the development section of the European Union (EU) **budget**, much to the dissatisfaction of many in the **European Parliament**. Under the **Cotonou Agreement** (which expires in 2020), the EDF was allocated €13,500m. for 2000–07. The 10th EDF, for 2008–13, was allocated €22,682m., of which €21,966m. was for the ACP countries. (See also **Development Aid**.) In 2011 the **European Commission** put forward a number of new proposals that would determine the future direction of the EDF. In negotiating the 11th EDF the Commission sought to maintain the EDF as a separate fund outside the EU budget; to increase the overall amount by some 13%, to €30,300m.; and to improve the democratic scrutiny of the EDF. In the agreement for the new financial perspective (2014–20) some €6,500m. was allocated towards the 11th EDF.

EUROPEAN DOCUMENTATION CENTRES (EDCs) are information centres that contain European Union (EU) documentation. Their function is to stimulate the development of European studies in academic institutions and to provide an information service on the EU to the public. They are usually based in university libraries, and can also be found in non-EU countries. (See also **Europe Direct Information Network**.)

The **EUROPEAN ECONOMIC AND SOCIAL COMMITTEE** (EESC), which was also known by the alternative acronyms of ESC and ECOSOC, is not to be confused with the **United Nations** Economic and Social Council, which also uses the abbreviation ECOSOC. It was one of the main European Communities (EC) bodies set up by the **Treaty of Rome**. It was established as a non-political body that enables those active in economic and social fields to voice opinions on EC policy formulation. It has a purely advisory function, but the **European Commission** and the **Council of the European Union** are mandated to consult it on a wide range of issues before they can arrive at a **decision**. The **Single European Act** and the **Treaty on European Union** extended the areas on which it had to be consulted (to environmental and regional issues). In practice, both the Council and the Commission have consulted the EESC on a number of other non-mandatory topics, though they do not always heed its advice. The **Treaty of Amsterdam** also allows for the EESC to be consulted by the **European Parliament**. The **Treaty of Lisbon** reinforced the position of the EESC in the overall EU architecture as a bridge between civil society and the European Union (EU) institutions. It gave the EESC the right to be consulted by the Commission on a new range of policy areas, such as sport, research and energy. The treaty also strengthens the EESC's consultative role vis-á-vis the European Parliament.

Its membership, which is drawn from national interest groups throughout the member states, increased from 222 to 317 with **enlargement** on 1 May 2004, and to 344 after the arrival of **Bulgaria** and **Romania** on 1 January 2007. The members are appointed for a four-year period, which is renewable. After **Croatia** joined the EU on 1 July 2013 the EESC expanded to 353 members. In the enlarged body, until late 2015, **Germany**, **France**, **Italy** and the **United Kingdom** each had 24 members; **Spain** and **Poland** 21 each; Romania had 15; **Belgium**, Bulgaria, the **Czech Republic**, **Greece**, **Hungary**, the **Netherlands**, **Portugal**, **Austria** and **Sweden** had 12 each; Croatia, **Denmark**, **Finland**, **Ireland**, **Lithuania** and **Slovakia** nine each; **Estonia**, **Latvia** and **Slovenia** seven each, **Cyprus** and **Luxembourg** six each, and **Malta** five. The membership was reduced to 350 for the current term, with Estonia's representation reduced to six members, and those of Cyprus and Luxembourg reduced to five. The President for 2015–18 is Georges Dassis from Greece. Each national delegation consists of three separate categories: workers, employers and a miscellany of other groups such as farmers, consumers and the self-employed. Members are nominated by national governments, normally after consultation with the major national interest groups, and appointed by the Council of the European Union. The Committee elects its own chair for a period of two years, and it is conventional for the role to rotate between the three categories of membership. Participation in the EESC is a part-time commitment, and appointees are expected to be granted time off from their employment to attend meetings. Much of its work is done in specialized working groups, which correspond to the major policy concerns of the EU. The groups provide draft opinions for approval in a plenary session of the Committee. The EESC can be divided into six main areas of interest and activity. These relate to agriculture, rural development and the environment; **economic and monetary union** and economic and social cohesion; **employment**, social affairs and **citizenship**; external relations; the **single market**, production and consumption; and finally, transport, energy, infrastructure and the **information society**. The EESC has often been divided between left and right, between workers and employers, on many social and economic questions. How effective it has been in directly influencing proposed EU **legislation** is debatable. Both the Commission and the Council have often sidelined its relevance, as the former prefers to deal directly with sectoral organizations.

Critics would argue that the impact of the EESC has been rather limited. It can be seen as representing an attempt at fostering a type of corporatist interest intermediation that suited the 1950s environment. More than 50 years later its influence has waned to a large degree, as many of the groups it seeks to represent have established more direct means to influence policy formulation. Nevertheless, it still has an important role in the formal EU policymaking process. Both the Commission and the Council are obliged to consult the EESC in certain cases. Later treaties from the **Single European Act** onwards have extended the range of issues that must be referred to the Committee, in particular new policy areas such as regional and **environmental policy**. The EESC can also adopt its own opinions. On average the EESC delivers 170 advisory documents and opinions a year (of which about 15% are issued on its own initiative). All opinions are forwarded to the EU's main decision making institutions and are published in the *Official Journal of the European Union*.

The **EUROPEAN ECONOMIC AREA** (EEA) is a trading area agreed upon in 1991 by the European Communities (EC) and members of the **European Free Trade Association** (EFTA). It was a consequence of fears by the EFTA countries that the development of the **internal market** might negatively affect their own economies. In 1989 they agreed upon a joint approach to the EC, using the phrase European Economic Space to describe the kind of structured partnership they wanted. Negotiations began in June 1990, and were completed by November 1991, largely upon EC terms, with an agreement on participation in the internal market. **Ratification** was delayed because of a query by the **Court of Justice** (ECJ) about the constitutional compatibility with the **founding treaties** of the proposed arbitration procedures. This led to the EFTA states having to create their own EFTA court and greater powers being placed in the hands of the ECJ. A referendum in **Switzerland** in 1992 rejected involvement in the EEA, and it came into existence without Swiss participation in January 1994. Although **Liechtenstein** had voted to join the EEA in a referendum held one week after the Swiss vote, the nature of its **customs union** with Switzerland made participation in the EEA problematic. When a number of necessary modifications had been made to the customs union, Liechtenstein voted again to join the EEA, in a second referendum held in April 1995. By this time, the EEA had lost three of its EFTA members, **Austria**, Finland and Sweden having joined the **European Union** (EU) on 1 January 1995. Indeed, from a positive perspective the EEA helped pave the way for their accession. However, the departure of these countries from EFTA turned the EEA into a rather more minor economic arrangement than the one originally envisaged. Despite expectations to the contrary, the EEA has survived and continues to expand its scope. It has therefore provided an adequate basis for relations between the EU and three of the most economically developed European non-EU states (**Iceland**, **Liechtenstein** and **Norway**). The EEA was one potential option for the **United Kingdom**, following the referendum vote by the British electorate in June 2016 in favour of leaving the EU (see **Brexit**).

EUROPEAN ECONOMIC COMMUNITY (EEC) was the official title of the organization established by the **Treaty of Rome** in 1958. The administrative network of the EEC was formally merged with that of the **European Coal and Steel Community** (ECSC) and the **European Atomic Energy Community** (EAEC or Euratom) in July 1967, after which the three bodies were collectively known as the European Communities or European Community (EC), although the abbreviation EEC remained in common usage, somewhat erroneously, to describe the Communities collectively. It also often carried a political connotation, being used by people who wished to emphasize that the EC should remain an economic organization without any implications of political union. The **Treaty on European Union** (TEU) confirmed that the EEC would in future be referred to as the European Community, and the founding Treaty of Rome was amended accordingly. The **Treaty of Lisbon** replaced the term European Community with the term **European Union**.

The **EUROPEAN ECONOMIC INTEREST GROUPING** (EEIG) is an arrangement established to enable European companies to collaborate more effectively on possible joint projects and enterprises. These EEIGs are not companies, but vehicles to allow individual companies to work together. They are legal entities in their own right and there are specific rules pertaining to their creation. The EEIG falls under the European Union's (EU) single market strategy and is designed to create more competitive consortia. One example of an EEIG is **Airbus**. Another is the creation of the Franco-German television channel *Arte*. An EEIG provides a legal structure for companies of different member states to link their activities while retaining economic and legal independence. Several thousand EEIGs were established in a variety of areas. The Regie initiative promotes EEIGs.

EUROPEAN ECONOMIC SPACE: See **European Economic Area**

EUROPEAN EMPLOYMENT STRATEGY: Each year, the **European Council** agrees on a series of guidelines setting out common priorities and individual objectives for member states' **employment** policies. The overall aims include creating jobs, improving job quality, making it easier for people to balance the demands of work and personal life, promoting active ageing and ensuring that race, gender or disabilities do not limit opportunities for employment in the formal economy.

Each EU government produces its own annual action plan describing how it is putting the guidelines into practice. Progress is measured against some 100 indicators, ranging from basic economic figures (e.g. gross domestic product—GDP—growth and unemployment levels) to the availability of career breaks and childcare.

EUROPEAN ENERGY CHARTER is the name of a document inspired by the European Communities (EC) and signed at The Hague in December 1991 by 38 countries. Its purpose was to make European energy supplies more secure by linking the natural resources of Eastern Europe with the West through a grid of supply lines. In return, Eastern Europe would receive investment from Western countries, and the EC proposed to extend the Organization of the Promotion of Energy Technology (OPET) scheme for the international transfer of energy-efficient and environmentally friendly technologies to Eastern Europe and the **Commonwealth of Independent States** (CIS). A further objective was to strengthen the Eastern democracies by easing their balance of payments problems, and to offer the **Russian Federation** an alternative to membership of the petroleum producers' **cartel**, the Organization of Petroleum Exporting Countries (OPEC). The wider aim of the Charter was the creation of a legally binding document, the Energy Charter Treaty. This Treaty aimed to enhance East-West industrial co-operation through a number of legal guarantees concerning investments, transit and trade. In December 1994 all signatories of the 1991 agreement, with the exception of Canada and the **USA**, signed the Energy Charter Treaty and the Energy Charter Protocol. There are 66 signatory states (plus the EU and **Euratom**), including all EU members, most European countries, including Russia, and the **USA**. In May 2015 72 countries plus the EU, Euratom and the Economic Community of West African States signed the International Energy Charter, a document based on the European Energy Charter and intended to make global energy supplies more secure, at a ministerial conference hosted by the government of the **Netherlands**.

The **EUROPEAN ENVIRONMENT AGENCY** (EEA) was established in May 1990 by the European Communities (EC) to collect and disseminate detailed information on environmental questions and problems, including air quality, water quality, state of the soil, land use, waste management, noise emissions and coastal erosion. Membership of this body is open also to non-European Union (EU) states. **France** blocked its inauguration because of its dispute with the EC over the future permanent location of the **European Parliament** and controversy over the siting of other European agencies. In November 1993, however, it was agreed that the EEA would be located in Copenhagen. The agency was the first EU body to have members from the 13 **candidate** states. Membership totals 33 countries, comprising the EU member states plus **Iceland, Liechtenstein, Norway, Switzerland** and **Turkey**.

The **EUROPEAN EXTERNAL ACTION SERVICE** (EEAS) was formally established in December 2010 following the entry into force of the **Treaty of Lisbon** in December 2009. The EEAS can be viewed as an embryonic European Union (EU) Ministry of Foreign Affairs, which seeks to work in close co-operation with the diplomatic services of the EU member states. It assists the **High Representative of the Union for Foreign Affairs and Security Policy** and is staffed by a mix of officials from the **European Commission**, the **Council Secretariat** and seconded diplomats from the member states. The first High Representative was Baroness Catherine Ashton, who was replaced in late 2014 by **Federica Mogherini**. In July 2016 Mogherini presented a new EU Global Strategy on Foreign and Security Policy, which acknowledged the changing security environment and sought to increase the efficacy of the EEAS in responding to issues such as energy security, migration, environmental concerns and terrorism. The Global Strategy stated that when united the joint resources of EU member states were 'unparalleled', thereby providing enormous potential for the EEAS to contribute to peace and security both regionally and worldwide.

The **EUROPEAN FEDERALIST MOVEMENT** has been the main proponent of the federalist ideal for Europe since the 1950s. Altiero Spinelli, who largely inspired it, led the movement until 1962. It had little impact upon European developments, although, thanks to Spinelli, some of its ideas were found in the **draft Treaty establishing the European Union**.

The **EUROPEAN FIGHTER AIRCRAFT PROGRAMME** was the first major joint European armaments project, although it was not a European Union project. It consisted of an agreement in 1985 by the arms procurement directors of **Germany**, **Italy**, **Spain** and the **United Kingdom** to work collectively towards the development of a replacement for aircraft that would be obsolete by the mid-1990s. The first aircraft were scheduled to be in service by 1997, but rising costs, technical problems, and the lower priority given to defence after the ending of the **Cold War** created doubts about the programme's viability and necessity. After 1992 the programme was scaled down in size and renamed the Eurofighter—Typhoon 2000 project. The first orders were placed in 1998. The project has proved very successful for the European aerospace industry and is, to date, Europe's largest military collaborative programme. Many regard the Eurofighter Typhoon as one of the world's most advanced fighter aircraft.

The **EUROPEAN FILM DISTRIBUTION OFFICE** (EFDO) was established under the MEDIA programme (see **Media Policy**) to sponsor and help to market European-produced films. The Office is based in Lisbon, **Portugal**.

The **EUROPEAN FINANCIAL STABILITY FACILITY** (EFSF) was established to provide emergency financial assistance to member states of the **eurozone** encountering financial difficulties. Agreed by eurozone member states in May 2010, it subsequently issued loans to **Ireland** and **Portugal**. EFSF loans were originally supported by eurozone member states (€440,000m.), the **European Financial Stabilization Mechanism** (€60,000m.) and the **International Monetary Fund** (€250,000m.). The permanent **European Stability Mechanism** (ESM) largely superseded the temporary facility, the EFSF. The EFSF was placed under the management of ESM personnel, and although it will not accept new country programmes, the Facility remains active for the purpose of financing existing loans.

The **EUROPEAN FINANCIAL STABILIZATION MECHANISM** (EFSM) was established as an emergency funding mechanism, allowing the **European Commission** to raise funds, up to a total of €60,000m., from financial markets to assist, via loan or credit guarantee, European Union (EU) member states experiencing or approaching serious financial difficulties. In raising funds, the European Commission has used the EU **budget** as collateral. The EFSM was activated for loans issued to both Ireland and Portugal in 2011–14. From 2013 members of the eurozone in need of financial assistance were able to make use of a new, permanent European institution, the **European Stability Mechanism**. The EFSM programme, managed by the Commission, remains available for specific tasks (such as bridging loans). For example, in July 2015 the EFSM was used to provide short-term lending of €7,160m. to Greece.

The **EUROPEAN FISHERIES FUND** (EFF) replaced the **Financial Instrument for Fisheries Guidance** (FIFG) on 1 January 2007. The scheme ran for the duration of the financial perspective to 2013 and had a budget of some €4,300m. The fund had many echoes of its predecessor. The EFF targeted five priority areas: the adaptation of the European Union (EU) fishing fleet; aquaculture, inland fishing, and processing and marketing of the products of fishing and aquaculture; measures of collective benefit; sustainable development of fisheries areas; and technical assistance to facilitate the delivery of aid. The fund was designed to assist the industry as it adapts its fleet to make it more competitive, and to encourage measures to protect and enhance the environment. As before, the fund sought to help the fisheries communities most affected by the changes by assisting them to diversify where possible. The fund existed to facilitate and support the major objectives of the **common fisheries policy** (CFP). This included, in particular, the sustainable exploitation of fisheries resources and achieving a stable balance between these resources and the capacity of the EU fishing fleet, as well as strengthening the **competitiveness** and viability of operators in the sector and fostering the sustainable development of fisheries areas.

A number of new and innovative measures were introduced to take account of the changing needs of the sector, including measures to encourage selective fishing methods and an emphasis on the sustainable development of fisheries areas. **Implementation** of the fund was considerably simplified. Whereas FIFG support for fisheries was divided among different programmes in a member state, there was a single EFF programme for each member state. A **European Maritime and Fisheries Fund** replaced the EFF from January 2014.

A **EUROPEAN FLAG** was adopted by the European Communities (EC) in 1986. Its design is a crown of 12 five-pointed stars set against an azure background. It is the same flag as that used by the **Council of Europe** since 1955; hence it was merely coincidental that the number of stars on the flag corresponded to the membership of the EC from 1986 to 1994. The stars were placed in a circle to represent the union of the European states. The flag is flown over the European Union (EU) headquarters in **Brussels**, and is otherwise used at national and international meetings and ceremonies where the EU is represented.

The **EUROPEAN FOOD SAFETY AUTHORITY** (EFSA) was established in Parma, **Italy**, in 2002 following various food safety scares in the 1990s, notably BSE (see **Bovine Spongiform Encephalopathy**). Its purpose is to provide independent scientific advice on all matters linked to food and feed safety, including animal health and welfare, and plant protection. It also provides scientific advice on nutrition in relation to EU **legislation**. (See also **Foodstuffs**.)

EUROPEAN FOUNDATION FOR THE IMPROVEMENT OF LIVING AND WORKING CONDITIONS (EUROFOUND) is the name of a **European Commission** agency established in 1975 and now based in Dublin, **Ireland**. It holds a broad mandate to provide information, advice and expertise—on the living and working environment of employees, industrial relations and managing change in Europe—for principal actors in the field of European Union (EU) social policy. Given the deteriorating economic situation following the onset of the global recession in 2008, Eurofound was particularly keen to place emphasis on measures to help create jobs and increase **competitiveness**, initiatives to help the young, and moves to reduce poverty and social exclusion. Eurofound appreciates that public sector reform will be a major issue to be dealt with over the next decade. The Foundation is staffed by representatives of the Commission, the member states and employers' and employees' organizations.

The **EUROPEAN FREE ALLIANCE** (EFA/ALE) forms part of the **Group of the Greens/European Free Alliance** in the **European Parliament**. It is made up of representatives of 'stateless nations' such as Wales (part of the **United Kingdom**) and Catalonia (officially part of **Spain**).

The **EUROPEAN FREE TRADE ASSOCIATION** (EFTA) was established by the **Stockholm Convention** of 4 January 1960. It consisted of seven states—**Austria**, **Denmark**, **Norway**, **Portugal**, **Sweden**, **Switzerland** and the **United Kingdom**—which were unwilling or, for various reasons, unable to accept the supranational and **common market** principles of the **Treaty of Rome** and the **European Economic Community** (EEC). EFTA's objectives were limited to securing a gradual elimination of **tariffs** on trade in most industrial goods between its members. It did not have an agricultural policy or any kind of **common external tariff** (CET), and its institutional structure was to be limited to a Council of Ministers which would meet only two or three times a year, although a council of heads of national delegations was to meet every two weeks. It brought together a disparate group of countries, which had reached consensus on two principal issues. First, they agreed on a rejection of the sequence of events postulated by the Treaty of Rome, apart from the establishment of a free trade area. Second, they believed that some form of unity would place them in an advantageous position vis-à-vis the EEC compared with the position they would be in if each country separately attempted to negotiate some accommodation with it.

Within its limited terms of reference, EFTA established its free trade area fairly quickly. After the late 1960s, it collaborated quite closely with the European Communities (EC). When **Denmark** and the UK joined the EC in 1973, they left EFTA. The remaining EFTA states, which now also included **Iceland** and **Liechtenstein**, with **Finland** as an associate, negotiated a series of **free trade agreements** with the EC, which came into force in 1973. With some variations from country to country, these agreements provided for the gradual introduction of free trade in industrial goods (but not in agriculture). The relationship was the province of a joint EC–EFTA executive committee meeting twice yearly. While the EFTA states avoided the obligations of full EC membership, the disadvantage was that they were not party to EC **decisions**, many of which had an important effect upon their own economies. The arrangement, however, worked quite well, and by the 1980s EFTA had moved very close to the EC in its economic practices.

In the late 1980s, the EFTA states felt obliged to review their situation in the light of the **Single European Act** and the EC decision to establish an **internal market**. In 1989 the creation of a broad European Economic Space was proposed, which, after protracted negotiations, came into being, albeit without Switzerland's participation, as the **European Economic Area** (EEA) in 1994. However, the EFTA states began to conclude that even EEA membership would leave them at a disadvantage and thus

Austria, Finland, Norway and Sweden all applied for membership of the EC. In January 1995 Austria, Sweden and Finland joined the European Union (EU), Norway having withdrawn its application following a referendum result that rejected EU membership. EFTA was left as a rump (comprising Iceland, Liechtenstein, Norway and Switzerland). The Association has nevertheless survived.

The **EUROPEAN FUSION DEVELOPMENT AGREEMENT** (EFDA) was created in 1999 and took over the operations of the **Joint European Torus**, one of the world's largest fusion experiments, in 2000. The Agreement has long aimed to promote collaboration in the field of nuclear fusion research by member states of the European Union (EU), **Switzerland** and certain **candidate countries** of **Central and Eastern Europe** (the **Czech Republic**, **Hungary** and **Romania**). The former two countries joined the EU in May 2004, and Romania in January 2007; 28 states were members of EFDA in 2013. Given that fusion energy is both a long term and highly costly undertaking, research collaboration is essential and the EU has been pursuing a strongly co-ordinated strategy in this area since 1958 (under **the European Atomic Energy Community** (Euroatom). EFDA also manages the **ITER** nuclear research project. Two support units are based in Garching, **Germany,** and Culham, **United Kingdom**; these units integrate research carried out in various centres into the European Fusion Programme. In 2008 a revised EFDA came into force and had two main objectives: to prepare for the operation and exploitation of ITER and to broaden further the knowledge base for overall fusion development, especially in relation to the proposed DEMO (the first electricity-producing experimental fusion power plant, which was planned to be built upon the expected success of the ITER experimental nuclear fusion reactor). In October 2014 the **European Commission** officially launched the **European Consortium for the Development of Fusion Energy** (EUROfusion), superseding the European Fusion Development Agreement and incorporating 29 bilateral association agreements between the Commission and research institutions.

The **EUROPEAN GROUP ON ETHICS IN SCIENCE AND NEW TECHNOLOGIES** (EGE) was established in 1998 to advise the **European Commission** on ethical aspects of science and technology. An independent and multidisciplinary group, the EGE has provided opinions on a range of issues, including: human embryo research, doping in sport, human stem cell research, clinical research in developing countries and genetic testing in the workplace.

EUROPEAN INFORMATION SYSTEM: See **Schengen Information System**

The **EUROPEAN INSTITUTE FOR GENDER EQUALITY** (EIGE) is an autonomous body of the **European Union** (EU) established in 2007 in **Brussels**, **Belgium**, to promote and monitor progress towards **gender equality** (equality between men and women) in all areas of EU and national policies. The EIGE is now based in Vilnius, Lithuania. EIGE is responsible for producing and maintaining the Gender Equality Index, and raising citizens' awareness about gender equality within the Union. In other words, it is a European gender equality knowledge centre. EIGE's main mechanism for ensuring gender quality is through the strategy of **gender mainstreaming**. The EIGE's budget for 2015 was €7.6m.

The **EUROPEAN INVENTORY OF EXISTING CHEMICAL SUBSTANCES** (EINECS) is a programme set up by the **European Commission** in 1986 as a response to widespread alarm about the hazards to both individuals and the environment of many chemical products. The inventory, which forms part of the **Environmental Chemicals Data Information Network**, is intended to record all commercially available chemical products. The Commission uses it to evaluate and control their application, and in the formulation of **consumer policy**, **environmental policy** and **health and safety** policy.

The **EUROPEAN INVESTMENT BANK** (EIB) was set up by the **Treaty of Rome** as a separate and autonomous institution within the European Communities. Based in **Luxembourg**, the EIB was designed to be a bank for the financing of capital investment that would benefit the process of European Union (EU) integration. In sum, the EIB finances viable capital projects and borrows on the world's financial markets to finance its projects. The EIB has evolved since 1958 in both importance and stature and today is the world's largest bank of its kind, with total subscribed capital of €243,284m. at the end of 2016. The member states are the basic members of the Bank, collectively subscribing to its capital. The EIB has a number of regional offices throughout Europe, as well as in other parts of the world (including Egypt, **Morocco**, **South Africa**, **Turkey** and Tunisia).

The ultimate decision making body of the EIB is the Board of Governors, normally consisting of the finance ministers of the member states. The Board of Governors normally meets only once a year. Supervision of the daily operations of the Bank is performed by a part-time Board of Directors, composed of nominees from the member states and from the **European Commission**. The management of operations is the responsibility of a Management Committee composed of the Bank's President and eight Vice-Presidents, nominated by the Board of Directors and appointed by the Board of Governors for renewable six-year terms. Werner Hoyer was appointed as the seventh President of the EIB on 1 January 2012, and was to take office for a second term on 1 January 2018.

In addition to its subscription capital, the EIB raises funds on the international capital markets, where it enjoys the highest possible credit rating. Its bonds are regularly rated 'AAA' by the leading rating agencies. As it works on a non-profit basis the EIB can pass on to projects the excellent conditions obtained as an AAA borrower. The EIB has three general aims: to assist less developed regions, to help to modernize the economy of the EU, and to support projects that are of interest to more than one member state. It provides fixed-rate loans, usually for periods of between five and 12 years (but up to 20 years for infrastructural projects), and occasionally also guarantees loans and credit.

National governments, regional authorities and companies may all apply for EIB loans or guarantees. The EIB never provides all the funding for a project. It considers only large-scale projects, and normally advances up to 50% of the projected costs. The balance has to be met by loans from other sources, the applicant's own resources or state assistance. Some 5% of EIB activity is devoted to external aid programmes, mainly benefiting the **African, Caribbean and Pacific (ACP) states** under the terms of the **Lomé Convention**. Under the terms of Lomé's successor, the **Cotonou Agreement**, €3,900m. was channelled to projects in ACP states between 2002 and 2006. The Bank publishes an annual report of its operations, with details of the projects it has funded. With a level of lending approaching that of the International Bank for Reconstruction and Development (IBRD—World Bank), it arguably constitutes the most successful of the funds available from the EU. After 1994 it administered a **European Investment Fund** (EIF), which was intended to promote economic growth and reduce unemployment through the provision of financial aid for major infrastructural projects, and for capital investments by smaller companies.

The responsibilities of the EIB were extended in June 1998 to include the Amsterdam Special Action programme, which allows the EIB to lend money for health and education projects and to provide risk capital for small and medium-sized companies, particularly in new high-technology areas. In recent years the EIB has tended to move its focus from long-term infrastructure projects towards supporting initiatives that increase employment and facilitate research and development across the EU. In 2008–09 the EIB increased its lending activities in the light of the financial crisis. Particular emphasis in recent years has been placed on supporting **small and medium-sized enterprises** (SMEs), environmental sustainability, the development of **Trans-European Networks** (**TENs**) and **cohesion** and convergence. In 2015 the EIB made disbursements totalling €60,419m., mainly within the EU. Its lending mandates are based on EU external co-operation arrangements and can be classified under the headings of Enlargement countries, European Free Trade Association countries, Mediterranean neighbourhood, EU Eastern Neighbours, ACP states and South Africa, and countries in Central Asia, and Asia and Latin America.

EUROPEAN INVESTMENT FUND (EIF) is the name of a body proposed by the **European Council** in 1992, as part of a collection of measures designed to combat the economic depression prevalent in the early 1990s, with the objective of providing additional aid for transnational infrastructural projects. The Fund was established in 1994 by the **European Investment Bank** (EIB), the European Union (EU), represented by the **European Commission**, and a group of 76 banks and financial institutions from throughout the EU. Its main task was to provide financial institutions with infrastructure and **small and medium-sized enterprise** (SME) guarantees. The EIB subscribed 40% of the EIF's **ecu** 2,000m. capital. The Fund assists SMEs and provides guarantees for the long-term financing of European infrastructure projects, in particular **Trans-European Networks** (TENs). The EIF became operational in 1995 and commenced its involvement in venture capital in 1997, as part of the **European Commission**'s 'Growth and Employment' initiative. In June 2000 the EIF's statutes were restructured and its shareholding structure was modified (with the EIB becoming the majority shareholder) so as to endorse the role of the EIF as the exclusive vehicle for venture capital of the EIB. The EIF is active in the member states of the EU as well as in countries that have applied to become members.

The **EUROPEAN JUDICIAL NETWORK IN CIVIL AND COMMERCIAL MATTERS** was established in 2001 as part of the European Union's activities in the area of **justice and home affairs** following the **Tampere summit** of the **European Council**. The network consists of representatives of the member states' judicial and administrative authorities and meets several times each year to exchange information and experience and promote co-operation in the areas of civil and commercial law. In 2013 a new European e-justice portal was opened, with the aim of making it easier for EU citizens to find out about information on justice systems throughout the EU and how to access these systems. The website contains information for businesses and legal practitioners. Materials are provided in 24 languages on themes such as going to court, legal aid, the rights of victims, costs and legal training.

The **EUROPEAN JUDICIAL NETWORK IN CRIMINAL MATTERS** (EJN) was established in 1998 and plays a major role in the European Union's efforts to promote **police and judicial co-operation in criminal matters**. It brings together experts from the member states dealing with criminal matters and has a Secretariat in The Hague linked to that of **Eurojust**.

The **EUROPEAN MARITIME AND FISHERIES FUND** (EMFF) came into existence in January 2014. It replaced the **European Fisheries Fund**. This fund aims to assist the fishing community in the current financial perspective (MFF) period that runs from 2014–20. This EMFF represents the social dimension of the newly reformed **Common Fisheries Policy** and focuses specifically on the development of sustainable fishing and aquaculture and seeks to secure and stimulate employment in coastal areas. It has been designed to help fishermen in their transition to sustainable fishing and aims to support coastal communities diversify into new areas of economic activity. Some €6,500m. was allocated to the EMFF for the period between 2014 and 2020.

The **EUROPEAN MARITIME SAFETY AGENCY** (EMSA) was created in 2002 to promote an improved maritime safety system within the European Union. One of the factors leading to the creation of the EMSA was in the form of a response to the environmental and economic damage caused by two major oil spills (Erika in 1999 and Prestige in 2002). The Agency moved to Lisbon, **Portugal**, from **Brussels**, **Belgium**, in 2006. It seeks to remind European Governments of the need to invest in better preparation for large-scale oil spills, as well as reducing the risk of maritime accidents, marine pollution from ships and the loss of human lives at sea.

The **EUROPEAN MEDICINES AGENCY** (EMA) was established as a decentralized agency of the European Communities by the **Council of the European Union**. Currently still located in London, **United Kingdom**, it began operations in early 1995 as the European Agency for the Evaluation of Medicinal Products (it was renamed as above in 2004). It is responsible for the licensing of all human and veterinary medicinal products in the European Union (EU), and for monitoring their efficacy. Once a **pharmaceuticals** company has obtained a licence, it may sell its products anywhere in the EU, in an arrangement that has brought to an end member states' former protective practices in the interests of their own companies. However, national regulatory bodies continue to operate and provide an alternative means for approving new drugs in the EU.

The **EUROPEAN MIGRATION CRISIS** arose from 2015, when some 1.35m. people travelled to European Union (EU) member states in an effort to claim asylum, with over 3,700 reported to have died crossing the Mediterranean Sea in 2016 and 2,512 estimated deaths in the first half of 2017. This figure was more than twice the 626,000 applications for asylum recorded in 2014; some 434,160 applications were made in 2013. Principal countries of origin for asylum seekers in 2015–16 included **Syria**, Afghanistan and Iraq, as well as other countries, such as Libya, **Kosovo**, Pakistan, Eritrea, Nigeria and Somalia, with many migrants seeking refuge from domestic conflict and instability, and others moving to seek economic opportunities. Some EU countries were more severely affected than others by the unprecedented numbers of migrants arriving at their borders, with some particularly exposed, such as **Greece**, which received more than 800,000 arrivals of migrants and refugees in 2015; meanwhile, **Denmark**, **Ireland**, **Sweden** and the **United Kingdom** had negotiated exemptions from fundamental aspects of EU **immigration policy**. In August German Chancellor **Angela Merkel** announced that **Germany** would accept unlimited asylum applicants from Syria, which was deeply mired in civil conflict, irrespective of their initial point of entry into the EU (in contravention of the **Dublin Regulation**), and offered Syrian refugees permanent leave to remain in Germany. As a result huge numbers of people began to cross Europe in order to reach Germany—some 800,000 were estimated to have arrived in 2015.

The refugee crisis challenged the functioning of the **Schengen Area** of free movement, as large-scale flows of migrants and refugees led some countries to reimpose border controls, and a number of member states (including **Austria**, **Hungary**, Denmark and Sweden) erected fences in order to dissuade immigrants. The continued viability of the **Schengen Agreement** was also questioned by those who feared that free movement and a lack of security checks risked undermining security and represented a contributory factor in terrorist attacks, such as those in Paris, **France**, in November 2015, as a result of which 130 people were killed by assailants linked to the so-called **Islamic State** organization, some of whom had reportedly travelled to fight in the civil war in Syria and subsequently returned to France and **Belgium** without being detained.

In March 2016 the EU reached an agreement with **Turkey**, which provided for undocumented asylum seekers who had not made an asylum application at their initial point of entry into the EU (usually Greece) to be returned to that country; the EU was to accept the same number of legitimately registered asylum seekers from Turkey's refugee camps—a so-called 'one in, one out' scheme. The Turkish Government pledged to increase efforts to prevent sea crossings, which witnessed a degree of success: less than 10,000 refugees travelled from Turkey to the EU in June–September 2016. In return, the EU announced that it would accelerate progress towards visa liberalization for Turkish citizens travelling to the EU and made available funding of up to €6,000m. by 2018, to help Turkey manage the crisis. The United Nations High Commissioner for Refugees expressed concern about the agreement, particularly the risks faced by asylum claimants in Greece and Turkey who might not receive necessary protection while in transit. Furthermore, migrant arrivals in **Italy** from North Africa had increased as the crossing from Turkey to Greece became less attractive for undocumented asylum seekers. Similar deals to that agreed with Turkey have been instigated with five countries under the new **Migration Partnership Framework**.

There was opposition in some member states, such as the members of the **Visegrad Group** (the **Czech Republic**, **Hungary**, **Poland** and **Slovakia**), to the imposition of mandatory quotas for the resettlement of refugees, on the grounds that member states should have ultimate control over the admission of asylum seekers into their territory, and amid popular protests in some countries about hosting refugees from Islamic countries. From mid-2015 migratory flows through southern Europe shifted direction according to which borders had been blocked. (For example, as Hungary's borders with Serbia and **Croatia** became harder to penetrate, pressure built up in **Slovenia**.)

EUROPEAN MONETARY AGREEMENT: See **European Payments Union**

The **EUROPEAN MONETARY CO-OPERATION FUND** (EMCF) was established in 1973. By the end of that decade it was the only survivor of plans made in the early 1970s for **economic and monetary union** (EMU). In 1979 it was incorporated into the **European Monetary System** (EMS), where it was the reserve fund that supported the European Currency Unit (**ecu**). Member states participating in the basket of currencies that determined the value of the ecu were required to deposit 20% of both their gold and dollar reserves with the Fund. The EMCF was used to regulate the interventions made on the exchange markets by the central banks of the member states to support the **exchange-rate mechanism** of the EMS, and it kept account of short-term borrowings used to support currencies. Its most important credit facility was its Very Short-Term Financing Facility (VSTF), which permitted borrowing by the central banks, with the proviso that credit must be settled within 45 days. The **European Monetary Institute** superseded it in January 1994, at the beginning of stage two of EMU.

The **EUROPEAN MONETARY INSTITUTE** (EMI) was established under the **Treaty on European Union** (TEU) and superseded the **European Monetary Co-operation Fund**. Its operations began with the commencement of stage two of **economic and monetary union** (EMU) and were completed shortly before stage three was launched on 1 January 1999. The EMI's role was to facilitate closer co-operation between the central banks of the member states, co-ordinate monetary policies, monitor the **European Monetary System** and eventually advise the **European Council** as to whether the conditions for stage three of EMU had been met. Located in Frankfurt am Main, **Germany**, it was the forerunner of the **European Central Bank** (ECB), which effectively replaced it in 1998.

The **EUROPEAN MONETARY SYSTEM** (EMS) constituted the second attempt by the European Communities (EC) to secure some form of monetary co-operation after the failure of the plans of 1970 for **economic and monetary union** (EMU). The EMS, established in 1979, was a more limited and practical attempt to secure, in the first instance, a zone of monetary stability in Western Europe. The core of the EMS was the **exchange-rate mechanism** (ERM), which linked the currencies of the participating member states and limited the amount by which each currency was permitted to fluctuate against its counterparts. If a currency went beyond these limits, the central banks, with the help of the **European Monetary Co-operation Fund**, intervened in the exchange markets, selling or buying as the case might be, to maintain the currency within the agreed limits. A central rate was calculated for each currency on the basis of the central rate of the European Currency Unit (**ecu**), a notional EC currency that existed alongside the national currencies. Special arrangements existed to provide help for countries that experienced short-term difficulties. Where a currency persistently had difficulty in staying within its agreed limits, the EMS made provision for its realignment.

The EMS had some considerable success in the 1980s. It was widely credited with contributing to the decline in inflation levels and to the increasing economic **convergence** of the member states. While the EMS was not a replacement for EMU, as it was unable to impose economic policy restraints upon the states, by the late 1980s it was widely felt that conditions were more appropriate for the EC to move on to full EMU. One weakness was that not all the member states were members of the ERM. The plans for EMU contained in the **Treaty on European Union** (TEU) were disrupted during the currency crises of 1992–93, with the **United Kingdom** and **Italy** leaving the ERM, which itself greatly extended the permissible limits of currency fluctuation. While these events may have delayed the EMU programme, they did not seriously affect the existence of the EMS, which remained essentially an instrument of co-operation in monetary policy until the formal establishment of EMU.

EUROPEAN MONITORING CENTRE FOR DRUGS AND DRUG ADDICTION (EMCDDA) is the name of a decentralized EU agency that resulted from the growing recognition by European leaders of the dangers of drugs and drug addiction. The **Treaty on European Union** provided the first references in the European Union treaty base to drugs. The EMCDDA was established in 1994 and subsequently secured greater European co-operation in this area under **CELAD**. The Centre itself opened in September 1995 and is located in Lisbon, **Portugal**. At the heart of its work is the promotion of scientific excellence. The data that the EMCDDA collects on drugs are passed to it from the relevant national authorities. Although much of its work is primarily focused on Europe, EMCDDA also works with partners in other parts of the world to exchange information and gather expertise.

The **EUROPEAN MONITORING CENTRE ON RACISM AND XENOPHOBIA** (EUMC) was established by the European Union (EU) in 1997 to study and review the extent and development of racism, xenophobia and anti-Semitism in Europe, and to report its findings to the EU. The EUMC works with the **Council of Europe**, the **United Nations** and other international organizations. It established a European Racism and Xenophobia Information Network (RAXEN), which collected statistics on racist incidents and passed them to the EUMC. The EUMC then used the materials gathered to construct a European database for conducting research and disseminating information on racism and how to combat it. EUMC set up a series of 'Round Table' discussions on racism and launched some of its own research initiatives. In December 2003 the European Council opted to extend the remit of the EUMC and converted it into a new **European Union Agency for Fundamental Rights** (FRA), which became fully operational in 2008.

EUROPEAN MOVEMENT is the name of an influential pressure group working for integration in the late 1940s and early 1950s. It was founded at the **Congress of Europe** of 1948. It was the Movement that drew up the first draft of what was to become the **Council of Europe**. Its influence faded after the early 1950s, but it remained active in supporting schemes for further political integration. With a membership that covers most European countries, it has come to act more as an umbrella organization, disseminating information to all groups, associations and institutions with an interest in European affairs, and liaising between them.

EUROPEAN NATO refers superficially to all members of the **North Atlantic Treaty Organization** (NATO) except the **USA** and Canada. It more precisely refers to the original European NATO membership of 1949, including **France**, despite the latter's partial membership of NATO, and with the addition of **Germany**. It is a descriptive expression rather than a specific subgroup within NATO, and has often been used in the context of the need to strengthen the European pillar of NATO.

The **EUROPEAN NEIGHBOURHOOD POLICY** (ENP) is the European Union's (EU) initiative to redefine relations with neighbouring regions (i.e. Eastern Europe, the Middle East and the Southern Mediterranean, but not **South-Eastern Europe** or the **Russian Federation**), following **enlargement** in 2004 and 2007. It aims to 'reduce poverty and create an area of shared prosperity and values based on deeper economic integration, intensified political and cultural relations, enhanced cross-border co-operation and shared responsibility for conflict prevention between the EU and its neighbours … [and to] anchor the EU's offer of concrete benefits and preferential relations within a differentiated framework which responds to progress made by the partner countries in political and economic reform'. There are 16 ENP countries. These contain an agenda of political and economic reforms with short- and medium-term priorities. Plans were agreed with Armenia, Azerbaijan, Egypt, Georgia, Israel, Jordan, Lebanon, **Moldova**, **Morocco**, the Palestinian Authority (now Palestinian Territories), Tunisia and **Ukraine**. Algeria was also negotiating an ENP plan. Belarus, Libya and **Syria** remained outside most of the ENP's scope, while Russia had 'special status'. The ENP is designed to cover increased trade relations, involvement in the EU's **internal market**, and co-operation on justice and home affairs, energy, transport, information society, environment and research and innovation, and social policy. 'Enhanced Agreements' were also envisaged and will involve more political dialogue, a free trade area and strengthened co-operation in these areas. Financial assistance worth almost €11,200m. was allocated through a European Neighbourhood and Partnership Instrument (ENPI) for the period 2007–13. From 2014 the European Neighbourhood Instrument (ENI) replaced the ENPI. EU membership, however, is not envisaged as part of either the Action Plans or the ENP more generally. The ENI was worth over €15,433m. for 2014–20.

The ENP attracted criticism from the EU's neighbours and others for lacking 'added value' compared with their existing relations and for being an essentially EU-imposed policy. In 2006 the **European Commission** published a set of proposals entitled 'Strengthening the European Neighbourhood Policy'. One year later it reported progress in developing the ENP, noting financial allocations under a Governance Facility, the establishment of a Neighbourhood Investment Facility worth €700m. in 2007–13, the launching of a regional dimension for the eastern neighbours through a new EU Black Sea Synergy initiative, and the opening up of EU programmes and agencies to ENP partners. The EU appeared nevertheless to be responding to criticism, by ensuring greater differentiation between partners, by allowing those more advanced in terms of political and economic reform and capacity to benefit from closer, upgraded relations, possibly through individual **deep and comprehensive free trade area** agreements, as well as improved mobility arrangements, enhanced political dialogue and greater participation in EU programmes. The EU also envisaged playing a greater role in conflict resolution.

In 2008 Sweden and **Portugal** proposed an **Eastern partnership** for the eastern European states, which included an offer of 'more profound integration'. This followed proposals for a **Union for the Mediterranean** from the French President, Nicolas Sarkozy. The Eastern partnership was eventually launched in May 2009. In 2010–11 the Commission undertook a routine review of the functioning of the ENP. This coincided with the so-called **Arab Spring** (the spring uprisings of revolutionary demonstrations and protests throughout several Middle Eastern and North African countries) in 2011, and the final report proposed a 'new response to a changing neighbourhood', comprising, *inter alia*, greater support for political reforms, enhanced EU involvement in solving protracted crises, increased support for economic and social development, visa facilitation measures, strengthened trade ties and more effective regional partnerships within the ENP. The Commission also proposed increasing financial assistance and advocated greater use of **conditionality**. Co-operation, improved market access and financial assistance would only be provided if political and economic reform programmes were implemented. A review of the ENP commenced in 2015, taking into account the increased security concerns that had emerged since the Arab Spring and the threat of terrorism following the rise of **Islamic State**, as well as the effect on **Turkey** and countries in the **Middle East** and **North Africa**, and EU member states to the south and east of the bloc, notably **Greece**, **Italy** and in South-Eastern Europe more generally, of the **European migration crisis**. In November 2015 a joint statement by the European Commission and the **High Representative of the Union for Foreign Affairs and Security Policy** on the future of the ENP proposed that a revised ENP should build on the new **European Agenda on Security**, to help combat terrorism and radicalization, to prevent organized cross-border crime, to ameliorate judicial co-operation, and to tackle so-called cybercrime, in compliance with international law.

The **EUROPEAN ORGANISATION FOR THE SAFETY OF AIR NAVIGATION**, commonly known as **Eurocontrol**, is an international organization, which seeks to ensure safe and seamless air traffic management across Europe. Founded in 1960, Eurocontrol has 41 member states, and its headquarters are located in Brussels, **Belgium**. Although Eurocontrol is not a European Union (EU) agency, the Union delegated elements of its Single European Sky regulations (see **Air Transport Policy**) to Eurocontrol, thereby making it the central organization for co-ordination and planning of air traffic control throughout Europe. The EU is a Eurocontrol signatory, and all EU member states are also members of Eurocontrol. The organization co-operates with national authorities, air navigation service providers, users of both civil and military airspace, airports and other aviation industry organizations.

EUROPEAN ORGANIZATION FOR THE EXPLOITATION OF METEOROLOGICAL SATELLITES: See **EUMETSAT**

EUROPEAN ORGANIZATION FOR NUCLEAR RESEARCH: See **CERN**

The **EUROPEAN PARLIAMENT** (EP) originated in the **Strasbourg**-based advisory Assembly of the **European Coal and Steel Community** (ECSC). With the establishment of the **European Economic Community** (EEC) and the **European Atomic Energy Community** (EAEC or Euratom) in 1958, one Parliamentary Assembly was created to serve all three Communities, with a membership of 142. The composition of the EP has changed repeatedly to reflect the waves of **enlargement**. Membership, for example, increased to 626 by January 1995, to 732 by June 2004 and after January 2007 increased further to 785 (to incorporate the accession of **Bulgaria** and **Romania**). The number of seats was altered again for the June 2009 EP elections, when candidates from across the 27 member states contested 736 places. With the entry into force of the **Treaty of Lisbon**, the number was temporarily increased to 754 for the period to 2014. In April 2013 **Croatia** (in advance of its accession to the EU on 1 July) held elections to the EP to elect 12 representatives to serve until 2014. The Treaty of Lisbon provided for 751 **Members of the European Parliament** (MEPs) thereafter. The eighth direct elections to the EP took place between 22 and 25 May 2014, and the EP now has 751 elected members. Its composition could potentially change before the EP elections due to take place in June 2019, as the **United Kingdom**'s withdrawal from the EU is due to take place by 29 March 2019.

Members were initially appointed by the **national parliaments** from among their own members, although the **Treaty of Rome** had called for the introduction of **direct elections**. The first direct elections to the EP took place in 1979. The powers of the Parliament were defined as the supervision of both the **European Commission** and the Council of Ministers (see **Council of the European Union**), and participation in the legislative and **budget** processes. Essentially, however, it was allotted a secondary position in the institutional framework, being more of an advisory and consultative body than a genuine decision making body.

From the outset, the Assembly (as it was then called), which was firmly in favour of rapid moves towards political union, was dissatisfied with its secondary role, campaigning for greater influence and authority. In 1962 it took the symbolic step of calling itself the European Parliament: although this was accepted by the European Commission (but not by the Council of Ministers), the EP was given a legal basis only in the **Single European Act** (SEA) of 1987. The EP also asserted a right to meet whenever it wished, circumventing the Treaty of Rome's provisions for an annual session by simply dividing the latter into several segments of time, spanning the whole calendar year. Some slight increases in powers were granted by the 1970 **Treaty of Luxembourg**, with a further modest rise in budgetary influence in 1975, when the EP was given the right to reject the budget in its entirety with effect from 1977. The SEA, the **Treaty on European Union** (TEU), the **Treaty of Amsterdam** and the **Treaty of Nice** extended the EP's competences further by introducing the **co-operation procedure** and assent procedure under the SEA and introducing the **co-decision procedure** under the TEU (extending the latter under both the Amsterdam and Nice Treaties).

Although the EP has to approve **accession treaties** and **association agreements**, it plays no active role in their negotiations, and has only a minor role in any constitutional revision of the EU treaties. However, the EP is the single major EU institution that has been gradually gaining power in terms of its involvement with EU decision making (e.g. through co-decision) with every successive treaty change.

The EP's representative character has also been criticized. Since 1979 the EP has been elected at five-yearly intervals. There is no standard electoral system across all the member states, although all states now use some form of proportional representation. The EP elections are generally deemed in the British context to represent second-order elections (with a reduced turnout and on a par with local and regional elections). The electorates tend to use the elections to express a verdict on their national governments and domestic problems: there has never been a true European election fought on exactly the same day by a series of European political parties running on a common manifesto. Furthermore, electorates tend to have only a vague perception of the EP, often seeing it as secondary to their own national legislatures. The fact that EP plenary sessions have often been attended by less than one-half of its members has not helped its cause, although this is changing.

The TEU strengthened the EP's right of scrutiny and supervision. The EP was given a formal right to establish committees of inquiry, to appoint an **Ombudsman** from among its members to investigate complaints of maladministration in EC institutions, and to be consulted on the nomination of a new President of the European Commission and to ratify the choice of President and members of the Commission. Furthermore, in accordance with the Treaty of Amsterdam, the EP had formally to approve the appointment of the President of the Commission. These powers came in addition to its right to put both oral and written questions to the Commission, a right it has taken seriously.

The EP has substantial budgetary powers, where it shares authority with the Council of the European Union. It must approve the budget: if it fails to do so, EU **expenditure** is frozen at the previous year's level, with only one-12th of the budgetary expenditure approved for the previous year being available each month until the issue is resolved. The EP's freedom of action is substantially greater on **non-compulsory expenditure**. However, while it can block a budget, it cannot substitute one of its own. The EP was to be provided with further powers under the proposed **Treaty establishing a Constitution for Europe**. Essentially, this would have extended the use of co-decision and, significantly, given the EP greater say over both the final settlement of the **budget** and the **common agricultural policy**. These changes, along with others contained in the abandoned Treaty establishing a Constitution for Europe, were built into the Treaty of Lisbon, which came into force in December 2009. The Treaty of Lisbon enhances the EP's powers in relation to the budget by removing the distinction between compulsory and non-compulsory expenditure. The Treaty also contained a clause that stated that the selection of the Commission president should be filled 'taking into account' the outcome of the European elections. This small phrase actually transformed the EP's role in the entire process and turned it into a proactive player. Rather than limiting the EP's role to either approving or rejecting the European Council's choice for president, this treaty alteration enabled the EP effectively to announce its candidates for the position of Commission president. The **Group of the European People's Party (Christian Democrats)** (EPP) had agreed upon the nomination of **Jean-Claude Juncker** as its candidate prior to the 2014 EP elections and pushed its claim after the EPP's emergence as the largest party. The European Council found itself in a reactive position, and opted to approve the Juncker candidacy on 27 June 2014, despite opposition from the Governments of the UK and Hungary. The EP formally adopted the Juncker candidacy in July 2014, and approved the Juncker Commission on 22 October; it took office on 1 November.

Members of the Commission and its bureaucracy attend meetings of the various EP committees. The EP has the right to submit questions to the Council of the European Union, which responds through ministers of the member state currently holding the Council presidency, who attend EP plenary sessions to deliver the Council's replies. Since 1981 the head of government currently occupying the presidency of the **Council of the European Union** attends the EP after each European Council **summit meeting** to report on its proceedings. The EP's most severe power—to censure and thus collectively dismiss the Commission—requires a two-thirds' majority of the votes cast, which must also be a majority of the total EP membership; there is no power to dismiss an individual Commissioner. A censure motion was initiated in January 1999 following allegations of financial and other irregularities against the European Commission, and although a compromise deal ensured that the motion was defeated, the concessions won by the EP during that dispute were felt to represent an important shift in the balance of power from Commission to Parliament.

The role of the EP was further enhanced by the TEU's introduction of a co-decision procedure, which builds upon the co-operation procedure introduced by the SEA. While these decision making procedures make the legislative process highly complex, they broadly follow five phases. The Commission first presents a proposal to both the Council of the European Union and the EP. The EP is entitled to give an opinion that must be considered by the Council. A suitably revised version approved by **qualified majority voting** is returned to the EP and, if the EP rejects the common position proposed by the Council, the issue is referred to a **Conciliation Committee** which may result in approval, rejection or further amendment. Amendments can lead to a repetition of the evaluation process by the Council and EP. The new procedure gives the EP a decision making role and a potential power of veto. The procedure applies only to those **Articles** of the treaty that specifically refer to its use. The co-operation procedure introduced by the SEA applies to other policy areas, mostly in the area of **economic and monetary union**: under the co-operation procedure, where the Council rejects an EP opinion, it must give a reasoned common position that will become law unless the EP proposes amendments. The Council can override such amendments only by a unanimous vote.

The Treaty of Amsterdam simplified the decision making process, while extending the EP's powers. Co-decision between the Council and the EP was extended into a wider range of policy areas, and the EP may be consulted in decisions taken by unanimity in Council. International agreements, treaty decisions and the accession of new member states all require the consent of the EP. The Treaty also calls for the EP to establish a formal code of conduct by which to regulate its members. On **ratification**, the Treaty of Nice was to introduce a new distribution of seats in the EP. With the exception of **Germany** and Luxembourg, the arrangements envisaged a reduction in the number of seats allocated to the **fifteen** member states at that time. This was deemed necessary for an enlarged EU.

Elections to the eighth EP took place in May 2014, and the centre right emerged with the most MEPs. These elections also recorded the highest number of **Eurosceptic** MEPs (from both the populist left and populist/far right political spectrums) in the history of the EP. These elections may have been the largest in the EU's history and the best example of transnational democracy in action, but the turnout was again disappointing. Only 42.5% of the total eligible electorate in the EU cast their vote— the lowest ever turnout in EP elections. Within the overall low turnout, there were wide discrepancies at the national level. **Belgium** recorded a turnout of 90%, and **Luxembourg** 86%. There was a high rate of participation in **Malta** (75%), but turnout declined in **Italy** to 57% (compared with 65% in 2009), and declined further in **Ireland** to 52% (59% in 2009). More ominously for pro-integrationists, the turnout in 20 EU member states fell below 50%. Although turnout increased in both **France** (42%) and Germany (48%) from the 2009 figures (41% and 43%, respectively), turnout was much lower in many of the newest member states from **Central and Eastern Europe**. Turnout fell sharply in **Latvia** from 54% in 2009 to 30% in 2014, and fell in the **Czech Republic** from 28% in 2009 to 18% in 2014. The lowest recorded turnout was recorded in **Slovakia** (13%), which by the time of its third EP elections had never attracted more than a 20% turnout. Arguably most disappointing was the turnout of 25% in the newest EU member state, Croatia.

Turnout in the UK increased slightly from 34.7% in 2009 to 35.4% in 2014. The lowest ever recorded turnout in the UK was 24% in 1999. Most of the 751 MEPs have opted to belong to one of the eight **party groups** within the EP. The remainder are unattached to any group.

The EP normally meets for one week each month (except in August), with further meetings in March and October when agricultural prices and the budget are considered. Most of its work is done in its 20 specialized committees, which correspond to different policy areas and European Commission agencies. Committee memberships are determined by the **party groups** in proportion to the number of seats they occupy in the EP. MEPs sit not by nationality, but in transnational party groups, which have official recognition and receive administrative expenses. MEPs who choose not to belong to a party group are each entitled to serve on one committee. Each committee appoints a *rapporteur*, who draws up the programme for discussion and prepares drafts for resolution by the committee, which are then presented to the full EP. The MEPs elect a president who serves for a two-and-a-half year term. The EP President is **Antonio Tajani**, who replaced **Martin Schulz** in January 2017. The EP's representative in negotiations with the UK, following its decision, in June 2016, to leave the EU (see **Brexit**), is the MEP **Guy Verhofstadt**.

In all its functions the effectiveness of the EP is diminished by two structural conditions. The first is the fact that it conducts its business in 24 officially recognized **languages**, with all the costs and consequences of translating its oral and written business. The second condition is that its operations are dispersed across three member states. Plenary sessions continue to be held mainly in **Strasbourg**. Most committees meet in **Brussels** in order to be close to the executive centre of the EU; after 1994 some plenary sessions were also held there. By contrast, much of the supporting secretariat is located in Luxembourg, and must move to Brussels or Strasbourg, along with the necessary documentation and paraphernalia, for EP sessions. France and Luxembourg have resisted the EP's efforts to relocate all its operations to Brussels, and in 1992 and 1997 it was confirmed that the present, unsatisfactory arrangements would remain until the member states could unanimously agree upon a change.

EUROPEAN PARTNERSHIPS were launched in 2003 and first adopted in 2004 by the European Union (EU) for the countries of the **Western Balkans**. They are similar to **accession partnerships** in that they identify short- and medium-term priorities that the countries need to address in order to integrate with the EU. It is envisaged that the successful fulfilment of the priorities will equip the countries with the institutional and legislative framework and administrative capacity required for a functioning democracy and market economy. It should also assist their progress towards EU membership.

A **EUROPEAN PASSPORT** was first proposed in 1974. In 1981 the member states agreed upon the size and layout of a common format burgundy-coloured passport that would be marked 'European Community'. It was due to be introduced in January 1985. While only three member states met the deadline, all began to comply over the next few years. European passports were marked 'European Union' from 1995.

EUROPEAN PATENT: See **Unitary Patent Convention**

The **EUROPEAN PAYMENTS UNION** (EPU) was established in 1950 under the auspices of the Organisation for European Economic Co-operation (OEEC). It was intended to tackle the problem of reciprocal credits and facilitate multilateral trade once the **Marshall Plan** had come to an end. The EPU proved to be highly successful, and in 1959 was replaced by a broader European Monetary Agreement, which fulfilled the same purpose. It contributed to the ability of the **Six** to co-operate economically in the 1950s, and it was used by the **European Economic Community** (EEC) during the latter's first year of operation.

EUROPEAN PEOPLE'S PARTY: See **Group of the European People's Party (Christian Democrats)**

EUROPEAN POLICE OFFICE: See **Europol**

EUROPEAN POLITICAL COMMUNITY was the name of a concept that arose out of the attempts to establish the **European Defence Community** (EDC) in the early 1950s; it was based on the view that a common defence structure ideally required a correspondingly unified foreign policy. It involved only the **Six** countries that had established the **European Coal and Steel Community** (ECSC) and had committed themselves to the EDC. The unratified EDC treaty required its proposed Common Assembly to study ways of establishing federal institutions. The ECSC Assembly was transformed into an ad hoc EDC Assembly to consider a more wide-ranging political co-operation than could be provided by the ECSC and EDC. The Assembly began its work in September 1952 and reported six months later in favour of a European Political Community that would go beyond **sectoral integration** and form the basis of a comprehensive political federation to which the ECSC and EDC would be subordinated. A draft treaty, with a proposed institutional structure based upon the ECSC model, was drawn up in March 1953. However, the EDC treaty had still not been ratified by any state when the Political Community treaty was published. Despite the significant implications of the proposed European Political Community, it was the subject of very little debate; its fate was totally dependent upon the EDC. The important arguments of the time concerned the EDC treaty, the **ratification** or rejection of which would determine the fate of the European Political Community. The refusal of **France** to ratify the EDC treaty in August 1954 effectively meant the abandonment of the draft Political Community treaty.

EUROPEAN POLITICAL CO-OPERATION (EPC), also known by the acronym POCO, was more of a concept than a structure. It was a term used to describe co-operation in foreign policy and foreign affairs by the member states of the European Communities (EC). Its origins lay in the **Davignon Report** of 1970, and its objectives were to ensure a better mutual understanding of international problems and issues among the member states through a regular process of consultation and exchange of information, to work towards a **harmonization** of views and a co-ordination of foreign policy positions, and, where appropriate, to attempt to establish a common EC position. The first ministerial meeting under EPC took place in 1970 and the first joint statement, on the **Middle East**, was issued in May 1971.

EPC was not based on the **founding treaties**, and its development occurred outside the institutional framework of the EC. It developed as an essentially intergovernmental operation involving close and continuing liaison between the national foreign ministries, with an ongoing consultation process involving ambassadors from the EC states to foreign countries and the **United Nations** (UN), and the issuing of common instructions by the foreign ministries to their diplomatic representatives abroad. Three major types of initiative emerged from EPC. The first was the practice for the EC, wherever possible, to have a single representation and single position in international meetings: the country occupying the presidency of the Council of Ministers normally presented the EC position (see **Council of the European Union**). In particular, great efforts were made to ensure that the member states agreed upon a common position on issues in the UN General Assembly. The second element of EPC involved the adoption of common policy statements and initiatives by the **European Council**, occasionally leading to action towards developing a common policy position. Finally, the most specific outcome of EPC was agreement to impose common economic **sanctions** on named countries.

The **Single European Act** regularized the position of EPC within the EC framework, committing the member states to 'endeavour jointly to formulate and implement a European foreign policy'. It also provided EPC with a small secretariat in **Brussels**, and made it responsible for the political and economic aspects of a security policy. Despite its intergovernmental character and the non-binding nature of its agreements, EPC proved to be a successful operation, although it was far from constituting a European foreign policy. It was the changing nature of world politics after 1989, as much as the desire for further integration, which led the EC to reconsider EPC. With the **Treaty on European Union** (TEU), EPC was replaced by the **common foreign and security policy** (CFSP).

The **EUROPEAN PRIVATE EQUITY AND VENTURE CAPITAL ASSOCIATION** (EVCA) was formed in 1983 and is intended to promote the discussion and study of the management and investment of venture capital. Supported by the **European Commission**, EVCA has as its broader aim to develop a European capital market. It has been particularly concerned with the development of small and medium-sized companies. Projects developed under EVCA have received a maximum of 30% funding from the European Union (EU), and are required, ideally, to complement other EC policies and programmes. (See also **European Business and Innovation Centre Network**.)

EUROPEAN PROGRAMME FOR HIGH TECHNOLOGY RESEARCH AND DEVELOPMENT: See **EUREKA**

A **EUROPEAN PUBLIC PROSECUTOR'S OFFICE** (EPPO) was originally envisaged in the **Treaty establishing a Constitution for Europe** and is actually provided for under Article 86 of the **Treaty of Lisbon**. This Treaty provides for a significant increase of European Union (EU) engagement in the field of criminal justice, and the possibility of establishing an EPPO for 'investigating, prosecuting and bringing to judgment ... the perpetrators of, and accomplices in, offences against the Union's financial interests'. Its powers can be extended, by unanimity, to include 'serious crime having a cross-border dimension'. Once established, the EPPO is expected to work closely with **Europol**, and may eventually move towards tackling cross-border crime. **Denmark**, **Ireland** and the **United Kingdom** do not participate in the EPPO, but Denmark and Ireland can opt to do so in the future.

The **EUROPEAN RAPID REACTION FORCE** (ERRF) was formed in 1999–2003 to support the European Union's (EU) efforts to move beyond a **common foreign and security policy** and establish a **European security and defence policy** (now **Common Security and Defence Policy**). Technically, the ERRF is not a standing force. Instead, it is based on commitments from the member states to ensure that the EU has at its disposal an ERRF of 60,000 troops that can be mobilized at 60 days' notice (the Helsinki Headline Goal). There is a resource of some 100,000 persons and approximately 400 combat aircraft and 100 vessels on which the EU can draw. The ERRF has been deployed to date in the **former Yugoslav republic of Macedonia** (Operation Concordia) and the Democratic Republic of the Congo (Operation Artemis). Subsequent to the development of the ERRF, the concept of **battlegroups** was adopted and developed.

EUROPEAN RECOVERY PROGRAMME: See **Marshall Plan**

The **EUROPEAN REGIONAL DEVELOPMENT FUND** (ERDF) or more commonly referred to as cohesion policy is one of the four **structural and cohesion funds**. It was established in 1975 and is the central element of efforts by the European Union (EU) to develop an effective **regional policy**. It is run by a Regional Fund Committee, structured along the lines of the **Management Committees** of the **common agricultural policy** (CAP), and a Regional Policy Committee consisting of two representatives from each member state and the **European Commission**, with a chairperson elected from among the government representatives, and with a secretariat provided by the Commission.

The bulk of ERDF **expenditure** is devoted to specific projects for regional infrastructural developments proposed by the member states, including grants to enterprises as well as for public works. While only national governments may bid for support from the Fund, these projects often originate from regional and local authorities, other public bodies, or private companies. Financial assistance from the ERDF is mainly focused on: supporting **small and medium-sized enterprises** (SMEs); promoting productive investment; and improving infrastructure and further local development. One of its prime aims is to create **employment** by fostering competitive and sustainable development.

The ERDF is also used to support EU programmes proposed by the Commission as being of particular importance, often to two or more regions, and it may also be used to support national programmes deemed to possess a value for the EU as a whole. Each member state must submit a list of the programmes and projects for which it is seeking support. The Regional Policy Committee evaluates national programmes and some major individual projects. The Regional Fund Committee may take decisions on smaller projects. To be considered by the

ERDF, national programmes must receive Commission endorsement. They must be located in those regions that the member state has designated as being eligible for support under its own regional aid schemes; they must be consistent with EU objectives; and they must appear to be economically worthwhile. The ERDF operates under the principle of **additionality**, providing a maximum of 50% of the costs, with the member state having to fund the remainder.

Originally, ERDF resources did not go exclusively to the poorest regions of the European Communities (EC). Each member state was allocated a percentage quota of the Fund, against which it could bid for support. This provided aid for the weakest regions in each country, no matter how healthy they might be in the context of the EC as a whole. The quota system was a constant source of contention among the member states. A limited non-quota element (totalling only 5%), to be utilized by the European Commission for its own programmes, was added in 1979, and in 1985 quotas were abandoned in favour of a percentile range of the ERDF budget being allocated to each member state; the range indicates the maximum and minimum levels of support a state can receive, provided that an appropriate number of eligible programmes submitted receive endorsement.

In 1987 the Commission introduced a five-year budgetary package to cover all EC expenditure. As part of this the Commission proposed the reform of, and increased resources for, the structural funds in the period from 1988 to 1992. This so-called proposal, which became known as **Delors I**, was supported at a special **European Council summit meeting** in **Brussels** in 1988. The issue had proved to be problematic, as the British Prime Minister, Margaret Thatcher, had strong reservations over aspects of regional funding and preferred to let market liberalization erode regional disparities within member states. However, the German Chancellor, Helmut Kohl, sympathized with the four poorest EC states (**Ireland, Greece, Portugal** and **Spain**) and wished to compensate them financially. Under the agreement reached, EC structural spending rose from 15% to 31% of total spending. Jacques Delors, then President of the Commission, described the European Council's decision as a 'second Marshall Plan'. The 1988 reform radically revised structural policy by introducing a number of new principles (**additionality**; partnership; programming; and concentration) and identified five priority objective areas (development of lagging regions under objective 1; conversion of regions facing industrial decline under objective 2; combating long-term unemployment under objective 3; combating youth unemployment under objective 4; and development of rural areas under objective 5).

In 1992 the Commission proposed an ambitious new five-year budgetary package (**Delors II**) to the European Council. At the Edinburgh summit in December the European Council agreed to double EC assistance to the least prosperous regions. The decision again reflected pressure from the four poorest states and the willingness of **Germany** (albeit more reluctant post-unification in 1990) largely to finance it. When **Austria, Finland** and **Sweden** joined the EU in 1995 a new objective was created to help low population density regions (objective 6). By 1999 **structural and cohesion funds** made up more than one-third of the EU **budget**. Spending had risen from **ecu** 18,000m. in 1992 to ecu 31,000m. by 1999.

The multi-annual programme for 2000–06 was determined at the European Council summit in Berlin in March 1999. This followed the Commission's action plan, **Agenda 2000**, which aimed to provide the EU with a new financial framework in preparation for **enlargement**. Under this framework, the funds available for spending on structural assistance were to decrease. Spending on such assistance was still to account for about one-third of the EU's total budget for this period, some €195,000m. (at 1999 prices). In 2003 spending on the EU's structural operations (including the **Cohesion Fund**) accounted for 34.3% of the EU budget (€33,164m.). Financial assistance was concentrated on the neediest areas and to this end the number of objective areas was reduced from seven to three and redefined. The bulk of the funds available was designated for the new objective 1 areas (i.e. towards the development and structural adjustment of the least-developed regions), the poorest EU areas, which consisted mainly of eastern regions of Germany, and **Greece, Italy**, Spain and **Portugal**. In 2003, for example, €21,577m. was directed to these areas. In contrast, €3,652m. was spent on objective 2 regions (to support the economic and social conversion of areas facing structural difficulties) and €3,719m. on the new objective 3 areas (supporting the adaptation and modernization of policies and systems of education, training and employment).

Negotiations for the multi-annual programme for 2007–13 commenced in early 2004 and agreement was reached at the end of 2005. The total amount of money allocated to the structural and cohesion funds for this period was (at 2007 prices) €347,410m. The ERDF constituted the largest part of the EU's structural and cohesion funds (at €201,000m.). The operations and aims of the structural and cohesion policy for that financing period were altered. Instead of the objective 1, 2 and 3 areas, the new policy focused its attention on three themes. These were **convergence**, regional **competitiveness** and **employment**, and territorial co-operation. The vast majority of the monies available were focused on the first aim of convergence. Some €283,000m. was directed here and was met by the ERDF, the **European Social Fund** and the **Cohesion Fund**. In the **United Kingdom**, the North-East region received some £255m. from the ERDF in the period up to 2013. In 2012 the European Commission began the process of framing a new ERDF for the new financial perspective, for 2014–20. Final agreement was reached on the new multi-annual perspective in late 2013. The ERDF now forms the largest category of the EU budget, 'Smart and Inclusive Growth'. Some 33.3% of the EU's annual budget for 2014 was directed towards economic, social and territorial cohesion. During 2014–20 it is estimated that a reformed cohesion policy will invest some €366,800m. in Europe's regions, cities and the real economy. This policy represents the EU's principal investment tool for delivering the objectives of the **Europe 2020** programme, in terms of creating economic growth jobs and reducing poverty and social exclusion. Small and medium-sized enterprises were to be assisted by doubling the financial resources available to them under the ERDF (from €70,000m. to €140,000m. over the seven-year period).

The **EUROPEAN RESEARCH AREA COMMITTEE** (ERAC) replaced the Scientific and Technical Research Committee (CREST) in May 2010. CREST was founded in the early 1970s as an **advisory committee** to the **European Commission** and the **Council of the European Union**, composed of scientific experts. The Committee is usually consulted on its opinions about proposals and funding for scientific research programmes. It meets on a regular basis, and also reviews progress reports on ongoing research programmes.

EUROPEAN RESEARCH CO-ORDINATION AGENCY: See **EUREKA**

EUROPEAN RIGHT (DR) was the name of one of the cross-national **party groups** in the **European Parliament** (EP) until 1994. It was formed after the 1984 **direct elections** by extreme right-wing and neo-Fascist groups. Because of the political attitudes of its members, the DR was the most isolated group in the EP, with no other group willing to be associated with it: indeed, in 1984 other party groups strove to avoid having to be seated beside it. Its share of the vote dwindled over the last decade or so to such an extent that it was represented neither in the 1999–2004 parliament nor in the sixth one (2004–09). However, the prospects for the **far right** in the EP seemed to have changed after the 2009 elections, when a number of far-right individuals were returned as **Members of the European Parliament** (MEPs). The creation of a new Alliance of European National Movements, which included members from the British National Party, the French Front National (FN) and the Hungarian Jobbik party seemed to signal closer co-operation. However, this alliance was not recognized as a political group within the EP, as it did not meet the necessary numbers (25) and had insufficient transnational membership (members must come from at least seven EU member states). Rivalries between the members ensured that the grouping was practically defunct by the end of 2012. Although the BNP lost its two seats at the 2014 EP elections, both the FN and Jobbik performed well. The FN emerged as the largest party in **France**, capturing nearly 25% of the votes and winning 24 seats, while Jobbik retained its three seats, with almost 15% of the votes. Other smaller extreme-right parties such as the German National Democratic Party and **Greece**'s Golden Dawn also won seats (one and three seats, respectively) at the 2014 EP elections. A new far-right grouping emerged in the EP in mid-2015, the **Europe of Nations and Freedom**.

The **EUROPEAN ROUND TABLE OF INDUSTRIALISTS** (ERT) is an influential **Brussels**-based organization that seeks to promote the interests of business in the strategic thinking of the European Union (EU) and in particular the **European Commission**. It was established in 1983 and comprises some 50 chief executives of the largest firms across the EU. These include representatives, for example, from the **United Kingdom** (AstraZeneca, British American Tobacco and BT), from **Germany** (Siemens, Volkswagen and Bayer), from **France** (Suez, Renault and Total) and from **Italy** (Pirelli and Fiat). ERT members strongly endorse the benefits of European economic integration and the role of business within it. Notably, they believe that a dynamic, wealth-producing industrial sector benefits society as a whole. Membership is personal and not corporate, but it is by invitation only. The ERT is funded by multinational firms and maintains some 10 personnel in Brussels. In terms of sectoral areas, the ERT has taken a particular interest in information technology and lifelong learning skills. It was highly influential in the development of plans to complete the **internal market** and to promote **Trans-European Networks**. (See also **interest groups**.) The ERT strongly encourages the promotion of the **Lisbon agenda**, but also recognizes that European industry cannot flourish unless it is competitive with other businesses around the world. The prevailing economic and social policy framework is, the ERT argues, crucially important and must be flexible enough to adapt to changes in global conditions. ERT constantly demands policies that provide flexibility and enable European companies to build and improve their competitive strengths. From 2009 until 2014 Leif Johansson (of the Swedish telecommunications company Ericsson) served as the chairperson of the ERT. Benoît Potier (Chairman of Air Liquide) succeeded him on 1 June 2014.

EUROPEAN SCHOOLS have been established by the **European Commission** in several countries. They are intended primarily for the children of European Union (EU) employees; in particular, those working in a member state other than their own. Subject to the availability of space, they are open to other pupils. The schools (of which there were 14 in 2016, with a total of around 20,000 pupils) seek to provide a European education by offering an international syllabus in which tuition is given in several EU **languages**. The syllabus leads to the European Baccalaureate, a recognized system of academic attainment that allows for entry to universities. An intergovernmental committee, on which the Commission is also represented, appoints the head teachers. Each national government appoints a proportion of the other teaching staff.

EUROPEAN SECURITY AND DEFENCE IDENTITY (ESDI) is often used to describe the goal of increased co-operation within the **North Atlantic Treaty Organization** (NATO) between its European members, particularly after 1994. Such co-operation was designed to complement the development of the **common foreign and security policy** of the European Union. More recently, efforts to develop a **European security and defence policy** have promoted the ESDI.

The **EUROPEAN SECURITY AND DEFENCE POLICY** (ESDP): See **Common Security and Defence Policy** (CSDP)

A **EUROPEAN SECURITY STRATEGY** entitled 'A Secure Europe in a Better World' and devised by the European Union (EU)'s **High Representative for the Common Foreign and Security Policy**, Javier Solana, was adopted by the **European Council** in December 2003. The strategy sought to guide the **common foreign and security policy** and the **European security and defence policy**. It comprised three main objectives: addressing threats posed by terrorism, nuclear proliferation and regional conflicts; building security in the EU's neighbourhood; and establishing an international order based on effective multilateralism. It committed the EU to greater activity in realizing these objectives, an enhancement of capabilities, greater coherence, and increased co-operation with other parties (e.g. the **USA** and the **Russian Federation**). A first five-year report adopted in December 2008 sought to reinforce the strategy. It noted, in particular, the increased complexity of the security challenges facing the EU and called on the EU to be more effective in addressing them.

EUROPEAN SOCIAL CHARTER: See **Charter of Fundamental Social Rights of Workers**

The **EUROPEAN SOCIAL FUND** (ESF) was established as required by the **Treaty of Rome** in order for the European Communities (EC) to develop 'employment opportunities for workers', to raise their standard of living, and to make 'the employment of workers easier', especially by 'increasing their geographical and occupational mobility within the Community'. From its inception in 1960, therefore, the ESF has been concerned with the specific field of **employment** and training rather than with broad issues of general social welfare. During the 1960s the Fund's operations were limited, being confined mainly to the retraining of workers made redundant by structural economic change. With the dramatic increase in unemployment after 1973, the role of the Fund was redefined and enhanced in terms of retraining, redeployment and the provision of vocational training for young people. Persisting high levels of unemployment, and budgetary restrictions, obliged the ESF to narrow its priorities, and it refocused its activities on retraining and the development of employment skills among young people, with particular attention paid to the long-term unemployed and women. In 1988 it was agreed that 75% of ESF resources would be spent on projects for people under 25 years of age. These funds included substantial amounts spent on the (now-defunct) Programme for the Vocational Training of Young People and their Preparation for Adult and Working Life (PETRA) and EUROFORM initiatives. In addition, the ESF was obliged to focus more intensively on the most economically disadvantaged regions of the EC.

In 1999 the **Council of the European Union** and the **European Parliament**, adopted a new regulation laying down general provisions on, and the three new objectives for, the structural funds. On the social front, the regulation provides for action in five general areas. These include: the development of active labour market policies to combat unemployment; the promotion of equal opportunities for all in terms of access to the market and particularly for those at risk from social exclusion; the promotion of vocational training; the promotion of a skilled, well-trained and flexible workforce; and specific measures to improve access to the labour market, especially for women. These objectives are in line with the European Union (EU) strategy and guidelines on employment.

ESF resources are available for both large- and small-scale projects proposed or accepted by a member state. It operates under the principle of **additionality**, normally providing only 50% of the projected costs of a scheme, the balance having to be met by the member state. In poor regions that have been given absolute priority status, the ESF contribution is permitted to rise to 75%. A small proportion (some 5%) of ESF expenditure is reserved for other more general purposes or special operations defined by the **European Commission**, which typically involve contributions from several EU sources combined into an integrated programme. The ESF is managed by a Social Fund Committee, and consumes some 8%–10% of the EU **budget**. The European Social Fund spent €60,000m. between 2000 and 2006. Special attention was paid to funding for areas of the EU with particularly high levels of unemployment or low average incomes. Around €3,000m. was reserved during this period for the EQUAL programme. The ESF remains focused on promoting employment, combating discrimination and supporting social inclusion. Funds are directed towards initiatives that develop human resources, secure better integration in the workplace and ensure equality between the sexes. The ESF has also been seeking to ensure that Europe's companies are better equipped to meet the new global challenges. For the period 2007–13, some €75,000m. was directed to the ESF. The Commission is placing an emphasis on increasing the adaptability of workers, enterprises and entrepreneurs. Lifelong learning, for example, is deemed to be an integral aspect of this drive. The ESF is considered a core element of the **Europe 2020** strategy. The Fund's main themes have been carried forward into the new financial perspective (2014–20). Final agreement was reached on the new multi-annual perspective for 2014–20 in late 2013. This financial period enables the EU to invest some €960,000m. in commitments and envisages some €908,400m. in payments. The creation of jobs remains a priority. Some €70,000m. (i.e. €10,000m. per year over the current financial framework from 2014–20) is allocated to the ESF. The Youth Employment Initiative is one of the latest developments under this fund.

The **EUROPEAN SPACE AGENCY** (ESA) was established in 1975. It represents a consortium of countries that produce the **ARIANE** rocket used to send commercial satellites into space. Its origins lie with the inadequacies of the first collaborative European organization for space research, the **European Space Research Organization** (ESRO), and its re-evaluation by a European Space Conference. Negotiations between 1971 and 1973 produced an agreement to establish ESA as a replacement for ESRO. ESA's 20 member states are **Austria**, **Belgium**, the **Czech Republic**, **Denmark**, **Finland**, **France**, **Germany**, **Greece**, **Ireland**, **Italy**, **Luxembourg**, the **Netherlands**, **Norway**, **Poland**, **Portugal**, **Romania**, **Spain**, **Sweden**, **Switzerland** and the **United Kingdom**. Canada is an associated member and participates in certain ESA projects. ESA is an independent European agency that employs more than 2,000 people and has its headquarters in Paris as well as a number of other centres such as ESTEC, the European Space Research and Technology Centre. ESTEC is the design hub for most ESA spacecraft and technology development, and is situated in Noordwijk, the Netherlands. ESA is governed by a Council, which comprises members from each of the ESA member states. ESA does not form part of the European Union (EU). There are, however, close ties between the two bodies and they are linked by a common aim: to strengthen Europe and benefit its citizens.

ESA is funded by its member countries, and its objective is 'to provide and to promote, for exclusively peaceful purposes, co-operation among European states in space research and technology and their space applications, with a view to their being used for scientific purposes and for operational space applications'. ESA has been active in satellite development, and in 1984 adopted the long-term 'Horizon 2000' programme to work towards manned European space flight. The 'Horizon 2000 Plus' extension programme, covering 2005–16, was initiated in 1994 for the inclusion of projects using new technologies and for participation in future international space activities. A further programme, 'Cosmic Vision 2015–25', was announced in 2005. In December 2012 ESA signed an agreement with the US National Aeronautics and Space Administration (NASA) to provide a service module for the Orion spacecraft's exploration mission in 2017. In September 2014 ESA signed a co-operation agreement with Sierra Nevada Corporation of the USA on the Dream Chaser project, for the creation of an unmanned, reusable cargo spacecraft. ESA's budget for 2016 amounted to €5,250m., and some 2,000 employees worked for the agency globally. (See also **EUMETSAT**.)

ESA's ties with the EU have developed considerably because of the increasing role of space in strengthening Europe's political and economic role. The necessity of ensuring Europe's guaranteed access to space is becoming ever more apparent as satellites are used to improve communications and navigation, monitor the environment, strengthen technology and increase scientific knowledge. To this end, ESA has also set up a liaison office in **Brussels** to facilitate relations between the two organizations. Joint initiatives include Galileo, a European global navigation satellite system, and the Global Monitoring for Environment and Security suite of services, known as GMES, as well as the European Geostationary Navigation Overlay Service (EGNOS), the first pan-European satellite navigation system, which extends the US Global Positioning System (GPS), and is suitable for use in challenging navigational situations in which safety is critical (for example, guiding boats through narrow channels). In April 2009 ownership of EGNOS was transferred to the European Commission. In October the European Commission announced the launch of the free EGNOS Open Service.

In January 2003 a **Green Paper** on European **space policy**, prepared in co-operation with ESA, sought to launch a debate on Europe's space policy and to increase awareness of the strategic importance of space and space policy for Europe and its citizens. In November the ESA Council adopted a Framework Agreement, previously endorsed by the EU Council of Ministers in October, marking a milestone in ESA/EU relations. It recognized that both parties had specific complementary strengths, and committed them to working together. The Agreement had two main aims: first, the establishment of a common basis and appropriate practical arrangements for efficient and mutually beneficial co-operation between ESA and the EU; and second, the progressive development of a European space policy to link the demand for services and applications in support of EU policies with the supply, through ESA, of the space systems and infrastructure needed to meet that demand. As a result, the EU adopted an action plan for implementing an enlarged European space policy in November 2003. Drafted by the EU and ESA, the **White Paper** included proposals for joint ESA-EU space activities and took the Framework Agreement as its basis for implementation.

In May 2007 the EU adopted a formal European Space Policy, which had been drafted by the **European Commission** and the Director-General of ESA. The 2009 Treaty of Lisbon strengthened the role of ESA as a research and development space agency. In October of that year the first EU-ESA International Conference on Human Space Exploration was held, in Prague, the Czech Republic.

In October 2016 a new Space Strategy for Europe was announced by the Commission, which aimed, *inter alia*, to encourage Galileo to be utilized by mobile devices and to increase connectivity in remote locations; to facilitate access to satellite data by companies, in order to develop new services and applications; to encourage private investment for relevant new businesses; and to support the development of industrial space hubs in European regions. The EU and ESA signed a joint declaration on a joint European space policy, demonstrating the importance to both institutions of close co-operation on space.

The **EUROPEAN SPACE RESEARCH ORGANIZATION** (ESRO) was a multi-purpose organization established in 1961 with the participation of 10 European countries. It was intended both to carry out scientific research and to design and develop European satellites built on a collaborative basis by its members. During its existence, it was beset with disputes between scientists, and arguments over both projects and costs between the participating countries. It became the core of the **European Space Agency** established in 1975.

The **EUROPEAN STABILITY MECHANISM** (ESM) is a permanent intergovernmental crisis mechanism designed to safeguard the financial stability of the **eurozone**. It is based on the temporary funding programme, the **European Financial Stability Facility** (EFSF), which it replaced (together with the temporary **European Financial Stabilization Mechanism**—EFSM) on 27 September 2012 when the **Treaty establishing the European Stability Mechanism** entered into force. The EFSF and the EFSM were, however, to continue to handle the money transfers and programme monitoring for the previously approved bailout loans to **Ireland**, **Portugal** and **Greece**. The ESM has total subscribed capital of €704,800m. (including €80,550m. in paid-up capital). Members of the eurozone can apply for bailouts from the ESM if they are in financial difficulty or their financial sector is a stability threat that requires recapitalization. Such applications are dependent, however, on two factors: the member state having first signed a memorandum of understanding outlining the requisite reforms to be undertaken to restore financial stability; and the member state having ratified the European Fiscal Compact. By April 2013 the ESM had approved two Financial Assistance Facility Agreements—€141,000m for the recapitalization of **Spain**'s banks and €9,000m in disbursements to **Cyprus** for a combined sovereign state bailout programme and financial sector recapitalization programme. The ESM has its headquarters in Luxembourg, has a staff of about 70 and is headed by a Managing Director, who holds this position for five years. In August 2015 the ESM Board of Governors approved a memorandum of understanding with Greece, which pledged to carry out reforms concentrating on four principal objectives: fiscal sustainability; financial stability; growth, competitiveness and investment; and public administration. The ESM is providing financial assistance to Greece over a three-year period, amounting to some €86,000m.

EUROPEAN STANDARDS COMMITTEE: See **CEN**

The **EUROPEAN STRATEGIC PROGRAMME FOR RESEARCH AND DEVELOPMENT IN INFORMATION TECHNOLOGY** (ESPRIT) was a European Communities (EC) initiative established in 1984. In order to foster and increase co-operation by the member states in science and technology **research and technological development**, the EC sponsored a pilot scheme involving 38 separate contracts that entailed co-operation between companies from at least two member states. On the basis of this experience, Esprit was launched as a five-year programme to develop EC resources in information technology to full-systems capability based on semiconductor technology. A series of projects were conducted under the auspices of Esprit in a number of technology areas. A specially commissioned Task Force defined the overall programme for Information Technology and Telecommunications, which in 1987 was fully absorbed within the **European Commission**. EC funding, which extended to a maximum level of only 50% of the projected research and development costs, was available only for applications that included companies, universities or research institutes from at least two member states. The programme was deemed to be a success in terms of the number of projects funded, the number of participants involved and the practical applications resulting from them, and it was agreed in 1994 to extend Esprit for a further five-year term. The extension was given funds triple those available for the first programme, and the new schedule called for a concentration of effort in applied technologies, information technology processing systems and microelectronics. As part of a new framework programme in 1998, Esprit was subsumed into the **Information Society Technologies** (IST) programme.

The **EUROPEAN SYSTEM OF CENTRAL BANKS** (ESCB) came into existence in 1998 once the date for the third and final stage of **economic and monetary union** (EMU) had been set. It coexists with the **European Central Bank** (ECB), having the responsibility of maintaining price stability, defining and implementing a common monetary policy, and supervising the foreign reserves and foreign exchange operations of the member states. It consists of the national central banks of the 28 **European Union** member states, along with the ECB, although those member states not participating in EMU are unable to take part in **decision making** in this area. The ESCB should not be confused with the **Eurosystem**.

The **EUROPEAN SYSTEM OF FINANCIAL SUPERVISION** (ESFS) was established in 2011 to supervise the EU's financial sector. Founded primarily to respond to the ongoing financial crisis, the ESFS comprises three supervisory bodies: the European Securities and Markets Authority (ESMA); the European Insurance and Occupational Pensions Authority (EIOPA); and the **European Banking Authority**. The main task of the ESFS is to improve the functioning of the **internal market** by ensuring appropriate, efficient and harmonized European regulation.

The **EUROPEAN SYSTEM OF INTEGRATED ECONOMIC ACCOUNTS** (ESA) was established to assist in the development of a European information system in connection with the **internal market**. This was to be compatible with the System of National Accounts (SNA), which was to be used to monitor the development of **economic and monetary union** (EMU).

EUROPEAN TELECOMMUNICATIONS SATELLITE ORGANIZATION: See **EUTELSAT**

The **EUROPEAN TRADE UNION CONFEDERATION** (ETUC) was created in 1973 and gave itself the task of promoting and defending the interests of working people throughout the European Union (EU). The ETUC has become the major overarching organization for member states' national trade unions, and for union federations outside the EU. The ETUC comprises 88 national trade union confederations from 37 countries in Europe, and 10 federations representing European industry, resulting in a total membership of some 60m. people. Other trade union structures such as Eurocadres (the Council of European Professional and Managerial Staff) and EFREP/FERPA (European Federation of Retired and Elderly Persons) operate under the auspices of the ETUC. In addition, the ETUC co-ordinates the activities of the 44 Interregional Trade Union Councils (IRTUCs), which organize trade union co-operation at cross-border level. Based in **Brussels**, the ETUC is represented on several EU committees and organizations, and is generally recognized as a body with a legitimate interest in EU affairs. the ETUC is recognized by the EU, by the **Council of Europe** and by the **European Free Trade Association** as the only representative cross-sectoral trade union organization at European level.

The ETUC exists to represent workers in Europe. It strives to promote the 'European Social Model', which the ETUC believes should embody a society combining sustainable economic growth with ever-improving living and working standards, full employment, social protection, equal opportunities and social inclusion. the ETUC campaigns constantly for the EU to have a strong social dimension. It has developed close relations with the **European Parliament**, has membership of a number of advisory bodies and consults other social partners. the ETUC has been particularly active in supporting EU initiatives on **workers' rights**, notably the **Charter of Fundamental Social Rights of Workers**, but less active in seeking to promote industrial development. Under the **Treaty on European Union** (TEU, as amended by the **Treaty of Amsterdam**) the ETUC is recognized as one of the three 'social partners', alongside industry associations such as **BUSINESSEUROPE** (formerly the **Union of Industrial and Employers' Confederations of Europe**, or UNICE), with which the **European Commission** negotiates draft social and economic **legislation**. In 2004 the ETUC was particularly vocal on a number of issues. For example, it strongly condemned calls for a longer working week, urged the Dutch presidency of the **Council of the European Union** to push for a greater social agenda and supported the **Treaty establishing a Constitution for Europe** as a starting point for progress towards greater social values in the EU. The ETUC has played a key role in helping to formulate principal parts of EC/EU legislation, for example the European Works Councils Directive of 1994 and the Information and Consultation Directive of 2002. More recently it has also been active in organizing a number of high-profile demonstrations or Action Days to coincide with **summit meetings** or to protest about the impact of policies that threaten to undermine the 'European Social Model'.

The **EUROPEAN TRAINING FOUNDATION** (ETF) was established by the Council of Ministers (see **Council of the European Union**) in 1990. The ETF, which is based in Turin, **Italy**, and has a staff of some 130, is open also to states outside the European Union (EU). Its aims are to develop vocational training and retraining, and to channel aid to training and life-long learning projects, particularly those concerning Eastern Europe, and especially the **candidate countries**. It was responsible for co-ordinating EU higher education programmes in the accession states of **Central and Eastern Europe**. (See also **European Centre for the Development of Vocational Training; Tempus**.)

EUROPEAN TREATIES is a term used to refer to the combination of **founding treaties** (see **Treaty of Paris**; **Treaty of Rome**), **accession treaties** and amending treaties (e.g. the **Single European Act, Treaty on European Union, Treaty of Amsterdam** and **Treaty of Nice**), which make up the treaty base of the European Union (EU). The latest addition is the **Treaty of Lisbon**, which entered into force on 1 December 2009 and which also renamed the **Treaty establishing the European Community** —one of the Treaties of Rome—as the **Treaty on the Functioning of the European Union**.

EUROPEAN UNION (EU) is the name of the body established in 1993 by the **Treaty on European Union** (TEU), although its exact status was not fully and clearly defined by the treaty. It had a notional structure consisting of three **pillars**. At the centre was pillar I, which comprised the European Communities (EC). Two pillars of intergovernmental co-operation complemented this: **common foreign and security policy** (pillar II) and **justice and home affairs** (pillar III). This pillar structure enhanced the powers of the **European Council**, whose role encompassed all the components of the EU. The supranational institutions, meanwhile, concerned themselves mainly with matters covered by pillar I. Hence, the **European Commission** had only a limited role in pillars II and III. The same was also true of the **Court of Justice** and the **European Parliament**. While the EU is a political entity that seeks to improve and deepen the relationships between the member states, and claims to have its own **citizenship**, it nevertheless accepts the principle of **subsidiarity** and recognizes national identity. In addition, it is not described by the TEU as a fixed structure, but as a 'new stage in the process of creating an ever closer union'. Further timetables and targets were therefore established, most of which were reviewed by an **intergovernmental conference** (IGC) in 1996. This produced the **Treaty of Amsterdam** which reformed elements of each of the EU's three pillars, notably pillar III, various activities of which were 'communitarized' (i.e. moved to the first supranational pillar) and whose title was consequently changed to **police and judicial co-operation in criminal matters**. Further reforms were introduced via the **Treaty of Nice** in 2003. The future shape of the EU was a key focus of debates within the **European Convention** in 2002–03 and the subsequent IGC launched in October 2003. The resulting **Treaty establishing a Constitution for Europe** never entered into force, however. Its replacement, the **Treaty of Lisbon**, which came into force on 1 December 2009, further reformed the EU, removed all references to the EC in favour of the EU and formally abandoned the pillar structure.

The **EUROPEAN UNION AGENCY FOR FUNDAMENTAL RIGHTS** (FRA) was established in Vienna, **Austria**, in March 2007 as the successor to the **European Monitoring Centre on Racism and Xenophobia** (EUMC). It became fully operational in 2008. The aims of the Agency are to provide assistance and expertise to the EU and its member states when implementing EU **legislation** on fundamental rights; and to produce objective, reliable and comparable data on racism, xenophobia and anti-Semitism. The FRA produces an annual report for the **European Parliament** in which it charts its activities and achievements. It has also assumed responsibility for the RAXEN network (an information-gathering network of experts in the field of racism and xenophobia in the EU member states).

EUROPEAN UNION LAW is a generic term to describe all the law produced by the European Union (EU). Prior to the **Treaty of Lisbon** and the abolition of the EU's 'community' **pillar**, there was, according to some, a need to distinguish between, on the one hand, the law of the supranational European Communities (EC) and the *acquis communautaire*—EC law—and, on the other, the law that was created under the EU's two intergovernmental pillars covering the **common foreign and security policy** and **police and judicial co-operation in criminal matters**.

The **EUROPEAN UNION MILITARY COMMITTEE** (EUMC) was created in 2000 as part of the development of the European Union's **European security and defence policy**. The EUMC is composed of the Chiefs of Defence of the member states, who are represented on a regular basis by their permanent military representatives in **Brussels**. The EUMC gives military advice to the **Political and Security Committee** and to the **High Representative of the Union for Foreign Affairs and Security Policy**. It also oversees the European Union Military Staff.

The **EUROPEAN UNION SATELLITE CENTRE** (EUSC) was established in 2002 to replace the Western European Union Satellite Centre. Situated in Torrejón de Ardoz in **Spain**, it is responsible for producing satellite imagery to aid decision making in the field of the **common foreign and security policy**, notably where crisis monitoring and conflict prevention are concerned. Although the EUSC is autonomous in its daily operations, the **High Representative of the Union for Foreign Affairs and Security Policy** is responsible for the Centre's operational direction.

The **EUROPEAN UNIT OF ACCOUNT** (EUA) was the bookkeeping device introduced by the European Communities (EC) for recording the relative value of payments into and from EC accounts. In 1981 it was replaced by the **ecu**, which, in turn, was replaced by the **euro** in 1999.

EUROPEAN UNITARIAN LEFT: See **Confederal Group of the European United Left/Nordic Green Left**

The **EUROPEAN UNIVERSITY INSTITUTE** (EUI) was founded in 1976 as part of the European Communities (EC) policy of encouraging co-operation in higher education. Based in Florence, **Italy**, the EUI is an establishment for research and training in postgraduate and post-doctoral education, offering programmes in economics, history and civilization, law, and political and social sciences. Entry for students is competitive. Those accepted on the programmes are funded by their national governments and are expected to have some competence in more than one **language** of the European Union (EU). Staff appointments, made on the basis of open competition, are funded by the EU and are for fixed terms of between three and seven years. The EUI is the depository for the historical archives of the EU institutions.

The **EUROPEAN VOLUNTARY SERVICE** (EVS) programme, which was piloted in 1996, enables young people between the ages of 18 and 30 years to participate in voluntary work (for a period of two to 12 months) within other member states of the European Union. EVS formed part of the **Youth in Action Programme** for 2007 to 2013, which had a total budget of €885m. From 2014 the EVS was incorporated in the **Erasmus+** programme.

The **EUROPEAN YOUTH FORUM** is the name of a body established in 1996 to advise and aid the **European Commission** on policy issues that concern young people. At April 2016 the Forum consisted of some 40 national youth councils and 60 international youth **non-governmental organizations** from across Europe. The Forum's impact has been limited, not least because, by its very nature, there is a lack of continuity in its membership.

EUROPEANIZATION (or arguably, and more accurately, EUization) is a popular theme of current academic research and is used most often to describe and assess the impact that the European Union (EU) exerts on both member states and non-member states, notably in terms of domestic legislation, policy priorities and administrative structures. Discussions of Europeanization can be measured by looking at the EU's impact on public policies, politics and the public. It affects much more than just member state governments, and can be applied to a whole range of non-governmental actors who have likewise adjusted their activities and responses to EU structures and activities. The term remains fashionable in contemporary academic literature, but it is often a disputed concept.

The **EUROPLUS PACT** (or the **Competitiveness** act) was adopted by the European Council in March 2011. The original idea behind this pact came from the Governments of **France** and **Germany**. It was designed as a more credible and stringent successor to the **Stability and Growth Pact**, the rules of which some member states had been able to flout. It sought to improve the fiscal strengths and competitiveness of the **eurozone** members, and contained four broad goals: fostering competitiveness; improving employment; securing sustainability of public finances and reinforcing financial stability. It referred to a fifth and much more problematic issue, tax policy co-ordination. Under the terms of the pact each member (of the eurozone) is expected to agree a set of annual actions and to keep one another informed about their own strategies.

EUROPOL (European Police Office) is now officially known as the European Union Agency for Law Enforcement Co-operation, and was first conceived under the terms of the **Treaty on European Union**. Its objective is to help create a safer Europe for all EU citizens. To this end, Europol supports national police activities in the member states, as an integral element of **justice and home affairs**, especially in combating drugs trafficking, fraud and terrorism. The Convention establishing the agency was signed in June 1995, but Europol only became fully operational on 1 July 1999 (although the Europol Drugs Unit was already in operation by this time). From January 2002 its mandate was extended to include all serious forms of international crime. The largest threats to internal security are posed by acts of terrorism, international drugs-trafficking, money laundering, organized fraud, counterfeiting of the **euro**, people smuggling, and the increasing occurrence of cybercrime. Europol is based in The Hague and has a staff of some 800, including about 150 Europol liaison officers (ELOs) seconded from the member state enforcement agencies. Europol covers all 28 EU member states, but it also works in conjunction with other countries, from **Albania** and Australia to the **Russian Federation** and **Turkey**, to tackle effectively cross-border and international crime. The directorate of Europol is appointed by the **Council of the European Union** and the Director (since 2009) is a British national, Rob Wainwright. Europol participates in some 500 cross-border investigations each year, resulting in an annual caseload of about 9,000 cases. According to Europol, its endeavours have helped to dismantle or disable many criminal and terrorist networks. In 2016 a new **European Counter Terrorism Centre** was established as a body overseen by Europol, in response to an upsurge in terrorist activity, notably attacks in **France** in 2015. A new Europol regulation entered into force with effect from 1 May 2017, amending its name and strengthening its capabilities in combating crime.

EUROSCEPTICS is a term used to describe those people who opposed the **Treaty on European Union** and attempts by the European Union (EU) to introduce further integration. Their preference is for intergovernmental and free trade co-operation only. However, the term is a rather loose concept and Eurosceptics can be divided into 'hard' and 'soft' variants. The former oppose all steps towards European integration—past, present and future—and normally advocate their country's **withdrawal** from the EU. In contrast, 'soft' Eurosceptics object to certain aspects of the EU, usually relating to policy competences that they would prefer to repatriate. Although opposition to the activities and aims of the EU can be traced back to the very early days of European Communities (EC) membership in many states, Euroscepticism emerged as a particular feature of British politics in the late 1980s, especially under the final years of Margaret Thatcher's premiership. Subsequently, opposition within Conservative ranks to the Maastricht Treaty (see **Treaty on European Union**) bedevilled the John Major Governments and continued to cast increasing shadows over the second and third administrations of Labour Prime Minister Tony Blair (1997–2007). The **United Kingdom**'s troubled relationship with the EU ultimately led to the end of the political career of **David Cameron**, during whose tenure as premier in 2010–16 the **UK Independence Party** became an influential political force, the threat from which arguably prompted Cameron to schedule a national referendum on the country's continued membership of the EU. It should be stressed that Euroscepticism has not been confined to the UK: there is strong evidence of similar tendencies in many other EU states such as, for example, in **France** with the Front National, and in **Germany** with the **Alternative für Deutschland**. Euroscepticism (both 'soft' and 'hard') remains a growing force in the current European Parliament. The Eurosceptic movement achieved its most notable success in the history of the EU in June 2016, when the British electorate voted in the national referendum in favour of leaving the bloc (see **Brexit**). The largely unexpected outcome led to concerns among senior EU officials of so-called 'contagion', with the possibility that the British vote would encourage Eurosceptic parties throughout the bloc to demand similar plebiscites, seeking either to renegotiate the terms of their membership, or to leave the Union altogether.

EUROSTAT is the abbreviated and popularized form of the Statistical Office of the European Union (EU). It is a Directorate-General of the **European Commission** (allocated to the portfolio of the European Commissioner for Taxation and Customs Union, Audit and Anti-Fraud), and is responsible for the collection and publication of statistics covering the whole range of the economic and social affairs of the European Union. Although the information is intended in the first instance for use by the Commission and its administration, its documentation is publicly available, both online and in printed form. The statistical database (available online) is divided into nine themes: general and regional statistics; economy and finance; population and social conditions; industry, trade and services; agriculture, forestry and fisheries; international trade; transport; environment and energy; and science, technology and digital society. These themes are themselves subdivided into various domains of information. The database comprises more than 100m. items of social and economic statistical data covering the EU member states, and, in some cases, the **USA**, **Japan** and other main economic partners, including countries that have applied for membership of the EU. Eurostat is located in Luxembourg. In January 2017 Mariana Kotzeva was appointed as Director-General of Eurostat, in an acting capacity.

The **EURO SUMMIT** comprises the heads of state or of government of the **eurozone** member states, the President of the Euro Summit and President of the **European Council Donald Tusk** and the President of the **European Commission**, currently **Jean-Claude Juncker**. It seeks to give guidance on the co-ordination of economic policy throughout the eurozone in order to enable **economic and monetary union** to run as smoothly as possible. The first Euro Summit took place in October 2008, in response to the incipient economic and financial crisis in Europe. Under the Treaty on Stability, Co-ordination and Governance in the Economic and Monetary Union, commonly known as the **Fiscal Compact**, Euro Summit meetings now take place at least twice a year, and are organized taking into account rules of procedure adopted in March 2013.

The **EUROSYSTEM** is the **eurozone**'s monetary authority, and comprises the **European Central Bank** (ECB) and the central banks of the member states participating in the eurozone. The principal goal of the Eurosystem is maintaining price stability, and it is also concerned with financial stability and financial integration. The Eurosystem should not be confused with the **European System of Central Banks**.

The **EUROZONE**, also called the euro area and sometimes more informally referred to as 'euroland', consists of those 19 member states that are full participants in **economic and monetary union**, have adopted the **euro** and are subject to the new rules established under the **banking union**.

EURYDICE is the commonly used name for the Education Information Network in the European Union (EU). It was established in 1980 and was one of the European Communities' first essays into both information technology and the development of collaboration in **education, vocational training and youth policy**. The Eurydice network became one of the strategic mechanisms run by the European Commission with the member states to support co-operation in the field of education. The networked information service is based upon databanks of educational statistics, and is available for use by the **European Commission** and national education officials. At 2016 the Eurydice network consisted of 42 national units based in all 38 countries participating in the EU's **Lifelong Learning Programme** (EU member states, **European Free Trade Association** countries, **Bosnia and Herzegovina**, the **former Yugoslav republic of Macedonia**, **Montenegro**, **Serbia** and **Turkey**). It is co-ordinated and managed by the EU Education, Audiovisual and Culture Executive Agency in **Brussels**, **Belgium**, which drafts its studies and provides a range of online resources. From 2014 Eurydice formed part of the **Erasmus+** programme.

EUTELSAT is the acronym of the European Telecommunications Satellite Organization, an intergovernmental organization that was established in 1977. The aim of Eutelsat was to foster collaboration in the development of a European communications satellite system, and in the co-ordination and implementation of requirements relating to satellites being developed by the **European Space Agency**. It was designed to operate a satellite-based telecommunications system infrastructure for Europe. Eutelsat launched its first satellite in 1983 and has since become the world's third largest satellite operator (in terms of revenue). Although created to meet the needs of Western Europe's demand for satellite communications, Eutelsat's interests now extend across all Europe, into Africa and the Middle East, and into large parts of Asia and the Americas. Eutelsat has no direct links with the European Union (EU), although all the EU member states are represented. In the wider context of telecommunications liberalization, Eutelsat was restructured in 2001 as a private company incorporated under French law and now it markets its services through a network of partners who include leading telecommunications operators and service providers.

EVCA: See **European Private Equity and Venture Capital Association**

EVS: See **European Voluntary Service**

The **EXCHANGE-RATE MECHANISM** (ERM), along with the **ecu**, was one of the core components of the **European Monetary System** (EMS) established in 1979. It was the central instrument by which the EMS sought to stabilize and limit currency fluctuations. Under the ERM, a currency received a central exchange rate against the ecu, the value of which was derived from a basket of currencies. From these central rates, a grid of cross-parities was constructed, within which bilateral central rates were calculated for each pair of currencies participating in the ERM. For each currency there was a permissible range of fluctuation around these central rates, as well as a divergence indicator (a threshold point that indicated that the margins of permissible fluctuation were in danger of being breached). The permissible range was set at ±2.25%, with a broader range of ±6.0% for some currencies. The divergence indicator was 75% of this range. Normally, a currency would have reached the divergence threshold before it hit its bilateral limit, but because each currency had a different weighting in the ecu basket, this was not always the case. When the limit for a currency was breached or its divergence indicator triggered, the central banks of the affected states intervened in the exchange markets to keep the currency within the prescribed limits. The **European Monetary Co-operation Fund** (EMCF) supported the banks, which supplied short-term credit facilities, but the national authorities could also have been required to take appropriate domestic measures to correct the situation, such as changing interest rates or adopting an incomes policy. Where it proved persistently difficult to hold a currency within its permissible range, mechanisms were available for realigning its central rate. There were 12 exchange rate realignments between 1979 and 1989.

The ERM was credited with contributing to the much lower levels of currency fluctuation in the 1980s, and to the increasing economic **convergence** of the member states. Its weakness was that not all the member states were part of it. **Greece** stayed outside the ERM until 1998; **Spain** joined the wider band in 1989, as did the **United Kingdom** in 1990 and **Portugal** in 1992. The 1989 **Delors Plan** saw the ERM as an integral element of **economic and monetary union** (EMU). It called for all member states to join the ERM as an essential condition for the first of three stages of progress towards full EMU. Partly because of the incorporation of the ERM into the EMU timetable, and partly because of the interpretation of the ERM's previous success, it became a more rigid mechanism after 1990, the scope for adjustments—at least without causing a crisis in the system—being greatly reduced. A more rigid system, however, tended to discount the substantial variations in national economic performance. Moreover, it also discounted currency strengths, as they were perceived by the international money markets. The Danish referendum result rejecting the **Treaty on European Union** in 1992 was a catalyst for great anxiety and uncertainties in the exchange markets, compounded by the dominance within the ERM of **Germany**, which, confronted with the escalating costs of reunification, was pursuing a strong domestic anti-inflation policy. The consequent high German interest rates forced other ERM members to pursue similar policies, leading to severe economic problems in several countries. In September 1992 a wave of speculation was unleashed against ERM currencies. Despite massive central bank intervention, there were several involuntary devaluations, and **Italy** and the UK withdrew from the ERM. Further speculative pressure in August 1993, especially against the French franc, resulted, after much acrimony, in an extension of the broad range of permissible fluctuation to such a degree that, with only Germany and the Netherlands agreeing to stay within the narrow band, the ERM effectively ceased to be a regulatory mechanism. These episodes cast severe doubts on the viability of the timetable for EMU. **Austria** joined the ERM in January 1995 and a further realignment of exchange rates took place in March 1995, when the Spanish peseta was devalued by 7% and the Portuguese escudo by 3.5% in relation to other currencies. **Finland** joined the ERM in October 1996, and Italy rejoined in November of that year. Greece entered the ERM in March 1998.

The need for the ERM, in its original form, ended when the final stage of EMU started on 1 January 1999 (with 11 of the member states taking part—**Denmark**, Greece, **Sweden** and the UK did not participate, although Greece subsequently met the **convergence criteria** and took part in EMU from 2001) and when the **euro** was introduced as a single currency. However, the ERM was to continue, as ERM II, from 1 January 1999, to regulate the relationship between the euro and the currencies of member states remaining outside EMU, although some of the non-participating member states indicated they would not take part in ERM II. European Union countries that have not adopted the euro are expected to participate for at least two years in ERM II before joining the eurozone. A currency in ERM II is allowed to float within a range of ±15% with respect to a central rate against the euro. Denmark is a member of ERM II. Former members of ERM II that have since joined the eurozone are Greece, **Slovenia**, **Cyprus**, **Estonia**, **Malta**, **Slovakia**, **Latvia** and **Lithuania**.

EXCHANGE RATES: See **Bretton Woods**; **Exchange-Rate Mechanism**; **European Monetary System**; **Snake**

EXCISE DUTIES: See **Competition Policy**; **Harmonization**; **Internal Market**; **White Paper**

EXCLUSIVE AGREEMENTS between companies have been banned under the European Union's **competition policy**. The ban covers exclusive purchasing agreements on a wide variety of products, several kinds of exclusive distribution agreements, including **market sharing** and **price-fixing agreements**, and the use of **patents** and **trademarks**.

EXPENDITURE relates to the **budget** of the European Union (EU). The budget itself is made up from the EU's **own resources**, and is expected to fund both the policies pursued by the EU, and administrative running costs. The budget in 2017 was divided into six separate headings and most planned expenditure was directed towards the two principal areas of smart and inclusive growth and sustainable growth; natural resources (including agricultural expenditure, rural development, environment and climate action, and fisheries). There were also four further budget categories, namely: security and citizenship; Global Europe; administration; and special instruments. The **European Court of Auditors** is responsible for ensuring that all EU expenditure has taken place legally.

The draft **EXTERNAL FRONTIERS CONVENTION** proposed determining controls on the crossing of the European Union's (EU) external borders by nationals of non-member states, thereby facilitating the implementation of common EU policies on visas and **immigration**. The draft was eventually abandoned because of **Spain**'s desire for Gibraltar to be excluded from the Convention. (See also **Schengen Agreement**, **Visa Policy**.)

EXTERNAL RELATIONS is a collective term which describes the formal bilateral and multilateral trading agreements made by the European Union (EU) with third countries, for example: **association agreements**, **co-operation agreements**, **Europe agreements**, **partnership and co-operation agreements** and the **Cotonou Agreement**. It also refers to attempts by the member states to develop, outside the institutional structures of the EU, a common set of foreign policies through **European political co-operation** and the **common foreign and security policy**.

F

The *FACTORTAME* **JUDGMENT** of 1990 (*R v Secretary of State for Transport, ex parte Factortame Ltd*) was an important verdict by the **Court of Justice**, confirming that national legislation in conflict with European Communities law must be suspended. More specifically, the Court ruled that a member state cannot be liable unless it can be established that the state has severely and deliberately disregarded EU **law**. In order to determine this the following criteria have to be considered: the clarity and precision of the **directive**; the level of discretion left to the member state to implement the directive; whether damages were intentional and whether the failure to implement EU law can be explained by other extenuating circumstances.

FAIR stands for Fisheries, Agriculture and agro-Industrial Research programme. Established in 1994, this programme replaced all previous agricultural research programmes: AIR, CAMAR, ÉCLAIR, FAR and FLAIR. The objectives of FAIR were: 'To contribute to the improvement of the **competitiveness** of European agro-industry and primary production by the development of new technologies compatible with sustainable growth and taking account of consumer needs; to improve the quality of agricultural, forestry and fish products in general and food products in particular; to contribute to the **implementation** of the Community's agriculture, rural development, fisheries, environment and **internal market** policies; to contribute to a better match between the production and utilization of biological primary materials.' It was subsumed into the **quality of life and management of living resources programme** in 1999.

The **FAR RIGHT** resurfaced as an element within the seventh **European Parliament** (EP) (2009–14) following a series of electoral gains across the European Union (EU), but especially in **Hungary**, **Italy**, the **Netherlands** and the **United Kingdom**. Such parties had generally campaigned on a range of issues, advocating explicitly anti-immigrant and anti-Islamic policies (leading to **Islamophobia**), maintaining ardent opposition to Turkish accession and stressing uncompromising nationalist positions, which included the **withdrawal** of their respective countries from the EU. Among these parties, the Italian Northern League practically doubled its vote (to 10.2%), and in Hungary the Jobbik party's anti-Roma and anti-immigration platform secured three seats. In the Netherlands the increasingly anti-

Islamic Freedom Party won four seats. In the UK, the British National Party (BNP) won (two) seats in the EP.

In October 2009 a number of nationalist and far-right parties, including Jobbik, attempted to foster a closer working relationship among elements of the far right in Europe through the creation of a new Alliance of European National Movements (Alliance Européenne des Mouvements Nationaux—AEMN). However, the AEMN could not be recognized as a formal political group within the EP as it fell far short of meeting the necessary numbers (25 **Members of the European Parliament** (MEPs) and had insufficient transnational membership (members must come from at least seven EU member states). Nevertheless, in February 2012 the alliance was awarded some €260,000 in funding as a pan-European bloc. The AEMN rejected all attempts to create a European 'superstate', demanded strong, pro-family policies and sought to fight against the destructive effects of **globalization**. As differences between the national delegations grew, the more unworkable the AEMN became, and it had collapsed by the beginning of 2013 following the decision of Marine Le Pen, the leader of the French Front National (FN), to sever contacts with the BNP. Although the BNP lost its two EP seats at the 2014 EP elections, both the FN and Jobbik performed well. The FN emerged as the largest party in **France**, capturing nearly 25% of the vote and winning 23 seats, while Jobbik retained its three seats with almost 15% of the vote. Other, smaller extreme-right parties such as the German National Democratic Party and **Greece**'s Golden Dawn also won seats (one and three seats, respectively) at the elections to the eighth EP. A new far-right grouping in the EP emerged in mid-2015, known as the **Europe of Nations and Freedom**.

The **FAROE ISLANDS** have internal autonomy under Danish sovereignty (see **Denmark**). The parliament of the Islands opposed entry into the European Communities (EC). After extensive negotiations, mainly over fishing rights, an agreement was reached in January 1972. The Islands were granted special status, with the option of applying for full membership by the end of 1975. The Islands, however, have continued to reject membership, and participate only in free trade arrangements with the European Union (EU). Thus, common EU policies do not apply to the Faroe Islands.

FEDERAL REPUBLIC OF GERMANY: See **Germany**

The **FEDERAL REPUBLIC OF YUGOSLAVIA** (FRY): See **Serbia**; **Montenegro**

FEDERALISM is a system of government whereby different levels of authority (usually national and regional) exercise responsibility for particular areas, and maintain their own institutions, and whose specific powers are constitutionally guaranteed. The term has been used loosely and confusingly in the context of the European Union (EU) to describe the result of both centralization and decentralization. **Eurosceptics** have used the term to criticize what they see as an undue concentration of power at the supranational level of the EU institutions, while others see federalism as the way of preventing such a concentration. In discussions of the **European Council**, it has been used vaguely to refer both to the acquisition of more authority by the supranational institutions and to decentralization, with respect not only to the member states, but also beyond them to the regions. However, by themselves, concepts such as the **Europe of the Regions** or **subsidiarity** do not fully represent a proper federal structure.

FEOGA: See **European Agricultural Guidance and Guarantee Fund**

FIFTEEN (EU15), or Europe of the Fifteen, is a term sometimes used to describe the membership of the European Union after January 1995, when **Austria**, **Finland** and **Sweden** joined the existing **Twelve** member states.

FIFTH DIRECTIVE is the name of the first of several major **European Commission** initiatives relating to the structure of industrial companies and the protection of **workers' rights**. The Directive was proposed in 1972, and its target was those limited companies in the European Communities with a payroll of more than 500 workers. The Directive established conditions for the structure of such companies which, modelled to some extent on the experience of the Federal Republic of **Germany** (West Germany), would entail obligatory worker representation on supervisory boards. It encountered strong opposition from employers' organizations and some member states, and failed to gain the necessary unanimous approval in the Council of Ministers (see **Council of the European Union**). The idea of worker representation was eventually incorporated into the **Charter of Fundamental Social Rights of Workers** (the Social Charter) and the Social Chapter.

FINALITÉ POLITIQUE is a term used to describe the possible end goals and structure of the European Union. Beyond the references to an 'ever closer union' in the **Treaty of Rome** and the **Treaty on European Union**, there is nothing specific written in the treaties regarding this *finalité politique*, although discussions on a **constitution**, particularly in the context of the **Laeken Declaration**, have led to increased pressure to define it. For many, however, the current situation where the *finalité politique* is left undefined is attractive, since it allows for greater flexibility within the process of European integration.

The **FINANCIAL INSTRUMENT FOR FISHERIES GUIDANCE** (FIFG) was established in 1992, and was the main instrument whereby the European Union (EU) afforded aid to the fisheries sector under the **common fisheries policy** (CFP). It ran until December 2006. It aimed to support the CFP and, in pursuance of that objective, it sought to help to achieve lasting balance between fish stocks and fishing; to strengthen the **competitiveness** of operating structures and develop economically viable firms in the sector; to improve supplies and enhance the commercial value of fishery and aquaculture products; and to help revitalize areas dependent on fisheries and aquaculture. It advocated a restructuring of the industry and encouraged a reduction in fishing in EU waters, the decommissioning of vessels, establishment of joint ventures with foreign investors, and increasing competitiveness and assistance for the aquaculture industry, while also promoting economic and social cohesion. National and regional authorities were obliged to contribute to projects, although increased funding was available for poorer regions of the EU. **Decision making** concerning the FIFG could be broken down into two stages. In the first, a member state submitted a draft programme to the Commission for structural interventions in the fisheries sector: this set out the strategy and priorities for assistance, as well as a request for funding, in the form of a coherent package of multi-annual measures.

Thereafter, the Commission negotiated the programme on the basis of this draft with the member state and, having reached an agreement with the member state, approved it. The competitiveness of the EU fishing fleet remains a crucial factor, and the FIFG provided support for building and modernizing vessels. FIFG support was also available for the aquaculture sector and for the creation of protected coastal areas. Port facilities, processing, marketing and promotional operations were also eligible for funding. In addition, the private sector, through the producers' organizations, could apply for funding for various measures relating to the management of the resource and/or fishing effort. Finally, financial contributions to redundancy payments and pensions for fishermen retiring early were also made. Programmed **expenditure** under the FIFG for 2000–06 amounted to €3,746m. Over this specific period the EU contribution accounted to 75% of the planned total cost of infrastructure in less-developed regions (objective 1) and 50% in other regions. Where the aid went to enterprises, the EU contributions were limited to 35% and 15%, respectively. The **European Fisheries Fund** (EFF) replaced the FIFG in January 2007. The establishment of the EFF aimed to heighten the competitiveness of the sector and its longer-term viability. The programme ran until the end of 2013 and had a budget of some €4,304m.; it was succeeded by a new **European Maritime and Fisheries Fund** (EMFF) from 2014. The EMFF has been designed to achieve the above-mentioned objectives of the CFP and is structured around four broad pillars: Smart, Green Fisheries; Smart, Green Aquaculture; Sustainable Development of Fisheries Areas; and an Integrated Maritime Policy. This last pillar is the most innovative and centres on marine spatial planning and integrated coastal zone management.

FINANCIAL PERSPECTIVES are the multi-annual **budget** programmes of the European Union (EU). The first, often referred to as the **Delors I** package, covered the period 1988–92 and was adopted in 1987 in an attempt to limit the annual wrangling over the budget between what is now the **Council of the European Union** and the **European Parliament** (EP) and provide a firmer foundation for medium-term policy planning. The second financial perspective, the so-called **Delors II** package, covered the years 1993–99. A further perspective was agreed at the Berlin **summit meeting** of the **European Council** in March 1999 and was designed to finance **enlargement**. It was to cover the period until 2006. Each financial perspective is accompanied by an **inter-institutional agreement**, an understanding between the **European Commission**, the Council of the European Union and the EP, by which they commit themselves in advance to observing agreed limits on the main budgetary priorities and establish a framework for EU **expenditure** in the form of the financial perspective over a particular time period. In other words, the financial perspective shows the maximum amount and the composition of foreseeable EU expenditure. The main categories of EU expenditure are divided into headings; each of these headings carries an amount of commitment appropriations for each year. The headings are: smart and inclusive growth (which includes **competitiveness** and cohesion); sustainable growth: natural resources (which includes agricultural policy and the environment); security and citizenship; global Europe; administration; and compensations. Negotiations among the member state governments for each new financial perspective prove contentious. The current financial perspective covers the seven-year period 2014–20. It was agreed by the European Parliament and the Council in November–December 2013, and came into effect in January 2014.

FINANCIAL POLICY: See **Economic and Financial Policy**

FINLAND has emerged as the most pro-European Union (EU) member state within Scandinavia and, unlike both **Denmark** and **Sweden**, signed up as one of the initial members of the **euro**. This identity with the EU and the wider Europe reflects Finland's somewhat troubled history, when its geographical position between both the **Russian Federation** and Sweden often curtailed the independence of this smaller state. In the immediate post-war period, for example, Finland was restricted in its relationships with other Western European countries by the Finno-Soviet Pact of Friendship, Co-operation and Mutual Assistance, which had been signed with the **USSR** in 1948. This in effect forced Finland to pursue a foreign policy based on neutrality, making its government wary of participation in any organization that the USSR might interpret as violating the terms of the treaty. Hence, for a number of years Finland played a minimal role in Western European developments. In the early 1960s it did not approach the European Communities (EC), as did the other Nordic states, for some form of association. Moreover, it became only an associate member of the **European Free Trade Association** (EFTA). However, it later joined the EFTA states in seeking some form of closer co-operation with the EC. The signing of a **free trade agreement** was delayed until 1973, again because of arguments over whether it violated Finland's neutrality, and doubts about its acceptability to the USSR. The Agreement came into force in January 1974 with an accelerated rate of tariff reductions, in order to synchronize the date for implementation with that for the other EFTA states. Finland became a full member of EFTA in 1986, and in the more relaxed atmosphere of the late 1980s and the collapse of the Iron Curtain felt able to join the other EFTA states in negotiations with the EC over a **European Economic Area**. In 1992, after much discussion, it formally submitted an application to join the EC. Negotiations were completed by 1994 and endorsed by a popular referendum, allowing Finland to join the EU on 1 January 1995. Finland remains the only Nordic EU member to have adopted the **euro** as its national currency, and is a signatory of the **Fiscal Compact**.

The **FISCAL COMPACT**, formally the Treaty on Stability, Coordination and Governance in the Economic and Monetary Union, was signed by all of the European Union (EU) member states on 2 March 2012, with the exception of the **Czech Republic** and the **United Kingdom**. The Fiscal Compact entered into force on 1 January 2013 for the 16 member states that had completed the **ratification** process prior to this date. For those member states that subsequently ratified the document, the Compact was to enter into force on the first day of the month following the deposit of ratification instruments. The Fiscal Compact, which is essentially a more stringent version and extension of the earlier **Stability and Growth Pact**, is designed to ensure improved financial discipline within the EU and especially within the **eurozone**. To this end, it stipulates that within one year of the Compact entering into force for it each signatory state has to introduce in primary law a so-called 'deficit brake' requiring the national budget to be in balance (i.e. with a deficit equivalent to less than 3% of gross domestic product—GDP) or in surplus, and for the annual structural deficit to be no greater than 0.5% or 1.0% of GDP (depending on a country's debt-to-GDP ratio). In addition, a 'debt brake' has to be legally implemented according to which the general government debt will not exceed 60% of GDP; if the debt is above this limit the member state is obliged to reduce it by at least one-twentieth each year. A breach of the agreed ceilings could result in a fine (of up to 0.1% of the offending member state's GDP) from the **Court of Justice**. The Fiscal Compact also reinforces commitments to improved economic and fiscal governance contained in existing agreements and legislation, notably the revised Stability and Growth Pact and the so-called 'six pack' of legislative measures designed to enforce budgetary discipline through, for example, increased budgetary surveillance. The Compact also provides for at least two summits per year of heads of government and state from the member countries of the eurozone; non-eurozone signatories will be permitted to attend at least one of these summits. The Fiscal Compact is not formally part of EU law, but an intergovernmental document. Only member states that have completed ratification of the Fiscal Compact are eligible for access to financial assistance from the **European Stability Mechanism**. At July 2014 25 of the 28 EU member states (19 eurozone members and six non-eurozone members) had ratified the Fiscal Compact. The UK was the only one of the former EU27 member states to have no intention of becoming a signatory to the treaty. The **Czech Republic** expressed its intention to do so in 2014, but by late 2017 had still not signed the compact. **Croatia**, the newest EU member state, had yet to sign the treaty at 2017.

FISHERIES: See **Common Fisheries Policy**; **North Atlantic Fisheries Organization**

FLANKING MEASURES is a term used in the European Union to describe measures or actions that are intended to support the implementation and objectives of a specific common policy or programme, but are not integral to it. The term is most often used in the context of the **internal market**. Among the most prominent flanking measures are those concerning **economic and monetary union**, **competition policy**, **social policy** and **environmental policy**.

FLEXIBILITY is a term used to describe the effects of different approaches to integration, such as **multi-speed Europe**, **à la carte Europe** and **two-speed Europe**. It is also used to describe the effects of the mechanisms for **enhanced co-operation** introduced by the **Treaty of Amsterdam**.

The **FONTAINEBLEAU SUMMIT** of the **European Council**, held in **France** in June 1984, was one of the most decisive in the history of **summit meetings**. It dealt conclusively with several major issues that had hindered the development of the European Communities (EC) for a number of years. A recurrent issue since the election of Margaret Thatcher as British Prime Minister in 1979 had been the **United Kingdom**'s contribution to the EC **budget**. Agreement was formally reached on the UK's budgetary position and on raising the limit of **value-added tax** contributions to the EC budget to avoid threatened insolvency; limits were placed upon **common agricultural policy** spending, and the way was opened for the entry into the EC of **Portugal** and **Spain**. By resolving such issues and authorizing the establishment of a **Committee for a People's Europe** and the **Dooge Committee**, the summit contributed to the EC's subsequent progress towards further integration.

FOOD AID: See **Development Aid**

The **FOOD FRAUD NETWORK** (FFN) was established in the wake of a scandal after it emerged in January–February 2013 that unregulated horsemeat had been used covertly in processed meat products widely supplied throughout Europe. In March the European Commissioner responsible for Health Policy, Antonio Borg, announced a five-point plan, which identified actions to be implemented over the short, medium and longer term in order to rectify shortcomings in the EU's food supply chain. The actions related to the following areas: food fraud; food testing; rules pertaining to the monitoring and issuing of horse passports (with which all horses are issued); official controls, implementation and penalties; and source of origin labelling. In May the Commission proposed new legislation to update and strengthen the agri-food chain, in an effort to improve food safety. In July the FFN was launched, comprising food fraud contact points in each of the 28 EU member states, as well as **Iceland**, **Norway** and **Switzerland**. The FFN, which held two meetings in 2013, provides cross-border administrative support and co-operation, on issues pertaining to financially motivated violations of legislation on food, and by 2014 had begun to examine potential food fraud cases and to act as a forum for discussion regarding the prioritization of action at the supranational level on food fraud.

FOODSTUFFS are the subject of several European Union **directives** intended to protect the **health and safety** of consumers and strengthen **consumer policy**. The directives govern the manufacturing, labelling and marketing of foodstuffs. Their provisions include: the publication of listings of permitted substances and additives along with the requisite purity standards; **regulations** governing the production of a range of foodstuffs; the fixing of maximum permitted levels for pesticide residues in fruit, vegetable and oil products; and regulations specifying that a list of ingredients and their quantities, as well as a 'best before' date, must be included on the labelling of foodstuffs. In addition, a general ban has been placed upon the use of animal growth promoters containing substances that might generate adverse hormonal or other side effects. The **European Parliament** in 2002 proposed stricter labelling regulations for foodstuffs containing genetically modified ingredients; these new regulations came into effect in April 2004. Following a proposal in the **European Commission**'s 2000 **White Paper** on food safety, a **European Food Safety Authority** was created in 2002. New legislation on food labelling came into effect in December 2014, and the application of the legislation was obligatory from December 2016. The new rules aimed to provide consumers with more transparent and comprehensive information on the content and composition of pre-packaged food.

FOREIGN POLICY: See **Common Foreign and Security Policy**; **European Political Co-operation**

FORESTRY has emerged as a salient aspect of environmental concerns over the last three decades. The European Union (EU) is home to some 5% of the world's forests and about 42% of the total land area of the EU is covered by forests or woodland. Although the design and implementation of forestry policy is very much a member state competence and most states have developed their own established forestry policy, the issue does, none the less, resonate at EU level. Forestry policy emerges in wider EU discussions about, for example, biodiversity, climate change, sources of clean water, energy and public amenities. Accordingly, the issue of forestry has been the subject of several EU initiatives designed to combine the economic development of the forestry industry with measures for environmental protection and conservation. The initiatives were first brought together in the Forestry Sectoral Research and Technology (FOREST) action programme of 1990. This was later absorbed into AIR in 1991, and then into FAIR, which was subsequently subsumed into the **quality of life and management of living resources programme**. In 1999 the **Council of the European Union** adopted a **resolution** on a Forestry Strategy for the EU, which focused on sustainable forest management and the multifunctional role of forests. Following a review of this strategy in 2005, the Commission adopted an EU Forest Action Plan in 2006, followed by a **Green Paper** on forest protection and information in 2010. The EU dedicates approximately €120m. a year to forest conservation and management projects in less developed countries. In September 2013 the **European Commission** adopted a communication on a new forest strategy.

FORTRESS EUROPE is a term popularized in the 1980s and early 1990s that summarizes the concerns expressed by politicians and economists in several countries about some of the possible consequences of the **internal market** including the free movement of goods, persons, services and capital. Then it referred to fears that while the European Union would have free trade within its borders, it might adopt a more protectionist attitude towards imports from the rest of the world. In more recent years, the term has become associated with the stringency of border controls and **immigration policies** in the member states whereby as internal **freedom of movement** has become realized within the EU, physical and metaphorical walls have been erected to keep those outside of Europe out. It has been suggested then that the phenomena of Fortress Europe have been at least partly to blame for the **European migration crisis**.

FOUCHET PLAN is the name commonly given to the outcome of a proposal by President Charles de Gaulle of **France** in 1961 that the **Six** members of the **European Economic Community** (EEC) should explore ways of achieving a 'Union of States'. A committee, headed by Christian Fouchet of France, considered the matter and produced a draft treaty in November 1961. A modified second version was produced the following year. The components of the Plan included a council of heads of government or of foreign ministers where decisions would be taken only by unanimous agreement, a permanent intergovernmental secretariat and four permanent intergovernmental committees to take responsibility for the policy fields of foreign affairs, defence, commerce and cultural affairs. The scheme was opposed by most of the other five states, especially the **Netherlands**. The Plan represented a considerable shift in direction from that envisaged by the **Treaty of Rome**, and in addition the smaller states wished first to settle the question of **enlargement**, particularly the possible entry into the EEC of the **United Kingdom**. With France unable to generate support among its partners, the Plan was abandoned in 1963. A truncated version survived in the form of the 1963 **Treaty of Friendship** between France and the Federal Republic of **Germany** (West Germany).

FOUNDING TREATIES is a phrase, like 'constitutive treaties', which refers to the four documents that established the European Communities and the European Union: the **Treaty of Paris** of 1951 establishing the **European Coal and Steel Community** (ECSC), the two treaties of 1957 (see **Treaty of Rome**) establishing the **European Atomic Energy Community** (EAEC or Euratom) and the **European Economic Community** (EEC), and the **Treaty on European Union** (TEU) of 1992. The founding treaties have all been amended by, among others, the **Single European Act**, the TEU, the **Treaty of Amsterdam** and the **Treaty of Nice**. The founding treaties and the amending treaties are increasingly referred to as the **European treaties**. If it had been ratified, the **Treaty establishing a Constitution for Europe** would have replaced the Treaty of Rome and the TEU. Its replacement, the **Treaty of Lisbon**, amended the founding treaties and renamed the **Treaty establishing the European Community** the **Treaty on the Functioning of the European Union**.

FRAMEWORK PROGRAMMES: See **Research Framework Programmes**.

FRANCE has been one of the most prominent supporters of European integration since 1948. It provided a location for the **Council of Europe** in 1949. The **European Coal and Steel Community** was initially conceived by **Jean Monnet** and was realized by Robert Schuman. France was a founder member of the European Communities (EC), and its involvement in their development has been such that French governments have taken an almost proprietorial interest in the EC. Their actions have had important consequences for the EC, even if not always to their benefit. The policies of President Charles de Gaulle (1959–69), for example, profoundly altered the nature of the EC and delayed its **enlargement**. His successor, Georges Pompidou (1969–74), opened the way to enlargement in return for obtaining the kind of **common agricultural policy** (CAP) that France wanted. President Valéry Giscard d'Estaing (1974–81) proposed the **European Council** and co-sponsored the **European Monetary System**. The tradition was maintained by François Mitterrand (1981–95), who campaigned strongly for further intensive integration, and by Jacques Chirac (1995–2007). In 2000 the French presidency of the European Council was responsible for bringing about the conclusion, albeit unsatisfactory, of the 2000 **intergovernmental conference** and the adoption of the **Treaty of Nice**.

France has benefited economically from the EC, above all from the CAP. Just as the EC provided the Federal Republic of **Germany** (FRG—West Germany) with an outlet for its export-orientated industry, so it gave France a bigger market for its large and variegated agriculture, although by the 1980s some French products faced severe competition from cheaper Mediterranean produce. On the whole, the French attitude towards the EC has been highly utilitarian, and governments have always been prepared to emphasize national interests should this seem advisable for domestic political and economic reasons. Nevertheless, its political influence within the EC has been great. To some extent, this was due to its close relationship with the FRG. The EC served one basic purpose of French foreign policy: to influence, even perhaps control, the FRG. That reason decreased in importance after German reunification. In particular, the currency crises of 1992–93 indicated that the two countries had different economic concerns. In the 1990s there emerged a stronger anti-integration mood, as exemplified by the results of the 1992 referendum on the **Treaty on European Union**. This was held by President Mitterrand to emphasize France's European commitment, but he narrowly escaped a humiliating defeat, because government policy, intended to enable the country to meet the criteria for participation in **economic and monetary union**, had contributed to high levels of unemployment. His successor, Jacques Chirac, proved less fortunate when in May 2005 the French people (with a rate of participation of 70%) rejected (by 55% to 45%) the **Treaty establishing a Constitution for Europe**. The final outcome owed much to a variety of concerns over issues such as the 2004 enlargement, the next wave of enlargement, a British economic blueprint being imposed on the European Union, and some dissatisfaction with Chirac's decade-long rule. Nicolas Sarkozy succeeded Chirac in May 2007. Sarkozy initially emerged as one of the most dynamic and flamboyant of the incumbent European leaders and as someone who was determined to reform and revive France's economic model, but he raised some concerns in his first six months of office over comments on both **competition policy** and the future of the **common fisheries policy**. France successfully completed **ratification** of the **Treaty of Lisbon** without holding a referendum. It was also noticeable that relations with Germany on European affairs and strategies reverted to the cordiality of the Helmut Schmidt/Giscard d'Estaing and Helmut Kohl/Mitterrand periods. However, François Hollande replaced Sarkozy following the latter's bid for a second term as French President in May 2012. Hollande's presidency coincided with perceptions by some observers of a cooling in relations between Germany and France. After what was largely deemed a tumultuous term of office, Hollande chose not run for another term, and in May 2017 newcomer **Emmanuel Macron** became the new President of France.

FRANCO-GERMAN MIXED BRIGADE: See **Eurocorps**

FRANCO-GERMAN TREATY OF FRIENDSHIP: See **Treaty of Friendship**

The *FRANCOVICH* JUDGMENT is the common name of a case (*Francovich et al.* v *Italy*) heard by the **Court of Justice** in 1992. The Italian Government was accused of not implementing European Communities rules. Specifically, it had failed to implement Directive 80/987/EEC, which seeks to protect employees in cases of insolvency, despite several reminders from the Commission. A worker named Francovich duly opted to initiate legal proceedings against the Italian Government for his lost pension rights when his company became insolvent. In finding against **Italy**, the Court established the principle that individuals could appeal against the non-implementation of European Union law by member states on the grounds that their individual rights had been infringed. It also confirmed that member states found guilty could be deemed liable and fined.

FRAUD rose to prominence on the political agenda of the European Communities (EC) in the 1990s. In particular, there were growing concerns about the amount of the EC **budget** that was being lost through fraud, concerns that were often reinforced by the annual reports of the **Court of Auditors** and criticisms coming from the **European Parliament**. On top of these came the allegations of corruption that led to the downfall of the **European Commission** under President Jacques Santer in 1999. Early concerns led to the creation in 1994 of an **Advisory Committee for the Co-ordination of Fraud Prevention**, which was followed in 1999 by the establishment of a **European Anti-Fraud Office** (OLAF) within the Commission. Beyond combating fraud within the institutions and policies of the European Union, much attention has also been focused since the early 1990s on the need to counter cross-border fraud. Hence, combating fraud features as one of the activities to be pursued as part of policy on **justice and home affairs**. Concerns about fraud were also instrumental in moves to create a **European Public Prosecutor's Office**.

FREE TRADE AGREEMENTS have been signed (or are currently under negotiation) by the European Union with many countries and regions, including European countries that, at the time of signing, were not applicants for membership. The agreements provide for a phased introduction of industrial free trade. Some examples include agreements signed as part of the **European Free Trade Association**, and the EU's free trade agreement with **South Africa**. There are provisional regional free trade agreements between the EU and countries in Africa and Central America, among others provided through **Economic Partnership Agreements**.

FREEDOM OF MOVEMENT lies at the heart of the objectives outlined in the **Treaty of Rome**, which required the abolition of barriers to the 'freedom of movement for persons, services and capital'. Frontier formalities and checks, different indirect tax rates, government appointive, contractual and procurement policies, and the national basis of many professional qualifications all effectively hindered the establishment of free movement. While some slight progress was taken towards removing the barriers, a significant impetus was not achieved until the decision to establish the **internal market** was made. The principle was reconfirmed and formally applied to goods by the **Treaty on European Union**, but the objective had still not been fully realized by the late 1990s. The **Treaty of Amsterdam** attempted to make improvements in this field by setting a timetable of five years within which an area of freedom, justice and security should be established. Common rules on **immigration**, **asylum** and **visa policy** were intended to promote greater freedom of movement between the member states. International crime was to be dealt with through improved co-operation between national police forces and customs authorities, and through the work of **Europol**. Moreover, the **Schengen Agreement** was incorporated into the Treaties, although **Bulgaria**, **Croatia**, **Cyprus**, **Ireland**, **Romania** and the **United Kingdom** remained outside the **Schengen Area**. The principle of freedom of movement became particularly controversial during the **European migration crisis** of 2015–16, when the movement of large numbers of migrants and asylum seekers along what became known as the Western Balkan route towards western and northern Europe prompted several member states to close their borders or to erect fences closing their borders with other European Union (EU) member states, effectively temporarily suspending their participation in the Schengen arrangement. At September 2017 five EU countries, as well as **Norway**, had temporarily reintroduced border controls, owing either to persistent irregular migratory flows or concerns relating to potential terrorist activity. Although the UK was outside the Schengen Area, the issue of freedom of movement became a topic of debate both prior to and after that country's referendum vote in June 2016 in favour of leaving the EU, as some British nationals voted to leave the Union in an attempt to halt inward migration by economic migrants from other EU member states, particularly Central and Eastern Europe.

FRONTEX (formally the European Border and Coast Guard Agency) is a European Union (EU) agency based in Warsaw, **Poland**. It was established in 2004, as the European Agency for the Management of Operational Co-operation at the External

Borders, to co-ordinate co-operation between EU member states on external border security issues. Its tasks included risk analysis, co-ordination of operational co-operation in the field of external border management and assistance in the training of national border guards, research relevant for the control and surveillance of external borders, technical and operational assistance at external borders, and support for member states in organizing joint return operations. It also pursued co-operation with non-member states to improve border security, and worked closely with the border control authorities of non-EU/**Schengen Area** countries, in particular countries that had been identified as a source or transit route for irregular migration, in order to ensure compliance with the EU's external relations policy. In September 2015, during his first State of the Union address, and amid the deepening **European migration crisis**, the President of the **European Commission**, **Jean-Claude Juncker**, called for FRONTEX to be strengthened and better funded in order to become a 'fully operational' border and coast guard. In December the Commission presented legislative proposals for the establishment of a new European Border and Coast Guard, building on FRONTEX as part of the **European Agenda on Migration**. The proposals, which sought to ensure improved management of migration, increased internal security, and the safeguarding of the principle of freedom of movement, were formally adopted in September 2016 and the European Border and Coast Guard Agency was officially launched in early October.

FUNCTIONALISM is an early theory of integration on which **neo-functionalism** draws. It holds that the creation of international agencies is the consequence of a shared need among states for technocratic management of policy.

FYRM: See **former Yugoslav republic of Macedonia**

G

G-7: The G-7 is officially the title of meetings between the finance ministers of Canada, **France**, **Germany**, **Italy**, **Japan**, the **United Kingdom** and the **USA**, a practice that was established in Tokyo, Japan, in May 1986. The term is also used more generally to describe the summit meetings of the heads of government of the same seven countries, which began at Rambouillet, France, in 1975 (although Canada did not become involved in the G-7 process until some months after the initial meeting). The European Union (EU) holds all the privileges and obligations of membership of the G-7, but does not have the right to host or chair a summit. The EU is represented at G-7 summits by the President of the **European Commission** and by the President of the **European Council**. Leaders of the **USSR** and, later, the **Russian Federation** were invited to attend the summits after 1991. Russia demanded equal representation and became a full member in 2002, thereby creating the G-8. Originally intended to discuss common economic problems, after 1989 the summit agendas became ever more political in tone and have sought to tackle issues such as trade with the Third World, global poverty, the environment, and, increasingly since 2008, the issue of taxation. In recent years these meetings of the world's richest countries have increasingly become a target for protesters to express their anger at politicians over issues such as the environment and capitalism. In March 2014 Russia was excluded from the G-8, owing to the controversy over its role in the secession of Crimea from **Ukraine**; the G-8 therefore reverted to its previous name, the G-7.

G-8: See **G-7**

GATT: See **General Agreement on Tariffs and Trade**

MARIYA GABRIEL (1979–) is the current Commissioner responsible for Digital Economy and Society, whose appointment was approved by the **European Parliament** in July 2017. Prior to holding this role, Gabriel was a **Member of the European Parliament** (MEP) from 2009, belonging to the **Group of the European People's Party**. As MEP Gabriel held particular interests in EU enlargement and **gender equality**, advocating the inclusion of women in all aspects of political life. Gabriel replaced **Kristalina Georgieva** as the Commissioner from Bulgaria.

GENDER EQUALITY is considered a foundational value of the European Union (EU) and it was first enshrined in the equal pay for equal work principle within the **Treaty of Rome**. It is the notion that men and women ought to be treated equally, while also acknowledging that women, in particular, are often confronted with discrimination in all spheres of society. To advance gender equality, the EU uses a three-pronged approach, including equal treatment legislation; **gender mainstreaming**; and specific measures for the advancement of women (promotion of **women's rights**). Although many EU member states show advancements in gender equality, there are still challenges within the Union. In 2010–15 the **European Commission** held the 'Strategy for Equality between Women and Men' as a guiding framework for advancing gender equality. It was succeeded by the 'Strategic Engagement for Gender Equality' for 2016–19, which was published in December 2015. This current strategy is especially committed to tackling gender-based violence and supporting victims both within and outside the EU. To achieve the aims of the Strategic Engagement, the **European Institute for Gender Equality** (EIGE) assists EU institutions and member states in the collection, analysis and dissemination of objective, reliable and comparable information and data on equality between women and men.

GENDER MAINSTREAMING was first advocated as a strategy for attaining **gender equality** at the Fourth World Conference on Women, held in Beijing, the People's Republic of China, in 1995. It is intended to integrate a gender perspective into all European Union (EU) policy domains. It was first brought to the fore of EU policy processes by the **Treaty of Amsterdam**. Gender mainstreaming is understood in this context as the preparation, design, implementation, monitoring and evaluation of policies, regulatory measures and spending programmes so that they achieve favourable, even if differentiated, outcomes for both men and women (so-called gender-responsive content). Gender mainstreaming advocates for gender representation, ensuring both men and women have equal and substantive influence in policy processes. It is the strategy for gender equality most advocated by the majority of international organizations and the **European Institute for Gender Equality** (EIGE).

The **GENERAL AGREEMENT ON TARIFFS AND TRADE** (GATT) was a convention signed in 1947 by 23 countries (although the number of contracting parties subsequently increased to several times that number), and maintained as a specialized agency of the **United Nations**. Its intention was to secure a pattern of free trade in the post-war world. GATT's objectives were to work towards an orderly framework for international trade, through the elimination of unilateral actions by states and the gradual reduction of tariff barriers. The organization was based upon the principle of non-discrimination: trade advantages offered by one country to another had to be extended to all. There were, however, many exceptions to the principle of non-discrimination. The **Treaty of Rome** specified that the European Communities (EC) should represent the member states and their interests in external trade affairs and negotiations. Accordingly, the **European Commission** represented the member states in all GATT rounds of negotiations after the **Kennedy Round** of the 1960s. While GATT was generally successful, the later negotiations were highly contentious as the agenda extended from manufactured products to cover, for example, agriculture, copyright and services. The **Uruguay Round** of negotiations of 1986–94 was dominated by arguments between the EC and the **USA**, which had been highly critical of what it perceived as EC protectionism in a variety of areas, particularly in relation to the **common agricultural policy** (CAP). **France**'s objections to lowering protection for its farmers caused considerable tension and the US Government threatened to walk away from the entire Round unless the CAP was tackled. This position found sympathy among some EC member states, including the **United Kingdom**. The Blair House Agreement of November 1992 between the EC and the USA greatly limited financial assistance to EC farmers and antagonized France. The French Government threatened to boycott the discussions until France secured concessions at a special EC **summit meeting** in December 1992. Negotiations on a successor to GATT were completed in 1993, and on 1 January 1995 the **World Trade Organization** was established.

The **GENERAL COURT** was formerly known as the Court of First Instance (CFI) and, after the **Treaty of Lisbon**, known as the General Court, and is an innovation of the late 1980s. Under the **Treaty of Rome**, the **Court of Justice** was made responsible for cases brought against the European Communities (EC) by their employees. These cases involved such issues as recruitment, promotion, salaries and disciplinary measures. They were, to a large degree, responsible for the increasing volume of work with which the Court had to cope, accounting for almost one-half of the cases heard. In order to reduce the Court's burden, by removing from its competence minor cases, including those involving EC staff that could easily be handled by a lower court, the **Single European Act** created the CFI. Composed of one judge from each member state, but chosen by common accord, the new Court began to operate in September 1989. Its role and status were further enhanced by the **Treaty on European Union** in 1991, but only after the **Treaty of Nice** was it instituted as a genuine court of first instance. Prior to this, it was competent primarily for cases relating to **competition policy** and the **European Coal and Steel Community**. Many other cases went directly to the Court of Justice, bypassing the CFI. Under the Treaty of Lisbon, the CFI was rebranded as the General Court on 30 November 2009. The treaty also introduced the term 'Court of Justice of the European Union' to describe the entire court system of the European Union (EU), comprising the Court of Justice, the General Court and the Civil Service Tribunal. The General Court, which is based in Luxembourg, deals with a range of cases covering, *inter alia*, actions for annulment of EU **legislation** and actions for failure to act by an EU institution. In all cases, appeals against its decisions can be directed to the Court of Justice on grounds of its lack of jurisdiction over a case or its misinterpretation of precedents. The General Court is divided into nine chambers, each of which consists of three or four judges; the Court includes at least one judge from each member state. In December 2015 the **Council of the European Union** adopted a regulation reforming the General Court. During the first stage of reform, the number of judges was to increase by 12, and in September 2016 the Civil Service Tribunal merged with the General Court, with its seven judges becoming part of the merged institution. Nine additional judges were to be appointed in September 2019, bringing the total number of judges to 56 (at late 2017 there were 47 judges). The current President of the General Court is Marc Jaeger, a jurist from Luxembourg.

The **GENERAL SECRETARIAT OF THE COUNCIL OF THE EUROPEAN UNION**: See **Council Secretariat**

PAOLO GENTILONI (1954–) has been the Prime minister of **Italy** since December 2016. He was born in Rome, and is a graduate in political science from the Sapienza University of Rome. His interest in politics was demonstrated early, and Gentiloni was a former member of the Student Movement and subsequently the Worker's Movement for Socialism. He was elected to the Italian parliament for the first time in the 2001 general election and went on to serve as Minister for Communications in the Government of Romano Prodi in 2006–08, and as Minister of Foreign Affairs under Matteo Renzi (succeeding **Federica Mogherini** who had left the post to become the **High Representative of the Union for Foreign Affairs and Security Policy**). In December 2016, following the defeat of the Italian constitutional referendum initiated by Renzi, the Italian President, Sergio Mattarella, asked Gentiloni to form a new Government, which was sworn in on 12 December 2016.

KRISTALINA GEORGIEVA (1953–) was nominated as the Bulgarian Commissioner to the new 28-member **European Commission** led by **Jean-Claude Juncker**, which took office on 1 November 2014. In September Juncker named Georgieva as one of the seven Vice-Presidents of the Commission and as Commissioner for **Budget** and Human Resources, subject to approval by the **European Parliament**. This constituted a reappointment to the European Commission, as immediately prior to this new position she had been one of the 28 Commissioners in 2010–14, when she had responsibility for international co-operation, humanitarian aid and crisis response. She is a Bulgarian national, who has an MA degree in Political Economy and holds a doctorate in environmental economics, both from the University of National and World Economy in Sofia, **Bulgaria**. Following postgraduate research, she held a range of academic and consultancy positions in Bulgaria and the **USA** and lectured in various universities around the world. In 1993 she launched her career as an environmental economist at the

World Bank, where she rose through the ranks to become Director in the Environment Department and then Vice-President and Corporate Secretary. Georgieva left her position in the Commission to take on the role of Chief Executive Officer at the World Bank. In July she was succeeded as the Commissioner from Bulgaria by **Mariya Gabriel**.

GERMANY was occupied after its military defeat in 1945 by the four victors: **France**, the **USSR**, the **United Kingdom** and the **USA**. Each of these states administered a part of Germany. The original intention was to demilitarize, de-Nazify and re-educate the German people before returning the reins of power to a German government. The onset of the **Cold War** between the USSR and the USA led to the division of Europe and the division of Germany in 1949. From then until October 1990 two separate countries, the Federal Republic of Germany (FRG—West Germany) and the German Democratic Republic (GDR—East Germany), existed in Germany. The FRG was a founder member of the European Communities (EC), and one of the most Europe-orientated of the member states, although there was not necessarily a strong correlation between this commitment and West German influence within the EC. German influence in the EC/European Union (EU) has been significant, although historically it has tended to focus on monetary and economic affairs rather than political issues. It was the largest and richest member state, with the strongest economy and manufacturing system, and after 1979 its currency dominated the **European Monetary System**. In the 1950s West German commitment to European integration was seen by then German Chancellor Konrad Adenauer not only as a means of access to important markets for its export-orientated economy, but also as a central element of his strategy to link the FRG firmly in a Western alliance, rehabilitating it in the eyes of its neighbours and allaying fears of a possible future resurgence of German militarism. Adenauer also saw European integration as being based upon a Franco-German rapprochement, even if this meant that the FRG would, because of post-war realities, be the junior partner. The rapprochement was formally acknowledged in the 1963 **Treaty of Friendship**.

It was not until the 1970s that the FRG began to seek to exert a political influence in the EC more commensurate with its economic strength. Its support was more tempered by an evaluation of the consequences of EC policies for West German national interests. Between 1974 and 1982 Chancellor Helmut Schmidt was particularly concerned, in a period of general economic downturn, about the cost of EC initiatives. His successor, the longest serving post-war German Chancellor, Helmut Kohl (1982–98), was a more unreserved supporter of further integration, and active in the initiatives of the 1980s—the single market (see **internal market**), **economic and monetary union** (EMU) and moves towards deeper political integration—which culminated in the **Treaty on European Union**.

The GDR had been given access to the EC for its products as a result of the **Ostpolitik** treaties, and upon German reunification automatically became part of the EC. The reunited Germany was subsequently the largest unit in the EC by an even greater margin, and Kohl increased the pressure for political union. His reasoning was much the same as that of Adenauer: the reduction of German sovereignty within a political Europe would also reduce fears abroad of German power and limit the effect of potential German nationalism. Nevertheless, there was resistance in Germany to Kohl's commitment to European union, especially over the replacement of the German mark by a single European currency. However, the coalition governments under Gerhard Schröder (1998–2002; 2002–05) maintained Germany's pro-EU stance and saw German entry into EMU in January 1999. Germany remains strongly in favour of the EU, but its Government is prepared to raise its concerns with the EU more often than it has in the past, as, for example, over its contributions to the EU **budget**. Both houses of the German parliament endorsed the **Treaty establishing a Constitution for Europe** in May 2005. In the Bundestag (lower house) some 569 votes were cast in favour of the treaty with only 23 against. In the latter part of 2005 **Angela Merkel** was elected the first female German Chancellor; she headed a 'grand coalition' Government between the Christian Democrats (CDU) and the Social Democrats (SPD). Merkel is largely credited with being responsible for both securing agreement on the budgetary settlement for the period 2007–13 and doing most of the groundwork prior to agreement in the **European Council** on the **Treaty of Lisbon**. Merkel has emerged as one of Europe's most substantial political personalities and successfully ran for re-election as Chancellor in the latter part of 2009. On this occasion the CDU, as it had hoped, was able to remove the 'problematic constraints' of the grand coalition with the SPD by disbanding it and entered instead into a coalition with the smaller Free Democratic Party. Merkel was also centrally involved in the appointment of her fellow Christian Democrat, the Belgian Herman Van Rompuy, as the first **President of the European Council** under the terms of the Treaty of Lisbon. In addition, Merkel was at the forefront of plans financially to address the perilous state of the Greek economy from 2010 as a means of stabilizing the **euro**. Merkel's efforts at safeguarding the stability of the **eurozone** and the future of the euro led directly to her key role in the drawing up of the 2012 **Fiscal Compact** (Treaty on Stability, Co-ordination and Governance in the Economic and Monetary Union). In October 2013 Merkel was re-elected as German Chancellor at the head of a grand coalition between her Christian Democrats/Christian Social Union and the Social Democrats. By that time she had earned the reputation of being perhaps the most influential politician in the EU.

In August 2015 Merkel aroused controversy by temporarily opening the German borders and announcing that Germany was willing to accept applications for asylum from Syrian refugees, irrespective of their initial point of entry into the EU (in contravention of the **Dublin Regulation**). Hundreds of thousands of people subsequently began to travel across Europe in order to reach Germany, with some 800,000 estimated to have arrived in 2015. The wave of migration led to the re-imposition of border controls and the erection of fences by a number of member states, including **Austria**, **Hungary**, **Denmark** and **Sweden**. In late September 2017 Merkel was re-elected as Chancellor, albeit with a weakened mandate.

GLOBALIZATION is one of the major challenges facing the European Union (EU). The phenomenon refers to a process of economic integration on a global level. The main characteristics and driving forces behind globalization are: the liberalization of international trade (through the **World Trade Organization**—WTO) and capital movements; developing technological progress and the advance of the **information society**; and the process of **deregulation**. These factors combined together stimulate international trade by removing barriers and promoting new forms of technology. Many EU policy areas have a global dimension, such as trade policy, **competition policy**, **environmental policy** and the **common foreign and security policy**. Some regard globalization with alarm and question how democratic, accountable and legitimate are some of these new forums such as the WTO, and who is taking decisions on the public's behalf. Recent years have seen the emergence of a well-co-ordinated anti-capitalist protest movement at gatherings of the WTO and, on occasion, at meetings of the **European Council**.

GOLDEN TRIANGLE is a phrase that has often been used to describe what is commonly perceived to be the economic centre and motivating force of the European Union, an area bounded by Paris (**France**), the German Ruhr area and Milan (**Italy**).

The **GONZÁLEZ GROUP** was a **reflection** group established in December 2008 with the goal of identifying how best the European Union (EU) can 'more effectively anticipate and meet challenges in the longer term horizon of 2020 to 2030'. Chaired by Felipe González Márquez, the 12-member group submitted its report to the European Council on 8 May 2010 during the **euro** crisis. The report—*Project Europe 2030: Challenges and Opportunities*—urged courageous leadership to address a range of challenges that the EU would face over the next 20 years to 2030. The challenges covered financial governance, social rights, education, research, migration and demographic change, foreign and security policy, and the engagement of EU citizens with the 'European project'.

The **GOVERNANCE WHITE PAPER** was launched by the **European Commission** in mid-2001 and sought to open up a debate on the nature and workings of European governance, and essentially contained a set of recommendations on how to enhance and open up democracy in the European Union (EU). The Paper considered how it might be possible to inject the EU institutions with greater legitimacy among the citizens of the EU. Two points should be made about it. First, the timing (late July) was unfortunate and restricted its impact in the media. Second, there was a degree of confusion as to the meaning of the term 'governance' across the member states (the word does not exist in some languages). Together these ensured less attention in the media for what amounted to the beginnings of a serious and far-reaching debate. On assuming the presidency of the European Commission in September 1999, Romano Prodi had placed considerable emphasis on the concept of governance and identified new forms of European governance as one of his four strategic priorities. Definitions of governance vary widely, but the European Commission adopted its own distinctive definition of the term governance, which it equated to the rules, processes and practices that affect how powers are exercised at the European level. It identified five principles of good governance, namely **openness**, participation, **accountability**, effectiveness and coherence. These five principles were supposed to reinforce those of **subsidiarity** and **proportionality**. The White Paper was followed by a public consultation that ended in March 2002 and the Commission pledged to report back with its conclusions by the end of that calendar year. Its findings were to be used to provide a firm basis for further inter-institutional co-operation on reforming European governance within the constraints imposed by the existing **founding treaties**.

The Governance White Paper was inevitably interwoven with and has formed part of the 'future of Europe' debate, and it was expected that both would inform and pave the way for further institutional changes at the **intergovernmental conference** (IGC) scheduled for 2004. The Commission, bound by the **Laeken Declaration**, was actively involved with the **European Convention** preceding the IGC and used this White Paper as its reference point.

GRAND CHAMBERS are an innovation of the **Treaty of Nice**. They are composed of the President and Vice-President of the **Court of Justice** and 13 other judges.

GREECE is a parliamentary republic and was one of the first countries to approach the **European Economic Community** (EEC) for some form of association in the late 1950s. An **association agreement** was signed in July 1961 and entered into force in November 1962. A **customs union** was to have been introduced gradually over a period of 10 years, but, in order to aid the development of Greek industry, a transitional period of 22 years was to have been applied to most Greek industrial goods. The EEC also agreed to provide loans to **Greece** during the first five years of the Agreement. The association was soon, however, frozen following the military coup of April 1967 in Greece, its provisions not being reactivated until the restoration of a civilian democratic regime in July 1974. Six months later, the new Greek Government notified the European Communities (EC) that it wished to apply for full membership, with similar transitional arrangements to those that had been part of the first **enlargement** process. The association agreement was restored in December 1974, and a formal application to join the EC submitted in June 1975. Negotiations took four years, and the **Treaty of Accession** was signed in Athens in May 1979, with **ratification** occurring the following month. Greece became the 10th member of the EC in January 1981.

After its electoral victory in October 1981 a new left-wing Government criticized the terms of membership accepted by its conservative predecessor for creating and exacerbating economic problems in Greece, and demanded a special status that, based upon a renegotiation of the terms, would take account of what was claimed to be the very different nature of the Greek economy. In 1983 the **European Council** recognized Greece's 'special problems', and negotiations culminated in several concessions to Greece and the adoption in 1985 of the Integrated Mediterranean Programmes. Greece had earlier indicated that its acceptance of the entry of **Portugal** and **Spain** was conditional upon a satisfactory resolution of its complaints.

As one of the poorer members of the European Union (EU), Greece has been a major beneficiary of EU programmes. More or less the whole country has priority status for the **structural and cohesion funds**, and it is a major recipient of the **cohesion policy**, in the form of the **Cohesion Fund**. Greece's attitude towards the EU, especially in terms of foreign policy, was more openly influenced by national interest than that of most member states, and this occasionally caused some irritation among its partners. This national interest often emerged over relations with **Turkey** and Cyprus. Greece joined the **exchange-rate mechanism** (ERM) in March 1998. However, Greece's inability to meet the criteria for **economic and monetary union** (EMU) was not in doubt, and in 1998 it was the only member state wishing to participate in EMU that was excluded from doing so. This did not dilute Greek determination to join, and the country acceded to EMU in 2001. Greece ratified the **Treaty establishing a Constitution for Europe** in April 2005. The document was backed by 268 votes in the 300-member parliament. Only 17 legislators voted against, while another 15 abstained. The New Democracy Party, led by Kostas Karamanlis, took control of government from the Panhellenic Socialist Movement (PASOK) following elections in March 2004. However, the party was returned to power by a much narrower margin in September 2007.

The Greek Conservative Government fared badly at the **European Parliament** (EP) 2009 elections, while the polls brought renewed success for both the Socialist and Communist parties. The Greek results ran very much against the general trend of the EP elections, which saw rising support for the centre-right. This national trend was confirmed when PASOK (under the leadership of George Papandreou) won the national elections in October and brought the five-year Conservative administration to an end. The new Government soon found itself confronting a severe economic crisis and was compelled to introduce austerity programmes to tackle the huge level of government debt. In so doing, it triggered social unrest and impacted on the stability of the **euro**. In April 2010 the Greek Government was offered a three-year financial rescue package by the EU, the **European Central Bank** (ECB) and the International Monetary Fund (IMF) 'troika' (totalling some €110,000m.) to assist it in its efforts at restoring confidence abroad and support at home. The sense of crisis was such, however, that many analysts were convinced that Greece would eventually default on its debt and come under increasing pressure to leave the eurozone. The economic situation deteriorated further in 2011 as political tensions and anger intensified as unemployment soared. The EU, the ECB and the IMF offered Greece a second bailout loan, worth €130,000m., in October on the condition that the country implemented further austerity measures and agreed to a restructuring of its debt. Papandreou resigned as Prime Minister in November to make way for a new national unity government. The second bailout was ratified by all parties (with a number of additional preconditions) in February 2012 and was activated the following month. After an indecisive general election in May failed to lead to the formation of a new government, fresh elections were scheduled for 17 June. At the polls the conservative New Democracy (ND) party, led by Antonis Samaras, won a narrow majority of seats and entered into a coalition government with PASOK and the Democratic Left. Samaras' party was pro-euro and fully supported the bailout programme.

However, Greek politics had undergone a major change as the 2012 elections heralded the rise of a new political force, the Coalition of the Radical Left (SYRIZA). SYRIZA had been a marginal actor in 2007, when it had secured only 5% of the vote, but, under the leadership of the charismatic Alexis Tsipras, it had emerged as the second largest party in Greece by June 2012 (with just under 27% of the vote). SYRIZA was opposed to the austerity programme and rejected a request to join a coalition government. By mid-2013 it was estimated that Greece had received a total of some €210,000m. as part of its bailout package from the troika. SYRIZA won nearly 27% of the Greek vote at the 2014 EP elections, placing it ahead of ND (which secured nearly 23%). SYRIZA's popularity continued to grow in 2014, and at national elections on 25 January 2015 SYRIZA was the winning party (with 36.3% of the votes), pushing ND firmly into second place (with 27.8%). Tsipras was sworn in as Prime Minister on 26 January, heading the first radical left administration in over 50 years. Tsipras initially aimed to renegotiate the terms of Greece's bailout agreement, to create some 300,000 new jobs and to improve relations with the **Russian Federation**, although strong opposition from within the eurozone, and fears that Greece might be compelled to abandon the euro, led the Government to dilute its pledges on the economy. Negotiations on the terms of Greece's bailout programme with the EU took place throughout the first half of the year. At the end of June, amid bank closures and default on a loan repayment to the IMF, Greece's imminent exit from the eurozone appeared increasingly likely. However, in July tentative agreement was reached between the Greek Government and the EU to negotiate a new lending arrangement, and in mid-August the Board of Governors of the **European Stability Mechanism** (ESM) approved new lending to Greece, worth €86,000m. over a period of three years. A Memorandum of Understanding with Greece was also adopted, according to which the Greek Government agreed to implement further widespread economic reforms. Amid internal conflict within SYRIZA over the adoption of austerity measures, Alexis Tsipras announced his resignation on 20 August. New legislative elections were held on 20 September, and a Tsipras-led Government was again appointed; Tsipras welcomed the results of the elections as a validation of the new bailout arrangement. In May 2016 the first review of the ESM programme, which had been due for completion in October 2015, was finished, following disagreement between the EU and the IMF over the depth of reform required for implementation by Greece in order to secure access to continuing debt relief. In mid-2017 a Eurogroup meeting of eurozone Ministers of Finance, together with the Managing Director of the IMF Christine Lagarde, reached agreement, in principle, on the next stages of the bailout arrangement.

Meanwhile, from the early months of 2015 Greece experienced a major refugee crisis, as large numbers of asylum seekers, many fleeing civil conflict in **Syria**, embarked on dangerous sea voyages in order to reach the Greek islands. By the end of June 2015 arrivals of seaborne migrants on the Aegean islands exceeded the total number for the whole of 2014. The Greek state did not have the capacity to respond satisfactorily, and some other EU members were reluctant to share responsibility. In March 2016 an EU-**Turkey** agreement was reached, providing for the return of undocumented migrants crossing into the territory of **Greece** and considered not to be in immediate need of international protection; the EU pledged to accept an officially documented Syrian refugee from inside Turkey for each migrant returned to that country. By June the European Commission reported that the number of migrants travelling between Turkey and Greece had declined significantly. Prior to the implementation of the agreement, around 1,740 migrants were crossing the Aegean Sea to Greek territory each day. From the beginning of May, average daily arrivals reportedly numbered some 47. According to the United Nations High Commissioner for Refugees, the number of migrants who arrived in Greece during 2016 fell to 173,208 (compared with 856,723 in 2015); an estimated 60,000 remained in the country at the end of the year.

GREEN GROUP: See **Group of the Greens/European Free Alliance**

A **GREEN PAPER** is a **European Commission** document that is intended to stimulate public debate and launch a process of consultation at European level on a particular topic. The Commission produces some 10 Green Papers every year. These consultations may then lead to a **White Paper** (e.g. **Governance White Paper**), which translates the conclusions of the debate into practical proposals for European Union action.

GREENLAND, a Danish colony since 1721, was incorporated into **Denmark** in 1953. It became part of the European Communities (EC) in 1973, even though in the 1972 Danish referendum some 70% of Greenland's electorate opposed membership. In 1978 Denmark accepted home rule for Greenland, and the enabling legislation included a provision for Greenland to withdraw from the EC if it wished. A narrow majority in favour of **withdrawal** (53%) was recorded in a 1982 referendum on the issue (fishing was a major issue) and Denmark, still responsible for Greenland's foreign affairs, requested that the **European Commission** revise the treaties to permit withdrawal and the inclusion of Greenland among the **Overseas Countries and Territories** (OCTs). Agreement on the final terms was reached in February 1985, with OCT status being conceded to the island. Greenland thus gained preferential access to EC markets; furthermore, all Greenlanders are recognized as EU citizens. However, Greenland's withdrawal from the European Community deprived it of EC **development aid**. This loss was compensated for by the revenue from the granting of fishing rights for Greenlandic waters to EU member states. Greenland, the EU and Denmark signed a new partnership agreement in June 2006, allowing Greenland to resume receiving its EU subsidy in return for EU control over policies such as scientific research and climate change. In 2011 current transfers from EU institutions to Greenland amounted to 312m. kroner. To date, Greenland remains the only territory to have left the European Union (EU), although it was due to be followed by the **United Kingdom** (see **Brexit**). Economic ties between Greenland and the EU have remained strong. In 2010 nearly 93% of all Greenland's exports went to the EU, while almost 70% of the island's imports came from the EU. A number of political and business leaders in Greenland have suggested that the country may opt to apply for full EU membership within a generation.

GREXIT is a popular term that was reportedly coined by economists in 2012, amid the economic and financial crisis in **Greece**, by combining the two words 'Greek' and 'exit'. It refers to the potential departure of Greece from the **eurozone**, which seemed increasingly inevitable at several points in the early to mid-2010s, most recently in mid-2015.

The **GROUP FOR A EUROPE OF DEMOCRACIES AND DIVERSITIES** (EDD) was a former **party group** in the **European Parliament** (EP). Its members favoured 'a stable and democratic Europe of Nation States' and were not in favour of further European integration and centralization. In 2002 the group had 18 members in the EP, from four countries (**Denmark**, **France**, the **Netherlands** and the **United Kingdom**). The group represented a varying **Eurosceptic** voice in the EP and re-formed as the **Independence and Democracy Group** in June 2004. This group, which included the **UK Independence Party** (UKIP), was deeply Eurosceptic, rejected the **Treaty of Lisbon** and all moves towards a federal superstate, and many members openly called for their own country's withdrawal from the European Union (EU). The group was led by Nigel Farage from UKIP, but, with only 21 members (13 of them from UKIP), it fell short of the 25 **Members of the European Parliament** needed to maintain a political group within the EP after the 2009 elections. The ethos and views of the EDD and the Independence and Democracy Group were quickly reborn and now reside within the **Europe of Freedom and Direct Democracy Group**.

The **GROUP OF THE ALLIANCE OF LIBERALS AND DEMOCRATS FOR EUROPE** (ALDE) was formed in July 2004 following the 2004 **European Parliament** (EP) elections. In 2007 this new group (which essentially emerged from the **Group of the European Liberal Democratic and Reform Party**) had 104 **Members of the European Parliament** (MEPs), who were drawn from 22 of the member states. After the 2009 elections the number of ALDE MEPs declined to 84 (from 19 member states) and it fell further to 67 following the May 2014 EP elections. At late 2017 the ALDE group consisted of 68 MEPs from 21 countries. The current President of ALDE is **Guy Verhofstadt**, a former Prime Minister of **Belgium**; seven Vice-Presidents assist him. Verhofstadt was selected by the ALDE group as its preferred candidate for the position of European Commission President in 2014. Following the EP elections and the success of the **Group of the European People's Party**, ALDE supported the candidacy of **Jean-Claude Juncker**. The group now constitutes the fourth-largest grouping in the EP. Traditionally, ALDE has been one of the most vocal groups in favour of **European Union** (EU) integration and seeks European solutions to many common challenges and problems. It is a firm supporter of the European single market and has been an advocate of neoliberalism and greater competition. Its interests have been presented in a 10-point programme that espouses, among other things, the need for the EU to: bridge the gap between its economic and political dimensions and be able to speak with one voice on the international stage; secure greater democratization of its functioning; demand the protection of all minorities; aspire to a common economic policy; and aim to make itself the world leader in environmental protection and ensure that **globalization** is effective and beneficial.

GROUP OF EIGHT: See **G-8**

The **GROUP OF THE EUROPEAN DEMOCRATIC ALLIANCE** (RDE) was a former **party group** in the **European Parliament**. It was established in 1973 (as the Progressive Democratic Group), largely as an arrangement of convenience, by the French Gaullist party (known as the Union des Démocrates until 1976, as the Rassemblement pour la République from then until 2002, and as the Union pour un Mouvement Populaire since then) and the nationalist Irish party Fianna Fáil, neither of which regarded any of the other available party groups as a natural home. While there were strains within the RDE, a common position was found in several policy areas, including agricultural, regional and social policy. In mid-1995 the RDE merged with Forza Europa to form what would become the **Union for Europe of the Nations Group**.

The **GROUP OF THE EUROPEAN LIBERAL DEMOCRATIC AND REFORM PARTY** (ELDR) was one of the oldest **party groups** in the **European Parliament** (EP). In 2002 it was the third largest group in the EP, containing 53 **Members of the European Parliament**, although the Group was considerably smaller than the **Group of the Party of European Socialists** and the **Group of the European People's Party**. The ELDR historically played a pivotal role between these two larger forces. Generally centrist in orientation, it experienced strains between its left- and right-wing elements, which reduced its cohesion and effectiveness. The arrival of the Nordic centre parties in the ELDR increased group heterogeneity. Throughout its existence the ELDR remained fully committed to deeper European Union integration. Following the 2004 European elections, the ELDR was replaced by the **Group of the Alliance of Liberals and Democrats for Europe**.

The **GROUP OF THE EUROPEAN PEOPLE'S PARTY (CHRISTIAN DEMOCRATS)** (EPP) is the formal name adopted by the **Group of the European People's Party (Christian Democrats) and European Democrats** after the 2009 elections to the **European Parliament** (EP) when the British Conservative Party and other European Democrat parties left to form the **European Conservatives and Reformists Group**. Despite these departures, the EPP remained the largest group within the EP after both the 2009 and 2014 elections. In 2014 221 **Members of the European Parliament** (MEPs) were returned to the EP under the EPP banner (compared with 265 in 2009). **Manfred Weber** was selected as the new Chairman of the EPP group in May 2014. The EPP is a centre-right group that supports the process of European integration, and by late 2017 it comprised 214 MEPs. The group seeks to advance the goal of a more competitive and democratic Europe. The **United Kingdom** was the only EU member state not to have representation in the EPP.

The **GROUP OF THE EUROPEAN PEOPLE'S PARTY (CHRISTIAN DEMOCRATS) AND EUROPEAN DEMOCRATS** (EPP-ED) united Christian Democrat, Conservative and other mainstream centre and centre-right political forces from across the 27-member European Union until the 2009 elections to the **European Parliament** (EP). The EPP-ED Group had its origins in the Group of the European People's Party (EPP), which was one of the first transnational **party groups** to emerge in the European Parliament. Christian Democrats had dominated the assembly from 1951 through to 1975 and, in anticipation of the introduction of **direct elections**, in 1976 they formed the EPP, self-consciously constituting a party rather than a federation of national groups. The EPP was strongly committed to European integration, desiring more powers to be given to the supranational institutions, and favoured a federalist structure for Europe. While broadly Christian Democrat and moderate centre-right in orientation, it contained both progressive and conservative strands, which were not always exactly consistent with national delegations. From 1979 it was generally one of the two largest party groups in the EP, and in 1992 it also absorbed the European Democratic Group (ED). Following the 1999 elections, it became the largest group, with 233 **Members of the European Parliament**. The results of the 2004 EP elections guaranteed the EPP-ED its relative majority with some 268 seats (out of 732), although by April 2006 this had declined to 264. Following the accession of **Bulgaria** and **Romania** in January 2007 membership increased again, to 278. The group remained the largest parliamentary group, and was the only one with deputies from all 27 member states of the Union at that time. Given its size, it was arguably in the best position to influence the EP's political agenda. Its strength was reflected in the fact that, from 1999, the EPP-ED Group was on the winning side of more votes than any other group in the EP's monthly plenary sessions. The size of this party also ensured that EPP-ED group members held a range of principal positions within the Parliament. For example, in the sixth parliament (2004–09), its members held the chairmanships of nine of the EP's 22 committees or subcommittees, seven of its 14 vice-presidencies and three of its five quaestorships. Within the parliamentary committees, EPP-ED group members were well placed to secure the right to author the EP's position on important draft **legislation** and other major reports. Moreover, the Group secured more of these rapporteurships, on more important subjects, than any other group.

GROUP OF THE EUROPEAN UNITARIAN LEFT: See **Confederal Group of the European United Left/Nordic Green Left**

The **GROUP OF THE GREENS/EUROPEAN FREE ALLIANCE** (or EFA) in the **European Parliament** (EP) was formed in July 1999, and is made up of two main groups—Greens and environmentalists on the one hand, and representatives of 'stateless nations' (i.e. Wales, Scotland and the Basque region) or regions on the other. This group first emerged after the 1984 **direct elections** when nine representatives of national Green parties were elected to the EP. Under EP rules, however, this was an insufficient number to be recognized as a separate party group, and consequently the Green representatives joined with a heterogeneous collection of other **Members of the European Parliament** (MEPs) to form the Rainbow Group. The Green Group did not become a separate **party group** until 1989, following a significant increase in membership. It has continued to evolve. The Group of the Greens/European Free Alliance in the EP is the product of the political will of two separate and progressive European political families to co-operate in order to strengthen their mutual political interests in the EP. The group has since established itself as one of the main voices within the Parliament. It has been an increasingly cohesive force and has focused its energies on environmental protection, the decentralization of power and gender equality. It is generally positively disposed today towards the European integration process. Following the May 2014 EP elections, it had 50 MEPs from 17 member states and represented some 25 different national parties. At late 2017 it had 51 MEPs. The MEPs came from **Austria**, **Belgium**, **Croatia**, **Denmark**, **Estonia**, **Finland**, **France**, **Germany**, **Hungary**, **Italy**, **Latvia**, **Luxembourg**, the **Netherlands**, **Slovenia**, **Spain**, **Sweden** and the **United Kingdom**. Over one-fifth of the MEPs (13) come from Germany. The Group's Bureau (or executive) is made up of nine members. Unlike all the other groups in the EP, the Greens/EFA have a co-presidency, i.e. two co-Presidents, always one male and one female. The two current co-Presidents are Ska Keller and Philippe Lamberts. There are seven vice-presidents.

The **GROUP OF THE PARTY OF EUROPEAN SOCIALISTS** (PSE) was the name of one of the **party groups** in the **European Parliament** (EP) before it was renamed the Socialist Group in the European Parliament in 2004 and the **Group of the Progressive Alliance of Socialists and Democrats in the European Parliament** in 2009. Between 1973 and the late 1990s the PSE was consistently the largest group in the EP. In terms of representation, the PSE became the second major party group following the 1999 EP elections when it secured 181 **Members of the European Parliament**. Despite an increase in representation (to 200) within the Parliament following the 2004 elections, reaching 218 after the accession of **Bulgaria** and **Romania** on 1 January 2007 the party group remained the second major force after the **European People's Party and European Democrats**.

The **GROUP OF THE PROGRESSIVE ALLIANCE OF SOCIALISTS AND DEMOCRATS IN THE EUROPEAN PARLIAMENT** (S&D) is the name adopted by the former Socialist Group in the **European Parliament** (EP—see **Group of the Party of European Socialists**) after the 2009 elections to the European Parliament. Despite the common political background of its representatives, the group (under its different nomenclatures over the years) has often been divided by major ideological and policy issues. While it permits free votes in debates, it makes great efforts to develop a common position on as many issues as possible, by means of pre-committee caucuses and working parties. The party group brings together the social democratic and socialist parties across the European Union (EU). The largest national groups within the party group have traditionally come from the Social Democratic Party in **Germany**, the French and Spanish Socialist Parties and the Labour Party in the **United Kingdom**. The S&D supports closer integration, particularly in the environmental and social fields. It campaigns on environmental issues, calls for social justice and reasonable minimum wages and supported the **Treaty of Lisbon**. The party group remained the second largest group (behind the **European People's Party**) in the EP after the May 2014 elections. The EP for 2014–19 had 189 S&D Members of the European Parliament (MEPs) at late 2017. The group has an MEP from each of the 28 EU member states; 20 come from the British Labour Party. The largest national delegation in the EP comes from **Italy** (30 MEPs), and in June 2014 Gianni Pittella was elected as the new President of the S&D group. Pittella is a member of the Italian Democratic Party. The S&D group is a major force and its input to, and support of, the legislative work of the EP is indispensable. Its activities are co-ordinated by the Bureau, which comprises the Group President, nine Vice-Presidents and the Treasurer. The S&D group strongly advocates its support for an inclusive European society and one that is based on the principles of freedom, equality, solidarity, diversity and fairness. The group remains pro-European in outlook and seeks to build a more democratic Europe, and aims for a better future for everyone and one where the EU can be seen to connect much better with the public. Combating unemployment remains a principal objective of the S&D.

GROUP OF SEVEN: See **G-7**

GROUPS IN THE EUROPEAN PARLIAMENT: See **Party Groups**

The **GRUNDTVIG** programme was designed to promote and encourage adult education. The Commission's action in this area was aimed at enhancing the European dimension of lifelong learning, and from 2007 Grundtvig was incorporated into the new **Lifelong Learning Programme** (LLP) 2007–13. It supports a wide range of activities designed to promote innovation and the improved availability, accessibility and quality of educational provision for adults, by means of European co-operation. A new programme, **Erasmus+**, replaced the LLP under the new financial perspective period for 2014–20. Erasmus+ has an integrated structure and focuses on three main actions: learning mobility, co-operation and policy reform.

GUARANTEE THRESHOLDS were introduced in 1986 as a means of limiting the open-ended nature of production **subsidies** in the **common agricultural policy** that had been a consequence of the guaranteed price system. With the imposition of guarantee thresholds on agricultural products, an upper limit has been placed upon automatic financial support, with no subsidies given for production that exceeds the thresholds.

GUE/NGL: See **Confederal Group of the European United Left/Nordic Green Left**

GUIDE PRICES are prices offered to farmers for beef and veal under the **common agricultural policy**. They are the same as target prices. Guide prices also apply under the **common fisheries policy**.

The first **GULF WAR** occurred in early 1991 when a **USA**-led coalition of states attacked Iraq. The origins of this international crisis date to August 1990 when Saddam Hussain, the Iraqi President, launched an invasion of Kuwait. At this point in the development of the European Union (EU), plans were being laid in the **intergovernmental conferences** that resulted in the **Treaty on European Union** (TEU). The Gulf War was significant as it focused the attention of member states on the issue of whether the EU should have some form of political role and even a military role. This would have been a major step in EU integration. The **European Defence Community** project of the early 1950s had proved just how controversial this area was, and little had changed some 40 years later. The Gulf War and the conflicts in **Yugoslavia** in the early 1990s could not persuade the governments of the member states to allow the EU a substantial military role. However, the TEU began the process, albeit tentatively. Throughout the 1990s doubts still lingered, principally in the USA, regarding Iraq's military capabilities and intentions and these were fuelled by Saddam Hussain's efforts to block several United Nations-backed searches for weapons of mass destruction. Frustrated and angered by Iraq's defiance, the US Government under George W. Bush, with the diplomatic and military support of the Governments of the **United Kingdom**, **Spain** and **Poland**, finally launched a second **Iraq War** in March 2003. Saddam Hussain's regime was overthrown with relative ease, but to the detriment of the UK's relations with both **France** and **Germany**, which strongly opposed the war.

GYMNICH MEETINGS is a term that refers to specialist ministerial meetings that are held in conjunction with the **summit meetings** of the **European Council**. They are designed to be informal and private sessions without any detailed agenda, in order to permit ministers to consider longer-term issues and problems without being pressurized to reach a decision. The name derives from Schloss Gymnich in **Germany** where the first such gathering was held.

H

HAGUE CONGRESS: See **Congress of Europe**

The **HAGUE SUMMIT** of December 1969 was only the third summit meeting of the **Six** since the **Treaty of Rome**, and the first since the French vetoes on British membership of the European Communities (EC) and the **empty chair crisis**. The newly elected French President, Georges Pompidou, took the initiative in calling for a summit meeting that would address directly the several problems and issues facing the Six. The summit opened the way to the **enlargement** of the EC; it established guidelines for the consolidation and development of common policies; and it reaffirmed political union as the ultimate objective of the EC. More specifically, it endorsed proposals for the financing of the **common agricultural policy**, for extending the budgetary powers of the **European Parliament**, for full **economic and monetary union** to be reached by 1980, and for the development of closer political co-ordination. It heralded the new style of **decision making** focusing on strategic leadership from heads of government and state (later institutionalized through the **European Council**), which would characterize the EC after 1970.

JOHANNES HAHN (1957–) was (re-)nominated as the Austrian Commissioner to the new 28-member **European Commission** led by **Jean-Claude Juncker**, which took office in November 2014. In September Juncker named Hahn as Commissioner for Neighbourhood Policy and **Enlargement**, subject to approval by the **European Parliament** and the **European Council**. Immediately prior to this appointment, Hahn had served as one of the 28 European Commissioners in the Commission of 2010–14, when he held responsibility for **regional policy**. Hahn was born in Vienna, **Austria**, and studied law and then philosophy at the city's university. He is a member of the Austrian People's Party and, prior to becoming a European Commissioner (since January 2007), he was the Minister for Science and Research in the Austrian Government. He assumed office on 1 November 2014.

HARD CORE: See **Core Europe**

HARMONIZATION is a term used to describe the process whereby national policies and standards are brought more closely in line with one another. To many, it is synonymous with **approximation**, although legally speaking it involves a greater degree of integration. The harmonization and approximation of **legislation** are central to the **internal market** programme. Legislative harmonization and approximation with the *acquis communautaire* also feature as an obligation placed on non-member states in their relations with the European Union.

HEADS OF GOVERNMENT: See **European Council**; **Summit Meetings**

HEALTH AND SAFETY, particularly with regard to the provision of satisfactory conditions for workers at their place of employment, have been a long-standing concern of the European Union (EU), as was reconfirmed in the **Treaty on European Union**. General policy initiation in the area of health and safety is the responsibility of two **European Commission** agencies, the Advisory Committee on Safety and Health at Work and the **European Foundation for the Improvement of Living and Working Conditions**. Health and safety also figure prominently in EU **consumer policy** and **environmental policy**. As a result of the **Single European Act**, **directives** and **regulations** on health and safety required only a **qualified majority vote** in the **Council of the European Union**. Hence supporters of several initiatives, notably the **Working Time Directive** and many deriving from the Social Chapter (see **Charter of Fundamental Social Rights of Workers**), attempted to have the Council consider them under the rubric of health and safety, before the **Treaty of Amsterdam** incorporated the **protocol** based on the Social Chapter into the **Treaty of Rome** and extended the use of qualified majority voting to this area.

The **HEALTH POLICY** competences of the European Union (EU) are mainly focused on incentive and co-operation measures. The EU does not have the capacity to organize health care provision independently. The majority of the EU's efforts have thus been restricted to co-ordinating and enhancing national policies on health awareness and health protection. This has led to campaigns on AIDS, cancer and drug dependence. For example, in October 2007 the **European Commission** presented a **White Paper** 'Together for Health: A Strategic Approach for the EU'. The three main objectives specified in the document were: fostering good health in an ageing Europe, protecting citizens from health threats, and supporting dynamic health systems and new technologies. The Together for Health strategy forms part of **Europe 2020**. In 2013 the Commission released a working document 'Investing in Health', which focused on the ways in with investment in health contributes to the broader aims of inclusive growth. Subsequently, a Commission communication titled 'On Effective, Accessible and Resilient Health Systems' (2014) called for closer co-operation among member states in terms of their health systems, in order better to support patient mobility while improving standards for all and maximizing the use of finite resources.

HELSINKI FINAL ACT: See **Organization for Security and Co-operation in Europe**

HIGH AUTHORITY: See **European Coal and Steel Community**

The **HIGH REPRESENTATIVE FOR THE COMMON FOREIGN AND SECURITY POLICY** was a post created under the terms of the **Treaty of Amsterdam** to provide a higher profile for the European Union's (EU) **common foreign and security policy** (CFSP). The **Secretary-General of the Council of the European Union** acted as the High Representative and, drawing on the French acronym for the CFSP, was often referred to as Monsieur or Madame PESC. The High Representative, along with the European Commissioner responsible for external relations and the representative of the **Council presidency**, constituted the EU's **Troika**, which represented the EU internationally. The first High Representative was Javier Solana. He was expected to become the first **Union Minister for Foreign Affairs**, once the **Treaty establishing a Constitution for Europe** was ratified. However, non-**ratification** of the treaty meant that the post was never created. Instead, the **Treaty of Lisbon** provided for the upgrading and cumbersome renaming of the post as **High Representative of the Union for Foreign Affairs and Security Policy**.

The **HIGH REPRESENTATIVE OF THE UNION FOR FOREIGN AFFAIRS AND SECURITY POLICY** superseded the role of **High Representative for the Common Foreign and Security Policy**, under the **Treaty of Lisbon**. The renaming of the post was accompanied by new powers. The first post-holder was Baroness Catherine Ashton, who was appointed by the **European Council** in late 2009 and held office until November 2014. At the end of August **Federica Mogherini**, the Italian Minister of Foreign Affairs, was named as the new High Representative of the Union for Foreign Affairs and Security Policy. She took office on 1 November. The High Representative chairs meetings of the Council of Ministers (see **Council of the European Union**) dealing with foreign affairs. She is also, *ex officio*, a Vice-President of the **European Commission**. The main responsibilities of the High Representative are to conduct and develop the **common foreign and security policy** (CFSP) and the **European security and defence policy**, with assistance in fulfilling these tasks from a **European External Action Service**. The creation of this dual responsibility post was designed to provide greater coherence and prominence to the role of the European Union (EU) in international affairs, although there was some concern over whether the High Representative's role in representing the EU had the potential to lead to conflict with that of the **President of the European Council**, who is also responsible for the external representation of the EU on issues concerning the CFSP.

PHIL HOGAN (1960–) was nominated in 2014 as the Irish Commissioner to the new 28-member **European Commission** led by **Jean-Claude Juncker**. In September Juncker named Hogan as Commissioner for Agriculture and Rural Development. Hogan was born in Kilkenny, Ireland, and graduated with a degree in Economics and Geography from University College Cork in 1981. He was elected to the Irish legislature for the first time in 1989. In 2002 he stood unsuccessfully for the leadership of Fine Gael, losing to Enda Kenny. Prior to his appointment to the Commission, Hogan held the position of Minister for the Environment, Community and Local Government in **Ireland** in 2011–14. Hogan passed his confirmation hearings and took up his post as Commissioner on 1 November 2014, after the Juncker Commission had secured the approval of both the **European Parliament** and the **European Council**.

HORIZON 2020 is an €80,000m. European Union (EU) research and innovation programme which is to run from 2014–20. The budget is 30% higher than for its immediate predecessor, Framework Programme 7. It is co-ordinated by the **European Commission** and brings all of the EU's research and innovation funding for this period under one umbrella. The programme comprises three main parts: some €24,600m. has been allocated to the European Research Council, which provides funds to university and scientific researchers; a further €17,900m. is to be allocated to secure European industry's leadership in innovation; and around €31,700m. is to be made available for other leading issues and concerns such as health and demographic change, secure, clean and efficient energy, smart, green and integrated transport, and climate action. Horizon 2020 is one manifestation of the EU's determination and drive to establish and foster greater growth opportunities in Europe. It anticipates funding some 65,000 researchers under its Marie Skłodowska-Curie Actions and a new European Institute of Innovation and Technology aims to develop closer links between the worlds of higher education and business and to foster specialized postgraduate training.

WERNER HOYER (1951–) assumed his current post as the seventh President of the **European Investment Bank** in January 2012. Hoyer was born in Wuppertal, **Germany**, and read economics at the University of Cologne. Following his attainment of a doctorate, he commenced his professional career as a senior research assistant/lecturer at the University of Cologne, specializing in international economics before being elected to the (West) German parliament in 1987 as a member of the Free Democratic Party (which he had joined in 1972). Hoyer served in Helmut Kohl's fifth and final administration as the Minister for State at the Foreign Office (1994–98) and held the same position in **Angela Merkel**'s second administration during 2009–11.

HUMAN RIGHTS have become an increasingly important issue in debates over the role and future of the European Union (EU) since reference to respect for fundamental rights was included in the **Treaty on European Union** (TEU) in 1993 and later expanded by the **Treaty of Amsterdam**, which declared the EU to be founded on respect for human rights and fundamental freedoms. The rights themselves are not explicitly listed anywhere in the EU's treaty base. Instead, reference is made to the **European Convention on Human Rights** (formally the Convention for the Protection of Human Rights and Fundamental Freedoms) adopted by the **Council of Europe** in 1950, and to the constitutional traditions of the member states. This did not prevent the drawing up in 2000 of a **Charter of Fundamental Rights** of the EU. Nor has it prevented the EU in its external relations from making respect for human rights a precondition for closer ties and, indeed, membership. The EU has not, however, signed the European Convention on Human Rights, the **European Court of Justice** ruling in 1996 that it did not have the competence to do so.

That human rights enjoy an increasingly higher profile in the EU is underlined by the fact that a member state's suspected breach of them may be investigated. Ultimately its voting rights, as well as other rights deriving from the TEU and **Treaty of Rome**, may be suspended where a serious and persistent breach is confirmed.

HUMANITARIAN ASSISTANCE is an area in which the European Union is active as part of the **common foreign and security policy**. Activities involving humanitarian assistance take place under the aegis of the **Directorate-General for European Civil Protection and Humanitarian Aid Operations (ECHO)**. Formal recognition of the EU's involvement in humanitarian assistance work appeared in the **Treaty establishing a Constitution for Europe** and is now contained in the **Treaty of Lisbon**.

HUNGARY indicated, soon after the fall of the communist regime in 1989, that it wished for a closer relationship with, and eventual membership of, the European Communities (EC) once it had adapted its economy to market conditions. A **Europe agreement** was signed in 1991, and the EC accepted in principle the possibility of membership, although not for a number of years. Hungary submitted a formal application for membership in March 1994. In **Agenda 2000** it was recognized as one of the best-placed applicants for membership and was invited to open **accession negotiations** in March 1998. These were concluded in December 2002 and in the following April almost 84% of those participating in a referendum opted for accession to the European Union (EU). The Hungarian Government welcomed the result and duly signed the **Treaty of Accession** on 16 April 2003. Following its entry into the EU on 1 May 2004, Hungary became the second country to ratify the **Treaty establishing a Constitution for Europe**, with a parliamentary vote (304 votes to 9) in December 2004. It was the first member state to ratify the **Treaty of Lisbon** in December 2007, the same month that the country became part of the EU's **Schengen Area**. Hungary held the rotating presidency of the Council of the European Union for the first time in January–June 2011. Relations between the EU and the Government of **Viktor Orbán**, the leader of the centre-right party Fidesz, which came to power as the head of a coalition following the general election in April 2010, have been increasingly strained. The Hungarian Prime Minister, and Fidesz, have systematically tightened state control over the media, the judiciary and banks, including through the implementation of highly controversial constitutional amendments in March 2013. Orbán's Government has increasingly acquired various media outlets to exert control over information in the country. In August EU **development aid** to Hungary was temporarily suspended over alleged failings in the country's financial management and control systems (although there was no evidence of fraud, according to the **European Commission**). Following Fidesz's win at the national elections held in May 2014, Orbán was re-elected as the Prime Minister of Hungary and formed his third administration. Since then, Orbán has been displaying a more **Eurosceptic** disposition with regard to many aspects of EU policy and policy priorities, with increasingly nationalistic and indeed xenophobic rhetoric. It is worth noting that Hungary and the **United Kingdom** were the only two countries to vote against **Jean-Claude Juncker**'s nomination within the **European Council** in June 2014.

The current Government's approach came to a head when the ruling party promoted a Higher Education Law that specifically targeted the Central European University, and its founder the philanthropist George Soros. Engaging the same nationalistic rhetoric, Orbán has claimed that Soros has an agenda to bring more Muslims into the EU, as a counterpoint to what he considers Europe, engaging simultaneously in anti-Semitic and Islamophobic rhetoric.

Amid what became widely known as the **European migration crisis**, in June 2015 the Hungarian Government's response to incoming refugees, predominantly from Syria, was to construct a razor wire fence along its border with **Serbia**, as a way of keeping refugees out. The fence was completed in September 2015 and resulted in Hungary effectively closing its border. Viktor Orbán, moreover, referred to refugees as poison. Although Hungary's new 'wall' met with disapproval from the Commission and other EU member states, the Hungarian Government argued that on joining the **Schengen Area** of free movement it had taken on an obligation to protect the EU's external borders. Although EU member countries have a duty to protect the welfare of refugees, Hungary argued that it was not the first safe country that the asylum seekers had passed through: most had landed in **Greece**, itself a member of both the EU and the Schengen Area, and had reached Hungary only because Greece had failed in its obligations under the **Dublin Regulation**. The Hungarian authorities subsequently authorized the erection of fences on the country's border with **Croatia**, as asylum seekers sought to find another way into Hungary in order to make their way to **Germany**, via **Austria**, and temporarily closed the border with **Slovenia**. In September 2016 the Minister of Foreign Affairs of **Luxembourg** reportedly called for the expulsion of Hungary from the EU for its attitude to refugees. Hungary was due to hold a controversial referendum in early October opposing the EU's plans for the mandatory imposition of refugee quotas on member states (except for those with exemptions), without approval from the national legislature; however, the referendum was invalidated by a low rate of participation by the electorate. In mid-2017 the EU announced that it was to launch **infringement procedures** against Hungary, the **Czech Republic** and **Poland**, in response to the refusal by the three countries to accept the arrival of mandatory quotas of immigrants under a relocation plan for immigrants who had entered the EU by way of Italy or Greece since mid-2015.

I

ICELAND played little part in European developments during the first two decades following the Second World War. It joined the **European Free Trade Association** (EFTA) only in March 1970. The following November it began talks with the European Communities (EC) along with the other non-applicant EFTA states, and formal negotiations began the following year. These were hindered by Iceland's unilateral decision in 1972 to expand its territorial fishing limits to 50 nautical miles (93 km). Although a **free trade agreement** was ratified in February 1973, the EC insisted that a satisfactory settlement of the fishing dispute had to be reached before Iceland would be allowed to obtain the full benefits of the Agreement, and an acceptable compromise was not reached until July 1976. After this, there were no significant qualitative changes in the relationship with the EC until the late 1980s, when discussions, followed by negotiations, on the **European Economic Area** (EEA) began. This arrangement satisfied Iceland's desire for access to the **internal market**. Hence, unlike most of its EFTA partners, Iceland did not apply for EC membership. Successive Icelandic governments remained rather sceptical on the subject of European Union (EU) entry. This attitude did not, however, prevent relations with the EU from developing further. Iceland, along with **Norway**, negotiated participation in the **Schengen Agreement** and regularly associated itself with EU positions adopted as part of the **common foreign and security policy**. The economic and financial turmoil unleashed in late 2008 had a heavy impact on Iceland, where banks had severely overstretched themselves on capital and bond markets. The crisis and ensuing 'credit crunch' shook the economic and political infrastructure of Iceland to its core, toppled the Government and led Iceland to consider for the first time the possibility of EU membership. A new centre-left (Social Democrats and Greens) coalition Government, formed after elections in April 2009, was determined to bring the issue before parliament for debate. In July, after intense debate, the Icelandic parliament voted in favour (33 votes to 28, with two abstentions) of initiating the process for EU membership. The application was submitted later that month. The application was generally welcomed within the EU, although it was clear that accession was not a foregone conclusion. The period prior to the Commission's generally positive *avis* in February 2010 was overshadowed by a dispute with the **United Kingdom** and the **Netherlands** over the level of compensation that Iceland should pay British and Dutch investors in the collapsed Icesave bank. Iceland opened **accession negotiations** in July, but these proved to be far more protracted than had been assumed, despite Iceland's already close integration with the EU through the EEA. Popular support in Iceland for membership began to decline following the application, raising the question of whether any successfully negotiated **accession treaty** would be passed in a referendum. Negotiations continued, however, although by mid-2012—the Icelandic Government's original target date for accession—only 10 of the 35 negotiating chapters had been closed. Following the defeat of the incumbent Government in legislative elections in April 2013, a new centre-right and Eurosceptic administration, under the premiership of Sigmundur Davíð Gunnlaugsson of the Progressive Party, came to power. In June the new Government confirmed that it was suspending the EU application process.

The **IDENTITY, TRADITION AND SOVEREIGNTY GROUP (ITS)** party group emerged in the sixth **European Parliament** (EP) (2004–09). It was established in January 2007 and had 23 members, thereby just surpassing the minimum requirement at that date (of 20) for an EP political group. It largely owed its creation to the arrival of a Bulgarian (one) and Romanian (six) **Members of the European Parliament** after accession on 1 January 2007. The ITS was a rather loose-knit group which belonged to the right of the party spectrum and included such personalities as Jean-Marie Le Pen, together with five other members of the French Front National, and Alessandra Mussolini. The group highlighted a number of core values including: the recognition of national interests, sovereignties, identities and differences; a commitment to Christian values, heritage, culture and the traditions of European civilization; a commitment to the traditional family as the natural unit within society; and strident opposition to a unitary and bureaucratic European superstate. It also espoused strong views on immigration and objected to Turkish accession to the European Union. The ITS represented another **Eurosceptic** voice in the EP. This group was always volatile and had been created through political opportunity. It disintegrated in November 2007 after Alessandra Mussolini was deemed to have made disparaging remarks about Romanians, whereupon the members from the Greater Romania Party withdrew from the ITS. This reduction in membership caused the disqualification of the ITS from its short-lived recognition as an official EP party group.

IFOP is the acronym (from Instrument financier d'orientation de la pêche) of a financial guidance instrument for fisheries that was established in 1994 and ran until 2006. It controlled the financing of adaptation and modernization of fisheries structures within the ambit of the **structural and cohesion funds**.

IGC: See **Intergovernmental Conference**

IMMIGRATION POLICY was a low priority for the European Communities (EC) until the 1980s, and member states were free to pursue their own policies. A more structured approach began to emerge after the creation of **TREVI** (Terrorisme, Radicalisme, Extrémisme, Violence Internationale), and an ad hoc Group on Immigration was established in 1986 to work for greater co-operation on improving controls at the external borders of the EC and on the granting of visas. Although the political changes in **Central and Eastern Europe** after 1989 contributed to greater immigration pressure, the member states were reluctant to relinquish total control of immigration policy to the EC. Under the **Treaty on European Union**, only visas became a **competence** of the EC, immigration being incorporated into the then intergovernmental **pillar** of **justice and home affairs**. Closer co-operation in immigration policies was also a feature of the **Treaty of Amsterdam**, which conferred powers on the European Union (EU) in areas of migration and asylum.

At the 1999 Tampere **European Council**, the member states set out the four principal areas for the development of a common policy on asylum and immigration. These were: a solid partnership with the countries of origin; the establishment of a common European asylum system; fair treatment of third-country nationals; and a more efficient management of migration flows. In 2000 and 2001 the European Commission proposed several new measures that would facilitate the development of a common policy on asylum and migration. For example, the Commission proposed a directive on family reunification and another on the status of third-country nationals who have been long-term residents. In addition, the **Council of the European Union** adopted **directives** on the mutual recognition of decisions on the expulsion of third-country nationals and on harmonizing financial penalties imposed on carriers transporting into the EU third-country nationals lacking the documents necessary for admission. To assist the member states in their examination of immigration, the Council established the Centre for Information, Discussion and Exchange on the Crossing of Frontiers and Immigration (CIREFI) in 1992. In December 2009 the **Committee of Permanent Representatives** decided to abolish CIREFI and to transfer its activities to **FRONTEX** and the Working Party on Frontiers.

By the beginning of 2004 the issue of immigration had emerged as a major theme, primarily linked to the implications of the **enlargement** of the EU in May 2004. Given public attitudes and the successes of extreme right-wing political movements in parts of Europe, most member states, with the notable exceptions of **Ireland** and the **United Kingdom**, decided to impose restrictions on the free movement of people from **Central and Eastern Europe**. The 2004 Hague programme reiterated the Tampere objectives. Immigration policy in the EU further developed as member states sought to secure greater intra-European co-operation on the issue of a common asylum and immigration policy. In June 2008 the European Commission published a communication on 10 common principles for the effective working of a common immigration policy for Europe. The Single Permit Directive, which was adopted in December 2011, created a set of rights for non-EU workers legally residing in an EU member state. The previous month the Commission had launched an EU Immigration Portal, providing clear information on migration procedures and migrant employment rights.

A directive adopted in November 2003 permits third-country nationals who have been resident in the EU for a period of five years to be granted the status of long-term residents. The Blue

Card Directive was adopted in 2009, regulating conditions for entry and residence of highly qualified workers from outside the EU and establishing an EU-wide permit for such workers; the UK, Ireland and Denmark were exempt from the provisions of the directive. In May 2016 the Parliament and the Council adopted a new directive regulating conditions for admission and residency for nationals from non-EU countries entering the EU for educational, research and training purposes (again, the UK, Ireland and Denmark were exempt).

Immigration became a key issue during the campaign of the 'Leave' side prior to the referendum on membership of the EU that took place in the UK on 23 June 2016, arguing that a vote in favour of **Brexit** was the only way for the UK fully to control its borders. The topic of immigration and EU **migration and asylum policy** also came to the fore during 2015–16 in the context of the **European migration crisis**.

IMPLEMENTATION is a crucial aspect of the process of European integration. As the European Union (EU) has evolved, so the body of laws and commitments aimed at establishing a genuine **internal market** has expanded. These laws have to be adhered to at national level, such as, for example, **environmental policy** and **competition policy**, if the project is to operate effectively and efficiently. However, this is not unproblematic, as member states may seek to delay or resist implementation for a variety of reasons, ranging from a dislike of a particular piece of **legislation** to a lack of sufficient technical expertise to apply EU rules. Implementation centres on the following three broad areas: transposition of EU law into national law; the application of EU law by the relevant national authorities; and the enforcement of EU law, including penalties for non-compliance. The **European Commission** has general responsibility for all implementation issues but, given its limited resources, it relies heavily on other specialized agencies (e.g. the **European Medicines Agency**) or on complaints from the wider public to inform it of cases of non-implementation. In order both to embarrass non-compliant member states and accelerate implementation relating to the completion of the single market, the **Directorate-General** responsible for the internal market initiated an internal market scoreboard to reveal the degree of implementation in each of the member states. This sort of **transparency** seems to work, but continues to reveal the existence of numerous infringements. Many questions remain over the ability of the **candidate countries** to implement the full *acquis communautaire* on joining the EU. Derogations or transitional periods are likely to be granted. Overall, the Commission does very little in the way of direct implementation and is much more concerned with indirect implementation, i.e. ensuring that the member states carefully transpose EU laws into national laws. One of its few areas of direct implementation is competition policy.

The **INDEPENDENCE AND DEMOCRACY GROUP** (ID) is a former **party group**. It was established in July 2004 following the 2004 **European Parliament** (EP) elections. It incorporated European Union (EU) critics, **Eurosceptics** and Eurorealists. It emerged following the rebranding of the former **Group for a Europe of Democracies and Diversities** (EDD) within the EP. The new group was numerically considerably stronger than the EDD, and in the 2004–09 Parliament initially had 37 deputies (from nine member states) as opposed to 17 (from four) in the 1999–2004 Parliament. In 2006, however, the delegation from **Italy** (Lega Nord) left the group, reducing the number of deputies to 24. The largest political party within the group was the **UK Independence Party** (UKIP), with 10 members, while other representatives were drawn from the **Czech Republic** (one), **Denmark** (one), **France** (three), **Greece** (one), **Ireland** (one), the **Netherlands** (two), **Poland** (three) and **Sweden** (two). The group was co-chaired by Jens-Peter Bonde, a Danish **Member of the European Parliament** (MEP), and Nigel Farage, a British MEP, and was essentially a marriage of convenience between two factions that had combined to fight and prevent the **ratification** of the **Treaty establishing a Constitution for Europe**. However, they had differing perspectives on the process of European integration. One, a more moderate wing, sought greater **transparency** in terms of EU **decision making** and certainly did not advocate leaving the EU, while the second sought nothing less than **withdrawal** from the EU. National groups, such as the June Movement in Denmark and the French Mouvement pour la France, represented elements of the former position, while UKIP was the best example of and the largest force in the latter group. Although at the 2009 elections UKIP secured 13 seats, the ID 'family' fell short of winning enough support and sufficient MEPs to obtain group status within the existing EP. UKIP MEPs now sit in the **Europe of Freedom and Direct Democracy Group**.

INDUSTRIAL POLICY was not developed by the European Communities (EC) in any comprehensive or integrated form, although the **European Commission** launched a discussion paper dealing with a general EC industrial policy in November 1990. This new emphasis represented nothing less than a complete transformation in Commission thinking as it moved away markedly from espousing direct intervention in the economy to seeking to stimulate European industrial **competitiveness**. The change was later reflected in the restructuring of the Commission in 2000 that saw the former **Directorate-General** (DG) III (Industry) being rebranded as DG Enterprise. Indeed, industrial policy was rebranded as **enterprise policy**. However, from 2014 the Directorate-General became known as the DG for Internal Market, Industry, Entrepreneurship and SMEs. The **Treaty on European Union** in 1993 provided industry with its own specific **article** in the **Treaty of Rome** (Article 157, now Article 173 of the **Treaty on the Functioning of the European Union**). This requires the member states to secure the conditions necessary for the competitiveness of European Union (EU) industry. The EU is empowered to take special measures to stimulate the sector, but only provided these measures do not interfere with or distort competition. In 1995 the Commission presented an action programme that contained four major priority areas to strengthen industrial competitiveness. These were: solidifying the **internal market**; encouraging **research and technological development**; promoting the **information society**; and promoting industrial co-operation. Collectively, however, EU enterprise policy, research and development policy, **regional policy**, **social policy**, **competition policy**, **workers' rights**, **energy policy**, **transport policy** and **environmental policy** can be said to constitute an industrial policy. The basic concern has been to increase the efficiency and competitiveness of any industry within a free-market ethos. Apart from policies aimed at specifically targeted industries such as coal and steel, further general objectives have been industrial development in the poorer regions of the EU, a restructuring of traditional, declining industries (including retraining for those workers needing to be redeployed), and the encouragement of transnational collaboration in new technology-orientated industries.

Innovation and entrepreneurship have emerged as central tenets of enterprise policy. The **European Commission** is the focal point for ensuring that innovation policy is coherent and cohesive across the EU, for benchmarking performance, for disseminating best practice, and for highlighting lessons to be learned from any failure of the market economy that might justify state intervention. In October 2010 as part of the **Europe 2020** strategy, the Commission adopted a communication on industrial policy. This document set out a strategy that aimed to encourage growth and the creation of jobs by maintaining and supporting a strong, diversified and competitive industrial base in Europe offering well-paid jobs while becoming more resource-efficient.

The EU's **small and medium-sized enterprises** (SMEs), which number more than 20m., are already the backbone of EU industry (representing around 99% of all EU enterprises and accounting for some 67% of employment), and are the main focus of proactive enterprise policies based on applying the principle 'think small first'. To this end, specific programmes have been devised to ensure that SMEs participate in EU-funded research and innovation projects. The rules on state aid (see **subsidies**) and other forms of funding are more generous for SMEs than for large firms. Entrepreneurs and SMEs, in particular, can obtain help in finding partners through the Enterprise Europe Network in more than 50 countries. This network, which was launched in 2008, is part-funded by the Commission.

Through its Entrepreneurship Action Plan, which was published in 2004, the Commission sought to promote an entrepreneurial mindset, encouraging more people to set up businesses, helping those businesses grow and become more competitive, improving the flow of finance and creating a more SME-friendly regulatory and administrative environment. Indeed, the EU granted some €90m. annually from 2001 to 2005 for SME-orientated projects in the EU and three **candidate countries**, **Bulgaria**, **Romania** and **Turkey**. Money was provided, for example, to facilitate the participation of European SMEs in a knowledge-based, internationalized economy and to give business easier access to networks such as the Euro Info Centres (which are, however, now closed down) in more than 40 countries. In June 2008 the Small Business Act for Europe was adopted by the European Commission, which, for the first time, put in place a comprehensive SME policy framework for the EU and its member states. In addition, in November 2011 the Commission presented a new approach to ensure that the EU responded better to the requirements of small businesses. Henceforth, the Commission would attempt wherever possible to exempt micro-enterprises from EU **legislation** or introduce special regimes so as to minimize the regulatory onus on them.

Enterprise policy is co-ordinated closely with other policies, in particular the single market (see **internal market**), research and innovation and information society policy. Conversely, when the EU is formulating policy on trade, education and training, or the environment, the business impacts are taken into account.

A new programme, COSME, for the Competitiveness of Enterprises and Small and Medium-sized Enterprises, was being implemented in 2014–20, with a budget of some €2,300m. COSME seeks to support SMEs by facilitating access to finance and to markets; providing support to entrepreneurs; and helping to ensure favourable conditions for the conception and growth of businesses.

The **INFORMATION SOCIETY** has been gradually emerging in Europe as a result of advances in technology and communication. One of the European Union's (EU) current priorities is to ensure that businesses, governments and citizens play an active role in shaping and participating in the global knowledge- and information-based economy. To achieve this, the **European Commission** wishes to stimulate research into the development and deployment of new information and communication technologies (ICT). It also wishes to set up and maintain a framework of regulation and standards that is designed to generate competition. In an attempt to encourage and promote a coherent information society within the EU, there have been a number of research and development programmes in the fields of information technology and telematics since 1984. Programmes within the different fields are considered essential to the economic growth and **competitiveness** of the EU, and to the creation of new jobs and markets. Maintaining and improving international competitiveness is an important element of the information society programmes, one of the earliest of which was the **European strategic programme for research and development in information technology** (ESPRIT). By the end of the 1990s the latest technological developments (such as the internet and the emerging knowledge-based economy) required a fresh impetus, which culminated in the 1999 Commission communication on 'eEurope—An information society for all'. An eEurope Action Plan was adopted at the 2000 Feira **summit meeting** of the **European Council**. The Commission's eEurope 2002 Action Plan identified a series of targets, which included securing a cheaper, faster and more secure internet; greater investment in people and skills; and finding ways to stimulate the use of the internet. The eEurope 2005 Action Plan was launched at the 2002 Seville summit of the European Council in Spain. In 2006 the Commission published the i2010 eGovernment Action Plan as part of the EU's i2010 strategy (launched in 2005), which aimed to stimulate the development of the digital economy in Europe. In order to foster an open and competitive **internal market** for the information society and the media, the primary objective of i2010 was to establish a Single European Information Space. In March 2010 the European Commission launched the **Europe 2020** strategy, which established the **Digital Agenda for Europe** as one of seven principal initiatives. The Digital Agenda for Europe replaced the i2010 initiative, and sought to utilize and develop the economic and social potential of ICT resources.

The importance of the information society cannot be overestimated as it has had a significant effect on certain areas of EU public policy and, for example, has accelerated the liberalization of the **telecommunications** sector. The EU's policy for the information society comprises the following four pillars: telecommunications policy; support to bring about technological development in information and communication technologies; creating the necessary conditions to ensure competitiveness exists; and to promote **Trans-European Networks** in transport, telecommunications and energy. The Connecting Europe Facility was to make available funds totalling some €1,000m. in 2014–20, for investment in areas including Digital Service Infrastructures and a number of broadband projects.

The **INFORMATION SOCIETY TECHNOLOGIES** (IST) programme was set up in 1998 as part of the European Communities information technology initiatives, and superseded various separate programmes, including the **European strategic programme for research and development in information technology**, in order to create a single integrated programme in this area. Four main topic areas were: systems and services for the citizen; new methods of work and electronic commerce;

multimedia content and tools; and essential technologies and infrastructures. The IST programme was subsequently restyled the Information and Communication Technologies (ICT) programme, which was allocated funding of €9,100m. for 2007–13. From 2014 ICT became part of the **Horizon 2020** programme.

INFRINGEMENT PROCEDURES relate specifically to the **implementation** of European Union (EU) laws. The **Treaty of Rome** charged the **European Commission** with the responsibility of ensuring that all laws and rules are applied. In its guise as guardian of the treaties, the Commission can initiate infringement proceedings under Article 226 (now Article 258 of the **Treaty on the Functioning of the European Union**) against a member state for failure to do so. Most of the infringement issues relate to the free movement of goods, free movement of people and free movement of capital as well as to decisions relating to **public procurement** and financial services. The Commission becomes aware of infringement by various means, as anyone residing in the EU or outside can lodge a complaint with the Commission against a member state on any issue that is deemed to be inconsistent with EU law. The Commission then decides whether to take the issue any further. If it does decide to do so, the Commission in the first instance may wish to bring the infringement to an end after presenting a letter of formal notice to the member state government concerned. This reasoned opinion alerts the member state concerned to the details of the infringement and asks the country to comply with EU law. If the state in question declines to end the infringement or ignores the letter, the Commission can then take the case to the **Court of Justice**. The **Treaty on European Union** gave the Courts the authority to levy fines against states infringing EU law. The Commission is also empowered under Regulation 1/2003 (an updated version of Regulation 17/62) to take action against a private company or a series of private companies for infringing the **competition policy** rules. This has led to the imposition of ever more substantial fines on the companies concerned.

INLAND WATERWAYS form an essential part of the transport network of much of the European Union (EU), especially for raw materials and industrial products. It is estimated that more than 37,000 km of waterways connect hundreds of towns and cities across the EU. Some 20 member states have inland waterways and 12 have interconnected waterways. The attraction of inland waterways as a means of transport has been growing in recent years in terms of reducing congestion on roads and railways and has also been pursued on account of the lower environmental costs (lower air and noise pollution) associated with this means of travel. This form of transport is also considered attractive as a means of transporting dangerous substances since waterway travel is safer than other modes. In 1976 the member states agreed to recognize, on a reciprocal basis, each other's decisions on the navigability and control of inland waterways. The type and technical specifications of commercial craft permitted to use the waterways have been subject to EU **regulations** since 1982, and the **European Commission** has continued to work towards broader international co-operation throughout the whole of Europe. Inland Navigation Europe is an independent organization, which acts as a platform for national and regional waterway managers and promotion bureaus within the EU.

INNER CORE is an expression used to refer to a group of member states that may wish to pursue deeper integration at a much quicker pace than would find agreement among all member states, where **unanimity** is required. The concept is an old one and can be traced back to discussions on differentiated integration that have surfaced since the founding of the European Communities. (See also **enhanced co-operation**; **flexibility**; **variable geometry**.)

INSTITUTIONS in the context of the European Union (EU) are the central decision making bodies of the organization. They possess a special status in EU treaties and practice. The **Treaty of Lisbon** identifies seven main EU institutions. These are the **Council of the European Union**, the **European Central Bank**, **the European Council**, the **European Commission**, the **European Parliament**, the European **Court of Justice** and the **European Court of Auditors**.

The **INSTRUMENT CONTRIBUTING TO STABILITY AND PEACE** (IcSP) replaced the Instrument for Stability (IfS) in March 2014. The IfS had, in turn, replaced the Rapid Reaction Mechanism in 2007. After the launch of the IfS, the **European Commission** considerably intensified its work in the area of conflict prevention, crisis management and peace building, and the instrument financed a large number of crisis response projects worldwide. An innovative part of it was the Peace-building Partnership, which was created to deepen the dialogue between civil society and the institutions of the **European Union** (EU). The IfS also enabled the EU to help build long-term international, regional and national capacity to address pervasive transregional and global threats.

The **INSTRUMENT FOR PRE-ACCESSION ASSISTANCE** (IPA) was launched at the beginning of 2007 (to run until the end of 2013) and replaced earlier pre-accession financial support programmes such as **PHARE**, **SAPARD**, **ISPA** (the **Instrument for Structural Policies for Pre-accession**) and **CARDS**. It was aimed at providing pre-accession assistance in five areas—transition assistance and institution building, cross-border co-operation, regional development, human resource development and rural development—and was available to countries of the **Western Balkans**, **Turkey** and **Iceland**. It was succeeded by IPA II, with a budget of €11,700m. for 2014–20.

The **INSTRUMENT FOR STRUCTURAL POLICIES FOR PRE-ACCESSION** (ISPA) was a European Communities initiative to strengthen the infrastructure of the **candidate countries** of **Central and Eastern Europe** in order to prepare them for membership of the European Union (EU). The ISPA operated in the area of transport and the environment. It was agreed by the Council of the European Union in June 1999 and stemmed directly from the **European Commission**'s **Agenda 2000** communication. The programme was scheduled to run from 2000 to 2006 and had an annual budget of €1,040m. for its duration. Financial assistance was granted to environmental projects that enabled the recipients to meet existing EU environmental standards and to initiatives in the transport sector that fostered **Trans-European Networks**. Between 2000 and the end of 2006 the Commission allocated some €1,040m. each year to ISPA projects. On accession to the EU a country automatically lost its entitlement to support under the ISPA. From 1 January 2007 the **instrument for pre-accession assistance** replaced the ISPA.

INSURANCE was identified by the **European Commission** in its 1985 **White Paper** on the **internal market** as one of the professional services that should be open to **freedom of movement** throughout the European Communities. While considerable liberalization has occurred, several national obstacles still hinder the emergence of a common insurance market and relatively little cross-border insurance business is actually carried out outside the field of large commercial risks.

INTEGRATION CAPACITY is, alongside the **accession criteria**, one of the criteria governing the **enlargement** of the European Union (EU). It relates to the institutional, financial and political ability of the EU to take in new members. Although as a term it only gained prominence following the EU's 2004 enlargement, questions about the EU's capacity to enlarge have always been present on the EU's agenda as part of the so-called '**widening** versus **deepening**' debate.

INTEGRATION THEORY refers to explanations, primarily produced by social scientists, to explain the logic and factors behind the European integration process. There now exists a huge and ever-expanding literature on European integration, but there is no single meta-theory that explains the entire process. These theories are intended to provide a better understanding of how the European Union (EU) works and how it has evolved. The distinction between the different integration theories often rest on specific assumptions. Over the years, some theories have come to dominate more than others. **Neofunctionalism** is considered one of the main theories of European integration, as developed by the political scientist Ernst Haas. **Intergovernmentalism** is another dominant approach that assumes the primacy of member states of the EU in decision making and, therefore, integration. **Liberal Intergovernmentalism** proposed by Andrew Moravcsik develops intergovernmentalism by highlighting the incorporation of the liberal model of preference formation wherein national governments will bargain through institutions to promote their preferences. New Institutionalism, developed outside the field of EU integration and EU studies more generally, has nevertheless been applied significantly to advance understanding of European integration. Through its three key strands, Rational Choice Institutionalism, Sociological Institutionalism and Historical Institutionalism, New Institutionalism contends that institutions understood as a system of rules, norms and preferences are important for understanding the function and processes of the EU.

While the majority of these theories focus on the institutions of the EU and the member states, the assumptions of these approaches are being challenged by a number of mid-range theories or approaches to EU integration and public policy studies that come under the headings of, for example, policy network analysis, multi-level governance and constructivism. Additionally, scholars such as Catherine Hoskyns and Annica Kronsell have introduced feminist theoretical approaches to broaden the relevance of the dominant theories and introduce new dimensions to the assumptions made about integration in Europe.

INTELLIGENT ENERGY EUROPE (IEE) is a support programme for non-technological actions in the field of energy (i.e. energy efficiency and renewable energy sources). It is intended to support the European Union's policies on energy as well as sustainable development. IEE had funding of some €730m. to cover the period 2007–13. From 2014 **Horizon 2020** funded the activities supported by IEE.

INTERACTIVE TERMINOLOGY FOR EUROPE (IATE) is the inter-institutional terminology database of the European Union (EU). The project was launched in 1999 and became operational throughout the EU in 2004. IATE incorporates all of the existing terminology databases of the EU's translation services into one inter-institutional database, and contains approximately 8.7m. multilingual entries in the 24 official languages.

INTEREST GROUPS seek to influence the European Union (EU) public policy process by forging close relations with the principal institutional actors, primarily the **European Commission** and, increasingly, the **European Parliament** (EP) since the **Treaty on European Union** and the arrival of the **co-decision procedure**; and also, to a lesser extent, the **Court of Justice**. The **Council of the European Union** cannot be lobbied directly and thus interest groups focus their attention on their national capitals. However, interest groups form a vital part of policy development, although their significance varies from group to group and from policy area to policy area. Some, such as the **European Round Table of Industrialists**, are clearly influential and have easy access to the institutions. Interest groups were a feature of European Communities (EC) business activity from the very outset. Given the EC's original economic activities, the first groups to establish themselves in **Brussels** were representatives from the business community (**BUSINESSEUROPE**, formerly the **Union of Industrial and Employers' Confederations of Europe**) and the agricultural community (**Committee of Professional Agricultural Organizations**). By the end of the 1970s trade unions and other new movements such as environmentalists had established a presence. Their influence was initially limited until the **Single European Act** and later treaties transformed **decision making** by enhancing the power of the EP and sought to establish a genuine **internal market** requiring EC-wide rules. By the late 1980s there was a noticeable expansion in the formation of interest groups. The emphasis on regions (see **Committee of the Regions**; **Europe of the Regions**) in the late 1980s and the 1990s added another dimension and led to the establishment of many offices representing sub-national authorities. In 2012 it was estimated that some 2,600 interest groups had permanent offices in Brussels, employing a combined total of around 15,000 people. The Commission has set up a database, CONECCS (Consultation, the European Commission and Civil Society), of around 1,000 organizations working at EU level, covering approximately 100 branches of activity. (See also **lobbying**.)

An **INTERGOVERNMENTAL CONFERENCE** (IGC) is the set of negotiations between the governments of the member states launched with a view to amending the **founding treaties**. The IGC provides a forum through which the European Communities (EC), or more specifically the **European Council**, has chosen to explore in detail new organizational and other infrastructural initiatives. They have become key events in the integration project and are used to seek agreement on **resolutions** approved in principle by the Council, and to plan their details. There have been seven major IGCs in the history of the European Union (EU) and five of these have occurred since the **Single European Act** was negotiated in the mid-1980s. The most important were the two conferences that began in 1990 to discuss **economic and monetary union** and **political union**, which formed the basis of the **Treaty on European Union**. Two further conferences on the future political integration of the EU were held in 1996 and 2000, and the measures suggested at these IGCs were formalized respectively in 1997 in the **Treaty of Amsterdam** and in 2000 in the **Treaty of Nice**. Following the December 2001 Laeken **summit meeting**, a new means for discussing and debating the future structure and powers of the EU—the **European Convention**—was launched. This allowed the views of a much wider range of interested parties to be brought together in preparation for the IGC that began its work in October 2003. This produced the **Treaty establishing a Constitution for Europe**. The most recent IGC was launched in July 2007 and produced the **Treaty of Lisbon**. The IGC is notable for, among other things, the exceptionally detailed mandate for its work agreed by the European Council.

INTERGOVERNMENTALISM relates primarily to one approach of academic discourse on European **integration theory**. It assumes the supremacy of national governments in the integration process and in treaty design, and downplays the role of the supranational institutions, the **European Commission**, the **European Parliament** and the **Court of Justice**, and other actors (e.g. the business community).

INTERIM AGREEMENTS are often concluded by the European Union (EU) to implement the trade provisions of international agreements that contain a mixture of EU and member state competences, such as **partnership and co-operation agreements** and **Europe agreements**, pending the **ratification** of such agreements.

INTER-INSTITUTIONAL AGREEMENTS are agreements made between the **Council of the European Union**, the **European Commission** and the **European Parliament** (EP) in order to run the European Union more efficiently. They involve a range of legal, organizational and budgetary arrangements. The most widely known are the Inter-institutional Agreements on the **budget** in 1988, 1993, 1999 and 2006, which determined levels of **expenditure** on multi-annual spending programmes. In March 2016 a new Inter-institutional Agreement on Better Law-Making, reached between the three legislative institutions, was adopted by the European Parliament, providing for the EP and the Council to be, hitherto, consulted on the withdrawal of legislative proposals.

An **INTERNAL MARKET** achieved by 'progressively approximating the economic policies of member states' was an immediate general objective of the **Treaty of Rome**. The Treaty set a specific timetable for the achievement of the **common market**. It was to be reached in a series of stages, and completed within 12 to 15 years. Although the **Six** successfully abolished **quota restrictions** and **tariffs** on internal trade, the broader objective was not attained within the stipulated time limit. It was not until the 1980s that the **European Communities** (EC) began to consider with greater urgency the need to tackle the numerous non-tariff barriers (so-called physical, technical and fiscal barriers) that restricted the **freedom of movement** of people, goods, services and capital. There was concern that the EC were not enjoying the economic advantage over their main trading rivals that their large population should provide. **European Commission** initiatives on economic liberalization were accumulating in the Council of Ministers (see **Council of the European Union**), where the effective requirement of unanimous agreement was seen as a major obstacle to any rapid progress. Jacques Delors, the incoming President of the Commission, had recognized the potential of pushing for a genuine internal market as a means not only of increasing trade and prosperity among the **Ten**, but also of re-launching the European integration project. In a tour of member state capital cities in the latter half of 1984 he found a general consensus in favour of the creation of an internal market, which he then presented to the **European Council** in **Brussels** in March 1985.

The Council accepted the principle of establishing a single market within a specified deadline, and instructed the European Commission to draw up a detailed programme, according to which the internal market would be completed by December 1992. The Commission responded with a **White Paper**, which listed some 300 actions (subsequently reduced to 282), with a timetable for each. Three months after its Brussels meeting, the European Council set in motion the developments that resulted in the **Single European Act**. This made the process of **harmonization** less subject to delay by amending the provisions relating to voting in the Council of Ministers. By 1992, most of the measures included in the White Paper had been adopted (although many still required **implementation** at national level). The effort to complete the internal market helped to revive the European project. It also persuaded the **European Free Trade Association** countries to seek a closer relationship with the European Union (EU), and possibly even membership. Furthermore, it led directly to renewed pressure for both **economic and monetary union** and closer political integration, and so indirectly to the **Treaty on European Union**. The **Treaty of Amsterdam** also introduced measures to improve freedom of movement within the EU, which could have an impact on the internal market. Other measures that had to be agreed at European level included greater combating of state aids (see **subsidies**), more market liberalization (especially in the energy sector), a more concerted **research and technological development** strategy, greater assistance for small and medium-sized businesses, better **Trans-European Networks**, greater labour mobility and, most controversially of all, fiscal harmonization. The **Treaty of Lisbon** deleted all references to the internal market, preferring the term '**single market**'.

INTERNATIONAL COMMITTEE OF THE MOVEMENTS FOR EUROPEAN UNITY was the name of an umbrella organization founded in December 1947 to co-ordinate and act as a link between the several bodies and the 1948 **Congress of Europe**.

The **INTERNATIONAL RUHR AUTHORITY** (IRA) was an agency established in April 1949 to supervise coal and steel production in the Ruhr region of **Germany**. It was intended to ensure that the Ruhr's resources in the new Federal Republic of Germany (FRG—West Germany) would not be used for aggressive purposes. As an alternative to keeping the FRG under military control, **France** had seen the IRA as a means of maintaining influence over German policy. The IRA was abandoned in 1950 as being unworkable. Its failure was one factor that made France look favourably upon the **Schuman Plan** as an alternative means of influencing German coal and steel production.

INTERNATIONAL SPACE STATION: See **Columbus**

INTERREG is the name of a **structural and cohesion funds** initiative, which was launched in 1989 with the aim of assisting border areas of the European Union (EU) to overcome problems of development caused by their relative isolation either within a national economy or within the EU as a whole. It is financed solely through the **European Regional Development Fund**. Interreg II was introduced in 1994 to encourage transnational spatial planning. Interreg III covered the period 2000–06, and was given a budget of €4,875m. This phase of Interreg was designed to strengthen economic and social cohesion throughout the EU. It aimed to do this through the promotion of balanced development of the Continent through cross-border, transnational and interregional co-operation. It placed particular emphasis on integrating remote regions and those that share external borders with **candidate countries** of **Central and Eastern Europe**. In 2007–13 some €7,800m. was allocated to the Interreg programme, distilled into three main areas of activity: cross-border co-operation, transnational co-operation (with 13 specific geographical programmes) and interregional co-operation (with no specific geographical boundaries for participation). The predominant theme of this latest phase is to strengthen and deepen cross-border co-operation, especially with regard to encouraging entrepreneurship and the development of **small and medium-sized enterprises** (SMEs), supporting links between rural and urban areas, promoting collaboration in health, culture and education, and sharing infrastructures (for example, in terms of waste management, energy systems and tourism). Since its inception, Interreg funding has always been available in Northern Ireland, but, whereas previous Interreg programmes operated on a Northern Ireland/**Ireland** cross-border basis, the Interreg IV programme redrew the operational borders to include Western Scotland for the first time. From 2014 Interreg became known as Interreg Europe.

INTERVENTION AGENCY is the name of the body that, under the **common agricultural policy**, intervenes to purchase produce when market prices fall below previously agreed **intervention prices**.

INTERVENTION PRICE has been the lynchpin of the **common agricultural policy**. It is a price support mechanism ensuring that if a product cannot be sold at an agreed price for that year then it goes into 'intervention' and is purchased and stored by the European Union. The cost is borne by the **budget**. In other words, intervention prices are fixed prices for farm commodities and are the minimum prices that producers are guaranteed for their commodities. When market prices fall below this level, an **Intervention Agency** purchases produce at the guaranteed price.

INVESTITURE is a term that refers to the process of conferring authority on the **European Commission** to act as a governmental body for the European Union. Because both the **Council of the European Union** and the **European Parliament** must now approve the membership of the Commission, the term 'double investiture' is used. (See **nomination procedure**.)

The **INVESTMENT SECURITIES DIRECTIVE** of 1989, introduced in 1993, is a **directive** designed to permit a company authorized in one **member state** to offer its services throughout the European Union without the need to acquire further authorization. It also set standards for solvency and the protection of investors.

INWARD INVESTMENT refers to the establishment of operations within the European Union (EU) by non-EU companies. The potential of the large EU market, the **common external tariff** and, more recently, the **internal market** and the **European Economic Area** have encouraged multinational companies to invest within the EU. On the whole, inward investment has been welcomed despite concerns that it might encourage over-capacity or weaken indigenous industries. To ensure that plants owned by external investors do not simply assemble components produced outside the EU, the EU has ruled that 60% of the manufactured product of such operations, measured by ex-factory prices, must be locally made.

The **IOANNINA COMPROMISE** takes its name from an informal meeting of foreign ministers in Ioannina, **Greece**, in March 1994, where political agreement was reached on the operation of **qualified majority voting** (QMV) rules to be applied within the **Council of the European Union** after the 1995 **enlargement** of the European Union (EU). With enlargement, the number of votes under QMV required to block a proposal—the 'blocking minority'—was set to increase from 23 to 26. The **United Kingdom** and **Spain** objected strongly and argued that the blocking minority should remain at 23. The agreed compromise stated that if members of the Council representing a total of between 23 and 25 votes indicated their desire to oppose the adoption of a decision by a qualified majority, the Council would do all in its powers to reach a satisfactory conclusion that could be adopted by at least 65 votes. The compromise was essentially a device for the British Government to preserve its dignity, and the compromise in effect has had little practical impact on EU **decision making**. A declaration annexed to the **Treaty of Amsterdam** extended the compromise until enlargement in 2004. With the new QMV rules agreed in the **Treaty of Nice**, it was anticipated that the Ioannina Compromise would be consigned to history. However, a new variant was adopted with the entry into force of the **Treaty of Lisbon**. It owed its existence to the insistence of **Poland** during the 2007 **intergovernmental conference** that it be compensated for the replacement of the—for Poland, very favourable—QMV provisions that had been introduced by the Treaty of Nice with the Treaty of Lisbon's less favourable **double majority** voting system. A new version of the Ioannina Compromise came into effect from November 2014, incorporating changes to the blocking minority threshold for EU member states wishing to demand the re-examination of EU **decisions** that they did not approve of; however, the previous weighting rules could continue to be applied on request until March 2017.

IPA: See **Instrument for Pre-accession Assistance**

The second **IRAQ WAR**, which commenced in March 2003, clearly revealed the sensitivities and difficulties within the European Union (EU) regarding efforts to create a **common foreign and security policy**. EU member states were deeply divided on the US invasion of Iraq and (leaving aside the four neutral countries—**Austria**, **Finland**, **Ireland** and **Sweden**) can be grouped into two camps. The first group supported the US attempt to remove President Saddam Hussain from power and included, among others, **Italy**, **Poland**, **Spain**, the **United Kingdom** and a number of the newest member states in **Central and Eastern Europe**. In contrast, the Governments of both **France** and **Germany** resolutely criticized the US move and led Donald Rumsfeld, the US Secretary of State for Defense, to talk of 'new' and 'old' Europe. Although the Hussain regime was swiftly defeated, all subsequent efforts to restore civil order and bring democracy to Iraq proved much harder to achieve. Sovereignty was transferred to an interim Government in June

2004, and six months later Iraqis voted in their country's first multi-party elections in 50 years. Saddam Hussain was caught and put on trial in 2005 for crimes against humanity. He was found guilty and was executed by hanging in December 2006. The security situation did not improve. On the ground, the US-led coalition forces faced armed rebellions and guerrilla-style attacks. They lost over 4,000 personnel in the process. Insurgents targeted civilians, Iraqi security forces and international agencies and suicide attacks became a regular reality and led to many thousands of civilian fatalities, and the dangers of the country spilling into full-scale civil war were not diminished. At the end of 2007 the UK handed over security of Basra province to Iraqi forces and effectively marked the end of nearly five years of British control of southern Iraq. During 2008–09 the violence abated as the security situation improved and there was notable progress in the 'Iraqization' of the governance of the country. The remaining US-led coalition forces ceased combat operations in 2010 and the final 50,000 US troops, who had stayed on in Iraq in an advisory capacity, had all withdrawn by the end of 2011. In May 2012 the EU and Iraq signed a **Partnership and Co-operation Agreement**. In August 2014 the European Council expressed dismay at the worsening security situation in Iraq and **Syria**, and the concomitant rise of the extremist Islamic State in Iraq and the Levant (ISIL, subsequently renamed **Islamic State**).

IRELAND did not become involved in most immediate post-war European developments (**ECSC, EDC, EEC** and **Euratom**), in part because of its neutral status, which itself in some ways reflected a very nationalistic and inward-looking focus in the late 1940s and 1950s. It also did not participate in the development of multilateral trading agreements, and became associated with the **European Free Trade Association** only in December 1965 through signing a free trade area agreement with the **United Kingdom**. Its application to join the European Communities (EC) was closely related with that of the UK, because of the strong economic links between the two countries. Its application was submitted several days before the original British application, but French President Charles De Gaulle's opposition to the latter ensured that the other membership applications, from Dublin (**Ireland**), Copenhagen (**Denmark**) and Oslo (**Norway**), ultimately failed. All four states were subsequently accepted to join the EC in January 1973 but Norway opted not to do so following the narrow rejection of membership in a **referendum**. Ireland has generally been a supporter of more economic and political integration, and the Irish electorate endorsed the **Single European Act**, the **Treaty on European Union** and the **Treaty of Amsterdam** in referenda. At least prior to 2004, Ireland was the greatest single net beneficiary of the **common agricultural policy** and the **structural funds**, which significantly helped to boost the Irish economy. The economic success of Ireland ensured that the country easily met the economic criteria to join **economic and monetary union**, and also meant that Ireland lost objective 1 status in relation to structural funds after 2006 (see **European Regional Development Fund**).

Interestingly, in the 1990s Ireland had one of the worst records among the member states on the implementation of EC **directives**. However, **Eurobarometer** frequently revealed Ireland remains to be one of the most pro-European Union (EU) member states, despite the much-publicized rejection of the **Treaty of Nice** in a referendum in June 2001. However, the outcome owed more to the low turnout (some 34%) and the inability of the major Irish political parties to campaign seriously on the issue than to any sudden change in opinion of the Irish public towards the EU. In a second referendum on the Nice Treaty, held in October 2002 the majority (some 62.9%) of those who participated supported the treaty, and thus paved the way for the **enlargement** of the EU. Nevertheless, the turnout for the referendum was still regarded as problematic, since only 48.5% of the electorate opted to vote.

Ireland was the only EU member state to hold a referendum on the **Treaty of Lisbon**. The outcome of the vote on 12 June 2008 was a victory for the treaty's opponents: 53.4% voted 'no' and 46.6% 'yes'. Given the relatively high turnout (53%), an early post-vote assumption was that there could be no second referendum as there had been with the Treaty of Nice. However, the Government greeted the result with disappointment. The Irish vote initially threatened to force the formal abandonment of the Treaty of Lisbon, which, in turn, could potentially have marginalized Ireland politically within the EU. After much deliberation on why the result had been a 'no', the former Irish Government under Brian Cowen finally agreed to hold a second referendum in the latter part of 2009, once it had secured some 'guarantees' from the European Council—most notably on retaining an Irish Commissioner and safeguarding neutrality—and thereby addressing 'no' voters' concerns. The onset of economic recession seemed to have refocused peoples' minds, and opinion polls from early 2009 displayed a turnaround in views and indicated a 'yes' vote. Despite growing public dissatisfaction with the Irish Government and its junior coalition partner, the Green Party, which led to heavy defeats for both parties at the local and European Parliament elections in June 2009, two-thirds of voters (67.1%) endorsed the Treaty of Lisbon in a second referendum which was held in October 2009. The electorate ultimately held the Cowen Government responsible for the economic difficulties that befell Ireland after 2008, and it was voted out of office on 25 February 2011 as Fianna Fáil experienced its worst election results since the founding of the Irish state. A coalition Government, comprising Fine Gael and the Labour Party, was appointed under the premiership of the leader of Fine Gael, Enda Kenny. On assuming power, Kenny stated that one of his top priorities was to renegotiate the terms of the €85,000m. bailout that had been agreed between the Irish Government and the **European Central Bank** and the International Monetary Fund in November 2010. This aspiration proved rather optimistic and **Angela Merkel** and Herman Van Rompuy expressed certain reservations about any such move. Kenny participated in discussions with his peers over the terms of the **Fiscal Compact** in the latter half of 2011 and signed the agreement in March 2012. It was decided to schedule a referendum on this treaty and on the Government's approach towards resolving the ongoing financial crisis. At the end of May 60.3% of those who participated in the referendum (around 50% of the electorate) voted in favour of the Government ratifying the Fiscal Compact. Ireland was the sole EU member state to hold a referendum on the treaty. The ratification process was completed by Ireland in December. From June 2017 the Irish Taoiseach was Leo Varadkar of Fine Gael.

IRISH REPUBLIC: See **Ireland**

ISDN stands for Integrated Services Digital Network. In 1989 the European Communities launched an initiative to raise the international **competitiveness** of the EC **telecommunications** industries through the provision of a range of compatible and harmonized services.

ISLAMIC STATE is an extremist Islamist militant organization, formerly known as Islamic State in Iraq and the Levant. In August 2014 the European Council expressed dismay at the deteriorating security situation in Iraq and **Syria**, caused by the declaration, in June, of an Islamic caliphate over parts of the two countries' territories by Islamic State, amid widespread human rights violations carried out against Christians and other minorities. The **European Council** noted that the ongoing civil conflict in Syria had facilitated the emergence of Islamic State, which it recognized as a threat to security in Europe, and announced its intention to co-operate with the **USA** and other countries in order to counter the threat posed by it and other organizations deemed to pose a terrorist threat. In December the new **High Representative of the Union for Foreign Affairs and Security Policy**, **Federica Mogherini**, attended the first meeting of the Global Coalition to Counter the Islamic State, which was held in Brussels, **Belgium**.

During 2015–17 several terrorist attacks took place in European Union (EU) member states, which caused fatalities and were attributed to supporters of Islamic State. In March 2016 suicide bombers claiming allegiance to Islamic State killed 35 people in attacks at Brussels international airport, and on an underground train in the city centre, in an apparently symbolic assault on Brussels as the heart of the EU. A new **European Counter Terrorism Centre** had been established in January, as part of **Europol**. In May a special envoy for the promotion of freedom of religion or belief was appointed, in an advisory role, to the **European Commission**, with an initial mandate of one year. The establishment of the role followed the adoption, in February, of a **European Parliament** resolution condemning the mass murder of religious minorities in Iraq and Syria by Islamic State, and sought to help to protect religious freedom in the context of the EU's programmes with countries outside the Union.

ISLAMOPHOBIA is a specific form of anti-Muslim racism directed at people who are or are perceived to be Muslim, and is an ongoing challenge to the European project. Islamophobia is often characterised by direct physical and social attack on individuals and communities. The rise in Islamophobia in recent times can be linked to incidents of jihadist terrorist violence in Europe; the rise of extreme right-wing politics; and the **European migration crisis**. Since 2015, a European Islamophobia Report (EIR) has been produced to document and analyse 'trends in the spread of Islamophobia' in Europe. Its main finding has been that incidents of Islamophobia have been linked to rhetoric fuelled by mass media, and have been demonstrated to undermine human rights and democracy.

The **ISOGLUCOSE CASE** relates to a 1980 ruling by the **Court of Justice**. This case represented one of the Court's landmark decisions in the development of the European Union. The case centred on a complaint brought to the Court by the **European Parliament** (EP) with specific reference to the **consultation procedure**. Although this procedure recognized the Council of Ministers (see **Council of the European Union**) as the sole decision maker, the **founding treaties** implied that the Council could only make legislative **decisions** once it had received the EP's opinion. In this particular instance, the Council had proceeded without waiting for the EP's response, which in this case went against the Council's decision. In Isoglucose, the Court upheld the EP's right to be consulted, and this marginally strengthened the EP's political position within the European Communities. Although following the case the EP still had few powers, this ruling enabled the EP to delay the Council in its decision making.

ISPA: See **Instrument for Structural Policies for Pre-accession**

IST: See **Information Society Technologies**

ISTC is the acronym for the International Science and Technology Centre, which was established in Moscow in 1994 in order to encourage scientists and engineers previously involved with weapons and warfare research in the former **USSR** to co-operate and to collaborate for peaceful purposes with their counterparts in the **USA**, **Japan** and the European Union.

ITALY was one of the founder members of the European Communities (EC) and has generally been a supporter of the principle of economic and political integration. Since 1957 it has favoured **supranationalism**, arguing for reforms that would strengthen the **European Commission** and the **European Parliament**. In 1986 it initially refused to sign the **Single European Act** as a protest against the inadequate nature of its proposed reforms. While the richer, more industrialized northern regions of the country benefited substantially from EC membership, the poorer south has remained relatively impoverished, despite the infusion of substantial EC funding. Nevertheless, Italy has been the subject of the greatest number of complaints against a member state (some one-third of the total) brought before the **Court of Justice**. The major reason has not been a reluctance to comply with EC **legislation**, but the cumbersome nature of the Italian parliament, which makes approval of any legislation a lengthy process. Most of the charges have related to Italy's failure to apply **directives** within the specified deadlines. Popular antipathy in Italy to the old political élites and parties, which were the subject of numerous national corruption charges after 1990, led to a new style of government that was more critical of the EC, the European Union (EU) and their objectives. In addition, speculative pressure in 1992 forced Italy to leave the **exchange-rate mechanism** (ERM). The country re-entered the ERM in November 1996, and Italy was one of the 11 member states to embrace **economic and monetary union** in January 1999. Critics questioned the degree to which Italy had actually met the **convergence criteria**, but there can be no doubting that the decision to join was politically motivated, and one that aroused a considerable degree of sensitivity in Rome.

The return of Silvio Berlusconi as Prime Minister in 2001 added an extra degree of controversy to the EU-Italian relationship as Berlusconi's unconventional style of leadership angered other heads of government. Italy became the first of the founding states of the EU to ratify the **Treaty establishing a Constitution for Europe** by parliamentary vote in April 2005. Berlusconi's premiership came to an end in May 2006 after his narrow defeat by his old adversary, Romano Prodi, in national elections. Prodi's tenure as Prime Minister, however, in the tradition of Italian post-war politics, was short-lived. He encountered difficulties, for example, over his foreign policy aspirations (especially the decision to allow the extension of a US military base) and some of his ministers were accused of corruption. He lost a vote of confidence in the Senate in January 2008 and immediately tendered his resignation as Prime Minister. Nevertheless, he remained in office for almost four months for routine business until early elections were held, and a new right-of-centre Government under Silvio Berlusconi was formed in April 2008. The Berlusconi Government's popularity with the electorate continued and it secured fairly impressive results in the 2009 EP elections, where it outscored the centre-left forces and captured 42% of the vote. It repeated its success in the regional elections of April 2010, but experienced a decline in support in a series of regional and local elections in 2011. Following the loss of his party's parliamentary majority and the continuing decline in the country's financial situation, Berlusconi stood down as Prime Minister in November. He was replaced by Mario Monti, a renowned economist and former EU commissioner, who appointed a cabinet of technocrats tasked with tackling the worsening economic crisis. At the parliamentary elections held in February 2013 Monti's party fared badly and fell short of securing even 10% of the vote. After two months of impasse, Enrico Letta, the deputy leader of the Democratic Party (Partito Democratico), was appointed as the new Prime Minister, at the head of a new 'grand coalition' Government in late April. Within 10 months Letta's position had become increasingly difficult and an internal challenge to his leadership by Matteo Renzi culminated in Letta's resignation and the creation of a new Government under Renzi in February 2014. Following a failed constitutional reform referendum campaign, Matteo Renzi left office on 12 December 2016, ushering in the premiership of **Paolo Gentiloni**, a member of the Democratic Party.

ITER stands for the International Thermonuclear Experimental Reactor (although this full title is no longer used), an international co-operation project comprising the member states of the **European Atomic Energy Community** (EAEC or Euratom), plus **Japan**, the **USA**, India, the People's Republic of China, the Republic of Korea and the **Russian Federation**. Completion of the nuclear fusion reactor, which is being built in Cadarache, **France**, is scheduled for 2019. (See also **European Fusion Development Agreement**; **Joint European Torus**.)

ITS: See the **Identity, Tradition and Sovereignty Group**

J

JAPAN has been regarded by the European Union (EU) as a major economic competitor, and perhaps also as an example to the EU, especially in terms of new technological industries. Much of EU **research and technological development policy** has been determined by the perceived need to compensate for the advantage that Japan is believed to hold. More generally, trade relations between the EU and Japan have been fraught with problems. The main reason was the large trade deficit that the EU incurred with Japan. In 1993–2000 Japanese exports to the EU increased by almost 84%, from €50,100m. to €92,100m., while EU exports to Japan rose from €28,800m. to €45,500m. Subsequently, however, the deficit narrowed considerably owing to a significant decline in Japan's share of total EU imports. In 2010 Japan accounted for 3.2% of the exports of the **Twenty-Seven** (EU27)—compared with 9.3% in 2000—and 4.3% of EU27 imports, and was the EU27's sixth most important trading partner. Japanese exports are concentrated in a few important consumer fields, such as cars, electronics and computers. Japan has traditionally been slow to ease the entry of imports to its domestic market by relaxing or removing a range of non-tariff barriers. However, the **European Commission** has regulated the entry of several Japanese products and has passed several anti-**dumping** measures. In addition, member states have imposed a number of restrictions on Japanese imports: the best known, perhaps, have been the so-called voluntary agreements limiting the volume of imports of Japanese cars. However, many Japanese companies have invested in the EU. In addition to the long-established bilateral negotiations and contacts on economic issues, a political dialogue between the EU and Japan also exists. This, dating back to a 1991 declaration, has gradually been developed through the holding of an annual summit meeting between the European Commission President, the European Council presidency and the Japanese Prime Minister. In 2001 a joint EU-Japan action plan entitled 'Shaping our Common Future' was adopted. In March 2013 Japan and the EU agreed to commence negotiations on an economic partnership agreement and a free trade agreement; the first round of talks was held in Brussels in April. In July 2017 the two sides reached agreement, in principle, on the terms of the two agreements, in what the Commission described as the most significant bilateral trade agreement agreed by the EU.

JEREMIE (JOINT EUROPEAN RESOURCES FOR MICRO TO MEDIUM ENTERPRISES) was established in 2007 as an initiative from the **European Commission**, the **European Investment Bank** and **the European Investment Fund** to enable European Union member states and regions to use part of their **structural and cohesion funds** to obtain a set of financial instruments specifically designed to support micro and small and medium-sized enterprises (SMEs). The initiative sought to contribute to growth and employment in line with the revised **Lisbon Agenda**.

JET: See **Joint European Torus**

JHA: See **Justice and Home Affairs**

JICS: See **Joint Interpreting and Conference Service**

JOINT ACTIONS are among the measures that can be adopted by the **Council of the European Union** under **common foreign and security policy** (CFSP). They commit the member states and are normally adopted unanimously. However, joint actions may in certain circumstances be adopted by a **qualified majority vote**. In all cases, the objectives of a joint action, its scope, the means to be made available to the European Union, and the conditions governing implementation, must be laid down.

JOINT EUROPEAN TORUS (JET) was one of the principal operations of the nuclear policy of the European Communities. Established in 1978, based at Culham in the **United Kingdom**, and built and funded by the **European Commission**, JET was the central institute for all West European research into nuclear fusion. Some non-member states also participated in the project (**Japan**, the **USA** and countries of the former **USSR**). JET was one of only four such centres in the world, and its objective was to develop nuclear fusion as a safer, cleaner, more efficient and economic source of energy than a nuclear fission reactor. It maintained links with similar institutes in other parts of the world. In 2000 the **European Fusion Development Agreement** took over JET's operations. In October 2014 the Commission officially launched the **European Consortium for the Development of Fusion Energy** (EUROfusion), superseding the European Fusion Development Agreement and incorporating 29 bilateral association agreements between the Commission and research institutions. (See also **ITER**.)

JOINT INTERPRETING AND CONFERENCE SERVICE (JICS), or Service Commun Interprétation-Conférences (SCIC), is a language service established by the European Union (EU) as an agency of the **European Commission** in 1985. In addition to providing appropriate support to EU institutions, one of its objectives is to assist in the training of conference interpreters. The JICS has now been restyled as the **Directorate-General** for Interpretation.

The **JOINT RESEARCH CENTRE** (JRC) is an organization established under the **European Atomic Energy Community** (EAEC or Euratom). Directed by the **European Commission**, but relying for much of its funding on individual contracts, it is, in fact, a collection of seven institutes based in Geel (**Belgium**), Karlsruhe (**Germany**), Ispra (**Italy**), Petten (**Netherlands**) and Seville (**Spain**). The Directorate-General of the JRC is located in **Brussels**. While nuclear research and development remain major concerns of the institutes, their research efforts have diversified to incorporate safety standards and measurements, systems engineering, safety technology, information technology, electronics, environmental protection, food and drug analysis, and space applications.

VERA JOUROVÁ (1964–) was nominated in 2014 as the Czech Commissioner to the new 28-member **European Commission** led by President-elect **Jean-Claude Juncker**, subject to approval from the **European Parliament**. In September Juncker named Jourová as Commissioner for Justice, Consumers and Gender Equality. Jourová took a Master's degree in Theory and Culture at Charles University in Prague before working in regional administration. She developed an expertise in European Union (EU) regional policy as Head of the Regional Department of Development of Vysočina region in 2001–03, before becoming deputy minister for regional development (2003–06) and working as an independent consultant specializing in EU accession in the Western Balkans from 2006–13. Prior to her appointment to the Commission Jourová was elected to the Czech legislature in October 2013 and became the Minister for Regional Development in January 2014. She took up her post as European Commissioner on 1 November.

JRC: See **Joint Research Centre**

JUDGES: See **General Court**; **Court of Justice**

JUDICIAL PANELS may be established by the **Council of the European Union** to exercise judicial competence in specific areas. The **Treaty of Nice** introduced provisions for the panels in an attempt to speed up legal proceedings. Explicit reference was made to establishing a judicial panel for cases brought by European Union personnel.

JEAN-CLAUDE JUNCKER (1954–) was selected to succeed José Manuel Durão Barroso as the President of the **European Commission** in November 2014. Juncker was born in Redange, **Luxembourg**, and educated in **Belgium** and Luxembourg, before completing a Master of Law degree at the University of **Strasbourg** in 1979. During his studies he had joined the Christian Social People's Party and after graduation he pursued a career in politics. Juncker worked as a parliamentary secretary before being elected to the Chamber of Deputies in Luxembourg in 1984. Juncker's rise within the party was extremely rapid. He first served as the Minister for Labour under Jacques Santer from 1984 until 1989 before becoming Minister of Finance in 1989. Juncker possessed strong European credentials from the outset and his time as Minister of Finance led to his involvement in the framing of the sections on **economic and monetary union** contained within the (Maastricht) **Treaty on European Union** (EU). He replaced Santer as the Prime Minister of Luxembourg in January 1995 and served as Prime Minister for some 18 years until December 2013. During that time he had always taken a deep interest in EU affairs and had steered the country to a majority vote (56%) in a referendum in favour of the **Treaty establishing a Constitution for Europe** in 2005. In March 2014 Juncker was selected by the Congress of the **Group of the European People's Party (Christian Democrats)** (EPP) meeting in Dublin (**Ireland**) as the EPP candidate for the position of European Commission president. A clause in the **Treaty of Lisbon** stipulated that presidents of the European Commission should be selected 'taking into account' the outcome of the **European Parliament** (EP) elections. This small alteration transformed the process, as it placed the EP in the role of a much more proactive actor in the selection of the Commission president than had been the case in the past. Until the Lisbon Treaty the EP's role had been limited to approving (or rejecting) the **European Council**'s candidate. The EP was effectively steering the process and despite some reservations within the European Council, Juncker was officially nominated as Barroso's successor on 27 June 2014. **David Cameron**, the then British Prime Minister, objected to Juncker's candidacy and urged a vote within the European Council. However, 26 of the 28 member states supported the choice of Juncker, with only **Hungary** supporting the **United Kingdom**. Juncker's position was formally secured following the majority support of the EP in July 2014. He presented his team of 27 fellow Commissioners in September. After the Slovenian Commissioner-designate was replaced, his Commission team was endorsed by the EP and the **European Council** in late October, and took office on 1 November. Shortly afterwards a number of Eurosceptic parties in the EP (including the **UK Independence Party**) launched an unsuccessful vote of no confidence in Juncker. Juncker made his first State of the Union address in September 2015, announcing that 'there is not enough Europe in this Union. And there is not enough Union in the Union'. He emphasized the need for solidarity and consensus with respect to major issues affecting the EU, such as the ongoing **European migration crisis**.

JUSTICE AND HOME AFFAIRS (JHA) was the title given to the then intergovernmental third **pillar** of the European Union (EU) when it was established by the **Treaty on European Union** in 1993. The origins of the pillar can be found in the co-operation on anti-terrorism measures and external border security being undertaken by the member states under the umbrella of **TREVI** (Terrorisme, Radicalisme, Extrémisme, Violence Internationale). Faced with increasing problems in the late 1980s and early 1990s in these and other areas such as asylum, immigration, drugs trafficking and fraud, many of the member states were persuaded that something more formal and structured than TREVI was desirable. A further factor was the difficulties faced by the countries that had signed the **Schengen Agreement** in their efforts to agree on a **harmonization** of policies. While the provisions for JHA often simply gave a more formal recognition to already well-established co-operative procedures, the socio-economic environment in the mid-1990s and difficulties in the operation of the pillar pushed the member states towards consideration of a less intergovernmental approach to JHA co-operation. Nevertheless, several member states were not prepared to consider incorporating JHA fully into the EU institutional structure, and this resistance inevitably placed limits upon its scope for action. The **Treaty of Amsterdam** transformed JHA by transferring a number of areas under the third pillar to the **Treaty of Rome**, and hence to the first, supranational, pillar of the EU as part of its aim of creating an **area of freedom, security and justice**. At the same time, pillar III was renamed **police and judicial co-operation in criminal matters** to reflect more precisely the areas of activity left for intergovernmental co-operation. (See also **Tampere summit**.) These residual issues were collapsed into the supranational activities of the EU with the entry into force of the **Treaty of Lisbon** and the abandonment of the pillar structure.

JUSTICIABLE means that, under the terms of the **European treaties**, a matter under dispute can be submitted to the **Court of Justice** or the **General Court** for resolution.

The **JUSTUS LIPSIUS** building in **Brussels** is the home of the **Council of the European Union** and the **European Council**. It is situated opposite the **Berlaymont** building, which is the home of the **European Commission**. Justus Lipsius (1547–1606) was a humanist and classical scholar.

K

KALININGRAD, formerly known as Königsberg, was part of German East Prussia until this territory was annexed by the **USSR** in 1946. The territory offered the USSR direct access to the Baltic Sea and was one of the most militarized places in Europe during the **Cold War**. However, the dissolution of the USSR in the early 1990s transformed the Kaliningrad region into what was effectively a Russian exclave that was cut off geographically from Russia by **Lithuania**, **Latvia** and Belarus, and whose economic situation has been desperate for much of the time since. In 1992 it was declared a 'free economic zone' in the hope of attracting foreign investment. The **enlargement** of the European Union (EU) and the **North Atlantic Treaty Organization** to include **Poland** and Lithuania heightened fears that the exclave could become completely isolated. Hence, the Russian Government was keen to ensure land access to Kaliningrad. Lithuania and the EU rejected its initial proposal of a closed land corridor during **accession negotiations**. Instead, agreement was reached in 2002 on introducing special transit arrangements for citizens of the **Russian Federation** from 1 July 2003.

JYRKI KATAINEN (1971–) was nominated in 2014 as the Finnish Commissioner-designate to the new 28-member **European Commission** led by **Jean-Claude Juncker**. Juncker named Katainen as Vice-President of the Commission for Jobs, Growth, Investment and Competitiveness. Katainen took a Master's degree in Social Sciences at the University of Tampere. He was elected to the Finnish parliament in 1999, and became Vice-President and then President of the Finnish Coalition party before serving as Minister of Finance in 2007–11. Prior to his appointment to the Commission Katainen held the position of Prime Minister of **Finland** between 2011 and 2014. The **Members of the European Parliament** (MEPs) approved Katainen's nomination, and the **European Parliament** and **European Council** approved the entire Juncker Commission in October 2014. Katainen took up his post as a European Commissioner on 1 November.

KENNEDY ROUND, named after President John F. Kennedy of the **USA**, was the name given to the sixth series of negotiations (1964–67) on tariff reductions held by the **General Agreement on Tariffs and Trade** (GATT). It was the first series of GATT talks where the **European Commission** was the sole representative of the European Communities (EC), according to the terms of the **Treaty of Rome**, which stipulated that the EC were to represent the member states in issues of external trade. As a result of the discussions, the EC **common external tariff** was reduced, on average, by some 35%.

GIOVANNI KESSLER (1956–) was born in Trento, **Italy**, and studied law at the University of Bologna. After finishing his studies, he pursued a legal career before being elected to the Italian parliament in 2001. His expertise in dealing with organized crime and corruption made him an ideal appointment for his current post as Director-General of the **European Anti-Fraud Office** (OLAF); he took up the post in 2011.

The **KIRCHBERG DECLARATION** dates from May 1994, when it was issued by the leaders of **Western European Union** (WEU). Essentially it established categories of WEU membership. The four categories listed were: full members, which were members of both the **North Atlantic Treaty Organization** (NATO) and the European Union (EU), such as the **United Kingdom**; associate members, which were members only of NATO and not the EU; associate partners, which were members of neither NATO nor the EU; and finally, observers, such as **Ireland**, which were members of the EU but not of NATO.

KOSOVO was formerly an autonomous region within **Serbia** and, before that, **Yugoslavia**. Following a three-year conflict in 1996–99 between Serbian and Yugoslav forces and the guerrilla Kosovo Liberation Army, the **North Atlantic Treaty Organization** (NATO) launched air strikes against Yugoslav forces in the region in an attempt to force a political settlement to the conflict. The Yugoslav and Serbian leaderships eventually accepted the presence of a NATO-led peacekeeping force—KFOR—in Kosovo. Over the next nine years, Kosovo was administered by the **United Nations** (UN), and pressure for independence grew within the province, culminating in a declaration of independence on 17 February 2008. This was strongly opposed by Serbia and by the **Russian Federation**. Within the European

Union (EU), opinion on recognizing the newly independent state was divided, although most member states moved quickly to recognition. The EU also assumed responsibility from the UN for the administration and security of Kosovo, deploying a mission of some 1,800 international administrators, lawyers, judges and police (subsequently increased to 2,000) under the European Union Rule of Law Mission in Kosovo (EULEX Kosovo, which also employs local personnel) in an attempt to ensure the functioning of the new state. Kosovo is gradually being integrated with the EU as part of both the **Stabilization and Association Process** and the EU's more general approach to the **Western Balkans**. However, the process is complicated by the fact that five EU member states—**Cyprus**, **Greece**, **Romania**, **Slovakia** and **Spain**—have so far refused to recognize Kosovo's independence and continue to consider it a breakaway province of Serbia. In June 2012 the Council of the European Union announced that the mandate of EULEX Kosovo had been extended for another two years until June 2014. A budget of €111m. was allocated for the first of these two additional years. Following a diplomatic rapprochement between Kosovo and Serbia in April 2013 in June the EU indicated its intention to commence negotiations with Kosovo on a **Stabilization and Association Agreement** (SAA). These began in October, and were concluded in May 2014; the SAA was initialled by both sides in July, and entered into force in April 2016. Meanwhile, in August 2015 the **High Representative of the Union for Foreign Affairs and Security Policy**, **Federica Mogherini**, announced that the Prime Ministers of Kosovo and Serbia had signed four agreements, which represented progress in the further normalization of relations. The agreements focused on energy, telecommunications, the introduction of additional rights for Serb-dominated municipalities in Kosovo and freedom of movement. However, subsequent progress was very limited.

L

The **LAEKEN DECLARATION** on the Future of the European Union was adopted by the **European Council** at its **summit meeting** in Laeken, **Belgium**, on 15 December 2001. The Declaration followed a similar Declaration on the Future of the Union adopted a year earlier at the same time as the **Treaty of Nice** and was significant for the issues it raised for consideration by the **European Convention**, which was launched in late February 2002. The Laeken Declaration begins by identifying the two key challenges facing Europe: the need to bring the European Union (EU) closer to its citizens; and defining the role for the EU in a fast-changing globalized world. It then proceeds to raise more than 50 questions and issues for the Convention to address. These include a better division and definition of the EU's competences; **simplification** of treaties and legislative measures; the need for more democracy, **transparency** and efficiency; and steps towards a **constitution** for the EU.

CHRISTINE LAGARDE (1956–) was appointed as the Managing Director of the International Monetary Fund, replacing Dominique Strauss-Kahn, in July 2011. Lagarde was born in Paris and studied law at university in the French capital before taking a Master's degree in English and political science at the Institute of Political Studies in Aix-en-Provence, **France**. After graduation she was admitted into the French legal profession. She started working for a major US law company (Baker & McKenzie) in 1981, where she specialized in antitrust and labour law. She rose rapidly through the firm and became a partner in 1987, the head of its European division in 1995 and its first female chair in 1999. She left Baker & McKenzie in 2005 to become Minister of Foreign Trade in the French Government of the centre-right Union pour un Mouvement Populaire. Under the presidency of Nicolas Sarkozy, Lagarde served as Minister of Agriculture (for a month) and then Minister of the Economy, Finance and Industry.

The **LAMFALUSSY PROCESS** refers to a novel approach to the process of European **legislation** and regulation. It originated in February 2001, when a 'Group of Wise Men' headed by Baron Alexandre Lamfalussy presented a Report on the Regulation of European Securities Markets to the **Council of the European Union**. The report provided a clear and coherent argument calling for a change in European legislative and regulatory structures. Essentially, the authors of the report identified the economic benefits of further financial market integration in Europe, highlighted the key factors slowing down that integration process and arrived at the conclusion that the then existing regulatory system was unable to cope with the accelerating pace of market change. To overcome and reduce the deficiencies, the Group agreed upon what has become known as the Lamfalussy process. It is a four-level approach to lawmaking, based partially on procedures existing (but not widely used before in the area of financial markets) in the European Union (EU) constitutional framework, and partially on experience in member states, but it is also partially new and innovative. According to the Lamfalussy proposals, financial markets legislation and regulation should usefully involve the following four levels: framework principles to be decided by normal EU legislative procedures, i.e. in co-decision between Council and Parliament (see **European Parliament**) upon a proposal by the Commission (see **European Commission**); **implementation** legislation by the Commission upon proposal by the newly established Council of European Securities Regulators (CESR) in consultation with member states through an EU Securities Committee; intense co-operation and networking between securities regulators in the CESR to ensure consistent and equivalent transposition of level I and II legislation; and strengthened enforcement, basically through Commission action, but with co-operation from member states, regulators, and the private sector. In the area of securities markets legislation, the Lamfalussy process was applied for the first time for the new **Directives** on Market Abuse and on Prospectuses. The first impressions were mixed; it appeared that not all of the parties involved had fully understood (or fully appreciated) the mechanics as intended by the 'Wise Men'. Proposals have been made to extend the application of the Lamfalussy process beyond securities markets into other financial areas (notably banking, insurance and investment funds).

LANGUAGES are both an indication of the diversity of the European Union (EU) and a barrier to effective integration.

Prior to **enlargement** in 2004, the EU had 11 official languages: Danish, Dutch, English, Finnish, French, German, Greek, Italian, Portuguese, Spanish and Swedish. With 10 countries joining, a further nine languages became official languages of the EU: Czech, Estonian, Hungarian, Latvian, Lithuanian, Maltese, Polish, Slovak and Slovenian. The total was thus raised to 20. In May 2005 the EU officially recognized the Irish language as a working language in the Union. Irish thus became the 21st language to be given such recognition by the EU. Prior to this development Irish had been recognized as a treaty language only. From January 2007 Bulgarian and Romanian also became official working languages, bringing the overall total to 23; this total increased again, to 24, following the accession of **Croatia** to the EU in July 2013. Any one official language may be used in EU meetings; all official documents from all EU institutions need to be translated into all languages; and simultaneous interpreting between all languages is provided for most EU meetings (e.g. of the **European Council**, the **Council of the European Union**, the **Court of Justice** and the **European Parliament**).

The cost of translation is considerable, there being more than 500 different translation combinations, but arguably necessary if the EU's citizens are to be able to understand the **decisions** and laws that affect them. Within the **European Commission**, costs are reduced since the administration conducts most of its daily business in English and French. Other institutions have yet to follow suit to the same extent although many committees do conduct their business in either English or French. (See also **Lingua**.)

LATIN AMERICA: See **South and Central America**

LATVIA regained its independence from the then **USSR** in 1991. Soon thereafter it began negotiations with the European Communities on a **free trade agreement**, which was concluded in 1994. However, by the time the subsequently negotiated **Europe agreement** was signed in 1995, attention was focusing on an application for membership of the European Union (EU), which was duly submitted on 27 October 1995. Although the **European Commission**'s *avis* in 1997 was supportive of Latvia's desire to join the EU, it did not recommend **accession negotiations**, primarily because of concerns over the insufficient progress made with economic reform. Instead, Latvia had to wait for the Helsinki **summit meeting** of the **European Council** in December 1999 before being invited to negotiate membership. Despite coming late to accession negotiations, Latvia was among the **candidate countries** that concluded negotiations at the **Copenhagen summit** in December 2002. The Latvian electorate subsequently endorsed the terms of accession in a referendum in September 2003. In a turnout of 72.5%, more than 67% voted in favour of EU membership. Latvia joined the EU in May 2004 and a year later approved (by parliamentary vote) the **Treaty establishing a Constitution for Europe**. The country became part of the EU's **Schengen Area** in December 2007. The Latvian Parliament approved the **Treaty of Lisbon** in early 2008. In March 2013 Latvia submitted an application to adopt the **euro** as its official currency. The European Commission approved the application in July, and Latvia became the 18th member of the **eurozone** in January 2014, when it also joined the **European Banking Authority** and the **Single Supervisory Mechanism**.

LAW in the context of the European Union (EU) derives originally from the provisions of the **Treaty of Rome** (1957), according to which EU law takes precedence over national law. EU law today stems from a series of treaties, **legislation** and court rulings. There are basically three sources of EU law, which can be identified as primary law, secondary law and supplementary law. Primary law relates directly to the EU treaty base, and specifically the **Treaty on the European Union** and the **Treaty on the Functioning of the European Union**. Secondary law comprises legal instruments based on these treaties and refers to the **regulations** and **directives**. Such law originates from initiatives taken by the **European Commission**, and is in most cases today adopted by the **Council of the European Union** and the **European Parliament** through the use of the **Ordinary Legislative Procedure** as established under the **Treaty of Lisbon** (2007). Supplementary law relates primarily to the body of case law that has been developed by the **Court of Justice** since the 1950s.

LDR: See **Group of the European Liberal Democratic and Reform Party**

The **LEGAL INSTRUMENTS** of the European Union include **directives**, **regulations** and **decisions**. The **Treaty establishing a Constitution for Europe** envisaged their replacement with a new range of instruments: European Laws and European Framework Laws, European Regulations and European Decisions. This was one of the few substantive elements of the treaty not carried forward into the **Treaty of Lisbon**.

LEGAL PERSONALITY is a concept that means that a body has the right under international law to take autonomous actions rather than relying upon governments to act on its behalf. The **Treaty of Rome** conferred legal personality upon the European Community (EC). This meant that the EC could act in law as an independent party, enter into legally binding agreements, and be subject to constitutional legal proceedings. The legal personality of the EC was distinct from that of the member states. By contrast, the **Treaty on European Union** did not explicitly confer legal personality on the European Union (EU). The fact that agreements could be and were concluded in the name of the EU strengthened the argument that the EU did in practice have legal personality. Had it entered into force, the **Treaty establishing a Constitution for Europe** would have resolved the situation by conferring legal personality on the EU. Legal personality for the EU has since been established with the entry into force of the **Treaty of Lisbon**.

The **LEGAL SERVICE** is a service of the **European Commission**. Its major task is to prepare and evaluate, from a legal perspective, European Union (EU) **legislation**; it also represents the Commission in all court cases. The Legal Service has to ensure that all legislation, before being printed in the *Official Journal of the European Union*, has the same precise legal meaning in all EU **languages**. The current Director-General of the Commission's Legal Service is Luis Romero Requena. The **Council of the European Union** also has a Legal Service, which advises the **Council Secretariat** and the **Council Presidency**.

LEGISLATION is enacted by complex procedures in the European Union (EU). The **Council of the European Union** and the **European Parliament** (EP) or the **European Commission** are empowered to issue three different kinds of legislation: **regulations**, **directives** and **decisions**. The **Court of Justice** institutes a fourth source of legislation: rulings given by the Court on the cases that come before it constitute a body of case law which affects the interpretation and **implementation** of European Communities (EC) and national **law**. In addition, there is so-called '**soft law**'.

The EU equivalent of national legislation is the combination of regulations and directives. The first stage of both lies with the Commission, which has the **right of initiative**. If adopted by the Council, the Commission's proposal becomes either a regulation or a directive. The distinction between the two is important. Regulations are more rigorous, the highest form of legislation. They are fairly detailed instructions, applicable throughout the EU, and directly binding upon all member states. Directives are also binding, but take the form of general instructions on the goal to be achieved, while leaving the way in which it will be attained to the discretion of each member state. The conditions of a directive are normally met by the member states introducing national legislation in conformity with EU stipulations.

Decisions by either the Commission or the Council are also binding upon the member states; they may be addressed to named individuals or enterprises. Decisions can be made by either of the EU executives on the basis of the direct authority they possess under the terms of the **Treaty of Rome** and its amendments, or on the basis of earlier regulations or directives. (Decisions made according to the provisions of the **Treaty of Paris** were slightly different: they were binding in their entirety upon member states and were thus more similar to regulations.)

Under the Treaty of Rome and its amendments, the Commission and the Council can also issue **recommendations**, which, like **opinions**, and in contrast to the pronouncements described above, do not constitute instructions but merely express an EU preference that member states are free to ignore. (However, recommendations made under the Treaty of Paris were binding as to the final result, but not the means to achieve it, rather like EU directives.)

Whereas originally decisions to adopt EC legislation involved either the Commission or the Council, the EP now has a significant role to play. In 1987 the **Single European Act** introduced the **co-operation procedure**, which allowed the EP to table amendments to and reject proposed legislation. It also made **ratification** of **association agreements** and **accession treaties** conditional on the assent of the EP. This was followed in 1993 by the introduction via the **Treaty on European Union** (TEU) of the **co-decision procedure**, along with a requirement that the Council and the EP jointly adopt certain legislative proposals. Since the TEU, the **Treaty of Amsterdam**, the **Treaty of Nice** and the **Treaty of Lisbon** have all extended use of the **ordinary legislative procedure** (formerly co-decision) and the consent (formerly assent) procedure, thus further enhancing the EP's role in the legislative process.

The **LEGITIMACY** of the European Communities (EC) prior to the early 1990s was hardly challenged thanks to the **permissive consensus** that surrounded the European integration project. Since then, and in particular since the establishment of the European Union (EU), the legitimacy of the EC and the EU has been increasingly challenged. This has been evident in the criticisms coming not just from politicians, but also from the citizens of the EU, as evidenced by the **ratification crises** surrounding the **Treaty on European Union** and the **Treaty of Nice**, and the low and falling turnout of voters in **European Parliament** elections. Major concerns focus on the perceived inability of the EU to deliver benefits to the people and to solve problems; lack of popular identification with and support for the EU; the alleged intrusiveness of the EU as it increasingly touches on areas traditionally viewed as being the preserve of national governments; and concern over the direction in which the integration project is heading. The question of how to remedy the declining legitimacy of the EU, as well as associated problems concerning the EU's **democratic deficit**, informed many of the issues on the agenda of the **European Convention** launched in February 2002.

LENIENCY NOTICES were first introduced by the Commission in 1996 in relation to its handling of **competition policy**. The Directorate-General for Competition revised its leniency procedures in 2002 and again in 2006. In an attempt to uncover **cartel** activity, the Commission devised its leniency initiative as a means to persuade and entice cartel members to break rank and supply the Commission with full details of a particular cartel's operations and management. A firm that does so can be given full immunity from any fine that the Commission imposes on the cartel. Cartels are by nature often unstable, and such an inducement to reveal wrongdoing can prove attractive and lead to more cartels being uncovered.

LEONARDO (full title: Leonardo da Vinci) was the name of a phased action programme on the implementation of a comprehensive European Communities **education, vocational training and youth policy** to absorb and replace all existing initiatives in the area of vocational education and training. The first phase of the programme started in 1995, superseding the vocational training programmes Eurotecnet, Comett and Force. In 1998 young people from **Hungary**, the **Czech Republic**, **Romania** and **Cyprus** were able to take part in vocational exchanges with European Union (EU) countries under the programme. The second phase of the Leonardo programme ran from January 2000 to 31 December 2006; with funding of €1,450m., this phase financed 21,000 projects involving about 3.7m. people. The Leonardo programme enabled more than 860,000 people to travel abroad for training or work experience, or for professionals to gain new skills and develop vocational education and training tools, methods and systems. During the five-year period 2007–11 it provided €1,270m. in grants. In 2007 Leonardo was incorporated into the new **Lifelong Learning Programme (LLP,** 2007–13); the LLP was superseded by **Erasmus+** in 2014.

LEVIES: See **Budget**; **Common Agricultural Policy**; **Own Resources**

LIBERAL INTERGOVERNMENTALISM is one of the most prominent approaches to understanding the major decisions in the history of the European Union. In contrast to **neo-functionalism**, it focuses on national preferences, interstate bargaining and institutional delegation. As a consequence, it tends to downplay the significance of geostrategic factors, ideology and supranational institutions in **decision making**.

LIBERALIZATION refers, in the context of the European Union, to the process of establishing the **internal market** by eliminating unnecessary obstacles and restraints to trade.

LIECHTENSTEIN is the fourth smallest country in Europe. It developed a customs union and common currency (the Swiss franc) with **Switzerland** in 1923, and therefore enjoyed a close relationship with the **European Free Trade Association** (EFTA) after that organization was formed in 1960, but only became a full member of EFTA in 1991. In December 1992 Liechtenstein voted in favour of the **European Economic Area** (EEA), one week after participation in the latter had been rejected by a Swiss referendum. The vote seemed to indicate that Liechtenstein saw the EEA as a way of preserving its prosperity and of becoming more politically independent of Switzerland. However, full membership of the EEA could not be realized until the 1923 agreement with Switzerland had been modified. When the necessary adjustments to the customs union had been completed, membership of the EEA was endorsed by 55.9% of the vote in a further referendum held on 9 April 1995. Liechtenstein signed the **Schengen Agreement** in February 2008 and became part of the **Schengen Area** in December 2011. Despite close ties with the European Union (EU), Liechtenstein has expressed scant interest in joining, not least because membership would most likely necessitate changes to its position as a tax haven, an issue that has resulted in tense relations with a number of EU member states, notably **Germany**.

LIFE is the name of the European Union's (EU) funding instrument for environmental and nature conservation projects. LIFE was agreed and commenced in 1992. To date, there have been four completed phases of the programme—LIFE I (1992–95), LIFE II (1996–99), LIFE III (2000–06) and LIFE+ (2007–13). Its objectives have been to provide financial aid for environmental activities, to support the implementation of various aspects of **environmental policy**, and to aid the EU in meeting the obligations of international environmental agreements and conventions to which it is a signatory. It also provided aid for certain non-EU states (those bordering the Mediterranean and the Baltic Sea) that applied to join the EU in the late 1990s. LIFE was also charged with the supervision of various EU environment programmes. It replaced a number of earlier programmes, including MEDSPA, which operated in the Mediterranean region, and NORSPA, which operated in the North European maritime regions. The third phase of LIFE began in January 2000 with an initial budget of €640m., and was originally scheduled to end in December 2004. However, this programme was extended until the end of 2006 with the provision of an additional €317m. of funding. The LIFE+ programme was agreed by the EU Environment Council meeting in Luxembourg in June 2006 and entered into force in 2007. LIFE+ ran from 2007–13 and had a budget of €2,143m. LIFE+ comprised three main themes: LIFE+ Nature and Biodiversity (and the conservation of natural habitats); LIFE+ Environment Policy and Governance (to promote new innovative methods and techniques to aid EU environmental policy); and LIFE+ Information and Communication. Since its inception in 1992 the LIFE programme has co-financed some 3,708 projects, contributing around €2,800m. to the protection of the environment. The programme is administered by the **European Commission**'s **Directorates-General** for Climate Change and the Environment. To cover the period from 2014 to 2020, the Commission adopted a new multi-annual work programme in April 2014. The new progamme has a budget of some €1,460m. for the two LIFE sub-programmes (environment and climate action).

The **LIFELONG LEARNING PROGRAMME** (LLP) for 2007–13 came into force on 14 December 2006 to foster lifelong learning opportunities for all citizens of the European Union (EU) from childhood to old age. The programme was distilled into four specific educational sectors or pillars. These were primary and secondary school education (**Comenius**), higher education exchanges (**Erasmus**), vocational education and training (**Leonardo** da Vinci) and adult education (**Grundtvig**). The LLP had a budget of some €6,970m. for 2007–13. The LLP was succeeded by the **Erasmus+** programme (following an initiative by the **European Commission** in 2011). The programme, covering all sectors of lifelong learning, education, training, youth and sport, has a budget of €14,774m. and runs during 2014–20.

LINGUA was the name of an action programme on the promotion and development of the teaching of the official **languages** of the European Union (EU), and the exchange of foreign-language teachers between the member states. It was a continuation of the 1984 commitment to ensure that schoolchildren would acquire a working knowledge of two other European Communities (EC) languages by the time they reached the statutory school-leaving age. More generally, it was intended as a contribution to increasing the cultural cohesion of the EC through creating awareness of languages and the notion of 'Europe' among the general public. Lingua was opposed in the Council of Ministers (see **Council of the European Union**) by the **United Kingdom** in 1989, on the grounds that the EC treaties did not provide for its objectives. In adopting Lingua by a **qualified majority**, the Council accepted that the UK would initially be excluded from the programme. In 1995 Lingua was incorporated into the **Socrates** and **Leonardo** programmes. Under these programmes, the Lingua action centred on language learning and teaching and had three main aims. These were: to encourage and support linguistic diversity throughout the EU; to contribute to an improvement in the quality of language teaching and learning; and to foster and facilitate access to lifelong language learning opportunities. To achieve these, action and activities were divided into two parts. Lingua 1 sought to raise citizens' awareness of the Union's multilingual wealth, encourage people to learn languages throughout their lifetime, and improve access to foreign language learning resources across Europe. Lingua 2 sought to ensure that a sufficiently wide range of language learning tools was available to language learners.

The **LISBON AGENDA** (or 2010 strategy) was the product of a special **European Council** held in the city of Lisbon, **Portugal**, in March 2000. It was decided on that occasion to set the European Union (EU) a 10-year strategic goal of becoming 'the most competitive and dynamic knowledge-based economy in the world, capable of sustaining and encouraging economic growth with more and better jobs (some 20m. more jobs) and greater social cohesion'. To this end, the Council established a series of targets, which included raising the employment rate and increasing the number of women in employment. Various mechanisms were subsequently developed to enable these goals to be achieved in areas such as **employment**, innovation, enterprise, liberalization and the environment.

Progress was reviewed on an annual basis and, where necessary, updated. In retrospect, these targets were over-ambitious. They were agreed at a time of growing economic and business confidence, but by 2005 it was clear that the EU was far from being a beacon of economic growth. In fact, growth rates in **France**, **Germany** and **Italy** had been disappointing. Instead of things getting better, in many European countries the economic outlook had actually deteriorated. In France and Germany, for example, unemployment was around 10%. Overall, the EU was struggling to compete with the **USA**, and European leaders were increasingly aware of the acute dangers and challenges to EU economic success that were presented by the rapidly growing competition from the Asian economies. The EU leaders realized that something had to be done to secure EU economic **competitiveness**, but also recognized some of the difficulties in trying to push for liberalization and greater economic reform. One of the clearest illustrations of such difficulties was revealed by the resistance to the EU's drive to open up the services market and, particularly, the fate of the **Bolkestein Directive** in 2005. The EU leaders agreed their determination to pursue the Lisbon objectives in early 2005, but scaled back their ambitious targets. In March 2010 the Commission launched the successor programme, **Europe 2020**.

LISBON TREATY: See **Treaty of Lisbon**

LITHUANIA, like its Baltic neighbours, **Estonia** and **Latvia**, regained its independence from the **USSR** in 1991. It then proceeded to conclude a **free trade agreement** (1994) and a **Europe agreement** (1995) with the European Union (EU) before applying to join the EU in December 1995. In its *avis* on the application, the **European Commission** expressed concern about the economic preparedness of Lithuania for membership. Consequently, Lithuania was not included among the countries of **Central and Eastern Europe** invited to open **accession negotiations** in early 1998. It did, however, start negotiations two years later, following a positive regular report from the Commission in October 1999 and an invitation to negotiate from the Helsinki **European Council** in December 1999. Although a latecomer to negotiations, by mid-2002 Lithuania had completed negotiations on more than two-thirds of the 31 negotiating chapters. As anticipated, the remaining chapters were closed by the time of the **Copenhagen summit** of the **European Council** in December. Lithuania therefore joined nine other **candidate countries** in signing the **Accession Treaty** in April 2003. In the following month, of the 63.4% of the electorate who participated in a referendum, 91.1% voted in favour of joining the EU. Lithuania joined the EU on 1 May 2004, and in November 2004 became the first EU member state successfully to ratify the **Treaty establishing a Constitution for Europe**. In March 2006 Lithuania applied to join the **eurozone**, seeking membership from 1 January 2007. In the event, this target proved just too ambitious, as the Lithuanian Government was unable to stabilize the country's inflation rate. The country did, however, become part of the EU's **Schengen Area** in December 2007. Successive governments remained firmly committed to joining the euro. **Estonia** was the first of the three **Baltic states** to join the eurozone in 2011. **Latvia**'s application to join the single currency was successful and in January 2014 Latvia became the 18th EU member state to accede to the eurozone. Successive Lithuanian governments had sought euro membership since 2004. The Lithuanian Government reapplied for membership of the euro in the first half of 2014 and both the **European Commission** and the **European Central Bank** approved its application in early June. The **European Council** and the **European Parliament** endorsed the application and Lithuania adopted the euro in January 2015.

LOBBYING of major institutions of the European Communities (EC) and the European Union (EU), such as the **European Commission** and the **European Parliament**, has grown dramatically since the mid-1980s, primarily as a consequence of the increase in the amount of **legislation** emanating from the EC and EU. In addition, a range of regional interests are represented in **Brussels**, Belgium, seeking to gain influence over the decision making process. (See also **interest groups**.)

The **LOMÉ CONVENTION**s is the title of a series of agreements named after the capital of Togo. Until the entry into force of the **Cotonou Agreement**, the Convention was the central element of the European Communities' (EC) relations with developing countries. It derived from a commitment in the original **Treaty of Rome** to develop a relationship between the original **Six** members of the **European Economic Community** (EEC) and their former colonies, in order to promote the interests of the latter and 'to lead them to the economic, social and cultural development to which they aspire'. The first agreements towards these ends were the **Yaoundé Convention** agreements of 1963 and 1969. The First Lomé Convention (Lomé I), signed in 1975, was an extension of the Yaoundé Convention to involve the EC more formally in development activities in more countries. The recipient states, some of which already had agreements with the EC (e.g. the Arusha Agreements with Kenya, Tanzania and Uganda), were known as the **African, Caribbean and Pacific** (ACP) **states**. Three further agreements under the Lomé Convention were signed in 1979, 1984 and 1989. Some 70 ACP countries were party to Lomé IV, compared with 46 signatories of Lomé I.

There are two central themes to the Lomé Convention. The first is the provision for duty-free access to the EC, on a non-reciprocal basis, for most ACP exports. There has always been discontent on the part of the ACP states over two major exceptions to the principle of free access: those agricultural products that would compete with European Union (EU) produce protected by the **common agricultural policy**; and textiles, which have been governed by the **multifibre arrangement**. However, exemptions have been made in the case of sugar, despite sugar beet over-production in the EU, according to which the EU buys an annual quota of ACP sugar at high EU prices. The second theme is **development aid** through grants from the **European Development Fund** (EDF) and low-interest loans from the **European Investment Bank**. Although funding has increased substantially since 1975, it has to be shared among a great number of eligible recipients. Lomé II introduced further assistance for ACP countries whose export earnings are heavily dependent on one or a few staple products, and which are consequently more exposed to market fluctuations, with the establishment of the System of Stabilization of Export Earnings (STABEX). More specialized assistance was subsequently provided through the System for Safeguarding and Developing Mineral Production (SYSMIN). Neither form of assistance survived the transition to the Cotonou Agreement. Under Lomé III, the EDF set agricultural and rural development as a first priority, with an emphasis on food crops as opposed to cash crops, small EC-based projects, and measures designed to combat drought and desertification. Lomé IV continued these broad emphases, but offered more money for shorter-term structural projects and increased the proportion of grants, as opposed to loans, made under STABEX.

The Lomé Convention created a legal framework for bilateral co-operation, and a series of joint institutions were made responsible for supervising the operation of the Convention and the **implementation** of its programmes: these were the ACP-EU Council of Ministers, a Committee of Ambassadors and a Joint Assembly of representatives from the ACP states and the **European Parliament**.

LUXEMBOURG participates with **Belgium** and the **Netherlands** in the **Benelux** Union and was a founder member of the European Communities (EC). Currently one of the smallest member states, and one that has always been exposed to external influences, it has perhaps had fewer reservations than most about diminution of national sovereignty and independence. Its governments have been strong supporters of initiatives for further integration, especially those relating to institutional reform, and several of its statesmen have figured prominently in the development of the EC. Several European institutions are based in Luxembourg rather than in **Brussels**: the **European Court of Justice**, the **General Court**, the **Court of Auditors**, the **European Investment Bank** and part of the **European Commission**'s staff, as well as part of the **European Parliament**'s. Luxembourg was also the headquarters of the **European Coal and Steel Community** before 1967. Luxembourg has been one of the most pro-European Union member states and was determined to go ahead as planned with its referendum on the **Treaty establishing a Constitution for Europe** in July 2005 even after the rejections in **France** and the **Netherlands**. A majority—56.5%—of Luxembourg's voters approved the draft constitution, and the then Prime Minister **Jean-Claude Juncker**, who had threatened to resign in the case of a 'no' vote, claimed the treaty had been resurrected by the vote. Luxembourg ratified the **Treaty of Lisbon** in May 2008. Juncker resigned as Prime Minister in December 2013 after some 18 years in office. He was succeeded by Xavier Bettel. Juncker succeeded José Manuel Durão Barroso as President of the European Commission in 2014, becoming the third person from Luxembourg to hold the post.

The **LUXEMBOURG COMPROMISE** is the name of the agreement reached by the **Six** in January 1966 that resolved the **empty chair crisis** between **France** and the five other member states. It was essentially acquiescence to French demands regarding **supranationalism**, and it specifically dealt with the operation of the Council of Ministers (see **Council of the European Union**) and the permissible use of **qualified majority voting** (QMV). The essential sentence of the Compromise states: 'Where, in the case of decisions which may be taken by a majority vote on a proposal from the Commission, very important interests of one or more partners are at stake, the Members of the Council will endeavour, within a reasonable time, to reach solutions which can be adopted by all the Members of the Council while respecting their mutual interests and those of the Community'. The member states also noted that 'there is a divergence of views on what should be done in the event of a failure to reach complete agreement', but that 'this divergence does not prevent the Community's work being resumed in accordance with the normal procedure'. In essence, the Six agreed to accept the right of any member state to veto proposals before the Council of Ministers whenever it believed its own national interests might be adversely affected.

The Compromise decisively altered the direction of the European Communities (EC) and the balance of power within it. It reduced the importance of the **European Commission**, emphasized the centrality of the member governments and delayed the completion of the **common market**. Despite all the rhetoric and initiatives for closer integration, it set the tone for EC developments until the mid-1980s. This is despite the fact that, as a document outside the framework of the treaties, the Compromise possesses no legal force. In practice, the phrase 'very important interests' has had an unrestricted definition. It was not that the member states chose to exercise a **veto** under the terms of the Compromise. Rather, the Council of Ministers chose to rely more upon unanimous agreement or consensus, being generally unwilling to proceed with any issue to the point where a veto might be invoked. This was a major factor in the steady accumulation of European Commission initiatives and proposals awaiting consideration by the Council of Ministers.

The widespread feeling that the Compromise was nevertheless hindering European developments was one of the factors that persuaded the member states to include institutional reform in the **Single European Act** (SEA) of 1986. By reducing the number and kinds of issues requiring unanimous approval in the Council of Ministers, the SEA succeeded in limiting the potential impact of the Luxembourg Compromise in the future. However, neither the SEA nor the subsequent **Treaty on European Union** disposed of or regularized the Compromise. Nevertheless, owing in part to a change in the rules of procedure of the Council, scant use of the Compromise has been made since. Indeed, many authorities contend that it is obsolete. However, the **Treaty of Amsterdam** introduced what has been referred to as a Luxembourg Compromise Mark II, where **decisions** are taken by QMV as part of the **common foreign and security policy**.

M

The **MAASTRICHT SUMMIT**, held in the town of that name in the **Netherlands** in December 1991, was one of the most decisive meetings of the **European Council**. It had been preceded by two **intergovernmental conferences** on political and monetary union. These provided the agenda of the **European Council**, which, after much and often acrimonious discussion, agreed upon a fundamental revision of the **Treaty of Rome** in the form of the **Treaty on European Union**.

MAASTRICHT TREATY: See **Treaty on European Union**

The **FORMER YUGOSLAV REPUBLIC OF MACEDONIA** (FYRM) was part of **Yugoslavia** from 1919 until its declaration of independence in 1991. The decision on the country's name drew a hostile response from **Greece**, which had a province of the same name, and the Greek Government feared that any international recognition of the new 'Macedonian' state might encourage a false claim to future territorial expansion. Greek opposition culminated in thwarting the European Union's (EU) recognition of Macedonia's independence from Yugoslavia until 1995, by which time the new state had become known as the FYRM. Once recognized, the FYRM concluded a **trade and co-operation agreement** with the EU in 1997. A **stabilization and association agreement** (SAA) followed in 2000, along with medium-term financial assistance via the former **CARDS** programme. Although it was keen to join the EU, civil unrest in 2001 excluded the FYRM from the chance of joining the countries of **Central and Eastern Europe** in **accession**

negotiations. The FYRM was nevertheless recognized as a **potential candidate state**. Successful **ratification** of its SAA in early 2004 was scheduled to be swiftly followed by the submission of an application for EU membership on 26 February 2004. The death in an air crash of the country's President, Boris Trajkovski, earlier that day meant that the application was postponed to 22 March. The **European Commission**'s response to the application came in November 2005 and was positive. The following month the European Council upgraded the status of the FYRM to **candidate country**, although no timetable was given for the opening of accession negotiations. The situation remained unchanged two years later when the Commission, in its progress report, noted that there was a general need in the FYRM to accelerate the domestic political and economic reform process, which had been undermined by political tensions in the country. The Commission did, however, propose the adoption of an **accession partnership** for the FYRM, thus upgrading relations from the **European partnership** of 2004 to a mechanism focused, symbolically, more squarely on accession. The country remains a candidate state alongside **Albania**, **Montenegro**, **Serbia** and **Turkey**. However, the European Commission acknowledged that the accession process had reached an impasse by the mid-2010s, and a severe political crisis in the country in 2015–16 led to EU concern. In mid-2015 cross-party talks between the FYRM Government and opposition leaders, mediated by the European Commissioner, responsible for European Neighbourhood Policy and Enlargement Negotiations, **Johannes Hahn**, resulted in an agreement, according to which early legislative elections were scheduled to take place in the FYRM in 2016 as part of efforts to resolve the crisis; however, the elections were repeatedly postponed owing to political disagreement. A new accord was reached in the FYRM in July 2016 with the mediation of the EU and the **USA**, which provided for electoral and media reforms to be undertaken. Legislative elections duly took place in December and, following intervention by, notably, the EU and US officials, at the end of May 2017 a new Government was formed under Zoran Zaev, and the party that had ruled the country for a decade was removed from power.

EMMANUEL MACRON (1977–) has been the President of **France** since May 2017, succeeding Socialist President François Hollande. Macron is the founder and leader of the centrist political party, En Marche!, which was established in 2016. The party fielded candidates for the first time during the June 2017 legislative elections, and achieved a majority. Macron is considered a newcomer to the French political landscape and he is indeed its youngest ever President. Prior to becoming President, Macron worked as an investment banker, but also served as Minister of the Economy, Industry and Digital Affairs (2014–16) under the prime ministership of Manuel Valls, and as Deputy Secretary-General in the Office of the President (2012–14). Macron is a philosophy graduate of Paris Nanterre University, and completed his Masters' degree in Public Administration at the Paris Institute of Political Studies (Sciences Po) before graduation from the prestigious Ecole National d'Administration (ENA) in 2004.

The **MAGHREB STATES** of Algeria, **Morocco** and Tunisia signed a collective bilateral trade and aid agreement with the European Communities (EC) in 1976, covering financial, industrial and technical affairs. The agreement allowed duty-free access to the EC for most industrial products from these states and special concessions for some of their agricultural produce. An **association agreement** was signed between the European Union (EU) and Tunisia in 1995, with Morocco in 1996 and with Algeria in 2002. The states also have access to EU **development aid**, and a new financial arrangement was negotiated in 1991. Since then, their relations with the EU have developed within the context of the **Euro-Mediterranean partnership** and the Joint Africa-EU Strategy (launched in 2007, and providing the overall long-term framework for Africa-EU relations).

MAJORITY VOTING is one of the ways in which **decisions** may be taken in the **Council of the European Union**. Simple majorities apply only to a limited number of minor issues, usually dealing with procedural matters. It is unlikely that the member states would accept it as the normal mode of **decision making**. Member states do, however, accept the use of **Qualified Majority Voting**.

CECILIA MALMSTRÖM (1968–) was nominated in 2014 as the Swedish Commissioner for Trade in the new 28-member **European Commission** led by **Jean-Claude Juncker**. Malmström holds a PhD in political science from Gothenburg University and worked as a lecturer at the same institution before entering the political arena. She was a member of Västra Götaland regional council (1998–2001), a member of the **European Parliament** (EP) (1999–2006) and Minister for European Affairs (2006–10). Malmström was first appointed as a Commissioner in 2010, when she held responsibility for Home Affairs. Malmström's reappointment to the Commission was approved by **Members of the European Parliament**. With the approval of the entire Juncker Commission by both the EP and the **European Council** in October 2014 she took up her new portfolio as Commissioner for Trade on 1 November.

MALTA initially played little part in the European integration process. It gained independence from the **United Kingdom** in 1964, joined the **Council of Europe** in 1965, and in 1970 concluded an **association agreement** with the European Communities (EC). The agreement was regarded by the EC as another element of their **Mediterranean policy**, and constituted a progressive move towards a **customs union**. Owing to domestic politics, however, little came out of the relationship. In July 1990, Malta formally applied for EC membership, receiving a favourable *avis* in 1993, but in 1996 the incoming Labour Government decided to freeze the country's application. A change of government in 1998 led Malta to revive its application, and in February 1999 the **European Commission** recommended that **accession negotiations** should begin, alongside those taking place with certain countries of **Central and Eastern Europe** and with Cyprus. Of all the **candidate countries**, Malta was often judged to be the one applicant state that was most likely to reject membership, and the outcome proved a difficult one to predict to the very end, as the country seemed evenly split on the issue. On 8 March 2003 91% of the Maltese electorate participated in a referendum on membership of the European Union (EU). The final result showed that 53.6% of those who participated in the referendum supported accession, while 46.4% voted against. This vote was further endorsed a month later when the pro-EU Nationalist Party defeated the Labour Party in a general election. This paved the way for Malta to join the EU (as the smallest member state, with some 380,000 citizens) in May 2004. Malta's accession to the EU posed very few policy-related problems. In June 2006 it was agreed that Malta would join the **eurozone** and adopt the **euro**, which it did on 1 January 2008. The previous month it joined the EU's **Schengen Area**. Malta's parliament unanimously ratified the **Treaty of Lisbon** in January 2008. The Maltese Prime Minister Lawrence Gonzi argued that the treaty was in Malta's interests and would provide Malta with an extra, sixth seat in the **European Parliament**. The Labour Party was returned to power in Malta, under the leadership of **Joseph Muscat**, after its victory in the general election of March 2013.

MANAGEMENT COMMITTEES, set up in 1962, are part of the structure of the **common agricultural policy** (CAP). The remit of the CAP is so broad, with varying economic and climatic conditions affecting different products that it has been divided according to product. Each commodity has its own Management Committee, composed of national government officials. The role of the Management Committees is to assist the **European Commission** in formulating **regulations** for the **implementation** of **decisions** made by the **Council of the European Union**, in order to achieve a uniform application of decisions that nevertheless takes account of different national circumstances. The Committees are also responsible for fixing levels of export refunds and import levies. Their opinions are not binding on the Commission but, if a Committee rejects a Commission proposal, the proposal must be presented to the Council for consideration.

MANSHOLT PLAN is the name of the document that was the origin of the **common agricultural policy** (CAP). Named after the Dutch statesman Sicco Mansholt, in its final version of 1968 it gave equal importance to price guarantees and to a restructuring and modernization of agriculture. Prior to this, the vast majority of agricultural expenditure was being directed towards price support rather than modernization schemes. The plan accepted that rationalization would incur heavy short-term costs, and proposed an extensive programme of compensation. In the longer term, it suggested that rationalization would produce a more cost-effective agriculture, so limiting the amount of **expenditure** required for price guarantees. The agricultural sector protested at the plans, and there were large demonstrations in **Brussels**. The CAP outline adopted by the European Communities (EC) in 1972 was a moderated version of the Mansholt Plan. It gave a greatly reduced emphasis to structural reform, an emphasis that disappeared almost completely when the policy began to operate. At the time, farming organizations almost everywhere in the EC rejected the plan, and Mansholt was much reviled by farmers.

A **MARKET ACCESS STRATEGY** was devised by the **European Commission** in 1996 as a means of promoting European Union (EU) exports. It aims to provide information for businesses regarding trade policy questions, to improve access for EU exporters to other markets and to increase the efficiency of EU **trade** policy.

MARKET-SHARING AGREEMENTS are banned by the **European Commission** on the grounds that they run contrary to the rules of European Union (EU) **competition policy**, and particularly to Article 81 of the **Treaty of Rome** (now Article 101 of the **Treaty on the Functioning of the European Union**), which targets restrictive agreements and **cartels**. Cartels remain an endemic feature of European business activity. The Commission, particularly since the early 1990s, has endeavoured to combat these agreements through the levying of fines on companies engaged in such practices.

The **MARSHALL PLAN** or the European Recovery Programme, named after US Secretary of State George Marshall (1880–1959), was an extensive programme of US aid to assist and stimulate economic reconstruction and recovery in Europe after the Second World War. It came into operation in 1948 and brought both economic and military stability and facilitated the reconstruction of Western Europe. The **USA** insisted that the allocation and operation of priorities had to be a European responsibility. The result was the formation of the Organisation for European Economic Co-operation (now the **Organisation for Economic Co-operation and Development**). The Marshall Plan played an instrumental role in promoting European integration, which indirectly can be said to have inspired the Schuman Declaration (see **Schuman Plan**). Reconciliation was an integral aspect of US foreign policy towards Western Europe, particularly given the onset of the **Cold War** in the late 1940s. By the time the Plan ended in 1952, some US $17,000m. had been given to Western Europe, to the latter's considerable financial and psychological benefit, as well as providing Western Europe with experience in intergovernmental co-operation.

MASHREQ STATES is a term used to describe Egypt, Jordan, Lebanon and **Syria**, with which the European Communities (EC) signed a collective bilateral trade and aid agreement in 1977. In addition to granting **development aid**, the agreement allowed the Mashreq states to export several manufactured products to the EC duty free. A further collection of financial aid measures was negotiated in 1991. Since then, relations between the European Union and the Mashreq states have developed within the context of the **Euro-Mediterranean partnership** and a proposal to establish a **Euro-Mediterranean Economic Area**.

THERESA MAY (1956–) is the Prime Minister of the **United Kingdom** and leader of the **Conservative Party**. She studied at Oxford University, and was employed at the Bank of England, before embarking on a political career, becoming British Secretary of State for Home Affairs in 2010–16. May took office as the UK's second female Prime Minister in mid-July 2016 (the first was fellow Conservative Margaret Thatcher), in succession to **David Cameron**, who resigned in late June, the day after the UK's referendum vote in favour of leaving the European Union (EU), also known as **Brexit**. In the leadership vote in July, to choose a successor to Cameron, Conservative MPs selected two candidates, Theresa May and Andrea Leadsom, to be put forward for election by the national party membership. However, following a controversial statement by Leadsom about the benefits of motherhood, which was widely perceived as thinly veiled criticism of May, she stood down, leaving May to be appointed unopposed as the new Conservative Party leader, and consequently Prime Minister. May, who had campaigned for the UK to remain in the EU, was regarded as a pragmatist, and she nevertheless appointed several leading proponents of Brexit to principal ministerial positions (notably stating 'Brexit means Brexit'), among them David Davis, who was appointed to the new position of Secretary of State for Exiting the European Union. In March 2017 May invoked **Article 50** of the **Treaty of Lisbon**. In the following month May called an early general election, despite repeatedly dismissing the possibility during the early days of her premiership. The result was not favourable to her authority, resulting in a hung parliament. May was forced to broker a deal with Northern Ireland's Democratic Unionist Party to support her minority Government.

MEDA was the acronym for a Mediterranean Special programme (launched in 1996 and amended in 2000 as MEDA II) that aimed to introduce financial and technical measures in parallel with economic and social structural reforms in the **Euro-Mediterranean partnership**. It was modelled on the aid programmes **PHARE** and **Technical Assistance to the Commonwealth of Independent States** (TACIS). The MEDA programme replaced all the bilateral **protocols** between the European Union (EU) and the so-called MED-12 non-EU member Mediterranean states (Algeria, **Cyprus**, Egypt, Israel, Jordan, Lebanon, **Malta**, **Morocco**, the Palestinian Authority (now Palestinian Territories), **Syria**, Tunisia and **Turkey**). MEDA was designed to support the economic transition in those Mediterranean non-EU member states and aimed for the establishment of a **Euro-Mediterranean** free trade area by promoting reforms that encouraged small and medium-sized businesses, opened up markets, and promoted private investment and industrial co-operation. It also supported the wider participation of civil society, the improvement of social and educational services, the upgrading of economic infrastructure and the protection of the environment, and placed emphasis on the strengthening of democracy and the rule of law. Both MEDA programmes encouraged regional co-operation. MEDA II was allocated some €5,350m. for 2000–06.

MEDIA 2007 was the fourth phase of the MEDIA Programme (Measures to Encourage the Development of the Audiovisual Production Industry—see **media policy**). The first phase of the programme, MEDIA I, covered the period 1991–95 and was succeeded in turn by MEDIA II (1996–2000) and MEDIA Plus (2001–06). The MEDIA Plus programme sought to aid and bolster the audiovisual industry by supporting the development, distribution and promotion of European audiovisual works (especially fiction in cinema and television, documentary making and the high-cost field of animation). The scheme also provided financial assistance and support for vocational training programmes to instruct audiovisual-industry professionals in business management, scriptwriting techniques and new technologies. In January 2005 the **European Commission** adopted Decision 2005/56/EC setting up a new **Education, Audiovisual and Culture Executive Agency**. This Agency is responsible for the management of certain parts of the European Union's (EU) programmes in the education, culture and audiovisual fields and it officially took over the operational management of the MEDIA programme as of 1 January 2006. MEDIA 2007 (2007–13) replaced Media Plus and had an initial budget of €755m. This new generational programme aimed to consolidate training with development and distribution and received an expanded budget of some €1,055m. Membership of the MEDIA 2007 programme comprised the 28 EU member states plus **Bosnia and Herzegovina** (which joined the programme in July 2013), **Iceland**, **Liechtenstein**, **Norway** and **Switzerland**. From 2014 MEDIA 2007 became part of the **Creative Europe** programme.

MEDIA POLICY, or at least that element that relates to film and television, represents the one area of **cultural policy** where the European Union (EU) has been noticeably active. While the **European Commission** aims to encourage co-operation within the EU, it has also been restrictive in seeking to control the effect on Europe of direct broadcasting by satellite and cable networks. The first draft **directive** in 1985 established a plan for the adoption by the member states of the television standards sponsored by the **European Broadcasting Union**, their immediate use in direct satellite broadcasting, and their gradual introduction into both cable and ground transmitter systems. This plan later encountered difficulties. A second and controversial directive, Television Without Frontiers, came into force in 1991. This was designed to ensure increasing co-ordination in broadcasting, and requires the member states to ensure that a specified and substantial proportion of their national production and broadcast programmes is of European origin. In May 2005 the Commission urged EU member states to accelerate the transition from analogue to digital broadcasting, and set a target of 2012 for shutting down analogue services. The modernized Television without Frontiers directive, renamed the Audiovisual Media Services without Frontiers directive, was adopted by the European Parliament in November 2007, with legislation to be implemented by member states by December 2009. In March 2010 the European Parliament and the Council adopted a directive on Audiovisual Media Services, with the aim of implementing a cross-border framework for audiovisual media services, thereby strengthening the EU's market for both production and distribution, and ensuring fair competition. In February 2017 the EU agreed new rules permitting consumers from EU member states to access digital culture and entertainment services online throughout the Union, as part of efforts to modernize EU digital copyright rules as part of the Digital Single Market strategy, adopted in May 2015. Through the MEDIA (Measures to Encourage the Development of the Audiovisual Production Industry) and SCRIPT (Support for Creative Independent Production Talent) programmes, the EU has also contributed to the financing, production and distribution of co-operative multilingual European broadcasting, and to the annual Geneva-Europe Prize for the best television scripts for fiction series. In addition, funding is provided for a media business school, a **European Film Distribution Office** and a European Group of Cinema and Audiovisual Financiers.

MEDITERRANEAN POLICY, sometimes known as the **Euro-Mediterranean Partnership** (EUROMED or EMP), is a term which is normally used to describe not a policy in the sense of a coherent integrated programme, but the varied collection of trade agreements that the European Union (EU) has signed with almost all the states that border the Mediterranean Sea, as well as various educational, economic and scientific initiatives that have the Mediterranean as their focus. A **European Commission** initiative of 1994 envisaged the creation of a **Euro-Mediterranean Economic Area**, which would include the **Maghreb** and **Mashreq** countries, Israel, the Palestinian Authority (now Palestinian Territories) and **Turkey**. Despite the initial enthusiasm accompanying the 1995 **Barcelona Declaration** that launched the process and laid the seeds for **MEDA**, there remains a great degree of scepticism as to how effective the EU's policy towards these Mediterranean countries has been and will be in the future. The primary reason for this is that distrust of and suspicion towards the EU still prevails among these states and greater efforts will be needed to ensure increased co-operation from them. Moreover, the benefits of relations have been viewed as primarily favouring the EU. Furthermore, despite the 2004 EU **enlargement** bringing two more Mediterranean states into the Union—**Cyprus** and **Malta**—there was limited enthusiasm for the **European Neighbourhood Policy** (launched in 2003). Some progress was made in developing a Euro-Mediterranean Energy Partnership and a further enhancement of relations resulted from the French-inspired **Union for the Mediterranean** (UfM) initiative, which was launched in July 2008.

The UfM, which was originally envisaged by former French President Nicolas Sarkozy, seeks to secure peace and prosperity within the region, including addressing pressing issues such as regional unrest, immigration and pollution.

MEDITERRANEAN UNION: See **Union for the Mediterranean**

MEMBER STATES is a term that is used to refer to the 28 countries that currently comprise the European Union. These are **Austria**, **Belgium**, **Bulgaria**, **Croatia**, **Cyprus**, the **Czech Republic**, **Denmark**, **Estonia**, **Finland**, **France**, **Germany**, **Greece**, **Hungary**, **Ireland**, **Italy**, **Latvia**, **Lithuania**, **Luxembourg**, **Malta**, the **Netherlands**, **Poland**, **Portugal**, **Romania**, **Slovakia**, **Slovenia**, **Spain**, **Sweden** and the **United Kingdom**.

MEMBERS OF THE EUROPEAN PARLIAMENT (MEPs) are elected for fixed five-year terms. The first direct elections occurred in 1979. In the **European Parliament** (EP), MEPs sit in transnational **party groups**, not by national party affiliations or in delegations, although a minority of MEPs prefers to sit as non-aligned independents. For a long time, MEPs were paid the same salary as the national parliamentary representatives in their own country, and there was therefore a substantial range in salary levels. This has now changed. All MEPs, however, have always received the same level of European Communities/Union resources, including allowances for research, secretarial assistance and travel. In the past many MEPs held a **dual mandate**, but could only draw on their salary and expenses as an MEP or as a member of their **national parliament**, but not as both. The dual mandate system has been phased out gradually. Over the last two decades the number of MEPs has altered to reflect EU **enlargement** and to keep the EP manageable as an institution (1999: 626; 2004: 732; 2007: 785; 2009: 736; 2014: 751).

MEPs: See **Members of the European Parliament**

MERCATOR is a European Union-funded network of five research and documentation centres connecting multilingual communities across Europe, promoting knowledge sharing and facilitating the structured exchange of best practice and groundbreaking initiatives through its programme of activities. The project is mainly focused on dealing with regional or minority **languages** in multilingual regions, but also on immigrant languages and smaller state languages, with emphasis on language needs arising from migration and **globalization**. The network builds on the achievements of the European Network for Regional or Minority Languages and Education, which was established in 1987.

MERGER POLICY became a leading aspect of European Union (EU) **competition policy**. However, it was omitted completely from the **Treaty of Rome**. The concept of a European merger control regime was first proposed by the **European Commission** as a draft **regulation** in 1973. Its aim was to give the Commission the ability to approve in advance any proposed transnational mergers, leaving the member states with the responsibility of policing mergers within their own territories. The Commission initiative and three subsequent efforts all failed to find any substantial favour within the Council of Ministers (see **Council of the European Union**). Finally, however, a renewed proposal was submitted in 1987, approved in 1989 and came into force in September 1990. The regulation owed much to growing demands from the business community for an integrated policy with regard to merger rules at the European level, thus avoiding the existing confusions and discrepancies in approach to mergers across the EU. Their demands were also vindicated by the business restructuring that was taking place prior to 1992 and the **internal market** initiative. The regulation required that all proposed mergers of companies with an aggregate world turnover of €5,000m., where at least two of the companies involved had a turnover within the EU of more than €250m. (unless they each realized more than two-thirds of their European turnover in one member state), and where the merger was likely to affect EU **competition policy**, should be submitted to the Commission for assessment and approval. As such, the regulation was designed to cover only the largest mergers, some 50 to 60 a year in the early years. Proposed mergers that fell below these levels, which constituted the majority of cases, remained the responsibility of the national authorities.

The number of proposed mergers notified to the Commission increased during the 1990s, so that by the end of that decade almost five times the number were being processed than at the outset. A 2001 Green Paper heralded a revised examination of merger thresholds that led the Commission to adopt a far-reaching reform of merger policy in December 2002, leading in turn to a new merger regulation that was agreed by the Council (for Economic and Monetary Affairs) in January 2004. The new merger regulation came into force on 1 May. The new package of reforms included guidelines on the assessment of mergers between competing firms and the Commission. The Commission had already introduced a set of best practices on the conduct of merger investigations, including the appointment of a chief economist in merger cases, which were designed to streamline **decision making** and to make it more transparent. These initiatives were designed to restore Commission credibility in merger cases, particularly after the Court of First Instance (now **General Court**) overturned for the first time in the history of EU merger policy three Commission prohibition orders in 2002, severely reprimanded the Commission for its methods and procedures, and emphasized the need for greater economic analysis capable of standing up to scrutiny.

MERGER TREATY is the name often given to the treaty that formally integrated the executives of the **European Atomic Energy Community**, the **European Coal and Steel Community** and the **European Economic Community** (EEC). While technically there were still three **European Communities**, it became commonplace thereafter to refer to them collectively as the **European Community**. The Treaty created a single **European Commission** and a single Council of Ministers (see **Council of the European Union**), and was signed on 8 April 1965, coming into effect on 1 July 1967. The degree of personal animosity between Charles de Gaulle and Walter Hallstein ensured that the latter, who by this stage was the outgoing President of the EEC Commission, was not nominated for the position of President of a single Commission.

ANGELA MERKEL (1954–) made history on 22 November 2005 when she was elected by the Bundestag (parliament) as **Germany**'s first ever female Chancellor. It should also be noted that her second claim to fame stems from the fact that she is the first citizen of the former German Democratic Republic (1949–90) to lead post-unification Germany (although she was actually born in Hamburg). In political terms, Merkel's rise has been meteoric. She was spotted and nurtured as a protégée by Helmut Kohl in the early 1990s and thereafter made a rapid advance through the Christian Democratic Union (CDU) party's ranks before being chosen to contest the 2005 federal elections as the CDU's candidate for Chancellor. Opinion polls in early 2005 pointed to a decisive Merkel victory, but, in the event, Gerhard Schröder's Social Democratic Party (SPD) staged a remarkable comeback. At the September 2005 elections Merkel's CDU/CSU (Christian Social Union) polled 35.2% of the vote, while the SPD obtained 34.2%. With these results, neither the incumbent SPD–Green coalition nor the CDU/CSU and its preferred coalition partner, the Free Democratic Party, was in a position to muster a majority in the Bundestag. Options for the parties were limited after such an inconclusive election and, after weeks of speculation and deliberation, Merkel led the CDU/CSU into a 'Grand Coalition' with the SPD. This arrangement supplied Merkel with the Chancellorship and the SPD with eight out of 16 seats in the cabinet, and it was the second time (the first occurred in 1966–69) in postwar German history that the two largest parties had formed a coalition government. The product of such negotiations had its critics, and some predicted a short history. Yet, in the event, it worked admirably well.

Merkel has emerged as a high-profile individual and, in terms of foreign policy, was generally given the credit for enabling the **Council of the European Union** to secure agreement on the European Union (EU) **budget** and the financing arrangements for 2007–13. Merkel remains an advocate of closer European co-operation and used the German presidency of the Council in the first half of 2007 to advance a number of ambitious targets. The most important was her determination to revive the debate on the **Treaty establishing a Constitution for Europe** and the necessity of agreeing some form of charter on EU **decision making** before the next **European Parliament** (EP) elections in June 2009. Merkel succeeded and presented the text of a draft mandate (which very much determined the content of the **Treaty of Lisbon**) at the concluding **European Council summit meeting** under the German presidency in June 2007. Merkel also committed herself to making further progress on energy security and climate change, a global trade deal, a new partnership agreement with the **Russian Federation**, and greater peace efforts for the **Middle East**. She successfully sought much better relations with the **USA**. The situation on the domestic front proved to be more contentious, and the coalition Government entered stormier seas as it sought to cut public spending and raise income tax. Accordingly, tensions between the two grand coalition partners became more apparent. The 2009 EP elections, when Merkel's CDU/CSU party comfortably beat the Social Democrats into second place, served as a barometer for support for the Government in the run-up to the 2009 federal elections. Merkel successfully ran again as the CDU candidate for Chancellor in the federal elections of September 2009. The election results gave the CDU/CSU a strong victory over its former grand coalition partner, the SPD, which was easily pushed into second place. Nevertheless, the percentage of the votes for both the CDU/CSU and the SPD was down, at 33.4% and 27.2%, respectively, and Merkel's CDU/CSU received its lowest share of the vote since 1949. The arithmetic of the election results enabled Merkel to form a new coalition with the Free Democrats (FDP), which had captured over 14% of the votes cast, their largest share in the party's history. Merkel's second administration was immediately beset with clashes between the governing parties over policy priorities, which damaged the Chancellor's popularity and reputation at home at the beginning of 2010. However, in European affairs, Merkel has been much more successful. She was instrumental in the appointment of Herman Van Rompuy as the first **President of the European Council**. She is viewed as having played a crucial role in managing the **eurozone** crisis from 2010, although her most trenchant critics have accused her of a lack of decisiveness and of acting very much in **Germany**'s, as opposed to the EU's, interests, accusations she has strongly denied. She was a principal architect of the **Fiscal Compact** (Treaty on Stability, Coordination and Governance in the Economic and Monetary Union), which was signed in March 2012. Merkel attracted some popular resentment in southern Europe for her insistence on austerity conditions for emergency assistance. However, the sense of strong leadership improved her personal ratings at home. At a general election in September 2013 the CDU/CSU obtained 41.5% of the votes, securing 311 seats in the Bundestag (five seats short of an overall majority). Support for the FDP collapsed: the party won no seats (previously having held 93). A new Eurosceptic party, **Alternative für Deutschland** (AFD), secured 4.7% of the votes but failed to secure representation in the federal parliament, as it had narrowly failed to reach the 5% threshold. Talks on a new 'grand coalition' between the CDU/CSU and the Social Democrats were successfully concluded in October 2013 and paved the way for Merkel's third administration. Merkel's CDU/CSU topped the polls at the 2014 EP elections with 36% of the votes. Merkel has earned the reputation of being possibly the most influential politician in the EU, and has succeeded in smoothing over any frictions between the centre-right and centre-left components of her Government; none the less, Merkel continued to attract some criticism outside Germany for her uncompromising stance towards Greece during negotiations in 2015.

Most controversially, in August 2015 Merkel announced that Germany would accept asylum applicants from Syria, irrespective of their initial point of entry into the EU, and that they would have permanent leave to remain in the country. Consequently, hundreds of thousands of people began to travel across Europe in an effort to reach Germany—some 800,000 were estimated to have arrived in 2015. It also subsequently led to the re-imposition of border controls and the erection of fences by a number of member states, including **Austria**, **Hungary**, **Denmark** and **Sweden**. US President Barack Obama responded positively to Merkel's announcement, describing the measure to be 'on the right side of history'. In federal elections in September 2017 Merkel won a fourth term of office, although with a weakened mandate. Notably, the AFD achieved legislative representation as the third largest party. Meanwhile, Merkel's stance with regard to the negotiations over the terms of the **United Kingdom**'s exit from the EU, following the referendum vote in June 2016 in favour of that country's withdrawal from the Union, may be crucial, both to their success and to the future direction of the Union.

The **MESSINA CONFERENCE** was the meeting of the foreign ministers of the **Six**, held in the Italian city of that name in June 1955. Its aim was to consider new initiatives in integration after the failure of the proposals for a **European Defence Community** and **European Political Community**. An invitation to participate officially was extended to the **United Kingdom**, but was not accepted. The ministers agreed to begin 'a fresh advance towards the building of Europe' and to create a market that was 'free from all customs duties and all quantitative restrictions'. They also proposed a pooling of information and work on the uses of nuclear energy. The meeting established an intergovernmental committee, headed by Paul-Henri Spaak of **Belgium**, which was to consider and elaborate upon the proposals before submitting its report. The conference was the first stage of the process that culminated in the two **Treaties of Rome**. They established the **European Economic Community** and the **European Atomic Energy Community**.

MFA: See **Multifibre Arrangement**

The **MIDDLE EAST** has, since the early 1970s, been a region that has attracted the attention of the European Communities/ Union. It was, for example, the focus of early attempts to forge closer foreign policy co-ordination among member states through **European political co-operation**. Trade agreements have also been signed with countries in the region, many of which have since been replaced by new arrangements agreed as part of the European Union's efforts to promote a **Euro-Mediterranean partnership** that includes the Middle East. See also **European Neighbourhood Policy**; **Union for the Mediterranean**.

MIGRATION AND ASYLUM POLICY did not formally exist for the European Communities (EC) before 1989, although matters relating to asylum had been discussed more informally within the **TREVI** process. The member states, except **Denmark**, signed the Dublin Convention on Asylum (later **Dublin Regulation**) in June 1990. Partly in response to growing unrest in the **USSR** and **Yugoslavia**, the member states agreed in June 1991 to establish a Quick Reaction Consultation Centre to deal with sudden and large-scale immigration pressures. After 1991 asylum procedures were generally tightened, and grants of asylum more restricted. Asylum and immigration policy were principal issues raised at the **Tampere summit** of the **European Council** in 1999, which urged the creation of a Common European Asylum System (CEAS). Between 1999 and 2005 the European Union (EU) established the CEAS and succeeded in passing a number of legislative acts that sought to harmonize minimum standards in the area of asylum, covering such issues as reception conditions for asylum seekers, qualifications for becoming a refugee and asylum procedures. Agreement was also reached on the Dublin Regulation that determined (when difficulties arose) which state held responsibility for dealing with asylum cases. As a means of further developing policy, the **European Commission** produced a **Green Paper** on Asylum Policy in 2007 and adopted its Policy Plan on Asylum in June 2008. The priorities of the CEAS were: making refinements to the existing legislation regarding reception and asylum procedures to secure further alignment; the creation of a European Support Office to facilitate European co-operation; and finding means to provide greater solidarity and responsibility among member states on asylum policy. A revised Asylum Procedures Directive, adopted in mid-2013, aimed specifically to provide fairer, faster and better decisions. Better processing was also to be paid to those asylum seekers with special needs and greater protection for unaccompanied minors and victims of torture. The revised Directive was fully implemented throughout the EU from July 2015. Other important legislation adopted in 2013 included the Reception Conditions Directive, which replaced a 2003 directive establishing minimum standards for the reception of asylum seekers. Meanwhile, a revised European Dactyloscopy (EURODAC) regulation enables law enforcement agencies to use the EU database containing the fingerprints of all asylum seekers to detect or investigate serious crimes, including murder and acts of terrorism.

An Asylum, Migration and Integration Fund (AMIF) was established to operate during 2014–20, with a budget of €3,137m. The AMIF works alongside the International Security Fund (ISF), and focuses on four principal objectives: strengthening the common European asylum system by ensuring the uniform application of EU legislation; facilitating legal migration to EU member states in compliance with labour market requirements, and assisting with the integration of non-EU nationals; implementing fair, sustainable and effective return strategies, while working to combat illegal migration; and ensuring that those EU member states most severely affected by migration and asylum issues can benefit from solidarity from other EU member states. Increased funding for search-and-rescue missions was announced, and in May 2015 the Commission published a new European Agenda on Migration, which incorporated proposals for the compulsory relocation within the EU of up to 20,000 refugees from the Middle East and North Africa. This plan encountered some opposition, as did proposals to redistribute up to 40,000 asylum applicants from Greece and Italy to other member states over a period of two years. In July the Justice and Home Affairs Council agreed to implement the European Agenda on Migration.

In September 2015, as the influx of migrants into the bloc increased significantly amid what became commonly known as the **European migration crisis**, the Commission sought to introduce further emergency measures, including proposals to relocate an additional 120,000 migrants, primarily from **Greece** and **Italy** (the countries most affected by unauthorized border crossings and applications for asylum), over a three-year period, to the rest of the EU (although Denmark, **Ireland** and the **United Kingdom** had exemptions). Distribution was to be calculated according to a key, which was to take into account factors such as the prevailing rate of gross domestic product per head, with richer states taking more than their poorer counterparts. It was agreed that 6,000 asylum applicants per month would be relocated from Greece and Italy to other EU member states; the Commission's proposals were supported by the **European Parliament** and adopted by the **Council of the European Union** in late September 2015.

Amid the huge burdens falling on Greece and Italy and the unwillingness of some member states to accept relocated asylum applicants, in 2016 the Commission formulated proposals to create a stronger Common European Asylum System, with common procedures and maximum harmonization, while presenting options to reform the Dublin Regulation. In April member states were presented with further proposals for reform, including the award of increased funding and resources to 'frontline' states. Furthermore, the European Asylum Support Office, based in **Malta**, was to be given a much greater role in monitoring the system and its effects.

In March 2016 the EU reached an agreement with **Turkey**, which provided for undocumented asylum seekers who had not made an asylum application at their initial point of entry into the EU (usually Greece) to be returned to that country; the EU was to accept the same number of legitimately registered asylum seekers from Turkey's refugee camps—a so-called 'one in, one out' scheme. This plan did indeed reduce the flow of refugees from Turkey to Greece. By mid-June some 511 Syrian refugees had been resettled from Turkey to the EU, while 462 migrants who had not made asylum applications in Greece were returned to Turkey. These were very small numbers, given the estimates of more than 2m. displaced Syrians within Turkey by that time. The Turkish Government pledged to increase efforts to prevent sea crossings, which witnessed a greater degree of success: 9,250 refugees travelled from Turkey to the EU in June–September

MIGRATION PARTNERSHIP FRAMEWORK

2016, a decline of over 90%. In return, the EU announced that it would accelerate progress towards visa liberalization for Turkish citizens travelling to the EU and made available funding of €6,000m. by 2018, to help Turkey manage the crisis. The **United Nations** High Commissioner for Refugees expressed concern about the agreement, particularly the risks faced by asylum claimants in Greece and Turkey who might not receive necessary protection while in transit. Furthermore, migrant arrivals in Italy from North Africa had increased as the crossing from Turkey to Greece became less attractive for undocumented asylum seekers. In June 2016 the Commission announced proposals for the establishment a new **Migration Partnership Framework** (MPF) to mobilize and focus EU action and resources on managing migration. The EU proposed to realize partnerships with key third countries of origin and transit, and identified a number of 'priority countries', including Jordan, Lebanon and Nigeria. Building on the European Agenda on Migration, the priorities included saving lives at sea, increasing the rate of repatriation of undocumented migrants, enabling migrants and refugees to remain closer to home and, in the long term, helping third countries' development in order to address the root causes of irregular migration.

Concerns about the free movement of migrants and asylum seekers were also a key factor in the British vote in June 2016 to leave the EU, despite the UK having an opt-out from the obligation to receive asylum seekers under the Commission's quota programme.

The **MIGRATION PARTNERSHIP FRAMEWORK** (MPF) is a new initiative launched in June 2016 by the **European Commission** as a means of managing the **European Migration Crisis**. MPFs aim to structure the European Union's (EU) relationship with third countries, many of them in Africa, to stem the flow of immigrants into the EU. At 2017 agreements had been signed with Ethiopia, Mali, Niger, Nigeria, and Senegal, identified as significant countries in terms of both origin and the transit of migrants. Under the MPF, these countries are not only encouraged to stop their citizens from making the journey to Europe, but are also obliged to ensure citizens of other countries do not make use of them as transit points. Moreover, these countries must receive citizens that are deported by the EU member states. As part of the MPF, a Trust Fund for Africa was established, following the Valletta summit on Migration, held in November 2015 in **Malta**, in order to discuss migration with African leaders. Funds were to be deployed to the mission of the MPF, drawing on the **European Development Fund**.

The **MILAN SUMMIT** held in **Italy** in June 1985 proved to be one of the more decisive sessions of the **European Council**. The Council was to consider the report from the **Dooge Committee** on institutional reform of the European Communities (EC) and the report from the **Committee for a People's Europe**, both of which had been commissioned at the 1984 **Fontainebleau summit**, as well as the decision at the Council's previous session in **Brussels** to establish a detailed timetable for the completion of an **internal market**. It was perhaps the first summit to be dominated by discussions on a comprehensive overhaul of the EC as established primarily by the **Treaty of Rome** almost 30 years earlier. In a way that was quite unprecedented for the European Council, which hitherto had always proceeded according to the principle of **unanimity**, a vote was called for on the establishment of an **intergovernmental conference** to discuss institutional reform; only a simple majority was needed. **Denmark**, **Greece** and the **United Kingdom** opposed the proposal, but were outvoted by the other seven member states and subsequently agreed to participate in the conference, which led, some six months later, to the **Single European Act**. At the time, the Milan summit seemed more of a failure than a success as it had clearly revealed a degree of opposition from Denmark, **Greece** and the UK towards any deeper integration. In retrospect, it is now recognized as a watershed in the history of European integration and one that relaunched the European integration project.

The United Nations' (UN) **MILLENNIUM DEVELOPMENT GOALS** (MDGs) were the eight development objectives agreed by UN members at the Millennium Summit in 2000. It expired at the end of 2015. The goals, which included targets to eradicate extreme poverty and hunger, to achieve universal primary education, to promote **gender equality**, to reduce child mortality, to combat HIV/AIDS and other diseases, and to ensure environmental sustainability, made a significant contribution to raising public awareness, increasing political will and mobilizing resources to end poverty in developing countries. The **European Union** (EU) supported the UN 2030 Agenda for Sustainable Development, which was approved unanimously by members of the UN in September 2015, and which builds on and extends the achievements of the MDGs, incorporating targets agreed at the UN Conference on Sustainable Development in 2012, and aiming to address poverty eradication together with the economic, social and environmental dimensions of sustainable development. The **European Commission** has been an active participant in contributing to this process, and is committed to it both inside the EU (such as through the Circular Economy Strategy adopted in 2014, designed to address more sustainable patterns of production and consumption) and through the EU's external policies, by supporting similar efforts in developing countries. The Sustainable Development Goals, also known as Global Goals, succeeded the MDGs.

NEVEN MIMICA (1953–) was nominated in 2014 as the Croatian Commissioner to the new 28-member **European Commission** led by **Jean-Claude Juncker**. In September Juncker named Mimica as Commissioner for International Co-operation and Development. Immediately prior to this appointment, Mimica had been a member of the Commission following **Croatia's** accession to the European Union (EU) in July 2013, holding responsibility for consumer policy. A politician and diplomat, Mimica graduated from the University of Zagreb with a degree in economics in 1976. After graduation he worked in a number of government departments dealing with trade and foreign policy. In 1997, as a member of the Croatian Social Democratic Party, he was appointed as assistant to the Croatian Minister of the Economy and served as **Croatia**'s chief negotiator during the country's accession to the **World Trade Organization** and to the EU association agreement. Prior to joining the Commission following Croatia's accession to the EU on 1 July 2013 Mimica was a member of the Croatian legislature and held the government posts of Minister for European Integration (2001–03) and Deputy Prime Minister (2011–13). He was approved by **Members of the European Parliament** (MEPs) and, after the full Juncker team was endorsed by both the **European Parliament** and the **European Council** in October 2014, Mimica took up a post as Commissioner once again on 1 November.

MINERVA was an action of the former **Socrates** programme. Minerva aimed to promote and assess the use of information and communication technologies (ICT) in education, and especially in open and distance learning (ODL). Minerva Action had three main objectives: first, to promote understanding among teachers, learners, decision makers and the public at large of the implications of the use of ICT in education, as well as the critical and responsible use of ICT for educational purposes; second, to ensure that pedagogical considerations were given proper weight in the development of ICT and multimedia-based educational products and services; and third, to promote access to improved methods and educational resources as well as to results and best practices in this field. To these ends it aimed to create a dialogue at the European level in order to exchange ideas and approaches for the use of ICT. Through Minerva, the **European Commission** supported four major types of activity: first, projects to better understand and foster innovation; second, activities to design new teaching methods and resources; third, activities intended to communicate and provide access to the results of projects in order to increase the publication of their findings; and last, projects intended to network and encourage the exchange of ideas. From 2007 Minerva was incorporated into the new **Lifelong Learning Programme 2007–13**, which was in turn succeeded by the **Erasmus+** programme in 2014.

MINORITY RIGHTS are referenced by the **Treaty on European Union**. The European Union (EU) insists in the **Copenhagen Criteria** for accession to the EU that respect for the rights of minorities is a prerequisite for membership. Article 21 of the EU's **Charter of Fundamental Rights** prohibits discrimination against members of national minorities.

CARLOS MOEDAS (1970–) was nominated in 2014 as the Portuguese Commissioner to the new 28-member **European Commission** led by **Jean-Claude Juncker**. In September Juncker named Moedas as Commissioner for Research, Science and Innovation, subject to approval by the **European Parliament** (EP). Moedas studied civil engineering at the University of Lisbon, and after graduating in 1993 took up a position with Suez in France. He subsequently returned to education and successfully completed an MBA at Harvard University, MA, USA (2000). He further developed his professional career in business, before moving into investment banking and establishing his own investment management company in 2008. Moedas was elected to the Portuguese parliament in 2011 and worked closely with the Portuguese Prime Minister's Office and was heavily involved in discussions with officials from both the **European Central Bank** and the **International Monetary Fund** over Portugal's economic bailout agreement. He passed his nomination hearing with **Members of the European Parliament** (MEPs) and, with the approval of the Juncker Commission by both the EP and the **European Council** in late October 2014, his term as Commissioner commenced on 1 November.

FEDERICA MOGHERINI (1973–) was appointed by the **European Council**, at the end of August 2013, as the new **High Representative of the Union for Foreign Affairs and Security Policy** at the **European External Action Service**. Her appointment took effect from November 2014, when she also became a Vice-President of the new **European Commission** led by **Jean-Claude Juncker**. An Italian, and a member of the Italian Democratic Party, prior to her appointment to the European Union (EU) Mogherini had held a number of roles in public life, most recently Minister of Foreign Affairs under Matteo Renzi. In mid-2016 Mogherini announced the launch of a new EU Global Strategy on Foreign and Security Policy.

MOLDOVA gained its independence from the **USSR** in 1991 and has since struggled with the political and economic challenges of the transition from Communist rule to democracy and a market economy. It also endured a civil war that left the country divided between Moldova proper and the separatist and pro-Russia Transnistria. Relations with the European Union (EU) have nevertheless developed, primarily on the basis of a **partnership and co-operation agreement** signed in 1994 (which came into effect in 1998) and financial assistance under the former **Technical Assistance to the Commonwealth of Independent States** programme. Since then, Moldova has sought some form of **association agreement** with the EU and it joined the **stability pact for South Eastern Europe** in 2001. The EU's response has been to include Moldova in its **European Neighbourhood Policy** and more recently its **Eastern partnership**. This resulted in an Action Plan designed to promote closer ties between the EU and Moldova. Evidence of the EU's increasing engagement with Moldova—now a country on the EU's border following **Romania**'s accession in 2007—came with the appointment in 2005 of an EU Special Representative on Moldova whose role is to strengthen the EU's contribution to the resolution of the Transnistria issue. There is a notional domestic political consensus in Moldova on the country eventually becoming a member of the EU. From the EU's point of view, such a goal can only be seriously contemplated if considerable progress is made in implementing democratic and market-focused economic reforms. The need for the former was amply highlighted by the political crisis triggered by the elections in April 2009. Since then, the Government's reform efforts have been rewarded with progress in negotiations—launched in January 2010—on an **association agreement** similar to that under discussion with **Ukraine**. In December 2011 the EU agreed to instigate negotiations with Moldova on a **deep and comprehensive free trade area** (DCFTA), as an integral part of the association agreement talks, although the EU remains steadfast in not offering Moldova a clear perspective of membership. Following the conclusion of the seventh round of negotiations in June 2013, the DCFTA negotiating process was technically completed. The European Council formally approved an association agreement with Moldova, providing for the gradual introduction of a DCFTA, in June 2014 (alongside similar agreements signed with both Georgia and **Ukraine**); the agreement entered into effect in July 2016. The **Russian Federation** had expressed strong reservations about such close ties between the EU and these three republics.

MONETARY POLICY is fundamental to **economic and monetary union** (EMU). **Decision making** in this area varies with regard to the topic in question: for the issue of coins by the member states the **co-operation procedure** applies, after consultation with the **European Central Bank** (ECB); for the formulation of exchange-rate policy guidelines, the **Council of the European Union** decides by **qualified majority voting** (QMV) following a recommendation from the ECB; for technical adjustments to the Statute of the **European System of Central Banks**, the Council decides by QMV on a recommendation from the ECB after consulting the **European Commission** and obtaining the assessment of the **European Parliament** (EP); for the exchange rate of the **euro** against non-EMU currencies, the Council decides by **unanimity**, following a recommendation from the ECB or the Commission and after consulting the EP.

MONETARY POLICY COMMITTEE

The **MONETARY POLICY COMMITTEE** is the name of an adjunct to the **Council of the European Union**. Along with the **Economic and Financial Affairs Council of Ministers** and the Economic Policy Committee, it is one of the bodies that provide a regular meeting place for representatives of the economic and finance ministers of the member states.

JEAN MONNET (1888–1979) probably contributed more than any other single individual to the post-war developments that established the building blocks that became the European Union (EU). Although he was pragmatic in his approach to integration, his contribution was in the form of ideas rather than as a practising politician. Monnet already had a distinguished diplomatic and business career when, in 1940, he contributed to the formulation of the plan for an Anglo-French Union subsequently advocated by British Prime Minister Winston Churchill. After the Second World War, Monnet was appointed head of the French Planning Commission in charge of the Modernization Plan. His experiences there persuaded him that no European country could, by itself and using its own resources, plan an effective programme of economic growth, development and prosperity. While Monnet's ultimate objective was a European political union, he tended to be suspicious of ostentatious political gestures. He believed that a programme of integration had to be practical and long-term: effective political integration could only be built on an accretion of proven and accepted experiences of co-operation. For Monnet, the means of achieving progress was a gradual integration of discrete economic sectors that would, through a process of **spillover**, lead in time to full economic and political union.

Monnet was the original conceiver of the **Schuman Plan**, and was appointed as the first President of the High Authority of the **European Coal and Steel Community**. He was the originator of the Pleven Plan that produced the ill-fated **European Defence Community** (EDC). When the EDC collapsed, Monnet resigned from the High Authority to found the Action Committee for a United States of Europe. He successfully sponsored the creation of the **European Atomic Energy Community**, which, after the collapse of the EDC, he thought had more chance of success than the proposal for a **common market**.

Monnet's vision of a united Europe was not exclusive. While he believed that reconciliation between **France** and **Germany** was essential, it was a matter of regret to him that only six countries were willing to participate in experiments in integration. He continually urged the **Six** to encourage other states to join them; in particular, he believed that European integration would be incomplete without the involvement of the **United Kingdom**. Monnet's labours are commemorated in several ways by the EU, mainly through the funding of Monnet fellowships and other positions in the field of education.

MONNET METHOD is the term used to describe a strategy of integration based on **spillover** from one area of activity to another. It proved successful in the early years of European integration and again under Jacques Delors in the late 1980s and early 1990s. Since then, it has proved more difficult to implement.

MONTENEGRO emerged again as a sovereign and independent European nation state (after nearly 90 years) in May 2006 when it severed its union with **Serbia** following the outcome of a referendum in which some 55% of the population opted for independence. The vote heralded the end of the former Union of Serbia and Montenegro, which came into being in 2003 and which was itself the rump of the former **Yugoslavia** that had been created in 1919. The Government expressed at the outset its intention to join the **European Union** (EU), and Montenegro has made some progress in this direction since the split with Serbia. (Montenegro had unilaterally adopted the **euro** as its state currency when it was launched in January 2002.) In January 2007 the EU adopted a **European partnership** for Montenegro and two months later it concluded negotiations on a **stabilization and association agreement**. This was then signed in September 2007 (and came into force in May 2010), as was a visa facilitation agreement. An Interim Agreement on free trade entered into force on 1 January 2008 and Montenegro applied for EU membership on 15 December. The Commission published its *avis* on the application in November 2010 and proposed the conferral of candidate status (which was officially granted on 17 December 2010). A year later it also recommended the opening of **accession negotiations**, which, following a decision of the European Council, were duly opened on 29 June 2012. At 2017 these negotiations were ongoing, and much more progress on closing the various policy chapters remained to be achieved before membership could be considered.

MOROCCO, one of the **Maghreb states**, entered into a bilateral trade and aid agreement with the European Communities (EC) in 1976. A decade later, in 1987, it submitted a formal application for membership, but was informed by the EC that because Morocco is not a European state it was not eligible for membership. An **association agreement** was signed with the European Union (EU) in 1996 (which came into effect in March 2000), and the country is now part of the **Euro-Mediterranean partnership**. The first EU-Morocco summit took place in Granada, **Spain**, in March 2010. Morocco received €580.5m. in EU financial aid, under the **European Neighbourhood Policy**, in 2011–13. Negotiations towards a **Deep and Comprehensive Free Trade Agreement** with Morocco commenced in April 2013 in the Moroccan capital, Rabat.

PIERRE MOSCOVICI (1957–) was nominated in 2014 as the French Commissioner to the new 28-member **European Commission** led by **Jean-Claude Juncker**. In September Juncker named Moscovici as Commissioner-designate for Economic and Financial Affairs, Taxation and Customs Union, subject to approval by the **European Parliament** (EP). He is a graduate of the Ecole National d'Administration (where he studied economics, philosophy and politics). Prior to his appointment to the Commission, Moscovici had held the role of Minister of Finance in France, and in earlier roles he had been a member of both the French National Assembly (2007–12) and the European Parliament (2004–07). Following his successful confirmation hearing with **Members of the European Parliament** (MEPs) and the endorsement of the Juncker Commission by both the EP and the **European Council**, he took up his post as Commissioner on 1 November 2014.

MULTIFIBRE ARRANGEMENT (MFA), the full title of which is the Arrangement regarding International Trade in Textiles, was first negotiated within the **General Agreement on Tariffs and Trade** (GATT) in 1973. It was an agreement between Western industrial states and suppliers of low-cost textile goods from developing countries. The textile industries of the developed world had already been severely damaged by low-cost imports, and the MFA was established as a means of controlling imports in such a way that Western markets would be gradually opened to developing countries as an orderly contraction and restructuring of the Western textile industries was taking place. In practice, the MFA operated as a protectionist mechanism restricting the level of low-cost imports. In the renegotiations of the MFA in 1977, 1981 and 1986, Western governments successfully imposed stricter quotas on the developing countries. Textiles were therefore generally excluded from GATT and the European Communities' commitment to free trade. However, as a result of the **Uruguay Round** of GATT trade negotiations, the MFA was progressively eliminated over a 10-year period. The agreement finally expired on 1 January 2005. Immediately, exports from the People's Republic of China into the European Union (EU) soared and this ultimately compelled the EU to bring in a quota system to protect some European manufacturers, especially in **Greece** and **Portugal**.

MULTI-SPEED EUROPE is a term that is used to describe the notion of differentiated integration, whereby common objectives are pursued by a group of member states that are both willing and able to advance them. The term assumes that the other member states, which may be temporarily unable or not willing to advance a given objective at that moment in time, will join the participating member states at a later date.

JOSEPH MUSCAT (1974–) was appointed Prime Minister of **Malta** in March 2013. Muscat took his first university degrees at the University of Malta before completing a doctorate in management research at the University of Bristol, **United Kingdom**. As a young member of the Maltese Labour Party he campaigned against Malta's accession to the European Union. However, in 2004 he successfully stood as a candidate for the elections to the **European Parliament**, but he resigned his seat when he was elected as leader of the Labour Party in 2008. He remained as leader of the opposition in Malta until assuming the premiership in March 2013, following his party's victory in the general election.

MUTUAL RECOGNITION, as a principle, is essential for the proper functioning of the **internal market**. It means that when a product is legally manufactured and marketed in one member state, it may be freely offered for sale in other member states, irrespective of whether it complies with the relevant national legislation in that country. The **Court of Justice** established the principle in 1979 in the *Cassis de Dijon* case.

N

NACC: See **North Atlantic Co-operation Council**

NAFO: See **North Atlantic Fisheries Organization**

The **NATIONAL ASSEMBLY FOR WALES EU OFFICE** was established in **Brussels** in 2000 and acts as a link for this region of the **United Kingdom** with the European Union (EU) and its institutions. The Office is staffed by Assembly officials and is directly accountable to the National Assembly of Wales. It is also part of the UK **Permanent Representation** (UKREP) family and works closely with officials from UKREP and alongside the **Office of the Northern Ireland Executive in Brussels** and **Scotland Europa**. The office was set up as a consequence of devolving powers to Wales in 1999. The Assembly seeks to engage directly with the EU across a broad front and the Brussels Office has several functions. These include: providing intelligence and information for ministers and committees from the Welsh Assembly; taking a policy lead on EU horizontal issues and constitutional developments; providing specialist support and acting as a focal point for Assembly visitors and staff based in Brussels; and representing the Assembly in Brussels, including as part of a number of Brussels-based working groups.

NATIONAL PARLIAMENTS have always played a role in the development of the European Communities (EC) and European Union (EU), not least in adopting the necessary implementing legislation for **directives**, undertaking the **ratification** of treaties and agreements, and scrutinizing the activities of the EU and national governments. To these ends, national parliaments have created specialized committees dealing with EU matters. These committees meet with a group of **Members of the European Parliament** every six months under the umbrella of **COSAC** (Conférence des Organes Spécialisés dans les Affaires Communautaires). Meetings of the Conference of Speakers of Parliaments in the EU are also held every six months. Less regular are the so-called **assizes** (or Conferences of the Parliaments) that are supposed to meet to discuss major developments in the EU.

Despite such involvement in EU affairs, concerns have long been voiced that closer integration at the EU level is leading to a reduction in the powers and roles of national parliaments. Moreover, there have been persistent concerns about the **democratic deficit** within the EU. Various, often half-hearted, attempts have been made to remedy the situation. Hence, the **Treaty of Amsterdam** sought to improve the flow of information on EC/EU matters to national parliaments, particularly on matters concerning **police and judicial co-operation in Criminal Matters**, and to encourage a greater input from COSAC on the legislative activities of the EC/EU. These did little, however, to assuage concerns. Consequently, one of the main issues highlighted in the Declaration on the Future of the Union, adopted at the Nice **European Council** meeting in December 2000, was the 'role of national parliaments in the European architecture'. This was developed in the **Laeken Declaration**, which called on the **European Convention** to look at what role national parliaments should play in the future, possibly as part of a new institution in which they would be represented alongside the **European Parliament** and the **Council of the European Union**. The hope was that an increased involvement of national parliaments might help improve the **legitimacy** of the EU and reduce the democratic deficit. The **Treaty of Lisbon**, which came into force on 1 December 2009, provides a more formal role for the national parliaments in the policymaking process and invites them to comment on and (if enough agree) to block certain policy proposals.

NATO: See **North Atlantic Treaty Organization**

TIBOR NAVRACSICS (1966–) was nominated in 2014 as the Hungarian Commissioner to the new 28-member **European Commission** led by **Jean-Claude Juncker**. Navracsics studied law at the University of Elte and secured a PhD in Political Science from Elte in 2000. Before entering the political arena he taught political science. He was elected to the Hungarian parliament in 2006 as a member of Fidesz. Immediately prior to his appointment to the Commission Navracsics held a number of senior political roles in **Hungary**, most recently that of Minister of Foreign Affairs and Trade from June 2014. He took up his post as the Commissioner for Education, Culture, Youth and Sport on 1 November following the approval of the Juncker Commission by both the **European Parliament** and the **European Council**.

NEGATIVE ASSENT is a phrase that has been used in the **United Kingdom** to describe the power of veto over **legislation** and the generally enhanced authority given to the **European Parliament** under the **Treaty on European Union** by the latter's implementation of the **co-decision procedure**, which created a joint **decision making** mechanism.

NEO-FUNCTIONALISM embodies one of the classical theories of European integration. It was devised in the 1950s as an attempt to explain and account for the political integration process that emerged in its unique form in Western Europe in that decade. According to the political scientist Ernst B. Haas regional integration was the process of how and why states cease to be wholly sovereign, and how and why they voluntarily mingle, merge and mix with their neighbours so as to lose the factual attributes of sovereignty while acquiring new techniques for resolving conflict themselves. For neo-functionalists the available evidence as manifest in the **European Coal and Steel Community**, the **European Economic Community** and the **European Atomic Energy Community** (Euratom) treaties seemed to suggest that the nation state was becoming redundant as an authoritative source of governance. In this European laboratory powers and sovereignty were being transferred from the nation states to a set of supranational institutions. Supranationality appeared to offer a new and definitive answer to resolving conflict through the pooling of sovereignty and the beginnings of a new Europe, but it was questioned whether a model could explain what was happening in such advanced countries and what the dynamics pushing the process onward were. Haas devised such a model. It refers to the placing of emphasis on a process of economic and political co-operation in limited and specified areas, rather than a commitment to a grand design such as **federalism**. Central to neo-functionalism is the idea of **spillover**, whereby co-operation in one area creates demands for, and leads to co-operation in, another. The appropriateness of neo-functionalism in explaining the process of integration has been challenged by, *inter alia*, **liberal intergovernmentalism**.

The **NETHERLANDS** has been deeply involved in European integration ever since 1945. Its Government-in-exile during the Second World War agreed on the establishment of the **Benelux** Economic Union (renamed the Benelux Union in 2010) and the Netherlands was also a founder member of the European Communities (EC). Several of its statesmen have made major contributions to European co-operative efforts. In the 1960s the Netherlands was a strong supporter of **enlargement**: it opposed the **Fouchet Plan**, wanting the question of enlargement to be settled first, and supported closer links between the EC and the **European Free Trade Association**. It also, albeit unsuccessfully, urged a reactivation of **Western European Union**. With its efficient agriculture, the Netherlands was a strong advocate of the **common agricultural policy**, of which it has been a major beneficiary. It later stressed the need for a stronger **environmental policy**, and after 1989 emphasized the importance of developing closer political links with **Central and Eastern Europe**. It has persistently supported closer economic and political collaboration, favouring institutional reform and a substantially greater role for the **European Parliament** (EP). As the host of the **Maastricht summit**, which was to consider a constitutional reform of the EC, it was responsible for constructing the summit agenda. The **Netherlands** produced a draft that went beyond what most member states were prepared to accept, and it had to moderate its position, making the **Treaty on European Union** less comprehensive than it desired. It proved more successful in handling the end stages of the 1996 **intergovernmental conference**, which led to the **Treaty of Amsterdam**. The Dutch Government took a bold decision when it opted to hold a referendum on the **Treaty establishing a Constitution for Europe**. Referenda are practically alien to Dutch political culture and it was assumed that the generally pro-European Union (EU) Dutch population would simply endorse the Government's position on the constitutional treaty. However, on 1 June 2005, three days after the French 'no' vote, some 62% voted against the treaty in the Netherlands, and so plunged the EU into a state of crisis. The Dutch Government decided not to hold a referendum on the **Treaty of Lisbon**. This treaty was ratified in the Dutch parliament in 2008.

NEUTRALITY, in some form, characterizes the foreign policies of six of the member states comprising the European Union: **Austria**, **Cyprus**, **Finland**, **Ireland**, **Malta** and **Sweden**. It means that in times of war the neutral states refrain from becoming engaged in the conflict and treat the belligerents equally. For most of the **Cold War**, this meant that Austria, Finland and Sweden felt unable to join the European Communities. Once they did apply for membership in 1989–92, concerns were raised about the impact that their membership and continued adherence to neutrality would have on plans for **common foreign and security policy** (CFSP). In practice, the neutral countries have not raised significant or insurmountable objections to the development of CFSP. The issue has surfaced as a controversial theme in the Irish **referenda** on European treaties.

The **NEW TRANSATLANTIC AGENDA** (NTA) of 1995 represented an extension of the 1990 **Transatlantic Declaration** and provided a framework for European Union (EU)–US partnership and co-operation across a wide range of activities. The NTA contained four main priorities: to promote peace and stability, democracy and development throughout the world (e.g. joint co-operation over the former **Yugoslavia** and the **Middle East**); to respond effectively to global challenges (e.g. co-operation in fields such as public health); to promote economic relations and contribute to the growth of world trade; and to build closer links between Europe and the **USA**. The last two aims have led to a number of transatlantic dialogues being established in areas such as the environment, consumer protection and business issues. The NTA was accompanied by an EU-US Joint Action Plan that contained some 150 specific areas of action. The aims were diverse and ranged from promoting economic reform in **Ukraine** and combating AIDS to developing closer links between universities and colleges on both sides of the Atlantic. Since 1995 the EU and the USA have made considerable progress in many of these areas, from combating illicit drugs to educational training. In May 1997 both parties reached agreement on Customs Co-operation and Mutual Assistance in Customs Matters, and in 1998 they signed a Mutual Recognition Agreement, which covers particular goods such as pharmaceuticals and medical devices and telecommunications equipment. In 1998 a further development included the launch of the Transatlantic Economic Partnership, which sought to develop a regular dialogue on multilateral trade issues.

The NTA launched an era of unprecedented co-operation on a wide range of political, economic and civil society issues between the EU and the USA, although this has not by any means resolved all differences between the two economic powers over issues such as the environment, the structure of labour markets and economic protection of the US steel industry. The EU–US partnership is a highly strategic relationship. It represents an ongoing means for dialogue on a range of issues that have evolved into formal biannual EU–US summits between the Presidents of the **European Council** and the **European Commission** and the President of the USA.

In May 2002 leaders from both the EU and the USA met in Washington, DC, USA, and agreed to establish a Positive Economic Agenda, which foresaw a highly developed scheme of bilateral co-operation in specific sectors, including financial markets, the insurance sector, organic farming, electronic tendering and electronic customs.

NGO: See **Non-governmental Organizations**

NICE TREATY: See **Treaty of Nice**

NINE is a popular term referring to the membership of the European Communities after the first **enlargement** of 1973. It is used to describe the collectivity of the nine member states between 1973 and 1981: the **Six** founder members, plus **Denmark**, **Ireland** and the **United Kingdom**.

NOISE is the subject of several European Union (EU) **directives** agreed as part of the EU's **environmental policy**. Maximum noise limits have been set for a wide range of commercial and domestic equipment. Manufacturers of many household appliances are required, moreover, to indicate the noise level on the packaging. Limits have also been set for decibel levels in the workplace.

NOMENCLATURE OF TERRITORIAL UNITS FOR STATISTICS (NUTS) describes a classification of regions in the European Union (EU) by the Statistical Office of the European Communities (**Eurostat**). The NUTS system has three levels: each level 1 unit is normally subdivided into a certain number of level 2 units, and level 2 units are composed of smaller level 3 units. NUTS units often correspond to national administrative divisions, but are sometimes ad hoc groupings of smaller national units for the purposes of EU regional statistics. Not all member states are subdivided at all three levels.

The **NOMINATION PROCEDURE** is used to nominate the **European Commission** and its President. Originally, nomination involved only the 'common accord' of the governments of the member states. Following the adoption of the **Treaty on European Union**, the **European Parliament** (EP) was involved more, and the procedure split into four stages: nomination of the Commission President; nomination of the remainder of the Commission; approval by the EP; and appointment by 'common accord' of the member states. The **Treaty of Amsterdam** further involved the EP, requiring its approval of the Commission President before the rest of the Commission was nominated. Under the terms of the **Treaty of Nice**, the **Council of the European Union** took over the responsibilities of the member states and makes **decisions** in this procedure by **qualified majority voting**.

NON-COMPULSORY EXPENDITURE referred to that part of the European Communities' (EC) **budget** (about 40%) that related to policies that were not directly provided for by the **Treaty of Rome** and its subsequent amendments. In practice, it included most EC **expenditure** except that on agriculture. After 1988 greater emphasis was placed upon 'privileged' non-compulsory expenditure, a phrase that refers to spending on long-term programmes. This development was criticized by the **European Parliament** (EP) for reducing its ability to influence the budget. The EP had greater influence over the non-compulsory part of the budget, and continually sought a redefinition and expansion of what that term covered. In practice, EP amendments to non-compulsory expenditure were not allowed to exceed an overall maximum figure previously set each year by the **Council of the European Union**. The criteria that determined the maximum level were the trend in gross national product, the average variation in the budgets of the member states, and the trend during the previous year in the cost of living. The **Treaty of Lisbon** ended the distinction between compulsory and non-compulsory expenditure as far as the EP was concerned and gave the **Members of the European Parliament** an equal voice with the Council on the entire European Union budget.

NON-GOVERNMENTAL ORGANIZATIONS (NGOs) is a term which, when used in the context of the European Union (EU), refers to **interest groups** that are involved with the EU and active in seeking to influence EU policy development, but have no formal connection with the EU. The majority of these groups represent business interests (e.g. ERT, **BUSINESSEUROPE**/UNICE) alongside a smaller number of non-business or more diffuse interests (e.g. trade unions, and consumers' and environmental associations). There are multiple points of access to the EU policy process, including the **European Commission**, the **European Parliament** (EP), the **Council of the European Union** and even the Courts. The EU system is very open to interest groups and, indeed, the European institutions consider interest group involvement to be essential in the development of legitimate and appropriate policies. The Commission has set up a database, CONECCS (Consultation, the European Commission and Civil Society), of around 1,000 NGOs working at EU level, covering approximately 100 branches of activity. Both the Commission and the EP have been seeking to regulate NGO activities in recent years in order to improve **transparency** and to establish minimum standards. (See also **lobbying**.)

NORDIC COUNCIL is the name of a body established in 1952 by the Nordic states as a loose association of intergovernmental co-operation. Despite its purely consultative character, the Nordic Council has achieved a high degree of co-operation and co-ordination in a wide range of policy fields. However, it failed, despite several initiatives, to secure an agreement on a Nordic economic union. After 1970 the Council created a limited institutional structure, with a small secretariat. In their membership applications to the European Communities (EC), **Denmark** and **Norway** made their continued membership of the Council an essential element of their submissions, a condition that was accepted by the EC. Denmark remained a member of the Council after joining the EC in 1973. It saw its role as one of liaison between the two organizations. Membership of both organizations has not created any serious policy problems for Denmark, and the Council's continued existence is currently in little doubt, despite the accession of **Finland** and **Sweden** to the European Union in 1995.

NORM PRICE is the term usually used to describe the price guaranteed to tobacco producers under the **common agricultural policy**.

The **NORTH ATLANTIC CO-OPERATION COUNCIL** (NACC) was a body linking the **North Atlantic Treaty Organization** with the new democracies of **Central and Eastern Europe** and the **Commonwealth of Independent States**. It was established in 1991 as a framework for co-operation in defence and security to ensure stability throughout the continent of Europe. Its formation was criticized by some for duplicating and confusing the role of the Conference on Security and Co-operation in Europe, now the **Organization for Security and Co-operation in Europe**. The **Euro-Atlantic Partnership Council** replaced the NACC in 1997.

The **NORTH ATLANTIC FISHERIES ORGANIZATION** (NAFO) is a body that consists of all those states with a major fisheries interest in the North Atlantic. NAFO was established in 1979 as a successor to the International Commission of the Northwest Atlantic Fisheries (ICNAF, 1949–78). The fisheries regulated by NAFO centre on those areas outside the coastal 200-mile exclusive economic zones in the North Atlantic. At 2016 12 states were operating in the area covered by NAFO, which deals with questions of fishing limits and zones, permissible quotas and catches, conservation of stocks and the types of equipment allowed. NAFO does not have responsibility for managing all fishery resources; notably, salmon, shellfish, tuna/marlins and whales are outside its remit. Given the existence of the **common fisheries policy**, the European Union member states are represented in the organization by the **European Commission**.

The **NORTH ATLANTIC TREATY ORGANIZATION** (NATO) owes its existence to the Washington Treaty of 4 April 1949 that brought the **USA** and Canada together with 10 European countries (**Belgium**, **Denmark**, **France**, **Iceland**, **Italy**, **Luxembourg**, the **Netherlands**, **Norway**, **Portugal** and the **United Kingdom**) in a military arrangement for the collective defence of Western Europe. During the **Cold War** the membership of NATO was enlarged to include **Greece** and **Turkey** in 1952, the Federal Republic of **Germany** in 1955, and **Spain** in 1986. France, however, withdrew from the integrated military command structure in 1966, although in 1996 it resumed participation in some of the military organs of NATO. Since then, NATO has undergone three further rounds of enlargement. As a result, only six of the **Twenty-Eight** European Union (EU) member states—**Austria**, **Cyprus**, **Finland**, **Ireland**, **Malta** and **Sweden**—are not NATO members. France returned to the integrated military command structure in 2009.

NATO member states are committed to providing military forces according to their means; these forces are subject to the NATO chain of military command. An attack upon one state is regarded as an attack upon all, although the treaty does not specify how the affected member state will receive assistance from its partners, who are required to take only such action as they deem necessary. The organization was not meant to be an agent of integration, but NATO and the other new international organizations of the late 1940s made an important contribution to integration by bringing Western European countries together in a series of institutional frameworks that obliged them to co-operate and liaise with each other on an intensive and continuous basis. After the end of the Cold War, there was some doubt over the future of NATO.

After 1990 it sought to redefine its role as a political and security alliance in association with the Conference on Security and Co-operation in Europe (now the **Organization for Security and Co-operation in Europe**—OSCE), and in 1992 it brought the former Communist states of Eastern Europe into its consultative processes through the formation of the **North Atlantic Co-operation Council** (since 1997 replaced by the **Euro-Atlantic Partnership Council**—EAPC). In 1994 the partnerships for peace programme was established under the aegis of NATO. This is open to EAPC and OSCE states and aims to promote political and military co-operation throughout Europe. By December 1997, 27 countries from **Central and Eastern Europe** and the former **USSR** had joined the initiative. Moreover, in March 1999 three Central and Eastern European countries—the **Czech Republic**, **Hungary** and **Poland**—joined NATO proper. At their Prague (Czech Republic) summit in November 2002 NATO leaders agreed to extend membership invitations to up to seven more countries from the former Soviet bloc: **Bulgaria**, **Estonia**, **Latvia**, **Lithuania**, **Romania**, **Slovakia** and **Slovenia**. These countries joined NATO in 2004. Further invitations were issued in 2008 to **Croatia** and **Albania**, and both joined on 1 April 2009. The **former Yugoslav republic of Macedonia**, Georgia and **Ukraine** have also expressed a desire to join NATO.

In general, relations between NATO and the EU have been close. NATO's protection permitted the European Communities (EC) to develop and consolidate themselves, while conversely the economic co-operation engendered by the EC contributed to a stronger Western Europe. Some states, especially France, wished to see **Western European Union** (WEU) reformed to become a European replacement for NATO. In establishing the **common foreign and security policy**, the **Treaty on European Union** re-emphasized the potential significance of WEU for the EU. The response of NATO was to build on regular joint NATO-WEU meetings and support the proposed improvement of WEU's operational capabilities. Fearful that such developments might undermine NATO, many member states insisted that NATO must remain the major European security organization. This has not, however, prevented the establishment of either the **Eurocorps** in 1992 or the **European Rapid Reaction Force**. Nor has it prevented the EU from developing a **European security and defence policy** and pursuing the goal of a common defence, flagged as part of the **common foreign and security policy** in the **Treaty on European Union** and most recently confirmed in the **Treaty of Lisbon**. Such developments have not always contributed to harmonious relations between the EU and NATO, despite their overlapping membership. However, despite misgivings in some NATO circles, more often than not voiced from within the USA, about the EU's aspirations regarding security and defence matters, the EU-NATO relationship has become closer over time. This is most evident in the Berlin-Plus Agreement of 2002, which provides for EU access to NATO assets and planning capabilities in the event of EU-led crisis management operations, and in the more institutionalized nature of dialogue. That there was scope for a closer relationship was evident in the call for a 'strategic partnership' from the then NATO Secretary-General, Jaap de Hoop Scheffer, in 2007. This and similar calls have not always been met with an enthusiastic response from the EU, which clearly has its own ambitions, as well as having some member states that are sceptical of NATO. However, **enlargement** to include the countries of **Central and Eastern Europe** in 2004 and 2007 certainly increased the ranks of pro-NATO member states within the EU. At a NATO summit meeting held in Lisbon, **Portugal**, in November 2010, a new Strategic Concept was adopted which committed NATO to working more closely with its international partners, including the United Nations and the EU. In July 2016, following a NATO summit held in Warsaw, **Poland**, the EU and NATO signed a joint declaration, which identified seven specific areas for enhanced co-operation. Building on this, in December more than 40 measures to strengthen co-operation were duly approved by the Ministers of Foreign Affairs of both organizations. The current Secretary-General of NATO is Jens Stoltenberg. NATO and the EU have 22 common members.

NORTHERN IRELAND EXECUTIVE OFFICE: See **Office of the Northern Ireland Executive in Brussels**

NORWAY has been, in general, suspicious of close European relations that involve anything more than intergovernmental co-operation. It first applied to join the European Communities (EC) in 1962, doing so out of necessity more than enthusiasm for European integration. Indeed, there was considerable disquiet in the country over what membership might mean in terms of national sovereignty and the 'special problems' arising from the country's 'geographical location and economic structure', which the Government had said would need to be resolved by the negotiations. Hence, **France**'s veto of the **United Kingdom**'s application in 1963 and again in 1967 was not wholly unwelcome. Opposition to membership increased after the resumption of negotiations in 1970, and the deep feelings aroused had widespread repercussions throughout Norway. In September 1972 a narrow majority (53%) voted against membership in a consultative referendum. Preparations for accession were halted and replaced by discussions on a **free trade agreement**, which entered into force in 1973. Thereafter, EC membership disappeared from the Norwegian political agenda until 1988, when it re-emerged because of concerns over the possible effect of the **internal market**. Initially, the preference was for the **European Economic Area** (EEA), but Norway soon found itself following its neighbours in applying for EC membership in 1992. **Accession negotiations** were concluded in 1994, but once again membership was rejected in a referendum. Since then, Norway's relations have been based on full participation in the EEA (which it joined in 1994) as well as involvement in the **Schengen Agreement**. Future membership of the European Union (EU) has not been ruled out, but the issue of EU membership is one that continues to divide public and political opinion in Norway.

NOUVELLES EQUIPES INTERNATIONALES was the name of a transnational association of Christian Democrat political parties formed in 1947. In 1965 it changed its name to the European Union of Christian Democrats, and in 1976 its members from member states of the European Communities founded the European People's Party (see **Group of the European People's Party—Christian Democrats**) as a transnational organization.

NOUVELLES FRONTIERES is the name of a French travel agency that challenged the price-fixing regulations of the French Civil Aviation Code in the **Court of Justice**. In April 1986 the Court ruled in favour of the company, declaring that air transport was not exempt from the **competition policy** of the European Communities, and that, under the **Treaty of Rome**, member states were not permitted to approve air fares that resulted from agreements between airlines. This was the first major challenge to the **cartel** arrangements on air fares pursued by both governments and airlines. The Court also pointed out that responsibility for determining whether an air-fare agreement transgresses the treaty rests with the **European Commission** and the national anti-trust authorities. The ruling gave the Commission greater powers, although subsequent progress on air transport liberalization was slow.

NUCLEAR ENERGY: See **Energy Policy**; **European Atomic Energy Community**; **European Fusion Development Agreement**; **Joint European Torus**

NUTS: See **Nomenclature of Territorial Units for Statistics**

O

OCTs: See **Overseas Countries and Territories**

OECD: See **Organisation for Economic Co-operation and Development**

GÜNTHER OETTINGER (1953–) was successfully nominated by the re-elected Merkel Government as the prospective German Commissioner in the **European Commission** (2010–14) in the latter part of 2009. Oettinger replaced the much-respected Günther Verheugen, and was responsible for the highly sensitive and important issue of energy (especially in terms of energy security). In September 2014 the President-elect of the Commission for 2014–19, **Jean-Claude Juncker**, named Oettinger as Commissioner-designate for the Digital Economy, subject to approval by the **European Parliament** (EP). Prior to Oettinger's appointment to the Commission, he had been active in German politics as a member of the Christian Democratic Union (CDU) for over 30 years. After reading law at the University of Tübingen and working in a legal firm he opted to focus his energies on a professional career in politics. He rapidly rose through the ranks. He became chair of his local CDU branch in Ditzingen in 1977 and first entered the state (regional) parliament of Baden-Württemberg in 1984. He became Minister President of this state (Land) in 2004 following the resignation of his predecessor and he remained in the post (being successfully re-elected to head a coalition government with the Free Democrats in 2006) until he became a Commissioner. After securing the support of **Members of the European Parliament** (MEPs) at his nomination hearing, and the approval of Juncker's Commission by both the EP and the **European Council** in late October 2014 Oettinger began his second term as a European Commissioner on 1 November. Oettinger became the Commissioner responsible for Budget and Human Resources from January 2017, following the appointment of Bulgarian Commissioner **Kristalina Georgieva** as Chief Executive Officer at the World Bank.

The **OFFICE FOR HARMONIZATION IN THE INTERNAL MARKET** (OHIM) is a decentralized European Union agency responsible for the **harmonization** of intellectual property rights, **trademarks** and design rights across the member states. It was established in 1994, and is located in Alicante, **Spain**.

OFFICE FOR OFFICIAL PUBLICATIONS OF THE EUROPEAN COMMUNITIES (EUR-OP): See **Publications Office of the European Union**

The **OFFICE OF THE NORTHERN IRELAND EXECUTIVE IN BRUSSELS** (ONIEB) was established in 2001 and is one of some 200 offices in **Brussels** that operate on behalf of regional and local authorities in the European Union (EU). The ONIEB was created, as part of the Belfast Agreement, as a means of enabling the newly devolved Northern Ireland executive to play a role in Europe. The functions of the ONIEB are essentially: to monitor the development by EU institutions of policies relevant to Northern Ireland; to provide up-to-date information to ministers and departments in Belfast; and to ensure that the interests of Northern Ireland are fully represented in policy developments by EU institutions. Moreover, the ONIEB seeks to raise the profile of Northern Ireland among European policymakers and to form interregional links with other regions in Europe. Technically the ONIEB forms part of the **United Kingdom**'s **Permanent Representation** (UKREP) and works closely with it and both the **Scottish Executive** Office and the **National Assembly for Wales EU Office**.

The *OFFICIAL JOURNAL OF THE EUROPEAN UNION* (OJ) is one of the principal publications of the **Publications Office of the European Union**, covering all of the major European Union (EU) **institutions**. The daily journal was first published in 1952. It contains the details of all EU (and, earlier, European Communities) **legislation**. Regulations become law throughout the EU as soon as they are published in the *Journal*. It also carries details of EU initiatives, and advertisements of staff vacancies. The OJ has three parts: the 'L' Series contains EU legislation, and the 'C' Series draft legislation, information and notices, while the 'S' Series is a supplement comprising notices and advertisements for public works, supplies, services and research contracts. Before the entry into force of the **Treaty of Nice**, the OJ was called the *Official Journal of the European Communities*. Since 1998 an electronic version of the OJ has been made available on **EUR-Lex** with every printed edition.

OHIM: See **Office for Harmonization in the Internal Market**

OJ: See *Official Journal of the European Union*

OLAF: See **European Anti-fraud Office**

An **OMBUDSMAN**, a post created by the **Treaty on European Union**, is appointed by the **European Parliament** (EP) to deal with complaints of maladministration in European Union (EU) **institutions** (with the exception of the **Court of Justice** and the **General Court**) and initiatives. Upon the receipt of complaints from citizens, or from business and other interests working in the EU, the Ombudsman launches an inquiry to try to resolve any particular issue of concern. The first Ombudsman, who took office in September 1995, was Jacob Söderman of **Finland**; he remained in the post until March 2003. His successor was Nikiforos Diamandouros, who, having served as the first ombudsman in his native **Greece**, was elected by the EP in January 2003. Diamandouros assumed the post on 1 April 2003 and was re-elected in 2005. In January 2010 Diamandouros was re-elected; after he announced his retirement, Emily O'Reilly of Ireland was elected Ombudsman in July 2013. The Ombudsman submits an annual report on his or her activities to the EP. The 2009 report, for example, indicated that the inability of citizens to see certain documents remained by far the most common complaint from EU citizens.

OMC: See **Open Method of Co-ordination**

ONIEB: See **Office of the Northern Ireland Executive in Brussels**

ONP stands for Open Network Provision, an initiative dating back to 1989 intended to harmonize the national regulations of the member states regarding telecommunications services.

OPEN METHOD OF CO-ORDINATION (OMC) is a policy method (introduced in 2000) that essentially involves the comparison of national policies across the European Union (EU) and the dissemination of best practices in such areas as social policy and employment policy. This instrument aims to facilitate the exchange of ideas and experiences between the member states and is intended to foster policy and learning. Under this method, member states seek to agree to and apply non-binding EU guidelines to national and regional policies, while avoiding the necessity of enacting new EU **legislation**.

OPENNESS relates primarily to increasing calls from the 1990s onwards for the provision of greater information about European Union (EU) policy debates and the EU decision making processes within the EU **institutions** and, in particular, the **Council of the European Union**. Openness is closely associated with the other concepts such as **transparency**, **legitimacy** and **accountability** that are familiar, recurrent themes of European governance. The EU institutions have promised greater openness in a serious effort both to reduce the criticisms of a '**democratic deficit**' and to enable the public to appreciate and understand much better the workings of the EU. The **Treaty of Amsterdam** included a chapter on transparency that gives 'any citizen … a right of access to **European Parliament**, Council and **European Commission** documents'. Despite these aspirations, access remains rather restricted, especially to the workings of the **Council of the European Union**. The launch of the **European Convention** in February 2002, following the meeting of the Laeken **European Council** of December 2001, was a further means of drawing the people of Europe closer to the EU, as are efforts to enable citizens to petition the EU institutions (under the **Treaty of Lisbon**) and also to have recourse to the European **Ombudsman**.

OPINIONS are one of two kinds of non-binding pronouncement that may be issued by the **Council of the European Union** and the **European Commission**. Like **recommendations** they do not constitute instructions, but merely express the preference of the European Union, and may be disregarded by the member states. (See also **Court of Justice**; **decisions**; **directives**; **law**; **legislation**; **regulations**; **resolutions**.)

OPTIMUM CURRENCY AREA is a term, attributed to the US economist Robert Mundell, which refers to a group of countries bound together by a system of fixed exchange rates. From 1970 such an area was an objective of the European Communities and was to be achieved through the establishment of **economic and monetary union**.

OPT-OUT is a term that came into common usage after the 1991 **Maastricht summit**. It refers to a decision to allow a member state the statutory right not to take part in any specific activity pursued by the European Union. Opt-outs are in fact exemptions from treaty provisions and have been granted to **Denmark** and the **United Kingdom** over **economic and monetary union**, and enabled the UK to remain outside the aspirations and all decisions pertaining to the Social Chapter of the **Treaty on European Union** (TEU) until the new Labour administration abandoned this opt-out in 1997. (See also **Charter of Fundamental Social Rights of Workers**.) Denmark also secured some political opt-outs from the defence elements of the **common foreign and security policy** following its initial rejection of the TEU in 1992. Denmark, the UK and Ireland were granted various opt-out and opt-in arrangements governing the area of freedom, security and justice and Schengen, which were both established by the **Treaty of Amsterdam**. These arrangements survived the **Treaty of Nice** and the **Treaty of Lisbon**, the latter updating those on the area of freedom, security and justice and Schengen and creating a new partial opt-out from the application of the **Charter of Fundamental Rights** for **Poland** and the UK. (See **Schengen Agreement**.)

VIKTOR ORBÁN (1963–) is the Prime Minister of **Hungary**, since 2010. He has also been the leader of the conservative party Fidesz since 2003 (as well as in 1993–2000). Orbán studied law at Eötvös Loránd University, Budapest, from where he graduated in 1987. Prior to entering politics, he also studied political science for a short time at Pembroke College, Oxford, the **United Kingdom**. Orbán's brand of politics is moderately Eurosceptic, quite nationalistic and increasingly populist. As such, the Orbán Administration has experienced some friction in its relations with the European Union (EU). During the **European migration crisis**, Orbán, like other leaders in the **Visegrad Group**, rejected the EU's plan for the compulsory re-distribution of immigrants between EU member states. Orbán has accused the EU, *inter alia*, of 'muslimizing' Europe, in what has been widely deemed a pattern of Islamophobic rhetoric.

The **ORDINARY LEGISLATIVE PROCEDURE** (formerly known as the co-decision procedure) is the European Union's main decision making procedure. It was introduced by the **Treaty on European Union**, being later simplified by the **Treaty of Amsterdam**, and requires all **legislation** adopted under the procedure to be approved by both the **Council of the European Union** and the **European Parliament**. Where the two institutions are initially unable to approve legislation, a **Conciliation Committee** is held. The co-decision procedure is used to adopt legislation in an increasing number of policy areas (e.g. the **internal market**, **social policy**, **transport policy** and **environmental policy**), although it does not apply to certain principal areas, such as the **common agricultural policy** (CAP), which is still governed by the **consultation procedure**, and matters of **economic and monetary union**, which are decided by the **co-operation procedure** introduced by the **Single European Act** of 1987. The **Treaty establishing a Constitution for Europe** envisaged the co-decision procedure being renamed the 'ordinary legislative procedure'. The **Treaty of Lisbon** copied this example and, in renaming the procedure, also further extended the areas in which co-decision would be utilized, notably to include decisions relating to the CAP.

The **ORDINARY REVISION PROCEDURE** is the means by which the European Union's member states amend the **founding treaties**. Traditionally it has involved an **intergovernmental conference** and **ratification** of the new treaty by **national parliaments** and/or **referenda**. With the entry into force of the **Treaty of Lisbon**, a new element has been included: a convention. This will examine proposed amendments and adopt recommendations, and follow structurally the model of the **European Convention** of 2002–04 which produced the **draft Treaty establishing a Constitution for Europe**. The Treaty of Lisbon also introduced a **simplified revision procedure**.

EMILY O'REILLY (1958–) became the **Ombudsman** in October 2013, when she succeeded Nikiforos Diamandouros. O'Reilly was born and grew up in **Ireland**. She graduated with a degree in Modern Languages and Literature from University College Dublin in 1979 before pursuing a career in journalism and broadcasting. She became Ireland's first female ombudsman in 2003 and was appointed Commissioner for Environmental Information and Freedom of Information in 2007.

The **ORGANISATION FOR ECONOMIC CO-OPERATION AND DEVELOPMENT** (OECD) was established under US leadership in 1961 as a successor to the Organisation for European Economic Co-operation. The **USA** sought a collaborative body that might mitigate some of the feared adverse consequences of the division of Western Europe into the **European Economic Community** and the **European Free Trade Association**. The USA and Canada became full members of the new organization, and **Japan** joined in 1964. The majority of European Union member states belong to OECD, which is a forum for the advanced industrial democracies, concerned not only with the effectiveness of the domestic economies of its members, but also with the broader and long-term problems of the international economic system. OECD membership increased in size with a spate of accessions in the mid-1990s (including Mexico in 1994, the **Czech Republic** in 1995 and **Hungary**, **Poland** and the Republic of Korea in 1996) and in 2010 (when Chile, **Estonia**, Israel and **Slovenia** joined). Today OECD has 34 member countries and is based in Paris, **France**, where it maintains a substantial organization staffed by economic experts. It has often acted as a pioneer in developing economic concepts, for example on **competition policy** and labour markets, and its regular economic reports and surveys on the international and national economies are detailed and highly regarded. The recommendations of its reports are often implemented, although OECD cannot impose a policy upon any one state. OECD seeks to foster good governance in the public service and in corporate activity. It also provides a forum to assist policymakers in adopting strategic orientations. OECD is currently headed by José Ángel Gurría Treviño (Ángel Gurría), who took up the post of Secretary-General on 1 June 2006.

The **ORGANIZATION FOR SECURITY AND CO-OPERATION IN EUROPE** (OSCE) was originally known as the Conference on Security and Co-operation in Europe (CSCE), a series of European conferences on security, science and technology, economic, environmental and **human rights** issues. A meeting place for all European countries, the **USSR**, the **USA** and Canada, it first convened in Helsinki, **Finland**, in July 1973. The conclusion of this first meeting was the Helsinki Final Act, which marked agreement in three main areas: economic co-operation, human rights and the exchange of information about military activities. Further meetings were held at regular intervals in Belgrade, **Serbia**, in 1977–78, Madrid, **Spain**, in 1980–83, Vienna, **Austria**, in 1986–89, Paris, **France**, in 1990, Helsinki again in 1992, and Budapest, **Hungary**, in 1994, in addition to a number of more specialized sessions, primarily on arms control, disarmament and human rights. The CSCE quickly assumed considerable importance as the principal opportunity for dialogue between East and West during the **Cold War**. Nevertheless, its significance as a pan-European forum could even be said to have increased after the ending of the Cold War.

Under the terms according to which the CSCE was established, and also at the insistence of the USSR, the European Communities (EC) were not allowed to have a common representation of their own at the first Helsinki meeting. However, the EC member states collaborated closely with one another in one of the first successful applications of **European political co-operation**, and the Helsinki Final Act was signed by Aldo Moro of **Italy** (the holder of the presidency of the Council of Ministers —see **Council of the European Union**—at the time) 'for Italy, and in the name of the European Community'. At the 1990 Paris meeting, which concluded with the signing of the **Charter of Paris for a New Europe**, endowing the CSCE with permanent institutions, the EC participated as a single entity rather than as separate states. In December 1994 the Budapest summit conference adopted the new name OSCE to indicate the organization's permanent nature and growing political role. The OSCE maintains a secretariat in Vienna and has 57 member states (if the European Union countries are counted separately), including all the former republics of the USSR. The abrupt rise in membership from 35 in 1990 to 55 by 1997 reflects the disintegration of the USSR and **Yugoslavia** in the early 1990s. The Federal Republic of Yugoslavia (now divided between Serbia and **Montenegro**), which was suspended from the CSCE in 1992, was admitted to the OSCE in 2000.

OSCE: See **Organization for Security and Co-operation in Europe**

OSTPOLITIK refers to the reorientation of the foreign policy of the Federal Republic of **Germany** (FRG—West Germany) after 1969 under the new left-of-centre Chancellor, Willy Brandt, which led to a series of treaties concluded by the FRG with the **USSR**, the German Democratic Republic (GDR—East Germany), **Poland**, and Czechoslovakia, and a Four Power agreement on Berlin. This change in policy was denounced by the Christian Democrats and their allies in Germany and caused a degree of concern in the West about Bonn's rapprochement with Moscow. To counter this, however, Brandt reinforced his support for European integration and strongly backed British membership of the European Communities (EC). As a result of the agreement with East Germany, the latter's products gained access to the EC in such great numbers that East Germany was sometimes described as the silent member of the EC.

OUTER SEVEN was a phrase often used in the 1960s to describe the member states of the **European Free Trade Association**.

OUTERMOST REGIONS were formally acknowledged in the **Treaty on European Union** (TEU). There are eight such regions: four French overseas departments (Guadeloupe, French Guiana, Martinique and Réunion), one French overseas collectivity (Saint Martin), the Azores, Madeira and the Canary Islands. All, by nature of their size, remoteness and climate, are dependent economically on a small number of export products. All the outermost regions are relatively depressed and receive substantial financial assistance through the European Union **budget**. The outermost regions are subject to a declaration drawn up at the time of the TEU, which acknowledges their major structural problems, and the **Council of the European Union**, acting under the rules of **qualified majority voting**, can give these areas exemption from the application of the provisions of the common policies.

The **OVERSEAS COUNTRIES AND TERRITORIES** (OCTs) are colonies or former colonies constitutionally subject to European Union (EU) member states and are the subject of Articles 182–187 of the **Treaty of Rome** (now Articles 198–204 of the **Treaty on the Functioning of the European Union**). Mainly French possessions when the treaty was signed in 1957, they were either overseas adjuncts to the metropolitan country or, in practice, colonies. A special convention annexed to the treaty specified the details of the association. Products from OCTs would have access to the European Communities (EC) market on the same terms as those of the member states, with a gradual removal of customs duties over five years. An Overseas Development Fund was established to finance development projects. After 1963 OCTs were absorbed into the broader EC agreements of the **Yaoundé Convention**, the **Lomé Convention** and the **Cotonou Agreement**. However, in 2001 a new **association agreement** was adopted, which provided a new co-operation framework for EU-OCT relations. There are 25 OCTs linked to the **United Kingdom**, **France**, the **Netherlands** and **Denmark**. Total EU funding (through the **European Development Fund**) amounted to €286m. for 2008–13. Funding of €364.5m. was to be allocated for the OCTs in 2014–20.

OWN RESOURCES is a term that refers to the possession by the European Union (EU) of financial resources that belong to it as of right and together form the **budget**. When the **European Economic Community** was established, its funding relied on the receipt of annual contributions from the member states. With the 1970 **Treaty of Luxembourg**, the member states agreed to move to a funding system of own resources, an independent source of income for the European Communities to spend as they wished within the limits of the obligations and decision making criteria set down by the treaties. Own resources were to be phased in over a period of five years. The own resources of the EU collected for it by the member states consist of **customs duties** on imports from third countries, levies on agricultural imports and the sugar and isoglucose levies, a contribution from the member states based on each country's share of total gross national product (GNP) in the EU and a proportion of the **value-added tax** levied by the member states.

P

PADOA-SCHIOPPA REPORT is the name of a report commissioned by the **European Commission** and submitted in April 1987 by a committee headed by Tommaso Padoa-Schioppa (1940–2010), the Deputy Director-General of the Bank of Italy. The committee had been asked to evaluate the effect of the entry into the European Communities (EC) of **Portugal** and **Spain**, and of the commitment to an **internal market** upon the EC's economic system. The Report contained four major recommendations: the establishment of a common monetary policy; the promotion of cohesion; the completion on schedule of the internal market; and the development of a macroeconomic strategy. These measures, it argued, were necessary to promote economic development while preventing an aggravation of regional economic differences within the EC.

A **PARAGRAPH** is a sub-element of an **Article** in the **European treaties**. Paragraphs within an Article are usually numbered.

A **PART** is a main sub-division in the **Treaty of Rome** and its successor, the **Treaty on the Functioning of the European Union**. Parts may in turn be sub-divided into **Titles**. The **Treaty on European Union** does not contain Parts, but is divided instead into Titles.

PARTNERSHIP AND CO-OPERATION AGREEMENTS (PCAs) were initially conceived to provide a framework for closer political, cultural and economic relations between the European Union (EU) and former republics of the **USSR**. In some cases, the agreements make reference to the possibility of eventual free trade with the EU. In all cases, emphasis is placed on the commitment of the contracting parties to **human rights** and democracy.

PARTY GROUPS are the basic organizational feature of the **European Parliament** (EP). While **Members of the European Parliament** (MEPs) normally belong to national political parties, in the EP they band together in transnational party groups. The EP originally laid down the criteria for what constitutes a party group in 1979. At that time, if a proposed group contained MEPs elected from at least five member states, then the minimum size required was 20 MEPs. The rules have changed as the European Union (EU) has enlarged, and currently party groups need to comprise at least 25 individuals from at least seven member states. A Member may not belong to more than one political group. Party groups cannot in theory be established if the proposed membership consists of MEPs from only one member state. However, in the past, it has been possible for one-party groups to be created. The first example, following the 1994 EP elections, was the Forza Europa group, which consisted exclusively of Italian MEPs. The President shall be notified in a statement when a political group is set up. This statement shall specify the name of the group, its members and its bureau. In each EP, a few MEPs have chosen to remain unaffiliated to any group, but, in general, groups are the basis of parliamentary procedure. They nominate and elect the President and Vice-President of the EP; the roles of committee chairperson and all memberships are filled on a group basis (although some provision is made for the few independent MEPs), and seating in the EP is by party group. The groups also receive funding, in proportion to their size and the number of countries represented, to enable them to maintain a secretariat and their various activities. The **Court of Justice** has ruled that these funds cannot be used for electoral purposes.

An examination of the history of party groups in the EP reveals a considerable degree of fluidity and instability as groups (with the exception of the Socialists) have become subject to regular change as they form, disband, amalgamate, constitute and reconstitute themselves. Consequently, the EP party groups can be said to be weakly institutionalized. There are currently eight political groups in the eighth parliament (2014–19). At late 2017 these were: the **Group of the European People's Party (Christian Democrats)** (EPP), with 214 members; the **Group of the Progressive Alliance of Socialists and Democrats in the European Parliament** (S&D—formerly the **Party of European Socialists**), with 189 members; the **European Conservatives and Reformists Group** (ECR), with 73 members; the **Group of the Alliance of Liberals and Democrats for Europe** (ALDE), with 68 members; the **Confederal Group of the European United Left/Nordic Green Left** (GUE/NGL), with 52 members; the **Group of the Greens/European Free Alliance**, with 51 members; the **Europe of Freedom and Direct Democracy** group (EFDD), with 41 members, and the **Europe of Nations and Freedom** group (founded in mid-2015), with 40 members. The remaining 18 MEPs were independents (the so-called *non-inscrits*).

The series of **enlargements** of the EU since 2004 entailed a degree of destabilization for the party group structure with the arrival of a host of new parties and MEPs. However, the real test for the party groups—and one that has not been successfully tackled to date—is the challenge to command loyalty and respect from EU citizens and to foster the idea and benefits of EU integration. Overall voter turnout at the 2004, 2009 and 2014 EP elections was lower than at preceding elections, at some 45%, 43% and 42.5%, respectively.

The **PARTY OF EUROPEAN SOCIALISTS (PES)** forms part of the **Group of the Progressive Alliance of Socialists and Democrats (S&D)** group in the **European Parliament**.

The **PASSERELLE CLAUSE** was originally found in Article 42 of the **Treaty on European Union** and allowed the **Council of the European Union**, acting unanimously, to transfer policy competences from the intergovernmental **pillar** III to the supranational European Community pillar of the European Union. Any transfer had first to be ratified by the member states. Since the abandonment of the pillar structure with the **Treaty of Lisbon**, the passerelle clause has been replaced by the **simplified revision procedure**.

PATENTS are not necessarily exempt from the **competition policy** of the European Union (EU). The **European Commission** has the authority to decide whether a patent or trademark violates the rules of competition. The **Court of Justice** has upheld the general principle of the non-exclusiveness of patents. Conversely, the Commission has launched several initiatives to facilitate the registration and protection of patents. In December 2012 all member states (with the exception of **Italy**, **Spain** and **Poland**) and the **European Parliament** agreed on a 'patent package'—a legislative initiative consisting of two regulations and an international agreement, laying the ground for the creation of unitary patent protection and a Unified Patent Court in the EU. (See also **Unitary Patent Convention; Office for Harmonization in the Internal Market**.)

PCAS: See **Partnership and Co-operation Agreements**

PEOPLE'S EUROPE: See **Citizenship; Committee for a People's Europe**

PERMANENT MISSION is the name given to the diplomatic representation of a non-member state to the European Union.

PERMANENT REPRESENTATION is the name given to the large delegation that each member state maintains in **Brussels**. It consists of both diplomats and administrative officials seconded from those national ministries whose work is affected by **decisions** of the European Union. A Permanent Representative, who possesses senior ambassadorial status, heads each delegation. Collectively, the Permanent Representatives meet at least weekly as the **Committee of Permanent Representatives** (COREPER).

PERMANENT STRUCTURED CO-OPERATION is a form of **enhanced co-operation** in the area of the **European security and defence policy**, originally envisaged in the **Treaty establishing a Constitution for Europe** and since provided for in the **Treaty of Lisbon**. It involves the pooling of military means and capabilities and measures to enhance the availability, interoperability, flexibility and deployability of the armed forces of participating member states.

The term **PERMISSIVE CONSENSUS** was coined by academics in the 1970s to describe the way in which European publics appeared to take for granted or readily accept the process of European integration. The permissive consensus has since been seriously challenged, as seen in: the rise of Euroscepticism; the **ratification crises** surrounding the **Treaty on European Union**, the **Treaty of Nice** and, more recently, the **Treaty establishing a Constitution for Europe** and the **Treaty of Lisbon**; and the concerns expressed about the **legitimacy** of the European Union (EU). The way in which a gap now exists between the political and economic élite and the wider populations of the former **Fifteen** and now **Twenty-Eight** member states cannot be disputed and has also been clearly displayed in the findings of **Eurobarometer** from 1992 onwards and in the **referenda** on the **euro** in **Denmark** (2000) and **Sweden** (2003). These have led to repeated demands for greater 'civic participation' in the EU project.

PES: See the **Party of European Socialists**

The **PETERSBERG TASKS** were originally set out in the Petersberg Declaration issued by foreign and defence ministers of the member states of **Western European Union** (WEU) in June 1992. They cover humanitarian and rescue operations, peacekeeping activities and tasks for combat forces in crisis management, including peacemaking. At the time, it was anticipated that WEU would undertake these tasks. Since then, however, the emphasis has shifted to the European Union (EU), notably through the **Treaty of Amsterdam** and, more recently, the further development of the **common foreign and security policy** and the creation of a **European Rapid Reaction Force**. With the de facto transfer of many of WEU's activities to the EU, the latter's responsibilities for, and commitment to, undertaking Petersberg tasks have increased.

PETITIONS may be referred to in the context of the right of citizens of the European Union (EU) to petition the **European Parliament** (EP) on any matter that falls within the EU's areas of authority, and that affects them directly. The right of petition was formalized by the **Treaty on European Union**, which empowered the EP to appoint an independent **Ombudsman** to receive and evaluate petitions and complaints. Where the Ombudsman upholds an allegation of maladministration, a report is submitted to both the institution concerned and the EP. The formalization of the right of petition was part of the attempt to develop a notion of EU **citizenship**.

PHARE, sometimes known as Operation PHARE, is the name originally given to the **Poland** and **Hungary** Assistance for Economic Restructuring programme, a system for co-ordinating economic aid set up by the **Organisation for Economic Co-operation and Development**, and co-ordinated by the European Communities. Established in 1989, it was subsequently extended to include **Albania**, **Bulgaria**, the **Czech Republic**, **Estonia**, **Latvia**, **Lithuania**, **Romania**, **Slovakia** and **Slovenia**. In March 1997 the **European Commission** agreed to the extension of PHARE in order to provide specific assistance to the **applicant countries** of **Central and Eastern Europe**, to help these countries implement the reforms required to fulfil the criteria for European Union membership. Assistance was to focus on building democratic institutions and administrations and financing investment (especially in the areas of the environment, transport, product quality, working conditions and major infrastructure projects). Among the new projects funded were **twinning**, the **instrument for structural policies for pre-accession** (ISPA) and the Special Accession Programme for Agriculture and Rural Development (SAPARD). A Technical Assistance Information Exchange Office (TAIEX) was opened in 1996 as part of PHARE operations. Overall annual funding available under PHARE, **SAPARD** and ISPA in the period 1999–2003 amounted to €2,645m. This compares with an annual figure for PHARE during 1995–99 of €730m. Assistance programmes similar to PHARE were established for the former **USSR** (see **Technical Assistance to the Commonwealth of Independent States**—TACIS) and the **Western Balkans** (see **CARDS**). On 1 January 2007 the **instrument for pre-accession assistance** replaced PHARE.

PHARMACEUTICALS have been a central concern of the **European Commission**. In pursuance of its **health and safety** policy, the Commission has been active in regulating pharmaceutical products, and a series of **directives** apply to their testing, patenting, production, marketing and labelling. Patenting in the use of brand names has also been held, in principle, to contravene **competition policy**, which has encouraged the growth of generic products that are often substantially cheaper than the branded product. In 1994 the European Agency for the Evaluation of Medicinal Products was established in London, the **United Kingdom**, as a decentralized agency of the European Union responsible for overseeing the registration of human and veterinary medicinal products; the agency was renamed the **European Medicines Agency** in 2004.

PILLAR is a term that was applied to the notional structure of the European Union (EU) prior to the **Treaty of Lisbon**, which came into force in December 2009. During this period the EU was held to consist of three pillars, the **European Council** being the only body capable of co-ordinating all three. The central pillar, the first pillar, was the European Communities (EC), where the **Community method** applied and the **European Commission**, **European Parliament** and the **Court of Justice** exercised their full powers. The two other pillars were **common foreign and security policy** (CFSP), pillar II, and **justice and home affairs** (JHA), pillar III. These were governed by principles of intergovernmental co-operation where the constitutional authority of the EC did not apply. The **Treaty of Amsterdam** amended the third pillar to the effect that it was now concerned with **police and judicial co-operation in criminal matters**. With the **Treaty of Lisbon**, the pillars were replaced by a more integrated structure, although the CFSP retains many of its intergovernmental characteristics.

POCO: See **European Political Co-operation**

POLAND entered into negotiations for association with the European Communities as a new democracy in 1989, and in December 1991 signed the **Europe agreement**. This was the first major step by Poland towards the ultimate objective of membership, and in April 1994 it submitted a formal application to join the European Union (EU). Three years later, the application received formal approval, although the **European Commission**'s report made clear that investment would be needed if the country was 'to comply with Community rules on agriculture, environment and transport', and that further administrative reform would be required for the application and enforcement of the *acquis communautaire*. **Accession negotiations** began in March 1998 and, despite some concerns within the EU about the capacity of the country to take on all the obligations of membership, were successfully concluded in December 2002. Six months later, in June 2003, 81.7% of those who participated in a national referendum (turnout was 58.8%) voted in favour of EU membership. Poland therefore joined the EU on 1 May 2004 as its largest new member.

Concerns that Poland might prove to be among the most difficult of the new members to integrate were borne out at the **European Council** meeting in December 2003, when the Polish and Spanish Governments opposed changes to **qualified majority voting** rules, thereby preventing conclusion of the **intergovernmental conference** that had begun work three months earlier. This Polish/Spanish alliance came to an abrupt end with the election of a new Spanish Government in early 2004. All member states reached agreement on a treaty text in June 2004. Poland was one of a number of states that adopted a very tough bargaining stance towards the financing of the new budgetary package (covering 2007–13), and was highly critical of the British rebate. Nevertheless, Poland readily accepted the deal struck in December 2005. The EU remains a contested issue within Polish politics. Poland possessed one of the most **Eurosceptic** governments in the run-up to agreement on the **Treaty of Lisbon**, and battled so hard to realize its own interests on issues such as voting rights and the place of Christianity within the treaty base that it often antagonized its fellow EU member states. The Eurosceptic Government of Jarosław Kaczyński was replaced in October 2007 by a new administration under **Donald Tusk**, which sought to steer a more EU-friendly (albeit with degrees of soft Euroscepticism) and pro-German course. Poland became part of the EU's **Schengen Area** in December 2007. The Polish parliament endorsed the Treaty of Lisbon in April 2008, but the then Polish President, Lech Kaczyński, waited until he knew the outcome of the second vote on the treaty in **Ireland** before he signed off the **ratification** process in Poland in October 2009. The Polish government coalition parties performed well in the 2009 **European Parliament** elections and received over 50% of the vote (with a turnout of some 28%) and were subsequently expected to play an even greater role within the **Group of the European People's Party**. Kaczyński's death in a plane crash in April 2010 precipitated a new presidential election over two rounds in June and July 2010, which was won by Bronisław Komorowski. The Polish parliament gave its support to the signing of the Treaty on Stability, Co-ordination and Governance in the Economic and Monetary Union (**Fiscal Compact**) in March 2013, which was formally approved by Komorowski in August. In September 2014 **Donald Tusk** announced the resignation of his Government, prior to assuming his new role as President of the European Council from December.

In September 2015 the Government agreed to accept several thousand refugees under a resettlement programme agreed by the EU, amid the **European migration crisis**, precipitated, in particular, by large numbers of migrants fleeing civil conflict in **Syria**. Poland, alone of the **Visegrad Group** of states, did not, at that time, vote against the imposition of mandatory quotas by the EU. This reflected the fact that the Government was still led by reformist centre-right party Civic Platform. However, with the election in late 2015 of a new, populist Government, under the Law and Justice party, pledges on immigration quotas were withdrawn. The new administration cited, in particular, security concerns in the wake of attacks linked to perpetrators affiliated with **Islamic State** in the French capital in mid-November. In January 2016 the new Polish Prime Minister, Beata Szydło, announced that Poland would take in no more than 400 refugees in that year.

Meanwhile, revisions to legislation on the judiciary and the media in late 2015 also prompted criticism from the European Commission. In 2017 judicial reforms that envisaged the dismissal of the entire Supreme Court, with the exception of those judges selected by the Minister of Justice, and the introduction of parliamentary powers permitting to the legislature to appoint members of the National Council of the Judiciary caused controversy. The proposed legislative changes directly challenged judicial independence and media freedom in Poland. In July 2017 the Commission threatened to halt Poland's voting rights within the EU if the judicial reform were passed. Poland's President, Andrzej Duma, intervened to veto two of three proposed pieces of legislation, but signed one into law. The bill receiving presidential approval allowed the Minister of Justice to select the heads of all lower courts, which the Polish public has widely judged still to limit judicial independence. Poland continues to challenge the EU, most recently dismissing EU demands temporarily to halt logging in a United Nations Educational, Scientific and Cultural Organization (UNESCO) World Heritage site, the ancient Białowieża forest.

POLICE AND JUDICIAL CO-OPERATION IN CRIMINAL MATTERS was the name given to Title VI of the **Treaty on European Union** prior to the **Treaty of Lisbon**. Originally known as **justice and home affairs**, this third pillar of the European Union (EU) was renamed by the **Treaty of Amsterdam**. The objective of police and judicial co-operation in criminal matters is to prevent and combat: problems of racism and xenophobia; terrorism; trafficking in human beings and crimes against children; drug trafficking; weapons trafficking; and corruption and fraud. Through **Europol**, the European Police Office, there is scope for closer co-operation between national police forces and customs and judicial authorities, co-operation in the latter area also being provided for through **Eurojust**. This co-operation may lead to closer approximation of rules on criminal matters in the member states. The Treaty of Lisbon transferred responsibility for such co-operation to the EU's supranational decision making procedures.

POLICY in the context of the European Union (EU) refers to the collectivity of proposals, initiatives and **legislation** intended to achieve EU aims in specific fields of activity.

The **POLICY PLANNING AND EARLY WARNING UNIT** was set up as part of the reforms to the **common foreign and security policy** (CFSP) introduced by the **Treaty of Amsterdam** in 1999. Its main role is to monitor and analyse developments in areas relevant to the CFSP, provide assessments of and early warning reports on issues of concern to the European Union, and prepare papers on options for policies. Personnel drawn from the member states, the **European Commission** and the **General Secretariat of the Council of the European Union** staff the unit.

The **POLITICAL AND SECURITY COMMITTEE** is the successor to the **Political Committee**. It was renamed and had its powers increased by the **Treaty of Nice**. Hence, acting under the responsibility of the **Council of the European Union**, the Committee exercises political control and strategic direction of crisis management operations undertaken by the European Union (EU). It may also be authorized to take specific implementing **decisions**. With the development of a more explicit defence dimension to the **common foreign and security policy**, the Committee has also provided support for the EU Military Staff, which is under the authority of the **European Union Military Committee**.

The **POLITICAL COMMITTEE** is the name of a body that had its origins in the committee of **Political Directors** originally charged with preparing the quarterly meetings of the member state foreign ministers under **European political co-operation**. It was formally established by the **Treaty on European Union** as part of the **common foreign and security policy** (CFSP). The tasks of the Political Committee, which was composed of the Political Directors, were to monitor the international situation in areas covered by the CFSP, and to advise and submit proposals to the **Council of the European Union** on foreign and security policy. In conjunction with the Council presidency, the Committee also had responsibility for implementing policies decided upon according to the CFSP structure. The **Treaty of Nice** enhanced the committee's powers and renamed it the **Political and Security Committee**.

POLITICAL CO-OPERATION: See **Common Foreign and Security Policy**; **European Political Co-operation**

POLITICAL DIRECTORS, each of whom is appointed by a member state as an aide to its foreign minister, are invariably senior diplomats. They formerly played an essential role in the operation of **European political co-operation**. Collectively, the Directors were responsible for the co-ordination and implementation of foreign policy initiatives, meeting monthly to review progress and urgent current issues. Under the **Single European Act**, the Directors were provided with their own secretariat in **Brussels**, and under the **Treaty on European Union**, they were formally constituted as a **Political Committee** with a major role in the **common foreign and security policy**. The **Treaty of Nice** enhanced the committee's powers and renamed it the **Political and Security Committee**. The responsibility for organizing the Directors belongs to the foreign ministry of the member state currently holding the presidency of the **Council of the European Union**, and therefore rotates between the Political Directors, changing every six months. The division of labour between the Directors and the **Committee of Permanent Representatives** is under constant review. The immediate subordinate of the Political Director, responsible for routine business, is known as the European Correspondent.

POLITICAL UNION: See **European Union**; **Maastricht Summit**; **Treaty on European Union**

PORTUGAL originally had no prospect of becoming a member of the European Communities (EC) as long as it remained under an authoritarian regime. In 1962, along with other members of the **European Free Trade Association**, Portugal approached the EC, but without specifying the form of association it desired. Negotiations had not begun when **France** vetoed the British application for entry, and Portugal's proposed schedule was abandoned. Discussions were not resumed until 1970, and a **free trade agreement** was signed in July 1972. After the 1974 revolution, the new Government expressed a desire for further co-operation with, and financial assistance from, the EC. A **protocol** to the free trade agreement, providing for financial aid, was signed in September 1976; further protocols were signed in 1979 and 1980. Portugal formally applied for full membership in March 1977. Progress on the negotiations was slow. Officially commencing in October 1978, they did not begin in earnest until 1980. While there were some problems between the two sides, the slowness of the negotiations was perhaps due more to the simultaneous negotiations with **Spain**, about whose application there were more substantive concerns among some member states. However, the two applications tended to be treated in conjunction with each other. The negotiations were concluded in March 1985, and Portugal joined the EC in January 1986. One of the poorest states in the European Union (EU), it has benefited substantially from the **structural funds**, the **Cohesion Fund** and other aid programmes. Portugal has generally been well disposed towards the EU, but in more recent times difficulties have arisen. In June 2005 the Portuguese Government was requested to cut its budget deficit to fall in line with EU rules on the **stability and growth pact**. Portugal's economy had certainly been in trouble, running into recession in 2003 and recording only 1% growth the following year. Unemployment reached an eight-year high (some 7.5%) in 2005. The Portuguese presidency of the **Council of the European Union** in the second half of 2007 culminated with the signing of the **Treaty of Lisbon**, which has since re-shaped the EU institutions and their decision making capabilities. The Portuguese Government decided not to hold a referendum on the treaty, and the Portuguese parliament ratified it with a strong majority in April 2008. The slump in Portugal's economy following the onset of the global financial crisis in 2008 led the Government to seek a bailout (of

€78,000m.) from the EU and the International Monetary Fund in April 2011—which was approved the following month—and to introduce a more stringent austerity programme in an attempt to bring the country's finances back under control. This move proved unpopular, especially given the drastic rise in the number of unemployed (which by April 2012 had almost reached 15%). Following the defeat in the legislature of further government austerity proposals, Prime Minister José Sócrates resigned in March 2011 and an early general election was scheduled for June. The Social Democrats, under Pedro Passos Coelho, triumphed in these polls, but remained committed to the austerity programme and participated in the negotiations leading to the signing of the Treaty on Stability, Co-ordination and Governance in the Economic and Monetary Union (**Fiscal Compact**) in March 2012. The current Prime Minister, following elections in 2015, is António Costa.

POTENTIAL CANDIDATE STATE, as opposed to candidate state, was the status assigned to the countries of the **Western Balkans** by the Feira **summit meeting** of the **European Council** in June 2000. The term has since been confirmed in the preambles to the **stabilization and association agreements**. It is to be assumed that a potential candidate state becomes a candidate state once it is admitted to the accession process.

A **PRE-ACCESSION STRATEGY** to help prepare countries from **Central and Eastern Europe** for membership of the European Union was launched in 1994 by the Essen **summit meeting** of the **European Council**. The idea was to build on the existing relationship based on the **Europe agreements** by intensifying co-operation and by outlining more precisely the steps necessary for meeting the obligations of membership, notably concerning adoption of the *acquis communautaire*. In 1998 the strategy was enhanced by the launch of **accession negotiations** and the conclusion of **accession partnerships**.

PREAMBLE refers to the opening recitals of a treaty. In the case of the European Union (EU), the preambles to the **founding treaties** outline the aims and purposes of the EU. The **Court of Justice**, in defining EU law, has often referred to preambles.

PREFERENTIAL TRADE AGREEMENTS signed by the European Union (EU) with other countries are intended to lead, within a reasonable period of time, to the establishment of either a free trade area or a **customs union**. This is a requirement that the **General Agreement on Tariffs and Trade** demanded of all preferential trade agreements. Those signed by the EU form part of the **common commercial policy** and fall into several categories: **trade and co-operation agreements**; **association agreements** (see also **Europe agreements** and **stabilization and association agreements**); the several individual and collective agreements signed with states bordering the Mediterranean; the **Cotonou Agreement** (see also the **Lomé Convention**); and **partnership and co-operation agreements**. In the majority of cases, the agreements are not restricted to purely economic matters.

The **PRELIMINARY RULING** procedure is a key element of the legal system of the European Union (EU). Under the procedure, a national court may refer a question about the meaning of an EU law to the **Court of Justice**. Once the Court issues its decision, it is applied to the relevant case by the national court.

PRESIDENCY: See **Council Presidency**

A **PRESIDENT OF THE EUROPEAN COUNCIL**, to be elected by the other members of the **European Council** for a term of two and a half years, was one of the institutional innovations originally contained in the **Treaty establishing a Constitution for Europe** and carried forward in the **Treaty of Lisbon**. The incumbent has five key tasks: chairing the European Council and driving forward its work; ensuring proper preparation for meetings and continuity in co-operation with the **European Commission** President; facilitating cohesion and consensus within the European Council; reporting to the **European Parliament** after each European Council meeting; and ensuring the external representation of the European Union on issues concerning the **common foreign and security policy**. The first person to occupy the position was Herman Van Rompuy, who assumed his post on 1 December 2009. He was re-elected to the post by the European Council on 1 March 2012, and his second (and last) term in office ran from 1 June 2012 to 30 November 2014. **Donald Tusk** of Poland succeeded him, and secured re-election to the post in March 2017.

PRICE-FIXING AGREEMENTS have been declared illegal by the **European Commission** on the grounds that they are contrary to the **competition policy** of the European Communities. The precedent was set in 1969 when the Commission successfully prosecuted the dyestuffs **cartel** that controlled some 80% of the European market at that time. Yet, price-fixing agreements remain an established fact of contemporary business activity across the European Union (EU). In recent years the European Commission has intensified its efforts to deter companies from engaging in such anti-competitive price-fixing arrangements. This resolve has seen a significant increase in the size of the fines imposed on companies that have deliberately sought to fix prices, as well as the adoption of **leniency notices**. In December 2002 the member states agreed to radical reforms (under regulation 1/2003) of the EU's anti-trust rules, which are designed to make it easier for the Commission to act against those seeking to fix prices. The new regime came into force in May 2004. The combating of cartels was identified by former Commissioner with responsibility for Competition, Neelie Kroes, as a particular focus of her term of office. One of the highest ever fines in the history of the Commission's war against cartel arrangements was levied against a number of truck manufacturers in 2017, and totalled some €2,966.5m. Price-fixing agreements remain a focus for the Commission.

The **PRIMACY OF EUROPEAN COMMUNITY LAW** is a doctrine established by the **European Court of Justice** in 1964. The case that provided this landmark decision was *Costa v Enel* and, when this decision is taken together with the doctrine of **direct effect**, it signifies nothing less than a complete metamorphosis of the nature and scope of European Communities (EC) law. These two doctrines transform the EC into a powerful means to advance the **supranational** idea and to challenge existing national law. A first formal reference to primacy of EU law was contained in a declaration adopted with the **Treaty of Lisbon**.

The **PRIVILEGES AND IMMUNITIES** of the European Communities (EC) were first laid down in a **protocol** of the 1965 **Merger Treaty**. It defined the privileges and immunities of all those who were members of, or who worked for, EC **institutions**. It further established the rights of the Communities themselves within the territory of the member states.

PRODUCTION QUOTAS can be imposed by the **European Commission** on the coal and steel industries. Under the powers it inherited from the High Authority of the **European Coal and Steel Community**, the Commission has the authority, if a state of manifest crisis is adopted, to impose quotas on individual companies. Severe production quotas were imposed upon steel companies in 1980, and were not abolished until June 1988. In the late 1980s, production quotas were also introduced into the **common agricultural policy**.

PROJECT EUROPE 2030: See **González Group**

PROPORTIONALITY, like **subsidiarity**, is a principle invoked to contain the accumulation of powers by the European Union (EU). In line with the principle of proportionality, the EU should not be taking any action that goes beyond the minimum necessary to achieve its objectives as laid down in the **European treaties**. Hence, proportionality is concerned with the scale and effect of any EU action.

A **PROTOCOL** is an additional element of a treaty. It either provides details of the implementation of treaty requirements or is too lengthy for inclusion in the treaty itself. However, protocols are equal in status to the main body of a treaty.

PROVISIONS is a term generally used in the context of the European Union to describe the contents of the **European treaties**.

The **PRÜM CONVENTION**, also known as the Treaty of Prüm or Schengen III, was signed in May 2005 by **Austria**, **Belgium**, **France**, **Germany**, **Luxembourg**, the **Netherlands** and **Spain**. It facilitates, for the purpose of combating terrorism, cross-border crime and illegal migration, the sharing between signatories of personal data (e.g. DNA, fingerprints). It builds on existing co-operation under the **Schengen Agreement** and on **police and judicial co-operation in criminal matters**.

PUBLIC HEALTH: See **Health Policy**

PUBLIC PROCUREMENT, although referred to in the **Treaty of Rome**, only emerged as a major objective after the Single European Market programme when a series of **directives** were introduced requiring all public contracts above a specific cost threshold to be open to competitive tender throughout the member states. The threshold varies according to the product or service involved, but is otherwise the same throughout the European Union.

PUBLIC SERVICES do not enjoy the privileged status within the European Union (EU) that some member states would like to see. Certainly their status often appears ambiguous. In principle, except where exemptions are approved, EU rules on **state aid** apply as much to public services as they do to commercial enterprises. That said, Article 16 of the **Treaty of Rome**, as introduced by the **Treaty of Amsterdam** (and now Article 14 of the **Treaty on the Functioning of the European Union**), draws particular attention to the role of 'services of general economic interest' and calls on the EU and the member states to 'take care that such services operate on the basis of principles and conditions which enable them to fulfil their missions'. The **Treaty of Lisbon** introduced a dedicated **protocol** on the subject.

The **PUBLICATIONS OFFICE OF THE EUROPEAN UNION**, which was formerly called the Office for Official Publications of the European Communities (EUR-OP), is based in Luxembourg. It is an agency of the **European Commission**, but provides services to, and is managed by, all European Union (EU) **institutions**. It is responsible for the publication and dissemination of EU publications, including official reports and pamphlets. These are available directly from the EU Bookshop and are also lodged in several educational institutions throughout the EU, which have been recognized as depositories for EU publications and are known as **European Documentation Centres**. The office also offers a number of online services giving free access to information on EU law (**EUR-Lex**), EU publications (EU Bookshop), public procurement (Tenders Electronic Daily —TED—the online format of the Supplement to the *Official Journal of the European Union*), and EU research and development (**CORDIS**—Community Research and Development Information Service).

Q

QMV: See **Qualified Majority Voting**

The **QUAD** comprises meetings between officials from the European Union, the **USA**, **Japan** and Canada, where multilateral trade issues are discussed. (See also **G-8**.)

QUAESTORS are five individuals elected from the ranks of the **Members of the European Parliament** (MEPs). They sit in an advisory capacity in the Bureau of the **European Parliament** and are responsible for financial and administrative matters affecting MEPs.

QUALIFIED MAJORITY VOTING (QMV) is one of the ways in which the **Council of the European Union** arrives at a decision on issues and proposals put before it. The vote is qualified in two ways. First, a qualified majority must be substantially in excess of 50%: traditionally, it has been more than two-thirds. Second, it is qualified in that it is based on a weighted voting system, where each member state has an indivisible block of votes at its disposal, the size of which is based roughly on the size of its population.

The **Treaty of Rome** envisaged that QMV would apply to most proposals after 1965. The **empty chair crisis** and the **Luxembourg Compromise** prevented the achievement of this objective. The possibilities for a greater use of QMV did not increase until the **Single European Act**. With the adoption of the **Treaty on European Union** and further **enlargement** of the European Union (EU), there was renewed pressure for an increase in the size of the minority that would be needed to obstruct a proposal, in the hope that this reform would speed up the process of integration. From January 1995, when the General Affairs and External Relations Council agreed on amendments to voting procedures in the Council which took into account the accession of three new member states, the total number of votes was 87, weighted as follows: **France**, **Germany**, **Italy** and the **United Kingdom** had 10 votes each; **Spain**, eight votes; **Belgium**, **Greece**, the **Netherlands** and **Portugal**, five votes each; **Austria** and **Sweden**, four votes each; **Denmark**, **Finland** and **Ireland**, three votes each; and **Luxembourg**, two votes. A qualified majority was constituted by 62 votes, and thus 26 votes were sufficient for a blocking minority. However, as a result of pressure from **Spain** and the UK, the so-called **Ioannina compromise** of March 1994 meant that 23–25 opposing votes ensured the continued discussion of proposed **legislation** by the Council for a 'reasonable' period until a consensus was obtained.

QMV was extended by the **Treaty of Amsterdam** into a number of areas previously subject to unanimous decision. The **European Parliament** was also to have the right of co-decision in these areas (see **co-decision procedure**). As the EU expanded, the use of qualified majority voting in a wider range of **decisions** was expected to minimize 'policy drag'. Under the terms of the **Treaty of Nice**, a further range of areas, mostly minor in nature and relating to appointments to various EU institutions (such as the **European Court of Auditors**), became subject to QMV. By 2002 most areas under pillar I were determined by QMV, although there were some notable exceptions, including decisions in the area of **economic and monetary union**.

With EU enlargement imminent there was general acceptance in the Council in the late 1990s that the voting procedures would have to be altered. Agreement would not be easy, given political sensitivities. Not surprisingly therefore, the issue was postponed at the Amsterdam **summit meeting** and agreement was finally reached, after a great deal of acrimony, at the Nice summit in December 2000. The Treaty of Nice had two major impacts. First, it complicated decision making by requiring a triple majority for a decision to be adopted by QMV. This comprises: first, a qualified majority of the weighted votes; second, a majority of the member states (which was already implicit under the existing regime); and, last, a demographic majority of at least 62% of the EU's total population. In effect, this new formula ensures that numbers and percentages have become more important in determining voting in the Council. It also increases the leverage of the larger EU states.

Second, the Treaty of Nice reformulated the votes for an EU of **Fifteen** and agreed the anticipated vote allocations for the **candidate countries** in an EU of **Twenty-Five**. These were subsequently confirmed in the **Accession Treaty**. Following the accession of **Romania** and **Bulgaria** in January 2007 and of **Croatia** in July 2013, the total number of votes in the Council was 352, weighted as follows: France, Germany, Italy and the UK had 29 votes each; Spain and **Poland**, 27 votes; Romania 14 votes; the Netherlands, 13; Belgium, the **Czech Republic**, Greece, **Hungary** and Portugal, 12 votes each; Austria, Bulgaria and Sweden, 10 votes each; Croatia, Denmark, Finland, Ireland, **Lithuania** and **Slovakia**, seven votes each; **Cyprus**, **Estonia**, **Latvia**, Luxembourg and **Slovenia**, four votes each; and **Malta**, three votes. A qualified majority could now be attained with 260 votes by at least 15 member states. From 1 November 2014, in accordance with the terms of the **Treaty of Lisbon**, the existing QMV system was replaced by a **double majority voting** system, under which an act is required to have the support of at least 55% of the member states (i.e. 16 member states in a Union of 28) and at least 65% of the population of the EU. A blocking minority must include at least four member states. However, the previous rules remained applicable until 2017 at the request of a member state.

The **QUALITY OF LIFE AND MANAGEMENT OF LIVING RESOURCES PROGRAMME** superseded existing programmes covering agricultural research (i.e. **FAIR**), biomedicine and health (Biomed) and biotechnology (**Biotech**) in 1998. The programme, which ran until 2002 and had a budget of €2,413m., supported research carried out by industry or educational establishments in member states and non-member states in all areas of the life sciences, including infectious diseases, nutrition, environment and health, sustainable agriculture, ageing, public health and neurosciences.

QUANTITATIVE RESTRICTIONS: See **Quota Restrictions**

QUOTA RESTRICTIONS on internal trade in the European Communities (EC) were abolished by the **Six** by 1968. Later entrants to the EC were allowed a transitional period of between four and six years in which to complete the process of abolition. In external trade, quota restrictions have been removed by many of the international agreements that the European Union has signed with other countries. They still exist, however, in certain areas such as agriculture and textiles, and for specified manufactured goods from some countries. For example, under the **common agricultural policy**, milk quotas were introduced in 1984 as a means of stabilizing milk production.

R

RACE (Research and Development in Advanced Communications Technologies in Europe) was a major **European Commission** initiative launched in 1987 and aimed at ensuring that the European Communities remained at the forefront of developments in the **telecommunications** sector and continued to be competitive. It complemented the **European strategic programme for research and development in information technology** (ESPRIT) and other more specific information technology projects; ACTS (Advanced Communications Technology and Services) replaced it in 1994.

RAILWAYS have not been a prominent element of European Union (EU) **transport policy**. While accepting that state subsidies are in conflict with **competition policy**, the EU has agreed to the public service function of railways, and policy has been designed to make the railways more competitive with other forms of transport. Infrastructure development has been at the centre of EU involvement in the railways, particularly within the context of efforts to develop **Trans-European Networks**.

RAPHAEL was a cultural programme that supported natural heritage activities, including co-operation between European Union museums, training for cultural heritage professionals, and the study, preservation and enhancement of European heritage. It was introduced in 1997 for three years (with a budget of €30m.), after which it was subsumed into the **Culture 2000** framework programme. (See also Kaleidoscope.).

RAPPORTEUR is the title given to the **Member of the European Parliament** responsible for drafting and presenting a report to a committee and to the plenary session of the **European Parliament**.

RATIFICATION refers to the process of approval of a treaty (such as one of the **European treaties**, or an **Accession Treaty**, or an external relations agreement) by the member states according to the rules and procedures established by their own constitutions. In certain member states (i.e. **Denmark**, **Ireland**) this has often involved a referendum. Treaties and agreements requiring ratification cannot come into force unless ratified by all the member states. In the case of an **accession treaty** or an **association agreement**, ratification also involves the **European Parliament** giving its approval via the consent procedure.

RATIFICATION CRISES is the term given to the political crises that have followed the popular rejection of a Treaty. The first ratification crisis came after the Danish 'no' to the **Treaty on European Union** (TEU) in June 1992, a crisis that intensified when the French people only narrowly gave their support to the TEU in a referendum three months later. The Danish 'no' was later overturned by popular endorsement of the TEU in a further referendum in May 1993. A second ratification crisis occurred following the rejection by Irish voters of the **Treaty of Nice** in June 2001. The response was to hold a second referendum in the latter half of 2002, when the original result was overturned by a vote in favour of the treaty. A third crisis, and the most major to date, occurred when the **Treaty establishing a Constitution for Europe** was rejected by French and Dutch voters in the first half of 2005. This led to the formal abandonment of the treaty. Much of its content was subsequently included in the **Treaty of Lisbon**. This treaty, in turn, was the focus of a fourth ratification crisis following a clear-cut 'no' in the Irish referendum in June 2008. This crisis involved various challenges and delays in three other states: **Germany**, **Poland** and the **Czech Republic**. All member states ultimately ratified the treaty, and it came into force on 1 December 2009.

RDE: See **Group of the European Democratic Alliance**

RECOMMENDATIONS are one of two kinds of non-binding pronouncement that may be issued by the **Council of the European Union** and the **European Commission**. Like **opinions**, they do not constitute instructions, but merely express the preference of the European Union (EU), and may be disregarded by the member states. Recommendations made according to the provisions of the **Treaty of Paris** were slightly different, however: they were binding upon member states as to the final result, but not the means of achieving it, and were thus more similar to EU **directives**. (See also **legislation**.)

REDISTRIBUTIVE POLICIES are those policies of the European Union (EU) that primarily involve the redistribution of resources from the richer to the less developed areas of the EU as part of the process of promoting economic and social cohesion. Such policies are generally financed from the **structural and cohesion funds**. Also included under the broad heading of redistributive policies are those policies that involve financial support being given to particular areas of production, for example, agriculture (via the **common agricultural policy**) and fisheries (via the **common fisheries policy**).

The **REFERENCE PRICE** is of importance in the **common agricultural policy**. It is the average price calculated from the market prices for fruit and vegetables in each member state. If the price of **foodstuffs** imported into the European Union is lower than the reference price, the imports incur a levy to raise their price to the same level.

REFERENDA on European Union (EU) issues play an increasingly important role in the European integration process. Countries joining the EU have tended to submit the terms of accession to their people for approval, while some member states have sought popular support, often in line with a constitutional requirement, for several of the more recent **European treaties** such as the **Treaty on European Union** (TEU) and the **Treaty of Nice**. In the case of referenda on accession to the EU, the outcome of a referendum has always been respected. The Norwegian Government, for example, has been forced twice to abandon plans to join the European Communities and the EU following a 'no' vote. By contrast, where a member state's electorate rejected the TEU or the Treaty of Nice and therefore brought about a **ratification crisis**, a second referendum was held. Nine of the 10 **candidate countries** that joined in May 2004 held a referendum on EU membership. In each case the outcome was positive.

Following the adoption of the **Treaty establishing a Constitution for Europe** in 2004 the EU geared itself up for what amounted to the most important series of referenda. A total of 10 member states (the **Czech Republic**, **Denmark**, **France**, **Ireland**, **Luxembourg**, the **Netherlands**, **Poland**, **Portugal**, **Spain** and the **United Kingdom**) had pledged to hold a referendum on **ratification** of the new treaty, and it was generally assumed, on the basis of early opinion polls, that the treaty would be endorsed by the public where and when it was put to a referendum. However, events took a rather different course. The first of the referenda took place in Spain in February 2005, with the treaty being approved, but the rejections of the treaty in France and the Netherlands (two of the founding member states of the EU) in the first half of 2005 put an end to the treaty altogether as all member states needed to endorse the Constitution, whether by referendum or by parliament or by both, in order for it to come into effect. The UK initially simply postponed its planned referendum after the French and Dutch votes. It was left to the **European Council** to consider how to proceed as the Treaty establishing a Constitution for Europe had held some very valuable alterations to existing decision making instruments. After much internal debate, it was decided to scale back the contents of the rejected treaty and to produce an amending treaty to incorporate many of the principal elements. A new text that bore considerable resemblance to the Treaty establishing a Constitution for Europe was agreed and the **Treaty of Lisbon** was signed in December 2007. Only Ireland was scheduled to hold a referendum on the text. Victory for the 'no' campaign in Ireland in June 2008 led to the latest in a succession of **ratification crises** for the EU. In the UK the Conservative Party continued to demand a referendum on the Treaty of Lisbon (even though the treaty had been approved by both Houses of Parliament) until the 'yes' vote in the second Irish referendum on the Treaty of Lisbon in October 2009.

On taking office in 2010, the Conservative-Liberal Democrat coalition Government in the UK introduced in Parliament an 'EU Bill' designed to subject future amending treaties and other major decisions affecting the UK's position within the EU to a referendum; this bill became law in July 2011. The move followed an amendment to the French Constitution to establish the referendum as the default means by which France would, once **Croatia** had joined the EU, ratify each future **accession treaty**. On 23 June 2016 the UK held a referendum to decide whether to remain a member of the EU; the unexpected vote in favour of **Brexit** prompted the immediate resignation of Prime Minister **David Cameron**.

REFERRALS: See **Court of Justice**

A **REFLECTION GROUP** (or Comité des Sages) is established by the **European Commission** to consider reforms to the European Union (EU). The first such group consisted of representatives of the ministers of foreign affairs of the member states and of the **European Parliament** and European Commission. It was responsible for preparing the agenda of the 1996 **intergovernmental conference**, which resulted in the **Treaty of Amsterdam**. A more recent group, the **González Group**, was established in December 2008 with the goal of identifying how best the EU could 'more effectively anticipate and meet challenges in the longer term horizon of 2020 to 2030'. It presented its report, called *Project Europe 2030*, to the European Council in May 2010. In another example, in April 2010 the European Commission set up a reflection group on the digitization, online accessibility and preservation of cultural works across Europe; the group presented its report, entitled *The New Renaissance*, in January 2011.

A **REFORM TREATY** was the planned outcome of the **intergovernmental conference** called by the **European Council** in June 2007. Having concluded negotiations, the **member states** dropped the 'Reform Treaty' title and instead decided to name the new treaty the **Treaty of Lisbon**.

REFUGEE POLICY forms part of the European Union's **migration and asylum policy** and is a relatively new area of competence of the European Union. Explicit reference to refugees in the **founding treaties** came with the **Treaty of Amsterdam** and the goal of creating an **area of freedom, security and justice**. This placed emphasis on adopting measures to ease the sharing of the burden of incoming refugees, and on proceeding in accordance with the 1951 Geneva Convention and the 1967 **protocol** concerning refugees, as well as on consulting with the United Nations High Commissioner for Refugees. (See also **European migration crisis; Immigration policy**.)

REGIONAL FUND COMMITTEE: See **European Regional Development Fund**

REGIONAL POLICY was not specifically covered by the **Treaty of Rome**, although the **Preamble** refers to the need to reduce 'the differences existing between the various regions and the backwardness of the less favoured regions', while a special **protocol** stated that the Italian *Mezzogiorno* (the southern half of the country) was a European responsibility. Pressure for a regional policy grew in the late 1960s and early 1970s, firstly because of increasing pessimism about the rate of economic growth, and secondly because of **enlargement**, with the **United Kingdom** and **Ireland** joining **Italy** in insisting upon a regional policy. Although formally established in 1973, regional policy did not acquire a high profile as a European Communities (EC) activity until the enlargements of the 1980s.

The **European Commission** has the responsibility of developing policy relating to the regions. The targets of European Union (EU) regional policy are two-fold: underdeveloped rural areas with low levels of agricultural modernization and high levels of unemployment or underemployment; and industrialized regions in rapid decline. The bulk of the spending is directed towards those regions with a gross domestic product below 75% of the EU average. To secure the modernization or renewal of these regions, EU policy has three strands. In addition to providing aid for the development of poorer regions, the Commission seeks to co-ordinate the regional policies of member states and secure a co-ordinated approach to regional problems in all relevant EU policy concerns.

The principal element of regional policy is the financial programme, channelled primarily through the **European Regional Development Fund** (ERDF), which was established in 1975 and funded from the EC **budget**. The other **structural and cohesion funds** of the EU are also required to maintain a strong regional focus in their own areas of concern. A number of further special regional programmes have been launched by the European Commission to deal with the problems of regions that are economically coherent, but divided politically between two or more member states, and several attempts have been made to ensure that the poorer regions benefit from, and participate in, technological developments and programmes. To ensure co-ordination across all these investment activities, the Commission monitors and reviews the socio-economic state of the regions on a regular basis, and undertakes analyses of the regional impact of all EU policies. With respect to the regional policies of the member states, the Commission is concerned to avoid duplication or waste of resources. Maximum limits have been established for the financial inducements that governments may offer to potential industrial investors in the poorer regions: the limits vary according to the nature of the particular regional problem. The resources of the structural funds have been directed more towards integrated programmes that link together various elements of a region's needs rather than isolated and discrete development projects. Financial resources are distributed under the terms of various agreements, or Community Support Frameworks, between the Commission and the member states. Regional policy was formally recognized in the **Single European Act**, which identified it as a major element in developing the socio-economic cohesion of the EC. Its centrality was further emphasized by the **Treaty on European Union**, particularly by the establishment of a **Cohesion Fund** and the commitment to **Trans-European Networks**.

The EU has used its more recent enlargements to re-examine its regional policy and to analyse where the monies are spent and whether they could be spent more effectively. Regional policy remains a commitment of the EU. In 2007–13 some 36% of the entire EU budget was allocated to this area, representing some €348,000m. over seven years, and regional policy was to be targeted to tackle convergence, **competitiveness**, employment and co-operation. These are known collectively as **cohesion policy**. Priority in terms of regional policy spending has shifted eastwards over the last decade or so and towards the countries of **Central and Eastern Europe**. Indeed, the 12 states that joined between 2004 and 2007 secured 51% of the overall receipts even though these countries made up only one-quarter of the entire

EU population. The money available is divided into three separate funds: the ERDF to enhance infrastructure projects; the **European Social Fund** to help provide vocational training projects and other employment assistance initiatives; and the Cohesion Fund, which targets environmental and transport projects.

REGIONAL POLICY COMMITTEE: See **European Regional Development Fund**

REGIONS: See **Cohesion Policy; Committee of the Regions; European Regional Development Fund; Nomenclature of Territorial Units for Statistics; Regional Policy**

REGULATIONS are one of three different types of **legal instrument** that the **European Commission** and **Council of the European Union** are empowered to issue. Regulations are the highest, most rigorous form of **legislation**. They are fairly detailed instructions, applicable throughout the European Union, and are directly binding upon all member states. (See also **decisions**; **directives; law; opinions; recommendations; resolutions**.)

REGULATORY POLICIES are those policies of the European Union based on regulations designed to achieve specific, and generally **internal market**-orientated, policies. Most prominent among them are **competition policy** and **environmental policy** and measures to promote **health and safety**.

RESEARCH AND DEVELOPMENT IN ADVANCED COMMUNICATIONS TECHNOLOGIES IN EUROPE: See **RACE**

RESEARCH AND TECHNOLOGICAL DEVELOPMENT (RTD) POLICY and the application of new technologies, apart from the sponsoring of research in the nuclear area through the **European Atomic Energy Community** (Euratom), received relatively little attention until the 1980s. They remained very much an issue, however, for the various member states. The lack of a European-level policy led to both duplication of effort and, often, missed opportunities. More importantly, high-level research is increasingly complex and costly. Observing that the majority of items such as microcomputers and video recorders used in the European Communities (EC) were imported, the **European Commission** intensified its efforts to encourage technological and collaborative research, to foster and promote research networks and teams at the European level in order to permit the EC to remain economically competitive.

The main objective of European Union (EU) research and development policy is to amalgamate the many projects and individuals conducting research in the member states into collaborative programmes that involve companies, universities and research institutes. The focus is not so much on basic research as on the development of new technologies that can more appropriately be co-ordinated at EU level, and that will provide products for existing and new markets. The **European Strategic Programme for Research and Development in Information Technology** (ESPRIT), adopted in 1984, marked a real turning point and was swiftly followed by the first framework for research and technological development. The **Single European Act** made science a Community responsibility. A second framework programme identifying several priority areas for research was adopted in 1987, and in 1988 a monitoring system was introduced in the form of Strategic Analysis, Forecasting and Evaluation in Matters of Research and Technology (MONITOR). The importance of research and development was confirmed by the **Treaty on European Union**, and further general framework programmes that extended the list of priority research areas were adopted in 1990, 1993 and 1998. In just over a decade the budgets for these programmes had grown substantially, from €3,250m. for the first programme to €13,215m. for the fourth (1994–98). Overall, the 1990s heralded the emergence and increasing salience of EU RTD policy and this ensured the inclusion of this theme on the agenda of a series of **European Council** summits. For example, the **summit meeting** in Lisbon in March 2000 acknowledged that European research and development needed to develop before the EU could legitimately claim to be the most competitive and dynamic knowledge-based economy in the world.

The Sixth Framework Programme (FP6), for 2002–06, allocated €15,000m. to RTD, and was much more ambitious in scope than its predecessors. It sought to integrate research in priority areas (through the creation of centres of excellence) and to create and structure a European Research Area. To maximize its impact, the framework programme focused its attention on a limited number of research areas—technological, economic, social and cultural, among others. These considered the quality of life; a user-friendly **information society**; competitive and sustainable growth; energy and the environment; improving human resource potential; and the promotion of innovation and growth of small and medium-sized enterprises. Since their launch in 1984 it is clear that the six framework programmes have played an instrumental role in producing multi-disciplinary research and forging cross-national research teams and networks across the EU and beyond. The Seventh Framework Programme (FP7), which covered the period 2007–13, was the biggest and most ambitious to date and RTD (or, as it was also referred to, research and innovation) was allocated a **budget** of €50,500m. The five designated RTD themes within FP7 were: co-operation (ensuring greater collaboration between industry and the university sector as a means of providing leadership in key technologies); ideas (supporting and fostering scientific research); people (especially supporting mobility and career development for researchers); capacities (developing the necessary means to create and maintain a thriving knowledge-based economy); and, lastly, nuclear research (where it was hoped to advance Europe's nuclear fission and fusion programmes). The programme also contained some significant differences from its predecessors, notably a substantially larger budget allocation. There was now also the first pan-European agency, the European Research Council, which was to take responsibility for funding scientific research. In addition, a new risk-sharing finance facility was created to assist private investors seeking to engage in research projects by providing them with greater access to loans from the **European Investment Bank**. Finally, a single helpdesk was set up to serve as the first point of contact for anyone who wished to find out more about the activities and operations of FP7. Under the Eighth Framework Programme (2014–20), the financial instrument for research and innovation was **Horizon 2020**, which was allocated a budget of some €80,000m. (See also **Biotech; ESPRIT; RACE**.)

RESEARCH FRAMEWORK PROGRAMMES are the principal means through which the European Union implements its **Research and Technological Development (RTD) Policy**. Each programme consists of a variety of specific projects.

RESOLUTIONS are statements of principle adopted by the **Council of the European Union** on the recommendation of the **European Commission**. While indicating governments' agreement or willingness to act, they have no basis in the **founding treaties** of the European Communities and are not legally binding upon the member states. (See also **opinions**; **recommendations**.)

RESTITUTIONS form an essential part of the **common agricultural policy** (CAP). They are the export **subsidies** or refunds that allow European Union (EU) agricultural produce to be competitive on world markets, where prices are usually lower. EU exporters receive restitutions to make up the difference between what they must pay to CAP producers and the lower prices at which they must sell on the world markets. Restitutions have been one of the most controversial elements of the CAP, because in the past they consumed up to 30% of the **expenditure** made through the Guarantee Section of the **European Agricultural Guidance and Guarantee Fund**. This figure was later reduced to some 15% of expenditure.

REVENUE accrues to the European Union (EU) from a variety of sources. Initially, the European Communities (EC) were financed by contributions from member states based upon the gross national product (GNP) of each member state. The **European Commission** argument that the EC should have their own sources of revenue was one of the contributing factors to the 1965 **empty chair crisis**. In 1970 the member states agreed that a system of **own resources** should progressively replace that of national contributions, with the change to be completed by 1975. The EU now has its own resources to finance its **expenditure**. These form the basis of the EU's own tax revenues, which automatically accrue to it without the need for any subsequent decision by national authorities. In other words, while the own resources would be collected by the member states, the revenue would belong as of right to the EU.

In terms of revenue, own resources consist of several elements. The first is levies and duties on imports, comprising customs duties on finished products and a levy on agricultural imports to raise their price to the level set by the **common agricultural policy** (CAP). The second, which soon became the most important source of revenue, was a proportion of the **value-added tax** (VAT) imposed by the member states. The VAT contributions that would accrue to the EC were set at a maximum of 1.0% of the final selling price of a common base of goods and services. By the early 1980s this revenue was proving insufficient to meet demands and, after much argument, the VAT maximum level was raised to 1.4% in 1986. This still proved to be insufficient, and annual deficits in the EC **budget** had to be covered by non-refundable contributions from the member states. The reform of the Community's finances took another step in June 1988 when the **European Council** approved a new category of revenue, which was based on GNP. This new revenue source provided the necessary funds for the **Delors I** package in 1989. To contain the growth of the resources taken up by the Community, the European Council decision set an overall ceiling rising to 1.2% of total Community GNP in 1992. This figure was applied for both 1993 and 1994. From 1994 a new decision on the own resources raised the ceiling of the GNP contribution to 1.21% and, in stages, to 1.27% of GNP by 1999. During this period the uniform VAT rate was gradually reduced from 1.4% to 1.0%.

In terms of EU budgetary calculations and expectations, gross national income (GNI) has widely replaced GNP in Commission documentation as an indicator of income. This alteration took effect in 2002. In order to maintain, unchanged, the cash value of the ceiling of EU revenue referred to as the 'own resources ceiling', it became necessary to recalculate it in percentage terms. It was established at 1.24% of GNI instead of the previous 1.27% of EU GNP. (By means of a definition, GNI at market prices represents total primary income receivable by resident institutional units: compensation of employees, taxes on production and imports less subsidies, property income—receivable less payable, operating surplus and mixed income. GNI equals GDP minus primary income payable by resident units to non-resident units plus primary income receivable by resident units from the rest of the world.)

Total revenue during the 1990s increased from **ecu** 47,000m. in 1990 to €93,000m. by 2002. With the prospect of **enlargement**, the estimated costs of admitting more member states ranged from €4,000m. to €38,000m. for the CAP alone, plus an estimated €30,000m. for the **structural and cohesion funds**. There was an expectation that total revenue would have to rise significantly. Reluctance on the part of member states to increase contributions meant, however, that greater emphasis was placed on reforming policies. Hence, according to the budgetary perspective for 2000–06 agreed at the Berlin European Council in March 1999, revenue was set to remain at or below existing levels. This **summit meeting** reached a political consensus on the EU budget and own resources and the Council adopted a new own resources decision in September 2000 that became effective in January 2002. This saw further reduction of the VAT resource ceiling, which in 2004 stood at 0.5%, and a reduction of the ceiling for GNI contribution to 1.24%. In 2010 the own resources ceiling stood at 1.23% of GNI. In the 2016 EU budget GNI-based own resources accounted for 72.9% of total revenue of €143,885m., while VAT-based own resources accounted for 13.1%. Owing to the ongoing **eurozone** financial crisis, in February 2013 the Council of the European Union agreed to reduce the budget for the Multi-Annual Financial Framework Programme (MFF) for 2014–20. In March 2013, however, the **European Parliament** (EP) rejected the budget agreement, demanding some €14,000m. from member states to cover arrears in payments, which had accumulated over the course of preceding budgets. Further negotiations subsequently took place, and new proposals for the MFF for 2014–20 were submitted unsuccessfully for endorsement by the European Parliament and the Council in late June 2013. Tensions between the Council and the EP persisted for the rest of the year and agreement on the arrangements for the new MFF were only finally approved in January 2014.

The **RIGHT OF ESTABLISHMENT**, as laid down in the **Treaty of Rome**, confers on nationals of one member state the right to set up business operations in another member state. It is a key principle underpinning the **internal market** and the free movement of services.

The **RIGHT OF INITIATIVE** within the European Union (EU) has traditionally been the preserve of the **European Commission**, it being the only institution that could formally initiate **legislation**. Since the **Treaty on European Union**, however, this is no longer technically the case. The **European Central Bank** has a right of initiative in certain areas concerning **economic and monetary union**, and member states were to enjoy a right of initiative over measures concerning asylum, immigration and border controls until 2004. The right of initiative under the common foreign and security policy and police and judicial co-operation in criminal matters pillars of the EU is shared by the European Commission and the member states. The **European Parliament** has no formal right of initiative, but can request that the European Commission submit a proposal under the **Treaty of Rome**. The **Treaty of Lisbon** introduced a right of initiative for EU citizens, thereby increasing their participation in the EU decision making process. It enables them, through the acquisition of at least 1m. signatures from a significant number of member states, to put proposals to the Commission.

ROAD TRANSPORT is the area of European Union **transport policy** where the **European Commission** has been most active. Most initiatives have been concerned with conditions of employment and road safety. Rules covering, for example, training and minimum rest periods have existed since the 1970s, and the ensuing decade saw the introduction of a common standard for the weight and dimensions of commercial vehicles, maximum limits for the axle weights of articulated vehicles, and several **directives** concerning road safety. More recently, the focus of road transport measures has been the deregulation of national licensing and quota systems governing inter-state road freight. A transitional road freight system of *cabotage* (the right to ply for hire in another country) was agreed to in 1993 (and updated in 2006 and 2010), and in 1999 a directive was issued introducing distance-related tolls and a *vignette* (a time-based user charge) for heavy goods vehicles, which would raise funds for distribution among the member states most affected by road transport.

ROMANIA concluded a trade and economic **co-operation agreement** with the European Communities in 1990, and a **Europe agreement** was signed in 1993, coming into effect in 1995. Although Romania applied for membership of the European Union (EU) in the same year, the **European Commission** recommended in 1997 that **accession negotiations** be deferred, owing to the need primarily for further economic reform in Romania. Its report stated that 'a considerable amount of work is still needed on environment, transport, employment, social affairs, home affairs, justice, and agriculture, and substantial reform is essential to provide Romania with the structures it needs for effective application and enforcement of the full body of Community law'. Subsequent reports made similar calls for further reform so that Romania could meet all the **accession criteria**. All the same, in 1999 Romania was invited to start accession negotiations. Despite the public commitment of a new Government elected in 2000 to speed up integration with the EU, progress in the negotiations was the slowest of all **candidate countries** involved. By the end of 2003, only 22 of the 31 negotiating chapters had been closed. As a consequence, Romania did not join the EU as part of the 2004 **enlargement**. By the end of that year, however, it had concluded the outstanding chapters. A **Treaty of Accession** followed in April 2005, which envisaged Romania joining the EU alongside **Bulgaria** on 1 January 2007. However, concerns persisted about the country's preparedness for membership. With this in mind, it was agreed that accession could be delayed, through a decision by a qualified majority of the member states, if Romania failed to address EU concerns, particularly regarding corruption, state aid (see **subsidies**) policy and border controls. Three monitoring reports followed before it was finally confirmed that accession would take place on 1 January 2007. Romania duly entered the EU on that date. Between 26 September 2005 and 31 December 2006 Romania had 35 observer members in the **European Parliament** (EP), who were appointed from government and opposition parties, as agreed by the Romanian Parliament. Following the country's accession on 1 January 2007 the observers became **Members of the European Parliament** (MEPs), who contested the elections to the EP held in June 2009. Upon Romania's accession to the EU, many existing EU member states imposed extensive labour market restrictions; only nine countries guaranteed unlimited access to migrant workers from Bulgaria and Romania; however, all transitional migration restrictions were lifted from 1 January 2014. Alongside Romania's membership, however, came domestic political crises, post-accession monitoring by the Commission of progress in terms of compliance with judicial reform and anti-corruption measures, and further demands for action to be taken in these areas. The Romanian parliament approved the Treaty on Stability, Co-ordination and Governance in the Economic and Monetary Union (**Fiscal Compact**) in May 2012 and it was granted presidential approval one month later. In early 2017 widespread protests took place in Romania against planned reforms, which had appeared to reverse anti-corruption legislation. In May, during a visit to the Romanian capital Bucharest, **Jean-Claude Juncker**, the President of the European Commission, praised those who participated in the protests, describing corruption as a 'national evil'.

The **ROYAUMONT PROCESS** was launched in 1995 as a European Union-sponsored effort to promote stability and good neighbourliness in the **Western Balkans**. It has since been subsumed within the **Stabilization and Association Process**.

RRF: See **European Rapid Reaction Force**

The **RUSSIAN FEDERATION**'s relations with the European Union (EU) were based on a **partnership and co-operation agreement** (PCA) concluded in June 1994, providing for closer political, cultural and economic relations, which entered into force in December 1997. This PCA followed an earlier agreement in 1993 on the establishment of regular political dialogue. This led to annual summits between the President of the **European Commission**, the EU's **High Representative for the Common Foreign and Security Policy** and the Russian President. The PCA was complemented by the adoption in 1999 by the **Council of the European Union** of a **common strategy** on EU-Russia relations. The strategy placed emphasis on assisting with the promotion of political and economic stability within Russia and the development of a market-based economy, as well as addressing common challenges relating to the environment, crime and illegal immigration. To these ends, financial assistance was made available under the **Technical Assistance to the Commonwealth of Independent States** programme, although there were demands for such assistance and the PCA to be suspended over Russia's handling of the Chechnya conflict; the EU generally resisted these. Nevertheless, the relationship—as a Commission report in 2004 highlighted—did not develop as positively as envisaged. There were major disagreements over whether negotiations should be opened on upgrading the EU-Russia trade relationship to a free trade area, over access in an enlarged EU for Russian citizens to the exclave of **Kaliningrad**, over **ratification** of the Kyoto Protocol, and over the extension of the PCA to the 10 **candidate countries** that joined the EU in 2004. Such differences threatened to undermine progress in achieving the strategic objective of EU-Russia relations as set out in St Petersburg in May 2003: a common economic space, a common space of freedom, security and justice, a common space of co-operation in the field of external security, and a common space of research and education, including culture. A set of Road Maps for the development of these common spaces (which Russia chose to pursue rather than joining the EU's **European Neighbourhood Policy**) was adopted in May 2005 at an EU-Russia summit in Moscow, but progress was limited. Initial plans for a replacement for the PCA also made little progress, leaving the PCA, renewed annually on a rolling basis, to continue to provide an inadequate legal basis for relations. At a summit held in the Russian town of Rostov in June 2010 the two sides drew up a Partnership for Modernisation, which covered all aspects of modernization—economic, technical (including standards and regulations), rule of law and the functioning of the judiciary. Meanwhile, a mandate for a new agreement covering trade and co-operation to replace the PCA was eventually agreed by EU member states in May 2008. Negotiations, expected to be protracted, began the following month. They were suspended, however, as a result of the Russia–Georgia conflict of 2008. Russia subsequently agreed to withdraw its troops from Georgia by mid-October. By 2011 Russia was the third largest trading partner of the **Twenty-Eight**, and the value of EU exports to Russia in that year was €108,400m., having been only €22,700m. in 2000. Russia's exports to the EU in 2011 were worth €199,500m. (€130,000m. of which was oil and €24,000m. natural gas), giving the EU a trade deficit of €91,100m. Relations between the EU and Russia have remained guarded, and have come under considerable strain following developments in **Ukraine** since 2013. In March 2014 the EU imposed travel bans and asset freezes against Russian and Ukrainian officials, in response to the destabilization of Ukraine and Russia's annexation of Crimea; these sanctions were later strengthened. Sanctions against the Russian Federation were extended in mid-2017. Regular bilateral talks with Russia have been suspended since 2014, as a result of that country's involvement in the conflict in eastern Ukraine.

S

SAA: See **Stabilization and Association Agreements**

SAFETY: See **Health and Safety**

SANCTIONS and their collective imposition against specific countries were accepted by the member states as a valuable element of their collaboration on foreign policy under **European political co-operation**. European Union (EU) sanctions have been applied on numerous occasions over the years. However, it is debatable whether any had the desired effect upon the embargoed countries, or whether they were not much more than symbolic gestures of EU solidarity. In addition, not all member states are willing to participate in a collective imposition of sanctions against a named country. In 2000 sanctions were imposed against Austria following the inclusion of the far-right Freedom Party under Jörg Haider in the Austrian Government. The sanctions were strongly resented in Austria and fuelled anti-EU feeling; they were lifted within six months. More recently, in March 2014 the EU imposed sanctions against officials from both the **Russian Federation** and **Ukraine**, in response to the destabilization of Ukraine and Russia's annexation of Crimea; the sanctions were subsequently strengthened.

SAPARD was the acronym of the Special Accession Programme for Agriculture and Rural Development, a programme of the European Union (EU) operating in the **candidate countries** of **Central and Eastern Europe** in order to prepare their agricultural sectors for membership of the EU. Following the **enlargement** of May 2004, when 10 candidate countries became members, SAPARD continued with a budget of €225.2m. for **Bulgaria** and **Romania** in 2004. SAPARD came under the remit of the Directorate-General for Agriculture, and covered 2000 to 2006. From 1 January 2007 SAPARD was replaced by the **instrument for pre-accession assistance**.

The **SCHENGEN AGREEMENT** is the name of a document originally signed by five founder members of the European Communities in the town of Schengen, Luxembourg, on 14 June 1985. The Schengen Convention was signed in June 1990. Under the Agreement, **Belgium**, **France**, the Federal Republic of **Germany**, **Luxembourg** and the **Netherlands** agreed in principle to work towards the formation of a border-free **Schengen Area**. The Agreement was implemented with effect from March 1995 by the original five signatories, along with **Portugal** and **Spain**. Frontier controls at airports on travellers between the countries were dismantled. However, France continued to impose border controls on countries other than Spain and Germany. **Italy**, **Austria**, **Greece**, **Denmark**, **Finland** and **Sweden** (along with non-member states **Norway** and **Iceland**) later became signatories. Of the then **Fifteen**, **Ireland** and the **United Kingdom** remained outside the Schengen Area.

Although the Schengen Agreement began as an international agreement outside the framework of the European Union (EU), it was incorporated into the **Treaty of Rome** and the **Treaty on European Union** following provisions contained in the **Treaty of Amsterdam** as part of moves to create a common area without frontiers. The UK and Ireland negotiated an **opt-out** and were allowed to retain jurisdiction over their borders and rules of asylum and immigration. In May 2000 the British Government secured agreement in the **Council of the European Union** that enabled the country to participate in substantial parts of the Schengen *acquis,* particularly in relation to the creation and operation of the **Schengen Information System**; Ireland did likewise. In 2005 seven member states signed the **Prüm Convention**, known as Schengen III, on data exchange for the purpose of combating terrorism, cross-border crime and illegal migration. On 21 December 2007 the Schengen Area was enlarged to include nine of the member states that joined the EU in 2004: the **Czech Republic**, **Estonia**, **Hungary**, **Latvia**, **Lithuania**, **Malta**, **Poland**, **Slovenia** and **Slovakia**. Initially internal land and sea border controls were abolished, and the abolition of air border controls followed in March 2008. Two non-EU states, Iceland and Norway, were officially classified as states associated with Schengen (and where Schengen rules apply) because of their involvement with the 1957 Nordic Passport Union, and also because of the lengthy land border between Norway and Sweden. **Switzerland** gained the status of a country associated with the Schengen activities in December 2008, following the approval in a referendum of that country's bilateral agreement with the EU to abolish passport controls. Its association with the Schengen Area offered the benefit to the Swiss authorities of access to a vast database on criminals, traffickers and stolen goods. **Liechtenstein** became the 26th member of the Schengen Area (as an associated state) in December 2011.

Nevertheless, the Schengen Agreement has attracted criticism from nationalists and **Eurosceptics** who have claimed that it facilitates illegal migration and the free movement of criminals. Large-scale terrorist attacks in Paris, France, in mid-November 2015, which resulted in the deaths of 130 people, and which were attributed to supporters of **Islamic State**, prompted demands for the revision of the Schengen Agreement. In mid-December the **European Commission** proposed an amendment, reinforcing checks at the EU's external borders against relevant databases (for example, police records) for both EU and non-EU travellers. Non-EU nationals with a Schengen visa have generally been exempt from identity checks within the Schengen Area, although such checks became more frequent from November 2015. If a serious threat to public policy or internal security is identified, a member of the Schengen Area may temporarily reintroduce border controls at its internal borders. At September 2017 five EU countries, and **Norway**, had temporarily reintroduced border restrictions, owing either to issues connected with irregular migration or concerns relating to terrorism.

The **SCHENGEN AREA** is the area in Europe in which the free movement of people has been realized on the basis of the **Schengen Agreement**. Following the European Union's (EU's) **enlargement** in July 2013 it covers all EU members, with the exception of **Bulgaria**, **Croatia**, **Cyprus**, **Ireland**, **Romania** and the **United Kingdom**, and also includes four non-members, **Iceland**, **Liechtenstein**, **Norway** and **Switzerland**, which have the status of countries associated with Schengen (and subject to Schengen rules and regulations). The Schengen Area also, de facto, includes Monaco, San Marino and the Vatican. Although not members of the Schengen Area, the UK and Ireland participate in substantial parts of the Schengen *acquis*. Since their accession to the EU in 2007 Bulgaria and Romania have been aiming to join the Schengen Area. However, political will is not sufficient in itself. In order to join the Schengen Area prospective members must fulfil a series of preconditions that include full control of external borders, close co-operation with law enforcement agencies in other states, the full application of the Schengen *acquis* (i.e. control of land, sea and air borders) and signing up to the **Schengen Information System**. Other member states continue to express concern over the readiness of both Bulgaria and Romania to join. The EU's newest member state, Croatia, also expressed a wish to join the Schengen Area. Nevertheless, the continued functioning of the Schengen Area was placed under considerable pressure by the **European migration crisis**. Under the **Dublin Regulation** migrants were expected to claim asylum in their point of entry, but were able to traverse Europe owing to the lack of internal border controls. Some politicians, notably German Chancellor **Angela Merkel**, argued that European countries should share responsibility for refugees or place the Schengen Agreement at risk.

The **SCHENGEN INFORMATION SYSTEM** (SIS), once also known as the European Information System, is a computer network that links the computer systems of immigration services and the police in signatory countries of the **Schengen Agreement**. A new network, SIS II, which has enhanced functionalities (including the possibility of using biometrics) and ensures stronger data protection, became operational in April 2013.

MARTIN SCHULZ (1955–) was elected as President of the **European Parliament** (EP) in January 2012. He resigned from his post in January 2017, in order to stand as a candidate of the Social Democratic Party of Germany (SPD) in the federal elections scheduled for September. Schulz was born in North Rhine-Westphalia, **Germany**, where he trained as a bookseller before entering politics. He has been a member of the SPD since the age of 19 and became the youngest mayor in North Rhine-Westphalia's history when he was appointed to the mayoralty in 1987 (at the age of 31). He was first elected to the EP in June 1994 and in 2004 was appointed as Chairman of the **Group of the Party of European Socialists** (renamed the **Group of the Progressive Alliance of Socialists and Democrats in the European Parliament—S&D**—in 2009). On assuming the presidency of the EP, Schulz was replaced as leader of the S&D by Hannes Swoboda. Schulz was the preferred candidate of the S&D group for the position of **European Commission** President in early 2014, but following the emergence of the **Group of the European People's Party (Christian Democrats)** (EPP) as the largest group within the EP after the May elections, the S&D supported the EPP's preferred candidate, **Jean-Claude Juncker**. The EPP reciprocated by backing the S&D group's choice of Schulz for President of the EP. Schulz was duly elected by a majority of the Members of Parliament in July to serve a second 30-month period as EP President, marking the first occasion on which a President of the EP had been re-elected to the post.

The **SCHUMAN PLAN**, named after Robert Schuman, was the original proposal for a consolidation of coal and steel resources that led to the **European Coal and Steel Community** (ECSC). In addition to the economic benefits, the Plan also argued that it would 'immediately provide for the establishment of common bases for economic development as a first step in the federation of Europe'; it went on to state explicitly that 'Europe must be organized on a federal basis'. The more specific political objective was to secure a rapprochement between **France** and the Federal Republic of **Germany** (West Germany). The Plan opened with the declaration that 'the French Government proposes that Franco-German coal and steel production should be placed under a common High Authority within the framework of an organization open to the participation of the other countries of Europe'. The Schuman Plan was first revealed at a press conference on 9 May 1950. It was immediately supported by West Germany and the **USA**. Only six countries entered the negotiations resulting in the **Treaty of Paris** of 18 April 1951, which formally established the ECSC.

SCIENTIFIC AND TECHNICAL RESEARCH COMMITTEE (CREST): See **European Research Area Committee** (ERAC)

SCOTLAND EUROPA is an innovative alliance of public, private and civil society bodies networking Scotland in Europe. Its aim is to promote Scotland's interests to the key institutions of the European Union (EU) and to the regions of the EU and beyond. It is located in Scotland House alongside the EU Office of the **Scottish Executive**.

The **SCOTTISH EXECUTIVE** established a European Union (EU) Office in 1999 to support and promote both itself and its EU-related work and to help increase Scotland's influence in the EU. The office is co-located in Scotland House, in **Brussels**, with **Scotland Europa** and provides a focal point for Scottish interests in the EU. The Office works closely with the **United Kingdom's Permanent Representation**, UKREP, which remains responsible for representing the views of the UK as a whole to the EU institutions, and alongside the **Office of the Northern Ireland Executive in Brussels** and the **National Assembly for Wales EU Office**.

SCREENING is an integral stage of the process leading to accession. In order to ensure as smooth a transition as possible into the European Union (EU) for the countries of **Central and Eastern Europe**, a 1995 **White Paper** drew up an initial list of EU **legislation** that had to be incorporated into the domestic legislation of all the applicant states before membership could be deemed possible. The negotiations on EU membership began formally in 1998 and have involved a careful examination of the compatibility of all existing legislation with current EU rules and the necessity of additional legislative action. This process conforms to a screening mechanism. It is conducted primarily by the **European Commission** and each of the **applicant countries**, which together analyse, sector by sector, the degrees of compatibility. The process has allowed outstanding measures to be identified and a timetable for their **implementation** to be drawn up.

SCRUTINY is the process whereby **national parliaments** monitor and try to influence **legislation** emanating from the European Union (EU). In the **United Kingdom**, for example, the procedure is centred on the 'scrutiny reserve', which prohibits a national minister from adopting any legislative proposal unless it has been examined by the House of Commons Select Committee on European Legislation. The **European Parliament** (EP) undertakes scrutiny of the EU policy process and of the annual **budget**. Members of the EP can put forward questions (orally and in writing) to both the **Council of the European Union** and the **European Commission**; they can, moreover, question individual Commissioners and national ministers in parliamentary committees. The EP also has the authority to draw up reports in particular policy areas and can pass **resolutions** on current themes. It can also hold public hearings and establish committees of inquiry. Ultimately, the EP can dismiss the Commission and can bring cases before the European courts.

SEA: See **Single European Act**

SEC DOCUMENTS are those produced by the **Secretariat-General** of the **European Commission**. Less formal than **COM Documents**, they consist of internal reports, discussion papers and draft **resolutions**.

SECRETARIAT-GENERAL is the name of the senior and central bureaucratic service of the **European Commission**. It sits alongside other services such as **Eurostat**, the **European Antifraud Office** and the **Directorate-General for European Civil Protection and Humanitarion Aid**. It is answerable to the President of the Commission, and is the major administrative link between the President and the various **Directorates-General** and other agencies. It comprises some 450 officials and is headed by the Secretary-General of the Commission, the most senior official within the Commission, whose post should not be confused with that of the **Secretary-General of the Council of the European Union**. The Secretariat-General is a highly important part of the Commission's machinery and ensures that all parts of the Commission co-ordinate their activities, act in accordance with established procedures and liaise properly with the other **institutions**.

The **SECRETARY-GENERAL OF THE COUNCIL OF THE EUROPEAN UNION** heads the administration of the Council. The structure of the General Secretariat was changed in the late 1990s to make the Secretary-General also the European Union's **High Representative for the Common Foreign and Security Policy**. The Council appoints the Secretary-General (although in reality they are selected by the **European Council** operating under **unanimity**). The appointment of Javier Solana in 1999 marked a significant departure from previous practice, since, for the first time, a politician was selected instead of the more customary senior diplomat. Solana, who was the fifth Secretary-General, stepped down in November 2009 and was replaced by Pierre de Boissieu, his deputy, as Secretary-General, while Baroness Catherine Ashton took over as the new **High Representative of the Union for Foreign Affairs and Security Policy** (in accordance with the **Treaty of Lisbon**, the two posts were now separate). In June 2011 Uwe Corsepius replaced de Boissieu as the new Secretary-General of the Council of the European Union. On 1 July 2015 he was replaced by **Jeppe Tranholm-Mikkelsen**, whose mandate runs until June 2020.

A **SECTION** is a subdivision of a **Chapter** within a European Union treaty.

SECTORAL INTEGRATION was the major alternative to the federalist approach to integration. **Jean Monnet** was the main proponent of the more gradualist sectoral approach. The strategy was to integrate national economies in stages, by taking one economic sector at a time. The process would be accelerated by '**spillover**', and would eventually create such an interlocking of national economies that a common political structure for their direction would be required and inevitable. Ultimately, the **European Coal and Steel Community** was the only successful example of sectoral integration, following which the **Six** directed their efforts instead to the development of a **common market**.

MAROŠ ŠEFČOVIČ (1966–) was nominated as the Slovakian Commissioner-designate to the new 28-member **European Commission** led by President-elect **Jean-Claude Juncker**. In September Juncker named Šefčovič as the Commissioner for Energy Union, subject to approval by the **European Parliament** (EP). The **Members of the European Parliament** (MEPs) duly endorsed Šefčovič, and with the approval of the entire Juncker Commission by both the EP and the **European Council** in late October, Šefčovič commenced his term as European Commissioner on 1 November. Prior to this appointment, Šefčovič had been one of the Commission Vice-Presidents in 2010–14, when he held the portfolio for Inter-institutional Relations and Administration. He had briefly also been Commissioner for Education, Training, Culture and Youth in the previous Commission. Šefčovič studied law and received his doctorate in law from Comenius University in Bratislava in 1990. After graduation he worked in the diplomatic service of the former Czechoslovakia and thereafter Slovakia. He became Slovakia's ambassador to Israel in 1999, the Director-General of European Affairs in the Slovakian Ministry of Foreign Affairs and then the Slovakian representative to the European Union in 2004–09.

SEPA: See **Single Euro Payments Area**

SERBIA emerged as an independent country from the former state of Serbia and **Montenegro** (which itself had previously been named the Federal Republic of **Yugoslavia**) in May 2006. For much of the 1990s, the former Federal Republic of Yugoslavia (FRY) underwent a process of disintegration, with Serbia, under Slobodan Milošević, being held responsible internationally for much of the ensuing conflict. After the departure from office of Milošević in October 2000 **sanctions** imposed by the European Union (EU) in the 1990s were lifted and the FRY was included in the EU's **Stabilization and Association Process** and financial assistance programme for the **Western Balkans** (**CARDS**). Despite fears of the disintegration of the FRY, agreement was reached in 2002 on maintaining the republic and renaming the country Serbia and Montenegro. However, in April 2002 the coalition Government in Montenegro collapsed, as a result of opposition to the agreement, although the Federal Assembly subsequently ratified this in May. Within Serbia, the assassination of the Prime Minister, Zoran Đinđić, in March 2003 reinforced concerns about organized crime and political stability in the country. Such concerns, along with continued unrest in **Kosovo**, which remains under international civilian and military administration, initially prevented the EU from opening negotiations on a **stabilization and association agreement** (SAA) with Serbia and Montenegro. However, progress with political and economic reforms in 2004 led the **European Commission** to propose such negotiations in April 2005 and these were later opened in October. Seven months later the negotiations were suspended owing to Serbia's lack of co-operation with the International Criminal Tribunal for the Former Yugoslavia (ICTY), notably regarding the arrest and handing over of alleged war criminals such as Ratko Mladić. Also overshadowing relations was the prospect of Montenegrin independence—on which a referendum had been scheduled for April 2006—and the future of Kosovo. In the referendum a majority (55%) of Montenegrin voters opted for independence, and the union with Serbia was soon dissolved. Kosovo was also moving towards independence, a development Serbia utterly opposed.

Disagreement on the future of Kosovo cast a shadow over Serbia's relations with the EU. However, improved co-operation with the ICTY led the EU to resume SAA negotiations in June 2007, and these were concluded at the technical level three months later. A process of 'enhanced permanent dialogue' was under way, focused on monitoring and encouraging the reforms set out in the **European partnership**, first adopted in 2004 and subsequently revised. Visa facilitation and readmission agreements were signed in September 2007, and in its progress report on Serbia in November the Commission, while critical of reforms in many areas, recorded encouraging progress in others. It also noted that Serbia was in receipt of financial assistance under the new **instrument for pre-accession assistance**. Formal conclusion of the negotiations and signature of the SAA were still outstanding, however, and in early 2008 relations entered a new period of strain following Kosovo's declaration of independence and pledges of support for the new state from many—but not all—of the EU's member states. However, in a subsequent move designed to bolster the electoral prospects of pro-EU forces around the then Serbian President, Boris Tadić, member states, demanding that Serbia improve its co-operation with the ICTY (notably by tracking down Mladić), agreed to lift their veto on finally concluding the SAA, and the agreement was signed on 29 April. The move was welcomed by supporters of integration in Serbia but widely criticized by nationalists and others as a cynical move to interfere with the election by manipulating public opinion. Victory for Tadić and his supporters led to a rapprochement with **Brussels** and, in December 2009 an application for EU membership. The Commission's **opinion** was published in October 2011 and, owing in part to the arrest by the Serbian authorities of Mladić and his transfer to the ICTY in May, was broadly positive. Conferral of candidate status followed in March 2012. Following further progress towards the normalization of relations between Serbia and Kosovo, in April 2013 the European Commission recommended the initiation of **accession negotiations** with Serbia. In June the Council of the European Union announced that negotiations would commence in 2014. The first EU-Serbia intergovernmental conference duly took place on 21 January. In August 2015 the **High Representative of the Union for Foreign Affairs and Security Policy**, Federica Mogherini, announced that the Prime Ministers of Kosovo and Serbia had signed four significant agreements, aiding the further normalization of relations. The agreements focused on energy, telecommunications, the introduction of additional rights for Serb-dominated municipalities in Kosovo, and freedom of movement. In December negotiations on the first two of the 35 policy areas of the *acquis communautaire* (on the normalization of relations with Kosovo and on financial control) were opened.

The **SET-ASIDE SCHEME** was adopted by the Council of Ministers of the European Communities in **Brussels** in 1988 as a means of improving the effectiveness of the **common agricultural policy** (CAP) through the elimination of surpluses of produce. Under the scheme, farmers receive financial compensation, on the condition that they undertake not to produce anything, leaving land uncultivated or destroying crops and livestock, on at least 15% (reduced to 10% in 1996) of their arable land for five years. The idea of set-aside became a fundamental part of the Ray MacSharry CAP reform package endorsed by the Council in 1992. In November 2008 the **European Commission** agreed to abolish the set-aside scheme completely as part of the so-called CAP Health Check.

SEVESO DIRECTIVES are the name given to European Communities **directives** first issued in 1982 on requirements relating to the accident risks of several industrial activities, and to the supervision and control of the transportation between member states of hazardous waste. They are named after Seveso, the Italian site of a major chemicals accident in 1976.

SHIPPING was not always regulated by the European Union (EU), despite the fact that almost 90% of EU external trade is carried by sea, short sea shipping represents around 40% of intra-EU exchanges in terms of ton-kilometres, and land links between member states on the geographical fringes of the EU are relatively indirect. A common shipping policy was adopted in December 1986, consisting of four **regulations**. The first regulation made sea transport subject to EU **competition policy**, from which it had been exempted in 1962; certain shipping consortia, however, remained exempt from competition rules. The second endorsed the right of EU-based ships to ply freely for trade within and beyond the EU. This was reinforced by a 1992 regulation on the liberalization of coastal shipping within the EU. The other two regulations dealt with **discrimination**. One permitted the **European Commission** to take anti-**dumping** measures against third parties: where the case was proved by a complaints investigation procedure, duties could be imposed upon vessels from the country concerned. The other regulation permitted the EU to retaliate against countries that reserved a proportion of the trade between themselves and the EU for their own vessels: the Commission was authorized to impose loading or discharging permits and quotas, and/or to levy duties. To maintain an adequate shipping fleet, the EU has, since the 1970s, had guidelines for state **subsidies** to shipping, in order to help it combat world competition, and proposals have been made for an EU system of vessel registration. In January 2009 the Commission presented its new Maritime Transport Strategy 2018, the two main goals of which were: the ability of the maritime transport sector to provide cost-efficient maritime transport services adapted to the needs of sustainable economic growth in the EU and other world economies; and the long-term competitiveness of the EU shipping sector, enhancing its capacity to generate value and employment in the EU, both directly and indirectly, through the whole spectrum of maritime industries.

SIMMENTHAL SPA V COMMISSION is the title of an important case heard by the **Court of Justice**, which ruled that national governments must apply European Union **law** in full, and that, where this is not done, individuals have the right to appeal to the Court.

SIMPLIFICATION relates to efforts to simplify **legislation** in order to make it much easier to comprehend, and to ensure greater effectiveness. The notion dates back to the 1985 **White Paper** on the Completion of the **Internal Market** and was explicitly dealt with at the December 1992 meeting of the **European Council** in Edinburgh, the **United Kingdom**. Since the 1980s the pursuit of a genuine single market based on the free movement of people, capital, services and goods has produced a substantial amount of European Union (EU) legislation. Simplifying this is a necessity. A pilot programme (SLIM—Simpler Legislation for the Internal Market) was launched in 1996 (running until 2002) and this could be extended to other areas. Simplification is also used to describe the process undertaken via the **Treaty of Amsterdam** to repeal or amend obsolete **articles** in the **founding treaties**. The **Treaty establishing a Constitution for Europe** should also be read as an attempt to simplify EU machinery and EU decision making. The same is true for the **Treaty of Lisbon**, which repealed or amended obsolete treaty provisions and saw the formal abandonment of the EU's **pillars** and the **European Community**.

The **SIMPLIFIED REVISION PROCEDURE** was introduced by the **Treaty of Lisbon** and allows the **European Council** to amend certain provisions of the **Treaty on the Functioning of the European Union** governing internal policies and how they are made, without recourse to a convention or an **intergovernmental conference**. Such amendments cannot involve any increase in the competences of the European Union and have to be ratified by **national parliaments** or by referendum.

SINGLE CURRENCY: See **Economic and Monetary Union**; **Euro**

The **SINGLE EURO PAYMENTS AREA** (SEPA) is a private-sector initiative, launched in early 2008 and involving about 4,000 banks in Europe representing approximately 80% of transactions, which facilitates cross-border payments made electronically within the **eurozone**. The SEPA Regulation adopted in 2012 set 1 February 2014 as the date for the migration to SEPA in the eurozone. However, as the migration rates for credit transfers and direct debits were not high enough to ensure a smooth transition to SEPA, in January the **European Commission** adopted a proposal to allow an additional transition period of six months, to 1 August. SEPA comprises 34 countries—all 28 European Union member states, the four **European Free Trade Association** member states, Monaco and San Marino.

The **SINGLE EUROPEAN ACT** (SEA) was an important amendment of the **founding treaties** of the European Communities (EC) that came into force in July 1987 after **ratification** by the national legislatures of the member states. The Act consisted of 34 Articles, divided into four sections. The first section (Articles 1–3) constituted the objective of the SEA—'making concrete progress towards European unity'—as well as legitimizing the status of the **European Council**. The second section (Articles 4–29) formed the greatest part of the SEA, dealing with the amendments to the founding treaties. The third section (Article 30) provided for a permanent secretariat for **European political co-operation** (EPC), while the final section (Articles 31–34) outlined the procedures necessary for the ratification and **implementation** of the Act.

The SEA had three main themes: the **internal market**, EPC and institutional reform. Its implications for the internal market were enormous. It obliged the EC to deal definitively with the whole range of national systems of **taxation** and law, national standards and **regulations** in a number of policy areas, and national social security and welfare systems. It specifically strengthened the role of the EC in several policy areas. It made the **European Commission** an equal partner in EPC, with the views of the **European Parliament** (EP) also needing to be taken into consideration; and it committed the EC to extending EPC to include collaboration on security policy issues. While its institutional reforms were limited, it provided for a more widespread use of **qualified majority voting** in the Council (see **Council of the European Union**), and required the latter to collaborate more with the EP in the legislative process according to a new **co-operation procedure**, whereby a rejection by the EP of a Council decision could be overturned only by unanimous agreement in the Council. A final amendment created a Court of First Instance (now **General Court**) to reduce the workload of the **Court of Justice**.

SINGLE MARKET: See **Internal Market**

The **SINGLE RESOLUTION MECHANISM** (SRM) applies to those banks covered by the **Single Supervisory Mechanism** (primarily those in the eurozone). It establishes that when banks fail—even following strong supervision—a Single Resolution Board and a Single Resolution Fund, financed by the banking sector, will respond and resolve the issue. The principal aim of the SRM is to ensure an orderly resolution in the case of a failing bank, and one that involves minimum costs for taxpayers and public funds. The SRM entered into force in 2014 and was signed by all member states except **Sweden** and the **United Kingdom**.

SINGLE RULEBOOK

The **SINGLE RULEBOOK** forms the foundations of the European Union's (EU) **banking union** and its origins lie in the financial crisis that hit Europe in 2008. The rulebook comprises a series of texts and rules that apply to all financial institutions (some 8,500) in the EU. The rulebook endeavours to provide rules on issues such as capital requirements for banks, and rules on giving greater protection for depositors, and also seeks to prevent and manage bank failures. Fundamentally, it seeks to prevent any reoccurrence of the banking crisis that took hold of Europe from the late 2000s, leading to huge public bailouts.

The **SINGLE SUPERVISORY MECHANISM** (SSM) is a powerful tool that made the **European Central Bank** (ECB) the main prudential supervisor of all financial institutions in the **eurozone** area and also in those countries that opt to participate in the SSM. The creation of an SSM was proposed by the **European Commission** in September 2012 and should be seen as a first step towards a **banking union** that also envisages other fundamental components, such as a **single rulebook**, common deposit protection and a single bank resolution system. The SSM was formally approved in October 2013 and aims to strengthen **economic and monetary union**. From November 2014 the ECB became responsible for the direct supervision of the largest banks in the European Union (EU), with responsibility for managing smaller banks falling to national supervisors. This mechanism seeks to ensure that banks comply with EU regulations and that any potential problems are identified and addressed much earlier than in the recent past.

SIS: See **Schengen Information System**

The **SIX**, or the Europe of the Six, is a popular way of referring to the membership of the European Communities from the **Schuman Plan** of 1950 until the first **enlargement** of 1973. It refers to the six founder members: **Belgium**, **France**, the Federal Republic of **Germany**, **Italy**, **Luxembourg** and the **Netherlands**.

SLOVAKIA applied for membership of the European Communities (EC) in early 1993, and subsequently signed a **Europe agreement** in October of that year. This agreement superseded the earlier Europe agreement signed between the EC and the former Czech and Slovak Federative Republic (Czechoslovakia) in 1991. The first Agreement had become obsolete in January 1993 with the creation of two separate states, the **Czech Republic** and Slovakia. Relations between Slovakia and the European Union (EU) can be divided into two periods. The early years of the new Slovak state under the authoritarian Prime Minister, Vladimír Mečiar, were characterized by a degree of friction between that country and the EU. The second period, following the election of a new Prime Minister, Mikuláš Dzurinda, in October 1998, constituted nothing less than a complete transformation in relations and contacts with the EU.

Despite the Europe agreement in force since the beginning of 1995, and Slovakia's application for EU membership, doubts about the country's potential membership persisted under the Mečiar regime because of reservations about the country's commitment to democracy. The **European Commission**'s 1997 report on Slovakia's membership application stated that the country's institutions were unstable and that there were shortcomings in the functioning of its democracy, a situation which was 'all the more regrettable as the country would be capable of meeting the economic criteria [for membership] in the medium term'. Considerable improvements were made under Dzurinda's leadership, particularly with regard to **minority rights**, but Slovakia continued to struggle on the economic front. Unemployment in the early 2000s stood at some 20%. However, progress was made in the **accession negotiations**, which were opened in 2000. By the end of 2002 Slovakia had closed all negotiating chapters. A national referendum in May 2003 then endorsed membership (92.5% of those who participated voted in favour), and paved the way for Slovakia to join the EU on 1 May 2004. The Slovakian parliament ratified the **Treaty establishing a Constitution for Europe** by 116 votes to 27, with four abstentions, in May 2005. Slovakia adopted the **euro** and thereby joined the **eurozone** in January 2009. It joined the EU's **Schengen Area** in December 2007. However, public support and interest in the EU seems low: Slovakia recorded the lowest turnout figures for the **European Parliament** elections among the **Twenty-Seven** (EU27) in both 2004 and 2009 (both were less than 20%). In October 2011 the Slovakian legislature failed to support plans by the EU to enhance the powers of the **European Financial Stability Facility**; the proposals required ratification by each EU member state prior to their implementation. The Government of Iveta Radičová subsequently collapsed, and the general election of March 2012 saw the return to the premiership of Robert Fico (who had been Prime Minister of Slovakia in 2006–10) at the head of the Direction-Social Democracy party. This new administration ensured the ratification of the Treaty on Stability, Co-ordination and Governance in the Economic and Monetary Union (**Fiscal Compact** treaty) in December 2012. Following legislative elections in March 2016, a new Government led by Fico took office.

SLOVENIA was the first of the former Yugoslav republics to declare independence, in 1991. The **European Communities** recognized the country in 1992. Slovenia is a small nation (with a population of some 2.1m. citizens) and in the early 1990s was clearly the most economically advanced of the former Yugoslav republics. Moreover, Slovenia found the transition from a socialist to a market economy easier than most. Nevertheless, relations with the European Union (EU)—primarily the conclusion of a **Europe agreement**—were initially held up by difficulties with **Italy**, which demanded compensation for Italian nationals who in 1947 had left territory now held by Slovenia. Once a compromise solution had been found and a Europe agreement concluded in 1995, Slovenia applied for EU membership in June 1996. The country subsequently received praise from the **European Commission** for its economic endeavours and political stability and, with strong political support from both **Austria** and **Germany**, opened **accession negotiations** with the EU in early 1998. These were successfully concluded just less than five years later and, following the successful outcome of a referendum on EU membership held in March 2003, when 89.61% of the electorate voted in favour of accession, Slovenia joined the EU on 1 May 2004. Slovenia's parliament voted overwhelmingly (79 votes for and four against) to ratify the **Treaty establishing a Constitution for Europe** in February 2005. Slovenia joined the **eurozone** and adopted the **euro** on 1 January 2007. In December of the same year it joined the EU's **Schengen Area** and the following month it became the first of the new members from the 2004 **enlargement** to hold the **Council presidency**.

In October 2015, after **Hungary** closed its border with **Croatia** at the peak of the **European migration crisis**, Croatia began to direct migrants, many of whom were seeking refuge from conflict in **Syria**, into Slovenia; according to official figures, within five days 50,400 immigrants had entered the country, leading the Slovenian Government to request EU assistance. Slovenia's erection of a razor wire fence on its border with Croatia in December in an effort to control the flow of migrants, prompted Croatia to submit a complaint against Slovenia to the Commission, on the grounds that the fence endangered wildlife.

The **'SLUICE-GATE' PRICE** is similar in its effect to the **threshold price**. It applies to pig meat and eggs and other poultry products. Imports of these products into the European Union are liable to a levy to raise them to the level of the sluice-gate price.

SMALL AND MEDIUM-SIZED ENTERPRISE TASK FORCE: See **SME Task Force**

SMALL AND MEDIUM-SIZED ENTERPRISES (SMEs) and their development in the **internal market** have been the subject of a number of European Union (EU) policies. In 1996 the **European Commission** agreed new guidelines for state assistance for SMEs: aid for the acquisition of licences, patents, etc., would be allowed at the same level as aid for tangible investment. SMEs have been financially assisted to invest in new technologies. Euro Info Centres were established primarily as a source of information for SMEs. The Commission has prioritized the simplification of the legislative, regulatory and administrative constraints on SMEs, and in 1997 a **European Council** meeting approved an action plan for the **European Investment Bank** to generate additional investments for SMEs. In November 1998 CREA (the French acronym for Risk Capital for Business Start-ups) was launched to offer investment to small businesses. Since 2009 the EU has also developed the **JEREMIE (Joint European Resources for Micro to Medium Enterprises)** initiative together with the **European Investment Fund** to support SMEs. JEREMIE promotes the use of financial engineering instruments to improve access to finance for SMEs via structural funds. There are currently more than 20m. SMEs in the EU, representing some 99% of businesses.

The **SME TASK FORCE** was an agency directed by the **European Commission**. It offered help and advice to **small and medium-sized enterprises** (SMEs) on **competition policy** and the **internal market**. It was later subsumed into the former **Directorate-General XXIII**. (See also **European Business and Innovation Centre Network**; **European Private Equity and Venture Capital Association**.)

SMES: See **Small and Medium-sized Enterprises**

SNAKE was the name given to an agreement in 1972 by several European states to establish a European system of exchange rates within the broader Smithsonian Agreement, with only one-half of the permissible fluctuation range of the latter. It proved to be ineffectual as an instrument of exchange-rate control. Many countries were forced to leave it because of their inability to stay within the prescribed parameters. The Snake was effectively abandoned by the mid-1970s, and its failure disappointed the European Communities' hope that it would enable them to achieve **economic and monetary union**.

SOCIAL CHAPTER: See **Charter of Fundamental Social Rights of Workers**

SOCIAL CHARTER: See **Charter of Fundamental Social Rights of Workers**

The **SOCIAL DIMENSION** is a concept that gained increasing significance from the second half of the 1980s. It was promoted by left-of-centre politicians, most notably by the then French President, François Mitterrand, the Spanish Prime Minister, Felipe González Márquez, and the President of the **European Commission**, Jacques Delors. They argued for the development of a social dimension at the European Communities level to protect and advance matters relating to workers. This new policy commitment was regarded as an essential complement to the **internal market** programme, which contained benefits for the business community. Social issues emerged as one of a series of policies that culminated in the 1989 **Charter of Fundamental Social Rights of Workers** and the **Social Protocol**, part of the **Treaty on European Union**. The concept forms a fundamental aspect of many policies relating to competitiveness and growth. The objectives of the **European Maritime and Fisheries Fund** (2014–20) provide one current example.

SOCIAL DUMPING is a phrase that has been used to describe the process whereby, taking advantage of the greater freedoms available under the **internal market**, manufacturers relocate their production sites within the European Union from high- to low-wage areas.

SOCIAL FUND COMMITTEE: See **European Social Fund**

SOCIAL PARTNERS refers to the organizations that the **European Commission** is obliged to consult when it wishes to pursue policy proposals in the field of **social policy**. This social dialogue takes place between the Commission and the following three main organizations that represent the social partners: the **European Trade Union Confederation**, BUSINESSEUROPE (formerly the **Union of Industrial and Employers' Confederations of Europe**), the European Association of Craft, Small and Medium-sized Enterprises and the European Centre of Enterprises with Public Participation and of Enterprises of General Economic Interest. The Commission encourages and facilitates discussion with each of these groups on issues relating primarily to the labour market. Alongside these cross-industry organizations the Commission consults many other socio-professional groups representing specific or sectoral interests. In addition, the Commission is also obliged, under the 1957 **Treaty of Rome**, to consult with the **European Economic and Social Committee** on a range of policy issues.

SOCIAL POLICY in the context of the European Union (EU) has a much narrower ambit than is usually implied by the phrase in the domestic context: it refers specifically to **employment** matters, education and vocational training, **health and safety** issues, equality matters and the part of social policy that relates to employer-worker relations. During the first decade of the European Communities' (EC) existence, social policy had a very low profile and priority. The **Treaty of Rome** contained very few references to a specific social policy. The provisions that did exist related to the free movement of workers and to the freedom of establishment and creation of a then-small **European Social Fund**. Social policy became much more important with the arrival of mass unemployment in the 1970s, and the EC adopted a Social Action Programme in 1974. From 1983, social policy had two priority areas: the training and employment of people aged 25 years or under, and the provision of training and employment in the most economically disadvantaged regions of the EC. The **European Commission** administers social policy through the **European Social Fund** (ESF).

The **United Kingdom** strongly resisted the development of EC **competences** in the field of social policy and was highly critical of the 1989 **Charter of Fundamental Social Rights of Workers**; the country, moreover, gained an **opt-out** at Maastricht from the new social policy **protocol** that was annexed to the **Treaty on European Union** (TEU). The UK opt-out caused a great deal of confusion and effectively meant the existence of two distinct legal bases for social policy measures: the TEU itself and a separate agreement (the **Social Protocol**) from which the UK was exempt. This situation came to an end only when the Labour Government led by Tony Blair signed the Charter soon after coming to power in May 1997.

The **Treaty of Amsterdam** marked an important step forward in this particular policy area, as it promoted a series of social policy priorities at EU level, particularly in the area of employment, which has now been designated as an EU objective (under Article 2) and a matter of common concern. The aim is to reach a 'high level of employment' throughout the EU and to this end the EU is charged with developing a 'co-ordinated strategy' for employment that should complement the activities of the member states. A new title on employment (125–130) spells out EU priorities in this area and provides for the creation of an **Employment Committee**. Furthermore, a new provision refers to the adoption of provisions on non-discrimination and enables the Council, acting unanimously, to take appropriate action to tackle any **discrimination** that is based on sex, race, ethnic origin, religion or belief, disability, age or sexual orientation. Now, as a result of changes introduced by the **Treaty of Amsterdam**, all social policy measures can be adopted on the basis of a new Chapter within the treaty. This has effectively created a new legal base for equal opportunities and equal treatment of men and women at work. Indeed, the Treaty of Rome explicitly states that the EU must strive to eliminate all inequalities and to promote equality. As regards **decision making**, the Council adopts **directives** by **qualified majority vote** and in conjunction with the **European Parliament** under the **co-decision procedure** in the following areas: workers' health and safety, working conditions, integration of persons excluded from the labour market, information and consultation of workers, and equality between men and women. **Unanimity** prevails, however, in relation to the following areas: social security and social protection of workers, conditions of employment for third-country nationals residing in the EU, and financial contributions for promotion of employment and job creation. It should be noted also that certain matters have not been brought into EU **competences**. These include pay issues, the right of association, the right to strike and the right to impose lockouts. Since the Treaty of Amsterdam, the **Charter of Fundamental Rights** has been drawn up. It restates many of the principles and goals underpinning social policy, including the aim of combating social exclusion.

More and better jobs as well as equal opportunities are the key watchwords of European employment and social policy. An employment body, European Employment Services (EURES), launched in 1994, maintains a web portal and operates as a network of more than 750 specialist advisers across Europe, who provide the three basic EURES services of information, guidance and placement to both job seekers and employers interested in the European job market. EURES has a particularly effective role to play in regions where there are significant degrees of cross-border commuting by employees. EURES, which also covers the countries of the **European Economic Area** and **Switzerland**, provides a public database of employment vacancies and a database through which job seekers can make their professional details available to a wide range of employers.

The framework of the Social Policy Agenda (2006–10) was designed to link economic, employment and social policies. The key strands of the agenda were: the **European Employment Strategy**; improving working conditions and standards; social inclusion and social protection; and equality of women and men. The EU has long sought to protect workers' rights by reaching agreement on common minimum rules on working conditions and health and safety at work. It has also attempted to promote better relations and an improved dialogue between worker representatives and employers. The European Commission also encouraged corporate social responsibility by promoting the concept that companies should include social and environmental concerns as an integral part of their business strategies. Common EU rules establish the baseline standards in a wide range of areas. These include protection against specific health risks, such as **noise** or exposure to chemicals, or in specific circumstances, such as pregnancy or where workers are under 18 years old. They also cover **workers' rights**. **Equal pay** for equal work, and protection against sexual harassment and all forms of discrimination, are fundamental tenets of the EU. The fight against discrimination and xenophobia was stepped up through an action programme to combat discrimination covering 2001–06. In 2008 the European Commission established a Governmental Expert Group in the field of non-discrimination and the promotion of equality. Moreover, the Strategy for Equality between Women and Men for 2010–15 sought to ensure that gender issues were taken into account in all EU policies. As part of the Seventh Framework Programme (2007–13), PROGRESS was the financial instrument supporting the development and co-ordination of EU policy in the following areas: employment; social inclusion and social protection; working conditions; anti-discrimination; and gender equality. PROGRESS was allotted a budget of €743m.

In December 2013 the Council adopted a regulation on a new programme for Employment and Social Innovation (EaSI), with a budget of €815m. for 2014–20. The EaSI programme aims to support measures by member states to develop and implement social reforms, and incorporates the PROGRESS and EURES programmes, and the European Progress Microfinance Facility (launched in 2010 to facilitate the provision of small loans for the establishment of businesses).

Four agencies provide essential technical input into EU work on employment, carry out research on social policy matters and disseminate best practice. They are the **European Agency for Safety and Health at Work** in Bilbao, **Spain**; the **European Foundation for the Improvement of Living and Working Conditions** in Dublin, **Ireland**; the European Institute for Gender Equality (which was established in 2007 and is now located in Vilnius, **Lithuania**); and the **European Union Agency for Fundamental Rights** (in Vienna, **Austria**). (See also **Disability Policy**; **Employment**.)

The **SOCIAL PROTOCOL** was an agreement, stemming from the **Charter of Fundamental Social Rights of Workers** (aiming to promote employment, improve living and working conditions and combat exclusion), reached between 11 of the **Twelve European Communities** member state governments at a meeting of the **European Council** in December 1991 at Maastricht, the **Netherlands**. The only hesitant state was the **United Kingdom**. On account of the UK's negotiated **opt-out**, the agreement was annexed to the **Treaty on European Union** as a **protocol** and became part of the treaty only when the UK finally signed up to the social charter in 1997.

SOCIALIST GROUP IN THE EUROPEAN PARLIAMENT: See **Group of the Progressive Alliance of Socialists and Democrats in the European Parliament** (S&D)

SOCRATES, a European Union programme, was introduced in 1995 to bring language, education and learning programmes together in order to promote co-operation and the exchange of information between member states with regard to education, as well as the mobility of students, especially in higher education. The 10-year programme, based in **Brussels**, combined a number of educational programmes, including **Erasmus**, **Grundtvig**, **Lingua**, **Minerva** and **Comenius**. According to the **European Commission**, nine out of 10 universities in Europe participated in the programme, with some 165,000 mobility scholarships being awarded each year. The Commission also encouraged the mobility of teachers, and some 23,000 received money in 2006 to enable them to benefit from cross-border educational exchanges. In 2007 the new **Lifelong Learning Programme** 2007–13 (LLP) replaced the Socrates, **Leonardo** da Vinci, and eLearning programmes, which expired at the end of 2006. The LLP was, in turn, succeeded by the **Erasmus+** programme which was to run from 2014–20.

SOFT LAWS are rules of conduct that in principle have no legally binding force, but which nevertheless may have practical effects in aiding policy development. This broad definition encompasses not only international agreements but also texts issued by the European Union (EU) **institutions**. In terms of the **European Commission**, soft law is usually equated with the following: codes of conduct, frameworks, **resolutions**, communications, **declarations**, guidance notes and circulars. Although the concept of soft law remains a highly problematic one for lawyers, it is generally regarded by policymakers as a useful instrument to encourage consistency in bureaucratic **decision making**, to enable speedy resolution of issues that would otherwise demand **legislation**, and to allow for regulation where no regulation would otherwise be possible. However, the use of soft law has its detractors, who emphasize the dangers and the undemocratic and illegitimate situations that might arise from such informal policymaking. When soft law is utilized, parliaments are bypassed, which, as far as the public is concerned, leads to opaque decision making, and the content of policies may often be vague, as well as possibly inconsistent with existing legislation. Moreover, it can be argued that because soft law is not legally binding, **implementation** must rest on the goodwill of those agreeing to it. Nevertheless, soft law is a fundamental part of EU policymaking (e.g. state aid—see also **subsidies**).

SOLEMN DECLARATION ON EUROPEAN UNION is the title of the general statement signed by the heads of government and foreign ministers at the conclusion of the meeting of the **European Council** held in Stuttgart, Federal Republic of **Germany**, in June 1983, which had discussed the Genscher–Colombo Plan. The Declaration reviewed the extent to which the potential of each institution of the European Communities (EC) had been implemented, and considered possibilities for their further co-ordination. It asserted a wish to work for further EC development as a nucleus of European union, to strengthen **European political co-operation** (EPC), to promote closer cultural co-operation, to launch a concerted action to deal with international problems of law and order, and to seek further **approximation** of the **legislation** of the member states. It also indicated the purpose of the Council and its relationship to the EC **institutions**. More a statement of belief than a plan of action, it nevertheless contributed to the movement in favour of change that developed during the 1980s.

SOUTH AFRICA over the last three decades or so has witnessed a transformation in its relations with the European Union (EU). For much of the 1980s it was the focus of **sanctions** adopted under **European political co-operation**, although a European Special Programme (ESP) was agreed to assist the victims of apartheid. Later, once the apartheid regime collapsed, the ESP was renamed the European Programme for Reconstruction and Development. This committed €500m. to South Africa for the period 1996–99. Further financial assistance has since been agreed. In addition, a trade, development and co-operation agreement was concluded in 1999 (which included the establishment of a free trade area and which entered into force in 2004), and the two sides signed a **Strategic Partnership** in 2007. South Africa is now the EU's largest trading partner in Africa (with total trade between the two countries amounting to €47,100m. in 2011). Total EU aid for South Africa over the period 2007–13 amounted to €980m. In accordance with the EU's 2011 'Agenda for Change', refocusing funding on the world's poorest countries, aid to South Africa for the period 2014–20 was reduced to €241m.

SOUTH AND CENTRAL AMERICA has not been, in general, the subject of a co-ordinated policy. However, the European Union (EU) has concluded economic and trade co-operation agreements with most of the countries in this area, which enable the latter to benefit from the EU Generalized System of Preferences. The arrangements allow duty-free access into the EU for some of their manufactured products. Between 1990 and 2009 regular ministerial meetings were held between the EU and the so-called 'Rio Group' (which started off with a membership of six countries but over the years expanded to 23 countries, including all the Latin American nations). From 1984 the San José dialogue has existed as the institutional forum between the EU and the six countries of Central America (Costa Rica, El Salvador, Guatemala, Honduras, Nicaragua and Panama). In 1998 the **European Commission** proposed negotiating mandates for the creation of a free trade area with the countries of Mercosur (Argentina, Brazil, Paraguay and Uruguay) and Chile. This was followed by a first summit between heads of state and government of the EU and the six above-named Central American countries at Rio de Janeiro, Brazil, in June 1999. At this meeting (the first EU-Latin America and Caribbean—LAC summit), a highly ambitious action plan, with 54 priorities covering institutional dialogue, trade liberalization and investment, was agreed. The Community of Latin American and Caribbean States (CELAC) was launched in 2010 as a regional mechanism for political dialogue and co-operation encompassing for the first time all 33 LAC countries. It merged the Rio Group and Cumbres América Latina y Caribe (the organizing body for internal LAC summits). In June 2012 the EU and the six Central American countries signed a comprehensive **association agreement**, which included an ambitious trade component. In the same month the EU signed a trade agreement with Colombia and Peru. In November 2016 Ecuador acceded to the trade agreement, and provisional application took place from January 2017. Meanwhile, the second EU-CELAC summit (the eighth EU-LAC summit) was held in Brussels, **Belgium**, in June 2015.

SOUTH-EASTERN EUROPE is a term used by the European Union when referring to **Bulgaria**, **Romania** and the countries of the **Western Balkans** collectively.

The **SOVEREIGNTY** of the member states has been significantly diminished by their acceptance of the principles of the **founding treaties** and their subsequent amendments. Encroachment on national sovereignty has further increased with the accumulation of the *acquis communautaire*. The net effect is that while the European Union (EU) may not be a sovereign body in the full political or legal sense, neither are the member states. The question of sovereignty has remained a contentious issue within the EU.

SOVIET UNION: See **USSR**

SPACE POLICY, until relatively recently, had been barely considered by the European Union (EU). While some of the member states were involved in space research and development as early as the 1960s, the European Communities (EC) was slow in developing a collaborative approach to space, despite retaining links with the **European Space Agency** (ESA). The **European Commission** produced a space policy document in July 1988. It identified six 'action lines': the promotion of co-ordination and complementary action between space programmes and EC **research and technological development policy (RTD)**; **telecommunications** and satellite technology; industrial development and the **internal market**; the development of observation of the Earth from space; the legal environment; and the development of space-related technology training programmes. Since 1988 the EC/EU has collaborated more closely with ESA. The **Treaty of Lisbon**, following the abandoned **Treaty establishing a Constitution for Europe**, envisages the EU adopting a more focused engagement, with space policy as part of its activities in the area of RTD policy. In October 2009 the first EU-ESA International Conference on Human Space Exploration was held, in Prague, **Czech Republic**. In October 2016 the Commission announced a new Space Strategy for Europe, which was to promote the use of the European global navigation satellite system Galileo by mobile devices and to support improved connectivity in remote locations; to ease business access to satellite data, in order to develop new services and applications; to encourage private investment; and to support the development of industrial space hubs in European regions. (See also **European Space Agency**.)

SPAIN first approached the European Communities (EC) in 1962, with a request for an **association agreement** that would, in time, permit full membership. The request was renewed in 1964. Negotiations on a **preferential trade agreement** began in 1967, and an agreement was signed in 1970. Full membership could not be considered by the EC as long as Spain continued to be governed by an authoritarian regime. Discussions on a new agreement for a free trade area were broken off by the EC in October 1975 in protest against executions in Spain that violated 'the principles of the rule of law and in particular the rights of the defence'. The new, democratic Spanish Government that emerged after General Francisco Franco's death in November 1975 submitted an application for full membership in July 1977, and negotiations began in February 1979. The negotiations proved to be difficult, particularly where agriculture and fishing were concerned, but were eventually concluded in March 1985, and Spain joined the EC the following January.

A beneficiary of EC **regional policy**, including the **Cohesion Fund**, and **social policy**, Spain was a strong supporter of further economic and political integration, even though its determination to meet some of the economic and monetary criteria set by the EC placed enormous strains on the Spanish economy. Spain successfully entered stage three of **economic and monetary union** in 1999. Under the premiership of the conservative José María Aznar (1996–2004), Spain's economic expansion continued. Little known outside Spain prior to his first election victory and appointment as Prime Minister in 1996, Aznar rapidly emerged as a leading figure on the European stage. Aznar's decision to stand down in 2004 may also have contributed to his determination to resist the proposals (which reduced Spain's position) outlined in the Draft Constitution on the new voting arrangements within the **Council of the European Union** after **enlargement**. This led to bitter recriminations from other European Union (EU) member states and the episode not only marginalized Spain but also helped to ensure that the 2003 Rome **intergovernmental conference** collapsed without agreement. A change in government in April 2004, when José Luis Rodríguez Zapatero became Prime Minister, brought a more accommodating Spanish approach to the EU. This approach helped the EU leaders to agree a treaty text in June 2004. Spain was the first EU member state to hold a referendum on the **Treaty establishing a Constitution for Europe** in February 2005 and a decisive majority (77%) approved the text. However, turnout was low, at just 42%. No referendum was held on the **Treaty of Lisbon**, Spain opting instead for parliamentary **ratification**, which was easily secured.

The Zapatero Government introduced an austerity programme in April 2010 to ease the country's debt burden and to help stabilize the **euro**. However, the country's economic situation deteriorated further throughout 2011 as the growth rate fell, the housing market collapsed and unemployment climbed steadily. Amid these economic problems, an early general election was held on 20 November. These elections saw the defeat (and worst ever electoral result since 1982) of the Socialist Party and the victory of the centre-right Peoples' Party. The new Spanish Prime Minister, Mariano Rajoy, assumed office on 22 December 2011. He participated in the negotiations with the EU that led to the signing of the **Fiscal Compact** (Treaty on Stability, Co-ordination and Governance in the Economic and Monetary Union) in March 2012 and supported the austerity agenda. By early 2012 nearly 25% of the country's workforce was unemployed and opposition was growing towards the Government's stringent austerity measures. Large protest rallies were held, notably in Madrid. The Spanish Government was compelled to bail out a number of leading Spanish banks in May and in July the **eurozone** finance ministers formally approved providing Spain with up to €100,000m. in loans in an attempt to support the country's ailing banking sector. Spain was able to exit its international bailout progamme in January 2014. Rajoy declared this development to be an important 'milestone' in Spain's economic recovery, but admitted that much work still had to be undertaken, especially with regard to the challenge of creating new jobs.

SPECIAL COMMITTEE ON AGRICULTURE is the name of a specialist committee within the **Committee of Permanent Representatives** (COREPER). It is the only COREPER body that deals with all agricultural issues that come before the plenary Committee.

SPIERENBURG REPORT is the name of a document produced for the **European Commission** in 1979. A group of experts headed by a former **Netherlands** diplomat, Dirk Spierenburg, was asked to review the structure and organization of the European Communities. The Report recommended a rationalization of the Commission—including a reduction in the number of Commissioners—and of its system of personnel management. It was opposed by the Council of Ministers (see **Council of the European Union**), and was never implemented.

SPILLOVER was a term widely used in the 1950s to describe how **sectoral integration** would lead to full European union. It had two components. Functional spillover was based on the principle that modern economies were based on interrelated sectors. Once one economic sector had been integrated, this complexity would generate pressure for the integration of other sectors. Political spillover suggested that once European institutions had been established for one sector, economic interest groups would look to that political level for the realization of their demands, and the advantages provided would lead them also to press for further sectoral integration. The notion largely fell into disfavour after the late 1950s as an explanation of, and strategy for, integration.

SPORT was identified by the **Committee for a People's Europe** as an area where, because of the mass interest and loyalties it generates, the European Communities (EC) could seek to encourage a sense of European identity and awareness. The **European Commission** had already sought, on a modest scale, to involve the EC in sporting events, most prominently through its sponsorship since 1976 of the Sail for Europe Association, a group which formed international crews of EC nationals to compete in round-the-world races and other sailing events. The Commission also sponsored the European Yacht Race in 1985, an event that now takes place on a biennial basis. Tennis and swimming championships have also been sponsored, along with a number of football, motor rally and walking events. The Eurathlon programme provided grants to sports projects during the 1990s. In 1997 the **European Parliament** passed a resolution requesting that a reference to sport be inserted into the **article** of the **Treaty of Rome** dealing with culture. This was not taken up, although the **Treaty of Lisbon**, following the abandoned **Treaty establishing a Constitution for Europe**, does envisage a greater role for the European Union (EU) in promoting European sporting issues as well as developing the European dimension in sport. This is to be done by 'promoting fairness and openness in sporting competitions and co-operation between bodies responsible for sports, and by protecting the physical and moral integrity of sportspeople'. As laid down in the 2007 White Paper on Sport, the EU Sport Forum, which coincides with an informal meeting of EU Sport Ministers, is held annually, bringing together some 250 delegates, including leading figures from the international and European Olympic Committees, European federations, 'sport for all' organizations, and organizations of leagues, clubs and athletes. The sixth EU Sport Forum took place in The Hague, the **Netherlands**, in March 2016.

SRM: See the **Single Resolution Mechanism**

SSM: See the **Single Supervisory Mechanism**

The **STABILITY AND GROWTH PACT** (SGP) emerged as an essential aspect of the third stage of plans for **economic and monetary union** (EMU). It was realized that if EMU were ultimately going to be successful, budgetary discipline across all **eurozone** members would have to be maintained after EMU had been launched in 1999. This demand was principally led by **Germany** and resulted in a **European Council** resolution (adopted at the Amsterdam European Council in 1997) and two subsequent Council regulations. The pact established clear and detailed arrangements for the surveillance of budgetary positions and for the co-ordination of economic policies, and procedures for dealing with excessive deficits and public debt. All eurozone members pledged to pursue budgets close to balance or in surplus for the foreseeable future and to present both the **European Commission** and the **Council of the European Union** with annual reports on their economic situation.

The SGP allows the Council to penalize any participating member state that fails to take the necessary measures to end an excessive deficit. In the first instance the penalty is more likely to constitute a non-interest-bearing deposit with the European Union (EU), but it could be converted into a fine if the deficit is not corrected within two years. The Commission is charged with supervising the economic policies of the participating countries and with alerting the member states to potential problems. The situation with Germany, the prime architect of the pact, deteriorated in 2003 as both Germany and France watched their economies remain locked in recession or stagnation. For the third successive year, both states breached one of the keystones of the pact—maintaining budget deficits at less than 3% of gross domestic product (GDP), the total value of goods and services the economy produces (the other keystone is maintaining public debt below a ceiling of 60% of GDP). With their economies stagnant, tax receipts were down, while public spending in terms of unemployment benefits had gone up. In November 2003 the SGP was effectively suspended through the reluctance of **France** and Germany to accept the recommendations of the **European Central Bank** and the Commission to reduce their budget deficits to below 3% of GDP. According to the rules, both states were therefore liable to pay substantial fines. However, the **Economic and Financial Affairs Council of Ministers** disregarded the Commission's recommendation and granted the eurozone's two largest economies an extra year's grace. France and Germany were therefore allowed to break the 3% rule again in 2004. The pact was thus severely undermined. Germany's wish at the time was to draw up additional EU fiscal rules that would lead to a 'better interpretation'—in other words, a less strict interpretation—of the pact, allowing more account to be taken of the economic situation, the impact of ageing on social security systems and the role played by public investment in modernizing the economy. The eurozone crisis from 2010 led to a stricter interpretation of the SGP generally being favoured. A revised pact, the Euro Plus Pact, was agreed in March 2011. It provides for more stringent commitments with emphasis on **competitiveness**, employment, sound public finances and financial stability.

The **STABILITY PACT FOR SOUTH EASTERN EUROPE** was launched in June 1999 following the **Kosovo** conflict to assist in the stabilization and reconstruction of the region, the European Union playing a lead role through its **Stabilization** and **Association Process** and the implementation of the former **CARDS** programme of financial assistance and its successor the **instrument for pre-accession assistance**. In April 2008 a Regional Co-operation Council, based in Sarajevo, **Bosnia and Herzegovina**, replaced the Stability Pact.

STABILIZATION AND ASSOCIATION AGREEMENTS (SAAs) are the **association agreements** that the European Union (EU) has devised for countries in the **Western Balkans** as part of the **Stabilization and Association Process**. The first was concluded with the **former Yugoslav republic of Macedonia** in 2001 and was soon followed by an agreement with **Croatia** and, later, one with **Albania** (2006). In March 2007 **Montenegro** concluded negotiations on an SAA. Agreements with **Bosnia and Herzegovina** and with **Serbia** followed in 2008. An SAA with **Kosovo** was signed in October 2015 and entered into force in April 2016. These are modelled very much on **Europe agreements**, but place a much greater emphasis on the pursuit of regional co-operation as a prerequisite for closer collaboration with the EU. They also confirm the associate country's status as potential candidate for EU membership (see **potential candidate state**).

The **STABILIZATION AND ASSOCIATION PROCESS** (SAP) was launched by the European Union as its contribution to the **stability pact for South Eastern Europe** following the **Kosovo** conflict in 1999. Its key elements are the **stabilization and association agreements**, the **CARDS** programme of financial assistance and its successor, the **instrument for pre-accession assistance**.

STABILIZERS were introduced into the **common agricultural policy** (CAP) in 1988. They are fixed ceilings, or upper limits, imposed on the production of several agricultural products. They involve production quotas, limits on both production and processing guarantees, and intervention ceilings, and have been supported by a system of **co-responsibility levies**. If the ceiling is exceeded, an automatic reduction in the level of price support provided by the CAP is triggered. The most significant effect, perhaps, has been upon cereal production.

The **STAFF** employed by the European Union (EU) number over 50,000—about 33,000 of these work for the **European Commission**, 6,000 for the **European Parliament** and 3,500 for the General Secretariat of the **Council of the European Union**. The total is substantially lower than staff employed by national bureaucracies. Formally, there are no quotas for each of the member states; in practice, however, an unofficial system of national allocation is employed, to ensure that each member state is adequately represented in all areas and at all levels of the administration. In principle, officials must be EU nationals and adequately bilingual, and those appointed as translators or interpreters must be proficient in two EU **languages** other than their own. Apart from these qualifications, most posts are filled by open competition, having been advertised in the *Official Journal of the European Union*. In addition, several senior posts are filled by nomination from the member states.

STAGIAIRE is the name given to a short-term trainee, usually a recent graduate, attached to a **European Commission** office. The position provides the appointee with an apprenticeship and in-service training, but does not guarantee subsequent employment with the European Union.

STANDARDIZATION: See **CEN**; **CENELEC**

The **STANDING COMMITTEE ON EMPLOYMENT** was established in 1970 to act in an advisory capacity. In 1996 the **European Commission** invited interested parties to consider how the Standing Committee could be reformed in order to improve social dialogue. Two years later the Commission presented a draft decision for reform to the **Council of the European Union**. In March 1999 the Council adopted the document entitled *Adapting and Promoting the Social Dialogue at Community Level*. The newly revised Committee served as a European forum, in effect a tripartite dialogue, between the Council, the Commission and European Union-level employer and employee organizations (including the **European Trade Union Confederation**, the **Committee of Professional Agricultural Organizations**, EUROCOMMERCE—representing wholesale and retail business—and the **Union of Industrial and Employers' Confederations of Europe**) to discuss **employment** strategy.

STATE AID: See **Subsidies**

STATISTICAL OFFICE OF THE EUROPEAN COMMUNITIES: See **Eurostat**

STOCKHOLM CONVENTION is the name of the document that in 1960 formally established the **European Free Trade Association**. The signatories accepted the economic aim of an elimination of tariffs on reciprocal trade in industrial goods, with special provisions for agriculture and fisheries. The Convention had no political implications.

The **STOCKHOLM PROGRAMME** was an initiative of the European Union (EU) to establish and develop its **area of freedom, security and justice**. Launched in 2009, it followed the Hague programme, and was designed 'to define the framework for EU police and customs co-operation, rescue services, criminal and civil law co-operation, asylum, migration and visa policy' for the period 2010–14.

STRASBOURG, France, is central to the theme of European unity because it is the home of the **Council of Europe**, and became the location of the plenary sessions of the **European Parliament** (EP) after 1958. Although the EP continues to meet in the city, many of its members would prefer it to be relocated in **Brussels**, where many EP committees meet. In recent years an absolute majority of **Members of the European Parliament** have repeatedly voted in favour of a single seat (i.e. Brussels). However, any decision to move must be agreed by all European Union member states and France is adamantly opposed to a move. The **Treaty of Amsterdam**, by means of a **protocol** on the location of the **institutions**, had tried to put an end to suggestions that the EP might relocate by confirming **Strasbourg** as its home and requiring that 12 plenary sessions be held in the city each year.

STRATEGIC PARTNERSHIPS (SPs) are European Union (EU) agreements that frame co-operation, collaboration and interdependence with third countries and regions. They are fundamental instruments of the EU's foreign policy. The EU has established 10 SPs with Brazil, Canada, the People's Republic of China, India, **Japan**, Mexico, the **Russian Federation**, **South Africa**, South Korea and the **USA**. Moreover, an SP exists, in effect between the **African Union** and the EU through the Joint

Africa-EU Strategy. These partnerships have attracted criticism for lacking strategy on the part of the EU in the sense of traditional foreign policy. Nevertheless, they now often serve as a framework for the relationships between signatories.

The **STRUCTURAL AND COHESION FUNDS** (see also the **Cohesion Fund**) have been designed to reduce the socioeconomic gap between the richest and poorest member states, and between rich and poor regions within states, through a coherent redistribution of financial resources. The strategy of reducing regional disparities has always been central to the European Union (EU) because such disparities clearly undermine the integrity of the single market and also run contrary to the aims of solidarity and assistance advocated by the European integration project. The **Treaty of Rome** explicitly, although briefly, referred to regional disparities; however, the initial assumption was that the operation of the free market would help reduce these. Attention was originally focused upon southern **Italy** and was subsequently widened to cover other Mediterranean regions as well as **Ireland**. The decision to create an **internal market** made resolution of the disparities more urgent, and the term 'cohesion' was first employed in the **Single European Act**. The inclusion of the relevant paragraph (title V) owed much to the efforts of the four poorest states (**Greece**, Ireland, **Portugal** and **Spain**), but was also promoted by richer states (notably **Germany**) as a means of presenting financial support and inducements to those regions that would not necessarily or immediately reap benefits from the prompt completion of the single market.

The term cohesion encompassed notions of solidarity and harmonious economic development that could not be secured by the free market alone, and the following structural funds were established: the **European Regional Development Fund** (ERDF), which was set up in 1975 and finances infrastructure, productive investment to create jobs, local development projects and assistance to small and medium-sized enterprises; and the **European Social Fund** (ESF), which was established in 1958 and is designed to help the workforce adapt to changes in the labour market. The term cohesion was further elaborated in the negotiations on the **European Economic Area** (EEA) and in the **Treaty on European Union**, which established a new structural fund, known as the Cohesion Fund, through which monies from the richer member states and the other members of the EEA would be directed to aid infrastructural developments in the poorer countries of the EU. The latter, in return, agreed to accept the provisions in the treaty relating to **economic and monetary union**. The major beneficiary of the Cohesion Fund has been **Spain**. Two other funds that contribute to regional development are the **European Agricultural Guarantee Fund** (EAGF), which finances rural development measures and provides assistance to farmers, the **European Agricultural Fund for Rural Development** and the **European Fisheries Fund**.

The financial assistance provided to counter regional disparities increased rapidly, from some 5% of the **budget** in 1975, and the structural and cohesion funds have accounted for over one-third of the EU budget since the late 1980s (see **Delors I** and **Delors II**). Spending in these areas has now more or less stabilized. Although politically successful, the funds themselves lack sufficient scope and scale to reduce the disparities completely.

The financial assistance for these programmes is calculated on a multi-annual basis, with the funds being used to tackle regional disparities and support regional development through actions including developing infrastructure and telecommunications, developing human resources and supporting research and development. They are subject to continuing changes of emphasis.

To facilitate the provision of financial assistance to the most needy areas and to prepare the EU for **enlargement** (see **Agenda 2000**), the EU's structural policy was substantially reformed and now focuses on a number of objective areas. The declared aim of the particular reform initiative was to concentrate aid where it was most needed, that is, on those regions that were falling furthest behind. In the 2000–06 financial perspective there were three main areas. Objective 1 areas were those regions that were lagging behind the rest of the EU in terms of development, i.e. regions in which gross national product (GNP) per head was less than 75% of the EU average. These objective 1 areas consumed 70% of structural funds expenditure. Objective 2 areas were those areas with structural difficulties, such as areas undergoing economic change, rural areas in decline and areas dependent on fishing. The third objective area related to the development of human resources outside those regions eligible for objective 1 aid.

In addition, there were four major structural funds initiatives. These were **Interreg** (1989–), which seeks to stimulate cross-border, transnational and interregional co-operation; Leader (1991–2006), which aimed to foster rural development through the initiatives of local action groups; EQUAL (2000–08), which provided assistance for the creation of new means to combat **discrimination** and inequalities in general; and **URBAN** (1994–2006), which promoted economic and social revitalization of cities and suburban areas in crisis.

As the candidate states moved closer to EU membership, it was decided to create two new funds to assist their progression for the period 2000–06. These funds (see Agenda 2000), namely the **instrument for structural policies for pre-accession** (ISPA) and the Special Accession Programme for Agriculture and Rural Development (**SAPARD**), were designed to support infrastructure projects, industry, services, **small and medium-sized enterprises** (SMEs), agriculture and the environment. ISPA and SAPARD were replaced in January 2007 by the **instrument for pre-accession assistance**.

At a **European Council** meeting in Berlin, Germany, in March 1999, although the member states agreed to maintain their levels of spending on these funds, a general consensus emerged that such spending should be regarded as promoting short- and medium-term solutions, and that, in the longer term, market mechanisms would have to reduce the inequalities. The 2006 budget was heralded by the Commission as a decisive step towards reforming EU spending, in that it placed emphasis on investment in growth and the necessity to create more and better jobs. As part of this objective, the funds for cohesion policy were linked to a new drive for **competitiveness**. Together, the initiatives that fell under these headings amounted to 39% of the planned budgetary **expenditure**. The bulk of this remained earmarked for regional development.

Together the funds are intended to support integrated, rather than individual, projects and increasingly are expected to have a regional focus. They are allocated through Community Support Frameworks that are negotiated between the regions, the **European Commission** and the member states. For example, in the **United Kingdom** context, the **Scottish Executive**, the Welsh Assembly Government and the Northern Ireland Administration are responsible for **regional policy**, including delivering the structural and cohesion funds in their territories.

STRUCTURAL POLICY

In December 2005 the European Council agreed a total structural and cohesion funds budget of €347,000m. (at 2007 prices) for 2007–13. Changes were made for the financial perspective period. The available funds were to be more tightly focused to help secure the targets laid down in the renewed Growth and Jobs (Lisbon) Agenda. It was also hoped to encourage and stimulate more ownership of the agenda at regional and local level. For instance, in the UK, 60% of expenditure for **convergence** regions and 75% of expenditure for regions under the regional competitiveness and **employment** objective were allocated to the **Lisbon agenda**. The new period also saw a simpler and more efficient operation of the funds. To this end, the number of instruments was reduced from six to three, and a new 'proportionality' principle was to provide for less bureaucracy.

The Commission defined new objectives for the financial perspective covering the period 2007–13. The greatest emphasis was placed on the first objective, which targeted **convergence**. The Commission sought to accelerate the economic convergence of the least developed countries and regions of the EU, which were home to some 35% of the EU's population. This area consumed the lion's share of the money, some 82%. To this end, monies were available through the ERDF, the ESF and the Cohesion Fund. This objective was very much concerned with developing human and physical capital, innovation, knowledge society, environment and administrative efficiency. The budget allocated to this instrument was €251,300m. The second objective centred on regional competitiveness and employment (where some €55,000m. was allocated for 2007–13). It applied to all parts of the EU and sought to ensure greater competitiveness and boost employment opportunities. The main themes here were innovation, entrepreneurship and environmental protection. The third and final objective focused on territorial co-operation. This built directly upon the Interreg initiatives of the previous years, which were originally planned to be fully incorporated into the main objectives of the structural funds. There was some €7,750m. available under the ERDF for this objective, which covered three distinct strands: cross-border co-operation, transnational co-operation and interregional co-operation. In total, some 423 programmes were financed by the structural and cohesion funds between 2007 and 2013.

Plans for the further development of policy in these areas commenced in 2011, but the legislative proposals for cohesion policy in 2014–20 were only finally approved in early 2014. The themes of economic, social and territorial cohesion form part of the category (one of six) 'Smart and Inclusive Growth' within the Multi-annual Financial Framework for 2014–20. This category now accounts for some 47% of overall spending and is the largest category of spending. The largest element within this category itself is cohesion, which takes some 34% of total spending; the remaining 13% is allocated to competitiveness.

STRUCTURAL POLICY: See **Structural and Cohesion Funds**

STUTTGART DECLARATION: See **Solemn Declaration on European Union**

CHRISTOS STYLIANIDES (1958–) was nominated in 2014 as the Cypriot Commissioner to the new 28-member **European Commission** led by **Jean-Claude Juncker**. In September Juncker named Stylianides as Commissioner-designate for Humanitarian Aid and Crisis Management, subject to approval by the **European Parliament** (EP). Prior to his appointment to the Commission, Stylianides was elected as a **Member of the European Parliament** (MEP) in May 2014, and was a Government Spokesperson in 2013–14, and a member of the House of Representatives in 2006–13. He trained as a dentist and holds a degree from Aristoteleion University in Thessaloníki, **Greece**. His position as Commissioner was endorsed by MEPs, and with the subsequent approval of the Juncker Commission by the EP and the **European Council** in late October 2014, Stylianides took up office on 1 November.

SUBSIDIARITY is a term that was first used in the context of the European Communities (EC) in the 1970s, but it only became politically contentious in the period preceding the signing of the **Treaty on European Union**. As defined by the **Treaty of Rome**, the term embodies the principles that the European Union (EU) can act only when it possesses the legal power to do so, that the EU should act only when an objective can be better achieved at the supranational level, and that the means employed by the EU when it does act should be proportional to the desired objective. It implies, therefore, that national powers are the norm, with EU action the exception. It remains, nevertheless, an ambiguous and controversial concept regarded by both those for and those against more intensive integration as supporting their own agenda. An attempt was made in a **protocol** introduced by the **Treaty of Amsterdam** to provide a clearer definition of subsidiarity. In the framework of the **intergovernmental conference** launched in February 2000, the **Committee of the Regions** asked for the principle of subsidiarity to be amended formally to recognize the role of the local and regional authorities. This did not happen at the Nice **summit meeting**. The **European Commission** produces, on an annual basis, a report (*Better Lawmaking*) that for the most part examines the application of the subsidiarity principle. The concept of subsidiarity was reaffirmed in the **Treaty establishing a Constitution for Europe** and more recently in the **Treaty of Lisbon**.

SUBSIDIES by the member states to either private companies or public enterprises are, in general, not permitted if the effect is likely to be contrary to the **competition policy** of the European Union (EU). **European Commission** guidelines permit subsidies for industries experiencing very severe economic difficulties, but in each instance the case should be demonstrated to be exceptional, the aid programme should be short-term only, and the objective should be the re-establishment of economic viability by a planned reduction in capacity. State aid is also permitted for natural disaster relief, depressed regions, and investment in new economic activities. In each instance, member states must inform the Commission of their intentions. Where member states have provided subsidies that do not conform to EU **regulations**, the Commission has the authority to demand their repayment and to levy fines on member states. Subsidies have always been controversial, and especially so in such sectors as agriculture and aircraft manufacture, and have led to ongoing disagreements within the EU and in relations with third states. The whole issue of subsidies became extremely controversial following the onset of the economic recession in 2008 and governments' subsequent moves to assist their respective banking sectors.

SUMMIT MEETINGS are gatherings of the heads of government of the member states. During the first decade of the three European Communities the **Six** held only three summits. Three further ad hoc summits were held between 1972 and 1974. In

1974 it was agreed to institutionalize summits with the establishment of the **European Council**, which was to meet three times a year. The frequency of summit meetings was reduced to twice yearly in 1985. Provisions also exist for the convocation of extraordinary or emergency sessions. Most summit meetings deal primarily with routine business and general reviews; a few, however, have been highly significant for European developments. (See, for example, **Fontainebleau summit**; **Hague summit**; **Maastricht summit**; **Milan summit**; **Tampere summit**.) It was traditionally the practice that summits were held in the country holding the presidency of the **Council of the European Union**. Since the second half of 2003, however, all scheduled summit meetings of the European Council have been held in **Brussels**, Belgium.

SUPRANATIONALISM is the condition whereby the structures and **decisions** of the European Union are superior to and, some would claim, independent of national governments. Supranationalism is completely different from intergovernmental **co-operation**.

The **SUSPENSION CLAUSE** was written into the **Treaty on European Union** by the **Treaty of Amsterdam**. Under this clause, some of the rights of a member state (e.g. voting in the **Council of the European Union**) can be suspended if that particular member state consistently or seriously contravenes the principles on which the European Union has been constructed, such as liberty, democracy, respect for **human rights** and the rule of law.

SUSTAINABILITY is the quality that may be ascribed to a form of economic growth that is self-maintaining without exhausting natural resources.

The **SUTHERLAND REPORT** dates from 1992 and was produced by a former Commissioner responsible for competition, Peter Sutherland, at the request of the **European Commission**. He was charged with producing a report on how the European Commission could develop a strategy to ensure that the **internal market** functioned properly and efficiently. The Report advocated a series of initiatives to achieve this goal. These included the necessity for greater **transparency** and much more monitoring and enforcement of European Union **legislation** at the national level. It also placed an emphasis on **subsidiarity**. The Commission responded to the report by promising to pursue many of the suggestions, particularly with regard to national enforcement. In addition, it promised to publish an annual report on the state of the single market and make more use of **Green Papers** to engage the wider public in suggestions on proposed legislation.

SWEDEN maintained a position of political and military **neutrality** after 1945, eschewing involvement in anything other than intergovernmental and economic co-operation. In 1961, it approached the European Communities (EC) for a form of economic association that did not imply full membership. Negotiations eventually began in 1970, and in 1971 Sweden ruled out full membership as being incompatible with its policy of neutrality. A **free trade agreement** was signed in 1972. Following the EC decision to implement the **internal market** by 1992, Sweden accepted the need for a closer economic relationship with the EC. This was eventually achieved through the **European Economic Area**. Before this was concluded, however, Sweden revised its view on membership, and in 1991 submitted a formal application to join the EC. Negotiations were completed in 1994 and, following approval in a popular referendum, Sweden joined the European Union (EU) on 1 January 1995. Sweden's transition to membership of the EU has been smooth, but the EU remains, according to **Eurobarometer**, less popular in the country than in other member states, and, like **Denmark** and the **United Kingdom**, Sweden opted not to enter **economic and monetary union** (EMU) in 1999. In a referendum held in September 2003 on joining EMU, a majority of those participating (56%) voted against replacing the krona with the **euro**. In November 2015, in the context of the **European migration crisis**, the Swedish Government announced that it was to reverse its hitherto liberal policy towards migrants and that henceforth the country would impose border controls and revert to EU minimum requirements in relation to asylum seekers. Prime Minister Stefan Löfven accused the EU of having failing to distribute the burden of the migrant crisis equitably between member states.

SWITZERLAND has historically adopted a strict position of **neutrality**, but it was a founder member of the **European Free Trade Association** (EFTA). It applied to the European Communities (EC) in 1961 for an economic association, but negotiations began only in 1970. A **free trade agreement** was signed in 1972 and subsequently ratified by a national referendum. In 1989 Switzerland accepted the need for EFTA to seek a new and closer relationship with the EC, and began examining the question of EC membership. However, in a referendum in December 1992, the Swiss rejected participation in the **European Economic Area**, thus forcing the Government to suspend the application for EC membership that had been submitted in the previous May. Subsequently Switzerland negotiated a series of sector-specific bilateral agreements with the European Union (EU) covering free movement of persons, air and land transport, agriculture, research, public procurement and the mutual recognition of conformity assessments; these were signed in June 1999 and entered into force two years later. In June 2002 negotiations on a further 10 bilateral agreements began. The negotiations lasted until 2003–04 and covered: pensions; trade in processed agricultural products; the environment; statistics; education, occupational training and youth; the media; taxation of savings; the fight against fraud; and co-operation in the fields of justice, police, asylum and migration. During their negotiation and **ratification**, official government policy was to seek EU membership. In a referendum held in March 2001, however, 77% of voters voted against commencing membership negotiations. In 2005 Switzerland voted in a referendum to join the **Schengen Agreement**. The decision meant that Switzerland would open its borders and become part of Europe's passport-free zone, and that the Swiss authorities would also share information with their EU colleagues on crime and on asylum applications. A year later, however, the Government, although it did not withdraw the 1992 membership application, dropped eventual EU membership from the objectives of its relations with the EU. Switzerland joined the **Schengen Area** in December 2008. By 2010 Switzerland had signed about 210 trade treaties with the EU, and its relations with the EU have been notably close for a non-member state. In September 2011 the Swiss Franc effectively switched to a euro peg: the franc had hitherto 'floated' independently until its currency appreciation became unsustainable during the financial crisis in the **eurozone**. By 2013 around 75% of Swiss imports came from EU member states, and more than 50% of its exports were purchased by EU countries.

However, in February 2014 some 50.3% of voters approved proposals that the country should renegotiate its freedom of movement agreement with the EU, and introduce immigration quotas. Switzerland subsequently failed to ratify an agreement on extending free movement to **Croatia**, the EU's most recent member state. In response, the EU excluded Switzerland from the **Erasmus+** student exchange programme, and suspended the country's participation in the **Horizon 2020** research programme. In April Switzerland announced that it would allow a limited number of Croatians into Switzerland under a new quota system. In December a renegotiated agreement for Switzerland's 'third country' participation in Horizon 2020 was finalized. In March 2016 Switzerland signed a treaty with the EU extending the principle of free movement of persons to Croatia. In June the Swiss legislature voted to terminate formally a long-dormant application to accede to EU membership. In December Switzerland passed legislation to ensure that employment vacancies gave priority to Swiss-based job seekers (particularly in areas with high levels of unemployment), but did not introduce quotas for workers from EU member states. The Swiss Government extended freedom of movement to Croatia from 1 January 2017.

SYRIA has been embroiled in civil conflict from 2011. From mid-March of that year anti-Government protests in Syria were forcibly quashed by the authorities. In response, the **European Union** (EU) imposed a number of restrictive measures, including an arms embargo and targeted **sanctions**, comprising a travel ban and the freezing of assets, against those deemed to be responsible for, or involved with, the repression. The Syrian authorities continued to implement harsh measures in an attempt to quell escalating demonstrations against the rule of President Bashar al-Assad. By August 2012 the EU had imposed 17 sets of sanctions on the Syrian authorities. In mid-November the Council expressed its continued support for on-going efforts to reach a political solution to the situation in Syria. The EU delegation to Syria closed in December, owing to security concerns. In that month the EU Foreign Affairs Council recognized the National Coalition for Syrian Revolutionary and Opposition Forces as the legitimate representatives of the Syrian people. In June 2013 the EU adopted a communication establishing a comprehensive approach to the crisis in Syria. In late August 2013 the **High Representative of the Union for Foreign Affairs and Security Policy** expressed deep concern at reports of the use of chemical weapons in Syria, and urged intensified diplomatic efforts to bring about a rapid resolution to the conflict. In mid-February 2014 the EU pledged €12m. to help to dismantle and destroy stockpiles of chemical weaponry in Syria. In August the European Council expressed dismay at the deterioration of the security situation in Iraq and Syria, and the rise of the extremist grouping **Islamic State** (formerly known as Islamic State in Iraq and the Levant), together with widespread **human rights** violations carried out against Christians and other minorities. The European Council noted that the ongoing civil conflict in Syria had facilitated the emergence of Islamic State, which it recognized as a threat to security in Europe, and announced its intention to co-operate with the USA and other countries in order to counter Islamic State and other organizations deemed to pose a terrorist threat. A comprehensive EU regional strategy for Syria, Iraq and the threat from Islamic State was adopted in March 2015, and subsequently reviewed in May 2016. Also in May a special envoy for the promotion of freedom of religion or belief was appointed, in an advisory role, to the **European Commission**, with an initial mandate of one year. The establishment of the role followed the adoption of a **European Parliament** resolution condemning the mass murder of religious minorities in Iraq and Syria by Islamic State, and sought to help to protect religious freedom in the context of the EU's programmes with countries outside the Union. According to an EU report published in January 2017, since the beginning of the Syrian conflict the EU and EU member states had allocated more than €9,200m. to the country in humanitarian and **development aid**, as well as economic and stabilization assistance.

T

TAC: See **Total Allowable Catch**

TACIS: See **Technical Assistance to the Commonwealth of Independent States**

ANTONIO TAJANI (1953–) has been President of the **European Parliament** (EP) since January 2017, succeeding **Martin Schulz**. Tajani was educated in Rome, **Italy**, and served in the Italian Air Force. He has also worked in broadcast and print media, and served as a diplomat. Tajani was a **Member of the European Parliament** in 1994–2008, and again from 2014. He was appointed to the **European Commission**, as Commissioner with responsibility for Transport, between 2008 and 2010, and was a Vice-Chairman of the Commission and Commissioner with responsibility for Industry and Entrepreneurship in 2010–14. He held the position of Vice-President of the EP in 2014–16.

The **TAMPERE SUMMIT** of the **European Council** in November 1999 represents a highly significant event in the development of European Union (EU) policy governing **justice and home affairs** (JHA). It was the first time that an area of loose intergovernmental co-operation had been propelled to the top of the political agenda. The origins of this agenda date back to early 1999 and a joint letter from the German Chancellor, Gerhard Schröder, and the Finnish Prime Minister, Paavo Lipponen, which called for European action in three broad areas. These all related to the then third pillar activities initiated by the **Treaty on European Union**, and covered asylum and **immigration policy**, the creation of a European **area of freedom, security and justice** and combating transnational crime. These became the main agenda items of the Tampere summit, where the heads of state and government reached agreement on the need for a 'common asylum system'. Tampere highlighted the expanding nature and position of the European Council as an agenda-setter and a driving force for EU integration. It led directly to a further extension of the EU's scope vis-à-vis policymaking in the field of JHA and resulted in several new initiatives and new bodies being set up in 2000, such as **Eurojust** and a European Police College.

With regard to the **European Commission**, Tampere was the first occasion for the post-Jacques Santer Commission to present itself as a credible and potent force to the leaders of the member states. However, the scandal surrounding the Santer regime and the growing determination of the European Council to control the policy agenda had already put the Commission on the defensive. The changing relationships among the EU **institutions** were epitomized by the European Council's rejection of the Commission's report on the restructuring of the EU institutions.

TARGET, or Trans-European Automated Real-time Gross Settlement Express Transfer, is a system of inter-bank payments established on 1 January 1999 at the start of the third stage of **economic and monetary union**, to regulate transactions between the **European Central Bank** and commercial banks of the participating member states. National central banks of non-participating member states also have some access to the settlement system. TARGET2 was launched in 2007. In 2016 TARGET2 processed a daily average of 342,008 payments, representing a daily average value of €1,700,000m.

The **TARGET PRICE** is the basic price set annually for each commodity covered by the **common agricultural policy**. The price support provided for farmers is calculated with reference to the target prices.

TARIC is the acronym for the Integrated Community Tariff established within the former Caddia (Co-operation in automation of data and documentation for imports/exports and agriculture) structure in 1988. It is similar to the **common external tariff**, but contains additional provisions relating to preferences and quotas. The tariff is published annually in the *Official Journal of the European Union*. The **European Commission** maintains an online, multilingual TARIC database.

TARIFFS on intra-European Communities (EC) trade were removed by the **Six** by 1968, well within the time limit set by the **Treaty of Rome**. New member states have been given a transitional period in which to remove their tariffs, although increasingly, acceding states already participate in free trade arrangements with the European Union (EU). The EU **common external tariff** has been progressively reduced (to a current 5%–9%) in line with decisions taken under the **General Agreement on Tariffs and Trade**, and now by the **World Trade Organization**.

TAX HARMONIZATION: See **Taxation**

TAXATION has, in general, been accepted by the European Union (EU) as a policy field that is the preserve of the member states and, normally, proposals relating to taxation that come before the **Council of the European Union** require unanimous approval. Despite the introduction of an **internal market** and **economic and monetary union**, an EU policy on taxation is still absent and this reflects the political sensitivity of fiscal policy and explains why the principle of unanimous **decision making** in this area was maintained in the **Single European Act** and beyond. The exceptions to the general rule are cases where national taxation policy is against EU **competition policy**, or where it discriminates against nationals of other member states. The problems of maintaining monetary union without economic and fiscal union were brought to the fore in early 2010, when the **euro** came under increasing strain on account of the financial difficulties throughout the EU and in particular in **Greece**, **Spain** and **Portugal**.

By contrast, the EU has an interest in indirect taxation and is bound to work for the **harmonization** of indirect taxation in order to enable the **internal market** to function properly. Currently, significant disparities exist in the levels of excise duty paid, for example, on alcohol and tobacco within the internal market. A code on corporate taxation was agreed in 1997 that would eliminate harmful tax competition between member states. Proposals made in December 1998 for the harmonization of taxes in the member states were rejected by the **United Kingdom**, which made it clear that a **veto** would be used to keep taxation within the realm of national governments. Such a position, shared by other member states, was emphatically restated during the **intergovernmental conference** in 2000. Consequently, the **Treaty of Nice** failed to extend **qualified majority voting** to tax harmonization. Nevertheless, it should be noted that the adoption of a single currency has intensified the pressure for a truly common rate of **value-added tax** (VAT) and for common rules in the area of corporate taxation in the EU. Moves in this direction were strongly resisted by both the UK and **Ireland**.

TECHNICAL ASSISTANCE TO THE COMMONWEALTH OF INDEPENDENT STATES (TACIS) was an aid programme for the successor states of the **USSR**, often referred to as the **Commonwealth of Independent States**, and also Mongolia. Established in 1991, TACIS had as its objective to assess and aid economic reform and privatization in a range of economic sectors and to foster the development of democratic societies. In 1995 the **European Commission** extended the programme until 1999, when a revised programme to promote democracy and encourage investment was proposed. A **PHARE** and TACIS Information Centre was opened in **Brussels** in 1998 to offer advice on the programmes. In the period 1991–99, the European Communities provided more than €4,000m. in assistance under the TACIS programme. A further €3,138m. was allocated for 2000–06. In January 2007 the European Neighbourhood and Partnership Instrument (ENPI) replaced TACIS (see **European Neighbourhood Policy**).

TED: See **Tenders Electronic Daily**

The **TELECOMMUNICATIONS** sector has been regarded by the **European Commission** as one of the real success stories of the single market and the European Union (EU) regulatory framework. It has come a long way since the time of the traditional national telecommunications monopolies that controlled telecommunications, both voice and data, in the mid- to late 1980s. In order genuinely to compete with their major world rivals and to reap the emerging benefits of this new multi-million dollar industry, the EU member states were compelled to collaborate more closely. Three factors propelled the Commission towards the liberalization of this sector. These were recognition of the radical changes in technology and the impact they would have on the industry, the shift towards globalized markets, and a growing trend towards greater liberalization and competition, especially in the **USA** and Scandinavia.

Several initiatives were launched in the fields of **media policy**, information networks, common standards and the **harmonization** of technical rules, and the development of satellite transmissions. Moreover, the telecommunications sector was targeted as part of efforts to develop **Trans-European Networks**. These initiatives, however, did not lead to an integrated policy. The push towards the creation of an **internal market** focused attention on the public monopolies, and, in particular, on telecommunications and energy. The former became a priority for the Commission. This led to a 1988 directive, which opened the telecommunications terminals market to competition. It was supplemented by a directive relating to the liberalization of satellite telecommunications equipment and services, which came into force in late 1994, but allowed for deferment until 1 January 1996. Telecommunications infrastructures in the EU, which had been operated mainly by state monopolies, also faced the arrival of competition. In 1993 the **Council of the European Union** decided to liberalize voice telephony services fully by January 1998 (although some states, such as **Ireland**, **Spain**, **Portugal** and **Greece**, were given **derogations** until 2003). Agreement by member states on common rules in the form of the Open Network Provision framework effectively meant the full harmonization of an EU-wide telecommunications market. It allowed new entrants into the market, and the growing ethos of competition completed the drive to create a genuine single telecommunications market. Simultaneously, the Commission defined the concept of universal service, detailing the provision and quality of the service, the charging principles and the dispute settlement procedures.

By 1998 the EU had liberalized all telecommunications goods and services and, as a result, the number of operators doubled between 1998 and 2003, investment intensified and greater levels of competition brought better deals for consumers in terms of both product specification and lower prices. Commission statistics revealed that telecommunications services grew cheaper (on average some 30% cheaper) between 1996 and 2002. The Commission adopted the i2010 agenda—a European Information Society for Growth and Employment—in 2005 and laid out an ambitious scheme to create a single European Information Space in the field of electronic communications and media services by 2010. In August 2010 the Commission launched a **Digital Agenda for Europe**, replacing the i2010 agenda, which highlighted the creation of a single market for content and telecommunications services as a vital tool to regain progress lost during the economic crisis. In particular, as part of the new agenda, the Commission aimed to remove the difference between roaming and national tariffs by 2014. It also set ambitious targets for fast and ultra-fast internet access in Europe. By July 2014 mobile roaming charges had been reduced significantly. In June 2015 agreement was reached to remove all roaming charges by June 2017, after a transitional period from April 2016.

In September 2015 the Commission launched public consultations on broadband needs and a review of the existing telecommunications framework. The Commission subsequently proposed a new European Electronic Communications Code to encourage businesses to invest in new infrastructure throughout the EU, thereby stimulating competition, and strengthening both the internal market and consumer rights. The Commission also presented an action plan to deploy 5G, the fifth generation of wireless communication systems, throughout the EU from 2018.

TELEVISION: See **Media Policy**

TEMPUS stands for the Trans-European Mobility Scheme for University Studies, a European Communities programme introduced in 1990. It sought to provide financial assistance for university education in, for the most part, the countries of the former **USSR** and the **Western Balkans**, and to facilitate courses taught in **Central and Eastern Europe** by European Union (EU) nationals, and student and staff exchanges with EU countries. Tempus featured also as part of the programmes providing assistance for the economic and social reform of the countries of Central and Eastern Europe (see **PHARE**) and the territories of the former USSR (see **Technical Assistance to the Commonwealth of Independent States**—TACIS), where it operated as an EU aid scheme to assist the restructuring of higher education in these states and to facilitate their development towards a market economy. The TEMPUS programme, as well as being open to the eligible countries under the former **CARDS** and TACIS programmes, was open to all EU member states, the EU **candidate countries**, and Australia, Canada, **Iceland**, **Japan**, **Liechtenstein**, New Zealand, **Norway**, **Switzerland** and the **USA**. Countries outside the EU were able to participate only through co-financing projects. From 1990 to 1999 Tempus/**PHARE** actions received €720.9m., and from 1993 to 1999 Tempus/TACIS actions amounted to approximately €130.2m. The third phase of Tempus expired on 31 December 2006; the programme was extended over the period 2007–13 under the name TEMPUS IV, financed partly under the European Neighbourhood and Partnership Instrument. TEMPUS, which in its fourth phase, had an annual budget of some €50m., facilitated joint European projects in higher education that supported joint teaching actions, the development of new courses, the promotion of links between universities and the wider community, and increasing the mobility of teachers and students. By 2012 some 120,000 teachers and 35,000 students from over 2,600 institutions had directly benefited from the Tempus programme, which covered 27 countries in the Western Balkans, Eastern Europe and Central Asia, North Africa and the Middle East. Tempus came to an end on 31 December 2013 and its activities now form part of the **Erasmus+** programme, which runs in 2014–20. Erasmus+ brings together all the EU's programmes relating to education, training and youth under one scheme.

The **TEN** (EU10), or the Europe of the Ten, are terms sometimes used to describe the membership of the European Communities (EC) between January 1981, when **Greece** became the 10th member state, and January 1986, when EC membership rose to **Twelve**.

TENDERS ELECTRONIC DAILY (TED) is an electronic information service detailing those **public procurement** contracts awarded by national and local authorities where bidding for the contract is open to any supplier within the European Union. It is the online version of the *Supplement to the Official Journal of the European Union*. TED is operated by the **Publications Office of the European Union**.

TENS: See **Trans-European Networks**

TESM: See **Treaty establishing the European Stability Mechanism**

TEU: See **Treaty on European Union**

TEXTILES: See **Multifibre Arrangement**

TFEU: See **Treaty on the Functioning of the European Union**

THRESHOLD PRICE is the name of the minimum price fixed for cereals, milk products and sugar within the **common agricultural policy**. Cheaper imports into the European Union (EU) are subject to a levy to raise their price to the level of the threshold price, which, unlike the **target price**, includes internal transportation costs from the port of entry into the EU.

MARIANNE THYSSEN (1956–) is a Belgian politician and **Member of the European Parliament** (MEP) who was nominated in 2014 as a Commissioner to the new 28-member **European Commission** led by **Jean-Claude Juncker**. In September Juncker named Thyssen as Commissioner-designate for Employment, Social Affairs, Skills and Labour Mobility, subject to approval by the **European Parliament** (EP). Thyssen holds a Master's degree in Law, and was first elected to the EP in 1991. She was the first Vice-President of the **Group of the European People's Party (Christian Democrats)** in the EP from 2004–09. She was approved at her confirmation hearing by MEPs and, with the endorsement of the Juncker Commission by both the EP and the **European Council** in late October 2014, she took up her new role on 1 November.

FRANS TIMMERMANS (1961–) was nominated in 2014 as the Dutch Commissioner to the new 28-member **European Commission** led by **Jean-Claude Juncker**. In September Juncker named Timmermans as First Vice-President of the Commission and Commissioner-designate for Better Regulation, Institutional Relations, the Rule of Law and the Charter of Fundamental Rights, subject to approval by the **European Parliament** (EP). Prior to his appointment to the Commission Timmermans was, most recently, the Dutch Minister of Foreign Affairs (2012–14). Timmermans studied French language and literature at Radboud University, Nijmegen and after graduation joined the Dutch diplomatic service. His subsequent career is steeped in mostly European Union (EU)-related affairs. He was elected to the Dutch parliament in 1997 and was Minister of European Affairs in 2007–10. Timmermans was approved at his confirmation hearing with **Members of the European Parliament**. Following the endorsement of the Juncker Commission by both the EP and the **European Council**, he took up his new role as a European Commissioner on 1 November.

TINDEMANS REPORT is the name of a document that originated at the 1974 **summit meeting** in Paris, where the heads of government commissioned Leo Tindemans, the Prime Minister of **Belgium**, to undertake a series of consultations in the national capitals examining what might be achievable by political co-operation. The Tindemans Report was published in 1976. It proposed a common foreign policy and defence collaboration, economic and monetary union, the development of regional and social policies, a common industrial policy and a strengthened **European Commission** elected by, and accountable to, a popularly elected European legislature. It also advanced the notion of a '**two-speed**' Europe, suggesting that the goals of the European Communities (EC) might be more easily achieved if all member states were not expected to proceed at the same rate in all policy areas. Despite remaining on the agenda of all its sessions until 1978, the Report was never discussed by the **European Council**. It did, however, serve as a basis for the several reviews of the EC that occurred in subsequent years.

A **TITLE** is a sub-division of a **Part** within a European Union treaty. Titles can in turn be divided into **Chapters**. In the **Treaty on European Union**, titles form the main sub-division of the treaty.

The **TOTAL ALLOWABLE CATCH** (TAC) is a central element of the **common fisheries policy**. It relates to the conservation and management of fish stocks. TACs are overall quotas, fixed annually by the **Council of the European Union**, for each species of fish that is thought to be threatened by overfishing. Within each overall quota for the European Union, each member state is allocated its own quota. The documentation of catches and other surveillance measures are the responsibility of the member states. The scheme is supervised by a team of inspectors who report directly to the **European Commission**, which has the authority to impose penalties for infringements of the TAC quotas.

TOURISM is a major industry in the European Union (EU) and an important growth area for **employment**. However, **European Commission** efforts to gain member state approval of a multi-annual programme for European tourism (Philoxenia) in 1996 failed. The major emphasis since has been focused on tourism within the context of employment. The **Treaty of Lisbon**, like the abandoned **Treaty establishing a Constitution for Europe**, did, however, envisage EU action complementing that of the member states in promoting the **competitiveness** of undertakings in the tourism sector.

TOURS DE TABLE refers to the procedure where each national delegation at a meeting of the **Council of the European Union** is allowed to make an opening statement on its views of a particular proposal or subject. In the enlarged European Union of 28 states, such interventions could be problematic in terms of time. For example, assuming each member state took five minutes to make its statement, this would mean that more than two hours would elapse before any discussions proper could commence.

TOWN TWINNING was launched by the **European Commission** in 1989. Through carefully targeted grants it seeks to foster and develop further existing links between the populations of the member states. It aims to raise awareness of other European cultures and to promote an understanding, through meetings of twinned towns and municipalities, of what European integration has achieved to date and what challenges remain. The Commission's work under this programme is divided into two areas. Under 'Town Twinning' the Commission promotes exchanges between towns across the European Union and projects that involve towns in current member states and in **applicant countries**. To this end, it supports financially exchanges between citizens and towns that are twinned, conferences and meetings on European subjects, and training seminars for organizers of town-twinning schemes. The second area deals with the so-called 'golden stars of town twinning', which is essentially an annual award presented to the towns that are judged to have done the most in forging closer links between their respective citizens.

TRADE and its development between the member states was the initial economic objective of the European Communities (EC). By 1968 internal **tariff** barriers had been removed by the **Six**, and new member states have been given a short transitional period in which to eliminate their tariffs. The process of free trade was not completed until the implementation of the **internal market**. The European Union (EU) has become the world's largest trader, accounting for some 20% of world trade. The EU has agreements of various kinds—**association agreements**, **free trade agreements** and **trade and co-operation agreements**—with over 120 countries, as well as some 30 multilateral arrangements.

TRADE AND CO-OPERATION AGREEMENTS take various forms and have been concluded with a variety of states, notably those in **Central and Eastern Europe** before the negotiation of **Europe agreements**. Such trade and co-operation agreements form part of the **common commercial policy** and normally involve preferential access to the European Union's **internal market** and the eventual establishment of an industrial free trade area. This is supplemented by co-operation in areas of mutual interest, often focused on facilitating trade and the economic development of the signatory state.

TRADEMARKS are important as indicators of the origin and quality of goods, but companies have had to make separate applications in each member state to secure protection for their trademarks. Since 1980 the **European Commission** has pursued a policy of **harmonization** that envisaged a common European Union trademark that would exist alongside the national ones. (See also **Office for Harmonization in the Internal Market**; **Unitary Patent Convention**.)

JEPPE TRANHOLM-MIKKELSEN (1962–) was appointed as the new **Secretary-General of the Council of the European Union** (EU) on 21 April 2015, with effect from 1 July. His mandate runs until 30 June 2020. His predecessor was Uwe Corsepius. Tranholm-Mikkelsen is Danish, and studied at the University of Aarhus before his MSc at the London School of Economic and Political Science in the **United Kingdom**. He then filled a number of diplomatic roles and was also an adviser on EU policy to the Danish Prime Minister and at the Ministry of Foreign Affairs. In 2007 he was appointed as ambassador to the People's Republic of China, a role that also included responsibility for Mongolia and the Democratic People's Republic of Korea. In 2010 he was appointed the Permanent Representative of Denmark to the EU, a post that he retained until being appointed to his current position.

The **TRANSATLANTIC DECLARATION** is the name of a document signed in November 1990 by the European Communities (EC) and the **USA**. It was intended, given the common heritage and the close historical, political, cultural and economic links between Europe and the USA, to form the basis of greater collaboration and co-operation between the two. The Declaration affirmed their desire for a partnership with specific goals and aspirations. These included openly supporting democracy and the rule of law and advancing respect for **human rights** and individual liberties. The signatories of the declaration sought to safeguard peace and promote international stability; to pursue policies that were targeted at advancing economic growth (such as greater liberalization and **competition policy**) and maintaining low inflation; to promote market principles; to reject all manner of protectionism; and to provide adequate support, in co-operation with other states and organizations, for the emerging liberal democracies of **Central and Eastern Europe**. The Declaration envisaged close consultation between the EC and the US Government on issues of mutual concern and common interest. For example, emphasis was placed on the need to strengthen the multilateral trading system and its organizations, on promoting liberalization and on pursuing bilateral dialogue in order to reduce and eventually eliminate other non-tariff barriers that impeded trade. Also within the Declaration, attention was focused on the need to develop joint scientific research projects in areas such as high-energy physics, **space policy** and environmental protection, as well as on extending youth and student exchanges. To facilitate such co-operation and networking the Declaration set up a regular system of biannual summits and ministerial meetings. (See also **New Transatlantic Agenda**.)

The **TRANSATLANTIC TRADE AND INVESTMENT PARTNERSHIP (TTIP)** is the name of a proposed EU-USA free trade agreement, under negotiation from July 2013. In August 2016 German Vice-Chancellor Sigmar Gabriel stated, after the 14th round of negotiations had taken place in **Brussels**, **Belgium**, in July, that neither side had succeeded in reaching agreement on a single common issue out of the total of 27 under discussion. The TTIP appeared to be moribund by the end of US President Barack Obama's term of office in January 2017, with the inauguration of the new President, Donald Trump, who was expected to introduce a policy of increased US protectionism.

TRANS-EUROPEAN MOBILITY SCHEME FOR UNIVERSITY STUDIES: See **Tempus**

TRANS-EUROPEAN NETWORKS or TENs is a concept introduced by the Treaty on European Union, which commits the European Union (EU) to developing such networks in energy (TEN-E or Ten-Energy), telecommunications (eTEN) and transport (TEN-T) through the interconnection and opening-up of national networks. The assumption has been that such networks aid both the **internal market** and social and economic cohesion within the EU. The EU has been expected to develop common projects and to provide financial assistance through, for example, the **Cohesion Fund**, while member states have been expected to co-ordinate national infrastructure projects that are likely to have a trans-European effect. Priority transport projects for development included high-speed rail links, such as a rail and road tunnel through the Brenner Pass in **Italy** and a motorway linking Lisbon (**Portugal**) and Valladolid (**Spain**). The TENs scheme was extended into **Central and Eastern Europe**, using financial assistance from the **PHARE** programme, with projects including a motorway link between Berlin (**Germany**) and Kyiv (**Ukraine**).

TRANSPARENCY is a term now used widely in the context of the need for more **openness** in and easier public access to the working of the institutions of the European Union (EU). It is hoped that increased transparency and openness will improve the **legitimacy** and **accountability** of the EU.

TRANSPORT POLICY was particularly slow to develop in the European Communities (EC), despite being identified as an objective by the **Treaty of Rome**. The vested interests of the member states in the domain of transport—for example, road haulage quotas and licences, customs documentation, **subsidies** for **railways** and **shipping**, and the protection of national airlines—meant that little progress was made towards a common transport policy until 1982. The catalyst was an action brought by the **European Parliament** in the **Court of Justice** against the Council of Ministers (see **Council of the European Union**) for failing to fulfil the requirements of the Treaty of Rome. The

Court upheld the complaint, arguing that the Council had an obligatory duty to liberalize international transport within the EC and to make it open to carriers of all member states, and recommended the establishment of a common transport policy. The Court ruling enabled the **European Commission** to act with more vigour. In 1983 the Commission formulated a list of policy objectives: a more effective integration of national transport policies; greater productivity and efficiency through reducing the number of bureaucratic constraints and the amount of documentation; greater competition within and between different modes of transport; and **harmonization** of rules relating to working conditions, **health and safety**, environmental protection and technical standards. However, because of the different problems and requirements of the various transport sectors, the Commission found it difficult to develop a common transport policy. Instead, it has sought common rules and harmonization within each major sector: **air transport**, **inland waterways**, **railways**, **road transport** and **shipping**. Common to all sectors is a programme of support for infrastructural developments and modernization. As part of the wider system of **Trans-European Networks** (TENS), the EU adopted a new policy in 1996. The transport network (TEN-T) guidelines envisaged co-ordinated improvements to primary roads, railways, inland waterways, airports, seaports, inland ports and traffic management systems, providing integrated and intermodal long-distance, high-speed routes throughout the EU. The projects undertaken under this initiative are now managed by the Trans-European Transport Executive Agency, which was established in 2006, but the majority of the projects are funded by national governments. The TEN-T was re-launched in January 2014.

The **TREATY ESTABLISHING A CONSTITUTION FOR EUROPE** was agreed in June 2004 and, had it been ratified, would have replaced the **Treaty of Rome** and the **Treaty on European Union** as the formal legal basis of the European Union (EU). Often referred to as a **Constitutional Treaty** or the European Constitution, the treaty emerged out of the deliberations of the **European Convention** that adopted the **draft Treaty establishing a Constitution for Europe** and the negotiations that took place in the subsequent **intergovernmental conference** (IGC).

The Treaty establishing a Constitution for Europe envisaged a range of reforms to the EU and its institutions. These included abolishing the existing **pillar** structure and granting the EU **legal personality**. New posts of **Union Minister for Foreign Affairs** and **President of the European Council** were planned, as were a new system of **qualified majority voting** (QMV) and a revised range of **legal instruments**. **Ratification** of the treaty would also have resulted in the **Charter of Fundamental Rights** being made legally binding, and in increased use of QMV, the extension and a renaming of the co-decision procedure as the '**ordinary legislative procedure**', an eventual reduction in the size of the **European Commission** and changes in the rotation of the **Council presidency**. The rules governing use of **enhanced co-operation** would also have been eased and a **European Public Prosecutor's Office** provided for and, for the first time, a formal mechanism for **withdrawal** from the EU would have existed.

Unlike the **Single European Act** or the Treaty on European Union, no significant expansion of the EU's policy competences would have occurred with the Treaty establishing a Constitution for Europe. All the same, the list of areas in which the EU enjoys a formal **competence** to act would have been increased, mainly in recognition of existing practice. Such areas include administrative co-operation, energy, **humanitarian assistance**, intellectual property, **public health**, **space policy**, **sport**, and **tourism**. One new area of competence was **civil protection**. In addition, the Treaty establishing a Constitution for Europe envisaged reforms to the **common foreign and security policy**, the **European security and defence policy**, EU activities regarding **police and judicial co-operation in criminal matters** and the **area of freedom, security and justice**.

The entry into force of the Treaty establishing a Constitution for Europe was thrown into question in mid-2005 when electorates in **France** and the **Netherlands** voted against its ratification. For some, such a dual rejection should have seen the immediate abandonment of the ratification process. Instead, it was agreed that member states could choose for themselves whether they wished to pause for 'reflection' as the **European Council** in June 2005 agreed or push ahead. **Cyprus**, **Luxembourg**, **Malta** and later **Belgium**, **Estonia** and **Finland** took the latter route, while others put on hold their ratification processes, pending clarification from the French and Dutch on how they intended to proceed. For states outside the EU seeking membership, the **ratification crisis** was worrying since it threatened to postpone or derail further **enlargement**. For others, there were concerns that it would lead to a period of introspection on the part of the EU as well as political weakness—two situations that the treaty had been designed to avoid. There were also concerns that the enlarged EU would not be able to function effectively without the reforms contained in the document. This led to suggestions that alternative mechanisms might be sought to allow key elements to enter into force. Any significant progress, it was widely held, would have to await the outcome of elections in **France** and the **Netherlands** in 2007. Following these, in June 2007 the European Council agreed a mandate for a new IGC that would subsequently adopt the **Treaty of Lisbon** incorporating key elements of the Treaty establishing a Constitution for Europe.

TREATY ESTABLISHING THE EUROPEAN ATOMIC ENERGY COMMUNITY: See **Treaty of Rome**; **European Atomic Energy Community**

TREATY ESTABLISHING THE EUROPEAN COAL AND STEEL COMMUNITY: See **Treaty of Paris**

TREATY ESTABLISHING THE EUROPEAN COMMUNITY: See **Treaty of Rome**

TREATY ESTABLISHING THE EUROPEAN ECONOMIC COMMUNITY: See **Treaty of Rome**

The **TREATY ESTABLISHING THE EUROPEAN STABILITY MECHANISM (TESM)** was signed by the 17 members of the **eurozone** on 11 July 2011 as part of their efforts to resolve the financial crisis in the eurozone. With additional decisions to strengthen the ESM being adopted in July and December 2011, the treaty was subsequently revised and a new version signed on 2 February 2012. With the crisis in the eurozone deepening, swift **ratification** was demanded. However, the scheduled date of 1 July 2012 for the entry into force of the treaty was not met, owing to delays in ratification in **Germany** and **Italy**. Germany's eventual ratification of the document on 27 September (Italy having ratified it on 23 July) brought the TESM into force on that date for the 16 eurozone members that had completed the ratification process; **Estonia** ratified the treaty on 3 October and the ESM commenced operations on 8 October.

A **TREATY OF ACCESSION** contains the **legal instruments** governing the accession of a state to the European Union (EU). Accession treaties have to be ratified by all existing member states as well as the acceding state or states. **Ratification** normally involves a referendum in the acceding country. Since the **Single European Act**, the approval of the **European Parliament** via the consent procedure has also been necessary. The most significant accession treaty of the past decade was signed in Athens, **Greece**, on 16 April 2003 between the EU's member states and 10 applicant states, mainly from **Central and Eastern Europe**: **Cyprus**, the **Czech Republic**, **Estonia**, **Hungary**, **Latvia**, **Lithuania**, **Malta**, **Poland**, **Slovakia** and **Slovenia**. With the exception of Cyprus, each of the applicant states held a referendum during 2003 on whether the country should join the EU. In each case, a majority of those voting voted in favour of membership. Successful ratification of the Accession Treaty in the member states ensured that **enlargement** took place, as planned, on 1 May 2004. An Accession Treaty was signed in **Luxembourg** on 25 April 2005, which governed the accession of **Bulgaria** and **Romania** to the EU. Neither country held a referendum to ratify the Accession Treaty. Its ratification was successfully completed in December 2006, allowing the two countries to accede to the EU on 1 January 2007. The most recent Accession Treaty was signed with **Croatia** on 9 December 2011 and membership was approved by a referendum held in Croatia on 22 January 2012. Croatia's accession to the EU took place on 1 July 2013.

The **TREATY OF AMSTERDAM** was agreed in June 1997 by the **Fifteen** heads of state and government of the European Union (EU). The Treaty was signed in October 1997 and, following **ratification** by the member states, came into force on 1 May 1999. The measures it introduced were discussed during the 1996 **intergovernmental conference** (IGC) review of the **Treaty on European Union** (TEU), which sought to address changing circumstances in **Central and Eastern Europe** and the new arrangements that would be required on **enlargement** of the EU. The IGC also highlighted measures introduced by the TEU that had not proved effective, particularly in relation to closing the gap between national governments and the people, regarding the way the EU was developing (see **democratic deficit**). The new Treaty therefore amended and updated the TEU. It also amended the **founding treaties**, removed many obsolete provisions and renumbered the **articles** of these treaties.

High priority was given in the Treaty of Amsterdam to measures combating high unemployment, extending **citizens' rights** and improving democratic **accountability** and participation in the institutions of the EU. In future, governments were to co-ordinate their employment strategies and a new **Employment Committee** was to be established to oversee the co-ordination process. Greater efforts were to be encouraged in the battle against **discrimination** on grounds of sex, race, ethnic origin, religion or belief, age, disability or sexual orientation. Member states were also required to address gender inequality, and to protect citizens against misuse of data stored in EU **institutions**. New and continued efforts in the fields of public health, the environment and sustainable development, and consumer protection were also to be encouraged. The **protocol** on social policy (see **Charter of Fundamental Social Rights of Workers**) was incorporated into the revised **Treaty of Rome**, following the decision of the British Labour Government to sign the Charter in 1997.

The **pillar**-based system brought in by the TEU was kept, although much of the province of the **justice and home affairs** pillar was transferred to the Treaty of Rome, thereby coming under the first, or Community, pillar, leaving the third pillar to deal primarily with **police and judicial co-operation in criminal matters**.

In an attempt to improve public accountability, the treaty introduced measures to ensure greater **openness** and **transparency** by improving public access to documents originating from the institutions of the European Communities and to the voting results of legislative **decisions** taken by the **Council of the European Union**. Moreover, in an attempt to counter criticisms that a democratic deficit existed within EU institutions, members of **national parliaments** were to become more involved in the **decision making** processes of the EU through the Conference of European Affairs Committees. This group was to be encouraged to voice its opinions in specific policy areas such as fundamental rights and freedoms, justice and security, and **subsidiarity**. National parliaments were also to be given more time to debate EU issues, as the treaty provided for a six-week interval between the tabling of legislative proposals and their placement on the Council agenda, thereby improving democratic participation.

Institutional reforms also featured in the treaty (see **Council of the European Union**; **European Commission**; **European Parliament**—EP), not only to improve democracy but for practical reasons as the EU prepared for expansion. The number of **Members of the European Parliament** elected to the EP was to be limited to 700, and decision making procedures were simplified. **Qualified majority voting** was extended, although **unanimity** was required for constitutional matters and certain policy areas, such as **taxation**. The authority of the Commission's President was also enhanced prior to a review of that institution before enlargement.

Moreover, membership of the EU was made more explicitly conditional. This means that successful applicants have to agree to abide by the principles of **human rights** and fundamental freedoms, liberty and democracy in relation to their citizens, as set down by the EU, or face suspension of certain membership rights, including the right to vote.

The Treaty also focused on creating a safer and stronger Europe by introducing new internal security measures, as well as measures that were intended to promote greater co-operation in foreign policy. A timetable was set within which a series of common immigration and asylum rules was to be established. Improved co-operation between national police forces and the legal systems of the member states was also required, as was incorporation of the **Schengen Agreement** *acquis* into the treaties (although the **United Kingdom** and **Ireland** were allowed an **opt-out**). Strict anti-**fraud** measures were to be introduced. The position of the **European Court of Auditors** was to be enhanced to assist in fraud prevention, and greater co-operation between customs authorities in the member states was to be developed. A stronger Europe in the world was also considered to be a priority, given the EU's failure to agree on a united policy during the 1990–91 hostilities in the Gulf, or in relation to the break-up of, and civil war in, the former **Yugoslavia**. The Secretary-General of the Council was simultaneously to hold the newly created post of **High Representative for the Common Foreign and Security Policy**. A new unit charged with early warning, planning and analysis in EU foreign affairs was also to be created. Closer co-operation between the EU and **Western European Union** (WEU) was called for, and the possibility of the integration of WEU into the EU was raised, but the **North**

Atlantic Treaty Organization was still seen by the EU to be the main security organization for Europe.

Despite its innovations and reforms, the treaty failed to introduce the institutional reforms necessary to prepare the EU for enlargement. Hence, even before it entered into force on 1 May 1999, preparations were being made for a further IGC that would lead to the **Treaty of Nice** in 2001.

The **TREATY OF BRUSSELS** was signed in March 1948 by the Governments of the **United Kingdom**, **France** and the **Benelux** countries. It was modelled on the 1947 **Treaty of Dunkirk** and, as such, was an agreement on mutual military assistance against military attack from either **Germany** or, more likely, the **USSR**. It also sought to foster greater economic, social and cultural issues between the five states. The Treaty was a precursor to establishment of the **North Atlantic Treaty Organization** (NATO) in 1949 and **Western European Union** in 1954. The Treaty was largely the creation of Ernest Bevin, the British Foreign Secretary. This initiative was endorsed warmly by the **USA**. Many Europeans who hoped that it promised greater British involvement in the construction of a new European order also welcomed the treaty. However, it was rendered almost meaningless with the creation of NATO under US hegemony in 1949.

TREATY OF DUNKIRK was the name of a document signed in 1947 by **France** and the **United Kingdom**. Although the pact called for bilateral economic assistance and co-operation, its justification was primarily military: a guarantee of mutual aid in the event of any future German aggression. It was superseded by the **Treaty of Brussels** in 1948.

TREATY OF FRIENDSHIP is the name of the pact, also known as the Elysée Treaty, signed by **France** and the Federal Republic of **Germany** (West Germany) on 22 January 1963. It was the only tangible result of the **Fouchet Plan** for greater political co-operation and integration, and provided for institutional co-operation between the two states in the four policy areas of defence, foreign affairs, education and culture. Strongly criticized at the time by the other members of the European Communities (EC), it became the basis of a considerable degree of liaison and regularized co-operation between the two states, and of a powerful Franco-German axis within the EC.

The **TREATY OF LISBON**, originally named the **Reform Treaty**, was agreed in October 2007 and signed on 13 December 2007. It was drawn up in an **intergovernmental conference** launched by the **European Council** in June 2007 and, having been ratified by all 27 member states, introduced a range of essentially institutional and political reforms originally contained in the abandoned **Treaty establishing a Constitution for Europe**. The Treaty of Lisbon was agreed with a view 'to enhancing the efficiency and democratic legitimacy' of the European Union (EU) and 'to improving the coherence of its action'. To these ends, it provided for increased use of **qualified majority voting** (QMV), the eventual replacement of QMV with a **double majority voting** system, the extension and a renaming of the co-decision procedure as the **'ordinary legislative procedure'**, an eventual reduction in the size of the **European Commission** and changes in the rotation of the **Council presidency**. It also eased the rules governing use of **enhanced co-operation**. In terms of the coherence of what the EU does, particularly externally, the Treaty of Lisbon introduced a number of reforms to the **common foreign and security policy** and was more explicit about what the EU envisages as the form and purpose of its **European security and defence policy**. It also developed the position of the **High Representative for the Common Foreign and Security Policy**, now retitled **High Representative of the Union for Foreign Affairs and Security Policy**, created the post of **President of the European Council**, and allowed for **permanent structured co-operation** on military matters.

Drawing also on what was envisaged in the Treaty establishing a Constitution for Europe, the Treaty of Lisbon abolished the EU's existing **pillar** structure, granted the EU **legal personality**, made the **Charter of Fundamental Rights** legally binding, provided for the establishment of a **European Public Prosecutor's Office** and, for the first time, established a formal mechanism for **withdrawal** from the EU. There was also clarification of the EU's formal **competence** and formal legal bases in a number of areas of existing practice, notably administrative co-operation, energy, **humanitarian assistance**, intellectual property, public health, space, **sport**, and **tourism**. One new area of competence was **civil protection**. EU activities regarding **police and judicial co-operation in criminal matters** and the **area of freedom, security and justice** also saw some reforms.

With the exception of **Ireland**, all member states were scheduled to pursue **ratification** using purely parliamentary means. By the end of May 2008 the parliaments of 16 member states had endorsed the treaty. The remaining member states were due to complete ratification by the end of the year, thereby allowing the treaty to enter into force on 1 January 2009. In the first half of June 2008 a further three parliaments—those of **Estonia**, **Finland** and **Greece**—ratified the treaty before attention switched on 12 June to Ireland, the only member state to hold a referendum. The outcome was a seemingly decisive victory for opponents of the treaty. However, the Irish came under considerable pressure to hold a second vote. Agreement to do so came following a commitment from the European Council to agree various clarifications and guarantees concerning the impact of the treaty on Irish neutrality, taxation powers, the right to life, family and education, and **workers' rights**. A second referendum was held in October 2009, at which voters endorsed the treaty by a two-thirds' majority. Following some last-minute delays in the **Czech Republic**, ratification was completed in time for the Treaty of Lisbon to enter into force on 1 December.

TREATY OF LUXEMBOURG is the name of a document signed by the member states in April 1970. An amendment to the **Treaty of Rome**, it incorporated the new budgetary system of **own resources** into the structure of the European Communities.

The **TREATY OF NICE** was agreed in December 2000 and signed in February 2001. **Ratification** took longer than expected after the process was thrown into doubt when, in June 2001, the Irish populace rejected the treaty in a referendum. As had been the case following the **ratification crisis** in 1992, when the Danish populace rejected the **Treaty on European Union** (TEU), a second referendum was scheduled. This took place in October 2002 and on this occasion the treaty was endorsed by 63% of those who voted. The Treaty was then successfully channelled through both Irish houses of parliament before finally coming into force on 1 February 2003.

The essential purpose of the treaty was explained in its preamble: to prepare the European Union (EU) for **enlargement**. It did this by introducing a series of staged reforms to the **institutions**, notably by: reducing the size of the **European Commission** to a maximum of one national from each member state; re-weighting votes within the **Council of the European Union**, essentially to the advantage of the larger member states; and re-allocating seats in the **European Parliament** (EP). Moreover, Council votes and EP seats were provisionally allocated to the **candidate countries** (albeit with the exception of **Turkey**), as were seats on the **Committee of the Regions** and the **Economic and Social Committee**. The **Court of Justice** and **Court of First Instance** were also to undergo some reform: innovations included the creation of **Grand Chambers** and **Judicial Panels** in an attempt to enable the courts to deal with an already large caseload. The existence and activities of **Eurojust** that enabled member states to co-operate in the area of cross-border crime were also formally recognized.

Beyond institutional reform, the Treaty of Nice introduced changes to the **common foreign and security policy** (CFSP), allowing for **enhanced co-operation** and essentially excising from the TEU references to **Western European Union**, a move that coincided with the establishment of the CFSP. More generally, enhanced co-operation was to be facilitated by reducing the number of member states needed to begin a project. Likewise, **decision making** generally was also facilitated through the extension of **qualified majority voting** to more than 40 provisions, although **unanimity** was still retained for the most sensitive areas (e.g. tax **harmonization**).

Unlike earlier treaties such as the **Single European Act** and the **Treaty of Amsterdam**, the Treaty of Nice did little in the way of increasing the competences of the EU. Little was included beyond a slight extension of the treaty making powers of the EU to include services and the insertion into the **Treaty of Rome** of a new **title** on economic, financial and technical co-operation with third countries. However, when adopting the treaty, the member states set in motion a process that could lead to significant increases in the activities of the EU. Equally, it could lead to limits being placed on them. The process in question was the debate on the future of Europe, which was later expanded in the **Laeken Declaration** and provided with a forum for expression in the **European Convention** launched in February 2002. Its conclusions informed a further **intergovernmental conference** that began work in October 2003.

TREATY OF PARIS is the commonly used name of the document, signed on 18 April 1951 and designated to remain in force for 50 years, which established the **European Coal and Steel Community**. This **founding treaty** committed the signatories to contribute to economic expansion through 'the development of employment and the improvement of the standard of living in the participating countries through the institution, in harmony with the general economy of the member states, of a common market'. Subsequent entrants to the European Communities and European Union had to accept the terms and obligations of the treaty, although after 2002 new members were no longer required to, as the Treaty of Paris expired in July 2002.

TREATY OF PRÜM: See **Prüm Convention**

TREATY OF ROME is the commonly used name of the document that established the **European Economic Community**. Signed on 25 March 1957, it is the most important of the **founding treaties** of the European Communities. It was concluded for an unlimited period of time and committed the signatories, 'by establishing a **common market** and progressively approximating the economic policies of member states, to promote throughout the Community a harmonious development of economic activities, a continuous and balanced expansion, an increase in stability, an accelerated raising of the standard of living, and closer relations between the States belonging to it'. The greater part of the treaty lists the actions and common policies to which the member states committed themselves, and the institutions of the new body. The Treaty has been amended on several occasions since 1957, most significantly by the **Single European Act**, the **Treaty on European Union**, the **Treaty of Amsterdam** (which renumbered the treaty's **articles**) and the **Treaty of Nice**. With the entry into force of the **Treaty of Lisbon**, the treaty was further amended and renamed the **Treaty on the Functioning of the European Union**. The **European Atomic Energy Community** was established by a separate document, also often referred to as the Treaty of Rome, which was signed at the same time. With the exception of its institutional provisions, this largely remains unamended, although there is currently support from some member states for a substantial revision.

TREATY OF ROME (EURATOM): See **European Atomic Energy Community**; **Treaty of Rome**

TREATY OF WESTMINSTER: See **Council of Europe**

The **TREATY ON EUROPEAN UNION** (TEU) is one of the main **European treaties**. Agreed at the **Maastricht summit** of the **European Council** in December 1991 and later signed by representatives of the member states of the European Communities (EC) on 7 February 1992, it formally established the European Union (EU), basing it on three **pillars**: the existing EC as the first pillar and two new pillars of intergovernmental co-operation covering a **common foreign and security policy** and **justice and home affairs**. In doing so, the TEU also brought about a significant revision of the **Treaty of Rome**, thereby increasing the powers of the EC. The member states, with the exception of the **United Kingdom**, agreed to further integration in social affairs in the form of a Social Chapter (see **Charter of Fundamental Social Rights of Workers**). Substantial institutional reforms to the EC were also introduced, as was the notion of EU **citizenship**. More significantly, the TEU laid down a detailed timetable and established **convergence criteria** for **economic and monetary union** (EMU), which was to be established by 1999 at the latest. Not all member states wished to be tied to the goal of EMU, however. Hence special **opt-outs** were agreed for **Denmark** and the UK, the latter also gaining an opt-out from the Social Chapter. The EMU opt-out did not assuage the concerns of the Danish people, however, who rejected the TEU in a referendum in June 1992. This led to a **ratification crisis** and the granting of further concessions to Denmark. In May 1993, the Danish people approved the TEU and it entered into force on 1 November 1993.

The Treaty was formally reviewed by an **intergovernmental conference** in 1996. The conference debated the measures required to address the shortfalls of the TEU, with the place of the EU in the world and its position vis-à-vis **enlargement** featuring prominently in debates. Measures required to move forward to a 'People's Europe' were also discussed and introduced via the **Treaty of Amsterdam**, which was signed in October 1997. Amendments to the TEU made in the Treaty of Amsterdam were soon to be followed by further revision via the **Treaty of Nice**. Had the **Treaty establishing a Constitution for Europe** been ratified, it would have replaced the TEU. Its replacement, the **Treaty of Lisbon**, further amended—and renumbered—the TEU's provisions.

The **TREATY ON THE FUNCTIONING OF THE EUROPEAN UNION** (TFEU) was the new name of the **Treaty establishing the European Community**—the Treaty of Rome—following the entry into force of the **Treaty of Lisbon** in December 2009. With this name change, all references to the **European Community** were replaced with 'European Union' and the European Community ceased to exist.

TREATY ON STABILITY, CO-ORDINATION AND GOVERNANCE IN THE ECONOMIC AND MONETARY UNION: See **Fiscal Compact**

TREVI stands for Terrorisme, Radicalisme, Extrémisme, Violence Internationale. It was established in 1975 as a forum for intergovernmental co-operation by the member states on matters relating to internal security, organized crime, terrorism and drug trafficking. It also worked for the co-ordination of **migration and asylum policy**. Its twice-yearly meetings of justice and home affairs ministers were held in secret. A more structured approach towards these policy areas was accepted as a consequence of the decision to establish an **internal market**, and in the late 1980s several more specialized subgroups were established within the TREVI framework. It formed the basis of the more formal **justice and home affairs** pillar of the European Union that was established by the **Treaty on European Union**.

TROIKA is a term that originally referred to the grouping that, prior to the **Treaty of Lisbon**, represented the European Union (EU) internationally as part of the **common foreign and security policy** and, previously, **European political co-operation**. Originally it comprised the member state occupying the presidency of the **Council of the European Union**, its immediate predecessor and its scheduled successor. The idea was that such a combination would achieve consistency in the activities and efforts of the EU and greater success in the attainment of their aims. Following the **Treaty of Amsterdam** the member state holding the presidency of the Council was accompanied by the **High Representative for the Common Foreign and Security Policy** and the member of the **European Commission** responsible for external relations. With the entry into force of the Treaty of Lisbon, representation fell to the **High Representative of the Union for Foreign Affairs and Security Policy**. The term troika was also used during the **eurozone** crisis to refer to the tripartite committee of the **European Commission**, the **European Central Bank** and the International Monetary Fund, which organized bailout packages for indebted states, contingent on the adoption of austerity measures.

TUNISIA: See **Maghreb States**

TURKEY, recognized by the European Communities as a European state, submitted an application for association in July 1959. Negotiations began in 1962 and concluded with an **association agreement** in 1963. This specified a transitional period of 22 years, commencing in 1970, that was designed to lead to a **customs union**. European opposition to the Turkish military coup of September 1980 further delayed developments. Talks were resumed in 1983, after the re-establishment of civilian government, and in 1987 Turkey submitted an application for full membership. The application did not progress within the European Union (EU) because of fears over Turkey's weak economy, doubts about its suitability in terms of democracy and **human rights**, and concern over the continuing partition of **Cyprus**. However, in March 1995 an agreement on a customs union was signed; it came into force in December 1995 following **ratification** by the **European Parliament**. In spite of persisting doubts over Turkey's progress in the economic, political and human rights fields and over the Cyprus issue, Turkey's eligibility for accession to the EU was confirmed in 1997: the country would be judged according to the same criteria as the other **applicant countries**. As a result, a number of measures were proposed by the **European Commission** in 1997 to assist the country in preparing for accession by extending its relations with the EU beyond the customs union. Turkey was not, however, invited to participate in the accession process launched in 1998.

In December 1999 the **European Council** held at Helsinki, **Finland**, agreed to recognize Turkey, alongside the applicant countries from **Central and Eastern Europe**, as a candidate state. Although Turkey was invited to become part of the accession process, **accession negotiations** did not begin. Instead, further progress with economic and political reforms was deemed necessary before they could be opened. Formal negotiations commenced on 3 October 2005 but progress proved to be slow. Although officially, from an EU perspective, progress was dependent on domestic reforms being undertaken in Turkey, the slow progress owed as much to the EU and the reluctance of some of its members (notably **Cyprus** and **France**, together with the **Netherlands**, **Austria** and **Germany**) to push forward towards Turkish accession. In some cases, national leaders were personally opposed to Turkish accession, and in some member states there has been evident popular disquiet at the prospect of Turkish membership. In the case of France, this led to a constitutional change, subjecting future EU enlargements to a referendum. Meanwhile, Cyprus has remained determined to see Turkey fulfil its obligations towards the EU and open up access to its ports to Cypriot vessels. By 1 July 2012 only 13 of the 35 negotiating chapters of the *acquis communautaire* had been opened (of which eight had been frozen) and only one had been closed. During the second half of 2012 Turkey suspended negotiations during Cyprus's tenure of the presidency of the **Council of the European Union**. Negotiations regarding EU accession had been due to recommence in June 2013, but, following a controversial crackdown by the Turkish security forces on anti-Government protesters that month, the EU postponed further talks until the presentation in October of a progress report on Turkey's bid, which recommended the resumption of talks. Negotiations recommenced in November. The Turkish accession issue remains highly contentious for a number of the EU's 28 member state governments. **Germany** remains lukewarm at best and one of **Angela Merkel**'s closest allies declared in April 2014 that the 'Erdoğan Turkey' was not fit for membership of the EU (referring to the controversial policies of then Turkish Prime Minister and, from August, President, Recep Tayyip Erdoğan). In mid-July 2016 the **High Representative of the Union for Foreign Affairs and Security Policy, Federica Mogherini**, and the Commissioner for European Neighbourhood Policy and Enlargement Negotiations, **Johannes Hahn**, condemned a coup attempt in Turkey. Although membership negotiations had opened in additional policy areas in December 2015 and June 2016, amid increased co-operation between the EU and Turkey on migration (see below), Turkey's eventual membership seemed no closer, and in late November 2016 the

European Parliament approved a non-binding resolution supporting the temporary suspension of accession negotiations with Turkey, owing to concerns over human rights and the rule of law following the suppression of an attempted coup in July. In mid-December the European Council confirmed that negotiations would not be launched in any new policy areas while the ongoing political situation in Turkey prevailed.

Meanwhile, in October 2015 a Joint Action Plan was negotiated between the European Commission and Turkey in an attempt to ameliorate co-operation in responding to the **European migration crisis**, caused, in particular, by the ongoing civil conflict in **Syria**. The agreement provided for political and financial engagement with Turkey to be deepened in several areas. In mid-March 2016 a new EU-Turkey agreement was reached, providing for the return of undocumented migrants crossing into the territory of **Greece** and considered not to be in immediate need of international protection; the EU pledged to accept an officially documented Syrian refugee from inside Turkey for each migrant returned to that country, and to provide assistance worth up to some €6,000m. by the end of 2018, together with the acceleration of visa liberalization for Turkish citizens. By June 2016 the European Commission reported there to have been a significant decline in the numbers of migrants leaving Turkey for Greek territory. Prior to the implementation of the agreement with Turkey, around 1,740 migrants were traversing the Aegean Sea to the Greek islands each day. From the beginning of May the average number of arrivals each day had reportedly declined to some 47, which represented a decline of more than 95%.

DONALD TUSK (1957–) was named at the end of August 2014 as the new President of the **European Council**, to hold office from 1 December until 31 May 2017 and as President of the **Euro Summit** (meetings of eurozone heads of state and of government) for the same period. Tusk, who was born in Gdánsk, Poland, was the leader of the liberal-conservative Platforma Obywatelska (Civic Platform) party, and had held the role of Prime Minister of Poland for seven years, which had been a period of relative political stability. He was the only Prime Minister to secure re-election for a second term in Poland since 1989. His Government resigned in September 2014. Tusk sees the USA as an important ally for Poland, and is in favour of increased European Union integration, primarily owing to security concerns. Owing to his reputation for pragmatism and tenaciousness, he has drawn comparisons from some observers with the German leader **Angela Merkel**. In March 2017 Polish Prime Minister Beata Szydło, who leads a populist Government, placed Poland in conflict with the **European Council** when she was the only national leader to oppose Tusk's re-election as Council President. Tusk was duly re-elected for s second term.

TWELVE (EU12), or the Europe of the Twelve, are terms sometimes used to describe the membership of the European Communities after 1986, when the accession of **Portugal** and **Spain** increased the number of member states from **Ten** to Twelve, and before 1995, when the accession of **Austria**, **Finland** and **Sweden** made the number **Fifteen**.

TWENTY-EIGHT (EU28), or Europe of the Twenty-Eight, is a term sometimes used to describe the membership of the European Union from July 2013, when **Croatia** joined the **Twenty-Seven** existing member states.

TWENTY-FIVE (EU25), or Europe of the Twenty-Five, is a term sometimes used to describe the membership of the European Union after May 2004, when **Cyprus**, the **Czech Republic**, **Estonia**, **Hungary**, **Latvia**, **Lithuania**, **Malta**, **Poland**, **Slovakia** and **Slovenia** joined the existing **Fifteen** member states.

TWENTY-SEVEN (EU27), or Europe of the Twenty-Seven, is a term sometimes used to describe the membership of the European Union from 2007, when **Bulgaria** and **Romania** joined the **Twenty-Five** existing member states, and before 2013, when the accession of **Croatia** made the number **Twenty-Eight**.

TWINNING is a programme directed at assisting the process of administrative reform in **candidate countries** in **Central and Eastern Europe**. The focus of the project is the development of the administrative capacity in these countries to implement effectively the *acquis communautaire*.

TWO-SPEED EUROPE is a more limited variant of **multi-speed Europe**.

U

UEN: See **Union for Europe of the Nations Group**

UK: See **United Kingdom**

The **UK INDEPENDENCE PARTY** (UKIP) was established in 1993 in opposition to any further European integration and, primarily, opposition to the **Maastricht Treaty**. The core principle uniting its members was a demand for the **United Kingdom** to leave the **European Union** (EU). For over a decade, however, UKIP remained very much a fringe party. With leadership changes it made its first major breakthrough at the 2004 elections to the **European Parliament** (EP), winning 12 seats and finishing third. In 2009 UKIP secured 13 seats and 16.5% of the votes cast to become the second largest British party in the EP. In the 2014 EP elections UKIP was the first-placed British party, with 27.5% of the votes cast, winning 24 seats. The successes at European level were not replicated at national level in the general elections of 2005 and 2010, at which UKIP polled 2.3% and 3.1%, respectively, and won no seats. In 2014 UKIP won its first seats in the House of Commons following two by-elections in Clacton (with some 59% of the votes) and in Rochester and Strood (with some 42% of the votes). Although UKIP continued to demand the UK's exit from the EU, it also benefited from strong opposition towards the UK's immigration policy and its anti-establishment rhetoric. Its growth was aided by Nigel Farage's charismatic leadership and ability to connect with particular sections of the electorate, although UKIP won only one seat at the May 2015 UK general election. At 2015 the party's representation in the EP stood at 23 seats, following the departure of one of its members, Amjad Bashir, to the

Conservatives and the **European Conservatives and Reformists Group**. Farage campaigned vociferously and sometimes controversially for the 'Leave' side prior to the referendum held in the UK in late June 2016 on British membership of the EU, in which a majority of participating voters chose to leave the Union (also referred to as **Brexit**). In early July Farage announced his intention to resign as leader of UKIP, stating that he had fulfilled his political ambitions; however, he remained a **Member of the European Parliament**. At the UK general election of June 2017, UKIP performed badly, securing no seats, having effectively fulfilled its purpose.

UKIP: See **UK Independence Party**

UKRAINE gained its independence from the **USSR** in 1991. In 1994 it concluded a **partnership and co-operation agreement** (PCA) with the European Union (EU), which entered into force in 1998. It is also a recipient of financial assistance from the EU under the **European Neighbourhood Policy** (ENP) (formerly the **Technical Assistance to the Commonwealth of Independent States**—TACIS—programme), and in 1999 was the focus of an EU **common strategy**. This is designed to support the democratic and economic transition process in Ukraine; to ensure co-operation in meeting common challenges in the areas of stability and security in Europe, the environment, energy and nuclear safety; to assist Ukraine's integration into the European and world economies; and to enhance co-operation in the field of **justice and home affairs**. With **enlargement** in 2004 meaning that Ukraine now shares a border with the EU, further developments in relations have taken place primarily within the framework of the ENP. Westward-looking governments in Ukraine, under Viktor Yushchenko's (2005–10) presidency, expressed strong interest in EU membership sometime in the future. However, the main focus was on implementing the ENP Action Plan agreed in 2005 and completing negotiations on an **association agreement** to replace the PCA (which expired in 2008). The new agreement was to involve more intense political dialogue, a **deep and comprehensive free trade area** and strengthened co-operation. Negotiations began in March 2007 and were eventually closed at the end of 2011 (without any agreement being signed). In the mean time, in May 2009 Ukraine became part of the EU's **Eastern partnership** project. Elections in early 2010 saw the defeat of Yushchenko, his replacement by Viktor Yanukovych and the start of a new period of less ambitious engagement with the EU. In fact, relations soon deteriorated as the EU strongly criticized the Ukrainian Government for its politicization of the country's judicial system. Particular criticism was reserved for the treatment of the imprisoned former Prime Minister, Yuliya Tymoshenko. The EU became increasingly concerned about developments within Ukraine and, although an association agreement was initialled with Ukraine in March 2012, its signature by the **Council of the European Union** and the **European Parliament** was indefinitely postponed until the Government in Kyiv made substantial progress regarding electoral, judicial and constitutional reform. In February 2013 the Ukrainian Government adopted a 'Plan on Priority Measures for European Integration of Ukraine' in a bid to facilitate the country meeting the EU stipulations for the signature of the association agreement by November.

However, events were to take a different direction, with Ukraine entering a period of real political uncertainty, when domestically relations between the people of Ukraine deteriorated, as did those between the **Russian Federation** and Ukraine.

The Ukrainian crisis emerged as a key European and international issue throughout 2014. The crisis commenced when the Ukrainian (and pro-Russian) Government of Yanukovych opted to suspend preparations for signing the Association Agreement with the EU, as had been planned, at a summit in Vilnius (**Lithuania**) in late November 2013. This decision led to immediate protests on the streets of Kyiv and culminated in the overthrow of Yanukovych in February 2014. These developments increased tensions within Ukraine and ultimately led to Crimea's annexation by Russia (following a referendum in the region). The EU tried to stabilize the situation and the new pro-European Government in Kyiv rapidly signed agreements with the EU on the political and economic aspects of association in March and June, respectively; parts of the agreement were provisionally applied in November. Meanwhile, in May EU ministers for foreign affairs, meeting in **Brussels**, Belgium, agreed to impose broader sanctions against those deemed to be threatening Ukrainian sovereignty. In mid-June the Council agreed to establish a Common Security and Defence Policy mission, the EU Advisory Mission for Civilian Security Sector Reform. In early July the EU extended the scope of the restrictive measures in place. Additional sanctions were imposed in late July, following the shooting down of a Malaysian Airlines aeroplane over Donetsk, and in September. In January 2015 the **European Commission** offered lending of some €1,800m. to Ukraine, in support of its reform programme. The deep and comprehensive free trade agreement, which formed part of the Association Agreement signed in 2014, entered into effect from January 2016. By late 2016 the Association Agreement had been ratified by all EU member states with the exception of the **Netherlands**; voters participating in a non-binding referendum held there in April rejected the deal. The deal was finally ratified in the Netherlands in May 2017, and in July the Council approved the Association Agreement with Ukraine, thereby permitting its full implementation from September of that year.

UNANIMITY applies to certain types of decision taken by the **Council of the European Union**. Its use is laid down in the **founding treaties**. Policies that are subject to unanimity require the agreement of all member states before a proposal can be adopted. For much of the early history of the European Communities, especially following the **Luxembourg Compromise**, unanimity was essential. Since the **Single European Act**, there has been a general shift away from unanimity towards greater use of **decisions** being taken under **qualified majority voting** (QMV). The **Treaty on European Union**, the **Treaty of Amsterdam** and the **Treaty of Nice** extended the use of QMV, and currently far fewer decisions are subject to unanimous agreement in the Council. This is particularly the case following the entry into force of the **Treaty of Lisbon**. For what were previously **pillar** I and pillar III matters—the pillars have since been abandoned—QMV became the general rule. By contrast, decisions relating to the **common foreign and security policy** are still generally subject to unanimity. However, even with QMV, the Council prefers to reach either unanimous agreement or consensus wherever possible.

UNICE: See **BUSINESSEUROPE**

UNIFORM ELECTORAL PROCEDURE relates to the method of elections to the **European Parliament** (EP). The idea that some form of uniform electoral procedure based on direct universal suffrage should be used across all member states dates back to the **Treaty of Paris** and can be found also in Article 190 of the **Treaty of Rome** (now Article 223 of the **Treaty on the Functioning of the European Union**). However, despite treaty commitments there has been little progress towards any uniform procedure. Elections in the member states and rules pertaining to them are decided at the national level. Elections to the EP first occurred in June 1979 but the procedures varied from state to state. Most countries opted for some form of proportional representation, while the **United Kingdom** maintained its 'first past the post' system that was used in elections to Parliament. The UK (with the exception of Northern Ireland, which was deemed a three-member constituency where the **Members of the European Parliament** are elected under the single transferable vote procedure) maintained this system until the Labour Government introduced legislation to use proportional representation in the European elections of June 1999. Currently there is no single electoral procedure throughout the member states, and voting continues to take place on different days (e.g. Thursday in the UK, Sunday in **France** and **Germany**, and both Sunday and Monday in **Italy**).

The **UNION FOR EUROPE OF THE NATIONS GROUP** (UEN/UPE) is a former **party group** of the **European Parliament** (EP). It was formed in 1999 as a conservative force that was largely sceptical towards the issue of any deeper European integration, although some of its member parties, such as the Irish Fianna Fáil, supported the Constitution for Europe. In stark contrast to the other EP groups, the UEN was a noticeably less cohesive force, reflecting the wide and often divergent views of its members. It grew gradually in membership following its establishment. In 2002 UEN had 21 members in the EP. After the 2004 elections it increased its representation in the parliament by securing 27 deputies, and its membership climbed to 35 immediately after the 2009 EP elections. However, the lack of internal cohesion not only ensured a lack of common purpose, but also created tensions. The group dissolved following the 2009 EP elections, as the representatives from the Polish Law and Conservative Party forged a new alliance (the **European Conservatives and Reformists Group**) with **David Cameron**'s British Conservatives, while Fianna Fáil had already left the group's ranks to join the **Group of the Alliance of Liberals and Democrats for Europe** (ALDE) (in April 2009).

The **UNION FOR THE MEDITERRANEAN** (UfM) is a relatively recent addition to the **Barcelona process**, hence its official title, Barcelona Process: Union for the Mediterranean. It was launched in July 2008 and follows from ideas promoted by Nicolas Sarkozy, the French President. Initially limited to littoral states of the Mediterranean, it now comprises all European Union (EU) member states plus **Albania**, Algeria, **Bosnia and Herzegovina**, Egypt, Israel, Jordan, Lebanon, Libya (observer status only), Mauritania, Monaco, **Montenegro**, **Morocco**, the Palestinian Territories, **Syria**, Tunisia and **Turkey**; it also includes the League of Arab States. In essence, the Union for the Mediterranean is a re-launch of the **Euro-Mediterranean partnership**, albeit with some additional elements, notably a dedicated Secretariat responsible for promoting co-operation projects in six designated areas: de-pollution of the Mediterranean Sea; the establishment of maritime and land highways; joint civil protection initiatives to combat natural and man-made disasters; a Mediterranean solar energy plan; the inauguration of the Euro-Mediterranean University in **Slovenia** (plans to construct a second such institution, in Fes, Morocco, were announced in June 2012); and the Mediterranean Business Development Initiative focusing on micro, **small and medium-sized enterprises**. The launch of the Union for the Mediterranean signalled a shift in the EU's approach to its immediate neighbours. Henceforth, as was underlined by the later launch in 2009 of the **Eastern partnership**, the **European Neighbourhood Policy** would essentially comprise distinct Mediterranean and Eastern elements. The Secretariat of the UfM was inaugurated in Barcelona, **Spain**, in March 2010; the Secretary-General is elected upon consensus from a non-EU country. The current holder of the post is Fathallah Sijilmassi of Morocco.

A **UNION MINISTER FOR FOREIGN AFFAIRS** was envisaged in the **Treaty establishing a Constitution for Europe** and would have replaced the **High Representative for the Common Foreign and Security Policy**. Under the terms of the **Treaty of Lisbon**, which came into force in December 2009 many of the powers planned for the Union Minister for Foreign Affairs have been passed to the renamed **High Representative of the Union for Foreign Affairs and Security Policy**, currently **Federica Mogherini**.

UNION OF EUROPEAN FEDERALISTS (UEF) is the name of an organization established in 1946 to harness and combine, on a transnational basis, the energy and ideas of the several groups and organizations that had emerged in 1945 to advocate a federal European state. The UEF is based in **Brussels** and consists of 20 constituent organizations.

UNION OF INDUSTRIAL AND EMPLOYERS' CONFEDERATIONS OF EUROPE (UNICE): See **BUSINESSEUROPE**

UNION OF SOVIET SOCIALIST REPUBLICS: See **USSR**

The **UNITARY PATENT CONVENTION** (UPC), formerly referred to as the Community Patent Convention (CPC), is an initiative aimed at overcoming some of the problems experienced by European companies in registering **patents** and **trademarks**. The European Patent Convention (EPC) was signed in 1973 and entered into force in 1977. In that year a European Patent Office was set up in Munich, **Germany**. The original Convention was not a European Communities (EC) instrument, since the member states could not agree on a common policy, and some did not join the scheme. The main problem was that, although it introduced a common registration procedure, where patent infringements occurred, the plaintiff had to pursue separate litigation in each country where the infringements were alleged to have taken place. Revisions to the EPC were agreed in November 2000 and a revised EPC entered into force on 13 December 2007. Meanwhile, in June 1997 the **European Commission** published proposals to simplify the European patent system through the introduction of a unitary Community patent, to remove the need to file patent applications with individual member states. Upon the entry into force in December 2009 of the **Treaty of Lisbon**, which provided a new legal basis for the establishment of unitary intellectual property titles within the European Union (EU), the proposed Community patent was renamed the EU patent. During that month the **European Council** agreed a draft regulation on the EU patent, in accordance with which it was envisaged that the EU would accede to the EPC (which would require further revision to the Convention), and the European Patent Office would grant EU patents with unitary effect throughout the territory of the

EU. Infringement and validity issues relating to the planned EU patent were to be addressed by a proposed European and EU Patents Court. In December 2012 the **European Parliament** approved the so-called patent package, comprising two draft regulations, on increased co-operation to facilitate unitary patent protection and associated translation arrangements, and an agreement on the establishment of a Unified Patent Court, which prepared the way for the introduction of a European patent with unitary effect. The agreement establishing the Unitary Patent Convention was signed in February 2013 and was to enter into force following its ratification by a minimum of 13 EU member states, including **France**, **Germany** and the **United Kingdom**. The UPC was legally adopted in December 2015, and by mid-2017 it had been ratified by nine countries. **Italy** and **Spain** did not intend to take part in the Convention.

The **UNITED KINGDOM** has played an important role in European Union (EU) affairs. However, the UK often had a troubled relationship with the EU, resisting further integration, often in opposition to **France** and **Germany**, and culminating in the referendum decision to leave the Union in June 2016 (see below).

In 1945 British prestige in Europe was high, and in many states there was an expectation that the UK would take the lead in developing European integration. However, British policy was to seek intergovernmental co-operation, and the UK avoided involvement in any partnership that might diminish its own sovereignty and affect its relations with the **USA** and the Commonwealth. Europe was seen as an important issue, but it ranked behind both of these. Consequently, the UK dismissed the European initiatives contained within the **European Coal and Steel Community**, the **European Economic Community** (EEC) and the **European Atomic Energy Community**. The UK finally applied for membership of the EEC in 1961 and again in 1967, but **France**, under President Charles de Gaulle, effectively vetoed both applications. Negotiations recommenced in 1970, and the UK became a member of the European Communities (EC) in January 1973.

After 1973, the UK was often seen as only a partial member of the EC. It demanded and obtained a renegotiation of its terms of entry in 1975, and waged a campaign until 1984 for a reduction of what it regarded as its excessive contribution to the EC **budget**. Although the UK was at the forefront of plans for the **internal market**, Prime Minister Margaret Thatcher grew increasingly hostile to the process of European integration by the late 1980s, and was particularly opposed to plans towards **economic and monetary union** (EMU). The UK frequently maintained a position of complete isolation in the **European Council** and the Council of Ministers (now the **Council of the European Union**). For example, the UK declined full membership of the **European Monetary System** until October 1990: even then, as a result of speculative pressure on sterling, it withdrew from the **exchange-rate mechanism** in September 1992. The UK also negotiated exemptions, or **opt-outs**, from parts of the **Treaty on European Union**, most notably from the Social Chapter (see **Charter of Fundamental Social Rights of Workers**), and from the **Treaty of Amsterdam**, which incorporated the **Schengen Agreement**. However, the Labour Government that came to power in 1997 agreed to sign the Social Charter shortly after coming into office, and hence the **protocol** on social policy was incorporated by the Treaty of Amsterdam into the revised **Treaty of Rome**. Although often hostile to moves towards political integration, the UK was a strong advocate of economic reform, supporting **freedom of movement** and the internal market. It refused, however, to join EMU, which came into operation in January 1999. The UK strongly supported **European political co-operation** and its replacement, the **common foreign and security policy**. The UK took up the presidency of the Council of the European Union in the latter half of 2005, and found itself trying to advance its arguments for more liberalization and economic reform while also having to deal with the issue of the budget, the reform of the **common agricultural policy** and the future direction and priorities of the EU itself. Agreement on securing the commencement of **accession negotiations** with **Turkey** was one of the successes of the British presidency, alongside a deal on the budget, both of which were achieved after much internal disagreement.

There can be little doubt that minimal debate among politicians and limited EU coverage from large sections of the popular media had a negative impact on voters in **European Parliament** (EP) elections. This was reflected in low turnout (34.5%, down from 38.4% in 2004) in the UK at the EP elections in 2009 and ongoing apathy and resistance towards European integration among the general public and large sections of the British media. The Labour Government lost power in May 2010 and a new, Conservative/Liberal Democrat coalition Government was formed under **David Cameron**'s leadership. As expected, the Liberal Democrat members of the coalition arrangement were able to dilute the more **Eurosceptic** tendencies of their Conservative partners. The coalition Government nevertheless proposed an 'EU Bill', which envisaged tighter parliamentary controls over transfers of power and competence from the UK to the EU and a referendum on the adoption of most future amending treaties as well as on principal decisions concerning the UK's position within the EU. The bill was passed into law on receiving Royal Assent in July 2011. The issue of closer EU integration resurfaced almost immediately as members of the **eurozone** endeavoured to respond to the ongoing instability with the **euro** by searching for greater co-ordination. To this end, most of the EU member states agreed to sign the Treaty on Stability, Co-ordination and Governance in the Economic and Monetary Union (**Fiscal Compact**). Neither the UK nor the **Czech Republic** signed this document, once again exemplifying the fact that these two countries appeared to be 'out of sync' with the majority of their counterparts. In June 2013 the British Government presented to Parliament draft legislation advocating the holding by the end of 2017 of an 'in/out' referendum on the issue of the country's continued membership of the EU. Following the EP elections in May 2014 and the success of the **UK Independence Party**, the pressure on the Government for a referendum (both from within and outside the Conservative Party) intensified. Meanwhile, in a referendum held in September 2014, which offered voters resident in Scotland the opportunity to vote for separation from the UK, some 55% voted in support of remaining part of the UK. Following the electoral success of the Conservatives in May 2015, and the subsequent formation of a single-party Government, again led by Cameron, the organization of an 'in/out' referendum and, therefore, the potential for **Brexit**, a term coined to describe the UK's potential departure from the EU, became a certainty.

On 18–19 February 2016 the European Council concluded a 'new settlement for the UK within the EU', exempting the UK from further political integration in the Union. The intention was to incorporate this into the various treaties and constitutional requirements of the member states. However, the settlement depended on the UK informing the Secretary-General of the Council that it was to remain a member of the EU, following the referendum, which was duly scheduled for 23 June.

The referendum campaign was divisive, and both sides were accused of being selective in their presentation of the facts. The 'Remain' side initially focused on the anticipated negative economic implications of leaving the EU, supported by negative forecasts by financial organizations. The 'Leave' campaign responded by arguing that the UK would have additional funds available for public spending if it left the EU and ceased its net payments to the Union. It also sought to focus attention on the controversial and emotive topic of immigration, asserting that Brexit would be the only way that the UK could regain control of its borders and its sovereignty.

At the referendum, 51.9% of voters expressed support for leaving the Union, while 48.1% voted in support of remaining. The results emphasized the deep divisions within the UK, with 62.0% of voters in Scotland, 55.8% of voters in Northern Ireland and 95.9% of voters in Gibraltar voting in support of remaining within the EU, as did many of those in some of England's major cities, including Liverpool, Manchester and the capital, London. The turnout was recorded at 72.2%. White British, the elderly and the less formally educated were also more likely to vote to leave (at 52%) compared with the 34% of those from Black and Minority Ethnic (BAME) backgrounds. Those who had suffered most from the global financial crisis and austerity politics after 2008 appeared most likely to favour a departure from the Union. The vote also appeared to have represented an opportunity for those who felt themselves to be largely powerless to express their disenchantment with the political élite. Cameron's accusers suggested that he had been irresponsible in scheduling a referendum without understanding the feelings and concerns of the electorate.

The unexpected vote to leave the EU created what appeared to be the most significant crisis in British politics since the end of the Second World War, and it rapidly became evident that neither side had planned for Brexit, and that policymakers lacked an understanding of how to bring about an exit from the EU and consensus over what they wished to achieve in the negotiations to leave the Union. The day after the referendum Prime Minister Cameron, who had campaigned for the UK to remain within the EU, announced that he was to resign; in September Cameron also announced that he was stepping down as an MP. In July **Theresa May** was invited to form a new Conservative Government.

The formal process of leaving the EU required the British Government to invoke **Article 50** of the **Treaty of Lisbon**, after which the UK would have a two-year period within which to negotiate its departure from the Union, prompting some EU officials, such as then EP President **Martin Schulz**, to demand that the UK waste no time in commencing the timetable for its departure; in late June 2016 ministers responsible for foreign affairs from the EU's six founding states also issued a statement demanding that the UK initiate the process of departure. Prime Minister May formally invoked Article 50 on 29 March 2017, and the UK was duly scheduled to leave the Union by 29 March 2019. May subsequently called an early election for June 2017, but during her election campaign failed to clarify how she planned to negotiate the terms of the UK's future relationship with the EU and was also forced to make a number of policy reversals. The elections resulted in reduced support for May's Government, which had to seek the support of Northern Ireland's Democratic Unionist Party. The election results were widely interpreted as a rejection of a so-called hard Brexit, involving a total rejection of the principle of freedom of movement and, therefore, a departure from the single market, and there were suggestions that a longer transition period might be feasible. However, by October 2017 widespread uncertainty remained over the implications of Brexit, and what form the UK's relationship with the EU would take after its exit from the Union.

The **UNITED KINGDOM BUDGET REBATE**, also known as the **United Kingdom** correction or the 'British budgetary question' (BBQ), resurfaced as a major and controversial issue in discussions over the future financing of the European Union (EU) at a **European Council summit meeting** in Luxembourg in June 2005. The issue had lain dormant for a number of years, but again became a major point of disagreement between the member states. French President Jacques Chirac persistently questioned the need for the UK rebate, but Labour Prime Minister Tony Blair (1997–2007) stated that he was unwilling to consider its curtailment unless major reforms were made to how agriculture was financed. This stance opened up an immediate battle with France, the largest recipient of spending under the EU's **Common Agricultural Policy** (CAP), and relations between Chirac and Blair took an extremely frosty turn for most of the British presidency of the Council of the European Union in the latter half of 2005. In December 2005 an agreement on the budget was finally reached, whereby the UK gave back some of its rebate in return for the promise of a wholesale review of the CAP in 2008.

The British rebate had been negotiated by Prime Minister Margaret Thatcher after a long battle between 1979 and 1984. In the end, a deal had been reached, essentially between François Mitterrand, Helmut Kohl and Margaret Thatcher, at the **Fontainebleau summit** in 1984 to settle the BBQ and to allow the EU time to pursue the **single market** programme. The UK's annual rebate is currently worth about £5,000m., but it was only designed or agreed to as a temporary measure. The rebate was intended to make up the shortfall between what the UK paid into the EU **budget** and what it received back. The UK argued that the difference was significant because some 80% of the EU budget in the early 1980s went towards the CAP, a fund from which the UK was not a major recipient. Another issue that should be factored into understanding the British arguments for the rebate was the much weaker economic position of the UK in the 1980s. The actuality and desirability of the UK rebate have appeared sporadically on the EU agenda over the course of the last 20 years or so—particularly whenever the member states have been considering the overall composition of the budget. It surfaced in March 1999 at the Berlin summit of the European Council and emerged again in the deliberations for the 2007–13 financial period. In December 2005 Prime Minister Blair agreed to give up some 20% of the rebate for this period, on the condition that the funds did not contribute to CAP payments, were matched by contributions from other countries and were only for the new member states. The issue of a rebate remained contentious. Despite some opposition from his peers to the level of the rebate, **David Cameron** secured a €3,100m. annual rebate for the UK in July 2013.

The **UNITED NATIONS** (UN) is one arena where **European political co-operation** and the **common foreign and security policy** have generally been applied successfully. The permanent representatives to the UN of the European Union (EU) member states continue to meet regularly, to ensure that the member states vote together in as many divisions within the UN General

Assembly as possible. In addition, since 2011 the President of the **European Council** has addressed the opening session of the General Assembly each September on behalf of the EU (a privilege previously held by the foreign minister of the member state currently holding the presidency of the **Council of the European Union**). In May 2011 the EU was granted an enhanced observer status at the UN. This means that the EU now has the right of reply, the right to speak in debates among representatives of major groups and before individual states, the right to submit proposals and amendments, and the right to raise points of order and to circulate documents. However, the EU does not have voting rights in the UN or the right to sit on the UN Security Council. In addition, the EU, which is the UN's largest financial contributor, holds an observer seat on the UN executive board for funds and programmes.

UNITED STATES OF AMERICA: See **USA**

UPE: See **Union for Europe of the Nations Group**

URBAN is the acronym of a 1994 initiative intended to promote the proliferation of innovative ideas and actions by means of their exchange between cities in the European Union, and to develop co-operative networks for the exchange of experience. Funded via the **European Regional Development Fund**, the subsequent initiative, URBAN II, covered the period 2000 until 2006. In the **United Kingdom**, Northern Ireland was a recipient of URBAN II funding, which was designed to assist urban regeneration of inner North Belfast.

URUGUAY ROUND is the name of a series of talks within the **General Agreement on Tariffs and Trade** (GATT). They began in 1986 and were initially due to be completed by the end of 1990. They were hindered by several disagreements over various aspects of the attempt to extend GATT rules beyond manufactured products to a variety of other areas, including services and intellectual copyright, and were eventually blocked by an impasse between the **USA** and the then European Communities (EC), primarily over agriculture (with **France** being the most vocal defender of the EC agricultural policy regime). Risking collapse on several occasions, the Round was eventually concluded in 1994, after France had agreed to accept the inclusion of agriculture in the agreement, resulting in a World Trade Agreement that led to the creation of a **World Trade Organization**.

The **US-EC DECLARATION** of 20 November 1990 was an attempt to place the relationship between the **USA** and the then European Communities on a more regularized base. Its major element was an agreement on the need for a framework within which consultations could be held on political and economic issues of interest to both sides, and since 1991 regular meetings have been held. (See **Transatlantic Declaration**.)

The **USA** (United States of America) made a major contribution to the development of European integration in the form of its strong involvement in European affairs after 1945, especially its provision of economic assistance (see **Marshall Plan**) and a defensive shield (see **North Atlantic Treaty Organization**), with the benefit of which the Western European states had the time to consider and explore ways of closer collaboration. Itself a federation, the USA encouraged efforts at integration until the 1960s, and did not seem to be averse to the notion of political union. After the 1960s, relations between the European Communities (EC) and the USA became more strained. While to some extent this was due to political arguments over foreign and defence policy, the major point of difference was economic. As the EC grew to be a more integrated economic entity, a conflict of interest developed with the USA, which was both a major economic rival and the EC's most important trading partner. Threats of action and retaliation from across the Atlantic, which reached their peak during the **Uruguay Round**, became commonplace, but disputes were usually resolved eventually by some form of compromise. (See **bananas**.)

During the 1990s, relations between the EC and the USA were institutionalized via a number of initiatives. The **Transatlantic Declaration** of 1990 provided a basis for greater collaboration and co-operation, and was followed in 1995 by the launch of a **New Transatlantic Agenda**. As a consequence of this, in May 1998 a Transatlantic Economic Partnership was initiated. In its draft Action Plan for the Partnership, the **European Commission** proposed that the European Union (EU) and the USA stimulate trade liberalization at worldwide level. Efforts to achieve such a goal have often been hindered by EU–US trade disputes. Equally, relations have often been soured as a consequence of major differences over, for example, the **Middle East** and the **Iraq War**. Annual summits nevertheless provide opportunities to stress the extent to which the EU and the USA do co-operate in an ever wider range of areas, including, for example, sharing information on **competition policy** cases. Following several years of discussion, in July 2013 the USA and the EU commenced official negotiations on the proposed creation of a **Transatlantic Trade and Investment Partnership**; total trade in goods between the USA and the EU amounted to some €500,000m. in 2012, while trade in services totalled around €280,000m. The talks had been expected to take up to three years to reach a conclusion, but the deal appeared moribund by the end of President Barack Obama's term of office in early 2017. Following the election of Donald Trump as US President in November 2016, President of the **European Council Donald Tusk** acknowledged that new challenges to the transatlantic relationship were likely to arise during the course of Trump's Administration, which was expected to introduce a policy of increased US protectionism. Tusk confirmed that the EU would seek to continue its co-operative relationship with the USA and maintain transatlantic unity.

The **USSR** (Union of Soviet Socialist Republics) was the major European military power after 1945 and unwittingly influenced the development of integration in Western Europe by arousing fears about its own power and intentions. Its actions in Eastern Europe between 1945 and 1948 and the dawning of the **Cold War** persuaded many Western states of the virtues of collaboration, at least in the form of a collective security system, and led them to urge greater involvement of the **USA** in Europe. The USSR remained hostile to Western European integration on both economic and political grounds, and only in 1988 did it declare a willingness to enter into discussions with the European Communities on a possible trading agreement. Since then, the USSR has disintegrated, with most of the successor states becoming members of the **Commonwealth of Independent States** and concluding **partnership and co-operation agreements** with the European Union (EU). The three **Baltic states—Estonia**, **Latvia** and **Lithuania**—are the main exceptions, having concluded **Europe agreements** and having now gained EU membership, which all three countries applied for in 1995.

V

V: See **Group of the Greens/European Free Alliance**

VAL DUCHESSE is a château on the outskirts of **Brussels** variously associated with the European Communities and the European Union. It was at Val Duchesse that the Spaak Report and the **Treaty of Rome** were drawn up in 1955–58. More recently, in 1985, the château gave its name to the process of social dialogue between the employers represented by the **Union of Industrial and Employers' Confederations of Europe** (now renamed BUSINESSEUROPE), employees represented by the **European Trade Union Confederation**, and the European Centre of Public Enterprises.

VALUE-ADDED TAX (VAT) is the second most important source of **revenue** for the European Union (EU), and represented 13.4% of the total revenue in the 2011 **budget**. (The most important source of revenue, based on gross national income (GNI), accounted for 75.6% of total EU revenue in that year.) Traditional **own resources** comprise customs duties, agricultural duties and sugar levies. In most cases, a uniform rate of 0.30% is levied on the harmonized VAT base of each member state. The taxable VAT base is capped at 50% of GNI for each country. The aim of this ceiling is to prevent less wealthy member states from having to pay a disproportionate amount (in low-income countries VAT generally accounts for a higher percentage of national income). In 1967 two **directives** obliged all member states that had not already done so to introduce a system of VAT as the third major element of indirect **taxation** by 1970. New members have also had to introduce a VAT system.

A second dimension to VAT is the issue of **harmonization**. As part of the **internal market** programme, an attempt to introduce a greater degree of harmonization was made by Francis Cockfield in his **White Paper** (see **Internal Market**). This was only partially successful, and the member states continued to contribute moderately different VAT rates. In 1992, however, formal agreement was reached on a minimum standard rate of 15%. This was subsequently confirmed in 1996 when informal agreement was also reached on a maximum rate of 25% (although **Hungary**'s VAT rate stood at 27% in 2012). Certain goods remain 'zero-rated' or appear on a special list subject to 'reduced rates' of VAT. Clearly, full harmonization is far from having been achieved. Moreover, the determination of several member states to make certain that the harmonization of VAT rates specifically, and indirect taxes in general, continues to be subject to voting by **unanimity** looks likely to ensure that it remains an elusive goal.

VAN GEND EN LOOS is the shortened name of a case, *Van Gend en Loos v Nederlandse Administratie der Belastingen*, which was heard by the **Court of Justice** in 1962. The Court ruled that European Communities **law** was a new legal order, directly applicable in the member states, and that individuals were required to be aware of this.

VARIABLE GEOMETRY is a phrase that was coined by Jacques Delors in the early 1980s and is widely used to refer to the possibility of common policies being developed and implemented at different rates by the member states, depending upon their degree of commitment to each policy. Reminiscent of the notion of a **two-speed Europe** raised by the 1976 **Tindemans Report**, it met with strong criticism from countries wary of political union. All the same, it has come to characterize aspects of the European Union's activities, notably **economic and monetary union** and the **area of freedom, security and justice** where certain member states enjoy **opt-outs**.

VAT: See **Value-added Tax**

KARMENU VELLA (1950–) was nominated in 2014 as the Maltese Commissioner to the new 28-member **European Commission** led by **Jean-Claude Juncker**. In September Juncker named Vella as Commissioner-designate for the Environment, Maritime Affairs and Fisheries, subject to approval by the **European Parliament**. Immediately prior to this appointment Vella had been a member of the Maltese Government and was Minister for Tourism and Aviation (2013−14). Vella holds a degree in engineering and architecture and was first elected to the Maltese Parliament in 1976. He was industry minister from 1984 to 1987 and tourism minister from 1996 to 1998. Vella was approved at his confirmation hearing with Members of the European Parliament and, with the endorsement of the Juncker Commission by both the European Parliament and the **European Council**, he took up his new role as a European Commissioner on 1 November 2014.

GUY VERHOFSTADT (1954–) is a politician and former Prime Minister of **Belgium**. He grew up in Ghent and studied law at the University of Ghent. As a university student he was active in politics and served as President of the Liberal Flemish Students Union. His career as an elected politician first began with his election to Ghent city council in 1976 and from there he rapidly rose within the ranks of the Party for Freedom and Progress, becoming a member of the House of Representatives, Deputy Prime Minister and Minister of the Budget. In July 1999 he became Prime Minister of Belgium. A decade later, in 2009, he ran successfully for the **European Parliament** (EP). He was elected as the leader of the **Group of the Alliance of Liberals and Democrats for Europe** (ALDE) within the EP in 2009 and was the group's preferred candidate for the position of European Commission President in 2014. The emergence of the **European People's Party** (EPP) as the largest group within the EP following the 2014 elections led ALDE to support the EPP's candidate, **Jean-Claude Juncker,** and also to support the re-election of **Martin Schulz** as President of the EP. In September 2016 Verhofstadt was appointed the EP's principal representative in the ongoing negotiations for **Brexit**, to which he had earlier expressed himself to be wholly opposed.

VERs: See **Voluntary Export Restraints**

MARGRETHE VESTAGER (1968–) was nominated in 2014 as the Danish Commissioner to the new 28-member **European Commission** led by **Jean-Claude Juncker**. In September Juncker named Vestager as Commissioner-designate for Competition, subject to approval by the **European Parliament** (EP). Prior to her appointment to the Commission Vestager most recently served as Deputy Prime Minister of **Denmark** and Danish Minister of the Economy and the Interior. She is an economist and holds a Master's degree in economics from Copenhagen University. She worked in the Ministry of Finance after graduation, became Education Minister in 1998 and was elected to parliament in 2001. Both the EP and the **European Council** approved Vestager at her confirmation hearing with **Members of the European Parliament**, and with the endorsement of the Juncker Commission she took up her new role as a European Commissioner on 1 November 2014.

VETO refers to the option available to each member state in the **Council of the European Union** to reject proposals put before it. Thanks to the **Luxembourg Compromise**, the option to veto survived almost unscathed until the mid-1980s. Since then, and owing mainly to the increased use and acceptance of **qualified majority voting**, the use of the veto is essentially restricted to areas (e.g. tax **harmonization**, the admission of new member states, treaty reform) where **unanimity** is still required under the treaties. In practice, the veto is rarely used.

A **VISA POLICY** was established by the **Treaty on European Union** (TEU), which declared the aim of developing such a policy, applicable throughout the European Union (EU), for nationals from third countries. The TEU demanded the establishment of a common format for all visas before January 1996 by which time visa policy decisions would require only a **qualified majority vote** in the **Council of the European Union**. The visa policy does not prevent member states from pursuing their own policies with regard to internal security and the maintenance of law and order. The **Treaty of Amsterdam** was also concerned that there should be greater co-operation over visa policies. Today, the majority of EU member states have a unified visa system as part of the **Schengen Area**. Of the six EU member states that do not form part of the Schengen Area, four —**Bulgaria**, **Croatia**, **Cyprus** and **Romania**—have a visa policy that is based on the Schengen *acquis*, while the other two—**Ireland** and the **United Kingdom**—operate a travel zone known as the Common Travel Area (which is different from that of the Schengen Area). The non-EU states of **Iceland**, **Norway**, **Liechtenstein** and **Switzerland** are part of the Schengen Area (with associated status). In April 2010 a new EU Visa Code (previously adopted in 2009 by the **Council of the European Union** and the **European Parliament**) came into force. This code, which represented an attempt to harmonize EU visa law, collected into one document all legal provisions governing the decisions on visas for those states belonging to the Schengen Area. It was hoped that the conditions for issuing visas to third-country nationals would now be more straightforward, transparent and fair.

The **VISEGRAD GROUP** originally consisted of Czechoslovakia, **Hungary** and **Poland** when it was created in 1991–92 as a mechanism for the three states to support each other in efforts to pursue closer integration with Western European organizations, notably the European Communities. In 1993 membership rose to four countries when the **Czech Republic** and **Slovakia** replaced the now-disbanded Czechoslovakia. Among the activities of the Visegrad group was the establishment of the **Central European Free Trade Association** (CEFTA). The extension of CEFTA to include other countries from **Central and Eastern Europe** and Slovakia's slower progress towards European Union (EU) membership during the mid-1990s led to the effective demise of the Visegrad Group. Multilateral co-operation between the members has nevertheless continued. Amid what became widely known as the **European migration crisis**, in early September 2015 the Visegrad Four countries adopted a joint statement on migrants at a summit in the Czech capital, Prague. The statement was prompted by the Commission's upcoming proposals for the resettlement of an additional 120,000 refugees. The scheme was to be compulsory for all states except those with exemptions, although the numbers to be taken by individual states were in some cases quite small: for example, 1,502 in the case of Slovakia, 2,978 for the Czech Republic and 9,287 for Poland. An Extraordinary Justice and Home Affairs Council (a meeting of the relevant ministers from the EU member states) adopted the plan in late September. Unanimity was not required for the decision to be binding and the Czech Republic, Hungary, Slovakia and **Romania** voted against it. The most extreme stance was adopted by Slovakia, whose Prime Minister Robert Fico said that he would take the decision on quotas to the **European Court of Justice** (ECJ). The complaint was duly filed in December, and supported by Hungary, a neighbour with which it had often disagreed on issues relating to the Hungarian ethnic minority in Slovakia; however, the ECJ rejected the case in September 2017. Meanwhile, in June of that year the EU warned the countries of the Visegrad Four that it might launch **infringement procedures** against them if they failed to adhere to the terms of the compulsory relocation scheme.

VOLUNTARY EXPORT RESTRAINTS (VERs) are bilateral agreements reached by the European Union (EU) with other countries, whereby the latter voluntarily agree to limit exports of particular products to the EU. The restraints are not in fact truly voluntary, but have been accepted by the exporting countries in preference to other restrictions that might be imposed. The best-known VERs have related to trade in steel and cars. The **European Commission** has a mandate to negotiate VERs on behalf of the EU.

W

The **WARSAW PACT** was the name of the **Cold War** alliance of Eastern European countries led by the **USSR** that regarded itself as a mutual defence organization against the ambitions of the **North Atlantic Treaty Organization**. It derived its name from the Warsaw Treaty of Friendship, Co-operation and Mutual Assistance, which was signed by the USSR, **Albania, Bulgaria**, Czechoslovakia, **Hungary, Poland** and **Romania** in May 1955. The Warsaw Pact was dissolved in 1991 following the fragmentation of the USSR.

WATER and its pollution are major European Union (EU) concerns, and a number of **European Commission directives** have been aimed at improving the quality and protection of water in all its aspects. High standards have been set for the quality of both drinking and bathing water, and member states risk punitive action if they do not meet the required standards within stipulated deadlines. Further directives relate to fish habitats and the discharge of pollutants. The EU has also signed several international conventions designed to reduce the level of water pollution. (See also **environmental policy**.)

MANFRED WEBER (1972–) was born in Wildenberg, in Bavaria. He studied physical technology/engineering at the University of Munich. He is a member of the Bavarian-based Christian Social Union party and was first elected to the **European Parliament** (EP) in 2004, after having developed his political activity at both local and regional level. He has taken a particular interest in and worked within the EP's committees on civil liberties and constitutional affairs and became a Vice-Chairman of the **Group of the European People's Party (Christian Democrats)** in 2009. He was elected as the new Chairman of the grouping in the EP in May 2014.

The **WERNER REPORT** is the name of a 1970 plan for **economic and monetary union** (EMU) prepared by a committee, headed by Pierre Werner (1913–2000), then Prime Minister of Luxembourg, which was appointed by the 1969 **Hague summit**. The Report emphasized the need for the European Communities to proceed simultaneously in co-ordinating and harmonizing economic policy, narrowing exchange-rate margins, integrating capital markets and establishing a common currency and a **European Central Bank**. It presented a three-stage programme for the implementation of full EMU by 1980, the deadline imposed by its remit. Although its views were accepted in a modified format by the Council of Ministers (see **Council of the European Union**), the economic difficulties of the 1970s led to the programme's abandonment. The question of full EMU was not considered again fully until Jacques Delors was appointed by the Council in 1988 to consider the EMU question, and this led directly on that occasion to a specific title on EMU being inserted into the **Treaty of Rome** by the **Treaty on European Union**.

WEST GERMANY: See **Germany**

The **WESTERN BALKANS**, as far as the European Union (EU) is concerned, comprises **Albania, Bosnia and Herzegovina, Croatia, Kosovo**, the **former Yugoslav republic of Macedonia** (FYRM), **Montenegro** and **Serbia**. Croatia became a member of the EU in July 2013, while the FYRM, Montenegro, Serbia and Albania have been granted the status of **candidate countries**. Membership negotiations with Montenegro began in June 2012, and the first EU-Serbia intergovernmental conference in January 2014 marked the formal start of Serbia's accession negotiations. Bosnia and Herzegovina and Kosovo remain potential candidate countries (**stabilization and association agreements** were signed with Bosnia and Herzegovina in June 2008 and initialled with Kosovo in July 2014). The EU continues to support political stabilization and economic development in this region, and provided more than €4,500m. to the above countries through the former **CARDS** programme in 2000–06 to anchor the democratization process and promote economic growth. Since early 2005 the Directorate-General for **Enlargement** has been responsible for managing all relations with the countries of the Western Balkans. Financial assistance is now provided via the **instrument for pre-accession assistance** (II) and amounts to €11,700m. for 2014–20.

WESTERN ECONOMIC SUMMITS: See **G-8**

WESTERN EUROPEAN UNION (WEU) originated in the 1948 **Treaty of Brussels** and was designed to promote co-operation in the fields of defence and security. After the collapse of the **European Defence Community** proposals in 1954, the treaty was used to establish a body 'to promote the unity and to encourage the progressive integration of Europe', which included the Federal Republic of **Germany** (West Germany) and **Italy** in addition to the original five signatories (**Belgium, France, Luxembourg**, the **Netherlands** and the **United Kingdom**). WEU had little infrastructure, and was only occasionally activated in the 1950s. The North Atlantic Treaty Organization absorbed its military functions more or less immediately after 1949, and it ceded its social and cultural responsibilities to the **Council of Europe** in 1960, in effect becoming moribund. Some attempts to revive it were made in the 1960s and 1970s, but it was not until 1984, partly as a result of the growing rapprochement between the **USA** and the **USSR**, that it was reactivated as a body that could provide a distinctive Western European voice on defence and security issues.

In 1987 it adopted a programme that called for the creation of a 'cohesive European defence identity', strengthening conventional capabilities while retaining nuclear potential, improving consultation and co-operative mechanisms, and establishing a common system of monitoring obligations. The **Treaty on European Union** (TEU) made WEU an integral part of the European Union (EU), identifying it as a de facto constituent of the pillar of **common foreign and security policy**. The EU was to 'foster closer institutional relations with the WEU with a view to the possibility of the integration of the WEU into the Union'. WEU moved its headquarters to **Brussels**, granted observer status to other Western European countries, and engaged in discussions on closer ties with countries from **Central and Eastern Europe**. Consequently, by 2002 28 countries enjoyed one of four different types of status with regard to WEU. These ranged from membership through associate membership and observer status to that of associate partner.

The pursuit of closer co-operation between the member states of the EU and WEU was further encouraged by the **Treaty of Amsterdam**. Moreover, the **Treaty of Nice** paved the way for the de facto incorporation of WEU into the EU by reducing the status of WEU and establishing a **European security and defence policy**. The Treaty effectively removed various references to WEU from the TEU, with the most visible representation of the incorporation of WEU into the EU being Javier Solana assuming the dual roles of Secretary-General of WEU and **Secretary-General of the Council of the European Union**. In December 2009 the entry into force of the **Treaty of Lisbon** transferred the mutual defence clause of WEU to the EU. WEU was formally dissolved in June 2011.

WEU: See **Western European Union**

WHITE PAPER is the term used to describe a **European Commission** document setting out proposed legislative initiatives, such as, for example, the 2001 **Governance White Paper** or the 2006 White Paper on a European Communication Policy. In some cases it follows a **Green Paper**, which is used by the Commission to launch a full-scale public discussion on a proposal. The document produced in 1985 by Francis Cockfield for the European Commission on the measures required to implement the **internal market** by 1992 is still the most widely known example. Entitled *Completing the Internal Market*, it listed some 300 separate measures that would need to be taken, for each of which a target date and a timetable were set. The measures related to the removal of physical, technical and fiscal barriers to a single market. To facilitate their **implementation**, appropriate provisions were incorporated into the 1987 **Single European Act** and, by 1992 most of the measures had been introduced. When a White Paper has been endorsed enthusiastically by the **Council of the European Union**, it becomes the action programme for the European Union in that specific policy area.

WIDENING involves extending the membership of the European Union (EU) through the process of **enlargement**. For much of the history of the EU, widening has been subordinate to **deepening**.

WITHDRAWAL from the European Union (EU) has rarely been seriously contemplated by any member state, although **Greenland**, as part of **Denmark**, did withdraw in 1985. With increasing evidence of Euroscepticism and concerns among some member states over the future path of integration, the **Treaty establishing a Constitution for Europe** included a dedicated withdrawal clause. This clause, inserted into the **Treaty on European Union** by the **Treaty of Lisbon**, allows a member state to withdraw from the EU provided it notifies the **European Council** of its intention. An agreement setting out the arrangements for withdrawal is then to be concluded by the Council, acting by a two-thirds' majority and after obtaining the consent of the **European Parliament**. Withdrawal will take place two years at the latest after the notification to withdraw has been received by the European Council. A former member state seeking to rejoin the EU would be subject to the same conditions as any other applicant country.

WITHDRAWAL PRICES: See **Common Fisheries Policy**

WOMEN'S RIGHTS have become a fundamental European Union (EU) concern, based initially upon Article 141 of the **Treaty of Rome** (now Article 157 of the **Treaty on the Functioning of the European Union**). The Article, as amended by the **Treaty of Amsterdam**, committed the member states to ensuring that 'the principle of **equal pay** for male and female workers for equal work or work of equal value is applied'. Various **directives** require the member states to amend their laws to exclude any form of sex **discrimination** and to ensure equality in training, appointments, promotion and pay. Workers who believe they are the victims of discrimination have the right to take their case to a tribunal without fear of dismissal: the **Court of Justice** can act as the final arbiter as to whether national laws conflict with EU rules. Discrimination in social security systems was banned in 1978, and in 1986 it was decreed that discrimination in occupational pension schemes had to end by 1993. In 1997 the **Council of the European Union** adopted a directive on sex-discrimination cases, whereby the plaintiff and defendant were to share the burden of proof. The **European Commission** has also launched a number of special action schemes. In May 1998 the EU's first conference on women's **employment** was held in Belfast (**United Kingdom**). The Committee on Women's Rights and Gender Equality (FEMM) is one of the standing committees in the **European Parliament**; the current Chairperson of FEMM is Vilija Blinkevičiūtė.

WORKER PARTICIPATION: See **Charter of Fundamental Social Rights of Workers**; **Fifth Directive**; **Workers' Rights**

WORKERS' RIGHTS were referred to in the **Treaty of Rome**, which obliged the member states to promote the improvement of living and working conditions for workers and required member states to collaborate on a number of questions relating to **employment**. Most European Communities/Union activity has been devoted to improving working conditions through the implementation of several **directives** on occupational **health and safety** (see **European Foundation for the Improvement of Living and Working Conditions**). Other directives relate to the principle of **freedom of movement**. Restrictions on free movement can be applied by the member states only on grounds of a risk to public order, safety or health, or where jobs are in a particular sector of public administration. Persistent efforts by the **European Commission** to establish worker participation in company decision making (see **Fifth Directive**) first achieved success when all the member states, except the **United Kingdom**, decided to implement the **Charter of Fundamental Social Rights of Workers**; the UK eventually signed up to the Charter in 1997 after the election of a Labour Government. Workers' rights are also prominent in the **Charter of Fundamental Rights** proclaimed in December 2000.

The **WORKING GROUP ON GENDER IN RESEARCH AND INNOVATION** was established in 2017. It was formerly known as the Helsinki Group on Women and Science, established in 1999 as an advisory group on gender issues to the **European Commission**. It comprises European Union member states and a number of associated countries (**Iceland**, Israel and **Norway**) and the European Commission. The Group provides advice to the **Council of the European Union** and Commission on policies and initiatives pertaining to **gender equality** in research and innovation so that they benefit scholars, research institutions, universities, business and society at large. The Group meets at least twice annually and a majority selects its

The **WORKING TIME DIRECTIVE** (WTD) aims to protect the **health and safety** of workers against the adverse effects of working long hours without adequate breaks. It also addresses disrupted working patterns and sets a maximum working week of 48 hours within any four-month period. Guidelines relating to daily rest times, weekly rest periods, minimum holiday entitlements and night-shift working are also included. Certain categories of workers, including those employed in oil extraction and transport, and junior doctors in training, were initially excluded from the **directive**.

The 1993 Working Time Directive had a treaty basis under Article 138 of the **Treaty of Rome** (now Article 154 of the **Treaty on the Functioning of the European Union**), which was incorporated into the treaty as part of the **Single European Act** in 1986. Approval of measures is by **qualified majority voting**. The **United Kingdom** opposed the directive and was successful in obtaining an **opt-out** of the 48-hour working week (under certain conditions). The original Working Time Directive (93/104/EC) covered all sectors of activity except transport, activities at sea and the activities of trainee doctors. The provisions of the WTD did not apply if other European Union (EU) law contained more specific provisions in a particular field or if national laws contained provisions that were more favourable to workers (for example, in February 2000 the French Government passed legislation adopting a 35-hour working week).

The WTD provided for: a maximum 48-hour working week averaged over a reference period; a minimum daily rest period of 11 consecutive hours a day; a rest break where the working day is longer than six hours; a minimum rest period of one day a week; and a statutory right to annual paid holiday of four weeks. Normal hours of work for night workers must not exceed an average of eight hours in any 24-hour period. Workers are entitled to a free medical examination before being employed on night work and at regular intervals thereafter. Anyone suffering from health problems connected with night work must be transferred, wherever possible, to day work. The issue of the WTD remained highly topical and controversial. In 2000 the scope of the WTD was extended to include some previously excluded professions (doctors in training, transport workers, activities at sea) to cover some 5m people. In 2003 the **European Commission** issued a Communication on the review of the directive, which analysed the **opt-outs** and **derogations** in member states, and summarized recent case law concerning the definition of working time. This consultation period ran until the end of March 2004 and fed into a new Commission proposal that still contained an opt-out, but one that made it more difficult for employers to press staff against their will to work for any longer than 48 hours. The sensitivities that working hours still caused for some member states, including especially the UK but also **Germany**, **Malta**, **Poland**, **Slovakia** and **Slovenia**, became apparent in early 2005 when the **European Parliament** voted in its first reading of the proposal to phase out the opt-out over a three-year period. The **European Trade Union Confederation** strongly supported the ending of the opt-out as did some of the UK's main trade unions, but UK Prime Minister Tony Blair consistently resisted any such moves and sought to garner enough support in other member states to form at least a blocking minority in the Council. In June 2005 the Council voted to maintain the opt-out.

The **WORLD TRADE ORGANIZATION** (WTO) was established on 1 January 1995 as the successor to the **General Agreement on Tariffs and Trade** (GATT). The origins of both GATT and the WTO can be traced back to the late 1940s and efforts to liberalize international trade by reducing the levels of tariffs. By the 1990s the agenda of international discourse on trade issues had widened considerably with a series of policy issues requiring consideration at a multilateral level. These included **competition policy**, **environmental policy** and approaches to labour market deregulation. GATT had been a fruitful exercise but was limited in its scope, and for this reason it was decided to establish a new organization that became the WTO. The WTO has a much broader scope than GATT. Whereas GATT regulated trade in merchandise goods, the WTO also covers trade in services, such as **telecommunications** and banking. The highest body of the WTO is the Ministerial Conference. This usually meets every two years and, among other things, elects the organization's chief executive—the director-general—and oversees the work of the General Council. The General Council is in charge of the day-to-day running of the WTO and is made up of ambassadors from member states that also serve on various subsidiary and specialist committees. The WTO has a crucial role to play in ensuring, promoting and protecting trade liberalization. It serves as a forum to settle disputes—these have occurred between the European Union (EU) and the **USA** over such issues as **bananas**, hormone-treated beef and hush kits (noise reduction devices) for aircraft—and may operate as the ideal body for settling cases on competition policy that involve European and North American companies.

Despite the apparent logic of such an international forum to resolve disputes, there has been growing unease and dissatisfaction among sections of the public about the democratic credentials of this body. Four main criticisms abound. These are: first, that the WTO is too powerful; second, that (it is believed) the WTO only serves the needs of the rich states and is largely indifferent to the needs of the economically less advanced states; third, that the WTO is indifferent to the impact of free trade on **workers' rights**, child labour, the environment and health; and last, that this organization lacks democratic **accountability**. This discontent was, in the early 2000s, manifest in street protests and a series of violent confrontations between protesters and the police at meetings of the WTO in response to the perceived threat of **globalization**. In September 2002 a former Thai Deputy Prime Minister, Dr Supachai Panitchpakdi, began a three-year term as Director-General and was charged with pursuing the **Doha Round**. He was the first WTO head to come from a developing nation. As a respected economist, he played a key role in leading Thailand out of the Asian currency crisis. In September 2003 the world trade talks in Cancún, Mexico, collapsed after four days of wrangling over farm **subsidies** and access to markets. Many commentators maintained that the failure to reach agreement would hit the poorest nations hardest. Pessimism intensified when the WTO announced that there was little hope of restarting the collapsed world trade talks in December of that year because both the developing countries and the rich nations seemed unable to agree on the scope of trade negotiations and the need to reduce agricultural subsidies. Nevertheless, agreement was attained in Geneva, Switzerland, in August 2004 when talks achieved consensus on a framework agreement on opening up global trade. The USA and the EU were to reduce agricultural subsidies, while developing nations would cut tariffs on manufactured goods. However, the future of the Doha Round appeared uncertain, with continuing disagreements over trade liberalization and protectionism remaining the major obstacles to progress.

In September 2005 the Frenchman Pascal Lamy became the fifth Director-General of the WTO, and he was re-elected to a new four-year term in 2009. Lamy's successor was the Brazilian Roberto Azevêdo, who became the new Director-General of the WTO on 1 September 2013. At September 2017 the WTO had 164 members.

WTO: See **World Trade Organization**

XYZ

YAOUNDÉ CONVENTION is the name of an agreement signed in 1963 and renegotiated in 1969. Named after the capital of Cameroon, the Convention provided for the former colonial territories of the member states to be associated with the **European Economic Community**. Eighteen countries, known collectively as the Associated African States and Madagascar, were signatories of the Convention. They were permitted duty-free access to the European Communities for most of their products on a non-reciprocal basis and were eligible for grants from the **European Development Fund** and loans from the **European Investment Bank**. The **Lomé Convention I** superseded the Yaoundé Convention in 1975.

The **YOUTH IN ACTION PROGRAMME** superseded the Youth Programme (2000–06) in 2007, and targeted young people aged between 13 and 30 years. The programme ran until 2013 and was given financial resources of €885m. in order to contribute to the education of young people, particularly through exchange activities and European voluntary service. The scheme involved 32 countries: the 28 European Union member states, plus **Iceland**, **Liechtenstein**, **Norway** and **Turkey**. The programme focused particularly on promoting co-operation in youth-related matters. The programme incorporated the **European Voluntary Service** programme and ran a Euro-Med partnership programme. From 2014 the activities of this programme formed part of the **Erasmus+** Programme.

YOUTH TRAINING: See **European Social Fund**; **Social Policy**

YUGOSLAVIA's disintegration in the 1990s was associated, as far as the European Union (EU) was concerned, with the early failure of efforts to develop an effective **common foreign and security policy**. From the outset of the conflict in the Balkans (see **Western Balkans**), the European Communities (EC) were involved in efforts to try to avert war and the disintegration of the Yugoslav federation. Initially, the EC offered the prospect of an **association agreement**, but this failed to prevent the secession of **Slovenia** and **Croatia** in 1991. Indeed, under pressure from **Germany**, the EC effectively sealed the fate of Yugoslavia by recognizing the two countries. Soon after this, **Bosnia and Herzegovina** was recognized, although Greek objections delayed recognition of the **former Yugoslav republic of Macedonia** until 1995. All that was now left of Yugoslavia was **Serbia** and **Montenegro**, which existed as the Federal Republic of Yugoslavia until adopting the name 'Serbia and Montenegro' in 2003. The dissolution was completed in June 2006 when, following a referendum, Montenegro declared its independence, a move officially recognized by the Serbian Government 10 days later.

In the mean time, the EC sought to avert further conflict in Bosnia and Herzegovina by sponsoring a Conference on Yugoslavia in August 1992 and seeking a new mandate for **sanctions** from the **United Nations**. Sanctions and renewed attempts to broker ceasefires failed to have much impact, and a plan for a confederal solution in 1993 had to be abandoned for lack of support within Bosnia and Herzegovina. The plan was replaced by a proposal to, in effect, divide the new state, but in 1994 the Bosnian Serbs rejected this too. Soon the **USA** became more deeply involved and, with the backing of the **North Atlantic Treaty Organization**, secured a peace deal at Dayton (Ohio, USA) in November 1995.

Post-Dayton, the role of the EU in the reconstruction of the former Yugoslavia was initially focused on the **Royaumont Process**, aimed at promoting stability and good neighbourliness between the successor states, and the administration of Mostar, a city divided between Croats and Muslims. In 1997 proposals on closer ties with the EU were put forward. In what was referred to as the 'regional approach', the EU required that the successor states co-operate with one another and commit themselves to respect minority and **human rights** as well as democratic principles as preconditions for financial aid and better trade access to the EU market. Following the **Kosovo** conflict in 1999, the need to promote stability in the region—now referred to as the **Western Balkans** and incorporating **Albania**—led to the creation of the **Stabilization and Association Process**. As part of this process, countries of the former Yugoslavia gained the status of **potential candidate state**, and in some cases, candidate state, as well as access to a new programme of financial assistance, **CARDS** (replaced in 2007 by the **instrument for pre-accession assistance**). Notably Croatia acceded to the Union in July 2013.

ESSAYS ON THE EUROPEAN UNION

THE LEGAL FRAMEWORK OF THE EUROPEAN UNION

Rose M. D'Sa

Historical Introduction to the Treaty Structure of the European Union

On 23 June 2016 the people of the United Kingdom voted in a nationwide referendum, by a narrow but clear majority of 51.9% to 48.1%, to leave the European Union (EU). The constitutional, economic, and legal consequences of this decision remain uncertain and unpredictable at the time of writing. Commentary on the subject of the UK's withdrawal from the EU (commonly known as Brexit) includes developments up to September 2017. The UK formally triggered the 'exit' procedure (see *Withdrawal of Membership*) in Article 50 of the Treaty on the European Union, and the relevant procedures therein on 29 March 2017. A two-year timeframe for negotiations is set out in Article 50 of the Treaty on European Union, with the possibility of additional prolongation. Until they are concluded, the UK remains a member state of the EU and the legal framework discussed below continues to apply to it.

The EU has a complex legal framework, which until now has supported its capacity for adaptability. The current legal framework is governed, in particular, by the Treaty of Lisbon, which was signed on 13 December 2007 and came into force on 1 December 2009. The provisions of the Lisbon Treaty are discussed further below. They had the effect of further amending the two (primary) treaties—the Treaty on European Union and the Treaty on the Functioning of the European Union which, although still distinct and of equal legal status, are now made much more interdependent and interrelated.

One measure of its success has been the Union's growing enlargement, from the original six founding member states (1957: France, the Federal Republic of Germany, Italy, the Netherlands, Belgium and Luxembourg) to nine (1973: Denmark, Ireland and the UK), 10 (1981: Greece), 12 (1986: Spain and Portugal), 15 (1995: Austria, Finland and Sweden), 25 (2004: involving states mainly from Central and Eastern Europe, namely Cyprus, the Czech Republic, Estonia, Hungary, Latvia, Lithuania, Malta, Poland, Slovakia and Slovenia), 27 (2007: Bulgaria and Romania) and 28, following the entry of Croatia to the EU on 1 July 2013. The current candidate countries comprise Albania, the former Yugoslav Republic of Macedonia, Montenegro, Serbia and Turkey. The EU and Turkey are already linked by a Customs Union Agreement, which came into force at the end of 1995. If Turkey became an EU member state, it would be the largest state to join since the EU's foundation in 1957, and also the first predominantly Islamic member. Other countries that may be considered as potential future candidates in the longer term are Bosnia and Herzegovina and Kosovo; Iceland has withdrawn from the accession process.

The EU includes eight 'Outermost Regions', which form an integral part of EU territory, such as the Canary Islands (Spain) and the Azores and Madeira (Portugal). It also has an intricate legal relationship with a web of some 25 Overseas Countries and Territories, which have associate status with their respective member states (namely Denmark, France, the Netherlands and the UK). In the case of the UK, withdrawal from the EU will, therefore, also affect the areas listed in the 12 last indents of Annex II to the Treaty on the Functioning of the European Union namely: Anguilla, the Cayman Islands, the Falkland Islands, South Georgia and the South Sandwich Islands, Montserrat, the Pitcairn Islands, Saint Helena and Dependencies, the British Antarctic Territory, the British Indian Ocean Territory, the Turks and Caicos Islands, the British Virgin Islands and Bermuda. Withdrawal of the UK from the EU will also directly affect Gibraltar. The latter, the sovereignty of which is disputed by the UK and Spain, voted overwhelmingly to remain in the EU in the June 2016 referendum and has a unique position within the EU, being a European territory to which certain parts of EU law do not apply (such as the Common Agricultural Policy—CAP, the Customs Union and the structure of EU value-added tax—VAT) and for the external relations of which the UK is responsible.

In 2010 the European Free Trade Association (EFTA) celebrated its 50th anniversary. It was founded to foster free trade and closer economic co-operation between the Western European countries, and was a response to the formation of the European Economic Community (EEC) in 1958. In 1990 negotiations took place with the (then) European Community (EC) for an agreement with EFTA to create the European Economic Area (EEA). Only three EFTA states, i.e. Norway, Iceland and Liechtenstein, continue to participate in the EEA. In July 2009 the parliament of Iceland voted to proceed with an application for its membership of the EU, but this was subsequently suspended. These countries enjoy a close relationship with the EU, with access to the EU internal market, but exemption from laws on agriculture and fisheries, and crucially no input into its political decision-making processes and, therefore, no direct influence over the future development of internal market law and policy. Hence, the so-called 'Norway' model has significant limitations if it were to be applied to any new relationship between the UK and the EU because it would involve the UK continuing to pay an annual financial contribution to the EU, accepting all the 'four freedoms' (including freedom of movement), being obligated to give effect to all EU law (without having first taken part in its adoption) and accepting jurisdiction of the EFTA court, which applies EU law and operates in parallel with the Court of Justice of the EU.

Switzerland voted by referendum in 1992 not to participate in the EEA, but remains a member of EFTA, is a signatory to the Schengen Agreement (discussed below) and concluded two sets of bilateral agreements with the EU in 1999 and 2004. The concept of free movement of persons, which is one of the so-called four fundamental freedoms of the EU treaties (the others being free movement of goods, services and capital), was placed in doubt by the outcome of a Swiss referendum on 'mass immigration' in February 2014. However, Switzerland subsequently signed a treaty with the EU in March 2016 to extend the principle of free movement of persons to Croatia, which had been uncertain after the 2014 referendum. Switzerland later passed a new law, which was crucially approved by the EU in December 2016, that further limits the effect of the 2014 referendum so that, although still seeking to give priority to Swiss-based job seekers, it now avoids imposing quotas on EU citizens. The outcome and effective compromise by the Swiss Government therefore preserves the EU principle of free movement of workers and represents a less dramatic precedent for Brexit talks, in relation to discussions on possible future curbs on EU migrants to the UK.

The EU also signs Association Agreements with a very wide range of third countries, which are international agreements aimed at establishing an all-embracing framework for the future conduct of bilateral relations. These agreements are concluded under a variety of names and normally provide for the progressive liberalization of trade to varying degrees, notably free trade areas or a customs union. The EU has indicated its wish to engage as early as practicable during its Brexit negotiations, in a constructive dialogue with the UK, on a possible common approach towards such third country partners, international organizations and conventions. This might avoid the UK having to negotiate independently in relation to each of these, but might also curtail the latter's ability then to agree better or more favourable terms for itself with such third parties.

DISTINCTION BETWEEN THE EU AND THE EC

The European Communities originally consisted of three separate Communities, each of which was established by treaty. These were the European Economic Community (EEC) established by the Treaty of Rome, the European Atomic Energy Community (Euratom), and the European Coal and Steel Community (ECSC[1]), both established by the Treaty of Paris. The ECSC Treaty expired in 2002, after a period of 50 years, and therefore the ECSC is no longer in existence. However, in order to preserve the experience and knowledge accumulated over the previous five decades, the ECSC Consultative Committee, composed of representatives of the coal and steel industries, which had assisted the (then) High Authority of the ECSC, was subsequently subsumed in an amended form into another EU advisory body, namely the European Economic and Social Committee (EESC, discussed further below), where it is known as the Consultative Commission on Industrial Change. The Euratom continues to exist alongside the EU. An orderly withdrawal or other arrangement with the Euratom must therefore also be negotiated within the terms of Brexit. The jurisdiction of the Court of Justice of the European Union (CJEU), also discussed below, is, in principle, the same for both the EU and Euratom.

The EU was first created and established by the original Treaty on European Union (TEU), frequently referred to as the Maastricht Treaty, which entered into force on 1 November 1993. The TEU brought into effect, *inter alia*, substantive amendments to the Treaty of Rome, including a change of name for the latter, from EEC Treaty to EC Treaty (i.e. the Treaty establishing the European Community). This European Union was originally founded on the European Communities, which in turn was supplemented by the policies and forms of co-operation established by the TEU. However, following the entry into force of the Treaty of Lisbon, the EU replaced and succeeded the EC.

The EU now has the legal personality of, and has acquired the competences previously conferred on, the EC. The latter is therefore redundant and the term EU covers and replaces all aspects of the (former) EC. Although the EC Treaty itself has survived the amendments made by the Treaty of Lisbon, it has been renamed the (unfamiliar sounding) Treaty on the Functioning of the European Union (TFEU). The term 'Community law' is nevertheless still habitually used where, for example, reference is being made to the case law of the European Court of Justice (ECJ) prior to the entry into force of the Treaty of Lisbon.

THE SINGLE EUROPEAN ACT

The Treaty of Rome, which came into force in 1958 and established the EEC, survived without major amendment for almost 30 years. However, it then became the subject of seemingly frequent revision,[2] notably beginning with amendments made by the treaty known as the Single European Act (SEA), signed in 1986, and which came into effect on 1 July 1987.

A principal element of the SEA was a commitment to 'adopt measures with the aim of progressively establishing the internal market over a period expiring on 31 December 1992', a date by which it was hoped that the necessary legislative reforms would be completed. To achieve this, the SEA, *inter alia*, altered some voting procedures, notably by replacing, in some areas, the requirement for unanimity in the Council of Ministers, with qualified majority voting (QMV), further described below. It also amended the legislative process by introducing what became known as the 'co-operation procedure', which significantly increased the powers of the (then) Assembly, which was officially renamed the Parliament. The SEA also formalized European political co-operation on foreign policy and introduced into the Treaty the first formal reference to the European Monetary System, which had been in operation since 1979.[3]

TREATY ON EUROPEAN UNION AGREED AT MAASTRICHT

The original version of the Treaty on European Union was signed in Maastricht on 7 February 1992 and is often referred to as the Maastricht Treaty. It is noteworthy that Article 1 of the TEU was intended to mark 'a new stage in the process of creating an ever closer union among the peoples of Europe'. The entire concept of the treaties, aimed ultimately at 'ever closer' Union, is arguably one of the most significant proactive legal, political and economic concepts of the post-war era. It is also an issue that gives rise to unpopularity in many EU states and was undoubtedly a factor in the UK's referendum result in favour of a British exit from the EU, referred to as Brexit. In response to British concerns related to the future development of the EU, the European Council, in the Conclusions of its summit of 25–27 June 2014 did, however, note (in paragraph 27 of those Conclusions) that 'the concept of ever closer union allows for different paths of integration for different countries, allowing those that want to deepen integration to move ahead, while respecting the wish of those who do not want to deepen any further'. This concession was further elaborated by the

European Council in a 'new settlement for the UK within the EU' in the Conclusions of its summit of 18–19 February 2016, to the effect that the UK 'is not committed to further political integration in the EU'.[4] The substance of this was intended to be incorporated into the treaties and the respective constitutional requirements of the member states, 'so as to make it clear that the references to ever closer union do not apply to the UK'. However, this 'settlement' was predicated on the UK informing the Secretary-General of the Council that the UK had decided to remain a member of the EU (following the anticipated in/out referendum). In the event, this political incentive did not succeed in persuading the UK population, which voted in June 2016 to leave the EU, and the so-called new settlement therefore no longer applies.

The Maastricht Treaty originally established a legal framework that consisted of three pillars. These were known as the European Community, Common Foreign and Security Policy (CFSP) and Justice and Home Affairs pillars, respectively, and frequently referred to as the first, second and third pillars. Following the implementation of the Treaty of Lisbon, the pillar concept was removed, although the CFSP still exists.

The CFSP is an area of intergovernmental activity within the EU, under which member states work together to achieve common objectives. The history of the evolution of the CFSP is intricate and includes Common Security and Defence Policy (CSDP), formerly known as European Security and Defence Policy (ESDP). It reflects a desire for closer EU co-operation on both foreign policy and defence policy, while *inter alia* also continuing to co-operate with the USA, within the North Atlantic Treaty Organization. The jurisdiction of the ECJ is restricted in relation to the CFSP.[5] The former third pillar known as the Justice and Home Affairs (or JHA) pillar, was renamed (by the Treaty of Amsterdam) as Police and Judicial Co-operation in Criminal Matters and again (by the Treaty of Lisbon) as the area of freedom, security and justice (AFSJ). The relevant treaty provisions have also been removed from the TEU and transferred into the TFEU. It essentially consists of a commitment to create an area without internal border controls but with a common external border, within which there are common measures in the fields of immigration, asylum and the rights of non-EU nationals, as well as judicial co-operation in civil and criminal matters, and police co-operation. The withdrawal agreement between the EU and the UK is expected to address potential issues arising from the departure of the UK in areas of co-operation such as judicial co-operation in civil, commercial and criminal matters, administrative and law enforcement co-operation procedures, and security. This might include rules, for example, on the protection of personal data and classified information, including security data. Both the EU and the UK have indicated a willingness to enter into partnership on areas unrelated to trade, such as the fight against terrorism and international crime, as well as security, defence and possibly foreign policy.

The special institutional arrangements surrounding the creation and operation of the original three pillars framework were necessitated in part by the insistence of member states that they should retain their legislative competences to act in the field of CFSP and on 'justice and home affairs' issues. However, successive treaties resulted in the gradual assimilation of third pillar issues into the first (i.e. Community, now Union) pillar, while leaving the CFSP pillar untouched as essentially intergovernmental in nature, addressing, for example, issues to do with foreign and security policy and military decisions.

The Maastricht Treaty made a number of novel and complex amendments. For example, it introduced the concept of citizenship of the Union and the rights of the EU citizen, with the corresponding obligations of the member states and the Community. It also established a timetable for progress towards economic and monetary union, or EMU (which led eventually to the establishment of a European Central Bank—ECB, based in Frankfurt, Germany) and the adoption of a Single Currency, the euro)[6] and introduced new procedures whereby (then) Community legislation could be adopted, including the 'co-decision procedure' (see below), as well as a new provision on subsidiarity (also discussed below).

TREATY OF AMSTERDAM

The Treaty of Amsterdam was signed on 2 October 1997 and entered into force on 1 May 1999. It amended the TEU, as well as each of the three treaties establishing the three European Communities (i.e. the EC, ECSC and Euratom Treaties, respectively), and certain related acts. The Treaty of Amsterdam retained the three-pillar structure of the EU, although it modified the contents of each pillar. In addition, it redistributed some contents between the pillars (most of all, from the third pillar to the first, EC, pillar). This emphasized the role of the Community and reduced the powers of the member states.

SCHENGEN AGREEMENT AND CONVENTION

'Schengen' is shorthand for measures originally agreed in 1985, in the village of Schengen, Luxembourg, by certain EU member states (Belgium, France, Germany, Luxembourg and the Netherlands) on the gradual elimination of border controls at their common frontiers and the introduction of freedom of movement for all individuals who were nationals of the signatory member states, other member states or third countries. To compensate for the eventual abolition of internal border checks, a series of implementing measures was put in place, providing for common entry controls at the external frontier of the Schengen area, enhanced police and judicial co-operation, and for the Schengen Information System (SIS, upgraded on 9 April 2013 to SIS II, with additional functions) to enable information exchange. These agreements, which were originally intergovernmental (i.e. created outside the framework of the treaties), were incorporated into the legal framework of the treaties by the Treaty of Amsterdam in 1999, as part of the effort to realize the AFSJ, discussed further below.

The Schengen Convention was signed by the same five states on 19 June 1990 and entered into force in 1995. It lays down the arrangement and guarantees for implementing freedom of movement. The Schengen area has gradually expanded to include Italy, Spain and Portugal, Greece, Austria, Denmark, Finland and Sweden, the non-EU member states of Norway, Iceland, Switzerland and Liechtenstein, and subsequently the member states from Central and Eastern Europe, although Bulgaria, Croatia, Cyprus and Romania are not yet full members. Hence, it is possible to travel overland from, for example, Lisbon, Portugal, to Tallinn, Estonia, without having to show a passport or travel identification. However, as a result of the migration crisis in Europe (where hundreds of thousands of migrants have sought refuge, largely owing to instability and conflict in the Middle East, mainly in Syria, Iraq and

Afghanistan) and terrorist attacks in a number of European cities in 2016–17, including Paris, France, and Brussels, Belgium, a significant number of countries temporarily reintroduced border controls. The Agreement and the Convention, the rules adopted on that basis and the related agreements together form the Schengen *acquis*. A Protocol to the Treaty of Amsterdam governs the incorporation of the Schengen *acquis* into the treaties. The absence of a comprehensive and co-ordinated migration policy and the need to ensure the security of the EU's external borders still poses a threat to the future operation of Schengen.

The UK and Ireland adhered to a passport-free Common Travel Area agreement long before the Schengen Agreements were concluded. These two 'island' states are not party to the Agreements, but under a Protocol to the Treaty of Amsterdam they may take part in some or all of the provisions of the *acquis* if the member states that are party to the Agreements and the representative of the Government of the country concerned vote unanimously in favour, within the Council. The UK, accordingly, has participated in certain fields of Schengen-based co-operation. The working and effect of the Common Travel Area will need to be reviewed, upon the UK's withdrawal from the EU. The latter intends to recognize such existing bilateral agreements and arrangements that are in conformity with EU law between Ireland and the UK. It is envisaged that the withdrawal agreement between the EU and the UK will also address issues arising from Ireland's unique geographic situation, including the transit of goods (to and from Ireland via the UK). There is also common ground between the UK and the EU on the need to support peace, stability and reconciliation on the island of Ireland, and not to undermine the objectives and commitments set out in the 1998 Good Friday Agreement (see below), although resolution of these issues will require flexible and imaginative solutions that had not been elaborated by August 2017.

Ireland also takes part in certain fields of Schengen activity, including all the provisions on the implementation and workings of the SIS. The latter (now upgraded to SIS II) enables competent national authorities such as border control, police forces, customs, visa, immigration, judicial and vehicle registration authorities (as well as the law enforcement agency Europol and the European Judicial Co-operation Unit—Eurojust, discussed further below) to exchange information and issue alerts for certain categories of persons, such as those who may have been involved in a serious crime, or who may not have the right to enter or stay in the EU, missing persons and so on, and generally to access and share data on law enforcement matters.

Denmark, although already a signatory to the Convention, may choose, in the context of the EU, whether or not to apply any new decision taken on the basis of the Schengen *acquis*.

TREATY OF NICE

The Treaty of Nice was the seventh principal European treaty since 1951 and the fourth since 1986. It entered into force on 1 February 2003. Like previous such treaties, it provided amendments and additions to the Treaty of Rome (EC Treaty). (Some 39 changes were made.)[7]

A notable feature of the EU has been the ability to adapt the legislative procedure over successive decades, in order to allow for laws to be adopted without the requirement for unanimity between an increasing number of member states, in particular through the creation of QMV. One of the most important aspects of the Treaty of Nice was the extension of the role of QMV, particularly in conjunction with the co-decision procedure between the Council and the European Parliament. (The co-decision procedure is now, after the Lisbon Treaty, known as the 'ordinary legislative procedure'.)

However, the use of QMV was not without complexity. This may be illustrated in relation to the issue of visas, asylum, immigration and other policies related to free movement of persons, wherein an additional paragraph was added to the EC Treaty by the Treaty of Nice (i.e. former Article 67(5) EC Treaty), so that whereas previously the Council had to act unanimously, it subsequently acted by QMV, using a co-decision procedure on specified matters, for example those concerning asylum, refugees, temporary protection of refugees and judicial co-operation in civil matters having cross-border implications, except for family law.

The Treaty of Nice also introduced four noteworthy Protocols, one of which replaced the previously existing Protocol on the ECJ, as well as provisions relating to the enlargement of the Union.

CONSTITUTIONAL TREATY

EC/EU treaty revisions are customarily prepared by an intergovernmental conference (IGC) bringing together representatives of the governments of the member states. The European Council meeting held in Laeken, Belgium, in December 2001 opted for an institutional innovation by establishing a Convention on the Future of Europe involving, in addition to EU government representatives, those of applicant (i.e. candidate) countries, national parliaments, the European Parliament, the European Commission and observers from the Economic and Social Committee, the Committee of the Regions and the European 'social partners'. This Convention reached a consensus on a draft Treaty establishing a Constitution for Europe, which was intended to replace the treaties accumulated over the previous 50 years by a single new Constitutional Treaty. This text served as a basis for the work of a subsequent IGC, which began work in October 2003.

Political agreement was reached in June 2004 and the draft Treaty establishing a Constitution for Europe was signed on 29 October by heads of state or government of the EU. It was later ratified by 18 of the then 25 member states, which included referenda endorsing it in Spain and Luxembourg. However, it never entered into force, in particular as a result of two negative referenda in France and the Netherlands, respectively. Following a period of reflection, followed by another IGC, a reform treaty for the EU (i.e. the Treaty of Lisbon) was drafted to replace the Constitutional Treaty. The latter was abandoned, although many of its provisions were subsumed, in one way or another, into the Treaty of Lisbon.

If the Constitutional Treaty had entered into force, it would have replaced in a single document the two existing principal treaties of the Union, namely the TEU and the EC Treaty, as well as the Charter of Fundamental Rights, while leaving the Treaty establishing the European Atomic Energy Community as a separate Treaty.

TREATY OF LISBON

The Treaty of Lisbon (also known as the Reform Treaty or simply as the Lisbon Treaty) has fundamentally amended the TEU and the EC Treaty. It was signed on 13 December 2007.

The process of ratification by all (then) 27 member states was intended to have been completed in time for its entry into force on 1 January 2009. However, this did not take place, *inter alia*, because of the negative outcome of a referendum in Ireland, in June 2008, on this issue. A second Irish referendum resulted in a positive outcome, finally enabling the Lisbon Treaty to enter into force on 1 December 2009.

An extremely complex document, this Treaty consists of some 271 pages, including 37 Protocols,[8] two Annexes, and 65 Declarations.[9] In the context of this essay, only a selective overview is possible.[10] The Lisbon Treaty remains in terms of content very similar to the abandoned Constitutional Treaty. However, among the provisions that were removed are symbols considered typical of a federal state, such as the terms 'Constitution' and 'European Foreign Affairs Minister', as well as a proposed Union flag, anthem and motto.

The Lisbon Treaty sought only to modify existing treaties.[11] Nevertheless, the modifications were substantial. It brought to an end the familiar legal entity called the EC and changed the name of the Treaty establishing the European Community (EC Treaty) to the TFEU. The term 'European Community' was replaced and succeeded throughout by the 'European Union'. The latter was expressly given legal personality. The current Treaty on European Union (TEU, as amended at Lisbon) and the TFEU remain distinct, but have equal legal status. They are also now much more interrelated. It is therefore necessary to have regard to both treaties for the legal provisions to be fully understood, and to be aware of the possible further implications of the Charter of Fundamental Rights, which has equal status with the treaties. The interpretation of EU law on issues of human rights may, in appropriate cases, also have to take into account relevant case law of the European Convention on Human Rights (referred to further below) and vice versa.

The EU Institutional Framework

Under Article 10 of the TEU, the Union's institutions are the European Parliament, the European Council (recognized for the first time as a formal institution by the Lisbon Treaty), the Council, the European Commission (known as the Commission), the Court of Justice of the European Union, the Court of Auditors and (as a result of the Lisbon Treaty) the European Central Bank, which, although in existence since 1 June 1998, did not become a fully fledged institution until the entry into force of the Lisbon Treaty. In addition, under Article 300 of the TFEU, the European Parliament, Council and Commission are assisted by the Economic and Social Committee and the Committee of the Regions, exercising advisory functions. The latter bodies previously had parity, but, under the Treaty of Lisbon, the latter alone acquired the right to bring an action before the Court of Justice for a relevant violation of the principle of subsidiarity (Article 263 of the TFEU). The Court of Auditors has the duty, *inter alia*, to audit the revenue and expenditure of the EC.

The EU institutions selected for analysis below are confined to those historically involved in the lawmaking processes of the EU.

EUROPEAN COUNCIL

One of the innovations introduced by the Maastricht Treaty was the granting of formal status to a (previously informal) forum for discussion with a pre-eminent political role, namely the European Council, which consists of the heads of state or of government of each of the member states, together with the President of the Commission. The High Representative of the Union for Foreign Affairs and Security Policy, a role created under the Lisbon Treaty, who is also a member of the Commission, also takes part in its work.

The European Council meets at least on a quarterly basis (Article 15 of the TEU). As a result of the Treaty of Lisbon, it is given, for the first time, formal recognition as a Union institution and is also made subject to the jurisdiction of the Court of Justice. Under the Treaty of Lisbon, the previous practice of a six-month (rotating) President chairing the meetings has been abolished in respect of the European Council (although it continues to exist for all configurations of another body, the Council—see immediately below), other than for the Foreign Affairs Council meetings, which are chaired by the High Representative. The former (rotating) President of the European Council has been replaced by a (permanent) President elected by members of the European Council, by QMV, for a term of two-and-a-half years, renewable once. This post of President of the European Council facilitates coherence and increased visibility to the outside world. This might imply greater effectiveness of action, but has introduced a rival centre of influence to both the Commission President and the High Representative of the Union for Foreign Affairs and Security Policy. It appears that, as a result of the economic and financial crisis, the then (first) President of the European Council, Herman Van Rompuy, did play a much more important co-ordinating role than had initially been expected, and the number of meetings of the European Council was increased.[12]

In addition to meetings of the European Council, there have also been numerous meetings of heads of state or of government of just the eurozone member states, sometimes referred to as Eurozone or Euro Area Summits. Protocol No. 14, which is annexed to the treaties, envisaged meetings of ministers of the Eurogroup of member states in which the currency is the euro, pending the euro becoming the currency of all member states of the EU. These countries subsequently agreed further, in the context of the Treaty on Stability, Co-ordination and Governance in the Economic and Monetary Union (TSCG—discussed below) and with the ambitious heading in its Title V of 'Governance of the Euro Area', to hold informal Euro Summit meetings of heads of state or of government of eurozone countries at least twice a year (with additional meetings as required). Such summits sometimes take place at the end of a formal European Council meeting. They have the same format (i.e. chaired by the President of the European Council and including the Commission President) but are restricted to the (currently 19) eurozone member states out of the overall total of 28 EU countries. As such, this situation arguably has the potential to divert and/or transfer co-ordinated political collaboration within the (official) European Council to a select group of member states, and away from those, among them the UK, that are outside the euro area.

COUNCIL

The Council has undergone several changes of name. After the Maastricht Treaty it was called the Council of the European Union, but should not be confused with the European Council (discussed above) or the Council of Europe. (The latter is a human rights organization consisting of 47 member states, 28 of which are members of the EU, and all of which have adopted the European Convention on Human Rights.) The Council is also sometimes still referred to as the Council of Ministers. After the Lisbon Treaty, however, it is formally known simply as the Council.

The Council retains the most important role in EU lawmaking. It is composed of representative ministers from the member states but is not, however, a fixed body. Instead, it has a fluctuating membership depending on the subject matter under discussion. It currently sits in one of 10 configurations, such as General Affairs, Foreign Affairs, Economic and Financial Affairs (including the budget), Justice and Home Affairs (including civil protection), etc. By the very nature of its composition it cannot be a permanently sitting body. The preparation of its discussions and decisions is undertaken by COREPER (a French acronym for Committee of Permanent Representatives), which is a permanent and full-time body of representatives (usually civil servants) from the member states. It is divided into two committees: COREPER I, which comprises the deputies of the ambassadors to the EU, and COREPER II, which comprises the ambassadors themselves and is therefore the more important of the two. The activities of COREPER are considered to be far from transparent. The Council, COREPER and a special Working Party on Article 50 will also play a role in the Brexit negotiations, in accordance with the EU terms of reference (discussed below).

The work of the Council, in so far as it relates to the functioning of the CFSP, has undergone significant reform.[13] By virtue of amendments made by the Treaty of Lisbon, it is significant that the Council is now required to meet in public when it legislates, so that relevant meetings can now be accessed via internet streaming, and also that the use of QMV (rather than the previous simple majority voting) in some 40 new areas of competence may make decision making faster.

When the Council votes on the basis of a qualified majority, the number of votes attributed to each member state is predetermined, according to a weighted voting system (applying a scale ranging from 29 votes each for the four largest member states, to three votes for the smallest). From 1 November 2014 a new and more intricate procedure for QMV applied in the Council (Article 16 of the TEU and Article 238 of the TFEU). A large number of acts now require a 'double majority' in order to be adopted, involving the support of at least 55% of the EU member states (in practice, 16 member states in a Union of 28) and at least 65% of the population of the EU (thereby strengthening the position of the larger EU states, such as the UK). In these cases, a 'blocking minority' must include at least four member states. However, between November 2014 and March 2017 any member state could request that the weighted voting system be applied, instead of the double majority system. After the UK withdraws from the EU, the voting weights and majority/minority thresholds in the Council will have to be revised.

The presidency of the Council (as opposed to the European Council) continues in traditional fashion to rotate every six months between the member states, in accordance with a Council Decision of 1 January 2007 (which had determined the relevant order until January–June 2020), and ensures a balance, in rotation, between large, small and newer states. A relevant minister from the member state that has the presidency chairs the various Council meetings, except for the Foreign Affairs Council, which is chaired by the High Representative for Foreign Affairs and Security Policy (unless the latter is unavailable). The UK had been scheduled (by Council decision) to hold the presidency of the Council in July–December 2017, but following the outcome of the June 2016 referendum on leaving the EU, did not take up the role. The Council subsequently decided to bring forward by six months the order of the presidencies, beginning on 1 July 2017. This meant that Estonia took the UK's 'slot'.[14]

The Council's rules of procedure provide that, for each period of 18 months, the respective three member-state presidencies during that time (known as the 'trio' system) work in close cooperation and consultation with the European Commission, so as to prepare a coherent and well-articulated draft programme for Council activities. This may ensure greater continuity and consistency in EU policies, while preserving some scope for manoeuvre for the country holding the presidency. The execution of Council presidency tasks is basically the responsibility of the relevant member state government, assisted mainly by its civil servants, diplomats, politicians and experts. The involvement of civil society organizations and citizens in this process is under-utilized but could yet become an additional means of furthering participatory democracy and civil dialogue within the EU.

EUROPEAN COMMISSION

The Commission[15] is both the institution and the 'college of commissioners'. There is currently one commissioner from each EU member state. Under the Lisbon Treaty, the post of High Representative of the Union for Foreign Affairs and Security Policy is created and combined with those of a Vice-President of the Commission. This post has been named 'First Vice-President' by the Commission of Jean-Claude Juncker, which will remain in place until 31 October 2019. The current College of Commissioners consists of the Commission President, seven Vice-Presidents (in particular policy areas), including the High Representative of the Union for Foreign Affairs and Security Policy and 20 Commissioners.

The Commission President must be proposed as a candidate by the European Council to the European Parliament and then approved by a majority of the latter's members. In the recent elections, each of the major European Parliament parties chose a candidate to lead their respective campaigns (known as the *Spitzenkandidaten* process). Juncker (a former Prime Minister of Luxembourg) was chosen by the European People's Party (EPP) to lead its campaign and it eventually won the highest number of seats in the European Parliament. Hence, the Parliament informed the European Council that Juncker was the preferred candidate for Commission President. Article 17(7) of the TEU requires that the European Council should first select its candidate 'taking into account the elections to the European Parliament and after having held the appropriate consultations'. At its meeting on 26–27 June 2014, the European Council adopted the decision (after a formal vote by qualified majority) to propose Juncker as its candidate for President of the European Commission in 2014–19. The European Council, by common accord with the President-elect, must then adopt the list of the other persons it proposes for appointment as members of the

Commission, on the basis of suggestions made by the member states. The college is then submitted collectively to the European Parliament for approval. The new Commission is officially appointed by the European Council, again acting by qualified majority.

The (current) 2014 Commission draws political legitimacy from the Parliament, to a far greater extent than previously, as a result of the *Spitzenkandidaten* process. This has arguably altered and more closely aligned the two institutions to the detriment of the political authority of the member states within the European Council and in a manner possibly unforeseen by the treaties.[16] There is, however, considerable speculation as to whether the *Spitzenkandidaten* will be used successfully next time (i.e. in 2019).

In the Brexit negotiations with the UK, the Commission, through its chief negotiator, Michel Barnier, will undertake most of the technical and legal negotiations, while at the same time working closely with the Council, and through the latter with the member states, in accordance with the terms of reference on Article 50 (discussed further below). Although the treaties do not give the Parliament a role in determining the substance of the negotiations, it has a crucial role to play at the end, since the final agreement requires its consent. The Commission's mandate and the negotiating guidelines are discussed in more detail below (see *Institutional Balance of Power in Brexit*).

The Commission has the general role of working for the good of the EU as a whole, not favouring any EU state or interest group. Except in specific cases, the Commission has the exclusive right to initiate draft Union legislation. Thus, although the Council and the Parliament, acting jointly, often take the final decisions on Union legislation, they can only act on the basis of a draft proposal from the Commission. In other words, the Commission possesses the considerable 'negative' powers of either withholding a proposal or withdrawing a proposal. However, by virtue of the new Inter-institutional Agreement on Better Law-Making between the three legislative institutions, adopted by the European Parliament on 9 March 2016, the Parliament and the Council are, hitherto, also to be consulted on withdrawals, and the follow-up to legislative initiative requests (pursuant to Article 225 or 241 of the TFEU) will also be improved. The Council, in addition to its main role of involvement in the passing of legislation, can (under Article 241 of the TFEU), and acting by a simple majority, ask the Commission to carry out studies and make proposals and can also confer power on the Commission to implement Union legislation (Article 291 of the TFEU).

The Commission also plays a significant role in relation to both the CFSP and the AFSJ. It also has important executive powers, such as the power to take a decision that a member state or undertaking (e.g. a company) is in breach of the competition rules. It also acts as the guardian of Union law, notably through its powers to begin infringement proceedings against a member state for failure to fulfil its Union law obligations.

The Commission is divided into several departments and services. The departments, known as Directorates-General (DGs), each have a specific mandate. For example, DG Trade is responsible, *inter alia*, for matters to do with trade policy (including areas of activity such as manufactured goods, services, intellectual property and investment). It also negotiates and concludes bilateral and multilateral trade agreements with a wide number of countries from all regions of the world, for example a new free trade agreement with the Republic of Korea entered into force in July 2011. The diverse range of countries with which the EU concluded trade agreements in 2012–13 included Armenia, Honduras, Nicaragua, Panama, Peru and Singapore (although ratification of the Singapore Trade Agreement is now subject to compliance with the ECJ ruling in Opinion 2/17 of 16 May 2017). A preliminary trade agreement was signed, in principle, with Canada in 2013, and received the approval of the European Parliament on 15 February 2017. New (and sensitive) negotiations were launched with the USA towards a Transatlantic Trade and Investment Partnership (TTIP), but failed following the election of US President Donald Trump, while talks are continuing with Japan. The Comprehensive Economic and Trade Agreement (CETA) with Canada might conceivably be a useful model or starting point on which any future relationship agreement between the UK and the EU is based, but the UK would have the added advantage of already being fully compliant with all EU regulatory and other norms.

EUROPEAN PARLIAMENT

The size of the European Parliament increased to 766, following the addition of a dozen Members of the European Parliament (MEPs) from Croatia after that state's accession to the EU in July 2013. This number declined to 751, in conformity with the provisions of the Lisbon Treaty, after the European Parliament elections of 2014. As a result of those elections, the political parties on the far right and far left increased their representation in the Parliament. However, the institution continues to be dominated by the two largest political groups, the EPP and the Group of the Progressive Alliance of Socialists & Democrats. The number of seats, as well as the relative majorities of the political groups in the Parliament, will necessarily be affected by Brexit, although the full implications are as yet unclear.

The powers of the European Parliament were significantly increased by the Lisbon Treaty, notably because of the extension of the previous co-decision legislative procedure (now renamed the ordinary legislative procedure) to a much larger range of areas, including the whole of the previous third pillar and also to agriculture and fisheries. The Maastricht Treaty ensured that the role (at that time) of both the Parliament and the Commission was limited, and that predominant power in all aspects of policymaking was held either by the Council or by the European Council. In the context of the Brexit negotiations, the role of the Parliament is significant because any withdrawal agreement with the UK will require its prior consent to be valid in accordance with Article 50(2) TEU.

Hence, historically, the quest for greater democratic accountability for the EU has centred, in large part, on an enhanced role for the European Parliament, which until 1986 had only a purely consultative role. By virtue of the Single European Act, its participation in the exercise of legislative power was introduced through the creation of the co-operation procedure. The introduction of a new co-decision procedure by the Maastricht Treaty, as amended by the Treaty of Amsterdam, subsequently placed the Parliament on an equal footing with the Council in the manner in which certain legislation is adopted, and considerably enhanced its authority as a legislative body.

The Parliament is now generally considered to be, together with the Council, a twin arm of the Union's budgetary and legislative authority.[17] It has three places of work. In 1992 the member states adopted the Edinburgh Decision on the location of the seats of the institutions and of certain bodies and departments of the (then) European Communities. This agreement is now in Protocol No. 6 to the treaties. It states that the European Parliament shall have its seat in Strasbourg, France, where the 12 periods of monthly plenary sessions, including the budget session, are held. Periods of additional plenary sessions are held in Brussels. The committees of the Parliament also meet in Brussels, but its administration (General Secretariat) is based in Luxembourg. In December 2012, in the Joined Cases C-237/11 and C-238/11, *France v. Parliament* (brought by France and supported by Luxembourg), the Court annulled an attempt by the Parliament to make a comparatively small procedural alteration to its calendar of sessions, the practical effect of which was to reduce from 12 to 11 the sessions scheduled in Strasbourg. The Court observed that, even if the disadvantages and significant costs engendered by the plurality of places of work are acknowledged, it is not for the Parliament or the Court to remedy that situation; rather it is for the member states to do so, if appropriate.

INSTITUTIONAL BALANCE OF POWER

The growth in the powers of the Parliament has altered the institutional balance of power. Originally, the Council was the sole legislator, but this role is now largely shared with the Parliament. The resulting compromises appear primarily to be aimed at achieving a political consensus in the passing of new legislation, rather than a focused attempt to lead and guide European public opinion along a particular course. In the context of the Brexit negotiations, the interplay between all the key institutions comes into greater focus, as well as, crucially, their relationship with the member states themselves. Only time will tell which political interests will ultimately hold the greatest sway.

The relatively low turnout in virtually all of the EU's (then) 27 member states during the 2009 European Parliament elections reflected a view of a continued lack of accountability of MEPs to the European public. In the 2014 elections turnout rates varied widely between member states and there was, in overall terms, a marginal further decline. About one-quarter of all seats were won by candidates of parties that were either sceptical of the EU or protest parties. The sense of either disaffection or disinterest by the European public with the Parliament may be in part the result of a lack of understanding, or interest, by European citizens in the political groupings to which MEPs belong in the context of their legislative work. Among these political groups, historically no single group has had an overall majority, and the various requirements to achieve a majority in the voting also oblige the major groupings in the European Parliament to work together to achieve a consensus, if they wish their institution to wield its powers effectively. At the 2014 elections the EPP won the most seats but was well short of an overall majority. Some public dissatisfaction with the Parliament may arguably also be indirectly intended for the European Commission, the EU's de facto 'executive', which cannot be voted out of office in the usual way, even if the public disagree with outcomes or any perceived performance failures.

In part, as a consequence of the use of the *Spitzenkandidaten* process (described above, see *European Commission*) to select the 2014 Commission President, there is now a stronger inter-institutional collaboration between the Parliament and the Commission than was previously the case. The current Juncker Commission has promised to legislate less, and this was immediately reflected in its 2015 work programme, in which the number of new proposals for legislation declined dramatically, compared with previous years, and were focused around 10 priority areas. These proposals have also been drawn up through a 'top-down', rather than 'bottom up', process, thus discontinuing the previous practice whereby the various Directorates-General of the Commission were encouraged to submit a 'shopping list' of proposals. It has also, as suggested by Martin Westlake,[18] succeeded in abandoning the previous inviolable linkage between Commissioners and portfolios. The various Vice-Presidents are to act as legislative 'filters', and each also plays a co-ordinating role in relation to teams or clusters of Commissioners. Some of the latter will be overseen by more than one Vice-President, depending on the subject matter under discussion. However, the general effect has been to bring the Commission under the more centralized control of its President.

There is also an increased focus on 'better regulation', which includes the repeal, consolidation and clarification of existing laws, and the carrying out of 'impact assessments' before proposing new laws. This portfolio is allocated as part of the new role of First Vice-President (Frans Timmermans, of the Netherlands), who is also made the ultimate arbiter on whether legislative proposals are forwarded to the College of Commissioners for consideration. This new structure is intended to facilitate the achievement of the 10 priorities of the Juncker Commission. However, the reduced legislative activity will doubtless have a major effect on the other main institutions, notably the Parliament and the Council, as well as the advisory bodies, such as the EESC, which have a treaty-based role to give opinions on proposed legislation. It has also caused some concern that it may be a mechanism for downplaying environmental and/or consumer legislation.

A new Inter-institutional Agreement on Better Law-Making was concluded by the three legislative institutions and adopted by the European Parliament on 9 March 2016.[19] It replaces the 2003 Agreement with the same name, but does not replace the 2010 Framework Agreement between the Parliament and the Commission and the privileged bilateral working relations between them established therein. Proposals for new legislation, although still largely the prerogative of the Commission, may continue, in practice, also to be drawn from the political decisions of the European Council or the requests of member states.

One of the aims of the 2016 Inter-institutional Agreement is to reaffirm the principle of sincere co-operation between the institutions, including information-sharing and dialogue and to emphasize that the Parliament and the Council, as co-legislators, shall exercise their powers on an equal footing. The Agreement also contains a commitment to enhanced transparency, which is to include 'appropriate handling of trilateral negotiations' (known as trilogues) with the aim, *inter alia*, of improving communication to the public during the whole legislative cycle and generally to facilitate the traceability of the various steps in the legislative process. Nevertheless, in May 2015 the European Ombudsman, Emily O'Reilly, launched a public consultation on the transparency of trilogues. She stated that: 'Trilogues are where the deals are done. The vast majority of draft EU laws now pass through the trilogue process before being finalized. Europeans have a right to an EU lawmaking process that is as open as possible, while elected representatives also need the space to negotiate. This public consultation will enable us to consider as many viewpoints as possible before deciding on the next step in the inquiry.' The consultation process for the submission of comments ended on 31 March 2016, and the Ombudsman adopted a decision on 12 July calling on the EU institutions to make specific reforms to trilogues, so her intervention may eventually result in improvements.

The Commission and the Council also produce numerous Action Plans, Strategies, Frameworks and Scoreboards on a wide array of subjects. Among such initiatives, the Lisbon Strategy (subsequently termed the Growth and Jobs Strategy), first agreed in March 2000, was a political commitment to bring about economic, social and environmental renewal in the EU, to be implemented broadly through the use of the open method of co-ordination (a concept that is discussed further below). It was largely considered to have been a failure and was replaced in March 2010 by 'Europe 2020: a strategy for smart, sustainable and inclusive growth'. The European integration process has led to the development of a distinctive jargon or 'Eurospeak', ranging from the familiar term *acquis*, to the less obvious, such as 'flexicurity' (which refers to a strategy for enhancing labour flexibility and security).

INSTITUTIONAL BALANCE OF POWER IN BREXIT

The complex inter-relationship described immediately above between the four key political institutions, namely the European Council, the Council, the Commission and the Parliament, is magnified in the context of Brexit, where, in accordance with both Article 50 of the TEU and Article 218 of the TFEU, all four play a part in the negotiations with the UK. After the UK triggered the exit procedure in Article 50 of the TEU in late March 2017, the European Council formally agreed negotiating guidelines in April, setting out its core principles for the negotiations. It then handed over the conduct of the negotiations to both the European Commission and the Council (of Ministers) of the EU.[20]

The European Commission appointed as its chief negotiator Michel Barnier, a former Vice-President of the Commission and former French Minister of Foreign Affairs. Within the Commission, he heads a task force for the preparation and conduct of the negotiations with the UK under Article 50 of the TEU. The Commission, drawing on its significant legal, technical and policy expertise, also drafts detailed position papers, outlining its stance on each area under negotiation, including the negotiating process itself and working arrangements between itself and the Council. The Commission's draft position or mandate is then discussed within the Council, which has a Working Party for this purpose, and ultimately must be agreed by the Council (excluding the UK) by a qualified majority vote. Once the mandate is agreed, the Commission takes over the actual negotiating process.

The Commission will continue to report back regularly to the Council, so that representatives of the individual member states are kept informed through the latter. However, the Council has also appointed a representative, Didier Seeuws, a Belgian diplomat, to head its own task force on Brexit. The European Parliament has further elected a representative, namely Guy Verhofstadt, a former Belgian Prime Minister and MEP.

Although the treaties appear to give in theory only a limited role in the substantive process to the Parliament, it must be kept immediately and fully informed at all stages of the procedure in accordance with Article 218(10). In reality, since the Parliament must give its consent under Article 50 to the eventual agreement, it therefore may be expected to wield significant influence and power over the negotiations in practice. The process of feedback will take place through the Parliament's own negotiator, who will report back to the various political group leaders in the latter institution.

However, the reality of Brexit will be felt not just within the EU institutions but primarily within the 27 remaining member states and by their citizens. Therefore, the input from all these states, some of which may be affected to a greater extent than others and in differing fields and sectors of the economy, will add to the complexity of balancing sometimes competing interests. Hence the Brexit negotiations, particularly when they become more embroiled in substantive detail, have the potential to create thorny political problems on all sides of the EU equation and not just for the UK.

There is also a potential further complication in that a future free trade agreement between the UK and the EU may, depending on its coverage, be regarded as a 'mixed competence agreement' that also requires the consent of all the other member states.[21] That, in turn, may require, in accordance with domestic constitutional requirements, the agreement of national and/or regional parliaments (as was the case in Belgium in the context of the EU-Canada trade agreement), hence also giving them oversight and an implicit say in the negotiations.

NATIONAL PARLIAMENTS

It was previously left to each individual member state to decide how far to involve its national parliament in European law-making, and very different practices have arisen. However, all the EU national legislatures have a European Affairs Committee and a system for examining European policies and documents.[22] Under the Lisbon Treaty, the role of national parliaments is substantially strengthened and formalized in relation to the EU legislative process, such as by giving national parliaments a role in helping to ensure compliance with the principle of 'subsidiarity' (the latter term is discussed further below).

The new procedures are known colloquially as 'yellow' and 'orange' cards. A proposal by the former British Prime Minister David Cameron (who resigned following the referendum in the UK in June 2016) to introduce a 'red card', if 55% of national parliaments wished to challenge a proposed European law for reasons based on 'subsidiarity', was agreed by the European Council in February 2016, but was not implemented, owing to the UK's vote in favour of Brexit. Under the current treaties, national parliaments gain the right to prior scrutiny, i.e. to be informed directly and in good time, *inter alia*, of all 'draft legislative acts', to express concerns directly to the institution that initiated the proposal (normally the Commission) within an eight-week time limit, and in this context to be able to consult regional parliaments 'where appropriate'.[23] The first use of the yellow card by national parliaments took place in May 2012, when the parliaments of several member states, notably Finland, Sweden and Denmark, complained about a proposed draft EU law (the 'Monti II' law) that concerned both the right to strike and the freedom of companies to offer services across the EU. The draft proposal was subsequently abandoned because it was politically controversial in any case, but the use of the yellow card procedure played its part in this reversal and demonstrated that, contrary to initial expectations, the national parliaments could and did have the ability and willingness to co-ordinate among themselves on EU-related issues.

The second use occurred in 2013 concerning the Commission's proposal for a Council Regulation on the establishment of a European Public Prosecutor's Office (EPPO) to investigate and prosecute the perpetrators of offences affecting the EU's financial interests. National parliaments issued 13 reasoned opinions on the proposal (representing 18 votes out of a possible 56). Under Article 7(2) of Protocol No. 2, 14 votes were needed to trigger a yellow card procedure. The Commission carried out a review of the proposal and issued a communication. In analysing the reasoned opinions, the Commission distinguished between arguments relating to the principle of subsidiarity and others relating, *inter alia*, to the principle of proportionality. It concluded that the proposal complied with the principle of subsidiarity and decided to maintain it. A third use of the procedure was triggered in May 2016 when national parliaments, mainly from Central and Eastern European countries, triggered a yellow card obliging the European Commission to reconsider its proposal to revise the Posting of Workers Directive, but the Commission opted to defend its original position and the legislative process continued.

These procedures, although novel, may not, in fact, be significant since breaches of the subsidiarity principle will almost certainly be rare. Scrutiny of the *substance* of legislative proposals by national parliaments is arguably more important, but may be neglected by default. Nevertheless, in the framework of the Lisbon Treaty, national parliaments are able to consider and examine EU policy initiatives early in the legislative process through the EC Annual Policy Strategy and Legislative and Work Programme.

National parliaments are also involved by the treaties, in consultations relating to agreements for changes to legislative procedures under the *passerelle* (bridge) clauses (referred to further below); the evaluation of EU policies in the area of freedom, security and justice (Article 70 of the TFEU) and the activities of Eurojust (Article 85 of the TFEU), as well as in the scrutiny of Europol's activities (Article 88 of the TFEU). They also have to be notified of the applications made by European states for Union membership (Article 49 of the TEU).[24] They may also have a national (but not a formal treaty) role to play in major EU events, e.g. the 2015 Greek bailout crisis, or the conclusion of certain EU trade agreements. For instance, if the TTIP between the EU and the USA had gone ahead and been deemed to be a 'mixed competence' trade agreement, i.e. involving both EU and member state competence, it would have required adoption by not just the Council and Parliament, but also ratification by all 28 EU member states, and hence a further potential involvement by national parliaments as part of their own national democratic processes (notably in Belgium in October 2016 the regional parliament of Wallonia initially withheld its consent to the EU-Canada CETA). A future EU-UK trade agreement may need to overcome similar obstacles.

COURT OF JUSTICE OF THE EUROPEAN UNION

The Court of Justice of the European Union, or CJEU, sometimes referred to as the European Court (Article 19 of the TEU), is seated in the city of Luxembourg and comprises three distinct courts. These are first, the Court of Justice, or ECJ; second, the General Court or GC (formerly known as the Court of First Instance); and third, the Civil Service Tribunal, which is a specialized court. The last was established in 2005 to deal with staff (civil servant) cases. In June 2015 the Council supported a proposal to reform the General Court, which was designed to speed up its ability to handle an increasing workload. This has resulted in a significant and progressive increase in the number of judges at the GC. A second regulation on the reform was also agreed by the Council. This resulted in the dissolution of the Civil Service Tribunal on 31 August 2016, with its first instance jurisdiction over staff cases being taken over by the General Court from 1 September. On the same date the Court of Justice regained jurisdiction over appeals in staff cases.

The ECJ made significant amendments to its Rules of Procedure in 2012.[25] The Lisbon Treaty has retained some existing provisions with regard to the creation of 'specialized courts' (formerly 'judicial panels'), but henceforth they are created in accordance with the ordinary legislative procedure, i.e. by co-decision with a qualified majority in the Council, rather than by unanimity among member states as was previously the case.

The ECJ was first established in 1952 as the Court of Justice of the European Coal and Steel Communities. It was later named, in 1958, as the Court of Justice of the European Communities, or CJEC. It has always been the highest court in the ECSC, EC and now EU, legal system, with the primary function of ensuring that (ECSC, subsequently EEC and now EU) legislation was interpreted and applied consistently by the member states. Subsequent treaty amendments have extended the ECJ's jurisdiction to new areas of EU competence. All cases heard by the General Court may be subject to appeal to the ECJ on questions of law. The General Court deals primarily with actions brought by individuals and undertakings against acts of the Union institutions, for example, appeals against European Commission decisions in competition cases or regulatory decisions (such as in the field of state aid).

The ECJ has been instrumental, through its judgments, in furthering the process of European integration. Some of its interventions in this context have been controversial. The ECJ gives 'preliminary rulings' when the national courts in the member states refer to it questions concerning the interpretation of the treaties, or the validity and interpretation of acts of the Union's institutions, bodies, offices or agencies (Article 267 of the TFEU).[26]

The ECJ is required (by Article 267 of the TFEU) to act with the minimum of delay if a question referred for a 'preliminary ruling' is raised in a case pending before any court or tribunal of a member state, with regard to a person in custody. It also has competence to hear cases brought by member states or the EU institutions against other member states or institutions. These may involve, for example, enforcement actions by the Commission against the member states for failing to implement EU legislation, or challenges by member states or institutions concerning the validity of EU legislation.

The ECJ currently consists of one judge from each member state. The GC has 47 judges, due to increase to 56 in 2019 (i.e. two per member state), unless Brexit changes the number. The ECJ is assisted by 11 Advocates-General. The Advocates-General have equal status to the judges and assist the Court in nearly all cases, by delivering independent and impartial opinions. These are not binding, and so leave the Court free to pronounce its own judgment. There is inconclusive evidence in current empirical research on the influence or impact of the opinions of Advocates-General, although some may be more influential than others, both on their colleague judges and/or the development of the doctrine of EU law more widely.

Following the entry into force of the Lisbon Treaty, the judges continue to be appointed by common accord of the governments of the member states for six years, but henceforth they will be appointed after consultation with a panel responsible for giving an opinion on candidates' suitability to perform the duties of Judge and Advocate-General of the Court of Justice and the GC. This panel is to comprise seven persons chosen from among former members of the two Courts, members of national supreme courts and lawyers of recognized competence, one of whom will be proposed by the European Parliament. The refusal of the Council to grant public access to the panel opinions regarding judicial candidates to the ECJ and the GC was made the subject of a complaint to the European Ombudsman (in Case 1011/2015/TN), which began on 13 July 2015. The Ombudsman's Decision on Case 1011/2015/TN was taken on 4 May 2016. As a result of the Ombudsman's inquiry and her preliminary views, the Council made a policy change and is now willing to reconsider the matter following a new access request by the complainants. The Ombudsman indicated that on the issue of striking the correct balance between the need to protect the personal data of persons being assessed for high public office with the need to ensure maximum transparency in relation to the process of making such senior appointments, she is in favour of greater openness.

In the context of Brexit, the future role of the Court of Justice is a key issue. The EU has indicated that the withdrawal agreement with the UK should respect the Union's autonomy and its legal order, including the supervisory role of the European Commission, but especially the role of the CJEU as regards, in particular, the interpretation and application of Union law. The Union therefore expects a continuing role for the Court in relation, *inter alia*, to the implementation and enforcement of any agreement after the withdrawal date. The UK, meanwhile, while indicating its commitment to minimizing legal uncertainty and disruption for individuals or businesses at and after the date of withdrawal, has also made it clear that leaving the EU will end the jurisdiction of the CJEU in the UK, which it contends is a position consistent with international legal precedent, placing the UK in the same position as all other third countries, including those with which the EU has deep and close relationships. The UK Government's introduction in Parliament of the proposed European Union (Withdrawal) Bill in July 2017 was in part intended to accomplish its objectives. However, some legal method of resolving future disputes or disagreements that may arise after withdrawal is nevertheless likely to be considered.

EUROPEAN EXTERNAL ACTION SERVICE (EEAS)

The role of the EU in the field of external relations, notably foreign and security policy, continues to evolve following the formation of the EEAS. The Lisbon Treaty established the EEAS in Article 27(3) of the TEU, as amended, and provided the legal basis for the Council to establish the organization and functioning of the service. It was formally introduced on 1 December 2010. It is a comparatively new service of a *sui generis* nature, with its own budget, independent from other EU institutions, though essentially formed by a merger of the external relations departments of the Council and the European Commission, as well as some staff seconded from national diplomatic services of the member states. What were previously designated European Commission Representations abroad have become EU Delegations (although member states retain their own embassies in many countries). The Commission continues to maintain its own representation offices *within* EU member states, *inter alia*, to monitor public opinion towards the EU.

The EEAS functions under the authority of the High Representative of the Union for Foreign Affairs and Security Policy (currently Federica Mogherini, a former Italian Minister of Foreign Affairs and International Co-operation), and conducts and implements the CFSP. The High Representative's combined role with that of Commission Vice-President is intended to ensure greater consistency between the different sectors of the EU's external action (i.e. not just the CFSP) and the Commission's responsibilities in external relations. Thus, for example, the EEAS manages the EU's response to external crises and co-operates with the Commission in areas of shared competence. However, management of trade policy (referred to above, see *European Commission*) remains the responsibility of the Commission. The creation of the EEAS and the multifaceted role of the High Representative for Foreign Affairs and Security Policy do not necessarily mean that the Union and its member states will thereby be united, or unanimous, in foreign policy matters, but it is a means towards that end.

ECONOMIC AND SOCIAL COMMITTEE

The Economic and Social Committee is one of two advisory bodies established under the treaties, the other being the Committee of the Regions (CoR). It is selected for discussion here on account of the writer's personal knowledge of it as the longest-serving female UK Committee Member, nominated by successive British Governments, for the period 1998–2020. Within the EU institutional framework, the Committee was previously known under the acronym ECOSOC or ESC, but is now colloquially known as the European Economic and Social Committee (EESC). [27]

The CoR provides EU subnational authorities such as regions, provinces and municipalities with a direct voice within the EU institutional framework. It was established by the Maastricht Treaty and is generally composed of elected local and regional government politicians. The EESC, in contrast, was first established in the founding EEC Treaty and its mandate was subsequently revised and expanded, notably by the Treaties of Maastricht and Amsterdam.

The EESC is notable because it largely consists not of elected politicians but of representatives of employers, of the employed and of other parties representative of civil society, notably in the socioeconomic, civic, professional and cultural areas (Article 300(2) of the TFEU). Specific mentions of certain interest groups, such as consumers, farmers and craftsmen, have been removed by the Lisbon Treaty. At the same time, the Treaty now provides that its composition may be reviewed at regular intervals by the Council (Article 300(5) of the TFEU). The main task of the EESC is to advise the three major institutions (Council, Commission and European Parliament, Article 3(4) of the TFEU). It therefore has a distinctive consultative role as an intermediary between the executive (the Commission) and the legislature (namely the Parliament and Council). The requirement for consultation by the Parliament has been made a formal legal requirement by the Lisbon Treaty, in respect of both this Committee and the CoR.

It is mandatory for the EESC to be consulted on most main legislative proposals, but it is important to note that the Council may impose a time limit, so that neither the EESC nor the CoR has the power of delay. However, the EESC is consulted facultatively on important proposals even where such consultation is not obligatory. It also has the right of 'own initiative' and may also be consulted at the request of another EU institution such as the European Commission or, more frequently, at the request of a member state that holds the presidency of the Council, to give its opinion in advance of a legislative proposal on various issues (known as an 'exploratory opinion').

In more recent years, the reduction of legislative activity within the EU has impacted on the Committee and it has responded by reforms aimed at anticipating referrals more effectively, improving the follow-up to its opinions, nurturing local ties with civil society in the member states, the award of an annual Civil Society prize to promote European values and the bolstering of the Committee's expertise by means of impact studies, fact-finding missions and the undertaking of projects. This newly structured role for the Committee was in part the result of an interinstitutional co-operation agreement with the European Parliament, signed in February 2014. In 2015 it published for the first time on its website its recommendations as input (in advance) to the European Commission's annual work programme 2016. It has thus made important changes to increase the influence of its work. The European Commission publishes quarterly reports indicating how it has taken the EESC's opinions into account.

The EESC arguably has a unique role in the institutional framework of the EU by helping to foster the concept of 'participatory democracy' and by facilitating a structured dialogue between civil society and Union institutions. This also extends to involvement in the newly created European Citizens' Initiative (ECI), which is discussed further below.

OMBUDSMAN

A minor body with a useful role to play, in part because he/she is impartial and independent, is the European Ombudsman. The first woman to hold the position, Emily O'Reilly, of Ireland, was elected in 2013 to replace the previous holder who resigned before the end of his term. She was re-elected in December 2014 for a five-year mandate. The Ombudsman investigates complaints about maladministration in the institutions and bodies of the EU.[28] She also undertakes inquiries on her own initiative. Two specific examples are discussed above (see *Institutional Balance of Power* and *Court of Justice of the European Union*). The Ombudsman is an appendix of the Parliament, which elected the first European Ombudsman in 1995. The Ombudsman has become an important element in rendering the EU institutions more open and accessible, and in obliging their administrations to aim to be both fairer and more 'user-friendly'. She also acts as an important link to the members of the European Network of Ombudsmen.

Selected Observations on the Evolution of the Treaties

Even though the UK decided to leave the EU, the fact that the Union has survived intact for over 50 years of development is a testament to its capacity for adaptation and survival.[29] As an international organization it has no parallel or precedent. The source of its success is arguably its ability to adjust to changing political and economic conditions, as well as its flexibility in the ongoing debate about the regulation of powers between different levels of governance, and also between its principal institutions. It has sought to strike the necessary balance between institutional and procedural efficiency and democratic accountability, as well as between the opposing objectives of supranationalism versus intergovernmentalism and between competitiveness and social cohesion.[30]

It has met these challenges through a variety of innovative, if at times elaborate, means, including frequent treaty revisions, political compromises, 'opt-ins' and 'opt-outs', clarifying declarations, as well as interinstitutional agreements such as the 2016 Inter-institutional Agreement on Better Law-Making, adopted by the European Parliament, the Council and the Commission, resulting in a highly complex and at times 'opaque legal apparatus'.[31] Its continued existence supports the view that it retains, by and large, the consent of various national political élites and, generally speaking, voluntary and widespread public agreement to comply with the duties imposed by Union law. At the same time, paradoxically, the EU referendum debate in the UK seemed to show that the public were suspicious, for instance, of institutions whose members it could not 'vote out' and of a Union that had proved itself capable, as in the eurozone crisis, of bypassing its own rules and/or the safeguard of a national veto. There may also have been a perception that it was capable of imposing austerity on member states against their will.[32]

It is significant that during the recent financial and economic crisis, and particularly given its impact on the eurozone, the majority of EU member states have resorted to the signature of new intergovernmental treaties, which are legal instruments concluded *outside* the scope of the EU treaties. These are namely the Treaty on Stability, Co-ordination and Governance in the Economic and Monetary Union (TSCG) and the Treaty on the European Stability Mechanism (TESM). In general, these treaties (which are discussed in more detail below) appear to have compromised the coherence of the EU legal framework. They have also been enacted without significant transparent or public debate within the main EU institutions and this has prompted some commentators, such as the British House of Commons European Scrutiny Committee, to question the legality of the approach taken by the EU and to draw attention to a possible conflict with the EU's own 'rule of law'. Some, but by no means all, of these broader EU constitutional issues were considered in a subsequent judgment of the ECJ in the *Pringle* case of 27 November 2012. This judgment (delivered exceptionally by a full Court, i.e. all the judges sitting together) concluded, *inter alia*, that various EU treaty articles under deliberation did not preclude the right of member states using the euro as their national currency from concluding an agreement such as the TESM.[33] (The significance of this ruling is also further considered below.)

The Lisbon Treaty seeks to involve the citizen more explicitly in the Union project. Article 10 of the TEU (as amended) confirms that the functioning of the Union shall be founded on 'representative democracy' (i.e. parliamentary democracy). Citizens will continue to be directly represented at Union level in the European Parliament. The right of every citizen to participate in the democratic life of the Union is now enshrined in Article 10(3) of the TEU. Furthermore, Article 11(1) of the TEU (as amended) requires that the 'institutions shall, by appropriate means, give citizens and representative associations the opportunity to make known and publicly exchange their views in all areas of Union actions'. In addition, under Article 11(2) of the TEU, the 'institutions shall maintain an open, transparent and regular dialogue with representative associations and civil society'. In this context, the EESC may be able to build on its existing role as a forum for facilitating European civil dialogue. To this end, a revised and reinforced Protocol on Co-operation between the European Commission and the EESC was signed in February 2012. A further interinstitutional co-operation agreement was signed in February 2014 with the European Parliament (referred to earlier).

One of the innovations of the Lisbon Treaty is the ECI, which is designed to promote direct (participatory) democracy in the EU by giving European citizens the right to invite the Commission to propose new legislation, within its areas of competence, provided that at least 1m. citizens, from a 'significant number' of EU member states, put forward such a proposal (Article 11(4) of the TEU).[34] This is the first time in the history of democracy that citizens of several countries have been given such a *transnational* right of democratic participation and is intended, *inter alia*, to help the public to identify more strongly with the EU.[35]

An expert group, composed of member state authorities, was set up by the Commission in order to exchange views and facilitate co-ordination among member states in relation to the implementation of the Regulation on the citizens' initiative. However, the conditions for submitting an ECI are onerous, requiring considerable time, effort and resources, and are therefore likely to be surmounted only by organized civil society; and even then, such initiatives will be heavily dependent upon the reaction and support of other Union institutions to turn such initiatives into law, so that their political influence may prove to be marginal, despite the initial novelty.[36] However, a General Court ruling on 10 May 2017 in Case T-754/14, *Michael Effer and Others v. Commission*, annulling a Commission decision refusing the registration of the proposed ECI 'Stop TTIP' may prove significant in the longer term.

The first ECI was accepted for attention by the European Commission in March 2014 on the 'Right 2 Water', which collected 1.68m. signatures and passed the minimum threshold of votes in 13 member states (far above the legally required minimum). The Commission's subsequent Communication on the subject was criticized by the European Parliament for simply reiterating existing commitments and its general lack of ambition. Other initiatives have generated legal proceedings before the General Court against Commission decisions refusing the registration of proposed initiatives and/or contesting the resulting Commission Communication. Still others have been the subject of complaints to the European Ombudsman. In general, the ECI in its current format is largely ineffective but it is too early to assess its longer-term impact on the EU legislative process. The ECI (which is addressed to the Commission) is to be distinguished from the other existing possibility of 'petition' by a citizen (which is addressed to the European Parliament).

ORIGINAL SCOPE OF THE TREATIES

The original aim of the Community project, as proclaimed in the Schuman Declaration of May 1950, was essentially to bind the nations of Europe together both politically and economically, so as to make the possibility of another war in Europe inconceivable. It is noteworthy, therefore, that the EU was awarded the Nobel Peace Prize in 2012. The aim and scope of the ECSC was the far more limited objective of establishing a common market for the products of coal and steel. The EEC, on the other hand, was tasked with the establishment of a much more general common market, to cover all sectors not covered by the ECSC and Euratom Treaties.

A wide range of policy sectors were covered including agriculture, transport, competition, tax, external trade policy, and social policy (including the principle of equal pay for equal work). These policy areas have been greatly added to, in the course of time, by subsequent treaties. For instance, under the Treaty of Amsterdam, the list of Community competences was further extended to include the creation of a Title on 'Employment'. The Protocol on Social Policy or 'Social Chapter' attached to the Maastricht Treaty was incorporated into the main body of the Treaty and social policy thereby became binding on all member states (including the UK, which had previously resisted it).

The Lisbon Treaty helpfully clarifies and lists the categories of Union competence (or powers),[37] i.e. whether 'exclusive', 'shared', or 'supporting', and establishes a more precise legal competence or basis for some areas in which the Union already undertakes action, such as the fields of energy,[38] public health, space, sport and tourism. It was always clear that the treaty provisions would be supplemented by subsequent legislative activity of the Community institutions. The articulation of the internal market programme in 1985, to have been created by the (notional and highly flexible) deadline of 31 December 1992, is one such example (and is discussed further below).

GENERAL LAW MATTERS

The current names for the different forms of laws, i.e. primary legislation adopted by the EU, are regulations, directives, decisions, recommendations and opinions, although the last two are not binding in nature. However, the Lisbon Treaty has introduced a somewhat complicated distinction between legislative acts, non-legislative acts, delegated acts and implementing acts (Articles 288–292, and Article 296 of the TFEU), which are discussed further below. For example, laws adopted in the form of a regulation or directive may constitute either a legislative act or, in some cases, a non-legislative act. The principal distinction is that a legislative act must have been adopted by a legislative procedure, either ordinary or special. However, in the EU context, both legislative and non-legislative acts are intended to have binding legal force.

The EU legal order differs from traditional public international law in that it can create rights for citizens that are enforceable before national courts. This is what is meant by direct effect.[39] The supremacy (or primacy) of European law, established by the case law of the ECJ,[40] remains a cornerstone principle in the Lisbon Treaty, where it is made the subject of a (new) Declaration (No. 17) as well as an Annex to the Treaty (which contains the opinion of the Council Legal Service on the continued existence of the principle of primacy, even though it is not stated explicitly in the treaties).

The principle of supremacy means that if a provision of Union law (previously Community law) is directly effective,[41] domestic courts not only must apply it but, following the primacy principle, must do so in priority over any conflicting provision of national law (including constitutional provisions). The principle is tempered by the fact that EU legislation itself must comply or be consistent with international law, general principles of Union law and fundamental rights, and also principles of good governance as defined by the treaties.[42] This principle has been widely accepted by the courts in the member states, despite some early resistance from national constitutional courts (such as in France and Germany), but can still be controversial, especially within the newer member states.[43] However, a future source of uncertainty is the exact relationship between and/or the priority to be given to the general principles of Union law (including fundamental rights), as developed in the case law of the ECJ, and those contained in the subsequently adopted Charter of Fundamental Rights.[44] (The latter instrument is made legally binding as a result of changes made by the Lisbon Treaty, and is discussed further below.)

The application of Union law within the UK after it leaves the EU, particularly in relation to EU citizens, as well as the jurisdiction of the ECJ to hear and settle disputes after that date, is a key issue to be resolved by the Brexit negotiations. The UK Government, meanwhile, also introduced new draft legislation in Parliament on 13 July 2017, namely the EU (Withdrawal) Bill (sometimes still referred to as the Great Repeal Bill), to create legal certainty and ensure an orderly exit. It envisages that the jurisdiction of the CJEU will end when Britain leaves the EU. However, the principle of supremacy of EU Law (referred to directly above) will continue, and pre-Brexit CJEU case law will nevertheless be applied and enforced and be binding in the UK, including on the UK Supreme Court, until the underlying law is itself repealed or amended. However, the Charter of Fundamental Rights is not envisaged in the Bill as remaining part of UK domestic law on or after the UK leaves the EU. This is not intended, however, to affect the retention in UK law of any corresponding fundamental rights or principles which exist irrespective of the Charter.

The innovations introduced by the ECJ, include in the case of *Francovich*,[45] the establishment of a new remedy, namely a claim in damages for breach of Community (now Union) law. The Court ruled that a member state is, in certain circumstances, obliged to make good damage to individuals arising from non-implementation of a directive. The remedy, described as a 'principle of Community law', was therefore to be available even for the failure to comply with Community measures which are not themselves directly effective.[46] The arguably weak legal basis for the obligation to compensate such damage[47] was, at the time, the subject of detailed analysis and criticism,[48] not least for having left many unanswered questions about the scope of the right to damages. Some of these queries were subsequently resolved by the Court, which also extended the remedy to include other types of breaches, but it has nevertheless had limited impact in practice, although it may have some deterrent effect. The scope of application of *Francovich* damages in the UK after its withdrawal from the EU is intended to be removed by the EU (Withdrawal) Bill, as introduced in the House of Commons in July 2017 (Bill 5).[49]

RENUMBERING OF TREATY PROVISIONS

The Treaty of Amsterdam began a trend of significant (and sometimes confusing) renumbering of the EC treaty provisions and also introduced the switch from the use of letters to numbers.[50] In particular, the Treaty of Amsterdam introduced a new numbering system for the articles of the TEU (Titles I, V, VI, VII and VIII) and the EC Treaty (Title II). As a consequence, there are two numbering systems, one for the TEU and a separate one for the EC Treaty (now the TFEU). Transparency and ease of use are impeded further by the fact that the Lisbon Treaty extensively changed as well as reordered (once again) the numbering of these treaty articles. The result is that it is difficult in some cases to trace the (old) original source of the article.

This necessitated a table of equivalences to be attached to the Lisbon Treaty, which is an integral part of that Treaty.[51]

AREA OF FREEDOM, SECURITY AND JUSTICE

By virtue of amendments made by the Lisbon Treaty, the 'Union shall constitute an area of freedom, security and justice with respect for fundamental rights and the different legal systems and traditions of the member states' (Article 67(1) of the TFEU). In order to achieve this area of freedom, security and justice (AFSJ), the TFEU sets out policies on border checks, asylum and immigration (Articles 77–80 of the TFEU); judicial co-operation in civil matters (Article 81 of the TFEU); judicial co-operation in criminal matters (Articles 82–86 of the TFEU); and police co-operation (Articles 87–89 of the TFEU).

Although the concept of AFSJ was originally launched only in 1997 by the Treaty of Amsterdam, it has already accumulated a significant volume of 'hard' and 'soft' law,[52] much of which is new and acquired as a result of new competences and institutional possibilities that came into existence as a result of the Treaty of Amsterdam.

It has been argued that the AFSJ lacks 'internal' coherence beyond its bare label, as it is not immediately apparent what the various issues collected under this label have in common; the assembled subject matter does not form a 'natural' unity in terms of a clearly defined overall project. The very presence of a plurality of values in the headline theme itself invites major problems of balance and militates against internal consistency.

There is arguably no *a priori* reason that compels the grouping of freedom, security and justice into a single project. One topic, in particular, stands out as possibly lacking policy or other coherence in relation to the AFSJ, namely the topic of judicial co-operation in civil matters, as specified in Article 81 of the TFEU. Apart from the principle of 'mutual recognition' between national authorities of legal decisions and judgments, judicial co-operation in civil matters is treated as a separate matter governed by quite distinct legal rules and a different academic community, whose domain of expertise is the conflict of (private) laws and of jurisdictions. The constitutional questions and the broader macro-political environment for the relevant issues are also, for the most part, arguably of a different order.

From 1999 the UK and Ireland had an opt-out from measures essentially relating to cross-border civil litigation and to family law.[53] In reality, the UK chose to opt in to most civil litigation measures, such as small claims and cross-border legal aid, although not to divorce and family law matters.[54] Family law matters still fall within the remit of the Lisbon Treaty, including, for example, cross-border divorce and parental responsibility, but remain subject to unanimity. In December 2015, as a result of the outcome of a public referendum, Denmark chose to retain the exemptions it negotiated in 1993, to remain outside large parts of the EU's criminal justice and home affairs system.

There are many areas of freedom, security and justice in which legislation is at the centre of the policy agenda. However, this is less evident in relation to police and criminal justice co-operation where there is instead a significant thrust towards executive action, whether in co-operation between existing national executive and operational agencies,[55] or in the development of new Europe-wide agencies such as Europol and Eurojust (discussed further below). Consequently, the Brexit negotiations will necessarily focus on complex matters concerning ongoing police, judicial and administrative co-operation in criminal, civil and commercial matters. The UK Government also intends to explore options, for instance, for continued co-operation with Europol, after the UK has left the EU.

PROPORTIONALITY AND SUBSIDIARITY

The ECJ has consistently held that the principle of proportionality is regarded as one of the general principles of Union (previously Community) law.[56] As British Judge Lord Diplock[57] put it, 'you must not use a steam hammer to crack a nut, if a nutcracker would do'.

Proportionality is now described in Article 5(4) of the TEU (as amended by the Lisbon Treaty), as follows: 'Under the principle of proportionality, the content and form of Union action shall not exceed what is necessary to achieve the objectives of the Treaties'. This is further elaborated in the Protocol (No. 2) on the application of the principles of subsidiarity and proportionality attached by the Lisbon Treaty (which replaced the Protocol on this subject originally introduced by the Treaty of Amsterdam).

The term subsidiarity is described in Article 5(3) of the TEU (as amended by the Lisbon Treaty). It refers to the principle that action should only be taken by the Union if, and insofar as, the objectives of the proposed action cannot be sufficiently achieved by the member states (either at central, regional or local level) and can therefore be better achieved, by reason of its scale or effects, at Union level. National parliaments are now required to ensure compliance with that principle, in accordance with the procedures laid down in Protocol No. 2. The Vienna European Council of December 1998 confirmed, *inter alia*, two underlying principles concerning subsidiarity: first, that decisions should be taken as closely as possible to the citizen; and second, that both subsidiarity and proportionality are legally binding on the Union institutions. The term 'subsidiarity' is usually used to convey the notion of a division of powers between various levels of public actors. However, it may also be used to convey the concept of 'horizontal' subsidiarity. This term is not explicitly used in the treaties, but gives recognition to the public role of *private* actors, e.g. citizens and civil society organizations, and their participation in the EU legislative process, as well as the role of the social partners in the context of European social dialogue (discussed further below).

Issues concerning subsidiarity and proportionality are inevitably closely related to the determination of legal competences,[58] over which the ECJ will have the final say. As a result of the Lisbon Treaty (Protocol No. 2, Article 8), it became possible for a member state to bring or notify an action before the ECJ, on behalf of a national parliament (or one of its chambers) for annulment of a legislative act on grounds of infringement of the principle of subsidiarity. This is in addition to a right to challenge proposed (i.e. draft) legislation (e.g. before the Commission) within an eight-week time limit for infringement of the principle of subsidiarity (already discussed above, under *National Parliaments*). The CoR also became able to invoke an infringement of this principle before the ECJ, provided that the acts in question are those on which it is required to be consulted.

'COMMUNITY METHOD'

The term 'Community method' emerged in the context of the (now defunct) three pillar structure of the EC. It referred to a number of principles including a well-defined decision-making process, an emphasis on binding legal rules, majority voting, the Commission's exclusive right to initiate legislation, and comprehensive judicial control by the ECJ.[59] This methodology still applies and can therefore be referred to as the 'Union method', or sometimes the 'EU method'. These principles all apply under the first pillar (now contained in the TFEU), and emphasize the role of the Union institutions in forming Union-wide laws that provide the basis for subsequent action by the member states. This contrasts with the approach taken in relation to the former second (CFSP) pillar, which constitutes a system in which the member states continue to instigate intergovernmental (rather than supranational) activity. The German Chancellor, Angela Merkel, in a speech to the College of Bruges in 2010,[60] implicitly cast doubt on the classical view and importance of the 'Community method' in the context of the European rule of law by seeming to suggest, in effect, that the intergovernmental method and the Community method are viable alternatives, within the EU context, if it comes to a political choice between a co-ordinated European position and nothing at all. This attitude would no doubt allow the member states and certain EU institutions, notably the European Council and the Council, to have maximum room for manoeuvre in situations where the treaties present a legal obstacle to the desired end result. It is, in the writer's view, however, not a desirable approach within the context of an EU properly governed by its founding treaties. However, it must be acknowledged that the enlargement of the EU to 28 member states certainly compounded the difficulty of reaching common positions, particularly on serious political and economic issues.

EUROPEAN SOCIAL DIALOGUE

Social dialogue may be considered as an embryonic form of participatory democracy. It was first introduced at European level by the Maastricht Treaty. In the specific field of social policy, Articles 152, 154 and 155 of the TFEU refer to and elaborate on the concept of 'social dialogue' at Union level. These provisions refer to the bipartite and tripartite processes whereby the 'social partners', namely the two sides of industry comprising representatives of management and of labour, may consult with each other and/or with the European Commission and which may lead to the adoption of legally or contractually binding agreements at European level. By virtue of Article 155 of the TFEU, under certain circumstances agreements signed at European level by entrepreneur and labour unions can be transferred into binding directives or regulations issued by the Council. This option of trying to achieve a legally binding instrument, though originally frequently used and actively requested by the European social partners[61] has, in more recent times, proved problematic for European social partners.

SECONDARY LEGISLATION

There is, however, a vast amount of EU law (estimated at least at 60%) that is passed with only limited intervention from the Council and the Parliament, which nevertheless plays a crucial role in almost all European policies and is therefore worthy of mention. The 'pre-Lisbon Treaty' term 'comitology' refers to a complex procedure and committee structure involved in the passing, by the Commission, of secondary (i.e. delegated) legislation. Indeed, the Commission adopts more legislation on its own each year than the Council and the European Parliament combined. Examples include the implementation of the CAP and Fisheries Policy, market authorizations for genetically modified organisms, detailed implementing rules in financial services, and the blocking of the export of British beef to the rest of the EU at the beginning of the 2007 outbreak of foot-and-mouth disease. Much of this law involved the use of (some 280) high-level committees, formed with representatives from each of the member states and a representative from the Commission.

The Lisbon Treaty radically altered the comitology procedures, which are now regulated by Articles 290 and 291 of the TFEU (replacing the former Article 202 of the EC Treaty). Two separate regimes (delegated and implementing acts) are created. These secondary laws often fill in important gaps deliberately left open by the primary or basic legislative act (usually a regulation or directive) under which they were adopted. Although the subject matter may be highly technical, these secondary laws are commonly applied in important areas, such as consumer safety, health and security.

Delegated acts, broadly speaking, address issues that the European Parliament and the Council did not deal with when adopting the original, underlying basic legal act but which were delegated to the Commission to be dealt with subsequently. Implementing acts are governed by Article 291 of the TFEU and by Regulation 182/2011[62] (sometimes known as the Comitology Regulation), which was adopted jointly by the European Parliament and the Council.

Implementing acts are intended to facilitate the implementation of the basic legal act *without* making any significant changes, e.g. to supplement or amend it. The traditional, 'old' comitology system, involving committees of member states' representatives, continues to exist for implementing acts. In relation to delegated acts, the previous comitology committees have been abolished (but may be substituted with other expert groups and EU agencies). One of the main differences between implementing acts and delegated acts is that only the Commission can adopt the latter, whereas implementing acts can be adopted by either the Commission or the Council (in specific circumstances). Delegated acts can also only relate to so-called non-essential elements of a legislative act, whereas there is no such restriction for implementing acts.

In general, post-Lisbon Treaty, the various procedures are intended to be simplified, there is greater involvement by the Council and the Parliament, and increased transparency and accessibility to information are envisaged, for example through the European Commission's Comitology Register. In accordance with the new Inter-institutional Agreement on Better Law-Making adopted in March 2016, some important novelties were introduced in relation to delegated and implementing acts.

For example, in order to safeguard the Council's interests, the Agreement commits the Commission to conducting a consultation of experts from member states, in addition to public consultations, prior to the adoption of delegated acts. Furthermore, the Parliament and the Council henceforth have equal access to information regarding such expert consultations as well as, and importantly, systematic access to the meetings of such expert groups. There are also to be further negotiations between the institutions to establish non-binding delineation criteria on when to use delegated and implementing acts respectively, and, finally, the establishment of a joint public register of delegated acts by the end of 2017 (similar to the existing Comitology Register for implementing acts, referred to above). The Annex to the agreement also contains some principles for the Commission's preparation of delegated acts.

In addition, under the Lisbon Treaty, the Parliament and the Council can include a veto provision in their (primary) legislation that allows them to block subsequent secondary legislation drafted by the Commission. This applies to delegated acts and the so-called regulatory procedure with scrutiny. The exercise of such a veto requires either a qualified majority vote in the Council or an absolute majority vote in the Parliament. These veto powers are little used formally, but may, nevertheless, have significant effect during informal negotiations between the EU institutions, although these take place behind 'closed doors' and may be 'off the record'.[63]

The Commission has also undertaken systematically to conduct an impact assessment on delegated and implementing acts with significant potential impact. The Agreement further called upon the Commission to make proposals by the end of 2016 for the prompt and further realignment of (pre-Lisbon) existing legislation, to adapt it to the new legal framework created by the Lisbon Treaty, in particular acts that provide for the use of the so-called regulatory procedure with scrutiny.

It remains to be seen whether these secondary laws continue to escape genuine, transparent and detailed scrutiny because of either the inherent complexity of the procedural rules that continue to apply to their creation[64] or the new mechanisms for monitoring their use and content, as well as the interinstitutional power struggle between the Commission, the Parliament and the Council that underlies the initial choice between delegated or implementing acts in respect of any specific legislation. Prior to the new Inter-institutional Agreement, it was suggested, for instance, that member states (acting through the Council) are arguably likely to favour the use of implementing rather than delegated acts because the former remain subject to the control of committees in which member state representatives take part and vote.[65]

OPEN METHOD OF CO-ORDINATION

It is significant that not all EU developments are legislative in nature. The open method of co-ordination (OMC) was first referred to in the Presidency Conclusions of the Lisbon European Council in March 2000.

The OMC is neither the traditional Community or Union method (discussed above) nor pure voluntarism (i.e. not mandated by law). Instead, the approach involves the member states in co-ordinating their activity through open dialogue, facilitated by the Commission. It was arguably devised as a 'third way' to advance the European cause and the Lisbon Strategy process (discussed further below), without giving the Commission the power to impose a reform programme on the member states.

The OMC is a way of encouraging co-operation, the exchange of best practice, and agreement on common targets and guidelines for the member states. It relies on regular monitoring of progress to meet those targets, allowing member states to compare their efforts and learn from each other's experience. Such parallel developments of national policy may conceivably eventually lead to new (national) law. However, in general, the OMC process results in member states being asked to submit National Action Plans on particular policy areas, which are evaluated by the Commission and from which a general set of recommendations emerge.

However, there appears to be little Commission documentation on the current extent or usage of OMC and the Commission's annual and other reports concerning this process regrettably appear to receive little journalistic or media analysis. Anecdotal evidence suggests that the OMC process does have a beneficial effect, *inter alia*, by making national civil servants more accountable to external review, concerning their efforts to implement EU policies. Nevertheless, after its initial popularity in the late 1990s, the OMC has in more recent years been criticized, particularly by the European Parliament, for a lack of democratic legitimacy. Although it is sometimes viewed as a threat to the use of the Community method (discussed above), its use has not been abandoned.

THE EUROPEAN SEMESTER

As a response to weakness in its economic governance system, revealed by the economic and financial crisis, the EU has taken a wide range of measures to strengthen economic governance and to achieve sustained convergence and economic growth. The European Semester, the EU's economic policy co-ordination calendar, introduced in 2010, ensures that member states discuss their budgetary and economic plans with their EU partners, at specific times throughout the year. This is an evolving and increasingly important process, which allows member states to comment on each other's plans and enables the Commission to give policy guidance before member states adopt final decisions. The Commission also monitors whether member states are working towards the jobs, education, innovation, climate, and poverty reduction targets of the EU's long-term growth strategy, Europe 2020. A distinction is made between eurozone and non-eurozone member states, with eurozone member states being subject to warnings and, ultimately, significant financial penalties for non-compliance.

Among other things, under the new rules, the draft budgets of eurozone member states must be sent to the Commission by mid-October each year, where they can be assessed by other member states and the Commission, *before* they are set before national parliaments. Some of the other non-eurozone states (other than the UK, Denmark and Sweden), are in the Exchange Rate Mechanism (ERM) with the euro and have opted into the draft budget process. The Commission is aware that this process represents a high level of intrusion in national affairs and therefore encourages member states' governments and social partners to engage in dialogue throughout the semester process and to set time aside for national parliamentary discussions with the Commission. Part of the added value of the exercise is the direct EU guidance it introduces into the (draft) national budgetary procedures. It represents a significant voluntary acceptance of 'pooling' of national sovereignty, arguably made necessary by membership of a single currency.

In 2014 the European Commission posted a specialist European Semester Officer (ESO) in each representation. In 2015 the number of officers in each representation was increased to two. The ESOs are economic policy experts who can help to explain the sometimes complex details of EU economic governance to national stakeholders. Their mission is also to obtain a balanced picture of the challenges that the member state is facing, so that the annual country specific recommendations will best reflect the realities on the ground. They work together with all relevant groups across society, including ministries, national, regional and local parliaments, social partners and other interest groups. Recognizing that persistent economic and social imbalances in one or several member states may put at risk the performance of the euro area as a whole, the European Commission's Directorate-General for Employment and Social Affairs launched, in March 2016, a consultation on a proposed European Pillar of Social Rights (the legal basis of which had yet to be decided), to build on and supplement existing social rights. The consultation concluded at the end of December, having involved, *inter alia*, conducting discussions through its representation offices in each member state, aided by the ESOs, with the social partners and other interested groups. The Commission subsequently presented its proposal for a Pillar of Social Rights on 26 April 2017.

The European Semester is part of a complex raft of procedures relating to economic policy co-ordination. The legal framework for these economic and fiscal issues is covered partly by Article 136 of the TFEU (relating to Economic and Monetary Union within the eurozone), which is itself of wide application. It also extends to a variety of EU legislation. This notably includes the Stability and Growth Pact (see below), the 'Six-Pack' (of five Regulations and one Directive on economic governance), the 'Two-Pack' (common budgetary rules for the euro area member states introduced in May 2013, which complement and reinforce the Six-Pack, but also integrate into EU law some of the content of the inter-governmental treaty known as the Fiscal Compact Treaty, discussed below), as well as certain Banking Union legislation. The Commission undertook an economic governance review of the operation of the seven regulations at the end of 2014 and invited comments from a wide range of interests. Further evolutions to the governance process have since been proposed, including establishing a timetable to 2025, to complete a move to full economic and monetary union.[66]

In October 2015 the Commission published a Communication *On Steps towards Completing Economic and Monetary Union*. The first stage ('deepening by doing'), scheduled to take place between 1 July 2015 and 30 June 2017, built on existing instruments. The measures included a revised approach to the European Semester; an improved toolbox of economic governance, including the introduction of independent national Competitiveness Boards and independent national Fiscal Councils; a more unified representation of the euro area in international organizations, notably the International Monetary Fund (IMF); and steps towards a Financial Union. Separately, a European Fiscal Board was set up as an independent advisory body to the Commission, to strengthen the European governance framework. The Board co-operates with the National Fiscal Councils and advises the Commission on the prospective fiscal stance appropriate for the euro area as a whole, as well as the appropriate national fiscal stances within the rules of the Stability and Growth Pact.

In June 2016 the Economic and Financial Affairs Council made, *inter alia*, changes to the National Competitiveness Boards, which included renaming them as National Productivity Boards, and agreed to improve co-ordination among eurozone member states to strengthen the euro area's communication on the global stage (particularly in the IMF) and to make further progress in developing the Banking Union and Capital Markets Union. It also agreed the more focused and targeted Country Specific Recommendations proposed by the Commission on 18 May. In order to simplify the European Semester process, the number of recommendations to all member states was reduced to 89, from 150. This package was considered at the European Council in July.

On the basis of more upward convergence in the euro area stage 2 ('completing EMU') from 1 July 2017, more fundamental reforms (possibly requiring treaty change) were recommended to be undertaken, moving to a medium-to-long-term vision for new growth perspectives. To prepare the transition from stage 1 to stage 2, on 1 March 2017 the Commission published a White Paper on *The Future of Europe*, which set out five scenarios on how the Union could evolve in the short term to 2019, and the medium term to 2025. The White Paper was followed by five Reflection Papers on: *The Social Dimension of Europe*; *Harnessing Globalisation*; *Deepening of the Economic and Monetary Union*; *The Future of European Defence*; and *The Future of EU Finances*.

The White Paper, which coincided with the 60th anniversary of the Treaties of Rome, is intended to start a large-scale debate across Europe on how deep the integration of Europe needs to be, to ensure that the euro area survives and that it is governed optimally to provide prosperity for all EU member states and their citizens. The proposed changes are suggested, mindful that the EU has tended towards divergence rather than convergence, resulting in European rules being decided by inter-governmental treaties rather than the Community method, and in creditor countries dictating terms to debtor countries, which would not happen in a deeper economic and monetary union. At the same time, creditor countries fear a transfer union and consequent moral hazard. There is growing recognition in some countries that optimal governance of the euro area requires a greater budget to ensure stability, but this in turn requires greater trust between the member states. There is also mention of creating a Minister for Finance to oversee such a budget and to represent the Union in international economic fora. There is concern that the austerity borne by some countries has given rise to disaffection with the EU and to the increase in protectionist and populist solutions. Therefore, deeper economic and fiscal integration will have to be accompanied by real and visible democratic accountability.

The translation of this ambitious programme into action requires, as noted in the Communication, 'a shared sense of purpose among all euro area member states and EU Institutions'. It is also possible that closer economic and monetary union may not be politically acceptable to some member states, for the foreseeable future. How the Brexit vote may have an impact on these developments is an open question. In the initial stages, at least, there is unity between all the remaining 27 member states with regard to Brexit, which may harness unity in other matters.

INTERNAL/SINGLE MARKET

Among the fundamental strengths of the EC/EU has been its ability to create and regulate the internal (single) market, which seeks to guarantee the free movement of goods, people, capital and services (also known as the 'four freedoms') between the EU's 28 member states. It is intended in part to promote economic integration, so that the various separate economies eventually become integrated within a single EU-wide economy, as well as to have an international dimension so that the EU market is represented as a whole in international trade negotiations. The creation of this market is an ongoing process and is intended to include the services industry. This provides a basis for greater economic prosperity based in part on the principle of free competition, which is one of the oldest Community (now Union) economic policies, but also one that is continuing to undergo reform, including in the field of state aid.[67] It is clear from the European Council (Article 50) guidelines for Brexit negotiations that preserving the integrity of the Single Market excludes participation in it based on a sector-by-sector approach. The European Council also welcomed the recognition by the British Government that the four freedoms of the Single Market (such as the free movement of people) are indivisible.

The Lisbon Treaty adds to the Union's objectives, stating that 'The Union shall establish an internal market', and some 40 TFEU Articles concern its functioning. In addition, four of the Protocols[68] introduced by the Lisbon Treaty may arguably have an effect on the internal market. It has been suggested that the Lisbon Treaty seems to give to the internal market more social aims by working towards 'a social market economy aiming at full employment and social progress'.[69] One of the ongoing and unresolved issues inherent in the internal market is whether and to what extent economic freedoms and the rules ensuring free competition take precedence over fundamental social rights relating, for example, to the protection of the employment rights of workers.

The Lisbon Treaty Protocol (No. 27) on the internal market and competition (which has the same legal status as treaty articles and is therefore legally binding) confirms that the internal market (as set out in Article 3 of the TEU as amended) 'includes a system ensuring that competition is not distorted'. This wording was nevertheless arguably more visible previously, when it was contained in a fundamental interpretative Article in the former EC Treaty (Article 3(1)(g) of the EC Treaty), which has been referred to the ECJ in numerous cases.[70] There may, therefore, still be a risk in the future, if it becomes necessary to strike a balance or resolve a conflict between preserving undistorted competition in the internal market and achieving social objectives, that there may be more scope for state-inspired circumvention measures to avoid the effect of the competition rules (including those prohibiting or restricting state aid). Such *lacunae* have historically often been left to the ECJ to arbitrate and resolve in appropriate cases, and can result in dissatisfaction for those on either side of the debate.

FUNDAMENTAL RIGHTS

The term 'fundamental rights' often refers to rights protected under domestic constitutional law, whereas 'human rights' is traditionally (but not exclusively) used in the field of public international law. The former can also encompass the rights of companies and other entities, not just human beings. It is used in the context of the EU to express the concept of human rights, but within the specific EU legal order. The principle that the Union is based, *inter alia*, on the principles of democracy, the rule of law and fundamental rights (DRF) was first introduced by the Maastricht Treaty and is now contained in Title I, Article 2 of the TEU as amended by the Lisbon Treaty. Breach of these values by a member state may cause the latter to lose certain rights, particularly voting rights (Title I, Article 7 of the TEU, as amended). Newer provisions (in Article 269 of the TFEU) state that the ECJ may, at the request solely of the member state concerned, decide on the legality of an act adopted by the European Council or by the Council pursuant to Article 7 of the TEU, determining that there is a clear risk of a serious breach of the values referred to in Article 2 of the TFEU (e.g. respect for human dignity, the rule of law and human rights, etc.). The intention is for the EU to intervene in situations, for example, where a member state no longer guarantees respect for DRF to its citizens and other residents, in order to protect the rights of the latter. No use has yet been made of the preventive or penalty-based mechanisms contained in Article 7 TEU, although political and legislative decisions taken in a number of post-accession Central and Eastern European countries have given rise to concerns about DRF.

However, the Commission adopted a new Framework to strengthen the Rule of Law (COM (2014) 158) in March 2014 in which it stated that it would seek to resolve future threats to the rule of law in member states *before* the conditions for activating the mechanisms foreseen in Article 7 of the TEU were met, i.e. a 'pre-Article 7' mechanism. The Council also launched a so-called Rule of Law Dialogue among EU member states in November 2015. The European Parliament has given consideration to the adoption of an EU pact for DRF in the form of an interinstitutional agreement that would provide, *inter alia*, for an integrated review mechanism applying to all member states as well as the three main EU institutions, to monitor the fundamental rights situation in member states on an ongoing and objective basis, possibly by means of a DRF Scoreboard, a DRF Semester and a DRF Policy Cycle in the EU institutions.

Meanwhile, the existing Commission Framework is intended to precede and complement Article 7 of the TEU mechanism, as well as existing infringement proceedings available to the Commission under Article 258 of the TFEU and may therefore apply when *national* rule of law safeguards do not seem capable of effectively addressing relevant issues. The European Commission activated this Framework for the first time on 13 January 2016, in connection with Poland, for alleged interference by the state in the independence and functioning of the Polish Constitutional Tribunal, and it issued a further Rule of Law recommendation to Poland on 26 July 2017.

The EU has also acquired legislative competence to combat discrimination based on sex, race or ethnic origin, religion or belief, disability, age or sexual orientation (Article 19(1) of the TFEU).[71] Various (non-legally binding) Declarations were also attached to the Treaty of Nice. One of these is the Charter of Fundamental Rights.[72] Following the entry into force of the Lisbon Treaty, this Charter remains a separate instrument, but has been declared to be legally binding[73] and to have the same legal value as the treaties. It therefore formally constitutes part of the body of constitutional rules and principles by reference to which the ECJ can adjudicate. It covers both traditional civil and political rights (such as the right to life, to a fair trial, etc.), as well as social and economic rights (such as the right to fair and just working conditions and the right of collective bargaining and action including strike action).[74] More modern rights (such as the protection of personal data, which in the case of the EU is also supported by an independent supervisory authority in the form of a European Data Protection Supervisor) also apply. A European Agency for Fundamental Rights has been established in Vienna, Austria, since 2007 as a decentralized agency of the EU to provide expert advice to the EU institutions and the member states on a range of fundamental rights issues, and also collects and analyses EU data on fundamental rights with reference to all rights listed in the Charter. It is the successor to the European Monitoring Centre on Racism and Xenophobia, but its remit is much broader.

The Lisbon Treaty makes provision for possible future accession by the EU to the European Convention on Human Rights 1950 (ECHR), although the EU and member states must already comply with the latter. However, the ECJ, in its Opinion 2/13 delivered on 18 December 2014 on the draft agreement on the accession of the EU to the ECHR, concluded that the draft agreement is not compatible with EU law. Notably, the Court pointed out that the EU cannot be considered to be a state and that, therefore, such an accession must take into account the particular characteristics of the EU. It found, *inter alia*, that the draft agreement on accession posed conflicts of jurisdiction and hierarchy between itself and the European Court of Human Rights, which effectively would undermine the autonomy of EU law, adversely affecting the competences of the EU, the powers of the Court, and the division of powers between the EU and its member states. Future accession of the EU to the ECHR therefore remains problematic and elusive and may arguably require treaty amendment to be achieved. It has been argued that the EU's Charter of Fundamental Rights contains in any case many and more 'up-to-date' rights than the ECHR, as well as the possibility of more extensive protection, so that if EU competences continue to grow, the ECHR may be rendered redundant as far as EU member states are concerned, or that the EU members should even withdraw from the ECHR.[75]

Under the Lisbon Treaty, the Charter of Fundamental Rights applies only to the European institutions and to the member states when they act to implement EU law, and does not apply to situations involving purely domestic law. Subject to that limitation, it offers citizens a further guarantee of the protection of fundamental rights within the EU. On 21 December 2011 the ECJ decided at a session of its Grand Chamber, in the Joined Cases C-411/10 and C-493/10, that the Charter, arguably, could be invoked, in principle, against the UK or Poland, which have opted out from the Charter of Fundamental Rights and are covered by a derogation (in Protocol No. 30), but that it cannot *extend* the ability of the ECJ or any national court or tribunal in those two respective countries to find them to be in breach of its provisions, nor does it create *new* rights or principles. In 2009 the European Council allowed for the possibility of extending the same derogation to the Czech Republic in the future.[76] The British House of Lords was not convinced that the Charter created or contained new rights differing from those in other relevant instruments, notably the European Convention on Human Rights 1950.[77] If so, such (old) rights are likely already to be binding upon the UK and therefore must be applied by the British courts, in any event, regardless of the derogation in the Protocol. In late January 2012 the UK Prime Minister, David Cameron, delivered a speech[78] in which he urged the ECHR to concentrate on *serious* abuses of human rights, maintaining that the Court had, in some cases, been too ready to substitute its own judgment for that of 'reasonable national processes'. There was some disquiet and dissatisfaction with certain rulings of the ECHR, notably in a case in which the UK's total denial of voting rights to prisoners was found by the Court to be a violation, despite the absence of any European consensus on the issue.[79] There has also been 'a call for judicial restraint by the Strasbourg Court, and a sharing by it of its responsibilities for judging whether a breach of human rights has occurred', and further that 'subsidiarity, including the margin of appreciation, is a concept the Strasbourg Court should strengthen in its jurisprudence'.[80]

ROLE OF THE EUROPEAN COURT OF JUSTICE IN THE DEVELOPMENT OF EU LAW

An important feature of the Union legal framework is the ability of the ECJ to interpret treaty provisions in the light of their object and purposes. This teleological or 'purposive' method of interpretation has since been applied to the interpretation of other forms of Union law, namely regulations, directives and decisions. The Court follows a line of reasoning based on the purpose, general aims and spirit of the treaty[81] and by doing so arguably resolves 'gaps' in EU law, while sometimes attempting to reconcile apparently conflicting issues.

Furthermore, the ability and capability of the ECJ to contribute to sensitive issues, such as immigration, asylum and cross-border criminal co-operation, as well as issues that concern the balance of powers between the member states and the Union or its institutions, have been a strength, but could become problematic in the future. It has also sometimes appeared to have engaged in judicial creativity, for instance through its jurisprudence on the issue of 'Union citizenship', and its judgments have given rise to controversy in certain areas.

The rights of individuals (i.e. natural persons or corporations) to challenge the legality of EU acts directly before the ECJ are made theoretically easier by the Lisbon Treaty (in Article 263 of the TFEU), so that a person will be able to institute proceedings against a 'regulatory' act that does not entail implementing measures, which is of 'direct concern' to him or her (and not of 'individual' concern to him or her, as previously, which was more difficult to satisfy).

The Lisbon Treaty has also amended and speeded up the powers of the ECJ to impose pecuniary sanctions on member states (i.e. lump sum and/or periodic penalty payments) in the event of non-compliance with a previous judgment of the Court establishing a failure to fulfil its obligations. This also extends to failures by a member state to notify the Commission when national measures could transpose a directive (Article 260 of the TFEU).[82] A position paper of 28 June 2017 on the subject of governance, transmitted by the European Commission Task Force on Brexit to member states and the Council Working Party on Brexit, envisages, on the part of the EU, a continuing role for the ECJ to impose, *inter alia*, a lump sum or penalty payment for relevant failures to comply with any withdrawal agreement between the EU and the UK.

ROLE OF THE EUROPEAN COURT OF JUSTICE IN RELATION TO 'FREEDOM, SECURITY AND JUSTICE'

The concept of an area of 'freedom, security and justice' (discussed above) first entered EU terminology in the Treaty of Amsterdam. The role of the ECJ in this area is significantly expanded by the Lisbon Treaty. It has gained jurisdiction over the subjects within the AFSJ (formerly 'police and judicial co-operation in criminal matters', Title VI of the TEU) as a result of the removal of the pillar structure, the effective merger of the third pillar with the first, and the repeal of other treaty provisions (i.e. Article 35 of the TEU and 68 of the EC Treaty) that imposed restrictions on its jurisdiction. Its jurisdiction in this field is, therefore, no longer subject to a declaration by each member state recognizing its jurisdiction and specifying the national courts that may request a preliminary ruling. Nevertheless, transitional measures apply (by virtue of Article 10, Protocol (No. 36) on transitional provisions), so that the powers of the ECJ are to remain the same with respect to acts in the field of police co-operation and judicial co-operation in criminal matters that have been adopted before the entry into force of the Lisbon Treaty, but this transitional measure ceased to have effect five years after that date (i.e. on 1 December 2014). Similarly, the Commission is now able to bring actions against member states for their failure to fulfil obligations in relation to measures concerned with police and judicial co-operation in criminal matters, which were adopted prior to the Lisbon Treaty entering into force.

Henceforth, any national court or tribunal (i.e. no longer just the higher courts) has been able to request preliminary rulings with regard to visas, asylum, immigration and other policies related to free movement of persons (formerly Title IV of the EC Treaty), which includes judicial co-operation in civil matters and the recognition and enforcement of judgments. The ECJ also has jurisdiction to rule on measures taken on grounds of public policy in connection with cross-border controls.

Decisions of the European Council are now also subject to the jurisdiction of the ECJ. However, its jurisdiction vis-à-vis the UK has differed from that of other member states, depending on the extent to which the UK has used its opt-in/opt-out from relevant legislation.[83]

The ECJ's review jurisdiction is restricted under the AFSJ in relation to Chapter 4 (judicial co-operation in criminal matters) and Chapter 5 (police co-operation), in that it may not review the legality or proportionality of operations carried out by the police or law enforcement services of a member state, nor the member state's responsibility to maintain law and order and the safeguarding of internal national security in any member state (Article 276 of the TFEU, formerly Article 35(5) of the TEU).

CRIMINAL MATTERS AND EUROJUST

Criminal justice policy[84] has hitherto been founded on matters such as police and judicial co-operation, minimum rules concerning the definition of criminal offences, sanctions in the areas of serious crime with a cross-border dimension, and the establishment of the bodies Europol and Eurojust, the purpose of which is to act as a judicial body to control cross-border crime. In general, the Lisbon Treaty reinforces current progress in these fields. Provision is made for the creation of the European Public Prosecutor from Eurojust to investigate and prosecute people involved in crimes affecting the financial interests of the Union (e.g. involving the EU budget), but could be extended to other crimes of a cross-border dimension, provided that all national governments agree (Article 86(4) of the TFEU). The scale of such fraud annually is thought to be significant, and may exceed €500m. In mid-July 2013 the Commission published a proposal for a regulation on a European Public Prosecutor's Office (EPPO), marking the beginning of detailed and sensitive negotiations on the form and role of the EPPO. Under the proposal, fraud or other illegal activity affecting the financial interests of the Union in participating member states could be investigated at the EPPO's request, and it would have the power to prosecute and bring cases to court. This will necessitate a change to the current role of the European Anti-Fraud Office, which was established in 1999 and the hybrid status and powers of which (it is effectively a directorate-general of the Commission) are the subject of ongoing discussions and proposals for reform.

Legislation in the field of judicial co-operation in criminal matters will now be decided by the ordinary legislative procedure in Article 82 of the TFEU (and no longer requires unanimity). However, a member state can also apply an 'emergency brake' procedure if it feels that fundamental aspects of its criminal justice system are unduly affected.

Under the Lisbon Treaty, the UK's opt-out (referred to above, see *Area of Freedom, Security and Justice*) was extended, on a case-by-case basis, to cover police and judicial co-operation, including matters such as the fight against organized crime and terrorism, cross-border prosecution and investigation, and individual rights and procedural guarantees.[85] The right of the UK and Ireland to opt in to criminal law measures (and therefore to be legally bound by them) was an innovation introduced by the Treaty of Lisbon. The UK and Ireland chose to exercise this right, by opting in, for example, to Directive 2010/64/EU of the European Parliament and of the Council of 20 October 2010 on the right to interpretation and translation in criminal proceedings (aimed generally at improving rights to a fair trial) and also to the Directive 2011/93/EU of the European Parliament and of the Council of 13 December 2011 on the European protection order, which is concerned with support measures for the victims, or possible victims, of crime. Following the referendum on the UK's membership of the EU, the British Government nevertheless indicated its intention to opt in to a new regulation on Europol, in order to remain part of this European law enforcement agency after May 2017 and presumably at least until Brexit takes effect.

CLOSER CO-OPERATION OR ENHANCED CO-OPERATION

The Treaty of Amsterdam introduced the process of 'closer co-operation' into the (then) third pillar, whereby a group of member states can develop policies separate from the other countries, while continuing to use the facilities of the Community. The Treaty of Nice extended this process, changed the name of the Title from 'Closer Co-operation' to 'Enhanced Co-operation' and also expanded its provisions, allowing member states to develop closer ties with a small number of other member states. This possibility has been retained by the Lisbon Treaty,[86] so that with regard to matters within the non-exclusive competence of the Union, (at least) nine EU member states may, subject to procedural conditions, proceed among themselves with a Commission proposal (if no agreement is ultimately reached with the rest), and with acts consequently adopted becoming binding only in the participating states. Other member states can, in principle, join in at any stage before or after enhanced co-operation has been launched. This procedure was used for the first time in the area of divorce and legal separation[87] and subsequently for the creation of unitary patent protection in the EU[88] as well as the proposed introduction of a financial transaction tax. However, another variation of this form of co-operation between a smaller group of member states may be seen in the creation of the eurozone and the Schengen area, as well as the previous use of either opt-outs, opt-ins or protocols to the treaties, in order to reflect and accommodate the unwillingness to participate, or distinct views of individual member states on specific measures, whilst allowing the rest to go ahead. However, the limits of such compromise have even extended to the adoption of new treaties *outside* the framework of the EU legal order. This development is discussed immediately below.

LEGAL IMPLICATIONS OF THE EU RESPONSE TO THE EUROZONE DEBT CRISIS: NEW INTERGOVERNMENTAL TREATIES

From the late 2000s European politics became increasingly focused on the economic, financial and sovereign debt crisis, particularly within the eurozone, triggered in part by the deteriorating situation in Greece. During this period there were a number of schemes, rescue packages and/or so-called bailouts, involving substantial payments to Greece, as well as to other EU member states. Under the founding treaties, these issues are largely governed by the rules of the European Monetary Union (EMU), originally set out in the Maastricht Treaty, as well as an intricate system of rules that entered into force on 1 January 1990, known as the Stability and Growth Pact (SGP). The latter was intended to maintain fiscal discipline, and includes both preventative and corrective elements, including the so-called Six-Pack of secondary legislation, which entered into force on 13 December 2011, composed of five Regulations and one Directive proposed by the European Commission and approved by all (the then 27) member states and the European Parliament. This has been supplemented by the Two-Pack, as well as by some Banking Union legislation.[89]

The economic and financial 'rescue' activity of the EU member states has naturally come under legal scrutiny and has provoked the criticism that it may be in breach of the substantive rules of the EMU, implying that the EU legal framework has, for practical purposes, been set aside in an 'EU State of Emergency'.[90] The general justification advanced by various politicians and representatives of the EU institutions is that the alternative is the collapse of the euro; perhaps even the whole 'European project'. In any event, there remain doubts as to whether the eurozone will be able to bear the political, financial and socio-economic costs of 'bridging the gap between a strong centre and a weak periphery which, ultimately, is undermining confidence in the future of the common currency'[91] and whether the measures taken will ultimately, or permanently, calm the financial markets and/or rescue, in particular, the Greek economy.

On 9 December 2011 the heads of state or of government of the eurozone member states agreed to create a new (additional) legal instrument relevant for the governance of the EMU under the EU treaties, namely the Treaty on Stability, Co-ordination and Governance in the Economic and Monetary Union (TSCG), sometimes referred to as the Fiscal Compact Treaty. The TSCG was supported by 25 of the then 27 EU member states, with allowances for two states (the Czech Republic and the UK), which had indicated their unwillingness to sign the Treaty, to accede at a later date.

The TSCG includes, *inter alia*, provisions that require each state to maintain a 'balanced budget', detailed rules concerning the level of annual structural deficit and for dealing with 'excessive deficit', as well as for governance of the eurozone, including the creation of the Euro Summit meetings. It should be observed that the EU treaties already provide for a Protocol (No. 12) on the 'excessive deficit procedure', which is annexed to the EU treaties and is an integral part of them.

The TSCG purports fully to respect, for example, the procedural requirements of the EU treaties and makes frequent cross-references to equivalent or related treaty rules and/or existing secondary legislation under EU law, including Article 126 of the TFEU (which sets out a procedure for dealing with excessive deficits). The detailed rules of the TSCG depend, to a considerable extent, on the implementation of existing EU law. This exacerbates the legal complexities caused by the creation of the TSCG, which is outside the framework of EU law but which relies on, and is interdependent with, various provisions that are within its scope.

The mechanism of Euro Summits is also likely further to blur and complicate the legal distinction between measures taken within the scope of the TSCG that are outside the scope of the EU treaties, and, therefore, binding only in public international (rather than EU) law, and measures that concern either the eurozone and/or the EMU that are governed partially or wholly by EU law. It is possible that over a period of time it might, therefore, no longer be possible to distinguish one from the other.

Contracting state parties are obliged, *inter alia*, to implement the fiscal compact rules in their national law, through provisions of binding force and permanent character, preferably of a constitutional or other guaranteed nature. In Ireland, this necessitated a referendum at the end of May 2012 to decide whether to proceed to ratification of the TSCG. The substantive content and economic approach of the TSCG is also not without its critics, who argue, *inter alia*, that it effectively prohibits member states from implementing an effective countercyclical fiscal policy, particularly after a recession, by prohibiting the public sector from using its spending powers to compensate for low or inadequate private demand. It remains to be seen whether the relevant TSCG provisions involve an actual or implied transfer, or other dilution of sovereign powers of the state, and hence their compliance and compatibility with the various national Constitutions of the signatory states. In the past, various such issues have resulted in litigation before national courts, in particular before the German Constitutional Court.[92]

In early February 2012 the member states of the eurozone also negotiated the final terms of the Treaty establishing the European Stability Mechanism (TESM, or ESM Treaty). The ESM is described by the European Council as an intergovernmental organization under public international law, with which EU institutions appear to collaborate on a voluntary basis. The ESM has an increased capitalization designed, in part, to fund future bailouts to eurozone members, under strict economic policy conditionality. EU member states that do not use the euro as their national currency may participate on an *ad hoc* basis, alongside the ESM, and/or accede formally to the TESM. The eurozone expanded to 19 member states with the admission of Lithuania in January 2015. The member states remaining outside the eurozone are Bulgaria, Croatia, the Czech Republic, Denmark, Hungary, Poland, Romania, Sweden and the UK.

The case law of the ECJ, confirmed by the tenor of the *Pringle* judgment of the ECJ in November 2012 (see *Selected Observations on the Evolution of the Treaties*) provides some support for the view that member states may retain some capacity and flexibility to meet within Union institutions, notably the Council, to discuss and conclude arrangements and mechanisms that may be strictly outside the scope of the EU treaties and to invite Union institutions, such as the Commission, to undertake tasks of an intergovernmental nature.[93] However, this flexibility must conform to the overall tasks, objectives and responsibilities of the EU and of its institutions.

Under its provisions, the TESM requires strict observance of the EU framework, in particular the SGP. It is also a requirement that contracting states ratify the TSCG and implement correctly the latter's fiscal compact and balanced budget provisions.

No doubt those who drew up the TESM have sought to improve economic governance as well as to deal with an emergency situation. Nevertheless, the creation by the TESM of a wholly new institutional structure that operates outside the EU's own institutional framework is questionable. Although, in principle, the member states are free to found new institutions, the manner and effect of their actions in this field though apparently condoned by the ECJ in the *Pringle* case, have considerably complicated and compromised the legal framework of the EU itself.

It is significant that both the TSCG and the TESM are intergovernmental in nature (i.e. they are treaties concluded under international law, rather than EU law). As such, they are outside the scope of the founding EU treaties. Although the political intention is eventually to incorporate the substance of both treaties into the legal framework of the EU, the mechanism for achieving this is unclear. Their provisions are, meanwhile, intended to apply insofar as they are compatible with the EU treaties and with EU law, implying that EU law has precedence over these international treaties. The TSCG requires, *inter alia*, that at least 12 contracting parties that use the euro as their national currency must ratify it before it can enter into force. This occurred on 1 January 2013 following its ratification by Finland. Ratification by Germany, a key signatory, was finally permitted, in principle, by a decision of the German Constitutional Court delivered on 12 September 2012, and the TESM entered into force on 27 September for the relevant euro member states.

The present writer has argued elsewhere that the existing EU treaties already provided an alternative legal framework for the achievement of the same or similar objectives, which could have been amended to achieve the same (new) objectives (notwithstanding inconvenient or even cumbersome political and/or procedural obstacles).[94] It is arguable that the perceived obstacles, including any requirement for unanimity among the member states, have been designed by the framers of the treaties to be a further democratic 'check and balance' to ensure that significant amendments to the founding EU treaties are not created without proper scrutiny. The European Parliament has alluded to the fact that the TSCG may not be compatible with the EU treaties, because it was not concluded in accordance with the 'Community method' of decision making (discussed above). The latter ordinarily includes the involvement of the European Parliament, within a single legal and institutional framework designed to strengthen democratic scrutiny and accountability of the decision-making process. However, no formal objection or court actions have to date been brought by any EU institution on these issues. The legal case brought before the ECJ by an Irish citizen in *Pringle* (referred to above) was unsuccessful. This judgment may be viewed as a largely pragmatic response by the Court not to obstruct actions taken to safeguard the financial stability of the eurozone, rather than promote transparent and democratic behaviour by the EU political institutions, or sustain strict legal coherence within the EU treaties.

FUTURE TREATY REVISIONS

The procedure for revising the treaties was substantially amended by the Lisbon Treaty (Article 48(1) and 48(6) of the TEU, as amended). Article 48(6) of the TEU provides for a Simplified

Revision Procedure, which allows the European Council, acting by unanimity after consulting the European Parliament, the Commission, and in certain cases, the ECB, to adopt a decision amending all or part of the provisions of Part Three of the TFEU (dealing with Union Policies and Internal Actions). Its first use by the European Council occurred on 25 March 2011, when the Council adopted Decision 2011/199 amending Article 136 of the TFEU by adding one paragraph to Article 136: 'The Member States whose currency is the euro may establish a stability mechanism to be activated if indispensable to safeguard the stability of the eurozone as a whole. The granting of any required financial assistance under the mechanism will be made subject to strict conditionality.' However, in order to enable member states of the eurozone to set up this permanent mechanism to safeguard the financial and economic stability of the eurozone as a whole—i.e. the ESM (referred to above), the relevant member states concluded a further (intergovernmental) treaty, the TESM (also discussed above), to clarify all the relevant details.

This wholly new institutional structure (the ESM), although originally based on an amendment to Article 136 of the TFEU, itself operates as a result of an intergovernmental treaty that had been concluded outside the EU's own institutional framework. This seems to be an extraordinary and constitutionally convoluted use of the Simplified Revision Procedure that was certainly not foreseen or envisaged when the Lisbon Treaty was adopted. Nevertheless, in the *Pringle* case, the ECJ came to the questionable conclusion on the issues specifically brought before it that there was nothing untoward in these events and decided, *inter alia*, that the right of a member state to conclude and ratify the TESM was not even subject to the prior entry into force of Decision 2011/199. This suggests, in effect, that even intricate constitutional amendments to the EU treaties may in substance be successfully achieved in future, without necessarily even requiring the support of all the EU member states. It remains to be seen whether such mechanisms could also be used to give effect to the anticipated changes to the EU institutions that will be necessary after Brexit, such as the number and allocation of seats by country in the European Parliament and/or relevant voting majorities in the Council, or allocation of the posts of advocate-general and judge in the CJEU once the UK has left, or whether a formal treaty revision will be necessary, with corresponding unanimous ratification required in the various member states (in accordance with their respective constitutional requirements, including the possible holding of referenda).

There are recent and significant '*passerelles*', i.e. provisions enabling procedural requirements to be reduced (such as a change to the method of voting of the Council in a given case from unanimity to QMV), or other amendments made, without formal treaty revision, including within the AFSJ. However, such revisions would require unanimity among member state governments in the European Council or the Council.[95] The revisions provide a mechanism for avoiding future formal (and potentially cumbersome) procedures for treaty amendments, but, if used, may also make future changes less visible to the European public. In the UK (while it remains a member state of the EU), however, the opposite situation may occur as a result of the passing of the European Union Act 2011 (sometimes known as the 'Referendum Lock' Act), in that a change from unanimity to majority voting in a particular area, despite not requiring domestic approval or ratification under the terms of the Lisbon Treaty, may nevertheless trigger a requirement under the Act for a prior domestic referendum in the UK before the British Government could give its support for such a change.

As a result of the Lisbon Treaty, the European Parliament and the national parliaments have to be informed of any new application for accession to the EU, and there is also a requirement for compliance with explicit eligibility criteria.

WITHDRAWAL OF MEMBERSHIP

For the first time, the TEU incorporated a mechanism for 'voluntary withdrawal from the Union' (Article 50 of the TEU, as amended), but it is arguable that such a move was already permissible under international treaty law. For instance, Greenland withdrew in 1985, after a transitional period, but since it was part of Denmark, a member state, and had a relatively small population, this may not provide a very useful precedent. However, a detailed procedure is now provided in the treaties for this situation and will apply to the withdrawal of the UK's membership.

Article 50(1) of the TEU affirms that any member state may decide to withdraw from the Union in accordance with its own constitutional requirements. On 24 January 2017 the UK Supreme Court (on appeal from the High Court), in the case of *R. (on the application of Miller and Dos Santos) v. Secretary of State for Exiting the European Union (and associated References)*, decided by a majority of eight to three judges that an Act of Parliament was first required to authorize Ministers to serve notice of the decision to withdraw from the EU and that, *inter alia*, the devolved legislatures of Scotland and Wales do not have a veto on that UK decision. The UK Parliament subsequently enacted the European Union (Notification of Withdrawal) Act 2017 and on 29 March 2017 Prime Minister Theresa May formally notified the European Council of the UK's intention to withdraw, in accordance with Article 50 TEU.

Article 50(2) of the TEU requires that the Union must negotiate and conclude an agreement with the withdrawing state, in the light of guidelines provided by the European Council, setting out the arrangements for its withdrawal, and taking account of the framework of its future relationship with the Union. This agreement is to be concluded on behalf of the Union by the Council, acting by a qualified majority, after obtaining the consent of the European Parliament. Some of the procedural formalities for the negotiation procedure are set out in Article 218(3) of the TFEU.

In accordance with Article 50 TEU and Article 218(3) TFEU, once the negotiations with the UK are concluded the draft final withdrawal agreement will be submitted by the Council to the European Parliament.[96] The consent of Parliament is required by a simple majority vote. The draft agreement then returns to the Council for the latter's vote, where a qualified majority in accordance with Article 238(3 (b) TFEU (i.e. 72% of the other 27 member states, representing 65% of the total population of the 27 member states), in effect 20 of the remaining 27 states, is sufficient for it to pass. The agreement, which would normally be in the form of a treaty, will also require signature and ratification by the UK, in accordance with general international law and its own constitutional requirements.

TWO-PHASED APPROACH TO THE BREXIT NEGOTIATIONS

The European Council has decided to proceed on the basis of a two-phased approach to Brexit negotiations. The first phase aims to clarify and give legal certainty to citizens, businesses and all relevant stakeholders on the immediate effects of the UK's withdrawal and generally settle its disentanglement from its rights and obligations as a member state, with a general aim of an orderly withdrawal, preventing a legal vacuum once the UK leaves. In the mean time, while the UK is still a member, all ongoing EU business is intended to proceed as normal, and the principle of sincere co-operation in the treaties will also continue to apply.

When sufficient progress on the first phase is considered to have been made, the European Council will make the decision to proceed with the next phase, which will focus on the future relationship between the Union and the UK. The European Council has welcomed and shares the UK's desire to establish a close partnership between the Union and the UK, after the latter's departure. While making clear that a non-member state cannot be offered the same benefits as Union membership, it considers that strong and constructive ties remain in both sides' interest and that it should encompass more than just trade. It is envisaged by the EU, as part of its negotiating position, that any future relationship agreement between the EU and the UK may not apply to the territory of Gibraltar without the agreement of Spain. For its part, the British Government has indicated that it will not seek to remain in the Single Market or Customs Union, but would like to pursue an ambitious free trade agreement with the EU.

It also appears that the EU intends to arrive at the totality of the Article 50 negotiations as a single package, i.e. on the basis that nothing is agreed until everything is agreed; and that individual items cannot be settled separately. The Union intends to approach the negotiations from a unified position, and on the basis that there will be no separate negotiations between individual member states and the UK on matters pertaining to withdrawal. However, it is nevertheless uncertain whether this single package might also include agreement on the future relationship with the EU. The European Parliament has taken the view that any agreement on such a future relationship with the UK as a third country can only be concluded once the UK has withdrawn from the EU. Article 50(2) TEU, on the other hand, states only that '...the Union shall negotiate and conclude an agreement with that State, setting out the arrangements for its withdrawal, *taking account of the framework for its future relationship* with the Union'. It may be the case that an agreement on future relations might form part of the withdrawal agreement or be contained in a separate treaty, in which case it might require unanimity in the Council and possibly even national ratification in each of the 27 member states.

FIRST PHASE PRIORITIES INCLUDING THE 'DIVORCE BILL'

In the first phase, both sides have identified as a priority the resolution of the rights of EU citizens and their family members to live, work or study in the UK and the corresponding rights and obligations of UK citizens in the Union countries, as well as the requirement for smooth and simple administrative procedures to accomplish this. The first phase also involves resolution of a single financial settlement (colloquially referred to as the 'exit or divorce bill'), including the UK's share of Union obligations resulting from the Multiannual Financial Frameworks (MFFs) for the period 2014–20 and the EU Own Resources Decision.[97] In other words, the EU seeks payment for obligations that might, in the normal course, have been intended to extend beyond the current expected date of UK withdrawal.[98] The EU position implies that even if the UK leaves in March 2019, it will be required to pay its relevant contributions at least until the end of 2020.

The final settlement would also include, *inter alia*, longer-term liabilities such as the pensions of staff working for the various EU institutions, contracts and other business arrangements and/or participation in EU-funded research and other programmes, including the European Development Fund and the Facility for Refugees in Turkey. Other relevant matters relate to the funding of the European Investment Bank (EIB) the European Development Fund (EDF) and the ECB. However, for its part, the UK may also want, in the course of negotiations, to take account of its share of EU financial and other *assets*, and not just its liabilities. The cost of relocating EU agencies located in the UK, for example the European Medicines Agency and the European Banking Authority, which are currently based in London, will also be discussed.

The EU expects the 'divorce bill' to be paid in euros; the significant devaluation of sterling after the UK referendum result may inflate the overall cost for the UK. The EU anticipates that a schedule and practical modalities of payments will also be agreed in advance, with the possibility that such obligations may also be subject to limited future technical adjustments. The overall size of the bill is a matter of intense speculation and serious estimates vary considerably, from €25,000m. to some €65,000m. or more.

TERMS OF REFERENCE FOR THE ARTICLE 50 BREXIT NEGOTIATIONS

At the time of writing, the UK and the European Commission, representing the EU, have agreed terms of reference for the Article 50 TEU negotiations. Three initial negotiating groups have been established, on the subject of citizens' rights, the financial settlement and other separation issues, respectively. In addition, a dialogue on Ireland and Northern Ireland has been launched. Ireland exports some 80% of its products, especially agricultural products, either directly to the UK or in transit to the rest of the EU. The effect of the UK leaving the Single Market, and especially the Customs Union, might, therefore, have a serious impact on the Irish economy, but also those of other countries in a similar situation, such as Denmark.

Both the UK and the EU have indicated a desire to take account of the unique circumstances on the island of Ireland, and accord paramount importance, in particular, to the terms of the Good Friday Agreement of 1998, which ended over 30 years of violence, and removed, for practical purposes, the meandering and at times contorted border between Northern Ireland and Ireland. Thus, flexible and imaginative solutions are required to avoid a 'hard border' between Northern Ireland and the Republic of Ireland, while continuing to respect the integrity of the Union's legal order and the four freedoms that are integral to the functioning of the EU Single Market. However, the Union has already indicated its acceptance of existing bilateral agreements and arrangements such as the Common Travel Area between the UK and Ireland, which are compatible with EU law, and by virtue of which Irish nationals have the right to travel, live and work freely in the UK and vice versa.

The Union will also seek to agree with the UK specific arrangements regarding the Sovereign Base Areas of the UK in Cyprus, and to recognize in that respect bilateral agreements and arrangements between Cyprus and the UK that are compatible with EU law, in particular with respect to safeguarding the rights and interests of EU citizens resident or working in the Sovereign Base Areas.

Following the withdrawal, the UK will no longer be covered by various agreements, such as trade agreements, either concluded by the Union, or by member states acting on its behalf, or by the Union and its member states acting jointly. The Union has indicated its willingness to agree a possible common approach towards such third country partners, international organizations and treaties or conventions. However, it is possible that the UK may retain an interest in remaining free to renegotiate trade deals on terms more favourable to itself with such third parties, in the longer term.

Negotiating rounds began on 19 June 2017 and are intended, in principle, to take place about once every four weeks. English and French are being used as working languages, with interpretation provided by the European Commission. There is expected to be a high level of transparency, unless the parties agree otherwise, and joint public statements after negotiating rounds, whenever possible.

Negotiating rounds consist of negotiating group meetings and plenary sessions. The latter are co-chaired by the Principals and/or Co-ordinators, who have overall responsibility for managing the negotiation process. The Principals may decide to establish additional working groups and sub-groups, or organize 'breakout' sessions. Each round of negotiations will only comprise public officials on both sides. At the beginning of October 2016 the European Commission appointed a former French Minister of Foreign Affairs, Michel Barnier, to act as its European negotiator with the UK on Brexit. The UK negotiator is David Davis, the Secretary of State for Exiting the EU, together with officials in his department, as well as Ambassador Tim Barrow, the UK's top diplomat in Brussels. The UK's general negotiating strategy was set out by Prime Minister Theresa May in a speech made at Lancaster House, London, in January 2017, and in the Brexit White Paper published on 2 February, entitled *The United Kingdom's exit from and new partnership with the European Union* (CM.9417). This was later supplemented by Prime Minister May in a speech in Florence, Italy, on Brexit on 22 September 2017.

The European Council remains permanently seized of the negotiations and will update its negotiating guidelines when necessary. Meanwhile, on 22 May 2017 the Council (of Ministers) of the EU promulgated a set of 'negotiating directives' intended for the first phase of the negotiations, which elaborate in more detail the European Council's initial guidelines and the Union's negotiating position, *inter alia*, on subjects such as citizens' rights, the financial settlement and other matters, including the future governance of the final agreement. The Council intends there to be new sets of negotiating directives issued to deal with the second phase of negotiations on the future relationship with the UK, in due course.

The negotiating directives may be amended and supplemented as necessary throughout the negotiations, in particular to reflect the European Council guidelines, as the latter themselves evolve. These documents are supplemented by working papers and position papers originating from the European Commission Task Force and addressed to the Council's Working Party on Article 50 on the same subjects. It is made clear in the negotiating directives that the Union negotiator will conduct negotiations with the UK in continuous co-ordination and permanent dialogue with the Council and its preparatory bodies, notably COREPER and the Working Party on Article 50.

The role of the European Parliament during the negotiations is not referred to in the negotiating directives, but its involvement and ultimately consent will have considerable influence. The Parliament passed on 5 April 2017 a (non-binding) Resolution on the negotiations. It reiterated, *inter alia*, the importance of the withdrawal agreement and any possible transition agreements entering into force well before the elections to the European Parliament due to take place in May 2019. The Parliament's resolution further stated that any transitional period should not exceed three years. It also anticipated that its consent is required not just for the withdrawal agreement but also any possible transitional agreement(s), as well as any future agreement on relations between the EU and the UK.

The withdrawal agreement might be expected to address complex matters, including the rights of EU citizens living and working in the withdrawing state and elsewhere in the EU, deriving from EU law, that might otherwise be extinguished by the withdrawal; the status of staff of the withdrawing state working for EU institutions; the phasing out of UK participation in various EU financial programmes, and so on. It might also address the future relationship between the UK and the EU, including the application, notably, of trade agreements made between the EU and third countries or international organizations.

Withdrawal Date

Article 50(3) provides that the treaties (including Euratom) shall cease to apply to the withdrawing state from the date of entry into force of the withdrawal agreement or, failing that, two years after the original notification (i.e. midnight on 30 March 2019, Brussels time), unless the European Council, in agreement with the member state concerned, unanimously decides to extend this period. Both sides intend to work hard to achieve a satisfactory agreement that is in their own best interests, while at the same time preparing to handle the situation if negotiations were to fail, given that the UK will become a 'third country' with respect to the EU from the withdrawal date.

At that point all primary law, i.e. the EU treaties (including the protocols and declarations thereto) and relevant international agreements would cease to apply in the withdrawing state, as well as all secondary law (e.g. regulations and directives), but any national law adopted to implement EU legislation remains valid in national law, until amended or repealed by national authorities. Hence the EU (Withdrawal) Bill 2017 before the UK Parliament is intended in effect to maintain the status quo in UK national law for the time being. In particular, pre-Brexit CJEU case law will continue to be binding on UK courts, including the Supreme Court, until the underlying law is itself repealed or amended. However, the Charter of Fundamental Rights, which is part of the EU Treaties, but is subject to a Protocol relating to its application to the UK, is not envisaged in the bill as remaining part of UK domestic law when the UK leaves the EU, although any corresponding fundamental rights or principles that exist in UK law irrespective of the Charter will continue to apply.

Enforcement, Governance and Transitional Matters

The Union has indicated that the withdrawal agreement should include appropriate dispute settlement and enforcement mechanisms regarding its application and interpretation, as well as institutional arrangements (which may involve the setting up of a 'Joint Committee') to allow for the adoption of future measures that may be necessary to deal with unforeseen situations. The Union will press for matters relating to the application and interpretation of the provisions of any agreement, particularly those relating to Union law, as well as those relating to EU citizens' rights, to include a continuing role for the ECJ (including the application of its future case law after the withdrawal date), and this is likely to be resisted by the UK. As the UK Government has reiterated, it is not the norm, under general international treaty law, for states to submit to the court(s) of the other party, for the simple reason that impartiality and independence of the adjudication may be compromised.

Any alternative dispute settlement mechanisms on matters not relating to Union law would, in the view of the EU, need to offer equivalent guarantees of independence and impartiality to the CJEU. The EU also envisages a continuing role for the ECJ to impose, *inter alia*, a lump sum or penalty payment for relevant failures to comply with any withdrawal agreement between the EU and the UK. The EU position is somewhat draconian and it has been pointed out elsewhere[99] that even the tiny states of San Marino or Andorra, i.e. third countries with trade and other economic co-operation agreements with the EU, do not submit to the jurisdiction of the CJEU.

The possibility that transitional arrangements may also be necessary is foreseen by the European Council, which takes the view that any such arrangements must be clearly defined, limited in time, and subject to effective enforcement mechanisms. For its part, the European Parliament intends that this should not exceed three years. Should a time-limited prolongation of Union *acquis* be considered, then the Union would require existing Union regulatory, budgetary, supervisory, judiciary and enforcement instruments and structures to apply. In other words, any transitional arrangement that involved the continued application of Union law would likely involve acceptance of the full application of the legal framework of the EU, including the jurisdiction of the ECJ, as well as continued payment of current financial contributions. In such a scenario, the UK would arguably still be fully bound by most, if not all, of its current rights and obligations as a member state (whether or not it had by then formally left the EU).

It is highly probable that the complexity of EU law—notably the extensive and intricate web of legal rights and duties, mutual dependencies and legitimate expectations that currently exist under EU law, in relation to individuals, companies, public authorities and other entities—and of the treaties themselves, may mean that an orderly withdrawal could be a difficult and possibly lengthy process with some resulting legal uncertainties for all, as well as having serious legal, political and economic consequences in the long term.[100]

Revocation of Withdrawal

Voluntary withdrawal should not be confused with suspension of membership (i.e. for serious breach of the values of the Union, discussed earlier). Article 50 does not provide expressly for the unilateral revocation of a notice of withdrawal or for suspension of the withdrawal process, once begun. One of the draftsmen of Article 50, (Lord) John Kerr, has argued that (as a matter of EU law) the Article 50 notification may be revoked at any moment, although he acknowledges that this would create a great deal of political confusion and, almost certainly, ill will. A state that withdraws from the Union may, by virtue of Article 50(5), ask to rejoin, but this would be subject to the procedure in Article 49 of the TFEU and require, *inter alia*, the unanimous approval of the Council and ultimately the ratification of an agreement by all the contracting states in accordance with their respective constitutional requirements.

Concluding Remarks

Until the dramatic UK referendum vote to leave the EU of 23 June 2016, the Union had generally continued to confound negative expectations. One of the original aims of the EU, which was to maintain peace in Europe, has been successful. There has been no armed conflict within the EU. The Balkans and Northern Ireland conflicts were also brought to an end in part through EU offices. However, the EU has been less successful in encouraging peace in the territories around it. Recent instability and conflict in the Middle East and North Africa, with the concomitant slaughter and mass migration to the EU, are major problems which have tested the ability of the EU to find solutions relating to the security of its external borders. The principle of free movement of EU nationals was effectively rejected by the majority in the 2016 UK referendum vote, and remains an unresolved issue for negotiation. In addition, events at the time of the banking collapse and financial turmoil of 2008 and since have also severely tested the capacity of the EU and, although the eurozone has survived so far, this is not to ignore the challenge of further consolidation.

Although the constitutional complexity of the EU is the basis for its success, its survival, and its capacity for future adaptation to differing political, economic or social priorities, it may paradoxically have distracted the Union into focusing on some lesser issues, rather than concentrating on major events. Now, the British decision to withdraw has dramatically refocused the EU's attention on its central goals, and possibly its own institutional survival. Some, therefore, see a possible silver lining in the Brexit cloud, in the form of possible further consolidation of the eurozone.

In terms of its internal governance, the growth in the powers of the European Parliament in relation to the Council has altered the institutional balance of power in favour of the former. However, the Commission, through its right of initiative in respect of legislative proposals, remains fundamental to the lawmaking process, though these powers have been seen to be capable of subsequent modification, even without treaty change, by the mechanism of a new Inter-institutional Agreement between the principal lawmaking institutions. Furthermore, the use of the *Spitzenkandidaten* process, whereby each of the major European Parliament parties chose a candidate to lead their respective campaigns in 2014, with the party winning the most seats effectively selecting the Commission President, may have altered the practical interinstitutional relationship and political collaboration between Commission and Parliament.[101] These instances demonstrate that the (formal) legal constitutional framework of the EU treaties cannot always fully be relied on to guarantee the course of EU politics. This creates legal and political uncertainty which, when compounded by a lack of transparency in how the EU actually works, and how laws are made, has given citizens disquiet and distrust in EU democracy. Part of the motivation in the UK to leave the EU was to 'take back' sovereignty, disengage from the jurisdiction of the ECJ and become more self-governing.

The improvements to the involvement and powers of the national parliaments in relation to the EU, particularly adherence to the principle of subsidiarity, are to be welcomed but are unlikely to prove significant since breaches of the subsidiarity principle will almost certainly be rare. Better scrutiny of the *substance* of EU legislative proposals by national parliaments, and at an early stage, may facilitate the removal of any perceived 'democratic deficit'. The innovative character of the ECI, although novel, has yet to be shown to have significant potential to engage European citizens fully in the European project as a whole.

The European Commission elected in 2014 made a commitment 'to do different things and to do things differently', recognizing that citizens now expect the EU to resolve significant economic and social challenges, notably high unemployment, slow growth, high levels of public debt, an investment gap and lack of competitiveness in the global marketplace. They are also perceived to want less EU interference in issues when member states are better equipped to respond at national and regional level, as well as more openness, transparency and accountability about what the EU does and how it does it.[102]

Notably, there is a lack of transparency in the EU legal framework that is in part a result of the successive amendments to the founding treaties—as exemplified by the Lisbon Treaty. In addition, a significant volume of EU law is passed not by primary law and openly debated by the main institutions, but by secondary legislation which may not be subject to sufficiently detailed monitoring or scrutiny. The Inter-institutional Agreement on Better Law-Making of 9 March 2016 seeks to remedy some of these deficiencies in relation to the so-called delegated and implementing acts. However, hitherto this constitutional weakness, when combined with the intricate interrelationship of the Union's institutions with each other and with the member states, as well as a sometimes problematic relationship between member states and their own regions, has inevitably led to continued identification of a 'democratic deficit' in the Union project as a whole. This has been further illustrated by the process of concluding the new intergovernmental treaties—the Treaty on Stability, Co-ordination and Governance in the Economic and Monetary Union (TSCG) and the Treaty on the European Stability Mechanism (TESM)—which took place largely behind closed doors and revealed a lack of transparency and political accountability of the actions of the main political institutions, notably in the context of their relationship with the European Parliament.

Thus, the limits otherwise imposed by the Lisbon Treaty in the field of EMU in this scenario have been avoided and evaded. No doubt this has been prompted by the impact of the global financial crisis, as well as significant economic uncertainty within the Union's eurozone. It does, however, demonstrate the determination of the national political élites and those in Brussels, to enable the Union to evolve further as required, without necessarily treating the founding treaties as a brake or restriction on their collective political priorities of the moment. Even if litigation were to take place on these issues in the future, the level of complexity and interaction between EU law and international law in this area is now arguably so great that the outcomes would be uncertain. Nevertheless, the EU is a union based on the rule of law, not of power (claimed by whomsoever), and it stands to reason that this principle, as a constant, must also apply in times of difficulty or distress.[103]

The continuing Greek crisis may arguably forestall, or delay, entry into the eurozone by other member states, particularly those from Central and Eastern Europe (such as Poland and Hungary). Nevertheless, there continues to be some momentum towards greater economic and monetary policy co-ordination, based in part on the dynamic created by the so-called European Semester. However, procedures for the latter are highly convoluted owing to their sheer number, their co-existence with intergovernmental agreements, which, although concluded outside the EU, nevertheless increasingly take effect within it, as well as the potential for different application as between eurozone and non-eurozone member states. Although these measures ostensibly seek to create a co-ordinated response to the achievement of the Europe 2020 goals, they also have the potential to intrude significantly on matters traditionally reserved for national sovereignty. However, for those member states within the eurozone, it may be argued that by relinquishing their national currencies and adopting a common currency they are now necessarily pooling their sovereignty to an increased extent to make it work. However, this concept of (increasing) shared sovereignty may have been one of the major reasons for the UK referendum vote in favour of leaving the EU and may stall momentum in other EU member states towards further political, economic and monetary union.

It also seems that as EU co-operation moved towards greater supranational decision making in fields beyond basic economic or trade co-operation, the more difficult became, in particular, its relationship with the UK. Previously, British preferences were largely accommodated through various forms of opt-outs, notably from the Schengen Agreement, the eurozone[104] and the AFSJ, and, more recently, the offer by the European Council in February 2016 of a 'new settlement for the UK' that, *inter alia*, would have effectively exempted it from any commitment to further political integration with the EU. It also included provisions on 'economic governance' designed to facilitate the further deepening of economic and monetary union by the eurozone members, while simultaneously seeking to guarantee the position of the British financial sector, without necessitating *immediate* treaty change. However, the latter settlement was decisively rejected by the British people in their in/out referendum of June 2016 and has since been withdrawn by the European Council.

The UK vote to leave the EU and the subsequent triggering of the Article 50 procedure has generated the clear need for negotiation of an orderly rearrangement of its future relationship with the EU, which is necessarily extremely complex and has created significant uncertainty in the legal, constitutional, political and economic spheres.[105] It is, however, certainly within the competence and experience of mature national and EU politicians and their legal and other advisers, to arrange an orderly withdrawal. This could include safeguards for existing rights and obligations of people living in other countries and businesses that have already invested on the basis of existing rules, thereby enabling systematic disengagement which would also serve to calm the economic repercussions on all sides. However, the insistence by the EU on a negotiating sequence that requires the terms of the UK's departure and 'divorce bill' to be sufficiently agreed first, before discussion of its future relationship with the EU can even be attempted, combined with its extremely complicated methodology for the conduct of the negotiations, as between the key EU political institutions, i.e.

the European Council, the Commission, the Council and the Parliament, may result in further inflexibility and the risk of 'too many cooks spoiling the broth'.

On the UK side of the equation, the outcome of the referendum has caused, *inter alia*, internal constitutional uncertainty and tensions, notably in Gibraltar and also with the UK-devolved nations, particularly in Scotland and Northern Ireland, where majorities of the electorate voted to remain in the EU. Nevertheless, the issue of Scottish independence is not necessarily relevant to the forthcoming negotiations with the EU and is a separate domestic matter for the UK Government to resolve. In this context, it should be noted that in the *Miller* case, brought on final appeal before the UK Supreme Court in 2017, the latter ruled that the devolved legislatures such as those of Scotland and Wales would not have a veto over a UK decision to trigger the Article 50 process. In relation to Gibraltar, it is currently envisaged by the EU that any future relationship agreement between the EU and the UK may not apply to the territory of Gibraltar without the agreement of Spain. This unilateral condition may also yet prove politically challenging. Furthermore, the maintenance of the long-standing relationship between the Republic of Ireland and the UK on the existing Common Travel Area (the continuation of which appears to have been accepted by the EU), when combined with the added intention to mitigate the effects of the UK withdrawal on the border between Ireland and Northern Ireland, and the safeguarding of the Good Friday Agreement, will nevertheless require special and innovative solutions.

The UK's economic performance is closely dependent on its trade in goods and services with European countries, which are in turn based on unimpeded movement across national borders. There is some confusion in the media between access to the Single Market (which would normally involve agreeing to the famous four freedoms of goods, services, people and capital) and simple trading access for goods, to the market of the EU, possibly under World Trade Organization rules, with or without (reciprocal) tariff or non-tariff barriers that apply to many countries outside the EU and the EEA. As discussed above, the EU has not sought to tackle the issue of the UK's future relationship first, or even in parallel. On the contrary, it has made that discussion contingent on satisfactory progress in other areas of the negotiations. This is a political choice, which may yet have serious repercussions for businesses, consumers and citizens in all parts of the EU and the UK, for whom the future agreement may in fact determine their medium- and longer-term prospects for economic prosperity. It is, nevertheless, not necessary that all parts of this complex negotiation should take place in one package or treaty, but can be achieved in stages. The more pragmatic and amicable the atmosphere of these negotiations, the more likely that markets will remain calm and any associated uncertainties will abate (for both sides).

The consequences of withdrawal have been likened to a long and expensive divorce.[106] None the less, the constitutional history of the EU, particularly in handling internal crisis, is one of relentless determination to maintain its ideals and to survive intact, without defeat of any of its fundamental objectives. This is made very evident in the EUs current negotiating position on Brexit. It remains to be seen whether such idealism can be maintained, while also creating a new, pragmatic and economically sound future relationship with a state that has long-standing and major economic, political and cultural ties, such as the UK.

The inherently complex interrelationship between the main political institutions of the EU is also further exposed in the Brexit process, wherein each claims a right to expound its own priorities and negotiating stance. The absence of clear and straightforward drafting in many EU treaty provisions is now exemplified by the absence in Article 50 TEU of a sufficiently clear process for withdrawal, notably in connection with negotiations for a future relationship with the withdrawing state. Perhaps the gaps reflect the likelihood that, when drafted, it was never envisaged that Article 50 would ever be invoked, and certainly not by a major country. However, it is entirely possible that the Brexit negotiations might yet result in an acceptable compromise, given the evident high stakes on all sides.

In its June 2014 meeting (two years before the UK Brexit referendum), the European Council, recognizing the increasing difficulty of maintaining unanimity in all areas, across 28 member states, but particularly in relation to the UK, conceded that: 'the concept of ever closer union allows for different paths of integration for different countries, allowing those that want to deepen integration to move ahead, while respecting the wish of those who do not wish to deepen any further' (para. 27 of the Conclusions). Perhaps other than within the euro area, the possibility of a 'multi-speed Europe'[107] could yet be the platform for the setting of a new direction within the EU after the UK withdrawal has taken place, in which all member states participate, but to varying degrees, eliminating pressure to participate in certain measures, and thereby removing any incentive to oppose them at all costs or attempt to withdraw from membership. Nevertheless, it is difficult to see how, if the UK leaves the EU, the founding treaties could continue to apply without significant revision in, for instance, the reallocation of voting powers and other rights in the various institutions, and rearrangement of financial contributions. This is likely, at some stage, to involve obtaining the agreement or consent of the other 27 member states, a process that once embarked upon may risk further significant complications.

It therefore remains to be seen, particularly during and after Brexit, whether growing disengagement by European citizens from the process of deeper European integration can be offset by the continuing broad consent of the vast majority of both national political parties and the European public, as well as the enhanced legitimacy the EU has gained by its enlargement to include countries of Central and Eastern Europe, most recently Croatia in mid-2013. However, this expansion to 28 member states, which will become 27 without the UK, and the unanimity required on many important issues, represents, paradoxically, both a triumph and an ongoing challenge to the future survival of the EU.

The success or otherwise of the Brexit negotiations may depend on whether the EU, in particular, can adhere to its core values, while nevertheless adopting a spirit of pragmatism on future economic issues, thus demonstrating flexibility, political sophistication and the will to create a new and special relationship with the UK. This may necessarily cover a wide range of issues, including trade and security matters. The outcome may be further influenced, in particular, by the results of the federal elections in Germany on 24 September 2017.

The achievement of a satisfactory compromise with the UK will serve to demonstrate how great a construction the EU really is. Whether during or after this process, it may also need to examine whether the principle of free movement, as developed in the aftermath of the Second World War, is still entirely appropriate in current times, in the face of both internal and external challenges such as mass migration and terrorism. The stage is set for genuine leaders to step forward in Europe and show the way towards continued peace, prosperity, progress and friendship, for the benefit of EU citizens in general, and not just the EU or its institutions.

The writer would like to thank Professor Martin Westlake (College of Europe and London School of Economics and former Secretary-General of the European Economic and Social Committee, Brussels) for sharing his considerable experience of the EU institutional framework and offering detailed comments on several earlier drafts; Professor Dr Michael Kaeding (Jean Monnet Chair for European Union Politics, Universität Duisburg-Essen, Institut für Politikwissenschaft) for his careful and insightful suggestions for further improvement of the current text; Dr Sara Drake (Senior Lecturer in Law, Cardiff University) for her knowledgeable assistance in updating it; Mr David Croughan (Co-Chair. of the Economists Working Group, Institute of International and European Affairs, Dublin and Irish Member of the European Economic and Social Committee) for his advice on economic and monetary issues; and the joint staff of the library of the European Economic and Social Committee and Committee of the Regions for their valued research support. However, the views expressed and any remaining flaws remain the author's own.

Notes

1. For an account of the history of the formation of the European Coal and Steel Community, see Westlake, M. *A Modern Guide to the European Parliament*, pp. 7–13. London, Pinter Publishers, 1994.
2. See generally, Chalmers, D., Davies, G., and Monti, G. *European Union Law: Text and Materials*. 3rd edn, Cambridge, Cambridge University Press, 2014; Dougan, M., and Currie, S. (Eds). *50 Years of the European Treaties: Looking Back and Thinking Forward*. Oxford, Hart Publishing, 2009.
3. Weatherill, S., and Beaumont, P. *EU Law: The Essential Guide to the Legal Workings of the European Union*, pp. 9–10. London, Penguin Books, 1999.
4. The Settlement was subsequently published in the *Official Journal of the European Union* on 23 Feb. 2016/C 69 1/01, Vol. 59, pp. 1–16.
5. See further, 'The Treaty of Lisbon and the Court of Justice of the European Union', Court of Justice of the European Communities, Press Release No. 104/09, Luxembourg, 30 November 2009. For a discussion of CFSP see Geddes, A. *Britain and the European Union*, pp. 191–196, Basingstoke and New York, Palgrave Macmillan, 2013. For analysis of CSDP see Koutrakos, P. *The EU Common Security and Defence Policy*. Oxford, Oxford University Press, 2013.
6. See further, *How the Euro Became Our Money: A Short History of the Euro Banknotes and Coins*. Frankfurt, European Central Bank, 2007. See also, Cedrone, C. et al. *Where is the Euro Headed?* pp. 1–169. Rome, Edizioni Nuova Cultura, 2015.
7. See further, Cowgill, A., and Cowgill, A., *The Treaty of Nice in Perspective*. Vol. 1, p. 27, *et seq*. Stroud, British Management Data Foundation, 2001.
8. The Protocols have the same legal status as the Treaties of which they form an integral part: see Article 36 of the TEU (as amended).
9. Unlike the Protocols, the Declarations are only an expression of political will rather than legal commitment, but may be used by the ECJ as evidence of the parties' intentions and therefore as an interpretative tool. In this essay, references to specific Protocols and Declarations utilize the relevant reference numbers that apply in the *Consolidated Versions of the Treaty on European Union and the Treaty on the Functioning of the European Union*, O.J. C 83/01, Vol. 53, 30 March 2010.
10. For a more detailed analysis, see D'Sa, R. M. 'The Treaty of Lisbon: An Overview', in *European Current Law*, pp. xi–xviii, June 2008. See also Piris, J.-C. *The Lisbon Treaty: A Legal and Political Analysis*. Cambridge and New York, Cambridge University Press, 2010; Information Report of the European Economic and Social Committee, *Impact of the Lisbon Treaty on the Functioning of the Internal Market*, INT/393 (SMO), CESE 241/2008, Rapporteur, Pegado Liz (hereinafter 'Pegado Liz Report') and its appended comparative study, INT/393—CESE 241/2008 fin Appendix; European Parliament *Report on the Treaty of Lisbon*, Committee on Constitutional Affairs, A6-0013/2008, 28 January 2008; House of Lords, European Union Committee, *The Treaty of Lisbon: An Impact Assessment*, Vol. 1: Report, 13 March 2008 (hereinafter 'HL Report'). The latter report, reaching some 275 pages and based on written and oral evidence received from more than 160 experts, non-governmental organizations, government departments, EU institutions and members of the public, can be found at: www.publications.parliament.uk/pa/ld200708/ldselect/ldeucom/62/62.pdf.
11. The Treaty establishing the European Atomic Energy Community (Euratom) is not affected in substance, but some provisions are altered by the Protocol amending the Euratom Treaty (to bring them in line with the new text). See also Cowgill, A. and Cowgill, A. *The Treaty of Lisbon in Perspective*, Vol. 1. Stroud, British Management Data Foundation, 2008, which provides an annotated consolidated text of the TEU and the TFEU, which attempts to display graphically all the relevant amendments made by the Lisbon Treaty.
12. See further, Van Rompuy, H. *Europe in the Storm: Promise and Prejudice*. Leuven, Davidsfonds, 2014. See also, Westlake, M. 'Chronicle of an Election Foretold: The Longer-Term Trends leading to the "*Spitzenkandidaten*" Procedure and the Election of Jean-Claude Juncker as European Commission President', in LEQS Paper No. 102/2016, London School of Economics *Europe in Question* Discussion Paper Series. Jan. 2016.
13. See further, Westlake, M., and Galloway, D. *The Council of the European Union*. London, John Harper Press, 2004; Dashwood, A. 'Issues of Decision-making in the European Union after Nice' in Arnull, A., and Wincott, D. (Eds). *Accountability and Legitimacy in the European Union*, p. 13. Oxford, Oxford University Press, 2002.
14. The same Council decision also added Croatia and extended the run until 2030. See: www.consilium.europa.eu/en/press/press-releases/2016/07/26-council-rotating-presidencies-revised-order/.

15. Szapiro, M., and Kaeding, M. *The European Commission: A Practical Guide*. London, John Harper, 2013.
16. There is, extraordinarily, a difference between certain language versions of the Treaty (Article 9D) as to whether 'the elections' or 'the result of the elections' need to be taken into account. See further: www.lse.ac.uk/european Institute/LEQS%20Discussion%20Paper%20Series/LEQS Paper102.pdf, especially pp. 39 and 40.
17. See further, Kaeding, M., and Stack, K. M. 'Legislative Scrutiny? The Political Economy and Practice of Legislative Vetoes in the European Union', Vol. 53, Issue 6, *Journal of Common Market Studies*, Nov. 2015, pp. 1268–84, first published online 5 May 2015, see below at footnote 63 for hyperlinks.
18. Opening address by Westlake, M., at the 10th University College Annual Seminar, Royal Society, London, 27 Nov. 2014, on the theme 'Beyond Fantasy or Fear, The Future of Britain Outside the European Union'.
19. See *Inter-institutional Agreement between the European Parliament, the Council of the European Union and the European Commission on Better Law-Making*, O.J. L123, 12.5.2016, pp. 1–14; eur-lex.europa.eu/legal-content/EN/TXT/?uri=uriserv:OJ.L_.2016.123.01.0001.01.ENG.
20. See further: europa.eu/rapid/press-release_IP-17-1405_en.htm.
21. See, in particular, the ECJ judgment in Opinion 2/17 of 16 May 2017 regarding the terms of the EU-Singapore Free Trade Agreement.
22. See Scanderbech, E. 'Can National Parliaments Contribute through the Early Warning System to the EU Decision Making Process?' in Cartabia, M., Lupo, N., and Simoncini, A. (Eds). *Democracy and Subsidiarity in the EU: National Parliaments, Regions and Civil Society in the Decision Making Process*, pp. 197–224 at p. 211. Bologna, Società Editrice Il Mulino, 2013. See further, Cooper, I. 'A Yellow Card for the Striker: National Parliaments and the Defeat of EU Legislation on the Right to Strike', in *Journal of European Public Policy*, Vol. 22, Issue 10, pp. 1406–1425, 2015.
23. See Article 12 of the TEU (as amended) and Protocols (No. 1) and (No. 2) annexed by the Lisbon Treaty. For analysis of the different mechanisms established for national parliamentary scrutiny of EU legislation, see further the website of the Conference of Community and European Affairs Committees of Parliaments of the European Union, available at: www.cosac.eu.
24. Scanderbech, *op. cit.*, p. 206.
25. See further, *Rules of Procedure of the Court of Justice*, O.J. L 265, Vol. 55, 29 September 2012; see also Annex 1 of *Protocol (No. 3) on the Statute of the Court of Justice of the European Union*, Consolidated Versions of the Treaty on European Union and the Treaty on the Functioning of the European Union, p. 210. O.J. C 83/01, Vol. 53, 30 March 2010.
26. See, for example, the German Constitutional Court decision of 18 March 2014, in a case involving issues to do, *inter alia*, with the European Stability Mechanism (ESM), the Fiscal Compact Treaty (TSCG), and the European Central Bank (ECB), available at: www.bundesverfassungsgericht.de/en/press/bvg14-009en.html.
27. For analysis of the EESC in general, see Westlake, M. *The European Economic and Social Committee: The House of European Organised Civil Society*. London, John Harper Publishing, June 2016; Westlake, M. 'The Antecedents, Origins and Creation of the European Economic and Social Committee', in *Bruges Political Research Papers*, 52/2016, pp. 1–27, Department of European Political and Administrative Studies, College of Europe. See also, *Shaping Europe: Recent EESC Achievements*. European Economic and Social Committee, 2015.
28. See further, Tsadiras, A. 'The European Ombudsman's Remedial Powers: An Empirical Analysis in Context' in *European Law Review*, Vol. 38, pp. 52–64, Feb. 2013.
29. See further, Dougan, M., and Currie, S. (Eds). *50 Years of the European Treaties: Looking Back and Thinking Forward*. Oxford and Portland, OR, Hart Publishing, 2009.
30. See Harpaz, G. 'European Integration in the Aftermath of the Ratification of the Treaty of Lisbon: Quo Vadis?' in *European Public Law*, Vol. 17, No. 1, pp. 73–89 at p. 89, 2011.
31. *Ibid.*, at p. 78. See also the document requested by the European Parliament's Constitutional Affairs Committee: Peers, S. *Trends in Differentiation of EU Law and Lessons for the Future*, European Parliament, European Union, 2015, available at: www.europarl.europa.eu/studies.
32. See further, Arnull, A., 'Broken Bats', *European Law Review*, 41, pp. 473–474, 2016.
33. See UK House of Commons European Scrutiny Committee, 62nd Report of Session 2010–12, *Treaty on Stability, Co-ordination and Governance: Impact on the Eurozone and the Rule of Law*, HC 1817, published 3 April 2012; available at: www.publications.parliament.uk. See also D'Sa, R. M. 'The Legal and Constitutional Nature of the New International Treaties on Economic and Monetary Union from the perspective of EU Law', in *European Current Law*, Issue 5, pp. xi–xxv, 2012; Ginter, C., and Narits, R. 'The Perspective of a Small Member State to the Democratic Deficiency of the ESM', in *Review of Central and East European Law*, Vol. 38, pp. 54–76, 2013; Menéndez, A. J. 'The EU's Unconstitutional Treaties' in European Voice, Vol. 18, No. 26 (28 June), p. 9, 2012; see also Case C-370/12, *Thomas Pringle v. The Government of Ireland, Ireland and the Attorney General*, Judgment of the Court (Full Court), 27 November 2012, available at: curia.europa.eu/juris. For analysis of the *Pringle* Judgment, see Van Malleghem, P.-A. '*Pringle*: A Paradigm Shift in the European Union's Monetary Constitution', in *German Law Journal*, Vol. 14, No. 1, pp. 141–168, 2013.
34. The detailed procedures and conditions for a European Citizens' Initiative (ECI) have been defined (in accordance with Article 24 of the TFEU) by *Regulation (EU) No. 211/2011 of the European Parliament and of the Council of 16 February 2011 on the citizens' initiative*, O.J. L 65/1, 11 March 2011 and by *Commission Implementing Regulation (EU) No. 1179/2011 of 17 November 2011 laying down technical specifications for online collection systems pursuant to Regulation (EU) No. 211/2011 of the European Parliament and of the Council on the citizens' initiative*, O.J. L 301/13, 18 Nov. 2011.
35. See further, the EESC Opinion on *The Implementation of the Lisbon Treaty: Participatory Democracy and the Citizens' Initiative (Article 11)*, (Own initiative Opinion), Rapporteur, Anne-Marie Sigmund, SC/032—CESE 465/

2010. See also Legg, J. *Effective Consultation with Citizens in the EU*, Volonteurope Report No. 2, April 2010.

36. See further, Dougan, M. 'What Are We to Make of the Citizens' Initiative?' in *Common Market Law Review*, Vol. 48, pp. 1807–1848, 2011; Kentmen-Cin, C. 'Explaining Willingness to Use the European Citizens' Initiative: Political Cynicism, anti-EU Attitudes and Voting Weight of Member States' in *Comparative European Politics*, Vol. 12, No. 3, pp. 301–318, 2014. Details on current citizens' initiatives may be found on the Commission's ECI website, available at: ec.europa.eu/citizens-initiative/public/welcome.

37. See Articles 1, 4, 5, 48(2) of the TEU (as amended by the Lisbon Treaty) and Articles 2–6 of the TFEU. See also the implicit relationship between the (amended) 'flexibility clause' in Article 352 of the TFEU and the issue of competences.

38. See Hawkes, L. W. N. 'Can the Lisbon Treaty Deliver Effective Energy Sector Reforms', in *Oil, Gas & Energy Law Intelligence (OGEL)*, Vol. 10, Issue 3, pp. 1–16, March 2012.

39. First established in Case 26/62, *Algemene Transport- en Expeditieonderneming van Gend & Loos NV v. Nederlandse Administratie der Belastingen* [1963] ECR 1. See D'Sa, R. M. *European Community Law and Civil Remedies in England and Wales*, at pp. 23–31. London, Sweet & Maxwell, 1994.

40. *Costa v Ente Nazionale per l'Energia Elettrica (ENEL)* (6/64) [1964] ECR. 585; [1964] C.M.L.R. 425.

41. Provisions of Community (now Union) law that are directly effective are understood as creating rights or obligations, which individuals may enforce in national courts without the requirement for any national measure of adoption or transformation into domestic law. Directly effective provisions of EC law are required to be clear and unambiguous, and unconditional, and must operate independently of further action by Community or national authorities: see Dashwood, A. 'The Principle of Direct Effect in European Community Law', in *Journal of Common Market Studies*, Vol. 16, No. 229, at p. 231 *et seq.*, 1978.

42. See, for example, Arnull, A. *The European Union and its Court of Justice*, 2nd edn. Oxford, Oxford University Press, 2006; Claes, M. *The National Courts' Mandate in the European Constitution*. Oxford, Hart Publishing, 2006.

43. See further, D'Sa, R. M., and Laffranque, J. 'Getting to Know You: the Developing Relationship between the National Courts of the "Newer" Member States and the European Court of Justice, with Particular Reference to Estonia', in *European Business Law Review*, Vol. 18, No. 2, pp. 311–320, 2008.

44. This is also related to the determination of the situations of whether and when member state action is deemed to fall 'within the scope of the Treaties'. See the Editorial Comments, 'The scope of application of the General Principles of Union law: An Ever Expanding Union?' in *Common Market Law Review*, pp. 1589–1596, 2010; see further, Case C-555/07, *Kücükdeveci*, judgment of 19 Jan. 2010, [2010] ECR I-365. For discussion of the difficulties in reconciling the existing case law of the ECJ with Article 47 of the Charter in the context of remedies, see Drake, S. 'More Effective Private Enforcement of EU Law Post-Lisbon: Aligning Regulatory Goals and Constitutional Values', in Drake, S., and Smith, M. (Eds). *New Directions in the Effective Enforcement of EU Law and Policy*. Cheltenham, Edward Elgar Publishing, 2016.

45. Joined Cases C-6/90 and C-9/90, *Francovich and Bonifaci v. Italy*, [1991] ECR I-5357, at para. 37.

46. Nevertheless, the ECJ made it clear that concepts similar to that of 'direct effect' may still be relevant in that the relevant provisions of the Directive must confer rights on individuals and second, these rights must be capable of identification and must therefore be sufficiently precise for that purpose.

47. This basis (originally found in Article 10 of the EC Treaty, as amended by the Nice Treaty) was repealed by the Lisbon Treaty and is now contained (with an additional first sentence) in Article 4(3) of the TEU (as amended).

48. See further, for example, Bebr, G. 'Francovich v. Italy, Bonifaci v Italy', in *Common Market Law Review*, p. 559 at p. 572, 1992; Ross, M. 'Beyond Francovich', in *Modern Law Review*, Vol. 56, No. 1, p. 55–73 at p. 71, 1993, in which he likens the contribution of *Francovich* to the framework of Community law to be 'constitutional in character'; and Drake, S. 'Scope of Courage and the Principle of "Individual Liability" for Damages: Further Development of the Principle of Effective Judicial Protection by the Court of Justice', in *European Law Review*, Vol. 6, pp. 841–864, 2006. See also, Krümmel, T., and D'Sa, R. M. 'Implementation by German Courts of the Jurisprudence of the European Court of Justice on State Liability for Breach of Community Law as Developed in *Francovich* and Subsequent Cases', in *European Business Law Review*, pp. 273–286, 2009. For a more recent assessment of the impact of the remedy see Lock, T. 'Is Private Enforcement of EU Law Through State Liability a Myth? An Assessment 20 years after *Francovich*', in *Common Market Law Review*, p. 1675, 2012.

49. See further, European Union (Withdrawal) Bill, Explanatory Notes, at paras 155–156. These Notes relate to the European Union (Withdrawal) Bill as introduced in the UK House of Commons on 13 July 2017 (Bill 5).

50. See Article 12, Treaty of Amsterdam.

51. See also Appendix 3 'Structure of the Treaties—A Rough Guide to What Goes Where' in the HL Report, cited above at footnote 10, pp. 289–292.

52. The legal literature on the area of freedom, security and justice is voluminous. See Walker, N. (Ed.). *Europe's Area of Freedom, Security and Justice*. Oxford, Oxford University Press, 2004, at p. 3; Sharpston, E. 'The Future of the Area of Freedom, Security and Justice' in Dougan, M. and Currie, S. *op. cit.*, at pp. 219–228; Peers, S. 'Mission Accomplished? EU Justice and Home Affairs Law after the Treaty of Lisbon', in *Common Market Law Review*, Vol. 48, No. 3, 2011, pp. 661–693.

53. See further, European Commission website available at: www.ec.europa.eu/civiljustice/index_en.htm.

54. See Article 3, *Protocol (No. 22) on the position of the United Kingdom and Ireland in respect of the area of freedom, security and justice,* Consolidated Versions of the Treaty on European Union and the Treaty on the Functioning of the European Union. See further, *A Guide to the Treaty of Lisbon: European Union Insight*, p. 10. The Law Society, Jan. 2008.

55. See the explanation of the word 'executive' in Walker, *op. cit.*, especially at p. 22.
56. See further, De Búrca, G. 'The Constitutional Challenge of New Governance in the European Union' in *European Law Review*, Vol. 28, No. 6, pp. 814–839, 2003.
57. In *R v. Goldstein* [1983] 1 WLR 151 at p. 155. See further, Arnull, A. 'Proportionality', in Monar, J. *et al.* (Eds). *Butterworths Expert Guide to the European Union*, p. 255. London, Butterworths Law, 1996.
58. See further, House of Lords, Constitution Committee, *European Union (Amendment) Bill and the Lisbon Treaty; Implications for the UK Constitution*, Report with Evidence, 6th Report of Session 2007–08, 28 March 2008, HL Paper 84, paras 108–113 (hereinafter 'HL/CCReport') available at: www.publications.parliament.uk/pa/ld200708/ldselect/ldconst/84/84.pdf.
59. See further, Monar, J. 'Maintaining the JHA *Acquis* in an Enlarged Europe', in Apap, J. (Ed.). *Justice and Home Affairs in the EU: Liberty and Security Issues after Enlargement*, pp. 37–53. Cheltenham, and Northampton, MA, Edward Elgar, 2004.
60. Speech by German Federal Chancellor Angela Merkel at the opening ceremony of the 61st academic year of the College of Europe in Bruges on 2 Nov. 2010, available at: www.bruessel.diplo.de/contentblob/2959854/Daten/.
61. See notably, directive 96/34 on parental leave, directive 99/63 on the working time of seafarers; directive 99/70 on fixed-term work and directive 2000/79 on the working time of mobile workers: see Simoncini, A. 'Beyond Representative Democracy: The Challenge of Participatory Democracy and the Boundless Galaxy of Civil Society', in Cartabia, C., Lupo, N., and Simoncini, A. (Eds). *Democracy and Subsidiarity in the EU*, pp. 45–74 at p. 54. Bologna, Società Editrice Il Mulino (2013).
62. Regulation 182/2011 laying down the rules and general principles concerning mechanisms for control by member states of the Commission's exercise of implementing powers, [2011] O.J. L 55/13 (Comitology Regulation). See also Decision 99/468 laying down the procedures for the exercise of implementing powers conferred on the Commission [1999] O.J. L 184/23 (Comitology Decision), which was amended in 2006 in order to strengthen the Parliament and the Council's powers of scrutiny, and which provides for the 'regulatory procedure with scrutiny' which has been used to adopt certain implementing measures. However, the use of the latter procedure is to be progressively withdrawn, post-Lisbon Treaty.
63. See Kaeding, M. and Stack, K. M., 'Legislative Scrutiny? The Political Economy and Practice of Legislative Vetoes in the European Union', *Journal of Common Market Studies* in Vol. 53, Issue 6, Nov. 2015, pp. 1268–84; onlinelibrary.wiley.com/doi/10.1111/jcms.12252/abstract/. See also concerning the same article, the London School of Economics blog: blogs.lse.ac.uk/europpblog/2016/10/25/a-dearth-of-legislative-vetoes/.
64. See Craig, Paul. 'Delegated Acts, Implementing Acts and the New Comitology Regulation', in *European Law Review*, Vol. 36, pp. 671–687, Oct. 2011. The European Court ruled on the distinction between implementing acts and delegated acts in the *Biocides* case, Case C 427/12, *Commission v. European Parliament and Council*, Judgment of 18 March 2014 by the Grand Chamber.
65. See further, Guéguen, D. and Marissen, V. *Handbook on EU Secondary Legislation: Navigating through Delegated and Implementing Acts, Comitology after Lisbon*, Brussels, PACT European Affairs, 1st edn, Jan. 2013; Draft Information Report of the Single Market Section of the European Economic and Social Committee, *Better Regulation: Implementing and Delegated Acts*, INT/656 and its Appendices, Brussels, 7 June 2013, Rapporteur, Pegado Liz; Hardacre, A., and Kaeding, M. *Delegated and Implementing Acts—The New Comitology*, European Institute of Public Administration (EIPA) Essential Guide, Version 2, March 2011.
66. See further, the Five Presidents' Report, *Completing Europe's Economic and Monetary Union* by Juncker, J.-C. *et al.* European Commission, 2015, available at: ec.europa.eu/priorities/economic-monetary-union/docs/5-presidents-report_en.pdf. See also, Grünewald, S. *The Resolution of Cross-Border Banking Crises in the European Union: A Legal Study from the Perspective of Burden Sharing*, pp. 245–251. Alphen aan den Rijn, Netherlands, Wolters Kluwer, 2014.
67. See generally, D'Sa, R. M. *European Community Law on State Aid*. London, Sweet & Maxwell, 1998; and Bacon, K. *European Union Law of State Aid*, 2nd edn. Oxford, Oxford University Press, 2013.
68. See for example Protocol (No. 2) on the application of the principles of subsidiarity and proportionality and Protocol (No. 25) on the exercise of shared competences. The internal market is an area of 'shared' competence and these Protocols concern the legal competences to be shared between the Union and the member states. See also the Declarations: No. 18, *Declaration in relation to the delimitation of competences* and No. 42, *Declaration on Article 352 of the Treaty on the Functioning of the European Union* (concerning the principle of conferral of powers).
69. See the Pegado Liz Report, cited above at footnote 10. Note also, the separate concept of 'social economy' which spans economic activity in the community, voluntary and social enterprise sectors: see further, a study commissioned by the EESC, *The Social Economy in the European Union* (Brussels, 2012), which examines the state of the social economy in the (then) 27 EU countries, plus Croatia and Iceland.
70. See further, Riley, A. 'The EU Reform Treaty and the Competition Protocol: Undermining EC Competition Law', in *European Competition Law Review*, Vol. 28, No. 12, 2007, pp. 703–707.
71. See further, Schiek, D. 'Age Discrimination Before the ECJ: Conceptual and Theoretical Issues', in *Common Market Law Review*, Vol. 48, No. 3, pp. 777–799, 2011.
72. The Charter of Fundamental Rights of the European Union was first proclaimed (in Nice) on 7 December 2000. The second proclamation (in Strasbourg), on 12 December 2007, was needed because explanations and footnotes had subsequently been added. The text of the Charter is now published together with the Consolidated Versions of the Treaty on European Union and the Treaty on the Functioning of the European Union, at O.J. C 83/02, Vol. 53, 30 March 2010.
73. Article 6(1) of the TEU. Despite the previous position concerning the non-legally binding nature of the Charter of Fundamental Rights, the ECJ had nevertheless referred

74. Article 28, Charter of Fundamental Rights.
75. See further, Douglas-Scott, S. 'The Court of Justice of the European Union and the European Court of Human Rights after Lisbon' (2012), in de Vries, S., Bernitz, U., and Weatherill, S. (Eds). *The Protection of Fundamental Rights in the EU after Lisbon*. Hart Publishing, 2013, pp. 153–179 at p. 164, citing, *inter alia*, Toth, A. G. 'The European Union and Human Rights: The Way Forward', in *Common Market Law Review*, Vol. 34, 1997, p. 491.
76. The Conclusions of the European Council of 29 and 30 October 2009 state that Protocol (No. 30) will apply to the Czech Republic (Doc. 15265/09, Concl. 3). See further, Nos. 1, 53, 61 and 62 of the *Declarations annexed to the Final Act of the Intergovernmental Conference which adopted the Treaty of Lisbon*, O.J. C 83/01, Vol. 53, p. 335 *et. seq.*, 30 March 2010.
77. HL Report, cited above at footnote 10, para. 12.44.
78. See www.number10.gov.uk/news/european-court-of-human-rights/.
79. Douglas-Scott, S., *op. cit.*, at p. 176, footnote 97, referring to the case *Hirst v. United Kingdom (No.2)* [2005] ECHR p. 681 and also *Greens and MT v. United Kingdom* [2010] ECHR p. 1826.
80. Paper by a UK judge, the Rt Hon. Lady Justice Arden, DBE, entitled 'Is the Convention Ours?' delivered at a seminar to mark the official opening of the judicial year of the ECHR in 2010, cited by Douglas-Scott, *op. cit.*, at pp. 176–177.
81. See generally, Steiner, J., Woods, L., and Twigg-Flesner, C. *EU Law*, p. 69, *et. seq.* 9th edn. Oxford, Oxford University Press, 2006.
82. For an analysis of the application of this provision in relation to penalties for non-compliance with the rules on state aid, see further, D'Sa, R. M., and Drake, S. 'Financial Penalties for Failure to Recover State Aid and their Relevance to State Liability for Breach of Union Law', in *European State Aid Law Quarterly*, Vol. 9, No. 1, 2010, pp. 33–46.
83. See further Chapter 6, HL Report, cited above at footnote 10.
84. See further European Commission website at www.ec.europa.eu/justice_home/fsj/criminal/network/fsj_criminal_network_en.htm.
85. See Title IV, Articles 67–89 TFEU, *Protocol (No. 21) on the position of the United Kingdom and Ireland in respect of the AFSJ*, and *Protocol (No. 19) on the Schengen acquis integrated into the framework of the EU*, which concerns in particular, Denmark, Ireland and the UK. See also HL/CC Report, cited above, paras 108–113.
86. See Article 20 of the TEU (as amended) and Articles 326–334 of the TFEU.
87. See the Commission's *Proposal for a Council Regulation (EU) implementing enhanced cooperation in the area of the law applicable to divorce and legal separation*, COM(2020) 105 final/2, Brussels, 30 March 2010. The Commission adopted the authorization Decision in July 2010, after obtaining the consent of the European Parliament: O.J. L 189/12, 2010.
88. The second authorization of enhanced co-operation, adopted in March 2011, concerns unitary patent protection: O.J. L 76/53, 2011.
89. See Dashwood, A. 'The United Kingdom in a Re-Formed European Union', in *European Law Review*, Vol. 38, Dec. 2013, pp. 737–756.
90. See further, Ruffert, Mathias, 'The European Debt Crisis and European Union Law', in *Common Market Law Review*, Vol. 48, No. 6, 2011, pp. 1777–1806. See also, Editorial Comment, 'The Greek Sovereign Debt Tragedy: Approaching the Final Act?', in *Common Market Law Review*, Vol. 48, pp. 1769–1776, 2011. For a similar discussion, but in the context of the EU state aid rules, see D'Sa, R. M. '"Instant" State Aid in a Financial Crisis: a U-turn?', in *European State Aid Law Quarterly*, Vol. 8, No. 2, 2008, pp. 139–144.
91. Zuleeg, F. and Emmanouilidis, J. A. 'Escaping Europe's Catch 22', European Policy Centre, Brussels, 2012, pp. 1–2, available at: www.epc.eu.
92. See further, Ziller, J. 'The German Constitutional Court's Friendliness Towards European Law: On the Judgment of *Bundesverfassungsgericht* over the Ratification of the Treaty of Lisbon', in *European Public Law*, Vol. 16, No. 1, 2010, pp. 53–73. For substantive criticism of the TSCG see, for example, Weeks, J., 'Time to repeal the "Six-Pack"', *E!Sharp*, April 2016.
93. D'Sa, R. M. 'The Legal and Constitutional Nature of the New International Treaties on Economic and Monetary Union from the Perspective of EU Law', in *European Current Law*, Issue 5, 2012, pp. xi–xxv, at p. xxiv.
94. *Ibid.*, at pp. xvi–xvii.
95. Two of the *passerelles*, i.e. the second simplified revision procedure (Article 48(7) TEU, as amended) and measures concerning family law with cross-border implications (Article 81(3) of the TFEU), are also subject to a veto by each national parliament, exercisable within six months of notification.
96. 'The EU's role in Brexit negotiations', Institute for Government, see www.instituteforgovernment.org.uk/explainers/brexit-explained-eu-role-brexit-negotiations/.
97. Council Decision 2014/335/EU, Euratom of 26 May 2014 on the system of own resources of the European Union: O.J. L 168, 7.6.2014, pp. 105–111.
98. See further, Working Paper, *Essential Principles on Financial Settlement*, European Commission Task Force for the Preparation and Conduct of the Negotiations with the UK under Article 50 TEU intended for discussion at the Council Working Party (Article 50) of 1 June 2017, 24 May 2017, Document No. 2.
99. See further, Beck, G., *EU Citizens' Rights after Brexit: The EU's extravagant demands for extra-territorial jurisdiction by the CJEU and reverse discrimination*, Judicial Power Project, June 2017, pp. 1–9, at p. 3.
100. See further, Poptcheva, E.-M. 'Article 50 TEU: Withdrawal of a Member State from the EU', Briefing,

Members' Research Service, European Parliamentary Research Service (EPRS), PE 577.971, pp. 1–8, February 2016; 'Wales and the EU: What does the Vote to Leave the EU Mean for Wales?', Research Briefing, Research Service, Legal Service and EU Office, National Assembly for Wales, Paper No. 16-037, June 2016, pp. 1–51.

101. See further the comments of Michael Kaeding, available at: www.euractiv.com/sections/eu-priorities-2020/eu-profes sor-juncker-decides-fate-european-parliament-316352.

102. *Communication from the Commission to the European Parliament, the Council, the European Economic and Social Committee and the Committee of the Regions, Commission Work Programme 2015: A New Start*, COM (2014) 910 final, European Commission, Strasbourg, 16.12.2014.

103. Ruffert, cited above at footnote 90, at p. 2.

104. For an authoritative analysis of the legal issues of the UK continuing to be a member of the EU, while remaining outside EMU, see House of Lords, *European Union Committee, 7th Report of Session 2012–13, European Banking Union: Key Issues and Challenges*, HL Paper 88 (12 Dec. 2012).

105. See further, Halligan, B. 'The Process of UK Withdrawal from the EU' in O'Ceallaigh, D., and Gillespie, P. (Eds). *Britain and Europe: The Endgame, an Irish Perspective*, Institute of International and European Affairs, Feb. 2015, pp. 119–130.

106. Emerson, M. (Ed.). *Britain's Future in Europe: Reform, Renegotiation, Repatriation or Secession?*, p. 155. Centre for European Policy Studies, 2015.

107. See Piris, J-C. *The Future of Europe*, p. 62. Cambridge, Cambridge University Press, 2012.

THE FUTURE OF THE EUROPEAN UNION

Juliet Lodge

Recent Developments and Background

The European Union (EU) celebrated its 60th anniversary in 2017 with renewed vigour. It was to focus on democratic and socioeconomic renewal and reform. This was occasioned by both the continuing overspill of previous years' preoccupations: Mediterranean immigration and border management, policing, terrorism, the war in Syria, steel, economic downturn in the People's Republic of China, the Trans-Atlantic Trade Agreement (TTIP), realizing the Digital Single Market, ongoing disputes with international corporations, continued conflict in Ukraine and the future of EU citizens. The previous year's tortuous arguments over the EU's attempts to pass updated legislation to protect citizens' data were resolved, but cybersecurity threats, the role of the Russian Federation, 'fake news', and a climate of political dishonesty were seen as threats not to EU unity but to the values underpinning the EU itself. The jejune pronouncements of the new US President Donald Trump and the, some felt, equally implausible posturing by British Prime Minister Theresa May (who succeeded David Cameron in July 2016) impelled both deeper appreciation of the achievements of European integration on the part of EU leaders and citizens alike, and a determination to deepen integration better to address internal and external challenges. The commitment to unity and common endeavour, reform and advance had never seemed stronger.

During 2015–17 the EU encountered major internal and external challenges. Some issues that had arisen in 2013 continued to cause problems as public concern over data protection and privacy across the board was discussed in the public domain. Its relevance to negotiations on an EU-US trade agreement grew as the 'right to be forgotten' (which differs from the right to privacy, and relates to an individual's right to remove data from the public domain) and Google's responses were debated, amid mounting disquiet and continuing legal challenges following the 2015 Schrems ruling by the European Court of Justice (ECJ) regarding the Safe Harbour Agreement (see below). Improving cybersecurity, updating Passenger Name Record (PNR) provisions, facilitating the Digital Single Market, and the growing role of the European law enforcement agency (Europol) in combating radicalization on the internet and in operational surveillance and anti-crime matters in the wake of terrorist attacks in Paris, France, and Brussels, Belgium, as well as elsewhere, were to some degree overshadowed by continuing lobbying by commercial interests and by third states and companies against elements of the EU's new regulation. All delayed but did not prevent its adoption. The TTIP, however, appeared doomed by mid-2016.

National elections in member states, along with the threat of the possible exits of the United Kingdom and Greece from the EU, served to underline Germany's central position on all matters relevant to the EU's future, consolidating the role of Chancellor Angela Merkel, notably after the UK referendum vote in June 2016 in favour of withdrawal (known as Brexit). Merkel was widely regarded as a courageous risk-taker, having faced rising criticism domestically and plaudits internationally for her 'open door' policy towards migrants She had been re-elected as Chancellor in December 2013 and was re-elected in September 2017. In mid-2017 polls showed that Germans were prioritizing equal education opportunities, improved pensions and health care provision far above immigration. In the wake of the pressures on Greece and Turkey, and later Italy, from the inflows of migrants, many of whom were not Syrian, Merkel had modified an earlier inflexible stance on Greek bailouts, culminating in May 2016 with the EU agreeing another round of measures to bolster the Greek economy. The EU had to reinforce the capacity of Greece and Turkey to manage migrants as successive Balkan EU members closed their borders and the Schengen Agreement on the freedom of movement came under threat. This led to funding increases and the negotiation of arrangements with Turkey on border controls, in exchange for promises that visa-free travel to the EU for Turkish citizens and Turkey's membership bid would be expedited. In early 2016 it was proposed that Turkish be recognized as an official EU language, but relations deteriorated sharply throughout 2017. The European Parliament opposed steps to relax previous agreements on Turkish compliance with EU requirements on liberal democratic practices and customs, in exchange for more consistent enforcement by Turkey of border controls to inhibit migration through its territory to the EU. By May 2016 more migrants were entering the EU via Italy than via the Greek islands and arrangements between the EU and an increasingly turbulent Turkey remained tense.

Amid the difficulties surrounding management of the migrant crisis, the EU found itself integrating more deeply than anticipated, primarily in response to the need to improve control of a common border, while at the same time the internal Schengen Agreement arrangements continued to be suspended unilaterally by many member states intent on closing their borders, and many others rejected the notion of the European Commission determining individual quotas of refugees for the member states. The aim was to have an EU border force in place by November 2016 and to improve information-sharing among the relevant agencies, partly in response to the terrorist atrocities in Belgium and France and partly in response to operational requirements. Lack of trust among the various agencies could not be readily overcome, given continuing reports as to the fitness for purpose and integrity of the agencies in some Balkan states, and deep concern over Poland's judicial system. The role of Europol was strengthened in May 2017. Growing concern over Russia's strategic intentions and tactics in the Middle East, as well as in response to EU sanctions applied with respect to Ukraine (see below), reverberated across policy sectors. The Common

Agricultural Policy (CAP), which had been subject to reform in June 2013, came under renewed pressure from Russian sanctions and France led calls for further change.

The prospect of adapting the EU's agenda to accommodate Euroscepticism led to calls to revive the 1970s ideas of an EU of concentric circles and multiple speeds with different degrees of integration. However, anti-democratic developments in Hungary and Poland, as well as the UK, deepened the commitment to integration. EU-wide public support for the EU grew significantly, with greater vociferous right-wing rhetoric on immigration and borders being combated by popular demonstrations in favour of democracy and the EU, exemplified by the 'Pulse of Europe', pro-EU marches, demonstrations and numerous citizen-led anti-Brexit movements in the UK. Criticism of the constitutional twists used to force through Brexit legislation, overt press and media pro-Brexit bias, and disinformation were derided by some when compared with the EU's open and carefully prepared and published position papers.

By mid-2017 there had been a change in public opinion: the sense that governments were widely out of touch with citizens had abated somewhat, as the EU came to be seen as a source of innovation, renovation in many of its member states and a bastion against neo-fascism. Following the referendum, however, the British Government had marginalized itself as a serious player inside the EU. It was increasingly among a minority of states outvoted by the others and was perceived to be out of touch with EU issues.

The Referendum on EU Membership in the UK

Initially, for many in the EU, the British referendum seemed relatively incidental, having been launched to appease internal Conservative Party divisions that had widened since the first membership referendum in 1975. At that time, the later notoriously Eurosceptic Prime Minister, Margaret Thatcher, had campaigned to remain in the European Community (EC). In 2015, when the Government led by David Cameron started to campaign for a 'yes' vote to remain in the EU, it was accused of wasting resources that tightened public finances could ill afford—a charge levelled at the creation in August 2016 of a ministerial department charged with facilitating the exit from the EU. This, along with the 'Panama Papers' scandal of April (in which leaked documents implicated numerous international figures in offshore tax evasion), was fuel to the well-funded, often flamboyant, pro-Brexit 'Vote Leave' campaign. The British public was assailed by international and national reports, political, economic and cultural leaders and experts warning about the profoundly negative anticipated consequences of Brexit for the British and EU economies. This begged the question as to why the Government had chosen to risk the UK's position in that manner, albeit shortly before it was due to take up the rotating presidency of the Council of the EU in 2017, the 60th anniversary year of the signature of the Treaty of Rome establishing the European Economic Community (EEC). In contrast to the earlier 'Britain in Europe' campaign on the single market during former Labour Prime Minister Tony Blair's Governments, it lacked all-party co-operation, which it tried to restore by rebranding itself as 'Open Britain' in mid-2016. Instead, the Labour Party ran a 'Labour In' campaign to stress the EU issues that it felt appealed to its electorate and demonstrated how the EU had protected values and socioeconomic policies opposed by the Conservatives. Without a strong Liberal Democrat presence in 2016, the Remain 'Britain Stronger In Europe' campaign appeared male-dominated, Westminster-centric and unconvincing.

The overall effect of all these factors was to undermine the credibility of the Government's claims. Public disenchantment and disaffection with both sides' campaigns and personality politics was marked well before June 2016. An opening claim that the referendum was to give the younger generation an opportunity to decide their future proved to be empty rhetoric. The 'Stronger In' campaign produced a video uploaded to social media based on a 14-month-old baby's future, yet 16–17 years olds were deprived of the opportunity to vote, unlike in Scotland's independence referendum of September 2014. When the Government's voter registration website failed at midnight on 7 June 2016, the registration deadline had to be extended by means of emergency legislation. This prompted Brexit campaigners to threaten a legal challenge.[1] Problems also arose with the delivery of postal ballots to and from eligible voters in other EU states.[2] For the Government, the fear of a break-up of the UK in the event of Brexit grew. Scotland indicated that it would seek to remain in the EU in the event of Brexit, and acted accordingly when the result—48% 'yes', 52% 'no'—was announced. Spain suggested joint sovereignty over Gibraltar. The subsequent dispute over when to invoke Article 50 to trigger secession from the EU, repealing the 1972 Treaty of Accession to the (then) EEC, and the use of the royal prerogative to bypass Parliament's majority in favour of remaining in the EU, caused extensive argument and a legal challenge that the Government lost. Nevertheless, the Repeal Bill put to Parliament in September 2017 was interpreted as a power grab by the executive.

International incredulity at the political situation in the UK increased steadily as the Government appeared to fail to comprehend the realities of trade negotiations and the unbreakable economic links of European integration. When former US President Barack Obama, Canadian Prime Minister Justin Trudeau and especially, perhaps, former Conservative Prime Minister John Major (who had been in office during the Maastricht Treaty's negotiation and ratification) stated emphatically that the UK's international standing would suffer in the event of exit from the EU, along with the standing of the EU itself, the sense that the British Government was floundering grew. The politico-economic impact from speculation surrounding Brexit was rapid: France overtook the UK within weeks as the world's fifth largest economy; sterling fell sharply to near-parity with the euro by mid-August 2017; dissension over the status of EU citizens in the UK was the subject of emergency debate; British applications for citizenship of other EU states escalated; and generally the sense that the 'Leave' campaign had been funded by a few rich, foreign businessmen and built on false information had deep repercussions throughout the UK and the EU. Meanwhile, member state government leaders advocated continuing EU reform, along with a second Constitutional Convention (see below).

Following the referendum, Prime Minister Cameron had delayed activating Article 50 and immediately resigned (being replaced shortly afterwards by Theresa May). In mid-2017 speculation about another change in leadership grew, fuelling suspicions that the referendum had been an exercise in settling the Conservative Party's internal divisions, not simply with respect to 'Europe', but regarding the successor to the Prime Minister (whether Chancellor of the Exchequer George Osborne or London Mayor Boris Johnson, who was succeeded in May 2016 by Labour's Sadiq Khan).

Public regret at the outcome from those who supported Remain was loud and immediate: an online petition to Parliament, originally launched by the 'Leave' campaign to set minimum participation standards in the event of a close vote (i.e. asking for a 75% voter turnout, and a 60% majority threshold), received over 3m. signatories within 48 hours of the result. The difference in the number of votes cast for 'Leave' over 'Remain' showed that if one-half of that 1.2m. had voted 'Remain', the outcome would not have triggered the politico-economic turbulence around the world that the presumption of exit did. Moreover, the large number of people disenfranchised in the UK was sufficient to query the legitimacy of the whole process and precipitate court action as to the constitutional status of the Government invoking Article 50 without prior approval by Parliament. This meant that the legitimacy of the outcome was immediately contested: a majority of MPs in the House of Commons favoured Remain but were constrained by party policy. Recriminations abounded and the Labour Party's leadership was challenged as many prominent Shadow Cabinet members resigned after leader Jeremy Corbyn dismissed Shadow Foreign Secretary Hilary Benn.

Although students were among those claiming to be Remain voters, a significant number failed to register in the constituencies where they were likely to be in late June 2016 (when many would have left university for the summer vacation). Somewhat surprisingly, it seemed that traditional non-voters were more inclined to participate to vote 'Leave', as a protest against the Government's and the Establishment's incomprehension of the extent of public anger outside the capital, London, over what they saw as unfair distribution of scare resources. Highly negative and contested forecasts regarding the impact of Brexit on the economy appeared daily, some of which the 'Leave' campaign quickly conceded after the result was announced. The 'Leave' campaign was accused of dishonesty and deception as it had focused on the pressures occasioned by migration, and sought to mobilize traditionally disinterested non-voters around this issue.[3] The Remain campaign led on more diverse matters, but these that lacked tangible meaning for the average person: crime, the environment, social and workers' rights, prosperity, cross-border mobility and the UK's standing in the world. Those themes had appeared in the Government's EU referendum pamphlet sent to all households in the UK.[4] Interventions by high-profile international organizations, international political leaders, trades unions, business and finance experts, British military leaders, celebrities and sports people, and other 'experts', including EU Commission President Jean-Claude Juncker (whom the British Government had opposed on the occasion of his nomination for election), did not seem significantly to persuade the electorate one way or the other. The EU's June 2016 summit was overshadowed by the implications of the referendum. The founding six member states initially sought a swift withdrawal for the UK but drew back as all realized the need to make plans and negotiate terms for Brexit, terms that could, potentially, be put to the electorate again, as had happened in France, Ireland and Denmark when past treaty change had led to negative referendum results, then, with changes, positive endorsement.

The apparent lack of credibility of the British Government's arguments grew. Somewhat implausible parallels with the situations of Norway, Switzerland and even Greenland were suggested by some as alternatives to remaining in the EU. Increasing awareness of the erosion of the UK's importance both inside the EU and internationally hit home, financial markets reacted negatively, and shortly before Prime Minister Theresa May called an early general election for June 2017 (having previously pledged not to), some areas of the pro-Brexit media began to modify their position.

Politically, it was hard to escape the impression of a government in disarray. Insufficient post-referendum planning had been undertaken: disputes erupted between the Foreign and Commonwealth Office and other departments with interests in UK international trade. Key governments stressed their desire for the UK to remain in the EU, but again, as in 2016, the Conservative Government (following the June 2017 election, backed by the Democratic Unionist Party) failed to adopt a pragmatic stance. This contrasted with the way both Labour Prime Minister Harold Wilson had managed divisions over Europe in 1974, on the eve of renegotiation followed by the first referendum on EEC membership in 1975,[5] and David Cameron's more nuanced call for 'better regulation' rather than wholesale treaty reform. Cameron had eventually abandoned strident calls for reform in favour of, among other things, a number of opt-outs, such as non-participation in the proposed establishment of a European Public Prosecutor's Office, to which the UK had long been opposed.

Unfavourable comparisons with former British Prime Minister Margaret Thatcher's confrontation with former German Chancellor Helmut Kohl were made. In the British media especially, these overshadowed informed discussion of the critical issues facing the EU, including the migration and asylum crises in the Mediterranean (where the British navy provided support to EU rescue operations to recover illegal migrants from unseaworthy boats—the border security Triton operation—together with humanitarian aid). From early 2015 Eurotunnel's freight terminal in Calais, France, had attracted migrants and asylum seekers seeking to enter the UK. Since they had already crossed many Schengen states that were safe, diplomatic divisions over their ultimate destination emerged. The UK continued to reject a proposed quota for many reasons, partly informed by its wider migration policy and the numbers arriving in the UK from other, third states. This did not endear the UK to its EU partners, many of which faced growing public opposition domestically to migrants and asylum seekers (as in Poland and Hungary). Public feeling that illegal migrants were receiving preferential treatment again benefited the media organizations that were supporting the 'Leave' campaign, but put intense extra public pressure on governments. This was only slightly dispelled by the ECJ's ruling in June 2016 in favour of the UK being permitted to set conditions regarding the payment of child benefit to the non-resident children of EU migrant workers. The UK's failure to implement relevant existing EU directives to permit temporary migration controls and limit freedom of movement were highlighted to undermine the Government's increasingly untenable position on Brexit.

By June 2017, days after the general election, four aides and junior ministers responsible for the Brexit brief had resigned and another had been dismissed. A large proportion of the public, and notably those aged 30–55 years, wanted freedom of movement and to remain in the EU. The Labour position was modified slightly initially to oppose a so-called 'hard' Brexit, and in August to imply support for staying in the single market and customs union as MPs came back to vote on the EU

Withdrawal Bill. Only the Liberal Democrats remained consistently pro-'Remain'; following the election the party's leader, Tim Farron, resigned and was replaced by experienced former minister Vince Cable. Government negotiations with the EU resumed in August. Objectively abandoning the focus on Brexit and focusing on pressing social welfare, National Health and economic issues was the course commended by many trade, business, commercial, health, education and scientific bodies and think tanks. However, the weakened May Government continued to devote inordinate resources (at an undisclosed cost) to, and was distracted by, Brexit, attracting criticism for its response to both international and domestic crises. Events such as terrorist attacks in mid-2017 and a fire at Grenfell Tower, a public housing tower block in London, in which some 80 died; threats to the 1998 Good Friday agreement on devolved government in Northern Ireland posed by Prime Minister May's deal with the DUP, and disingenuous proposals for a post-Brexit 'special border'; and May's stated preference to depart the EU without a deal if negotiations were unsuccessful, all exacerbated a sense of turmoil in the UK. While impervious to this, the EU's open, public and clear negotiating strategy of prioritizing a resolution of the situation of EU citizens across the EU over everything else was accepted in part by May. None the less, the government team working on Brexit had apparently misunderstood the full meaning of freedom of movement, and seemed at times uncertain as to what integration and the single market really indicated. Party dogma seemed to triumph over fact at every turn.

Beyond the Borders of the EU

To the east of the EU, relations with Russia deteriorated further. The continuing conflict in eastern Ukraine and the Russian Government's support for separatists alleged to have been responsible for the shooting down of Malaysian Airlines flight MH17 in July 2014 precipitated ever more serious suspicions as to Russia's intentions on the world stage, including in respect to the Syrian crisis. Its sanctions and threats against Western Europe continued. Russian economic sanctions came in response to a series of low-, medium- and high-intensity sanctions imposed by the EU, including further targeted measures against Russian individuals and some companies; the cessation of loans from the European Investment Bank; the suspension of EU grants to Russian projects; restrictions on imports of luxury Russian goods and exports; and the reconsideration of Russia's right to host the 2018 Fédération Internationale de Football Association (FIFA) World Cup, which other states also contested after corruption revelations in 2015. Threats regarding energy supplies were made, and recently concluded Russian-Chinese agreements on energy supplies for the next 30 years took on greater significance.

Meanwhile, EU-US relations deteriorated somewhat following the election of US President Trump in late 2016, amid allegations of Russian interference in elections, as well as US and Russian media manipulation, social media 'bots' and fake news. Closer co-operation on trade between the EU and the USA remains an aspiration and the arrangement reached with Canada is presented by some as a possible model. The EU-Canada Comprehensive Economic and Trade Agreement (CETA) was concluded in October 2013 (the first such agreement between the EU and a Group of Eight—G8—countries) and was widely regarded as a landmark deal and a template for the TTIP. However, internal opposition to clauses in both agreements, including those relating to third country use of so-called big data and the transmission of data from within the EU to outside it—US companies would be allowed to sue EU states for loss, in effect, of profits under certain circumstances—slowed their conclusion. The CETA entered into force in September 2017, but the negotiations on the proposed TTIP had been suspended.

The turmoil on the international stage also demonstrated the need for concerted action by the EU-28 both through the EU itself and in conjunction with allies. The EU-Russian sanctions highlighted the importance to credible EU foreign action of public co-operation by the leaders of Germany, the UK and France with the USA. Former President Obama (but initially not Trump), Juncker and other EU leaders had stated that British membership of the EU helped create and sustain a viable, credible EU foreign policy: the EU would be weaker on the international stage without it, and British policy on combating international crime and terrorism would be seriously hindered by any separation from the EU agencies on which it relied, including Europol, FRONTEX, Eurojust, the European Community Humanitarian Office (ECHO) and many others. The British Government's stated intention to leave the European Atomic Energy Community (Euratom) was also widely condemned. Meanwhile, other EU states began to compete over which should host the European Medicines Agency upon its departure from the UK. Franco-German co-operation intensified, as did the commitment to deepen integration by dint of, in effect, expanding the EU's competence in more policy areas (increasingly those linked to defence) and widening the scope of federal authority.

EU public support for European integration continued to rise. British support for remaining in the EU also rose by mid-2017, and there was a growing belief among some observers that Brexit simply would not happen, and that the referendum was advisory not mandatory, as the British courts were called on to affirm, and that Brexit would deny a generation of young people their birth right: the 'four freedoms' of free movement of persons, capital, services and goods had existed since 1992. Conservative ministers' apparent indecisiveness and speculation over potential Brexit negotiation 'bargains' fuelled a degree of public disillusionment, and pro-EU sentiment followed, while the value of sterling and the British economy declined. The other EU states, having a veto over any Brexit deal, meanwhile turned to examining the EU's future shape.

The Future Shape of the EU

For over 30 years, EU member states have been debating constitutional reform: does the EU have or need a Constitution? How should it be written and what should it say? At the beginning of the 2000s, the EU faced one of the greatest challenges in its history. Not only was it confronted by states seeking rapid accession, but its own internal policymaking procedures and legitimacy were contested, and the territorial integrity and capacity of its member states to resist international terrorism—either singly or together as the EU per se—were challenged. Many of these issues persist today, exacerbated by the international economic crisis and the weakness of several EU member states' economies. This makes more urgent the need to augment the EU's capacity to find common solutions to the priorities of the day—climate change, migration, agricultural trade and social justice—and to adapt appropriately to new demands on governance arising from the monetary and economic crisis, digitization, and advances in information and communications technology. Fiscal and economic union has been placed firmly on the agenda, with federal institutional reforms being regarded as ineluctable for eurozone members, and the idea of a Eurozone minister of finance, endowed with appropriate funding, is now being discussed publicly by EU leaders. The federal imperative has been made all the more relevant by the additional pressure for the EU to have a genuine external defence and security capacity. Combating radicalism and terrorism, and securing borders against illegal migration as part of a common policy to regulate migration remain elusive. Steps to strengthen common endeavour during 2015–16 were confirmed with the issue of the EU's Internal Security Strategy and the strengthened role of Europol's European Cybercrime Centre (EC3) in addressing and responding to cybercrime. By June 2016 pressure for a second Convention on the Future of Europe, one to reform and renew the EU, gained momentum. Former concerns surrounding treaty and constitutional change have given way to a more nuanced appreciation of the need to accommodate challenges more effectively and with less political posturing than in the past. Even so, right-wing and authoritarian domestic politics (notably in Poland and Hungary) also drove forward appraisal of how the EU was to maintain democratic values when a member state seemed reluctant to observe them.

This issue cannot be entirely separated from domestic strains in UK politics as Brexit unravelled. The British Government's statements came to accept that materially the UK was bound to the EU, no matter how much it protested at the jurisdiction of the ECJ, and all the safeguards and protections that being in the EU gave all members. It was disingenuous to suggest otherwise. It undoubtedly valued EU support and wanted to be a leading player in shaping EU external policy. However, it objects (at least rhetorically) to the kind of internal, constitutional implications and arrangements needed to facilitate this. Accordingly, it has become trapped in pseudo-constitutional circuitous wrangling reminiscent of the 1950s. The referendum outcome allowed old divisions far greater voice but could not be considered representative of public opinion. Whereas initially, in both the Labour and the Conservative parties, pro-EU MPs had been dismissed or silenced, as senior civil servants and policy advisers resigned or publicly expressed their deep misgivings, talk of a centrist party alarmed both. The tone and content of unrealistic claims began to be modified. The UK's political position over European integration has always been somewhat contradictory: it has simultaneously eschewed federal union, but argued for greater influence in areas where the EU per se lacked legal powers.

The original treaties have been revised each time the EU has been enlarged, and in 2012 relatively smaller changes were anticipated to accommodate yet more states on the brink of entry. A return to the prospect of a 'two-speed' Europe has been raised periodically since the mid-1970s, most recently by French President Emmanuel Macron in mid-2017. Meanwhile, Germany insists on giving the EU the genuine capacity and political will to address serious economic problems, with every state adhering to existing rules, commitments and obligations, and reducing malpractice and corruption, for which Bulgaria and Romania, in particular, continue to be criticized, together with their law enforcement and legal systems. This precluded them from being allowed full participation in the EU's internal, policing, security and Schengen systems. This issue persisted in 2013–17, not least because Ukraine sought a special relationship with the EU, and Georgia pushed for association. With Serbia and Albania, *inter alia*, seeking accession, difficulties mounted. For its part, Russia suggested that a legal review was needed of the process by which the Baltic states had gained independence and, by implication, been able to seek EU membership.

EU constitutional change, however, has been a largely intergovernmental process since the European Council meeting held in Milan, Italy, in 1985, which led to the single market programme of 1992 and subsequently to the Treaty on European Union (also known as the Maastricht Treaty). What has changed since then has been the interest and capacity of EU institutions to engage with the public in seeking feedback for reform ideas, both those directly prompted by citizens' initiatives and calls for input from the European Commission itself, whether by means of questionnaires relating to policy initiatives and draft papers, photography competitions (of the EU 'in your region'), or youth and cultural events. Since the 2014 elections to the European Parliament, when average turnout across the EU fell slightly, to 42.5% (compared with a peak of 61.9% at the first Euro-elections in 1979), public attitudes towards the EU have been problematic, partly because governments have successfully portrayed the EU as 'distant', unresponsive to or 'disconnected' from the people. The Brexit referendum reversed this, especially when the British Government started to use citizens' rights as a bargaining chip in the negotiations, in direct opposition to the agreed position of member states. Until then, it had been easier for governments to blame domestic problems on the EU and to use sometimes acute scepticism (especially in some member states) over the impact of enlargement to include Bulgaria and Romania in 2007, Croatia in 2013, and prospectively Turkey and others. Turkey exploited its pivotal position in the migration crisis and its potential EU membership in exchange for tougher policing of its borders. This issue also featured in the UK referendum.

As historic as the 2004 enlargement was, many of the issues that plagued the earlier IGCs remain problematic. Public disillusionment seemed to be manipulated by external media interests. The EU's image as cumbersome was not erased by the ratification of treaties amending the treaties on the basis of which the Communities and the EU were founded—namely the Single European Act (1986), TEU (1992), the Treaty of Amsterdam (1997), the Treaty of Nice (2001) and, most recently, the Lisbon Treaty signed in December 2007, which entered into force on 1 December 2009. Further reform was intended to be unnecessary for many years, but the eurozone crisis impelled further action.[6] The economic recession added a further imperative, as the older EU member states increasingly saw themselves as the paymasters for policies sought and voted for by newer states under majority voting rules. The implicit resource distribution and the commitment to economic prosperity placed a premium on governments advancing research and innovation, at a time when the public was not inclined to endorse enlargement at all, especially when polls suggested far higher degrees of unemployment and consequent demands on social welfare, health and education provision among migrant EU citizens in some member states. The widespread introduction of 'e-government' services, including weblogs and online discussions with politicians, failed to convince the public that the political class was listening to their concerns or taking measures to respond adequately to them.

However, by the time of the EU's 60th anniversary celebrations, EU leaders more keenly sought to close the gap between themselves and the public in terms of what the EU's priorities should be, to inform a political agenda, and to engineer sustainable prosperity and peace for the EU. This was not simply a response to the Brexit impact (and the UK's perceived self-importance). Rather, it responded to a generational change (as EU architect Jean Monnet's vision of integration had foreseen) in belatedly adjusting to the concerns of a generation adversely affected by austerity and unemployment, and the dynamics of digital politico-socioeconomic innovation. This meant that the EU talked about reform both in terms of artificial intelligence and great transformative opportunities in a Digital Single Market and measures to combat so-called fake news that deceived citizens at the same time as it revisited much older ideas of how diversity in government approaches to the challenges of integration could be accommodated constitutionally. As a result, the old idea of a two-speed, multi-tier Europe resurfaced, if somewhat more adapted to the 21st century. Above all, however, leaders seek to ensure the EU's capacity to act credibly in existing areas, as well as future new ones. Chancellor Merkel's resolve to advance a unified EU position in the face of challenges from both sides of the Atlantic showed how Germany was giving the Union the means and capabilities to 'speak with one voice' in the international arena, enhancing them in such a way as to make the EU a respected, credible, independent force for peaceful conflict resolution and prevention in its own right.

Accordingly, its remit on foreign affairs and internal security continued to be strengthened. The Ukrainian–Russian flashpoint and pressure from refugees on its borders highlighted the continuing significance of the EU approach to seeking peace through practical, enduring conflict resolution measures.

The approach to reform continues patterns set in the past. Both at Maastricht and earlier[7] it had been argued that reforms should be gradual, modest and relatively cost-free. By 2008 it was accepted that this was overly optimistic, given several international crises, such as the growing number of states seeking EU membership (including some on its flanks and adjacent to the Mediterranean basin and the Middle East); the pressures of asylum seekers and economic migration; and, subsequently, terrorist attacks in EU cities. In addition, continuing regional conflict, the wars in Syria, Iraq and Afghanistan, and the international community's campaign against international terrorism, the economic recession and an isolationist US foreign policy precipitated rethinking of the EU's security capabilities, and its capacity to act collectively and integrate, in a supranational way, aspects of foreign and security policy that years earlier would have provoked concern at the implicit greater pooling of sovereignty. Internal and external security integration deepened. These actions had provided the legitimizing rationale for ever more resources being provided in these areas during 2014–17. The pro-Brexit arguments that leaving the EU would enable the UK to regain 'sovereignty' and 'democratic control' over its future seemed not merely vacuous after the terrorist atrocities in 2016–17, but deeply flawed. Even Prime Minister Theresa May had threatened to withdraw from security and judicial co-operation if the EU did not accede to the UK's Brexit demands.

The other 27 EU member states were unimpressed. Judicial co-operation continued to proceed, both as a means of enhancing the member states' collective ability to engage, apprehend and extradite terrorist suspects and to augment their ability to combat international organized crime in all its various guises:

from people trafficking (the majority of whom were used in the sex trade, and 12% of whom were forced into begging or used for their organs)[8], to the trade in illegal drugs, money laundering, fraud and cross-border crime. Europol's operational capabilities were progressively enhanced (see below) and its status changed, giving it greater authority and widening its remit. The British authorities had always adopted a somewhat contradictory approach to Europol's enhancement, but warned against withdrawal from such co-operative arrangements. Negative experiences with the European Arrest Warrant (EAW)—notably for British nationals accused of relatively minor offences—led the British Government to argue in favour of a conditional opt-in to the EAW after the UK had in effect withdrawn from all 133 EU provisions, under the Lisbon Treaty, in the area of police and judicial affairs, and continued conditional work with Europol and Eurojust. Opting in to areas of particular interest to individual member states continued during 2014–15, when Denmark explored this facility.

Brexit poses a major logistical threat to all this, which, in turn, makes Brexit materially impossible. The effectiveness of co-operation among lawyers and judges and the various legal services, such as Eurojust and FRONTEX (the role of which in border management intensified swiftly), influenced co-operation on cross-border civil law matters. Under the principle of availability established by The Hague Programme (and its successors), greater co-operation and mutual access to and exchange of data for combating crime and enhancing customs and fiscal processes accelerated. Automated information exchange and the growth of e-services and e-government, from the highest to the most local levels in the member states, was improved in the face of growing public fears over the use of information technologies (IT) for border control, biometric passports and live capture digital photographs for visas, and the cross-border transfer of personal data for unclear government and private purposes. A proximity paradox arose: the EU was becoming ever closer to its citizens (through biometric identifiers such as facial recognition) at the very time that the public was becoming increasingly distrustful of and alienated from governments. In February 2014 member governments continued their discussions on smart border initiatives and guidelines for cross-border law enforcement information exchange. Europol's EC3 unit assumed greater visibility from 2015. The series of terrorist attacks unmasked the implausibility of the suggestion that security co-operation could be at risk if the EU did not concede to the British Government's demands by way of Brexit.

In April 2016, following the adoption of the highly controversial updated PNR arrangements, the EU Commissioner for Migration, Home Affairs and Citizenship, Dimitris Avramopoulos, announced plans to create a single searchable interface to facilitate the work of law enforcement authorities. This again provoked objections, as police can already access the Advanced Passenger Information (API) database. The EU seeks an interoperable system to allow all police on the street immediate access to track entry and exit data, while the main such Entry-Exit System (EES) is being finalized to complement and bridge the Schengen Information System (SIS), Eurodac (see below), the PNR, Visa Information System and Automatic Number Plate Recognition (ANPR) systems, *inter alia*.[9]

Public suspicions over who collected and exchanged personal data grew as the media too picked up the issue of 'consent', ethical processing, the opportunity to have data deleted and amended. The European Data Protection Supervisor (who had published his *Guidelines on the Rights of Individuals with regard* to the Processing of Personal Data in February 2014) was less well known. Data loss by public and private agencies continued to exercise the public and national governments. In 2015 the French Commission Nationale de l'Informatique et des Libertés (National Commission for Informatics and Liberty) issued new rules on internet cookies, and the Belgian authorities gained more power in respect of issuing fines for data loss and breaches. These seemed small recompense for losses, both actual and anticipated, which some felt were increasingly likely given the rise in financial fraud, big data commercialization, identity theft and the exponential growth in cybercrime. By 2017 stringent German requirements and EU investment in research and measures to combat this were beginning to yield results. Policy sectors ceased to be seen as information silos.

The need for vigilance on related issues of transparency and public participation was reiterated in July 2014 in the European Ombudsman's letter to outgoing European Commission President José Manuel Barroso regarding weak provisions for public participation (compared to that of external stakeholders) in the ongoing, often tense, TTIP negotiations. The data protection issues were highlighted when the ECJ ruled that the Safe Harbour Agreement allowing the USA to process EU citizens' data was inadequate. It was superseded by an interim arrangement, the 'Privacy Shield', which was also criticized increasingly in 2016 and again in 2017 as inadequate compared with the EU's new regulation.[10] Accordingly, it was made subject to annual review. EU-US relations more generally were to become increasingly uneasy thereafter with the election of President Trump, who seemed to have a somewhat less nuanced appreciation of the issues in the TTIP, the North Atlantic Treaty Organization (NATO) and the EU than President Obama. He clashed immediately with Chancellor Merkel and new French President Macron and seemed to be widely disliked in the EU: online protests followed the announcement of what seemed to many to be a premature and precipitate official invitation to the UK after the referendum. The public mood seemed more aligned to that elsewhere in the EU than to the professed position of the May Governments. Whereas President Trump demanded that the EU 'pay more' towards defence as his own position became increasingly isolationist, the EU seemed to become more united. This was both in response to the UK referendum and to a deep-held belief that the EU was under threat from both the Russian Federation and the USA.

The EU's capacity to act credibly, both on the world stage and internally, evolves incrementally and sometimes in response to external threats. However, the existential threat that, according to British allegations, faced the EU was a British delusion. The EU became increasingly aware of how much public expectations exceeded its legal capacity to regulate in areas where the public appears to favour action—notably in respect of corporate tax evasion (where the EU is to boost regulation and action, against considerable UK and US pressure to desist), a genuine social pillar, possibly based on universal basic income, and measures to combat market dominance in some sectors. EU action over Facebook and Google was sometimes seen as dilatory and insufficient, but led to continued EU-Irish wrangling in resolving fines. However, the 60th anniversary celebrations resulted in a more thorough commitment to re-engage with a review of the future of the EU, and a reappraisal of reforms likely to meet the approval of a younger generation encumbered with, in some member states, falling socioeconomic expectations, unemployment and debt.

The EU is in a constant state of evolution. Reform in the scope of the EU's competence is necessary if it is to meet domestic and external expectations that it can act with unity and is willing, and financially and politically able, to undertake greater responsibilities commensurate with its pretensions to being a major international player. In addition, while the EU still clings to the notion of itself as a civilian power devoid of military intention or capacity, political rhetoric suggests that it should assume responsibility for preserving socioeconomic and political stability and promoting peaceful resolution of conflicts inside the EU and on its immediate eastern flanks, using member states' military resources and through assistance from policing agencies. This still sits most uneasily with its far more limited preferred role and competences, defined first by the Treaty of Rome and then by the amendments introduced through the Single European Act (SEA). The development of a more coherent, autonomous diplomatic capacity became inevitable, even if controversial, following the Lisbon Treaty's introduction of the EU's External Action Service (EEAS) and reform of the Council presidency.

External Involvement and Security Concerns

The EU is an international player in its own right. Its strategic partnerships with principal international players, presence in the UN and the General Agreement on Tariffs and Trade (GATT), and range of bilateral Association Agreements with a number of states in its vicinity are reflected in its network of some 140 EU delegations and offices around the world, which have a similar function to those of an embassy. The EU's strong attachment to safeguarding human rights, working multilaterally to find peaceful resolutions to conflicts, reflects the underlying ethos on which the EU was itself founded. It also attests to the fact that the EU per se has not replaced the foreign offices, embassies and consulates overseas of EU member states. They have increasingly pooled their functions and collaborated, notably to assist each other's citizens. The internal–external dimension, however, has become increasingly indistinct. Expectations of what the EU should deliver continue to exceed by a long way what it can feasibly deliver, given its limited capacity and capabilities. This is a situation that third states can exploit. The extent of the EU's external involvement, whether by dint of the growing presence and support for Rapid Reaction forces or its civilian emergency relief and policing role—as initially in Bosnia and Herzegovina and elsewhere—adds to multi-agency involvement in the presentation of the EU's role in the world. The operational requirements appear to outstrip the political institutions and accountability mechanisms that make expenditure and action in these areas subject to appropriate controls and legitimation.

Such issues have become increasingly hidden in the rhetoric of European integration as implying the demise of the nation state and the creation of a European super state. Their impact has been presented as being dealt with through the semantic nuances of subsidiarity. This cannot obscure, however, the qualitative change in European integration that is gradual and responds, often, to an external agenda and external expectations as to what role would be appropriate for the EU to play on the world stage as much as internally. Every new enlargement has brought in states with additional external concerns, priorities and agenda for enlargement and spending.[11]

Concern remains over the implications of further integration for security. This continues to be problematic for Norway (a non-EU state even though it participates in many EU forums) and for initiatives designed to improve the EU's capacity to sustain freedom, security and justice in the wake of further enlargement and the application of the Hague Programme principles of availability and proportionality in the exchange of information by law enforcement bodies seeking to combat international crime.[12] These principles include non-EU states and continue to extend the EU's reach into internal security. This has precipitated public fears concerning the access of law enforcement agencies to personal data, data retention, data protection and privacy. There has been corresponding criticism and some successful intervention on behalf of the citizen by the EU Ombudsman, the Office of the European Data Protection Supervisor (EDPS) and the European Parliament's Committee on Civil Liberties (known as LIBE). However, in 2012–17 the proposed reform of the EU Directive on data protection and its transformation into a Regulation[13]—to ensure consistency, among other things, in its application across the EU-28—elicited fierce opposition from vested interests outside the EU, as well as blatant filibustering from national governments. Over 3,500 amendments had been tabled by mid-2013, leading the then EU Commissioner for Justice, Fundamental Rights and Citizenship, Viviane Reding, in the wake of revelations regarding the USA's clandestine mass electronic surveillance programme known as PRISM, to urge swift resolution and a review of the 2000 Safe Harbour Agreement on data exchange between the EU and the USA.[14] The agreement had been poorly enforced and its data protection principles were weak. In February the EDPS insisted on responsibility for effective IT security and EU action to lead education on security of data processed on the internet.[15] Challenges in the courts to Google and Facebook underlined the attendant issues and problematic nature of resolution in the face of a patchwork of rules and laws.

National parliaments too have begun to take a more critical and vigilant stance as e-government and e-administration encroach on many of the elements of privacy in a way that citizens now suspect leaves them open to international fraud (online), and tracking and surveillance by invisible state and non-state agencies, whether territorially or virtually. However, confusion over large and complex data and the intentions of governments selling public data to private companies persists. Both the European Parliament and national parliaments are given more information since 2012 following the establishment of the Standing Committee on Operational Co-operation in Internal Security (COSI) under Article 71 of the TFEU and Article 6(2) of Council Decision 2010/131/EU. In a report to COSI covering July 2014 to December 2015, growing support for data exchange had been observed in the light of the terrorist attacks in France in January and November 2015). Two extraordinary COSI meetings were convened immediately to prepare and monitor a series of counter-terrorism measures. The related EU Internal Security Strategy (ISS) had been adopted in December 2014 and informed the Commission's Communication on the European Agenda on Security (COM (2015) 185 final). COSI prepared the conclusions on the renewed EU ISS 2015–20, adopted by the Council in June 2015, and it discussed the implementation of the EU Policy Cycle as a model in the fight against organized crime.

Europol issued its first Interim EU Serious and Organised Crime Threat Assessment (SOCTA) in March 2015, which determined priorities for the 2014–17 Policy Cycle, changed the funding arrangements (known as EMPACT) to support action against illegal immigration and firearms in the wake of the continuing migration crisis and terrorism, and strengthened the use of Interpol's Stolen and Lost Travel Documents database. Operational information exchange was augmented and monitored. This involved the European Network of Law Enforcement Technology Services (ENLETS), the informal network of contact points and the Maritime Analysis and Operations Centre—Narcotics (MAOC—N). Representatives from justice and home affairs agencies (Europol, Eurojust, FRONTEX and the European Police College—CEPOL) were regularly involved in relevant discussions. Occasional input was provided by the European Agency for the operational management of large-scale IT systems in the area of freedom, security and justice (eu-LISA), the Fundamental Rights Agency (FRA) and the European Asylum Support Office (EASO).

Customs agencies were also involved. A new action plan for 2016–17 focusing on co-operation among law enforcement authorities was adopted to strengthen the link with the EU Policy Cycle, especially in respect of action to combat illegal firearms and drug trafficking, counterfeit goods and excise fraud. This mirrored priorities on reinforced Schengen work, information sharing and operational co-operation. Europol was charged with developing an EU Internet Referral Unit (EU IRU) by July 2015 as an integral part of its European Counter Terrorism Centre, officially launched on 25 January 2016.[16] Efforts to achieve interoperability between the Second Generation Schengen Information System (SIS II), Interpol's Stolen and Lost Travel Documents (SLTD) database and its Illicit Arms Records and tracing Management System (iARMS) continue (Council of the EU 5299/2/16 Rev2).

National, regional and local police and law enforcement agencies work increasingly with their EU counterparts, as well as with Europol and Eurojust, both of which were the subject of reform in 2016,[17] to try to combat cybercrime. An EU cybercrime capacity has been established to combat e-crime. Co-operation on justice and law enforcement (home affairs) has grown exponentially in highly contentious and sensitive policy areas in the field of freedom, security and justice.[18]

Whereas the draft Constitutional Treaty aimed to expand democratic accountability and scrutiny powers to national parliaments as well as, crucially, the European Parliament under these areas, operational requirements could fall prey to continuing divisions over the implications of treating such sensitive issues under intergovernmental or supranational decision-making rules. By 2008 the growing feeling among politicians and thinktanks alike, that the balance between liberty and security was out of kilter, led to successful pressure for the introduction of the post of Commissioner for Justice in the new Commission to bolster the work of the EU Ombudsman, EDPS and the ever vigilant civil liberties committee of the European Parliament. Nevertheless, concerns that the British government planned to use the EU Withdrawal Bill to remove protection for citizens merely reinforced pressure for the EU to have a distinctive, independent voice in these areas, not least because the EU approach to data protection seeks greater protection for EU citizens, regardless of place of residence, than many third countries and organizations want, owing to their less stringent arrangements.

This accounts for the continuing debate over the enforceability of the misleadingly termed 'right to be forgotten' (a principle of EU data protection since 1995 that in May 2014 was extended by the ECJ to search engines). Facebook's privacy policy changes to the WhatsApp messaging service subsequently came under scrutiny. In complying with the ECJ ruling, Google undertook to remove pages breaching EU privacy laws on request, subject to certain ambiguous qualifications, such as whether the host was under Irish or other jurisdiction. While the European Parliament adopted the draft Regulation, the Council prevaricated. The UK sought the deletion of this 'right'. However, when the British House of Lords in July 2014 termed it 'unworkable, unreasonable and wrong in principle,'[19] the EU Commissioner for Justice, Martine Reicherts, disputed this assessment, stating that the 'right to be forgotten' was not a 'super right' trumping others, such as the freedom of expression and of the media, but one empowering citizens to manage their personal data. When, in August 2016, Socialist member of the European Parliament (MEP) Marc Tarabella signalled his intention to query the conformity of location-based mobile application game Pokémon Go with the EU's new General Data Protection Regulation, the EU's position as an advocate for the rights of citizens not to become commercial resources for companies in the age of the Internet of Things and People placed a significant burden on it. Keeping pace with technological innovation placed exceptional new demands on its capacity to respond with appropriate legislation. The goal of realizing the potential of the Digital Single Market, however, served to push the issue up the agenda.

When the new, post-Treaty of Lisbon European Commission took office in 2010, the drive for reforms to match policy developments—including, crucially, greater concentration of effort among the portfolios concerned with advancing e-government service delivery, e-commerce, the proposed single e-payments system (which eventually entered into force in August 2014), e-judicial co-operation and easy access to services for citizens—resulted in a renewed emphasis on advancing the digital economy, harnessing the potential of the internet for cross-border information exchange and automating as many transactions as possible by pushing for 'interoperability'. The European Digital Single Market strategy was formalized in April 2015. Associated Commission Directorates-General responsible for related areas were reformed in June 2016.

The European Digital Single Market strategy dovetails with the EU's ISS because both have a strong interest in resilient, trustworthy, credible, authentic identity management. They address the question of facilitating 'convenient anytime anywhere' access to private and domestic services in the age of the Internet of Things, and smart environments, complete with the attendant risks and opportunities. They recognize the hype but are committed to enabling each citizen to use an electronic identity token or card (probably containing at least some biometric data) to access services of whatever type, wherever they happened to be, without having to input repeatedly the same information. They also tie in with the hopes of governments that administrative costs could be reduced by overcoming barriers to access to information posed by incompatible legacy systems. The implementation of 'interoperability' measures, however, is not risk-free, and there is growing concern, and ever greater criticism from the EDPS and LIBE over lax data handling by companies and public agencies, erratic application of data privacy and data protection laws, side-stepping of the principles of data proportionality and data minimization, purpose limitation, 'function creep' and 'mission creep' (when projects are expanded beyond their original goals), outsourcing, and public-private outsourcing arrangements that save public money but expose individuals to greater risk of identity and data theft. Since late 2009, the ethical implications for citizens of practices that compromise the integrity and security of their personal data have been increasingly highlighted: Google, Swift, and advertisers tracking online behaviour (including automated facial recognition applications) are among those that have been taken to task (with some modest success) by the EU.

At the same time, the EU and the EDPS have adopted a far more critical position with regard to data exchange with non-EU states. For example, the review of the US-EU PNR data exchange arrangement in 2010 emphasized EU dissatisfaction with the inadequate reciprocity involved. The USA was criticized both for not sharing data with the EU and for embedding 'mission creep' in the use of personal data derived from the PNR that facilitated both profiling and pictures of passengers' 'associates' who had not even travelled to the USA.[20] The issue continues to hamper discussions on border management as well as wider discussions over data 'harvesting' and 'linkage'.

Although the automated border controls introduced as part of this were not as reliable as had been anticipated, the principle has been established. In July 2013 the European Commission discussed aspects of data exchange with the USA with a view to tightening provisions and, specifically, enforcing the seven core principles of the binding Safe Harbour Agreement: notice, choice, onward enforcement, security, integrity, access and enforcement. Since the drawing up of the Agreement in 2000 only one court case had been launched regarding non-compliance. When it was ruled in 2015 that the Safe Harbour Agreement was deficient compared with the EU's new draft regulation, and that its successor, the Privacy Shield, left much to be desired, EU-US tensions over privacy and access to data created by EU citizens and those in the EU remained problematic. With the German and French authorities adopting strong privacy-preserving positions, the EU began to be accepted as an authoritative, independent, ethical voice in international fora. By 2017 the EU was widely regarded as a 'model'.

The appearance of the EU as a more independent player on the international stage has advanced even though clusters of regional states (such as in the Balkans) continued to have particular points of view reflecting geopolitical concerns. At the same time, efforts continued to improve interaction and multilateral diplomacy with emerging powers, such as the People's Republic of China, India and Brazil. Bilateral and multilateral progress on trade and commerce broadened in scope. The furore in mid-2013 over the US PRISM programme, and alleged associated espionage within and on EU governments, organizations and individuals, delayed but has not entirely halted the commitment to facilitating EU-US trade. Difficulties over climate change targets, the EU's vision of an energy union driving a circular economy, and 'dumping' and human rights periodically rise to the top of the agenda, but have been increasingly swamped by the demands of managing the continued impact of the economic crisis and illegal immigration into the EU. The ideas of 'interoperability' took on greater salience as the old artificial divisions between policy areas associated with domestic activities (commerce and policing) were clearly linked to external activities (border controls of all types, diplomacy and trafficking). The Commission's 2015 Communication confirmed this.

The Ministerial Declaration published in November 2009 in Malmö under the Swedish presidency had emphasized goals to be attained by capitalizing on e-government and interoperable service delivery by 2015. This had been unanimously agreed by ministers responsible for e-government policy of the EU member states, accession states and candidate countries, and of the EFTA countries, who were to collaborate closely with the European Commission in order to define new actions based on EU policy priorities for the period 2011–15, underpinned by obligations under national and European legislation, in particular those on privacy and data protection and administrative procedures. Again, the hype risks outstripping capacity to deliver: e-government costs and capabilities, together with data loss and spiralling cost scandals, e-payments, and the rising use of near field communication, contactless cards and service delivery via mobile telephony, raise new concerns. The growth of cybercrime placed significant sociolegal and, especially, political demands on those responsible for gaining legislative acceptance of operationally vital measures. As the EC3 unit stated in April 2015: 'Law enforcement needs to invest in capacity building with a view to acquiring the necessary skills, expertise, knowledge and tools to perform cybercrime investigations, Big Data analysis and Internet of Everything related digital forensics. This should range from first responder training on the basic principles of cybercrime, to team leaders managing international cybercrime investigations and ideally be co-ordinated at an EU level to ensure harmonization'. Cybercrime as a business model is to be disrupted by cross-border co-operation of a type that would have politically too sensitive even a decade ago.

Then, as in the 1990s, the functioning of the single market imposed new demands for supranational action on areas that had hitherto been the preserve of national governments. Labour mobility rules under the SEA's provisions on the 'four freedoms' of movement—of goods, people, capital and services—to realize the single market meant that if internal frontiers were removed and the external frontier around the EC strengthened, there would be consequences for internal and external border controls of legal and illegal movement of people and goods, as well as customs formalities. Among such issues were immigration, refugees, asylum, police and anti-crime activities.[21] From this point onwards, the EU's competences in combating crime grew rapidly, often covertly through the soft law options that introduced Europol and progressively expanded its remit from a data-gathering body to an agency with real operational capacity, missions and tasks by 2003, and a recognized EU Agency in 2007. Other agencies (for example, FRONTEX) charged with managing the EU's external borders have become increasingly important reference points even though their formal powers and budgets remain limited. FRONTEX presaged the controversial goal to create an operational EU Border Guard, also dealing with the pressures of illegal migration on the EU's flanks, and with the associated maritime problems in relation to irregular trade in people and goods. Its role has grown, as regional wars and instability in the Middle East and Africa led to waves of illegal immigrants arriving in states ill-equipped to deal with them, and with states responding in vastly different ways.

As long ago as the 1990s, the pressures of illegal immigration necessitated a review of the notion of EC or EU citizenship. The European Parliament linked the idea of political rights and obligations (such as the right to contest and vote in direct elections) with the far more limited concept of citizenship,[22] deriving solely from a concept of economic rights—that is, those relating to labour mobility—customarily inferred from the Treaty of Rome and later the SEA and single market programme. In 2003 disagreement persisted over citizenship. On the one hand, possession of EU citizenship rested on the conferment of, or entitlement to, the citizenship/nationality of one of the member states. On the other hand, this created inequalities between citizens and 'non-citizens', i.e. others, whether legal or illegal residents, asylum seekers or refugees. Measures to promote social inclusion, racial harmony and family unification were adopted over the next 10 years and pressure to have a common immigration policy led to action. An increasing number of states came to be concerned about the respective rights of residents, citizens, asylum seekers and third country nationals who had illegally settled inside the EU's borders. Amnesties did not overcome these problems and suspicion grew that member states were offloading the problem of economic migrants or asylum seekers onto their neighbours, thereby shifting onto them the burden of border management and of providing social welfare and health services to the migrants and asylum seekers. This is illustrated by the situation at the Brussels Eurostar terminal, where Belgian exit controls are followed by British passport entry controls before baggage checks. Such practices exist elsewhere in the world, for example in northern Africa and in Asia. The French and British Governments struggle more now with the pressures arising from illegal migrant camps near the Channel Tunnel terminal in Calais. In 2015–16 the UK provided more physical assistance and fencing to the French authorities amid increasingly strenuous efforts by those seeking to board trains and lorries to enter the UK without transport documents or tickets. Such pressure induced greater understanding of the need for an EU policy on asylum and migration shaped in line with member states' interests. This had been controversial since the time of the Treaty of Amsterdam, and increasingly so with issues such as the Irish border, endangered by Brexit.

The Treaty of Amsterdam reformed the third pillar in such a way as to bring asylum, visa and immigration policy into the first pillar (covering economic, social and environmental policies), which was where it logically fitted in view of the single market and its four freedoms. The Schengen Agreement was incorporated into the treaty (with qualifications and exceptions for a few states, notably the UK), as was the Prüm Convention (which made provision for sharing of information to combat cross-border crime, and mutual access to fingerprint and DNA data).[23] Pursuant to Article 13 of the 'Prüm implementing Decision' (Council Decision 2008/616/JHA of 23 June 2008), member states provide statistics to the presidency of the Council of the European Union on how often they access data held in another state. This is designed to ensure that forensic searches of, for example, DNA databases, are not off-loaded onto other states, thereby overstretching their management capacity. Bilateral agreements among heavy users are permitted. Overall, however, there has been an ongoing problem regarding the capacity of different IT systems to manage and become interoperable, the costs of new systems (the SIS II and Visa Information System II), ethical issues and access rights. By the early 2010s there was far greater recognition of the implications of public and private services that required the enrolment of biometric data before people could access services of various kinds. Issues of disproportionality, ethics, equality and dignity assumed greater prominence, as concern grew over the trend for several governments to outsource the handling of sensitive citizen data to private companies, some of which were based outside the EU and therefore potentially outside the scope of the

EU's data protection rules. As a result, the European Commission revised the existing 1995 Directive and proposed its replacement with a Regulation, which would bind not only member states but any individual based anywhere in the world who was handling data about EU citizens. It was finally adopted in April 2016 following a number of delaying tactics and revisions to dilute its provisions, and is expected to come into force in 2018. It creates a single set of rules, with a separate component on data protection rules for the police and criminal justice sectors. Mass surveillance or indiscriminate bulk collection of data is not permitted. Encryption and data protection (privacy) by design are enabled. Non-EU companies have to apply the same rules as EU companies and thus may not use differential 'cheaper' less privacy-compliant rules to gain competitive advantages. The General Data Protection Regulation is seen as setting a high standard internationally.

Insistence on EU values and norms continues to be reflected in discussions with third states seeking EU accession. Human rights remain problematic in these terms and also in relation to trade and international agreements. All countries seeking membership have to comply; respect for human rights is a condition of EU membership. Clear signals are given to would-be members that respect for the rule of law and democratic principles taken for granted in the older 15 member states remain a precondition of entry: the common treaty provisions refer to liberty, democracy, human rights and the rule of law. EU accession to the European Convention on Human Rights is vital.

The overarching preoccupation remains border management as part of the progressive establishment of an area of freedom, security and justice, in which the free movement of people is assured in conjunction with appropriate measures on external borders, immigration, asylum and the prevention and combating of crime (particularly international organized crime). Measures have been approved to strengthen administrative co-operation, and police and judicial co-operation to these ends, including Eurodac (the EU's first experiment with collating biometric data—fingerprints of illegal immigrants), harmonized measures on short stays in the EU for less than three months (a highly charged area that overlaps with member states' rights to conclude or uphold bilateral agreements with third countries), common codes on visas and consular co-operation, and citizen 'tests' (with preconditions relating to the would-be migrant citizen's linguistic competence and appreciation of the local norms and cultures). Agreement also covers biometric identity cards and tracking for third country nationals crossing into the EU, and monitoring their entry and exit (notably at universities and colleges) to combat the practice of colleges being a vehicle for illegal migration or trafficking.

Based on a proposal by the European Commission, the European Council statement of 23 April 2015 committed member states to taking rapid action to save lives and boost EU action on migration. It prescribed relocation (making use of the emergency response mechanism under Article 78(3) of the TFEU) and resettlement arrangements, and economic inducements, which had to be adapted as migration increased throughout 2015–16. The controversial idea of quotas for all EU states, following Germany's announcement of an 'open door' policy, was met with resistance. Turkey was encouraged to manage borders and migrants more effectively and given greater assistance accordingly, which was exploited politically.

Nevertheless, progress has been outstripped by demand. The EU Action plan (2015–20) against migrant trafficking needs to be reviewed. It began listing suspicious vessels; facilitating dedicated programmes to enhance co-operation and the exchange of information with financial institutions; and co-operating with internet service providers and social media platforms to ensure swift detection and removal of internet content used by traffickers to advertise their activities. Other measures recommended systematic fingerprinting of migrants on arrival to enable the EU's common asylum system to work effectively. 'Hotspot' teams from EASO, FRONTEX and Europol identify, register and fingerprint incoming migrants and assess those needing protection. The Commission also sought to improve the EU Blue Card scheme, designed to ease entry for highly skilled people, which has been under-utilized. A new Operational Plan for Operation Triton set out maritime, land, air, and human 'assets'; and extended Triton southwards to the borders of the Maltese search and rescue zone to cover the area of the former Italian Mare Nostrum operation.[24]

It is clear that the EU's long-held conviction that it is no more than a civilian power is being increasingly challenged as it is called upon by third parties to engage in policing, knowledge transfer and conflict prevention-type roles in troubled areas. Inevitably, this affects the EU's self-image, its role conception and its vision of what contribution its members may hope to make to world prosperity and peace. That the EU as such is expected to play a role shows the extent to which it has become externally accepted and how, in the member states, governments increasingly see the EU as their reference point for external action. This would have been inconceivable 20 years ago.

However, it cannot be inferred that the EU is a state, is akin to one or is attempting to become one. Rather, the major changes that have taken place without formal treaty reform symbolize a growth in mutual trust and understanding, recognition of the relative weakness of the member states individually (as opposed to the EU collectively) to play major influential roles in the world by themselves, and a more realistic assessment of what is feasible against overly optimistic aspirations. Moreover, the exponential impact of ICTs and scientific advances places a premium on the EU being able to encourage research, innovation and development for the benefit of all. Mobilizing that kind of capacity requires governments to rethink even more radically what the purpose is of the EU and how they can contribute to shaping and giving effect to a new agenda in a changing world.

The EU's independence would be compromised without a strong role for the European Parliament, which plays a largely unrecognized, but extremely important, role in constitution-building, especially in ensuring that new areas of competence and responsibility bestowed by the member governments on the EU are subject to appropriate scrutiny, for example in respect of anti-terrorism measures—often impelled by US pressure (such as the exchange of passenger name records)—and that sensitive matters concerning data protection, civil liberties, co-operation in relation to drug trafficking, asylum and police affairs, and the proper role and supervision of Europol increase in salience. These were presaged in the 1990s with the pressure among some governments for a charter of fundamental human rights and freedoms to be accepted by the EU, either by accession to the Council of Europe's Convention (the European Convention for the Protection of Human Rights and Fundamental Freedoms), or in a separate bill of rights.[25]

The European Parliament can innovate even where the treaty framework seems more restrictive, by means of inter-institutional agreements. These work on the European Parliament's principle that anything not expressly forbidden by the treaties is allowed. Although designed to improve harmonious working and interinstitutional relations, they and other informal changes have significant implications over the longer term for constitutional amendments to enhance the European Parliament's authority, its legislative capacity and its supervisory powers, which are designed to ensure the democratic accountability of the EU's executive bodies and of the Court of Auditors, the ECJ, the European Council, the European Central Bank (ECB) and the Ombudsman (elected for the first time by the European Parliament in July 1995).[26]

Openness and Transparency

A declaration annexed to the TEU (the Declaration on the Right of Access to Information) affirmed member governments' acceptance of transparency as a condition of democracy. On 25 October 1993 the Council, European Commission and European Parliament concluded an inter-institutional agreement on democracy, transparency and subsidiarity, which was designed to enhance openness. In practice, however, the impression was left—and remains to this day—of a democratic deficit residing primarily within the ranks of a Commission that is perceived as closed, and by the mid-2010s as out of touch with a public disenchanted with austerity. The British Government's initial refusal to publish its position on Brexit, however, helped to demonstrate how open and transparent the EU was. Its leading negotiators (Michel Barnier for the European Commission and Guy Verhofstadt for the European Parliament, along with the European Council President Donald Tusk) immediately published statements and their papers on the public webpage.

Throughout 2014–17 the Commission continued to address issues over lobbying, transparency, citizen responsive initiatives and more recent concerns over media concentration and censorship in some EU states.

Democratic Legitimacy

Ensuring democratic legitimacy is not simply a question of elections, and of reforming the current electoral provisions to bring national provisions broadly into line under a system of proportional representation. Nor is it only a matter of improving the transparency, efficiency, accountability and democratic nature of EU institutions. Inadequate parliamentary control over the European Commission, and especially over the Council of the European Union, coupled with the absence of direct elections, originally lay at the heart of the democratic deficit. However, the democratic deficit is not just a problem of the distribution of power among EU institutions, but also affects interactions at all levels of government, especially as the implementation of policy is carried out at those levels.

The authority of EU institutions is open to challenge, notably by dissatisfied national political élites, which can manipulate dissent and blame the supranational institutions for their own failings. The increase in the European Parliament's powers paradoxically made its actions more visible, but not necessarily more tangible or intelligible. Further confusion as to the extent of popular authority persists given the role of a Committee of the Regions (CoR) with negligible powers. This compounds the problem of national parliaments having a small role, and one which Eurosceptics plausibly condemned as inadequate. The Commission and member governments are addressing this, not simply because of its relevance to Brexit and the different roles member governments have allowed their national parliaments to play in scrutinizing their own actions in EU decision making. Institutionalizing national parliaments at EU level would be costly and reminiscent of the days when MEPs were unelected appointees from national parliaments to a European Parliament devoid of any real legislative power but having the right to issue opinions. The CoR has not done much to help to bring the EU 'closer to the citizen' and has to work with MEPs in a mutually constructive way.

There is need for the nature and purpose of European Union to be clarified. The European Parliament's role remains contested, but it has perhaps the greatest responsibility—as the legatee of Altiero Spinelli's Draft Treaty establishing the European Union—to ensure that appropriate practices are enshrined in a representative, pluralist, democratic parliamentary system at EU level.[27] British Prime Minister David Cameron secured for the UK the deletion of a reference to commitment to forge 'an ever closer union' (in the preamble to the founding Treaty of Rome). This was considered disingenuous by some, and the British public were not convinced that it meant anything tangible. The outcome of the 2016 Brexit referendum, however, did provoke a degree of reflection in the EU-27 as to what the policy priorities should be for the EU in the coming decade. The principle of integration and an ever closer union remained uncontested as an ideal.

European Union: A Federal Future?

The progress of European integration towards some presumed federal destiny, analogous to the federal system of government in Germany, has often been measured by reference to the range of policies under the exclusive competence of the EC or EU institutions and to the powers of the European Parliament. The disagreement over the selection of the Commission President in 2014 exemplified this. MEPs and the ECJ have been seen to be the guardians of a federal destiny, and the ECJ's remit has also expanded. The treaty reforms have introduced measures to prevent a dilution of integration. The work on simplifying and consolidating the treaties into one—constitutional—document underscored this not only as a method to advance integration, but as a way to experiment with and set the principles for new legislation later to be adopted by all in the shape of the Treaty of Lisbon.[28] This put in place institutional arrangements and democratic controls that would allow the EU member states to meet those ideals more effectively than ever before. The prospect of further enlargement and the need to manage the economic crises afflicting many EU states have heightened appreciation among leaders of the necessity for co-operation and commonality if the EU is to have any impact at all on shaping the future world. Although adjustments would have to be made to withdraw UK officials and MEPs in the event of Brexit, in September 2016 the European Parliament endorsed the candidacy of the new British Commissioner for the Security Union.

The Future: Money, Money, Money

The Lisbon Treaty introduced innovations—such as the longer presidency of the European Council, headed by someone governments thought would be more of a civil servant than a politician (Herman Van Rompuy, who became the first permanent President of the European Council), and the creation of the EEAS. This was to be the EU's diplomatic corps, with its own staff, as well as a very large number drawn from the member states. The European Parliament quickly insisted that the EEAS must complement national ministries of foreign affairs and that it should ensure that the EU become what the veteran German Christian Democrat Elmar Brok, MEP and rapporteur, termed a 'global player, not just a global payer'. The significance of this lies not only in the aim to ensure that the EU develops diplomatic capacity and weight in line with its economic influence, but in the fact that the European Parliament has the power to veto the EEAS budget. The power of budgetary concerns is one that cannot be overestimated as the various EU institutions and agencies vie for authority in overlapping areas of interest and competence. MEPs seek to guard against incoherence and have lobbied for experienced politicians, rather than civil servants, to assume senior EEAS posts, given that the EEAS structurally mirrors foreign offices, complete with directorates-general divided into geographical desks and 'multilateral and thematic' desks. It takes on consular work on behalf of smaller states unable to afford their own embassies around the world—something presaged in the earlier commitments to citizens that as EU citizens they would be able to call on the services abroad of states other than those of which they are nationals, in times of need, when their own state lacks a diplomatic post. That, too, is something that many British citizens fear has been lost since the referendum.

Increasingly, the EU is playing a role on the world stage that is founded on its commitment to realising peace and sustaining freedom and democracy on the basis of functional (often socio-economic) common endeavour. Migration flows and the pervasive securitization agenda mean that it will be difficult for member states to act coherently, consistently and accountably unless they deal with constitutional power-sharing and recognize how new technologies and new policy demands have undermined their ability to govern territorially. Digital borders raise questions about identity and also about the relevance of identity in territorially governed spaces[29]. Those questions at present cannot be answered without reference to more traditional forms of institutional means of ensuring that measures are in place to guard against the abuse of power. The EU also needs to be more overtly political in acknowledging why it may fall far short of the international system's expectations of it on climate change (as it did in 2015–17), carbon dioxide (CO_2) and diesel emissions, the fragmented digital market inside the EU, financial stability (exemplified by the threat in the mid-2010s of a Greek exit from the EU), sustainable water and food supplies, biometrics, ethical scientific endeavour, biodiversity, agriculture, world trade, poverty, migration and social justice. In addition, intra-EU mobility and access to welfare benefits became key issues in negotiations and bilateral talks surrounding Brexit.

The overarching question for the future, however, is how effective and how soon will be the introduction of reforms to increase the EU's capacity to deal with its member states' crises. European Commission President Barroso stressed in 2012 and again in 2013 the need for the EU institutions themselves to have greater powers in this respect. The fear expressed in 2012 highlighted concern over whether a eurozone banking union was feasible in the absence of comprehensive political union. By 2015 the fear was related to averting eurozone implosion and managing, rather than querying, a eurozone banking union. France, adopting its historical wariness of Germany, repudiates political union, a precondition of genuine economic union.

The ECB's role and ability to recapitalize EU banks has preoccupied EU policymakers, and attention also turned in the early 2010s to the need for a single banking supervisory mechanism for Europe, based on the ECB, in order to break the 'vicious circle' link between the debt crisis in the eurozone and struggling banks.[30] Concerns persist over the UK's budgetary contributions during any transitional Brexit period. It is clear that Brexit will cost the UK more than would remaining a full EU member.

In 2012 non-eurozone countries (such as the UK and Sweden) were to be invited to opt in voluntarily to ECB oversight. In a report on the vision of of Economic and Monetary Union, published in June 2012, the ECB accepted the need for what it delicately termed 'possible changes to the EU treaties at some point in time'. This did not, however, satisfy Chancellor Merkel, who mooted the idea of a second European Convention to expedite progress based on the consent of stakeholders and citizens. Several years later this was again on the agenda.

In the mean time, British rhetoric and demands for opt-outs and opt-ins have created a sense of confusion. The EU would welcome the UK remaining a member. Legal action against the soundness of the actual and contestable invocation of Article 50 is pending. Ireland has pointedly noted that it can veto any Brexit agreement (and clearly does not want a return to an internal border on the island of Ireland).[31] Both third state and EU leaders wish the UK to play a role commensurate with its position as an international financial centre and as a state known for finding pragmatic solutions to difficult questions in multilateral bodies. For the UK, many fear that leaving the EU will prove catastrophic. Remaining would require it to resume its place, this time in a spirit of collective endeavour, renewal and commitment.

Notes

1. www.euractiv.com (accessed 9 June 2016).
2. www.connexionfrance.com (accessed 6 June 2016).
3. Lodge, J. 'Done to death by slanderous tongue and ignorance in action', available at: www.univiennamedialab.wordpress.com/26/06/2016/done-to-death-by-slanderous-tongue-and-ignorance-in-action, 28 June 2016.
4. HM Government, 'Why the Government believes that voting to remain in the European Union is the best decision for the UK: the EU referendum', available at: www.gov.uk/government/uploads/system/uploads/attachment_data/file/515068/why-the-government-believes-that-voting-to-remain-in-the-european-union-is-the-best-decision-for-the-uk.pdf, 23 June 2016.
5. Lodge, J. 'Britain and the EEC: Exit, Voice or Loyalty?' in *Cooperation and Conflict*, Vol. 10, No. 4, Nov. 1975, pp. 199–216.
6. The Treaty on European Union includes a provision for amending the treaties. Under Article 48 any member state, the European Parliament or the Commission can submit proposals for amending the treaties to the Council. The Council then forwards proposals to the European Council, and the national parliaments are notified. If the European Council agrees to examine the proposed amendments, its President convenes a Convention composed of representatives of the national parliaments, the heads of state or of

government of the member states, the European Parliament and the Commission. The Convention examines the proposals for amendment and adopts by consensus a recommendation to an Intergovernmental Conference (IGC), which is convened by the President of the Council. Alternatively, and subject to the consent of the European Parliament, the European Council can also decide by a simple majority not to convene a Convention if a Convention is not justified by the extent of the proposed amendments, in which case it is the European Council itself that defines the terms of reference of an IGC, which is then convened by the President of the Council. In any case, an IGC composed of all the member states is convened (whether preceded by a Convention or not) and any amendment to the Treaties must be ratified by all the member states in accordance with their own constitutional requirements (see www.consilium.europa.eu/treaty-of-lisbon.aspx).

7. Corbett, R. *The Treaty of Maastricht*. London, Longman, 1993.
8. EUObserver, https://euobserver.com (accessed 19 May 2016).
9. EUObserver. 'EU wants single-click police access to personal data' (accessed 22 April 2016).
10. Under the proposed 'Privacy Shield', the USA is to provide an independent 'ombudsperson' to address complaints. US companies processing EU data must resolve complaints within 45 days. Data protection authorities in EU member states will have to work with the FTC to ensure these are resolved. A draft adequacy decision was also published. Privacy campaigner Max Schrems called it 'lipstick on a pig'. Dutch MEP Sophie in't Veld wondered how a US government official could be 'independent'. Orlowski, A. 'Safe Harbour v2.0 greenlights six bulk data collection excuses', available at: www.theregister.co.uk/2016/03/01/safe_harbour_20_oks_six_bulk_collection_excuses. 1 March 2016.
11. Lodge, J. 'Negotiating the European Union', in *Journal of International Negotiation*, Fall 1998; and Lodge, J. 'The European Parliament', in S. Andersen and K. Eliassen (Eds). *The European Union: How Democratic Is It?* London, Sage, 1996, pp. 187–214.
12. Lodge, J. 'eJustice, Security and Biometrics: the EU's Proximity Paradox', in *European Journal of Crime, Criminal Law and Criminal Justice*, Vol. 13, No. 4, 2005, pp. 533–564; and Lodge, J. '"Fortress Europe": Borders and the Power of Information in the European Union', in Magone, J. (Ed.). *Routledge Handbook on European Politics*, London, Routledge, 2015, pp. 132–152.
13. Proposal for a Regulation of the European Parliament and of the Council on protection of individuals with regard to the processing of personal data and on the free movement of such data (General Data Protection Regulation), proposed by the European Commission on 25 Jan. 2012, Brussels, COM (2012) 11 final. This seeks to amend Directive 95/46/EC; House of Lords, European Union Committee, 2nd Report of Session 2014–15, EU Data Protection law: A 'right to be forgotten'? London, Stationery Office Ltd, HL Paper 40.
14. Busch, A. 'From Safe Harbor to Rough Sea', in SCRIPTed, 2006, 3:4; Thompson, M. W., and van Wagonen Magee, P. 'US/EU Safe Harbor Agreement', Privacy Regulation, 2003, available at: www.ftc.gov.speeches/Thompson/Thompson.safeharbor.pdf.
15. Opinion of the European Data Protection Supervisor on the Communication from the Commission to the European Parliament and the Council on 'Rebuilding Trust in EU-US data Flows' and on the Communication from the Commission to the European Parliament and the Council on 'the Functioning of the Safe Harbor from the Perspective of EU Citizens and Companies established in the EU', Brussels, 20 Feb. 2014.
16. Council of the European Union. Draft report to the European Parliament and national Parliaments on the proceedings of the Standing Committee on operational cooperation on internal security for the period July 2014–Dec. 2015, 5299/2/16. data.consilium.europa.eu/doc/document/ST-5299-2016-REV-2/en/pdf, 26 Feb. 2016.
17. European Parliament. The European Public Prosecutor's Office (EPPO) and Eurojust, Public Hearing, Brussels, 24 May 2016.
18. See Europol EC3 The Internet Organised Crime Threat Assessment (iOCTA), Brussels, 2014; and Lodge, J. 'Justice and Home Affairs: Internal Security, Maastricht and the 1996 IGC', in A. Leicht (Ed.). *Wohin steuert die EU: Regierungskonferenz 1996*. Vienna, Signum, 1996, pp. 317–344.
19. House of Lords, European Union Committee, 2nd Report of Session 2014–15, EU Data Protection Law: a 'right to be forgotten'?, London, Stationery Office Ltd, HL Paper 40.
20. 'Trends in Biometrics' (2010), report for the LIBE Committee of the European Parliament by J. Lodge, and 'Quantum surveillance and shared secrets: a biometric step too far?' Brussels, CEPS, 2010, available at: ceps.eu.
21. *Berlin Declaration of Increased Co-operation in Combating Drug Crime and Organised Crime in Europe*. Brussels, Council Secretariat, 1994.
22. Closa, C. 'The Concept of Citizenship in the Treaty on European Union', in *Common Market Law Review*, No. 29, 1992, pp. 1137–1169.
23. Council of the EU Presidency note to the Ad Hoc Group on Information Exchange, Implementation of the Prüm Decisions regarding fingerprints—search capacities, Brussels, 27 April 2010; Lodge, J. 'Dark Side of the Moon: Accountability, Ethics and New Biometrics', in E. Mordini and D. Tzovaras (Eds). *Behavioural, Electrophysiological, Multimodal and Soft Biometrics: the Ethical, Legal and Social Context*. New York, Springer, 2013.
24. European Commission. Communication from the Commission to the European Parliament, the Council, the European Economic and Social Committee and the Committee of the Regions: A European Agenda on Migration, COM(2015) 240 final, 13 May 2015.
25. See Newman report on Human Rights in the EU, which was rejected by MEPs by 210 to 176, with six abstentions, on 18 May 1995, EP Working Document A4-76/95; Copenhagen European Council, *Déclaration sur la Démocratie*, 8 April 1978, Bulletin of the EC, 4-1978; Dublin European Council, *Déclaration sur l'Antisémitisme, le Racisme et la Xénophobie*, 25–26 June 1990, Bulletin of the EC, 6-1990; Luxembourg European Council, *Déclaration sur les Droits de l'Homme*, 28–29 June 1991, Bulletin of the EC, 6-1991; Maastricht European Council, *Déclaration sur le Racisme et la Xénophobie*, 9–10 Dec. 1991, Bulletin of the EC, 12-1991; Conseil et Etats Membres, réunis au sein du Conseil, *Résolution sur les Droits de l'Homme, la Démocratie et le Développement*, 28 Nov. 1991, Bulletin of

the EC, 11-1991; EP, *Le Parlement Européen et Les Droits de l'Homme,* Brussels, 1994; EP, *Déclaration sur les Droits et Libertés Fondamentaux,* 12 April 1989, Official Journal C120, 16 May 1989; EP, Council and Commission, *Déclaration Commune sur les Droits Fondamentaux,* Official Journal C103, 27 April 1977; Schermers, H. G. 'The European Communities Bound by Fundamental Human Rights', in *Common Market Law Review,* No. 27, 1990, pp. 249–258.

26. Millar, D. 'A Weak Ombudsman, a Weaker Parliament', in *European Brief,* 2, 1994.

27. Lodge, J. (Ed.). *The 2009 Elections to the European Parliament.* London, Palgrave Macmillan, 2010; Lodge, J. and Sarikakis, K. (Eds) *Communication, Mediation and Culture in the Making of Europe.* Rome, Il Mulino, 2013.

28. *Draft Treaty establishing a Constitution for Europe,* The European Convention, 20 June 2003.

29. Lodge, J. 'EU Homeland Security: Citizens or Suspects?', in *Journal of European Integration,* Vol. 26, Issue 3, 2004, pp. 253–279; Lodge, J. (Ed.). 'Are You Who You Say You Are?', in *The EU and Biometric Borders,* Nijmegen, Wolf Legal Publishers, 2007.

30. Euro Area Summit Statement, 29 June 2012, available at: www.consilium.europa.eu/uedocs/cms_data/docs/pressdata/en/ec/131359.pdf.

31. 'Just the Facts: EU and UK Documents and Position Papers on Brexit', available at: www.europeanmovement.ie.

FOREIGN AND SECURITY POLICY IN THE 21ST CENTURY: CHALLENGES AND OPPORTUNITIES

Ana E. Juncos

Introduction

The European Security Strategy, the first strategic reflection at the European Union (EU) level adopted in 2003, opened with the sentence 'Europe has never been so prosperous, so secure nor so free' (European Council, 2003). The optimism contained in this statement contrasts starkly with the opening remarks of the new EU Global Strategy, presented in June 2016 to the European Council by the EU's High Representative for Foreign Affairs and Security Policy, Federica Mogherini. The new security strategy states: 'We live in times of existential crisis, within and beyond the European Union. Our Union is under threat. Our European project, which has brought unprecedented peace, prosperity and democracy, is being questioned.' (EEAS, 2016). One year later this assessment still remains valid. Indeed, despite the institutional reforms brought forward by the Lisbon Treaty (2009), which included the establishment of the post of High Representative of the Union for Foreign Affairs and Security Policy and the European External Action Service (EEAS), there is agreement among both observers and policy-makers that the EU faces increasing political, economic and existential challenges.

Nothing reflects this environment better than the problems encountered by the EU's foreign and security policy. As described by another strategic review of the EU's global environment: we live in 'a more connected, contested and complex world' (EEAS, 2015). These challenges, however, also bring with them opportunities, as increasing interdependence allows for increased co-operation on issues of common interest, not only at the EU level, but also at the global level. This essay examines the principal challenges and opportunities confronted by the EU in the 21st century. In particular, it explores the EU's efforts to foster peace and democracy in its neighbourhood, and takes stock of the main achievements and failures thus far. The essay also examines the EU's attempts to build an autonomous security and defence policy, in particular in the area of crisis management, and the EU's role in a more multipolar world. Finally, this essay reflects on the prospects for the EU's foreign and security policy in the aftermath of the June 2016 referendum vote in the United Kingdom in favour of a British exit from the EU (commonly referred to as Brexit).

Securing the EU's Neighbourhood to the East and the South

As the EU has expanded over the years through the process of enlargement, it has come closer to new neighbours to the East and the South, but also to new threats emanating from these countries (conflicts, failed states, terrorism, human trafficking and organized crime). Thus, one of the main priorities for the EU has been to promote security and stability beyond its borders, particularly through the promotion of peace and democracy. First and foremost, the EU's enlargement policy has been the main mechanism to achieve this policy goal, as exemplified by the enlargements to admit countries from, *inter alia*, Central and Eastern Europe in 2004 and 2007, with the newest member being Croatia, which was admitted in 2013. The fact that other Western Balkan countries and Turkey have applied to become members of the EU testifies to the historic success of the enlargement policy, which was widely deemed the EU's most successful foreign policy initiative. By July 2017 five countries had been granted official candidate status: the former Yugoslav republic of Macedonia (FYRM), Montenegro, Serbia, Turkey and Albania. Bosnia and Herzegovina submitted an application for EU membership in February 2016. Meanwhile, the status of Kosovo remains unclear, as five EU member countries (Cyprus, Greece, Romania, Slovakia and Spain) have yet to recognize its independence. This has not prevented the EU from developing its relations with Kosovo through the signature of a Stabilization and Association Agreement in 2015. EU mediation between Serbia and Kosovo also constitutes one of the few major foreign policy successes of recent years, resulting in an historic political agreement that was signed in April 2013.

In recent years, however, the success of enlargement has been questioned by both internal and external events. Internally, 'enlargement fatigue' and the rise of Euroscepticism and populism in some European countries, as illustrated by the results of the 2014 European Parliament elections and the Brexit referendum, have eroded support for enlargement. Enlargement has thus disappeared from the EU's list of foreign policy priorities. This also explains the fact that the new European Commission led by Jean-Claude Juncker stressed that no further enlargement would take place during its five-year term. For countries wishing to join the EU, these developments call into question the EU's long-standing commitment to enlargement. The fact that the adoption of reforms in many of the candidate countries has been slow has also contributed to this state of affairs. In particular, the possibility of Turkish accession remains a divisive issue among the EU member states, especially given the increasingly authoritarian style of President and former Prime Minister Recep Tayyip Erdoğan. The crackdown that followed a failed coup attempt in July 2016, together with Erdoğan's calls to reinstate the death penalty, have worsened EU-Turkey relations. Finally, the result of the referendum on the UK's membership of the EU has added to this disenchantment with the EU project as, for the first time in the Union's history, a country is seeking to leave (rather than to join) the EU. However, Brexit could also provide an opportunity for the EU to show that the

EU project is alive and well by re-energizing the enlargement process.

Externally, enlargement and, more generally, the EU's policies for promoting democracy have been thwarted by the emergence of an 'arc of instability' from the East to the South (EEAS, 2015). Long gone are the EU's ambitions to create 'a ring of well governed countries to the East of the European Union and on the borders of the Mediterranean with whom we can enjoy close and co-operative relations' (European Council, 2003). Adopted in 2004, the European Neighbourhood Policy (ENP) was the EU's attempt to spread democracy beyond its borders. Governing relations between the EU and 16 neighbours to the East and the South, the ENP sought to promote reforms in exchange for financial incentives and closer relations with the EU, with the major exception that the offer of membership was explicitly excluded. It soon became apparent that this approach was not going to create the necessary momentum for reform and that at least some differentiation between the Eastern and Southern countries was needed. The conflict in August 2008 between Georgia and the Russian Federation contributed to the creation of a sense of urgency regarding the need for the EU to work to promote stability and prosperity in its Eastern neighbourhood. Hence, the Eastern Partnership, which was approved by the European Council in March 2009, was designed to advance the EU's relations with Armenia, Azerbaijan, Belarus, Georgia, Moldova and Ukraine.

The EU's troubles in the neighbourhood were only beginning, however. The so-called Arab Spring of popular uprisings in 2011 and the subsequent conflicts that engulfed the region from Egypt to Libya to Syria provided more evidence of the failure of the EU (and the West) to promote 'deep' democracy in the South. The revised ENP strategy adopted by the EU in 2011 constituted another attempt to respond to these events, by placing increased emphasis on the need to support the promotion of democracy and the use of positive and negative conditionality, including the creation of a new European Endowment for Democracy. Nevertheless, recent events, such as the deterioration of the situation in Libya and Yemen, the civil war in Syria, and the rise of the Islamic State in Iraq and the Levant (ISIL, subsequently renamed Islamic State) suggest that the ENP remains a dysfunctional policy that lacks real impact, and has led to a rethinking of the EU's policy. By proclaiming the idea of 'principled pragmatism', the EU Global Strategy of 2016 seems to suggest that the EU should focus on promoting peace and stability in the neighbourhood first, rather than democracy promotion. It is too early to say whether this change in strategy might be enough to solve some of these intractable conflicts.

The turn to a more realist or pragmatic foreign policy is also linked to Europe's attempt to safeguard its 'homeland security', particularly in relation to the threat of Islamic State terrorist attacks and the refugee crisis. Although the EU has a long history of fighting terrorism, efforts to combat Islamic State emerged as a new and pressing security issue in the Southern neighbourhood for the Union in 2014. Many European countries did not consider Islamic State to be a direct security threat at the time, but there were growing concerns about EU nationals travelling to the Middle East to join Islamic State and coming back to their home countries as radicalized jihadists. The EU did not take a leadership role in military efforts to counter the threat posed by Islamic State in Syria, Iraq and the wider region in the first year. Instead, the USA led the fight against Islamic State through an international coalition that carried out air strikes in Syria and Iraq, with most EU countries pledging support for the global coalition. Serious terrorist attacks in France in 2015 and 2016 were to change the situation, however. France became actively involved in the fight against Islamic State in 2015 and requested the support of other EU member states. The refugee crisis caused by the ongoing civil conflict in Syria only contributed to exacerbating the feeling of insecurity of many EU citizens (fuelled by Eurosceptic populist parties and the media). EU member states and institutions were caught both unprepared and divided regarding how to accommodate the hundreds of thousands of people fleeing one of the worst civil wars in the 21st century. Although by 2017 the high volume of refugee flows that affected Europe from 2015 had been reduced, some European countries, such as Italy, continue to receive more refugees than they can accommodate, and this also provides evidence of the lack of solidarity across the Union when it comes to the relocation of refugees.

Meanwhile, the deterioration of the political situation in Ukraine under President Viktor Yanukovych led to a new conflict on the EU's Eastern flank. In November 2013 the Government of Ukraine decided to suspend its preparations for the signature of an Association Agreement (including free trade arrangements) with the EU, for which negotiations had been concluded. This led to anti-Government demonstrations opposing Yanukovych and the occupation of Independence Square in the centre of the capital, Kyiv. The protests had dramatic consequences, ultimately leading to the collapse of the Yanukovych regime, Russia's annexation of the Crimean Peninsula in March 2014 and the ongoing conflict in the Donbass region.

Although the EU-Russia partnership had traditionally been difficult, as a result of the crisis in Ukraine relations reached a new low in 2014–15 and the current state of relations can be said to be anything but a 'partnership'. On the positive side, the EU member states managed to achieve a more cohesive stance towards the Russian Federation, including the adoption of several packages of sanctions. Nevertheless, there is still a lack of agreement among the EU member states over a post-sanctions strategy and how relations with Russia should be conducted in the medium and long term. Tensions between EU member states and Russia also relate to the latter's intervention in Syria and accusations of Russian efforts to undermine the electoral process in a number of states (so-called election hacking). In terms of EU-Ukraine relations, the EU has continued to support the new Government with the signature of an Association Agreement, which was finally ratified by the Dutch legislature in May 2017 after a controversial, non-binding referendum the previous year; the Agreement entered into force from the beginning of September. The crisis in Ukraine has led to a reinvigoration of the role of the North Atlantic Treaty Organization (NATO) in Europe and renewed concerns among some EU member states about territorial defence. It has also led to increased calls for the EU to strengthen its role in security and defence matters. It is to these issues that the following section turns.

Developing Autonomous Defence Capabilities and EU Relations with NATO

With open conflicts to the East and the South, discussions about the need for a strong EU security and defence policy came back to the table. In December 2013 the European Council discussed defence issues, for the first time in seven years. The opening sentence of the Council conclusions—'Defence matters'—symbolized what was at stake. The financial crisis of 2008 and the austerity policies that followed had reduced what were already very small defence budgets (only three EU member states meet the NATO target of 2% of defence expenditure as a percentage of GDP). The problem lies not only in the amount of money that European states spend on defence, but in the quality of their armed forces. Of a total of almost 2m. troops, fewer than 20% are deployable abroad. Other shortfalls in European capabilities relate to lack of intelligence, surveillance and reconnaissance (ISR) systems, strategic air-lift and air-refuelling capabilities, and unmanned vehicles. The election in November 2016 of US President Donald Trump, who had urged Europeans to do more on defence, and preparations for the exit of the UK from the EU brought new urgency to this debate, with EU leaders and the Commission adopting a new package of measures to improve the EU's defence capabilities. In November 2016 the European Commission proposed the European Defence Fund initiative to provide funding for research projects on defence technologies and for the development and acquisition of defence equipment and technologies. Other recent initiatives agreed by the EU member states include the establishment of a Military Planning and Conduct Capability for non-executive military capacity-building missions, the implementation of the Permanent Structured Cooperation initiatives, providing for increased co-operation in defence between particular countries, and ways to make better use of the EU Battlegroups.

Meanwhile, as mentioned above, the Ukrainian crisis has also had the effect of revitalizing NATO and its role in territorial defence in the European continent. At NATO summits in Newport, Wales, UK (2014) and Warsaw, Poland (2016), the Alliance emphasized its commitment to collective defence in the face of a resurgent Russian threat. It also supported these declarations with some concrete operational measures, such as the deployment of US troops to Eastern Europe. At the Warsaw summit of June 2016, the EU and NATO also declared their intention to co-operate more closely, for instance in the area of hybrid threats, cyber security and maritime security, and by co-ordinating exercises. The security challenges currently confronting NATO and the EU in Europe and beyond have provided new impetus for co-operation between the two organizations.

Russia's annexation of Crimea and the revival of NATO's security role in Europe has had the unintended consequence of bridging the gap between Atlanticists and Europeanists within the EU. Increasing insecurity in the continent and beyond has led some EU member states (such as Spain, Italy and Sweden) to become more pragmatic (and realistic) in their approach to the Common Security and Defence Policy (CSDP). Eastern European states such as Poland and Lithuania have pledged to increase their defence budgets to reach the NATO target within the next five years, and have supported the strengthening of both the EU and NATO. In other cases, this change of attitude pre-dates the events in Ukraine. A case in point here is France, which has adopted a much more pragmatic attitude towards the Alliance. This culminated with France's return to NATO's integrated command in 2009 during the presidency of Nicolas Sarkozy. The participation of France in NATO's Libya mission in 2011 was also reflective of this change of attitude. The UK and France jointly led the international intervention in Libya and closely co-operated within a NATO framework, demonstrating how the positions of the two countries have come closer in recent years. Nevertheless, as mentioned earlier, the election of Donald Trump as US President, has led to some tensions between the EU and the USA as a result of differing approaches to international crises such as those in Syria, Iran and North Korea, and also because of Trump's vacillating commitment to NATO's Article 5 (the mutual defence guarantee).

The EU has also continued to be actively involved in conflict prevention and crisis management with the deployment of CSDP operations. In July 2017 the EU had a total of 16 civilian and military operations deployed in Europe, Africa and Asia. For instance, in 2014 the EU deployed the Advisory Mission for Civilian Security Sector Reform in Ukraine (EUAM) to provide advice to the Ukrainian authorities in improving their security structures. For its part, EUNAVFOR MED Operation Sophia was deployed in 2015 as another element in the EU's response to the refugee crisis. The mission's mandate is to identify, capture and dispose of vessels used by migrant smugglers in order to disrupt the business model of human trafficking networks in the Southern Central Mediterranean and prevent the further loss of life at sea. The most recent CSDP mission was agreed in mid-July 2017 to support the Iraqi authorities with security sector reform. These examples demonstrate that the EU is well placed to deal with a wide variety of security challenges and, in particular, support peacebuilding and capacitybuilding in the security sector in countries that have recently undergone a period of conflict. However, these and other CSDP missions also demonstrate the EU's weaknesses in responding to more challenging security threats beyond 'soft' security issues and, in particular, in being a relevant defence actor. In this area, EU member states still rely on NATO—and, more generally, on the USA—as demonstrated by responses to the crisis in Ukraine. Whether the initiatives mentioned earlier can actually improve the EU's defence capabilities in a context of increasing insecurity in the neighbourhood is still unclear. Much will also depend on the impact of Brexit (see *Conclusion*).

Responding to the Rise of the Emerging Economies

Western countries, including the EU, have struggled to deal with the challenges associated with the rise of emerging economies. The global financial crisis accelerated the shift in the international balance of power from the West to 'the rest'. As a result, European countries were confronted not only by the prospect of a relative decline in power—as other world powers emerged—but also by an absolute decline in power as a consequence of the effects of the crisis in the eurozone. The eurozone crisis also highlighted the increasing gap in global governance structures, which led some EU member states to give up some of their decision-making power at international forums in reforms agreed between 2008 and 2010. Hence, the demands of the emerging economies for greater democratization of the international system have been partially addressed in the International Monetary Fund (IMF) and the World Bank, and with the increasing role of the Group of 20 leading industrialized and developing nations (G20) in global economic and financial issues. However, these reforms have not fully redressed the under-representation of emerging and developing economies in global governance structures, in particular in the United Nations

(UN) system. The issue of representation at the UN Security Council continues to be routinely raised by India, Brazil and Japan, but has not received the support of other Security Council members, including the People's Republic of China.

Given the inability of individual countries to deal with this challenge on its own, the EU acting as a bloc and as a single political entity could thus become an important force, as it has demonstrated in the past in trade issues. However, too often the EU's position is undermined by the existence of disagreements among its member states and a preference among them for conducting bilateral, rather than multilateral, relations. Moreover, the EU's response to the emergence of a multipolar world and the rise of the BRICS (Brazil, Russia, India, China and South Africa) has been characterized by 'ad hocism', an emphasis on trade issues—rather than political and security matters—and the lack of a clear strategy. As a result, the EU's attempts to establish strategic partnerships with emerging powers have so far failed to deliver concrete results. Relations with China best exemplify some of these problems.

Relations with China are of crucial importance to the EU, especially in a post-Brexit and post-Trump context. The strategic partnership with China can be seen as a way to contain the rise of the Asian power, as well as to respond to a less predictable US Presidency (for instance, after the announcement by the USA in June 2017 of its intended withdrawal from the Paris Agreement on climate change—see below). However, although institutional relations between the EU and China have intensified in recent years, the partnership has failed to deliver substantive outcomes in political and security matters. For instance, the member states are still divided on how best to deal with the impact of China's rapid development in the European economy. Member states have expressed concerns about economic competition from cheap Chinese exports, but at the same time they have sought to benefit from the opportunities offered by a growing Chinese economy in the form of exports and investments through bilateral deals. In political terms, the question has been how to engage China strategically and how to deal with the authorities' human rights violations. For instance, there have been tensions between China and the EU over several issues, including the long-standing arms embargo, China's status as a market economy, and accusations of violations of the human rights of religious minorities. In addition, the issue of the Republic of China (Taiwan) remains sensitive. There have also been concerns about increasing tensions in the South China Sea, intensified by China's island-building in 2015. On these and other issues, the EU has remained cautious and divided, and China has not hesitated to exploit these divisions, favouring the conclusion of bilateral deals with member states.

Despite these problems, there are also opportunities for the EU to play a stronger role in reshaping global governance. When the EU demonstrates leadership and unity, it can achieve important goals. For instance, by ensuring better diplomatic co-ordination within the EU and with other international actors, agreement was reached at the UN climate change summit held in Paris, France, in December 2015. The EU and China have vowed to support the implementation of the Paris climate agreement, despite the USA's withdrawal.

They have also expressed their joint commitment to free trade in the context of increasing hostility by the Trump Administration towards multilateral trade agreements, such as the now-abandoned, proposed Transatlantic Trade and Investment Partnership with the EU and the Trans-Pacific Partnership, from which the USA withdrew in January 2017. Negotiations with Iran on its nuclear programme and the conclusion of a Joint Comprehensive Plan of Action in January 2016 provided another successful example of EU common foreign policy and leadership. There is also recognition that the emerging economies do not constitute a united or coherent bloc, despite the institutionalization of BRICS summits, and that the EU can exploit some of these divergences in order to promote its own goals at the international level, whether in the World Trade Organization or the United Nations. Some of these emerging economies have also shown weaknesses, with their economic growth slowing down in recent years (China, South Africa), or even contracting (Russia, Brazil). It is in the interest of the EU, however, that these economies continue to grow smoothly and to ensure stronger co-operation at the economic and political level. Nevertheless, the EU has sought to pursue other avenues, such as the negotiation of trade deals with other Western powers like Canada (the EU-Canada Comprehensive Economic and Trade Agreement was signed in October 2016) and Japan (currently under negotiation) as a way to counterbalance the rise of the emerging economies and the potential effects of Brexit.

Conclusion

Over the last decade the EU has had to deal with the accumulated impact of a number of crises, from the financial and economic crisis in the eurozone to security crises in the neighbourhood, or the recent refugee crisis. Despite the institutional innovations introduced by the Lisbon Treaty, the EU's response to these crises has continued to be very much fragmented, reactive and characterized by divisions among the member states—with the exception perhaps of the sanctions agreed against the Russian Federation. It is true that there have been some very important successes, such as progress on the normalization of relations between Serbia and Kosovo, and Iran's nuclear deal, but these seem to represent the exception rather than the norm.

In many cases, this undesirable state of affairs reflects the absolute and relative decline in power of European states. In other cases, the problems are self-inflicted, as a result of a failure to invest in security and defence capabilities, or of the continuing disagreements among the EU member states, which prevent it from speaking with one voice. In this regard, the impact of Brexit could exacerbate some of these problems, for instance by reducing the total resources available for EU foreign policy initiatives. This could be particularly true in matters of security and defence, since the UK's defence budget is the largest among the EU member states. However, we should not overestimate the UK's actual contribution to the CSDP, as the country underperformed relative to its capabilities. (Despite its military capabilities, it was sixth in terms of troop deployments on military missions and seventh in the context of civilian missions.) Of course, this has much to do with the UK's suspicion of the CSDP as a political project, which led in recent times to the UK's absence from many EU initiatives or, even worse, to it openly blocking them. Hence, the removal of a major veto player could ultimately improve security integration among the remaining EU member states, political will permitting. In this regard, there were some positive signs in 2016 and 2017 in support of this view, including the implementation of the EU Global Strategy and plans to move forward in the area of defence. The election of the pro-European centrist Emmanuel

Macron as French President in May 2017, and the potential for increased Franco-German co-operation have also improved the prospects for a stronger EU role in the world.

References

European Council. 'A Secure Europe in a Better World. European Security Strategy.' Brussels, 12–13 Dec. 2003, available at: www.eeas.europa.eu/csdp/about-csdp/european-security-strategy.

European External Action Service. 'The European Union in a Changing Global Environment. A More Connected, Contested and Complex World', Brussels, June 2015, available at: https://eeas.europa.eu/docs/strategic_review/eu-strategic-review_strategic_review_en.pdf.

European External Action Service. 'Shared Vision, Common Action: A Stronger Europe. A Global Strategy for the European Union's Foreign and Security Policy', Brussels, June 2016, available at: https://europa.eu/globalstrategy/sites/globalstrategy/files/eugs_review_web.pdf.

Howorth, J. *Security and Defence Policy in the European Union.* Basingstoke, Palgrave Macmillan, 2014.

Juncos, A. E 'Resilience as the New EU Foreign Policy Paradigm: A Pragmatist Turn?', *European Security*, Vol. 26 (1), pp. 1–18, 2017, available at: 10.1080/09662839.2016.1247809.

Juncos, A. E. and Whitman, R. G. 'Europe as a Regional Actor: Neighbourhood Lost?', *Journal of Common Market Studies*, Vol. 53, Annual Review, pp. 200–215, 2015.

Keukeleire, S. and Delreux, T. *The Foreign Policy of the European Union.* Basingstoke, Palgrave Macmillan, 2014.

Pomorska, K. and Vanhoonacker, S. 'Europe as a Global Actor: the (Un)Holy Trinity of Economy, Diplomacy and Security', *Journal of Common Market Studies*, Vol. 53, Annual Review, pp. 216–229, 2015.

EUROSCEPTICISM IN TIMES OF CRISIS

Sofia Vasilopoulou

Introduction

The European Union (EU) is a unique political and economic partnership of sovereign states, aiming to promote peace, stability and prosperity among its members. Over the years, EU member states have pooled resources and adopted common policies in a number of core areas, including trade, agriculture, the single market, the euro currency, human rights, and citizenship. They have also taken steps to co-operate in other policy domains, such as justice and home affairs, and foreign and security policy. This increased economic and political integration has been accompanied by the growing politicization of the EU, as well as public and party Euroscepticism. Although opposition to the EU, its policies, and its institutional structures is not necessarily a new phenomenon, the economic and migration crises have placed it at the forefront of political and journalistic discussions alike. European citizens are increasingly sceptical of the benefits of European integration and its policies, and political parties with critical and anti-EU agendas have been gaining political representation in both the EU and domestic parliaments. Euroscepticism is no longer a marginal project limited to fringe political actors. It has instead developed into a fundamental feature of European integration. It is increasingly salient among European citizens and is often expressed in government circles. The referendum held in the United Kingdom in 2016, which resulted in a decision for the country to leave the EU (so-called Brexit), is one of the most tangible examples of Euroscepticism becoming a core political issue with substantial impact on both domestic British politics and the EU as a whole.

This contribution examines the ways in which the eurozone and migration crises have altered the dynamics of Euroscepticism across the EU and its member states. Taking into consideration the changing nature of European integration, it highlights new patterns of division between European citizens and EU member states. It focuses on political parties and public opinion, paying specific attention to the different dimensions of Euroscepticism that have arisen as a result of the crisis.

What is Euroscepticism?

Euroscepticism may be defined as a sentiment of disapproval towards the EU. It is a multi-faceted phenomenon that relates to multiple objects of opposition and can be attributed to different political ideologies. In its hardest form, Euroscepticism tends to be an outright rejection of a country's EU membership, opposition to the principle of co-operation at a European multilateral level, and hostility towards the entire system of European political governance. Other, more 'qualified', forms of Euroscepticism may include criticisms of specific EU policies, including Economic and Monetary Union (EMU), the single market, the Schengen Agreement on the abolition of internal border controls, and EU enlargement. Some Eurosceptic actors may support a level of intergovernmental co-operation at the EU level, while opposing any shift towards supranational governance and the deepening of European integration (Szczerbiak and Taggart, 2008; Vasilopoulou, 2011). Targets of discontent may be diffuse, such as the EU regime and its mode of co-operation, or specific, related to policy transfer to the EU, an evaluation of the functioning of European institutions, and the direction of how the EU is developing. Euroscepticism may have an affective component, i.e. denoting a feeling of fear or anger against the EU; and an identity dimension, related to a lack of political or cultural identification with the European community, the EU project, and its symbols. Eurosceptic criticisms may include a focus on the EU's undemocratic structures; a utilitarian component related to the EU's negative effect on a country's or an individual's economic wellbeing; and a dimension related to the EU's weak crisis management and unsatisfactory response capabilities.

The ideological foundations of Euroscepticism tend to differ. One the one hand, right-wing Eurosceptics are mainly motivated by nationalist and identity considerations. They oppose European integration from a predominantly sovereignty-based perspective justified on ethnocultural grounds. They view the EU as posing a threat to the nation and its sovereignty, and promoting cultural diversity at the expense of the cultural homogeneity of European nation states. Left-wing Eurosceptics, on the other hand, tend primarily to anchor their opposition in socioeconomic concerns. They tend to view the EU as a capitalist project at the service of banking and neoliberal interests. While they often support the deepening of integration, they tend to oppose the way in which the EU functions.

That being said, we may observe some similarities towards the extremes of the political spectrum. Nationalism is the common driver of both far-right and far-left Euroscepticism (Halikiopoulou et al., 2012). Far-right Euroscepticism tends to have a stronger ethnic and cultural nationalist basis, prioritizing questions of national belonging; far-left Euroscepticism is mostly founded on economic and territorial nationalism, portraying the EU as an imperialist project, which favours the neoliberal ruling classes and poses a threat to the economic and territorial integrity of the nation-state. Far-right and far-left parties tend to increasingly compete for a similar pool of voters, i.e. those low-educated, low-skilled, and culturally insecure individuals who feel threatened by international competition. They offer a similar programme in their opposition to denationalization and deregulation, which targets the so-called 'losers of globalization' and is linked to their criticisms of the EU project as a regional form of globalization.

Pre-crisis Patterns of Euroscepticism

Although Euroscepticism has become a buzzword in both policy circles and academic literature, it is far from a new phenomenon. Euroscepticism is a core feature of the EU project, present since the very early stages of European integration. It is a dynamic phenomenon, changing in nature and scope over time. In fact, we may observe distinct phases of European integration overlapping with a different character of Euroscepticism (Vasilopoulou, 2013). The first phase, which broadly ranges from the end of the Second World War until the late 1980s, is characterized by élite-driven Euroscepticism structured mainly along national lines. During this period, European leaders put forward different, and often conflicting, visions of integration. Examples include the failure of the Pleven and Fouchet Plans, former French President Charles de Gaulle's veto of British membership, the so-called 'empty chair crisis', the British rebate and opposition to a European political union, and the Greek centre-right Panhellenic Socialist Movement's overt challenge of Greece's European Economic Community orientation. Given that economic liberalization was the primary focus of integration during the 1970s and 1980s, opposition to the project was mostly observed among left-wing and socialist actors.

The Maastricht Treaty in the early 1990s marks the beginning of the second phase of integration. It is considered a turning point when it comes to anti-EU sentiment, as it altered the nature of European integration in the direction of political integration, giving rise to an additional form of opposition that focused on the defence of national interests and sovereignty. Euroscepticism was, however, mostly an expression of public protest limited to single-issue or anti-establishment parties in the margins of European political systems. This period is also associated with the rise of plebiscitary politics and direct democracy on EU enlargement and treaty change. European citizens were given the opportunity to express their EU preferences in a variety of EU referenda, although often citizens employed this platform to voice concerns related to domestic politics. New conceptions of integration, such as multi-speed, variable geometry and à la carte Europe, were coined for the first time during this period.

New Divisions in the Context of Multiple EU Crises

The financial and migration crises signal a new period in the process of European integration and mark a significant change in Eurosceptic politics. These developments may be considered as 'critical junctures', as they have contributed to the emergence of a transnationalist cleavage (Hooghe and Marks, 2017). They have—more than ever before—brought to the forefront issues of transnational economic redistribution, have weakened European solidarity, and have increased political contestation in and about the EU. They have resulted in political divisions within mainstream parties, and the rise of EU 'issue entrepreneurs', i.e. Eurosceptic parties that have placed the EU issue on the political agenda by increasing its salience and polarizing public opinion (De Vries and Hobolt, 2012). In contrast to the pre-crisis period, Euroscepticism has developed into a widespread cross-European phenomenon not confined to particular value and belief systems and encountered in both the centre and the periphery of political systems.

The EU's inability promptly to resolve the crises contributed to the rise of anti-EU sentiment among European citizens, further eroding the project's credibility. Public opinion towards the EU worsened, albeit with country level variations (Eurobarometer, 2014). The image of the EU suffered considerably, with 28% of Europeans having a negative image of the EU in 2013, compared with 15% in 2009. Trust in the EU was at a record low in 2013–14, with only about one-third of Europeans expressing such trust, in comparison with 57% in 2007. Pessimism about the future of the EU increased dramatically, with 46% of Europeans being pessimistic in 2013, in comparison with 24% in 2007.

Beyond general disillusionment and lack of optimism with the EU project, the two crises have contributed to the rise of multiple dimensions of anti-EU sentiment that go beyond simply opposing the EU project. These include dissatisfaction with EU initiatives such as European Economic Governance, or EU bailout programmes initiated by the European Financial Stabilization Mechanism and the European Stability Mechanism, opposition to freedom of movement of persons as a fundamental principle of EU integration, and scepticism towards a common EU migration and anti-terrorism policy. The crises have contributed to the rise of nationalism and identity politics across the EU. They have exacerbated divisions between highly skilled and highly educated individuals who reap the benefits from integrated economics on the one hand, and those individuals who lack the skills and education to compete in a highly competitive environment on the other. They have also created tensions between richer and poorer, creditor and debtor, and Eastern and Western EU member states.

ECONOMIC PROSPERITY AND TRANSNATIONAL INCOME REDISTRIBUTION

The European sovereign debt crisis called into question the viability of the EMU. The necessity of fiscal transfers as a means of preventing the demise of the eurozone revealed that income redistribution in the EU takes place not only within member states, but also across member states. Financial bailouts and adjustment programmes triggered Eurosceptic sentiment not only among creditor countries, which have transferred their wealth to the less affluent countries, but also among debtor countries, which have been obliged to delegate more national sovereignty to European institutions.

In 2011 only 37% of Europeans thought that the euro had cushioned the effects of the economic crisis. Respondents in the eurozone were more likely to agree with this statement, at 42%, compared with those outside it at 30%. Although a large majority of Europeans living in eurozone countries supported measures to strengthen the co-ordination of economic policy within the EU, this number substantially decreased among those living in non-eurozone countries (Eurobarometer, 2011). Economic concerns persisted during 2013–14. The three most important issues confronting the EU included economic themes, namely the economic situation, unemployment and the state of member states' public finances. The number of Europeans judging that their country's economic situation was good declined from 48% in 2007 to between 26% and 34% during 2013–14.

The percentage of positive evaluations of the national economy was below 10% in a number of EU member states, including Spain, Greece, Portugal, Italy, Bulgaria, Hungary, Slovenia, Cyprus and France. In 2013 more than 50% of Europeans thought that the worst of the negative impact of the economic crisis on the job market was still to come and over one-third believed that there was a risk that they could fall into poverty. In the same year only 28% of Europeans felt that their voice counted in the EU, compared with 38% in 2009 (Eurobarometer, 2014). In crisis-affected countries, such as Cyprus and Greece, this percentage declined to 11% and 13%, respectively, in 2013.

TRANSNATIONAL MOBILITY

One of the unintended consequences of the European sovereign debt crisis relates to increased labour mobility, particularly from poorer to richer EU member states. Although intra-EU migration flows also took place following the EU's enlargement to Central and Eastern Europe, the financial crisis served to increase the salience of this issue. The crisis initially reduced internal EU mobility, but this trend was reversed from 2011 onwards, with an overall 14% increase in the number of EU nationals working in another EU country during 2008–12 (Eurofound, 2014).

This change in intra-EU migration flows may be interpreted in two distinct ways. On the one hand, it may be understood as a positive means through which EU member states can meet labour demand and cover skills shortages. On the other hand, it may be seen as placing a strain on recipient countries' labour market and welfare institutions. Some individuals may view EU migrants as posing a threat to wages, decreasing employment standards, and disproportionately relying on the welfare state. This is especially the case during times of economic crisis, which entail more competition for scarce national resources. Concerns about intra-EU migration may have a cultural component related to a potential change in demographics. They may also be portrayed through a security perspective whereby the weakening of territorial boundaries and border controls is thought to contribute to the rise of criminality and terrorist attacks across Europe.

Although support for the free movement of persons within the EU was strong across member states, at 78% on average in 2015, opposition to it was fairly weak in countries such as the UK, Austria and Denmark, at 29%, 28% and 23%, respectively (Eurobarometer, 2015). In fact, the question of EU migration was prominent in the official 'Vote Leave' UK referendum campaign, which argued that the EU's immigration system had put pressure on the country's schools and hospitals and that open borders had created an 'international passport-free zone for terrorists'.[1] Immigration and sovereignty were the two most important issues in deciding how to vote among Leave voters.

MIGRATION AND EUROPEAN SOLIDARITY

The migration crisis further deepened political divisions within the EU and called European unity into question. Frontline states, such as Greece and Italy, and destination states in the north, such as Germany and Sweden, have criticized other EU member states for lack of solidarity. In an unprecedented sign of inter-state acrimony, Greece withdrew its ambassador to Austria in February 2016, criticizing Austria's unilateral decision to host a meeting with Balkan states on the question of migration, without inviting Greece.

Other European governments, particularly in Central and Eastern Europe, have complained about Germany's asylum policies, arguing that they serve as 'pull' factors, and have fiercely criticized the European Commission's quota system for migrants' relocation and resettlement. The question was highly politicized in Hungary, where the Prime Minister, Viktor Orbán, openly questioned the EU's right to impose quotas on EU member states. In a government-initiated referendum in October 2016, Hungarians were asked to vote on the question 'Do you want the European Union to be able to mandate the obligatory resettlement of non-Hungarian citizens into Hungary even without the approval of the National Assembly?'. The result was a resounding victory for Orbán's rejection of the EU quota scheme. However, the turnout was below the required 50% threshold, which rendered the referendum invalid. In the same year the Visegrad Group—the Czech Republic, Hungary, Poland and Slovakia—put forward a statement calling for an EU migration policy based on the principle of 'flexible solidarity', i.e. voluntary participation in the quota system and each EU member state contributing to the scheme in different ways, 'taking into account their experience and potential'.[2]

Among European citizens, immigration and terrorism replaced economics as the most important issues facing the EU during 2015–16. In addition, whereas approximately 70% of Europeans supported a common European policy on migration in 2017, there was significant variation across EU member states. For example, support for such a scheme was over 80% in Spain, the Netherlands, Germany, Cyprus and Luxembourg. It was, however, below 50% in the Czech Republic, Hungary, Estonia and Poland. In the Czech Republic, for example, the percentage of those who supported the common policy was 39%, compared with 56% 'against' (Eurobarometer, 2017).

Euroscepticism in the European Parliament

The trend of dissatisfaction and socioeconomic insecurity was also manifested in the 2014 European Parliament (EP) elections, with Eurosceptic parties from both the right and the left of the political spectrum claiming victory across EU member states. For example, far-right parties with a strong anti-EU agenda were the main winners in Denmark and the UK, which are non-eurozone members. The Eurosceptic far-right also headed the polls in France, which is a eurozone member and one of the 'inner six' founding member states of the European Communities. Euroscepticism was electorally manifested even in countries such as Germany, which is a leading eurozone creditor with no significant history of anti-EU sentiment. The Eurosceptic Alternative für Deutschland (Alternative for Germany) received 7.1% of the German vote, securing seven seats in the EP. In Hungary, the extreme nationalist Jobbik was the second most successful party, although it experienced some decline in support compared with the 2009 EP elections. Eurosceptic parties of the right that did not head the polls in their respective countries but experienced a rise in support in 2014 compared with the 2009 EP elections include the Freiheitliche Partei Österreichs (FPÖ—Freedom Party of Austria), Perussuomalaiset (Finns Party—formerly True Finns), Sverigedemokraterna (Sweden Democrats) and the Greek Chrysi Avgi (Golden Dawn).

Despite this success, co-operation between Eurosceptic right groups remained limited, with parties divided into three EP groups—the European Conservatives and Reformists, the Europe of Freedom and Direct Democracy (EFDD), and the Europe of Nations and Freedom. A number of Eurosceptic right MEPs were also 'non-inscrits', i.e. they did not sit in one of the recognized EP groups. A remarkable development was the creation of the Europe of Nations and Freedom group, which joined together radical forces of the right, including the French Front National (FN—National Front), the Italian Lega Nord (Northern League), the Dutch Partij voor de Vrijheid (Party for Freedom), the FPÖ, the Belgian Vlaams Belang (Flemish Interest), the Polish Kongres Nowej Prawicy (Congress of the New Right), and independent MEPs from Germany, Romania and the UK. The substantive success of this group in terms of policy making, however, remains debatable, as MEPs from such parties tend to limit their engagement in those legislative activities that attract most attention, such as parliamentary speeches. The establishment of this group may be considered a financial success, as it qualified for up to €17.5m. in EU funds. It has also been accompanied by setbacks. Crucially, Marine Le Pen, the leader of the French FN, was placed under investigation in mid-2017 for alleged embezzlement and misappropriation of EU funds, amounting to approximately €5m. during 2012–17. The allegations included spending EP money reserved for the salaries of EP staff to fund instead France-based party aides and members.

Far-left Eurosceptic parties did not enjoy similarly widespread success. In Greece and Spain, beset by crisis, the successes they did have, however, had far-reaching domestic implications. In Greece, the Synaspismos Rizospastikis Aristeras (SYRIZA—Coalition of the Radical Left) was placed first, increasing its support by over 20 percentage points. This electoral achievement was of a strong symbolic value, and paved the way towards the party's eventual victory in Greece's national elections in January and September 2015. In Spain, the newly formed Podemos (We Can) group was placed fourth with approximately 8% of the vote and the La Izquierda Plural (Plural Left) electoral coalition was placed third with 10%. The rise of Podemos contributed to a climate of uncertainty in domestic party politics, with both the 2015 and 2016 national elections failing to produce a clear winner and a functioning government.

A significant development was the success of the Eurosceptic Italian MoVimento 5 Stelle (Five Star Movement). The party was placed second with approximately 22% of the vote, obtaining 22 seats in the EP. The party has a populist agenda that transcends left–right politics by attacking traditional political parties and élites for corruption. It attracts support across the board, tapping into the different political orientations held by citizens. It puts forward a critical—yet often contradictory—position on European integration and the euro, calling for a referendum on Italy's continued membership of the eurozone. It challenges EU austerity rules, and calls for the dismantling of the troika, i.e. the decision group of international lenders formed by the European Commission, the European Central Bank and the International Monetary Fund. It also rejects the EU's proposed Transatlantic Trade and Investment Partnership agreement with the USA (suspended following the election as US President of Donald Trump) and the EU-Canada Comprehensive Economic and Trade Agreement. Following the 2014 EP elections, the party allied with the right-wing, Eurosceptic EFDD in the EP. It subsequently sought to join the Alliance of Liberals and Democrats for Europe EP group, but its request was rejected.

Conclusion

The eurozone and migration crises revealed a tension between, on the one hand, the need for European solidarity and further integration in order to resolve them, and growing public and party dissatisfaction with the EU on the other. They have served to weaken the legitimacy of European integration and placed the EU under serious stress. They increased the importance of European integration, economic prosperity and migration in the hearts and minds of Europeans, and raised concerns not only about the EU's crisis management capabilities, but also about the viability of the entire project. They amplified divisions between countries inside and outside the eurozone, between creditor and debtor countries, and between those countries that agree to host migrants and those that do not.

At the same time, the context of multiple crises made clear that EU competence goes far beyond trade liberalization. EU decision making affects highly politicized and controversial domestic policy areas, such as national budgets, decisions on how many non-EU migrants an EU member state should receive, and who should have access to domestic labour markets. Euroscepticism in times of crisis, thus, consists of a number of dimensions encompassing questions of economic prosperity and transnational income redistribution, transnational mobility among European citizens, terrorism and international migration. These new patterns of division in Europe are cross-cutting and may depend on a number of factors, including individuals' skills, education and mobility prospects, their country of residence, and the extent to which they perceive common European policies as a threat to national policies.

Is this growing Euroscepticism a sign of a weakening EU? In its lifetime, the EU has undergone a series of challenges, and history has shown that its structures tend to be resilient. None the less, in an era of continuing internal and external geopolitical crises, EU initiatives need to be backed up by member states' political will, if they are to succeed.

Notes

1. www.voteleavetakecontrol.org/briefing_immigration.html/.
2. www.euractiv.com/section/justice-home-affairs/news/flexible-solidarity-becomes-new-tool-in-response-to-refugee-crisis/.

References

De Vries, C. E. and Hobolt, S. B. 'When dimensions collide: The electoral success of issue entrepreneurs', *European Union Politics*, Vol. 13, No 2, 2012, pp. 246–268.

Eurobarometer. *Europeans, the European Union and the Crisis.* Standard Eurobarometer 75, Spring 2011. Available at: ec.europa.eu/public_opinion/archives/eb/eb75/eb75_cri_en.pdf (accessed 14 Aug. 2017).

Eurobarometer. *Public Opinion in the European Union.* Standard Eurobarometer 81, Spring 2014. Available at: ec.europa

.eu/public_opinion/archives/eb/eb81/eb81_publ_en.pdf (accessed 11 Aug. 2017).

Eurobarometer. *Public Opinion in the European Union*. Standard Eurobarometer 84.3, Autumn 2015. Available at: ec.europa.eu/commfrontoffice/publicopinion/index.cfm/Survey/getSurveyDetail/instruments/STANDARD/surveyKy/2099 (accessed 14 Aug. 2017).

Eurobarometer. *Public Opinion in the European Union*. Standard Eurobarometer 87, Spring 2017. Available at ec.europa.eu/commfrontoffice/publicopinion/index.cfm/Survey/getSurveyDetail/instruments/STANDARD/surveyKy/2142 (accessed 14 Aug. 2017).

Eurofound. 'Labour mobility in the EU: Recent trends and policies'. Publications Office of the European Union, Luxembourg, 2014.

Halikiopoulou, D., Nanou, K. and Vasilopoulou, S. 'The Paradox of Nationalism: The Common Denominator of Radical Right and Radical Left Euroscepticism', *European Journal of Political Research*, Vol. 51, No 4, 2012, pp. 504–39.

Hooghe, L. and Marks, G. 'Cleavage Theory meets Europe's Crises: Lipset, Rokkan, and the Transnational Cleavage', *Journal of European Public Policy*, doi: 10.1080/13501763.2017.1310279, 2017.

Szczerbiak, A. and Taggart, P. A. *Opposing Europe? The Comparative Party Politics of Euroscepticism*. Oxford, Oxford University Press, 2008.

Vasilopoulou, S. 'European Integration and the Radical Right: Three Patterns of Opposition', *Government and Opposition*, Vol. 46, No 2, 2011, pp. 223–44.

Vasilopoulou, S. 'Continuity and Change in the Study of Euroscepticism: Plus Ça Change?', *JCMS: Journal of Common Market Studies*, Vol. 57, No 1, 2013, pp. 153–168.

THE SOCIAL FRAMEWORK OF THE EUROPEAN UNION

Emil J. Kirchner

Introduction

Social solidarity in the context of the European Union (EU) implies the promotion of fraternity among its citizens and a redistributive mechanism in the allocation of scarce resources and values. It constitutes an important component of the meaning of 'Union'. Labour market mobility, although important, is only one element of social solidarity, which needs to be complemented by active social policy interventions in such areas as education and vocational training, social security, health and safety, and working conditions generally. Equally, to avoid labour market mobility resulting in regional imbalances, such as heavy congestion (in terms of the workforce) in highly industrialized or urbanized areas and heavy depletion in the economically less-developed regions, structural funds are required. Thus, in practice, social solidarity implies that, for example, unemployment compensation, vocational training programmes and social security remunerations are available throughout the EU and are accessible to groups irrespective of category, including migrants (from other member states), ethnic minorities, or people with disabilities. However, the combined effects of the financial and economic crisis in the eurozone and rising anti-immigration sentiment in several EU countries have placed severe strains on the credibility of the social solidarity principles. These factors contributed to the United Kingdom's referendum decision of 23 June 2016 to leave the EU.

The Evolution of Social Policy

The evolution of EU social policy has been dichotomous. On the one hand, lofty social policy aims have been stipulated, together with a belief held by some of the original member states that economic convergence would generally produce social convergence. On the other hand, the various EU treaties have been less specific on the actions to be taken and on the competences to be held by EU institutions towards the establishment of a common social, regional or labour market policy.

In substantive terms, little progress was made on EU social policy until the 1969 summit of heads of state and of government, in The Hague, Netherlands, which sought to complement the introduction of Economic and Monetary Union with a regional policy component. Further such efforts were initiated at the 1972 summit in Paris, France, with demands for a Social Action Programme, which enabled the European Commission to develop a new range of active social policies.[1] This involved 40 priority measures such as full and better employment, improved living and working conditions, and closer collaboration between employers and employees in the decision making of the EU.

However, the preparation of this Social Action Programme, as of the other programmes envisaged by the Paris Summit, was overshadowed by the emerging energy crisis in late 1973 and the subsequent economic crisis during the remaining part of the 1970s. Consequently, only a few proposals were put forward or adopted by the Council of Ministers. These included provisions on workers' rights in situations of mass dismissal; transfer of undertakings and insolvencies; a strengthening of the European Social fund (ESF); equal pay for men and women; and health and safety provisions in mining industries.

Overcoming the deep-seated economic problems of the 1970s and accompanying factors caused by self-serving attitudes, the EU revived its interest in social and regional policy, and in labour market policy, through the Single European Act (SEA), signed in 1986. Economic liberalism largely prevailed in the SEA, especially in the British view, according to which economic convergence would result in greater social convergence. However, there were also strong views, particularly espoused by the Mediterranean countries and Ireland, that the EU should become more interventionist in social and regional policy. In other words, the completion of the internal market should be complemented by the principle of economic and social cohesion, avoiding an excessively detrimental impact on the peripheral or economically deprived regions and peoples of the EU by providing them with financial aid.

These differences reappeared in the negotiations on the Treaty on European Union (TEU) in December 1991. With the UK unwilling to accept proposals for a common social policy, the other 11 member states agreed to accept a social protocol outside the Treaty. The protocol on social policy of December 1991 extended the use of Qualified Majority Voting (QMV) beyond health and safety issues to hitherto contentious social policy issues, namely working conditions, worker information and consultation rights, gender equality and help for the unemployed. It should be noted, however, that the application of QMV with regard to health and safety at the workplace, or where it involves interference with the single market, is subject to conflict between those who want to extend EU activity in the social dimension and those who want to keep such activity to a minimum. The social protocol stipulated unanimity on matters relating to social security, redundancy, collective representation for non-EU workers and job creation schemes.

The Treaty of Amsterdam of 1997 gave further impetus to social policy, by incorporating the protocol on social policy into EU policymaking proper. This helped to strengthen EU efforts as well as achievements in the areas of social protection, especially in relation to health and safety, and equal opportunities between men and women. Also, with regard to Article 119 concerning equal pay for equal value, QMV was introduced and the European Parliament was given co-decision participation. (This Article was amended by the Treaty of Amsterdam, and is now known as Article 141.) A new Article 118c (now Article 140) was added, giving the European Commission the task of co-ordinating member states' policies relating to employment, labour law, social security and collective bargaining.

In another important development, following the election of a Labour Government, the UK, in June 1997, decided that it would forthwith be party to measures taken in this area. Directives already adopted on the basis of the protocol were extended to the UK. These included, for example, directives concerning the European works council and parental leave. However, the UK retained the 'opt-out' on the directive for a 48-hour working week, which still applies.

From 1998 EU efforts in the social policy field primarily concentrated on labour market mobility, employment and social protection. In pursuit of this, a number of so-called co-ordination processes were initiated and subsequently monitored at European Council meetings, involving economic, employment and social policy. Among these was the so-called Lisbon process, which aims to make the EU 'the most competitive and dynamic knowledge-based economy in the world capable of sustainable economic growth with better and more jobs and greater social cohesion'. Significantly, the Lisbon process introduced a new method of EU decision making, known as the open method of co-ordination. The aims of these processes were also outlined in the Social Agenda for 2000–05, which was adopted at the Nice European Council in December 2000. Similar objectives can be found in the subsequent Social Agenda (2005–10). Although the Lisbon Treaty (2009) made a number of changes in social policy, these predominantly reinforced existing EU social policy developments rather than set substantial new guidelines. However, the Treaty provided for more shared competences between the European Parliament and the Council, such as in Article 149 (employment policy), Article 153 (co-ordination of member states' social policies), Articles 155 and 156 (industrial relations), Article 157 (equal opportunities and treatment for men and women in matters of employment) and Article 164 (European Social Fund).

Current Trends in Social Policy Development

Largely owing to the impact of the financial and economic crisis in the eurozone, the EU has in recent years been confronted with a number of important challenges or concerns in the field of social policy. Foremost among these have been persistently high levels of unemployment. There were 19m. unemployed people in the EU in July 2017, with particularly high rates of unemployment among young people and women and in the numbers of long-term unemployed. Coinciding with the unemployment trends have been challenges arising from changing work patterns, an ageing population, and growing welfare demands. The following paragraphs examine how the EU is responding to these trends and concerns.

EMPLOYMENT

The onset of the financial and economic crisis in 2008 resulted in a steady rise in the rate of unemployment, which reached 11.9% of the active population of the eurozone, or some 26.6m. people, in July 2013. The rate of unemployment in the eurozone declined slowly, and fell from 10.2% in May 2016 to 9.3% in May 2017. Of particular concern was youth unemployment. In July 2017 the youth unemployment rate was 16.9% in the 28 EU member states (the EU-28—down from 20.7% in April 2015) and 19.1% in the eurozone (down from 22.3% in April 2015). Meanwhile, there was a persistent gap of some 40% between the member states with the highest (Greece, 44.4%) and lowest rates (Germany, 6.5%) of youth unemployment at mid-2017. The overall rate of unemployment for the EU-28 had declined to 7.7% by July 2017, compared with 8.5% in July 2016. At July 2017 the total number of unemployed persons was 18.9m. in the EU-28 and 14.9m. in the eurozone.

In response to the economic downturn, the European Commission launched a number of combative measures. Foremost among these was the Commission's Europe 2020 Strategy[2] (COM(2010) 2020), published in March 2010, which addressed the challenges of the economic crisis and defined the priorities for action for the following 10 years. According to the Strategy, the crisis had 'wiped out 20 years of progress', with some 7m. workers losing their jobs in less than a year. The Europe 2020 Strategy set a number of targets, which were representative of three priorities for smart, sustainable and inclusive growth. The targets sought, among other things, to raise the employment rate among the population aged 20–64 years from 69% to at least 75% by 2020; to reduce the share of early school leavers to 10% from the current 15%; to increase the share of the population aged 30–34 years having completed tertiary education from 31% to at least 40%; and to reduce the number of Europeans living below the national poverty line by 25%, lifting 20m. people out of poverty.[3] Overall, the Strategy focuses on growth from knowledge, creating an inclusive society, and building a greener economy. In an attempt to alleviate the unemployment situation, the European Commission proposed two further measures. One was the Youth Employment Package of December 2012, and the other involved the allocation of €6,000m. for a Youth Employment Initiative.[4] In turn, the European Council, meeting in Berlin, Germany, in June 2013, decided to upgrade the amount to a projected €8,000m., with most of the money concentrated in the subsequent two years. The aim was to ensure that within four months of leaving school or becoming unemployed, every young European would receive a good offer for employment, education or training.[5] This measure was strengthened in March 2014, when the Council adopted a recommendation on a quality framework for traineeships, addressing two shortcomings: insufficient learning content and inadequate working conditions. In terms of employment initiatives, the Council also adopted, in December 2013, a regulation on the new EU programme for employment and social innovation (EaSI) (80/13). EaSI, with a budget of €815m. for 2014–20, seeks to support member states in carrying out employment and social policy activities at European and national, as well as regional and local, levels by means of policy co-ordination, and the identification, analysis and sharing of best practices.[6]

The continued combined effects of high unemployment rates and stagnant economic growth caused the EU to undertake further economic stimulus initiatives in 2014. The European Council meeting of December called for the establishment of a European Fund for Strategic Investments (EFSI) in the European Investment Bank Group, with the aim of mobilizing €315,000m. in new investment between 2015 and 2017.[7] In addition, the European Central Bank announced an expanded stimulus programme amounting to €60,000m. (US $69,000m.) per month in asset purchases, in an effort to revive the eurozone's struggling economy.[8]

The structural funds, in particular the European Social Fund (ESF), are the most important financial instruments available at

European level to invest in people and promote social progress. The ESF has a budget cost of €80,000m. between 2014 and 2020. Its main aims are to train people and help them get into work; promote social inclusion; improve education and training; and improve the quality of public services in EU countries. A related fund is the European Globalization Adjustment Fund (EGF), which was established in 2006,[9] with €500m. available annually to provide personalized support to workers made redundant as a result of global trade liberalization and increased competition. The fund can also be used to help workers who have lost their jobs owing to the financial crisis to retrain and find new employment. Further funding is provided via the European Regional Development Fund (ERDF), which assisted programmes designed to promote convergence, regional competitiveness and employment, and European territorial co-operation in 2007–13; a renewed ERDF covers the period 2014–20.

SOCIAL PROTECTION: HEALTH AND SAFETY

Since the late 1980s a legislative framework for minimum European health and safety standards has been put in place, underpinned by successive EU programmes on health and safety at work. Attention now needs to be focused on adapting these programmes to new risks and changing work practices brought about by technological developments and scientific advances.

Work-related accidents are a major concern. Every year over 4,000 workers in the EU die from work-related accidents, with hazardous substances such as asbestos being a main cause, and more than 3m. workers suffer serious accidents. About 25% of workers feel that their health and safety is at risk because of their work.[10] Studies show that work accidents and occupational diseases cost national economies between 1.5% and 4.0% of gross domestic product (GDP). To help to alleviate this problem a Council Directive (2006/25/CE) was adopted on the minimum health and safety requirements regarding the exposure of workers to the risks arising from physical agents (optical radiation). Furthermore, existing EU provisions specify that pregnant women should not be exposed to certain dangerous substances. During 2007–12 a new strategy on health and safety at work was implemented, which aimed for a 25% reduction in the total incidence rate of accidents at work in the EU-27 by 2012 through improved health and safety protection for workers. The Commission published an evaluation of the strategy in mid-2013, and a new Strategic Framework on Health and Safety at Work was adopted for 2014–20.

Meanwhile, the European Agency for Health and Safety at Work, located in Bilbao, Spain, and the European Foundation for Living and Working Conditions, in Dublin, Ireland, played an important role. Under Article 144 of the Treaty of Nice, a Social Protection Committee was established, comprising two members from each member state and the European Commission. Its task was defined as to 'monitor the social situation and the development of social protection policies in the member states and the Community; to promote exchanges of information, experience and good practice between member states and the Commission; and to prepare reports, formulate opinions or undertake other work within its field of competence, at the request of either the Council of Ministers or the Commission or on its own initiative'.[11] The Commission has also launched initiatives on public health, including areas such as HIV/AIDS, communicable diseases, cancer, drugs dependence, health monitoring and health promotion. Furthermore, in March and April 2014, respectively, the Council adopted a directive aimed at making tobacco products less attractive, and a regulation on speeding up the authorization procedure for clinical trials.[12] It also introduced a directive in 2017 to help protect workers from exposure to carcinogens or mutagens in the workplace. The aim is to help save up to 100,000 lives over the next 50 years.[13]

In February 2014 the EU launched an Action Plan on Childhood Obesity for 2014–20, which is expected to contribute to promoting healthy nutrition and physical activity, and to curtail current obesity trends through co-ordinated voluntary action by the member states and stakeholders.

The ageing of the population and the related problem of sufficient pension coverage have become a prominent issue in EU circles. By 2020 it is estimated that 25% of the Union's population will be aged over 60 years, and by 2030 roughly two active people (aged 15–65 years) will be required to take care of one inactive person (65+).[14] Responsibility for designing and managing pension systems remains with the member states. However, the EU has a role to play in promoting co-operation between member states in this field. To this end, in December 2016 the Council adopted a directive on institutions for occupational retirement provision (IORPs), aimed at facilitating their development and at better protecting pension scheme members and beneficiaries. The directive seeks to improve the governance and transparency of IORPs and facilitate their cross-border activities. Safer and more efficient occupational pensions will enhance the contribution of complementary savings to retirement income.[15]

From 1 May 2010 new legislation in the field of social security co-ordination came into effect. In particular, Regulation (EC) No. 987/2009 specified the procedure for the implementation of Regulation (EC) No. 883/2004 on the co-ordination of social security systems. The changes affected the quality and quantity of information available to citizens and led to the simplification of procedures, including the introduction of the Electronic Exchange of Social Security Information (EESSI), for the exchange of information between European national institutions. Meanwhile, social security, and social policy in general, remained the exclusive competence of member states; the provisions aimed to facilitate the free movement of workers through co-ordination rather than harmonization of national policies.

The procedure for receiving medical care abroad was further strengthened through the introduction of the European Health Insurance Card, which replaced the complicated E111 document. Furthermore, under a European Commission directive introduced in October 2005, European citizens are able to move between jobs and member states without losing pension benefits. Prior to 2005, changing jobs or country of residence could mean losing occupational pension benefits in some member states.

A further attempt to promote EU mobility was enshrined with the introduction of the Europass (Decision No. 2241/2004/EC), which consists of a portfolio of five documents. The Europass enables citizens to provide evidence of their qualifications and skills clearly and easily throughout the EU member states, candidate countries, Iceland, Liechtenstein, Norway and Switzerland. It complements the Ploteus (Portal on Learning Opportunities throughout the European Space) website, launched in 2002, which provides information on education and vocational training opportunities throughout Europe.

In the wider context of social protection, a number of EU legislative measures are noteworthy, such as the Working Time

Directive (June 2008). The main agreement of the latter directive was the introduction of a 48-hour maximum working week, unless a member state introduces an opt-out clause and a worker decides to use that clause. In the case of workers who opt for the derogation, the directive provides for a maximum of 60 hours of work a week on average over a three-month period. This can be increased to 65 hours a week on average over three months where there is no collective bargaining agreement and where the inactive period of on-call time is regarded as working time. The agreement also stipulates various safeguards for workers who use the opt-out clause. A further adoption relates to the Temporary Agency Worker Directive, which sought to ensure the appropriate protection of temporary agency workers through the application of the principle of equal treatment. It stipulated working conditions for such workers, as well as regular workers, in terms of pay, leave and maternity leave, while also including clauses on information for temporary agency workers about permanent employment opportunities in the user enterprise, equal access to training and other collective facilities (such as canteen, childcare facilities and transport services). The directive also ruled on the need for penalties for non-compliance by temporary agencies and enterprises. It was complemented by the Directive on Temporary Agency Work. Additional legislation guarantees adequate health and safety at work for pregnant women, prohibits dismissal on the grounds of maternity, and ensures a minimum period of maternity leave of 14 weeks (two of which are mandatory).

The process of defining a set of common European social rights and values is to be further promoted through the Charter on Fundamental Rights (CFR).[16] However, the legally binding nature of the CFR was a controversial issue in the UK, which, together with Poland, was granted a partial opt-out clause from this charter.

SOCIAL INTEGRATION AND EQUAL OPPORTUNITIES

Complementing health and safety concerns are efforts to relate to people with disabilities and to promote the principle of equal opportunities. Approximately one in 10 EU citizens, according to the European Commission, has a significant disability—psychological, physical or mental. The EU has sought to ensure that disabled people are able to become fully integrated members of their communities. The Helios II programme (Handicapped People in the European Community Living Independently in an Open Society) performed the main function in this respect, focusing from 1994 on the functional rehabilitation of disabled people, educational integration, vocational training, social integration and independent living. It linked to other programmes, and aimed to encourage increased exchanges of information between national governments, non-governmental organizations (NGOs) and disabled people's representatives, so that successful and innovatory practices could be shared.[17] The EU is a signatory, since January 2011, of the UN Convention on the Rights of People with Disabilities, which is intended to guarantee respect for the rights and freedoms of disabled people. The Convention also aims to ensure their social welfare and legal protection. In line with this, a Council Decision (2010/48/EC) was adopted, to ensure the full enjoyment of all human rights and fundamental freedoms by persons with disabilities. In November 2010 the Commission also introduced the European Disability Strategy 2010–20 (COM 2010/636final), which aims to improve the social inclusion and the well-being of people with disabilities and to enable them to exercise their rights fully.

The EU, especially the European Commission, has long had a commitment to equal opportunities, and it is widely recognized that this has been a catalyst for major change in the member states. It has issued directives on equal pay, upholding the principle of 'equal pay for work of equal value'; equal treatment in access to employment, training, promotion and working conditions; and equal treatment in social security and for the self-employed. A further development was the adoption of a Council Regulation (1922/2006) in December 2006 for the establishment of a European Institute for Gender Equality. In September 2010 the Commission launched a new strategy for equality between women and men for 2010–15 (COM 2010/491). In accordance with the main action planned, the Commission and the European Parliament have both strongly supported legislative measures on binding quotas to improve the gender balance in boardrooms. Along similar lines, the Council, at its meeting in June 2015, took up the issue of equal income opportunities for women and men, seeking to close the gender gap in pensions. By that time the average gender gap in pensions in the EU was 38.5% and the gender pay gap average was 16.5%.[18] In June 2016 the Council passed Conclusions on equality between women and men and on equality for lesbian, gay, bisexual, transsexual and/or intersex people.

In the sphere of social integration, the EU has introduced measures to combat racial discrimination. In June 1997 the Council adopted a regulation to establish, in Vienna, Austria, a European Monitoring Centre on Racism and Xenophobia. The Lisbon Treaty (Articles 9 and 10) aims at social protection, the fight against social exclusion, and a high level of education, training and protection of human health; it also combats discrimination based on sex, racial or ethnic origin, religion or belief, disability, age or sexual orientation. The Council, at a meeting in December 2013, recommended that member states should do more to improve the economic and social integration of Europe's 10m.–12m. Roma.

In terms of equal opportunities, the European Commission considered a proposal to give equal pay to seconded workers in the EU, arguing that the same rules on remuneration should apply for the same work at the same location, irrespective of who carries out that work: a local worker or a posted worker. A posted worker, as defined by EU law, is an employee sent by his or her company to carry out a service in another member state for a limited period. The Commission had claimed that the existing rules needed to be better applied when putting forward an enforcement directive. However, the proposal was criticized by some member states as being premature. There are 1.9m. posted workers in the EU, representing 0.7% of total EU employment. One-half of these workers go to three countries: Germany, France and Belgium. Poland is the largest source of posted workers in the EU, followed by Germany and France.

DEVELOPMENTS IN INDUSTRIAL RELATIONS

Highly divergent economic conditions in European countries give rise to different and sometimes conflicting interests where a European industrial relations system and its economic consequences are concerned. The trend since the late 1990s has been towards joint consultation at a transnational level, rather than collective bargaining. Works councils have become increasingly common in a more interdependent European economy, even if national governments and the EU failed to develop the capacity necessary to impose them by law. However, such councils will, for some time, continue to serve as information forums on narrowly defined subjects, rather than involve consultation or co-determination. This is in line with a Directive (2009/38/EC) adopted by the European Parliament and the Council on the establishment of a European Works Council or a procedure in Union-scale undertakings and Union-scale groups of undertakings for the purpose of informing and consulting employees. It aims at Union-scale undertakings that employ at least 1,000 employees within the member states and at least 150 employees in two different states.

Efforts towards the universal establishment of works councils have been promoted through what is known as the 'social dialogue', which was initiated in the mid-1980s between union and employer representatives under the auspices of the European Commission. Since the late 1980s the social dialogue has made important contributions in the form of its joint opinions. These have covered, for example, new technology, training, and the quality and motivation of work, and are particularly significant with respect to developing high-technology-based industries—an area of high priority for the EU. The result of extensive consultation and discussion between representatives of the European Trade Union Confederation (ETUC), the Union of Industrial and Employers' Confederations of Europe (UNICE) and the European Centre of Public Enterprises (CEEP), the social dialogue can be considered as contributing towards the establishment of some degree of consensus at a European level. By 2015 43 sectoral social dialogue committees (SSDCs) had been established. SSDCs are forums for discussion and consultation on employment and social policy proposals in some specific sectors. They often comprise several working groups and committees. Several agreements have also been produced under cross-industry social dialogue, including (a) four agreements signed by European social partners that have been transformed into directives under the social dialogue procedure set out in Articles 154 and 155 of the Treaty on the Functioning of the European Union; and (b) four cross-industry agreements concluded by social partners on the basis of their own work programme.

The European Commission consults the Social Dialogue Steering Group regularly. The Lisbon Treaty introduced Article 136a to signify the Union's aim to promote dialogue between social partners, to which the Tripartite Social Summit[19] for Growth and Employment was to contribute. For example, the Tripartite Social Summit of March 2017 focused on the future of Europe: charting the course towards growth, employment and fairness. Moreover, there was the possibility that training, on which most of the discussions in the social dialogue have centred since the early 1990s, would help to prime negotiations on other substantive issues.[20]

In recent years a new phenomenon has entered the social dialogue, known as 'flexicurity', which represents an integrated strategy for enhancing flexibility and security in the labour market. Flexicurity attempts to reconcile employers' need for a flexible workforce with workers' need for security—confidence that they will not experience long periods of unemployment. The areas of application are flexible and reliable contractual arrangements; comprehensive lifelong learning strategies; effective active labour market policies; and modern social security systems.[21]

It is apparent that European-level social partner organizations, of employers and trade unions, are not yet sufficiently equipped to play as effective a role as they might in promoting the establishment and dissemination of EU norms in the context of industrial relations. There is a tendency for affiliated bodies of European interest groups to demand action in Brussels without, however, ceding to their European-level organizations the necessary mandates. However, partly in response to the ongoing European economic crisis, there has been a significant increase in joint actions, statements and recommendations between the social partners, reaching a total of 42 in 2012.[22] Moreover, the establishment of a European Alliance of Apprenticeships in July 2013 marks the first ever joint Declaration by the European Commission, the Presidency of the EU's Council of Ministers and European level trade union and employer organizations—the ETUC, BUSINESSEUROPE, CEEP and the UEAPME. The Alliance will help to fight youth unemployment by improving the quality and supply of apprenticeships across the EU through a broad partnership of principal employment and education stakeholders. It also seeks to change attitudes to apprenticeships. It will, in particular, identify the most successful apprenticeship schemes in the EU and apply appropriate solutions in each member state. Public authorities, businesses, trade unions, chambers of commerce, providers of vocational education and training, youth representatives and employment services are all invited to join the scheme. The Alliance promotes measures which will be supported by the European Social Fund, the Youth Employment Initiative and Erasmus, and the new EU programme for education, training and youth.[23]

Europe-wide co-operation has been assisted by the establishment of an online service to the European Industrial Relations Observatory database, which is a project of the Dublin-based European Foundation for the Improvement of Living and Working Conditions. This project covers developments in industrial relations in the various EU member states and at the European level. New records are added to the database—and the online service—at monthly intervals. The database contains both shorter news and more in-depth features, plus comparative overviews of how particular issues have been dealt with in the industrial relations systems of the member states.

Future Trends

EU social policy is entering a new phase, reflecting the changing socioeconomic situation and, in particular, the high levels of unemployment in the EU, which in May 2017 were recorded at 7.8% of the active population in the EU-28 (down from 8.6% in May 2016) and 9.3% in the eurozone (down from 10.2%)[24] but which affected countries experiencing severe economic difficulties, such as Greece and Spain, disproportionately more severely. The EU and its member states also have to adapt to 'new family and working patterns, changing values, weakening bonds between generations, new job opportunities, demands for new skills, mobility and diversity'.[25] While increased opportunities, more choices, open society, and longer and healthier lives are positive indicators that European social changes have improved living conditions, there are also challenges linked to increasing unemployment, especially among youths, an ageing population, child poverty and diseases of affluence (i.e. obesity and stress). There is a growing awareness within the EU that social progress and economic growth are mutually complementary. After all, only a high employment rate can ensure coverage of the rising costs of pensions and health care. Social policy should therefore promote a decent quality of life and standard of living for all in an active, inclusive and healthy society that encourages access to employment, good working conditions and equality of opportunity.[26] Articles in the Lisbon Treaty seek to promote full employment; social justice; social peace; sustainable development; economic, social and territorial cohesion; social market economy; quality of work; lifelong learning; social inclusion; a high degree of social protection; equality between men and women; non-discrimination on the basis of racial or ethnic origin, religious or sexual orientation, disability and age; children's rights; a high level of health; and efficient and high-quality social services and services of general interest. Another recommendation in the treaty is to enlarge Article 152 in order to give the Union more competences in the field of public health and to cover matters such as serious cross-border threats, communicable diseases, bioterrorism and World Health Organization agreements.

In this context, a number of short-term predictions can be made in relation to social affairs and social policy in the EU. The first of these is that different national socioeconomic conditions and industrial relations will continue to prevail. Economic heterogeneity renders social integration difficult, and there are both positive and negative factors to consider in relation to this heterogeneity. Nearly 3m. wage-earners and some 7m. EU citizens live outside their countries of origin. There is also an increasing trend towards mobility among professionals. Conversely, language and culture are factors that will always impede migration. Other current barriers derive from the fact that unemployed workers cannot migrate from the country where they were last employed without forfeiting their unemployment benefits in that country. Pension portability also continues to present some difficulties, since some member states have separate social security schemes for public sector employees. However, progress is being made on the elimination of technical barriers to labour mobility, such as the achievement of mutual recognition of vocational certificates, provisional qualifications and higher education diplomas. In addition, EU programmes such as the Socrates programme (replaced in December 2006 by the EU Lifelong Learning Programme, which was incorporated into the Erasmus+ programme from 2014) were designed to encourage mobility within the education system itself, as well as to improve the quality of educational systems through increased co-operation.

A second prognosis that can be made is that regional differences within the EU will continue: around 15% of the people in the EU live in regions where income per head is lower than 75% of the EU average, but the figure is around 90% for the newer member states from Central and Eastern Europe.

Third, rather than being able to find the means to either achieve labour market regulation or create an EU-wide social policy, the most the European Commission is likely to attain is to secure a gradual strengthening of the EU social dimension. The Commission will try to pursue the twin objectives of economic growth and social progress by striking a balance between what is economically necessary and what is socially desirable in the formulation of a social policy. In other words, it will attempt a balance between social protection and job creation. Issues of pay, the right of association, and the rights to strike and to impose lockouts will remain distant goals of EU social policy legislation.

Fourth, the constituent parts of European partnerships such as the ETUC, UNICE and CEEP will only slowly cede autonomy and authority to the EU level.

Fifth, the introduction into EU decision making of the principles of both mutual recognition and subsidiarity, as well as the open method of co-ordination, will make the European social dialogue an instrument for the exchange of information, and perhaps for consultation, rather than for collective bargaining agreements.

Sixth, European works councils appear to be the most likely mechanism for European-level management-union arrangements in transnational companies. Their success, in terms of transnational information and consultative arrangements, is particularly heightened where there is a unified ownership and management structure, homogeneity of product and service, and integrated production arrangements.

Seventh, the provisions of the Charter of Fundamental Rights in the Lisbon Treaty (although only partially legally binding in Poland and the UK) will continue to have an important exemplary effect, helping to inform the debate and shaping the form of eventual solutions, whether legal or collectively negotiated. In addition, the social dimension may set in motion unforeseen developments in industrial relations at the EU level and within member states. However, although transnational laws and rules will become increasingly important, for the foreseeable future national political circumstances will determine labour market policy. The determination expressed by many to have greater control over immigration or labour market policy was one of the main motivations behind the UK Government's decision to hold a referendum on EU membership.

Finally, differences remain as to which European social model should be adopted EU-wide. The Belgian economist André Sapir outlined differences between four different European social models: on the one hand, the Nordic and the Anglo-Saxon models, both efficient and (the former only) promoting equality; on the other, the Continental and Mediterranean models, which, while pursuing equality, have proven to be ineffective and outdated, and in need of reform.[27] The financial and economic crisis, which severely affected Greece, Ireland, Portugal and Spain, and resulted in a number of EU-International Monetary Fund bailout arrangements, is likely to continue to affect the welfare models in one way or another. Severe financial cuts tend to strain social protection and pensions and impact unemployment and poverty levels.

Conclusion

The EU has undertaken modest direct efforts to develop an activist social policy. However, additional, if not substantial, progress in the social policy field has been made through the adjustments national governments have had to make to their welfare programmes, as a consequence of the unhindered labour mobility introduced with the internal market. Hence there has been increasing supranational influence over the design of national social policy.[28]

Unlike national situations, where social policies have grown in response to the shortcomings of market arrangements, EU social policy interventions have expanded as part of the process of marketbuilding itself. As Leibfried and Pierson explain, these extensive interventions reveal that national welfare state regimes are now part of a large, multi-tiered system of social policy. Member states profoundly influence this structure, but they no longer fully control it. While the governance of social policy occurs at multiple levels, however, the EU's peculiar arrangement is also different in many respects from traditional federal states, distinguished by a weak policymaking centre, court-driven regulation, and strong links with marketmaking processes.[29] However, as Scharpf suggests, European integration has created a constitutional asymmetry between policies promoting market efficiencies and policies promoting social protection and equality. In his opinion, European social policies are politically impeded by the diversity of national welfare states, differing not only in levels of economic development and hence in their abilities to pay for social transfers and services but, even more significantly, in their normative aspirations and institutional structures. The aspirations of 'social Europe' can, in his opinion, no longer be realized through purely national solutions.[30]

To achieve economic and social cohesion within the EU requires a reduction of regional disparities and the creation of comparable social conditions for the population generally and for the workforce in particular. Some success has been achieved in these areas by means of EU social policy and education and vocational training policy, especially through the operations of the European structural funds, which represent approximately one-third of the total EU budget. However, available EU structural fund resources, which are much less than national resources, are unable to cope with the huge unemployment problem. EU enlargement, to include Central and Eastern European countries, has further exacerbated the existing problem of regional disparities. Moreover, the impact of structural funds is somewhat limited as long as member states insist on the principle of subsidiarity, or the principle of additionality on ESF and ERDF applications (the ESF and ERDF finance only 50% of the cost of projects, the rest of which is to be borne by national authorities).

EU social policy and solidarity constitute more than labour market policies. They include protective measures for the economically deprived regions; an upgrading of social standards generally; an active dialogue between the social partners; and effective procedures for informing and consulting workers and encouraging their participation in companies. The EU has achieved some notable results in this area, but has many further challenges to meet before social solidarity in the Union becomes a reality.

Notes

1. Shanks, M. *European Social Policy Today and Tomorrow.* Oxford, Pergamon, 1977.
2. ec.europa.eu/eu2020.
3. European Social Fund (ESF) European Employment, ec.europa.eu/social/main.jsp?catId=325
4. See European Commission, 'Communication from the Commission to the European Parliament, the European Council, the Council, the European Economic and Social Committee and the Committee of the Regions: Working together for Europe'.
5. See statement by the President of the European Council, EUCO 161/13 1, Berlin, 3 July 2013, EUCO 161/13 PRESSE 317 PR PCE 142.
6. Council of the European Union, Brussels, 5 Dec. 2013, 17421/13 (OR.en) Presses 543.
7. European Council, Brussels, 18 Dec. 2014, italia2014.eu/media/4478/european-council-conclusions-on-fostering-investment-in-europe-18-december-2014.pdf.
8. Davidson, P., Hjelmgaard K., and Leinwand Leger, D., 'European Central Bank announces huge stimulus program' in USA Today, 22 Jan. 2015.
9. europa.eu/legislation_summaries/employment_and_social_policy/social_agenda/c10155_en.htm.
10. eur-lex.europa.eu/legal-content/EN/TXT/?uri=URISERV:170904_1&qid=1465984067850.
11. See European Commission, ec.europa.eu/social/main.jsp?catId=758.
12. Council of the European Union, 7763/14 (OR.en) Presse 152, Brussels, 14 March 2014 and 8891/14 (OR.en) PRESSE 232, Luxembourg, 14 April 2014.
13. https://www.eu2017.mt/en/news/Pages/Carcinogens-or-mutagens-at-work-Council-and-European-Parliament-reach-agreement.aspx.
14. See European Commission, 'Europe's population is getting older', europa.eu/rapid/pressReleasesAction.do?reference=IP/05/322&format=HTML&aged=1&language=EN&guiLanguage=en.
15. See www.lexology.com/library/detail.aspx?g=5aaba5ea-06a0-4ed8-ba20-9d7eb874287d.
16. See De Burca, G. 'Fundamental Rights and Citizenship', in B. de Witte (Ed.) *Ten Reflections on the Constitutional Treaty for Europe.* Florence, Robert Schuman Centre for Advanced Studies and Academy of European Law, 2003.
17. See European Commission, *How is the European Union Meeting Social and Regional Needs?* Luxembourg, Office for Official Publications of the European Communities, 1996.
18. Council of the European Union, Outcome of the Council Meeting, Luxembourg, 18–19 June 2015, www.consilium.europa.eu/en/meetings/epsco/2015/06/18-19.
19. The Tripartite Social Summit is a forum for dialogue between the EU institutions at the level of President and the European social partners at top management level. The Summit is co-chaired by the President of the European Council, the President of the European Commission and the Head of State or Government of the incumbent Presidency.
20. Gold, M., and Hall, M. *European Level Information and Consultation in Multinational Companies: An Evaluation of Practice.* Brussels, European Commission, 1992.
21. See ec.europa.eu/social/main.jsp?catId=102&langId=en.
22. See European Commission, 'Overview of EU Social Dialogue Liaison Forum'—Newsletter. Jan. 2013.
23. European Commission, Employment and Social Affairs Inclusion, News, 2.7.2013, ec.europa.eu/social/main.jsp?langId=en&catId=89&newsId=1934&furtherNews.
24. Eurostat statistics explained: Unemployment statistics, ec.europa.eu/eurostat/statistics-explained/index.php/Unemployment_statistics.
25. Barroso, J. M., President of the European Commission, 'Shaping a modern social agenda for Europe', Social Agenda Forum, Brussels, 6 May 2008, europa.eu/rapid/pressReleasesAction.do?reference=SPEECH/08/230&format=HTML&aged=0&language=EN&guiLanguage=fr.

26. See Sapir, A. 'Globalization and the reform of European Social Models', in *Journal of Common Market Studies*, Vol. 44, No. 2, pp. 369–390, June 2006.
27. Leibfried, S., and Pierson, P. European Social Policy. Washington, DC, Brookings Institution, 1995; Martinsen, D.S. 'The Europeanization of Welfare—The Domestic Impact of Intra-European Social Security', in Journal of Common Market Studies, Vol. 43, No. 5, pp. 1027–54, Dec. 2005.
28. See Polanyi, K. The Great Transformation. Boston, MA, Beacon, 1992.
29. See Leibfried, S., and Pierson, P. *ibid.*
30. See Scharpf, F. 'The European Social Model', in *Journal of Common Market Studies,* Vol. 40, No. 4, pp. 645–70, Nov. 2002.

EUROPEAN UNION ENVIRONMENTAL POLICY

Susan Baker

Introduction

As high consumption economies, the European Union (EU) and its member states have a major impact on the environment, both internally and globally. Around 8.8% of the greenhouse gases emitted worldwide come from the EU and it creates around 2,500m. metric tons of waste each year, some 95m. tons of it hazardous.[1] At the same time, environmental policy is one of the most important and far-reaching areas of EU legislation. Since the early 1970s, the EU has developed an ever-expanding policy agenda and regulatory regime, dealing with the protection of air and water quality, the conservation of natural resources and of biodiversity, waste management and the control of industrial activities that have adverse environmental impact. It also has a major impact on the environmental policy of its near neighbours and plays an ever-growing role in global environmental governance.

This chapter explores environmental policy in the EU. It begins by looking at the Union's strong legal commitment to environmental protection and then examines the policy and strategy documents that frame the EU's approach. Exploring the challenge of environmental policy integration at the sectoral level provides insight into the difficulties surrounding implementation efforts. We conclude with some reflections on the wider political and economic context within which environmental policy is embedded and the consequences of this for policy progress.

Treaty Basis and Regulatory Developments

Environmental protection was not mentioned in the Treaty of Rome (1958) and EU initiatives in the field did not begin until the 1970s, a time when member states were influenced by growing domestic and international concerns about the environment. The EU declared that economic expansion is not an end in itself, but should result not only in improvements in the standard of living but also in quality of life (Baker, 2000). However, it was not until the Single European Act of 1986 that the EU's role in environmental protection was formally recognized. By this time, the European Commission, the main body that initiates new policy proposals in the EU, feared that the strengthening of environmental legislation by member states in response to increasing societal mobilization around environmental issues would act as a barrier to European free trade. The Commission, in particular the administrative division responsible for the environment, the Directorate-General for the Environment (DG Environment), was keen to ensure that environmental policy was more fully Europeanized.

EU environmental policy initially focused on legislating against pollution, particularly that of a transboundary nature, and then on supporting the completion of the internal market, including by setting EU trading standards, such as in relation to environmental standards for products. Some developments were in reaction to major pollution events, such as the Seveso Directives (Council Directive 96/82/EC; Seveso II & III 2012/18/EU), dealing with the control of major accident hazards involving dangerous substances, while others were in response to the obligations incurred under international agreements. Gradually, there was a shift of policy focus from general environmental protection measures to the promotion of sustainable development. This shift was reflected in treaty modifications, including the Treaty on European Union or Maastricht Treaty (signed in 1992) and the Treaty of Amsterdam (signed in 1997), the latter making sustainable development, along with economic and social progress, one of the objectives of the Community. The Treaty of Nice (signed in 2001) confirmed this. The Treaty of Lisbon (signed in 2007) reinforced the EU's pledge to pursue sustainable development both within and beyond its borders. In 2009 the European Council reaffirmed that sustainable development remained a fundamental objective of the EU under the Lisbon Treaty. Owing to these treaty modifications, there is probably no single government or other association of states with such a strong 'constitutional' commitment to sustainable development as the EU. Sustainable development is now a *norm* of EU politics, both domestically and internationally (Baker and McCormick, 2004). The Lisbon Treaty also commits the EU to work towards the adoption of international measures to preserve and improve the quality of the environment and the sustainable management of global natural resources.[2] The Treaty also makes combating climate change on an international level a specific objective of EU environmental policy, recognizing that the EU has a leading international role to play.

Treaties of the EU establish the remit, procedures and objectives of the European integration process. Guided by these, the EU has played an ever-stronger role in regulating economic behaviour to address the negative environmental consequences of production, and, to a lesser extent, consumption activities. This has resulted in a wide body of legislation, mostly in the form of directives governing an ever-growing array of issues.[3] There are several hundred environmental directives aimed at improving the quality of water, including in the marine environment; tackling air and noise pollution, including from transport and industrial sources; assuring the safety of chemicals; setting standards for the prevention and recycling of waste; protecting soil, native wildlife and plants; and the maintenance of biodiversity (Swords, 2010). One of the most complicated of these directives is the EU Water Framework Directive (WFD, 2000), which requires member states to establish river basin districts and, for each of these, a river basin management plan (CEC, 2014a). The Directive utilizes a cyclical process where river basin management plans are prepared, implemented and reviewed every six years, and it sets a series of implementation deadlines up to 2027. In response to concerns about weak implementation of the WFD, in 2012 the Commission published a Blueprint to Safeguard Europe's Water Resources, outlining actions to improve implementation (CEC, 2012). The Blueprint is expected to shape EU water policy up to 2050 (CEC, 2014b). In keeping with trends towards making greater use of market instruments in environmental policy, it also explains how to apply economic instruments through the internalization of costs for water use and water pollution. To support the continued use of market instruments, the Commission subsequently undertook research into the application of payments for ecosystem services to support the implementation of the WFD (European Union, 2014). The Blueprint also introduced new water-related green infrastructure measures, such as reforestation, floodplains restoration, soil management and sustainable urban drainage systems. Ways to integrate water management issues into the Common Agricultural Policy (CAP) and Cohesion Policy were also detailed.

Progress, however, has been slow. A 2015 report on the implementation of the WFD found that only 23% of WFD-specific basic measures were reported as completed, while 66% were ongoing and 11% not started (CEC, 2015a). Furthermore, two-thirds of the river basin districts established under the WFD reported that the basic measures were not sufficient to tackle diffuse pollution from agriculture. Funding shortfalls were also shown to hamper implementation. More recently, the lack of systems thinking, seen as a prerequisite to effective WFD implementation, has been highlighted, as too has the departure of implementation efforts from the WFD's original intentions (Voulvoulis et al, 2017).

Greater use of market-based instruments is also evident in the use of quota trading schemes, voluntary agreements and ecolabels, as seen, for example, in the development of the EU Emissions Trading Scheme (ETS) for trading greenhouse gas emissions. Increased use of these instruments was demanded by the sixth Environment Action Programme (EAP), the renewed Sustainable Development Strategy and the Lisbon Strategy, and is also reflected in the seventh EAP, as discussed below. The use of these environmental policy instruments forms part of the shift to new styles of governance in the EU, a neoliberal approach that sees greater involvement of economic partners and stakeholder networks in both the design and delivery of policy. Several criticisms of these instruments have been mounted, including concerns that the ETS, for example, may pass on costs to customers through price increases and that the scheme may result in 'carbon leakage' to companies outside the EU (Muûls et al, 2016). More seriously, corruption has enabled and facilitated the resale and misreporting of used carbon offsets, sophisticated computer hacking schemes for the theft from national carbon emission registries, and continuing value-added tax fraud. In 2010 European authorities uncovered several cases of so-called 'carousel fraud' in the trading of emissions, which amounted to an estimated US \$6,450m. in lost revenues across at least 11 countries (UNEP, 2013).

In addition to using both market-based and so-called 'command and control' legislative and regulatory instruments, reliance is also made on 'soft' procedural tools. These include the 2001 Convention on Access to Information, Public Participation in Decision-Making and Access to Justice in Environmental Matters (the Aarhus Convention), and the use of environmental impact assessments (EIA) and strategic environmental assessments (SEA) in certain planning decisions. The revised 2014 Environmental Impact Assessment (EIA) Directive (2014/52/EU) simplifies the rules for assessing the potential effects of projects on the environment. This simplification is in line with the drive for smarter regulation to reduce the administrative burden, especially on the private sector (CEC, 2015b). Similarly, proposals for the amendment of directives on waste policy were also tabled (CEC, 2014c). These planned reforms were driven by concerns to improve resource efficiency, including through waste capture and reuse. This, it was hoped, would create a more circular economy, in turn supporting further economic growth. They were also designed to support the objectives of the Resource Efficiency Roadmap and the seventh EAP, as discussed below. However, the proposals for the amendments were withdrawn. The official reason given was that the proposals needed to be redrafted to make them more ambitious, but some MEPs believed that the decision was a result of lobbying by big business (Crisp, 2015).

Closing the Loop—an EU Action Plan for the Circular Economy (COM/2015/0614 final) was adopted by the EU in 2015. This addressed the need to ensure that product design and related production processes, alongside waste management strategies, promoted the circular economy. This is considered to require action to boost the market for secondary raw materials and water reuse, with plastics, food waste, critical raw materials, construction and demolition, biomass and bio-based products regarded as priority areas for action. The implementation of this action plan was reviewed and a report published in January 2017, giving progress on action taken to date, and setting out the key initiatives for 2017, in particular with respect to the identification of synergies between the WFD to integrate water reuse in water management and planning (CEC, 2017a).

The EU is also party to a number of international conventions and protocols, including the UN Framework Convention on Climate Change (UNFCCC) and the related Kyoto Protocol, the UN Convention on Biological Diversity. It is also a member of several international governance regimes, such as those developed under the World Trade Organization, the trade policies of which have both direct and indirect environmental effects. International engagement plays a fundamental role in shaping EU policy. In the lead-up to the UNFCCC Conference of the Parties (COP21) in Paris, France, in 2015, for example, the EU agreed to cut its emissions by 40%, compared with 1990 levels, by 2030. Targets for 2020, 2030 and 2050 are broadly the same (CEC, 2016a). The Paris Agreement also included a five-year, so-called 'ambition cycle', providing for parties to reconvene to take stock and re-examine their commitments, strengthening them if necessary (CEC, 2017b).

These targets have major consequences for sectoral policy, including for the energy sector, as discussed below, as well as for internal relations between the EU and its member states. There are tensions between the EU and the Visegrad group (the Czech Republic, Hungary, Poland and Slovakia), for example. Czech proposals to limit energy efficiency savings from 1.5% a year to 0.35%, and Poland's proposal to carry over unused carbon credits into the next market phase, which would depress prices and reduce the incentive to scale back CO_2 emissions, are cases in point (Neslen, 2017).

The European Environment Agency (EEA) 2015 Trends Report indicated that the EU is on track to meet the 2020 target for reducing greenhouse gas emissions by 20%, with calculations showing that the Union could achieve a 24% reduction, in comparison with 1990 levels, by 2020 (EEA, 2015a; see also CEC, 2016b).

Targets for individual member states were set in July 2016, and these were already seeing resistance from at least Poland, where the Government has advocated a 0% reduction target, while the Commission has calculated a target of a 7% reduction. The longer-term goal is to achieve reductions of 80%–95% by 2050, compared with 1990 levels. This is discussed further below.

Developments over time also saw the EU enlarge to 28 member states. Enlargement introduced a more diverse range of ecosystem types and environmental conditions that had to be taken into account in policy formulation. However, the increased number of jurisdictions, with different national policy styles and political cultures, has not only made negotiations more complex and time-consuming across the 28 member states, but has often resulted in policy outcomes that are a weak compromise. Ensuring effective implementation of policy also poses new challenges. Several of the newer member states have retained their historical tendency to give low priority to environmental considerations, with the countries of the Visegrad Group, for example, able to win concessions on a range of environmental issues, including their individual country emissions reduction targets. Implementation capacity is also weak among the newer member states, particularly those from South-Eastern Europe.

Policy Developments

EU environmental policy is framed by medium-term Environment Action Programmes (EAPs), which translate declaratory and legal commitments into policy actions. They provide a forward-looking framework for policy developments, which are drawn up by the European Commission's Environment Directorate-General (DG Environment). The first EAP (1973–76) acknowledged that economic growth was not an end in itself, while the second EAP (1977–81) referred to the limits to growth stemming from natural resource availability and affirmed that 'economic growth should not be viewed solely in its quantitative aspects'. The third EAP (1982–86) forged links between environmental policy and the Community's industrial strategy, arguing that environmental protection measures could stimulate technological innovation. This argument proved decisive and, since the third EAP, environmental protection has come to be seen as having the potential to enhance the competitiveness of the EU's economy. The fourth EAP (1987–92) further developed this idea, drawing upon, while also helping to promote, the principle of ecological modernization, with a twin focus on efficiency and technological innovation as solutions to environmental problems (Baker, 2007).

The fifth EAP, *Towards Sustainability* (1993–2000), made the first explicit policy pledge to the promotion of sustainable development. It was drawn up in parallel with preparations for the Rio Earth Summit. This EAP has been the subject of extensive reviews, which have shown that up to 2000 there was no reversal in economic and social trends harmful to the environment, particularly in relation to the transport, energy and tourism sectors (EEA, 1995). The EU is responsible for 15%–20% of the world's consumption of resources; the balance remained unchanged during this period.

The sixth EAP, *Our Future, Our Choice* (2001–10), attempted to address some of these shortcomings by developing a more strategic and targeted approach (CEC, 2001a). It identified four environmental areas for priority action: climate change; nature and biodiversity; environment, health and quality of life; and natural resources and waste. Detailed measures were set out in seven Thematic Strategies, in turn used to identify further proposals for legislation. Under the sixth EAP, the EU adopted a number of new environmental policies and measures, set ambitious targets in various areas, and developed several 'cross-cutting' strategies and plans. However, the failure to set concrete targets, and limited monitoring and reporting mechanisms compromised the sixth EAP. Furthermore, coherence between the different strands of EU policy was also weak. Environmental policy integration has proved particularly elusive for the Commission, especially at the sectoral level. Transport, for example, continues to impose a significant environmental burden and environmental pressures from unsustainable consumption and production continue to grow (CEC, 2011). The prioritization of road building in EU transport policy in Eastern Europe provides a good example of the failure of policy integration (CEE Bankwatch Network, 2007; Baker, 2012) and has given rise to conflicts where road-building programmes are at odds with EU biodiversity protection policy.

The CAP, to take another policy sector, has also led to serious environmental deterioration. The high level of support given to maintaining agricultural prices has encouraged intensive agriculture. The resultant increased use of fertilizers and pesticides has polluted water and led to soil contamination. It has also resulted in the destruction of some important ecosystems through the removal of hedges, stone walls and ditches, and the drainage of wetlands. This has reduced natural habitats for a large number of birds, plants and other forms of wildlife. In some regions, intensification has resulted in over-consumption of water and has accelerated soil erosion. The CAP has undergone a series of reforms in order to address both mounting environmental concerns and to enable it better to support rural livelihoods. Reforms include the introduction of agri-environmental and, more recently, climate change measures. The 2013 reforms, for example, introduced direct payments to farmers given by way of so-called 'greening payments': that is, they must support farming practices that are beneficial to both the climate and the environment (CEC, 2016c). In 2017 the Commission planned to begin wide consultation on the 2013 reforms, seen as necessary because of several developments, including falling agricultural prices, the new emphasis on bilateral deals in trade negotiations, and the EU's international environmental commitments under the UNFCCC following COP21 and under the United Nations (UN) Sustainable Development Goals (SDGs), and the need to address growing concerns about food security (CEC, 2017c). However, pressures from intensive agriculture continue and protection of high nature value farmland remains limited.

Efforts to integrate environmental considerations into the Common Fisheries Policy (CFP) have also proved difficult. The CFP was reformed in 2013, when the practice of discards (throwing away fish that would take a boat over its quota, or are not covered by the quota) was replaced by a landing obligation. However, sufficient integration between fisheries management and environmental conservation has not yet been achieved (IEEP, 2016). In addition, it is unlikely that the current period will see much improvement, as since under the Commission led by President Jean-Claude Juncker, the DG for Maritime Affairs and Fisheries has been encouraged to prioritize 'respect for the principles of subsidiarity, proportionality and better regulation … [and to] … always look for the most efficient and least burdensome approach' (Juncker, 2014). Greater commitment to the sustainable development obligations with respect to the marine environment are needed, both under the CFP and the Marine Strategy Framework Directive of 2008. This Marine Directive forms part of the Integrated Maritime Policy introduced in 2007 to develop a management framework to promote 'blue growth' and spatial planning in the maritime environment at the EU level. The Directive legally binds member states to achieve good environmental status of their waters by 2020. However, implementation plans remain weak, especially at the member state level (IEEP, 2016; EEA, 2015b). In addition, over time the discourse on the commitment to sectoral integration has tended to be replaced by more general discussion on the need to 'reflect' environmental considerations in EU policies.

In 2013 the EU adopted the seventh EAP, *Living Well, within the Limits of our Planet*, to guide environment policy up to 2020 (OJ, 2013) The seventh EAP identifies a series of challenges facing the EU and seeks to enhance Europe's ecological resilience in the face of these by transforming the EU into an inclusive and sustainable green economy. It differs from previous action programmes in that it is designed to address the increasingly interlinked nature of environmental, economic and social challenges, especially in the context of climate change. It also indicates that the body of EU legislation has reached maturity, both in terms of its spread and coverage, and that attention now needs to be focused on both implementation and on non-legislative engagements. In addition, the seventh EAP emphasizes the need for the EU to take a leadership role in international environmental governance, in particular with respect to climate change. This reflects the fact that the Treaty of Lisbon adds the support of international action for fighting climate change to the list of objectives defining environmental policy at the EU level. This requires, in turn, that the increased growth in the demand for natural resources and the impact this has for the environment is addressed both internally by the EU and externally in the Union's international engagements.

However, claims that EU legislation has reached maturity may be premature, especially given new evidence about the health impact of poor air quality standards within the EU, particularly in urban settings, and the growing policy challenges arising from climate change and biodiversity loss, including natural resource scarcity. Regulation supporting the maintenance of the environmental quality of soils is also needed, especially given that promises to address this in the sixth EAP are still outstanding. Proposals for a Soil Framework Directive were withdrawn in May 2014, due to lack of support in the Council (CEC, 2016d). In the absence of a common policy framework, there is no EU-level political or legislative framework supporting an integrated and coherent approach to soil management (Ecologic, 2017).

Nevertheless, the seventh EAP reflects a shift from support for binding legislation in favour of a focus on setting long-term environmental strategies, such as seen in the *Roadmap to a Low Carbon Economy in 2050* (COM(2011) 122), the *EU Biodiversity Strategy to 2020* (COM(2011) 0244), the *Roadmap to a Resource-Efficient Europe* (COM(2011) 0244) and the *Europe 2020 Strategy* (COM(2010) 2020), some of which are discussed further below. The shift from a legislative approach is also in keeping with the 'Better Regulation' package (COM(2014)368), which investigates whether EU legislation is fit for purpose.

Nature protection policy, built around the construction of a Natura 2000 network of protected areas and the Birds (2009/147/EC) and Habitats Directives (92/43/EEC) is currently the subject of this regulation 'fitness check'. Such a check is necessary, given that biodiversity remains under severe threat, not least because of pressure from agricultural pollution, overfishing, land taken for roads and urban development, and from climate change. The EEA's report entitled *State of Nature in the EU* confirmed the negative impact of these pressures across different biogeographical and marine regions in the EU (EEA, 2015b). The failure to make effective progress towards meeting the EU 2020 Biodiversity Strategy targets has also been highlighted (EEA, 2015c). Such failures illustrate the need not only for enhanced efforts in implementing existing legislation, but also the need to take major and consequential steps to integrate environmental considerations into EU sectoral policy (particularly within agricultural and transport policy), and to update legislation to take account of new issue areas, for example, in relation to the conservation of biodiversity outside the protected areas network. The Review of the EU's Biodiversity Strategy in 2015 (CEC, 2015c), for example, led to demands from the European Parliament to address urgently the social, ecological and economic consequence of biodiversity loss in Europe and for the EU not to fail as it did in relation to meeting the 2010 biodiversity targets (EP, 2016).

The seventh EAP identified nine priority objectives up to 2020, including protecting nature and strengthening ecological resilience; stimulating sustainable, resource-efficient, low-carbon growth; and addressing environment-related threats to health. The programme set out a framework to support the achievement of these objectives through, *inter alia*, better implementation of EU environment law; enhancement in scientific knowledge; securing the necessary investments in support of environment and climate change policy; and improving the way in which environmental concerns are reflected in other policies. The programme also aims to help EU cities to become more sustainable.[4] Nearly 75% of Europeans live in cities and urban areas, and by 2020 this is expected to have risen to 80%. Cities encounter several environmental challenges, including ensuring security of food supplies while at the same time reducing their environmental impact, and trying to balance the need for green spaces for both healthy living and the maintenance of biodiversity amid the ever-growing demand for land required by city expansion. The 2016 Amsterdam Pact outlines the main features of the Urban Agenda for the EU. Initial priorities include addressing air quality, supporting climate adaptation through the extension of green infrastructure solutions, and the promotion of energy transition (NLU, 2016).

Although the seventh EAP was only adopted in 2013, concerns have already been expressed by the European Environmental Bureau (EEB), Europe's largest federation of environmental organizations, with over 143 member organizations, about its weakness, in particular the lack of specific targets and clear commitments to further binding measures (EEB, 2013). Such criticisms already beset the sixth EAP.[5] However, the seventh programme explicitly recognizes the importance of environmental policy integration and the need to make cross-thematic linkages with other policy areas. This is a critical first step in developing a comprehensive approach towards integrating environmental, social and economic concerns into policy-making. Yet the programme has not explicitly identified the trade-offs that will have to be made between the different priorities it has set, making it difficult to negotiate between different actors, such as individual stakeholders or institutions, and concerns, such as in relation to social and environmental matters, and to take appropriate action (Endl and Berger, 2014). A 2016 review of the seventh EAP by the EEA made it clear that 'dealing with the complex, inter-related priorities of the 7th EAP requires more integrated and systemic approaches to knowledge. The opportunities for knowledge synergies across these policy domains are potentially considerable' (EEA, 2016). The report also concluded that the EU's natural capital is not yet being protected, and that environmental pressures continue to contribute significantly to the overall burden of disease and that further efforts are needed to implement existing environment and heath legislation and policies (EEA, 2016).

An overview of the implementation of EU environmental laws and policies, *The Environmental Implementation Review*, was published in 2017 (CEC, 2017d). The report highlighted that waste prevention remains an important challenge in all member states, including those with high recycling rates. Decoupling of waste production from economic growth is still required. It also found that the overall status of protected species and habitats has not significantly improved. Across the EU, more than three-quarters of the habitat assessments indicate an unfavourable conservation status and a significant proportion is continuing to deteriorate. Although there has been progress in many areas and there are local success stories, there are significant gaps in implementation, financing and policy integration. Furthermore, while air quality in the EU has improved over the past few decades, natural surface water bodies have good or high ecological status in only one-third of member states. While sustainable development strategies exist, including at regional level, in some cases these are not updated. In some member states there continue to be obstacles to access to justice in environmental matters. These implementation deficits were attributed to ineffective co-ordination among local, regional and national authorities; lack of administrative capacity and insufficient financing; lack of knowledge and data; insufficient compliance assurance mechanisms; and lack of integration and policy coherence.

In summary, the use of EAPs has allowed the EU to engage in forward planning and has enabled it to set up a process of periodic review, which has helped to highlight both its achievements and its failings, and to identify its future challenges. Over time, this has proved beneficial in several ways. It has given a strategic focus to legislative developments that has, in turn, helped to improve ambient quality, including European water quality, reduce air pollution, transform waste management, improve the safety of handing of chemicals and is beginning to address the pressures on the marine environment. Longer-term planning has also enabled the European Commission to keep environmental issues on the policy agenda, despite the fluctuations in its political salience. It has also served to push several reluctant EU member states towards taking greater care of their environment, including in relation to nature protection. Meeting the objectives of the UN SDGs by 2030, and EU priorities, such as the Circular Economy energy transition, will also require that the EU address both the synergies and trade-offs between the economy, the environment and human well-being.

The Sustainable Development Strategy

In addition to being guided by EAPs, environmental policy in the EU is framed within the context of specific strategic initiatives, such as the Resource Efficiency Roadmap, the 2020 Biodiversity Strategy, and the Low Carbon Economy Roadmap.[6] In addition, policy is guided by *A Sustainable Europe for a Better World: A European Union Strategy for Sustainable Development* (EU SDS) (CEC, 2001b), which was renewed in June 2006 following the enlargement of the EU (CEC, 2005).

Since it was adopted at the European Council meeting held in Göteborg (Gothenburg), Sweden in 2001, the EU Sustainable Development Strategy (SDS) is sometimes called the Gothenburg Strategy. Its development followed from the 1992 Rio Earth Summit, when governments agreed to formulate national strategies, and the 1997 Rio+5 Summit, which set the objective for all countries to have their SDSs in place by the 2002 Johannesburg World Summit for Sustainable Development. In part, the SDS was designed to show how the Union is contributing to global efforts to promote sustainable development.

The renewed 2005 SDS focuses on seven principal challenges, in particular as they relate to climate change, contains detailed arrangements for implementation, monitoring and follow-up, and specifies what is expected, not only of other EU institutions, but also of member states. Specific quantitative targets and measures have been laid down, for example with respect to greenhouse gas emissions and energy efficiency. Policy integration has a central role in this strategy. These targets and objectives are, to a large extent, based on international commitments at the time, for example, under the Kyoto Protocol, the Johannesburg World Summit on Sustainable Development and the Millennium Development Goals, or reflect internal policy developments, such as on biofuels (IEEP, 2010). In 2016 the EU presented its response to the UN 2030 Agenda (CEC, 2016e). However, a more detailed response to the 17 SDGs, including how the EU will implement them, remains at a very general level (CEC, 2016f). Nevertheless, some of the environmental objectives include vaguely formulated ambitions, for example to decouple economic growth from environmental degradation. Although at the declaratory level the Strategy reflects a relatively strong commitment to promoting fundamental changes in policy, implementation remains the challenge. Limited attention has been given in the strategy to conceptual clarification and to the necessary revision of the traditional hierarchy of policy objectives, which give precedent to economic growth over and above environmental considerations. This leads to a confusing variety of methods for integrating environmental concerns in sector policies across the strategy as a whole (IEEP, 2010).

The SDS also reflects new thinking on environmental issues, as seen, for example, in its recognition of the value of ecosystem services, placing more emphasis on promoting sustainable consumption and production patterns, and demanding that environmental and health aspects be integrated in transport policy. The external dimension is also addressed in the renewed SDS. Attention should also be drawn to a European Commission communication published in 2014 and entitled *A Decent Life for All: From Vision to Collective Action*, which addresses the UN SDGs developed under the auspices of the UN 2030 Agenda. This communication is strong in its recognition of the international dimension of the EU's engagement, and the importance of addressing the promotion of sustainable development at a global level (CEC, 2014e). However, it is unlikely that the contribution of the EU to the attainment of the SDGs will be achieved without substantial changes to the status quo, particularly in relation to high consumption, and without substantial additional financial contributions to developing countries.

The third theme of the strategy, 'progress reviews', involves a review at each spring European Council meeting concerning progress in implementing the SDS. This lends a high-level political weight to the review process. In order to contribute to these progress reports, Eurostat has developed a set of Sustainable Development Indicators (SDIs).[7] However, reviews tend to be negative, concluding that, while the EU has taken the international lead in the fight against climate change and the promotion of a low-carbon economy, unsustainable trends persist in the EU in several areas, including in relation to transport, consumption and natural resource use (CEC, 2009; EU, 2015).

Taken together, the EAPs and strategy documents represent the environmental policy framework of the EU and serve to put legal obligations and declaratory intent into practice. They frame the context within which actions, secondary legislation, specific programmes and funding are structured. It is clear from our review that new issues continue to arise on the EU's environmental policy agenda and that over time these have stretched concerns beyond the EU border, particularly given global environmental change, especially climate change. In recent years, the EU has played an ever-greater role in ensuring more effective international environmental governance to address global environmental change. It is also clear, however, that domestic achievements continue to fall far short of the declaratory intent of policy, particularly when it comes to the integration of environmental considerations into sectoral policies.

Tensions at the Heart of the Integration Process

Much has changed since the EU began its active engagement in the environmental policy arena, including enlargement, which resulted in the EU expanding to 28 members, and the entry into force of the Treaty of Lisbon, which changed the institutional architecture of the EU. Over time, despite an early and strong commitment to environmental policy, political priorities have veered more and more towards a prioritization of economic and social issues to the detriment of environmental considerations, a trend further exacerbated by the post-2008 financial and economic crises. The implementation of EU environmental policy has to be seen as embedded within this wider political and economic context. The tensions between the EU's environmental and economic policy are evident in the EU's 10-year growth strategy, Europe 2020.

It is the Commission's view that current environmental policy, as reflected in the seventh EAP, for example, should contribute to the objectives of the Europe 2020 Strategy of obtaining high levels of employment, productivity and social cohesion for 2020. The aim of the 2020 Strategy, introduced in 2010, is to help Europe to overcome the ongoing economic and financial crisis through a 10-year programme of growth. Europe 2020 is closely related to the earlier, so-called Lisbon Strategy, the objective of which was to make the EU the most competitive and dynamic knowledge-based economy in the world. The 2020 Strategy builds on the aspirations of Lisbon by addressing the shortcomings of the Union's current growth model, replacing it with a new type of growth that is smart, sustainable and inclusive. It focuses on three themes: smart growth, which fosters knowledge, innovation, education and the digital society; sustainable growth, which involves making production more resource-efficient while improving competitiveness; and inclusive growth that raises participation in the labour market, the acquisition of skills, and seeks to combat poverty. The Europe 2020 Strategy has set five objectives to be reached by 2020 on employment, innovation, education, social inclusion and climate/energy. These include the so-called '20/20/20' climate and energy targets: a 20% reduction in EU greenhouse gas emissions from 1990 levels; raising the share of energy consumption produced from renewable resources to 20%; and a 20% improvement in energy efficiency. Targets are also set for 2030 to achieve at least a 40% cut in greenhouse gas emissions compared with 1990, at least 27% of total energy consumption from renewable energy and at least a 27% increase in energy efficiency. The 2009 Renewable Energy Directive (2009/28/EC) sets binding targets of the share of renewables in each member state to 2020, while the Energy Efficiency Directive of 2012 (2012/27/EU) sets targets for energy savings. This covers all sectors except transport and includes, for the first time in an energy efficiency directive, measures for supply side efficiency. The Europe 2020 Strategy also includes seven 'flagship initiatives',[8] including the roadmap to a resource-efficient Europe that supports the shift towards a resource-efficient, low-carbon economy to achieve sustainable growth.[9] The Revised Renewable Energy Directive, published in 2016, aims for at least a 27% renewable energy share by 2030 (CEC, 2016g). A Progress Report, published in 2017, found that the majority of member states are on track to fulfil the original objective of 20% by 2020 (CEC, 2017e). A proposed update, the Energy Efficiency Directive of 2016, aims to achieve a 30% energy efficiency target by 2030 (CEC, 2016h).

Progress is monitored through the so-called European Semester, an annual cycle that submits member states to analyses of their economic and structural reforms, with potential policy warnings and enforcement through incentives and/or sanctions (CEC, 2014f; see also CEC, 2017f).

However, the roadmap tends to prioritize only those environmental actions that help to promote growth and jobs, to the detriment of wider environmental considerations. Community negotiations on growth and competitiveness now routinely include discussion on moving to a low-carbon economy and creating 'green' jobs, emphasizing the 'win-win' potential of addressing climate change, especially through energy initiatives. Security of supply is also a principal focus, particularly in the context of geopolitical concerns over Russian control of gas exports to the EU. Energy policy, both through promoting decarbonization and market liberalization, is seen as the key tool not only to support climate change objectives but also wider economic and social achievements (IEEP, 2010). Emphasizing the need for a so-called Energy Union, Juncker regards energy policy as fundamental to the construction of a resilient Union: 'This is not only a matter of a responsible climate change policy. It is, at the same time, an industrial policy imperative if we still want to have affordable energy at our disposal in the medium term' (European People's Party, not dated).

Within both the roadmap and the 2020 Strategy, environmental protection is increasingly considered dependent on achieving a dynamic European economy, thus making it subservient to shorter-term economic goals. The emphasis on energy policy has been at the expense of both environmental policy and a wider understanding of the imperatives associated with climate change adaptation and mitigation. Recent restructuring of the Commission under the Juncker presidency, which saw the loss of a dedicated Climate Change portfolio, has led to criticism from the EEB that environmental and climate change actions have been marginalized (Energy Post, 2016). This approach runs counter to the basic tenets of sustainable development, which hold that long-term sustainability can be achieved only through policies that integrate environmental, economic and social considerations from the outset of policy developments.

Because of the strong focus on economic growth, implementation of environmental policy has often had to confront opposition within the EU institutions, at times leading to delays in the adoption of specific implementation measures, and in some cases to a lowering of their level of ambition (IEEP, 2010). The consequences of this can be seen in the regularity with which assessments of EU environmental policy indicate the failure to bring about effective reductions in the stresses that sectoral policies place on the natural resource base and on the global ecological system. The proposed Transatlantic Trade and Investment Partnership (TTIP) with the USA (suspended following the election of US President Donald Trump in November 2016) was a case in point. It was criticized as exemplifying the deepening neoliberal approach of the EU, and in this case for its potential to lead to weakened environmental standards and consumer protection measures.

The shift under the current Juncker Commission away from environmental issues to a focus on job creation, competitiveness and economic growth was also reflected in the Commission's Work Programme for 2016. This mentioned the environment in only two places: once in the context of the development of the circular economy where 'The aim is to address economic and environmental concerns by maximizing efficiency in the use of resources, covering the whole value chain (including sustainable consumption, production, waste management) and through innovation, thereby enabling the development of new markets and business models'; and in the second case in relation to the external implementation of the UN SDGs (CEC, 2015c). In both cases, environmental matters are linked to growth and in the latter case no new legislation is envisaged. This mirrored the Commission's Work Programme of 2015, which offered 23 new policy proposals, only one of which was environmental (Gravey, 2016).

The impact of austerity on EU environmental policy has also to be taken into account. The global financial crisis of 2008–09 and new austerity measures introduced following the EU debt crisis in 2011 led some member states to impose severe restrictions on public expenditure, not only on environment-related policy. In other countries, most notably Sweden, this resulted in a redirection of policy towards a green economic approach, giving the state a greater role in the creation of jobs through 'greening' the economy. It has also been used as an opportunity to transfer the responsibility for managing environmental issues to the private sector (EPSU, 2012).

The impact on EU environmental policy of a British exit from the EU, supported by the results of a referendum held in the United Kingdom in June 2016, and commonly referred to as 'Brexit', remains more uncertain. On the one hand, the British Government can be seen as having had a negative impact on the formulation of EU environmental policy, and thus Brexit could result in an environmentally stronger Union. The UK, for example, which is in favour of the release of genetically modified organisms, has tried to prevent the adoption of stronger pesticide regulations, and, more recently, has called for weaker habitats protection, has sought to block strict rules limiting the imports of tar sands at the EU level, tried to dilute the terms of the EU energy efficiency directive, successfully blocked the adoption of binding national renewable energy targets for 2030, and threatened to block an EU pesticide ban protecting bees (Burns, 2015). On the other hand, the need to address obligations incurred under the UNFCCC continues to bring out tensions between those member states that are keen to address climate change and those for whom it is less of a policy priority; and between member states that wish climate change to be dealt with under the principle of subsidiarity and those that wish the EU to play a greater role, including in international negotiations. The UK has provided strong leadership on climate change issues, including at the international level, and Brexit may see a weakening of EU international environmental leadership in this area (Oberthür, 2015). However, the UK has been less keen to introduce binding targets, particularly at the sectoral level, including within the energy sector, instead favouring market-based approaches, such as the ETS. Without the strong neoliberal push from the UK, a push that is not necessarily favourable for the advancement of EU environmental policy, a new opportunity may be created. An EU without the UK could be more willing to accept regulatory measures, for example, for promoting the circular economy (Dupont et al, 2016), and more willing to support efforts to promote policies to address climate change other than through the dysfunctional ETS.

Conclusion

Environmental policy is a well-developed field in the EU, backed by treaty obligations, a comprehensive range of legislation, strategy documents and action programmes. However, while it would appear that the EU is making a certain amount of progress, this is not enough to reduce pressure on the environment and even less so to promote sustainable development. It is also clear that the environmental policy of the EU cannot be wholly separated from other influences, such as the state of the European economy and shifting political mandates. These result in tensions at the heart of the European integration process, between the stimulation of growth-orientated economic policy and environmental protection measures. In this context, environmental policy integration remains a daunting challenge, especially given the current marginalization of environmental and sustainable development considerations. The current period, with the prioritization of economic growth and the imposition of harsh austerity measures, risks the EU losing the environmental leadership role that it has developed over the past several decades. In addition, without accelerated efforts and commitment, pressure on the environment will continue to exceed the limited carrying capacity of the environment, including at the global level.

Notes

1. See Boden, T. A., Marland, G., and Andres, R. J. (2015). *National CO_2 Emissions from Fossil-Fuel Burning, Cement Manufacture, and Gas Flaring: 1751-2011*, Carbon Dioxide Information Analysis Center, Oak Ridge National Laboratory, US Department of Energy, doi 10.3334/CDIAC/00001_V2015; CEC, *Report from the Commission to the European Parliament and the Council: Progress Towards Achieving the Kyoto and EU 2020 Objectives* (Brussels, 28.10.2014, COM(2014) 689 final available at ec.europa.eu/transparency/regdoc/rep/1/

2014/EN/1-2014-689-EN-F1-1.pdf.2014; *Annex to the Report from the Commission to the European Parliament and the Council: Progress Towards Achieving the Kyoto and EU 2020 Objectives*, available at ec.europa.eu/transparency/regdoc/rep/1/2014/EN/1-2014-689-EN-F1-1-ANNEX-1.pdf.2014; Eurostat, *Waste Statistics*, available at ec.europa.eu/eurostat/statistics-explained/index.php/Waste_statistics#Further_Eurostat_information.

2. See eur-lex.europa.eu/JOHtml.do?uri=OJ:C:2007:306:SOM:EN:HTM.
3. EU directives lay down certain end results that must be achieved in every member state. National authorities have to adapt their laws to meet these goals, but are free to decide how to do so. Each directive specifies the date by which the national laws must be adapted, giving national authorities the room for manoeuvre within the deadlines necessary to take account of differing national situations(ec.europa.eu/eu_law/directives/directives_en.htm).
4. See ec.europa.eu/environment/newprg.
5. See www.eeb.org/index.cfm/news-events/news/eeb-welcomes-respect-for-planatory-limits-in-7th-eap-proposal-but-misses-concrete-targets.
6. See ec.europa.eu/environment/newprg/index.htm.
7. See www.ieep.eu/assets/443/sdi_review.pdf.
8. See ec.europa.eu/europe2020/europe-2020-in-a-nutshell.
9. See ec.europa.eu/resource-efficient-europe.

Select Bibliography

Baker, S. 'The European Union: Integration, Competition, Growth—and Sustainability', in W. M. Lafferty and J. Meadowcroft (Eds), *Implementing Sustainable Development: Strategies and Initiatives in High Consumption Societies*, pp. 303–336. Oxford, Oxford University Press, 2000.

Baker, S. 'Sustainable Development as Symbolic Commitment: Declaratory Politics and the Seductive Appeal of Ecological Modernisation in the European Union', *Environmental Politics*, March 2007.

Baker, S. 'Environmental Governance: Influence of the European Union beyond its Borders', in Gladman, I. (Ed.) *Central and South-Eastern Europe 2013*, 13th edn, Abingdon, Routledge, 2012.

Baker, S., and McCormick, J. 'Sustainable Development: Comparative Understandings and Responses', in Vig, N. J., and Faure, M. C. (Eds). *Green Giants? Environmental Policy of the United States and the European Union*. Cambridge, MA, MIT Press, 2004.

Burns, C. *The EU Referendum and the Environment*. London, Friends of the Earth, 2015, available at: www.foe.co.uk/sites/default/files/downloads/eu_referendum_environment.pdf.

CEC. 'First Programme of Action on the Environment', *Official Journal of the European Communities*, Vol. 16, No. C 112, 20 Dec. 1973.

CEC. 'Second Environmental Action Programme, 1977–1981', *Official Journal of the European Communities*, No. C 139, 13 June 1977.

CEC. 'Third Environmental Action Programme', *Official Journal of the European Communities*, No. C 46, 17 Feb. 1983.

CEC. *Towards Sustainability: A European Community Programme of Policy and Action in Relation to the Environment (1992–2000)*, COM(92) 23 final. Brussels, Commission of the European Communities, 1992.

CEC. *Environment 2010: Our Future, Our Choice*, COM(2001) 31 final. Brussels, Commission of the European Communities, 2001a.

CEC. *A Sustainable Europe for a Better World: A European Union Strategy for Sustainable Development*, COM(2001) 264 final. Brussels, Commission of the European Communities, 2001b.

CEC. *Review of the Sustainable Development Strategy—A Platform for Action*, COM(2005) 658 final. Brussels, Commission of the European Communities, 2005.

CEC. *Mainstreaming Sustainable Development into EU Policies: 2009 Review of the European Union Strategy for Sustainable Development*, COM(2009) 400 final. Brussels, Commission of the European Communities, 2009.

CEC. *EUROPE 2020 A Strategy for Smart, Sustainable and Inclusive Growth*, COM(2011) 0531 final. Brussels, Commission of the European Communities, **2011**.

CEC. 'The Sixth Community Environment Action Programme: Final Assessment', COM(2011) 531 final. Brussels, Commission of the European Communities, 2011.

CEC. *A Blueprint to Safeguard Europe's Water Resources*, COM(2012) 673, final. Brussels, Commission of the European Communities, 2012.

CEC. *Review of Waste Policy and Legislation: Roadmap*, available at: ec.europa.eu/smart-regulation/impact/planned_ia/docs/2014_env_005_waste_review_en.pdf. Brussels, Commission of the European Communities, 2013.

CEC. *River Basin Management Plans 2009–2015: Information on Availability by Country*, available at: ec.europa.eu/environment/water/participation/map_mc/map.htm. Brussels, Commission of the European Communities, 2014a.

CEC. *A Water Blueprint: Taking Stock, Moving Forward*, available at: ec.europa.eu/environment/water/blueprint/index_en.htm. Brussels, Commission of the European Communities, 2014b.

CEC. *Proposal for a Directive of the European Parliament and of the Council amending Directives 2008/98/EC on Waste, 94/62/EC on Packaging and Packaging Waste, 1999/31/EC on the landfill of waste, 2000/53/EC on end-of-life vehicles, 2006/66/EC on Batteries and Accumulators and Waste Batteries and Accumulators, and 2012/19/EU on Waste Electrical and Electronic Equipment*, COM(2014) 0397, final, available at: eur-lex.europa.eu/legal-content/EN/TXT/?uri=celex:52014PC0397. Brussels, Commission of the European Communities, 2014c.

CEC. *2030 Framework for Climate and Energy Policies*. Brussels, Commission of the European Communities, 2014d.

CEC. Communication from the Commission to the European Parliament, the Council, the European Economic and Social Committee and the Committee of the Regions, *A Decent Life for All: From Vision to Collective Action*, COM/2014/0335 final, available at: eur-lex.europa.eu/legal-content/EN/TXT/?uri=CELEX:52014DC0335. Brussels, Commission of the European Communities, 2014e.

CEC. *Making It Happen: The European Semester*, available at: ec.europa.eu/europe2020/making-it-happen/index_en.htm. Brussels, Commission of the European Communities, 2014f.

CEC. *The Fourth Implementation Report—Assessment of the Water Framework Directive Programmes of Measures and the Flood Directive*, available at: ec.europa.eu/environment/water/water-framework/impl_reports.htm#fourth. Brussels, Commission of the European Communities, 2015a.

CEC. *Review of the Environmental Impact Assessment (EIA) Directive*, available at: ec.europa.eu/environment/eia/review.htm. Brussels, Commission of the European Communities, 2015b.

CEC. *Mid-term Review of the EU Biodiversity Strategy to 2020* (COM(2015) 0478 final. Brussels, Commission of the European Communities, 2015c.

CEC. Annex to the Communication from the Commission to the European Parliament, the Council, the European Economic and Social Committee and the Committee of the Regions, *Commission Work Programme 2016: No Time for Business as Usual*. Brussels, Commission of the European Communities, COM(2015) 610 final, available at: ec.europa.eu/atwork/pdf/cwp_2016_annex_i_en.pdf ANNEX 1, 2015d.

CEC. *Implementing the Paris Agreement: Progress of the EU towards the at least -40% target*. Brussels, ECE, 2016a, available at: https://ec.europa.eu/clima/sites/clima/files/eu_progress_report_2016_en.pdf, 2016a.

CEC. *Report from the Commission to the European Parliament and the Council on Evaluating the Implementation of Decision No. 406/2009/EC pursuant to its Article 14*. Brussels, Commission of the European Communities, COM(2016) 0483 final, 2016b.

CEC. *The Common Agricultural Policy after 2013*. Brussels, Commission of the European Communities, available at: ec.europa.eu/agriculture/cap-post-2013, 2016c.

CEC. *Addressing Soil Quality Issues in the EU*, available at: ec.europa.eu/environment/soil/process_en.htm, 2016d.

CEC. *Sustainable Development: EU Sets out its Priorities*. Brussels, Commission of the European Communities, Press Release, Strasbourg, 22 Nov. 2016, available at: europa.eu/rapid/press-release_IP-16-3883_en.htm, 2016e.

CEC. *Key European Action supporting the 2030 Agenda and the Sustainable Development Goals Accompanying the Document Communication from the Commission to the European Parliament, the Council, the European Economic and Social Committee and the Committee of the Regions. Next Steps for a Sustainable European Future: European Union Action for Sustainability*. Brussels, Commission of the European Communities, COM(2016) 739 final, available at: ec.europa.eu/europeaid/sites/devco/files/swd-key-european-actions-2030-agenda-sdgs-390-20161122_en.pdf, 2016f.

CEC. *Proposal for a Directive of the European Parliament and of the Council on the Promotion of the Use of Energy from Renewable Sources (Recast)*. Brussels, Commission of the European Communities, COM(2016) 0767 final/2 (2016) 0382 (COD), available at: eur-lex.europa.eu/legal-content/EN/TXT/?uri=CELEX:52016PC0767R%2801%29.0, 2016g.

CEC. *Proposal for a Directive of the European Parliament and of the Council amending Directive 2012/27/EU on Energy Efficiency*. Brussels, Commission of the European Communities, 2016, COM(2016) 761 final, available at: ec.europa.eu/energy/sites/ener/files/documents/1_en_act_part1_v16.pdf, 2016h.

CEC. Report from the Commission to the European Parliament, the Council, the European Economic and Social Committee and the Committee of the Regions, *On the Implementation of the Circular Economy Action Plan*. Brussels, Commission of the European Communities, COM(2017) 33 final, available at: ec.europa.eu/environment/circular-economy/implementation_report.pdf, 2017a.

CEC. *Paris Agreement*, available at: https://ec.europa.eu/clima/policies/international/negotiations/paris_en, 2017b.

CEC. *Consultation on Modernisation and Simplifying the Common Agricultural Policy (CAP)*, available at: https://ec.europa.eu/agriculture/consultations/cap-modernising/2017_en, 2017c.

CEC. *The Environmental Implementation Review (EIR)*, available at: ec.europa.eu/environment/eir/index_en.htm, 2017d.

CEC. Report from the Commission to the European Parliament, the Council, the European Economic and Social Committee and the Committee of the Regions, *Renewable Energy Progress Report*. Brussels: Commission of the European Communities, COM(2017) 57 final, available at: eur-lex.europa.eu/legal-content/EN/TXT/PDF/?uri=CELEX:52017DC0057&qid=1488449105433&from=E, 2017e.

CEC. *Eurostat: Headline Indictors Score Board*, available at: ec.europa.eu/eurostat/web/europe-2020-indicators/europe-2020-strategy/headline-indicators-scoreboard, 2017f.

CEE Bankwatch Network. 'Lost in Transportation', available at: bankwatch.org/documents/lost_in_transport.pdf. Prague, CEE Bankwatch Network, March 2007.

Crisp, J. 'Waste Laws will be Binned, Despite Protests', *Euroactiv*, 23 Jan. 2015, available at: www.euractiv.com/section/sustainable-dev/news/waste-laws-will-be-binned-despite-protests.

Dupont, C., Groen, L., and Oberthür, S. 2016 'The UK in EU Environmental Policy: Common Responses to Common Problems', in Dupont, C. and Trauner, F. (Eds), IES, April 2016, available at: www.ies.be/files/Brexit%20Project.pdf.

EAP. 'Living Well, within the Limits of Our Planet', *Official Journal* L354, pp. 171–200. Brussels, EAP, 28 Dec. 2013.

EEA. *Environment in the European Union 1995—Report for the Review of the Fifth Environmental Action Programme*, State of the environment report No 1/1995, available at: www.eea.europa.eu/publications/92-827-5263-1. Copenhagen, EEA, 1995.

EEA. *Trends and Projections in Europe 2015—Tracking Progress towards Europe's Climate and Energy Targets*, EEA Report No 4/2015. Copenhagen, EEA, 2015a, available at: www.eea.europa.eu/publications/trends-and-projections-in-europe-2015.

EEA. *Results from Reporting under the Nature Directives 2007–2012*, Technical Report No 2/2015, 2015b.

EEA. *Marine Protected Areas in Europe's Seas—An Overview and Perspectives for the Future*, EEA Report No 3/2015, 2015c, available at: www.eea.europa.eu/publications/marine-protected-areas-in-europes.

EEA. *Environmental Indicator Report 2016, In Support to the Monitoring of the 7th Environmental Action Programme*, EEA Report No 30/2016. Copenhagen, EEA, available at: https://www.eea.europa.eu/publications/environmental-indicator-report-2016.

EEB. *Future of EU Environmental Policy: Towards the 7th Environmental Action Programme*, available at: www.eeb.org/index.cfm/activities/sustainability/7th-environmental-action-programme. Brussels, EEB, 2013.

Ecologic. *Updated Inventory and Assessment of Soil Protection Policy Instruments in EU Member States*. Final Report. Berlin, Ecologic Institute, 2017, available at: ec.europa.eu/environment/soil/pdf/Soil_inventory_report.pdf.

Endl, A., and Berger, G. *The 7th Environment Action Programme: Reflections on Sustainable Development and Environmental Policy Integration*, ESDN Quarterly Report 32, March 2014, available at: www.sd-network.eu/quarterly%20reports/report%20files/pdf/2014-March-The_7th_Environment_Action_Programme.pdf. Vienna, ESDN, 2014.

Energy Post 2016 'Team Juncker: EU unveils new Energy Commissioner(s)', available at: www.energypost.eu/team-juncker-eu-unveils-new-energy-commissioners.

EPSU. *Environmental Protection Agencies Study: Syndex Report for the European Federation of Public Service Unions*. Brussels, SPSU Secretariat, 2012.

EU. *Sustainable Development in the European Union: 2015 Monitoring Report of the EU Sustainable Development Strategy*, Brussels, European Union, available at: ec.europa.eu/eurostat/documents/3217494/6975281/KS-GT-15-001-EN-N.pdf/5a20c781-e6e4-4695-b33d-9f502a30383f

European Parliament, *European Parliament Resolution of 2 February 2016 on the Mid-Term Review of the EU's Biodiversity Strategy* (2015/2137(INI)), available at: www.europarl.europa.eu/sides/getDoc.do?type=TA&reference=P8-TA-2016-0034&format=XML&language=EN.

European People's Party, 'My Priorities', (J.-C. Juncker, European People's Party), available at: juncker.epp.eu/my-priorities (not dated).

European Union Communication and Information Resource Centre for Administrations, Businesses and Citizens. *Support Policy Development for Integration of Ecosystem Service Assessments into WFD and FD Implementation*, available at: circabc.europa.eu/sd/a/95c93149-0093-473c-bc27-1a69cface404/Ecosystem%20service_WFD_FD_Main%20Report_Final.pdf. Brussels, 2014.

European Union Delegation to the United Nations. *EU Statement: United Nations Open Working Group on Sustainable Development Goals*, EUUN14–089EN, 20 June, available at www.eu-un.europa.eu/articles/en/article_15185_en.htm. New York, 2014.

Gravey, V. 'Reforming EU Policy', in Burns, C., Jordan, A., Gravey, V., Berny, N., Bulmer, S., Carter, N., Cowell, R., Dutton, J., Moore, B., Oberthür, S., Owens, S., Rayner, T., Scott, J., and Stewart, B. (2016) *The EU Referendum and the UK Environment: An Expert Review. How has EU membership affected the UK and what might change in the event of a vote to Remain or Leave?*, pp. 125–134, available at: environmentEUref.blogspot.co.uk/.

Institute for European Environmental Policy (IEEP). *Strategic Orientations of EU Environmental Policy under the Sixth Environment Action Programme and Implications for the Future*, Final Report', available at: www.ieep.eu/assets/556/Strategic_Orientations_of_6EAP-Revised_report-May_2010.pdf. Brussels, IEEP, May 2010.

IEEP. *The Potential Policy and Environmental Consequences for the UK of a Departure from the European Union*. London, IEEP, 2016.

Juncker, J.-C., President of the European Commission, *Mission Letter to Karmenu Vella, Commissioner for Environment, Maritime Affairs and Fisheries*, 1 Nov. 2014, available at: efaep.org/sites/enep/files/President%20Juncker%27s%20Mission%20Letter%20to%20Karmenu%20Vella.pdf.

Muûls, M., Colmer, J., Martin, R., and Wagner, U. J. *Evaluating the EU Emissions Trading System: Take it or Leave it? An Assessment of the Data after Ten Years*. Imperial College London, Grantham Institute Briefing Paper No 21, Oct. 2016, available at: https://www.imperial.ac.uk/media/imperial-college/grantham-institute/public/publications/briefing-papers/Evaluating-the-EU-emissions-trading-system_Grantham-BP-21_web.pdf.

Neslen, A. 'EU climate laws undermined by Polish and Czech revolt, documents reveal', *Climate Home*, 29 May 2017, available at: www.climatechangenews.com/2017/05/29/eu-climate-targets-undermined-polish-czech-revolt-documents-reveal.

NLU. *Establishing the Urban Agenda for the EU: Pact of Amsterdam*, 30 May 2016, available at: https://ec.europa.eu/futurium/en/system/files/ged/pact-of-amsterdam_en.pdf.

Oberthür, S. *How Would a Brexit Affect the Environment?* London School of Economics, 2015, available at: bit.ly/28Q7Qdf.

Official Journal of the European Union, Decision No 1386/2013/EU of the European Parliament and of the Council of 20 Nov. 2013 on a General Union Environment Action Programme to 2020, 'Living well, within the limits of our planet'. Brussels, EU, L 354/171.

Swords, P. *The Failures to Properly Implement EU Environmental Legislation in Ireland*, Correspondence with Party Concerned, 28 June, Regarding Communication to Aarhus Convention Compliance Committee, ACCC/C/2010/54, available at: www.unece.org/fileadmin/DAM/env/pp/compliance/C2010-UN Economic Commission for Europe, 54/Communication/CommunicationACCC.pdf. Geneva, 2011.

UNEP. *The Impact of Corruption on Climate Change: Threatening Emissions Trading Mechanisms?* 2013, available at: https://na.unep.net/geas/getUNEPPageWithArticleIDScript.php?article_id=97.

Voulvoulis, N., Arpon, K. D., and Giakoumis, T. 'The EU Water Framework Directive: From Great Expectations to Problems with Implementation', *Science of The Total Environment*, Vol. 575, No 1, pp. 358–366, Jan. 2017.

MIGRATION AND ASYLUM POLICY

Andrew Geddes

Introduction

Recent debate about immigration in Europe has been dominated by the 'migration crisis'. This crisis has been seen by many as a crisis of numbers linked to those arriving via Mediterranean routes to Europe, fleeing in particular conflict, poverty, oppression and inequality. It is, however, also a wider crisis of politics and institutions in the European Union (EU). The tensions and stresses linked to migration have spread within the EU governance system and opened schisms between member states, as well as animating debates about solidarity and responsibility-sharing between member states.

It is important to bear in mind that most people moving to Europe do so via regular routes to work, join family members or to study: but such migration is not high on the news agenda. Rather, migration and refugee flows to Europe, and the loss of life in the Mediterranean Sea have created powerful images viewed by millions of people. Between January 2016 and August 2017 data gathered by the International Organization for Migration (IOM) showed that around 520,000 people moved across the Mediterranean to Europe. During this time a shift occurred from an 'eastern' route, via Greece, to a 'central' route, via Italy. The Mediterranean was also the world's most deadly 'migration corridor', with the IOM reporting 7,685 people dead or missing between January 2016 and August 2017. Although migration and asylum are frequently identified as principal priorities of the EU, with various initiatives launched both by the EU and by member states, it is evident that collective European responses and solidarity have been lacking, while the EU is widely seen as having failed to deal effectively with the crisis. In many member states, 'immigration' has become a fundamental concern for electorates. In the United Kingdom, voting in the June 2016 referendum on EU membership, which resulted in a decision in favour of a departure from the EU—so-called Brexit—was powerfully influenced by migration issues linked both to intra-EU free movement and to migration from outside the Union. A key point is that high levels of migration to the UK activated existing high levels of Euroscepticism in that country. This means that the UK experience might not necessarily apply to other European countries, where the level of latent Euroscepticism is not as high. It does demonstrate, however, the potential for concern about immigration to send shockwaves through political systems.

EU efforts to respond to the migration crisis have included calls for solidarity between member states and the relocation of asylum seekers more equitably across the EU by means of quotas. The EU concluded an agreement with Turkey in March 2016 (see *Asylum* below) to stem the flow of migrants crossing via the eastern Mediterranean route (from Turkey into Greece and on through the Balkan states into central and western Europe), and in July the European Commission proposed reform of the Common European Asylum System to make it more efficient and humane.

Migration in its many forms—to work, to join family members, to study and to seek refuge—is salient and politically controversial, both globally and within the EU. The European refugee crisis is only part of a global crisis of displacement. According to the United Nations High Commissioner for Refugees (UNHCR), there were more than 63m. displaced people worldwide in 2015, of whom 26m. were internationally displaced as either asylum seekers or refugees. Of the 63m. displaced persons, it is important to bear in mind that only around 6% of them were in the EU. Of the world's displaced people in 2015, 84% were in developing countries, overwhelmingly in sub-Saharan Africa and South Asia. Adjacent to the EU, Turkey hosted around 2.5m. people, again largely individuals who had fled the conflict in neighbouring Syria.

In May 2015 the European Commission published the European Agenda on Migration, which noted the importance of countering 'misguided and stereotyped narratives' that mean that the 'inherent complexity' of migration can be missed in public debate, while also noting that no member state can effectively address migration by acting alone. The European Agenda proposed a series of immediate measures and identified four 'pillars' focused on longer-term, structural factors that can cause migration and refugee flows. These are:

- Reducing incentives for irregular migration, including addressing root causes such as underdevelopment and poverty, combating people smugglers and traffickers, co-operating with non-EU countries, and ensuring the return of people residing irregularly in Europe.
- Border management to build capacity to deal with pressures on the borders of EU member states, such as Greece, Italy, Malta and Spain, given that such pressures are unlikely to dissipate.
- A common EU asylum policy based on existing legislation, with effective monitoring of implementation and reinforced measures to promote practical co-operation. Fundamental to this is the effective implementation of the so-called Dublin system (see below) and the sharing of responsibility between member states.
- A new policy on legal migration to deal with longer-term economic and demographic challenges, given that the EU working-age population is expected to decline by 17.5m. people by the mid-2020s.

EU efforts have been directed towards making the asylum process more efficient, improving border security, and preventing irregular and illegal migration. However, the EU has no jurisdiction over the number of migrants to be admitted, which is ultimately a matter for the member states. The four pillars have been consistent themes in EU migration and asylum policy and can help in understanding both the development of policy and future challenges. The political debate about the European

Agenda on Migration demonstrated the preference for EU member states to focus on the more repressive and restrictive aspects of migration and asylum policy rather than on measures that might create new routes for legal migration to Europe.

Informal Co-operation on Immigration and Asylum

In order to understand contemporary EU migration and asylum policy, it is necessary to explore its origins. This helps to show why the EU approach is *partial,* in that it covers some aspects of policy (asylum, irregular migration and border controls) and not others (admissions policy). It is also *differential* in its effects, as some countries are more affected than others, with some exposed to high migration and refugee flows, such as Greece, which received more than 800,000 migrants and refugees in 2015, while Sweden, Ireland and the UK have negotiated exemptions from fundamental aspects of EU migration policy, such as membership of the Schengen Area, which provides for free movement between signatory member states, without the need for internal border checks.

By the 1980s it was becoming clear that there were links between international migration and a range of economic and security issues that were common European concerns and that could require some form of action on immigration and asylum. This did not mean that immigration and asylum would inevitably become competencies of the European Community (EC—which became the EU in 1993). The form that this action was to take remained an open question. Some member states (such as the UK and Denmark) preferred an intergovernmental vision to minimize the influence of the Commission. Other member states (such as France, Germany and the Benelux countries) favoured common EU policies. The informal co-operation—i.e. outside the treaty framework—that developed on immigration and asylum during the 1980s and into the early 1990s demonstrated the intention of the member states to use new European structures as a way of attaining domestic objectives; in other words, they saw the EC as a means to reassert immigration controls rather than ceding control to supranational institutions. Cross-border co-operation was a way to reassert controls through new forms of collaborative action, but even this looser form of co-operation began to change the meaning and practice of national sovereignty in Europe.

Until 1993 Commission attempts to create limited competencies in the area of immigration policy were rebuffed by member states. More informal routes were chosen. An Ad Hoc Working Group on Immigration created in 1986 was a forum for senior Ministry of the Interior officials to consult on asylum, external frontiers, forged papers, admissions, deportations, and the exchange of information. A Group of Co-ordinators, created in 1988, was charged with the task of co-ordinating free movement measures (which lay within the treaty framework) and internal security co-operation (including immigration and asylum that were outside the treaty framework). The outcome of their labours was the Palma Programme, but this was widely regarded as ineffectual, as the member states did not have any real decision-making powers. Although there was agreement among the EU-15 member states that links existed between single market integration, security, and immigration and asylum, they could only seek to co-operate through conventions in international law. Not only was it difficult to reach agreement on such conventions, they also required ratification in each member state. The best example of the problems this caused was the External Frontiers Convention agreed in September 1991, which reached an impasse because of a disagreement between the UK and Spain over the status of Gibraltar, and meant that the convention was not signed by all member states, let alone ratified.

Although it was difficult to reach agreement on measures to be adopted, the late 1980s and early 1990s did begin to see the emergence of ideas and some more concrete measures relating to the future form of a common EU approach. Frequent interaction between interior ministry officials helped to develop shared understandings of common problems and focused minds on the future shape of common EU policies. Indeed, the links between migration and internal security evolved from a framework established within the Trevi Group, which was originally set up in 1975 to discuss terrorism, and the remit of which expanded to cover other security issues. This 'framing' of migration and asylum as security issues has shaped EC, and subsequently, EU policy responses.

A key example of the ways in which informal co-operation shaped later action is the Dublin Convention on Asylum, agreed in Ireland in September 1991, which sought to impose common provisions on every state responsible for processing an asylum application and to rule that a rejection in one member state applied to the whole EC/EU. This Dublin system is central to the EU response to the post-2011 refugee crisis. The basic idea is quite simple: to prevent multiple applications by the same person within the EU as they move from state to state in search of one that would provide refuge. Usually, the member state responsible for offering asylum to the claimant would be the state through which the asylum seeker first entered the EU. The Dublin Convention, which was signed in 1990 and came into effect in 1997, was an agreement in international law, which meant that it limped through a six-year ratification process, while also excluding EC institutions from scrutinizing measures. The ideas put in place by the Dublin Convention were to form the core of 'Dublin II', introduced in 2002 using the provisions of the Amsterdam Treaty, and then further revised in the form of the 'Dublin III' regulation in 2013. By 2015 it had become evident that the Dublin Convention was inadequate in the face of the refugee crisis emanating from the eastern Mediterranean. One dimension of this inadequacy was evident when German Chancellor Angela Merkel announced in August that Germany would accept asylum applicants from Syria in unlimited numbers, irrespective of their initial point of entry into the EU, and that they would have permanent leave to remain in the country. The result of this was that hundreds of thousands of people began often chaotic journeys across Europe by whatever means available in a bid to reach Germany—some 800,000 were estimated to have arrived in 2015. This led to scenes in mid-2015 of hundreds of thousands of men, women and children moving across Europe on foot. It also led to the re-imposition of border controls and the erection of fences by a number of member states, including Austria, Hungary, Denmark and Sweden. Given their geographical proximity to the Middle East, Greece and Italy were, as part of the European mainland, overwhelmingly the countries of first arrival, but could not cope with the sheer numbers of people arriving. The Dublin Convention seemed loaded against such countries and thus unfair.

Linked to the refugee crisis was the future of the Schengen Area of free movement that had been established in 1985. At that time Schengen was seen not only as a realization of the European ideal of free movement, but also as a laboratory for the kinds of internal security measures that would be needed if free movement were to be realized. The Schengen Agreement was initially signed by France, Germany and the Benelux countries, but was extended to include all 15 EU member states, except Ireland and the UK, by 1997, with non-EU member states Iceland and Norway having observer status. The legacies of this early period of informal co-operation in the 1990s were profound: Schengen and the Dublin Convention have shaped the common EU response until the present day. The Schengen principle sought to move more quickly towards free movement and the removal of internal frontiers within its signatory states. On one level it dealt with liberalization, but on another it was concerned with the internal security implications of free movement. The refugee crisis called into question the Schengen system because large-scale and uncontrolled flows of migrants and refugees had led to the re-imposition of 'internal' border controls within the Schengen Area. Schengen was also questioned by those who saw free movement and lack of security checks as a contributing factor to terrorist attacks, such as those that took place in the French cities of Paris and Nice, in Brussels (Belgium), Berlin (Germany), Stockholm (Sweden), the British cities of Manchester and London, and in Barcelona (Spain) between 2015 and 2017. There was evidence that some of the terrorists had been able to travel to Syria and other conflict regions to fight with Islamist militant groups, and return to Europe without being detected by the intelligence agencies in their home countries.

The Treaty on European Union and Formalized Co-operation

Co-operation became more formalized between 1992 and 1999, but this was still a relatively weak form of intergovernmental co-operation without binding decision-making procedures. The 1992 Treaty on European Union or Maastricht Treaty created a 'Justice and Home Affairs' (JHA) pillar, dealing with immigration and asylum, along with other internal security issues. The JHA pillar recognized immigration and asylum as matters of 'common interest' (i.e. not as matters requiring a common policy). Asylum, external frontiers and immigration policy were located within the JHA pillar. There was some confusion because visa policy was covered by Article 100c of the Maastricht Treaty and, at the same time, by the immigration provisions of the JHA pillar. Decisions within the JHA pillar required unanimity. The Commission could participate in meetings, but had limited powers of proposal, which it shared with member states. Within the JHA pillar the measures that could be introduced were not directives, regulations and the other regular components of EC law. Member states could agree on non-binding joint positions, on joint actions that could have binding effects—but only if all member states agreed on this—and on conventions agreed in international law. The reason for this was disagreement about the form and content of an EU approach.

The post-Maastricht framework demonstrated the disadvantages of intergovernmental co-operation in terms of decision-making, accountability and effective scrutiny. Immigration and asylum were processed within a framework that centred on control. EU member states were not particularly open to new migration and this was reflected in the approach that they adopted to immigration and asylum.

From Amsterdam to Lisbon

The 1999 Treaty of Amsterdam shifted the focus of the EU immigration and asylum debate from competencies to the content of legislation, but for some rather than all elements of policy. The notable omission was and still is admissions policy, which remains the prerogative of the member states. The Treaty of Amsterdam did two things. First, it moved immigration and asylum from the JHA pillar to a new Title IV of the main treaty dealing with free movement, immigration and asylum. Second, it 'normalized' immigration and asylum as EU issues in the sense that they could henceforth be covered by the regular EU legal devices, namely directives and regulations. The UK, Ireland and Denmark opted out of Title IV.

A parallel background development at this time was debate in some member states about new economic migration to address labour market shortages in some sectors and to offset longer-term effects of population change. The tone of this debate changed as economic crisis hit after 2008, but a need for both higher- and lower-skilled migrant workers is still evident, as demographic change within the EU affects the labour market, particularly an increasing ageing population, and a falling birth rate in most of Western Europe, which falls below the 'replacement rate' of around two children per woman.

The Treaty of Amsterdam added a new EU objective to become an 'Area of Freedom, Security and Justice'. The new Title IV henceforth dealt with free movement, immigration and asylum. Article 61 of the Treaty specified that within five years the member states were to ensure the free movement of persons and 'directly related flanking measures' relating to external frontier controls, asylum and immigration. Until 2004 immigration and asylum would be covered by unanimity. After 2004, asylum moved to 'co-decision', with the Council and European Parliament sharing responsibility for decision-making.

A meeting held in Tampere, Finland, in October 1999 was highly significant in setting the parameters for EU action that remained in force in terms of EU policy in 2016. A fundamental component of the approach was to build closer relations with non-EU countries that were either the point of origin or transit for many refugees. This blurred the distinction between domestic and foreign policy and has led to closer links between interior, foreign and development policies. The heads of government agreed to a four-point plan for common migration and asylum policies, comprising partnership with countries of origin; a common asylum system; 'more vigorous' integration policies for third country nationals; and the management of migration flows with the emphasis on illegal immigration, smuggling and trafficking. The Tampere agenda covering 1999–2004 launched a series of five-year plans, and was followed by the Hague Programme, agreed in November 2004, which covered the period until 2010 and sought: a common European asylum system with a common procedure and a uniform status for those granted asylum or protection by 2009; measures for foreigners to work legally in the EU in accordance with labour market requirements; a European framework to guarantee the successful integration of migrants into host societies; partnerships with third countries on asylum, irregular migration, border controls, resettlement and return; a policy to expel and return illegal immigrants to their countries of origin; a fund for the management of external borders; the SIS II—a database of people issued with arrest warrants and of stolen objects, to be operational from 2007; and common visa rules (common application centres and the introduction of biometrics in the visa information system). The Stockholm agenda then sought further to develop EU action until 2014 with a range of measures, including strengthened action on external border controls, development of a common asylum system and greater efforts to promote dialogue with non-member states, as part of what the EU calls the Global Approach to Migration and Mobility.

For the period 2015–19, the Strategic Guidelines for the Area of Freedom, Security and Justice (adopted by the European Council in June 2014) reaffirmed the commitment to the development of a common EU migration and asylum policy. The 2011 Global Approach to Migration and Mobility emphasized the need to seek co-operation and dialogue with neighbouring states and sending countries, while the broadening of the issue agenda has also raised concerns about policy coherence. The principal obstacle to progress is the divergence between EU interests and those of the sending or so-called 'transit' countries, because the EU seeks to export control measures to these countries, while they may be reluctant to assume responsibility for complex migration issues on the EU's behalf.

Meanwhile, the Treaty of Lisbon, which was finally ratified in November 2009, represented the consolidation of EU action through a strengthened legal base. Its entry into force on 1 December marked the full incorporation of migration and asylum within the Treaty framework. Migration and asylum became 'normal' EU issues with Qualified Majority Voting in the Council, co-decision with the European Parliament and a full role for the Court of Justice to consider annulment of legislation, to rule on failure to act on the part of EU institutions and in cases of infringement where member states have failed to fulfil their obligations. The Treaty of Amsterdam had only allowed reference to be made to the Court of Justice by a court in a member state if it were the final court of appeal in that state. The Treaty of Lisbon allows all national courts and tribunals to make preliminary reference to the Court of Justice. Articles 77–80 set out provisions on borders, asylum and migration.

Legal Immigration

At the core of immigration policy is the number of migrants to be admitted, or admissions policy. Article 79(5) of the Treaty of Lisbon very clearly states that the determination of numbers of migrants to be admitted remains a prerogative of the member states. The Commission has established a foothold with measures that seek co-ordination with regard to, for example, the admission of highly qualified migrant workers—the so-called Blue Card—agreed in 2009, and directives agreed in 2014 on the rights of migrants who are seasonal workers and intra-corporate transferees. The rationale for this action is that the EU needs migrant workers and that the demand for migrant workers is likely to grow because of population ageing in the Union. In its 2014 annual report on immigration and asylum in 2012, the Commission argued that legal migration can be a tool for growth, helping to mitigate the impact of an ageing population, and offsetting skills and labour market shortages.

EU measures have centred on attempts to establish mechanisms for the co-ordination of national policies, rather than, for example, seeking to establish EU-level quotas for new immigrants. The formal position remains that both entry and the numbers of entrants for the purposes of employment are matters regulated by the national laws of member states. Although there is also a clear demand for unskilled labour, entry conditions for unskilled migrants have been generally more restrictive. A Commission green paper on economic migration, published in November 2004, outlined the issues at stake and was designed to serve as a basis for more developed policy recommendations in the future. A December 2005 Commission policy plan defined a roadmap for the development of a common approach to economic migration with four elements: conditions of entry and residence of third country nationals; the provision of better information on immigration; the development of a common agenda for migrant integration; and co-operation with third countries on the management of migration flows. A Commission communication in May 2007 on 'Circular Migration and Mobility Partnerships between the EU and Third Countries' focused on partnerships with non-EU member states designed to counter illegal immigration by offering paths for nationals of non-EU states to enter the EU, for example on short-term visas. There was also discussion of circular migration as a means of allowing people to enter EU states, leave and then re-enter. This has been viewed as a device that could facilitate economic development in both sending and receiving states. Indeed, this theme of migration and development has been at the fore.

The European Commission, through the Blue Card scheme and seasonal workers' directive, has focused its efforts on a sectoral approach. The Blue Card provides a fast-track admissions procedure that allows non-EU nationals to be issued with a residence permit granting them a range of socio-economic rights, mobility within the EU after an established waiting period, and more favourable conditions governing family reunification. In 2014 some 13,800 Blue Cards were issued, of which 87% were granted in Germany. However, only 31% of highly qualified migrants who moved to countries in the Organisation for Economic Co-operation and Development in 2014 settled in the EU. This low take-up led the European Commission in June 2016 to announce plans to strengthen the Blue Card system.

This discussion of labour migration also needs to be located within the context of EU enlargement and the right to free movement. Prior to the 2004 enlargement, all member states except Ireland, Sweden and the UK agreed a formula that would impose restrictions on movement within the EU by nationals of new accession states (known as the A8 states) of Eastern and South-Eastern Europe. The final agreement involved a 2+3+2 formula from 2004 until 2011, which stated that the situation would be reviewed after two years, and again after a further three, until the end of the seven-year transition period in May 2011. All EU-15 member states opened their labour markets to Bulgaria and Romania by January 2014, although, once again, there was concern about the potential scale of movement. Free movement was also a key factor in the British vote in June 2016 to leave the EU, although significant uncertainty remained about what shape the so-called Brexit would eventually take and whether the UK could maintain single market access without allowing free movement of people.

The Commission has encountered difficulties when seeking to develop a comprehensive approach to labour migration, as member states have not been prepared to agree to such a significant extension of the EU's role in such a sensitive policy area. As noted, the preferred path for the Commission has been a sectoral approach focused on the highly qualified, seasonal workers and intra-corporate transferees. It has also maintained its interest in temporary and circular migration. Although it has been argued that temporary and circular routes could contribute to a 'triple win' for sending countries, destination countries and migrants themselves, the evidence base to inform policy is weak, and there are widely differing approaches to temporary migration in member states, and little practical experience of circular migration.

Irregular Immigration

EU action on irregular migration falls under the heading of 'EU Action on Migratory Pressures: A Strategic Response'. This strategy has seven priority areas: strengthening co-operation with third countries of origin and transit; enhanced border management; preventing irregular migration from Turkey; curbing abuse of legal migration channels; protecting free movement from abuse; enhancing migration management, including return; and preventing irregular flows from and via southern Mediterranean countries. These priorities reflected an issue that has been at the top of the EU migration policy agenda for more than 20 years. Operational co-operation was enhanced in 2005 when the European agency for the operational co-ordination of border controls, FRONTEX, was established. In December 2015 the European Commission announced plans to create a European Border and Coast Guard greatly to strengthen the EU's commitment to border security.

Although ministries of the interior typically manage migration as a 'domestic' concern, the issue also possesses clear international implications. Irregular flows are a fundamental issue because they relate very directly to the EU's relations with third countries. For example, the EU seeks the insertion of a standard readmission clause into all future association or co-operation agreements, whereby third countries resolve to take back illegal immigrants or rejected asylum applicants. Readmission agreements are designed to facilitate the expulsion of illegal immigrants by obliging the non-EU country to readmit its own nationals, as well as those who have passed through it on the way to the EU. Readmission agreements have been signed with Albania, Cabo Verde, Hong Kong, Macao, Sri Lanka, Pakistan, Turkey, Bosnia and Herzegovina, Russia, Ukraine, Moldova, Serbia, Montenegro, the former Yugoslav republic of Macedonia, Georgia, Armenia and Azerbaijan.

The 'foreign policy' dimension of migration and asylum also became apparent through the activities of the EU's High-Level Working Group on Migration and Asylum, which drafted reports on countries including Afghanistan, Iraq, Pakistan, Sri Lanka, Morocco and Somalia. Migration and asylum have also been recognized as strategic priorities within the European Neighbourhood Policy, which reinforces the foreign policy dimension of migration and asylum.

A significant development was an agreement between the European Parliament and Council on a directive dealing with the return of illegal immigrants. The return directive allows EU member states to detain illegal immigrants for up to 12 months prior to their expulsion and bans re-entry for five years. It does, however, remain for each member state to decide whether to regularize or return an illegal immigrant (the UK and Ireland are not affected by the return directive because they have not opted into this area of EU law).

The post-2011 refugee crisis heightened concern at both government and popular levels about border controls and irregular migration. The European Agenda on Migration put forward the EU's intention to tackle human trafficking. So-called 'Operation Sophia', also known as EUNAVFOR MED, enlisted naval support for anti-trafficking operations in the Mediterranean Sea. Such efforts can, however, form only part of a response because they deal with the symptoms and not the causes of migration. Moreover, if the effects of more stringent controls are to force migrants and refugees to take more dangerous routes, then they could ultimately be counter-productive.

In 2012 the Italian Government sought co-operation with Libya in the form of a secret agreement (subsequently leaked to the press) on the return of irregular migrants, but the effective absence of state authority in Libya facilitated growth of the people-smuggling industry from its shores. There is also evidence of serious abuses of migrants' human rights in Libya.

Asylum

Asylum is an area in which there has been significant development at EU level. The 1.20m. applications made in 2016 were fewer than the 1.35m. made in 2015, but were almost twice the 626,000 applications made in 2014—in which year there had been an increase of more than 190,000 compared with the 434,160 applications made in 2013. Principal countries of origin included Syria, Afghanistan, Eritrea, Nigeria and Somalia.

The Dublin Convention had been put in place in the early 1990s and was the cornerstone of the EU asylum system. It was the end of the Cold War, as well as and civil conflict in the former Yugoslavia, that impelled co-operation on asylum in the 1990s and the movement towards common policies in the 2000s. Between 2002 and 2004 the first phase of the Common European Asylum System was put in place, and the second phase was ongoing in the 2010s.

The October 1999 Tampere Declaration identified four building blocks of the EU asylum system: determination of the state responsible for the examination of an application (agreed in 2002); conditions for the reception of asylum seekers (agreed in 2002); minimum standards on asylum procedures (agreed in 2003); and the qualification and content of refugee and subsidiary protection status (agreed in 2004). The next step, identified by the Commission in 2008, was movement towards a Common European Asylum System, with three pillars: improved harmonization on protection standards through further alignment of national legislation; improved capacity at EU level to gather and manage information and to offer assistance to member states; and increased solidarity between member states for member states 'under pressure'. In 2013 negotiations were concluded on the revised Reception Conditions and Procedures directives, and on the Dublin and Eurodac (European fingerprint database) regulations. In 2016 the Commission produced plans to create a stronger common European asylum system with common procedures and maximum harmonization. The Commission also presented options to reform the Dublin Convention. The need for change had been made manifest by the refugee crisis, with huge burdens falling on Greece and Italy and an unwillingness among member states to accept relocated asylum applicants. In September 2015 the EU Council agreed a temporary emergency relocation scheme to bring about the mandatory relocation of some 160,000 asylum applicants from

Greece and Italy (and other countries if necessary) throughout the EU (with the exception of the UK, Ireland and Denmark). Distribution was to be calculated according to a 'key', taking into account factors such as the prevailing rate of gross domestic product (GDP) per head, with richer states taking more than their poorer counterparts. It was agreed to relocate 6,000 asylum applicants per month from Greece and Italy to other EU member states, but by July 2016 only 843 applicants had actually been relocated over a period of nine months. In April 2016 member states were presented with further proposals for reform, including the award of increased funding and resources to 'front-line' states. Furthermore, the European Asylum Support Office (EASO), based in Malta, was to be given a much greater role in monitoring the system and its effects. In May the Commission threatened to impose fines of €250,000 for each refugee that a member state refused to accommodate. By the second half of 2017, member states were a long way from achieving their objectives. In July the European Commission reported an increased rate of relocation: although the total number of people who had been relocated by means of the system stood at just over 24,000, this remained some way short of the objective. In September the Court of Justice rejected claims by the Hungarian and Slovakian Governments that the relocation system was unlawful, and ruled that they must abide by the terms of the relocation agreement.

The migration crisis also raised questions about relations between the EU and non-member states, particularly the EU-Turkey agreement that was concluded in March 2016. Central to the plan was a so-called 'one in, one out' scheme to arrest the flow of undocumented refugees crossing the Mediterranean into Europe, and to introduce a scheme whereby legitimate asylum seekers, who had already been registered in Turkey, would be relocated from that country to the EU, instead of risking a perilous crossing by sea; in return, non-documented refugees who had not made an asylum application at their initial point of entry into the EU (usually Greece) would be returned to Turkey. The Turkish Government pledged to increase efforts to prevent sea crossings, which witnessed a greater degree of success. In return, the EU announced that it would accelerate progress towards visa liberalization for Turkish citizens travelling to the EU and made available funding to help Turkey to manage the crisis. UNHCR expressed concern about the agreement, particularly about the risks faced by asylum claimants in Greece and Turkey who might not receive necessary protection while in transit.

In July 2016 the EU further developed its global approach when it identified 'priority countries', including Jordan, Lebanon and Nigeria, with which it sought to develop partnerships on migration and refugee flows. A partnership approach requires the EU to broaden its focus beyond the return and readmission of irregular migrants, to consider routes for regular migration, as well as the relationship between migration and development, or lack thereof, in the migrants' countries of origin.

Financial Resources

There has been a considerable expansion in resources devoted to capacity building in the areas of border control and border security since 2000. The EU has also worked through various regional programmes. In 2003 spending on asylum, immigration and the management of external frontiers amounted to just under 1% of Community internal policies expenditure. Between 2001 and 2004 a specific €42.5m. budget line (called B7-667) funded projects relating to co-operation with non-EU states. Between 2002 and 2004 Morocco received around €50m. to assist with border control development. In March 2004 the AENEAS programme was established to provide financial and technical assistance to non-EU states in the areas of migration and asylum. Between 1 January 2004 and 31 December 2008 €250m. was allocated to promote more efficient management of migration flows, in co-operation with third countries engaged in preparing or implementing a readmission agreement. The 2007–13 budget settlement allocated €4,020m. to Solidarity and Management of Migration Flows, including €1,820m. to external borders, €676m. to the return fund (mentioned above), €699m. to the European Refugee Fund and €825m. to an Integration Fund. In late 2013 the European Parliament and the Council reached agreement on the Multiannual Financial Framework for 2014–20, which included an Asylum, Migration and Integration Fund amounting to €3,100m., an Internal Security Fund with a border control and visa component amounting to €3,800m., and €2,500m. allocated to FRONTEX and EASO.

Conclusion: the Politicization of EU Migration and Asylum Policy

The migration and refugee crisis has raised questions about the Schengen Area of free movement and the basic principle of the EU asylum system as it has developed since the 1990s. In the 2014 European Parliament elections around 30% of seats were won by Eurosceptics on the left and the right, although the balance of power within the official EU institutions remains centred on a commitment to free movement and the continued development of migration and asylum policies. The Commission President, Jean-Claude Juncker, has made it clear that the Commission would not accept a reversal of the Schengen free movement framework, but new fences have been erected within the Schengen Area, and controls imposed. A principal tension is between what many member states see as the strong political argument for working together at EU level and the domestic strains around immigration that are clearly evident at national level. Nevertheless, confronted with the refugee crisis, the Commission has been keen to promote arguments for much stronger solidarity and sharing of responsibility. A principal difficulty is that member states have not always been receptive to these demands and have resisted the introduction of compulsory schemes to relocate or redistribute refugees and asylum seekers. This demonstrates significant limits to EU co-operation on migration and asylum.

Select Bibliography

Boswell, C. and Geddes, A. *Migration and Mobility in the European Union*. London, Palgrave Macmillan, 2011.

European Commission. 'A European Agenda on Migration' (2015) COM (2015) 240 final, ec.europa.eu/dgs/home-affairs/what-we-do/policies/european-agenda-migration/background-information/docs/communication_on_the_european_agenda_on_migration_en.pdf.

DIRECTORY OF THE EUROPEAN UNION

COUNCIL OF THE EUROPEAN UNION

Presidency

HOLDER OF THE OFFICE OF PRESIDENT OF THE COUNCIL

From 1 July 2017 to 31 December 2017: Estonia
From 1 January 2018 to 30 June 2018: Bulgaria
From 1 July 2018 to 31 December 2018: Austria
From 1 January 2019 to 30 June 2019: Romania
From 1 July 2019 to 31 December 2019: Finland
From 1 January 2020 to 30 June 2020: Croatia
From 1 July 2020 to 31 December 2020: Germany

Members of the Council of the European Union

AUSTRIA

Federal Chancellor: Christian Kern.

Vice-Chancellor and Federal Minister of Justice: Dr Wolfgang Brandstetter.

Federal Minister of Defence and Sports: Hans Peter Doskozil.

Federal Minister of Arts and Culture, Constitution and Media: Thomas Drozda.

Federal Minister of Education: Dr Sonja Hammerschmid.

Federal Minister of Family and Youth: Dr Sophie Karmasin.

Federal Minister of Europe, Integration and Foreign Affairs: Sebastian Kurz.

Federal Minister of Transport, Innovation and Technology: Jörg Leichtfried.

Federal Minister for Science, Research and Economy: Dr Harald Mahrer.

Federal Minister of Health and Women's Affairs: Pamela Rendi-Wagner.

Federal Minister of Agriculture, Forestry, Environment and Water Management: Andrä Rupprechter.

Federal Minister of Finance: Dr Hans Jörg Schelling.

Federal Minister of the Interior: Wolfgang Sobotka.

Federal Minister of Labour, Social Affairs and Consumer Protection: Alois Stöger.

Ministries

Office of the Federal Chancellor: Ballhauspl. 2, 1014 Vienna; tel. (+43 1) 531-15-0; fax (+43 1) 535-03-38-0; e-mail post@bka.gv.at; internet www.bka.gv.at.

Federal Ministry of Agriculture, Forestry, Environment and Water Management: Stubenring 1, 1010 Vienna; tel. (+43 1) 711-00-0; e-mail service@bmlfuw.gv.at; internet www.bmlfuw.gv.at.

Federal Ministry of Defence and Sports: Rossauer Lände 1, 1090 Vienna; tel. (+43 1) 502-01-0; e-mail presse@bmlvs.gv.at; internet www.bundesheer.at.

Federal Ministry of Education: Minoritenpl. 5, 1010 Vienna; tel. (+43 1) 531-20-0; fax (+43 1) 531-20-30-99; e-mail ministerium@bmbf.gv.at; internet www.bmbf.gv.at.

Federal Ministry of Europe, Integration and Foreign Affairs: Minoritenpl. 8, 1010 Vienna; tel. (+43 5) 011-50-0; fax (+43 5) 011-59-0; e-mail post@bmeia.gv.at; internet www.bmeia.gv.at.

Federal Ministry of Family and Youth: Untere Donaustr. 13–15, 1020 Vienna; tel. (+43 1) 711-00-0; e-mail office@bmfj.gv.at; internet www.bmfj.gv.at.

Federal Ministry of Finance: Johannesgasse 5, 1010 Vienna; tel. (+43 1) 514-33-0; e-mail zollinfo@bmf.gv.at; internet www.bmf.gv.at.

Federal Ministry of Health and Women's Affairs: Radetzkystr. 2, 1030 Vienna; tel. (+43 1) 711-00-0; fax (+43 1) 713-44-04-10-00; e-mail buergerservice@bmg.gv.at; internet www.bmg.gv.at.

Federal Ministry of the Interior: Herrengasse 7, Postfach 100, 1010 Vienna; tel. (+43 1) 531-26-0; fax (+43 1) 531-26-10-86-13; e-mail post@bmi.gv.at; internet www.bmi.gv.at.

Federal Ministry of Justice: Museumstr. 7, 1070 Vienna; tel. (+43 1) 521-52-0; internet www.justiz.gv.at.

Federal Ministry of Labour, Social Affairs and Consumer Protection: Stubenring 1, 1010 Vienna; tel. (+43 1) 711-00-0; e-mail post@sozialministerium.at; internet www.bmask.gv.at.

Federal Ministry of Science, Research and Economy: Stubenring 1, 1010 Vienna; tel. (+43 1) 711-00-0; fax (+43 1) 710-85-73; e-mail service@bmwfw.gv.at; internet www.bmwfw.gv.at.

Federal Ministry of Transport, Innovation and Technology: Radetzkystr. 2, Postfach 201, 1030 Vienna; tel. (+43 1) 711-62-65-0; e-mail kbm@bmvit.gv.at; internet www.bmvit.gv.at.

BELGIUM

Prime Minister: Charles Michel.

Deputy Prime Minister and Minister of Employment, Economic Affairs and Consumer Protection, in charge of Foreign Trade: Kris Peeters.

Deputy Prime Minister and Minister of the Interior and Public Security, in charge of Public Buildings: Jan Jambon.

Deputy Prime Minister and Minister of Development Co-operation, Digital Agenda, Telecommunications and Postal Services: Alexander De Croo.

Deputy Prime Minister and Minister of Foreign and European Affairs, in charge of Beliris and Federal Cultural Institutions: Didier Reynders.

Minister of Justice: Koen Geens.

Minister of Social Affairs and Public Health: Maggie De Block.

Minister of Pensions: Daniel Bacquelaine.

Council

Minister of Finance, in charge of Combating Tax Fraud: Johan Van Overtveldt.

Minister of the Middle Classes, the Self-employed, Small and Medium-sized Enterprises, Agriculture and Social Integration: Denis Ducarme.

Minister of Energy, Environment and Sustainable Development: Marie Christine Marghem.

Minister of Defence, in charge of the Civil Service: Steven Vandeput.

Minister of the Budget, in charge of the National Lottery: Sophie Wilmès.

Minister of Mobility, in charge of Belgocontrol and the Société Nationale des Chemins de Fer Belges/Nationale Maatschappij der Belgische Spoorwegen: François Bellot.

There are four Secretaries of State.

Federal Public Services and Ministries

Federal Public Service Chancellery of the Prime Minister: 16 rue de la Loi, 1000 Brussels; tel. (+32) 2-5010211; fax (+32) 2-5126953; e-mail info@premier.fed.be; internet www.premier.be.

Federal Public Service of the Budget and Management Control: 138/2 rue Royale, 1000 Brussels; tel. (+32) 2-2123711; fax (+32) 2-2123937; e-mail info.bb@budget.fed.be; internet www.budgetfederal.be.

Ministry of Defence: 1 rue d'Evere, 1140 Evere, Brussels; tel. (800) 333-48; internet www.mil.be.

Federal Public Service of the Economy, Small and Medium-sized Enterprises, the Self-Employed and Energy: 50 rue du Progrès, 1210 Brussels; tel. (+32) 2-80012033; e-mail info.eco@economie.fgov.be; internet economie.fgov.be.

Federal Public Service of Employment, Labour and Social Dialogue: 1 rue Ernest Blerot, 1070 Brussels; tel. (+32) 2-2334111; e-mail spf@emploi.belgique.be; internet www.emploi.belgique.be.

Federal Public Service of Finance: 33 blvd du Roi Albert II, BP 70, 1030 Brussels; tel. (+32) 2-5725757; e-mail info.tax@minfin.fed.be; internet www.financien.belgium.be.

Federal Public Service of Foreign Affairs, Foreign Trade and Development Co-operation: 15 rue des Petits Carmes, 1000 Brussels; tel. (+32) 2-5018111; e-mail info@diplobel.fed.be; internet www.diplomatie.be.

Federal Public Service of Health, Food Chain Safety and Environment: Eurostation II, 40 pl. Victor Horta, BP 10, 1060 Brussels; tel. (+32) 2-5249797; fax (+32) 2-5249527; e-mail info@health.fgov.be; internet www.health.belgium.be.

Federal Public Service of Information and Communication Technology: WTC III, blvd Simon Bolivar, 1000 Brussels; tel. (+32) 2-2129600; fax (+32) 2-2129699; e-mail info@fedict.be; internet www.fedict.belgium.be.

Federal Public Service of the Interior: 1 rue de Louvain, 1000 Brussels; tel. (+32) 2-5002111; fax (+32) 2-5002028; e-mail info@ibz.fgov.be; internet www.ibz.be.

Federal Public Service of Justice: 115 blvd de Waterloo, 1000 Brussels; tel. (+32) 2-5426511; fax (+32) 2-5427039; e-mail info@just.fgov.be; internet justice.belgium.be.

Federal Public Service of Mobility and Transport: 56 rue du Progrès, 1210 Brussels; tel. (+32) 2-2773111; e-mail info@mobilit.fgov.be; internet mobilit.belgium.be.

Federal Public Service of Personnel and Organization: 51 rue de la Loi, 1040 Brussels; tel. (+32) 2-7905800; fax (+32) 2-7905899; e-mail info@po.belgium.be; internet www.fedweb.belgium.be.

Federal Public Service of Social Security: Centre Administratif Botanique, Finance Tower, 50 blvd du Jardin Botanique, bte 100, 1000 Brussels; tel. (+32) 2-5286011; fax (+32) 2-5286953; e-mail social.security@minsoc.fed.be; internet socialsecurity.fgov.be.

BULGARIA

Prime Minister: Boyko Borisov.

Deputy Prime Minister: Tomislav Donchev.

Deputy Prime Minister for Economic and Demographic Policy: Valeri Simeonov.

Deputy Prime Minister for Public Order and Security and Minister of Defence: Krasimir Karakachanov.

Deputy Prime Minister for Justice Reforms and Minister of Foreign Affairs: Ekaterina Zaharieva.

Minister of Finance: Vladislav Goranov.

Minister of the Interior: Valentin Radev.

Minister of Regional Development and Public Works: Nikolai Nankov.

Minister of Labour and Social Policy: Biser Petkov.

Minister of Justice: Tsetska Tsacheva.

Minister of Education and Science: Krasimir Valchev.

Minister of Health: Nikolai Petrov.

Minister for the Bulgarian Presidency of the Council of the European Union in 2018: Lilyana Pavlova.

Minister of Culture: Boil Banov.

Minister of the Environment and Water: Neno Dimov.

Minister of Agriculture, Food and Forestry: Rumen Porozhanov.

Minister of Transport, Information Technology and Communications: Ivaylo Moskovski.

Minister of the Economy: Emil Karanikolov.

Minister of Energy: Temenuzhka Petkova.

Minister of Tourism: Nikolina Angelkova.

Minister of Youth and Sports: Krasen Kralev.

Ministries

Office of the Council of Ministers: 1594 Sofia, bul. Dondukov 1; tel. (+359 2) 940-29-99; fax (+359 2) 980-21-01; e-mail gis@government.bg; internet www.government.bg.

Ministry of Agriculture, Food and Forestry: 1040 Sofia, bul. Hristo Botev 55; tel. (+359 2) 985-11-338; fax (+359 2) 980-62-56; e-mail press@mzh.government.bg; internet www.mzh.government.bg.

Ministry of Culture: 1040 Sofia, bul. A. Stamboliyski 17; tel. (+359 2) 940-09-00; fax (+359 2) 981-81-45; e-mail press@mc.government.bg; internet mc.government.bg.

Ministry of Defence: 1092 Sofia, ul. Dyakon Ignatiy 3; tel. (+359 2) 922-09-22; fax (+359 2) 987-96-93; e-mail pressentr@mod.bg; internet www.mod.bg.

Ministry of the Economy: 1000 Sofia, ul. Slavyanska 8; tel. (+359 2) 940-70-01; fax (+359 2) 987-21-90; e-mail e-docs@mi.government.bg; internet www.mi.government.bg.

Ministry of Education and Science: 1540 Sofia, bul. Knyaz Dondukov 2A; tel. (+359 2) 921-77-99; fax (+359 2) 988-24-85; e-mail press_mon@mon.bg; internet www.mon.bg.

Ministry of Energy: 1000 Sofia, ul. Triaditsa 8; tel. (+359 2) 926-31-52; fax (+359 2) 980-76-30; e-mail e-energy@me.government.bg; internet www.me.government.bg.

Ministry of the Environment and Water: 1000 Sofia, bul. Maria Luiza 22; tel. (+359 2) 940-61-94; fax (+359 2) 986-25-33; e-mail minister@moew.government.bg; internet www5.moew.government.bg.

Ministry of Finance: 1040 Sofia, ul. G. S. Rakovski 102; tel. (+359 2) 985-92-684; fax (+359 2) 980-68-63; e-mail feedback@minfin.bg; internet www.minfin.bg.

Ministry of Foreign Affairs: 1113 Sofia, ul. Al. Zhendov 2; tel. (+359 2) 948-29-99; fax (+359 2) 971-36-20; e-mail crisis@mfa.bg; internet www.mfa.bg.

Ministry of Health: 1000 Sofia, pl. Sv. Nedelya 5; tel. (+359 2) 930-11-71; fax (+359 2) 981-18-33; e-mail press@mh.government.bg; internet www.mh.government.bg.

Ministry of the Interior: 1000 Sofia, ul. 6-ti Septemvri 29; tel. (+359 2) 982-50-00; fax (+359 2) 987-79-67; e-mail press@mvr.bg; internet www.mvr.bg.

Ministry of Justice: 1040 Sofia, ul. Slavyanska 1; tel. (+359 2) 923-75-55; e-mail pr@justice.government.bg; internet www.justice.government.bg.

Ministry of Labour and Social Policy: 1051 Sofia, ul. Triaditsa 2; tel. (+359 2) 811-94-43; fax (+359 2) 988-44-05; e-mail mlsp@mlsp.government.bg; internet www.mlsp.government.bg.

Ministry of Regional Development and Public Works: 1202 Sofia, ul. Kiril i Metodij 17–19; tel. (+359 2) 940-59-00; fax (+359 2) 987-25-17; e-mail mrrb@mrrb.government.bg; internet www.mrrb.government.bg.

Ministry of Tourism: 1000 Sofia, ul. Saborna 1; tel. (+359 2) 904-68-09; fax (+359 2) 447-08-99; e-mail tourism@tourism.government.bg; internet www.tourism.government.bg.

Ministry of Transport, Information Technology and Communications: 1000 Sofia, ul. Dyakon Ignatiy 9; tel. (+359 2) 988-50-94; e-mail mail@mtitc.government.bg; internet www.mtitc.government.bg.

Ministry of Youth and Sports: 1040 Sofia, ul. V. Levski 75; tel. (+359 2) 930-05-55; fax (+359 2) 930-06-61; e-mail question@mpes.government.bg; internet mpes.government.bg.

CROATIA

Prime Minister: Andrej Plenković.

Deputy Prime Minister and Minister of the Economy, Small and Medium-sized Enterprises and Crafts: Martina Dalić.

Deputy Prime Minister and Minister of Foreign and European Affairs: Marija Pejčinović Burić.

Deputy Prime Minister and Minister of Defence: Damir Krstičević.

Deputy Prime Minister and Minister of Construction and Physical Planning: Predrag Štromar.

Minister of Finance: Zdravko Marić.

Minister of Internal Affairs: Davor Božinović.

Minister of Environment and Energy: Tomislav Corić.

Minister of Labour and Pensions: Marko Pavić.

Minister of Agriculture: Tomislav Tolušić.

Minister of Justice: Dražen Bošnjaković.

Minister of Health: Milan Kujundžić.

Minister of Regional Development and EU Funds: Gabrijela Žalac.

Minister of Veterans' Affairs: Tomo Medved.

Minister of Maritime Affairs, Transport and Infrastructure: Oleg Butković.

Minister of State Property: Goran Marić.

Minister of Tourism: Gari Cappelli.

Minister of Public Administration: Lovro Kuščević.

Minister of Science and Education: Blaženka Divjak.

Minister of Culture: Nina Obuljen Koržinek.

Minister of Demography, Family, Youth and Social Policy: Nada Murganić.

Ministries

Office of the Prime Minister: 10000 Zagreb, trg sv. Marka 2; tel. (+385 1) 4569239; fax (+385 1) 6303022; e-mail press@vlada.hr; internet vlada.gov.hr.

Ministry of Agriculture: 10000 Zagreb, ul. grada Vukovara 78; tel. (+385 1) 6106111; fax (+385 1) 6109201; e-mail kabinet@mps.hr; internet www.mps.hr.

Ministry of Construction and Physical Planning: 10000 Zagreb, ul. Republike Austrije 20; tel. (+385 1) 3782444; fax (+385 1) 3772822; e-mail glasnogovornica@mgipu.hr; internet www.mgipu.hr.

Ministry of Culture: 10000 Zagreb, Runjaninova 2; tel. (+385 1) 4866666; fax (+385 1) 4816755; e-mail press@min-kulture.hr; internet www.min-kulture.hr.

Ministry of Defence: 10000 Zagreb, trg kralja Petra Krešimira IV; tel. (+385 1) 4567111; fax (+385 1) 4568109; e-mail infor@morh.hr; internet www.morh.hr.

Ministry of Demography, Family, Youth and Social Policy: 10000 Zagreb, trg Nevenke Topalušić 1; tel. (+385 1) 5557111; fax (+385 1) 5557222; e-mail ministarstvo@mdomsp.hr; internet www.mspm.hr.

Ministry of the Economy, Small and Medium-sized Enterprises and Crafts: 10000 Zagreb, ul. grada Vukovara 78; tel. (+385 1) 6106111; fax (+385 1) 6109110; e-mail info@mingo.hr; internet www.mingo.hr.

Ministry of Environment and Energy: 10000 Zagreb, ul. Radnička cesta 80; tel. (+385 1) 3717111; fax (+385 1) 3717149; e-mail ministar@mzoe.hr; internet www.mzoip.hr.

Ministry of Finance: 10000 Zagreb, ul. Katančićeva 5; tel. (+385 1) 4591333; fax (+385 1) 4922583; e-mail kabinet@mfin.hr; internet www.mfin.hr.

Ministry of Foreign and European Affairs: 10000 Zagreb, trg Nikole Šubića Zrinskog 7–8; tel. (+385 1) 4569964; fax (+385 1) 4551795; e-mail ministarstvo@mvep.hr; internet www.mvep.hr.

Ministry of Health: 10000 Zagreb, Ksaver 200A; tel. (+385 1) 4607555; fax (+385 1) 4677076; e-mail pitajtenas@miz.hr; internet zdravstvo.gov.hr.

Ministry of Internal Affairs: 10000 Zagreb, ul. grada Vukovara 33; tel. (+385 1) 6122111; fax (+385 1) 6122452; e-mail pitanja@mup.hr; internet www.mup.hr.

Ministry of Justice: 10000 Zagreb, ul. grada Vukovara 49; tel. (+385 1) 3714000; fax (+385 1) 3714507; e-mail ministar@pravosudje.hr; internet pravosudje.gov.hr.

Ministry of Labour and Pensions: 10000 Zagreb, ul. grada Vukovara 78; tel. (+385 1) 6106835; fax (+385 1) 6109638; e-mail info@mrms.hr; internet www.mrms.hr.

Ministry of Maritime Affairs, Transport and Infrastructure: 10000 Zagreb, Prisavlje 14; tel. (+385 1) 6169111; fax (+385 1) 3784580; e-mail ministar@mmpi.hr; internet www.mmpi.hr.

Ministry of Public Administration: 10000 Zagreb, Maksimirska 63; tel. (+385 1) 2357555; fax (+385 1) 2357607; e-mail kontakt-uprava@uprava.hr; internet uprava.gov.hr.

Minister of Regional Development and EU Funds: 10000 Zagreb, Račkoga 6; tel. (+385 1) 6400660; fax (+385 1) 6400644; e-mail kabinet@mrrfeu.hr; internet razvoj.gov.hr.

Ministry of Science and Education: 10000 Zagreb, Donje Svetice 38; tel. (+385 1) 4569000; fax (+385 1) 4594301; e-mail ministrica@mzos.hr; internet public.mzos.hr.

Ministry of State Property: 10000 Zagreb, Ivana Dežmana 10; tel. (+385 1) 6346286; fax (+385 1) 6448906; e-mail pisarnica@midim.hr; internet imovina.gov.hr.

Ministry of Tourism: 10000 Zagreb, Prisavlje 14; tel. (+385 1) 6169180; fax (+385 1) 6169181; e-mail ministar@mint.hr; internet www.mint.hr.

Ministry of Veterans' Affairs: 10000 Zagreb, trg Nevenke Topalušić 1; tel. (+385 1) 2308888; fax (+385 1) 2308941; e-mail ministarstvo@branitelji.hr; internet branitelji.gov.hr.

CYPRUS

President: Nikos Anastasiades.

Minister of Foreign Affairs: Ioannis Kasoulides.

Minister of Finance: Haris Georgiades.

Minister of the Interior: Constantinos Petrides.

Minister of Defence: Christoforos Fokaides.

Minister of Education and Culture: Costas Kadis.

Minister of Transport, Communications and Works: Marios Demetriades.

Minister of Energy, Commerce, Industry and Tourism: Georgios Lakkotrypis.

Minister of Agriculture, Rural Development and the Environment: Nikos Kouyalis.

Minister of Labour, Welfare and Social Insurance: Georgia (Zeta) Emilianidou.

Minister of Justice and Public Order: Ionas Nicolaou.

Minister of Health: Dr George Pamboridis.

Government Spokesman: Nikos Christodoulides.

Ministries

Office of the President: Presidential Palace, Demosthenis Severis Ave, 1400 Nicosia; tel. (+357) 22867400; fax (+357) 22663799; e-mail info@presidency.gov.cy; internet www.presidency.gov.cy.

Ministry of Agriculture, Rural Development and the Environment: 6 Amfipoleos St, 2025 Strovolos, Nicosia; tel. (+357) 22408305; fax (+357) 22408352; e-mail registry@moa.gov.cy; internet www.moa.gov.cy.

Ministry of Defence: 4 Emmanuel Roides Ave, 1432 Nicosia; tel. (+357) 22807500; fax (+357) 22304135; e-mail defence@mod.gov.cy; internet www.mod.gov.cy.

Ministry of Education and Culture: Kimonos and Thoukididis, 1434 Nicosia; tel. (+357) 22800600; fax (+357) 22426349; e-mail moec@moec.gov.cy; internet www.moec.gov.cy.

Ministry of Energy, Commerce, Industry and Tourism: 6 Andreas Araouzos St, 1421 Nicosia; tel. (+357) 22867100; fax (+357) 22375120; e-mail perm.sec@mcit.gov.cy; internet www.mcit.gov.cy.

Ministry of Finance: Cnr Michalakis Karaolis St and Gregoriou Afxentiou St, 1439 Nicosia; tel. (+357) 22602723; fax (+357) 22602741; e-mail registry@mof.gov.cy; internet www.mof.gov.cy.

Ministry of Foreign Affairs: Presidential Palace Ave, 1447 Nicosia; tel. (+357) 22651000; fax (+357) 22661881; e-mail info@mfa.gov.cy; internet www.mfa.gov.cy.

Ministry of Health: 1 Prodomou and 17 Chilonos, 1448 Nicosia; tel. (+357) 22605300; fax (+357) 22605487; e-mail perm.sec@moh.gov.cy; internet www.moh.gov.cy.

Ministry of the Interior: Demosthenis Severis Ave, Ex Secretariat Compound, 1453 Nicosia; tel. (+357) 22867800; fax (+357) 22671465; e-mail info@moi.gov.cy; internet www.moi.gov.cy.

Ministry of Justice and Public Order: 125 Athalassa Ave, 1461 Nicosia; tel. (+357) 22805950; fax (+357) 22518356; e-mail registry@mjpo.gov.cy; internet www.mjpo.gov.cy.

Ministry of Labour, Welfare and Social Insurance: 7 Byron Ave, 1463 Nicosia; tel. (+357) 22805950; fax (+357) 22518356; e-mail administration@mlsi.gov.cy; internet www.mlsi.gov.cy.

Ministry of Transport, Communications and Works: 28 Achaeon St, Agios Andreas, 1424 Nicosia; tel. (+357) 22800100; fax (+357) 22776266; e-mail ipiresia.politi@mcw.gov.cy; internet www.mcw.gov.cy.

CZECH REPUBLIC

Prime Minister: Bohuslav Sobotka.

First Deputy Prime Minister and Minister of the Environment: Richard Brabec.

Deputy Prime Minister, responsible for Science, Research and Innovation: Pavel Bělobrádek.

Minister of Finance: Ivan Pilný.

Minister of Foreign Affairs: Lubomír Zaorálek.

Minister of Defence: Martin Stropnický.

Minister of the Interior: Milan Chovanec.

Minister of Industry and Trade: Jiří Havlíček.

Minister of Justice: Robert Pelikán.

Minister of Labour and Social Affairs: Michaela Marksová.

Minister of Transport: Dan Ťok.

Minister of Agriculture: Marian Jurečka.

Minister of Health: Miloslav Ludvík.

Minister of Education, Youth and Sports: Stanislav Štech.

Minister of Regional Development: Karla Šlechtová.

Minister of Culture: Daniel Herman.

Minister of Human Rights, Equal Opportunities and Legislation, and Chairman of the Government Legislative Council: Jan Chvojka.

Ministries

Office of the Government: náb. E. Beneše 4, 118 01 Prague 1; tel. (+420) 224002111; fax (+420) 257531283; e-mail posta@vlada.cz; internet www.vlada.cz.

Ministry of Agriculture: Těšnov 65/17, 110 00 Prague 1; tel. (+420) 221811111; fax (+420) 224810478; e-mail info@mze.cz; internet www.eagri.cz.

Ministry of Culture: Maltéské nám. 1, 118 11 Prague 1; tel. (+420) 257085111; fax (+420) 224318155; e-mail epodatelna@mkcr.cz; internet www.mkcr.cz.

Ministry of Defence: Tychonova 221/1, 160 00 Prague 6; tel. (+420) 973201111; e-mail e-podatelnamo@army.cz; internet www.army.cz.

Ministry of Education, Youth and Sports: Karmelitská 529/5, 118 12 Prague 1; tel. (+420) 234811111; e-mail posta@msmt.cz; internet www.msmt.cz.

Ministry of the Environment: Vršovická 1442/65, 100 10 Prague 10; tel. (+420) 267121111; fax (+420) 267310308; e-mail info@mzp.cz; internet www.mzp.cz.

Ministry of Finance: Letenská 15, 118 10 Prague 1; tel. (+420) 257041111; fax (+420) 257042788; e-mail podatelna@mfcr.cz; internet www.mfcr.cz.

Ministry of Foreign Affairs: Loretánské nám. 5, 118 00 Prague 1; tel. (+420) 224181111; e-mail epodatelna@mzv.cz; internet www.mzv.cz.

Ministry of Health: Palackého nám. 4, 128 01 Prague 2; tel. (+420) 224971111; fax (+420) 224972111; e-mail mzcr@mzcr.cz; internet www.mzcr.cz.

Ministry of Industry and Trade: Na Františku 32, 110 15 Prague 1; tel. (+420) 224851111; fax (+420) 224811089; e-mail posta@mpo.cz; internet www.mpo.cz.

Ministry of the Interior: Nad Štolou 3, POB 21, 170 34 Prague 7; tel. (+420) 974811111; fax (+420) 974833582; e-mail posta@mvcr.cz; internet www.mvcr.cz.

Ministry of Justice: Vyšehradská 16, 128 10 Prague 2; tel. (+420) 221997111; fax (+420) 224919927; e-mail posta@msp.justice.cz; internet portal.justice.cz.

Ministry of Labour and Social Affairs: Na poříčním právu 1/376, 128 01 Prague 2; tel. (+420) 221921111; fax (+420) 224918391; e-mail posta@mpsv.cz; internet www.mpsv.cz.

Ministry of Regional Development: Staroměstské nám. 6, 110 15 Prague 1; tel. (+420) 224861111; fax (+420) 224861333; e-mail posta@mmr.cz; internet www.mmr.cz.

Ministry of Transport: nábř. L. Svobody 1222/12, POB 9, 110 15 Prague 1; tel. (+420) 225131111; fax (+420) 225131184; e-mail posta@mdcr.cz; internet www.mdcr.cz.

DENMARK

Prime Minister: Lars Løkke Rasmussen.

Minister of Foreign Affairs: Anders Samuelsen.

Minister of Justice: Søren Pape Poulsen.

Minister of Finance: Kristian Jensen.

Minister of Defence: Claus Hjort Frederiksen.

Minister of Business: Brian Mikkelsen.

Minister of Economic Affairs and the Interior: Simon Emil Ammitzbøll.

Minister of Development Co-operation: Ulla Tørnæs.

Minister of Employment: Troels Lund Poulsen.

Minister of Immigration and Integration: Inger Støjberg.

Minister of Fisheries, Equality Opportunities, and of Nordic Co-operation: Karen Ellemann.

Minister of Higher Education and Research: Søren Pind.

Minister of Energy, Utilities and Climate: Lars Christian Lilleholt.

Minister of Health: Ellen Trane Nørby.

Minister of Public Sector Innovation: Sophie Løhde.

Minister of Taxation: Karsten Lauritzen.

Minister of Environment and Food: Esben Lunde Larsen.

Minister of Children and Social Affairs: Mai Mercado.

Minister of Education: Merete Riisager.

Minister of Culture and of Ecclesiastical Affairs: Mette Bock.

Minister of Transport, Building and Housing: Ole Birk Olesen.

Minister of the Elderly: Thyra Frank.

Ministries

Prime Minister's Office: Christiansborg, Prins Jørgens Gård 11, 1218 Copenhagen K; tel. (+45) 33-92-33-00; fax (+45) 33-11-16-65; e-mail stm@stm.dk; internet www.stm.dk.

Ministry of Business: Slotsholmsgade 10–12, 1216 Copenhagen K; tel. (+45) 33-92-33-50; fax (+45) 33-12-37-78; e-mail evm@evm.dk; internet www.evm.dk.

Ministry of Children and Social Affairs: Holmens Kanal 22, 1060 Copenhagen K; tel. (+45) 33-92-93-00; fax (+45) 33-93-25-18; e-mail sim@sim.dk; internet socialministeriet.dk.

Ministry of Culture: Nybrogade 2, 1203 Copenhagen K; tel. (+45) 33-92-33-70; fax (+45) 33-91-33-88; e-mail kum@kum.dk; internet www.kum.dk.

Ministry of Defence: Holmens Kanal 42, 1060 Copenhagen K; tel. (+45) 72-81-00-00; fax (+45) 72-81-03-00; e-mail fmn@fmn.dk; internet www.fmn.dk.

Ministry of Ecclesiastical Affairs: Frederiksholms Kanal 21, 1220 Copenhagen K; tel. (+45) 33-92-33-90; e-mail km@km.dk; internet www.km.dk.

Ministry of Economic Affairs and the Interior: Slotsholmsgade 10, 1216 Copenhagen K; tel. (+45) 72-28-24-00; e-mail oim@oim.dk; internet www.oim.dk.

Ministry of Education: Frederiksholms Kanal 21, 1220 Copenhagen K; tel. (+45) 33-92-50-00; e-mail uvm@uvm.dk; internet www.uvm.dk.

Ministry of Employment: Ved Stranden 8, 1061 Copenhagen K; tel. (+45) 72-20-50-00; fax (+45) 33-12-13-78; e-mail bm@bm.dk; internet www.bm.dk.

Ministry of Energy, Utilities and Climate: Stormgade 2–6, 1470 Copenhagen K; tel. (+45) 33-92-28-00; fax (+45) 33-92-28-01; e-mail efkm@efkm.dk; internet www.efkm.dk.

Ministry of Environment and Food: Slotsholmsgade 12, 1216 Copenhagen K; tel. (+45) 38-14-21-42; e-mail mfvm@mfvm.dk; internet mfvm.dk.

Ministry of Finance: Christiansborg Slotspl. 1, 1218 Copenhagen K; tel. (+45) 33-92-33-33; e-mail fm@fm.dk; internet www.fm.dk.

Ministry of Foreign Affairs: Asiatisk Pl. 2, 1448 Copenhagen K; tel. (+45) 33-92-00-00; fax (+45) 32-54-05-33; e-mail um@um.dk; internet www.um.dk.

Ministry of Health and the Elderly: Holbergsgade 6, 1057 Copenhagen K; tel. (+45) 72-26-90-00; e-mail sum@sum.dk; internet www.sum.dk.

Ministry of Higher Education and Research: Børsgade 4, 1215 Copenhagen K; tel. (+45) 33-92-97-00; fax (+45) 33-32-35-01; e-mail ufm@ufm.dk; internet ufm.dk.

Ministry of Immigration and Integration: Gammel Slotsholmsgade 10, 1216 Copenhagen K; tel. (+45) 61-98-40-00; e-mail uim@uim.dk; internet uim.dk.

Ministry of Justice: Slotsholmsgade 10, 1216 Copenhagen K; tel. (+45) 72-26-84-00; fax (+45) 33-93-35-10; e-mail jm@jm.dk; internet www.justitsministeriet.dk.

Ministry of Taxation: Nicolai Eigtveds Gade 28, 1402 Copenhagen K; tel. (+45) 33-92-33-92; e-mail skm@skm.dk; internet www.skm.dk.

Ministry of Transport, Building and Housing: Frederiksholms Kanal 27, 1220 Copenhagen K; tel. (+45) 41-71-27-00; fax (+45) 33-12-38-93; e-mail trm@trm.dk; internet www.trm.dk.

ESTONIA

Prime Minister: Jüri Ratas.

Minister of Health and Labour: Jevgeni Ossinovski.

Minister of Defence: Jüri Luik.

Minister of Education and Research: Mailis Reps.

Minister of Foreign Affairs: Sven Mikser.

Minister of the Environment: Siim Kiisler.

Minister of Rural Affairs: Tarmo Tamm.

Minister of Finance: Toomas Tõniste.

Minister of Social Protection: Kaia Iva.

Minister of Culture: Indrek Saar.

Minister of Justice: Urmas Reinsalu.

Minister of Economic Affairs and Infrastructure: Kadri Simson.

Minister of Entrepreneurship and Information Technology: Urve Palo.

Minister of the Interior: Andres Anvelt.

Minister of Public Administration: Jaak Aab.

Ministries

Office of the Prime Minister: Stenbocki maja, Rahukohtu 3, Tallinn 15161; tel. (+372) 693-5555; fax (+372) 693-5554; e-mail riigikantselei@riigikantselei.ee; internet valitsus.ee.

Ministry of Culture: Suur Karja 23, Tallinn 15076; tel. (+372) 628-2222; fax (+372) 628-2200; e-mail min@kul.ee; internet www.kul.ee.

Ministry of Defence: Sakala 1, Tallinn 15094; tel. (+372) 717-0022; fax (+372) 717-0001; e-mail info@kaitseministeerium.ee; internet www.kaitseministeerium.ee.

Ministry of Economic Affairs and Infrastructure: Harju 11, Tallinn 15072; tel. (+372) 625-6342; fax (+372) 631-3660; e-mail info@mkm.ee; internet www.mkm.ee.

Ministry of Education and Research: Munga 18, Tartu 50088; tel. (+372) 735-0222; fax (+372) 730-1080; e-mail hm@hm.ee; internet www.hm.ee.

Ministry of the Environment: Narva mnt. 7A, Tallinn 15172; tel. (+372) 626-2802; fax (+372) 626-2801; e-mail keskkonnaministeerium@envir.ee; internet www.envir.ee.

Ministry of Finance: Endla 13, Tallinn 10122; tel. (+372) 611-3558; fax (+372) 611-3664; e-mail info@fin.ee; internet www.fin.ee.

Ministry of Foreign Affairs: Islandi Väljak 1, Tallinn 15049; tel. (+372) 637-7000; fax (+372) 637-7099; e-mail vminfo@vm.ee; internet www.vm.ee.

Ministry of the Interior: Pikk 61, Tallinn 15065; tel. 612-5008; e-mail info@siseministeerium.ee; internet www.siseministeerium.ee.

Ministry of Justice: Tõnismägi 5A, Tallinn 15191; tel. (+372) 620-8100; fax (+372) 620-8109; e-mail info@just.ee; internet www.just.ee.

Ministry of Rural Affairs: Lai 39/41, Tallinn 15056; tel. (+372) 625-6101; fax (+372) 625-6200; e-mail info@agri.ee; internet www.agri.ee.

Ministry of Social Protection: Gonsiori 29, Tallinn 15027; tel. (+372) 626-9301; fax (+372) 699-2209; e-mail info@sm.ee; internet www.sm.ee.

FINLAND

Prime Minister: Juha Sipilä.

Deputy Prime Minister and Minister for Foreign Affairs: Timo Soini.

Minister for Foreign Trade and Development: Kai Mykkänen.

Minister of Justice: Antti Häkkänen.

Minister of the Interior: Paula Risikko.

Minister of Defence: Jussi Niinistö.

Minister of Finance: Petteri Orpo.

Minister of Local Government and Public Reforms: Anu Vehviläinen.

Minister of Education: Sanni Grahn-Laasonen.

Minister of European Affairs, Culture and Sport: Sampo Terho.

Minister of Agriculture and Forestry: Jari Leppä.

Minister of Transport and Communications: Anne Berner.

Minister of Economic Affairs: Mika Lintilä.

Minister of Employment: Jari Lindström.

Minister of Social Affairs and Health: Pirkko Mattila.

Minister of Family Affairs and Social Services: Annika Saarikko.

Minister of Housing, Energy and the Environment: Kimmo Tiilikainen.

Ministries

Prime Minister's Office: Snellmaninkatu 1A, Helsinki; POB 23, 00023 Government; tel. (+358 9) 16001; fax (+358 9) 16022165; e-mail info@vnk.fi; internet www.vnk.fi.

Ministry of Agriculture and Forestry: Hallituskatu 3A, Helsinki; POB 30, 00023 Government; fax (+358 9) 16054202; e-mail kirjaamo@mmm.fi; internet www.mmm.fi.

Ministry of Defence: Eteläinen Makasiinikatu 8, POB 31, 00131 Helsinki; fax (+358 9) 16088244; e-mail tiedotus@defmin.fi; internet www.defmin.fi.

Ministry of Economic Affairs and Employment: Aleksanterinkatu 4, 00170 Helsinki; POB 32, 00023 Government; fax (+358 9) 16062160; e-mail kirjaamo@tem.fi; internet www.tem.fi.

Ministry of Education: Meritullinkatu 10, Helsinki; POB 29, 00023 Government; fax (+358 9) 1359335; e-mail kirjaamo@minedu.fi; internet www.minedu.fi.

Ministry of Finance: Snellmaninkatu 1A, Helsinki; POB 28, 00023 Government; e-mail valtiovarainministerio@vm.fi; internet www.vm.fi.

Ministry for Foreign Affairs: Merikasarmi, Laivastokatu 22, POB 176, 00023 Government; fax (+358 9) 629840; e-mail kirjaamo.um@formin.fi; internet formin.finland.fi.

Ministry of Housing, Energy and the Environment: Aleksanterinkatu 7, Helsinki; POB 35, 00023 Government; fax (+358 9) 16039320; e-mail kirjaamo@ym.fi; internet www.ym.fi.

Ministry of the Interior: Erottajankatu 2, Helsinki; POB 26, 00023 Government; fax (+358 9) 16044635; e-mail kirjaamo@intermin.fi; internet www.intermin.fi.

Ministry of Justice: Eteläesplanadi 10, Helsinki; POB 25, 00023 Government; fax (+358 9) 16067730; e-mail oikeusministerio@om.fi; internet www.oikeusministerio.fi.

Ministry of Social Affairs and Health: Meritullinkatu 8, 00170 Helsinki; POB 33, 00023 Government; fax (+358 9) 6980709; e-mail kirjaamo@stm.fi; internet www.stm.fi.

Ministry of Transport and Communications: Eteläesplanadi 16, Helsinki; POB 31, 00023 Government; fax (+358 9) 16028596; e-mail kirjaamo@lvm.fi; internet www.lvm.fi.

FRANCE

Prime Minister: Edouard Philippe.

Minister of the Interior: Gérard Collomb.

Minister of Ecological and Solidarity Transition: Nicolas Hulot.

Keeper of the Seals, Minister of Justice: Nicole Belloubet.

Minister of the Armed Forces: Florence Parly.

Minister for Europe and Foreign Affairs: Jean-Yves Le Drian.

Minister of Territorial Cohesion: Jacques Mézard.

Minister of Solidarity and Health: Agnès Buzyn.

Minister of Culture: Françoise Nyssen.

Minister of Economy and Finance: Bruno Le Maire.

Minister of Labour: Muriel Pénicaud.

Minister of National Education: Jean-Michel Blanquer.

Minister of Agriculture and Food: Stéphane Travert.

Minister of Public Affairs and Public Accounts: Gérald Darmanin.

Minister of Higher Education, Research and Innovation: Frédérique Vidal.

Minister of Overseas Territories: Annick Girardin.

Minister of Sports: Laura Flessel.

Secretary of State for Relations with Parliament and Government Spokesperson, attached to the Prime Minister: Christophe Castaner.

Secretary of State for Equality between Women and Men, attached to the Prime Minister: Marlène Schiappa.

Secretary of State for the Disabled, attached to the Prime Minister: Sophie Cluzel.

Secretary of State for the Digital Economy, attached to the Prime Minister: Mounir Mahjoubi.

Minister, attached to the Minister of the Interior: Jacqueline Gourault.

Minister of Transport, attached to the Minister of Ecological and Solidarity Transition: Elisabeth Borne.

Secretary of State to the Minister of Ecological and Solidarity Transition: Sébastien Lecornu.

Secretary of State to the Minister of Ecological and Solidarity Transition: Brune Poirson.

Minister for European Affairs, attached to the Minister for Europe and Foreign Affairs: Nathalie Loiseau.

Secretary of State to the Minister for Europe and Foreign Affairs: Jean-Baptiste Lemoyne.

Secretary of State to the Minister of the Armed Forces: Geneviève Darrieussecq.

Secretary of State to the Minister of Territorial Cohesion: Julien Denormandie.

Secretary of State to the Minister of Economy and Finance: Benjamin Griveaux.

Ministries

Office of the Prime Minister: Hôtel de Matignon, 57 rue de Varenne, 75007 Paris; tel. (+33) 1-42-75-80-00; e-mail premier-ministre@premier-ministre.gouv.fr; internet www.gouvernement.fr.

Ministry of Agriculture and Food: 78 rue de Varenne, 75349 Paris Cedex 07; tel. (+33) 1-49-55-49-55; e-mail ministere.presse@agriculture.gouv.fr; internet agriculture.gouv.fr.

Ministry of the Armed Forces: 14 rue Saint Dominique, 75007 Paris; tel. (+33) 1-80-50-14-00; fax (+33) 1-47-05-40-91; e-mail courrier-ministre@sdbc.defense.gouv.fr; internet www.defense.gouv.fr.

Ministry of Culture: 182 rue Saint-Honoré, 75001 Paris; tel. (+33) 1-40-15-80-00; internet www.culturecommunication.gouv.fr.

Ministry of Ecological and Solidarity Transition: 246 blvd Saint Germain, 75700 Paris; tel. (+33) 1-40-81-21-22; internet www.developpement-durable.gouv.fr.

Ministry of Economy and Finance: 139 rue de Bercy, 75572 Paris Cedex 12; tel. (+33) 1-40-04-04-04; internet www.economie.gouv.fr.

Ministry for Europe and Foreign Affairs: 37 quai d'Orsay, 75351 Paris Cedex 07; tel. (+33) 1-43-17-53-53; fax (+33) 1-43-17-47-53; internet www.diplomatie.gouv.fr.

Ministry of Higher Education, Research and Innovation: 1 rue Descartes, 75231 Paris Cedex 05; tel. (+33) 1-55-55-90-90; e-mail sup-info@education.gouv.fr; internet www.enseignementsup-recherche.gouv.fr.

Ministry of the Interior: place Beauvau, 75008 Paris; tel. (+33) 1-49-27-49-27; fax (+33) 1-43-59-89-50; e-mail sirp@interieur.gouv.fr; internet www.interieur.gouv.fr.

Ministry of Justice: 13 place Vendôme, 75042 Paris Cedex 01; tel. (+33) 1-44-77-60-60; e-mail cyberjustice@justice.gouv.fr; internet www.justice.gouv.fr.

Ministry of Labour: 127 rue de Grenelle, 75700 Paris; tel. (+33) 1-44-38-38-38; internet travail-emploi.gouv.fr.

Ministry of National Education: 110 rue de Grenelle, 75357 Paris Cedex 07; tel. (+33) 1-55-55-10-10; internet www.education.gouv.fr.

Ministry of Overseas Territories: 27 rue Oudinot, 75007 Paris; tel. (+33) 1-53-69-20-00; e-mail ministere@outre-mer.gouv.fr; internet www.outre-mer.gouv.fr.

Ministry of Solidarity and Health: 14 ave Duquesne, 75007 Paris; tel. (+33) 1-40-56-60-00; internet social-sante.gouv.fr.

Ministry of Sports: Hôtel de Broglie, 35 rue Saint-Dominique, 75007 Paris; tel. (+33) 1-49-55-34-00; e-mail presse@ville-jeunesse-sports.gouv.fr; internet www.jeunes.gouv.fr.

Ministry of Territorial Cohesion: Hôtel de Castries, 72 rue de Varenne, 75007 Paris; tel. (+33) 1-40-81-21-22; internet www.territoires.gouv.fr.

GERMANY

A new Govenment was to be formed following federal elections on 24 September 2017.

Federal Chancellor: Angela Merkel.

Federal Vice-Chancellor and Federal Minister of Foreign Affairs: Sigmar Gabriel.

Federal Minister of Economic Affairs and Energy: Brigitte Zypries.

Federal Minister of the Interior: Thomas de Maizière.

Federal Minister of Justice and Consumer Protection: Heiko Maas.

Federal Minister of Finance: Wolfgang Schäuble.

Federal Minister of Labour and Social Affairs: Andrea Nahles.

Federal Minister of Food and Agriculture: Christian Schmidt.

Federal Minister of Defence: Ursula von der Leyen.

Federal Minister of Family Affairs, Senior Citizens, Women and Youth: Katarina Barley.

Federal Minister of Health: Herrmann Gröhe.

Federal Minister of Transport and Digital Infrastructure: Alexander Dobrindt.

Federal Minister of the Environment, Nature Conservation, Building and Nuclear Safety: Barbara Hendricks.

Federal Minister of Education and Research: Johanna Wanka.

Federal Minister of Economic Co-operation and Development: Gerd Müller.

Head of the Federal Chancellery and Federal Minister for Special Tasks: Peter Altmaier.

Ministries

Office of the Federal President: Bundespräsidialamt, Spreeweg 1, 10557 Berlin; tel. (+49 30) 20000; fax (+49 30) 20001999; e-mail bundespraesidialamt@bpra.bund.de; internet www.bundespraesident.de.

Federal Chancellery: Bundeskanzler-Amt, Willy-Brandt Str. 1, 10557 Berlin; tel. (+49 30) 40000; fax (+49 30) 40002357; e-mail internetpost@bpa.bund.de; internet www.bundeskanzlerin.de.

Press and Information Office of the Federal Government: Dorotheenstr. 84, 10117 Berlin; 11044 Berlin; tel. (+49 30) 182720; fax (+49 30) 182722555; e-mail internetpost@bundesregierung.de; internet www.bundesregierung.de.

Federal Ministry of Defence: Stauffenbergstr. 18, 10785 Berlin; tel. (+49 30) 182424242; fax (+49 30) 182422197; e-mail bmvgprinfoab2@bmvg.bund.de; internet www.bmvg.de.

Federal Ministry of Economic Affairs and Energy: 11019 Berlin; Scharnhorststr. 34–37, 10115 Berlin; tel. (+49 30) 186150; fax (+49 30) 186157010; e-mail kontakt@bmwi.bund.de; internet www.bmwi.de.

Federal Ministry of Economic Co-operation and Development: Dahlmannstr. 4, 53113 Bonn; Postfach 120322, 53045 Bonn; tel. (+49 228) 995350; fax (+49 228) 995353500; e-mail info@bmz.bund.de; internet www.bmz.de.

Federal Ministry of Education and Research: Heinemannstr. 2, 53175 Bonn; tel. (+49 228) 99570; fax (+49 228) 995783601; e-mail information@bmbf.bund.de; internet www.bmbf.de.

Federal Ministry of the Environment, Nature Conservation, Building and Nuclear Safety: Stresemannstr. 128–130, 10117 Berlin; tel. (+49 30) 183050; fax (+49 30) 183052044; e-mail service@bmub.bund.de; internet www.bmub.bund.de.

Federal Ministry of Family Affairs, Senior Citizens, Women and Youth: Glinkastr. 24, 10117 Berlin; tel. (+49 30) 185550; fax (+49 30) 185551145; e-mail poststelle@bmfsfj.bund.de; internet www.bmfsfj.de.

Federal Ministry of Finance: 11016 Berlin; Wilhelmstr. 97, 10117 Berlin; tel. (+49 30) 186820; fax (+49 30) 186823260; e-mail poststelle@bmf.bund.de; internet www.bundesfinanzministerium.de.

Federal Ministry of Food and Agriculture: 11055 Berlin; Wilhelmstr. 54, 10117 Berlin; tel. (+49 30) 185290; fax (+49 30) 185294262; e-mail poststelle@bmel.bund.de; internet www.bmel.de.

Federal Ministry of Foreign Affairs: 11013 Berlin; Werderscher Markt 1, 10117 Berlin; tel. (+49 30) 18170; fax (+49 30) 18173402; e-mail poststelle@auswaertiges-amt.de; internet www.auswaertiges-amt.de.

Federal Ministry of Health: 53107 Bonn; Rochusstr. 1, 53123 Bonn; tel. (+49 228) 994410; fax (+49 228) 994414900; e-mail poststelle@bundesgesundheitsministerium.de-mail.de; internet www.bundesgesundheitsministerium.de.

Federal Ministry of the Interior: Alt-Moabit 140, 10557 Berlin; tel. (+49 30) 186810; fax (+49 30) 1868112926; e-mail poststelle@bmi.bund.de; internet www.bmi.bund.de.

Federal Ministry of Justice and Consumer Protection: Mohrenstr. 37, 10117 Berlin; tel. (+49 30) 185800; fax (+49 30) 185809525; e-mail postelle@bmjv.bund.de; internet www.bmjv.de.

Federal Ministry of Labour and Social Affairs: Wilhelmstr. 49, 10117 Berlin; tel. (+49 30) 185270; fax (+49 30) 185271830; e-mail info@bmas.bund.de; internet www.bmas.de.

Federal Ministry of Transport and Digital Infrastructure: Invalidenstr. 44, 10115 Berlin; tel. (+49 30) 183003060; fax (+49 30) 183001942; e-mail buergerinfo@bmvi.bund.de; internet www.bmvi.de.

GREECE

Prime Minister and Chairman of the Government: Alexis Tsipras.

Deputy Prime Minister: Ioannis Dragasakis.

Minister of the Interior: Panagiotis Skourletis.

Minister of the Economy and Development: Dimitris Papadimitrou.

Minister of Digital Policy, Telecommunications and Media: Nikolaos Pappas.

Minister of National Defence: Panos Kammenos.

Minister of Education, Research and Religious Affairs: Kostas Gavroglou.

Minister of Foreign Affairs: Nikos Kotzias.

Minister of Justice, Transparency and Human Rights: Stavros Kontonis.

Minister of Labour, Social Security and Social Welfare: Effie Achtsioglou.

Minister of Health: Andreas Xanthos.

Minister of Culture and Sport: Lydia Koniordou.

Minister of Finance: Euclid Tsakalotos.

Minister of Administrative Reform: Olga Gerovasili.

Minister of the Environment and Energy: Giorgos Stathakis.

Minister of Infrastructure and Transport: Christos Spirtzis.

Minister of Migration Policy: Ioannis Mouzalas.

Minister of Shipping and Island Policy: Panagiotis Kouroublis.

Minister of Rural Development and Food: Evangelos Apostolou.

Minister of Tourism: Elena Kountoura.

Ministers of State: Christoforos Vernardakis, Alexandros Flambouraris, Dimitrios Tzanakopoulos.

Ministries

Office of the President: Odos Vassileos Georgiou 2, 100 28 Athens; tel. (+30 210) 7283111; fax (+30 210) 7248938; internet www.presidency.gr.

Office of the Prime Minister: Maximos Mansion, Herodou Atticou 19, 106 74 Athens; tel. (+30 210) 3385491; fax (+30 210) 3238129; e-mail primeminister@primeminister.gr; internet www.primeminister.gr.

Ministry of Culture and Sport: Mpoympoylínas 20–22, 106 82 Athens; tel. (+30 213) 1322100; fax (+30 210) 8201138; e-mail grplk@culture.gr; internet new.culture.gr.

Ministry of Digital Policy, Telecommunications and Media: Athens.

Ministry of the Economy and Development: Nikhs 5–7, 101 80 Athens; tel. (+30 210) 3332637; fax (+30 210) 3332775; e-mail public@mnec.gr; internet www.mindev.gov.gr.

Ministry of Education, Research and Religious Affairs: Andreas Papandreou 37, 151 80 Athens; tel. (+30 210) 3442000; internet www.minedu.gov.gr.

Ministry of the Environment and Energy: Odos Amalia 17, 115 23 Athens; tel. (+30 210) 1515000; fax (+30 210) 6447608; e-mail service@dorg.minenv.gr; internet www.ypeka.gr.

Ministry of Finance: Karageorgi Servias 10, 105 62 Athens; tel. (+30 210) 3375000; fax (+30 210) 3332608; e-mail minister@minfin.gr; internet www.minfin.gr.

Ministry of Foreign Affairs: Odos Sofias 1, 106 71 Athens; tel. (+30 210) 3681000; fax (+30 210) 3681717; e-mail mfa@mfa.gr; internet www.mfa.gr.

Ministry of Health: Odos Aristotelous 17, 101 87 Athens; tel. (+30 210) 5232821; e-mail secretary.gen@yyka.gov.gr; internet www.moh.gov.gr.

Ministry of Infrastructure and Transport: Resurrection 2 and Tsigante, 101 91 Athens; tel. (+30 210) 6508000; e-mail yme@yme.gov.gr; internet www.yme.gr.

Ministry of the Interior: Odos Stadiou 27, 10183 Athens; tel. (+30 213) 1364000; fax (+30 213) 1364130; e-mail info@ypes.gr; internet www.ypes.gr.

Ministry of Justice, Transparency and Human Rights: Odos Mesogeion 96, 115 27 Athens; tel. (+30 210) 7767300; fax (+30 210) 7767187; e-mail ypdipimi@otenet.gr; internet www.ministryofjustice.gr.

Ministry of Labour, Social Security and Social Welfare: Odos Pireos 40, 104 37 Athens; tel. (+30 210) 5295248; fax (+30 210) 5249805; e-mail info@ypakp.gr; internet www.ypakp.gr.

Ministry of Migration Policy: Odos P. Kanellopoulou 2, 10177 Athens; tel. (+30 210) 6988500; e-mail asylo@asylo.gov.gr; internet asylo.gov.gr.

Ministry of National Defence: Odos Mesogeion 227–231, Holargos, 155 61 Athens; tel. (+30 210) 6598100; fax (+30 210) 850060; e-mail minister@mod.mil.gr; internet www.mod.mil.gr.

Ministry of Rural Development and Food: Acharnon 2, 101 76 Athens; tel. (+30 210) 2124000; e-mail info@minagric.gr; internet www.minagric.gr.

Ministry of Shipping and Island Policy: 18510 Piraeus; tel. (+30 213) 1371700; fax (+30 210) 4191562; e-mail info@yen.gr; internet www.yen.gr.

Ministry of Tourism: Lewforos Amalias 12, 105 57 Athens; tel. (+30 210) 3736001; fax (+30 210) 8707635; e-mail mailbox@mintour.gr; internet www.mintour.gov.gr.

HUNGARY

Prime Minister: Viktor Orbán.

Deputy Prime Minister for Hungarian Communities Abroad: Dr Zsolt Semjén.

Minister in charge of the Prime Minister's Office: János Lázár.

Minister of Human Resources: Zoltán Balog.

Minister of Agriculture: Dr Sándor Fazekas.

Minister of the Interior: Dr Sándor Pintér.

Minister of National Development: Miklós Seszták.

Minister of Defence: István Simicskó.

Minister of Foreign Affairs and Trade: Péter Szijjártó.

Minister of Justice: László Trócsányi.

Minister of the National Economy: Mihály Varga.

Head of the Cabinet of the Prime Minister: Antal Rogán.

Minister without Portfolio: János Süli.

Ministries

Office of the Prime Minister: 1357 Budapest, pf. 6; tel. (+36 1) 896-1747; fax (+36 1) 795-0893; e-mail mk@mk.gov.hu; internet www.kormany.hu.

Ministry of Agriculture: 1055 Budapest, Kossuth Lajos tér 11; tel. (+36 1) 795-2000; fax (+36 1) 795-0200; e-mail info@fm.gov.hu; internet www.kormany.hu/hu/foldmuvelesugyi-miniszterium.

Ministry of Defence: 1055 Budapest, Balaton u. 7–11; tel. (+36 1) 236-5111; fax (+36 1) 474-1335; e-mail hmugyfelszolgalat@hm.gov.hu; internet www.kormany.hu/hu/honvedelmi-miniszterium.

Ministry of Foreign Affairs and Trade: 1027 Budapest, Bem rakpart 47; tel. (+36 1) 458-1000; fax (+36 1) 212-5918; e-mail konz@mfa.gov.hu; internet www.kormany.hu/hu/kulgazdasagi-es-kulugyminiszterium.

Ministry of Human Resources: 1054 Budapest, Akadémia u. 3; tel. (+36 1) 795-1200; e-mail ugyfelszolgalat@emmi.gov.hu; internet www.kormany.hu/hu/emberi-eroforrasok-miniszteriuma.

Ministry of the Interior: 1051 Budapest, József Attila u. 2–4; tel. (+36 1) 441-1000; fax (+36 1) 441-1437; e-mail ugyfelszolgalat@bm.gov.hu; internet www.kormany.hu/hu/belugyminiszterium.

Ministry of Justice: 1055 Budapest, Kossuth Lajos tér 2–4; tel. (+36 1) 795-1000; fax (+36 1) 795-0359; e-mail lakossag@im.gov.hu; internet www.kormany.hu/hu/igazsagugyi-miniszterium.

Ministry of National Development: 1011 Budapest, F u. 44–50; tel. (+36 1) 795-1700; fax (+36 1) 795-0697; e-mail ugyfelszolgalat@nfm.gov.hu; internet www.kormany.hu/hu/nemzeti-fejlesztesi-miniszterium.

Ministry of the National Economy: 1051 Budapest, József Nádor tér 2–4; tel. (+36 1) 795-5010; fax (+36 1) 795-0716; e-mail ugyfelszolgalat@ngm.gov.hu; internet www.kormany.hu/hu/nemzetgazdasagi-miniszterium.

IRELAND

Taoiseach (Prime Minister) and Minister of Defence: Leo Varadkar.

Tánaiste (Deputy Prime Minister) and Minister for Enterprise and Innovation: Frances Fitzgerald.

Minister for Finance, and for Public Expenditure and Reform: Paschal Donohoe.

Minister for Education and Skills: Richard Bruton.

Minister for Foreign Affairs and Trade, with responsibility for Brexit: Simon Coveney.

Minister for Justice and Equality: Charles Flanagan.

Minister for Culture, Heritage and the Gaeltacht: Heather Humphreys.

Minister for Health: Simon Harris.

Minister for Agriculture, Food and the Marine: Michael Creed.

Minister for Communications, Climate Action and Environment: Denis Naughten.

Minister for Transport, Tourism and Sport: Shane Ross.

Minister for Children and Youth Affairs: Katherine Zappone.

Minister for Rural and Community Development: Michael Ring.

Minister for Employment and Social Protection: Regina Doherty.

Minister for Housing, Planning and Local Government: Eoghan Murphy.

Ministries

Department of the Taoiseach: Government Bldgs, Upper Merrion St, Dublin 2, D02 R583; tel. (+353 1) 6194000; fax (+353 1) 6763302; e-mail webmaster@taoiseach.gov.ie; internet www.taoiseach.gov.ie.

Department of Agriculture, Food and the Marine: Agriculture House, Kildare St, Dublin 2, D02 WK12; tel. (+353 1) 6072000; fax (+353 1) 6616263; e-mail info@agriculture.gov.ie; internet www.agriculture.gov.ie.

Department of Children and Youth Affairs: 43–49 Mespil Rd, Dublin 4, D04 YP52; tel. (+353 1) 6473000; fax (+353 1) 6473101; e-mail contact@dcya.gov.ie; internet www.dcya.gov.ie.

Department of Communications, Climate Action and Environment: 29–31 Adelaide Rd, Dublin, D02 X285; tel. (+353 1) 6782000; e-mail press.office@dccae.gov.ie; internet www.dccae.gov.ie.

Department of Culture, Heritage and the Gaeltacht: 23 Kildare St, Dublin 2, D02 TD30; tel. (+353 1) 6313807; e-mail press.office@ahg.gov.ie; internet www.chg.gov.ie.

Department of Defence: Station Rd, Newbridge, Co Kildare, W12 AD93; tel. (4+353 5) 492000; fax (+353 45) 492017; e-mail info@defence.ie; internet www.defence.ie.

Department of Education and Skills: Marlborough St, Dublin 1, D01 RC96; tel. (+353 1) 8896400; e-mail info@education.gov.ie; internet www.education.ie.

Department of Finance: Government Bldgs, Upper Merrion St, Dublin 2, D02 R583; tel. (+353 1) 6767571; fax (+353 1) 6789936; e-mail webmaster@finance.gov.ie; internet www.finance.gov.ie.

Department of Foreign Affairs and Trade: 80 St Stephen's Green, Dublin 2, D02 VY53; tel. (+353 1) 4082000; internet www.dfa.ie.

Department of Health: Hawkins House, Hawkins St, Dublin 2, D02 VW90; tel. (+353 1) 6353000; e-mail info@health.gov.ie; internet health.gov.ie.

Department of Housing, Planning, Community and Local Government: Custom House, Dublin, D01 W6XO; tel. (+353 1) 8882000; e-mail qcsofficer@housing.gov.ie; internet www.housing.gov.ie.

Department of Jobs, Enterprise and Innovation: 23 Kildare St, Dublin 2, D02 TD30; tel. (+353 1) 6312121; e-mail info@djei.ie; internet www.djei.ie.

Department of Justice and Equality: 51 St Stephen's Green, Dublin 2, D02 HK52; tel. (+353 1) 6028202; fax (+353 1) 6615461; e-mail info@justice.ie; internet www.justice.ie.

Department of Public Expenditure and Reform: Government Bldgs, Upper Merrion St, Dublin 2, D02 R583; tel. (+353 1) 6767571; fax (+353 1) 6789936; e-mail pressoffice@per.gov.ie; internet per.gov.ie.

Department of Rural and Community Development: 25 Clare St, Dublin 2, D02 TD30; tel. (+353 1) 631-3800; internet drcd.gov.ie/.

Department of Social Protection: Áras Mhic Dhiarmada, Store St, Dublin 1; tel. (+353 1) 7043000; e-mail info@welfare.ie; internet www.welfare.ie.

Department of Transport, Tourism and Sport: Leeson Lane, Dublin 2, D02 TR60; tel. (+353 1) 6707444; e-mail info@dttas.ie; internet www.dttas.ie.

ITALY

Prime Minister and acting Minister for Regional Affairs: Paolo Gentiloni Silveri.

Minister of Foreign Affairs and International Co-operation: Angelino Alfano.

Minister of the Interior: Domenico (Marco) Minniti.

Minister of Justice: Andrea Orlando.

Minister of Defence: Roberta Pinotti.

Minister of the Economy and Finance: Pier Carlo Padoan.

Minister of Economic Development: Carlo Calenda.

Minister of Agricultural, Food and Forestry Policies: Maurizio Martina.

Minister of the Environment, Land Management and the Sea: Gian Luca Galletti.

Minister of Infrastructure and Transport: Graziano Delrio.

Minister of Labour and Social Policies: Giuliano Poletti.

Minister of Education, Universities and Research: Valeria Fedeli.

Minister of Cultural Assets and Activities and of Tourism: Dario Franceschini.

Minister of Health: Beatrice Lorenzin.

Minister without Portfolio for Relations with Parliament: Anna Finocchiaro.

Minister without Portfolio for Territorial Cohesion and for the Mezzogiorno: Claudio De Vincenti.

Minister without Portfolio for Sport: Luca Lotti.

Minister without Portfolio for Legislative Simplification and Public Administration: Maria Anna Madia.

Ministries

Office of the Prime Minister: Palazzo Chigi, Piazza Colonna 370, 00187 Roma; tel. (+39 06) 67791; e-mail ufficio_stampa@governo.it; internet www.governo.it.

Ministry of Agricultural, Food and Forestry Policies: Via XX Settembre 20, 00187 Roma; tel. (+39 06) 46651; fax (+39 06) 4742314; e-mail urp@politicheagricole.it; internet www.politicheagricole.gov.it.

Ministry of Cultural Assets and Activities and of Tourism: Via del Collegio Romano 27, 00186 Roma; tel. (+39 06) 67235338; e-mail urp@beniculturali.it; internet www.beniculturali.it.

Ministry of Defence: Palazzo Baracchini, Via XX Settembre 8, 00187 Roma; tel. (+39 06) 4882126; internet www.difesa.it.

Ministry of Economic Development: Via Molise 2, 00187 Roma; tel. (+39 06) 47051; fax (+39 06) 47887770; e-mail segreteria.capogabinetto@mise.gov.it; internet www.sviluppoeconomico.gov.it.

Ministry of the Economy and Finance: Via XX Settembre 97, 00187 Roma; tel. (+39 06) 476111; e-mail ufficio.stampa@mef.gov.it; internet www.mef.gov.it.

Ministry of Education, Universities and Research: Via Trastevere 76A, 00153 Roma; tel. (+39 06) 58491; e-mail urp@istruzione.it; internet www.istruzione.it.

Ministry of the Environment, Land Management and the Sea: Via Cristoforo Colombo 44, 00147 Roma; tel. (+39 06) 57221; e-mail segr.ufficiostampa@minambiente.it; internet www.minambiente.it.

Ministry of Foreign Affairs and International Co-operation: Piazzale della Farnesina 1, 00194 Roma; tel. (+39 06) 36911; fax (+39 06) 3236210; e-mail ministero.affariesteri@cert.esteri.it; internet www.esteri.it.

Ministry of Health: Viale Giorgio Ribotta 5, 00144 Roma; tel. (+39 06) 59941; e-mail ufficiostampa@sanita.it; internet www.salute.gov.it.

Ministry of Infrastructure and Transport: Piazzale Porta Pia 1, 00198 Roma; tel. (+39 06) 44122100; fax (+39 06) 44267283; e-mail segreteria.ministro@pec.mit.gov.it; internet www.mit.gov.it.

Ministry of the Interior: Piazzale del Viminale, Via Agostino Depretis 7, 00184 Roma; tel. (+39 06) 4651; fax (+39 06) 46549599; e-mail gabinetto.ministro@pec.interno.it; internet www.interno.gov.it.

Ministry of Justice: Via Arenula 70, 00186 Roma; tel. (+39 06) 68851; fax (+39 06) 68891493; e-mail ufficio.stampa@giustizia.it; internet www.giustizia.it.

Ministry of Labour and Social Policies: Via Veneto 56, 00187 Roma; tel. (+39 06) 48161; e-mail ufficiostampa@lavoro.gov.it; internet www.lavoro.gov.it.

LATVIA

Prime Minister: Māris Kučinskis.

Deputy Prime Minister, Minister of the Economy: Arvils Ašeradens.

Minister of Defence: Raimonds Bergmanis.

Minister of Foreign Affairs: Edgars Rinkēvičs.

Minister of Finance: Dana Reizniece-Ozola.

Minister of the Interior: Rihards Kozlovskis.

Minister of Education and Science: Kārlis Šadurskis.

Minister of Culture: Dace Melbārde.

Minister of Welfare: Jānis Reirs.

Minister of Transport: Uldis Augulis.

Minister of Health: Anda Čakša.

Minister of Justice: Dzintars Rasnačs.

Minister of Environmental Protection and Regional Development: Kaspars Gerhards.

Minister of Agriculture: Jānis Dūklavs.

Ministries

Office of the Cabinet of Ministers: Brīvības bulv. 36, Rīga 1520; tel. (+371) 6708-2800; fax (+371) 6728-0469; e-mail vk@mk.gov.lv; internet www.mk.gov.lv.

Ministry of Agriculture: Republikas lauk. 2, Rīga 1981; tel. (+371) 6702-7010; fax (+371) 6702-7512; e-mail zm@zm.gov.lv; internet www.zm.gov.lv.

Ministry of Culture: K. Valdemāra iela 11A, Rīga 1364; tel. (+371) 6733-0200; fax (+371) 6733-0293; e-mail kontakti@km.gov.lv; internet www.km.gov.lv.

Ministry of Defence: K. Valdemāra iela 10–12, Rīga 1473; tel. (+371) 6733-5114; fax (+371) 6721-2307; e-mail kanceleja@mod.gov.lv; internet www.mod.gov.lv.

Ministry of the Economy: Brīvības iela 55, Rīga 1519; tel. (+371) 6701-3100; fax (+371) 6728-0882; e-mail pasts@em.gov.lv; internet www.em.gov.lv.

Ministry of Education and Science: Vaļņu iela 2, Rīga 1050; tel. (+371) 6722-6209; fax (+371) 6722-3905; e-mail pasts@izm.gov.lv; internet www.izm.gov.lv.

Ministry of Environmental Protection and Regional Development: Peldu iela 25, Rīga 1494; tel. (+371) 6702-6533; fax (+371) 6782-0442; e-mail pasts@varam.gov.lv; internet www.varam.gov.lv.

Ministry of Finance: Smilšu iela 1, Rīga 1919; tel. (+371) 6709-5405; fax (+371) 6709-5503; e-mail pasts@fm.gov.lv; internet www.fm.gov.lv.

Ministry of Foreign Affairs: K. Valdemāra iela 3, Rīga 1395; tel. (+371) 6701-6201; fax (+371) 6782-8121; e-mail mfa.cha@mfa.gov.lv; internet www.mfa.gov.lv.

Ministry of Health: Brīvības iela 72, Rīga 1011; tel. (+371) 6787-6000; fax (+371) 6787-6002; e-mail vm@vm.gov.lv; internet www.vm.gov.lv.

Ministry of the Interior: Čiekurkalna 1, līnija 1, korp. 2, Rīga 1026; tel. (+371) 6721-9263; fax (+371) 6782-9686; e-mail kanceleja@iem.gov.lv; internet www.iem.gov.lv.

Ministry of Justice: Brīvības bulv. 36, Rīga 1536; tel. (+371) 6703-6801; fax (+371) 6721-0823; e-mail tm.kanceleja@tm.gov.lv; internet www.tm.gov.lv.

Ministry of Transport: Gogoļa iela 3, Rīga 1743; tel. (+371) 6702-8205; fax (+371) 6782-0630; e-mail satiksmes.ministrija@sam.gov.lv; internet www.sam.gov.lv.

Ministry of Welfare: Skolas ielā 28, Rīga 1331; tel. (+371) 6702-1600; fax (+371) 6727-6445; e-mail lm@lm.gov.lv; internet www.lm.gov.lv.

LITHUANIA

Prime Minister: Saulius Skvernelis.

Minister of the Environment: Kęstutis Navickas.

Minister of Energy: Žygimantas Vaičiūnas.

Minister of Finance: Vilius Šapoka.

Minister of National Defence: Raimondas Karoblis.

Minister of Culture: Liana Ruokytė-Jonsson.

Minister of Social Security and Labour: Linas Kukuraitis.

Minister of Transport and Communications: Rokas Masiulis.

Minister of Health: Aurelijus Veryga.

Minister of Education and Science: Jurgita Petrauskienė.

Minister of Justice: Milda Vainiutė.

Minister of the Economy: Mindaugas Sinkevičius.

Minister of Foreign Affairs: Linas Linkevičius.

Minister of the Interior: Eimutis Misiūnas.

Minister of Agriculture: Bronius Markauskas.

Ministries

Office of the Prime Minister: Gedimino pr. 11, Vilnius 01103; tel. (+370 8) 706-63711; fax (+370 8) 706-63895; e-mail lrvkanceliarija@lrv.lt; internet ministraspirmininkas.lrv.lt.

Ministry of Agriculture: Gedimino pr. 19, Vilnius 01103; tel. (+370 5) 239-1111; fax (+370 5) 239-1212; e-mail zum@zum.lt; internet zum.lrv.lt.

Ministry of Culture: J. Basanavičiaus 5, Vilnius 01118; tel. (+370 5) 219-3400; fax (+370 5) 262-3120; e-mail dmm@lrkm.lt; internet lrkm.lrv.lt.

Ministry of the Economy: Gedimino pr. 38, Vilnius 01104; tel. (+370 8) 706-64845; fax (+370 8) 706-64762; e-mail kanc@ukmin.lt; internet ukmin.lrv.lt.

Ministry of Education and Science: A. Volano 2, Vilnius 01516; tel. (+370 5) 219-1190; fax (+370 5) 261-2077; e-mail smmin@smm.lt; internet www.smm.lt.

Ministry of Energy: Gedimino pr. 38, Vilnius 01104; tel. (+370 8) 706-64991; fax (+370 8) 706-64820; e-mail info@enmin.lt; internet enmin.lrv.lt.

Ministry of the Environment: A. Jakšto 4, Vilnius 01105; tel. (+370 5) 266-3661; fax (+370 5) 266-3663; e-mail info@am.lt; internet www.am.lt.

Ministry of Finance: Lukiškių g. 2, Vilnius 01512; tel. (+370 5) 239-0000; fax (+370 5) 279-1481; e-mail finmin@finmin.lt; internet finmin.lrv.lt.

Ministry of Foreign Affairs: J. Tumo-Vaižganto g. 2, Vilnius 01511; tel. (+370 5) 236-2444; fax (+370 5) 231-3090; e-mail urm@urm.lt; internet www.urm.lt.

Ministry of Health: Vilniaus g. 33, Vilnius 01506; tel. (+370 5) 268-5110; fax (+370 5) 266-1402; e-mail ministerija@sam.lt; internet sam.lrv.lt.

Ministry of the Interior: Šventaragio 2, Vilnius 01510; tel. (+370 5) 271-7130; fax (+370 5) 271-8551; e-mail bendrasisd@vrm.lt; internet vrm.lrv.lt.

Ministry of Justice: Gedimino pr. 30, Vilnius 01104; tel. (+370 5) 266-2981; fax (+370 5) 262-5940; e-mail rastine@tm.lt; internet www.tm.lt.

Ministry of National Defence: Totorių 25, Vilnius 01121; tel. (+370 8) 706-70750; fax (+370 5) 264-8517; e-mail kam@kam.lt; internet www.kam.lt.

Ministry of Social Security and Labour: A. Vivulskio g. 11, Vilnius 03610; tel. (+370 5) 266-4201; fax (+370 5) 266-4209; e-mail post@socmin.lt; internet www.socmin.lt.

Ministry of Transport and Communications: Gedimino pr. 17, Vilnius 01505; tel. (+370 5) 261-2363; fax (+370 5) 212-4335; e-mail sumin@sumin.lt; internet sumin.lrv.lt.

LUXEMBOURG

Prime Minister, and Minister of State, of Communications and Media, of Religious Affairs, and of Culture: Xavier Bettel.

Deputy Prime Minister and Minister of the Economy, of Internal Security, and of Defence: Etienne Schneider.

Minister of Foreign and European Affairs, and of Immigration and Asylum: Jean Asselborn.

Minister of Justice: Félix Braz.

Minister of Labour, Employment, and Social Economy and Solidarity: Nicolas Schmit.

Minister of Social Security, of Co-operation and Humanitarian Action, and of Sports: Romain Schneider.

Minister of Sustainable Development and Infrastructure: François Bausch.

Minister of Agriculture, Viticulture and Consumer Protection, and of Relations with Parliament: Fernand Etgen.

Minister of Finance: Pierre Gramegna.

Minister of Health and of Equal Opportunities: Lydia Mutsch.

Minister of the Interior, and of the Civil Service and Administrative Reform: Daniel Kersch.

Minister of Education, Children and Youth, and of Higher Education and Research: Claude Meisch.

Minister of Family Affairs, Integration and the Greater Region: Corinne Cahen.

Minister of the Environment: Carole Dieschbourg.

Minister of Housing: Marc Hansen.

Ministries

Office of the Prime Minister: 4 rue de la Congrégation, 1352 Luxembourg; tel. (+352) 247-82100; e-mail ministere.etat@me.etat.lu; internet www.gouvernement.lu.

Ministry of Agriculture, Viticulture and Consumer Protection: 1 rue de la Congrégation, 1352 Luxembourg; tel. (+352) 247-82500; fax (+352) 46-40-27; e-mail info@ma.public.lu; internet www.ma.public.lu.

Ministry of the Civil Service and Administrative Reform: 63 ave de la Liberté, BP 1807, 1931 Luxembourg; tel. (+352) 247-83100; e-mail info@fonction-publique.public.lu; internet www.fonction-publique.public.lu.

Ministry of Culture: 4 blvd Roosevelt, 2450 Luxembourg; tel. (+352) 247-86600; fax (+352) 29-21-86; e-mail info@mc.public.lu; internet www.mc.public.lu.

Ministry of the Economy: 19–21 blvd Royal, 2449 Luxembourg; tel. (+352) 247-84137; fax (+352) 46-04-48; e-mail info@eco.public.lu; internet www.eco.public.lu.

Ministry of Education, Children and Youth: 29 rue Aldringen, 2926 Luxembourg; tel. (+352) 247-85100; fax (+352) 247-85113; e-mail info@men.lu; internet www.men.public.lu.

Ministry of Equal Opportunities: 6A blvd Roosevelt, 2921 Luxembourg; tel. (+352) 247-85806; fax (+352) 24-18-86; e-mail info@mega.public.lu; internet www.mega.public.lu.

Ministry of Family Affairs, Integration and the Greater Region: 12–14 ave Emile Reuter, 2420 Luxembourg; tel. (+352) 247-86500; fax (+352) 247-86570; e-mail info@mfi.public.lu; internet www.mfi.public.lu.

Ministry of Finance: 3 rue de la Congrégation, 1352 Luxembourg; tel. (+352) 247-82600; fax (+352) 47-52-41; internet www.mf.public.lu.

Ministry of Foreign and European Affairs: Hôtel St Maximin, 5 rue Notre-Dame, 2240 Luxembourg; tel. (+352) 247-82300; fax (+352) 22-31-44; e-mail boite.officielle@mae.etat.lu; internet www.mae.lu.

Ministry of Health: Villa Louvigny, allée Marconi, 2120 Luxembourg; tel. (+352) 247-85500; e-mail info@sante.public.lu; internet www.sante.public.lu.

Ministry of Higher Education and Research: 18–20 montée de la Pétrusse, 2327 Luxembourg; tel. (+352) 247-86619; e-mail guy.loos@mesr.etat.lu; internet www.mesr.public.lu.

Ministry of Housing: 4 place de l'Europe, 1499 Luxembourg; tel. (+352) 247-84819; fax (+352) 247-84840; e-mail info@ml.public.lu; internet www.ml.public.lu.

Ministry of the Interior: 19 rue Beaumont, 1219 Luxembourg; tel. (+352) 247-84600; fax (+352) 22-11-25; e-mail info@miat.public.lu; internet www.miat.public.lu.

Ministry of Internal Security: 19–21 blvd Royal, 2449 Luxembourg; tel. (+352) 247-84659; fax (+352) 22-72-76; e-mail secretariat@msi.etat.lu; internet www.gouvernement.lu/msi.

Ministry of Justice: Centre 13 rue Erasme, 2934 Luxembourg; tel. (+352) 247-84537; fax (+352) 266-84861; e-mail info@mj.public.lu; internet www.mj.public.lu.

Ministry of Labour, Employment, and Social Economy and Solidarity: 26 rue Ste Zithe, 2939 Luxembourg; tel. (+352) 247-86100; fax (+352) 247-86108; e-mail info@mte.public.lu; internet www.mte.public.lu.

Ministry of Social Security: 26 rue Ste Zithe, 2763 Luxembourg; tel. (+352) 247-86311; fax (+352) 247-86328; e-mail mss@mss.etat.lu; internet www.mss.public.lu.

Ministry of Sports: 66 rue de Trèves, BP 180, 2011 Luxembourg; tel. (+352) 247-83400; fax (+352) 247-83440; internet www.sport.public.lu.

Ministry of State: 4 rue de la Congrégation, 1352 Luxembourg; tel. (+352) 247-82100; fax (+352) 46-17-20; e-mail ministere.etat@me.etat.lu; internet www.etat.public.lu.

Ministry of Sustainable Development and Infrastructure: Bâtiment Alcide de Gasperi, 4 place de l'Europe, 1499 Luxembourg; tel. (+352) 247-82478; fax (+352) 46-27-09; e-mail info@developpement-durable-infrastructures.public.lu; internet www.developpement-durable-infrastructures.public.lu.

MALTA

Prime Minister: Dr Joseph Muscat.

Minister for the Economy, Investment and Small Business: Dr Christian Cardona.

Minister for Education and Employment: Evarist Bartolo.

Minister for Energy and Water Management: Joe Mizzi.

Minister for European Affairs and Equality: Dr Helena Dalli.

Minister for Finance: Prof. Edward Scicluna.

Minister for Tourism: Dr Konrad Mizzi.

Minister for Home Affairs and National Security: Dr Michael Farrugia.

Minister for Justice, Culture and Local Government: Dr Owen Bonnici.

Minister for the Environment, Sustainable Development and Climate Change: Dr José A. Herrera.

Minister for Health: Chris Fearne.

Minister for Foreign Affairs and Trade Promotion: Carmelo Abela.

Minister for Transport, Infrastructure and Capital Projects: Dr Ian Borg.

Minister for Gozo: Dr Justyne Caruana.

Minister for the Family, Children's Rights and Social Solidarity: Dr Michael Falzon.

Ministries

Office of the Prime Minister: Auberge de Castille, Valletta VLT 1061; tel. (+356) 22000000; e-mail joseph.muscat@gov.mt; internet opm.gov.mt/en/Pages/primeministerhome.aspx.

Ministry for the Economy, Investment and Small Business: Palazzo Zondadori, 197–198 Merchants St, Valletta VLT 2000; tel. (+356) 22209500; e-mail christian.cardona@gov.mt; internet economy.gov.mt.

Ministry for Education and Employment: Great Siege Rd, Floriana VLT 2000; tel. (+356) 25980000; e-mail evarist.bartolo@gov.mt; internet education.gov.mt.

Ministry for Energy and Water Management: Valletta VLT.

Ministry for the Environment, Sustainable Development and Climate Change: Casa Leone, St Venera SVR 1012; tel. (+356) 23886110; fax (+356) 21494813; e-mail jose.herrera@gov.mt; internet msdec.gov.mt.

Ministry for European Affairs and Equality: Auberge d'Aragon, Valletta VLT 2000; tel. (+356) 22957423; e-mail eufunds@gov.mt; internet eufunds.gov.mt.

Ministry for the Family, Children's Rights and Social Solidarity: Palazzo Ferreria, Republic St, Valletta VLT 1101; tel. (+356) 25903062; e-mail michael.a.falzon@gov.mt; internet mfcs.gov.mt.

Ministry for Finance: 30 Maison Demandols, South St, Valletta VLT 1102; tel. (+356) 25998259; fax (+356) 25998429; e-mail info.mfin@gov.mt; internet mfin.gov.mt.

Ministry for Foreign Affairs and Trade Promotion: Palazzo Parisio, Merchants St, Valletta VLT 1171; tel. (+356) 21242191; e-mail info.mfa@gov.mt; internet foreignaffairs.gov.mt.

Ministry for Gozo: St Francis Sq., Victoria VCT 1335, Gozo; tel. (+356) 22156400; e-mail gozo@gov.mt; internet mgoz.gov.mt.

Ministry for Health: 15 Palazzo Castellania, Merchants St, Valletta VLT 1171; tel. (+356) 21224071; e-mail customercare.mecw@gov.mt; internet health.gov.mt.

Ministry for Home Affairs and National Security: 201 Strait St, Valletta VLT 1433; tel. (+356) 25689000; e-mail customercare.mhas@gov.mt; internet homeaffairs.gov.mt.

Ministry for Justice, Culture and Local Government: 30 Old Treasury St, Valletta VLT 1410; tel. (+356) 22013000; e-mail owen.bonnici@gov.mt; internet mjcl.gov.mt.

Ministry for Tourism: 233 Republic St, Valletta VLT 1116; tel. (+356) 22915900; fax (+356) 22915039; e-mail tourism@gov.mt; internet tourism.gov.mt.

Ministry for Transport, Infrastructure and Capital Projects: Francesco Buonamici St, Floriana FRN 1700; tel. (+356) 22922200; e-mail joe.mizzi@gov.mt; internet mti.gov.mt.

THE NETHERLANDS

A new Government under Mark Rutte had still to be formed following legislative elections in March 2017.

Prime Minister, Minister of General Affairs: Mark Rutte.

Deputy Prime Minister, Minister of Social Affairs and Employment: Lodewijk Asscher.

Minister of Foreign Affairs: Bert Koenders.

Minister of the Interior and Kingdom Relations: Ronald Plasterk.

Minister of Security and Justice: Stef Blok.

Minister of Education, Culture and Science: Jet Bussemaker.

Minister of Finance: Jeroen Dijsselbloem.

Minister of Defence: Jeanine Hennis-Plasschaert.

Minister of Infrastructure and the Environment: Melanie Schultz van Haegen-Maas Geesteranus.

Minister of Economic Affairs: Henk Kamp.

Minister of Health, Welfare and Sport: Edith Schippers.

Minister for Foreign Trade and Development Co-operation: Lilianne Ploumen.

State Secretary for Security and Justice: Klaas Dijkhoff.

State Secretary for Education, Culture and Science: Sander Dekker.

State Secretary for Finance: Eric Wiebes.

State Secretary for Infrastructure and the Environment: Sharon Dijksma.

State Secretary for Economic Affairs: Martijn van Dam.

State Secretary for Social Affairs and Employment: Jetta Klijnsma.

State Secretary for Health, Welfare and Sport: Martin van Rijn.

Ministries

Office of the Prime Minister, Ministry of General Affairs: Binnenhof 19, POB 20001, 2500 EA The Hague; tel. (+31 70) 3564100; fax (+31 70) 3564683; internet www.rijksoverheid.nl/ministeries/az.

Ministry of Defence: Plein 4, POB 20701, 2500 ES The Hague; tel. (+31 70) 3188188; fax (+31 70) 3187888; e-mail defensievoorlichting@mindef.nl; internet www.rijksoverheid.nl/ministeries/def.

Ministry of Economic Affairs: Bezuidenhoutseweg 30, POB 20401, 2500 EK The Hague; tel. (+31 70) 3798911; internet www.rijksoverheid.nl/ministeries/eleni.

Ministry of Education, Culture and Science: Rnstraat 50, POB 16375, 2500 BJ The Hague; tel. (+31 70) 4123456; fax (+31 70) 4123450; internet www.rijksoverheid.nl/ministeries/ocw.

Ministry of Finance: Korte Voorhout 7, POB 20201, 2500 EE The Hague; tel. (+31 70) 3428000; fax (+31 70) 3427900; e-mail webmaster@minfin.nl; internet www.rijksoverheid.nl/ministeries/fin.

Ministry of Foreign Affairs: Bezuidenhoutseweg 67, POB 20061, 2500 EB The Hague; tel. (+31 70) 3486486; fax (+31 70) 3484848; internet www.rijksoverheid.nl/ministeries/bz.

Ministry of Health, Welfare and Sport: Parnassusplein 5, POB 20350, 2500 EJ The Hague; tel. (+31 70) 3407911; fax (+31 70) 3407834; internet www.rijksoverheid.nl/ministeries/vws.

Ministry of Infrastructure and the Environment: Plesmanweg 1–6, POB 20901, 2500 EX The Hague; tel. (+31 70) 4560000; internet www.rijksoverheid.nl/ministeries/ienm.

Ministry of the Interior and Kingdom Relations: Turfmarkt 147, POB 20011, 2500 EA The Hague; tel. (+31 70) 4266426; internet www.rijksoverheid.nl/ministeries/bzk.

Ministry of Security and Justice: Turfmarkt 147, POB 20301, 2500 EH The Hague; tel. (+31 70) 3707911; internet www.rijksoverheid.nl/ministeries/venj.

Ministry of Social Affairs and Employment: Parnassusplein 5, POB 90801, 2509 LV The Hague; tel. (+31 70) 3334444; internet www.rijksoverheid.nl/ministeries/szw.

POLAND

Prime Minister: Beata Szydło.

Deputy Prime Minister and Minister of Culture and National Heritage: Piotr Gliński.

Deputy Prime Minister and Minister of Science and Higher Education: Jarosław Gowin.

Deputy Prime Minister and Minister of Development and of Finance: Mateusz Morawiecki.

Minister of Infrastructure and Construction: Andrzej Adamczyk.

Minister of Sport and Tourism: Witold Bańka.

Minister of the Interior and Administration: Mariusz Błaszczak.

Minister of Maritime Economy and Inland Waterways: Marek Gróbarczyk.

Minister of Agriculture and Rural Development: Krzysztof Jurgiel.

Minister of National Defence: Antoni Macierewicz.

Minister of Health: Konstanty Radziwiłł.

Minister of Family, Labour and Social Policy: Elżbieta Rafalska.

Minister of Digital Affairs: Anna Streżyńska.

Minister of the Environment: Jan Szyszko.

Minister of Energy: Krzysztof Tchórzewski.

Minister of Foreign Affairs: Witold Waszczykowski.

Minister of National Education: Anna Zalewska.

Minister of Justice: Zbigniew Ziobro.

Minister without Portfolio and Special Services Co-ordinator: Mariusz Kamiński.

Minister without Portfolio and Head of the Chancellery of the Prime Minister: Beata Kempa.

Minister without Portfolio and Chairman of the Permanent Committee of the Council of Ministers: Henryk Kowalczyk.

Minister without Portfolio: Elżbieta Witek.

Ministries

Chancellery of the Prime Minister: 00-583 Warsaw, Al. Ujazdowskie 1/3; tel. (+48 22) 2500115; fax (+48 22) 8403810; e-mail kontakt@kprm.gov.pl; internet www.premier.gov.pl.

Ministry of Agriculture and Rural Development: 00-930 Warsaw, ul. Wspólna 30; tel. (+48 22) 6231000; fax (+48 22) 6232750; e-mail kanceleria@minrol.gov.pl; internet www.minrol.gov.pl.

Ministry of Culture and National Heritage: 00-071 Warsaw, ul. Krakowskie Przedmieście 15/17; tel. (+48 22) 4210100; fax (+48 22) 4210131; e-mail minister@mkidn.gov.pl; internet www.mkidn.gov.pl.

Ministry of Development: 00-507 Warsaw, pl. Trzech Krzyży 3/5; tel. (+48 22) 25500130; e-mail kancelaria@mr.gov.pl; internet www.mr.gov.pl.

Ministry of Digital Affairs: 00-060 Warsaw, ul. Królewska 27; tel. (+48 22) 2500110; e-mail mc@mc.gov.pl; internet www.gov.pl/cyfryzacja.

Ministry of Energy: 00-507 Warsaw, pl. Trzech Krzyży 3/5; tel. (+48 22) 6935000; fax (+48 22) 6934048; e-mail me@me.gov.pl; internet www.me.gov.pl.

Ministry of the Environment: 00-922 Warsaw, ul. Wawelska 52/54; tel. (+48 22) 3692900; fax (+48 22) 36929224; e-mail info@mos.gov.pl; internet www.mos.gov.pl.

Ministry of Family, Labour and Social Policy: 00-513 Warsaw, ul. Nowogrodzka 1/3/5; tel. (+48 22) 2500108; fax (+48 22) 6611336; e-mail info@mrpips.gov.pl; internet www.mpips.gov.pl.

Ministry of Finance: 00-916 Warsaw, ul. Świętokrzyska 12; tel. (+48 22) 6945555; e-mail kancelaria@mf.gov.pl; internet www.mf.gov.pl.

Ministry of Foreign Affairs: 00-580 Warsaw, Al. Szucha 23; tel. (+48 22) 5239000; e-mail dabw.sekretariat@msz.gov.pl; internet www.msz.gov.pl.

Ministry of Health: 00-952 Warsaw, ul. Miodowa 15; tel. (+48 22) 6349600; e-mail kancelaria@mz.gov.pl; internet www.mz.gov.pl.

Ministry of Infrastructure and Construction: 00-926 Warsaw, ul. Chałubińskiego 4/6; tel. (+48 22) 6301000; e-mail kancelaria@mib.gov.pl; internet mib.gov.pl.

Ministry of the Interior and Administration: 02-591 Warsaw, ul. Stefana Batorego 5; tel. (+48 22) 2500112; fax (+48 22) 6013988; e-mail kancelaria.glowna@mswia.gov.pl; internet www.mswia.gov.pl.

Ministry of Justice: 00-950 Warsaw, Al. Ujazdowskie 11; tel. (+48 22) 5212888; e-mail skargi@ms.gov.pl; internet ms.gov.pl.

Ministry of Maritime Economy and Inland Waterways: 00-400 Warsaw, ul. Nowy Świat 6/12; tel. (+48 22) 5838500; fax (+48 22) 5838501; e-mail sekretariatmgrobarczyka@mgm.gov.pl; internet www.mgm.gov.pl.

Ministry of National Defence: 00-909, ul. Klonowa 1; tel. (+48 22) 6280031; e-mail newsroom@mon.gov.pl; internet www.mon.gov.pl.

Ministry of National Education: 00-918 Warsaw, Al. Szucha 25; tel. (+48 22) 3474100; fax (+48 22) 3474261; e-mail informacja@men.gov.pl; internet men.gov.pl.

Ministry of Science and Higher Education: 00-529 Warsaw, ul. Wspólna 1/3; tel. (+48 22) 5292718; fax (+48 22) 5017865; e-mail sekretariat.bm@nauka.gov.pl; internet www.nauka.gov.pl.

Ministry of Sport and Tourism: 00-082 Warsaw, ul. Senatorska 14; tel. (+48 22) 2443264; fax (+48 22) 2443255; e-mail kontakt@msport.gov.pl; internet www.msport.gov.pl.

PORTUGAL

Prime Minister: António Costa.

Minister of Foreign Affairs: Augusto Santos Silva.

Minister of the Presidency and of Administrative Modernization: Maria Manuel Leitão Marques.

Minister of Finance: Mário Centeno.

Minister of National Defence: José Alberto Azeredo Lopes.

Minister of Internal Administration: Constança Urbano de Sousa.

Minister of Justice: Francisca Van Dunem.

Minister in the Cabinet of the Prime Minister: Eduardo Cabrita.

Minister of Culture: Castro Mendes.

Minister of Science, Technology and Higher Education: Manuel Heitor.

Minister of Education: Tiago Brandão Rodrigues.

Minister of Labour, Solidarity and Social Security: José António Vieira da Silva.

Minister of Health: Adalberto Campos Fernandes.

Minister of Planning and Infrastructure: Pedro Marques.

Minister of the Economy: Manuel Caldeira Cabral.

Minister of the Environment: João Pedro Matos Fernandes.

Minister of Agriculture, Forestry and Rural Development: Luís Capoulas Santos.

Minister of Sea: Ana Paula Vitorino.

Ministries

Office of the Prime Minister, Presidency of the Council of Ministers: Rua da Imprensa à Estrela 4, 1200-888 Lisbon; tel. (+351 21) 3923500; e-mail pm@pm.gov.pt; internet www.portugal.gov.pt.

Ministry of Agriculture, Forestry and Rural Development: Praça do Comércio, 1149-010 Lisbon; tel. (+351 21) 3234600.

Ministry of Culture: Palácio Nacional da Ajuda, 1300-018 Lisbon; tel. (+351 21) 3614500.

Ministry of the Economy: Rua da Horta Seca 15, 1200-221 Lisbon; tel. (+351 21) 3245400.

Ministry of Education: Av. 5 de Outubro 107, 1069-018 Lisbon; tel. (+351 21) 7811800.

Ministry of the Environment: Rua de 'O Século' 63, 2°, 1200-433 Lisbon; tel. (+351 21) 3231500.

Ministry of Finance: Av. Infante D. Henrique 1, 1149-009 Lisbon; tel. (+351 21) 8816800.

Ministry of Foreign Affairs: Palácio das Necessidades, Largo do Rilvas, 1399-030 Lisbon; tel. (+351 21) 3946000.

Ministry of Health: Av. João Crisóstomo 9, 1000-179 Lisbon; tel. (+351 21) 3305000.

Ministry of Internal Administration: Praça do Comércio, 1149-015 Lisbon; tel. (+351 21) 3233000.

Ministry of Justice: Praça do Comércio, 1149-019 Lisbon; tel. (+351 21) 3222300.

Ministry of Labour, Solidarity and Social Security: Praça de Londres 2, 1049-056 Lisbon; tel. (+351 21) 5963800.

Ministry of National Defence: Av. Ilha da Madeira 1, 1400-204 Lisbon; tel. (+351 21) 3034500.

Ministry of Planning and Infrastructure: Av. Barbosa du Bocage, 5, 2°, 1049-039 Lisbon; tel. (+351 21) 0426200.

Ministry of Science, Technology and Higher Education: Palácio das Laranjeiras, Estrada das Laranjeiras 205, 1649-018 Lisbon; tel. (+351 21) 7231000.

Ministry of the Sea: Praça do Comércio, 1499-010 Lisbon; tel. (+351 21) 3234600.

ROMANIA

Prime Minister: Mihai Tudose.

Deputy Prime Minister and Minister of Regional Development, Public Administration and European Union Funds: Sevil Shhaideh.

Deputy Prime Minister and Minister of the Environment: Grațiela-Leocadia Gavrilescu.

Deputy Prime Minister: Ion-Marcel Ciolacu.

Minister of Internal Affairs: Carmen Daniela Dan.

Minister of Foreign Affairs: Teodor-Viorel Meleșcanu.

Minister of National Defence: Mihai-Viorel Fifor.

Minister of Public Finance: Ionuț Mişa.

Minister of Justice: Tudorel Toader.

Minister of Agriculture and Rural Development: Petre Daea.

Minister of National Education: Liviu-Marian Pop.

Minister of Labour and Social Protection: Lia-Olguța Vasilescu.

Minister of the Economy: Gheorghe Şimon.

Minister of Energy: Toma-Florin Petcu.

Minister of Transport: Alexandru-Răzvan Cuc.

Minister of Business, Commerce and Entrepreneurship: Ilan Laufer.

Minister of Health: Florian-Dorel Bodog.

Minister of Culture and National Identity: Lucian Romaşcanu.

Minister of Water and Forests: Adriana-Doina Pană.

Minister of Research and Innovation: Puiu Lucian Georgescu.

Minister of Communications and the Information Society: Lucian Şova.

Minister of Youth and Sports: Marius-Alexandru Dunca.

Minister of Tourism: Mircea-Titus Dobre.

Minister for the Romanian Diaspora: Andreea Păstîrnac.

Minister of Public Consultation and Civic Dialogue: Gabriel Petrea.

Minister for Relations with Parliament: Viorel Ilie.

Minister-delegate responsible for European Funds: Rovana Plumb.

Minister-delegate for European Affairs: Victor Negrescu.

Ministries

Office of the Prime Minister: 011791 Bucharest 1, Piața Victoriei 1; tel. (+40 21) 3143400; fax (+40 21) 3139846; e-mail drp@gov.ro; internet www.gov.ro.

Ministry of Agriculture and Rural Development: 030163 Bucharest 3, Bd. Carol I 2–4, POB 37; tel. (+40 21) 3072446; fax (+40 21) 3078554; e-mail relatii.publice@madr.ro; internet www.madr.ro.

Ministry of Business, Commerce and Entrepreneurship: Bucharest; tel. (+40 21) 4010529; e-mail directia.imm@imm.gov.ro; internet www.aippimm.ro.

Ministry of Communications and the Information Society: 050706 Bucharest 5, Bd. Libertății 14; tel. (+40 21) 4001190; fax (+40 21) 3114131; e-mail cabinetministru@msinf.ro; internet www.comunicatii.gov.ro.

Ministry of Culture and National Identity: 030833 Bucharest 3, Bd. Unirii 22; tel. (+40 21) 2242510; fax (+40 21) 2234951; e-mail cabinet.ministru@cultura.ro; internet www.cultura.ro.

Ministry of the Economy: 010096 Bucharest 1, Calea Victoriei 152; tel. (+40 21) 2025426; fax (+40 21) 2025108; e-mail birou.presa@economie.gov.ro; internet economie.gov.ro.

Ministry of Energy: Bucharest; e-mail comunicare@energie.gov.ro; internet energie.gov.ro.

Ministry of the Environment: 040129 Bucharest 5, Bd. Libertății 12; tel. (+40 21) 4089642; fax (+40 21) 4089615; e-mail srp@mmediu.ro; internet www.mmediu.ro; internet www.mmediu.gov.ro.

Ministry of Foreign Affairs: 011822 Bucharest, Al. Alexandru 31; tel. (+40 21) 3192108; fax (+40 21) 3196862; e-mail opinia_ta@mae.ro; internet www.mae.ro.

Ministry of Health: 010024 Bucharest 1, Str. Cristian Popişteanu 1–3; tel. (+40 21) 3072500; e-mail presa@ms.ro; internet www.ms.ro.

Ministry of Internal Affairs: 010086 Bucharest 1, Piața Revoluției 1A; tel. (+40 21) 3037080; fax (+40 21) 2648677; e-mail petitii@mai.gov.ro; internet www.mai.gov.ro.

Ministry of Justice: 050741 Bucharest 5, Str. Apolodor 17; tel. (+40 37) 2041999; fax (+40 37) 2871140; e-mail relatiipublice@just.ro; internet www.just.ro.

Ministry of Labour and Social Protection: 010026 Bucharest 1, Str. Demetru I. Dobrescu 2–4; tel. (+40 21) 3158556; fax (+40 21) 3158812; e-mail relatiicupublicul@mmuncii.ro; internet www.mmuncii.ro.

Ministry of National Defence: 050561 Bucharest 5, Str. Izvor 110; tel. (+40 21) 4104040; fax (+40 21) 3195689; e-mail secretariat_general@mapn.ro; internet www.mapn.ro.

Ministry of National Education: 010168 Bucharest 1, Str. Gen. Berthelot 28–30; tel. (+40 21) 4056200; fax (+40 21) 3124719; e-mail cabinet@edu.gov.ro; internet www.edu.ro.

Ministry of Public Consultation and Civic Dialogue: 011791 Bucharest 1, Palatul Victoria, Piaţa Victoriei 1; tel. (+40 21) 3143400; fax (+40 21) 3181186; e-mail cabinet.ministru@dialogsocial.gov.ro; internet dialogsocial.gov.ro.

Ministry of Public Finance: 050741 Bucharest 5, Str. Apolodor 17; tel. (+40 21) 3199759; fax (+40 21) 3122509; e-mail presa.mfp@mfinante.gov.ro; internet www.mfinante.gov.ro.

Ministry of Regional Development, Public Administration and European Union Funds: 050706 Bucharest 5, Str. Libertăţii 16, North Wing; tel. (+40 37) 2111409; e-mail info@mdrap.ro; internet www.mdrap.ro.

Ministry of Relations with Parliament: 011731 Bucharest 1, Piaţa Victoriei 1; tel. (+40 21) 3163677; fax (+40 21) 3163652; e-mail contact.drp@gov.ro; internet mrp.gov.ro.

Ministry of Research and Innovation: 010362 Bucharest 1, Str. Mendeleev 21–25; tel. (+40 21) 3034198; fax (+40 21) 3126617; e-mail contact@research.gov.ro; internet www.research.gov.ro.

Ministry of Romanian Diaspora: 011972 Bucharest 1, Bd Primăverii 22; tel. (+40 21) 2339687; fax (+40 21) 2339599; e-mail cabinet.ministru@mprp.gov.ro; internet www.dprp.gov.ro.

Ministry of Tourism: 010873 Bucharest 1, Bd Dinicu Golescu 38; tel. (+40 21) 3037875; fax (+40 21) 3037870; e-mail cabinet.ministru@mturism.ro; internet turism.gov.ro.

Ministry of Transport: 010873 Bucharest 1, Bd. Dinicu Golescu 38; tel. (+40 21) 3196124; fax (+40 21) 3138869; e-mail presa@mt.ro; internet mt.gov.ro.

Ministry of Water and Forests: 010233 Bucharest 1, Calea Plevnei 46–48; tel. (+40 21) 3160215; fax (+40 21) 3194609; e-mail petitii@map.gov.ro; internet apepaduri.gov.ro.

Ministry of Youth and Sports: 020954 Bucharest 2, Str. Vasile Conta 16; tel. (+40 21) 3076417; fax (+40 21) 3076418; e-mail cabinet.ministru@mts.ro; internet mts.ro.

Office of Secretary-General of the Government: 011791 Bucharest 1, Piaţa Victoriei 1; tel. (+40 21) 3143400; fax (+40 21) 3139846; e-mail drp@gov.ro; internet sgg.gov.ro.

SLOVAKIA

Prime Minister: Robert Fico.

Deputy Prime Minister, responsible for Investment: Peter Pellegrini.

Minister of the Interior: Robert Kaliňák.

Minister of Justice: Lucia Žitňanská.

Minister of Finance: Peter Kažimír.

Minister of Foreign Affairs: Miroslav Lajčák.

Minister of the Economy: Peter Žiga.

Minister of Transport, Construction and Regional Development: Árpád Érsek.

Minister of Agriculture and Rural Development: Gabriela Matečná.

Minister of Defence: Lt-Gen. Peter Gajdoš.

Minister of Labour, Social Affairs and the Family: Ján Richter.

Minister of the Environment: László Solymos.

Minister of Education, Science, Research and Sport: Martina Lubyová.

Minister of Culture: Marek Maďarič.

Minister of Health: Tomáš Drucker.

Ministries

Office of the Government: nám. Slobody 1, 813 70 Bratislava; tel. (+421 2) 2092-5111; fax (+421 2) 5249-7595; e-mail uvsrinfo@vlada.gov.sk; internet www.vlada.gov.sk.

Ministry of Agriculture and Rural Development: Dobrovičova 12, 812 66 Bratislava; tel. (+421 2) 5926-6114; fax (+421 2) 5296-3871; e-mail press@land.gov.sk; internet www.mpsr.sk.

Ministry of Culture: nám. SNP 33, 813 31 Bratislava; tel. (+421 2) 2048-2111; fax (+421 2) 2048-2271; e-mail info@culture.gov.sk; internet www.culture.gov.sk.

Ministry of Defence: Kutuzovova 8, 832 47 Bratislava; tel. (+421 2) 4425-8861; fax (+421 2) 4425-8904; e-mail minister@mod.gov.sk; internet www.mosr.sk.

Ministry of the Economy: Mierová 19, 827 15 Bratislava; tel. (+421 2) 4854-1111; fax (+421 2) 4333-7827; e-mail minister@mhsr.sk; internet www.economy.gov.sk.

Ministry of Education, Science, Research and Sport: Stromová 1, 813 30 Bratislava; tel. (+421 2) 5937-4111; fax (+421 2) 5937-4333; e-mail info@minedu.sk; internet www.minedu.sk.

Ministry of the Environment: nám. Ľ. Štúra 1, 812 35 Bratislava; tel. (+421 2) 5956-1111; fax (+421 2) 5956-2481; e-mail info@enviro.gov.sk; internet www.minzp.sk.

Ministry of Finance: Štefanovičova 5, POB 82, 817 82 Bratislava; tel. (+421 2) 5958-1111; fax (+421 2) 5958-3048; e-mail info@mfsr.sk; internet www.finance.gov.sk.

Ministry of Foreign Affairs: Hlboká cesta 2, POB 37, 833 36 Bratislava; tel. (+421 2) 5978-1111; fax (+421 2) 5978-3333; e-mail info@mzv.sk; internet www.mzv.sk.

Ministry of Health: Limbová 2, POB 52, 837 52 Bratislava; tel. (+421 2) 5937-3111; fax (+421 2) 5477-7983; e-mail office@health.gov.sk; internet www.health.gov.sk.

Ministry of the Interior: Pribinova 2, 812 72 Bratislava; tel. (+421 2) 5094-1111; fax (+421 2) 5094-4397; internet www.minv.sk.

Ministry of Justice: Župné nám. 13, 813 11 Bratislava; tel. (+421 2) 8889-1111; fax (+421 2) 5935-3602; e-mail ms.kvsu.sek@justice.sk; internet www.justice.gov.sk.

Ministry of Labour, Social Affairs and the Family: Špitálska 4–6, 816 43 Bratislava; tel. (+421 2) 2046-0000; e-mail minister@employment.gov.sk; internet www.employment.gov.sk.

Ministry of Transport, Construction and Regional Development: nám. Slobody 6, POB 100, 810 05 Bratislava; tel. (+421 2) 5949-4111; fax (+421 2) 5249-4794; e-mail info@mindop.sk; internet www.telecom.gov.sk.

SLOVENIA

Prime Minister: Miro Cerar.

Deputy Prime Minister and Minister of Public Administration: Boris Koprivnikar.

Deputy Prime Minister and Minister of Foreign Affairs: Karl Erjavec.

Deputy Prime Minister and Minister of Agriculture, Forestry and Food: Dejan Židan.

Minister of the Interior: Vesna Györkös Žnidar.

Minister of Defence: Andreja Katič.

Minister of Finance: Mateja Vraničar Erman.

Minister of Economic Development and Technology: Zdravko Počivalšek.

Minister of Justice: Goran Klemenčič.

Minister of Labour, the Family, Social Affairs and Equal Opportunities: Anja Kopač Mrak.

Minister of Health: Milojka Kolar Celarc.

Minister of Education, Science and Sport: Maja Makovec Brenčič.

Minister of Infrastructure: Peter Gašperšič.

Minister of Culture: Anton Peršak.

Minister of the Environment and Spatial Planning: Irena Majcen.

Minister of Development, Strategic Projects and Cohesion: Alenka Smerkolj.

Minister of Relations with the Indigenous Slovenian National Communities in Neighbouring Countries and with Slovenians Abroad: Gorazd Žmavc.

Ministries

Office of the Prime Minister: 1000 Ljubljana, Gregorčičeva 20–25; tel. (+386 1) 4781000; fax (+386 1) 4781721; e-mail gp.kpv@gov.si; internet www.kpv.gov.si.

Government Office for Development and European Cohesion Policy: 1000 Ljubljana, Kotnikova 5; tel. (+386 1) 4003680; e-mail gp.svrk@gov.si; internet www.svrk.gov.si.

Government Office for Slovenes Abroad: 1000 Ljubljana, Erjavčeva 15; tel. (+386 1) 2308000; fax (+386 1) 2308017; e-mail urad.slovenci@gov.si; internet www.uszs.gov.si.

Ministry of Agriculture, Forestry and Food: 1000 Ljubljana, Dunajska 22; tel. (+386 1) 4789000; fax (+386 1) 4789021; e-mail gp.mkgp@gov.si; internet www.mkgp.gov.si.

Ministry of Culture: 1000 Ljubljana, Maistrova 10; tel. (+386 1) 3695900; fax (+386 1) 3695901; e-mail gp.mk@gov.si; internet www.mk.gov.si.

Ministry of Defence: 1000 Ljubljana, Vojkova cesta 55; tel. (+386 1) 4712211; e-mail glavna.pisarna@mors.si; internet www.mo.gov.si.

Ministry of Economic Development and Technology: 1000 Ljubljana, Kotnikova 5; tel. (+386 1) 4003311; e-mail gp.mgrt@gov.si; internet www.mgrt.gov.si.

Ministry of Education, Science and Sport: 1000 Ljubljana, Masarykova 16; tel. (+386 1) 4005200; e-mail gp.mizs@gov.si; internet www.mizs.gov.si.

Ministry of the Environment and Spatial Planning: 1000 Ljubljana, Dunajska 48; tel. (+386 1) 4787000; fax (+386 1) 4787425; e-mail gp.mop@gov.si; internet www.mop.gov.si.

Ministry of Finance: 1000 Ljubljana, Župančičeva 3; tel. (+386 1) 3696300; fax (+386 1) 3696659; e-mail gp.mf@gov.si; internet www.mf.gov.si.

Ministry of Foreign Affairs: 1001 Ljubljana, Prešernova 25; tel. (+386 1) 4782000; e-mail info.mzz@gov.si; internet www.mzz.gov.si.

Ministry of Health: 1000 Ljubljana, Štefanova 5; tel. (+386 1) 4786001; fax (+386 1) 4786058; e-mail gp.mz@gov.si; internet www.mz.gov.si.

Ministry of Infrastructure: 1535 Ljubljana, Langusova 4; tel. (+386 1) 4788000; fax (+386 1) 4788139; e-mail gp.mzi@gov.si; internet www.mzi.gov.si.

Ministry of the Interior: 1501 Ljubljana, Štefanova 2; tel. (+386 1) 4284000; e-mail gp.mnz@gov.si; internet www.mnz.gov.si.

Ministry of Justice: 1000 Ljubljana, Županičeva 3; tel. (+386 1) 3695200; fax (+386 1) 3695783; e-mail gp.mpju@gov.si; internet www.arhiv.mp.gov.si.

Ministry of Labour, the Family, Social Affairs and Equal Opportunities: 1000 Ljubljana, Kotnikova 28; tel. (+386 1) 3697700; fax (+386 1) 3697832; e-mail gp.mddsz@gov.si; internet www.mddsz.gov.si.

Ministry of Public Administration: 1000 Ljubljana, Tržaška cesta 21; tel. (+386 1) 4788330; fax (+386 1) 4788331; e-mail gp.mju@gov.si; internet www.mju.gov.si.

SPAIN

President of the Government (Prime Minister): Mariano Rajoy.

Deputy Prime Minister, Minister of the Presidency and of the Regional Administrations: María Soraya Sáenz de Santamaría Antón.

Minister of Foreign Affairs and Co-operation: Alfonso Dastis Quecedo.

Minister of Justice: Rafael Catalá Polo.

Minister of Defence: María Dolores de Cospedal García.

Minister of the Treasury and Public Administration: Cristóbal Montoro Romero.

Minister of Home Affairs: Juan Ignacio Zoido Álvarez.

Minister of Public Works: Íñigo de la Serna Hernáiz.

Minister of Education, Culture and Sport, and Government Spokesperson: Iñigo Méndez de Vigo y Montojo.

Minister of Employment and Social Security: Fátima Báñez García.

Minister of Energy, Tourism and Digital Agenda: Álvaro Nadal Belda.

Minister of Agriculture and Fisheries, Food, and Environmental Affairs: Isabel García Tejerina.

Minister of Economic Affairs, Industry and Competitiveness: Luis de Guindos Jurado.

Minister of Health, Social Services and Equality: Dolors Montserrat Montserrat.

Ministries

Office of the President of the Government: Complejo de la Moncloa, Avda de Puerta de Hierro s/n, 28071 Madrid; tel. (+34 91) 3214000; e-mail secretariapresidente@presidencia.gob.es; internet www.lamoncloa.gob.es.

Ministry of Agriculture and Fisheries, Food and Environmental Affairs: Paseo Infanta Isabel 1, 28014 Madrid; tel. (+34 91) 3474580; fax (+34 91) 3475580; e-mail qprensa@magrama.es; internet www.mapama.gob.es.

Ministry of Defence: Paseo de la Castellana 109, 28046 Madrid; tel. (+34 91) 3955000; e-mail infodefensa@mde.es; internet www.defensa.gob.es.

Ministry of Economic Affairs, Industry and Competitiveness: Alcalá 9, Paseo de la Castellana 162, 28046 Madrid; tel. (+34 91) 5837400; internet www.mineco.gob.es.

Ministry of Education, Culture and Sport: Alcalá 34, 28014 Madrid; tel. (+34 91) 7018000; e-mail prensa@mecd.es; internet www.mecd.gob.es.

Ministry of Employment and Social Security: Agustín de Bethencourt 4, 28071 Madrid; tel. (+34 91) 3630000; e-mail informacionmtin@meyss.es; internet www.empleo.gob.es.

Ministry of Energy, Tourism and Digital Agenda: Paseo de la Castellana 160, 28046 Madrid; tel. (+34 91) 3494640; internet www.minetad.gob.es.

Ministry of Foreign Affairs and Co-operation: Plaza de la Provincia 1, 28012 Madrid; tel. (+34 91) 3799700; e-mail informaec@maec.es; internet www.exteriores.gob.es.

Ministry of Health, Social Services and Equality: Paseo del Prado 18–20, 28014 Madrid; tel. (+34 91) 5961089; fax (+34 91) 5964480; e-mail oiac@msssi.es; internet www.msps.es.

Ministry of Home Affairs: Paseo de la Castellana 5, 28046 Madrid; tel. (+34 91) 5371000; fax (+34 91) 3085566; e-mail estafeta@mir.es; internet www.interior.gob.es.

Ministry of Justice: San Bernardo 45, 28071 Madrid; tel. (+34 91) 3902247; fax (+34 91) 3902244; e-mail prensa@mjusticia.es; internet www.mjusticia.gob.es.

Ministry of the Presidency: Complejo de la Moncloa, Avda de Puerta de Hierro s/n, 28071 Madrid; tel. (+34 91) 3214000; e-mail sec@mpr.es; internet www.mpr.gob.es.

Ministry of Public Works: Paseo de la Castellana 67, 28071 Madrid; tel. (+34 91) 5977000; fax (+34 91) 5978503; e-mail fomento@fomento.es; internet www.fomento.es.

Ministry of the Treasury and Public Administration: Calle Alcalá 9, 28014 Madrid; tel. (+34 91) 5958000; fax (+34 91) 5958486; e-mail secretaria.prensa@minhap.es; internet www.minhafp.gob.es.

SWEDEN

Prime Minister: Stefan Löfven.

Minister of Policy Co-ordination and Energy, Prime Minister's Office: Ibrahim Balyan.

Minister of Employment and Integration: Ylva Johansson.

Minister of Finance: Magdalena Andersson.

Minister of Financial Markets and Consumer Affairs, and Deputy Minister of Finance: Per Bolund.

Minister of Public Administration: Ardalan Shekarabi.

Minister of Defence: Peter Hultqvist.

Minister of Justice and Home Affairs: Morgan Johansson.

Minister of Migration and Deputy Minister of Justice: Heléne Fritzon.

Minister of Culture and Democracy: Alice Bah Kuhnke.

Minister of the Environment: Karolina Skog.

Minister of Enterprise and Innovation: Mikael Damberg.

Minister of Rural Affairs: Sven-Erik Bucht.

Minister of Housing and Digital Development: Peter Eriksson.

Minister of Infrastructure: Tomas Eneroth.

Minister of Health and Social Affairs: Annika Strandhäll.

Minister of Children, the Elderly and Gender Equality: Åsa Regnér.

Minister of Education: Gustav Fridolin.

Minister of Upper Secondary School and Adult Education and Training: Anna Ekström.

Minister of Higher Education and Research: Helene Hellmark Knutsson.

Minister of Foreign Affairs: Margot Wallström.

Minister of European Union Affairs and Trade: Ann Linde.

Minister of International Development Co-operation and Climate, and Deputy Prime Minister: Isabella Lövin.

Ministries

Prime Minister's Office: Rosenbad 4, 103 33 Stockholm; tel. (+46 8) 405-10-00; fax (+46 8) 723-11-71; e-mail sb.registrator@regeringskansliet.se; internet www.regeringen.se.

Ministry of Culture: Drottninggt. 16, 103 33 Stockholm; tel. (+46 8) 405-10-00; e-mail kulturdepartementet.registrator@regeringskansliet.se; internet www.regeringen.se/sveriges-regering/kulturdepartementet.

Ministry of Defence: Jakobsgt. 9, 103 33 Stockholm; tel. (+46 8) 405-10-00; fax (+46 8) 723-11-89; e-mail forsvarsdepartementet.registrator@regeringskansliet.se; internet www.regeringen.se/sveriges-regering/forsvarsdepartementet.

Ministry of Education and Research: Drottninggt. 16, 103 33 Stockholm; tel. (+46 8) 405-10-00; e-mail u.registrator@regeringskansliet.se; internet www.regeringen.se/sveriges-regering/utbildningsdepartementet.

Ministry of Employment: Fredsgt. 8, 103 33 Stockholm; tel. (+46 8) 405-10-00; fax (+46 8) 411-36-16; e-mail arbetsmarknadsdepartementet.registrator@regeringskansliet.se; internet www.regeringen.se/sveriges-regering/arbetsmarknadsdepartementet.

Ministry of Enterprise and Innovation: Mäster Samuelsgt. 70, 103 33 Stockholm; tel. (+46 8) 405-10-00; e-mail n.registrator@regeringskansliet.se; internet www.regeringen.se/sveriges-regering/naringsdepartementet.

Ministry of the Environment and Energy: Malmtorgsgt. 3, 103 33 Stockholm; tel. (+46 8) 405-10-00; fax (+46 8) 24 16 29; e-mail m.registrator@regeringskansliet.se; internet www.regeringen.se/sveriges-regering/miljo-och-energidepartementet.

Ministry of Finance: Jakobsgt. 24, 103 33 Stockholm; tel. (+46 8) 405-10-00; e-mail finansdepartementet.registrator@regeringskansliet.se; internet www.regeringen.se/sveriges-regering/finansdepartementet.

Ministry for Foreign Affairs: Gustav Adolfs torg 1, 103 39 Stockholm; tel. (+46 8) 405-10-00; e-mail utrikesdepartementet.registrator@regeringskansliet.se; internet www.regeringen.se/sveriges-regering/utrikesdepartementet.

Ministry of Health and Social Affairs: Fredsgt. 8, 103 33 Stockholm; tel. (+46 8) 405-10-00; fax (+46 8) 723-11-91; e-mail socialdepartementet.registrator@regeringskansliet.se; internet www.regeringen.se/sveriges-regering/socialdepartementet.

Ministry of Justice: Rosenbad 4, 103 33 Stockholm; tel. (+46 8) 405-10-00; e-mail justitiedepartementet.registrator@regeringskansliet.se; internet www.regeringen.se/sveriges-regering/justitiedepartementet.

UNITED KINGDOM

Prime Minister, First Lord of the Treasury and Minister for the Civil Service: Theresa May.

First Secretary of State and Minister for the Cabinet Office: Damian Green.

Chancellor of the Exchequer: Philip Hammond.

Secretary of State for the Home Department: Amber Rudd.

Secretary of State for Foreign and Commonwealth Affairs: Boris Johnson.

Secretary of State for Exiting the European Union: David Davis.

Secretary of State for Defence: Sir Michael Fallon.

Secretary of State for Health: Jeremy Hunt.

Lord Chancellor and Secretary of State for Justice: David Lidington.

Secretary of State for Education and Minister for Women and Equalities: Justine Greening.

Secretary of State for International Trade and President of the Board of Trade: Liam Fox.

Secretary of State for Business, Energy and Industrial Strategy: Greg Clark.

Secretary of State for Environment, Food and Rural Affairs: Michael Gove.

Secretary of State for Transport: Chris Grayling.

Secretary of State for Communities and Local Government: Sajid Javid.

Leader of the House of Lords and Lord Privy Seal: Baroness Evans of Bowes Park.

Secretary of State for Scotland: David Mundell.

Secretary of State for Wales: Alun Cairns.

Secretary of State for Northern Ireland: James Brokenshire.

Secretary of State for International Development: Priti Patel.

Secretary of State for Culture, Media and Sport: Karen Bradley.

Secretary of State for Work and Pensions: David Gauke.

Chancellor of the Duchy of Lancaster: Patrick McLoughlin.

Ministries

Prime Minister's Office: 10 Downing St, London, SW1A 2AA; tel. (+44 20) 7270-3000; internet www.gov.uk/government/organisations/prime-ministers-office-10-downing-street.

Cabinet Office: 70 Whitehall, London, SW1A 2AS; tel. (+44 20) 7276-1234; e-mail publiccorrespondence@cabinetoffice.gov.uk; internet www.gov.uk/government/organisations/cabinet-office.

Attorney-General's Office: 20 Victoria St, London, SW1H 0NF; tel. (+44 20) 7271-2492; e-mail correspondence@attorneygeneral.gsi.gov.uk; internet www.gov.uk/government/organisations/attorney-generals-office.

Department for Business, Energy and Industrial Strategy: 1 Victoria St, London, SW1H 0ET; tel. (+44 20) 7215-5000; e-mail enquiries@beis.gov.uk; internet www.gov.uk/government/organisations/department-for-business-energy-and-industrial-strategy.

Department for Communities and Local Government: 2 Marsham St, London, SW1P 4DF; tel. (+44 30) 3444-0000; e-mail newsdesk@communities.gsi.gov.uk; internet www.gov.uk/government/organisations/department-for-communities-and-local-government.

Department for Culture, Media and Sport: 100 Parliament St, London, SW1A 2BQ; tel. (+44 20) 7211-6000; e-mail enquiries@culture.gov.uk; internet www.gov.uk/government/organisations/department-for-culture-media-sport.

Ministry of Defence: Main Bldg, 5th Floor, Whitehall, London, SW1A 2HB; tel. (+44 20) 7218-9000; e-mail parlibranch-treat-official@mod.uk; internet www.gov.uk/government/organisations/ministry-of-defence.

Department for Education: Sanctuary Bldgs, Great Smith St, London, SW1P 3BT; tel. (+44 870) 000-2288; internet www.gov.uk/government/organisations/department-for-education.

Department for Environment, Food and Rural Affairs: Nobel House, 17 Smith Sq., London, SW1P 3JR; tel. (+44 20) 7238-6951; e-mail defra.helpline@defra.gsi.gov.uk; internet www.gov.uk/government/organisations/department-for-environment-food-rural-affairs.

Department for Exiting the European Union: 9 Downing St, London, SW1A 2AS; tel. (+44 20) 7276-0432; e-mail dexeu.correspondence@cabinetoffice.gov.uk; internet www.gov.uk/government/organisations/department-for-exiting-the-european-union.

Foreign and Commonwealth Office: King Charles St, London, SW1A 2AH; tel. (+44 20) 7008-1500; e-mail fcocorrespondence@fco.gov.uk; internet www.gov.uk/government/organisations/foreign-commonwealth-office.

Department of Health: Richmond House, 79 Whitehall, London, SW1A 2NS; tel. (+44 20) 7210-4850; internet www.gov.uk/government/organisations/department-of-health.

Home Office: 2 Marsham St, London, SW1P 4DF; tel. (+44 20) 7035-4848; e-mail public.enquiries@homeoffice.gsi.gov.uk; internet www.gov.uk/government/organisations/home-office.

Department for International Development: 22 Whitehall, London, SW1A 2EG; tel. (+44 20) 7023-0000; fax (+44 20) 7023-0012; e-mail enquiry@dfid.gov.uk; internet www.gov.uk/government/organisations/department-for-international-development.

Department for International Trade: King Charles St, Whitehall, London, SW1A 2AH; tel. (+44 20) 7215-5000; e-mail enquiries@trade.gsi.gov.uk; internet www.gov.uk/government/organisations/department-for-international-trade.

Ministry of Justice: 102 Petty France, London, SW1H 9AJ; tel. (+44 20) 3334-3555; e-mail general.queries@justice.gsi.gov.uk; internet www.gov.uk/government/organisations/ministry-of-justice.

Northern Ireland Office: 1 Horse Guards Rd, London, SW1A 2HQ; tel. (+44 28) 9052-0700; e-mail niowebeditor.mailbox@nio.gov.uk; internet www.gov.uk/government/organisations/northern-ireland-office.

Office of the Leader of the House of Commons: 70 Whitehall, London, SW1A 2AS; tel. (+44 20) 7276-1005; fax (+44 20) 7276-1006; e-mail commonsleader@cabinetoffice.gov.uk; internet www.gov.uk/government/organisations/the-office-of-the-leader-of-the-house-of-commons.

Office of the Leader of the House of Lords: House of Lords, Room 20, London, SW1A 0PW; tel. (+44 20) 7219-3200; fax (+44 20) 7219-3051; e-mail psleaderofthelords@cabinetoffice.gov.uk; internet www.gov.uk/government/organisations/office-of-the-leader-of-the-house-of-lords.

Scotland Office: Dover House, Whitehall, London, SW1A 2AU; tel. (+44 131) 244-9010; e-mail pressoffice@scotlandoffice.gsi

.gov.uk; internet www.gov.uk/government/organisations/scotland-office.

Department for Transport: Great Minster House, 33 Horseferry Rd, London, SW1P 4DR; tel. (+44 300) 330-3000; internet www.gov.uk/government/organisations/department-for-transport.

HM Treasury: 1 Horse Guards Rd, London, SW1A 2HQ; tel. (+44 20) 7270-5000; e-mail public.enquiries@hmtreasury.gsi.gov.uk; internet www.gov.uk/government/organisations/hm-treasury.

Wales Office: Gwydyr House, Whitehall, London, SW1A 2NP; tel. (+44 29) 2092-4220; e-mail correspondence@walesoffice.gsi.gov.uk; internet www.gov.uk/government/organisations/office-of-the-secretary-of-state-for-wales.

Department for Work and Pensions: Caxton House, Tothill St, London, SW1H 9NA; tel. (+44 20) 3267-5144; e-mail ministers@dwp.gsi.gov.uk; internet www.gov.uk/government/organisations/department-for-work-pensions.

EU Member States' Permanent Representations

AUSTRIA

30 ave de Cortenbergh, 1040 Brussels, Belgium; tel. (+32) 2-2345100; fax (+32) 2-2356300; e-mail bruessel-ov@bmeia.gv.at; internet www.bmeia.gv.at/oev-bruessel

Ambassador Extraordinary and Plenipotentiary, Permanent Representative (Coreper II): Nikolaus Marschik; tel. (+32) 2-2345130; fax (+32) 2-2345318; e-mail nikolaus.marschik@bmeia.gv.at.

Minister Plenipotentiary, Deputy Permanent Representative (Coreper I): Thomas Oberreiter; tel. (+32) 2-2345122.

Political and Security Committee

Ambassador, Representative of Austria to the Political and Security Committee (PSC) of the European Union: Alexander Kmentt; tel. (+32) 2-2345202; fax (+32) 2-2356202.

Press and Communication

Press Officer: Alexander Paier; tel. (+32) 2-2345344; e-mail alexander.paier@bmeia.gv.at.

BELGIUM

61–63 rue de la Loi, 1040 Brussels, Belgium; tel. (+32) 2-2332111; fax (+32) 2-2311075; e-mail dispatch.belgoeurop@diplobel.fed.be; internet europeanunion.diplomatie.belgium.be

Ambassador Extraordinary and Plenipotentiary, Permanent Representative (Coreper II): François Roux; tel. (+32) 2-2332120.

Deputy Permanent Representative (Coreper I): Jan Hoogmartens; tel. (+32) 2-2332124.

Political and Security Committee

Ambassador, Representative of Belgium to the PSC: François Cornet d'Elzius; tel. (+32) 2-2330303.

Press and Communication

Spokesperson: Nico Van Dijck; tel. (+32) 2-2330392.

BULGARIA

49 sq. Marie-Louise, 1000 Brussels, Belgium; tel. (+32) 2-2358301; fax (+32) 2-3749188; e-mail mission.brusselseu@bg-permrep.eu; internet www.bg-permrep.eu

Ambassador Extraordinary and Plenipotentiary, Permanent Representative (Coreper II): Dimiter Tzantchev; tel. (+32) 2-2358307; e-mail mission.brusselseu@bg-permrep.eu.

Ambassador, Deputy Permanent Representative (Coreper I): Maria Koleva; tel. (+32) 2-2358305; e-mail mission.brusselseu@bg-permrep.eu.

Political and Security Committee

Minister-Counsellor, Representative of Bulgaria to the PSC: Gergana Karadjova; tel. (+32) 2-2358315; e-mail mission.brusselseu@bg-permrep.eu.

Press and Information

Press Officer: Genoveva Chervenakova; tel. (+32) 2-2358347; e-mail genoveva.chervenakova@bg-permrep.eu.

CROATIA

50 ave des Arts 50, 1000 Brussels, Belgium; tel. (+32) 2-5075411; fax (+32) 2-6465664; e-mail hr.perm.rep@mvep.hr; internet eu.mfa.hr/hr

Ambassador Extraordinary and Plenipotentiary (Coreper II): Mato Škrabalo; tel. (+32) 2-5075401.

Deputy Permanent Representative (Coreper I): Goran Štefanić; tel. (+32) 2-5075413; e-mail goran.stefanic@mvep.hr.

Political and Security Committee

Permanent Representative of Croatia to the PSC: Tomislav Car; tel. (+32) 2-5075480; e-mail tomislav.car@mvep.hr.

Press and Information

Minister Plenipotentiary (Spokesperson, Public Relations, Press, Information): Vesna Lončarić; tel. (+32) 2-5075416; e-mail vesna.loncaric@mvep.hr.

CYPRUS

61 ave de Cortenbergh, 1000 Brussels, Belgium; tel. (+32) 2-7395111; fax (+32) 2-7354552; e-mail cy.perm.rep@mfa.gov.cy; internet www.mfa.gov.cy/mfa/PermRep

Ambassador Extraordinary and Plenipotentiary, Permanent Representative (Coreper II): Nicholas Emiliou; tel. (+32) 2-7395137; e-mail nemiliou@mfa.gov.cy.

Deputy Permanent Representative (Coreper I): Olympia Neocleous; tel. (+32) 2-7395102; e-mail oneocleous@mfa.gov.cy.

Political and Security Committee

Ambassador, Representative of Cyprus to the PSC: Spyros Attas; tel. (+32) 2-7395159; e-mail sattas@mfa.gov.cy.

Press

Press Officer: Maria Stavropoulou; tel. (+32) 2-7395150; e-mail mstavropoulou@mfa.gov.cy.

CZECH REPUBLIC

15 rue Caroly, 1050 Brussels, Belgium; tel. (+32) 2-2139111; fax (+32) 2-2139186; e-mail eu.brussels@embassy.mzv.cz; internet www.czechrep.be

Ambassador Extraordinary and Plenipotentiary, Permanent Representative (Coreper II): Martin Povejsil; tel. (+32) 2-2139114; fax (+32) 2-2139185.

Ambassador, Deputy Permanent Representative (Coreper I): Jaroslav Zajíček; tel. (+32) 2-2139120.

Political and Security Committee

Ambassador, Representative to the Political and Security Committee: David Konecký; tel. (+32) 2-2139106.

Press and Communication

Spokesperson: Michal Bucháček; tel. (+32) 2-2139245.

DENMARK

73 rue d'Arlon 73, 1040 Brussels, Belgium; tel. (+32) 2-2330811; fax (+32) 2-2309384; e-mail brurep@um.dk; internet eu.um.dk/da.aspx

Ambassador Extraordinary and Plenipotentiary, Permanent Representative (Coreper II): Kim Jørgensen; tel. (+32) 2-2330865.

Ambassador, Deputy Permanent Representative (Coreper I): Vibeke Pasternak Jørgensen; tel. (+32) 2-2330866.

Political and Security Committee

Ambassador, Representative of Denmark to the PSC: Lisbet Zilmer-Johns; tel. (+32) 2-2330970.

Press and Communication

Spokesperson: Tanne Krogh Bertelsen; tel. (+32) 2-2330855.

ESTONIA

11–13 rue Guimard, 1040 Brussels, Belgium; tel. (+32) 2-2273910; fax (+32) 2-2273925; e-mail permrep.eu@mfa.ee; internet www.eu.estemb.be

Ambassador Extraordinary and Plenipotentiary, Permanent Representative (Coreper II): Kaja Tael; tel. (+32) 2-2274312; fax (+32) 2-2274343.

Deputy Permanent Representative (Coreper I): Clyde Kull; tel. (+32) 2-2274303; fax (+32) 2-2274343.

Political and Security Committee

Representative of Estonia to the PSC: Lembit Uibo; tel. (+32) 2-2274318; fax (+32) 2-2274381.

Press and Information

First Secretary (Spokesperson): Marika Post; tel. (+32) 2-2273928.

FINLAND

80 ave de Cortenbergh, 1000 Brussels, Belgium; tel. (+32) 2-2878411; fax (+32) 2-2878405; e-mail sanomat.eue@formin.fi; internet www.finland.eu

Ambassador Extraordinary and Plenipotentiary, Permanent Representative (Coreper II): Marja Rislakki; tel. (+32) 2-2878422.

Ambassador, Deputy Permanent Representative (Coreper I): Minna Kivimäki; tel. (+32) 2-2878624.

Political and Security Committee

Ambassador, Permanent Representative of Finland to the PSC: Sofie From-Emmesberger; tel. (+32) 2-2878485.

Press Relations

Press Counsellor: Leena Brandt; tel. (+32) 2-2878502.

FRANCE

14 place de Louvain, 1000 Brussels, Belgium; tel. (+32) 2-2298211; fax (+32) 2-22309950; e-mail courrier.bruxelles-dfra@diplomatie.gouv.fr; internet www.rpfrance.eu

Ambassador Extraordinary and Plenipotentiary, Permanent Representative (Coreper II): Pierre Sellal.

Deputy Permanent Representative (Coreper I): Fabrice Dubreil.

Political and Security Committee

Ambassador, Permanent Representative of France to the PSC: Nicolas Suran.

Press and Information

Press Counsellor, Spokesperson: Frédéric Jung; tel. (+32) 2-2298277; e-mail frederic.jung@diplomatie.gouv.fr.

GERMANY

8–14 rue Jacques de Lalaing, 1040 Brussels, Belgium; tel. (+32) 2-7871000; fax (+32) 2-7872000; e-mail info@bruessel-eu.diplo.de; internet www.eu-vertretung.de

Ambassador Extraordinary and Plenipotentiary, Permanent Representative (Coreper II): Reinhard Silberberg.

Ambassador, Deputy Permanent Representative (Coreper I): Peter Rösgen.

Political and Security Committee

Ambassador, Representative of Germany to the PSC: Michael Flügger.

Press Office

Spokesperson (Coreper II): Hardy Böckle; tel. (+32) 2-7871071.

Deputy Spokesperson (Coreper I): Helge Holleck; tel. (+32) 2-7871071.

GREECE

19–21 rue Jacques de Lalaing, 1040 Brussels, Belgium; tel. (+32) 2-5515611; fax (+32) 2-5515651; e-mail mea.bruxelles@rp-grece.be; internet www.mfa.gr/brussels

Ambassador Extraordinary and Plenipotentiary, Permanent Representative (Coreper II): Andreas Papastavrou; tel. (+32) 2-5515637; fax (+32) 2-5515711; e-mail rp@rp-grece.be.

Ambassador, Deputy Permanent Representative (Coreper I): Argyris Makris; tel. (+32) 2-5515601; e-mail rp-adj@rp-grece.be.

Political and Security Committee

Minister Plenipotentiary, Representative of Greece to the PSC: Roussos Koundouros; tel. (+32) 2-5515797; e-mail r.koundouros@mfa.gr.

Press Office

Counsellor (Press), Spokesperson: Panagiotis Agrafiotis; tel. (+32) 2-2350375; e-mail pagrafiotis@gpo.be.

HUNGARY

92–98 rue de Trèves, 1040 Brussels, Belgium; tel. (+32) 2-2341200; fax (+32) 2-2304351; e-mail sec.beu@mfa.gov.hu; internet www.hunrep.be

Ambassador Extraordinary and Plenipotentiary, Permanent Representative (Coreper II): Olivér Várhelyi; tel. (+32) 2-2341203; e-mail cor2.beu@mfa.gov.hu.

Ambassador, Deputy Permanent Representative: Tibor Stelbaczky; tel. (+32) 2-2341205; e-mail deputy.beu@mfa.gov.hu.

Political and Security Committee

Ambassador Extraordinary and Plenipotentiary, Representative to the PSC: Harry Alex Rusz; tel. (+32) 2-2341416; e-mail psc.beu@mfa.gov.hu.

Press and Communication

Spokesperson: Dóra Bókay; tel. (+32) 2-2341281; e-mail dora.bokay@mfa.gov.hu.

IRELAND

50 rue Froissart, 1040 Brussels, Belgium; tel. (+32) 2-2823211; fax (+32) 2-2303203; e-mail irlprb@dfa.ie; internet www.irelandrepbrussels.be

Ambassador Extraordinary and Plenipotentiary, Permanent Representative (Coreper II): Declan Kelleher.

Ambassador, Deputy Permanent Representative (Coreper I): Joe Hackett.

Political and Security Committee

Ambassador, Representative of Ireland to the PSC: Noel White.

Press and Communication

Counsellor (Press and Information): Ed Brannigan.

ITALY

Chancery, 7–15 rue du Marteau, 1000 Brussels, Belgium; tel. (+32) 2-2200411; fax (+32) 2-2200426; e-mail rpue@rpue.esteri.it; internet www.italiaue.esteri.it

Ambassador Extraordinary and Plenipotentiary, Permanent Representative (Coreper II): Maurizio Massari.

Ambassador, Deputy Permanent Representative (Coreper I): Giovanni Pugliese.

Political and Security Committee

Ambassador, Representative of Italy to the PSC: Luca Franchettipardo.

Press

Spokesperson: Davide Bonvicini; tel. (+32) 2-2200432; e-mail stampa@rpue.esteri.it.

LATVIA

23 ave des Arts, 1000 Brussels, Belgium; tel. (+32) 2-2383100; fax (+32) 2-2383250; e-mail permrep.eu@mfa.gov.lv; internet www.mfa.gov.lv/brussels

Ambassador Extraordinary and Plenipotentiary, Permanent Representative (Coreper II): Sanita Pavļuta-Deslandes; tel. (+32) 2-2383201.

Ambassador, Deputy Permanent Representative (Coreper I): Alise Balode; tel. (+32) 2-2383203.

Political and Security Committee

Ambassador, Representative of Latvia to the PSC: Andžejs Vilumsons; tel. (+32) 2-2383205.

Press and Communication

Spokesperson: Baiba Čamane; tel. (+32) 2-2383134.

LITHUANIA

41–43 rue Belliard, 1040 Brussels, Belgium; tel. (+32) 2-7710140; fax (+32) 2-4019877; e-mail office@eu.mfa.lt; internet www.eu.mfa.lt

Ambassador Extraordinary and Plenipotentiary, Permanent Representative (Coreper II): Jovita Neliupšienė; tel. (+32) 2-4019844.

Ambassador-at-large, Deputy Permanent Representative (Coreper I): Robertas Rosinas.

Political and Security Committee

Ambassador, Permanent Representative to the PSC: Dainius Petras Kamaitis; tel. (+32) 2-4019825.

Information and Press

Counsellor (Press, Communication): Žana Tarasė; tel. (+32) 2-7881875; e-mail press@eu.mfa.lt.

LUXEMBOURG

75 ave de Cortenbergh, 1000 Brussels, Belgium; tel. (+32) 2-7375600; fax (+32) 2-7361429; e-mail bruxelles.rpue@mae.etat.lu; internet bruxelles-rpue.mae.lu/fr

Ambassador Extraordinary and Plenipotentiary, Permanent Representative (Coreper II): Georges Friden.

Ambassador, Deputy Permanent Representative (Coreper I): Mike Hentges.

Political and Security Committee

Ambassador Extraordinary and Plenipotentiary, Permanent Representative of Luxembourg to the PSC: Stephan Muller.

Press and Communication

Counsellor, Press Officer, Working Party on Information: Carole Ensch; tel. (+32) 2-7375673.

MALTA

25 rue Archimède, 1000 Brussels, Belgium; tel. (+32) 2-3430195; fax (+32) 2-3430106; e-mail maltarep@gov.mt; internet www.eu2017.mt/en/Pages/home.aspx

Ambassador Extraordinary and Plenipotentiary, Permanent Representative (Coreper II): Marlene Bonnici; tel. (+32) 2-2382603; fax (+32) 2-3430106; e-mail pr.maltarep@gov.mt.

Deputy Permanent Representative (Coreper I): Neil Kerr; tel. (+32) 2-2382781; fax (+32) 2-3430106; e-mail dpr.maltarep@gov.mt.

Political and Security Committee

Representative to the Political and Security Committee: Alan Bugeja; tel. (+32) 2-2382766; fax (+32) 2-3430106; e-mail alan-john.bugeja@gov.mt.

Press and Communication

Spokesperson (Coreper II): Wendy Borg; tel. (+32) 2-23827862; e-mail wendy.borg@gov.mt.

Spokesperson (Coreper I): Pablo Micallef; tel. (+32) 2-2382620; e-mail pablo.micallef@gov.mt.

THE NETHERLANDS

4–10 ave de Cortenbergh, 1040 Brussels, Belgium; tel. (+32) 2-6791511; fax (+32) 2-6791775; e-mail bre@minbuza.nl; internet eu.nlvertegenwoordiging.org

Ambassador Extraordinary and Plenipotentiary, Permanent Representative (Coreper II): Robert de Groot; tel. (+32) 2-6791502; fax (+32) 2-6791795; e-mail bre-cdp@minbuza.nl.

Minister Plenipotentiary, Deputy Permanent Representative (Coreper I): Ronald van Roeden; tel. (+32) 2-6791508; fax (+32) 2-6791775; e-mail bre-cdp@minbuza.nl.

Political and Security Committee

Representative of the Netherlands to the PSC: Joanneke Balfoort; tel. (+32) 2-6791602; fax (+32) 2-7263299; e-mail bre-psc-secretariat@minbuza.nl.

Press and Information Service

Spokesperson, Counsellor: Dirk-Jan Vermeij; tel. (+32) 2-6791509; fax (+32) 2-6791774; e-mail dirk-jan.vermeij@minbuza.nl.

POLAND

139 rue Stevin, 1000 Brussels, Belgium; tel. (+32) 2-7804200; fax (+32) 2-7804297; e-mail bebrustpe@msz.gov.pl; internet www.brukselaeu.mzv.gov.pl/pl

Ambassador Extraordinary and Plenipotentiary, Permanent Representative (Coreper II): (vacant).

First Counsellor, Deputy Permanent Representative (Coreper I): Sebastian Barkowski.

Political and Security Committee

Representative of Poland to the PSC (acting): Maciej Karasiński.

Press and Communication

Spokesperson: Adrian Biernacki; tel. (+32) 2-7804225.

PORTUGAL

12 ave de Cortenbergh, 1040 Brussels, Belgium; tel. (+32) 2-2864211; fax (+32) 2-2310026; e-mail reper@reper-portugal.be; internet www.ue.missaoportugal.mne.pt/pt

Ambassador Extraordinary and Plenipotentiary, Permanent Representative (Coreper II): Nuno Brito.

Ambassador, Deputy Permanent Representative (Coreper I): Pedro Lourtie.

Political and Security Committee

Ambassador, Representative of Portugal to the PSC: Rui Vinhas.

Press and Information

Spokesperson: António Esteves Martins; tel. (+32) 2-2864281; e-mail aem@reper-portugal.be.

ROMANIA

12 rue Montoyer, 1000 Brussels, Belgium; tel. (+32) 2-7000640; fax (+32) 2-7000641; e-mail bru@rpro.eu; internet www.ue.mae.ro

Ambassador Extraordinary and Plenipotentiary, Permanent Representative to the EU (Coreper II): Luminiţa Teodora Odobescu; tel. (+32) 2-7000640; e-mail bru@rpro.eu.

Minister Plenipotentiary, Deputy Permanent Representative (Coreper I): Cosmin Boiangiu; tel. (+32) 2-7000640; e-mail cosmin.boiangiu@rpro.eu.

Political and Security Committee

Minister Plenipotentiary, Representative of Romania to the PSC: Adrian-Cristian Bradu; tel. (+32) 2-7000601; e-mail adrian.bratu@rpro.eu.

Press and Communication

Spokesperson: Carmen Raluca Norel; tel. (+32) 2-7000303; e-mail raluca.norel@rpro.eu.

SLOVAKIA

107 ave de Cortenbergh, 1000 Brussels, Belgium; tel. (+32) 2-7436811; fax (+32) 2-7436888; fax (+32) 2-7436889; e-mail eu.brussels@mzv.sk; internet www.mzv.sk/szbrusel

Ambassador Extraordinary and Plenipotentiary, Permanent Representative (Coreper II): Peter Javorčik; tel. (+32) 2-7436800.

Ambassador, Deputy Permanent Representative (Coreper I): Alexander Micovčin; tel. (+32) 2-7436801; e-mail alexander.micovcin@mzv.sk.

Political and Security Committee

Ambassador, Permanent Representative of Slovakia to the Political and Security Committee: Ľubomír Čaňo; tel. (+32) 2-7436861; e-mail lubomir.cano@mzv.sk.

Media Service

Spokesperson: Renáta Goldirova; tel. (+32) 4-73523824; e-mail renata.goldirova@mzv.sk.

SLOVENIA

44 rue du Commerce, 1000 Brussels, Belgium; tel. (+32) 2-2136300; fax (+32) 2-2136301; e-mail spbr@gov.si; internet brussels.representation.si

Ambassador Extraordinary and Plenipotentiary, Permanent Representative (Coreper II): Janez Lenarčič; tel. (+32) 2-2136431.

Deputy Permanent Representative (Coreper I): Metka Ipavić; tel. (+32) 2-2136374.

Political and Security Committee

Ambassador, Representative of Slovenia to the Political and Security Committee: Matjaž Šinkovec; tel. (+32) 2-2136417.

Press and Communication

Public and Media Relations: Helena Vodušek; tel. (+32) 2-2136340.

SPAIN

52 blvd du Régent, 1000 Brussels, Belgium; tel. (+32) 2-5098611; fax (+32) 2-5111940; e-mail reper.bruselasue@reper.maec.es; internet www.representacionpermanente.eu

Ambassador Extraordinary and Plenipotentiary, Permanent Representative (Coreper II): Pablo García-Berdoy.

Ambassador, Deputy Permanent Representative (Coreper I): Juan Aristegui.

Political and Security Committee

Ambassador, Permanent Representative of Spain to the PSC: Nicolás Pascual de la Parte.

Press

Spokesperson: Julio Fenoy Muñoz; tel. (+32) 2-5098724.

SWEDEN

30 sq. de Meeûs, 1000 Brussels, Belgium; tel. (+32) 2-2895611; fax (+32) 2-2895600; e-mail representationen.bryssel@gov.se; internet www.regeringen.se/eu-representationen

Ambassador Extraordinary and Plenipotentiary, Permanent Representative (Coreper II): Lars Danielsson; tel. (+32) 2-2895645; e-mail lars.danielsson@gov.se.

Ambassador, Deputy Permanent Representative (Coreper I): Åsa Webber; tel. (+32) 2-2895642; e-mail asa.webber@gov.se.

Political and Security Committee

Ambassador, Representative of Sweden to the PSC: Anna Jardfelt Melvin; tel. (+32) 2-2895657; e-mail anna.jardfelt@gov.se.

Press and Communication

Press Adviser: Helena Zimmerdahl; tel. (+32) 2-2895655; e-mail helena.zimmerdahl@gov.se.

UNITED KINGDOM

Chancery, 10 ave d'Auderghem, 1040 Brussels, Belgium; tel. (+32) 2-2878211; fax (+32) 2-2828900; e-mail ukrep@fco.gov.uk; internet www.ukeu.fco.gov.uk

Ambassador Extraordinary and Plenipotentiary, Permanent Representative (Coreper II): Tim Barrow; tel. (+32) 2-2878211; fax (+32) 2-2828900.

Deputy Permanent Representative (Coreper I): Katrina Williams; tel. (+32) 2-2878211.

Political and Security Committee

Representative of the UK to the PSC: Angus Lapsley.

Press and Communication

Spokesperson: Alexandra Knapton; tel. (+32) 2-2878212.

Administrative Units

175 rue de la Loi, 1048 Brussels, Belgium; tel. (+32) 2-2816111; fax (+32) 2-2816934; internet www.consilium.europa.eu

SECRETARIAT-GENERAL

Secretary-General: Jeppe Tranholm-Mikkelsen; tel. (+32) 2-2816215.

Secretary-General's Private Office

Head of the Secretary-General's Private Office: Agnieszka Bartol; tel. (+32) 2-2816694.

GENERAL AND INSTITUTIONAL POLICY

Deputy Director-General: Jim Cloos; tel. (+32) 2-2819330.

Directorate 1—General Policy

Director: Ivan Gabor; tel. (+32) 2-2814277.

1A—European Council and Strategic Planning

Head of Unit: Jan van Elst; tel. (+32) 2-2818252.

1B—Council and Presidency Preparation

Head of Unit: Klaus Schwab; tel. (+32) 2-2817293.

Directorate 2—Interinstitutional Relations

Director: Geneviève Tuts; tel. (+32) 2-2817474.

COUNTER-TERRORISM CO-ORDINATION

Director: Gilles de Kerchove D'Ousselghem; tel. (+32) 2-2817933.

INTERNAL AUDIT

Head of Unit: Fernando Sendra; tel. (+32) 2-2817582.

DATA PROTECTION

Head of Unit (Data Protection Officer): Reyes Otero Zapata; tel. (+32) 2-2817178.

LEGAL SERVICE

Director-General: Hubert Legal; tel. (+32) 2-2817322.

Co-ordination

Head of Unit: Fernando Florindo Gijón; tel. (+32) 2-2816196.

Directorate 1—Competitiveness, Environment, Transport, Telecommunications, Energy
Director: Tim Middleton; tel. (+32) 2-2817919.

Directorate 2—Employment, Social Affairs, Education, Agriculture, Fisheries
Director: Emer Finnegan; tel. (+32) 2-2815283.

Directorate 3—External Relations
Director: Paul Richard Berman; tel. (+32) 2-2816878.

Directorate 4—Institutional Questions, Litigation and Staff Regulations
Director: Jean-Baptiste Laignelot; tel. (+32) 2-2812744.

Directorate 5—Justice and Home Affairs
Director: Thérèse Blanchet; tel. (+32) 2-2818775.

Directorate 6—Economic and Financial Affairs, Budget, Structural Funds
Director: Alberto de Gregorio Merino; tel. (+32) 2-2819353.

Directorate 7—Quality of Legislation
Director: Andreas Lernhart; tel. (+32) 2-2816241.

CO-ORDINATION AND OFFICIAL JOURNAL
Head of Office: Erzsebet Toth; tel. (+32) 2-2816390.

INTERNATIONAL AGREEMENTS/RESOURCES
Head of Unit: Helio Gómez de Mayora Rojas; tel. (+32) 2-2816946.

LEGISLATIVE ACTS/PLANNING
Head of Unit: Manuela Guggeis; tel. (+32) 2-2818359.

NON-LEGISLATIVE ACTS/FOLLOW-UP
Head of Unit: Ieva Lejasisaka; tel. (+32) 2-2815147.

DIRECTORATE-GENERAL A— ADMINISTRATION
Director-General: William Shapcott; tel. (+32) 2-2815824.

Directorate 1—Human Resources and Personnel Administration
Director: Cesira D'Aniello; tel. (+32) 2-2818253.

STAFFING AND MOBILITY UNIT
Head of Unit: Kim Freidberg; tel. (+32) 2-2817729.

Staffing
Head of Office: Hilary Majewska; tel. (+32) 2-2817657.

Traineeships
Head of Office: Tamas Zahonyi; tel. (+32) 2-2816461.

Recruitment
Head of Sector: Saskia Hermann; tel. (+32) 2-2812466.

Selection of Officials
Head of Sector: Cristina Zucchi; tel. (+32) 2-2816329.

Temporary Staffing Services
Head of Sector: Cristina Cirieco; tel. (+32) 2-2816057.

STAFF DEVELOPMENT
Head of Unit: Elizabeth Willocks; tel. (+32) 2-2816216.

Budget and Programming
Head of Sector: Bruno Pereira Lagos; tel. (+32) 2-2814925.

INTERNAL COMMUNICATION
Head of Unit: Małgorzata Stecko; tel. (+32) 2-2817647.

LEGAL ADVISERS TO THE ADMINISTRATION
Head of Unit: Eleonora Botar; tel. (+32) 2-2819359.

INDIVIDUAL ENTITLEMENTS
Head of Unit: Sonia Fumagalli; tel. (+32) 2-2818943.

Internal Support
Head of Sector: Jean-Éric Roland; tel. (+32) 2-2817866.

Operational Secretariat
Head of Office: Christian Braun; tel. (+32) 2-2816668.

Working Time and Privileges
Head of Sector: Ulrike Rackow; tel. (+32) 2-2817504.

Time Management
Head of Office: Maria Rosario Marin Villar; tel. (+32) 2-2818289.

Privileges
Head of Office: Christine van Vijle; tel. (+32) 2-2818054.

Individual Entitlements
Head of Sector: Pascal Mary; tel. (+32) 2-2819636.

Active Staff
Head of Office: Linda Rogers; tel. (+32) 2-2817288.

SALARIES AND MISSIONS
Head of Unit: Piet Schelling; tel. (+32) 2-2814967.

Salaries
Head of Sector: Vincent Yacoub; tel. (+32) 2-2818721.

Missions
Head of Sector: Alberto Baronio; tel. (+32) 2-2811914.

HEALTH CARE AND SOCIAL SERVICES
Head of Unit: Nessa Delaney; tel. (+32) 2-2817330.

Crèche and Childcare
Head of Office: Celia Costa e Silva; tel. (+32) 2-2817156.

Social Insurance
Head of Office: Elena Forcano; tel. (+32) 2-2818986.

MEDICAL SECTOR
Head of Unit: (vacant).

Management, Co-ordination and Accounts
Head of Office: Marianne Fieve Dieu; tel. (+32) 2-2816970.

Directorate 2—Protocol, Meetings, Buildings, Logistics
Deputy Director-General: (vacant).

DIRECTORATE 2A—PROTOCOL AND MEETINGS
Director: Dominique-Georges Marro; tel. (+32) 2-2816423.

Protocol
Head of Sector: Paulo Vidal; tel. (+32) 2-2815802.

Meetings
Head of Unit: Silvia Bianchi; tel. (+32) 2-2817737.

Catering
Head of Unit: Jarosław Zaczykiewicz; tel. (+32) 2-2815389.

Support
Head of Unit: Nathalie Terrana; tel. (+32) 2-2813285.

DIRECTORATE 2B—BUILDINGS, LOGISTICS
Director: Kristin Van Hoolst; tel. (+32) 2-2815454.

Buildings
Head of Unit: Marc De Feu; tel. (+32) 2-2816243.

Electrical, Electromechanical and Security Installations
Head of Office: Nicolas Debrulle; tel. (+32) 2-2815677.

Thermal and Sanitary Installations
Head of Office: Enrico Morello; tel. (+32) 2-2815497.

General Maintenance, Monitoring of Operating Conditions
Head of Office: Vincent Bouillez; tel. (+32) 2-2814926.

Buildings Policy and Environmental Management
Head of Sector: Stefano Venanzi; tel. (+32) 2-2815344.

Projects
Head of Sector: Stéphane Magnette; tel. (+32) 2-2813069.

Technical Management
Head of Sector: Marco Sereno; tel. (+32) 2-2813293.

Logistics
Head of Unit: Aleksandra Krysztofiak; tel. (+32) 2-2818788.

Equipment and Operations
Head of Sector: Javier López Ariza; tel. (+32) 2-2816331.

Furniture, Removals, Events Equipment
Head of Office: Eddy Ceuleers; tel. (+32) 2-2818906.

Stores, Stocktaking
Head of Office: Maria Tur Tur; tel. (+32) 2-2819568.

Service Vehicles
Head of Office: Gian S. Palmeri; tel. (+32) 2-2812369.

Finances
Head of Unit: Nicolas Papadopoulos; tel. (+32) 2-2815893.

Budget Implementation
Head of Sector: Nicolas Bourgeois; tel. (+32) 2-2815874.

Public Procurement Contracts
Head of Sector: Anna Świda; tel. (+32) 2-2813075.

Directorate 3—Translation Service
Deputy Director-General: (vacant).

DIRECTORATE 3A—TRANSLATION
Director: Minna Vuorio; tel. (+32) 2-2818662.

Bulgarian Language Unit
Head of Unit: Vladimir Karakashov; tel. (+32) 2-2814415.

Czech Language Unit
Head of Unit: Karl-Heinz Walker; tel. (+32) 2-2817412.

German Language Unit
Head of Unit: David Zelinger; tel. (+32) 2-2812540.

Irish Language Unit
Head of Unit: Seán Hade; tel. (+32) 2-2813061.

Greek Language Unit
Head of Unit: Ioannis Dimolistas; tel. (+32) 2-2817323.

Spanish Language Unit
Head of Unit: Guillermo Troncoso González; tel. (+32) 2-2818217.

Italian Language Unit
Head of Unit: Lucia Ceccarelli; tel. (+32) 2-2819910.

Latvian Language Unit
Head of Unit: Baiba Aleksejuka; tel. (+32) 2-2815388.

Lithuanian Language Unit
Head of Unit: Viktorija Tichonova-Zurbiene; tel. (+32) 2-2813765.

Portuguese Language Unit
Head of Unit: Orlando Gamboa Dos Santos; tel. (+32) 2-2815495.

Slovak Language Unit
Head of Unit: Mari Linnapuomi; tel. (+32) 2-2811741.

English Language Unit
Head of Unit: Jennifer Lockett; tel. (+32) 2-2815414.

DIRECTORATE 3B—TRANSLATION
Director: Sabine Ehmke-Gendron; tel. (+32) 2-2818569.

Council

Resources
Head of Unit: Katelijn Serlet; tel. (+32) 2-2817285.

Danish Language Unit
Head of Unit: (vacant); tel. (+32) 2-2817908.

Estonian Language Unit
Head of Unit: Heiki Pisuke; tel. (+32) 2-2813968.

French Language Unit
Head of Unit: Eric Thoraval; tel. (+32) 2-2815432.

Croatian Language Unit
Head of Unit: Gordana Mlacak.

Hungarian Language Unit
Head of Unit: (vacant).

Maltese Language Unit
Head of Unit: Paul Saliba; tel. (+32) 2-2815196.

Dutch Language Unit
Head of Unit: Andreea Ivanescu; tel. (+32) 2-2812332.

Polish Language Unit
Head of Unit: Agata Kłopotowska; tel. (+32) 2-2816027.

Romanian Language Unit
Head of Unit: Dan Marasescu; tel. (+32) 2-2814402.

Slovenian Language Unit
Head of Unit: Patrick Langlois; tel. (+32) 2-2815907.

Finnish Language Unit
Head of Unit: Hannu Poysti.

Swedish Language Unit
Head of Unit: Ragnheidur Roubineau; tel. (+32) 2-2817135.

Directorate 4—Finances

Director: Hans-Werner Grenzhäuser; tel. (+32) 2-2816462.

PROJECTS AND FINANCE UNIT
Head of Unit: Uwe Harms; tel. (+32) 2-2815012.

BUDGET MANAGEMENT UNIT
Head of Unit: Wolfgang Ploch; tel. (+32) 2-2817771.

PROCUREMENT CO-ORDINATION UNIT
Head of Unit: Hans Nilsson; tel. (+32) 2-2817915.

ACCOUNTING UNIT
Head of Unit: Lucy Hess; tel. (+32) 2-2817568.

Security, Safety and Communication and Information Systems

Deputy Director-General: David Galloway; tel. (+32) 2-2816194.

SAFETY AND SECURITY
Director: Francis Morgan.

Security Strategy and Business Continuity
Head of Unit: Siegfried Van den Enden; tel. (+32) 2-2812131.

Risk Management and Business Continuity Planning
Head of Sector: Philip Meulenberghs; tel. (+32) 2-2818034.

Investigation and Technical Surveillance Counter-Measures
Head of Sector: Philip Vanassche; tel. (+32) 2-2815644.

Operational Security Unit
Head of Unit: Yves Deceuninck; tel. (+32) 2-2817050.

Access
Head of Office: Serge Adan; tel. (+32) 2-2818345.

Planning and Performance
Head of Sector: Isabelle Dirkx; tel. (+32) 2-2813576.

Security Contracts
Head of Office: Joaquín Aguado Alonso; tel. (+32) 2-2815856.

Physical Security
Head of Sector: Nicola Notari; tel. (+32) 2-2819635.

Security Centres
Head of Office: Francisco J. Fernández Villa Villa; tel. (+32) 2-2813830.

Physical Protection
Head of Office: Loutphi Gharbi; tel. (+32) 2-2817292.

Information Security
Head of Unit: Ulrich van Essen; tel. (+32) 2-2819840.

EUCI Management and National Security Authorities Liaison (NSA)
Head of Sector: Bruno Desloover; tel. (+32) 2-2816826.

Security Clearance
Head of Office: Annabelle Gauci; tel. (+32) 2-2813658.

Information Assurance
Head of Sector: Stefan Wittmann; tel. (+32) 2-2815741.

Safety
Head of Unit: (vacant).

Directorate 5—Information and Communication Systems

Director: Dirk Schilders; tel. (+32) 2-2819989.

Resources
Head of Sector: Kalenga d'Almeida; tel. (+32) 2-2815460.

Systems Security
Head of Unit: Sébastien Leonnet; tel. (+32) 2-2815538.

Systems Validation
Head of Unit: Benoit Verreet; tel. (+32) 2-2815148.

Study and Documentation
Head of Unit: Patrice Baguet; tel. (+32) 2-2816575.

Crypto Operations and Security Administration Sector
Head of Unit: Thierry Manté; tel. (+32) 2-2815087.

Operational Management
Head of Office: Raul Martinez Lopez; tel. (+32) 2-2815234.

Network Defence Capability
Head of Unit: Jean-Luc Auboin; tel. (+32) 2-2816877.

Architecture, Projects Portfolio and Services Management (PLAN)
Head of Unit: Philippe Vleminckx; tel. (+32) 2-2817138.

Project Portfolio Management
Head of Sector: Manuel Del Castillo; tel. (+32) 2-2813316.

Enterprise Architecture, IT Strategy Sector
Head of Unit: Sonia Riano; tel. (+32) 2-2816671.

IT Service Management/Service Desk
Head of Sector: Ovidiu Gheorghita; tel. (+32) 2-2812581.

IT Service Specialists
Head of Office: Carlos Simon Saiz; tel. (+32) 2-2819225.

Design and Development (BUILD)
Head of Unit: Fabrice Drezet; tel. (+32) 2-2819390.

Human Resources
Head of Sector: Sébastien Le Roquais; tel. (+32) 2-2816841.

Finances
Head of Sector: Ivan Enev; tel. (+32) 2-2818183.

Back Office Applications
Head of Unit: Wout Dekeyser; tel. (+32) 2-2819151.

Front Office Applications
Head of Sector: Gunter Vanuytsel; tel. (+32) 2-2814751.

Events, Security and Logistics
Head of Sector: (vacant).

Infrastructure and Operations (RUN)
Head of Unit: Jan Stuer; tel. (+32) 2-2812871.

Corporate Networks
Head of Sector: Panagiotis Saragiotis; tel. (+32) 2-2816198.

Middleware and Applications
Head of Sector: Paul Gordebeke; tel. (+32) 2-2816762.

Database and Applications
Head of Office: Benedikt Luyckx; tel. (+32) 2-2816281.

E-mail
Head of Office: Roberto Sabatini; tel. (+32) 2-2816750.

Telecommunications
Head of Sector: Cuong Ly; tel. (+32) 2-2819188.

Telecom Operations
Head of Office: Toufiq Zioui; tel. (+32) 2-2817116.

Digital Workplace Sector
Head of Sector: Frank Hoogervorst; tel. (+32) 2-2819936.

Digital Printing Solutions
Head of Office: Juan Marcos; tel. (+32) 2-2818346.

Digital Workplace Systems
Head of Office: (vacant).

Digital End Point Solutions
Head of Office: José López González; tel. (+32) 2-2815520.

Member States' Networks
Head of Sector: Mohammed Amri; tel. (+32) 2-2815071.

Member States' Network Operations
Head of Unit: Donato Curioni; tel. (+32) 2-2819581.

Central Infrastructure
Head of Sector: Michel Kasica; tel. (+32) 2-2817208.

Servers
Head of Office: Bart Vanneste; tel. (+32) 2-2819483.

Storage and Back-up
Head of Office: Hans Rooselaer; tel. (+32) 2-2817613.

IT Facilities
Head of Office: Christophe Delhaye; tel. (+32) 2-2816318.

DIRECTORATE-GENERAL B—AGRICULTURE, FISHERIES, SOCIAL AFFAIRS AND HEALTH

Director-General: Ángel Boixareu Carrera; tel. (+32) 2-2816234.

Directorate 1—Agriculture (Special Committee on Agriculture) and Social Policy

Director: Petr Blizkovsky; tel. (+32) 2-2815130.

UNIT 1A—DIRECT PAYMENTS AND MARKET SUPPORT
Head of Unit: Jean-Paul Decaestecker; tel. (+32) 2-2816807.

UNIT 1B—RURAL DEVELOPMENT
Head of Unit: César Cortes; tel. (+32) 2-2816114.

UNIT 1C—EMPLOYMENT AND SOCIAL POLICY
Head of Unit: Maria-Luise Lindorfer; tel. (+32) 2-2819280.

Directorate 2—Fisheries, Food and Health

Director: Marta Arpio; tel. (+32) 2-2816183.

UNIT 2A—FISHERIES
Head of Unit: Dirk Hellwig; tel. (+32) 2-2816958.

UNIT 2B—VETERINARY AND PLANT HEALTH QUESTIONS, FOOD CHAIN, FORESTRY
Head of Unit: Jean Recalde; tel. (+32) 2-2819440.

UNIT 2C—PUBLIC HEALTH AND FOODSTUFFS
Head of Unit: Jakob Thomsen; tel. (+32) 2-2819417.

DIRECTORATE-GENERAL C—FOREIGN AFFAIRS, ENLARGEMENT AND CIVIL PROTECTION

Director-General: Leonardo Schiavo; tel. (+32) 2-2815575.

Directorate 1—Trade, Development, Horizontal Issues, Foreign Affairs Council Support

Director: Alda Silveira Reis; tel. (+32) 2-2816093.

UNIT 1A—TRADE
Head of Unit: David Johns; tel. (+32) 2-2818600.

UNIT 1B—DEVELOPMENT
Head of Unit: Boštjan Šporar; tel. (+32) 2-2813902.

UNIT 1C—HORIZONTAL ISSUES
Head of Unit: Petr Hrdlicka; tel. (+32) 2-2817477.

Directorate 2—Enlargement, Security, Civil Protection, Foreign Affairs Council Support

Director: Zoltán Martinusz; tel. (+32) 2-2815327.

UNIT 2A—ENLARGEMENT
Head of Unit: Matthew Reece; tel. (+32) 2-2815994.

UNIT 2B—SECURITY
Head of Unit: Luís Amorim; tel. (+32) 2-2816136.

UNIT 2C—CIVIL PROTECTION
Head of Unit: Jan Alhadeff; tel. (+32) 2-2815799.

DIRECTORATE-GENERAL D—JUSTICE AND HOME AFFAIRS

Director-General: Christine Roger; tel. (+32) 2-2815047.

Directorate 1—Home Affairs

Director: Raoul Ueberecken; tel. (+32) 2-2814789.

UNIT 1A—SCHENGEN, VISAS AND BORDERS
Head of Unit: Bent Mejborn; tel. (+32) 2-2816722.

UNIT 1B—EXTERNAL RELATIONS, ASYLUM AND MIGRATION
Head of Unit: Paulo Oliveira; tel. (+32) 2-2816619.

UNIT 1C—POLICE AND CUSTOMS CO-OPERATION
Head of Unit: Guy Stessens; tel. (+32) 2-2816711.

Directorate 2—Justice

Director: Nathalie Pensaert; tel. (+32) 2-2815425.

UNIT 2A—JUDICIAL CO-OPERATION IN CIVIL MATTERS AND E-JUSTICE
Head of Unit: Alain Pilette; tel. (+32) 2-2818989.

UNIT 2B—JUDICIAL CO-OPERATION IN CRIMINAL MATTERS
Head of Unit: Gilles Duval; tel. (+32) 2-2818142.

UNIT 2C—FUNDAMENTAL RIGHTS, DATA PROTECTION AND DRUGS POLICIES
Head of Unit: Ralph Kaessner; tel. (+32) 2-2819422.

DIRECTORATE-GENERAL E—ENVIRONMENT, EDUCATION, TRANSPORT AND ENERGY

Director-General: Jarosław Pietras; tel. (+32) 2-2817421.

Directorate 1—Environment, Education, Youth, Culture, Audiovisual and Sport

Director: Berthold Berger; tel. (+32) 2-2816392.

UNIT 1A—ENVIRONMENT, INCLUDING INTERNATIONAL AFFAIRS
Head of Unit: Maria Marotta; tel. (+32) 2-2816225.

UNIT 1B—CLIMATE CHANGE, CO-ORDINATION AND HORIZONTAL AFFAIRS
Head of Unit: Jacob Vries; tel. (+32) 2-2815619.

UNIT 1C—EDUCATION, YOUTH, CULTURE, AUDIOVISUAL AND SPORT
Head of Unit: Nicolas Platten; tel. (+32) 2-2817431.

Directorate 2—Transport, Telecommunications and Energy

Director: Didier Seeuws; tel. (+32) 2-2816883.

UNIT 2A—TRANSPORT
Head of Unit: Luís Manuel Teixeira da Costa; tel. (+32) 2-2819808.

UNIT 2B—ENERGY POLICIES, ATOMIC QUESTIONS, INFORMATION SOCIETY
Head of Unit: Janusz Bielecki; tel. (+32) 2-2816003.

DIRECTORATE-GENERAL F—COMMUNICATION AND INFORMATION

Director-General: Reijo Kemppinen; tel. (+32) 2-2815825.

Directorate 1—Media and Communication

Director: Paul Reiderman; tel. (+32) 2-2818704; fax (+32) 2-2812700.

UNIT 1A—MEDIA RELATIONS
Head of Unit: Guy Milton; tel. (+32) 2-2818519.

Media Monitoring

Head of Unit: René Smeets; tel. (+32) 2-2817589.

UNIT 1B—MEDIA OPERATIONS
Head of Unit: Erik Schultz-Nielsen; tel. (+32) 2-2817372.

Audiovisual

Head of Sector: Isabelle Brusselmans; tel. (+32) 2-2815713.

UNIT 1C—WEB COMMUNICATION
Head of Unit: Margarita Comamala; tel. (+32) 2-2817039.

Editorial Office

Head of Sector: Maciej Bury; tel. (+32) 2-2814456.

UNIT 1D—PUBLIC RELATIONS
Head of Unit: Inés Hempel; tel. (+32) 2-2815688.

Relations with the Public

Head of Sector: Liina Parve; tel. (+32) 2-2816473; fax (+32) 2-2814810.

Public Information

Head of Office: Pilar Roza Manzano; tel. (+32) 2-2819441.

Publications, Documentation

Head of Sector: Elena Neculcea; tel. (+32) 2-2812385.

Publications

Head of Office: Isabelle Beyney; tel. (+32) 2-2818337.

Directorate 2—Information and Knowledge Management

Director: Roland Genson; tel. (+32) 2-2815822; fax (+32) 2-2816934.

UNIT 2A—INFORMATION MANAGEMENT
Head of Unit: Juan Pallares; tel. (+32) 2-2819922.

Document Processing

Head of Office: Riikka Ikaheimo; tel. (+32) 2-2819194.

Mail

Head of Office: Olivier Lanove; tel. (+32) 2-2816531.

Notifications and Official Acts

Head of Office: Mario Ortega Barquero; tel. (+32) 2-2816384.

Technical Production Services

Head of Sector: Bernard Philippart; tel. (+32) 2-2819619.

Information and Planning

Head of Sector: Laura Amore; tel. (+32) 2-2816820.

UNIT 2B—KNOWLEDGE MANAGEMENT
Head of Unit: Fernando Rui Paulino Pereira; tel. (+32) 2-2816621.

Library and Research

Head of Sector: Ausra Aleliunaitė; tel. (+32) 2-2816938.

Archives

Head of Office: Kerstin Reinhardt; tel. (+32) 2-2816426.

UNIT 2C—INNOVATION AND PROJECTS
Head of Unit: Juraj Sykora; tel. (+32) 2-2819385.

CLASSIFIED INFORMATION OFFICE
Head of Sector: Javier Torijano Montero; tel. (+32) 2-2815632.

DIRECTORATE-GENERAL G—ECONOMIC AFFAIRS AND COMPETITIVENESS

Director-General: Carsten Pillath; tel. (+32) 2-2816213.

Directorate 1—Economic and Financial Affairs

Director: Johannes Gilbers; tel. (+32) 2-2819891.

UNIT 1A—ECONOMIC POLICY, INCLUDING EUROGROUP
Head of Unit: Olaf Prüssmann; tel. (+32) 2-2812124.

UNIT 1B—INSURANCE AND SECURITIES
Head of Unit: Ana Ramírez Fueyo; tel. (+32) 2-2817004.

UNIT 1C—BANKING SECTOR
Head of Unit: Mariano Abad Menéndez; tel. (+32) 2-2815093.

Directorate 2—Budget, Tax and Regional Policy

Director: (vacant); tel. (+32) 2-2816383.

UNIT 2A—BUDGET AND FINANCIAL REGULATIONS
Head of Unit: Eva Veivo; tel. (+32) 2-2819588.

UNIT 2B—TAX POLICY, EXPORT CREDITS AND REGIONAL POLICY
Head of Unit: Andreas Strub; tel. (+32) 2-2818321.

Directorate 3—Competitiveness

Director: Marius Hirte; tel. (+32) 2-2819407.

UNIT 3A—INTERNAL MARKET, CONSUMER POLICY, BETTER REGULATION
Head of Unit: Bodil Nielsen; tel. (+32) 2-2816195.

UNIT 3B—COMPETITION, CUSTOMS UNION, COMPANY LAW, INTELLECTUAL PROPERTY, PUBLIC PROCUREMENT
Head of Unit: Thomas Brandtner; tel. (+32) 2-2817072.

UNIT 3C—EU 2020, INDUSTRY, SPACE, RESEARCH, INNOVATION
Head of Unit: Ilkka Saarilahti; tel. (+32) 2-2815524.

The Council's Committees and Working Parties

The Council is assisted in its work by a series of committees and working parties, the most important being the Committee of Permanent Representatives (Coreper), which prepares the Council's work and carries out any instructions given to it by the Council. The Committee meets in two parts—Deputy Permanent Representatives (Part I) and Ambassadors (Part II).

COMMITTEE OF PERMANENT REPRESENTATIVES—PART 1 (COREPER I)

Minister Plenipotentiary, Deputy Permanent Representative of Austria: Thomas Oberreiter. 30 ave de Cortenbergh, 1040 Brussels, Belgium; tel. (+32) 2-2345122; e-mail bruessel-ov@bmeia.gv.at.

Deputy Permanent Representative of Belgium: Jan Hoogmartens. 61–63 rue de la Loi, 1040 Brussels, Belgium; tel. (+32) 2-2332111; fax (+32) 2-2311075; e-mail dispatch.belgoeurop@diplobel.fed.be.

Ambassador, Deputy Permanent Representative of Bulgaria: Maria Koleva. 49 sq. Marie-Louise, 1000 Brussels, Belgium; tel. (+32) 2-2358300; fax (+32) 2-3749188; e-mail mission.brusselseu@bg-permrep.eu.

Ambassador, Deputy Permanent Representative of Croatia: Goran Štefanić. 50 ave des Arts, 1000 Brussels, Belgium; tel. (+32) 2-5075413; e-mail goran.stefanic@mvep.hr.

Ambassador, Deputy Permanent Representative of Cyprus: Olympia Neocleous. 61 ave de Cortenbergh, 1000 Brussels, Belgium; tel. (+32) 2-7404042; e-mail cy.perm.rep@mfa.gov.cy.

Ambassador, Deputy Permanent Representative of the Czech Republic: Jaroslav Zajíček. 15 rue Caroly, 1050 Brussels, Belgium; tel. (+32) 2-2139120; e-mail eu.brussels@embassy.mzv.cz.

Ambassador, Deputy Permanent Representative of Denmark: Vibeke Pasternak Jørgensen. 73 rue d'Arlon, 1040 Brussels, Belgium; tel. (+32) 2-2330811; fax (+32) 2-2309384; e-mail brurep@um.dk.

Ambassador, Deputy Permanent Representative of Estonia: Clyde Kull. 11–13 rue Guimard, 1040 Brussels, Belgium; tel. (+32) 2-2273910; fax (+32) 2-2273925; e-mail permrep.eu@mfa.ee.

Ambassador, Deputy Permanent Representative of Finland: Minna Kivimäki. 80 ave de Cortenbergh, 1000 Brussels, Belgium; tel. (+32) 2-2878411; fax (+32) 2-2878400; e-mail sanomat.eue@formin.fi.

Deputy Permanent Representative of France: Fabrice Dubreil. 14 Place de Louvain, 1000 Brussels, Belgium; tel. (+32) 2-2298211; fax (+32) 2-2298282; e-mail courrier.bruxelles-dfra@diplomatie.gouv.fr.

Ambassador, Deputy Permanent Representative of Germany: Peter Rösgen. 8–14 rue Jacques de Lalaing, 1040 Brussels, Belgium; tel. (+32) 2-7871000; fax (+32) 2-7872000; e-mail info@bruessel-eu.diplo.de.

Ambassador, Deputy Permanent Representative of Greece: Argyris Makris. 19–21 rue Jacques de Lalaing, 1040 Brussels, Belgium; tel. (+32) 2-5515611; e-mail mea.bruxelles@rp-grece.be.

Ambassador, Deputy Permanent Representative of Hungary: Tibor Stelbaczky. 92–98 rue de Trèves, 1040 Brussels, Belgium; tel. (+32) 2-2341205; fax (+32) 2-2340784; e-mail deputy.beu@kum.hu.

Ambassador, Deputy Permanent Representative of Ireland: Joe Hackett. 50 rue Froissart, 1040 Brussels, Belgium; tel. (+32) 2-2308580; fax (+32) 2-2303203; e-mail irlprb@dfa.ie.

Ambassador, Deputy Permanent Representative of Italy: Giovanni Pugliese. 7–15 rue du Marteau, 1000 Brussels, Belgium; tel. (+32) 2-2200411; fax (+32) 2-2200426; e-mail rpue@rpue.esteri.it.

Ambassador, Deputy Permanent Representative of Latvia: Alise Balode. 23 ave des Arts, 1000 Brussels, Belgium; tel. (+32) 2-2383203; fax (+32) 2-2383250; e-mail permrep.eu@mfa.gov.lv.

Ambassador-at-large, Deputy Permanent Representative of Lithuania: Robertas Rosinas. 41–43 rue Belliard, 1040 Brussels, Belgium; tel. (+32) 2-4019844; fax (+32) 2-7714597; e-mail office@eurep.mfa.lt.

Ambassador, Deputy Permanent Representative of Luxembourg: Mike Hentges. 75 ave de Cortenbergh, 1000 Brussels, Belgium; tel. (+32) 2-7375600; fax (+32) 2-7361429; e-mail secretariat@rpue.etat.lu.

Ambassador, Deputy Permanent Representative of Malta: Neil Kerr. 25 rue Archimède, 1000 Brussels, Belgium; tel. (+32) 2-3430195; fax (+32) 2-3430106; e-mail dpr.maltarep@gov.mt.

Minister Plenipotentiary, Deputy Permanent Representative of the Netherlands: Ronald van Roeden. 4–10 ave de Cortenbergh, 1040 Brussels, Belgium; tel. (+32) 2-6791508; fax (+32) 2-6791775; e-mail bre-gm@minbuza.nl.

First Counsellor, Deputy Permanent Representative of Poland: Sebastian Barkowski. 139 rue Stevin, 1000 Brussels, Belgium; tel. (+32) 2-7804200; fax (+32) 2-7804297; e-mail bebrustpe@msz.gov.pl.

Ambassador, Deputy Permanent Representative of Portugal: Pedro Lourtie. 12 ave de Cortenbergh, 1040 Brussels, Belgium; tel. (+32) 2-2864211; fax (+32) 2-2310026; e-mail reper@reper-portugal.be.

Minister Plenipotentiary, Deputy Permanent Representative of Romania: Cosmin Boiangiu. 12 rue Montoyer, 1000 Brussels, Belgium; tel. (+32) 2-7000640; fax (+32) 2-7000641; e-mail cosmin.boiangiu@rpro.eu.

Ambassador, Deputy Permanent Representative of Slovakia: Alexander Micovčin. 107 ave de Cortenbergh, 1000 Brussels, Belgium; tel. (+32) 2-7436811; fax (+32) 2-7436888; e-mail eu.brussels@mzv.sk.

Ambassador, Deputy Permanent Representative of Slovenia: Metka Ipavić. 44 rue du Commerce, 1000 Brussels, Belgium; tel. (+32) 2-2136300; fax (+32) 2-2136301; e-mail spbr@gov.si.

Ambassador, Deputy Permanent Representative of Spain: Juan Aristegui. 52 blvd du Régent, 1000 Brussels, Belgium; tel. (+32) 2-5098611; fax (+32) 2-5111940; e-mail reperue@reper.maec.es.

Ambassador, Deputy Permanent Representative of Sweden: Åsa Webber. 30 sq. de Meeûs, 1000 Brussels, Belgium; tel. (+32) 2-2895642; fax (+32) 2-2895600; e-mail asa.webber@gov.se.

Ambassador, Deputy Permanent Representative of the United Kingdom: Katrina Williams. 10 ave d'Auderghem, 1040 Brussels, Belgium; tel. (+32) 2-2878211; fax (+32) 2-2878900; e-mail ukrep@fco.gov.uk; internet www.ukrep.be.

COMMITTEE OF PERMANENT REPRESENTATIVES—PART 2 (COREPER II)

Ambassador Extraordinary and Plenipotentiary, Permanent Representative of Austria: Nikolaus Marschik. 30 ave de Cortenbergh, 1040 Brussels, Belgium; tel. (+32) 2-2345100; fax (+32) 2-2345300; e-mail bruessel-ov@bmeia.gv.at.

Ambassador Extraordinary and Plenipotentiary, Permanent Representative of Belgium: François Roux. 61–63 rue de la Loi, 1040 Brussels, Belgium; tel. (+32) 2-2332111; fax (+32) 2-2311075; e-mail dispatch.belgoeurop@diplobel.fed.be.

Ambassador Extraordinary and Plenipotentiary, Permanent Representative of Bulgaria: Dimiter Tzantchev. 49 sq. Marie-Louise, 1000 Brussels, Belgium; tel. (+32) 2-2358300; fax (+32) 2-23749188; e-mail mission.brusselseu@bg-permrep.eu.

Ambassador Extraordinary and Plenipotentiary, Permanent Representative of Croatia: Mato Škrabalo. 50 ave des Arts, 1000 Brussels, Belgium; tel. (+32) 2-25075411; fax (+32) 2-25075664; e-mail hr.pr@mvep.hr.

Ambassador Extraordinary and Plenipotentiary, Permanent Representative of Cyprus: Nicholas Emiliou. 61 ave de Cortenbergh, 1000 Brussels, Belgium; tel. (+32) 2-7395137; e-mail cy.perm.rep@mfa.gov.cy.

Ambassador Extraordinary and Plenipotentiary, Permanent Representative of the Czech Republic: Martin Povejsil. 15 rue Caroly, 1050 Brussels, Belgium; tel. (+32) 2-2139111; fax (+32) 2-2139186; e-mail eu.brussels@embassy.mzv.cz.

Ambassador Extraordinary and Plenipotentiary, Permanent Representative of Denmark: Kim Jørgensen. 73 rue d'Arlon, 1040 Brussels, Belgium; tel. (+32) 2-2330811; fax (+32) 2-2309384; e-mail brurep@um.dk.

Ambassador Extraordinary and Plenipotentiary, Permanent Representative of Estonia: Kaja Tael. 11–13 rue Guimard, 1040 Brussels, Belgium; tel. (+32) 2-2274312; fax (+32) 2-2274343; e-mail permrep.eu@mfa.ee.

Ambassador Extraordinary and Plenipotentiary, Permanent Representative of Finland: Marja Rislakki. 80 ave de Cortenbergh, 1000 Brussels, Belgium; tel. (+32) 2-2878411; fax (+32) 2-2878400; e-mail sanomat.eue@formin.fi.

Ambassador Extraordinary and Plenipotentiary, Permanent Representative of France: Pierre Sellal. 14 Place de Louvain, 1000 Brussels, Belgium; tel. (+32) 2-2298211; fax (+32) 2-2298282; e-mail courrier.bruxelles-dfra@diplomatie.gouv.fr; internet www.rpfrance-ue.org.

Ambassador Extraordinary and Plenipotentiary, Permanent Representative of Germany: Reinhard Silberberg. 8–14 rue Jacques de Lalaing, 1040 Brussels, Belgium; tel. (+32) 2-7871000; fax (+32) 2-7872000; e-mail info@bruessel-eu.diplo.de.

Ambassador Extraordinary and Plenipotentiary, Permanent Representative of Greece: Andreas Papastavrou. 19–21 rue Jacques de Lalaing, 1040 Brussels, Belgium; tel. (+32) 2-5515611; fax (+32) 2-5126951; e-mail mea.bruxelles@rp-grece.be.

Ambassador Extraordinary and Plenipotentiary, Permanent Representative of Hungary: Olivér Várhelyi. 92–98 rue de Trèves, 1040 Brussels, Belgium; tel. (+32) 2-2341203; fax (+32) 2-2340784; e-mail cor2.beu@mfa.gov.hu.

Ambassador Extraordinary and Plenipotentiary, Permanent Representative of Ireland: Declan Kelleher. 50 rue Froissart, 1040 Brussels, Belgium; tel. (+32) 2-2308580; fax (+32) 2-2303203; e-mail permanentrepresentativesoffice@dfa.ie.

Ambassador Extraordinary and Plenipotentiary, Permanent Representative of Italy: Maurizio Massari. 7–11 rue du Marteau, 1000 Brussels, Belgium; tel. (+32) 2-2200411; fax (+32) 2-2200426; e-mail rpue@rpue.esteri.it.

Ambassador Extraordinary and Plenipotentiary, Permanent Representative of Latvia: Sanita Pavļuta-Deslandes. 23 ave des Arts, Brussels, Belgium; tel. (+32) 2-2383100; fax (+32) 2-2383250; e-mail permrep.eu@mfa.gov.lv.

Ambassador Extraordinary and Plenipotentiary, Permanent Representative of Lithuania: Jovita Neliupšienė. 41–43 rue Belliard, 1040 Brussels, Belgium; tel. (+32) 2-24019830; fax (+32) 2-27714597; e-mail office@eurep.mfa.lt.

Ambassador Extraordinary and Plenipotentiary, Permanent Representative of Luxembourg: Georges Friden. 75 ave de Cortenbergh, 1000 Brussels, Belgium; tel. (+32) 2-7352060; fax (+32) 2-7361429; e-mail secretariat@mae.etat.lu.

Ambassador Extraordinary and Plenipotentiary, Permanent Representative of Malta: Marlene Bonnici. 25 rue Archimède, 1040 Brussels, Belgium; tel. (+32) 2-3430195; fax (+32) 2-3430106; e-mail pr.maltarep@gov.mt.

Ambassador Extraordinary and Plenipotentiary, Permanent Representative of the Netherlands: Robert de Groot. 4–10 ave de Cortenbergh, 1040 Brussels, Belgium; tel. (+32) 2-6791511; fax (+32) 2-6791795; e-mail bre-cdp@minbuza.nl.

Ambassador Extraordinary and Plenipotentiary, Permanent Representative of Poland: (vacant). 139 rue Stevin, 1000 Brussels, Belgium; tel. (+32) 2-7804200; fax (+32) 2-7804297; e-mail bebrustpe@msz.gov.pl.

Ambassador Extraordinary and Plenipotentiary, Permanent Representative of Portugal: Nuno Brito. 12 ave de Cortenbergh, 1040 Brussels, Belgium; tel. (+32) 2-2864211; fax (+32) 2-2310026; e-mail reper@reper-portugal.be.

Ambassador Extraordinary and Plenipotentiary, Permanent Representative of Romania: Luminiţa Teodora Odobescu. 12 rue Montoyer, 1000 Brussels, tel. (+32) 2-7000640; fax (+32) 2-7000641; e-mail bru@rpro.eu.

Ambassador Extraordinary and Plenipotentiary, Permanent Representative of Slovakia: Peter Javorčik. 79 ave de Cortenbergh, 1000 Brussels, Belgium; tel. (+32) 2-7436811; fax (+32) 2-7436888; e-mail eu.brussels@mzv.sk.

Ambassador Extraordinary and Plenipotentiary, Permanent Representative of Slovenia: Janez Lenarčič. 44 rue du Commerce, 1000 Brussels, Belgium; tel. (+32) 2-2136300; fax (+32) 2-2136301; e-mail spbr@gov.si.

Ambassador Extraordinary and Plenipotentiary, Permanent Representative of Spain: Pablo García-Berdoy. 52 blvd du Régent, 1000 Brussels, Belgium.

Ambassador Extraordinary and Plenipotentiary, Permanent Representative of Sweden: Lars Danielsson. 30 sq. de Meeûs, 1000 Brussels, Belgium; tel. (+32) 2-2895645; fax (+32) 2-2895600; e-mail lars.danielsson@gov.se.

Ambassador Extraordinary and Plenipotentiary, Permanent Representative of the United Kingdom: Tim Barrow. 10 ave d'Auderghem, 1040 Brussels, Belgium; tel. (+32) 2-2878211; fax (+32) 2-2878900; e-mail ukrep@fco.gov.uk.

ACP-EU Council

ACP-EU INSTITUTIONS

The ACP (African Caribbean and Pacific) states are:

Angola
Antigua and Barbuda
Bahamas
Barbados
Belize
Benin
Botswana
Burkina Faso
Burundi
Cabo Verde
Cameroon
Central African Republic
Chad
Comoros
Congo, Democratic Republic
Congo, Republic
Cook Islands
Côte d'Ivoire
Cuba
Djibouti
Dominica
Dominican Republic
Equatorial Guinea
Eritrea
Ethiopia
Fiji
Gabon
The Gambia
Ghana
Grenada
Guinea
Guinea-Bissau
Guyana
Haiti
Jamaica
Kenya
Kiribati
Lesotho
Liberia
Madagascar
Malawi
Mali
Marshall Islands
Mauritania
Mauritius
Federated States of Micronesia
Mozambique
Namibia
Nauru
Niger
Nigeria
Niue
Palau
Papua New Guinea
Rwanda
Saint Christopher and Nevis
Saint Lucia
Saint Vincent and the Grenadines
Samoa
São Tomé e Príncipe
Senegal
Seychelles
Sierra Leone
Solomon Islands
Somalia
South Africa
Sudan
Suriname
Swaziland
Tanzania
Timor-Leste
Togo
Tonga
Trinidad and Tobago
Tuvalu
Uganda
Vanuatu
Zambia
Zimbabwe

General Secretariat of the ACP-EU Council of Ministers

rue de la Loi 175, 1048 Brussels, Belgium; tel. (+32) 2-2816111; fax (+32) 2-2858411; e-mail info@acp.int; internet www.acp.int.

Co-Secretaries (from each of the two groups) run the Secretariat of the ACP-EU Council of Ministers, the Committee of Ambassadors, Committees, Sub-Committees and the Permanent Joint Group:

Dr Patrick Ignatius Gomes (Sec.-Gen. of the ACP Group of States): Gen. Secretariat of the ACP Group of States, 451 ave Georges Henri, 1200 Brussels, Belgium; tel. (+32) 2-7430600; fax (+32) 2-7355573; e-mail info@acp.int.

Council of Ministers

EU members comprise members of the Council of the European Union and members of the European Commission; ACP members comprise one minister from each signatory state; one Co-President from each of the two groups; meets twice annually; Presidency of the Council of Ministers is held by the EU from 1 Oct. to 31 March (held by the Member State holding the Presidency of the EU) and by the ACP from 1 April to 30 Sep. (ACP Presidencies are chosen on a regional basis and are held from 1 Feb. to 31 July and from 1 Aug. to 31 Jan.).

Committee of Ambassadors

EU members comprise the permanent representative of each EU member state and a representative of the European Commission; ACP members comprise the head of mission to the European Union from each signatory state; chairmanship alternates between the two groups; meets at least every six months; Presidency of the Committee of Ambassadors is held by the EU from 1 Oct. to 31 March and by the ACP from 1 April to 30 Sept.

Joint Parliamentary Assembly

EU and ACP are equally represented; attended by parliamentary delegates from each of the ACP countries and an equal number of members of the European Parliament; one co-chair from each group; meets twice a year.

Centre for the Development of Enterprise (CDE)

ave Edmond Van Nieuwenhuyse 2, 1160 Brussels, Belgium; tel. (+32) 2-6791811; fax (+32) 2-6752603; e-mail info@cde.int; internet www.cde.int; f 1977 to encourage and support the creation, expansion and restructuring of industrial companies (mainly in the fields of manufacturing and agro-industry) in the ACP states by promoting co-operation between ACP and European companies, in the form of financial, technical or commercial partnerships, management contracts, licensing or franchise agreements, sub-contracts, etc.; financial resources come mainly from the European Development Fund (EDF); manages the Pro€Invest programme; Dir Ilse Van de Mierop.

Technical Centre for Agricultural and Rural Co-operation (CTA)

Agro Business Park 2, Postbus 380, 6708 PW Wageningen, Netherlands; tel. (+31 317) 467100; fax (+31 317) 460067; e-mail info@cta.int; internet www.cta.int; f 1984 to provide ACP states with better access to information, research, training and innovations in agricultural development and extension; under the authority of the Committee of Ambassadors; Dir Michael Hailu.

EUROPEAN COUNCIL

175 rue de la Loi, 1048 Brussels, Belgium; tel. (+32) 2-2816111; fax (+32) 2-2816934; internet www.consilium.europa.eu/en/european-council

President of the European Council

President of the European Council: Donald Tusk.

PRESIDENT'S CABINET

Head of Cabinet: Piotr Serafin.

Deputy Head of Cabinet: André Gillissen.

Senior Political and Communication Adviser: Paweł Graś.

Special Adviser on Energy Union: Łukasz Koliński.

Adviser: Emilia Surowska.

Head of Private Office: Łukasz Broniewski.

Horizontal Team

Advisers: Katarzyna Smyk, Paweł Karbownik.

Foreign Policy Team

Chief Foreign Policy Adviser: Riina Kionka.

Senior Adviser: Carl Hartzell.

Advisers: Zusana Michalcová Sutiaková, Leila Brahimi, Alina Butuliga.

Economic Team

Chief Economic Adviser: João Nogueira Martíns.

Senior Adviser: Alfredo Panarella.

Advisers: Christina Jordan, Wouter Coussens.

Press and Communication Team

Spokesperson: Preben Aamann.

Speechwriter: Hugo Brady.

Adviser: Beata Turska.

EUROPEAN COMMISSION

THE COMMISSIONERS

The Commission is the executive of the European Union. It currently has 28 members and is appointed for a five-year period.

President: Jean-Claude Juncker.

High Representative of the Union for Foreign Affairs and Security Policy, and Vice-President: Federica Mogherini.

First Vice-President (Better Regulation, Inter-institutional Relations, the Rule of Law, the Charter of Fundamental Rights): Frans Timmermans.

Vice-President (Digital Single Market): Andrus Ansip.

Vice-President (Energy Union): Marcos Šefčovič.

Vice-President (Euro and Social Dialogue) and Member of the Commission (Financial Stability, Financial Services and Capital Markets Union): Valdis Dombrovskis.

Vice-President (Jobs, Growth, Investment and Competitiveness): Jyrki Katainen.

Member of the Commission (Budget and Human Resources): Günther Oettinger.

Member of the Commission (European Neighbourhood Policy and Enlargement Negotiations): Johannes Hahn.

Member of the Commission (Trade): Cecilia Malmström.

Member of the Commission (International Co-operation and Development): Neven Mimica.

Member of the Commission (Climate Action and Energy): Miguel Arias Cañete.

Member of the Commission (Environment, Maritime Affairs and Fisheries): Karmenu Vella.

Member of the Commission (Health and Food Safety): Vytenis Andriukaitis.

Member of the Commission (Migration, Home Affairs and Citizenship): Dimitris Avramopoulos.

Member of the Commission (Employment, Social Affairs, Skills and Labour Mobility): Marianne Thyssen.

Member of the Commission (Economic and Financial Affairs, Taxation and Customs): Pierre Moscovici.

Member of the Commission (Humanitarian Aid and Crisis Management): Christos Stylianides.

Member of the Commission (Agriculture and Rural Development): Phil Hogan.

Member of the Commission (Security Union): Julian King.

Member of the Commission (Transport): Violeta Bulc.

Member of the Commission (Internal Market, Industry, Entrepreneurship and SMEs): Elżbieta Bieńkowska.

Member of the Commission (Justice, Consumers and Gender Equality): Věra Jourová.

Member of the Commission (Education, Culture, Youth and Sport): Tibor Navracsics.

Member of the Commission (Regional Policy): Corina Crețu.

Member of the Commission (Competition): Margrethe Vestager.

Member of the Commission (Research, Science and Innovation): Carlos Moedas.

Member of the Commission (Digital Economy and Society): Mariya Gabriel.

SECRETARIAT-GENERAL OF THE COMMISSION

200 rue de la Loi, 1049 Brussels, Belgium; tel. (+32) 2-2991111; internet ec.europa.eu/info/departments/secretariat-general

Secretary-General: Alexander Italiener; tel. (+32) 2-2994393.

Assistant to the Secretary-General: Tom Snels; tel. (+32) 2-2964058.

Principal Adviser Institutional and Administrative Policies

Principal Adviser: Hubert Szlaszewski; tel. (+32) 2-2995171.

Directorate R—Resources

Director: Tatjana Verrier; tel. (+32) 2-2992535.

HR BUSINESS CORRESPONDENT, FINANCE, CORPORATE TRAINING

Head of Unit: Christopher Curran; tel. (+32) 2-2962407.

MAIL MANAGEMENT

Head of Unit: Viviane D'udekem D'Acoz; tel. (+32) 2-2961919.

INFORMATION TECHNOLOGY

Head of Unit: Martin Gritsch; tel. (+32) 2-2959467.

Directorate A—Decision-Making Process

Director: Jordi Ayet Puigarnau; tel. (+32) 2-2951528.

ADVICE AND DEVELOPMENT

Head of Unit: Martine Deprez; tel. (+32) 2-2962236.

ORAL PROCEDURE

Head of Unit: Ghislaine Allouis-Le Lostec; tel. (+32) 2-2990979.

WRITTEN, EMPOWERMENT AND DELEGATION PROCEDURE, EXTERNAL TRANSMISSION

Head of Unit: Robert Andrecs; tel. (+32) 2-2956072.

BUSINESS CONTINUITY

Head of Unit: Florin Urseanu; tel. (+32) 2-2962666.

LEGAL SERVICE

200 rue de la Loi, 1049 Brussels, Belgium; tel. (+32) 2-2991111; internet ec.europa.eu/info/departments/legal-service

Director-General: Luís Romero Requena; tel. (+32) 2-2995150.

Deputy Director-General in charge of Quality of Legislation (Directorate K), Infringements and Information: Karen Banks; tel. (+32) 2-2952824.

Head of HR Business Correspondent, IT and Finance Unit: William O'Leary; tel. (+32) 2-2966221.

Legal Adviser: Bernhard Schima; tel. (+32) 2-2960372.

Legal Adviser: Bernd Martenczuk; tel. (+32) 2-2965058.

Principal Adviser for Migration Issues and Strategic Horizontal Matters: Clemens Ladenburger; tel. (+32) 2-2952444.

Reporting directly to the Deputy Director-General in charge of Quality of Legislation (Directorate K), Infringements and Information

K—LEG Team (Quality of Legislation)

Principal Legal Adviser (acting): Karen Banks; tel. (+32) 2-2962043.

MAREC—PROCUREMENT AND RECOVERIES

Head of Unit (acting): Olivier Verheecke; tel. (+32) 2-2986954.

B—AGRI Team (Agriculture and Fisheries)

Principal Legal Adviser: Fernando Castillo De La Torre; tel. (+32) 2-2960064.

Legal Adviser: André Bouquet; tel. (+32) 2-2952541.

Legal Adviser: Alexandre Xavier Pierre Lewis; tel. (+32) 2-2968749.

Legal Adviser: Dimitrios Triantafyllou; tel. (+32) 2-2961570.

C—AIDE Team (State Aid and Dumping)

Principal Legal Adviser: Paolo Stancanelli; tel. (+32) 2-2961808.

Legal Adviser: Bruno Stromsky; tel. (+32) 2-2951705.

D—BUDG Team (Budget, Customs, Taxation)

Principal Legal Adviser: Richard Lyal; tel. (+32) 2-2954814.

E—CONC Team (Competition)

Principal Legal Adviser: Theofanis Christoforou; tel. (+32) 2-2950168.

F—INST Team (Institutions)

Principal Legal Adviser: Pieter Van Nuffel; tel. (+32) 2-2950029.

Legal Adviser: Hannes Kraemer; tel. (+32) 2-2950686.

Legal Adviser: Maria-Isabel Martínez Del Peral; tel. (+32) 2-2965039.

G—JLS Team (Justice, Freedom and Security, Private Law and Criminal Law)

Principal Legal Adviser: Enrico Traversa; tel. (+32) 2-2955921.

Legal Adviser: Maria Condou; tel. (+32) 2-2958342.

Legal Adviser: Dominique Maidani; tel. (+32) 2-2994913.

Legal Adviser: Elisabetta Montaguti; tel. (+32) 2-2952972.

Legal Adviser: Rudi Troosters; tel. (+32) 2-2954109.

Legal Adviser: Michael Wilderspin; tel. (+32) 2-2966713.

H—MIME Team (Internal Market for Goods, Energy including Euratom, Enterprise, Customs Union, Environment)

Principal Legal Adviser: Eva Kruzikova; tel. (+32) 2-2990785.

I—CFSP Team (CFSP and External Relations)

Principal Legal Adviser: Lucio Gussetti; tel. (+32) 2-2964168.

Legal Adviser: Antonio Aresu; tel. (+32) 2-2953309.

Legal Adviser: Esa Paasivirta; tel. (+32) 2-2961769.

J—SOC Team (Employment and Social Affairs, Education and Culture, Health and Consumer Protection)

Principal Legal Adviser: Marc van Hoof; tel. (+32) 2-2950625.

Legal Adviser: Denis Martin; tel. (+32) 2-2965296.

Legal Adviser: Michel van Beek; tel. (+32) 2-2951990.

L—TRADE Team (Trade Policy and World Trade Organization)

Principal Legal Adviser: Ulrich Woelker; tel. (+32) 2-2962268.

M—Team ECS (European Civil Service Law)

Principal Legal Adviser: Laura Pignataro; tel. (+32) 2-2954905.

N—Team EEI (Eurozone and Economic Issues)

Principal Legal Adviser: Jean-Paul Keppenne; tel. (+32) 2-2998377.

DG COMM—DIRECTORATE-GENERAL FOR COMMUNICATION

56 rue de la Loi, 1049 Brussels, Belgium; tel. (+32) 2-2991111; internet ec.europa.eu/info/departments/communication

Director-General: Timo Pesonen; tel. (+32) 2-2957995.

Assistant to the Director-General: Carsten Lietz; tel. (+32) 2-2954119.

Deputy Director-General: Sixtine Bouygues; tel. (+32) 2-2951718.

SPOKESPERSON'S SERVICE

European Commission Chief Spokesperson: Margaritis Schinas; tel. (+32) 2-2960524.

European Commission Deputy Chief Spokesperson: Mina Alexandrova Andreeva; tel. (+32) 2-2991382.

European Commission Deputy Chief Spokesperson: Alexander Winterstein; tel. (+32) 2-2993265.

Jobs, Growth and Investment, EMU and the European Semester

Head of Unit, Co-ordinating Spokesperson: Annika Breidthardt; tel. (+32) 2-2956153.

Head of Unit, Co-ordinating Spokesperson: Natasha Bertaud; tel. (+32) 2-2967456.

Directorate A—Strategy and Corporate Communication

Director: Mikel Landabaso Alvarez; tel. (+32) 2-2965256.

STRATEGIC COMMUNICATION
Head of Unit: Tina Zournatzi; tel. (+32) 2-2956092.

CORPORATE SERVICES
Head of Unit: Jens Mester; tel. (+32) 2-2963973.

MEDIA MONITORING AND ANALYSIS
Head of Unit (acting): Maria Letizia Albergati; tel. (+32) 2-2950481.

AUDIOVISUAL SERVICES
Head of Unit: Nathalie Davies; tel. (+32) 2-2964933.

EUROPA WEBSITE
Head of Unit: Krisztina Nagy; tel. (+32) 2-2988663.

Directorate B—Representations

Director: Pia Ahrenkilde Hansen; tel. (+32) 2-2953070.

COUNTRY STRATEGIES AND CAPACITY BUILDING
Head of Unit (acting): Paavo Makinen; tel. (+32) 2-2986547.

POLITICAL INTELLIGENCE AND COMMUNICATION ACTIONS
Head of Unit: Jan Michal; tel. (+32) 2-2964032.

REPRESENTATIONS IN THE MEMBER STATES

Athens, Greece

Head of Representation: Panayotis Carvounis; tel. (+210) 7272000.

Berlin, Germany

Head of Representation: Richard Kuehnel; tel. (+49 30) 2-2802000.

Bratislava, Slovakia

Head of Representation: Dusan Chrenek; tel. (+421 2) 5443-1718.

Brussels, Belgium

Head of Representation: Joseph Jamar; tel. (+32) 2-2952082.

Bucharest, Romania

Head of Representation: Angela Cristea; tel. (+40 21) 2035400.

Budapest, Hungary

Head of Representation: Gabor Zupko; tel. (+36) 1-2099710.

Copenhagen, Denmark

Head of Representation: Stina Soewarta; tel. (+45) 33-41-40-10.

Dublin, Ireland

Head of Representation: Gerard Kiely; tel. (+353) 1-6341111.

The Hague, the Netherlands

Head of Representation: Peter Bekx; tel. (+31 70) 3135300.

Helsinki, Finland

Head of Representation: Sari Artjoki; tel. (+358 9) 62265450.

Lisbon, Portugal

Head of Representation: Sofia Alves; tel. (+351) 213509815.

Ljubljana, Slovenia

Head of Representation: Zoran Stancic; tel. (+386 1) 2528800.

London, United Kingdom

Head of Representation (acting): Christine Dalby; tel. (+44 20) 7973-1931.

Luxembourg, Luxembourg

Head of Representation: Yuriko Backes; tel. (+352) 430132925.

Madrid, Spain

Head of Representation: Aranzazu Beristain; tel. (+34) 914238030.

Nicosia, Cyprus

Head of Representation: Georgios Markopouliotis; tel. (+357) 22817770.

Paris, France

Head of Representation: Isabelle Jegouzo; tel. (+33) 1-40-63-38-21.

Prague, Czech Republic

Head of Representation (acting): Dana Kovarikova; tel. (+420) 2-55708244.

Rīga, Latvia

Head of Representation: Inna Steinbuka; tel. (+371) 67085400.

Rome, Italy

Head of Representation: Beatrice Covassi; tel. (+39) 06-699991.

Sofia, Bulgaria

Head of Representation: Ognian Zlatev; tel. (+35) 9-29335252.

Stockholm, Sweden

Head of Representation: Katarina Areskoug; tel. (+46 8) 56-24-44-11.

Tallinn, Estonia

Head of Representation: Keit Kasemets; tel. (+372) 6264400.

Valletta, Malta

Head of Representation: Elena Grech; tel. (+356) 23425000.

Vienna, Austria

Head of Representation: Jörg Wojahn; tel. (+43 1) 516180.

Vilnius, Lithuania

Head of Representation: Arnoldas Pranckevicius; tel. (+370 523) 13191.

Warsaw, Poland

Head of Representation: Marek Prawda; tel. (+48) 22-5568989.

Zagreb, Croatia

Head of Representation: Branko Baricević; tel. (+385) 1-4681300.

Directorate C—Communication with Citizens

Director: Viviane Hoffman; tel. (+32) 2-2960305.

Adviser: Jaime Andreu Romeo; tel. (+32) 2-2999252.

CITIZENS' INFORMATION
Head of Unit: Ierotheos Papadopoulos; tel. (+32) 2-2956239.

CITIZENS' DIALOGUES
Head of Unit: Joachim Ott; tel. (+32) 2-2961471.

CITIZENS' CONTACT
Head of Unit (acting): Marie-Thérèse Duffy-Haeusler; tel. (+32) 2-2955212.

VISITORS' CENTRE
Head of Unit: Benoît Woringer; tel. (+32) 2-2963498.

Directorate D—Resources

Director: Fabrizia De Rosa; tel. (+32) 2-2993739.

BUDGET, ACCOUNTING AND EVALUATION
Head of Unit: Sonja Ziemer; tel. (+32) 2-2990748.

INFRASTRUCTURE, SECURITY AND DOCUMENT MANAGEMENT
Head of Unit: Marc Sievers; tel. (+32) 2-2993666.

FINANCE AND CONTROLS
Head of Unit: Philippe Cattoir; tel. (+32) 2-2955692.

TECHNOLOGIES
Head of Unit: Jean-Jacques Cavez; tel. (+32) 2-2961336.

LOGISTICS
Head of Unit (acting): Carsten Lietz; tel. (+32) 2-2954119.

EUROPEAN POLITICAL STRATEGY CENTRE (EPSC)

200 rue de la Loi, 1049 Brussels, Belgium; internet ec.europa.eu/info/departments/european-political-strategy-centre

Head of EPSC: Ann Mettler; tel. (+32) 2-2962328.

Principal Adviser for European Social Policy: Patrick Develtere; tel. (+32) 2-2967476.

Deputy Head of EPSC 1

Deputy Head: Mihnea Ioan Motoc; tel. (+32) 2-2963042.

INSTITUTIONAL TEAM
Legal Adviser: Christian Calliess; tel. (+32) 2-2986984.

FOREIGN AFFAIRS TEAM
Representative: Sylvia Hartleif; tel. (+32) 2-2966091.

Deputy Head of EPSC 2

Deputy Head of EPSC: Pawel Swieboda; tel. (+32) 2-2966097.

BC—MANAGEMENT AND RESOURCES UNIT
Head of Management and Resource Unit of the EPSC: Agnieszka Skuratowicz; tel. (+32) 2-2965082.

OUTREACH AND COMMUNICATION TEAM
Representative: Elisabeth Ardaillon-Poirier; tel. (+32) 2-2981625.

TF 50—ARTICLE 50 TASK FORCE

200 rue de la Loi, 1049 Brussels, Belgium

Chief Negotiatior—Task Force for the Preparation and Conduct of the Negotiations with the United Kingdom under Article 50 TEU: Michel Barnier; tel. (+32) 2-2994060.

Principal Adviser for Strategy, Co-ordination and Communication (acting): Stephanie Riso; tel. (+32) 2-2967476.

DG ECFIN—DIRECTORATE-GENERAL FOR ECONOMIC AND FINANCIAL AFFAIRS

170 rue de la Loi, 1049 Brussels, Belgium; tel. (+32) 2-2991111; internet ec.europa.eu/info/departments/economic-and-financial-affairs

Director-General: Marco Buti; tel. (+32) 2-2962246; fax (+32) 2-2998497.

Assistant to the Director-General: Angela D'Elia; tel. (+32) 2-2972650.

Assistant to the Director-General: Alexandr Hobza; tel. (+32) 2-2986658.

Deputy Director-General, responsible for Directorates C, D, F and G: Servaas Deroose; tel. (+32) 2-2994375.

Deputy Director-General, responsible for Directorates B, E and L: Kerstin Jorna; tel. (+32) 2-2961326.

Directorate A—Policy, Strategy and Communication

Director: Jose Eduardo Leandro; tel. (+32) 2-2995430.

POLICY AND ECONOMIC SURVEILLANCE
Head of Unit: Jakob Wegener Friis; tel. (+32) 2-2984832.

EMU DEEPENING AND MACROECONOMY OF THE EURO AREA
Head of Unit: Gabriele Giudice; tel. (+32) 2-2963654.

ECONOMIC SITUATION, FORECASTS, BUSINESS AND CONSUMER SURVEYS
Head of Unit: Björn Döhring; tel. (+32) 2-2998160.

INTER-INSTITUTIONAL RELATIONS AND COMMUNICATION
Head of Unit: Philip Tod; tel. (+32) 2-2920811.

Directorate C—Fiscal Policy and Policy Mix

Director: Lucio Pench; tel. (+32) 2-2993433.

Reporting to the Director

Adviser: Nicolas Vincent Carnot; tel. (+32) 2-2969021.

FISCAL POLICY AND SURVEILLANCE
Head of Unit: Gilles Mourre; tel. (+32) 2-2963225.

European Commission

SUSTAINABILITY OF PUBLIC FINANCES
Head of Unit: Giuseppe Carone; tel. (+32) 2-2992295.

MONETARY POLICY, EXCHANGE RATE POLICY OF THE EURO AREA, ERM II AND EURO ADOPTION
Head of Unit: Eric Ruscher; tel. (+32) 2-2966488.

FISCAL GOVERNANCE
Head of Unit: Stefan Ciobanu; tel. (+32) 2-2990092.

EURO PROTECTION AND EURO CASH
Head of Unit: Johan Khouw; tel. (+32) 2-2995946.

Directorate D—International Economic and Financial Relations, Global Governance
Director: Elena Flores; tel. (+32) 2-2993461.
Adviser: Heinz Scherrer; tel. (+32) 2-2957914.

CANDIDATE COUNTRIES AND PRE-CANDIDATE COUNTRIES
Head of Unit: Uwe Stamm; tel. (+32) 2-2955813.

NEIGHBOURHOOD COUNTRIES—MACROFINANCIAL ASSISTANCE
Head of Unit: Heliodoro Temprano Arroyo; tel. (+32) 2-2961858.

IMF AND G-GROUPS
Head of Unit: Santiago Loranca Garcia; tel. (+32) 2-2966800.

GLOBAL ECONOMY
Head of Unit: Norbert Wunner; tel. (+32) 2-2953283.

Directorate F—Economies of Member States I
Director: Manfred Bergmann; tel. (+32) 2-2993479.
Economic Adviser: Peter Weiss; tel. (+32) 2-2954350.

GERMANY, AUSTRIA, CYPRUS
Head of Unit: Moises Orellana; tel. (+32) 2-2969933.

GREECE
Head of Unit: Paul Kutos; tel. (+32) 2-2960923.

ESTONIA, LATVIA, LITHUANIA, THE NETHERLANDS
Head of Unit: Heinz Jansen; tel. (+32) 2-2953894.

SPAIN, CROATIA
Head of Unit: Laura Bardone; tel. (+32) 2-2967436.

Directorate G—Economies of Member States II
Director: Carlos Martínez Mongay; tel. (+32) 2-2961228.
Adviser: Martin Hallet; tel. (+32) 2-2993438.

FRANCE, BELGIUM, LUXEMBOURG
Head of Unit (acting): Javier Yaniz Igal; tel. (+32) 2-2966926.

CZECH REPUBLIC, SLOVAKIA, UNITED KINGDOM
Head of Unit (acting): Florian Woehlbier; tel. (+32) 2-2984123.

PORTUGAL, DENMARK, IRELAND
Head of Unit: Christian Weise; tel. (+32) 2-2984327.

Directorate B—Investment, Growth and Structural Reforms
Director: Mary Veronica Tovsak Pleterski; tel. (+32) 2-2952034.
Senior Adviser: Karl Pichelmann; tel. (+32) 2-2993365.

MACROECONOMIC IMBALANCES AND ADJUSTMENT
Head of Unit: Alessandro Turrini; tel. (+32) 2-2995072.

ASSESSMENT AND BENCHMARKING OF NATIONAL REFORMS
Head of Unit: Emmanuelle Maincent; tel. (+32) 2-2990654.

MODELS AND DATABASES
Head of Unit: Werner Röger; tel. (+32) 2-2993362.

IMPACT OF EU POLICIES ON NATIONAL ECONOMIES
Head of Unit: Andrea Mairate; tel. (+32) 2-2950298.

Directorate E—Economies of the Member States III
Director: Istvan Pal Szekely; tel. (+32) 2-2958674.

ITALY, MALTA, POLAND
Head of Unit: Marie Donnay; tel. (+32) 2-2965308.

FINLAND, HUNGARY, SLOVENIA
Head of Unit: Outi Slotboom; tel. (+32) 2-2967296.

BULGARIA, ROMANIA, SWEDEN
Head of Unit: Isabel Grilo; tel. (+32) 2-2951502.

Directorate L—Treasury and Financial Operations
Director: Benjamin Angel; tel. (+352) 430135263.

CO-ORDINATION WITH THE EIB GROUP, THE EBRD AND THE INTERNATIONAL FINANCIAL INSTITUTIONS
Head of Unit: Anna Krzyzanowska; tel. (+352) 430133453.

FINANCING OF INNOVATION, COMPETITIVENESS AND EMPLOYMENT POLICIES
Head of Unit: Merete Clausen; tel. (+352) 430134310.

FINANCING OF CLIMATE CHANGE, INFRASTRUCTURE POLICIES AND EURATOM
Head of Unit: Giorgio Chiarion Casoni; tel. (+352) 430136404.

BORROWING, LENDING, ACCOUNTING AND BACK OFFICE
Head of Unit: Jean-Pierre Raes; tel. (+352) 430130070.

TREASURY AND ASSET MANAGEMENT
Head of Unit: Patrick Steimer; tel. (+352) 430136301.

STABILITY MECHANISMS AND LEGAL AFFAIRS
Head of Unit: Irmantas Šimonis; tel. (+352) 430130213.

Directorate R—Resources
Director: Michaela Di Bucci; tel. (+32) 2-2996284.
Adviser: Francesco Contesso; tel. (+32) 2-2995965.
Adviser: Johan Verhaeven; tel. (+32) 2-2993443.

HR BUSINESS CORRESPONDENT, BUSINESS CONTINUITY AND CONTROL
Head of Unit: Linda Rowan; tel. (+32) 2-2992289.

FINANCE

Head of Unit: Henrik Kersting; tel. (+32) 2-2964900.

MANAGEMENT OF IT RESOURCES

Head of Unit: Tomek Pietrzak; tel. (+32) 2-2994392.

DG GROW—DIRECTORATE-GENERAL FOR INTERNAL MARKET, INDUSTRY, ENTREPRENEURSHIP AND SMEs

45 ave d'Auderghem, 1049 Brussels, Belgium; tel. (+32) 2-2991111; fax (+32) 2-2969930; internet ec.europa.eu/info/departments/internal-market-industry-entrepreneurship-and-smes

Director-General: Lowri Evans; tel. (+32) 2-2965029.

Deputy Director-General 1, responsible for Directorates B, C, D and F: Antti Ilmari Peltomaki; tel. (+32) 2-2952847.

Deputy Director-General 2, responsible for Directorates E, G, H and Unit B4: Irmfried Schwimann; tel. (+32) 2-2967002.

Deputy Director-General 3, responsible for Directorates I and J: Pierre Delsaux; tel. (+32) 2-2965472.

Directorate R—Resources

Director: Valentina Superti; tel. (+32) 2-2965403.

FINANCIAL RESOURCES AND INTERNAL CONTROL

Head of Unit: Maarit Viljanen; tel. (+32) 2-2996306.

BUSINESS CONTINUITY, SECURITY AND ADMINISTRATIVE CO-ORDINATION

Head of Unit: Alessandro Buttice; tel. (+32) 2-2965425.

INFORMATION SYSTEMS FOR GROWTH

Informatics Resource Manager: Konstantin Pashev; tel. (+32) 2-2984687.

SINGLE MARKET SERVICE CENTRE

Head of Unit: Laurence De Richemont; tel. (+32) 2-2951996.

Directorate A—Competitiveness and European Semester

Director: Eric Mamer; tel. (+32) 2-2994073.

COMMUNICATION, ACCESS TO DOCUMENTS AND DOCUMENT MANAGEMENT

Head of Unit: Bonifacio García Porras; tel. (+32) 2-2968721.

EUROPEAN SEMESTER AND COMPETITIVENESS OF MEMBER STATES

Head of Unit: Francisco Caballero Sanz; tel. (+32) 2-2951168.

INTER-INSTITUTIONAL RELATIONS

Head of Unit: Stéphane Lebrun; tel. (+32) 2-2962530.

INTERNATIONAL AFFAIRS

Head of Unit (acting): Christos Kyriatzis; tel. (+32) 2-2961049.

Directorate B—Single Market Policy, Regulation and Implementation

Director: Joaquim Nunes De Almeida; tel. (+32) 2-2955428.

SINGLE MARKET POLICY, MUTUAL RECOGNITION AND SURVEILLANCE

Head of Unit: Hans Ingels; tel. (+32) 2-2966441.

PREVENTION OF TECHNICAL BARRIERS

Head of Unit: Giuseppe Casella; tel. (+32) 2-2956396.

STANDARDS FOR GROWTH

Head of Unit: Radek Maly; tel. (+32) 2-2920868.

ENFORCEMENT OF THE INTERNAL MARKET

Head of Unit: Maciej Górka; tel. (+32) 2-2954714.

Directorate C—Industrial Transformation and Advanced Value Chains

Director: Gwenole Cozigou; tel. (+32) 2-2951304.

Adviser: Victoria Petrova; tel. (+32) 2-2965732.

CLEAN TECHNOLOGIES AND PRODUCTS

Head of Unit: Fulvia Raffaelli; tel. (+32) 2-29-59409.

RESOURCE EFFICIENCY AND RAW MATERIALS

Head of Unit: Mattia Pellegrini; tel. (+32) 2-2954138.

ADVANCED ENGINEERING AND MANUFACTURING SYSTEMS

Head of Unit (acting): Birgit Weidel; tel. (+32) 2-2986931.

AUTOMOTIVE AND MOBILITY INDUSTRIES

Head of Unit: Joanna Szychowska; tel. (+32) 2-2988632.

Directorate D—Consumer, Environmental and Health Technologies

Director: Carlo Pettinelli; tel. (+32) 2-2994037.

Adviser: Renate Weissenhorn; tel. (+32) 2-2952014.

REACH

Head of Unit: Michael Flueh; tel. (+32) 2-2992257.

CHEMICALS

Head of Unit: Luisa Prista; tel. (+32) 2-2961598.

BIOTECHNOLOGY AND FOOD SUPPLY CHAIN

Head of Unit: Stefano Soro; tel. (+32) 2-2967543.

HEALTH TECHNOLOGY AND COSMETICS

Head of Unit: Salvatore D'Acunto; tel. (+32) 2-2950798.

Directorate E—Modernization of the Single Market

Director: Hubert Gambs; tel. (+32) 2-2993990.

SERVICE POLICY FOR CONSUMERS

Head of Unit: Robert Strauss; tel. (+32) 2-2960531.

PUBLIC INTEREST SERVICES

Head of Unit: Raphael Goulet; tel. (+32) 2-2992470.

DIGITALIZATION OF THE SINGLE MARKET

Head of Unit: Marian Grubben; tel. (+32) 2-2990079.

BUSINESS-TO-BUSINESS SERVICES

Head of Unit: Maria Rehbinder; tel. (+32) 2-2990007.

PROFESSIONAL QUALIFICATIONS AND SKILLS
Head of Unit: Martin Frohn; tel. (+32) 2-2996420.

Directorate F—Innovation and Advanced Manufacturing

Director: Slawomir Tokarski; tel. (+32) 2-2988630.

Reporting to the Director

Adviser: Kim Henrik Holmstrom; tel. (+32) 2-2991852.

INNOVATION POLICY AND INVESTMENT FOR GROWTH
Head of Unit: Mark Nicklas; tel. (+32) 2-2954181.

CLUSTERS, SOCIAL ECONOMY AND ENTREPRENEURSHIP
Head of Unit: Ulla Engelmann; tel. (+32) 2-2957624.

KETS, DIGITAL MANUFACTURING AND INTEROPERABILITY
Head of Unit: Kirsi Ekroth-Manssila; tel. (+32) 2-2950708.

TOURISM, EMERGING AND CREATIVE INDUSTRIES
Head of Unit: Iuliana Gabriela Aluas; tel. (+32) 2-2983179.

INTELLECTUAL PROPERTY AND FIGHT AGAINST COUNTERFEITING
Head of Unit (acting): Michael Koenig; tel. (+32) 2-2992108.

Directorate G—Single Market for Public Administrations

Director (acting): Irmfried Schwimann; tel. (+32) 2-2967002.

PUBLIC PROCUREMENT STRATEGY
Head of Unit: Marzena Rogalska; tel. (+32) 2-2959772.

ACCESS TO PROCUREMENT MARKETS
Head of Unit: Jean-Yves Muylle; tel. (+32) 2-2967537.

PROCUREMENT LEGISLATION AND ENFORCEMENT
Head of Unit: Alvydas Stancikas; tel. (+32) 2-2963857.

INNOVATIVE AND E-PROCUREMENT
Head of Unit (acting): Thomas Spoormans; tel. (+32) 2-2955743.

Directorate H—COSME Programme

Director: Kristin Schreiber; tel. (+32) 2-2965823.

COSME PROGRAMME, SME ENVOYS AND RELATIONS WITH EASME
Head of Unit: Costas Andropoulos; tel. (+32) 2-2956601.

ENTERPRISE EUROPE NETWORK AND INTERNATIONALISATION OF SMEs
Head of Unit: Giacomo Mattinò; tel. (+32) 2-2957563.

COSME FINANCIAL INSTRUMENTS
Head of Unit: Claudiu Ciprian Cristea; tel. (+32) 2-2959314.

Directorate I—Space Policy, Copernicus and Defence

Director: Philippe Brunet; tel. (+32) 2-2954128.

SPACE POLICY AND RESEARCH
Head of Unit: Sabine Lecrenier; tel. (+32) 2-2955738.

SPACE DATA FOR SOCIETAL CHALLENGES AND GROWTH
Head of Unit: Andreas Veispak; tel. (+32) 2-2984033.

DEFENCE, AERONAUTIC AND MARITIME INDUSTRIES
Head of Unit: Alain Alexis; tel. (+32) 2-2955303.

Directorate J—EU Satellite Navigation Programmes

Director: Matthias Petschke; tel. (+32) 2-2964697.

GALILEO AND EGNOS—PROGRAMME MANAGEMENT
Head of Unit: Paul Flament; tel. (+32) 2-2956342.

GALILEO AND EGNOS—LEGAL AND INSTITUTIONAL ASPECTS
Head of Unit: Philippe Jean; tel. (+32) 2-2950539.

GALILEO AND EGNOS—APPLICATIONS, SECURITY, INTERNATIONAL CO-OPERATION
Head of Unit: Ekaterini Kavvada; tel. (+32) 2-2954902.

DG COMP—DIRECTORATE-GENERAL FOR COMPETITION

1 place Madou, 1210 Brussels, Belgium; tel. (+32) 2-2991111; internet ec.europa.eu/info/departments/competition

Director-General: Johannes Laitenberger; tel. (+32) 2-2965745.

Assistant to the Director-General: Andrea Bomhoff; tel. (+32) 2-2987100.

Principal Adviser to the Director-General: Fabienne Ilzkovitz; tel. (+32) 2-2993379.

Deputy Director-General (General Anti-trust Activities): Cecilio Madero Villarejo; tel. (+32) 2-2960949; fax (+32) 2-2969809.

Deputy Director-General (General Mergers): Carles Esteva Mosso; tel. (+32) 2-2969721.

Deputy Director-General (State Aid): Gert-Jan Koopman; tel. (+32) 2-2993381.

Chief Economist: Tommaso Valletti; tel. (+32) 2-2964270.

MERGERS
Head of Unit: Giulio Federico; tel. (+32) 2-2997954.

COMMUNICATIONS POLICY AND INTER-INSTITUTIONAL RELATIONS
Head of Unit: Jonathan Todd; tel. (+32) 2-2994107.

STATE AID POLICY AND CASE SUPPORT
Head of Unit: Koen Van De Casteele; tel. (+32) 2-2969419.

STRATEGY, DELIVERY AND EVALUATION
Head of Unit: Téa Katarina Broms; tel. (+32) 2-2954436.

Directorate A—Policy and Strategy

Director: Kris Dekeyser; tel. (+32) 2-2954206.

ANTI-TRUST CASE SUPPORT AND POLICY
Head of Unit: Maria Jaspers; tel. (+32) 2-2962577.

MERGERS CASE SUPPORT AND POLICY
Head of Unit: José María Carpi Badia; tel. (+32) 2-2993721.

STATE AID STRATEGY
Head of Unit: Barbara Brandtner; tel. (+32) 2-2951563.

EUROPEAN COMPETITION NETWORK
Head of Unit: Anna Vernet; tel. (+32) 2-2968049.

INTERNATIONAL RELATIONS
Head of Unit: Eddy De Smijter; tel. (+32) 2-2951380.

Directorate B—Markets and Cases I: Energy and Environment

Director: Céline Gauer; tel. (+32) 2-2963919.

ANTI-TRUST: ENERGY, ENVIRONMENT
Head of Unit: Johannes Luebking; tel. (+32) 2-2959851.

STATE AID I
Head of Unit: Anna Jarosz-Friis; tel. (+32) 2-2993733.

STATE AID II
Head of Unit: Christof Lessenich; tel. (+32) 2-2966690.

MERGERS
Head of Unit: Hanna Anttilainen; tel. (+32) 2-2953692.

Directorate C—Markets and Cases II: Information, Communication and Media

Director: Guillaume Loriot; tel. (+32) 2-2984988.

ANTI-TRUST: TELECOMMUNICATIONS
Head of Unit: Rita Wezenbeek; tel. (+32) 2-2998939.

ANTI-TRUST: MEDIA
Head of Unit: Krzysztof Kuik; tel. (+32) 2-2953631.

ANTI-TRUST: IT, INTERNET AND CONSUMER ELECTRONICS
Head of Unit: Nicholas Banasević; tel. (+32) 2-2966569.

STATE AID
Head of Unit: Ewoud Sakkers; tel. (+32) 2-2966352.

MERGERS
Head of Unit: Michele Piergiovanni; tel. (+32) 2-2986577.

Directorate E—Markets and Cases IV: Basic Industries, Manufacturing and Agriculture

Director: Paul Csiszar; tel. (+32) 2-2984669.

ANTI-TRUST: PHARMA AND HEALTH SERVICES
Head of Unit (acting): Philipp Gasparon; tel. (+32) 2-2996114.

ANTI-TRUST: CONSUMER GOODS, BASIC INDUSTRIES, AGRICULTURE AND MANUFACTURING
Head of Unit: Natalia Lazarova; tel. (+32) 2-2958857.

STATE AID: INDUSTRIAL RESTRUCTURING
Head of Unit: Eduardo Martínez Rivero; tel. (+32) 2-2964977.

MERGERS
Head of Unit: Thomas Deisenhofer; tel. (+32) 2-2985081.

Directorate D—Markets and Cases III: Financial Services

Director: Maria Velentza; tel. (+32) 2-2951723.

ANTI-TRUST: PAYMENTS SYSTEMS
Head of Unit: Sari Suurnakki; tel. (+32) 2-2991828.

ANTI-TRUST: FINANCIAL SERVICES
Head of Unit: Jean Bergevin; tel. (+32) 2-2951639.

STATE AID I: TASK FORCE FINANCIAL CRISIS
Head of Unit: Peer Ritter; tel. (+32) 2-2966490.

STATE AID II: TASK FORCE FINANCIAL CRISIS
Head of Unit (acting): Maria Velentza; tel. (+32) 2-2951723.

STATE AID III: TASK FORCE FINANCIAL CRISIS
Head of Unit: Christophe Galand; tel. (+32) 2-2988458.

MERGERS
Head of Unit: Alberto Bacchiega; tel. (+32) 2-2956398.

Directorate F—Markets and Cases V: Transport, Post and Other Services

Director: Henrik Morch; tel. (+32) 2-2950766.

ANTI-TRUST: TRANSPORT, POST AND OTHER SERVICES
Head of Unit: Hubert de Broca; tel. (+32) 2-2996660.

STATE AID: TRANSPORT
Head of Unit: Sophie Moonen; tel. (+32) 2-2981807.

STATE AID: POST AND OTHER SERVICES
Head of Unit: Monique Negenman; tel. (+32) 2-2955228.

MERGERS
Head of Unit: Daniel Boeshertz; tel. (+32) 2-2966437.

Directorate G—Cartels

Director: Eric van Ginderachter; tel. (+32) 2-2954427.

CARTELS I
Head of Unit: Gerald Miersch; tel. (+32) 2-2996504.

CARTELS II
Head of Unit: Brigitta Renner-Loquenz; tel. (+32) 2-2954569.

CARTELS III
Head of Unit: Zsuzsanna Jambor; tel. (+32) 2-2987436.

CARTELS IV
Head of Unit: Corinne Dussart-Lefret; tel. (+32) 2-2961223.

CARTELS V
Head of Unit: Flavio Laina; tel. (+32) 2-2969669.

Directorate H—State Aid: General Scrutiny and Enforcement

Director: Karl Soukup; tel. (+32) 2-2967442.

INFRASTRUCTURE AND REGIONAL AID
Head of Unit: Miek Van Der Wee; tel. (+32) 2-2960216.

ACCESS TO FINANCE, R&D&I AND ENVIRONMENT
Head of Unit: Demos Spatharis; tel. (+32) 2-2996839.

FISCAL AID
Head of Unit: Christina Siaterli; tel. (+32) 2-2967053.

ENFORCEMENT AND MONITORING
Head of Unit: Kristine Liljeberg; tel. (+32) 2-2984630.

TAX PLANNING PRACTICES
Head of Unit: Max Lienemeyer; tel. (+32) 2-2986243.

Directorate R—Horizontal Management
Director: Isabelle Benoliel; tel. (+32) 2-2960198.

REGISTRY AND TRANSPARENCY
Head of Unit: Marc Ekelmans; tel. (+32) 2-2956873.

FINANCE AND INTERNAL COMPLIANCE
Head of Unit: Kristine Vlagsma; tel. (+32) 2-2987328.

INFORMATION TECHNOLOGY
Head of Unit: Manuel Pérez Espín; tel. (+32) 2-2961691.

DG EMPL—DIRECTORATE-GENERAL FOR EMPLOYMENT, SOCIAL AFFAIRS AND INCLUSION

27 rue Joseph II, 1000 Brussels, Belgium; tel. (+32) 2-2991111; internet ec.europa.eu/info/departments/employment-social-affairs-and-inclusion

Director-General: Michel Servoz; tel. (+32) 2-2956891.

Deputy Director-General: Zoltán Kazatsay; tel. (+32) 2-2959172; fax (+32) 2-2951405.

Assistant to the Director-General: Gelu Calacean; tel. (+32) 2-2969658.

Reporting directly to the Director-General

Principal Adviser: Viktorija Šmatko; tel. (+32) 2-2994537.

Co-ordination

Head of Unit: María Luisa Llano Cardenal; tel. (+32) 2-2992759.

BC—HR Business Correspondent

Head of Unit: Fabienne Levy; tel. (+32) 2-2994002.

Directorate A—Employment and Social Governance
Director: Barbara Kauffmann; tel. (+32) 2-2993489.

EMPLOYMENT AND SOCIAL ASPECTS OF EUROPEAN SEMESTER
Head of Unit: Jeroen Jutte; tel. (+32) 2-2961972.

SOCIAL DIALOGUE
Head of Unit: David Dion; tel. (+32) 2-2988269.

COUNTRY REFORM
Head of Unit: Nathalie Darnaut; tel. (+32) 2-2966575.

THEMATIC ANALYSIS
Head of Unit: Loukas Stemitsiotis; tel. (+32) 2-2993366.

CYPRUS, GREECE
Head of Unit: Jiri Svarc; tel. (+32) 2-2981346.

Directorate B—Employment
Director: Stefan Olsson; tel. (+32) 2-2953569.

EMPLOYMENT STRATEGY
Head of Unit—Youth employment, Entrepreneurship, Microfinance Facility: Max Uebe; tel. (+32) 2-2968272.

WORKING CONDITIONS
Head of Unit: Adam Pokorny; tel. (+32) 2-2963988.

HEALTH AND SAFETY
Head of Unit: Charlotte Grevfors Ernoult; tel. (+351) 430135916.

SPAIN, MALTA
Head of Unit: Emma Toledano Laredo; tel. (+32) 2-2966204.

ROMANIA, BULGARIA
Head of Unit: Cendrine De Buggenoms; tel. (+32) 2-2998529.

Directorate C—Social Affairs
Director (acting): Manuela Geleng; tel. (+32) 2-2962102.

SOCIAL INVESTMENT STRATEGY
Head of Unit: Manuela Geleng; tel. (+32) 2-2962102.

MODERNIZATION OF SOCIAL PROTECTION SYSTEMS
Head of Unit: Ana Carla Pereira; tel. (+32) 2-2962631.

DISABILITY AND INCLUSION
Head of Unit: Emmanuelle Grange; tel. (+32) 2-2958795.

HUNGARY, UK, IRELAND, PORTUGAL
Head of Unit: Nicolas Gibert-Morin; tel. (+32) 2-2991120.

FINLAND, LATVIA, ESTONIA, LITHUANIA
Head of Unit: Muriel Guin; tel. (+32) 2-2960013.

Directorate D—Labour Mobility
Director: Jordi Curell Gotor; tel. (+32) 2-2990478.

FREE MOVEMENT OF WORKERS, EURES
Head of Unit: Jackie Morin; tel. (+32) 2-2961145; fax (+32) 2-2998077.

SOCIAL SECURITY CO-ORDINATION
Head of Unit (acting): Jörg Tagger; tel. (+32) 2-2992366.

INTERNATIONAL ISSUES
Head of Unit: Lluís Prats; tel. (+32) 2-2966994.

FRANCE, NETHERLANDS, BELGIUM, LUXEMBOURG
Head of Unit: Jiri Plecity; tel. (+32) 2-2986660.

GERMANY, AUSTRIA, SLOVENIA, CROATIA
Head of Unit: Egbert Holthuis; tel. (+32) 2-2993953.

Directorate E—Skills
Director: Detlef Eckert; tel. (+32) 2-2963197.

JOB CREATION
Head of Unit: Ann Branch; tel. (+32) 2-2985340.

SKILLS AND QUALIFICATIONS
Head of Unit: Alison Crabb; tel. (+32) 2-2959223.

VET, APPRENTICESHIPS AND ADULT LEARNING

Head of Unit: Dana-Carmen Bachmann; tel. (+32) 2-2991277.

ITALY, DENMARK, SWEDEN

Head of Unit: Denis Genton; tel. (+32) 2-2969965.

POLAND, CZECH REPUBLIC, SLOVAKIA

Head of Unit: Wallis Goelen Vandebrock; tel. (+32) 2-2951827.

Directorate F—Investment

Director: Andriana Sukova-Tosheva; tel. (+32) 2-2962903.

ESF AND FEAD: POLICY AND LEGISLATION

Head of Unit: Loris Di Pietrantonio; tel. (+32) 2-2965470.

EGF, SHARED MANAGEMENT

Head of Unit: Szilard Tamas; tel. (+32) 2-2963560.

PROGRAMMING AND PLANNING

Head of Unit: Brigitte Fellahi-Brognaux; tel. (+32) 2-2958565.

PROGRAMME MANAGEMENT AND IMPLEMENTATION

Head of Unit: Anne Grisard; tel. (+32) 2-2984103.

INFORMATION TECHNOLOGIES

Head of Unit: Octavian Purcarea; tel. (+32) 2-2987704.

Directorate G—Audit, Evaluation and Communication

Director: Francisco Merchan Cantos; tel. (+32) 2-2996730.

Adviser: Vincent Widdershoven; tel. (+32) 2-2953330.

AUDIT DIRECT MANAGEMENT, DISCHARGE

Head of Unit: Stefan De Keermaecker; tel. (+32) 2-2984680.

AUDIT SHARED MANAGEMENT I

Head of Unit: Mark Schelfhout; tel. (+32) 2-2959518.

AUDIT SHARED MANAGEMENT II

Head of Unit: Androulla Ioannou; tel. (+32) 2-2961794.

EVALUATION AND IMPACT ASSESSMENT

Head of Unit: Maria-José Cueto Faus; tel. (+32) 2-2965277.

COMMUNICATION

Head of Unit: Roberta Persichelli Scola; tel. (+32) 2-2950428.

DG AGRI—DIRECTORATE-GENERAL FOR AGRICULTURE AND RURAL DEVELOPMENT

130 rue de la Loi, 1049 Brussels, Belgium; tel. (+32) 2-2991111; fax (+32) 2-2950130; internet ec.europa.eu/info/departments/agriculture-and-rural-development

Director-General: Jerzy Bogdan Plewa; tel. (+32) 2-2980125.

Deputy Director-General, responsible for Directorates A, B and C: María De Los Angeles Benítez Salas; tel. (+32) 2-2995472.

Deputy Director-General, responsible for Directorates D, E and F: Mihail Dumitru; tel. (+32) 2-2955666.

Deputy Director-General, responsible for Directorates G, H and I: Rudolf Mögele; tel. (+32) 2-2962930; fax (+32) 2-2920166.

Reporting directly to the Director-General

Assistant to the Director-General: Gijs Schilthuis; tel. (+32) 2-2954341.

Assistant to the Director-General: Christina Gerstgrasser; tel. (+32) 2-286829.

Directorate A—International

Director: John Clarke; tel. (+32) 2-2950048.

Adviser: Isabelle Peutz; tel. (+32) 2-2952331.

GLOBAL ISSUES AND RELATIONS WITH ACP

Head of Unit: Willi Schulz-Greve; tel. (+32) 2-2960945.

WORLD TRADE ORGANIZATION (WTO)

Head of Unit: John Bedford; tel. (+32) 2-2981200.

THE AMERICAS

Head of Unit: Jean-Marc Trarieux; tel. (+32) 2-2998770.

ASIA AND AUSTRALASIA

Head of Unit: Antonia Gamez Moreno; tel. (+32) 2-2965795.

NEIGHBOURHOOD AND ENLARGEMENT

Head of Unit: Susana Marazuela Azpiroz; tel. (+32) 2-2965725.

Directorate B—Quality, Research and Innovation, Outreach

Director (acting): Lene Naesager; tel. (+32) 2-2950015.

Adviser: Georges Vassilakis; tel. (+32) 2-2965711.

EXTERNAL COMMUNICATION AND PROMOTION POLICY

Head of Unit: Lene Naesager; tel. (+32) 2-2950015.

RESEARCH AND INNOVATION

Head of Unit: Rob Peters; tel. (+32) 2-2962624.

GEOGRAPHICAL INDICATIONS

Head of Unit: Francis Fay; tel. (+32) 2-2962974.

ORGANICS

Head of Unit: Nicolas Verlet; tel. (+32) 2-2961508.

Directorate C—Strategy, Simplification and Policy Analysis

Director: Tassos Haniotis; tel. (+32) 2-2991381; fax (+32) 2-2987186.

Adviser: Florence Buchholzer; tel. (+32) 2-2962332.

POLICY PERSPECTIVES

Head of Unit: Flavio Coturni; tel. (+32) 2-2967585; fax (+32) 2-2959236.

ANALYSIS AND OUTLOOK

Head of Unit: Pierluigi Londero; tel. (+32) 2-2991255.

FARM ECONOMICS

Head of Unit: Mariusz Stefan Migas; tel. (+32) 2-2959305.

MONITORING AND EVALUATION

Head of Unit: Adelina Dos Reis; tel. (+32) 2-2961454.

Directorate D—Sustainability and Income Support
Director: Pierre Bascou; tel. (+32) 2-2950846.

DIRECT PAYMENTS
Head of Unit: Marie Bourjou; tel. (+32) 2-2964271.

GREENING, CROSS-COMPLIANCE AND POSEI
Head of Unit: Richard Etievant; tel. (+32) 2-2994468.

IMPLEMENTATION SUPPORT AND IACS
Head of Unit: Owen Jones; tel. (+32) 2-2953200.

ENVIRONMENT, CLIMATE CHANGE, FORESTRY AND BIOECONOMY
Head of Unit: Mauro Poinelli; tel. (+32) 2-2985475.

Directorate E—Rural Development I and Pre-Accession Assistance
Director: Mario Milouchev; tel. (+32) 2-2962150.

BELGIUM, FRANCE, LUXEMBOURG, THE NETHERLANDS
Head of Unit: Barbara Lücke; tel. (+32) 2-2963223.

DENMARK, ESTONIA, LATVIA, LITHUANIA, FINLAND, SWEDEN; ENRD
Head of Unit: Neda Skakelja; tel. (+32) 2-2988561.

GERMANY, AUSTRIA
Head of Unit: Vesselina Komitska; tel. (+32) 2-2951049.

CZECH REPUBLIC, HUNGARY, ROMANIA, SLOVAKIA; BROADBAND AND INCLUSION
Head of Unit: Bruno Chauvin; tel. (+32) 2-2955174.

PRE-ACCESSION ASSISTANCE
Head of Unit: Liam Breslin; tel. (+32) 2-2950477.

Directorate F—Rural Development II
Director: Josefine Loriz-Hoffmann; tel. (+32) 2-2957977.

CONCEPTION AND CONSISTENCY OF RURAL DEVELOPMENT
Head of Unit: Martin Scheele; tel. (+32) 2-2963970.

CYPRUS, GREECE, ÉIRE/IRELAND, UK
Head of Unit: Alexander Bartovic; tel. (+32) 2-2962807.

BULGARIA, CROATIA, POLAND, SLOVENIA; FINANCIAL INSTRUMENTS
Head of Unit: Michael Pielke; tel. (+32) 2-2965707.

ITALY, MALTA
Head of Unit: Filip Busz; tel. (+32) 2-2990923.

SPAIN, PORTUGAL
Head of Unit: Efthimios Bokias; tel. (+32) 2-2962023.

Directorate G—Markets and Observatories
Director: Jens Schaps; tel. (+32) 2-2953034.
Economic adviser: Fabien Santini; tel. (+32) 2-2955248.

GOVERNANCE OF THE AGRI-FOOD MARKETS
Head of Unit: Bruno Buffaria; tel. (+32) 2-2963144.

WINE, SPIRITS AND HORTICULTURAL PRODUCTS
Head of Unit: João Onofre; tel. (+32) 2-2969788.

ANIMAL PRODUCTS
Head of Unit: Luís Carazo Jiménez; tel. (+32) 2-2960066; fax (+32) 2-2953310.

ARABLE CROPS AND OLIVE OIL
Head of Unit: Silke Boger; tel. (+32) 2-2964936.

Directorate H—Assurance and Audit
Director: Christina Borchmann; tel. (+32) 2-2953259.

COMPETENCY CENTRE FOR ASSURANCE AND AUDIT
Head of Unit: Margaret Bateson-Missen; tel. (+32) 2-2966117.

ASSURANCE AND AUDIT—EXPENDITURE ON MARKET MEASURES
Head of Unit (acting): Fernando Domínguez Perals; tel. (+32) 2-2987139.

ASSURANCE AND AUDIT—DIRECT PAYMENTS
Head of Unit: Philippe Coenjaarts; tel. (+32) 2-2967095.

ASSURANCE AND AUDIT—RURAL DEVELOPMENT
Head of Unit: Horea-Silviu Todoran; tel. (+32) 2-2950264.

ASSURANCE AND FINANCIAL AUDIT
Head of Unit: Katia Philaniotou; tel. (+32) 2-2957825.

Directorate I—Legal, Institutional and Procedural Matters
Director: Nathalie Sauze-Vandevyer; tel. (+32) 2-2954765.

AGRICULTURAL LAW; SIMPLIFICATION
Head of Unit: Michael Niejahr; tel. (+32) 2-2969576.

STATE AID
Head of Unit: Gereon Thiele; tel. (+32) 2-2952901.

ENFORCEMENT OF LEGISLATION, RELATIONS WITH THE EUROPEAN OMBUDSMAN AND ACCESS TO DOCUMENTS
Head of Unit: Karl Von Kempis; tel. (+32) 2-2968809.

ADOPTION PROCEDURES, COMMITTEES, EXPERT GROUPS AND CIVIL DIALOGUE GROUPS
Head of Unit: Péter Bokor; tel. (+32) 2-2997889.

STRATEGIC PLANNING, INTERNAL CONTROL, AND INTER-INSTITUTIONAL RELATIONS
Head of Unit: Ico Von Wedel; tel. (+32) 2-2957327.

Directorate R—Resources
Director: Georg Häusler; tel. (+32) 2-2961082.

BUDGET MANAGEMENT, BFOR
Head of Unit: Frank Bollen; tel. (+32) 2-2998320.

DIRECT FINANCIAL MANAGEMENT AND ACCOUNTING
Head of Unit: Alexis Loncke; tel. (+32) 2-2993805.

DIGITAL SOLUTIONS
Head of Unit: Éric Müller; tel. (+32) 2-2952257.

DIRECTORY *European Commission*

FINANCIAL MANAGEMENT OF EAGF AND EAFRD

Head of Unit: Silvia Michelini; tel. (+32) 2-2962447.

DOCUMENT MANAGEMENT, SECURITY AND HR BUSINESS CORRESPONDENT

Head of Unit: Carmen Naranjo Sánchez; tel. (+32) 2-2953120.

DG ENER—DIRECTORATE-GENERAL FOR ENERGY

24 rue Demot, 1040 Brussels, Belgium; tel. (+32) 2-2991111; internet ec.europa.eu/info/departments/energy

Director-General: Dominique Ristori; tel. (+32) 2-2992460.

Deputy Director-General (External Policy and Development of Financial Instruments): Christopher Jones; tel. (+32) 2-2965030.

Deputy Director-General, responsible for Directorates D and E: Gerassimos Thomas; tel. (+32) 2-2974611.

Reporting directly to the Director-General

Assistant to the Director-General: Agnija Rasa; tel. (+32) 2-22995475.

Principal Adviser: Tudorel Constantinescu; tel. (+32) 2-2969416.

Legal Adviser: Ben van Houtte; tel. (+32) 2-2950494.

Resource Management and Support Luxembourg

Head of Unit: Benoît Morisset; tel. (+32) 2-2932458.

Directorate A—Energy Policy

Director: Megan Richards; tel. (+32) 2-2962443.

ENERGY POLICY CO-ORDINATION

Head of Unit: Paula Pinho; tel. (+32) 2-2920815.

COMMUNICATION AND INTER-INSTITUTIONAL RELATIONS

Assistant to the Director-General: Alejandro Ulzurrun de Asanza y Muñoz; tel. (+32) 2-2954867.

INTERNATIONAL RELATIONS AND ENLARGEMENT

Head of Unit: Anne-Charlotte Bournoville; tel. (+32) 2-2967304.

ECONOMIC ANALYSIS AND FINANCIAL INSTRUMENTS

Head of Unit (acting): Tom Howes; tel. (+32) 2-2988139.

Directorate B—Internal Energy Market

Director: Klaus-Dieter Borchhardt; tel. (+32) 2-2994011.

NETWORKS AND REGIONAL INITIATIVES

Head of Unit: Catharina Sikow-Magny; tel. (+32) 2-2962125.

WHOLESALE MARKETS; ELECTRICITY AND GAS

Head of Unit: Florian Ermacora; tel. (+32) 2-2985126.

RETAIL MARKETS; COAL AND OIL

Head of Unit: Anna Colucci; tel. (+32) 2-2968319.

SECURITY OF SUPPLY

Head of Unit: Stefan Moser; tel. (+32) 2-2965880.

Directorate C—Renewables, Research and Innovation, Energy Efficiency

Director: Mechthild Woersdoerfer; tel. (+32) 2-2990030.

Adviser: Hans Van Steen; tel. (+32) 2-2953798.

RENEWABLES AND CARBON CAPTURE STORAGE POLICY

Head of Unit: Paula Abreu Marques; tel. (+32) 2-2953805.

NEW ENERGY TECHNOLOGIES, INNOVATION AND CLEAN COAL

Head of Unit: Magdalena Andreea Strachinescu Olteanu; tel. (+32) 2-2962488.

ENERGY EFFICIENCY

Head of Unit: Paul Hodson; tel. (+32) 2-2991258.

Directorate D—Nuclear Energy, Safety and ITER

Director: Massimo Garribba; tel. (+352) 430133861.

EURATOM CO-ORDINATION, LEGAL MATTERS AND INTERNATIONAL RELATIONS

Head of Unit: Hans Rhein; tel. (+32) 2-2958232.

NUCLEAR ENERGY, NUCLEAR WASTE AND DECOMMISSIONING

Head of Unit: Ioanna Metaxopoulou; tel. (+352) 430133685.

RADIATION PROTECTION AND NUCLEAR SAFETY

Head of Unit: Michael Hübel; tel. (+352) 430134023.

ITER

Head of Unit: Jan Panek; tel. (+32) 2-2969955.

Directorate E—EURATOM Safeguards

Director: Stephan Lechner; tel. (+352) 430134705.

POLICY, QUALITY AND TECHNOLOGY

Head of Unit (acting): Nicole Erdmann; tel. (+352) 430136792.

INSPECTIONS: REPROCESSING PLANTS

Head of Unit: Pavel Jirsa; tel. (+352) 430134860.

INSPECTIONS: FUEL FABRICATION AND ENRICHMENT PLANTS

Head of Unit: Peter Beuseling; tel. (+352) 430135590.

INSPECTIONS: REACTORS, GEOLOGICAL REPOSITORIES AND OTHER INSTALLATIONS

Head of Unit (acting): Valentí Canadell Bofarull; tel. (+352) 430135376.

NUCLEAR ACCOUNTANCY AND INTERNATIONAL OBLIGATIONS

Head of Unit: Stefano Ciccarello; tel. (+352) 430136227.

DG MOVE—DIRECTORATE-GENERAL FOR MOBILITY AND TRANSPORT

28 rue Demot, 1049 Brussels, Belgium; tel. (+32) 2-2991111; internet ec.europa.eu/info/departments/mobility-and-transport

Director-General: Henrik Hololei; tel. (+32) 2-2988764.

Deputy Director-General with responsibility for Directorate B: Maja Bakran; tel. (+32) 2-2987773.

Deputy Director-General with responsibility for Directorates C, D and E: Matthew Baldwin; tel. (+32) 2-2981304.

European Commission

Reporting directly to the Director-General

Adviser: Peter Vis; tel. (+32) 2-2984804.

Directorate A—Policy Co-ordination

Director: Per Haugaard; tel. (+32) 2-2960140.

CO-ORDINATION AND PLANNING
Head of Unit: Elisabeth Werner; tel. (+32) 2-2959506.

INTERNATIONAL RELATIONS
Head of Unit: Harvey Rouse; tel. (+32) 2-2962326.

ECONOMIC ANALYSIS AND BETTER REGULATION
Head of Unit: Rolf Diemer; tel. (+32) 2-2961075.

LEGAL ISSUES AND ENFORCEMENT
Head of Unit: Barbara Jankovec; tel. (+32) 2-2957809.

SECURITY
Head of Unit: Carlos Mestre Zamarreño; tel. (+32) 2-2987145.

Directorate B—Investment, Innovate and Sustainable Transport

Director: Herald Ruijters; tel. (+32) 2-2968372.
Adviser: Helmut Morsi; tel. (+32) 2-2950844.

TRANSPORT NETWORKS
Head of Unit: Jean-Louis Colson; tel. (+32) 2-2960995.

TRANSPORT INVESTMENT
Head of Unit: Olivier Silla; tel. (+32) 2-2966597.

INNOVATION AND RESEARCH
Head of Unit: Robert Missen; tel. (+32) 2-2955201.

SUSTAINABLE AND INTELLIGENT TRANSPORT
Head of Unit: Claire Depre; tel. (+32) 2-2998463.

SOCIAL ASPECTS, PASSENGER RIGHTS AND EQUAL OPPORTUNITIES
Head of Unit (acting): Jean-Louis Colson; tel. (+32) 2-2960995.

Directorate C—Land

Director (acting): Matthew Baldwin; tel. (+32) 2-2981304.

ROAD TRANSPORT
Head of Unit: Eddy Liegeois; tel. (+32) 2-2951839.

ROAD SAFETY
Head of Unit: Fotini Ioannidou; tel. (+32) 2-2955548.

SINGLE EUROPEAN RAIL AREA
Head of Unit: Sian Prout; tel. (+32) 2-2968240.

RAIL SAFETY AND INTEROPERABILITY
Head of Unit: Keir Fitch; tel. (+32) 2-2959316.

Directorate D—Waterborne

Director: Magda Kopczynska; tel. (+32) 2-2955609.

MARITIME TRANSPORT AND LOGISTICS
Head of Unit: Sandro Santamato; tel. (+32) 2-2955609.

MARITIME SAFETY
Head of Unit: Christine Berg; tel. (+32) 2-2991922.

PORTS AND INLAND NAVIGATION
Head of Unit: Daniela Rosca; tel. (+32) 2-2995640.

Directorate E—Aviation

Director (acting): Filip Cornelis; tel. (+32) 2-2969219.

AVIATION POLICY
Head of Unit: Filip Cornelis; tel. (+32) 2-2969219.

AVIATION AGREEMENTS
Head of Unit: Carlos Bermejo Acosta; tel. (+32) 2-2967376.

SINGLE EUROPEAN SKY
Head of Unit: Maurizio Castelletti; tel. (+32) 2-2991915.

AVIATION SAFETY
Head of Unit: Joachim Luecking; tel. (+32) 2-2966545.

Directorate SRD—Shared Resources MOVE/ENER

Director: Agnieszka Kazmierczak; tel. (+32) 2-2990868.
Adviser: Eleni Kopanezou; tel. (+32) 2-2996768.

ASSURANCE AND SUPERVISION
Head of Unit: Alessandro D'Atri; tel. (+32) 2-2959301.

INFORMATION MANAGEMENT AND SYSTEMS
Head of Unit: André Mambourg; tel. (+32) 2-2969222.

BUDGET AND FINANCIAL MANAGEMENT
Head of Unit (acting): Marcos Roamn Parra; tel. (+32) 2-2955492.

DG CLIMA—DIRECTORATE-GENERAL FOR CLIMATE ACTION

24 ave de Beaulieu, 1160 Brussels, Belgium; tel. (+32) 2-2991111; internet ec.europa.eu/info/departments/climate-action

Director-General: Jos Delbeke; tel. (+32) 2-2968804.

Reporting directly to the Director-General

Assistant to the Director-General: Christian Holzleitner; tel. (+32) 2-2996452.

Principal Adviser: Jacob David Werksman; tel. (+32) 2-2954087.

Directorate A—International and Mainstreaming

Director: Yvon Slingenberg; tel. (+32) 2-2992036.

INTERNATIONAL AND INTER-INSTITUTIONAL RELATIONS
Head of Unit: Elina Bardram; tel. (+32) 2-2993305.

CLIMATE FINANCE, MAINSTREAMING, MONTREAL PROTOCOL
Head of Unit: Philip Owen; tel. (+32) 2-2965562.

ADAPTATION
Head of Unit (acting): Claus Kondrup; tel. (+32) 2-2981615.

Directorate B—European and International Carbon Markets

Director: Beatriz Yordi; tel. (+32) 2-2953970.

Adviser: Damien Meadows; tel. (+32) 2-2996319.

ETS POLICY DEVELOPMENT AND AUCTIONING
Head of Unit: Peter Zapfel; tel. (+32) 2-2959195.

ETS IMPLEMENTATION
Head of Unit: Mette Koefoed Quinn; tel. (+32) 2-2991241.

INTERNATIONAL CARBON MARKET, AVIATION AND MARITIME
Head of Unit: Laurence Graff; tel. (+32) 2-2960518.

Directorate C—Climate Strategy, Governance and Emissions from Non-Trading Sectors

Director: Artur Runge-Metzger; tel. (+32) 2-2956898.

Adviser: Stefaan Vergote; tel. (+32) 2-2969696.

STRATEGY AND ECONOMIC ASSESSMENT
Head of Unit: Willem Van Ierland; tel. (+32) 2-2997810.

GOVERNANCE AND EFFORT SHARING
Head of Unit: Hans Bergman; tel. (+32) 2-2966546.

LAND USE AND FINANCE FOR INNOVATION
Head of Unit: Peter Wehrheim; tel. (+32) 2-2988578.

ROAD TRANSPORT
Head of Unit: Alexandre Paquot; tel. (+32) 2-2996130.

DG ENV—DIRECTORATE-GENERAL FOR ENVIRONMENT

5 ave de Beaulieu, 1160 Brussels, Belgium; tel. (+32) 2-2991111; internet ec.europa.eu/info/departments/environment

Director-General: Daniel Calleja Crespo; tel. (+32) 2-2961386.

Policy Assistant to the Director-General: Natalie Pauwels; tel. (+32) 2-2980992.

Directorate A—Policy

Director: Gilles Gantelet; tel. (+32) 2-2994896.

CO-ORDINATION, INTER-INSTITUTIONAL RELATIONS AND PLANNING
Head of Unit (acting): Helen McCarthy-O'Kelly; tel. (+32) 2-2990113.

COMMUNICATION
Head of Unit: Gilles Laroche; tel. (+32) 2-2991122.

ENVIRONMENTAL KNOWLEDGE, ECO-INNOVATION AND SMES
Head of Unit: Claudia Fusco; tel. (+32) 2-2951394.

Directorate B—Circular Economy and Green Growth

Director: Kestutis Sadauskas; tel. (+32) 2-2951862.

SUSTAINABLE PRODUCTION, PRODUCTS AND CONSUMPTION
Head of Unit: Hugo-Maria Schally; tel. (+32) 2-2958569.

SUSTAINABLE CHEMICALS
Head of Unit: Björn Hansen; tel. (+32) 2-2965015.

WASTE MANAGEMENT AND SECONDARY MATERIALS
Head of Unit: Sarah Nelen; tel. (+32) 2-2957695.

Directorate C—Quality of Life

Director (acting): François Wakenhut; tel. (+32) 2-2965380; fax (+32) 2-2968824.

CLEAN WATER
Head of Unit: Bettina Doeser; tel. (+32) 2-2967050.

MARINE ENVIRONMENT AND WATER INDUSTRY
Head of Unit: Matjaž Malgaj; tel. (+32) 2-2988674.

CLEAN AIR
Head of Unit: François Wakenhut; tel. (+32) 2-2965380; fax (+32) 2-2968824.

INDUSTRIAL EMISSIONS AND SAFETY
Head of Unit: Aneta Willems; tel. (+32) 2-2951393.

Directorate D—Natural Capital

Director: Humberto Delgado Rosa; tel. (+32) 2-2958604.

LAND USE AND MANAGEMENT
Head of Unit: Claudia Olazabal; tel. (+32) 2-2990441.

BIODIVERSITY
Head of Unit: Stefan Leiner; tel. (+32) 2-2995068.

NATURE PROTECTION
Head of Unit: Nicola Notaro; tel. (+32) 2-2990499.

LIFE PROGRAMME
Head of Unit: Jean-Claude Merciol; tel. (+32) 2-2953504.

Directorate E—Implementation and Support to Member States

Director: Aurel Ciobanu-Dordea; tel. (+32) 2-2999871.

MAINSTREAMING AND ENVIRONMENTAL ASSESSMENTS
Head of Unit: Georges-Stavros Kremlis; tel. (+32) 2-2966526.

ENVIRONMENTAL IMPLEMENTATION
Head of Unit: Ion Codescu; tel. (+32) 2-2990214.

LIFE—NATURE
Head of Unit: Angelo Salsi; tel. (+32) 2-2969376.

ENVIRONMENTAL ENFORCEMENT
Head of Unit: Paul Speight; tel. (+32) 2-2964135.

COMPLIANCE AND BETTER REGULATION
Head of Unit: Robert Konrad; tel. (+32) 2-2998633.

Directorate F—Global Sustainable Development

Director: Astrid Schomaker; tel. (+32) 2-2969641.

Adviser: Jill Hanna; tel. (+32) 2-2953232.

Adviser: Véronique Hyeulle; tel. (+32) 2-2990235.

European Commission — DIRECTORY

SUSTAINABLE DEVELOPMENT GOALS, GREEN FINANCE AND ECONOMIC ANALYSIS

Head of Unit (acting): Manfred Rosenstock; tel. (+32) 2-2954887.

BILATERAL AND REGIONAL ENVIRONMENTAL CO-OPERATION

Head of Unit (acting): Astrid Schomaker; tel. (+32) 2-2969641.

MULTILATERAL ENVIRONMENTAL CO-OPERATION

Head of Unit: Emmanuelle Maire; tel. (+32) 2-2991586.

Directorate SRD—Shared Resources Directorate ENV/CLIMA

Director: Robert Bruno Pragnell; tel. (+32) 2-2991100.

ADMINISTRATION AND SUPPORT SERVICES

Head of Unit (acting): José Torcato; tel. (+32) 2-2963537.

FINANCE

Head of Unit (acting): Alexandra Vakrou; tel. (+32) 2-2996133.

INFORMATION TECHNOLOGY

Head of Unit: José Torcato; tel. (+32) 2-2963537.

DG RTD—DIRECTORATE-GENERAL FOR RESEARCH AND INNOVATION

8 sq. Frère-Orban, 1050 Brussels, Belgium; tel. (+32) 2-2991111; internet ec.europa.eu/info/departments/research-and-innovation

Director-General: Robert-Jan Smits; tel. (+32) 2-2963296.

Deputy Director-General, with responsibility for Directorates A, B and C: Wolfgang Burtscher; tel. (+32) 2-2996898.

Deputy Director-General (acting), with responsibility for Directorates D, E, F, G, H and I: Jack Metthey; tel. (+32) 2-2968870.

Deputy Director-General, with responsibility for Directorates J and R: Patrick Child; tel. (+32) 2-2959891.

Assistant to the Director-General: Anne Mallaband; tel. (+32) 2-2999945.

Principal Adviser (REA—Director of the Agency): Marc Tachelet; tel. (+32) 2-2967827.

Principal Adviser (ERC—Director of the Agency): Pablo Amor; tel. (+32) 2-2980167.

Adviser (Scientific Culture): Gábor Mihály Nagy; tel. (+32) 2-2968367.

Directorate A—Policy Development and Co-ordination

Director: Kurt Vandenberghe; tel. (+32) 2-2969207.

COMMUNICATION

Head of Unit: Minna Wilkki; tel. (+32) 2-2995573.

INTER-INSTITUTIONAL RELATIONS AND INTERNAL CO-ORDINATION

Head of Unit: María Olivan Aviles; tel. (+32) 2-2994975.

HORIZON 2020 POLICY AND FORESIGHT

Head of Unit: Renzo Tomellini; tel. (+32) 2-2960136.

ANALYSIS AND MONITORING OF NATIONAL RESEARCH AND INNOVATION POLICIES

Head of Unit: Roman Arjona Gracía; tel. (+32) 2-2994570.

BETTER REGULATION

Head of Unit: Rosalinde Van der Vlies; tel. (+32) 2-2990295.

OPEN DATA POLICY AND SCIENCE CLOUD

Head of Unit: Jean-Claude Burgelman; tel. (+32) 2-2980006.

Directorate B—Open Innovation and Open Science

Director: Jean-David Malo; tel. (+32) 2-2993842.

OPEN INNOVATION

Head of Unit: Matthew King; tel. (+32) 2-2955077.

OPEN SCIENCE AND ERA POLICY

Head of Unit: Fabienne Gautier; tel. (+32) 2-2993781.

SMES, FINANCIAL INSTRUMENTS AND STATE AID

Head of Unit: Stephane Ouaki; tel. (+32) 2-2967286.

RESEARCH INFRASTRUCTURE

Head of Unit: Antonio di Giulio; tel. (+32) 2-2995886.

SPREADING OF EXCELLENCE AND WIDENING PARTICIPATION

Head of Unit: Magda de Carli; tel. (+32) 2-2990512.

OPEN AND INCLUSIVE SOCIETIES

Head of Unit: Elisabeth Lipiatou; tel. (+32) 2-2966286.

SCIENCE WITH AND FOR SOCIETY

Head of Unit: Ana Arana Antelo; tel. (+32) 2-2964263.

ADMINISTRATION AND FINANCE

Head of Unit: Pascale Cid; tel. (+32) 2-2986226.

Directorate C—International Co-operation

Director: Maria Cristina Russo; tel. (+32) 2-2955975.

STRATEGY, EFTA AND ENLARGEMENT COUNTRIES, RUSSIA, ASIA AND PACIFIC

Head of Unit: Konstantinos Glinos; tel. (+32) 2-2969577; fax (+32) 2-2993127.

NORTH AMERICA, LATIN AMERICA AND CARIBBEAN

Head of Unit: Begona Arano; tel. (+32) 2-2992040.

EUROPEAN NEIGHBOURHOOD POLICY, AFRICA AND THE GULF

Head of Unit: Andrea Carignani di Novoli; tel. (+32) 2-2990095.

Directorate D—Industrial Technologies

Director: Peter Droell; tel. (+32) 2-2990348.

STRATEGY

Head of Unit: Doris Schroecker; tel. (+32) 2-2955869.

ADVANCED MANUFACTURING SYSTEMS AND BIOTECHNOLOGIES

Head of Unit: Jürgen Tiedje; tel. (+32) 2-2950525.

ADVANCED MATERIALS AND NANOTECHNOLOGIES

Head of Unit: Hélène Chraye; tel. (+32) 2-2989469.

DIRECTORY

European Commission

COAL AND STEEL
Head of Unit: Hervé Martin; tel. (+32) 2-2965444.

ADMINISTRATION AND FINANCE
Head of Unit: Patrik Kolar; tel. (+32) 2-2985161.

Directorate E—Health

Director (acting): Line Matthiessen; tel. (+32) 2-2952853.

STRATEGY
Head of Unit: Cornelius Schmaltz; tel. (+32) 2-2958984.

INNOVATIVE AND PERSONALIZED MEDICINE
Head of Unit: Irene Norstedt; tel. (+32) 2-2969527.

FIGHTING INFECTIOUS DISEASES AND ADVANCING PUBLIC HEALTH
Head of Unit: Line Matthiessen; tel. (+32) 2-2952853.

NON-COMMUNICABLE DISEASES AND THE CHALLENGE OF HEALTHY AGEING
Head of Unit: Maria Jose Vidal-Ragout; tel. (+32) 2-2965789.

INNOVATIVE TOOLS, TECHNOLOGIES AND CONCEPTS IN HEALTH RESEARCH
Head of Unit: Arnd Hoeveler; tel. (+32) 2-2956801.

ADMINISTRATION AND FINANCE
Head of Unit: Mila Bas Sánchez; tel. (+32) 2-2998391.

Directorate F—Bioeconomy

Director: John Bell; tel. (+32) 2-2991940.

STRATEGY
Head of Unit: Waldemar Kütt; tel. (+32) 2-2994145.

BIOBASED PRODUCTS AND PROCESSING
Head of Unit: Gaia Fantechi; tel. (+32) 2-2986217.

AGRI-FOOD CHAIN
Head of Unit: Barend Verachtert; tel. (+32) 2-2955311.

MARINE RESOURCES
Head of Unit: Sieglinde Grüber; tel. (+32) 2-2984342.

ADMINISTRATION AND FINANCE
Head of Unit: István László Narai; tel. (+32) 2-2966348.

Directorate G—Energy

Director (acting): Patrick Child; tel. (+32) 2-2959891.

ADMINISTRATION AND FINANCE STRATEGY
Head of Unit: Gwennael Joliff-Botrel; tel. (+32) 2-2965774.

ADVANCED ENERGY PRODUCTION
Head of Unit: Jose Cotta; tel. (+32) 2-2966407; fax (+32) 2-2969131.

RENEWABLE ENERGY SOURCES
Head of Unit: Piotr Tulej; tel. (+32) 2-2999732.

FISSION ENERGY
Head of Unit: Rita Lecbychova; tel. (+32) 2-2966038.

FUSION ENERGY
Head of Unit: Elena Righi Steele; tel. (+32) 2-2995213.

ADMINISTRATION AND FINANCE
Head of Unit: Marisa Atienza Morales; tel. (+32) 2-2966762.

Directorate H—Transport

Director: Clara de la Torre; tel. (+32) 2-2995827.

STRATEGY
Head of Unit: Tiit Jurimae; tel. (+32) 2-2992059.

SURFACE TRANSPORT
Head of Unit: Jean-François Aguinaga; tel. (+32) 2-2951442.

AVIATION
Head of Unit: Sebastiano Fumero; tel. (+32) 2-2969688.

ADMINISTRATION AND FINANCE
Head of Unit: Silvia Bojinova; tel. (+32) 2-2985891.

Directorate I—Climate Action and Resource Efficiency

Director: Jack Metthey; tel. (+32) 2-2968870.

STRATEGY
Head of Unit: Jean-François Hulot; tel. (+32) 2-2952991.

ECO-INNOVATION
Head of Unit: Pavel Misiga; tel. (+32) 2-2994420.

SUSTAINABLE MANAGEMENT OF NATURAL RESOURCES
Head of Unit: Birgit de Boissezon; tel. (+32) 2-2994715.

CLIMATE ACTION AND EARTH OBSERVATION
Head of Unit: Andrea Tilche; tel. (+32) 2-2996342.

ADMINISTRATION AND FINANCE
Head of Unit: Vincent Favrel; tel. (+32) 2-2993710.

Directorate J—Common Support Centre

Director: Anna Panagopoulou; tel. (+32) 2-2967894.

COMMON LEGAL SUPPORT SERVICE
Head of Unit (acting): Reinhard Schulte; tel. (+32) 2-2993750.

COMMON AUDIT SERVICE
Head of Unit: Marina Zanchi; tel. (+32) 2-2953814.

COMMON SERVICE FOR BUSINESS PROCESSES
Head of Unit (acting): Peter Haertwich; tel. (+32) 2-2950622.

COMMON IT SERVICE
Head of Unit: Stephane Ndong; tel. (+32) 2-2958151.

COMMON SERVICE FOR HORIZON 2020 INFORMATION AND DATA
Head of Unit (acting): Gabor Mihály Nagy; tel. (+32) 2-2968367.

Directorate R—Resources

Director: Priscila Fernández-Cañadas; tel. (+32) 2-2955945.

KNOWLEDGE AND INFORMATION SERVICES
Head of Unit: Bernardus Tubbing; tel. (+32) 2-2957142.

European Commission   DIRECTORY

BUDGET
Head of Unit: Jacques van Oost; tel. (+32) 2-2968523.

STRATEGIC PROGRAMMING, PLANNING AND COMPLIANCE
Head of Unit: Paul Webb; tel. (+32) 2-2954533.

NEW MANAGEMENT MODES
Head of Unit (acting): José-Lorenzo Valles; tel. (+32) 2-2991757.

JOINT RESEARCH CENTRE (JRC)

21 rue du Champ de Mars, 1050 Brussels, Belgium; tel. (+32) 2-2991111; fax (+32) 2-2950146; e-mail jrc-info@ec.europa.eu; internet ec.europa.eu/info/departments/joint-research-centre

Director-General: Vladimír Sucha; tel. (+32) 2-2995548.

Deputy Director-General: Maive Rute; tel. (+32) 2-2959159.

Reporting directly to the Director-General

Assistant to the Director-General: Margarita Nikolova; tel. (+32) 2-2988242.

Deputy Director-General, responsible for Directorates B, C, D, E, F and G

Deputy Director-General: Charlina Vitcheva; tel. (+32) 2-2950483.

Adviser for Policy Communication: Geraldine Barry; tel. (+32) 2-2990266.

Directorate A—Strategy and Work Programme Co-ordination (Brussels)

Director: Delilah al-Khudhairy; tel. (+32) 2-2999158.

Adviser for Public Tendering and Compliance: Eric Fischer; tel. (+32) 2-2958683.

Adviser for Talent Management: Josephina Pijls; tel. (+31) 2-24565332; fax (+31) 2-24565602.

RESOURCE MANAGEMENT, SEVILLE
Head of Unit: Vincenzo Cardarelli; tel. (+34) 9544-88324; fax (+34) 9544-88300.

RESOURCE MANAGEMENT, PETTEN
Head of Unit: Francesco Scaffidi-Argentina; tel. (+31) 2-24565208.

LOGISTICS
Head of Unit: Raymond Crandon; tel. (+39) 0332-789828.

MAINTENANCE AND UTILITIES
Head of Unit (acting): Maurizio Bavetta; tel. (+39) 0332-785571.

RESOURCE MANAGEMENT, GEEL
Head of Unit: Marc Wellens; tel. (+32) 1-4571327.

RESOURCE MANAGEMENT, KARLSRUHE
Head of Unit: Jacqueline Ribeiro; tel. (+49) 7247951-356.

BUDGET AND ACCOUNTING
Head of Unit: Stanislav Drapal; tel. (+31) 2-22960663.

FINANCE AND PROCUREMENT
Head of Unit: Iain Formosa; tel. (+39) 0332-786091.

INFRASTRUCTURE DEVELOPMENT
Head of Unit: François Augendre; tel. (+39) 0332-789541.

INFORMATION AND COMMUNICATION TECHNOLOGY
Head of Unit: Philippe Bierlaire; tel. (+32) 2-2994682.

Directorate B—Growth and Innovation (Seville)

Director (acting): Luis Delgado Sancho; tel. (+34) 9544-88218; fax (+34) 9544-88426.

FINANCE AND ECONOMY
Head of Unit: Francesca Campolongo; tel. (+39) 0332-785476; fax (+39) 0332-785752.

FISCAL POLICY ANALYSIS
Head of Unit: Daniel Daco; tel. (+34) 9544-88224.

TERRITORIAL DEVELOPMENT
Head of Unit: Alessandro Rainoldi; tel. (+34) 9544-88316; fax (+34) 9544-88326.

HUMAN CAPITAL AND EMPLOYMENT
Head of Unit: Ioannis Maghiros; tel. (+34) 9544-88281; fax (+34) 9544-88208.

CIRCULAR ECONOMY AND INDUSTRIAL LEADERSHIP
Head of Unit: Luis Delagado Sancho; tel. (+34) 9544-88218; fax (+34) 9544-88426.

DIGITAL ECONOMY
Head of Unit: Alessandro Annoni; tel. (+39) 0332-786166; fax (+39) 0332-786086.

KNOWLEDGE FOR FINANCE, INNOVATION AND GROWTH
Head of Unit: Xabier Goenaga Beldarrain; tel. (+32) 2-2965263.

Directorate C—Energy, Transport and Climate (Petten)

Director: Piotr Szymanski; tel. (+31) 2-24565401.

ENERGY STORAGE
Head of Unit (acting): Pietro Moretto; tel. (+31) 2-24565269.

ENERGY EFFICIENCY AND RENEWABLES
Head of Unit (acting): Diana Rembges; tel. (+39) 0332-785953; fax (+39) 0332-789453.

ENERGY SECURITY, DISTRIBUTION AND MARKETS
Head of Unit: Marcelo Masera; tel. (+31) 2-24565403.

SUSTAINABLE TRANSPORT
Head of Unit: Alois Krasenbrink; tel. (+39) 0332-785474.

AIR AND CLIMATE
Head of Unit: Elisabetta Vignati; tel. (+39) 0332-789414.

AIR AND CLIMATE: ECONOMICS OF CLIMATE CHANGE, ENERGY AND TRANSPORT
Head of Unit: Antonio Soria Ramírez; tel. (+34) 9544-88294.

KNOWLEDGE FOR THE ENERGY UNION
Head of Unit: Efstathios Peteves; tel. (+31) 2-24565245.

Directorate D—Sustainable Resources (ISPRA)

Director: David Wilkinson; tel. (+39) 0332-786541; fax (+39) 0332-789222.

Adviser: Peeter Part; tel. (+39) 0332-785496; fax (+39) 0332-789222.

BIO-ECONOMY
Head of Unit: Guido Schmuck; tel. (+39) 0332-785313; fax (+39) 0332-785230.

WATER AND MARINE RESOURCES
Head of Unit: Giovanni Bidoglio; tel. (+39) 0332-789383; fax (+39) 0332-785601.

LAND RESOURCES
Head of Unit: Constantin Ciupagea; tel. (+39) 0332-785132; fax (+39) 0332-786645.

ECONOMICS OF AGRICULTURE
Head of Unit: Giampiero Genovese; tel. (+34) 9544-87160; fax (+34) 9544-88434.

FOOD SECURITY
Head of Unit: Neil Hubbard; tel. (+39) 0332-785725; fax (+39) 0332-785162.

KNOWLEDGE FOR SUSTAINABLE DEVELOPMENT AND FOOD SECURITY
Head of Unit: Alan Belward; tel. (+39) 0332-789298; fax (+39) 0332-789073.

Directorate E—Space, Security and Migration (ISPRA)

Director: Dan Chirondojan; tel. (+39) 0332-789947; fax (+39) 0332-789923.

DISASTER RISK MANAGEMENT
Head of Unit: Ian Clark; tel. (+39) 0332-783585; fax (+39) 0332-785154.

TECHNOLOGY INNOVATION IN SECURITY
Head of Unit: Georg Peter; tel. (+39) 0332-789089; fax (+39) 0332-785469.

CYBER AND DIGITAL CITIZENS' SECURITY
Head of Unit: Jean-Pierre Nordvik; tel. (+39) 0332-785021; fax (+39) 0332-785813.

SAFETY AND SECURITY OF BUILDINGS
Head of Unit: Artur Pinto; tel. (+39) 0332-789294; fax (+39) 0332-789049.

TRANSPORT AND BORDER SECURITY
Head of Unit: Bartel Meersman; tel. (+32) 1457-1404; fax (+32) 1457-1539.

DEMOGRAPHY, MIGRATION AND GOVERNANCE
Head of Unit: Alessandra Zampieri; tel. (+39) 0332-783894; fax (+39) 0332-789156.

KNOWLEDGE FOR SECURITY AND MIGRATION
Head of Unit: Giacinto Tartaglia; tel. (+39) 0332-789338; fax (+39) 0332-786543.

Directorate F—Health, Consumers and Reference Materials (Geel)

Director: Elke Anklam; tel. (+32) 14-571292.

HEALTH IN SOCIETY
Head of Unit: Ciaran Nicholl; tel. (+39) 0332-789523; fax (+39) 0332-789059.

CONSUMER PRODUCTS SAFETY
Head of Unit: María Pilar Aguar Fernández; tel. (+39) 0332-785950; fax (+39) 0332-789453.

CHEMICALS SAFETY AND ALTERNATIVE METHODS
Head of Unit: Maurice Whelan; tel. (+39) 0332-786234; fax (+39) 0332-789963.

FRAUD DETECTION AND PREVENTION
Head of Unit: Franz Ulberth; tel. (+32) 14-571316.

FOOD AND FEED COMPLIANCE
Head of Unit: Hendrik Emons; tel. (+32) 14-571722.

REFERENCE MATERIALS
Head of Unit: Doris Florian; tel. (+32) 14-571272; fax (+32) 14-571864.

KNOWLEDGE FOR HEALTH AND CONSUMER SAFETY
Head of Unit: Guy van den Eede; tel. (+32) 14-571481.

Directorate G—Nuclear Safety and Security (Karlsruhe)

Director: Maria Betti; tel. (+49 7247) 951350; fax (+49 7247) 951591.

JRC SITES, RADIO PROTECTION AND SECURITY
Head of Unit: Ralph Maier; tel. (+49 7247) 951330.

STANDARDS FOR NUCLEAR SAFETY, SECURITY AND SAFEGUARDS
Head of Unit: Willy Mondelaers; tel. (+32) 14-571478.

NUCLEAR FUEL SAFETY
Head of Unit: Rudy Konings; tel. (+49 7247) 951391.

NUCLEAR REACTOR SAFETY AND EMERGENCY PREPAREDNESS
Head of Unit (acting): Michael Fütterer; tel. (+31) 2-24565158.

ADVANCED NUCLEAR KNOWLEDGE
Head of Unit: Roberto Caciuffo; tel. (+49 7247) 951382; fax (+49 7247) 95199382.

NUCLEAR SAFEGUARDS AND FORENSICS
Head of Unit: Klaus Lützenkirchen; tel. (+49 7247) 951424.

NUCLEAR SECURITY
Head of Unit: Stefan Nonneman; tel. (+39) 0332-783631.

WASTE MANAGEMENT
Head of Unit: Joseph Somers; tel. (+49 7247) 951359.

JRC NUCLEAR DECOMMISSIONING
Head of Unit: Paolo Peerani; tel. (+39) 0332-785625; fax (+39) 0332-785072.

European Commission

KNOWLEDGE FOR NUCLEAR SECURITY AND SAFETY
Head of Unit: Franck Wastin; tel. (+31) 2-24565066; fax (+31) 2-24565637.

Directorate A—Strategy and Work Programme Co-ordination (Brussels)
Director: Delilah Al Khudhairy; tel. (+32) 2-2999158.

ADVISER FOR BIO-ECONOMY
Adviser: Joachim Kreysa; tel. (+32) 2-2952959.

RESOURCE PLANNING
Head of Unit: Patrice Lemaitre; tel. (+32) 2-2961464.

WORK PROGRAMME
Head of Unit: Margareta Theelen; tel. (+32) 2-2993184.

INTER-INSTITUTIONAL, INTERNATIONAL RELATIONS AND OUTREACH
Head of Unit: Emanuela Bellan; tel. (+32) 2-2953134.

LEGAL AFFAIRS
Head of Unit: Carina Røhl Søberg; tel. (+32) 2-2953724.

SCIENTIFIC DEVELOPMENT
Head of Unit: Jutta Thielen-Del Pozo; tel. (+39) 0332-785455; fax (+39) 0332-785704.

QUALITY ASSURANCE AND EVALUATION
Head of Unit: Jens Otto; tel. (+32) 2-2969468.

EURATOM CO-ORDINATION
Head of Unit: Said Abousahl; tel. (+32) 2-2990133.

Directorate H—Knowledge Management (Ispra)
Director: Krzysztof Maruszewski; tel. (+39) 0332-786514; fax (+39) 0332-789059.

GEOGRAPHIC CO-ORDINATION
Head of Unit: David Mair; tel. (+32) 2-2950489.

THEMATIC CO-ORDINATION
Head of Unit: Marc Wilikens; tel. (+39) 0332-789737; fax (+39) 0332-789991.

Directorate I—Competencies (ISPRA)
Director: Giovanni de Santi; tel. (+39) 0332-789482; fax (+39) 0332-785869.

MODELLING, INDICATORS AND IMPACT EVALUATION
Head of Unit: Sven Langedijik; tel. (+39) 0332-789103; fax (+39) 0332-785752.

FORESIGHT, BEHAVIOURAL INSIGHTS AND DESIGN FOR POLICY
Head of Unit: Xavier Troussard; tel. (+32) 2-2999126.

TEXT AND DATA MINING
Head of Unit: Margarida Abecasis; tel. (+39) 0332-783571; fax (+39) 0332-786369.

INTELLECTUAL PROPERTY AND TECHNOLOGY TRANSFER
Head of Unit: Giancarlo Caratti Di Lanzacco; tel. (+32) 2-2961516.

DG CNECT—DIRECTORATE-GENERAL FOR COMMUNICATIONS NETWORKS, CONTENT AND TECHNOLOGY

25 ave de Beaulieu, 1049 Brussels, Belgium; tel. (+32) 2-2991111; fax (+32) 2-2999499; e-mail cnect-desk@ec.europa.eu; internet ec.europa.eu/digital-single-market/dg-connect

Director-General: Roberto Viola; tel. (+32) 2-2960240.

Deputy Director-General, responsible for Directorates A, C, E and H: Khalil Rouhana; tel. (+32) 2-2968057.

Deputy Director-General, responsible for Directorates B, D, F, G and I: Claire Bury; tel. (+32) 2-2960499.

Reporting directly to the Director-General

Assistant to the Director-General: Olivier Bringer; tel. (+32) 2-2992067.

Principal Adviser: Florin Lupescu; tel. (+32) 2-2968538.

Adviser (International Relations linked to Future Networks): Per Axel Blixt; tel. (+32) 2-2968048.

Adviser (Digital Single Market International Outreach): Tonnie de Koster; tel. (+32) 2-2968501.

Adviser (Societal Challenges): Ilias Iakovidis; tel. (+32) 2-2952329.

Adviser (Societal Issues): Nicole Dewandre; tel. (+32) 2-2994925.

Adviser (Innovation Systems): Bror Salmelin; tel. (+32) 2-2969564.

Directorate A—Digital Industry
Director (acting): Khalil Rouhana; tel. (+32) 2-2968057.

ROBOTICS AND ARTIFICIAL INTELLIGENCE
Head of Unit: Juha Heikkilä; tel. (+32) 2-2935325.

TECHNOLOGIES AND SYSTEMS FOR DIGITIZING INDUSTRY
Head of Unit: Max Lemke; tel. (+32) 2-2991575.

COMPETITIVE ELECTRONICS INDUSTRY
Head of Unit (acting): Colette Maloney; tel. (+32) 2-2969082.

PHOTONICS
Head of Unit: Philippe Vannson; tel. (+32) 2-2956921.

ADMINISTRATION AND FINANCE
Head of Unit: Ales Fiala; tel. (+32) 2-2964787.

Directorate C—Digital Excellence and Science Infrastructure
Director: Thomas Skordas; tel. (+32) 2-2968908.

E-INFRASTRUCTURE AND SCIENCE CLOUD
Head of Unit: Augusto Burgueno Arjona; tel. (+32) 2-2992471.

HIGH PERFORMANCE COMPUTING AND QUANTUM TECHNOLOGY
Head of Unit: Gustav Kalbe; tel. (+32) 2-2952117.

FUTURE AND EMERGING TECHNOLOGIES (FET)
Head of Unit: Viorel Peca; tel. (+32) 2-2957843.

FLAGSHIPS

Head of Unit (acting): Aymard de Touzalin; tel. (+32) 2-2968540.

Directorate E—Future Networks

Director (acting): Pearse O'Donohue; tel. (+32) 2-2991280; fax (+32) 2-2961775.

FUTURE CONNECTIVITY SYSTEMS

Head of Unit: Peter Stuckmann; tel. (+32) 2-2921097.

CLOUD AND SOFTWARE

Head of Unit: Pearse O'Donohue; tel. (+32) 2-2991280; fax (+32) 2-2961775.

NEXT-GENERATION INTERNET

Head of Unit (acting): Peter Fatelnig; tel. (+32) 2-2991890.

INTERNET OF THINGS

Head of Unit: Mechthild Rohen; tel. (+32) 2-2963674.

Directorate H—Digital Society, Trust and Cybersecurity

Director: Despina Spanou; tel. (+32) 2-2975979.

CYBERSECURITY AND DIGITAL PRIVACY

Head of Unit: Jakub Boratynski; tel. (+32) 2-2969452.

SMART MOBILITY AND LIVING

Head of Unit: Eddy Hartog; tel. (+32) 2-2990084.

E-HEALTH, WELL-BEING AND AGEING

Head of Unit: Miguel González-Sancho; tel. (+32) 2-2952918.

E-GOVERNMENT AND TRUST

Head of Unit: Andrea Servida; tel. (+32) 2-2958186.

ADMINISTRATION AND FINANCE

Head of Unit: Griet van Caenegem; tel. (+32) 2-2961895.

Directorate B—Electronic Communications Networks and Services

Director: Anthony Whelan; tel. (+32) 2-2950941.

IMPLEMENTATION OF THE REGULATORY FRAMEWORK

Head of Unit: Wolf-Dietrich Grussmann; tel. (+32) 2-2958559.

MARKETS

Head of Unit: Reinald Krueger; tel. (+32) 2-2961555.

RADIO SPECTRUM POLICY

Head of Unit: Andreas Geiss; tel. (+32) 2-2959466.

INVESTMENT IN HIGH-CAPACITY NETWORKS

Head of Unit (acting): Hervá Dupuy; tel. (+32) 2-2995258.

Directorate D—Policy Strategy and Outreach

Director: Linda Corugedo Steneberg; tel. (+32) 2-2996383.

RESEARCH STRATEGY AND PROGRAMME CO-ORDINATION

Head of Unit: Morten Fjalland; tel. (+32) 2-2950021.

POLICY IMPLEMENTATION AND PLANNING

Head of Unit: Lorena Boix Alonso; tel. (+32) 2-2990009.

POLICY OUTREACH AND INTERNATIONAL AFFAIRS

Head of Unit: David Ringrose; tel. (+32) 2-2993913.

COMMUNICATION

Head of Unit (acting): Anna Katrami; tel. (+32) 2-2991870; fax (+32) 2-2969037.

Directorate F—Digital Single Market

Director: Gerard de Graaf; tel. (+32) 2-2968466.

DIGITAL POLICY DEVELOPMENT AND CO-ORDINATION

Head of Unit: Martin Bailey; tel. (+32) 2-2969176.

E-COMMERCE AND PLATFORMS

Head of Unit: Werner Stengg; tel. (+32) 2-2969159.

START-UPS AND INNOVATION

Head of Unit: Peteris Zilgalvis; tel. (+32) 2-2950935.

DIGITAL ECONOMY AND SKILLS

Head of Unit: Lucilla Sioli; tel. (+32) 2-2951262.

Directorate G—Data

Director: Gail Kent; tel. (+352) 430135160.

DATA POLICY AND INNOVATION

Head of Unit: Yvo Volman; tel. (+352) 430131959.

DATA APPLICATIONS AND CREATIVITY

Head of Unit (acting): Federico Milani; tel. (+352) 430138155.

LEARNING, MULTILINGUALISM AND ACCESSIBILITY

Head of Unit: Marco Marsella; tel. (+352) 430132750.

ADMINISTRATION AND FINANCE

Head of Unit: June Lowery-Kingston; tel. (+352) 430131555.

Directorate I—Media Policy

Director: Giuseppe Abbamonte; tel. (+32) 2-2993573.

AUDIOVISUAL AND MEDIA SERVICES POLICY

Head of Unit (acting): Giuseppe Abbamonte; tel. (+32) 2-2993573.

COPYRIGHT

Head of Unit (acting): Marco Giorello; tel. (+32) 2-2969563.

AUDIOVISUAL INDUSTRY AND MEDIA SUPPORT PROGRAMMES

Head of Unit: Lucia Recalde Langarica; tel. (+32) 2-2991281.

MEDIA CONVERGENCE AND SOCIAL MEDIA

Head of Unit: Paolo Cesarini; tel. (+32) 2-2951286.

Directorate R—Resources and Support

Director (acting): Ingrid Marien-Dusak; tel. (+32) 2-2992376.

HR BUSINESS CORRESPONDENT AND SUPPORT SERVICES

Head of Unit: Ingrid Marien-Dusak; tel. (+32) 2-2992376.

BUDGET AND FINANCE
Head of Unit: Marie-Christine Laffineur; tel. (+32) 2-2968515.

KNOWLEDGE MANAGEMENT AND SUPPORT SYSTEMS
Head of Unit: Franco Accordino; tel. (+32) 2-2998272.

COMPLIANCE AND PLANNING
Head of Unit: Katleen Engelbosch; tel. (+32) 2-2954693.

PROGRAMME OPERATIONS AND COMMON SERVICES
Head of Unit (acting): Peter Diry; tel. (+32) 2-2969252.

DG MARE—DIRECTORATE-GENERAL FOR MARITIME AFFAIRS AND FISHERIES

99 rue Joseph II, 1000 Brussels, Belgium; tel. (+32) 2-2991111; internet ec.europa.eu/info/departments/maritime-affairs-and-fisheries

Director-General: João Aguiar Machado; tel. (+32) 2-2996310.

Principal Adviser (CFP Policy Development): Ernesto Penas Lado; tel. (+32) 2-2963744.

Principal Adviser (Development of Fisheries Law): Fabrizio Donatella; tel. (+32) 2-2968038.

Assistant to the Director-General: Stijn Billiet; tel. (+32) 2-2957641.

Assistant to the Director-General: Céline Idil; tel. (+32) 2-2966900.

Directorate A—Maritime Policy and Blue Economy

Director: Bernhard Friess; tel. (+32) 2-2956038.

MARITIME INNOVATION, MARINE KNOWLEDGE AND INVESTMENT
Head of Unit: Haitze Siemers; tel. (+32) 2-2990185.

BLUE ECONOMY SECTORS, AQUACULTURE AND MARITIME SPATIAL PLANNING
Head of Unit: Felix Leinemann; tel. (+32) 2-2983093.

SEA-BASIN STRATEGIES, MARITIME REGIONAL CO-OPERATION AND MARITIME SECURITY
Head of Unit: Christos Economou; tel. (+32) 2-2966310.

ECONOMIC ANALYSIS, MARKETS AND IMPACT ASSESSMENT
Head of Unit: Frangiscos Nikolian; tel. (+32) 2-2956208.

Directorate B—International Ocean Governance and Sustainable Fisheries

Director: Stefaan Depypere; tel. (+32) 2-2990713.

Adviser (International Affairs): Kristofer du Rietz; tel. (+32) 2-2966434.

OCEAN GOVERNANCE, LAW OF THE SEA, ARCTIC POLICY
Head of Unit: Andreas Papaconstantinou; tel. (+32) 2-2982008.

REGIONAL FISHERIES MANAGEMENT ORGANIZATIONS
Head of Unit: Anders Jessen; tel. (+32) 2-2992457.

TRADE NEGOTIATIONS AND SUSTAINABLE FISHERIES PARTNERSHIP AGREEMENTS
Head of Unit: Christian Rambaud; tel. (+32) 2-2960545.

ILLEGAL, UNREPORTED AND UNREGULATED FISHERIES POLICY
Head of Unit: Roberto Cesari; tel. (+32) 2-2994276.

Directorate C—Fisheries Policy Atlantic, North Sea, Baltic and Outermost Regions

Director: Helene Clark; tel. (+32) 2-2952957.

Adviser (Norway): Jacques Verborgh; tel. (+32) 2-2951352.

FISHERIES MANAGEMENT ATLANTIC, NORTH SEA AND BALTIC SEA
Head of Unit: Maja Kirchner; tel. (+32) 2-2980508.

STRUCTURAL SUPPORT ATLANTIC, NORTH SEA, BALTIC SEA AND OUTERMOST REGIONS
Head of Unit: Isabelle Garzon; tel. (+32) 2-2956301.

SCIENTIFIC ADVICE AND DATA COLLECTION
Head of Unit: Ilona Jepsena; tel. (+32) 2-2969149.

DATA MANAGEMENT
Head of Unit: Bernardus Kloppenborg; tel. (+32) 2-2987540.

Directorate D—Fisheries Policy Mediterranean and Black Sea

Director: Veronika Veits; tel. (+32) 2-2967224.

Adviser (Mediterranean Strategy): Franz Lamplmair; tel. (+32) 2-2957765.

FISHERIES MANAGEMENT MEDITERRANEAN AND BLACK SEA
Head of Unit: Valerie Laine; tel. (+32) 2-2965341.

STRUCTURAL SUPPORT MEDITERRANEAN, BLACK SEA AND LANDLOCKED MEMBER STATES
Head of Unit: Fabrizia Benini; tel. (+32) 2-2966417.

CFP AND STRUCTURAL SUPPORT, POLICY DEVELOPMENT AND CO-ORDINATION
Head of Unit: Elisa Roller; tel. (+32) 2-2986951.

FISHERIES CONTROL AND INSPECTIONS
Head of Unit (acting): Francesca Arena; tel. (+32) 2-2961364.

Directorate E—General Affairs and Resources

Director: Dora Correra; tel. (+32) 2-2950101.

BUDGET, AUDIT AND PUBLIC PROCUREMENT
Head of Unit: Andrew Mathison; tel. (+32) 2-2956051.

INTER-INSTITUTIONAL MATTERS, STRATEGIC PROGRAMMING AND COMMUNICATION
Head of Unit: Carmen Preising; tel. (+32) 2-2986983.

HR BUSINESS CORRESPONDENT, IT AND ELECTRONIC DOCUMENT MANAGEMENT
Head of Unit: Simona Lupu; tel. (+32) 2-2966224.

LEGAL AFFAIRS
Head of Unit: Valérie Tankink; tel. (+32) 2-2987430.

DG FISMA—DIRECTORATE-GENERAL FOR FINANCIAL STABILITY, FINANCIAL SERVICES AND CAPITAL MARKETS UNION

2 rue de Spa, 1000 Brussels, Belgium; tel. (+32) 2-2991111; internet ec.europa.eu/info/departments/financial-stability-financial-services-and-capital-markets-union

Director-General: Olivier Guersent; tel. (+32) 2-2965414.

Deputy Director-General, in charge of Directorates B, C, D and E: John Berrigan; tel. (+32) 2-2993580.

Policy Assistant to the Director-General: Anne Schaedle; tel. (+32) 2-2995612.

Directorate B—Investment and Company Reporting

Director: Nathalie de Basaldua; tel. (+32) 2-2956189.

FREE MOVEMENT OF CAPITAL AND APPLICATION OF EU LAW
Head of Unit: Chantal Hughes; tel. (+32) 2-2964450.

ECONOMIC ANALYSIS AND EVALUATION
Head of Unit: Martin Spolc; tel. (+32) 2-2986535.

ACCOUNTING AND FINANCIAL REPORTING
Head of Unit: Alain Deckers; tel. (+32) 2-2992348.

AUDIT AND CREDIT RATING AGENCIES
Head of Unit: Dorota Kalina Zaliwska; tel. (+32) 2-2966943.

Directorate C—Financial Markets

Director: Ugo Bassi; tel. (+32) 2-2953118.

CAPITAL MARKETS UNION
Head of Unit: Niall Bohan; tel. (+32) 2-2963007.

FINANCIAL MARKETS INFRASTRUCTURE
Head of Unit: Patrick Pearson; tel. (+32) 2-2955758.

SECURITIES MARKETS
Head of Unit: Tilman Lueder; tel. (+32) 2-2991548.

ASSET MANAGEMENT
Head of Unit: Sven Gentner; tel. (+32) 2-2985365.

Directorate D—Regulation and Prudential Supervision of Financial Institutions

Director: Martin Merlin; tel. (+32) 2-2958947.

BANK REGULATION AND SUPERVISION
Head of Unit: Klaus Wiedner; tel. (+32) 2-2967125.

BANKS AND FINANCIAL CONGLOMERATES
Head of Unit: Didier Millerot; tel. (+32) 2-2969782.

RETAIL FINANCIAL SERVICES AND PAYMENTS
Head of Unit: Ralf Jacob; tel. (+32) 2-2990483.

INSURANCE AND PENSIONS
Head of Unit: Nathalie Berger; tel. (+32) 2-2996503.

Directorate E—Financial System Surveillance and Crisis Management

Director: Mario Nava; tel. (+32) 2-2964235.

Adviser: Nigel Nagarajan; tel. (+32) 2-2987509.

EU/EURO AREA FINANCIAL SYSTEM
Head of Unit: Peter Grasmann; tel. (+32) 2-2993417.

NATIONAL FINANCIAL SYSTEMS
Head of Unit: Filip Keereman; tel. (+32) 2-2993490.

MACROPRUDENTIAL POLICY AND RELATIONS WITH THE ESRB
Head of Unit: Almoro Rubin de Cervin; tel. (+32) 2-2955008.

RESOLUTION AND CRISIS MANAGEMENT
Head of Unit (acting): Emiliano Tornese; tel. (+32) 2-2985400.

Directorate A—Resources and Communication

Director: Pamela Brumter-Coret; tel. (+32) 2-2959408.

HR BUSINESS CORRESPONDENT AND INFORMATION TECHNOLOGY
Head of Unit: Florence François-Poncet; tel. (+32) 2-2993816.

FINANCIAL RESOURCES AND INTERNAL CONTROL
Head of Unit: Nathalie Stefanowicz; tel. (+32) 2-2962213.

COMMUNICATION AND DOCUMENT MANAGEMENT
Head of Unit: Henning Arp; tel. (+32) 2-2957310.

DG REGIO—DIRECTORATE-GENERAL FOR REGIONAL AND URBAN POLICY

1 rue Pére de Deken, 1049 Brussels, Belgium; tel. (+32) 2-2991111; fax (+32) 2-2966003; internet ec.europa.eu/info/departments/regional-and-urban-policy

Director-General: Marc Lemaître; tel. (+32) 2-2990902.

Deputy Director-General with responsibility for Implementation: Normunds Popens; tel. (+32) 2-2980690.

Reporting directly to the Director-General

Assistant to the Director-General: Eva Maria Szavuj; tel. (+32) 2-2967448.

Northern Ireland Task Force and International Relations

Principal Adviser: Ronald Hall; tel. (+32) 2-2954401.

Policy and Implementation

Principal Adviser: Natalija Kazlauskienė; tel. (+32) 2-2963130.

Co-ordination and Policy Dialogue Eastern Partnership and Russia

Adviser: Michael Ralph; tel. (+32) 2-2955023.

Directorate A—Budget, Communication and General Affairs

Director: Dana Spinant; tel. (+32) 2-2990150.

OUTERMOST REGIONS
Head of Unit: Sabine Bourdy; tel. (+32) 2-2980291.

COMMUNICATION
Head of Unit: Agnès Monfret; tel. (+32) 2-2965402.

European Commission

BUDGET AND FINANCIAL MANAGEMENT
Head of Unit: Philippe Jouret; tel. (+32) 2-2965768.

IT IMPLEMENTATION AND IT GOVERNANCE
Head of Unit: Rik Vooges; tel. (+32) 2-2968108.

Directorate B—Policy
Director: Eric Von Breska; tel. (+32) 2-2995149.

POLICY DEVELOPMENT AND ECONOMIC ANALYSIS
Head of Unit: Moray Gilland; tel. (+32) 2-2969289.

EVALUATION AND EUROPEAN SEMESTER
Head of Unit: Mariana Hristcheva; tel. (+32) 2-2960840.

FINANCIAL INSTRUMENTS AND INTERNATIONAL FINANCIAL INSTITUTIONS RELATIONS
Head of Unit: Stefan Appel; tel. (+32) 2-2954596.

LEGAL AFFAIRS
Head of Unit: Erik Nooteboom; tel. (+32) 2-2960348.

Directorate C—Audit
Director: Franck Sébert; tel. (+32) 2-2969590.

CO-ORDINATION, RELATIONS WITH THE COURT OF AUDITORS AND OLAF
Head of Unit: Lothar Kuhl; tel. (+32) 2-2963925.

AUDIT 1
Head of Unit: Caroline Callens; tel. (+32) 2-2993927.

AUDIT 2
Head of Unit: Claude Tourner; tel. (+32) 2-2951644.

AUDIT 3
Head of Unit: Ilse van den Abeele; tel. (+32) 2-2998962.

Directorate D—European Territorial Co-operation, Macro-regions, Interreg and Programme Implementation I
Director: Lena Andersson Pench; tel. (+32) 2-2959819.

MACRO-REGIONS, TRANSNATIONAL/INTERREGIONAL CO-OPERATION, IPA, ENLARGEMENT
Head of Unit: Jean-Pierre Halkin; tel. (+32) 2-2957042.

INTERREG, CROSS-BORDER CO-OPERATION, INTERNAL BORDERS
Head of Unit: Ana-Paula Laissy; tel. (+32) 2-2953258.

BELGIUM, FRANCE AND LUXEMBOURG
Head of Geographical Unit France, Belgium and Luxembourg: Agnes Lindemans; tel. +32 229-60528.

DENMARK, IRELAND, SWEDEN AND THE UK
Head of Unit for Regional Operations in Denmark, Ireland, Sweden and the UK (acting): Lena Andersson Pench; tel. (+32) 2-2959819.

ESTONIA, FINLAND, LATVIA AND LITHUANIA
Head of Unit: Angela Martínez Sarasola; tel. (+32) 2-2951711.

Directorate E—Administrative Capacity Building and Programme Implementation II
Director: Vittoria Alliata-Di Villafranca; tel. (+32) 2-2958386.

ROMANIA
Head of Unit: Carsten Rasmussen; tel. (+32) 2-2963446.

BULGARIA, CROATIA AND SLOVENIA
Head of Unit: Aurelio Cecilio; tel. (+32) 2-2962806.

HUNGARY
Head of Unit: Thomas Bender; tel. (+32) 2-2969917.

Directorate F—Closure, Major Projects and Programme Implementation III
Director: Erich Unterwurzacher; tel. (+32) 2-2966721.

CLOSURE AND MAJOR PROJECTS
Head of Unit: Jonathan Denness; tel. (+32) 2-2965038.

AUSTRIA, GERMANY AND THE NETHERLANDS
Head of Unit: Leo Maier; tel. (+32) 2-2998195.

POLAND
Head of Unit: Christopher Todd; tel. (+32) 2-2957776.

CZECH REPUBLIC AND SLOVAKIA
Head of Unit: Andreas von Busch; tel. (+32) 2-2955108.

Directorate G—Smart and Sustainable Growth and Programme Implementation IV
Director: Rudolf Niessler; tel. (+32) 2-2995280.

SMART AND SUSTAINABLE GROWTH
Head of Unit: Peter Berkowitz; tel. (+32) 2-2962017.

SPAIN
Head of Unit: Aderito Pinto; tel. (+32) 2-2959781.

PORTUGAL
Head of Unit: Georgios Yannoussis; tel. (+32) 2-2960585.

ITALY AND MALTA
Head of Unit (acting): Rudolf Niessler; tel. (+32) 2-2995280.

CYPRUS AND GREECE
Head of Unit: Willibrordus Sluijters; tel. (+32) 2-2954667.

DG TAXUD—DIRECTORATE-GENERAL FOR TAXATION AND CUSTOMS UNION

79 rue Joseph II, 1000 Brussels, Belgium; tel. (+32) 2-2991111; internet ec.europa.eu/info/departments/taxation-and-customs-union

Director-General: Stephen Quest; tel. (+32) 2-2965897.

Harmonization IT Co-ordination
Principal Adviser: Paulo José Santos; tel. (+32) 2-2985084.

Directorate R—Resources
Director: Sabine Henzler; tel. (+32) 2-2992441.

FINANCES AND HR BUSINESS CORRESPONDENT
Head of Unit: Stéphane Mail Fouilleul; tel. (+32) 2-2995050.

INTER-INSTITUTIONAL RELATIONS, CO-ORDINATION, COMMUNICATION AND STRATEGIC PLANNING
Head of Unit: Momchil Sabev; tel. (+32) 2-2952135.

MANAGEMENT OF PROGRAMMES AND EU TRAINING
Head of Unit: Michèle Perolat; tel. (+32) 2-2952451.

Directorate A—Customs Policy, Legislation, Tariff
Director: Philip Kermode; tel. (+32) 2-2961371.

CUSTOMS POLICY
Head of Unit: Ilze Kuniga; tel. (+32) 2-2980567.

CUSTOMS LEGISLATION
Head of Unit: Susanne Aigner; tel. (+32) 2-2966795.

CUSTOMS PROCESSES AND PROJECT MANAGEMENT
Head of Unit (acting): Sophie de Coster; tel. (+32) 2-2986134.

COMBINED NOMENCLATURE, TARIFF CLASSIFICATION, TARIC AND INTEGRATION OF TRADE MEASURES
Head of Unit: Antti Suortti; tel. (+32) 2-2967258.

ENTERPRISE ARCHITECTURE AND IT OPERATIONS
Head of Unit (acting): Paul-Hervé Theunissen; tel. (+32) 2-2963095.

CUSTOMS IT SYSTEMS FOR THE UNION CUSTOMS CODE
Head of Unit: Paul-Hervé Theunissen; tel. (+32) 2-2963095.

Directorate B—Security, Safety, Facilitation of Trade, Rules of Origin and International Co-operation
Director: Antonis Kastrissianakis; tel. (+32) 2-2957380.

PROTECTION OF CITIZENS AND ENFORCEMENT OF IPR
Head of Unit: Pierre-Jacques Larrieu; tel. (+32) 2-2959489.

RISK MANAGEMENT AND SECURITY
Head of Unit: Lina Papamichalopoulou; tel. (+32) 2-2986493.

TRADE FACILITATION, RULES OF ORIGIN AND INTERNATIONAL CO-ORDINATION: EUROPE AND NEIGHBOURING COUNTRIES
Head of Unit: Peter Kovacs; tel. (+32) 2-295948971918.

TRADE FACILITATION, RULES OF ORIGIN AND INTERNATIONAL CO-ORDINATION: AMERICAS, AFRICA, FAR EAST AND SOUTH ASIA, OCEANIA AND INTERNATIONAL ORGANIZATIONS
Head of Unit: Jean-Michel Grave; tel. (+32) 2-2951520.

Directorate C—Indirect Taxation and Tax Administration
Director: Maria Teresa Fabregas Fernández; tel. (+32) 2-2995177.

VALUE-ADDED TAX
Head of Unit: Maria Elena Scoppio; tel. (+32) 2-2954129.

INDIRECT TAXES OTHER THAN VAT
Head of Unit: Thomas Carroll; tel. (+32) 2-2955842.

CONTROL OF THE APPLICATION OF EU LEGISLATION AND STATE AID/INDIRECT TAXES
Head of Unit: Patrice Pillet; tel. (+32) 2-2991993.

TAX ADMINISTRATION AND THE FIGHT AGAINST TAX FRAUD
Head of Unit: Caroline Edery; tel. (+32) 2-2969906.

TAXATION SYSTEMS AND IT COMPLIANCE
Head of Unit: Theodoros Vassiliadis; tel. (+32) 2-2961739.

Directorate D—Direct Taxation, Tax Co-ordination, Economic Analysis and Evaluation
Director: Valère Moutarlier; tel. (+32) 2-2962162.

COMPANY TAXATION INITIATIVES
Head of Unit: Bernardus Zuijdendorp; tel. (+32) 2-2960321.

DIRECT TAX POLICY AND CO-OPERATION
Head of Unit: Thomas Neale; tel. (+32) 2-2954705.

CONTROL OF THE APPLICATION OF EU LEGISLATION AND STATE AID/DIRECT TAXATION
Head of Unit: Wolfgang Mederer; tel. (+32) 2-2953584.

ECONOMIC ANALYSIS, EVALUATION AND IMPACT ASSESSMENT SUPPORT
Head of Unit: Gaëtan Nicodeme; tel. (+32) 2-2969751.

DG EAC—DIRECTORATE-GENERAL FOR EDUCATION, YOUTH, SPORT AND CULTURE

70 rue Joseph II, 1049 Brussels, Belgium; tel. (+32) 2-2991111; e-mail eac-info@ec.europa.eu; internet ec.europa.eu/info/departments/education-and-culture

Director-General: Martine Reicherts; tel. (+32) 2-2987121.

Adviser: Giorgio Sonnino; tel. (+32) 2-2990463.

Deputy Director-General, in charge of Directorates C and D: Jens Nymand Christenen; tel. (+32) 2-2993317.

Reporting directly to the Director-General

Policy Co-ordination and Inter-Institutional Relations

Head of Unit: Filip Van Depoele; tel. (+32) 2-2995667.

Assistant to the Director-General: Luca Perego; tel. (+32) 2-2990064.

Principal Adviser: Tamás Szücs; tel. (+32) 2-2992273.

Directorate A—Policy Strategy and Evaluation
Director: Stefaan Hermans; tel. (+32) 2-2969288; fax (+32) 2-2975168.

Adviser: Luca Dalpozzo; tel. (+32) 2-2951771.

Adviser: Sergej Koperdak; tel. (+32) 2-2969375.

STRATEGY AND INVESTMENTS
Head of Unit (acting): Stefaan Hermans; tel. (+32) 2-2969288; fax (+32) 2-2975168.

COUNTRY ANALYSIS
Head of Unit: Denis Crowley; tel. (+32) 2-2995943.

STAKEHOLDER ENGAGEMENT AND PROGRAMME IMPACT
Head of Unit: Francesca Pagnossin; tel. (+32) 2-2994954.

EVIDENCE-BASED POLICY AND EVALUATION
Head of Unit: Jan Pakulski; tel. (+32) 2-2953699.

Directorate B—Youth, Education and Erasmus+
Director: Sophia Eriksson Waterschoot; tel. (+32) 2-2969044.

Adviser: Belen Bernaldo De Quiros; tel. (+32) 2-2960312.

HIGHER EDUCATION
Head of Unit: Adam Tyson; tel. (+32) 2-2966056.

SCHOOLS AND MULTILIGUALISM
Head of Unit: Michael Teutsch; tel. (+32) 2-2992317.

YOUTH, VOLUNTEER SOLIDARITY AND TRAINEESHIPS OFFICE
Head of Unit: Florencia van Houdt; tel. (+32) 2-2991228.

ERASMUS+ CO-ORDINATION
Head of Unit: Barbara Nolan; tel. (+32) 2-2950857.

Directorate C—Innovation, International Co-operation and Sport
Director: Antoaneta Angelova-Krasteva; tel. (+32) 2-2991145.

INNOVATION AND EIT
Head of Unit: Harald Hartung; tel. (+32) 2-2965450.

MARIE SKŁODOWSKA-CURIE ACTIONS
Head of Unit: Sophie Beernaerts; tel. (+32) 2-2966315.

INTERNATIONAL CO-OPERATION
Head of Unit: Claire Morel; tel. (+32) 2-2993925.

SPORT
Head of Unit: Yves le Lostecque; tel. (+32) 2-2965232.

Directorate D—Culture and Creativity
Director: Michel Magnier; tel. (+32) 2-2956199.

Adviser: Catherine Magnant; tel. (+32) 2-2965376.

Adviser: João Delgado; tel. (+32) 2-253781.

CULTURAL POLICY
Head of Unit: Walter Zampieri; tel. (+32) 2-2998974.

CREATIVE EUROPE
Head of Unit: Barbara Gessler; tel. (+32) 2-2956738.

LIBRARY AND E-RESOURCES
Head of Unit: Theo Duivenvoorde; tel. (+32) 2-2994484.

Directorate R—Performance Management, Supervision and Resources
Director: Arturo Caballero Bassedas; tel. (+32) 2-2953974.

ORGANIZATIONAL PERFORMANCE AND LEGAL AFFAIRS
Head of Unit: Ulrich Sondermann; tel. (+32) 2-2985311.

BUDGET, PLANNING AND SUPERVISION
Head of Unit: Frederic Fimeyer; tel. (+32) 2-2995296.

ACCOUNTING AND FINANCE
Head of Unit: Ioannis Malekos; tel. (+32) 2-2952902.

IT PROJECTS AND SUPPORT
Head of Unit: Dimitrios Athanasiadis; tel. (+32) 2-2958826.

DG SANTE—DIRECTORATE-GENERAL FOR HEALTH AND FOOD SAFETY

4 rue Breydel, 1049 Brussels, Belgium; tel. (+32) 2-2991111; internet ec.europa.eu/info/departments/health-and-food-safety

Director-General: Xavier Prats Monne; tel. (+32) 2-2961230.

Deputy Director-General, responsible for Directorates B and C: Martin Seychell; tel. (+32) 2-2950675.

Deputy Director-General for the food chain, responsible for Directorates D, E, F and G: Ladislav Miko; tel. (+32) 2-2987237.

Reporting directly to the Director-General

Assistant to the Director-General: Bruno Gautrais; tel. (+32) 2-2956465.

Assistant to the Director-General: Roberto Reig Rodrigo; tel. (+32) 2-2995716.

STRATEGY AND CO-ORDINATION
Adviser: Annukka Ojala; tel. (+32) 2-2966213.

COMMUNICATION
Head of Unit: Roser Domenech Amado; tel. (+32) 2-2962759.

HEALTH AND CRISIS MANAGEMENT
Principal Adviser: Isabel de la Mata Barranco; tel. (+352) 4301-31454; fax (+352) 4301-34511.

Directorate A—Resource Management and Better Regulation
Director: David Matthew Hudson; tel. (+32) 2-2964671.

BETTER REGULATION
Head of Unit: Carmen Garau; tel. (+32) 2-2958937.

LEGAL AFFAIRS
Head of Unit (acting): Rossella Delfino; tel. (+32) 2-2996084.

FINANCE, BUDGET AND CONTROLS
Head of Unit: Guido de Clercq; tel. (+32) 2-2955096.

INFORMATION: SYSTEMS
Head of Unit: Herman Brand; tel. (+32) 2-2950141.

Directorate B—Health Systems, Medical Products and Innovation
Director: Andrzej Jan Rys; tel. (+32) 2-2969667.

PERFORMANCE OF NATIONAL HEALTH SYSTEMS
Head of Unit: Sylvain Giraud; tel. (+32) 2-2961767.

HEALTH IN ALL POLICIES, GLOBAL HEALTH, TOBACCO CONTROL
Head of Unit (acting): Andrzej Jan Rys; tel. (+32) 2-2969667.

CROSS BORDER HEALTHCARE, E-HEALTH
Head of Unit: Tapani Piha; tel. (+32) 2-2985487.

MEDICAL PRODUCTS: QUALITY, SAFETY, INNOVATION
Head of Unit: Anna Eva Ampelas; tel. (+32) 2-2960541.

MEDICINES: POLICY, AUTHORIZATION AND MONITORING
Head of Unit: Olga Solomon; tel. (+32) 2-2955959.

Directorate C—Public Health, Country Knowledge, Crisis Management

Director (acting): John Ryan; tel. (+352) 430134658.

HEALTH PROGRAMME AND CHRONIC DISEASES
Head of Unit: Stefan Schreck; tel. (+352) 430138520.

COUNTRY KNOWLEDGE AND SCIENTIFIC COMMITTEES
Head of Unit: Philippe Roux; tel. (+352) 430135056.

CRISIS MANAGEMENT AND PREPAREDNESS IN HEALTH
Head of Unit: Wolfgang Philipp; tel. (+352) 430138243.

HEALTH DETERMINANTS AND INEQUALITY
Head of Unit: Wojciech Kalamarz; tel. (+352) 430134658.

Directorate D—Food Chain: Stakeholder and International Relations

Director: Michael Scannell; tel. (+32) 2-2974943.

SANITARY AND PHYTOSANITARY ISSUES
Adviser: Carlos Álvarez Antolinez; tel. (+32) 2-2994968.

SCIENCE, STAKEHOLDERS, ENFORCEMENT
Head of Unit: Lorenzo Terzi; tel. (+32) 2-2968555.

MULTILATERAL INTERNATIONAL RELATIONS
Head of Unit: Dirk Lange; tel. (+32) 2-2952837.

BILATERAL INTERNATIONAL RELATIONS
Head of Unit: Koen Van Dyck; tel. (+32) 2-2984334.

FOOD SAFETY PROGRAMME, EMERGENCY FUNDING
Head of Unit: Christophe Bertrand; tel. (+32) 2-2999524.

Directorate E—Food and Feed Safety, Innovation

Director: Sabine Juelicher; tel. (+32) 2-2962587.

FOOD INFORMATION AND COMPOSITION, FOOD WASTE
Head of Unit: Alexandra Nikolakopoulou; tel. (+32) 2-2986854.

FOOD PROCESSING TECHNOLOGIES AND NOVEL FOODS
Head of Unit: Maria Iglesia; tel. (+32) 2-2953036.

BIOTECHNOLOGY
Head of Unit: Chantal Bruetschy; tel. (+32) 2-2962362.

PESTICIDES AND BIOCIDES
Head of Unit: Klaus Berend; tel. (+32) 2-2994860.

ANIMAL NUTRITION, VETERINARY MEDICINES
Head of Unit: Christian Siebert; tel. (+32) 2-2966244.

Directorate F—Health and Food Audits and Analysis

Director: Paola Colombo; tel. (+353) 469061858.

FOOD
Head of Unit: Stefan Hönig; tel. (+353) 469061616.

ANIMALS
Head of Unit: Ana Ramírez Vela; tel. (+353) 469061615.

PLANTS AND ORGANICS
Head of Unit: Andrew Owen-Griffiths; tel. (+353) 469061847.

FEED, IMPORTS AND EXPORTS
Head of Unit: Kenneth Elliott; tel. (+353) 469061837.

HEALTH PROTECTION
Head of Unit: Ruben Tascon; tel. (+353) 469061830.

INTERNAL CONTROL AND SERVICES
Head of Unit: Brona Carton; tel. (+353) 469061800.

COUNTRY KNOWLEDGE AND WORK PROGRAMME
Head of Unit: Frank Andriessen; tel. (+353) 469061714.

Directorate G—Crisis Management in Food, Animals and Plants

Director: Bernard van Goethem; tel. (+32) 2-2953143.

CRISIS MANAGEMENT
Adviser: Francisco Reviriego Gordejo; tel. (+32) 2-2984799.

PLANT HEALTH
Head of Unit: Dorothée André; tel. (+32) 2-2962315.

ANIMAL HEALTH AND WELFARE
Head of Unit: Eva María Zamora Escribano; tel. (+32) 2-2998682.

OFFICIAL CONTROLS AND ERADICATION OF DISEASES IN ANIMALS
Head of Unit: Andrea Gavinelli; tel. (+32) 2-2966426.

FOOD HYGIENE
Head of Unit: Eric Thévenard; tel. (+32) 2-2969966.

ALERTS, TRACEABILITY AND COMMITTEES
Head of Unit: Philippe Loopuyt; tel. (+32) 2-2990572.

DG HOME—DIRECTORATE-GENERAL FOR MIGRATION AND HOME AFFAIRS

46 rue de Luxembourg, 1050 Brussels, Belgium; tel. (+32) 2-2991111; internet ec.europa.eu/info/departments/migration-and-home-affairs

Director-General: Matthias Ruete; tel. (+32) 2-2950734.

Reporting directly to the Director-General

Assistant to the Director-General: Catherine Delacour; tel. (+32) 2-2980753.

Assistant to the Director-General: Kertu Kaera; tel. (+32) 2-2969209.

Adviser: Frank Paul; tel. (+32) 2-2954875.

Deputy Director-General responsible for Directorates C and E

Deputy Director-General: Simon Mordue; tel. (+32) 2-2984970.

European Commission

Deputy Director-General responsible for Directorates D and Units B3 and B4

Director: Olivier Onidi; tel. (+32) 2-2956040.

Anti-Trafficking Co-ordinator

Principal Adviser: Myria Vassiliadou; tel. (+32) 2-2981228.

Migratory Crisis

Principal Adviser: Alain Scriban; tel. (+32) 2-2963343.

Directorate C—Migration and Policy

Director: Laurent Muschel; tel. (+32) 2-2994708.

IRREGULAR MIGRATION AND RETURN POLICY
Head of Unit: Ioan-Dragos Tudorache; tel. (+32) 2-2984903.

BORDER MANAGEMENT AND SCHENGEN
Head of Unit: Joannes de Ceuster; tel. (+32) 2-2961072.

ASYLUM
Head of Unit: Henrik Nielsen; tel. (+32) 2-2991641.

MIGRATION MANAGEMENT SUPPORT
Head of Unit: Martin Schieffer; tel. (+32) 2-2991313.

Directorate B—Migration and Security Funds; Financial Resources and Monitoring

Director (acting): Simon Mordue; tel. (+32) 2-2984970.

UNION ACTIONS
Head of Unit: Stephanie Carillon; tel. (+32) 2-2998815.

NATIONAL PROGRAMMES FOR SOUTH AND EAST EUROPE; AMIF/ISF COMMITTEE
Head of Unit: Bernadette Frederick; tel. (+32) 2-2995877.

NATIONAL PROGRAMMES FOR NORTH AND WEST EUROPE; EVALUATIONS; MFF
Head of Unit: Francisco Gaztelu Mezquiriz; tel. (+32) 2-2992546.

BUDGET AND CONTROL
Head of Unit: Donatella Ineichen; tel. (+32) 2-2962609.

Directorate D—Security

Director: Luigi Soreca; tel. (+32) 2-2962116.

POLICE CO-OPERATION AND INFORMATION EXCHANGE
Head of Unit: Victoria Amici; tel. (+32) 2-2966081.

TERRORISM AND RADICALISATION
Head of Unit: Hans Das; tel. (+32) 2-2990436.

ORGANIZED CRIME AND DRUGS POLICY
Head of Unit: Ute Stiegel; tel. (+32) 2-2964591.

CYBERCRIME
Head of Unit: Graham Willmott; tel. (+32) 2-2952056.

Directorate D—Strategy and General Affairs

Director: Marta Cygan; tel. (+32) 2-2959927.

INTER-INSTITUTIONAL RELATIONS AND CITIZENSHIP
Head of Unit: Christine Grau; tel. (+32) 2-2955716.

LEGAL AFFAIRS
Head of Unit: Dimitrios Giotakos; tel. (+32) 2-2954474.

INTERNATIONAL CO-ORDINATION
Head of Unit: Blanca Rodriguez Galindo; tel. (+32) 2-2952920.

KNOWLEDGE HUB FOR MIGRATION AND SECURITY
Head of Unit: Pawel Busiakiewicz; tel. (+32) 2-2959423.

Directorate B—Migration, Mobility and Innovation

Director: Matthias Oel; tel. (+32) 2-2992728.

LEGAL MIGRATION AND INTEGRATION
Head of Unit: Laura Corrado; tel. (+32) 2-2950831.

VISA POLICY AND DOCUMENT SECURITY
Head of Unit: Yolanda Gallego-Casilda Grau; tel. (+32) 2-2993987.

INFORMATION SYSTEMS FOR BORDERS AND SECURITY
Head of Unit: Rob Rozenburg; tel. (+32) 2-2961831.

INNOVATION AND INDUSTRY FOR SECURITY
Head of Unit: Anabela Gago; tel. (+32) 2-2961022.

DG JUST—DIRECTORATE-GENERAL FOR JUSTICE AND CONSUMERS

59 rue Montoyer, 1049 Brussels, Belgium; tel. (+32) 2-2991111; internet ec.europa.eu/info/departments/justice-and-consumers

Director-General: Tiina Astola; tel. (+32) 2-2920678.

Reporting directly to the Director-General

Assistant to the Director-General: Juan González Mellizo; tel. (+32) 2-2962687.

Assistant to the Director-General: Johanna Engström; tel. (+32) 2-2968097.

Deputy Director-General responsible for Directorates B and E: Francisco Fonseca Morillo; tel. (+32) 2-2961119.

Strategies for Cross-cutting Justice Policies or Legal Actions

Principal Adviser: Paul Nemitz; tel. (+32) 2-2969135.

Directorate B—Criminal Justice

Director: Alexandra Jour-Schroeder; tel. (+32) 2-2951553.

GENERAL CRIMINAL LAW AND JUDICIAL TRAINING
Head of Unit: Peter Jozsef Csonka; tel. (+32) 2-2966563.

PROCEDURAL CRIMINAL LAW
Head of Unit: Isabelle Perignon; tel. (+32) 2-2950532.

FINANCIAL CRIME
Head of Unit (acting): Despina Vassiliadou; tel. (+32) 2-2999763.

EE-JSTICE, IT AND DOCUMENT MANAGEMENT
Head of Unit: Cristian Nicolau; tel. (+32) 2-2996961.

Directorate E—Consumers

Director (acting): Francisco Fonseca Morillo; tel. (+32) 2-2961119.

CONSUMER POLICY
Head of Unit: Renatas Mazeika; tel. (+32) 2-2962152.

CONSUMER AND MARKETING LAW
Head of Unit: Veronica Manfredi; tel. (+32) 2-2953936.

CONSUMER ENFORCEMENT AND REDRESS
Head of Unit: Marie-Paule Benassi; tel. (+32) 2-2989432.

PRODUCT SAFETY AND RAPID ALERT SYSTEM
Head of Unit: Pinuccia Contino; tel. (+32) 2-2965230.

Directorate A—Civil and Commercial Justice
Director: Salla Saastamoinen; tel. (+32) 2-2969463.

CIVIL JUSTICE
Head of Unit: Andréas Stein; tel. (+32) 2-295292198393.

CONTRACT LAW
Head of Unit: Dirk Staudenmayer; tel. (+32) 2-2954552.

COMPANY LAW
Head of Unit: Maija Laurila; tel. (+32) 2-2967879.

Directorate C—Fundamental Rights and Rule of Law
Director (acting): Emmanuel Crabit; tel. (+32) 2-2958114.

JUSTICE POLICY AND RULE OF LAW
Head of Unit: Emmanuel Crabit; tel. (+32) 2-2958114.

FUNDAMENTAL RIGHTS POLICY
Head of Unit: Chiara Adamo; tel. (+32) 2-2996797.

DATA PROTECTION
Head of Unit: Olivier Micol; tel. (+32) 2-2981417.

INTERNATIONAL DATA FLOWS AND PROTECTION
Head of Unit: Bruno Gencarelli; tel. (+32) 2-2963163.

Directorate D—Equality and Union Citizenship
Director: Irena Moozova; tel. (+32) 2-2990470.

NON-DISCRIMINATION AND ROMA CO-ORDINATION
Head of Unit: Szabolcs Schmidt; tel. (+32) 2-2969958.

GENDER EQUALITY
Head of Unit: Karen Vandekerckhove; tel. (+32) 2-2960114.

UNION CITIZENSHIP RIGHTS AND FREE MOVEMENT
Head of Unit: Marie-Hélène Boulanger; tel. (+32) 2-2969408.

SERVICE FOR FOREIGN POLICY INSTRUMENTS

Rond point Schuman, 1049 Brussels, Belgium; e-mail fpi-info@ec.europa.eu; internet ec.europa.eu/info/departments/foreign-policy-instruments

Director: Hilde Hardeman; tel. (+32) 2-2965077.

Adviser: Gary Miller; tel. (+32) 2-2957046.

BUDGET, FINANCE, RELATIONS WITH OTHER INSTITUTIONS
Head of Unit: Christian Meunier; tel. (+32) 2-2960789.

INSTRUMENT CONTRIBUTING TO STABILITY AND PEACE (ICSP)
Head of Unit: Oliver Nette; tel. (+32) 2-2957402.

CFSP OPERATIONS
Head of Unit (acting): Raimondo Bussi; tel. (+32) 2-2986542.

PARTNERSHIP INSTRUMENT
Head of Unit: Nona Deprez; tel. (+32) 2-2986489.

EU FOREIGN POLICY REGULATORY INSTRUMENTS AND ELECTION OBSERVATION
Head of Unit: Georgios Tsitsopoulos; tel. (+32) 2-2969915.

DG TRADE—DIRECTORATE-GENERAL

170 rue de la Loi, 1049 Brussels, Belgium; tel. (+32) 2-2991111; internet ec.europa.eu/info/departments/trade

Director-General: Jean-Luc Demarty; tel. (+32) 2-2956126.

Deputy Director-General responsible for Directorates B, C and D: Mauro Raffaele Petriccione; tel. (+32) 2-2961666.

Deputy Director-General, responsible for Directorates E, F, G and H: Joost Korte; tel. (+32) 2-2965900.

Reporting directly to the Director-General

Assistant to the Director-General: Stephanie Leupold; tel. (+32) 2-2961669.

Assistant to the Director-General: Eoin O'Malley; tel. (+32) 2-2987058.

Directorate A—Resources, Information and Policy Co-ordination
Director: Peter Sandler; tel. (+32) 2-2968645.

RESOURCES, HR BUSINESS CORRESPONDENT AND PLANNING
Head of Unit: Sofia Muñoz Albarran; tel. (+32) 2-2969575.

POLICY CO-ORDINATION AND INTER-INSTITUTIONAL RELATIONS
Head of Unit: Jorge Vitorino; tel. (+32) 2-2986054.

INFORMATION, COMMUNICATION AND CIVIL SOCIETY
Head of Unit: Lutz Güller; tel. (+32) 2-2964641.

INFORMATION TECHNOLOGY AND IT SYSTEMS
Head of Unit: Fabrice van Oost; tel. (+32) 2-2969550.

TRANSPARENCY AND EVALUATION
Head of Unit: Delphine Sallard; tel. (+32) 2-2993547.

Directorate B—Services and Investment, Intellectual Property and Public Procurement
Director: Maria Martin-Prat; tel. (+32) 2-2965157.

SERVICES
Head of Unit: Christophe Kiener; tel. (+32) 2-2984581.

INVESTMENT
Head of Unit: Carlo Pettinato; tel. (+32) 2-2980445.

INTELLECTUAL PROPERTY AND PUBLIC PROCUREMENT
Head of Unit: Fernando Perreau De Pinninck; tel. (+32) 2-2961932.

European Commission

Directorate C—Asia and Latin America

Director: Helena Konig; tel. (+32) 2-2960205.

FAR EAST
Head of Unit: Philippe Duponteil; tel. (+32) 2-2992155.

SOUTH AND SOUTH EAST ASIA, AUSTRALIA, NEW ZEALAND
Head of Unit: Peter Berz; tel. (+32) 2-2963083.

LATIN AMERICA
Head of Unit (acting): Peter Matthias Jorgensen; tel. (+32) 2-2988567.

Directorate D—Sustainable Development; Economic Partnership Agreements—Africa, Caribbean and Pacific; Agri-food and Fisheries

Director: Sandra Gallina; tel. (+32) 2-2958745.

Director: Nikolaos Zaimis; tel. (+32) 2-2962290.

TRADE AND SUSTAINABLE DEVELOPMENT, GENERALIZED SYSTEM OF PREFERENCES
Head of Unit: Madelaine Tuininga; tel. (+32) 2-2990151.

ECONOMIC PARTNERSHIP AGREEMENTS: AFRICAN, CARIBBEAN AND PACIFIC, OVERSEAS COUNTRIES AND TERRITORIES
Head of Unit: Diana Acconcia; tel. (+32) 2-2963064.

AGRICULTURE, FISHERIES, SANITARY AND PHYTOSANITARY MARKET ACCESS, BIOTECHNOLOGY
Head of Unit: Zoltán Somogyi; tel. (+32) 2-2961234.

Directorate E—Neighbouring Countries, USA and Canada

Director: Ignacio García Bercero; tel. (+32) 2-2995661.

USA AND CANADA
Head of Unit: Hiddo Houben; tel. (+32) 2-2956293.

RUSSIA, COMMONWEALTH OF INDEPENDENT STATES, UKRAINE, WEST BALKANS, EFTA, EEA AND TURKEY
Head of Unit: Petros Sourmelis; tel. (+32) 2-2987935.

SOUTH MEDITERRANEAN AND MIDDLE EAST
Head of Unit: Monika Hencsey; tel. (+32) 2-2986051.

Directorate F—WTO, Legal Affairs and Trade in Goods

Director: Denis Redonnet; tel. (+32) 2-2955424.

WTO CO-ORDINATION, OECD, EXPORT CREDITS AND DUAL USE
Head of Unit: Myrto Zambarta; tel. (+32) 2-2980562.

DISPUTE SETTLEMENT AND LEGAL ASPECTS OF TRADE POLICY
Head of Unit: Martin Lukas; tel. (+32) 2-2954506.

TARIFF AND NON-TARIFF NEGOTIATIONS, RULES OF ORIGIN
Head of Unit: Ignacio Iruarrizaga Díez; tel. (+32) 2-2952863.

Directorate G—Trade Strategy and Analysis, Market Access

Director: Signe Ratso; tel. (+32) 2-2993776.

Adviser: Marjut Hannonen; tel. (+32) 2-2961768.

TRADE STRATEGY
Head of Unit: Tomas Baert; tel. (+32) 2-2956277.

CHIEF ECONOMIST AND TRADE ANALYSIS
Head of Unit: Lucian Cernat; tel. (+32) 2-2951446.

MARKET ACCESS, INDUSTRY, ENERGY AND RAW MATERIALS
Head of Unit: Francisco Perez Canado; tel. (+32) 2-2963851.

Directorate H—Trade Defence

Director: Leopoldo Rubinacci; tel. (+32) 2-2990303.

Adviser: Piotr Ogonowski; tel. (+32) 2-2990958.

GENERAL POLICY, WTO RELATIONS, RELATIONS WITH INDUSTRY
Head of Unit: Wolfgang Müller; tel. (+32) 2-2963010.

INVESTIGATIONS I: RELATIONS WITH MEMBER STATES FOR COMMERCIAL DEFENCE AFFAIRS
Head of Unit: Claudia de Cesaris; tel. (+32) 2-2961733.

INVESTIGATIONS II: ANTI-CIRCUMVENTION
Head of Unit: Frank Hoffmeister; tel. (+32) 2-2993727.

INVESTIGATIONS III: MONITORING OF IMPLEMENTATION
Head of Unit: Joanna Krzeminska-Vamvaka; tel. (+32) 2-2950299.

INVESTIGATIONS IV: RELATIONS WITH THIRD COUNTRIES FOR TRADE DEFENCE MATTERS
Head of Unit: Joaquin Fernández Martin; tel. (+32) 2-2951041.

DG NEAR—DIRECTORATE-GENERAL FOR NEIGHBOURHOOD AND ENLARGEMENT NEGOTIATIONS

15 rue de la Loi, 1049 Brussels, Belgium; tel. (+32) 2-2991111; internet ec.europa.eu/info/departments/european-neighbourhood-policy-and-enlargement-negotiations

Director-General: Christian Danielsson; tel. (+32) 2-2950228.

Deputy Director-General, responsible for Eastern Neighbourhood, Economic Transformation and Relations with IFIs: Katarina Mathernová; tel. (+32) 2-2962873.

Deputy Director-General, responsible for Southern Neighbourhood, Turkey, Migration/Refugees and Security Issues: Maciej Popowski; tel. (+32) 2-2959910.

Reporting directly to the Director-General

Assistant to the Director-General: Simone Rave; tel. (+32) 2-2985046.

Principal Adviser (Civil Society and Media): Andris Kesteris; tel. (+32) 2-2921318.

Directorate C—Neighbourhood East

Director: Lawrence Meredith; tel. (+32) 2-2957538.

GEORGIA, MOLDOVA AND NEIGHBOURHOOD CROSS-BORDER CO-OPERATION
Head of Unit: Mathieu Bousquet; tel. (+32) 2-2980861.

ARMENIA, AZERBAIJAN, BELARUS AND EASTERN PARTNERSHIP
Head of Unit: Vassilis Maragos; tel. (+32) 2-2957198.

INSTITUTION-BUILDING, TECHNICAL ASSISTANCE AND INFORMATION EXCHANGE INSTRUMENT (TAIEX), TWINNING
Head of Unit: Heike Gerstbrein; tel. (+32) 2-2990161.

Directorate A—Strategy and Turkey

Director (acting): Maciej Popowski; tel. (+32) 2-2959910.

Adviser (Economic Governance): Andreas Papadopoulos; tel. (+32) 2-2996919.

STRATEGY, POLICY; EEA/ EFTA
Head of Unit: Allan Jones; tel. (+32) 2-2952211.

INTER-INSTITUTIONAL RELATIONS AND COMMUNICATION
Head of Unit: Claus Giering; tel. (+32) 2-2960389.

THEMATIC SUPPORT, MONITORING AND EVALUATION
Head of Unit: Bernard Brunet; tel. (+32) 2-2955727.

FINANCIAL ASSISTANCE: POLICY AND STRATEGY
Head of Unit (acting): Isabelle Combes; tel. (+32) 2-2958147.

TURKEY
Head of Unit: Myriam Ferran; tel. (+32) 2-2969119.

Directorate B—Neighbourhood South

Director: Michael Koehler; tel. (+32) 2-2990753.

MIDDLE EAST
Head of Unit: Michael Miller; tel. (+32) 2-2962771.

REGIONAL PROGRAMMES, NEIGHBOURHOOD SOUTH
Head of Unit: Irène Mingasson; tel. (+32) 2-2959959.

MAGHREB
Head of Unit: Jean-Christophe Filori; tel. (+32) 2-2965660.

Directorate D—Western Balkans

Director: Genoveva Ruíz Calavera; tel. (+32) 2-2950793.

MONTENEGRO
Head of Unit: Thomas Hagleitner; tel. (+32) 2-2967203.

SERBIA
Head of Unit: Catherine Wendt; tel. (+32) 2-2998257.

THE FORMER YUGOSLAV REPUBLIC OF MACEDONIA, KOSOVO
Head of Unit: David Cullen; tel. (+32) 2-2993174.

ALBANIA, BOSNIA AND HERZEGOVINA
Head of Unit: Michela Matuella; tel. (+32) 2-2957047.

WESTERN BALKANS REGIONAL CO-OPERATION AND PROGRAMMES
Head of Unit: Colin Wolfe; tel. (+32) 2-2990516.

Directorate R—Resources

Director: Mark Johnston; tel. (+32) 2-2968513.

RESOURCE PLANNING AND IT
Head of Unit (acting): Farid Rahmi; tel. (+32) 2-2995147.

LEGAL ISSUES
Head of Unit: Christos Komninos; tel. (+32) 2-2959208.

AUDIT AND INTERNAL CONTROL
Head of Unit: Nicole Smith; tel. (+32) 2-2992121.

CONTRACTS AND FINANCE ENI
Head of Unit (acting): Tuuli Virtanen; tel. (+32) 2-2967185.

CONTRACTS AND FINANCE (IPA)
Head of Unit: Maria Farrar-Hockley; tel. (+32) 2-2980385.

DG DEVCO—DIRECTORATE-GENERAL FOR INTERNATIONAL CO-OPERATION AND DEVELOPMENT

41 rue de la Loi, 1040, Brussels, Belgium; tel. (+32) 2-2965802; internet ec.europa.eu/info/departments/international-cooperation-and-development

Director-General: Stefano Manservisi; tel. (+32) 2-2957169.

Deputy Director-General, responsible for Directorates D, E, F and G: Klaus Rudischhauser; tel. (+32) 2-2990421.

Deputy Director-General, responsible for Directorates B, C, R; TF Knowledge, Performance and Results: Marjeta Jager; tel. (+32) 2-2980322.

Reporting directly to the Director-General

General Co-ordination and Inter-Institutional Relations
Head of Unit: Philippe Latriche; tel. (+32) 2-2987128.

Communication
Head of Unit: Hannah Cole; tel. (+32) 2-2967930.

Directorate A—International Co-operation and Development Policy

Director: Gustavo Martin; tel. (+32) 2-2956300.

SDGS, POLICY AND COHERENCE
Head of Unit: Gaspar Frontini; tel. (+32) 2-2992682.

DEVELOPMENT FINANCING EFFECTIVENESS, RELATIONS WITH MEMBER STATES
Head of Unit: Laurent Sarazin; tel. (+32) 2-2999621.

INTERNATIONAL ORGANIZATIONS AND DEVELOPMENT DIALOGUE WITH OTHER DONORS
Head of Unit: Maria Francesca Spatilosano; tel. (+32) 2-2980287.

BUDGET SUPPORT, PUBLIC FINANCE MANAGEMENT, DOMESTIC REVENUE MOBILIZATION
Head of Unit: Erica Gerretsen; tel. (+32) 2-2965208.

CIVIL SOCIETY ORGANIZATIONS, FOUNDATIONS
Head of Unit: Rosario Bento Pais; tel. (+32) 2-2952228.

CO-ORDINATION AND PROGRAMMING OF EXTERNAL FINANCING INSTRUMENTS
Head of Unit: Vincent Grimaud; tel. (+32) 2-2963320.

Directorate B—People and Peace

Director (acting): Jean-Louis Ville; tel. (+32) 2-2962256.

European Commission — DIRECTORY

GENDER EQUALITY, HUMAN RIGHTS AND DEMOCRATIC GOVERNANCE
Head of Unit: Jean-Louis Ville; tel. (+32) 2-2962256.

RESILIENCE, FRAGILITY
Head of Unit: María Manuela Cabral; tel. (+32) 2-2954259.

MIGRATION, EMPLOYMENT
Head of Unit: Stefano Signore; tel. (+32) 2-2996559.

CULTURE, EDUCATION, HEALTH
Head of Unit: Aida Liha Matejicek; tel. (+32) 2-2991625.

SECURITY, NUCLEAR SAFETY
Head of Unit: Olivier Luyckx; tel. (+32) 2-2964110.

FINANCE AND CONTRACTS
Head of Unit: Daniele D'Amico; tel. (+32) 2-2963292.

Directorate C—Planet and Prosperity
Director: Roberto Ridolfi; tel. (+32) 2-2954859.

RURAL DEVELOPMENT, FOOD SECURITY, NUTRITION
Head of Unit: Leonard Mizzi; tel. (+32) 2-2980477.

ENVIRONMENT, NATURAL RESOURCES, WATER
Head of Unit: Chantal Marijnissen; tel. (+32) 2-2986565.

INVESTMENT AND INNOVATIVE FINANCING
Head of Unit: Kay Parplies; tel. (+32) 2-2980104.

PRIVATE SECTOR, TRADE
Head of Unit: Antti Pekka Karhunen; tel. (+32) 2-2960281.

CITIES, LOCAL AUTHORITIES, DIGITALIZATION, INFRASTRUCTURE
Head of Unit: Paolo Ciccarelli; tel. (+32) 2-2960347.

SUSTAINABLE ENERGY, CLIMATE CHANGE
Head of Unit: Felice Zaccheo; tel. (+32) 2-2966856.

Directorate D—EU-Africa Relations, East and Southern Africa
Director: Koen Doens; tel. (+32) 2-2981566.

SOUTHERN AFRICA, INDIAN OCEAN
Head of Unit: Jobst Von Kirchmann; tel. (+32) 2-2957614.

EASTERN AFRICA, HORN OF AFRICA
Head of Unit: Hans Stausboll; tel. (+32) 2-2991681.

EU-AFRICA, AFRICAN PEACE FACILITY
Head of Unit: Domenico Rosa; tel. (+32) 2-2999815.

REGIONAL SECTOR POLICY ANALYSIS
Head of Unit (acting): Marzia Pietrelli; tel. (+32) 2-2991863.

Directorate E—West and Central Africa
Director: Carla Montesi; tel. (+32) 2-2961453.

CENTRAL AFRICA
Head of Unit: Francesca di Mauro; tel. (+32) 2-2961411.

WESTERN AFRICA
Head of Unit: Didier Verse; tel. (+32) 2-2968547.

FINANCE AND CONTRACTS
Head of Unit: Enrique Lobera Arguelles; tel. (+32) 2-2963085.

Directorate F—Asia, Central Asia, Middle East/Gulf and Pacific
Director: Pierre Amilhat; tel. (+32) 2-2992054.

MIDDLE EAST, CENTRAL ASIA, SOUTH ASIA
Head of Unit: Raffaella Iodice; tel. (+32) 2-2966175.

EAST, SOUTH-EAST ASIA AND THE PACIFIC
Head of Unit: Henriette Geiger; tel. (+32) 2-2984063.

FINANCE AND CONTRACTS
Head of Unit: Carlos Eduardo M. Filipe; tel. (+32) 2-2960862.

Directorate G—Latin America and Caribbean
Director: Jolita Butkevicienė; tel. (+32) 2-2959279.

LATIN AMERICA AND CARIBBEAN
Head of Unit: Jorge de la Caballeria; tel. (+32) 2-2959123.

REGIONAL OPERATIONS, LATIN AMERICA AND CARIBBEAN
Head of Unit: Fermín J. Melendro Arnaiz; tel. (+32) 2-2962501.

REGIONAL SECTOR POLICY ANALYSIS
Head of Unit (acting): Milko Van Gool; tel. (+32) 2-2963788.

Directorate R—Resources
Director: Luc Bagur; tel. (+32) 2-2991845.

PLANNING, BUDGET AND REPORTING
Head of Unit: Carlo Eich; tel. (+32) 2-2957864.

AUDIT AND CONTROL
Head of Unit: Emmanouil-Georgios Papaioannou; tel. (+32) 2-2969988.

LEGAL AFFAIRS
Head of Unit: Sandra Bartelt; tel. (+32) 2-2956828.

INFORMATION TECHNOLOGY, DOCUMENT MANAGEMENT
Head of Unit: Fernando Centurione; tel. (+32) 2-2960641.

FINANCE, CENTRE OF GRAVITY, HR BUSINESS CORRESPONDENT
Head of Unit: Jean-Hervé Ramat; tel. (+32) 2-2952621.

DG ECHO—DIRECTORATE-GENERAL FOR EUROPEAN CIVIL PROTECTION AND HUMANITARIAN AID OPERATIONS

86 rue d'Arlon, 1040 Brussels, Belgium; tel. (+32) 2-2991111; fax (+32) 2-2954544; internet ec.europa.eu/info/departments/humanitarian-aid-and-civil-protection

Director-General: Monique Pariat; tel. (+32) 2-2953188.

Assistant to the Director-General: Gosia Pearson; tel. (+32) 2-2963473.

Assistant to the Director-General: Francisco Javier Pérez Aparicio; tel. (+32) 2-2999229.

Directorate A—Emergency Management

Director: Johannes Luchner; tel. (+32) 2-296496868811.

Adviser: Rodrigo Vila de Benavent; tel. (+32) 2-2968828.

EMERGENCY RESPONSE CO-ORDINATION CENTRE (ERCC)
Head of Unit: Antoine Lemasson; tel. (+32) 2-2994691.

EMERGENCY PREPAREDNESS AND SECURITY
Head of Unit: Peter Billing; tel. (+32) 2-2968671.

DISASTER RISK REDUCTION, EUROPEAN VOLUNTARY HUMANITARIAN CORPS
Head of Unit: Nacira Boulehouat; tel. (+32) 2-2955263.

CIVIL PROTECTION POLICY
Head of Unit: Julia Stewart-David; tel. (+32) 2-2956432.

Directorate B—Europe, Eastern Neighbourhood and Middle East

Director: Jean-Louis De Brouwer; tel. (+32) 2-2961964.

POLICY DEVELOPMENT AND REGIONAL STRATEGY
Head of Unit: Leonor Nieto Leon; tel. (+32) 2-2968713.

EMERGENCY SUPPORT INSIDE EU
Head of Unit: Joe Murran; tel. (+32) 2-2958338.

EASTERN NEIGHBOURHOOD
Head of Unit: Juha Auvinen; tel. (+32) 2-2991072.

MIDDLE EAST
Head of Unit: Hervé Delphin; tel. (+32) 2-2951820.

Directorate C—Africa, Asia, Latin America, Caribbean and Pacific

Director: Androulla Kaminara; tel. (+32) 2-2987225.

Adviser: Giuseppe Anglini; tel. (+32) 2-2964342.

POLICY DEVELOPMENT AND REGIONAL STRATEGY II
Head of Unit: Henrike Trautmann; tel. (+32) 2-2957423.

NORTH, WEST AND CENTRAL AFRICA
Head of Unit: Susanne Mallaun; tel. (+32) 2-2955010.

EAST AND SOUTHERN AFRICA, GREAT LAKES
Head of Unit: Dominique Albert; tel. (+32) 2-2957188.

ASIA, LATIN AMERICA, CARIBBEAN, PACIFIC
Head of Unit (acting): Martin Landgraf; tel. (+32) 2-2980795.

Directorate D—General Affairs and HR Business Correspondent

Director: Chiara Gariazzo; tel. (+32) 2-2999255.

POLICY CO-ORDINATION, INTERNATIONAL AND MULTILATERAL RELATIONS, LEGAL AFFAIRS
Head of Unit: Kim Eling; tel. (+32) 2-2964149.

INTER-INSTITUTIONAL RELATIONS AND COMMUNICATION
Head of Unit: Mihela Zupancic; tel. (+32) 2-2980086.

BUDGET, FINANCE AND CONTROL
Head of Unit: Marco Panigalli; tel. (+32) 2-2954441.

FIELD NETWORK
Head of Unit: Andrea Koulaimah; tel. (+32) 2-2993761.

INFORMATION SYSTEM MANAGEMENT AND REPORTING
Head of Unit: Andrea Stella Zarkali; tel. (+32) 2-2966851.

EUROSTAT

5 rue Alphonse Weicker, 2721 Luxembourg, Luxembourg; internet   ec.europa.eu/info/departments/eurostat-european-statistics

Director-General (acting): Mariana Kotzeva; tel. (+352) 430133407.

Deputy Director-General responsible for Directorates B, E, F and G: Mariana Kotzeva; tel. (+352) 430133407.

Reporting directly to the Director-General

Assistant to the Director-General: Jukka Jalava; tel. (+352) 430134317.

Principal Adviser: Laurs Norlund; tel. (+352) 430132755.

Adviser: Marleen de Smedt; tel. (+352) 430133673.

Adviser: Guillermo Davila Muro; tel. (+32) 2-2993434.

Adviser: Pierre Bischoff; tel. (+32) 2-2980762.

Communication

Head of Unit (acting): Timothy Allen; tel. (+352) 430135098.

Directorate A—Co-operation in the European Statistical System, International Co-operation, Resources

Director: Pieter Everaers; tel. (+352) 430136847.

EUROPEAN STATISTICAL SYSTEM GOVERNANCE AND EXTERNAL RELATIONS
Head of Unit: Cristina Pereira de Sa; tel. (+352) 430132378.

STRATEGY AND PLANNING
Head of Unit: Annika Näslund Fogelberg; tel. (+352) 430133055.

STATISTICAL CO-OPERATION
Head of Unit: James Whitworth; tel. (+352) 430136857.

BUDGET, FINANCIAL MANAGEMENT AND INTERNAL CONTROL
Head of Unit: Luc Briol; tel. (+352) 430134450.

LEGAL AND INSTITUTIONAL AFFAIRS, RELATIONS WITH THE EP, DOCUMENT MANAGEMENT
Head of Unit: Helena Ottoson; tel. (+352) 430132771.

Directorate B—Methodology; Corporate Statistical and IT services

Director: Emanuele Baldacci; tel. (+352) 430132739.

METHODOLOGY AND CORPORATE ARCHITECTURE
Head of Unit: Martina Hahn; tel. (+352) 430135031.

IT GOVERNANCE, SERVICE AND RELATIONSHIP MANAGEMENT
Head of Unit: Christian Goedert; tel. (+352) 430133275.

IT SOLUTIONS FOR STATISTICAL PRODUCTION
Head of Unit: Giorgio Benali; tel. (+352) 430133680.

DISSEMINATION
Head of Unit: Philippe Bautier; tel. (+352) 430133556.

DATA AND METADATA SERVICES AND STANDARDS
Head of Unit: Márta Nagy-Rothengass; tel. (+352) 430131680.

Directorate C—National Accounts; Prices and Key Indicators
Director: Silke Stapel-Weber; tel. (+352) 430135586.

NATIONAL ACCOUNTS METHODOLOGY, INDICATORS
Head of Unit: John Verrinder; tel. (+352) 430134185.

NATIONAL ACCOUNTS PRODUCTION
Head of Unit: Ani Todorova; tel. (+352) 430135912.

STATISTICS FOR ADMINISTRATIVE PURPOSES
Head of Unit: Jean-Pierre Poncelet; tel. (+352) 430134317.

PRICE STATISTICS, PURCHASING POWER PARITIES, HOUSING STATISTICS
Head of Unit: Joachim Recktenwald; tel. (+352) 430134103.

INTEGRATED GLOBAL ACCOUNTS AND BALANCE OF PAYMENTS
Head of Unit: Aleš Čapek; tel. (+352) 430136045.

Directorate D—Government Finance Statistics (GFM) and Quality
Director: Eduardo Barredo Capelot; tel. (+352) 430135402.

EXCESSIVE DEFICIT PROCEDURE AND METHODOLOGY
Head of Unit: Luca Ascoli; tel. (+352) 430132707.

EXCESSIVE DEFICIT PROCEDURE (EDP) I
Head of Unit: Lena Frej Ohlsson; tel. (+352) 430135161.

EXCESSIVE DEFICIT PROCEDURE (EDP) II
Head of Unit (acting): Eduardo Barredo Capelot; tel. (+352) 430135402.

QUALITY MANAGEMENT; GFS
Head of Unit: Claudia Junker; tel. (+352) 430135774.

Directorate E—Sectoral and Regional Statistics
Director: Marcel Jortay; tel. (+352) 430134235.

AGRICULTURE AND FISHERIES
Head of Unit: Christine Wirtz; tel. (+352) 430134994.

ENVIRONMENTAL STATISTICS AND ACCOUNTS; SUSTAINABLE DEVELOPMENT
Head of Unit: Anton Steurer; tel. (+352) 430137339; fax (+352) 430130755.

TRANSPORT
Head of Unit: Ruxandra Roman Enescu; tel. (+352) 430135813.

REGIONAL STATISTICS AND GEOGRAPHICAL INFORMATION
Head of Unit: Gunter Schäfer; tel. (+352) 430133566.

ENERGY
Head of Unit: Gita Bergère; tel. (+352) 430137644.

Directorate F—Social Statistics
Director: Gallo Gueye; tel. (+352) 430134859.

SOCIAL INDICATORS: METHODOLOGY AND DEVELOPMENT; RELATIONS WITH USERS
Head of Unit: Jean-Louis Mercy; tel. (+352) 430134862.

POPULATION AND MIGRATION
Head of Unit: Adam Wronski; tel. (+352) 430135285.

LABOUR MARKET AND LIFELONG LEARNING
Head of Unit: Anne Clemenceau; tel. (+352) 430134880.

INCOME AND LIVING CONDITIONS; QUALITY OF LIFE
Head of Unit: Didier Dupre; tel. (+352) 430135034.

EDUCATION, HEALTH AND SOCIAL PROTECTION
Head of Unit: Christine Coin; tel. (+352) 430133722.

Directorate G—Global Business Statistics
Director: Maria-Helena Figueira; tel. (+352) 430134730.

CO-ORDINATION AND INFRASTRUCTURE DEVELOPMENT
Head of Unit: Merja Rantala; tel. (+352) 430136080.

STRUCTURAL BUSINESS STATISTICS AND GLOBAL VALUE CHAINS
Head of Unit: Axel Behrens; tel. (+352) 430135142.

BUSINESS CYCLE, TOURISM AND REGISTERS
Head of Unit: August Götzfried; tel. (+352) 430134432.

INNOVATION AND INFORMATION SOCIETY
Head of Unit: Carsten Olsson; tel. (+352) 430134208.

GOODS—PRODUCTION AND INTERNATIONAL TRADE
Head of Unit: Sophie Limpach; tel. (+352) 430134570.

DG HR—DIRECTORATE-GENERAL FOR HUMAN RESOURCES AND SECURITY

11 rue de la Science, 1049 Brussels, Belgium; tel. (+32) 2-2991111; internet ec.europa.eu/info/departments/human-resources-and-security

Director-General: Irène Souka; tel. (+32) 2-2957206.

Reporting directly to the Director-General

Assistant to the Director-General: Guillaume Laplatte; tel. (+32) 2-2984436.

Planning and Policy Steering

Head of Unit: Bertrand Saint Aubin; tel. (+32) 2-2987655.

Luxembourg Site Co-ordination

Principal Adviser: Georges Bingen; tel. (+352) 430133928.

HR Professionalisation and Customer Orientation

Principal Adviser (acting): Fernando García Ferreiro; tel. (+32) 2-2950283.

Deputy Director-General, responsible for Directorates AMC, A and B and Unit R.1: Bernard Magenhann; tel. (+32) 2-2999482.

Directorate AMC—Account Management Centre

Director (acting): Bernard Magenhahn; tel. (+32) 2-296660699482.

ACCOUNT MANAGEMENT CENTRE 1—SERVING COMP, ECFIN, EMPL, FISMA, GROW, TAXUD, TRADE

Head of Unit: Anette Mandler; tel. (+32) 2-2950221.

ACCOUNT MANAGEMENT CENTRE 2—SERVING AGRI, EAC, ENER, MARE, MOVE, RTD, SANTE

Head of Unit: Harald Spitzer; tel. (+32) 2-2991633.

ACCOUNT MANAGEMENT CENTRE 3—ERVINSG CLIMA, CNECT, ENV, REGIO

Head of Unit: Manuela Veiga; tel. (+32) 2-2960810.

ACCOUNT MANAGEMENT CENTRE 4—SERVING DEVCO, ECHO, FPI, NEAR

Head of Unit: Nancy Vanhavebeke-Merckx; tel. (+32) 2-2954178.

ACCOUNT MANAGEMENT CENTRE 5—SERVING COLLEGE, COMM, EPSC, HOME, IAS, JUST, OLAF, SG, SJ

Head of Unit: Emiel Weizenbach; tel. (+32) 2-2994953.

ACCOUNT MANAGEMENT CENTRE 6—SERVING DGT, ESTAT, OIL, OP

Head of Unit (acting): Benoît Vermeersch; tel. (+32) 2-2934768.

ACCOUNT MANAGEMENT CENTRE 7—SERVING BUDG, DIGIT, EPSO, HR, OIB, PMO, SCIC

Head of Unit: Giancarlo Granero; tel. (+32) 2-2999311.

ACCOUNT MANAGEMENT CENTRE 8—SERVING JRC

Head of Unit: James Gray; tel. (+32) 2-295875.

Directorate A—Organisational Development

Director: Matthias Will; tel. (+32) 2-2957387.

ORGANISATIONAL PERFORMANCE, RESOURCE ALLOCATION AND STRUCTURES

Head of Unit: Alexander Gemberg-Weisike; tel. (+32) 2-2960882.

ORGANISATIONAL DEVELOPMENT PROJECTS AND KNOWLEDGE MANAGEMENT

Head of Unit: Stephen Collins; tel. (+32) 2-2998436.

HR PROCESSES, IT AND REPORTING

Head of Unit: Marta Silva Mendes; tel. (+32) 2-2952261.

INTERNAL COMMUNICATION

Head of Unit: Norman Jardine; tel. (+32) 2-2992852.

Directorate B—Talent Management and Diversity

Director: Christian Levasseur; tel. (+32) 2-2965580.

Adviser (Talent Management): Enrico Maria Armani; tel. (+32) 2-2993371.

Adviser (Diversity): Thinam Jakob; tel. (+32) 2-2962933.

SELECTION, RECRUITMENT AND END OF SERVICE

Head of Unit: Roberto Carlini; tel. (+32) 2-2964512.

PERFORMANCE MANAGEMENT

Head of Unit: Stefan Tostmann; tel. (+32) 2-2968833.

LEARNING AND DEVELOPMENT

Head of Unit: Geraldine Dufort; tel. (+32) 2-2988040.

CAREER MANAGEMENT AND MOBILITY

Head of Unit: Marie-Hélène Pradines; tel. (+32) 2-2990167.

Directorate C—Talent Management and Diversity—Executive Staff

Director: Henk Post; tel. (+32) 2-2966606.

Legal Adviser: Michael Berger; tel. (+32) 2-2984509.

SENIOR MANAGEMENT AND CCA

Head of Unit: Susan Panter; tel. (+32) 2-2981755.

MIDDLE MANAGEMENT

Head of Unit: Flaminia Bussacchini; tel. (+32) 2-2969488.

Directorate D—Health and Wellbeing—Working Conditions

Director: Fernando García Ferreiro; tel. (+32) 2-2950283.

Adviser (Corporate Social Responsibility): Janette Sinclair; tel. (+32) 2-2966674.

WORKING CONDITIONS AND WELLBEING

Head of Unit: Koen Binon; tel. (+32) 2-2980669.

WORKING ENVIRONMENT AND SAFETY

Head of Unit: Robert Vanhoorde; tel. (+32) 2-2959928.

MEDICAL SERVICE—BRUSSELS

Head of Unit (acting): Elisabeth de Meulder; tel. (+32) 2-2962490.

MEDICAL SERVICE—LUXEMBOURG

Head of Unit: Danielle Depiesse; tel. (+352) 430132592.

MEDICAL SERVICE—ISPRA

Head of Unit: Italo Lombardi; tel. (+39 033) 2786775.

Directorate E—Legal Affairs and Partnerships

Director: Marco Umberto Moricca; tel. (+32) 2-2961654.

EUROPEAN CIVIL SERVICE LAW AND SOCIAL DIALOGUE

Head of Unit: Christian Roques; tel. (+32) 2-2995079.

APPEALS AND CASE MONITORING

Head of Unit: Lars Albath; tel. (+32) 2-2969401.

ETHICS AND OMBUDSMAN

Head of Unit: Nathalie Creste; tel. (+32) 2-2981027.

AGENCIES, EUROPEAN SCHOOLS AND INTERNATIONAL AFFAIRS

Head of Unit: Mariana Saude; tel. (+32) 2-2963204.

Investigation and Disciplinary Office

Director: Karen Williams; tel. (+32) 2-2965575.

DISCIPLINARY AFFAIRS

Head of Unit: Georgeta Luminita Nicolaie; tel. (+32) 2-2964789.

Directorate DS—Security

Director: Ilkka Salmi; tel. (+32) 2-2959224.

Principal Adviser: Richard Sonnenschein; tel. (+32) 2-2987253.

OPERATIONS
Head of Unit (acting): Richard Sonnenschein; tel. (+32) 2-2987253.

TECHNICAL SECURITY
Head of Unit (acting): Nicholas Kaye; tel. (+32) 2-2955030.

INFORMATION SECURITY
Head of Unit: Maresa Meissl; tel. (+32) 2-2956214.

HORIZONTAL TASKS
Head of Unit: Leszek Madeja; tel. (+32) 2-2963455.

DG DIGIT—DIRECTORATE-GENERAL FOR INFORMATICS

12 rue G. Kroll, 2920 Luxembourg, Luxembourg; internet ec.europa.eu/info/departments/informatics

Director-General: Gertrud Ingestad; tel. (+352) 430132194.

Deputy Director-General, responsible for Directorates C and D: Mario Campolargo; tel. (+352) 430163479.

Directorate A—Digital Workplace and Infrastructure

Director: Philippe Van Dame; tel. (+352) 430135350.

CLOUD AND SERVICE MANAGEMENT CAPABILITIES
Head of Unit: Olivier Altenhoven; tel. (+352) 430130673.

HOSTING AND PLATFORMS
Head of Unit: Michael Sønderskov; tel. (+352) 430133772.

DATA CENTRES
Head of Unit (acting): Miguel Angel González González; tel. (+32) 2-2952807.

NETWORKS AND TELECOMMUNICATIONS
Head of Unit (acting): Bernard Vanderperren; tel. (+32) 2-2984136.

DIGITAL WORKPLACE SUPPORT
Head of Unit: Guy Drowart; tel. (+32) 2-2999273.

DIGITAL WORKPLACE ENGINEERING
Head of Unit (acting): Yves Paternoster; tel. (+352) 430134983.

Directorate D—Digital Services

Director (acting): Mario Campolargo; tel. (+32) 2-2963479.

DATA SERVICES
Head of Unit: Roberto Barcellan; tel. (+32) 2-2935802.

INTEROPERABILITY
Head of Unit: Natalia Aristimuño Pérez; tel. (+32) 2-2966382.

TRANS-EUROPEAN SERVICES
Head of Unit: Dirk Stockmans; tel. (+352) 430132610.

Directorate A—Strategy and Resources

Director: Petra Kneuer; tel. (+32) 2-2950056.

CUSTOMERS, COMMUNICATION AND GOVERNANCE
Head of Unit: Isabelle Krauss; tel. (+32) 2-2966929.

STRATEGIC PLANNING AND MONITORING
Head of Unit: Anne-Catherine Simeon; tel. (+32) 2-2962010.

ICT PROCUREMENT AND CONTRACTS
Head of Unit: José-Martín Bilbao Zabala; tel. (+32) 2-2952544.

BUDGET AND FINANCE
Head of Unit: Paul Detilleux; tel. (+32) 2-2995293.

Directorate B—Digital Business Solutions

Director: Thomas Gageik; tel. (+32) 2-2962119.

SOLUTIONS FOR GRANTS AND PROCUREMENT
Head of Unit: Joaquín Pérez Echague; tel. (+32) 2-2993685.

SOLUTIONS FOR LEGISLATION, POLICY AND HR
Head of Unit: Willy van Puymbroeck; tel. (+32) 2-2968138.

REUSABLE SOLUTIONS
Head of Unit: Eric Derruine; tel. (+32) 2-2990497.

Directorate S—IT Security

Director: Ken Ducatel; tel. (+32) 2-2956867.

IT SECURITY POLICY
Head of Unit: Grzegorz Minczakiewicz; tel. (+32) 2-2968164.

IT SECURITY OPERATIONS
Head of Unit (acting): Grzegorz Minczakiewicz; tel. (+32) 2-2968164.

DG BUDG—DIRECTORATE-GENERAL FOR BUDGET

19 ave d'Auderghem, 1040 Brussels, Belgium; tel. (+32) 2-2991111; internet ec.europa.eu/info/departments/budget

Director-General: Nadia Calvino; tel. (+32) 2-2955067.

Assistant to the Director-General: Antoine Koppe; tel. (+32) 2-2990121.

Assistant to the Director-General: Ana María Gomez Mascarell; tel. (+32) 2-2986450.

Deputy Director-General (acting), in charge of Directorate C, Accounting Officer of the Commission: María Rosa Aldea Busquets; tel. (+32) 2-2950848.

Deputy Director-General (acting), in charge of Directorate A, B and D: Silvano Presa; tel. (+32) 2-2952221.

Directorate R—Resources

Director: Daniela Gheorghe; tel. (+32) 2-2954561.

INFORMATION AND COMMUNICATION
Head of Unit: Petr Mooz; tel. (+32) 2-2986232.

GENERAL CO-ORDINATION, FINANCE AND HR BUSINESS CORRESPONDENT
Head of Unit: Raluca Blanaru; tel. (+32) 2-2968581.

FINANCIAL INFORMATION SYSTEMS IMPLEMENTATION
Head of Unit: André Pening; tel. (+32) 2-2999307.

IT INFRASTRUCTURE AND USER SUPPORT
Head of Unit: Marc Parmentier; tel. (+32) 2-2984310.

IT PROGRAMME AND ARCHITECTURE OFFICE
Head of Unit: Dirk Lapage; tel. (+32) 2-2961982.

Directorate C—Budget Execution (General Budget and EDF)
Director: María Rosa Aldea Busquets; tel. (+32) 2-2956873.

TREASURY MANAGEMENT
Head of Unit: Vincenzo Curiale; tel. (+32) 2-2959234.

ACCOUNTING
Head of Unit: Derek Dunphy; tel. (+32) 2-2952450.

BUDGETARY STRUCTURE AND VALIDATION OF LOCAL SYSTEMS
Head of Unit: José Antonio Lopez Sánchez; tel. (+32) 2-2990105.

RECOVERY OF DEBTS
Head of Unit: Kristian Vangrieken; tel. (+32) 2-2965452.

USER SERVICE MANAGEMENT
Head of Unit: Hans Gevaert; tel. (+32) 2-2994703.

FINANCIAL REPORTING AND STRATEGY
Head of Unit: Yiannos Asimakis; tel. (+32) 2-2968752.

Directorate A—Expenditure
Director (acting): Johan Ureel; tel. (+32) 2-2966609.

BUDGETARY PROCEDURE AND EXECUTION, RELATIONS WITH THE BUDGET COMMITTEES
Head of Unit: Johan Ureel; tel. (+32) 2-2966609.

COMMON AGRICULTURAL POLICY (CAP) AND STRUCTURAL POLICIES
Head of Unit: Juan José López Lledo; tel. (+32) 2-2951289.

INTERNAL POLICIES
Head of Unit: Olivier Salles; tel. (+32) 2-2956954.

EXTERNAL POLICIES
Head of Unit (acting): Lars Jorgen Magnusson; tel. (+32) 2-2951614.

ADMINISTRATIVE APPROPRIATIONS AND ALLOCATION OF IT RESOURCES
Head of Unit: Jennifer Brown; tel. (+32) 2-2954644.

Directorate B—Own Resources and Financial Programming
Director: Stefan Lehner; tel. (+32) 2-2993383.

MULTIANNUAL FINANCIAL FRAMEWORK, FUNDING SYSTEMS AND FORECASTS, BUDGETARY ASPECTS OF ENLARGEMENT
Head of Unit: Andreas Schwarz; tel. (+32) 2-2985476.

REVENUE MANAGEMENT
Head of Unit: Charles Groutage; tel. (+32) 2-2991090.

CONTROL OF TRADITIONAL OWN RESOURCES AND ASSISTANCE FOR CANDIDATE COUNTRIES
Head of Unit: José Madeira; tel. (+32) 2-2965440.

CONTROL OF VAT AND GNI OWN RESOURCES
Head of Unit: Tomás Kucirek; tel. (+32) 2-2953616.

Directorate D—Central Financial Service
Director: Olivier Waelbroeck; tel. (+32) 2-2999803.

FINANCIAL RULES AND GOVERNANCE
Head of Unit: Michael Erhart; tel. (+32) 2-2959617.

PROGRAMME MANAGEMENT AND IMPLEMENTING CONTRACTS
Head of Unit: Victoria Gil Casado; tel. (+32) 2-2985626.

FINANCIAL PROCEDURES AND CONTROL SYSTEMS
Head of Unit: Catherine Heldmaier-Regnier; tel. (+32) 2-2952208.

BUDGWEB, FINANCIAL TRAINING, HELPDESK FOR INSTITUTIONS AND AGENCIES
Head of Unit: Ana Sofia Silva; tel. (+32) 2-2966826.

DG IAS—INTERNAL AUDIT SERVICE

1 place Madou, 1210 Brussels, Belgium; e-mail ias-europa@ec.europa.eu; internet ec.europa.eu/info/departments/internal-audit-service

Director-General: Manfred Kraff; tel. (+32) 2-2966413.

Assistant to the Director-General: Adrian Mircea; tel. (+32) 2-2953385.

Principal Adviser: Ciaran Spillane; tel. (+32) 2-2981263.

SECRETARIAT OF THE APC
Adviser: Migle Halauko; tel. (+32) 2-2961251.

Directorate A—Audit in EU Agencies and Other Autonomous Bodies
Director: Reinder Van Der Zee; tel. (+32) 2-2965734.

AUDIT UNIT A.1
Head of Unit: Ilian Komitski; tel. (+32) 2-2963612.

AUDIT UNIT A.2
Head of Unit: Friedrich Bräuer; tel. (+32) 2-2996070.

Directorate B—Audit of the Commission and Executive Agencies I
Director: Jeffrey Mason; tel. (+32) 2-2958969.

AUDIT UNIT B.1
Head of Unit: Carlo Billi; tel. (+32) 2-2996924.

AUDIT UNIT B.2
Head of Unit: Doriane Givord-Strassel; tel. (+32) 2-2950799.

European Commission — DIRECTORY

AUDIT UNIT B.3
Head of Unit: Filip Verhoeven; tel. (+32) 2-2962059.

AUDIT UNIT B.4
Head of Unit: Christoph Nerlich; tel. (+32) 2-2951437.

Directorate C—Audit of the Commission and Executive Agencies II

Director: Cristiana Giacobbo; tel. (+32) 2-2995085.

AUDIT UNIT C.1
Head of Unit: Laura Candeloro; tel. (+32) 2-2984542.

AUDIT UNIT C.2
Head of Unit: Volker Rokos; tel. (+32) 2-2965017.

AUDIT UNIT C.3
Head of Unit (acting): Rudi Dries; tel. (+32) 2-2999481.

AUDIT UNIT C.4
Head of Unit: Edwin Croonen; tel. (+32) 2-2961867.

OLAF—EUROPEAN ANTI-FRAUD OFFICE

30 rue Joseph II, 1000 Brussels, Belgium; tel. (+32) 2-2991111; fax (+32) 2-2960853; internet ec.europa.eu/info/departments/european-anti-fraud-office

Director-General: Giovanni Kessler; tel. (+32) 2-2964690.

Reporting directly to the Director-General

Assistant to the Director-General: Marco D'Ambrisio; tel. (+32) 2-2993765.

Principal dviserA: Nicholas Ilett; tel. (+32) 2-2984986.

INVESTIGATION, SELECTION AND REVIEW
Head of Unit: Corinna Ullrich; tel. (+32) 2-2994856.

BUDGET AND HR BUSINESS CORRESPONDENT
Head of Unit (acting): Ludo Bedeer; tel. (+32) 2-2994827.

Directorate A—Investigations I

Director: Dominik Schnichels; tel. (+32) 2-2966937.

Adviser: Joaquín González-Herrero González; tel. (+32) 2-2991466.

EU STAFF
Head of Unit: Lara Dobinson; tel. (+32) 2-2964276.

NEW FINANCIAL INSTRUMENTS
Head of Unit: Antonio Miceli; tel. (+32) 2-2963783.

CENTRALIZED EXPENDITURE
Head of Unit: Vasil Kirov; tel. (+32) 2-2965438.

EXTERNAL AID
Head of Unit: Marco Pecoraro; tel. (+32) 2-2951350.

Directorate B—Investigations II

Director: Ernesto Bianchi; tel. (+32) 2-2994316.

Adviser (acting): Konstantinos Chatzipazarlis; tel. (+32) 2-2966749.

CUSTOMS AND TRADE FRAUD
Head of Unit: James Sweeney; tel. (+32) 2-2956037.

TOBACCO AND COUNTERFEIT GOODS
Head of Unit: Vincent Sauvalère; tel. (+32) 2-2951420.

AGRICULTURAL AND STRUCTURAL FUNDS I
Head of Unit: Cvetelina Cholakova; tel. (+32) 2-2955525.

AGRICULTURAL AND STRUCTURAL FUNDS II
Head of Unit (acting): James Sweeney; tel. (+32) 2-2956037.

AGRICULTURAL AND STRUCTURAL FUNDS III
Head of Unit: Francesco Albore; tel. (+32) 2-2958797.

Directorate C—Investigation Support

Director: Beatriz Sanz Redrado; tel. (+32) 2-2950051.

INVESTIGATION WORKFLOW
Head of Unit: Claire Scharf-Kroener; tel. (+32) 2-2959581.

INFORMATION SYSTEMS DEVELOPMENT
Head of Unit: Jean-Philippe Lienard; tel. (+32) 2-2954083.

OPERATIONAL ANALYSIS AND DIGITAL FORENSICS
Head of Unit: Eduardo Cano Romera; tel. (+32) 2-2961502.

LEGAL ADVICE
Head of Unit: Dorothe Dalheimer; tel. (+32) 2-2950049.

INFORMATION SYSTEMS INFRASTRUCTURE
Head of Unit (acting): Vasile Dumitrescu; tel. (+32) 2-2959924.

Directorate D—Policy

Director: Margarete Hofmann; tel. (+32) 2-2981710.

POLICY DEVELOPMENT AND HERCULE
Head of Unit: Irene Sacristán Sánchez; tel. (+32) 2-2950278.

FRAUD PREVENTION, REPORTING AND ANALYSIS
Head of Unit: Frank Michlik; tel. (+32) 2-2992797.

INTER-INSTITUTIONAL AND EXTERNAL RELATIONS
Head of Unit: Charlotte Arwidi; tel. (+32) 2-2987797.

CUSTOMS AND TOBACCO ANTI-FRAUD POLICY; AFIS
Head of Unit: Georg Roebling; tel. (+32) 2-2958976.

DG SCIC—DIRECTORATE-GENERAL FOR INTERPRETATION

100 rue Belliard, 1000 Brussels, Belgium; tel. (+32) 2-2991111; internet ec.europa.eu/info/departments/interpretation

Director-General: Florika Fink-Hooijer; tel. (+32) 2-2964968.
Deputy Director-General: Carlos Alegria; tel. (+32) 2-2963394.

Reporting directly to the Director-General

Principal Adviser: Jarek Porejski; tel. (+32) 2-2987440.

Inter-institutional Relations and International Co-operation
Head of Unit: François Génisson; tel. (+32) 2-2958036.

DIRECTORY

European Commission

Strategic Communication and Outreach, HR Business Correspondent

Head of Unit: Miklós András Mátyássy; tel. (+32) 2-2988140.

Directorate A—Interpreters

Director: Alexandra Panagakou; tel. (+32) 2-2959319.

INTERPRETATION DEPARTMENT I

Head of Language Department (acting): Leszek Skibniewski; tel. (+32) 2-2980014.

Czech Interpretation

Head of Unit: Hana Jungová; tel. (+32) 2-2980012.

French Interpretation

Head of Unit: Franz Lemaître; tel. (+32) 2-2993694.

Lithuanian Interpretation

Head of Unit: Ramūnas Česonis; tel. (+32) 2-2991766.

Swedish Interpretation

Head of Unit: Nuria Bonel Canadell; tel. (+32) 2-2988886.

Bulgarian Interpretation

Head of Unit (acting): Daniela Sabeva; tel. (+32) 2-2991791.

INTERPRETATION DEPARTMENT II

Head of Language Department: Francine Goffaux; tel. (+32) 2-2991613.

German Interpretation

Head of Unit: Carlota Jovani; tel. (+32) 2-2956139.

Estonian Interpretation

Head of Unit: Karl Lepa; tel. (+32) 2-2991836.

Hungarian Interpretation

Head of Unit: Katalin Vittay Fedineczné; tel. (+32) 2-2950777.

Finnish Interpretation

Head of Unit: Veijo Kruth; tel. (+32) 2-2953786.

Romanian Interpretation

Head of Unit: Maria Koroknai; tel. (+32) 2-2992128.

INTERPRETATION DEPARTMENT III

Head of Language Department: Leszek Skibniewski; tel. (+32) 2-2980014.

English Interpretation

Head of Unit: John Swales; tel. (+32) 2-2996515.

Latvian Interpretation

Head of Unit: Ieva Zauberga; tel. (+32) 2-2991975.

Portuguese Interpretation

Head of Unit: Anabela Frade; tel. (+32) 2-2997669.

Slovak Interpretation

Head of Unit: Katarina Skacaniová; tel. (+32) 2-2995212.

INTERPRETATION DEPARTMENT IV

Head of Language Department (acting): Francine Goffaux; tel. (+32) 2-2991613.

Danish Interpretation

Head of Unit: Peter Aagaard; tel. (+32) 2-2980011.

Italian Interpretation

Head of Unit: Paolo Torrigiani; tel. (+32) 2-2980015.

Netherlands Interpretation

Head of Unit: Dominique Stevens; tel. (+32) 2-2987031.

Slovenian Interpretation

Head of Unit: Marjanca Rupnik; tel. (+32) 2-2991998.

INTERPRETATION DEPARTMENT V

Head of Language Department: Luisa Castellani; tel. (+32) 2-2998265.

Greek Interpretation

Head of Unit: Evgenia Paparouni; tel. (+32) 2-2987652.

Spanish Interpretation

Head of Unit: María Natalia Sánchez-Calero Guilarte; tel. (+32) 2-2977434.

Maltese Interpretation

Head of Unit: Peter Mifsud; tel. (+32) 2-2992237.

Polish Interpretation

Head of Unit: Dorota Nofska-Sierant; tel. (+32) 2-2990650.

Croatian Interpretation

Head of Unit (acting): Tatjana Zagajski; tel. (+32) 2-2981515.

Directorate C—Provision of Interpretation

Director: Filip Majcen; tel. (+32) 2-2958728.

MULTILINGUALISM AND INTERPRETER TRAINING SUPPORT

Head of Unit: Javier Hernández Saseta; tel. (+32) 2-2985377.

PROGRAMMING OF INTERPRETATION

Head of Unit: Anne-Laure Hubert; tel. (+32) 2-2996600.

PROFESSIONAL SUPPORT FOR INTERPRETERS

Head of Unit: Paula Ovaska-Romano; tel. (+32) 2-2952403.

JOINT MANAGEMENT OF EXTERNAL CONFERENCE INTERPRETING STAFF

Head of Unit: Maria do Pilar Moreira Ribeiro; tel. (+32) 2-2953549.

Directorate S—Resources and Support

Director: Gianluca Pecchi; tel. (+32) 2-2998666.

CONFERENCE ORGANIZATION

Head of Unit: José Manuel Bastos; tel. (+32) 2-2968111.

BUDGET AND FINANCIAL MANAGEMENT

Head of Unit: Valérie de Leeuw; tel. (+32) 2-2987446.

European Commission

SUPPORT TO MANAGEMENT AND CORE PROCESSES, IT DEVELOPMENTS

Head of Unit: Marc Berthiaume; tel. (+32) 2-2959493.

MANAGEMENT OF TECHNICAL INFRASTRUCTURE

Head of Unit: Angelo Tosetti; tel. (+32) 2-2968924.

IT NETWORKS, INTERPRETATION STREAMING AND VIDEO SERVICES

Head of Unit: Lode de Raedt; tel. (+32) 2-2959142.

DG DGT—DIRECTORATE-GENERAL FOR TRANSLATION

1 rue de Genève, 1140 Brussels, Belgium; tel. (+32) 2-2991111; internet ec.europa.eu/info/departments/translation

Director-General (acting): Rytis Martikonis.

Deputy Director-General, in charge of Directorates A, B and C: Christos Ellinides; tel. (+32) 2-2988476.

Assistant to the Director-General: Roslyn Bottoni; tel. (+32) 2-2959433.

Assistant to the Director-General: Kerstin Kettig-Bauer; tel. (+32) 2-2935531.

Reporting directly to the Director-General

Audit

Co-ordination and Institutional Affairs

Head of Unit: Alicia Fracchia-Fernández; tel. (+32) 2-2964873.

Communication and Relations with Stakeholders

Head of Unit: Elisabetta Degiampietro; tel. (+32) 2-2990589.

Directorate A—Translation

Director: Klaus Meyer-Koeken; tel. (+352) 430130660.

BULGARIAN LANGUAGE DEPARTMENT

Head of Department: Olga Manafová; tel. (+352) 430133565.

Bulgarian Language Unit 1

Head of Department: Rusana Bardarska; tel. (+32) 2-2987052.

Bulgarian Language Unit 2

Head of Department: Tatiana Telkedjiyska; tel. (+352) 430136154.

CZECH LANGUAGE DEPARTMENT

Head of Department: Otto Pacholik; tel. (+352) 430136523.

Czech Language Unit 1

Head of Department: Kamila Adamková; tel. (+352) 430137540.

Czech Language Unit 2

Head of Department: Jakub Chab; tel. (+352) 430137842.

DANISH LANGUAGE DEPARTMENT

Head of Department (acting): Stig Pilgaard Olsen; tel. (+32) 2-2951410.

Danish Language Unit 1

Head of Unit: Stig Pilgaard Olsen; tel. (+32) 2-2951410.

Danish Language Unit 2

Head of Department: Erling Nielsen; tel. (+352) 430133030.

FINNISH LANGUAGE DEPARTMENT

Head of Department (acting): Tiina Lohikko; tel. (+32) 2-295279.

Finnish Language Unit 1

Head of Unit: Tiina Lohikko; tel. (+32) 2-295279.

FINNISH LANGUAGE UNIT 2

Head of Unit: Kati Niemi; tel. (+352) 430133253.

ITALIAN LANGUAGE DEPARTMENT

Head of Department: Paola Rizzotto; tel. (+32) 2-2991152.

Italian Language Unit 1

Head of Unit: Sonia Peressini; tel. (+32) 2-2956884.

Italian Language Unit 2

Head of Unit: Alessandra Recchioni; tel. (+352) 430134804.

LITHUANIAN LANGUAGE DEPARTMENT

Head of Department: Arunas Butkevičius; tel. (+352) 430135693.

Lithuanian Language Unit 1

Head of Unit: Rita Dedonienė; tel. (+352) 430137844.

Lithuanian Language Unit 2

Head of Unit: Vitalija Spokienė; tel. (+352) 430137847.

MALTESE LANGUAGE DEPARTMENT

Head of Department: Helga Josette Zahra; tel. (+352) 430134496.

Maltese Language Unit 1

Head of Department: Carmel Attard; tel. (+352) 430138022.

Maltese Language Unit 2

Head of Unit (acting): Helga Josette Zahra; tel. (+352) 430134496.

Directorate B—Translation

Director: Maria Cristina de Preter; tel. (+32) 2-2959323.

GREEK LANGUAGE DEPARTMENT

Head of Department: Basile Koutsivitis; tel. (+32) 2-2958478.

Greek Language Unit 1

Head of Department: Anastassios Anagnostu; tel. (+32) 2-2965915.

Greek Language Unit 2

Head of Department: George Mathioudakis; tel. (+352) 430134362.

ESTONIAN LANGUAGE DEPARTMENT

Head of Department (acting): Epp Vihterpal; tel. (+352) 430135576.

Estonian Language Unit 1

Head of Unit: Epp Vihterpal; tel. (+352) 430135576.

Estonian Language Unit 2

Head of Unit: Leila Anupold; tel. (+352) 430137473.

POLISH LANGUAGE DEPARTMENT

Head of Department: Marcin Stryjecki; tel. (+352) 430130637.

Polish-Language Unit 1

Head of Unit (acting): Agnieszka Zukowska; tel. (+352) 430137248.

Polish Language Unit 2

Head of Unit: Mirosław Szpakowski; tel. (+352) 430134303.

PORTUGUESE LANGUAGE DEPARTMENT

Head of Department: María Cristina de Preter; tel. (+32) 2-2959323.

Portuguese Language Unit 1

Head of Unit: María Fortunato de Almeida; tel. (+32) 2-2950788.

Portuguese Language Unit 2

Head of Department: João Coelho; tel. (+352) 430131500.

ROMANIAN LANGUAGE DEPARTMENT

Head of Department: Viorel Serbanescu; tel. (+352) 430136383.

RomanianLanguage Unit 1

Head of Unit: Viorel Florean; tel. (+32) 2-2951478.

Romanian Language Unit 2

Head of Department: Margareta Felicia Negru; tel. (+352) 430133547.

SLOVAK-LANGUAGE DEPARTMENT

Head of Department: Jozef Stefanik; tel. (+352) 430133897.

Slovak Language Unit 1

Head of Unit (acting): Sergej Skackov; tel. (+352) 430136068.

SlovakLanguage Unit 2

Head of Unit: Karin Milkovicová; tel. (+352) 430136680.

SWEDISH LANGUAGE DEPARTMENT

Head of Department (acting): Andreas Larsson; tel. (+32) 2-2959151.

SWEDISH LANGUAGE UNIT 1

Head of Unit: Andreas Larsson; tel. (+32) 2-2959151.

Swedish Language Unit 2

Head of Department (acting): Katarina Hyllienmark; tel. (+352) 430135948.

Directorate C—Translation

Director: Merit-Ene Ilja; tel. (+32) 2-2980255.

Adviser: Hiie Tamm; tel. (+352) 430137754.

SPANISH LANGUAGE DEPARTMENT

Head of Department (acting): María José González Gayoso; tel. (+32) 2-2954709.

Spanish Language Unit 1

Head of Unit: María José González Gayoso; tel. (+32) 2-2954709.

Spanish Language Unit 2

Head of Unit (acting): José Luis Vega Expósito; tel. (+32) 2-2960472.

IRISH LANGUAGE DEPARTMENT

Head of Unit: Colmcille O'Monacháin; tel. (+32) 2-2952839.

CROATIAN LANGUAGE DEPARTMENT

Head of Department: Mirna Zelić Pokaz; tel. (+32) 2-2955848.

Croatian Language Unit 1

Head of Unit: Natalija Lujo; tel. (+32) 2-2955795.

Croatian Language Unit 2

Head of Unit: Saša Sirovec; tel. (+352) 430134550.

HUNGARIAN LANGUAGE DEPARTMENT

Head of Department (acting): Jan Bednarich; tel. (+352) 430136963.

Hungarian Language Unit 1

Head of Unit: Balint Vanyi; tel. (+352) 430133603.

Hungarian Language Unit 2

Head of Unit: Sándor Kovács; tel. (+352) 430131654.

LATVIAN LANGUAGE DEPARTMENT

Head of Department: Mareks Kovalevskis; tel. (+352) 430133971.

Latvian Language Unit 1

Head of Unit: Liena Muskare; tel. (+352) 430131533.

Latvian Language Unit 2

Head of Unit: Iveta Rancane-Abarte; tel. (+352) 430137596.

DUTCH LANGUAGE DEPARTMENT

Head of Department (acting): Betsie Klein Brinke; tel. (+32) 2-2950751.

Dutch Language Unit 1

Head of Unit: Betsie Klein Brinke; tel. (+32) 2-2950751.

Dutch Language Unit 2

Head of Unit: Sabine Scheirsen; tel. (+352) 430135658.

SLOVENIAN LANGUAGE DEPARTMENT

Head of Department: Jan Bednarich; tel. (+352) 430136963.

Slovenian Language Unit 1

Head of Unit: Tanja Baraga; tel. (+352) 430137714.

Slovenian Language Unit 2

Head of Unit: Tina Kosir; tel. (+352) 430137084.

Directorate D—Translation

Director: Gurli Hauschildt; tel. (+32) 2-2959893.

Adviser: José Luis Vega Expósito; tel. (+352) 430130663.

GERMAN LANGUAGE DEPARTMENT
Head of Department: Josefine Oberhausen; tel. (+32) 2-2955934.

German Language Unit 1

Head of Unit: Myriam Laurent-Gatz; tel. (+32) 2-2952820.

German Language Unit 2

Head of Unit: Levke King-Elsner; tel. (+32) 2-2958260.

German Language Unit 3

Head of Unit: Hannelore Schwabbauer; tel. (+352) 430133269.

German Language Unit 4

Head of Unit: Wolfgang Kilb; tel. (+352) 430131994.

ENGLISH LANGUAGE DEPARTMENT
Head of Department: Klaus Ahrend; tel. (+32) 2–2956610.

English Language Unit 1

Head of Unit: Martin Turley; tel. (+32) 2–2955253.

English Language Unit 2

Head of Unit: Stella Clarke; tel. (+32) 2–2984006.

English Language Unit 3

Head of Unit: Valda Selga Liepina; tel. (+352) 430134388.

FRENCH-LANGUAGE DEPARTMENT
Head of Department: Isabelle Tranchant; tel. (+32) 2–2956196.

French Language Unit 1

Head of Unit: Emmanuel Jacquin; tel. (+32) 2–2955798.

French Language Unit 2

Head of Unit: Ludovic Laporte; tel. (+32) 2–2951757.

French Language Unit 3

Head of Unit: Bruno Stas; tel. (+32) 2-2960653.

French Language Unit 4

Head of Unit: Michel Baut; tel. (+352) 430132627.

TERMINOLOGY CO-ORDINATION
Head of Unit: Konstantinos Zacharis; tel. (+352) 430133460.

Directorate R—Resources

Director: Piet Verleysen; tel. (+352) 430134523.

INTERNAL ADMINISTRATIVE MATTERS
Head of Unit: Paschalis Papachristopoulos; tel. (+32) 2-2950820.

BUDGET AND FINANCE
Head of Unit: Olivier Rouland; tel. (+32) 2-2966218.

INFORMATICS
Head of Unit: Dieter Rummel; tel. (+352) 430135174.

PROFESSIONAL AND ORGANIZATIONAL DEVELOPMENT
Head of Unit: Fabian Diego Luís; tel. (+352) 430131580.

Directorate S—Customer Relations

Director: Miroslav Adamis; tel. (+32) 2-2920836.

Adviser: Raymund Berners; tel. (+32) 2-2994626.

Adviser: Klaudia Zagorowicz; tel. (+32) 2-2994166.

DEMAND MANAGEMENT
Head of Unit: Valéria Daro; tel. (+32) 2-2956251.

EXTERNAL TRANSLATION
Head of Unit: Werner Grünewald; tel. (+32) 2-2991408.

EDITING
Head of Unit: David Baker; tel. (+32) 2-2985078.

EVALUATION AND ANALYSIS
Head of Unit: Anne Paternoster; tel. (+352) 430134002.

PUBLICATIONS OFFICE

2 rue Mercier, 2985 Luxembourg, Luxembourg; tel. (+352) 29291; fax (+352) 292944619; e-mail info@publications.europa.eu; internet publications.europa.eu

Director-General: Rudolf Strohmeier; tel. (+352) 292944070.

Assistant to the Director-General: Luca Martinelli; tel. (+352) 292942768.

Reporting directly to the Director-General

Internal Control and Evaluation

Head of Unit: László Szabó; tel. (+352) 292944195.

Directorate R—Resources and Logistics

Director: Eva Beňová; tel. (+352) 292942868.

CALLS FOR TENDER, CONTRACTS AND COPYRIGHT
Head of Unit: Jan Planovsky; tel. (+352) 292944415.

FINANCE
Head of Unit: Raymond Pisani; tel. (+352) 292942882.

DISTRIBUTION
Head of Unit (acting): Corinna Paysan-Huens; tel. (+352) 292942615.

Directorate A—Core Business Services

Director (acting): Peter Schmitz; tel. (+352) 292942605.

ENTERPRISE ARCHITECTURE, METHODS AND FORMATS
Head of Unit: Roberto Pappalardo; tel. (+352) 292942798.

POST-PRODUCTION RECEPTION, VALIDATION AND CELLAR MANAGEMENT
Head of Unit: Peter Schmitz; tel. (+352) 292942605.

IT PROJECTS
Head of Unit (acting): Pavel Borkovec; tel. (+352) 292944200.

IT INFRASTRUCTURE AND SECURITY
Head of Unit: Pavel Borkovec; tel. (+352) 292944200.

Directorate B—Official Journals and Publications Production

Director: Harolds Celms; tel. (+352) 292944969.

OFFICIAL JOURNALS AND CASE LAW
Head of Unit: Valeria Sciarrino; tel. (+352) 292944011.

PUBLICATIONS
Head of Unit: Patricia Ruggiu; tel. (+352) 292944621.

CO-ORDINATION AND QUALITY CONTROL A
Head of Unit: António Reis; tel. (+352) 292942970.

QUALITY CONTROL B
Head of Unit (acting): Dana Molnar Andreica; tel. (+32) 2-2944031.

QUALITY CONTROL C
Head of Unit: Margaret Warton-Woods; tel. (+32) 2-2944682.

Directorate C—Dissemination and Reuse

Director: António Carneiro; tel. (+352) 292942310.

COMMON PORTAL AND OPEN DATA PORTAL
Head of Unit: Cécile Adam; tel. (+352) 292942516.

EUR-LEX AND TED
Head of Unit: María Manuela Cruz; tel. (+352) 292944164.

EU BOOKSHOP AND CORDIS
Head of Unit: Ventsislav Voikov; tel. (+352) 292942916.

DOCUMENTARY MANAGEMENT AND METADATA
Head of Unit: Maria Westermann; tel. (+352) 292942992.

OFFICE FOR INFRASTRUCTURE AND LOGISTICS—BRUSSELS (OIB)

23 Cours Saint-Michel, 1040 Brussels, Belgium; internet ec.europa.eu/info/departments/infrastructure-and-logistics-brussels

Director: Marc Mouligneau; tel. (+32) 2-2956731.

Adviser: Luc Latouche; tel. (+32) 2-2993690.

Adviser: Peter Bensuka; tel. (+32) 2-2981321.

HR BUSINESS CORRESPONDENT, INFORMATICS AND COMMUNICATION
Head of Unit: Marie Soder Higgins; tel. (+32) 2-2993347.

BUDGET, PUBLIC PROCUREMENT, INTERNAL CONTROL AND PROGRAMMING
Head of Unit: Pierre-Olivier Bindels; tel. (+32) 2-2987435.

MANAGEMENT OF REAL ESTATE
Head of Department: Marc Seguinot; tel. (+32) 2-2959771.

Implementation of Real Estate Policy, Real Estate Assets and Project Management

Head of Unit: Jacky Marteau; tel. (+32) 2-2950457.

Management of Buildings and Technical Installations

Head of Unit: Michel Durand; tel. (+32) 2-2986265.

Energy, EMAS, IT systems and logistical support

Head of Unit: Stephen Price; tel. (+32) 2-2956625.

OPERATIONS AND SERVICES
Head of Department: Marie-Pierre Darchy; tel. (+32) 2-2984169.

Historical Archives, Mail, Reproduction

Head of Unit: Konstantin Kostantinou; tel. (+32) 2-2963818.

Transport, Mobility and Support Services

Head of Unit: Cristina Querol Carceller; tel. (+32) 2-2960363.

Social Infrastructure—Ispra

Head of Unit: Antonios Koletsos; tel. (+39) 0332786200; fax (+39) 0332786148.

Catering

Head of Unit: Carole Micmacher; tel. (+32) 2-2961002.

CHILDCARE FACILITIES
Head of Department: Christiane Bardoux; tel. (+32) 2-2954547.

Nurseries

Head of Unit (acting): Graziano Scatozza; tel. (+32) 2-2990159.

Kindergarten and Childminding Facilities

Head of Unit: Philippe Loop; tel. (+32) 2-2993720.

Enrolments, Operational Management and Support

Head of Unit: Jacek Pasternak; tel. (+32) 2-2958334.

OFFICE FOR ADMINISTRATION AND PAYMENT OF INDIVIDUAL ENTITLEMENTS (PMO)

41 ave de Tervuren, 1040 Brussels, Belgium; tel. (+32) 2-2991111; internet ec.europa.eu/info/departments/administration-and-payment-individual-entitlements

Director: Veronica Gaffey; tel. (+32) 2-2969596.

SUPCOM—SECRETARIAT OF THE OLAF SUPERVISORY COMMITTEE
Secretary of the OLAF Supervisory Committee: Marek Kaduczak; tel. (+32) 2-29684022.

SALARIES AND ADMINISTRATION OF INDIVIDUAL RIGHTS
Head of Unit: Horacio Barata; tel. (+32) 2-2951641.

MISSIONS, LAISSEZPASSER AND VISAS
Head of Unit: Fernanda Serra; tel. (+32) 2-2960406.

SICKNESS AND ACCIDENT INSURANCE
Head of Unit: Bruno Fetelian; tel. (+32) 2-2967255.

PENSIONS AND RELATIONS WITH FORMER STAFF
Head of Unit: Giuseppe Scognamiglio; tel. (+32) 2-2952799.

PMO—LUXEMBOURG
Head of Unit: Luc Dooms; tel. (+352) 430134924.

PMO—ISPRA
Head of Unit: Anna-Maria Silvano; tel. (+39) 0332-785508.

BUDGET, INTERNAL CONTROL AND IT CO-ORDINATION
Head of Unit: Jean-Pierre Vanderstraeten; tel. (+32) 2-2966499.

OFFICE FOR INFRASTRUCTURE AND LOGISTICS—LUXEMBOURG (OIL)

400 route d'Esch, 2920 Luxembourg, Luxembourg; internet ec.europa.eu/info/departments/infrastructure-and-logistics-luxembourg

Director: Marc Becquet; tel. (+352) 430137127.

BUILDINGS PROJECTS, EMAS, TRANSPORT, PRINTSHOP
Head of Unit (acting): Delia Morea; tel. (+352) 430138312.

COMMUNICATION, IT, CONFERENCES, HEALTH AND SAFETY, MAIL SERVICE
Head of Unit: Milagros Gallego Perez; tel. (+352) 430132895.

GENERAL MAINTENANCE AND FACILITY MANAGEMENT
Head of Unit: Thomas Kirchner; tel. (+352) 430135351.

CATERING SERVICES, FOYER, FITNESS CENTRE
Head of Unit: Daniel Necsa; tel. (+352) 430138290.

INTER-INSTITUTIONAL CHILDCARE CENTRE
Head of Unit: Hilde van Loon; tel. (+352) 430138998.

FINANCE, PROCUREMENT, REPORTING
Head of Unit (acting): Xavier Gilquin; tel. (+352) 430131938.

EUROPEAN PERSONNEL SELECTION OFFICE (EPSO)

25 ave de Cortenbergh, 1040 Brussels, Belgium; internet europa.eu/epso/about

Director: Nicholas Bearfield; tel. (+32) 2-2954126.

Adviser: Antonio Friz; tel. (+32) 2-2959484.

E-SELECTION AND TEST DEVELOPMENT
Head of Unit: Angela Heberling; tel. (+32) 2-2990386.

ASSESSMENT CENTRES MANAGEMENT
Head of Unit: Jaime Reis Conde; tel. (+32) 2-2966879.

RESOURCES AND ADMINISTRATIVE SUPPORT
Head of Unit: Gilles Guillard; tel. (+32) 2-2995020.

STAKEHOLDER RELATIONS AND SELECTION MANAGEMENT
Head of Unit: Sari Lehkonen; tel. (+32) 2964886.

COMMUNICATION AND ATTRACTIVENESS
Head of Unit: Claudine Camilleri; tel. (+32) 2-2998790.

EUSA—EUROPEAN SCHOOL OF ADMINISTRATION
Head of EUSA: Anna Smedeby; tel. (+32) 2-2955774.

Diplomatic Corps Accredited to the European Union

The diplomatic missions of non-member states accredited to the European Union are valuable information sources for companies, authorities and socioprofessional organizations. Their various advisers have, each within their own sector, a thorough knowledge of the different mechanisms applicable in commercial, technical, financial and cultural exchanges between their country and the EU.

Afghanistan: 61 ave de Wolvendael, 1180 Brussels, Belgium; tel. (+32) 2-7613166; fax (+32) 2-7613167; e-mail info@embassyafghanistan.be; Head of Mission Wali J. Monawar.

Albania: 30 rue Tenbosch, 1000 Brussels, Belgium; tel. (+32) 2-6443329; fax (+32) 2-6403177; e-mail mission.eu@mfa.gov.al; Head of Mission Suela Janina.

Algeria: 207–209 ave Molière, 1050 Brussels, Belgium; tel. (+32) 2-3435078; fax (+32) 2-3435168; e-mail info@algerian-embassy.be; internet www.algerian-embassy.be; Head of Mission Amar Belani.

Andorra: Bte 1, 1000 Brussels, Belgium; tel. (+32) 2-5132806; fax (+32) 2-5130741; e-mail ambaixada_belgica@govern.ad; internet www.andorra.be; Head of Mission (vacant).

Angola: 182 rue Franz Merjay, 1050 Brussels, Belgium; tel. (+32) 2-3461880; fax (+32) 2-3440894; e-mail angola.embassy.belgium@skynet.be; Head of Mission Maria Elizabeth Augusto Simbrão de Carvalho.

Argentina: Bte 2, 1050 Brussels, Belgium; tel. (+32) 2-6489371; fax (+32) 2-6480804; e-mail eceur@mrecic.gov.ar; Head of Mission Mario Raúl Verón Guerra.

Armenia: 28 rue Montoyer, 1000 Brussels, Belgium; tel. (+32) 2-3484400; fax (+32) 2-3484401; e-mail info@armeniamission.eu; Head of Mission Tatoul Markarian.

Australia: 56 ave des Arts, 1000 Brussels, Belgium; tel. (+32) 2-2860500; fax (+32) 2-2860576; e-mail austemb.brussels@dfat.gov.au; internet www.eu.mission.gov.au; Head of Mission Mark William Christopher Higgie.

Azerbaijan: 464 ave Molière, 1050 Brussels, Belgium; tel. (+32) 2-3452660; fax (+32) 2-3459158; e-mail office@azembassy.be; internet www.azembassy.be; Head of Mission Fuad Edgar oglu Isgandarov.

Bahamas: 23 ave de France, 1202 Geneva, Switzerland; tel. (+44 22) 7492-2080; fax (+44 22) 7492-2089; e-mail info@bahamasmission.ch; Head of Mission Rhoda Jackson.

Bahrain: 250 ave Louise, 1050 Brussels, Belgium; tel. (+32) 2-6270030; fax (+32) 2-6472274; e-mail brussels.mission@mofa.gov.bh; Head of Mission Bahiya Jawad Aljishi.

Bangladesh: 29–31 rue Jacques Jordaens, 1000 Brussels, Belgium; tel. (+32) 2-6405500; fax (+32) 2-6465998; e-mail bdootbrussels@skynet.be; internet www.bangladesh-embassy.be; Head of Mission Mohammed Shahdat Hossain.

Barbados: 166 Ave F. D. Roosevelt, 1050 Brussels, Belgium; tel. (+32) 2-7321737; fax (+32) 2-7323266; e-mail brussels@foreign.gov.bb; Head of Mission Samuel Jefferson Chandler.

Belarus: 192 ave Molière, 1050 Brussels, Belgium; tel. (+32) 2-3400270; fax (+32) 2-3400287; e-mail belgium@mfa.gov.by; Head of Mission Aleksandr Mikhnevich.

Belize: 87–93 Blvd Brand Whitlock, 1200 Brussels, Belgium; tel. (+32) 2-7326204; fax (+32) 2-7326246; e-mail embelize@skynet.be; Head of Mission Dylan Vernon.

Benin: 5 Ave de l'Observatoire, 1180 Brussels, Belgium; tel. (+32) 2-3749192; fax (+32) 2-3758326; e-mail ambabenin_benelux@yahoo.fr; Head of Mission Richard Zacharie Akplogan.

Bhutan: 70 ave Jules César, 1150 Brussels, Belgium; e-mail infobhutan@bhutanembassy.be; Head of Mission Pema Choden.

Bolivia: 176 ave Louise, Bte 6, 1050 Brussels, Belgium; tel. (+32) 2-6270010; fax (+32) 2-6474782; e-mail info@embajadadebolivia.eu; internet www.embajadadebolivia.eu; Head of Mission Nestor Gabriele Bellavite.

Bosnia and Herzegovina: 22 Rue de l'Industrie 22, 1040 Brussels, Belgium; tel. (+32) 2-6442008; fax (+32) 2-6441698; e-mail info@bhmeu.be; Head of Mission Lidija Topić.

Botswana: 169 ave de Tervuren, 1150 Brussels, Belgium; tel. (+32) 2-7352070; fax (+32) 2-7356318; e-mail boteur@gov.bw; internet www.botswana-brussels.com; Head of Mission Samuel Otsile Outlule.

Brazil: 30 ave F. D. Roosevelt, 1050 Brussels, Belgium; tel. (+32) 2-6402040; fax (+32) 2-6488040; e-mail braseuropa@itamaraty.gov.br; Head of Mission Everton Vieira Vargas.

Brunei: 238 ave F. D. Roosevelt, 1050 Brussels, Belgium; tel. (+32) 2-6750878; fax (+32) 2-6729358; e-mail info@bruneiembassy.be; Head of Mission Abu Sufian bin Haji Ali.

Burkina Faso: 16 Place Guy d'Arezzo 16, 1180 Brussels, Belgium; tel. (+32) 2-3459912; fax (+32) 2-3450612; e-mail ambassade.burkina@skynet.be; internet www.ambassadeduburkina.be; Head of Mission Jacqueline Marie Zaba.

Burundi: 46 Sq. Marie-Louise, 1000 Brussels, Belgium; tel. (+32) 2-2304535; fax (+32) 2-2307883; e-mail ambassade.burundi@gmail.com; internet www.ambaburundi.be; Head of Mission Jérémie Banigwaninzigo.

Cabo Verde: 29 ave Jeanne, 1050 Brussels, Belgium; tel. (+32) 2-6436270; fax (+32) 2-6463385; e-mail emb.caboverde@skynet.be; internet www.embcv.be; Head of Mission José Filomeno De Carvalho Dias Monteiro.

Cambodia: 264A Ave de Tervuren, 1150 Brussels, Belgium; tel. (+32) 2-7720372; fax (+32) 2-7720376; e-mail amcambel@skynet.be; Head of Mission Thireak Chea.

Cameroon: 131–133 ave Brugmann, 1190 Brussels, Belgium; tel. (+32) 2-3451870; fax (+32) 2-3445735; e-mail embassy@cameroon.be; internet www.cameroon.be; Head of Mission Daniel Evina Abe'e.

Canada: 58 ave des Arts, 1000 Brussels, Belgium; tel. (+32) 2-7410611; fax (+32) 2-7410643; e-mail breu@international.gc.ca; internet www.belgium.gc.cy; Head of Mission Dan Costello.

Central African Republic: 64 rue de la Fusée, 1130 Brussels, Belgium; tel. (+32) 2-7055603; fax (+32) 2-7055602; e-mail contact@ambassaderca.be; internet www.ambassaderca.be; Head of Mission Daniel Emery Dede.

Chad: 52 Blvd Lambermont, 1030 Brussels, Belgium; tel. (+32) 2-2151975; fax (+32) 2-2163526; e-mail contact@ambassadutchad.be; Chargé d'affaires a.i. Oumar Noury Abdelkerim.

Chile: 106 rue des Aduatiques, 1040 Brussels, Belgium; tel. (+32) 2-7433660; fax (+32) 2-7881621; e-mail echilebelgica@minrel.gov.cl; internet www.embachile.be; Head of Mission Raúl Fernández Daza.

China, People's Republic: 100 blvd de la Woluwé, 1200 Brussels, Belgium; tel. (+32) 2-7729572; fax (+32) 2-7728542; e-mail chinamission_eu@mfa.gov.cn; internet www.chinamission.be; Head of Mission Yanyi Yang.

Colombia: 96A ave F. D. Roosevelt, 1050 Brussels, Belgium; tel. (+32) 2-6495679; fax (+32) 2-6465491; e-mail ebruselas@cancilleria.gov.co; internet www.belgica.embajada.gov.co; Head of Mission Rodrigo Rivera Salazar.

Comoros: 64 rue de la Fusée, 1130 Brussels, Belgium; tel. (+32) 2-7795838; fax (+32) 2-7795838; e-mail ambacom.bxl@skynet.be; Head of Mission Siad Mdhoma Ali.

Congo, Democratic Republic: 30 rue Marie de Bourgogne, 1000 Brussels, Belgium; tel. (+32) 2-2134980; fax (+32) 2-2134995; e-mail secretariat@ambardc.be; internet www.ambardc.eu; Chargé d'affaires a.i. Paul-Crispin Kakhozi Bin Bulongo.

Congo, Republic: 16–18 Ave F. D. Roosevelt, 1050 Brussels, Belgium; tel. (+32) 2-6483856; fax (+32) 2-6484213; Head of Mission Roger Julien Menga.

Cook Islands: 10 rue Berckmans, 1060 Brussels, Belgium; tel. (+32) 2-5431000; fax (+32) 2-5431001; e-mail cookislands@prmltd.com; Head of Mission (vacant).

Costa Rica: Bte 23, 1050 Brussels, Belgium; tel. (+32) 2-6405541; fax (+32) 2-6483192; e-mail info@costaricaembassy.be; internet www.costaricaembassy.be; Head of Mission István Alfaro Solano.

Côte d'Ivoire: 234 ave F. D. Roosevelt, Bte 3, 1050 Brussels, Belgium; tel. (+32) 470-6613450; fax (+32) 2-6720491; e-mail mailbox@ambacibnl.be; internet www.ambacibnl.be; Head of Mission Jean-Vincent Zinsou.

Cuba: 80 ave Brugman, 1190 Brussels, Belgium; tel. (+32) 2-3497626; fax (+32) 2-3449691; e-mail mision@embacuba.be; Head of Mission Norma Miguelina Goicochea Estenoz.

Djibouti: 204 ave F. D. Roosevelt, 1050 Brussels, Belgium; tel. (+32) 2-3476967; fax (+32) 2-3476963; e-mail ambdjib@yahoo.be; Head of Mission Omar Abdi Said.

Dominica: 42 rue de Livourne, 1000 Brussels, Belgium; tel. (+32) 2-5342611; fax (+32) 2-5394009; e-mail ecs.embassies@oecs.org; internet www.oecs.org; Chargé d'affaires a.i. Sharlene Shillingford-McKimon.

Dominican Republic: 251 ave Louise, 1050 Brussels, Belgium; tel. (+32) 2-3464935; fax (+32) 2-3465152; e-mail mission.eu@dominicanembassy.be; Head of Mission Alejandro González Pons.

Ecuador: Bte 1, 1050 Brussels, Belgium; tel. (+32) 2-6499545; fax (+32) 2-6482611; e-mail mission.equateur@skynet.be; Head of Mission Pablo Villagómez Reinel.

Egypt: 19 ave de l'Uruguay, 1000 Brussels, Belgium; tel. (+32) 2-6635800; fax (+32) 2-6755888; e-mail eg.sec.be@hotmail.com; Head of Mission Ehab Fawzy.

El Salvador: 171 ave de Tervuren, 7ème étage, 1150 Brussels, Belgium; tel. (+32) 2-7330485; fax (+32) 2-7326574; e-mail embajadabruselas@rree.gob.sv; Head of Mission Julia Emma Villatoro Tario.

Equatorial Guinea: 6 place Guy d'Arezzo, 1180 Brussels, Belgium; tel. (+32) 2-3462509; fax (+32) 2-3463309; e-mail guineaecuatorial.brux@skynet.be; Head of Mission Carmelo Nvono-Ncá.

Eritrea: 15–17 ave de Wolvendael, 1180 Brussels, Belgium; tel. (+32) 2-3744434; fax (+32) 2-3720730; e-mail emba.eri.brusssels@skynet.be; Head of Mission Negassi Kassa Tekle.

Ethiopia: 64 ave de Tervuren, 1040 Brussels, Belgium; tel. (+32) 2-7713294; fax (+32) 2-7714914; e-mail info@ethiopianembassy.be; internet www.ethiopianembassy.be; Head of Mission Teshome Toga Chanka.

Fiji: 92–94 sq. Plasky, 1030 Brussels, Belgium; tel. (+32) 2-7369050; fax (+32) 2-7361458; e-mail info@fijiembassy.be; internet www.fijiembassy.be; Head of Mission Deo Saran.

Gabon: 112 ave Winston Churchill, 1180 Brussels, Belgium; tel. (+32) 2-3406210; fax (+32) 2-3464669; e-mail ambagabbel@yahoo.fr; Head of Mission Félicité Ongouori Ngoubili.

Gambia: 126 ave F. D. Roosevelt, 1050 Brussels, Belgium; tel. (+32) 2-6401049; fax (+32) 2-6463277; e-mail info@gambiaembassybrussels.be; Head of Mission Teneng Mba Jaiteh.

Georgia: 245 rue Père Eudore Devroye, 1150 Brussels, Belgium; tel. (+32) 2-7611190; fax (+32) 2-7611199; e-mail geomission.eu@mfa.gov.ge; internet www.belgium.mfa.gov.ge; Head of Mission Natalie Sabanadze.

Ghana: 7 blvd Général Wahis, 1030 Brussels, Belgium; tel. (+32) 2-7058220; fax (+32) 2-7056653; e-mail info@ghanaembassy.be; internet www.ghanaemb.be; Head of Mission Novisi Aku Abaidoo.

Guatemala: 185 ave Winston Churchill, 1180 Brussels, Belgium; tel. (+32) 2-3459047; fax (+32) 2-3446499; e-mail guatemala@skynet.be; Head of Mission José Alberto Briz Gutiérrez.

Guinea: 108 blvd Auguste Reyers, 1030 Brussels, Belgium; tel. (+32) 2-7710126; fax (+32) 2-7626036; e-mail ambaguinee.bruxelles@yahoo.fr; Head of Mission Ousmane Sylla.

Guinea-Bissau: 114 blvd Brand Whitlock, 1200 Brussels, Belgium; tel. (+32) 2-2905181; fax (+32) 2-2905156; e-mail ambaguibissaubrux@hotmail.com; Head of Mission Alfredo Lopes Cabral.

Guyana: 114 blvd Brand Whitlock, 1200 Brussels, Belgium; tel. (+32) 2-6756216; fax (+32) 2-6725598; e-mail ambassguybruss@skynet.be; Head of Mission David Hales.

Haiti: 139 chaussée de Charleroi, 1060 Brussels, Belgium; tel. (+32) 2-6497381; fax (+32) 2-6406080; e-mail ambassade@amb-haiti.be; Chargé d'affaires a.i. Monesty Junior Fanfil.

Holy See: 289 ave Brugmann, 1180 Brussels, Belgium; tel. (+32) 2-3407700; fax (+32) 2-3407704; e-mail nuncioeuropa@nuncioeuropa.org; Head of Mission Alain Paul Lebeaupin.

Honduras: 89 ave de Cortenbergh, 1000 Brussels, Belgium; tel. (+32) 2-7340000; fax (+32) 2-7352626; e-mail info@hondurasembassy.be; Head of Mission Roberto Ochoa Madrid.

Iceland: 11 Rond-Point Schuman, 1040 Brussels, Belgium; tel. (+32) 2-2385000; fax (+32) 2-2306938; e-mail emb.brussels@mfa.is; internet www.iceland.org/be; Head of Mission Bergdís Ellertsdóttir.

India: 217 chaussée de Vleurgat, 1050 Brussels, Belgium; tel. (+32) 2-6451850; fax (+32) 2-6489638; e-mail admin@indembassy.be; internet www.indembassy.be; Head of Mission Gaitri Issar Kumar.

Indonesia: 38 blvd de la Woluwé, 1200 Brussels, Belgium; tel. (+32) 2-7750120; fax (+32) 2-7728210; e-mail kbri.brussel@skynet.be; internet www.embassyofindonesia.eu; Head of Mission Yuri Octavian Thamrin.

Iran: 15 ave F. D. Roosevelt, 1050 Brussels, Belgium; tel. (+32) 2-6270350; fax (+32) 2-7623915; e-mail secretariat@iranembassy.be; Head of Mission Peiman Seadat.

Iraq: 115 ave F. D. Roosevelt, 1050 Brussels, Belgium; tel. (+32) 2-3745992; fax (+32) 2-3747615; e-mail ambassade.irak@skynet.be; Head of Mission Jawad Khadim Jawad Al-Chlaihawi.

Israel: 40 ave de l'Observatoire, 1180 Brussels, Belgium; tel. (+32) 2-3735500; fax (+32) 2-3735617; e-mail info-eu@brussels.mfa.gov.il; Head of Mission Aharon Leshno-Yaar.

Jamaica: 77 ave Hansen-Soulie, 1040 Brussels, Belgium; tel. (+32) 2-2301170; fax (+32) 2-2346969; e-mail emb.jam.brussels@skynet.be; Head of Mission Vilma McNish.

Japan: 1 rue Van Maerlant, 1040 Brussels, Belgium; tel. (+32) 2-5007711; fax (+32) 2-5133241; e-mail info@eu.mofa.go.jp; internet www.eu.emb-japan.go.jp; Head of Mission Kazuo Kodama.

Jordan: 104 ave F. D. Roosevelt, 1050 Brussels, Belgium; tel. (+32) 2-6407755; fax (+32) 2-6467737; e-mail joremb.amb.office@jordanembassy.be; internet www.jordanembassy.be; Head of Mission Yousef R. Bataineh.

Kazakhstan: 30 ave Van Bever, 1180 Brussels, Belgium; tel. (+32) 2-3749562; fax (+32) 2-3745091; e-mail brussels@mfa.kz; internet www.kazakhstanembassy.be; Head of Mission Almaz Khamzayev.

Kenya: 208 ave Winston Churchill, 1180 Brussels, Belgium; tel. (+32) 2-3401040; fax (+32) 2-3401050; e-mail info@kenyabrussels.com; internet www.kenyabrussels.com; Head of Mission Johnson Mwangi Weru.

Korea, Democratic People's Republic: 73 ave Gunnersbury, W5 4LP London, United Kingdom; tel. (+44 20) 8992-4965; fax (+44 20) 89922053; Third Sec. and Chargé d'affaires a.i. Kyong Jun Ryu.

Korea, Republic): 173–175 chaussée de La Hulpe, 1170 Brussels, Belgium; tel. (+32) 2-6755777; fax (+32) 2-6755221; e-mail eukorea@mofat.go.kr; internet www.koreanmissiontoeu.org; Head of Mission Hyoung-zhin Kim.

Kuwait: 43 ave F. D. Roosevelt, 1050 Brussels, Belgium; tel. (+32) 2-6477950; fax (+32) 2-6461298; e-mail embassy.kwt@skynet.be; Head of Mission Jasem Mohamed Albudaiwi.

Kyrgyzstan: 47 rue de l'Abbaye, 1050 Brussels, Belgium; tel. (+32) 2-6401868; fax (+32) 2-6400131; e-mail kyrgyz.embassy@skynet.be; Head of Mission Asein Kuseinovich Isayev.

Laos: 19–21 ave de la Brabançonne, 1000 Brussels, Belgium; tel. (+32) 2-7400950; fax (+32) 2-7341666; Head of Mission Khamkheuang Bounteum.

Lebanon: 101 ave F. D. Roosevelt, 1050 Brussels, Belgium; tel. (+32) 2-6457765; fax (+32) 2-6457769; e-mail ambliban@yahoo.fr; Head of Mission Rami Mortada.

Lesotho: 45 blvd Général Wahis, 1030 Brussels, Belgium; tel. (+32) 2-7053976; fax (+32) 2-7056779; e-mail lesothobrussels@hotmail.com; Head of Mission Mpeo Mahase-Moiloa.

Liberia: 11 rue Archimède, 1000 Brussels, Belgium; tel. (+32) 2-4110112; fax (+32) 2-4110912; e-mail info@embassyofliberia.be; Head of Mission Isaac Wehyee Nyenabo.

Libya: 1 rue Paul Lauters, 1050 Brussels, Belgium; tel. (+32) 2-6493737; fax (+32) 2-6409076; e-mail libyanmission.eu@gmail.com; Head of Mission (vacant).

Liechtenstein: 1 place du Congrès, 1000 Brussels, Belgium; tel. (+32) 2-2293900; fax (+32) 2-2193545; e-mail ambassade.liechtenstein@bru.llv.li; Head of Mission Sabine Monauni.

Macedonia, former Yugoslav republic: 38 rue de la Loi, 1040 Brussels, Belgium; tel. (+32) 2-2350350; fax (+32) 2-2800949; e-mail mission.eu@mfa.gov.mk; internet eu.missions.gov.mk; Chargé d'affaires a.i. Vlatko Stankovski.

Madagascar: 276 ave de Tervuren, 1150 Brussels, Belgium; tel. (+32) 2-7701726; fax (+32) 2-7723731; e-mail info@madagascar-embassy.eu; internet www.madagascar-embassy.eu; First Counsellor and Chargé d'affaires a.i. Ibrahim Norbert Richard.

Malawi: 46 ave Herman Debroux, 1160 Brussels, Belgium; tel. (+32) 2-2310980; fax (+32) 2-2311066; e-mail embassy.malawi@skynet.be; Head of Mission Tedson Aubrey Kalebe.

Malaysia: 414A Ave de Tervuren, 1150 Brussels, Belgium; tel. (+32) 2-7760340; fax (+32) 2-7625049; e-mail malbrussels@kln.gov.my; Head of Mission Hasnudin bin Hamzah.

Maldives: 11 Rond-Point Schuman, 1040 Brussels, Belgium; tel. (+32) 2-2567567; fax (+32) 2-2567569; e-mail info@maldivesembassy.be; internet www.maldivesmission.eu; Head of Mission Ahmed Shiaan.

Mali: 487 ave Molière, 1050 Brussels, Belgium; tel. (+32) 2-3457432; fax (+32) 2-3445700; e-mail info@amba-mali.be; internet www.amba-mali.be; Head of Mission Sékou dit Gaoussou Cissé.

Mauritania: 6 ave de la Colombie, 1000 Brussels, Belgium; tel. (+32) 2-6724747; fax (+32) 2-6722051; e-mail info@amb-mauritania.be; Head of Mission Abdallahi Bah Nagi Kebd.

Mauritius: 68 rue des Bollandistes, 1040 Brussels, Belgium; tel. (+32) 2-7339988; fax (+32) 2-7344021; e-mail ambsec@mubru.org; Head of Mission Haymandoyal Dillum.

Mexico: 94 ave F. D. Roosevelt, 1050 Brussels, Belgium; tel. (+32) 2-6290777; fax (+32) 2-6440819; e-mail embamex@embamex.eu; Head of Mission Eloy Cantu Segovia.

Moldova: 55 ave F. D. Roosevelt, 1050 Brussels, Belgium; tel. (+32) 2-7400660; fax (+32) 2-7400669; e-mail mission.bru@mfa.md; internet www.eumission.mfa.gov.md; Head of Mission Eugen Caras.

Monaco: 17 place Guy d'Arezzo, 1180 Brussels, Belgium; tel. (+32) 2-3474987; fax (+32) 2-3434920; Head of Mission Sophie Thevenoux.

Mongolia: 18 ave Besme, 1190 Brussels, Belgium; tel. (+32) 2-3446974; fax (+32) 2-3443215; e-mail brussels@embmongolie.be; internet www.embassyofmongolia.be; Head of Mission Od Och.

Montenegro: 117 rue du Trône, 1050 Brussels, Belgium; tel. (+32) 2-2235561; fax (+32) 2-2236028; e-mail eu@mfa.gov.me; internet www.mip.gov.me; Head of Mission Bojan Šarkić.

Morocco: 2 ave F. D. Roosevelt, 1050 Brussels, Belgium; tel. (+32) 2-6263410; fax (+32) 2-6263434; e-mail mission.ue@maec.gov.ma; Head of Mission Ahmed Réda Chami.

Mozambique: 97 blvd Saint-Michel, 1040 Brussels, Belgium; tel. (+32) 2-7360096; fax (+32) 2-7320664; e-mail info@embassyofmozambique.be; internet www.embassyofmozambique.be; Head of Mission Ana Nemba Uaiene.

Myanmar: 9 blvd Général Wahis, 1030 Brussels, Belgium; tel. (+32) 2-7019380; fax (+32) 2-7055048; e-mail mebrussels@skynet.be; internet www.embassyofmyanmar.be; Head of Mission Paw Lwin Sein.

Namibia: 454 ave de Tervuren, 1150 Brussels, Belgium; tel. (+32) 2-7711410; fax (+32) 2-7719689; e-mail nam.emb@brutele.be; Head of Mission Kaire Munionganda Mbuende.

Nepal: 210 ave Brugman, 1050 Brussels, Belgium; tel. (+32) 2-3462658; fax (+32) 2-3441361; e-mail embn@skynet.be; internet www.nepalembassybrussels.be; Head of Mission Lok Bahadur Thapa.

New Zealand: 9/31 ave des Nerviens, 7ème étage, 1000 Brussels, Belgium; tel. (+32) 2-5121040; fax (+32) 2-5134856; e-mail nzemb.brussels@mfat.govt.nz; internet www.nzembassy.com/belgium; Head of Mission David Taylor.

Nicaragua: 55 ave de Wolvendael, 1180 Brussels, Belgium; tel. (+32) 2-3756434; fax (+32) 2-3757188; e-mail sky77706@skynet.be; Head of Mission Mauricio Lautaro Sandino Montes.

Niger: 78 ave F. D. Roosevelt, 1050 Brussels, Belgium; tel. (+32) 2-6486140; fax (+32) 2-6482784; e-mail ambassadeduniger belgique@yahoo.be; Head of Mission Ousmane Alhassane Abba.

Nigeria: 288 ave de Tervuren, 1150 Brussels, Belgium; tel. (+32) 2-7625200; fax (+32) 2-7623763; e-mail nigeriabrussels@belgacom.net; internet www.nigeriabrussels.be; Chargé d'affaires a.i. Suleiman Umar.

Niue: 10 rue Berckmans, 1060 Brussels, Belgium; tel. (+32) 2-5431000; fax (+32) 2-5431001; e-mail cookislands@prmltd.com; Head of Mission (vacant).

Norway: 17 rue Archimède, 1000 Brussels, Belgium; tel. (+32) 2-2387400; fax (+32) 2-2387490; e-mail eu.brussels@mfa.no; internet www.eu-norway.org; Head of Mission Oda Helen Sletnes.

Oman: 236 ave F. D. Roosevelt, 1050 Brussels, Belgium; tel. (+32) 2-6797010; fax (+32) 2-5347992; e-mail oman@omanembassy.be; Head of Mission Najeem Bin Suleiman Al-Abri.

Pakistan: 57 ave Delleur, 1170 Brussels, Belgium; tel. (+32) 2-6738007; fax (+32) 2-6758394; e-mail secretary.parkbrussels@yahoo.co.uk; Head of Mission Naghmana A. Hashmi.

Palau: 6 Rond-Point Robert Schuman, 1050 Brussels, Belgium; tel. (+32) 2-2346345; e-mail office@palaueu.com; internet palaugov.pw; Head of Mission Ngedikes Olai Uludong.

Panama: 475 ave Louise, 1050 Brussels, Belgium; tel. (+32) 2-6490729; fax (+32) 2-6484833; e-mail info@embpanamabxl.be; internet www.embpanamabxl.be; Head of Mission Darío Ernesto Chirú Ochoa.

Papua New Guinea: 430 ave de Tervuren, 1150 Brussels, Belgium; tel. (+32) 2-7790609; fax (+32) 2-7727088; Head of Mission Joshua Rimarkindu Kalinoe.

Paraguay: 475 ave Louise, 12ème étage, 1050 Brussels, Belgium; tel. (+32) 2-6499055; fax (+32) 2-6474248; e-mail embapar@skynet.be; Head of Mission Rigoberto Gauto.

Peru: 212 ave de Tervuren, 1150 Brussels, Belgium; tel. (+32) 2-7333319; fax (+32) 2-7334819; e-mail info@embaperu.be; Head of Mission Gonzalo Gutiérrez Reinel.

Philippines: 297 ave Molière, 1050 Brussels, Belgium; tel. (+32) 2-3403377; fax (+32) 2-3456425; e-mail brusselspe@gmail.com; internet www.philembassy.be; Head of Mission(vacant).

Qatar: 79 ave Franklin Roosevelt, 1050 Brussels, Belgium; tel. (+32) 2-6434730; fax (+32) 2-2231166; e-mail brussels@mofa.gov.qa; internet www.qatarembassy.be; Head of Mission Abdulrahman Mohammed al-Khulaifi.

Russian Federation: 45 drève de Lorraine, 1180 Brussels, Belgium; tel. (+32) 2-3756629; fax (+32) 2-3756650; e-mail misrusce@numericable.be; internet www.russiaeu.mid.ru; Head of Mission Vladimir A. Chizhov.

Rwanda: 1 ave des Fleurs, 1150 Brussels, Belgium; tel. (+32) 2-7630721; fax (+32) 2-7630753; e-mail ambarwanda@gmail.com; internet www.ambarwanda.be; Chargé d'affaires a.i. Faustin Musare.

Saint Christopher and Nevis: 42 rue de Livourne, 1000 Brussels, Belgium; tel. (+32) 2-5342611; fax (+32) 2-5394009; e-mail ecs.embassies@oecs.org; internet www.oecs.org; Chargé d'affaires a.i. Sharlene Shillingford-McKimon.

Saint Lucia: 42 rue de Livourne, 1000 Brussels, Belgium; tel. (+32) 2-5342611; fax (+32) 2-5394009; e-mail ecs.embassies@oecs.org; internet www.oecs.org; Chargé d'affaires a.i. Sharlene Shillingford-McKimon.

Saint Vincent and the Grenadines: 42 rue de Livourne, 1000 Brussels, Belgium; tel. (+32) 2-5342611; fax (+32) 2-5394009; e-

European Commission DIRECTORY

mail ecs.embassies@oecs.org; internet www.oecs.org; Chargé d'affaires a.i. Sharlene Shillingford-McKimon.

Samoa: 1 ave Commandant Lothaire, 1040 Brussels, Belgium; tel. (+32) 2-6608454; fax (+32) 2-6750336; e-mail samoaembassy@skynet.be; Head of Mission Fatumanava Dr Pa'olelei H. Luteru.

San Marino: 62 ave F. D. Roosevelt, 1050 Brussels, Belgium; tel. (+32) 2-6442224; fax (+32) 2-6442057; Head of Mission Antonella Benedettini.

São Tomé e Príncipe: 175 ave de Tervuren, 1150 Brussels, Belgium; tel. (+32) 2-7348966; fax (+32) 2-7348815; e-mail ambassade@saotomeeprincipe.be; Chargé d'affaires a.i. Horácio Fernandes Da Fonseca.

Saudi Arabia: 326 ave Louise, 1050 Brussels, Belgium; tel. (+32) 2-6492044; fax (+32) 2-6472492; e-mail beemb@mofa.gov.sa; internet www.mofa.gov.sa; Head of Mission Abdulrahman Sulaiman Alahmed.

Senegal: 196 ave F. D. Roosevelt, 1050 Brussels, Belgium; tel. (+32) 2-6730097; fax (+32) 2-6750460; e-mail ambassadesenegal@skynet.be; Head of Mission Amadou Diop.

Serbia: 53 blvd du Régent, 1000 Brussels, Belgium; tel. (+32) 2-6498242; fax (+32) 2-6490878; e-mail mission.serbia.eu@mfa.rs; internet www.eu-brussels.mfa.gov.rs; Head of Mission Ana Hrustanović.

Seychelles: Bte 23, 1040 Brussels, Belgium; tel. (+32) 2-7336055; fax (+32) 2-7326022; e-mail brussels@seychellesgov.com; Head of Mission Thomas Selby Pillay.

Sierra Leone: 410 ave de Tervuren, 1150 Brussels, Belgium; tel. (+32) 2-7710053; fax (+32) 2-7718230; e-mail sierraleoneembassy@brutele.be; Head of Mission Ibrahim Sorie.

Singapore: 85 ave F. D. Roosevelt, 1050 Brussels, Belgium; tel. (+32) 2-6602979; fax (+32) 2-6608685; e-mail singemb_bru@sgmfa.gov.sg; internet www.mfa.gov.sg/brussels; Head of Mission Jaya Ratnam.

Solomon Islands: 17 ave Edouard Lacomble, 1040 Brussels, Belgium; tel. (+32) 2-7327085; fax (+32) 2-7326885; e-mail siembassy@skynet.be; Head of Mission Moses Kouni Mose.

Somalia: 66 ave F. D. Roosevelt, 1050 Brussels; tel. (+32) 2-6466488; fax (+32) 2-6492888; e-mail somalrep@gmail.com; Head of Mission Ali Said Faqi.

South Africa: 17–19 rue Montoyer, 1000 Brussels, Belgium; tel. (+32) 2-2854400; fax (+32) 2-5147803; e-mail publicdiplomacy@southafrica.be; internet www.southafrica.be; Head of Mission Baso Sangqu.

South Sudan: 30 blvd Brand Whitlock, 1040 Brussels, Belgium; tel. (+32) 2-2802355; fax (+32) 2-2803144; e-mail info@goss-brussels.com; Head of Mission Emmanuel Lomoro Lo Willa.

Sri Lanka: 27 rue Jules Lejeune, 1050 Brussels, Belgium; tel. (+32) 2-3445394; fax (+32) 2-3446737; e-mail secretariat@srilankaembassy.be; Head of Mission E. Rodney M. Perera.

Sudan: 124 ave F. D. Roosevelt, 1050 Brussels, Belgium; tel. (+32) 2-6479494; fax (+32) 2-6483499; e-mail sudanbx@yahoo.com; Head of Mission Mutrif Siddig Ali.

Suriname: 200 ave F. D. Roosevelt, 1050 Brussels, Belgium; tel. (+32) 2-6401172; fax (+32) 2-6463962; e-mail amb.belgie@foreignaffairs.gov.sr; Chargé d'affaires a.i. Milton A. Castelen.

Swaziland: 188 ave Winston Churchill, 1180 Brussels, Belgium; tel. (+32) 2-3474771; fax (+32) 2-3474623; e-mail brussels@swaziembassy.be; internet www.swaziembassy.be; Head of Mission Sibusisiwe Mngomezulu.

Switzerland: 1 place du Luxembourg, 1050 Brussels, Belgium; tel. (+32) 2-2861311; fax (+32) 2-2304509; e-mail vertretung@brm.rep.admin.ch; internet www.eda.admin.ch/mission.eu; Head of Mission Urs Bucher.

Syria: 1 ave F. D. Roosevelt, 1050 Brussels, Belgium; tel. (+32) 2-5541920; fax (+32) 2-6481485; e-mail syria.mission@skynet.be

Tajikistan: 16 blvd Général Jacques, 1050 Brussels, Belgium; tel. (+32) 2-6406933; fax (+32) 2-6490195; Head of Mission Erkinkhon Rahmatullozoda.

Tanzania: 72 ave F. D. Roosevelt, 1050 Brussels, Belgium; tel. (+32) 2-6406500; fax (+32) 2-6468026; e-mail tanzania@skynet.be; Chargé d'affaires a.i. Agnes R. Kayola.

Thailand: 876 chaussée de Waterloo, 1000 Brussels, Belgium; tel. (+32) 2-6406810; fax (+32) 2-6483066; e-mail thaibxl@thaiembassy.be; internet www.thaiembassy.be; Head of Mission Manasvi Srisodapol.

Timor-Leste: 102 ave de Tervuren, 1040 Brussels, Belgium; tel. (+32) 2-7359671; fax (+32) 2-7339003; e-mail info@timor-leste.be; Head of Mission Francisco Tilman Cepeda.

Togo: 264 ave de Tervuren, 1150 Brussels, Belgium; tel. (+32) 2-7701791; fax (+32) 2-7715075; e-mail belgique@diplomatie.gouv.tg; internet www.ambatogobruxelles.be; Head of Mission Kokou Nayio Atsumikoa M'Beou.

Tonga: 36 Molyneux St, 1150 London W1H 5BQ, United Kingdom; tel. (+44 20) 7724-5828; fax (+44 20) 7723-9074; e-mail snkioa@tongahighcom.co.uk; Head of Mission (vacant).

Trinidad and Tobago: 14 ave de la Faisanderie, 1150 Brussels, Belgium; tel. (+32) 2-7629400; fax (+32) 2-7722783; e-mail info@embtrinbago.be; Head of Mission Colin Michael Connelly.

Tunisia: 278 ave de Tervuren, 1150 Brussels, Belgium; tel. (+32) 2-7717395; fax (+32) 2-7719433; e-mail at.belgique@diplomatie.gov.tn; Head of Mission Tahar Chérif.

Turkey: 36–38 ave des Arts, 1000 Brussels, Belgium; tel. (+32) 2-2896240; fax (+32) 2-5110450; e-mail tr-delegation.eu@mfa.gov.tr; internet www.avbir.dt.mfa.gov.tr; Head of Mission Faruk Kaymakci.

Turkmenistan: 15 blvd Général Jacques, 1050 Brussels, Belgium; tel. (+32) 2-6481874; fax (+32) 2-6481906; e-mail turkmenistan@skynet.be; Head of Mission Ata Oveznepesovich Serdarov.

Tuvalu: 17 ave Edouard Lacomble, 1040 Brussels, Belgium; tel. (+32) 2-7421067; fax (+32) 2-7422869; e-mail tuvaluembassy@skynet.be; Head of Mission Tine Leuelu.

Uganda: 317 ave de Tervuren, 1150 Brussels, Belgium; tel. (+32) 2-7625825; fax (+32) 2-7630438; e-mail contactugandaembassy@gmail.com; internet www.ugandamission-benelux.org; Head of Mission Mirjam Blaak Sow.

Ukraine: 99–101 ave Louis Lepoutre, 1050 Brussels, Belgium; tel. (+32) 2-3409860; fax (+32) 2-3409879; e-mail pm_eu@mfa.gov.ua; internet www.ukraine-eu.mfa.gov.ua; Head of Mission Mykola Tochytskiy.

United Arab Emirates: 11 rue des Colonies, 1000 Brussels, Belgium; tel. (+32) 2-6406000; fax (+32) 2-6462473; e-mail info@uaeembassy.be; Head of Mission Mohamed Issa Hamad Abushahab.

USA: 13 rue Zinner, 1000 Brussels, Belgium; tel. (+32) 2-8114100; fax (+32) 2-8115154; Head of Mission Anthony Luzzatto Gardner.

Uruguay: 22 ave F. D. Roosevelt, 1050 Brussels, Belgium; tel. (+32) 2-6401169; fax (+32) 2-6482909; e-mail urucomun@mrree.gub.uy; Head of Mission Carlos Perez Del Castillo.

Uzbekistan: 99 ave F. D. Roosevelt, 1050 Brussels, Belgium; tel. (+32) 2-6728844; fax (+32) 2-6723946; e-mail eumission@uzbekistan.be; Chargé d'affaires a.i. Karomiddin Gadoev.

Vanuatu: Chemin de Ronde, 1150 Brussels, Belgium; tel. (+32) 2-7717494; fax (+32) 2-7717494; e-mail info@vanuatuembassy.net; Head of Mission Roy Mickey Joy.

Venezuela: 10 ave F. D. Roosevelt, 1050 Brussels, Belgium; tel. (+32) 2-6390340; fax (+32) 2-6478820; e-mail embve.bebrs@mppre.gob.ve; internet belgica.embajada.gob.ve; Head of Mission Claudia Salerno Caldera.

Viet Nam: 1 blvd Général Jacques, 1050 Brussels, Belgium; tel. (+32) 2-3792737; fax (+32) 2-3749376; e-mail vnemb.brussels@skynet.be; Head of Mission Thua Phong Vuong.

Yemen: 114 ave F. D. Roosevelt, 1050 Brussels, Belgium; tel. (+32) 2-6465290; fax (+32) 2-6462911; e-mail mofa@yemen-embassy.be; Head of Mission Mohamed Taha Mustafa.

Zambia: 469 ave Molière, 1050 Brussels, Belgium; tel. (+32) 2-3435649; fax (+32) 2-3474333; e-mail gov@zebru.org; internet www.zebru.org; Head of Mission Grace Musonda Mutale Kabwe.

Zimbabwe: 11 sq. Joséphine-Charlotte, 1200 Brussels, Belgium; tel. (+32) 2-7625808; fax (+32) 2-7756510; e-mail zimbrussels@skynet.be; Head of Mission Tadeous Tafirenyika Chifamba.

EUROPEAN EXTERNAL ACTION SERVICE (EEAS)

Rond Point Schuman 9A, 1046 Brussels, Belgium; tel. (+32) 2-584-1111; internet eeas.europa.eu

High Representative of the Union for Foreign Affairs and Security Policy and Vice-President of the European Commission: Federica Mogherini.

Secretariat-General

Executive Secretary-General: Helga Maria Schmid.

Deputy Secretary-General for Political Affairs

Deputy Secretary-General: Jean-Christophe Belliard.

CHAIR. OF POLITICAL AND SECURITY COMMITTEE

Director and Permanent Chair.: Walter Stevens.

MD-ASIAPAC—ASIA AND THE PACIFIC

Managing Director: Gunnar Wiegand.
Deputy Managing Director: Paola Pampaloni.

Regional Affairs, India, Nepal, Bhutan, Bangladesh
Head of Division: Veronica Cody.

Pakistan, Afghanistan, Sri Lanka, Maldives
Head of Division: Dietmar Krissler.

South-East Asia
Head of Division: David Daly.

China, Hong Kong, Macao, Taiwan, Mongolia
Head of Division: Ellis Matthews.

Japan, Korea, Australia and New Zealand, Pacific
Head of Division: Reinhold Brender.

MD-EURCA—EUROPE AND CENTRAL ASIA

Managing Director: Thomas Mayr Harting.

Western Europe, Western Balkans and Turkey
Head of Division: Angelina Eichhorst.
Head of Division (Western Europe): Claude Maerten.
Head of Division (Western Balkans): Eduard Auer.
Head of Division (Turkey): Javier Niño Perez.

Russia, Eastern Partnership, Central Asia and Regional Co-operation and Organization for Security and Co-operation in Europe
Head of Division: Luc Pierre Devigne.
Head of Division (Eastern Partnership, Regional Co-operation and Organization for Security and Co-operation in Europe): Boris Jarochevtich.
Head of Division (Eastern Partnership Bilateral): Dirk Schuebel.
Head of Division (Russia): Fernando Andresen Guimaraes.

MD-MENA—MIDDLE EAST AND NORTH AFRICA

Managing Director: Nick Westcott.
Deputy Managing Director: Colin Scicluna.

Middle East I—Egypt, Syria, Lebanon, Jordan
Head of Division: Patrick Costello.

Middle East II—Israel, Occupied Palestinian Territories and Middle East Peace Process
Head of Division: Raul Fuentes Milani.

Arabian Peninsula, Iraq and Regional Policies
Head of Division: Rosamaria Gili.

Maghreb
Head of Division: Vincent Piket.

GCC Countries, Iraq and Yemen
Head of Division: John O'Rourke.

Strategy and Instruments of the European Neighbourhood Policy
Head of Division: Gianluca Grippa.

Deputy Secretary-General for Economic and Global Issues

Deputy Secretary-General: Christian Leffler.

MD-GLOBAL—HUMAN RIGHTS, GLOBAL AND MULTILATERAL ISSUES

Managing Director: Lotte Knudsen.
Deputy Managing Director: Marc Giacomini.

Human Rights
Head of Division: Mercedes García Pérez.

Economic and Global Issues
Head of Division: Dominic Porter.

Democracy and Electoral Observation
Head of Division: Emanuele Giaufret.

Migration and Human Security
Head of Division: Leonello Gabrici.

Development Co-operation Co-ordination
Head of Division: Filiberto Ceriani Sebregondi.

Multilateral Relations
Head of Division: Jonas Jonsson.

MD-AFRICA—AFRICA
Director: Koen Vervaeke.
Deputy Managing Director: Birgitte Markussen.

Horn of Africa and East Africa
Head of Division: Patrick Simmonet.

Southern Africa and Indian Ocean
Head of Division: Girolama Erminia Notarangelo.

West Africa
Head of Division: Hans-Peter Schadek.

Central Africa
Head of Division: Patrick Spirlet.

Pan-African Affairs
Head of Division: Kristin de Peyron.

MD-AMERICAS—AMERICAS
Managing Director: Edita Hrda.
Deputy Managing Director: Roland Schaefer.

USA and Canada
Head of Division: Richard Tibbels.

Mexico, Central America and Caribbean
Head of Division: Aldo dell'Ariccia.

South America
Head of Division: Adrianus Koetsenruijter.

Regional Affairs
Head of Division: Manfredo Fanti.

Deputy Secretary-General for Common Security and Defence Policy and Crisis Response

Deputy Secretary-General: Pedro Serrano.

Prevention of Conflicts, Rule of Law, Integrated Approach, Stabilization and Mediation
Head of Division: Stefano Tomat.

Security Policy
Director: Pawel Herczynski.

European Union Intelligence and Situation Centre
Director: Gerhard Conrad.

Crisis Management and Planning
Head of Division: Gábor Iklody.

Civilian Planning and Conduct Capability
Head of Division: Kenneth Deane.

European Union Military Staff

Managing Director: Esa Pulkkinen.
Deputy Head of the European Union Military Staff: Giovanni Manione.

Budget and Administration

Managing Director: Gianmarco Di Vita.

External Delegations to Non-Member States

Afghanistan: Chahari Sedarat, Ministry of the Interior Rd, Shar-e-Naw, Kabul; tel. (+93) 799095004; e-mail delegation-afghanistan@eeas.europa.eu; internet www.eeas.europa.eu/delegations/afghanistan; Franz-Michael Mellbin (Head of Delegation).

Albania: ABA Business Centre, Rr. Papa Gjon Pali II, 17th Floor, Tirana; tel. (+355 4) 2228320; fax (+355 4) 2230752; e-mail delegation-albania@eeas.europa.eu; internet www.eeas.europa.eu/delegations/albania; Romana Vlahutin (Head of Delegation).

Algeria: Domaine Benouadah, Rue du 11, El-Biar, Algiers; tel. (+213 21) 923641; fax (+213 21) 923681; e-mail delegation-algeria@eeas.europa.eu; internet www.eeas.europa.eu/delegations/algeria; John O'Rourke (Head of Delegation).

Angola: Rua Rainha Ginga 45 (3°), Caixa Postal 2669, Luanda; tel. (+244 925) 978332; e-mail delegation-angola@eeas.europa.eu; internet www.eeas.europa.eu/delegations/angola; Ulicný Tomas (Head of Delegation).

Argentina: Ayacucho 1537, C1112AAA, Buenos Aires; tel. (+54 11) 48053759; fax (+54 11) 48011594; e-mail delegation-argentina@eeas.europa.eu; internet www.eeas.europa.eu/delegations/argentina; François Roudie (Head of Delegation (acting)).

Armenia: 21 Frik Str., 0002, Yerevan; tel. (+374 10) 54-64-94; fax (+374 10) 54-64-95; e-mail delegation-armenia@eeas.europa.eu; internet www.eeas.europa.eu/delegations/armenia Piotr Antoni Switalski (Head of Delegation).

Australia: 18 Arkana St, Yarralumla, Canberra ACT 2600; tel. (+61 2) 6271-2777; fax (+61 2) 6273-4445; e-mail delegation-australia@eeas.europa.eu; internet www.eeas.europa.eu/delegations/australia; Sem Fabrizi (Head of Delegation).

Azerbaijan: 11th Floor, Landmark 3 Bldg, Nizami 90A, 1010 Baku; tel. (+994 12) 4972063; fax (+994 12) 4972069; e-mail delegation-azerbaijan@eeas.europa.eu; internet eeas.europa.eu/delegations/azerbaijan; Anna Malena Mard (Head of Delegation).

Bangladesh: Plot 7, Rd 84, Gulshan 2, POB GN 6086, Dhaka 1212; tel. (+880 2) 8824730; fax (+880 2) 8823118; e-mail delegation-bangladesh@eeas.europa.eu; internet www.eeas.europa.eu/delegations/bangladesh; Pierre Mayaudon (Head of Delegation).

Barbados and the Eastern Caribbean: Palm Beach Corporate Centre, Hastings, Christ Church, 15156, Bridgetown; tel. (+1 246) 4348501; fax (+1 246) 4277687; e-mail delegation-barbados@eeas.europa.eu; internet www.eeas.europa.eu/delegations/barbados; Daniela Tramacere (Head of Delegation).

Belarus: Engels St 34A, 220030, Minsk; tel. (+375 17) 3286613; fax (+375 17) 2891281; e-mail delegation-belarus@eeas.europa.eu; internet www.eeas.europa.eu/delegations/belarus; Andrea Wiktorin (Head of Delegation).

Benin: Ave Clozel, Bâtiment Administratif, 01 BP 910, Cotonou; tel. (+229) 21-31-30-99; fax (+229) 21-31-53-28; e-mail delegation-benin@eeas.europa.eu; internet www.eeas.europa.eu/delegations/benin; Josep Coll i Carbó (Head of Delegation).

Bolivia: Ave Costanera Nº 300 entre Calle 10 y, Nardos, Calacoto 10747, La Paz; tel. (+591 2) 2782244; fax (+591 2) 2784550; e-mail delegation-bolivia@eeas.europa.eu; internet www.eeas.europa.eu/delegations/bolivia; Leon de la Torre Krais (Head of Delegation).

Bosnia and Herzegovina: Skenderia 3A, 71000, Sarajevo; tel. (+387) 33666044; fax (+387) 33666037; e-mail delegation-bih@eeas.europa.eu; internet europa.ba; Lars-Gunnar Wigemark (Head of Delegation).

Botswana: Robinson Rd, Plot 758, POB 1253, Gaborone; tel. (+267) 3914455; fax (+267) 3913626; e-mail delegation-botswana@eeas.europa.eu; internet www.eeas.europa.eu/delegations/botswana; Alexander Baum (Head of Delegation).

Brazil: SHIS QI 7, Bl. A, Lago Sul, Brasília DF 71615-205; tel. (+55 61) 2104-3122; fax (+55 61) 2104-3141; e-mail delegation-brazil@eeas.europa.eu; internet www.eeas.europa.eu/delegations/brazil; João Cravinho (Head of Delegation).

Burkina Faso: Ave Kwame N'Krumah, en face de la Sonatur, BP 352, Ouagadougou 01; tel. (+226) 50-49-29-00; fax (+226) 50-49-29-99; e-mail delegation-burkina-faso@eeas.europa.eu; internet www.eeas.europa.eu/delegations/burkina_faso; Jean Lamy (Head of Delegation).

Burundi: Bât. Old East, Place de l'Indépendence, BP 103, Bujumbura; tel. (+257) 22-22-34-26; fax (+257) 22-22-46-12; e-mail delegation-burundi@ec.europa.eu; internet www.eeas.europa.eu/delegations/burundi; Wolfram Vetter (Head of Delegation).

Cabo Verde: Rua Largo de Europa, CP 122, Praia; tel. (+238) 2621393; fax (+238) 2621391; e-mail delegation-cape-verde@eeas.europa.eu; internet www.eeas.europa.eu/delegations/cape_verde; José Manuel Pinto Texeira (Head of Delegation).

Cambodia: 100A Norodom Blvd, Sangkat Chaktomuk, Khan Daun Penh, POB 2301, 12207 Phnom Penh; tel. (+855) 23216996; fax (+855) 23216997; e-mail delegation-cambodia@ec.europa.eu; internet www.eeas.europa.eu/delegations/cambodia; George Edgar (Head of Delegation).

Cameroon: Immeuble le Belvédère, 1068 rue Onambele Nkou, Quartier Nlongkak, BP 847, Yaoundé; tel. (+237) 22-21-00-28; fax (+237) 22-20-21-49; e-mail delegation-cameroun@eeas.europa.eu; internet www.eeas.europa.eu/delegations/cameroon; Françoise Collet (Head of Delegation).

Canada: 150 Metcalfe, Suite 1900, Ottawa ON K2P 1P1; tel. (+1 613) 238-6464; fax (+1 613) 238-5191; e-mail delegation-canada@eeas.europa.eu; internet www.eeas.europa.eu/delegations/canada; Marie-Anne Coninsx (Head of Delegation).

Central African Republic: Ave Barthélémy Boganda, BP 1298, Bangui; tel. (+236) 21-61-30-53; fax (+236) 21-61-65-35; e-mail delegation-central-african-rep@eeas.europa.eu; internet eeas.europa.eu/central_africa; Jean-Pierre Reymondet-Commoy (Head of Delegation).

Chad: Ave Moll 150, BP 552, N'Djamena; tel. (+235) 22527276; fax (+235) 22527105; e-mail delegation-tchad@eeas.europa.eu; internet www.eeas.europa.eu/delegations/tchad; Denisa-Elena Ionete (Head of Delegation).

Chile: Torre Paris, Avda Ricardo Lyon 222 (3°), Casilla 10093, Providencia, Santiago; tel. (+56 2) 3352450; fax (+56 2) 3351779; e-mail delegation-chile@eeas.europa.eu; internet www.eeas.europa.eu/chile Styliani Zervoudaki (Head of Delegation).

China (Hong Kong): 19/F St John's Bldg, 33 Garden Rd, Central, Hong Kong; tel. (+852) 25376083; fax (+852) 25221302; e-mail delegation-hong-kong@eeas.europa.eu; internet www.eeas.europa.eu/delegations/hong_kong; Carmen Cano de Lasala (Head of Delegation).

China, People's Republic: 15 Dong Zhi Men Wai Dajie, Sanlitun, 100600, Beijing; tel. (+86 10) 84548000; fax (+86 10) 84548011; e-mail delegation-china@eeas.europa.eu; internet www.eeas.europa.eu/delegations/china; Hans Dietmar Schweisgut (Head of Delegation).

Colombia: Calle 116, 7–15, piso 12, 94046, Bogotá 8; tel. (+57 1) 6581150; fax (+57 1) 6581179; e-mail delegation-colombia@eeas.europa.eu; internet www.eeas.europa.eu/delegations/colombia; Ana Paula Zacarias (Head of Delegation).

Congo, Democratic Republic: Immeuble BCDC, Blvd du 30 Juin, BP 2699, Kinshasa-Gombe; tel. (+243) 815567401; fax (+243) 815554634; e-mail delegation-dem-rep-of-congo@eeas.europa.eu; internet www.eeas.europa.eu/delegations/congo_kinshasa; Bart Ouvry (Head of Delegation).

Congo, Republic: Impasse Auxence Ickonga (face à l'Ambassade d'Italie), BP 2149, Brazzaville; tel. (+242) 521-74-00; fax (+242) 669-99-29; e-mail delegation-rep-congo@eeas.europa.eu; internet www. eeas.europa.eu/delegations/congo; Saskia De Lang (Head of Delegation).

Costa Rica: Ofiplaza del Este, Edificio D, 3°, De la Rotonda de la Bandera, Apdo. 836-1007, San José; tel. (+506) 2832959; fax (+506) 2832960; e-mail delegation-costa-rica@ec.europa.eu; internet eeas.europa.eu/delegations/costa_rica; Pelayo Castro Zuzuarregui (Head of Delegation).

Côte d'Ivoire: Ave Terrasson de Fougères, Immeuble Union européenne, BP 1821, Abidjan 01; tel. (+225 20) 31-83-50; fax (+225 20) 21-40-89; e-mail delegation-ivory-coast@eeas.europa.eu; internet www.eeas.europa.eu/delegations/cote_ivoire; Jean-François Valette (Head of Delegation).

Cuba: 5ta Avda 2007, E/22, Miramar, Ciudad de la Habana; tel. (+537) 2040327; fax (+537) 2040328; e-mail delegation-cuba@eeas.europa.eu; internet www.eeas.europa.eu/delegations/cuba; Herman Portocarero (Head of Delegation).

Djibouti: Quartier du Héron, BP 2477, Djibouti; tel. (+253) 35-26-15; fax (+253) 35-00-36; e-mail delegation-djibouti@eeas.europa.eu; internet www.eeas.europa.eu/delegations/djibouti; Adam Kulach (Head of Delegation).

Dominican Republic: Ave Abraham Lincoln 1063, Serralles, Apdo Postal 226-2, Santo Domingo; tel. (+1 809) 227-0525; fax (+1 809) 227-0510; e-mail delegation-dominican-rep@eeas.europa.eu; internet eeas.europa.eu/delegations/dominican; Alberto Navarro González (Head of Delegation).

Ecuador: Edificio Schuman, Orellana E11-160 y Whymper, Quito, (+593 2) 2523912; tel. (+593 2) 2527511; e-mail delegation-ecuador@eeas.europa.eu; internet www.eeas.europa.eu/delegations/ecuador; Marianne Van Steen (Head of Delegation).

Egypt: Nile City Towers, North Tower, 2005 C Corniche El Nil, 10th Floor, Ramlet Boulaq, Giza, Cairo; tel. (+20 2) 24619860; fax (+20 2) 24619884; e-mail delegation-egypt@eeas.europa.eu; internet www.eeas.europa.eu/delegations/egypt; Ivan Surkos (Head of Delegation).

El Salvador: Calle Cortez Blanco Poniente y Pasaje 'H' Norte 2, Urbanización Madre Selva, Tercera Etapa, Antiguo Cuscatlán, San Salvador; tel. (+503) 22432424; fax (+503) 22432525; e-mail delegation-el-salvador@eeas.europa.eu; internet eeas.europa.eu/delegations/el_salvador; Jaume Segura Socías (Head of Delegation).

Eritrea: 192 Marsa Teklai, Zone 2, Subzone 03, House No 20/22, POB 5710, Asmara; tel. (+291 1) 126566; fax (+291 1) 126578; e-mail delegation-eritrea@eeas.europa.eu; internet eeas.europa.eu/delegations/eritrea; Christian Manahl (Head of Delegation).

Ethiopia: Cape Verde Rd, POB 5570, Addis Ababa; tel. (+251 11) 6612511; fax (+251 11) 6612877; e-mail delegation-ethiopia@eeas.europa.eu; internet www.eeas.europa.eu/delegations/ethiopia; Chantal Hebberecht (Head of Delegation).

Fiji and the Pacific: Development Bank Centre, 4th Floor, 360 Victoria Parade, Private Mail Bag, GPO, Suva; tel. (+679) 3313633; fax (+679) 3300370; e-mail delegation-fiji@eeas.europa.eu; internet www.eeas.europa.eu/delegations/fiji; Andrew Jacobs (Head of Delegation) (also responsible for Cook Islands, French Polynesia, Kiribati, Marshall Islands, Micronesia, Nauru, New Caledonia, Niue, Palau, Pitcairn, Samoa, Tonga, Tuvalu, and Wallis and Futuna Islands).

Gabon: Bas de Gué-Gué, BP 321, Libreville; tel. (+241) 732250; fax (+241) 736554; e-mail delegation-gabon@eeas.europa.eu; internet www.eeas.europa.eu/delegations/gabon; Helmut Rudolf Kulitz (Head of Delegation) (also responsible for Equatorial Guinea and São Tomé and Príncipe).

The Gambia: 74 Atlantic Rd, Fajara, POB 512, Banjul; tel. (+220) 4495146; fax (+220) 4497848; e-mail delegation-gambia@eeas.europa.eu; internet eeas.europa.eu/delegations/gambia; Attila Lajos (Head of Delegation).

Georgia: Nino Chkheidze St 38, Diplomatic Bag Brussels EC Del. Georgia, 0102 Tbilisi; tel. (+995 32) 943763; fax (+995 32) 943768; e-mail delegation-georgia@eeas.europa.eu; internet www.eeas.europa.eu/delegations/georgia; Janos Herman (Head of Delegation).

Ghana: The Round House, 81 Cantonments Rd, POB 9505 KIA, Accra; tel. (+233 30) 2774201; fax (+223 30) 2774154; e-mail delegation-ghana@eeas.europa.eu; internet www.eeas.europa.eu/delegations/ghana; William Hanna (Head of Delegation).

Guatemala: 5 Avda 5-55, Zona 14, Edificio Europlaza (Torre II, Nivel 17), Guatemala, (+502) 23842500; tel. (+502) 23842596; e-mail delegation-guatemala@ec.europa.eu; internet www.eeas.europa.eu/delegations/guatemala; Stefano Gatto (Head of Delegation).

Guinea: Immeuble Le Golfe, Lanséboundji, Matam, BP 730, Conakry; tel. (+224) 64352070; fax (+32) 2-664352070; e-mail delegation-guinee-conakry@eeas.europa.eu; internet www.eeas.europa.eu/delegations/guinea; Gerardus Gielen (Head of Delegation).

Guinea-Bissau: Bairro da Penha, CP 359, Bissau; tel. (+245) 3251469; fax (+245) 3251044; e-mail delegation-guinee-bissau@eeas.europa.eu; internet www.eeas.europa.eu/delegations/guinea_bissau; Victor Madeira Dos Santos (Head of Delegation).

Guyana: 11 Sendall Place, Stabroek, PO Box 10847, Georgetown; tel. (+592 22) 64004; fax (+592 22) 62615; e-mail delegation-guyana@eeas.europa.eu; internet www.eeas.europa.eu/delegations/guyana; Jernej Videtic (Head of Delegation).

Haiti: 4, Impasse Oriol, Morne Calvaire, BP 15588, Petion Ville, Port-au-Prince, (+509) 29494949; e-mail delegation-haiti@ec.europa.eu; internet www.eeas.europa.eu/delegations/haiti; Vincent Degert (Head of Delegation).

Honduras: 4ta Avenida, 2da Calle, Colonia Altos Lomas del Guijarro Sur, Tegucigalpa, (+504) 22399991; tel. (+504) 22399994; e-mail delegation-honduras@eeas.europa.eu; internet eeas.europa.eu/delegations/honduras; Ketil Karlsen (Head of Delegation).

Iceland: Adalstraeti 6, 101 Reykjavik; tel. (+354) 5203399; fax (+354) 5203398; e-mail delegation-iceland@eeas.europa.eu; internet www.eeas.europa.eu/delegations/Iceland; Matthias Brinkmann (Head of Delegation).

India: 65 Golf Links, New Delhi, 110003; tel. (+91 11) 49496565; fax (+91 11) 49496555; e-mail delegation-india@eeas.europa.eu; internet www.eeas.europa.eu/delegations/india; Tomasz Kozlowski (Head of Delegation).

Indonesia: Intiland Tower (formerly Wisma Dharmala Sakti), 16th fl., Jl. Jendral Sudirman 32, POB 6454 JKPDS, Jakarta 10220; tel. (+62 21) 25546200; fax (+62 21) 25546201; e-mail delegation-indonesia@eeas.europa.eu; internet www.eeas.europa.eu/delegations/indonesia; Vincent Guereno (Head of Delegation).

Iraq: Baghdad, e-mail delegation-iraq@eeas.europa.eu; internet www.eeas.europa.eu/delegations/iraq; Patrick Simonnet (Head of Delegation).

European External Action Service

Israel: Paz Tower, 15th–16th Floors, 5–7 Shoham St, POB 3513, 52136 Ramat Gan; tel. (+972 3) 6137799; fax (+972 3) 6137770; e-mail delegation-israel@eeas.europa.eu; internet www.eeas.europa.eu/delegations/israel; Lars Faaborg-Andersen (Head of Delegation).

Jamaica: 8 Olivier Rd, POB 463, Kingston 8; tel. (+1 876) 9246333; fax (+1 876) 9246339; e-mail delegation-jamaica@eeas.europa.eu; internet www.eeas.europa.eu/delegations/jamaica; Malgorzata Wasiewska (Head of Delegation).

Japan: Europa House, 4-6-28 Minami-Azabu, Minato-Ku, Tokyo 106-0047; tel. (+81 3) 54226001; fax (+81 3) 54205544; e-mail delegation-japan@eeas.europa.eu; internet www.euinjapan.jp; Viorel Isticioaia-Budura (Head of Delegation).

Jordan: Al-Ameerah Basma St, North Abdoun, POB 852099, 11185 Amman; tel. (+962 6) 4607000; fax (+962 6) 4607001; e-mail delegation-jordan@eeas.europa.eu; internet www.eeas.europa.eu/delegations/jordan; Andrea Matteo Fontana (Head of Delegation).

Kazakhstan: 62 Kosmonavtov Str., Renco Business Centre, 010000, Astana; tel. (+7 717) 2971040; fax (+7 717) 2979563; e-mail delegation-kazakhstan@eeas.europa.eu; internet www.eeas.europa.eu/delegations/kazakhstan; Traian Hristea (Head of Delegation).

Kenya: Union Insurance Bldg, Ragati Rd, POB 45 119, Nairobi; tel. (+245 20) 2802000; fax (+245 20) 2716481; e-mail delegation-kenya@eeas.europa.eu; internet eeas.europa.eu/delegations/kenya; Stefano-Antonio Dejak (Head of Delegation).

Korea, Republic: Sean Bldg, 16th Floor, 116 Shinmoonro 1-ka, Chongro-ku, POB 911, Seoul 110-700; tel. (+82 2) 3704-1700; fax (+82 2) 735-1211; e-mail delegation-rep-of-korea@eeas.europa.eu; internet www.eeas.europa.eu/delegations/south_korea; Michael Reiterer (Head of Delegation).

Kosovo: Kosova St 1, POB 331, 10000 Prishtina; tel. (+381 38) 5131200; fax (+381 38) 5131304; e-mail delegation-kosovo@eeas.europa.eu; internet www.eeas.europa.eu/delegations/kosovo; Nataliya Apostolova (Head of Delegation).

Kyrgyzstan: 21 Erkindik Blvd, 5th Floor, Business Centre Orion, 720040 Bishkek; tel. (+996 312) 26-10-00; fax (+996 312) 26-10-07; e-mail delegation-kyrgyzstan@ec.europa.eu; internet eeas.europa.eu/delegations/kyrgyzstan; Cesare de Montis (Head of Delegation).

Laos: Sihom Commerce Center Bldg, Souphanouvong Ave, POB 9325, Vientiane; tel. (+856) 21 241134; fax (+856) 21 241125; e-mail delegation.laos@ec.europa.eu; internet www.eeas.europa.eu/delegations/laos; Léon Paul Faber (Head of Delegation).

Lebanon: 490 Harbor Drive, Ave Charles Helou Saifi, BP 11-4008, Riad el Solh, 11072150 Beirut; tel. (+961 1) 569400; fax (+961 1) 569415; e-mail delegation-lebanon@eeas.europa.eu; internet www.eeas.europa.eu/delegations/lebanon; Christina Lassen (Head of Delegation).

Lesotho: 167 Constitutional Rd, POB MS 518, Maseru 100; tel. (+266) 22272200; fax (+266) 22272255; e-mail delegation-lesotho@eeas.europa.eu; internet eeas.europa.eu/delgations/lesotho; Michael Gerard Doyle (Head of Delegation).

Liberia: 100 UN Drive, Mamba Point, POB 10-3049, 1000 Monrovia; tel. (+231 7) 7757826; fax (+231 7) 7001062; e-mail delegation-liberia@eeas.europa.eu; internet www.eeas.europa.eu/delegations/liberia; Tiina Intelmann (Head of Delegation).

Libya: Palm City Compound, Janzour; tel. (+218 214) 873661; fax (+218 214) 873663; e-mail delegation-libya@eeas.europa.eu; internet www.eeas.europa.eu/delegations/libya; Bettina Muscheidt (Head of Delegation).

Macedonia, former Yugoslav republic: Mito Hadzivasilev Jasmin 52v, 1000, Skopje; tel. (+389 2) 3248500; fax (+389 2) 3248501; e-mail delegation-fyrmacedonia@eeas.europa.eu; internet www.eeas.europa.eu/delegations/the_former_yugoslav_republic_of_macedonia; Samuel Žbogar (Head of Delegation).

Madagascar: Tour Zital, 9ème étage, Ankorondrano, BP 746, Antananarivo101; tel. (+261 20) 2224216; fax (+261 20) 2264562; e-mail delegation-madagascar@eeas.europa.eu; internet www.eeas.europa.eu/delegations/madagascar; Antonio Sánchez-Benedito Gaspar (Head of Delegation).

Malawi: Area 18 Roundabout, Corner Presidential Way and M1, POB 30102, Capital City, Lilongwe; tel. (+265) 1773199; fax (+265) 1773534; e-mail delegation-malawi@eeas.europa.eu; internet www.eeas.europa.eu/delegations/malawi; Marcel Gerrmann (Head of Delegation).

Malaysia: Menera Tan & Tan 207, Jalan Tun Razak, Suite 10.01, 50400 Kuala Lumpur; tel. (+603) 27237373; fax (+603) 27237337; e-mail delegation-malaysia@eeas.europa.eu; internet www.eeas.europa.eu/delegations/malaysia; Maria Castillo Fernandez (Head of Delegation).

Mali: Immeuble UATT, Quartier du Fleuve, BP 115, Bamako; tel. (+223) 44929292; fax (+223) 44919191; e-mail delegation-mali@ec.europa.eu; internet www.eeas.europa.eu/delegations/mali; Alain Holleville (Head of Delegation).

Mauritania: Rue 42–163 Tevragh Zeina, BP 213, Nouakchott; tel. (+222) 45252724; fax (+222) 54253524; e-mail delegation-mauritania@ec.europa.eu; internet www.eeas.europa.eu/delegations/mauritania; José-Antonio Sabadell (Head of Delegation).

Mauritius: 8th Floor, St James Court Bldg, St Denis St, BP 1148, Port Louis; tel. (+230) 2071515; fax (+230) 2116624; e-mail delegation-mauritius@eeas.europa.eu; internet eeas.europa.eu/delegations/mauritius; Iina Marjaana Sall (Head of Delegation).

Mexico: Paseo de la Reforma 1675, Lomas de Chapultepec, CP 11000, Mexico, DF; tel. (+52 55) 55403345; fax (+52 55) 55406564; e-mail delegation-mexico@eeas.europa.eu; internet www.eeas.europa.eu/delegations/mexico; Andrew Standley (Head of Delegation).

Moldova: Str. Kogălniceanu 12, 2001, Chișinău; tel. (+373 22) 50-52-10; fax (+373 22) 27-26-22; e-mail delegation-moldova@eeas.europa.eu; internet www.eeas.europa.eu/delegations/moldova; Pirkka Tapiola (Head of Delegation).

Montenegro: Vuka Karadzika 12, 81000, Podgorica; tel. (+382) 20444600; fax (+382) 20444666; e-mail delegation-montenegro@ec.europa.eu; internet www.delmne.ec.europa.eu; Aivo Orav (Head of Delegation).

Morocco: Riad Business Centre, Aile Sud, Blvd Er-Riad, BP 1302, Rabat; tel. (+212 537) 579800; fax (+212 537) 579810; e-mail delegation-morocco@eeas.europa.eu; internet www.eeas.europa.eu/delegations/morocco; Raul De Lezenberger (Head of Delegation).

Mozambique: Avda Julius Nyerere, CP 1306, 2820 Maputo; tel. (+258 21) 481000; fax (+258 21) 491866; e-mail delegation

-mozambique@eeas.europa.eu; internet eeas.europa.eu/delegations/mozambique; Sven Kühn von Burgsdorff (Head of Delegation).

Myanmar: Villa No 45, Inya Myaing, Rd, Golden Valley, Bahan Township, Yangon; tel. (+95 01) 537823; internet eeas.europa.eu/delegations/myanmarburma_en; Roland Kobia (Head of Delegation).

Namibia: 2 Newton St, POB 24.443, Windhoek; tel. (+264 61) 2026000; fax (+264 61) 2026224; e-mail delegation-namibia@eeas.europa.eu; internet www.eeas.europa.eu/delegations/namibia; Jana Hybaskova (Head of Delegation).

Nepal: Uttar Dhoka Sadak, Lainchaur, POB 6754, Kathmandu; tel. (+977 1) 4429445; fax (+977 1) 4423541; e-mail delegation-nepal@eeas.europa.eu; internet www.eeas.europa.eu/delegations/nepal; Rensje Teerink (Head of Delegation).

New Zealand: 119 Featherston St, Level 7, POB 5106, Featherston House, 6011, Wellington; tel. (+64) 44729145; fax (+64) 44729147; e-mail delegation-new-zealand@eeas.europa.eu; internet www.eeas.europa.eu/delegations/new_zealand; Bernard Savage (Head of Delegation).

Nicaragua: Carretera a Masaya, del Colegio Teresiano una cuadra al Este, Apartado postal 2654, Managua; tel. (+505) 22704499; fax (+505) 22709569; e-mail delegation-nicaragua@ec.europa.eu; internet eeas.europa.eu/delegations/nicaragua; Kenneth Bell (Head of Delegation).

Niger: Rue du Commerce, Immeuble BIA, 3e étage, BP 10388, Niamey; tel. (+227) 738583; fax (+227) 732322; e-mail delegation-niger@eeas.europa.eu; internet www.eeas.europa.eu/delegations/niger; Raul Mateus Paula (Head of Delegation).

Nigeria: 21st Crescent, off Constitution Ave, Central Business District, PMB 280, Garki, Abuja; tel. (+234 9) 4617800; fax (+234 9) 4617836; e-mail delegation-nigeria@eeas.europa.eu; internet www.eeas.europa.eu/delegations/nigeria; Michel Arrion (Head of Delegation).

Norway: Klingenberggaten 7A, 5th Fl., 0161, Oslo; tel. (+47) 22-83-35-83; fax (+47) 22-83-40-55; e-mail delegation-norway@eeas.europa.eu; internet www.eeas.europa.eu/delegations/norway; Helen Campbell (Head of Delegation).

Pakistan: House No 9, St No 88, Sector G-6/3, POB 1608, Islamabad; tel. (+92 51) 2271828; fax (+92 51) 2822604; e-mail delegation-pakistan@eeas.europa.eu; internet eeas.europa.eu/delegations/pakistan; Jean-François Cautain (Head of Delegation).

Papua New Guinea: BSP Haus, 6th Floor, Harbour City, POB 76, Port Moresby; tel. (+675) 3213544; fax (+675) 3217850; e-mail delegation-papua-new-guinea@eeas.europa.eu; internet eeas.europa.eu/delegations/papua_new_guinea; Martin Dihm (Head of Delegation).

Paraguay: Calle America 404, Asunción, (+595) 21206069; tel. (+595) 21213975; e-mail delegation-paraguay@eeas.europa.eu; internet www.eeas.europa.eu/delegations/paraguay; Alessandro Palmero (Head of Delegation).

Peru: Avda Comandante Espinar 719, Miraflores, Casilla Postal 18-0792, Lima 18; tel. (+511) 4150800; fax (+511) 4465100; e-mail delegation-peru@eeas.europa.eu; internet www.eeas.europa.eu/delegations/peru; Irène Horejs (Head of Delegation).

Philippines: 30/F Tower II, RCBC Plaza, 6819 Ayala Ave, corner Sen Gil Puyat, 1200 Makati City; tel. (+63 2) 8595100; fax (+63 2) 8595109; e-mail delegation-philippines@eeas.europa.eu; internet www.eeas.europa.eu/delegations/philippines; Franz Jessen (Head of Delegation).

Russian Federation: Kadashevskaya Nab. 14/1, 109017 Moscow; tel. (+7 495) 721-20-00; fax (+7 495) 721-20-20; e-mail delegation-russia@eeas.europa.eu; internet www.eeas.europa.eu/delegations/russia; Vygaudas Ušackas (Head of Delegation).

Rwanda: Bd Umuganda 1807, BP 515, Kigali; tel. (+250) 252-58-57-38; fax (+250) 252-58-57-36; internet delegation-rwanda@eeas.europa.eu; internet www.eeas.europa.eu/delegations/rwanda; Michael Ryan (Head of Delegation).

Saudi Arabia: Thabet Al Loghawi St, Al-Maathar area, POB 65995, Riyadh 11566; tel. (+966 1) 4827057; fax (+966 1) 4821427; e-mail delegation-saudi-arabia@eeas.europa.eu; internet www.eeas.europa.eu/delegations/gulf_countries; Michele Cervone D'Urso (Head of Delegation).

Senegal: 12 Ave Hassan II, BP 3345, Dakar; tel. (+221) 338891100; fax (+221) 338426338; e-mail delegation-senegal@ec.europa.eu; internet www.eeas.europa.eu/delegations/senegal; Joaquin González-Ducay (Head of Delegation).

Serbia: Ave 19A, Vladimira Popovića 40A, 11070, Belgrade; tel. (+381) 113083200; fax (+381) 113083201; e-mail delegation-serbia@eeas.europa.eu; internet www.europa.rs/en/o_nama/uloga_delegacije_eu.html; Michael Davenport (Head of Delegation).

Sierra Leone: Leicester Peak, POB 1399, Freetown; tel. (+232-88) 136000; fax (+232-76) 541153; e-mail delegation-sierra-leone@eeas.europa.euinternet eeas.europa.eu/delegations/sierra_leone; Peter Versteeg (Head of Delegation).

Singapore: 250 North Bridge Rd, 38-03/04 Raffles City Tower, Singapore, 179101; tel. (+65) 63367919; fax (+65) 63363394; e-mail delegation-singapore@eeas.europa.eu; internet www.eeas.europa.eu/delegations/singapore; Michael Pulch (Head of Delegation).

Solomon Islands: Mendana Ave, 2nd Floor, City Centre Bldg, POB 840, Honiara; tel. (+677) 22765; fax (+677) 23318; e-mail delegation-solomon@eeas.europa.eu; internet eeas.europa.eu/delegations/solomon; Leonidas Tezapsidis (Head of Delegation).

Somalia: POB 30475, Nairobi; tel. (+254 020) 2712830; fax (+254 020) 2710997; e-mail delegation-somalia@eeas.europa.eu; internet eeas.europa.eu/delegations/Somalia; Veronique Lorenzo (Head of Delegation).

South Africa: 1–2 Green Park Estates, 27 George Storrar Drive, POB 945, Groenkloof, 0027 Pretoria; tel. (+27-12) 4525200; fax (+27-12) 4609923; e-mail delegation-s-africa@eeas.europa.eu; internet www.eeas.europa.eu/delegations/south_africa; Markus Cornaro (Head of Delegation).

Sri Lanka: 26 Sir Marcus Fernando Mawatha, Colombo 7; tel. (+94-11) 2674413; fax (+94 11) 2665983; e-mail delegation-sri-lanka@eeas.europa.eu; internet www.eeas.europa.eu/delegations/sri_lanka; Tung-Lai Margue (Head of Delegation).

Sudan: Block 1B, Plot 10, Gamhoria St, POB 2363, Khartoum; tel. (+249 183) 799393; fax (+249 183) 799391; internet delegation-soudan@eeas.europa.eu; internet www.eeas.europa.eu/delegations/sudan; Jean-Michel Dumond (Head of Delegation).

Swaziland: Lilunga House, 4th Floor, Somhlolo Rd, POB A36, Swazi Plaza H101, Mbabane; tel. (+268) 4042018; fax (+268) 4046729; e-mail delegation-swaziland@eeas.europa.eu; internet eeas.europa.eu/delegations/swaziland; Nicola Bellomo (Head of Delegation).

Switzerland: Bundesgasse 18, POB 264, Bern 3000; tel. (+41) 313101530; fax (+41) 313101549; e-mail delegation-bern@eeas.europa.eu; internet eeas.europa.eu/delegations/switzerland; Michael Matthiessen (Head of Delegation).

Syria: Abou Roumaneh, Najeeb Al-Rayyes St, Bldg No. 3, BP 11269, Damascus; tel. (+963 11) 3320683; fax (+963 11) 3320683; e-mail delegation-syria@eeas.europa.eu; internet eeas.europa.eu/delegations/Syria; Simon Bojsen-Moller (Head of Delegation (acting)).

Tajikistan: 74 Adhamov St, 734013, Dushanbe; tel. (+992 372) 217407; fax (+992 372) 2143321; e-mail delegation-tajikistan@eeas.europa.eu; internet www.eeas.europa.eu/delegations/tajikistan; Hidajet Biscević (Head of Delegation).

Tanzania: Umoja House, Garden Ave, POB 9514, Dar es Salaam; tel. (+255) 222117473; fax (+255) 222113277; e-mail delegation-tanzania@eeas.europa.eu; internet www.eeas.europa.eu/delegations/tanzania; Roeland Van de Geer (Head of Delegation).

Thailand: Kian Gwan House II, 19th Floor, Wireless Rd 140/1, Bangkok 10330; tel. (+66 2) 3052600; fax (+66 2) 2559113; e-mail delegation-thailand@eeas.europa.eu; internet www.eeas.europa.eu/delegations/thailand; Jesús Miguel Sanz Escorihuela (Head of Delegation).

Timor-Leste: Casa Europa, Avenida Presidente Nicolou Lobato, Acait, Dili; tel. (+670) 3311580; fax (+670) 3311581; e-mail delegation-timor-leste@eeas.europa.eu; internet eeas.europa.eu/delegations/timor_leste; Alexandre José Dos Reis Leitao (Head of Delegation).

Togo: Cité Oua, BP 1657, Lomé; tel. (+228) 2536000; fax (+228) 2265720; e-mail delegation-togo@eeas.europa.eu; internet www.eeas.europa.eu/delegations/togo; Nicolas Berlanga Martínez (Head of Delegation).

Trinidad and Tobago: The Sagicor Financial Centre, Queen's Park West 16, POB 1144, Port of Spain; tel. (+1) 8686226628; fax (+1) 8686226355; e-mail delegation-trinidad-and-tobago@eeas.europa.eu; internet www.eeas.europa.eu/delegations/trinidad; Arend Biesebroek (Head of Delegation).

Tunisia: Rue du Lac Biwa, Les Berges du Lac, BP 150, 1053 Tunis; tel. (+216 71) 960330; fax (+216 71) 960302; e-mail delegation-tunisia@eeas.europa.eu; internet www.eeas.europa.eu/delegations/tunisia; Patrice Bergamini (Head of Delegation).

Turkey: Uğur Mumcu Cad. 88, 4th Floor, 06700, Gaziosmanpasa, Ankara; tel. (+90 312) 4598700; fax (+90 312) 4466737; e-mail delegation-turkey@eeas.europa.eu; internet www.avrupa.info.tr; Christian Berger (Head of Delegation).

UAE: Etihad Tower 3, 15th Floor, Corniche Rd, POB 63870, Abu Dhabi; tel. (+971) 22-05-11-11; internet eeas.europa.eu/delegation/uae; Patrizio Fondi (Head of Delegation).

Uganda: Crested Towers 15F, Plot 17-23, Hannington Rd, POB 5244, Kampala; tel. (+256 41) 4701000; fax (+256 41) 4233708; e-mail delegation-uganda@ec.europa.eu; internet www.eeas.europa.eu/delegations/uganda; Kristian Schmidt (Head of Delegation).

Ukraine: 101 Volodymyrska St, 01033, Kyiv; tel. (+380 44) 3908010; fax (+380 44) 3908015; e-mail delegation-ukraine@eeas.europa.eu; internet www.eeas.europa.eu/delegations/ukraine; Hugues Mingarelli (Head of Delegation).

USA: 2175 K St NW, Washington, DC 20037-1831; tel. (+1 202) 862-9500; fax (+1 202) 429-1766; e-mail delegation-usa-info@eeas.europa.eu; internet www.eurunion.org; David O'Sullivan (Head of Delegation).

Uruguay: Blvd Artigas 1300, 11300, Montevideo; tel. (+598 2) 19440101; fax (+598 2) 19440122; e-mail delegation-uruguay@eeas.europa.eu; internet www.eeas.europa.eu/delegations/uruguay; Juan Fernández Trigo Paraguay (Head of Delegation).

Uzbekistan: International Business Centre, 11th Floor, 107B, Amir Temur St, Tashkent 100084; tel. (+998) 711201601; fax (+998) 711201608; e-mail delegation-uzbekistan@eeas.europa.eu; internet www.eeas.europa.eu/delegations/uzbekistan; Eduards Stiprais (Head of Delegation).

Venezuela: Edificio Comisión Europea, Avenida Orinoco, Las Mercedes, Apartado de Correos 67076, Plaza Las Americas, 1061-A Caracas; tel. (+58 212) 9586611; fax (+58 212) 9935573; e-mail delegation-venezuela@eeas.europa.eu; internet www.eeas.europa.eu/delegations/venezuela; Aude Maio-Coliche (Head of Delegation).

Viet Nam: Pacific Place Bldg, 17th–18th Floor, Office 83B, Ly Thuong Kiet, Hanoi; tel. (+844) 39410099; fax (+844) 39461701; e-mail delegation-vietnam@eeas.europa.eu; internet www.eeas.europa.eu/delegations/vietnam; Bruno Angelet (Head of Delegation).

West Bank and Gaza Strip: Al-Mashtal Hotel, First Floor Salah Khalaf St, POB 576, Gaza; tel. (+972 2) 5415888; fax (+972 2) 5415848; e-mail delegation-west-bank-gaza@ec.europa.eu; internet eeas.europa.eu/delegations/westbank; Ralph-Joseph Tarraf (Head of Delegation).

Yemen: Mujahed St, next to French Embassy, POB 11408, Sana'a; tel. (+967 1) 570200; fax (+967 1) 570194; e-mail delegation-yemen@eeas.europa.eu; internet www.eeas.europa.eu/delegations/yemen; Antonia Calvo Puerta (Head of Delegation).

Zambia: Plot 4899, Los Angeles Boulevard, POB 34871, Lusaka; tel. (+260 211) 255583; fax (+260 211) 252336; e-mail delegation-zambia@eeas.europa.eu; internet www.eeas.europa.eu/delegations/zambia; Alessandro Mariani (Head of Delegation).

Zimbabwe: EU House, 1 Norfolk Rd, Mount Pleasant, POB MP 620, Harare; tel. (+263 4) 338158; fax (+263 4) 338165; e-mail delegation-zimbabwe-hod@eeas.europa.eu; internet www.eeas.europa.eu/delegations/zimbabwe; Philippe Van Damme (Head of Delegation).

EUROPEAN PARLIAMENT

60 Rue Wiertz, 1047 Brussels, Belgium; tel. (+32) 2-2842111; fax (+32) 2-2846974; internet www.europarl.europa.eu

Plateau du Kirchberg, BP 1601, 2929 Luxembourg, Luxembourg; tel. (+352) 43001; fax (+352) 430024842

Allée du Printemps, BP 1024, 67070 Strasbourg Cedex, France; tel. (+33) 3-88-17-40-01; fax (+33) 3-88-17-48-60

BUREAU

President: Antonio Tajani (EPP).

Vice-Presidents Mairead McGuinness (EPP), Bogusław Liberadzki (S&D), Rainer Wieland (EPP), Ramón Luis Valcárcel (EPP), Evelyne Gebhardt (S&D), Sylvie Guillaume (S&D), Ioan Mircea Paşcu (S&D), David-Maria Sassoli (S&D), Pavel Telička (ALDE), Alexander Graf Lambsdorff (ALDE), Ulrike Lunacek (Greens/EFA), Dimitrios Papadimoulis (GUE/NGL), Ryszard Czarnecki (ECR).

Quaestors Élisabeth Morin-Chartier (EPP), Catherine Bearder (ALDE), Andrey Kovatchev (EPP), Karol Karski (ECR), Vladimír Maňka (EPP).

FORMER PRESIDENTS

1958–60: Robert Schuman.
1960–62: Hans Furler.
1962–64: Gaetano Martino.
1964–65: Jean Duvieusart.
1965–66: Victor Leemans.
1966–69: Alain Poher.
1969–71: Mario Scelba.
1971–73: Walter Behrendt.
1973–75: Cornelis Berkhouwer.
1975–77: Georges Spenale.
1977–79: Emilio Colombo.
1979–82: Simone Veil.
1982–84: Pieter Dankert.
1984–87: Pierre Pflimlin.
1987–89: Lord Henry Plumb.
1989–92: Enrique Barón Crespo.
1992–94: Egon Klepsch.
1994–97: Dr Klaus Hänsch.
1997–99: José Maria Gil-Robles Gil-Delgado.
1999–2002: Nicole Fontaine.
2002–04: Pat Cox.
2004–07: Josep Borrell Fontelles.
2007–09: Hans-Gert Pöttering.
2009–12: Jerzy Buzek.
2012–17: Martin Schulz.

Members of the European Parliament

Name	Member State	Telephone	E-mail	Political Group
Adaktusson, Lars	Sweden	(+33) 3-88-17-51-55	lars.adaktusson@europarl.europa.eu	EPP
Adinolfi, Isabella	Italy	(+33) 3-88-17-57-14	isabella.adinolfi@europarl.europa.eu	EFDD
Affronte, Marco	Italy	(+33) 3-88-17-57-11	marco.affronte@europarl.europa.eu	Greens/EFA
Agea, Laura	Italy	(+33) 3-88-17-55-46	laura.agea@europarl.europa.eu	EFDD
Agnew, John Stuart	UK	(+33) 3-88-17-54-04	johnstuart.agnew@europarl.europa.eu	EFDD
Aguilera García, Clara Eugenia	Spain	(+33) 3-88-17-57-83	claraeugenia.aguileragarcia@europarl.europa.eu	S&D
Aiuto, Daniela	Italy	(+33) 3-88-17-54-22	daniela.aiuto@europarl.europa.eu	EFDD
Aker, Tim	UK	(+33) 3-88-17-51-09	tim.aker@europarl.europa.eu	EFDD
Albiol Guzmán, Marina	Spain	(+33) 3-88-17-59-98	marina.albiol@europarl.europa.eu	GUE/NGL
Albrecht, Jan Philipp	Germany	(+33) 3-88-17-50-60	jan.albrecht@europarl.europa.eu	Greens/EFA
Ali, Nedzhmi	Bulgaria	(+33) 3-88-17-56-08	nedzhmi.ali@europarl.europa.eu	ALDE
Alliot-Marie, Michèle	France	(+33) 3-88-17-52-82	michele.alliot-marie@europarl.europa.eu	EPP
Anderson, Lucy	UK	(+33) 3-88-17-54-96	lucy.anderson@europarl.europa.eu	S&D
Anderson, Martina	UK	(+33) 3-88-17-52-22	martina.anderson@europarl.europa.eu	GUE/NGL
Andersson, Max	Sweden	(+33) 3-88-17-54-57	max.andersson@europarl.europa.eu	Greens/EFA
Andrieu, Eric	France	(+33) 3-88-17-51-70	eric.andrieu@europarl.europa.eu	S&D
Andrikienė, Laima Liucija	Lithuania	(+33) 3-88-17-55-50	laimaliucija.andrikiene@europarl.europa.eu	EPP
Androulakis, Nikos	Greece	(+33) 3-88-17-53-40	nikos.androulakis@europarl.europa.eu	S&D
Annemans, Gerolf	Belgium	(+33) 3-88-17-57-00	gerolf.annemans@europarl.europa.eu	ENF
Arena, Maria	Belgium	(+33) 3-88-17-56-90	maria.arena@europarl.europa.eu	S&D
Arimont, Pacal	Belgium	(+33) 3-88-17-57-78	pascal.arimont@europarl.europa.eu	EPP
Arnautu, Marie-Christine	France	(+33) 3-88-17-55-29	marie-christine.arnautu@europarl.europa.eu	ENF
Arnott, Jonathan	UK	(+33) 3-88-17-53-30	jonathan.arnott@europarl.europa.eu	EFDD
Arthuis, Jean	France	(+33) 3-88-17-57-74	jean.arthuis@europarl.europa.eu	ALDE
Ashworth, Richard	UK	(+33) 3-88-17-53-09	richard.ashworth@europarl.europa.eu	ECR

Name	Member State	Telephone	E-mail	Political Group
Assis, Francisco	Portugal	(+33) 3-88-17-54-35	francisco.assis@europarl.europa.eu	S&D
Atkinson, Janice	UK	(+33) 3-88-17-55-37	janice.atkinson@europarl.europa.eu	ENF
Auken, Margrete	Denmark	(+33) 3-88-17-53-27	margrete.auken@europarl.europa.eu	Greens/EFA
Auštrevičius, Petras	Lithuania	(+33) 3-88-17-56-11	petras.austrevicius@europarl.europa.eu	ALDE
Ayala Sender, Inés	Spain	(+33) 3-88-17-55-08	ines.ayalasender@europarl.europa.eu	S&D
Ayuso, Pilar	Spain	(+33) 3-88-17-53-98	pilar.ayuso@europarl.europa.eu	EPP
Baalen, Johannes Cornelis van	Netherlands	(+33) 3-88-17-56-15	hans.vanbaalen@europarl.europa.eu	ALDE
Bach, Georges	Luxembourg	(+33) 3-88-17-51-13	georges.bach@europarl.europa.eu	EPP
Balas, Guillaume	France	(+33) 3-88-17-54-12	guillaume.balas@europarl.europa.eu	S&D
Balčytis, Zigmantas	Lithuania	(+33) 3-88-17-54-27	zigmantas.balcytis@europarl.europa.eu	S&D
Balczó, Zoltán	Hungary	(+33) 3-88-17-52-34	zoltan.balczo@europarl.europa.eu	NI
Balz, Burkhard	Germany	(+33) 3-88-17-51-19	burkhard.balz@europarl.europa.eu	EPP
Barekov, Nikolay	Bulgaria	(+33) 3-88-17-53-17	nikolay.barekov@europarl.europa.eu	ECR
Bashir, Amjad	UK	(+33) 3-88-17-53-19	amjad.bashir@europarl.europa.eu	ECR
Batten, Gerard	UK	(+33) 3-88-17-59-20	gerard.batten@europarl.europa.eu	EFDD
Bay, Nicholas	France	(+33) 3-88-17-58-48	nicolas.bay@europarl.europa.eu	ENF
Bayet, Hugues	Belgium	(+33) 3-88-17-57-91	hugues.bayet@europarl.europa.eu	S&D
Bearder, Catherine	UK	(+33) 3-88-17-56-32	catherine.bearder@europarl.europa.eu	ALDE
Becerra Basterrechea, Beatriz	Spain	(+33) 3-88-17-53-12	beatriz.becerra@europarl.europa.eu	ALDE
Becker, Heinz K.	Austria	(+33) 3-88-17-52-88	heinzk.becker@europarl.europa.eu	EPP
Beghin, Tiziana	Italy	(+33) 3-88-17-59-24	tiziana.beghin@europarl.europa.eu	EFDD
Belder, Bas	Netherlands	(+33) 3-88-17-52-70	bastiaan.belder@europarl.europa.eu	ECR
Belet, Ivo	Belgium	(+33) 3-88-17-56-23	ivo.belet@europarl.europa.eu	EPP
Bendtsen, Bendt	Denmark	(+33) 3-88-17-51-25	bendt.bendtsen@europarl.europa.eu	EPP
Benifei, Brando Maria	Italy	(+33) 3-88-17-56-44	brando.benifei@europarl.europa.eu	S&D
Benito Ziluaga, Xabier	Spain	(+33) 3-88-17-52-81	xabier.benitoziluaga@europarl.europa.eu	GUE/NGL
Beňová, Monika	Slovakia	(+33) 3-88-17-51-60	monika.benova@europarl.europa.eu	S&D
Berès, Pervenche	France	(+33) 3-88-17-57-77	pervenche.beres@europarl.europa.eu	S&D
Bergeron, Joëlle	France	(+33) 3-88-17-52-95	joelle.bergeron@europarl.europa.eu	EFDD
Bettini, Goffredo Maria	Italy	(+33) 3-88-17-53-13	goffredo.bettini@europarl.europa.eu	S&D
Bilbao Barandica, Izaskun	Spain	(+33) 3-88-17-55-28	izaskun.bilbaobarandica@europarl.europa.eu	ALDE
Bilde, Dominique	France	(+33) 3-88-17-57-42	dominique.bilde@europarl.europa.eu	ENF
Bizzotto, Mara	Italy	(+33) 3-88-17-57-29	mara.bizzotto@europarl.europa.eu	ENF
Björk, Malin	Sweden	(+33) 3-88-17-53-74	malin.bjork@europarl.europa.eu	GUE/NGL
Blanco López, José	Spain	(+33) 3-88-17-53-78	jose.blancolopez@europarl.europa.eu	S&D
Blinkevičiūtė, Vilija	Lithuania	(+33) 3-88-17-54-28	vilija.blinkeviciute@europarl.europa.eu	S&D
Bocskor, Andrea	Hungary	(+33) 3-88-17-58-29	andrea.bocskor@europarl.europa.eu	EPP
Böge, Reimer	Germany	(+33) 3-88-17-53-26	reimer.boege@europarl.europa.eu	EPP
Bogovič, Franc	Slovenia	(+33) 3-88-17-55-83	franc.bogovic@europarl.europa.eu	EPP
Bonafè, Simona	Italy	(+33) 3-88-17-55-95	simona.bonafe@europarl.europa.eu	S&D
Boni, Michał	Poland	(+33) 3-88-17-54-51	michal.boni@europarl.europa.eu	EPP
Borghezio, Mario	Italy	(+33) 3-88-17-57-04	mario.borghezio@europarl.europa.eu	ENF
Borrelli, David	Italy	(+33) 3-88-17-51-94	david.borrelli@europarl.europa.eu	EFDD
Borzan, Biljana	Croatia	(+33) 3-88-17-59-32	biljana.borzan@europarl.europa.eu	S&D
Boştinaru, Victor	Romania	(+33) 3-88-17-58-32	victor.bostinaru@europarl.europa.eu	S&D
Bours, Louise	UK	(+33) 3-88-17-55-52	louise.bours@europarl.europa.eu	EFDD
Boutonnet, Marie-Christine	France	(+33) 3-88-17-56-02	marie-christine.boutonnet@europarl.europa.eu	ENF
Bové, José	France	(+33) 3-88-17-53-52	jose.bove@europarl.europa.eu	Greens/EFA
Boylan, Lynn	Ireland	(+33) 3-88-17-52-57	lynn.boylan@europarl.europa.eu	GUE/NGL
Brannen, Paul	UK	(+33) 3-88-17-57-95	paul.brannen@europarl.europa.eu	S&D
Bresso, Mercedes	Italy	(+33) 3-88-17-51-48	mercedes.bresso@europarl.europa.eu	S&D
Briano, Renata	Italy	(+33) 3-88-17-56-34	renata.briano@europarl.europa.eu	S&D
Briois, Steeve	France	(+33) 3-88-17-85-50	steeve.briois@europarl.europa.eu	ENF
Brok, Elmar	Germany	(+33) 3-88-17-53-23	elmar.brok@europarl.europa.eu	EPP
Buchner, Klaus	Germany	(+33) 3-88-17-57-39	klaus.buchner@europarl.europa.eu	Greens/EFA
Buda, Daniel	Romania	(+33) 3-88-17-51-10	daniel.buda@europarl.europa.eu	EPP
Bullmann, Udo	Germany	(+33) 3-88-17-53-42	udo.bullmann@europarl.europa.eu	S&D
Bullock, Jonathan	UK	(+33) 3-88-17-57-64	jonathan.bullock@europarl.europa.eu	EFDD
Buşoi, Cristian-Silviu	Romania	(+33) 3-88-17-56-09	cristiansilviu.busoi@europarl.europa.eu	EPP
Bütikofer, Reinhard	Germany	(+33) 3-88-17-58-16	reinhard.buetikofer@europarl.europa.eu	Greens/EFA
Buzek, Jerzy	Poland	(+33) 3-88-17-56-31	jerzy.buzek@europarl.europa.eu	EPP
Cabezón Ruiz, Soledad	Spain	(+33) 3-88-17-55-96	soledad.cabezonruiz@europarl.europa.eu	S&D
Cadec, Alain	France	(+33) 3-88-17-57-65	alain.cadec@europarl.europa.eu	EPP

DIRECTORY *European Parliament*

Name	Member State	Telephone	E-mail	Political Group
Calvet Chambon, Enrique	Spain	(+33) 3-88-17-57-94	enrique.calvetchambon@europarl.europa.eu	ALDE
Camp, Wim van de	Netherlands	(+33) 3-88-17-52-98	wim.vandecamp@europarl.europa.eu	EPP
Campbell Bannerman, David	UK	(+33) 3-88-17-57-33	david.campbellbannerman@europarl.europa.eu	ECR
Caputo, Nicola	Italy	(+33) 3-88-17-57-63	nicola.caputo@europarl.europa.eu	S&D
Carthy, Matt	Ireland	(+33) 3-88-17-58-38	matt.carthy@europarl.europa.eu	GUE/NGL
Carver, James	UK	(+33) 3-88-17-57-44	james.carver@europarl.europa.eu	EFDD
Casa, David	Malta	(+33) 3-88-17-54-45	david.casa@europarl.europa.eu	EPP
Caspary, Daniel	Germany	(+33) 3-88-17-59-78	daniel.caspary@europarl.europa.eu	EPP
Castaldo, Fabio Massimo	Italy	(+33) 3-88-17-54-78	fabiomassimo.castaldo@europarl.europa.eu	EFDD
Castillo Vera, Pilar del	Spain	(+33) 3-88-17-59-82	pilar.delcastillo@europarl.europa.eu	EPP
Cavada, Jean-Marie	France	(+33) 3-88-17-53-67	jean-marie.cavada@europarl.europa.eu	ALDE
Cesa, Lorenzo	Italy	(+33) 3-88-17-52-18	lorenzo.cesa@europarl.europa.eu	EPP
Charanzová, Dita	Czech Republic	(+33) 3-88-17-55-06	dita.charanzova@europarl.europa.eu	ALDE
Chauprade, Aymeric	France	(+33) 3-88-17-55-68	aymeric.chauprade@europarl.europa.eu	NI
Childers, Nessa	Ireland	(+33) 3-88-17-51-80	nessa.childers@europarl.europa.eu	S&D
Chinnici, Caterina	Italy	(+33) 3-88-17-53-87	caterina.chinnici@europarl.europa.eu	S&D
Chountis, Nikolaos	Greece	(+33) 3-88-17-57-73	nikolaos.chountis@europarl.europa.eu	GUE/NGL
Christensen, Ole	Denmark	(+33) 3-88-17-54-64	ole.christensen@europarl.europa.eu	S&D
Christoforou, Lefteris	Cyprus	(+33) 3-88-17-58-76	lefteris.christoforou@europarl.europa.eu	EPP
Chrysogonos, Kostas	Greece	(+33) 3-88-17-54-05	konstantinos.chrysogonos@europarl.europa.eu	GUE/NGL
Cicu, Salvatore	Italy	(+33) 3-88-17-56-75	salvatore.cicu@europarl.europa.eu	EPP
Ciocca, Angelo	Italy	(+33) 3-88-17-58-47	angelo.ciocca@europarl.europa.eu	ENF
Cirio, Alberto	Italy	(+33) 3-88-17-52-59	alberto.cirio@europarl.europa.eu	EPP
Clune, Deirdre	Ireland	(+33) 3-88-17-52-92	deirdre.clune@europarl.europa.eu	EPP
Coburn, David	UK	(+33) 3-88-17-54-81	david.coburn@europarl.europa.eu	EFDD
Coelho, Carlos	Portugal	(+33) 3-88-17-55-51	carlos.coelho@europarl.europa.eu	EPP
Cofferati, Sergio Gaetano	Italy	(+33) 3-88-17-55-13	sergio.cofferati@europarl.europa.eu	S&D
Collin-Langen, Birgit	Germany	(+33) 3-88-17-58-26	birgit.collin-langen@europarl.europa.eu	EPP
Collins, Jane	UK	(+33) 3-88-17-51-04	jane.collins@europarl.europa.eu	EFDD
Comi, Lara	Italy	(+33) 3-88-17-51-35	lara.comi@europarl.europa.eu	EPP
Corazza Bildt, Anna Maria	Sweden	(+33) 3-88-17-51-28	annamaria.corazzabildt@europarl.europa.eu	EPP
Corbett, Richard	UK	(+33) 3-88-17-54-84	richard.corbett@europarl.europa.eu	S&D
Cornillet, Thierry	France	(+33) 3-88-17-54-50	thierry.cornillet@europarl.europa.eu	ALDE
Corrao, Ignazio	Italy	(+33) 3-88-17-56-10	ignazio.corrao@europarl.europa.eu	EFDD
Costa, Silvia	Italy	(+33) 3-88-17-55-14	silvia.costa@europarl.europa.eu	S&D
Couso Permuy, Javier	Spain	(+33) 3-88-17-55-57	javier.cousopermuy@europarl.europa.eu	GUE/NGL
Cozzolino, Andrea	Italy	(+33) 3-88-17-55-17	andrea.cozzolino@europarl.europa.eu	S&D
Cramer, Michael	Germany	(+33) 3-88-17-57-79	michael.cramer@europarl.europa.eu	Greens/EFA
Cristea, Andi-Lucian	Romania	(+33) 3-88-17-56-05	andi.cristea@europarl.europa.eu	S&D
Crowley, Brian	Ireland	(+33) 3-88-17-57-51	brian.crowley@europarl.europa.eu	ECR
Csáky, Pál	Slovakia	(+33) 3-88-17-56-01	pal.csaky@europarl.europa.eu	EPP
Czarnecki, Ryszard	Poland	(+33) 3-88-17-54-41	ryszard.czarnecki@europarl.europa.eu	ECR
Czesak, Edward	Poland	(+33) 3-88-17-52-10	edward.czesak@europarl.europa.eu	ECR
Dalen, Peter van	Netherlands	(+33) 3-88-17-57-19	peter.vandalen@europarl.europa.eu	ECR
Dalli, Miriam	Malta	(+33) 3-88-17-56-35	miriam.dalli@europarl.europa.eu	S&D
Dalton, Daniel	UK	(+33) 3-88-17-58-97	daniel.dalton@europarl.europa.eu	ECR
Dalunde, Jakop	Sweden	(+33) 3-88-17-57-52	jakop.dalunde@europarl.europa.eu	Greens/EFA
D'Amato, Rosa	Italy	(+33) 3-88-17-55-93	rosa.damato@europarl.europa.eu	EFDD
Dance, Seb	UK	(+33) 3-88-17-58-33	seb.dance@europarl.europa.eu	S&D
Dăncilă, Viorica	Romania	(+33) 3-88-17-58-08	vasilicaviorica.dancila@europarl.europa.eu	S&D
Danjean, Arnaud	France	(+33) 3-88-17-58-52	arnaud.danjean@europarl.europa.eu	EPP
Danti, Nicola	Italy	(+33) 3-88-17-51-43	nicola.danti@europarl.europa.eu	S&D
Dantin, Michel	France	(+33) 3-88-17-55-33	michel.dantin@europarl.europa.eu	EPP
Dartmouth, William	UK	(+33) 3-88-17-57-35	william.dartmouth@europarl.europa.eu	EFDD
Dati, Rachida	France	(+33) 3-88-17-58-96	rachida.dati@europarl.europa.eu	EPP
De Castro, Paolo	Italy	(+33) 3-88-17-55-20	paolo.decastro@europarl.europa.eu	S&D
Delahaye, Angélique	France	(+33) 3-88-17-54-09	angelique.delahaye@europarl.europa.eu	EPP
Deli, Andor	Hungary	(+33) 3-88-17-53-60	andor.deli@europarl.europa.eu	EPP
Delli, Karima	France	(+33) 3-88-17-53-62	karima.delli@europarl.europa.eu	Greens/EFA
Delvaux, Mady	Luxembourg	(+33) 3-88-17-51-36	mady.delvaux-stehres@europarl.europa.eu	S&D
De Masi, Fabio	Germany	(+33) 3-88-17-56-67	fabio.demasi@europarl.europa.eu	GUE/NGL
Demesmaeker, Mark	Belgium	(+33) 3-88-17-58-62	mark.demesmaeker@europarl.europa.eu	ECR

Name	Member State	Telephone	E-mail	Political Group
De Monte, Isabella	Italy	(+33) 3-88-17-53-58	isabella.demonte@europarl.europa.eu	S&D
Denanot, Jean-Paul	France	(+33) 3-88-17-52-13	jean-paul.denanot@europarl.europa.eu	S&D
Deprez, Gérard	Belgium	(+33) 3-88-17-54-97	gerard.deprez@europarl.europa.eu	ALDE
Dess, Albert	Germany	(+33) 3-88-17-52-31	albert.dess@europarl.europa.eu	EPP
Deutsch, Tamás	Hungary	(+33) 3-88-17-51-56	tamas.deutsch@europarl.europa.eu	EPP
Deva, Nirj	UK	(+33) 3-88-17-52-45	nirj.deva@europarl.europa.eu	ECR
Diaconu, Mircea	Romania	(+33) 3-88-17-58-23	mircea.diaconu@europarl.europa.eu	ALDE
Díaz de Mera García Consuegra, Agustín	Spain	(+33) 3-88-17-56-24	agustin.diazdemera@europarl.europa.eu	EPP
Dlabajová, Martina	Czech Republic	(+33) 3-88-17-58-57	martina.dlabajova@europarl.europa.eu	ALDE
Dodds, Diane	UK	(+33) 3-88-17-57-70	diane.dodds@europarl.europa.eu	NI
Dohrmann, Jørn	Denmark	(+33) 3-88-17-57-21	jorgen.dohrmann@europarl.europa.eu	ECR
Dorfmann, Herbert	Italy	(+33) 3-88-17-51-58	herbert.dorfmann@europarl.europa.eu	EPP
D'Ornano, Mireille	France	(+33) 3-88-17-52-41	mireille.dornano@europarl.europa.eu	ENF
Drăghici, Damian	Romania	(+33) 3-88-17-51-14	damian.draghici@europarl.europa.eu	S&D
Durand, Pascal	France	(+33) 3-88-17-51-61	pascal.durand@europarl.europa.eu	Greens/EFA
Dzhambazki, Angel	Bulgaria	(+33) 3-88-17-56-97	angel.dzhambazki@europarl.europa.eu	ECR
Eck, Stefan	Germany	(+33) 3-88-17-55-90	stefan.eck@europarl.europa.eu	GUE/NGL
Ehler, Christian	Germany	(+33) 3-88-17-53-25	christian.ehler@europarl.europa.eu	EPP
Eickhout, Bas	Netherlands	(+33) 3-88-17-53-65	bas.eickhout@europarl.europa.eu	Greens/EFA
Elissen, André	Netherlands	(+33) 3-88-17-58-14	andre.elissen@europarl.europa.eu	ENF
Engel, Frank	Luxembourg	(+33) 3-88-17-51-62	frank.engel@europarl.europa.eu	EPP
Engström, Linnéa	Sweden	(+33) 3-88-17-53-94	linnea.engstrom@europarl.europa.eu	Greens/EFA
Epitideios, Georgios	Greece	(+33) 3-88-17-56-41	georgios.epitideios@europarl.europa.eu	NI
Erdős, Norbert	Hungary	(+33) 3-88-17-57-16	norbert.erdos@europarl.europa.eu	EPP
Ernst, Cornelia	Germany	(+33) 3-88-17-56-60	cornelia.ernst@europarl.europa.eu	GUE/NGL
Ertug, Ismail	Germany	(+33) 3-88-17-55-47	ismail.ertug@europarl.europa.eu	S&D
Estaràs Ferragut, Rosa	Spain	(+33) 3-88-17-51-63	rosa.estaras@europarl.europa.eu	EPP
Etheridge, Bill	UK	(+33) 3-88-17-54-53	bill.etheridge@europarl.europa.eu	EFDD
Evans, Jill	UK	(+33) 3-88-17-51-03	jill.evans@europarl.europa.eu	Greens/EFA
Evi, Eleonora	Italy	(+33) 3-88-17-52-90	eleonora.evi@europarl.europa.eu	EFDD
Fajon, Tanja	Slovenia	(+33) 3-88-17-54-93	tanja.fajon@europarl.europa.eu	S&D
Farage, Nigel	UK	(+33) 3-88-17-58-55	nigel.farage@europarl.europa.eu	EFDD
Faria, José Inácio	Portugal	(+33) 3-88-17-54-54	joseinacio.faria@europarl.europa.eu	EPP
Federley, Fredrick	Sweden	(+33) 3-88-17-58-67	fredrick.federley@europarl.europa.eu	ALDE
Ferber, Markus	Germany	(+33) 3-88-17-52-30	markus.ferber@europarl.europa.eu	EPP
Fernandes, José Manuel	Portugal	(+33) 3-88-17-51-65	josemanuel.fernandes@europarl.europa.eu	EPP
Fernández Álvarez, Jonás	Spain	(+33) 3-88-17-51-74	jonas.fernandezalvarez@europarl.europa.eu	S&D
Ferrand, Édouard	France	(+33) 3-88-17-58-06	edouard.ferrand@europarl.europa.eu	ENF
Ferrara, Laura	Italy	(+33) 3-88-17-54-10	laura.ferrara@europarl.europa.eu	EFDD
Ferreira, João	Portugal	(+33) 3-88-17-76-51	joao.ferreira@europarl.europa.eu	GUE/NGL
Finch, Raymond	UK	(+33) 3-88-17-55-94	raymond.finch@europarl.europa.eu	EFDD
Fisas Ayxelà, Santiago	Spain	(+33) 3-88-17-51-69	santiago.fisasayxela@europarl.europa.eu	EPP
Fitto, Raffaele	Italy	(+33) 3-88-17-58-12	raffaele.fitto@europarl.europa.eu	ECR
Fjellner, Christofer	Sweden	(+33) 3-88-17-55-36	christofer.fjellner@europarl.europa.eu	EPP
Flack, John	UK	(+33) 3-88-17-56-72	john.flack@europarl.europa.eu	ECR
Flanagan, Luke Ming	Ireland	(+33) 3-88-17-52-38	lukeming.flanagan@europarl.europa.eu	GUE/NGL
Flašíková-Beňová, Monika	Slovakia	(+33) 3-88-17-51-60	monika.flasikovabenova@europarl.europa.eu	S&D
Fleckenstein, Knut	Germany	(+33) 3-88-17-55-48	knut.fleckenstein@europarl.europa.eu	S&D
Florenz, Karl-Heinz	Germany	(+33) 3-88-17-53-20	karl-heinz.florenz@europarl.europa.eu	EPP
Fontana, Lorenzo	Italy	(+33) 3-88-17-52-78	lorenzo.fontana@europarl.europa.eu	ENF
Forenza, Eleonora	Italy	(+33) 3-88-17-57-15	eleonora.forenza@europarl.europa.eu	GUE/NGL
Foster, Jacqueline	UK	(+33) 3-88-17-56-74	jacqueline.foster@europarl.europa.eu	ECR
Fotyga, Anna Elżbieta	Poland	(+33) 3-88-17-53-56	annaelzbieta.fotyga@europarl.europa.eu	ECR
Fountoulis, Lampros	Greece	(+33) 3-88-17-57-55	lampros.fountoulis@europarl.europa.eu	NI
Fox, Ashley	UK	(+33) 3-88-17-56-77	ashley.fox@europarl.europa.eu	ECR
Freund, Eugen	Austria	(+33) 3-88-17-51-39	eugen.freund@europarl.europa.eu	S&D
Frunzulică, Doru Claudian	Romania	(+33) 3-88-17-55-42	doru.frunzulica@europarl.europa.eu	S&D
Gahler, Michael	Germany	(+33) 3-88-17-59-77	michael.gahler@europarl.europa.eu	EPP
Gál, Kinga	Hungary	(+33) 3-88-17-55-99	kinga.gal@europarl.europa.eu	EPP
Gambús, Francesc	Spain	(+33) 3-88-17-51-02	francesc.gambus@europarl.europa.eu	EPP
García Pérez, Iratxe	Spain	(+33) 3-88-17-56-46	iratxe.garcia-perez@europarl.europa.eu	S&D
Gardiazábal Rubial, Eider	Spain	(+33) 3-88-17-53-33	eider.gardiazabalrubial@europarl.europa.eu	S&D
Gardini, Elisabetta	Italy	(+33) 3-88-17-53-93	elisabetta.gardini@europarl.europa.eu	EPP
Gasbarra, Enrico	Italy	(+33) 3-88-17-54-21	enrico.gasbarra@europarl.europa.eu	S&D

Name	Member State	Telephone	E-mail	Political Group
Gebhardt, Evelyne	Germany	(+33) 3-88-17-54-66	evelyne.gebhardt@europarl.europa.eu	S&D
Geier, Jens	Germany	(+33) 3-88-17-58-74	jens.geier@europarl.europa.eu	S&D
Gentile, Elena	Italy	(+33) 3-88-17-52-50	elena.gentile@europarl.europa.eu	S&D
Gerbrandy, Gerben-Jan	Netherlands	(+33) 3-88-17-56-16	gerben-jan.gerbrandy@europarl.europa.eu	ALDE
Gericke, Arne	Germany	(+33) 3-88-17-51-67	arne.gericke@europarl.europa.eu	ECR
Geringer de Oedenberg, Lidia Joanna	Poland	(+33) 3-88-17-58-09	lidiajoanna.geringerdeoedenberg@europarl.europa.eu	S&D
Giegold, Sven	Germany	(+33) 3-88-17-53-69	sven.giegold@europarl.europa.eu	Greens/EFA
Gierek, Adam	Poland	(+33) 3-88-17-57-81	adam.gierek@europarl.europa.eu	S&D
Gieseke, Jens	Germany	(+33) 3-88-17-55-56	jens.gieseke@europarl.europa.eu	EPP
Gill, Nathan	UK	(+33) 3-88-17-53-41	nathan.gill@europarl.europa.eu	EFDD
Gill, Neena	UK	(+33) 3-88-17-51-93	neena.gill@europarl.europa.eu	S&D
Giménez Barbat, María Teresa	Spain	(+33) 3-88-17-55-92	teresa.gimenezbarbat@europarl.europa.eu	ALDE
Girling, Julie	UK	(+33) 3-88-17-56-78	julie.girling@europarl.europa.eu	ECR
Giuffrida, Michela	Italy	(+33) 3-88-17-55-31	michela.giuffrida@europarl.europa.eu	S&D
Goddyn, Sylvie	France	(+33) 3-88-17-51-49	sylvie.goddyn@europarl.europa.eu	ENF
Goerens, Charles	Luxembourg	(+33) 3-88-17-56-12	charles.goerens@europarl.europa.eu	ALDE
Gollnisch, Bruno	France	(+33) 3-88-17-52-65	bruno.gollnisch@europarl.europa.eu	NI
Gomes, Ana	Portugal	(+33) 3-88-17-58-24	anamaria.gomes@europarl.europa.eu	S&D
González Peñas, Tania	Spain	(+33) 3-88-17-51-41	tania.gonzalezpenas@europarl.europa.eu	GUE/NGL
González Pons, Esteban	Spain	(+33) 3-88-17-53-72	esteban.gonzalezpons@europarl.europa.eu	EPP
Gosiewska, Beata Barbara	Poland	(+33) 3-88-17-57-99	beatabarbara.gosiewska@europarl.europa.eu	ECR
de Graaff, Marcel	Netherlands	(+33) 3-88-17-53-70	marcel.degraaff@europarl.europa.eu	ENF
Grammatikakis, George	Greece	(+33) 3-88-17-54-86	giorgos.grammatikakis@europarl.europa.eu	S&D
de Grandes Pascual, Luis	Spain	(+33) 3-88-17-55-12	luis.degrandespascual@europarl.europa.eu	EPP
Grapini, Maria	Romania	(+33) 3-88-17-55-26	maria.grapini@europarl.europa.eu	S&D
Grässle, Ingeborg	Germany	(+33) 3-88-17-58-68	ingeborg.graessle@europarl.europa.eu	EPP
Graswander-Hainz, Karoline	Austria	(+33) 3-88-17-54-36	karoline.graswander-hainz@europarl.europa.eu	S&D
Griesbeck, Natalie	France	(+33) 3-88-17-53-91	nathalie.griesbeck@europarl.europa.eu	ALDE
Griffin, Theresa	UK	(+33) 3-88-17-52-71	theresa.griffin@europarl.europa.eu	S&D
Grigule, Iveta	Latvia	(+33) 3-88-17-52-76	iveta.grigule@europarl.europa.eu	ALDE
Grossetête, Françoise	France	(+33) 3-88-17-59-52	francoise.grossetete@europarl.europa.eu	EPP
Grzyb, Andrzej	Poland	(+33) 3-88-17-51-85	andrzej.grzyb@europarl.europa.eu	EPP
Gualtieri, Roberto	Italy	(+33) 3-88-17-55-23	roberto.gualtieri@europarl.europa.eu	S&D
Guerrero Salom, Enrique	Spain	(+33) 3-88-17-53-34	enrique.guerrerosalom@europarl.europa.eu	S&D
Guillaume, Sylvie	France	(+33) 3-88-17-54-33	sylvie.guillaume@europarl.europa.eu	S&D
Guoga, Antanas	Lithuania	(+33) 3-88-17-55-22	antanas.guoga@europarl.europa.eu	EPP
Guteland, Jytte	Sweden	(+33) 3-88-17-56-94	jytte.guteland@europarl.europa.eu	S&D
Gutiérrez Prieto, Sergio	Spain	(+33) 3-88-17-53-31	sergio.gutierrezprieto@europarl.europa.eu	S&D
Gyürk, András	Hungary	(+33) 3-88-17-57-27	andras.gyurk@europarl.europa.eu	EPP
Hadjigeorgiou, Takis	Cyprus	(+33) 3-88-17-56-57	takis.hadjigeorgiou@europarl.europa.eu	GUE/NGL
Halla-Aho, Jussi	Finland	(+33) 3-88-17-51-21	jussi.halla-aho@europarl.europa.eu	ECR
Händel, Thomas	Germany	(+33) 3-88-17-56-58	thomas.haendel@europarl.europa.eu	GUE/NGL
Hannan, Daniel	UK	(+33) 3-88-17-51-37	daniel.hannan@europarl.europa.eu	ECR
Harkin, Marian	Ireland	(+33) 3-88-17-57-97	marian.harkin@europarl.europa.eu	ALDE
Harms, Rebecca	Germany	(+33) 3-88-17-56-95	rebecca.harms@europarl.europa.eu	Greens/EFA
Häusling, Martin	Germany	(+33) 3-88-17-58-20	martin.haeusling@europarl.europa.eu	Greens/EFA
Hautala, Heidi	Finland	(+33) 3-88-17-55-18	heidi.hautala@europarl.europa.eu	Greens/EFA
Hayes, Brian	Ireland	(+33) 3-88-17-52-75	brian.hayes@europarl.europa.eu	EPP
Hazekamp, Anja	Netherlands	(+33) 3-88-17-56-29	anja.hazekamp@europarl.europa.eu	GUE/NGL
Hedh, Anna	Sweden	(+33) 3-88-17-55-27	anna.hedh@europarl.europa.eu	S&D
Henkel, Hans-Olaf	Germany	(+33) 3-88-17-51-32	hans-olaf.henkel@europarl.europa.eu	ECR
Herranz García, Esther	Spain	(+33) 3-88-17-52-74	esther.herranzgarcia@europarl.europa.eu	EPP
Hetman, Krzysztof	Poland	(+33) 3-88-17-57-67	krzysztof.hetman@europarl.europa.eu	EPP
Heubuch, Maria	Germany	(+33) 3-88-17-53-35	maria.heubuch@europarl.europa.eu	Greens/EFA
Hoc, Czesław	Poland	(+33) 3-88-17-58-64	czeslaw.hoc@europarl.europa.eu	ECR
Hoffmann, Iris	Germany	(+33) 3-88-17-55-67	iris.hoffmann@europarl.europa.eu	S&D
Hohlmeier, Monika	Germany	(+33) 3-88-17-51-91	monika.hohlmeier@europarl.europa.eu	EPP
Hökmark, Gunnar	Sweden	(+33) 3-88-17-58-22	gunnar.hokmark@europarl.europa.eu	EPP
Hölvényi, György	Hungary	(+33) 3-88-17-51-97	gyorgy.holvenyi@europarl.europa.eu	EPP
Honeyball, Mary	UK	(+33) 3-88-17-52-09	mary.honeyball@europarl.europa.eu	S&D
Hookem, Mike	UK	(+33) 3-88-17-55-61	mike.hookem@europarl.europa.eu	EFDD
Hortefeux, Brice	France	(+33) 3-88-17-52-86	brice.hortefeux@europarl.europa.eu	EPP
Howarth, John	UK	(+33) 3-88-17-52-73	john.howarth@europarl.europa.eu	S&D

Name	Member State	Telephone	E-mail	Political Group
Hübner, Danuta Maria	Poland	(+33) 3-88-17-51-92	danuta.huebner@europarl.europa.eu	EPP
Hudghton, Ian	UK	(+33) 3-88-17-54-99	ian.hudghton@europarl.europa.eu	Greens/EFA
Huitema, Jan	Netherlands	(+33) 3-88-17-51-31	jan.huitema@europarl.europa.eu	ALDE
Hyusmenova, Filiz	Bulgaria	(+33) 3-88-17-59-03	filizhakaeva.hyusmenova@europarl.europa.eu	ALDE
in 't Veld, Sophia	Netherlands	(+33) 3-88-17-57-96	sophie.intveld@europarl.europa.eu	ALDE
Iturgaiz, Carlos	Spain	(+33) 3-88-17-52-91	carlos.iturgaiz@europarl.europa.eu	EPP
Ivan, Cătălin Sorin	Romania	(+33) 3-88-17-54-56	catalin-sorin.ivan@europarl.europa.eu	S&D
Iwaszkiewicz, Robert Jarosław	Poland	(+33) 3-88-17-55-77	robertjaroslaw.iwaszkiewicz@europarl.europa.eu	EFDD
Jaakonsaari, Liisa	Finland	(+33) 3-88-17-55-40	liisa.jaakonsaari@europarl.europa.eu	S&D
Jäätteenmäki, Anneli	Finland	(+33) 3-88-17-56-14	anneli.jaatteenmaki@europarl.europa.eu	ALDE
Jadot, Yannick	France	(+33) 3-88-17-53-75	yannick.jadot@europarl.europa.eu	Greens/EFA
Jahr, Peter	Germany	(+33) 3-88-17-51-95	peter.jahr@europarl.europa.eu	EPP
Jakovčić, Ivan	Croatia	(+33) 3-88-17-56-39	ivan.jakovcic@europarl.europa.eu	ALDE
Jalkh, Jean-François	France	(+33) 3-88-17-52-52	jean-francois.jalkh@europarl.europa.eu	ENF
James, Diane	UK	(+33) 3-88-17-55-41	diane.james@europarl.europa.eu	NI
Jamet, France	France	(+33) 3-88-17-51-66	france.jamet@europarl.europa.eu	ENF
Jáuregui Atondo, Ramón	Spain	(+33) 3-88-17-55-82	ramon.jaureguiatondo@europarl.europa.eu	S&D
Jávor, Benedek	Hungary	(+33) 3-88-17-55-73	benedek.javor@europarl.europa.eu	Greens/EFA
Jazłowiecka, Danuta	Poland	(+33) 3-88-17-51-96	danuta.jazlowiecka@europarl.europa.eu	EPP
Ježek, Petr	Czech Republic	(+33) 3-88-17-54-15	petr.jezek@europarl.europa.eu	ALDE
Jiménez-Becerril Barrio, Teresa	Spain	(+33) 3-88-17-51-98	teresa.jimenez-becerril@europarl.europa.eu	EPP
Joly, Eva	France	(+33) 3-88-17-53-76	eva.joly@europarl.europa.eu	Greens/EFA
de Jong, Dennis	Netherlands	(+33) 3-88-17-56-64	dennis.dejong@europarl.europa.eu	GUE/NGL
Jongerius, Agnes	Netherlands	(+33) 3-88-17-56-99	agnes.jongerius@europarl.europa.eu	S&D
Joulaud, Marc	France	(+33) 3-88-17-52-43	marc.joulaud@europarl.europa.eu	EPP
Juaristi Abaunz, Josu	Spain	(+33) 3-88-17-56-28	josu.juaristi@europarl.europa.eu	GUE/NGL
Jurek, Marek	Poland	(+33) 3-88-17-52-39	marek.jurek@europarl.europa.eu	ECR
Juvin, Philippe	France	(+33) 3-88-17-51-99	philippe.juvin@europarl.europa.eu	EPP
Kadenbach, Karin	Austria	(+33) 3-88-17-54-75	karin.kadenbach@europarl.europa.eu	S&D
Kaili, Eva	Greece	(+33) 3-88-17-56-13	eva.kaili@europarl.europa.eu	S&D
Kalinowski, Jarosław	Poland	(+33) 3-88-17-52-03	jaroslaw.kalinowski@europarl.europa.eu	EPP
Kallas, Kaja	Estonia	(+33) 3-88-17-54-79	kaja.kallas@europarl.europa.eu	ALDE
Kalniete, Sandra	Latvia	(+33) 3-88-17-52-04	sandra.kalniete@europarl.europa.eu	EPP
Kamall, Syed	UK	(+33) 3-88-17-57-92	syed.kamall@europarl.europa.eu	ECR
Kammerevert, Petra	Germany	(+33) 3-88-17-55-54	petra.kammerevert@europarl.europa.eu	S&D
Kappel, Barbara	Austria	(+33) 3-88-17-55-76	barbara.kappel@europarl.europa.eu	ENF
Karas, Othmar	Austria	(+33) 3-88-17-56-27	othmar.karas@europarl.europa.eu	EPP
Kari, Rina Ronja	Denmark	(+33) 3-88-17-51-52	rinaronja.kari@europarl.europa.eu	GUE/NGL
Karim, Sajjad	UK	(+33) 3-88-17-56-40	sajjad.karim@europarl.europa.eu	ECR
Kariņš, Krišjānis	Latvia	(+33) 3-88-17-52-05	krisjanis.karins@europarl.europa.eu	EPP
Karlsson, Rikke	Denmark	(+33) 3-88-17-58-21	rikke.karlsson@europarl.europa.eu	ECR
Karski, Karol Adam	Poland	(+33) 3-88-17-76-63	karol.karski@europarl.europa.eu	ECR
Kaufmann, Sylvia-Yvonne	Germany	(+33) 3-88-17-57-88	sylvia-yvonne.kaufmann@europarl.europa.eu	S&D
Kefalogiannis, Manolis	Greece	(+33) 3-88-17-55-70	manolis.kefalogiannis@europarl.europa.eu	EPP
Kelam, Tunne	Estonia	(+33) 3-88-17-52-79	tunne.kelam@europarl.europa.eu	EPP
Keller, Jan	Czech Republic	(+33) 3-88-17-54-25	jan.keller@europarl.europa.eu	S&D
Keller, Ska	Germany	(+33) 3-88-17-53-79	franziska.keller@europarl.europa.eu	Greens/EFA
Kelly, Seán	Ireland	(+33) 3-88-17-52-06	sean.kelly@europarl.europa.eu	EPP
Khan, Wajid	UK	(+33) 3-88-17-54-37	wajid.khan@europarl.europa.eu	S&D
Kirton-Darling, Jude	UK	(+33) 3-88-17-51-05	jude.kirton-darling@europarl.europa.eu	S&D
Klosowski, Sławomir	Poland	(+33) 3-88-17-53-57	slawomir.klosowski@europarl.europa.eu	ECR
Koch, Dieter-Lebrecht	Germany	(+33) 3-88-17-57-61	dieter-lebrecht.koch@europarl.europa.eu	EPP
Kofod, Jeppe	Denmark	(+33) 3-88-17-54-63	jeppe.kofod@europarl.europa.eu	S&D
Kohlíček, Jaromír	Czech Republic	(+33) 3-88-17-59-07	jaromir.kohlicek@ep.europa.eu	GUE/NGL
Kohn, Arndt	Germany	(+33) 3-88-17-58-69	arndt.kohn@europarl.europa.eu	S&D
Kölmel, Bernd	Germany	(+33) 3-88-17-57-01	bernd.koelmel@europarl.europa.eu	ECR
Konečná, Kateřina	Czech Republic	(+33) 3-88-17-51-68	katerina.konecna@europarl.europa.eu	GUE/NGL
Korwin-Mikke, Janusz Ryszard	Poland	(+33) 3-88-17-55-75	janusz.korwin-mikke@europarl.europa.eu	NI
Kósa, Ádám	Hungary	(+33) 3-88-17-52-08	adam.kosa@europarl.europa.eu	EPP
Köster, Dietmar	Germany	(+33) 3-88-17-56-07	dietmar.koester@europarl.europa.eu	S&D
Köstinger, Elisabeth	Austria	(+33) 3-88-17-52-11	elisabeth.koestinger@europarl.europa.eu	EPP
Kouloglou, Stelios	Greece	(+33) 3-88-17-55-35	stelios.kouloglou@europarl.europa.eu	GUE/NGL

Name	Member State	Telephone	E-mail	Political Group
Kovács, Béla	Hungary	(+33) 3-88-17-57-89	bela.kovacs@europarl.europa.eu	NI
Kovatchev, Andrey	Bulgaria	(+33) 3-88-17-56-62	andrey.kovatchev@europarl.europa.eu	EPP
Kozłowska-Rajewicz, Agnieszka	Poland	(+33) 3-88-17-54-20	agnieszka.kozlowska-rajewicz@europarl.europa.eu	EPP
Krasnodębski, Zdzisław Marek	Poland	(+33) 3-88-17-55-10	zdzislaw.krasnodebski@europarl.europa.eu	ECR
Krehl, Constanze	Germany	(+33) 3-88-17-51-34	constanze.krehl@europarl.europa.eu	S&D
Krupa, Urszula	Poland	(+33) 3-88-17-58-02	urszula.krupa@europarl.europa.eu	ECR
Kudrycka, Barbara	Poland	(+33) 3-88-17-55-19	barbara.kudrycka@europarl.europa.eu	EPP
Kuhn, Werner	Germany	(+33) 3-88-17-52-15	werner.kuhn@europarl.europa.eu	EPP
Kukan, Eduard	Slovakia	(+33) 3-88-17-52-16	eduard.kukan@europarl.europa.eu	EPP
Kumpula-Natri, Miapetra	Finland	(+33) 3-88-17-52-94	miapetra.kumpula-natri@europarl.europa.eu	S&D
Kuneva, Kostadinka	Greece	(+33) 3-88-17-58-91	kostadinka.kuneva@europarl.europa.eu	GUE/NGL
Kuźmiuk, Zbigniew Krzysztof	Poland	(+33) 3-88-17-55-64	zbigniew.kuzmiuk@europarl.europa.eu	ECR
Kyenge, Cécile Kashetu	Italy	(+33) 3-88-17-51-23	kashetu.kyenge@europarl.europa.eu	S&D
Kyllönen, Merja	Finland	(+33) 3-88-17-55-43	merja.kyllonen@europarl.europa.eu	GUE/NGL
Kyrkos, Miltiadis	Greece	(+33) 3-88-17-54-89	miltiadis.kyrkos@europarl.europa.eu	S&D
Kyrtsos, Georgios	Greece	(+33) 3-88-17-58-56	georgios.kyrtsos@europarl.europa.eu	EPP
Kyuchyuk, Ilhan	Bulgaria	(+33) 3-88-17-51-78	ilhan.kyuchyuk@europarl.europa.eu	ALDE
Lalonde, Patricia	France	(+33) 3-88-17-52-97	patricia.lalonde@europarl.europa.eu	ALDE
Lamassoure, Alain	France	(+33) 3-88-17-57-06	alain.lamassoure@europarl.europa.eu	EPP
Lambert, Jean	UK	(+33) 3-88-17-55-07	jean.lambert@europarl.europa.eu	Greens/EFA
Lamberts, Philippe	Belgium	(+33) 3-88-17-53-88	philippe.lamberts@europarl.europa.eu	Greens/EFA
Lambsdorff, Alexander Graf	Germany	(+33) 3-88-17-51-18	alexandergraf.lambsdorff@europarl.europa.eu	ALDE
Lange, Bernd	Germany	(+33) 3-88-17-55-55	bernd.lange@europarl.europa.eu	S&D
de Lange, Esther	Netherlands	(+33) 3-88-17-59-54	esther.delange@europarl.europa.eu	EPP
Langen, Werner	Germany	(+33) 3-88-17-53-85	werner.langen@europarl.europa.eu	EPP
Lauristin, Marju	Estonia	(+33) 3-88-17-54-74	marju.lauristin@europarl.europa.eu	S&D
La Via, Giovanni	Italy	(+33) 3-88-17-52-17	giovanni.lavia@europarl.europa.eu	EPP
Lavrilleux, Jérôme	France	(+33) 3-88-17-54-55	jerome.lavrilleux@europarl.europa.eu	EPP
Lebreton, Gilles	France	(+33) 3-88-17-58-17	gilles.lebreton@europarl.europa.eu	ENF
Lechevalier, Christelle	France	(+33) 3-88-17-57-09	christelle.lechevalier@europarl.europa.eu	ENF
Le Grip, Constance	France	(+33) 3-88-17-51-20	constance.legrip@europarl.europa.eu	EPP
Legutko, Ryszard Antoni	Poland	(+33) 3-88-17-57-22	ryszardantoni.legutko@europarl.europa.eu	ECR
Le Hyaric, Patrick	France	(+33) 3-88-17-56-56	patrick.lehyaric@europarl.europa.eu	GUE/NGL
Leinen, Jo	Germany	(+33) 3-88-17-58-42	jo.leinen@europarl.europa.eu	S&D
Lenaers, Jeroen	Netherlands	(+33) 3-88-17-55-60	jeroen.lenaers@europarl.europa.eu	EPP
Le Pen, Jean-Marie	France	(+33) 3-88-17-57-20	jean-marie.lepen@europarl.europa.eu	NI
Lewandowski, Janusz	Poland	(+33) 3-88-17-52-42	janusz.lewandowski@europarl.europa.eu	EPP
Liberadzki, Bogusław	Poland	(+33) 3-88-17-54-23	boguslaw.liberadzki@europarl.europa.eu	S&D
Liese, Peter	Germany	(+33) 3-88-17-59-81	peter.liese@europarl.europa.eu	EPP
Lietz, Arne	Germany	(+33) 3-88-17-52-96	arne.lietz@europarl.europa.eu	S&D
Lins, Norbert	Germany	(+33) 3-88-17-58-19	norbert.lins@europarl.europa.eu	EPP
Lochbihler, Barbara	Germany	(+33) 3-88-17-53-92	barbara.lochbihler@europarl.europa.eu	Greens/EFA
Loiseau, Philippe	France	(+33) 3-88-17-52-27	philippe.loiseau@europarl.europa.eu	ENF
Lokkegaard, Morten	Denmark	(+33) 3-88-17-57-66	morten.lokkegaard@europarl.europa.eu	ALDE
Loones, Sander	Belgium	(+33) 3-88-17-57-18	sander.loones@europarl.europa.eu	ECR
Lope Fontagné, Verónica	Spain	(+33) 3-88-17-52-23	veronica.lopefontagne@europarl.europa.eu	EPP
López, Javi	Spain	(+33) 3-88-17-56-25	javi.lopez@europarl.europa.eu	S&D
López Aguilar, Juan Fernando	Spain	(+33) 3-88-17-53-36	juanfernando.lopezaguilar@europarl.europa.eu	S&D
López Bermejo, Paloma	Spain	(+33) 3-88-17-54-95	paloma.lopez@europarl.europa.eu	GUE/NGL
López-Istúriz White, Antonio	Spain	(+33) 3-88-17-57-13	antonio.lopezisturiz@europarl.europa.eu	EPP
Lösing, Sabine	Germany	(+33) 3-88-17-58-94	sabine.loesing@europarl.europa.eu	GUE/NGL
Lucke, Bernd	Germany	(+33) 3-88-17-52-68	bernd.lucke@europarl.europa.eu	ECR
Ludvigsson, Olle	Sweden	(+33) 3-88-17-54-42	olle.ludvigsson@europarl.europa.eu	S&D
Łukacijewska, Elżbieta Katarzyna	Poland	(+33) 3-88-17-53-29	elzbieta.lukacijewska@europarl.europa.eu	EPP
Lunacek, Ulrike	Austria	(+33) 3-88-17-53-95	ulrike.lunacek@europarl.europa.eu	Greens/EFA
Lundgren, Peter	Sweden	(+33) 3-88-17-56-73	peter.lundgren@europarl.europa.eu	EFDD
Łybacka, Krystyna Maria	Poland	(+33) 3-88-17-51-50	krystyna.lybacka@europarl.europa.eu	S&D
Matthews, Rupert	UK	(+33) 3-88-17-55-98	rupert.matthews@europarl.europa.eu	ECR
McAllister, David	Germany	(+33) 3-88-17-51-30	david.mcallister@europarl.europa.eu	EPP
McAvan, Linda	UK	(+33) 3-88-17-54-38	linda.mcavan@europarl.europa.eu	S&D

Name	Member State	Telephone	E-mail	Political Group
McClarkin, Emma	UK	(+33) 3-88-17-56-84	emma.mcclarkin@europarl.europa.eu	ECR
McGuinness, Mairead	Ireland	(+33) 3-88-17-52-14	mairead.mcguinness@europarl.europa.eu	EPP
McIntyre, Anthea	UK	(+33) 3-88-17-51-06	anthea.mcintyre@europarl.europa.eu	ECR
Macovei, Monica Luisa	Romania	(+33) 3-88-17-52-25	monica.macovei@europarl.europa.eu	ECR
Maletić, Ivana	Croatia	(+33) 3-88-17-57-34	ivana.maletic@europarl.europa.eu	EPP
Malinov, Svetoslav Hristov	Bulgaria	(+33) 3-88-17-54-90	svetoslav.malinov@europarl.europa.eu	EPP
Maltese, Curzio	Italy	(+33) 3-88-17-54-52	curzio.maltese@europarl.europa.eu	GUE/NGL
Mamikins, Andrejs	Latvia	(+33) 3-88-17-53-73	andrejs.mamikins@europarl.europa.eu	S&D
Mănescu, Ramona Nicole	Romania	(+33) 3-88-17-54-39	ramonanicole.manescu@europarl.europa.eu	EPP
Maňka, Vladimír	Slovakia	(+33) 3-88-17-54-49	vladimir.manka@europarl.europa.eu	S&D
Mann, Thomas	Germany	(+33) 3-88-17-53-18	thomas.mann@europarl.europa.eu	EPP
Manscour, Louis-Joseph	France	(+33) 3-88-17-52-28	louis-joseph.manscour@europarl.europa.eu	S&D
Marcellesi, Florent	Spain	(+33) 3-88-17-57-43	florent.marcellesi@europarl.europa.eu	Greens/EFA
Marias, Notis	Greece	(+33) 3-88-17-51-51	notis.marias@europarl.europa.eu	ECR
Marinescu, Marian-Jean	Romania	(+33) 3-88-17-54-16	marian-jean.marinescu@europarl.europa.eu	EPP
Marinho e Pinto, António	Portugal	(+33) 3-88-17-54-03	antonio.marinhoepinto@europarl.europa.eu	ALDE
Martin, David	UK	(+33) 3-88-17-55-39	david.martin@europarl.europa.eu	S&D
Martin, Dominique	France	(+33) 3-88-17-54-02	dominique.martin@europarl.europa.eu	ENF
Martin, Edouard	France	(+33) 3-88-17-54-72	edouard.martin@europarl.europa.eu	S&D
Martusciello, Fulvio	Italy	(+33) 3-88-17-57-45	fulvio.martusciello@europarl.europa.eu	EPP
Marusik, Michał	Poland	(+33) 3-88-17-53-68	michal.marusik@europarl.europa.eu	ENF
Mašťálka, Jiří	Czech Republic	(+33) 3-88-17-59-05	jiri.mastalka@europarl.europa.eu	GUE/NGL
Matera, Barbara	Italy	(+33) 3-88-17-52-36	barbara.matera@europarl.europa.eu	EPP
Matias, Marisa	Portugal	(+33) 3-88-17-56-69	marisa.matias@europarl.europa.eu	GUE/NGL
Mato, Gabriel	Spain	(+33) 3-88-17-52-37	gabriel.mato@europarl.europa.eu	EPP
Maullu, Stefano	Italy	(+33) 3-88-17-52-19	stefano.maullu@europarl.europa.eu	EPP
Maurel, Emmanuel	France	(+33) 3-88-17-57-47	emmanuel.maurel@europarl.europa.eu	S&D
Mavrides, Costas	Cyprus	(+33) 3-88-17-56-48	costas.mavrides@europarl.europa.eu	S&D
Maydell, Eva	Bulgaria	(+33) 3-88-17-57-71	eva.maydell@europarl.europa.eu	EPP
Mayer, Alex	UK	(+33) 3-88-17-54-77	alex.mayer@europarl.europa.eu	S&D
Mayer, Georg	Austria	(+33) 3-88-17-52-77	georg.mayer@europarl.europa.eu	ENF
Mazuronis, Valentinas	Lithuania	(+33) 3-88-17-52-55	valentinas.mazuronis@europarl.europa.eu	ALDE
Meissner, Gesine	Germany	(+33) 3-88-17-55-78	gesine.meissner@europarl.europa.eu	ALDE
Mélin, Joëlle	France	(+33) 3-88-17-53-10	joelle.melin@europarl.europa.eu	ENF
Melior, Susanne	Germany	(+33) 3-88-17-51-83	susanne.melior@europarl.europa.eu	S&D
Melo, Nuno	Portugal	(+33) 3-88-17-52-40	nuno.melo@europarl.europa.eu	EPP
Messerschmidt, Morten	Denmark	(+33) 3-88-17-57-38	morten.messerschmidt@europarl.europa.eu	ECR
Meszerics, Tamás	Hungary	(+33) 3-88-17-52-80	tamas.meszerics@europarl.europa.eu	Greens/EFA
Metsola, Roberta	Malta	(+33) 3-88-17-56-86	roberta.metsola@europarl.europa.eu	EPP
Michel, Louis	Belgium	(+33) 3-88-17-55-32	louis.michel@europarl.europa.eu	ALDE
Michels, Martina	Germany	(+33) 3-88-17-58-34	martina.michels@europarl.europa.eu	GUE/NGL
Mihaylova, Iskra	Bulgaria	(+33) 3-88-17-58-58	iskra.mihaylova@europarl.europa.eu	ALDE
Mikolášik, Miroslav	Slovakia	(+33) 3-88-17-52-89	miroslav.mikolasik@europarl.europa.eu	EPP
Millán Mon, Francisco José	Spain	(+33) 3-88-17-54-30	francisco.millanmon@europarl.europa.eu	EPP
van Miltenburg, Matthijs	Netherlands	(+33) 3-88-17-57-24	matthijs.vanmiltenburg@europarl.europa.eu	ALDE
Mineur, Anne-Marie	Netherlands	(+33) 3-88-17-51-29	anne-marie.mineur@europarl.europa.eu	GUE/NGL
Mizzi, Marlene	Malta	(+33) 3-88-17-52-35	marlene.mizzi@europarl.europa.eu	S&D
Mlinar, Angelika	Austria	(+33) 3-88-17-58-51	angelika.mlinar@europarl.europa.eu	ALDE
Mobarik, Baroness Nosheena	UK	(+33) 3-88-17-52-49	nosheena.mobarik@europarl.europa.eu	ECR
Moi, Giulia	Italy	(+33) 3-88-17-51-71	giulia.moi@europarl.europa.eu	EFDD
Moisă, Ionel-Sorin	Romania	(+33) 3-88-17-57-05	sorin.moisa@europarl.europa.eu	S&D
Molnár, Csaba	Hungary	(+33) 3-88-17-55-71	csaba.molnar@europarl.europa.eu	S&D
Monot, Bernard	France	(+33) 3-88-17-52-20	bernard.monot@europarl.europa.eu	ENF
Monteiro de Aguiar, Cláudia	Portugal	(+33) 3-88-17-54-58	claudia.monteirodeaguiar@europarl.europa.eu	EPP
Montel, Sophie	France	(+33) 3-88-17-51-26	sophie.montel@europarl.europa.eu	ENF
Moody, Clare	UK	(+33) 3-88-17-53-08	clare.moody@europarl.europa.eu	S&D
Moraes, Claude	UK	(+33) 3-88-17-55-53	claude.moraes@europarl.europa.eu	S&D
Morano, Nadine	France	(+33) 3-88-17-54-46	nadine.morano@europarl.europa.eu	EPP
Morgano, Luigi	Italy	(+33) 3-88-17-56-45	luigi.morgano@europarl.europa.eu	S&D
Morin-Chartier, Élisabeth	France	(+33) 3-88-17-56-30	elisabeth.morinchartier@europarl.europa.eu	EPP

Name	Member State	Telephone	E-mail	Political Group
Morvai, Krisztina	Hungary	(+33) 3-88-17-57-86	krisztina.morvai@europarl.europa.eu	NI
Mosca, Alessia Maria	Italy	(+33) 3-88-17-57-46	alessia.mosca@europarl.europa.eu	S&D
Müller, Ulrike	Germany	(+33) 3-88-17-58-43	ulrike.mueller@europarl.europa.eu	ALDE
Mureşan, Siegfried	Romania	(+33) 3-88-17-51-54	siegfried.muresan@europarl.europa.eu	EPP
Muselier, Renaud	France	(+33) 3-88-17-55-16	renaud.muselier@europarl.europa.eu	EPP
Mussolini, Alessandra	Italy	(+33) 3-88-17-55-21	alessandra.mussolini@europarl.europa.eu	EPP
Nagy, József	Slovakia	(+33) 3-88-17-52-12	jozsef.nagy@europarl.europa.eu	EPP
Nart, Javier	Spain	(+33) 3-88-17-58-11	javier.nart@europarl.europa.eu	ALDE
Nekov, Momchil	Bulgaria	(+33) 3-88-17-52-01	momchil.nekov@europarl.europa.eu	S&D
Neuser, Norbert	Germany	(+33) 3-88-17-58-92	norbert.neuser@europarl.europa.eu	S&D
Nica, Dan	Romania	(+33) 3-88-17-54-48	dan.nica@europarl.europa.eu	S&D
Nicholson, James	UK	(+33) 3-88-17-59-33	james.nicholson@europarl.europa.eu	ECR
Nicolai, Norica	Romania	(+33) 3-88-17-56-19	norica.nicolae@europarl.europa.eu	ALDE
Niebler, Angelika	Germany	(+33) 3-88-17-53-90	angelika.niebler@europarl.europa.eu	EPP
Niedermayer, Luděk	Czech Republic	(+33) 3-88-17-55-74	ludek.niedermayer@europarl.europa.eu	EPP
Niedermüller, Péter	Hungary	(+33) 3-88-17-54-68	peter.niedermueller@europarl.europa.eu	S&D
van Nieuwenhuizen, Cora	Netherlands	(+33) 3-88-17-52-21	cora.vannieuwenhuizen@europarl.europa.eu	ALDE
Nilsson, Jens	Sweden	(+33) 3-88-17-58-27	jens.nilsson@europarl.europa.eu	S&D
Ní Riada, Liadh	Ireland	(+33) 3-88-17-53-22	liadh.niriada@europarl.europa.eu	GUE/NGL
van Nistelrooij, Lambert	Netherlands	(+33) 3-88-17-54-34	lambert.vannistelrooij@europarl.europa.eu	EPP
Noichl, Maria	Germany	(+33) 3-88-17-51-57	maria.noichl@europarl.europa.eu	S&D
Novakov, Andrey	Bulgaria	(+33) 3-88-17-57-10	andrey.novakov@europarl.europa.eu	EPP
Nuttall, Paul	UK	(+33) 3-88-17-57-40	paul.nuttall@europarl.europa.eu	EFDD
Obermayr, Franz	Austria	(+33) 3-88-17-56-80	franz.obermayr@europarl.europa.eu	ENF
O'Flynn, Patrick	UK	(+33) 3-88-17-53-37	patrick.oflynn@europarl.europa.eu	EFDD
Olbrycht, Jan Marian	Poland	(+33) 3-88-17-55-11	jan.olbrycht@europarl.europa.eu	EPP
Omarjee, Younous	France	(+33) 3-88-17-56-43	younous.omarjee@europarl.europa.eu	GUE/NGL
Ożóg, Stanisław	Poland	(+33) 3-88-17-56-53	stanislaw.ozog@europarl.europa.eu	ECR
Pabriks, Artis	Latvia	(+33) 3-88-17-58-10	artis.pabriks@europarl.europa.eu	EPP
Paet, Urmas	Estonia	(+33) 3-88-17-59-30	urmas.paet@europarl.europa.eu	ALDE
Pagazaurtundua Ruiz, Maite	Spain	(+33) 3-88-17-57-30	maite.pagaza@europarl.europa.eu	ALDE
Paksas, Rolandas	Lithuania	(+33) 3-88-17-56-71	rolandas.paksas@europarl.europa.eu	EFDD
Panzeri, Pier Antonio	Italy	(+33) 3-88-17-53-49	pierantonio.panzeri@europarl.europa.eu	S&D
Paolucci, Massimo	Italy	(+33) 3-88-17-53-11	massimo.paolucci@europarl.europa.eu	S&D
Papadakis, Demetris	Cyprus	(+33) 3-88-17-56-04	demetris.papadakis@europarl.europa.eu	S&D
Papadakis, Konstantinos	Greece	(+33) 3-88-17-54-94	konstantinos.papadakis@europarl.europa.eu	NI
Papadimoulis, Dimitrios	Greece	(+33) 3-88-17-53-99	dimitrios.papadimoulis@europarl.europa.eu	GUE/NGL
Pargneaux, Gilles	France	(+33) 3-88-17-54-40	gilles.pargneaux@europarl.europa.eu	S&D
Parker, Margot	UK	(+33) 3-88-17-51-82	margot.parker@europarl.europa.eu	EFDD
Paşcu, Ioan Mircea	Romania	(+33) 3-88-17-58-13	ioanmircea.pascu@europarl.europa.eu	S&D
Patriciello, Aldo	Italy	(+33) 3-88-17-54-18	aldo.patriciello@europarl.europa.eu	EPP
Pavel, Emilian	Romania	(+33) 3-88-17-58-44	emilian.pavel@europarl.europa.eu	S&D
Pedicini, Piernicola	Italy	(+33) 3-88-17-53-82	piernicola.pedicini@europarl.europa.eu	EFDD
Peillon, Vincent	France	(+33) 3-88-17-59-28	vincent.peillon@europarl.europa.eu	S&D
Peterle, Alojz	Slovenia	(+33) 3-88-17-56-38	alojz.peterle@europarl.europa.eu	EPP
Petersen, Morten Helveg	Denmark	(+33) 3-88-17-56-83	mortenhelveg.petersen@europarl.europa.eu	ALDE
Petir, Marijana	Croatia	(+33) 3-88-17-54-29	marijana.petir@europarl.europa.eu	EPP
Philippot, Florian	France	(+33) 3-88-17-57-58	florian.philippot@europarl.europa.eu	ENF
Picierno, Giuseppina (Pina)	Italy	(+33) 3-88-17-52-29	giuseppina.picierno@europarl.europa.eu	S&D
Picula, Tonino	Croatia	(+33) 3-88-17-59-48	tonino.picula@europarl.europa.eu	S&D
Piecha, Bolesław Grzegorz	Poland	(+33) 3-88-17-53-66	boleslaw.piecha@europarl.europa.eu	ECR
Pieper, Markus	Germany	(+33) 3-88-17-53-05	markus.pieper@europarl.europa.eu	EPP
Pietikäinen, Sirpa	Finland	(+33) 3-88-17-52-64	sirpa.pietikainen@europarl.europa.eu	EPP
Pimenta Lopes, João	Portugal	(+33) 3-88-17-54-65	joao.pimentalopes@europarl.europa.eu	GUE/NGL
Piotrowski, Mirosław	Poland	(+33) 3-88-17-55-88	miroslaw.piotrowski@europarl.europa.eu	ECR
Piri, Kati	Netherlands	(+33) 3-88-17-51-38	kati.piri@europarl.europa.eu	S&D
Pirinski, Georgi	Bulgaria	(+33) 3-88-17-52-54	georgi.pirinski@europarl.europa.eu	S&D
Pitera, Julia	Poland	(+33) 3-88-17-53-86	julia.pitera@europarl.europa.eu	EPP
Pittella, Gianni	Italy	(+33) 3-88-17-51-59	gianni.pittella@europarl.europa.eu	S&D
Plura, Marek Mirosław	Poland	(+33) 3-88-17-57-12	marek.plura@europarl.europa.eu	EPP
Poc, Pavel	Czech Republic	(+33) 3-88-17-54-11	pavel.poc@europarl.europa.eu	S&D
Poche, Miroslav	Czech Republic	(+33) 3-88-17-53-28	miroslav.poche@europarl.europa.eu	S&D
Pogliese, Salvatore Domenico	Italy	(+33) 3-88-17-51-88	salvatoredomenico.pogliese@europarl.europa.eu	EPP

Name	Member State	Telephone	E-mail	Political Group
Polčák, Stanislav	Czech Republic	(+33) 3-88-17-54-85	stanislav.polcak@europarl.europa.eu	EPP
Ponga, Maurice	France	(+33) 3-88-17-52-56	maurice.ponga@europarl.europa.eu	EPP
Poręba, Tomasz Piotr	Poland	(+33) 3-88-17-58-66	tomasz.poreba@europarl.europa.eu	ECR
Pospíšil, Jiří	Czech Republic	(+33) 3-88-17-55-86	jiri.pospisil@europarl.europa.eu	EPP
Post, Soraya	Sweden	(+33) 3-88-17-55-84	soraya.post@europarl.europa.eu	S&D
Preda, Cristian Dan	Romania	(+33) 3-88-17-52-61	cristiandan.preda@europarl.europa.eu	EPP
Pretzell, Marcus	Germany	(+33) 3-88-17-57-72	marcus.pretzell@europarl.europa.eu	ENF
Preuss, Gabriele	Germany	(+33) 3-88-17-58-45	gabriele.preuss@europarl.europa.eu	S&D
Procter, John	UK	(+33) 3-88-17-53-21	john.procter@europarl.europa.eu	ECR
Proust, Franck	France	(+33) 3-88-17-58-41	franck.proust@europarl.europa.eu	EPP
Punset, Carolina	Spain	(+33) 3-88-17-57-84	carolina.punset@europarl.europa.eu	ALDE
Quisthoudt-Rowohl, Godelieve	Germany	(+33) 3-88-17-53-38	godelieve.quisthoudt-rowohl@europarl.europa.eu	EPP
Radev, Emil	Bulgaria	(+33) 3-88-17-51-89	emil.radev@europarl.europa.eu	EPP
Radoš, Jozo	Croatia	(+33) 3-88-17-55-87	jozo.rados@europarl.europa.eu	ALDE
Radtke, Dennis	Germany	(+33) 3-88-17-56-50	dennis.radtke@europarl.europa.eu	EPP
Rangel, Paulo	Portugal	(+33) 3-88-17-52-63	paulo.rangel@europarl.europa.eu	EPP
Rebega, Constantin-Laurenţiu	Romania	(+33) 3-88-17-54-69	laurentiu.rebega@europarl.europa.eu	ENF
Reda, Julia	Germany	(+33) 3-88-17-57-32	julia.reda@europarl.europa.eu	Greens/EFA
Reding, Viviane	Luxembourg	(+33) 3-88-17-54-60	viviane.reding@europarl.europa.eu	EPP
Regner, Evelyn	Austria	(+33) 3-88-17-54-76	evelyn.regner@europarl.europa.eu	S&D
Reid, Julia	UK	(+33) 3-88-17-57-41	julia.reid@europarl.europa.eu	EFDD
Reimon, Michel	Austria	(+33) 3-88-17-56-81	michel.reimon@europarl.europa.eu	Greens/EFA
Reintke, Terry	Germany	(+33) 3-88-17-57-60	terry.reintke@europarl.europa.eu	Greens/EFA
Revault d'Allonnes-Bonnefoy, Christine	France	(+33) 3-88-17-58-53	christine.revaultdallonnesbonnefoy@europarl.europa.eu	S&D
Ribeiro, Sofia	Portugal	(+33) 3-88-17-53-45	sofia.ribeiro@ep.europa.eu	EPP
Ries, Frédérique	Belgium	(+33) 3-88-17-55-49	frederique.ries@europarl.europa.eu	ALDE
Riquet, Dominique	France	(+33) 3-88-17-52-66	dominique.riquet@europarl.europa.eu	ALDE
Rivasi, Michèle	France	(+33) 3-88-17-53-97	michele.rivasi@europarl.europa.eu	Greens/EFA
Rochefort, Robert	France	(+33) 3-88-17-58-30	robert.rochefort@europarl.europa.eu	ALDE
Rodrigues, Liliana	Portugal	(+33) 3-88-17-57-59	liliana.rodrigues@europarl.europa.eu	S&D
Rodrígues, María João	Portugal	(+33) 3-88-17-58-63	mariajoao.rodrigues@europarl.europa.eu	S&D
Rodríguez-Piñero Fernández, Inmaculada	Spain	(+33) 3-88-17-54-67	inma.rodriguezpinero@europarl.europa.eu	S&D
Rodust, Ulrike	Germany	(+33) 3-88-17-55-02	ulrike.rodust@europarl.europa.eu	S&D
Rohde, Jens	Denmark	(+33) 3-88-17-55-69	jens.rohde@europarl.europa.eu	ALDE
Rolin, Claude	Belgium	(+33) 3-88-17-51-16	claude.rolin@europarl.europa.eu	EPP
Ropė, Bronis	Lithuania	(+33) 3-88-17-53-84	bronis.rope@europarl.europa.eu	Greens/EFA
Rosati, Dariusz	Poland	(+33) 3-88-17-54-82	dariusz.rosati@europarl.europa.eu	EPP
Rozière, Virginie	France	(+33) 3-88-17-54-08	virginie.roziere@europarl.europa.eu	S&D
Ruas, Fernando	Portugal	(+33) 3-88-17-52-62	fernando.ruas@europarl.europa.eu	EPP
Rübig, Paul	Austria	(+33) 3-88-17-57-49	paul.ruebig@europarl.europa.eu	EPP
Ruohonen-Lerner, Pirkko	Finland	(+33) 3-88-17-57-57	pirkko.ruohonen-lerner@europarl.europa.eu	ECR
Saïfi, Tokia	France	(+33) 3-88-17-55-62	tokia.saifi@europarl.europa.eu	EPP
Sakorafa, Sofia	Greece	(+33) 3-88-17-57-25	sofia.sakorafa@europarl.europa.eu	GUE/NGL
Salafranca Sánchez-Neyra, José Ignacio	Spain	(+33) 3-88-17-53-07	joseignacio.salafranca@europarl.europa.eu	EPP
Salini, Massimiliano	Italy	(+33) 3-88-17-55-04	massimiliano.salini@europarl.europa.eu	EPP
Sánchez Caldentey, Lola	Spain	(+33) 3-88-17-51-24	mariadoloreslola.sanchezcaldentey@europarl.europa.eu	GUE/NGL
Sander, Anne	France	(+33) 3-88-17-75-25	anne.sander@europarl.europa.eu	EPP
Sant, Alfred	Malta	(+33) 3-88-17-52-87	alfred.sant@europarl.europa.eu	S&D
Dos Santos, Manuel António	Portugal	(+33) 3-88-17-51-64	manuel.dossantos@europarl.europa.eu	S&D
Sârbu, Daciana Octavia	Romania	(+33) 3-88-17-58-05	dacianaoctavia.sarbu@europarl.europa.eu	S&D
Sargentini, Judith	Netherlands	(+33) 3-88-17-58-81	judith.sargentini@europarl.europa.eu	Greens/EFA
Sarvamaa, Petri	Finland	(+33) 3-88-17-56-47	petri.sarvamaa@europarl.europa.eu	EPP
Saryusz-Wolski, Jacek	Poland	(+33) 3-88-17-53-71	jacek.saryusz-wolski@europarl.europa.eu	NI
Sassoli, David-Maria	Italy	(+33) 3-88-17-55-30	david.sassoli@europarl.europa.eu	S&D
Saudargas, Algirdas	Lithuania	(+33) 3-88-17-52-72	algirdas.saudargas@europarl.europa.eu	EPP
Schaake, Marietje	Netherlands	(+33) 3-88-17-56-17	marietje.schaake@europarl.europa.eu	ALDE
Schaffhauser, Jean-Luc	France	(+33) 3-88-17-57-26	jean-luc.schaffhauser@europarl.europa.eu	ENF
Schaldemose, Christel	Denmark	(+33) 3-88-17-54-91	christel.schaldemose@europarl.europa.eu	S&D
Schlein, Elena Ethel	Italy	(+33) 3-88-17-57-62	elly.schlein@europarl.europa.eu	S&D
Schmidt, Claudia	Austria	(+33) 3-88-17-51-81	claudia.schmidt@europarl.europa.eu	EPP
Scholz, Helmut	Germany	(+33) 3-88-17-58-93	helmut.scholz@europarl.europa.eu	GUE/NGL

Name	Member State	Telephone	E-mail	Political Group
Schöpflin, György	Hungary	(+33) 3-88-17-58-84	gyorgy.schopflin@europarl.europa.eu	EPP
Schreijer-Pierik, Annie	Netherlands	(+33) 3-88-17-55-38	annie.schreijer-pierik@europarl.europa.eu	EPP
Schulze, Sven	Germany	(+33) 3-88-17-52-07	sven.schulze@europarl.europa.eu	EPP
Schuster, Joachim	Germany	(+33) 3-88-17-54-13	joachim.schuster@europarl.europa.eu	S&D
Schwab, Andreas	Germany	(+33) 3-88-17-59-38	andreas.schwab@europarl.europa.eu	EPP
Scott Cato, Molly	UK	(+33) 3-88-17-57-37	molly.scottcato@europarl.europa.eu	Greens/EFA
Sehnalová, Olga	Czech Republic	(+33) 3-88-17-54-17	olga.sehnalova@europarl.europa.eu	S&D
Selimović, Jasenko	Sweden	(+33) 3-88-17-56-21	jasenko.selimovic@europarl.europa.eu	ALDE
Senra Rodríguez, Maria Lidia	Spain	(+33) 3-88-17-54-14	lidia.senra@europarl.europa.eu	GUE/NGL
Sernagiotto, Remo	Italy	(+33) 3-88-17-52-69	remo.sernagiotto@europarl.europa.eu	ECR
Serrão Santos, Ricardo	Portugal	(+33) 3-88-17-56-55	ricardo.serraosantos@europarl.europa.eu	S&D
Seymour, Jill	UK	(+33) 3-88-17-58-03	jill.seymour@europarl.europa.eu	EFDD
Siekierski, Czesław Adam	Poland	(+33) 3-88-17-57-93	czeslaw.siekierski@europarl.europa.eu	EPP
Silva Pereira, Pedro	Portugal	(+33) 3-88-17-57-07	pedro.silvapereira@europarl.europa.eu	S&D
Simon, Peter	Germany	(+33) 3-88-17-55-58	peter.simon@europarl.europa.eu	S&D
Simon, Siôn	UK	(+33) 3-88-17-55-05	sion.simon@europarl.europa.eu	S&D
Sippel, Birgit	Germany	(+33) 3-88-17-55-59	birgit.sippel@europarl.europa.eu	S&D
Škripek, Branislav	Slovakia	(+33) 3-88-17-55-09	branislav.skripek@europarl.europa.eu	ECR
Škrlec, Davor	Croatia	(+33) 3-88-17-58-28	davor.skrlec@europarl.europa.eu	Greens/EFA
Smith, Alyn	UK	(+33) 3-88-17-51-87	alyn.smith@europarl.europa.eu	Greens/EFA
Smolková, Monika	Slovakia	(+33) 3-88-17-54-83	monika.smolkova@europarl.europa.eu	S&D
Sógor, Csaba	Romania	(+33) 3-88-17-53-89	csaba.sogor@europarl.europa.eu	EPP
Šojdrová, Michaela	Czech Republic	(+33) 3-88-17-55-65	michaela.sojdrova@europarl.europa.eu	EPP
Solé, Jordi	Spain	(+33) 3-88-17-56-06	jordi.sole@europarl.europa.eu	Greens/EFA
Šoltes, Igor	Slovenia	(+33) 3-88-17-58-18	igor.soltes@europarl.europa.eu	Greens/EFA
Sommer, Renate	Germany	(+33) 3-88-17-53-83	renate.sommer@europarl.europa.eu	EPP
Sonneborn, Martin	Germany	(+33) 3-88-17-57-56	martin.sonneborn@europarl.europa.eu	NI
Soru, Renato	Italy	(+33) 3-88-17-53-51	renato.soru@europarl.europa.eu	S&D
Spinelli, Barbara	Italy	(+33) 3-88-17-51-07	barbara.spinelli@europarl.europa.eu	GUE/NGL
Spyraki, Maria	Greece	(+33) 3-88-17-51-76	maria.spyraki@europarl.europa.eu	EPP
Staes, Bart	Belgium	(+33) 3-88-17-56-42	bart.staes@europarl.europa.eu	Greens/EFA
Stanishev, Sergei	Bulgaria	(+33) 3-88-17-56-54	sergey.stanishev@europarl.europa.eu	S&D
Starbatty, Joachim	Germany	(+33) 3-88-17-53-54	joachim.starbatty@europarl.europa.eu	ECR
Štefanec, Ivan	Slovakia	(+33) 3-88-17-56-76	ivan.stefanec@europarl.europa.eu	EPP
Steinruck, Jutta	Germany	(+33) 3-88-17-55-63	jutta.steinruck@europarl.europa.eu	S&D
Štětina, Jaromír	Czech Republic	(+33) 3-88-17-54-92	jaromir.stetina@europarl.europa.eu	EPP
Stevens, Helga	Belgium	(+33) 3-88-17-53-43	helga.stevens@europarl.europa.eu	ECR
Stihler, Catherine	UK	(+33) 3-88-17-54-62	catherine.stihler@europarl.europa.eu	S&D
Stolojan, Theodor Dumitru	Romania	(+33) 3-88-17-56-70	theodordumitru.stolojan@europarl.europa.eu	EPP
von Storch, Beatrix	Germany	(+33) 3-88-17-58-36	beatrix.vonstorch@europarl.europa.eu	EFDD
Stuger, Olaf	Netherlands	(+33) 3-88-17-53-14	olaf.stuger@europarl.europa.eu	ENF
Šuica, Dubravka	Croatia	(+33) 3-88-17-51-75	dubravka.suica@europarl.europa.eu	EPP
Sulík, Richard	Slovakia	(+33) 3-88-17-53-81	richard.sulik@europarl.europa.eu	ECR
Šulin, Patricija	Slovenia	(+33) 3-88-17-54-70	patricija.sulin@europarl.europa.eu	EPP
Svoboda, Pavel	Czech Republic	(+33) 3-88-17-53-03	pavel.svoboda@europarl.europa.eu	EPP
Swinburne, Kay	UK	(+33) 3-88-17-56-87	kay.swinburne@europarl.europa.eu	ECR
Sylikiotis, Neoklis	Cyprus	(+33) 3-88-17-57-54	neoklis.sylikiotis@europarl.europa.eu	GUE/NGL
Synadinos, Eleytherios	Greece	(+33) 3-88-17-55-15	eleytherios.synadinos@europarl.europa.eu	NI
Szájer, József	Hungary	(+33) 3-88-17-58-71	jozsef.szajer@europarl.europa.eu	EPP
Szanyi, Tibor	Hungary	(+33) 3-88-17-52-84	tibor.szanyi@europarl.europa.eu	S&D
Szejnfeld, Adam	Poland	(+33) 3-88-17-57-76	adam.szejnfeld@europarl.europa.eu	EPP
Tajani, Antonio	Italy	(+33) 3-88-17-57-50	antonio.tajani@europarl.europa.eu	EPP
Takkula, Hannu	Finland	(+33) 3-88-17-53-61	hannu.takkula@europarl.europa.eu	ALDE
Tamburrano, Dario	Italy	(+33) 3-88-17-55-24	dario.tamburrano@europarl.europa.eu	EFDD
Tănăsescu, Claudiu Ciprian	Romania	(+33) 3-88-17-57-90	claudiuciprian.tanasescu@europarl.europa.eu	S&D
Tang, Paul	Netherlands	(+33) 3-88-17-56-26	paul.tang@europarl.europa.eu	S&D
Tannock, Charles	UK	(+33) 3-88-17-58-70	charles.tannock@europarl.europa.eu	ECR
Tapardel, Ana-Claudia	Romania	(+33) 3-88-17-55-91	ana-claudia.tapardel@europarl.europa.eu	S&D
Tarabella, Marc	Belgium	(+33) 3-88-17-54-44	marc.tarabella@europarl.europa.eu	S&D
Tarand, Indrek	Estonia	(+33) 3-88-17-54-01	indrek.tarand@europarl.europa.eu	Greens/EFA
Taylor, Keith	UK	(+33) 3-88-17-51-53	keith.taylor@europarl.europa.eu	Greens/EFA
Telička, Pavel	Czech Republic	(+33) 3-88-17-57-87	pavel.telicka@europarl.europa.eu	ALDE
Terricabras, Josep-Maria	Spain	(+33) 3-88-17-57-48	josep-maria.terricabras@europarl.europa.eu	Greens/EFA

Name	Member State	Telephone	E-mail	Political Group
Theocharous, Eleni	Cyprus	(+33) 3-88-17-52-93	eleni.theocharous@europarl.europa.eu	ECR
Theurer, Michael	Germany	(+33) 3-88-17-55-72	michael.theurer@europarl.europa.eu	ALDE
Thomas, Isabelle	France	(+33) 3-88-17-54-32	isabelle.thomas@europarl.europa.eu	S&D
von Thun und Hohenstein, Róża Gräfin	Poland	(+33) 3-88-17-53-01	roza.thun@europarl.europa.eu	EPP
Toia, Patrizia	Italy	(+33) 3-88-17-51-27	patrizia.toia@europarl.europa.eu	S&D
Tőkés, László	Hungary	(+33) 3-88-17-58-01	laszlo.tokes@europarl.europa.eu	EPP
Tolić, Ivica	Croatia	(+33) 3-88-17-59-55	ivica.tolic@europarl.europa.eu	EPP
Tomaševski, Valdemar	Lithuania	(+33) 3-88-17-56-98	valdemar.tomasevski@europarl.europa.eu	ECR
Tomašić, Ruža	Croatia	(+33) 3-88-17-56-36	ruza.tomasic@europarl.europa.eu	ECR
Tomc, Romana	Slovenia	(+33) 3-88-17-56-65	romana.tomc@europarl.europa.eu	EPP
Toom, Yana	Estonia	(+33) 3-88-17-55-81	yana.toom@europarl.europa.eu	ALDE
Torres Martínez, Estefanía	Spain	(+33) 3-88-17-52-02	estefania.torresmartinez@europarl.europa.eu	GUE/NGL
Torvalds, Nils	Finland	(+33) 3-88-17-55-85	nils.torvalds@europarl.europa.eu	ALDE
Tošenovský, Evžen	Czech Republic	(+33) 3-88-17-57-17	evzen.tosenovsky@europarl.europa.eu	ECR
Trebesius, Ulrike	Germany	(+33) 3-88-17-54-98	ulrike.trebesius@europarl.europa.eu	ECR
Tremosa i Balcells, Ramon	Spain	(+33) 3-88-17-55-80	ramon.tremosa@europarl.europa.eu	ALDE
Troszczynski, Mylène	France	(+33) 3-88-17-55-89	mylene.troszczynski@europarl.europa.eu	ENF
Trüpel, Helga	Germany	(+33) 3-88-17-51-40	helga.truepel@europarl.europa.eu	Greens/EFA
Ţurcanu, Mihai	Romania	(+33) 3-88-17-58-65	mihai.turcanu@europarl.europa.eu	EPP
Turmes, Claude	Luxembourg	(+33) 3-88-17-52-46	claude.turmes@europarl.europa.eu	Greens/EFA
Ujazdowski, Kazimierz Michał	Poland	(+33) 3-88-17-52-47	kazimierzmichal.ujazdowski@europarl.europa.eu	ECR
Ujhelyi, István	Hungary	(+33) 3-88-17-56-49	istvan.ujhelyi@europarl.europa.eu	S&D
Ulvskog, Marita	Sweden	(+33) 3-88-17-54-43	marita.ulvskog@europarl.europa.eu	S&D
Ungureanu, Traian	Romania	(+33) 3-88-17-57-85	traian.ungureanu@europarl.europa.eu	EPP
Urbán Crespo, Miguel	Spain	(+33) 3-88-17-56-82	miguel.urbancrespo@europarl.europa.eu	GUE/NGL
Urtasun, Ernest	Spain	(+33) 3-88-17-57-98	ernest.urtasun@europarl.europa.eu	Greens/EFA
Urutchev, Vladimir	Bulgaria	(+33) 3-88-17-51-45	vladimir.urutchev@europarl.europa.eu	EPP
Uspaskich, Viktor	Lithuania	(+33) 3-88-17-53-39	viktor.uspaskich@europarl.europa.eu	ALDE
Vaidere, Inese	Latvia	(+33) 3-88-17-54-24	inese.vaidere@europarl.europa.eu	EPP
Vajgl, Ivo	Slovenia	(+33) 3-88-17-56-20	ivo.vajgl@europarl.europa.eu	ALDE
Valcárcel, Ramón Luís	Spain	(+33) 3-88-17-58-15	ramonluis.valcarcel@europarl.europa.eu	EPP
Vălean, Adina-Ioana	Romania	(+33) 3-88-17-58-61	adinaioana.valean@europarl.europa.eu	EPP
Valenciano, Elena	Spain	(+33) 3-88-17-58-46	elena.valenciano@europarl.europa.eu	S&D
Valero, Bodil	Sweden	(+33) 3-88-17-57-68	bodil.valero@europarl.europa.eu	Greens/EFA
Valli, Marco	Italy	(+33) 3-88-17-53-96	marco.valli@europarl.europa.eu	EFDD
Vallina, Ángela	Spain	(+33) 3-88-17-56-92	angela.vallina@europarl.europa.eu	GUE/NGL
Vana, Monika	Austria	(+33) 3-88-17-57-03	monika.vana@europarl.europa.eu	Greens/EFA
Van Bossuyt, Anneleen	Belgium	(+33) 3-88-17-51-08	anneleen.vanbossuyt@europarl.europa.eu	ECR
Van Brempt, Kathleen	Belgium	(+33) 3-88-17-54-47	kathleen.vanbrempt@europarl.europa.eu	S&D
Vandenkendelaere, Tom	Belgium	(+33) 3-88-17-59-18	tom.vandenkendelaere@europarl.europa.eu	EPP
Van Orden, Geoffrey	UK	(+33) 3-88-17-53-32	geoffrey.vanorden@europarl.europa.eu	ECR
Vaughan, Derek	UK	(+33) 3-88-17-54-19	derek.vaughan@europarl.europa.eu	S&D
Vautmans, Hilde	Belgium	(+33) 3-88-17-56-61	hilde.vautmans@europarl.europa.eu	ALDE
Väyrynen, Paavo	Finland	(+33) 3-88-17-51-33	paavo.vayrynen@europarl.europa.eu	ALDE
Vergiat, Marie-Christine	France	(+33) 3-88-17-58-31	marie-christine.vergiat@europarl.europa.eu	GUE/NGL
Verheyen, Sabine	Germany	(+33) 3-88-17-52-99	sabine.verheyen@europarl.europa.eu	EPP
Verhofstadt, Guy	Belgium	(+33) 3-88-17-55-66	guy.verhofstadt@europarl.europa.eu	ALDE
Viegas, Miguel	Portugal	(+33) 3-88-17-53-44	miguel.viegas@europarl.europa.eu	GUE/NGL
Vieu, Marie-Pierre	France	(+33) 3-88-17-56-59	marie-pierre.vieu@europarl.europa.eu	GUE/NGL
Vilimsky, Harald	Austria	(+33) 3-88-17-53-24	harald.vilimsky@europarl.europa.eu	ENF
Viotti, Daniele	Italy	(+33) 3-88-17-56-52	daniele.viotti@europarl.europa.eu	S&D
Virkkunen, Henna	Finland	(+33) 3-88-17-52-26	henna.virkkunen@europarl.europa.eu	EPP
Vistisen, Anders Primdahl	Denmark	(+33) 3-88-17-58-59	anders.vistisen@europarl.europa.eu	ECR
Voigt, Udo	Germany	(+33) 3-88-17-51-22	udo.voigt@europarl.europa.eu	NI
Voss, Axel	Germany	(+33) 3-88-17-53-02	axel.voss@europarl.europa.eu	EPP
Vozemberg, Elissavet	Greece	(+33) 3-88-17-52-32	elissavet.vozemberg@europarl.europa.eu	EPP
Wałęsa, Jarosław Leszek	Poland	(+33) 3-88-17-53-04	jaroslaw.walesa@europarl.europa.eu	EPP
Ward, Julie	UK	(+33) 3-88-17-57-02	julie.ward@europarl.europa.eu	S&D
Weber, Manfred	Germany	(+33) 3-88-17-58-90	manfred.weber@europarl.europa.eu	EPP
Weber, Renate	Romania	(+33) 3-88-17-58-49	renate.weber@europarl.europa.eu	ALDE
Weidenholzer, Josef	Austria	(+33) 3-88-17-54-73	josef.weidenholzer@europarl.europa.eu	S&D
von Weizsäcker, Jakob	Germany	(+33) 3-88-17-52-67	jakob.vonweizsaecker@europarl.europa.eu	S&D
Wenta, Bogdan Brunon	Poland	(+33) 3-88-17-51-90	bogdan.wenta@europarl.europa.eu	EPP
Werner, Martina	Germany	(+33) 3-88-17-57-82	martina.werner@europarl.europa.eu	S&D

Name	Member State	Telephone	E-mail	Political Group
Westphal, Kerstin	Germany	(+33) 3-88-17-55-34	kerstin.westphal@europarl.europa.eu	S&D
Wieland, Rainer	Germany	(+33) 3-88-17-55-45	rainer.wieland@europarl.europa.eu	EPP
Weirinck, Lieve	Belgium	(+33) 3-88-17-51-11	lieve.wierinck@europarl.europa.eu	ALDE
Wikström, Cecilia	Sweden	(+33) 3-88-17-56-22	cecilia.wikstrom@europarl.europa.eu	ALDE
Willmott, Dame Glenis	UK	(+33) 3-88-17-54-59	glenis.willmott@europarl.europa.eu	S&D
Winberg, Kristina	Sweden	(+33) 3-88-17-51-72	kristina.winberg@europarl.europa.eu	EFDD
Winkler, Hermann	Germany	(+33) 3-88-17-53-06	hermann.winkler@europarl.europa.eu	EPP
Winkler, Iuliu	Romania	(+33) 3-88-17-54-06	iuliu.winkler@europarl.europa.eu	EPP
Wiśniewska, Jadwiga	Poland	(+33) 3-88-17-54-71	jadwiga.wisniewska@europarl.europa.eu	ECR
Wölken, Tiemo	Germany	(+33) 3-88-17-54-31	tiemo.woelken@europarl.europa.eu	S&D
Woolfe, Steven	UK	(+33) 3-88-17-51-15	steven.woolfe@europarl.europa.eu	NI
Záborská, Anna	Slovakia	(+33) 3-88-17-59-23	anna.zaborska@europarl.europa.eu	EPP
Zagorakis, Theodoros	Greece	(+33) 3-88-17-54-61	theodoros.zagorakis@europarl.europa.eu	EPP
Zahradil, Jan	Czech Republic	(+33) 3-88-17-56-66	jan.zahradil@europarl.europa.eu	ECR
Zala, Boris	Slovakia	(+33) 3-88-17-54-80	boris.zala@europarl.europa.eu	S&D
Zammit Dimech, Francis	Malta	(+33) 3-88-17-58-35	francis.zammitdimech@europarl.europa.eu	EPP
Zanni, Marco	Italy	(+33) 3-88-17-55-97	marco.zanni@europarl.europa.eu	ENF
Zanonato, Flavio	Italy	(+33) 3-88-17-53-63	flavio.zanonato@europarl.europa.eu	S&D
Zarianopoulos, Sotirios	Greece	(+33) 3-88-17-51-12	sotirios.zarianopoulos@europarl.europa.eu	NI
Ždanoka, Tatjana	Latvia	(+33) 3-88-17-59-12	tatjana.zdanoka@europarl.europa.eu	Greens/EFA
Zdechovský, Tomáš	Czech Republic	(+33) 3-88-17-57-80	tomas.zdechovsky@europarl.europa.eu	EPP
Zdrojewski, Bogdan Andrzej	Poland	(+33) 3-88-17-52-51	bogdan.zdrojewski@europarl.europa.eu	EPP
Zeller, Joachim	Germany	(+33) 3-88-17-59-10	joachim.zeller@europarl.europa.eu	EPP
Zemke, Janusz Władysław	Poland	(+33) 3-88-17-54-26	janusz.zemke@europarl.europa.eu	S&D
Zijlstra, Auke	Netherlands	(+33) 3-88-17-59-22	auke.zijlstra@europarl.europa.eu	ENF
Zīle, Roberts	Latvia	(+33) 3-88-17-52-24	roberts.zile@europarl.europa.eu	ECR
Zimmer, Gabriele	Germany	(+33) 3-88-17-51-01	gabriele.zimmer@europarl.europa.eu	GUE/NGL
Žitňanská, Jana	Slovakia	(+33) 3-88-17-53-64	jana.zitnanska@europarl.europa.eu	ECR
Złotowski, Kosma Tadeusz	Poland	(+33) 3-88-17-57-75	kosma.zlotowski@europarl.europa.eu	ECR
Zoffoli, Damiano	Italy	(+33) 3-88-17-53-53	damiano.zoffoli@europarl.europa.eu	S&D
Żółtek, Stanisław Józef	Poland	(+33) 3-88-17-56-03	stanislawjozef.zoltek@europarl.europa.eu	ENF
Zorrinho, Carlos	Portugal	(+33) 3-88-17-52-60	carlos.zorrinho@europarl.europa.eu	S&D
Zovko, Željana	Croatia	(+33) 3-88-17-55-79	zeljana.zovko@europarl.europa.eu	EPP
Zullo, Marco	Italy	(+33) 3-88-17-53-48	marco.zullo@europarl.europa.eu	EFDD
Zver, Milan	Slovenia	(+33) 3-88-17-53-15	milan.zver@europarl.europa.eu	EPP
Zwiefka, Tadeusz	Poland	(+33) 3-88-17-52-58	tadeusz.zwiefka@europarl.europa.eu	EPP

TRANSNATIONAL PARTY GROUPS—ACRONYMS

ALDE	Group of the Alliance of Liberals and Democrats for Europe
ECR	European Conservatives and Reformists Group
EFDD	Europe of Freedom and Direct Democracy Group
ENF	Europe of Nations and Freedom Group
EPP	Group of the European People's Party
Greens/EFA	Group of the Greens/European Free Alliance
GUE/NGL	Confederal Group of the European United Left/Nordic Green Left
NI	Non-attached members
S&D	Group of the Progressive Alliance of Socialists and Democrats

Committees and Delegations

STANDING COMMITTEES

AFCO—Committee on Constitutional Affairs

Chair.: Danuta Maria Hübner.
Vice-Chair.: Morten Messerschmidt, Pedro Silva Pereira, Barbara Spinelli, Markus Pieper.

AFET—Committee on Foreign Affairs

Chair.: David McAllister.
Vice-Chair.: Javier Couso Permuy, Andi Cristea, Dubravka Šuica, Anders Primdahl Vistisen.

DROI—Sub-Committee on Human Rights

Chair.: Pier Antonio Panzeri.
Vice-Chair.: Barbara Lochbihler, Cristian Dan Preda, László Tökés, Beatriz Becerra Basterrechea.

SEDE—Sub-Committee on Regional Development

Chair.: Anna Elżbieta Fotyga.
Vice-Chair.: Christian Ehler, Clare Moody, Sabine Lösing, Jaromír Štětina.

AGRI—Committee for Agriculture and Rural Development

Chair.: Czesław Adam Siekierski.
Vice-Chair.: Clara Eugenia Aguilera García, Paolo de Castro, Viorica Dăncilă, Zbigniew Kuzmiuk.

BUDG—Committee on Budgets

Chair.: Jean Arthius.

Vice-Chair.: Jens Geier, Monika Hohlmeier, Siegfried Mureşan, Petri Sarvamaa.

CONT—Committee on Budgetary Control

Chair.: Ingeborg Grässle.
Vice-Chair.: Martina Dlabajová, Cătălin Sorin Ivan, Indrek Tarand, Derek Vaughan.

CULT—Committee on Culture and Education

Chair.: Petra Kammerevert.
Vice-Chair.: Andrea Bocskor, Mircea Diaconu, Stefano Maullu, Helga Trüpel.

DEVE—Committee on Development

Chair.: Linda McAvan.
Vice-Chair.: Stelios Kouloglou, Nirj Deva, Maurica Ponga, Paavo Väyrynen.

ECON—Committee on Economic and Monetary Affairs

Chair.: Roberto Gualtieri.
Vice-Chair.: Markus Ferber, Luděk Niedermayer, Peter Simon, Kay Swinburne.

EMPL—Committee on Employment and Social Affairs

Chair.: Thomas Händel.
Vice-Chair.: Renate Weber, Agnes Jongerius, Claude Rolin, Marita Ulvskog.

ENVI—Committee on the Environment, Public Health and Food Safety

Chair.: Adina-Ioana Vălean.
Vice-Chair.: Benedek Jávor, Gilles Pargneaux, Pavel Poc, Daciana Octavia Sârbu.

FEMM—Committee on Women's Rights and Gender Equality

Chair.: Vilija Blinkevičiūtė.
Vice-Chair.: Mary Honeyball, Barbara Matera, Jana Žitňanská, João Pimenta Lopes.

IMCO—Committee on the Internal Market and Consumer Protection

Chair.: Dita Charanzová.
Vice-Chair.: Anna Maria Corazza Bildt, Nicola Danti, Catherine Stihler.

INTA—Committee on International Trade

Chair.: Bernd Lange.
Vice-Chair.: Yannick Jadot, Tokia Saïfi, Iuliu Winkler, Jan Zahradil.

ITRE—Committee on Industry, Research and Energy

Chair.: Jerzy Buzek.
Vice-Chair.: Hans-Olaf Henkel, Morten Helveg Petersen, Jaromír Kohlícek, Patrizia Toia.

JURI—Committee on Legal Affairs

Chair.: Pavel Svoboda.
Vice-Chair.: Jean-Marie Cavada, Mady Delvaux, Lidia Joanna Geringer de Oedenberg, Laura Ferrara.

LIBE—Committee on Civil Liberties, Justice and Home Affairs

Chair.: Claude Moraes.
Vice-Chair.: Jan Philipp Albrecht, Kinga Gál, Sergei Stanishev, Barbara Kudrycka.

PECH—Committee on Fisheries

Chair.: Alain Cadec.
Vice-Chair.: Renata Briano, Linnéa Engström, Werner Kuhn, Jarosław Wałęsa.

PETI—Committee on Petitions

Chair.: Cecilia Wikström.
Vice-Chair.: Pál Csáky, Rosa Esteràs Ferragut, Roberta Metsola, Marlene Mizzi.

REGI—Committee on Regional Development

Chair.: Iskra Mihaylova.
Vice-Chair.: Pascal Arimont, Andrea Cozzolino, Younous Omarjee, Joachim Zeller.

TRAN—Committee on Transport and Tourism

Chair.: Karima Delli.
Vice-Chair.: Dieter-Lebrecht Koch, Tomasz Piotr Poręba, Dominique Riquet, István Ujhelyi.

DELEGATIONS

Delegation for Relations with South Africa

Chair.: Johannes Cornelis van Baalen.
Vice-Chair.: Boris Zala, Sabine Verheyen.

Delegation to the EU-former Yugoslav republic of Macedonia Joint Parliamentary Committee

Chair.: Alojz Peterle.
Vice-Chair.: Angel Dzhambazki, Sergei Stanishev.

Delegation to the EU-Turkey Joint Parliamentary Committee

Chair.: Manolis Kefalogiannis.
Vice-Chair.: Takis Hadjigeorgiou, Miltiadis Kyrkos.

Delegation to the EU-Mexico Joint Parliamentary Committee

Chair.: Teresa Jiménez-Becerril Barrio.
Vice-Chair.: José Blanco López, Pina Picierno.

Delegation to the EU-Chile Joint Parliamentary Committee

Chair.: Constanze Krehl.
Vice-Chair.: Eleonora Forenza, Renate Weber.

Delegation to the Cariforum-EU Parliamentary Committee

Chair.: Bolesław G. Piecha.
Vice-Chair.: Maurica Ponga, Anna Záborská.

Delegation to the ACP-EU Joint Parliamentary Assembly

Chair.: Louis Michel.
Vice-Chair.: Michèle Rivasi, João Ferreira, Cécile Kashetu Kyenge, Renaud Muselier, Daniel Hannan, Louis-Joseph Manscour, Piernicola Pedicini, Edward Czesak, Paulo Rangel, Javier Nart, Juan Fernando López Aguilar, Jadwiga Wiśniewska.

Delegation to the EU-Serbia Stabilization and Association Parliamentary Committee

Chair.: Eduard Kukan.
Vice-Chair.: Igor Šoltes, Paul Tang.

Delegation to the EU-Albania Stabilization and Association Parliamentary Committee

Chair.: Monica Macovei.
Vice-Chair.: Ivan Jakovčić, Elly Schlein.

Delegation to the EU-Montenegro Stabilization and Association Parliamentary Committee

Chair.: David Martin.
Vice-Chair.: Peter Kouroumbashev, Mairead McGuinness.

Delegation for Relations with Switzerland and Norway and to the EU-Iceland Joint Parliamentary Committee and the European Economic Area (EEA) Joint Parliamentary Committee
Chair.: Jørn Dohrmann.
Vice-Chair.: Anna Hedh, Jasenko Selimović.

Delegation for Relations with Bosnia and Herzegovina, and Kosovo
Chair.: Tonino Picula.
Vice-Chair.: Ulrike Lunacek, Dubravka Šuica.

Delegation to the EU-Russia Parliamentary Co-operation Committee
Chair.: Othmar Karas.
Vice-Chair.: Liisa Jaakonsaari, Jiří Maštálka.

Delegation to the EU-Ukraine Parliamentary Association Committee
Chair.: Dariusz Rosati.
Vice-Chair.: Kaja Kallas, Tibor Szanyi.

Delegation to the EU-Moldova Parliamentary Association Committee
Chair.: Andi Cristea.
Vice-Chair.: Michał Boni, Sławomir Kłosowski.

Delegation for Relations with Belarus
Chair.: Bogdan Andrzej Zdrojewski.
Vice-Chair.: Andrejs Mamikins, Valdemar Tomaševski.

Delegation to the EU-Armenia and EU-Azerbaijan Parliamentary Co-operation Committees and the EU-Georgia Parliamentary Association Committee
Chair.: Sajjad Karim.
Vice-Chair.: Antanas Guoga, Elisabeth Köstinger.

Delegation for Relations with Israel
Chair.: Fulvio Martusciello.
Vice-Chair.: Bas Belder, Olga Sehnalová.

Delegation for Relations with Palestine
Chair.: Neoklis Sylikiotis.
Vice-Chair.: Margrete Auken, Marita Ulvskog.

Delegation for Relations with the Maghreb Countries and the Arab Maghreb Union
Chair.: Inés Ayala Sender.
Vice-Chair.: María Teresa Gimenez Barbat, Tokia Saïfi.

Delegation for Relations with the Mashreq Countries
Chair.: Marisa Matias.
Vice-Chair.: Ramona Nicole Mănescu, Gilles Pargneaux.

Delegation for Relations with the Pan-African Parliament
Chair.: Michael Gahler.
Vice-Chair.: Fredrick Federley, Maria Heubuch.

Delegation for Relations with the Arab Peninsula
Chair.: Michèle Alliot-Marie.
Vice-Chair.: Salvatore Cicu, Alessia Maria Mosca.

Delegation for Relations with Iraq
Chair.: David Campbell Bannerman.
Vice-Chair.: Javier Couso Permuy, Brian Hayes.

Delegation for Relations with Iran
Chair.: Janusz Lewandowski.
Vice-Chair.: Cornelia Ernst, Damiano Zoffoli.

Delegation for Relations with the USA
Chair.: Christian Ehler.
Vice-Chair.: Jeppe Kofod, Marietje Schaake.

Delegation for Relations with Canada
Chair.: Bernd Kölmel.
Vice-Chair.: Godelieve Quisthoudt-Rowohl, Paul Brannen.

Delegation for Relations with Brazil
Chair.: Fernando Ruas.
Vice-Chair.: António Marinho e Pinto, Carlos Zorrinho.

Delegation for Relations with the countries of Central America
Chair.: Sofia Sakorafa.
Vice-Chair.: Caterina Chinnici, Gabriel Mato.

Delegation for Relations with the countries of the Andean Community
Chair.: Luis de Grandes Pascual.
Vice-Chair.: Izaskun Bilbao Barandica, Tania González Peñas.

Delegation for Relations with Mercosur
Chair.: Francisco Assis.
Vice-Chair.: Elisabetta Gardini, Xabier Benito Ziluaga.

Delegation for Relations with Japan
Chair.: Petr Ježek.
Vice-Chair.: Karin Kadenbach, Romana Tomc.

Delegation for Relations with the People's Republic of China
Chair.: Jo Leinen.
Vice-Chair.: Reinhard Bütikofer, Frank Engel.

Delegation for Relations with India
Chair.: Geoffrey Van Orden.
Vice-Chair.: Neena Gill, Cora Van Nieuwenhuizen.

Delegations to the EU-Kazakhstan, EU-Kyrgyzstan, EU-Uzbekistan and EU-Tajikistan Parliamentary Co-operation Committees and for Relations with Turkmenistan and Mongolia
Chair.: Iveta Grigule.
Vice-Chair.: Laima Liucija Andrikienė, Tatjana Ždanoka.

Delegation for Relations with Afghanistan
Chair.: Petras Auštrevičius.
Vice-Chair.: Lars Adaktusson, Eva Joly.

Delegation for Relations with the countries of South Asia
Chair.: Jean Lambert.
Vice-Chair.: Richard Corbett, James Nicholson.

Delegation for Relations with the countries of Southeast Asia and the Association of Southeast Asian Nations (ASEAN)
Chair.: Werner Langen.
Vice-Chair.: Jeroen Lenaers, Marc Tarabella.

Delegation for Relations with Australia and New Zealand
Chair.: Michael Theurer.
Vice-Chair.: Axel Voss, Jacqueline Foster.

European Parliament DIRECTORY

Delegation for Relations with the Korean Peninsula

Chair.: Nirj Deva.
Vice-Chair.: Nedzhmi Ali, Paul Rübig.

Delegation to the Parliamentary Assembly of the Union for the Mediterranean

Chair.: Antonio Tajani.

Delegation to the Euronest Parliamentary Assembly

Chair.: Rebecca Harms.
Vice-Chair.: Zigmantas Balčytis, Ryszard Czarnecki, Andrea Bocskor, Rolandas Paksas.

Delegation to the Euro-Latin American Parliamentary Assembly

Chair.: Ramón Jáuregui Atondo.
Vice-Chair.: Tomasz Piotr Poręba, Ernest Urtasun, Miroslav Mikolášik, João Pimenta Lopes, Gérard Deprez, Agustín Díaz de Mera García Consuegra, Karoline Graswander-Hainz.

Delegation for Relations with the NATO Parliamentary Assembly

Chair.: Eva Kaili.
Vice-Chair.: Arnaud Danjean, Georgios Kyrtsos.

Political Groups' Secretariats

GROUP OF THE ALLIANCE OF LIBERALS AND DEMOCRATS FOR EUROPE (ALDE)

Brussels office: tel. (+32) 2-2842111; fax (+32) 2-2302485

Chair.: Guy Verhofstadt.

Secretary-General: Alexander Beels; tel. (+32) 2-2842561; e-mail alexander.beels@europarl.europa.eu.

Deputy Secretary-General: François Pauli; tel. (+32) 2-2841415; e-mail francois.pauli@europarl.europa.eu.

Deputy Secretary-General: Marieta Colera; tel. (+32) 2-2842089; e-mail marieta.colera@europarl.europa.eu.

EUROPEAN CONSERVATIVES AND REFORMISTS GROUP (ECR)

Brussels office: tel. (+32) 2-2845792

Chair.: Syed Kamall.

Secretary-General: Frank Barrett; tel. (+32) 2-2842971; e-mail frank.barrett@europarl.europa.eu.

Assistant to the Secretary-General: Alessia Piccarolo; tel. (+32) 2-2844581; e-mail alessia.piccarolo@europarl.europa.eu.

EUROPE OF FREEDOM AND DIRECT DEMOCRACY GROUP

Brussels office: tel. (+32) 2-2845855; fax (+32) 2-2849855

Chair.: Nigel Farage.

Secretary-General: Aurelie Laloux; tel. (+32) 2-2846388; e-mail aurelie.laloux@europarl.europa.eu.

Deputy Secretary-General: Tobias Teuscher; tel. (+32) 2-2843259; e-mail tobias.teuscher@europarl.europa.eu.

Deputy Secretary-General: Dovile Rucyte; tel. (+32) 2- 2842186; e-mail dovile.rucyte@europarl.europa.eu.

EUROPE OF NATIONS AND FREEDOM (ENF)

Brussels office: tel. (+32) 2-2832053

Co-Chair.: Nicolas Bay.
Co-Chair.: Marcel de Graaff.

GROUP OF THE EUROPEAN PEOPLE'S PARTY (CHRISTIAN DEMOCRATS) (EPP)

Brussels office: tel. (+32) 2-2842111; tel. (+32) 2-2844001 (Parliamentary work); tel. (+32) 2-2844144 (Press); fax (+33) 8-8176954 (Parliamentary work); fax (+33) 8-8176926 (Press)

Chair.: Manfred Weber.

Secretary-General: Martin Kamp; tel. (+32) 2-2843265; e-mail martin.kamp@europarl.europa.eu.

GROUP OF THE GREENS/EUROPEAN FREE ALLIANCE (GREENS/EFA)

Brussels office: tel. (+32) 2-2843045; fax (+32) 2-2307837

Co-Chair.: Ska Keller.
Co-Chair.: Philippe Lamberts.

Secretary-General: Paraskevi Tsetsi; tel. (+32) 2-2842117; e-mail paraskevi.tsetsi@ep.europa.eu.

Deputy Secretary-General: Aurélie Brochard; tel. (+32) 2-2842557; e-mail aurelie.brochard@europarl.europa.eu.

CONFEDERAL GROUP OF THE EUROPEAN UNITED LEFT—NORDIC GREEN LEFT (GUE/NGL)

Brussels office: tel. (+32) 2-2842683; fax (+32) 2-2841774

Chair.: Gabriele Zimmer.

Secretary-General: Maria D'Alimonte.

Deputy Secretary-General: Sannaleena Lepola-Honig; tel. (+32) 2-2842570; e-mail sanna.lepola@europarl.europa.eu.

Deputy Secretary-General: Soultana Pantazidou; tel. (+32) 2-2843316; e-mail soultana.pantazidou@europarl.europa.eu.

GROUP OF THE PROGRESSIVE ALLIANCE OF SOCIALISTS AND DEMOCRATS IN THE EUROPEAN PARLIAMENT (S&D)

Brussels office: tel. (+32) 2-2842309

Chair.: Gianni Pittella.

Secretary-General: Javier Moreno Sanchez; tel. (+32) 2-2841156; e-mail javier.morenosanchez@europarl.europa.eu.

NON-ATTACHED MEMBERS (NI)

Secretary-General: Emmanuel Bordez; tel. (+32) 2-2846385; e-mail emmanuel.bordez@europarl.europa.eu.

National Parties and Lists Represented in the European Parliament

(Parties obtaining seats in the 2014 elections to the European Parliament—EP)

AUSTRIA

Freiheitliche Partei Österreichs (FPÖ/Die Freiheitlichen) (Freedom Party of Austria): Friedrich Schmidt-Pl. 4/3A, 1080 Vienna; tel. (+43 1) 51235350; fax (+43 1) 51235359; e-mail bgst@fpoe.at; internet www.fpoe.at; f. 1955; populist, Eurosceptic right-wing party, advocating the participation of workers in management, stricter immigration controls and deregulation in the business sector; won four seats in the EP elections in 2014; Chair. Heinz-Christian Strache.

Grünen, Die—Grüne Alternativa (Greens): Rooseveltplatz 4–5/Top 5, 1090 Vienna; tel. (+43 1) 23639980; fax (+43 1) 5269110; e-mail bundesbuero@gruene.at; internet www.gruene.at; f. 1986; campaigns for environmental protection, peace and social justice; won three seats in the EP elections in 2014; Chair. Ingrid Felipe.

Neue Österreich und Liberales Forum, Das (NEOS) (The New Austria): Neustiftgasse 73–75/7, 1070 Vienna; e-mail kontakt@neos.eu; internet ichtuwas.neos.eu; f. 2012 as Das Neue Österreich; renamed as present in 2014; won one seat in the EP elections in 2014; Chair. Matthias Strolz.

Österreichische Volkspartei (ÖVP) (Austrian People's Party): Lichtenfelsgasse 7, 1010 Vienna; tel. (+43 1) 51543-200; fax (+43 1) 51543-200; e-mail info@wien.oevp.at; internet oevp-wien.at; f. 1945; Christian-Democratic party; advocates an ecologically orientated social market economy; won five seats in the EP elections in 2014; Chair. Gernot Blümel.

Sozialdemokratische Partei Österreichs (SPÖ) (Social Democratic Party of Austria): Löwelstr. 18, 1014 Vienna; tel. (+43 1) 0810-810-211; e-mail direkt@spoe.at; internet www.spoe.at; f. 1889; f. as the Social-Democratic Party, subsequently renamed the Socialist Party, reverted to its original name in June 1991; advocates democratic socialism and Austria's permanent neutrality; won five seats in the EP elections in 2014; Chair. Christian Kern.

BELGIUM

Centre Démocrate Humaniste (CDH) (Humanist Democratic Centre): 41 rue des Deux Eglises, 1000 Brussels; tel. (+32) 2-2380111; fax (+32) 2-2380129; e-mail info@lecdh.be; internet www.lecdh.be; f. 1945; f. as the Parti Social Chrétien/Christelijke Volkspartij (PSC/CVP); PSC separated from CVP by 1972, name changed as above in May 2002; secured one seat in the 2014 EP elections; Pres. Benoît Lutgen.

Christen-Democratisch en Vlaams Partij (CD&V) (Christian Democratic and Flemish Party): Wetstraat 89, 1040 Brussels; tel. (+32) 2-2383811; fax (+32) 2-2304360; e-mail info@cdenv.be; internet www.cdenv.be; f. 1945; fmrly known as Christelijke Volkspartij; Christian Social Party's Dutch-speaking wing; secured two seats in the EP elections of 2014; Chair. Wouter Beke.

Christlich Soziale Partei (CSP) (Christian Social Party): Platz des Parlaments 1, 4700 Eupen; tel. (+32) 87-318447; fax (+32) 87-318448; e-mail info@csp.pdg.be; internet www.csp-dg.be; f. 1972; Christian democratic party operating in German-speaking areas of Belgium; secured one seat in the EP elections of 2014; Pres. Luc Frank.

Ecologistes Confédérés pour l'Organisation de Luttes Originales (ECOLO) (Ecologist Party): 52 ave Marlagne, 5000 Namur; tel. (+32) 81-227871; fax (+32) 81-230603; e-mail info@ecolo.be; internet www.ecolo.be; f. 1980; ecologist party; French-speaking; secured one seat in the elections to the EP in 2014; Joint Pres. Zakia Khattabi; Joint Pres. Patrick Dupriez.

Groen (Greens): Sergeant De Bruynestraat 78–82, 1070 Anderlecht; tel. (+32) 2-2191919; e-mail info@groen.be; internet www.groen.be; f. 1982; fmrly known as Anders Gaan Leven (Agalev), name changed 2003; secured one seat in the EP elections of 2014; Chair. Meyrem Almaci.

Mouvement Réformateur (MR) (Reform Movement): 84-86 ave de la Toison, 1060 Brussels; tel. (+32) 2-5003511; fax (+32) 2-5003500; e-mail contact@mr.be; internet www.mr.be; f. 2002; formed through alliance of the Partei für Freiheit und Fortschritt (PFF), Front Démocratique des Francophones (FDF), Mouvement des Citoyens pour le Changement (MCC) and Parti Réformateur Libéral (PRL); secured three seats in the 2014 EP elections; Pres. Olivier Chastel.

Nieuw-Vlaamse Alliantie (N-VA) (New Flemish Alliance): Koningsstraat 47 bus 6, 1000 Brussels; tel. (+32) 2-2194930; e-mail info@n-va.be; internet www.n-va.be; f. 2001 as breakaway group; Flemish nationalist party advocating a federal structure for Belgium and a European federation of nations and regions; secured four seats in the EP elections in 2014; Chair. Bart De Wever; Gen. Sec. Louis Ide.

Open Vlaamse Liberalen en Demokraten (Open VLD) (Flemish Liberals and Democrats): Melsensstraat 34, 1000 Brussels; tel. (+32) 2-5490020; fax (+32) 2-5126025; e-mail contact@openvld.be; internet www.openvld.be; f. 1961; Liberal Party's Flemish-speaking wing; describes its stance as broad-minded, liberal democrat; secured three seats in the 2014 EP elections; Chair. Gwendolyn Rutten.

Parti Socialiste (PS) (Socialist Party): Maison du PS, Blvd de l'Empereur 13, 1000 Brussels; tel. (+32) 2-5483211; fax (+32) 2-5483380; e-mail info@ps.be; internet www.ps.be; f. 1885 as Parti Ouvrier Belge; Socialist Party's French-speaking wing; secured three seats in the 2014 EP elections; Pres. Elio Di Rupo; Sec.-Gen. Jacques Braggaar.

SP.A—Socialistische Partij Anders (SP.A) (Socialist Party—Different): Grasmarkt 105/37, 1000 Brussels; tel. (+32) 2-5520200; fax (+32) 2-5520255; e-mail info@s-p-a.be; internet www.s-p-a.be; f. 1885 as Parti Ouvrier Belge; Socialist Party's Flemish wing; secured one seat in the national vote in the 2014 EP elections; Chair. John Crombez.

Vlaams Belang (Flemish Interest): Madouplein 8, bus 9, Brussels, 1210 Brussels; tel. (+32) 2-2196009; e-mail info@vlaamsbelang.org; internet www.vlaamsbelang.org; f. 2004; f. by the former leadership and members of Vlaams Bloc after that party was convicted of incitement to discrimination; advocates Flemish separatism and strict limits on immigration, has sought recently to adopt a conservative rather than radical ideology; secured one seat in the EP elections in 2014; Chair. Tom Van Grieken.

BULGARIA

Balgariya bez tsenzura (BBTs) (Bulgaria without Censorship): Cherni Vrah Blvd, Sofia; e-mail bulgariabezcenzura@gmail.com; internet bulgariabezcenzura.bg; f. 2014; centre-right, populist party; secured one seat in the elections to EP in 2014, and formed part of a coalition that secured 11% of the elections' national vote overall; Chair. Nikolay Barekov.

Balgariya na grazhdanite (Bulgaria for Citizens): ul. G. Benkovski 7, 2nd Floor, 1000 Sofia; tel. (+359 2) 843-38-00; e-mail office@grajdani.bg; internet grajdani.bg; f. 2012; secured one seat in the elections to the EP in 2014, heading a coalition that secured 6% of the national vote; Chair. Maglena Kuneva.

Bălgarska Socialističeska Partija (BSP) (Bulgarian Socialist Party): Pozitano Str. 20, 1000 Sofia; tel. (+359 2) 810-72-00; fax (+359 2) 981-21-85; e-mail bsppress@bsp.bg; internet bsp.bg; f. 1990; successor party to the communist Bulgarian Social Democratic Party (BSDP; f. 1891); secured four seats in the 2014 elections to the EP; Chair. Kornelia Ninova Petrova.

Demokrati za silna Balgariya (DSB) (Democrats for a Strong Bulgaria): bul. Vitosha 18, 1000 Sofia; tel. (+359 2) 400-99-21; fax (+359 2) 400-99-48; e-mail dsb@dsb.bg; internet dsb.bg; f. 1990; right-wing, contested 2014 EP elections as mem. of Reformatorsky Blok, winning one seat; Chair. Radan Kanev.

Dvizhenie za Prava i Svobodi (DPS) (Movement for Rights and Freedoms): Al Stamboliyski Blvd 45A, 1301 Sofia; tel. (+359 2) 811-44-42; fax (+359 2) 811-44-53; e-mail dps@dps.bg; internet www.dps.bg; f. 1990; centrist party originally f. to protect the rights of Turkish and other minorities during communism; secured four seats in the 2014 elections to the EP; Chair. Mustafa Karadaya.

Grazhdani za Evropeysko Razvitie na Balgariya (GERB) (Citizens for European Development of Bulgaria): NDK Administration Bldg, 17th Floor, Bulgaria Pl. 1, 1000 Sofia; tel. (+359 2) 490-13-13; fax (+359 2) 490-09-51; e-mail pr@gerb.bg; internet www.gerb.bg; f. 2005; f. from the Mayor of Sofia's political movement; centre-right; prioritizes fighting crime and corruption, the family as cornerstone of society and achieving energy independence; secured six seats in the 2014 EP elections; Chair. Boyko Borisov.

VMRO—Balgarsko natsionalno dvizhenie (VMRO—BND) (IMRO) (Bulgarian National Movement): ul. Pirotska 5, 1301 Sofia; tel. (+359 2) 980-25-82; fax (+359 2) 980-25-83; e-mail vmro@vmro.bg; internet www.vmro.bg; f. 2000; secured one seat in the EP elections of 2014, forming part of a coalition that secured 11% of the votes overall; Chair. Krasimir Karakachanov.

CROATIA

Hrvatska demokratska zajednica (HDZ) (Croatian Democratic Union): Trg črtava fašizma 4, 10000 Zagreb; tel. (+385 1) 4553-000; fax (+385 1) 4552-600; e-mail hdz@hdz.hr; internet www.hdz.hr; f. 1989; Christian democratic and conservative; the main centre-right party in Croatia; contested EP elections of 2014 as part of alliance, winning six seats; Pres. Andrej Plenković.

Hrvatska Narodna Stranka-Liberalni Demokrati (HNS) (Croatian People's Party-Liberal Democrats): Kneza Mislava 8, 10000 Zagreb; tel. (+385 1) 4629111; fax (+385 1) 4629110; e-mail ured@hns.hr; internet www.hns.hr; f. 1990; 43,000 mems (2016); formed part of the SDP-led alliance in 2014; Chair. Ivan Vrdoljak.

Odrčivi Razvoj Hrvatske (ORaH) (Sustainable Development of Croatia): Ilica 48, 10000 Zagreb; e-mail info.ured@orah.hr; internet www.orah.hr; f. 2013; left-wing, environmentalist; secured one seat in the EP in 2014; Pres. Luka Keller.

Socijaldemokratska partija Hrvatske (SDP) (Social Democratic Party of Croatia): Trg Drage Iblera 9, 10000 Zagreb; tel. (+385 1) 4552-055; fax (+385 1) 4552-842; e-mail info@sdp.hr; internet www.sdp.hr; f. 1990; centre-left; contested EP elections of 2014 heading an alliance, and winning four seats; Pres. Davor Bernardić; Sec.-Gen. Zvane Brumnić.

CYPRUS

Anorthotiko Komma Ergazomenou Laou (AKEL) (Progressive Party for the Working People): Ezekias Papaioannou 4, 1075 Nicosia; tel. (+357) 22761121; fax (+357) 22761574; e-mail grafeiotypou@akel.org.cy; internet www.akel.org.cy; f. 1926; socialist; supports an independent, demilitarized and non-aligned Cyprus; secured two seats in the 2014 EP elections; Sec.-Gen. Andros Kyprianou.

Dimokratiko Komma (DIKO) (Democratic Party): POB 23979, Gr. Dhigenis Ave 50, 1080 Nicosia; tel. (+357) 22873800; fax (+357) 22873801; e-mail diko@diko.org.cy; internet www.diko.org.cy; f. 1976; centre-left, but with a strong nationalist tendency; won one seat in the 2014 EP elections; Pres. Nicolas Papadopoulos.

Dimokratikos Synagermos (DISY) (Democratic Rally): Pindarou 25, POB 25305 1308 Nicosia; tel. (+357) 22883000; fax (+357) 22752751; e-mail epikinonia@disy.org.cy; internet disy.org.cy; f. 1976; won two seats in the EP in 2014; Pres. Averof Neophytou.

Kinima Sosialdimokraton EDEK (EDEK) (Movement for Social Democracy EDEK): 40 Byron Ave, 4th Floor, 1096 Nicosia; tel. (+357) 22476000; fax (+357) 22678894; e-mail tipos@cytanet.com.cy; internet edek.org.cy; f. 1969; won one seat in the EP election of 2014; Pres. Marinos Sizopoulos.

CZECH REPUBLIC

Akce Nespokojených Občanů (ANO) (Action of Dissatisfied Citizens): Babická 2329/2, 149 00 Prague 4; tel. (+420) 272192122; e-mail duchanova@anobudelip.cz; internet www.anobudelip.cz; f. 2011; liberal; secured four seats in the EP in 2014; Leader Andrej Babiš.

Česká strana sociálně demokratická (ČSSD) (Czech Social Democratic Party): Lidový dům, Hybernská 1033/7, 110 00 Prague 1; tel. (+420) 296522111; fax (+420) 296522292; e-mail kmalina@socdem.cz; internet www.cssd.cz; f. 1878; re-established 1989; fmrly the Czechoslovak Social Democratic Party; secured four seats in the EP in 2014; Chair. Bohuslav Sobotka.

Komunistická strana Čech a Moravy (KSČM) (Communist Party of Bohemia and Moravia): Politických vězňů 9, 111 21 Prague 1; tel. (+420) 222897111; fax (+420) 222897207; e-mail press@kscm.cz; internet www.kscm.cz; f. 1991; f. as a result of the reorganization of the fmr Communist Party of Czechoslovakia; secured three seats in the EP in 2014; Chair. Vojtěch Filip.

Křesťanská a demokratická unie-Československá strana lidová (KDU-ČSL) (Christian and Democratic Union-Czechoslovak People's Party): Palác Charitas, Karlovo nám. 5, 128 01 Prague 2; tel. (+420) 226205111; fax (+420) 226205100; e-mail info@kdu.cz; internet www.kdu.cz; f. 1992; conservative, Christian democratic, centre-right party; secured three seats in the EP in 2014; Chair. Pavel Bělobrádek; Sec.-Gen. Pavel Hořava.

Občanská demokratická strana (ODS) (Civic Democratic Party): Polygon House, Truhlářská 1106/9, 110 00 Prague 1; tel. (+420) 234707111; e-mail hk@ods.cz; internet www.ods.cz; f. 1991; moderate right-wing; secured two seats in the EP in 2014; Leader Petr Fiala.

Starostové a Nezávislí (STAN) (Mayors and Independents): V Rovinách 40, 140 00 Prague 4; tel. (+420) 241412091; e-mail info@stan.cz; internet www.starostove-nezavisli.cz; f. 2004; localism; contested EP elections of 2014 as part of an alliance that won four seats (with TOP 09); Pres. Petr Gazdík.

Strana Svobodných Občanů (Svobodní) (Party of Free Citizens): Perucká 2196/14, 120 00 Prague 2; tel. (+420) 773697986; e-mail mach@svobodni.cz; internet web.svobodni.cz; f. 2009; secured one seat in the EP in 2014; Chair. Petr Mach.

Tradice, Odpovědnost, Prosperita 09 (TOP 09) (Tradition, Responsibility, Prosperity 09): Michnův palác, budova č. 2, Újezd 450/40, Malá Strana, 118 00 Prague 1; tel. (+420) 255790999; fax (+420) 255790899; e-mail info@top09.cz; internet www.top09.cz; f. 2009; conservative; contested EP elections of 2014 as part of an alliance that won four seats (with STAN); Chair. Miroslav Kalousek.

DENMARK

Dansk Folkeparti (DF) (Danish People's Party): Christiansborg, 1240 Copenhagen K; tel. (+45) 33-37-51-99; e-mail df@ft.dk; internet www.danskfolkeparti.dk; f. 1995; f. by defectors from the Progress Party; right-wing; aims to assert Denmark's independence, to guarantee the freedom of the Danish people in their own country and to preserve and promote representative government and the monarchy; secured four seats in the EP in 2014; Leader Kristian Thulesen Dahl.

Det Radikale Venstre (RV) (Social Liberals): Christiansborg, Slotsplads 1, 1240 Copenhagen K; tel. (+45) 33-37-47-47; fax (+45) 33-13-72-51; e-mail radikale@radikale.dk; internet www.radikale.dk; f. 1905; supports international détente and co-operation within regional and world orgs, social reforms without socialism, income policy, workers' participation in industry, state intervention in industrial disputes, state control of trusts and monopolies, strengthening private enterprise; obtained one seat in the EP in 2014; Nat. Chair. Svend Thorhauge.

Folkebevægelsen mod EU: Tordenskjoldsgade 21, st.th., 1055 Copenhagen K; tel. (+45) 35-36-37-40; fax (+45) 35-82-18-06; e-mail fb@folkebevaegelsen.dk; internet www.folkebevaegelsen.dk; f. 1972; opposes membership of the EU, in favour of self-determination for Denmark and all European countries; collective leadership; won one seat in the EP in 2014; Sec.-Gen. Poul Gerhard Kristiansen.

Konservative Folkeparti (KF) (Conservative People's Party): Christiansborg, 1240 Copenhagen K; tel. (+45) 33-13-41-44; e-mail info@konservative.dk; internet konservative.dk; f. 1916; conservative ideology; won one seat in the EP in 2014; Leader Søren Pape Poulsen.

Socialdemokraterne (SD) (Social Democratic Party): Vester Voldgade 96, 1552 Copenhagen V; tel. (+45) 72-30-08-00; fax (+45) 72-30-08-50; e-mail partikontoret@socialdemokraterne.dk; internet www.socialdemokraterne.dk; f. 1871; advocates democratic socialism; approx. 38,000 mems; also known as Socialdemokratiet; secured three seats in the EP in 2014; Leader Mette Frederiksen; Sec.-Gen. Jan Juul Christensen.

Socialistisk Folkeparti (SF) (Socialist People's Party): Christiansborg, 1240 Copenhagen K; tel. (+45) 33-37-44-44; fax (+45) 33-32-72-48; e-mail sf@sf.dk; internet sf.dk; f. 1959; unites Red and Green perspectives and a democratic outlook; won one seat in the EP in 2014; Chair. Pia Olsen Dyhr.

Venstre (Liberal Party): Søllerødvej 30, 2840 Holte; tel. (+45) 45-80-22-33; e-mail venstre@venstre.dk; internet www.venstre.dk; f. 1870; free market liberal party; obtained two seats in the EP in 2014; Chair. Lars Løkke Rasmussen; Sec.-Gen. Claus Søgaard-Richter.

ESTONIA

Eesti Keskerakond (EK) (Estonian Centre Party): Toom-Rüütli 3/5, 10130 Tallinn; tel. (+372) 6273460; fax (+352) 6273461; e-mail keskerakond@keskerakond.ee; internet www.keskerakond.ee; f. 1991; absorbed the Estonian Green Party in 1998 and the Estonian Pensioners' Party in 2005; obtained one seat in the EP in 2014; Chair. Jüri Ratas; Sec.-Gen Mikhail Korb.

Eesti Reformierakond (Estonian Reform Party): Tõnismägi 9, 10119 Tallinn; tel. (+372) 6808080; fax (+372) 6808081; e-mail info@reform.ee; internet www.reform.ee; f. 1994; free-market liberal party; won two seats in the EP in 2014; Chair. Hanno Pevkur.

Erakond Isamaa ja Res Publica Liit (IRL) (Union of Pro Patria and Res Publica): Paldiski 13, 10137 Tallinn; tel. (+372) 6240403; e-mail info@irl.ee; internet www.irl.ee; f. 2006; f. by merger of Erakond Ismaaliit and Res Publica; conservative nationalist party; secured one seat in the EP in 2014; Chair. Helir-Valdor Seeder; Sec.-Gen. Priit Sibul.

Sotsiaaldemokraatlik Erakond (SDE) (Social Democratic Party): Toompuiestee 16, 10137 Tallinn; tel. (+372) 6116040; fax (+352) 6116050; e-mail kantselei@sotsdem.ee; internet www.sotsdem.ee; f. 1999; f. as the People's Party Moderates, by merger of the People's Party and the Moderates' Party; name changed in 2004; some 6,000 mems; secured one seat in the 2014 EP elections; Chair. Jevgeni Ossinovski; Sec.-Gen. Kristen Kanarik.

FINLAND

Kansallinen Kokoomus (Kok) (National Coalition Party): Kansakoulukuja 3A, 2 krs, 00100 Helsinki; tel. (+358 20) 7488488; fax (+358 20) 7488505; e-mail petteri.orpo@eduskunta.fi; internet www.kokoomus.fi; f. 1918; moderate conservative political ideology; won three seats in the EP in 2014; Chair. Petteri Orpo; Sec.-Gen. Janne Pesonen.

Perussuomalaiset (PS) (True Finns): Yrjönkatu 8–102 B 12, 00120 Helsinki; tel. (+358 20) 7430800; fax (+358 20) 7430801; e-mail riikka.poutsalo@perussuomalaiset.fi; internet www.perussuomalaiset.fi; f. 1995; on the dissolution of the Finnish Rural Party; is critical of the EU and advocates a large welfare state; secured two seats in the 2014 EP elections; Chair. Jussi Halla-aho; Sec. Riikka Slunga-Poutsalo.

Suomen Keskusta (Kesk) (Centre Party of Finland): Apollonkatu 11A, 00100 Helsinki; tel. (+358 10) 2897000; fax (+358 10) 2897240; e-mail puoluetoimisto@keskusta.fi; internet www.keskusta.fi; f. 1906; radical centre party founded to promote the interests of the rural population; now a reformist 'green' movement favouring individual enterprise, equality and decentralization; won three seats in the EP elections in 2014; Chair. Juha Sipilä; Sec. Jouni Ovaska.

Suomen Sosialidemokraattinen Puolue (SDP) (Finnish Social Democratic Party): Siltasaarenkatu 18-20 C, 6 krs., 00530 Helsinki; tel. (+358 9) 478988; fax (+358 9) 712752; e-mail antti.rinne@sdp.fi; internet sdp.fi; f. 1899; constitutional socialist programme; c. 50,000 mems; secured two seats in the EP in 2014; Chair. Antti Rinne; Sec.-Gen. Antton Rönnholm.

Svenska Folkpartiet (SFP) (Swedish People's Party): Simonsgatan 8A, POB 430, 00101 Helsinki; tel. (+358 9) 693070; e-mail info@sfp.fi; internet www.sfp.fi; f. 1906; liberal party representing the interests of the Swedish-speaking minority; obtained one seat in the EP elections in 2014; Chair. Anna-Maja Henriksson.

Vasemmistoliitto (VAS) (Left Alliance): Lintulahdenkatu 10, 3rd Floor, 00500 Helsinki; tel. (+358 9) 7737700; e-mail marianna.rautiainen@vasemmistoliitto.fi; internet www.vasemmisto.fi; f. Founded 1990 by merger of the Finnish People's Democratic League (f. 1944), the Communist Party of Finland (f. 1918), the Democratic League of Finnish Women, and left-wing groups; won one seat in the EP elections in the 2014; Chair. Li Andersson; Sec.-Gen. Joonas Leppänen.

Vihreä Liitto (VIHR) (Green League): 33A Fredrikinkatu, 00120 Helsinki; tel. (+358 9) 58604160; fax (+358 9) 58604161; e-mail vihreat@vihreat.fi; internet www.vihrealiitto.fi; f. 1987; environmental and liberal party; secured one seat in the 2014 EP elections; Chair. Touko Aalto; Sec.-Gen. Lasse Miettinen.

FRANCE

Europe Écologie—Les Verts (EELV) (Greens): 3 rue de Vincennes, 93100 Montreuil; tel. (+33) 1-53-19-53-19; fax (+33) 1-53-19-03-93; e-mail contact@eelv.fr; internet eelv.fr; f. 1984; ecologist; fmrly called Europe Ecologie; name changed to above following merger with Les Verts in 2010; secured six seats in the EP elections in 2014; Nat. Sec. David Cormand.

Front National (FN) (National Front): 76–78 rue des Suisses, 92000 Nanterre; tel. (+33) 1-41-20-20-00; e-mail marine.lepen@frontnational.com; internet www.frontnational.com; f. 1972; extreme right-wing nationalist party; won 23 seats in the EP elections in 2014; Leader Marine Le Pen; Sec.-Gen. Nicolas Bay.

Génération citoyens (GC): 20 rue Cambon, 750001 Paris; e-mail contact@generationcitoyens.fr; internet www.generationcitoyens.fr; f. 2015; Leader Jean-Marie Cavada.

Mouvement Démocrate (MoDEM) (Democratic Movement): 133 bis rue de l'Université, 75007 Paris; tel. (+33) 1-53-59-20-64; internet www.mouvementdemocrate.fr; f. 2007; founded by François Bayrou as a successor party to Union pour la Démocratie Française; centrist, pro-European; formed L'Altervative (The Alternative) coalition with the Union des Démocrates et Indépendants in 2013, contested EP elections of 2014 as part of alliance and secured seven seats; Pres. François Bayrou.

Parti Communiste Français (PCF) (French Communist Party): 2 place du Colonel Fabien, 75019 Paris; tel. (+33) 1-40-40-12-22; e-mail pcf@pcf.fr; internet www.pcf.fr; f. 1920; advocates independent foreign policy; part of the Front de Gauche coalition for the 2014 EP elections; secured three seats as part of alliance; Nat. Sec. Pierre Laurent.

Parti de Gauche (PG) (Left Party): 20–22 rue Doudeauville, 75018 Paris; tel. (+33) 1-55-28-92-20; e-mail contact@lepartidegauche.fr; internet www.lepartidegauche.fr; f. 2008; by its leader and other dissident members of the Parti Socialiste; part of the Front de Gauche coalition for the 2014 EP elections; won three seats in the EP as part of alliance; Co-Chair. Eric Coquerel; Co-Chair. Danielle Simonnet.

Parti Socialiste (PS) (Socialist Party): 10 rue de Solférino, 75333 Paris Cedex 07; tel. (+33) 1-45-56-77-00; fax (+33) 1-47-05-15-78; e-mail interps@parti-socialiste.fr; internet www.parti-socialiste.fr; f. 1971; subscribed to common programme of United Left (with PCF) until 1977; advocates solidarity, full employment and the eventual attainment of socialism through a mixed economy; contested the 2014 EP elections as part of alliance and secured 13 seats; First Sec. Jean-Christophe Cambadélis.

Les Républicains (The Republicans): 238 rue de Vaugirard, 75015 Paris; tel. (+33) 1-40-76-27-32; e-mail federation@les-republicains.paris; internet www.republicains.fr; f. 2002; ecologist; fmrly called Union pour un Mouvement Populaire (UMP); name changed as above in May 2015; secured 20 seats in the EP elections in 2014; Sec.-Gen. Bernard Accover.

Union des Démocrates et Indépendants (UDI): 22 bis rue des Volontaires, 75015 Paris; tel. (+33) 1-53-71-20-17; e-mail contact@parti-udi.fr; internet www.parti-udi.fr; f. 2012; centrist; comprises several ind. parties, incl. Alliance Centriste, Force Européenne Démocrate, La Gauche Moderne, Nouveau Centre, Parti Radical, Parti Libéral Démocrate; formed L'Altervative (The Alternative) coalition with the Mouvement Démocrate in 2013, contested EP elections of 2014 as part of alliance, winning seven seats; Pres. Laurent Hénart.

GERMANY

Allianz für Fortschritt und Aufbruch (ALFA) (Alliance for Progress and Renewal): Mierendorffstr. 10, 10589 Berlin; tel. (+49 30) 55572662; fax (+49 30) 55572693; e-mail geschaeftsstelle@lkr.de; internet lkr.de; f. 2015; formerly known as Allianz für Fortschritt und Aufbruch (ALFA), present name adopted in 2016, following divisions within Alternative für Deutschland (AfD) and the split into two parties; Chair. Christian Kott; Gen. Sec. Jürgen Joost.

Alternative für Deutschland (AfD) (Alternative for Germany): Schillstr. 9, 10785 Berlin; tel. (+49 30) 22056960; fax (+49 30) 220569629; e-mail bgs@alternativefuer.de; internet www.afd.de; f. 2013; anti-euro; secured seven seats in the EP in 2014; Spokespersons Dr Frauke Petry, Prof. Dr Jörg Meuthen.

Bündnis 90/Die Grünen (Grüne) (Alliance 90/The Greens): Platz vor dem Neuen Tor 1, 10115 Berlin; tel. (+49 30) 284420; fax (+49 30) 28442210; e-mail info@gruene.de; internet www.gruene.de; f. 1993; f. by merger of Bündnis 90 (f. 1990, as an electoral political asscn of citizens' movements of the former GDR) and Die Grünen (f. 1980); essentially left-wing programme includes ecological issues, democratization of society, social justice, comprehensive disarmament; won 11 seats in the 2014 EP elections; Joint Chair. Cem Özdemir, Simone Peter.

Christlich Demokratische Union Deutschlands (CDU) (Christian Democratic Union of Germany): Konrad-Adenauer-Haus, Klingelhöferstr. 8, 10785 Berlin; tel. (+49 30) 220700; fax (+49

30) 22070111; e-mail info@cdu.de; internet www.cdu.de; f. 1945; became a federal party in 1950; moderate Christian party; incorporated the CDU of the former German Democratic Republic in Oct 1990; c. 520,000 mems, contested the 2014 EP elections as part of alliance and secured 34 seats; Chair. Dr Angela Merkel; Sec.-Gen. Dr Peter Tauber.

Christlich-Soziale Union in Bayern e.V. (CSU) (Christian Social Union of Bavaria): Franz Josef Strauss-Haus, Mies-van-der-Rohe-Str. 1, 80807 Munich; tel. (+49 89) 12430; fax (+49 89) 1243299; e-mail landesleitung@csu-bayern.de; internet www.csu.de; f. 1946; operates only in Bavaria; sister party of CDU; combines national consciousness with support for a united Europe; contested the 2014 EP elections as part of alliance, winning 34 seats; Chair. Horst Seehofer; Gen.-Sec. Andreas Scheuer.

Familienpartei Deutschlands (FAMILIE) (Family Party of Germany): Landesverband Saarland, 66376 St. Ingbert; e-mail info@familien-partei-saarland.de; internet www.familien-partei.de; f. 1981; conservative; secured one seat in the 2014 EP elections; Chair. Roland Körner.

Freie Demokratische Partei (FDP) (Free Democratic Party): Bundesgeschäftsstelle, Reinhardtstr. 14, 10117 Berlin; tel. (+49 30) 28495880; fax (+49 30) 28495822; e-mail info@fdp.de; internet www.fdp.de; f. 1948; represents democratic and social liberalism and makes the individual the focal point of the State and its laws and economy; c. 54,000 mems, won three seats in the EP elections in 2014; Chair. Christian Lindner; Sec.-Gen. Nicola Beer.

Freie Wähler (FW) (Independent Voters): Mühlenstr. 1, 27777 Ganderkesee; tel. (+49 22) 2094925; fax (+49 22) 2094923; e-mail office@freiewaehler.eu; internet www.freiewaehler.eu; f. 1946; non-ideological, centrist; regional orgs in all 16 Länder; obtained one seat in the EP in 2014; Chair. Hubert Aiwanger.

Die, Linke (The Left): Karl-Liebnecht-Haus, Kleine Alexanderstr. 28, 10178 Berlin; tel. (+49 30) 24009397; fax (+49 30) 24009999; e-mail bundesgeschaeftsstelle@die-linke.de; internet www.die-linke.de; f. 2007; formed from the merger of Die Linkspartei.PDS (formerly Partei des Demokratischen Sozialismus, PDS) and Arbeit und Soziale Gerechtigkeit—Die Wahlalternative, WASG; secured seven seats in the EP elections in 2014; Joint Chair. Katja Kipping, Bernd Riexinger.

Nationaldemokratische Partei Deutschlands (NPD) (National Democratic Party of Germany): Seelenbinderstr. 42, 12555 Berlin; tel. (+49 30) 650110; fax (+49 30) 65011140; e-mail parteizentrale@npd.de; internet www.npd.de; f. 1964; right-wing; secured one seat in the 2014 EP election; Chair. Frank Franz.

Die Ökologisch-Demokratische Partei (ÖDP) (The Ecological Democratic Party): Pommer Gasse 1, 97070 Würzburg; e-mail info@oedp.de; internet www.oedp.de; f. 1982; won a single seat in the 2014 EP elections; Leader Gabriela Shimmer Göresz.

Sozialdemokratische Partei Deutschlands (SPD) (Social Democratic Party of Germany): Willy-Brandt-Haus, Wilhelmstr. 141, 10963 Berlin; tel. (+49 30) 25991500; fax (+49 30) 25991375; e-mail parteivorstand@spd.de; internet www.spd.de; f. 1863; incorporated the SPD of the former German Democratic Republic in Sept 1990; maintains that a vital democracy can be built only on the basis of social justice; advocates for the economy as much competition as possible, as much planning as necessary to protect the individual from uncontrolled economic interests; favours a positive attitude to national defence, while supporting controlled disarmament; rejects any political ties with communism; secured 27 seats in the 2014 EP elections; Chair. Martin Schulz.

GREECE

Anexartitoi Ellines (ANEL) (Independent Greeks): Charokopou 2 & Siggrou, 196 Kallithea, 176 71 Athens; tel. (+30) 210-9545000; internet www.anexartitoiellines.gr; f. 2012; obtained one seat in the 2014 EP elections; Leader Panos Kammenos.

Chrysi Avgi (Golden Dawn): Diligiannis 50, 10439 Athens; tel. (+30) 210-6985121; fax (+30) 210-3706579; e-mail info@xryshaygh.com; internet www.xryshaygh.com; f. 1993; extreme nationalist; gained three seats in the EP in 2014; Leader Nikolaos Michaloliakos.

Kommounistikó Kómma Elládas (KKE) (Communist Party of Greece): Leoforos Irakliou 145, Nea Ionia, 142 31 Athens; tel. (+30) 210-2592111; fax (+30) 210-2592298; e-mail cpg@int.kke.gr; internet inter.kke.gr; f. 1918; banned 1947, reappeared 1974; secured two seats in the EP in 2014; Gen.-Sec. Dimitris Koutsoumpas.

Laiki Enotita (LE) (Popular Unity): Patission 14, 8th Floor, Athens; tel. (+30) 210-3800067; fax (+30) 210-3800015; e-mail organotiko@laiki-enotita.gr; internet www.laiki-enotita.gr; f. 2015 by members formerly affiliated with SYRIZA; Leader Panagiotis Lafazanis.

Nea Dimokratia (ND) (New Democracy): Leoforos Syngrou 340, 176 73 Kallithea; tel. (+30) 210-9444000; fax (+30) 210-7251491; e-mail proedros@nd.gr; internet nd.gr; f. 1974; f. by Konstantinos Karamanlis; centre-right party advocating social reform in the framework of a liberal economy; led and completed Greece's accession to the EU; won five seats in the EP in 2014; Chair. Kyriakos Mitsotakis.

Olive Tree—Democratic Alignment (ELIA DA); internet www.elia-dimokratikiparataxi.gr; f. 2014; centre-left; gained two seats in the EP in 2014.

Panellinio Socialistiko Kinima (PASOK) (Panhellenic Socialist Movement): Trikoupi 50, 106 80 Athens; tel. (+30) 210-3665000; fax (+30) 210-3665209; e-mail pasok@pasok.gr; internet www.pasok.gr; f. 1974; incorporates Democratic Defence and Panhellenic Liberation Movement resistance organizations; supports social welfare, decentralization and self-management, aims at a Mediterranean socialist development through international co-operation; contested the 2014 EP elections as part of alliance, winning two seats; Pres. Fofi Gennimata; Sec.-Gen. Stefanos Xekalakis.

To Potami (The River): Sevastoupoleos 22, 115 26 Athens; tel. (+30) 210-7470100; fax (+30) 210-7470115; e-mail info@topotami.gr; internet topotami.gr; f. 2014; secured two seats in the EP in 2014; Pres. Stavros Theodorakis.

Synaspismos Rizospastikis Aristeras (SYRIZA) (Coalition of the Radical Left): 1 Liberty Sq., 105 53 Athens; tel. (+30) 210-3378400; fax (+30) 210-3217003; e-mail info@syriza.gr; internet www.syriza.gr; f. 2004; far-left; won six seats in the EP in 2014; Chair. Alexis Tsipras.

HUNGARY

Demokratikus Koalíció (DK) (Democratic Coalition): Victor Hugo u. 11–15, 1132 Budapest; tel. (+36 1) 3001000; e-mail info@dkp.hu; internet web.dkp.hu; f. 2011; social democratic; won two seats in the EP in 2014; Chair. Ferenc Gyurcsány.

Együtt 2014 (Together 2014): Alkota u. 17-19, 1123 Budapest; tel. (+36 1) 2400613; e-mail hello@egyuttpart.hu; internet egyuttpart.hu; f. 2013; alliance of three civil society organizations, secured a single seat in the EP in 2014; Chair. Peter Juhasz.

Fidesz—Magyar Polgári Szövetség (FIDESZ—MPSZ) (Hungarian Civic Union): Lendvay u. 28, 1062 Budapest; tel. (+36 1) 5552100; fax (+36 1) 2998061; e-mail polgarokhaza@chello.hu; internet www.fidesz.hu; f. 1988; f. as the Federation of Young Democrats; renamed April 1995; re-formed as an alliance in 2003, with a new charter; conservative; 10,000 mems; secured 12 seats in the EP in 2014; Pres. Viktor Orbán.

Jobbik Magyarországért Mozgalom (Jobbik) (Movement for a Better Hungary): Villányi út 20A, 1113 Budapest; tel. (+36 1) 3651488; internet www.jobbik.hu; f. 2003; radical conservative party with a strong commitment to nationalism; secured three seats in the EP in 2014; Chair. Gábor Vona.

Lehet Más a Politika! (LMP) (Politics Can Be Different!): Hegedus Gyula u. 36, 1136 Budapest; tel. (+36 1) 7827120; fax (+36 1) 7994304; e-mail info@lehetmas.hu; internet lehetmas.hu; f. 2009; environmentalist, won one seat in the EP in 2014; Co-Chair. Szél Bernadetttársalnök; Co-Chair. Ákos Hadházy; Sec. Sallai R. Benedektitkár.

Magyar Szocialista Párt (MSZP) (Hungarian Socialist Party): Jokai u. 6, 1066 Budapest; tel. (+36 1) 4597200; e-mail info@mszp.hu; internet mszp.hu; f. 1989 to replace the Hungarian Socialist Workers' Party; won two seats in the 2014 EP elections; Pres. Molnár Gyula.

IRELAND

Fianna Fáil (FF) (Soldiers of Destiny): 65–66 Lower Mount St, Dublin 2; tel. (+353 1) 6761551; fax (+353 1) 6785690; e-mail info@fiannafail.ie; internet www.fiannafail.ie; f. 1926; Republican party; centrist; secured one seat in the EP in 2014; Leader Micheál Martin.

Fine Gael (FG) (Family of the Irish): 51 Upper Mount St, Dublin 2; tel. (+353 1) 6198444; fax (+353 1) 6764048; e-mail finegael@finegael.com; internet www.finegael.ie; f. 1933; United Ireland Party; centrist; won four seats in the 2014 EP elections; Leader Leo Varadkar.

Sinn Féin (SF) (We Ourselves): 44 Parnell Sq., Dublin 1; tel. (+353 1) 8726100; fax (+353 1) 8733441; e-mail admin@sinnfein.ie; internet www.sinnfein.ie; f. 1905; advocates the termination of British rule in Northern Ireland; seeks a mandate to establish a democratic socialist republic in a reunified Ireland; secured three seats in the EP in 2014; Pres. Gerry Adams.

ITALY

L'Altra Europa con Tsipras (The Other Europe): www.listatsipras.eu; f. 2014; left-wing; won three seats in the EP in 2014; Leader Massimo Torelli.

Forza Italia (FI) (Forward Italy): Via dell'Umiltà 36, 00187 Rome; internet www.forzaitalia.it; f. 2013 following the splitting of Popolo della Libertà into two parties; secured 13 seats in the 2014 EP elections; Pres. Silvio Berlusconi.

Lega Nord per l'Indipendenza della Padania (LN) (Northern League for the Independence of Padania): Via Carlo Bellerio 41, 20161 Milan; internet www.leganord.org; f. 1991; advocates federalism in Italy and transfer of control of resources to regional govts; in 1996 declared the 'Independent Republic of Padania'; opposes immigration; won five seats in the EP in 2014; Leader Umberto Bossi; Sec. Matteo Salvini.

MoVimento 5 Stelle (M5S) (Five Star Movement): internet www.movimento5stelle.it; f. 2009; populist, anti-corruption; secured 17 seats in the EP in 2014; Leader Beppe Grillo.

Partito Democratico (PD) (Democratic Party): Via Sant'Andrea delle Fratte 16, 00187 Rome; tel. (+39) 06-675471; e-mail privacy@partitodemocratico.it; internet www.partitodemocratico.it; f. 2007; centre-left; formed by the merger of Democrazia è Libertà —La Margherita, Democratici di Sinistra and other smaller centrist and left-wing parties and movements that fmrly were part of the Unione di Centro coalition; Nat. Sec. Matteo Renzi.

Südtiroler Volkspartei (SVP) (South Tyrolean People's Party): Brennerstraße 7/a, 39100 Bolzano; tel. (+39) 471-304000; fax (+39) 471-981473; e-mail info@svp.eu; internet www.svp.eu; f. 1945; regional party representing the German-speaking population of northern Italy; secured one seat in the EP in 2014; Pres. Philipp Achammer.

Unione dei Democratici Cristiani e Democratici di Centro (UDC) (Union of Christian and Centre Democrats): Via del Tritone 102, 00182 Rome; tel. (+39) 06-42010118; fax (+39) 06-42821164; e-mail info@udc-italia.it; internet www.udc-italia.it; f. 2002; f. by merger of the former Centro Cristiano Democratico and Cristiani Democratici Uniti; advocates centre-right policies; fought the 2009 EP elections within the Unione di Centro coalition as part of the broader Pole of Autonomy coalition, which includes the Partito Pensionati (Pensioners' Party) among others; contested the 2014 EP elections as part of alliance, winning three seats; Nat. Sec. Lorenzo Cesa; Pres. Antonio De Poli.

LATVIA

Latvijas Krievu savienība (LKS) (Latvian Russian Union): Rūpniecības iela 9, 1010 Rīga; tel. (+371) 67320290; e-mail pctvl.info@gmail.com; internet www.pctvl.lv; f. 1998; secured a single seat in the EP in 2014; Joint Chair. Miroslav Mitrofanov, Tatjana Zdanoka.

Latvijas Zaļā Partija (LZP) (Latvian Green Party): Latvian Green Party): Kalnciema iela 30, 1046 Rīga; tel. (+371) 67614272; fax (+371) 66015268; e-mail birojs@zp.lv; internet www.zp.lv; f. 1990; forms part of the ZZS; contested the 2014 EP elections as part of alliance, winning one seat; Joint Chair. Ingmar Pike; Joint Chair. Viesturs Silenieks.

Nacionālā Apvienība (NA) (National Alliance): Torna iela 4/1B, 1050 Rīga; tel. (+371) 27755997; e-mail info@nacionalaapvieniba.lv; internet www.nacionalaapvieniba.lv; f. 2011; f. by merger of the Conservative Union for Fatherland and Freedom and All for Latvia; secured one seat in the 2014 EP elections; Joint Chair. Gaidis Bērziņš, Raivis Dzintars.

Sociāldemokrātiskā Partija 'Saskaņa' (SDPS) (Social Democratic Party 'Harmony'): Maskavas iela 4, 1050 Rīga; tel. (+371) 67333515; e-mail sekretare@partijasaskana.lv; internet www.saskana.info; f. 2010; f. by Tautas Saskaņas Partija and other members of the Saskaņas Centrs (Harmony Centre) alliance; advocates social democracy, liberalizing Latvian citizenship rules and teaching in minority languages, particularly Russian; stands in the EP under the banner of the Saskaņas Centrs alliance; secured a single seat in the EP in 2014; Leader Nils Ušakovs.

Vienotība (Unity): Meierovica bulvāris 12-3, 1050 Rīga; tel. (+371) 67205472; e-mail sekretare@vienotiba.lv; internet vienotiba.lv; f. 2011; formed from the centre-right electoral alliance of the New Era Party, Civic Union and the Society for Other Politics (f. as a proposed political counterweight to the leftist Harmony Centre alliance); secured four seats in the EP in 2014; Pres. Andris Piebalgs; Sec. Artis Kampars.

LITHUANIA

Darbo Partija (Labour Party): Ankštoji 3, Penktas Aukstas, 01109 Vilnius; tel. (+370 5) 2107152; fax (+370 5) 2107153; e-mail info@darbopartija.lt; internet www.darbopartija.lt; f. 2003; absorbed the New Union (Social Liberals) in 2011, 25,227 mems (2014), centrist policies; secured one seat in the 2014 EP elections; Pres. Živilė Pinskuvienė.

Lietuvos lenkų rinkimų akcija—Krikščioniškų šeimų sąjunga (Lithuania (LLRA-KŠS) (Electoral Action of Poles in Lithuania): Naugarduko g. 76, 03202 Vilnius; tel. (+370 5) 2333103; fax (+370 5) 2331266; e-mail info@awpl.lt; internet www.awpl.lt; f. 1994; centrist, representing interests of Poles in Lithuania; secured one seat in the 2014 EP elections under the name Akcja Wyborcza Polaków na Litwie; Leader Valdemar Tomaševski.

Lietuvos Respublikos Liberalų Sąjūdis (LRLS) (Lithuanian Republic Liberal Movement): Vašingtono aikštė 1, 1108 Vilnius; tel. (+370 5) 2496959; fax (+370 5) 2121083; e-mail info@liberalai.lt; internet www.liberalai.lt; f. 2006; f. by dissident members of Liberalų ir Centro Sąjunga, liberal policies; secured two seats in the EP in 2014; Leader Remigijus Šimašius.

Lietuvos Socialdemokratų Partija (LSDP) (Lithuanian Social Democratic Party): Barboros Radvilaitės g. 1, 2600 Vilnius; tel. (+370 5) 2613907; fax (+370 5) 2615420; e-mail info@lsdp.lt; internet www.lsdp.lt; f. 2001; absorbed the Lithuanian Democratic Labour Party in 2001; some 21,150 mems; won two seats in the EP in 2014; Chair. Gintautas Paluckas.

Lietuvos Valstiečių ir Žaliųjų Sąjunga (LZVS) (Lithuanian Peasants' and Greens' Union): Pamėnkalnio g. 26, 01114 Vilnius; tel. (+370 5) 2120821; fax (+370 5) 2120822; e-mail info@lvzs.lt; internet www.lvls.lt; f. 2001; obtained one seat in the EP in 2014; Chair. Ramūnas Karbauskis.

Tėvynės Sąjunga—Lietuvos krikščionys demokratai (TS-LKD) (Homeland Union—Lithuanian Christian Democrats): L. Stuokos-Gucevičiaus 11, 1122 Vilnius; tel. (+370 5) 2121657; fax (+370 5) 2784722; e-mail sekretoriatas@tsajunga.lt; internet www.tsajunga.lt; f. 1993; right-wing, Christian democrat; secured two seats in the 2014 EP elections; Chair. Gabrielius Landsbergis.

Tvarka ir Teisingumas (TT) (Order and Justice): Gedimino pr. 10/Totorių g. 1, 1103 Vilnius; tel. (+370) 852691618; fax (+370) 852691618; e-mail tt@tvarka.lt; internet www.tvarka.lt; f. 2002; centre-right; changed its name from Liberalų Demokratų Partija in 2006; secured two seats in the EP in 2014; Leader Rolandas Paksas.

LUXEMBOURG

Déi Gréng (Green Party): 3 rue du Fossé, 1563 Luxembourg; tel. (+352) 2748271; fax (+352) 27482722; e-mail greng@greng.lu; internet www.greng.lu; f. 1983 as Gréng Alternativ Partei; joined with Gréng Lëscht Ekologesch Initiativ in 1994 to form Déi Gréng; advocates 'grass-roots' democracy, environmental protection, social concern and increased aid to developing countries; won one seat in the 2014 EP elections; Co-Pres. Françoise Folmer, Christian Kmiotek.

Parti Chrétien Social/Chrëschtlech Sozial Vollekspartei (PCS/CSV) (Christian Social Party): 4 rue de l'Eau, 1449 Luxembourg; tel. (+352) 2257311; e-mail csv@csv.lu; internet www.csv.lu; f. 1914; advocates political stability, sustained economic expansion, ecological and social progress; secured three seats in the EP in 2014; Pres. Marc Spautz; Sec.-Gen. Laurent Zeimet.

Parti Démocratique/Demokratesch Partei (DP/PD) (Democratic Party): 5 rue du St Esprit, 1475 Luxembourg; tel. (+352) 221021; fax (+352) 221013; e-mail secretariat@dp.lu; internet www.dp.lu; f. 1955; liberal; obtained a single seat in the EP in 2014; Leader Corinne Cahen; Sec.-Gen. Marc Ruppert.

Parti Ouvrier Socialiste Luxembourgeois/Lëtzebuerger Sozialistesch Arbechterpartei (POSL/LSAP) (Socialist Workers' Party): 68 rue de Gasperich, 1617 Luxembourg; tel. (+352) 4565731; fax (+352) 456575; e-mail info@lsap.lu; internet www.lsap.lu; f. 1902; social democrat; secured one seat in the 2014 EP elections; Pres. Claude Haagen; Sec.-Gen. Yves Cruchten.

MALTA

Partit Laburista/Malta Labour Party (MLP) (Centru Nazzjonali Laburista): Triq Milend, Hamrun HMR 1717; tel. (+356) 21249900; fax (+356) 21244204; e-mail info@partitlaburista.org; internet josephmuscat.com; f. 1921; democratic socialist won three seats in the EP in 2014; Pres. Daniel Micallef; Leader Dr Joseph Muscat.

Partit Nazzjonalista (PN) (Nationalist Party): Herbert Ganado St, Pieta, Tal-Pietà PTA 1450; tel. (+356) 21243641; fax (+356) 21243640; e-mail info@pn.org.mt; internet www.pn.org.mt; f. 1880; Christian democratic; advocated full membership of the EU; 33,000 mems, secured three seats in the EP in 2014; Leader Simon Busuttil.

NETHERLANDS

Christen Democratisch Appèl (CDA) (Christian Democratic Appeal): Buitenom 18, POB 30453, 2500 GL The Hague; tel. (+31 70) 3424888; fax (+31 70) 3643417; e-mail cda@cda.nl; internet www.cda.nl; f. 1980; by merger of three 'confessional' parties; 55,000 mems; centre-right; won five seats in the EP in 2014; Pres. Ruth Peetoom; Sec. Rutger Ploum.

ChristenUnie (CU) (Christian Union): Johan van Oldenbarneveltlaan 46, POB 439, 3800 AK Amersfoort; tel. (+31 33) 4226969; fax (+31 33) 4226968; e-mail info@christenunie.nl; internet www.christenunie.nl; f. 2000 by merger of two evangelical parties, the Gereformeerd Politiek Verbond and the Reformatische Politieke Federatie; interdenominational, based on biblical precepts; stood in the 2014 EP elections jointly with the

SGP, and secured two seats; Chair. Piet Adema; Leader Gert-Jan Segers.

Democraten 66 (D66) (Democrats '66): Hoge Nieuwstraat 30, Postbus 660, 2501 CR The Hague; tel. (+31 70) 3566066; fax (+31 70) 3641917; e-mail info@d66.nl; internet d66.nl; f. 1966; social liberal; promotes free personal development; secured four seats in the 2014 EP elections; Chair. Letty Demmers; Leader Alexander Pechtold.

GroenLinks (Green Left): Oudegracht 312, POB 8008, 3503 PK Utrecht; tel. (+31 30) 2399900; internet www.groenlinks.nl; f. 1990 by merger of the Communistische Partij van Nederland, Evangelische Volkspartij, Pacifistisch Socialistische Partij and Politieke Partij Radikalen; leftist liberal party, obtained two seats in the EP in 2014; Chair. Marjolein Meijer; Leader Jesse Klaver.

Partij van de Arbeid (PvdA) (Labour Party): Haarlemmerweg 516, Building C, 1014 BL Amsterdam; tel. (+31 20) 5512155; fax (+31 20) 5512250; e-mail voorzitter@pvda.nl; internet www.pvda.nl; f. 1946 by merger of progressive and liberal organizations; democratic socialist; 50,000 mems; secured three seats in the EP in 2014; Chair. Hans Spekman; Sec. Lodewijk Asscher.

Partij voor de Dieren (PvdD) (Party for the Animals): POB 17622, 1001 Amsterdam; tel. (+31 70) 5203870; e-mail administratie@partijvoordedieren.nl; internet www.partijvoordedieren.nl; f. 2002; promotes animal rights and animal welfare; secured a single seat in the EP in 2014; Chair. Floriske van Leeuwen; Sec. Elze Boshart.

Partij voor de Vrijheid (PVV) (Party for Freedom): POB 20018, 2500 EA The Hague; tel. (+31) 70 3182867; fax (+31) 70 3183836; e-mail webmaster@pvv.nl; internet www.pvv.nl; f. 2006 by its leader on leaving the VVD; right-wing; conservative stance on immigration; secured four seats in the EP in 2014; Leader Geert Wilders.

Socialistische Partij (SP) (Socialist Party): Snouckaertlaan 70, 3811 MB Amersfoort; tel. (+31 10) 2435555; fax (+31 10) 2435512; e-mail sp@sp.nl; internet www.sp.nl; f. 1972; 46,000 mems; secured two seats in the 2014 EP elections; Chair. Ron Meyer; Leader Emile Roemer.

Staatkundig Gereformeerde Partij (SGP) (Political Reformed Party): Dinkel 7, 3068 HB Rotterdam; tel. (+31 182) 7200770; e-mail voorlichting@sgp.nl; internet www.sgp.nl; f. 1918; Calvinist; female membership banned from 1993 until 2006; stood in the 2014 EP elections jointly with the CU and won two seats; Chair. M.F. van Leeuwen; Leader Kees van der Staaij.

Volkspartij voor Vrijheid en Democratie (VVD) (People's Party for Freedom and Democracy): Mauritskade 21, POB 30836, 2500 GV The Hague; tel. (+31 70) 3613061; fax (+31 70) 3608276; e-mail info@vvd.nl; internet www.vvd.nl; f. 1948; economically liberal and advocates free enterprise, individual freedom and responsibility, but its programme also supports social security and recommends the participation of workers in profits and management; 38,000 mems, won three seats in EP in 2014; Chair. Henry Keizer.

POLAND

Platforma Obywatelska (PO) (Civic Platform): ul. Wiejska 12A, piętro IV, 00-490 Warsaw; tel. (+48 22) 635-78-79; fax (+48 22) 635-76-41; e-mail biuro@platforma.org; internet www.platforma.org; f. 2001 by a popular independent presidential candidate and factions of the UW and the AWS; also known as the Citizens' Platform; secured 19 seats in the 2014 EP elections; Chair. Grzegorz Schetyna.

Poland (KNP) (Congress of the New Right): Szklanych Domów 3, 04-346 Warsaw; tel. (+48 79) 500-85-00; e-mail centrala@knp.org.pl; internet knp.org.pl; f. 2011; secured four seats in the 2014 EP elections; Pres. Michał Marusik.

Polskie Stronnictwo Ludowe (PSL) (Polish People's Party): ul. Piękna 3A, 00-539 Warsaw; tel. (+48 22) 620-60-20; fax (+48 22) 654-35-83; e-mail biuronkw@psl.org.pl; internet www.psl.pl; f. 1990; to replace United Peasant Party (Zjednoczone Stronnictwo Ludowe; f. 1949) and Polish Peasant Party-Rebirth (Polskie Stronnictwo Ludowe-Odrodzenie; f. 1989); centrist, stresses development of agriculture and social-market economy; 140,000 mems (2015); won four seats in the EP in 2014; Chair. Wladyslaw Kosiniak-Kamysz.

Prawo i Sprawiedliwość (PiS) (Law and Justice Party): ul. Nowogrodzka 84/86, 02-018 Warsaw; tel. (+48 22) 621-50-35; fax (+48 22) 621-67-67; e-mail biuro@pis.org.pl; internet www.pis.org.pl; f. 2001; conservative; 30,000 mems (2015); secured 19 seats in the EP in 2014; Pres. Jarosław Kaczyński.

Sojusz Lewicy Demokratycznej (SLD) (Alliance of the Democratic Left): Złota 9, 00-019 Warsaw; tel. (+48 22) 621-03-41; e-mail sld@sld.org.pl; internet www.sld.org.pl; f. 1993; left-wing; formed a coalition with Unia Pracy for the 2004 and 2009 EP elections; secured five seats in the EP in 2014; Chair. Włodzimierz Czarzasty.

PORTUGAL

Bloco de Esquerda (Esquerda) (Left-Wing Bloc): Rua da Palma 268, 1100-394 Lisbon; tel. (+351) 213510510; fax (+351) 213510519; e-mail bloco.esquerda@bloco.org; internet www.bloco.org; f. 1999; originally founded as coalition of left-wing political groups, before acquiring full party status; left-wing; secured a single seat in the EP in 2014; Leader Catarina Martins.

Partido Comunista Português (PCP) (Portuguese Communist Party): Rua Soeiro Pereira Gomes 3, 1600-196 Lisbon; tel. (+351) 217813800; fax (+351) 217969126; e-mail pcp@pcp.pt; internet www.pcp.pt; f. 1921; legalized 1974; theoretical foundation is Marxism-Leninism; aims are the defence and consolidation of the democratic regime and the revolutionary achievements, and ultimately the building of, a socialist society in Portugal; stood for the 2014 EP elections as the Democrática Unitária coalition with Partido Ecologista Os Verdes (PEV) and secured three seats in the EP; Sec.-Gen. Jerónimo de Sousa.

Partido Popular (CDS-PP) (Popular Party): Largo Adelino Amaro da Costa 5, 1149-063 Lisbon; tel. (+351) 218814700; fax (+351) 218860454; e-mail cds-pp@cds.pt; internet www.cds.pt; f. 1974; formerly Centro Democrático Social; centre-right; mem. of International Democratic Union; supports social market economy and reduction of public-sector intervention in the economy; contested the 2014 EP elections in alliance with Partido Social Democrata and won seven seats; Pres. Assunção Cristas.

Partido Social Democrata (PSD) (Social Democratic Party): Rua de São Caetano 9, 1249-087 Lisbon; tel. (+351) 213918500; fax (+351) 213976967; e-mail psd@psd.pt; internet www.psd.pt; f. 1974; formerly Partido Popular Democrático (PPD); centre-right; supports EU membership; contested the 2014 EP elections in coalition with Partido Popular and secured seven seats; Leader Pedro Passos Coelho.

Partido Socialista (PS) (Socialist Party): Largo do Rato 2, 1269-143 Lisbon; tel. (+351) 213822000; fax (+351) 213822022; e-mail portal@ps.pt; internet www.ps.pt; f. 1973; from former Acção Socialista Portuguesa (Portuguese Socialist Action); advocates a society of greater social justice and co-operation between public, private and co-operative sectors, while respecting public liberties and the will of the majority attained through free elections; won eight seats in the 2014 EP elections; Pres. Carlos César; Sec.-Gen. António Costa.

Partido da Terra (MPT) (The Earth Party): Rua da Beneficência 111, 1°, Apdo 43050, 1600-018 Lisbon; tel. (+351) 211341068; fax (+351) 215917414; e-mail mpt@mpt.pt; internet www.mpt.pt; f. 1993; secured two seats in the EP elections in 2014; Pres. José Inácio Faria.

ROMANIA

Alianţa Liberalilor şi Democraţilor (ALDE Romania) (Alliance of Liberals and Democrats): Str. Kiseleff 57, Sec. 1, Bucharest; tel. (+40 31) 4251101; fax (+40 31) 4251102; e-mail secretariat@alde.ro; internet www.alde.ro; f. 2015; f. by merger of Partidul Coservator (Conservative Party), which had obtained 16 seats in the EP in 2014, and Partidul Liberal Reformator (Liberal Reformist Party); Co-Pres. Călin Popescu-Tăriceanu, Daniel Constantin.

Partidul Mişcarea Populară (PMP) (People's Movement Party): str. Iorga 11, 010432 Bucharest; e-mail secretariat@pmponline.ro; f. 2014; centre-right; won two seats in the 2014 EP elections; Chair. Traian Băsescu.

Partidul Naţional Liberal (PNL) (National Liberal Party): Aleea Modrogan 1, Bucharest; tel. (+40 21) 2310795; fax (+40 21) 2310796; e-mail pnl.ro; f. 1875; advocates both economic and social liberalism; secured six seats in the EP in 2014; in Nov. 2014 absorbed Partidul Democrat Liberal (Democratic Liberal Party), which had secured five seats in the EP in 2014; Pres. Ludovic Orban.

Partidul Social Democrat (PSD) (Social Democratic Party): Şos. Kiseleff 10, 011346 Bucharest 1; tel. (+40 31) 4135155; e-mail psd@psd.ro; internet www.psd.ro; f. 2001 from the merger of the Romanian Social Democratic Party (PSDR) and the Party of Social Democracy in Romania (PDSR; f. 1993); formed an alliance with Partidul Conservator and Uniunea Nationala pentru Progresul Romaniei for the 2014 EP elections and won 16 seats; Chair. Liviu Nicolae Dragnea; Sec.-Gen. Marian Neacsu.

Romániai Magyar Demokrata Szövetség/Uniunea Democrată Maghiară din România (RMDSZ/UDMR) (Democratic Alliance of Hungarians in Romania): Str. Dr. Lister 57, 050 542 Bucharest; e-mail internationalsecretary@rmdsz.ro; internet www.rmdsz.ro; f. 1989; f. to represent the interests of the Hungarian minority in Romania; secured two seats in the EP in 2014; Chair. Hunor Kelemen.

SLOVAKIA

Kresťanskodemokratické hnutie (KDH) (Christian Democratic Alliance): Safarikovo 4, 811 02 Bratislava; tel. (+421 2) 58233431; fax (+421 2) 58233434; e-mail sekretariat@kdh.sk; internet kdh.sk; f. 1990; applies Christian and conservative values; obtained two seats in EP in 2014; Chair. Alojz Hlina.

Magyar Koalíció Pártja—Strana mad'arskej koalície (MKP—SMK) (Party of the Hungarian Coalition): Cajaková 8, 811 05 Bratislava; tel. (+421 2) 57106013; fax (+421 2) 57106015; e-mail admin@smk.sk; internet www.mkp.sk; f. 1998; f. by merger of Coexistence, the Hungarian Christian Democratic Movement and the Hungarian Civic Party; represents the interests of the Hungarian community in Slovakia; secured a single seat in the EP in 2014; Chair. József Menyhart.

Most-Híd (Bridge): Trnavská cesta 37, 831 04 Bratislava; tel. (+421 2) 49114555; fax (+421 2) 49114500; e-mail office@most-hid.sk; internet www.most-hid.sk; f. 2009; promotes co-operation between all sections of society; obtained one seat in the EP in 2014; Chair. Béla Bugár.

Nová väčšina—Dohoda (NOVA) (New Majority—Agreement): Ručová dolina 6, 821 08 Bratislava; e-mail nova@nova.sk; internet www.nova.sk; f. 2012; conservative, anti-corruption; won one seat in the EP in 2014; Chair. Daniel Lipšic.

Obyčajní ľudia a nezávislé osobnosti (OĽaNO) (Ordinary People and Independent Personalities): Študentská 2, 917 01 Trnava; e-mail kontakt@obycajniludia.sk; internet www.obycajniludia.sk; f. 2011; conservative; secured a single seat in the EP in 2014; Leader Igor Matovič.

Sloboda a Solidarita (SaS) (Freedom and Solidarity): Priemyselná 8, 821 09 Bratislava; e-mail sas@strana-sas.sk; internet www.strana-sas.sk; f. 2009; liberal; secured one seat in the EP in 2014; Chair. Richard Sulík.

Slovenská demokratická a kresťanská únia—Demokratická strana (SDKÚ—DS) (Slovak Democratic and Christian Union): Šancová 70, 811 05 Bratislava; tel. (+421 9) 15982625; e-mail sdku-ds@sdku-ds.sk; internet www.sdku-ds.sk; f. 2000; centre-right; secured two seats in the EP in 2014; Chair. Pavol Frešo.

SMER—Sociálna Demokracia (SMER-SD) (Direction—Social Democracy): Súmračná 25, 821 02 Bratislava; tel. (+421 2) 43426297; fax (+421 2) 43426300; e-mail sekretariat.predseda@strana-smer.sk; internet www.strana-smer.sk; f. 1999; absorbed the Party of Civic Understanding in 2003; centre-right, pro-EU, pro-NATO; won four seats in the 2014 EP elections; Chair. Robert Fico.

SLOVENIA

Demokratična Stranka Upokojencev Slovenije (DeSUS) (Democratic Party of Pensioners of Slovenia): Kersnikova 6/VI, 1000 Ljubljana; tel. (+386 1) 4397350; fax (+386 1) 4314113; e-mail info@desus.si; internet www.desus.si 12,000 mems (2015); obtained one seat in the EP in 2014; Pres. Karl Erjavec.

Nova Slovenija—Krščanska ljudska stranka (Nsi) (New Slovenia—Christian People's Party): Dyorakova 11A, 1000 Ljubljana; tel. (+386 1) 2416650; fax (+386 1) 2416670; e-mail tajnistvo@nsi.si; internet nsi.si; f. 2000 by disaffected mems of the Slovenian People's Party; right-wing; contested the 2014 EP elections in coalition with Slovenska ljudska stranka, securing two seats; Pres. Ljudmila Novak.

Slovenska demokratska stranka (SDS) (Slovenian Democratic Party): Trstenjakova 8, 1000 Ljubljana; tel. (+386 1) 4345450;

fax (+386 1) 4345452; e-mail tajnistvo@sds.si; internet www.sds.si; f. 1994 by mems of Democratic Party who opted not to join the LDS; 30,000 mems (2013); won three seats in the EP in 2014; Pres. Janez Janša; Sec.-Gen. Janez Mežan.

Socialni demokrati (SD) (Social Democrats): Levstikova 15, 1000 Ljubljana; tel. (+386 1) 2444100; e-mail info@socialnidemokrati.si; internet socialnidemokrati.si; f. 1992 as the United List, an electoral alliance of the Democratic Party of Pensioners, the Party of Democratic Reform of Slovenia, the Social Democratic Union and the Workers' Party of Slovenia; became a single party in 1993; secured a single seat in the EP in 2014; Pres. Dejan Zidan.

Verjamem (I Believe): Domčale cesta 104, 1230 Ljubljana; tel. (+031) 356970; e-mail drustvo.verjamem.vate@gmail.com; internet www.verjamem.si; seeks to raise living standards, and to promote self-sufficiency in food and energy; secured one seat in the EP in 2014; Leader Igor Šoltes.

Zares—Socialno Liberalni (Zares) (For Real—Social Liberals): Dunajska cesta 106, 1000 Ljubljana; e-mail info@zares.si; internet www.zares.si; f. 2007 as a result of a split within LDS; centre-left policies; Pres. Dr Pavel Gantar.

SPAIN

Bloque Nacionalista Galego (BNG) (Bloque Nacionalista Gallego): Avda. Rodriguez de Viguri, 16, 15703 Santiago de Compostela; e-mail sedenacional@bng.gal; internet www.bng.gal; f. 1982; contested the 2014 EP elections as part of alliance, winning one seat; Leader Xavier Vence.

Ciudadanos—Partido de la Ciudadanía (The Citizens—Party of the Citizenry): Gran Vía, 751A, 1°, 2ª, 08013 Barcelona; e-mail info@ciudadanos-cs.org; internet www.ciudadanos-cs.org; f. 2006; won two seats in the EP in 2014; Pres. Albert Rivera.

Convergència Democràtica de Catalunya (CDC) (Democratic Convergence of Catalonia): C/ Còrsega 331–333, 08037 Barcelona; tel. (+34) 93-2363100; e-mail cdc@convergencia.cat; internet www.convergencia.cat; f. 1974; allied with Unió Democràtica de Catalunya (UDC) under the name Convergència i Unió (CiU) for the purposes of national elections; Catalan nationalist; centre; stood for the 2014 EP elections as part of the Coalición por Europa and secured three seats in the EP; Pres. Jacint Borràs.

Euzko Alderdi Jeltzalea/Partido Nacionalista Vasco (EAJ/PNV) (Basque Nationalist Party): Ibáñez de Bilbao 16, 48001 Bilbao; tel. (+34) 94-4039400; fax (+34) 94-4039415; e-mail idazkaritza.abb@eaj-pnv.eus; internet www.eaj-pnv.com; f. 1895; Basque nationalist; seeks to achieve autonomous region through peaceful means; stood for the 2014 EP elections as part of the Coalición por Europa, securing three seats; Pres. Andoni Ortuzar Arruabarrena.

Iniciativa per Catalunya Verds (ICV) (Initiative for Catalonia—Greens): Passatge del Rellotge 3, 08002 Barcelona; tel. (+34) 93-3010612; e-mail iniciativa@iniciativa.cat; internet www.iniciativa.cat; f. 1987; f. as a federation of parties with the aim of fostering an alternative left-leaning project; contested the 2014 EP elections as part of alliance, winning six seats; Joint Nat. Co-ordinator David Cid, Marta Ribas; Sec.-Gen. Nuria Buenaventura.

Izquierda Unida (IU) (United Left): Olimpo 35, 28043 Madrid; tel. (+34) 91-7227500; fax (+34) 91-3880405; e-mail info@izquierda-unida.es; internet www.izquierda-unida.es; f. 1986 by left-wing parties to contest elections; includes Candidatura Unitaria de Trabajadores (CUT), Izquierda Republicana (IR), Partido de Acción Socialista (PASOC), Partido Comunista de España (PCE); contested the 2014 EP elections as part of alliance, winning six seats; Fed. Co-ordinator Cayo Lara Moya.

Partido Popular (PP) (Popular Party): Calle Génova 13, 1ª planta, 28004 Madrid; tel. (+34) 91-5577200; e-mail atencion2@pp.es; internet www.pp.es; f. 1976; fmrly Alianza Popular, name changed 1989; absorbed Democracia Cristiana (fmrly Partido Demócrata Popular) and Partido Liberal in 1989; centre-right, Christian Democrat; 860,818, mems (2016), secured 16 seats in the EP in 2014; Pres. Mariano Rajoy Brey; Sec.-Gen. María Dolores de Cospedal García.

Partit dels Socialistes de Catalunya (PSC-PSOE) (Socialists' Party of Catalonia): Nicaragua 75–77, 08029 Barcelona; tel. (+34) 93-4955400; e-mail info@socialistes.org; internet www.socialistes.ca; f. 1978; Catalan social democratic party; secured 14 seats in the EP in 2014; Pres. Àngel Ros i Domingo.

Podemos (We Can): C/ Zurita 21, 28005 Madrid; e-mail contacto@podemos.info; internet podemos.info; f. 2014; 489,039 mems (2017); secured five seats in the EP in 2014; Leader Pablo Iglesias.

Unión Progreso y Democracia (UPyD) (Union, Progress and Democracy): Desengaño 12, Madrid; tel. (+34) 91-5982286; e-mail informacion@upyd.es; internet upyd.es; f. 2007 to oppose the two main Spanish political parties; stresses the idea of Spain as a nation-state, opposing regional nationalist movements; won four seats in the EP in 2014; Spokesperson Cristiano Brown.

SWEDEN

Centerpartiet (Centre Party): Stora Nygatan 4, POB 2200103 15 Stockholm; tel. (+46 8) 617-38-00; e-mail info@centerpartiet.se; internet www.centerpartiet.se; f. 1910 as an agrarian party; previously known as Centerpartiets Riksorganisation; advocates social, environmental and progressive development and decentralization; secured one seat in the EP in 2014; Leader Annie Lööf.

Feministiskt initiativ (Fi) (Feminist Initiative): Östervångsplan 15, 26 144 Landskrona; e-mail info@feministisktinitiativ.se; internet feministisktinitiativ.se; f. 2005; secured one seat in the EP in 2014; Pres. Gita Nabavi; Sec Maria Pettersson.

Folkpartiet Liberalerna (FP) (Liberal Party): Stora Nygatan 2A, POB 2253, 103 16 Stockholm; tel. (+46 8) 41-02-42-00; e-mail info@folkpartiet.se; internet www.folkpartiet.se; f. 1902; advocates market-orientated economy and social welfare system; won two seats in the EP in 2014; Leader Jan Björklund.

Kristdemokraterna (Kd) (Christian Democratic Party): Munkbron 1, Box 2373, 103 18 Stockholm; tel. (+46 8) 723-25-00; e-mail info@kristdemokraterna.se; internet www.kristdemokraterna.se; f. 1964; f. as Kristdemokratiska Samhällspartiet (KdS), to promote emphasis on Christian values in political life; obtained one seat in the EP in 2014; Chair. Ebba Busch Thor.

Miljöpartiet de Gröna (MP) (Green Party): Pustegränd 1–3, 118 20 Stockholm; tel. (+46 8) 545-224-50; fax (+46 8) 545-224-60; e-mail info@mp.se; internet www.mp.se; f. 1981; environmentalist; opposes EU membership; 9,400 mems; secured four seats in the EP in 2014; Joint Leaders Gustav Fridolin, Isabella Lövin.

Moderata Samlingspartiet (Moderaterna) (Moderate Coalition Party): Stora Nygatan 30, Box 2080, 103 12 Stockholm; tel. (+46 8) 676-80-00; e-mail info@moderaterna.se; internet moderaterna.se; f. 1904; advocates liberal-conservative market-orientated economy; obtained three seats in the EP in 2014; Chair. Anna Kinberg.

Piratpartiet (Pirate Party): POB 307, 101 26 Stockholm; tel. (+46 076) 314-99-82; e-mail info@piratpartiet.se; internet www.piratpartiet.se; f. 2006; seeks fundamental reform of copyright law, abolition of the patent system and respect for citizens' rights to privacy as its sole agenda; Leader Magnus Andersson; Sec. Anton Nordenfur.

Sverigedemokraterna (SD) (Sweden Democrats): POB 26, 291 21 Kristianstad; e-mail info@sverigedemokraterna.se; internet sd.se; f. 1988; nationalist, anti-immigration; won two seats in the EP in 2014; Leader Jimmie Åkesson.

Vänsterpartiet (V) (Left Party): POB 12660, 112 93 Stockholm; tel. (+46 8) 654-08-20; e-mail info@vansterpartiet.se; internet www.vansterpartiet.se; f. 1917 as Left Social Democratic Party of Sweden; affiliated to the Communist International 1919; renamed the Communist Party in 1921; renamed Left Party/Communists in 1967; renamed Left Party in 1990; policies based on the principles of Marxism, feminism and other theories; secured one seat in the EP in 2014; Chair. Jonas Sjöstedt.

UNITED KINGDOM

Conservative Party (Conservative and Unionist Party) (Con): Conservative Campaign Headquarters, 4 Matthew Parker St, London SW1H 9HQ; tel. (+44 20) 7222-9000; fax (+44 20) 7222-1135; internet www.conservatives.com; f. 1870; formed an electoral alliance, Ulster Conservatives and Unionists—New Force, with the UUP for the 2009 EP elections; secured 19 seats in the EP in 2014; Leader Theresa May; Chair. Patrick McLoughlin.

Democratic Unionist Party (DUP): 91 Dundela Ave, Belfast BT4 3BU; tel. (+44 28) 9047-1155; fax (+44 28) 9052-1289; e-mail info@mydup.com; internet www.mydup.com; f. 1905; the larger of the two main unionist political parties in Northern Ireland; secured one seat in the EP in 2014; Leader Arlene Foster.

Green Party: The Biscuit Factory, Unit 201A Block, 100 Clements Rd, London SE16 4DG; tel. (+44 20) 3691-9400; e-mail office@greenparty.org.uk; internet www.greenparty.org.uk; f. 1973 as the Ecology Party; present name adopted in 1985; campaigns for the protection of the environment and the promotion of social justice; 12,000 mems; secured three seats in the EP in 2014; Co-Leaders Jonathan Bartley, Caroline Lucas.

Labour Party (Lab): Labour Central, Kings Manor, Newcastle NE1 6PA; tel. (+44 845) 092-2299; internet www.labour.org.uk; f. 1900; democratic socialist party; 517,000 mems (2017); won 20 seats in the EP in 2014; Leader Jeremy Corbyn.

Liberal Democrats (Lib Dems): 8–10 Great George St, London SW1P 3AE; tel. (+44 20) 7022-0988; e-mail info@libdems.org.uk; internet www.libdems.org.uk; f. 1988; 82,000 mems (2017); secured a single seat in the EP in 2014; Leader Vince Cable.

Plaid Cymru (Plaid) (The Party of Wales): Tŷ Gwynfor, Marine Chambers, Anson Court, Atlantic Wharf, Cardiff CF10 4AL; tel. (+44 29) 2047-2272; e-mail post@plaidcymru.org; internet www2.plaid.cymru; f. 1925; promotes Welsh interests and seeks national status for Wales; 8,300 mems (2016); secured one seat in the EP in 2014; Leader Leanne Wood; Chair. Alun Ffred Jones.

Scottish National Party (SNP): Gordon Lamb House, 3 Jackson's Entry, Edinburgh EH8 8PJ; tel. (+44 800) 633-5432; e-mail info@snp.org; internet www.snp.org; f. 1934; advocates independence for Scotland as a mem. of the EU, and Scottish control of national resources; 120,000 mems (2016); won two seats in the EP in 2014; Leader Nicola Sturgeon.

Sinn Féin (SF) (We Ourselves): 53 Falls Rd, Belfast BT12 4PD; tel. (+44 28) 9034-7350; fax (+44 28) 9022-3001; e-mail admin@sinnfein.ie; internet www.sinnfein.ie; f. 1905; has seats in the Northern Ireland Assembly; advocates the termination of British rule in Northern Ireland; seeks the establishment of a democratic socialist republic in a reunified Ireland; obtained a single seat in the EP in the 2014 elections; Pres. Gerry Adams.

Ulster Unionist Party (UUP): Strandtown Hall, 2-4 Belmont Rd, Belfast BT4 2AN; tel. (+44 28) 9047-4630; fax (+44 28) 9065-2149; e-mail uup@uup.org; internet uup.org; f. 1905; formally allied to the Conservative Party until 1985; supports devolution for N. Ireland within the context of union with Great Britain; formed an electoral alliance, Ulster Conservatives and Unionists—New Force, with the Conservative Party for the 2009 EP elections; secured one seat in the EP in 2014; Leader Robin Swann.

UK Independence Party (UKIP): Lexdrum House, King Charles Business Park, Newton Abbot, Devon TQ12 6UT; tel. (+44 0333) 8006800; e-mail mail@ukip.org; internet www.ukip.org; f. 1993; opposed British membership of the EU; 39,000 mems; secured 24 seats in the EP in 2014; Chair. Henry Bolton.

Member Parties of Political Groups

GROUP OF THE ALLIANCE OF LIBERALS AND DEMOCRATS FOR EUROPE (ALDE)

Member Parties

Alianța Liberalilor și Democraților (Romania)

Ano 2011 (Czech Republic)

Centerpartiet (Sweden)

Ciudadanos (Spain)

Darbo Partija (Lithuania)

Democraten 66 (D66—Netherlands)

Drasi (Greece)

Dvizhenie za Prava i Svobodi (Bulgaria)

Eesti Keskerakond (Estonia)

Eesti Reformierakond (Estonia)

Fianna Fáil (Ireland)

Freie Demokratische Partei (Germany)

Hrvatska Narodna Stranka-Liberalni Demokrati (Croatia)

Hrvatska Socijalno-Liberalna Stranka (Croatia)

Istarski Demokratski Sabor (Croatia)

Latvijas Attistibai (Latvia)

Liberal Democrats (United Kingdom)

Liberalisok—Magyar Liberális Párt (Hungary)

Liberalna (Sweden)

Lietuvos Laisvės Sajunga (Lithuania)

Mouvement Réformateur (Belgium)

NEOS (Austria)

Nowoczesna (Poland)

Open Vlaamse Liberalen en Democraten (Belgium)

Parti Démocratique/Demokratesch Partei (DP/PD—Luxembourg)

Partit Demòcrata Europeu Català (Spain)

Radicali Italiani (Italy)

Radikale Venstre (Denmark)

Stranka Modernega Centra (Slovenia)

Suomen Keskusta (Kesk—Finland)

Svenska Folkpartiet (Finland)

Union of Democrats and Independents (France)

United Democrats (Cyprus)

Venstre–Danmarks Liberale Parti (Denmark)

Volkspartij voor Vrijheid en Democratie (Netherlands)

EUROPEAN CONSERVATIVES AND REFORMISTS GROUP (ECR)

Member Parties

ChristenUnie (Netherlands)

Conservative Party (United Kingdom)

Dansk Folkeparti (Denmark)

Direzione Italia (Italy)

Fianna Fáil (Ireland)

Familien-Partei Deutschlands (FAMILIE-Germany)

Hrvatska Konzervativna Stranka (Croatia)

Liberal-Konservative Reformer (Germany)

Lietuvos lenkų rinkimų akcija—Krikščioniškų šeimų sąjunga (Lithuania)

Nacionālā apvienība 'Visu Latvijai!'—'Tēvzemei un Brīvībai/LNNK' (Latvia)

Nieuw-Vlaamse Alliantie (Belgium)

Nová väčšina (NOVA—Slovakia)

Občanská Demokratická Strana (Czech Republic)

Obyčajní ľudia (OĽaNO—Slovakia)

Partidul M10 (M10—Romania)

Perussuomalaiset (Finland)

Prawica Rzeczypospolitej (Poland)

Reload Bulgaria (Bulgaria)

Prawo i Sprawiedliwość (Poland)

Sloboda a Solidarita (Slovakia)

Solidarity (Cyprus)

Ulster Unionist Party (United Kingdom)

VMRO—Balgarsko Natsionalno Dvizhenie (Bulgaria)

EUROPE OF FREEDOM AND DIRECT DEMOCRACY (EFDD)

Member Parties

Alternative für Deutschland (Germany)

MoVimento 5 Stelle (M5S—Italy)

Strana svobodných občanů (Czech Republic)

Sverigedemokraterna (Sweden)

Tvarka ir Teişingumas (Lithuania)

UK Independence Party (United Kingdom)

GROUP OF THE EUROPEAN PEOPLE'S PARTY (CHRISTIAN DEMOCRATS) (EPP)

Member Parties

Centre Démocrate Humaniste (Belgium)

Christen Democratisch Appèl (Netherlands)

Christen-Demokratisch en Vlaams Partij (Belgium)

Christlich Demokratische Union Deutschlands (Germany)

Christlich Soziale Partei (Belgium)

Christlich-Soziale Union in Bayern e.V (Germany)

Demokrati za Silna Bălgarija (DSB—Bulgaria)

Det Konservative Folkeparti (Denmark)

Dimokratikos Synagermos (Cyprus)

Erakond Isamaa ja Res Publica Liit (Estonia)

Fidesz—Magyar Polgári Szövetség (FIDESZ—MPSZ—Hungary)

Fine Gael (Ireland)

Forza Italia (Italy)

Grazhdani za Evropeysko Razvitie na Balgariya (GERB—Bulgaria)

Hrvatska demokratska zajednica (Croatia)

Hrvatska Seljačka Stranka (Croatia)

Kansallinen Kokoomus (Kok—Finland)

Kereszténydemokrata Néppárt (Hungary)

Křesťanská a Demokratická Unia—československá Strana Lidová (Czech Republic)

Kresťanskodemokratické Hnutie (Slovakia)

Kristdemokraterna (Denmark)

Moderata Samlingspartiet (Moderaterna—Sweden)

Most-Híd (Slovakia)

Nea Dimokratia (Greece)

Nova Slovenija—Krščanska ljudska stranka (Slovenia)

Nuovo Centrodestra-Unione di Centro (Italy)

Österreichische Volkspartei (Austria)

Parti Chrétien Social Luxembourgeois (Luxembourg)
Partido da Terra (Portugal)
Partido Popular (Portugal)
Partido Popular (Spain)
Partido Social Democrata (Portugal)
Partidul Mişcarea Populară (Romania)
Partidul Naşional Liberal (Romania)
Partit Nazzjonalista (Malta)
Platforma Obywatelska (Poland)
Polskie Stronnictwo Ludowe (Poland)
Les Républicains (France)
Slovenska Demokratska Stranka (Slovenia)
Slovenska Ljudska Stranka (Slovenia)
Starostové a Nezávisli (Czech Republic)
Strana Mad'arskej Komunity-Magyar Közösség Pártja (Slovakia)
Südtiroler Volkspartei (Italy)
Tėvynės Sąjunga—Lietuvos Krikščionys Demokratai (Lithuania)
TOP 09 (Czech Republic)
Uniunea Democrată Maghiară din România (Romania)
Vienotība (Latvia)

GROUP OF THE GREENS/EUROPEAN FREE ALLIANCE (GREENS/EFA)

Member Parties

Bündnis 90/Die Grünen (Germany)
Ecologistes Confédérés pour l'Organisation de Luttes Originales (ECOLO—Belgium)
EQUO (Spain)
Esquerra Republicana de Catalunya (Spain)
Europe Écologie—Les Verts (France)
Green Party (United Kingdom)
Gréng, Déi (Luxembourg)
Groen! (Belgium)
GroenLinks (Netherlands)
Die Grünen (Belgium)
Iniciativa per Catalunya Verds (Spain)
Lehet Más a Politika (Hungary)
Lietuvos valstiečių ir čaliųjų sąjunga (Lithuania)
Miljöpartiet de Gröna (Sweden)
Odrčivi Razvoj Hrvatske (Croatia)
Ökologisch-Demokratische Partei (Germany)
Párbeszéd Magyarországért (Hungary)
Par Cilvžka Tiesībām Vienotā Latvijā (Latvia)
Piratenpartei (Germany)
Plaid Cymru (Plaid—United Kingdom)
Scottish National Party (SNP—United Kingdom)
Socialistisk Folkeparti (SF—Denmark)
Verjamem (Slovenia)
Vihreät (Vihr—Finland)

CONFEDERAL GROUP OF THE EUROPEAN UNITED LEFT/NORDIC GREEN LEFT (GUE/NGL)

Member Parties

Anorthotiko Komma Ergazomenou Laou (Cyprus)
Bloco de Esquerda (Left Bloc—Portugal)
Euskal Herria Bildu (Spain)
Folkebevægelsen mod EU (Denmark)
Front de Gauche (France)
Izquierda Plural (Spain)
Komunistická Strana čech a Moravy (Czech Republic)
L'Altra Europa con Tsipras (Italy)
Die Linke (Germany)
Partido Comunista Português (Portugal)
Partij voor de Dieren (Netherlands)
Podemos (Spain)
Popular Unity (Greece)
Sinn Féin (United Kingdom)
Socialistische Partij (Netherlands)
Synaspismos Rizospastikis Aristeras (SYRIZA—Greece)
Union pour les Outre-Mer (France)
VänsterPartiet (Sweden)
Vasemmistoliitto (Finland)

EUROPE OF NATIONS AND FREEDOM (ENF)

Member Parties

Alternative für Deutschland (Germany)
Freiheitliche Partei Österreichs (Austria)
Front National (France)
Kongres Nowej Prawicy (Poland)
Lega Nord (Italy)
Partij voor de Vrijheid (Netherlands)
Vlaams Belang (Belgium)

GROUP OF THE PROGRESSIVE ALLIANCE OF SOCIALISTS AND DEMOCRATS IN THE EUROPEAN PARLIAMENT (S&D)

Member Parties

Arbetarepartiet-Socialdemokraterna (Sweden)
Articolo UNO: Movimento Democratico e Progressista (Italy)
Bălgarska Socialističeska Partija (Bulgaria)
Bezpartyjna (Poland)

European Parliament

česká strana sociálně demokratická (Czech Republic)

Demokratikus Koalíció (Hungary)

Dimokratiko Komma (Cyprus)

Feministiskt initiative (Sweden)

Kinima Sosialdimokraton EDEK (Cyprus)

Labour Party (United Kingdom)

Lietuvos Socialdemokrat Partija (Lithuania)

Magyar Szocialista Párt (Hungary)

Panellinio Socialistiko Kinima-Olive Tree (Greece)

Parti Ouvrier Socialiste Luxembourgeois/Lëtzebuerger Sozialistesch Arbechterpartei (Luxembourg)

Parti Radicale de Gauche (France)

Parti Socialiste (Belgium)

Parti Socialiste (France)

Partido Socialista (Portugal)

Partido Socialista Obrero Español (Spain)

Partidul Puterii Umaniste (Romania)

Partidul Social Democrat (Romania)

Partij van de Arbeid (Netherlands)

Partit dels Socialistes de Catalunya (Spain)

Partit Laburista/Malta Labour Party (Malta)

Partito Democratico (Italy)

SMER—Sociálna Demokracia (Slovakia)

Socialdemokratiet (Denmark)

Sociāldemokrātiskā Partija 'Saskaņa' (Latvia)

Socialni Demokrati (Slovenia)

Socijaldemokratska Partija Hrvatske (Croatia)

Sojusz Lewicy Demokratycznej (Poland)

Sotsiaaldemokraatlik Erakond (Estonia)

Sozialdemokratische Partei Deutschlands (Germany)

Sozialdemokratische Partei Österreichs (Austria)

SP.A—Socialistische Partij Anders (Belgium)

Suomen Sosialidemokraattinen Puolue/Finlands Socialdemokratiska Parti (Finland)

To Potami (The River—Greece)

Unia Pracy (Poland)

Administrative Units

SECRETARIAT

60 rue Wiertz, 1047 Brussels, Belgium; tel. (+32) 2-2842111
Plateau du Kirchberg, 2929 Luxembourg, Luxembourg; tel. (+352) 43001
1 ave du Président Robert Schuman, CS 91024, 67070 Strasbourg, France; tel. (+33) 3-88-17-40-01

DIRECTORY

Secretary-General

Secretary-General: Klaus Welle; tel. (+32) 2-2846242; e-mail klaus.welle@europarl.europa.eu.

Deputy Secretary-General and Director-General: Markus Winkler; tel. (+32) 2-2840737; e-mail markus.winkler@europarl.europa.eu.

SECRETARY-GENERAL'S OFFICE

Head of Office: Christian Mangold; tel. (+32) 2-2840770; e-mail christian.mangold@europarl.europa.eu.

Cabinet Member: Piotr Bartoszewicz-Malicki; tel. (+32) 2-2843199; e-mail piotr.bartoszewicz-malicki@europarl.europa.eu.

Team Leader: Franck Debie; tel. (+32) 2-2841307; e-mail franckrene.debie@europarl.europa.eu.

Adviser: Ana María Fernández Perles; tel. (+32) 2-2832084; e-mail ana.fernandez@europarl.europa.eu.

Adviser: Karen Fredsgaard; tel. (+32) 2-2832503; e-mail karen.fredsgaard@europarl.europa.eu.

Team Leader: Lars Vind Sørensen; tel. (+32) 2-2843123; e-mail lars.soerensen@europarl.europa.eu.

Legal Administrator: Piero Cavicchi; tel. (+352) 430022477; e-mail piero.cavicchi@europarl.europa.eu.

Legal Administrator: Gabriele Mazzini; e-mail gabriele.mazzini@europarl.europa.eu.

Conference of Presidents' Secretariat

Head of Unit: Sonia Wollny; tel. (+32) 2-2841065; e-mail sonia.wollny@europarl.europa.eu.

Bureau and Quaestors' Secretariat

Head of Unit: Nikolaos Tziorkas; tel. (+32) 2-2842341; e-mail nikolaos.tziorkas@europarl.europa.eu.

Internal Audit Unit

Head of Unit/Internal Auditor: Robert Galvin; tel. (+32) 2-2842331; e-mail robert.galvin@europarl.europa.eu.

Management Team Support Office

Head of Unit: Lucinia Bal; tel. (+32) 2-2846607; e-mail lucinia.bal@europarl.europa.eu.

Eco-Management and Audit Scheme Unit

Head of Unit: Siegfried Breier; tel. (+32) 2-2831283; e-mail siegfried.breier@europarl.europa.eu.

Data Protection

Data Protection Officer: Secondo Sabbioni; tel. (+32) 2-2846392; e-mail secondo.sabbioni@europarl.europa.eu.

DIRECTORATE FOR RELATIONS WITH THE POLITICAL GROUPS

Director: Mario Schwetz; tel. (+32) 2-2843992; e-mail mario.schwetz@europarl.europa.eu.

LEGAL SERVICE

Jurisconsult: Freddy Drexler; tel. (+32) 2-2843620; e-mail jurisconsultus@europarl.europa.eu.

Resources Service

Head of Service: Brigitte Müller-Reck; tel. (+352) 430024354.

Legislative and Judicial Co-ordination Unit

Head of Unit/Lawyer Manager: Maria Gomez-Leal; tel. (+32) 2-2843209; e-mail maria.gomez@europarl.europa.eu.

Directorate for Institutional and Parliamentary Affairs

Jurisconsult: Freddy Drexler; tel. (+32) 2-2843620; e-mail jurisconsultus@europarl.europa.eu.

Unit for Institutional and Budgetary Law

Head of Unit (acting): Ulrich Rosslein; tel. (+32) 2-2842618 e-mail ulrich.rosslein@europarl.europa.eu.

Unit for External Relations

Lawyer Manager: Anders Neergaard; tel. (+32) 2-2843970 e-mail anders.neergaard@europarl.europa.eu.

Unit for Rules and Parliamentary Law

Lawyer Manager: Niklas Goerlitz; tel. (+32) 2-2830442; e-mail niklas.goerlitz@europarl.europa.eu.

Directorate for Legislative Affairs

Director, Legal Affairs: María José Martínez Iglesias; tel. (+32) 2-2843150; e-mail mariajose.martinez@europarl.europa.eu.

Unit for Economic and Scientific Policies

Lawyer Manager: Luca Visaggio; tel. (+32) 2-2832589; e-mail luca.visaggio@europarl.europa.eu.

Unit for Structural and Cohesion Policies

Lawyer Manager: Lisbeth Grodum Knudsen; tel. (+32) 2-2832311; e-mail lisbeth.knudsen@europarl.europa.eu.

Unit for Justice and Civil Liberties

Lawyer Manager: Antonio Caiola; tel. (+32) 2-2840518; e-mail antonio.caiola@europarl.europa.eu.

Directorate for Administrative and Financial Affairs

Director, Legal Affairs: Norbert Lorenz; tel. (+32) 2-2843870 e-mail norbert.lorenz@europarl.europa.eu.

Unit for Staff Rights and Obligations

Lawyer Manager: Olivier Caisou-Rousseau; tel. (+352) 430020103; e-mail olivier.caisou-rousseau@europarl.europa.eu.

Unit for Staff Careers

Lawyer Manager: Valérie Montebello-Demogeot; tel. (+352) 430022178; e-mail valerie.montebellodemogeot@europarl.europa.eu.

Unit for Contract and Financial Law

Lawyer Manager: Paloma López-Carceller; tel. (+352) 430022801; e-mail paloma.lopez-carceller@europarl.europa.eu.

Real Estate Projects Unit

Head of Unit/Lawyer Manager: Jean-Marie Stenier; tel. (+352) 430027167; e-mail jean-marie.stenier@europarl.europa.eu.

DIRECTORATE-GENERAL FOR THE PRESIDENCY

Director-General: Markus Winkler; tel. (+32) 2-2840737; e-mail markus.winkler@europarl.europa.eu.

Resources Unit

Head of Unit: Josep María Ribot Igualada; tel. (+32) 2-2842354; e-mail josep.ribot@europarl.europa.eu.

Protocol Unit

Head of Unit: Carmen Castillo Del Carpio; tel. (+32) 2-2840538; e-mail carmen.castillo@europarl.europa.eu.

Directorate for the Plenary

Director (acting): Maria Gandolfo; tel. (+32) 2-2833064; e-mail maria.gandolfo@europarl.europa.eu.

PLENARY RECORDS UNIT

Head of Unit: José González Holguera; tel. (+32) 2-2840860 e-mail jose.holguera@europarl.europa.eu.

MEMBERS' ACTIVITIES UNIT

Head of Unit: Francisco Peyró Llopis; tel. (+32) 2-2844063 e-mail fran.peyro@europarl.europa.eu.

PLENARY ORGANIZATION AND FOLLOW-UP UNIT

Head of Unit: Carla Sailis; tel. (+32) 2-2843317; e-mail carla.sailis@europarl.europa.eu.

TABLING DESK

Head of Unit: Steven Wicker; tel. (+32) 2-2842420; e-mail steven.wicker@europarl.europa.eu.

OFFICIAL MAIL UNIT

Head of Unit: Milvia Priano; tel. (+32) 2-2843760; e-mail milvia.priano@europarl.europa.eu.

UNIT FOR RECEPTION AND REFERRAL OF OFFICIAL DOCUMENTS

Head of Unit: Libor Bohac; tel. (+32) 2-2831736; e-mail libor.bohac@europarl.europa.eu.

European Parliament DIRECTORY

MEMBERS' ADMINISTRATION UNIT

Head of Unit: Maria Gandolfo; tel. (+32) 2-2843064; e-mail maria.gandolfo@europarl.europa.eu.

Directorate for Legislative Acts

Director: Ellen Robson; tel. (+32) 2-2831408; e-mail ellen.robson@europarl.europa.eu.

LEGISLATIVE PLANNING AND CO-ORDINATION UNIT

Head of Unit: Patricia Jiminez Lozano; tel. (+32) 2-2834174 e-mail patricia.jimenez@europarl.europa.eu.

LEGISLATIVE QUALITY UNIT A—ECONOMIC AND SCIENTIFIC POLICY

Head of Unit: Peter Vavrik; tel. (+32) 2-2831726; e-mail peter.vavrik@europarl.europa.eu.

LEGISLATIVE QUALITY UNIT B—STRUCTURAL AND COHESION POLICY

Head of Unit (acting): Alina Monica Medeleanu; tel. (+32) 2-2832783; e-mail monica.medeleanu@europarl.europa.eu.

LEGISLATIVE QUALITY UNIT C—CITIZENS' RIGHTS

Head of Unit: Philipp Reifenrath; tel. (+32) 2-2844013; e-mail philipp.reifenrath@europarl.europa.eu.

LEGISLATIVE QUALITY UNIT D—BUDGET AFFAIRS

Head of Unit: Ellen Heinemann; tel. (+32) 2-2831716; e-mail ellen.heinemann@europarl.europa.eu.

LEGISLATIVE QUALITY UNIT E—EXTERNAL POLICIES

Head of Unit: Peter Norman; tel. (+32) 2-2841366; e-mail peter.norman@europarl.europa.eu.

Directorate for Relations with National Parliaments

Director-General: Markus Winkler; tel. (+32) 2-2840737; e-mail markus.winkler@europarl.europa.eu.

INSTITUTIONAL CO-OPERATION UNIT

Head of Unit: Pekka Nurminen; tel. (+32) 2-2840572; e-mail pekka.nurminen@europarl.europa.eu.

LEGISLATIVE DIALOGUE UNIT

Head of Unit: Patrizia María Prode; tel. (+32) 2-2843510; e-mail patrizia.prode@europarl.europa.eu.

DIRECTORATE-GENERAL FOR INTERNAL POLICIES OF THE UNION

Director-General: Riccardo Ribera D'Alcala; tel. (+32) 2-2843923; e-mail riccardo.ribera@europarl.europa.eu.

Strategic Planning Unit

Director-General: Riccardo Ribera D'Alcala; tel. (+32) 2-2843923; e-mail riccardo.ribera@europarl.europa.eu.

Directorate for Economic and Scientific Policies

Director: Karl-Peter Repplinger; tel. (+32) 2-2832235; e-mail karl-peter.repplinger@europarl.europa.eu.

SECRETARIAT FOR THE COMMITTEE ON EMPLOYMENT AND SOCIAL AFFAIRS

Head of Unit: Andreas Huber; tel. (+32) 2-2842418; e-mail andreas.huber@europarl.europa.eu.

SECRETARIAT FOR THE COMMITTEE ON ECONOMIC AND MONETARY AFFAIRS

Head of Unit: Adolfo Barbera del Rosal; tel. (+32) 2-2832160; e-mail adolfo.barbera@europarl.europa.eu.

SECRETARIAT FOR THE COMMITTEE ON THE INTERNAL MARKET AND CONSUMER PROTECTION

Head of Unit: Panayotis Konstantopoulos; tel. (+32) 2-2844550; e-mail panos.konstantopoulos@europarl.europa.eu.

SECRETARIAT FOR THE COMMITTEE ON INDUSTRY, RESEARCH AND ENERGY

Head of Unit: Klaus Baier; tel. (+32) 2-2844873; e-mail klaus.baier@europarl.europa.eu.

SECRETARIAT FOR THE COMMITTEE ON THE ENVIRONMENT, PUBLIC HEALTH AND FOOD SAFETY

Head of Unit: Sabina Magnano; tel. (+32) 2-2843685; e-mail sabina.magnano@europarl.europa.eu.

POLICY DEPARTMENT FOR ECONOMIC, SCIENTIFIC AND QUALITY OF LIFE POLICIES

Head of Unit: Patricia Silveira da Cunha; tel. (+32) 2-2843069; e-mail patricia.silveira@europarl.europa.eu.

ECONOMIC GOVERNANCE SUPPORT UNIT

Head of Unit: Kajus Hagelstam; tel. (+32) 2-2832856; e-mail kajus.hagelstam@europarl.europa.eu.

COMMITTEE OF INQUIRY INTO MONEY LAUNDERING, TAX AVOIDANCE AND TAX EVASION

Administrator: Anje Bultena; tel. (+32) 2-2832532; e-mail anje.bultena@europarl.europa.eu.

Directorate for Structural and Cohesion Policies

Director: Susanne Oberhauser; tel. (+32) 2-2843048; e-mail susanne.oberhauser@europarl.europa.eu.

SECRETARIAT FOR THE COMMITTEE ON AGRICULTURE AND RURAL DEVELOPMENT

Head of Unit: Philippe Musquar; tel. (+32) 2-2832078; e-mail philippe.musquar@europarl.europa.eu.

SECRETARIAT FOR THE COMMITTEE ON FISHERIES

Head of Unit: Claudio Quaranta; tel. (+32) 2-2832281; e-mail claudio.quaranta@europarl.europa.eu.

SECRETARIAT FOR THE COMMITTEE ON REGIONAL DEVELOPMENT

Head of Unit: Stephen Salter; tel. (+32) 2-2842772; e-mail stephen.salter@europarl.europa.eu.

SECRETARIAT FOR THE COMMITTEE ON TRANSPORT AND TOURISM

Head of Unit: Walter Goetz; tel. (+32) 2-2832587; e-mail walter.goetz@europarl.europa.eu.

SECRETARIAT FOR THE COMMITTEE ON CULTURE AND EDUCATION

Head of Unit: Nils Danklefsen; tel. (+32) 2-2832681; e-mail nils.danklefsen@europarl.europa.eu.

POLICY DEPARTMENT FOR STRUCTURAL AND COHESION POLICIES

Head of Unit: Iain Watt; tel. (+32) 2-2843113; e-mail iain.watt@europarl.europa.eu.

Directorate for Citizens' Rights and Constitutional Affairs

Director: Michael Alexander Speiser; tel. (+32) 2-2842475 e-mail michael.speiser@europarl.europa.eu.

SECRETARIAT FOR THE COMMITTEE ON CIVIL LIBERTIES, JUSTICE AND HOME AFFAIRS

Head of Unit: Antoine Cahen; tel. (+32) 2-2840660; e-mail antoine.cahen@europarl.europa.eu.

SECRETARIAT FOR THE COMMITTEE ON LEGAL AFFAIRS

Head of Unit: Robert Bray; tel. (+32) 2-2846337; e-mail robert.bray@europarl.europa.eu.

SECRETARIAT FOR THE COMMITTEE ON CONSTITUTIONAL AFFAIRS

Head of Unit: José Luís Pacheco; tel. (+32) 2-2843454; e-mail joseluis.pacheco@europarl.europa.eu.

SECRETARIAT FOR THE COMMITTEE ON WOMEN'S RIGHTS AND GENDER EQUALITY

Head of Unit (acting): Chiara Tamburini; tel. (+32) 2-2831735; e-mail chiara.tamburini@europarl.europa.eu.

SECRETARIAT FOR THE COMMITTEE ON PETITIONS

Head of Unit: Virpi Koykka; tel. (+32) 2-2846222; e-mail virpi.koykka@europarl.europa.eu.

POLICY DEPARTMENT FOR CITIZENS' RIGHTS AND CONSTITUTIONAL AFFAIRS

Head of Unit: Miguel Tell Cremades; tel. (+32) 2-2842433; e-mail miguel.tell@europarl.europa.eu.

Directorate for Budgetary Affairs

Director: Monika Strasser; tel. (+32) 2-2840623; e-mail monika.strasser@europarl.europa.eu.

SECRETARIAT FOR THE COMMITTEE ON BUDGETS

Head of Unit: Elisa Daffarra; tel. (+32) 2-2831387; e-mail elisa.daffarra@europarl.europa.eu.

SECRETARIAT FOR THE COMMITTEE ON BUDGETARY CONTROL

Head of Unit: Evelyn Waldherr; tel. (+32) 2-2842345; e-mail evelyn.waldherr@europarl.europa.eu.

POLICY DEPARTMENT FOR BUDGETARY AFFAIRS

Head of Unit: Niels Fischer; tel. (+32) 2-2841012; e-mail niels.fischer@europarl.europa.eu.

Directorate for Legislative Co-ordination and Conciliations

Director: Els Vandenbosch; tel. (+32) 2-2842736; e-mail els.vandenbosch@europarl.europa.eu.

CONCILIATIONS AND CO-DECISION UNIT

Head of Unit: Sarah Blau; tel. (+32) 2-2832504; e-mail sarah.blau@europarl.europa.eu.

UNIT FOR CO-ORDINATION OF EDITORIAL AND COMMUNICATION ACTIVITIES

Head of Unit: Federico Rossetto; tel. (+32) 2-2840955; e-mail federico.rossetto@europarl.europa.eu.

UNIT FOR LEGISLATIVE CO-ORDINATION AND PROGRAMMING

Head of Unit: Stephan Huber; tel. (+32) 2-2841301; e-mail stephan.huber@europarl.europa.eu.

Directorate for Resources

Director: Raquel De Vicente; tel. (+32) 2-2841040; e-mail raquel.devicente@europarl.europa.eu.

PERSONNEL UNIT

Head of Unit: Johannes Litzelmann; tel. (+32) 2-2832219 e-mail johannes.litzelmann@europarl.europa.eu.

INFORMATICS UNIT

Head of Unit: Juho Eskelinen; tel. (+32) 2-2842267; e-mail juho.eskelinen@europarl.europa.eu.

FINANCE UNIT

Head of Unit: Richard Wester; tel. (+32) 2-2842432; e-mail richard.wester@europarl.europa.eu.

DIRECTORATE-GENERAL FOR EXTERNAL POLICIES OF THE UNION

Director-General: Luís Marco Aguiriano Nalda; tel. (+32) 2-2843036; e-mail marco.aguiriano@europarl.europa.eu.

DIRECTORATE FOR COMMITTEES

Director: Alexandre Stutzmann; tel. (+32) 2-2843439; e-mail alexandre.stutzmann@europarl.europa.eu.

Secretariat for the Committee on Foreign Affairs

Head of Unit: Armelle Douaud; tel. (+32) 2-2843806; e-mail armelle.douaud@europarl.europa.eu.

SECRETARIAT FOR THE SUBCOMMITTEE ON SECURITY AND DEFENCE

Head of Unit: Maximilian Schroeder; tel. (+32) 2-2832250; e-mail maximilian.schroeder@europarl.europa.eu.

SECRETARIAT FOR THE SUBCOMMITTEE ON HUMAN RIGHTS/ HUMAN RIGHTS UNIT

Head of Unit: Rosemary Opacic; tel. (+32) 2-2842498; e-mail rosemary.opacic@europarl.europa.eu.

SECRETARIAT FOR THE COMMITTEE ON DEVELOPMENT

Head of Unit: Anne Louise McLauchlan; tel. (+32) 2-2846060; e-mail anne.mclauchlan@europarl.europa.eu.

SECRETARIAT FOR THE COMMITTEE ON INTERNATIONAL TRADE

Head of Unit: Alberto Rodas; tel. (+32) 2-2843514; e-mail alberto.rodas@europarl.europa.eu.

Directorate for Regions

Director: Ciril Stokelj; tel. (+32) 2-2842979; e-mail ciril.stokelj@europarl.europa.eu.

UNIT FOR EUROPE: ENLARGEMENT AND EUROPEAN ECONOMIC AREA

Head of Unit: Tatiana Mrazikova; tel. (+32) 2-2831739; e-mail tatiana.mrazikova@europarl.europa.eu.

UNIT FOR ASIA, AUSTRALIA AND NEW ZEALAND

Head of Unit: Niccolò Rinaldi; tel. (+32) 2-2830644; e-mail niccolo.rinaldi@europarl.europa.eu.

POLICY DEPARTMENT FOR EXTERNAL RELATIONS

Head of Unit: Pekka Hakala; tel. (+32) 2-2846273; e-mail pekka.hakala@europarl.europa.eu.

EUROMED AND MIDDLE EAST UNIT

Head of Unit: François Massoulie; tel. (+32) 2-2843688; e-mail francois.massoulie@europarl.europa.eu.

LATIN AMERICA UNIT

Head of Unit: José Javier Fernández Fernández; tel. (+32) 2-2842381; e-mail josejavier.fernandez@europarl.europa.eu.

UNIT FOR EUROPE: EASTERN PARTNERSHIP AND RUSSIA

Head of Unit: Sabina Mazzi-Zissis; tel. (+32) 2-2842643; e-mail sabina.mazzi@europarl.europa.eu.

UNIT FOR AFRICA, CARIBBEAN AND PACIFIC

Head of Unit: Donatella Pribaz; tel. (+32) 2-2840723; e-mail donatella.pribaz@europarl.europa.eu.

TRANSATLANTIC RELATIONS AND G8 UNIT

Head of Unit: Adam Isaacs; tel. (+32) 2-2842603; e-mail adam.isaacs@europarl.europa.eu.

Directorate for Resources

Director: Bernard Hellot; tel. (+32) 2-2843715; e-mail bernard.hellot@europarl.europa.eu.

PERSONNEL UNIT

Head of Unit: Emilia Gallego Perona; tel. (+32) 2-2844061 e-mail emilia.gallego@europarl.europa.eu.

FINANCE UNIT

Head of Unit: Mauro De Oliveira; tel. (+32) 2-2841866; e-mail mauro.deoliveira@europarl.europa.eu.

INFORMATICS UNIT

Director: Claudio Fabiani; tel. (+32) 2-2844778; e-mail claudio.fabiani@europarl.europa.eu.

Directorate for Democracy Support

Director: Pietro Ducci; tel. (+32) 2-2846656; e-mail pietro.ducci@europarl.europa.eu.

EUROPEAN PARLIAMENT MEDIATION SUPPORT SERVICE

Parliamentary Research Administrator: Doichin Cholakov; tel. (+32) 2-2832303; e-mail doichin.cholakov@europarl.europa.eu.

DEMOCRACY AND ELECTIONS ACTIONS

Head of Unit: Cristina Castagnoli; tel. (+32) 2-2832782; e-mail cristina.castagnoli@europarl.europa.eu.

PRE-ACCESSION ACTIONS UNIT

Head of Unit: Krzysztof Bernacki; tel. (+32) 2-2832685; e-mail krzysztof.bernacki@europarl.europa.eu.

HUMAN RIGHTS ACTION UNIT

Head of Unit (acting): Inga Rosinska; tel. (+32) 2-2846014 e-mail inga.rosinska@europarl.europa.eu.

DIRECTORATE-GENERAL FOR COMMUNICATION

Director-General: Jaume Duch Guillot; tel. (+32) 2-2843000 e-mail jaume.duch@europarl.europa.eu.

Public Opinion Monitoring Unit

Head of Unit: Philipp Schulmeister; tel. (+32) 2-2841381; e-mail philipp.schulmeister@europarl.europa.eu.

Directorate for Media

Director (acting): Ioannis Darmis; tel. (+32) 2-2843816; e-mail ioannis.darmis@europarl.europa.eu.

PRESS UNIT

Head of Unit: Marjory van den Broeke; tel. (+32) 2-2844304 e-mail marjory.vandenbroeke@europarl.europa.eu.

MEDIA SERVICES UNIT

Head of Unit: Ioannis Darmis; tel. (+32) 2-2843816; e-mail ioannis.darmis@europarl.europa.eu.

AUDIOVISUAL UNIT

Head of Unit/Audiovisual Manager: Fernando Carbajo; tel. (+32) 2-2844816; e-mail fernando.carbajo@europarl.europa.eu.

WEB COMMUNICATION UNIT

Head of Unit (acting): Thibault Lesenecal; tel. (+32) 2-2840709; e-mail thibault.lesenecal@europarl.europa.eu.

EUROPARL WEBMASTER UNIT

Head of Unit: Manuel Fernández Ponce; tel. (+32) 2-2846029 e-mail manuel.fernandez-ponce@europarl.europa.eu.

MEDIA INTELLIGENCE UNIT

Head of Unit: Paula Fernández-Hervas; tel. (+32) 2-2842535 e-mail paula.fernandez-hervas@europarl.europa.eu.

Directorate for Information Offices

Director: Katrin Ruhrmann; tel. (+32) 2-2842573; e-mail katrin.ruhrmann@europarl.europa.eu.

EP-US CONGRESS LIAISON OFFICE IN WASHINGTON, DC

Director: Antoine Ripoll.

CO-ORDINATION AND PROGRAMMING UNIT

Head of Unit: Pablo Ibanez López-Pozas; tel. (+32) 2-2832015; e-mail pablo.ibanez@europarl.europa.eu.

HORIZONTAL AND THEMATIC MONITORING UNIT

Head of Unit: Jesús Gómez; tel. (+32) 2-2832157; e-mail jesus.gomez@europarl.europa.eu.

EUROPEAN PARLIAMENT INFORMATION OFFICE IN GREECE

Head of Unit: Leonidas Antonakopoulos; tel. (+30) 210-350024; e-mail epathinai@europarl.europa.eu.

EUROPEAN PARLIAMENT INFORMATION OFFICE IN GERMANY

Head of Unit: Frank Piplat; tel. (+49 30) 22801000; e-mail epberlin@europarl.europa.eu.

EUROPEAN PARLIAMENT INFORMATION OFFICE IN BELGIUM

Head of Unit: Sjerp Pieter Van Der Vaart; tel. (+32) 2-2842006; e-mail sjerp.vandervaart@europarl.europa.eu.

EUROPEAN PARLIAMENT INFORMATION OFFICE IN DENMARK

Head of Unit: Anne Mette Vestergaard; tel. (+45) 33-14-90-03; e-mail epkobenhavn@europarl.europa.eu.

EUROPEAN PARLIAMENT INFORMATION OFFICE IN IRELAND

Head of Unit: James Temple-Smithson; tel. (+353 1) 60552904; e-mail james.temple-smithson@europarl.europa.eu.

EUROPEAN PARLIAMENT INFORMATION OFFICE IN FINLAND

Head of Unit: Jarmo Oikarinen; tel. (+358 9) 6229406; e-mail ephelsinki@europarl.europa.eu.

EUROPEAN PARLIAMENT INFORMATION OFFICE IN THE NETHERLANDS

Head of Unit: Eduardus Slootweg; tel. (+31 70) 36251402 e-mail epdenhaag@europarl.europa.eu.

EUROPEAN PARLIAMENT INFORMATION OFFICE IN PORTUGAL

Head of Unit: Pedro Valente da Silva; tel. (+351) 213504900 e-mail eplisboa@europarl.europa.eu.

EUROPEAN PARLIAMENT INFORMATION OFFICE IN THE UNITED KINGDOM

Head of Unit: Björn Kjellström; tel. (+44 20) 7227-4300; e-mail eplondon@europarl.europa.eu.

EUROPEAN PARLIAMENT INFORMATION OFFICE IN LUXEMBOURG

Head of Unit: Christoph Schroeder; tel. (+352) 430022596 e-mail epluxembourg@europarl.europa.eu.

EUROPEAN PARLIAMENT INFORMATION OFFICE IN SPAIN

Head of Unit: María Andres Marin; tel. (+34) 91-4364747 e-mail epmadrid@europarl.europa.eu.

EUROPEAN PARLIAMENT INFORMATION OFFICE IN FRANCE

Head of Unit: Isabelle Coustet; tel. (+33) 1-40-63-40-00; e-mail epparis@europarl.europa.eu.

EUROPEAN PARLIAMENT INFORMATION OFFICE IN ITALY

Head of Unit: Gianpaolo Meneghini; tel. (+39) 06-699501 e-mail eproma@europarl.europa.eu.

EUROPEAN PARLIAMENT INFORMATION OFFICE IN SWEDEN

Head of Unit: Markus Bonekamp; tel. (+46 8) 56-24-44-55 e-mail epstockholm@europarl.europa.eu.

EUROPEAN PARLIAMENT INFORMATION OFFICE IN STRASBOURG, FRANCE

Head of Unit: Luís Martínez Guillen; tel. (+33) 3-88-17-23-80; e-mail epstrasbourg@europarl.europa.eu.

EUROPEAN PARLIAMENT INFORMATION OFFICE IN AUSTRIA

Head of Unit: Georg Pfeifer; tel. (+43 1) 5169375; e-mail epwien@europarl.europa.eu.

EUROPEAN PARLIAMENT INFORMATION OFFICE IN CYPRUS

Head of Unit: Andreas Kettis; tel. (+357) 2228750583; e-mail andreas.kettis@europarl.europa.eu.

EUROPEAN PARLIAMENT INFORMATION OFFICE IN ESTONIA

Head of Unit: Kadi Herkuel; tel. (+372) 6306969; e-mail eptallinn@europarl.europa.eu.

EUROPEAN PARLIAMENT INFORMATION OFFICE IN HUNGARY

Head of Unit: Andrea Lovei; tel. (+36 1) 4113540; e-mail epbudapest@europarl.europa.eu.

EUROPEAN PARLIAMENT INFORMATION OFFICE IN LATVIA

Head of Unit: Marta Ribele; tel. (+371) 7085460; e-mail epriga@europarl.europa.eu.

EUROPEAN PARLIAMENT INFORMATION OFFICE IN LITHUANIA

Head of Unit: Daiva Jakaitė; tel. (+370 521) 20766; e-mail epvilnius@europarl.europa.eu.

EUROPEAN PARLIAMENT INFORMATION OFFICE IN MALTA

Head of Unit: Katrin Ruhrmann; tel. (+32) 2-2842573; e-mail katrin.ruhrmann@europarl.europa.eu.

EUROPEAN PARLIAMENT INFORMATION OFFICE IN POLAND

Head of Unit: Jacek Safuta; tel. (+48 22) 595-24-70; e-mail epwarszawa@europarl.europa.eu.

EUROPEAN PARLIAMENT INFORMATION OFFICE IN THE CZECH REPUBLIC

Head of Unit: Jiří Kubiček; tel. (+420) 2559169; e-mail eppraha@europarl.europa.eu.

EUROPEAN PARLIAMENT INFORMATION OFFICE IN SLOVAKIA

Head of Unit: Robert Hajsel; tel. (+421 2) 59203296; e-mail epbratislava@europarl.europa.eu.

EUROPEAN PARLIAMENT INFORMATION OFFICE IN SLOVENIA

Head of Unit: Klemen Zumer; tel. (+386 1) 2528830; e-mail epljubljana@europarl.europa.eu.

EUROPEAN PARLIAMENT INFORMATION OFFICE IN BULGARIA

Head of Unit: Teodor Stoychev; tel. (+359 2) 98553540; e-mail epsofia@europarl.europa.eu.

EUROPEAN PARLIAMENT INFORMATION OFFICE IN ROMANIA

Head of Unit: Madalina Beatrice Mihalache; tel. (+40 21) 4050880; e-mail epbucarest@europarl.europa.eu.

EUROPEAN PARLIAMENT INFORMATION OFFICE IN CROATIA

Head of Unit: Violeta Staničić; tel. (+385 1) 4619-180; e-mail epzagreb@ep.europa.eu.

SUPPORT UNIT FOR INFORMATION OFFICES

Head of Unit: Delia Carro; tel. (+32) 2-2843237; e-mail delia.carro@europarl.europa.eu.

MINI-PARLAMENTARIUM BERLIN, GERMANY

Director: Katrin Ruhrmann; tel. (+32) 2-2842573; e-mail katrin.ruhrmann@europarl.europa.eu.

Directorate for Relations with Citizens

Director: Stephen Clark; tel. (+32) 2-2843281; e-mail stephen.clark@europarl.europa.eu.

PARLIAMENTARIUM

Head of Unit: Alexander Kleinig; tel. (+32) 2-2844397; e-mail alexander.kleinig@europarl.europa.eu.

VISITS AND SEMINARS UNIT

Head of Unit (acting): Mariana Cosac; tel. (+32) 2-2831210; e-mail mariana.cosac@europarl.europa.eu.

EVENTS AND EXHIBITIONS UNIT

Head of Unit: Tasos Georgiou; tel. (+32) 2-2832023; e-mail tasos.georgiou@europarl.europa.eu.

INFORMATION CAMPAIGNS UNIT

Head of Unit: Alain Crespinet; tel. (+32) 2-2842861; e-mail alain.crespinet@europarl.europa.eu.

HOUSE OF EUROPEAN HISTORY

Head of Unit: Constanze Itzel; tel. (+32) 2-2832265; e-mail constanze.itzel@europarl.europa.eu.

EUROPEAN UNION VISITORS PROGRAMME UNIT

Head of Unit: Beatriz Oliveira-Goumas; tel. (+32) 2-29908150326; e-mail beatriz.oliveiragoumas@europarl.europa.eu.

EYE UNIT

Head of Unit: Klaus Löffler; tel. (+32) 2-2842103; e-mail klaus.loeffler@europarl.europa.eu.

DIRECTORY

VISITORS SERVICES CO-ORDINATION UNIT

Head of Unit: Nastja Klemencic Schmidt; tel. (+32) 2-2844642; e-mail nastja.klemencic@europarl.europa.eu.

Directorate for Resources

Director: Christina Rupp; tel. (+32) 2-2843794; e-mail christina.rupp@europarl.europa.eu.

PERSONNEL UNIT

Head of Unit: Renate Feiler; tel. (+32) 2-2840762; e-mail renate.feiler@europarl.europa.eu.

FINANCE UNIT

Head of Unit: Paul de Spiegeleer; tel. (+32) 2-2841159; e-mail paul.despiegeleer@europarl.europa.eu.

INFORMATICS UNIT

Head of Unit: Flemming Sorensen; tel. (+32) 2-2841429; e-mail flemming.sorensen@europarl.europa.eu.

MEASUREMENT, EVALUATION AND RISK UNIT

Head of Unit: Rebecca West; tel. (+32) 2-2840539; e-mail rebecca.west@europarl.europa.eu.

DIRECTORATE-GENERAL FOR PERSONNEL

Director-General (acting): Kristian Knudsen; tel. (+32) 2-2841731; e-mail kristian.knudsen@europarl.europa.eu.

Internal Communication Service

Head of Service: Jean-Yves Loog; tel. (+32) 2-2844652; e-mail jean-yves.loog@europarl.europa.eu.

Equality and Diversity Unit

Head of Unit: Alberto Rossetti; tel. (+352) 430022032.

Directorate for Human Resources Development

Director: Jesús Moreno Diaz; tel. (+32) 2-2842766; e-mail jesus.morenodiaz@europarl.europa.eu.

UNIT FOR INTERNAL ORGANIZATION AND HUMAN RESOURCES PLANNING

Head of Unit: Rik Hugelier; tel. (+32) 2-2843303; e-mail rik.hugelier@europarl.europa.eu.

COMPETITIONS AND SELECTION PROCEDURES UNIT

Head of Unit: Frédéric Anton; tel. (+32) 2-2846095; e-mail frederic.anton@europarl.europa.eu.

CONTRACT STAFF AND ACCREDITED PARLIAMENTARY ASSISTANTS RECRUITMENT UNIT

Head of Unit: Pierre-Antoine Barthélémy; tel. (+352) 430023029.

STAFF MANAGEMENT AND CAREERS UNIT

Head of Unit: Ekaterini Despotopoulou; tel. (+352) 430022912; e-mail ekaterini.despotopoulou@europarl.europa.eu.

PROFESSIONAL TRAINING UNIT

Head of Unit: Sarita Kaujaoja; tel. (+32) 2-2844231; e-mail sarita.kaukaoja@europarl.europa.eu.

OFFICIALS AND TEMPORARY STAFF RECRUITMENT UNIT

Head of Unit: Christine Bahr; tel. (+352 4) 30021224; e-mail christine.bahr@europarl.europa.eu.

Directorate for Administrative Management

Director: Suzanne König; tel. (+32) 2-2843695; e-mail suzanne.koenig@europarl.europa.eu.

INDIVIDUAL ENTITLEMENTS AND PAYROLL UNIT

Head of Unit: Fernando Arroyo Redondo; tel. (+352) 430022652; e-mail fernando.arroyoredondo@europarl.europa.eu.

MISSIONS UNIT

Head of Unit: Michiel Janssens; tel. (+352) 430025902; e-mail michiel.janssens@europarl.europa.eu.

PENSIONS AND SOCIAL INSURANCE UNIT

Head of Unit: Jean-Marie Weissenberger; tel. (+352) 430022741; e-mail jeanmarie.weissenberger@europarl.europa.eu.

UNIT FOR RELATIONS WITH PERSONNEL

Head of Unit: Fabio Galatioto; tel. (+32) 2-2841310; e-mail fabio.galatioto@europarl.europa.eu.

Directorate for Management of Support and Social Services

Director: Erika Landi-Gietema; tel. (+32) 2-2842062; e-mail erika.landi@europarl.europa.eu.

MEDICAL LEAVE SERVICE

Doctor: Fabienne Suzanne Maria Peters; tel. (+352) 430022691; e-mail fabienne.peters@europarl.europa.eu.

MEDICAL SERVICE, LUXEMBOURG

Head of Unit (acting): Alexander Baumgartel; tel. (+352) 430024644.

MEDICAL SERVICE, BRUSSELS

Head of Unit: Petra Claes; tel. (+32) 2-2842123; e-mail petra.claes@europarl.europa.eu.

SOCIAL SERVICES UNIT

Head of Unit, Doctor: Pietro Alba; tel. (+352) 430022546.

European Parliament — DIRECTORY

RISK PREVENTION AND WELLBEING AT WORK UNIT

Director: Philip Scott; tel. (+32) 2-2844078; e-mail philip.scott@europarl.europa.eu.

Directorate for Resources

Director: Carlos Neto; tel. (+32) 2-2843471; e-mail carlos.neto@europarl.europa.eu.

HUMAN RESOURCES UNIT

Head of Unit/Lawyer Manager: Poul Runge Nielsen; tel. (+352) 430024414.

FINANCIAL RESOURCES MANAGEMENT AND CONTROLS UNIT

Head of Unit: Stéphane Vivard; tel. (+352) 430027789; e-mail stephane.vivard@europarl.europa.eu.

INFORMATION TECHNOLOGY AND IT SUPPORT UNIT

Head of Unit: Ana Juste Gilabert; tel. (+352) 430023609; e-mail ana.juste@europarl.europa.eu.

DIRECTORATE-GENERAL FOR INFRASTRUCTURE AND LOGISTICS

Director-General: Leena Maria Linnus; tel. (+32) 2-2842825 e-mail leena.linnus@europarl.europa.eu.

ONE-STOP SHOP FOR MEMBERS UNIT

Head of Unit: Christine Kyst; tel. (+32) 2-2831384; e-mail christine.kyst@europarl.europa.eu.

Directorate for Infrastructure

Director: Olivier Pesesse; tel. (+32) 2-2843905; e-mail olivier.pesesse@europarl.europa.eu.

MAINTENANCE ASSISTANCE SERVICE

Director: Olivier Pesesse; tel. (+32) 2-2843905; e-mail olivier.pesesse@europarl.europa.eu.

LUXEMBOURG BUILDINGS MANAGEMENT AND MAINTENANCE UNIT

Head of Unit: Anna María Vago; tel. (+352) 430025314.

INFORMATION OFFICES BUILDINGS MANAGEMENT AND MAINTENANCE UNIT

Head of Unit: Bernd Lippert; tel. (+352) 430025154.

BRUSSELS BUILDINGS MANAGEMENT AND MAINTENANCE UNIT

Head of Unit: Claude Champetter; tel. (+32) 2-2831323; e-mail claude.champetter@europarl.europa.eu.

STRASBOURG BUILDINGS MANAGEMENT AND MAINTENANCE UNIT

Head of Unit: Eric Ricca; tel. (+33) 3-88-17-30-37.

Directorate for Logistics

PROCUREMENT SERVICE

Head of Service: Jakub Kodym; tel. (+352) 430022733; e-mail jakub.kodym@europarl.europa.eu.

FINANCIAL INITIATION SERVICE

Head of Service: Patrick Bega; tel. (+352) 430020338; e-mail patrick.bega@europarl.europa.eu.

PURCHASES, MANAGEMENT OF GOODS AND INVENTORY UNIT

Head of Unit: Paolo Colantonio; tel. (+32) 2-2831860; e-mail paolo.colantonio@europarl.europa.eu.

CATERING AND STAFF SHOP UNIT

Head of Unit: Denitza Bogomilova; tel. (+32) 2-2844286; e-mail denitza.bogomilova@europarl.europa.eu.

OFFICE ALLOCATION AND MOVES UNIT

Head of Unit: Elina Kaartinen; tel. (+32) 2-2832388; e-mail elina.kaartinen@europarl.europa.eu.

MAIL USHERS UNIT

Head of Unit: Koenraad Snijders; tel. (+32) 2-2842193; e-mail koenraad.snijders@europarl.europa.eu.

Directorate for Resources

Director: Ute Kassnitz; tel. (+32) 2-2844269; e-mail ute.kassnitz@europarl.europa.eu.

PERSONNEL UNIT

Head of Unit: Maria Haerdin Howat; tel. (+32) 2-2843933 e-mail maria.haerdin@europarl.europa.eu.

FINANCE UNIT

Head of Unit: Lothar Bauer; tel. (+32) 2-2844520; e-mail lothar.bauer@europarl.europa.eu.

EX-ANTE CONTROL AND PUBLIC PROCUREMENT CO-ORDINATION UNIT

Head of Unit (acting): Attila Gemes; tel. (+352) 430023314 e-mail attila.gemes@europarl.europa.eu.

INFORMATION TECHNOLOGY AND IT SUPPORT UNIT

Head of Unit: Alain Donadoni; tel. (+32) 2-2840913; e-mail alain.donadoni@europarl.europa.eu.

COMMUNICATION UNIT

Head of Unit (acting): Thomas Cantarella; tel. (+352) 430022293; e-mail thomas.cantarella@europarl.europa.eu.

CENTRAL SUPPORT UNIT

Head of Unit: Hans Torrekens; tel. (+352) 430022197; e-mail hans.torrekens@europarl.europa.eu.

Directorate for Building Projects

Director: Kirsten Luddecke; tel. (+32) 2-2841384; e-mail kirsten.luddecke@europarl.europa.eu.

LUXEMBOURG BUILDING PROJECTS UNIT

Head of Unit: Xavier Bilger; tel. (+352) 430024527; e-mail xavier.bilger@europarl.europa.eu.

BRUSSELS BUILDING PROJECTS UNIT

Head of Unit: Xavier Lacroix; tel. (+32) 2-2841352; e-mail xavier.lacroix@europarl.europa.eu.

STRASBOURG BUILDING PROJECTS UNIT

Head of Unit: Dimitrios Tenezakis; tel. (+33) 3-88-17-44-26 e-mail dimitrios.tenezakis@europarl.europa.eu.

DIRECTORATE-GENERAL FOR TRANSLATION

Director-General: Valter Mavrič; tel. (+32) 2-2844948; e-mail valter.mavric@europarl.europa.eu.

Multilingualism and External Relations Unit

Head of Unit: Alison Graves; tel. (+32) 2-2831026; e-mail alison.graves@europarl.europa.eu.

QUALITY CO-ORDINATION SERVICE

Head of Unit (acting): Angelika Vaasa; e-mail angelika.vaasa@europarl.europa.eu.

Directorate for Support and Technological Services for Translation

Director: Jochen Richter; tel. (+32) 2-2841796; e-mail jochen.richter@europarl.europa.eu.

APPLICATIONS AND IT SYSTEMS DEVELOPMENT UNIT

Head of Unit: Pascale Chartier-Brun; tel. (+352) 430024584 e-mail pascale.chartierbrun@europarl.europa.eu.

EXTERNAL TRANSLATION UNIT

Head of Unit: Tom Skinner; tel. (+352) 430023345.

EURAMIS PRE-TRANSLATION UNIT

Head of Unit: Maria-Paula Marginean; e-mail paula.marginean@europarl.europa.eu.

TERMINOLOGY CO-ORDINATION UNIT

Director: Rodolfos Maslias; tel. (+352) 430023872; e-mail rodolfos.maslias@europarl.europa.eu.

Directorate for Translation

Director (acting): Veronique Rosenkranz; tel. (+32) 2-2844222; e-mail veronique.rosenkranz@europarl.europa.eu.

DANISH TRANSLATION UNIT

Head of Unit/Translation Manager: Hans Drangsfeldt; tel. (+352) 430023165; e-mail hans.drangsfeldt@europarl.europa.eu.

GERMAN TRANSLATION UNIT

Head of Unit/Translation Manager: Michael Fuchs; tel. (+352) 430023291; e-mail michael.fuchs@europarl.europa.eu.

GREEK TRANSLATION UNIT

Head of Unit/Translation Manager: Maria Bali; tel. (+352) 430023857; e-mail maria.bali@europarl.europa.eu.

ENGLISH TRANSLATION UNIT

Head of Unit: Mark Smith; tel. (+352) 430025441.

SPANISH TRANSLATION UNIT

Head of Unit: María Teresa Ruíz; tel. (+352) 430024242.

FRENCH TRANSLATION UNIT

Head of Unit/Translation Manager: Michel Catuhe; tel. (+352) 430024755; e-mail michel.catuhe@europarl.europa.eu.

ITALIAN TRANSLATION UNIT

Head of Unit/Translation Manager: Luisa Forsingdal; tel. (+352) 430023422; e-mail luisa.forsingdal@europarl.europa.eu.

DUTCH TRANSLATION UNIT

Head of Unit/Translation Manager: Frans de Groot; tel. (+352) 430023462; e-mail frans.degroot@europarl.europa.eu.

PORTUGUESE TRANSLATION UNIT

Head of Unit/Translation Manager: Vitor Bastos; tel. (+352) 430023798; e-mail vitor.bastos@europarl.europa.eu.

FINNISH TRANSLATION UNIT

Head of Unit/Translation Manager: Timo Sulkanen; tel. (+352) 430024806.

SWEDISH TRANSLATION UNIT

Head of Unit/Translation Manager: Christian Wolmerud; tel. (+352) 430023926; e-mail christian.wolmerud@europarl.europa.eu.

CZECH TRANSLATION UNIT

Head of Unit/Translation Manager: Karel Hruska; tel. (+352) 430022388; e-mail karel.hruska@europarl.europa.eu.

ESTONIAN TRANSLATION UNIT

Head of Unit/Translation Manager: Marek Dreving; tel. (+352) 430025115; e-mail marek.dreving@europarl.europa.eu.

HUNGARIAN TRANSLATION UNIT

Head of Unit: József Villányi; tel. (+352) 430025784.

LITHUANIAN TRANSLATION UNIT

Head of Unit/Translation Manager: Ieva Mainardi; tel. (+352) 430023914.

LATVIAN TRANSLATION UNIT

Head of Unit/Translation Manager: Uldis Krastiņš; tel. (+352) 430022038; e-mail uldis.krastins@europarl.europa.eu.

MALTESE TRANSLATION UNIT

Head of Unit/Translation Manager: Joseph Caruana; tel. (+352) 430027779; e-mail joseph.caruana@europarl.europa.eu.

POLISH TRANSLATION UNIT

Head of Unit/Translation Manager: Dariusz Chmiel; tel. (+352) 430022180; e-mail dariusz.chmiel@europarl.europa.eu.

SLOVENE TRANSLATION UNIT

Head of Unit/Translation Manager: Tadeja Zdenka Tomšič; tel. (+352) 430025296; e-mail tadeja.tomsic@europarl.europa.eu.

SLOVAK TRANSLATION UNIT

Head of Unit/Translation Manager: Pavol Tvarozek; tel. (+352) 430025321; e-mail pavol.tvarozek@europarl.europa.eu.

BULGARIAN TRANSLATION UNIT

Head of Unit/Translation Manager: Daniela Dimova; tel. (+352) 430024160; e-mail daniela.dimova@europarl.europa.eu.

ROMANIAN TRANSLATION UNIT

Head of Unit (acting)/Translation Manager: Maria-Paula Marginean; tel. (+352) 430025479; e-mail paula.marginean@europarl.europa.eu.

CROATIAN TRANSLATION UNIT

Head of Unit/Translation Manager: Marijana Nikolić; tel. (+352) 430024677.

IRISH TRANSLATION SERVICE

Head of Service (acting): Labhras O. Finneadha; tel. (+352) 430023093; e-mail labhras.finneadha@europarl.europa.eu.

PLANNING UNIT

Head of Unit (acting): István Soos-Petek; tel. (+352) 430023043; e-mail istvan.soos-petek@europarl.europa.eu.

EDITING UNIT

Head of Unit (acting): Patrick Byrne; tel. (+352) 430023318.

Directorate for Resources

Director: Bernadette Ligeti; tel. (+32) 2-2831840; e-mail bernadette.ligeti@europarl.europa.eu.

HUMAN RESOURCES UNIT

Head of Unit: Bernadette Ligeti; e-mail bernadette.ligeti@europarl.europa.eu.

FINANCIAL RESOURCES MANAGEMENT AND CONTROLS UNIT

Head of Unit: Christian Bastien; tel. (+352) 430022890; e-mail christian.bastien@europarl.europa.eu.

TRAINING AND TRAINEESHIPS UNIT

Head of Unit: Alessandro Pettini; tel. (+352) 430023379; e-mail alessandro.pettini@europarl.europa.eu.

INFORMATION TECHNOLOGY AND IT SUPPORT UNIT

Head of Unit: Erik De Becker; tel. (+352) 430024271; e-mail erik.debecker@europarl.europa.eu.

DIRECTORATE-GENERAL FOR INTERPRETATION AND CONFERENCES

Director-General: Agnieszka Walter-Drop; tel. (+32) 2-2834477; e-mail agnieszka.walter-drop@europarl.europa.eu.

ACI Payment Unit

Head of Unit: Constantin Paleologos; tel. (+32) 2-2843102; e-mail constantin.paleologos@europarl.europa.eu.

Strategy Unit

Head of Unit: Nick Gheysen; tel. (+32) 2-2832061; e-mail nick.gheysen@europarl.europa.eu.

Quality Management Unit

Head of Unit: Francis Clergeaud; tel. (+32) 2-2846126; tel. francis.clergeaud@europarl.europa.eu.

Directorate for Interpretation

Director: Nick Gheysen; tel. (+32) 2-2832061; e-mail nick.gheysen@europarl.europa.eu.

DANISH INTERPRETATION UNIT

Head of Unit (acting): Florian Heines; tel. (+32) 2-2831833; e-mail florian.heines@europarl.europa.eu.

GERMAN INTERPRETATION UNIT

Interpretation manager: Viviane Ramponi; tel. (+32) 2-2843672; e-mail viviane.ramponi@europarl.europa.eu.

GREEK INTERPRETATION UNIT

Interpretation Manager: Konstantinos Mastoros; tel. (+32) 2-2843482; e-mail konstantinos.mastoros@europarl.europa.eu.

ENGLISH INTERPRETATION UNIT

Interpretation Manager: Miguel Gomes; tel. (+32) 2-2843301; e-mail miguel.gomes@europarl.europa.eu.

SPANISH INTERPRETATION UNIT

Head of Unit (acting): Konstantinos Mastoros; tel. (+32) 2-2843482; e-mail konstantinos.mastoros@europarl.europa.eu.

FINNISH INTERPRETATION UNIT

Interpretation Manager: Mirja Bouchard; tel. (+32) 2-2842719; e-mail mirja.bouchard@europarl.europa.eu.

FRENCH INTERPRETATION UNIT

Interpretation Manager: Serge Levenheck; tel. (+32) 2-2843404; e-mail serge.levenheck@europarl.europa.eu.

ITALIAN INTERPRETATION UNIT

Interpretation Manager: Giancarlo Zucchetto; tel. (+32) 2-2844622; e-mail giancarlo.zucchetto@europarl.europa.eu.

DUTCH INTERPRETATION UNIT

Interpretation Manager: Leonardus Hendrikx; tel. (+32) 2-2846034; e-mail leonardus.hendrikx@europarl.europa.eu.

PORTUGUESE INTERPRETATION UNIT

Interpretation Manager: Francisco Falcao; tel. (+32) 2-2834444; e-mail francisco.falcao@europarl.europa.eu.

SWEDISH INTERPRETATION UNIT

Interpretation Manager: Florian Heines; tel. (+32) 2-2831833; e-mail florian.heines@europarl.europa.eu.

POLISH INTERPRETATION UNIT

Head of Unit (acting): Mirja Bouchard; tel. (+32) 2-2842719; e-mail mirja.bouchard@europarl.europa.eu.

CZECH INTERPRETATION UNIT

Interpretation Manager: Ivana Hlavacova; tel. (+32) 2-2843661; e-mail ivana.hlavacova@europarl.europa.eu.

HUNGARIAN INTERPRETATION UNIT

Head of Unit (acting): Leonardus Hendrikx; tel. (+32) 2-2836034; e-mail leonardus.hendrikx@europarl.europa.eu.

SLOVAK INTERPRETATION UNIT

Interpretation Manager: Miroslava Petrovská; tel. (+32) 2-2831066; e-mail miroslava.petrovska@europarl.europa.eu.

SLOVENE INTERPRETATION UNIT

Head of Unit (acting): Ivana Hlaváčová; tel. (+32) 2-2843661; e-mail ivana.hlavacova@europarl.europa.eu.

ESTONIAN INTERPRETATION UNIT

Head of Unit: Michael Short; tel. (+32) 2-2846446; e-mail michael.short@europarl.europa.eu.

LITHUANIAN INTERPRETATION UNIT

Interpretation Manager: Gintaras Morkunas; tel. (+32) 2-2831242; e-mail gintaras.morkunas@europarl.europa.eu.

LATVIAN INTERPRETATION UNIT

Head of Unit: Ilga Bērziņa; tel. (+32) 2-2831494; e-mail ilga.berzina@europarl.europa.eu.

MALTESE INTERPRETATION UNIT

Head of Unit (acting): Giancarlo Zucchetto; tel. (+32) 2-2844622; e-mail giancarlo.zucchetto@europarl.europa.eu.

BULGARIAN INTERPRETATION UNIT

Head of Unit (acting): Michael Short; tel. (+32) 2-2846446; e-mail michael.short@europarl.europa.eu.

ROMANIAN INTERPRETATION UNIT

Interpretation manager: Izabella Badiu; tel. (+32) 2-2843882; e-mail izabella.badiu@europarl.europa.eu.

CROATIAN INTERPRETATION UNIT

Head of Unit (acting): Gintaras Morkunas; tel. (+32) 2-2831242; e-mail gintaras.morkunas@europarl.europa.eu.

Directorate for Organization and Planning

Director: Juan-Carlos Jiménez Marín; tel. (+32) 2-2846427; e-mail juan-carlos.jimenezmarin@europarl.europa.eu.

UNIT FOR THE RECRUITMENT OF AUXILIARY CONFERENCE INTERPRETERS

Head of Unit: Jyrki Tuononen; tel. (+32) 2-2842192; e-mail jyrki.tuononen@europarl.europa.eu.

PROGRAMMING UNIT

Head of Unit: Carine Smets; tel. (+32) 2-2846533; e-mail carine.smets@europarl.europa.eu.

MEETINGS AND CONFERENCES UNIT

Head of Unit: Anna Grzybowska; tel. (+32) 2-2842112; e-mail anna.grzybowska@europarl.europa.eu.

CONFERENCE TECHNICIANS UNIT

Head of Unit: Philip Tulkens; tel. (+32) 2-2846150; e-mail philip.tulkens@europarl.europa.eu.

MULTILINGUALISM AND SUCCESSION PLANNING UNIT

Head of Unit (acting): Marcin Feder; tel. (+32) 2-2832611; e-mail marcin.feder@europarl.europa.eu.

INTERPRETER SUPPORT AND TRAINING UNIT

Head of Unit: Marcin Feder; tel. (+32) 2-2832611; e-mail marcin.feder@europarl.europa.eu.

E-LEARNING UNIT

Head of Unit: Ekaterini Dara-Lepoura; tel. (+32) 2-2846637; e-mail ekaterini.dara-lepoura@europarl.europa.eu.

Directorate for Resources

Director: Izabela Wisniewska; tel. (+32) 2-2842822; e-mail izabela.wisniewska@europarl.europa.eu.

HUMAN RESOURCES UNIT

Head of Unit: Laura Tarragona Saez; tel. (+32) 2-2843653 e-mail laura.tarragona-saez@europarl.europa.eu.

INFORMATION TECHNOLOGY AND IT SUPPORT UNIT

Head of Unit: Bernard Gevaert; tel. (+32) 2-2842333; e-mail bernard.gevaert@europarl.europa.eu.

BUDGET UNIT

Head of Unit (acting): Marion Breen; tel. (+32) 2-2843297 e-mail marion.breen@europarl.europa.eu.

DIRECTORATE-GENERAL FINANCE

Director-General: Didier Klethi; tel. (+32) 2-2844862; e-mail didier.klethi@europarl.europa.eu.

Budget and Verification Service

Head of Unit: Corinne Nicolai; tel. (+352) 430022865; e-mail corinne.nicolai@europarl.europa.eu.

Directorate for Budget and Financial Services

Director: Miguel Papi-Boucher; tel. (+32) 2-2830979; e-mail miguel.papi@europarl.europa.eu.

BUDGET UNIT

Head of Unit (acting): Gábor Motika; tel. (+32) 2-2846563 e-mail gabor.motika@europarl.europa.eu.

ACCOUNTING AND TREASURY UNIT

Head of Unit/Accountant: Ville-Veikko Timberg; tel. (+32) 2-2830673; e-mail ville.timberg@europarl.europa.eu.

CENTRAL FINANCIAL UNIT

Head of Unit: Auke Baas; tel. (+32) 2-2842369; e-mail auke.baas@europarl.europa.eu.

UNIT FOR RE-ENGINEERING OF THE FINANCIAL INFORMATION SYSTEMS

Director: Miguel Papi Boucher; tel. (+32) 2-2830979; e-mail miguel.papi@europarl.europa.eu.

Directorate for Members' Financial and Social Entitlements

Director: Lorenzo Mannelli; tel. (+32) 2-2842435; e-mail lorenzo.mannelli@europarl.europa.eu.

PARLIAMENTARY ASSISTANTS' SERVICE

Head of Department (acting): María Del Río Camarero Rioseco; tel. (+32) 2-2843426; e-mail mariadelrio.camarero@europarl.europa.eu.

Portal

Head of Service: María Angeles Martínez Valls; tel. (+32) 2-2842007; e-mail mariaangeles.martinez@europarl.europa.eu.

MEMBERS' SALARIES AND SOCIAL ENTITLEMENTS UNIT

Head of Unit: Sune Hansen; tel. (+32) 2-2842642; e-mail sune.hansen@europarl.europa.eu.

PARLIAMENTARY ASSISTANCE AND MEMBERS' GENERAL EXPENDITURE UNIT

Head of Unit: Frank Antoine-Poirel; tel. (+32) 2-2846655; e-mail frank.antoine-poirel@europarl.europa.eu.

MEMBERS' TRAVEL AND SUBSISTENCE EXPENSES UNIT

Head of Unit (acting): Oliver Martin Leon; tel. (+32) 2-2844654; e-mail oliver.martin@europarl.europa.eu.

Directorate for Political Structures' Financing and Resources

Director: Eduard Reijnders; tel. (+32) 2-2832531; e-mail eduard.reijnders@europarl.europa.eu.

TRAVEL ORGANIZATION SERVICE

Head of Unit: Martina Giering; tel. (+32) 2-2842465; e-mail martina.giering@europarl.europa.eu.

Political Structures Financing Unit

Head of Unit: Helmut Betz; tel. (+32) 2-2843183; e-mail helmut.betz@europarl.europa.eu.

Information Technology and Inventory Unit

Head of Unit (acting): Georg Becker; tel. (+32) 2-2846511 e-mail georg.becker@europarl.europa.eu.

Human Resources and Members' Professional Training Unit

Head of Unit: Judith Ecker; tel. (+32) 2-2842629; e-mail judith.ecker@europarl.europa.eu.

DIRECTORATE-GENERAL FOR INNOVATION AND TECHNOLOGICAL SUPPORT

Director-General: Giancarlo Vilella; tel. (+32) 2-2841348; e-mail giancarlo.vilella@europarl.europa.eu.

Directorate for Development and Support

Director: Steen Eilertsen; tel. (+32) 2-2832520; e-mail steen.eilertsen@europarl.europa.eu.

USER SUPPORT UNIT

Head of Unit (acting): Stéphan Janssens; tel. (+32) 2-2846171 e-mail stephan.janssens@europarl.europa.eu.

UNIT ICT CONCEPTION AND DEVELOPMENT

Head of Unit: Ludovic Delepine; tel. (+352) 430022091; e-mail ludovic.delepine@europarl.europa.eu.

EVOLUTION AND MAINTENANCE

Head of Unit: Gerrit Potoms; tel. (+32) 2-22840969; e-mail gerrit.potoms@europarl.europa.eu.

Directorate for Infrastructure and Equipment

Director: Pascal Paridans; e-mail pascal.paridans@europarl.europa.eu.

Infrastructure Management Unit

Head of Unit: Jean-Marc Mariotti.

INDIVIDUAL EQUIPMENT AND LOGISTICS UNIT

Head of Unit: Gilbert Schilt; tel. (+32) 2-2843475; e-mail gilbert.schilt@europarl.europa.eu.

ICT OPERATIONS AND HOSTING UNIT

Head of Unit: Rafael Ruíz de la Torre; tel. (+32) 2-2844525; e-mail rafael.ruiz@europarl.europa.eu.

Directorate for Publishing and Distribution

Director: Roger-Marie Dubois; tel. (+32) 2-2843356; e-mail roger-marie.dubois@europarl.europa.eu.

INTRANET AND MULTIMEDIA UNIT

Head of Unit: Takis Panagiotis Ageladarakis; tel. (+32) 2-2846170; e-mail takis.ageladarakis@europarl.europa.eu.

DOCUMENT PRODUCTION UNIT

Head of Unit: Andrea Bartolini; tel. (+352) 430022480.

PRINTING UNIT

Head of Unit: Michael Lamour; tel. (+32) 2-2846765; e-mail michael.lamour@europarl.europa.eu.

CLIENTS, TOOLS AND METHODS UNIT

Director: Adriana Jansen; e-mail adriana.jensen@europarl.europa.eu.

Directorate for Innovation and Resources

Director: Walter Petrucci; tel. (+32) 2-2843537; e-mail walter.petrucci@europarl.europa.eu.

HUMAN RESOURCES UNIT

Head of Department: Philippe Van Avermaet; tel. (+32) 2-2844775; e-mail philippe.vanavermaet@europarl.europa.eu.

INNOVATION, PERFORMANCE AND INTERNAL CONTROL UNIT

Head of Unit (acting): Pierfrancesco Sabbatucci; e-mail pierrefrancesco.sabbatucci@europarl.europa.eu.

FINANCIAL RESOURCES MANAGEMENT UNIT

Head of Unit: Jesper Madsen; tel. (+352) 430024517.

PROCUREMENT AND CONTACT MANAGEMENT UNIT

Head of Unit: Karin Collin; tel. (+352) 430020321.

CUSTOMER RELATIONSHIP AND COMMUNICATION UNIT

Head of Unit/IT Manager: Wouter Offereins; tel. (+32) 2-2842523; e-mail wouter.offereins@europarl.europa.eu.

Chief Information Systems Security Officer

Director, Information Technology: Pascal Paridans; tel. (+32) 2-2843080; e-mail pascal.paridans@europarl.europa.eu.

ICT SECURITY UNIT

Head of Unit: Luca Rettore; tel. (+32) 2-2842058; e-mail luca.rettore@europarl.europa.eu.

DIRECTORATE-GENERAL FOR PARLIAMENTARY RESEARCH SERVICES

Director-General: Anthony Teasdale; tel. (+32) 2-2841678; e-mail anthony.teasdale@europarl.europa.eu.

Resources Unit

Head of Unit: Jutta Schulze-Hollmen; tel. (+32) 2-2842615; e-mail jutta.schulze@europarl.europa.eu.

HUMAN RESOURCES SERVICE

Head of Service: Maria Grazia Tanese; tel. (+32) 2-2842716.

FINANCE SERVICE

Head of Service: Alfonso García-Miguel Casanueva; tel. (+32) 2-2832968; e-mail alfonso.garciamiguel@europarl.europa.eu.

INFORMATION TECHNOLOGY SERVICE

Head of Service: Lars De Nul; tel. (+32) 2-2844658; e-mail lars.denul@europarl.europa.eu.

Strategy and Co-ordination Unit

Head of Unit: Eschel Claus Alpermann; tel. (+32) 2-2834324; e-mail eschel.alpermann@europarl.europa.eu.

Directorate Members' Research Service

Director: Etienne Bassot; tel. (+32) 2-2844741; e-mail etienne.bassot@europarl.europa.eu.

ECONOMIC POLICIES UNIT

Head of Unit: Alessandro Piccioli; tel. (+32) 2-2832967; e-mail alessandro.piccioli@europarl.europa.eu.

STRUCTURAL POLICIES UNIT

Head of Unit: Sarah Sheil; tel. (+32) 2-2834046; e-mail sarah.sheil@europarl.europa.eu.

CITIZENS' POLICIES UNIT

Head of Unit: Jesus Carmona Nuñez; tel. (+32) 2-2830406; e-mail jesus.carmona@europarl.europa.eu.

EXTERNAL POLICIES UNIT

Head of Unit (acting): Monika Nogaj; tel. (+32) 2-2840635; e-mail monika.nogaj@europarl.europa.eu.

BUDGETARY POLICIES UNIT

Head of Unit (acting): Sidonia Elżbieta Jedrzejewska; tel. (+32) 2-2830477; e-mail sidonia.jedrzejewska@europarl.europa.eu.

PUBLICATIONS MANAGEMENT AND EDITORIAL UNIT

Head of Unit: Alison Davies; tel. (+32) 2-2831705; e-mail alison.davies@europarl.europa.eu.

Directorate for the Library

Director: Joseph Dunne; tel. (+32) 2-2842491; e-mail joseph.dunne@europarl.europa.eu.

ON-SITE AND ONLINE LIBRARY SERVICES UNIT

Head of Unit: Elke Ballon; tel. (+32) 2-2840649; e-mail elke.ballon@europarl.europa.eu.

HISTORICAL ARCHIVES UNIT

Head of Unit (acting): Aurora Parraga Gimenez; tel. (+32) 2-2846233; e-mail aurora.parragagimenez@europarl.europa.eu.

CITIZENS' ENQUIRIES UNIT

Head of Unit: Aurora Parraga Gimenez; tel. (+32) 2-2846233; e-mail aurora.parraga-gimenez@europarl.europa.eu.

COMPARATIVE LAW LIBRARY UNIT

Head of Unit: Ignacio Diez Parra; tel. (+32) 2-2842281; e-mail idp@europarl.europa.eu.

Directorate for Impact Assessment and European Added Value

Director: Wolfgang Hiller; tel. (+32) 2-2843405; e-mail wolfgang.hiller@europarl.europa.eu.

EX-ANTE IMPACT ASSESSMENT UNIT

Head of Unit (acting): Alexia Maniaki-Griva; tel. (+32) 2-2846690; e-mail alexia.maniaki@europarl.europa.eu.

EUROPEAN ADDED VALUE UNIT

Head of Unit (acting): Astrid Worum; tel. (+32) 2-2841333; e-mail astrid.worum@europarl.europa.eu.

SCIENTIFIC FORESIGHT UNIT

Head of Service: Lieve Van Woensel; tel. (+32) 2-2834048; e-mail lieve.vanwoensel@europarl.europa.eu.

EX-POST EVALUATION UNIT

Head of Unit: José Luís Rufas Quintana; tel. (+32) 2-2843956; e-mail jrufas@europarl.europa.eu.

EUROPEAN COUNCIL OVERSIGHT UNIT

Head of Unit (acting): Astrid Worum; tel. (+32) 2-2841333 e-mail astrid.worum@europarl.europa.eu.

GLOBAL TRENDS UNIT

Head of Unit: Daniele Rechard; tel. (+32) 2-2843730; e-mail daniele.rechard@europarl.europa.eu.

DIRECTORATE-GENERAL FOR SECURITY AND SAFETY

Director-General: Elio Carozza; tel. (+32) 2-2840936; e-mail elio.carozza@europarl.europa.eu.

Risk Assessment Unit

Head of Unit: Juan Ignacio Sole Andres; tel. (+32) 2-2834217; e-mail ignacio.sole-andres@europarl.europa.eu.

Directorate for Proximity and Assistance, Security and Safety

Director: Guy Mols; tel. (+32) 2-2846017; e-mail guy.mols@europarl.europa.eu.

ACCREDITATION UNIT

Head of Unit: Niall O'Neill; tel. (+32) 2-2843944; e-mail niall.oneill@europarl.europa.eu.

SECURITY AND SAFETY BRUSSELS UNIT

Head of Unit (acting): Gert Van Bastelaere; tel. (+32) 2-2832283; e-mail gert.vanbastelaere@europarl.europa.eu.

SECURITY AND SAFETY STRASBOURG UNIT

Head of Unit: Karel Van De Weyer; tel. (+33 3) 88164705; e-mail karel.vandeweyer@europarl.europa.eu.

SECURITY AND SAFETY LUXEMBOURG UNIT

Head of Unit: Xavier Gros; tel. (+352) 430022576; e-mail xavier.gros@europarl.europa.eu.

PROTECTION UNIT

Head of Unit: Alessio Nardi; tel. (+32) 2-2846495; e-mail alessio.nardi@europarl.europa.eu.

Directorate for Prevention, First Aid and Fire Safety

Director: Mathieu Thomann; tel. (+32) 2-2844927; e-mail mathieu.thomann@europarl.europa.eu.

FIRE PREVENTION BRUSSELS UNIT

Director: Mathieu Thomann; tel. (+32) 2-2844927; e-mail mathieu.thomann@europarl.europa.eu.

FIRE PREVENTION STRASBOURG UNIT

Head of Unit: Catherine Schaal; tel. (+33 3) 88172106.

FIRE PREVENTION LUXEMBOURG UNIT

Head of Unit: Pascal De Backer; tel. (+352) 430021653.

FIRE AND SAFETY TRAINING UNIT

Head of Unit: Christopher Sanchez Ozols; tel. (+32) 2-2834095; e-mail christopher.sanchez@europarl.europa.eu

Directorate for Strategy and Resources

Director: Elio Carozza; tel. (+32) 2-2840936; e-mail elio.carozza@europarl.europa.eu..

DISPATCHING UNIT

Head of Unit: Jean Luca Cocci; tel. (+32) 2-2841903; e-mail jean-luca.cocci@europarl.europa.eu.

PERSONNEL AND PLANNING UNIT

Head of Unit: Fabien Durand; tel. (+32) 2-2843727; e-mail fabien.durand@europarl.europa.eu.

BUDGET UNIT

Head of Unit: Marie-Cécile Bernard; tel. (+32) 2-2842075; e-mail marie-cecile.bernard@europarl.europa.eu.

TECHNOLOGIES AND INFORMATION SECURITY UNIT

Head of Unit: Victor Manuel Dias Fernandes; tel. (+32) 2-2844245; e-mail victor.dias-fernandes@europarl.europa.eu.

COURT OF JUSTICE AND GENERAL COURT

COURT OF JUSTICE

rue du Fort Niedergrünewald, 2925 Luxembourg, Luxembourg; tel. (+352) 4303-1; fax (+352) 4303-2600; e-mail info@curia.europa.eu; internet curia.europa.eu

Members

President: Koen Lenaerts.

Vice-President: Antonio Tizzano.

President of the First Chamber: Rosario Silva de Lapuerta.

President of the Second Chamber: Marko Ilešič.

President of the Third Chamber: Lars Bay Larsen.

President of the Fourth Chamber: Thomas von Danwitz.

President of the Fifth Chamber: José Luís da Cruz Vilaça.

First Advocate-General: Melchior Wathelet.

President of the Sixth Chamber: Eugene Regan.

President of the Seventh Chamber: Alexandra Prechal.

President of the Eighth Chamber: Michail Vilaras.

President of the Ninth Chamber: Maria Berger.

President of the Tenth Chamber: Endre Juhász.

Judge: Allan Rosas.

Advocate-General: Juliane Kokott.

Judge: Anthony E. Borg Barthet.

Judge: Jiří Malenovský.

Judge: Egils Levits.

Advocate-General: Eleanor Sharpston.

Advocate-General: Paolo Mengozzi.

Advocate-General: Yves Bot.

Judge: Jean-Claude Bonichot.

Judge: Marek Safjan.

Judge: Alexander Arabadjiev.

Judge: Camille Toader.

Judge: Daniel Šváby.

Judge: Egidijus Jarašiūnas.

Judge: Carl Gustav Fernlund.

Judge: Christopher Vajda.

Advocate-General: Nils Wahl.

Judge: Siniša Rodin.

Judge: François Biltgen.

Judge: Küllike Jürimäe.

Advocate-General: Maciej Szpunar.

Judge: Constantinos Lycourgos.

Advocate-General: Manuel Campos Sánchez-Bordona.

Advocate-General: Henrik Saugmandsgaard Øe.

Advocate-General: Michal Bobek.

Advocate-General: Evgeni Tanchev.

Registrar: Alfredo Calot Escobar.

GENERAL COURT

rue du Fort Niedergrünewald, 2925 Luxembourg, Luxembourg; tel. (+352) 4303-1; fax (+352) 4303-2600; e-mail info@curia.europa.eu; internet curia.europa.eu

Members

President: Marc Jaeger.

Vice-President: Marc van der Woude.

President of Chamber: Irena Pelikánová.

President of Chamber: Miro Prek.

President of Chamber: Sten Frimodt Nielsen.

President of Chamber: Heikki Kanninen.

President of Chamber: Dimitrios Gratsias.

President of Chamber: Guido Berardis.

President of Chamber: Vesna Tomljenović.

President of Chamber: Anthony Michael Collins.

President of Chamber: Stéphane Gervasoni.

Judge: Ingrida Labucka.

Judge: Savvas Papasavvas.

Judge: Alfred Dittrich.

Judge: Juraj Schwarcz.

Judge: Mariyana Kancheva.

Judge: Eugène Buttigieg.

Judge: Egidijus Bieliūnas.

Judge: Viktor Kreuschitz.

Judge: Ignacio Ulloa Rubio.

Judge: Lauri Madise.

Judge: Ian Stewart Forrester.

Judge: Constantinos Iliopoulos.

Judge: Leopoldo Calvo-Sotelo Ibáñez-Martín.

Judge: Dean Spielmann.

Judge: Virgilijus Valančius.

Judge: Zoltán Csehi.

Judge: Nina Półtorak.

Judge: Anna Marcoulli.

Judge: Peter George Xuereb.

Judge: Fredrik Schalin.

Judge: Inga Reine.

Judge: Ezio Perillo.

Judge: René Barents.

Judge: Ricardo da Silva Passos.

Judge: Paul Nihoul.

Judge: Barna Berke.

Judge: Jesper Svenningsen.

Judge: Ulf Christophe Öberg.

Judge: Octavia Spineanu-Matei.

Judge: Maria José Costeira.

Judge: Jan M. Passer.

Judge: Krystyna Kowalik-Bańczyk.

Judge: Alexander Kornezov.

Judge: Colm Mac Eochaidh.

Registrar: Emmanuel Coulon.

EUROPEAN COURT OF AUDITORS

12 rue Alcide de Gasperi, 1615 Luxembourg, Luxembourg; tel. (+352) 43981; fax (+352) 439342; e-mail eca-info@eca.europa.eu; internet www.eca.europa.eu

COMPOSITION

President of the Court: Klaus-Heiner Lehne; tel. (+352) 439845271.

Head of Private Office: Thomas Arntz; tel. (+352) 439847556.

Attaché: Edouard Dirrig; tel. (+352) 439845214.

Attaché: Marc-Oliver Heidkamp; tel. (+352) 439847622.

Member of the Court: Karel Pinxten; tel. (+352) 439845295.

Head of Private Office: Gerard Madden; tel. (+352) 439845516.

Attaché: Mila Strahilova; tel. (+352) 439847771.

Member of the Court: Henri Grethen; tel. (+352) 439845376; fax (+352) 439846819.

Head of Private Office: Marc Hostert; tel. (+352) 439847711.

Attaché: Ildikó Preiss; tel. (+352) 439847340.

Member of the Court: Ladislav Balko; tel. (+352) 439847201.

Head of Private Office: Branislav Urbanič; tel. (+352) 439847127.

Attaché: Zuzana Franková; tel. (+352) 439847205.

Member of the Court: Lazaros S. Lazarou; tel. (+352) 439847241.

Head of Private Office: Johan Adriaan Lok; tel. (+352) 439845415.

Attaché: Agathoclis Argyrou; tel. (+352) 439845714.

Member of the Court: Hans Gustaf Wessberg; tel. (+352) 439845958.

Head of Private Office: Peter Eklund; tel. (+352) 439845668.

Attaché: Emmanuel-Douglas Hellinakis; tel. (+352) 439845032.

Member of the Court: Pietro Russo; tel. (+352) 439845374.

Head of Private Office: Chiara Cipriani; tel. (+352) 439845218.

Attaché: Benjamin Jakob; tel. (+352) 439847056.

Member of the Court: Ville Itälä; tel. (+352) 439845965.

Head of Private Office: Turo Hentilä; tel. (+352) 439845925.

Attaché: Helka Nykänen; tel. (+352) 439845246.

Member of the Court: Kevin Cardiff; tel. (+352) 439845931.

Head of Private Office: Gediminas Mačys; tel. (+352) 439847263.

Attaché: Shane Enright; tel. (+352) 439847043.

Member of the Court: Baudilio Tomé Muguruza; tel. (+352) 439845592.

Head of Private Office: Daniel Costa de Magalhães; tel. (+352) 439845174.

Attaché: Ignacio García de Parada; tel. (+352) 439845006.

Member of the Court: Iliana Ivanova; tel. (+352) 439847141.

Head of Private Office: Mihail Stefanov; tel. (+352) 439847023.

Attaché: Peter Borsos; tel. (+352) 439847787.

Member of the Court: George Pufan; tel. (+352) 439847506.

Head of Private Office: Patrick Weldon; tel. (+352) 439845335.

Attaché: Mircea Rădulescu; tel. (+352) 439845431.

Member of the Court: Neven Mates; tel. (+352) 439847439.

Head of Private Office: Georgios Karakatsanis; tel. (+352) 439845929.

Attaché: Marko Mrkalj; tel. (+352) 439847417.

Member of the Court: Alex Brenninkmeijer; tel. (+352) 439845236.

Head of Private Office: Raphael Debets; tel. (+352) 439845081.

Attaché: Di Hai; tel. (+352) 439845838.

Member of the Court: Danièle Lamarque; tel. (+352) 439845203.

Head of Private Office: Dirk Pauwels; tel. (+352) 439845229.

Attaché: Stéphanie Girard; tel. (+352) 439845847.

Member of the Court: Nikolaos Milionis; tel. (+352) 439845258.

Head of Private Office: Ioulia Papatheodorou; tel. (+352) 439847299.

Attaché: Kristian Sniter; tel. (+352) 439847355.

Member of the Court: Phil Wynn Owen; tel. (+352) 439845372.

Head of Private Office: Gareth Roberts; tel. (+352) 439845724.

Attaché: Katharina Bryan; tel. (+352) 439845211.

Member of the Court: Oskar Herics; tel. (+352) 439847558.

Head of Private Office: Margit Spindelegger; tel. (+352) 439845955.

Attaché: Thomas Obermayer; tel. (+352) 439847406.

Member of the Court: Bettina Jakobsen; tel. (+352) 439847144.

Head of Private Office: Katja Mattfolk; tel. (+352) 439847428.

Attaché: Kim Storup; tel. (+352) 439847551.

Member of the Court: Janusz Wojciechowski; tel. (+352) 4398445567.

Head of Private Office: Kinga Wiśniewska-Danek; tel. (+352) 439845753.

Attaché: Katarzyna Radecka-Moroz; tel. (+352) 439847253.

Member of the Court: Samo Jereb; tel. (+352) 439845570.

Head of Private Office: Kathrine Henderson; tel. (+352) 439847213.

Attaché: Jerneja Vrabič; tel. (+352) 439845606.

Member of the Court: Jan Gregor; tel. (+352) 439845559.

Head of Private Office: Werner Vlasselaer; tel. (+352) 439845434.

Attaché: Bernard Moya; tel. (+352) 439845916.

Member of the Court: Mihails Kozlovs; tel. (+352) 439845569.

Head of Private Office: Edite Dzalbe; tel. (+352) 439845583.

Attaché: Laura Graudina; tel. (+352) 439845691.

Member of the Court: Rimantas Šadžius; tel. (+352) 439847261.

Head of Private Office: Mindaugas Pakštys; tel. (+352) 439845755.

Attaché: Tomas Mackevičius; tel. (+352) 439847133.

Member of the Court: Leo Brincat; tel. (+352) 439845162.

Head of Private Office: Neil Baldacchino Kerr; tel. (+352) 439847108.

Attaché: Annette Farrugia; tel. (+352) 439845185.

Member of the Court: João Figuiredo; tel. (+352) 439845154.

Head of Private Office: Manuel Lourenço de Oliveira; tel. (+352) 439845160.

Attaché: Paula Betencourt; tel. (+352) 439845059.

Member of the Court: Juhan Parts; tel. (+352) 439845299.

Head of Private Office: Ken-Marti Vaher; tel. (+352) 439845917.

Attaché: Margus Kurm; tel. (+352) 439845912.

Member of the Court: Ildikó Gáll-Pelcz; tel. (+352) 439847053.

Head of Private Office: Zoltán Lavos; tel. (+352) 439847150.

Attaché: Claudia Bara; tel. (+352) 439847131.

PRESIDENCY

Liaison Officer and Protocol, Communications and Institutional Relations and Strategy

Director: Martin Weber; tel. (+352) 439845151.

Chief Institutional Relations Officer: Helena Piron Mäki-Korvela; tel. (+352) 439845314.

Spokesperson: Mark Rogerson; tel. (+352) 439847063.

Press Officer: Damijan Fišer; tel. (+352) 439847300.

Legal Service

Head of Unit: Christophe Lesauvage; tel. (+352) 439845803.

Internal Audit

Head of Unit: Meletios Stavrakis; tel. (+352) 439845261.

CHAMBERS

Chamber I—Sustainable Use of Natural Resources

Dean: Phil Wynn Owen; tel. (+352) 439845372.

Director: Peter Welch; tel. (+352) 439845272.

Member: Janusz Wojciechowski; tel. (+352) 439845567.

Member: Nikolaos Milionis; tel. (+352) 439845258.

Member: Samo Jereb; tel. (+352) 439845570.

Member: João Figuiredo; tel. (+352) 439845154.

Principal Manager: Michael Bain; tel. (+352) 439845438.

Principal Manager: Hélder Faria Viegas; tel. (+352) 439845249.

Principal Manager: Robert Markus; tel. (+352) 439845371.

Principal Manager: Colm Friel; tel. (+352) 439845023.

Principal Manager: Richard Hardy; tel. (+352) 439845625.

Chamber II—Investment for Cohesion, Growth and Inclusion

Dean: Iliana Ivanova; tel. (+352) 439847141.

Director: Gerhard Ross; tel. (+352) 439845988.

Member: Ladislav Balko; tel. (+352) 439847201.

Member: Henri Grethen; tel. (+352) 439845376.

Member: George Pufan.

Member: Oskar Herics.

Principal Manager: Juan Ignacio González Bastero; tel. (+352) 439845117.

Principal Manager: Niels-Erik Brokopp-Spiermann; tel. (+352) 439845579.

Principal Manager: Pietro Puricella; tel. (+352) 439845674.

Principal Manager: Emmanuel Rauch; tel. (+352) 439845919.

Principal Manager: Myriam Cazzaniga; tel. (+352) 439845641.

Chamber III—External Action, Security and Justice

Dean: Karel Pinxten; tel. (+352) 439845295.

Director: Philippe Froidure; tel. (+352) 439845302.

Member: Ville Itälä; tel. (+352) 439845965.

Member: Bettina Jakobsen; tel. (+352) 439847144.

Member: Juhan Parts; tel. (+352) 439845299.

Member: Hans Gustaf Wessberg; tel. (+352) 439845959.

Principal Manager: Sabine Hiernaux-Fritsch; tel. (+352) 439845454.

Principal Manager: Alejandro Ballester Gallardo; tel. (+352) 439845272.

Principal Manager: Beatrix Lesiewicz; tel. (+352) 439845920.

Chamber IV—Regulation of Markets and Competitive Economy

Dean: Baudilio Tomé Muguruza; tel. (+352) 439845592; fax (+352) 439846818.

Director: Tony Murphy; tel. (+352) 439847784.

Member: Kevin Cardiff; tel. (+352) 439845931; fax (+352) 439846493.

Member: Neven Mates; tel. (+352) 439847439; fax (+352) 439848439.

Member: Alex Brenninkmeijer; tel. (+352) 439845236; fax (+352) 439846236.

Member: Rimantas Šadžius; tel. (+352) 439847261.

Principal Manager: Marion Colonerus; tel. (+352) 439845237.

Principal Manager: Paul Stafford; tel. (+352) 439845494.

Principal Manager: Friedemann Zippel; tel. (+352) 439845488.

Head of Unit: Fred Michael Zippel; tel. (+352) 439845488.

Chamber V—Financing and Administering the Union

Dean: Lazaros S. Lazarou; tel. (+352) 439847241.

Director: Mariusz Pomieński; tel. (+352) 439847671.

Member: Pietro Russo; tel. (+352) 439845374.

European Court of Auditors — DIRECTORY

Member: Jan Gregor; tel. (+352) 439845559.
Member: Mihails Kozlovs; tel. (+352) 439845569.
Member: Leo Brincat; tel. (+352) 439845162.
Principal Adviser: Gabriele Cipriani; tel. (+352) 439845556.
Principal Manager: Bertrand Albugues; tel. (+352) 4398645769.
Principal Manager: Ralph Otte; tel. (+352) 439845255.
Principal Manager: Alberto Gasperoni; tel. (+352) 439845110.
Principal Manager: Davide Lingua; tel. (+352) 439845555.

Audit Quality Control Committee

Member for Audit Quality Control: Danièle Lamarque; tel. (+352) 439845203.
Director: Geoffrey Simpson; tel. (+352) 439845347.
Member: Bettina Jakobsen; tel. (+352) 439847144.
Member: Samo Jereb; tel. (+352) 439845570.
Principal Manager: John Sweeney; tel. (+352) 439845526.
Principal Manager: Bogna Kuczyńska; tel. (+352) 439845526.

ADMINISTRATIVE COMMITTEE

President: Klaus-Heiner Lehne; tel. (+352) 439845271.
Dean of Chamber I: Phil Wynn Owen; tel. (+352) 439845372.
Dean of Chamber II: Iliana Ivanova; tel. (+352) 439847141.
Dean of Chamber III: Karel Pinxten; tel. (+352) 439845295.
Dean of Chamber IV: Baudilio Tomé Muguruza; tel. (+352) 439845592.
Dean of Chamber V: Lazaros S. Lazarou; tel. (+352) 439847241.

SECRETARIAT-GENERAL

Secretary-General: Eduardo Ruiz García; tel. (+352) 439845620.
Head of Private Office: Alfonso de La Fuente; tel. (+352) 439845681.
Attaché: Nirina Robinson; tel. (+352) 439845944.

Directorate of Human Resources, Finance and General Services

Director: Zacharias Kolias; tel. (+352) 439845907.
Principal Manager: Isidoro Rodriguez De Las Parras; tel. (+352) 439847175.
Principal Manager: Pilar Calvo Fuentes; tel. (+352) 439845787.

DATA PROTECTION AND INFORMATION SECURITY

Data Protection Officer: Johan Van Damme; tel. (+352) 439845279; fax (+352) 439342.
Principal Manager: Christine Stark; tel. (+352) 439845191.

Directorate of Information, Workplace and Innovation

Director: Magdalena Cordero Valdavida; tel. (+352) 439845007.
Principal Manager: José Carrascosa Moreno; tel. (+352) 439847307.
Principal Manager: Franck Noël; tel. (+352) 439847313.
Principal Manager: Spyridon Pilos; tel. (+352) 439847939.

Directorate of Translation and Language Services

Director: Gailė Dagilienė; tel. (+352) 439847351.

CO-ORDINATION

Planning and Technical Pool
Principal Manager: José Ortiz Pintor; tel. (+352) 439845321.

Linguistic/Administrative Pool
Principal Manager: Alain Verkaeren; tel. (+352) 439845512.

IT Co-ordinator
Principal Manager: Paweł Szuba; tel. (+352) 439847259.

Communication Co-ordinator
Principal Manager: Veronica Ardelean; tel. (+352) 439847193.

LANGUAGE TEAMS

Bulgarian Language Team
Principal Manager: Miroslava Chakalova-Siddy; tel. (+352) 439845978.

Spanish Language Team
Principal Manager: Pilar Cano de Gardoqui; tel. (+352) 439845670.

Czech Language Team
Principal Manager: Martin Krejza; tel. (+352) 439847360.

Danish Language Team
Principal Manager: Dorte Remaoun; tel. (+352) 439845582.

German Language Team
Principal Manager: Monika Krumnau; tel. (+352) 439845544.

Estonian Language Team
Principal Manager: Madis Rausi; tel. (+352) 439847827.

Greek Language Team
Principal Manager: Zoe Bolanki; tel. (+352) 439845701.

English Language Team
Principal Manager: Adrian Williams; tel. (+352) 439845982.

French Language Team
Principal Manager: Alain Verkaeren; tel. (+352) 439845512.

Croatian Language Team
Principal Manager: Ljupče Stojkovski; tel. (+352) 439847567.

Italian Language Team
Principal Manager: Elisabetta Palla; tel. (+352) 439845509.

Latvian Language Team
Principal Manager: Inta Šmite; tel. (+352) 439847618.

Lithuanian Language Team
Principal Manager: Kęstutis Žilionis; tel. (+352) 439845192.

Hungarian Language Team
Principal Manager: Madis Rausi; tel. (+352) 439847827.

Dutch Language Team
Principal Manager: Ingrid van Gent; tel. (+352) 439845521.

Maltese Language Team
Principal Manager: Anna Maria Attard Montalto; tel. (+352) 439847252.

Polish Language Team
Principal Manager: Paweł Szuba; tel. (+352) 439847259.

Portuguese Language Team
Principal Manager: Maria de Lurdes Rodrigues; tel. (+352) 439845525.

Romanian Language Team
Principal Manager: Veronica Ardelean; tel. (+352) 439847193.

Slovak Language Team
Principal Manager: Miroslav Pikna; tel. (+352) 439845205.

Slovenian Language Team
Principal Manager: Vesna Marn; tel. (+352) 439845113.

Finnish Language Team
Principal Manager: Eija Raittinen; tel. (+352) 439845675.

Swedish Language Team
Principal Manager: Carolina Ask; tel. (+352) 439845939.

EUROPEAN ECONOMIC AND SOCIAL COMMITTEE (EESC)

99 rue Belliard, 1040 Brussels, Belgium; tel. (+32) 2-5469011; fax (+32) 2-5134893; internet www.eesc.europa.eu

Bureau

President: Georges Dassis.

Vice-Presidents: Gonçalo Lobo Xavier, Michael Smyth.

MEMBERS OF THE BUREAU

Gunta Anča, Dorthe Andersen, Krzysztof Stanisław Balon, Gabriele Bischoff, Brendan Burns, Miguel Ángel Cabra de Luna, Patricia Círez Miqueleiz, Pierre Jean Coulon, David Croughan, Georges Dassis, Bernd Dittmann, Raymond Hencks, Luca Jahier, Jacek Krawczyk, Daiva Kvedaraitė, Tellervo Kylä-Harakka-Ruonala, Ronny Lannoo, Gonçalo Lobo Xavier, Emil Machyna, Reine-Claude Mader, Daniel Mareels, Dragica Martinović Džamonja, Manthos Mavrommatis, Arno Metzler, Ellen Nygren, Stefano Palmieri, Cristian Pîrvulescu, Ariane Rodert, Oliver Röpke, Martin Siecker, Dilyana Slavova, Michael Smyth, Lucie Studničná, Reet Teder, Ákos Topolánszky, Pavel Trantina, Joost van Iersel, Charles Vella, Andrej Zorko.

Members

INTEREST GROUPS

Employers (Group I)

President: Jacek Krawczyk.

Workers (Group II)

President: Gabriele Bischoff.

Various Interests (Group III)

President: Luca Jahier.

SECTIONS

The specialized sections for the principal fields covered by the Treaty on the Functioning of the European Union, and additional bodies, are:

1. Economic and Monetary Union and Economic and Social Cohesion (ECO)

President: Joost van Iersel.

2. Single Market, Production and Consumption (INT)

President: Martin Siecker.

3. Agriculture, Rural Development and the Environment (NAT)

President: Brendan Burns.

4. External Relations (REX)

President: Dilyana Slavova.

5. Employment, Social Affairs and Citizenship (SOC)

President: Pavel Trantina.

6. Transport, Energy, Infrastructure and the Information Society (TEN)

President: Pierre Jean Coulon.

7. Consultative Commission on Industrial Change (CCMI)

President: Lucie Studničná.

EESC Members

Name	Member State	Group	Sections
Ābeltiņa, Ariadna	Latvia	II	1, 4, 5
Abildgaard, Ask Løvbjerg	Denmark	III	2, 5, 6
Abrahamsson, Tomas	Sweden	II	3, 6
Adamczyk, Andrzej	Poland	II	2, 4
Ahtela, Jukka	Finland	I	1, 4, 5
Albu, Octavian Cătălin	Romania	I	1, 4
Alistar, Victor	Romania	III	2, 5
Almeida Freire, Pedro Augusto	Portugal	I	2, 6, 7
Anča, Gunta	Latvia	III	1, 5, 6, 7
Andersen, Dorthe	Denmark	I	1, 5
Andersson, Krister	Sweden	I	1, 2
Angelova, Milena	Bulgaria	I	1, 2
Antoniou, Michalis	Cyprus	I	3, 5, 6, 7
Babrauskienė, Tatjana	Lithuania	II	1, 4, 5
Back, Stefan	Sweden	I	3, 6
Báleš, Vladimír	Slovakia	III	4, 5, 6
Balon, Krzysztof Stanisław	Poland	III	2, 5
Baráth, Etele	Hungary	III	1, 6
Barbieri, Pietro Vittorio	Italy	III	4, 5
Barbucci, Giulia	Italy	II	5, 6
Barceló Delgado, Andrés	Spain	I	4, 6, 7
Barker, Roger	UK	I	1, 2, 7
Barros Vale, Paulo	Portugal	I	1, 2
Basáñez Villaluenga, Josep Manuel	Spain	I	1, 6
Basset, Christiane	France	III	5, 6
Batut, Laure	France	II	5, 6
Bäumler, Christian	Germany	II	4, 5
Bergrath, Dirk	Germany	II	2, 6, 7
Bischoff, Gabriele	Germany	II	1, 5
Björnsson, Sofia	Sweden	III	2, 3
Bobrowski, Franciszek	Poland	II	3, 6
Boland, Seamus	Ireland	III	1, 3, 5, 7
Bontea, Ana	Romania	I	1, 5

DIRECTORY

Name	Member State	Group	Sections
Broniarz, Wincenty Sławomir	Poland	II	2, 4
Bryan, John	Ireland	III	2, 3, 4
Brzobohatá, Zuzana	Czech Republic	III	1, 6, 7
Buffetaut, Stéphane	France	I	3, 6
Bulk, Marjolijn	Netherlands	II	1, 5
Burns, Brendan	UK	I	3, 6
Buschi, Claudia	Italy	II	2, 3
Butaud-Stubbs, Emmanuelle	France	I	2, 4
Buzek, Tanja	Germany	II	4, 6
Cabra de Luna, Miguel Ángel	Spain	III	2, 4
Calderone, Marina Elvira	Italy	III	2, 5
Caño Aguilar, Isabel	Spain	II	3, 6
Carr, Liina	Estonia	II	1, 3, 6
Catsambis, Constantine	Greece	I	4, 6
Cetica, Stefano	Italy	II	1, 3
Chassagnette, Anne	France	I	3, 6
Círez Miqueleiz, Patricia	Spain	I	1, 5
Clever, Peter	Germany	I	4, 5
Coheur, Alain	Belgium	III	2, 5, 7
Comer, John	Ireland	III	1, 3, 4
Coulon, Pierre Jean	France	II	4, 6
Coumont, Raymond	Belgium	II	4, 5, 7
Crook, Nicholas	UK	II	3, 4
Croughan, David	Ireland	I	1, 2, 4
Cser, Ágnes	Hungary	III	4, 6
Curtis, Brian	UK	II	3, 6, 7
Curylo, Lukáš	Czech Republic	III	4, 5
Dandea, Petru Sorin	Romania	II	1, 5
Danev, Bojidar	Bulgaria	I	1, 6
Dassis, Georges	Greece	II	
de Brauer, Philippe	France	I	1, 6, 7
de Buck, Philippe	Belgium	I	1, 4
de Felipe Lehtonen, Helena	Spain	I	4, 5
Delapina, Thomas	Austria	II	1, 6
De Leeuw, Rudy	Belgium	II	4, 6
Dell'Alba, Gianfranco	Italy	I	1, 2
De Lotto, Pietro Francesco	Italy	I	2, 4
Del Rio, Cinzia	Italy	II	2, 5, 7
Demelenne, Anne	Belgium	II	1, 5
Dias da Silva, João	Portugal	II	4, 5
Di Fazio, Tommaso	Spain	III	4, 6, 7
Dimitriadis, Dimitris	Greece	I	1, 2
Dimitrov, Plamen	Bulgaria	II	1, 6
Dirx, Jan	Netherlands	III	3, 6
Dittmann, Bernd	Germany	I	2, 6
Doz Orrit, Javier	Spain	II	1, 4
Drbalová, Vladimíra	Czech Republic	I	2, 5
Dreszer-Smalec, Karolina	Poland	III	1, 5
D'Sa, Rose	UK	III	2, 4, 7
Dubravská, Jarmila	Slovakia	I	2, 3, 4
Dubromel, Michel	France	III	3, 6
Dufek, Bohumír	Czech Republic	II	3, 6
Dulevski, Lalko	Bulgaria	III	1, 5
Durante, Giancarlo	Italy	I	2, 5
Dutto, Diego	Italy	III	5, 6
Edelényi, András	Czech Republic	I	1, 6, 7
Ekenger, Karin	Sweden	I	4, 5
Epistithiou, Nicos	Cyprus	II	3, 4, 5
Etherington, Stuart	UK	III	1, 5
Fallenkamp, Bernt	Denmark	II	1, 2, 5
Fatovic, Emilio	Italy	II	3, 6
Federspiel, Benedicte	Denmark	III	2, 4, 6
Floria, Irinel Eduard	Romania	I	5, 6
Fornea, Dumitru	Romania	II	4, 6, 7
Gajdosik, Alfred	Austria	III	4, 6
García Arriola, Andoni	Spain	III	3, 4
García del Riego, Antonio	Spain	I	1, 2
García Magarzo, Ignacio	Spain	I	2, 3
Gardias, Dorota	Poland	II	3, 5
Gavrilovs, Vitālijs	Latvia	I	1, 4, 6
Geisen, Norbert	Luxembourg	III	1, 2, 3, 7
Gkofas, Panagiotis	Greece	III	2, 3
Gondard-Argenti, Marie-Françoise	France	I	2, 5
González de Txabarri Etxaniz, Laura	Spain	II	4, 5
Götz, Nadja	Slovenia	II	1, 3, 5
Greif, Wolfgang	Austria	II	1, 5, 7
Grevsen, Arne	Denmark	II	6
Guerini, Giuseppe	Italy	III	1, 2
Haken, Roman	Czech Republic	III	1, 3
Handke, Gerhard	Germany	I	1, 4
Hansen, Christophe	Luxembourg	I	1, 2, 6
Hanževački, Marija	Croatia	II	4, 5
Heinisch, Renate	Germany	III	2, 6
Hemmerling, Udo	Germany	I	3, 6
Hencks, Raymond	Luxembourg	II	2, 5, 6
Hernández Bataller, Bernardo	Spain	III	2, 6
Hillairet, Christophe	France	III	3, 4
Houwing, Hester	Netherlands	II	1, 6
Ikrath, Michael	Austria	I	1, 6
Indjova, Diana	Bulgaria	III	4, 5
Iuliano, Giuseppe Antonio Maria	Italy	II	4, 5
Ivanov, Evgeniy	Bulgaria	I	4, 5
Ivaşcu, Mihai	Romania	III	1, 2, 7
Ivaşcu, Minel	Romania	II	2, 6
Jahier, Luca	Italy	III	1, 5
Janoszka, Wioletta	Poland	II	2, 6
Jansson, Bo	Sweden	I	4, 5
Jelić, Violeta	Croatia	I	1, 2, 3
Jones, Tom	UK	III	3, 5
Jonuška, Alfredas	Lithuania	I	2, 4, 5
Joó, Kinga	Hungary	III	4, 5
Joost, Meelis	Estonia	III	1, 4, 5
Kállay, Piroska	Hungary	II	3, 4
Kamieniecki, Krzysztof	Poland	III	3, 6
Kattnig, Thomas	Austria	II	4, 6
Kekeleki, Evangelia	Greece	III	2, 6
Kelly, Diane	UK	II	5, 6
Kessler, Jürgen	Germany	III	1, 2
Kindberg, Mette	Denmark	III	1, 4, 5
King, Brenda	UK	I	3, 5
Klimek, Jan	Poland	I	2, 5
Kluge, Norbert	Germany	II	2, 6
Kokalov, Ivan	Bulgaria	II	1, 5
Kolbe, Rudolf	Austria	III	2, 4
Koller, Erika	Hungary	II	4, 5
Kolyvas, Ioannis	Greece	III	3, 6
Komoróczki, István	Hungary	I	3, 4
Körzell, Stefan	Germany	II	1, 2
Krawczyk, Jacek	Poland	I	4, 6

Name	Member State	Group	Sections
Krīgers, Pēteris	Latvia	II	2, 3, 6, 7
Kropil, Rudolf	Slovakia	III	1, 3, 4
Kropp, Thomas	Germany	I	5, 6, 7
Krzaklewski, Marian	Poland	II	1, 6, 7
Kvedaraitė, Daiva	Lithuania	II	2, 6, 4
Kylä-Harakka-Ruonala, Tellervo	Finland	I	2, 3, 6
Ladefoged, Anders	Denmark	I	2, 4, 6
Lambertz, Günter	Germany	I	2, 5
Lannoo, Ronny	Belgium	III	1, 2
Lasiauskas, Linas	Lithuania	I	2, 4, 6, 7
Lefèvre, Christophe	France	II	2, 4
Leirião, José Custódio	Portugal	III	1, 5
Lemercier, Jacques	France	II	2, 3, 7
Le Roux, Jocelyne	France	III	1, 2
Libaert, Thierry	France	III	2, 3
Liebus, Patrick	France	I	2, 5
Lindberg Madsen, Niels	Denmark	I	2, 3, 6
Lobo Xavier, Gonçalo	Portugal	I	2, 6
Lohan, Cillian	Ireland	III	1, 6, 3
Longo, Antonio	Italy	III	2, 6
Luca, Liviu	Romania	II	1, 6
Lustenhouwer, Colin	Netherlands	I	2, 6
Lyon, George Traill	UK	I	2, 5
McDonogh, Thomas	Ireland	I	2, 4, 6
Machyna, Emil	Slovakia	II	1, 6, 7
Maciulevičius, Mindaugas	Lithuania	III	2, 3, 6, 7
Mačiulis, Vitas	Lithuania	III	3, 4, 6
McKeown, Patricia	Ireland	II	4, 5
McKnight, Judy	UK	II	4, 5
McLoughlin, Michael	Ireland	III	1, 4, 5
Mader, Reine-Claude	France	III	2, 3
Maier, Ferdinand	Austria	I	4, 6
Majetić, Davor	Croatia	I	1, 2, 6
Malinowski, Andrzej	Poland	I	1, 6
Mallia, Stefano	Malta	I	1, 4, 5
Malosse, Henri	France	I	1, 3
Manoliu, Mihai	Romania	I	4, 6
Manolov, Dimitar	Bulgaria	II	4, 6
Mareels, Daniel	Belgium	I	1, 2
Martinović Džamonja, Dragica	Croatia	I	2, 4, 6
Mascia, Sandro	Italy	I	3, 4
Matthiesen, Klaus	Denmark	II	5
Mavrommatis, Manthos	Cyprus	I	1, 2, 4
Mayer, Martin	UK	II	1, 6
Mayerová, Mária	Slovakia	II	5, 6
Mazzola, Alberto	Italy	I	4, 6
Mendoza Castro, Juan	Spain	II	1, 2
Metzler, Arno	Germany	III	2, 4
Meynent, Denis	France	II	2, 5
Michel, Dominique	Belgium	I	2, 3
Mihók, Peter	Slovakia	I	1
Milićević-Pezelj, Anica	Croatia	II	5, 7
Miltoviča, Baiba	Latvia	III	1, 2, 6
Mira, Luís Miguel	Portugal	I	2, 3
Mitov, Vesselin	Bulgaria	II	2, 3, 7
Modrzejewski, Michał Grzegorz	Poland	III	2, 3
Moisio, Pasi	Finland	III	2, 5, 6
Moos, Christian	Germany	III	4, 5, 7
Moreno Díaz, José Antonio	Spain	II	2, 5
Morkis, Gintaras	Lithuania	I	1, 4, 6
Morrice, Jane	UK	III	4, 5
Mulewicz, Jarosław	Poland	I	1, 4
Muller, Catelijne	Netherlands	II	1, 2
Nikolov, Bogomil	Bulgaria	III	2, 6, 7
Norkārklis, Gustavs	Latvia	III	1, 2, 3
Novotný, Vladimír	Czech Republic	I	3, 6, 7
Nygren, Ellen	Sweden	II	4, 5
O'Connor, Jack	Ireland	II	1, 5, 6
Oldfather, Irene	UK	III	4, 5
Öngörur, Berivan	Sweden	II	2, 4
Opran, Marius Eugen	Romania		2, 6
Osinga, Klaas Johan	Netherlands	III	3
Ostrowski, Krzysztof	Poland	I	1, 6
Päärendson, Eve	Estonia	I	1, 4, 5, 7
Palmieri, Stefano	Italy	II	1, 2
Panagopoulos, Ioannis	Greece	II	1, 5, 7
Papaspyros, Spyridon	Greece	II	3, 4
Pari, Irini Ivoni	Greece	I	1, 5
Pásztor, Miklós	Hungary	II	1, 2
Pater, Krzysztof	Poland	III	1, 5
Pavić Rogošić, Lidija	Croatia	III	3, 4
Pavlikkas, Andreas	Cyprus	II	1, 2, 6
Peel, Jonathan	UK	I	3, 4
Pegado Liz, Jorge	Portugal	III	2, 6, 7
Penttinen, Markus	Finland	II	1, 3, 4
Petersen, Volker J.	Germany	I	3, 6
Petraitienė, Irena	Lithuania	II	1, 3, 5
Petropoulos, Georgios	Greece	II	2, 5
Pezzini, Antonello	Italy	I	5, 6, 7
Pietkiewicz, Janusz	Poland	I	2, 4, 7
Pilawski, Lech	Poland	I	2, 5
Pîrvulescu, Cristian	Romania	III	4, 5
Ploşceanu, Aurel Laurenţiu	Romania	I	4, 6, 7
Počivavšek, Jakob Krištof	Slovenia	II	1, 2, 6, 7
Popelková, Hana	Czech Republic	II	1, 5
Puech d'Alissac, Arnold	France	I	3, 6
Puxeu Rocamora, Josep	Spain	I	3, 4
Quaedvlieg, Winand	Netherlands	I	3, 6
Quarez, Christophe	France	II	4, 6
Ramos, Carlos	Portugal	III	5, 6
Raunemaa, Pirkko	Finland	III	1, 3, 4
Ravnik, Branko	Slovenia	III	1, 3, 6
Reale, Maurizio	Italy	I	1, 3
Reding, Jean-Claude	Luxembourg	II	1, 2, 5, 7
Ribbe, Lutz	Germany	III	3, 6
Ribić, Vilim	Croatia	II	1, 2, 4
Riemer, Gerhard	Austria	I	1, 5
Ristelä, Pekka	Finland	II	5
Rizzo, Benjamin	Malta	III	1, 2, 5, 7
Roche Ramo, José Manuel	Spain	III	3, 4
Rodert, Ariane	Sweden	III	2, 5
Rogalewski, Adam	Poland	II	4, 5
Roirant, Jean-Marc	France	III	4, 5
Röpke, Oliver	Austria	II	2, 5
Rotti, Claudio	Italy	I	1, 4
Rusu, Sabin	Romania	II	2, 3
Salis-Madinier, Franca	France	II	2, 5
Samm, Ulrich	Germany	I	3, 6
Sarró Iparraguirre, Gabriel	Spain	III	3, 4
Savigny, Geneviève	France	III	3
Schackmann-Fallis, Karl-Peter	Germany	I	1, 2
Schlüter, Bernd	Germany	III	2, 5
Schmidt, Peter	Germany	II	3, 4
Schwannecke, Holger	Germany	III	1, 2
Schwartz, Arnaud	France	III	3, 6

Name	Member State	Group	Sections
Schweng, Christa	Austria	I	2, 5, 7
Sears, David	UK	I	5, 6
Serra Arias, Ricardo	Spain	I	3, 4
Sharma, Madi	UK	I	4, 5
Sibian, Ionuț	Romania	III	4, 5
Siecker, Martin	Netherlands	II	2, 3
Silva, Carlos	Portugal	II	1, 5
Silva, Francisco	Portugal	III	3, 4
Simons, Jan	Netherlands	I	4, 6
Singh, Amarjite	UK	II	1, 2
Sipko, Juraj	Slovakia	III	1, 2, 4
Širhalová, Martina	Slovakia	I	1, 4, 6
Škrabalo, Marina	Croatia	III	2, 4, 5
Slavova, Dilyana	Bulgaria	III	3, 4
Smole, Jože	Slovenia	I	2, 4, 5
Smyth, Michael	UK	III	1, 2
Soares, Mário	Portugal	II	3, 4
Soete, Paul	Belgium	I	5, 6
Somville, Yves	Belgium	III	3, 4
Srmus, Roomet	Estonia	III	2, 3, 6
Šporar, Primož	Slovenia	III	2, 4, 5, 7
Spragg Nilsson, Imse	Sweden	III	4, 5
Stoev, Georgi	Bulgaria	I	2, 6, 7
Stojan, Dare	Slovenia	I	1, 3, 6
Strautmanis, Gundars	Latvia	I	1, 3, 6, 7
Studničná, Lucie	Czech Republic	II	2, 4, 7
Süle, Katalin Elza	Hungary	I	3, 6
Svensson, Erik	Sweden	I	1, 2
Szadzińska, Elżbieta	Poland	III	2, 3, 7
Szalay, Anton	Slovakia	II	5, 6
Teder, Reet	Estonia	I	1, 2, 6
Thomopoulos, Aristotelis	Greece	I	2, 4
Thurner, Andreas	Austria	III	3, 4
Tiainen, Simo	Finland	III	3, 4, 6
Tiszbierek, Teresa	Poland	III	5, 6
Tolmie, Agnes	UK	II	1, 4
Topolánszky, Ákos	Hungary	III	4, 5
Trantina, Pavel	Czech Republic	III	5, 6
Trías Pinto, Carlos	Spain	III	1, 2, 7
Trindade, Carlos Manuel	Portugal	II	4, 5
Ungerman, Jaroslav	Czech Republic	II	1, 2
Vadász, Borbála	Hungary	I	1, 5
Valentin, Olivier	Belgium	II	1, 4
Vallander, Taina	Finland	II	5, 6
van Iersel, Joost	Netherlands	I	1, 6, 7
van Wezel, Annie	Netherlands	II	4, 6
Vardakastanis, Ioannis	Greece	III	4, 5
Vareikytė, Indrė	Lithuania	III	4, 5, 6
Vella, Charles	Malta	II	1, 4, 5
Vezzani, Marco	Italy	II	4, 6
Vicens Guillén, Katiana	Spain	II	3, 6
Vidan, Toni	Croatia	III	3, 6
Viies, Mare	Estonia	II	1, 2, 5
Vitale, Ester	Italy	II	1, 3
von Brockdorff, Philip	Malta	II	1, 5
Vuori, Timo	Finland	I	2, 4
Wagnsonner, Thomas	Austria	II	2, 4
Walker, John	UK	I	2, 5
Walker Shaw, Kathleen	UK	II	2, 5
Watson, Graham	UK	III	4, 6
Weltner, János	Hungary	II	2, 5
Westendorp, Dirk	Netherlands	III	2, 6
Westerlund, Ulrika	Sweden	III	4, 5
Willems, Josiane	Luxembourg	III	3, 4, 6
Wilms, Hans-Joachim	Germany	II	2, 3
Wyckmans, Ferre	Belgium	II	1, 2
Yannakoudakis, Marina	UK	III	3, 5
Yiapanis, Anastasis	Cyprus	III	2, 3, 4, 7
Yildirim, Ozlem	France	II	3, 4
Zahra, Tony	Malta	I	1, 2, 4
Zahradník, Petr	Czech Republic	I	1, 6
Zorko, Andrej	Slovenia	II	2, 4, 5
Zufiaur Narvaiza, José María	Spain	II	4, 5, 7
Zvolská, Marie	Czech Republic	I	2, 5

Administrative Units

99 rue Belliard, 1040 Brussels, Belgium; tel. (+32) 2-5469011; fax (+32) 2-5134893; internet www.eesc.europa.eu

PRESIDENCY

President's Office

Head of Cabinet: Nicolas Alexopoulos; tel. (+32) 2-5469370.

GROUP SECRETARIATS

Group I—Employers

Head of Unit: Marco Thyssen; tel. (+32) 2-5468411; e-mail gr1@eesc.europa.eu.

Group II—Workers

Head of Unit: Susanna Florio; tel. (+32) 2-5469932; e-mail gr2@eesc.europa.eu.

Group III—Various Interests

Head of Unit: Marc Beffort; tel. (+32) 2-5469547; e-mail gr3@eesc.europa.eu.

SECRETARY-GENERAL

Secretary-General: Luis Planas Puchades; tel. (+32) 2-25469022.

Deputy Secretary-General: Livia Gruia; tel. (+32) 2-5134843.

Directorate A—Legislative Planning, Relations with Institutions and Civil Society

Director: María Echevarría; tel. (+32) 2-5469393.

REGISTRY
Head of Unit: John Power; tel. (+32) 2-5469035.

RELATIONS WITH THE INSTITUTIONS AND THE NATIONAL ESCS
Head of Unit: Tatiana Adamisova; tel. (+32) 2-5468110.

RELATIONS WITH ORGANIZED CIVIL SOCIETY AND FORWARD STUDIES
Head of Unit: Pierluigi Brombo; tel. (+32) 2-5469718.

LEGAL SERVICE
Head of Unit: Marta Carmen Pascua Mateo; tel. (+32) 2-5469086.

Directorate B—Legislative Works

Director: Alan Hick; tel. (+32) 2-5469302.

EXTERNAL RELATIONS
Head of Unit: Beatriz Porres; tel. (+32) 2-5469131.

ECONOMIC AND MONETARY UNION, ECONOMIC AND SOCIAL COHESION
Head of Unit: Gilbert Marchwelewitz; tel. (+32) 2-5469358.

TRANSPORT, ENERGY, INFRASTRUCTURE AND THE INFORMATION SOCIETY
Head of Unit: Birgit Fulhar; tel. (+32) 2-5469044.

CONSULTATIVE COMMISSION ON INDUSTRIAL CHANGE
Head of Unit: (vacant).

Directorate C—Legislative Works

Director: Jean-François Bence; tel. (+32) 2-5469399.

EMPLOYMENT, SOCIAL AFFAIRS AND CITIZENSHIP
Head of Unit: Johannes Kind; tel. (+32) 2-5469111.

AGRICULTURE, RURAL DEVELOPMENT AND THE ENVIRONMENT
Head of Unit: Eric Ponthieu; tel. (+32) 2-5468771.

SINGLE MARKET, PRODUCTION AND CONSUMPTION
Head of Unit: Luis Lobo; tel. (+32) 2-5469717.

POLICY ASSESSMENT
Head of Unit: Philippe Cuisson; tel. (+32) 2-5469961.

Directorate D—Communication

Head of Unit: Peter Lindvald-Nielsen; tel. (+32) 2-5469888.

PRESS
Head of Unit: Alun Jones; fax (+32) 2-5468641.

ONLINE INFORMATION
Head of Unit: Karin Fussl; tel. (+32) 2-5468722.

VISITS/PUBLICATIONS
Head of Unit: Eleonora Di Nicolantonio; tel. (+32) 2-5469454.

CONFERENCES, INTERNAL SERVICES AND PROTOCOL
Head of Unit: Dominique-François Bareth; tel. (+32) 2-5469089.

Directorate E—Human Resources and Finance

Director: Gianluca Brunetti; tel. (+32) 2-5469695.

RECRUITMENT AND SALARIES
Head of Unit: Marie-Hélène Burhin; tel. (+32) 2-5469539.

WORKING CONDITIONS, RIGHTS AND OBLIGATIONS, PENSIONS
Head of Unit: Lotte Berg; tel. (+32) 2-5469388.

HR PLANNING AND TRAINING
Head of Unit: Monika Lernhart; tel. (+32) 2-5469287.

BUDGET
Head of Unit: Torben Bach Nielsen; tel. (+32) 2-5469619.

FINANCE AND FINANCIAL VERIFICATION
Head of Unit: Federico Rossi; tel. (+32) 2-5469733.

SERVICE TO MEMBERS
Head of Unit: Gerardus Nijiborg; tel. (+32) 2-5469807.

JOINT SERVICES OF THE EUROPEAN ECONOMIC AND SOCIAL COMMITTEE AND THE COMMITTEE OF THE REGIONS

Directorate for Logistics

Director: Paulo Campilho; tel. (+32) 2-5469813.

SECURITY
Administrator: Philippe Guebels; tel. (+32) 2-5468662.

PROGRAMMING/FINANCIAL AND CONTRACTUAL MANAGEMENT
Head of Unit: Livia Gruia; tel. (+32) 2-5469714.

INFRASTRUCTURE
Head of Unit: Patrick de Schrijver; tel. (+32) 2-5468665.

IIT—INFORMATION TECHNOLOGIES, TELECOMMUNICATION
Head of Unit: Niall O'Higgins; tel. (+32) 2-5469668.

PRINTING/DIFFUSION
Head of Unit: Annette Orth; tel. (+32) 2-5469967.

Directorate for Translation

Director: Ineta Strautina; tel. (+32) 2-25468243.

TRANSLATION MANAGEMENT
Head of Unit: Éric Lavigne; tel. (+32) 2-2822032.

BULGARIAN TRANSLATION
Head of Unit: Katia Pankova; tel. (+32) 2-2822117.

SPANISH TRANSLATION
Head of Unit: Joaquín Calvo Basarán; tel. (+32) 2-5468866.

CROATIAN TRANSLATION
Head of Unit: Suzanna Matvejevic; tel. (+32) 2-5469726.

CZECH-SLOVAK TRANSLATION
Head of Unit: Markéta Franková; tel. (+32) 2-5469742.

DANISH TRANSLATION
Head of Unit (acting): Marie Heising; tel. (+32) 2-5468380.

GERMAN TRANSLATION
Head of Unit: Giovanni Di Carlo; tel. (+32) 2-5469502.

ESTONIAN TRANSLATION
Head of Unit: Aivar Paidla; tel. (+32) 2-5468664.

GREEK TRANSLATION
Head of Unit: Nikolaos Papanikolaou; tel. (+32) 2-5469508.

ENGLISH TRANSLATION
Head of Unit: David Schlesinger; tel. (+32) 2-5469005.

FRENCH TRANSLATION
Head of Unit: Florence Maelerts; tel. (+32) 2-5469184.

ITALIAN TRANSLATION
Head of Unit: Luisa Celino; tel. (+32) 2-2359584.

LATVIAN TRANSLATION
Head of Unit: Edite Kruze; tel. (+32) 2-5468150.

LITHUANIAN TRANSLATION
Head of Unit: Marius Daskus; tel. (+32) 2-5468914.

HUNGARIAN TRANSLATION
Head of Unit: Andras Laszlo Egyedi; tel. (+32) 2-2822463.

MALTESE TRANSLATION
Head of Unit: Paul Anthony Buhagiar; tel. (+32) 2-5468022.

DUTCH TRANSLATION
Head of Unit: Francis Taillieu; tel. (+32) 2-5468735.

POLISH TRANSLATION
Head of Unit: Joanna Kaduczak; tel. (+32) 2-2822360.

PORTUGUESE TRANSLATION
Head of Unit: Sónia Rocha; tel. (+32) 2-5468795.

ROMANIAN TRANSLATION
Head of Unit (acting): Genoveva Bartha; tel. (+32) 2-5468283.

SLOVENIAN TRANSLATION
Head of Unit (acting): Marjan Pogacnik; tel. (+32) 2-5468930.

FINNISH-SWEDISH TRANSLATION
Head of Unit: Päivi Seppanen; tel. (+32) 2-5469811.

COMMITTEE OF THE REGIONS (CoR)

Bâtiment Jacques Delors, 99–101 rue Belliard, 1040 Brussels, Belgium; tel. (+32) 2-2822211; fax (+32) 2-2822325; internet cor.europa.eu

Bureau

President: Karl-Heinz Lambertz.

First Vice-President: Markku Markkula.

MEMBERS OF THE BUREAU

(including alternate members of the CoR)

Austria: Hanspeter Wagner, Heinz Schaden, Herwig Van Staa, Christian Illedits.

Belgium: Alain Hutchinson, Hicham Imane, Luc Van Den Brande, Marc Hendrickx, Karl Vanlouwe, Bartolomeus Somers.

Bulgaria: Zlatko Zhivkov, Malina Edreva, Vladimir Moskov, Lyudmil Vesselinov.

Croatia: Bruno Hranić, Danijel Marušić, Vojko Obersnel, Nikola Dobroslavić.

Cyprus: Eleni Loukaidou, Stavros Stavrinides, Louis Koumenides.

Czech Republic: Petr Osvald, Adriana Krnáčová, Roman Línek, Jan Mares.

Denmark: Jess Laursen, Per Bodker Andersen, Henrik Ringbæk Madsen.

Estonia: Mihkel Juhkami, Kurmet Müürsepp.

Finland: Anne Karjalainen, Antti Liikkanen, Pauliina Haijanen, Sirpa Hertell.

France: Danièle Boeglin, Stéphan Rossignol, Martine Vassal, Christophe Rouillon, Christophe Clergeau.

Germany: Ulrike Hiller, Heinz Lehmann, Helma Kuhn-Theis, Babette Winter, Michael Schneider.

Greece: Apostolos Tzitzikostas, Ioannis Sgouros, Dimitrios Kalogeropoulos, Georgios Patoulis.

Hungary: József Ribányi, Anna Magyar, Zoltán Varga, Kata Tüttö.

Ireland: Mary Freehill, Hughie McGrath.

Italy: Raffaele Cattaneo, Giovanni Ardizzone, Luciano D'Alfonso, Piero Fassino, Micaelo Fanelli, Catiuscia Marini.

Latvia: Andris Jaunsleinis, Gints Kaminskis.

Lithuania: Arnoldas Abramavičius, Vytautas Grubliauskas, Ričardas Malinauskas, Andrius Kupcinskas.

Luxembourg: Roby Biwer, Simone Beissel.

Malta: Joseph Cordina, Mario Fava.

Netherlands: Annemiek Jetten, Hans Janssen, Rob Jonkman, Wim Van De Donk, Theo Bovens.

Poland: Adam Banaszak, Adam Struzik, Adam Sebastian Jarubas, Stanisław Szwabski, Marek Woźniak, Olgierd Geblewicz, Marek Olszewski, Ludwik Węgrzyn.

Portugal: Álvaro Amaro, Rui Bettencourt, Vasco Ilídio Alves Cordeiro, António Bragança Fernandes.

Romania: Robert Sorin Negoiţă, Mariana Gâju, Adrian Ovidiu Teban, Ion Prioteasa.

Slovakia: Jaroslav Hlinka, Milan Belica, Jozef Dvonč, Pavel Frešo.

Slovenia: Ivan Žagar, Andreja Potočnik.

Spain: Juan Vicente Herrera Campo, María de Diego Durántez, Susana Díaz Pacheco, Angel Luis Sánchez Muñoz, Emiliano García-Page Sánchez, Ximo Puig I Ferrer, Joan Calabuig Rull.

Sweden: Anders Knape, Jelena Drenjanin, Ilmar Reepalu, Yoomi Renström, Ulrika Carlefall Landergren.

United Kingdom: Albert Bore, Jennette Arnold.

President of the Group of the European People's Party (EPP): Michael Schneider.

President of the Group of the Party of European Socialists (PES): Catiuscia Marini.

President of the European Alliance group (EA): Karl Vanlouwe.

President of the Alliance of Liberals and Democrats for Europe (ALDE): Bartolomeus (Bart) Somers.

President of the European Conservatives and Reformists Group (ECR): Rob Jonkman.

Members of the CoR

COMMISSIONS

1. COTER: Commission for Territorial Cohesion Policy and EU Budget

President: Petr Osvald.

First Vice-President: Spyros Spyridon.

2. ECON: Commission for Economic Policy

President: Michel Delebarre.

First Vice-President: Arnoldas Abramavičius.

3. CIVEX: Commission for Citizenship, Governance and Institutional and External Affairs

President: Barbara Duden.

First Vice-President: François Decoster.

4. SEDEC: Commission for Social Policy, Education, Employment, Research and Culture

President: José Ignacio Ceniceros González.

First Vice-President: Alin-Adrian Nica.

5. ENVE: Commission for the Environment, Climate Change and Energy

President: Cor Lamers.

First Vice-President: Roby Biwer.

6. NAT: Commission for Natural Resources

President: Ossi Martikainen.

First Vice-President: Christophe Clerceau.

CoR MEMBERS

Name	Member State	Commissions
Abramavičius, Arnoldas	Lithuania	2, 3
Adamowicz, Paweł	Poland	1, 2
Agorastos, Konstantinos	Greece	1, 4
Alambritis, Stephen	UK	1, 2
Albuquerque, Miguel Filipe	Portugal	3, 6
Alves, Miguel	Portugal	3, 6
Alves Cordeiro, Vasco Ilídio	Portugal	5, 6
Amaro, Álvaro	Portugal	1, 5
Anastasiou, Nikos	Cyprus	4, 6
Andreasson, Martin	Sweden	3, 4
Ardizzone, Giovanni	Italy	3, 5
Árgyelán, János	Hungary	3, 4
Armengol i Socias, Francina	Spain	2, 6
Arnaoutakis, Stavros	Greece	5, 6
Arnold, Jennette	UK	3, 5
Arsene, Ionel	Romania	1, 4
Azevedo, João	Portugal	4, 6
Azis, Hasan	Bulgaria	2, 3
Azzopardi, Samuel M.	Malta	1, 3, 6
Badia i Cutchet, Maria	Spain	2, 3
Ballaré, Andrea	Italy	2, 3
Barcos Berruezo, Miren Uxue	Spain	4, 5
Barnier, Jean-François	France	1, 3
Beissel, Simone	Luxembourg	2, 3
Belica, Milan	Slovakia	2, 4
Benešík, Ondřej	Czech Republic	3, 5
Bērziņa, Inga	Latvia	3, 6
Besozzi, Matteo	Italy	5, 6
Bianchi, Matteo Luigi	Italy	3, 4
Bianco, Vincenzo	Italy	3, 4
Bille, Kirstine Helene	Belgium	5, 6
Biwer, Roby	Luxembourg	5, 6
Blanc, Jacques	France	4, 6
Bødker Andersen, Per	Denmark	1, 3
Boeglin, Danièle	France	1, 4
Bóka, István	Hungary	1, 5
Borboly, Csaba	Romania	4, 5
Bore, Albert	UK	1, 2
Bossman, Peter	Slovenia	2, 3
Boudineau, Isabelle	France	1, 5
Bovens, Theo	Denmark	3, 4
Bragança Fernandes, António	Portugal	3, 4
Branda, Pavel	Czech Republic	5, 6
Bright, Robert	UK	1, 6
Brzezin, Gustaw Marek	Poland	2, 5
Buchanan, Anthony Gerard	UK	1, 6
Budde, Katrin	Germany	4, 6
Caballero Álvarez, Abel	Spain	2, 4
Calderoli-Lotz, Martine	France	2, 4
Carlefall Landergren, Ulrika	Sweden	1, 4
Cattaneo, Raffaele	Italy	1, 6
Ceniceros González, José Ignacio	Spain	4, 6
Chiotakis, Nikolaos	Greece	3, 6
Cifuentes Cuencas, Cristina	Spain	2, 5
Clavijo Batlle, Fernando	Spain	1, 6
Clergeau, Christophe	France	4, 6
Cooney, Joseph	UK	2, 3
Cooper, Andrew Varah	UK	4, 5
Cordina, Joseph	Malta	2, 5, 6
Crocetta, Rosario	Italy	1, 6
Cummings, Trevor	UK	1, 6
Da Cunha Costa, José	Portugal	2, 5
D'Alfonso, Luciano	Italy	1, 2
D'Attis, Mauro	Italy	4, 5
Decoster, François	France	1, 3
de Heer, René	Netherlands	1, 3
Delebarre, Michel	France	1, 2
De Meo, Salvatore	Italy	2, 6
Díaz Pacheco, Susana	Spain	1, 6
Díaz Tezanos, Rosa Eva	Spain	3, 4
di Laura Frattura, Paolo	Italy	5, 6
Dobroslavić, Nikola	Croatia	1, 3
Drăghici, Emil	Romania	3, 6
Drenjanin, Jelena	Sweden	2, 3
Dudás, Róbert	Hungary	3, 4
Duden, Barbara	Germany	1, 3
Durdu, Agnès	Luxembourg	1, 4
Durnez, Jan	Belgium	4, 6
Dvonč, Jozef	Slovakia	2, 4
Dworzański, Jarosław	Slovakia	2, 6
Edreva, Malina	Bulgaria	1, 4
Espadas Cejas, Juan	Spain	1, 5
Făgădău, Decebal	Romania	3, 4
Falcă, Gheorghe	Romania	1, 6
Falque, Rose-Marie	France	5, 6
Fanelli, Micaela	Italy	1, 2
Farrugia, Paul	Malta	1, 2, 5
Fassino, Piero	Italy	2, 3
Fava, Mario	Malta	3, 6
Feeney, Kate	Ireland	2, 4
Ferenčák, Ján	Slovakia	3, 5
Fernández Fernández, Javier	Spain	2, 3
Fernández Vara, Guillermo	Spain	1, 6
Flego, Valter	Croatia	1, 6
Flyvholm, Erik	Denmark	4, 6
Forde, Deirdre	Ireland	1, 2
Fortier, Mélanie	France	2, 5
Fraňková, Štěpánka	Czech Republic	4, 6
Freehill, Mary	Ireland	4, 5

Name	Member State	Commissions
Frešo, Pavol	Slovakia	1, 3
Gabrić, Jasna	Slovenia	4, 5
Gâju, Mariana	Romania	2, 5
Gambacorta, Domenico	Italy	4, 5
García-Page Sánchez, Emiliano	Spain	1, 2
Geblewicz, Olgierd	Poland	3, 6
Gintere, Ligita	Latvia	3, 4
Gjesing, Jens Christian	Denmark	3, 4
Gomes, Luís	Portugal	3, 4
Gougen, Mairi Angela	UK	3, 5
Gordon, Robert Ian Neilson	UK	1, 2
Grubliauskas, Vytautas	Lithuania	1, 6
Grzybowski, Paweł	Poland	4, 6
Gundlack, Tilo	Germany	2, 6
Guninski, Rumen	Bulgaria	1, 6
Hackenschmidt, Barbara	Germany	2, 5
Haijanen, Pauliina	Finland	1, 2
Hambálek, Augustín	Slovakia	4, 6
Häupl, Michael	Austria	1, 4
Herrera Campo, Juan Vicente	Spain	4, 5
Hertell, Sirpa	Finland	5, 6
Hiller, Ulrike	Germany	4, 5
Hlinka, Jaroslav	Slovakia	3, 5
Honé, Birgit	Germany	3, 5
Horta, Basílio	Portugal	2, 3
Horváth, Jácint	Hungary	2, 4
Hranić, Bruno	Croatia	2, 5
Hristova, Tanya	Bulgaria	1, 4
Hughes, Judith	UK	3, 4
Hutchinson, Alain	Belgium	4, 6
Iacop, Franco	Italy	3, 5
Illedits, Christian	Austria	1, 5
Imane, Hicham	Belgium	1, 2
Istasse, Jean-François	Belgium	4, 6
Ive, Jens Bo	Denmark	2, 5
Janson, Camilla	Sweden	3, 6
Janssen, Hans	Netherlands	3, 4
Jarubas, Adam Sebastian	Poland	2, 4
Jaunsleinis, Andris M.	Latvia	2, 5
Jaworski, Lech	Poland	2, 4
Jetten, Annemiek	Netherlands	1, 6
Jevšek, Aleksander	Slovenia	3, 6
Jiránek, Dan	Czech Republic	4, 5
Jonkman, Rob	Netherlands	2, 4
Juhkami, Mihkel	Estonia	1, 2
Juránek, Stanislav	Czech Republic	4, 6
Kaes, Ali	Luxembourg	1, 5, 6
Kahrimanis, Alexandros	Greece	2, 6
Kaiser, Peter	Austria	2, 4
Kalafatis, Stavros	Greece	2, 5
Kallo, Kalev	Estonia	2, 5
Kalogeropoulos, Dimitrios	Greece	3, 5
Kaminis, Georgios	Greece	2, 6
Kanevičius, Vytautas	Lithuania	1, 5
Karayiannis, Andros	Cyprus	3, 5
Karjalainen, Anne	Finland	1, 4
Karlsson, Ewa-May	Sweden	5, 6
Katsifaras, Apostolos	Greece	1, 4
Keresztes, László Lóránt	Hungary	2, 6
Kielstra, Klaas	Netherlands	2, 4
Knape, Anders	Sweden	1, 5
Kompatscher, Arno	Italy	4, 6
Komskis, Virginijus	Lithuania	4, 6
Koumenides, Louis	Cyprus	2, 5, 6
Kourakis, Ioannis	Greece	1, 2
Kovács, Raymund	Hungary	4, 5
Krnáčová, Adriana	Czech Republic	2, 3
Kuhn-Theis, Helma	Germany	4, 6
Kupčinskas, Andrius	Lithuania	1, 3
Lahellec, Gérard	France	2, 6
Lambán Montañés, Francisco Javier	Spain	1, 5
Lambertz, Karl-Heinz	Belgium	3, 4
Lamers, Cor	Netherlands	5, 6
Larsson, Joakim	Sweden	5, 6
Laursen, Jess	Denmark	4, 5
Lebrun, Michel	Belgium	1, 5
Lehmann, Heinz	Germany	2, 5
Lielmežs, Aleksandrs	Latvia	4, 6
Liikkanen, Antti	Finland	3, 5
Lindholm, Gun-Mari	Finland	3, 4
Lindquist, Paul	Sweden	2, 6
Línek, Roman	Czech Republic	2, 3
Linhart, Markus	Austria	2, 5
Lishman, Margaret	UK	2, 4
Loggen, Cees	Netherlands	5, 6
Loukaidou, Eleni	Cyprus	1, 3, 2
Lundy, Jerry	Ireland	3, 6
McCarthy, Kieran	Ireland	1, 4
McGrath, Hughie	Ireland	3, 5
Madsen, Henrik Ringbæk	Denmark	1, 3
Magyar, Anna	Hungary	1, 3
Majthényi, László	Hungary	3, 6
Malinauskas, Ričardas	Lithuania	2, 5
Mangin, Pascal	France	1, 5
Marini, Catiuscia	Italy	1, 2
Markkula, Markku	Finland	3, 4
Martikainen, Ossi	Finland	1, 6
Marušić, Danijel	Croatia	3, 6
Maupertuis, Marie-Antoinette	France	1, 6
Medina, Fernando	Portugal	1, 2
Merk, Beate	Germany	1, 2
Mesnard, Françoise	France	4, 5
Mifsud, Anthony	Malta	4, 5
Mikl-Leitner, Johanna	Austria	1
Moraru, Victor	Romania	1, 3
Moskov, Vladimir	Bulgaria	2, 4
Murphy, Michael	Ireland	2, 3
Murray, Gerry	Ireland	1, 6
Müürsepp, Kurmet	Estonia	3, 4
Negoiţă, Robert Sorin	Slovakia	2, 5
Nesrovnal, Ivo	Slovakia	1, 6
Nica, Alin Adrian	Romania	1, 4
Nuñez Feijoo, Alberto	Spain	3, 6
Obersnel, Vojko	Croatia	1, 5
Olszewski, Marek	Poland	4, 5
Oprea, Emilian	Romania	3, 4
Ortyl, Władysław	Poland	3, 5
Osvald, Petr	Czech Republic	1, 3
Ovcharova, Diana	Bulgaria	1, 3
Pavičić Vukičević, Jelena	Croatia	4
Peel, Kevin	UK	1, 3
Perera Christensen, Marc	Denmark	1, 2
Petersen, Karsten Uno	Denmark	2, 6
Pigliaru, Francesco	Italy	4, 5

Name	Member State	Commissions
Pinto de Sá, Carlos	Portugal	2, 4
Placé, Jean-Vincent	France	3, 4
Podraza, Zbigniew	Poland	4, 6
Poersch, Regina	Germany	1, 6
Pokorná Jermanová, Jaroslava	Czech Republic	2, 4
Potočnik, Andreja	Slovenia	1, 2
Pourquier, Jean-Paul	France	5, 6
Prioteasa, Ion	Romania	2, 6
Puig I Ferrer, Ximo	Spain	1, 2
Půta, Martin	Czech Republic	1, 2
Quart, Anne	Germany	2, 6
Raab, Heike	Germany	4, 5
Radev, Stefan	Bulgaria	5, 6
Reepalu, Ilmar	Sweden	1, 5
Renström, Yoomi	Sweden	2, 4
Repaský, Miloslav	Slovakia	2, 6
Ribányi, József	Hungary	1, 5
Ribau Esteves, José	Portugal	1, 5
Rinaldi, Giuseppe	Italy	1, 5
Riste, Tomas	Sweden	1, 4
Robert, Didier	France	4, 6
Rokavec, Franci	Slovenia	4, 6
Román Jasanada, Antonio	Spain	3, 4
Rossi, Enrico	Italy	2, 4
Rossignol, Stéphan	France	3, 5
Rouillon, Christophe	France	2, 3
Salcevičs, Leonīds	Latvia	1, 5
Sali, Beytula	Bulgaria	3, 6
Saliera, Simonetta	Italy	3, 4
Sarrabezolles, Nathalie	France	4, 6
Schaden, Heinz	Austria	3
Schaefer, Marc	Luxembourg	3, 4
Schausberger, Franz	Austria	3, 4
Scheffer, Michiel	Netherlands	1, 6
Schmidt, Wolfgang	Germany	2, 4
Schneider, Michael	Germany	1, 3
Seszták, Oszkár	Hungary	2, 6
Sgouros, Ioannis	Greece	4, 5
Sharpe, Dee	UK	4, 6
Siggs, Harvey	UK	5, 6
Silberg, Uno	Estonia	1, 6
Simmonds, David	UK	1, 3
Smrdelj, Robert	Slovenia	1, 3
Solere, Thierry	France	2, 3
Somers, Bartolomeus	Belgium	3, 5
Sosnowski, Sławomir	Poland	4, 5
Spyridon, Spyros	Greece	1, 3
Stavrinides, Stavros	Cyprus	1, 4
Stenson, Enda	Greece	5, 6
Stępień, Witold	Poland	1, 5
Strugała, Dariusz Antoni	Poland	5, 6
Strugl, Michael	Austria	5
Struk, Mieczysław	Poland	1, 6
Struzik, Adam	Poland	1, 5
Sukles, Urmas	Estonia	3, 6
Szabó, Róbert	Hungary	2, 6
Szwabski, Stanisław	Poland	1, 3
Teban, Adrian Ovidiu	Romania	1, 2
Tietari, Satu	Finland	2, 5
Todorov, Zhivko	Bulgaria	2, 5
Tramś, Marek	Poland	3, 4
Truskolaski, Tadeusz	Poland	1, 2
Turk, Željko	Croatia	3, 6
Turlais, Dainis	Latvia	1, 2
Tzitzikostas, Apostolos	Greece	3, 4
Urkullu Renteria, Iñigo	Spain	3, 5
Ursăciuc, Marius Ioan	Romania	5, 6
Van De Donk, W. B. H. J.	Netherlands	1, 3
Van De Nadort, André	Netherlands	2, 5
Van Den Brande, Luc	Belgium	1, 3
Van Der Sande, Rogier	Netherlands	2, 5
Vanlouwe, Karl	Belgium	2, 3
Van Overmeire, Karim	Belgium	1, 5
Vanraes, Jean-Luc	Belgium	2, 6
Van Staa, Herwig	Austria	1, 3
Varga, Zoltán	Hungary	1, 5
Vassal, Martine	France	2, 3
Verfaillie, Jean-Noël	France	2, 5
Vesselinov, Lyudmil	Bulgaria	5, 6
Vigelis, Vytautas	Lithuania	2, 5
Viola, André	France	1, 3
Vītoliņš, Jānis	Lithuania	1, 2
Vlasák, Oldřich	Czech Republic	1, 5
Vogel, Hans-Josef	Germany	3, 4
Võrklaev, Mart	Estonia	4, 5
Wagner, Hanspeter	Austria	5, 6
Wallace, Judith Anne	UK	5, 6
Wallner, Markus	Austria	2, 3
Walsmann, Marion	Germany	1, 6
Watson, Paul	UK	2, 6
Węgrzyn, Ludwik Kajetan	Poland	2, 3
Weinmeister, Mark	Germany	5, 6
Westley, Emily	UK	4, 6
Winter, Babette	Germany	4, 5
Wolbergs, Joachim	Germany	5, 6
Wolf, Guido	Belgium	1, 3
Woop, Gerry	Germany	1, 3
Woźniak, Marek	Poland	1, 3
Wróbel, Dariusz	Poland	3, 6
Zachariaš, István	Slovakia	1, 5
Žagar, Ivan	Slovenia	1, 5
Žagunis, Povilas	Lithuania	4, 6
Zaia, Luca	Lithuania	2, 6
Zaychev, Nikolay	Bulgaria	3, 5
Zhivkov, Zlatko	Bulgaria	2, 4
Zimola, Jiří	Czech Republic	1, 6
Zingaretti, Nicola	Italy	1, 3
Zrihen, Olga	Belgium	2, 5

Administrative Units

SECRETARIAT-GENERAL OF THE CoR

Secretary-General

Secretary-General: Jiří Buriánek.

Political Groups' Secretariats

GROUP OF THE EUROPEAN PEOPLE'S PARTY (EPP)

Secretary-General: Heinz-Peter Knapp; tel. (+32) 2-2822221; fax (+32) 2-2822329.

Administrator: Inès Roseta; tel. (+32) 2-2822247; fax (+32) 2-2822329.

Administrator: Vasileios Antoniou; tel. (+32) 2-2822388; fax (+32) 2-2822329.

Administrator: Marko Juvancić; tel. (+32) 2-2822520.

Administrator: Agnieszka Bidzinska; tel. (+32) 2-2822078.

Administrator: Simone Brusadin; tel. (+32) 2-2822091.

Administrator: Grigor Asenov; tel. (+32) 2-2822536.

Administrator: Saara Mattero; tel. (+32) 2-2822373.

GROUP OF THE ALLIANCE OF LIBERALS AND DEMOCRATS FOR EUROPE (ALDE)

Secretary-General: Sean O'Curneen; tel. (+32) 2-2822226; fax (+32) 2-2822331.

Administrator: Johanna Lindblom; tel. (+32) 2-2822238; fax (+32) 2-2822331.

Administrator: Abdoul Diallo; tel. (+32) 2-2822282; fax (+32) 2-2822331.

Administrator: Marc-Fabien Naether; tel. (+32) 2-2822569.

GROUP OF THE PARTY OF EUROPEAN SOCIALISTS (PES)

Secretary-General: Jordi Harrison; tel. (+32) 2-2822312; fax (+32) 2-2822318.

Administrator: Chiara Malagodi; tel. (+32) 2-2822224; fax (+32) 2-2822069.

Administrator: Aliona Fornea; tel. (+32) 2-2822570.

Administrator: Matthieu Hornung; tel. (+32) 2-2822578; fax (+32) 2-2822069.

Administrator: Santiago Mondragón Vial; tel. (+32) 2-2822283.

Administrator: Olga Fotinou; tel. (+32) 2-2822086; fax (+32) 2-2822069.

Administrator: Justus Schönlau; tel. (+32) 2-2822227; fax (+32) 2-2822069.

GROUP OF THE EUROPEAN ALLIANCE

Secretary-General: Michael O'Conchuir; tel. (+32) 2-2822251; fax (+32) 2-2822334.

Administrator: Bogna Rodziewicz; tel. (+32) 2-2822158; fax (+32) 2-2822334.

Administrator: Endrik Marfia; tel. (+32) 2-2822204.

Administrator: Pavle Licina; tel. (+32) 2-2822168.

GROUP OF THE EUROPEAN CONSERVATIVES AND REFORMISTS

Secretary-General: Neva Sadikoglu; tel. (+32) 2-2822263.

Administrator: Adam Lazarski; tel. (+32) 2-2822423.

Administrator: Jacopo Piccinetti; tel. (+32) 2-2822441.

Cabinet of the President

Head of Cabinet: Aurel Trandafir; tel. (+32) 2-2822094.

Administrator: Julien De Ridder; tel. (+32) 2-2822309; fax (+32) 2-2822069.

Administrator: Monika Kapturska; tel. (+32) 2-2822579.

Administrator: Kathryn Owens; tel. (+32) 2-2822400; fax (+32) 2-2822329.

Administrator: Filippo Terruso; tel. (+32) 2-2822291.

Administrator: Taina Tukiainen; tel. (+32) 2-2822303.

Secretariat-General

Secretary-General: Jiří Buriánek; tel. (+32) 2-2822005; fax (+32) 2-2822007.

Head of Cabinet: Gianluca Spinaci; tel. (+32) 2-2822541; fax (+32) 2-2822442.

Administrator: Marie-Pierre Jouglain; tel. (+32) 2-2822566.

Administrator: Boris Essender; tel. (+32) 2-2822390; fax (+32) 2-2822180.

Administrator: Boele Klaus; tel. (+32) 2-2822594.

Administrator: Anna Passera; tel. (+32) 2-2995619.

Adviser to the Secretary-General: Christian Gsodam; tel. (+32) 2-2822121; fax (+32) 2-2822150.

Internal Audit Service

Head of Unit: Pascale Van Outryve d'Ydewalle; tel. (+32) 2-2822456; fax (+32) 2-2822150.

Administrator: Barbara Masotti; tel. (+32) 2-2822398; fax (+32) 2-2822150.

Protocol Service

Head of Unit: Lambrini Yalamboukidou; tel. (+32) 2-2822154; fax (+32) 2-2822338.

Directorate A—Members and Plenaries

Director: Pedro Cervilla; tel. (+32) 2-2822189; fax (+32) 2-2822072.

Deputy Director: Juan Carlos Cañoto Argüelles; tel. (+32) 2-28222547.

Administrator: Oana Stinga; tel. (+32) 2-28228367.

UNIT A1—SERVICES TO MEMBERS AND ECOR

Head of Unit: Pierre-Alexis Feral; tel. (+32) 2-2822055; fax (+32) 2-2822050.

Administrator: Lina Grebliuniene; tel. (+32) 2-2822550.

Administrator: Athanasios Kaskamanidis; tel. (+32) 2-2822068.

Administrator: Dimitrios Katsanidis; tel. (+32) 2-5469703; fax (+32) 2-2822119.

Administrator: Patrick Schaumans; tel. (+32) 2-2822292; fax (+32) 2-282287.

Administrator: Mihaela Lafont; tel. (+32) 2-2822365.

Administrator: Cintia Da Luz Tanqueiro Dias; tel. (+32) 2-2828124.

UNIT A2—STATUTORY BODIES AND MEETINGS

Head of Unit: Caroline Bouquerel; tel. (+32) 2-5469019; fax (+32) 2-5469080.

Administrator: Saskia Beljaars-Verhoeven; tel. (+32) 2-2822315; fax (+32) 2-2822119.

Administrator: Elena Bravo Casado; tel. (+32) 2-2822506.

Administrator: Julianna Szabo; tel. (+32) 2-2822029.

Administrator: Erica Savazzi; tel. (+32) 2-2822370.

UNIT A3—LEGAL AFFAIRS

Head of Unit: Sophie Bachotet; tel. (+32) 2-2822180; fax (+32) 2-2823334.

Administrator: Michele Antonini; tel. (+32) 2-2822489.

Administrator: Manuel Esparrago Arzadun; tel. (+32) 2-2822120.

Administrator: Antonio Figueira; tel. (+32) 2-2822016.

Directorate B—Legislative Work 1

Director: Laurent Thieule; tel. (+32) 2-2822199; fax (+32) 2-2822338.

Deputy Director: Michael Collins; tel. (+32) 2-2822105; fax (+32) 2-282515.

Administrator: Iris Urban; tel. (+32) 2-2822096.

Administrator: Piotr Paweł Zajaczkowski; tel. (+32) 2-2822401.

UNIT B1—COMMISSION NAT

Head of Unit: Christof Kienel; tel. (+32) 2-2822521.

Administrator: Anemarija Kosjek; tel. (+32) 2-2828480.

Administrator: Helene Moraut; tel. (+32) 2-2822161.

Administrator: Dimo Stoyanov; tel. (+32) 2-2822296.

Administrator: Dorota Tomalak; tel. (+32) 2-5104007.

UNIT B2— COMMISSION ENVE

Head of Unit: Elisa Garosi; tel. (+32) 2-2822246; fax (+32) 2-2822087.

Administrator: Carsten Brauns; tel. (+32) 2-2822585.

Administrator: Jens Zvirgzdgrauds; tel. (+32) 2-2822137.

Administrator: Nicola Di Pietrantonio; tel. (+32) 2-2822106.

Administrator: Radim Dvorak; tel. (+32) 2-2822095.

UNIT B3—COMMISSION CIVEX

Head of Unit: Silke Tönshoff; tel. (+32) 2-2822455; fax (+32) 2-2828366.

Administrator: Simona-Elena Livideanu; tel. (+32) 2-2822583.

Constitutional Affairs (CONST)

Administrator: Kristina Charrad; tel. (+32) 2-2828950.

Administrator: Paulo Rocha Trindade; tel. (+32) 2-2822166.

Administrator: Pavla Danisova; tel. (+32) 2-2822011.

Administrator: Benedetta Pricolo; tel. (+32) 2-2822446.

Administrator: Katerina Stamati; tel. (+32) 2-2822273; fax (+32) 2-2822325.

Administrator: Monika Weymann; tel. (+32) 2-2822509.

Administrator: Oskar Whyte; tel. (+32) 2-2822319.

External Relations (RELEX)

Administrator: Tatiana Dimitrova; tel. (+32) 2-5468381.

Administrator: Darja Gontsarova-Parvulescu; tel. (+32) 2-2822545.

Administrator: Gudrun Niedorf; tel. (+32) 2-2822444.

Administrator: Milica Neacsu; tel. (+32) 2-2822207; fax (+32) 2-2822075.

Administrator: Victor Tilea; tel. (+32) 2-2822395.

Directorate C—Legislative Work 2

Director: Thomas Wobben; tel. (+32) 2-2822577; fax (+32) 2-2822007.

Deputy Director: Béatrice Taulegne; tel. (+32) 2-2822175.

Administrator: Karina Suleimanova; tel. (+32) 2-2822478.

Administrator: Emmanouil Vergis; tel. (+32) 2-2822529.

UNIT C1—COMMISSION FOR TERRITORIAL COHESION POLICY AND EU BUDGET (COTER/BUDG)

Head of Unit: Marie-Claire Neill-Cowper; tel. (+32) 2-2822185.

Administrator: Alfonso Alcolea Martinez; tel. (+32) 2-2822015; fax (+32) 2-2822087.

Administrator: Marek Bobis; tel. (+32) 2-2822527.

Administrator: Gustavo José Lopez Cutillas; tel. (+32) 2-2822503.

Administrator: Slaven Klobucar; tel. (+32) 2-2822466.

Administrator: Oliver Heiden; tel. (+32) 2-2822405.

Administrator: Gordon Modro; tel. (+32) 2-2822434.

Administrator: Lucy Tober; tel. (+32) 2-2822372.

Administrator: Petr Votoupal; tel. (+32) 2-2822214.

UNIT C2—COMMISSION FOR ECONOMIC POLICY (ECON)

Head of Unit: Bert Kuby; tel. (+32) 2-2822571.

Administrator: John Bennett; tel. (+32) 2-2822305.

Administrator: Nils Brunelet; tel. (+32) 2-2822565.

Administrator: Claudia Moser; tel. (+32) 2-2822002.

Administrator: Effrosyni Kossyvaki; tel. (+32) 2-2822241.

Administrator: Robert Rönstrom; tel. (+32) 2-2822192.

Administrator: Hana Slepickova; tel. (+32) 2-2822152.

Europe 2020

Administrator: Andrea Forti; tel. (+32) 2-2822084; fax (+32) 2-2822087.

Administrator: Marc Kiwitt; tel. (+32) 2-2822378.

Administrator: Audrey Parizel; tel. (+32) 2-2822512.

UNIT C3—COMMISSION FOR SOCIAL POLICY, EDUCATION, EMPLOYMENT, RESEARCH AND CULTURE (SEDEC)

Head of Unit: Kyriakos Tsirimiagos; tel. (+32) 2-2822122; fax (+32) 2-2822330.

Administrator: Svetlozar Andreev; tel. (+32) 2-2822039.

Administrator: Ilaria Babolin; tel. (+32) 2-2822337.

Administrator: Daniele Berno; tel. (+32) 2-2822316.

Administrator: Doru-Iulian Hobjila; tel. (+32) 2-2822064.

Administrator: Anna Kerekgyarto; tel. (+32) 2-2822248.

Administrator: Maria Lozano Uriz; tel. (+32) 2-2822274.

Administrator: Petri Mirala; tel. (+32) 2-2822136.

Administrator: Alexander Popov; tel. (+32) 2-2822351.

Administrator: Valeria Satta; tel. (+32) 2-2822495.

Administrator: Rita Soares; tel. (+32) 2-2822098.

Administrator: Pawel Zamojski; tel. (+32) 2-2822590.

Directorate D—Communication

Director: Ian Barber; tel. (+32) 2-2822013.

Deputy Director: Wolfgang Petzold; tel. (+32) 2-2822358; fax (+32) 2-2822075.

UNIT D1—PRESS OFFICERS AND RELATIONS WITH MEDIA

Head of Unit: Serafino Nardi; tel. (+32) 2-2822508; fax (+32) 2-2822109.

Administrator: David Crous Duran; tel. (+32) 2-2822409.

Administrator: Nathalie Vandelle; tel. (+32) 2-2822499.

Administrator: Andrew Gardner; tel. (+32) 2-2822429.

Administrator: Coralie Guillot; tel. (+32) 2-2822299.

Administrator: Lauri Ouvinen; tel. (+32) 2-2822063.

Administrator: Carmen Schmidle; tel. (+32) 2-2822366.

Administrator: Stephanie Paillet; tel. (+32) 2-2822532.

Administrator: Pierluigi Boda; tel. (+32) 2-2822461.

Administrator: Wioleta Wojewodzka; tel. (+32) 2-2822289.

Administrator: Nina Paukovic; tel. (+32) 2-2822533.

Administrator: Laura Serassio; tel. (+32) 2-2822275.

UNIT D2—EVENTS

Head of Unit: Michele Cercone; fax (+32) 2-2822164; fax (+32) 2-2822075.

Head of Unit: Amelie Cousin; fax (+32) 2-2822492.

Administrator: Klaus Hullmann; tel. (+32) 2-2822124; fax (+32) 2-2822075.

Administrator: Pauliina Makarainen; tel. (+32) 2-2822304.

Administrator: Andrea Bodova; tel. (+32) 2-2822010.

Administrator: Ginevra Del Vecchio; tel. (+32) 2-2822534.

Administrator: Martin Gosset; tel. (+32) 2-2822330.

UNIT D3—SOCIAL AND DIGITAL MEDIA, PUBLICATIONS

Head of Unit: Achim Ladwig; tel. (+32) 2-2822581.

Administrator: Emmanuelle Martins; tel. (+32) 2-2822364.

Administrator: Jens Nordmeyer; tel. (+32) 2-2822347; fax (+32) 2-2822075.

Administrator: Eszter Wirth; tel. (+32) 2-2828655.

Administrator: Nicole Zandi; tel. (+32) 2-2822553.

Directorate E—Human Resources and Finance

Director: Agnieszka Kudlinska; tel. (+32) 2-25104002.

Deputy Director: Reinhold Gnan; tel. (+32) 2-2822335; fax (+32) 2-2822180.

Deputy Director: Florence Thome; tel. (+32) 2-2822147.

UNIT E1—BUDGET AND FINANCE

Head of Unit: Peder Jakobsson; tel. (+32) 2-2822055; fax (+32) 2-2822332.

Administrator: Éric Leurquin; tel. (+32) 2-2822286; fax (+32) 2-2829922.

Administrator: Elmars Kronbergs; tel. (+32) 2-2822592; fax (+32) 2-2829922.

Administrator: Tamara Hoffman; tel. (+32) 2-2822591.

UNIT E2—RECRUITMENT AND CAREER

Head of Unit: François Filipek; tel. (+32) 2-2828486; fax (+32) 2-2822013.

Administrator: Stefan Bäckman; tel. (+32) 2-2829854.

Administrator: Adina Mariasiu; tel. (+32) 2-2822525; fax (+32) 2-2822013.

UNIT E3—WORKING CONDITIONS

Head of Unit: Tom Haenebalcke; tel. (+32) 2-2822228; fax (+32) 2-2822118.

Administrator: Benjamin Janicaud; tel. (+32) 2-2828126.

Medical Adviser: Eveline Madrid; tel. (+32) 2-5462505.

Administrator: Anna Mitelman; tel. (+32) 2-2829840.

Administrator: Beatrice Rentmeister; tel. (+32) 2-2822376.

Administrator: Gie Werkers; tel. (+32) 2-2822568.

UNIT E4—GENERAL ADMINISTRATION AND PUBLIC PROCUREMENT

Head of Unit: Sybren Singelsma; tel. (+32) 2-2829362; fax (+32) 2-2822213.

Administrator: Erwan Gery; tel. (+32) 2-2822557; fax (+32) 2-2822213.

Administrator: Nikolaos Petras; tel. (+32) 2-2828221; fax (+32) 2-2822213.

Administrator: Almudena Garcia Perez; tel. (+32) 2-2822437.

Administrator: Thierry Firmin; tel. (+32) 2-2822076; fax (+32) 2-2822213.

Administrator: Maartje Wouters; tel. (+32) 2-2822111.

EUROPEAN INVESTMENT BANK (EIB)

98–100 blvd Konrad Adenauer, 2950 Luxembourg, Luxembourg; tel. (+352) 43791; fax (+352) 437704; e-mail press@eib.org; internet www.eib.org

Other Offices

Caribbean: César Nicolás Penson 85A, Leopoldo Navarro, Santo Domingo, Dominican Republic; tel. (+809) 473-44-96; fax (+809) 473-40-31; e-mail santodomingo@eib.org.

Central and Eastern Africa: Africa Re Centre, 5th Floor, Hospital Road, POB 40193, 00100 Nairobi, Kenya; tel. (+254 20) 2735260; fax (+254 20) 2713278; e-mail nairobi@eib.org.

Egypt: 2005c Corniche El Nil, Ramlet, Boulak 11221, Cairo, Egypt; tel. (+20 2) 24619890; fax (+20 2) 24619891.

Morocco: Riad Business Center, Aile Sud, Immeuble S3, 4 étage, blvd Er-Riad, Rabat, Morocco; tel. (+212) 5-37-56-54-60; fax (+212) 5-37-56-53-93; e-mail rabat@eib.org.

Pacific: Level 25, 88 Phillip St, Sydney, NSW 2000, Australia; tel. (+61 2) 8211-0536; fax (+61 2) 8211-0538; e-mail sydney@eib.org.

Russian Federation: 14/1 Kadashevskaya Embankment, 119017 Moscow, Russia; tel. (+7) 49572120-30; fax (+7) 49572120-36; e-mail moscow@eib.org.

Senegal: 3 rue du Docteur Roux, BP 6935, Dakar-Plateau, Senegal; tel. (+221) 338894300; fax (+221) 338429712; e-mail dakar@eib.org.

Southern Africa and the Indian Ocean: 5 Greenpark Estates, 27 George Storrar Drive, Groenkloof 0181, Tshwane (Pretoria), South Africa; tel. (+27 12) 4250460; fax (+27 12) 4250470; e-mail pretoria@eib.org.

Tunisia: 70 ave Mohamed V, 1002 Tunis, Tunisia; tel. (+216) 71-11-89-00; fax (+216) 71-28-09-98; e-mail tunis@eib.org.

West Africa and Sahal: 3 rue du Docteur Roux, BP 6935, Dakar-Plateau, Senegal; tel. (+221) 338894300; fax (+221) 338429712; e-mail dakar@eib.org.

European Investment Fund: 37B ave J. F. Kennedy, 2968 Luxembourg, Luxembourg; tel. (+352) 24851; fax (+352) 248581200; e-mail info@eif.org; internet www.eif.org.

Board of Governors

The Board of Governors comprises ministers (usually ministers of finance) representing each of the 28 member states.

Chairman: Mário Centeno (Portugal).

Members: Hans Jörg Schelling (Austria), Johan Van Overtveldt (Belgium), Vladislav Goranov (Bulgaria), Zdravko Marić (Croatia), Ivan Pilný (Czech Republic), Harris Georgiades (Cyprus), Brian Mikkelsen (Denmark), Toomas Tõniste (Estonia), Petteri Orpo (Finland), Bruno Lemaire (France), Wolfgang Schäuble (Germany), Euclid Tsakalotos (Greece), Mihály Varga (Hungary), Paschal Donohue (Ireland), Pier Carlo Padoan (Italy), Dana Reizniece-Ozola (Latvia), Vilius Šapoka (Lithuania), Pierre Gramegna (Luxembourg), Edward Scicluna (Malta), Jeroen Dijsselbloem (Netherlands), Mateusz Morawiecki (Poland), Ionuţ Mişa (Romania), Peter Kažimír (Slovakia), Mateja Vraničar Erman (Slovenia) Luis de Guindos (Spain), Magdalena Andersson (Sweden), Philip Hammond (United Kingdom).

Audit Committee

Chairman: Pierre Krier.

Members: Duarte Pitta Ferraz, John Sutherland, Jacek Dominik, Mindaugas Macijauskas.

Observers: Uldis Cerps, Jens Henrik, Myllerup Laursen.

Board of Directors

Directors: Werner Hoyer (Chairman, non-voting), Karin Rysavy (Austria), Marc Descheemaecker (Belgium), Marinela Petrova (Bulgaria), Vladimira Ivandić (Croatia), Kyriacos Kakouris (Cyprus), Petr Pavelek (Czech Republic), Julie Sonne (Denmark), Andres Kuningas (Estonia), Kristina Sarjo (Finland), Emmanuel Masse (France), Thomas Westphal (Germany), Konstantin J. Andreopoulos (Greece), László Baranyay (Hungary), John Moran (Ireland), (vacant) (Italy), Armands Eberhards (Latvia), Miglė Tuskienė (Lithuania), Arsène Jacoby (Luxembourg), Stanley Mifsud (Malta), Mickie Schoch (Netherlands), Piotr Nowak (Poland), (vacant) (Portugal), Attila György (Romania), Ivan Lesay (Slovakia), (vacant) (Slovenia), Carlos San Basilio Pardo (Spain), Mattias Hector (Sweden), Jonathan Black (United Kingdom), Kerstin Jorna (European Commission).

Management Committee

President: Werner Hoyer.

Vice-Presidents: Dario Scannapieco, Pim van Ballekom, Jonathan Taylor, Román Escolano, Ambroise Fayolle, Alexander Stubb, Andrew McDowell, Vazil Hudák.

Administrative Units

GENERAL SECRETARIAT

Secretary-General: Klaus Trömel.

Deputy Secretary-General: Marjut Santoni.

European Investment Bank

Governing Bodies

Director: Frank Schuster.

SECRETARIAT
Head of Division: Katarina Kaszasová.

LINGUISTIC SERVICES
Head of Division: Christi Schraut.

PROTOCOL—EVENTS
Head of Division: Dieter Bachlmair.

Institutional Strategy

Director: Guido Bichisao.

PLANNING, BUDGET AND ANALYTICS
Head of Division: Janette Foster.

EIB EXTERNAL REPRESENTATION
Head of Division: Jane Macpherson.

STRATEGY
Head of Division: Jane Macpherson.

Communication

Director: Matteo Maggiore.

MEDIA RELATIONS
Head of Division: Dirk Heilmann.

EDITORIAL, PUBLISHING AND PRODUCTION
Head of Division: Rainer Schlitt.

Head of Design, Production and Distribution: Marc Bello.

ONLINE AND MULTIMEDIA
Head of Division: Raquel González Dalmau.

Economics

Director: Debora Revoltella.

COUNTRY AND FINANCIAL SECTOR ANALYSIS
Head of Division: Barbara Marchitto.

POLICY AND STRATEGY
Head of Division: Natacha Valla.

ECONOMIC STUDIES
Head of Division: Natacha Valla.

Advisory Services

Director: Simon Barnes.

STRATEGY AND CO-ORDINATION
Head of Division: Jean-Luc Revéreault.

EUROPEAN INVESTMENT ADVISORY HUB
Head of Division: Mark Mawhinney.

EUROPEAN PPP EXPERTISE CENTRE
Head of Division: Chris Blades.

DECENTRALIZED FINANCIAL INSTRUMENTS ADVISORY
Head of Division: Frank Lee.

CONSULTANT PROCUREMENT AND CONTRACT MANAGEMENT
Head of Division: Simona Bovha Padilla.

INNOVATION FINANCE ADVISORY
Head of Division: Shiva Dustdar.

PROJECT ADVISORY SUPPORT
Head of Division: (vacant).

JASPERS

Director: Antonio Almagro.

NETWORKING AND COMPETENCE CENTRE
Head of Division: Norbert Hahn.

WATER AND WASTEWATER
Head of Division: Eckart Tronnier.

ENERGY AND SOLID WASTE
Head of Division: Ralf Goldmann.

SMART DEVELOPMENT
Head of Division: Eugenia Kazamaki-Ottersten.

RAIL, AIR AND MARITIME
Head of Division: Alan Lynch.

ROADS
Head of Division: Pasquale Staffini.

INDEPENDENT QUALITY REVIEW
Head of Division: (vacant).

Corporate Responsibility

Director: (vacant).

CIVIL SOCIETY
Head of Division: Hakan Lucius.

CORPORATE SOCIAL RESPONSIBILITY
Head of Division: (vacant).

EIB Institute

Dean of the Institute: Francisco de Paulo Coelho.

LEGAL DIRECTORATE

Director-General and General Counsel: Nicola Barr.

Legal Department, Operations
Director: Pierre Albouze.

RESTRUCTURING, NEW PRODUCTS AND FUND MANAGEMENT
Head of Division: Donald Fitzpatrick.

WESTERN EUROPE
Head of Division: Emer Falvey.

BALTIC SEA
Head of Division: Hanna Karczewska.

CENTRAL EUROPE, EASTERN NEIGHBOURS AND CENTRAL ASIA
Head of Division: Wiebke Jardet.

SOUTH-EAST EUROPE
Head of Division: Massimo Novo.

SPAIN AND PORTUGAL
Head of Division: Ignacio Lacorzana.

OUTSIDE EUROPE
Associate Director: Patrick Hugh Chamberlain.

Legal Department, Corporate
Director: Barbara Balke.

FINANCIAL ISSUES
Head of Division: Richard Schnopfhagen.

INSTITUTIONAL, CORPORATE AND LITIGATION
Head of Division: Tom Gilliams.

OPERATIONAL PROGRAMMES AND TECHNICAL ASSISTANCE
Head of Division: Stephen Sturmer.

PROCUREMENT, DECENTRALIZED FINANCIAL INSTRUMENTS AND ADMINISTRATIVE LAW
Head of Division: Ruth Niland.

REGULATORY MATTERS
Head of Division: Tero Pietila.

CORPORATE SERVICES DIRECTORATE
Director-General: Patrick Klaedtke.

Resource Management and Co-ordination
Head of Division: Geneviève Dewulf.

Information Management and Procurement
Director: Nicholas Barclay.

CORPORATE INFORMATION AND PROCESSES
Head of Division: Dennis Kessler.

INFORMATION MANAGEMENT
Head of Division: Alan Murdock.

PROCUREMENT AND PURCHASING
Head of Division: Jacinta Ryan.

Buildings and Logistics
Director: Silvia Sierra.

BUILDINGS MANAGEMENT OFFICE
Head of Division: Maritta Paajanen.

FACILITIES MANAGEMENT—TECHNICAL
Head of Division: Philipp Horn.

FACILITIES MANAGEMENT—SERVICES
Head of Division: Michael Schmitt.

BUILDING TASK FORCE
Head of Division: Jacques Margue.

Information Technology
Director: Derek Barwise.

BUSINESS SERVICES
Director: Jean-Yves Pirnay.

Finance and Lending
Head of Division: Jean-Yves Pirnay.

Enterprise Applications
Head of Division: Jean-Yves Pirnay.

Risk Management and Best Banking Practices
Head of Division: Jean-Marc Dalimier.

TRANSVERSAL SERVICES
Director: Sonia Hidalgo.

Information Technology Management Office
Head of Division: Sonia Hidalgo.

Information and Reporting
Head of Division: Jean-Marie Orosco.

Infrastructure and Operations
Head of Division: Jean-Marie Orosco.

Personnel
Director-General and Head of Personnel: Cheryl Fisher.

QUALITY, MANAGEMENT SUPPORT AND SYSTEMS
Director: Dominique Courbin.

Analytics, Compensation and Benefits; Budget
Head of Division: Filippo Zanzi.

European Investment Bank

Quality and Systems
Head of Division: Filippo Zanzi.

EMPLOYEE RELATIONS AND ADMINISTRATION
Director: José María Fernández Martín.

Benefits Administration
Head of Division: Catherine Albrecht.

Employee Relations and Wellbeing
Head of Division: Jean-Philippe Birckel.

Salaries, Pensions and Health Insurance
Head of Division: Jaroslav Salac.

STAFFING AND DEVELOPMENT
Director: Jürgen Mührke.

Staffing
Head of Division: Claudio Pasqui.

Development and Performance
Head of Unit: Stephen McCafferty.

DIRECTORATE FOR OPERATIONS

Director-General; Head of Operations: Jean-Christophe Laloux.
Director-General; Deputy Head of Operations: Luca Lazzaroli.

Investment Team for Greece
Deputy Director-General: Nicholas Jennett.

Operational Strategy and Business Development
Head of Division: Markus Berndt.

Project Finance—Global Partners and Neighbouring Countries
Head of Division: Paloma Pérez De Vega.

PROJECT FINANCE—BALTIC SEA AND NORTHERN EUROPE AND CENTRAL AND SOUTH EASTERN EUROPE
Head of Division: Matthias Woitok.

Operations Support
Director: Monique Koning.

OPERATIONAL MANAGEMENT
Head of Division: Loïc Le Ruyet.

INFORMATION SYSTEMS AND APPLICATIONS
Head of Division: Patrick Wortmann.

BUSINESS DEVELOPMENT AND SUPPORT
Head of Division: Nina Van Doren.

Mandate Management
Director: Christoph Kuhn.

MANDATE PORTFOLIO MANAGEMENT
Head of Division: Edvardas Bumsteinas.

RISK SHARING MANDATES
Head of Division: Manuel Neto Pinto.

TRUST FUNDS AND BLENDING
Head of Division: Jesper Persson.

DEVELOPMENT AND IMPACT FINANCE
Head of Division: Heike Rüttgers.

MANDATE SERVICES
Head of Division: Eugenio Leanza.

Equity, New Products and Special Transactions
Director: Adrian Kamenitzer.

INFRASTRUCTURE, NEW PRODUCTS AND SPECIAL TRANSACTIONS
Head of Division: Pilar Solano.

GROWTH CAPITAL AND INNOVATION FINANCE
Head of Division: Hristo Stoykov.

INFRASTRUCTURE FUNDS AND CLIMATE ACTION
Data Protection Officer: Christopher Knowles.

INTERMEDIATED FINANCE FOR MICRO, SMALL AND MEDIUM-SIZED COMPANIES
Head of Division: Milena Messori.

Western Europe
Director: Anita Fürstenberg-Lucius.

BANKS
Head of Division: Gilles Badot.

PROJECT FINANCE
Head of Division: Alessandro Izzo.

PUBLIC SECTOR AND UTILITIES
Head of Unit: Gemma Feliciani.

PUBLIC SECTOR AND TRANSACTION SUPPORT
Head of Division: Tanguy Desrousseaux.

CORPORATES
Head of Division: Christine Garburg.

Iberia
Director: Birthe Bruhn-Léon.

PUBLIC SECTOR—SPAIN
Head of Division: Juan Basora.

DIRECTORY

PUBLIC SECTOR—PORTUGAL
Head of Division: Nuno Ascenso Pires.

BANKS AND CORPORATES
Head of Division: Fernando Torija.

IMPLEMENTATION
Head of Division: Peter Bandilla.

Central and South-Eastern Europe
Director: Flavia Palanza.

INTERNATIONAL BANKS
Head of Divison: Kristin Lang.

PRIVATE LOCAL BANKS AND PRIVATE CORPORATES
Head of Division: Anders Risberg.

PUBLIC SECTOR—AUSTRIA, CZECH REPUBLIC, HUNGARY AND SLOVAKIA
Head of Division: Manuel Dueñas.

PUBLIC SECTOR—BULGARIA, ROMANIA AND TURKEY
Head of Division: Dietmar Dumlich.

PUBLIC SECTOR—CYPRUS AND GREECE
Head of Division: Ioannis Kaltsas.

Adriatic Sea
Director: Miguel Morgado.

PUBLIC SECTOR AND REGULATED OPERATIONS—ITALY AND MALTA
Head of Division: Andrea Tinagli.

BANKS AND CORPORATES
Head of Division: Marguerite McMahon.

PUBLIC SECTOR—SLOVENIA, CROATIA AND THE WESTERN BALKANS
Head of Division: Matteo Rivellini.

FINANCIAL INSTRUMENTS AND IMPLEMENTATION
Head of Division: Monika Mroczek-Comparetto.

Baltic Sea and Northern Europe
Deputy Director-General: Romualdo Massa Bernucci.

BANKS AND CORPORATES—POLAND AND BALTICS
Head of Division: Angel Ferrero.

CORPORATES—GERMANY AND NORDICS
Head of Division: Elina Kamenitzer.

PUBLIC SECTOR—POLAND AND BALTICS
Head of Division: Rafal Rybacki.

PUBLIC SECTOR—GERMANY AND NORDICS
Head of Division: Eric Gällstad.

Neighbouring Countries
Director: Heinz Olbers.

PUBLIC SECTOR—SOUTH NEIGHBOURHOOD
Head of Division: Kristina Kanapinskaitė.

PUBLIC SECTOR—EASTERN NEIGHBOURHOOD
Head of Division: Lionel Rapaille.

CORPORATES
Head of Division: Nathalie Climence.

BANKS
Head of Division: Marion Hoenicke.

Global Partners
Director: Maria Shaw-Barragan.

PUBLIC SECTOR—LATIN AMERICA AND CARIBBEAN
Head of Division: Philippe Szymcak.

PUBLIC SECTOR—AFRICA
Head of Division: Diederick Zambon.

PUBLIC SECTOR—ASIA AND PACIFIC
Head of Division: Angela Marcarino Paris.

FINANCIAL SECTOR
Head of Division: Robert Schofield.

CORPORATES, BUSINESS DEVELOPMENT AND IMPLEMENTATION
Head of Division: Paolo Munini.

TRANSACTION MANAGEMENT AND RESTRUCTURING DIRECTORATE
Director-General: Carlos Guille.

Systems, Data and Compliance
Head of Division: Pekka Myllymäki.

Counterparty Management
Director: Sandrine Croset.

INFRASTRUCTURE AND BASIC INDUSTRIES
Head of Division: Nikolaus Bahn.

PUBLIC SECTOR
Head of Division: Nikolaus Bahn.

MANUFACTURING INDUSTRIES
Head of Division: Yves Khali.

European Investment Bank

FINANCIAL INSTITUTIONS
Head of Division: Luigi Armeli.

IMPLEMENTATION
Head of Division: Petra Cutková.

Transaction Management
Director: Volkmar Bruhn-Léon.

PROJECT FINANCE
Head of Division: Francisco Quevedo.

RESTRUCTURING AND RESOLUTIONS
Head of Division: Jitka Bures.

EQUITY AND SUB-ORDINATED DEBTS
Head of Division: Aleksander Skórnik.

FINANCE DIRECTORATE
Director-General: Bertrand de Mazières.

Co-ordination and Financial Policies
Head of Division: Nicola Santini.

Capital Markets
Director: Eila Kreivi.

EURO
Head of Division: Carlos Ferreira da Silva.

EUROPE (EXCLUDING EURO), AFRICA
Head of Division: Richard Teichmeister.

AMERICA, ASIA, PACIFIC
Head of Division: Sandeep Dhawan.

INVESTOR RELATIONS AND MARKETING
Head of Division: Irene Sánchez Aizpurúa.

Treasury
Director: Éric Lamarcq.

LIQUIDITY MANAGEMENT
Head of Division: Timothy O'Connell.

ASSET/LIABILITY MANAGEMENT
Head of Division: Jean-Dominique Potocki.

PORTFOLIO MANAGEMENT
Head of Division: Jean-Erik de Zagon.

FINANCIAL ENGINEERING AND ADVISORY SERVICES
Head of Division: Thomas Ribarits.

Planning and Settlement of Operations
Director: Peggy Nylund Green.

BACK OFFICE TREASURY
Head of Division: Francisco Castro Gutierrez.

BACK OFFICE BORROWINGS
Head of Division: Antonío Vieira.

FINANCIAL SUPPORT CENTRE
Head of Division: Lorenzo Cicchelli.

LOAN ADMINISTRATION AND REFLOWS
Head of Division: Georgia Koutsiana.

PROJECTS DIRECTORATE
Director-General: Christopher Hurst.

Safeguards and Quality Management
Director: Maj Theander.

ENVIRONMENT, CLIMATE AND SOCIAL OFFICE
Head of Environment, Climate and Social Policy: Monica Scatasta.

PROCUREMENT OFFICE
Head of Procurement: José-Luis Alfaro.

QUALITY MANAGEMENT
Head of Division: Ann-Louise Aktiv Vimont.

PROJECT IMPACT AND REPORTING
Head of Division: Timo Välilä.

Mobility
Director: Gavin Dunnett.

SUSTAINABLE URBAN MOBILITY
Head of Division: Max Jensen.

AIR, MARITIME AND INNOVATIVE TRANSPORT
Head of Division: Stephen O'Driscoll.

STRATEGIC ROADS
Head of Division: Neil Valentine.

STRATEGIC RAILWAYS
Head of Division: Pierre Poinsignon.

Energy
Director: François Trevoux.

ENERGY EFFICIENCY AND SMALL-SCALE ENERGY PROJECTS
Head of Division: Dirk Roos.

ENERGY SECURITY
Head of Division: Sanjoy Rajan.

RENEWABLE ENERGY
Head of Division: Alessandro Boschi.

ELECTRICITY NETWORKS
Head of Division: Nicola Pochettino.

Innovation and Competitiveness
Director: Gunnar Muent.

LIFE SCIENCES
Head of Division: Felicitas Riedl.

DIGITAL ECONOMY
Head of Division: Harald Gruber.

INNOVATIVE INDUSTRIES
Head of Division: Laura Piovesan.

EDUCATION AND PUBLIC RESEARCH
Head of Division: Laura Piovesan.

Environment and Sustainable Territorial Development
Director: Werner Schmidt.

WATER MANAGEMENT
Head of Division: Thomas Van Gilst.

AGRIBUSINESS AND RURAL DEVELOPMENT
Head of Division: Hans-Harald Jahn.

URBAN DEVELOPMENT
Head of Division: Gerald Muscat.

REGIONAL DEVELOPMENT
Head of Division: Leonard Reinard.

RISK MANAGEMENT DIRECTORATE
Director-General: Alain Godard.

Co-ordination
Head of Division: Antonio Roca Iglesias.

MANAGEMENT AND BUSINESS SUPPORT
Head of Division: Ewen McMillan.

Operations
Director: Paolo Lombardo.

CORPORATES
Head of Division: Boryana Radeva.

STRUCTURED FINANCE AND EQUITY
Head of Division: James Whitall.

PUBLIC SECTOR ENTITIES AND FINANCIAL INSTITUTIONS
Head of Division: Giancarlo Sardelli.

PRICING AND SUPPORT
Head of Division: Florence Gaboreaud.

Financial Risk
Director: Stuart Rowlands.

ALM—ASSETS LIABILITY MANAGEMENT AND MARKET RISK
Head of Division: Michéle Liebermann.

DERIVATIVES
Head of Division: Guy Mertens.

TREASURY AND LIQUIDITY RISK
Head of Division: Giovanni Gentili.

APPLICATIONS AND DATA MANAGEMENT
Head of Division: Marie-Carmen González.

Regulation and EIB Group Risk
Director: Marie-Carmen González.

REGULATION AND BEST BANKING PRACTICES
Head of Division: Vincent Thunus.

EIB GROUP CAPITAL AND REPORTING
Head of Division: Pierre Tychon.

EIB GROUP INTERNAL MODELLING
Head of Division: Pedro De Lima.

EIB GROUP MODEL VALIDATION
Head of Division: Sergio Scandizzo.

INSPECTORATE-GENERAL
Inspector-General: Jan Willem van der Kaaij.

Fraud Investigation
Head of Division: Bernard O'Donnell.

Operations Evaluation
Head of Division: Ivory Lorena Yong-Protzel.

Complaints Mechanism
Head of Division: Felismino Alcarpe.

Internal Audit—EIB
Head of Division: Ciaran Hollywood.

Internal Audit—EIB
Head of Division: Sonja Derkum.

Internal Audit—EIF and Information Technology
Head of Division: Yves Decoster.

COMPLIANCE DIRECTORATE
Director-General and EIB Group Chief Compliance Officer: Gerhard Hütz.

Director and Deputy Chief Compliance Officer: Luigi La Marca.

Compliance Operations
Head of Division: Emeram Binder.

Compliance Corporate
Head of Division: Kamil Sugar.

Compliance Monitoring
Head of Division: Maria Leonides Esser Diaz.

Data Protection Office
Data Protection Officer: Pelopidas Donos.

FINANCIAL CONTROL DIRECTORATE
Director-General and Financial Controller: Patrick Klaedtke.

Financial Reporting
Director and Deputy Financial Controller: Frank Tassone.

Financial Reporting
Head of Division: Gwenael Robert.

THIRD PARTY ACCOUNTING AND ADMINISTRATIVE EXPENSES
Head of Division: Susanne Sternagel.

EUROPEAN CENTRAL BANK (ECB)

Sonnemannstr. 20, 60311 Frankfurt am Main, Germany; tel. (+49 69) 1344-0; fax (+ 49 69) 1344-6000; e-mail info@ecb.europa.eu; internet www.ecb.europa.eu

Governing Council

President: Mario Draghi.

Vice-President: Vítor Constâncio.

Members from the Executive Board: Benoît Cœuré, Sabine Lautenschläger, Yves Mersch, Peter Praet.

National Representatives: Ewald Nowotny (Governor, Oesterreichische Nationalbank), Jan Smets (Governor, Nationale Bank van België/Banque Nationale de Belgique), Chrystalla Georghadji (Governor, Central Bank of Cyprus), Ardo Hansson (Governor, Eesti Pank), Erkki Liikanen (Governor, Suomen Pankki—Finlands Bank), François Villeroy de Galhau (Governor, Banque de France), Jens Weidmann (President, Deutsche Bundesbank), Yannis Stournaras (Governor, Bank of Greece), Philip R. Lane (Governor, Central Bank of Ireland), Ignazio Visco (Governor, Banca d'Italia), Ilmārs Rimšēvičs (Governor, Latvijas Banka), Vitas Vasiliauskas (Chairman of the Board, Lietuvos Bankas), Gaston Reinesch (Governor, Banque Centrale du Luxembourg), Mario Vella (Governor, Central Bank of Malta), Klaas Knot (President, De Nederlandsche Bank), Carlos Costa (Governor, Banco de Portugal), Boštjan Jazbec (Governor, Banka Slovenije), Jozef Makúch (Governor, Národná Banka Slovenska), Luis María Linde (Governor, Banco de España).

Executive Board

Members: Mario Draghi, Vítor Constâncio, Benoît Cœuré, Sabine Lautenschläger, Yves Mersch, Peter Praet.

General Council

Members: Mario Draghi (President of the ECB), Vítor Constâncio (Vice-President of the ECB), Ewald Nowotny (Governor, Oesterreichische Nationalbank), Jan Smets (Governor, Nationale Bank van België/Banque Nationale de Belgique), Dimitar Radev (Governor, Balgarska Narodna Banka), Boris Vujčić (Governor, Hrvatska Narodna Banka), Chrystalla Georghadji (Governor, Central Bank of Cyprus), Jiří Rusnok (Governor, Česká Národní Banka), Lars Rohde (Governor, Danmarks Nationalbank), Ardo Hansson (Governor, Eesti Pank), Erkki Liikanen (Governor, Suomen Pankki—Finlands Bank), François Villeroy de Galhau (Governor, Banque de France), Yannis Stournaras (Governor, Bank of Greece), Jens Weidmann (President, Deutsche Bundesbank), György Matolcsy (Governor, Magyar Nemzeti Bank), Philip R. Lane (Governor, Central Bank of Ireland), Ignazio Visco (Governor, Banca d'Italia), Ilmārs Rimšēvičs (Governor, Latvijas Banka), Vitas Vasiliauskas (Chairman of the Board, Lietuvos Bankas), Gaston Reinesch (Governor, Banque Centrale du Luxembourg), Mario Vella (Governor, Central Bank of Malta), Klaas Knot (President, De Nederlandsche Bank), Adam Glapiński (President, Narodowy Bank Polski), Carlos Costa (Governor, Banco de Portugal), Mugur Constantin Isărescu (Governor, Banca Națională a României), Boštjan Jazbec (Governor, Banka Slovenije), Jozef Makúch (Governor, Národná Banka Slovenska), Luis María Linde (Governor, Banco de España), Stefan Ingves (Governor, Sveriges Riksbank), Mark Carney (Governor, Bank of England).

Administrative Units

DIRECTORATE-GENERAL ADMINISTRATION

Director-General: Werner Studener.

Deputy Director-General: Klaus Riemke.

Administrative Services Division

Head of Division: Erich Niederdorfer.

Premises Division

Head of Division: Holger Hansel.

Security Division

Head of Division: Jean-Marie Connes.

DIRECTORATE BANKNOTES

Director: Ton Roos.

CURRENCY DEVELOPMENT DIVISION

Head of Division: Jean-Michel Grimal.

CURRENCY MANAGEMENT DIVISION

Head of Division: Doris Schneeberger.

DIRECTORATE-GENERAL COMMUNICATIONS AND LANGUAGE SERVICES

Director-General: Christine Graeff.

Deputy Director-General: Thierry Bracke.

GLOBAL MEDIA RELATIONS DIVISION

Head of Division: Michael Steen.

WEB AND DIGITAL DIVISION

Head of Division: Joellen Perry.

OUTREACH AND PROTOCOL DIVISION

Head of Division: Valérie Saintot.

LANGUAGE SERVICES DIVISION

Head of Division: Rossana Villani.

European Central Bank

COUNSEL TO THE EXECUTIVE BOARD

Counsellor to the President and Co-ordinator of the Counsel to the Executive Board: Roland Straub.

ESRB SECRETARIAT

Head of Secretariat: Francesco Mazzaferro.

ECB REPRESENTATION IN WASHINGTON, DC, USA

Director-General: Rasmus Rüffer.

DIRECTORATE-GENERAL ECONOMICS

Director-General: Frank Smets.

Fiscal Policies Division
Head of Division: Christophe Kamps.

DIRECTORATE ECONOMIC DEVELOPMENTS

Director-General: Hans-Joachim Klöckers.

PRICES AND COSTS DIVISION
Head of Division: Christiane Nickel.

OUTPUT AND DEMAND DIVISION
Head of Division: Diego Rodríguez-Palenzuela.

COUNTRY SURVEILLANCE DIVISION
Head of Division: Isabel Vansteenkiste.

CONVERGENCE AND COMPETITIVENESS DIVISION
Head of Division: Ettore Dorrucci.

DIRECTORATE MONETARY POLICY

Director: Massimo Rostagno.

CAPITAL MARKETS/FINANCIAL STRUCTURE DIVISION
Head of Division: Thomas Werner.

MONETARY ANALYSIS DIVISION
Head of Division: João Sousa.

DIRECTORATE-GENERAL MACRO-PRUDENTIAL POLICY AND FINANCIAL STABILITY

Director-General: Sergio Nicoletti-Altimari.
Deputy Director-General: John Fell.

Macro-Prudential Policy Division
Head of Division: Carsten Detken.

Stress Test Modelling Division
Head of Division: Carmelo Salleo.

Financial Regulation and Policy Division
Head of Division: Fátima Pires.

Macro-Financial Policies Division
Head of Division: Carmelo Salleo.

DIRECTORATE-GENERAL HUMAN RESOURCES

Director-General: Anne-Sylvie Catherin.
Deputy Director-General: Peter Rennpferdt.

Employee Services Division
Head of Division: Søren Beier.

Talent Management Division
Head of Division: Manfred Koch.

DIRECTORATE-GENERAL FINANCE

Director-General: Roberto Schiavi.
Deputy Director-General: Claudia Mann.

Accounting Division
Head of Division: Pär Dickman.

Central Procurement Division
Head of Division: Juan Prieto Fernández.

Financial Reporting Division
Head of Division: Kevin Yeung.

Budgeting and Controlling Division
Head of Division: Carin Pronk.

DIRECTORATE-GENERAL INFORMATION SYSTEMS

Director-General: Koenraad de Geest.
Deputy Director-General: Magí Clavé.
Deputy Director-General: Dirk Robijns.

Security and Architecture Division
Head of Division: Alvise Grammatica.

Enterprise Systems Division
Head of Division: Gerard Salou.

Analytical Domain Applications Division
Head of Division: Patrick Maccury.

Executional Domain Applications Division
Head of Division: Michail Christidis.

Infrastructure and Operations Division
Head of Division: Christoph Schaper.

IT Governance and Business Relations Division
Head of Division: Danièle Krebs.

DIRECTORATE INTERNAL AUDIT
Director: Klaus Gressenbauer.

AUDIT SERVICES DIVISION
Head of Division: Jan Wapperom.

AUDIT MISSIONS DIVISION
Head of Division: Éric Vermeir.

DIRECTORATE-GENERAL INTERNATIONAL AND EUROPEAN RELATIONS
Director-General: Frank Moss.
Deputy Director-General: Gilles Noblet.

EU Institutions and Fora Division
Head of Division: Johannes Lindner.

International Relations and Co-operation Division
Head of Division: Benjamin Vonessen.

International Policy Analysis Division
Head of Division: Livio Stracca.

External Developments Division
Head of Division: Stylianos Makrydakis.

DIRECTORATE-GENERAL LEGAL SERVICES
Director-General: Chiara Zilioli.
Deputy Director-General: Christian Kroppenstedt.
Deputy Director-General: Roberto Ugena.

Financial Law Division
Head of Division: Otto Heinz.

Institutional Law Division
Head of Division: Frederik Malfrère.

Legislation Division
Head of Division: Mikael Stenström.

Supervisory Law Division
Head of Division: Eleni Koupepidou.

DIRECTORATE-GENERAL MARKET OPERATIONS
Director-General: Ulrich Bindseil.
Deputy Director-General: Cornelia Holthausen.
Deputy Director-General: Torsti Silvonen.

Financial Operations Services Division
Head of Division: Michael Stubbe.

Money Market and Liquidity Division
Head of Division: Holger Neuhaus.

Bond Markets and International Operations Division
Head of Division: Michail Christidis.

Market Operations Analysis Division
Head of Division: Benjamin Sahel.

Market Operations Systems Division
Head of Division: Christian Reynders.

DIRECTORATE-GENERAL MARKET INFRASTRUCTURE AND PAYMENTS
Director-General: Marc Bayle.
Deputy Director-General: Pierre Petit.

Oversight Division
Head of Division: Fiona Van Echelpoel.

Market Integration Division
Head of Division: Helmut Wacket.

Market Infrastructure Management Division
Head of Division: Sylvain Debeaumont.

Market Infrastructure Development Division
Head of Division: Mehdi Manaa.

DIRECTORATE-GENERAL RESEARCH
Director-General: Luc Laeven.
Deputy Director-General: Philipp Hartmann.

Monetary Policy Research Division
Head of Division: Günter Coenen.

Financial Research Division
Head of Division: Simone Manganelli.

DIRECTORATE RISK MANAGEMENT
Director: Carlos Bernadell.

Risk Analysis Division
Head of Division: Michail Christidis.

Risk Strategy Division
Head of Division: Alessandro Calza.

DIRECTORATE-GENERAL SECRETARIAT
Director-General: Pedro Gustavo Teixeira.

Compliance and Governance Office
Director-General: Roman Schremser.

Secretariat Division
Head of Division: Roman Schremser.

European Central Bank

Information Management Services Division
Head of Division: Roman Schremser.

DIRECTORATE-GENERAL STATISTICS

Director-General: Aurel Schubert.

Deputy Director-General: Werner Bier.

External Statistics and Sector Accounts Division
Head of Division: Caroline Willeke.

External Statistics Division
Head of Division: Remigio Echeverría.

Analytical Credit and Master Data Division
Head of Division: Jean-Marc Israël.

Statistical Application and Tools Division
Head of Division: Alessandro Binara.

Monetary and Economic Statistics Division
Head of Division: Ioannis Ganoulis.

Banking Supervision Data Division
Head of Division: Giancarlo Pellizzari.

DIRECTORATE-GENERAL MICRO-PRUDENTIAL SUPERVISION I

Director-General: Stefan Walter.

Deputy Director-General: Margarita Delgado.

Deputy Director-General: Patrick Amis.

DIRECTORATE-GENERAL MICRO-PRUDENTIAL SUPERVISION II

Director-General: Ramón Quintana.

Deputy Director-General: Rolf Klug.

Deputy Director-General: Paolo Corradino.

DIRECTORATE-GENERAL MICRO-PRUDENTIAL SUPERVISION III

Director-General: Jukka Vesala.

Deputy Director-General: Linette Field.

DIRECTORATE-GENERAL MICRO-PRUDENTIAL SUPERVISION IV

Director-General: Korbinian Ibel.

Deputy Director-General: François-Louis Michaud.

Deputy Director-General: Giuseppe Siani.

DIRECTORATE SECRETARIAT TO THE SUPERVISORY BOARD

Director-General: Petra Senković.

European System of Central Banks (ESCB)

(comprises the ECB and the national central banks of European Union member states)

CENTRAL BANKS OF EUROPEAN UNION MEMBER STATES

Oesterreichische Nationalbank: POB 61, 1011 Vienna, Austria; premises at: Otto-Wagner-Platz 3, 1090 Vienna, Austria; tel. (+43 1) 40420-0; fax (+43 1) 40420-2399; internet www.oenb.at; f. 1922; Pres. Claus J. Raidl; Gov. Ewald Nowotny.

Banque Nationale de Belgique (National Bank of Belgium): 14 blvd de Berlaimont, 1000 Brussels, Belgium; tel. (+32) 2-2212111; e-mail info@nbb.be; internet www.nbb.be; f. 1850; Gov. Jan Smets.

Balgarska Narodna Banka (Bulgarian National Bank): Pl. Knyaz Aleksandar I 1, 1000 Sofia, Bulgaria; tel. (+359 2) 9-14-59; fax (+359 2) 980-24-25; e-mail press_office@bnbank.org; internet www.bnb.bg; f. 1879; Gov. Dimitar Radev; Gen. Sec. Snezhanka Deyanova.

Hrvatska Narodna Bank (HNB) (Croatian National Bank): 10002 Zagreb, trg Hrvatskih velikana 3, Croatia; tel. (+385) 1-4564555; fax (+385) 1-4550726; e-mail info@hnb.hr; internet www.hnb.hr; Gov. Boris Vujčić.

Central Bank of Cyprus: POB 25529, 1395 Nicosia, Cyprus; premises at: Kennedy Ave 80, 1076 Nicosia, Cyprus; tel. (+357) 22714100; fax (+357) 22714959; internet www.centralbank.gov.cy; f. 1963; Gov. Chrystalla Georghadji.

Česká Národní Banka (Czech National Bank): Na Příkopě 28, 115 03 Prague 1, Czech Republic; tel. (+420) 224411111; fax (+420) 224412404; internet www.cnb.cz; Gov. Jiří Rusnok.

Danmarks Nationalbank: Havnegade 5, 1093 Copenhagen K, Denmark; tel. (+45) 33-63-63-63; fax (+45) 33-63-71-03; e-mail kommunikation@nationalbanken.dk; internet www.nationalbanken.dk; f. 1818; Chair. Søren Bjerre-Nielsen; Govs Lars Rohde, Hugo Frey Jensen, Per Callesen.

Eesti Pank: Estonia pst 13, 15095 Tallinn, Estonia; tel. (+372) 6680719; fax (+372) 6680836; e-mail info@eestipank.ee; internet www.eestipank.info; Chair. Mart Laar; Gov. Ardo Hansson.

Suomen Pankki/Finlands Bank (Bank of Finland): POB 160, 00101 Helsinki, Finland; tel. (+358 9) 1832626; fax (+358 9) 658424; e-mail info@bof.fi; internet www.suomenpankki.fi; f. 1811; Gov. Erkki Liikanen; Dep. Gov. Seppo Honkapohja.

Banque de France: 31 rue Croix-des-Petits-Champs, 75001 Paris, France; tel. (+33) 1-42-92-42-92; fax (+33) 1-42-92-39-40; e-mail infos@banque-france.fr; internet www.banque-france.fr; f. 1800; Gov. François Villeroy de Galhau.

Deutsche Bundesbank: Postfach 100602, 60006 Frankfurt am Main, Germany; premises at: Wilhelm-Epstein-Str. 14, 60431 Frankfurt am Main, Germany; tel. (+49 69) 9566-3512; e-mail info@bundesbank.de; internet www.bundesbank.de; f. 1957; Pres. Jens Weidmann; Vice-Pres. Claudia M. Buch.

Bank of Greece: Leoforos E. Venizelos 21, 102 50 Athens, Greece; tel. (+30) 210-3201111; fax (+30) 210-3232239; internet www.bankofgreece.gr; f. 1928; Gov. Yannis Stournaras.

Magyar Nemzeti Bank: Szabadság tér 9, 1054 Budapest; tel. (+36 1) 4282600; fax (+36 1) 4298000; e-mail info@mnb.hu; internet www.mnb.hu; f. 1921; Gov. Dr György Matolcsy.

Banc Ceannais na héireann (Central Bank of Ireland): POB 559, Dame St, Dublin 1, Ireland; tel. (+353 1) 2246000; fax (+353 1) 6715550; e-mail enquiries@centralbank.ie; internet www.centralbank.ie; f. 1942; Gov. Philip R. Lane; Dep. Govs Sharon Donnery, Bernard Sheridan (acting).

Banca d'Italia (Bank of Italy): Via Nazionale 91, 00184 Rome, Italy; tel. (+39) 06-47921; e-mail email@bancaditalia.it; internet www.bancaditalia.it; f. 1893; Gov. Ignazio Visco; Dir-Gen. Salvatore Rossi.

Latvijas Banka (Bank of Latvia): K. Valdemara iela 2a, 1050 Riga, Latvia; tel. (+371) 67022300; fax (+371) 67022420; e-mail info@bank.lv; internet www.bank.lv; f. 1992; Gov. Ilmārs Rimšēvičs; Dep. Gov. Zoja Razmusa.

Lietuvos Bankas (Bank of Lithuania): Totoriu St 4, 01121 Vilnius, Lithuania; premises at: Gedimino pr. 6, 01103 Vilnius, Lithuania; tel. (+370 8) 2680029; fax (+370 5) 2680038; e-mail info@lb.lt; internet www.lb.lt; Chair. Vitas Vasiliauskas; Dep. Chair. Raimondas Kuodis, Ingrida Šimonytė.

Banque Centrale du Luxembourg: 2 blvd Royal, 2983 Luxembourg, Luxembourg; tel. (+352) 4774-1; fax (+352) 47744910; e-mail info@bcl.lu; internet www.bcl.lu; f. 1998 as successor to the Institut Monétaire Luxembourgeois; Gov. Gaston Reinesch.

Bank Ċentrali ta' Malta (Central Bank of Malta): Pjazza Kastilja, Valletta VLT 1060, Malta; tel. (+356) 25500000; fax (+356) 25502500; e-mail info@centralbankmalta.org; internet www.centralbankmalta.org; Gov. Mario Vella; Dep. Govs Alfred Mifsud, Alexander Demarco.

Nederlandsche Bank NV: POB 98, 1000 AB Amsterdam, Netherlands; premises at: Westeinde 1, 1017 ZN Amsterdam, Netherlands; tel. (+31 20) 5249111; fax (+31 20) 5242500; e-mail info@dnb.nl; internet www.dnb.nl; f. 1814; Pres. Prof. Klaas Knot; Exec. Dirs Jan Sijbrand, Frank Elderson, Job Swank.

Narodowy Bank Polski (National Bank of Poland): ul. Świętokrzyska 11/21, 00-919 Warsaw, Poland; tel: (+48 22) 185-10-00; fax (+48 22) 185-10-10; e-mail listy@nbp.pl; internet www.nbp.pl; f. 1828; Pres. Adam Glapiński; First Vice-Pres. Piotr Wiesiołek.

Banco de Portugal: Rua do Comércio 148, 1100-150 Lisbon, Portugal; tel: (+351) 213130000; e-mail info@bportugal.pt; internet www.bportugal.pt; f. 1846; Gov. Carlos da Silva Costa; Vice-Govs José Joaquim Berberan e Santos Ramalho, Pedro Miguel de Seabra Duarte Neves.

Banca Națională a României (National Bank of Romania): Str. Lipscani 25, Sector 3, 030031 Bucharest, Romania; tel. (+40 21) 3130410; (+40 21) 3123831; e-mail info@bnro.ro; internet www.bnro.ro; f. 1880; Gov. Mugur Constantin Isărescu; First Dep. Gov. Florin Georgescu.

Národná Banka Slovenska (National Bank of Slovakia): Imricha Karvaša 1, 813 25 Bratislava, Slovakia; tel. (+421 2) 57871111; fax (+421 2) 57871100; e-mail info@nbs.sk; internet www.nbs.sk; f. 1993; Gov. Jozef Makúch.

Banka Slovenije (Bank of Slovenia): Slovenska 35, 1505 Ljubljana, Slovenia; tel. (+386 1) 4719000; fax (+386 1) 2515516; internet www.bsi.si; f. 1991; Gov. Boštjan Jazbec; Vice-Govs Irena Vodopivec Jean, Marko Bošnjak, Primož Dolenc, Jožef Bradeško.

Banco de España: C/ Alcalá 48, 28014 Madrid, Spain; tel. (+34) 91-3385000; e-mail comunicacion@bde.es; internet www.bde.es; f. 1829; Gov. Luis María Linde; Dep. Gov. Javier Alonso.

Sveriges Riksbank: Brunkebergstorg 11, 103 37 Stockholm, Sweden; tel. (+46 8) 787-00-00; fax (+46 8) 21-05-31; e-mail registratorn@riksbank.se; internet www.riksbank.se; f. 1668; Gov. Stefan Ingves; First Dep. Gov. Kerstin af Jochnick.

Bank of England: Threadneedle St, London, EC2R 8AH, United Kingdom; tel. (+44 20) 7601-4444; fax (+44 20) 7601-4771; e-mail enquiries@bankofengland.co.uk; internet www.bankofengland.co.uk; inc. by Royal Charter in 1694 and nationalized by Act of Parliament on 1 March 1946; Gov. Mark Carney; Dep. Govs Sam Woods, Ben Broadbent, Sir Jon Cunliffe.

EUROPEAN OMBUDSMAN

1 ave du Président Robert Schuman, 67001 Strasbourg Cedex, France; tel. (+33) 3-88-17-23-13; fax (+33) 3-88-17-90-62; e-mail eo@ombudsman.europa.eu; internet www.ombudsman.europa.eu

European Ombudsman

European Ombudsman: Emily O'Reilly; tel. (+33) 3-88-17-23-13.

CABINET OF THE EUROPEAN OMBUDSMAN

Head of Cabinet: Aidan O'Sullivan; tel. (+32) 2-2846868.

Adviser to the European Ombudsman: Fintan Butler; tel. (+33) 3-88-17-67-27.

Adviser to the European Ombudsman: Graham Smith; tel. (+32) 2-22843897.

SECRETARIAT-GENERAL

Secretary-General: Beate Gminder; tel. (+33) 3-88-17-23-84.

Assistant to the Secretary-General and Principal Administrator: Murielle Richardson; tel. (+33) 3-88-17-23-88.

Communication Unit

Head of Unit: Gundi Gadesmann.

Communication Officer: Richard More O'Ferrall; tel. (+32) 2-2843044.

Legal Officer: Peter Dyrberg; tel. (+32) 2-2832752.

ICT and Inquiries Unit 1

Head of Unit: Marta Hirsch-Ziembińska; tel. (+33) 3-88-17-27-46.

Principal Legal Officer: Maria Depasquale; tel. (+33) 3-88-17-29-77.

Investigator: Zina Assimakopoulou; tel. (+33) 3-88-17-22-62.

Legal Officer: Josef Nejedlý; tel. (+33) 3-88-16-41-68.

Legal Officer: Eija Salonen; tel. (+33) 3-88-17-24-29.

ICT Sector

Head of ICT sector: Marc Kamran Amir-Tahmasseb; tel. (+33) 3-88-17-44-10.

Co-ordination and Inquiries Unit 2

Head of Inquiry Co-ordination, Unit 2: Fergal Ó Regan; tel. (+32) 2-2843548.

Legal Officer: Katrin Metz-Van Issem; tel. (+32) 2-2842543.

Legal Officer: Jakub Pawlowicz; tel. (+32) 2-28433332.

Inquiries Unit 3

Head of Inquiries, Unit 3: Lambros Papadias; tel. (+32) 2-2846769.

Principal Legal Officer: Juliano Franco; tel. (+32) 2-2843858.

Principal Legal Officer: Antonios Antoniadis; tel. (+33) 3-88-17-37-68.

Legal Officer: Diana Riochet; tel. (+32) 2-2830280.

Legal Officer: Patricia López Martín; tel. (+32) 2-2834731.

Inquiries Unit 4

Head of Inquiries, Unit 4: Tina Nilsson; tel. (+32) 2-2841417.

Legal Officer: Nastaja Fuxa; tel. (+32) 2-2830784.

Legal Officer: Angela Marcos-Figueruelo; tel. (+32) 2-2841030.

Legal Officer: Jan Stadler; tel. (+32) 2-2843586.

Legal Officer: Philipp-Maximilian Chaimowicz; tel. (+32) 2-2846768.

Inquiries Unit 5

Head of Unit 5: Peter Bonnor; tel. (+33) 3-88-17-25-41.

Principal Legal Officer: Juliano Franco; tel. (+32) 2-2843858.

Legal Officer: Daniel Koblencz; tel. (+32) 2-2843831.

Strategic Inquiries

Head of Strategic Inquiries: Rosita Hickey; tel. (+32) 2-2842542.

Own Initiative Inquiries Officer: Alice Bossieré; tel. (+32) 2-2833401.

Case Handler: Koen Roovers; tel. (+32) 2-2841141.

Personnel, Administration and Budget Unit

Head of Administration and Personnel Unit: Alessandro de Bon; tel. (+33) 3-88-17-23-82; fax (+33) 3-88-17-90-62.

Legal Adviser: Marjorie Fuchs; tel. (+33) 3-88-17-40-78.

Accounting Officer: Véronique Vandaele; tel. (+32) 2-2842300.

DATA PROTECTION OFFICER

Data Protection Officer: Juliano Franco; tel. (+32) 2-2843858.

EU AGENCIES

Agency for the Co-operation of Energy Regulators (ACER)

Trg republike 3, 1000 Ljubljana, Slovenia; tel. (+386 8) 2053400; fax (+386 8) 2053413; e-mail info@acer.europa.eu; internet www.acer.europa.eu

ADMINISTRATIVE UNITS

Director: Alberto Pototschnig.

Head of Electricity Dept: Christophe Gence-Creux.

Head of Gas Dept: Dennis Hesseling.

Head of Administration Dept: Olga Borissova.

Head of Market Monitoring Dept: Volker Zuleger.

Body of European Regulators for Electronic Communications (BEREC)

2nd Floor, Z. A. Meierovica Bulv. 14, 1050 Rīga, Latvia; tel. (+371) 66117590; fax (+371) 67117560; e-mail berec@berec.europa.eu; internet berec.europa.eu

Administrative Manager: László Igneczi.

Community Plant Variety Office (CPVO)

3 blvd du Maréchal Foch, CS 10121, 49101 Angers Cedex 02, France; tel. (+33) 2-41-25-64-00; fax (+33) 2-41-25-64-10; e-mail cpvo@cpvo.europa.eu; internet www.cpvo.europa.eu

ADMINISTRATIVE UNITS

Chairman of the Management Board: Martin Ekvad; e-mail ekvad@cpvo.europa.eu.

Vice-President: Carlos Godinho.

Head of the Legal Unit: Francesco Mattina.

Head of the Technical Unit: Dirk Theobald; tel. (+33) 2-41-25-64-42; e-mail theobald@cpvo.europa.eu.

Head of the Administration and Finance Unit: James Moran; tel. (+33) 2-41-25-64-51; e-mail moran@cpvo.europa.eu.

Management Board

Chairman: Andrew Mitchell.

Vice-Chairman: Bistra Pavlovska.

European Agency for the Operational Management of Large-scale IT Systems in the Area of Freedom, Security and Justice (EU-LISA)

EU House, Rävala pst 4, 10143 Tallinn, Estonia; e-mail info@eulisa.europa.eu; internet eulisa.europa.eu

Executive Director: Krum Garkov.

European Agency for Safety and Health at Work (EU-OSHA)

Edif. Miribilla, 5th Floor, Santiago de Compostela 12, 48003 Bilbao, Spain; tel. (+34) 94-4358400; fax (+34) 94-4358401; e-mail information@osha.europa.eu; internet osha.europa.eu

ADMINISTRATIVE UNITS

Chairman of the Governing Board: Christa Schweng.

Director and Head of Network Secretariat Unit: Christa Sedlatschek; tel. (+34) 94-4358302; e-mail sedlatschek@osha.europa.eu.

Prevention and Research Unit

Head of Unit: William Cockburn; tel. (+34) 94-4358373; e-mail cockburn@osha.europa.eu.

Communication and Promotion Unit

Head of Unit: Andrew Smith; tel. (+34) 94-4358341; e-mail smith@osha.europa.eu.

Resource and Service Centre

Head of Unit: Françoise Murillo; tel. (+34) 94-4794321; e-mail murillo@osha.europa.eu.

European Asylum Support Office (EASO)

MTC Block A, Winemakers Wharf, Grand Harbour, MRS 1917 Valletta, Malta; tel. (+356) 22487500; e-mail info@easo.europa.eu; internet www.easo.europa.eu

Executive Director: José Carreira.

European Aviation Safety Agency (EASA)

POB 101253, 50452 Cologne, Germany; tel. (+49 221) 89990000; fax (+49 221) 89990999; e-mail info@easa.europa.eu; internet www.easa.europa.eu

ADMINISTRATIVE UNITS

Executive Director: Patrick Ky.

Management Board
Chairman: Pekka Hentu.
Deputy Chairman: Piotr Ołowski.

Executive Directorate
Executive Section Manager: Marieke Van Hijum.
Head of Communication and Quality Dept: Dominique Fouda.
Head of Legal Dept: Frank Manuhutu.
Chief Engineer: Pascal Medal.

Strategy and Safety Management
Director: Luc Tytgat.
Deputy Director: Rachel Daeschler.

Certification
Director: Trevor Woods.
Deputy Director: Ralf Erckmann.

Flight Standards
Director: Ricardo Genova Galvan.
Deputy Director: Wilfried Schulze.

Resources and Support
Director: Olivier Ramsayer.

European Bank Authority (EBA)

1 Canada Square, 46th Floor, Canary Wharf, London E14 5AA, United Kingdom; tel. (+44) 2073821776; e-mail info@eba.europa.eu; internet www.eba.europa.eu

Director: Adam Farkas.

European Border and Coast Guard Agency (FRONTEX)

Plac Europejski 6, 00-844 Warsaw, Poland; tel. (+48 22) 544-95-00; fax (+48 22) 544-95-01; e-mail frontex@frontex.europa.eu; internet www.frontex.europa.eu

ADMINISTRATIVE UNITS

Executive Director: Fabrice Leggeri.
Deputy Executive Director: Berndt Körner.
Spokesperson: Izabella Cooper; tel. (+48 22) 544-95-35; e-mail press@frontex.europa.eu.
Spokesperson: Ewa Moncure; tel. (+48 22) 544-95-00; e-mail frontex@frontex.europa.eu.

European Centre for the Development of Vocational Training (Cedefop)

570 02 Thessaloniki, Greece; tel. (+30) 2310-490111; fax (+30) 2310-490049; e-mail info@cedefop.europa.eu; internet www.cedefop.europa.eu

ADMINISTRATIVE UNITS

Chairman of the Governing Board: Micheline Scheys.
Director: James Calleja; tel. (+30) 2310-490140; e-mail joachim.james.calleja@cedefop.europa.eu.
Deputy Director: Mara Brugia; tel. (+30) 2310-490125; fax (+30) 2310-490120; e-mail mara.brugia@cedefop.europa.eu.
Assistant to the Director: Steven Bainbridge.
Assistant to the Deputy Director: Eleanora Schmid; tel. (+30) 2310-490027; e-mail lore.schmid@cedefop.europa.eu.
Legal Adviser: Miriam Fuchs; tel. (+30) 2310-490011; e-mail miriam.fuchs@cedefop.europa.eu.

Department for Skills and Labour Market
Head of Dept: Pascaline Descy; tel. (+30) 2310-490187; e-mail pascaline.descy@cedefop.europa.eu.

Department for VET Systems and Institutions
Head of Dept: Loukas Zahilas; tel. (+30) 2310-490044; e-mail loukas.zahilas@cedefop.europa.eu.

Department for Learning and Employability
Head of Dept: Antonio Ranieri; tel. (+30) 2310-490074; e-mail antonio.ranieri@cedefop.europa.eu.

Department for Communication
Head of Dept: Gerd Oskar Bausewein; tel. (+30) 2310-490288; e-mail gerd-oskar.bausewein@cedefop.europa.eu.

Department for Resources and Support
Head of Dept: Michail Christidis.

Human Resources
Head of Service: Ginette Manderscheid; tel. (+30) 2310-490072; e-mail ginette.manderscheid@cedefop.europa.eu.

Finance and Procurement
Head of Service: Michail Christidis; e-mail michail.christidis@cedefop.europa.eu.

Accountancy
Accounting Officer: Stephen Temkow; tel. (+30) 2310-490013; e-mail stephen.temkow@cedefop.europa.eu.

Brussels Office

1er étage, rue Joseph II-6, 1049 Brussels, Belgium; tel. (+32) 2-2991207; fax (+30) 23-10490049

Senior Expert: Jens Bjørnåvold; tel. (+32) 2-2991093; e-mail jens.bjornavold@cedefop.europa.eu.

European Centre for Disease Prevention and Control (ECDC)

Tomtebodavägen 11A, 171 65 Solna, Sweden; tel. (+46 8) 58-60-10-00; fax (+46 8) 58-60-10-01; e-mail info@ecdc.europa.eu; internet ecdc.europa.eu

DIRECTOR'S OFFICE

Director (acting): Andrea Ammon.

Office of the Chief Scientist

Chief Scientist: Michael Catchpole.

Public Health Capacity and Communication Unit

Head of Unit: Karl Ekdahl.

Surveillance and Response Support Unit

Head of Unit: Denis Coulombier.

Resource Management and Co-ordination Unit

Head of Unit (acting): Jean-Claude Brival.

Information and Communication Technologies Unit

Head of Unit: Caroline Aguado.

European Chemicals Agency (ECHA)

Annankatu 18, 00121 Helsinki, Finland; tel. (+358 9) 686180; fax (+358 9) 68618210; e-mail info@echa.europa.eu; internet echa.europa.eu

ADMINISTRATIVE UNITS

Executive Director: Geert Dancet; e-mail executive-director@echa.europa.eu.

Directorate of Co-operation

Director: Andreas Herdina.

Directorate of Regulatory Affairs

Director: Jukka Malm.

Directorate of Registration

Director: Christel Musset.

Directorate of Risk Management

Director: Jack de Bruijn.

Directorate of Evaluation

Director: Leena Ylä-Mononen.

Directorate of Information Systems

Director: Luisa Consolini.

Directorate of Resources

Director: Shay O'Malley.

Management Board

Chairman: Nina Cromnier; e-mail mb-secretariat@echa.europa.eu.

Vice-Chairman: Karel Blaha.

Committee for Risk Assessment

Chairman: Timothy Bowmer.

Committee for Socioeconomic Analysis

Chairman: Tomas Öberg.

Member State Committee

Chairman: Watze De Wolf.

Biocidal Products Committee

Chairman: Erik Van De Plassche.

Forum for Exchange of Information on Enforcement

Chairman: Szilvia Deim.

Vice-Chairman: Katja Vom Hofe.

Vice-Chairman: Eugen Anwander.

Board of Appeal

Chairman: Mercedes Ortuño.

Technically Qualified Member: Andrew Fasey.

Legally Qualified Member: Sari Haukka.

Registrar: Alen Mocilnikar.

European Defence Agency (EDA)

Rue des Drapiers 17–23, 1050 Brussels, Belgium; tel. (+32) 2-5042800; fax (+32) 2-5042815; e-mail info@eda.europa.eu; internet www.eda.europa.eu

ADMINISTRATIVE UNITS

Director-General: Jorge Domencq.

Deputy Chief Executive: Rini Goos.

Strategy and Policy Unit

Head of Unit: Graham Muir.

Co-operation, Planning and Support Directorate

Director: Roland Van Reybroeck.

Capability, Armament and Technology Directorate

Director: Peter Round.

European Synergies and Innovation Directorate

Director: Denis Roger.

Corporate Services Directorate

Director: Luigi Sandrin.

European Environment Agency (EEA)

Kongens Nytorv 6, 1050 Copenhagen, Denmark; tel. (+45) 33-36-71-00; fax (+45) 33-36-71-99; e-mail eea@eea.europa.eu; internet www.eea.europa.eu

ADMINISTRATIVE UNITS

Executive Director's Office

Executive Director: Hans Bruyninckx; e-mail hans.bruyninckx@eea.europa.eu.

Air and Climate Change

Head of Programme: Paul McAleavey; e-mail paul.mcaleavey@eea.europa.eu.

Administrative Services

Head of Administration: Søren Nielsen; e-mail soren.nielsen@eea.europa.eu.

Communications

Head of Programme: Katja Rosenbohm; e-mail katja.rosenbohm@eea.europa.eu.

Partnerships and Networks

Head of Programme: Peder Jensen; e-mail peder.jensen@eea.europa.eu.

Integrated Environmental Assessments

Head of Programme: Jock Martin; e-mail jock.martin@eea.europa.eu.

Natural Systems and Vulnerability

Head of Programme: Ronan Uhel; e-mail ronan.uhel@eea.europa.eu.

Operational Services

Head of Programme: Sigfús Bjarnason; e-mail sigfus.bjarnason@eea.europa.eu.

IDM—ICT and Data Management

Head of Programme: Chris Steenmans; e-mail chris.steenmans@eea.europa.eu.

European Fisheries Control Agency (EFCA)

Edificio Odriozola, Avda García Barbón 4, 36201 Vigo, Spain; tel. (+34) 986-120610; fax (+34) 986-125237; e-mail efca@efca.europa.eu; internet efca.europa.eu

ADMINISTRATIVE UNITS

Director: Pascal Savouret; e-mail pascal.savouret@efca.europa.eu.

Unit A—Resources and IT

Head of Unit: Niall McHale; tel. (+34) 986-120618; e-mail niall.mchale@efca.europa.eu.

Unit B—Operations

Head of Unit: Karin Hermansson; tel. (+34) 986-120614; e-mail karin.hermansson@efca.europa.eu.

Unit C—Programmes and Assistance

Head of Unit: Pedro Galache; tel. (+34) 986-120633; fax (+34) 886-125237; e-mail pedro.galache@efca.europa.eu.

European Food Safety Authority (EFSA)

Via Carlo Magno 1A, 43126 Parma, Italy; tel. (+39) 0521-036111; fax (+39) 0521-036110; internet www.efsa.europa.eu

ADMINISTRATIVE UNITS

Directorate

Executive Director: Bernard Url; e-mail bernhard.url@efsa.europa.eu.

Management Board

Chairman: Jaana Huso-Kallio.

Vice-Chairman: Raymond O'Rourke.

Vice-Chairman: Robert Van Gorcom.

Risk Assessment and Scientific Assistance

Head of Dept: Hans Verhagen; e-mail hans.verhagen@efsa.europa.eu.

Scientific Evaluation of Regulated Products

Head of Dept: Guilhem de Seze; e-mail guilhem.deseze@efsa.europa.eu.

Communications and External Relations

Head of Dept: Barbara Gallani.

Business Services

Head of Dept: Selomey Yamadjako; e-mail elomsey.yamadjako@efsa.europa.eu.

European Foundation for the Improvement of Living and Working Conditions (Eurofound)

Wyattville Rd, Loughlinstown, Dublin 18, Ireland; tel. (+353 1) 2043100; fax (+353 1) 2826456; e-mail postmaster@eurofound.europa.eu; internet www.eurofound.europa.eu

ADMINISTRATIVE UNITS

Chairman of the Governing Board: Herman Fonck.

Director: Juan Menéndez-Valdés; e-mail jme@eurofound.europa.eu.

Deputy Director: Erika Mezger; e-mail eme@eurofound.europa.eu.

Liaison Office, Brussels

Head of Unit: Sylvie Jacquet; e-mail sja@eurofound.europa.eu.

Research Programmes

EMPLOYMENT AND CHANGE

Head of Unit: Donald Storrie; e-mail dst@eurofound.europa.eu.

WORKING CONDITIONS AND INDUSTRIAL RELATIONS

Head of Unit: David Foden; e-mail dfo@eurofound.europa.eu.

LIVING CONDITIONS AND QUALITY OF LIFE

Head of Unit: Robert Anderson; e-mail rma@eurofound.europa.eu.

Information and Communication

Head of Unit: Mary McCaughey; e-mail mcu@eurofound.europa.eu.

PRESS OFFICE

Media and Promotions Manager: Måns Mårtensson; e-mail mma@eurofound.europa.eu.

COMMUNICATION PRODUCTS

Managing Editor: Fiachra Ó Marcaigh; e-mail fma@eurofound.europa.eu.

Web Manager: Fiona Murray; e-mail fmm@eurofound.europa.eu.

Events Co-ordinator: Cristina Arigho; e-mail car@eurofound.europa.eu.

Administration and Research Support Services

ADMINISTRATION AND FINANCE

Head of Unit: Markus Grimmeisen; e-mail mgr@eurofound.europa.eu.

HUMAN RESOURCES

Head of Unit: Raymond Comerford; e-mail rac@eurofound.europa.eu.

INFORMATION AND COMMUNICATION TECHNOLOGIES

Head of Unit: Jim Halpenny; e-mail jim@eurofound.europa.eu.

OPERATIONAL SUPPORT UNIT

Head of Unit: Mattanja de Boer; e-mail mdb@eurofound.europa.eu.

European Global Navigation Satellite Systems (GNSS) Agency (GSA)

Janovského 438/2, 170 00 Prague 7, Czech Republic; tel. (+420) 234766600; e-mail info@gsa.europa.eu; internet www.gsa.europa.eu

ADMINISTRATIVE UNITS

Executive Director: Carlo des Dorides; tel. (+420) 234766601; e-mail carlo.desdorides@gsa.europa.eu.

Head of the Market Development Dept: Gian Gherardo Calini; tel. (+420) 234766603; fax (+32) 2-2967238; e-mail gian-gherardo.calini@gsa.europa.eu.

GNSS Exploitation Programme Manager: Jean-Marc Piéplu; tel. (+420) 22962413; e-mail jean-marc.pieplu@gsa.europa.eu.

Head of the Security Dept: Stefano Iannitti; tel. (+420) 234766666.

Head of Communication: Donna Reay; tel. (+420) 22985210; e-mail donna.reay@gsa.europa.eu.

Head of the Galileo Security Monitoring Centre: Olivier Crop; tel. (+420) 22958426; e-mail olivier.crop@gsa.europa.eu.

Head of Project Control Dept: Patrick Hamilton; tel. (+420) 234766708; e-mail patrick.hamilton@gsa.europa.eu.

Head of Legal Dept: Ezio Villa; tel. (+420) 234766666.

Head of Legal Dept: Olivier Lambinet; tel. (+420) 234766727; e-mail olivier.lambinet@gsa.europa.eu.

European Institute for Gender Equality (EIGE)

Gedimino pr. 16, 01103 Vilnius, Lithuania; tel. (+370 5) 2157400; e-mail eige.sec@eige.europa.eu; internet eige.europa.eu

ADMINISTRATIVE UNITS

Chairman of the Management Board: Pauline Moreau; tel. (+49 30) 185551200; e-mail eige-mb-chair@eige.europa.eu.

Director: Virginija Langbakk; tel. (+370 5) 2157401; e-mail virginija.langbakk@eige.europa.eu.

Head of Administration: (vacant).

Head of Operations: Therese Murphy; tel. (+370 5) 2157404; e-mail therese.murphy@eige.europa.eu.

Head of Knowledge Management and Communications: Mira Banerjee; tel. (+370 5) 2157408; e-mail mira.banerjee@eige.europa.eu.

EU Agencies

European Insurance and Occupational Pensions Authority (EIOPA)

Westhafenplatz 1, 60327 Frankfurt am Main, Germany; tel. (+49 699) 5111920; fax (+49 699) 5111919; e-mail info@eiopa.europa.eu; internet eiopa.europa.eu

Executive Director: Fausto Parente.

Chairman: Gabriel Bernardino.

European Judicial Co-operation Unit (Eurojust)

Maanweg 174, 2500 AB The Hague, Netherlands; tel. (+31 70) 4125000; fax (+31 70) 4125005; e-mail info@eurojust.europa.eu; internet www.eurojust.europa.eu

ADMINISTRATIVE UNITS

President of Eurojust and National Member for Belgium: Michèle Coninsx.

Administrative Director: Klaus Rackwitz.

Head of Human Resources: Nikolaos Panagiotopoulos; tel. (+31 70) 4125000.

Head of Budget and Finance (acting): Natalie Groves.

Head of Legal Service: Catherine Deboyser.

Head of Operational Services: Alfredo García Miravete.

Head of Information Management: Jon Broughton.

Head of Communications and External Relations: Ulf Bergström.

Head of Corporate Services: Jacques Vos.

Head of Case Analysis: Alinde Verhaag.

Head of Data Protection: Diana Alonso Blas; tel. (+31 70) 4125510.

Head of College Secretariat: Carla García Bello.

Head of EJN Secretariat: Ola Löfgren; tel. (+31 70) 4125000.

JITs Network Secretariat Co-ordinator: Vincent Jamin.

Genocide Network Co-ordinator: Matevz Pezdirk.

European Maritime Safety Agency (EMSA)

Cais do Sodré 4, 1249-206 Lisbon, Portugal; tel. (+351) 211209200; fax (+351) 211209210; internet www.emsa.europa.eu

ADMINISTRATIVE UNITS

Chairman of the Administrative Board: Frans van Rompuy.

Executive Director: Markku Mylly.

Bureau of the Executive Director

Policy Adviser, including Communication: Andrea Tassoni.

Accounting Officer: Michel Metzger.

Department A—Corporate Services

Head of Dept (acting): Manuela Tomassini.

HUMAN RESOURCES
Head of Unit: Cristina Romay-Lopez.

LEGAL AND FINANCIAL AFFAIRS
Head of Unit: Dominika Lempicka Fichter.

OPERATIONS SUPPORT
Head of Unit: Steve Deighton.

Department B—Safety and Standards

Head of Dept: Manuela Tomassini.

VISITS AND INSPECTIONS
Head of Unit: Mario Mifsud.

SHIP SAFETY
Head of Unit: Michael Hunter.

MARINE ENVIRONMENT AND PORT STATE CONTROL
Head of Unit: Georgios Christophi.

Department C—Operations

Head of Dept: Leendert Bal.

POLLUTION RESPONSE SERVICES
Head of Unit: Bernd Bluhm.

VESSEL TRAFFIC AND REPORTING SERVICES
Head of Unit: Lazaros Aichmalotidis.

SATELLITE-BASED MONITORING SERVICES
Head of Unit: Leendert Bal.

European Medicines Agency (EMA)

30 Churchill Place, Canary Wharf, London E14 5EU, United Kingdom; tel. (+44 20) 3660-6000; fax (+44 20) 3660-5555; e-mail press@ema.europa.eu; internet www.ema.europa.eu

ADMINISTRATIVE UNITS

Executive Director: Guido Rasi; tel. (+44 20) 3660-8406; e-mail guido.rasi@ema.europa.eu.

Deputy Executive Director: Noël Wathion; tel. (+44 20) 3660-8592; e-mail noel.wathion@ema.europa.eu.

Advisory Functions

Senior Medical Officer: Hans-Georg Eichler; tel. (+44 20) 3660-7491; e-mail hans-georg.eichler@ema.europa.eu.

INTERNATIONAL AFFAIRS
Head of Unit: Emer Cooke; tel. (+44 20) 3660-7075; e-mail emer.cooke@ema.europa.eu.

LEGAL DEPT

Head of Unit: Stefano Marino; tel. (+44 20) 3660-7677; e-mail stefano.marino@ema.europa.eu.

AUDIT

Head of Unit: Edit Weidlich; tel. (+44 20) 3660-7039; e-mail edit.weidlich@ema.europa.eu.

PROGRAMME DESIGN BOARD DIVISION

Head of Unit: Agnès Saint Raymond; tel. (+44 20) 3660-7017; e-mail agnes.saint-raymond@ema.europa.eu.

Human Medicines Research and Development Support Division

Head of Division: Zaïde Frias; tel. (+44 20) 3660-7019; e-mail zaide.frias@ema.europa.eu.

PRODUCT DEVELOPMENT SCIENTIFIC SUPPORT DEPT

Head of Unit: Jordi Llinares-Garcia; tel. (+44 20) 3660-7126; e-mail jordi.llinares@ema.europa.eu.

Procedure Management and Committees Support Division

Head of Division (acting): Anthony Humphreys; tel. (+44 20) 3660-8583; e-mail anthony.humphreys@ema.europa.eu.

PROCEDURE MANAGEMENT DEPT

Head of Unit: Evdokia Korakianiti; tel. (+44 20) 3660-7150; e-mail evdokia.korakianiti@ema.europa.eu.

SCIENTIFIC COMMITTEE SUPPORT DEPT

Head of Unit: Anthony Humphreys; tel. (+44 20) 3660-8583; e-mail anthony.humphreys@ema.europa.eu.

Human Medicines Evaluation Division

Head of Division: Enrica Alteri; tel. (+44 20) 3660-7577; e-mail enrica.alteri@ema.europa.eu.

SCIENTIFIC AND REGULATORY MANAGEMENT DEPT

Head of Unit: Michael Berntgen; tel. (+44 20) 3660-7498; e-mail michael.berntgen@ema.europa.eu.

SPECIALIZED SCIENTIFIC DISCIPLINES DEPT

Head of Unit: Ana Hidalgo-Simon; tel. (+44 20) 3660-8467; e-mail ana.hidalgo-simon@ema.europa.eu.

Inspections and Human Medicines Pharmacovigilance Division

Head of Division: Fergus Sweeney; tel. (+44 20) 3660-7026; e-mail fergus.sweeney@ema.europa.eu.

COMPLIANCE AND INSPECTIONS DEPT

Head of Unit: Anabela Luís de Lima Marçal; tel. (+44 20) 3660-8449; e-mail anabela.marcal@ema.europa.eu.

PHARMACOVIGILANCE DEPT

Head of Unit: Peter Arlett; tel. (+44 20) 3660-7108; e-mail peter.arlett@ema.europa.eu.

Veterinary Medicines Division

Head of Unit: David Mackay; tel. (+44 20) 3660-8413; e-mail david.mackay@ema.europa.eu.

VETERINARY MEDICINES DEPT

Head of Unit: Fia Westerholm.

Stakeholders and Communication Division

Head of Division (acting): Melanie Carr; tel. (+44 20) 3660-8575; e-mail melanie.carr@ema.europa.eu.

Information Technology Division

Head of Unit (acting): Alexis Nolte; tel. (+44 20) 3660-7188; e-mail alexis.nolte@ema.europa.eu.

IT OPERATIONS DEPT

Head of Unit: Pedro José Borges Pina Ferreira; tel. (+44 20) 3660-8383; e-mail pedro.ferreira@ema.europa.eu.

Administration and Corporate Management Division

Head of Unit (acting): Nerimantas Steikūnas; tel. (+44 20) 3660-7220; e-mail nerimantas.steikunas@ema.europa.eu.

Deputy Head of Division: Agneta Brandt; tel. (+44 20) 3660-7550; e-mail agneta.brandt@ema.europa.eu.

HUMAN RESOURCES

Head of Unit: Manuel José Camara Ramalho Ortigao; tel. (+44 20) 3660-7731; e-mail manuel.ortigao@ema.europa.eu.

FINANCE AND BUDGET

Head of Unit: Michael Lenihan; tel. (+44 20) 3660-7088; e-mail michael.lenihan@ema.europa.eu.

European Monitoring Centre for Drugs and Drug Addiction (EMCDDA)

Cais do Sodré, 1249-289 Lisbon, Portugal; tel. (+351) 211210200; fax (+351) 218131711; e-mail info@emcdda.europa.eu; internet www.emcdda.europa.eu

ADMINISTRATIVE UNITS

Chairman of the Management Board: Laura D'Arrigo.

Vice-Chairman of the Management Board: Franz Pietsch.

Director: Alexis Goosdeel; e-mail alexis.goosdeel@emcdda.europa.eu.

Executive Office

Head of Unit: Fabián Pereyra; e-mail fabian.pereyra@emcdda.europa.eu.

Senior Policy Officer to the Management Board: Monika Blum; e-mail monika.blum@emcdda.europa.eu.

Scientific Division

Scientific Director: Paul Griffiths; e-mail paul.griffiths@emcdda.europa.eu.

Prevalence, Data Management and Content Co-ordination

Head of Unit: Julián Vicente; e-mail julian.vicente@emcdda.europa.eu.

EU Agencies   DIRECTORY

Supply Reduction and New Drugs

Head of Unit: Roumen Sedefov; e-mail roumen.sedefov@emcdda.europa.eu.

Consequences, Interventions and Best Practices

Head of Unit: Roland Simon; e-mail roland.simon@emcdda.europa.eu.

Reitox and International Co-operation

Head of Unit: Gonçalo Felgueiras E. Sousa; e-mail goncalo.felgueiras@emcdda.europa.eu.

Communication

Head of Unit: Rosemary de Sousa; e-mail rosemary.de.sousa@emcdda.europa.eu.

Information and Communication Technologies

Head of Unit: Pedro Ribeiro; e-mail pedro.ribeiro@emcdda.europa.eu.

Administration

Head of Unit: Dante Storti; e-mail dante.storti@emcdda.europa.eu.

European Securities and Markets Authority (ESMA)

103 rue de Grenelle, 75007 Paris, France; e-mail info@esma.europa.eu; internet www.esma.europa.eu

Executive Director: Verena Ross.

Chairman: Steven Maijoor.

Vice-Chairperson: Anneli Tuominen.

European Training Foundation (ETF)

Villa Gualino, Viale Settimio Severo 65, 10133 Turin, Italy; tel. (+39) 011-6302282; fax (+39) 011-6302200; e-mail info@etf.europa.eu; internet www.etf.europa.eu

ADMINISTRATIVE UNITS

Director: Madlen Serban; tel. (+39) 011-6302248; e-mail madlen.serban@etf.europa.eu.

Operations Department

Head of Dept: Anastasia Fetsi; e-mail anastasia.fetsi@etf.europa.eu.

Corporate Performance Department

Head of Dept: Peter Greenwood; e-mail peter.greenwood@etf.europa.eu.

Communication Department

Head of Dept: Alastair Macphail; e-mail alastair.macphail@etf.europa.eu.

Administration Department

Head of Dept: Henrik Faudel; e-mail henrik.faudel@etf.europa.eu.

European Union Agency for Fundamental Rights (FRA)

Schwarzenbergplatz 11, 1040 Vienna, Austria; tel. (+43-1) 580300; e-mail info@fra.europa.eu; internet fra.europa.eu

ADMINISTRATIVE UNITS

Director: Michael O'Flaherty; tel. (+43-1) 58030651; e-mail michael.oflaherty@fra.europa.eu.

Administration

Head of Unit: Constantinos Manolopoulos; tel. (+43-1) 58030810; e-mail constantinos.manolopoulos@fra.europa.eu.

Human Resources and Planning

Head of Unit (acting): Xavier Catala; tel. (+43-1) 58030670; e-mail personnel@fra.europa.eu.

Equality and Citizens' Rights

Head of Unit: Ioannis Dimitrakopoulos; tel. (+43-1) 58030856; e-mail ioannis.dimitrakopoulos@fra.europa.eu.

Freedoms and Justice

Head of Unit: Joanna Goodey; tel. (+43-1) 58030629; e-mail joanna.goodey@fra.europa.eu.

Communication and Outreach

Head of Unit: Friso Roscam Abbing; tel. (+43-1) 58030671; e-mail info@fra.europa.eu.

European Union Agency for Law Enforcement Co-operation (Europol)

Eisenhowerlaan 73, 90850 The Hague, Netherlands; tel. (+31 70) 3025000; internet www.europol.europa.eu

ADMINISTRATIVE UNITS

Director: Rob Wainwright.

Deputy Director: Oldřich Martinů.

Management Board

MANAGEMENT BOARD SECRETARIAT

Secretary: Alfredo Nunzi.

JOINT SUPERVISORY BODY

Chairman: Vana Palumbo.

European Union Agency for Law Enforcement Training (CEPOL)

27 Ó utca, 1066 Budapest, Hungary; tel. (+36 1) 8038030; fax (+36 1) 8038032; e-mail info@cepol.europa.eu; internet www.cepol.europa.eu

ADMINISTRATIVE UNITS

Executive Director: Ferenc Bánfi; tel. (+36 1) 8038033; e-mail ferenc.banfi@cepol.europa.eu.

Deputy Director: Detlef Schröder; tel. (+36 1) 8038035; e-mail detlef.schroeder@cepol.europa.eu.

European Union Agency for Network and Information Security (ENISA)

Science and Technology Park of Crete (ITE), Vassilika Vouton, 700 13 Heraklion, Greece; tel. (+30) 2814-409710; fax (+30) 2810-391410; e-mail info@enisa.europa.eu; internet www.enisa.europa.eu

ADMINISTRATIVE UNITS

Executive Director: Udo Helmbrecht; tel. (+30) 2814-409591; fax (+30) 2810-391410; e-mail udo.helmbrecht@enisa.europa.eu.

Administration and Support Dept

Head of Unit: Paulo Empadinhas; tel. (+30) 2814-409521; e-mail paulo.empadinhas@enisa.europa.eu.

Core Operations Dept

Head of Unit: Steve Purser; tel. (+30) 2814-409611; e-mail steve.purser@enisa.europa.eu.

European Union Agency for Railways (ERA)

120 rue Marc Lefrancq, 59307 Valenciennes, Cedex, France; tel. (+33) 3-27-09-65-00; fax (+33) 3-27-33-40-65; e-mail directorate-info@era.europa.eu; internet www.era.europa.eu

ADMINISTRATIVE UNITS

Chairman of the Administrative Board: Mats Andersson.

Executive Director: Josef Doppelbauer; e-mail josef.doppelbauer@era.europa.eu.

Cross Acceptance

Head of Unit: Richard Lockett; e-mail richard.lockett@era.europa.eu.

Accountancy

Stefan Meert; tel. (+33) 3-27-09-65-00; e-mail stefan.meert@era.europa.eu.

Communications and Public Relations

Thorsten Hahn; tel. (+33) 3-27-09-65-95; fax (+33) 3-27-09-66-95; e-mail communication@era.europa.eu.

Economic Evaluation Unit

Head of Unit: Jens Engelmann; e-mail jens.engelmann@era.europa.eu.

ERTMS Unit

Head of Unit: Pio Guido; e-mail pio.guido@era.europa.eu.

Interoperability

Head of Unit: Anna Gigantino; e-mail anna.gigantino@era.europa.eu.

Safety

Head of Unit: Chris Carr; e-mail chris.carr@era.europa.eu.

Administration

Mikkel Emborg; e-mail mikkel.emborg@era.europa.eu.

European Union Institute for Security Studies (EUISS)

100 ave de Suffren, 75015 Paris, France; tel. (+33) 1-56-89-19-30; fax (+33) 1-56-89-19-31; e-mail info@iss.europa.eu; internet www.iss.europa.eu

ADMINISTRATIVE UNITS

Director: Antonio Missiroli.

Administration

Head of Unit: Philippe Zinopoulos.

Publications

Head of Unit: Gearóid Cronin.

Public Information

Head of Unit: John-Joseph Wilkins.

Brussels Liaison Office

Head of Unit: Jackie Granger.

European Union Intellectual Property Office (EUIPO)

Avda de Europa 4, 03008 Alicante, Spain; tel. (+34) 96-5139100; fax (+34) 96-5131344; e-mail information@euipo.europa.eu; internet www.euipo.europa.eu

ADMINISTRATIVE UNITS

Administrative Board

Chairman: Mihály Ficsor.

EU Agencies DIRECTORY

Budget Committee
Chairman: Anne Rejnhold Jørgensen.

Executive Director of the Office
Executive Director: António Campinos.
Deputy Executive Director: Christian Archambeau.

Boards of Appeal

FIRST BOARD OF APPEAL
Chairman: Theophilos Margellos.

SECOND BOARD OF APPEAL
Chairman: Tomás de las Heras Lorenzo.

THIRD BOARD OF APPEAL
Chairman: Theophilus Margellos.

FOURTH BOARD OF APPEAL
Chairman: Detlef Schennen.

FIFTH BOARD OF APPEAL
Chairman: Gordon Humphreys.

REGISTRY
Head of Service: Erik Dijkema.

KNOWLEDGE AND INFORMATION SUPPORT SERVICE
Head of Service: Jakub Pinkowski.

Cabinet
Head of Cabinet: Fabrice Claireau.

CORPORATE GOVERNANCE SERVICE
Head of Service (acting): Miguel Gusmao.

COMMUNICATIONS SERVICE
Head of Service: Luis Berenguer.

Internal Audit
Head of Service: Reiner Tretter.

Academy
Director: Hugues Bello.

Operations Department
Director: Ralph Pethke.

Customer Support Department
Director: Alain Rassat.

Infrastructure and Buildings Department
Director: Miguel Angel Villarroya.

COMMON SERVICES
Head of Service: Jean-Marc Nicolaï.

Facility Management

Head of Service: Vincent Polomé.

Business Information Technology Department
Director: Niloofar Simon.

ARCHITECTURE AND PLANNING
Head of Service: Diego Eguidazu.

APPLICATIONS DEVELOPMENT AND MAINTENANCE
Head of Service: Raymond Klaasen.

OPERATIONS AND INFRASTRUCTURE
Head of Service: Angel Aledo.

HUMAN RESOURCES DEPT
Director: Susana Pérez Ferreras.

STAFFING, DEVELOPMENT AND RECOGNITION SERVICE
Head of Service: François Femia.

ENTITLEMENTS AND STAFF WELFARE SERVICE
Head of Service: Patricia López Fernández de Corres.

International Co-operation and Legal Affairs Department
Director: João Negrao.

INTERNATIONAL CO-OPERATION
Deputy Director: José Izquierdo Peris.

EUROPEAN CO-OPERATION
Head of Service: Simon White.

INSTITUTIONAL RELATIONS SERVICE
Head of Service: Kirsten Bauch Edner.

LEGAL AFFAIRS
Deputy Director: Dimitris Botis.

LITIGATION SERVICE
Head of Service: Giuseppe Bertoli.

LEGAL PRACTICE SERVICE
Head of Service: Oscar Mondejar.

Finance Dept
Director: Juan Ramón Rubio.

European Union Satellite Centre (EU SatCen)

Apdo de Correos 511, 28850 Torrejon de Ardoz, Madrid, Spain; tel. (+34) 91-6786000; fax (+34) 91-6786006; e-mail info@satcen.europa.eu; internet www.satcen.europa.eu

ADMINISTRATIVE UNITS
Director: Pascal Legai.
Deputy Director: Guiseppe D'Amico.

Administration Division
Head of Division: Paul Cozzi.

Operations Division

Head of Division: Adriano Baptista.

Capability Development Division

Head of Division: Andrea Patrono.

Information Technology Division

Head of Division: Alexis Letulier.

Finance Section

Head of Section: Lorenzo Mulero.

Brussels Office

Head of Office: Oliver Rajan; tel. (+32) 25849400.

Single Resolution Board

Treurenberg 22, 1049 Brussels, Belgium; tel. (+32) 24903000; internet srb.europa.eu

Chairman: Elke König.

Translation Centre for the Bodies of the European Union (CdT)

Bâtiment Drosbach 12, rue Guillaume Kroll, 1882 Luxembourg, Luxembourg; tel. (+352) 4217111; fax (+352) 421711220; e-mail cdt@cdt.europa.eu; internet www.cdt.europa.eu

ADMINISTRATIVE UNITS

Chairman of the Management Board: Rytis Martikonis; tel. (+32) 229-67825.

Director: Máire Killoran; tel. (+352) 421711200; e-mail maire.killoran@cdt.europa.eu.

Director's Assistant: Catherine Steinmetz; tel. (+352) 421711213; e-mail catherine.steinmetz@cdt.europa.eu.

Translation Department

Head of Dept: Thierry Fontenelle; tel. (+352) 421711209; e-mail thierry.fontenelle@cdt.europa.eu.

EXTERNAL RELATIONS AND COMMUNICATION SECTION

Head of Unit: Stephanie Busse; tel. (+352) 421711389; e-mail stephanie.busse@cdt.europa.eu.

Translation Support Departmentt

Head of Dept: Jean-Luc Verbruggen; tel. (+352) 421711465; e-mail jean-luc.verbruggen@cdt.europa.eu.

DEMAND MANAGEMENT SECTION

Head of Section: Jacky Nazac; tel. (+352) 421711399; e-mail jacky.nazac@cdt.europa.eu.

LANGUAGE AND TECHNOLOGY SUPPORT SECTION

Head of Section: Denis Dechandon; tel. (+352) 421711295; e-mail denis.dechandon@cdt.europa.eu.

Administration Department

Head of Dept: Silvana Miggiano; tel. (+352) 421711335; e-mail silvana.miggiano@cdt.europa.eu.

Accounting Officer: Kamil Kolembus; tel. (+352) 421711337; e-mail kamil.kolembus@cdt.europa.eu.

BUDGETARY AND STRATEGIC PLANNING SECTION

Head of Group: Luc Vanheel.

HUMAN RESOURCES SECTION

Head of Section: Mauro Bubnic; tel. (+352) 421711307; e-mail mauro.bubnic@cdt.europa.eu.

LEGAL AFFAIRS SECTION

Head of Group: Anne-Marie Rikkert; tel. (+352) 421711267; e-mail anne-marie.rikkert@cdt.europa.eu.

FACILITIES AND SECURITY GROUP

Head of Group: Robert Lanners; tel. (+352) 4217111; e-mail cdt@cdt.europa.eu.

IT Department

Head of Dept: Benoît Vitale; tel. (+352) 421711374; e-mail benoit.vitale@cdt.europa.eu.

IT INFRASTRUCTURE SECTION

Head of Section: Pascal Dufour; tel. (+352) 421711224; e-mail pascal.dufour@cdt.europa.eu.

SERVICE DESK SECTION

Head of Section: Marc Maréchal; tel. (+352) 421711277; e-mail marc.marechal@cdt.europa.eu.

DEVELOPMENT SECTION

Head of Section: Salvatore Sanfilippo; tel. (+352) 421711325; e-mail salvatore.sanfilippo@cdt.europa.eu.

EU EXECUTIVE AGENCIES

Consumers, Health and Food Executive Agency (Chafea)

DRB A3/042, 2920 Luxembourg, Luxembourg; tel. (+352) 430132015; fax (+352) 430130359; e-mail chafea@ec.europa.eu; internet ec.europa.eu/chafea

ADMINISTRATIVE UNITS

Director: Véronique Wasbauer; tel. (+352) 430138102.

Administrative Unit

Head of Unit: Robert Geeraerts; tel. (+352) 430132090.

Health Unit

Head of Unit: Jacques Remacle; tel. (+352) 430137237.

Consumers and Food Safety Unit

Head of Unit: Salvatore Maguzzu; tel. (+352) 430134096.

EU Agencies   DIRECTORY

European Research Council Executive Agency (ERCEA)

Place C. Rogier 16, 1049 Brussels, Belgium; e-mail erc-info@ec.europa.eu; internet erc.europa.eu

ADMINISTRATIVE UNITS

Director: Pablo Amor; tel. (+32) 2-2980167.

Communications

Head of Communication Unit: Massimo Gaudina; tel. (+32) 2-298879.

Department B—Scientific Management

Head of Department: José Labastida; tel. (+32) 2-2967935.

B1—ETHICS REVIEW AND EXPERT MANAGEMENT

Head of Unit: Michel Vanbiervliet; tel. (+32) 2-2999336.

B2—CALL AND PROJECT FOLLOW-UP CO-ORDINATION

Head of Unit: Alejandro Martin-Hobdey; tel. (+32) 2-2994589.

B3—LIFE SCIENCES

Head of Unit: Anna Lonnroth; tel. (+32) 2-2994210.

B4—PHYSICAL SCIENCES AND ENGINEERING

Head of Unit: Martin Penny; tel. (+32) 2-2954504.

B5—SOCIAL SCIENCES AND HUMANITIES

Head of Unit: Angela Liberatore; tel. (+32) 2-2952229.

Department C—Grant Management

Head of Department: Mechtild May; tel. (+32) 2-2963824.

C1—STARTING GRANTS

Head of Unit: Niki Atzoulatou; tel. (+32) 2-2995992.

C2—CONSOLIDATOR GRANTS

Head of Unit: Marja Hennessy; tel. (+32) 2-2995449.

C3—ADVANCED GRANTS

Head of Unit: Thierry Prost; tel. (+32) 2-2950790.

C4—AUDIT AND EX-POST CONTROLS

Head of Unit: Anisoara Ulceluse-Pirvan; tel. (+32) 2-2975176.

Department D—Resources and Support

Head of Unit: Georges Te Kolste; tel. (+32) 2-2964735.

D1—IT TOOLS DEVELOPMENT AND MANAGEMENT

Head of Unit: Dirk Costens; tel. (+32) 2-2954524.

D2—HUMAN RESOURCES, INFRASTRUCTURE AND DOCUMENT MANAGEMENT

Head of Unit: Sari Vartiainen; tel. (+32) 2-2957909.

D3—LEGAL AFFAIRS AND INTERNAL CONTROL

Head of Unit: Laurence Moreau; tel. (+32) 2-2981448.

Innovation and Networks Executive Agency (INEA)

Chaussée de Wavre 910, 1049 Brussels, Belgium; e-mail inea@ec.europa.eu; internet inea.ec.europa.eu

ADMINISTRATIVE UNITS

Director: Dirk Beckers; tel. (+32) 2-2954261.

Department C—Connecting Europe Facility

Head of Department: Anderas Boschen; tel. (+32) 2-2959654.

CEF TRANSPORT: BALTIC SEA, MOS AND ERTMS

Head of Unit (acting): Morten Jensen.

CEF TRANSPORT: EAST MEDITERRANEAN, BLACK SEA, SE EUROPE AND MARCO POLO

Head of Unit: Cristóbal Millán de la Lastra.

CEF TRANSPORT: WEST MEDITERRANEAN, ATLANTIC, ITS, RIS AND INNOVATION

Head of Unit: Christian Faure; tel. (+32) 2-2954290.

CEF ENERGY AND ICT

Head of Unit: Olivier Silla; tel. (+32) 2-2966597.

Department H—Horizon 2020

Head of Department: Alan Haigh.

ENERGY RESEARCH

Head of Unit: Robert Goodchild; tel. (+32) 2-2990137.

TRANSPORT RESEARCH

Head of Unit: Marcel Rommerts; tel. (+32) 2-2955334.

Department R—Programme Support and Resources

Head of Department: Anna Panagopoulou; tel. (+32) 2-2967894.

PROGRAMME SUPPORT, CO-ORDINATION AND COMMUNICATION

Head of Unit: Bernadette Frederick; tel. (+32) 2-2995877.

ADMINISTRATIVE FINANCE, LEGAL AND FINANCIAL MANAGEMENT

Head of Unit: Philippe Stalins.

OPERATIONAL FINANCE

Head of Unit: Joachim Ball; tel. (+32) 2-2955951.

HR, IT AND LOGISTICS

Head of Unit: Maria Novak; tel. (+32) 2-2995635.

Education, Audiovisual and Culture Executive Agency (EACEA)

139 rue Colonel Bourg, 1049 Brussels, Belgium; tel. (+32) 2-2991111; e-mail eacea-info@ec.europa.eu; internet eacea.ec.europa.eu

ADMINISTRATIVE UNITS

Director: Brian Holmes; tel. (+32) 2-2993672.

Executive Agency for Small and Medium-sized Enterprises (EASME)

Covent Garden Bldg, Place Rogier 16, 1210 Brussels, Belgium; e-mail easme-communication@ec.europa.eu; internet ec.europa.eu/easme

ADMINISTRATIVE UNITS

Director (acting): Marco Malacarne; tel. (+32) 2-2955277.

Department A—Cosme, H2020 SME and EMFF

Head of Unit: Marco Malacarne; tel. (+32) 2-2955277.

UNIT A1—COSME
Head of Unit: José Puigpelat; tel. (+32) 2-2961494.

UNIT A2—H2020 SME
Head of Unit: Bernd Reichart; tel. (+32) 2-2954617.

UNIT A3—EMFF
Head of Unit: Alenka Kampl; tel. (+32) 2-2968773.

Department B—LIFE and H2020 Energy, Environment, Resources

Head of Unit (acting): Angelo Salsi; tel. (+32) 2-2969376.

Unit B1—H2020 Energy
Head of Unit: Vincent Berrutto; tel. (+32) 2-2968642.

Unit B2—H2020 Environment and Resources
Head of Unit: Arnoldas Milukas; tel. (+32) 2-2998414.

Unit B3—Life and CIP Eco-Innovation
Head of Unit: Angelo Salsi; tel. (+32) 2-2969376.

Department C—Finance and Administration

Team Leader: S. Anthis; tel. (+32) 2-2958491.

UNIT C1—H2020 FINANCE
Head of Unit (acting): Anne Burrill; tel. (+32) 2-2954388.

UNIT C2—ADMINISTRATION
Head of Unit: Natalia Martínez Páramo; tel. (+32) 2-2962543.

Research Executive Agency (REA)

1049 Brussels, Belgium; e-mail rea-info@ec.europa.eu; internet ec.europa.eu/rea

ADMINISTRATIVE UNITS

Director: Marc Tachelet; tel. (+32) 2-2967827.

Head of Department Excellent Science: Alessandra Luchetti; tel. (+32) 2-2960874.

Head of Department Industrial Leadership and Societal Challenges: Marc Bellens; tel. (+32) 2-2950942.

Head of Department of Administration, Finance and Support: Wilfried Beurms; tel. (+32) 2-2967357.

A1—Marie Skłodowska-Curie—Innovative Training Networks
Head of Unit: Klaus-Günther Barthel; tel. (+32) 2-2951242.

A2—Marie Skłodowska-Curie—Individual Fellowships: European
Head of Unit: Jean-Bernard Veyret; tel. (+32) 2-2990622.

A3—Marie Skłodowska-Curie—Research and Innovation Staff Exchange
Head of Unit: Fredrik Olsson Hector; tel. (+32) 2-2964255.

A4—Marie Skłodowska-Curie—COFUND, Researchers' Night and Individual Fellowships: Global
Head of Unit: François Willekens; tel. (+32) 2-2952596.

A5—Fostering Novel Ideas: FET-Open
Head of Unit: Timo Hallantie; tel. (+32) 2-2968167.

B1—Space Research
Head of Unit: Marko Curavić; tel. (+32) 2-2987425.

B2—Sustainable Resources for Food Security and Growth
Head of Unit: Kerstin Rosenow; tel. (+32) 2-2992807.

B3—Inclusive, Innovative and Reflective Societies
Head of Unit: Corinna Amting; tel. (+32) 2-2967542.

B4—Safeguarding Secure Society
Head of Unit: Angelo Marino; tel. (+32) 2-2966657.

B5—Spreading Exellence, Widening Participation, Science with and for Society
Head of Unit: Peter van der Zandt; tel. (+32) 2-2969505.

C1—Administration
Head of Unit: Bruno Wastin; tel. (+32) 2-2953138.

C2—Finance
Head of Unit: Hubert Cousin; tel. (+32) 2-2996377.

C3—Participant Validation
Head of Unit: Rita Bultynck-Lepoudre; tel. (+32) 2-2961340.

C4—Expert Management and Support
Head of Unit: Anya Oram; tel. (+32) 2-2997805

EURATOM AGENCIES

Euratom Supply Agency

EUFO 2161, rue Alcide de Gaspari, 2920 Luxembourg, Luxembourg; tel. (+352) 4301–34229; e-mail esa-aae@ec.europa.eu; internet ec.europa.eu/euroatom/index.html

Director-General: Marian O'Leary.

European Joint Undertaking for ITER and the Development of Fusion Energy

2 Josep Bla, Torres Diagonal Litoral, Edificio B3, 08019 Barcelona, Spain; tel. (+34) 93-3201800; e-mail info@f4e.europa.eu; internet fusionforenergy.europa.eu

Director: Johannes Schwemmer.

TREATIES

Summary of the Treaty of Paris establishing the European Coal and Steel Community (ECSC)

(effective 25 July 1952–23 July 2002; as amended by subsequent treaties, including the Merger Treaty, the Treaty on European Union, the Treaty of Amsterdam and the Treaty of Nice)

TITLE I: THE EUROPEAN COAL AND STEEL COMMUNITY

Articles 1–6

By this Treaty, the High Contracting Parties establish among themselves a European Coal and Steel Community, founded upon a common market, common objectives and common institutions. The European Coal and Steel Community shall have as its task to contribute, in harmony with the general economy of the Member States and through the establishment of a common market as provided in this Treaty, to economic expansion, growth of employment and a rising standard of living in the Member States. The Community shall bring about conditions which will of themselves ensure the most rational distribution of production at the highest possible level of productivity, while safeguarding continuity of employment and taking care not to provoke fundamental and persistent disturbances in the economies of Member States.

The institutions of the Community shall, within the limits of their respective powers, in the common interest:

(a) ensure an orderly supply to the common market, taking into account the needs of third countries;
(b) ensure that all comparably placed consumers in the common market have equal access to the sources of production;
(c) ensure the establishment of the lowest prices under such conditions that these prices do not result in higher prices charged by the same undertakings in other transactions or in a higher general price level at another time, while allowing necessary amortization and normal return on invested capital;
(d) ensure the maintenance of conditions which will encourage undertakings to expand and improve their production potential and to promote a policy of using natural resources rationally and avoiding their unconsidered exhaustion;
(e) promote improved working conditions and an improved standard of living for the workers in each of the industries for which it is responsible, so as to make possible their harmonization while the improvement is being maintained;
(f) promote the growth of international trade and ensure that equitable limits are observed in export pricing;
(g) promote the orderly expansion and modernization of production, and the improvement of quality, with no protection against competing industries that is not justified by improper action on their part or in their favour.

The following are recognized as incompatible with the common market for coal and steel and shall accordingly be prohibited within the Community, as provided in this Treaty:

(a) import and export duties, or charges having equivalent effect, and quantitative restrictions on the movement of products;
(b) measures or practices which discriminate between producers, between purchasers or between consumers, especially in prices and delivery terms or transport rates and conditions, and measures or practices which interfere with the purchaser's free choice of supplier;
(c) subsidies or aids granted by States, or special charges imposed by States, in any form whatsoever;
(d) restrictive practices which tend towards the sharing or exploiting of markets.

TITLE II: THE INSTITUTIONS OF THE COMMUNITY

Articles 7–45

The institutions of the Community shall be:

a Commission;
a European Parliament;
a Council;
a Court of Justice;
a Court of Auditors.

The Commission shall be assisted by a Consultative Committee.

In order to carry out the tasks assigned to it the Commission shall, in accordance with the provisions of this Treaty, take decisions, make recommendations or deliver opinions. Decisions shall be binding in their entirety. Recommendations shall be binding as to the aims to be pursued but shall leave the choice of the appropriate methods for achieving these aims to those to whom the recommendations are addressed. Opinions shall have no binding force.

TITLE III: ECONOMIC AND SOCIAL PROVISIONS

GENERAL PROVISIONS

Articles 46–48

To provide guidance, in line with the tasks assigned to the Community, on the course of action to be followed by all concerned, and to determine its own course of action, in accordance with the provisions of this Treaty, the Commission shall, in consultation:

(a) conduct a continuous study of market and price trends;
(b) periodically draw up programmes indicating foreseeable developments in production, consumption, exports and imports;
(c) periodically lay down general objectives for modernization, long-term planning of manufacture and expansion of productive capacity;

(d) take part, at the request of the Governments concerned, in studying the possibilities for re-employing, in existing industries or through the creation of new activities, workers made redundant by market developments or technical changes;

(e) obtain the information it requires to assess the possibilities for improving working conditions and living standards for workers in the industries within its province, and the threats to those standards.

FINANCIAL PROVISIONS

Articles 49–53

The Commission is empowered to procure the funds it requires to carry out its tasks by imposing levies on the production of coal and steel and by contracting loans. It may receive gifts. The levies shall be assessed annually on the various products according to their average value; the rate thereof shall not, however, exceed 1% unless previously authorized by the Council, acting by a two-thirds' majority. The mode of assessment and collection shall be determined by a general decision of the Commission taken after consulting the Council; cumulative imposition shall be avoided as far as possible.

INVESTMENT AND FINANCIAL AID

Articles 54–56

The Commission may facilitate the carrying out of investment programmes by granting loans to undertakings or by guaranteeing other loans which they may contract. It shall promote technical and economic research relating to the production and increased use of coal and steel and to occupational safety in the coal and steel industries. To this end it shall organize all appropriate contacts among existing research bodies.

If the introduction, within the framework of the general objectives of the Commission, of new technical processes or equipment should lead to an exceptionally large reduction in labour requirements in the coal or the steel industry, making it particularly difficult in one or more areas to re-employ redundant workers, the Commission, on application by the Governments concerned:

(a) shall obtain the opinion of the Consultative Committee;

(b) may facilitate, either in the industries within its jurisdiction or, with the assent of the Council, in any other industry, the financing of such programmes as it may approve for the creation of new and economically sound activities capable of reabsorbing the redundant workers into productive employment;

(c) shall provide: non-repayable aid towards the payment of tideover allowances to workers, the payment of resettlement allowances to workers, the financing of vocational retraining for workers having to change their employment.

PRODUCTION

Articles 57–59

In the sphere of production, the Commission shall give preference to the indirect means of action at its disposal, such as co-operation with Governments to regularize or influence general consumption, particularly that of the public services, and intervention in regard to prices and commercial policy as provided for in this Treaty.

In the event of a decline in demand, if the Commission considers that the Community is confronted with a period of manifest crisis and that the means of action provided for above are not sufficient to deal with this, it shall, after consulting the Consultative Committee and with the assent of the Council, establish a system of production quotas.

The Commission may impose fines upon undertakings which do not comply with decisions taken by it.

PRICES

Articles 60–64

Pricing practices contrary to the Articles of this Treaty shall be prohibited, in particular:

(a) unfair competitive practices, especially purely temporary or purely local price reductions tending towards the acquisition of a monopoly position within the common market;

(b) discriminatory practices involving, within the common market, the application by a seller of dissimilar conditions to comparable transactions, especially on the grounds of the nationality of the buyer.

The Commission may, for one or more of the products within its jurisdiction:

(a) fix maximum prices within the common market, if it finds that such a decision is necessary to attain the objectives set out in this Treaty;

(b) fix minimum prices within the common market, if it finds that a manifest crisis exists or is imminent and that such a decision is necessary to attain the objectives of the Treaty;

(c) fix, by methods appropriate to the nature of the export markets, minimum or maximum export prices.

AGREEMENTS AND CONCENTRATIONS

Articles 65–66

All agreements between undertakings, decisions by associations of undertakings and concerted practices tending directly or indirectly to prevent, restrict or distort normal competition within the common market shall be prohibited, and in particular those tending to fix or determine prices, to restrict or control production, technical development or investment, and to share markets, products, customers or sources of supply. However, the Commission shall authorize specialization agreements or joint-buying or joint-selling agreements in respect of particular products if it finds that:

(a) such specialization or such joint-buying or -selling will make for substantial improvement in the production or distribution of those products;

(b) the agreement in question is essential in order to achieve these results and is not more restrictive than is necessary for that purpose; and

(c) the agreement is not liable to give the undertakings concerned the power to determine the prices, or to control or restrict the production or marketing, of a substantial part of the products in question within the common market, or to shield them against effective competition from other undertakings within the common market.

If the Commission finds that public or private undertakings which, in law or in fact, hold or acquire in the market for one of the products within its jurisdiction a dominant position shielding them against effective competition in a substantial part of the common market, are using that position for purposes contrary to the objectives of the Treaty, it shall make to them such recommendations as may be appropriate to prevent the position from being so used. If these recommendations are not implemented satisfactorily within a reasonable time, the Commission shall, by decisions taken in consultation with the Government concerned, determine the prices and conditions of sale to be applied by the undertaking in question or draw up production or delivery programmes with which it must comply, subject to liability to the penalties provided for in this Treaty.

INTERFERENCE WITH CONDITIONS OF COMPETITION

Article 67

Any action by a Member State which is liable to have appreciable repercussions on conditions of competition in the coal or the steel industry shall be brought to the knowledge of the Commission by the Government concerned. If the action taken by that State is having harmful effects on the coal or steel undertakings within the jurisdiction of that State, the Commission may authorize it to grant aid to these undertakings. If the action taken by that State is having harmful effects on the coal or steel undertakings within the jurisdiction of other Member States, the Commission shall make a recommendation to that State with a view to remedying these effects by such measures as that State may consider most compatible with its own economic equilibrium.

WAGES AND MOVEMENT OF WORKERS

Articles 68–69

The methods used for fixing wages and welfare benefits in the several Member States shall not, in the case of the coal and steel industries, be affected by this Treaty, subject to provisions.

Member States undertake to remove any restriction based on nationality upon the employment in the coal and steel industries of workers who are nationals of Member States and have recognized qualifications in a coal mining or steel making occupation, subject to the limitations imposed by the basic requirements of health and public policy. They shall prohibit any discrimination in remuneration and working conditions between nationals and immigrant workers.

TRANSPORT

Article 70

It is recognized that the establishment of the common market necessitates the application of such rates and conditions for the carriage of coal and steel as will afford comparable price conditions to comparably placed consumers. Any discrimination in rates and conditions of carriage of every kind which is based on the country of origin or destination of products shall be prohibited in traffic between Member States.

COMMERCIAL POLICY

Articles 71–75

The powers of the Governments of Member States in matters of commercial policy shall not be affected by this Treaty, save as otherwise provided therein. The powers conferred on the Community by this Treaty in matters of commercial policy towards third countries may not exceed those accorded to Member States under international agreements to which they are parties. The Governments of Member States shall afford each other such mutual assistance as is necessary to implement measures recognized by the Commission as being in accordance with this Treaty and with existing international agreements.

Minimum rates below which Member States undertake not to lower their customs duties on coal and steel as against third countries, and maximum rates above which they undertake not to raise them, may be fixed by decision of the Council acting on a proposal from the Commission.

TITLE IV: GENERAL PROVISIONS

Articles 76–100

The Community shall enjoy in the territories of the Member States such privileges and immunities as are necessary for the performance of its tasks, under the conditions laid down in the Protocol annexed to this Treaty on the privileges and immunities of the European Communities.

The financial year shall run from 1 January to 31 December. Each institution of the Community shall, before 1 July, draw up estimates of its administrative expenditure. The Commission shall consolidate these estimates in a preliminary draft administrative budget.

This Treaty shall apply to the European territories of the High Contracting Parties. It shall also apply to European territories for whose external relations a signatory State is responsible, subject to certain exceptions stipulated in Treaties of Accession of new Member States. Each High Contracting Party undertakes to extend to the other Member States the preferential treatment which it enjoys with respect to coal and steel in the non-European territories under its jurisdiction.

The establishment of the Community shall in no way prejudice the system of ownership of the undertakings to which this Treaty applies.

Member States undertake to take all appropriate measures, whether general or particular, to ensure fulfilment of the obligations resulting from decisions and recommendations of the institutions of the Community and to facilitate the performance of the Community's tasks.

Officials of the Commission entrusted by it with tasks of inspection shall enjoy in the territories of Member States, to the full extent required for the performance of their duties, such rights and powers as are granted by the laws of these States to their own revenue officials.

If a State has not fulfilled its obligation under this Treaty by the time limit set by the Commission, or if it brings an action which is dismissed, the Commission may, with the assent of the Council acting by a two-thirds' majority:

(a) suspend the payment of any sums which it may be liable to pay to the State in question under this Treaty;

(b) take measures, or authorize the other Member States to take measures, in order to correct the effects of the infringement of the obligation.

Decisions of the Commission which impose a pecuniary obligation shall be enforceable.

Where a decision has been taken to suspend the voting rights of the representative of the government of a Member State in accordance with Article F.1(2) of the Treaty on European Union, these voting rights shall also be suspended with regard to this Treaty.

Summary of the Treaty of Rome establishing the European Atomic Energy Community (Euratom)

(effective from 1 January 1958; as amended by subsequent treaties, including the Merger Treaty, the Treaty on European Union, the Treaty of Amsterdam and the Treaty of Nice)

TITLE I: THE TASKS OF THE COMMUNITY

Articles 1–3

By this Treaty the High Contracting Parties establish among themselves a European Atomic Energy Community (Euratom). It shall be the task of the Community to contribute to the raising of the standard of living in the Member States and to the development of relations with the other countries by creating the conditions necessary for the speedy establishment and growth of nuclear industries. In order to perform its task, the Community shall, as provided in this Treaty:

(a) promote research and ensure the dissemination of technical information;
(b) establish uniform safety standards to protect the health of workers and of the general public and ensure that they are applied;
(c) facilitate investment and ensure, particularly by encouraging ventures on the part of undertakings, the establishment of the basic installations necessary for the development of nuclear energy in the Community;
(d) ensure that all users in the Community receive a regular and equitable supply of ores and nuclear fuels;
(e) make certain, by appropriate supervision, that nuclear materials are not diverted to purposes other than those for which they are intended;
(f) exercise the right of ownership conferred upon it with respect to special fissile materials;
(g) ensure wide commercial outlets and access to the best technical facilities by the creation of a common market in specialized materials and equipment, by the free movement of capital for investment in the field of nuclear energy and by freedom of employment for specialists within the Community;
(h) establish with other countries and international organizations such relations as will foster progress in the peaceful uses of nuclear energy.

The tasks entrusted to the Community shall be carried out by the following institutions:

a European Parliament;
a Council;
a Commission;
a Court of Justice;
a Court of Auditors.

The Council and the Commission shall be assisted by an Economic and Social Committee acting in an advisory capacity.

TITLE II: PROVISIONS FOR THE ENCOURAGEMENT OF PROGRESS IN THE FIELD OF NUCLEAR ENERGY

PROMOTION OF RESEARCH

Articles 4–11

The Commission shall be responsible for promoting and facilitating nuclear research in the Member States and for complementing it by carrying out a Community research and training programme. To encourage the carrying out of research programmes communicated to it the Commission may:

(a) provide financial assistance within the framework of research contracts, without, however, offering subsidies;
(b) supply, either free of charge or against payment, for carrying out such programmes, any source materials or special fissile materials which it has available;
(c) place installations, equipment or expert assistance at the disposal of Member States, persons or undertakings, either free of charge or against payment;
(d) promote joint financing by the Member States, persons or undertakings concerned.

After consulting the Scientific and Technical Committee, the Commission shall establish a Joint Nuclear Research Centre. The Centre shall ensure that a uniform nuclear terminology and a standard system of measurements are established.

DISSEMINATION OF INFORMATION

Articles 12–29

Information over which the Community has power of disposal

Member States, persons or undertakings shall have the right, on application to the Commission, to obtain non-exclusive licences under patents, provisionally protected patent rights, utility models or patent applications owned by the Community, where they are able to make effective use of the inventions covered thereby. Under the same conditions, the Commission shall grant sub-licences under patents, provisionally protected patent rights, utility models or patent applications, where the Community holds contractual licences conferring power to do so.

Security provisions

Information which the Community acquires as a result of carrying out its research programme, and the disclosure of which is liable to harm the defence interests of one or more Member States, shall be subject to a security system in accordance with the provisions of this Treaty.

HEALTH AND SAFETY

Articles 30–39

Basic standards shall be laid down within the Community for the protection of the health of workers and the general public against the dangers arising from ionizing radiations. Each Member State shall lay down the appropriate provisions, whether by legislation, regulation or administrative action, to ensure compliance with the basic standards which have been established and shall take the necessary measures with regard to teaching, education and vocational training; shall establish the facilities necessary to carry out continuous monitoring of the level of radioactivity in the air, water and soil and to ensure compliance with the basic standards; and shall provide the Commission with such general data relating to any plan for the disposal of radioactive waste in whatever form as will make it possible to determine whether the implementation of such a plan is liable to result in the radioactive contamination of the water, soil or airspace of another Member State.

INVESTMENT

Articles 40–44

In order to stimulate action by persons and undertakings and to facilitate co-ordinated development of their investment in the nuclear field, the Commission shall periodically publish illustrative programmes indicating, in particular, nuclear energy production targets and all the types of investment required for their attainment.

JOINT UNDERTAKINGS

Articles 45–51

Undertakings which are of fundamental importance to the development of the nuclear industry in the Community may be established as Joint Undertakings. Every project for establishing a Joint Undertaking, whether originating from the Commission, a Member State or any other quarter, shall be the subject of an inquiry by the Commission, and shall be established by Council decision.

SUPPLIES

Articles 52–76

The supply of ores, source materials and special fissile materials shall be ensured, in accordance with the provisions of this Treaty, by means of a common supply policy on the principle of equal access to sources of supply. For this purpose all practices designed to secure a privileged position for certain users shall be prohibited, and an Agency is hereby established; it shall have a right of option on ores, source materials and special fissile materials produced in the territories of Member States and an exclusive right to conclude contracts relating to the supply of ores, source materials and special fissile materials coming from inside the Community or from outside.

The Agency

The Agency shall be under the supervision of the Commission, which shall issue directives to it, possess a right of veto over its decisions and appoint its Director-General and Deputy Director-General. The Member States shall be responsible for ensuring that the Agency may operate freely in their territories.

Ores, source materials and special fissile materials coming from inside the Community

Special fissile materials may be exported only through the Agency. Potential users shall periodically inform the Agency of the supplies they require, specifying the quantities, the physical and chemical nature, the place of origin, the intended use, delivery dates and price terms, which are to form the terms and conditions of the supply contract which they wish to conclude. Similarly, producers shall inform the Agency of offers which they are able to make, stating all the specifications, and, in particular, the duration of contracts, required to enable their production programmes to be drawn up. The Agency shall inform all potential users of the offers and of the volume of applications which it has received, and when the Agency has received all such orders, it shall make known the terms on which it can meet them. If the Agency cannot meet in their entirety all the orders received, it shall share out the supplies proportionately among the orders relating to each offer. Agency rules, which shall require approval by the Commission, shall determine the manner in which demand is to be balanced against supply.

Ores, source materials and special fissile materials coming from outside the Community

The Agency, acting where appropriate within the framework of agreements concluded between the Community and a third State or an international organization, shall, subject to the exceptions provided for in this Treaty, have the exclusive right to enter into agreements or contracts whose principal aim is the supply of ores, source materials or special fissile materials coming from outside the Community.

Prices

Save where exceptions are provided for in this Treaty, prices shall be determined as a result of balancing supply against demand. Pricing practices designed to secure a privileged position for certain users in violation of the principle of equal access laid down in the provisions of this Chapter shall be prohibited. The Council may fix prices.

Provisions relating to supply policy

The Commission may give financial support to prospecting programmes in the territories of Member States. If, although the prospects for extraction appear economically justified on a long-term basis, prospecting activities and the expansion of mining operations continue to be markedly inadequate, the Member State concerned shall, for as long as it has failed to remedy this situation, be deemed to have waived, both for itself and for its nationals, the right of equal access to other sources of supply within the Community.

SAFEGUARDS

Articles 77–85

The Commission shall satisfy itself that, in the territories of Member States:

(a) ores, source materials and special fissile materials are not diverted from their intended uses as declared by the users;

(b) the provisions relating to supply and any particular safeguarding obligations assumed by the Community under an agreement concluded with a third State or an international organization are complied with.

The Commission may send inspectors into the territories of Member States, who shall at all times have access to all places and data and to all persons who, by reason of their occupation, deal with materials, equipment or installations. In the event of an infringement on the part of persons or undertakings of the obligations imposed on them by these conditions, the Commission may impose sanctions on such persons or undertakings. Decisions taken by the Commission shall be enforceable.

Treaties

PROPERTY OWNERSHIP

Articles 86–91

Special fissile materials shall be the property of the Community, and Member States, persons or undertakings shall have the unlimited right of use and consumption of special fissile materials which have properly come into their possession.

THE NUCLEAR COMMON MARKET

Articles 92–100

Member States shall prohibit between themselves all customs duties on imports and exports or charges having equivalent effect, and all quantitative restrictions on imports and exports for the goods and products covered by this Treaty. Non-European territories under the jurisdiction of a Member State may, however, continue to levy import and export duties or charges having equivalent effect where they are of an exclusively fiscal nature. The rates of such duties and charges and the system governing them shall not give rise to any discrimination between that State and the other Member States.

The Member States shall abolish all restrictions based on nationality affecting the right of nationals of any Member State to take skilled employment in the field of nuclear energy, subject to the limitations resulting from the basic requirements of public policy, public security or public health.

EXTERNAL RELATIONS

Articles 101–106

The Community may, within the limits of its powers and jurisdiction, enter into obligations by concluding agreements or contracts with a third State, an international organization or a national of a third State. No person or undertaking concluding or renewing an agreement or contract with a third State, an international organization or a national of a third State after 1 January 1958 or, for acceding States, after the date of their accession, may invoke that agreement or contract in order to evade the obligations imposed by this Treaty.

TITLE III: PROVISIONS GOVERNING THE INSTITUTIONS

Articles 107–160

The Council and the Commission shall consult each other and shall settle by common accord their methods of co-operation. The Commission shall adopt its rules of procedure so as to ensure that both it and its departments operate in accordance with the provisions of this Treaty. It shall ensure that these rules are published.

PROVISIONS COMMON TO SEVERAL INSTITUTIONS

Articles 161–164

In order to carry out their task the Council and the Commission shall, in accordance with the provisions of this Treaty, make regulations, issue directives, take decisions, make recommendations or deliver opinions. A regulation shall have general application. It shall be binding in its entirety and directly applicable in all Member States. A directive shall be binding, as to the result to be achieved, upon each Member State to which it is addressed, but shall leave to the national authorities the choice of form and methods. A decision shall be binding in its entirety upon those to whom it is addressed. Recommendations and opinions shall have no binding force.

THE ECONOMIC AND SOCIAL COMMITTEE

Articles 165–170

An Economic and Social Committee is hereby established. It shall have advisory status. The committee shall consist of representatives of the various categories of economic and social activity. The Committee may be consulted by the European Parliament.

TITLE IV: FINANCIAL PROVISIONS

Articles 171–183

Estimates shall be drawn up for each financial year of all revenue and expenditure of the Community, other than those of the Agency and the Joint Undertakings, and such revenue and expenditure shall be shown either in the operating budget or in the research and investment budget. The revenue and expenditure shown in each budget shall be in balance. The revenue and expenditure of the Agency, which shall operate in accordance with commercial principles, shall be budgeted for in a special account. Without prejudice to other revenue, the budget shall be financed wholly from own resources.

TITLE V: GENERAL PROVISIONS

Articles 184–208

In each of the Member States, the Community shall enjoy the most extensive legal capacity accorded to legal persons under their laws; it may, in particular, acquire or dispose of movable and immovable property and may be a party to legal proceedings. To this end, the Community shall be represented by the Commission.

The officials and other servants of the European Coal and Steel Community, the European Economic Community and the European Atomic Energy Community shall, at the date of entry into force of this Treaty, become officials and other servants of the European Communities and form part of the single administration of these Communities.

The European Communities shall enjoy in the territories of the Member States such privileges and immunities as are necessary for the performance of their tasks, under the conditions laid down in the Protocol annexed to this Treaty. The same shall apply to the European Investment Bank.

Member States shall take all appropriate measures, whether general or particular, to ensure fulfilment of the obligations arising out of this Treaty or resulting from action taken by the institutions of the Community. They shall facilitate the achievement of the Community's tasks. They shall abstain from any measure which could jeopardize the attainment of the objectives of this Treaty. The institutions of the Community, the Agency and the Joint Undertakings shall, in applying this Treaty, comply with the conditions of access to ores, source materials and special fissile materials laid down in national rules and regulations made for reasons of public policy or public health.

Save as otherwise provided, this Treaty shall apply to the European territories of Member States and to non-European territories under their jurisdiction. It shall also apply to the European territories for whose external relations a Member

State is responsible, subject to certain exceptions stipulated in Treaties of Accession of new Member States.

It shall be for the Commission to ensure the maintenance of all appropriate relations with the organs of the United Nations, of its specialized agencies and of the World Trade Organization; it shall also maintain such relations as are appropriate with all international organizations. The Community shall establish all appropriate forms of co-operation with the Council of Europe, and shall establish close co-operation with the Organisation for Economic Co-operation and Development, the details to be determined by common accord. The provisions of this Treaty shall not preclude the existence or completion of regional unions between Belgium and Luxembourg, or between Belgium, Luxembourg and the Netherlands, to the extent that the objectives of these regional unions are not attained by application of this Treaty.

Where a decision has been taken to suspend the voting rights of the representative of the government of a Member State in accordance with Article 7(2) of the Treaty on European Union, these voting rights shall also be suspended with regard to this Treaty.

The Community may conclude with one or more States or international organizations agreements establishing an association involving reciprocal rights and obligations, common action and special procedures. These agreements shall be concluded by the Council, acting unanimously after consulting the European Parliament.

This Treaty is concluded for an unlimited period.

Summary of the Treaty of Rome establishing the European Economic Community (EEC)

(effective from 1 January 1958; as amended by subsequent treaties, including the Merger Treaty, the Single European Act, the Treaty on European Union, the Treaty of Amsterdam, the Treaty of Rome and the Treaty of Nice)

Note: The Treaty of Amsterdam, as well as providing in its Part One for substantive amendments to the Treaty of Rome, in its Part Two amended the Treaty and its annexes and protocols, for the purpose of deleting lapsed provisions of the Treaty and adapting in consequence the text of certain of its provisions. It also renumbered the Articles of the Treaty to take into account those Articles that had been inserted or had lapsed.

The first paragraphs of Article 8 of the Treaty on European Union read as follows:

The Treaty establishing the European Economic Community shall be amended in accordance with the provisions of this Article, in order to establish a European Community.

Throughout the Treaty: The term 'European Economic Community' shall be replaced by the term 'European Community'.

Under the Terms of the Treaty of Lisbon, the Treaty establishing the European Community has been renamed as the Treaty on the Functioning of the European Union (TFEU).

PART ONE: PRINCIPLES

Articles 1–16

The Community shall have as its task, by establishing a common market and an economic and monetary union and by implementing the common policies or activities referred to in Articles 3 and 4, to promote throughout the Community a harmonious, balanced and sustainable development of economic activities, a high level of employment and of social protection, equality between men and women, sustainable and non-inflationary growth, a high degree of competitiveness and convergence of economic performance, a high level of protection and improvement of the quality of the environment, the raising of the standard of living and quality of life, and economic and social cohesion and solidarity among Member States. With these aims in view, the activities of the Community will include:

(a) the prohibition between Member States of customs duties and of quantitative restrictions in regard to the importation and exportation of goods, as well as of all other measures with equivalent effect;
(b) a common commercial policy;
(c) an internal market characterized by the abolition, as between Member States, of obstacles to the free movement of goods, persons, services and capital;
(d) measures concerning the entry and movement of persons as provided for in Title IV;
(e) a common policy in the sphere of agriculture and fisheries;
(f) a common policy in the sphere of transport;
(g) a system ensuring that competition in the internal market is not distorted;
(h) the approximation of the laws of Member States to the extent required for the functioning of the common market;
(i) the promotion of co-ordination between employment policies of the Member States with a view to enhancing their effectiveness by developing a co-ordinated strategy for employment;
(j) a policy in the social sphere comprising a European Social Fund;
(k) the strengthening of economic and social cohesion;
(l) a policy in the sphere of the environment;
(m) the strengthening of the competitiveness of Community industry;
(n) the promotion of research and technological development;
(o) encouragement for the establishment and development of trans-European networks;
(p) a contribution to the attainment of a high level of health protection;
(q) a contribution to education and training of quality and to the flowering of the cultures of the Member States;
(r) a policy in the sphere of development co-operation;
(s) the association of the overseas countries and territories in order to increase trade and promote jointly economic and social development;
(t) a contribution to the strengthening of consumer protection;
(u) measures in the spheres of energy, civil protection and tourism.

In all the activities referred to in this Article, the Community shall aim to eliminate inequalities, and to promote equality, between men and women.

Environmental protection requirements must be integrated into the definition and implementation of the Community policies and activities referred to in Article 3, in particular with a view to promoting sustainable development.

Member States which intend to establish closer co-operation between themselves may be authorized, subject to Articles 43 and 44 of the Treaty on European Union, to make use of the institutions, procedures and mechanisms laid down by this Treaty.

The activities of the Member States and the Community shall include the adoption of an economic policy which is based on the close co-ordination of Member States' economic policies, on the internal market and on the definition of common objectives, and conducted in accordance with the principle of an open market economy with free competition. These activities shall include the irrevocable fixing of exchange rates leading to the introduction of a single currency, the European Currency Unit, and the definition and conduct of a single monetary policy and exchange-rate policy, the primary objective of both of which shall be to maintain price stability and, without prejudice to this objective, to support the general economic policies in the Community, in accordance with the principle of an open market economy with free competition. These activities of the Member States and the Community shall entail compliance with the following guiding principles: stable prices, sound public finances and monetary conditions and a sustainable balance of payments.

The Community shall act within the limits of the powers conferred upon it by this Treaty and of the objectives assigned to it therein.

In areas which do not fall within its exclusive competence, the Community shall take action, in accordance with the principle of subsidiarity, only if and in so far as the objectives of the proposed action cannot be sufficiently achieved by the Member States and can therefore, by reason of the scale or effects of the proposed action, be better achieved by the Community.

Any action by the Community shall not go beyond what is necessary to achieve the objectives of this Treaty.

The tasks entrusted to the Community shall be carried out by the following institutions: a European Parliament; a Council; a Commission; a Court of Justice; a Court of Auditors. A European System of Central Banks (ESCB) and a European Central Bank (ECB) shall be established. A European Investment Bank is hereby established.

The Council, acting unanimously on a proposal from the Commission and after consulting the European Parliament, may take appropriate action to combat discrimination based on sex, racial or ethnic origin, religion or belief, disability, age or sexual orientation.

The Community shall adopt measures with the aim of progressively establishing the internal market over a period expiring on 31 December 1992.

PART TWO: CITIZENSHIP OF THE UNION

Articles 17–22

Citizenship of the Union is hereby established. Every person holding the nationality of a Member State shall be a citizen of the Union. Citizenship of the Union shall complement and not replace national citizenship. Every citizen of the Union shall have the right to move and reside freely within the territory of the Member States, subject to the limitations and conditions laid down in this Treaty and by the measures adopted to give it effect. Every citizen of the Union residing in a Member State of which he is not a national shall have the right to vote and to stand as a candidate at municipal elections and elections to the European Parliament in the Member State in which he resides, under the same conditions as nationals of that State. Every citizen of the Union shall, in the territory of a third country in which the Member State of which he is a national is not represented, be entitled to protection by the diplomatic or consular authorities of any Member State, on the same conditions as the nationals of that State.

PART THREE: COMMUNITY POLICIES

TITLE I: FREE MOVEMENT OF GOODS

The Customs Union

Articles 23–27

Customs duties on imports and exports and charges having equivalent effect shall be prohibited between Member States. This prohibition shall also apply to customs duties of a fiscal nature.

Common Customs Tariff duties shall be fixed by the Council acting by a qualified majority on a proposal from the Commission.

Prohibition of Quantitative Restrictions between Member States

Articles 28–31

Quantitative restrictions on imports and all measures having equivalent effect shall be prohibited between Member States. Quantitative restrictions on exports, and all measures having equivalent effect, shall be prohibited between Member States. These provisions shall not be an obstacle to prohibitions or restrictions in respect of importation, exportation or transit which are justified on grounds of public morality, health or safety, the protection of human or animal life or health, the preservation of plant life, the protection of national treasures of artistic, historic or archaeological value or the protection of industrial and commercial property. Such prohibitions or restrictions shall not, however, constitute either a means of arbitrary discrimination or a disguised restriction on trade between Member States. Member States shall adjust any state monopolies of a commercial character in such a manner as will ensure the exclusion of all discrimination between the nationals of Member States in regard to conditions of supply and marketing of goods. These provisions shall apply to any body by means of which a Member State shall de jure or de facto, either directly or indirectly, control or appreciably influence importation or exportation between Member States, and also to monopolies assigned by the State. In the case of a commercial monopoly which is accompanied by regulations designed to facilitate the marketing or the valorization of agricultural products, it should be ensured that in the application of these provisions equivalent guarantees are provided in respect of the employment and standard of living of the producers concerned.

TITLE II: AGRICULTURE

Articles 32–38

The common market shall extend to agriculture and trade in agricultural products. The common agricultural policy shall have as its objectives:

(a) the increase of agricultural productivity by developing technical progress and by ensuring the rational

development of agricultural production and the optimum utilization of the factors of production, particularly labour;
(b) the ensurance thereby of a fair standard of living for the agricultural population;
(c) the stabilization of markets;
(d) regular supplies;
(e) reasonable prices in supplies to consumers.

Due account must be taken of the particular character of agricultural activities, arising from the social structure of agriculture and from structural and natural disparities between the various agricultural regions; of the need to make the appropriate adjustments gradually; and of the fact that in Member States agriculture constitutes a sector which is closely linked with the economy as a whole. In order to attain the objectives of a common agricultural policy, a common organization of agricultural markets shall be effected.

TITLE III: FREE MOVEMENT OF PERSONS, SERVICES AND CAPITAL

Workers

Articles 39–42

The free movement of workers shall be ensured within the Community, involving the abolition of any discrimination based on nationality between workers of the Member States as regards employment, remuneration and other working conditions. This shall include the right to accept offers of employment actually made, to move about freely for this purpose within the territory of the Member States, to stay in any Member State in order to carry on an employment in conformity with the legislative and administrative provisions governing the employment of the workers of that State, and to live, on conditions which shall be the subject of implementing regulations laid down by the Commission, in the territory of a Member State after having been employed there. (These provisions do not apply to employment in the public administration.)

In the field of social security, the Council shall adopt the measures necessary to effect the free movement of workers. To this end, it shall make arrangements to secure for migrant workers and their dependants aggregation, for the purpose of acquiring and retaining the right to benefit and of calculating the amount of benefit, of all periods taken into account under the laws of the several countries; and payment of benefits to persons resident in the territories of Member States.

Right of Establishment

Articles 43–48

Restrictions on the freedom of establishment of nationals of a Member State in the territory of another Member State shall be prohibited, nor may any new restrictions of a similar character be introduced. Such prohibition shall also extend to restrictions on the setting-up of agencies, branches or subsidiaries. Freedom of establishment shall include the right to engage in and carry on non-wage-earning activities and also to set up and manage enterprises and companies under the conditions laid down by the law of the country of establishment for its own nationals, subject to the provisions of this Treaty relating to capital.

Services

Articles 49–55

Restrictions on the free supply of services within the Community shall be prohibited in respect of nationals of Member States who are established in a state of the Community other than that of the person to whom the services are supplied; no new restrictions of a similar character may be introduced.

The Council, acting by a qualified majority on a proposal of the Commission, may extend the benefit of these provisions to cover services supplied by nationals of any third country who are established within the Community.

Particular services involved are activities of an industrial or artisan character and those of the liberal professions.

Capital

Articles 56–60

Within the framework of the provisions set out in this Chapter, all restrictions on the movement of capital between Member States and between Member States and third countries shall be prohibited.

TITLE IV: VISAS, ASYLUM, IMMIGRATION AND OTHER POLICIES RELATED TO FREE MOVEMENT OF PERSONS

Articles 61–69

In order to establish progressively an area of freedom, security and justice, the Council shall adopt within a period of five years after the entry into force of the Treaty of Amsterdam, measures aimed at ensuring the free movement of persons, in conjunction with directly related flanking measures with respect to external border controls, asylum and immigration, and measures to prevent and combat crime; other measures in the fields of asylum, immigration and safeguarding the rights of nationals of third countries; measures in the field of judicial co-operation in civil matters; appropriate measures to encourage and strengthen administrative co-operation; and measures in the field of police and judicial co-operation in criminal matters aimed at a high level of security by preventing and combating crime within the Union.

The Council shall, within a period of five years after the entry into force of the Treaty of Amsterdam, adopt measures with a view to ensuring the absence of any controls on the persons, be they citizens of the Union or nationals of third countries, when crossing internal borders; and measures on the crossing of the external borders of the Member States.

The Council shall, within a period of five years after the entry into force of the Treaty of Amsterdam, adopt measures on asylum, in accordance with the Geneva Convention of 28 July 1951 and the Protocol of 31 January 1967 relating to the status of refugees and other relevant treaties; measures on refugees and displaced persons who cannot return to their country of origin or who otherwise need international protection; measures on immigration policy; and measures defining the rights and conditions under which nationals of third countries who are legally resident in a Member State may reside in other Member States.

The application of this Title shall be subject to the provisions of the Protocol on the position of the United Kingdom and Ireland and to the Protocol on the position of Denmark.

TITLE V: TRANSPORT

Articles 70–80

With a view to establishing a common transport policy, the Council of Ministers shall, acting in accordance with the procedure referred to in Article 251 and after consulting the Economic and Social Committee and the Committee of the Regions, lay down common rules applicable to international transport to or from the territory of a Member State or passing across the territory of one or more Member States, conditions under which non-resident carriers may operate transport services within a Member State, measures to improve transport safety and any other appropriate provisions. Until these have been enacted and unless the Council of Ministers gives its unanimous consent, no Member State shall apply the various provisions governing this subject on 1 January 1958 or, for acceding States, the date of their accession in such a way as to make them less favourable, in their direct or indirect effect, for carriers of other Member States by comparison with its own national carriers.

Any discrimination which consists in the application by a carrier, in respect of the same goods conveyed in the same circumstances, of transport rates and conditions which differ on the ground of the country of origin or destination of the goods carried, shall be abolished in the traffic of the Community.

A Committee with consultative status, composed of experts appointed by the Governments of the Member States, shall be established and attached to the Commission, without prejudice to the powers of the Economic and Social Committee.

TITLE VI: COMMON RULES ON COMPETITION, TAXATION AND APPROXIMATION OF LAWS

Rules on Competition

Articles 81–89

Rules applying to undertakings:

The following practices by enterprises are prohibited: the direct or indirect fixing of purchase or selling prices or of any other trading conditions; the limitation of control of production, markets, technical development of investment; market-sharing or the sharing of sources of supply; the application to parties to transactions of unequal terms in respect of equivalent supplies, thereby placing them at a competitive disadvantage; the subjection of the conclusion of a contract to the acceptance by a party of additional supplies which, either by their nature or according to commercial usage, have no connection with the subject of such contract. The provisions may be declared inapplicable if the agreements neither impose on the enterprises concerned any restrictions not indispensable to the attainment of improved production, distribution or technical progress, nor enable enterprises to eliminate competition in respect of a substantial proportion of the goods concerned.

Aids granted by States:

Any aid granted by a Member State or granted by means of state resources which is contrary to the purposes of the Treaty is forbidden. The following shall be deemed to be compatible with the common market:

(a) aids of a social character granted without discrimination to individual consumers;

(b) aids intended to remedy damage caused by natural calamities or other extraordinary events;

(c) aids granted to the economy of certain regions of the Federal German Republic affected by the division of Germany, to the extent that they are necessary to compensate for the economic disadvantages caused by the division.

The following may be deemed to be compatible with the common market:

(a) aids intended to promote the economic development of regions where the standard of living is abnormally low or where there exists serious underemployment;

(b) aids intended to promote the execution of important projects of common European interest or to remedy a serious economic disturbance of the economy of a Member State;

(c) aids intended to facilitate the development of certain activities or of certain economic regions, provided that such aids do not change trading conditions to such a degree as would be contrary to the common interest;

(d) aid to promote culture and heritage conservation where such aid does not affect trading conditions and competition in the Community to an extent that is contrary to the common interest;

(e) such other categories of aids as may be specified by a decision of the Council of Ministers acting on a proposal of the Commission.

The Commission is charged to examine constantly all systems of aids existing in the Member States, and may require any Member State to abolish or modify any aid which it finds to be in conflict with the principles of the common market.

Tax Provisions

Articles 90–93

A Member State shall not impose, directly or indirectly, on the products of other Member States, any internal charges of any kind in excess of those applied directly or indirectly to like domestic products. Furthermore, a Member State shall not impose on the product of other Member States any internal charges of such a nature as to afford indirect protection to other productions. Products exported to any Member State may not benefit from any drawback on internal charges in excess of those charges imposed directly or indirectly on them.

Approximation of Laws

Articles 94–97

The Council shall, acting unanimously on a proposal of the Commission and after consulting the European Parliament and the Economic and Social Committee, issue directives for the approximation of such laws, regulations or administrative provisions of the Member States as directly affect the establishment or functioning of the common market.

Where the Commission finds that a difference between the provisions laid down by law, regulation or administrative action in Member States is distorting the conditions of competition in the common market and that the resultant distortion needs to be eliminated, it shall consult the Member States concerned. If such consultation does not result in an agreement, the Council shall, on a proposal from the Commission, acting by a qualified majority, issue the necessary directives.

TITLE VII: ECONOMIC AND MONETARY POLICY

Economic Policy

Articles 98–104

Member States shall conduct their economic policies with a view to contributing to the achievement of the objectives of the Community. The Member States and the Community shall act in accordance with the principle of an open market economy with free competition, favouring an efficient allocation of resources.

Member States shall regard their economic policies as a matter of common concern and shall co-ordinate them within the Council. The Council shall, acting by a qualified majority on a recommendation from the Commission, formulate a draft for the broad guidelines of the economic policies of the Member States and of the Community, and shall report its findings to the European Council; the European Council shall discuss a conclusion on the broad guidelines of the economic policies of the Member States and of the Community; on the basis of this conclusion, the Council shall, acting by a qualified majority, adopt a recommendation setting out these broad guidelines. In order to ensure closer co-ordination of economic policies and sustained convergence of the economic performances of the Member States, the Council shall, on the basis of reports submitted by the Commission, monitor economic developments in each of the Member States and in the Community as well as the consistency of economic policies, and regularly carry out an overall assessment. Where it is established that the economic policies of a Member State are not consistent with the broad guidelines referred to above or that they risk jeopardizing the proper functioning of economic and monetary union, the Council may, acting by a qualified majority on a recommendation from the Commission, make the necessary recommendations to the Member State concerned.

The Council may, acting unanimously on a proposal from the Commission, decide upon the measures appropriate to the economic situation, in particular if severe difficulties arise in the supply of certain products. Where a Member State is in difficulties or is seriously threatened with severe difficulties caused by exceptional occurrences beyond its control, the Council may, acting unanimously on a proposal from the Commission, grant, under certain conditions, Community financial assistance to the Member State concerned. Where the severe difficulties are caused by natural disasters, the Council shall act by qualified majority.

Overdraft facilities or any other type of credit facility with the ECB or with the central banks of the Member States in favour of Community institutions or bodies, central governments, regional, local or other public authorities, other bodies governed by public law, or public undertakings of Member States shall be prohibited, as shall the purchase directly from them by the ECB or national central banks of debt instruments. This shall not apply to publicly owned credit institutions which, in the context of the supply of reserves by central banks, shall be given the same treatment by national central banks and the ECB as private credit institutions.

Any measure, not based on prudential considerations, establishing privileged access by Community institutions or bodies, central governments, regional, local or other public authorities, other bodies governed by public law, or public undertakings of Member States to financial institutions shall be prohibited.

The Community shall not be liable for or assume the commitments of central governments, regional, local or other public authorities, other bodies governed by public law, or public undertakings of any Member State, without prejudice to mutual financial guarantees for the joint execution of a specific project. A Member State shall not be liable for or assume the commitments of central governments, regional, local or other public authorities, other bodies governed by public law or public undertakings of another Member State, without prejudice to mutual financial guarantees for the joint execution of a specific project.

Member States shall avoid excessive government deficits. The Commission shall monitor the development of the budgetary situation and of the stock of government debt in the Member States with a view to identifying gross errors. Where the existence of an excessive deficit is decided by the Council, acting by a qualified majority on a recommendation from the Commission, the Council shall make recommendations to the Member State concerned with a view to bringing that situation to an end within a given period. If a Member State persists in failing to put into practice the recommendations of the Council, the Council may decide to give notice to the Member State to take, within a specified time-limit, measures for the deficit reduction which is judged necessary by the Council in order to remedy the situation. As long as a Member State fails to comply with a decision taken in accordance with the above, the Council may decide to apply or, as the case may be, intensify one or more of the following measures: to require the Member State concerned to publish additional information, to be specified by the Council, before issuing bonds and securities; to invite the European Investment Bank to reconsider its lending policy towards the Member State concerned; to require the Member State concerned to make a non-interest-bearing deposit of an appropriate size with the Community until the excessive deficit has, in the view of the Council, been corrected; to impose fines of an appropriate size.

Monetary Policy

Articles 105–111

The primary objective of the European System of Central Banks (ESCB) shall be to maintain price stability. Without prejudice to the objective of price stability, the ESCB shall support the general economic policies in the Community with a view to contributing to the achievement of the objectives of the Community. The ESCB shall act in accordance with the principle of an open market economy with free competition, favouring an efficient allocation of resources, and in compliance with the principles set out in the Treaty. The basic tasks to be carried out through the ESCB shall be to define and implement the monetary policy of the Community, to conduct foreign-exchange operations, to hold and manage the official foreign reserves of the Member States and to promote the smooth operation of payment systems.

The ECB shall have the exclusive right to authorize the issue of banknotes within the Community. The ECB and the national central banks may issue such notes. Member States may issue coins subject to approval by the ECB of the volume of the issue.

In order to carry out the tasks entrusted to the ESCB, the ECB shall make regulations, take decisions, make recommendations and deliver opinions.

Institutional Provisions

Articles 112–115

In order to promote co-ordination of the policies of Member States to the full extent needed for the functioning of the internal market, a Monetary Committee with advisory status is hereby set up to keep under review the monetary and financial situation of the Member States and of the Community and the general payments system of the Member States and to report regularly thereon to the Council and to the Commission; to deliver opinions at the request of the Council or of the Commission, or on its own initiative for submission to those institutions; and to examine, at least once a year, the situation regarding the movement of capital and the freedom of payments, as they result from the application of this Treaty and of measures adopted by the Council. The Member States and the Commission shall each appoint two members of the Monetary Committee. At the start of the third stage, an Economic and Financial Committee shall be set up; the Monetary Committee shall be dissolved.

Transitional Provisions

Articles 116–124

The second stage for achieving economic and monetary union shall begin on 1 January 1994. Each Member State shall adopt, if necessary, multiannual programmes intended to ensure the lasting convergence necessary for the achievement of economic and monetary union, in particular with regard to price stability and sound public finances. Each Member State shall endeavour to avoid excessive government deficits, and shall, as appropriate, start the process leading to the independence of its central bank.

A European Monetary Institute (EMI) shall be established to strengthen co-operation between the national central banks; strengthen the co-ordination of monetary policies of the Member States, with the aim of ensuring price stability; monitor the functioning of the European Monetary System; hold consultations concerning issues falling within the competence of the national central banks and affecting the stability of financial institutions and markets; take over the tasks of the European Monetary Co-operation Fund, which shall be dissolved; and facilitate the use of the ECU and oversee its development, including the smooth functioning of the ECU clearing system. For the preparation of the third stage, the EMI shall prepare the instruments and the procedures necessary for carrying out a single monetary policy in the third stage; promote the harmonization, where necessary, of the rules and practices governing the collection, compilation and distribution of statistics in the areas within its field of competence; prepare the rules for operations to be undertaken by the national central banks within the framework of the ESCB; promote the efficiency of cross-border payments; and supervise the technical preparation of ECU banknotes.

The EMI may formulate opinions or recommendations; submit opinions or recommendations to governments and to the Council; and make recommendations to the monetary authorities of the Member States.

From the start of the third stage, the value of the ECU shall be irrevocably fixed in accordance with this Treaty.

Where a Member State is in difficulties or is seriously threatened with difficulties as regards its balance of payments, and where such difficulties are liable in particular to jeopardize the functioning of the common market or the progressive implementation of the common commercial policy, the Commission shall immediately investigate the position of the State in question and the action which, making use of all the means at its disposal, that State has taken or may take in accordance with the provisions of this Treaty. The Commission shall state what measures it recommends the State concerned to take.

The Commission and the EMI shall report to the Council on the progress made in the fulfilment by the Member States of their obligations regarding the achievement of economic and monetary union. The reports shall examine the achievement of a high degree of sustainable convergence. Taking due account of the reports and the opinion of the European Parliament, the Council, meeting in the composition of heads of state or Government, shall, acting by a qualified majority, not later than 31 December 1996 decide whether a majority of the Member States fulfil the necessary conditions for the adoption of a single currency; decide whether it is appropriate for the Community to enter the third stage; and if so set the date for the beginning of the third stage.

If the Council has confirmed which Member States fulfil the necessary conditions for the adoption of a single currency, those Member States which do not fulfil the conditions shall have a derogation.

At the starting date of the third stage, the Council shall, acting with the unanimity of the Member States without a derogation, on a proposal from the Commission and after consulting the ECB, adopt the conversion rates at which their currencies shall be irrevocably fixed and at which irrevocably fixed rate the ECU shall be substituted for these currencies, and the ECU will become a currency in its own right.

TITLE VIII: EMPLOYMENT

Articles 125–130

Member States and the Community shall work towards developing a co-ordinated strategy for employment and particularly for promoting a skilled, trained and adaptable workforce and labour markets responsive to economic change.

The European Council shall each year consider the employment situation in the Community and adopt conclusions thereon, on the basis of a joint annual report by the Council and the Commission. On the basis of the conclusions of the European Council, the Council, acting by a qualified majority on a proposal from the Commission and after consulting the European Parliament, the Economic and Social Committee, the Committee of the Regions and the Employment Committee referred to in Article 130, shall each year draw up guidelines which the Member States shall take into account in their employment policies.

The Council, after consulting the European Parliament, shall establish an Employment Committee with advisory status to promote co-ordination between Member States on employment and labour market policies. Each Member State and the Commission shall appoint two members of the Committee.

TITLE IX: COMMON COMMERCIAL POLICY

Articles 131–134

The common commercial policy shall be based on uniform principles, particularly in regard to changes in tariff rates, the conclusion of tariff and trade agreements, the achievement of uniformity in measures of liberalization, export policy and measures to protect trade such as those to be taken in the event of dumping or subsidies. Where agreements with one or more States or international organizations need to be negotiated, the Commission shall make recommendations to the Council, which shall authorize the Commission to open the necessary negotiations.

In order to ensure that the execution of measures of commercial policy taken in accordance with this Treaty by any Member State is not obstructed by deflection of trade, or where differences between such measures lead to economic difficulties in one or more Member States, the Commission shall recommend the methods for the requisite co-operation between Member States. Failing this, the Commission may authorize Member States to take the necessary protective measures.

TITLE X: CUSTOMS CO-OPERATION

Article 135

Within the scope of application of this Treaty, the Council shall take measures in order to strengthen customs co-operation between Member States and between the latter and the Commission. These measures shall not concern the application of national criminal law or the national administration of justice.

TITLE XI: SOCIAL POLICY, EDUCATION, VOCATIONAL TRAINING AND YOUTH

Social Provisions

Articles 136–145

The Community and the Member States, having in mind fundamental social rights such as those set out in the European Social Charter signed at Turin on 18 October 1961 and in the 1989 Community Charter of the Fundamental Social Rights of Workers, shall have as their objectives the promotion of employment, and improved living and working conditions, so as to make possible their harmonization while the improvement is being maintained, proper social protection, dialogue between management and labour, the development of human resources with a view to lasting high employment and the combating of exclusion. To this end the Community and the Member States shall implement measures which take account of the diverse forms of national practices, in particular in the field of contractual relations, and the need to maintain the competitiveness of the Community economy.

The Commission shall have the task of promoting the consultation of management and labour at Community level and shall take any relevant measure to facilitate their dialogue by ensuring balanced support for the parties.

Each Member State shall ensure that the principle of equal pay for male and female workers for equal work or work of equal value is applied. With a view to ensuring full equality in practice between men and women in working life, the principle of equal treatment shall not prevent any Member State from maintaining or adopting measures providing for specific advantages in order to make it easier for the under-represented sex to pursue a vocational activity or to prevent or compensate for disadvantages in professional careers.

The European Social Fund

Articles 146–148

In order to improve employment opportunities for workers in the internal market and to contribute thereby to raising the standard of living, a European Social Fund is hereby established; it shall have the task of rendering the employment of workers easier and of increasing their geographical and occupational mobility within the Community, and to facilitate their adaptation to industrial changes and to changes in production systems, in particular through vocational training and retraining. The Fund shall be administered by the Commission. The Council, acting in accordance with the procedure referred to in Article 251 and after consulting the Economic and Social Committee and the Committee of the Regions, shall adopt implementing decisions relating to the European Social Fund.

Education, Vocational Training and Youth

Articles 149–150

The Community shall contribute to the development of quality education by encouraging co-operation between Member States and, if necessary, by supporting and supplementing their action. The Community shall implement a vocational training policy which shall support and supplement the action of the Member States.

TITLE XII: CULTURE

Article 151

The Community shall contribute to the flowering of the cultures of the Member States, while respecting their national and regional diversity and at the same time bringing the common cultural heritage to the fore. The Community shall take cultural aspects into account in its action under other provisions of this Treaty, in particular in order to respect and to promote the diversity of its cultures.

TITLE XIII: PUBLIC HEALTH

Article 152

A high level of human health protection shall be ensured in the definition and implementation of all Community policies and activities. Community action, which shall complement national policies, shall be directed towards improving public health, preventing human illness and diseases, and obviating sources of danger to human health. Such action shall cover the fight against the major health scourges, by promoting research into their causes, their transmission and their prevention, as well as health information and education. The Community shall complement the Member States' action in reducing drugs-related health damage, including information and prevention. The Community and the Member States shall foster co-operation with third countries and the competent international organizations in the sphere of public health. Community action in the field of public health shall fully respect the responsibilities of the Member States for the organization and delivery of health services and medical care.

TITLE XIV: CONSUMER PROTECTION

Article 153

In order to promote the interests of consumers and to ensure a high level of consumer protection, the Community shall contribute to protecting the health, safety and economic interests of consumers, as well as to promoting their right to information and education and to organize themselves in order to safeguard their interests.

TITLE XV: TRANS-EUROPEAN NETWORKS

Articles 154–156

The Community shall contribute to the establishment and development of trans-European networks in the areas of transport, telecommunications and energy infrastructures. Action by the Community shall aim at promoting the interconnection and interoperability of national networks, as well as access to such networks. It shall take account, in particular, of the need to link island, landlocked and peripheral regions with the central regions of the Community.

TITLE XVI: INDUSTRY

Article 157

The Community and the Member States shall ensure that the conditions necessary for the competitiveness of the Community's industry exist. Their action shall be aimed at speeding up the adjustment of industry to structural changes; encouraging an environment favourable to initiative and the development of undertakings throughout the Community, particularly small and medium-sized undertakings; encouraging an environment favourable to co-operation between undertakings; and fostering better exploitation of the industrial potential of policies of innovation, research and technological development. The Member States shall consult each other in liaison with the Commission and, where necessary, shall co-ordinate their action.

TITLE XVII: ECONOMIC AND SOCIAL COHESION

Articles 158–162

The Community shall develop and pursue its actions leading to the strengthening of its economic and social cohesion. In particular, the Community shall aim at reducing disparities between the levels of development of the various regions and the backwardness of the least favoured regions or islands, including rural areas.

Implementing decisions relating to the European Regional Development Fund shall be taken by the Council, acting in accordance with the procedure referred to in Article 251 and after consulting the Economic and Social Committee and the Committee of the Regions.

TITLE XVIII: RESEARCH AND TECHNOLOGICAL DEVELOPMENT

Articles 163–173

The Community shall have the objective of strengthening the scientific and technological bases of Community industry and encouraging it to become more competitive at international level. The Community shall carry out the following activities, complementing the activities carried out in the Member States: implementation of research, technological development and demonstration programmes, by promoting co-operation with and between undertakings, research centres and universities; promotion of co-operation in the field of Community research, technological development and demonstration with third countries and international organizations; dissemination and optimization of the results of activities in Community research, technological development and demonstration; stimulation of the training and mobility of researchers in the Community.

A multiannual framework programme shall be adopted by the Council.

TITLE XIX: ENVIRONMENT

Articles 174–176

Community policy on the environment shall aim at a high level of protection taking into account the diversity of situations in the various regions of the Community. It shall be based on the precautionary principle and on the principles that preventive action should be taken, that environmental damage should, as a priority, be rectified at source and that the polluter should pay. In this context, harmonization measures answering environmental protection requirements shall include, where appropriate, a safeguard clause allowing Member States to take provisional measures, for non-economic environmental reasons, subject to a Community inspection procedure.

TITLE XX: DEVELOPMENT CO-OPERATION

Articles 177–181

Community policy in the sphere of development co-operation, which shall be complementary to the policies pursued by the Member States, shall foster the sustainable economic and social development of the developing countries, and, more particularly, the most disadvantaged among them; the smooth and gradual integration of the developing countries into the world economy; and the campaign against poverty in the developing countries. Community policy in this area shall contribute to the general objective of developing and consolidating democracy and the rule of law, and to that of respecting human rights and fundamental freedoms. The community and the Member States shall comply with the commitments and take account of the objectives they have approved in the context of the United Nations and other competent international organizations.

The Community and the Member States shall co-ordinate their policies on development co-operation and shall consult each other on their aid programmes, including in international organizations and during international conferences. They may undertake joint action. Member States shall contribute if necessary to the implementation of Community aid programmes.

PART FOUR: ASSOCIATION OF THE OVERSEAS COUNTRIES AND TERRITORIES

Articles 182–188

The Member States agree to bring into association with the Community the non-European countries and territories which have special relations with Denmark, France, the Netherlands and the United Kingdom in order to promote the economic and social development of these countries and territories and to establish close economic relations between them and the Community as a whole. Association shall serve primarily to further the interests and prosperity of the inhabitants of these countries and territories in order to lead them to the economic, social and cultural development to which they aspire.

Member States shall, in their commercial exchanges with the countries and territories, apply the same rules which they apply among themselves pursuant to the Treaty. Each country or territory shall apply to its commercial exchanges with Member States and with other countries and territories the same rules which it applies in respect of the European States with which it has special relations. Member States shall contribute to the investments required by the progressive development of these countries and territories.

Customs duties on trade between Member States and the countries and territories are to be prohibited according to the same timetable as for trade between the Member States themselves. The countries and territories may, however, levy customs duties which correspond to the needs of their development and to the requirements of their industrialization or which, being of a fiscal nature, have the object of contributing to their budgets.

PART FIVE: INSTITUTIONS OF THE COMMUNITY

TITLE I: PROVISIONS GOVERNING THE INSTITUTIONS

Articles 189–267

In order to carry out their task and in accordance with the provisions of this Treaty, the European Parliament acting jointly with the Council and the Commission shall make regulations and issue directives, take decisions, make recommendations or deliver opinions. A regulation shall have general application. It shall be binding in its entirety and directly applicable in all Member States. A directive shall be binding, as to the result to be achieved, upon each Member State to which it is addressed, but shall leave to the national authorities the choice of form and methods. A decision shall be binding in its entirety upon those to whom it is addressed. Recommendations and opinions shall have no binding force.

Where reference is made in this Treaty to this Article [Article 251] for the adoption of an act, the following procedure shall apply. The Commission shall submit a proposal to the European Parliament and the Council. The Council, acting by a qualified majority after obtaining the opinion of the European Parliament:

(a) if it approves all the amendments contained in the European Parliament's opinion, may adopt the proposed act thus amended;
(b) if the European Parliament does not propose any amendments, may adopt the proposed act;
(c) shall otherwise adopt a common position and communicate it to the European Parliament. The Commission shall inform the European Parliament fully of its position.

If, within three months of such communication, the European Parliament:

(a) approves the common position or has not taken a decision, the act in question shall be deemed to have been adopted in accordance with that common position;
(b) rejects, by an absolute majority of its component members, the common position, the proposed act shall be deemed not to have been adopted;
(c) proposes amendments to the common position by an absolute majority of its component members, the amended text shall be forwarded to the Council and to the Commission, which shall deliver an opinion on those amendments.

If, within three months of the matter being referred to it, the Council, acting by a qualified majority, approves all the amendments of the European Parliament, the act shall be deemed to have been adopted in the form of the common position; however, the Council shall act unanimously on the amendments on which the Commission has delivered a negative opinion. If the Council does not approve all the amendments, the President of the Council, in agreement with the President of the European Parliament, shall within six weeks convene a meeting of the Conciliation Committee. If, within six weeks of its being convened, the Conciliation Committee approves a joint text, the European Parliament, acting by an absolute majority of the votes cast, and the Council, acting by a qualified majority, shall each have a period of six weeks in which to adopt the act in accordance with the joint text. If either of the two institutions fails to approve the proposed act, it shall be deemed not to have been adopted. Where the Conciliation Committee does not approve a joint text, the proposed act shall be deemed not to have been adopted.

TITLE II: FINANCIAL PROVISIONS

Articles 268–280

All items of revenue and expenditure of the Community, including those relating to the European Social Fund, shall be included in estimates to be drawn up for each financial year and shall be shown in the budget. Administrative expenditure occasioned for the institutions by the provisions of the Treaty on European Union relating to common foreign and security policy and to co-operation in the fields of justice and home affairs shall be charged to the budget. The operational expenditure occasioned by the implementation of the said provisions may, under the conditions referred to therein, be charged to the budget. The revenue and expenditure shown in the budget shall be in balance.

Without prejudice to other revenue, the budget shall be financed wholly from own resources.

The Commission shall implement the budget, in accordance with the provisions of the regulations made pursuant to Article 279, on its own responsibility and within the limits of the appropriations, having regard to the principles of sound financial management. Member States shall co-operate with the Commission to ensure that the appropriations are used in accordance with the principles of sound financial management.

The Council, acting unanimously on a proposal from the Commission and after consulting the European Parliament and obtaining the opinion of the Court of Auditors, shall:

(a) make Financial Regulations specifying, in particular, the procedure to be adopted for establishing and implementing the budget and for presenting and auditing accounts;
(b) determine the methods and procedure whereby the budget revenue provided under the arrangements relating to the Community's own resources shall be made available to the Commission, and determine the measures to be applied, if need be, to meet cash requirements;
(c) lay down rules concerning the responsibility of financial controllers, authorizing officers and accounting officers, and concerning appropriate arrangements for inspection.

The Community and the Member States shall counter fraud and any other illegal activities affecting the financial interests of the Community.

PART SIX: GENERAL AND FINAL PROVISIONS

Articles 281–312

Member States shall, in so far as is necessary, engage in negotiations with each other with a view to ensuring for the benefit of their nationals:

(a) the protection of persons as well as the enjoyment of protection of rights under the conditions granted by each State to its own nationals;
(b) the elimination of double taxation within the Community;
(c) the mutual recognition of companies, the maintenance of their legal personality in cases where the registered office is transferred from one country to another, and the possibility for companies subject to the municipal law of different Member States to form mergers;
(d) the simplification of the formalities governing the reciprocal recognition and execution of judicial decisions and arbitral awards.

Within a period of three years after the date of the entry into force of the Treaty, Member States shall treat nationals of other Member States in the same manner, as regards financial participation by such nationals in the capital of companies, as they treat their own nationals, without prejudice to the application of the other provisions of the Treaty.

The Treaty shall in no way prejudice the system existing in Member States in respect of property.

The provisions of the Treaty shall not detract from the following rules:

(a) no Member State shall be obliged to supply information the disclosure of which it considers contrary to the essential interests of its security;
(b) any Member State may take the measures which it considers necessary for the protection of the essential interests of its security, and which are connected with the production of, or the trade in, arms, ammunition and war material; such measures shall not, however, prejudice conditions of competition in the common market in respect of products not intended for specifically military purposes.

The list of products to which (b) applies shall be determined by the Council in the course of the first year after the date of entry into force of the Treaty. The list may be subsequently amended by the unanimous vote of the Council on a proposal of the Commission.

Member States shall consult one another for the purpose of enacting in common the necessary provisions to prevent the functioning of the common market from being affected by measures which a Member State may be called upon to take in case of serious internal disturbances affecting public order, in case of war or in order to carry out undertakings into which it has entered for the purpose of maintaining peace and international security.

Where this Treaty provides for the conclusion of agreements between the Community and one or more States or international organizations, the Commission shall make recommendations to the Council, which shall authorize the Commission to open the necessary negotiations. The Commission shall conduct these negotiations in consultation with special committees appointed by the Council to assist it in this task and within the framework of such directives as the Council may issue to it. The agreements shall be concluded by the Council, after consulting the European Parliament, acting by a qualified majority on a proposal from the Commission. The Council shall act unanimously when the agreement covers a field for which unanimity is required.

The provisions of the Treaty shall not affect those of the Treaty establishing the European Coal and Steel Community, nor those of the Treaty establishing the European Atomic Energy Community; nor shall they be an obstacle to the existence or completion of regional unions between Belgium and Luxembourg, and between Belgium, Luxembourg and the Netherlands, in so far as the objectives of these regional unions are not achieved by the application of this Treaty.

Where a decision has been taken to suspend the voting rights of the representative of the government of a Member State in accordance with Article 7(2) of the Treaty on European Union, these voting rights shall also be suspended with regard to this Treaty.

The Community may conclude with one or more States or international organizations agreements establishing an association involving reciprocal rights and obligations, common action and special procedures.

The Treaty is concluded for an unlimited period.

The Single European Act (SEA)

On 1 July 1987 amendments to the Treaties of Paris and Rome, in the form of the Single European Act (SEA), came into effect, following ratification by all the Member States. The Act contained provisions which aimed to complete by 31 December 1992 the creation of a single Community market—'an area without internal frontiers in which the free movement of goods, persons, services and capital is ensured'. Other provisions increased Community co-operation in research and technology, social policy (particularly the improvement of working conditions), economic and social cohesion (reduction of disparities between regions), environmental protection, creation of economic and monetary union, and foreign policy. It allowed the Council of Ministers to take decisions by a qualified majority vote on matters which previously, under the Treaty of Rome, had required unanimity; this applied principally to matters relating to the establishment of the internal market. The Act increased the powers of the European Parliament to delay and amend legislation, by introducing a new co-operation procedure for major decisions concerned with the completion of the internal market, although the Council retained final decision-making powers. The Act provided for the establishment of the Court of First Instance. The Act also provided for the establishment of a secretariat for European political co-operation on matters of foreign policy.

Summary of the Treaty on European Union (Maastricht Treaty)

(effective from 1 November 1993; as amended by the Treaty of Amsterdam and the Treaty of Nice)

At the meeting of the European Council in December 1992, it was agreed that Denmark was to be exempted from certain central provisions of the Treaty, including those regarding monetary union, European citizenship and defence (subject to approval by a second Danish referendum, which ratified the Treaty in May 1993).

A protocol to the Treaty was approved and a separate agreement signed by all Member States except the United Kingdom on social policy, based on the Charter of Fundamental Social Rights (the Social Charter) of 1989.

TITLE I: COMMON PROVISIONS

Article 1

By this Treaty, the High Contracting Parties establish among themselves a European Union, hereinafter called 'the Union'.

This Treaty marks a new stage in the process of creating an ever closer union among the peoples of Europe, in which decisions are taken as openly as possible and as closely as possible to the citizen.

The Union shall be founded on the European Communities, supplemented by the policies and forms of co-operation established by this Treaty. Its task shall be to organize, in a manner demonstrating consistency and solidarity, relations between the Member States and between their peoples.

Article 2

The Union shall set itself the following objectives:

(a) to promote economic and social progress and a high level of employment and to achieve balanced and sustainable development, in particular, through the creation of an area without internal frontiers, through the strengthening of economic and social cohesion and through the establishment of economic and monetary union, ultimately including a single currency in accordance with the provisions of this Treaty;
(b) to assert its identity on the international scene, in particular, through the implementation of a common foreign and security policy, including the progressive framing of a common defence policy, which might lead to a common defence;
(c) to strengthen the protection of the rights and interests of the nationals of its Member States through the introduction of a citizenship of the Union;
(d) to maintain and develop the Union as an area of freedom, security and justice, in which the free movement of persons is assured in conjunction with appropriate measures with respect to external border controls, asylum, immigration and the prevention and combating of crime;
(e) to maintain in full the *acquis communautaire* and build on it with a view to considering to what extent the policies and forms of co-operation introduced by this Treaty may need to be revised with the aim of ensuring the effectiveness of the mechanisms and the institutions of the Community.

The objectives of the Union shall be achieved as provided in this Treaty and in accordance with the conditions and the timetable set out therein while respecting the principle of subsidiarity as defined in Article 3b of the Treaty establishing the European Community.

Article 3

The Union shall be served by a single institutional framework which shall ensure the consistency and the continuity of the activities carried out in order to attain its objectives while respecting and building upon the *acquis communautaire*.

The Union shall, in particular, ensure the consistency of its external activities as a whole in the context of its external relations, security, economic and development policies. The Council and the Commission shall be responsible for ensuring such consistency and shall co-operate to this end. They shall ensure the implementation of these policies, each in accordance with its respective powers.

Article 4

The European Council shall provide the Union with the necessary impetus for its development and shall define the general political guidelines thereof.

The European Council shall bring together the heads of state or Government of the Member States and the President of the Commission. They shall be assisted by the Ministers for Foreign Affairs of the Member States and by a Member of the Commission. The European Council shall meet at least twice a year, under the chairmanship of the head of state or Government of the Member State which holds the Presidency of the Council.

The European Council shall submit to the European Parliament a report after each of its meetings and a yearly written report on the progress achieved by the Union.

Article 5

The European Parliament, the Council, the Commission, the Court of Justice and the Court of Auditors shall exercise their powers under the conditions and for the purposes provided for, on the one hand, by the provisions of the Treaties establishing the European Communities and of the subsequent Treaties and Acts modifying and supplementing them and, on the other hand, by the other provisions of this Treaty.

Article 6

(a) The Union is founded on the principles of liberty, democracy, respect for human rights and fundamental freedoms, and the rule of law, principles which are common to the Member States.
(b) The Union shall respect fundamental rights, as guaranteed by the European Convention for the Protection of Human Rights and Fundamental Freedoms signed in Rome on 4 November 1950 and as they result from the constitutional traditions common to the Member States, as general principles of Community law.
(c) The Union shall respect the national identities of its Member States.
(d) The Union shall provide itself with the means necessary to attain its objectives and carry through its policies.

Article 7

(a) The Council, meeting in the composition of the heads of state or Government and acting by unanimity on a proposal by one-third of the Member States or by the Commission and after obtaining the assent of the European Parliament, may determine the existence of a serious and persistent breach by a Member State of principles mentioned in Article 6(1).
(b) The Council, acting by a qualified majority, may decide to suspend certain of the rights deriving from the application of this Treaty to the Member State in question.

TITLE II: PROVISIONS AMENDING THE TREATY ESTABLISHING THE EUROPEAN ECONOMIC COMMUNITY WITH A VIEW TO ESTABLISHING THE EUROPEAN COMMUNITY

Article 8

The Treaty establishing the European Economic Community shall be amended in accordance with the provisions of this Article, in order to establish a European Community.

Throughout the Treaty: the term 'European Economic Community' shall be replaced by the term 'European Community'.

TITLE III: PROVISIONS AMENDING THE TREATY ESTABLISHING THE EUROPEAN COAL AND STEEL COMMUNITY

Article 9

The Treaty establishing the European Coal and Steel Community shall be amended in accordance with the provisions of this Article.

TITLE IV: PROVISIONS AMENDING THE TREATY ESTABLISHING THE EUROPEAN ATOMIC ENERGY COMMUNITY

Article 10

The Treaty establishing the European Atomic Energy Community shall be amended in accordance with the provisions of this Article.

TITLE V: PROVISIONS ON A COMMON FOREIGN AND SECURITY POLICY

Articles 11–28

The Union shall define and implement a common foreign and security policy covering all areas of foreign and security policy. The objectives of this policy shall be: to safeguard the common values, fundamental interests, independence and integrity of the Union in conformity with the principles of the United Nations Charter; to strengthen the security of the Union in all ways; to preserve peace and strengthen international security, in accordance with the principles of the United Nations Charter, as well as the principles of the Helsinki Final Act and the objectives of the Paris Charter, including those on external borders; to promote international co-operation; to develop and consolidate democracy and the rule of law, and respect for human rights and fundamental freedoms. The Member States shall support the Union's external and security policy actively and unreservedly in a spirit of loyalty and mutual solidarity. They shall refrain from any action which is contrary to the interests of the Union or likely to impair its effectiveness as a cohesive force in international relations.

The Union shall pursue its objectives by defining the principles of and general guidelines for the common foreign and security policy; deciding on common strategies; adopting joint actions; adopting common positions; strengthening systematic co-operation between Member States in the conduct of policy.

The European Council shall define the principles of and general guidelines for the common foreign and security policy, including for matters with defence implications. The Council shall ensure the unity, consistency and effectiveness of action by the Union.

The Council shall adopt common positions, which shall define the approach of the Union to a particular matter of a geographical or thematic nature. Member States shall ensure that their national policies conform to the common positions.

The common foreign and security policy shall include all questions relating to the security of the Union, including the progressive framing of a common defence policy, which might lead to a common defence, should the European Council so decide. Western European Union (WEU) is an integral part of the development of the Union providing the Union with access to an operational capability. The Union shall accordingly foster closer institutional relations with WEU with a view to the possibility of the integration of WEU into the Union, should the European Council so decide. The progressive framing of a common defence policy will be supported, as Member States consider appropriate, by co-operation between them in the field of armaments. Questions referred to shall include humanitarian and rescue tasks, peacekeeping tasks and tasks of combat forces in crisis managment, including peacemaking. The provisions of this Article shall not prevent the development of closer co-operation between two or more Member States on a bilateral level.

The Presidency shall represent the Union in matters coming within the common foreign and security policy.

Member States shall co-ordinate their action in international organizations and at international conferences.

The diplomatic and consular missions of the Member States and the Commission Delegations in third countries and international conferences, and their representations to international organizations, shall co-operate in ensuring that the common positions and joint actions adopted by the Council are complied with and implemented.

The Presidency shall consult the European Parliament and shall ensure that the views of the European Parliament are duly taken into consideration.

Decisions under this Title shall be taken by the Council acting unanimously. Abstentions by members present in person or represented shall not prevent the adoption of such decisions.

A Political Committee shall monitor the international situation in the areas covered by the common foreign and security policy and contribute to the definition of policies by delivering opinions to the Council. It shall also monitor the implementation of agreed policies.

TITLE VI: PROVISIONS ON POLICE AND JUDICIAL CO-OPERATION IN CRIMINAL MATTERS

Article 29

Without prejudice to the powers of the European Community, the Union's objective shall be to provide citizens with a high level of safety within an area of freedom, security and justice by developing common action among the Member States in the fields of police and judicial co-operation in criminal matters and by preventing and combating racism and xenophobia. That objective shall be achieved by preventing and combating crime, organized or otherwise, in particular, terrorism, trafficking in persons and offences against children, illicit drug trafficking and illicit arms trafficking, corruption and fraud, through:

(a) closer co-operation between police forces, customs authorities and other competent authorities in the Member States,

both directly and through the European Police Office (Europol);
(b) looser co-operation between judicial and other competent authorities of the Member States;
(c) approximation, where necessary, of rules on criminal matters in the Member States.

Article 30

Common action in the field of police co-operation shall include:

(a) operational co-operation between the competent authorities, including the police, customs and other specialized law enforcement services of the Member States in relation to the prevention, detection and investigation of criminal offences;
(b) the collection, storage, processing, analysis and exchange of relevant information, in particular through Europol;
(c) co-operation and joint initiatives in training, the exchange of liaison officers, secondments, the use of equipment, and forensic research;
(d) the common evaluation of particular investigative techniques in relation to the detection of serious forms of organized crime.

The Council shall promote co-operation through Europol.

Article 31

Common action on judicial co-operation in criminal matters shall include facilitating and accelerating co-operation between competent ministries and judicial or equivalent authorities of the Member States in relation to proceedings and the enforcement of decisions; facilitating extradition between Member States; ensuring compatibility in rules applicable in the Member States, as may be necessary to improve such co-operation; preventing conflicts of jurisdiction between Member States; progressively adopting measures establishing minimum rules relating to the constituent elements of criminal acts and to penalties in the fields of organized crime, terrorism and illicit drug trafficking.

Article 34

Member States shall inform and consult one another within the Council with a view to co-ordinating their action.

Article 35

The Court of Justice of the European Communities shall have jurisdiction to give preliminary rulings on the validity and interpretation of framework decisions and decisions, on the interpretation of conventions and on the validity and interpretation of the measures implementing them.

Article 39

The Council shall consult the European Parliament before adopting any measures referred to in subsections of Article 34. The Presidency and the Commission shall regularly inform the European Parliament of discussions in the areas covered by this Title. The European Parliament may ask questions of the Council or make recommendations to it.

TITLE VII: PROVISIONS ON CLOSER CO-OPERATION

Article 43

Member States which intend to establish closer co-operation between themselves may make use of the institutions, procedures and mechanisms laid down by this Treaty and the Treaty establishing the European Community.

TITLE VIII: FINAL PROVISIONS

Articles 46–53

Any European State which respects the principles set out in Article 7 may apply to become a member of the Union.

This Treaty is concluded for an unlimited period.

Summary of the Treaty of Amsterdam

(effective from 1 May 1999; as amended by the Treaty of Nice)

Note: Following the decision of the Government of the United Kingdom to subscribe to the Charter of Fundamental Social Rights (the Social Charter) of 1989 with effect from May 1997, the Treaty incorporated the protocol based on the Charter (by amending the Treaty of Rome establishing the European Economic Community).

A Protocol to the Treaty also incorporated the Schengen *acquis* on the freedom of movement of persons across internal European Union boundaries in order to integrate it into the framework of the European Union. The *acquis* includes the Schengen Agreement, signed on 14 June 1985 between the Governments of the States of the Benelux Economic Union, the Federal Republic of Germany and France; the Convention, signed in Schengen on 19 June 1990 between Belgium, the Federal Republic of Germany, France, Luxembourg and the Netherlands; the Accession Protocols and Agreements to the 1985 Agreement and the 1990 Implementation Convention with Italy, Spain and Portugal, Greece, Austria, Denmark, Finland and Sweden; and decisions and declarations adopted by the Executive Committee established by the Implementation Convention, as well as acts adopted for the implementation of the Convention by the organs upon which the Executive Committee has conferred decision-making powers.

PART ONE: SUBSTANTIVE AMENDMENTS

Article 1

The Treaty on European Union shall be amended in accordance with the provisions of this Article.

Article 2

The Treaty establishing the European Community shall be amended in accordance with the provisions of this Article.

Article 3

The Treaty establishing the European Coal and Steel Community shall be amended in accordance with the provisions of this Article.

Article 4

The Treaty establishing the European Atomic Energy Community shall be amended in accordance with the provisions of this Article.

Article 5

The Act concerning the election of the representatives of the European Parliament by direct universal suffrage annexed to the Council Decision of 20 September 1976 shall be amended in accordance with the provisions of this Article.

In Article 2, the following paragraph shall be added:

In the event of amendments to this Article, the number of representatives elected in each Member State must ensure appropriate representation for the peoples of the States brought together in the Community.

Article 7(2) shall be replaced by the following:

Pending the entry into force of a uniform electoral procedure or a procedure based on common principles and subject to the other provisions of this Act, the electoral procedure shall be governed in each Member State by its national provisions.

PART TWO: SIMPLIFICATION

Articles 6–11

Article 6

The Treaty establishing the European Community, including the annexes and protocols thereto, shall be amended in accordance with the provisions of this Article for the purpose of deleting lapsed provisions of the Treaty and adapting in consequence the text of certain of its provisions.

Article 7

The Treaty establishing the European Coal and Steel Community, including the annexes, protocols and other acts annexed thereto, shall be amended in accordance with the provisions of this Article for the purpose of deleting lapsed provisions of the Treaty and adapting in consequence the text of certain of its provisions.

Article 8

The Treaty establishing the European Atomic Energy Community, including the annexes and protocols thereto, shall be amended in accordance with the provisions of this Article for the purpose of deleting lapsed provisions of the Treaty and adapting in consequence the text of certain of its provisions.

Article 9

The Convention of 25 March 1957 on certain institutions common to the European Communities and the Treaty of 8 April 1965 establishing a Single Council and a Single Commission of the European Communities shall be repealed. This is with the exception of the Protocol of 8 April 1965 on the privileges and immunities of the European Communities, to which is added an Article 23, applying the Protocol to the European Central Bank, to the members of its organs and to its staff.

The powers conferred on the European Parliament, the Council, the Commission, the Court of Justice and the Court of Auditors by the Treaty establishing the European Community, the Treaty establishing the European Coal and Steel Community and the Treaty establishing the European Atomic Energy Community shall be exercised by the single institutions under the conditions laid down respectively by the said Treaties and this Article.

The functions conferred on the Economic and Social Committee by the Treaty establishing the European Community and the Treaty establishing the European Atomic Energy Community shall be exercised by a single committee.

The European Communities shall enjoy in the territories of the Member States such privileges and immunities as are necessary for the performance of their tasks. The position shall be the same as regards the European Central Bank, the European Monetary Institute and the European Investment Bank.

Article 10

The repeal or deletion of lapsed provisions of the Treaty establishing the European Community, the Treaty establishing the European Coal and Steel Community and the Treaty establishing the European Atomic Energy Community and the adaptation of certain of their provisions shall not bring about any change in the legal effects of the provisions of those Treaties.

PART THREE: GENERAL AND FINAL PROVISIONS

Articles 12–15

Article 12

The articles, titles and sections of the Treaty on European Union and of the Treaty establishing the European Community, as amended by the provisions of this Treaty, shall be renumbered in accordance with the tables of equivalences set out in the Annex to this Treaty.

Article 13

This Treaty is concluded for an unlimited period.

Article 14

This Treaty shall be ratified by the High Contracting Parties in accordance with their respective constitutional requirements. This Treaty shall enter into force on the first day of the second month following that in which the instrument of ratification is deposited by the last signatory State to fulfil that formality.

Summary of the Treaty of Nice

(amending the Treaty on European Union, the Treaties establishing the European Communities and Certain Related Acts— effective from 1 February 2003)

PART ONE: SUBSTANTIVE AMENDMENTS

Article 1

The Treaty on European Union shall be amended in accordance with the provisions of this Article.

Article 7 shall be replaced by the following (abbreviated):

On a reasoned proposal by one third of the Member States, by the European Parliament or by the Commission, the Council, acting by a majority of four-fifths of its members after obtaining the assent of the European Parliament, may determine that there is a clear risk of a serious breach by a Member State of principles mentioned in Article 6(1) (i.e. liberty, democracy, respect for human rights and fundamental freedoms, and the rule of law) and address appropriate recommendations to that State. The Council, meeting in the composition of the heads of state or Government and acting by unanimity on a proposal by one-third of the Member States or by the Commission and after obtaining the assent of the European Parliament, may determine the existence of a serious and persistent breach by a Member State of principles mentioned in Article 6(1). The Council, acting by a qualified majority, may decide to suspend certain of the rights deriving from the application of this Treaty to the Member State in question, including the voting rights of the representative of the government of that Member State in the Council.

Article 17 shall be replaced by the following (abbreviated):

The common foreign and security policy shall include all questions relating to the security of the Union, including the progressive framing of a common defence policy, which might lead to a common defence, should the European Council so decide. It shall in that case recommend to the Member States the adoption of such a decision in accordance with their respective constitutional requirements. The policy of the Union in accordance with this Article shall not prejudice the specific character of the security and defence policy of certain Member States and shall respect the obligations of certain Member States, which see their common defence realized in the North Atlantic Treaty Organization (NATO), under the North Atlantic Treaty and be compatible with the common security and defence policy established within that framework. The progressive framing of a common defence policy will be supported, as Member States consider appropriate, by co-operation between them in the field of armaments. Questions referred to in this Article shall include humanitarian and rescue tasks, peacekeeping tasks and tasks of combat forces in crisis management, including peacemaking. The provisions of this Article shall not prevent the development of closer co-operation between two or more Member States on a bilateral level, in the framework of Western European Union (WEU) and NATO, provided such co-operation does not run counter to or impede that provided for in this Title.

Article 24 shall be replaced by the following (abbreviated):

When it is necessary to conclude an agreement with one or more States or international organizations in implementation of this Title (i.e. concerning a common foreign and security policy), the Council may authorize the Presidency, assisted by the Commission as appropriate, to open negotiations to that effect. Such agreements shall be concluded by the Council on a recommendation from the Presidency. The provisions of this Article shall also apply to matters falling under Title VI (police and judicial co-operation).

Article 25 shall be replaced by the following (abbreviated):

A Political and Security Committee shall monitor the international situation in the areas covered by the common foreign and security policy and contribute to the definition of policies by delivering opinions to the Council. It shall also monitor the implementation of agreed policies. This Committee shall exercise, under the responsibility of the Council, political control and strategic direction of crisis management operations. The Council may authorize the Committee, for the purpose and for the duration of a crisis management operation, as determined by the Council, to take the relevant decisions concerning the political control and strategic direction of the operation.

Articles 27a–27e shall be inserted:

Enhanced co-operation in any of the areas referred to in this Title (i.e. provisions on a common foreign and security policy) shall be aimed at safeguarding the values and serving the interests of the Union as a whole by asserting its identity as a coherent force on the international scene. It shall respect: the principles, objectives, general guidelines and consistency of the common foreign and security policy and the decisions taken within the framework of that policy; the powers of the European Community, and consistency between all the Union's policies and its external activities. Enhanced co-operation pursuant to this Title shall relate to implementation of a joint action or a common position. It shall not relate to matters having military or defence implications.

Article 29 is to stipulate:

Closer co-operation between judicial and other competent authorities of the Member States, including co-operation through the European Judicial Co-operation Unit (Eurojust).

Article 31 is to include the following:

The Council shall encourage co-operation through Eurojust by: enabling Eurojust to facilitate proper co-ordination between Member States' national prosecuting authorities; promoting support by Eurojust for criminal investigations in cases of serious cross-border crime, particularly in the case of organized crime, taking account, in particular, of analyses carried out by Europol; facilitating close co-operation between Eurojust and the European Judicial Network.

The heading of Title VII shall be 'Provisions on enhanced co-operation'.

Article 43 shall be replaced by the following (abbreviated):

Member States which intend to establish enhanced co-operation between themselves may make use of the institutions, procedures and mechanisms laid down by this Treaty and by the Treaty establishing the European Community provided that the proposed co-operation: is aimed at furthering the objectives of the Union and of the Community, at protecting and serving their interests and at reinforcing their process of integration; respects the said Treaties and the single institutional framework of the Union; does not undermine the internal market or economic and social cohesion; does not constitute a barrier to or discrimination in trade between Member States or distort competition between them; involves a minimum of eight Member States; respects the competences, rights and obligations of non-participating Member States; and is open to all the Member States.

Article 2

The Treaty establishing the European Community shall be amended in accordance with the provisions of this Article.

Many of the amendments under this Article concern the decision-making procedure. The following provisions were formerly required to be approved unanimously by the Council, but, following the entry into force of the Treaty of Nice, they may now be approved by a qualified majority vote in the Council (see below for definition of qualified majority voting):

Incentive measures for countering discrimination (Article 13 of the Treaty Establishing the European Community).

Facilitating freedom of movement for EC citizens (Article 18).

Judicial co-operation in civil proceedings (Article 65).

Financial assistance to a Member State in the event of serious difficulties (Article 100).

Representation of the Community at international level as regards issues of particular relevance to economic and monetary union (Article 111).

Measures necessary for the introduction of the Euro as a single currency (Article 123).

Negotiation and conclusion of international agreements on services and the commercial aspects of intellectual property (with some exceptions) (Article 133).

Specific support measures in the industrial field (Article 157).

Specific actions outside the Structural Funds (Article 159).

Economic, financial and technical co-operation with third countries (Article 181a).

Regulations and general conditions governing the duties of members of the European Parliament (except aspects relating to taxation) (Article 190).

Regulations governing political parties at European level (Article 191).

Appointment of the Secretary-General and Deputy Secretary-General of the Council (Article 207).

Appointment of the President and members of the Commission (Article 214).

Approval of the rules of procedure of the Court of Justice (Article 223) and of the Court of First Instance (Article 224).

Appointment of the members of the Court of Auditors (Article 247) and approval of the internal rules of the Court of Auditors (Article 248).

Appointment of the members of the Economic and Social Committee (Article 259) and of the Committee of the Regions (Article 263).

The change to qualified majority voting was deferred until 2007 for decisions relating to the Structural Funds and the Cohesion Funds (Article 161), and for the adoption of Financial Regulations (Article 279). The change to qualified majority voting was also deferred for certain measures concerning visas, asylum, immigration and the free movement of persons (Articles 62 and 63), either until 2004 or until after the adoption of new legislation.

Other amendments under Article 2 concern the following Articles of the Treaty establishing the European Community (abbreviated versions of the new text):

Article 137. The Community shall support and complement the activities of the Member States in the following fields: improvement of the working environment to protect workers' health and safety; working conditions; social security and protection of workers; protection of workers where their employment contract is terminated; information and consultation of workers; representation and collective defence of the interests of workers and employers; conditions of employment for third country nationals legally residing in Community territory; integration of persons excluded from the labour market; equality between men and women with regard to labour market opportunities and treatment at work; combating of social exclusion; and the modernization of social protection systems. To this end the Council may adopt measures designed to encourage co-operation between Member States, and directives on minimum requirements for gradual implementation, having regard to the conditions and technical rules obtaining in each of the Member States. Such directives shall avoid imposing constraints in a way which would hold back the creation and development of small and medium-sized undertakings.

Article 144. The Council, after consulting the European Parliament, shall establish a Social Protection Committee with advisory status to promote co-operation on social protection policies between Member States and with the Commission. Each Member State and the Commission shall appoint two members of the Committee.

The following Title shall be added:

Title XXI: Economic, Financial and Technical Co-operation with Third Countries.

Article 181a. The Community shall carry out economic, financial and technical co-operation measures with third countries. Such measures shall be complementary to those carried out by the Member States and consistent with the development policy of the Community. Community policy in this area shall contribute to the general objective of developing and consolidating democracy and the rule of law, and to the objective of respecting human rights and fundamental freedoms.

Article 189. The number of members of the European Parliament shall not exceed 732.

Article 191. The Council, acting in accordance with the procedure referred to in Article 251, shall lay down the regulations governing political parties at European level and in particular the rules regarding their funding.

Article 217. The Commission shall work under the political guidance of its President, who shall decide on its internal organization. The responsibilities incumbent upon the Commission shall be structured and allocated among its members by its President. The President may reshuffle the allocation of these responsibilities during the Commission's term of office.

Articles 220–245. The Court of Justice and the Court of First Instance, each within its own jurisdiction, shall ensure that in the interpretation and application of this Treaty the law is observed. In addition, judicial panels may be attached to the Court of the First Instance. The Court of Justice shall consist of one judge per Member State; it shall sit in chambers or in a Grand Chamber, and may also sit as a full Court. The Court of Justice shall be assisted by eight Advocates-General. The Court of First Instance shall comprise at least one judge per Member State. The Court of First Instance shall have jurisdiction to hear and determine at first instance actions or proceedings referred to in Articles 230 (proceedings against a decision), 232 (failure to act), 235 (actions for damages), 236 and 238, with the exception of those assigned to a judicial panel and those reserved for the Court of Justice. The Statute of the Court of Justice shall be laid down in a separate Protocol (annexed to the Treaty).

Articles 247–248. The Court of Auditors shall consist of one national from each Member State. The Court shall examine the accounts of all revenue and expenditure of the Community, and of all bodies set up by the Community.

Articles 258–263. The number of members of the Economic and

Social Committee and of the Committee of the Regions shall not exceed 350 each. Members of the Committee of the Regions either hold a regional or local authority mandate or are politically accountable to an elected assembly.

Articles 3 and 4

The Treaty establishing the European Atomic Energy Community and the Treaty establishing the European Coal and Steel Community (ECSC) shall be amended in accordance with the provisions of Article 3 and Article 4 respectively. (These amendments correspond with amendments already listed under Articles 1 and 2.)

Article 5

The Protocol on the Statute of the European System of Central Banks and of the European Central Bank (ECB) shall be amended in accordance with the provisions of this Article.

Article 10 is to include the following:

Article 10.2 (rules on decision-making) may be amended by the Council, acting unanimously either on a recommendation from the ECB and after consulting the European Parliament and the Commission, or on a recommendation from the Commission and after consulting the European Parliament and the ECB. These amendments shall enter into force after having been ratified by all the Member States.

Article 6

This Article amends Article 21 of the Protocol on the privileges and immunities of the European Communities (applying to the Court of Justice and the Court of First Instance).

PART TWO: TRANSITIONAL AND FINAL PROVISIONS

Articles 7–13

Articles 7–9. These refer to the Protocol on the Statute of the Court of Justice annexed by this Treaty to the Treaty on European Union, to the Treaty establishing the European Community and to the Treaty establishing the European Atomic Energy Community. This Protocol replaces the previous Protocols on the Statute of the Court of Justice.

This Treaty is concluded for an unlimited period.

PROTOCOL ON THE ENLARGEMENT OF THE EUROPEAN UNION

Provisions concerning the European Parliament

With effect from the start of the 2004–09 term the number of representatives elected in each Member State shall be as follows: Belgium 22; Denmark 13; Germany 99; Greece 22; Spain 50; France 72; Ireland 12; Italy 72; Luxembourg 6; Netherlands 25; Austria 17; Portugal 22; Finland 13; Sweden 18; United Kingdom 72.

The total number of representatives in the European Parliament for the 2004–09 term is to include representatives of new Member States resulting from the accession treaties signed by 1 January 2004 at the latest. If the total number of members is less than 732, a pro rata correction shall be applied to the number of representatives to be elected in each Member State, so that the total number is as close as possible to 732. In the event of the entry into force of later accession treaties the number of members may temporarily exceed 732.

Provisions concerning the weighting of votes in the Council

From 1 January 2005, where the Council is required to act by a qualified majority, the votes of its members shall be weighted as follows: Belgium 12; Denmark 7; Germany 29; Greece 12; Spain 27; France 29; Ireland 7; Italy 29; Luxembourg 4; Netherlands 13; Austria 10; Portugal 12; Finland 7; Sweden 10; United Kingdom 29.

Acts of council shall require for their adoption at least 169 votes in favour, cast by a majority of the members, where this Treaty requires them to be adopted on a proposal from the Commission. In other cases, for their adoption acts of Council shall require at least 169 votes in favour, cast by at least two-thirds of the members. Acts of council shall require for their adoption at least 169 votes in favour cast by a majority of the members where this Treaty requires them to be adopted on a proposal from the Commission. In other cases, for their adoption acts of Council shall require at least 169 votes in favour, cast by at least two-thirds of the members. When a decision is to be adopted by the Council by a qualified majority, a member of the Council may request verification that the Member States constituting the qualified majority represent at least 62% of the total population of the Union. If that condition is shown not to have been met, the decision in question shall not be adopted.

Provisions concerning the Commission

With effect from when the first Commission after 1 January 2005 takes up its duties, the Commission shall include one national of each of the Member States; the number of members of the Commission may be altered by the Council, acting unanimously. When the Union consists of 27 Member States, the number of members of the Commission shall be less than the number of Member States: they shall be chosen according to a rotation system based on the principle of equality, the implementing arrangements for which shall be adopted by the Council, acting unanimously.

Note: The 10 countries listed below signed a Treaty of Accession on 16 April 2003 and were admitted as full members of the EU on 1 May 2004. The figures in parentheses represent, respectively, the number of members to be returned by each new entrant to the European Parliament, and each new entrant's quota of votes in the European Council: Czech Republic (20; 12); Estonia (6; 4); Cyprus (6; 4); Latvia (8; 4); Lithuania (12; 7); Hungary (20; 12); Malta (5; 3); Poland (50; 27); Slovenia (7; 4); Slovakia (13; 7).

OTHER PROTOCOLS

The Protocol on the Statute of the Court of Justice describes the functions of the Court of Justice under the following Titles: Judges and Advocates-General; Organization; Procedure; The

Court of First Instance of the European Communities; and Final Provisions.

The Protocol on the financial consequences of the expiry of the ECSC Treaty and on the Research Fund for Coal and Steel provides for the transfer of all assets and liabilities of the ECSC to the European Community on 24 July 2002. The net worth of these assets and liabilities shall be considered as assets intended for research in the sectors related to the coal and steel industry.

Principal Elements of the Treaty of Lisbon

In an effort to revive the constitutional reform process, following the rejection of the Draft Constitutional Treaty in national referendums in France and the Netherlands in May and June 2005, a new treaty was drawn up. The Treaty of Lisbon (formally known as the Treaty of Lisbon amending the Treaty on European Union and the Treaty establishing the European Community) was signed in Lisbon on 13 December 2007 by the heads of state or government of the 27 Member States. The Treaty entered into force on 1 December 2009.

The Treaty of Lisbon sought to redefine the functions and procedures of the institutions of the EU. It created a High Representative of the Union for Foreign Affairs and Security Policy (appointed by the European Council by qualified majority with the agreement of the President of the Commission) to represent the EU internationally, combining the former roles of EU Commissioner responsible for external relations and EU High Representative for the Common Foreign and Security Policy (although foreign policy remains subject to a national veto). The High Representative of the Union for Foreign Affairs and Security Policy is mandated by the Council, but is also one of the Vice-Presidents of the Commission and chairs the External Relations Council. The Lisbon Treaty also provided for the creation of a new permanent president of the European Council, elected by the European Council for a period of two years and six months, renewable once; the creation of this role aimed to promote coherence and continuity in policymaking.

The system of a six-month rotating presidency was retained for the different Council formations (except for the External Relations Council, chaired by the High Representative of the Union for Foreign Affairs and Security Policy). A new system of fixed 18-month troikas (groups of three presidencies) was introduced, sharing the presidencies of most configurations of the Council, to facilitate overall co-ordination and continuity of work. The Lisbon Treaty provided for a revised system of qualified majority voting in the Council.

The European Parliament's legislative powers are consolidated under the Treaty, which grants the Parliament the right of co-decision with the Council of the European Union in an increased number of policy areas, giving it a more prominent role in framing legislation. The maximum number of seats in the European Parliament was raised to 751 (fully effective from 2014).

The European Commission retains its composition of one commissioner for each member state. The Treaty establishing the European Community (also known as the Treaty of Rome) is renamed as the Treaty on the Functioning of the European Union, with references to the 'Community' replaced by 'Union'. The Lisbon Treaty attempts to improve democracy and transparency within the Union, introducing the right for EU citizens to petition the Commission to introduce new legislation and enshrining the principles of subsidiarity (that the EU should only act when an objective can be better achieved at supranational level, implying that national powers are the norm) and proportionality (that the action should be proportional to the desired objective). National parliaments are given the opportunity to examine EU legislation to ensure that it rests within the EU's remit, and legislation may be returned to the Commission for reconsideration if one-third of Member States find that a proposed law breaches these principles. The Treaty of Lisbon enables enhanced co-operation for groups numbering at least one-third (i.e. currently nine) of the Member States.

The Treaty provides a legal basis for the EU defence force, with a mutual defence clause, and includes the stipulation that the EU has the power to sign treaties and sit on international bodies as a legal entity in its own right. The new framework also provides for the establishment of a European public prosecutor's office to combat EU fraud and cross-border crime and the right to dual citizenship (i.e. of the EU as well as of a Member State), and includes arrangements for the formal withdrawal of a Member State from the EU.

Other Treaties

Additional treaties have also been signed by Member States of the European Union:

Treaty Instituting a Single Council and a Single Commission of the European Communities (Merger Treaty): signed in Brussels on 8 April 1965 by the six original members. This Treaty was repealed by the Treaty of Amsterdam.

Treaty Modifying Certain Budgetary Arrangements of the European Communities and of the Treaty Instituting a Single Council and a Single Commission of the European Communities: signed in Luxembourg on 22 April 1970 by the six original members.

Treaty Concerning the Accession of the Kingdom of Denmark, Ireland, the Kingdom of Norway and the United Kingdom of Great Britain and Northern Ireland to the European Economic Community and the European Atomic Energy Community: signed in Brussels on 22 January 1972 (amended on 1 January 1973, owing to the non-accession of Norway).

Treaty of Accession of the Hellenic Republic to the European Economic Community and to the European Atomic Energy Community: signed in Athens on 28 May 1979.

Treaty of Accession of the Portuguese Republic and the Kingdom of Spain to the European Economic Community and to the European Atomic Energy Community: signed in Lisbon and Madrid on 12 June 1985.

Note: Accession of new members to the European Coal and Steel Community was enacted separately, by a Decision of the European Council.

Treaty Concerning the Accession of the Kingdom of Norway, the Republic of Austria, the Republic of Finland and the Kingdom of Sweden to the European Union: signed in Corfu on 24 June

1994 (amended on 1 January 1995, owing to the non-accession of Norway).

Treaty of Accession of the Czech Republic, Estonia, Cyprus, Latvia, Lithuania, Hungary, Malta, Poland, Slovenia and Slovakia: signed in Athens on 16 April 2003.

Treaty of Accession of Bulgaria and Romania: signed in Luxembourg on 25 April 2005.

Treaty of Accession of Croatia: signed in Brussels on 9 December 2011.

Treaty Establishing the European Stability Mechanism: signed in Brussels on 2 February 2012.

Treaty on Stability, Coordination and Governance in the Economic and Monetary Union: signed in Brussels on 2 March 2012.

TRADE AND PROFESSIONAL ORGANIZATIONS

AAPA (Audiovisual Anti-Piracy Alliance): 65 ave Louise, 1050 Brussels, Belgium; e-mail contact@aapa.eu; internet www.aapa.eu; 24 mem. cos; f. 1997; Contact Sheila Cassells (Exec. Dir); Philip Davies (Vice-Pres.).

ACE (Alliance for Beverage Cartons and the Environment): 250 ave Louise, POB 106, 1050 Brussels, Belgium; tel. (+32) 2-5040710; fax (+32) 2-5040719; e-mail secretariat@beveragecarton.eu; internet www.ace.be; f. 1990; Pres. Kristian Hall; Contact Annick Carpentier (Dir-Gen.).

ACE/CAE (Architects' Council of Europe/Conseil des Architectes d'Europe): 29 rue Paul Emile Janson, 1050 Brussels, Belgium; tel. (+32) 2-5431140; fax (+32) 2-5431141; e-mail info@ace-cae.eu; internet www.ace-cae.eu; f. 1990; Pres. Luciano Lazzari; Sec.-Gen. Ian Pritchard.

ACEA (Association of European Automobile Manufacturers/Association des Constructeurs Européens d'Automobiles): 85 ave des Nerviens, 1040 Brussels, Belgium; tel. (+32) 2-7325550; fax (+32) 2-7387310; e-mail info@acea.be; internet www.acea.be; f. 1991; Pres. Dieter Zetsche; Sec.-Gen. Erik Jonnaert; Contact Cara McLaughlin (Dir, Communications).

ACEM (Association des Constructeurs Européens de Motocycles/Motorcycle Industry in Europe): 1 ave de la Joyeuse Entrée, 1040 Brussels, Belgium; tel. (+32) 2-2309732; e-mail acem@acem.eu; internet www.acem.eu; f. 1994; Pres. Stephan Pierer; Sec.-Gen. Antonio Perlot; Contact Manuel Ordonez de Barraicua (Communications Officer).

ACF Europe (Association of Career Firms Europe): c/o Slooter & Partners, Badhuisweg 84, 2587 CL, The Hague, Netherlands; tel. (+31 70) 3588184; fax (+31 70) 3585880; e-mail acfeurope@gmail.com; internet www.acf-europe.org; f. 1996; Pres. Bev White; Contact Herbert Mühlenhoff (Treasurer).

ACI EUROPE (Airports Council International—European Region/Conseil International des Aéroports—Région Europe/Internationaler Flughafenrat—Region Europa): 10 rue Montoyer, 1000 Brussels, Belgium; tel. (+32) 2-5520977; fax (+32) 2-5025637; e-mail communique@aci-europe.org; internet www.aci-europe.org; f. 1991; Pres. Dr Michael Kerkloh; Contact Olivier Jankovec (Dir-Gen.).

ACME (Association of Mutual Insurers and Insurance Co-operatives in Europe/Association des Assureurs Mutuels et Coopératifs en Europe): 98 rue du Trône, 1050 Brussels, Belgium; tel. (+32) 2-5033878; fax (+32) 2-5033055; e-mail secretariat@amice-eu.org; internet www.amice-eu.org; f. 1978; Pres. Grzegorz Buczkowski; Sec.-Gen. Sarah Goddard; Contact Tatiana Paraskeva (Communications Officer).

ACT (Association of Commercial Television in Europe/Association des Télévisions Commerciales Européennes): 26 rue des Deux Eglises, 1000 Brussels, Belgium; tel. (+32) 2-7360052; e-mail gp@acte.be; internet www.acte.be; f. 1989; Contact Grégoire Polad (Dir-Gen.).

ACTIP (Animal Cell Technology Industrial Platform): POB 256, 03580 La Nucia (Alicante), Spain; tel. (+34) 687-967080; e-mail actip-secretariat@telefonica.net; internet www.actip.org; f. 1990; Contact Dr Chantra Eskes (Exec. Sec.).

ACTUARIES (European Actuarial Consultative Group/Groupe Consultatif Actuariel Européen): Maison des Actuaires, 1 Place du Samedi, 1000 Brussels, Belgium; tel. (+32) 2-2016021; e-mail moniques@actuary.eu; internet actuary.eu; f. 1978; Contact Kristoffer Bork (Chair.).

ADDE (Association of Dental Dealers in Europe/Association des Dépôts Dentaires en Europe): Ten Houte 13, 8500 Kortrijk, Belgium; tel. (+32) 4-75831908; e-mail info@adde.info; internet www.adde.info; f. 1950; Pres. Dominique Deschietere; Contact Dr Maurizio Quaranta (Vice-Pres.).

AECM (Association of European Candle Manufacturers/Association Européenne des Syndicats de Fabricants de Bougies et de Cierges): 142 ave Jules Bordet, 1140 Brussels, Belgium; tel. (+32) 2-7611654; fax (+32) 2-7611699; e-mail aecm@kelleneurope.com; internet europecandles.org; f. 1962; Pres. Miquel Roura; Sec.-Gen. Dani Kolb.

AEDE (European Association of Teachers/Association Européenne des Enseignants/Europäische Erzieherbund): 21 rue Marie Thérèse, 1000 Brussels, Belgium e-mail jeanclaude.gonon@gmail.com; internet www.aede.eu; f. 1956; Pres. Prof. Silvano Marseglia; Sec.-Gen. Jean-Claude Gonon.

AEEBC (Association of European Experts in Building and Construction/Association d'Experts Européens du Bâtiment et de la Construction): 67 rue Ducale, 1000 Brussels, Belgium e-mail aeebcorg@gmail.com; internet www.aeebc.org; f. 1991; Pres. Gert Johansen; Sec.-Gen. Kevin Sheridan; Contact Martin Russell-Croucher (Gen. Man.).

AEGPL (European LPG Association/Association Européenne des Gaz de Pétrole Liquéfiés/Europäischer Flüssiggasverband): 15–17 Rue Belliard, Etterbeek, 1040 Brussels, Belgium; tel. (+32) 2-5669120; fax (+32) 2-5669129; e-mail aegpl@aegpl.be; internet www.aegpl.eu; f. 1968; Pres. Paul Ladner.

AEGRAFLEX (European Association of Engravers and Flexographers/Association Européenne des Graveurs et des Flexographes/Europäische Vereinigung der Graveure und Flexografen): Jakobsplatz 11–15, 90402 Nürnberg, Germany; tel. (+49 911) 205620; fax (+49 911) 2056240; e-mail info@aegraflex.org; internet aegraflex.org; f. 1966; Pres. Geo Wulf Müller; Contact Andrzej Kruszena (Vice-Pres.).

AEJ/AJE (Association of European Journalists/Association des Journalistes Européens/Vereinigung Europäischer Journalisten): 261/19 Panská, 811 01 Staré Mesto, Slovakia; e-mail tibor.macak@gmail.com; internet www.aej.org; f. 1962; Pres. Otmar Lahodynsky; Sec.-Gen. Tibor Macak.

AER (Association of European Radios/Association Européenne des Radios): 26 rue des Deux Eglises, 1000 Brussels, Belgium; tel. (+32) 2-7369131; e-mail vincent.sneed@aereurope.org; internet www.aereurope.org; f. 1992; Pres. Stefan Möller; Sec.-Gen. Julia Maier-Hauff.

AEROBAL (European Association of Aluminium Aerosol Container Manufacturers/Association Européenne des Fabricants de Boîtes en Aluminium pour Aérosol/Europäische Vereinigung der Hersteller von Aluminium-Aerosoldosen): Haus der Metalle, 2nd Floor, Rooms 213 & 214, Am Bonneshof 5, 40474 Düsseldorf, Germany; tel. (+49 211) 4796-144; fax (+49 211) 4796-25141; e-mail aerobal@aluinfo.de; internet www.aerobal.org; f. 1976; Pres. Eric Olivier Frantz; Sec.-Gen. Gregor Spengler; Contact Heike Heckmann-Hardy (Assistant).

AESGP (Association of the European Self-Medication Industry/Association Européenne des Spécialités Pharmaceutiques Grand Public/Europäischer Fachverband der Arzneimittel-

Hersteller): 7 ave de Tervuren, 1040 Brussels, Belgium; tel. (+32) 2-7355130; fax (+32) 2-7355222; e-mail info@aesgp.eu; internet www.aesgp.eu; f. 1964; Pres. Birgit Schuhbauer; Contact Dr Hubertus Cranz (Dir-Gen.).

AEXEA (Association of European Registered Experts/Association des Experts Européens Agréés/Arbeitsgemeinschaft der Europäischen Anerkannten Sachverständigen): 3 rue du Col Moll, 75017 Paris, France; tel. (+33) 4-67-64-37-10; e-mail aexea.contact@aexea.fr; internet www.aexea.org; f. 1990; Pres. Bernard Robert; Contact Lygia Negrier Dormont (Vice-Pres.).

AFECOR (European Control Manufacturers' Association/Association des Fabricants Européens d'Appareils de Contrôle et de Régulation/Verband Europäischer Kontrollgerätehersteller): 16 Luchthavenlaan, 1800 Vilvoorde, Belgium; e-mail afecor@din.de; internet www.afecor.org; f. 1963; Pres. Dr Martin Bergemann; Sec.-Gen. Dr T. Norbert Burger.

AFEMS (Association of European Manufacturers of Sporting Ammunition/Association des Fabricants Européens de Munitions de Sport/Vereinigung der Europäischen Sportmunitionshersteller): Viale dell'Astronomia 30, 00144 Rome, Italy; tel. (+39 06) 5903510; fax (+39 06) 54282691; e-mail secretariat@afems.org; internet www.afems.org; f. 1951; Pres. Torbjorn Lindskog.

AFERA (European Association for the Self Adhesive Tape Industry/Association des Fabricants Européens de Rubans Auto-Adhésifs/Verband des Europäischen Klebebandhersteller): Laan Copes van Nieuw Oost-Indië 131-G, 2593 BM The Hague, Netherlands; tel. (+31 70) 3123916; fax (+31 70) 3636348; e-mail mail@afera.com; internet www.afera.com; f. 1958; Pres. Mete Konuralp; Sec.-Gen. Astrid Lejeune; Contact Evert Smit (Technical Committee Chair.).

AFILIATYS 105 ave des Nerviens, 1040 Brussels, Belgium; tel. (+32) 2-2985000; e-mail info@afiliatys.eu; internet www.afiliatys.eu; f. 2006; Pres. Pierre Eveillard; Sec.-Gen. Daniel Germain.

AICV (Association of the Cider and Fruit Wine Industry of the EU/Association des Industries des Cidres et Vins de Fruits de l'UE/Vereinigung der Obst- und Fruchtweinindustrie der EG): 221 rue de la Loi, POB 5, 1040 Brussels, Belgium; tel. (+32) 2-2350620; fax (+32) 2-2829420; e-mail aicv@aicv.org; internet www.aicv.org; f. 1968; Pres. Jean-Pierre Stassen; Sec.-Gen. Jan Hermans; Contact Karin Batstra (Office Man.).

AIDA (International Association for the Distributive Trade/Association Internationale de la Distribution/Internationale Vereinigung des Handels): 34 rue Marianne 34, 1180 Brussels, Belgium; tel. (+32) 2-3459923; fax (+32) 2-3460204; e-mail info@aida-int.org; f. 1952; Pres. Pierre Jeanmart; Sec.-Gen. Léon F. Wegnez.

AIECE (Association of European Conjuncture Institutes/Association d'Instituts Européens de Conjoncture Economique/Vereinigung der Europäischen Wirtschaftsprognoseinstitute): 3 Place Montesquieu, 1348 Louvain-La-Neuve, Belgium; tel. (+32) 10-474143; fax (+32) 10-473945; e-mail severine.dinjar@uclouvain.be; internet sites.uclouvain.be/aiece; f. 1957; Sec.-Gen. Severine Dinjar; Contact C. Mathieu (Chair.).

AIJN (Association of the Industry of Juices and Nectars from Fruits and Vegetables of the EU/Association de l'Industrie des Jus et Nectars de Fruits et de Légumes de l'UE): 221 rue de la Loi, Bte 5, 1040 Brussels, Belgium; tel. (+32) 2-2350620; fax (+32) 2-2829420; e-mail aijn@aijn.org; internet www.aijn.org; f. 1958; Pres. Marjan Skotnicki-Hoogland; Sec.-Gen. Jan Hermans; Contact Karin Batstra (Office Man.).

AIM (Association des Industries de Marque/European Brands Association): 9 ave des Gaulois, 1040 Brussels, Belgium; tel. (+32) 2-7360305; fax (+32) 2-7346702; internet www.aim.be; f. 1967; Pres. Jan Zijderveld; Contact Alain Galaski (Dir-Gen.).

AIMA (Alternative Investment Management Association Limited): 167 Fleet St, 2nd Floor, London EC4A 2EA, United Kingdom; tel. (+44 20) 7822-8380; e-mail info@aima.org; internet www.aima.org; f. 1997; Contact Jack Inglis (CEO).

AIPCE (EU Fish Processors' Association/Association des Industries du Poisson de l'UE): c/o AGEP, 142B ave Jules Bordet, 1140 Brussels, Belgium; tel. (+32) 2-7611649; fax (+32) 2-7611699; e-mail aipcee@kellencompany.com; internet www.aipce-cep.org; f. 1959; Pres. Guus Pastoor; Sec.-Gen. A. Vicente.

AISE (Association Internationale de la Savonnerie, de la Détergence et des Produits d'Entretien/International Association of Soap, Detergent and Maintenance Products): 165 blvd du Souverain, 4th Floor, 1160 Brussels, Belgium; tel. (+32) 2-6796260; fax (+32) 2-6796279; e-mail aise.main@aise.eu; internet www.aise.eu; f. 1952; Pres. Arndt Scheidgen; Contact Susanne Zänker (Dir-Gen.).

AMFEP (Association of Manufacturers and Formulators of Enzyme Products): 142 ave Jules Bordet 142, 1140 Brussels, Belgium; tel. (+32) 2-7611677; fax (+32) 2-7611699; e-mail amfep@kellencompany.com; internet www.amfep.org; f. 1977; Sec.-Gen. Patrick Fox; Contact Karl-Heinz Maurer (Treasurer).

ANEC (European Association for the Co-ordination of Consumer Representation in Standardization/Porte-parole des Consommateurs Européens dans la Normalisation): 32 ave de Tervuren, POB 27, 1040 Brussels, Belgium; tel. (+32) 2-7432470; fax (+32) 2-7065430; e-mail anec@anec.eu; internet www.anec.org; f. 1995; Pres. Arnold Pindar; Sec.-Gen. Stephen Russell.

APAG (European Oleochemicals & Allied Products Group/Groupement Européen des Produits Oléochimiques & Associés): 4 ave E. Van Nieuwenhuyse, Bte 1, 1160 Brussels, Belgium; tel. (+32) 2-6767211; fax (+32) 2-6767300; e-mail oleosurfactant@cefic.be; internet www.apag.org; Pres. Eddy Feijen; Sec.-Gen. Chantal de Cooman.

APEAL (Association of European Producers of Steel for Packaging/Association Professionnelle des Producteurs Européens d'Acier pour Emballage): 5 ave Ariane, Bldg 'Integrale' E3, 4th Floor, 1200 Brussels, Belgium; tel. (+32) 2-5379151; fax (+32) 2-5357200; e-mail info@apeal.be; internet www.apeal.org; f. 1986; Pres. Stéphane Tondo; Sec.-Gen. Alexis Van Maercke.

APFE (European Glass Fibre Producers' Association/Association des Producteurs de Fibres de Verre Européens): 89 ave Louise, Bte 2, 1050 Brussels, Belgium; tel. (+32) 2-5384446; fax (+32) 2-5378469; e-mail info@glassfibreeurope.eu; internet www.glassfibreeurope.eu; f. 1987; Pres. Mauro Malanchini; Sec.-Gen. Axel C. Jorns.

APME (Association of Plastics Manufacturers in Europe (Plastics Europe)/Association des Producteurs de Matières Plastiques en Europe): 4 ave E. Van Nieuwenhuyse, POB 3, Auderghem, 1160 Brussels, Belgium; tel. (+32) 2-6753297; fax (+32) 2-6753935; e-mail info@plasticseurope.org; internet www.plasticseurope.org; f. 1976; Pres. Daniele Ferrari; Contact Karl-H. Foerster (Exec. Dir).

APPE (Association of Petrochemical Producers in Europe/Association des Producteurs de Produits Pétroléochimiques en Europe): 4 ave E. Van Nieuwenhuyse, 1160 Brussels, Belgium; tel. (+32) 2-6767257; fax (+32) 2-6767216; e-mail info@petrochemistry.eu; internet www.petrochemistry.eu; f. 1985; Contact Arns Dorothée (Exec. Dir).

AQUA (European Association of Water Meter Manufacturers/Association Européenne des Fabricants de Compteurs d'Eau):

39–41 rue Louis Blanc, 92038 Paris La Défense, Cedex, France; tel. (+33) 1-43-34-76-81; fax (+33) 1-43-34-76-86; e-mail mesure@syndicat-mesure.fr; internet www.syndicat-mesurev2.fr; f. 1959; Pres. Patrick Antoine; Contact Lance McGowan (Treasurer).

AQUA EUROPA (European Water Conditioning Association/ Fédération Européenne du Traitement de l'Eau): 80 blvd A. Reyers, 1030 Brussels, Belgium; tel. (+32) 10-245236; fax (+32) 10-225659; e-mail henderyckx.aqua@skynet.be; internet www.britishwater.co.uk/aqua-europa.aspx; Pres. Peter-Lorenz Schmidt; Sec.-Gen. David Neil-Gallacher.

AREA (Air Conditioning & Refrigeration European Association): Diamant Bldg, 5th Floor, 80 blvd A. Reyers, 1030 Brussels, Belgium; tel. (+32) 2-2066866; e-mail info@area-eur.be; internet www.area-eur.be; f. 1989; Pres. Per Jonasson; Sec.-Gen. Olivier Janin; Contact Wolfgang Zaremski (Treasurer).

ARGE (European Federation of Associations of Lock and Builders' Hardware Manufacturers/Fédération Européenne des Associations de Fabricants de Serrures et de Ferrures): Offerstr. 12, 42551 Velbert, Germany; tel. (+49 2051) 950636; e-mail j.kieker@arge.org; internet arge.org; f. 1956; Sec.-Gen. Joachim Kieker; Contact Hans Weissenböck (Chair.).

ARTGLACE (Confederation of Associations of Ice-Cream Makers of the EC/Confédération des Associations des Artisans Glaciers de la Communauté Européenne/Konföderation der Eishersteller der EG): Via del Parco 3, 32013 Longarone (Belluno), Italy; tel. (+39 04) 37577577; fax (+39 04) 37770340; e-mail info@artglace.org; internet www.artglace.com; f. 1989; Pres. Ferdinando Buonocore; Sec.-Gen. Giuseppina Cascone; Contact Fausto Bortolot (Vice-Pres.).

ASD (AeroSpace and Defence Industries Association of Europe): 10 rue Montoyer, 1000 Brussels, Belgium; tel. (+32) 2-7758110; e-mail info@asd-europe.org; internet www.asd-europe.org; f. 2004; Pres. Eric Trappier; Sec.-Gen. Jan Pie; Contact Marine d'Hollander (Communications Man.).

ASERCOM (Association of European Refrigeration Compressor and Controls Manufacturers): 194 rue de Chataignières, 38890 Vignieu, France; tel. (+33) 4-74-80-64-53; fax (+33) 4-74-80-64-53; e-mail office@asercom.org; internet asercom.org; f. 1992; Pres. Claude Blanc; Contact Stephane Nassau (Chair.).

ASSIFONTE (Association of the Processed Cheese Industry in the EU/Association de l'Industrie de la Fonte de Fromage de l'UE): Euromilk, 22–28 ave d'Auderghem, 1040 Brussels, Belgium; tel. (+32 2) 5-495041; fax (+32 4) 7-5590422; e-mail aanton@euromilk.org; internet eda.euromilk.org; f. 1964; Pres. Ludwig Rupp; Sec.-Gen. Alexander Anton.

ASSUC (Association of Professional Organizations of the Sugar Trade in the EU/Association des Organisations Professionnelles du Commerce des Sucres pour les Pays de l'Union Européenne): 49–51 rue de Trèves, POB 14, 1040 Brussels, Belgium; tel. (+32) 2-2310638; fax (+32) 2-7326766; e-mail assuc@assuc.eu; internet www.assuc.eu; f. 1959; Pres. Julian Price; Sec.-Gen. Daniel Pérez Vega.

AVEC (Association of Poultry Processors and Poultry Import and Export Trade in the EU countries/Association des Centres d'Abattage de Volailles et du Commerce d'Importation et d'Exportation de Volailles des Pays de l'UE): 47–51 rue du Luxembourg, 1050 Brussels, Belgium; tel. (+32) 2-2381082; fax (+32) 2-2381084; e-mail avec@avec-poultry.eu; internet www.avec-poultry.eu; f. 1966; Pres. Paul Lopez; Sec.-Gen. Cees Vermeeren.

BEDA (Bureau of European Designers' Associations/Bureau des Associations de Designers Européens): Koloniënstraat 56, 7th Floor, 1000 Brussels, Belgium; tel. (+32) 2-2173977; fax (+32) 2-2179972; internet www.beda.org; f. 1969; Pres. Robin Edman; Contact John Mathers (Vice-Pres.).

BIBM (Bureau International du Béton Manufacturé/International Bureau for Precast Concrete): 55 rue d'Arlon, 6th Floor, 1040 Brussels, Belgium; tel. (+32) 2-3401828; fax (+32) 2-5880649; e-mail info@bibm.eu; internet www.bibm.eu; f. 1954; Pres. Claus Bering; Sec.-Gen. Alessio Rimoldi.

BIPAR (Bureau International des Producteurs d'Assurances et de Réassurances/European Federation of Insurance Intermediaries): 40 ave Albert-Elisabeth, 1200 Brussels, Belgium; tel. (+32) 2-7356048; fax (+32) 2-7321418; e-mail bipar@bipar.eu; internet www.bipar.eu; f. 1937; Sec.-Gen. Juan Ramon Pla.

CAEF (European Foundry Association): c/o Bundesverband der Deutschen Gie.-Industrie Hansaallee 203, 40549 Düsseldorf, Germany; tel. (+49 211) 6871-217; fax (+49 211) 6871-40217; e-mail info@caef.eu; internet www.caef.org; f. 1953; Pres. Borut Triplat; Sec.-Gen. Max Schumacher.

CAFIM/BDMH (Confederation of European Music Industries/Bundesverband der Deutschen Musikinstrumenten-Hersteller eV): Brunnenstr. 31, 65191 Wiesbaden, Germany; tel. (+49 611) 9545-886; fax (+49 611) 9545-885; e-mail mail@cafim.org; internet www.cafim.org; f. 2000; Pres. Claudio Formisano; Contact Emmanuel Tonnelier (Vice-Pres.).

CAOBISCO (Association of the Chocolate, Biscuit and Confectionery Industries of the EU/Association des Industries de la Chocolaterie, Biscuiterie et Confiserie de l'UE): 9–31 ave des Nerviens, 1040 Brussels, Belgium; tel. (+32) 2-5081021; internet caobisco.eu; f. 1959; Pres. Alessandro Cagli; Contact Laurence Vicca (Communications and Project Man.).

CAPIEL (Co-ordinating Committee for the Associations of Manufacturers of Industrial Electrical Switchgear and Controlgear in the European Union/Comité de Coordination des Associations de Constructeurs d'Appareillage Industriel Electrique de l'Union Européenne): 11–17 rue de l'Amiral Hamelin, 75783 Paris, France; tel. (+33) 1-45-05-70-77; fax (+33) 1-47-04-68-57; e-mail info@capiel.eu; internet www.capiel.eu; f. 1959; Pres. Karlheinz Kaul; Sec.-Gen. Delphine Eyraud-Galant.

CARTOON (European Association of Animation Film/Association Européenne du Film d'Animation): 105 ave Huart Hamoir, 1030 Brussels, Belgium; tel. (+32) 2-2451200; fax (+32) 2-2454689; e-mail info@cartoon-media.eu; internet cartoon-media.com; f. 1988; Pres. Christian Davin; Contact Marc Vandeweyer (Dir-Gen.).

CBMC (Brewers of Europe/Brasseurs Européens/Europäischen Brauer): 23–25 rue Caroly, 1050 Brussels, Belgium; tel. (+32) 2-5511810; fax (+32) 2-6609402; e-mail info@brewersofeurope.org; internet www.brewersofeurope.org; f. 1958; Pres. Pavlos Photiades; Sec.-Gen. Pierre-Olivier Bergeron; Contact Jan de Grave (Dir, Communications).

CCA-EUROPE (Calcium Carbonate Association-Europe): c/o IMA-Europe, 26 rue des Deux Eglises, Bte 2, 1000 Brussels, Belgium; tel. (+32) 2-2104410; fax (+32) 2-2104429; e-mail secretariat@ima-europe.eu; internet www.cca-europe.eu; f. 1995; Pres. Catherine Delfaux; Sec.-Gen. Dr Roger Doome.

CCBE (Council of Bars and Law Societies of Europe/Conseil des Barreaux de l'Union Européenne/Rat der Anwaltschaften der Europäischen Union): 40/8 rue Joseph II, 1000 Brussels, Belgium; tel. (+32) 2-2346510; fax (+32) 2-2346511; e-mail ccbe@ccbe.eu; internet www.ccbe.org; f. 1960; Pres. Ruthven Gemmell; Sec.-Gen. Philip Buisseret; Contact Antonín Mokry (Vice-Pres.).

CEA-PME/ECA-SME (Confédération Européenne des Associations de Petites et Moyennes Entreprises/European Confederation of Associations of Small and Medium-sized

Enterprises): 60 ave de Tervuren, 1000 Brussels, Belgium; tel. (+32) 2-74020278; fax (+32) 2-7396279; e-mail info@cea-pme.org; internet www.cea-pme.com; f. 1992; Pres. Mario Ohoven; Sec.-Gen. Walter G. Grupp; Contact Valérie Guimard (Vice-Pres.).

CEAB (Confédération Européenne des Administrateurs de Biens/European Confederation of Property Managers): 36 ave de Tervuren, Bte 2, 1040 Brussels, Belgium; tel. (+32) 2-7354990; fax (+32) 2-7359988; e-mail secretariat@cepi.eu; internet www.cepi.eu; f. 1990; Pres. Jaroslaw Zielinski; Sec.-Gen. Elisabeth Rohr; Contact Guy Valkenborg (Man. Dir).

CEC (Confédération Européenne des Cadres/European Confederation of Executives and Managerial Staff): 81A rue de la Loi, 1040 Brussels, Belgium; tel. (+32) 2-4201051; fax (+32) 2-4201292; e-mail info@cec-managers.org; internet www.cec-managers.org; f. 1989; Pres. Ludger Ramme; Sec.-Gen. Luigi Caprioglio; Contact Catherine Houlmann (Deputy Sec.-Gen.).

CEC (Confédération Européenne de l'Industrie de la Chaussure/European Confederation of the Footwear Industry): 14B rue de la Science, 1040 Brussels, Belgium; tel. (+32) 2-8084452; fax (+32) 2-8088464; e-mail info@cec-footwearindustry.eu; internet cec-footwearindustry.eu; f. 1981; Pres. Cleto Sagripanti; Contact Carmen Arias Castellano (Gen. Sec.).

CECAPI (Comité Européen des Constructeurs d'Appareillage Electrique d'Installation/European Committee of Electrical Installation Equipment Manufacturers): c/o Orgalime, Diamant Bldg, 80 blvd A. Reyers, 1030 Brussels, Belgium; tel. (+32) 2-7068237; fax (+32) 2-7068253; e-mail cecapi@orgalime.org; internet www.cecapi.org; f. 1967; Pres. Concha García Concepción; Contact Terry Rowbury (Gen. Sec.).

CECCM (Confederation of European Community Cigarette Manufacturers/Confédération des Fabricants de Cigarettes de la Communauté Européenne): 375 ave Louise, 1050 Brussels, Belgium; tel. (+32) 2-5410030; fax (+32) 2-5410035; e-mail ceccm@ceccm.eu; internet www.ceccm.eu; f. 1988; Sec.-Gen. Alisdair Gray; Contact Amani Kessi (Chair.).

CECE (Committee for European Construction Equipment/Comité Européen des Matériels de Génie Civil/Europäisches Baumaschinen Komitee): BluePoint, 80 blvd A. Reyers, 1030 Brussels, Belgium; tel. (+32) 2-7068226; fax (+32) 2-7068210; e-mail info@cece.eu; internet www.cece.eu; f. 1959; Pres. Bernd Holz; Sec.-Gen. Riccardo Viaggi; Contact Enrico Prandini (Vice-Pres.).

CECED (Federation of European Manufacturers of Domestic Appliances/Conseil Européen des Constructeurs d'Appareils Ménagers): 114 blvd Brand Whitlock, 1200 Brussels, Belgium; tel. (+32) 2-7387810; fax (+32) 2-4030841; e-mail secretariat@ceced.eu; internet www.ceced.eu; f. 1959; Pres. Reinhard Zinkann; Contact Paolo Falcioni (Dir-Gen.).

CECIMO (European Committee for Co-operation of the Machine Tools Industries/Europäisches Komitee für die Zusammenarbeit der Werkzeugmaschinenindustrien): 66 ave Louise, 1050 Brussels, Belgium; tel. (+32) 2-5027090; fax (+32) 2-5026082; e-mail information@cecimo.eu; internet www.cecimo.eu; f. 1950; Pres. Luigi Galdabini; Contact Giorgia Zia (Communication Officer).

CECIP (Comité Européen des Constructeurs d'Instruments de Pesage/European Committee of Scale and Weighing Machines Manufacturers): Bluepoint Bldg, 80 blvd A. Reyers, 1030 Brussels, Belgium; tel. (+32) 2-7068215; fax (+32) 2-7068210; e-mail info@cecip.eu; internet www.cecip.eu; f. 1958; Pres. Urs Widmer; Sec.-Gen. Bárbara Morales Pascual.

CECOD (Committee of European Manufacturers of Petroleum Measuring and Distributing Equipment/Comité de Fabricants Européens d'Installation et de Distribution de Pétrole): 39–41 rue Louis Blanc, 92400 Courbevoie, Paris, France; tel. (+33) 1-43-34-76-81; fax (+33) 1-43-34-76-82; e-mail cecod@cecod.eu; internet www.cecod.eu; f. 1969; Contact Damian Tracey (Chair.).

CECOF (Comité Européen des Constructeurs de Fours et d'Equipements Thermiques Industriels/European Committee of Industrial Furnace and Heating Equipment Manufacturers): Lyoner Str. 18, 60528 Frankfurt am Main, Germany; tel. (+49 69) 6603-1413; fax (+49 69) 6603-2413; e-mail cecof@vdma.org; internet www.cecof.org; f. 1972; Pres. René Branders; Sec.-Gen. Dr Timo Würz; Contact Dr Karl Nolte (Vice-Pres.).

CECOMAF/EUROVENT (European Committee of Air Handling and Air Conditioning Equipment Manufacturers/Comité Européen des Constructeurs de Matériel Aéraulique): Diamant Bldg, 80 blvd A. Reyers, 1030 Brussels, Belgium; tel. (+32) 2-466900401; e-mail secretariat@eurovent.eu; internet eurovent.eu; f. 1958; Pres. Alex Rasmussen; Sec.-Gen. Felix Van Eyken.

CECOP (European Confederation of Workers' Co-operatives, Social Co-operatives and Social and Participative Enterprises/Confédération Européenne des Coopératives de Travail Associé, des Coopératives Sociales et des Entreprises Sociales et Participatives): 105 ave Milcamps 105, 1030 Brussels, Belgium; tel. (+32) 2-5431033; fax (+32) 2-5431037; e-mail cecop@cecop.coop; internet www.cecop.coop; f. 1979; Pres. Beppe Guerini; Sec.-Gen. Bruno Roelants; Contact Leire Luengo (Communications Officer).

CECRA (European Council for Motor Trades and Repairs/Conseil Européen du Commerce et de la Réparation Automobiles): 46 blvd de la Woluwe, Bte 9, 1200 Brussels, Belgium; tel. (+32) 2-7719656; fax (+32) 2-7726567; e-mail mail@cecra.org; internet www.cecra.eu; f. 1983; Pres. Jean-Charles Herrenschmidt; Contact Arnold Koopmans (Vice-Pres.).

CECT (Comité Européen de la Chaudronnerie et de la Tuyauterie/European Committee of Boiler, Vessel and Pipework Manufacturers): c/o SNCT, 39–41 rue Louis Blanc, 92038 Courbevoie, France; tel. (+33) 1-47-17-62-71; fax (+33) 1-47-17-62-77; e-mail snct@snct.org; internet www.snct.org; Pres. François Rieffel; Sec.-Gen. Yolande Bufquin.

CED (Council of European Dentists): 1 ave de la Renaissance, 1000 Brussels, Belgium; tel. (+32) 2-7363429; fax (+32) 2-7402026; e-mail ced@cedentists.eu; internet www.cedentists.eu; f. 1961; Pres. Dr Marco Landi; Sec.-Gen. Nina Brandelet-Bernot; Contact Cecilia Prunas (Communications Officer).

CED/VDD (Confédération Européenne de la Droguerie/Verband Deutscher Drogisten): Am Mühleacker 59, 50259 Pulheim-Brauweiler, Cologne, Germany; tel. (+49 2234) 9673-260; fax (+49 2234) 9673-270; e-mail drogistenverband@t-online.de; internet www.drogistenverband.de; f. 1873; Pres. Martin Dälken; Contact Michael Bastian (Chief Exec. Officer).

CEDEC (Confédération Européenne des Distributeurs d'Energie Publics Communaux/European Federation of Local Energy Companies): 55 rue Royale, 1000 Brussels, Belgium; tel. (+32) 2-2178117; e-mail info@cedec.com; internet www.cedec.com; f. 1992; Pres. Rudi Oss; Sec.-Gen. Gert de Block; Contact Catherine Biren (Management Asst).

CEDI (European Confederation of Independents/Confédération Européenne des Indépendants/Europaverband der Selbständigen): Wilhelmstr. 77, 10117 Berlin, Germany; tel. (+49 030) 20459854; fax (+49 030) 20455320; e-mail info@esd-ev.de; internet www.esd-ev.de; f. 1973; Pres. Kuni Ludwig Both.

Trade and Professional Organizations DIRECTORY

CEDIP (European Committee of Professional Diving Instructors/Comité Européen des Moniteurs de Plongée Professionnels/Europäischer Verband der Berufstauchlehrer): Via L.Cagnola 7, 24050 Ghisalba, Italy; tel. (+39 03) 296263749; e-mail info@insias.it; internet www.cedip.org; f. 1993; Pres. Pierangello Martinelli.

CEEC (Comité Européen des Economistes de la Construction/European Committee of Construction Economists): POB 5078, 5800 Venray, the Netherlands; tel. (+31) 478691616; e-mail info@ceecorg.eu; internet www.ceecorg.eu; f. 1979; Pres. Tarmo Savolainen; Contact Micheál O'Connor (Gen. Sec.).

CEEP (European Centre for Enterprises with Public Participation and of Enterprises of General Economic Interest/Centre Européen des Entreprises à Participation Publique et des Entreprises d'Intérêt Economique Général): 26 rue des Deux Eglises, bte 5, 1000 Brussels, Belgium; tel. (+32) 2-2192798; internet (+32) 2-2181213; e-mail ceep@ceep.eu; internet www.ceep.eu; f. 1961; Pres. Katherina Reiche; Sec.-Gen. Valeria Ronzitti; Contact Manuela Mattiello (Office Man.).

CEEREAL (European Breakfast Cereal Association): 9–31 ave des Nerviens, 1040 Brussels, Belgium; tel. (+32) 2-5495640; e-mail info@ceereal.eu; internet www.ceereal.eu; f. 1992; Pres. John Athanatos; Sec.-Gen. Alexander Jess.

CEETTAR (Confédération Européenne des Entrepreneurs de Travaux Agricoles et Ruraux et Forestiers/European Organization of Agricultural, Rural and Forestry Contractors/Europäische Konföderation der Technischen, Landwirtschaftlichen und Ländlichen Unternehmen): 31B/2 rue de l'Hôpital, 1000 Brussels, Belgium; tel. (+32) 2-2742206; fax (+32) 2-4007126; e-mail ceettar@ceettar.eu; internet www.ceettar.eu; f. 1961; Pres. Klaus Pentzlin; Sec.-Gen. Eric Dresin.

CEEV (Comité Européen des Entreprises Vins/European Committee of Wine Companies): 43/5E ave des Arts, 1040 Brussels, Belgium; tel. (+32) 2-2309970; fax (+32) 2-5130218; e-mail ceev@ceev.eu; internet www.ceev.eu; f. 1960; Pres. Jean Marie-Barillère; Sec.-Gen. Ignacio Sánchez Recarte; Contact Julie Bouveret (Office Man.).

CEFACD (Comité Européen des Fabricants d'Appareils de Chauffage et de Cuisine Domestique/European Committee of Manufacturers of Domestic Heating and Cooking Appliances/Europäischer Auschuss der Heiz- und Kochgeräte Industrie): Lyoner Str. 9, D-60528, Frankfurt am Main, Germany; tel. (+32) 2-8924625; fax (+32) 2-8924629; e-mail secretary.general@cefacd.eu; internet www.cefacd.eu; f. 1950; Pres. Jean-François Sidler; Sec.-Gen. Dorothea Kadenbach.

CEFIC (Conseil Européen de l'Industrie Chimique/European Chemical Industry Council/Europäischer Rat der Chemischen Industrie): 4 ave E. Van Nieuwenhuyse, Bte 1, 1160 Brussels, Belgium; tel. (+32) 2-6767211; fax (+32) 2-6767300; e-mail jpi@cefic.be; internet www.cefic.org; f. 1972; Pres. Hariolf Kottmann; Contact Marco Mensink (Dir-Gen.).

CEFS (Comité Européen des Fabricants de Sucre/European Committee for Sugar Manufacturers): 182 ave de Tervuren, 1150 Brussels, Belgium; tel. (+32) 2-7620760; fax (+32) 2-7710026; e-mail cefs@cefs.org; internet www.comitesucre.org; f. 1954; Sec.-Gen. Nicole Lejeune; Contact Marie-Christine Ribera (Dir.-Gen.).

CEI-BOIS (Confédération Européenne des Industries du Bois/European Confederation of Woodworking Industries/Zentralverband der Europäischen Holzindustrie): 24 rue Montoyer, Bte 20, 1000 Brussels, Belgium; tel. (+32) 2-5562585; e-mail info@cei-bois.org; internet www.cei-bois.org; f. 1952; Sec.-Gen. Patrizio Antonicoli; Contact Anders Ek (Chair.).

CEIR (Comité Européen de l'Industrie de la Robinetterie/European Association for the Taps and Valves Industry/Europäisches Komitee der Armaturenindustrie): c/o Orgalime, 80 blvd A. Reyers, 1030 Brussels, Belgium; tel. (+32) 2-2066866; e-mail secretariat@ceir.eu; internet www.ceir.eu; f. 1959; Pres. Ugo Pettinaroli; Sec.-Gen. Anne Claire Rasselet; Contact Carlos Velazquez (Vice-Pres.).

CEJA (Conseil Européen des Jeunes Agriculteurs/European Council of Young Farmers/Europäischer Rat der Junglandwirte): 67 rue de la Loi, 1040 Brussels, Belgium; tel. (+32) 2-2304210; e-mail ceja@ceja.be; internet www.ceja.eu; f. 1958; Pres. Alan Jagoe; Sec.-Gen. Alessia Musumarra.

CEJH (Communauté Européenne des Jeunes de l'Horticulture/European Community of Young Horticulturists/Europäische Gemeinschaft der Jungen Gartenbauer): Giessener Stra. 47, D-35305 Grunberg, Germany; tel. (+49 6401) 910-150; fax (+49 6401) 910-176; e-mail info@cejh.org; internet www.cejh.org; f. 1965; Pres. Rikard Jansson; Sec.-Gen. Sandro Beutnagel.

CELCAA (Comité Européen de Liaison des Commerces Agricoles et Agro-Alimentaires/European Liaison Committee for the Agri-Food Trade/Europäischer Verbindungsausschuss für den Handel mit Landwirtschaftlichen Produkten und Lebensmitteln): 10 rue de Tamines, 1060 Brussels, Belgium; tel. (+32) 2-5373711; e-mail p.rouhier@celcaa.eu; internet www.celcaa.eu; f. 1979; Pres. Paul Rooke; Sec.-Gen. Pascale Rouhier; Contact Ignacio Sanchez Recarte (Vice-Pres.).

CEMA (Comité Européen des Groupements de Constructeurs du Machinisme Agricole/European Committee of Associations of Manufacturers of Agricultural Machinery/Europäisches Komitee der Verbände der Landmaschinenhersteller): Diamant Bldg, 80 blvd A. Reyers, 1030 Brussels, Belgium; tel. (+32) 2-7068173; fax (+32) 2-7068210; e-mail secretariat@cema-agri.org; internet www.cema-agri.org; f. 1959; Pres. Richard Markwell; Sec.-Gen. Ulrich Adam.

CEMAFON (European Committee for Materials and Products for Foundries/Comité Européen des Matériels et Produits pour la Fonderie/Europäisches Komitee der Hersteller von Giessereimaschinen und Giessereiausrüstungen): Lyoner Str. 18, 60528 Frankfurt am Main, Germany; tel. (+49 69) 6603-1413; fax (+49 69) 6603-2413; e-mail cemafon@vdma.org; internet www.cemafon.org; f. 1972; Pres. Gabriele Galante; Sec.-Gen. Timo Würz.

CEMATEX (Comité Européen des Constructeurs de Machines Textiles/European Committee of Textile Machinery Manufacturers/Europäisches Komitee der Textilmaschinenhersteller): c/o UCMTF, 92038 Paris La Défense Cedex, France; tel. (+33) 1-47-17-63-45; fax (+33) 1-47-17-63-48; e-mail info@cematex.com; internet cematex.org; f. 1953; Pres. Fritz P. Mayer; Sec.-Gen. Maria Avery.

CEMBUREAU (European Cement Association/Association Européenne du Ciment): 55 rue d'Arlon 55, 1040 Brussels, Belgium; tel. (+32) 2-2341011; fax (+32) 2-2304720; e-mail communications@cembureau.eu; internet www.cembureau.be; f. 1947; Pres. Gonçalo Salazar Leite; Contact Jessica Johnson (Dir, Communications Dept).

CEMEP (Comité Européen de Constructeurs de Machines Electriques et d'Electronique de Puissance/European Committee of Manufacturers of Electrical Machines and Power Electronics/Europäisches Komitee der Hersteller von Elektrischen und Kraftelektronischen Maschinen): Diamant Bldg, 80 blvd A. Reyers, 1030 Brussels, Belgiume-mail cemep@cemep.eu; internet cemep.eu; f. 1990; Pres. Jürgen Sander; Sec.-Gen. Marco Vecchio.

CEN (Comité Européen de Normalisation/European Committee for Standardization/Europäisches Komitee für Normung): 17 ave Marnix, 1000 Brussels, Belgium; tel. (+32) 2-5500811;

fax (+32) 2-5500819; internet www.cen.eu; f. 1961; Pres. Vincent Laflèche; Sec.-Gen. Elena Santiago Cid.

CENELEC (European Committee for Electrotechnical Standardization/Comité Européen de Normalisation Electrotechnique/Europäisches Komitee für Elektrotechnische Normung): 17 ave Marnix, 1000 Brussels, Belgium; tel. (+32) 2-5500811; fax (+32) 2-5500819; e-mail info@cenelec.eu; internet www.cenelec.eu; f. 1973; Pres. Bernhard Thies; Sec.-Gen. Elena Santiago Cid.

CEOAH (Comité Européen de l'Outillage Agricole et Horticole/European Committee for Agricultural and Horticultural Tools and Implements/Europäisches Komitee der Gerätehersteller für Landwirtschaft und Garten): Light Trades House, 3 Melbourne Ave, Sheffield S10 2QJ, United Kingdom; e-mail light.trades@virgin.net; Pres. C. A. Thomashoff; Sec.-Gen. J. G. Till.

CEOC (Confédération Européenne des Organismes de Contrôle Technique, d'Inspection, de Certification et de Prévention/International Confederation of Inspection and Certification Organizations/Europäische Vereinigung der Organisationen für Prüfung, Überwachung, Zertifizierung und Prävention): 20–22 rue du Commerce, 1000 Brussels, Belgium; tel. (+32) 2-5115065; fax (+32) 2-5025047; e-mail info@ceoc.com; internet www.ceoc.com; f. 1961; Pres. Stefan Haas; Sec.-Gen. Drewin Nieuwenhuis; Contact Van Phuc Lê (Vice-Pres.).

CEP (Comité des Organisations Nationales des Importateurs et Exportateurs de Poisson/Federation of National Organizations of Importers and Exporters of Fish): 142 ave Jules Bordet, 1140 Brussels, Belgium; tel. (+32) 2-7611649; fax (+32) 2-7611699; e-mail aipcee@kellencompany.com; internet www.aipce-cep.org; f. 1959; Pres. P. Bamberger; Sec.-Gen. A. Vincete; Contact Matthias Keller (Vice-Pres.).

CEPA (Confederation of European Pest Control Associations/Confédération Européenne des Associations de Pesticides Appliqués): 37 Seringenstraat, 1950 Kraainem, Belgium; tel. (+32) 2-7313281; fax (+32) 2-7315843; e-mail roland@cepa-europe.org; internet www.cepa-europe.org; f. 1974; Contact Henry Mott (Chair.).

CEPE (European Council of Paint, Printing Ink and Artists' Colours Industry/Conseil Européen de l'Industrie des Peintures, des Encres d'Imprimerie et des Couleurs d'Art/Europäische Vereinigung der Lack-, Druckfarben und Künstlerfarbenindustrie): 6 ave Van Nieuwenhuyse, 1160 Brussels, Belgium; tel. (+32) 2-6767480; fax (+32) 2-6767490; e-mail secretariat@cepe.org; internet www.cepe.org; f. 1951; Sec.-Gen. Jean Schoder; Contact Paul Keymolen (Asst Sec.-Gen.).

CEPEC (Confédération Européenne Professionelle des Esthéticiennes Cosméticiennes/European Confederation of Beauticians and Cosmeticians): 36–38 rue Joseph II, 1000 Brussels, Belgium; tel. (+32) 2-2307429; fax (+32) 2-2307219; e-mail info@cepec-eu.org; internet www.cepec-eu.org; f. 1995; Pres. Laura Grilli; Sec.-Gen. Magda Magri Naudi.

CEPI (Confederation of European Paper Industries/Confédération des Industries Papetières Européennes/Europäische Konföderation der Papierindustrien): 250 ave Louise, Bte 80, 1050 Brussels, Belgium; tel. (+32) 2-6274911; fax (+32) 2-6468137; e-mail mail@cepi.org; internet www.cepi.org; f. 1992; Contact Sylvain Lhôte (Dir-Gen.).

CEPI-CEI (Conseil Européen des Professions Immobilières/European Association of Real Estate Professions): Ave de Tervuren 36, Bte 2, 1040 Brussels, Belgium; tel. (+32) 2-7354990; fax (+32) 2-7359988; e-mail secretariat@cepi-cei.eu; internet www.cepi-cei.eu; f. 2015 by merger of two real estate asscns; Pres. Luc Machon; Sec.-Gen. Elisabeth Rohr; Contact Guy Valkenborg (Man. Dir).

CEPIS (Council of European Professional Informatics Societies): 18 ave Roger Vandendriessche, 1150 Brussels, Belgium; tel. (+32) 2-7721836; fax (+32) 2-6463032; e-mail info@cepis.org; internet www.cepis.org; f. 1989; Pres. Byron Nicolaides; Sec.-Gen. Fiona Fanning.

CEPLIS (European Council of the Liberal Professions/Conseil Européen des Professions Libérales): 70 Coudenberg, 1000 Brussels, Belgium; tel. (+32) 2-5114439; fax (+32) 2-5110124; e-mail ceplis@scarlet.be; internet www.ceplis.org; f. 1974; Pres. Rudolf Kolbe; Contact Gaetano Stella (Vice-Pres.).

CEPM/AGPM (General Association of Maize Growers/Confédération Européenne des Producteurs de Maïs/Association Générale des Producteurs de Maïs): 21 chemin de Pau, 64121 Montardon, France; tel. (+33) 5-59-12-67-00; fax (+33) 5-59-12-67-10; internet www.maizeurop.com; f. 1934; Pres. Daniel Peyraube; Sec.-Gen. Anne-Claire Vial; Contact Céline Duroc (Dir-Gen.).

CEPMC (Council of European Producers of Materials for Construction/Conseil Européen des Producteurs de Matériaux de Construction/Vereinigung Europäischer Baustoffhersteller): 68 blvd du Souverain, 1170 Brussels, Belgium; tel. (+32) 2-6455207; fax (+32) 2-6455213; e-mail info@construction-products.eu; internet www.construction-products.eu; f. 1988; Pres. Heimo Scheuch; Contact Christophe Skyes (Dir-Gen.).

CEPS (Confédération Européenne des Producteurs de Spiritueux/European Spirits Organization): 12 rue Belliard, POB 5, 1040 Brussels, Belgium; tel. (+32) 2-7792423; e-mail info@spirits.eu; internet www.spirits.eu; f. 1993; Pres. Joep Stassen; Contact Paul Skehan (Dir-Gen.).

CEPT (European Conference of Postal and Telecommunications Administrations/Conférence Européenne des Administrations des Postes et des Télécommunications/Europäische Konferenz der Verwaltungen für Post und Telekommunikation): Nyropsgade 37, 1602 Copenhagen K, Denmark; tel. (+45) 33-89-63-00; fax (+45) 33-89-63-30; e-mail eco@eco.cept.org; internet cept.org; f. 1959; Pres. Germán Vázquez.

CER/CCFE (Community of European Railways/Communauté Européenne du Rail/Gemeinschaft der Europäischen Bahnen): 53 ave des Arts, 1000 Brussels, Belgium; tel. (+32) 2-2130870; fax (+32) 2-5125231; e-mail contact@cer.be; internet www.cer.be; f. 1988; Contact Libor Lochman (Exec. Dir).

CERAME-UNIE (Liaison Office of the European Ceramic Industries/Bureau de Liaison des Industries Céramiques Européennes/Verbindungsbüro der Europäischen Keramikindustrie): 12 rue Belliard, 1000 Brussels, Belgium; tel. (+32) 2-8083880; fax (+32) 2-5115174; e-mail sec@cerameunie.eu; internet cerameunie.eu; f. 1962; Contact Renaud Batier (Dir-Gen.).

CERP/DPRG (European Public Relations Confederation/Confédération Européenne des Relations Publiques/Deutsche Public Relations Gesellschaft eV): 443 chaussée de Gand, Bte 4, 1080 Brussels, Belgium; tel. (+32) 2-4140432; fax (+32) 2-4149605; f. 1959; Pres. Roberto Zangrandi; Sec.-Gen. Colin Farrington; Contact Dr Serra Görpe (Vice-Pres.).

CESA (Community of European Shipyards Association): 52–54 rue Marie de Bourgogne, 3rd Floor, 1000 Brussels, Belgium; tel. (+32) 2-2302791; fax (+32) 2-2304332; e-mail info@cesa.eu; internet www.cesa-shipbuilding.org; f. 1937; Sec.-Gen. Douwe Cunningham; Contact Costas Kokkalas (Vice-Chair.).

CESCE (Comité Européen des Services de Soutien aux Entreprises/European Committee for Business Support Services): Kanselarijstraat 19, 1000 Brussels, Belgium; tel. (+32) 2-2276390; fax (+32) 2-2276391; f. 1969; Pres. Jean-Claude Bachelot.

Trade and Professional Organizations DIRECTORY

CESI (Confédération Européenne des Syndicats Indépendants/European Confederation of Independent Trade Unions/Europäische Union der Unabhängigen Gewerkschaften): 1–5 ave de la Joyeuse Entrée, 1040 Brussels, Belgium; tel. (+32) 2-2821870; fax (+32) 2-2821871; e-mail info@cesi.org; internet www.cesi.org; f. 1990; Pres. Romain Wolff; Sec.-Gen. Klaus Heeger; Contact Péterné Erzsébet Boros (Vice-Pres.).

CET (European Ceramic Tile Manufacturers' Federation/Fédération Européenne des Producteurs de Carreaux/Europäischer Industrieverband der Keramikfliesen): 17 rue de la Montagne, 1000 Brussels, Belgium; tel. (+32) 2-5113012; fax (+32) 2-5115174; e-mail sec@cerameunie.eu; internet www.cerameunie.eu; f. 1959; Pres. José Luís Lanuza; Sec.-Gen. Renaud Batier.

CET (Confédération Européenne des Taxis/Taxi Radio Bruxellois S.A./Europäische Konföderation der Taxis): 54–56 rue des Carburants, 1190 Brussels, Belgium; tel. (+32) 2-3494949; fax (+32) 2-3494900; internet www.taxisverts.be.

CETOP (Comité Européen des Transmissions Oléohydrauliques et Pneumatiques/European Oil Hydraulic and Pneumatic Committee/Europäisches Komitee Ölhydraulik und Pneumatik): Lyoner Str. 18, 60528 Frankfurt am Main, Germany; tel. (+49 69) 66031-201; fax (+49 69) 66032-201; e-mail info@cetop.org; internet www.cetop.org; f. 1962; Pres. Stefan König; Sec.-Gen. Sylvia Grohmann-Mundschenk.

CFE (Confédération Fiscale Européenne): 188A ave de Tervuren, 1150 Brussels, Belgium; tel. (+32) 2-7610092; e-mail brusselsoffice@cfe-eutax.org; internet www.cfe-eutax.org; f. 1959; Pres. Piergiorgio Valente; Sec.-Gen. Andrew Clarke; Contact Petra Pospisilova (Vice-Pres.).

CIBE (Confédération Internationale des Betteraviers Européens/International Confederation of European Beet Growers/Internationale Vereinigung Europäischer Rübenanbauer): 111/9 blvd Anspachlaan, 1000 Brussels, Belgium; tel. (+32) 2-5046090; fax (+32) 2-5046099; e-mail cibeoffice@cibe-europe.eu; internet www.cibe-europe.eu; f. 1925; Pres. Bernhard Conzen; Sec.-Gen. Elisabeth Lacoste; Contact Eric Lane (Vice-Pres.).

CIDE (Commission Intersyndicale des Déshydrateurs Européens/European Dehydrators' Association/Arbeitsgemeinschaft Europäischer Trockungsbetriebe): 57 rue Froissart, 1040 Brussels, Belgium; e-mail ericguillemot@aol.com; f. 1959; Pres. Eiko Jan Duursema; Sec.-Gen. M. Eric Guillemot.

CIELFFA (Comité International d'Etude du Laminage à Froid du Feuillard d'Acier/European Federation of the National Associations of Cold Rolled Narrow Steel Strip Producers/Europäische Verband der Nationalen Fachverbände der Kaltbandhersteller): Kaiserswerther Str. 137, 40474 Düsseldorf, Germany; tel. (+49 211) 456412-0; fax (+49 211) 456412-2; e-mail info@cielffa.org; internet www.cielffa.org; f. 1953; Pres. Dr Rolf Jansen; Sec.-Gen. Martin Kunkel.

CIMO (Freshfel Europe/European Fresh Produce Asscn): 49–51 rue de Trèves, 1040 Brussels, Belgium; tel. (+32) 2-7771580; fax (+32) 2-7771581; e-mail info@freshfel.org; internet freshfel.org; Pres. Luc Clerx; Contact Stephan Weist (Vice-Pres.).

CIRCCE (Confédération Internationale de la Représentation Commerciale de la Communauté Européenne/International Confederation of the Commercial Representation of the European Community/Internationale Vereinigung der Handelsvertretung der Europäischen Gemeinschaft): 2 rue d'Hauteville, 75010 Paris, France; tel. (+33) 1-48-24-97-59; internet www.csn.fr; Pres. Nelly Froger; Contact Michel Boccacci (Gen. Sec.).

CIRFS (Comité International de la Rayonne et des Fibres Synthétiques/International Rayon and Synthetic Fibres Committee/Internationale Chemiefaservereinigung): 6 ave E. Van Nieuwenhuyse, 1160 Brussels, Belgium; tel. (+32) 2-6767455; fax (+32) 2-6767454; e-mail secretariat@cirfs.org; internet www.cirfs.org; f. 1950; Pres. Heinz Meierkord; Contact Frédéric van Houte (Dir-Gen.).

CLCCR (Comité de Liaison de la Construction de Carrosseries et de Remorques/Liaison Committee of the Body and Trailer Building Industry/Verbindungsausschuss der Aufbauen- und Anhängerindustrie): c/o Verband der Automobilindustrie eV (VDA), Behrenstr. 35, 10117 Berlin, Germany; tel. (+49 30) 897842-0; fax (+49 30) 897842-600; e-mail info@vda.de; internet www.vda.de; f. 1961; Pres. Matthias Wissmann; Sec.-Gen. Thomas Fabian.

CLECAT (European Association for Forwarding, Transport, Logistic and Customs Services): 77 rue du Commerce, 1040 Brussels, Belgium; tel. (+32) 2-5034705; fax (+32) 2-5034752; e-mail info@clecat.org; internet www.clecat.org; f. 1958; Pres. Steve Parker; Sec.-Gen. Ivan Petrov; Contact Nicolette van der Jagt (Dir-Gen.).

CLEO/ELCO (Comité de Liaison Européen des Ostéopathes/European Liaison Committee of Osteopaths/Europäisches Verbindungskomitee der Osteopathen): 116 ave des Champs Elysées, 75008 Paris, France; tel. (+33) 1-44-21-80-75; fax (+33) 1-44-21-82-99; Pres. J. Barkworth; Sec.-Gen. F. P. Berthenet.

CLEPA (European Association of Automotive Suppliers/Association Européenne des Equipementiers Automobiles/Verband der Europäischen Autozulieferer): 30G Cours Saint-Michel, 1040 Brussels, Belgium; tel. (+32) 2-7439130; fax (+32) 2-7320055; e-mail info@clepa.be; internet clepa.eu; f. 1959; Pres. Roberto Vavassori; Sec.-Gen. Sigrid de Vries.

CLGE (Comité de Liaison des Géomètres Européens/Council of European Geodetic Surveyors): 76 rue du Nord, 1000 Brussels, Belgium; tel. (+32) 2-2196281; fax (+32) 2-2193147; e-mail info@ubg-bul.be; internet www.clge.eu; f. 1972; Pres. Maurice Barbieri; Sec.-Gen. Vasile Chiriac.

CLITRAVI (Centre de Liaison des Industries Transformatrices de Viandes de l'UE/Liaison Centre for the Meat Processing Industries in the EU): 18 blvd Baudoin, Bte 4, 1000 Brussels, Belgium; tel. (+32) 2-2035141; fax (+32) 2-2033244; e-mail info@clitravi.eu; internet www.clitravi.eu; f. 1958; Sec.-Gen. Dirk Dobbelaere; Contact Paolo Patruno (Deputy Sec.-Gen.).

CLPEU (Comité de Liaison des Podologues de l'UE/Liaison Committee of Podiatrists of the EU/Verbindungskomitee für Podologen der EU): St. Bernardse Steenweg 1000, 2620 Hemiksen, Belgium; tel. (+32) 3-8773938; fax (+32) 3-8775902; e-mail serge.coimbra@clpue.org; internet www.clpue.org; f. 1969; Pres. Neil Simmonite; Contact José Rooftfooth (Adviser).

CNUE/CNEU (Conférence des Notariats de l'Union Européenne/Council of the Notariats of the European Union): 120 ave de Cortenbergh, 1000 Brussels, Belgium; tel. (+32) 2-5139529; fax (+32) 2-5139382; e-mail info@cnue.be; internet www.cnue.be; f. 1993; Pres. José Manuel García Collantes; Sec.-Gen. Raul Radoi.

COCERAL (Committee of Cereals, Oilseeds, Animal Feed, Olive Oil, Oils and Fats and Agrosupply Trade in the EU/Comité du Commerce des Céréales, Aliments du Bétail, Oléagineux, Huile d'Olive, Huiles et Graisses et Agrofournitures/Komitee des Getreide-, Futtermittel-, Ölsaaten, Olivenöl, Ölen und Fetten und Landwirtschaftsliche Betriebsmittelhandels in der EG): 98 rue du Trône, 4th Floor, 1050 Brussels, Belgium; tel. (+32) 2-5020808; fax (+32) 2-5026030; e-mail secretariat@coceral.com; internet www.coceral.com; f. 1958; Pres. Jaana Kleinschmit; Sec.-Gen. Teresa Babuscio.

COCIR (European Co-ordination Committee of the Radiological, Electromedical and Healthcare IT Industry/Comité Européen de Coordination des Industries Radiologiques et

Electromédicales): Diamant Bldg, 80 blvd A. Reyers, 1030 Brussels, Belgium; tel. (+32) 2-7068960; fax (+32) 2-7068969; e-mail info@cocir.org; internet www.cocir.org; f. 1959; Pres. Joost Leeflang; Sec.-Gen. Nicole Denjoy; Contact Barbara Pes (Communications Man.).

COFALEC (Committee of Bakers Yeast Manufacturers of the EU/Comité des Fabricants de Levure Panification de l'UE/Komitee der Hefeindustrie in der EG): 9 blvd Malesherbes, 75008 Paris, France; tel. (+33) 1-45-08-54-82; internet www.cofalec.com; f. 1959; Pres. Marc Casier; Sec.-Gen. Emmanuel Guichard.

COGECA (Comité Général de la Coopération Agricole de l'UE/General Committee for Agricultural Co-operation in the EU/Allgemeiner Ausschuss des Ländlichen Genossenschaftswesens der Europäischen Union): 61 rue de Trèves, 1040 Brussels, Belgium; tel. (+32) 2-2872711; fax (+32) 2-2872700; e-mail mail@copa-cogeca.eu; internet www.copa-cogeca.be; f. 1959; Pres. Thomas Magnusson; Sec.-Gen. Pekka Pesonen.

COGEN EUROPE (European Association for the Promotion of Cogeneration/Association Européenne de Promotion de la Cogénération/Europese Vereniging voor de Promotie van Warmtekrachtkoppeling): 3–5 ave des Arts, 1210 Brussels, Belgium; tel. (+32) 2-7728290; fax (+32) 2-7725044; e-mail info@cogeneurope.eu; internet www.cogeneurope.eu; f. 1993; Contact Roberto Francia (Man. Dir).

CONCAWE (Oil Companies' European Association for Environment, Health and Safety in Refining and Distribution/Organisation Européenne des Compagnies Pétrolières pour l'Environnement, la Santé et Sécurité/Europäische Organisation der Ölgesellschaften für Umwelt, Gesundheit und Sicherheit): 165 blvd du Souverain, 1160 Brussels, Belgium; tel. (+32) 2-5669160; fax (+32) 2-5669181; e-mail info@concawe.org; internet www.concawe.eu; f. 1963; Pres. Bela Kelemen; Contact John Cooper (Dir-Gen.).

CONEBI (Confederation of the European Bicycle Industry): 46 blvd de la Woluwe 46, Bte 16, 1200 Brussels, Belgium; tel. (+32) 2-3044887; e-mail manuel.marsilio@conebi.eu; internet www.conebi.eu; f. 2014 as a result of merger; Pres. René Takens; Sec.-Gen. Greet Engelen; Contact Massimo Panzeri (Co-Vice-Pres); Erhard Büchel.

COPA (Committee of Professional Agricultural Organizations in the European Union/Comité des Organisations Professionnelles Agricoles de l'Union Européenne/Comité de las Organizaciones Profesionales Agrarias de la Unión Europea): 61 rue de Trèves, 1040 Brussels, Belgium; tel. (+32) 2-2872711; fax (+32) 2-2872700; e-mail mail@copa-cogeca.be; internet www.copa-cogeca.be; f. 1959; Pres. Martin Merrild; Sec.-Gen. Pekka Pesonen.

Cosmetics Europe (European Cosmetic, Toiletry and Perfumery Association): 40 ave Hermann Debroux, Auderghem, 1160 Brussels, Belgium; tel. (+32) 2-2276610; fax (+32) 2-2276627; e-mail cosmeticseurope@cosmeticseurope.eu; internet www.cosmeticseurope.eu; f. 1962 as COLIPA; Pres. Loïc Armand; Contact John Chave (Dir-Gen.).

COTANCE (Confederation of National Associations of Tanners and Dressers of the European Community/Confédération des Associations Nationales des Tanneurs et Mégissiers de la Communauté Européenne/Vereinigung der Nationalen Verbänden der Lederindustrie): 40 rue Washington, 1050 Brussels, Belgium; tel. (+32) 2-5127703; e-mail cotance@euroleather.com; internet www.euroleather.com; f. 1981; Pres. Thomas Bee; Sec.-Gen. Gustavo Gonzalez-Quijano.

CPIV (Comité Permanent des Industries du Verre Européennes/Standing Committee of the European Glass Industries/Ständiger Ausschuss der Europäischen Glasindustrien): 89 ave Louise, Bte 1, 1050 Brussels, Belgium; tel. (+32) 2-5384446; fax (+32) 2-5378469; e-mail info@cpivglass.be; internet www.cpivglass.be; f. 1967; Pres. Paolo Giacobbo; Sec.-Gen. Frédéric van Houte; Contact Véronique Favry Dupuis (Asst).

CPLOL (Comité Permanent de Liaison des Orthophonistes/Logopèdes de l'Union Européenne/Standing Liaison Committee of EU Speech and Language Therapists and Logopedists): 145 blvd Magenta, 75010 Paris, France; tel. (+33) 1-40-35-63-75; fax (+33) 1-40-37-41-42; e-mail info@cplol.org; internet www.cplol.eu; f. 1988; Pres. Michèle Kaufmann-Meyer; Sec.-Gen. Ulrika Guldstrand.

CPME (Comité Permanent des Médecins Européens/Standing Committee of European Doctors): 15 rue Guimard, 1040 Brussels, Belgium; tel. (+32) 2-7327202; fax (+32) 2-7327344; e-mail secretariat@cpme.eu; internet www.cpme.eu; f. 1959; Pres. Dr Jacques de Haller; Sec.-Gen. Annabel Seebohm; Contact Markus Kujawa (EU Policy Adviser).

CRIET (European Textile Finishers' Organization/Comités Réunis de l'Industrie de l'Ennoblissement Textile dans les Communautés Européennes): POB 314, 6700 AH Wageningen, Netherlands; tel. (+31 318) 564488; fax (+31 318) 564487; e-mail criet@criet.org; internet www.criet.org; f. 1956; Sec.-Gen. Cees Lodiers; Contact Koen Buyse (Vice-Pres.).

DIGITALEUROPE 14 rue de la Science, 1040 Brussels, Belgium; tel. (+32) 2-6095310; fax (+32) 2-4310489; e-mail info@digitaleurope.org; internet www.digitaleurope.org; f. 1999; Pres. Markus Borchert; Contact Cecilia Bonefeld-Dahl (Dir-Gen.).

EAAP/FEZ/EVT (European Association for Animal Production/Fédération Européenne de Zootechnie/Europäische Vereinigung für Tierproduktion): Via G. Tomassetti 3 A/1, 00161 Rome, Italy; tel. (+39 06) 44202639; e-mail eaap@eaap.org; internet www.eaap.org; f. 1949; Pres. Matthias Gauly; Sec.-Gen. Andrea Rosati; Contact Mike Coffey; Barac Zdravko (Vice-Pres.).

EACA (European Association of Communications Agencies): 152 blvd Brand Whitlock, 1200 Woluwe-Saint-Lambert, Belgium; tel. (+32) 2-7400710; e-mail info@eaca.eu; internet eaca.eu; f. 1959; Pres. Dominic Grainger; Contact Dominic Lyle (Dir-Gen.).

EACB/GEBC (European Association of Cooperative Banks/Groupement Européen des Banques Coopératives/Europäische Vereinigung der Genossenschaftsbanken): 26–38 rue de l'Industrie, 1040 Brussels, Belgium; tel. (+32) 2-2301124; fax (+32) 2-2300649; e-mail secretariat@eacb.coop; internet www.eacb.coop; f. 1970; Pres. G. Hofmann; Contact Hervé Guider (Gen. Man.).

EADTU (European Association of Distance Teaching Universities/Association Européenne des Universités d'Enseignement à Distance/Europäischer Verband der Universitaten für Fernstudien): Parkweg 27, 5th Floor, 6212 XN Maastricht, Netherlands; tel. (+31 43) 3118712; e-mail secretariat@eadtu.eu; internet eadtu.eu; f. 1987; Pres. Prof. Anja Oskamp; Contact George Ubachs (Man. Dir).

EAEVE/AEEEV (European Association of Establishments for Veterinary Education/Association Européenne des Etablissements d'Enseignement Vétérinaire/Europäischer Verband der Veterinarmedizinischen Ausbildungsstatten): Hietzinger Kai 87, 1130 Vienna, Austria; tel. (+43 1) 5123394; fax (+43 1) 5127710; e-mail office@eaeve.org; internet www.eaeve.org; f. 1988; Pres. Prof. Dr. Ana Bravo del Moral; Contact Dr Gerhard Greif (Vice-Pres.).

EAFE (European Association of Fisheries Economists): Research Institute of National Gendarmerie Criminal Department, 5 blvd Hautil, 95000 Pontoise, France; e-mail

Trade and Professional Organizations

webmaster@eafe.org; internet www.eafe.org; f. 1989; Pres. Luc Bourguignon.

EAHP / AEPH / EJHP (European Association of Hospital Pharmacists/Association Européenne des Pharmaciens des Hôpitaux/Europäische Vereinigung der Krankenhaus Apotheker): 3B rue de l'Abbé Cuypers, 1040 Brussels, Belgium; tel. (+32) 2-7412436; fax (+32) 2-7347910; e-mail info@eahp.eu; internet www.eahp.eu; f. 1972; Pres. Joan Peppard; Contact Aida Batista (Vice-Pres.).

EALM / AEMB (European Association of Livestock Markets/Association Européenne des Marchés aux Bestiaux/Europäischer Viehmärkteverband): c/o UECBV, 81A rue de la Loi, Bte 9, 1040 Brussels, Belgium; tel. (+32) 2-2304603; fax (+32) 2-2309400; e-mail info@uecbv.eu; internet www.uecbv.eu; f. 1983; Pres. Philippe Borremans; Sec.-Gen. Jean-Luc Mériaux.

EANPC / AECNP (European Association of National Productivity Centres/Association Européenne des Centres Nationaux de Productivité): c/o Prevent, Kolonel Begaultlaan 1A/51, 3012 Leuven, Belgium; tel. (+32) 1-6910910; fax (+32) 1-6910901; e-mail eanpc@prevent.be; internet www.eanpc.eu; f. 1966; Pres. John Heap; Sec.-Gen. Dr Marc De Greef; Contact Anil Yilmaz (Vice-Pres.).

EAPA (European Animal Protein Association/Association Européenne de Protéine Animale/Europäische Vereinigung für Tierprotein): 18 blvd Baudouin, 4th Floor, 1000 Brussels, Belgium; tel. (+32) 2-2035141; fax (+32) 2-2033244; e-mail info@eapa.biz; internet eapa.biz; f. 1988; Pres. Albert Gilbert; Sec.-Gen. Dirk Dobbelaere; Contact Geert van der Velden (Vice-Pres.).

EAPA (European Asphalt Pavement Association/Association Européenne des Producteurs des Enrobés/Europäische Asphalt Verband): 77 rue du Commerce, 1040 Brussels, Belgium; tel. (+32) 2-5025888; fax (+32) 2-5022358; e-mail info@eapa.org; internet www.eapa.org; f. 1973; Pres. John Kruse Larsen; Sec.-Gen. Egbert Beuving; Contact Christoph Hagemeier (Vice-Pres.).

EAPO / AEOP (European Association of Fish Producers Organizations/Association Européenne des Organisations de Producteurs dans le Secteur de la Pêche/Europese Vereniging van Visproducerende Organisaties): 20 Hendrik Baelskaai, 8400 Oostende, Belgium; tel. (+32) 59-432005; fax (+32) 59-322840; e-mail info@eapo.com; internet www.eapo.com; f. 1980; Pres. Pim Visser; Sec.-Gen. Emiel Brouckaert; Contact José A. Suárez-Llanos (Sec.).

EARTO (European Association of Research and Technology Organizations): 36–38 rue Joseph II, 1000 Brussels, Belgium; tel. (+32) 2-5028698; fax (+32) 2-5028693; e-mail secretariat@earto.eu; internet www.earto.eu; f. 1999; Pres. Frank Treppe; Sec.-Gen. Muriel Attané; Contact Antti Vasara (Vice-Pres.).

EAS (European Aquaculture Society/Société Européenne d'Aquaculture/Europäische Gesellschaft für Wasserlandwirtschaft): Slijkensesteenweg 4, 8400 Oostende, Belgium; tel. (+32) 5-9323859; fax (+32) 5-9321005; internet www.aquaeas.eu; f. 1976; Pres. Björn Myrseth; Contact Margriet Drouillon (Treas.).

EASA (European Advertising Standards Alliance/Alliance Européenne pour l'Ethique en Publicité): 26 rue de Deux Eglises, 1000 Brussels, Belgium; tel. (+32) 2-5137806; fax (+32) 2-5132861; e-mail info@easa-alliance.org; internet www.easa-alliance.org; f. 1992; Contact Stéphane Martin (Chair.).

EATP (European Association for Textile Polyolefins/Association Européenne des Textiles Polyolefines/Europäischer Verband der Polyolefintextilien): 46 ave E. Van Nieuwenhuyse, 1160 Brussels, Belgium; tel. (+32) 2-6767472; fax (+32) 2-6767474; e-mail secretariat@eatp.org; internet www.eatp.org; f. 1971; Contact Frédéric Van Houte (Dir-Gen.).

EAZA (European Association of Zoos and Aquaria/Association Européenne des Zoos et des Aquariums): POB 20164, 1000 HD Amsterdam, Netherlands; tel. (+31 20) 5200750; fax (+31 20) 5200752; e-mail info@eaza.net; internet www.eaza.net; f. 1992; Contact Myfanwy Griffith (Exec. Dir).

EBA (European Borates Association): c/o IMA-Europe, 26 rue des Deux Eglises, 1000 Brussels, Belgium; tel. (+32) 2-2104410; fax (+32) 2-2104429; e-mail secretariat@ima-europe.eu; internet www.ima-europe.eu/about-ima-europe/associations/eba; f. 1998; Pres. Muhittin Gündüz; Sec.-Gen. Dr Roger Doome.

EBC (European Brewery Convention/Convention Européenne de la Brasserie/Europäische Brauereikonvention): POB 510, 2380 BB Zoeterwoude, Netherlands; tel. (+31 71) 5456047; fax (+31 71) 5410013; e-mail secretariat@ebc-nl.com; internet www.ebc-nl.com; f. 1946; Pres. Dr Tiago M. Brandão; Sec.-Gen. John Brauer.

EBC (European Builders' Confederation/Confédération Européenne de l'Artisanat, des Petites et Moyennes Entreprises du Bâtiment/Europäische Konföderation des Handwerks und der Kleinen und Mittleren Bauunternehmen): 4 rue Jacques de Lalaing, 1040 Brussels, Belgium; tel. (+32) 25142323; fax (+32) 25140015; e-mail secretariat@ebc-construction.eu; internet www.ebc-construction.eu; f. 1990; Pres. Patrick Liébus; Sec.-Gen. Eugenio Quintieri.

EBF / FBE (European Banking Federation/Fédération Bancaire de l'Union Européenne): 56 ave des Arts, 1000 Brussels, Belgium; tel. (+32) 25083711; fax (+32) 25112328; e-mail ebf@ebf-fbe.eu; internet www.ebf-fbe.eu; f. 1960; Pres. Frédéric Oudéa; Contact Giovanni Sabatini (Chair.).

EBU / UER (European Broadcasting Union/Union Européenne de Radio-Télévision): L'Ancienne-Route 17A, 1218 Grand-Saconnex, Switzerland; tel. (+41) 22-717-21-11; fax (+41) 22-747-40-00; e-mail ebu@ebu.ch; internet www.ebu.ch; f. 1950; Pres. Jean-Paul Philippot; Contact Monica Maggioni (Vice-Pres.).

ECA (European Carpet Association/Association Européenne du Tapis/Europäischer Teppichverband): 24 rue Montoyer, 1000 Brussels, Belgium; tel. (+32) 2-2854883; fax (+32) 2-2306054; e-mail info@euratex.eu; internet www.euratex.org; f. 1994; Contact Francesco Marchi (Dir-Gen.).

ECA / USC (European Chimney Association/Union Syndicale des Cheminées): 3941 rue Louis Blanc, 92400 Courbevoie Paris Cedex, France; tel. (+33) 1-47-17-62-92; fax (+33) 1-47-17-64-27; e-mail office@eca-europe.org; internet www.eca-europe.org; f. 1989; Pres. Heinrich Göddeke; Sec.-Gen. Thomas Mühl; Contact Jean-Jaques Adam (Vice-Pres.).

ECA (European Cockpit Association/Association Européenne du Cockpit/Europäischer Cockpitverband): 20–22 rue du Commerce, 1000 Brussels, Belgium; tel. (+32) 27053293; fax (+32) 27050877; e-mail eca@eurocockpit.be; internet www.eurocockpit.be; f. 1990; Pres. Dirk Polloczek; Sec.-Gen. Philip von Schöppenthau; Contact Jon Horne (Vice-Pres.).

ECCA (European Cable Communications Association/Cable Europe): 41 ave des Arts 41, 1040 Brussels, Belgium; tel. (+32) 25211763; fax (+32) 25217976; e-mail info@cable-europe.eu; internet www.cable-europe.eu; f. 1955; Pres. Manuel Kohnstamm; Contact Virginia Lee (Dir of Communications).

ECCA (European Coil Coating Association): 19–21 rue du Luxembourg, 1000 Brussels, Belgium; tel. (+32) 25150020; fax (+32) 25114361; e-mail info@prepaintedmetal.eu; internet www.prepaintedmetal.eu; f. 1967; Pres. Vincent van Offeren; Contact Nick Brown (Vice-Pres.).

ECCO (European Confederation of Conservators and Restorers Organizations/Confédération Européenne des Organisations de Conservateurs-Restaurateurs): 70 rue Coudenberg, 1000 Brussels, Belgium; e-mail info@ecco-eu.org; internet www.ecco-eu.org; f. 1991; Pres. Susan Corr; Contact BarbaraAnja Davidson (Deputy Sec.-Gen.).

ECCO (European Consulting Company/Groupement des Associations Meunières des Pays de l'UE/Arbeitsgemeinschaft der Handelsmühlenverbände in den EG-Ländern): 13A ave de Tervueren, 1040 Brussels, Belgium; tel. (+32) 2-7365354; fax (+32) 2-7323427; e-mail info@ecco-eu.com; internet www.ecco-eu.com; f. 1975; Contact Frances Hunt (Man. Dirs); Maryse Hervé.

ECCS / CECM / EKS (European Convention for Constructional Steelwork/Convention Européenne de la Construction Métallique/Europäische Konvention für Stahlbau): 32 ave des Ombrages, Bte 20, 1200 Brussels, Belgium; tel. (+32) 27620429; fax (+32) 27620935; e-mail eccs@steelconstruct.com; internet www.steelconstruct.com; f. 1955; Contact Ernest Hendrickx (Chair.).

ECED (European Confederation of Equipment Distributors/Confédération Européenne des Distributeurs d'Equipment aisbl): 9–13 rue d'Idalie, 1050 Brussels, Belgium; tel. (+32) 26396247; fax (+32) 26449017; e-mail tom.antonissen@eced-association.org; Pres. Dr José Manuel L. Gameiro; Sec.-Gen. Tom Antonissen; Contact Philippe Papin (Vice-Pres.).

ECETOC (European Centre for Ecotoxicology and Toxicology of Chemicals/Centre Européen d'Ecotoxicologie et de Toxicologie de Produits Chimiques/Europäisches Zentrum für Ökotoxikologie und Chemietoxikologie): 2 ave Edmond Van Nieuwenhuyse, Bte 8, 1160 Brussels, Belgium; tel. (+32) 26753600; fax (+32) 26753625; e-mail info@ecetoc.org; internet www.ecetoc.org; f. 1978; Sec.-Gen. Alan Poole; Contact Dr Geneviève Gérits (Office Man.).

ECF (European Coffee Federation/Fédération Européenne du Café): 9–31 ave des Nerviens, 1040 Brussels, Belgium; tel. (+32) 25495641; fax (+32) 25081025; e-mail ecf@ecf-coffee.org; internet www.ecf-coffee.org; f. 1981; Sec.-Gen. Roel Vassen.

ECMA (European Carton Makers' Association): POB 85612, 2508 CH The Hague, Netherlands; tel. (+31 70) 3123911; fax (+31 70) 3636348; e-mail mail@ecma.org; internet www.ecma.org; f. 1973; Pres. Andreas Blaschke; Contact Hans van Schaik (Man. Dir).

ECMA (European Computer Manufacturers' Association): 114 rue du Rhône 114, 1204 Geneva, Switzerland; tel. (+41) 22-849-60-00; fax (+41) 22-849-60-01; e-mail istvan@ecma-international.org; internet www.ecma-international.org; f. 1961; Pres. Dr K. Yamashita; Sec.-Gen. Istvan Sebestyen.

ECNAIS (European Council of National Associations of Independent Schools/Conseil Européen d'Associations Nationales d'Ecoles Indépendantes/Europäischer Rat Nationaler Verbande von Freien Schulen): Ny Kongensgade 10, 1472 Copenhagen K, Denmark; tel. (+45) 70-20-26-42; fax (+45) 70-20-26-43; e-mail chairman@ecnais.org; internet www.ecnais.org; f. 1988; Sec.-Gen. Rodrigo Queiroz e Melo; Contact Simon J. Steen (Chair.).

ECOO (European Council of Optometry and Optics/Conseil Européen de l'Optométrie et de l'Optique/Europäischer Rat für Optometrie und Optik): 227 rue de la Loi, Bte 4, 1040 Brussels, Belgium; tel. (+32) 25800532; e-mail secretariat@ecoo.info; internet www.ecoo.info; f. 1992; Pres. Peter Folkesson; Sec.-Gen. Fabienne Eckert; Contact Dr Cindy Tromans (Vice-Pres.).

ECPA (European Crop Protection Association/Association Européenne pour la Protection des Cultures/Europäischer Pflanzenschutzverband): 6 ave E. Van Nieuwenhuyse, 1160 Brussels, Belgium; tel. (+32) 26631550; fax (+32) 26631560; e-mail ecpa@ecpa.eu; internet www.ecpa.eu; f. 1992; Pres. Eric Dereudre; Contact Jean-Philippe Azoulay (Dir-Gen.).

ECPCI (Association of the European Cigarette Paper Converting Industry/Association Européenne de l'Industrie de Transformation du Papier à Cigarettes/Verband der Europäischen Zigaretten Papier Verarbeitenden Industrie): Jägerstr. 51, 10117 Berlin, Germany; tel. (+49 030) 2096565-0; e-mail info@verband-rauchtabak.de; internet www.verband-rauchtabak.de; f. 1995; Contact Michael von Foerster (CEO).

ECSA (European Community Shipowners' Associations): 67 rue Ducale, 1000 Brussels, Belgium; tel. (+32) 25113940; fax (+32) 25118092; e-mail mail@ecsa.eu; internet www.ecsa.eu; f. 1965; Pres. Niels Smedegaard; Sec.-Gen. Patrick Verhoeven.

ECSLA (European Cold Storage and Logistics Association): sq. de Meeûs 35, 1000 Brussels, Belgium; tel. (+32) 28939737; fax (+32) 2-8939788; e-mail info@ecsla.eu; internet www.ecsla.eu; f. 1967; Pres. Rainer Wittenfeld; Sec.-Gen. Christine Weiker; Contact Manuel Cabrera Kabana (Vice-Pres.).

ECTA (European Communities Trade Mark Association/Association Communautaire du Droit des Marques/Vereinigung für Warenzeichen der Europäischen Gemeinschaften): 18/24 rue des Colonies, 8th Floor, 1000 Brussels, Belgium; tel. (+32) 2-5135285; fax (+32) 2-5130914; e-mail ecta@ecta.org; internet www.ecta.org; f. 1980; Pres. Ruta Olmane; Sec.-Gen. Carolin Kind; Contact Sozos-Christos Theodoulou (Vice-Pres.).

ECTA (European Cutting Tools Association/Association Européenne d'Outillage Mécanique/Europäischer Verband der Hersteller für Ausrüstungen von Schneidewerkzeugen): Lyoner Str. 18, 60528 Frankfurt am Main, Germany; tel. (+49 69) 6603-1467; fax (+49 69) 6603-2467; e-mail ecta@vdma.org; internet www.ecta-tools.org; Pres. Marc Schuler; Sec.-Gen. Dr Markus Heseding; Contact Alexandre Fernandez I Grau (Vice-Pres.).

ECTAA (Group of National Travel Agents' and Tour Operators' Associations within the EU/Groupement des Unions Nationales des Agences et Organisateurs de Voyages de l'UE): 36 rue Dautzenberg 36, 1050 Brussels, Belgium; tel. (+32) 2-6443450; fax (+32) 2-6442421; e-mail secretariat@ectaa.eu; internet www.ectaa.org; f. 1961; Pres. Merike Hallik; Sec.-Gen. Michel de Blust.

ECTP / CEU (European Council of Spatial Planners/Conseil Européen des Urbanistes/Europäischer Rat der Stadt- Regional- und Landesplaner): 63 ave d'Auderghem 63, 1040 Brussels, Belgium; tel. (+32) 0470350432; e-mail secretariat@ectp-ceu.eu; internet www.ectp-ceu.eu; f. 1985; Pres. Joris Scheers; Sec.-Gen. Dominique Lancrenon; Contact Michael Stein (Treasurer).

ECYC (European Confederation of Youth Club Organizations/Confédération Européenne des Organisations des Centres de Jeunes): 30 rue des Capucins, 1000 Brussels, Belgiumfax (+32) 2-5023917; e-mail ecyc@fcjmp.be; internet www.ecyc.org; f. 1976; Pres. Tor Haave; Sec.-Gen. Rares Craiut; Contact Pierre Evrard (Treasurer).

EDA (European Dairy Association/Association Laitière Européenne/Europäischer Milchindustrieverband): 22–28 ave d'Auderghem, 1040 Brussels, Belgium; tel. (+32) 2-5495040; e-mail eda@euromilk.org; internet www.euromilk.org; f. 1995; Pres. Michel Nalet; Sec.-Gen. Alexander Anton; Contact Claudine Hansen (Office Man.).

EDA (European Decaffeinators' Association/Association Européenne des Décaféineurs/Europäischer Verband der Entcoffeinierer): 18 rue de la Pépinière, 75008 Paris, France; tel. (+33) 1-53-42-13-38; fax (+33) 1-53-42-13-39; e-mail b-dufrene@wanadoo.fr; f. 1969; Pres. Dr Bernhard Bichsel.

EDA (European Demolition Association/Association Européenne de Démolition/Europäischer Abbruchverband): 11 rue des Colonies, 1000 Brussels, Belgium; tel. (+32) 2-8082760; e-mail info@europeandemolition.org; internet www.europeandemolition.org; f. 1978; Pres. William Sinclair; Sec.-Gen. José Blanco; Contact Francisco Cobo (Vice-Pres.).

EDANA (European Disposables and Non-wovens Association): 46 ave Herrmann Debroux, 1160 Brussels, Belgium; tel. (+32) 2-7349310; fax (+32) 2-7333518; e-mail info@edana.org; internet www.edana.org; f. 1971; Contact Paul Eevers (Treasurer).

EDIMA (European Digital Media Association/Association Européenne des Médias Numériques): 60 rue du Trône, 1050 Brussels, Belgium; tel. (+32) 2-6261990; fax (+32) 2-6269501; e-mail info@edima-eu.org; internet www.edima-eu.org; f. 2000; Pres. Stefan Krawczyk; Contact Siada El Ramly (Dir-Gen.).

EDTNA/ERCA (European Dialysis and Transplant Nurses' Association/European Renal Care Association/Association Européenne du Personnel Soignant en Dialyse et Greffes/Association Européenne des Soins Rénaux/Verband des Europäischen Dialyse- und Transplantationspflegepersonals/Verband des Europäischen Nierenpflegepersonals): Högs Byväg 118, 24655 Löddeköpinge, Sweden; tel. (+46 4) 670-96-24; e-mail edtna_erca@adexcellentbranding.com; internet www.edtnaerca.org; f. 1971; Contact Edita Noruisiene (Interim Sec. and Treasurer).

EEA (European Elevator Association): 44 ave Herrmann-Debroux, 1160, Brussels, Belgium; tel. (+32) 2-7721093; fax (+32) 2-7718661; e-mail info@eea-geie.org; internet www.eea-eeig.org; f. 1990; Pres. Jorge Estévez; Sec.-Gen. Robert Wright; Contact Gaëtane Van Laethem (Sec.).

EEA (European Express Association): 35 sq. de Meeûs, 1000 Brussels, Belgium; tel. (+32) 2-2854604; fax (+32) 2-2305706; e-mail info@euroexpress.org; internet www.euroexpress.org; f. 2000; Sec.-Gen. Russell Patten.

EECA (European Electronic Component Manufacturers' Association/Association Européenne des Fabricants de Composants Electroniques/Europäische Vereinigung der Elektronischen Komponentenhersteller): 11/13 rue de la Duchesse, 1150 Brussels, Belgium; e-mail secretariat@eusemiconductors.eu; internet www.eusemiconductors.eu; f. 1973; Pres. Thierry Tingaud; Contact Reinhard Sperlich (Vice-Pres.).

EEPA (European Egg Processors' Association/Association des Producteurs Européens d'Ovoproduits/Euro Eiprodukten Fabrikanten Verband): Bilkske 93, 8000 Brugge, Belgium; tel. (+32) 50-440070; fax (+32) 50-440077; e-mail info@eepa.info; internet www.eepa.info; f. 1995; Pres. Matthieu Justeau; Sec.-Gen. Clara Hagen.

EFA (European Driving Schools Association/Fédération Européenne des Auto-Ecoles/Europäische Fahrlehrer-Assoziation eV): 101 Wellington Rd North, Stockport, Cheshire SK4 2LP, United Kingdom; tel. (+44 161) 8831665; fax (+44 161) 4299779; e-mail info@efa-eu.com; internet efa-eu.com; Pres. John Lepine; Contact Manuel Picardi (Vice-Pres.); René Arnt.

EFAA (European Federation of Accountants and Auditors for SMEs): 4 rue Jacques de Lalaing, 1040 Brussels, Belgium; tel. (+32) 2-7368886; fax (+32) 2-7362964; e-mail info@efaa.com; internet www.efaa.com; f. 1994; Pres. Bodo Richardt.

EFAMA/FEFSI (European Fund and Asset Management Association/Fédération Européenne des Fonds et Sociétés d'Investissement): 47 rue Montoyer, 1000 Brussels, Belgium; tel. (+32) 2-5133969; fax (+32) 2-5132643; e-mail info@efama.org; internet www.efama.org; f. 1974; Pres. William Nott; Contact Bernard Delbecque (Dir of Economics and Research).

EFAMRO (European Federation of Associations of Market Research Organizations/Fédération Européenne des Associations d'Instituts de Marketing/Europäische Föderation der Marktforschungsinstitutsverbände): Overtocht 29, NL-2411 BS Bodegraven, the Netherlands; tel. (+31 10) 2894505; fax (+31 10) 2894400; e-mail efamro@wanadoo.nl; internet www.efamro.com; f. 1992; Pres. Andrew Cannon; Contact Debrah Harding (Vice-Pres.).

EFAPIT (Royal Dutch Grain and Feed Trade Association/Fédération Européenne des Importateurs et Négociants en Protéine Animale/Europäische Föderation der Tierproteinimporteure und -Händler): 80 Louis Braillelaan 80, 2719 EK Zoetermeer, the Netherlands; tel. (+31 10) 4673188; e-mail cvg@graan.com; internet www.graan.com; f. 1961; Sec.-Gen. Paulien D. van de Graaff; Contact Anton van Eck (Vice-Chair.).

EFB (European Federation of Biotechnology/Fédération Européenne de Biotechnologie/Europäische Föderation Biotechnologie): Baldiri Reixac 4–8, 08028 Barcelona, Spain; tel. (+34) 93-4020599; fax (+34) 93-4020434; e-mail efb@efb-central.org; internet www.efb-central.org; f. 1978; Pres. Prof. Mathias Uhlen.

EFBS/FEECL/EuBV (European Federation of Bldg Societies/Fédération Européenne d'Epargne et de Crédit pour le Logement/Europäische Bausparkassenvereinigung): 28 rue Jacques de Lalaing, 1040 Brussels, Belgium; tel. (+32) 2-2310371; fax (+32) 2-2308245; e-mail info@efbs-bausparkassen.org; internet www.efbs.org; f. 1962; Pres. Mag. Jan Jeníček; Contact Andreas J. Zehnder (Man. Dir).

EFBWW/FETBB (European Federation of Building and Woodworkers/Fédération Européenne des Travailleurs du Bâtiment et du Bois/Europäische Föderation der Bau- und Holzarbeiter): 45 rue Royale, Bte 1, 1000 Brussels, Belgium; tel. (+32) 2-2271040; fax (+32) 2-2198228; e-mail info@efbh.be; internet www.efbww.org; f. 1957; Pres. Dietmar Schäfers; Sec.-Gen. Sam Hägglund; Contact Marina Saegerman (Off. Man.).

EFCA (European Federation of Engineering Consultancy Associations/Fédération Européenne des Associations d'Ingénieurs-Conseils et Bureaux d'Ingénierie/Europäische Vereinigung der Verbände Beratender Ingenieure): 3–5 ave des Arts, 1210 Brussels, Belgium; tel. (+32) 2-2090770; fax (+32) 2-2090771; e-mail efca@efca.be; internet www.efcanet.org; f. 1992; Pres. Kevin Rudden; Sec.-Gen. Jan van der Putten; Contact Maximilian Grauvogl (Vice-Pres.); Liv Kari Skudal Hansteen.

EFCE (European Federation of Chemical Engineering/Fédération Européenne du Génie Chimique/Europäische Föderation für Chemie-Ingenieurwesen): c/o Dechema eV, Theodor-Heuss-Allee 25, 60486 Frankfurt am Main, Germany; tel. (+49 69) 7564-143; fax (+49 69) 7564-418; e-mail honndorf@dechema.de; internet efce.info; f. 1953; Pres. Prof. Rafiqul Gani; Sec.-Gen. Prof. Willi Meier; Contact Prof. Mike Considine (Exec. Vice-Pres.).

EFCEM (European Federation of Catering Equipment Manufacturers/Fédération Européenne des Constructeurs d'Equipement de Grandes Cuisines/Europäischer Verband der Hersteller von Grosskochanlagen): Via Matteo Bandello 5, 20123 Milan, Italy; tel. (+39 02) 43518826; e-mail garganti@inwind.it; internet www.efcem.info; f. 1969; Pres. Steve Loughton; Contact Drewry Pearson (Vice-Pres.).

EFCF (European Federation of City Farms): Schapenstraat 14, 1750 Sint-Martens-Lennik, Belgium; e-mail info@cityfarms.org; internet www.cityfarms.org; f. 1990; Contact Pauline Wolters (Sec.).

EFCI/FENI (European Federation of Cleaning Industries/Fédération Européenne du Nettoyage Industriel/Europäischer Dachverband der Gebäudereinigung): 27 rue de l'Association,

1000 Brussels, Belgium; tel. (+32) 2-2258330; fax (+32) 2-2258339; e-mail office@feni.be; internet www.feni.be; f. 1988; Pres. Yvan Fieremans; Contact Andreas Lill (Dir).

EFCLIN (European Federation of the Contact Lens Industry/Fédération Européenne de l'Industrie de l'Optique de Contact/Europäische Föderation der Kontaktlinsen-Industrie): POB 140, Winkelbüel 2, CH-6043 Adligenswil, Switzerland; tel. (+41 0) 413721010; e-mail info@efclin.com; internet www.efclin.com; Pres. Armin Duddek; Contact Marion Beeler (Exec. Dir).

EFEMA (European Food Emulsifiers Manufacturers' Association/Association des Fabricants Européens d'Emulsifiants Alimentaires/Verband Europäischer Hersteller von Nahrungsmittel-emulgatoren): 13A ave de Tervueren, Bte 7, 1040 Brussels, Belgium; tel. (+32) 2-7365354; fax (+32) 2-7323427; e-mail efema@ecco-eu.com; internet www.emulsifiers.org; f. 1973; Pres. Robert Graf; Sec.-Gen. Frances Hunt.

EFF (European Franchise Federation/Fédération Européenne de la Franchise/Europäische Franchiseföderation): 65/11 ave Louise, 1050 Brussels, Belgium; tel. (+32) 2-5201607; fax (+32) 2-5201735; e-mail info@eff-franchise.com; internet www.eff-franchise.com; f. 1972; Contact Carol Chopra (Exec. Dir).

EFFA (European Flavour and Fragrance Association/Association des Industries d'Arômes et de Parfums): 6 ave des Arts, 1210 Brussels, Belgium; tel. (+32) 2-2142040; fax (+32) 2-2300265; e-mail secretariat@effa.eu; internet www.effa.eu; f. 1961; Pres. Jean Robello; Contact Alexander Mohr (Exec. Dir).

EFFAT (European Federation of Trade Unions in the Food, Agriculture and Tourism Sectors and Allied Branches/Fédération Européenne des Syndicats des Secteurs de l'Alimentation, de l'Agriculture et du Tourisme et des Branches Connexes/Europäische Föderation der Gewerkschaften des Lebens-, Genussmittel-, Landwirtschafts- und Tourismussektors und Verwandter Branchen): 38 rue Fossé-aux-Loups, Bte 3, 1000 Brussels, Belgium; tel. (+32) 2-2187730; fax (+32) 2-2183018; e-mail effat@effat.org; internet www.effat.org; f. 2000; Pres. Malin Ackholt; Sec.-Gen. Harald Wiedenhofer.

EFFC (European Federation of Foundation Contractors/Fédération Européenne des Entreprises de Fondations/Europäischer Verband der Spezialtiefbauer): Forum Court, 83 Copers Cope Rd, Beckenham BR3 1NR, United Kingdom; tel. (+44 20) 8663-0948; fax (+44 20) 8663-0949; e-mail fionamcw@talktalk.net; internet www.foundationworld.org.uk; f. 1988; Pres. Patrice Runacher; Contact Peter de Kort (Vice-Pres.).

EFFCA (European Food and Feed Cultures Association/Association Européenne des Fabricants de Ferments à Usage Agroalimentaire/Europäische Vereinigung der Fermenthersteller für Nahrungsmittelindustriegebrauch): 142 ave Jules Bordet, 1140 Brussels, Belgium; tel. (+32) 2-7611671; e-mail effca@kellencompany.com; internet www.effca.com; f. 1992; Pres. Paul Tenning; Sec.-Gen. Patrick Fox; Contact Christoffer Lorenzen (Vice-Pres.).

EFFCM/FEPF (European Federation of Fibre Cement Manufacturers/Fédération Européenne des Producteurs de Fibres-Ciment/Europäische Vereinigung der Faserzement-Hersteller): 361 ave de Tervuren, 1150 Brussels, Belgium; tel. (+32) 2-7781211; fax (+32) 2-7781212; e-mail info@etexgroup.com; internet www.etexgroup.com; f. 1984; Contact Paul Van Oyen (CEO).

EFFOST (European Federation of Food Science and Technology/Fédération Européenne de la Science et de la Technologie Alimentaire/Europäische Föderation der Nahrungsmittelwissenschaft und -Technologie): POB 557, 6700 AN Wageningen, Netherlands; tel. (+31 88) 3663700; e-mail info@effost.org; internet www.effost.org; f. 1986; Pres. Lilia Ahrné; Contact Rachid Belkhir (Communication Officer).

EFFS (European Federation of Funeral Services/Fédération Européenne de Services Funéraires/Europäischer Vereinigung für Bestattungsdienste): Simmeringer Hauptstr. 339, 1110 Vienna, Austria; tel. (+43 0211) 1600849; fax (+43 0211) 16008949; e-mail teraa@effs.eu; internet www.effs.eu; Pres. Giovanni Primavesi; Contact Anke Teraa (Exec. Dir).

EFIP/FEPI (European Federation of Inland Ports/Fédération Européenne des Ports Intérieurs/Europäischer Verband der Binnenhafen): Treurenberg 6, 1000 Brussels, Belgium; tel. (+32) 2-2198207; fax (+32) 2-7366325; e-mail info@inlandports.be; internet www.inlandports.eu; f. 1994; Pres. Roland Hörner; Contact Alexander van den Bosch (Dir).

EFLA/FEAP (European Federation of Landscape Architecture/Fondation Européenne pour l'Architecture du Paysage): 149/24 ave Louise, 12th Floor, 1050 Brussels, Belgium; tel. (+32) 2-319451; e-mail secretariat@iflaeurope.eu; internet iflaeurope.eu; f. 1989; Pres. Tony Williams; Sec.-Gen. Urszula Forczek-Brataniec; Contact Emilia Weckman (Vice-Pres. Education).

EFLA/AEDA (European Food Law Association/Association Européenne pour le Droit de l'Alimentation/Europäische Vereinigung für Lebensmittelrecht): 13A ave de Tervueren, Bte 7, 1040 Brussels, Belgium; tel. (+32) 2-7365354; fax (+32) 2-7323427; e-mail secretariat@efla-aeda.org; internet www.efla-aeda.org; f. 1973; Pres. Andreas Natterer; Sec.-Gen. Frances Hunt.

EFMA (European Fertilizer Manufacturers' Association/Association Européenne des Producteurs d'Engrais/Europäischer Verband der Düngemittelhersteller): 4–6 ave E. Van Nieuwenhuyse, 1160 Brussels, Belgium; tel. (+32) 2-6753550; fax (+32) 2-6753961; e-mail main@fertilizerseurope.com; internet www.fertilizerseurope.com; f. 1987; Pres. Javier Goñi del Cacho; Contact Jacob Hansen (Dir-Gen.).

EFMD (European Foundation for Management Development/Fondation Européenne pour le Développement de la Gestion/Europäische Management-Entwicklungsstiftung): 88 rue Gachard, Bte 3, 1050 Brussels, Belgium; tel. (+32) 2-6290810; fax (+32) 2-6290811; internet www.efmd.org; Pres. Alain Dominique Perrin; Contact Eric Cornuel (Dir-Gen. and CEO).

EFOMP (European Federation of Organizations for Medical Physics): Fairmount House, 230 Tadcaster Rd, York YO24 1ES, United Kingdom; tel. (+44 1904) 61-0821; fax (+44 1904) 61-2279; e-mail office@efomp.org; internet www.efomp.org; f. 1980; Pres. Prof. John Damilakis; Sec.-Gen. Dr Marco Brambilla.

EFPIA (European Federation of Pharmaceutical Industries and Associations/Fédération Européenne d'Associations et d'Industries Pharmaceutiques): 108 rue du Trône, Leopold Plaza Bldg, 1050 Brussels, Belgium; tel. (+32) 2-6262555; fax (+32) 2-6262566; e-mail reception@efpia.eu; internet www.efpia.eu; f. 1978; Pres. Stefan Oschmann; Contact Nathalie Moll (Dir-Gen.).

EFPRA (European Fat Processors' and Renderers' Association): 18 blvd Baudouin, Bte 4, 1000 Brussels, Belgium; tel. (+32) 2-2035141; fax (+32) 2-2033244; e-mail info@efpra.eu; internet efpra.eu; Pres. Niels Leth Nielsen; Sec.-Gen. Dirk Dobbelaere; Contact Sjors Beerendonk (Vice-Pres.).

EFQM (European Foundation for Quality Management/Fondation Européenne du Contrôle de la Qualité): 2 ave des Olympiades, 1140 Brussels, Belgium; tel. (+32) 2-7753511; fax (+32) 2-7753535; e-mail info@efqm.org; internet www.efqm.org; f. 1989; Contact Léon Tossaint (Chief Exec. Officer).

EFTC/EVH (Federation of Craftsmen/Fédération des Artisans/Europäische Vereinigung des Holzbaus): 2 circuit de la Foire Internationale, BP 1604, 1016 Luxembourg-Kirchberg, Luxembourg; tel. (+352) 4245111; e-mail m.reckinger@fda.lu; internet www.fda.lu; Pres. Michel Reckinger; Sec.-Gen. Romain Schmit.

Trade and Professional Organizations DIRECTORY

EGA (European Generic Medicines Association/Association Européenne des Médicaments Génériques/Europäischer Verband der Generikaindustrie): 50 rue d'Arlon, 1000 Brussels, Belgium; tel. (+32) 2-7368411; fax (+32) 2-7367438; e-mail info@medicinesforeurope.com; internet www.medicinesforeurope.com; f. 1993; Pres. Jacek Glinka; Contact Pierluigi Antonelli (Treasurer).

EGGA (European General Galvanizers' Association/Association Européenne des Galvanisateurs/Europäische Vereinigung für Allgemeine Verzinkung): 11 Emmanuel Court, 14–16 Reddicroft, B73 6AZ, United Kingdom; tel. (+44 121) 355-2119; fax (+44 121) 354-4895; e-mail mail@egga.com; internet www.egga.com; f. 1990; Pres. M. Kopf; Contact Murray Cook (Dir).

EGOLF (European Group of Organizations for Fire Testing, Inspection and Certification): La Chavade, Quartier Laval, 07230 Planzolles, France; tel. (+33) 4-75-39-10-18; e-mail christine.roszykiewicz@egolf.org.uk; internet www.egolf.org.uk; f. 1988; Pres. Anne Steen-Hansen; Sec.-Gen. Christine Roszykiewicz.

EGTA (European Group of Television Advertising/Groupe Européen de la Publicité Télévisée/Europäische Gruppe für Fernsehwerbung): 22 rue des Comédiens, 1000 Brussels, Belgium; tel. (+32) 2-2903131; fax (+32) 2-2903139; internet www.egta.com; f. 1974; Pres. Fabrice Mollier; Contact Katty Roberfroid (Dir-Gen.).

EHA/GEH (European Helicopter Association/Groupement Européen de l'Hélicoptère/Europäischer Hubschrauberverband): Altenberger Str. 19–21, 50668 Cologne, Germany; tel. (+49 221) 29082908; e-mail office@eha-heli.eu; internet www.eha-heli.eu; Contact Jaime Arqué (Chair.).

EHI (Association of the European Heating Industry): 40 ave des Arts 40, 1040 Brussels, Belgium; tel. (+32) 2-8803070; fax (+32) 2-8803069; internet www.ehi.eu; f. 20022; Sec.-Gen. Federica Sabbati; Contact Ettore Riello (Treasurer).

EHIMA (European Hearing Instrument Manufacturers' Association/Association Européenne des Fabricants d'Audioprothèses/Europäische Vereinigung der Hörgerätehersteller): 523 Ave Louise, 1050 Brussels, Belgium; tel. (+45) 40-45-71-35; e-mail sh@ehima.com; internet www.ehima.com; f. 1985; Pres. Lukas Braunschweiler; Sec.-Gen. Stefan Zimmer.

EHMA (European Health Management Association/Association Européenne de Gestion des Systèmes de Santé/Europäische Vereinigung für Management im Gesundheitswesen): 15–17 rue Belliard, 6th Floor, 1040 Brussels, Belgium; tel. (+32) 2-5026525; e-mail info@ehma.org; internet ehma.org; f. 1966; Contact Usman Khan (Dir).

EHPM (European Federation of Associations of Health Product Manufacturers/Groupement Européen des Associations des Fabricants de Produits de Réforme/Europäische Vereinigung der Verbände der Reformwaren-Hersteller): 4 rue Jacques de Lalaing, 1040 Brussels, Belgium; tel. (+32) 2-7216495; internet www.ehpm.org; f. 1975; Contact Patrick Ahern (Dir-Gen.).

EIBF/FEL (European and International Booksellers' Federation/Fédération Européenne des Libraires): 69 sq. Marie-Louise, 1000 Brussels, Belgium; tel. (+32) 22234940; e-mail info@europeanbooksellers.eu; internet www.europeanbooksellers.eu; f. 1968; Contact Françoise Dubruille (Dir).

EIGA (European Industrial Gases Association/Association Européenne des Gaz Industriels/Europäischer Verband für Technische Gase): 3–5 ave des Arts, 1210 Brussels, Belgium; tel. (+32) 2-2177098; fax (+32) 2-2198514; e-mail info@eiga.org; internet www.eiga.eu; f. 1991; Pres. Marco Annoni; Sec.-Gen. Philip Brickell.

EIHSA/IEACS/EIJS (European Institute for Hunting and Sporting Arms/Institut Européen des Armes de Chasse et de Sport/Europäisches Institut für Jagd- und Sportwaffen): Viale dell'Astronomia 30, 00144 Rome, Italy; tel. (+39 06) 5903510; fax (+39 06) 54282691; e-mail ieacs@anpam.it; internet www.ieacs.eu; f. 1976; Pres. Carlo Peroni; Sec.-Gen. Mauro Silvis.

EIPG/GPIE (European Industrial Pharmacy Group/Groupe des Pharmaciens de l'Industrie en Europe): 4 ave Ruysdaël, 75379 Paris, France; e-mail info@eipg.eu; internet eipg.eu; f. 1966; Pres. Claude Farrugia; Contact Jane Nicholson (Exec. Dir).

EIRMA (European Industrial Research Management Association/Association Européenne pour l'Administration de la Recherche Industrielle/Asociación Europea para la Administración de la Investigación Industrial): Rue de la Loi 81A, 1040 Brussels, Belgium; tel. (+32) 2-2331180; fax (+32) 2-2310835; e-mail news@eirma.asso.fr; internet www.eirma.org; f. 1966; Pres. Ernst Lutz; Sec.-Gen. Michel Crispi; Contact Carla Hilhorst (Vice-Pres.).

ELA (European Lift Association): 44/1 ave Herrmann-Debroux, 1160 Brussels, Belgium; tel. (+32) 2-7795082; fax (+32) 2-7721685; e-mail info@ela-aisbl.org; internet www.ela-aisbl.eu; f. 2002; Pres. Jorge Ligüerre; Sec.-Gen. Robert Wright; Contact Gaëtane van Laethem (Sec.).

ELA (European Logistics Association/Association Européenne de Logistiques/Europäische Logistikvereinigung): Handelsstr. 77, 1040 Brussels, Belgium; tel. (+32 471) 832989; e-mail ela@elalog.org; internet www.elalog.eu; f. 1985; Pres. Paolo Bisogni; Sec.-Gen. Adriana Palasan; Contact Péter Kiss (Treasurer).

ELC (Federation of European Speciality Food Ingredients Industries/Fédération des Industries Européennes d'Additifs et d'Enzymes Alimentaires/Föderation der Europäischen Industrien für Nahrungszusätze und -Enzyme): 13A ave Tervueren, 1040 Brussels, Belgium; tel. (+32) 2-7365354; fax (+32) 2-7323427; e-mail secretary@elc-eu.org; internet www.elc-eu.org; f. 1983; Pres. Franck Monmont; Sec.-Gen. Maryse Hervé.

ELCA (European Landscape Contractors' Association/Union Européenne des Entrepreneurs du Paysage/Europäische Vereinigung des Garten-, Landschafts- und Sportplatzbaus): Robert Schuman 6, bte 5, 1040 Brussels, Belgium; tel. (+32) 351191; e-mail eline.vidts@elca.info; internet elca.info; f. 1963; Pres. Emmanuel Mony; Sec.-Gen. Dr Hermann J. Kurth; Contact Neil Huck (Vice-Pres.).

ELF (European Locksmith Federation): c/o Suomen Turvaurakoitsijaliitto, Hämeentie 157, 6th Floor, 00560 Helsinki, Finland; tel. (+358 29) 0074920; e-mail ona@lukkoliikkeet.fi; internet www.eurolockfed.com; f. 1984; Pres. Dave O'Toole; Contact Ona Gardemeister (Sec.).

ELO/Propriété Rurale (European Landowners' Organization/Organisation Européene de la Propriété Rurale/Europäische Grundbesitzerorganisation): 67 rue de Trèves, 1040 Brussels, Belgium; tel. (+32) 2-2343000; fax (+32) 2-2343009; e-mail elo@elo.org; internet www.europeanlandowners.org; f. 1972; Pres. Pierre Olivier Drège; Sec.-Gen. Thierry de l'Escaille.

ELVHIS (European Leading Association of Luminous Radiant Gas Heaters Manufacturers/Association Européenne Principale des Fabricants de Panneaux Infrarouges Lumineux à Gaz/Europäischer Leit-Verband der Hersteller von Gaz-Infrarot-Hellstrahlern eV): Marienburgerstr. 15, 50968 Cologne, Germany; tel. (+49 221) 3766-857; fax (+49 221) 3766-860; e-mail info@figawa.de; internet www.elvhis.eu; f. 1994; Pres. Prof. Friedhelm Schlösser; Sec.-Gen. Harald Petermann.

EMA (European Medical Association): 19 ave des Volontaires, 1160 Brussels, Belgium; tel. (+32) 2-7342980; fax (+32) 2-

7342135; e-mail contact@emanet.org; internet emanet.org; f. 1990; Pres. Dr Vincenzo Costigliola; Sec.-Gen. Angelo Manenti; Contact Prof. Winrich Breipohl (Vice-Pres.).

EMA / ASFE (European Midwives' Association/Association des Sages-Femmes Européennes): Haantjeslei 185, 2018 Antwerpen, Belgium; e-mail board@europeanmidwives.com; internet www.europeanmidwives.com; f. 1968; Pres. Mervi Jokinen; Contact Joris Vermeulen (Sec.).

EMAA (European Management Accountants' Association eV/Association Européenne de Comptables Agréés/Europäischer Verband der Bilanbuchhalter): Am Propsthof 15–17, 53121 Bonn, Germany; tel. (+49 228) 9639-318; fax (+49 228) 9639-314; e-mail kontakt@emaa.de; internet emaa.de; f. 1994; Pres. Uwe Jüttner; Contact Günter Hendrich (Vice-Pres.).

EMB / EMF / FEM (European Metalworkers' Federation/Fédération Européenne des Métallurgistes/Europäischer Metallgewerkschaftsbund): 5 blvd du Roi Albert II, Bte 10, 1210 Brussels, Belgium; tel. (+32) 2-2271010; fax (+32) 2-2175963; e-mail emf@emf-fem.org; internet www.emf-fem.org; f. 1971; Pres. Renzo Ambrosetti; Sec.-Gen. Ulrich Eckelmann; Contact William Slade (Communications and Admin. Officer).

EMBO (European Molecular Biology Organization): Meyerhofstrasse 1, 69117 Heidelberg, Germany; tel. (+49 6221) 8891-0; fax (+49 6221) 8891-200; e-mail embo@embo.org; internet www.embo.org; f. 1964; Sec.-Gen. Paul Nurse; Contact Prof. Maria Leptin (Dir).

EMC (European Marketing Confederation): 35 sq. du Meeûs, 1000 Brussels, Belgium; tel. (+32) 2-7421780; e-mail info@emc.be; internet emc.be; Contact Andrew Harvey (Chair.); Uwe Tännler (Vice-Chair.); Martin Huisman.

EMF / FHE / EHV (European Mortgage Federation/Fédération Hypothécaire Européenne/Europäischer Hypothekenverband): 14A rue de la Science, 2nd Floor, 1040 Brussels, Belgium; tel. (+32) 2-2854030; e-mail info@hypo.org; internet hypo.org; f. 1967; Pres. Bruno Deletré; Sec.-Gen. Luca Bertalot; Contact Jean-Michel Corbisier (Communication Adviser).

EMMA (European Magazine Media Association): 73A rue de Namur, 1000 Brussels, Belgium; tel. (+32) 2-5360606; fax (+32) 2-5360601; e-mail info@magazinemedia.eu; internet www.magazinemedia.eu; f. 1974; Pres. Auke Visser; Contact Max von Abendroth (Exec. Dir).

EMO (European Mortar Industry Organization/Association de l'Industrie Européenne des Mortiers/Verband der Europäischen Mortelindustrie): 68 blvd du Souverain, 1170 Brussels, Belgium; tel. (+49 2408) 599-6207; fax (+49 408) 599-6208; e-mail info@euromortar.com; internet www.euromortar.com; f. 1991; Pres. Andreas Weier; Sec.-Gen. Antonio Caballero González; Contact Sebastian L. M. Huysmans (Vice-Pres.); Guillaume Latil.

EMOTA / AEVPC (European Distance Selling Trade Association/Association Européenne de Vente par Correspondance/Europäische Vereinigung des Versandverkaufs): 30 ave Marnix, 1000 Brussels, Belgium; tel. (+32) 2-2137423; e-mail info@emota.eu; internet www.emota.org; f. 1977; Pres. Jörgen Bödmar; Sec.-Gen. Maurits Bruggink; Contact Borislava Markova (European Affairs).

EMU (European Metal Union/Union Européenne du Métal/Europäische Metall-Union): Gasthuisstraat 31 B2, 1000 Brussels, Belgium; tel. (+32) 2-2742207; fax (+32) 2-4007126; e-mail office@emu-sme.eu; internet www.emu-online.eu; Pres. Erwin Kostyra; Sec.-Gen. Eric Dresin.

ENERO (European Network of Environmental Research Organizations): c/o ISSeP, 200 rue du Chéra 200, 4000 Liège, Belgium; tel. (+32) 4-2298311; fax (+32) 4-2524665; e-mail jcl.maquinay@issep.be; internet enero.nilu.no; f. 1992; Pres. Ignacio Calleja; Sec.-Gen. Jean-Claude Maquinay; Contact Ronald Albers (Vice-Pres.).

ENGAGE (European Network of Engineering for Agriculture and Environment): 17 Chandos Rd, Ampthill MK45 2LD, United Kingdom; tel. (+44 1525) 861096; fax (+44 1525) 861660; e-mail rbrunsch@atb-potsdam.de; internet www.eurageng.eu/engage; f. 1988; Pres. Reiner Brunsch; Sec.-Gen. David Tinker.

ENGVA (European Natural Gas Vehicle Association): 172 ave de Cortenbergh, 1000 Brussels, Belgium; tel. (+32 2) 8944839; e-mail info@ngva.eu; internet www.ngva.eu; f. 1994; Pres. Dr Gerhard Holtmeier; Sec.-Gen. Andrea Gerini; Contact Hans Wach (Sec.).

ENPA (European Newspaper Publishers' Association/Association Européenne des Editeurs de Journaux/Verband Europäischer Zeitungsverleger): 73A rue de Namur, 1050 Brussels, Belgium; tel. (+32) 2-5510190; fax (+32) 2-5510199; e-mail enpa@enpa.be; internet www.enpa.eu; f. 1961; Pres. Pres, Ivar Rusdal; Contact Sophie Scrive (Exec. Dir); Valdo Lehari, Jr (Vice-Pres); Bruno Pachent.

ENS / SEEN (European Nuclear Society/Société Européenne de l'Energie Nucléaire/Europäische Kernenergie Gesellschaft): 56 ave des Arts, 1000 Brussels, Belgium; tel. (+32) 2-5053050; fax (+32) 2-5023902; e-mail info@euronuclear.org; internet www.euronuclear.org; f. 1975; Pres. Roger Schène; Sec.-Gen. Jean-Pol Poncelet.

ENSCA (European Natural Sausage-casing Association/Association Européenne des Industries et Commerces de Boyauderie/Europejskie Stowarzyszenie Naturalnych Osłonek do Wędlin): 81A rue de la Loi, Bte 9, 1040 Brussels. Belgium; tel. (+32) 2-2304603; fax (+32) 2-2309400; e-mail info@ensca.eu; internet www.ensca.eu; f. 1952; Pres. Jan Roelsgaard; Sec.-Gen. Ingrid Morvan.

EOQ (European Organization for Quality/Organisation Européenne pour la Qualité/Europäische Organisation für Qualität): 36–38 rue Joseph II, 1000 Brussels, Belgium; tel. (+32) 4-74240800; e-mail eoq@eoq-org.eu; internet www.eoq.org; f. 1956; Pres. Torolf Paulshus; Contact Dr Konrad Scheiber (Vice-Pres.).

EOS / OES (European Organization of the Sawmill Industry/Organisation Européenne des Scieries/Europäische Organisation der Sägewerke): 24 rue Montoyer, Bte 20, 1000 Brussels, Belgium; tel. (+32) 2-5562597; fax (+32) 2-2870875; e-mail info@eos-oes.eu; internet www.eos-oes.eu; f. 1958; Pres. Sampsa Auvinen; Sec.-Gen. Silvia Melegari; Contact Alfred Jechart (Chair.).

EOTA (European Organization for Technical Assessment/Organisation Européenne pour l'Agrément Technique/Europäische Organisation für Technische Zulassungen): 40 ave des Arts, 1040 Brussels, Belgium; tel. (+32) 2-5026900; fax (+32) 2-5023814; e-mail info@eota.eu; internet www.eota.be; f. 1990; Pres. Karsten Kathage; Sec.-Gen. Sergio Vazquez Jimenez; Contact Carlo de Pauw (Chair.).

EPA (European Association of Polyol Producers): 13A ave de Tervuren, 1040 Brussels, Belgium; tel. (+32) 2-7365354; fax (+32) 2-7323427; e-mail epa@ecco-eu.com; internet www.polyols-eu.com; f. 1991; Sec.-Gen. Maryse Hervé.

EPAG (European Property Agents Group): 36 ave de Tervuren, Bte 2, 1040 Brussels, Belgium; tel. (+32) 2-7354990; fax (+32) 2-7359988; e-mail cepi@cepi.eu; internet www.cepi.eu; f. 1990; Pres. Claudine Speltz; Sec.-Gen. Jens-Ulrich Kiessling; Contact Xavier Ortegat-Consorte (Man. Dir).

EPBA (European Portable Battery Association/Association Européenne des Piles Portables/Europäische Vereinigung der

Trade and Professional Organizations DIRECTORY

Tragbaren Batterien): 142 ave Jules Bordet, 1140 Brussels, Belgium; tel. (+32) 2-7611602; fax (+32) 2-7611699; e-mail epba@kelleneurope.com; internet www.epbaeurope.net; f. 1958; Pres. Rémy Burel; Sec.-Gen. Hans Craen; Contact Bénédicte Lambert (Man. Asst).

EPC (European Publishers' Council/Conseil Européen des Editeurs/Europäischer Verlegerrat): 26 ave Livingstone, 1000 Brussels, Belgium; tel. (+32) 2-2311299; fax (+32) 2-2307658; e-mail info@epceurope.eu; internet epceurope.eu; f. 1991; Pres. Francisco Pinto Balsemão; Sec.-Gen. Michel Viaud; Contact Angela Mills Wade (Exec. Dir).

EPDCC (European Pressure Die Casting Committee/Comité Européen des Fondeurs/Europäisches Komitee der Metallgiessereien): Sohnstr. 70, 40237 Düsseldorf, Germany; tel. (+49 211) 6871-154; fax (+49 211) 6871-409; e-mail gerhard.kluegge@bdguss.de; Pres. Bernd Voigtländer; Sec.-Gen. Gerhard Klügge; Contact Michael Grund (Dir).

EPEGA/UEVG/EUWEP (European Egg, Poultry and Game Association/Union Européenne de la Volaille et du Gibier/Europäische Vereinigung des Eier, Wild- und Geflügelgross- und Aussenhandels eV): Zuse-Platz 5, 53227 Bonn, Germany; tel. (+49 228) 95960-0; fax (+49 228) 95960-50; e-mail info@epega.org; internet www.epega.org; Pres. Wolfgang Christ.

EPF (European Panel Federation/Fédération Européenne des Panneaux à Base de Bois/Europäischer Holswerkstoffverband): 24 rue Montoyer, Bte 20, 1000 Brussels, Belgium; tel. (+32) 2-5562589; fax (+32) 2-2870875; e-mail info@europanels.org; internet europanels.org; f. 1958; Contact Katia Thiebaut (Communication Adviser).

EPHA (European Public Health Alliance/Alliance Européenne de la Santé Publique/Europäische Allianz für Öffentliche Gesundheit): 49–51 rue de Trèves, 1040 Brussels, Belgium; tel. (+32) 2-2303056; fax (+32) 2-2333880; e-mail epha@epha.org; internet www.epha.org; f. 1994; Pres. Archie Turnbull; Sec.-Gen. Nina Renshaw; Contact Giulia Vettore (Communications Co-ordinator).

EPIA (European Photovoltaic Industry Association): 69–71 rue d'Arlon, 1040 Brussels, Belgium; tel. (+32) 2-7095520; fax (+32) 2-7253284; e-mail info@solarpowereurope.org; internet www.solarpowereurope.org; f. 1986; Pres. Christian Westermeier; Contact James Watson (CEO).

EPMA (European Powder Metallurgy Association/Association Européenne de Poudre Métallurgique/Europäische Vereinigung des Metallpuders): 2nd Floor, Talbot House, Market St, Shrewsbury SY1 1LG, United Kingdom; tel. (+44 1743) 248899; fax (+44 1743) 362968; e-mail info@epma.com; internet www.epma.com; f. 1989; Pres. Philippe Gundermann; Contact Lionel Aboussouan (Exec. Dir).

EPSU/FSESP (European Federation of Public Service Unions/Fédération Syndicale Européenne des Services Publics/Europäischer Gewerkschaftsverband für den Öffentlichen Dienst): 40 rue Joseph II, POB 9, 1000 Brussels, Belgium; tel. (+32) 2-2501080; fax (+32) 2-2501099; e-mail epsu@epsu.org; internet www.epsu.org; f. 1978; Pres. Isolde Kunkel-Weber; Sec.-Gen. Jan Willem Goudriaan.

EPTA (European Power Tool Association/Elektrowerkzeuge): 58 rue Marie de Bourgogne, 1000 Brussels, Belgium; tel. (+32) 2-8924623; e-mail eckert@epta.eu; internet www.epta.eu; f. 1984; Pres. Horst W. Garbrecht; Sec.-Gen. Christian Eckert; Contact Josef M. Ortolf (Dir-Gen.).

ERA (European Rotogravure Association/Association Européenne de Héliogravure/Verband des Europäischen Tiefdruchindustrie): Swakopmunder Str. 3, 81827 Munich, Germany; tel. (+49 89) 43950-51; fax (+49 89) 43941-07; e-mail info@era.eu.org; internet www.era.eu.org; f. 1956; Pres. Manfred Janoschka; Sec.-Gen. James Siever; Contact Max Rid (Vice-Pres.).

ERAA (European Regions Airline Association/Association des Compagnies d'Aviation des Régions d'Europe/Verband der Fluglinien Europäischer Regionen): Park House, 127 Guildford Rd, Lightwater, Surrey GU18 5RA, United Kingdom; tel. (+44 1276) 856495; fax (+44 1276) 857038; e-mail info@eraa.org; internet www.eraa.org; f. 1980; Pres. Boet Kreiken; Contact Simon McNamara (Dir-Gen.).

ERF (European Road Federation): 6/B Place Stephanie, 1050 Brussels, Belgium; tel. (+32) 2-6445877; fax (+32) 2-6475934; e-mail info@erf.be; internet www.erf.be; f. 1998; Pres. Rik Nuyttens; Contact José Díez (Dir of Public Affairs and Communication).

ERMCO (European Ready Mixed Concrete Organization/Association Européenne du Béton Prêt à l'Emploi/Europäischer Transportbetonverband): 68 blvd du Souverain, 1170 Brussels, Belgium; tel. (+32) 2-6455212; fax (+32) 2-7351467; e-mail secretariat@ermco.eu; internet www.ermco.eu; f. 1967; Pres. Stein Tosterud; Sec.-Gen. Francesco Biasioli.

ESA (European Sealing Association eV/Association Européenne de l'Etanchéité): 310 route de la Plagne Morzine, 74110 Haute Savoie, France; tel. (+33) 631941600; e-mail markneal@europeansealing.com; internet europeansealing.com; f. 1992; Sec.-Gen. Mark Neal; Contact Dr Wolfgang Bommes (Vice-Chair.).

ESA (European Snacks Association): 26 rue des Deux Eglises, 1000 Brussels, Belgium; tel. (+32) 2-5382039; fax (+32) 2-2181213; e-mail esa@esasnacks.eu; internet www.esasnacks.eu; f. 1961; Pres. Valentina Maglio; Contact Dr Andrew Curtis (Regulatory Affairs).

ESA (European Spice Association/Association Européenne de l'Epice/Europäische Vereinigung des Gewürzes): Reuterstr. 151, 53113 Bonn, Germany; tel. (+49 228) 2101-80; fax (+49 228) 2294-60; e-mail esa@verbaendebuero.de; internet www.esa-spices.org; Pres. Simon Cripps; Sec.-Gen. Gerhard Weber.

ESBG/GECE/ESV (European Savings Banks Group): 11 rue Marie-Thérèse, 1000 Brussels, Belgium; tel. (+32) 2-2111111; fax (+32) 2-2111199; e-mail info@wsbi-esbg.org; internet www.esbg.eu; f. 1963; Pres. François Perol; Sec.-Gen. Henning Schoppmann; Contact Chris de Noose (Man. Dir).

ESBO (European Solid Board Organization): Laan Copes van Cattenburch 79, POB 85612, 2508 CH The Hague, Netherlands; tel. (+31 70) 3603837; fax (+31 70) 3636348; e-mail mail@esbo.nl; internet www.esbo.nl; f. 1961; Pres. Dirk Schut; Sec.-Gen. Mans Lejeune; Contact Ad Smit (Vice-Pres.).

ESDREMA (European Surgical Dressings Manufacturers' Association): Tastarellogasse 31, 1130 Vienna, Austria; tel. (+43 1) 8777012; fax (+43 1) 8777013; internet www.esdrema.eu; f. 1974; Contact Giangiacomo Zabban (Vice-Chair.).

ESF (European Safety Federation): Bavikhoofsestraat 190, 8531 Harelbeke, Belgium; tel. (+32) 5-6701103; fax (+32) 3-4600213; e-mail info@eu-esf.org; internet eu-esf.org; f. 1991; Sec.-Gen. Henk Vanhoutte; Contact Gwin Steenhoudt (Co-ordinator).

ESF (European Spring Federation): Goldene Pforte 1, 58093 Hagen, Germany; tel. (+49 2331) 958-851; fax (+49 2331) 958-751; e-mail contact@esf-springs.com; internet www.esf-springs.com; Pres. Michel Fauconnier; Sec.-Gen. Wolfgang Hermann; Contact Anton Svensson (Vice-Pres.).

ESGG/FNAMS (European Seed Growers Group/Fédération Nationale des Agriculteurs Multiplicateurs de Semences): 74 rue Jean-Jacques Rousseau, 75001 Paris, France; tel. (+33) 1-44-82-

73-33; fax (+33) 1-44-82-73-40; e-mail tgk@thorkofoed.dk; Pres. G. Matteucci; Contact Sebastien Prin.

ESHA (European School Heads' Association/Association Européenne des Chefs d'Etablissement/Europäische Schulleitervereinigung): Herenstraat 35, 3512 KB Utrecht, Netherlands; tel. (+31 30) 2361010; fax (+31 30) 2361036; e-mail fredverboon@gmail.com; internet www.esha.org; Pres. Clive Byrne; Contact Fred Verboon (Dir).

ESHP/SEG/EGS (European Society of Handwriting Psychology/Société Européenne de Graphologie/Europäische Gesellschaft für Schriftpsychologie und Schriftexpertise e. V.): Martha Ringier-Str. 11, CH-5600 Lenzburg, Switzerland; e-mail bolliger.grapho@bluewin.ch; internet egs-graphologie.org; f. 1972; Pres. Rosmarie Bolliger; Contact Barbara Maria Buzzi (Sec.).

ESOMAR (European Society for Opinion and Marketing Research/Association Européenne pour les Etudes d'Opinion et de Marketing/Europäische Gesellschaft für Meinungs- und Marketing-Forschung): Hoogoorddreef 5, 1101 BA Amsterdam, Netherlands; tel. (+31 20) 6642141; fax (+31 20) 6642922; e-mail info@esomar.org; internet www.esomar.org; f. 1948; Pres. Niels Schillewaert; Contact Finn Raben (Dir-Gen.).

ESPO (European Sea Ports Organization/Organisation des Ports Maritimes Européens): Treurenberg 6, 1000 Brussels, Belgium; tel. (+32) 2-7363463; fax (+32) 2-7366325; e-mail mail@espo.be; internet www.espo.be; f. 1993; Sec.-Gen. Isabelle Ryckbost; Contact Robin Guillon (Policy Adviser).

ESTA (European Security Transport Association/Association Européenne du Transport et Convoyage de Valeurs/Europäische Vereinigung für Geldtransport und -Begleitung): 6 Rond Point Schuman, 1040 Brussels, Belgium; tel. (+32) 2-2347820; fax (+32) 2-3009023; e-mail contact@esta.biz; internet www.esta-cash.eu; f. 1975; Pres. Kenneth Högman; Sec.-Gen. Thierry Lebeaux; Contact Carlo Weisen (Exec. Vice-Pres.).

ESTA (European Smoking Tobacco Association/Association Européenne de Tabac à Fumer): 9 Rond Point Schumanplein, 1040 Brussels, Belgium; tel. (+32) 2-2308092; fax (+32) 2-2308214; e-mail info@esta.be; internet www.esta.be; Sec.-Gen. Peter van der Mark; Contact William Meyer (EU Policy Officer).

ESTA (European Steel Tube Association/Association Européenne du Tube d'Acier): 79 rue Marcel Dassault, 92100 Boulogne-Billancourt, France; tel. (+33) 1-41-31-56-40; fax (+33) 1-41-31-00-24; e-mail esta.info@orange.fr; f. 1994; Sec.-Gen. Dominique Richardot.

ESTA (European Surgical Trade Association): Hanikerweg 16, 5943 NB Lomm, Netherlands; tel. (+31 77) 3525215; e-mail info@estahealthcare.com; internet www.estahealthcare.com; f. 1959; Pres. Eric Knuiman; Contact Robert Lelieveld (Man. Dir).

ESTOC (European Smokeless Tobacco Council/Conseil Européen du Tabac sans Fumée/Europäischer Rat für Rauchlosen Tabak): 108 rue du Trône, 1050 Brussels, Belgium; tel. (+32) 2-6463497; fax (+32) 2-6463597; e-mail inge.delfosse@estoc.org; internet www.estoc.org; f. 1989; Pres. Patrik Hildingsson; Sec.-Gen. Inge Delfosse.

ETA/ETMA (European Tube Association/Association Européenne des Fabricants de Tubes Souples/Europäische Tuben Vereinigung): Haus der Metalle, 2nd Floor, Am Bonneshof 5, 40474 Düsseldorf, Germany; tel. (+49 211) 4796-144; fax (+49 211) 479625141; e-mail info@etma-online.org; internet www.etma-online.org; f. 1959; Pres. Oliver Höll; Sec.-Gen. Gregor Spengler; Contact Martin Hintz (Vice-Pres.).

ETAD (Ecological and Toxicological Association of Dyes and Organic Pigments Manufacturers): Stadthausgasse 18, 4051 Basel, Switzerland; tel. (+41) 61-690-99-66; fax (+41) 61-691-42-78; e-mail info@etad.com; internet etad.com; f. 1974; Pres. Ravi Kapoor; Contact Dr Walther Hofherr (Exec. Dir).

ETC/CET (European Travel Commission/Commission Européenne du Tourisme/Comisión Europea del Turismo): 19A ave Marnix, Bte 25, 1000 Brussels, Belgium; tel. (+32) 2-5489000; fax (+32) 2-5141843; e-mail info@etc-corporate.org; internet www.etc-corporate.org; f. 1948; Pres. Peter de Wilde; Contact Eduardo Santander (Exec. Dir).

ETF (European Transport Workers' Federation/Fédération Européenne des Travailleurs des Transports/Europäische Transportarbeiter-Föderation): 105 rue du Marché aux Herbes, Boîte 11B, 1000 Brussels, Belgium; tel. (+32) 2-2854660; fax (+32) 2-2800817; e-mail etf@etf-europe.org; internet www.etf-europe.org; f. 1999; Pres. Frank Moreels; Sec.-Gen. Eduardo Chagas; Contact Ekaterina Yordanova (Vice-Pres.).

ETNO (European Telecommunications Network Operators' Association): 43–44 blvd du Régent, 1000 Brussels, Belgium; tel. (+32) 2-2193242; fax (+32) 2-2196412; e-mail info@etno.eu; internet etno.eu; f. 1992; Contact Lise Fuhr (Dir Gen.).

ETRMA (European Association of the Rubber Industry): 2 ave des Arts, POB 12, 1210 Brussels, Belgium; tel. (+32) 2-2184940; fax (+32) 2-2186162; e-mail info@etrma.org; internet www.etrma.org; f. 1959; Pres. Christian Lepercq; Sec.-Gen. Fazilet Cinaralp; Contact Thierry du Granrut (Vice-Pres.).

ETRTO/ETWTC (European Tyre and Rim Technical Organization/Technische Organisation der Europäischen Reifen- und Felgenhersteller): 78–80 rue Defacqz, 1060 Brussels, Belgium; tel. (+32) 2-3444059; fax (+32) 2-3440084; e-mail info@etrto.org; internet www.etrto.org; f. 1964; Pres. J. Burfien; Sec.-Gen. Nicolas de Mahieu; Contact P. Roest (Vice-Pres.).

ETSA (European Telecommunication Services Association/Association Européenne des Entreprises de Service en Télécommunication): 4 rue Jacques de Lalaing, 1040 Brussels, Belgium; tel. (+32) 2-2850705; fax (+32) 2-2307861; e-mail info@etsa.org; internet www.etsa.org; f. 1988; Pres. Maurizio Esitini; Sec.-Gen. Baronne Dominique de Coninck de Merckem.

ETSA (European Textile Services Association): 24 rue Montoyer, Bte 7, 1000 Brussels, Belgium; tel. (+32) 2-2820990; fax (+32) 2-2820999; e-mail etsa@etsa-europe.org; internet www.etsa-europe.org; f. 1994; Pres. Juha Laurio; Sec.-Gen. Robert Long; Contact Thomas Krautschneider (Vice-Pres.).

ETUC/CES/EGB (European Trade Union Confederation/Confédération Européenne des Syndicats/Europäischer Gewerkschaftsbund): 5 Blvd du Roi Albert II, 9th Floor, 1210 Brussels, Belgium; tel. (+32) 2-2240411; fax (+32) 2-2240454; e-mail etuc@etuc.org; internet www.etuc.org; f. 1973; Pres. Rudy de Leeuw; Sec.-Gen. Luca Visentini.

ETUCE/CSEE (European Trade Union Committee for Education/Comité Syndical Européen de l'Education/Education International Pan-European Structure): 5 blvd du Roi Albert II, 9th Floor, 1210 Brussels, Belgium; tel. (+32) 2-2240691; fax (+32) 2-2240694; e-mail secretariat@csee-etuce.org; internet www.csee-etuce.org; f. 1975; Pres. Christine Blower; Sec.-Gen. Martin Romer; Contact Odile Cordelier (Vice-Pres.).

ETUI-REHS (European Trade Union Institute—Research, Education, Health and Safety): 5 blvd du Roi Albert II, POB 4, 1210 Brussels, Belgium; tel. (+32) 2-2240470; fax (+32) 2-2240502; e-mail etui@etui.org; internet www.etui.org; Contact Philippe Pochet (Man. Dir).

ETV (European Tobacco Wholesalers' Association/Association Européenne des Grossistes en Produits du Tabac/Europäischer Tabakwaren-Grosshandels-Verband): Stadtwaldgürtel 44, 50931 Cologne, Germany; tel. (+49 221) 4007-00; e-mail info@

Trade and Professional Organizations DIRECTORY

etv-online.eu; internet www.etv-online.eu; f. 1973; Pres. Paul Heinen; Sec.-Gen. Carsten Zenner.

EUBA (European Bentonite Association): c/o IMA-Europe, 26 rue des Deux Eglises, 1000 Brussels, Belgium; tel. (+32) 2-2104410; fax (+32) 2-2104429; e-mail secretariat@ima-europe.eu; internet www.ima-europe.eu/about-ima-europe/associations/euba; f. 1999; Pres. Klaus Langer; Sec.-Gen. Dr Roger Doome.

EUCAR (European Council for Automotive Research and Development/Conseil Européen pour la Recherche et Développement dans le Secteur Automobile): 85 ave des Nerviens, 1040 Brussels, Belgium; tel. (+32) 2-7387352; fax (+32) 2-7387312; e-mail eucar@eucar.be; internet www.eucar.be; f. 1994; Contact Stefan Deix (Dir).

EUCARPIA (European Association for Research on Plant Breeding/Association Européenne pour l'Amélioration des Plantes/Europäische Gesellschaft für Züchtungsforschung): Vossenburchkade 68, NL-2805 PC Gouda, the Netherlands; tel. (+31 182) 688668; fax (+31 182) 688667; e-mail t.simons@plantum.nl; internet www.eucarpia.org; f. 1956; Pres. Richard Visser; Sec.-Gen. Thijs Simons; Contact Stefan van der Heijden (Treasurer).

EUCEPA (European Liaison Committee for Pulp and Paper/Comité Européen de Liaison pour la Cellulose et le Papier/Europäischer Verband für Zellstoff- und Papiertechnik): 23 rue d'Aumale, 75009 Paris, France; tel. (+33) 1-45-62-11-91; fax (+33) 1-45-63-53-09; e-mail eucepa@yahoo.fr; internet www.eucepa.eu; f. 1956; Pres. Barry Read; Sec.-Gen. Virginie Batais.

EuCheMS (European Association for Chemical and Molecular Sciences/Fédération des Sociétés Chimiques Européennes/Föderation Europäischer Chemiker Gesellschaften): 62 rue du Trône, 1050 Brussels, Belgium; tel. (+32) 2-2892567; e-mail secretariat@euchems.eu; internet www.euchems.eu; f. 1970; Pres. Prof. David Cole-Hamilton; Sec.-Gen. Nineta Majcen.

EuCIA (European Composites Industry Association/Groupement Européen des Plastiques Renforcés/Matériaux Composites): Diamond Bldg, 80 blvd A. Reyers, 1030 Brussels, Belgium; tel. (+32) 2-7068906; e-mail info@eucia.eu; internet www.eucia.eu; f. 1960; Pres. Roberto Frassine; Sec.-Gen. Julie Leroy; Contact Jan Verhaeghe (Vice-Pres.).

EUCOLAIT (European Union of Dairy Trade/Union Européenne du Commerce des Produits Laitiers et Dérivés/Europäische Union des Handels mit Milcherzeugnissen): 199 rue Belliard, 1040 Brussels, Belgium; tel. (+32) 2-2304448; fax (+32) 2-2304044; e-mail info@eucolait.eu; internet www.eucolait.be; f. 1959; Pres. Jack F. Baines; Sec.-Gen. Jukka Likitalo; Contact Julie Collard (Office Man.).

EUDA (European Dredging Association/Association Européenne de Dragage): 148 ave Grandchamp, 1150 Brussels, Belgium; tel. (+32) 2-6468183; fax (+32) 2-6466063; e-mail info@euda.be; internet www.european-dredging.info; f. 1993; Sec.-Gen. Paris Sansoglou; Contact Peter van der Linde (Treasurer).

EUF (Federation of European Tile Fixers' Associations/Union Européenne des Fédérations des Entreprises de Carrelage/Europäische Union der Fliesen Fachverbände): Keramikweg 3, 6252 Dagmersellen, Switzerland; tel. (+41 062) 7484272; fax (+41 062) 7484250; e-mail info@eufgs.com; internet www.eufgs.com; f. 1958; Sec.-Gen. Werner Altmayer; Contact Bob Howard (Chair.).

EUFED (European Union Federation of Youth Hostel Associations/Fédération des Auberges de Jeunesse de l'Union Européenne): 25 rue Haute, 1000 Brussels, Belgium; tel. (+32) 2-5028066; fax (+32) 2-5025578; e-mail info@eufed.org; internet www.eufed.org; f. 1987; Pres. Gerhard Koller; Contact Viktorija Ramasauskaitė (Dir).

EULA (European Lime Association/Association Européenne de la Chaux/Europäischer Kalkverband): c/o IMA-Europe aisbl, Twin Gardens, 26 rue des Deux Eglises, 6th Floor, 1000 Brussels, Belgium; tel. (+32) 2-2104410; fax (+32) 2-2104429; e-mail secretariat@ima-europe.eu; internet www.eula.eu; f. 1990; Pres. Ludwig de Mot; Sec.-Gen. Eleni Despotou; Contact Amina Langedijk (Senior Adviser, Communications).

EUMABOIS (European Federation of Woodworking Machinery Manufacturers): Centro Direzionale Milanofiori, 1a Strada Palazzo F3, 20090 Assago (Milan), Italy; tel. (+39 02) 89210200; fax (+39 02) 8259009; e-mail info@eumabois.com; internet www.eumabois.com; f. 1960; Pres. Jürgen Köppel; Contact Luigi De Vito (Vice-Pres.).

EUMETSAT (European Organization for the Exploitation of Meteorological Satellites/Organisation Européenne pour l'Exploitation des Satellites Météorologiques/Europäische Organisation zur Nutzung Meteorologischer Satelliten): Eumetsat Allee 1, 64295 Darmstadt, Germany; tel. (+49 6151) 807-3660; fax (+49 6151) 807-3790; e-mail ops@eumetsat.int; internet www.eumetsat.int; f. 1986; Contact Prof. Neil Fletcher (Communications Man.).

EUMU/UEME (European Union for Small and Medium-Sized Enterprises/Union Européenne des Petites et Moyennes Entreprises/Europäischen Union Mittelständischer Unternehmen): Edelsbergstr. 8, 80686 Munich, Germany; tel. (+49 89) 5700-70; fax (+49 89) 5700-7260; e-mail info@eumu.net; internet eumu.net; f. 1989; Pres. Hatto Brenner; Contact Hermann Sturm (Treas.).

EUnited (European Association of Municipal Equipment Manufacturers): Diamant Bldg, 80 blvd A. Reyers, 1030 Brussels, Belgium; tel. (+32) 2-7068205; fax (+32) 2-7068210; e-mail info@eu-nited.net; internet eu-nited.net; Contact Frank Diedrich (Dir).

EUPC (European Plastics Converters/Confédération Européenne de la Plasturgie): 71 ave de Cortenbergh, 1000 Brussels, Belgium; tel. (+32) 2-7324124; fax (+32) 2-7324218; e-mail info@eupc.org; internet www.plasticsconverters.eu; f. 1989; Pres. Michael Kundel; Contact Alexandre Dangis (Man. Dir).

EUPPA (European Potato Processors' Association): 142 ave Jules Bordet, 1140 Brussels; tel. (+32) 2-7611670; fax (+32) 2-7611699; e-mail mail@euppa.eu; internet www.euppa.eu; Pres. Kees Meijer; Sec.-Gen. Adriana Nosewicz.

EURACOAL (European Association for Coal and Lignite/Association Européenne du Charbon et du Lignite/Europäische Stein- und Braunkohleverband): 168 ave de Tervuren, Bte 11, 1150 Brussels, Belgium; tel. (+32) 2-7753170; fax (+32) 2-7714104; e-mail euracoal@euracoal.org; internet euracoal.org; Pres. Dr Wolfgang Cieslik; Sec.-Gen. Brian Ricketts; Contact Vladimír Budinský (Vice-Pres.).

EURADA (European Association of Development Agencies/Association Européenne des Agences de Développement/Europäischer Verband der Wirtschaftsförderungsagenturen): 12 ave des Arts, Bte 7, 1210 Brussels, Belgium; tel. (+32) 2-2184313; fax (+32) 2-2184583; e-mail info@eurada.org; internet www.eurada.org; f. 1992; Pres. Roberta Dall'Olio; Contact Esteban Pelayo (Dir).

EURATEX (European Apparel and Textile Organization/Organisation Européenne de l'Habillement et du Textile): 24 rue Montoyer, Bte 10, 1000 Brussels, Belgium; tel. (+32) 2-2854883; fax (+32) 2-2854881; e-mail info@euratex.eu; internet www.euratex.org; f. 1996; Pres. Serge Piolat; Sec.-Gen. Pascale Maupertuis; Contact Francesco Marchi (Dir-Gen.).

EUREAU (European Union of National Associations of Water Suppliers and Waste Water Services/Union Européenne des

Associations Nationales de Distributeurs d'Eau et de Services d'Assainissement): 47–51 rue du Luxembourg, 1050 Brussels, Belgium; tel. (+32) 2-7064080; fax (+32) 2-7064081; e-mail info@eureau.org; internet www.eureau.org; f. 1975; Pres. Bruno Tisserand; Sec.-Gen. Oliver Loebel; Contact Louise Hoogenhout (Office Man.).

EUREL (Convention of National Societies of Electrical Engineers of Europe): 18 ave Roger Vandendriessche, 1150 Brussels, Belgium; tel. (+32) 2-6467600; fax (+32) 2-6463032; e-mail eurel@eurel.org; internet www1.vde.com/eurel/; f. 1972; Pres. Prof. Jerzy Barglik; Contact Margaretha Eriksson (Vice-Pres.).

EURELECTRIC (Union of the Electricity Industry/Groupement Européen des Entreprises d'Electricité/Europäische Vereinigung der Elektrizitätsversorgung): 66 blvd de l'Impératrice, 1000 Brussels, Belgium; tel. (+32) 2-5151000; fax (+32) 2-5151010; e-mail nrega@eurelectric.org; internet www.eurelectric.org; Pres. Dr Francesco Starace; Sec.-Gen. Kristian Ruby; Contact Anne-Marie Rego (Communication Man.).

EURIC (European Recycling Industries' Confederation): 80 blvd A. Reyers, 1030 Brussels, Belgium; tel. (+32) 2-7068720; e-mail euric@euric-aisbl.eu; internet www.euric-aisbl.eu; f. 1972; Pres. Michael Schuy; Sec.-Gen. Emmanuel Katrakis.

EURIMA (European Insulation Manufacturers' Association/Association Européenne des Fabricants de Produits Isolants/Europäische Vereinigung von Dämmstoff-Herstellern): 375 ave Louise, Bte 4, 1050 Brussels, Belgium; tel. (+32) 2-6262090; fax (+32) 2-6262099; e-mail info@eurima.org; internet www.eurima.org; f. 1959; Pres. Pascal Eveillard; Contact Jan te Bos (Dir-Gen.).

EURO-AIR (European Association of Air Heater Manufacturers): Marienbürger Str. 15, 50968 Cologne, Germany; tel. (+49 221) 3764-830; fax (+49 221) 3764-861; e-mail info@figawa.de; internet www.euro-air.com; f. 1995; Pres. Ing. L. B. G. Looman; Sec.-Gen. Harald Petermann; Contact Ferdinand Ehard (Vice-Pres.).

EURO-CASE (European Council of Applied Sciences Technology and Engineering): Grand Palais des Champs Elysées, Porte C, Ave Franklin D. Roosevelt, 75008 Paris, France; tel. (+33) 1-53-59-53-40; fax (+33) 1-53-59-53-41; e-mail mail@euro-case.org; internet www.euro-case.org; f. 1992; Sec.-Gen. Yves Caristan; Contact Reinhard Hüttl (Chair.).

EURO CHLOR (European Chlorine Industry): 4 ave E. van Nieuwenhuyse, POB 2, 1160 Brussels, Belgium; tel. (+32) 2-6767320; fax (+32) 2-6767241; e-mail eurochlor@cefic.be; internet www.eurochlor.org; f. 1991; Contact Dolf van Wijk (Exec. Dir.).

EURO COOP (European Community of Consumer Co-operatives/Communauté Européenne des Coopératives de Consommateurs/Europäische Gemeinschaft der Verbrauchergenossenschaften): 12 ave de Tervuren, Bte 3, 1040 Brussels, Belgium; tel. (+32) 2-2850073; e-mail info@eurocoop.coop; internet www.eurocoop.coop; f. 1957; Pres. Massimo Bongiovannin; Sec.-Gen. Todor Ivanov; Contact Jan Schiettecatte (Dir Communications).

EUROALLIAGES (Association of European Ferro-alloy Producers/Comité de Liaison des Industries de Ferro-Alliages): 12 ave de Broqueville, 1150 Brussels, Belgium; tel. (+32) 2-7756301; e-mail euroalliages@euroalliages.be; internet www.euroalliages.com; f. 1993; Pres. Johan Svensson; Sec.-Gen. Inès van Lierde; Contact Catherine Conty (Exec. Assistant).

EUROBAT (Association of European Storage Battery Manufacturers/Association de Fabricants Européens d'Accumulateurs/Vereinigung Europäischer Akkumulatoren-Hersteller): 142 ave Jules Bordet, 1140 Brussels, Belgium; tel. (+32) 2-7611653; fax (+32) 2-7611699; e-mail eurobat@eurobat.org; internet eurobat.org; f. 1968; Contact Veerle Guns (Man. Asst).

EUROCADRES (Council of European Professional Managerial Staff/Conseil des Cadres Européens/Rat der Europäischen Fach- und Führungskrafte): 5 blvd du Roi Albert II, 1210 Brussels, Belgium; tel. (+32) 2-2240730; fax (+32) 2-2240733; e-mail secretariat@eurocadres.org; internet www.eurocadres.org; f. 1993; Pres. Martin Jefflén; Contact Slavica Uzelac (Exec. Officer).

EUROCAE (European Organization for Civil Aviation Equipment/Organisation Européenne pour l'Equipement de l'Aviation Civile): 9–23 rue Paul Lafargue, 93200 Saint-Denis, France; tel. (+33) 1-49-92-79-30; fax (+33) 1-46-55-62-65; e-mail eurocae@eurocae.net; internet www.eurocae.net; f. 1963; Pres. Francis Schubert; Sec.-Gen. Christian Schleifer-Heingärtner; Contact Jean-Christophe Albouy (Chair.).

EUROCHAMBRES (Association of European Chambers of Commerce and Industry/Association des Chambres Européennes de Commerce et d'Industrie/Vereinigung der Europäischen Industrien- und Handelskammern): 19A/D ave des Arts, 1000 Brussels, Belgium; tel. (+32) 2-2820850; fax (+32) 2-2300038; e-mail eurochambres@eurochambres.eu; internet www.eurochambres.eu; f. 1958; Contact Arnaldo Abruzzini (CEO).

EUROCINEMA (Association of Producers of Cinema and Television/Association de Producteurs de Cinéma et de Télévision): 19 rue des Chartreux, Bte 12, 1000 Brussels, Belgium; tel. (+32) 2-7325830; fax (+32) 2-7333657; e-mail eurocinema@eurocinema.eu; internet www.eurocinema.eu; f. 1991; Contact Fabienne Burton (Assistant).

EUROCOMMERCE (Association for Retail, Wholesale and International Trade Sectors in Europe/Commerce de Détail, de Gros et International en Europe/Gegründet und Vertritt den Einzel-, Gross- und Aussenhandel in Europa): 9 ave des Nerviens, 5th Floor, 1040 Brussels, Belgium; tel. (+32) 2-7370598; fax (+32) 2-2300078; e-mail bastings@eurocommerce.be; internet www.eurocommerce.be; f. 1993; Pres. Dame Lucy Neville-Rolfe; Contact Fabienne Bastings (Office Man.).

EUROCOP (European Confederation of Police): 59A rue Principale, 5480 Wormeldange, Luxembourg; tel. (+352) 4349611; fax (+352) 43496133; e-mail contact@eurocop-police.org; internet www.eurocop-police.org; f. 2002; Pres. Angels Bosch Camprecios; Contact Roger Mercatoris (Vice-Pres.).

EUROCORD (Federation of European Rope, Twine and Netting Industries/Fédération Européenne des Industries de Corderie-Ficellerie et de Filets/EG-Verbindungsausschuss der Hartfaser- und Tauwerkindustrie): 65 ave Victor Hugo, 75116 Paris, France; tel. (+33) 1-53-75-10-04; fax (+33) 1-53-75-10-02; e-mail eurocord@eurocord.com; internet www.eurocord.com; f. 1959; Pres. Rui Faria; Sec.-Gen. Philippe Verschueren; Contact Giancarlo Badinotti (Vice-Pres.).

EUROCOTON (Committee of the Cotton and Allied Textile Industries/Komitee der Baumwoll- und Verwandten Textilindustriën der EG): 24 rue Montoyer, Bte 13, 1000 Brussels, Belgium; tel. (+32) 2-2303239; fax (+32) 2-2303622; e-mail michele.anselme@eurocoton.org; Pres. Benoît Hacot; Sec.-Gen. Michèle Anselme; Contact Tito Burgi (Vice-Pres.).

EUROFEDOP (European Federation of Public Service Employees/Fédération Européenne du Personnel des Services Publics/Europäische Föderation der Öffentlichbediensteten): 39 rue Montoyer, 1000 Brussels, Belgium; tel. (+32) 2-2303865; fax (+32) 2-2821871; e-mail eurofedop@eurofedop.org; internet www.eurofedop.org; f. 1966; Pres. Fritz Neugebauer; Sec.-Gen. Bert van Caelenberg; Contact Valentin Rasking (Translator).

Trade and Professional Organizations DIRECTORY

EUROFEL (European Association of Feldspar Producers): c/o IMA-Europe, 26 rue des Deux Eglises, 6th Floor, Bte 2, 1000 Brussels, Belgium; tel. (+32) 2-2104410; fax (+32) 2-2104429; e-mail secretariat@ima-europe.eu; internet www.ima-europe.eu; f. 1996; Pres. Sinan Ozman; Sec.-Gen. Dr Roger Doome.

EUROFER (European Confederation of Iron and Steel Industries/Association Européenne de la Sidérurgie/Europäische Wirtschaftsvereinigung der Eisen- und Stahlindustrie): 172 ave de Cortenbergh, 1000 Brussels, Belgium; tel. (+32) 2-7387920; fax (+32) 2-7387955; e-mail mail@eurofer.be; internet www.eurofer.org; f. 1976; Contact Axel Eggert (Dir-Gen.).

EUROFEU (European Committee of the Manufacturers of Fire Protection Equipment and Fire Fighting Vehicles/Comité Européen des Constructeurs de Matériels d'Incendie et de Secours/Europäisches Komitee der Hersteller von Fahrzeugen, Geräten und Anlagen für den Brandschutz): Koellikerstr. 13, 97070 Würzburg, Germany; tel. (+49 931) 35292-0; fax (+49 931) 35292-29; e-mail info@eurofeu.org; internet www.eurofeu.org; f. 1969; Pres. Jan Witte; Sec.-Gen. Wolfram Krause.

EUROFINAS (European Federation of Finance House Associations/Fédération Européenne des Instituts de Crédit/Europäische Vereinigung der Verbände von Finanzierungsbanken): 87 blvd Louis Schmidt, 1040 Brussels, Belgium; tel. (+32) 2-7780560; fax (+32) 2-7780578; e-mail j.debruyne@eurofinas.org; internet www.eurofinas.org; f. 1960; Pres. Valentino Ghelli; Contact Anne Valette (Head, Communications).

EUROFORGE (European Forging Associations/Comité de Liaison des Industries Européennes de l'Estampage et de la Forge/Europäischer Schmiedeverband): blvd A. Reyers 80, 1030 Brussels, Belgium; tel. (+49 2331) 9588028; fax (+49 2331) 958728; e-mail hain@euroforge.org; internet www.euroforge.org; f. 1953; Pres. José Yudego; Sec.-Gen. Dr Theodor L. Tutmann; Contact Friederike Schnittker (Asst).

EUROGAS (European Union of the Natural Gas Industry/Union Européenne de l'Industrie du Gaz Naturel/Europäische Vereinigung der Erdgaswirtschaft): 172 ave de Cortenbergh, Bte 6, 1000 Brussels, Belgium; tel. (+32) 2-8944848; fax (+32) 2-8944800; e-mail eurogas@eurogas.org; internet www.eurogas.org; f. 1990; Pres. Klaus Schäfer; Sec.-Gen. Beate Raabe; Contact Martin Herrmann (Vice-Pres.).

EUROGIRO (Giro and Postbank Organizations in Europe): Telegade 1, 1st Floor, 2630 Taastrup, Denmark; tel. (+45) 43-71-27-72; fax (+45) 43-71-26-62; e-mail eurogiro@eurogiro.com; internet www.eurogiro.com; f. 1992; Contact Michel Stuijt (CEO).

EUROGLACES (European Ice Cream Association): c/o FEVIA, 14 rue de la Science, 1040 Brussels, Belgium; tel. (+32) 2-2138478; fax (+32) 2-5081021; e-mail info@euroglaces.eu; internet euroglaces.eu; f. 1957; Pres. Albert Bricall; Sec.-Gen. Myriam Goffings; Contact Clive Gristwood (Vice-Pres.).

EUROGYPSUM (Association of European Gypsum Industries/Association des Industries Européennes du Plâtre/Verband der Europäischen Gipsindustrien): 4 rue de la presse, 1000 Brussels, Belgium; tel. (+32) 2-2271130; fax (+32) 2-2273141; e-mail secretariat@eurogypsum.org; internet www.eurogypsum.org; f. 1961; Pres. Bernard Lekien; Sec.-Gen. Christine Marlet.

EUROHEAT & POWER (International Association for District Heating, District Cooling and Combined Heat and Power): Cours Saint Michel 30A, 1040 Brussels, Belgium; tel. (+32) 2-7402110; fax (+32) 2-7402119; e-mail office@euroheat.org; internet www.euroheat.org; f. 1954; Pres. Werner Lutsch; Contact Paul Voss (Man. Dir).

EUROLAB (European Federation of National Associations of Measurement, Testing and Analytical Laboratories): 20–22 rue du Commerce, 1000 Brussels, Belgium; tel. (+32) 2-5115065; fax (+32) 2-5025047; e-mail info@eurolab.org; internet www.eurolab.org; f. 1990; Pres. Álvaro Silva Ribeiro; Contact Dr Bernd Kroon (Treas.); Contact Dr Kurt Ziegler (Vice-Pres.); Paolo Moscatti.

EUROM (European Federation of Precision Mechanical and Optical Industries/Fédération Européenne de l'Industrie de l'Optique et de la Mécanique de Précision/Europäische Industrie-Vereinigung Feinmechanik und Optik): c/o Spectaris, Saarbrücker Str. 38, 10405 Berlin, Germany; tel. (+49 30) 414021-0; fax (+49 30) 41402133; e-mail pposso@worldcom.ch; internet eurom.org; f. 1958; Pres. Dr Patrick Posso; Sec.-Gen. Nadine Benad.

EUROM II (Optics Laser and Laboratory Instrumentation Group within the European Federation of Precision Mechanical and Optical Industries): 39 rue L. Blanc, Courbevoie, 92038 Paris La Défense Cedex, France; tel. (+33) 1-47-17-64-05; fax (+33) 1-47-17-61-05; e-mail eurom2@blwa.co.uk; internet www.fabrilabo.com/eurom2.htm; Pres. Michel Leclercq; Sec.-Gen. Francis Pithon.

EUROMALT (Working Committee of the EU Malting Industry/Comité de Travail des Malteries de l'UE/Arbeitskomitee der Malzereien in der EG): 98 rue du Trône, 1050 Brussels, Belgium; tel. (+32) 2-5020808; fax (+32) 2-5026030; e-mail euromalt@grainindustry.com; internet www.euromalt.be; f. 1959; Pres. Nicholas King; Sec.-Gen. Teresa Babuscio; Contact Tim Stonehouse (Vice-Pres.).

EUROMAT (European Gaming and Amusement Federation/Fédération Européenne des Jeux et d'Amusement/Europäische Vereinigung der Automaten-Verbände): 22–24 rue du Luxembourg, 1000 Brussels, Belgium; tel. (+32) 2-7616684; fax (+32) 2-2131363; e-mail secretariat@euromat.org; internet euromat.org; f. 1979; Pres. Jason Frost; Sec.-Gen. Kieran O'Keeffe; Contact Uwe Christiansen (Vice-Pres.).

EUROMETAL (European Federation of Associations of Steel, Tubes and Metal Merchants/Fédération Européenne des Associations de Négociants en Aciers, Tubes et Métaux/Europäischer Federation der Nationalen Verbande der Stahl-, Rohre- und Metall-Handlers): 46 blvd de la Woluwe, Bte 7, 1200 Brussels, Belgium; tel. (+32) 2-7715340; fax (+32) 2-7721977; e-mail office@eurometal.net; internet www.eurometal.net; f. 1964; Pres. Jens Lauber; Contact Robert Kay (Vice-Pres.).

EUROMETAUX (European Association of Metals/Association Européenne des Métaux): 12 ave de Broqueville, 1150 Brussels, Belgium; tel. (+32) 2-7756311; fax (+32) 2-7790523; e-mail eurometaux@eurometaux.be; internet eurometaux.org; f. 1981; Pres. Dirk Vandenberghe; Contact Anne Heymans-Cornelissen (Office Man.).

EUROMOT (European Association of Internal Combustion Engine Manufacturers): 7 rue Joseph Stevens, 14th Floor, 1000 Brussels, Belgium; tel. (32) 2-8932142; e-mail info@euromot.eu; internet www.euromot.org; f. 1991; Pres. Georg Diderich; Sec.-Gen. Dr Peter Scherm; Contact Dr Giancarlo Dellora (Deputy Pres.).

EUROPABIO (European Association for Bioindustries/Association Européenne des BioIndustries): 6 ave de l'Armée, 1040 Brussels, Belgium; tel. (+32) 2-7350313; fax (+32) 2-7354960; e-mail communications@europabio.org; internet www.europabio.org; f. 1996; Sec.-Gen. John Brennan; Contact Dr Petra Laux (Treas.).

EUROPACABLE (European Confederation of National Associations of Manufacturers of Insulated Wires and Cable/Confédération Européenne des Associations de Fabricants de Fils et de Câbles Isolés/Europäische Konföderation der Vereinigungen der Kabel- und Isolierdrahthersteller): 58 rue Marie Bourgogne,

1000 Brussels, Belgium; tel. (+32) 2-2908996; fax (+32) 2-7068733; e-mail contact@europacable.com; internet www.europacable.com; f. 1990; Pres. Valerio Battista; Sec.-Gen. Thomas Neesen.

EUROPATAT (European Union of the Potato Trade/Union Européenne du Commerce des Pommes de Terre/Europäische Union des Kartoffelhandels): 49–51 rue de Trèves, Bte 8, 1040 Brussels, Belgium; tel. (+32) 9-7771585; fax (+32) 9-7771586; e-mail secretariat@europatat.eu; internet europatat.eu; f. 1952; Pres. Jos Muyshondt; Sec.-Gen. Raquel Izquierdo de Santiago; Contact Domenico Citterio (Vice-Pres.).

European Region of WCPT (European Region of the World Confederation for Physical Therapy): 36 rue de Pascale, 1040 Brussels, Belgium; tel. (+32) 2-2315063; fax (+32) 2-2315064; e-mail info@erwcpt.eu; internet www.erwcpt.eu; f. 1998; Pres. Sarah Bazin; Sec.-Gen. David Gorria; Contact Roland Craps (Vice-Chair.).

EUROPECHE (Association of the National Organizations of Fishing Enterprises in the European Union/Association des Organisations Nationales d'Entreprises de Pêche de l'UE/Vereinigung der Nationalen Verbände von Fischereiunternehmen in der Europäischen Union): 24 rue Montoyer, 1000 Brussels, Belgium; tel. (+32) 2-2304848; fax (+32) 2-2302680; e-mail europeche@europeche.org; internet www.europeche.org; f. 1962; Pres. Javier Garat; Contact Barrie Deas (Vice-Pres.).

EUROPEN (European Organization for Packaging and the Environment/Organisation Européenne pour l'Emballage et l'Environnement/Europäische Vereinigung für Verpackung und Umwelt): Le Royal Tervuren, 6 ave de l'Armée, 1040 Brussels, Belgium; tel. (+32) 2-7363600; fax (+32) 2-7363521; e-mail packaging@europen.be; internet www.europen.be; f. 1992; Contact Virginia Janssens (Man. Dir).

EUROPGEN (European Generating Set Association/Comité de Coordination du Groupe Electrogène en Europe/Koordinierungskomitee der Kraftwerksfachverbände in Europa): c/o VDMA, Lyoner Str. 18, 60528 Frankfurt am Main, Germany; tel. (+44) 1787226995; e-mail info@europgen.com; internet www.europgen.eu; f. 1989; Pres. Lenaik Andrieux; Contact Paul Blything (Gen. Sec.).

EUROPLANT (European Plantmakers' Committee/Comité Européen des Ensembliers Industriels/Europäisches Komittee der Grossanlangen Bauwerk): c/o VDMA, Lyoner Str. 18, 60528 Frankfurt am Main, Germany; tel. (+49 69) 66031472; fax (+49 69) 66031814; e-mail thomas.waldmann@vdma.org; Contact Thomas Waldmann (Man. Dir).

EUROPUMP (European Association of Pump Manufacturers/Association Européenne des Constructeurs de Pompes/Europäische Vereinigung der Pumpenhersteller): Diamant Bldg, 80 blvd A. Reyers, 1030 Brussels, Belgium; tel. (+32) 2-7068230; fax (+32) 2-7068253; e-mail secretariat@europump.org; internet europump.net; f. 1960; Pres. Martijn van den Born; Sec.-Gen. Pierre Lucas; Contact Frank Ennenbach (Commission Chair.).

EUROPUR (European Association of Flexible Polyurethane Foam Blocks Manufacturers/Association Européenne des Fabricants de Blocs de Mousse Souple de Polyuréthane/Verband der Europäischen Hersteller von Polyurethan Weichblockschann): 71 ave de Cortenbergh, 1000 Brussels, Belgium; tel. (+32) 2-7418281; fax (+32) 2-7366072; e-mail info@europur.org; internet www.europur.com; f. 1965; Pres. Bart J. ten Brink; Sec.-Gen. Michael Baumgartner; Contact Raffaella Salerno (Asst).

EUROSAFE (European Committee of Safe Manufacturers' Associations/Comité Européen des Associations de Fabricants de Coffres-Forts): Lundbyvägen 8, 311 68 Slöinge, Sweden; tel. (+46 34) 626-02-50; fax (+46 34) 626-02-22; e-mail peter.blomdahl@robursafe.com; internet www.eurosafe-online.com; f. 1988; Sec.-Gen. Peter Blomdahl.

EUROSEED (European Seed Association): 52 ave des Arts, 7th Floor, 1000 Brussels, Belgium; tel. (+32) 2-7432860; fax (+32) 2-7432869; e-mail secretariat@euroseed.org; internet www.euroseeds.org; f. 2001; Pres. Nigel Moore; Sec.-Gen. Garlich von Essen; Contact Christophe Rouillard (Technical Man.).

EUROSIL (European Association of Silica Producers): c/o IMA-Europe, 26 rue des Deux Eglises, 6th Floor, Bte 2, 1000 Brussels, Belgium; tel. (+32) 2-2104410; fax (+32) 2-2104429; e-mail f.lumen@ima-europe.eu; internet www.eurosil.eu; f. 1991; Pres. Laurence Boens; Sec.-Gen. Florence Lumen.

EUROSMART (European Smart Card Association Network): 19–21 rue du Luxembourg, 1000 Brussels, Belgium; tel. (+32) 2-5068838; fax (+32) 2-5068825; e-mail info@eurosmart.com; internet www.eurosmart.com; f. 1994; Pres. Timothée Mangenot; Sec.-Gen. Bruno Dupont; Contact Nicholas Raffin; Stefane Mouille (Vice-Pres.).

EUROTALC (Scientific Association of European Talc Producers): 26 rue des Deux Eglises, 1000 Brussels, Belgium; tel. (+32) 2-2104410; fax (+32) 2-2104429; e-mail secretariat@ima-europe.eu; internet www.eurotalc.eu; f. 2006; Pres. José Manuel Dominguez; Sec.-Gen. Florence Lumen.

EUROVENT (European Committee of Air Handling and Air Conditioning Equipment Manufacturers/Comité Européen des Constructeurs de Matériel Aéraulique): Diamant Bldg, 80 blvd A. Reyers, 1030 Brussels, Belgium; tel. (+32) 4-66900401; fax (+32) 2-7067966; e-mail secretariat@eurovent.eu; internet eurovent.eu; f. 1958; Pres. Alex Rasmussen; Sec.-Gen. Felix Van Eyken; Contact Naci Şahin (Vice-Pres.).

EUROVIA/ECVC (European Co-ordination Via Campesina/Coordination Européenne Via Campesina/Coordinadora Europea Vía Campesina): 18 rue de la Sablonnière, 1000 Brussels, Belgium; tel. (+32) 2-2173112; fax (+32) 2-2184509; e-mail info@eurovia.org; internet www.eurovia.org; f. 1986; Contact Gérard Choplin (Co-ordinator).

EuSalt (European Salt Producers' Association/Association Européenne des Producteurs de Sel/Europäische Vereinigung der Salzhersteller): 38/40 sq de Meeûs, 1000 Brussels, Belgium; tel. (+32) 2-4016133; fax (+32) 2-4016135; e-mail info@eusalt.com; internet www.eusalt.com; f. 1957; Pres. Hubert François; Contact Wouter Lox (Man. Dir).

EUSP/UEPS (European Union of Social Pharmacies/Union Européenne des Pharmacies Sociales): 900 route de Lennik, 1070 Brussels, Belgium; tel. (+32) 2-5299240; fax (+32) 2-5299376; e-mail ophaco@ophaco.org; internet www.eurosocialpharma.org; f. 1961; Pres. William Janssens; Sec.-Gen. Marc-Henry Cornely; Contact Venanzio Gizzi (Vice-Pres.).

EUTECA (European Technical Caramel Colour Association/Association Européenne de Caramels Colorants/Europäischer Verband der Hersteller von Farbstoffkaramel): 13A ave de Tervueren, Bte 7, 1040 Brussels, Belgium; tel. (+32) 2-7365354; fax (+32) 2-7323427; internet www.euteca.org; f. 1978; Pres. Barry Foley; Sec.-Gen. Dionne Heijnen.

EUTECER (Federation of the EU Manufacturers of Technical Ceramics): 17 rue de la Montagne, 1000 Brussels, Belgium; tel. (+32) 2-8083880; fax (+32) 2-5115174; e-mail sec@cerameunie.net; internet www.cerameunie.net; f. 1966; Sec.-Gen. Astrid Volckaert; Contact Renaud Batier (Dir-Gen.).

EUTO (European Union of Tourist Officers/Union Européenne des Cadres du Tourisme/Europäischer Verband für Tourismusfachleute): 200 Chemin du Bois d'Andrieu, 34800 Canet, France; tel. (+44 1294) 313006; fax (+44 1294) 313016; e-mail

Trade and Professional Organizations

presidency@euto.org; internet www.euto.org; f. 1975; Pres. Liz Buchanan; Sec.-Gen. John T. Owen; Contact Julian Zarb (Vice-Pres.).

EUTS (European Union of Tapestries and Saddlers/Union Européenne des Tapissiers-Décorateurs et Selliers/Europäische Union der Tapeziere-Dekorateure und Sattler): Eichholzstrasse 11, 2545 Selzach, Switzerland; tel. (+41) 32-641-66-10; e-mail info@interieursuisse.ch; internet www.interieursuisse.ch; Pres. Reto Eilinger; Sec.-Gen. Peter Platzer.

EUVEPRO (European Vegetable Protein Federation/Fédération Européenne des Protéines Végétales/Europäische Vereinigung für Pflanzliches Eiweiss): 142 ave Jules Bordet, 1140 Brussels, Belgium; tel. (+32) 2-7611650; fax (+32) 2-7611699; e-mail euvepro@kellencompany.com; internet www.euvepro.eu; f. 1977; Sec.-Gen. Susanne Meyer; Contact Yves Goemans (Chair.).

EUWEP (EU Association for Egg Packers and Traders, Egg Processors, Poultry and Game/Union Européenne du Commerce du Gros des Oeufs, Produits d'Oeufs, Volaille et Gibier/Europäische Union des Grosshandels mit Eiern, Eiprodukten, Geflügel und Wild): 89 Charterhouse St, 2nd Floor, London EC1M 6HR, United Kingdom; tel. (+44 20) 7608-3760; fax (+44 20) 7608-3860; e-mail info@euwep.org; internet www.euwep.info; f. 1959; Pres. Jan Lahde; Sec.-Gen. Mark Williams.

EVA (European Vending Association): 44 rue Van Eyck, 1000 Brussels, Belgium; tel. (+32) 2-5120075; fax (+32) 2-5022342; e-mail vending@vending-europe.eu; internet www.vending-europe.eu; f. 1976; Pres. Jan-Marck Vrijlandt; Contact Erwin Wetzel (Dir-Gen.).

EWA (European Water Association): Theodor-Heuss-Allee 17, 53773 Hennef, Germany; tel. (+49 2242) 872-189; fax (+49 2422) 872-135; e-mail info@ewa-online.eu; internet www.ewa-online.eu; f. 1981; Pres. José Saldanhas Matos; Sec.-Gen. Johannes Lohaus; Contact Bjørn Kaare Jensen (Vice-Pres.).

EWA (European Welding Association/Association Européenne des Fabricants de Matériel de Soudage/Europäischer Verband der Hersteller von Schweisselektrodenapparaten): c/o Symop Maison de la mécanique, 45 rue Louis Blanc, 92038 La Défense, Paris, France; e-mail guy.missiaen@european-welding.org; internet european-welding.org; f. 1987; Pres. Robert Stoeckl; Contact Nicolas Parascandolo; Emil Schubert (Vice-Pres.); Guy Missiaen (Gen. Man.).

EWPA (European Whey Products Association/Association Européenne des Produits de Lactosérum/Europäischer Whey-Produkte-Verband): 22–28 ave d'Auderghem, 1040 Brussels, Belgium; tel. (+32) 2-5495047; fax (+32) 2-5495049; e-mail ewpa@euromilk.org; internet ewpa.euromilk.org; f. 1996; Pres. Jeroen Derks; Sec.-Gen. Bénédicte Masure; Contact Angela Aris (Office Man.).

EWPM (European Wood Preservative Manufacturers Group): 4A Mallard Way, Pride Park, Derby DE24 8GX, United Kingdom; tel. (+44 1423) 500720; fax (+44 7092) 072214; e-mail info@ewpm.org; internet ewpm.org; f. 1977; Pres. Dr Finn Imsgard; Sec.-Gen. Dr Christopher Coggins.

EWRIS (European Federation of Wire Rope Industries/Fédération Européenne des Industries de Câbles d'Acier/Europäische Informationsdienststelle für Drahtseil): 65 ave Victor Hugo, 75116 Paris, France; tel. (+33) 1-53-75-10-04; fax (+33) 1-53-75-10-02; e-mail ewris@ewris.com; internet www.ewris.com; f. 1962; Pres. Maurizio Prete; Sec.-Gen. Dr Anne Jourdain; Contact Valérie Excoffon (Sec.).

FACE (Federation of Associations for Hunting and Conservation of the EU/Fédération des Associations de Chasse et Conservation de la Faune Sauvage de l'UE/Federación de las Asociaciones de Caza y Conservación de la Fauna Silvestre de la UE): 82 rue F. Pelletier, 1030 Brussels, Belgium; tel. (+32) 2-7326900; fax (+32) 2-7327072; e-mail info@face.eu; internet www.face.eu; f. 1977; Pres. Gilbert de Turckheim; Sec.-Gen. Filippo Segato; Contact Charlotte Nyffels (Office Man.).

FAECF (Federation of European Window and Curtain Wall Manufacturers' Associations/Fédération des Associations Européennes des Constructeurs de Fenêtres et de Façades/Föderation der Europäischen Fenster- und Fassadenhersteller-Verbände): 54 Ayres St, London SE1 1EU, United Kingdom; tel. (+44 20) 7939-9101; e-mail general.secretariat@faecf.org; internet www.faecf.org; f. 1968; Pres. Nico Kremers; Sec.-Gen. Giles Willson; Contact Patrick England (Technical Sec.).

FAFPAS (Federation of the Associations of EU Frozen Food Producers/Fédération des Associations de Fabricants de Produits Alimentaires Surgelés de l'UE/Föderation der Tiefgefriernahrungsmittelhersteller-Verbände der EG): 30 ave de Roodebeek, 1030 Brussels, Belgium; tel. (+32) 2-7438730; fax (+32) 2–7368175; e-mail fafpas@sia-dvi.be; f. 1962; Sec.-Gen. Michel Coenen.

FARECOGAZ (Association of European Gas Meter Manufacturers): Allée Broc à l'Aye 14, 1400 Nivelles, Belgium; tel. (+32) 6-7214602; fax (+32) 6-7443251; e-mail jsenave@skynet.be; internet www.farecogaz.eu; f. 2011; Pres. Dr Cristiano Nardi; Sec.-Gen. Dr Norbert Burger.

FCC (Federation of Cocoa Commerce Ltd/Fédération du Commerce des Cacaos): Cannon Bridge House, 1 Cousin Lane, London EC4R 3XX, United Kingdom; tel. (+44 20) 7379-2884; fax (+44 20) 7379-2389; e-mail fcc@nyx.com; internet www.cocoafederation.com; f. 2002; Sec.-Gen. Silde Lauand; Contact Philip M Sigley (Chief Exec.).

FEA (European Aerosol Federation/Fédération Européenne des Aérosols/Europäischer Aerosolverband): 15A ave Hermann Debroux, 1160 Brussels, Belgium; tel. (+32) 2-6796280; fax (+32) 2-6796283; e-mail info@aerosol.org; internet www.aerosol.org; f. 1959; Pres. Dr Rolf Bayersdörfer; Sec.-Gen. Alain d'Haese; Contact Valérie Boulet (Projects and Communications).

FEACO (European Federation of Management Consulting Associations/Fédération Européenne des Associations de Conseils en Management/Europäische Föderation der Unternehmensberaterverbände): 3–5 ave des Arts, 1210 Brussels, Belgium; tel. (+32) 2-2500650; fax (+32) 2-2500651; e-mail feaco@feaco.org; internet www.feaco.org; f. 1960; Sec.-Gen. David Ifrah; Contact Ezio Lattanzio (Chair.).

FEAD (European Federation of Waste Management and Environmental Services/Fédération Européenne des Activités du Déchet et de l'Environnement/Europäische Föderation der Entsorgungswirtschaft): 15 rue Philippe le Bon, 1000 Brussels, Belgium; tel. (+32) 2-7323213; fax (+32) 2-7349592; e-mail info@fead.be; internet www.fead.be; f. 1981; Pres. Peter Kurth; Sec.-Gen. Nadine De Greef; Contact Milda Basiulyte (Legal and Communications Officer).

FEANI (European Federation of National Engineering Associations/Fédération Européenne d'Associations Nationales d'Ingénieurs/Föderation Europäischer Nationaler Ingenieurverbände): 18 ave Roger Vandendriessche, 1150 Brussels, Belgium; tel. (+32) 2-6390390; fax (+32) 2-6390399; e-mail secretariat.general@feani.org; internet www.feani.org; f. 1951; Pres. Rafael Aller; Sec.-Gen. Dirk Bochar.

FEAP (Federation of European Aquaculture Producers/Fédération Européenne des Producteurs Aquacoles): 9 rue de Paris, 4020 Liège, Belgium; tel. (+32) 4-3382995; fax (+32) 4-3379846; e-mail secretariat@feap.info; internet www.feap.info; f. 1969;

Pres. Arnault Chaperon; Sec.-Gen. Courtney Hough; Contact Marco Gilmozzi (Vice-Pres.).

FEB (Fellowship of European Broadcasters): 23 The Service Rd, Potters Bar, Hertfordshire EN6 1QA, United Kingdom; tel. (+44 1707) 649910; fax (+44 1707) 662653; e-mail feb@feb.org; internet www.feb.org; Pres. Harvey Thomas; Contact Jackie Sibuns (Administrator).

FEC (Federation of the European Cutlery, Flatware, Holloware and Cookware Industries/Fédération de l'Industrie Européenne de la Coutellerie et des Couverts de Table, de l'Orfèvrerie et des Articles Culinaires/Föderation der Europäischen Schneidwaren-, Besteck-, Tafelgeräte-, Küchengeschirr und Haushaltgeräteindustrie): c/o IVSH, Neuenhofer Str. 24, 42657 Solingen, Germany; tel. (+49 212) 2267-320; fax (+49 212) 2267-329; e-mail ivsh@fecinfo.org; internet www.fecinfo.org; f. 1952; Pres. Maurits Demeyere; Sec.-Gen. Jens-Heinrich Beckmann; Contact Fred Hollaender (Vice-Pres.).

FECC (Fédération Européenne du Commerce Chimique/European Association of Chemical Distributors/Europäische Föderation des Chemischen Handels): 16B rue du Luxembourg, 1000 Brussels, Belgium; tel. 6790260; fax 6727355; e-mail vle@fecc.org; internet www.fecc.org; Pres. Nordmann Edgar; Contact Uta Jensen-Korte (Dir-Gen.).

FECC (European Federation of Managers in the Construction Industry/Fédération Européenne des Cadres de la Construction): 15 rue de Londres, 75009 Paris, France; tel. (+33) 1-55-31-76-76; fax (+33) 1-55-31-76-33; e-mail contact@cgcbtp.com; f. 1993; Pres. Janert Martineau.

FECS (European Federation of Ceramic Sanitary Ware Manufacturers/Fédération Européenne des Fabricants de Céramiques Sanitaires/Europäische Föderation der Sanitär-Keramik-Hersteller): 3 rue La Boétie, 75008 Paris, France; tel. (+33) 1-58-18-30-40; fax (+33) 1-42-66-09-00; e-mail sanitaire@ceramique.org; f. 1954; Pres. Miguel Angel Munar Saura; Sec.-Gen. François de la Tour.

FEDARENE (European Federation of Regional Energy and Environment Agencies/Fédération Européenne des Agences Régionales de l'Energie et de l'Environnement/Europäische Dachorganisation Regionale Energie- und Umweltbehorden): 11 rue du Beau-Site, 1000 Brussels, Belgium; tel. (+32) 2-6468210; fax (+32) 2-6468975; e-mail fedarene@fedarene.org; internct www.fedarene.org; f. 1990; Pres. Julije Domac; Sec.-Gen. Michael Geissler; Contact Gerhard Dell (Vice-Pres.).

FEDEMAC (European Organization of National Removals Associations): Schulstr. 53, 65795 Hattersheim am Main, Germany; tel. (+49 6190) 989-811; fax (+49 6190) 989-820; e-mail headquarters@fedemac.com; internet www.fedemac.com; f. 1959; Pres. Aivars Usans; Sec.-Gen. Dr Ellen Troska; Contact Tony Richman (European Affairs Representative).

FEDFA (Federation of European Deer Farmers' Associations): Kuytegemstraat 66/2, 2890 Synt Amands, Belgium; tel. (+32) 5-2341788; fax (+32) 5-0500667; e-mail marc.peelman@skynet.be; internet www.fedfa.com; f. 1990; Pres. Morten Nystad; Sec.-Gen. Radim Kotrba; Contact Tomás Landete-Castillejos (Vice-Pres.).

FEDIAF (European Pet Food Industry Federation/Fédération Européenne de l'Industrie des Aliments pour Animaux Familiers/Europäischer Verband der Heimtiernahrungsindustrie): 89/2 ave Louise, 1050 Brussels, Belgium; tel. 2-5360520; fax 2-5378469; e-mail fediaf@fediaf.org; internet www.fediaf.org; f. 1974; Pres. Robert Kaczmarek; Sec.-Gen. Thomas Meyer.

FEDIMA (Federation of European Union Manufacturers and Suppliers of Ingredients to the Bakery, Confectionery and Patisserie Industries): c/o AGEP S.A., 77–79 blvd St Michel, 1040 Brussels, Belgium; tel. (+32) 2-7402965; fax (+32) 2-7325102; e-mail fedima@agep.eu; internet www.fedima.org; f. 1969; Pres. Sofia Barbosa; Sec.-Gen. Jean Christophe Kremer; Contact Gilles Morelle (Chair.).

FEDIOL (EU Oil and Proteinmeal Industry): 168 ave de Tervuren, Bte 12, 1150 Brussels, Belgium; tel. (+32) 2-7715330; fax (+32) 2-7713817; e-mail fediol@fediol.be; internet www.fediol.be; f. 1957; Pres. Alain Brinon; Sec.-Gen. Nathalie Lecocq; Contact Rob Freeriks (Vice-Pres.).

FEDMA (Federation of European Direct and Interactive Marketing/Fédération Européenne du Marketing Direct): 5 ave Ariane, 4th Floor, 1200 Brussels, Belgium; tel. (+32) 2-7794268; fax (+32) 2-7789922; e-mail info@fedma.org; internet www.fedma.org; f. 1997; Pres. Dieter Weng; Sec.-Gen. Sébastien Houzé.

FEE (Federation of European Accountants/Fédération des Experts Comptables Européens/Föderation der Europäischen Wirtschaftsprüfer): 22–28/8 Ave d'Auderghem, 1040 Brussels, Belgium; tel. (+32) 2-2854085; fax (+32) 2-2311112; e-mail secretariat@fee.be; internet www.fee.be; f. 1986; Pres. André Kilesse; Sec.-Gen. Henri Olivier; Contact Olivier Boutellis-Taft (Chief Exec.).

FEEDM (European Federation of Honey Packers and Distributors/Fédération Européenne des Emballeurs et Distributeurs de Miel/Europäischer Verband der Honig-Verpacker und -Händler): Grosse Baeckerstr. 4, 20095 Hamburg, Germany; tel. (+49 40) 3747-1913; fax (+49 40) 3747-1926; e-mail feedm@waren-verein.de; internet www.feedm.com; f. 1958; Pres. Thomas Heck; Sec.-Gen. Dr Katrin Langner; Contact Hanna Liebig.

FEEM (Federation of European Explosives Manufacturers): c/o CEFIC, 4 ave de Niewenhuyse, Bte 1, 1160 Brussels, Belgium; tel. (+32) 2-6767211; fax (+32) 2-6767300; e-mail contact@feem-europe.org; internet www.feem-europe.org; f. 1975; Sec.-Gen. Hans H. Meyer; Contact Mara Caboara.

FEFAC (European Feed Manufacturers' Federation/Fédération Européenne des Fabricants d'Aliments Composés/Europäischer Verband der Mischfutterindustrie): 223 rue de la Loi, POB 3, 1040 Brussels, Belgium; tel. (+32) 2-2850050; fax (+32) 2-2305722; e-mail fefac@fefac.org; internet www.fefac.org; f. 1959; Pres. Ruud Tijssens; Sec.-Gen. Alexander Doring; Contact Arnaud Bouxin (Deputy Sec.-Gen.).

FEFANA (EU Association of Feed Additives and Premixtures Operators/Fédération Européenne des Fabricants d'Adjuvants pour la Nutrition Animale/Europäischer Verband für Wirkstoffe in der Tierernährung): 130A ave Louise, POB 1, 1050 Brussels, Belgium; tel. (+32) 2-6396660; fax (+32) 2-6404111; e-mail info@fefana.org; internet www.fefana.org; f. 1963; Pres. Marco Bruni; Sec.-Gen. Dr Didier Jans; Contact Dieter Greissinger (Vice-Pres.).

FEFCO (European Federation of Corrugated Board Manufacturers/Fédération Européenne des Fabricants de Carton Ondulé/Europäische Föderation der Wellpappefabrikanten): 250 ave Louise, 1050 Brussels, Belgium; tel. (+32) 2-6464070; fax (+32) 2-6466460; e-mail information@fefco.org; internet www.fefco.org; f. 1952; Pres. Roberto Villaquiran; Sec.-Gen. Angelika Christ; Contact Nathalie Schneegans (Dir Communications).

FEFPEB (Fédération Européenne des Fabricants de Palettes et Emballages en Bois/European Federation of Wooden Pallet and Packaging Manufacturers/Europäischer Verband der Holzpackmittel und Palettenhersteller): POB 90154, 5000 LG Tilburg, Netherlands; tel. (+31 13) 5944802; fax (+31 13) 5944749; e-mail fefpeb@wispa.nl; internet www.fefpeb.eu; f. 1947; Pres. Rob van

Trade and Professional Organizations DIRECTORY

Hoesel; Sec.-Gen. Fons J. M. Ceelaert; Contact Michael van Hoesel (Vice-Pres.).

FEIBP (European Brushware Federation/Fédération Européenne de l'Industrie de la Brosserie et de la Pinceauterie/Europäische Föderation der Pinsel- und Burstenindustrie): POB 90154, 5000 LG Tilburg, Netherlands; tel. (+31 13) 5944678; fax (+31 13) 5944749; e-mail feibp@wispa.nl; internet www.eurobrush.com; f. 1958; Pres. Evert Zuiddam; Contact Thorsten W. Stollberg (Vice-Pres.).

FEIC (Fédération Européenne de l'Industrie du Contreplaqué/European Federation of the Plywood Industry/Europäische Föderation der Sperrholzindustrie): 24 rue Montoyer, POB 20, 1000 Brussels, Belgium; tel. (+32) 2-5562584; fax (+32) 2-2870875; e-mail info@europlywood.org; internet www.europlywood.org; Pres. Jean-Charles Thébault; Sec.-Gen. Kris Wijnendaele; Contact Nathalie Godichiabois (Sec.).

FEICA (Fédération Européenne des Industries de Colles et Adhésifs/Association of European Adhesives Manufacturers/Verband Europäischer Klebstoffindustrien): 4 ave Van Nieuwenhuyse, 1160 Brussels, Belgium; tel. (+32) 2-6767320; fax 2 6767399; e-mail info@feica.eu; internet www.feica.com; f. 1972; Pres. Phil Derby; Sec.-Gen. Bernard Ghyoot; Contact Mara Um (Office Administrator).

FELASA (Federation of European Laboratory Animal Science Associations/Fédération des Associations Européennes Scientifiques d'Expérimentation Animale/Föderation der Europäischen Versuchstierkundeverbände): POB 951, Needham Market, Ipswich IP6 8WH, United Kingdom; tel. (+44 20) 7405-0463; fax (+44 20) 7831-9489; e-mail info@felasa.eu; internet www.felasa.eu; f. 1978; Pres. Jan-Bas Prins; Sec.-Gen. Javier Guillen.

FEMB (Fédération Européenne du Mobilier de Bureau/European Federation of Office Furniture): Bierstadter Str. 39, 65189 Wiesbaden, Germany; tel. (+49 611) 1736-0; fax (+49 611) 1736-20; e-mail info@femb.org; internet www.femb.org; f. 1994; Pres. Julian Roebuck; Sec.-Gen. Colin Watson.

FEMFM (Federation of European Manufacturers of Friction Materials/Fédération Européenne des Fabricants de Matériaux de Friction/Europäischer Verband der Hersteller von Reibmaterialen): 79 rue Jean-Jacques Rousseau, 92158 Suresnes Cedex, France; tel. (+33) 1-46-25-02-30; fax (+33) 1-46-97-00-80; e-mail office@femfm.com; internet www.femfm.com; f. 1971; Sec.-Gen. Dietmar K. Leicht.

FEMIB (Federation of the European Building Joinery Associations/Fédération Européenne des Syndicats de Menuiseries Industrielles du Bâtiment/Vereinigung der Europäischen Verbände der Holzindustrie im Baubereich): Walter-Kolb-Str. 1–7, 60594 Frankfurt am Main, Germany; tel. (+49 69) 95505435; fax (+49 69) 95505411; e-mail femib@femib.com; internet www.femib.com; f. 1958; Pres. Helle Carlsen Nielsen; Sec.-Gen. Frank Koos; Contact Anders Isaksson (Vice-Pres.).

FEMIN (European Federation of Manufacturers and Traders of Cleaning Machines, Material and Accessories): Lyoner Str. 18, 60528 Frankfurt am Main, Germany; tel. (+49 69) 6603-1240; e-mail rs@vdma.org; internet www.femin.eu.com; f. 1998; Pres. Michele Redi; Sec.-Gen. Toni d'Andrea; Contact Christian Bodard (Vice-Pres.).

FEP/FEE (Federation of European Publishers/Fédération des Editeurs Européens): 31 rue Montoyer, Bte 8, 1000 Brussels, Belgium; tel. (+32) 2-7701110; fax (+32) 2-7712071; e-mail info@fep-fee.eu; internet www.fep-fee.eu; f. 1967; Pres. Piotr Marciszuk; Sec.-Gen. Anne Bergman-Tahon; Contact Laura Houlgatte (Policy Adviser).

FEPA (Federation of European Producers of Abrasives/Fédération Européenne des Fabricants de Produits Abrasifs/Vereinigung der Europäische Schleifmittel-Hersteller): 20 ave Reille, 75014 Paris, France; tel. (+33) 1-45-81-25-90; fax (+33) 1-45-81-62-94; e-mail fepa@fepa-abrasives.org; internet www.fepa-abrasives.org; f. 1955; Pres. Steffen Neu; Sec.-Gen. Franck Verguet.

FEPD (European Federation of Perfume Retailers/Fédération Européenne des Parfumeurs Détaillants/Bundesverband Parfümerien): An der Engelsburg 1, Postfach 100 225, 45657 Recklinghausen, Germany; tel. (+49 2361) 92480; fax (+49 2361) 924888; e-mail info@parfuemerieverband.de; internet www.bvpkw.de; f. 1960; Pres. Barbara Summerer.

FEPE (European Envelope Manufacturers' Association/Fédération Européenne des Producteurs d'Enveloppes/Europäische Vereinigung der Briefumschlagfabrikanten): 250 ave Louise, POB 81, 1050 Brussels, Belgium; tel. (+32) 2-7794001; fax (+32) 2-7794901; e-mail info@fepe.org; internet www.fepe.org; f. 1957; Pres. Yves Peiffer; Contact Lisa Kretschmann (Man. Dir).

FEPF (European Federation for Table- and Ornamentalware/Fédération Européenne des Industries de Porcelaine et de Faïence de Table et d'Ornementation): 17 rue de la Montagne, 1000 Brussels, Belgium; tel. (+32) 2-8083880; fax (+32) 2-5115174; e-mail sec@cerameunie.eu; internet www.cerameunie.eu; f. 1958; Pres. Gérard Zink; Sec.-Gen. Rogier Chorus.

FEPORT (Federation of European Private Port Operators/Fédération Européenne des Opérateurs Portuaires Privés/Vereinigung Europäischer Privater Hafenumschlag Betriebe): 3–5 ave des Arts, 1210 Brussels, Belgium; tel. (+32) 2-7367552; fax (+32) 2-7323149; e-mail info@feport.be; internet www.feport.eu; f. 1993; Pres. Günther Bonz; Sec.-Gen. Lamia Kerdjoudj Belkaid; Contact Conor Feighan (Policy Adviser).

FEPPD (Fédération Européenne et Internationale des Patrons Prothésistes Dentaires/International and European Federation of European Dental Laboratory Owners): 4 rue Jacques de Lalaing, 1040 Brussels, Belgium; tel. (+32) 2-2310573; fax (+32) 2-2305027; e-mail feppd@kmonet.org; internet www.feppd.eu; f. 1953; Pres. Hilde Wahlen; Sec.-Gen. Jan Eric Gyllenram; Contact Richard Koffu (Vice-Pres.).

FESE (Federation of European Securities Exchanges): 116 ave de Cortenbergh, 1000 Brussels, Belgium; tel. (+32) 2-5510180; fax (+32) 2-5124905; e-mail info@fese.eu; internet www.fese.eu; f. 1974; Pres. Christian Katz; Sec.-Gen. Judith Hardt; Contact Sandra De Sutter (Exec. Asst).

FESI (European Federation of Associations of Insulation Contractors/Fédération Européenne des Syndicats d'Entreprises d'Isolation/Europäische Vereinigung der Verbände der Isolierunternehmen): c/o Thermal Insulation Contractors' Association, Tica House, Allington Way, Yarm Rd Business Park, Darlington DL1 4QB, United Kingdom; tel. (+44 1325) 466704; fax (+44 1325) 487691; e-mail bfa.wksb@bauindustrie.de; internet www.fesi.eu; f. 1970; Pres. Lorenzo Borsini; Sec.-Gen. Andreas Gürtler; Contact Tatiana Goneou (Vice-Pres.).

FETRATAB (European Federation of Tobacco Transformers/Fédération Européenne des Transformateurs de Tabac): 23 rue de Frémicourt, 75015 Paris, France; tel. (+33) 1-45-66-86-43; fax (+33) 1-45-66-00-06; e-mail maisontabac.tobaccohouse@hebel.net; Pres. A. Matossian; Sec.-Gen. Carlo Sacchetto.

FETSA (Federation of European Tank Storage Associations): 11 rue des Colonies, 1000 Brussels, Belgium; tel. (+32) 2-5176261; fax (+32) 2-5176500; e-mail info@fetsa.org; internet www.fetsa.org; f. 1993; Pres. G. Bonetti; Sec.-Gen. M. de Witte; Contact M. Teeuwens (Vice-Pres.).

FEUGRES (European Federation for the Vitrified Clay Pipe Industry/Fédération Européenne des Fabricants de Tuyaux en Grès/Europäische Vereinigung der Steinzeugröhrenindustrie): 18–24 rue des Colonies, Bte 17, 1000 Brussels, Belgium; tel. (+32) 2-5113012; fax (+32) 2-5115174; e-mail sec@cerameunie.net; internet www.feugres.eu; Pres. Gernot Schoebitz; Sec.-Gen. Rogier Chorus.

FEVE (European Container Glass Federation/Fédération Européenne du Verre d'Emballage/Europäischer Behälterglasindustrie-Verband): 89 ave Louise, Bte 4, 1050 Brussels, Belgium; tel. (+32) 2-5360080; fax (+32) 2-5393752; e-mail secretariat@feve.org; internet www.feve.org; f. 1977; Pres. Stefan Jaenecke; Sec.-Gen. Adeline Farrelly; Contact Michael Delle Selve (Communications Man.).

FIDE (Federation of the European Dental Industry/Fédération de l'Industrie Dentaire en Europe/Vereinigung der Europäischen Dental-Industrie): Aachener Str. 1053–1055, 50858 Cologne, Germany; tel. (221) 500687-23; fax (221) 500687-21; e-mail info@fide-online.org; internet www.fide-online.org; f. 1957; Pres. Dr Jürgen Eberlein; Sec.-Gen. Dr Markus Heibach; Contact Dr Alessandro Gamberini (Vice-Pres.).

FIDE (International Federation for European Law/Fédération Internationale pour le Droit Européen/Internationale Föderation für Europarecht): 113 ave Louise, 1050 Brussels, Belgium; tel. (+32) 2-5347163; fax (+32) 2-5342858; e-mail pia.conseil@euronet.be; internet www.fide-europe.eu; Pres. Ulla Neergaard; Sec.-Gen. Dr Catherine Jacqueson.

FIEC (Fédération de l'Industrie Européenne de la Construction/European Construction Industry Federation/Verband der Europäischen Bauwirtschaft): 225 ave Louise, 1050 Brussels, Belgium; tel. (+32) 2-5145535; fax (+32) 2-5110276; e-mail info@fiec.eu; internet www.fiec.eu; f. 1905; Pres. Thomas Schleicher; Contact Ulrich Paetzold (Dir-Gen.).

FIGIEFA (Fédération Internationale des Grossistes, Importateurs & Exportateurs en Fournitures Automobiles/International Federation of Automotive Aftermarket Distributors/Europäischer Verbindungsausschuss der Selbsständigen Verteilung von Ersatzteilen & Ausrüstungen für Kraftwagen): 42 blvd de la Woluwe, POB 5, 1200 Brussels, Belgium; tel. (+32) 2-7619510; fax (+32) 2-7621255; e-mail figiefa.secretariat@figiefa.eu; internet www.figiefa.org; f. 1982; Pres. Hartmut Röhl; Sec.-Gen. Sylvia Gotzen; Contact Michel Vilatte (Vice-Pres.).

FITCE (Federation of the Telecommunications Engineers of the European Community/Fédération des Ingénieurs des Télécommunications de la Communauté Européenne): 80 blvd A. Reyers, 1030 Brussels, Belgium; tel. (+32) 2-7067805; fax (+32) 2-7068009; e-mail filip.geerts@agoria.be; internet www.fitce.org; f. 1961; Pres. Wojciech Halka; Sec.-Gen. Walter Van Hemeledonck; Contact Barry Reynolds (Information Man.).

FLORINT (International Florist Organization): Hoofdweg 119, 1424 PE De Kwakel, the Netherlands; tel. 682-800075; e-mail info@florint.org; internet www.florint.org; f. 1958; Pres. Mark Ward; Sec.-Gen. Simon Ogrizek.

FOODDRINKEUROPE (Confédération des Industries Agro-Alimentaires de l'UE/Confederation of the Food and Drink Industries of the EU): 9–31 ave des Nerviens, 1040 Brussels, Belgium; tel. (+32) 2-5141111; fax (+32) 2-5112905; e-mail info@fooddrinkeurope.eu; internet www.fooddrinkeurope.eu; f. 1982; Pres. Jesús Serafín Pérez; Contact Mella Frewen (Dir-Gen.).

FOODSERVICEEUROPE 27 rue du Collège, 1050 Brussels, Belgium; tel. (+32) 2-8080644; fax (+32) 2-2301737; e-mail info@foodserviceeurope.org; internet www.foodserviceeurope.org; f. 1990; Pres. Norbert Hummel; Sec.-Gen. Rocco Renaldi; Contact Antonio Llorens (Vice-Pres.).

FORATOM (European Atomic Forum/Forum Atomique Européen/Europäisches Atomforum): 56 ave des Arts, 1000 Brussels, Belgium; tel. (+32) 2-5024595; fax (+32) 2-5023902; e-mail foratom@foratom.org; internet www.foratom.org; f. 1960; Pres. Mats Ladeborn; Contact Berta Picamal (Exec. Asst).

FRESHFEL (Freshfel Europe): 49–51 rue de Trèves, Bte 8, 1040 Brussels, Belgium; tel. (+32) 2-7771580; fax (+32) 2-7771581; e-mail info@freshfel.org; internet www.freshfel.org; f. 1959; Pres. Philippe Henri; Contact Philippe Binard (Gen. Delegate).

FRUCOM (European Federation of the Trade in Dried Fruit, Edible Nuts, Preserved Foods, Spices, Honey and Similar Foodstuffs/Fédération Européenne du Commerce en Fruits Secs, Conserves, Epices et Miel/Europäische Vereinigung des Handels mit Trockenfrüchten, Konserven, Gewürzen und Honig und verwandten Waren): 49–51 rue de Trèves, POB 14, 1040 Brussels, Belgium; tel. (+32) 2-2310638; fax (+32) 2-7326766; e-mail info@frucom.eu; internet www.frucom.eu; f. 1959; Pres. Martin Rome; Sec.-Gen. Cristina Moser.

FTA (Foreign Trade Association/Association de Commerce Extérieur): 168 ave de Cortenbergh, 1000 Brussels, Belgium; tel. (+32) 2-7620551; fax (+32) 2-7627506; e-mail info@fta-intl.org; internet www.fta-eu.org; f. 1977; Pres. Ferry den Hoed; Sec.-Gen. Jan Eggert; Contact Véronique Debroux (Office Man.).

FuelsEurope (European Petroleum Industry Association/Association de l'Industrie Pétrolière Européenne): 165 blvd du Souverain, 3rd Floor, 1160 Brussels, Belgium; tel. (+32) 2-5669100; fax (+32) 2-5669111; e-mail info@fuelseurope.eu; internet www.fuelseurope.eu; f. 1989; Pres. Bela Kelemen; Contact Alain Mathuren (EU Communications Man.).

FVE (Federation of Veterinarians of Europe/Fédération Vétérinaire Européenne/Europäische Föderation der Tierärtze): 12 ave de Tervueren, 1040 Brussels, Belgium; tel. (+32) 2-5337020; fax (+32) 2-5372828; e-mail info@fve.org; internet www.fve.org; f. 1953; Pres. Christophe Buhot; Contact Karin Östensson (Vice-Pres.).

GAFTA (Grain and Feed Trade Association): 9 Lincoln's Inn Fields, London WC2A 3BP, United Kingdom; tel. (+44 20) 7814-9666; fax (+44 20) 7814-8383; e-mail post@gafta.com; internet www.gafta.com; f. 1878; Pres. Lucien Agniel; Contact Pamela Kirby Johnson (Dir-Gen.).

GERA-Europe (Global Entertainment Retail Association-Europe): Colonnade House, 1st Floor, 2 Westover Rd, Bournemouth, Dorset BH1 2BY, United Kingdom; tel. (+44) 1202-292063; fax (+44) 1202-292067; e-mail beth@eraltd.org; internet www.gera-europe.org; f. 2000; Pres. Martin De Wilde.

GERG (European Gas Research Group/Groupe Européen de Recherches Gazières): 4 ave Palmerston, 1000 Brussels, Belgium; tel. (+32) 2-2308017; fax (+32) 2-2306788; e-mail robertjudd@gerg.eu; internet www.gerg.eu; f. 1961; Pres. David Salisbury; Sec.-Gen. Robert Judd.

GIRP (Groupement International de la Répartition Pharmaceutique/European Association of Pharmaceutical Full-Line Wholesalers/Internationaler Verband der Europäischen Pharmazeutischen Grosshandelsverbände): 26 rue de la Loi, 10th Floor, POB 14B, 1040 Brussels, Belgium; tel. (+32) 2-7779977; fax (+32) 2-7703601; e-mail girp@girp.org; internet www.girp.eu; f. 1960; Pres. René Jenny; Sec.-Gen. Monika Derecque-Pois; Contact Lisa McGowan (Communications Man.).

Glass for Europe 199/33 rue Belliard, 1040 Brussels, Belgium; tel. (+32) 2-5384377; fax (+32) 2-2800281; e-mail info@glassforeurope.com; internet www.glassforeurope.com; f. 1978; Pres. Houchan Shoeibi; Sec.-Gen. Bertrand Cazes.

HDE (The German Retail Federation/Handelsverband Deutschland): Weidendamm 1A, 10117 Berlin, Germany; tel.

(+49 30) 726250-0; fax (+49 30) 726250-99; e-mail hde@einzelhandel.de; internet www.einzelhandel.de; f. 1919; Pres. Josef Sanktjohanser.

HOPE (European Hospital and Healthcare Federation/Comité Permanent des Hôpitaux de l'Union Européenne/Ständiger Ausschuss der Krankenhäuser der Europäischen Union): 30 ave Marnix, 3rd Floor, 1000 Brussels, Belgium; tel. (+32) 2-7421320; fax (+32) 2-7421325; e-mail sg@hope.be; internet www.hope.be; f. 1995; Pres. Dr Georg Baum; Sec.-Gen. Pascal Garel; Contact Dr Sara C. Pupato Ferrari (Vice-Pres.).

HOTREC (Hotels, Restaurants and Cafés in Europe): 111 blvd Anspach, Bte 4, 1000 Brussels, Belgium; tel. (+32) 2-5136323; fax (+32) 2-5024173; e-mail hotrec@hotrec.eu; internet www.hotrec.eu; Pres. Kent Nyström; Contact Christian de Barrin (Chief Exec.).

IATM (International Association of Tour Managers Ltd): 397 Walworth Rd, London SE17 2AW, United Kingdom; tel. (+44 20) 7703-9154; fax (+44 20) 7703-0358; e-mail iatm@iatm.co.uk; internet www.iatm.co.uk; f. 1962; Pres. Carole-Anne Seidelman; Contact Ron Julian (Gen. Man.).

IBC/CIBC/IMV (International Butchers' Confederation/Confédération Internationale de la Boucherie et de la Charcuterie/Internationaler Metzgermeister Verband): 4 rue Jacques de Lalaing, 1040 Brussels, Belgium; tel. (+32) 2-2303876; fax (+32) 2-2303451; e-mail info@cibc.be; internet www.cibc-imv.de; f. 1907; Pres. Jean-Marie Oswald; Sec.-Gen. Martin Fuchs; Contact Kirsten Diessner (Man. Dir).

IDF/FIL (International Dairy Federation/Fédération Internationale de Laiterie): Diamant Bldg, 80 Blvd A. Reyers, 1030 Brussels, Belgium; tel. (+32) 2-3256740; fax (+32) 2-3256741; e-mail info@fil-idf.org; internet www.fil-idf.org; f. 1903; Pres. Dr Jeremy Hill; Contact Dr Nico van Belzen (Dir-Gen.).

IFAH/FEDESA (European Federation of Animal Health/Fédération Européenne de la Santé Animale/Europäische Föderation für Tiergesundheit): 1 rue Defacqz, 1000 Brussels, Belgium; tel. (+32) 2-5437560; fax (+32) 2-5370049; e-mail info@ifaheurope.org; internet www.ifaheurope.org; f. 1987; Pres. Pedro Lichtinger; Contact Declan O'Brien (Man. Dir).

IFEAT (International Federation of Essential Oils and Aroma Trades/Fédération Internationale des Huiles Essentielles et du Commerce des Arômes/Internationale Föderation der Ätherischen Öle und des Aromahandels): Dorfstr. 40, 86470 Thannhausen, Germany; tel. (+49 8281) 7994-044; fax (+49 8281) 7994-050; e-mail secretariat@ifeat.org; internet www.ifeat.org; f. 1977; Pres. Michael Boudjouk; Contact Alain Frix (Chair.).

IFJ/FIJ/EJF (International Federation of Journalists/Fédération Internationale des Journalistes/Europäische Journalisten-Föderation): Résidence Palace, Bloc C, 155 rue de la Loi, 1040 Brussels, Belgium; tel. (+32) 2-2352200; fax (+32) 2-2352219; e-mail ifj@ifj.org; internet www.ifj.org; f. 1989; Pres. Jim Boumelha; Sec.-Gen. Beth Costa; Contact Younes M'Yahed (Vice-Pres.).

IFSW (International Federation of Social Workers/Fédération Internationale des Travailleurs Sociaux): Schwarztorstr. 22, POB 6875, 3001 Berne, Switzerland; tel. (+41) 31-382-60-15; fax (+41) 31-382-11-25; e-mail europe@ifsw.org; internet www.ifsw.org; f. 1928; Pres. Cristina Martins; Sec.-Gen. Rory Truell; Contact Ana Radulescu (Sec.).

IMA-EUROPE (Industrial Minerals Association—Europe IMA): 26 rue des Deux Eglises, 6th Floor, Bte 2, 1000 Brussels, Belgium; tel. (+32) 2-2104410; fax (+32) 2-2104429; e-mail secretariat@ima-europe.eu; internet www.ima-europe.eu; f. 1993; Sec.-Gen. Michelle Wyart-Remy; Contact Amina Langedijk (Senior Adviser, Communications).

IMACE (International Margarine Association of the Countries of Europe/Association des Industries Margarinières de la CE/Vereinigung der Margarine-Industrie der EG-Lander): 168 ave de Tervuren, Bte 12, 1150 Brussels, Belgium; tel. (+32) 2-7723353; fax (+32) 2-7714753; e-mail imace.ifma@imace.org; internet www.imace.org; f. 1958; Pres. Didier van Dallemagne; Sec.-Gen. Inneke Herreman.

Independent Retail Europe 3 ave des Gaulois, Bte 3, 1040 Brussels, Belgium; tel. (+32) 2-7324660; fax (+32) 2-7358623; e-mail else.groen@independentretaileurope.eu; internet www.independentretaileurope.eu; f. 1963; Pres. R. Gerking; Contact F. Julen (Vice-Pres.).

Insurance Europe 51 rue Montoyer, 1000 Brussels, Belgium; tel. (+32) 2-8943000; fax (+32) 2-8943001; internet www.insuranceeurope.eu; f. 1953; Pres. Sergio Balbinot; Contact Michaela Koller (Dir-Gen.).

Invest Europe (European Private Equity and Venture Capital Association/Association Européenne des Investissements en Capital à Risque/Europäischer Venture Capital Verband): Bastion Tower, 5 Place du Champ de Mars, 1050 Brussels, Belgium; tel. (+32) 2-7150020; fax (+32) 2-7250704; e-mail info@investeurope.eu; internet www.investeurope.eu; f. 1983; Sec.-Gen. Dörte Höppner; Contact Michael Collins (CEO).

INTERGRAF (International Confederation for Printing and Allied Industries Aisbl): 130A ave Louise, 1050 Brussels, Belgium; tel. (+32) 2-2308646; fax (+32) 2-2311464; e-mail bklose@intergraf.eu; internet www.intergraf.eu; Pres. Havard Grjotheim; Sec.-Gen. Beatrice Klose; Contact Hilda Salah (Office Administration).

IPPA (International Pectin Producers' Association): Turnstr. 37, 75305 Neuenbuerg, Germany; tel. (+49 7082) 7913-700; fax (+49 7082) 7913-701; e-mail secretary-general@ippa.info; internet www.ippa.info; f. 1969; Pres. Didier Viala; Sec.-Gen. Dr Hans-Ulrich Endress; Contact Steen Hoejgaard Christensen (Exec. Sec.).

IPTIC/CICILS (International Pulse Trade and Industry Confederation/Confédération Internationale du Commerce et des Industries des Légumes Secs/Ständiger EG Ausschuss der Internationalen Konföderation des Handels und der Trockengemüseindustrien): 2 rue de Viarmes, Bureau 267, Bourse de Commerce, 75040 Paris Cedex 01, France; tel. (+33) 1-42-36-84-35; fax (+33) 1-42-36-44-93; e-mail cicilsiptic@cicilsiptic.org; internet www.cicilsiptic.org; f. 1964; Pres. Hakan Bahceci; Contact Huseyin Arslan (Exec. Vice-Pres.).

IRU (International Road Transport Union/Union Internationale des Transports Routiers): 3 rue de Varembé, 1211 Geneva 20, Switzerland; tel. (+41) 22-918-27-00; fax (+41) 22-918-27-41; e-mail iru@iru.org; internet www.iru.org; f. 1958; Pres. Janusz Lacny; Sec.-Gen. Umberto de Pretto; Contact Juliette Ebélé (Communications).

ISA/AIE/ISV (International Sweeteners Association/Association Internationale pour les Edulcorants/Internationaler Süsstoff Verband): 9 ave des Gaulois, 1040 Brussels, Belgium; tel. (+32) 2-7365354; fax (+32) 2-7323427; e-mail isa@ecco-eu.com; internet www.sweeteners.org; f. 1972; Pres. Hugues Pitre; Sec.-Gen. Frances Hunt.

ISOPA (European Diisocyanates and Polyol Producers' Association): 4 ave E. Van Nieuwenhuyse, 1160 Brussels, Belgium; tel. (+32) 2-6767475; fax (+32) 2-6767479; e-mail main@isopa.org; internet www.isopa.org; f. 1987; Pres. Frank Grunert; Sec.-Gen. Jörg Palmersheim.

ITTFA (International Tourism Trade Fairs Association/Association des Foires Touristiques Européennes/Europäischer Fremdenverkehrsmessenverband): POB 585, Richmond, Surrey

TW9 1YQ, United Kingdom; tel. (+44 20) 8939-9000; fax (+44 20) 8948-8097; e-mail secretariat@ittfa.org; Pres. Zeljka Tomljenović; Sec.-Gen. M. Lapter; Contact Tom Nutley (Chair.).

IUCAB (International Union of Commercial Agents and Brokers/Union Internationale des Agents Commerciaux et des Courtiers): De Lairessestraat 131–135, 1075 HJ Amsterdam, Netherlands; tel. (+31 20) 4700177; fax (+31 20) 6710974; e-mail info@iucab.nl; internet www.iucab.nl; f. 1953; Pres. Kriton Phitidis; Sec.-Gen. J. W. B. Baron van Till; Contact J. Bjornum (Vice-Pres.).

IVTIP (In Vitro Testing Industrial Platform): POB 70, 4797 ZH Willemstad, Netherlands; tel. (+31 6) 54757261; fax (+31 168) 471249; e-mail ivtip@planet.nl; internet www.ivtip.org; f. 1993; Pres. Dr Erwin Roggen; Contact Dr Bart de Wever (Exec. Sec.).

IWTO (International Wool Textile Organization): 4 rue de l'Industrie, 1000 Brussels, Belgium; tel. (+32) 2-5054010; fax (+32) 2-5034785; e-mail info@iwto.org; internet www.iwto.org; f. 1961; Pres. Peter Ackroyd; Contact Henrik Kuffner (Dir-Gen.).

IZA (International Zinc Association): 168 ave de Tervuren, Bte 4, 1150 Brussels, Belgium; tel. (+32) 2-7760070; fax (+32) 2-7760089; e-mail contact@zinc.org; internet www.zinc.org; f. 1990; Pres. Stephen Wilkinson; Contact Berit Wirths (Man. Communications).

KPC-Europe (European Kaolin and Plastic Clays Association): c/o IMA-Europe, 26 rue des Deux Eglises, Bte 2, 1000 Brussels, Belgium; tel. (+32) 2-2104410; fax (+32) 2-2104429; e-mail secretariat@ima-europe.eu; internet www.ima-europe.eu; f. 1986; Pres. Dr Otto Hieber; Sec.-Gen. Dr Roger Doome.

LEASEUROPE (European Federation of Leasing Company Associations/Fédération Européenne des Associations des Etablissements de Crédit-Bail/Europäische Vereinigung der Verbände von Leasing-Gesellschaften): 87 blvd Louis Schmidt, 1040 Brussels, Belgium; tel. (+32) 2-7780560; fax (+32) 2-7780578; e-mail i.vermeersch@leaseurope.org; internet www.leaseurope.org; f. 1972; Pres. J. Salonen; Contact Tanguy van de Werve (Dir-Gen.).

Lighting Europe (European Lamp Companies' Federation/Fédération Européenne des Entreprises d'Eclairage): Diamant Bdg, 80 blvd A. Reyers, 1030 Brussels, Belgium; tel. (+32) 2-7068608; fax (+32) 2-7068609; e-mail juergen.sturm@elcfcd.org; internet www.elcfed.org; f. 2012; Pres. Jan Denneman; Sec.-Gen. Jürgen Sturm.

MARCOGAZ (Technical Association of the European Natural Gas Industry): 4 ave Palmerston, 1000 Brussels, Belgium; tel. (+32) 2-2371111; fax (+32) 2-2304480; e-mail marcogaz@marcogaz.org; internet www.marcogaz.org; f. 1968; Pres. M. Florette; Sec.-Gen. Daniel Hec; Contact Carol Morales (Exec. Asst).

MARINALG (Marinalg International): 12A ave Brugmann, POB 12, 1060 Brussels, Belgium; tel. (+32) 2-5383825; fax (+32) 2-5383826; e-mail info@marinalg.org; internet www.marinalg.org;.

Metal Packaging Europe 40 sq. de Meeûs, 1000 Brussels, Belgium; tel. (+32) 2-5357651; e-mail info@metalpackagingeurope.org; internet www.metalpackagingeurope.org; f. 1973.

NATCOL (Natural Food Colours Association/Association de Colorants Alimentaires Naturels/Natürliche Nahrungsmittelfarbstoffvereinigung): POB 3255, Boycestown, Carrigaline, Co. Cork, Ireland; tel. (+353 21) 4919673; fax (+353 21) 4919673; e-mail secretariat@natcol.org; internet www.natcol.org; f. 1979; Pres. Dr B. S. Henry; Sec.-Gen. Dr Mary O'Callaghan; Contact Paul Collins (Chair.).

OCE (Standing Liaison Committee of Orthoptists within the European Community/Comité de Liaison des Orthoptistes de la Communauté Européenne): Bierbeekstraat 14, 3001 Heverlee, Belgium; tel. (+32) 16-239524; fax (+33) 16-291809; e-mail info@euro-orthoptics.com; internet www.euro-orthoptics.com; f. 1989; Pres. Gail Stephenson; Contact Maria-Luise Lenk-Schaefer (Treasurer).

OEA (Organization of European Aluminium Refiners and Remelters): Am Bonneshof 5, 40474 Düsseldorf, Germany; tel. (+49 211) 4796-441; fax (+49 211) 4796-447; e-mail office@oea-alurecycling.org; internet www.oea-alurecycling.org; f. 1960; Pres. Jim Morrison; Sec.-Gen. Günter Kirchner; Contact John Gardner (Vice-Pres.).

OEB/ESO (Organisation Européenne des Bateliers/European Skippers Organization): Sint-Pieterskaai 74, 8000 Brugge, Belgium; tel. (+32) 50-470720; fax (+32) 50-335337; e-mail secretariat@eso-oeb.org; internet www.eso-oeb.org; f. 1975; Pres. Christiaan van Lancker.

ORGALIME (European Engineering Industries Association representing the interests of the Mechanical, Electrical, Electronic, Metalworking & Metal Articles Industries/Organisme de Liaison des Industries Métalliques Européennes/Verbindungsstelle der Europäischen Maschinenbau-, Metall Verarbeitenden und Elektroindustrie): Diamant Bldg, 80 blvd A. Reyers, 1030 Brussels, Belgium; tel. (+32) 2-7068235; fax (+32) 2-7068250; e-mail secretariat@orgalime.org; internet www.orgalime.org; f. 1954; Pres. Sandro Bonomi; Contact Mark Redgrove (Communications Manager).

Pack2Go Europe 13–15 ave Livingstone, 1000 Brussels, Belgium; tel. (+32) 2-2869496; fax (+32) 2-2869495; e-mail info@pack2go-europe.com; internet www.pack2go-europe.com; f. 1974; Pres. Jan Schuermann; Sec.-Gen. Eamonn Bates; Contact David Schisler (Chair.).

PGEU/GPUE (Pharmaceutical Group of the European Union/Groupement Pharmaceutique de l'Union Européenne): 19–21 rue du Luxembourg, 1000 Brussels, Belgium; tel. (+32) 2-2380818; fax (+32) 2-2380819; e-mail pharmacy@pgeu.eu; internet www.pgeu.eu; f. 1959; Pres. Štefan Krchňák; Sec.-Gen. John Chave; Contact Jan Smits (Vice-Pres.).

PNEUROP (European Committee of Manufacturers of Compressors, Vacuum Pumps and Pneumatic Tools/Comité Européen des Constructeurs de Compresseurs, Pompes à Vide et Outils à Air Comprimé/Europäisches Komitee der Hersteller von Kompressoren, Vakuumpumpen und Druckluftwerkzeugen): Diamant Bldg, 80 blvd A. Reyers, 1030 Brussels, Belgium; tel. (+32) 2-7068237; fax (+32) 2-7068253; e-mail secretariat@pneurop.org; internet www.pneurop.eu; f. 1960; Pres. Dr Paul Frigne; Sec.-Gen. Guy van Doorslaer.

POSTEUROP (Association of 48 European Public Postal Operators/Association Représentant 48 Opérateurs Postaux Publics Européens/Vereinigung der Öffentlichen Europäischen Postdienstbetreiber): 114 blvd Brand Whitlock, 1200 Brussels, Belgium; tel. (+32) 2-7619650; fax (+32) 2-7714856; e-mail info@posteurop.org; internet www.posteurop.org; f. 1993; Sec.-Gen. Botond Szebeny; Contact Cynthia Wee (Communications Manager).

PPTA (Plasma Protein Therapeutics Association Europe): 114–115 Blvd Brand Whitlock, 1200 Brussels, Belgium; tel. (+32) 2-7055811; fax (+32) 2-7055820; e-mail pptaeu@pptaglobal.be; internet www.pptaglobal.org; f. 1994; Pres. Jan M. Bult; Contact Joachim Herborg (Chair.).

PRE (European Refractories Producers' Federation/Fédération Européenne des Fabricants de Produits Réfractaires/Europäische Industrieverband der Feuerfestkeramik): 17 rue de la Montagne, 1000 Brussels, Belgium; tel. (+32) 2-8083880; fax

Trade and Professional Organizations DIRECTORY

(+32) 2-5115174; e-mail sec@cerameunie.net; internet www.pre.eu; f. 1953; Pres. François Wanecq; Sec.-Gen. Astrid Volckaert.

PROFEL (European Association of Fruit and Vegetable Processing Industries/Organisation Européenne des Industries Transformatrices de Fruits et de Légumes): 77–79 blvd Saint-Michel, 1040 Brussels, Belgium; tel. (+32) 2-7402968; fax (+32) 2-7325102; e-mail profel@agep.eu; internet www.profel-europe.eu; f. 1978; Pres. Jean-Bernard Bonduelle; Sec.-Gen. Aline Rutsaert; Contact Costas Apostolou (Vice-Pres.).

REHVA (Federation of European Heating and Airconditioning Associations/Fédération des Associations Européennes de Chauffage et Conditionnement d'Air): 40 rue Washington, 1050 Brussels, Belgium; tel. (+32) 2-5141171; fax (+32) 2-5129062; e-mail info@rehva.com; internet www.rehva.eu; f. 1963; Pres. Prof. Dr-Ing. Karel Kabele; Sec.-Gen. Jan Aufderheijde; Contact Stefano P. Corgnati (Vice-Pres.).

RIAE (Recording Media Industry Association of Europe): 42 rue Notre Dame, 2951 Luxembourg-Ville, Luxembourg; e-mail info@riae.org; Pres. Joe Gote; Sec.-Gen. Maria Laptev; Contact Alina Burea (EU and Country Man.).

RICS EUROPE (European Society of Chartered Surveyors): 67 rue Ducale, 1000 Brussels, Belgium; tel. (+32) 2-7331019; fax (+32) 2-7429748; e-mail ricseurope@rics.org; internet www.rics.org; f. 1993; Pres. Jörn Stobbe; Contact Liliane Van Cauwenbergh (Gen. Man.).

Rural Youth Europe Karjalankatu 2A, 00520 Helsinki, Finland; tel. (+358 45) 2345629; fax (+358 20) 7552627; e-mail office@ruralyoutheurope.com; internet www.ruralyoutheurope.com; f. 1957; Pres. Kadri Toomingas; Sec.-Gen. Pia Nurmio-Perälä; Contact Lukas Helfenstein (Vice-Chair.).

SCEPEA (Standing Committee of European Port Employers' Associations/Comité Permanent des Entreprises de Manutention dans les Ports Européens/Zentralverband der deutschen Seehafenbetriebe): Am Sandtorkai 2, 20457 Hamburg, Germany; tel. (+49 40) 366203-4; fax (+49 40) 3663-77; e-mail info@zds-seehaefen.de; internet www.zds-seehaefen.de; Pres. Detthold Aden; Contact Dr Ulrich Bauermeister (Vice-Pres.).

SEFA (European Association of Steel Drum Manufacturers/Syndicat Européen de l'Industrie des Fûts en Acier/Verband der Europäischen Stahlfassindustrie): c/o Agoria, Diamant Bldg, 80 blvd A. Reyers, 1030 Brussels, Belgium; tel. (+32) 2-7067963; fax (+32) 2-7068130; e-mail info@sefa.be; internet www.sefa.be; f. 1953; Pres. Patrick Moet; Sec.-Gen. Hugo Dejonghe; Contact G. Boom (Chair.).

SEFEL (European Secretariat of Manufacturers of Light Metal Packaging/Secrétariat Européen des Fabricants d'Emballages Métalliques Légers/Europäisches Sekretariat der Hersteller von Leichten Metallverpackungen): Diamant Bldg, 80 blvd A. Reyers, 1030 Brussels, Belgium; tel. (+32) 2-7067953; fax (+32) 2-7067966; e-mail sefel@agoria.be; internet www.sefel.net; f. 1959; Sec.-Gen. Pierre Diederich.

SELDIA (European Direct Selling Association): 14 ave de Tervuren, 1040 Brussels, Belgium; tel. (+32) 2-7361014; fax (+32) 2-7363497; e-mail seldia@seldia.eu; internet www.seldia.eu; f. 1968; Pres. Magnus Brännström; Contact Maurits Bruggink (Exec. Dir.).

SITS (Surface Treatment Manufacturers and Suppliers Trade Association/Syndicat Général des Industries de Matériels et Procédés pour les Traitements de Surfaces): 39–41 rue Louis Blanc, 92038 Paris La Défense Cedex, France; tel. (+33) 1-47-17-63-73; fax (+33) 1-47-17-63-74; e-mail info@sits.fr; internet www.sits.fr; f. 1963; Pres. Daniel Odille; Sec.-Gen. Françoise Leclerc; Contact Louis-Marie Girard (Vice-Pres.).

SNE (Specialised Nutrition Europe): 9–31 ave de Nerviens, 5th Floor, 1040 Brussels, Belgium; tel. (+32) 2-5081070; fax (+32) 2-5081025; e-mail secretariat@specialisednutritioneurope.eu; internet www.specialisednutritioneurope.eu; Pres. Roger Clarke.

Starch Europe (European Starch Industry Association): 43 ave des Arts, 1040 Brussels, Belgium; tel. (+32) 2-2896760; fax (+32) 2-5135592; e-mail veronique.deridder@starch.eu; internet www.starch.eu; f. 1988; renamed in Oct. 2014; Pres. Gianfranco Patrucco; Contact Jamie Fortescue (Man. Dir).

TBE (European Federation of Brick and Tile Manufacturers/Fédération Européenne des Fabricants de Tuiles et de Briques/Europäischer Verband der Mauerziegel- und Dachziegelhersteller): 17 rue de la Montagne, 1000 Brussels, Belgium; tel. (+32) 2-8083880; fax (+32) 2-5115174; e-mail sec@cerameunie.net; internet www.cerameunie.eu; f. 1952; Pres. Yiannis Maliouris; Sec.-Gen. Magdalena Vallebona.

TEGOVA (European Group of Valuers' Associations): 45 blvd Saint-Michel, 1040 Brussels, Belgium; tel. (+32) 2-5033234; fax (+32) 2-5033232; e-mail info@tegova.org; internet www.tegova.org; f. 1977; Sec.-Gen. Alexander Benedetti; Contact François Isnard (Man. Dir).

THIE (Tea and Herbal Infusions Europe): Sonninstr. 28, 20097 Hamburg, Germany; tel. (+49 40) 23601621; fax (+49 40) 23601610; e-mail thie@wga-hh.de; internet www.thie-online.eu; f. 2015 as successor to the European Tea Committee (ETC) and the European Herbal Infusions Association (EHIA); Pres. Nick Revett; Sec.-Gen. Dr Monika Beutgen.

TIE (Toy Industries of Europe): 20 rue des Deux Eglises, 1000 Brussels, Belgium; tel. (+32) 2-2134190; fax (+32) 2-2134199; e-mail info@tietoy.org; internet www.tietoy.org; f. 1997; Pres. John Harper; Contact Mateo Romano (Vice-Chair.).

TII (European Association for the Transfer of Technologies, Innovation and Industrial Information/Association Européenne pour le Transfert des Technologies, de l'Innovation et de l'Information Industrielle/Europäische Vereinigung für den Transfer von Technologien, Innovation und Industrieller Information): 3 rue Aldringen, 1118 Luxembourg-Ville, Luxembourg; tel. (+352) 4630351; fax (+352) 462185; e-mail tii@tii.org; internet www.tii.org; f. 1984; Pres. Joachim Hafkesbrink; Sec.-Gen. Christine Robinson; Contact José Syne (European Project Man.).

TRAXIO 164 ave Jules Bordet, 1140 Brussels, Belgium; tel. (+32) 2-7786200; fax (+32) 2-7786222; e-mail mail@traxio.be; internet www.traxio.be; Contact Luc Missante (Man. Dir).

UAE (Union des Avocats Européens/European Lawyers' Union/Europäischer Anwaltsverein): Via Cassa di Risparmio 3, 39100 Bolzano, Italy; tel. (+39 04) 71063506; fax (+39 04) 71063507; e-mail eb@saintyvesavocats.com; internet www.uae.lu; f. 1986; Pres. Carlos Botelho Moniz; Sec.-Gen. Elisabeth de Boissieu; Contact Agustin Cruz (Vice-Pres.).

UEA (Union Européenne de l'Ameublement/European Furniture Manufacturers' Federation/Verband der Europäischen Möbelindustrie): 26 rue de la Loi, 1040 Brussels, Belgium; tel. (+32) 2-2181889; fax (+32) 2-2192701; e-mail secretary@ueanet.com; internet www.ueanet.com; f. 1952; Pres. John Alston; Sec.-Gen. Bart de Turck.

UEAPME (European Association of Craft, Small and Medium-Sized Enterprises/Union Européenne de l'Artisanat et des Petites et Moyennes Entreprises/Europäische Union des Handwerks und der Klein- und Mittelbetriebe): 4 rue Jacques de Lalaing, 1040 Brussels, Belgium; tel. (+32) 2-2307599; fax (+32) 2-2307861; e-mail info@ueapme.com; internet www.ueapme.com; f. 1979; Pres. Gunilla Almgren; Sec.-Gen. Peter Faross; Contact Luca Crosetto (Vice-Pres.).

UEATC (European Union of Agrément/Union Européenne pour l'Agrément Technique dans la Construction/Europäische Union für das Agrement im Bauwesen): 42 rue de Lombard, 1000 Brussels, Belgium; e-mail mail@ueatc.com; internet www.ueatc.eu; f. 1960; Pres. Ángel Arteaga; Sec.-Gen. Joe Blaisdale.

UECBV (European Livestock and Meat Trading Union/Union Européenne du Commerce du Bétail et de la Viande/Europäische Vieh- und Fleischhandelsunion): 81A rue de la Loi, Bte 9, 4th Floor, 1040 Brussels, Belgium; tel. (+32) 2-2304603; fax (+32) 2-2309400; e-mail info@uecbv.eu; internet www.uecbv.eu; f. 1952; Pres. Philippe Borremans; Sec.-Gen. Jean-Luc Meriaux; Contact Heinz Osterloh (Vice-Pres.).

UEEIV (Union of European Railway Engineer Associations/Union des Associations Européennes des Ingénieurs Ferroviaires/Union Europäischer Eisenbahn-Ingenieur-Verbände): Kaiserstr. 61, 60329 Frankfurt am Main, Germany; tel. (+49 69) 2593-29; fax (+49 69) 2592-20; e-mail ueeiv@t-online.de; internet www.ueeiv.eu; Pres. Klaus Riessberger; Contact Frans Heijnen (Sec.).

UEHP (European Union of Private Hospitals/Union Européenne de l'Hospitalisation Privée): 1 ave de la Joyeuse Entrée, Bte 11, 1040 Brussels, Belgium; tel. (+32) 2-2861237; fax (+32) 2-2306908; e-mail paolo.giordano@uehp.org; internet www.uehp.org; f. 1991; Pres. Dr Paul Garassus; Sec.-Gen. Paolo Giordano; Contact Andrzej Sokolowski (Sec.).

UEIL (Independent Union of the European Lubricant Industry/Union Indépendante de l'Industrie Européenne des Lubrifiants): 22–24 rue du Luxembourg, 1000 Brussels, Belgium; tel. (+32) 2-7616685; fax (+32) 2-2131363; e-mail info@ueil.org; internet www.ueil.org; f. 1963; Pres. Fabio Dalla Giovanna; Sec.-Gen. Milagros Mostaza-Corral.

UEMO (European Union of General Practitioners/Union Européenne des Médecins Omnipraticiens/Europäische Vereinigung der Omnipraktizierenden Ärzte): Villagatan 5, POB 5610, 114 86 Stockholm, Sweden; tel. (+46 8) 790-33-00; fax (+46 8) 20-57-18; e-mail info@uemo.org; internet www.uemo.eu; f. 1967; Pres. Aldo Lupo; Sec.-Gen. Giuseppe Enrico Rivolta; Contact Claudia Ventura (Exec. Sec.).

UEMS (European Union of Medical Specialists/Union Européenne des Médecins Spécialistes/Europäische Vereinigung der Fachärzte): 24 rue de l'Industrie, 1040 Brussels, Belgium; tel. (+32) 2-6495164; fax (+32) 2-6403730; e-mail sg@uems.net; internet www.uems.net; f. 1958; Pres. Dr Romuald Krajewski; Sec.-Gen. Dr Edwin Borman; Contact Dr Hans Hjelmqvist (Vice-Pres.).

UEMV (European Glaziers' Association/Union Européenne des Miroitiers Vitriers/Europäischer Dachverband des Gläserhandwerks): Gothersgade 160, 1123 Copenhagen, Denmark; tel. (+45) 33-13-65-10; fax (+45) 33-13-65-60; e-mail mail@uemv.org; internet www.uemv.org; f. 1967; Pres. Hans-Georg Nielsen; Sec.-Gen. Pim H. K. de Ridder.

UEPC (European Union of Developers and House Builders/Union Européenne des Promoteurs-Constructeurs/Europäische Union der Freien Wohnungsunternehmen): 43 rue de la Violette, 1000 Brussels, Belgium; tel. (+32) 2-8939750; fax (+32) 2-8939791; e-mail info@uepc.org; internet www.uepc.org; f. 1958; Pres. Terry Roydon; Contact Filiep Loosveldt (Man. Dir.).

UEPG (European Aggregates Association/Union Européenne des Producteurs de Granulats/Europäischer Gesteinsverband): 21 rue d'Arlon, 1050 Brussels, Belgium; tel. (+32) 2-2335300; fax (+32) 2-2335301; e-mail secretariat@uepg.eu; internet www.uepg.eu; f. 1987; Pres. Arnaud Colson; Sec.-Gen. Dirk Fincke; Contact Elisabeth Gammelsæter (Vice-Pres.).

UFEMAT (European Association of National Builders Merchants' Associations/Union Européenne des Fédérations Nationales des Négociants en Matériaux de Construction/Europäische Vereinigung der Nationalen Baustoffhändler-Verbände): Brusselsesteenweg 524 B 6, 1731 Zellik, Belgium; tel. (+32) 2-4662483; fax (+32) 2-4632646; e-mail ufemat@ufemat.eu; internet www.ufemat.eu; f. 1959; Pres. Géraud Spire; Sec.-Gen. Marnix Van Hoe; Contact Geert Segers (Vice-Pres.).

UIB (International Union of Bakers and Bakers-Confectioners/Confédération Européenne des Organisations Nationales de la Boulangerie et de la Pâtisserie/Internationaler Verband der Bäcker und Bäcker-Konditoren): Calle Raimundo Fernández Villaverde 61, 6A Planta Izquierda, 28003 Madrid, Spain; tel. (+34) 91-5346996; fax (+34) 91-337267; e-mail admin@worldbakersconfectioners.org; internet www.worldbakersconfectioners.org/uibc; f. 1992; Pres. Peter Becker; Sec.-Gen. Dr José Maria Fernandez del Vallado; Contact Gerhard Schenk (Deputy Pres.).

UITP-EuroTeam (International Association of Public Transport/Union Internationale des Transports Publics/Internationaler Verband für Öffentliches Verkehrswesen): 6 rue Sainte Marie, Quai des Charbonnages, 1080 Brussels, Belgium; tel. (+32) 2-6736100; fax (+32) 2-6601072; e-mail info@uitp.org; internet www.uitp.org; f. 1865; Pres. Nicolas Blain; Sec.-Gen. Alain Flausch; Contact Robert Huber (Vice-Pres.).

UNESDA-CISDA (Union of EU Soft Drinks Associations-Confederation of International Soft Drinks Associations): 79 blvd Saint Michel, 1040 Brussels, Belgium; tel. (+32) 2-7434050; fax (+32) 2-7325102; e-mail mail@unesda.org; internet www.unesda.org; f. 1959; Pres. Dominique Reiniche; Contact Sam Rowe (Communications).

UNI Europa (Regional European Organization of Union Network International/Organisation Régionale Européenne d'Union Network International/Europäische Regionalorganisation von Union Network International): 40 rue Joseph II, 1000 Brussels, Belgium; tel. (+32) 2-2345656; fax (+32) 2-2350870; e-mail uni-europa@uniglobalunion.org; internet www.uniglobalunion.org; f. 2000; Pres. Frank Bsirske; Sec.-Gen. Philip Jennings; Contact Oliver Roethig (Regional Sec.).

UNICE (Business Europe/Union des Confédérations de l'Industrie et des Employeurs d'Europe): 168 ave de Cortenbergh, 1000 Brussels, Belgium; tel. (+32) 2-2376511; fax (+32) 2-2311445; e-mail main@businesseurope.eu; internet www.businesseurope.eu; f. 1958; Pres. Dr Emma Marcegaglia; Contact P. Sennekamp (Dir Communications).

UNIFE (Association of the European Rail Industry): 221 ave Louise, Bte 11, 1050 Brussels, Belgium; tel. (+32) 2-6261260; fax (+32) 2-6261261; e-mail general@unife.org; internet www.unife.org; f. 1992; Contact Massimo Marianeschi (Gen. Man.).

UNISTOCK (European Association of Professional Storekeepers for Agribulk Commodities within the European Union): 98 rue du Trône, 4th Floor, 1050 Brussels, Belgium; tel. (+32) 2-5020808; fax (+32) 2-5026030; e-mail info@unistock.be; internet www.unistock.be; f. 1969; Pres. Julian Scott; Sec.-Gen. Dr Teresa Babuscio.

UPEI (Union of European Petroleum Independents/Union Pétrolière Européenne Indépendante): 1 ave de la Renaissance, 1000 Brussels, Belgium; tel. (+32) 2-7402020; fax (+32) 2-7402023; e-mail info@upei.org; internet www.upei.org; f. 1960; Sec.-Gen. Yvonne Stausbøll.

USSPE (Union Syndicale—European Public Service/Union Syndicale—Service Public Européen): 36 ave des Gaulois, 1040 Brussels, Belgium; tel. (+32) 2-7339800; fax (+32) 2-7330533; e-mail web@unionsyndicale.eu; internet www.unionsyndicale.eu; f. 1974; Pres. Günther Lorenz; Sec.-Gen. Olivier Petsch; Contact Palmina Di Meo (Communication Sec.).

VDMA (Committee of Apparel Machinery Manufacturers in Europe): c/o VDMA, Richard Strauss Str. 56/III, 81677 Munich, Germany; tel. (+49 69) 6603-1648; fax (+49 69) 6603-2648; e-mail ingo.elste@vdma.org; internet www.vdma.org; Pres. Dr Reinhold Festge; Contact Thilo Brodtmann (Exec. Dir).

WEI/IEO (Western European Institute for Wood Preservation/Institut de l'Europe Occidentale pour l'Imprégnation du Bois/West-Europäisches Institut für Holzimprägnierung): 24/20 rue Montoyer, 1000 Brussels, Belgium; tel. (+32) 2-5562586; fax (+32) 2-2870875; e-mail info@wei-ieo.org; internet www.wei-ieo.org; f. 1951; Pres. Willie Clason; Sec.-Gen. Frederik Lauwaert; Contact Cindy Asselman (Sec.).

WFA/FMA (World Federation of Advertisers/Fédération Mondiale des Annonceurs): 166 ave Louise, 1050 Brussels, Belgium; tel. (+32) 2-5025740; fax (+32) 2-5025666; e-mail info@wfanet.org; internet www.wfanet.org; f. 1953; Pres. David Wheldon.

YES (European Confederation of Young Entrepreneurs/Confédération des Jeunes Entrepreneurs pour l'Europe/Junge Unternehmer für Europa): 40 ave de Broqueville, 1200 Woluwe-Saint-Lambert, Brussels, Belgium; tel. (+32) 2-2803425; fax (+32) 2-2803317; e-mail secretariat@yes.be; internet www.yes.be; f. 1990; Pres. Dimitris Tsigos; Sec.-Gen. Philippe Léonard; Contact Chiara de Caro (Co-ordination Man.).

INDEX OF KEYWORDS
relating to the list of EU-Level Trade and Professional Associations

Keywords are shown below in **bold**, while associations are represented by their acronym, followed by the number of the page on which their entry appears

Abrasives ... FEPA 526
Accountants ... EFAA 514, EMAA 517, FEE 525
Actuaries ... ACTUARIES 504
Additives ... FEFANA 525
Adhesive Tape ... AFERA 505
Adhesives ... FEICA 526
Advertising ... EGTA 516, WFA 532
Advertising Standards ... EASA 512
Aerosols ... FEA 524
Aerospace ... ASD 506
Aggregates ... UEPG 531
Agrement ... UEATC 531
Agri-Food ... FOODDRINKEUROPE 527
Agri-Food Trade ... CELCAA 508
Agribulk Commodities ... UNISTOCK 531
Agricultural Co-operation ... COGECA 511
Agricultural Contractors ... CEETTAR 508
Agricultural Machinery ... CEMA 508
Agricultural Tools ... CEOAH 509
Agriculture ... COPA 511, ENGAGE 517, IPTIC 528
Air Conditioning ... AREA 506, EUROVENT 523, REHVA 530
Air Conditioning Equipment ... CECOMAF 507
Air Heaters ... EURO-AIR 521
Airlines ... ERAA 518
Airports ... ACI EUROPE 504
Alcohol ... AICV 505, CBMC 506, CEEV 508, CEPS 509, EBC 512
Aluminium ... AEROBAL 504, OEA 529
Animal Cells ... ACTIP 504
Animal Feed ... COCERAL 510, EFAPIT 514, EFFCA 515, FEFAC 525, GAFTA 527
Animal Health ... IFAH 528
Animal Protein ... EAPA 512
Apparel Machinery ... VDMA 532
Applied Sciences ... EURO-CASE 521
Aquaculture ... EAS 512
Aquariums ... EAZA 512
Architects ... ACE 504
Asphalt ... EAPA 512
Asset Management ... EFAMA 514
Atomic Forum ... FORATOM 527
Audiovisual ... AAPA 504, AER 504, CAFIM 506, CARTOON 506, EBU 512, FEB 525, RIAE 530
Automobiles ... ACEA 504, CLEPA 510, EUCAR 520, FIGIEFA 527, TRAXIO 530

Bakery ... COFALEC 511, FEDIMA 525, UIB 531
Banking ... EACB 511, EBF 512, ESBG 518, EUROFINAS 522
Batteries ... EPBA 517, EUROBAT 521
Beet ... CIBE 510
Bentonite ... EUBA 520
Beverages ... ACE 504, AICV 505, AIJN 505, CBMC 506, CEEV 508, CEPS 509, ECF 513, THIE 530, UNESDA-CISDA 531
Bicycles ... CONEBI 511
Bioindustries ... EUROPABIO 522
Biotechnology ... EFB 514
Biscuits ... CAOBISCO 506
Board (Corrugated) ... FEFCO 525
Booksellers ... EIBF 516
Borates ... EBA 512
Brands ... AIM 505
Breweries ... EBC 512
Broadcasting ... ACT 504, AER 504, EBU 512
Brokers ... IUCAB 529
Brushware ... FEIBP 526
Builders ... EBC 512, UEPC 531
Builders Merchants ... UFEMAT 531
Building ... AEEBC 504, ARGE 506, EFBWW 514, FEMIB 526
Building Materials ... TBE 530
Building Societies ... EFBS 514
Business ... CEA-PME 506, CEC 507, CESCE 509, EUMU 520, UEAPME 530, UNICE 531, YES 532
Businesses ... CEDI 507
Cable Communications ... ECCA 512
Cables ... EUROPACABLE 522
Calcium Carbonate ... CCA-EUROPE 506
Candles ... AECM 504
Cans ... Metal Packaging Europe 529
Careers ... ACF Europe 504
Carpets ... ECA 512
Carton Makers ... ECMA 513
Catering ... FOODSERVICEEUROPE 527
Catering Equipment ... EFCEM 514
Cement ... CEMBUREAU 508
Ceramics ... CERAME-UNIE 509, CET 510, EUTECER 523, FECS 525
Cereals ... CEEREAL 508, CEPM 509, COCERAL 510, EFAPIT 514, GAFTA 527
Chambers of Commerce and Industry ... EUROCHAMBRES 521
Chartered Surveyors ... RICS EUROPE 530
Cheese ... ASSIFONTE 506

Chemical Engineering ... EFCE 514
Chemicals ... ECETOC 513, EuCheMS 520, FECC 525
Chemistry ... CEFIC 508
Chimneys ... ECA 512
Chlorine ... EURO CHLOR 521
Chocolate ... CAOBISCO 506
Cigarette Paper ... ECPCI 513
City Farms ... EFCF 514
Civil Aviation ... EUROCAE 521
Cleaning Industries ... EFCI 514
Cleaning Machines and Materials ... FEMIN 526
Clothing ... EURATEX 520
Co-operatives ... CECOP 507
Co-ordination ... EUROVIA 523
Coal ... EURACOAL 520
Cockpit ... ECA 512
Cocoa ... FCC 524
Coffee ... ECF 513
Cogeneration ... COGEN EUROPE 511
Coil Coating ... ECCA 512
Cold Storage ... ECSLA 513
Colour ... EUTECA 523
Commercial Agents ... IUCAB 529
Commercial Representation ... CIRCCE 510
Communications ... EACA 511
Computers ... ECMA 513
Concrete ... BIBM 506, ERMCO 518
Confectionery ... CAOBISCO 506, FEDIMA 525, UIB 531
Conjuncture Institutes ... AIECE 505
Conservation ... ECCO 513
Construction ... AEEBC 504, CECE 507, CEPMC 509, EBC 512, FECC 525, FEMIB 526, FIEC 527, TBE 530, UEPC 531, UFEMAT 531
Construction Economists ... CEEC 508
Consultancy ... ECCO 513
Consulting ... FEACO 524
Consumer Co-operatives ... EURO COOP 521
Consumers ... ANEC 505
Contact Lenses ... EFCLIN 515
Control Manufacturers ... AFECOR 505
Controlgear ... CAPIEL 506
Cookware ... FEC 525
Cosmetics ... CEPEC 509, Cosmetics Europe 511
Cotton ... EUROCOTON 521
Craftsmen ... EFTC 515
Crop Protection ... ECPA 513
Cutlery ... FEC 525
Cutting Tools ... ECTA 513

Index of Keywords   DIRECTORY

Dairy ... EDA 513, EUCOLAIT 520, IDF 528, IMACE 528
Decaffeinators ... EDA 513
Defence ... ASD 506
Dehydrators ... CIDE 510
Demolition ... EDA 514
Dental Dealers ... ADDE 504
Dentists ... CED 507, FEPPD 526, FIDE 527
Designers ... BEDA 506
Detergent ... AISE 505
Development Agencies ... EURADA 520
Dialysis ... EDTNA 514
Die Casting ... EPDCC 518
Digital Media ... EDIMA 514
Digital Technology ... DIGITALEUROPE 511
Direct Selling ... SELDIA 530
Disposables ... EDANA 514
Distance Selling ... EMOTA 517
Distance Teaching ... EADTU 511
Distribution ... ECED 513
Diving ... CEDIP 508
Doctors ... CPME 511
Domestic Appliances ... CECED 507, CEFACD 508
Dredging ... EUDA 520
Driving Schools ... EFA 514
Dyes ... ETAD 519
Ecotoxicology ... ECETOC 513
Education ... ETUCE 519
Eggs ... EEPA 514, EPEGA 518, EUWEP 524
Electrical Engineers ... EUREL 521
Electrical Installation Equipment ... CECAPI 507
Electrical Machines ... CEMEP 508
Electricity ... EURELECTRIC 521
Electronic Components ... EECA 514
Electronics ... DIGITALEUROPE 511
Elevators ... EEA 514
Employees ... UNI Europa 531
Employers ... UNICE 531
Energy ... CEDEC 507, FEDARENE 525
Engineering ... ENGAGE 517, FEANI 524
Engineering Consultancy ... EFCA 514
Engines ... EUROMOT 522
Entertainment ... GERA-Europe 527
Envelopes ... FEPE 526
Environment ... CONCAWE 511, ENERO 517, ENGAGE 517, EUROPEN 523, FACE 524, FEAD 524, FEDARENE 525
Enzymes ... AMFEP 505
Equipment ... ECED 513
Essential Oils ... IFEAT 528
Estate Agents ... CEAB 507, CEPI-CEI 509, EPAG 517
European Securities ... FESE 526
Experts ... AEXEA 505
Explosives ... FEEM 525
Express Carriers ... EEA 514
Farmers ... CEJA 508, COPA 511, FEDFA 525, Rural Youth Europe 530
Farming ... EAAP 511
Fat Processors ... EFPRA 515
Feldspar ... EUROFEL 522

Ferro-alloys ... EUROALLIAGES 521
Ferrous Metals ... EURIC 521
Fertilizers ... EFMA 515
Fibre Cement ... EFFCM 515
Fibres ... CIRFS 510
Film ... CARTOON 506, EUROCINEMA 521
Fire Protection ... EUROFEU 522
Fire Testing ... EGOLF 515
Fish ... AIPCE 505, CEP 509, EAFE 511, EAPO 512, EAS 512, EUROPECHE 523, FEAP 524
Fixed Assets ... TEGOVA 530
Florists ... FLORINT 527
Foam Blocks ... EUROPUR 523
Food ... EFFCA 515, ESA 518, UIB 531
Food Colours ... NATCOL 529
Food Emulsifiers ... EFEMA 515
Food Ingredients (Speciality) ... ELC 516
Food Law ... EFLA 515
Food Science ... EFFOST 515
Footwear ... CEC 507
Foreign Trade ... FTA 527
Forging ... EUROFORGE 522
Forwarding ... CLECAT 510
Foundations ... EFFC 515
Foundries ... CAEF 506, CEMAFON 508
Franchises ... EFF 515
Fresh Produce ... CIMO 510, FRESHFEL 527
Friction Materials ... FEMFM 526
Frozen Food ... FAFPAS 524
Fruit ... AIJN 505, FRUCOM 527, PROFEL 530
Fuel ... AEGPL 504, MARCOGAZ 529
Funeral Services ... EFFS 515
Furniture ... FEMB 526, UEA 530
Galvanizers ... EGGA 516
Gas ... FARECOGAZ 524, GERG 527
Gas Meters ... FARECOGAZ 524
Generating ... EUROPGEN 523
Generic Medicines ... EGA 516
Glass ... CPIV 511, FEVE 527, Glass for Europe 527, UEMV 531
Glass Fibre ... APFE 505
Glaziers ... UEMV 531
Grain ... EFAPIT 514
Gypsum ... EUROGYPSUM 522
Handwriting ... ESHP 519
Health Care ... CLEO 510, CLPEU 510, CPLOL 511, CPME 511, EAHP 512, EDTNA 514, EHIMA 516, EMA 516, EPHA 518, HOPE 528, IVTIP 529, OCE 529, UEHP 531, UEMO 531, UEMS 531
Health Management ... EHMA 516
Health Products ... EHPM 516
Hearing Aids ... EHIMA 516
Heaters ... ELVHIS 516
Heating ... EHI 516, EUROHEAT & POWER 522, REHVA 530
Heating Equipment ... CECOF 507
Helicopters ... EHA 516
Herbal Infusions ... THIE 530
Honey ... FEEDM 525, FRUCOM 527
Horticulturalists ... CEJH 508
Hunting ... EIHSA 516, FACE 524

Ice-cream ... ARTGLACE 506, EUROGLACES 522
In Vitro Testing ... IVTIP 529
Independent Schools ... ECNAIS 513
Industrial Gases ... EIGA 516
Industrial Research ... EIRMA 516
Informatics ... CEPIS 509
Information Technology ... DIGITALEUROPE 511
Innovation ... TII 530
Inspection Organization ... CEOC 509
Insulation ... EURIMA 521, FESI 526
Insurance ... ACME 504, BIPAR 506, Insurance Europe 528
International Trade ... EUROCOMMERCE 521
Investment ... AIMA 505
Iron ... EUROFER 522
Journalism ... AEJ 504
Journalists ... EMMA 517, ENPA 517, IFJ 528
Kaolin ... KPC-Europe 529
Laboratories ... FELASA 526
Lamps ... Lighting Europe 529
Landowners ... ELO 516
Landscape Architecture ... EFLA 515
Landscaping ... ELCA 516
Lasers ... EUROM II 522
Law ... CCBE 506, EFLA 515, FIDE 527, UAE 530
Leasing ... LEASEUROPE 529
Liberal Professions ... CEPLIS 509
Lifts ... ELA 516
Lignite ... EURACOAL 520
Lime ... EULA 520
Livestock ... EALM 512, UECBV 531
Locks ... ARGE 506, ELF 516
Logistics ... ECSLA 513, ELA 516
Lubricants ... UEIL 531
Machine Tools ... CECIMO 507
Machines (Coin-operated) ... EUROMAT 522
Magazines ... EMMA 517
Maize ... CEPM 509
Malting ... EUROMALT 522
Management Development ... EFMD 515
Managerial Staff ... EUROCADRES 521
Margarine ... IMACE 528
Market Research ... EFAMRO 514, ESOMAR 519
Marketing ... EMC 517, FEDMA 525
Measurement ... EUROLAB 522
Meat ... AVEC 506, CLITRAVI 510, EALM 512, ENSCA 517, EPEGA 518, IBC 528, UECBV 531
Mechanical Industries ... EUROM 522, ORGALIME 529
Media ... EMMA 517
Medical Physics ... EFOMP 515
Metal Packaging ... SEFEL 530
Metals ... AEROBAL 504, CIELFFA 510, EMU 517, EUROFER 522, EUROMETAL 522, EUROMETAUX 522, IZA 529, Metal Packaging Europe 529, OEA 529
Metalworkers ... EMB 517

Meteorological Satellites ... EUMETSAT 520
Midwives ... EMA 517
Minerals ... IMA-EUROPE 528
Molecular Biology ... EMBO 517
Mortar ... EMO 517
Mortgages ... EMF 517
Motor Trade and Repairs ... CECRA 507
Motorcycles ... ACEM 504
Music ... CAFIM 506
National Productivity ... EANPC 512
Natural Gas ... ENGVA 517, EUROGAS 522, MARCOGAZ 529
Netting ... EUROCORD 521
Newspapers ... ENPA 517
Non-wovens ... EDANA 514
Notaries ... CNUE 510
Nuclear Energy ... ENS 517
Nutrition ... SNE 530
Nuts ... FRUCOM 527
Oil ... FEDIOL 525
Oleochemicals ... APAG 505
Optics ... ECOO 513
Ornaments ... FEPF 526
Orthoptists ... OCE 529
Osteopaths ... CLEO 510
Packacking ... EUROPEN 523
Packaging ... ECMA 513, FEFPEB 525, Pack2Go Europe 529
Paint ... CEPE 509
Panels ... EPF 518
Paper ... CEPI 509, EUCEPA 520, FEPE 526
Pectin ... IPPA 528
Perfume ... Cosmetics Europe 511
Perfumes ... EFFA 515, FEPD 526
Pest Control ... CEPA 509
Pet Food ... FEDIAF 525
Petrochemicals ... APPE 505
Petroleum ... CECOD 507, FuelsEurope 527, UPEI 531
Pharmaceuticals ... AESGP 504, CED 507, EFPIA 515, EIPG 516, GIRP 527, PGEU 529
Pharmacies ... EUSP 523
Pharmacists ... EAHP 512
Photovoltaic Industry ... EPIA 518
Physical Therapy ... European Region of WCPT 523
Pigments ... ETAD 519
Pipes ... FEUGRES 527
Pipework ... CECT 507
Plant Breeding ... EUCARPIA 520
Plantmakers ... EUROPLANT 523
Plasma Protein ... PPTA 529
Plastic Clays ... KPC-Europe 529
Plastics ... EUPC 520
Pneumatic Tools ... PNEUROP 529
Pneumatics ... CETOP 510
Podiatrists ... CLPEU 510
Police ... EUROCOP 521
Polyol ... EPA 517, ISOPA 528
Port Employers ... SCEPEA 530
Ports ... EFIP 515, ESPO 519, FEPORT 526
Postal Operators ... POSTEUROP 529
Postal Services ... CEPT 509, EUROGIRO 522

Potatoes ... EUPPA 520, EUROPATAT 523
Poultry ... AVEC 506, EPEGA 518, EUWEP 524
Powder Metallurgy ... EPMA 518
Power ... EUROHEAT & POWER 522
Power Tools ... EPTA 518
Printing ... CEPE 509, ERA 518, INTERGRAF 528
Private Equity ... Invest Europe 528
Public Participation (Enterprises) ... CEEP 508
Public Relations ... CERP 509
Public Service ... USSPE 531
Public Services ... EPSU 518, EUROFEDOP 521
Publishers ... FEP 526
Publishing ... EPC 518
Pulp ... EUCEPA 520
Pulses ... IPTIC 528
Pump Manufacturers ... EUROPUMP 523
Quality ... EOQ 517
Quality Management ... EFQM 515
Radio ... AER 504
Radiological Industries ... COCIR 510
Rail ... CER 509, UEEIV 531, UNIFE 531
Refractories ... PRE 529
Refrigeration ... AREA 506, ASERCOM 506
Removals ... FEDEMAC 525
Renal Care ... EDTNA 514
Renderers ... EFPRA 515
Research ... EARTO 512, GERG 527
Restaurants ... HOTREC 528
Restoration ... ECCO 513
Retail ... EUROCOMMERCE 521
Retail Trade ... HDE 527
Retailers ... Independent Retail Europe 528
Roads ... ERF 518
Rope ... EUROCORD 521
Rubber ... ETRMA 519
Saddlers ... EUTS 524
Safe Manufacturers ... EUROSAFE 523
Safety ... ESF 518
Salt ... EuSalt 523
Sanitary Ware ... FECS 525
Sausage Casing ... ENSCA 517
Sawmills ... EOS 517
School Heads ... ESHA 519
Sealing ... ESA 518
Seaweeds ... MARINALG 529
Security ... ESTA 519
Seeds ... ESGG 518, EUROSEED 523
Shipowners ... ECSA 513
Shipyards ... CESA 509
Silica ... EUROSIL 523
Skippers ... OEB 529
Smart Cards ... EUROSMART 523
Snacks ... ESA 518
Soap ... AISE 505
Social Workers ... IFSW 528
Spatial Planners ... ECTP 513
Speech Therapists ... CPLOL 511
Spices ... ESA 518, FRUCOM 527
Spirits ... CEPS 509
Sporting Goods ... AFEMS 505

Springs ... ESF 518
Standardization ... CEN 508, CENELEC 509
Starch ... Starch Europe 530
Steel ... APEAL 505, CIELFFA 510, EUROFER 522
Steel Drums ... SEFA 530
Steel Tubes ... ESTA 519
Steelwork ... ECCS 513
Sugar ... ASSUC 506, CEFS 508
Surface Treatment ... SITS 530
Surgical Goods ... ESDREMA 518, ESTA 519
Surveyors ... CLGE 510
Sweeteners ... ISA 528
Switchgear ... CAPIEL 506
Tableware ... FEPF 526
Talc ... EUROTALC 523
Tank Storage ... FETSA 526
Tanners ... COTANCE 511
Tapestries ... EUTS 524
Taps ... CEIR 508
Taxation ... CFE 510
Taxis ... CET 510
Teaching ... AEDE 504
Technical Assessment ... EOTA 517
Technology ... EARTO 512, TII 530
Telecommunications ... ETNO 519, ETSA 519, FITCE 527
Television ... ACT 504, EUROCINEMA 521, FEB 525
Textiles ... CEMATEX 508, CRIET 511, EATP 512, ETSA 519, EURATEX 520, EUROCOTON 521
Tiles ... EUF 520
Tobacco ... CECCM 507, ESTA 519, ESTOC 519, ETV 519, FETRATAB 526
Tour Operators ... ECTAA 513
Tourism ... ITTFA 528
Toxicology ... ECETOC 513
Toys ... TIE 530
Trade ... AIDA 505
Trade Marks ... ECTA 513
Trade Unions ... CESI 510, EFFAT 515, ETUC 519, ETUCE 519, ETUI-REHS 519
Trailers ... CLCCR 510
Transport ... CER 509, CESA 509, CET 510, CLECAT 510, EHA 516, ENGVA 517, ERAA 518, ESPO 519, ESTA 519, ETF 519, IRU 528, UEEIV 531, UITP-EuroTeam 531, UNIFE 531
Travel ... ETC 519, EUFED 520, EUTO 523, HOTREC 528, IATM 528
Travel Agents ... ECTAA 513
Tubes ... ETA 519
Twine ... EUROCORD 521
Tyres ... ETRTO 519
Valves ... CEIR 508
Vegetable Protein ... EUVEPRO 524
Vegetables ... CIBE 510, EUPPA 520, EUROPATAT 523, PROFEL 530
Vehicles ... ENGVA 517
Vending ... EVA 524
Venture Capital ... Invest Europe 528
Veterinarians ... EAEVE 511, FVE 527
Waste ... FEAD 524

Index of Keywords

Water ... AQUA 505, AQUA EUROPA 506, EUREAU 520, EWA 524
Weighing Machines ... CECIP 507
Welding ... EWA 524
Welfare ... AFILIATYS 505
Whey ... EWPA 524
Wholesale ... EUROCOMMERCE 521

Windows ... FAECF 524
Wine ... CEEV 508
Wire Rope ... EWRIS 524
Wood ... EPF 518, EWPM 524, FEFPEB 525, FEIC 526, WEI 532
Wood Textiles ... IWTO 529
Woodworkers ... EFBWW 514

Woodworking ... CEI-BOIS 508
Woodworking Machinery ... EUMA-BOIS 520
Youth ... EUFED 520
Youth Clubs ... ECYC 513
Zinc ... IZA 529
Zoos ... EAZA 512

STATISTICAL SURVEY OF THE EUROPEAN UNION

Except where otherwise stated, the following tables/data are reproduced from the official website of the Statistical Office of the European Union (Eurostat)
ec.europa.eu/eurostat
© European Union, 1995–2017
Responsibility for the reproduction of the data lies entirely with Routledge

Notes
n.a. = not applicable or not available
Figures for Cyprus apply to the government-controlled area only
(i.e. excluding the 'Turkish Republic of Northern Cyprus')
Note: Totals may not be equal to the sum of the components, due to rounding.

Contents
Population, Labour and Health and Welfare
Agriculture, Forestry and Fishing
Energy and Industry
The Environment
Finance, Consumer Prices and National Accounts
Balance of Payments and External Trade
Transport and Communications
Tourism
Education

POPULATION

TOTAL POPULATION

Area, Population and Density (1 January 2016)

	Surface area (sq km)	Population	Density (per sq km)		Surface area (sq km)	Population	Density (per sq km)
Austria	83,879*	8,690,076	103.6	Latvia	64,490*	1,968,957	30.5
Belgium	30,530*	11,311,117	370.5	Lithuania	65,286*	2,888,558	44.2
Bulgaria	110,000*	7,153,784	65.0	Luxembourg	2,590*	576,249	222.5
Croatia	56,590*	4,190,669	74.1	Malta	320*	434,403	1,357.5
Cyprus	5,896†	848,319	143.9	Netherlands	41,540*	16,979,120	408.7
Czech Republic	78,870*	10,553,843	133.8	Poland	312,680*	37,967,209	121.4
Denmark	42,922*	5,707,251	133.0	Portugal	92,225*	10,341,330	112.1
Estonia	45,230*	1,315,944	29.1	Romania	238,390*	19,760,314	82.9
Finland	338,420*	5,487,308	16.2	Slovakia	49,035*	5,426,252	110.7
France	549,087*	66,759,950	121.6	Slovenia	20,270*	2,064,188	101.8
Germany	357,380*	82,175,684	229.9	Spain	505,940*	46,445,828	91.8
Greece	131,960*	10,783,748	81.7	Sweden	447,420*	9,851,017	22.0
Hungary	93,030*	9,830,485	105.7	United Kingdom	243,610*	65,382,556	268.4
Ireland	70,280*	4,724,720	67.2				
Italy	301,340*	60,665,551	201.3	**Total (EU-28)**	4,463,600‡	510,284,430	114.3

* Source: World Bank. † Source: Department of Statistics and Research, Ministry of Finance, Nicosia, Cyprus. ‡ Source: Eurostat.
Note: Figures for density are calculated from surface area and population data.
© European Union. Source: Eurostat, 2017, Population and social conditions, table *DEMO_PJANBROAD*—Population on 1 January by broad age-group and sex.

Total population at 1 January

	2014	2015	2016		2014	2015	2016
Austria	8,506,889	8,576,261	8,690,076	Latvia	2,001,468	1,986,096	1,968,957
Belgium	11,180,840	11,237,274	11,311,117	Lithuania	2,943,472	2,921,262	2,888,558
Bulgaria	7,245,677	7,202,198	7,153,784	Luxembourg	549,680	562,958	576,249
Croatia	4,246,809	4,225,316	4,190,669	Malta	425,384	429,344	434,403
Cyprus	858,000	847,008	848,319	Netherlands	16,829,289	16,900,726	16,979,120
Czech Republic	10,512,419	10,538,275	10,553,843	Poland	38,017,856	38,005,614	37,967,209
Denmark	5,627,235	5,659,715	5,707,251	Portugal	10,427,301	10,374,822	10,341,330
Estonia	1,315,819	1,314,870	1,315,944	Romania	19,947,311	19,870,647	19,760,314
Finland	5,451,270	5,471,753	5,487,308	Slovakia	5,415,949	5,421,349	5,426,252
France	65,942,093	66,488,186	66,759,950	Slovenia	2,061,085	2,062,874	2,064,188
Germany	80,767,463	81,197,537	82,175,684	Spain	46,512,199	46,449,565	46,445,828
Greece	10,926,807	10,858,018	10,783,748	Sweden	9,644,864	9,747,355	9,851,017
Hungary	9,877,365	9,855,571	9,830,485	United Kingdom	64,351,155	64,875,165	65,382,556
Ireland	4,605,501	4,628,949	4,724,720				
Italy	60,782,668	60,795,612	60,665,551	**Total (EU-28)**	506,973,868	508,504,320	510,284,430

© European Union. Source: Eurostat, 2017, Population and social conditions, table *DEMO_PJANBROAD*—Population on 1 January by broad age-group and sex.

Population by sex (1 January 2016)

	Males	Females	Total		Males	Females	Total
Austria	4,265,369	4,424,707	8,690,076	Latvia	904,299	1,064,658	1,968,957
Belgium	5,569,264	5,741,853	11,311,117	Lithuania	1,329,607	1,558,951	2,888,558
Bulgaria	3,477,177	3,676,607	7,153,784	Luxembourg	289,193	287,056	576,249
Croatia	2,022,797	2,167,872	4,190,669	Malta	217,569	216,834	434,403
Cyprus	412,692	435,627	848,319	Netherlands	8,417,135	8,561,985	16,979,120
Czech Republic	5,186,330	5,367,513	10,553,843	Poland	18,377,040	19,590,169	37,967,209
Denmark	2,837,887	2,869,364	5,707,251	Portugal	4,901,509	5,439,821	10,341,330
Estonia	616,708	699,236	1,315,944	Romania	9,649,811	10,110,503	19,760,314
Finland	2,701,490	2,785,818	5,487,308	Slovakia	2,646,082	2,780,170	5,426,252
France	32,340,016	34,419,934	66,759,950	Slovenia	1,023,333	1,040,855	2,064,188
Germany	40,514,123	41,661,561	82,175,684	Spain	22,809,420	23,636,408	46,445,828
Greece	5,224,210	5,559,538	10,783,748	Sweden	4,930,966	4,920,051	9,851,017
Hungary	4,688,519	5,141,966	9,830,485	United Kingdom	32,224,529	33,158,027	65,382,556
Ireland	2,335,733	2,388,987	4,724,720				
Italy	29,456,321	31,209,230	60,665,551	**Total (EU-28)**	249,369,129	260,915,301	510,284,430

© European Union. Source: Eurostat, 2017, Population and social conditions, table *DEMO_PJANBROAD*—Population on 1 January by broad age-group and sex.

Population by age-groups at 1 January 2016 (completed years of age at last birthday)

	0 to 14	15 to 64	65 and over		0 to 14	15 to 64	65 and over
Austria	1,245,179	5,839,708	1,605,189	Latvia	300,260	1,282,112	386,585
Belgium	1,921,342	7,326,873	2,062,902	Lithuania	423,747	1,916,284	548,527
Bulgaria	998,206	4,693,792	1,461,786	Luxembourg	94,891	399,401	81,957
Croatia	611,472	2,774,312	804,885	Malta	61,889	289,773	82,741
Cyprus	139,538	580,541	128,240	Netherlands	2,799,772	11,094,040	3,085,308
Czech Republic	1,623,716	6,997,715	1,932,412	Poland	5,708,855	26,198,877	6,059,477
Denmark	960,274	3,672,555	1,074,422	Portugal	1,460,832	6,739,674	2,140,824
Estonia	211,445	854,174	250,325	Romania	3,064,993	13,258,901	3,436,420
Finland	896,023	3,468,182	1,123,103	Slovakia	832,043	3,810,273	783,936
France	12,328,769	41,871,421	12,559,760	Slovenia	306,390	1,377,696	380,102
Germany	10,881,126	53,994,380	17,300,178	Spain	7,025,400	30,720,536	8,699,892
Greece	1,556,763	6,934,132	2,292,853	Sweden	1,717,143	6,186,647	1,947,227
Hungary	1,424,448	6,609,458	1,796,579	United Kingdom	11,587,390	42,069,267	11,725,899
Ireland	1,036,938	3,063,359	624,423				
Italy	8,281,859	39,013,938	13,369,754	**Total (EU-28)**	79,500,703	333,038,021	97,745,706

© European Union. Source: Eurostat, 2017, Population and social conditions, table *DEMO_PJANBROAD*—Population on 1 January by broad age-group and sex.

Population aged 0 to 14 years by sex (1 January 2016)

	Males	Females	Total		Males	Females	Total
Austria	640,128	605,051	1,245,179	Latvia	154,373	145,887	300,260
Belgium	982,958	938,384	1,921,342	Lithuania	217,110	206,637	423,747
Bulgaria	513,597	484,609	998,206	Luxembourg	48,773	46,118	94,891
Croatia	314,532	296,940	611,472	Malta	31,956	29,933	61,889
Cyprus	71,678	67,860	139,538	Netherlands	1,433,087	1,366,685	2,799,772
Czech Republic	832,609	791,107	1,623,716	Poland	2,930,232	2,778,623	5,708,855
Denmark	492,349	467,925	960,274	Portugal	748,017	712,815	1,460,832
Estonia	108,461	102,984	211,445	Romania	1,575,366	1,489,627	3,064,993
Finland	458,048	437,975	896,023	Slovakia	426,954	405,089	832,043
France	6,304,922	6,023,847	12,328,769	Slovenia	157,674	148,716	306,390
Germany	5,594,051	5,287,075	10,881,126	Spain	3,619,502	3,405,898	7,025,400
Greece	798,355	758,408	1,556,763	Sweden	882,875	834,268	1,717,143
Hungary	731,304	693,144	1,424,448	United Kingdom	5,934,059	5,653,331	11,587,390
Ireland	528,987	507,951	1,036,938				
Italy	4,261,296	4,020,563	8,281,859	**Total (EU-28)**	40,793,253	38,707,450	79,500,703

© European Union. Source: Eurostat, 2017, Population and social conditions table *DEMO_PJANBROAD*—Population on 1 January by broad age-group and sex.

Population aged 15 to 64 years by sex (1 January 2016)

	Males	Females	Total		Males	Females	Total
Austria	2,937,557	2,902,151	5,839,708	Latvia	623,457	658,655	1,282,112
Belgium	3,690,158	3,636,715	7,326,873	Lithuania	927,968	988,316	1,916,284
Bulgaria	2,372,870	2,320,922	4,693,792	Luxembourg	203,988	195,413	399,401
Croatia	1,387,827	1,386,485	2,774,312	Malta	148,509	141,264	289,773
Cyprus	281,894	298,647	580,541	Netherlands	5,578,377	5,515,663	11,094,040
Czech Republic	3,550,303	3,447,412	6,997,715	Poland	13,086,380	13,112,497	26,198,877
Denmark	1,854,792	1,817,763	3,672,555	Portugal	3,262,355	3,477,319	6,739,674
Estonia	423,458	430,716	854,174	Romania	6,689,337	6,569,564	13,258,901
Finland	1,756,787	1,711,395	3,468,182	Slovakia	1,915,715	1,894,558	3,810,273
France	20,668,814	21,202,607	41,871,421	Slovenia	708,132	669,564	1,377,696
Germany	27,415,031	26,579,349	53,994,380	Spain	15,437,204	15,283,332	30,720,536
Greece	3,410,016	3,524,116	6,934,132	Sweden	3,152,192	3,034,455	6,186,647
Hungary	3,281,899	3,327,559	6,609,458	United Kingdom	20,977,472	21,091,795	42,069,267
Ireland	1,516,439	1,546,920	3,063,359				
Italy	19,431,527	19,582,411	39,013,938	**Total (EU-28)**	166,690,458	166,347,563	333,038,021

© European Union. Source: Eurostat, 2017, Population and social conditions, table *DEMO_PJANBROAD*—Population on 1 January by broad age-group and sex.

Population aged 65 years and over by sex (1 January 2016)

	Males	Females	Total		Males	Females	Total
Austria	687,684	917,505	1,605,189	Latvia	126,469	260,116	386,585
Belgium	896,148	1,166,754	2,062,902	Lithuania	184,529	363,998	548,527
Bulgaria	590,710	871,076	1,461,786	Luxembourg	36,432	45,525	81,957
Croatia	320,438	484,447	804,885	Malta	37,104	45,637	82,741
Cyprus	59,120	69,120	128,240	Netherlands	1,405,671	1,679,637	3,085,308
Czech Republic	803,418	1,128,994	1,932,412	Poland	2,360,428	3,699,049	6,059,477†
Denmark	490,746	583,676	1,074,422	Portugal	891,137	1,249,687	2,140,824
Estonia	84,789	165,536	250,325	Romania	1,385,108	2,051,312	3,436,420
Finland	486,655	636,448	1,123,103	Slovakia	303,413	480,523	783,936
France	5,366,280	7,193,480	12,559,760	Slovenia	157,527	222,575	380,102
Germany	7,505,041	9,795,137	17,300,178	Spain	3,752,714	4,947,178	8,699,892
Greece	1,015,839	1,277,014	2,292,853	Sweden	895,899	1,051,328	1,947,227
Hungary	675,316	1,121,263	1,796,579	United Kingdom	5,312,998	6,412,901	11,725,899
Ireland	290,307	334,116	624,423				
Italy	5,763,498	7,606,256	13,369,754	**Total (EU-28)**	41,885,418	55,860,288	97,745,706

© European Union. Source: Eurostat, 2017, Population and social conditions, table *DEMO_PJANBROAD*—Population on 1 January by broad age-group and sex.

Economically active population (age 15–64) by citizenship in fourth quarter of 2016 ('000)

	Nationals	Foreigners	Total		Nationals	Foreigners	Total
Austria	3,714	701	4,415	Latvia	834	116	950
Belgium	4,415	573	4,989	Lithuania	1,418	7	1,425
Bulgaria	3,149	n.a.*	3,149	Luxembourg	134	146	280
Croatia	1,797	5	1,802	Malta	190	8	198
Cyprus	340	82	421	Netherlands	8,303	375	8,678
Czech Republic	5,141	117	5,258	Poland	16,912	58	16,970
Denmark	2,637	289	2,926	Portugal	4,817	121	4,938
Estonia	556	97	652	Romania	8,624	n.a.*	8,624
Finland	2,478	88	2,568	Slovakia	2,734	8	2,742
France	27,343	1,877	29,220	Slovenia	949	44	993
Germany	37,462	4,940	42,401	Spain	19,923	2,652	22,575
Greece	4,403	295	4,699	Sweden	4,687	378	5,065
Hungary	4,536	31	4,567	United Kingdom	28,482	3,637	32,119
Ireland	1,788	339	2,127				
Italy	22,576	2,835	25,411	**Total (EU-28)**	220,342	19,819	240,298

* Unreliable data.

© European Union. Source: Eurostat, 2017, Population and social conditions, table *LFSQ_AGAN*—Active population by sex, age and citizenship.

POPULATION CHANGE

Total population increase or decrease ('000)

	2014	2015	2016		2014	2015	2016
Austria	69.4	113.8	82.8*	Latvia	−15.4	−17.1	−18.8
Belgium	56.4	73.8	54.7	Lithuania	−22.2	−32.7	−40.7
Bulgaria	−43.5	−48.4	−51.9	Luxembourg	13.3	13.3	11.5†
Croatia	−21.5	−34.6	−36.5	Malta	4.0	5.1	6.0*
Cyprus	−11.0	1.3	6.5*	Netherlands	71.4	78.4	102.4
Czech Republic	25.9	15.6	25.0	Poland	−12.2	−38.4	5.8
Denmark	32.5	47.5	41.5	Portugal‡	−52.5	−33.5	−31.8
Estonia	−2.5	1.1†	−0.3	Romania‡	−76.7	−110.3	−122.0*
Finland	20.5	15.6	16.0	Slovakia	5.4	4.9	9.1
France	319.2	271.8*†	264.5*	Slovenia	1.8	1.3	1.7
Germany	430.1	978.1	624.3‡	Spain	−62.6	−9.5	88.9*
Greece	−68.8	−74.3	−26.5*‡	Sweden	102.5	103.7	144.1
Hungary	−21.8	−25.1	−32.9	United Kingdom‡	524.0	507.4	426.0
Ireland	23.4	35.2	50.1				
Italy	12.9*	−130.1*	−76.1†‡	**Total (EU-28)*‡**	1,301.9	1,713.8	1,523.5

* Provisional. † Break in series. ‡ Estimate.

© European Union. Source: Eurostat, 2017, Population and social conditions, table *DEMO_GIND*—Population change: demographic balance and crude rates at national level.

Natural increase or decrease (births minus deaths, '000)

	2014	2015	2016		2014	2015	2016
Austria	3.5	1.3	7.0	Latvia	−6.7	−6.5	−6.6
Belgium	20.3	11.7	13.8	Lithuania	−9.9	−10.3	−10.5
Bulgaria	−41.4	−44.2	−42.6	Luxembourg	2.2	2.1	2.1
Croatia	−11.3	−16.7	−14.0*	Malta	0.9	0.9	1.1*
Cyprus	4.0	3.3	4.0	Netherlands	36.0	23.4	23.5
Czech Republic	4.2	−0.4	4.9	Poland	−1.3	−25.6	−5.8
Denmark	5.5	5.7	8.8	Portugal	−22.5	−23.0	−23.4
Estonia	−1.9	−1.3	−1.3	Romania	−61.1	−63.8	−68.1*
Finland	5.0	3.0	−1.1	Slovakia	3.7	1.8	5.2
France	259.9	205.9	198.6*	Slovenia	2.3	0.8	0.7
Germany	−153.4	−187.6	−150.0†	Spain	32.3	−2.0	−0.3*
Greece	−21.6	−29.4	−26.0*	Sweden	25.9	24.0	26.4
Hungary	−33.0	−39.4	−31.7	United Kingdom	207.1†	175.5†	177.6*
Ireland	38.0	35.5	33.5*				
Italy	−95.8	−161.8	−141.8	**Total (EU-28)***	191.0	−117.3	−15.9*

* Provisional. † Estimate.
© European Union. Source: Eurostat, 2017, Population and social conditions, table *DEMO_GIND*—Population change: demographic balance and crude rates at national level.

Net inward migration (including statistical adjustment) ('000)

	2014	2015	2016		2014	2015	2016
Austria	65.9	112.5	75.8*	Latvia	−8.7	−10.6	−12.2
Belgium	36.2	62.1	40.9	Lithuania	−12.3	−22.4	−30.2
Bulgaria	−2.1	−4.2	−9.3	Luxembourg	11.0	11.2	9.4†
Croatia	−10.2	−17.9	−22.5	Malta	3.0	4.2	4.9*
Cyprus	−15.0	−2.0	2.5*	Netherlands	35.5	55.0	78.9
Czech Republic	21.7	16.0	20.1	Poland	−10.9	−12.8	11.5
Denmark	27.0	41.9	32.7	Portugal‡	−30.0	−10.5	−8.3
Estonia	−0.6	2.4	1.0	Romania‡	−15.5	−46.5	−53.9*
Finland	15.4	12.6†	17.1	Slovakia	1.7	3.1	3.9
France	59.3	65.9*	65.9*	Slovenia	−0.5	0.5	1.1
Germany	583.5	1,165.8*	774.3‡	Spain	−95.0	−7.5	89.1*
Greece	−47.2	−44.9	−0.5*‡	Sweden	76.6	79.7	117.7
Hungary	11.2	14.4	−1.2	United Kingdom‡	316.9	331.9	248.4*
Ireland*	−14.6	−0.3	16.6‡				
Italy	108.7	31.7	65.7	**Total (EU-28)* ‡**	1,111.0	1,831.2	1,539.4

* Provisional. † Break in series. ‡ Estimate(s).
© European Union. Source: Eurostat, 2017, Population and social conditions, table *DEMO_GIND*—Population change: demographic balance and crude rates at national level.

Live births ('000)

	2014	2015	2016		2014	2015	2016
Austria	81.7	84.4	87.7	Latvia	21.7	22.0	22.0
Belgium	125.0	122.3	121.9	Lithuania	30.4	31.5	30.6
Bulgaria	67.6	66.0	65.0	Luxembourg	6.1	6.1	6.1
Croatia	39.6	37.5	37.5	Malta	4.2	4.3	4.5*
Cyprus	9.3	9.2	9.5*	Netherlands	175.2	170.5	172.5
Czech Republic	109.9	110.8	112.7	Poland	375.2	369.3	382.3
Denmark	56.9	58.2	61.6	Portugal	82.4	85.5	87.1
Estonia	13.6	13.9	14.1	Romania	193.1	197.5	188.4*
Finland	57.2	55.5	52.8	Slovakia	55.0	55.6	57.6
France	819.3	799.7	785.7*	Slovenia	21.2	20.6	20.3
Germany	714.9	737.6	770.0†	Spain	426.1	418.4	406.6*
Greece	92.1	91.8	92.8*	Sweden	114.9	114.9	117.4
Hungary	93.3	92.1	95.4	United Kingdom	775.9†	776.7	774.8*
Ireland	67.3	65.5	63.9*				
Italy	502.6	485.8	473.4	**Total (EU-28)**	5,131.5†	5,103.2	5,114.1*†

* Provisional. † Estimate.
© European Union. Source: Eurostat, 2017, Population and social conditions, table *DEMO_GIND*—Population change: demographic balance and crude rates at national level.

STATISTICAL SURVEY — Population

Crude birth rate (live births per 1,000 inhabitants)

	2014	2015	2016		2014	2015	2016
Austria	9.6	9.8	10.0*	Latvia	10.9	11.1	11.2
Belgium	11.2	10.8	10.8	Lithuania	10.4	10.8	10.7
Bulgaria	9.4	9.2	9.1	Luxembourg	10.9	10.7	10.4‡
Croatia	9.3	8.9	9.0	Malta	9.8	10.0	10.2*
Cyprus	10.9	10.8	11.1*	Netherlands	10.4	10.1	10.1
Czech Republic	10.4	10.5	10.7	Poland	9.9	9.7	10.1
Denmark	10.1	10.2	10.8	Portugal†	7.9	8.3	8.4
Estonia	10.3	10.6‡	10.7	Romania†	9.7	10.0	9.6*
Finland	10.5	10.1	9.6	Slovakia	10.2	10.3	10.6
France	12.4	12.0*	11.7*	Slovenia	10.3	10.0	9.9
Germany	8.8	9.0	9.3†	Spain	9.2	9.0	8.7*
Greece	8.5	8.5	8.6†*	Sweden	11.9	11.7	11.8
Hungary	9.5	9.4	9.7	United Kingdom†	12.0	11.9	11.8*
Ireland*	14.6	14.1	13.5†‡				
Italy	8.3	8.0	7.8	**Total (EU-28)*†**	10.1	10.0	10.0

* Provisional. † Estimate(s). ‡ Break in series.
© European Union. Source: Eurostat, 2017, Population and social conditions, table *DEMO_GIND*—Population change: demographic balance and crude rates at national level.

Total fertility rate (children per woman)

	2013	2014	2015		2013	2014	2015
Austria	1.44	1.47	1.49	Latvia	1.52	1.65	1.70
Belgium	1.75	1.74	1.70	Lithuania	1.59	1.63	1.70
Bulgaria	1.48	1.53	1.53	Luxembourg	1.55	1.50	1.47
Croatia	1.46	1.46	1.40	Malta	1.38	1.42	1.45
Cyprus	1.30	1.31	1.32	Netherlands	1.68	1.71	1.66
Czech Republic	1.46	1.53	1.57	Poland	1.29	1.32	1.32
Denmark	1.67	1.69	1.71	Portugal	1.21	1.23	1.31
Estonia	1.52	1.54	1.58*	Romania	1.46	1.52	1.58
Finland	1.75	1.71	1.65	Slovakia	1.34	1.37	1.40
France	1.99	2.01*	1.96*‡	Slovenia	1.55	1.58	1.57
Germany	n.a.	1.47*	1.50	Spain	1.27	1.32	1.33
Greece	1.29	1.30	1.33	Sweden	1.89	1.88	1.85
Hungary	1.35	1.44	1.45	United Kingdom	1.83	1.81†	1.80†
Ireland‡	1.96	1.94	1.92				
Italy	1.39	1.37	1.35	**Total (EU-28)† ‡**	1.55	1.58*	1.58*

* Break in series. † Estimate(s). ‡ Provisional.
© European Union. Source: Eurostat, 2017, Population and social conditions, table *DEMO_FIND*—Fertility indicators.

Deaths ('000)

	2014	2015	2016		2014	2015	2016
Austria	78.3	83.1	80.7	Latvia	28.5	28.5	28.6
Belgium	104.8	110.5	108.1	Lithuania	40.3	41.8	41.1
Bulgaria	109.0	110.1	107.6	Luxembourg	3.8	4.0	4.0
Croatia	50.8	54.2	51.5	Malta	3.3	3.4	3.3*
Cyprus	5.3	5.9	5.5*	Netherlands	139.2	147.1	149.0
Czech Republic	105.7	111.2	107.8	Poland	376.5	394.9	388.0
Denmark	51.3	52.6	52.8	Portugal	104.8	108.5	110.5
Estonia	15.5	15.2	15.4	Romania	254.2	261.3	256.5*
Finland	52.2	52.5	53.9	Slovakia	51.3	53.8	52.4
France	559.4	593.8	587.1*	Slovenia	18.9	19.8	19.7
Germany	868.4	925.2	920.0†	Spain	393.7	420.4	406.8*
Greece	113.7	121.2	118.8*	Sweden	89.0	90.9	91.0
Hungary	126.3	131.6	127.1	United Kingdom	568.8†	601.3†	597.2*
Ireland	29.3	30.1	30.4*				
Italy	598.4	647.6	615.3	**Total (EU-28)†**	4,940.5	5,220.5	5,130.0*

* Provisional. † Estimate(s).
© European Union. Source: Eurostat, 2017, Population and social conditions, table *DEMO_GIND*—Population change: demographic balance and crude rates at national level.

Crude death rate (deaths per 1,000 inhabitants)

	2014	2015	2016		2014	2015	2016
Austria	9.2	9.6	9.2*	Latvia	14.3	14.4	14.6
Belgium	9.3	9.8	9.5	Lithuania	13.7	14.4	14.3
Bulgaria	15.1	15.3	15.1	Luxembourg	6.9	7.0	6.8‡
Croatia	12.0	12.9	12.4	Malta	7.7	8.0	7.6*
Cyprus	6.2	6.9	6.4*	Netherlands	8.3	8.7	8.7
Czech Republic	10.0	10.5	10.2	Poland	9.9	10.4	10.2
Denmark	9.1	9.2	9.2	Portugal†	10.1	10.5	10.7
Estonia	11.8	11.6‡	11.7	Romania†	12.8	13.2	13.0*
Finland	9.6	9.6	9.8	Slovakia	9.5	9.9	9.6
France	8.5	8.9*‡	8.8*	Slovenia	9.2	9.6	9.5
Germany	10.7	11.3	11.2	Spain	8.5	9.1	8.8*
Greece	10.4	11.2	11.0*†	Sweden	9.2	9.3	9.2
Hungary	12.8	13.4	13.0	United Kingdom†	8.8	9.2	9.1*
Ireland*	6.3	6.5	6.4				
Italy	9.8	10.7	10.1*‡	**Total (EU-28)***†	9.7	10.2	10.0

* Provisional. † Estimate(s). ‡ Break in series.
© European Union. Source: Eurostat, 2017, Population and social conditions, table *DEMO_GIND*—Population change: demographic balance and crude rates at national level.

Infant mortality (deaths of children under one year of age)

	2013	2014	2015		2013	2014	2015
Austria	245	249	259	Latvia	91	83	90
Belgium	436	423	400	Lithuania	110	118	132
Bulgaria	489	517	434	Luxembourg	24	17	17
Croatia	162	199	154	Malta	27	21	25
Cyprus	15	13	25	Netherlands	645	630	561
Czech Republic	265	263	272	Poland	1,684	1,583	1,476
Denmark	194	229	216	Portugal	243	236	250
Estonia	28	36	35	Romania	1,677	1,628	1,500
Finland	102	124	97	Slovakia	301	318	285
France	2,936	2,880*	2,944	Slovenia	62	39	33
Germany	2,250	2,284	2,405	Spain	1,149	1,202	1,117
Greece	345	345	364	Sweden	306	251	282
Hungary	448	418	383	United Kingdom	3,030	2,990	3,005
Ireland	243	224	224				
Italy	1,493	1,429	1,398	**Total (EU-28)**	19,000	18,749*	18,383†

* Break in series. † Estimate.
© European Union. Source: Eurostat, 2017, Population and social conditions, table *DEMO-MINF*—Infant mortality.

Infant mortality rate (deaths under one year per 1,000 live births)

	2013	2014	2015		2013	2014	2015
Austria	3.1	3.0	3.1	Latvia	4.4	3.8	4.1
Belgium	3.5	3.4	3.3	Lithuania	3.7	3.9	4.2
Bulgaria	7.3	7.6	6.6	Luxembourg	3.9	2.8	2.8
Croatia	4.1	5.0	4.1	Malta	6.7	5.0	5.8
Cyprus	1.6	1.4	2.7	Netherlands	3.8	3.6	3.3
Czech Republic	2.5	2.4	2.5	Poland	4.6	4.2	4.0
Denmark	3.5	4.0	3.7	Portugal	2.9	2.9	2.9
Estonia	2.1	2.7	2.5	Romania	8.9	8.4	7.6
Finland	1.8	2.2	1.7	Slovakia	5.5	5.8	5.1
France	3.6	3.5	3.7	Slovenia	2.9	1.8	1.6
Germany	3.3	3.2	3.3	Spain	2.7	2.8	2.7
Greece	3.7	3.7	4.0	Sweden	2.7	2.2	2.5
Hungary	5.0	4.5	4.2	United Kingdom	3.9	3.9	3.9
Ireland	3.5	3.3	3.4				
Italy	2.9	2.8	2.9	**Total (EU-28)**	3.7	3.7	3.6

© European Union. Source: Eurostat, 2017, Population and social conditions, table *DEMO_MINFIND*—Infant mortality rates.

STATISTICAL SURVEY — Population

Expectation of life (years at birth)

	2014 Males	2014 Females	2015 Males	2015 Females		2014 Males	2014 Females	2015 Males	2015 Females
Austria	79.1	84.0	78.8	83.7	Latvia	69.1	79.4	69.7	79.5
Belgium	78.8	83.9	78.7	83.4	Lithuania	69.2	80.1	69.2	79.7
Bulgaria	71.1	78.0	71.2	78.2	Luxembourg	79.4	85.2	80.0	84.7
Croatia	74.7	81.0	74.4	80.5	Malta	79.8	84.2	79.7	84.0
Cyprus	80.9	84.7	79.9	83.7	Netherlands	80.0	83.5	79.9	83.2
Czech Republic	75.8	82.0	75.7	81.6	Poland	73.7	81.7	73.5	81.6
Denmark	78.7	82.8	78.8	82.7	Portugal	78.0	84.4	78.1	84.3
Estonia	72.4	81.9	73.2	82.2	Romania	71.4	78.7	71.5	78.7
Finland	78.4	84.1	78.7	84.4	Slovakia	73.3	80.5	73.1	80.2
France	79.5	86.0	79.2	85.5	Slovenia	78.2	84.1	77.8	83.9
Germany	78.7	83.6	78.3	83.1	Spain	80.4	86.2	80.1	85.8
Greece	78.8	84.1	78.5	83.7	Sweden	80.4	84.2	80.4	84.1
Hungary	72.3	79.4	72.3	79.0	United Kingdom	79.5	83.2	79.2	82.8
Ireland	79.3	83.5	79.6	83.4					
Italy	80.7	85.6	80.3	84.9	**Total (EU-28)**	78.1	83.6	77.9	83.3

© European Union. Source: Eurostat, 2017, Population and social conditions, table *DEMO_MLEXPEC*—Life expectancy by sex and age.

Applications for asylum (annual aggregated data)

	2014	2015	2016		2014	2015	2016
Austria	28,065	88,180	42,285	Latvia	375	330	350
Belgium	22,850	44,760	18,325	Lithuania	440	315	430
Bulgaria	11,080	20,365	19,420	Luxembourg	1,150	2,505	2,160
Croatia	450	210	2,225	Malta	1,350	1,845	1,930
Cyprus	1,745	2,265	2,940	Netherlands	24,535	44,970	20,945
Czech Republic	1,155	1,525	1,480	Poland	8,025	12,190	12,305
Denmark	14,715	20,970	6,195	Portugal	445	895	1,465
Estonia	155	230	175	Romania	1,545	1,260	1,880
Finland	3,625	32,345	5,625	Slovakia	330	330	145
France	64,310	76,165	84,270	Slovenia	385	275	1,310
Germany	202,815	476,620	745,265	Spain	5,615	14,785	15,755
Greece	9,435	13,205	51,110	Sweden	81,325	162,550	28,860
Hungary	42,775	177,135	29,430	United Kingdom	33,010	40,410	38,870
Ireland	1,450	3,275	2,245				
Italy	64,625	83,540	122,960	**Total (EU-28)**	627,780	1,323,450	1,260,350

© European Union. Source: Eurostat, 2017, Population and social conditions, table *MIGR_ASYAPPCTZA*—Asylum and new asylum applicants by citizenship, age and sex.

MARRIAGE AND DIVORCE

Registered marriages

	2013	2014	2015		2013	2014	2015
Austria	36,140	37,458	44,502	Latvia	11,436	12,515	13,617
Belgium	37,854	39,878	40,049	Lithuania	20,469	22,142	21,987
Bulgaria	21,943	24,596	27,720	Luxembourg	1,722	1,657	2,052
Croatia	19,169	19,501	19,834	Malta	2,578	2,871	3,002
Cyprus	5,493	5,378	6,092	Netherlands	64,549	65,333	64,308
Czech Republic	43,499	45,575	48,191	Poland	180,396	188,488	188,832
Denmark	27,503	28,331	28,853	Portugal	31,998	31,478	32,393
Estonia	5,630	6,220	6,815	Romania	107,507	118,075	125,454
Finland	25,119	24,462	24,708	Slovakia	25,491	26,737	28,775
France	238,720	241,425	236,432	Slovenia	6,254	6,571	6,449
Germany	373,655	385,952	400,115	Spain	154,470	160,256	166,651
Greece	51,256	53,105	53,672	Sweden	51,610	53,113	52,314
Hungary	36,986	38,780	46,137	United Kingdom	276,527	293,647	n.a.
Ireland	20,680	22,045	22,116				
Italy	194,057	189,765	194,377	**Total (EU-28)**	2,072,711	2,145,354	n.a.

© European Union. Source: Eurostat, 2017, Population and social conditions, table *DEMO_NIND*—Marriage indicators.

Crude marriage rate (marriages per 1,000 inhabitants)

	2013	2014	2015		2013	2014	2015
Austria	4.3	n.a.	n.a.	Latvia	5.7	6.3	6.9
Belgium	3.4	3.6	3.6	Lithuania	6.9	7.6	7.6
Bulgaria	3.0	3.4	3.9	Luxembourg	3.2	3.0	3.6
Croatia	4.5	4.6	4.7	Malta	6.1	6.7	7.0
Cyprus	6.4	6.3	7.2	Netherlands	3.8	3.9	3.8
Czech Republic	4.1	4.3	4.6	Poland	4.7	5.0	5.0
Denmark	4.9	5.0	5.1	Portugal	3.1	3.0	3.1
Estonia	4.3	4.7	5.2	Romania	5.4	5.9	6.3
Finland	4.6	4.5	4.5	Slovakia	4.7	4.9	5.3
France	n.a.	n.a.	n.a.	Slovenia	3.0	3.2	3.1
Germany	4.6	4.8	4.9	Spain	3.3	3.4	3.6
Greece	4.7	4.9	5.0	Sweden	5.4	5.5	5.3
Hungary	3.7	3.9	4.7	United Kingdom	4.3	n.a.	n.a.
Ireland	4.5	4.8	4.8				
Italy	3.2	3.1	3.2	**Total (EU-28)**	n.a.	n.a.	n.a.

© European Union. Source: Eurostat, 2017, Population and social conditions, table *DEMO_NIND*—Marriage indicators.

Registered divorces

	2013	2014	2015		2013	2014	2015
Austria	15,958	16,647	16,351	Latvia	7,031	6,271	5,151
Belgium	24,872	24,310	24,414	Lithuania	9,974	9,806	9,371
Bulgaria	10,908	10,584	10,483	Luxembourg	1,163	1,453	1,345
Croatia	5,992	6,140	6,010	Malta	338	323	372
Cyprus	1,857	1,884	1,807	Netherlands	33,636	35,409	34,232
Czech Republic	27,895	26,764	26,083	Poland	66,132	65,761	67,296
Denmark	18,875	19,435	16,343	Portugal	22,525	n.a.	n.a.
Estonia	3,343	3,218	3,382	Romania	28,507	27,188	31,527
Finland	13,766	13,682	13,939	Slovakia	10,946	10,514	9,786
France	124,948	123,537	123,668	Slovenia	2,351	2,469	2,432
Germany	169,833	166,199	163,335	Spain	95,427	100,746	96,562
Greece	16,717	14,427	n.a.	Sweden	26,933	26,143	24,876
Hungary	20,209	19,576	20,315	United Kingdom	126,716	122,556	n.a.
Ireland	2,949	n.a.	n.a.				
Italy	52,943	52,355	82,469	**Total (EU-28)**	942,744	n.a.	n.a.

© European Union. Source: Eurostat, 2017, Population and social conditions, table *DEMO_NDIVIND*—Divorce indicators.

Crude divorce rate (divorces per 1,000 inhabitants)

	2013	2014	2015		2013	2014	2015
Austria	1.9	1.9	1.9	Latvia	3.5	3.1	2.6
Belgium	2.2	2.2	2.2	Lithuania	3.4	3.3	3.2
Bulgaria	1.5	1.5	1.5	Luxembourg	2.1	2.6	2.4
Croatia	1.4	1.4	1.4	Malta	0.8	0.8	0.9
Cyprus	2.2	2.2	2.1	Netherlands	2.0	2.1	2.0
Czech Republic	2.7	2.5	2.5	Poland	1.7	1.7	1.8
Denmark	3.4	3.4	2.9	Portugal	2.2	n.a.	n.a.
Estonia	2.5	2.4	2.6	Romania	1.4	1.4	1.6
Finland	2.5	2.5	2.5	Slovakia	2.0	1.9	1.8
France	1.9	1.9	1.9	Slovenia	1.1	1.2	1.2
Germany	2.1	2.1	2.0	Spain	2.0	2.2	2.1
Greece	1.5	1.3	n.a.	Sweden	2.8	2.7	2.5
Hungary	2.0	2.0	2.1	United Kingdom	2.0	1.9	n.a.
Ireland	0.6	n.a.	n.a.				
Italy	0.9	0.9	1.4	**Total (EU-28)**	1.9	n.a.	n.a.

© European Union. Source: Eurostat, 2017, Population and social conditions, table *DEMO_NDIVIND*—Divorce indicators.

LABOUR

LABOUR FORCE

Total active population aged 15 to 64 years ('000 persons)

	2014	2015	2016		2014	2015	2016
Austria	4,278	4,319	4,412	Latvia	966	965	957
Belgium	4,920	4,921	4,929	Lithuania	1,445	1,434	1,433
Bulgaria	3,309	3,276	3,200	Luxembourg	258	274	277
Croatia	1,868	1,865	1,806	Malta	189	193	198
Cyprus	425	413	413	Netherlands	8,677	8,719	8,754
Czech Republic	5,206	5,201	5,226	Poland	17,153	17,112	16,961
Denmark	2,831	2,859	2,934	Portugal	4,976	4,949	4,940
Estonia	648	654	658	Romania	8,883	8,858	8,696
Finland	2,617	2,619	2,615	Slovakia	2,707	2,719	2,738
France	29,148	29,164	29,204	Slovenia	991	992	982
Germany	40,990	41,117	42,019	Spain	22,814	22,767	22,657
Greece	4,747	4,738	4,732	Sweden	5,005	5,044	5,100
Hungary	4,413	4,483	4,543	United Kingdom	31,534	31,754	32,017
Ireland	2,098	2,102	2,125				
Italy	25,039	24,997	25,243				

© European Union. Source: Eurostat, 2017, Population and social conditions, table *LFSI_EMP_A*—Employment and activity by sex and age—Annual data.

Active population aged 15 to 64 years by sex in 2016 ('000 persons)

	Males	Females	Total		Males	Females	Total
Austria	2,340	2,072	4,412	Latvia	479	478	957
Belgium	2,649	2,281	4,929	Lithuania	709	724	1,433
Bulgaria	1,710	1,490	3,200	Luxembourg	151	126	277
Croatia	968	838	1,806	Malta	120	78	198
Cyprus	211	202	413	Netherlands	4,645	4,109	8,754
Czech Republic	2,906	2,321	5,226	Poland	9,315	7,646	16,961
Denmark	1,532	1,402	2,934	Portugal	2,498	2,441	4,940
Estonia	343	315	658	Romania	5,006	3,689	8,696
Finland	1,350	1,265	2,615	Slovakia	1,499	1,239	2,738
France	15,128	14,077	29,204	Slovenia	524	458	982
Germany	22,420	19,599	42,019	Spain	12,120	10,536	22,657
Greece	2,613	2,119	4,732	Sweden	2,658	2,442	5,100
Hungary	2,465	2,079	4,543	United Kingdom	16,976	15,041	32,017
Ireland	1,156	969	2,125				
Italy	14,464	10,779	25,243				

© European Union. Source: Eurostat, 2017, Population and social conditions, table *LFSI_EMP_A*—Employment and activity by sex and age—Annual data.

Active population aged 15 to 64 years by labour status in 2016 ('000 persons)

	Employed	Unemployed	Total		Employed	Unemployed	Total
Austria	4,143	270	4,412	Latvia	862	95	957
Belgium	4,541	389	4,929	Lithuania	1,318	116	1,433
Bulgaria	2,954	245	3,200	Luxembourg	259	18	277
Croatia	1,567	240	1,806	Malta	188	9	198
Cyprus	359	55	413	Netherlands	8,223	530	8,754
Czech Republic	5,016	211	5,226	Poland	15,902	1,059	16,961
Denmark	2,748	186	2,934	Portugal	4,371	568	4,940
Estonia	612	46	658	Romania	8,166	530	8,696
Finland	2,380	236	2,615	Slovakia	2,472	266	2,738
France	26,243	2,962	29,204	Slovenia	902	80	982
Germany	40,256	1,763	42,019	Spain	18,183	4,474	22,657
Greece	3,610	1,122	4,732	Sweden	4,736	365	5,100
Hungary	4,309	234	4,543	United Kingdom	30,436	1,581	32,017
Ireland	1,953	172	2,125				
Italy	22,241	3,002	25,243				

© European Union. Source: Eurostat, 2017, Population and social conditions, tables *LFSI_EMP_A*—Employment and activity by sex and age—Annual data and *LFSA_UGAN*—Unemployment by sex, age and citizenship ('000).

EMPLOYMENT

Employed persons aged 15 to 64 years ('000)

	2014	2015	2016		2014	2015	2016
Austria	4,034	4,068	4,143	Latvia	859	868	862
Belgium	4,497	4,499	4,541	Lithuania	1,288	1,301	1,318
Bulgaria	2,927	2,974	2,954	Luxembourg	243	255	259
Croatia	1,542	1,559	1,567	Malta	178	182	188
Cyprus	355	350	359	Netherlands	8,028	8,115	8,223
Czech Republic	4,883	4,934	5,016	Poland	15,591	15,812	15,902
Denmark	2,640	2,678	2,748	Portugal	4,254	4,309	4,371
Estonia	600	613	612	Romania	8,254	8,235	8,166
Finland	2,386	2,368	2,380	Slovakia	2,349	2,405	2,472
France	26,129	26,118	26,243	Slovenia	892	902	902
Germany	38,908	39,176	40,256	Spain	17,211	17,717	18,183
Greece	3,480	3,548	3,610	Sweden	4,597	4,660	4,736
Hungary	4,070	4,176	4,309	United Kingdom	29,560	30,028	30,436
Ireland	1,856	1,899	1,953				
Italy	21,810	21,973	22,241				

© European Union. Source: Eurostat, 2017, Population and social conditions, table *LFSI_EMP_A*—Employment and activity by sex and age—Annual data.

Employed persons aged 15 to 64 years by sex in 2016 ('000)

	Males	Females	Total		Males	Females	Total
Austria	2,187	1,956	4,143	Latvia	425	437	862
Belgium	2,433	2,107	4,541	Lithuania	643	674	1,318
Bulgaria	1,569	1,385	2,954	Luxembourg	142	117	259
Croatia	845	721	1,567	Malta	114	74	188
Cyprus	184	175	359	Netherlands	4,383	3,840	8,223
Czech Republic	2,806	2,210	5,016	Poland	8,737	7,165	15,902
Denmark	1,440	1,307	2,748	Portugal	2,210	2,161	4,371
Estonia	317	295	612	Romania	4,668	3,499	8,166
Finland	1,225	1,154	2,380	Slovakia	1,367	1,105	2,472
France	13,561	12,681	26,243	Slovenia	484	419	902
Germany	21,401	18,855	40,256	Spain	9,910	8,272	18,183
Greece	2,092	1,519	3,610	Sweden	2,457	2,278	4,736
Hungary	2,337	1,972	4,309	United Kingdom	16,112	14,325	30,436
Ireland	1,048	905	1,953				
Italy	12,853	9,388	22,241				

© European Union. Source: Eurostat, 2017, Population and social conditions, table *LFSI_EMP_A*—Employment and activity by sex and age—Annual data.

Employed persons by professional status in fourth quarter of 2016 ('000 persons aged 15 to 64 years)

	Employees	Self-employed	Family workers	No response	Total
Austria	3,657	448	38	n.a.	4,143
Belgium	3,895	614	32	n.a.	4,541
Bulgaria	2,617	320	17	n.a.	2,954
Croatia	1,363	185	19	n.a.	1,567
Cyprus	312	43	3	n.a.	359
Czech Republic	4,180	811	25	n.a.†	5,016
Denmark	2,521	210	16	n.a.	2,748
Estonia	554	58	n.a.*	n.a.	612
Finland	2,076	296	8	n.a.	2,380
France	23,255	2,890	96	n.a.*	26,243
Germany	36,401	3,742	112	n.a.	40,256
Greece	2,409	1,064	137	n.a.	3,610
Hungary	3,862	432	12	3.4*	4,309
Ireland	1,656	285	13	n.a.	1,953
Italy	17,183	4,774	284	n.a.	22,241
Latvia	753	102	7	n.a.*	862
Lithuania	1,160	147	11	n.a.	1,318
Luxembourg	233	23	2	0.6*	259
Malta	163	25	n.a.†	n.a.	188
Netherlands	6,910	1,278	36	n.a.	8,223
Poland	12,681	2,809	412	n.a.	15,902
Portugal	3,740	609	23	n.a.	4,371
Romania	6,182	1,344	641	n.a.	8,166
Slovakia	2,093	376	3*	n.a.	2,472
Slovenia	782	104	17	n.a.	903
Spain	15,161	2,930	85	6.2	18,183
Sweden	4,319	410	7	n.a.†	4,736
United Kingdom	25,996	4,296	70	61.1	30,424
Total (EU-28)	186,114	30,624	2,126	72.9	218,937

* Unreliable or uncertain figure. † Confidential.
© European Union. Source: Eurostat, 2017, Population and social conditions, table *LFSQ_EGAPS*—Employment by sex, age and professional status.

Employment by branch of economic activity: European Union (EU-28) ('000 persons aged 15 years and over)

	2014	2015	2016
Agriculture, forestry and fishing	10,264	9,934	9,557
Mining and quarrying	840	817	767
Manufacturing	33,676	33,959	34,606
Electricity, gas, steam and air conditioning supply	1,593	1,563	1,566
Water supply; sewerage, waste management and remediation activities	1,662	1,706	1,706
Construction	14,830	14,857	15,009
Wholesale and retail trade; repair of motor vehicles and motorcycles	30,594	30,894	31,415
Transportation and storage	11,152	11,391	11,737
Accommodation and food service activities	9,938	10,337	10,743
Information and communication	6,391	6,615	6,759
Financial and insurance activities	6,443	6,484	6,561
Real estate activities	1,826	1,839	1,834
Professional, scientific and technical activities	11,857	12,099	12,517
Administrative and support service activities	9,016	9,268	9,451
Public administration and defence; compulsory social security	15,097	15,198	15,370
Education	16,533	16,814	17,008
Human health and social work activities	23,618	23,953	24,360
Arts, entertainment and recreation	3,704	3,865	3,920
Other service activities	5,347	5,385	5,491
Activities of households as employers; undifferentiated goods- and services-producing activities of households for own use	2,479	2,335	2,330
Activities of extraterritorial organizations and bodies	195	180	192
Unknown	1,280	1,337	1,379
Total	218,333	220,830	224,276

© European Union. Source: Eurostat, 2017, Population and social conditions, table *LFSA_EGAN2*—Employment by sex, age and economic activity (NACE Rev. 2).

Employment by branch of economic activity: Austria and Belgium ('000 persons aged 15 years and over)

	Austria			Belgium		
	2014	2015	2016	2014	2015	2016
Agriculture, forestry and fishing	199	188	184	55	54	57
Mining and quarrying	6	7	8	5	4*	5*
Manufacturing	643	663	673	582	589	571
Electricity, gas, steam and air conditioning supply	31	30	29	25	23	26
Water supply; sewerage, waste management and remediation activities	21	21	18	36	37	39
Construction	357	348	350	325	323	335
Wholesale and retail trade; repair of motor vehicles and motorcycles	602	599	608	609	617	607
Transportation and storage	202	206	208	247	249	252
Accommodation and food service activities	235	239	258	155	156	152
Information and communication	121	117	132	144	142	140
Financial and insurance activities	137	134	133	153	149	138
Real estate activities	36	39	42	30	29	32
Professional, scientific and technical activities	236	234	236	233	234	238
Administrative and support service activities	139	135	137	265	260	264
Public administration and defence; compulsory social security	273	280	272	380	380	395
Education	281	284	289	432	422	430
Human health and social work activities	405	421	435	653	668	682
Arts, entertainment and recreation	71	82	74	65	65	73
Other service activities	104	106	119	99	105	101
Activities of households as employers; undifferentiated goods- and services-producing activities of households for own use	9	9	10	10	4*	4*
Activities of extraterritorial organizations and bodies	6	8	5*	42	43	45
Unknown	n.a.	n.a.	n.a.	n.a.	n.a.	n.a.
Total	4,113	4,148	4,220	4,544	4,552	4,587

* Unreliable or uncertain figure.
© European Union. Source: Eurostat, 2017, Population and social conditions, table *LFSA_EGAN2*—Employment by sex, age and economic activity (NACE Rev. 2).

Employment by branch of economic activity: Bulgaria and Croatia ('000 persons aged 15 years and over)

	Bulgaria			Croatia		
	2014	2015	2016	2014	2015	2016
Agriculture, forestry and fishing	209	208	204	149	146	121
Mining and quarrying	26	26	26	8*	8*	5*
Manufacturing	585	598	589	269	264	271
Electricity, gas, steam and air conditioning supply	37	39	40	16	14	13
Water supply; sewerage, waste management and remediation activities	34	30	29	25	28	27
Construction	215	214	215	104	109	112
Wholesale and retail trade; repair of motor vehicles and motorcycles	519	520	516	215	224	220
Transportation and storage	178	185	196	115	104	99
Accommodation and food service activities	155	158	158	96	102	109
Information and communication	73	88	88	42	42	49
Financial and insurance activities	61	62	59	37	38	38
Real estate activities	11	12	10	6*	7*	7*
Professional, scientific and technical activities	94	103	112	57	65	70
Administrative and support service activities	112	111	109	35	38	48
Public administration and defence; compulsory social security	223	224	220	110	110	104
Education	189	186	173	118	118	118
Human health and social work activities	163	163	161	106	104	107
Arts, entertainment and recreation	42	43	48	24	24	25
Other service activities	49	56	56	30	36	43
Activities of households as employers; undifferentiated goods- and services-producing activities of households for own use*	6	6	7	1	2	2
Activities of extraterritorial organizations and bodies*	n.a.	n.a.	n.a.	1	n.a.	n.a.
Unknown	n.a.	n.a.	n.a.	3*	3*	3*
Total	2,981	3,032	3,017	1,566	1,585	1,590

* Unreliable or uncertain figure(s).
© European Union. Source: Eurostat, 2017, Population and social conditions, table *LFSA_EGAN2*—Employment by sex, age and economic activity (NACE Rev. 2).

Employment by branch of economic activity: Cyprus and the Czech Republic ('000 persons aged 15 years and over)

	Cyprus			Czech Republic		
	2014	2015	2016	2014	2015	2016
Agriculture, forestry and fishing	16	14	13	137	148	149
Mining and quarrying	n.a.*	1*	1*	36	38	39
Manufacturing	30	28	26	1,330	1,377	1,429
Electricity, gas, steam and air conditioning supply	2	2	2	57	49	53
Water supply; sewerage, waste management and remediation activities	3	2	3	55	57	50
Construction	25	25	30	414	396	386
Wholesale and retail trade; repair of motor vehicles and motorcycles	64	67	66	590	616	606
Transportation and storage	14	14	16	296	298	314
Accommodation and food service activities	28	29	33	195	197	183
Information and communication	10	9	10	149	142	148
Financial and insurance activities	21	17	20	122	118	117
Real estate activities	2*	2	3	46	45	39
Professional, scientific and technical activities	26	26	25	222	238	252
Administrative and support service activities	9	10	10	130	129	129
Public administration and defence; compulsory social security	27	29	30	319	316	330
Education	33	29	28	326	323	339
Human health and social work activities	18	18	20	354	352	360
Arts, entertainment and recreation	5	6	7	81	82	93
Other service activities	10	10	11	88	90	87
Activities of households as employers; undifferentiated goods- and services-producing activities of households for own use	20	18	12	27	32	36
Activities of extraterritorial organizations and bodies*	1	1	1	1	1	1
Unknown	n.a.	n.a.	n.a.	n.a.*	n.a.*	1*
Total	363	358	367	4,974	5,042	5,139

* Unreliable or uncertain figure(s).
© European Union. Source: Eurostat, 2017, Population and social conditions, table *LFSA_EGAN2*—Employment by sex, age and economic activity (NACE Rev. 2).

Employment by branch of economic activity: Denmark and Estonia ('000 persons aged 15 years and over)

	Denmark			Estonia		
	2014	2015	2016	2014	2015	2016
Agriculture, forestry and fishing	67	69	71	24	25	25
Mining and quarrying	6	6	5	4	3	3
Manufacturing	322	329	332	114	121	121
Electricity, gas, steam and air conditioning supply	15	14	15	8	8	6
Water supply; sewerage, waste management and remediation activities	16	16	15	3	3	3
Construction	163	165	157	59	62	58
Wholesale and retail trade; repair of motor vehicles and motorcycles	378	398	426	81	84	84
Transportation and storage	132	126	128	51	47	51
Accommodation and food service activities	105	119	121	26	26	27
Information and communication	110	114	120	22	26	28
Financial and insurance activities	78	74	77	8	10	11
Real estate activities	27	32	34	12	10	12
Professional, scientific and technical activities	142	148	156	27	26	25
Administrative and support service activities	97	105	107	19	19	21
Public administration and defence; compulsory social security	150	145	152	45	42	40
Education	257	262	254	55	61	58
Human health and social work activities	505	479	491	39	39	39
Arts, entertainment and recreation	66	69	72	17	14	18
Other service activities	69	71	75	11	15	14
Activities of households as employers; undifferentiated goods- and services-producing activities of households for own use	3*	3*	n.a.*	n.a.	n.a.	n.a.
Activities of extraterritorial organizations and bodies*	n.a.	n.a.	n.a.	n.a.	n.a.	n.a.
Unknown	7	9	28	n.a.*	1*	2*
Total	2,714	2,752	2,840	625	641	645

* Unreliable or uncertain figure(s).
© European Union. Source: Eurostat, 2017, Population and social conditions, table *LFSA_EGAN2*—Employment by sex, age and economic activity (NACE Rev. 2).

Employment by branch of economic activity: Finland and France ('000 persons aged 15 years and over)

	Finland			France		
	2014	2015	2016	2014	2015	2016
Agriculture, forestry and fishing	104	103	94	744	716	754
Mining and quarrying	6	7	6	29	28	28
Manufacturing	332	328	327	3,211	3,225	3,231
Electricity, gas, steam and air conditioning supply	14	13	17	200	176	175
Water supply; sewerage, waste management and remediation activities	13	11	12	188	192	192
Construction	169	168	178	1,748	1,697	1,699
Wholesale and retail trade; repair of motor vehicles and motorcycles	291	284	290	3,396	3,371	3,428
Transportation and storage	140	137	141	1,430	1,475	1,463
Accommodation and food service activities	86	87	85	934	995	1,022
Information and communication	101	106	101	720	745	740
Financial and insurance activities	51	49	51	863	879	865
Real estate activities	23	24	24	424	399	359
Professional, scientific and technical activities	169	171	163	1,474	1,497	1,526
Administrative and support service activities	101	107	109	1,017	999	1,042
Public administration and defence; compulsory social security	106	106	111	2,446	2,430	2,431
Education	180	179	173	1,967	1,996	1,995
Human health and social work activities	403	405	409	3,835	3,880	3,868
Arts, entertainment and recreation	64	61	63	424	441	446
Other service activities	76	74	75	687	642	656
Activities of households as employers; undifferentiated goods- and services-producing activities of households for own use	10	9	10	368	298	300
Activities of extraterritorial organizations and bodies	n.a.*	n.a.*	n.a.*	22	17	19
Unknown	11	9	8	269	327	344
Total	2,447	2,437	2,448	26,396	26,424	26,583

* Unreliable or uncertain figure(s).
© European Union. Source: Eurostat, 2017, Population and social conditions, table *LFSA_EGAN2*—Employment by sex, age and economic activity (NACE Rev. 2).

Employment by branch of economic activity: Germany and Greece ('000 persons aged 15 years and over)

	Germany			Greece		
	2014	2015	2016	2014	2015	2016
Agriculture, forestry and fishing	570	561	541	480	466	455
Mining and quarrying	88	82	85	11	10	14
Manufacturing	7,808	7,759	7,923	316	335	348
Electricity, gas, steam and air conditioning supply	336	341	324	28	26	28
Water supply; sewerage, waste management and remediation activities	221	227	230	23	23	23
Construction	2,732	2,724	2,762	152	145	147
Wholesale and retail trade; repair of motor vehicles and motorcycles	5,613	5,671	5,838	626	661	658
Transportation and storage	1,925	1,958	2,023	172	168	185
Accommodation and food service activities	1,528	1,549	1,569	297	326	341
Information and communication	1,164	1,199	1,262	76	73	81
Financial and insurance activities	1,274	1,248	1,305	93	88	94
Real estate activities	196	214	217	4	6	6
Professional, scientific and technical activities	2,167	2,223	2,353	196	209	202
Administrative and support service activities	1,954	2,022	2,066	84	86	88
Public administration and defence; compulsory social security	2,797	2,758	2,895	311	313	331
Education	2,595	2,638	2,698	290	294	295
Human health and social work activities	4,970	5,106	5,302	209	214	218
Arts, entertainment and recreation	537	561	559	47	45	50
Other service activities	1,148	1,135	1,172	72	74	67
Activities of households as employers; undifferentiated goods- and services-producing activities of households for own use	231	217	227	49	47	40
Activities of extraterritorial organizations and bodies	21	18	19	1*	2*	3*
Unknown	n.a.	n.a.	n.a.	n.a.	n.a.	n.a.
Total	39,871	40,211	41,367	3,536	3,611	3,674

* Unreliable or uncertain figure.
© European Union. Source: Eurostat, 2017, Population and social conditions, table *LFSA_EGAN2*—Employment by sex, age and economic activity (NACE Rev. 2).

STATISTICAL SURVEY   *Labour*

Employment by branch of economic activity: Hungary and Ireland ('000 persons aged 15 years and over)

	Hungary			Ireland		
	2014	2015	2016	2014	2015	2016
Agriculture, forestry and fishing	191	206	219	109	110	113
Mining and quarrying	11	10	9	6	7	5
Manufacturing	886	902	944	212	221	232
Electricity, gas, steam and air conditioning supply	36	34	33	10	10	11
Water supply; sewerage, waste management and remediation activities	56	58	60	11	11	9
Construction	258	272	278	109	126	136
Wholesale and retail trade; repair of motor vehicles and motorcycles	551	541	543	272	274	277
Transportation and storage	259	267	276	89	92	95
Accommodation and food service activities	172	188	198	137	138	147
Information and communication	104	103	118	81	83	87
Financial and insurance activities	95	88	95	90	89	90
Real estate activities	20	18	21	10	12	11
Professional, scientific and technical activities	155	159	153	116	117	119
Administrative and support service activities	148	160	167	64	65	68
Public administration and defence; compulsory social security	384	423	445	97	100	101
Education	324	318	326	150	151	152
Human health and social work activities	275	275	284	247	251	253
Arts, entertainment and recreation	63	81	81	42	44	49
Other service activities	93	96	90	45	48	49
Activities of households as employers; undifferentiated goods- and services-producing activities of households for own use	3*	4*	5	6	9	7
Activities of extraterritorial organizations and bodies	n.a.*	n.a.*	n.a.*	6	3*	n.a.*
Unknown	16	7	3*	3*	6	7
Total	**4,101**	**4,211**	**4,352**	**1,914**	**1,964**	**2,020**

* Unreliable or uncertain figure.
© European Union. Source: Eurostat, 2017, Population and social conditions, table *LFSA_EGAN2*—Employment by sex, age and economic activity (NACE Rev. 2).

Employment by branch of economic activity: Italy and Latvia ('000 persons aged 15 years and over)

	Italy			Latvia		
	2014	2015	2016	2014	2015	2016
Agriculture, forestry and fishing	812	843	884	66	71	69
Mining and quarrying	39	34	33	4	4	3
Manufacturing	4,134	4,122	4,149	119	116	124
Electricity, gas, steam and air conditioning supply	108	114	126	10	13	14
Water supply; sewerage, waste management and remediation activities	228	238	235	5	7	8
Construction	1,484	1,468	1,404	73	72	66
Wholesale and retail trade; repair of motor vehicles and motorcycles	3,227	3,194	3,242	132	129	124
Transportation and storage	1,039	1,033	1,085	85	85	83
Accommodation and food service activities	1,269	1,334	1,395	29	30	31
Information and communication	551	562	562	26	26	24
Financial and insurance activities	612	644	649	18	21	24
Real estate activities	126	132	141	21	21	21
Professional, scientific and technical activities	1,404	1,416	1,459	36	36	34
Administrative and support service activities	907	968	991	24	25	24
Public administration and defence; compulsory social security	1,280	1,293	1,262	59	59	62
Education	1,513	1,509	1,543	85	83	82
Human health and social work activities	1,804	1,796	1,831	52	56	54
Arts, entertainment and recreation	298	303	324	22	22	25
Other service activities	652	659	667	15	18	20
Activities of households as employers; undifferentiated goods- and services-producing activities of households for own use	776	787	763	2*	n.a.*	3*
Activities of extraterritorial organizations and bodies	16	17	15	n.a.*	n.a.*	n.a.*
Unknown	n.a.	n.a.	n.a.	n.a.*	n.a.*	n.a.*
Total	**22,279**	**22,465**	**22,758**	**885**	**896**	**893**

* Unreliable or uncertain figure.
© European Union. Source: Eurostat, 2017, Population and social conditions, table *LFSA_EGAN2*—Employment by sex, age and economic activity (NACE Rev. 2).

Employment by branch of economic activity: Lithuania and Luxembourg ('000 persons aged 15 years and over)

	Lithuania			Luxembourg		
	2014	2015	2016	2014	2015	2016
Agriculture, forestry and fishing	121	121	109	3	3	2
Mining and quarrying	n.a.	n.a.	n.a.	n.a.	n.a.	n.a.
Manufacturing	199	203	210	13	12	11
Electricity, gas, steam and air conditioning supply	10	11	12	1	2	1
Water supply; sewerage, waste management and remediation activities	14	14	14	1*	1	1
Construction	99	105	104	11	15	15
Wholesale and retail trade; repair of motor vehicles and motorcycles	233	225	234	21	21	19
Transportation and storage	101	100	97	10	10	11
Accommodation and food service activities	34	34	36	8	10	9
Information and communication	24	27	29	11	9	8
Financial and insurance activities	18	19	20	31	26	28
Real estate activities	15	15	14	1	2	2
Professional, scientific and technical activities	50	52	56	20	19	19
Administrative and support service activities	46	48	54	6	8	8
Public administration and defence; compulsory social security	80	82	83	28	27	25
Education	128	132	137	21	20	20
Human health and social work activities	85	90	92	27	27	28
Arts, entertainment and recreation	30	28	30	3	2	3
Other service activities	27	26	29	4	5	5
Activities of households as employers; undifferentiated goods- and services-producing activities of households for own use	n.a.*	n.a.*	n.a.*	4	4	3
Activities of extraterritorial organizations and bodies	n.a.*	n.a.*	n.a.*	17	14	15
Unknown	n.a.	n.a.	n.a.	5	23	29
Total	**1,319**	**1,335**	**1,361**	**246**	**258**	**261**

*Unreliable or uncertain figure(s).
© European Union. Source: Eurostat, 2017, Population and social conditions, table *LFSA_EGAN2*—Employment by sex, age and economic activity (NACE Rev. 2).

Employment by branch of economic activity: Malta and the Netherlands ('000 persons aged 15 years and over)

	Malta			Netherlands		
	2014	2015	2016	2014	2015	2016
Agriculture, forestry and fishing	2	3	3	174	178	175
Mining and quarrying	0*	n.a.*	n.a.*	10	13	11
Manufacturing	24	23	24	765	786	802
Electricity, gas, steam and air conditioning supply	1*	n.a.*	n.a.*	27	28	33
Water supply; sewerage, waste management and remediation activities	2	2	2	33	31	33
Construction	11	11	11	398	403	398
Wholesale and retail trade; repair of motor vehicles and motorcycles	29	30	30	1,235	1,233	1,242
Transportation and storage	10	10	11	358	356	374
Accommodation and food service activities	14	13	14	325	352	357
Information and communication	7	7	7	245	256	272
Financial and insurance activities	8	9	9	280	268	264
Real estate activities	1	1	1	64	67	66
Professional, scientific and technical activities	8	9	9	581	585	578
Administrative and support service activities	7	8	9	410	429	445
Public administration and defence; compulsory social security	15	16	15	490	485	483
Education	17	18	19	544	557	561
Human health and social work activities	16	17	18	1,299	1,291	1,293
Arts, entertainment and recreation	5	5	5	160	169	169
Other service activities	5	4	4	186	181	181
Activities of households as employers; undifferentiated goods- and services-producing activities of households for own use	n.a.*	n.a.*	0*	10	4	4
Activities of extraterritorial organizations and bodies*	1	1	1	n.a.	2	2
Unknown	n.a.	n.a.	n.a.	643	646	686
Total	**182**	**186**	**191**	**8,236**	**8,319**	**8,427**

* Unreliable or uncertain figure(s).
© European Union. Source: Eurostat, 2017, Population and social conditions, table *LFSA_EGAN2*—Employment by sex, age and economic activity (NACE Rev. 2).

Employment by branch of economic activity: Poland and Portugal ('000 persons aged 15 years and over)

	Poland			Portugal		
	2014	2015	2016	2014	2015	2016
Agriculture, forestry and fishing	1,820	1,849	1,708	389	343	318
Mining and quarrying	268	230	229	12	12	12
Manufacturing	3,036	3,107	3,279	739	769	777
Electricity, gas, steam and air conditioning supply	176	175	173	15	19	18
Water supply; sewerage, waste management and remediation activities	170	178	171	31	29	31
Construction	1,187	1,207	1,223	276	278	290
Wholesale and retail trade; repair of motor vehicles and motorcycles	2,296	2,329	2,353	670	702	702
Transportation and storage	927	944	970	175	172	189
Accommodation and food service activities	334	340	376	276	259	279
Information and communication	356	369	360	106	104	111
Financial and insurance activities	376	395	384	100	108	112
Real estate activities	158	172	161	30	28	33
Professional, scientific and technical activities	555	561	584	181	193	203
Administrative and support service activities	456	440	429	161	154	153
Public administration and defence; compulsory social security	1,063	1,075	1,085	316	306	288
Education	1,249	1,233	1,193	357	380	381
Human health and social work activities	935	947	970	381	404	424
Arts, entertainment and recreation	208	213	216	57	67	61
Other service activities	239	245	246	107	103	108
Activities of households as employers; undifferentiated goods- and services-producing activities of households for own use	26	25	27	117	117	114
Activities of extraterritorial organizations and bodies	n.a.*	n.a.*	n.a.*	n.a.†	n.a.†	n.a.†
Unknown	27	50	62	n.a.	n.a.	n.a.
Total	15,862	16,084	16,197	4,500	4,549	4,605

* Confidential. † Unreliable or uncertain figure.

© European Union. Source: Eurostat, 2017, Population and social conditions, table *LFSA_EGAN2*—Employment by sex, age and economic activity (NACE Rev. 2).

Employment by branch of economic activity: Romania and Slovakia ('000 persons aged 15 years and over)

	Romania			Slovakia		
	2014	2015	2016	2014	2015	2016
Agriculture, forestry and fishing	2,442	2,184	1,952	83	77	72
Mining and quarrying	75	73	69	10	12	11
Manufacturing	1,595	1,551	1,598	550	598	610
Electricity, gas, steam and air conditioning supply	92	83	82	27	25	30
Water supply; sewerage, waste management and remediation activities	90	86	98	28	26	28
Construction	640	636	678	223	214	230
Wholesale and retail trade; repair of motor vehicles and motorcycles	1,112	1,149	1,177	284	297	311
Transportation and storage	432	475	472	152	161	164
Accommodation and food service activities	181	186	205	119	115	114
Information and communication	148	173	168	57	66	67
Financial and insurance activities	113	105	111	51	39	47
Real estate activities	21	22	18	15	13	16
Professional, scientific and technical activities	193	186	196	76	73	79
Administrative and support service activities	184	204	207	61	65	60
Public administration and defence; compulsory social security	392	442	434	211	217	222
Education	312	355	346	167	175	177
Human health and social work activities	368	388	390	176	181	182
Arts, entertainment and recreation	55	57	61	38	35	34
Other service activities	117	127	129	32	32	37
Activities of households as employers; undifferentiated goods- and services-producing activities of households for own use	53.6	54.3	57.4	3.9	n.a.*	n.a.*
Activities of extraterritorial organizations and bodies	n.a.†	n.a.†	n.a.†	n.a.*	n.a.*	n.a.*
Unknown	n.a.	n.a.	n.a.	n.a.*	n.a.*	n.a.*
Total	8,614	8,535	8,449	2,363	2,424	2,492

* Unreliable or uncertain figure(s). † Confidential.

© European Union. Source: Eurostat, 2017, Population and social conditions, table *LFSA_EGAN2*—Employment by sex, age and economic activity (NACE Rev. 2).

Employment by branch of economic activity: Slovenia and Spain ('000 persons aged 15 years and over)

	Slovenia			Spain		
	2014	2015	2016	2014	2015	2016
Agriculture, forestry and fishing	88	64	46	736	737	775
Mining and quarrying	3*	3*	3*	32	34	31
Manufacturing	206	215	230	2,141	2,225	2,284
Electricity, gas, steam and air conditioning supply	11	10	8	94	92	84
Water supply; sewerage, waste management and remediation activities	9	9	9	113	131	124
Construction	52	53	51	994	1,074	1,074
Wholesale and retail trade; repair of motor vehicles and motorcycles	110	111	117	2,867	2,921	2,969
Transportation and storage	42	45	48	853	871	932
Accommodation and food service activities	40	47	41	1,404	1,505	1,604
Information and communication	31	34	31	516	530	546
Financial and insurance activities	24	23	22	453	454	458
Real estate activities	3*	2*	2*	100	104	114
Professional, scientific and technical activities	45	42	44	851	891	924
Administrative and support service activities	23	20	23	899	928	940
Public administration and defence; compulsory social security	57	55	55	1,309	1,325	1,266
Education	76	81	82	1,152	1,182	1,268
Human health and social work activities	57	60	67	1,417	1,442	1,511
Arts, entertainment and recreation	18	18	16	350	365	377
Other service activities	15	14	13	406	424	435
Activities of households as employers; undifferentiated goods- and services-producing activities of households for own use	n.a.*	n.a.*	n.a.*	657	628	624
Activities of extraterritorial organizations and bodies	n.a.	n.a.	n.a.	3.0*	2.4*	3.5*
Unknown	5	11	7	n.a.	n.a.	n.a.
Total	917	917	915	17,344	17,866	18,342

* Unreliable or uncertain figure.
© European Union. Source: Eurostat, 2017, Population and social conditions, table *LFSA_EGAN2*—Employment by sex, age and economic activity (NACE Rev. 2).

Employment by branch of economic activity: Sweden and the United Kingdom ('000 persons aged 15 years and over)

	Sweden			United Kingdom		
	2014	2015	2016	2014	2015	2016
Agriculture, forestry and fishing	94	98	92	382	352	354
Mining and quarrying	10	9	9	132	154	115
Manufacturing	509	503	501	3,007	2,992	2,991
Electricity, gas, steam and air conditioning supply	25	30	29	182	184	186
Water supply; sewerage, waste management and remediation activities	21	23	21	210	215	221
Construction	317	313	328	2,236	2,234	2,294
Wholesale and retail trade; repair of motor vehicles and motorcycles	556	563	564	4,019	4,065	4,166
Transportation and storage	245	245	243	1,475	1,557	1,611
Accommodation and food service activities	159	167	173	1,598	1,637	1,708
Information and communication	197	203	207	1,201	1,263	1,264
Financial and insurance activities	98	98	98	1,179	1,234	1,245
Real estate activities	75	71	75	351	341	354
Professional, scientific and technical activities	402	413	425	2,143	2,177	2,281
Administrative and support service activities	218	227	232	1,441	1,500	1,511
Public administration and defence; compulsory social security	307	313	324	1,825	1,846	1,907
Education	532	551	562	3,182	3,279	3,310
Human health and social work activities	733	735	745	4,090	4,147	4,126
Arts, entertainment and recreation	121	119	118	794	844	825
Other service activities	124	124	131	838	865	873
Activities of households as employers; undifferentiated goods- and services-producing activities of households for own use	n.a.*	n.a.*	n.a.*	84	55	70
Activities of extraterritorial organizations and bodies	2*	n.a.*	n.a.*	43	39	50
Unknown	27	32	31	260	214	168
Total	4,772	4,837	4,910	30,671	31,193	31,628

* Unreliable or uncertain figure.
© European Union. Source: Eurostat, 2017, Population and social conditions, table *LFSA_EGAN2*—Employment by sex, age and economic activity (NACE Rev. 2).

UNEMPLOYMENT

Unemployed persons aged 15 to 64 years ('000)

	2014	2015	2016		2014	2015	2016
Austria	244	252	270	Latvia	107	97	95
Belgium	423	421	389	Lithuania	158	134	116
Bulgaria	381	303	245	Luxembourg	15	18*	18
Croatia	326	306	240	Malta	11	11	9
Cyprus	69	63	55	Netherlands	649	604	530
Czech Republic	322	267	211	Poland	1,562	1,300	1,059
Denmark	191	180	186*	Portugal	722	640	568
Estonia	49	41	46	Romania	628	623	530
Finland	231	251	236	Slovakia	358	314	266
France	3,019	3,045	2,962	Slovenia	98	90	80
Germany	2,082	1,941	1,763	Spain	5,603	5,050	4,474
Greece	1,268	1,190	1,122	Sweden	407	384	365
Hungary	343	307	234	United Kingdom	1,974	1,726	1,581
Ireland	242	202	172				
Italy	3,230	3,024	3,002	**Total (EU-28)**	24,712	22,785	20,820

* Break in series.
© European Union. Source: Eurostat, 2017, Population and social conditions, table *LFSA_UGAN*—Unemployment by sex, age and citizenship.

Unemployment by sex in 2016 ('000 persons aged 15 to 64 years)

	Males	Females	Total		Males	Females	Total
Austria	153	116	270	Latvia	54	41	95
Belgium	216	173	389	Lithuania	66	50	116
Bulgaria	141	105	245	Luxembourg	9	8	18
Croatia	123	117	240	Malta	5	4	9
Cyprus	27	28	55	Netherlands	262	268	530
Czech Republic	100	110	211	Poland	578	481	1,059
Denmark	91	95	186	Portugal	288	280	568
Estonia	26	20	46	Romania	339	191	530
Finland	125	110	236	Slovakia	132	134	266
France	1,566	1,395	2,962	Slovenia	40	40	80
Germany	1,019	744	1,763	Spain	2,210	2,264	4,474
Greece	521	600	1,122	Sweden	201	164	365
Hungary	127	107	234	United Kingdom	864	717	1,581
Ireland	108	64	172				
Italy	1,611	1,391	3,002	**Total (EU-28)**	11,004	9,817	20,820

© European Union. Source: Eurostat, 2017, Population and social conditions, table *LFSA_UGAN*—Unemployment by sex, age and citizenship.

Unemployment rate (% of active population aged 15 to 64 years)

	2014	2015	2016		2014	2015	2016
Austria	5.7	5.8	6.1	Latvia	11.1	10.1	9.9
Belgium	8.6	8.6	7.9	Lithuania	10.9	9.3	8.1
Bulgaria	11.5	9.2	7.7	Luxembourg	5.9	6.7*	6.3
Croatia	17.5	16.4	13.3	Malta	5.9	5.5	4.8
Cyprus	16.3	15.2	13.2	Netherlands	7.5	6.9	6.1
Czech Republic	6.2	5.1	4.0	Poland	9.1	7.6	6.2
Denmark	6.8	6.3	6.3*	Portugal	14.5	12.9	11.5
Estonia	7.5	6.3	7.0	Romania	7.1	7.0	6.1
Finland	8.8	9.6	9.0	Slovakia	13.2	11.5	9.7
France	10.4	10.4	10.1	Slovenia	9.9	9.1	8.1
Germany	5.1	4.7	4.2	Spain	24.6	22.2	19.7
Greece	26.7	25.1	23.7	Sweden	8.1	7.6	7.1
Hungary	7.8	6.8	5.1	United Kingdom	6.3	5.4	4.9
Ireland	11.5	9.6	8.1				
Italy	12.9	12.1	11.9	**Total (EU-28)**	10.4	9.6	8.7

* Break in series.
© European Union. Source: Eurostat, 2017, Population and social conditions, table *LFSA_URGAN*—Unemployment rates by sex, age and nationality (%).

Unemployment rate by sex in 2016 (% of active population, aged 15 to 64 years)

	Males	Females	Total		Males	Females	Total
Austria	6.6	5.6	6.1	Latvia	11.2	8.6	9.9
Belgium	8.1	7.6	7.9	Lithuania	9.3	6.8	8.1
Bulgaria	8.2	7.0	7.7	Luxembourg	6.0	6.6	6.3
Croatia	12.7	13.9	13.3	Malta	4.5	5.2	4.8
Cyprus	12.8	13.7	13.2	Netherlands	5.6	6.5	6.1
Czech Republic	3.4	4.8	4.0	Poland	6.2	6.3	6.2
Denmark	6.0	6.8	6.3	Portugal	11.5	11.5	11.5
Estonia	7.6	6.3	7.0	Romania	6.8	5.2	6.1
Finland	9.3	8.7	9.0	Slovakia	8.8	10.8	9.7
France	10.4	9.9	10.1	Slovenia	7.6	8.7	8.1
Germany	4.5	3.8	4.2	Spain	18.2	21.5	19.7
Greece	19.9	28.3	23.7	Sweden	7.6	6.7	7.1
Hungary	5.2	5.1	5.1	United Kingdom	5.1	4.8	4.9
Ireland	9.3	6.6	8.1				
Italy	11.1	12.9	11.9	**Total (EU-28)**	8.5	8.9	8.7

© European Union. Source: Eurostat, 2017, Population and social conditions, table *LFSA_URGAN*—Unemployment rates by sex, age and nationality (%).

HEALTH AND WELFARE

HEALTH PERSONNEL

Medical doctors

	2013	2014	2015		2013	2014	2015
Austria	42,302	43,126	44,002	Latvia	6,423	6,412	6,324
Belgium	32,999	33,353	34,020	Lithuania	12,650	12,631	12,605
Bulgaria	28,891	28,801	29,038	Luxembourg	1,525	1,589	1,656*
Croatia	12,906	13,302	13,430	Malta	1,466	1,566	1,636
Cyprus	2,754	2,880*	3,032	Netherlands	n.a.	57,762	58,858
Czech Republic	38,776	n.a.	n.a.	Poland	85,246	87,687	88,437
Denmark	20,519	20,639	n.a.	Portugal	n.a.	n.a.	n.a.
Estonia	4,326	4,364	4,502	Romania	52,828	53,720	54,807
Finland†	17,116	17,511	n.a.	Slovakia	n.a.	n.a.	n.a.
France	203,490	206,159	207,789	Slovenia	5,416	5,712	5,830
Germany	325,407	332,695	338,129	Spain	177,665	176,665	178,600
Greece	n.a.	n.a.	n.a.	Sweden	39,638	40,637	n.a.
Hungary	31,748	32,791	30,486*	United Kingdom	177,663	180,533	181,673*
Ireland†	12,367	12,982	13,446				
Italy	234,918	235,889	233,102	**Total (EU-28)**	n.a.	n.a.	n.a.

* Break in series. † Estimates.

© European Union. Source: Eurostat, 2017, Population and social conditions, table *HLTH_RS_PRS1*—Health personnel (excluding nursing and caring professionals).

Medical doctors per 100,000 inhabitants

	2013	2014	2015		2013	2014	2015
Austria	499	505	510	Latvia	319	322	320
Belgium	295	298	302	Lithuania	428	431	434
Bulgaria	398	399	405	Luxembourg	281	286	291*
Croatia	303	314	319	Malta	346	366	379
Cyprus	320	338*	358	Netherlands	n.a.	343	347
Czech Republic	369	n.a.	n.a.	Poland	224	231	233
Denmark	365	366	n.a.	Portugal	n.a.	n.a.	n.a.
Estonia	328	332	342	Romania	264	270	277
Finland†	315	321	n.a.	Slovakia	n.a.	n.a.	n.a.
France	310	311	312	Slovenia	263	277	283
Germany	400	411	414	Spain	381	380	385
Greece	n.a.	n.a.	n.a.	Sweden	413	419	n.a.
Hungary	321	332	310*	United Kingdom	277	279	279*
Ireland†	269	281	288				
Italy	390	388	384	**Total (EU-28)**	n.a.	n.a.	n.a.

* Break in series. † Estimates.

© European Union. Source: Eurostat, 2017, Population and social conditions, table *HLTH_RS_PRS1*—Health personnel (excluding nursing and caring professionals).

Dentists

	2013	2014	2015		2013	2014	2015
Austria	4,853	4,893	4,906	Latvia	1,459	1,400	1,419
Belgium	7,965	8,108	8,291	Lithuania	2,678	2,669	2,644
Bulgaria	7,293	7,054	7,547	Luxembourg	472	476*	506
Croatia	3,225	3,327	3,347	Malta	197	201	206
Cyprus	829	839*	874	Netherlands	n.a.	8,596*	8,561
Czech Republic	7,426	7,906*†	8,461	Poland	12,322	13,088	12,603
Denmark	4,295	4,244	n.a.	Portugal	n.a.	n.a.	n.a.
Estonia	1,182	1,215	1,239	Romania	14,248	14,846	15,389
Finland	3,885	3,925	n.a.	Slovakia	n.a.	n.a.	n.a.
France	42,084	42,281	42,602	Slovenia	1,337	1,365	1,392
Germany	68,268	69,135	69,863	Spain	n.a.	n.a.	n.a.
Greece	n.a.	n.a.	n.a.	Sweden	7,731	7,777	n.a.
Hungary	5,963	6,203	5,936*	United Kingdom	33,999	34,638	34,621*
Ireland	n.a.	n.a.	n.a.				
Italy†	47,038	47,610	47,604	**Total (EU-28)**	n.a.	n.a.	n.a.

* Break in series. † Estimate(s).

© European Union. Source: Eurostat, 2017, Population and social conditions, table *HLTH_RS_PRS1*—Health personnel (excluding nursing and caring professionals).

Dentists per 100,000 inhabitants

	2013	2014	2015		2013	2014	2015
Austria	57	57	57	Latvia	72	70	72
Belgium	71	72	74	Lithuania	91	91	91
Bulgaria	100	98	105	Luxembourg	87	86*	89
Croatia	76	79	80	Malta	47	47	48
Cyprus	96	98*	103	Netherlands	n.a.	51*	51
Czech Republic	71	75*†	80	Poland	32	34	33
Denmark	76	75	n.a.	Portugal	n.a.	n.a.	n.a.
Estonia	90	92	94	Romania	71	75	78
Finland	71	72	n.a.	Slovakia	n.a.	n.a.	n.a.
France	64	64	64	Slovenia	65	66	67
Germany	84	85	86	Spain	n.a.	n.a.	n.a.
Greece	n.a.	n.a.	n.a.	Sweden	81	80	n.a.
Hungary	60	63	60*	United Kingdom	53	54	53*
Ireland	n.a.	n.a.	n.a.				
Italy†	78	78	78	**Total (EU-28)**	n.a.	n.a.	n.a.

* Break in series. † Estimate(s).
© European Union. Source: Eurostat, 2017, Population and social conditions, table *HLTH_RS_PRS1*—Health personnel (excluding nursing and caring professionals).

HEALTH FACILITIES

Hospital beds

	2013	2014	2015		2013	2014	2015
Austria	64,825	64,815	65,138	Latvia	11,673	11,279	11,261
Belgium	69,940	69,924	69,730	Lithuania	21,538	21,176	20,236
Bulgaria	49,522	51,505	51,933	Luxembourg	2,746	2,746	2,746
Croatia	24,933	25,036	23,409	Malta	2,034	1,994	2,041
Cyprus	2,938	2,912	2,895	Netherlands	70,310	n.a.	n.a.
Czech Republic	67,888	67,937*	68,392	Poland	251,383	251,904	252,029
Denmark	17,241	15,174*†	14,380	Portugal	35,478	34,522	35,223†
Estonia	6,597	6,584	6,524	Romania	133,354	133,619	134,572
Finland	26,499	24,741	23,854	Slovakia	31,416	31,348	31,172
France	413,206	410,921	408,245	Slovenia	9,377	9,356	9,315
Germany	667,560	666,337	664,364	Spain	138,153	137,877	138,368
Greece	46,510	46,160	45,945	Sweden	24,905	24,612	23,885
Hungary	69,621	68,910	68,843	United Kingdom	176,791	176,324	169,995
Ireland	11,837	11,989	12,169				
Italy	199,474	195,189	194,065	**Total (EU-28)**	2,647,749	2,635,201	2,621,039

Note: Figures refer to available beds in hospitals.
* Break in series. † Estimate.
© European Union. Source: Eurostat, 2017, Population and social conditions, table *HLTH_RS_BDS*—Hospital beds by type of care.

Hospital beds per 100,000 inhabitants

	2013	2014	2015		2013	2014	2015
Austria	764.5	758.8	754.5	Latvia	580.0	565.7	569.5
Belgium	625.4	623.8	618.5	Lithuania	728.2	722.2	696.6
Bulgaria	681.6	713.0	723.5	Luxembourg	505.4	493.6	482.1
Croatia	586.0	591.0	556.3	Malta	480.4	466.6	472.6
Cyprus	340.9	341.6	341.5	Netherlands	418.4	n.a.	n.a.
Czech Republic	645.7	645.5*	648.5	Poland	660.8	662.7	663.5
Denmark	307.1	268.9*	253.0	Portugal	339.3	331.9	340.1†
Estonia	500.5	500.6	496.0	Romania	667.3	671.2	679.1
Finland	487.2	453.0	435.3	Slovakia	580.3	578.5	574.7
France	628.5	620.6	612.8	Slovenia	455.2	453.7	451.4
Germany	820.2	822.8	813.3	Spain	296.3	296.6	297.9
Greece	424.2	423.8	424.6	Sweden	259.4	253.8	243.7
Hungary	703.7	698.4	699.4	United Kingdom	275.7	272.9	261.0
Ireland	257.4	259.7	260.2				
Italy	331.2	321.1	319.6	**Total (EU-28)**	522.4	519.0	514.5

Note: Figures refer to available beds in hospitals.
* Estimate. † Break in series.
© European Union. Source: Eurostat, 2017, Population and social conditions, table *HLTH_RS_BDS*—Hospital beds by type of care.

FINANCING OF SOCIAL PROTECTION

Total expenditure of social protection schemes (million euros)

	2012	2013	2014		2012	2013	2014
Austria	92,967.7	96,003.9	99,244.6	Latvia	3,165.7	3,341.7	3,418.4
Belgium	114,643.1	117,996.6	121,264.2	Lithuania	5,411.6	5,344.9	5,550.4
Bulgaria	6,956.9	7,389.6	7,921.0	Luxembourg	10,014.8	10,739.2	11,197.5
Croatia	9,283.8	9,548.2	9,286.1	Malta	1,370.8	1,443.2	1,535.4
Cyprus	4,343.2	4,381.6	4,036.9	Netherlands	199,724.0	203,593.0	205,176.0
Czech Republic	32,996.2	31,828.6	30,805.4	Poland	73,478.3	76,519.1	78,599.4
Denmark	81,442.0	84,182.8	87,181.8	Portugal	44,424.7	47,017.6	46,492.1
Estonia	2,693.5	2,810.0	2,988.6	Romania	20,512.7	21,455.6	22,185.2
Finland	60,156.3	63,317.1	65,552.7	Slovakia	13,090.4	13,556.3	14,046.2*
France	699,500.6	717,008.3	734,126.6	Slovenia	8,966.7	8,959.0	8,991.2*
Germany	790,976.7	819,745.9	849,792.0*	Spain*	264,874.7	264,611.6	263,135.4
Greece*	53,863.9	48,208.9	46,203.2	Sweden	124,041.0	130,873.6	127,692.2
Hungary	21,182.3	21,154.0	20,926.9	United Kingdom	603,948.7	582,081.5	619,930.4*
Ireland	40,742.4	40,122.6	39,815.2				
Italy	472,505.0	478,719.0*	485,522.0*	**Total (EU-28)***	3,857,295.8	3,911,950.0	4,012,635.1

* Provisional.

© European Union. Source: Eurostat, 2017, Population and social conditions, table *SPR_EXP_SUM*—Social protection expenditure—Main results.

Expenditure by function in 2014 (million euros)

	Social protection benefits	Administration costs	Other expenditure		Social protection benefits	Administration costs	Other expenditure
Austria	96,627.3	1,912.7	704.6	Latvia	3,369.9	47.6*	0.9
Belgium	116,266.2	3,678.0	1,320.0	Lithuania	5,268.0	118.9	163.5
Bulgaria	7,663.5	166.4*	91.1	Luxembourg	11,025.0	158.2	14.3
Croatia	9,113.1	161.7	11.3	Malta	1,519.4	16.0*	0.0
Cyprus	3,894.2	36.7	106.0	Netherlands	191,827.0	11,284.0	2,065.0
Czech Republic	29,910.3	895.2*	0.0	Poland	76,821.0	1,735.1	43.3
Denmark	83,900.0	3,281.8	0.0	Portugal	44,103.6	683.6	1,704.9
Estonia	2,952.4	36.2	0.0	Romania	21,712.0	456.9	16.3
Finland	63,915.9	1,636.8	0.0	Slovakia†	13,660.7	366.5	19.0
France	689,830.2	29,693.5	14,602.9	Slovenia†	8,829.6	142.5	19.1
Germany†	812,680.1	32,684.2	4,427.8	Spain†	258,355.4	4,755.5	24.5
Greece†	45,370.7	730.3	102.2	Sweden	125,228.9	2,463.3	0.0
Hungary	20,656.1	270.7	0.0	United Kingdom†	613,942.0	5,988.4	0.0
Ireland	37,350.4	2,411.9	52.8				
Italy†	467,147.0	10,108.0	8,267.0	**Total (EU-28)†**	3,862,959.0	115,919.6	33,756.5

* Estimate. † Provisional.

© European Union. Source: Eurostat, 2017, Population and social conditions, table *SPR_EXP_SUM*—Social protection expenditure—Main results.

Health and Welfare STATISTICAL SURVEY

Classification of social benefits in 2014 (million euros)

	Sickness/ Health care	Disability	Old age	Survivors	Family/ Children	Unemployment	Housing	Other social exclusion
Austria	24,410.7	6,736.7	43,020.7	5,990.7	9,149.1	5,391.0	404.6	1,524.0
Belgium	33,604.6	9,626.7	39,083.4	7,818.9	8,756.2	13,534.5	1,001.3	2,840.7
Bulgaria	2,115.4	596.1	3,372.1	420.1	811.8	222.0	5.6	120.6
Croatia	3,057.6	1,113.9	3,089.1	894.3	656.5	204.9	10.6	86.2
Cyprus	781.9	125.8	1,907.0	253.4	243.5	334.4	47.6	200.7
Czech Republic	9,381.1	1,973.5	13,091.5	1,035.8	2,593.7	900.9	443.2	490.7
Denmark	16,764.6	10,794.8	31,277.5	5,864.3	9,415.1	4,358.9	1,855.8	3,568.9
Estonia	865.7	349.3	1,294.1	12.3	321.4	83.3	6.4	19.9
Finland	15,349.8	6,971.3	24,833.4	1,803.1	6,621.2	5,252.1	1,240.2	1,844.8
France	196,100.3	45,347.2	275,548.3	37,819.5	54,095.8	42,794.3	17,982.9	20,142.0
Germany*	282,562.6	65,498.6	263,594.8	54,993.8	91,651.3	31,757.7	16,789.2	5,832.2
Greece*	8,898.0	2,937.4	24,951.8	4,553.1	1,981.6	1,938.9	1.6	108.4
Hungary	5,102.5	1,517.2	9,534.4	1,218.2	2,464.8	390.4	303.3	125.4
Ireland*	12,906.5	2,251.7	10,320.5	811.5	4,895.5	5,140.7	714.1	310.0
Italy*	109,758.0	27,618.0	230,130.0	43,513.0	25,359.0	27,069.0	517.0	3,183.0
Latvia	815.4	308.1	1,706.9	46.1	306.4	134.4	22.8	29.9
Lithuania	1,498.9	494.5	2,439.8	157.2	396.4	122.6	1.9	156.8
Luxembourg	2,789.8	1,250.9	3,262.3	894.6	1,719.0	716.5	153.0	239.0
Malta	499.0	57.3	654.2	131.3	100.8	43.6	10.8	22.4
Netherlands	66,457.0	14,740.0	73,707.0	7,896.0	6,021.0	10,662.0	2,834.0	9,510.0
Poland	16,352.5	6,359.2	38,147.2	7,863.4	6,304.0	1,009.2	232.1	553.4
Portugal	10,522.8	3,253.6	22,068.2	3,301.5	2,025.2	2,542.0	5.1	385.3
Romania	5,831.2	1,622.3	10,951.8	1,012.3	1,801.9	208.4	26.3	257.8
Slovakia*	4,224.1	1,230.9	5,528.1	701.7	1,271.4	397.1	30.2	277.1
Slovenia*	2,722.7	541.3	3,752.3	572.7	695.1	268.1	9.1	268.3
Spain*	67,329.3	18,989.0	101,335.0	25,544.1	13,651.4	27,794.4	1,106.5	2,605.7
Sweden	32,633.0	14,991.3	52,627.1	1,613.6	13,265.6	4,810.1	2,010.3	3,277.9
United Kingdom*	195,228.4	32,895.2	262,677.7	2,167.2	63,662.4	10,249.8	31,485.2	15,576.2

* Provisional.

© European Union. Source: Eurostat, 2017, Population and social conditions, table *SPR_EXP-SUM*—Social protection expenditure—Main results.

Social protection expenditure as % of GDP

	2012	2013	2014		2012	2013	2014
Austria	29.3	29.8	30.0	Latvia	14.4	14.6	14.5
Belgium	29.6	30.1	30.3	Lithuania	16.2	15.3	15.2
Bulgaria	16.6	17.6	18.5	Luxembourg	22.8	23.2	22.7
Croatia	21.1	22.0	21.6	Malta	19.1	18.9	18.2
Cyprus	22.3	24.2	23.0	Netherlands	31.0	31.2	30.9
Czech Republic	20.4	20.2	19.7	Poland	18.9	19.4	19.1
Denmark	32.0	32.5	32.9	Portugal	26.4	27.6	26.9
Estonia	15.0	14.9	15.1	Romania	15.4	14.9	14.8
Finland	30.1	31.1	31.9	Slovakia	18.0	18.3	18.5*
France	33.5	33.9	34.3	Slovenia	24.9	24.9	24.1*
Germany	28.7	29.0	29.1*	Spain*	25.5	25.8	25.4
Greece*	28.2	26.7	26.0	Sweden	29.3	30.0	29.5
Hungary	21.4	20.8	19.9	United Kingdom	29.2	28.4	27.4*
Ireland	23.2	22.3	20.6				
Italy	29.3	29.8*	29.9*	**Total (EU-28)***	28.7	28.9	28.7

* Provisional.

© European Union. Source: Eurostat, 2017, Population and social conditions, table *SPR_EXP-SUM*—Social protection expenditure—Main results.

STATISTICAL SURVEY — Health and Welfare

Social protection expenditure per inhabitant (euros at current prices)

	2012	2013	2014		2012	2013	2014
Austria	11,028.2	11,322.1	11,619.0	Latvia	1,556.1	1,660.4	1,714.5
Belgium	10,302.0	10,551.6	10,818.4	Lithuania	1,811.2	1,807.1	1,892.8
Bulgaria	952.2	1,017.1	1,096.5	Luxembourg	18,862.1	19,764.5	20,127.8
Croatia	2,174.7	2,244.3	2,192.1	Malta	3,268.0	3,408.8	3,592.8
Cyprus	5,027.2	5,083.5	4,735.3	Netherlands	11,920.3	12,115.4	12,165.8
Czech Republic	3,139.3	3,027.2	2,926.8	Poland	1,930.4	2,011.5	2,067.8
Denmark	14,565.1	14,992.7	15,448.2	Portugal	4,225.0	4,496.2	4,469.9
Estonia	2,036.4	2,132.1	2,273.5	Romania	1,022.7	1,073.7	1,114.3
Finland	11,111.3	11,641.4	12,002.7	Slovakia	2,420.7	2,504.2	2,592.2*
France	10,689.4	10,901.6	11,106.0	Slovenia	4,358.8	4,349.1	4,360.4*
Germany	9,834.9	10,164.8	10,493.5*	Spain*	5,663.0	5,675.9	5,661.2
Greece*	4,876.8	4,396.5	4,241.8	Sweden	13,030.4	13,632.1	13,169.4
Hungary	2,135.2	2,138.3	2,121.0	United Kingdom	9,481.1	9,076.8	9,594.5*
Ireland	8,882.4	8,725.5	8,623.2				
Italy	7,936.0	7,947.7*	7,987.0*	**Total (EU-28)***	7,644.1	7,729.9	7,904.7

* Provisional.
© European Union. Source: Eurostat, 2017, Population and social conditions, table *SPR_EXP-SUM*—Social protection expenditure—Main results.

Expenditure on pensions in 2014 (million euros)

	Old age pension	Anticipated old age pension	Partial pension	Disability pension	Early retirement benefit (a)*	Survivor's pension	Early retirement benefit (b)*	Total
Austria	36,189.6	2,833.7	0.0	4,233.0	0.0	5,953.6	72.3	49,282.1
Belgium	34,165.3	6.2	0.0	7,022.6	0.0	7,414.0	1,555.7	50,163.7
Bulgaria	2,890.3	386.1	0.0	343.8	0.0	137.5	0.0	3,757.7
Croatia	2,460.2	593.1	0.0	833.6	0.0	849.6	0.0	4,736.4
Cyprus	1,536.1	6.4	0.0	60.5	0.1	249.8	0.0	1,853.0
Czech Republic	11,329.6	269.8	0.0	1,425.2	9.8	1,017.8	0.0	14,052.2
Denmark	23,326.2	2,319.8	0.0	19.9	5,620.8	5,844.5	0.0	37,131.2
Estonia	947.7	319.6	0.0	230.3	0.0	12.3	0.0	1,509.9
Finland	20,916.1	1,269.4	164.9	3,369.0	0.0	1,762.6	7.2	27,489.1
France	264,019.1	0.0	0.0	24,030.2	259.5	36,077.5	574.3	324,960.6
Germany†	250,407.4	12,049.8	0.0	4,687.1	22,584.5	54,289.4	1,312.4	345,330.5
Greece†	23,723.9	0.0	0.0	2,173.2	0.0	4,457.8	80.3	30,435.3
Hungary	7,696.1	531.4	0.0	0.0	0.0	1,213.6	0.0	9,441.0
Ireland	9,481.9	73.8	0.0	1,981.2	0.0	789.2	24.3	12,350.4
Italy†	189,204.0	22,645.0	0.0	4,416.0	6,985.0	43,410.0	1,203.0	267,863.0
Latvia	1,600.6	44.4	0.0	185.3	0.0	30.1	0.0	1,860.5
Lithuania	1,994.0	94.0	0.0	330.0	0.0	125.1	0.5	2,543.6
Luxembourg	2,276.9	973.4	0.0	402.8	0.0	889.5	81.2	4,623.7
Malta	541.0	0.0	0.0	36.4	0.0	116.9	3.9	698.2
Netherlands	65,847.0	1,484.0	0.0	769.0	0.0	7,896.0	0.0	75,996.0
Poland	32,451.0	4,405.8	0.0	4,244.7	71.3	7,104.0	77.0	48,353.8
Portugal	19,854.2	874.7	0.0	2,998.7	0.0	3,179.5	76.5	26,983.6
Romania	10,309.6‡	54.2	165.0	499.1‡	535.4	807.6	0.0	12,370.8
Slovakia†	4,848.6	196.8	0.0	793.5	0.0	684.8	102.9	6,626.7
Slovenia†	2,501.9	1,000.7	4.8	193.9	0.0	498.4	0.0	4,199.7
Spain†	83,397.2	9,125.2	0.0	14,487.9	0.0	25,241.9	118.6	132,370.7
Sweden	40,027.9	2,710.0	0.0	5,190.1	0.0	1,613.6	0.0	49,541.6
United Kingdom†	231,897.4	0.0	0.0	20,859.3	17.3	2,109.3	0.0	254,883.2
Total (EU-28)†	1,376,070.8	64,267.2	334.7	105,816.0	36,083.7	213,775.7	5,290.0	1,801,408.0

* Benefits (a) owing to reduced capacity to work; or (b) for labour market reasons.
† Provisional. ‡ Estimate.
© European Union. Source: Eurostat, 2017, Population and social conditions, table *SPR_EXP_PENS*—Pensions.

Social protection receipts in 2014 (million euros)

	Social contributions				General government contributions	Other receipts	Total
	by employers	by employees	by the self-employed	by other protected persons			
Austria	35,686.5	20,550.9	2,867.6	2,342.4	35,921.3	1,260.2	98,628.9
Belgium	48,849.5	18,617.5	3,792.9	1,526.4	47,450.1	2,781.3	123,017.7
Bulgaria	2,727.0	1,265.8*	201.7	40.3*	4,192.6	166.7	8,594.1
Croatia	2,664.2	2,889.2	248.4	21.7	3,512.2	258.1	9,593.8
Cyprus	918.3	659.0	49.2	1.0	1,940.0	160.4	3,727.9
Czech Republic	15,034.0	5,914.0	1,476.7	5.6	9,135.4	486.0	32,051.6
Denmark	10,127.3	6,700.6	591.1	0.0	73,282.1	1,165.8	91,867.0
Estonia	2,335.2	31.7	0.0	0.0	525.2	4.2	2,896.4
Finland	23,755.9	6,801.0*	1,385.7*	685.4*	32,313.1	3,479.0	68,420.1
France	311,147.2	91,284.9	25,420.5	24,094.6	257,265.4	23,101.5	732,314.0
Germany†	310,299.2	205,319.1	16,153.7	51,874.4	298,415.1	15,501.6	897,563.2
Greece†	14,870.0	8,277.6	2,245.5	0.6	18,276.2	2,217.8	45,887.6
Hungary	8,360.0	4,827.3	137.0	1.1	7,771.3	427.5	21,524.3
Ireland	10,851.9	3,073.2	406.3	0.0	24,034.0	1,378.6	39,743.9
Italy†	172,173.0	41,182.0	31,274.0	662.0	243,339.0	9,854.0	498,484.0
Latvia	1,443.1*	561.2	2.7	35.3	1,375.5*	22.7	3,440.5
Lithuania	2,935.9	831.6	102.1	0.0	1,523.0	41.9	5,434.4
Luxembourg	3,174.9	2,351.1	271.1	227.3	5,442.5	1,537.7	13,004.5
Malta	453.8	152.7	36.4	0.0	864.0	32.1	1,539.0
Netherlands	72,767.0	76,481.0	464.0	0.0	45,237.0	32,779.0	227,728.0
Poland	32,830.0	15,822.6	0.0	0.0	16,872.5	12,018.2	77,543.5
Portugal	13,871.6	5,720.2	751.9	1,333.3	22,026.3	4,116.8	47,820.1
Romania	7,635.9	3,278.2	52.8	6.1	11,139.9	312.6	22,425.5
Slovakia†	6,471.5	2,423.4	528.2	83.7	4,691.4	620.4	14,818.5
Slovenia†	2,340.2	2,836.9	260.7	471.6	3,084.9	128.0	9,122.2
Spain†	103,092.8	19,824.1	11,193.7	1,194.9	111,383.3	6,646.7	253,335.5
Sweden	52,158.1	11,911.1	602.4	0.0	69,836.9	2,845.7	137,354.2
United Kingdom†	200,175.1	68,155.3	2,796.5	29.5	356,959.8	106,519.2	734,635.3
Total (EU-28)†	1,465,691.8	627,655.5	103,242.2	84,637.1	1,707,971.7	229,905.9	4,219,104.2

* Provisional. † Estimates.
© European Union. Source: Eurostat, 2017, Population and social conditions, table *SPR_REC_SUMT*—Receipts by type.

CHILDCARE

Formal childcare by age group and duration in 2015: between one and 29 hours a week (% of the population of each age group)

	Less than 3 years	Between 3 years and compulsory school age	Between compulsory school age and 12 years		Less than 3 years	Between 3 years and compulsory school age	Between compulsory school age and 12 years
Austria	14	58	54	Latvia	1	3	16
Belgium	23	22	13	Lithuania	2	5	58
Bulgaria	1	3	26	Luxembourg	17	27	41
Croatia	2	7	62	Malta	11	35	11
Cyprus	9	49	74	Netherlands	41	78	73
Czech Republic	1	23	39	Poland	1	8	43
Denmark	8	9	0	Portugal	4	6	7
Estonia	4	7	50	Romania	4	51	87
Finland	8	23	83	Slovakia	0	14	24
France	16	37	34	Slovenia	3	9	23
Germany	10	35	40	Spain	19	47	48
Greece	5	41	38	Sweden	21	26	1
Hungary	5	10	19	United Kingdom	26	49	3
Ireland	22	73	52				
Italy	10	23	22	**Total (EU-28)**	15	34	33

© European Union. Source: Eurostat, 2017, Population and social conditions, table *ILC_CAINDFORMAL*—Formal childcare by age group and duration (% of the population of each age group).

Formal childcare by age group and duration in 2015: 30 hours or more a week (% of the population of each age group)

	Less than 3 years	Between 3 years and compulsory school age	Between compulsory school age and 12 years		Less than 3 years	Between 3 years and compulsory school age	Between compulsory school age and 12 years
Austria	9	28	46	Latvia	22	79	83
Belgium	27	77	78	Lithuania	8	69	40
Bulgaria	8	68	71	Luxembourg	35	55	57
Croatia	10	46	28	Malta	7	54	89
Cyprus	11	32	26	Netherlands	5	13	28
Czech Republic	2	55	52	Poland	4	36	53
Denmark	70	88	100	Portugal	43	84	93
Estonia	18	86	50	Romania	5	7	1
Finland	25	60	17	Slovakia	1	54	41
France	26	57	66	Slovenia	35	82	70
Germany	16	55	51	Spain	21	45	51
Greece	7	26	53	Sweden	43	70	99
Hungary	11	80	81	United Kingdom	4	24	96
Ireland	9	19	47				
Italy	17	63	78	**Total (EU-28)**	16	49	63

© European Union. Source: Eurostat, 2017, Population and social conditions, table *ILC_CAINDFORMAL*—Formal childcare by age group and duration (% of the population of each age group).

AGRICULTURE, FORESTRY AND FISHING

LAND USE

Utilized agricultural area ('000 hectares, excluding inland waters)

	2013	2014	2015		2013	2014	2015
Austria	2,862.4	2,716.2	2,720.4	Latvia	1,877.7	1,872.5	1,884.8
Belgium	1,338.6	1,333.4	1,330.9	Lithuania	2,891.4	2,952.4	3,006.0
Bulgaria	4,995.1	4,976.8	5,011.5	Luxembourg	131.0	131.1	131.4
Croatia	1,300.8	1,240.9	1,537.6	Malta	11.7	11.7	11.7
Cyprus	107.1	107.0	126.5	Netherlands	1,847.6	1,839.0	1,845.8
Czech Republic	3,521.0	3,515.6	3,493.7	Poland	14,409.9	14,424.2	14,398.2
Denmark	2,627.8	2,652.0	2,633.0	Portugal	3,716.4	3,701.3	3,700.0
Estonia	965.9	974.8	993.6	Romania	13,904.6	13,830.4	13,835.5
Finland	2,258.6	2,267.2	2,273.3	Slovakia	1,928.5	1,924.7	1,921.6
France	28,976.0	28,929.8	29,115.3	Slovenia	478.9	482.2	476.9
Germany	16,699.6	16,724.8	16,730.7	Spain	23,494.6	23,571.8	23,897.1
Greece	5,315.0	5,138.9	5,091.9	Sweden	3,036.1	3,036.1	3,028.4
Hungary	5,339.5	5,346.3	5,346.5	United Kingdom	17,259.0	17,240.0	17,147.0
Ireland	4,477.4	4,465.4	4,429.1				
Italy	12,426.0	12,720.2	12,660.9	**Total (EU-28)**	178,198.3	178,126.5	178,778.9

© European Union. Source: Eurostat, 2017, Agriculture, forestry and fisheries, table *APRO_ACS_A*—Crop statistics (from 2000 onwards).

Distribution of utilized agricultural land, 2015 ('000 hectares)

	Arable land	Permanent grassland	Land under permanent crops	Kitchen gardens		Arable land	Permanent grassland	Land under permanent crops	Kitchen gardens
Austria	1,346.0	1,306.9	65.5	2.0	Latvia	1,229.8	648.3	6.7	n.a.
Belgium	836.4	476.0	18.6	0.0	Lithuania	2,169.8	798.0	30.3	7.9
Bulgaria	3,494.1	1,368.7	133.1	15.7	Luxembourg	62.9	66.9	1.6	0.0
Croatia	841.9	618.1	75.5	2.2	Malta	9.0	0.0	1.3	1.5
Cyprus	98.2	1.9	26.3	0.1	Netherlands	1,033.0	766.0	38.0	n.a.
Czech Republic	2,495.9	957.8	38.6	1.4	Poland	10,887.0	3,092.8	391.0	27.4
Denmark	2,348.7	254.8	29.5	0.0	Portugal	1,117.0	1,816.6	751.0	15.4
Estonia	665.9	314.9	3.3	9.6	Romania	8,757.2	4,655.3	317.3	105.7
Finland	2,240.9	27.8	3.3	1.0	Slovakia	1,349.9	520.6	18.7	n.a.
France	18,659.1	9,528.2	1,009.7	149.1	Slovenia	171.2	278.7	27.0	n.a.
Germany	11,846.4	4,677.1	204.7	2.4	Spain	12,656.8	6,399.1	4,728.2	113.1
Greece	2,893.0	930.1	1,268.9	0.0	Sweden	2,575.2	449.8	3.3	0.0
Hungary	4,331.7	761.5	179.1	80.5	United Kingdom	5,761.0	11,079.0	38.0	0.0
Ireland	452.1	3,975.3	1.7	0.0					
Italy	6,601.7	3,579.2	2,447.1	32.9	**Total (EU-28)**	106,931.9	59,349.1	11,857.0	n.a.

© European Union. Source: Eurostat, 2017, Agriculture, forestry and fisheries, table *APRO_ACS_A*—Crop statistics (from 2000 onwards).

STATISTICAL SURVEY

Agriculture, Forestry and Fishing

CROP PRODUCTION

Note: Figures refer to harvested production, excluding fruits and vegetables.

Principal crops: European Union (EU-28) ('000 metric tons)

	2014	2015	2016
Wheat	157,061.2	n.a.	n.a.
Rye and maslin	9,366.4	8,195.0	7,833.9
Barley	60,773.4	61,924.6	60,226.3
Oats and mixed grain other than maslin	10,803.7	n.a.	n.a.
Grain maize and corn-cob-mix	77,460.3	58,905.6	60,614.5
Triticale (wheat-rye hybrid)	13,074.7	12,615.5	11,646.4
Sorghum	940.1	728.7	687.8
Rice	2,852.7	2,995.4	n.a.
Potatoes	59,036.2	53,159.9	n.a.
Sugar beet	131,021.8	101,866.9	n.a.
Rapeseed	24,127.0	21,701.0	n.a.
Cotton seed	n.a.	n.a.	n.a.

© European Union. Source: Eurostat, 2017, Agriculture, forestry and fisheries, table *APRO_ACS_A*—Crop statistics (from 2000 onwards).

Principal crops: Austria ('000 metric tons)

	2014	2015	2016
Wheat	1,804.0	1,725.7	1,977.0
Rye and maslin	250.2	186.0	202.5
Rye	232.5	171.1	188.4
Barley	845.7	840.4	859.7
Oats and mixed grain other than maslin	121.1	109.3	106.8
Oats	105.9	96.3	94.8
Mixed grain other than maslin	15.2	13.0	12.0
Grain maize and corn-cob-mix	2,334.4	1,637.9	2,179.6
Triticale (wheat-rye hybrid)	302.6	284.1	322.6
Other cereals	33.8	39.6	26.5
Dried pulses (grain equivalent)	50.9	54.9	59.6
Peas	17.4	18.7	19.2
Potatoes	750.6	536.5	767.3
Sugar beet	4,244.2	2,853.3	3,534.4
Rapeseed	198.3	111.8	141.9
Sunflower seed	57.8	38.1	59.9
Soya beans	118.1	136.2	152.6

© European Union. Source: Eurostat, 2017, Agriculture, forestry and fisheries, table *APRO_ACS_A*—Crop statistics (from 2000 onwards).

Principal crops: Belgium ('000 metric tons)

	2014	2015	2016
Wheat	1,919.0	2,076.3	1,430.5
Barley	400.0	434.1	342.2
Oats and mixed grain other than maslin	17.7	22.2	16.5
Grain maize and corn-cob-mix	778.6	693.0	533.2
Triticale (wheat-rye hybrid)	39.8	40.6	30.5
Potatoes	4,121.5	3,665.5	3,372.5
Sugar beet	5,162.1	4,453.6	3,999.7
Rapeseed	53.3	48.3	39.3
Flax (straw)	72.8	80.5	85.2
Chicory	39.3	354.5	340.2

© European Union. Source: Eurostat, 2017, Agriculture, forestry and fisheries, table *APRO_ACS_A*—Crop statistics (from 2000 onwards).

Principal crops: Bulgaria ('000 metric tons)

	2014	2015	2016
Wheat	5,347.1	5,140.1	5,798.1
Barley	852.2	714.8	713.0
Oats and mixed grain other than maslin	27.1	21.7	31.4
Grain maize and corn-cob-mix	3,137.5	2,696.9	2,218.8
Triticale (wheat-rye hybrid)	60.4	38.4	49.3
Potatoes	132.7	164.9	128.1
Rapeseed	527.9	422.1	506.8

© European Union. Source: Eurostat, 2017, Agriculture, forestry and fisheries, table *ACS_A*—Crop statistics (from 2000 onwards).

Principal crops: Croatia ('000 metric tons)

	2014	2015	2016
Wheat	650.8	763.0	927.7
Barley	175.6	193.5	263.8
Oats and mixed grain other than maslin	56.6	71.7	75.8
Grain maize and corn-cob-mix	2,047.0	1,709.2	2,103.0
Triticale (wheat-rye hybrid)	61.3	54.6	81.1
Potatoes	160.9	171.2	192.0
Sugar beet	1,392.0	756.5	1,103.0
Oilseeds	n.a.	349.8	476.0
Sunflower seed	99.5	94.1	118.0
Soya beans	131.4	196.4	239.0
Tobacco (raw)	9.2	10.1	9.0

© European Union. Source: Eurostat, 2017, Agriculture, forestry and fisheries, table *APRO_ACS_A*—Crop statistics (from 2000 onwards).

Principal crops: Cyprus ('000 metric tons)

	2014	2015	2016
Wheat	4.4	35.4	18.9
Barley	2.7	52.2	8.8
Dried pulses (grain equivalent)	0.9	0.9	1.0
Potatoes	117.5	95.9	84.2

© European Union. Source: Eurostat, 2017, Agriculture, forestry and fisheries, table *APRO_ACS_A*—Crop statistics (from 2000 onwards).

Principal crops: Czech Republic ('000 metric tons)

	2014	2015	2016
Wheat	5,442.4	5,274.3	5,454.7
Rye	129.1	107.9	104.4
Barley	1,967.1	1,991.4	1,845.3
Oats	152.2	154.6	132.2
Grain maize and corn-cob-mix	832.2	442.7	845.8
Triticale (wheat-rye hybrid)	243.9	202.7	193.2
Dried pulses (grain equivalent)	53.8	95.9	84.6
Peas	42.8	78.2	68.7
Potatoes	697.5	505.0	699.6
Sugar beet	4,424.6	3,421.0	4,118.4
Oilseeds	1,644.1	1,355.0	1,476.5
Rapeseed	1,537.3	1,256.2	1,359.1
Sunflower seed	42.3	31.6	44.6

© European Union. Source: Eurostat, 2017, Agriculture, forestry and fisheries, table *APRO_ACS_A*—Crop statistics (from 2000 onwards).

Principal crops: Denmark ('000 metric tons)

	2014	2015	2016
Wheat	5,153.3	5,030.0	4,201.5
Rye	n.a.	772.0	577.2
Barley	3,547.6	3,856.0	3,949.6
Oats	184.9	206.8	277.8
Triticale (wheat-rye hybrid)	95.9	82.0	56.2
Dried pulses (grain equivalent)	33.2	51.0	55.5
Potatoes	964.5	1,748.0	1,954.0
Sugar beet	2,266.1	2,429.0	1,696.1
Rapeseed	708.9	826.0	506.2

© European Union. Source: Eurostat, 2017, Agriculture, forestry and fisheries, table *APRO_ACS_A*—Crop statistics (from 2000 onwards).

Principal crops: Estonia ('000 metric tons)

	2014	2015	2016
Wheat	615.5	812.6	455.5
Rye	49.6	54.7	32.4
Barley	458.1	556.6	357.4
Oats and mixed grain other than maslin	72.6	75.1	67.1
Oats	65.0	67.8	64.5
Mixed grain other than maslin	7.6	7.3	2.6
Triticale (wheat-rye hybrid)	25.2	35.1	18.9
Dried pulses (grain equivalent)	39.5	86.2	109.5
Potatoes	82.3	80.7	62.9
Rapeseed	166.2	196.3	102.5

© European Union. Source: Eurostat, 2017, Agriculture, forestry and fisheries, table *APRO_ACS_A*—Crop statistics (from 2000 onwards).

Principal crops: Finland ('000 metric tons)

	2014	2015	2016
Wheat	1,088.2	992.1	810.5
Rye	n.a.	107.5	86.5
Barley	1,854.8	1,569.0	1,555.4
Oats and mixed grain other than maslin	1,109.9	1,014.2	1,068.0
Oats	1,039.0	979.6	1,028.5
Mixed grain other than maslin	70.9	34.6	39.5
Dried pulses (grain equivalent)	35.6	52.2	65.0
Potatoes	600.3	532.1	587.6
Sugar beet	626.3	406.5	433.6
Rapeseed	62.1	85.3	92.9

© European Union. Source: Eurostat, 2017, Agriculture, forestry and fisheries, table *APRO_ACS_A*—Crop statistics (from 2000 onwards).

Principal crops: France ('000 metric tons)

	2014	2015	2016
Wheat	38,991.6	42,715.9	29,479.0
Rye	n.a.	123.5	n.a.
Barley	11,775.3	13,027.6	10,139.0
Oats and mixed grain other than maslin	665.3	600.6	523.6
Oats	443.6	399.4	346.2
Mixed grain other than maslin	221.7	201.3	177.4
Grain maize and corn-cob-mix	18,541.8	13,738.2	12,191.8
Triticale (wheat-rye hybrid)	2,022.5	1,863.6	1,482.0
Sorghum	395.6	277.8	232.2
Other cereals	111.3	205.0	166.6
Rice	83.4	80.9	80.3
Dried pulses (grain equivalent)	863.9	930.4	812.2
Peas	526.9	661.7	525.0
Broad and field beans	278.7	251.4	198.3
Potatoes	8,054.5	7,114.5	1,864.5
Sugar beet	37,931.5	33,503.4	33,794.9
Rapeseed	5,509.8	5,307.2	4,302.4
Sunflower seed	1,559.1	1,185.8	1,189.8
Soya beans	223.2	334.2	29.1
Flax (straw)	506.4	478.2	587.1

© European Union. Source: Eurostat, 2017, Agriculture, forestry and fisheries, table *APRO_ACS_A*—Crop statistics (from 2000 onwards).

Principal crops: Germany ('000 metric tons)

	2014	2015	2016
Wheat	27,784.8	26,549.5	24,594.8
Rye and maslin	3,854.4	3,487.8	3,190.2
Barley	11,562.8	11,629.9	10,829.6
Oats and mixed grain other than maslin	694.2	628.3	579.6
Oats	627.1	566.3	532.9
Mixed grain other than maslin	67.1	62.0	46.7
Grain maize and corn-cob-mix	5,142.1	3,973.0	3,658.7
Triticale (wheat-rye hybrid)	2,972.2	2,598.3	2,406.8
Dried pulses (grain equivalent)	300.4	466.4	n.a.
Broad and field beans	87.6	133.2	160.0
Potatoes	11,607.3	10,370.2	10,176.6
Sugar beet	29,748.1	22,572.0	n.a.
Sunflower seed	46.0	35.3	37.1

© European Union. Source: Eurostat, 2017, Agriculture, forestry and fisheries, table *APRO_ACS_A*—Crop statistics (from 2000 onwards).

Principal crops: Greece ('000 metric tons)

	2014	2015	2016
Wheat	1,655.3	1,138.6	1,148.6
Rye	47.9	23.0	23.6
Barley	459.6	353.9	357.6
Oats	79.7	83.1	81.6
Grain maize and corn-cob-mix	1,778.1	1,542.3	1,552.3
Rice	229.9	251.2	266.2
Potatoes	583.2	556.3	552.2
Sugar beet	537.1	270.7	265.1
Cotton seed	828.5	1,337.2	1,349.9
Cotton fibre	273.4	441.3	445.5
Tobacco (raw)	34.3	30.6	28.7

© European Union. Source: Eurostat, 2017, Agriculture, forestry and fisheries, table *APRO_ACS_A*—Crop statistics (from 2000 onwards).

Principal crops: Hungary ('000 metric tons)

	2014	2015	2016
Wheat	5,261.9	5,331.4	5,592.1
Rye	95.9	104.0	80.8
Barley	1,274.7	1,408.6	1,608.2
Oats	135.6	128.7	101.4
Grain maize and corn-cob-mix	9,315.1	6,632.8	8,806.9
Triticale (wheat-rye hybrid)	486.5	502.3	472.1
Dried pulses (grain equivalent)	50.4	68.2	51.4
Peas	46.3	63.6	46.5
Potatoes	567.4	452.0	402.9
Sugar beet	1,066.8	910.9	1,075.6
Rapeseed	699.8	590.4	882.0
Sunflower seed	1,597.3	1,557.0	1,892.5
Soya beans	115.6	145.9	181.3

© European Union. Source: Eurostat, 2017, Agriculture, forestry and fisheries, table *APRO_ACS_A*—Crop statistics (from 2000 onwards).

Principal crops: Ireland ('000 metric tons)

	2014	2015	2016
Wheat	717.0	696.6	647.8
Barley	1,731.2	1,739.2	1,479.9
Oats	149.7	197.7	183.3
Dried pulses (grain equivalent)	20.6	69.3	70.6
Potatoes	383.0	360.1	352.0
Rapeseed	34.2	39.9	34.1

© European Union. Source: Eurostat, 2017, Agriculture, forestry and fisheries, table *APRO_ACS_A*—Crop statistics (from 2000 onwards).

Principal crops: Italy ('000 metric tons)

	2014	2015	2016
Wheat	7,141.9	n.a.	8,037.9
Barley	848.7	955.1	944.9
Oats	241.1	261.4	229.6
Grain maize and corn-cob-mix	9,250.1	7,073.9	6,839.5
Sorghum	368.8	294.2	315.7
Rice	1,415.7	1,518.3	1,518.3
Dried pulses (grain equivalent)	123.8	118.2	176.6
Broad and field beans	85.8	92.0	100.0
Potatoes	1,365.4	1,355.4	1,397.2
Sugar beet	3,784.4	2,183.9	2,183.9
Sunflower seed	250.4	248.0	268.3
Soya beans	933.1	1,117.0	1,081.4
Tobacco (raw)	53.9	51.4	51.4

© European Union. Source: Eurostat, 2017, Agriculture, forestry and fisheries, table *APRO_ACS_A*—Crop statistics (from 2000 onwards).

Principal crops: Latvia ('000 metric tons)

	2014	2015	2016
Wheat	1,467.5	2,250.1	2,062.3
Rye	114.3	159.6	140.9
Barley	418.8	385.1	283.2
Oats and mixed grain other than maslin	191.2	175.7	160.4
Oats	155.1	160.4	146.1
Mixed grain other than maslin	36.1	15.3	14.3
Triticale (wheat-rye hybrid)	26.9	41.2	37.3
Potatoes	209.9	203.6	203.6
Rapeseed	186.4	293.2	283.0

© European Union. Source: Eurostat, 2017, Agriculture, forestry and fisheries, table *APRO_ACS_A*—Crop statistics (from 2000 onwards).

Principal crops: Lithuania ('000 metric tons)

	2014	2015	2016
Wheat	3,230.6	4,380.3	3,798.4
Rye	85.3	107.8	76.0
Barley	1,018.5	811.5	543.1
Oats and mixed grain other than maslin	241.8	205.4	188.0
Oats	183.8	163.4	153.3
Mixed grain other than maslin	58.0	42.1	34.8
Triticale (wheat-rye hybrid)	395.2	468.5	329.5
Dried pulses (grain equivalent)	200.9	454.7	640.0
Peas	101.1	228.8	400.5
Potatoes	460.9	391.6	333.5
Sugar beet	1,014.4	619.5	933.5
Rapeseed	501.5	512.2	392.5

© European Union. Source: Eurostat, 2017, Agriculture, forestry and fisheries, table *APRO_ACS_A*—Crop statistics (from 2000 onwards).

Principal crops: Luxembourg ('000 metric tons)

	2014	2015	2016
Wheat	77.9	91.1	70.1
Rye	n.a.	5.6	4.2
Barley	46.0	44.4	34.0
Oats and mixed grain other than maslin	6.5	6.4	6.5
Oats	5.5	5.9	5.3
Mixed grain other than maslin	1.0	0.5	1.2
Grain maize and corn-cob-mix	1.7	0.9	0.8
Triticale (wheat-rye hybrid)	30.1	27.4	22.8
Potatoes	19.0	13.0	18.7
Rapeseed	15.7	13.8	10.9

© European Union. Source: Eurostat, 2017, Agriculture, forestry and fisheries, table *APRO_ACS_A*—Crop statistics (from 2000 onwards).

Principal crops: Malta ('000 metric tons)

	2014	2015	2016
Potatoes	10.8	8.0	7.0

© European Union. Source: Eurostat, 2017, Agriculture, forestry and fisheries, table *APRO_ACS_A*—Crop statistics (from 2000 onwards).

Principal crops: Netherlands ('000 metric tons)

	2014	2015	2016
Wheat	1,304.0	1,287.8	1,018.5*
Rye	n.a.	6.1	6.7*
Barley	197.0	226.7	233.7*
Oats	10.0	8.0	8.7*
Grain maize and corn-cob-mix	240.0	171.0	96.2*
Triticale (wheat-rye hybrid)	9.0	6.8	5.9*
Other cereals	n.a.	0.0	0.0
Dried pulses (grain equivalent)	0.0	5.5	2.6
Potatoes	7,100.0	6,651.7	6,702.9
Sugar beet	6,822.0	4,868.3	5,489.5
Flax (straw)	10.0	14.2	13.8
Chicory	51.0	222.1	221.3

* Provisional

© European Union. Source: Eurostat, 2017, Agriculture, forestry and fisheries, table *APRO_ACS_A*—Crop statistics (from 2000 onwards).

Principal crops: Poland ('000 metric tons)

	2014	2015	2016
Wheat	11,628.7	10,957.8	11,047.1*
Rye and maslin	3,228.8	2,331.5	2,514.6*
Rye	n.a.	2,013.1	2,237.5*
Maslin	n.a.	318.4	277.1*
Barley	3,274.8	2,960.7	3,603.2*
Oats and mixed grain other than maslin	3,944.9	3,151.2	3,577.7
Oats	1,458.6	1,219.6	1,358.1
Mixed grain other than maslin	2,486.3	1,931.6	2,219.7
Grain maize and corn-cob-mix	4,468.4	3,156.2	4,170.0*
Triticale (wheat-rye hybrid)	5,246.6	5,339.4	5,007.6*
Other cereals	153.2	105.9	n.a.
Dried pulses (grain equivalent)	483.2	714.8	n.a.
Peas	9.7	23.0	n.a.
Potatoes	7,424.7	6,151.8	n.a.
Sugar beet	13,488.9	9,364.5	n.a.
Other root crops	n.a.	337.7	n.a.
Rapeseed	3,275.8	2,700.8	n.a.
Chicory	33.7	30.1	26.1

* Provisional.

© European Union. Source: Eurostat, 2017, Agriculture, forestry and fisheries, table *APRO_ACS_A*—Crop statistics (from 2000 onwards).

Principal crops: Portugal ('000 metric tons)

	2014	2015	2016
Wheat	98.8	80.4	95.0
Rye	17.6	15.5	16.3
Barley	37.9	44.4	55.5
Oats	67.4	49.0	67.0
Grain maize and corn-cob-mix	897.0	827.5	707.6
Triticale (wheat-rye hybrid)	47.2	38.5	41.9
Rice	167.3	184.9	166.4
Potatoes	539.9	486.8	455.3
Sugar beet	13.3	5.8	5.1
Sunflower seed	16.4	24.7	23.5

© European Union. Source: Eurostat, 2017, Agriculture, forestry and fisheries, table *APRO_ACS_A*—Crop statistics (from 2000 onwards).

Principal crops: Romania ('000 metric tons)

	2014	2015	2016
Wheat	7,584.8	7,962.4	8,382.6
Rye	24.4	24.3	27.7
Barley	1,712.5	1,623.2	1,927.4
Oats	381.6	344.2	337.0
Grain maize and corn-cob-mix	11,988.6	8,984.7	8,901.9
Triticale (wheat-rye hybrid)	275.2	262.1	274.3
Rice	45.2	49.8	42.6
Potatoes	3,519.3	2,625.0	2,687.1
Sugar beet	1,398.6	1,040.7	965.9
Sunflower seed	2,189.3	1,785.8	1,953.9

© European Union. Source: Eurostat, 2017, Agriculture, forestry and fisheries, table *APRO_ACS_A*—Crop statistics (from 2000 onwards).

Principal crops: Slovakia ('000 metric tons)

	2014	2015	2016
Wheat	2,072.4	2,082.1	n.a.
Rye	n.a.	41.6	n.a.
Barley	675.9	668.7	602.8
Oats	38.7	43.0	38.1
Grain maize and corn-cob-mix	1,814.1	929.2	1,566.1
Triticale (wheat-rye hybrid)	49.4	38.5	30.7
Dried pulses (grain equivalent)	14.5	26.8	26.3
Peas	12.1	23.4	22.4
Potatoes	178.8	144.6	177.2
Sugar beet	1,550.2	1,205.5	1,506.9
Rapeseed	448.9	320.6	430.6
Sunflower seed	200.7	174.3	246.5
Soya beans	83.9	62.1	92.5

© European Union. Source: Eurostat, 2017, Agriculture, forestry and fisheries, table *APRO_ACS_A*—Crop statistics (from 2000 onwards).

Principal crops: Slovenia ('000 metric tons)

	2014	2015	2016
Wheat	173.2	157.1	163.2
Barley	89.7	93.2	91.7
Oats	4.5	5.0	4.3
Grain maize and corn-cob-mix	350.7	338.7	352.0
Triticale (wheat-rye hybrid)	20.1	20.9	24.7
Potatoes	97.2	91.0	84.9
Sugar beet	0.0	0.0	0.0
Rapeseed	19.9	3.6	8.6

© European Union. Source: Eurostat, 2017, Agriculture, forestry and fisheries, table *APRO_ACS_A*—Crop statistics (from 2000 onwards).

Principal crops: Spain ('000 metric tons)

	2014	2015	2016*
Wheat	6,471.4	6,362.7	7,943.0
Rye and maslin	291.0	331.9	448.2
Rye	n.a.	281.4	390.7
Barley	6,983.1	6,705.1	9,289.8
Oats and mixed grain other than maslin	659.0	790.4	1,125.3
Oats	649.1	781.1	1,115.7
Grain maize and corn-cob-mix	4,776.2	4,564.4	3,981.8
Triticale (wheat-rye hybrid)	449.7	450.1	540.8
Rice	861.1	847.0	821.5
Dried pulses (grain equivalent)	450.5	503.3	641.1
Peas	141.9	193.4	297.1
Broad and field beans	38.9	65.5	55.0
Potatoes	2,543.9	2,284.1	2,244.3
Sugar beet	3,723.3	3,605.1	3,149.8
Sunflower seed	953.0	769.2	713.3
Cotton seed	n.a.	71.6	71.6
Cotton fibre	74.9	61.8	50.8

* Provisional.

© European Union. Source: Eurostat, 2017, Agriculture, forestry and fisheries, table *APRO_ACS_A*—Crop statistics (from 2000 onwards).

Principal crops: Sweden ('000 metric tons)

	2014	2015	2016
Wheat	3,086.4	3,300.4	2,834.5
Rye	173.6	149.2	101.3
Barley	1,574.2	1,672.3	1,530.4
Oats and mixed grain other than maslin	714.8	796.7	824.1
Oats	665.9	744.7	767.9
Mixed grain other than maslin	48.9	52.0	56.2
Triticale (wheat-rye hybrid)	226.4	243.8	157.0
Dried pulses (grain equivalent)	108.7	183.3	198.1
Potatoes	822.1	802.5	862.5
Sugar beet	2,517.8	1,178.3	1,988.4
Rapeseed	325.4	359.3	268.1

© European Union. Source: Eurostat, 2017, Agriculture, forestry and fisheries, table *APRO_ACS_A*—Crop statistics (from 2000 onwards).

Principal crops: United Kingdom ('000 metric tons)

	2014	2015	2016*
Wheat	16,606.0	16,444.0	14,383.0
Barley	6,911.0	7,370.0	6,655.0
Oats and mixed grain other than maslin	820.0	799.0	816.0
Oats	820.0	799.0	816.0
Triticale (wheat-rye hybrid)	46.0	43.0	43.0
Dried pulses (grain equivalent)	574.0	920.0	838.0
Peas	126.0	180.0	189.0
Broad and field beans	448.0	740.0	649.0
Potatoes	5,921.0	5,598.0	5,373.0
Sugar beet	9,310.0	6,218.0	5,687.0
Rapeseed	2,460.0	2,542.0	1,775.0
Linseed (oil flax)	39.0	29.0	48.0

* Provisional.

© European Union. Source: Eurostat, 2017, Agriculture, forestry and fisheries, table *APRO_ACS_A*—Crop statistics (from 2000 onwards).

PRODUCTION OF FRUIT AND VEGETABLES

Note: Figures refer to harvested production, including, where known, the output of kitchen gardens.

Fruit and vegetables: Austria ('000 metric tons)

	2014	2015	2016
Brassicas	95.6	70.2	70.3
Cabbages	62.5	45.5	44.8
Other leafy or stalked vegetables	70.3	62.2	76.7
Lettuce	39.8	34.6	43.7
Spinach	11.9	11.0	12.8
Vegetables cultivated for fruit	154.2	147.7	156.3
Tomatoes	57.3	55.7	55.1
Cucumbers	34.7	32.0	35.6
Gherkins	10.9	11.7	11.9
Gourds and pumpkins	13.9	15.1	17.5
Red pepper, capsicum	18.6	15.9	14.6
Root, tuber and bulb vegetables	351.8	266.4	298.9
Carrots	106.9	66.8	98.5
Onions	206.0	168.1	163.3
Beetroot	8.1	4.8	8.5
Celeriac	14.5	12.2	13.1
Pulses	17.2	13.7	13.5
Apples (including cider apples)	310.3	287.6	101.7
Pears (including perry pears)	50.7	51.1	23.5
Stone fruit	34.0	35.8	18.3
Peaches	3.0	2.9	1.3
Apricots	8.6	8.7	5.3
Cherries (including sour cherries)	8.2	7.5	4.0
Plums	14.3	16.7	7.8
Walnuts	3.4	4.9	1.4
Strawberries	14.5	13.4	9.8
Currants	3.3	3.3	1.8
Redcurrants	1.9	2.0	1.3

© European Union. Source: Eurostat, 2017, Agriculture, forestry and fisheries, table *APRO_ACS_A*—Crop statistics (from 2000 onwards).

Fruit and vegetables: Belgium ('000 metric tons)

	2014	2015	2016
Brassicas	n.a.	238.1	221.6
Cauliflower and broccoli	99.2	110.1	112.7
Brussels sprouts	n.a.	52.6	37.7
Cabbages	31.5	58.3	54.7
Other cabbages	n.a.	17.2	16.5
Other leafy or stalked vegetables	n.a.	736.0	648.1
Leeks	190.0	168.0	130.7
Celery	25.4	22.3	21.2
Lettuce	52.7	54.8	52.6
Endive	7.5	7.3	6.7
Spinach	107.1	115.6	80.9
Chicory	39.3	354.5	340.2
Vegetables cultivated for fruit	n.a.	346.9	370.9
Tomatoes	249.3	253.1	259.5
Cucumbers	17.6	16.9	23.6
Courgettes	34.2	37.4	42.5
Gourds and pumpkins	n.a.	6.0	10.1
Red pepper, capsicum	25.2	25.5	27.1
Root, tuber and bulb vegetables	n.a.	436.5	596.4
Kohlrabi	n.a.	n.a.	n.a.
Carrots	328.0	243.0	385.4
Onions	102.3	108.3	130.8
Celeriac	48.8	46.0	48.0
Pulses	191.7	185.0	175.9
Peas	79.1	72.8	65.0
Beans	112.6	112.2	110.9
Cultivated mushrooms	0.0	28.0	28.0
Apples (including cider apples)	318.4	284.9	238.2
Pears (including perry pears)	374.3	369.1	331.6
Stone fruit	10.3	8.0	5.7
Cherries (including sour cherries)	8.3	8.0	5.7
Strawberries	39.3	48.0	45.0

© European Union. Source: Eurostat, 2017, Agriculture, forestry and fisheries, table *APRO_ACS_A*—Crop statistics (from 2000 onwards).

Fruit and vegetables: Bulgaria ('000 metric tons)

	2014	2015	2016
Brassicas	n.a.	45.1	77.8
Cauliflower and broccoli	3.2	2.6	2.1
Cabbages	42.4	42.5	75.7
Other leafy or stalked vegetables	n.a.	6.7	7.9
Leeks	1.8	0.7	1.9
Lettuce	5.5	2.5	2.4
Spinach	1.7	0.5	1.1
Vegetables cultivated for fruit	n.a.	353.7	540.7
Tomatoes	120.5	121.7	141.4
Cucumbers	51.3	45.8	59.6
Courgettes and marrows	3.5	4.4	5.0
Red pepper, capsicum	49.9	67.8	72.0
Root, tuber and bulb vegetables	n.a.	22.6	25.8
Carrots	9.6	7.9	7.4
Onions	13.3	8.9	14.9
Pulses	5.1	5.7	12.1
Peas	2.4	3.4	7.4
Beans	2.6	2.3	4.7
Cultivated mushrooms	2.2	2.5	1.5
Apples (including cider apples)	54.5	58.4	44.8*
Pears (including perry pears)	2.2	3.0	2.0*
Stone fruit	n.a.	138.5	136.6*
Cherries (including sour cherries)	37.1	52.9	42.0*
Strawberries	4.2	5.0	5.2

* Definition differs.

© European Union. Source: Eurostat, 2017, Agriculture, forestry and fisheries, table *APRO_ACS_A*—Crop statistics (from 2000 onwards).

Fruit and vegetables: Croatia ('000 metric tons)

	2014	2015	2016
Brassicas	26.7	40.2	36.8
Cauliflower and broccoli	2.0	1.8	3.0
Cabbages	21.0	34.7	31.4
Other cabbages	3.7	3.7	2.4
Other leafy or stalked vegetables	4.2	9.5	8.0
Leeks	0.5	0.9	1.2
Lettuce	1.8	4.5	4.0
Vegetables cultivated for fruit	69.3	80.6	77.8
Tomatoes	19.6	36.3	24.0
Cucumbers	6.6	6.6	6.9
Courgettes and marrows	2.6	1.6	2.9
Red pepper, capsicum	10.9	14.4	17.0
Root, tuber and bulb vegetables	38.6	45.8	43.1
Carrots	7.2	10.9	12.8
Onions	27.8	29.4	25.0
Pulses	4.5	4.6	5.7
Peas	3.5	3.6	2.9
Beans	1.1	1.1	2.8
Apples (including cider apples)	96.7	96.2	44.0
Pears (including perry pears)	2.9	3.8	3.7
Stone fruit	47.2*	21.4	22.1
Peaches	3.2	3.7	3.3
Cherries (including sour cherries)	10.7	6.8	8.3
Plums	5.7	9.1	8.5
Strawberries	3.2	2.4	3.2

* Estimate.

© European Union. Source: Eurostat, 2017, Agriculture, forestry and fisheries, table *APRO_ACS_A*—Crop statistics (from 2000 onwards).

Fruit and vegetables: Cyprus ('000 metric tons)

	2014	2015	2016*
Brassicas	6.3	5.5	6.7
Cauliflower and broccoli	1.6	1.1	2.0
Cabbages	4.7	4.4	4.7
Artichokes	2.2	2.1	2.3
Vegetables cultivated for fruit	70.1	64.5	78.2
Tomatoes	16.6	16.1	20.1
Cucumbers	12.4	8.1	11.2
Aubergines	2.8	2.1	4.1
Melons	10.0	12.0	15.4
Water melons	22.8	20.1	20.8
Root, tuber and bulb vegetables	12.9	12.8	13.5
Carrots	2.0	2.3	2.1
Onions	7.2	7.0	8.1
Beetroot	1.3	1.4	1.4
Beans	4.1	2.6	2.9
Apples	4.9	4.9	3.6
Stone fruit	6.3	7.7	4.7
Peaches	2.2	2.3	1.6
Apricots	0.8	1.1	0.8
Figs	3.7	3.5	6.0
Nuts	0.5	0.5	0.5
Almonds	0.4	0.4	0.3
Strawberries	1.4	1.4	1.9
Citrus fruit	103.9	117.0	n.a.
Lemons	n.a.	n.a.	n.a.
Pomelos and grapefruit	20.5	24.5	n.a.
Oranges	33.3	32.8	42.6
Fresh grapes	20.2	21.7	20.1
Olives	17.3	13.4	n.a.
Table olives	3.5	2.1	3.0
Olives for oil	13.8	11.3	10.5

* Provisional.

© European Union. Source: Eurostat, 2017, Agriculture, forestry and fisheries, table *APRO_ACS_A*—Crop statistics (from 2000 onwards).

Fruit and vegetables: Czech Republic ('000 metric tons)

	2014	2015	2016
Brassicas	63.7	50.5	57.6
Cauliflower and broccoli	3.9	3.7	2.6
Cabbages	57.6	43.6	52.1
Vegetables cultivated for fruit	25.7	23.2	35.4
Tomatoes	8.5	5.6	14.4
Cucumbers	4.3	3.6	4.2
Gherkins	12.9	14.0	16.8
Root, tuber and bulb vegetables	80.4	65.2	92.0
Carrots	26.1	23.5	26.6
Onions	38.2	27.2	42.0
Celeriac	8.9	7.6	10.9
Peas	5.7	4.2	4.6
Apples (including cider apples)	128.3	155.4	125.0
Pears (including perry pears)	3.7	8.9	6.5
Stone fruit	17.0	21.2	16.3
Peaches	1.1	1.6	0.3
Apricots	2.3	2.2	0.8
Cherries (including sour cherries)	7.5	8.3	9.2
Plums	6.1	9.1	6.0
Currants	1.9	2.9	1.8

© European Union. Source: Eurostat, 2017, Agriculture, forestry and fisheries, table *APRO_ACS_A*—Crop statistics (from 2000 onwards).

Fruit and vegetables: Denmark ('000 metric tons)

	2014	2015	2016
Brassicas	n.a.	44.7	42.5
Cauliflower and broccoli	4.4	6.0	5.1
Cabbages	26.3	27.1	33.3
Other leafy or stalked vegetables	n.a.	16.3	23.1
Leeks	6.3	6.4	5.8
Lettuce	10.2	9.2	15.5
Vegetables cultivated for fruit	n.a.	31.0	30.9
Tomatoes	12.8	10.6	10.6
Cucumbers	19.6	19.5	19.5
Root, tuber and bulb vegetables	n.a.	174.1	203.2
Carrots	107.3	89.2	117.6
Onions	51.9	53.4	62.0
Beetroot	n.a.	12.4	12.5
Apples (including cider apples)	35.4	35.7	36.5
Cherries (including sour cherries)	4.2	4.0	3.7
Blackcurrants	3.9	7.1	4.5

© European Union. Source: Eurostat, 2017, Agriculture, forestry and fisheries, table *APRO_ACS_A*—Crop statistics (from 2000 onwards).

Fruit and vegetables: Estonia ('000 metric tons)

	2014	2015	2016
Cabbages	11.8	14.3	11.6
Tomatoes	0.8	0.9	0.4
Cucumbers	5.3	7.8	5.2
Root, tuber and bulb vegetables	18.9	24.8	17.2
Carrots	12.8	18.1	11.1
Beetroot	5.0	5.6	4.9
Apples (including cider apples)	1.2	1.6	2.8
Strawberries	1.1	1.3	1.0

© European Union. Source: Eurostat, 2017, Agriculture, forestry and fisheries, table *APRO_ACS_A*—Crop statistics (from 2000 onwards).

Fruit and vegetables: Finland ('000 metric tons)

	2014	2015	2016
Brassicas	n.a.	29.0	25.9
Cabbages	24.2	21.6	20.3
Other leafy or stalked vegetables	n.a.	19.0	18.5
Lettuce	16.5	15.7	15.1
Vegetables cultivated for fruit	n.a.	90.0	92.7
Tomatoes	39.9	38.9	40.6
Cucumbers	38.4	40.5	39.1
Gherkins	9.7	8.1	10.3
Root, tuber and bulb vegetables	n.a.	116.3	128.3
Carrots	74.4	63.9	73.0
Onions	26.3	27.9	26.2
Beetroot	n.a.	10.0	11.4
Peas	7.1	5.9	7.2
Strawberries	12.9	14.5	12.0

© European Union. Source: Eurostat, 2017, Agriculture, forestry and fisheries, table *APRO_ACS_A*—Crop statistics (from 2000 onwards).

Fruit and vegetables: France ('000 metric tons)

	2014	2015	2016
Brassicas	521.9	523.6	484.6
Cauliflower and broccoli	326.4	341.5	308.5
Cabbages	69.5	57.9	55.2
Other cabbages	112.8	110.9	108.0
Other leafy or stalked vegetables	1,035.1	1,004.4	992.5
Leeks	165.9	159.8	150.9
Lettuce	238.0	229.1	228.4
Endive	59.2	64.1	61.3
Spinach	118.1	117.4	106.5
Chicory	242.1	222.9	223.4
Artichokes	38.4	38.5	45.9
Vegetables cultivated for fruit	1,485.1	1,501.5	1,580.3
Tomatoes	786.1	787.9	822.7
Cucumbers	130.6	134.7	135.7
Courgettes and marrows	132.4	123.0	128.4
Gourds and pumpkins	99.5	96.9	95.6
Melons	253.2	273.5	251.6
Root, tuber and bulb vegetables	1,317.2	1,322.8	1,411.4
Carrots	543.2	560.0	578.5
Onions	376.8	368.7	458.1
Shallots	50.3	48.9	49.4
Beetroot	132.7	131.9	133.7
Celeriac	59.4	59.0	57.3
Pulses	613.9	541.7	568.5
Peas	236.1	203.3	233.1
Beans	338.0	300.3	299.9
Cultivated mushrooms	108.6	107.4	101.9
Apples (including cider apples)	1,847.6	1,968.2	1,819.8
Pears (including perry pears)	132.6	140.8	129.6
Stone fruit	668.0	593.1	576.9
Peaches	121.5	114.7	108.9
Nectarines	113.1	102.9	98.9
Apricots	175.8	159.4	110.9
Cherries (including sour cherries)	47.3	42.0	34.7
Plums	199.6	163.0	211.3
Strawberries	58.8	56.9	58.7
Kiwi fruit	60.4	66.9	65.0
Wine grapes	6,156.9	6,212.8	6,197.9
Table grapes	43.8	41.6*	44.8*

* Estimate.

© European Union. Source: Eurostat, 2017, Agriculture, forestry and fisheries, table *APRO_ACS_A*—Crop statistics (from 2000 onwards).

Fruit and vegetables: Germany ('000 metric tons)

	2014	2015	2016
Brassicas	952.1	823.8	838.0
Cauliflower and broccoli	149.2	134.9	122.4
Cabbages	666.2	550.3	586.7
Other leafy or stalked vegetables	656.2	640.5	645.1
Leeks	108.2	89.5	85.9
Lettuce	214.6	215.7	206.8
Spinach	62.9	62.8	69.1
Asparagus	114.1	113.6	120.0
Vegetables cultivated for fruit	483.3	459.7	511.1
Tomatoes	84.5	80.9	85.3
Gherkins	197.9	190.1	207.1
Root, tuber and bulb vegetables	1,471.5	1,334.7	1,529.2
Kohlrabi	n.a.	n.a.	n.a.
Carrots	609.4	526.9	641.6
Onions	589.7	553.3	616.5
Beetroot	73.4	65.5	76.1
Celeriac	79.0	68.6	81.3
Radishes	120.1	120.5	113.7
Pulses	79.3	77.5	77.0
Cultivated mushrooms	59.9	62.6	72.1
Apples (including cider apples)	1,115.9	973.5	1,032.9
Pears (including perry pears)	45.0	43.1	34.6
Stone fruit	120.0	100.0	87.4
Cherries (including sour cherries)	56.9	48.6	45.3
Plums	63.1	51.4	42.1
Strawberries	168.8	172.6	143.2
Currants	12.9	13.9	14.0
Gooseberries	n.a.	n.a.	n.a.
Wine grapes	1,244.8	1,199.0	1,225.6

© European Union. Source: Eurostat, 2017, Agriculture, forestry and fisheries, table *APRO_ACS_A*—Crop statistics (from 2000 onwards).

Fruit and vegetables: Greece ('000 metric tons)

	2014	2015	2016
Brassicas	176.0	190.5	168.5
Cauliflower and broccoli	57.7	66.9	55.3
Cabbages	118.3	123.6	113.2
Other leafy or stalked vegetables	164.6	194.4	155.7
Leeks	23.5	34.0	29.3
Lettuce	50.5	71.6	59.8
Endive	4.4	4.1	3.9
Spinach	33.2	38.7	33.7
Asparagus	7.8	8.0	8.0
Artichokes	11.4	6.6	4.7
Vegetables cultivated for fruit	2,167.2	2,168.7	2,055.8
Tomatoes	1,042.1	1,050.4	1,014.4
Cucumbers	165.1	146.6	127.0
Aubergines	53.3	69.0	63.8
Gourds and pumpkins	0.0	0.0	0.0
Melons	97.1	99.7	79.5
Water melons	572.5	546.6	535.8
Red pepper, capsicum	147.9	153.6	151.7
Root, tuber and bulb vegetables	271.9	289.3	269.4
Carrots	44.1	36.4	34.9
Onions	204.2	229.3	217.5
Beetroot	8.8	10.4	9.3
Garlic	13.2	10.8	6.0
Pulses	80.7	93.8	84.1
Beans	60.5	73.5	68.6
Apples (including cider apples)	280.7	290.0	278.9
Pears (including perry pears)	70.2	66.1	65.3
Stone fruit	1,197.9	979.3	936.5
Peaches	829.1	631.4	627.8
Nectarines	145.4	145.6	135.4
Apricots	117.3	87.7	84.5
Cherries (including sour cherries)	73.0	82.2	67.3
Nuts	78.5	81.0	80.1
Walnuts	22.3	24.0	21.3
Almonds	20.4	20.5	19.1
Figs	10.5	9.7	8.0
Kiwi fruit	140.3	158.5	145.7
Citrus fruit	1,081.1	1,104.1	1,135.5
Oranges	859.4	880.9	916.7
Clementines	140.3	158.5	145.7
Lemons	64.5	44.8	69.1
Fresh grapes	1,046.0	1,082.2	998.8
Raisins (in fresh weight)	153.5	259.4	140.3
Wine grapes	598.9	574.1	541.6
Table grapes	293.5	248.7	316.9
Olives	1,781.1	1,269.9	1,203.0
Table olives	206.6	304.1	247.1
Olives for oil	1,574.5	965.8	955.9

© European Union. Source: Eurostat, 2017, Agriculture, forestry and fisheries, table *APRO_ACS_A*—Crop statistics (from 2000 onwards).

STATISTICAL SURVEY — Agriculture, Forestry and Fishing

Fruit and vegetables: Hungary ('000 metric tons)

	2014	2015	2016
Brassicas	96.9	102.6	102.3
Cauliflower and broccoli	19.9	19.0	18.6
Cabbages	69.6	75.2	75.2
Other leafy or stalked vegetables	33.5	32.1	33.2
Lettuce	12.3	12.1	12.1
Vegetables cultivated for fruit	538.8	601.8	607.0
Tomatoes	153.2	200.4	201.2
Cucumbers	15.6	14.9	15.1
Gourds and pumpkins	21.7	12.0	11.9
Melons	12.2	15.9	16.1
Watermelons	218.5	196.0	196.4
Red pepper, capsicum	83.6	117.1	119.1
Root, tuber and bulb vegetables	221.4	227.8	224.8
Carrots	119.3	78.2	79.7
Onion	61.9	60.3	61.5
Garlic	7.2	6.9	6.8
Pulses	105.2	115.5	118.9
Peas	87.7	94.6	96.5
Beans	17.5	20.9	22.4
Cultivated mushrooms	22.1	28.6	29.0
Apples (including cider apples)	779.9	511.5	485.9
Pears (including perry pears)	20.8	36.8	40.5
Stone fruit	209.5	192.9	186.4
Peaches	38.7	37.4	37.4
Apricots	23.1	19.9	21.1
Cherries (including sour cherries)	101.3	88.1	83.9
Plums	45.1	46.0	42.5
Berries (excluding strawberries)	18.4	22.2	21.3
Currants	2.6	3.6	4.7
Raspberries	1.6	1.5	1.3
Fresh grapes	406.0	472.4	449.2
Wine grapes	390.5	457.9	433.3
Table grapes	15.6	11.6	13.2

© European Union. Source: Eurostat, 2017, Agriculture, forestry and fisheries, table *APRO_ACS_A*—Crop statistics (from 2000 onwards).

Fruit and vegetables: Ireland ('000 metric tons)

	2014	2015	2016
Brassicas	36.4	35.0	34.7
Cauliflower and broccoli	12.1	11.1	10.8
Cabbages	22.1	22.3	22.3
Other leafy or stalked vegetables*	13.1	12.7	15.1
Lettuce	7.9	7.4	7.6
Vegetables cultivated for fruit	5.8	6.5	5.8
Tomatoes	4.3	4.4	4.0
Root, tuber and bulb vegetables	72.0	71.2	85.0
Carrots	40.2	40.2	52.2
Onions	5.1	4.6	6.0
Cultivated mushrooms	69.6	72.2	70.0
Apples (including cider apples)	19.6	18.8	21.8

* Definition differs.
© European Union. Source: Eurostat, 2017, Agriculture, forestry and fisheries, table *APRO_ACS_A*—Crop statistics (from 2000 onwards).

Fruit and vegetables: Italy ('000 metric tons)

	2014	2015	2016
Brassicas	n.a.	n.a.	n.a.
Cauliflower and broccoli	405.1	386.0	343.6
Cabbages	76.9	177.5	76.2
Other leafy or stalked vegetables	n.a.	n.a.	3,525.6
Celery	113.5	112.2*	100.9
Lettuce	484.9	438.0	322.2
Endive	215.4	214.7	209.7
Spinach	96.7	97.5*	92.3
Chicory	224.4	n.a.	260.7
Artichokes	451.5	401.3	400.6
Vegetables cultivated for fruit	n.a.	n.a.	9,476.5
Tomatoes	4,498.1	6,410.3	6,580.0
Cucumbers	59.9	55.6	435.8
Aubergines	308.7	300.2	317.6
Courgettes and marrows	540.0	533.5	554.1
Melons	560.3	595.6	632.3
Watermelons	453.2	494.5	534.0
Red pepper, capsicum	285.2	282.9	173.8
Root, tuber and bulb vegetables	n.a.	n.a.	n.a.
Carrots	539.2	533.0	530.8
Onions	418.6	378.3	450.7
Pulses	301.2	n.a.	308.5
Peas	80.0	74.7	99.1
Beans	169.7	148.7	163.0
Cultivated mushrooms	n.a.	n.a.	68.3
Apples (including cider apples)	2,473.6	2,488.0	2,455.6
Pears (including perry pears)	701.6	789.9	701.9
Stone fruit	n.a.	n.a.	1,986.0
Peaches	860.0	921.2	912.1
Nectarines	519.5	501.7	515.4
Apricots	222.7	216.8	237.0
Cherries (including sour cherries)	110.8	110.7	94.9
Plums	214.9	199.9	220.7
Nuts	n.a.	n.a.	244.9
Hazelnuts	75.5	101.6	120.6
Almonds	74.0	70.4	74.6
Strawberries	135.3	143.2	34.4
Kiwi fruit	507.0	578.9	523.6
Citrus fruit	2,661.6	n.a.	n.a.
Oranges	1,668.7	1,668.3	n.a.
Clementines	478.3	613.8	n.a.
Lemons	n.a.	n.a.	n.a.
Fresh grapes	6,930.8	8,050.2	8,247.9
Wine grapes	5,932.2	7,005.6	7,204.2
Table grapes	998.6	1,044.6	997.0
Olives	1,963.7*	3,171.0	n.a.
Olives for oil	1,903.4*	n.a.	2,022.5

* Estimate.
© European Union. Source: Eurostat, 2017, Agriculture, forestry and fisheries, table *APRO_ACS_A*—Crop statistics (from 2000 onwards).

Fruit and vegetables: Latvia ('000 metric tons)

	2014	2015	2016
Brassicas	30.1	28.2	27.6
Cabbages	29.6	27.7	27.3
Vegetables cultivated for fruit	14.5	14.8	16.5
Cucumbers	7.8	6.8	7.6
Root, tuber and bulb vegetables	39.4	31.2	31.4
Carrots	19.0	8.8	14.8
Onions*	n.a.	5.7	5.2
Beetroot	11.9	14.6	10.3
Apples (including cider apples)	0.9	1.4	1.1
Stone fruit	9.6	7.8	9.8
Strawberries	0.2	0.3	0.2
Currants	0.3	0.6	0.4

* Definition differs.
© European Union. Source: Eurostat, 2017, Agriculture, forestry and fisheries, table *APRO_ACS_A*—Crop statistics (from 2000 onwards).

Fruit and vegetables: Lithuania ('000 metric tons)

	2014	2015	2016
Brassicas	68.5	58.2	57.1
Cauliflower and broccoli	1.8	1.7	1.3
Cabbages	65.2	55.4	54.4
Vegetables cultivated for fruit	37.6	28.3	29.3
Cucumbers	22.9	18.2	15.9
Root, tuber and bulb vegetables	139.5	102.0	101.2
Carrots	61.2	38.0	38.1
Onions	25.9	22.2	23.4
Beetroot	50.0	38.9	37.5
Cultivated mushrooms	12.2	13.8	1.6
Apples (including cider apples)	52.0	65.0	60.4
Stone fruit	1.3	1.0	1.7
Strawberries	3.2	3.2	2.7
Blackcurrants	2.7	3.3	2.9

© European Union. Source: Eurostat, 2017, Agriculture, forestry and fisheries, table *APRO_ACS_A*—Crop statistics (from 2000 onwards).

Fruit and vegetables: Luxembourg ('000 metric tons)

	2014	2015	2016
Vegetables	2.6	2.6	2.6
Apples (including cider apples)	2.6	2.4	2.4
Pears (including perry pears)	0.3	0.3	0.3
Stone fruit	n.a.	0.2	0.2
Fresh grapes	16.6	14.7	11.0

© European Union. Source: Eurostat, 2017, Agriculture, forestry and fisheries, table *APRO_ACS_A*—Crop statistics (from 2000 onwards).

Fruit and vegetables: Malta ('000 metric tons)

	2014	2015	2016
Brassicas	12.2	10.8	12.0
Cauliflower and broccoli	6.7	5.8	6.8
Cabbages	4.4	3.9	4.1
Other leafy or stalked vegetables	7.1	7.3	6.6
Lettuce	4.2	4.1	3.8
Vegetables cultivated for fruit	32.8	30.2	29.6
Tomatoes	12.9	12.0	12.4
Courgettes and marrows	3.7	3.2	3.1
Melons	3.5	3.0	2.5
Watermelons	3.7	3.6	3.2
Root, tuber and bulb vegetables	10.5	10.3	10.5
Carrots	1.2	1.3	1.5
Onions	8.3	8.1	8.2
Table grapes	0.4	0.4	0.4

© European Union. Source: Eurostat, 2017, Agriculture, forestry and fisheries, table *APRO_ACS_A*—Crop statistics (from 2000 onwards).

Fruit and vegetables: Netherlands ('000 metric tons)

	2014	2015	2016
Brassicas	319.0	335.2	309.0
Cauliflower and broccoli	52.0	65.5	62.3
Brussels sprouts	55.0	60.0	46.6
Cabbages	206.0	209.8	182.0
Other cabbages	6.0	0.0	18.1
Other leafy or stalked vegetables	313.0	519.0	521.6
Leeks	106.0	86.3	82.2
Lettuce	89.0	119.5	118.0
Endive	17.0	16.0	17.6
Spinach	35.0	47.0	44.8
Asparagus	18.0	17.1	18.6
Chicory	51.0	222.1	221.3
Vegetables cultivated for fruit	1,647.0	1,729.4	1,708.1
Tomatoes	900.0	890.0	890.0
Cucumbers	440.0	405.0	370.0
Aubergines	51.0	53.0	54.0
Courgettes and marrows	18.0	18.4	16.9
Red pepper, capsicum	340.0	345.0	365.0
Root, tuber and bulb vegetables	2,181.0	2,216.1	2,205.5
Carrots	548.0	563.4	600.4
Onions	1,379.0	1,504.1*	1,449.4*
Beetroot	38.0	33.5	40.3
Celeriac	74.0	71.4	75.2
Radishes	26.0	24.0	24.0
Pulses	75.0	54.8	52.1
Peas	19.0	17.7	15.6
Beans	32.0	37.1	33.0
Cultivated mushrooms	310.0	310.0	300.0
Apples (including cider apples)	353.0	335.9	317.4
Pears (including perry pears)	349.0	349.0	373.8
Strawberries	54.0	57.7	57.5

* Definition differs.

© European Union. Source: Eurostat, 2017, Agriculture, forestry and fisheries, table *APRO_ACS_A*—Crop statistics (from 2000 onwards).

Fruit and vegetables: Poland ('000 metric tons)

	2014	2015	2016
Brassicas	1,539.1	1,185.5	1,406.4
Cauliflower and broccoli	320.6	252.9	314.7
Cabbages	1,156.4	875.0	1,017.7
Vegetables cultivated for fruit	1,548.8	1,498.1	1,651.7
Tomatoes	810.6	789.6	867.0
Cucumbers	454.1	419.5	457.5
Root, tuber and bulb vegetables	2,142.4	1,773.0	2,113.8
Carrots	822.6	677.7	822.0
Onions	651.1	548.4	651.4
Beetroot	357.8	297.0	341.1
Apples (including cider apples)	3,195.3	3,168.8	3,604.3
Pears (including perry pears)	73.7	69.6	81.5
Stone fruit	n.a.	336.1	371.8
Cherries (including sour cherries)	224.6	227.5	248.6
Plums	106.1	94.9	109.5
Strawberries	213.7	214.6	207.6
Berries (excluding strawberries)	n.a.	305.0	373.3
Currants	163.0	159.9	166.1
Raspberries	125.9	79.9	129.1

© European Union. Source: Eurostat, 2017, Agriculture, forestry and fisheries, table *APRO_ACS_A*—Crop statistics (from 2000 onwards).

Fruit and vegetables: Portugal ('000 metric tons)

	2014	2015	2016
Brassicas	236.0	198.8	241.0
Cauliflower and broccoli	39.0	47.7	46.5
Other leafy or stalked vegetables	144.1	154.1	110.1
Lettuce	63.3	56.9	52.0
Vegetables cultivated for fruit	1,679.8	1,641.6	1,938.2
Tomatoes	1,399.5	1,407.0	1,693.9
Melons	88.6	61.0	45.1
Watermelons	24.0	29.1	31.7
Red pepper, capsicum	43.1	23.3	34.1
Root, tuber and bulb vegetables	198.0	187.3	210.1
Carrots	104.5	97.5	95.7
Onions	57.1	59.4	69.9
Pulses	26.3	32.9	24.0
Beans	13.5	9.7	9.4
Apples (including cider apples)	273.7	325.0	228.0
Pears (including perry pears)	210.0	141.2	113.0
Stone fruit	79.2	93.2	72.5
Peaches	31.2	35.6	26.7
Cherries (including sour cherries)	10.8	17.9	9.0
Plums	24.2	24.5	24.5
Nuts*	32.0	42.1	38.2
Almonds	9.0	10.1	7.6
Chestnuts	18.5	27.6	26.2
Strawberries	14.8	9.7	10.8
Kiwi fruit	18.2	28.3	21.3
Citrus fruit	304.0	301.5	n.a.
Oranges	251.5	246.6	283.0
Lemons	14.7	15.5	n.a.
Fresh grapes	818.5	935.1	793.0
Wine grapes	804.1	916.1	778.6
Table grapes	14.4	19.0	14.4
Olives	455.4	722.9	n.a.
Table olives	17.4	20.8	17.6
Olives for oil	438.0	702.1	491.5

* Definition differs.

© European Union. Source: Eurostat, 2017, Agriculture, forestry and fisheries, table *APRO_ACS_A*—Crop statistics (from 2000 onwards).

Fruit and vegetables: Romania ('000 metric tons)

	2014	2015	2016
Brassicas	729.0	687.2	654.8
Cauliflower and broccoli	45.1	43.2	39.9
Other leafy or stalked vegetables	6.5	5.7	6.2
Lettuce	2.1	2.2	2.3
Vegetables cultivated for fruit	1,431.1	1,351.6	1,250.6
Tomatoes	473.9	464.8	421.7
Melons	56.0	56.9	59.1
Water melons	474.6	449.2	418.5
Red pepper, capsicum	149.5	145.5	119.7
Root, tuber and bulb vegetables	445.0	392.4	347.5
Carrots	139.2	122.1	108.5
Onions	249.5	218.2	183.4
Pulses	33.0	31.2	29.1
Beans	27.5	26.8	25.0
Apples (including cider apples)	502.4	459.1	450.4
Pears (including perry pears)	58.5	41.8	50.0
Stone fruit	630.6	588.8	607.7
Peaches	23.3	20.5	22.3
Cherries (including sour cherries)	79.7	71.1	69.9
Plums	484.3	467.3	485.4
Almonds	0.0	0.0	0.0
Strawberries	21.8	21.5	22.9
Fresh grapes	779.8	794.9	732.8
Table grapes	36.0	42.1	38.8

© European Union. Source: Eurostat, 2017, Agriculture, forestry and fisheries, table *APRO_ACS_A*—Crop statistics (from 2000 onwards).

Fruit and vegetables: Slovakia ('000 metric tons)

	2014	2015	2016
Brassicas	n.a.	13.2	18.5
Cauliflower and broccoli	1.0	2.9	1.2
Cabbages	16.0	9.8	16.9
Vegetables cultivated for fruit	n.a.	36.6	39.6
Tomatoes	21.5	19.5	18.9
Cucumbers	2.6	3.4	4.1
Gherkins	0.7	0.9	1.2
Melons	0.4	0.3	0.4
Water melons	3.0	3.0	2.5
Red pepper, capsicum	5.1	5.8	6.0
Root, tuber and bulb vegetables	n.a.	31.9	41.6
Carrots	6.5	10.1	6.4
Onions	24.3	16.9	29.9
Pulses	2.3	2.8	3.2
Peas	2.8	2.8	3.2
Apples (including cider apples)	48.5	46.3	20.7
Stone fruit	n.a.	n.a.	n.a.
Peaches	2.0	2.1	1.1
Plums	2.4	2.2	0.5
Fresh grapes	38.5	50.2	37.8
Wine grapes	38.2	49.7	37.4

© European Union. Source: Eurostat, 2017, Agriculture, forestry and fisheries, table *APRO_ACS_A*—Crop statistics (from 2000 onwards).

Fruit and vegetables: Slovenia ('000 metric tons)

	2014	2015	2016
Brassicas	n.a.	24.8	28.0
Cabbages	16.2	20.9	22.7
Other leafy or stalked vegetables	n.a.	24.9	23.4
Lettuce	10.5	11.7	12.2
Chicory	4.2	5.7	5.2
Vegetables cultivated for fruit	n.a.	17.2	21.2
Tomatoes	6.6	5.7	8.7
Red pepper, capsicum	3.6	4.0	4.5
Root, tuber and bulb vegetables	n.a.	22.5	29.4
Carrots	3.5	3.4	5.6
Onions	7.6	7.2	10.9
Beetroot	n.a.	2.7	4.0
Pulses	n.a.	3.3	3.4
Beans	3.4	3.1	3.2
Apples (including cider apples)	71.0	83.9	42.7
Pears (including perry pears)	3.5	3.7	3.2
Stone fruit	n.a.	8.2	6.6
Peaches	4.2	5.6*	4.7*
Cherries (including sour cherries)	1.1	1.5	1.0
Plums	0.4	0.3	0.3
Nuts	n.a.	1.0	0.8

* Definition differs.
© European Union. Source: Eurostat, 2017, Agriculture, forestry and fisheries, table *APRO_ACS_A*—Crop statistics (from 2000 onwards).

Fruit and vegetables: Spain ('000 metric tons)

	2014	2015	2016
Brassicas	n.a.	813.9	891.8
Cauliflower and broccoli	597.0	607.2	640.1
Cabbages	150.5	165.8	162.8
Other cabbages	0.0	39.6	86.9
Other leafy or stalked vegetables	n.a.	1,698.1	1,724.2
Leeks	90.5	92.6	81.8
Celery	91.7	96.2	93.8
Lettuce	902.9	927.4	929.9
Endive	75.7	71.5	67.6
Artichokes	234.1	204.1	225.6
Vegetables cultivated for fruit	n.a.	9,285.3	9,767.1
Tomatoes	4,888.9	4,832.7	5,233.5
Cucumbers	775.9	705.2	630.5
Aubergines	208.2	244.5	242.6
Gourds and pumpkins	53.9	82.7	97.2
Melons	750.2	692.1	649.8
Water melons	858.6	1,039.7	1,092.1
Red pepper, capsicum	1,130.3	1,105.1	1,175.6
Root, tuber and bulb vegetables	n.a.	1,909.9	2,109.5
Carrots	376.3	410.9	405.0
Onions	1,364.6	1,247.6	1,407.9
Garlic	177.4	178.4	209.8
Pulses	337.8	314.1	356.3
Peas	98.6	84.7	117.1
Beans	188.2	180.0	181.7
Cultivated mushrooms	149.9	218.8	148.0
Apples (including cider apples)	620.8	598.2	621.2
Pears (including perry pears)	429.6	355.4	349.3
Stone fruit	n.a.	2,048.1	1,856.9
Peaches	931.1	964.1	902.9
Nectarines	642.6	617.4	518.8
Apricots	136.5	153.7	139.6
Cherries (including sour cherries)	111.8	94.2	100.5
Plums	232.8	217.3	193.6
Nuts	n.a.	409.8	391.0
Almonds	195.7	211.1	199.2
Avocados	77.4	86.6	91.5
Strawberries	291.9	397.4	377.6
Citrus fruit	7,043.4	5,970.6	n.a.
Oranges	3,494.5	3,098.3	3,629.7*
Satsumas	135.8	120.5	n.a.
Clementines	1,694.5	1,361.3	n.a.
Lemons	n.a.	775.5	n.a.
Fresh grapes	6,221.7	5,799.1	6,102.9*
Wine grapes	5,978.5	5,527.1	5,819.6*
Table grapes	241.8	270.7	282.0*
Olives	4,577.8	7,344.8	n.a.
Table olives	434.8	540.5	528.0*
Olives for oil	4,143.0	6,804.3	6,501.3*

* Provisional.
© European Union. Source: Eurostat, 2017, Agriculture, forestry and fisheries, table *APRO_ACS_A*—Crop statistics (from 2000 onwards).

Fruit and vegetables: Sweden ('000 metric tons)

	2014	2015	2016
Cauliflower and broccoli	9.4	9.3	7.7
Cabbages	16.5	15.2	15.6
Leeks	5.4	4.9	2.9
Lettuce	37.8	32.2	32.7
Tomatoes	14.6	14.8	14.6
Cucumbers	28.2	28.0	32.6
Gherkins	10.0	9.1	9.6
Carrots	119.0	115.6	111.7
Apples (including cider apples)	24.6	25.4	26.8
Strawberries	16.0	17.1	15.3

© European Union. Source: Eurostat, 2017, Agriculture, forestry and fisheries, table *APRO_ACS_A*—Crop statistics (from 2000 onwards).

Fruit and vegetables: United Kingdom ('000 metric tons)

	2013	2014	2015
Brassicas	n.a.	447.0	444.3
Cauliflower and broccoli	88.0	163.0	163.0
Brussels sprouts	n.a.	52.0	50.9
Other leafy or stalked vegetables	0.0	258.0	279.7
Celery	51.0	54.0	53.7
Leeks	35.0	35.0	33.9
Lettuce	126.0	124.0	160.1
Vegetables cultivated for fruit	0.0	178.7	191.3
Tomatoes	0.0	98.5	97.2
Cucumbers	0.0	56.5	53.6
Root, tuber and bulb vegetables	n.a.	1,445.0	1,398.9
Carrots	696.0	786.0	731.0
Onions	354.0	374.0	408.1
Beetroot	n.a.	72.0	71.7
Pulses	n.a.	195.0	176.6
Peas	120.9	165.0	162.7
Cultivated mushrooms	0.0	79.0	103.2
Apples (including cider apples)	385.5	268.0	459.6
Pears (including perry pears)	34.0	26.0	26.5

© European Union. Source: Eurostat, 2017, Agriculture, forestry and fisheries, table *APRO_ACS_A*—Crop statistics (from 2000 onwards).

LIVESTOCK POPULATION

Cattle ('000 head at December)

	2014	2015	2016		2014	2015	2016
Austria	1,961	1,958	1,954	Latvia	422	419	412
Belgium	2,477	2,503	2,499	Lithuania	737	723	695
Bulgaria	562	561	570	Luxembourg	201	201	202
Croatia	441	455	462	Malta	15	15	14
Cyprus	60	59*	63*	Netherlands	4,169	4,315	4,294
Czech Republic	1,373	1,366	1,340	Poland	5,660	5,763	5,970
Denmark	1,553	1,566	1,554	Portugal	1,549	1,606	1,635*
Estonia	265	256	248	Romania	2,069	2,092	2,050
Finland	907	903	887	Slovakia	466	457	446
France	19,271	19,406	19,004	Slovenia	468	484	489
Germany	12,742	12,635	12,467	Spain	6,079	6,183	6,257
Greece	659	582	554	Sweden	1,436	1,428	1,436
Hungary	802	821	838	United Kingdom	9,693	9,816	9,806
Ireland	6,243	6,422	6,613				
Italy	6,125	6,156	6,315	**Total (EU-28)**	88,406	89,152	89,075*

* Provisional.

© European Union. Source: Eurostat, 2017, Agriculture, forestry and fisheries, table *APRO_MT_LSCATL*—Cattle population—Annual data.

Goats ('000 head at December)

	2014	2015	2016		2014	2015	2016
Austria	71	77	83	Latvia	12	13	13
Belgium	n.a.	n.a.	n.a.	Lithuania	13	14	13
Bulgaria	293	277	238	Luxembourg	n.a.	n.a.	n.a.
Croatia	61	62	75	Malta	5	5	5
Cyprus	240	237*	n.a.	Netherlands	441	468	504
Czech Republic	n.a.	n.a.	n.a.	Poland	n.a.	n.a.	n.a.
Denmark	n.a.	n.a.	n.a.	Portugal	382	373	347*
Estonia	n.a.	n.a.	n.a.	Romania	1,417	1,440	1,483
Finland	n.a.	n.a.	n.a.	Slovakia	35	36†	36
France	1,271	1,230	1,204	Slovenia	n.a.	n.a.	n.a.
Germany	117†	110†	139	Spain	2,704	2,801	3,088
Greece	4,254	4,017	3,888	Sweden	0	n.a.	n.a.
Hungary	70	72	78	United Kingdom	100	101	104
Ireland	n.a.	n.a.	n.a.				
Italy	937	962	1,026	**Total (EU-28)**	n.a.	n.a.	n.a.

* Provisional. † Estimate.

© European Union. Source: Eurostat, 2017, Agriculture, forestry and fisheries, table *APRO_MT_LSGOAT*—Goat population—Annual data.

Agriculture, Forestry and Fishing

Sheep ('000 head at December)

	2014	2015	2016		2014	2015	2016
Austria	349	354	378	Latvia	93	102	107
Belgium	n.a.	n.a.	n.a.	Lithuania	124	147	164
Bulgaria	1,335	1,332	1,360	Luxembourg	n.a.	n.a.	n.a.
Croatia	605	608	619	Malta	11	11	12
Cyprus	322	332*	n.a.	Netherlands	1,070	1,032	1,040
Czech Republic	n.a.	n.a.	n.a.	Poland	n.a.	n.a.	n.a.
Denmark	n.a.	n.a.	n.a.	Portugal	2,033	2,043	2,068*
Estonia	n.a.	n.a.	n.a.	Romania	9,518	9,810	9,876
Finland	n.a.	n.a.	n.a.	Slovakia	391	381†	369
France	7,168	7,057	7,157	Slovenia	n.a.	n.a.	n.a.
Germany	1,601	1,580	1,574	Spain	15,432	16,026	15,963
Greece	9,072	8,852	8,739	Sweden	589	595	578
Hungary	1,185	1,190	1,158	United Kingdom	22,687	23,103	23,819
Ireland	3,325	3,325	3,438				
Italy	7,166	7,149	7,285	**Total (EU-28)**	n.a.	n.a.	n.a.

* Provisional. † Estimate.
© European Union. Source: Eurostat, 2017, Agriculture, forestry and fisheries, table *APRO_MT_LSSHEEP*—Sheep population—Annual data.

Pigs ('000 head at December)

	2014	2015	2016		2014	2015	2016
Austria	2,868	2,845	2,793	Latvia	349	334	336
Belgium	6,350	6,364	6,181*	Lithuania	714	688	664
Bulgaria	553	600	616	Luxembourg	93	89	95
Croatia	1,156	1,167	1,163	Malta	47	44	41
Cyprus	342	328*	353	Netherlands	12,065	12,453	11,881
Czech Republic	1,607	1,555	1,479	Poland	11,266	10,590	11,107
Denmark	12,709	12,702	12,281	Portugal	2,127	2,247	2,151*
Estonia	358	305	266	Romania	5,042	4,927	4,708
Finland	1,223	1,239	1,197	Slovakia	642	633	586
France*	13,300	13,307	12,793	Slovenia	282	271	266
Germany	28,339	27,652	27,376	Spain	26,568	28,367	29,232
Greece	1,046	877	743	Sweden	1,458	1,435	1,471
Hungary	3,136	3,124	2,887	United Kingdom	4,510	4,422	4,538
Ireland	1,506	1,475	1,528				
Italy	8,676	8,675	8,478	**Total (EU-28)**	148,331	148,716	147,209*

* Provisional.
© European Union. Source: Eurostat, 2017, Agriculture, forestry and fisheries, table *APRO_MT_LSPIG*—Pig population—Annual data.

Laying hens ('000 head)

	2007	2010	2013
Austria	6,700	6,400	5,980
Belgium	11,990	11,680	n.a.
Bulgaria	6,910	7,880	n.a.
Croatia	3,230	4,650	n.a.
Cyprus	540	550	460
Czech Republic	8,850	8,990	n.a.
Denmark	4,160	3,900	n.a.
Estonia	850	860	850
Finland	4,260	4,680	n.a.
France	73,670	78,060	n.a.
Germany	51,430	35,280	n.a.
Greece	8,400	8,240	n.a.
Hungary	13,090	10,300	n.a.
Ireland	2,380	2,700	n.a.
Italy	37,030	44,100	n.a.
Latvia	2,850	3,460	3,190
Lithuania	4,650	3,080	3,030
Luxembourg	60	70	100
Malta	560	300	n.a.
Netherlands	49,410	56,500	53,480
Poland	51,530	51,080	50,490
Portugal	9,140	11,980	9,760
Romania	39,350	39,070	n.a.
Slovakia	4,490	5,850	5,560
Slovenia	1,270	1,500	1,180
Spain	59,940	59,480	n.a.
Sweden	7,080	7,710	n.a.
United Kingdom	48,450	46,950	n.a.
Total (EU-28)	n.a.	n.a.	n.a.

© European Union. Source: Eurostat, 2017, Agriculture, forestry and fisheries, table *EF_LSAYHENAA*—Laying hens: number of farms and heads of poultry by agricultural size of farm (UAA) and size of laying hen flock.

PRODUCTION OF MEAT

Note: Figures refer to slaughterings.

Meat production: Austria ('000 metric tons)

	2014	2015	2016
Beef and veal	221.6	228.8	227.4
Pig meat	525.6	527.8	511.5
Mutton and lamb	7.2	7.0	6.4
Goat meat	0.8	0.8	0.9
Poultry meat	n.a.	n.a.	n.a.

© European Union. Source: Eurostat, 2017, Agriculture, forestry and fisheries, table *APRO_MT_PANN*—Slaughtering in slaughterhouses—Annual data.

Meat production: Belgium ('000 metric tons)

	2014	2015	2016
Beef and veal	257.7	267.9	278.4
Pig meat	1,118.3	1,124.3	1,060.5
Mutton and lamb	2.4	2.5	2.8
Horse meat	n.a.	n.a.	n.a.
Poultry meat	433.3	452.9	461.3

© European Union. Source: Eurostat, 2017, Agriculture, forestry and fisheries, table *APRO_MT_PANN*—Slaughtering in slaughterhouses—Annual data.

Meat production: Bulgaria ('000 metric tons)

	2014	2015	2016
Beef and veal	4.8	5.3	6.7
Pig meat	53.7	60.7	65.7
Mutton and lamb	n.a.	n.a.	n.a.
Poultry meat	97.9	101.3	106.5

© European Union. Source: Eurostat, 2017, Agriculture, forestry and fisheries, table *APRO_MT_PANN*—Slaughtering in slaughterhouses—Annual data.

Meat production: Croatia ('000 metric tons)

	2014	2015	2016
Beef and veal	44.4	42.3	44.4
Pig meat	68.7	73.0	79.9
Mutton and lamb	0.8	1.0	1.1
Poultry meat	59.1	63.4	64.0

© European Union. Source: Eurostat, 2017, Agriculture, forestry and fisheries, table *APRO_MT_PANN*—Slaughtering in slaughterhouses—Annual data.

Meat production: Cyprus ('000 metric tons)

	2014	2015	2016
Beef and veal	4.6	5.0	7.7
Pig meat	42.6	43.4	43.9
Mutton and lamb	3.1	3.4	3.0
Goat meat	2.1	2.0	1.6
Poultry meat	21.7	23.8	24.0

© European Union. Source: Eurostat, 2017, Agriculture, forestry and fisheries, table *APRO_MT_PANN*—Slaughtering in slaughterhouses—Annual data.

Meat production: Czech Republic ('000 metric tons)

	2014	2015	2016
Beef and veal	65.5	68.3	71.9
Pig meat	236.0	227.7	220.3
Mutton and lamb	0.2	0.2	0.2
Poultry meat	149.4	151.4	156.5

© European Union. Source: Eurostat, 2017, Agriculture, forestry and fisheries, table *APRO_MT_PANN*—Slaughtering in slaughterhouses—Annual data.

Meat production: Denmark ('000 metric tons)

	2014	2015	2016
Beef and veal	125.6	120.6	129.4
Pig meat	1,593.9	1,598.7	1,566.6
Mutton and lamb	1.7	1.8	1.6
Poultry meat	143.0	134.4	144.3

© European Union. Source: Eurostat, 2017, Agriculture, forestry and fisheries, table *APRO_MT_PANN*—Slaughtering in slaughterhouses—Annual data.

Meat production: Estonia ('000 metric tons)

	2014	2015	2016
Beef and veal	n.a.	9.6	9.4
Pig meat	40.6	42.4	42.8
Mutton and lamb	0.1	0.1	0.1
Poultry meat	n.a.	n.a.	n.a.

© European Union. Source: Eurostat, 2017, Agriculture, forestry and fisheries, table *APRO_MT_PANN*—Slaughtering in slaughterhouses—Annual data.

Meat production: Finland ('000 metric tons)

	2014	2015	2016
Beef and veal	82.3	85.8	86.4
Pig meat	186.1	191.9	190.1
Mutton and lamb	1.0	1.2	1.3
Horse meat	n.a.	n.a.	n.a.
Poultry meat	113.4	117.3	125.4

© European Union. Source: Eurostat, 2017, Agriculture, forestry and fisheries, table *APRO_MT_PANN*—Slaughtering in slaughterhouses—Annual data.

Meat production: France ('000 metric tons)

	2014	2015	2016
Beef and veal	1,420.4	1,451.0	1,461.7
Pig meat	1,943.6	1,967.6	1,987.8
Mutton and lamb	80.5	80.7	82.9
Goat meat	6.2	6.2	6.5
Horse meat	n.a.	n.a.	n.a.
Poultry meat	1,678.0	1,718.0	1,669.0

© European Union. Source: Eurostat, 2017, Agriculture, forestry and fisheries, table *APRO_MT_PANN*—Slaughtering in slaughterhouses—Annual data.

Meat production: Germany ('000 metric tons)

	2014	2015	2016
Beef and veal	1,128.0	1,124.0	1,148.0
Pig meat	5,507.0	5,562.0	5,579.0
Mutton and lamb	19.0	21.0	22.0
Goat meat	0.0	0.0	0.0
Horse meat	n.a.	n.a.	n.a.
Poultry meat	1,527.0	1,511.0	1,525.0

© European Union. Source: Eurostat, 2017, Agriculture, forestry and fisheries, table *APRO_MT_PANN*—Slaughtering in slaughterhouses—Annual data.

Meat production: Greece ('000 metric tons)

	2014	2015	2016
Beef and veal	46.0	41.9	40.2
Pig meat	96.2	90.0	93.5
Mutton and lamb	58.4	54.9	53.6
Goat meat	23.9	21.9	20.9
Poultry meat	190.5	189.6	212.7

© European Union. Source: Eurostat, 2017, Agriculture, forestry and fisheries, table *APRO_MT_PANN*—Slaughtering in slaughterhouses—Annual data.

Meat production: Hungary ('000 metric tons)

	2014	2015	2016
Beef and veal	23.1	26.4	28.1
Pig meat	368.6	409.3	431.8
Mutton and lamb	0.3	0.4	0.6
Poultry meat	430.1	478.7	507.9

© European Union. Source: Eurostat, 2017, Agriculture, forestry and fisheries, table *APRO_MT_PANN*—Slaughtering in slaughterhouses—Annual data.

Meat production: Ireland ('000 metric tons)

	2014	2015	2016
Beef and veal	581.8	564.1	588.4
Pig meat	254.1	276.4	282.7
Mutton and lamb	57.6	58.4	61.0
Poultry meat	115.9	128.0	145.5

© European Union. Source: Eurostat, 2017, Agriculture, forestry and fisheries, table *APRO_MT_PANN*—Slaughtering in slaughterhouses—Annual data.

Meat production: Italy ('000 metric tons)

	2014	2015	2016
Beef and veal	709.4	788.3	809.7
Pig meat	1,327.8	1,485.8	1,544.1
Mutton and lamb	25.3	33.6	31.3
Goat meat	1.3	1.8	1.6
Horse meat	n.a.	n.a.	n.a.
Poultry meat	1,242.8	1,295.0	1,366.3

© European Union. Source: Eurostat, 2017, Agriculture, forestry and fisheries, table *APRO_MT_PANN*—Slaughtering in slaughterhouses—Annual data.

Meat production: Latvia ('000 metric tons)

	2014	2015	2016
Beef and veal	17.0	17.4	17.7
Pig meat	28.2	29.3	31.2
Mutton and lamb	0.2	0.3	0.4
Poultry meat	28.6	29.5	30.0

© European Union. Source: Eurostat, 2017, Agriculture, forestry and fisheries, table *APRO_MT_PANN*—Slaughtering in slaughterhouses—Annual data.

Meat production: Lithuania ('000 metric tons)

	2014	2015	2016
Beef and veal	39.3	44.1	42.3
Pig meat	66.7	66.2	60.4
Mutton and lamb	0.1	0.1	0.2
Poultry meat	94.4	95.8	104.1

© European Union. Source: Eurostat, 2017, Agriculture, forestry and fisheries, table *APRO_MT_PANN*—Slaughtering in slaughterhouses—Annual data.

Meat production: Luxembourg ('000 metric tons)

	2014	2015	2016
Beef and veal	8.5	9.1	9.4
Pig meat	11.9	12.3	13.8
Mutton and lamb	0.0	0.0	0.1
Poultry meat	0.0	0.0	0.0

© European Union. Source: Eurostat, 2017, Agriculture, forestry and fisheries, table *APRO_MT_PANN*—Slaughtering in slaughterhouses—Annual data.

Meat production: Malta ('000 metric tons)

	2014	2015	2016
Pig meat	6.2	5.6	4.9
Poultry meat	3.9	3.9	3.8

© European Union. Source: Eurostat, 2017, Agriculture, forestry and fisheries, table *APRO_MT_PANN*—Slaughtering in slaughterhouses—Annual data.

Meat production: Netherlands ('000 metric tons)

	2014	2015	2016
Beef and veal	376.2	382.5	416.1
Pig meat	1,370.9	1,456.2	1,452.8
Mutton and lamb	12.7	13.0	12.6
Poultry meat	n.a.	n.a.	n.a.

© European Union. Source: Eurostat, 2017, Agriculture, forestry and fisheries, table *APRO_MT_PANN*—Slaughtering in slaughterhouses—Annual data.

Meat production: Poland ('000 metric tons)

	2014	2015	2016
Beef and veal	412.7	471.0	501.5
Pig meat	1,838.5	1,906.1	1,963.0
Horse meat	n.a.	n.a.	n.a.
Poultry meat	1,804.1	2,011.0	2,268.4

© European Union. Source: Eurostat, 2017, Agriculture, forestry and fisheries, table *APRO_MT_PANN*—Slaughtering in slaughterhouses—Annual data.

Meat production: Portugal ('000 metric tons)

	2014	2015	2016
Beef and veal	79.8	88.6	91.1
Pig meat	360.0	377.5	375.4
Mutton and lamb	10.2	10.5	10.1
Poultry meat	295.2	308.7	326.4

© European Union. Source: Eurostat, 2017, Agriculture, forestry and fisheries, table *APRO_MT_PANN*—Slaughtering in slaughterhouses—Annual data.

Meat production: Romania ('000 metric tons)

	2014	2015	2016
Beef and veal	29.2	44.5	57.5
Pig meat	324.9	330.5	337.0
Mutton and lamb	4.8	9.2	8.4
Poultry meat	345.6	374.8	390.7

© European Union. Source: Eurostat, 2017, Agriculture, forestry and fisheries, table *APRO_MT_PANN*—Slaughtering in slaughterhouses—Annual data.

Meat production: Slovakia ('000 metric tons)

	2014	2015	2016
Beef and veal	8.8	8.4	8.3
Pig meat	33.8	45.2	48.3
Poultry meat	n.a.	n.a.	n.a.

© European Union. Source: Eurostat, 2017, Agriculture, forestry and fisheries, table *APRO_MT_PANN*—Slaughtering in slaughterhouses—Annual data.

Meat production: Slovenia ('000 metric tons)

	2014	2015	2016
Beef and veal	31.6	33.6	35.7
Pig meat	20.2	20.2	22.7
Poultry meat	59.8	58.8	64.0

© European Union. Source: Eurostat, 2017, Agriculture, forestry and fisheries, table *APRO_MT_PANN*—Slaughtering in slaughterhouses—Annual data.

Meat production: Spain ('000 metric tons)

	2014	2015	2016
Beef and veal	578.6	626.1	637.8
Pig meat	3,620.2	3,854.7	4,058.9
Mutton and lamb	114.2	115.9	116.5
Goat meat	8.6	9.1	9.8
Horse meat	n.a.	n.a.	n.a.
Poultry meat	1,436.7	1,447.0	1,523.9

© European Union. Source: Eurostat, 2017, Agriculture, forestry and fisheries, table *APRO_MT_PANN*—Slaughtering in slaughterhouses—Annual data.

Meat production: Sweden ('000 metric tons)

	2014	2015	2016
Beef and veal	142.0	144.0	131.3
Pig meat	236.2	233.5	233.9
Mutton and lamb	5.1	5.1	5.0
Poultry meat	135.2	145.8	153.9

© European Union. Source: Eurostat, 2017, Agriculture, forestry and fisheries, table *APRO_MT_PANN*—Slaughtering in slaughterhouses—Annual data.

Meat production: United Kingdom ('000 metric tons)

	2014	2015	2016
Beef and veal	877.6	883.2	911.7
Pig meat	862.1	898.3	919.2
Mutton and lamb	298.2	300.3	289.6
Poultry meat	1,642.6	1,688.8	1,791.3

© European Union. Source: Eurostat, 2017, Agriculture, forestry and fisheries, table *APRO_MT_PANN*—Slaughtering in slaughterhouses—Annual data.

MILK AND DAIRY PRODUCTS

Total production of milk on farms ('000 metric tons, whole milk)

	2013	2014	2015		2013	2014	2015
Austria	3,425	3,525	3,569	Latvia	915	972	978
Belgium	3,529	3,710	3,826	Lithuania	1,723	1,795*	1,739
Bulgaria	1,306	1,231	1,153	Luxembourg	299	320	349
Croatia	739	728	707	Malta	44	45	44
Cyprus	206	213	214	Netherlands	12,640	12,905	13,784
Czech Republic	2,849	2,934	3,027	Poland	12,735	13,002	13,253
Denmark	5,082	5,162	5,336	Portugal	1,951	2,044	2,114
Estonia	772	805	783	Romania	4,619	4,804	4,677
Finland	2,328	2,400	2,437	Slovakia	922	942	942
France	25,329	26,603*	26,713*	Slovenia	597	619	634
Germany	31,338	32,395	32,685	Spain	7,631	7,854*	8,105*
Greece	1,817	1,892	1,915	Sweden	2,870	2,932	2,933
Hungary	1,778	1,881	1,947	United Kingdom	13,943	15,088	15,457*
Ireland	5,601	5,821	6,634				
Italy	12,040	12,217	12,192	**Total (EU-28)**	159,026	164,837	168,145*

* Provisional.

© European Union. Source: Eurostat, 2017, Agriculture, forestry and fisheries, table *APRO_MK_FARM*—Production and utilization of milk on the farm—Annual data.

Milk production on farms by source, 2015 ('000 metric tons)

	Cows' milk	Ewes' milk	Goats' milk	Buffalo milk		Cows' milk	Ewes' milk	Goats' milk	Buffalo milk
Austria	3,538	11	21	0	Latvia	975	0	3	0
Belgium	3,826	0	0	0	Lithuania	1,735	0	4	0
Bulgaria	1,028	74	41	9	Luxembourg	346	n.a.	3	0
Croatia	694	6	7	n.a.	Malta	42	2	1	0
Cyprus	165*	26	23	0	Netherlands	13,522	n.a.	261	1
Czech Republic	3,026	0	1	0	Poland	13,236	0	16	0
Denmark	5,336	0	0	0	Portugal	2,014	72	29	0
Estonia	783	0	1	0	Romania	3,981	425	246	25
Finland	2,437	0	0	0	Slovakia	931	11	0	0
France†	25,820	279	613	0	Slovenia	632	0	2	n.a.
Germany	32,671	0	14	0	Spain†	7,029	581	495	0
Greece	770	804	341	0	Sweden	2,933	0	0	0
Hungary	1,941	2	4	n.a.	United Kingdom†	15,457	0	0	0
Ireland	6,634	0	0	0					
Italy	11,426	475	64	227	**Total (EU-28)†**	162,928	n.a.	2,187	n.a.

* Provisional.

© European Union. Source: Eurostat, 2017, Agriculture, forestry and fisheries, table *APRO_MK_FARM*—Production and utilization of milk on the farm—Annual data.

Production of butter ('000 metric tons)

	2014	2015	2016		2014	2015	2016
Austria	32.4	32.5	n.a.	Latvia	6.9	6.3	7.0
Belgium	30.1	32.2	36.9	Lithuania	16.0	13.6	16.6
Bulgaria	1.0	1.0	0.9	Luxembourg†	n.a.	n.a.	n.a.
Croatia	3.9	3.7	3.7	Malta†	n.a.	0.0	0.0
Cyprus	0.0	0.0	0.0	Netherlands†	n.a.	n.a.	n.a.
Czech Republic	21.9	24.6	24.2	Poland	147.8	170.1	186.1
Denmark	42.8	44.7	n.a.	Portugal	28.1	32.3	30.8
Estonia	4.5	5.0	5.0	Romania	10.6	11.2	11.9
Finland	48.7	54.7	55.5	Slovakia	6.8	6.8	7.0
France*	364.9	367.8	363.9	Slovenia†	n.a.	n.a.	n.a.
Germany	441.1	456.1	451.2	Spain*	30.7	31.9	31.7
Greece	1.2	1.2	1.3	Sweden	16.9	16.5	n.a.
Hungary	4.3	4.6	5.6	United Kingdom	n.a.†	n.a.†	125.3
Ireland	166.4	187.5	n.a.				
Italy	99.7	95.2	93.8	**Total (EU-28)†**	n.a.	n.a.	n.a.

* Provisional. † Confidential.

© European Union. Source: Eurostat, 2017, Agriculture, forestry and fisheries, table *APRO_MK_POBTA*—Milk collection (all milks) and dairy products obtained—Annual data.

Production of cheese ('000 metric tons)

	2014	2015	2016		2014	2015	2016
Austria	172.4	184.9	n.a.	Latvia	34.7	38.4	38.6
Belgium	84.8	103.1	110.2	Lithuania	102.5	101.0	97.5
Bulgaria	77.4	76.8	79.6	Luxembourg*	n.a.	n.a.	n.a.
Croatia	32.2	34.0	36.1	Malta*	n.a.	n.a.	n.a.
Cyprus	20.0	23.2	26.6	Netherlands	771.9	845.0	888.0
Czech Republic	116.6	123.0	141.7	Poland	743.7	772.7	806.0
Denmark	368.9	391.3	n.a.	Portugal	73.4	73.3	76.3
Estonia	40.5	43.1	43.3	Romania	74.7	81.7	87.6
Finland	n.a.*	88.4	83.8	Slovakia	33.3	35.8	38.3
France†	1,946.3	1,949.8	1,918.6	Slovenia	16.6	15.2	15.2
Germany	1,892.8	1,899.5	1,862.7	Spain†	387.7	465.4	461.0
Greece	190.0	188.3	203.8	Sweden	88.1	90.2	n.a.
Hungary	74.8	80.5	80.5	United Kingdom	377.8	403.4	403.9
Ireland	188.4	207.1	n.a.				
Italy	1,176.0	1,206.7	1,232.2	**Total (EU-28)***	n.a.	n.a.	n.a.

* Confidential. † Provisional.

© European Union. Source: Eurostat, 2017, Agriculture, forestry and fisheries, table *APRO_MK_POBTA*—Milk collection (all milks) and dairy products obtained—Annual data.

PRODUCTION OF WINE

Total wine production ('000 hectolitres)

	2014	2015	2016		2014	2015	2016
Austria	2,392	1,999	2,268	Latvia	26	n.a.	n.a.
Belgium	6	7	10	Lithuania	0	0	0
Bulgaria	1,913	881	1,568	Luxembourg	101	125	111
Croatia	1,249	842	992	Malta	21	21	n.a.
Cyprus	108	94	79	Netherlands	n.a.	n.a.	n.a.
Czech Republic	520	536	783	Poland	n.a.	n.a.	n.a.
Denmark	n.a.	n.a.	n.a.	Portugal	6,231	6,206	7,045
Estonia	n.a.	n.a.	0	Romania	n.a.	n.a.	n.a.
Finland	n.a.	n.a.	n.a.	Slovakia	373	286	343
France	42,316	47,423	47,857	Slovenia	n.a.	659	823
Germany	8,493	9,294	8,907	Spain	53,550	45,015	43,284
Greece	3,343	2,800	2,501	Sweden	0	n.a.	n.a.
Hungary	n.a.	n.a.	n.a.	United Kingdom	33	27	38
Ireland	0	0	0				
Italy	47,966	42,088	50,700	**Total (EU-28)**	n.a.	n.a.	n.a.

Note: Year ending 31 July.

© European Union. Source: Eurostat, 2017, Agriculture, forestry and fisheries, table *APRO_CPB_WINE*—Wine balance sheet—Marketing year.

FORESTRY

Roundwood removals ('000 cubic metres, excluding bark)

	2013	2014	2015		2013	2014	2015
Austria	17,390	17,089	17,550	Latvia	n.a.	12,885	12,294
Belgium	n.a.	n.a.	n.a.	Lithuania	7,053	7,351	6,414
Bulgaria	6,155	5,570	6,372	Luxembourg	n.a.	n.a.	381
Croatia	5,436*	5,926	5,178	Malta	0	0	n.a.
Cyprus	9	9	11	Netherlands	1,108	8	1,173
Czech Republic	15,331	15,476	16,163	Poland	38,940	40,862	41,375
Denmark	3,180	3,180	n.a.	Portugal	10,610	11,152	11,533
Estonia	7,655	8,000	7,736	Romania	15,195	15,330	15,315
Finland	56,992*	57,033	59,411	Slovakia	8,063	9,168	8,995
France	51,304	51,866	51,005	Slovenia	3,415	5,099	5,054
Germany	53,207	54,356	55,613	Spain	15,560*	16,395	16,719
Greece	1,092	1,217*	n.a.	Sweden	69,600	73,300	74,300
Hungary	6,027	5,798	n.a.	United Kingdom	10,821	11,184	10,550
Ireland	2,760	2,828	2,908				
Italy	n.a.	5,759	5,052	**Total (EU-28)***	432,975	436,843	446,819

* Estimate(s).

© European Union. Source: Eurostat, 2017, Agriculture, forestry and fisheries, table *FOR_BASIC*—Roundwood, fuelwood and other basic products.

Roundwood removals by species groups, 2015 ('000 cubic metres, excluding bark)

	Coniferous	Non-coniferous	Total		Coniferous	Non-coniferous	Total
Austria	14,571	2,979	17,550	Latvia	8,246	4,049	12,294
Belgium	n.a.	n.a.	n.a.	Lithuania	3,452	2,962	6,414
Bulgaria	3,031	3,341	6,372	Luxembourg	188	193	381
Croatia	838	4,341	5,178	Malta	n.a.	n.a.	n.a.
Cyprus	9	2	11	Netherlands	592	581	1,173
Czech Republic	14,385	1,778	16,163	Poland	30,632	10,743	41,375
Denmark	n.a.	n.a.	n.a.	Portugal	2,994	8,540	11,533
Estonia	4,636	3,100	7,736	Romania	6,024	9,290	15,315
Finland	46,871	12,540	59,411	Slovakia	4,662	4,332	8,995
France	19,087	31,918	51,005	Slovenia	3,063	1,992	5,054
Germany	42,050	13,563	55,613	Spain	7,414	9,305	16,719
Greece	n.a.	n.a.	n.a.	Sweden	67,260	7,040	74,300
Hungary	n.a.	n.a.	n.a.	United Kingdom	10,088	462	10,550
Ireland	2,807	101	2,908				
Italy	1,948	3,105	5,052	**Total (EU-28)***	301,645	145,174	446,819

* Estimates.

© European Union. Source: Eurostat, 2017, Agriculture, forestry and fisheries, table *FOR_REMOV*—Roundwood removals by type of wood and assortment.

Removals of fuel wood ('000 cubic metres, excluding bark)

	2013	2014	2015		2013	2014	2015
Austria	4,957	5,059	4,979	Latvia	1,258	1,299	1,200
Belgium	n.a.	n.a.	n.a.	Lithuania	2,431	2,316	2,110
Bulgaria	2,758	2,534	2,848	Luxembourg	n.a.	n.a.	70
Croatia	1,400	2,300	1,769	Malta	0	0	n.a.
Cyprus	6	5	7	Netherlands	290	4	357
Czech Republic	2,182	2,111	2,336	Poland	5,145	5,185	5,152
Denmark	1,950	1,950	n.a.	Portugal	600	600	600
Estonia	2,439	2,257	2,179	Romania	5,103	4,859	5,079
Finland	7,660*	7,832	7,964	Slovakia	690	560	560
France	26,853	26,116	25,962	Slovenia	1,127	1,589	1,242
Germany	11,155	11,114	10,494	Spain	3,435*	3,709	3,709
Greece	765	894	n.a.	Sweden	5,900	5,900	7,000
Hungary	2,858	2,679	n.a.	United Kingdom	1,578	1,823	1,921
Ireland	209	206	203				
Italy	n.a.	3,717	3,004	**Total (EU-28)***	99,921	96,617	97,745

* Estimate(s).

© European Union. Source: Eurostat, 2017, Agriculture, forestry and fisheries, table *FOR_BASIC*—Roundwood, fuelwood and other basic products.

Removals of industrial roundwood ('000 cubic metres, excluding bark)

	2013	2014	2015		2013	2014	2015
Austria	12,433	12,030	12,570	Latvia	n.a.	11,586	11,094
Belgium	n.a.	n.a.	n.a.	Lithuania	4,622	5,035	4,304
Bulgaria	3,396	3,036	3,524	Luxembourg	n.a.	n.a.	311
Croatia	4,036	3,626	3,410	Malta	0	0	n.a.
Cyprus	4	4	3	Netherlands	818	4	816
Czech Republic	13,149	13,365	13,827	Poland	33,795	35,677	36,223
Denmark	1,230	1,230	n.a.	Portugal	10,010	10,552	10,933
Estonia	5,216	5,743	5,558	Romania	10,091	10,471	10,235
Finland	49,331*	49,202	51,446	Slovakia	7,373	8,608	8,435
France	24,451	25,750	25,043	Slovenia	2,288*	3,511	3,812
Germany	42,052	43,243	45,119	Spain	12,125*	12,686	13,010
Greece	328	323*	n.a.	Sweden	63,700	67,400	67,300
Hungary	3,169	3,119	n.a.	United Kingdom	9,243	9,361	8,629
Ireland	2,550	2,622	2,705				
Italy	n.a.	2,042	2,048	**Total (EU-28)***	333,054	340,225	349,074

* Estimate(s).

© European Union. Source: Eurostat, 2017, Agriculture, forestry and fisheries, table *FOR_BASIC*—Roundwood, fuelwood and other basic products.

Industrial roundwood removals by species groups, 2015 ('000 cubic metres, excluding bark)

	Coniferous	Non-coniferous	Total		Coniferous	Non-coniferous	Total
Austria	11,571	999	12,570	Latvia	8,046	3,049	11,094
Belgium	3,136	979	n.a.	Lithuania	2,713	1,591	4,304
Bulgaria	2,428	1,096	3,524	Luxembourg	160	151	311
Croatia	775	2,634	3,410	Malta	n.a.	n.a.	n.a.
Cyprus	3	0	3	Netherlands	521	295	816
Czech Republic	12,871	956	13,827	Poland	28,003	8,220	36,223
Denmark	n.a.	n.a.	n.a.	Portugal	2,794	8,140	10,933
Estonia	3,791	1,767	5,558	Romania*	5,007	5,229	10,235
Finland	42,925	8,522	51,446	Slovakia	4,425	4,010	8,435
France	16,491	8,553	25,043	Slovenia	2,860	952	3,812
Germany	36,740	8,379	45,119	Spain	6,126	6,884	13,010
Greece	211	112	n.a.	Sweden	63,760	3,540	67,300
Hungary	834	2,214	n.a.	United Kingdom	8,517	112	8,629
Ireland	2,702	3	2,705				
Italy	1,292	756	2,048	**Total (EU-28)***	269,743	79,331	349,074

* Estimates.

© European Union. Source: Eurostat, 2017, Agriculture, forestry and fisheries, table *FOR_BASIC*—Roundwood, fuelwood and other basic products.

Production of sawnwood ('000 cubic metres)

	2013	2014	2015		2013	2014	2015
Austria	8,534	8,460	8,807	Latvia	3,367	3,657	3,479
Belgium	n.a.	n.a.	n.a.	Lithuania	1,120	1,345	1,248
Bulgaria	803	838	908*	Luxembourg	n.a.	n.a.	n.a.
Croatia	1,192	1,294	1,488	Malta	0	0	n.a.
Cyprus	2	2	2	Netherlands	216	228	185
Czech Republic	4,037	3,861	4,150	Poland	4,321	4,725	4,835
Denmark	358	358	n.a.	Portugal	854	1,035	1,134
Estonia	1,558	1,554	1,650	Romania	5,532	6,019	5,936
Finland	10,440	10,920	10,640	Slovakia	1,430	1,750	1,600
France	7,901	7,697	7,514	Slovenia	660	700	725
Germany	21,459	21,772	21,490	Spain	2,047	2,245	2,453
Greece†	109	108	n.a.	Sweden	16,074	17,500	18,174
Hungary	109	121	n.a.	United Kingdom	3,581	3,764	3,493
Ireland	825	907	905				
Italy	1,360	1,430	1,470	**Total (EU-28)†**	99,695	102,288	102,890

* Provisional.   †Estimates.
© European Union. Source: Eurostat, 2017, Agriculture, forestry and fisheries, table *FOR_SWPAN*—Sawnwood and panels.

Sawnwood production by species groups, 2015 ('000 cubic metres)

	Coniferous	Non-coniferous	Total		Coniferous	Non-coniferous	Total
Austria	8,681*	126*	8,807	Latvia	2,809	670	3,479
Belgium	n.a.	n.a.	n.a.	Lithuania	783	465	1,248
Bulgaria*	748	160	908	Luxembourg	n.a.	n.a.	n.a.
Croatia	267	1,221	1,488	Malta	n.a.	n.a.	n.a.
Cyprus	2	0	2	Netherlands	129	56	185
Czech Republic	3,920	230	4,150	Poland	4,315	520	4,835
Denmark	n.a.	n.a.	n.a.	Portugal	1,101	33	1,134
Estonia	1,500	150	1,650	Romania†	n.a.	n.a.	5,936
Finland†	10,600	40	10,640	Slovakia	1,150	450	1,600
France†	6,223	1,291	7,514	Slovenia	625	100	725
Germany	20,433	1,056	21,490	Spain†	2,062	392	2,453
Greece†	n.a.	n.a.	n.a.	Sweden	18,074	100	18,174
Hungary	n.a.	n.a.	n.a.	United Kingdom	3,449	44	3,493
Ireland	904	2	905				
Italy	920	550	1,470	**Total (EU-28)†**	93,694	9,195	102,890

* Provisional.   † Estimates.
© European Union. Source: Eurostat, 2017, Agriculture, forestry and fisheries, table *FOR_SWPAN*—Sawnwood and panels.

FISHING

Note: Figures exclude the products of aquaculture (see below) and the catch of aquatic mammals (whales, seals etc.).

Total catch of fishery products (metric tons, live weight)

	2013	2014	2015		2013	2014	2015
Austria	n.a.	n.a.	n.a.	Latvia	115,759	119,293	81,305
Belgium	25,377	26,509	24,463	Lithuania	74,803	148,843	72,432
Bulgaria	9,535	8,565	8,747	Luxembourg	n.a.	n.a.	n.a.
Croatia	75,267	78,928	72,264	Malta	2,355	2,403	2,437
Cyprus	1,166	1,249	1,475	Netherlands	324,370	375,441	364,990
Czech Republic	n.a.	n.a.	n.a.	Poland	195,477	169,574	187,051
Denmark	668,338	745,019	868,890	Portugal	194,610	177,231	185,217
Estonia	66,763	66,103	70,753	Romania	1,617	2,200	4,843
Finland	144,297	153,488	153,394	Slovakia	n.a.	n.a.	n.a.
France	528,732	543,525	497,435	Slovenia	232	247	191
Germany	219,001	216,166	251,268	Spain	904,126	1,108,830	901,512
Greece	63,638	60,319	64,431	Sweden	176,789	171,889	202,946
Hungary	n.a.	n.a.	n.a.	United Kingdom	617,592	751,979	701,769
Ireland	246,240	276,847	234,772				
Italy	172,907	177,019	191,634	**Total (EU-28)**	4,828,990	5,382,310	5,144,219

© European Union. Source: Eurostat, 2017, Agriculture, forestry and fisheries, table *FISH_CA_MAIN*—Catches—Major fishing areas.

Catch by major fishing areas: European Union (EU-28) (metric tons, live weight)

	2013	2014	2015
Atlantic, North-West	65,196	54,932	48,028
Atlantic, North-East	3,600,950	3,829,901	3,959,232
Atlantic, Eastern Central	379,677	476,934	259,284
Atlantic, South-West	125,491	206,330	135,162
Atlantic, South-East	44,869	90,037	116,605
Indian Ocean, Western	187,815	300,344	194,128
Mediterranean and Black Sea	424,993	423,832	431,780
Pacific, Eastern Central	n.a.	n.a.	n.a.
Pacific, South-East	n.a.	n.a.	n.a.
Total fishing areas	4,828,990	5,382,310	5,144,219

© European Union. Source: Eurostat, 2017, Agriculture, forestry and fisheries, table *FISH_CA_MAIN*—Catches—Major fishing areas.

Catch by product group: European Union (EU-28) (metric tons, live weight)

	2013	2014	2015
Aquatic animals	4,758,401	5,321,018	5,122,247
Finfish	4,207,219	4,755,666	4,557,877
Freshwater fishes	n.a.	n.a.	n.a.
Diadromous fishes	n.a.	n.a.	n.a.
Marine fishes	4,182,643	4,731,210	4,535,352
Total fishery products	4,828,990	5,382,310	5,144,219

© European Union. Source: Eurostat, 2017, Agriculture, forestry and fisheries, table *FISH_CA_MAIN*—Catches—Major fishing areas.

Catch by principal species: European Union (EU-28) (metric tons, live weight)

	2007	2008	2009
European anchovy	109,485	99,596	102,212
Atlantic cod	117,750	119,041	127,189
Atlantic herring	684,115	577,516	531,443
Atlantic horse mackerel	153,288	173,828	154,813
Atlantic mackerel	302,075	278,566	346,850
Blue mussel	62,773	44,440	43,310
European pilchard (sardine)	234,792	237,092	243,359
European plaice	65,605	63,139	66,053
Round sardinella	42,801	104,599	86,935
Sandeels (Sandlances)	180,068	280,047	339,270
Skipjack tuna	87,650	251,084	114,490
European sprat	498,819	468,174	543,389
Blue whiting (Poutassou)	337,290	240,287	85,158
Yellowfin tuna	116,541	145,714	72,244

© European Union. Source: Eurostat, 2017, Agriculture, forestry and fisheries, table *FISH_CA_MAIN*—Catches—Major fishing areas.

AQUACULTURE

Total catch of fishery products (metric tons, live weight)

	2013	2014	2015		2013	2014	2015
Austria	n.a.*	3,393†	3,503	Latvia	644	686	863
Belgium	n.a.	214	32	Lithuania	3,841	3,350	4,083
Bulgaria	6,292	6,883	10,652	Luxembourg	n.a.	n.a.	n.a.
Croatia	13,720	13,768	16,875	Malta	9,077	8,606	10,800
Cyprus	5,339	4,835	5,459	Netherlands	46,605	63,089†	62,204†
Czech Republic	19,360	20,163	20,200	Poland	31,258	36,336	33,560
Denmark	31,790	33,624	35,990	Portugal†	9,612	10,795	9,322
Estonia	n.a.*	865	798	Romania†	10,147	10,677	11,016
Finland	n.a.*	13,324	14,879	Slovakia	1,085	1,214	1,248
France	200,330	180,344	n.a.	Slovenia	n.a.*	1,441	1,590
Germany	n.a.*	26,223	26,867	Spain	226,221	284,977	293,510
Greece	n.a.*	104,452	105,934	Sweden	13,366	12,899	12,277
Hungary	14,383	15,366	17,337	United Kingdom	203,263	214,627	211,568
Ireland	32,664	29,327†	37,581†				
Italy	140,880	148,730	n.a.	**Total (EU-28)**	1,178,197†	1,250,207†	n.a.

* Confidential. † Estimate.

© European Union. Source: Eurostat, 2017, Agriculture, forestry and fisheries, table *FISH_AQ2A*—Production from aquaculture excluding hatcheries and nurseries (from 2008 onwards).

Catch by culture environment: European Union (EU-28) (metric tons, live weight)

	2010	2011	2012
Brackish water	14,966	14,133	14,779*
Freshwater†	n.a.	n.a.	n.a.
Seawater	726,468	n.a.†	778,477*
Total	n.a.†	1,247,982*	1,221,304*

* Estimate. † Confidential.

© European Union. Source: Eurostat, 2017, Agriculture, forestry and fisheries, table *FISH_AQ2A*—Production from aquaculture excluding hatcheries and nurseries (from 2008 onwards).

Catch by product group: European Union (EU-28) (metric tons, live weight)

	2007	2008	2009*
Aquatic animals	1,306,592	1,271,603	1,317,976
Finfish	629,060	647,681	665,566
Freshwater fishes	95,229	105,285	107,681
Diadromous fishes	362,181	364,081	373,570
Marine fishes	171,651	178,314	184,316
Aquatic invertebrates	n.a.	55	n.a.
Crustaceans	212	222	250
Molluscs	677,319	623,646	652,159
Aquatic plants	60	67	111
Total fishery products	1,306,652	1,271,671	1,318,087

* Estimates.

© European Union. Source: Eurostat, 2017, Agriculture, forestry and fisheries, table *FISH_AQ2A*—Production from aquaculture excluding hatcheries and nurseries (from 2008 onwards).

Catch by principal species: European Union (EU-28) (metric tons, live weight)

	2008	2009	2010
European seabass	60,701	60,279	65,358
Japanese carpet shell	1,147	1,606	36,981
Common carp	72,237	72,819	n.a.*
Mediterranean mussel	295,451	317,171	288,399
Blue mussel	166,448	147,112	139,280
Pacific cupped oyster	115,787	106,065	88,740
Atlantic salmon	139,325	156,898	170,406
Gilthead seabream	87,519	98,478	92,686
Rainbow trout	172,678	166,085†	n.a.*

* Confidential. † Estimate.

© European Union. Source: Eurostat, 2017, Agriculture, forestry and fisheries, table *FISH_AQ2A*—Production from aquaculture excluding hatcheries and nurseries (from 2008 onwards).

ENERGY

MINING OF ENERGY MATERIALS

Production of solid fuels (coal and lignite, '000 metric tons)

	2013	2014	2015		2013	2014	2015
Austria	1	1	1	Latvia	10	5	0
Belgium	0	0	0	Lithuania	84	100	74
Bulgaria	28,621	31,268	35,859	Luxembourg	0	0	0
Croatia	0	0	0	Malta	n.a.	n.a.	n.a.
Cyprus	0	0	0	Netherlands	0	0	0
Czech Republic	48,979	46,857	46,419	Poland	142,315	136,417	135,304
Denmark	0	0	0	Portugal	0	0	0
Estonia	20,774	21,256	19,734	Romania	24,722	23,567	25,497
Finland	7,388	6,722	3,489	Slovakia	2,353	2,188	1,939
France	0	0	0	Slovenia	3,876	3,108	3,168
Germany	190,956	186,515	184,714	Spain	4,368	3,899	3,064
Greece	53,924	50,845	46,246	Sweden	624	450	369
Hungary	9,558	9,551	9,261	United Kingdom	12,673	11,647	8,598
Ireland	6,657	4,604	3,546				
Italy	73	86	81	**Total (EU-28)**	557,956	539,086	527,363

© European Union. Source: Eurostat, 2017, Environment and energy, table *NRG_101A*—Supply, transformation and consumption of solid fuels—Annual data.

Production of hard coal and derivatives ('000 metric tons)

	2013	2014	2015		2013	2014	2015
Austria	0	0	0	Latvia	0	0	0
Belgium	0	0	0	Lithuania	0	0	0
Bulgaria	6	0	0	Luxembourg	0	0	0
Croatia	0	0	0	Malta	n.a.	n.a.	n.a.
Cyprus	0	0	0	Netherlands	0	0	0
Czech Republic	8,594	8,680	8,314	Poland	76,466	72,540	72,176
Denmark	0	0	0	Portugal	0	0	0
Estonia	0	0	0	Romania	47	80	10
Finland	0	0	0	Slovakia	0	0	0
France	0	0	0	Slovenia	0	0	0
Germany	8,260	8,337	6,649	Spain	4,368	3,899	3,064
Greece	0	0	0	Sweden	0	0	0
Hungary	0	0	0	United Kingdom	12,673	11,647	8,598
Ireland	0	0	0				
Italy	73	86	81	**Total (EU-28)**	110,487	105,269	98,892

© European Union. Source: Eurostat, 2017, Environment and energy, table *NRG_101A*—Supply, transformation and consumption of solid fuels—Annual data.

Production of lignite ('000 metric tons, including brown coal)

	2013	2014	2015		2013	2014	2015
Austria	0	0	0	Latvia	0	0	0
Belgium	0	0	0	Lithuania	0	0	0
Bulgaria	28,615	31,268	35,859	Luxembourg	0	0	0
Croatia	0	0	0	Malta	n.a.	n.a.	n.a.
Cyprus	0	0	0	Netherlands	0	0	0
Czech Republic	40,385	38,177	38,105	Poland	65,849	63,877	63,128
Denmark	0	0	0	Portugal	0	0	0
Estonia	0	0	0	Romania	24,674	23,485	25,483
Finland	0	0	0	Slovakia	2,353	2,188	1,939
France	0	0	0	Slovenia	3,876	3,108	3,168
Germany	182,696	178,178	178,065	Spain	0	0	0
Greece	53,924	50,845	46,246	Sweden	0	0	0
Hungary	9,558	9,551	9,261	United Kingdom	0	0	0
Ireland	0	0	0				
Italy	0	0	0	**Total (EU-28)**	411,930	400,677	401,254

© European Union. Source: Eurostat, 2017, Environment and energy, table *NRG_101A*—Supply, transformation and consumption of solid fuels—Annual data.

Production of crude petroleum ('000 metric tons)

	2013	2014	2015		2013	2014	2015
Austria	843	953	854	Latvia	n.a.	n.a.	n.a.
Belgium	n.a.	n.a.	n.a.	Lithuania	86	82	75
Bulgaria	28	26	25	Luxembourg	n.a.	n.a.	n.a.
Croatia	536	541	619	Malta	n.a.	n.a.	n.a.
Cyprus	n.a.	n.a.	n.a.	Netherlands	1,122	1,525	1,396
Czech Republic	154	150	128	Poland	962	951	928
Denmark	8,683	8,131	7,690	Portugal	n.a.	n.a.	n.a.
Estonia	n.a.	n.a.	n.a.	Romania	4,043	3,963	3,902
Finland	n.a.	n.a.	n.a.	Slovakia	10	9	10
France	793	766	835	Slovenia	n.a.	n.a.	n.a.
Germany	2,636	2,435	2,414	Spain	368	305	232
Greece	70	64	62	Sweden	n.a.	n.a.	n.a.
Hungary	599	584	623	United Kingdom	38,456	37,474	42,826
Ireland	n.a.	n.a.	n.a.				
Italy	5,502	5,765	5,470	**Total (EU-28)**	64,891	63,724	68,089

© European Union. Source: Eurostat, 2017, Environment and energy, table *NRG_102A*—Supply, transformation and consumption of oil—Annual data.

Production of natural gas (net calorific value, terajoules)

	2013	2014	2015		2013	2014	2015
Austria	49,849	45,428	43,437	Latvia	0	0	0
Belgium	0	0	0	Lithuania	0	0	0
Bulgaria	9,791	6,677	3,538	Luxembourg	0	0	0
Croatia	63,107	60,447	61,605	Malta	n.a.	0	0
Cyprus	0	0	0	Netherlands	2,586,100	2,099,445	1,632,983
Czech Republic	8,621	8,873	8,576	Poland	160,067	156,014	154,196
Denmark	179,275	173,259	173,510	Portugal	0	0	0
Estonia	0	0	0	Romania	360,068	366,995	367,820
Finland	0	0	0	Slovakia	4,370	3,510	3,258
France	12,114	525	801	Slovenia	108	108	108
Germany	371,190	287,384	265,238	Spain	2,086	871	2,264
Greece	243	228	197	Sweden	0	0	0
Hungary	64,656	60,177	57,319	United Kingdom	1,376,212	1,387,840	1,492,983
Ireland	6,076	5,140	4,490				
Italy	265,234	245,139	232,178	**Total (EU-28)**	5,519,168	4,908,060	4,504,502

© European Union. Source: Eurostat, 2017, Environment and energy, table *NRG_103A*—Supply, transformation and consumption of gas—Annual data.

ENERGY SUPPLY AND CONSUMPTION

Primary production of all energy products ('000 metric tons of oil equivalent)

	2013	2014	2015		2013	2014	2015
Austria	12,165	11,966	11,932	Latvia	2,144	2,381	2,338
Belgium	14,650	12,318	10,367	Lithuania	1,414	1,487	1,585
Bulgaria	10,548	11,264	11,986	Luxembourg	132	152	147
Croatia	4,438	4,353	4,393	Malta	9	13	15
Cyprus	109	118	121	Netherlands	69,253	58,496	47,593
Czech Republic	30,422	29,611	28,756	Poland	70,580	66,885	67,347
Denmark	16,404	15,735	15,709	Portugal	5,751	5,981	5,304
Estonia	5,653	5,782	5,554	Romania	26,111	26,572	26,656
Finland	18,000	18,105	17,538	Slovakia	6,408	6,307	6,320
France	134,474	135,925	136,699	Slovenia	3,595	3,665	3,391
Germany	120,575	119,881	119,770	Spain	34,576	34,942	33,441
Greece	9,312	8,805	8,473	Sweden	34,671	34,171	33,643
Hungary	11,391	10,983	11,188	United Kingdom	110,099	108,155	118,274
Ireland	2,251	2,011	1,912				
Italy	36,864	36,809	36,134	**Total (EU-28)**	791,998	772,870	766,583

© European Union. Source: Eurostat, 2017, Environment and energy, table *NRG_100A*—Simplified energy balances—Annual data.

Total imports of all energy products ('000 metric tons of oil equivalent)

	2013	2014	2015		2013	2014	2015
Austria	28,453	27,981	29,473	Latvia	4,345	3,780	4,504
Belgium	77,920	78,265	81,502	Lithuania	14,169	12,692	14,370
Bulgaria	11,778	11,528	12,513	Luxembourg	4,387	4,262	4,199
Croatia	6,798	6,408	7,162	Malta	2,288	2,249	2,761
Cyprus	2,333	2,291	2,476	Netherlands	193,919	196,074	220,509
Czech Republic	20,405	21,165	21,944	Poland	45,275	46,657	48,930
Denmark	18,512	17,379	18,565	Portugal	23,117	21,869	26,070
Estonia	2,515	2,738	2,589	Romania	10,576	11,321	11,635
Finland	26,421	26,431	23,121	Slovakia	15,325	14,736	15,344
France	154,502	147,536	149,670	Slovenia	4,966	5,267	5,757
Germany	252,053	244,283	255,760	Spain	118,778	122,542	124,531
Greece	31,010	33,083	35,286	Sweden	28,122	31,500	32,551
Hungary	17,081	19,079	17,875	United Kingdom	165,656	152,549	143,184
Ireland	13,630	13,023	14,583				
Italy	149,720	138,141	151,070	**Total (EU-28)**	1,444,053	1,414,826	1,477,933

© European Union. Source: Eurostat, 2017, Environment and energy, table *NRG_100A*—Simplified energy balances—Annual data.

Total exports of all energy products ('000 metric tons of oil equivalent)

	2013	2014	2015		2013	2014	2015
Austria	7,673	6,501	9,259	Latvia	1,718	1,881	2,134
Belgium	29,349	31,137	30,876	Lithuania	8,865	7,460	8,888
Bulgaria	5,421	5,371	5,928	Luxembourg	177	189	192
Croatia	2,760	2,821	3,045	Malta	150	199	531
Cyprus	0	0	24	Netherlands	169,671	166,479	173,725
Czech Republic	8,354	8,376	8,400	Poland	20,109	19,612	20,909
Denmark	16,262	15,232	16,264	Portugal	6,455	5,724	7,770
Estonia	1,667	2,113	2,106	Romania	4,557	5,822	6,093
Finland	9,776	9,375	7,461	Slovakia	5,259	4,880	5,702
France	29,186	32,206	32,827	Slovenia	1,716	2,283	2,524
Germany	47,165	49,535	59,745	Spain	29,731	31,881	30,103
Greece	14,620	15,723	16,474	Sweden	12,102	15,506	18,310
Hungary	5,202	4,956	4,421	United Kingdom	71,340	64,966	70,990
Ireland	1,273	1,342	1,867				
Italy	25,485	22,020	29,240	**Total (EU-28)**	536,041	533,587	575,809

© European Union. Source: Eurostat, 2017, Environment and energy, table *NRG_100A*—Simplified energy balances—Annual data.

Gross inland consumption of all energy products ('000 metric tons of oil equivalent)

	2013	2014	2015		2013	2014	2015
Austria	33,695	32,468	33,250	Latvia	4,466	4,452	4,380
Belgium	56,574	53,549	54,217	Lithuania	6,687	6,695	6,913
Bulgaria	16,756	17,745	18,511	Luxembourg	4,336	4,222	4,177
Croatia	8,586	8,195	8,525	Malta	876	886	756
Cyprus	2,188	2,229	2,272	Netherlands	80,286	76,359	77,557
Czech Republic	43,519	42,241	42,442	Poland	97,986	94,326	95,434
Denmark	17,814	16,803	16,766	Portugal	22,381	22,085	22,997
Estonia	6,703	6,677	6,255	Romania	32,428	32,158	32,414
Finland	34,146	34,769	33,155	Slovakia	16,996	16,181	16,426
France	258,917	248,454	252,615	Slovenia	6,865	6,653	6,579
Germany	324,533	313,239	314,203	Spain	119,329	116,681	121,418
Greece	24,242	24,370	24,449	Sweden	49,122	48,209	45,474
Hungary	23,942	23,815	25,200	United Kingdom	201,197	189,707	190,745
Ireland	13,705	13,561	14,178				
Italy	159,515	151,027	156,169	**Total (EU-28)**	1,667,791	1,607,754	1,627,475

© European Union. Source: Eurostat, 2017, Environment and energy, table *NRG_100A*—Simplified energy balances—Annual data.

Energy available for final consumption ('000 metric tons of oil equivalent)

	2013	2014	2015		2013	2014	2015
Austria	29,774	28,764	29,295	Latvia	3,961	3,987	3,893
Belgium	43,969	42,725	44,463	Lithuania	5,743	5,900	5,985
Bulgaria	8,691	8,953	9,654	Luxembourg	4,154	4,034	4,018
Croatia	7,111	6,781	7,117	Malta	532	555	575
Cyprus	1,628	1,649	1,674	Netherlands	68,492	63,606	64,586
Czech Republic	27,722	26,579	27,369	Poland	68,582	66,193	66,520
Denmark	14,371	13,710	14,103	Portugal	17,237	17,176	17,288
Estonia	3,047	3,148	3,029	Romania	22,906	22,758	23,041
Finland	25,172	26,387	25,430	Slovakia	11,705	10,976	11,162
France	167,224	157,053	160,337	Slovenia	4,925	4,727	4,820
Germany	239,265	229,869	233,136	Spain	84,787	81,441	83,179
Greece	15,569	16,230	17,150	Sweden	34,479	33,825	32,660
Hungary	17,897	17,705	19,095	United Kingdom	143,090	136,743	139,193
Ireland	11,167	11,072	11,629				
Italy	125,182	118,585	121,994	**Total (EU-28)**	1,208,380	1,161,131	1,182,392

© European Union. Source: Eurostat, 2017, Environment and energy, table *NRG_100A*—Simplified energy balances—Annual data.

Available energy by source, 2015 ('000 metric tons of oil equivalent)

	Gross inland consumption	Less Transformation input	Transformation output	Exchanges, transfers, returns	Less Consumption – Energy sector	Less Distribution losses	Energy available for final consumption
Austria	33,250	16,759	14,777	13	1,500	485	29,295
Belgium	54,217	50,549	43,279	118	2,238	364	44,463
Bulgaria	18,511	19,062	11,856	-8	1,154	489	9,654
Croatia	8,525	4,598	4,031	1	622	220	7,117
Cyprus	2,272	923	362	0	20	19	1,674
Czech Republic	42,442	32,495	20,406	6	2,312	679	27,369
Denmark	16,766	14,153	13,403	13	1,157	769	14,103
Estonia	6,255	4,344	1,476	0	226	130	3,029
Finland	33,155	28,478	22,714	-3	1,300	657	25,430
France	252,615	190,945	109,455	-27	7,034	3,727	160,337
Germany	314,203	234,006	169,538	56	12,835	3,821	233,136
Greece	24,449	36,599	31,920	-3	2,187	429	17,150
Hungary	25,200	16,860	12,214	5	947	516	19,095
Ireland	14,178	7,340	5,279	1	249	239	11,629
Italy	156,169	124,140	99,549	-46	7,559	1,980	121,994
Latvia	4,380	1,194	919	0	87	124	3,893
Lithuania	6,913	10,392	10,329	-10	668	188	5,985
Luxembourg	4,177	237	144	0	47	19	4,018
Malta	756	264	104	0	6	15	575
Netherlands	77,557	85,866	76,089	2,539	5,165	568	64,586
Poland	95,434	77,647	56,714	27	6,472	1,537	66,520
Portugal	22,997	22,355	18,517	-8	1,434	429	17,288
Romania	32,414	23,329	17,384	-3	2,347	1,077	23,041
Slovakia	16,426	15,066	11,196	-10	1,020	363	11,162
Slovenia	6,579	2,678	1,130	0	109	103	4,820
Spain	121,418	110,687	84,412	139	9,533	2,570	83,179
Sweden	45,474	43,466	32,854	178	1,626	754	32,660
United Kingdom	190,745	129,767	92,722	13	11,291	3,229	139,193
Total (EU-28)	1,627,475	1,304,201	962,772	2,991	81,146	25,500	1,182,392

© European Union. Source: Eurostat, 2017, Environment and energy, table *NRG_100A*—Simplified energy balances—Annual data.

Final energy consumption ('000 metric tons of oil equivalent)

	2013	2014	2015		2013	2014	2015
Austria	27,971	26,742	27,370	Latvia	3,855	3,885	3,788
Belgium	36,404	34,196	35,780	Lithuania	4,794	4,893	4,869
Bulgaria	8,778	9,012	9,508	Luxembourg	4,121	4,001	3,988
Croatia	6,573	6,241	6,587	Malta	525	545	572
Cyprus	1,614	1,616	1,660	Netherlands	51,583	47,322	48,505
Czech Republic	24,310	23,625	24,187	Poland	63,259	61,599	62,251
Denmark	14,052	13,515	13,946	Portugal	15,854	15,770	16,038
Estonia	2,870	2,816	2,765	Romania	21,834	21,721	21,893
Finland	24,680	24,503	24,181	Slovakia	10,608	9,983	10,077
France	151,243	140,345	144,123	Slovenia	4,796	4,589	4,689
Germany	217,654	208,881	212,124	Spain	80,771	79,225	80,461
Greece	15,282	15,520	16,502	Sweden	31,582	31,192	31,759
Hungary	16,562	16,191	17,309	United Kingdom	136,735	129,623	131,370
Ireland	10,738	10,766	11,214				
Italy	118,519	113,350	116,444	**Total (EU-28)**	1,107,567	1,061,668	1,083,957

© European Union. Source: Eurostat, 2017, Environment and energy, table *NRG_100A*—Simplified energy balances—Annual data.

Final energy consumption by sector, 2015 ('000 metric tons of oil equivalent)

	Industry	Transport	Other sectors*		Industry	Transport	Other sectors*
Austria	9,117	9,000	9,252	Latvia	788	1,147	1,853
Belgium	11,891	10,444	13,445	Lithuania	983	1,832	2,054
Bulgaria	2,713	3,402	3,392	Luxembourg	651	2,420	918
Croatia	1,090	2,107	3,390	Malta	46	311	215
Cyprus	201	867	591	Netherlands	14,266	14,273	19,966
Czech Republic	7,474	6,489	10,225	Poland	15,047	17,241	29,963
Denmark	2,110	4,949	6,886	Portugal	4,451	6,613	4,975
Estonia	524	785	1,457	Romania	6,472	5,577	9,844
Finland	10,698	4,791	8,692	Slovakia	4,427	2,212	3,438
France	28,639	50,077	65,407	Slovenia	1,227	1,799	1,663
Germany	60,951	63,168	88,004	Spain	18,915	33,595	27,952
Greece	3,128	6,577	6,797	Sweden	11,528	8,668	11,563
Hungary	4,236	4,354	8,719	United Kingdom	24,731	51,766	54,873
Ireland	2,414	4,624	4,177				
Italy	26,023	39,541	50,880	**Total (EU-28)**	274,737	358,629	450,591

* Households, services, etc.

© European Union. Source: Eurostat, 2017, Environment and energy, table *NRG_100A*—Simplified energy balances—Annual data.

NUCLEAR ENERGY

Primary production of nuclear energy ('000 metric tons of oil equivalent)

	2013	2014	2015
Belgium	11,000	8,694	6,733
Bulgaria	3,671	4,107	3,983
Czech Republic	7,952	7,843	6,945
Finland	6,089	6,083	5,996
France	109,291	112,590	112,836
Germany	25,096	25,055	23,677
Hungary	3,977	4,055	4,104
Netherlands	746	1,055	1,052
Romania	2,997	3,012	3,003
Slovakia	4,106	4,041	3,954
Slovenia	1,367	1,643	1,457
Spain	14,633	14,782	14,782
Sweden	17,143	16,735	14,535
United Kingdom	18,213	16,444	18,146
Total (EU-28)	226,282	226,140	221,202

Note: Only countries producing nuclear energy are listed.

© European Union. Source: Eurostat, 2017, Environment and energy, table *NRG_104A*—Supply and transformation of nuclear energy—Annual data.

ELECTRICAL ENERGY

Gross electricity generation (million kWh)

	2013	2014	2015		2013	2014	2015
Austria	68,312	65,442	65,299	Latvia	6,209	5,141	5,533
Belgium	83,488	72,672	70,648	Lithuania	4,762	4,397	4,933
Bulgaria	43,784	47,485	49,228	Luxembourg	2,888	2,966	2,762
Croatia	14,052	13,554	11,403	Malta	2,251	2,245	1,303
Cyprus	4,290	4,350	4,533	Netherlands	101,736	103,418	110,070
Czech Republic	86,913	86,148	83,892	Poland	164,580	159,059	164,944
Denmark	34,743	32,184	28,947	Portugal	51,672	52,802	52,420
Estonia	13,275	12,446	10,417	Romania	58,888	65,676	66,296
Finland	71,257	68,094	68,598	Slovakia	28,832	27,401	26,903
France	571,372	563,694	568,454	Slovenia	16,103	17,437	15,100
Germany	638,729	627,795	646,888	Spain	285,632	278,749	281,020
Greece	57,152	50,474	51,874	Sweden	153,166	153,662	162,058
Hungary	30,294	29,392	30,342	United Kingdom	358,377	338,176	339,095
Ireland	25,920	26,087	28,387				
Italy	289,807	279,827	282,994	**Total (EU-28)**	3,268,484	3,190,773	3,234,341

© European Union. Source: Eurostat, 2017, Environment and energy, table *NRG_105A*—Supply, transformation and consumption of electricity—Annual data.

Gross electricity generation by principal source, 2015 (million kWh)

	Nuclear power plants	Hydro power plants	Geothermal power plants	Wind turbines	Conventional thermal power plants (combustible fuels)
Austria	0	40,113	0	4,840	6,643
Belgium	26,103	1,418	0	5,543	19,410
Bulgaria	15,383	6,147	0	1,452	20,881
Croatia	0	6,550	0	796	2,596
Cyprus	0	0	0	221	4,128
Czech Republic	26,841	2,505	0	573	8,649
Denmark	0	18	0	14,133	14
Estonia	0	27	0	701	8,325
Finland	23,245	15,690	0	2,327	3,796
France	437,428	58,801	0	19,795	21,369
Germany	91,786	24,741	134	79,206	281,591
Greece	0	6,150	0	4,621	27,127
Hungary	0	234	0	693	8,708
Ireland	0	1,095	0	6,573	18,559
Italy	0	46,361	6,185	14,844	95,124
Latvia	0	1,858	0	143	0
Lithuania	0	1,024	0	810	0
Luxembourg	0	1,524	0	102	680
Malta	0	0	0	0	1,203
Netherlands	4,077	93	0	6,369	48,946
Poland	0	2,432	0	10,858	4,349
Portugal	0	9,784	204	11,607	21,883
Romania	11,640	16,603	0	6,696	13,927
Slovakia	4,241	4,052	0	1	345
Slovenia	5,648	3,937	0	6	11
Spain	57,305	30,620	0	49,312	96,474
Sweden	56,348	75,428	0	16,268	23
United Kingdom	70,345	7,646	0	33,257	177,866
Total (EU-28)	830,390	364,851	6,523	291,747	892,627

© European Union. Source: Eurostat, 2017, Environment and energy, table *NRG_105A*—Supply, transformation and consumption of electricity—Annual data.

Final consumption of electrical energy (million kWh)

	2013	2014	2015		2013	2014	2015
Austria	61,011	60,678	60,813	Latvia	6,576	6,582	6,461
Belgium	83,029	81,153	81,714	Lithuania	8,955	9,237	9,342
Bulgaria	27,532	27,674	28,326	Luxembourg	6,201	6,182	6,221
Croatia	15,072	14,833	15,343	Malta	1,950	2,005	2,114
Cyprus	3,921	3,965	4,091	Netherlands	104,373	101,630	103,112
Czech Republic	53,587	53,420	54,474	Poland	123,557	125,347	127,819
Denmark	31,106	30,530	30,700	Portugal	45,257	45,195	45,812
Estonia	6,820	6,906	6,852	Romania	40,628	41,905	43,030
Finland	79,946	79,143	78,466	Slovakia	25,084	24,157	24,371
France	440,710	414,810	424,919	Slovenia	12,479	12,459	12,788
Germany	523,201	512,835	514,731	Spain	230,087	226,897	232,038
Greece	48,791	49,500	50,787	Sweden	125,016	122,191	124,859
Hungary	34,873	34,737	36,193	United Kingdom	316,384	303,018	302,850
Ireland	24,201	24,136	25,070				
Italy	287,398	281,498	287,483	**Total (EU-28)**	2,767,745	2,702,623	2,740,779

© European Union. Source: Eurostat, 2017, Environment and energy, table *NRG_105A*—Supply, transformation and consumption of electricity—Annual data.

Electricity consumption by sector, 2015 (million kWh)

	Industry	Transport	Other sectors*		Industry	Transport	Other sectors*
Austria	27,228	3,109	30,476	Latvia	1,703	106	4,652
Belgium	37,936	1,616	42,162	Lithuania	3,313	67	5,962
Bulgaria	8,946	352	19,028	Luxembourg	3,160	124	2,937
Croatia	3,429	245	11,669	Malta	415	0	1,699
Cyprus	459	0	3,632	Netherlands	34,247	1,752	67,113
Czech Republic	22,642	1,609	30,223	Poland	49,482	3,107	75,230
Denmark	8,397	397	21,906	Portugal	15,481	308	30,023
Estonia	2,059	47	4,746	Romania	20,525	1,082	21,423
Finland	37,893	703	39,870	Slovakia	11,605	602	12,164
France	107,019	10,178	307,722	Slovenia	6,199	152	6,437
Germany	224,880	11,279	278,572	Spain	76,045	6,072	149,921
Greece	12,668	388	37,731	Sweden	50,281	2,595	71,983
Hungary	15,390	1,162	19,641	United Kingdom	92,452	4,476	205,922
Ireland	9,844	41	15,185				
Italy	112,665	10,856	163,962	**Total (EU-28)**	996,363	62,425	1,681,991

* Households, services, etc.

© European Union. Source: Eurostat, 2017, Environment and energy, table *NRG_105A*—Supply, transformation and consumption of electricity—Annual data.

Electricity: Net installed capacity by main activity producers, 2015 ('000 kW)

	Combustible fuels	Nuclear	Hydro	Geothermal	Wind
Austria	5,964	0	12,814	1	2,489
Belgium	7,199	5,913	1,422	0	2,161
Bulgaria	3,854	1,975	3,219	0	700
Croatia	1,959	0	2,205	0	418
Cyprus	1,481	0	0	0	158
Czech Republic	11,275	4,290	2,069	0	281
Denmark	7,520	0	7	0	5,075
Estonia	2,526	0	6	0	294
Finland	7,031	2,752	3,063	0	1,005
France	20,934	63,130	25,075	2	9,536
Germany	86,552	10,799	11,356	26	44,670
Greece	10,294	0	3,392	0	2,091
Hungary	5,856	2,000	57	:	329
Ireland	6,242	0	529	0	2,440
Italy	60,575	0	22,099	768	9,137
Latvia	1,234	0	1,587	0	69
Lithuania	1,931	0	877	0	436
Luxembourg	451	0	1,328	0	64
Malta	590	0	0	0	0
Netherlands	23,400	485	37	0	2,854
Poland	27,929	0	2,369	0	4,886
Portugal	6,205	0	6,162	25	4,936
Romania	8,895	1,411	6,619	0	2,684
Slovakia	2,119	1,940	2,495	0	1
Slovenia	1,086	688	1,179	0	5
Spain	49,350	7,399	20,053	0	22,943
Sweden	7,751	9,688	16,321	0	5,840
United Kingdom	53,038	9,487	4,221	0	11,453
Total (EU-28)	423,241	121,957	150,561	822	136,955

© European Union. Source: Eurostat, 2017, Environment and energy, table *NRG_113A*—Infrastructure—electricity—Annual data.

RENEWABLE ENERGIES

Primary production of renewables ('000 metric tons of oil equivalent)

	2013	2014	2015		2013	2014	2015
Austria	9,453	9,217	9,303	Latvia	2,137	2,371	2,330
Belgium	2,966	2,945	2,959	Lithuania	1,288	1,358	1,466
Bulgaria	1,826	1,842	2,033	Luxembourg	98	119	113
Croatia	2,313	2,292	2,228	Malta	9	13	15
Cyprus	109	111	118	Netherlands	4,373	4,555	4,810
Czech Republic	4,118	4,198	4,279	Poland	8,521	8,072	8,635
Denmark	3,048	3,133	3,528	Portugal	5,607	5,835	5,182
Estonia	1,122	1,186	1,286	Romania	5,561	6,090	5,935
Finland	9,930	10,118	10,394	Slovakia	1,467	1,441	1,592
France	22,545	21,013	21,417	Slovenia	1,115	1,158	1,026
Germany	33,680	36,018	38,886	Spain	17,562	18,003	16,874
Greece	2,487	2,329	2,641	Sweden	16,770	16,709	18,375
Hungary	3,314	2,981	3,240	United Kingdom	8,920	9,859	11,835
Ireland	757	854	981	**Total (EU-28)**	194,594	197,464	205,043
Italy	23,500	23,644	23,564				

Note: Biomass, hydropower, geothermal energy, wind and solar energy are included in renewable energies.
© European Union. Source: Eurostat, 2017, Environment and energy, table *NRG_107A*—Supply, transformation and consumption of renewable energies—Annual data.

Share of renewable energy in gross final energy consumption (%)

	2013	2014	2015
Austria	32.3	32.8	33.0
Belgium	7.5	8.0	7.9
Bulgaria	19.0	18.0	18.2
Croatia	28.0	27.9	29.0
Cyprus	8.1	8.9	9.4
Czech Republic	13.8	15.1	15.1
Denmark	27.4	29.3	30.8
Estonia	25.6	26.3	28.6
Finland	36.7	38.7	39.3
France	14.1	14.7	15.2
Germany	12.4	13.8	14.6
Greece	15.0	15.3	15.4
Hungary	16.2	14.6	14.5
Ireland	7.7	8.7	9.2
Italy	16.7	17.1	17.5
Latvia	37.1	38.7	37.6
Lithuania	22.7	23.6	25.8
Luxembourg	3.5	4.5	5.0
Malta	3.7	4.7	5.0
Netherlands	4.8	5.5	5.8
Poland	11.4	11.5	11.8
Portugal	25.7	27.0	28.0
Romania	23.9	24.8	24.8
Slovakia	10.1	11.7	12.9
Slovenia	22.4	21.5	22.0
Spain	15.3	16.1	16.2
Sweden	52.0	52.5	53.9
United Kingdom	5.7	7.1	8.2
Total (EU-28)	15.2	16.1	16.7

© European Union. Source: Eurostat, 2017, Environment and energy, table *NRG_IND_335A*—Share of energy from renewable sources.

INDUSTRY

INDUSTRIAL ENTERPRISES

Mining and quarrying: number of enterprises

	2012	2013	2014		2012	2013	2014
Austria	355	353	349	Latvia	230	236	236
Belgium	203	214	192	Lithuania	90	97	116
Bulgaria	382	386	359	Luxembourg	10	10	10
Croatia	281	257	245	Malta*	n.a.	n.a.	n.a.
Cyprus*	n.a.	n.a.	n.a.	Netherlands	321	417	437
Czech Republic	359	363	380	Poland	1,944	1,657	1,852
Denmark	218	210	207	Portugal	1,176	1,157	1,102
Estonia	128	138	142	Romania	1,098	1,072	1,112
Finland	888	895†	897	Slovakia	125	157	193
France	1,718	1,861	1,888†	Slovenia	106	105	99
Germany	1,902	1,706	1,916	Spain	2,357	1,967	1,911
Greece	380	372	369	Sweden	753	749	740
Hungary	448	448	429	United Kingdom	1,263	1,303	1,263
Ireland	411	421	411				
Italy	2,451	2,336	2,257	**Total (EU-28)**	19,000‡	19,000‡	19,237

* Confidential. † Break in series. ‡ Estimate.
© European Union. Source: Eurostat, 2017, table *SBS_NA_SCA_R2*—Annual enterprise statistics for special aggregates of activities (NACE Rev. 2).

Manufacturing: number of enterprises

	2012	2013	2014		2012	2013	2014
Austria	25,003	25,129	25,524	Latvia	8,981	9,537	9,806
Belgium	33,972	33,468	35,747	Lithuania	15,133	16,120	17,975
Bulgaria	29,715	30,091	30,374	Luxembourg	822	839	812
Croatia	21,330	20,673	20,087	Malta†	n.a.	n.a.	n.a.
Cyprus	5,283	5,243	5,076	Netherlands	53,319	60,506	61,394
Czech Republic	173,889	167,688	170,041	Poland	174,700	174,414	180,639
Denmark	15,524	15,062	15,007	Portugal	67,485	66,423	66,201
Estonia	5,927	6,381	6,613	Romania	46,004	46,761	48,091
Finland	21,848	21,582*	21,042	Slovakia	66,683	63,208	64,975
France	217,865	226,372	235,092†	Slovenia	17,182	18,148	18,561
Germany	203,664	202,824	212,602	Spain	175,919	168,935	166,589
Greece	64,582	57,736	58,211	Sweden	54,615	53,681	53,896
Hungary	49,798	47,475	47,614	United Kingdom	124,599	127,943	125,967
Ireland	14,533	14,649	14,628				
Italy	417,306	407,344	396,422	**Total (EU-28)‡**	2,100,000	2,080,000	2,110,000

* Break in series. † Confidential. ‡ Estimates.
© European Union. Source: Eurostat, 2017, table *SBS_NA_SCA_R2*—Annual enterprise statistics for special aggregates of activities (NACE Rev. 2).

Electricity, gas, steam and air conditioning supply: number of enterprises

	2012	2013	2014		2012	2013	2014
Austria	2,142	2,256	2,271	Latvia	454	480	506
Belgium	533	618	693	Lithuania	488	1,214	1,434
Bulgaria	1,703	1,784	1,743	Luxembourg	74	74	82
Croatia	388	513	560	Malta*	n.a.	n.a.	n.a.
Cyprus*	n.a.	n.a.	n.a.	Netherlands	765	950	1,191
Czech Republic	5,991	8,446	10,414	Poland	2,730	2,546	2,583
Denmark	1,902	1,845	1,784	Portugal	888	925	941
Estonia	231	226	226	Romania	1,050	1,345	1,501
Finland	783	816†	849	Slovakia	358	430	487
France	18,554	20,756	24,883†	Slovenia	1,305	1,526	1,570
Germany	1,899	1,974	2,058	Spain	13,986	13,867	14,244
Greece	18	32	28	Sweden	2,182	2,287	2,470
Hungary	670	675	668	United Kingdom	1,829	2,577	3,285
Ireland	456	485	483				
Italy	8,926	10,169	10,459	**Total (EU-28)**	70,066‡	78,601‡	n.a.

* Confidential. † Break in series. ‡ Estimate.
© European Union. Source: Eurostat, 2017, table *SBS_NA_SCA_R2*—Annual enterprise statistics for special aggregates of activities (NACE Rev. 2).

Construction: number of enterprises

	2012	2013	2014		2012	2013	2014
Austria	32,174	33,518	34,227	Latvia	8,000	8,767	9,424
Belgium	95,549	96,791	105,998	Lithuania	20,242	22,736	27,543
Bulgaria	19,068	18,738	18,908	Luxembourg	3,365	3,512	3,542
Croatia	20,170	19,236	18,359	Malta	3,835	3,623	3,758
Cyprus	8,640	7,603	7,197	Netherlands	134,589	152,519	154,748
Czech Republic	175,799	170,494	170,806	Poland	233,731	223,794	230,497
Denmark	31,300	30,707	31,281	Portugal	87,592	81,335	77,844
Estonia	8,376	8,870	9,029	Romania	44,607	45,382	47,813
Finland	42,781	42,844*	41,827	Slovakia	86,412	81,902	83,927
France	512,864	536,488	575,733*	Slovenia	18,392	18,066	18,133
Germany	274,002	267,849	338,535	Spain	320,872	320,086	346,822
Greece	86,873	84,622	84,672	Sweden	93,598	94,368	96,694
Hungary	60,284	55,471	56,765	United Kingdom	257,192	262,586	270,770
Ireland	49,530	48,502	47,349				
Italy	572,412	549,846	529,103	**Total (EU-28)**	3,280,371†	3,269,946†	3,441,304

* Break in series. † Estimate.
© European Union. Source: Eurostat, 2017, table *SBS_NA_SCA_R2*—Annual enterprise statistics for special aggregates of activities (NACE Rev. 2).

INDUSTRIAL EMPLOYMENT

Mining and quarrying: number of persons employed (enterprise statistics)

	2012	2013	2014		2012	2013	2014
Austria	6,069	6,138	6,265	Latvia	3,101	3,096	3,213
Belgium	2,739	2,713	2,911	Lithuania	2,530	2,592	2,723
Bulgaria	25,030	24,635	24,066	Luxembourg	275	266	252
Croatia	14,254	13,799	13,278	Malta*	n.a.	n.a.	n.a.
Cyprus*	n.a.	n.a.	n.a.	Netherlands	8,704	10,378	11,326
Czech Republic	34,072	33,015	30,854	Poland	175,220	171,468	164,037
Denmark	5,937	4,448	4,456	Portugal	10,297	9,628	9,355
Estonia	5,288	5,104	4,875	Romania	58,216	51,826	47,223
Finland	5,968	6,494†	6,318	Slovakia	7,316	7,407	7,137
France	24,423	24,108	21,523†	Slovenia	2,473	2,400	2,410
Germany	66,139	61,061	60,841	Spain	24,547	20,988	20,082
Greece	5,083	5,842	6,037	Sweden	10,498	10,857	10,847
Hungary	4,403	4,337	4,298	United Kingdom	75,136	65,557	66,637
Ireland	4,180	4,146	4,058				
Italy	32,569	31,231	31,222	**Total (EU-28)‡**	614,400	583,400	566,936

* Confidential. † Break in series. ‡ Estimates.
© European Union. Source: Eurostat, 2017, table *SBS_NA_SCA_R2*—Annual enterprise statistics for special aggregates of activities (NACE Rev. 2).

Manufacturing: number of persons employed (enterprise statistics)

	2012	2013	2014		2012	2013	2014
Austria	616,087	617,441	620,993	Latvia	118,289	120,760	121,746
Belgium	523,818	514,258	504,879	Lithuania	192,085	197,923	207,060
Bulgaria	525,257	524,041	536,216	Luxembourg	34,021	33,558	33,311
Croatia	263,154	261,749	254,850	Malta*	n.a.	n.a.	n.a.
Cyprus	32,031	28,861	27,680	Netherlands	687,218	681,619	673,456
Czech Republic	1,225,264	1,212,459	1,230,099	Poland	2,361,455	2,347,504	2,425,350
Denmark	364,334	354,054	360,983	Portugal	647,947	637,427	650,628
Estonia	103,196	104,564	107,870	Romania	1,167,452	1,166,313	1,180,098
Finland	362,966	351,985*	347,713	Slovakia	449,880	440,479	467,686
France	3,029,253	3,005,971	3,014,251*	Slovenia	190,851	188,750	188,697
Germany	7,169,663	7,220,296	7,269,135	Spain	1,805,808	1,736,652	1,724,072
Greece	311,615	289,188	283,215	Sweden	654,989	635,788	622,950
Hungary	670,653	664,724	678,247	United Kingdom	2,492,378	2,482,898	2,491,437
Ireland	178,700	181,091	189,966				
Italy	3,846,840	3,733,694	3,654,887	**Total (EU-28)‡**	30,000,000	29,700,000	29,900,000

* Break in series. † Confidential. ‡ Estimates.
© European Union. Source: Eurostat, 2017, table *SBS_NA_SCA_R2*—Annual enterprise statistics for special aggregates of activities (NACE Rev. 2).

Electricity, gas and water supply: number of persons employed (enterprise statistics)

	2012	2013	2014		2012	2013	2014
Austria	29,129	29,402	29,297	Latvia	10,792	11,109	10,624
Belgium	18,605	20,181	20,907	Lithuania	12,712	13,781	13,912
Bulgaria	33,243	32,809	32,573	Luxembourg	1,341	1,435	1,470
Croatia	16,494	15,472	14,739	Malta*	n.a.	n.a.	n.a.
Cyprus*	n.a.	n.a.	n.a.	Netherlands	26,458	27,056	27,153
Czech Republic	32,886	33,495	33,849	Poland	147,917	139,998	136,068
Denmark	11,160	11,265	14,308	Portugal	9,264	8,913	8,703
Estonia	5,444	5,218	5,097	Romania	79,663	77,393	76,016
Finland	13,805	13,729†	13,645	Slovakia	18,547	17,885	18,104
France	178,012	181,335	190,297†	Slovenia	8,713	8,942	9,069
Germany	222,351	219,936	228,179	Spain	50,383	38,974	38,514
Greece	21,478	20,481	21,598	Sweden	31,469	31,264	31,811
Hungary	25,244	24,608	24,782	United Kingdom	120,535	129,496	129,335
Ireland	8,735	8,246	8,496				
Italy	88,208	87,908	88,476	**Total (EU-28)**	1,227,300	1,216,300	1,230,152

* Confidential. † Break in series.
© European Union. Source: Eurostat, 2017, table *SBS_NA_SCA_R2*—Annual enterprise statistics for special aggregates of activities (NACE Rev. 2).

Construction: number of persons employed (enterprise statistics)

	2012	2013	2014		2012	2013	2014
Austria	285,320	283,165	288,074	Latvia	59,775	61,248	68,027
Belgium	317,544	314,116	323,140	Lithuania	93,448	96,779	103,200
Bulgaria	150,381	145,504	147,163	Luxembourg	41,066	41,092	41,694
Croatia	111,447	106,214	102,296	Malta	10,217	10,232	9,992
Cyprus	28,486	21,309	18,514	Netherlands	474,618	450,148	429,255
Czech Republic	395,214	376,377	368,547	Poland	890,864	830,679	831,226
Denmark	166,230	164,878	169,288	Portugal	340,913	307,907	294,458
Estonia	43,437	44,157	43,597	Romania	410,340	378,331	365,320
Finland	182,778	190,164*	189,792	Slovakia	153,110	144,544	146,448
France	1,772,057	1,705,993	1,813,280*	Slovenia	62,357	60,852	60,690
Germany	1,962,860	1,971,082	2,202,152	Spain	1,112,233	982,095	991,202
Greece	197,363	193,633	196,024	Sweden	353,468	353,646	363,586
Hungary	198,317	187,872	194,532	United Kingdom	1,293,991	1,301,497	1,337,324
Ireland	89,351	91,122	99,860				
Italy	1,553,237	1,445,485	1,356,571	**Total (EU-28)†**	12,730,700	12,238,100	12,555,252

* Break in series. † Estimates.
© European Union. Source: Eurostat, 2017, table *SBS_NA_SCA_R2*—Annual enterprise statistics for special aggregates of activities (NACE Rev. 2).

INDUSTRIAL PRODUCTION

Mining and quarrying: value of production (million euros)

	2012	2013	2014		2012	2013	2014
Austria	2,606.6	2,500.5	2,325.7	Latvia	193.2	211.6	219.0
Belgium	857.3	846.8	902.7	Lithuania	195.6	217.0	215.7
Bulgaria	1,518.4	1,307.4	1,243.9	Luxembourg	74.8	74.9	71.0
Croatia	3,953.4	3,727.3	3,357.7	Malta*	n.a.	n.a.	n.a.
Cyprus*	n.a.	n.a.	n.a.	Netherlands	24,932.9	26,162.2	21,585.3
Czech Republic	3,449.1	2,944.4	2,614.9	Poland	15,186.0	13,628.6	12,982.6
Denmark	8,399.2	7,612.2	6,538.0	Portugal	1,104.1	1,027.5	1,000.0
Estonia	395.1	457.7	459.2	Romania	6,379.5	6,083.0	6,396.6
Finland	1,886.9	1,722.8†	1,506.9	Slovakia	497.6	528.0	533.0
France	7,434.4	7,575.9	6,610.9†	Slovenia	250.5	252.5	262.4
Germany	12,455.8	11,686.2	11,767.8	Spain	4,341.3	3,613.7	3,455.1
Greece	622.1	672.9	870.3	Sweden	5,241.2	4,742.2	4,221.5
Hungary	369.6	418.1	387.4	United Kingdom	58,949.9	60,123.2	53,499.6
Ireland	1,303.9	1,070.0	1,007.3				
Italy	71,869.8	47,950.2	46,765.3	**Total (EU-28)**	234,000.0‡	207,000.0‡	190,897.0

* Confidential. † Break in series. ‡ Estimates.
© European Union. Source: Eurostat, 2017, table *SBS_NA_SCA_R2*—Annual enterprise statistics for special aggregates of activities (NACE Rev. 2).

Manufacturing: value of production (million euros)

	2012	2013	2014		2012	2013	2014
Austria	166,931.2	166,674.2	167,255.5	Latvia	7,688.0	7,480.6	7,332.8
Belgium	254,096.5	253,620.1	245,052.8	Lithuania	18,742.5	19,098.9	18,379.5
Bulgaria	25,506.8	26,115.2	26,783.3	Luxembourg	9,091.9	8,774.9	9,127.9
Croatia	14,882.6	14,471.7	14,873.4	Malta†	n.a.	n.a.	n.a.
Cyprus	2,953.0	2,558.5	2,518.5	Netherlands	283,180.0	273,812.6	294,154.7
Czech Republic	139,632.2	136,544.7	142,705.2	Poland	244,432.0	245,039.2	255,244.8
Denmark	95,178.0	94,535.6	95,895.0	Portugal	75,232.6	75,262.3	76,428.7
Estonia	9,766.1	10,359.8	10,929.2	Romania	60,231.5	62,207.7	65,635.1
Finland	109,558.4	105,717.7†	102,620.7	Slovakia	61,003.5	61,848.5	63,660.3
France	765,885.0	743,807.5	783,987.9*	Slovenia	21,603.2	21,418.4	22,438.2
Germany	1,755,199.3	1,748,343.8	1,787,369.6	Spain	431,644.4	421,276.5	431,705.8
Greece	52,604.6	51,014.1	51,449.6	Sweden	192,533.9	185,790.4	181,820.9
Hungary	82,299.0	82,353.7	86,891.6	United Kingdom	593,095.9	575,745.2	599,303.1
Ireland	106,334.0	105,621.6	116,927.0				
Italy	868,846.3	853,491.4	849,097.1	**Total (EU-28)**‡	6,440,000.0	6,300,000.0	6,510,000.0

* Break in series.   † Confidential.   ‡ Estimates.
© European Union. Source: Eurostat, 2017, table *SBS_NA_SCA_R2*—Annual enterprise statistics for special aggregates of activities (NACE Rev. 2).

Electricity, gas, steam and air conditioning supply: value of production (million euros)

	2012	2013	2014		2012	2013	2014
Austria	38,679.7	38,779.7	34,590.6	Latvia	1,690.5	1,743.6	1,511.9
Belgium	41,251.6	42,099.2	39,171.4	Lithuania	1,921.0	2,038.8	1,983.5
Bulgaria	4,932.1	4,623.7	3,719.8	Luxembourg	950.0	958.6†	1,054.8
Croatia	4,231.1	4,426.4	4,393.9	Malta*	n.a.	n.a.	n.a.
Cyprus*	n.a.	n.a.	n.a.	Netherlands	27,395.8	25,572.2	20,274.2
Czech Republic	40,354.7	38,314.2	32,034.7	Poland	27,721.9	27,502.2	27,969.0
Denmark	17,758.6	22,716.2	18,432.6	Portugal	13,414.3	13,005.2	12,439.3
Estonia	1,157.7	1,303.6	1,398.9	Romania	14,125.8	13,920.5	12,479.5
Finland	7,915.8	7,861.1†	7,752.6	Slovakia	12,180.2	11,560.1	9,609.1
France	122,254.7	122,083.3	116,406.8†	Slovenia	2,800.7	2,812.1	2,661.1
Germany*	n.a.	n.a.	n.a.	Spain	61,581.2	73,719.3	74,551.9
Greece	9,310.1	9,804.3	8,452.5	Sweden	20,091.1	19,482.9	18,312.5
Hungary	6,058.2	5,210.9	4,698.1	United Kingdom	59,278.0	58,594.7	65,449.3
Ireland	7,253.7	7,372.7	6,989.8				
Italy	131,876.6	97,637.4	98,660.5	**Total (EU-28)**	1,256,914.0	1,226,098.0	1,178,922.0

* Confidential.   † Break in series.
© European Union. Source: Eurostat, 2017, table *SBS_NA_SCA_R2*—Annual enterprise statistics for special aggregates of activities (NACE Rev. 2).

Construction: value of production (million euros)

	2012	2013	2014		2012	2013	2014
Austria	42,190.4	42,335.2	43,373.8	Latvia	3,871.2	4,259.4	4,155.1
Belgium	56,613.7	56,018.1	59,022.6	Lithuania	3,569.6	3,998.8	4,840.4
Bulgaria	6,595.7	6,492.6	7,641.1	Luxembourg	4,351.7	4,349.0	4,807.9
Croatia	5,384.1	5,159.6	5,127.5	Malta	801.6	815.5	961.4
Cyprus	2,637.8	1,893.5	1,716.1	Netherlands	81,883.2	77,553.5	77,125.0
Czech Republic	27,481.5	25,336.1	24,981.4	Poland	49,362.7	49,061.2	59,974.8
Denmark	26,457.9	25,803.8	27,501.9	Portugal	20,838.9	18,295.1	16,899.4
Estonia	2,706.6	2,804.5	2,766.1	Romania	18,134.0	17,983.3	16,726.5
Finland	29,047.0	28,720.7*	29,315.1	Slovakia	7,226.8	6,232.8	6,641.1
France	284,007.8	282,296.4	290,927.1*	Slovenia	4,485.8	4,194.1	4,536.4
Germany	213,720.2	217,858.4	242,724.3	Spain	119,303.4	99,206.3	103,533.1
Greece	10,858.4	10,238.0	10,873.4	Sweden	60,975.8	62,105.5	62,838.8
Hungary	6,477.1	7,313.1	8,356.8	United Kingdom	228,994.7	235,051.8	272,192.5
Ireland	7,903.5	9,757.8	14,102.7				
Italy	202,692.7	181,368.1	168,117.1	**Total (EU-28)**	1,528,954.0	1,485,741.0	1,571,780.0

* Break in series.
© European Union. Source: Eurostat, 2017, table *SBS_NA_SCA_R2*—Annual enterprise statistics for special aggregates of activities (NACE Rev. 2).

INDICES OF INDUSTRIAL PRODUCTION

Note: Data are adjusted according to the number of working days in each year.

Total industry (excluding construction) (volume index; base: 2010 = 100)

	2014	2015	2016		2014	2015	2016
Austria	108.4	110.7	113.0	Latvia	114.0	118.0	123.8
Belgium	104.7	104.7	109.2*	Lithuania	114.3	119.5	122.9
Bulgaria	107.3	110.2	113.1	Luxembourg	97.9	98.8	98.8
Croatia	92.9	95.3	100.0	Malta	94.1	100.1*	96.5*
Cyprus	71.6	74.1	80.0*	Netherlands	96.4	93.2	95.2
Czech Republic	110.2	115.5	118.8	Poland	114.4	119.6	123.3
Denmark	103.2	104.5	108.2	Portugal	95.1	96.7	97.6
Estonia	131.7	131.9	134.3	Romania	127.8	131.6*	133.3*
Finland	94.8	93.7	95.9	Slovakia	122.2	131.2	137.4
France	99.0	100.7	101.0	Slovenia	101.3	106.5	114.9*
Germany	107.9	108.8	109.9	Spain*	91.1	94.2	95.9
Greece	87.4	88.3	90.6*	Sweden	94.5	97.1	98.2
Hungary	113.3	121.4	122.2	United Kingdom	97.5	98.8	100.4
Ireland	116.0	158.9	159.9				
Italy	91.3	92.3	93.9	**Total (EU-28)**	101.7	103.9	105.6

* Provisional.

© European Union. Source: Eurostat, 2017, Industry, trade and services, table *STS_INPR_A*— Production in industry—Annual data (2010 = 100).

Mining and quarrying (volume index; base: 2010 = 100)

	2014	2015	2016		2014	2015	2016
Austria	101.4	92.1	94.5	Latvia	115.7	123.3	123.0
Belgium	88.1	103.7	106.6*	Lithuania	125.3	107.1	112.5
Bulgaria	98.2	98.4	100.6	Luxembourg	101.3	104.8	95.6
Croatia	73.3	76.9	75.6	Malta	96.5	93.9*	106.3*
Cyprus	35.4	36.1	47.5*	Netherlands	81.5	65.6	63.1
Czech Republic	83.4	81.4	73.9	Poland	96.2	96.5	92.1
Denmark	64.5	62.3	59.7	Portugal	58.0	60.1	53.9
Estonia	111.3	105.6	89.6	Romania	117.5	102.8*	86.7*
Finland	100.8	81.5	109.6	Slovakia	97.4	97.8	94.8
France	91.4	93.0	93.5	Slovenia	82.9	82.7	84.7*
Germany	82.3	78.0	71.6	Spain*	53.2	48.9	43.6
Greece	85.7	80.2	68.4*	Sweden	107.1	104.8	112.4
Hungary	110.2	94.7	75.6	United Kingdom	74.8	81.4	82.2
Ireland	114.1	82.2	72.0				
Italy	92.5	88.3	83.6	**Total (EU-28)**	81.1	79.6	78.0

* Provisional.

© European Union. Source: Eurostat, 2017, Industry, trade and services, table *STS_INPR_A*—Production in industry—Annual data (2010 = 100).

Manufacturing (volume index; base: 2010 = 100)

	2014	2015	2016		2014	2015	2016
Austria	108.9	111.4	113.7	Latvia	122.4	127.6	133.9
Belgium	109.0	109.2	111.7*	Lithuania	122.4	129.1	133.2
Bulgaria	109.8	114.2	118.9	Luxembourg	99.4	100.4	100.9
Croatia	94.0	97.3	102.5	Malta	92.9	99.2*	95.1*
Cyprus	70.2	72.6	78.0*	Netherlands	102.6	103.2	106.1
Czech Republic	114.8	122.0	126.4	Poland	117.4	123.6	129.1
Denmark	112.9	115.7	120.8	Portugal	99.3	100.6	99.4
Estonia	136.5	138.1	140.4	Romania	130.9	135.1*	139.2*
Finland	96.0	94.9	97.0	Slovakia	131.1	141.6	149.0
France	99.9	101.6	101.9	Slovenia	101.2	106.8	116.5*
Germany	109.7	110.2	111.6	Spain*	91.8	95.5	97.9
Greece	88.3	89.8	93.6*	Sweden	92.0	94.5	96.1
Hungary	115.4	124.4	125.8	United Kingdom	102.6	102.5	103.9
Ireland	117.7	165.8	166.6				
Italy	91.8	92.9	94.6	**Total (EU-28)**	104.0	106.5	108.3

* Provisional.

© European Union. Source: Eurostat, 2017, Industry, trade and services, table *STS_INPR_A*—Production in industry—Annual data (2010 = 100).

Electricity, gas, steam and air conditioning supply (volume index; base: 2010 = 100)

	2014	2015	2016		2014	2015	2016
Austria	98.6	97.2	90.7	Latvia	89.3	89.2	94.9
Belgium	77.7	75.7	90.7*	Lithuania	71.3	69.7	69.4
Bulgaria	106.0	105.3	102.9	Luxembourg	82.2	81.9	77.8
Croatia	95.5	90.1	96.4	Malta	102.7	106.8*	106.4*
Cyprus	81.6	84.9	91.3	Netherlands	83.2	90.5	95.3
Czech Republic	93.6	91.1	92.0	Poland	98.9	96.3	89.5
Denmark	98.2	92.6	97.3	Portugal	79.5	82.8	95.9
Estonia	94.8	83.2	95.2	Romania	100.4	101.8*	100.2*
Finland	83.8	84.5	84.6	Slovakia	82.1	84.6	86.3
France	92.5	95.0	95.1	Slovenia	103.5	105.7	102.4*
Germany	93.8	99.8	99.2	Spain*	90.4	90.6	88.2
Greece	85.1	85.6	87.1*	Sweden	104.1	109.2	104.0
Hungary	86.3	91.6	91.7	United Kingdom	87.3	87.7	90.1
Ireland	102.4	102.2	108.0				
Italy	86.2	87.9	88.9	**Total (EU-28)**	91.0	93.2	93.8

* Provisional.

© European Union. Source: Eurostat, 2017, Industry, trade and services, table *STS_INPR_A*—Production in industry—Annual data (2010 = 100).

THE ENVIRONMENT

RESOURCE PRODUCTIVITY

Resource productivity (index, 2000 = 100)

	2014	2015	2016*†		2014	2015	2016*†
Austria	121.12	124.85	122.49	Latvia	141.54	137.98	135.32
Belgium*	121.42	130.66	133.80	Lithuania*	121.02	123.20	131.08
Bulgaria*	119.26	111.19	120.03	Luxembourg	137.96	136.26	143.04
Croatia*	106.58	102.60	102.46	Malta*	100.55	97.51	99.10
Cyprus*	171.17	181.07	166.53	Netherlands	134.80	128.00	152.94
Czech Republic	161.78	163.47	172.46	Poland	135.30	142.95	149.53
Denmark*	124.99	125.42	121.48	Portugal	125.32	126.23	129.63
Estonia*	99.62	102.91	114.33	Romania*	63.39	62.35	64.39
Finland*	121.60	123.50	115.53	Slovakia	139.92	144.13	151.47
France*	133.66	140.26	145.50	Slovenia	164.44	165.76	177.48
Germany	124.14	133.92	137.02	Spain*	210.40	221.36	225.48
Greece*	107.56	108.99	114.12	Sweden	104.07	108.67	104.29
Hungary*	123.79	147.16	155.28	United Kingdom	157.91	165.61	170.35
Ireland	191.71	241.64	230.62				
Italy	223.20	224.77	224.97	**Total (EU-28)***	133.22	137.32	140.98

Note: Resource productivity is defined as gross domestic product (GDP) divided by domestic material consumption (DMC).
* Eurostat estimates.   † Provisional.
© European Union. Source: Eurostat, 2017, Environment and energy, table *ENV_AC_RP*—Resource productivity.

ENVIRONMENTAL PROTECTION EXPENDITURE

Environmental protection expenditure by the public sector (% of GDP)

	2011	2012	2013		2011	2012	2013
Austria	0.42	0.44	n.a.	Latvia	0.68	0.73	n.a.
Belgium	0.70	0.63	n.a.	Lithuania	0.94	0.90	0.56
Bulgaria	0.60	0.73	1.06	Luxembourg	0.53	0.56	0.57
Croatia	0.32	0.26	0.32	Malta	1.20	1.38	n.a.
Cyprus	0.58	0.43	0.51	Netherlands	1.44	n.a.	n.a.
Czech Republic	0.51	0.56	0.48	Poland	0.53	0.53	0.48
Denmark	0.54	0.55	0.64	Portugal	0.48	0.51	0.44
Estonia	0.31	n.a.	n.a.	Romania	0.95	0.6	0.46
Finland	0.59	0.64	n.a.	Slovakia	0.31	0.32	0.28
France	0.58	0.59	n.a.	Slovenia	0.80	0.70	n.a.
Germany	n.a.	n.a.	n.a.	Spain	0.26	0.22	n.a.
Greece	n.a.	n.a.	n.a.	Sweden	0.33	0.34	0.33
Hungary	0.39	0.42	n.a.	United Kingdom	0.93	0.91	n.a.
Ireland	n.a.	n.a.	n.a.				
Italy	0.88	n.a.	n.a.	**Total (EU-28)***	0.68	0.67	0.67

* Estimates.

© European Union. Source: Eurostat, 2017, Environment and energy, table *ENV_AC_EXP2*—Environmental protection expenditure in Europe—euros per head and % of GDP.

Environmental protection expenditure by industry (% of GDP)

	2011	2012	2013		2011	2012	2013
Austria	0.28	0.29	n.a.	Latvia	0.23	0.26	0.28
Belgium	0.29	0.29	n.a.	Lithuania	0.46	0.26	0.22
Bulgaria	0.69	0.61	0.76	Luxembourg	n.a.	n.a.	n.a.
Croatia	0.80	0.50	0.51	Malta	n.a.	n.a.	n.a.
Cyprus	0.18	0.17	n.a.	Netherlands	0.29	n.a.	n.a.
Czech Republic	0.86	0.86	0.96	Poland	0.84	0.95	0.85
Denmark	n.a.	n.a.	n.a.	Portugal	0.23	0.19	0.19
Estonia	n.a.*	0.47	n.a.	Romania	0.76	1.16	1.20
Finland	0.43	0.44	n.a.	Slovakia	0.55	0.54	n.a.*
France	n.a.	n.a.	n.a.	Slovenia	0.99	1.17	n.a.
Germany	n.a.	n.a.	n.a.	Spain	0.23	0.23	n.a.
Greece	n.a.	n.a.	n.a.	Sweden	0.36	0.38	0.34
Hungary	0.70	0.71	n.a.	United Kingdom	0.20	0.20	n.a.
Ireland	n.a.	n.a.	n.a.				
Italy	0.76	n.a.	n.a.	**Total (EU-28)†**	0.40	0.40	0.40

* Confidential.   † Estimates.
© European Union. Source: Eurostat, 2017, Environment and energy, table *ENV_AC_EXP2*—Environmental protection expenditure in Europe—euros per caput and % of GDP.

FINANCE

EXCHANGE RATES

Value of the euro in relation to selected currencies (European Central Bank rates at end of December each year)

	2014	2015	2016
Bulgarian lev	1.9558	1.9558	1.9558
Croatian kuna	7.6682	7.6397	7.5404
Czech koruna	27.6400	27.0270	27.0310
Danish krone	7.4402	7.4612	7.4362
Hungarian forint	310.8300	314.4000	312.2400
Yen (Japan)	147.0600	132.3600	122.3900
Norwegian krone	8.9802	9.4642	9.0252
Polish złoty	4.2155	4.2900	4.4357
Romanian leu	4.4583	4.5033	4.5164
Swedish krona	9.4043	9.2451	9.7095
Swiss franc	1.2026	1.0827	1.0750
Turkish lira	2.8304	3.1800	3.6917
Pound sterling (United Kingdom)	0.7883	0.7260	0.8444
United States dollar	1.2331	1.0877	1.0543

Note: From 1 January 1999 exchange rates were fixed for 11 EU members: Austria, Belgium, Finland, France, Germany, Ireland, Italy, Luxembourg, the Netherlands, Portugal and Spain. From 1 January 2001 the exchange rate was fixed for Greece. On 1 January 2002 these 12 countries began using euro notes and coins, and their national currencies were replaced at the fixed rates hitherto in operation. Slovenia joined the system from 1 January 2007, Cyprus and Malta from 1 January 2008, Slovakia from 1 January 2009 and Estonia from 1 January 2011. Latvia joined the eurozone on 1 January 2014 and Lithuania on 1 January 2015.
© European Union. Source: Eurostat, 2017, General and regional statistics, table *EI_MFRT_M*—Exchange rates—Monthly data.

PUBLIC FINANCE

Total revenue of general government (million euros)

	2014	2015	2016		2014	2015	2016
Austria	165,233	171,943	173,077	Latvia	8,486	8,720	9,097
Belgium	208,571	210,734	214,063	Lithuania	12,475	13,036	13,315
Bulgaria	15,654	17,681	16,810	Luxembourg	21,566	22,335	23,147
Croatia	18,523	19,818	21,672	Malta	3,333	3,703	3,871
Cyprus	6,953	6,917	7,019	Netherlands	291,176	292,596	307,004
Czech Republic	63,151	69,190	70,597	Poland	159,334	167,691	164,828
Denmark	150,516	145,357	145,948	Portugal	77,196	78,913	79,613
Estonia	7,731	8,195	8,507	Romania	50,373	56,043	53,718
Finland	112,796	113,648	116,047	Slovakia	29,855	33,691	32,345
France	1,141,981	1,165,302	1,181,278	Slovenia	16,682	17,433	17,352
Germany	1,306,759	1,354,784	1,411,381	Spain	403,431	415,539	421,672
Greece	83,532	84,820	87,473	Sweden	216,147	225,603	235,507
Hungary	49,266	53,170	51,280	United Kingdom	860,553	993,873	926,638
Ireland	65,932	70,547	73,029				
Italy	776,480	785,938	788,502	**Total (EU-28)**	6,323,683	6,607,219	6,654,791

© European Union. Source: Eurostat, 2017, Economy and finance, table *GOV_10A_MAIN*—Government revenue, expenditure and main aggregates.

Government expenditure by function: Austria, Belgium and Bulgaria (million euros)

	Austria			Belgium			Bulgaria		
	2013	2014	2015	2013	2014	2015	2013	2014	2015
General public services	23,338	22,725	23,283	33,967	33,753	33,296	1,521	1,209	1,439
Defence	2,013	1,929	1,952	3,667	3,546	3,458	500	588	632
Public order and safety	4,280	4,460	4,700	7,331	7,405	7,226	1,098	1,176	1,246
Economic affairs	18,326	24,559	20,928	27,098	27,957	26,499	2,289	3,571	2,742
Environment protection	1,636	1,567	1,527	4,583	3,880	3,567	384	295	358
Housing and community amenities	1,184	1,206	1,194	1,582	1,544	1,362	550	699	962
Health	25,195	26,067	27,172	31,397	32,333	31,454	1,897	2,341	2,471
Recreation, culture and religion	4,062	4,018	4,203	5,047	5,078	4,900	318	630	766
Education	16,270	16,406	16,855	25,020	25,449	26,348	1,545	1,746	1,801
Social protection	68,953	71,378	73,599	78,605	79,899	82,909	5,675	5,731	6,009
Total	165,257	174,313	175,412	218,296	220,845	221,018	15,777	17,986	18,426

© European Union. Source: Eurostat, 2017, Economy and finance, table *GOV_10A_EXP*—General government expenditure by function (COFOG).

Government expenditure by function: Croatia, Cyprus and Czech Republic (million euros)

	Croatia			Cyprus			Czech Republic		
	2013	2014	2015	2013	2014	2015	2013	2014	2015
General public services	3,858	3,907	4,000	1,818	1,763	1,807	7,469	7,405	7,232
Defence	607	626	587	288	251	245	1,210	1,096	1,539
Public order and safety	950	890	970	387	304	300	2,752	2,649	3,066
Economic affairs	2,584	2,481	2,183	526	1,980	614	9,239	9,524	10,955
Environment protection	184	160	199	81	46	63	1,596	1,629	1,829
Housing and community amenities	431	392	367	348	388	319	1,303	1,336	1,124
Health	2,940	2,906	2,899	554	462	451	12,062	11,893	12,737
Recreation, culture and religion	640	554	643	164	151	160	2,148	2,141	2,237
Education	2,215	2,036	2,076	1,178	1,003	1,008	8,059	8,011	8,240
Social protection	6,605	6,825	6,637	2,143	2,121	2,113	21,365	20,483	21,124
Total	21,012	20,777	20,561	7,486	8,467	7,080	67,202	66,167	70,083

© European Union. Source: Eurostat, 2017, Economy and finance, table *GOV_10A_EXP*—General government expenditure by function (COFOG).

Government expenditure by function: Denmark, Estonia and Finland (million euros)

	Denmark			Estonia			Finland		
	2013	2014	2015	2013	2014	2015	2013	2014	2015
General public services	19,466	19,414	20,158	769	806	868	16,862	17,023	17,835
Defence	3,393	3,025	3,055	343	355	384	2,981	2,890	2,808
Public order and safety	2,624	2,685	2,672	352	385	366	2,754	2,658	2,618
Economic affairs	9,018	9,670	9,953	880	939	966	9,734	9,916	9,952
Environment protection	1,224	1,233	1,213	118	123	140	522	521	501
Housing and community amenities	722	598	669	99	87	73	809	813	855
Health	22,026	22,745	23,263	946	1,021	1,116	16,869	17,076	15,009
Recreation, culture and religion	4,694	4,654	4,789	382	395	401	2,992	3,022	3,099
Education	17,810	18,938	19,140	1,136	1,125	1,235	13,011	13,122	13,090
Social protection	63,454	63,770	64,097	2,254	2,362	2,619	50,388	52,250	53,611
Total	144,431	146,732	149,008	7,279	7,597	8,168	116,922	119,291	119,378

© European Union. Source: Eurostat, 2017, Economy and finance, table *GOV_10A_EXP*—General government expenditure by function (COFOG).

STATISTICAL SURVEY
Finance

Government expenditure by function: France, Germany and Greece (million euros)

	France			Germany			Greece		
	2013	2014	2015	2013	2014	2015	2013	2014	2015
General public services	144,670	141,444	137,219	182,798	189,074	180,394	17,854	17,925	17,365
Defence	37,523	35,835	38,319	30,592	29,323	30,491	3,879	4,757	4,792
Public order and safety	34,546	35,113	35,606	44,372	45,711	47,465	3,372	3,763	3,694
Economic affairs	104,867	115,147	124,481	94,141	92,040	95,191	29,718	7,350	15,619
Environment protection	21,651	21,984	21,930	17,447	17,791	18,468	3,082	2,628	2,603
Housing and community amenities	26,931	25,806	23,337	11,677	11,431	11,614	530	494	430
Health	170,238	175,485	178,239	199,004	209,440	217,241	9,313	8,364	7,973
Recreation, culture and religion	30,905	30,052	28,999	28,901	30,251	30,831	1,179	1,221	1,223
Education	116,295	118,001	119,173	120,903	123,926	127,394	8,257	7,800	7,593
Social protection	517,641	527,775	535,481	533,883	549,220	574,772	35,354	35,712	36,055
Total	1,205,267	1,226,643	1,242,785	1,263,718	1,298,207	1,333,861	112,538	90,014	97,347

© European Union. Source: Eurostat, 2017, Economy and finance, table *GOV_10A_EXP*—General government expenditure by function (COFOG).

Government expenditure by function: Hungary, Ireland and Italy (million euros)

	Hungary			Ireland			Italy		
	2013	2014	2015	2013	2014	2015	2013	2014	2015
General public services	10,287	10,231	9,756	11,510	11,306	10,433	145,747	144,536	137,769
Defence	687	622	602	777	784	897	18,998	19,549	19,711
Public order and safety	2,059	1,996	2,260	2,626	2,685	2,778	31,247	30,761	30,728
Economic affairs	6,972	7,655	9,472	5,151	6,036	8,657	62,448	66,803	66,695
Environment protection	928	1,230	1,347	1,100	1,056	1,018	15,494	15,326	15,876
Housing and community amenities	801	963	1,186	1,266	1,612	1,478	11,260	10,247	10,056
Health	5,110	5,096	5,827	14,220	14,463	14,569	115,140	116,031	117,012
Recreation, culture and religion	1,830	2,103	2,357	1,470	1,472	1,481	12,072	11,821	12,170
Education	4,668	5,336	5,659	8,994	9,330	9,374	65,696	65,534	65,193
Social protection	16,728	16,213	16,405	24,601	24,256	24,633	337,585	344,557	352,570
Total	50,069	51,444	54,870	71,715	73,000	75,320	815,687	825,165	827,780

© European Union. Source: Eurostat, 2017, Economy and finance, table *GOV_10A_EXP*—General government expenditure by function (COFOG).

Government expenditure by function: Latvia, Lithuania and Luxembourg (million euros)

	Latvia			Lithuania			Luxembourg		
	2013	2014	2015	2013	2014	2015	2013	2014	2015
General public services	1,099	1,166	1,267	1,848	1,715	1,631	2,253	2,222	2,256
Defence	203	210	245	342	385	500	162	151	143
Public order and safety	439	476	490	578	613	593	479	489	512
Economic affairs	1,132	1,186	1,034	1,217	1,173	1,356	2,195	2,387	2,563
Environment protection	152	161	169	164	206	201	514	531	557
Housing and community amenities	277	261	238	88	123	119	244	280	265
Health	836	898	926	1,971	2,014	2,164	2,342	2,370	2,341
Recreation, culture and religion	359	399	393	287	328	348	599	603	608
Education	1,310	1,393	1,466	1,964	1,963	2,022	2,491	2,606	2,668
Social protection	2,636	2,704	2,794	3,971	4,184	4,155	8,855	9,215	9,659
Total	8,443	8,854	9,023	12,429	12,703	13,090	20,136	20,852	21,573

© European Union. Source: Eurostat, 2017, Economy and finance, table *GOV_10A_EXP*—General government expenditure by function (COFOG).

Government expenditure by function: Malta, Netherlands and Poland (million euros)

	Malta			Netherlands			Poland		
	2013	2014	2015	2013	2014	2015	2013	2014	2015
General public services	537	584	625	33,472	34,764	33,961	22,530	20,676	21,102
Defence	49	63	78	7,541	7,325	7,719	6,542	6,048	6,736
Public order and safety	107	111	113	12,880	12,353	12,264	8,814	9,188	9,509
Economic affairs	386	431	473	25,062	27,639	26,873	16,669	19,795	19,781
Environment protection	104	126	187	10,076	9,770	9,675	2,462	2,556	2,619
Housing and community amenities	26	28	34	3,437	3,051	2,174	2,918	2,945	3,035
Health	435	484	540	53,561	54,044	54,078	18,298	19,066	20,001
Recreation, culture and religion	68	88	109	10,024	9,644	9,502	4,480	4,996	4,847
Education	440	470	508	35,268	35,727	36,786	20,803	21,606	22,394
Social protection	1,054	1,110	1,148	110,715	111,887	112,323	63,975	66,187	68,344
Total	3,206	3,496	3,815	302,036	306,204	305,355	167,490	173,063	178,366

© European Union. Source: Eurostat, 2017, Economy and finance, table *GOV_10A_EXP*—General government expenditure by function (COFOG).

Government expenditure by function: Portugal, Romania and Slovakia (million euros)

	Portugal			Romania			Slovakia		
	2013	2014	2015	2013	2014	2015	2013	2014	2015
General public services	15,167	14,896	14,580	7,091	7,041	7,729	3,990	4,140	5,095
Defence	1,873	1,786	1,902	1,132	1,250	1,538	670	695	834
Public order and safety	3,909	3,727	3,714	3,167	3,163	3,630	1,618	1,706	1,866
Economic affairs	6,475	12,567	9,076	8,963	8,062	8,507	3,472	3,699	4,987
Environment protection	788	675	692	1,159	1,193	1,609	595	641	814
Housing and community amenities	1,070	931	890	1,680	1,755	2,244	446	465	668
Health	10,883	10,692	11,067	5,788	6,013	6,731	5,079	5,346	5,635
Recreation, culture and religion	1,538	1,291	1,348	1,448	1,641	1,932	667	705	810
Education	10,638	10,558	10,739	4,032	4,499	4,911	2,934	3,128	3,329
Social protection	32,690	32,475	32,818	16,565	17,142	18,351	11,267	11,387	11,814
Total	85,032	89,598	86,825	51,024	51,759	57,180	30,737	31,911	35,850

© European Union. Source: Eurostat, 2017, Economy and finance, table *GOV_10A_EXP*—General government expenditure by function (COFOG).

Government expenditure by function: Slovenia, Spain and Sweden (million euros)

	Slovenia			Spain			Sweden		
	2013	2014	2015	2013	2014	2015*	2013	2014	2015
General public services	2,394	2,737	2,637	74,082	72,683	69,935	34,035	32,560	31,596
Defence	347	320	327	9,862	8,969	10,425	6,378	5,574	5,072
Public order and safety	655	611	603	21,048	20,832	21,818	5,986	5,850	5,832
Economic affairs	5,507	2,327	2,305	47,510	47,410	47,163	18,925	18,780	18,760
Environment protection	273	365	389	8,621	9,096	9,293	1,445	1,353	1,304
Housing and community amenities	269	334	232	4,681	5,174	5,197	3,230	3,352	3,330
Health	2,480	2,442	2,590	63,307	63,492	66,632	30,472	30,324	31,059
Recreation, culture and religion	646	616	624	11,810	11,958	12,113	4,911	4,903	4,889
Education	2,352	2,250	2,147	42,081	42,520	43,979	28,623	28,494	29,173
Social protection	6,747	6,686	6,706	184,448	183,476	184,147	94,387	91,832	93,432
Total	21,669	18,688	18,559	467,450	465,610	470,702	228,392	223,022	224,446

* Provisional.

© European Union. Source: Eurostat, 2017, Economy and finance, table *GOV_10A_EXP*—General government expenditure by function (COFOG).

Government expenditure by function: United Kingdom (million euros)

	United Kingdom		
	2013	2014	2015
General public services	110,108	114,801	117,023
Defence	46,309	48,825	54,914
Public order and safety	44,435	46,131	51,550
Economic affairs	63,937	68,647	78,820
Environment protection	15,916	18,357	20,286
Housing and community amenities	9,603	10,249	12,464
Health	152,932	170,811	196,619
Recreation, culture and religion	14,984	15,025	16,771
Education	110,102	121,154	131,980
Social protection	346,957	373,530	423,863
Total	915,282	987,530	1,104,290

© European Union. Source: Eurostat, 2017, Economy and finance, table *GOV_10A_EXP*—General government expenditure by function (COFOG).

Gross debt of general government (consolidated, million euros at 31 December)

	2014	2015	2016		2014	2015	2016
Austria	278,968	290,466	295,719	Latvia	9,660	8,899	10,038
Belgium	427,515	434,800	446,824	Lithuania	14,825	15,940	15,536
Bulgaria	11,532	11,772	13,969	Luxembourg	11,208	11,314	10,853
Croatia	37,109	37,913	38,239	Malta	5,421	5,622	5,767
Cyprus	18,818	18,961	19,298	Netherlands	450,487	441,011	434,090
Czech Republic	65,589	67,952	64,946	Poland	202,182	215,666	228,166
Denmark	116,799	107,447	104,673	Portugal	226,031	231,540	241,061
Estonia	2,108	2,036	1,984	Romania	58,703	59,708	63,008
Finland	123,696	133,381	136,054	Slovakia	40,725	41,295	42,053
France	2,038,011	2,098,185	2,147,418	Slovenia	30,199	32,071	31,677
Germany	2,189,564	2,158,814	2,140,368	Spain	1,041,624	1,073,894	1,106,952
Greece	319,728	311,668	314,897	Sweden	189,584	199,896	190,559
Hungary	77,690	80,395	83,665	United Kingdom	2,060,356	2,269,874	2,022,241
Ireland	203,326	201,384	200,569				
Italy	2,137,240	2,172,850	2,217,909				

© European Union. Source: Eurostat, 2017, Economy and finance, table *GOV_10DD_EDPT1*—Government deficit/surplus, debt and associated data.

General government debt as percentage of annual GDP (consolidated gross debt at 31 December)

	2014	2015	2016		2014	2015	2016
Austria	84.4	85.5	84.6	Latvia	40.9	36.5	40.1
Belgium	106.7	106.0	105.9	Lithuania	40.5	42.7	40.2
Bulgaria	27.0	26.0	29.5	Luxembourg	22.4	21.6	20.0
Croatia	86.6	86.7	84.2	Malta	64.3	60.6	58.3
Cyprus	107.1	107.5	107.8	Netherlands	67.9	65.2	62.3
Czech Republic	42.2	40.3	37.2	Poland	50.2	51.1	54.4
Denmark	44.0	39.6	37.8	Portugal	130.6	129.0	130.4
Estonia	10.7	10.1	9.5	Romania	39.4	38.0	37.6
Finland	60.2	63.7	63.6	Slovakia	53.6	52.5	51.9
France	94.9	95.6	96.0	Slovenia	80.9	83.1	79.7
Germany	74.9	71.2	68.3	Spain	100.4	99.8	99.4
Greece	179.7	177.4	179.0	Sweden	45.2	43.9	41.6
Hungary	75.7	74.7	74.1	United Kingdom	88.1	89.0	89.3
Ireland	105.3	78.7	75.4				
Italy	131.8	132.1	132.6	**Total (EU-28)**	86.7	84.9	83.5

© European Union. Source: Eurostat, 2017, Economy and finance, table *GOV_10DD_EDPT1*—Government deficit/surplus, debt and associated data.

OFFICIAL RESERVES

Total reserves (million euros at 31 December, including gold)

	2010	2011	2012		2010	2011	2012
Austria	16,688	19,446	20,626	Latvia	5,736	4,966	5,726
Belgium	20,094	22,748	23,326	Lithuania	4,988	6,348	6,438
Bulgaria	12,977	13,349	15,553	Luxembourg	637	784	751
Croatia	n.a.	n.a.	n.a.	Malta	402	386	522
Cyprus	858	932	904	Netherlands	34,649	39,623	41,553
Czech Republic	31,794	31,155	34,005	Poland	69,732	75,022	82,865
Denmark	57,634	65,735	68,040	Portugal	15,717	16,490	17,174
Estonia	29,933	n.a.	n.a.	Romania	36,143	37,221	35,287
Finland	7,155	7,991	8,397	Slovakia	1,621	1,869	1,901
France	124,472	133,091	139,875	Slovenia	803	767	722
Germany	162,100	184,603	188,630	Spain	23,905	36,402	38,347
Greece	4,777	5,332	5,500	Sweden	36,199	38,878	39,650
Hungary	33,771	37,360	33,764	United Kingdom	57,688	67,950	75,597
Ireland	1,587	1,317	1,295				
Italy	118,939	133,937	137,701	**Total (EU-28)**	n.a.	n.a.	n.a.

© European Union. Source: Eurostat, 2016, Economy and finance, table *MNY_FOR_A*—Foreign official reserves—Annual data.

Finance   STATISTICAL SURVEY

Reserves of foreign exchange (million euros at 31 December)

	2010	2011	2012		2010	2011	2012
Austria	4,621	5,465	6,042	Latvia	5,331	4,553	5,293
Belgium	5,897	6,177	6,405	Lithuania	4,629	5,956	6,043
Bulgaria	10,864	11,023	13,183	Luxembourg	202	141	114
Croatia	n.a.	n.a.	n.a.	Malta	255	224	360
Cyprus	207	126	108	Netherlands	6,662	7,079	8,188
Czech Republic	28,431	27,244	28,364	Poland	60,722	66,541	73,125
Denmark	48,499	58,353	58,055	Portugal	1,506	263	424
Estonia	22,462	n.a.	n.a.	Romania	31,807	32,710	30,981
Finland	3,682	4,102	4,318	Slovakia	39	55	13
France	27,100	20,208	23,003	Slovenia	407	254	205
Germany	27,957	29,433	28,774	Spain	9,958	19,972	21,384
Greece	81	23	37	Sweden	28,422	30,034	30,571
Hungary	32,389	34,730	31,663	United Kingdom	32,819	38,344	45,360
Ireland	375	21	3				
Italy	26,701	26,399	26,388	**Total (EU-28)**	n.a.	n.a.	n.a.

© European Union. Source: Eurostat, 2016, Economy and finance, table *MNY_FOR_A*—Foreign official reserves—Annual data.

CONSUMER PRICES

Harmonized indices of consumer prices (HICP): All items (annual averages; base: 2015 = 100)

	2014	2015	2016		2014	2015	2016
Austria	99.2	100.0	101.0	Latvia	99.8	100.0	100.1
Belgium	99.4	100.0	101.8	Lithuania	100.7	100.0	100.7
Bulgaria	101.1	100.0	98.7	Luxembourg	99.9	100.0	100.0
Croatia	100.3	100.0	99.4	Malta	98.8	100.0	100.9
Cyprus	101.6	100.0	98.8	Netherlands	99.8	100.0	100.1
Czech Republic	99.8	100.0	100.7	Poland	100.7	100.0	99.8
Denmark	99.8	100.0	100.0	Portugal	99.5	100.0	100.6
Estonia	99.9	100.0	100.8	Romania	100.4	100.0	98.9
Finland	100.2	100.0	100.4	Slovakia	100.4	100.0	99.5
France	99.9	100.0	100.3	Slovenia	100.8	100.0	99.9
Germany	99.9	100.0	100.4	Spain	100.6	100.0	99.7
Greece	101.1	100.0	100.0	Sweden	99.3	100.0	101.1
Hungary	99.9	100.0	100.5	United Kingdom	100.0	100.0	100.7
Ireland	100.0	100.0	99.8				
Italy	99.9	100.0	99.9	**Total (EU-28)**	100.0	100.0	100.3

© European Union. Source: Eurostat, 2017, Economy and finance, table *PRC_HICP_AIND*—HICP (2015 = 100)—Annual data (average index and rate of change).

Inflation: All items (percentage) (annual average rate of change in HICP)

	2014	2015	2016		2014	2015	2016
Austria	1.5	0.8	1.0	Latvia	0.7	0.2	0.1
Belgium	0.5	0.6	1.8	Lithuania	0.2	−0.7	0.7
Bulgaria	−1.6	−1.1	−1.3	Luxembourg	0.7	0.1	0.0
Croatia	0.2	−0.3	−0.6	Malta	0.8	1.2	0.9
Cyprus	−0.3	−1.5	−1.2	Netherlands	0.3	0.2	0.1
Czech Republic	0.4	0.3	0.6	Poland	0.1	−0.7	−0.2
Denmark	0.4	0.2	0.0	Portugal	−0.2	0.5	0.6
Estonia	0.5	0.1	0.8	Romania	1.4	−0.4	−1.1
Finland	1.2	−0.2	0.4	Slovakia	−0.1	−0.3	−0.5
France	0.6	0.1	0.3	Slovenia	0.4	−0.8	−0.2
Germany	0.8	0.1	0.4	Spain	−0.2	−0.6	−0.3
Greece	−1.4	−1.1	0.0	Sweden	0.2	0.7	1.1
Hungary	0.0	0.1	0.4	United Kingdom	1.5	0.0	0.7
Ireland	0.3	0.0	−0.2				
Italy	0.2	0.1	−0.1	**Total (EU-28)**	0.5	0.0	0.3

© European Union. Source: Eurostat, 2017, Economy and finance, table *PRC_HICP_AIND*—HICP (2015 = 100)—Annual data (average index and rate of change).

HICP by category: European Union (EU-28) (annual averages; base: 2015 = 100)

	2014	2015	2016
Food and non-alcoholic beverages	100.0	100.0	100.2
Alcoholic beverages, tobacco and narcotics	97.9	100.0	101.7
Clothing and footwear	100.0	100.0	100.2
Housing, water, electricity, gas and other fuels	100.4	100.0	99.3
Furnishings, household equipment and routine maintenance of the house	99.8	100.0	100.2
Health	99.1	100.0	100.8
Transport	102.7	100.0	98.8
Communications	100.4	100.0	100.1
Recreation and culture	99.8	100.0	100.4
Education	97.2	100.0	102.2
Restaurants and hotels	98.3	100.0	101.8
Miscellaneous goods and services	99.1	100.0	101.3
All items	100.0	100.0	100.3

© European Union. Source: Eurostat, 2017, Economy and finance, table *PRC_HICP_AIND*—HICP (2015 = 100)—Annual data (average index and rate of change).

HICP by category: Austria, Belgium and Bulgaria (annual averages; base: 2015 = 100)

	Austria			Belgium			Bulgaria		
	2014	2015	2016	2014	2015	2016	2014	2015	2016
Food and non-alcoholic beverages	99.2	100.0	100.7	98.8	100.0	102.0	99.4	100.0	100.1
Alcoholic beverages, tobacco and narcotics	96.9	100.0	101.5	96.4	100.0	106.8	99.2	100.0	101.7
Clothing and footwear	99.9	100.0	100.7	99.4	100.0	100.8	99.3	100.0	99.9
Housing, water, electricity, gas and other fuels	98.8	100.0	101.0	101.2	100.0	101.5	96.8	100.0	99.2
Furnishings, household equipment and routine maintenance of the house	98.7	100.0	101.4	99.1	100.0	101.0	100.0	100.0	98.9
Health	98.3	100.0	102.4	98.5	100.0	100.6	101.2	100.0	100.0
Transport	103.6	100.0	98.0	102.7	100.0	100.1	108.8	100.0	93.9
Communications	99.4	100.0	97.9	100.1	100.0	104.2	103.2	100.0	96.1
Recreation and culture	98.3	100.0	101.3	99.5	100.0	101.3	99.3	100.0	98.9
Education	97.6	100.0	101.3	92.4	100.0	120.2	97.4	100.0	102.3
Restaurants and hotels	97.2	100.0	103.5	97.3	100.0	103.1	98.7	100.0	101.1
Miscellaneous goods and services	98.2	100.0	101.5	98.0	100.0	101.7	99.9	100.0	98.9
All items	99.2	100.0	101.0	99.4	100.0	101.8	101.1	100.0	98.7

© European Union. Source: Eurostat, 2017, Economy and finance, table *PRC_HICP_AIND*—HICP (2015 = 100)—Annual data (average index and rate of change).

HICP by category: Croatia, Cyprus and Czech Republic (annual averages; base: 2015 = 100)

	Croatia			Cyprus			Czech Republic		
	2014	2015	2016	2014	2015	2016	2014	2015	2016
Food and non-alcoholic beverages	99.7	100.0	99.6	100.0	100.0	100.0	100.9	100.0	99.2
Alcoholic beverages, tobacco and narcotics	98.2	100.0	100.7	98.5	100.0	100.8	95.6	100.0	104.4
Clothing and footwear	100.1	100.0	100.2	101.0	100.0	100.6	96.7	100.0	101.9
Housing, water, electricity, gas and other fuels	101.6	100.0	97.2	109.7	100.0	93.4	98.9	100.0	100.2
Furnishings, household equipment and routine maintenance of the house	100.3	100.0	100.1	100.5	100.0	99.3	99.8	100.0	99.9
Health	96.1	100.0	104.7	99.8	100.0	101.1	108.2	100.0	102.6
Transport	106.4	100.0	96.4	104.9	100.0	92.5	104.3	100.0	98.2
Communications	99.1	100.0	97.7	99.8	100.0	99.3	101.5	100.0	99.5
Recreation and culture	98.8	100.0	98.3	101.8	100.0	99.4	98.5	100.0	101.4
Education	100.5	100.0	99.9	101.0	100.0	100.4	98.9	100.0	101.4
Restaurants and hotels	98.1	100.0	100.6	100.6	100.0	100.4	98.9	100.0	101.5
Miscellaneous goods and services	99.9	100.0	100.5	100.6	100.0	99.9	98.4	100.0	101.1
All items	100.3	100.0	99.4	101.6	100.0	98.8	99.8	100.0	100.7

© European Union. Source: Eurostat, 2017, Economy and finance, table *PRC_HICP_AIND*—HICP (2015 = 100)—Annual data (average index and rate of change).

HICP by category: Denmark, Estonia and Finland (annual averages; base: 2015 = 100)

	Denmark			Estonia			Finland		
	2014	2015	2016	2014	2015	2016	2014	2015	2016
Food and non-alcoholic beverages	99.0	100.0	100.1	100.3	100.0	100.2	101.9	100.0	98.9
Alcoholic beverages, tobacco and narcotics	99.7	100.0	100.3	95.1	100.0	106.5	98.9	100.0	101.0
Clothing and footwear	99.6	100.0	97.5	97.3	100.0	103.6	99.5	100.0	99.4
Housing, water, electricity, gas and other fuels	101.3	100.0	100.1	101.4	100.0	98.5	97.8	100.0	101.8
Furnishings, household equipment and routine maintenance of the house	99.2	100.0	99.8	98.7	100.0	100.4	100.4	100.0	99.7
Health	99.4	100.0	99.7	96.9	100.0	101.9	96.9	100.0	106.6
Transport	100.8	100.0	98.5	106.6	100.0	97.2	103.0	100.0	98.4
Communications	104.4	100.0	93.6	98.9	100.0	98.8	104.4	100.0	100.9
Recreation and culture	98.9	100.0	100.8	97.8	100.0	101.2	101.2	100.0	99.1
Education	97.1	100.0	102.7	119.9	100.0	94.9	101.0	100.0	102.4
Restaurants and hotels	98.9	100.0	102.7	98.3	100.0	103.6	98.6	100.0	101.7
Miscellaneous goods and services	97.8	100.0	101.9	97.4	100.0	102.0	99.5	100.0	100.6
All items	99.8	100.0	100.0	99.9	100.0	100.8	100.2	100.0	100.4

© European Union. Source: Eurostat, 2017, Economy and finance, table *PRC_HICP_AIND*—HICP (2015 = 100)—Annual data (average index and rate of change).

HICP by category: France, Germany and Greece (annual averages; base: 2015 = 100)

	France			Germany			Greece		
	2014	2015	2016	2014	2015	2016	2014	2015	2016
Food and non-alcoholic beverages	99.6	100.0	100.6	99.3	100.0	100.9	98.4	100.0	99.9
Alcoholic beverages, tobacco and narcotics	99.4	100.0	100.5	97.4	100.0	102.3	97.7	100.0	101.3
Clothing and footwear	100.8	100.0	100.2	99.4	100.0	100.6	103.0	100.0	97.1
Housing, water, electricity, gas and other fuels	99.6	100.0	99.9	101.1	100.0	99.3	107.5	100.0	96.8
Furnishings, household equipment and routine maintenance of the house	100.1	100.0	99.9	99.3	100.0	100.6	101.7	100.0	99.1
Health	100.7	100.0	99.4	98.3	100.0	101.4	100.5	100.0	101.7
Transport	101.7	100.0	99.0	101.4	100.0	99.2	101.2	100.0	100.7
Communications	99.6	100.0	100.7	101.3	100.0	99.0	100.0	100.0	100.4
Recreation and culture	99.8	100.0	101.1	99.5	100.0	100.7	101.7	100.0	99.7
Education	98.1	100.0	102.0	100.8	100.0	101.5	102.5	100.0	98.9
Restaurants and hotels	98.6	100.0	101.7	97.5	100.0	102.0	98.6	100.0	101.9
Miscellaneous goods and services	99.0	100.0	101.2	99.0	100.0	101.8	103.0	100.0	98.7
All items	99.9	100.0	100.3	99.9	100.0	100.4	101.1	100.0	100.0

© European Union. Source: Eurostat, 2017, Economy and finance, table *PRC_HICP_AIND*—HICP (2015 = 100)—Annual data (average index and rate of change).

HICP by category: Hungary, Ireland and Italy (annual averages; base: 2015 = 100)

	Hungary			Ireland			Italy		
	2014	2015	2016	2014	2015	2016	2014	2015	2016
Food and non-alcoholic beverages	99.5	100.0	100.3	102.2	100.0	98.7	98.9	100.0	100.2
Alcoholic beverages, tobacco and narcotics	96.7	100.0	101.9	99.6	100.0	101.5	97.4	100.0	101.4
Clothing and footwear	100.0	100.0	100.5	103.9	100.0	97.5	99.9	100.0	100.5
Housing, water, electricity, gas and other fuels	101.0	100.0	100.6	94.8	100.0	101.5	100.8	100.0	98.4
Furnishings, household equipment and routine maintenance of the house	99.6	100.0	100.6	102.4	100.0	96.8	99.6	100.0	100.2
Health	95.9	100.0	102.2	100.0	100.0	100.7	98.9	100.0	101.0
Transport	106.1	100.0	97.0	105.5	100.0	96.5	102.8	100.0	98.6
Communications	99.7	100.0	100.9	98.4	100.0	98.8	101.2	100.0	99.8
Recreation and culture	99.0	100.0	101.7	100.3	100.0	98.9	99.7	100.0	100.7
Education	98.9	100.0	100.3	95.5	100.0	103.3	98.3	100.0	100.6
Restaurants and hotels	97.2	100.0	102.7	98.4	100.0	102.0	98.8	100.0	100.7
Miscellaneous goods and services	98.5	100.0	101.0	99.4	100.0	100.5	99.9	100.0	100.4
All items	99.9	100.0	100.5	100.0	100.0	99.8	99.9	100.0	99.9

© European Union. Source: Eurostat, 2017, Economy and finance, table *PRC_HICP_AIND*—HICP (2015 = 100)—Annual data (average index and rate of change).

HICP by category: Latvia, Lithuania and Luxembourg (annual averages; base: 2015 = 100)

	Latvia			Lithuania			Luxembourg		
	2014	2015	2016	2014	2015	2016	2014	2015	2016
Food and non-alcoholic beverages	101.2	100.0	101.1	100.7	100.0	101.3	99.4	100.0	101.5
Alcoholic beverages, tobacco and narcotics	98.3	100.0	103.3	98.3	100.0	103.7	96.7	100.0	102.5
Clothing and footwear	100.5	100.0	100.0	99.4	100.0	101.4	99.7	100.0	101.2
Housing, water, electricity, gas and other fuels	96.6	100.0	97.1	103.7	100.0	98.4	100.9	100.0	98.4
Furnishings, household equipment and routine maintenance of the house	99.1	100.0	99.8	98.6	100.0	101.1	98.6	100.0	100.7
Health	98.5	100.0	102.6	97.4	100.0	102.8	100.0	100.0	100.1
Transport	104.0	100.0	97.4	107.7	100.0	96.2	104.2	100.0	96.7
Communications	99.2	100.0	102.1	100.0	100.0	96.1	101.1	100.0	100.2
Recreation and culture	99.2	100.0	101.4	98.1	100.0	101.6	99.0	100.0	100.5
Education	98.5	100.0	101.7	97.8	100.0	103.6	98.8	100.0	102.2
Restaurants and hotels	98.5	100.0	100.7	95.4	100.0	105.1	96.0	100.0	101.3
Miscellaneous goods and services	98.6	100.0	100.8	97.5	100.0	103.0	99.0	100.0	101.1
All items	99.8	100.0	100.1	100.7	100.0	100.7	99.9	100.0	100.0

© European Union. Source: Eurostat, 2017, Economy and finance, table *PRC_HICP_AIND*—HICP (2015 = 100)—Annual data (average index and rate of change).

HICP by category: Malta, the Netherlands and Poland (annual averages; base: 2015 = 100)

	Malta			Netherlands			Poland		
	2014	2015	2016	2014	2015	2016	2014	2015	2016
Food and non-alcoholic beverages	97.7	100.0	101.9	99.4	100.0	101.0	101.7	100.0	101.0
Alcoholic beverages, tobacco and narcotics	95.2	100.0	104.5	97.9	100.0	101.9	98.5	100.0	101.0
Clothing and footwear	98.0	100.0	98.6	102.1	100.0	100.6	104.8	100.0	95.8
Housing, water, electricity, gas and other fuels	102.0	100.0	101.2	99.3	100.0	99.3	99.6	100.0	99.6
Furnishings, household equipment and routine maintenance of the house	98.9	100.0	102.9	100.3	100.0	101.0	100.3	100.0	99.9
Health	98.6	100.0	102.2	101.1	100.0	98.1	98.1	100.0	99.0
Transport	101.6	100.0	98.8	101.8	100.0	99.0	107.5	100.0	96.9
Communications	101.2	100.0	98.4	103.1	100.0	95.1	97.5	100.0	99.7
Recreation and culture	98.3	100.0	97.7	99.4	100.0	101.1	99.3	100.0	96.7
Education	94.1	100.0	105.6	97.7	100.0	100.9	98.8	100.0	100.6
Restaurants and hotels	98.2	100.0	102.0	97.8	100.0	102.4	98.1	100.0	101.4
Miscellaneous goods and services	97.5	100.0	101.0	98.1	100.0	99.5	98.8	100.0	104.2
All items	98.8	100.0	100.9	99.8	100.0	100.1	100.7	100.0	99.8

© European Union. Source: Eurostat, 2017, Economy and finance, table *PRC_HICP_AIND*—HICP (2015 = 100)—Annual data (average index and rate of change).

HICP by category: Portugal, Romania and Slovakia (annual averages; base: 2015 = 100)

	Portugal			Romania			Slovakia		
	2014	2015	2016	2014	2015	2016	2014	2015	2016
Food and non-alcoholic beverages	99.0	100.0	100.5	103.7	100.0	97.6	100.3	100.0	97.3
Alcoholic beverages, tobacco and narcotics	96.1	100.0	102.6	97.1	100.0	102.5	99.3	100.0	100.6
Clothing and footwear	102.1	100.0	99.6	98.0	100.0	101.3	99.1	100.0	100.3
Housing, water, electricity, gas and other fuels	99.8	100.0	100.4	97.4	100.0	97.8	101.4	100.0	98.5
Furnishings, household equipment and routine maintenance of the house	99.4	100.0	100.4	98.7	100.0	99.7	98.2	100.0	100.2
Health	99.6	100.0	99.4	99.1	100.0	99.9	99.3	100.0	101.1
Transport	100.9	100.0	99.4	103.2	100.0	97.1	106.7	100.0	97.6
Communications	96.0	100.0	103.2	99.9	100.0	98.6	100.2	100.0	100.0
Recreation and culture	101.6	100.0	100.2	98.4	100.0	100.3	99.2	100.0	101.4
Education	99.4	100.0	100.9	98.1	100.0	101.3	97.8	100.0	101.3
Restaurants and hotels	98.1	100.0	102.3	98.7	100.0	100.8	98.3	100.0	102.3
Miscellaneous goods and services	99.6	100.0	100.6	96.7	100.0	101.8	98.7	100.0	101.4
All items	99.5	100.0	100.6	100.4	100.0	98.9	100.4	100.0	99.5

© European Union. Source: Eurostat, 2017, Economy and finance, table *PRC_HICP_AIND*—HICP (2015 = 100)—Annual data (average index and rate of change).

HICP by category: Slovenia, Spain and Sweden (annual averages; base: 2015 = 100)

	Slovenia			Spain			Sweden		
	2014	2015	2016	2014	2015	2016	2014	2015	2016
Food and non-alcoholic beverages	99.5	100.0	100.6	98.8	100.0	101.4	97.7	100.0	101.1
Alcoholic beverages, tobacco and narcotics	97.9	100.0	100.2	98.7	100.0	100.5	96.2	100.0	101.3
Clothing and footwear	101.3	100.0	99.6	99.5	100.0	100.9	98.8	100.0	103.6
Housing, water, electricity, gas and other fuels	101.9	100.0	98.8	102.3	100.0	95.8	100.6	100.0	101.6
Furnishings, household equipment and routine maintenance of the house	101.5	100.0	99.9	100.2	100.0	100.2	100.0	100.0	100.8
Health	99.2	100.0	100.5	99.9	100.0	100.4	99.4	100.0	100.4
Transport	105.7	100.0	96.6	105.5	100.0	97.2	100.5	100.0	100.6
Communications	99.2	100.0	103.2	101.9	100.0	102.6	104.1	100.0	95.3
Recreation and culture	99.0	100.0	100.2	100.4	100.0	99.1	99.5	100.0	101.0
Education	99.1	100.0	100.3	99.0	100.0	100.6	96.6	100.0	99.3
Restaurants and hotels	99.5	100.0	102.2	99.0	100.0	101.1	97.5	100.0	102.3
Miscellaneous goods and services	98.7	100.0	101.3	99.0	100.0	100.9	98.8	100.0	102.0
All items	100.8	100.0	99.9	100.6	100.0	99.7	99.3	100.0	101.1

© European Union. Source: Eurostat, 2017, Economy and finance, table *PRC_HICP_AIND*—HICP (2015 = 100)—Annual data (average index and rate of change).

HICP by category: United Kingdom (annual averages; base: 2015 = 100)

	United Kingdom		
	2014	2015	2016
Food and non-alcoholic beverages	102.7	100.0	97.6
Alcoholic beverages, tobacco and narcotics	97.9	100.0	101.4
Clothing and footwear	99.7	100.0	100.2
Housing, water, electricity, gas and other fuels	99.5	100.0	100.2
Furnishings, household equipment and routine maintenance of the house	100.0	100.0	99.9
Health	98.1	100.0	102.1
Transport	102.2	100.0	100.5
Communications	98.6	100.0	102.7
Recreation and culture	100.6	100.0	100.4
Education	92.2	100.0	104.7
Restaurants and hotels	98.1	100.0	102.4
Miscellaneous goods and services	99.7	100.0	101.1
All items	100.0	100.0	100.7

© European Union. Source: Eurostat, 2017, Economy and finance, table *PRC_HICP_AIND*—HICP (2015 = 100)—Annual data (average index and rate of change).

NATIONAL ACCOUNTS

EUROPEAN UNION TOTALS (EU-28)

Expenditure on the gross domestic product (GDP) at current prices (million euros)

	2014	2015	2016
Final consumption expenditure	10,860,951	11,307,725	11,344,569
Households and non-profit institutions serving households	7,945,046	8,288,327	8,312,495
General government	2,915,905	3,019,398	3,032,075
Gross capital formation	2,775,119	2,915,858	2,969,648
Gross fixed capital formation	2,714,578	2,876,598	2,920,633
Changes in inventories; acquisitions, less disposals, of valuables	60,541	39,261	49,015
Domestic demand	n.a.	n.a.	n.a.
Exports of goods and services	6,036,076	6,462,331	6,512,670
Less Imports of goods and services	5,661,220	5,957,478	6,002,128
Gross domestic product at market prices	14,010,925	14,728,435	14,824,759

© European Union. Source: Eurostat, 2017, Economy and finance, table *NAMA_10_GDP*—GDP and main components (output, expenditure and income).

Index of expenditure on the GDP at constant 2010 prices (chain-linked volumes, index 2010 = 100)

	2014	2015	2016
Final consumption expenditure	100.8	102.7	104.9
Households and non-profit institutions serving households	100.6	102.7	105.1
General government	101.4	102.7	104.4
Gross capital formation	102.0	105.1	107.7
Gross fixed capital formation	100.6	104.2	106.9
Changes in inventories and acquisitions, less disposals of valuables	n.a.	n.a.	n.a.
Domestic demand	n.a.	n.a.	n.a.
Exports of goods and services	116.4	123.6	127.6
Imports of goods and services	111.2	118.1	123.0
Gross domestic product at market prices	103.1	105.4	107.4

© European Union. Source: Eurostat, 2017, Economy and finance, table *NAMA_10_GDP*—GDP and main components (output, expenditure and income).

Gross value added (GVA) by branch of activity (million euros at current prices)

	2013	2014	2015
Agriculture, forestry and fishing	207,585	201,686	201,109
Industry (except construction)	2,334,160	2,397,534	2,541,072
Construction	649,959	665,831	696,880
Wholesale and retail trade, transport, accommodation and food service activities	2,280,353	2,366,173	2,490,161
Information and communication	591,949	610,430	651,018
Financial and insurance activities	650,957	680,622	695,568
Real estate activities	1,371,200	1,414,237	1,478,906
Professional, scientific and technical activities; administrative and support service activities	1,274,897	1,337,480	1,430,249
Public administration, defence, education, human health and social work activities	2,351,581	2,413,964	2,510,609
Arts, entertainment and recreation; other service activities; activities of household and extraterritorial organizations and bodies	427,258	440,560	459,328
Total GVA (all NACE activities)	12,139,900	12,528,516	13,154,898

© European Union. Source: Eurostat, 2017, Economy and finance, table *NAIDA_10_A10*—Gross value added by A*10 industry—Selected international annual data.

Index of GVA by branch of activity (chain-linked volumes, index 2010 = 100)

	2013	2014	2015
Agriculture, forestry and fishing	100.4	103.2	102.2
Industry (except construction)	100.4	102.7	106.6
Construction	90.8	91.8	93.1
Wholesale and retail trade, transport, accommodation and food service activities	102.0	103.9	106.5
Information and communication	109.1	112.7	117.1
Financial and insurance activities	100.3	99.1	99.3
Real estate activities	103.9	105.2	106.4
Professional, scientific and technical activities; administrative and support service activities	105.5	109.1	113.0
Public administration, defence, education, human health and social work activities	101.3	101.9	102.7
Arts, entertainment and recreation; other service activities; activities of household and extraterritorial organizations and bodies	99.5	101.0	101.5
Total gross value added (all NACE activities)	101.6	103.3	105.5

© European Union. Source: Eurostat, 2017, Economy and finance, table *NAIDA_10_A10*—Gross value added by A*10 industry—Selected international annual data.

DISTRIBUTION BY COUNTRY

Gross domestic product (GDP) at current market prices (million euros)

	2014	2015	2016		2014	2015	2016
Austria	330,418	339,896	349,344	Latvia	23,631	24,368	25,021
Belgium	400,797	410,247	421,611	Lithuania	36,590	37,331	38,637
Bulgaria	42,762	45,287	47,364*	Luxembourg	49,971	52,340	54,195
Croatia	42,978	44,068	45,819	Malta	8,443	9,273	9,896
Cyprus	17,567	17,637	17,901*	Netherlands	663,008	683,457	702,641*
Czech Republic	156,660	168,473	176,564	Poland	410,990	430,038	424,269
Denmark	265,233	271,786	277,339	Portugal	173,079	179,504†	184,934†
Estonia	19,758	20,252	20,916	Romania	150,358	159,964*	169,578*
Finland	205,474	209,581	215,615	Slovakia	75,946	78,686	80,958
France	2,147,609	2,194,243*	2,228,857*	Slovenia	37,332	38,570	39,769
Germany	2,923,930	3,032,820	3,134,070	Spain*	1,037,025	1,075,639	1,113,851
Greece*	177,941	175,697	175,888	Sweden	432,691	447,010	462,058
Hungary	104,953	109,674	112,399	United Kingdom	2,260,805	2,580,065	2,366,912
Ireland	193,160	255,815	265,835				
Italy	1,621,827	1,645,439	1,672,438				

* Provisional. † Estimate.

© European Union. Source: Eurostat, 2017, Economy and finance, table *NAMA_10_GDP*—GDP and main components (output, expenditure and income).

Gross domestic product at market prices (million euros, chain-linked volumes, reference year 2010)

	2014	2015	2016		2014	2015	2016
Austria	307,509	310,470	315,068	Latvia	20,627	21,186	21,600
Belgium	378,061	383,641	388,218	Lithuania	33,062	33,650	34,423
Bulgaria	39,833	41,274	42,695*	Luxembourg	45,093	46,899	48,859
Croatia	43,215	44,187	45,504	Malta	7,763	8,327	8,743
Cyprus	17,364	17,656	18,156*	Netherlands	643,024	657,561	672,093*
Czech Republic	161,739	170,292	174,709	Poland	404,277	419,819	431,065
Denmark	253,457	257,528	261,857	Portugal	169,108	171,805†	174,207†
Estonia	17,223	17,472	17,746	Romania	137,564	142,982*	149,871*
Finland	186,553	186,537	190,132	Slovakia	73,530	76,347	78,855
France	2,075,016	2,097,166*	2,122,073*	Slovenia	36,212	37,050	37,974
Germany	2,743,894	2,791,109	2,843,226	Spain*	1,035,111	1,068,283	1,102,850
Greece*	184,873	184,468	184,490	Sweden	392,477	408,509	421,491
Hungary	104,582	107,874	109,982	United Kingdom	1,980,128	2,023,577	2,060,123
Ireland	181,164	228,767	240,694				
Italy	1,542,924	1,555,009	1,568,691				

* Provisional. † Estimate.

© European Union. Source: Eurostat, 2017, Economy and finance, table *NAMA_10_GDP*—GDP and main components (output, expenditure and income).

Index of GDP at market prices (chain-linked volumes, index 2010 = 100)

	2014	2015	2016		2014	2015	2016
Austria	104.4	105.4	106.9	Latvia	116.0	119.1	121.4
Belgium	103.5	105.1	106.3	Lithuania	118.0	120.1	122.8
Bulgaria	104.2	108.0	111.7*	Luxembourg	112.2	116.7	121.6
Croatia	96.0	98.2	101.1	Malta	117.6	126.2	132.5
Cyprus	90.0	91.5	94.1*	Netherlands	101.8	104.1	106.4*
Czech Republic	103.2	108.7	111.5	Poland	111.7	116.0	119.1
Denmark	104.2	105.9	107.7	Portugal	94.0	95.5†	96.8†
Estonia	117.0	118.7	120.6	Romania	108.5	112.8*	118.2*
Finland	99.7	99.7	101.6	Slovakia	108.8	113.0	116.7
France	103.8	104.9*	106.2*	Slovenia	99.9	102.2	104.7
Germany	106.4	108.2	110.2	Spain*	95.8	98.8	102.0
Greece*	81.8	81.6	81.6	Sweden	106.3	110.7	114.2
Hungary	106.4	109.7	111.9	United Kingdom	108.0	110.4	112.4
Ireland	108.4	136.9	144.0				
Italy	96.2	96.9	97.8	**Total (EU-28)**	103.1	105.4†	107.4†

* Provisional. † Estimate.

© European Union. Source: Eurostat, 2017, Economy and finance, table *NAMA_10_GDP*—GDP and main components (output, expenditure and income).

Percentage change in GDP at market prices (chain-linked volumes, compared with previous period)

	2014	2015	2016		2014	2015	2016
Austria	0.6	1.0	1.5	Latvia	2.1	2.7	2.0
Belgium	1.6	1.5	1.2	Lithuania	3.5	1.8	2.3
Bulgaria	1.3	3.6	3.4*	Luxembourg	5.6	4.0	4.2
Croatia	-0.5	2.2	3.0	Malta	8.3	7.3	5.0
Cyprus	-1.5	1.7	2.8*	Netherlands	1.4	2.3	2.2*
Czech Republic	2.7	5.3	2.6	Poland	3.3	3.8	2.7
Denmark	1.7	1.6	1.7	Portugal	0.9	1.6†	1.4†
Estonia	2.8	1.4	1.6	Romania	3.1	3.9*	4.8*
Finland	-0.6	0.0	1.9	Slovakia	2.6	3.8	3.3
France	0.9	1.1*	1.2*	Slovenia	3.1	2.3	2.5
Germany	1.6	1.7	1.9	Spain*	1.4	3.2	3.2
Greece*	0.4	-0.2	0.0	Sweden	2.6	4.1	3.2
Hungary	4.0	3.1	2.0	United Kingdom	3.1	2.2	1.8
Ireland	8.5	26.3	5.2				
Italy	0.1	0.8	0.9	**Total (EU-28)**	1.7	2.2	1.9

* Provisional. † Estimate.
© European Union. Source: Eurostat, 2017, Economy and finance, table *NAMA_10_GDP*—GDP and main components (output, expenditure and income).

GDP per inhabitant at current prices (rounded figures, euros)

	2014	2015	2016		2014	2015	2016
Austria	38,700	39,400	40,000	Latvia	11,800	12,300	12,800
Belgium	35,900	36,600	37,400	Lithuania	12,500	12,900	13,500
Bulgaria*	5,900	6,300	6,600	Luxembourg	89,500	91,900	92,900
Croatia	10,100	10,500	11,000	Malta	19,800	21,500	22,700
Cyprus	20,600	20,800*	21,000*	Netherlands	39,300	40,400*	41,300*
Czech Republic	14,900	16,000	16,700	Poland†	10,700	11,200	11,000
Denmark	47,000	47,800	48,400	Portugal	16,600	17,300†	17,900†
Estonia	15,000	15,400	15,900	Romania	7,600	8,100*	8,600*
Finland	37,600	38,200	39,200	Slovakia	14,000	14,500	14,900
France	32,400	33,000*	33,300*	Slovenia	18,100	18,700	19,300
Germany	36,100	37,100	38,000	Spain*	22,300	23,200	24,000
Greece*	16,300	16,200	16,300	Sweden	44,600	45,600	46,600
Hungary	10,600	11,100	11,500	United Kingdom	35,000	39,600	36,100
Ireland	41,900	55,100	56,800				
Italy	26,700	27,100	27,600	**Total (EU-28)**	27,600	28,900	29,000

* Provisional. † Estimate(s).
© European Union. Source: Eurostat, 2017, Economy and finance, table *NAMA_10_PC*—Main GDP aggregates per capita.

Gross national income (GNI)/Balance of primary incomes (million euros at current prices)

	2013	2014	2015		2013	2014	2015
Austria	323,366	331,092	338,041	Latvia	22,768	23,577	24,290
Belgium	398,187	402,933	410,500	Lithuania	34,092	36,115	35,824
Bulgaria	41,087	42,392	44,377	Luxembourg	31,153	33,018	33,335
Croatia	42,700	42,276	43,988	Malta	7,306	7,907	8,674
Cyprus	17,279	16,920	17,575*	Netherlands	661,879	661,287	679,610
Czech Republic	148,326	146,073	155,990	Poland	381,485	395,768	413,909
Denmark	266,935	274,848	280,894	Portugal	167,975	170,117	174,353†
Estonia	18,452	19,225	19,833	Romania	141,538	148,871	156,904*
Finland	204,034	207,342	211,265	Slovakia	73,477	74,608	77,403
France	2,144,749	2,168,271*	2,216,484*	Slovenia	35,721	37,294	37,685
Germany	2,893,930	2,988,943	3,098,834	Spain	1,020,307	1,033,690	1,074,859
Greece*	180,437	178,332	176,300	Sweden	445,769	442,307	453,863
Hungary	98,828	100,554	104,530	United Kingdom	2,036,152	2,231,323	2,544,598
Ireland	153,100	164,490	203,888				
Italy	1,601,864	1,621,888	1,636,304				

* Provisional. † Estimate.
© European Union. Source: Eurostat, 2017, Economy and finance, table *NASA_10_NF_TR*—Non-financial transactions.

GNI per inhabitant at current market prices (rounded figures, euros)

	2011	2012	2013
Austria	35,400	36,200	36,700
Belgium	33,900	34,100	34,400
Bulgaria	5,100	5,400	5,400
Croatia	10,000	9,900	9,900
Cyprus	21,400	19,900	18,600
Czech Republic	13,800	13,500	13,300
Denmark	44,400	45,200	46,100
Estonia	11,500	12,400	13,300
Finland	35,100	35,700	35,800
France	31,400	31,600	31,900
Germany	32,600	33,300	34,300
Greece	18,200	17,600	n.a.
Hungary	9,400	9,200	n.a.
Ireland	28,800	29,200	n.a.
Italy	25,900	25,600	25,400
Latvia	9,900*	10,900*	11,600*
Lithuania	9,800	10,700	11,300
Luxembourg	55,300	55,000	n.a.
Malta	15,200	15,400	16,100
Netherlands	36,000	36,100	35,700
Poland	9,200	9,500	n.a.
Portugal	15,500	15,200	15,500
Romania	6,400	6,400	n.a.
Slovakia	12,500	12,800	13,000
Slovenia	17,400	17,000	17,000
Spain	22,200	22,000	22,100
Sweden	41,700	43,900	45,100
United Kingdom	28,600	30,000	29,300†
Total (EU-28)	25,200	25,600	25,700‡

* Break in series. † Provisional. ‡ Estimate.
© European Union. Source: Eurostat, 2017, Economy and finance, table *NAMA_INC_C*—Income, saving and net lending/net borrowing—Current prices.

INDIVIDUAL COUNTRIES

Main aggregates at current prices: Austria, Belgium and Bulgaria (million euros)

	Austria			Belgium			Bulgaria		
	2013	2014	2015	2013	2014	2015	2013	2014	2015
Gross domestic product at market prices...	322,539	330,418	339,896	391,712	400,805	410,351	42,011	42,762	45,286
Gross national income at market prices.....	323,366	331,092	338,041	398,187	402,933	410,500	41,087	42,392	44,377

© European Union. Source: Eurostat, 2017, Economy and finance, table *NASA_10_NF_TR*—Non-financial transactions.

Expenditure on the GDP at current prices: Austria, Belgium and Bulgaria (million euros)

	Austria			Belgium			Bulgaria		
	2014	2015	2016	2014	2015	2016	2014	2015	2016*
Final consumption expenditure	242,022	246,806	254,117	304,518	308,215	315,636	33,999	35,624	36,298
Households and non-profit institutions serving households	176,696	179,090	184,061	207,243	210,154	215,974	26,788	28,319	28,796
General government	65,325	67,716	70,056	97,276	98,061	99,662	7,211	7,305	7,502
Gross capital formation	78,163	79,899	83,149	92,606	95,180	95,869	9,166	9,596	9,618
Gross fixed capital formation	75,133	76,845	80,235	91,644	94,324	96,920	9,026	9,517	9,035
Changes in inventories; acquisitions, less disposals, of valuables	3,030	3,055	2,914	961	856	-1,051	140	80	584
Domestic demand	n.a.	n.a.	n.a.	n.a.	n.a.	n.a.	n.a.	n.a.	n.a.
Exports of goods and services	175,175	180,350	182,354	333,478	340,295	356,092	27,801	29,032	30,107
Less Imports of goods and services	164,271	166,726	169,742	329,805	333,443	345,985	28,204	28,965	28,659
Gross domestic product at market prices	330,418	339,896	349,344	400,797	410,247	421,611	42,762	45,287	47,364

* Provisional.

© European Union. Source: Eurostat, 2017, Economy and finance, table *NAMA_10_GDP*—GDP and main components (output, expenditure and income).

Gross value added (GVA) by branch of activity: Austria, Belgium and Bulgaria (million euros at current prices)

	Austria			Belgium			Bulgaria		
	2014	2015	2016	2014	2015	2016	2014	2015	2016
Agriculture, forestry and fishing	4,034	3,905	3,939	2,565	2,745	2,775	1,952	1,873	1,800
Industry (except construction)	64,246	66,363	67,138	59,107	61,520	63,001	8,428	9,210	9,719
Construction	19,003	19,412	20,088	19,716	19,957	20,700	1,647	1,699	1,732
Wholesale and retail trade, transport, accommodation and food service activities	67,729	69,249	71,099	70,692	72,034	73,173	7,918	8,633	9,086
Information and communication	10,357	10,676	10,778	14,606	15,183	15,697	2,063	2,073	2,183
Financial and insurance activities	12,826	12,810	12,652	22,883	23,094	23,196	2,545	2,738	2,956
Real estate activities	28,890	30,557	32,295	30,442	31,226	31,851	3,829	3,853	4,089
Professional, scientific and technical activities; administrative and support service activities	27,799	28,437	29,514	48,937	50,698	52,754	2,117	2,462	2,571
Public administration, defence, education, human health and social work activities	51,181	52,684	54,422	81,323	82,403	84,503	5,665	5,643	5,749
Arts, entertainment and recreation; other service activities; activities of household and extraterritorial organizations and bodies	8,379	8,560	8,849	8,201	8,432	8,488	961	955	987
Total GVA (all NACE activities)	294,443	302,653	310,774	358,473	367,292	376,138	37,126	39,138	40,872

© European Union. Source: Eurostat, 2017, Economy and finance, table *NAIDA_10_A10*—Gross value added by A*10 industry—Selected international annual data.

STATISTICAL SURVEY

National Accounts

Main aggregates at current prices: Croatia, Cyprus and the Czech Republic (million euros)

	Croatia			Cyprus			Czech Republic		
	2010	2011	2012	2013	2014	2015*	2013	2014	2015
Gross domestic product at market prices....	45,004	44,709	43,934	18,118	17,567	17,637	157,742	156,660	166,964
Gross national income at market prices......	43,693	43,464	42,799	17,279	16,920	17,575	148,326	146,073	155,990

* Provisional.

© European Union. Source: Eurostat, 2017, Economy and finance, table *NASA_10_NF_TR*—Non-financial transactions.

Expenditure on the GDP at current prices: Croatia, Cyprus and the Czech Republic (million euros)

	Croatia			Cyprus			Czech Republic		
	2014	2015	2016	2014	2015	2016*	2014	2015	2016
Final consumption expenditure	34,143	34,283	35,339	15,042	15,027	15,190	106,145	111,269	116,845
Households and non-profit institutions serving households	25,514	25,742	26,536	12,235	12,255	12,468	75,307	78,895	82,920
General government	8,629	8,541	8,803	2,807	2,772	2,722	30,838	32,374	33,925
Gross capital formation	8,003	8,729	9,086	2,165	2,551	2,870	40,544	47,098	46,507
Gross fixed capital formation	8,357	8,721	9,202	2,052	2,341	3,087	39,369	44,588	44,076
Changes in inventories; acquisitions, less disposals, of valuables.	-354	8	-115	112	210	-216	1,175	2,510	2,431
Domestic demand	n.a.	n.a.	n.a.	n.a.	n.a.	n.a.	n.a.	n.a.	n.a.
Exports of goods and services	19,661	21,472	22,754	10,926	10,797	11,102	130,718	138,182	142,086
Less Imports of goods and services	18,829	20,416	21,361	10,565	10,738	11,177	120,747	128,076	128,873
Gross domestic product at market prices	42,978	44,068	45,819	17,567	17,637	17,901	156,660	168,473	176,564

* Provisional.

© European Union. Source: Eurostat, 2017, Economy and finance, table *NAMA_10_GDP*—GDP and main components (output, expenditure and income).

Gross value added (GVA) by branch of activity: Croatia, Cyprus and the Czech Republic (million euros at current prices)

	Croatia			Cyprus			Czech Republic		
	2014	2015	2016	2014	2015	2016*	2014	2015	2016
Agriculture, forestry and fishing	1,504	1,557	1,566	321	353	360	3,876	3,753	3,895
Industry (except construction)	7,763	7,890	8,143	1,090	1,083	1,118	45,855	48,753	51,038
Construction	1,905	1,933	2,009	562	556	607	7,795	8,514	8,668
Wholesale and retail trade, transport, accommodation and food service activities	7,731	8,184	8,637	3,851	3,908	4,080	25,217	28,015	29,587
Information and communication	1,593	1,620	1,680	731	774	765	7,106	7,778	8,160
Financial and insurance activities...................................	2,391	2,372	2,419	1,888	1,896	1,689	6,105	6,492	6,711
Real estate activities..	3,796	3,817	3,870	1,613	1,590	1,607	12,120	12,767	13,346
Professional, scientific and technical activities; administrative and support service activities................	2,952	2,971	3,081	1,481	1,525	1,591	9,201	9,959	10,559
Public administration, defence, education, human health and social work activities	5,526	5,539	5,721	3,188	3,156	3,187	21,206	22,224	23,352
Arts, entertainment and recreation; other service activities; activities of household and extraterritorial organizations and bodies..	1,150	1,162	1,209	686	681	684	3,101	3,347	3,462
Total GVA (all NACE activities)	36,312	37,045	38,334	15,409	15,521	15,688	141,582	151,603	158,778

* Provisional.

© European Union. Source: Eurostat, 2017, Economy and finance, table *NAIDA_10_A10*— Gross value added by A*10 industry—Selected international annual data.

National Accounts STATISTICAL SURVEY

Main aggregates at current prices: Denmark, Estonia and Finland (million euros)

	Denmark			Estonia			Finland		
	2014	2015	2016	2013	2014	2015	2013	2014	2015
Gross domestic product at market prices...	265,232	271,786	276,805	18,890	19,758	20,252	203,338	205,474	209,511
Gross national income at market prices.....	274,848	280,894	284,280	18,452	19,225	19,833	204,034	207,342	211,265

© European Union. Source: Eurostat, 2017, Economy and finance, table *NASA_10_NF_TR*—Non-financial transactions.

Expenditure on the GDP at current prices: Denmark, Estonia and Finland (million euros)

	Denmark			Estonia			Finland		
	2014	2015	2016	2014	2015	2016	2014	2015	2016
Final consumption expenditure	193,750	197,979	202,313	13,942	14,710	15,464	164,346	166,977	170,771
Households and non-profit institutions serving households	125,082	128,155	131,732	10,124	10,604	11,150	113,635	115,856	119,056
General government	68,668	69,824	70,581	3,818	4,106	4,315	50,711	51,121	51,715
Gross capital formation	53,025	53,691	56,382	5,356	5,011	4,992	43,039	43,853	47,123
Gross fixed capital formation	50,811	52,277	55,621	4,814	4,790	4,604	42,235	42,713	46,423
Changes in inventories; acquisitions, less disposals, of valuables .	2,214	1,414	761	542	222	388	804	1,140	700
Domestic demand	n.a.	n.a.	n.a.	n.a.	n.a.	n.a.	n.a.	n.a.	n.a.
Exports of goods and services	144,599	150,099	147,978	16,411	16,057	16,702	76,482	76,431	75,967
Less Imports of goods and services	126,142	129,983	129,333	15,715	15,217	15,881	78,393	77,481	78,616
Gross domestic product at market prices	265,233	271,786	277,339	19,758	20,252	20,916	205,474	209,581	215,615

© European Union. Source: Eurostat, 2017, Economy and finance, table *NAMA_10_GDP*—GDP and main components (output, expenditure and income).

Gross value added (GVA) by branch of activity: Denmark, Estonia and Finland (million euros at current prices)

	Denmark			Estonia			Finland		
	2014	2015	2016	2014	2015	2016	2014	2015	2016
Agriculture, forestry and fishing	3,633	2,901	2,617	615	592	526	4,934	4,591	4,961
Industry (except construction)	41,121	43,053	45,085	3,829	3,709	3,717	36,313	37,341	37,615
Construction	10,644	11,032	11,688	1,094	1,092	1,075	11,081	11,552	12,695
Wholesale and retail trade, transport, accommodation and food service activities	47,464	47,466	46,412	3,831	3,768	3,898	28,504	28,770	29,238
Information and communication	10,420	10,999	10,996	966	1,051	1,135	9,825	10,303	10,708
Financial and insurance activities	14,318	14,542	14,256	668	693	726	5,230	5,204	5,240
Real estate activities	22,846	23,418	24,259	1,680	1,764	1,773	21,663	22,814	23,885
Professional, scientific and technical activities; administrative and support service activities	19,485	21,308	22,815	1,490	1,589	1,659	14,832	15,124	15,837
Public administration, defence, education, human health and social work activities	52,277	53,113	53,570	2,592	2,785	2,939	39,054	39,449	39,477
Arts, entertainment and recreation; other service activities; activities of household and extraterritorial organizations and bodies	7,871	8,075	8,507	429	453	489	5,551	5,637	5,811
Total GVA (all NACE activities)	230,079	235,908	240,205	17,194	17,497	17,937	176,987	180,785	185,467

© European Union. Source: Eurostat, 2017, Economy and finance, table *NAIDA_10_A10*—Gross value added by A*10 industry—Selected international annual data.

STATISTICAL SURVEY — National Accounts

Main aggregates at current prices: France, Germany and Greece (million euros)

	France			Germany			Greece*		
	2013	2014*	2015*	2013	2014	2015	2013	2014	2015
Gross domestic product at market prices..	2,115,257	2,139,964	2,181,063	2,826,240	2,923,930	3,032,820	180,655	177,941	175,698
Gross national income at market prices....	2,144,749	2,168,271	2,216,484	2,893,930	2,988,943	3,098,834	180,437	178,332	176,300

* Provisional.

© European Union. Source: Eurostat, 2017, Economy and finance, table *NASA_10_NF_TR*—Non-financial transactions.

Expenditure on the GDP at current prices: France, Germany and Greece (million euros)

	France			Germany			Greece*		
	2014	2015*	2016*	2014	2015	2016	2014	2015	2016
Final consumption expenditure	1,701,788	1,727,373	1,759,625	2,155,414	2,219,674	2,296,809	161,228	158,175	158,573
Households and non-profit institutions serving households	1,186,111	1,206,492	1,232,883	1,594,361	1,635,974	1,681,479	125,087	122,833	124,032
General government............................	515,677	520,881	526,742	561,053	583,700	615,330	36,141	35,341	34,542
Gross capital formation	488,207	499,936	512,647	577,789	583,607	598,506	21,046	17,270	18,494
Gross fixed capital formation................	469,072	473,219	489,359	585,147	603,820	626,064	20,625	20,285	20,118
Changes in inventories; acquisitions, less disposals, of valuables................	19,135	26,717	23,288	-7,358	-20,213	-27,558	421	-3,015	-1,624
Domestic demand......................................	n.a.	n.a.	n.a.	n.a.	n.a.	n.a.	n.a.	n.a.	n.a.
Exports of goods and services	620,855	651,088	652,178	1,334,833	1,418,789	1,442,213	57,838	56,074	53,037
Less Imports of goods and services...........	663,241	684,154	695,593	1,144,106	1,189,250	1,203,458	62,171	55,821	54,216
Gross domestic product at market prices....	2,147,609	2,194,243	2,228,857	2,923,930	3,032,820	3,134,070	177,941	175,697	175,888

* Provisional.

© European Union. Source: Eurostat, 2017, Economy and finance, table *NAMA_10_GDP*—GDP and main components (output, expenditure and income).

Gross value added (GVA) by branch of activity: France, Germany and Greece (million euros at current prices)

	France			Germany			Greece*		
	2014	2015*	2016*	2014	2015	2016	2014	2015	2016
Agriculture, forestry and fishing	33,458	34,647	32,689	20,436	17,351	18,011	5,843	6,386	6,173
Industry (except construction)	267,166	278,030	279,973	685,143	707,459	722,313	21,113	20,639	20,538
Construction	110,903	107,501	109,593	118,196	124,755	134,648	3,935	3,697	3,655
Wholesale and retail trade, transport, accommodation and food service activities	338,289	344,511	350,580	413,879	430,167	443,074	37,612	37,780	37,580
Information and communication	95,029	98,329	103,648	125,372	131,632	136,936	5,238	5,290	5,262
Financial and insurance activities............	86,923	87,966	82,071	109,951	110,930	110,826	7,656	7,473	7,218
Real estate activities................................	246,856	253,038	259,147	285,979	297,278	306,953	28,787	27,825	27,143
Professional, scientific and technical activities; administrative and support service activities	246,432	253,404	262,521	289,623	303,258	316,420	7,558	7,734	7,369
Public administration, defence, education, human health and social work activities...	442,099	446,711	452,113	476,643	497,154	518,957	33,045	32,145	32,290
Arts, entertainment and recreation; other service activities; activities of household and extraterritorial organizations and bodies......................	57,920	59,207	60,009	106,046	109,678	114,052	6,400	6,130	6,197
Total GVA (all NACE activities)	1,925,074	1,963,342	1,992,345	2,631,268	2,729,662	2,822,190	157,187	155,098	153,426

* Provisional.

© European Union. Source: Eurostat, 2017, Economy and finance, table *NAIDA_10_A10*—Gross value added by A*10 industry—Selected international annual data.

National Accounts STATISTICAL SURVEY

Main aggregates at current prices: Hungary, Ireland and Italy (million euros)

	Hungary			Ireland			Italy		
	2013	2014	2015	2013	2014	2015	2014	2015	2016
Gross domestic product at market prices...	101,483	104,953	109,674	180,209	193,159	255,815	1,621,827	1,645,439	1,672,438
Gross national income at market prices.....	98,828	100,554	104,530	153,100	164,490	203,888	1,621,888	1,636,304	1,675,309

© European Union. Source: Eurostat, 2017, Economy and finance, table *NASA_10_NF_TR*—Non-financial transactions.

Expenditure on the GDP at current prices: Hungary, Ireland and Italy (million euros)

	Hungary			Ireland			Italy		
	2014	2015	2016	2014	2015	2016	2014	2015	2016
Final consumption expenditure	73,681	76,086	79,360	114,240	119,362	124,615	1,299,306	1,312,653	1,330,112
Households and non-profit institutions serving households	52,678	54,113	56,631	82,566	87,260	90,811	985,995	1,001,014	1,014,117
General government...............................	21,003	21,973	22,729	31,674	32,101	33,805	313,311	311,639	315,995
Gross capital formation	23,987	23,816	21,448	42,399	55,397	79,723	276,246	284,894	284,444
Gross fixed capital formation.................	22,883	23,764	20,004	39,574	54,235	77,926	271,516	276,537	284,338
Changes in inventories; acquisitions, less disposals, of valuables.................	1,104	51	1,443	2,825	1,162	1,796	4,730	8,357	106
Domestic demand......................................	n.a.	n.a.	n.a.	n.a.	n.a.	n.a.	n.a.	n.a.	n.a.
Exports of goods and services	93,047	99,504	103,977	219,790	317,197	318,817	475,301	493,934	501,473
Less Imports of goods and services...........	85,761	89,731	92,386	185,182	235,985	257,159	429,026	446,042	443,590
Gross domestic product at market prices....	104,953	109,674	112,399	193,160	255,815	265,835	1,621,827	1,645,439	1,672,438

© European Union. Source: Eurostat, 2017, Economy and finance, table *NAMA_10_GDP*—GDP and main components (output, expenditure and income).

Gross value added (GVA) by branch of activity: Hungary, Ireland and Italy (million euros at current prices)

	Hungary			Ireland			Italy		
	2014	2015	2016	2014	2015	2016	2014	2015	2016
Agriculture, forestry and fishing	4,154	3,801	4,310	2,585	2,398	2,378	31,477	33,358	31,567
Industry (except construction)	23,465	25,525	25,594	41,948	92,619	95,406	270,481	280,115	289,728
Construction	3,778	3,816	3,217	5,434	6,025	6,444	70,387	70,655	71,479
Wholesale and retail trade, transport, accommodation and food service activities	16,326	17,010	17,909	29,024	30,317	31,570	295,601	303,713	313,228
Information and communication	4,603	4,550	4,692	18,719	19,166	19,855	53,760	52,579	52,464
Financial and insurance activities.......................	3,455	3,431	3,359	15,560	14,966	14,872	84,880	84,297	78,900
Real estate activities..	6,943	7,088	7,357	14,392	15,873	16,898	203,588	204,880	207,924
Professional, scientific and technical activities; administrative and support service activities	7,920	8,173	8,768	18,713	22,752	24,047	138,401	139,508	142,474
Public administration, defence, education, human health and social work activities...........	15,167	15,951	16,905	27,735	29,154	30,136	250,550	251,522	254,090
Arts, entertainment and recreation; other service activities; activities of household and extraterritorial organizations and bodies ..	2,630	2,635	2,774	3,431	3,546	3,672	58,736	57,844	58,731
Total GVA (all NACE activities)	88,440	91,978	94,884	177,540	236,814	245,280	1,457,859	1,478,470	1,500,585

© European Union. Source: Eurostat, 2017, Economy and finance, table *NAIDA_10_A10*—Gross value added by A*10 industry—Selected international annual data.

STATISTICAL SURVEY — National Accounts

Main aggregates at current prices: Latvia, Lithuania and Luxembourg (million euros)

	Latvia			Lithuania			Luxembourg		
	2013	2014	2015	2013	2014	2015	2013	2014	2015
Gross domestic product at market prices....	22,816	23,608	24,348	35,002	36,590	37,331	46,353	49,273	51,216
Gross national income at market prices......	22,768	23,577	24,290	34,092	36,115	35,824	31,153	33,018	33,335

© European Union. Source: Eurostat, 2017, Economy and finance, table *NASA_10_NF_TR*—Non-financial transactions.

Expenditure on the GDP at current prices: Latvia, Lithuania and Luxembourg (million euros)

	Latvia			Lithuania			Luxembourg		
	2014	2015	2016	2014	2015	2016	2014	2015	2016
Final consumption expenditure	18,602	19,259	19,900	29,046	30,148	31,991	23,591	24,302	24,688
Households and non-profit institutions serving households	14,457	14,864	15,516	22,853	23,586	25,144	15,236	15,659	15,840
General government................................	4,146	4,395	4,384	6,193	6,563	6,847	8,355	8,643	8,848
Gross capital formation	5,477	5,385	4,985	6,844	7,425	6,319	9,399	9,877	9,780
Gross fixed capital formation..................	5,337	5,242	4,578	6,770	7,195	7,197	9,447	9,503	9,655
Changes in inventories; acquisitions, less disposals, of valuables...................	139	143	407	73	230	-878	-49	374	125
Domestic demand..	n.a.	n.a.	n.a.	n.a.	n.a.	n.a.	n.a.	n.a.	n.a.
Exports of goods and services	14,068	14,361	14,510	29,599	28,320	28,725	103,091	118,871	123,531
Less Imports of goods and services	14,515	14,636	14,373	28,899	28,563	28,398	86,110	100,710	103,803
Gross domestic product at market prices.....	23,631	24,368	25,021	36,590	37,331	38,637	49,971	52,340	54,195

© European Union. Source: Eurostat, 2017, Economy and finance, table *NAMA_10_GDP*—GDP and main components (output, expenditure and income).

Gross value added (GVA) by branch of activity: Latvia, Lithuania and Luxembourg (million euros at current prices)

	Latvia			Lithuania			Luxembourg		
	2014	2015	2016	2014	2015	2016	2014	2015	2016
Agriculture, forestry and fishing	728	724	710	1,252	1,221	1,139	127	113	114
Industry (except construction)	3,465	3,555	3,668	7,630	7,580	7,678	3,304	3,535	3,560
Construction	1,397	1,382	1,137	2,425	2,440	2,280	2,446	2,366	2,505
Wholesale and retail trade, transport, accommodation and food service activities	5,429	5,457	5,493	10,590	10,544	11,189	7,920	8,321	8,412
Information and communication	920	990	1,060	1,052	1,160	1,222	2,672	3,411	3,537
Financial and insurance activities.................	943	1,010	1,243	663	700	775	11,733	12,624	13,399
Real estate activities......................................	2,759	2,874	2,863	2,128	2,256	2,328	3,641	3,647	3,671
Professional, scientific and technical activities; administrative and support service activities	1,457	1,532	1,633	2,026	2,186	2,278	4,799	5,255	5,646
Public administration, defence, education, human health and social work activities....	3,223	3,392	3,501	4,600	4,772	5,035	7,070	7,353	7,539
Arts, entertainment and recreation; other service activities; activities of household and extraterritorial organizations and bodies...........................	614	650	680	680	719	772	827	789	805
Total GVA (all NACE activities)	20,934	21,566	21,989	33,046	33,577	34,697	44,541	47,412	49,186

© European Union. Source: Eurostat, 2017, Economy and finance, table *NAIDA_10_A10*—Gross value added by A*10 industry—Selected international annual data.

Main aggregates at current prices: Malta, the Netherlands and Poland (million euros)

	Malta			Netherlands			Poland		
	2013	2014	2015	2014	2015	2016*	2013	2014	2015
Gross domestic product at market prices	7,671	8,093	8,788	663,008	683,457	702,641	394,721	410,990	429,794
Gross national income at market prices	7,306	7,907	8,674	661,287	679,610	694,231	381,485	395,768	413,909

* Provisional.

© European Union. Source: Eurostat, 2017, Economy and finance, table *NASA_10_NF_TR*—Non-financial transactions.

Expenditure on the GDP at current prices: Malta, the Netherlands and Poland (million euros)

	Malta			Netherlands			Poland		
	2014	2015	2016	2014	2015	2016*	2014	2015	2016
Final consumption expenditure	5,948	6,322	6,446	468,668	475,147	484,374	321,358	328,699	324,621
Households and non-profit institutions serving households	4,343	4,630	4,775	296,682	303,470	310,692	246,788	251,305	248,777
General government	1,605	1,691	1,671	171,986	171,677	173,682	74,570	77,394	75,844
Gross capital formation	1,384	2,218	2,308	122,455	136,175	140,919	83,707	88,031	83,159
Gross fixed capital formation	1,453	2,299	2,328	119,530	132,464	140,049	81,110	86,396	76,616
Changes in inventories; acquisitions, less disposals, of valuables	-69	-81	-20	2,925	3,711	870	2,597	1,635	6,542
Domestic demand	n.a.	n.a.	n.a.	n.a.	n.a.	n.a.	n.a.	n.a.	n.a.
Exports of goods and services	12,682	13,355	13,924	547,415	570,178	579,317	195,586	212,967	221,816
Less Imports of goods and services	11,570	12,622	12,783	475,530	498,043	501,969	189,661	199,659	205,327
Gross domestic product at market prices	8,443	9,273	9,896	663,008	683,457	702,641	410,990	430,038	424,269

* Provisional.

© European Union. Source: Eurostat, 2017, Economy and finance, table *NAMA_10_GDP*—GDP and main components (output, expenditure and income).

Gross value added (GVA) by branch of activity: Malta, the Netherlands and Poland (million euros at current prices)

	Malta			Netherlands			Poland		
	2014	2015	2016	2014	2015	2016*	2014	2015	2016
Agriculture, forestry and fishing	96	104	117	10,996	11,102	11,543	10,740	9,472	9,047
Industry (except construction)	866	901	933	95,277	96,515	96,214	92,405	99,715	99,385
Construction	302	352	347	27,223	28,201	29,965	28,602	30,468	25,744
Wholesale and retail trade, transport, accommodation and food service activities	1,621	1,769	1,814	121,772	128,679	133,940	91,890	96,163	98,356
Information and communication	476	535	596	28,473	29,736	30,253	14,374	15,411	14,681
Financial and insurance activities	505	547	587	48,526	47,145	44,375	16,501	15,515	15,223
Real estate activities	383	440	477	34,716	35,935	37,880	19,123	18,735	18,716
Professional, scientific and technical activities; administrative and support service activities	858	984	1,103	83,331	89,890	95,131	27,683	30,829	30,546
Public administration, defence, education, human health and social work activities	1,356	1,448	1,540	131,453	131,508	134,851	54,521	56,396	55,056
Arts, entertainment and recreation; other service activities; activities of household and extraterritorial organizations and bodies	947	1,073	1,177	15,647	16,275	16,880	8,605	8,812	8,549
Total GVA (all NACE activities)	7,409	8,153	8,691	597,414	614,986	631,032	364,443	381,515	375,303

* Provisional.

© European Union. Source: Eurostat, 2017, Economy and finance, table *NAIDA_10_A10*—Gross value added by A*10 industry—Selected international annual data.

STATISTICAL SURVEY — National Accounts

Main aggregates at current prices: Portugal, Romania and Slovakia (million euros)

	Portugal			Romania			Slovakia		
	2014	2015*	2016*	2013	2014	2015†	2013	2014	2015
Gross domestic product at market prices...	173,079	179,504	184,934	144,253	150,357	159,964	74,170	75,946	78,686
Gross national income at market prices.....	170,117	174,353	181,110	141,538	148,872	156,904	73,477	74,608	77,403

* Estimates. † Provisional.
© European Union. Source: Eurostat, 2017, Economy and finance, table *NASA_10_NF_TR*—Non-financial transactions.

Expenditure on the GDP at current prices: Portugal, Romania and Slovakia (million euros)

	Portugal			Romania			Slovakia		
	2014	2015*	2016*	2014	2015†	2016†	2014	2015	2016
Final consumption expenditure	146,266	150,431	155,115	113,894	121,017	128,736	56,770	58,521	60,070
Households and non-profit institutions serving households	114,060	117,821	121,768	92,717	99,086	104,852	42,348	43,213	44,314
General government	32,206	32,610	33,347	21,177	21,931	23,884	14,422	15,308	15,756
Gross capital formation	26,486	27,768	27,645	37,125	39,931	42,433	16,468	18,257	17,417
Gross fixed capital formation	25,993	27,417	27,478	36,549	39,614	38,440	15,495	18,108	16,332
Changes in inventories; acquisitions, less disposals, of valuables	493	352	167	576	317	3,993	973	149	1,086
Domestic demand	n.a.	n.a.	n.a.	n.a.	n.a.	n.a.	n.a.	n.a.	n.a.
Exports of goods and services	69,360	72,808	74,504	61,935	65,759	70,182	69,721	73,562	75,950
Less Imports of goods and services	69,033	71,503	72,330	62,597	66,743	71,773	67,012	71,654	72,929
Gross domestic product at market prices	173,079	179,504	184,934	150,358	159,964	169,578	75,946	78,686	80,958

* Estimates. † Provisional.
© European Union. Source: Eurostat, 2017, Economy and finance, table *NAMA_10_GDP*—GDP and main components (output, expenditure and income).

Gross value added (GVA) by branch of activity: Portugal, Romania and Slovakia (million euros at current prices)

	Portugal			Romania			Slovakia		
	2014	2015*	2016*	2014	2015†	2016†	2014	2015	2016
Agriculture, forestry and fishing	3,512	3,654	3,612	7,104	6,651	6,604	3,005	2,601	2,760
Industry (except construction)	26,488	28,484	29,727	38,021	38,071	39,085	18,422	19,143	19,907
Construction	6,278	6,364	6,284	9,367	9,273	10,196	5,302	5,577	5,501
Wholesale and retail trade, transport, accommodation and food service activities	37,274	38,690	40,067	22,502	26,845	30,807	14,740	15,484	15,736
Information and communication	5,192	5,328	5,419	7,284	8,167	9,360	2,769	2,844	3,001
Financial and insurance activities	8,089	8,500	8,028	5,425	6,122	6,304	2,859	3,084	3,207
Real estate activities	18,891	19,052	19,531	12,221	13,653	13,905	4,513	4,621	4,661
Professional, scientific and technical activities; administrative and support service activities	10,856	11,135	11,562	9,546	11,026	12,595	5,383	5,446	5,554
Public administration, defence, education, human health and social work activities	30,391	30,843	31,646	17,428	15,809	17,829	9,300	9,471	9,794
Arts, entertainment and recreation; other service activities; activities of household and extraterritorial organizations and bodies	4,395	4,563	4,740	4,146	4,953	5,524	2,474	2,724	2,813
Total GVA (all NACE activities)	151,365	156,612	160,614	133,044	140,569	152,208	68,766	70,994	72,933

* Estimates. † Provisional.
© European Union. Source: Eurostat, 2017, Economy and finance, table *NAIDA_10_A10*—Gross value added by A*10 industry—Selected international annual data.

National Accounts STATISTICAL SURVEY

Main aggregates at current prices: Slovenia, Spain and Sweden (million euros)

	Slovenia			Spain			Sweden		
	2013	2014	2015	2013	2014	2015	2014	2015	2016
Gross domestic product at market prices	35,917	37,332	38,570	1,025,634	1,037,025	1,075,639	432,691	447,009	462,057
Gross national income at market prices	35,721	37,294	37,685	1,020,307	1,033,690	1,074,859	442,307	453,863	470,105

© European Union. Source: Eurostat, 2017, Economy and finance, table *NASA_10_NF_TR*—Non-financial transactions.

Expenditure on the GDP at current prices: Slovenia, Spain and Sweden (million euros)

	Slovenia			Spain*			Sweden		
	2014	2015	2016	2014	2015	2016	2014	2015	2016
Final consumption expenditure	27,153	27,315	28,104	810,919	833,524	854,148	312,984	317,585	326,647
Households and non-profit institutions serving households	20,153	20,112	20,574	608,945	625,035	643,840	199,613	201,440	205,852
General government	7,000	7,204	7,530	201,974	208,489	210,308	113,371	116,145	120,796
Gross capital formation	7,398	7,738	7,833	201,035	215,769	227,289	101,033	108,207	114,059
Gross fixed capital formation	7,316	7,525	7,322	198,335	212,069	221,966	99,736	105,709	111,408
Changes in inventories; acquisitions, less disposals, of valuables	82	214	511	2,700	3,700	5,323	1,298	2,498	2,651
Domestic demand	n.a.	n.a.	n.a.	n.a.	n.a.	n.a.	n.a.	n.a.	n.a.
Exports of goods and services	28,518	30,060	31,440	338,769	356,873	368,322	194,854	203,792	205,245
Less Imports of goods and services	25,736	26,543	27,608	313,698	330,527	335,908	176,181	182,574	183,894
Gross domestic product at market prices	37,332	38,570	39,769	1,037,025	1,075,639	1,113,851	432,691	447,010	462,058

* Provisional.
© European Union. Source: Eurostat, 2017, Economy and finance, table *NAMA_10_GDP*—GDP and main components (output, expenditure and income).

Gross value added (GVA) by branch of activity: Slovenia, Spain and Sweden (million euros at current prices)

	Slovenia			Spain*			Sweden		
	2014	2015	2016	2014	2015	2016	2014	2015	2016
Agriculture, forestry and fishing	779	794	775	23,560	25,004	26,028	5,144	5,212	5,165
Industry (except construction)	8,810	9,082	9,496	165,978	176,102	179,527	77,358	80,676	81,269
Construction	1,837	1,826	1,623	53,524	54,554	56,540	21,303	23,273	24,803
Wholesale and retail trade, transport, accommodation and food service activities	6,506	6,802	7,126	219,194	226,553	236,475	69,260	71,322	73,159
Information and communication	1,352	1,395	1,462	40,445	40,501	41,962	21,868	22,902	23,917
Financial and insurance activities	1,297	1,388	1,329	37,910	38,282	39,618	17,700	18,313	17,161
Real estate activities	2,218	2,306	2,378	112,596	109,202	110,781	34,002	33,463	35,432
Professional, scientific and technical activities; administrative and support service activities	3,191	3,319	3,425	73,768	82,058	88,380	42,458	44,446	46,937
Public administration, defence, education, human health and social work activities	5,378	5,497	5,813	177,669	183,882	191,047	82,464	83,893	87,801
Arts, entertainment and recreation; other service activities; activities of household and extraterritorial organizations and bodies	865	903	931	39,135	39,657	40,648	11,680	12,002	12,513
Total GVA (all NACE activities)	32,231	33,311	34,359	943,779	975,795	1,011,006	383,237	395,501	408,156

* Provisional.
© European Union. Source: Eurostat, 2017, Economy and finance, table *NAIDA_10_A10*—Gross value added by A*10 industry—Selected international annual data.

Main aggregates at current prices: United Kingdom (million euros)

	United Kingdom		
	2014	2015	2016
Gross domestic product at market prices	2,260,805	2,580,064	2,366,912
Gross national income at market prices	2,231,323	2,544,598	2,338,688

© European Union. Source: Eurostat, 2017, Economy and finance, table *NASA_10_NF_TR*—Non-financial transactions.

Expenditure on the GDP at current prices: United Kingdom (million euros)

	United Kingdom		
	2014	2015	2016
Final consumption expenditure	1,912,161	2,173,380	1,990,097
Households and non-profit institutions serving households	1,467,402	1,673,491	1,540,252
General government	444,759	499,888	449,845
Gross capital formation	393,579	443,251	403,026
Gross fixed capital formation	375,248	436,813	394,429
Changes in inventories; acquisitions, less disposals, of valuables	18,331	6,438	8,597
Domestic demand	n.a.	n.a.	n.a.
Exports of goods and services	634,712	712,893	668,216
Less Imports of goods and services	679,647	753,932	713,399
Gross domestic product at market prices	2,260,805	2,580,065	2,366,912

© European Union. Source: Eurostat, 2017, Economy and finance, table *NAMA_10_GDP*—GDP and main components (output, expenditure and income).

Gross value added (GVA) by branch of activity: United Kingdom (million euros at current prices)

	United Kingdom		
	2014	2015	2016
Agriculture, forestry and fishing	13,643	14,981	12,870
Industry (except construction)	285,964	304,788	274,579
Construction	120,027	141,519	130,367
Wholesale and retail trade, transport, accommodation and food service activities	370,269	425,467	392,792
Information and communication	125,824	149,234	141,368
Financial and insurance activities	151,223	166,698	151,506
Real estate activities	254,614	297,951	271,455
Professional, scientific and technical activities; administrative and support service activities	243,403	282,934	260,845
Public administration, defence, education, human health and social work activities	370,724	425,328	383,891
Arts, entertainment and recreation; other service activities; activities of household and extraterritorial organizations and bodies	79,241	90,769	86,493
Total GVA (all NACE activities)	2,014,931	2,299,669	2,106,165

© European Union. Source: Eurostat, 2017, Economy and finance, table *NAIDA_10_A10*—Gross value added by A*10 industry—Selected international annual data.

BALANCE OF PAYMENTS

EUROPEAN UNION TOTALS (EU-28)

Current transactions with non-EU partners (million euros)

	2014	2015	2016
Exports of goods f.o.b.	1,699,009	1,824,740	1,799,389
Imports of goods c.i.f	−1,651,317	−1,682,778	−1,622,296
Trade balance	47,692	141,962	177,093
Exports of services	753,832	821,716	819,817
Imports of services	−592,652	−674,697	−692,653
Balance on services	161,180	147,019	127,165
Primary income received	596,128	604,375	588,659
Primary income paid	−588,954	−637,304	−565,289
Balance on primary income	7,175	−32,928	23,370
Secondary income received	80,916	88,431	86,350
Secondary income paid	−159,877	−168,270	−165,469
Balance on secondary income	−78,961	−79,839	−79,119
Total current receipts	3,129,885	3,339,262	3,294,215
Total current payments	−2,992,799	−3,163,048	−3,045,707
Balance on current account	137,086	176,214	248,509

© European Union. Source: Eurostat, 2017, Economy and finance, table *BOP_EU6_Q*—European Union and euro area balance of payments—Quarterly data (BPM6).

Trade in services with non-EU partners (million euros)

	2014	2015	2016
Transportation receipts	137,584	145,576	135,998
Transportation payments	−117,787	−124,227	−118,522
Balance on transportation	19,797	21,349	17,476
Travel receipts	109,947	115,014	113,576
Travel payments	−97,752	−101,590	−102,268
Balance on travel	12,195	13,425	11,308
Other services: receipts	n.a.	n.a.	n.a.
Other services: payments	n.a.	n.a.	n.a.
Balance on other services	n.a.	n.a.	n.a.
Unallocated services: receipts	209	590	839
Unallocated services: payments	−141	−197	−175
Balance on unallocated services	69	393	665
Total services: receipts	753,832	821,716	819,817
Total services: payments	−592,652	−674,697	−692,653
Balance on total services	161,180	147,019	127,165

© European Union. Source: Eurostat, 2017, Economy and finance, table *BOP_EU6_Q*—European Union and euro area balance of payments—Quarterly data (BPM6).

STATISTICS BY COUNTRY

Transactions with the rest of the world: Austria, Belgium and Bulgaria (million euros)

	Austria			Belgium			Bulgaria		
	2014	2015	2016	2014	2015	2016	2014	2015	2016
Exports of goods f.o.b.	124,976	128,150	129,077	236,851	229,698	250,986	21,027	21,920	22,556
Imports of goods c.i.f.	−123,935	−126,651	−129,262	−241,431	−227,119	−245,106	−23,803	−24,542	−24,401
Trade balance	1,041	1,499	−185	−4,580	2,579	5,880	−2,777	−2,622	−1,845
Exports of services	50,707	52,396	54,323	94,260	101,957	100,350	6,738	6,967	7,500
Imports of services	−41,300	−42,380	−44,054	−88,026	−95,187	−97,170	−4,224	−3,964	−4,054
Balance on services	9,407	10,016	10,269	6,234	6,770	3,180	2,514	3,004	3,447
Primary income received	23,133	28,552	28,524	50,717	46,070	40,469	929	972	1,102
Primary income paid	−22,436	−30,193	−29,133	−48,658	−46,939	−43,808	−2,248	−3,054	−2,301
Balance on primary income	697	−1,641	−609	2,059	−869	−3,339	−1,318	−2,082	−1,199
Secondary income received	2,784	4,403	4,523	7,333	7,713	8,330	2,267	2,406	2,285
Secondary income paid	−6,034	−7,787	−7,995	−13,746	−14,379	−15,719	−651	−765	−700
Balance on secondary income	−3,250	−3,384	−3,472	−6,413	−6,666	−7,389	1,616	1,640	1,585
Total current receipts	201,600	213,499	216,445	389,160	385,437	400,135	30,961	32,265	33,444
Total current payments	−193,704	−207,012	−210,443	−391,863	−383,625	−401,804	−30,926	−32,325	−31,455
Balance on current account	7,895	6,487	6,002	−2,702	1,813	−1,670	35	−61	1,989
Capital account (net)	n.a.	n.a.	n.a.	n.a.	n.a.	n.a.	n.a.	n.a.	n.a.
Financial account (net)	2,604	4,901	6,665	−3,321	2,794	−2,728	−282	2,654	3,416
Net errors and omissions	−4,939	163	1,291	433	867	−793	−1,277	1,293	361

© European Union. Source: Eurostat, 2017, Economy and finance, table *BOP_C6_Q*—Balance of payments by country—Quarterly data (BPM6).

Transactions with the rest of the world: Croatia, Cyprus and the Czech Republic (million euros)

	Croatia			Cyprus			Czech Republic		
	2014	2015	2016	2014	2015	2016	2014	2015	2016
Exports of goods f.o.b.	9,753	10,701	11,004	2,808	2,482	2,440	110,401	115,573	118,494
Imports of goods c.i.f.	−16,107	−17,365	−18,070	−5,620	−5,650	−6,287	−102,406	−108,701	−109,224
Trade balance	−6,354	−6,664	−7,066	−2,812	−3,168	−3,847	7,995	6,872	9,270
Exports of services	10,212	11,246	12,146	8,118	8,316	8,868	18,915	20,603	21,618
Imports of services	−2,988	−3,347	−3,527	−4,945	−5,090	−5,020	−16,892	−17,742	−17,880
Balance on services	7,224	7,899	8,619	3,173	3,226	3,848	2,023	2,861	3,738
Primary income received	818	958	1,189	4,358	4,559	4,165	5,551	6,623	7,093
Primary income paid	−1,691	−1,237	−2,809	−4,995	−4,620	−4,647	−15,022	−15,979	−17,145
Balance on primary income	−874	−279	−1,621	−637	−61	−482	−9,470	−9,357	−10,053
Secondary income received	1,921	2,253	2,313	232	249	313	2,924	3,221	2,593
Secondary income paid	−1,023	−987	−1,047	−716	−759	−774	−3,176	−3,228	−3,603
Balance on secondary income	898	1,266	1,266	−484	−510	−461	−252	−8	−1,010
Total current receipts	22,704	25,158	26,652	15,517	15,604	15,785	137,791	146,019	149,798
Total current payments	−21,809	−22,936	−25,459	−16,278	−16,119	−16,727	−137,495	−145,651	−147,852
Balance on current account	895	2,223	1,193	−760	−514	−942	296	368	1,946
Capital account (net)	n.a.	n.a.	n.a.	n.a.	n.a.	n.a.	n.a.	n.a.	n.a.
Financial account (net)	414	1,874	1,022	−1,251	355	−1,060	2,166	6,394	4,352
Net errors and omissions	−547	−626	−221	−636	420	−156	695	2,306	427

© European Union. Source: Eurostat, 2017, Economy and finance, table *BOP_C6_Q*—Balance of payments by country—Quarterly data (BPM6).

Transactions with the rest of the world: Denmark, Estonia and Finland (million euros)

	Denmark			Estonia			Finland		
	2014	2015	2016	2014	2015	2016	2014	2015	2016
Exports of goods f.o.b.	89,313	92,553	94,025	11,089	10,853	11,213	56,461	53,792	52,709
Imports of goods c.i.f.	−77,895	−78,965	−78,091	−12,092	−11,714	−12,073	−55,295	−51,828	−52,127
Trade balance	11,418	13,588	15,934	−1,003	−861	−860	1,166	1,964	582
Exports of services	55,288	57,548	53,438	5,322	5,204	5,514	20,333	23,361	22,987
Imports of services	−48,247	−51,019	−50,366	−3,623	−3,502	−3,786	−22,822	−25,410	−25,655
Balance on services	7,041	6,528	3,072	1,699	1,702	1,729	−2,489	−2,049	−2,669
Primary income received	24,978	26,286	24,203	1,116	991	1,199	16,381	14,632	15,152
Primary income paid	−15,360	−17,178	−16,778	−1,649	−1,409	−1,515	−15,150	−13,470	−13,405
Balance on primary income	9,618	9,108	7,424	−534	−418	−316	1,232	1,162	1,747
Secondary income received	2,903	3,270	3,212	446	481	472	1,099	1,053	1,556
Secondary income paid	−7,370	−7,613	−7,159	−426	−456	−467	−3,595	−3,374	−3,506
Balance on secondary income	−4,468	−4,343	−3,947	20	25	5	−2,496	−2,321	−1,951
Total current receipts	172,481	179,656	174,878	17,972	17,528	18,398	94,274	92,838	92,404
Total current payments	−148,872	−154,774	−152,393	−17,790	−17,082	−17,841	−96,861	−94,082	−94,694
Balance on current account	23,609	24,882	22,484	182	447	557	−2,587	−1,244	−2,290
Capital account (net)	n.a.	n.a.	n.a.	n.a.	n.a.	n.a.	n.a.	n.a.	n.a.
Financial account (net)	20,239	18,606	19,896	254	1,006	554	−7,990	−2,178	−5,159
Net errors and omissions	−2,820	−5,311	−2,635	n.a.	n.a.	−181	n.a.*	n.a.*	n.a.*

* Confidential.
© European Union. Source: Eurostat, 2017, Economy and finance, table *BOP_C6_Q*—Balance of payments by country—Quarterly data (BPM6).

Transactions with the rest of the world: France, Germany and Greece (million euros)

	France			Germany			Greece		
	2014	2015	2016	2014	2015	2016	2014	2015	2016
Exports of goods f.o.b.	437,979	460,654	458,416	1,115,751	1,179,208	1,195,022	26,785	24,787	24,486
Imports of goods c.i.f.	−478,457	−484,659	−485,737	−887,390	−918,027	−923,355	−49,040	−42,019	−41,070
Trade balance	−40,478	−24,005	−27,321	228,361	261,181	271,667	−22,255	−17,232	−16,584
Exports of services	207,115	217,774	213,856	224,464	246,160	254,299	31,052	27,920	25,016
Imports of services	−190,221	−208,971	−212,985	−249,786	−264,762	−276,719	−12,781	−10,987	−9,703
Balance on services	16,894	8,803	871	−25,322	−18,602	−22,420	18,271	16,933	15,313
Primary income received	157,016	160,747	155,536	189,380	192,836	188,853	8,457	7,519	6,647
Primary income paid	−109,263	−108,774	−106,274	−133,203	−135,467	−136,716	−7,056	−6,493	−5,899
Balance on primary income	47,753	51,973	49,262	56,177	57,369	52,137	1,401	1,026	748
Secondary income received	14,437	17,099	21,643	61,951	65,206	65,014	2,551	1,911	1,804
Secondary income paid	−61,400	−58,220	−64,829	−103,139	−105,194	−105,037	−2,885	−2,432	−2,401
Balance on secondary income	−46,963	−41,121	−43,186	−41,188	−39,988	−40,023	−334	−521	−597
Total current receipts	816,548	856,275	849,451	1,591,545	1,683,413	1,703,189	68,846	62,136	57,954
Total current payments	−839,341	−860,625	−869,824	−1,373,519	−1,423,450	−1,441,827	−71,762	−61,929	−59,072
Balance on current account	−22,793	−4,352	−20,374	218,026	259,963	261,361	−2,916	206	−1,118
Capital account (net)	n.a.	n.a.	n.a.	n.a.	n.a.	n.a.	n.a.	n.a.	n.a.
Financial account (net)	−7,543	−7,025	−31,831	238,631	234,602	231,252	1,464	3,430	−137
Net errors and omissions	13,081	−4,751	−12,568	18,248	−24,725	−31,222	1,867	1,235	−55

© European Union. Source: Eurostat, 2017, Economy and finance, table *BOP_C6_Q*—Balance of payments by country—Quarterly data (BPM6).

Transactions with the rest of the world: Hungary, Ireland and Italy (million euros)

	Hungary			Ireland			Italy		
	2014	2015	2016	2014	2015	2016	2014	2015	2016
Exports of goods f.o.b.	74,421	79,611	82,785	114,461	195,592	186,251	389,511	405,420	410,446
Imports of goods c.i.f.	−72,047	−75,204	−77,533	−73,730	−85,024	−83,268	−342,104	−354,690	−349,783
Trade balance	2,374	4,408	5,253	40,731	110,568	102,983	47,407	50,730	60,663
Exports of services	18,639	20,283	21,195	105,327	121,605	132,566	85,902	88,599	91,568
Imports of services	−13,731	−14,881	−14,853	−111,453	−150,963	−173,891	−86,919	−91,349	−95,158
Balance on services	4,908	5,402	6,342	−6,126	−29,358	−41,325	−1,017	−2,750	−3,590
Primary income received	10,706	10,407	10,899	62,705	61,665	68,282	62,121	53,009	56,550
Primary income paid	−15,065	−15,541	−15,294	−91,353	−113,581	−114,696	−62,167	−62,226	−53,776
Balance on primary income	−4,359	−5,133	−4,395	−28,648	−51,916	−46,414	−46	−9,217	2,774
Secondary income received	1,989	2,072	1,450	2,923	4,010	4,572	15,202	14,839	15,301
Secondary income paid	−2,761	−3,174	−3,207	−5,674	−7,149	−7,273	−31,043	−29,867	−32,062
Balance on secondary income	−772	−1,102	−1,757	−2,751	−3,139	−2,701	−15,841	−15,028	−16,761
Total current receipts	105,755	112,373	116,329	285,414	382,873	391,671	552,736	561,866	573,864
Total current payments	−103,605	−108,799	−110,886	−282,212	−356,716	−379,129	−522,234	−538,131	−530,780
Balance on current account	2,150	3,574	5,442	3,203	26,157	12,544	30,503	23,734	43,084
Capital account (net)	n.a.	n.a.	n.a.	n.a.	n.a.	n.a.	n.a.	n.a.	n.a.
Financial account (net)	4,463	6,755	3,754	−5,404	22,782	5,080	43,820	27,440	63,382
Net errors and omissions	−1,639	−1,950	−2,257	−1,839	−2,120	−1,905	9,931	1,077	22,415

© European Union. Source: Eurostat, 2017, Economy and finance, table *BOP_C6_Q*—Balance of payments by country—Quarterly data (BPM6).

Transactions with the rest of the world: Latvia, Lithuania and Luxembourg (million euros)

	Latvia			Lithuania			Luxembourg		
	2014	2015	2016	2014	2015	2016	2014	2015	2016
Exports of goods f.o.b.	10,214	10,322	10,265	23,750	22,310	21,906	18,476	15,853	14,791
Imports of goods c.i.f.	−12,414	−12,364	−12,008	−24,686	−24,296	−23,816	−18,711	−18,465	−18,053
Trade balance	−2,200	−2,042	−1,743	−936	−1,986	−1,910	−235	−2,612	−3,262
Exports of services	3,853	4,038	4,244	5,850	6,011	6,819	75,888	86,207	85,485
Imports of services	−2,101	−2,273	−2,365	−4,212	−4,266	−4,582	−59,264	−65,849	−64,866
Balance on services	1,752	1,765	1,879	1,638	1,744	2,238	16,624	20,358	20,619
Primary income received	1,229	1,391	1,484	763	741	803	182,208	200,676	192,190
Primary income paid	−1,260	−1,449	−1,425	−1,274	−2,292	−2,256	−196,485	−216,618	−207,613
Balance on primary income	−31	−58	59	−511	−1,552	−1,454	−14,277	−15,942	−15,423
Secondary income received	813	903	899	2,058	1,754	1,595	7,944	8,511	8,831
Secondary income paid	−797	−758	−725	−931	−832	−812	−7,545	−7,631	−8,210
Balance on secondary income	16	145	174	1,127	923	783	399	880	621
Total current receipts	16,110	16,654	16,894	32,420	30,815	31,122	284,515	311,246	301,297
Total current payments	−16,574	−16,843	−16,523	−31,103	−31,687	−31,465	−282,005	−308,565	−298,743
Balance on current account	−463	−189	369	1,317	−872	−343	2,510	2,680	2,555
Capital account (net)	n.a.	n.a.	n.a.	n.a.	n.a.	n.a.	n.a.	n.a.	n.a.
Financial account (net)	647	−194	536	467	656	−107	1,432	1,974	1,868
Net errors and omissions	357	−690	−84	−1,829	404	−326	−14	−110	45

© European Union. Source: Eurostat, 2017, Economy and finance, table *BOP_C6_Q*—Balance of payments by country—Quarterly data (BPM6).

Transactions with the rest of the world: Malta, the Netherlands and Poland (million euros)

	Malta			Netherlands			Poland		
	2014	2015	2016	2014	2015	2016	2014	2015	2016
Exports of goods f.o.b.	2,618	2,667	2,461	429,655	427,415	429,636	158,657	172,150	176,716
Imports of goods c.i.f.	−3,736	−4,544	−4,333	−353,737	−351,268	−351,093	−161,911	−169,937	−174,767
Trade balance	−1,117	−1,877	−1,872	75,918	76,147	78,543	−3,255	2,214	1,949
Exports of services	10,026	10,689	11,538	117,762	130,618	132,268	36,743	40,663	44,260
Imports of services	−7,841	−8,082	−8,481	−121,829	−133,798	−135,132	−27,679	−29,745	−30,560
Balance on services	2,184	2,608	3,057	−4,067	−3,180	−2,864	9,064	10,918	13,699
Primary income received	10,428	10,265	9,936	251,165	230,238	195,539	11,611	11,198	10,981
Primary income paid	−10,901	−10,744	−10,596	−250,974	−232,671	−203,426	−25,572	−26,135	−26,842
Balance on primary income	−473	−479	−661	191	−2,433	−7,887	−13,962	−14,937	−15,860
Secondary income received	992	996	991	11,079	11,708	10,953	5,944	5,808	5,666
Secondary income paid	−832	−753	−731	−24,178	−22,673	−20,050	−6,321	−6,657	−6,728
Balance on secondary income	221	243	259	−13,099	−10,965	−9,097	−377	−848	−1,062
Total current receipts	24,064	24,617	24,925	809,661	799,977	768,395	212,954	229,819	237,623
Total current payments	−23,310	−24,122	−24,141	−750,716	−740,411	−709,701	−221,483	−232,473	−238,897
Balance on current account	815	495	783	58,944	59,568	58,697	−8,529	−2,654	−1,275
Capital account (net)	n.a.	n.a.	n.a.	n.a.	n.a.	n.a.	n.a.	n.a.	n.a.
Financial account (net)	672	311	1,976	61,678	22,475	61,455	−4,680	1,311	873
Net errors and omissions	−284	−351	1,114	3,299	−3,127	4,548	−6,187	−6,196	−2,359

© European Union. Source: Eurostat, 2017, Economy and finance, table *BOP_C6_Q*—Balance of payments by country—Quarterly data (BPM6).

STATISTICAL SURVEY — Balance of payments

Transactions with the rest of the world: Portugal, Romania and Slovakia (million euros)

	Portugal			Romania			Slovakia		
	2014	2015	2016	2014	2015	2016	2014	2015	2016
Exports of goods f.o.b.	47,296	49,115	49,499	46,839	49,097	52,164	62,581	66,089	68,253
Imports of goods c.i.f.	−56,783	−58,386	−58,574	−53,375	−56,888	−61,412	−59,823	−64,073	−65,975
Trade balance	−9,487	−9,271	−9,075	−6,536	−7,791	−9,248	2,016	2,278	2,278
Exports of services	23,421	25,178	26,281	15,104	16,640	18,014	6,889	7,301	7,588
Imports of services	−12,043	−12,742	−13,140	−9,236	−9,849	−10,356	−6,713	−7,144	−7,180
Balance on services	11,378	12,436	13,141	5,868	6,791	7,658	176	157	407
Primary income received	8,419	8,232	8,451	2,304	2,321	2,754	3,699	3,808	2,880
Primary income paid	−11,824	−12,780	−12,432	−4,322	−6,092	−7,578	−4,450	−4,619	−4,786
Balance on primary income	−3,405	−4,548	−3,981	−2,019	−3,771	−4,824	−750	−812	−1,906
Secondary income received	6,169	5,766	5,589	4,552	5,697	5,104	486	551	326
Secondary income paid	−4,550	−4,260	−4,115	−2,869	−2,907	−2,646	−1,799	−1,782	−1,695
Balance on secondary income	1,619	1,506	1,474	1,684	2,789	2,458	−1,313	−1,231	−1,369
Total current receipts	85,306	88,293	89,818	68,799	73,755	78,036	73,655	77,748	79,047
Total current payments	−85,202	−88,167	−88,261	−69,802	−75,736	−81,992	−72,785	−77,617	−79,637
Balance on current account	105	125	1,556	−1,004	−1,982	−3,956	871	131	−590
Capital account (net)	n.a.	n.a.	n.a.	n.a.	n.a.	n.a.	n.a.	n.a.	n.a.
Financial account (net)	2,827	2,164	3,142	2,924	2,204	1,578	−324	863	241
Net errors and omissions	220	−69	−12	−26	289	1,300	−1,924	−2,058	−799

© European Union. Source: Eurostat, 2017, Economy and finance, table *BOP_C6_Q*—Balance of payments by country—Quarterly data (BPM6).

Transactions with the rest of the world: Slovenia, Spain and Sweden (million euros)

	Slovenia			Spain			Sweden		
	2014	2015	2016	2014	2015	2016	2014	2015	2016
Exports of goods f.o.b.	22,961	24,039	24,952	238,578	250,176	253,571	135,278	137,159	137,071
Imports of goods c.i.f.	−21,780	−22,541	−23,416	−260,955	−271,922	−271,367	−122,129	−124,974	−126,402
Trade balance	1,181	1,498	1,536	−22,377	−21,746	−17,796	13,149	12,185	10,670
Exports of services	5,558	6,025	6,513	100,429	106,695	114,821	57,945	65,569	64,883
Imports of services	−3,862	−4,006	−4,227	−52,544	−58,722	−64,149	−52,115	−55,611	−55,060
Balance on services	1,697	2,019	2,286	47,885	47,973	50,672	5,830	9,957	9,823
Primary income received	1,396	1,632	1,602	52,696	52,516	54,332	46,673	43,929	43,523
Primary income paid	−1,521	−2,614	−2,233	−55,951	−53,177	−53,480	−37,901	−37,666	−36,347
Balance on primary income	−125	−982	−630	−3,255	−661	852	8,772	6,262	7,176
Secondary income received	709	725	712	13,431	13,642	14,529	4,503	4,666	4,941
Secondary income paid	−1,137	−1,262	−1,205	−24,442	−24,483	−26,472	−12,208	−12,095	−11,158
Balance on secondary income	−428	−537	−493	−11,011	−10,841	−11,943	−7,705	−7,429	−6,217
Total current receipts	30,624	32,420	33,779	405,134	423,029	437,254	244,398	251,322	250,418
Total current payments	−28,299	−30,422	−31,081	−393,890	−408,305	−415,469	−224,352	−230,347	−228,967
Balance on current account	2,325	1,998	2,698	11,245	14,724	21,785	20,046	20,975	21,451
Capital account (net)	n.a.	n.a.	n.a.	n.a.	n.a.	n.a.	n.a.	n.a.	n.a.
Financial account (net)	2,377	1,772	936	11,510	25,185	30,420	13,888	9,354	−11,806
Net errors and omissions	−105	−596	−1,449	−4,783	3,452	6,783	−5,538	−10,733	−32,882

© European Union. Source: Eurostat, 2017, Economy and finance, table *BOP_C6_Q*—Balance of payments by country—Quarterly data (BPM6).

Transactions with the rest of the world: United Kingdom (million euros)

	United Kingdom		
	2014	2015	2016
Exports of goods f.o.b.	363,381	396,257	368,078
Imports of goods c.i.f.	−515,639	−561,008	−531,702
Trade balance	−152,259	−164,751	−163,623
Exports of services	271,568	316,709	300,517
Imports of services	−164,233	−192,964	−182,078
Balance on services	107,335	123,745	118,439
Primary income received	176,586	184,155	174,331
Primary income paid	−206,300	−219,728	−203,355
Balance on primary income	−29,714	−35,573	−29,025
Secondary income received	23,825	27,354	24,898
Secondary income paid	−54,857	−61,342	−54,708
Balance on secondary income	−31,032	−33,988	−29,810
Total current receipts	835,360	924,475	867,824
Total current payments	−941,029	−1,035,041	−971,843
Balance on current account	−105,670	−110,566	−104,019
Capital account (net)	n.a.	n.a.	n.a.
Financial account (net)*	n.a.	n.a.	n.a.
Net errors and omissions*	n.a.	n.a.	n.a.

* Confidential.

© European Union. Source: Eurostat, 2017, Economy and finance, table *BOP_C6_Q*—Balance of payments by country—Quarterly data (BPM6).

EXTERNAL TRADE

SUMMARY STATISTICS

Total imports c.i.f. ('000 million euros)

	2014	2015	2016		2014	2015	2016
Austria	137.0	140.7	142.4	Italy	356.9	370.5	365.6
Belgium	342.2	338.1	331.5	Latvia	13.3	13.1	12.9
Bulgaria	26.1	26.3	26.1	Lithuania	25.9	25.4	24.8
Croatia	17.2	18.6	19.8	Luxembourg	20.1	21.0	19.6
Cyprus	5.1	5.0	5.9	Malta	5.1	5.2	5.6
Czech Republic	116.2	127.5	128.7	Netherlands	443.7	462.6	455.6
Denmark	75.0	77.2	77.3	Poland	168.4	177.2	178.2
Estonia	13.8	13.1	13.5	Portugal	59.0	60.3	61.1
Finland	57.8	54.5	54.7	Romania	58.6	63.0	67.3
France	509.3	516.8	517.5	Slovakia	61.7	66.2	68.2
Germany	908.6	947.6	953.1	Slovenia	25.6	26.9	27.6
Greece	48.3	43.6	44.0	Spain	270.2	281.2	279.7
Hungary	79.0	82.9	84.6	Sweden	122.1	124.8	127.1
Ireland	60.7	69.0	69.5	United Kingdom	519.7	564.6	574.6

© European Union. Source: Eurostat, 2017, International trade, table *EXT_LT_INTERTRD*—International trade of EU, the euro area and the member states by SITC product group.

Total exports f.o.b. ('000 million euros)

	2014	2015	2016		2014	2015	2016
Austria	134.2	137.8	137.5	Italy	398.9	412.3	417.1
Belgium	355.5	357.7	357.5	Latvia	11.0	10.9	10.9
Bulgaria	22.0	22.9	23.5	Lithuania	24.4	22.9	22.6
Croatia	10.4	11.7	12.5	Luxembourg	14.5	15.5	14.3
Cyprus	1.4	1.7	1.7	Malta	2.2	2.3	2.7
Czech Republic	131.8	142.4	147.1	Netherlands	506.3	513.5	514.5
Denmark	83.9	86.1	86.1	Poland	165.7	179.5	183.0
Estonia	12.1	11.6	11.9	Portugal	48.1	49.8	50.3
Finland	56.0	54.0	52.2	Romania	52.5	54.6	57.4
France	436.9	455.9	452.8	Slovakia	65.1	67.8	70.1
Germany	1,125.0	1,195.8	1,209.6	Slovenia	27.1	28.8	29.7
Greece	27.1	25.9	25.4	Spain	244.3	254.6	260.0
Hungary	83.3	88.8	92.1	Sweden	123.9	126.3	126.0
Ireland	91.8	111.7	116.4	United Kingdom	380.3	414.7	370.1

© European Union. Source: Eurostat, 2017, International trade, table *EXT_LT_INTERTRD*—International trade of EU, the euro area and the member states by SITC product group.

Total trade balances: Exports f.o.b. less Imports c.i.f. ('000 million euros)

	2014	2015	2016		2014	2015	2016
Austria	−2.8	−2.9	−4.9	Italy	41.9	41.8	51.5
Belgium	13.3	19.6	26.0	Latvia	−2.3	−2.1	−2.0
Bulgaria	−4.1	−3.5	−2.6	Lithuania	−1.5	−2.5	−2.2
Croatia	−6.7	−6.9	−7.3	Luxembourg	−5.6	−5.5	−5.3
Cyprus	−3.7	−3.4	−4.2	Malta	−2.9	−2.9	−2.9
Czech Republic	15.6	14.9	18.4	Netherlands	62.7	50.9	58.9
Denmark	8.9	8.9	8.8	Poland	−2.7	2.4	4.7
Estonia	−1.7	−1.5	−1.6	Portugal	−11.0	−10.5	−10.8
Finland	−1.8	−0.5	−2.4	Romania	−6.1	−8.4	−10.0
France	−72.4	−60.9	−64.7	Slovakia	3.4	1.7	1.9
Germany	216.5	248.2	256.5	Slovenia	1.5	1.9	2.2
Greece	−21.2	−17.7	−18.6	Spain	−25.9	−26.6	−19.8
Hungary	4.3	5.9	7.5	Sweden	1.8	1.5	−1.1
Ireland	31.1	42.7	46.9	United Kingdom	−139.5	−149.8	−204.5

© European Union. Source: Eurostat, 2017, International trade, table *EXT_LT_INTERTRD*—International trade of EU, the euro area and the member states by SITC product group.

Total imports c.i.f. from other EU-28 countries ('000 million euros)

	2014	2015	2016		2014	2015	2016
Austria	105.2	108.0	111.1	Italy	203.9	217.4	221.3
Belgium	222.5	212.3	208.9	Latvia	10.7	10.4	10.4
Bulgaria	16.1	17.0	17.3	Lithuania	17.0	17.2	17.5
Croatia	13.1	14.4	15.2	Luxembourg	16.1	15.2	15.1
Cyprus	3.6	3.7	4.3	Malta	3.2	3.4	3.1
Czech Republic	89.9	98.5	102.1	Netherlands	203.4	212.4	213.8
Denmark	52.1	53.6	55.0	Poland	117.3	125.3	128.5
Estonia	11.3	10.7	11.0	Portugal	44.1	46.2	47.5
Finland	39.4	39.8	39.9	Romania	44.1	48.6	51.9
France	344.6	353.8	357.7	Slovakia	46.9	52.1	54.6
Germany	594.8	621.6	632.6	Slovenia	17.7	18.8	19.5
Greece	23.3	23.1	24.1	Spain	154.8	170.8	172.5
Hungary	59.4	63.5	65.7	Sweden	84.0	87.4	90.5
Ireland	40.4	45.6	46.9	United Kingdom	275.4	302.8	290.4

© European Union. Source: Eurostat, 2017, International trade, table *EXT_LT_INTRATRD*—Intra- and extra-EU trade by member state and by product group.

Total exports f.o.b. to other EU-28 countries ('000 million euros)

	2014	2015	2016		2014	2015	2016
Austria	93.8	96.5	97.0	Italy	218.8	226.0	233.0
Belgium	251.4	257.1	258.1	Latvia	7.5	7.6	7.7
Bulgaria	13.8	14.9	15.9	Lithuania	13.4	14.0	13.7
Croatia	6.6	7.7	8.2	Luxembourg	12.0	13.1	11.8
Cyprus	0.8	0.9	0.8	Malta	1.1	1.0	1.1
Czech Republic	108.4	118.6	123.2	Netherlands	384.2	388.8	388.7
Denmark	53.5	52.8	53.1	Poland	128.3	142.4	145.6
Estonia	8.7	8.7	8.8	Portugal	34.0	36.3	37.9
Finland	32.1	31.8	30.7	Romania	37.3	40.2	43.1
France	262.6	268.1	269.1	Slovakia	54.9	58.0	59.9
Germany	648.6	692.8	708.2	Slovenia	20.4	21.9	22.4
Greece	13.1	14.0	14.3	Spain	155.8	165.6	173.2
Hungary	66.6	72.2	75.0	Sweden	72.4	73.8	74.5
Ireland	50.5	59.3	59.3	United Kingdom	182.1	184.2	175.7

© European Union. Source: Eurostat, 2017, International trade, table *EXT_LT_INTRATRD*—Intra- and extra-EU trade by member state and by product group

TRADE BY COMMODITY GROUPS

Food, drink and tobacco (SITC Sections 0 and 1): Imports c.i.f. ('000 million euros)

	2014	2015	2016		2014	2015	2016
Austria	10.1	10.4	10.7	Italy	34.4	35.4	35.5
Belgium	27.8	28.2	28.9	Latvia	2.0	1.9	2.1
Bulgaria	2.2	2.4	2.5	Lithuania	3.3	3.2	3.0
Croatia	2.1	2.3	2.4	Luxembourg	2.2	2.2	2.2
Cyprus	1.0	1.0	1.0	Malta	0.6	0.6	0.6
Czech Republic	6.5	7.2	7.4	Netherlands	41.8	45.8	46.7
Denmark	10.1	10.6	10.8	Poland	13.3	14.2	14.9
Estonia	1.4	1.3	1.4	Portugal	7.7	8.0	8.4
Finland	4.2	4.3	4.3	Romania	4.5	5.4	5.9
France	44.0	46.0	47.5	Slovakia	3.4	3.5	3.8
Germany	67.2	71.6	74.1	Slovenia	2.1	2.3	2.4
Greece	5.7	5.6	6.0	Spain	25.5	27.9	28.9
Hungary	4.1	4.3	4.5	Sweden	12.3	13.3	14.2
Ireland	7.0	7.6	7.6	United Kingdom	48.1	53.6	51.1

© European Union. Source: Eurostat, 2017, International trade, table *EXT_LT_INTERTRD*—International trade of EU, the euro area and the member states by SITC product group.

Food, drink and tobacco: Exports f.o.b. ('000 million euros)

	2014	2015	2016		2014	2015	2016
Austria	9.7	10.0	10.3	Italy	31.0	33.4	34.7
Belgium	31.8	33.5	34.5	Latvia	2.0	1.9	2.0
Bulgaria	2.8	2.9	3.1	Lithuania	4.3	4.0	4.0
Croatia	1.2	1.5	1.7	Luxembourg	1.2	1.2	1.1
Cyprus	0.3	0.3	0.3	Malta	0.2	0.2	0.3
Czech Republic	5.7	6.4	6.6	Netherlands	64.9	66.3	69.4
Denmark	15.5	15.6	16.1	Poland	20.6	22.4	22.8
Estonia	1.1	1.1	1.0	Portugal	5.3	5.6	5.8
Finland	1.4	1.4	1.4	Romania	4.5	4.8	4.8
France	53.6	54.8	54.2	Slovakia	2.3	2.4	2.4
Germany	62.4	64.3	66.3	Slovenia	1.3	1.5	1.6
Greece	4.4	4.6	5.0	Spain	34.4	38.0	39.9
Hungary	6.4	6.6	6.6	Sweden	7.3	7.8	8.5
Ireland	10.4	11.1	11.4	United Kingdom	23.4	25.2	24.7

© European Union. Source: Eurostat, 2017, International trade, table *EXT_LT_INTERTRD*—International trade of EU, the euro area and the member states by SITC product group.

Mineral fuels, lubricants and related materials (SITC Section 3): Imports c.i.f. ('000 million euros)

	2014	2015	2016		2014	2015	2016
Austria	13.0	10.5	8.9	Italy	58.3	47.2	37.6
Belgium	55.9	41.1	33.9	Latvia	1.8	1.4	1.1
Bulgaria	5.2	4.1	3.2	Lithuania	6.0	5.1	4.4
Croatia	3.2	2.8	2.4	Luxembourg	2.3	1.7	1.3
Cyprus	1.3	1.1	1.1	Malta	1.5	1.2	1.1
Czech Republic	9.8	8.4	6.2	Netherlands	98.8	74.2	62.9
Denmark	6.3	5.0	4.0	Poland	17.6	12.8	10.7
Estonia	1.7	1.4	1.1	Portugal	10.2	8.0	6.2
Finland	11.3	7.7	7.2	Romania	5.5	4.0	3.8
France	72.3	53.8	42.8	Slovakia	6.3	5.3	4.4
Germany	113.1	88.8	70.4	Slovenia	3.0	2.6	2.1
Greece	16.3	11.3	9.7	Spain	54.6	38.5	29.6
Hungary	9.3	6.7	5.3	Sweden	16.6	12.1	11.3
Ireland	6.5	5.1	3.7	United Kingdom	60.6	45.8	35.5

© European Union. Source: Eurostat, 2017, International trade, table *EXT_LT_INTERTRD*—International trade of EU, the euro area and the member states by SITC product group.

Mineral fuels, lubricants and related materials: Exports f.o.b. ('000 million euros)

	2014	2015	2016		2014	2015	2016
Austria	3.2	2.7	2.3	Italy	15.9	14.1	11.4
Belgium	40.5	29.9	24.7	Latvia	0.8	0.7	0.5
Bulgaria	2.8	2.4	2.1	Lithuania	4.3	3.8	3.2
Croatia	1.4	1.3	1.2	Luxembourg	0.1	0.1	0.0
Cyprus	0.2	0.4	0.5	Malta	0.2	0.3	0.1
Czech Republic	3.6	4.3	2.9	Netherlands	88.3	67.0	58.4
Denmark	6.4	5.2	4.0	Poland	6.9	5.9	4.6
Estonia	1.3	1.1	0.9	Portugal	4.0	3.9	3.2
Finland	6.4	3.9	4.2	Romania	3.3	2.6	2.2
France	18.2	14.7	11.2	Slovakia	3.1	2.5	2.3
Germany	29.9	29.1	23.5	Slovenia	1.5	1.4	1.2
Greece	10.3	7.6	6.9	Spain	24.4	17.0	13.3
Hungary	2.8	2.1	1.7	Sweden	10.9	8.3	7.6
Ireland	1.2	1.1	0.8	United Kingdom	41.8	29.9	23.8

© European Union. Source: Eurostat, 2017, International trade, table *EXT_LT_INTERTRD*—International trade of EU, the euro area and the member states by SITC product group.

Chemicals and related products (SITC Section 5): Imports c.i.f. ('000 million euros)

	2014	2015	2016		2014	2015	2016
Austria	18.1	18.8	19.0	Italy	55.3	58.9	59.1
Belgium	81.8	87.8	84.6	Latvia	1.6	1.6	1.7
Bulgaria	3.3	3.7	3.9	Lithuania	3.6	3.9	3.8
Croatia	2.3	2.6	3.0	Luxembourg	2.0	2.1	2.2
Cyprus	0.6	0.6	0.6	Malta	0.4	0.4	0.4
Czech Republic	13.3	14.2	14.7	Netherlands	55.8	60.9	61.3
Denmark	9.4	9.7	9.6	Poland	24.2	24.8	26.3
Estonia	1.5	1.5	1.5	Portugal	8.0	8.5	8.7
Finland	6.5	7.0	6.7	Romania	8.0	8.6	9.1
France	71.4	72.0	70.7	Slovakia	5.4	5.8	6.1
Germany	121.8	130.8	134.6	Slovenia	3.5	3.8	3.9
Greece	6.7	6.8	6.9	Spain	39.0	42.3	41.0
Hungary	9.4	10.4	10.6	Sweden	14.6	14.6	14.2
Ireland	11.4	13.8	14.6	United Kingdom	62.8	69.3	66.1

© European Union. Source: Eurostat, 2017, International trade, table *EXT_LT_INTERTRD*—International trade of EU, the euro area and the member states by SITC product group.

Chemicals and related products: Exports f.o.b. ('000 million euros)

	2014	2015	2016		2014	2015	2016
Austria	18.2	18.3	18.2	Italy	49.9	50.4	52.5
Belgium	104.1	108.3	105.6	Latvia	0.9	0.9	1.0
Bulgaria	2.0	2.3	2.4	Lithuania	3.3	3.4	3.5
Croatia	1.1	1.4	1.6	Luxembourg	1.3	1.6	1.6
Cyprus	0.3	0.3	0.3	Malta	0.3	0.3	0.9
Czech Republic	8.4	8.5	8.6	Netherlands	81.6	86.3	85.7
Denmark	15.5	17.1	17.9	Poland	15.1	15.8	16.7
Estonia	0.7	0.7	0.7	Portugal	4.3	4.4	4.6
Finland	4.6	5.7	5.4	Romania	2.7	2.6	2.5
France	82.5	84.7	83.7	Slovakia	3.1	3.2	3.2
Germany	179.4	189.9	193.1	Slovenia	4.4	4.5	4.6
Greece	2.7	2.7	2.7	Spain	32.8	34.6	34.5
Hungary	9.3	10.2	10.3	Sweden	14.8	16.1	15.7
Ireland	51.6	64.2	66.3	United Kingdom	59.9	71.9	64.4

© European Union. Source: Eurostat, 2017, International trade, table *EXT_LT_INTERTRD*—International trade of EU, the euro area and the member states by SITC product group.

Machinery and transport equipment (SITC Section 7): Imports c.i.f. ('000 million euros)

	2014	2015	2016		2014	2015	2016
Austria	47.1	49.9	52.7	Italy	87.2	100.5	107.8
Belgium	76.5	81.2	85.1	Latvia	3.7	4.0	3.9
Bulgaria	6.4	7.0	7.2	Lithuania	6.3	6.4	6.8
Croatia	3.9	4.5	5.1	Luxembourg	7.0	8.2	7.2
Cyprus	1.0	1.0	1.8	Malta	1.9	2.3	2.7
Czech Republic	50.3	58.3	59.1	Netherlands	129.6	154.3	156.9
Denmark	23.5	25.1	25.7	Poland	56.9	64.7	63.6
Estonia	5.0	4.9	5.1	Portugal	15.2	16.8	18.6
Finland	17.1	18.6	19.6	Romania	20.9	23.5	25.6
France	169.3	184.4	195.1	Slovakia	27.2	31.2	32.8
Germany	317.3	349.2	362.5	Slovenia	8.3	9.1	9.7
Greece	8.6	8.8	9.7	Spain	74.8	88.8	93.4
Hungary	36.7	40.9	42.3	Sweden	44.6	48.1	49.9
Ireland	22.3	27.2	27.9	United Kingdom	183.9	213.9	211.3

© European Union. Source: Eurostat, 2017, International trade, table *EXT_LT_INTERTRD*—International trade of EU, the euro area and the member states by SITC product group.

External Trade STATISTICAL SURVEY

Machinery and transport equipment: Exports f.o.b. ('000 million euros)

	2014	2015	2016		2014	2015	2016
Austria	53.1	55.8	56.4	Italy	141.1	150.4	153.1
Belgium	72.7	77.3	80.6	Latvia	2.5	2.7	2.6
Bulgaria	4.3	4.7	4.9	Lithuania	4.9	4.2	4.3
Croatia	2.3	2.8	2.9	Luxembourg	4.9	5.5	4.7
Cyprus	0.2	0.4	0.3	Malta	1.0	0.9	0.9
Czech Republic	72.5	78.9	82.8	Netherlands	148.7	165.1	168.7
Denmark	22.0	22.6	22.6	Poland	62.7	69.0	69.7
Estonia	4.1	4.0	4.2	Portugal	12.2	12.9	13.4
Finland	16.3	17.1	15.9	Romania	22.2	24.3	26.9
France	164.9	178.3	181.0	Slovakia	37.4	40.0	42.5
Germany	546.8	593.5	602.9	Slovenia	10.2	11.1	11.6
Greece	2.3	2.6	2.6	Spain	77.8	86.6	90.9
Hungary	44.8	49.8	52.3	Sweden	46.8	49.6	50.3
Ireland	12.0	16.6	19.0	United Kingdom	132.5	147.5	146.1

© European Union. Source: Eurostat, 2017, International trade, table *EXT_LT_INTERTRD*—International trade of EU, the euro area and the member states by SITC product group.

Other manufactured products (SITC Sections 6 and 8): Imports c.i.f. ('000 million euros)

	2014	2015	2016		2014	2015	2016
Austria	41.0	42.8	43.7	Italy	97.3	103.9	102.5
Belgium	81.5	81.9	81.4	Latvia	3.6	3.5	3.5
Bulgaria	6.4	6.4	6.9	Lithuania	5.5	5.5	5.7
Croatia	5.3	5.9	6.3	Luxembourg	5.3	5.5	5.5
Cyprus	1.2	1.3	1.2	Malta	0.7	0.7	0.7
Czech Republic	32.6	35.7	37.7	Netherlands	93.0	102.6	104.4
Denmark	21.6	22.8	23.2	Poland	47.2	51.8	54.3
Estonia	3.5	3.4	3.6	Portugal	15.3	16.3	16.6
Finland	11.7	12.1	12.3	Romania	17.7	19.3	20.5
France	136.9	145.2	146.0	Slovakia	17.3	18.5	19.1
Germany	236.5	253.9	257.2	Slovenia	7.1	7.6	8.1
Greece	9.5	9.5	10.3	Spain	62.2	69.0	72.4
Hungary	17.5	18.8	19.8	Sweden	29.7	32.2	33.0
Ireland	11.0	12.6	12.7	United Kingdom	127.6	142.0	137.5

© European Union. Source: Eurostat, 2017, International trade, table *EXT_LT_INTERTRD*—International trade of EU, the euro area and the member states by SITC product group.

Other manufactured products: Exports f.o.b. ('000 million euros)

	2014	2015	2016		2014	2015	2016
Austria	44.9	45.7	44.9	Italy	146.0	149.0	150.0
Belgium	88.4	91.0	91.7	Latvia	3.2	3.2	3.2
Bulgaria	8.0	8.3	8.2	Lithuania	6.4	6.2	6.5
Croatia	3.4	3.7	4.0	Luxembourg	6.3	6.6	6.3
Cyprus	0.2	0.2	0.2	Malta	0.5	0.5	0.5
Czech Republic	36.9	39.6	41.7	Netherlands	93.1	98.8	102.3
Denmark	19.0	19.7	20.1	Poland	55.8	61.5	64.3
Estonia	3.6	3.7	3.8	Portugal	19.5	20.2	20.7
Finland	18.8	19.9	19.6	Romania	16.6	17.4	18.1
France	99.5	104.3	103.6	Slovakia	17.6	18.2	18.2
Germany	260.4	272.0	276.3	Slovenia	8.4	8.9	9.4
Greece	5.6	6.0	5.9	Spain	61.3	64.8	66.7
Hungary	17.4	17.8	18.7	Sweden	33.2	34.2	33.7
Ireland	13.9	16.1	16.4	United Kingdom	80.7	91.5	84.1

© European Union. Source: Eurostat, 2017, International trade, table *EXT_LT_INTERTRD*—International trade of EU, the euro area and the member states by SITC product group.

TRANSPORT

RAILWAYS

Total length of lines (kilometres)

	2013	2014	2015		2013	2014	2015
Austria	5,531	5,531	5,522	Latvia	1,859	1,860	1,860
Belgium	n.a.	n.a.	n.a.	Lithuania	1,768	1,768	1,877
Bulgaria	4,032	4,023	n.a.	Luxembourg	275	275	275
Croatia	2,722	2,604	2,604	Malta	–	–	–
Cyprus	–	–	–	Netherlands	3,013	3,032	n.a.
Czech Republic	9,560	9,559	9,566	Poland	19,328	19,240	19,231
Denmark	n.a.	n.a.	n.a.	Portugal	2,544.4	2,546	n.a.
Estonia	1,166	1,166	1,164	Romania	10,768	10,777	10,770
Finland	5,944	5,944	5,923	Slovakia	3,631	3,627	3,626
France	30,318	29,335	28,987	Slovenia	1,209	1,209	1,209
Germany	37,860	37,775	n.a.	Spain*	15,312	15,182	15,384
Greece	2,586	n.a.	2,240	Sweden	10,957	10,881	10,908
Hungary	7,357	8,017	7,197	United Kingdom	16,202	16,209	16,248
Ireland	1,931	1,931	1,931				
Italy	16,752	n.a.	n.a.	**Total (EU-28)**	n.a.	n.a.	n.a.

Note: There are no railways in Cyprus or Malta.
* Definition differs.
© European Union. Source: Eurostat, 2017, Transport, table *RAIL_IF_LINE_TR*—Railway transport—Length of lines, by number of tracks.

Lines by number of tracks, 2015 (kilometres)

	Single track	Double track or more	Total		Single track	Double track or more	Total
Austria	3,405	2,116	5,522	Latvia	1,493	367	1,860
Belgium	n.a.	n.a.	n.a.	Lithuania	1,447	431	1,877
Bulgaria	n.a.	n.a.	n.a.	Luxembourg	128	147	275
Croatia	2,350	254	2,604	Malta	–	–	–
Cyprus	–	–	–	Netherlands	n.a.	n.a.	n.a.
Czech Republic	7,602	1,964	9,566	Poland	10,505	8,726	19,231
Denmark	n.a.	n.a.	n.a.	Portugal	n.a.	n.a.	n.a.
Estonia	1,062	102	1,164	Romania	7,715	2,917	10,770
Finland	5,280	643	5,923	Slovakia	2,609	1,017	3,626
France	12,096	16,826	28,987	Slovenia	879	330	1,209
Germany	n.a.	n.a.	n.a.	Spain*	9,647	5,737	15,384
Greece	1,716	524	2,240	Sweden	8,945	1,964	10,908
Hungary	5,992	1,205	7,197	United Kingdom	n.a.	n.a.	16,248
Ireland	1,208	723	1,931				
Italy	n.a.	n.a.	n.a.	**Total (EU-28)**	n.a.	n.a.	n.a.

* Definition differs.
© European Union. Source: Eurostat, 2017, Transport, table *RAIL_IF_LINE_TR*—Railway transport—Length of lines, by number of tracks.

Electrification of lines, 2015 (kilometres)

	Electrified	Non-electrified	Total		Electrified	Non-electrified	Total
Austria	3,905	1,617	5,522	Latvia	251	1,609	1,860
Belgium	n.a.	n.a.	n.a.	Lithuania	122	1,755	1,877
Bulgaria	n.a.	n.a.	n.a.	Luxembourg	262	13	275
Croatia	970	1,634	2,604	Malta	–	–	–
Cyprus	–	–	–	Netherlands	n.a.	n.a.	n.a.
Czech Republic	3,237	6,329	9,566	Poland	11,865	7,366	19,231
Denmark	n.a.	n.a.	n.a.	Portugal	n.a.	n.a.	n.a.
Estonia	132	1,032	1,164	Romania	4,030	6,740	10,770
Finland	3,262	2,661	5,923	Slovakia	1,587	2,039	3,626
France	16,008	12,979	28,987	Slovenia	500	709	1,209
Germany	n.a.	n.a.	n.a.	Spain*	9,717	5,667	15,384
Greece	494	1,746	2,240	Sweden	8,235	2,673	10,908
Hungary	2,963	4,234	7,197	United Kingdom	5,440	10,808	16,248
Ireland	145	1,786	1,931				
Italy	n.a.	n.a.	n.a.	**Total (EU-28)**	n.a.	n.a.	n.a.

* Definition differs.
© European Union. Source: Eurostat, 2017, Transport, table *RAIL_IF_LINE_TR*—Railway transport—Length of lines, by number of tracks.

Total number of locomotives in use

	2013	2014	2015		2013	2014	2015
Austria	1,366	1,367	1,314	Latvia	257	254	255
Belgium	n.a.	n.a.	n.a.	Lithuania	267	239	229
Bulgaria	458	n.a.	n.a.	Luxembourg	n.a.	n.a.	n.a.
Croatia	266	266	263	Malta	—	—	—
Cyprus	—	—	—	Netherlands	n.a.	n.a.	n.a.
Czech Republic	1,932	1,895	n.a.	Poland	4,032	4,143	4,033
Denmark	n.a.	n.a.	n.a.	Portugal	n.a.	170	n.a.
Estonia	294	297	287	Romania	1,795	1,779	1,795
Finland	465	459	456	Slovakia	984	973	952
France	3,601	3,558	3,569	Slovenia	156	156	156
Germany	n.a.	n.a.	n.a.	Spain	n.a.	n.a.	n.a.
Greece	179	n.a.	n.a.	Sweden	647	648	622
Hungary	1,131	1,166	1,153	United Kingdom	n.a.	n.a.	n.a.
Ireland	56	56	56				
Italy	n.a.	n.a.	n.a.	**Total (EU-28)**	n.a.	n.a.	n.a.

© European Union. Source: Eurostat, 2017, Transport, table *RAIL_EQ_LOCON*—Number of locomotives and railcars, by source of power.

Total number of railcars in use

	2013	2014	2015		2013	2014	2015
Austria	657	666	658	Latvia	104	104	104
Belgium	n.a.	n.a.	n.a.	Lithuania	53	51	48
Bulgaria	102	n.a.	n.a.	Luxembourg	n.a.	n.a.	n.a.
Croatia	129	129	145	Malta	—	—	—
Cyprus	—	—	—	Netherlands	n.a.	n.a.	n.a.
Czech Republic	1,002	994	n.a.	Poland	1,489	1,472	1,493
Denmark	n.a.	n.a.	n.a.	Portugal	n.a.	257	n.a.
Estonia	65	71	71	Romania	327	346	300
Finland	187	194	194	Slovakia	228	236	251
France	3,725	3,866	4,045	Slovenia	109	109	108
Germany	n.a.	n.a.	n.a.	Spain	n.a.	n.a.	n.a.
Greece	129	n.a.	n.a.	Sweden	1,684	1,768	1,800
Hungary	431	460	515	United Kingdom	n.a.	n.a.	n.a.
Ireland	426	426	426				
Italy	n.a.	n.a.	n.a.	**Total (EU-28)**	n.a.	n.a.	n.a.

© European Union. Source: Eurostat, 2017, Transport, table *RAIL_EQ_LOCON*—Number of locomotives and railcars, by source of power.

Passenger coaches in use

	2013	2014	2015		2013	2014	2015
Austria	n.a.	n.a.	n.a.	Latvia	n.a.	n.a.	136
Belgium	n.a.	n.a.	n.a.	Lithuania*	30	28	27
Bulgaria	760	n.a.	n.a.	Luxembourg	n.a.	n.a.	n.a.
Croatia	364	356	356	Malta	—	—	—
Cyprus	—	—	—	Netherlands	n.a.	n.a.	n.a.
Czech Republic	1,993	n.a.	n.a.	Poland	2,700	2,404	2,193
Denmark	n.a.	n.a.	n.a.	Portugal	n.a.	890	n.a.
Estonia	63	63	63	Romania	291	291	291
Finland	505	498	449	Slovakia	803	769	780
France	6,318	6,291	6,290	Slovenia	102	102	100
Germany	n.a.	n.a.	n.a.	Spain	n.a.	n.a.	n.a.
Greece	n.a.	n.a.	n.a.	Sweden	371	354	365
Hungary	2,293	2,254	2,245	United Kingdom	n.a.	n.a.	n.a.
Ireland	n.a.	n.a.	n.a.				
Italy	n.a.	n.a.	n.a.	**Total (EU-28)**	n.a.	n.a.	n.a.

* Definition differs.

© European Union. Source: Eurostat, 2017, Transport, table *RAIL_EQ_PA_NTY*—Passenger railway vehicles, by type of vehicle.

STATISTICAL SURVEY — Transport

Railcar trailers for passenger transport

	2013	2014	2015		2013	2014	2015
Austria	n.a.	n.a.	n.a.	Latvia	238	238	238
Belgium	n.a.	n.a.	n.a.	Lithuania*	156	133	121
Bulgaria	102	n.a.	n.a.	Luxembourg	n.a.	n.a.	n.a.
Croatia	129	129	145	Malta	—	—	—
Cyprus	—	—	—	Netherlands	n.a.	n.a.	n.a.
Czech Republic	2,180	n.a.	n.a.	Poland	4,395	4,600	4,820
Denmark	n.a.	n.a.	n.a.	Portugal	n.a.	108	n.a.
Estonia	80	85	85	Romania	3,296	3,336	3,234
Finland	512	546	546	Slovakia	0	0	0
France	9,389	9,913	10,646	Slovenia	253	253	249
Germany	n.a.	n.a.	n.a.	Spain	n.a.	n.a.	n.a.
Greece	n.a.	n.a.	n.a.	Sweden	2,206	2,307	2,347
Hungary	204	184	281	United Kingdom	n.a.	n.a.	n.a.
Ireland	n.a.	n.a.	n.a.	**Total (EU-28)**	n.a.	n.a.	n.a.
Italy	n.a.	n.a.	n.a.				

* Definition differs.

© European Union. Source: Eurostat, 2017, Transport, table *RAIL_EQ_PA_NTY*—Passenger railway vehicles, by type of vehicle.

Railway wagons in use

	2013	2014	2015		2013	2014	2015
Austria	20,108	19,771	19,294	Latvia	11,092	12,420	11,888
Belgium	n.a.	n.a.	n.a.	Lithuania	13,369	13,018	12,792
Bulgaria	9,907	n.a.	n.a.	Luxembourg	3,255	n.a.	n.a.
Croatia	5,959	5,518	5,519	Malta	—	—	—
Cyprus	—	—	—	Netherlands	n.a.	n.a.	n.a.
Czech Republic	33,289	n.a.	n.a.	Poland	87,726	87,538	86,364
Denmark	n.a.	n.a.	n.a.	Portugal	n.a.	3,283	n.a.
Estonia	22,285	21,188	21,501	Romania	39,832	35,385	34,254
Finland	9,457	9,078	8,854	Slovakia	15,982	14,970	15,533
France	90,638	85,539	80,915	Slovenia	3,550	3,483	3,386
Germany	n.a.	n.a.	n.a.	Spain	n.a.	n.a.	n.a.
Greece	3,184	n.a.	n.a.	Sweden	n.a.	n.a.	n.a.
Hungary	10,217	9,509	8,916	United Kingdom	n.a.	n.a.	n.a.
Ireland	254	254	254	**Total (EU-28)**	n.a.	n.a.	n.a.
Italy	n.a.	n.a.	n.a.				

© European Union. Source: Eurostat, 2017, Transport, table *RAIL_EQ_WAGON_N*—Number of wagons, by status of enterprise.

Total railway passenger journeys (national transport) ('000)

	2013	2014	2015		2013	2014	2015
Austria	225,063	222,381	230,921	Latvia	19,419	18,938	16,885
Belgium	n.a.	n.a.	n.a.	Lithuania	3,807	3,672	3,430
Bulgaria	25,727	24,325	22,284	Luxembourg	14,838	15,466	16,133
Croatia	23,810	21,528	21,331	Malta	—	—	—
Cyprus	—	—	—	Netherlands*	n.a.	n.a.	n.a.
Czech Republic	170,790	172,255	171,976	Poland	255,619	250,460	263,178
Denmark	181,151	197,549	n.a.	Portugal	125,945	128,139	130,195
Estonia	4,077	5,808	6,604	Romania	56,188	64,525	61,001
Finland	68,720	67,744	75,524	Slovakia	42,608	45,706	56,991
France	1,122,265	1,114,684	1,197,822	Slovenia	15,563	14,054	13,792
Germany	2,597,616	2,678,025	n.a.	Spain	558,239	558,301	560,934
Greece	13,191	13,356	16,008	Sweden	188,450	195,022	201,745
Hungary	145,575	143,407	n.a.	United Kingdom	1,579,843	1,659,637	1,702,234
Ireland	36,361	37,804	39,347	**Total (EU-28)**	n.a.	n.a.	n.a.
Italy	811,391	818,577	826,020				

* Confidential.

© European Union. Source: Eurostat, 2017, Transport, table *RAIL_PA_TYPEPAS*—Railway transport—Passenger transport by type of transport (detailed reporting only).

Total railway passenger traffic (million passenger-kilometres)

	2013	2014	2015		2013	2014	2015
Austria	11,188	11,345	11,433	Latvia	721	644	590
Belgium	n.a.	n.a.	n.a.	Lithuania	278	270	262
Bulgaria	1,821	1,698	1,549	Luxembourg	394	366	418
Croatia	935	917	941	Malta	—	—	—
Cyprus	—	—	—	Netherlands*	n.a.	n.a.	n.a.
Czech Republic	7,512	7,644	8,125	Poland	16,453	15,479	17,024
Denmark	6,566	6,804	n.a.	Portugal	3,649	3,852	3,957
Estonia	223	280	286	Romania	4,352	4,971	4,910
Finland	4,053	3,874	4,114	Slovakia	2,485	2,583	3,411
France	90,485	89,499	91,653	Slovenia	679	620	628
Germany	89,450	90,978	n.a.	Spain	23,660	24,915	26,018
Greece	1,056	1,072	1,263	Sweden	11,842	12,121	12,741
Hungary	7,806	7,710	n.a.	United Kingdom	61,950	64,711	66,399
Ireland	1,569	1,728	1,918				
Italy	47,707	48,881	51,121	**Total (EU-28)**	n.a.	n.a.	n.a.

* Confidential.

© European Union. Source: Eurostat, 2017, Transport, table *RAIL_PA_TYPEPKM*—Railway transport—Passenger transport by type of transport.

Goods carried in national railway transport ('000 metric tons)

	2013	2014	2015		2013	2014	2015
Austria	28,769	29,384	28,918	Latvia	1,178	1,257	1,672
Belgium*	n.a.	n.a.	n.a.	Lithuania	15,129	14,487	14,426
Bulgaria	10,152	10,361	10,296	Luxembourg	1,050	956	1,579
Croatia	3,395	2,858	3,038	Malta	—	—	—
Cyprus	—	—	—	Netherlands	3,247	3,267	3,133
Czech Republic	37,270	40,656	42,069	Poland	180,412	173,563	171,709
Denmark	711	932	1,111	Portugal	7,908	8,593	9,363
Estonia	22,451	20,523	15,119	Romania	41,268	41,549	43,431
Finland	22,791	22,742	20,692	Slovakia	8,182	10,434	8,055
France	60,369	57,754	60,729	Slovenia	3,318	3,196	2,953
Germany	247,472	238,687	241,671	Spain	20,771	23,797	23,987
Greece	174	232	129	Sweden	36,514	37,331	36,303
Hungary	12,461	15,020	14,409	United Kingdom	114,824	104,966	95,813
Ireland	589	578	362				
Italy	30,832	32,318	33,149	**Total (EU-28)**	911,238	n.a.	n.a.

* Confidential.

© European Union. Source: Eurostat, 2017, Transport, table *RAIL_GO_TYPEALL*—Goods transported by type of transport.

Goods traffic in national railway transport (million ton-kilometres)

	2013	2014	2015		2013	2014	2015
Austria	4,634	4,717	4,579	Latvia	286	315	453
Belgium*	n.a.	n.a.	n.a.	Lithuania	3,645	3,513	3,500
Bulgaria	2,376	2,557	2,514	Luxembourg	23	21	19
Croatia	914	836	909	Malta	—	—	—
Cyprus	—	—	—	Netherlands	538	542	466
Czech Republic	5,544	5,617	5,534	Poland	36,273	35,288	36,318
Denmark	141	168	203	Portugal	1,815	1,896	2,105
Estonia	678	609	515	Romania	10,410	9,809	9,957
Finland	6,503	6,336	5,847	Slovakia	1,197	1,384	1,148
France	20,289	20,137	21,373	Slovenia	652	661	599
Germany	57,585	56,387	59,433	Spain	7,445	8,614	9,136
Greece	35	70	50	Sweden	13,129	13,456	12,800
Hungary	1,606	2,049	1,784	United Kingdom	21,955	21,583	21,529
Ireland	99	100	46				
Italy	9,122	10,092	10,509	**Total (EU-28)**	n.a.	n.a.	n.a.

* Confidential.

© European Union. Source: Eurostat, 2017, Transport, table *RAIL_GO_TYPEALL*—Goods transported by type of transport.

ROAD TRANSPORT

Length of motorways (kilometres)

	2013	2014	2015		2013	2014	2015
Austria	1,719	1,719	n.a.	Latvia	0	0	0
Belgium	n.a.	n.a.	n.a.	Lithuania	309	309	309
Bulgaria	605	610	n.a.	Luxembourg	152	152	161
Croatia	1,289	1,290	1,310	Malta	n.a.	n.a.	n.a.
Cyprus	257	257	272	Netherlands	2,666	2,678	2,730
Czech Republic	776	776	776	Poland	1,482	1,556	1,559
Denmark	n.a.	n.a.	n.a.	Portugal*	3,035	3,065	n.a.
Estonia	140	141	147	Romania	644	683	747
Finland	810	881	881	Slovakia	420	420	463
France	11,552	11,560	11,599	Slovenia	770	770†	773‡
Germany	12,917	12,949	12,993	Spain*	14,981	15,049	15,336
Greece	n.a.	n.a.	n.a.	Sweden	2,044	2,088	2,119
Hungary	1,767	1,782	1,884	United Kingdom‡	3,756	3,760	3,768
Ireland	897	897	916				
Italy	6,751	6,844	n.a.	**Total (EU-28)**	n.a.	n.a.	n.a.

* Definition differs. † Provisional. ‡ Estimate(s).
© European Union. Source: Eurostat, 2017, Transport, table *ROAD_IF_MOTORWA*—Length of motorways and e-roads.

Length of e-roads* (kilometres)

	2013	2014	2015		2013	2014	2015
Austria	2,248	2,248	n.a.	Latvia	202	202	202
Belgium	n.a.	n.a.	n.a.	Lithuania	1,639	1,639	1,639
Bulgaria	2,899	2,926	n.a.	Luxembourg	n.a.	n.a.	n.a.
Croatia	2,200	2,251	2,251	Malta	n.a.	n.a.	n.a.
Cyprus	n.a.	n.a.	n.a.	Netherlands	n.a.	n.a.	n.a.
Czech Republic	2,632	2,628	2,628	Poland	5,500	5,500	5,500
Denmark	n.a.	n.a.	n.a.	Portugal	2,241	2,241	n.a.
Estonia	995	995	953	Romania	6,269	6,194	6,193
Finland	4,210	4,216	4,286	Slovakia	1,528	1,524	1,520
France	1,071,823	1,081,664	1,086,219	Slovenia	729	729	728
Germany	n.a.	n.a.	n.a.	Spain	n.a.	n.a.	n.a.
Greece	n.a.	n.a.	n.a.	Sweden	6,745	6,742	6,744
Hungary	2,352	2,345	2,348	United Kingdom	n.a.	n.a.	n.a.
Ireland	n.a.	n.a.	n.a.				
Italy	n.a.	n.a.	n.a.	**Total (EU-28)**	n.a.	n.a.	n.a.

* The international e-road network consists of a system of reference roads as laid down in the European Agreement on Main International Arteries (Geneva, Switzerland, 15 November 1975) and its amendments.
© European Union. Source: Eurostat, 2017, Transport, table *ROAD_IF_MOTORWA*—Length of motorways and e-roads.

Length of other roads (kilometres)

	2013	2014	2015		2013	2014	2015
Austria	122,872	122,869	n.a.	Latvia	58,573	58,628	58,243
Belgium	n.a.	n.a.	n.a.	Lithuania	84,159	84,725	84,624
Bulgaria	19,073	19,118	n.a.	Luxembourg	2,899	2,899	n.a.
Croatia	25,525	25,488	25,396	Malta†	2,410	2,854	2,854
Cyprus	12,590	12,605	12,614	Netherlands‡	129,204	129,436	n.a.
Czech Republic	129,904	129,891	129,880	Poland	413,530	415,470	419,636
Denmark	n.a.	n.a.	n.a.	Portugal‡	11,245	11,245	n.a.
Estonia	58,827	58,984	58,828	Romania	84,243	84,679	85,333
Finland	106,760	106,809	105,118	Slovakia	42,943	42,938	42,951
France	1,060,271	1,070,103	1,074,619	Slovenia	38,104	38,110*	38,124†
Germany	n.a.	n.a.	n.a.	Spain‡	150,380	151,235	150,667
Greece	n.a.	n.a.	n.a.	Sweden	212,836	212,964	212,972
Hungary	203,309	204,057	202,998	United Kingdom†	417,193	417,367	417,491
Ireland	95,102*	95,102	97,982				
Italy	249,288	248,846	n.a.	**Total (EU-28)**	n.a.	n.a.	n.a.

* Provisional. † Estimate(s).
‡ Definition differs.
© European Union. Source: Eurostat, 2017, Transport, table *ROAD_IF_ROADSC*—Length of other roads by category of roads.

Stock of road vehicles: Mopeds ('000)

	2013	2014	2015		2013	2014	2015
Austria	293	287	281	Latvia	25	27	28
Belgium	n.a.	n.a.	n.a.	Lithuania	21	10	11
Bulgaria	65	69	n.a.	Luxembourg	9	n.a.	n.a.
Croatia	97	94	90	Malta	0	0	0
Cyprus	15	14	13	Netherlands	1,102	n.a.	n.a.
Czech Republic*	480	479	485	Poland	1,163	1,217	1,259
Denmark	n.a.	n.a.	n.a.	Portugal	n.a.	n.a.	n.a.
Estonia	14	15	16	Romania*	7	7	7
Finland	303	311	317	Slovakia	32	32	32
France	n.a.	n.a.	n.a.	Slovenia	41	41	42
Germany	n.a.	n.a.	n.a.	Spain*	2,107	2,061	2,023
Greece	n.a.	n.a.	n.a.	Sweden*	73	75	76
Hungary	n.a.	n.a.	n.a.	United Kingdom*	75	n.a.	64
Ireland	2	2	2				
Italy	2,256	2,517	n.a.	**Total (EU-28)**	n.a.	n.a.	n.a.

* Definition differs.
© European Union. Source: Eurostat, 2017, Transport, table *ROAD_EQS_MOPEDS*—Mopeds and motorcycles, by type of motor energy.

Stock of road vehicles: Motorcycles ('000)

	2013	2014	2015		2013	2014	2015
Austria	450	468	485	Latvia	19	20	21
Belgium	451	457	466	Lithuania	46	23	27
Bulgaria	82	88	n.a.	Luxembourg	17	n.a.	n.a.
Croatia	60	61	63	Malta	17	18	20
Cyprus	25	27	26	Netherlands	654	n.a.	n.a.
Czech Republic	977	999	1,046	Poland	1,153	1,190	1,272
Denmark	n.a.	n.a.	n.a.	Portugal	n.a.	n.a.	n.a.
Estonia	25	27	n.a.	Romania	95	100*	106*
Finland	252	257	260	Slovakia	74	81	89
France	n.a.	n.a.	n.a.	Slovenia	52	55	58
Germany	4,055	4,145	4,228	Spain*	2,891	2,972	3,079
Greece	1,569	1,593	1,620	Sweden	285	289	292
Hungary	157	162	163	United Kingdom	1,145	n.a.	1,167*
Ireland	35	35	35				
Italy	6,482	6,506	n.a.	**Total (EU-28)**	n.a.	n.a.	n.a.

* Definition differs.
© European Union. Source: Eurostat, 2017, Transport, table *ROAD_EQS_MOTORC*—Motorcycles, by power of vehicles.

Stock of road vehicles: Passenger motor cars ('000)

	2013	2014	2015		2013	2014	2015
Austria	4,641	4,695	4,748	Latvia	635	658	679
Belgium	5,493	5,555	5,624	Lithuania	1,809	1,206	1,244
Bulgaria	2,910	3,014	n.a.	Luxembourg	363	373	381
Croatia	1,448	1,474	1,500	Malta	256	266	275
Cyprus	475	478	488	Netherlands	7,932	n.a.	n.a.
Czech Republic	4,729	4,833	5,115	Poland	19,389	20,004	20,723
Denmark	n.a.	n.a.	n.a.	Portugal	4,327	4,700	n.a.
Estonia	629	653	677	Romania*	4,696	4,908	5,155
Finland	3,106	3,173	3,235	Slovakia	1,880	1,949	2,035
France	32,858	32,531	32,326	Slovenia	1,064	1,068	1,079
Germany	43,851	44,403	45,071	Spain*	22,025	22,030	22,356
Greece	5,124	5,111	5,108	Sweden	4,495	4,585	4,668
Hungary	3,041	3,108	3,197	United Kingdom	n.a.	n.a.	30,250*
Ireland	1,985	2,018	2,060				
Italy	36,963	37,081	n.a.	**Total (EU-28)**	n.a.	n.a.	n.a.

* Definition differs.
© European Union. Source: Eurostat, 2017, Transport, table *ROAD_EQS_CARMOT*—Passenger cars, by motor energy.

STATISTICAL SURVEY

Transport

Passenger motor cars per 1,000 inhabitants

	2013	2014	2015		2013	2014	2015
Austria	546	547	546	Latvia	317	331	345
Belgium	491	494	497	Lithuania	615	413	431
Bulgaria	402	418	n.a.	Luxembourg	661	662	661
Croatia	341	349	358	Malta	602	619	634
Cyprus	553	565	575	Netherlands	471	n.a.	n.a.
Czech Republic	450	459	485	Poland	510	526	546
Denmark	n.a.	n.a.	n.a.	Portugal	415	453	n.a.
Estonia	478	497	514	Romania	235	247	261
Finland	570	580	590	Slovakia	347	360	375
France	498	489	484	Slovenia	516	518	523
Germany	543	547	548	Spain	474	474	481
Greece	469	471	474	Sweden	466	470	474
Hungary	308	315	325	United Kingdom	n.a.	n.a.	463
Ireland	431	436	436				
Italy	608	610	n.a.	**Total (EU-28)**	n.a.	n.a.	n.a.

© European Union. Source: Eurostat, 2017, Transport, table *ROAD_EQS_CARHAB*—Passenger cars per 1,000 inhabitants.

Stock of road vehicles: Motor coaches, buses and trolley buses (number)

	2013	2014	2015		2013	2014	2015
Austria	9,579	9,585	9,679	Latvia	5,253	5,102	5,066
Belgium	15,822	15,976	16,094	Lithuania	13,063	7,371	7,286
Bulgaria	23,259	23,603	n.a.	Luxembourg	1,759	1,778	1,857
Croatia	4,789	5,040	5,276	Malta	1,705	1,789	1,955
Cyprus	3,495	2,581	2,712	Netherlands	9,922	n.a.	n.a.
Czech Republic	20,318	20,511	20,667	Poland	n.a.	106,387	110,186
Denmark	n.a.	n.a.	n.a.	Portugal	12,111	14,941	n.a.
Estonia	4,587	4,706	4,845	Romania	42,836	44,283	47,347
Finland	15,485	16,202	16,812	Slovakia	9,071	9,159	9,270
France	95,743	96,467	98,746	Slovenia	2,465	2,559	2,631
Germany	76,794	77,501	78,345	Spain*	59,892	59,799	60,252
Greece	27,149	27,047	26,942	Sweden	13,981	13,987	14,109
Hungary*	17,569	17,923	18,135	United Kingdom*	n.a.	n.a.	162,696
Ireland	10,155	10,407	10,878				
Italy	98,551	97,914	n.a.	**Total (EU-28)**	n.a.	n.a.	n.a.

* Definition differs.

© European Union. Source: Eurostat, 2017, Transport, table *ROAD_EQS_BUSMOT*—Motor coaches, buses and trolley buses, by type of motor energy.

Stock of road vehicles: Lorries (number)

	2013	2014	2015		2013	2014	2015
Austria	53,346	52,908	52,352	Latvia	33,976*	20,021	19,198
Belgium	n.a.	n.a.	n.a.	Lithuania	34,628	20,493*	20,770
Bulgaria*	348,834	369,189	n.a.	Luxembourg	5,298	5,311	5,404
Croatia	130,547*	132,045*	29,473	Malta	9,830	9,920	9,941
Cyprus	10,142	9,407	9,473	Netherlands	65,046	n.a.	n.a.
Czech Republic	187,864	n.a.	221,650	Poland	627,649	638,104	650,612
Denmark	n.a.	n.a.	n.a.	Portugal	50,111	51,562	n.a.
Estonia	24,521	24,807	24,974	Romania	n.a.	n.a.	n.a.
Finland	n.a.	137,285	141,197	Slovakia*	288,436	293,118	302,455
France	348,715	344,215	337,159	Slovenia	n.a.	n.a.	n.a.
Germany	531,000	n.a.	n.a.	Spain*	n.a.	332,568	332,422
Greece	n.a.	n.a.	n.a.	Sweden	66,807	67,313	67,599
Hungary	46,874	46,258	45,166	United Kingdom	n.a.	n.a.	360,695*
Ireland	n.a.	19,731	19,143				
Italy	619,035	n.a.	n.a.	**Total (EU-28)**	n.a.	n.a.	n.a.

Note: Excludes light goods road vehicles.
* Definition differs.

© European Union. Source: Eurostat, 2017, Transport, table *ROAD_EQS_LORNUM*—Lorries by permissible maximum gross weight.

New registrations of passenger motor cars (number)

	2013	2014	2015		2013	2014	2015
Austria	319,035	303,318	308,555	Latvia	55,808	13,173*	14,291
Belgium	490,369	487,711	506,284	Lithuania*	155,855	136,098	131,606
Bulgaria	199,963	211,033	n.a.	Luxembourg	46,624	49,793	46,473
Croatia	46,563	68,522	74,181	Malta	13,094	15,439	16,803
Cyprus	14,771	17,933	21,462	Netherlands	416,717	n.a.	n.a.
Czech Republic	164,627	192,923	229,731	Poland	987,809	1,047,598	1,145,506
Denmark	n.a.	n.a.	n.a.	Portugal	n.a.	199,288	n.a.
Estonia	19,690	21,128	21,064	Romania	279,740	n.a.	332,223
Finland	103,450	106,235	108,819	Slovakia	113,876	125,813	137,751
France	1,756,953	1,765,855	1,886,229	Slovenia	51,968	54,086	60,668
Germany	2,952,431	3,036,773	3,206,042	Spain*	742,305	890,125	1,094,117
Greece*	64,932	84,445	96,151	Sweden	292,162	324,030	361,908
Hungary*	126,937	164,420	199,906	United Kingdom*	n.a.	n.a.	2,602,146
Ireland	74,960	84,136	129,959				
Italy	1,311,334	n.a.	n.a.	**Total (EU-28)**	n.a.	n.a.	n.a.

* Definition differs.
© European Union. Source: Eurostat, 2017, Transport, table *ROAD_EQR_CARMOT*—New registrations of passenger cars by type of motor energy and engine size.

New registrations of passenger motor cars by type of motor energy, 2015 ('000)

	Petrol	Diesel	Total		Petrol	Diesel	Total
Austria	125,656	180,510	308,555	Latvia	7,211	6,923	14,291
Belgium	198,299	305,838	506,284	Lithuania*	33,550	97,813	131,606
Bulgaria	n.a.	n.a.	n.a.	Luxembourg	n.a.	n.a.	46,473
Croatia	16,311	56,807	74,181	Malta	11,395	5,312	16,803
Cyprus	14,786	6,667	21,462	Netherlands	n.a.	n.a.	n.a.
Czech Republic	n.a.	n.a.	229,731	Poland	571,541	481,006	1,145,506
Denmark	n.a.	n.a.	n.a.	Portugal	n.a.	n.a.	n.a.
Estonia	14,069	6,949	21,064	Romania	148,062	181,809	332,223
Finland	69,469	38,844	108,819	Slovakia	n.a.	n.a.	137,751
France	777,645	1,089,403	1,886,229	Slovenia	29,038	31,031	60,668
Germany	1,611,389	1,538,451	3,206,042	Spain*	394,777	694,161	1,094,117
Greece*	n.a.	n.a.	96,151	Sweden	145,383	207,091	361,908
Hungary*	92,477	103,928	199,906	United Kingdom*	1,334,875	1,257,152	2,602,146
Ireland	35,311	92,436	129,959				
Italy	n.a.	n.a.	n.a.	**Total (EU-28)**	n.a.	n.a.	n.a.

* Definition differs.
© European Union. Source: Eurostat, 2017, Transport, table *ROAD_EQR_CARMOT*—New registrations of passenger cars by type of motor energy and engine size.

Goods carried in national road transport ('000 metric tons)

	2013	2014	2015		2013	2014	2015
Austria	300,241	323,229	325,651	Latvia	53,573	55,572	53,174
Belgium	248,857	250,707	211,577	Lithuania	31,637	34,919	34,564
Bulgaria	138,756	134,264	134,361	Luxembourg	22,585	28,518	25,502
Croatia	60,376	57,605	55,904	Malta	n.a.	n.a.	n.a.
Cyprus	16,099	14,569	14,384	Netherlands	505,018	502,743	508,461
Czech Republic	289,114	324,080	375,533	Poland	1,117,001	1,107,702	1,060,300
Denmark	165,532	171,259	175,131	Portugal	122,577	124,164	126,967
Estonia	25,544	21,446	22,285	Romania	169,710	165,670	167,909
Finland	269,473	273,911	267,495	Slovakia	92,402	101,173	100,698
France	1,953,814	1,871,576	1,756,053	Slovenia	42,608	50,698	43,530
Germany	2,809,778	2,924,711	2,910,116	Spain	1,059,727	1,116,693	1,186,869
Greece	477,627	400,465	416,675	Sweden	276,659	375,707	416,940
Hungary	136,738	159,797	164,198	United Kingdom	1,486,847	1,488,393	1,650,109
Ireland	101,151	106,577	110,207				
Italy	998,420	937,415	934,839	**Total (EU-28)**	n.a.	n.a.	n.a.

© European Union. Source: Eurostat, 2017, Transport, table *ROAD_GO_NA_TGTT*—National annual transport by group of goods and type of transport.

Goods traffic in national road transport (million ton-kilometres)

	2013	2014	2015		2013	2014	2015
Austria	13,486	14,077	14,782	Latvia	2,742	2,671	2,678
Belgium	23,412	23,698	23,230	Lithuania	2,519	2,748	2,893
Bulgaria	7,305	6,921	7,233	Luxembourg	777	1,127	698
Croatia	4,281	3,927	4,053	Malta	n.a.	n.a.	n.a.
Cyprus	618	526	548	Netherlands	33,091	32,993	32,527
Czech Republic	15,391	16,812	21,227	Poland	100,316	96,624	104,675
Denmark	12,218	12,944	12,532	Portugal	9,709	9,863	10,775
Estonia	1,587	1,532	1,511	Romania	12,503	12,132	12,061
Finland	20,969	20,299	21,434	Slovakia	4,532	5,046	5,211
France	155,727	151,124	141,250	Slovenia	1,869	2,030	2,033
Germany	246,957	253,907	260,161	Spain	126,994	128,154	137,233
Greece	14,291	14,886	15,028	Sweden	28,147	35,749	37,550
Hungary	9,124	9,518	10,227	United Kingdom	146,725	142,421	160,282
Ireland	6,980	7,469	7,522				
Italy	111,971	102,348	104,101	**Total (EU-28)**	n.a.	n.a.	n.a.

© European Union. Source: Eurostat, 2017, Transport, table *ROAD_GO_NA_TGTT*—National annual transport by group of goods and type of transport.

INLAND WATERWAYS

Number of self-propelled vessels

	2013	2014	2015		2013	2014	2015
Austria	n.a.	n.a.	n.a.	Latvia	n.a.	n.a.	n.a.
Belgium	922	874	n.a.	Lithuania*	33	36	35
Bulgaria*	24	31	n.a.	Luxembourg	n.a.	n.a.	n.a.
Croatia	13	17	19	Malta	n.a.	n.a.	n.a.
Cyprus	n.a.	n.a.	n.a.	Netherlands	n.a.	n.a.	n.a.
Czech Republic*	32	33	30	Poland	71	79	89
Denmark	n.a.	n.a.	n.a.	Portugal	n.a.	n.a.	n.a.
Estonia	9	n.a.	n.a.	Romania	120	128	154
Finland	151	194	197	Slovakia	31	23	23
France	876	851	804	Slovenia	n.a.	n.a.	n.a.
Germany	1,253	1,204	1,168	Spain	n.a.	n.a.	n.a.
Greece	n.a.	n.a.	n.a.	Sweden	n.a.	n.a.	n.a.
Hungary	72	71	70	United Kingdom†	158	158	158
Ireland	n.a.	n.a.	n.a.				
Italy	58	66	n.a.	**Total (EU-28)**	n.a.	n.a.	n.a.

* Definition differs. † Estimates.
© European Union. Source: Eurostat, 2017, Transport, table *IWW_EQ_LOADCAP*—Self-propelled vessels, dumb and pushed vessels by load capacity.

Number of dumb and pushed vessels

	2013	2014	2015		2013	2014	2015
Austria	n.a.	n.a.	n.a.	Latvia	n.a.	n.a.	n.a.
Belgium	265	263	n.a.	Lithuania*	41	50	50
Bulgaria*	127	117	n.a.	Luxembourg	n.a.	n.a.	n.a.
Croatia	119	109	111	Malta	n.a.	n.a.	n.a.
Cyprus	n.a.	n.a.	n.a.	Netherlands	n.a.	n.a.	n.a.
Czech Republic*	119	114	107	Poland	500	504	511
Denmark	n.a.	n.a.	n.a.	Portugal	n.a.	n.a.	n.a.
Estonia	3	n.a.	n.a.	Romania	1,152	1,137	1,134
Finland	34	40	46	Slovakia	141	122	104
France	416	379	363	Slovenia	n.a.	n.a.	n.a.
Germany	894	833	861	Spain	n.a.	n.a.	n.a.
Greece	n.a.	n.a.	n.a.	Sweden	n.a.	n.a.	n.a.
Hungary	264	256	252	United Kingdom	287	n.a.	n.a.
Ireland	n.a.	n.a.	n.a.				
Italy	83	81	n.a.	**Total (EU-28)**	n.a.	n.a.	n.a.

* Definition differs.
© European Union. Source: Eurostat, 2017, Transport, table *IWW_EQ_LOADCAP*—Self-propelled vessels, dumb and pushed vessels by load capacity.

OIL AND GAS PIPELINES

Length of oil pipelines operated (kilometres)

	2013	2014	2015		2013	2014	2015
Austria	1,214	1,214	n.a.	Latvia*	417	417	417
Belgium	n.a.	n.a.	n.a.	Lithuania	500	500	500
Bulgaria	570	570	n.a.	Luxembourg	n.a.	n.a.	n.a.
Croatia	610	610	610	Malta	n.a.	n.a.	n.a.
Cyprus	n.a.	n.a.	n.a.	Netherlands	n.a.	n.a.	n.a.
Czech Republic	674	n.a.	n.a.	Poland	2,444	2,483	2,483
Denmark	n.a.	n.a.	n.a.	Portugal	n.a.	n.a.	n.a.
Estonia	n.a.	n.a.	n.a.	Romania	2,951	3,048	2,715
Finland	n.a.	n.a.	n.a.	Slovakia	n.a.†	506	506
France	n.a.	6,400	n.a.	Slovenia	n.a.	n.a.	n.a.
Germany	2,370	2,370	2,370	Spain*	4,735	n.a.	n.a.
Greece	n.a.	n.a.	n.a.	Sweden	n.a.	n.a.	n.a.
Hungary	2,217	2,215	2,215	United Kingdom	n.a.	n.a.	n.a.
Ireland	n.a.	n.a.	n.a.				
Italy	4,303	4,304	n.a.	**Total (EU-28)**	n.a.	n.a.	n.a.

* Definition differs. † Estimate.
© European Union. Source: Eurostat, 2017, Transport, table *PIPE_IF_LENGHT*—Length of pipelines operated.

MARITIME TRANSPORT

Total passengers transported ('000 passengers, all ports)

	2013	2014	2015		2013	2014	2015
Austria	–	–	–	Latvia	932	862	661
Belgium	859	821	844	Lithuania	280	280	286
Bulgaria	2	1	2	Luxembourg	–	–	–
Croatia	27,355	23,523	27,271	Malta	9,170	9,669	9,910
Cyprus	99	76	68	Netherlands	1,738	1,819	1,910
Czech Republic	–	–	–	Poland	2,201	2,224	2,421
Denmark	41,266	41,353	41,647	Portugal	555	551	583
Estonia	13,146	13,654	14,164	Romania	n.a.	1	1
Finland	18,524	18,487	18,884	Slovakia	–	–	–
France	25,634	26,638	26,133	Slovenia	28	27	34
Germany	29,848	30,780	30,087	Spain	22,871	23,486	24,522
Greece	72,918	66,533	65,680	Sweden	29,146	29,244	29,500
Hungary	–	–	–	United Kingdom	27,472	28,135	27,805
Ireland	2,747	2,755	2,751				
Italy	73,238	72,225	70,268	**Total (EU-28)**	400,029	393,143	395,432

Note: Austria, the Czech Republic, Hungary, Luxembourg and Slovakia are landlocked countries, with no coastal ports.
© European Union. Source: Eurostat, 2017, Transport, table *MAR_PA_AA*—Maritime transport—Passengers embarked and disembarked in all ports by direction—Annual data.

Passenger traffic at ports by direction of flow, 2015 ('000 passengers)

	Inwards	Outwards	Total		Inwards	Outwards	Total
Austria	–	–	–	Latvia	317	344	661
Belgium	422	422	844	Lithuania	136	150	286
Bulgaria	0	2	2	Luxembourg	–	–	–
Croatia	13,974	13,297	27,271	Malta	4,956	4,954	9,910
Cyprus	35	33	68	Netherlands	941	969	1,910
Czech Republic	–	–	–	Poland	1,205	1,217	2,421
Denmark	20,854	20,793	41,647	Portugal	292	291	583
Estonia	7,062	7,102	14,164	Romania	0	0	1
Finland	9,480	9,404	18,884	Slovakia	–	–	–
France	13,113	13,020	26,133	Slovenia	17	17	34
Germany	14,944	15,143	30,087	Spain	12,300	12,222	24,522
Greece	32,852	32,828	65,680	Sweden	14,985	14,516	29,500
Hungary	–	–	–	United Kingdom	13,845	13,961	27,805
Ireland	1,359	1,392	2,751				
Italy	35,145	35,123	70,268	**Total (EU-28)**	198,233	197,199	395,432

Note: Austria, the Czech Republic, Hungary, Luxembourg and Slovakia are landlocked countries, with no coastal ports.
© European Union. Source: Eurostat, 2017, Transport, table *MAR_PA_AA*—Maritime transport—Passengers embarked and disembarked in all ports by direction—Annual data.

STATISTICAL SURVEY — Transport

Seaborne freight handled ('000 metric tons, all ports)

	2013	2014	2015		2013	2014	2015
Austria	–	–	–	Latvia	67,148	71,836	67,811
Belgium	228,130	237,852	241,459	Lithuania	39,757	41,105	43,128
Bulgaria	28,841	27,235	27,166	Luxembourg	–	–	–
Croatia	19,366	18,603	18,930	Malta	3,101	3,460	3,705
Cyprus	7,172	7,186	10,268	Netherlands	557,929	570,489	594,272
Czech Republic	–	–	–	Poland	64,282	68,744	69,530
Denmark	88,406	92,244	95,098	Portugal	78,244	80,156	86,769
Estonia	42,908	43,578	34,965	Romania	43,577	43,753	44,533
Finland	105,117	105,537	99,962	Slovakia	–	–	–
France	303,031	298,203	297,880	Slovenia	17,184	18,012	19,931
Germany	297,281	303,742	295,918	Spain	397,462	427,672	447,048
Greece	160,986	168,501	167,036	Sweden	161,570	167,530	169,685
Hungary	–	–	–	United Kingdom	503,324	503,171	496,708
Ireland	46,722	47,483	50,666				
Italy	457,078	443,141	458,020	**Total (EU-28)**	3,718,618	3,789,235	3,840,488

Note: Austria, the Czech Republic, Hungary, Luxembourg and Slovakia are landlocked countries, with no coastal ports.
© European Union. Source: Eurostat, 2017, Transport, table *MAR_GO_AA*—Maritime transport—Gross weight of goods handled in all ports by direction—Annual data.

Seaborne freight traffic at ports by direction of flow, 2015 ('000 metric tons)

	Inwards	Outwards	Total		Inwards	Outwards	Total
Austria	–	–	–	Latvia	6,774	61,037	67,811
Belgium	128,946	112,513	241,459	Lithuania	14,615	28,513	43,128
Bulgaria	12,622	14,544	27,166	Luxembourg	–	–	–
Croatia	12,484	6,446	18,930	Malta	3,409	296	3,705
Cyprus	6,433	3,835	10,268	Netherlands	406,668	187,604	594,272
Czech Republic	–	–	–	Poland	39,834	29,696	69,530
Denmark	54,627	40,471	95,098	Portugal	50,841	35,928	86,769
Estonia	10,331	24,634	34,965	Romania	19,579	24,954	44,533
Finland	49,896	50,066	99,962	Slovakia	–	–	–
France	196,574	101,305	297,880	Slovenia	13,175	6,756	19,931
Germany	173,401	122,517	295,918	Spain	255,238	191,810	447,048
Greece	91,137	75,899	167,036	Sweden	92,143	77,542	169,685
Hungary	–	–	–	United Kingdom	314,172	182,535	496,708
Ireland	33,638	17,028	50,666				
Italy	292,505	165,515	458,020	**Total (EU-28)**	2,279,042	1,561,446	3,840,488

Note: Austria, the Czech Republic, Hungary, Luxembourg and Slovakia are landlocked countries, with no coastal ports.
© European Union. Source: Eurostat, 2017, Transport, table *MAR_GO_AA*—Maritime transport—Gross weight of goods handled in all ports by direction—Annual data.

AVIATION

International air passenger arrivals (number of passengers carried)

	2014	2015	2016		2014	2015	2016
Austria	12,850,394	13,055,442	13,286,309	Latvia	2,403,895	2,575,805	2,697,898
Belgium	14,361,416	15,464,845	15,072,271	Lithuania	1,897,351	2,110,375	2,397,541
Bulgaria	3,650,039	3,696,502	4,554,836	Luxembourg	1,209,353	1,318,094	1,483,897
Croatia	2,815,972	3,039,248	3,481,370	Malta	2,144,199	2,310,486	n.a.
Cyprus	3,662,657	3,796,773	4,489,416	Netherlands	30,459,132	32,207,973	35,094,099
Czech Republic	5,971,262	6,269,420	6,786,783	Poland	12,066,944	13,658,371	n.a.
Denmark	13,546,142	14,090,097	15,399,145	Portugal	14,877,261	16,279,729	18,356,334
Estonia	990,970	1,053,828	1,081,278	Romania	5,165,961	5,990,845	7,080,901
Finland	7,317,088	7,430,818	7,688,890	Slovakia	820,579	962,139	1,061,871
France	54,182,194	56,321,517	58,257,458	Slovenia	652,606	716,311	700,250
Germany	82,072,343	85,657,516	88,746,522	Spain	67,916,974	71,787,146	80,170,866
Greece	16,285,099	17,158,136	n.a.	Sweden	12,714,416	13,277,920	n.a.
Hungary	4,495,411	5,068,931	5,783,067	United Kingdom	99,482,311	105,137,832	n.a.
Ireland	13,110,050	14,717,088	16,215,853				
Italy	45,851,056	48,892,809	n.a.	**Total (EU-28)**	532,973,075	564,045,996	n.a.

© European Union. Source: Eurostat, 2017, Transport, table *AVIA_PAOC*—Air passenger transport by reporting country.

Transport   STATISTICAL SURVEY

International air passenger departures (number of passengers carried)

	2014	2015	2016		2014	2015	2016
Austria	12,949,287	13,168,955	13,384,624	Latvia	2,398,242	2,569,877	2,685,288
Belgium	14,374,645	15,466,022	15,031,829	Lithuania	1,900,515	2,116,671	2,389,641
Bulgaria	3,702,352	3,751,118	4,605,536	Luxembourg	1,224,003	1,332,696	1,499,673
Croatia	2,859,615	3,065,712	3,506,240	Malta	2,145,829	2,308,812	n.a.
Cyprus	3,665,884	3,794,014	4,472,401	Netherlands	30,503,161	32,361,354	35,222,259
Czech Republic	6,019,743	6,294,828	6,802,941	Poland	12,169,298	13,661,418	n.a.
Denmark	13,505,738	14,074,956	15,352,380	Portugal	14,721,109	16,063,714	18,101,895
Estonia	1,012,206	1,087,591	1,116,350	Romania	5,239,525	6,083,714	7,177,458
Finland	7,338,649	7,449,292	7,722,184	Slovakia	828,521	959,931	1,071,490
France	54,258,569	56,379,944	58,047,722	Slovenia	654,522	719,560	703,902
Germany	81,584,315	85,122,000	88,165,827	Spain	68,230,863	71,984,244	80,266,533
Greece	16,565,578	17,456,260	n.a.	Sweden	12,695,886	13,286,491	n.a.
Hungary	4,559,278	5,159,421	5,884,889	United Kingdom	98,677,645	104,303,777	n.a.
Ireland	13,139,159	14,756,780	16,298,068				
Italy	46,129,937	49,115,765	n.a.	**Total (EU-28)**	533,054,074	563,894,917	n.a.

© European Union. Source: Eurostat, 2017, Transport, table *AVIA_PAOC*—Air passenger transport by reporting country.

International air transport of freight and mail: goods loaded (metric tons)

	2014	2015	2016		2014	2015	2016
Austria	94,381	102,079	102,328	Latvia	22,432	10,345	10,928
Belgium	536,395	632,989	603,838	Lithuania	5,174	5,857	6,177
Bulgaria	12,944	21,288	22,751	Luxembourg	383,824	409,264	436,340
Croatia	2,595	2,619	2,980	Malta	5,854	6,471	n.a.
Cyprus	13,103	13,230	12,455	Netherlands	840,176	844,352	897,518
Czech Republic	30,768	32,313	41,235	Poland	36,684	42,631	n.a.
Denmark	114,158	118,966	114,292	Portugal	66,770	63,672	63,112
Estonia	3,491	3,578	5,668	Romania	12,531	14,340	17,271
Finland	91,401	89,995	94,292	Slovakia	8,877	10,775	11,802
France	1,131,953	1,170,143	1,217,480	Slovenia	3,575	3,554	3,697
Germany	2,220,286	2,226,620	2,294,028	Spain	266,278	278,557	298,286
Greece	27,173	29,979	n.a.	Sweden	66,281	69,988	n.a.
Hungary	27,039	29,672	36,985	United Kingdom	1,092,580	1,099,391	n.a.
Ireland	62,006	67,905	66,102				
Italy	464,057	512,840	n.a.	**Total (EU-28)**	7,642,786	7,913,412	n.a.

© European Union. Source: Eurostat, 2017, Transport, table *AVIA_GOOC*—Freight and mail air transport by reporting country.

International air transport of freight and mail: goods unloaded (metric tons)

	2014	2015	2016		2014	2015	2016
Austria	123,164	114,318	120,942	Latvia	9,007	6,464	6,994
Belgium	477,839	492,213	484,817	Lithuania	8,036	9,047	8,005
Bulgaria	10,097	10,210	10,196	Luxembourg	323,326	327,616	364,716
Croatia	3,619	3,934	4,162	Malta	9,748	9,935	n.a.
Cyprus	14,992	14,397	15,975	Netherlands	887,248	867,680	934,245
Czech Republic	27,230	26,020	36,386	Poland	43,669	46,991	n.a.
Denmark	93,591	90,833	85,682	Portugal	53,461	55,395	59,241
Estonia	15,941	12,456	8,200	Romania	18,555	19,033	19,880
Finland	96,787	89,724	89,315	Slovakia	9,620	10,440	11,226
France	969,774	1,008,892	1,104,655	Slovenia	4,988	5,337	5,273
Germany	1,998,569	1,982,018	2,050,622	Spain	266,701	258,236	280,990
Greece	27,066	26,470	n.a.	Sweden	60,402	61,064	n.a.
Hungary	34,931	36,111	40,549	United Kingdom	1,203,690	1,199,506	n.a.
Ireland	71,166	76,173	70,922				
Italy	356,097	358,931	n.a.	**Total (EU-28)**	7,219,312	7,219,443	n.a.

© European Union. Source: Eurostat, 2017, Transport, table *AVIA_GOOC*—Freight and mail air transport by reporting country.

COMMUNICATIONS

TELECOMMUNICATIONS

Number of main telephone lines ('000)

	2011	2012	2013		2011	2012	2013
Austria	3,388	3,380	3,349	Latvia	516	501	480
Belgium	4,634	4,635	4,588†	Lithuania	712	675	625
Bulgaria	2,273	2,133	1,942	Luxembourg	279	267	268
Croatia	1,761	1,633	1,577	Malta	232	230	231
Cyprus	405	373	349	Netherlands	7,133	7,182	7,125
Czech Republic	2,204	2,117*	1,997*	Poland	6,853	5,951	5,299
Denmark	2,481	2,299	2,104	Portugal	4,543	4,558	4,530
Estonia	472	448	426	Romania	4,680	4,650	4,740
Finland	1,080	890	752	Slovakia	1,056	975	967
France	40,370	39,674	39,079	Slovenia	878	830	792
Germany	51,400	50,100	48,700*	Spain	19,889	19,575	19,105
Greece	5,745	5,461	5,333	Sweden	4,482	4,169	3,887
Hungary	2,933	2,961	2,978	United Kingdom	33,252	33,197	33,384
Ireland	2,047	2,008	2,034				
Italy	22,105	21,656	20,926	**Total (EU-28)**	227,804	222,528*	217,569*

* Estimate.
© European Union. Source: Eurostat, 2017, Industry, trade and services, table *ISOC_TC_FTTELI*—Fixed telephony—Main telephone lines.

Number of mobile telephone subscriptions ('000)

	2011	2012	2013		2011	2012	2013
Austria	12,654	13,382	13,212	Latvia	3,530	3,881	4,683
Belgium	12,584	13,104	13,162	Lithuania	4,927	4,953	4,988
Bulgaria	10,864	11,733	11,867	Luxembourg	731	765	798
Croatia	n.a.	5,263	5,151	Malta	526	542	555
Cyprus	1,088	1,131	1,114	Netherlands	20,839	21,946	20,153
Czech Republic	13,531	13,608	13,297	Poland	45,990	50,519	51,947
Denmark	8,189	8,610	8,407	Portugal	16,632	16,628	16,734
Estonia	1,795	1,986	2,013	Romania	23,590	22,697	22,600
Finland	8,780	9,150	9,310	Slovakia	6,033	6,232	6,551
France	65,060	68,987	72,571	Slovenia	2,163	2,198	2,252
Germany	99,020	101,657	104,119	Spain	58,299	57,138	55,349
Greece	12,472	13,350	13,643	Sweden	12,997	13,684	14,057
Hungary	11,003	10,991	11,262	United Kingdom	85,207	82,983	82,908
Ireland	5,185	5,486	5,615				
Italy	95,903	98,358	99,097	**Total (EU-28)**	n.a.	660,964	667,413

© European Union. Source: Eurostat, 2017, Industry, trade and services, table *ISOC_TC_MCSUPE*—Mobile communications: Subscriptions and penetration.

Fixed broadband penetration rate (percentage of households)

	2014	2015	2016		2014	2015	2016
Austria	64	65	68	Latvia	63	65	61*
Belgium	81	78	80	Lithuania	58	60	63
Bulgaria	54	55	57	Luxembourg	91	94	96
Croatia	61	70	70	Malta	79	80	80
Cyprus	68	69	72	Netherlands	n.a.	94	95
Czech Republic	76	76	71	Poland	60	57	59
Denmark	79	77	83	Portugal	53	61	68
Estonia	69	77	77	Romania	54	60	63
Finland	61	59	61	Slovakia	70	72	72
France	74	71	72	Slovenia	71	75	77
Germany	83	84	86	Spain	65	69	71
Greece	63	66	66	Sweden	67	68	72*
Hungary	66	69	72	United Kingdom	82	85	87
Ireland	62	65	69				
Italy	51	53	55	**Total (EU-28)**	70	72	74

* Break in series.
© European Union. Source: Eurostat, 2017, Industry, trade and services, table *ISOC_BDE15B_H*—Broadband and connectivity—Households.

INFORMATION TECHNOLOGY

Percentage of all individuals using a computer in the last year

	2013	2014	2015		2013	2014	2015
Austria	83	83	85	Latvia	76	77	79
Belgium	85	87	86	Lithuania	70	73	72
Bulgaria	57	60	60	Luxembourg	95	95	98
Croatia	69	69	70	Malta	72	75	76
Cyprus	67	71	71	Netherlands	95	94	94
Czech Republic	76	81	82	Poland	66	70	70
Denmark	96	97	97	Portugal	67	69	71
Estonia	81	85	89	Romania	55	60*	63
Finland	93	93	94	Slovakia	82	83	81
France	82	84	85	Slovenia	75	74	76
Germany	87	89	90	Spain	75	76	77
Greece	62	65	68	Sweden	95	94	92
Hungary	75	77	75	United Kingdom	91	92	92
Ireland	80	81	79				
Italy	60	61	64	**Total (EU-28)**	78	79	80

* Break in series.
© European Union. Source: Eurostat, 2017, Industry, trade and services, table *ISOC_CI_CFP_CU*—Individuals—Computer use.

Percentage of households with access to a computer

	2012	2013	2015		2012	2013	2015
Austria	81	81	82	Latvia	70	72	76
Belgium	80	82	82	Lithuania	62	66	68
Bulgaria	52	55	59	Luxembourg	92	94	95
Croatia	68	66	77	Malta	78	80	81
Cyprus	70	70	71	Netherlands	95	95	96
Czech Republic	67	74	79	Poland	73	75	78
Denmark	92	93	92	Portugal	66	67	71
Estonia	74	79	88	Romania	57	61	69
Finland	88	89	89	Slovakia	79	80	80
France	81	82	82	Slovenia	76	76	78
Germany	87	89	91	Spain	73	73	76
Greece	57	60	69	Sweden	92	92	88
Hungary	70	71	75	United Kingdom	87	88	90
Ireland	83	84	84				
Italy	67	71	73	**Total (EU-28)**	78	80	82

Note: No data available for 2014.
© European Union. Source: Eurostat, 2017, Industry, trade and services, table *ISOC_CI_CM_H*—Households—Availability of computers.

Level of internet access (percentage of households)

	2014	2015	2016		2014	2015	2016
Austria	81	82	85	Latvia	73	76	77
Belgium	83	82	85	Lithuania	66	68	72
Bulgaria	57	59	64	Luxembourg	96	97	97
Croatia	68	77	77	Malta	81	82	82
Cyprus	69	71	74	Netherlands	96	96	97
Czech Republic	78	79	82	Poland	75	76	80
Denmark	93	92	94	Portugal	65	70	74
Estonia	83	88	86	Romania	61	68	72
Finland	90	90	92	Slovakia	78	79	81
France	83	83	86	Slovenia	77	78	78
Germany	89	90	92	Spain	74	79	82
Greece	66	68	69	Sweden	90	91	94
Hungary	73	76	79	United Kingdom	90	91	93
Ireland	82	85	87				
Italy	73	75	79	**Total (EU-28)**	81	83	85

© European Union. Source: Eurostat, 2017, Industry, trade and services, table *ISOC_CI_IN_H*—Households—Level of internet access.

Internet access of households, by access device, 2014 (percentage)

	Desktop computer	Portable computer*	Other mobile device†	Connected TV (Smart TV)	Games console		Desktop computer	Portable computer*	Other mobile device†	Connected TV (Smart TV)	Games console
Austria	42	66	58	11	9	Latvia	42	50	27	5	2
Belgium	41	69	48	11	12	Lithuania	35	46	25	2	0
Bulgaria	41	32	17	2	0	Luxembourg	58	83	72	25	22
Croatia	43	47	45	10	5	Malta	45	65	52	19	14
Cyprus	23	63	44	3	8	Netherlands	59	84	74	39	20
Czech Republic	47	54	19	3	1	Poland	40	56	32	6	4
Denmark	41	87	76	27	23	Portugal	25	57	43	9	11
Estonia	40	66	50	12	6	Romania	51	21	12	2	1
Finland	38	72	66	18	15	Slovakia	50	56	39	6	4
France	46	62	48	16	13	Slovenia	54	57	51	11	6
Germany	53	71	63	33	15	Spain	40	54	61	12	16
Greece	40	46	24	3	1	Sweden	43	78	70	21	22
Hungary	53	45	45	8	4	United Kingdom	40	77	62	19	21
Iceland	19	72	51	8	8						
Italy	32	47	34	2	3	**Total (EU-28)**	43	62	50	16	12

* Laptop, netbook, tablet. † Mobile device other than portable computer.
© European Union. Source: Eurostat, 2016, Industry, trade and services, table *ISOC_CI_ID_H*—Households—Devices to access the internet.

Regular use of the internet by individuals (percentage of individuals)

	2014	2015	2016		2014	2015	2016
Austria	77	81	82	Latvia	72	75	77
Belgium	83	83	84	Lithuania	69	69	72
Bulgaria	54	55	58	Luxembourg	93	97	97
Croatia	65	66	71	Malta	70	74	76
Cyprus	65	70	74	Netherlands	91	91	92
Czech Republic	76	77	79	Poland	63	65	70
Denmark	92	93	94	Portugal	61	65	68
Estonia	82	86	85	Romania	48	52	56
Finland	90	90	91	Slovakia	76	74	78
France	80	81	82	Slovenia	68	71	73
Germany	82	84	87	Spain	71	75	76
Greece	59	63	66	Sweden	91	89	91
Hungary	74	72	78	United Kingdom	89	90	93
Ireland	76	78	79				
Italy	59	63	67	**Total (EU-28)**	75	76	79

Note: Regular use: at least once a week on average within the last three months before the survey.
© European Union. Source: Eurostat, 2016, Industry, trade and services, table *ISOC_BDE15CUA*—Internet use and activities.

Use of the internet to buy goods or services (percentage of individuals)

	2014	2015	2016		2014	2015	2016
Austria	43	46	48	Latvia	24	27	31
Belgium	41	42	46	Lithuania	19	22	24
Bulgaria	10	12	11	Luxembourg	62	63	69
Croatia	22	26	25	Malta	41	43	41
Cyprus	23	19	22	Netherlands	59	59	63
Czech Republic	25	26	29	Poland	24	24	31
Denmark	66	67	71	Portugal	17	23	23
Estonia	37	46	45	Romania	6	8	8
Finland	53	49	48	Slovakia	31	35	41
France	49	49	52	Slovenia	26	28	30
Germany	61	64	64	Spain	28	32	35
Greece	20	24	23	Sweden	62	56	63
Hungary	20	23	27	United Kingdom	72	75	78
Ireland	43	44	41				
Italy	15	18	20	**Total (EU-28)**	41	43	45

Note: refers to individuals who have ordered/bought goods or services for private use over the internet in the three months before the survey.
© European Union. Source: Eurostat, 2017, Industry, trade and services, table *ISOC_EC_IBUY*—Internet purchases by individuals.

Percentage of all individuals who have never used the internet

	2014	2015	2016		2014	2015	2016
Austria	15	13	13	Latvia	21	18	17
Belgium	13	13	11	Lithuania	25	25	22*
Bulgaria	37	35	33	Luxembourg	4	2	2
Croatia	28	26	23	Malta	25	22	21
Cyprus	28	26	23	Netherlands	5	4	5
Czech Republic	16	13	13	Poland	28	27	22
Denmark	3	3	2	Portugal	30	28	26
Estonia	12	9	10	Romania	39	32	30
Finland	6	5	4	Slovakia	15	16	15
France	12	11	10	Slovenia	24	22	22
Germany	11	10	8	Spain	21	19	17
Greece	33	30	28	Sweden	6	5	3*
Hungary	22	21	19	United Kingdom	6	6	4
Ireland	16	16	15				
Italy	32	28	25	**Total (EU-28)**	18	16	14

* Break in series.

© European Union. Source: Eurostat, 2017, Industry, trade and services, table *ISOC_CI_IFP_IU*—Individuals—Internet use.

TOURISM

ACCOMMODATION

Hotels and similar establishments (number)

	2014	2015	2016		2014	2015	2016
Austria	12,839	12,625	12,366	Latvia	258	332	343
Belgium	1,653	1,557	1,522	Lithuania	421	418	420
Bulgaria	2,166	2,180	n.a.	Luxembourg	236	236	n.a.
Croatia	909	938	1,011	Malta	149	161	164
Cyprus	799	786	783	Netherlands	3,561	3,525	3,585
Czech Republic	5,833	5,992	6,022	Poland	3,646	3,723	3,965
Denmark	533	525	537	Portugal	2,331	2,430	n.a.
Estonia	410	414	413	Romania	2,500	2,626	2,638
Finland	785	777	772	Slovakia	1,397	1,509	1,475
France	17,336	18,328	n.a.	Slovenia	647	681	692
Germany	33,997	33,635	33,061	Spain	19,563	19,718	19,524
Greece	10,123	10,111	n.a.	Sweden	2,033	1,992	n.a.
Hungary	2,123	2,185	2,202	United Kingdom	n.a.	n.a.	n.a.
Ireland	2,438	n.a.	n.a.				
Italy	33,290	33,202	n.a.	**Total (EU-28)***	202,248	186,890	n.a.

* Estimates.

© European Union. Source: Eurostat, 2017, Industry, trade and services, table *TOUR_CAP_NAT*—Number of establishments, bedrooms and bedplaces—National—Annual data.

Other collective accommodation establishments (number)

	2014	2015	2016		2014	2015	2016
Austria	7,490	7,690	8,253	Latvia	386	345	416
Belgium	3,486	6,433	6,688	Lithuania	1,641	1,901	2,266
Bulgaria	997	1,022	n.a.	Luxembourg	198	195	n.a.
Croatia	66,815	72,501	82,222	Malta	17	17	20
Cyprus	3	2	2	Netherlands	5,653	5,576	5,365
Czech Republic	3,180	3,171	3,146	Poland	6,239	6,301	6,544
Denmark	585	588	599	Portugal	1,098	1,055	n.a.
Estonia	1,009	1,003	1,041	Romania	3,691	4,323	4,390
Finland	623	615	596	Slovakia	1,290	1,399	1,280
France	11,559	11,717	n.a.	Slovenia	2,253	2,323†	2,568†
Germany	16,928	16,937	17,091	Spain	28,126	28,610	29,177
Greece*	24,399	24,570	n.a.	Sweden	2,236	2,192	n.a.
Hungary	2,053	2,171	2,234	United Kingdom	n.a.	n.a.	n.a.
Ireland	4,136	n.a.	n.a.				
Italy	125,122	134,495	n.a.	**Total (EU-28)***	368,020	391,203	n.a.

Note: refers to holiday and other short-stay accommodation; camping grounds, recreational vehicle parks and trailer parks.
*Estimates. † Low reliability.

© European Union. Source: Eurostat, 2017, Industry, trade and services, table *TOUR_CAP_NAT*—Number of establishments, bedrooms and bedplaces—National—Annual data.

Bedplaces in hotels and similar establishments (number)

	2014	2015	2016		2014	2015	2016
Austria	598,742	600,342	601,945	Latvia	22,781	25,398	26,164
Belgium	127,835	129,307	129,232	Lithuania	28,459	28,585	28,665
Bulgaria	271,526	279,090	n.a.	Luxembourg	14,787	14,542	n.a.
Croatia	161,875	164,675	167,380	Malta	40,222	41,283	41,684
Cyprus	85,150	84,426	83,251	Netherlands	252,115	254,589	261,164
Czech Republic	306,430	314,210	317,756	Poland	292,521	301,555	325,776
Denmark	90,433	89,371	90,503	Portugal	309,918	328,186	n.a.
Estonia	32,437	32,620	32,404	Romania	217,721	225,227	213,635
Finland	133,785	134,107	135,177	Slovakia	91,663	96,997	95,774
France	1,274,920	1,304,692	n.a.	Slovenia	44,567	45,274	45,716
Germany	1,763,742	1,778,206	1,784,654	Spain	1,875,912	1,906,827	1,893,978
Greece	800,022	801,787	n.a.	Sweden	238,852	236,555	n.a.
Hungary	173,914	177,182	181,407	United Kingdom	n.a.	n.a.	n.a.
Ireland	151,258	n.a.	n.a.				
Italy	2,241,239	2,250,816	n.a.	**Total (EU-28)***	13,660,998	13,522,493	n.a.

* Estimates.

© European Union. Source: Eurostat, 2017, Industry, trade and services, table *TOUR_CAP_NAT*—Number of establishments, bedrooms and bedplaces—National—Annual data.

OCCUPANCY

Arrivals of national residents at hotels and similar establishments

	2013	2014	2015		2013	2014	2015
Austria	9,366,270	9,574,431	9,861,284	Latvia	377,441	442,127	492,757
Belgium	3,947,228	4,175,387	4,304,415	Lithuania	647,376	708,361	777,021
Bulgaria	2,610,602	2,726,631	2,937,839	Luxembourg	68,401	69,747	68,923
Croatia	889,283	873,818	946,008	Malta	146,891	153,989	156,040
Cyprus	438,104	431,992	441,137	Netherlands	11,504,042	12,143,198	12,410,086
Czech Republic	5,045,667	5,052,889	5,736,436	Poland	12,428,807	13,772,799	15,061,959
Denmark	2,454,332	2,606,932*	2,827,006*	Portugal	6,142,385	6,893,425	7,336,203
Estonia	756,251	818,257	880,083	Romania	4,961,498	5,189,322	6,020,451
Finland	6,856,916	6,743,345	6,960,237	Slovakia	1,703,947	1,629,260	1,910,028
France	78,660,790	76,972,426	78,799,599	Slovenia	613,019	625,630	674,631
Germany	94,618,956	97,846,589	100,982,801	Spain	42,569,374	44,682,747	47,523,598
Greece	5,518,835	5,536,719	5,744,134	Sweden	14,069,313	14,645,511	15,514,466
Hungary	3,625,777	4,054,154	4,450,377	United Kingdom	53,129,000	n.a.	n.a.
Ireland*	7,012,298	7,570,342	7,713,240				
Italy	42,650,052	43,470,802	45,898,875	**Total (EU-28)**	412,812,855	422,539,830*	n.a.

* Estimate(s).
© European Union. Source: Eurostat, 2017, Industry, trade and services, table *TOUR_OCC_ARNAT*—Arrivals at tourist accommodation establishments.

Arrivals of national residents at other collective accommodation establishments

	2013	2014	2015		2013	2014	2015
Austria	1,791,258	1,825,964	1,944,434	Latvia	211,986	225,216	171,871
Belgium	2,520,847	2,578,257	3,187,758	Lithuania	552,538	608,335	640,300
Bulgaria	416,014	427,699	476,826	Luxembourg	31,589	34,670	37,618
Croatia	541,425	570,198	667,509	Malta	1,771	1,389	1,227
Cyprus	2,449	1,987	415	Netherlands	9,763,241	9,787,995	9,901,217
Czech Republic	2,510,139	2,438,302	2,752,201	Poland	5,729,359	5,840,844	6,190,527
Denmark	1,653,865	1,636,082*	1,706,660*	Portugal	1,358,620	1,320,560	1,604,067
Estonia	284,484	285,498	302,896	Romania	1,242,499	1,342,891	1,643,874
Finland	1,186,673	1,185,505	1,152,565	Slovakia	646,367	600,402	663,261
France	29,032,056	29,912,237	31,895,634	Slovenia	500,884	475,232	534,388
Germany	23,368,868	24,221,775	25,079,934	Spain	9,304,832	10,503,132	11,498,198
Greece	1,847,024	1,890,856*	1,855,239*	Sweden	5,509,004	5,751,494	6,274,241
Hungary	1,303,976	1,461,011	1,534,362	United Kingdom	28,150,000	n.a.	n.a.
Ireland	n.a.†	550,097*	375,560*				
Italy	10,949,242	11,446,050	12,422,117	**Total (EU-28)**	140,938,226	145,073,678*	n.a.

Note: refers to holiday and other short-stay accommodation; camping grounds, recreational vehicle parks and trailer parks.
* Estimate. † Unreliable data.
© European Union. Source: Eurostat, 2017, Industry, trade and services, table *TOUR_OCC_ARNAT*—Arrivals at tourist accommodation establishments.

Arrivals of non-residents at hotels and similar establishments

	2013	2014	2015		2013	2014	2015
Austria	18,163,665	18,588,441	19,627,356	Latvia	1,131,839	1,305,554	1,372,532
Belgium	6,227,649	6,388,967	6,439,780	Lithuania	1,098,496	1,166,466	1,182,212
Bulgaria	2,754,493	2,732,212	2,805,760	Luxembourg	762,760	834,129	870,390
Croatia	4,672,944	4,911,252	5,250,645	Malta	1,292,763	1,369,656	1,407,062
Cyprus	1,946,893	1,934,727	1,873,550	Netherlands	10,017,355	10,978,473	11,765,596
Czech Republic	7,326,692	7,513,226	8,023,523	Poland	4,686,963	4,886,042	5,073,855
Denmark	1,699,027	1,825,660*	1,821,779*	Portugal	7,783,145	8,963,700	9,808,271
Estonia	1,798,392	1,816,317	1,765,561	Romania	1,594,591	1,792,483	2,077,353
Finland	2,458,332	2,396,997	2,332,623	Slovakia	1,422,658	1,251,559	1,469,042
France	34,067,189	34,393,532	35,093,619	Slovenia	1,639,871	1,761,729	1,930,683
Germany	27,603,412	28,878,052	30,691,278	Spain	41,251,545	43,131,783	45,693,370
Greece	10,490,113	11,882,134	12,734,567	Sweden	3,469,061	3,767,943	4,240,483
Hungary	4,006,962	4,186,556	4,437,504	United Kingdom	21,255,703	n.a.	n.a.
Ireland*	1,830,935	1,856,431	2,260,323				
Italy	39,989,184	40,769,577	43,093,324	**Total (EU-28)**	262,442,632*	272,539,301*	n.a.

* Estimate(s).
© European Union. Source: Eurostat, 2017, Industry, trade and services, table *TOUR_OCC_ARNAT*—Arrivals at tourist accommodation establishments.

Tourism

Arrivals of non-residents at other collective accommodation establishments

	2013	2014	2015		2013	2014	2015
Austria	3,619,072	3,657,756	3,917,028	Latvia	117,975	125,484	102,233
Belgium	1,456,636	1,498,459	1,914,973	Lithuania	161,840	190,369	206,275
Bulgaria	66,180	59,366	58,611	Luxembourg	181,586	204,346	219,186
Croatia	6,102,056	6,527,554	7,292,864	Malta	19,220	29,645	21,739
Cyprus	943	914	773	Netherlands	2,765,545	2,946,408	3,241,539
Czech Republic	525,173	582,659	683,390	Poland	556,009	584,293	615,715
Denmark	629,791	639,787*	809,159*	Portugal	617,107	724,612	1,031,654
Estonia	141,738	166,998	163,603	Romania	119,947	119,334	156,879
Finland	338,507	334,259	289,416	Slovakia	230,128	208,415	231,704
France	11,934,304	11,680,410	11,704,089	Slovenia	586,546	612,261	738,521
Germany	3,804,059	3,981,488	4,139,734	Spain	8,547,339	9,227,347	9,733,245
Greece	2,259,282	2,519,761*	2,765,904*	Sweden	1,560,595	1,687,420	2,027,383
Hungary	380,730	431,195	491,007	United Kingdom†	n.a.	n.a.	n.a.
Ireland	n.a.†	386,384*	406,525*				
Italy	10,274,052	10,865,923	11,940,358	**Total (EU-28)**	60,649,238*	66,257,829*	n.a.

Note: refers to holiday and other short-stay accommodation; camping grounds, recreational vehicle parks and trailer parks.
* Estimate. † Unreliable data.
© European Union. Source: Eurostat, 2017, Industry, trade and services, table *TOUR_OCC_ARNAT*—Arrivals at tourist accommodation establishments.

Nights spent by national residents at hotels and similar establishments

	2013	2014	2015		2013	2014	2015
Austria	23,634,952	23,481,554	23,938,781	Latvia	659,799	777,895	820,891
Belgium	6,525,416	6,926,111	7,047,847	Lithuania	1,230,428	1,292,253	1,366,560
Bulgaria	5,926,849	6,219,194	6,559,421	Luxembourg	156,506	160,508	151,836
Croatia	2,192,934	2,112,138	2,305,130	Malta	325,025	350,228	371,007
Cyprus	880,959	816,655	823,689	Netherlands	19,038,980	19,679,902	19,909,913
Czech Republic	11,824,827	11,715,863	13,290,176	Poland	22,604,694	24,982,015	27,502,446
Denmark	6,871,591	7,298,891	7,914,982	Portugal	12,682,529	14,400,193	15,152,615
Estonia	1,220,369	1,290,216	1,379,100	Romania	13,369,830	13,813,061	15,649,121
Finland	11,455,281	11,170,690	11,464,457	Slovakia	4,151,302	4,137,568	4,784,423
France	131,480,572	128,341,140	131,209,905	Slovenia	1,972,671	1,945,189	2,051,804
Germany	196,498,770	201,846,444	207,127,423	Spain	100,633,927	104,729,889	110,254,905
Greece	13,007,272	13,049,668	13,201,273	Sweden	22,557,815	23,652,182	25,116,876
Hungary	8,596,983	9,419,008	10,125,570	United Kingdom	101,806,000	n.a.	n.a.
Ireland*	14,725,825	15,114,322	14,655,156				
Italy	128,429,060	127,567,695	133,270,279	**Total (EU-28)***	864,461,166	878,096,472	904,862,511

* Estimates.
© European Union. Source: Eurostat, 2017, Industry, trade and services, table *TOUR_OCC_NINAT*—Nights spent at tourist accommodation establishments.

Nights spent by national residents at other collective accommodation establishments

	2013	2014	2015		2013	2014	2015
Austria	8,618,875	8,860,126	9,122,164	Latvia	475,959	504,589	415,134
Belgium	8,411,043	8,610,698	12,480,481	Lithuania	1,952,427	2,138,925	2,203,905
Bulgaria	1,320,199	1,401,399	1,486,114	Luxembourg	167,851	193,718	171,895
Croatia	2,846,462	2,940,192	3,350,860	Malta	3,714	2,505	2,235
Cyprus	14,980	14,287	828	Netherlands	45,264,643	45,648,108	46,326,801
Czech Republic	9,338,556	9,120,954	10,517,215	Poland	27,883,490	28,605,333	29,974,318
Denmark	11,714,973	11,739,889	11,722,942	Portugal	5,126,957	4,948,899	5,369,994
Estonia	604,338	599,949	632,563	Romania	2,460,786	2,654,719	3,336,148
Finland	2,925,329	2,904,630	2,763,316	Slovakia	2,916,741	2,791,300	3,007,052
France	144,394,327	143,065,326	148,377,985	Slovenia	1,611,038	1,520,640	1,643,317
Germany	87,180,293	89,875,701	92,092,888	Spain	36,130,294	39,597,339	42,553,368
Greece	7,105,533	7,391,572*	7,161,761*	Sweden	15,709,922	16,367,477	16,882,047
Hungary	3,846,282	4,283,535	4,454,933	United Kingdom	91,264,000	n.a.	n.a.
Ireland	n.a.†	2,775,637*	1,592,550*				
Italy	63,563,173	63,410,604	66,885,677	**Total (EU-28)**	585,540,988	593,232,051*	n.a.

Note: refers to holiday and other short-stay accommodation; camping grounds, recreational vehicle parks and trailer parks.
* Estimate. † Unreliable data.
© European Union. Source: Eurostat, 2017, Industry, trade and services, table *TOUR_OCC_NINAT*—Nights spent at tourist accommodation establishments.

Nights spent by non-residents at hotels and similar establishments

	2013	2014	2015		2013	2014	2015
Austria	62,137,088	61,829,801	63,327,453	Latvia	2,294,596	2,529,942	2,553,177
Belgium	11,624,497	12,081,835	12,034,552	Lithuania	2,169,087	2,251,173	2,246,829
Bulgaria	13,987,515	13,763,998	13,095,720	Luxembourg	1,413,420	1,538,265	1,586,274
Croatia	18,900,602	18,891,924	19,851,214	Malta	7,940,350	8,182,364	8,302,348
Cyprus	13,141,237	12,872,854	12,548,278	Netherlands	18,350,969	20,183,788	21,707,565
Czech Republic	20,071,692	19,970,831	20,970,266	Poland	10,129,465	10,667,222	11,302,368
Denmark	6,010,083	6,481,576	6,487,067	Portugal	29,824,569	33,050,064	35,474,514
Estonia	3,536,875	3,515,676	3,367,951	Romania	3,167,791	3,503,522	4,100,387
Finland	4,906,135	4,795,215	4,676,645	Slovakia	3,528,739	3,171,407	3,642,146
France	73,619,897	73,552,947	74,456,927	Slovenia	4,202,067	4,294,013	4,540,345
Germany	58,322,664	61,311,889	64,890,191	Spain	185,396,233	190,530,741	197,980,823
Greece	57,058,282	60,901,973	63,570,840	Sweden	6,874,759	7,421,430	8,401,002
Hungary	10,367,322	10,653,116	11,092,521	United Kingdom	76,419,113	n.a.	n.a.
Ireland*	8,658,824	8,668,203	10,789,960				
Italy	126,330,288	127,373,740	129,680,864	**Total (EU-28)***	840,384,159	860,408,622	896,705,749

* Estimates.

© European Union. Source: Eurostat, 2017, Industry, trade and services, table *TOUR_OCC_NINAT*—Nights spent at tourist accommodation establishments.

Nights spent by non-residents at other collective accommodation establishments

	2013	2014	2015		2013	2014	2015
Austria	16,296,458	16,269,295	16,977,503	Latvia	344,838	345,992	320,708
Belgium	4,887,224	4,987,037	6,817,535	Lithuania	737,114	782,653	763,898
Bulgaria	382,911	313,800	256,561	Luxembourg	899,704	975,320	1,069,459
Croatia	40,478,294	42,180,737	45,831,796	Malta	232,058	245,851	239,707
Cyprus	11,352	11,545	2,043	Netherlands	13,419,540	14,239,764	15,590,022
Czech Republic	2,073,204	2,139,281	2,316,249	Poland	2,341,803	2,325,019	2,455,289
Denmark	3,904,190	4,126,543	4,684,349	Portugal	2,254,204	2,580,281	3,422,815
Estonia	372,451	403,623	402,256	Romania	303,361	258,943	359,630
Finland	954,312	915,487	833,705	Slovakia	748,859	680,740	742,654
France	58,631,238	57,355,753	56,008,070	Slovenia	1,685,795	1,710,610	1,988,741
Germany	12,869,278	13,493,364	13,937,582	Spain	67,051,532	69,105,054	71,437,279
Greece	11,934,358	13,773,183*	14,683,684*	Sweden	4,567,931	4,839,282	5,211,922
Hungary	1,615,561	1,698,214	1,869,874	United Kingdom†	n.a.	n.a.	n.a.
Ireland	n.a.†	2,608,221*	2,672,388*				
Italy	58,463,094	59,418,767	62,927,066	**Total (EU-28)**	351,208,796*	350,655,533*	n.a.

Note: refers to holiday and other short-stay accommodation; camping grounds, recreational vehicle parks and trailer parks.

* Estimate. † Unreliable data.

© European Union. Source: Eurostat, 2017, Industry, trade and services, table *TOUR_OCC_NINAT*—Nights spent at tourist accommodation establishments.

TOURIST ARRIVALS BY COUNTRY

Austria: Total arrivals at hotels and similar establishments (geographical breakdown by country of residence)

	2014	2015	2016
European Union (EU-28)	23,443,671	24,225,234	25,487,957
Belgium	380,948	378,420	399,028
Czech Republic	388,058	411,414	467,329
Denmark	203,163	210,871	226,493
France	426,329	424,952	434,949
Germany	8,099,430	8,304,366	8,809,113
Hungary	334,645	332,239	355,592
Italy	869,750	919,558	899,216
Netherlands	856,977	894,677	964,830
Poland	285,332	303,236	308,923
Spain	276,805	311,883	317,479
Sweden	165,843	180,647	195,710
United Kingdom	667,561	729,091	755,380
European Free Trade Association	1,211,415	1,286,686	1,315,779
Switzerland	1,123,100	1,195,623	1,223,762
Russian Federation	398,687	264,833	225,645
Africa	56,109	64,735	68,031
North America	654,815	726,848	711,384
USA	569,240	636,652	625,333
Asia	1,553,666	2,028,363	2,023,957
China, People's Republic	476,693	689,415	702,683
Japan	237,551	230,148	200,499
Oceania	123,006	138,619	130,601
Total (incl. others)	28,162,872	29,488,640	30,765,260

© European Union. Source: Eurostat, 2017, Industry, trade and services, table *TOUR_OCC_ARNRAW*—Arrivals at tourism accommodation establishments by country/world region of residence of the tourist.

Belgium: Total arrivals at hotels and similar establishments (geographical breakdown by country of residence)

	2013	2014	2015
European Union (EU-28)	8,790,453	9,070,579	9,169,788
France	1,009,822	1,009,350	958,867
Germany	657,785	667,288	698,056
Italy	259,112	276,201	267,713
Netherlands	1,093,336	1,053,476	1,044,476
Spain	313,681	340,432	329,234
United Kingdom	847,770	880,480	872,759
European Free Trade Association	134,541	140,688	148,840
Africa	67,517	69,579	67,545
North America	354,170	393,612	414,715
USA	306,495	342,609	361,948
Asia	447,477	502,003	570,550
Japan	107,027	107,045	92,350
Oceania	44,129	50,987	55,794
Total (incl. others)	10,174,877	10,564,354	10,744,195

© European Union. Source: Eurostat, 2017, Industry, trade and services, table *TOUR_OCC_ARNRAW*—Arrivals at tourism accommodation establishments by country/world region of residence of the tourist.

Bulgaria: Total arrivals at hotels and similar establishments (geographical breakdown by country of residence)

	2013	2014	2015
European Union (EU-28)	4,266,151	4,368,447	4,705,862
Germany	344,876	356,393	363,443
Greece	112,861	110,225	109,605
Romania	349,895	302,616	369,799
European Free Trade Association	64,059	64,205	61,141
Russian Federation	354,571	285,200	176,506
Turkey	89,403	96,227	119,046
Africa	2,668	4,373	4,343
North America	48,587	54,748	63,219
Asia	117,691	142,503	170,533
Oceania	8,370	9,248	9,233
Total (incl. others)	5,365,095	5,458,843	5,743,599

© European Union. Source: Eurostat, 2017, Industry, trade and services, table *TOUR_OCC_ARNRAW*—Arrivals at tourism accommodation establishments by country/world region of residence of the tourist.

Croatia: Total arrivals at hotels and similar establishments (geographical breakdown by country of residence)

	2013	2014	2015
European Union (EU-28)	4,310,201	4,345,546	4,605,448
Austria	529,991	543,951	595,858
Denmark	26,545	25,100	23,991
France	238,466	222,878	219,580
Germany	647,169	634,031	658,982
Italy	362,114	371,740	389,636
Netherlands	91,715	91,426	92,482
Spain	107,770	117,799	124,610
United Kingdom	228,457	242,335	268,320
European Free Trade Association	155,783	150,385	151,630
Russian Federation	103,194	77,456	52,570
Africa	12,405	13,008	13,220
North America	192,691	212,450	248,900
USA	153,431	168,966	199,776
Asia	392,525	602,410	719,184
China, People's Republic	47,099	60,719	89,220
Japan	147,775	161,826	145,213
Oceania	71,811	71,801	74,263
Total (incl. others)	5,562,227	5,785,070	6,196,653

© European Union. Source: Eurostat, 2017, Industry, trade and services, table *TOUR_OCC_ARNRAW*—Arrivals at tourism accommodation establishments by country/world region of residence of the tourist.

Cyprus: Total arrivals at hotels and similar establishments (geographical breakdown by country of residence)

	2013	2014	2015
European Union (EU-28)	1,590,587	1,540,144	1,617,414
Germany	102,822	98,150	101,731
United Kingdom	623,522	600,628	657,579
European Free Trade Association	109,731	97,284	83,659
Russian Federation	532,588	544,861	402,222
Total (incl. others)	2,384,997	2,366,719	2,314,687

© European Union. Source: Eurostat, 2017, Industry, trade and services, table *TOUR_OCC_ARNRAW*—Arrivals at tourism accommodation establishments by country/world region of residence of the tourist.

Czech Republic: Total arrivals at hotels and similar establishments (geographical breakdown by country of residence)

	2013	2014	2015
European Union (EU-28)	9,511,207	9,696,525	10,827,019
Austria	218,074	231,234	254,283
France	274,569	256,706	249,736
Germany	1,382,292	1,444,365	1,640,033
Italy	344,434	356,884	356,015
Netherlands	152,624	160,031	161,966
Poland	381,577	400,834	422,624
Slovakia	392,201	433,509	508,338
Spain	179,513	185,276	195,996
United Kingdom	360,117	372,627	409,207
European Free Trade Association	160,191	160,897	167,369
Russian Federation	767,103	647,360	402,594
Africa	36,008	41,021	40,582
North America	482,837	508,397	573,325
USA	389,392	407,260	462,911
Asia	834,701	933,661	1,180,572
China, People's Republic	166,476	203,295	278,196
Japan	133,096	122,059	120,485
Oceania	90,265	99,762	94,233
Total (incl. others)	12,372,359	12,566,115	13,759,959

© European Union. Source: Eurostat, 2017, Industry, trade and services, table *TOUR_OCC_ARNRAW*—Arrivals at tourism accommodation establishments by country/world region of residence of the tourist.

Denmark: Total arrivals at hotels and similar establishments (geographical breakdown by country of residence)

	2013	2014*	2015*
European Union (EU-28)	3,400,022	3,616,198	3,802,740
Germany	130,354	143,820	136,280
Netherlands	48,992	52,976	54,105
Sweden	377,435	379,279	353,356
United Kingdom	123,318	133,598	142,845
European Free Trade Association	274,759	284,666	282,304
Norway	231,116	234,217	230,621
North America	139,187	147,474	163,514
USA	119,084	127,890	144,724
Asia	142,895	152,872	165,919
China, People's Republic	48,387	51,891	61,883
Total (incl. others)	4,153,359	4,432,592	4,648,785

* Estimates.

© European Union. Source: Eurostat, 2017, Industry, trade and services, table *TOUR_OCC_ARNRAW*—Arrivals at tourism accommodation establishments by country/world region of residence of the tourist.

Estonia: Total arrivals at hotels and similar establishments (geographical breakdown by country of residence)

	2013	2014	2015
European Union (EU-28)	2,096,450	2,194,819	2,272,791
Finland	858,802	874,424	865,231
Germany	90,521	99,382	103,903
Latvia	89,651	95,722	108,029
European Free Trade Association	44,843	43,812	47,127
Russian Federation	280,297	243,794	161,301
Africa	1,462	1,673	1,894
North America	28,277	33,210	44,983
Asia	33,915	45,645	58,091
Oceania	5,258	6,632	5,052
Total (incl. others)	2,554,643	2,634,574	2,645,644

© European Union. Source: Eurostat, 2017, Industry, trade and services, table *TOUR_OCC_ARNRAW*—Arrivals at tourism accommodation establishments by country/world region of residence of the tourist.

Finland: Total arrivals at hotels and similar establishments (geographical breakdown by country of residence)

	2013	2014	2015
European Union (EU-28)	7,944,107	7,879,248	8,165,570
Estonia	66,052	67,646	66,394
France	67,909	69,739	76,362
Germany	207,227	208,421	225,918
Sweden	249,750	262,038	278,259
United Kingdom	167,373	169,722	179,160
European Free Trade Association	123,040	126,104	137,874
Russian Federation	655,556	503,251	284,330
Africa	6,808	7,418	8,426
North America	100,601	105,252	110,358
Asia	270,398	283,912	354,340
Oceania	23,554	27,163	27,911
Total (incl. others)	9,315,248	9,140,342	9,292,860

© European Union. Source: Eurostat, 2017, Industry, trade and services, table *TOUR_OCC_ARNRAW*—Arrivals at tourism accommodation establishments by country/world region of residence of the tourist.

France: Total arrivals at hotels and similar establishments (geographical breakdown by country of residence)

	2013	2014	2015
European Union (EU-28)	98,978,804	97,665,842	99,546,847
Belgium	2,926,033	2,957,774	2,938,798
Germany	3,322,194	3,262,162	3,232,258
Italy	2,427,317	2,490,874	2,339,570
Netherlands	1,715,307	1,722,876	1,724,461
Portugal	311,186	356,274	335,430
Spain	1,913,750	2,004,869	2,185,234
Sweden	314,395	281,734	298,541
United Kingdom	5,526,000	5,685,977	5,636,015
European Free Trade Association	1,779,742	1,772,621	1,810,994
Switzerland	1,552,099	1,561,271	1,608,925
Russian Federation	894,657	786,395	540,096
Africa	602,540	633,407	675,086
North America	3,652,890	3,791,418	3,994,461
Canada	480,226	469,513	481,175
USA	3,171,720	3,321,151	3,513,286
Central and South America	1,109,839	1,076,681	1,046,823
Asia	4,433,803	4,503,807	5,176,105
China, People's Republic	1,246,779	1,292,479	1,936,951
Japan	1,172,935	1,101,304	847,603
Total (incl. others)	112,727,979	111,365,958	113,893,218

© European Union. Source: Eurostat, 2017, Industry, trade and services, table *TOUR_OCC_ARNRAW*—Arrivals at tourism accommodation establishments by country/world region of residence of the tourist.

Tourism

Germany: Total arrivals at hotels and similar establishments (geographical breakdown by country of residence)

	2013	2014	2015
European Union (EU-28)	110,422,948	114,419,526	118,425,963
Austria	1,515,620	1,599,512	1,644,699
Belgium	1,064,641	1,093,246	1,136,134
Czech Republic	359,909	388,463	418,392
Denmark	1,133,266	1,189,149	1,260,288
France	1,384,068	1,428,480	1,447,028
Italy	1,443,223	1,494,138	1,552,160
Netherlands	2,803,924	2,901,235	2,997,991
Poland	704,246	773,910	804,847
Spain	804,204	846,238	1,065,664
Sweden	815,053	814,630	850,901
United Kingdom	2,043,672	2,157,616	2,285,965
European Free Trade Association	2,714,961	2,872,678	3,080,585
Norway	377,334	379,869	373,246
Switzerland	2,308,603	2,463,044	2,675,175
Turkey	247,772	262,868	292,453
Russian Federation	986,401	902,923	640,925
Africa	221,892	231,521	252,381
North America	2,470,515	2,526,775	2,694,165
Canada	269,810	257,016	261,957
USA	2,200,705	2,248,149	2,405,424
Central and South America	527,677	529,279	563,726
Asia	3,258,174	3,555,460	4,216,341
China, People's Republic	837,269	993,995	1,346,185
Japan	692,637	651,626	629,818
Oceania	297,765	300,721	309,404
Total (incl. others)	122,222,368	126,724,641	131,674,079

© European Union. Source: Eurostat, 2017, Industry, trade and services, table *TOUR_OCC_ARNRAW*—Arrivals at tourism accommodation establishments by country/world region of residence of the tourist.

Greece: Total arrivals at hotels and similar establishments (geographical breakdown by country of residence)

	2013	2014	2015
European Union (EU-28)	12,149,245	13,169,214	14,153,487
Austria	162,972	179,697	197,241
Belgium	245,012	263,194	291,913
Bulgaria	172,068	196,410	222,943
Denmark	177,776	194,390	209,245
France	779,927	896,598	1,039,674
Germany	1,156,193	1,373,910	1,488,417
Italy	576,038	642,476	649,225
Netherlands	377,445	429,539	433,288
Sweden	345,611	409,374	427,383
United Kingdom	1,281,594	1,427,060	1,656,014
European Free Trade Association	436,827	478,593	475,178
Norway	264,436	281,211	251,404
Switzerland	166,480	191,261	218,037
Russian Federation	1,141,086	1,039,711	705,724
Africa	66,229	63,911	63,871
North America	600,679	748,494	905,643
USA	494,695	626,709	762,624
Asia	639,688	869,094	1,059,070
Oceania	188,211	220,288	238,375
Total (incl. others)	16,008,948	17,418,853	18,478,701

© European Union. Source: Eurostat, 2017, Industry, trade and services, table *TOUR_OCC_ARNRAW*—Arrivals at tourism accommodation establishments by country/world region of residence of the tourist.

Hungary: Total arrivals at hotels and similar establishments (geographical breakdown by country of residence)

	2013	2014	2015
European Union (EU-28)	6,276,784	6,821,244	7,348,961
Austria	260,618	265,094	265,664
France	136,435	138,296	148,015
Germany	489,359	489,006	479,564
Italy	221,127	226,536	237,994
Romania	199,860	216,387	232,907
Spain	124,710	133,635	140,135
United Kingdom	255,525	277,621	323,709
European Free Trade Association	110,224	109,935	116,166
Russian Federation	194,390	184,345	143,772
Africa	16,449	19,063	25,651
North America	231,460	258,544	289,632
USA	197,915	222,582	250,597
Asia	378,009	433,999	520,114
Oceania	33,087	32,711	37,245
Total (incl. others)	7,632,739	8,240,710	8,887,881

© European Union. Source: Eurostat, 2017, Industry, trade and services, table *TOUR_OCC_ARNRAW*—Arrivals at tourism accommodation establishments by country/world region of residence of the tourist.

Ireland: Total arrivals at hotels and similar establishments (geographical breakdown by country of residence)

	2013*	2014*	2015*
European Union (EU-28)	8,288,318	8,854,061	9,286,860
France	118,444	111,605	136,143
Germany	157,183	167,415	199,568
Italy	62,162	66,430	91,577
Netherlands	36,655	38,908	59,195
United Kingdom	649,456	653,211	796,787
European Free Trade Association	47,168	44,681	59,991
Africa	10,185	9,384	11,412
North America	376,761	399,309	473,000
Canada	42,966	66,054	71,973
USA	329,865	329,324	396,337
Asia	36,970	39,951	51,455
Oceania	54,639	50,275	59,407
Australia	49,445	44,872	51,984
Total (incl. others)	8,843,233	9,426,773	9,973,563

* Estimates.

© European Union. Source: Eurostat, 2017, Industry, trade and services, table *TOUR_OCC_ARNRAW*—Arrivals at tourism accommodation establishments by country/world region of residence of the tourist.

Tourism STATISTICAL SURVEY

Italy: Total arrivals at hotels and similar establishments (geographical breakdown by country of residence)

	2013	2014	2015
European Union (EU-28)	64,730,800	65,992,163	69,272,066
Austria	1,616,711	1,682,685	1,750,171
Belgium	875,174	855,856	897,984
Czech Republic	385,291	386,434	418,432
Denmark	359,724	344,502	357,053
France	3,120,628	3,104,639	3,371,199
Germany	7,094,037	7,132,089	7,223,429
Greece	273,558	279,669	232,138
Hungary	259,329	285,977	316,160
Ireland	297,695	302,247	262,903
Netherlands	931,599	941,618	966,947
Poland	730,935	832,041	892,346
Spain	1,398,327	1,467,437	1,489,827
Sweden	506,766	502,893	522,710
United Kingdom	2,498,185	2,612,349	2,756,726
European Free Trade Association	2,138,321	2,179,704	2,368,627
Norway	338,409	333,386	299,607
Switzerland	1,780,438	1,823,760	2,047,162
Turkey	305,028	318,997	384,508
Russian Federation	1,753,193	1,592,380	1,032,899
Africa	344,209	349,858	448,283
North America	4,600,356	4,742,675	4,541,431
Canada	605,987	608,385	624,354
USA	3,984,822	4,126,484	3,907,273
Central and South America	1,576,002	1,548,031	1,904,708
Asia	4,989,037	5,429,747	6,998,151
China, People's Republic	1,760,320	2,180,295	3,152,726
Japan	1,361,430	1,236,817	1,050,508
South Korea	398,919	477,435	700,401
Oceania	804,255	816,473	838,865
Australia	702,333	692,006	708,036
Total (incl. others)	82,639,236	84,240,379	88,992,199

© European Union. Source: Eurostat, 2017, Industry, trade and services, table *TOUR_OCC_ARNRAW*—Arrivals at tourism accommodation establishments by country/world region of residence of the tourist.

Latvia: Total arrivals at hotels and similar establishments (geographical breakdown by country of residence)

	2013	2014	2015
European Union (EU-28)	1,004,980	1,205,872	1,379,386
Estonia	96,179	110,145	131,517
Finland	59,303	70,118	79,177
Germany	108,883	152,255	163,118
Lithuania	82,678	94,789	118,786
European Free Trade Association	76,495	83,681	93,067
Russian Federation	288,841	277,769	193,522
Africa	1,815	3,398	3,003
North America	28,494	29,774	34,024
Asia	44,664	61,782	76,919
Oceania	4,839	6,808	5,507
Total (incl. others)	1,509,280	1,747,681	1,865,289

© European Union. Source: Eurostat, 2017, Industry, trade and services, table *TOUR_OCC_ARNRAW*—Arrivals at tourism accommodation establishments by country/world region of residence of the tourist.

Lithuania: Total arrivals at hotels and similar establishments (geographical breakdown by country of residence)

	2013	2014	2015
European Union (EU-28)	1,248,318	1,340,087	1,471,895
Germany	128,620	140,674	146,096
Poland	117,133	105,880	111,906
European Free Trade Association	34,585	39,969	50,028
Russian Federation	208,004	187,223	123,977
Africa	1,772	1,815	3,097
North America	28,672	35,904	33,895
Asia	40,762	55,807	73,720
Oceania	4,156	5,022	4,171
Total (incl. others)	1,745,872	1,874,827	1,959,233

© European Union. Source: Eurostat, 2017, Industry, trade and services, table *TOUR_OCC_ARNRAW*—Arrivals at tourism accommodation establishments by country/world region of residence of the tourist.

Luxembourg: Total arrivals at hotels and similar establishments (geographical breakdown by country of residence)

	2013	2014	2015
European Union (EU-28)	682,275	731,078	756,717
Belgium	165,711	171,307	175,027
France	117,507	131,621	131,102
Germany	112,086	120,260	121,332
Netherlands	66,714	69,455	71,257
European Free Trade Association	23,032	27,304	25,933
Africa	4,416	5,999	5,226
North America	29,045	31,868	36,710
Asia	53,534	62,384	68,748
Oceania	3,057	3,652	4,119
Total (incl. others)	831,161	903,876	939,313

© European Union. Source: Eurostat, 2017, Industry, trade and services, table *TOUR_OCC_ARNRAW*—Arrivals at tourism accommodation establishments by country/world region of residence of the tourist.

Malta: Total arrivals at hotels and similar establishments (geographical breakdown by country of residence)

	2013*	2014*	2015*
European Union (EU-28)	1,226,721	1,308,441	1,373,237
Germany	128,736	125,035	121,117
Italy	195,670	211,835	215,076
United Kingdom	351,463	385,236	420,182
European Free Trade Association	41,997	44,234	41,512
Africa	65,387	64,771	15,133
North America	16,944	21,769	25,927
Asia	21,137	22,817	53,240
Oceania	13,658	14,087	16,054
Total (incl. others)	1,439,654	1,523,645	1,563,102

* Estimates.

© European Union. Source: Eurostat, 2017, Industry, trade and services, table *TOUR_OCC_ARNRAW*—Arrivals at tourism accommodation establishments by country/world region of residence of the tourist.

Netherlands: Total arrivals at hotels and similar establishments (geographical breakdown by country of residence)

	2014	2015	2016
European Union (EU-28)	19,587,080	20,427,503	21,913,539
Belgium	1,092,542	1,192,916	1,317,080
Denmark	126,521	135,773	127,588
France	651,970	669,628	706,170
Germany	2,036,036	2,210,650	2,425,342
Italy	482,437	522,887	510,327
Spain	384,869	420,263	432,751
Sweden	135,401	146,641	149,403
United Kingdom	1,752,593	1,854,949	1,924,229
European Free Trade Association	365,108	385,260	364,204
Switzerland	234,492	247,519	240,510
Russian Federation	185,569	143,023	122,873
Africa	132,029	127,241	134,765
North America	1,126,453	1,179,126	1,327,912
Canada	142,246	153,590	153,573
USA	984,207	1,025,536	1,174,339
Central and South America	294,555	316,195	307,483
Asia	964,605	1,109,715	1,071,707
China, People's Republic	245,410	324,054	289,007
Japan	144,694	136,096	106,102
Oceania	184,887	185,422	196,572
Total (incl. others)	23,121,671	24,175,682	25,758,232

© European Union. Source: Eurostat, 2017, Industry, trade and services, table *TOUR_OCC_ARNRAW*—Arrivals at tourism accommodation establishments by country/world region of residence of the tourist.

Poland: Total arrivals at hotels and similar establishments (geographical breakdown by country of residence)

	2013	2014	2015
European Union (EU-28)	15,379,468	16,896,599	18,416,724
France	180,558	187,059	197,508
Germany	1,087,300	1,159,850	1,234,149
Italy	203,213	206,115	212,925
Slovakia	47,283	52,368	56,434
United Kingdom	355,828	343,359	388,378
European Free Trade Association	191,060	219,917	247,548
Russian Federation	376,891	316,028	204,374
Ukraine	233,473	226,996	230,055
Africa	16,296	16,568	16,263
North America	234,056	256,719	274,518
USA	205,400	225,307	244,112
Asia	345,347	377,128	386,744
Oceania	27,225	27,418	27,801
Total (incl. others)	17,115,770	18,658,841	20,135,814

© European Union. Source: Eurostat, 2017, Industry, trade and services, table *TOUR_OCC_ARNRAW*—Arrivals at tourism accommodation establishments by country/world region of residence of the tourist.

Portugal: Total arrivals at hotels and similar establishments (geographical breakdown by country of residence)

	2013	2014	2015
European Union (EU-28)	11,916,148	13,520,087	14,677,278
Belgium	164,745	211,820	232,075
France	803,369	996,499	1,132,036
Germany	821,398	920,297	1,037,870
Ireland	192,092	213,760	232,115
Italy	317,229	359,510	429,108
Netherlands	389,200	394,113	425,342
Spain	1,227,456	1,426,857	1,521,965
United Kingdom	1,232,853	1,405,039	1,554,618
European Free Trade Association	228,525	245,583	273,994
Russian Federation	157,682	142,693	94,286
Africa	122,019	149,034	142,967
North America	453,234	522,151	607,373
USA	328,644	364,292	429,300
Central and South America	582,291	665,609	636,630
Brazil	506,251	579,559	551,687
Asia	330,390	442,903	537,504
Oceania	52,907	70,613	75,567
Total (incl. others)	13,925,530	15,857,125	17,144,474

© European Union. Source: Eurostat, 2017, Industry, trade and services, table *TOUR_OCC_ARNRAW*—Arrivals at tourism accommodation establishments by country/world region of residence of the tourist.

Romania: Total arrivals at hotels and similar establishments (geographical breakdown by country of residence)

	2013	2014	2015
European Union (EU-28)	6,049,463	6,356,104	7,322,520
Bulgaria	41,643	45,265	53,357
Hungary	74,730	77,107	84,833
European Free Trade Association	33,508	30,733	37,541
Russian Federation	27,062	26,648	22,822
Ukraine	15,729	20,967	22,609
Africa	13,438	18,244	18,065
North America	102,107	127,616	145,593
Asia	162,453	219,727	310,128
Oceania	9,404	12,261	12,480
Total (incl. others)	6,557,110	6,981,805	8,097,804

© European Union. Source: Eurostat, 2017, Industry, trade and services, table *TOUR_OCC_ARNRAW*—Arrivals at tourism accommodation establishments by country/world region of residence of the tourist.

Slovakia: Total arrivals at hotels and similar establishments (geographical breakdown by country of residence)

	2013	2014	2015
European Union (EU-28)	2,778,705	2,603,523	3,061,600
Czech Republic	388,848	346,847	405,739
Germany	142,431	128,452	147,049
Poland	125,531	121,536	127,727
European Free Trade Association	23,987	19,403	22,120
Russian Federation	47,173	34,779	26,144
Africa	6,065	4,845	6,490
North America	39,317	33,877	44,699
Asia	93,781	71,207	111,189
Oceania	5,666	5,095	6,827
Total (incl. others)	3,126,605	2,880,037	3,379,070

© European Union. Source: Eurostat, 2017, Industry, trade and services, table *TOUR_OCC_ARNRAW*—Arrivals at tourism accommodation establishments by country/world region of residence of the tourist.

Slovenia: Total arrivals at hotels and similar establishments (geographical breakdown by country of residence)

	2013	2014	2015
European Union (EU-28)	1,758,764	1,845,788	1,991,819
Austria	198,847	218,222	229,615
Germany	141,387	147,559	156,746
Italy	339,930	367,128	394,030
European Free Trade Association	34,022	34,370	40,074
North America	56,610	61,394	67,881
Asia	146,839	205,528	258,322
Oceania	18,106	17,104	20,732
Total (incl. others)	2,252,890	2,387,359	2,605,314

© European Union. Source: Eurostat, 2017, Industry, trade and services, table *TOUR_OCC_ARNRAW*—Arrivals at tourism accommodation establishments by country/world region of residence of the tourist.

Spain: Total arrivals at hotels and similar establishments (geographical breakdown by country of residence)

	2013	2014	2015
European Union (EU-28)	72,268,928	75,842,823	80,633,699
Austria	375,363	411,885	446,689
Belgium	1,121,392	1,177,339	1,276,536
Denmark	475,730	500,599	512,905
Finland	327,868	393,817	366,027
France	4,546,021	4,811,600	5,309,416
Germany	7,035,130	7,274,553	7,261,343
Ireland	585,472	631,547	696,065
Italy	2,195,871	2,329,343	2,588,733
Netherlands	1,497,341	1,524,507	1,670,956
Poland	494,162	557,934	667,053
Portugal	1,009,310	1,138,568	1,205,309
Sweden	919,171	911,029	903,642
United Kingdom	8,099,534	8,369,634	8,993,074
European Free Trade Association	1,457,074	1,506,647	1,514,960
Norway	614,088	614,605	562,751
Switzerland	803,763	847,357	898,300
Russian Federation	1,484,739	1,283,778	753,830
Africa	501,349	527,410	589,499
North America	2,614,835	2,751,673	3,085,263
Canada	376,993	364,851	409,976
USA	1,942,857	2,069,346	2,303,035
Central and South America	1,535,426	1,540,394	1,629,179
Asia	1,994,038	2,448,323	2,906,641
China, People's Republic	441,055	574,835	777,883
Japan	683,383	649,743	592,636
Oceania	319,280	316,028	339,401
Australia	281,822	278,065	296,141
Total (incl. others)	83,820,917	87,814,530	93,216,968

© European Union. Source: Eurostat, 2017, Industry, trade and services, table *TOUR_OCC_ARNRAW*—Arrivals at tourism accommodation establishments by country/world region of residence of the tourist.

Sweden: Total arrivals at hotels and similar establishments (geographical breakdown by country of residence)

	2013*	2014*	2015*
European Union (EU-28)	15,740,520	16,432,803	17,498,676
Denmark	223,968	238,467	274,843
Finland	189,408	196,905	207,686
Germany	386,815	428,067	451,059
United Kingdom	265,612	292,013	342,723
European Free Trade Association	688,865	682,367	725,537
Norway	604,024	588,556	614,887
North America	241,405	264,485	276,799
USA	212,449	234,673	248,400
Asia	263,035	297,820	360,551
Oceania	27,228	31,319	31,427
Total (incl. others)	17,538,374	18,413,454	19,754,949

* Estimates.

© European Union. Source: Eurostat, 2017, Industry, trade and services, table *TOUR_OCC_ARNRAW*—Arrivals at tourism accommodation establishments by country/world region of residence of the tourist.

United Kingdom: Total arrivals at hotels and similar establishments (geographical breakdown by country of residence)

	2011	2012*	2013
European Union (EU-28)	n.a.	n.a.	65,399,849
Austria	180,188	224,164	249,450
Belgium	558,989	624,266	782,342
Denmark	446,101	481,867	630,631
France	1,666,557	1,722,158	1,941,126
Germany	2,262,948	2,136,764	2,358,725
Ireland	1,146,369	1,092,773	1,043,791
Italy	1,028,947	960,762	1,061,073
Netherlands	1,120,591	1,094,759	1,250,336
Spain	1,026,346	894,317	932,790
Sweden	665,226	556,776	681,182
European Free Trade Association	1,107,694	1,180,637	1,393,749
Norway	580,811	596,459	754,452
Switzerland	495,113	546,467	595,211
Russian Federation	138,988	154,518	184,390
Africa	269,936	315,629	368,656
North America	3,111,673	3,116,241	3,522,556
Canada	587,369	536,236	670,852
USA	2,524,304	2,489,265	2,719,976
Central and South America	436,083	360,494	448,325
Asia	1,533,818	1,596,716	2,324,479
China, People's Republic	114,070	222,603	322,373
Japan	203,383	204,744	220,863
Oceania	1,085,932	966,836	1,172,780
Australia	979,204	846,360	1,037,337
Total (incl. others)	60,730,955	74,280,089	75,010,155

* Break in series.

© European Union. Source: Eurostat, 2017, Industry, trade and services, table *TOUR_OCC_ARNRAW*—Arrivals at tourism accommodation establishments by country/world region of residence of the tourist.

EDUCATION

Note: Reference years relate to the latter part of the relevant school or academic year.
For example, 2015 refers to the school year 2014/15.

ENROLMENT

Total number of pupils and students at all levels of education (full-time and part-time)

	2013	2014	2015		2013	2014	2015
Austria	1,713,630	1,705,895	1,710,122	Latvia	418,674	408,588	401,491
Belgium	2,978,165	3,012,779	3,032,451	Lithuania	671,942	650,334	634,107
Bulgaria	1,294,682	1,303,836	1,284,910	Luxembourg	n.a.	n.a.	107,346
Croatia	809,004	805,517	795,154	Malta	78,485	78,474	79,572
Cyprus	169,786	168,581	172,007	Netherlands	n.a.	n.a.	4,175,715
Czech Republic	2,137,200	2,139,286	2,138,012	Poland	8,381,197	8,126,967	8,018,013
Denmark	1,508,185	1,513,888	1,523,180	Portugal	2,139,977	2,081,827	2,049,662
Estonia	298,957	294,848	n.a.	Romania	3,887,891	3,805,043	3,716,940
Finland	1,417,102	1,413,461	1,417,675	Slovakia	1,075,588	1,051,484	1,031,920
France	15,018,514	15,141,701	15,292,567	Slovenia	412,721	414,892	404,867
Germany	15,995,657	15,969,735	15,965,088	Spain	n.a.	9,674,213	9,713,547
Greece	n.a.	n.a.	2,203,291*	Sweden	2,461,050	2,478,059	2,529,956
Hungary	2,049,730	1,985,790	1,915,960	United Kingdom	14,763,504	14,849,255	14,993,815
Ireland	1,203,790	1,223,826	1,266,320				
Italy	11,022,228	10,985,398	10,927,554	**Total (EU-28)**	n.a.	n.a.	n.a.

* Estimate.
Note: refers to all ISCED 2011 levels, excluding early childhood educational development.
© European Union. Source: Eurostat, 2017, Population and social conditions, table *EDUC_UOE_ENRA01*—Pupils and students enrolled by education level, sex, type of institution and intensity of participation.

Distribution of pupils and students by level of education*, 2015

	Level 1	Level 2	Level 3	Level 4	Level 5	Level 6	Total (Levels 1–6)
Austria	327,817	333,535	357,536	20,011	77,877	183,768	1,710,122
Belgium	782,606	444,573	773,339	66,118	24,414	365,925	3,032,451
Bulgaria	261,793	223,664	277,734	1,643	n.a.	186,702	1,284,910
Croatia	162,355	178,650	181,555	n.a.	118	100,879	795,154
Cyprus	53,773	27,142	30,019	347	3,128	19,994	172,007
Czech Republic	534,932	370,387	400,050	65,424	994	236,887	2,138,012
Denmark	468,536	241,669	311,594	n.a.	34,973	195,054	1,523,180
Estonia	79,594	37,202	40,708	10,248	n.a.	36,299	n.a.
Finland	355,231	178,389	361,678	23,012	n.a.	219,370	1,417,675
France	4,255,988	3,376,340	2,606,528	33,691	495,472	991,175	15,292,567
Germany	2,879,394	4,543,318	2,569,631	764,460	394	1,792,434	15,965,088
Greece	643,762	320,754	341,987	55,945	n.a.	598,990	2,203,291
Hungary	395,549	385,299	441,327	75,144	11,655	214,737	1,915,960
Ireland	544,856	189,681	164,989	81,064	16,505	161,302	1,266,320
Italy	2,856,247	1,772,841	2,833,176	1,703	6,548	1,076,667	10,927,554
Latvia	117,303	55,331	62,430	4,477	16,105	50,634	401,491
Lithuania	108,038	182,697	80,545	19,903	n.a.	108,083	634,107
Luxembourg	35,920	21,660	25,367	752	587	3,231	107,346
Malta	24,624	12,533	16,901	3,081	2,537	7,026	79,572
Netherlands	1,208,038	816,476	797,021	n.a.	18,687	646,851	4,175,715
Poland	2,306,102	1,116,897	1,431,508	261,921	2,721	1,104,364	8,018,013
Portugal	656,727	384,971	393,618	12,179	395	203,836	2,049,662
Romania	947,205	785,100	777,860	105,557	n.a.	354,186	3,716,940
Slovakia	216,266	253,671	200,361	15,326	2,847	102,434	1,031,920
Slovenia	115,560	54,595	88,652	n.a.	11,485	48,893	404,867
Spain	3,010,404	1,624,793	1,688,334	27,985	372,356	1,204,409	9,713,547
Sweden	791,893	333,721	510,391	22,468	25,244	246,400	2,529,956
United Kingdom	4,621,192	2,334,679	4,039,996	n.a.	272,487	1,523,902	14,993,815
Total (EU-28)	n.a.	n.a.	n.a.	n.a.	n.a.	n.a.	n.a.

* Definitions: Level 1—Primary; Level 2—Lower secondary; Level 3—Upper secondary; Level 4—Post-secondary non-tertiary; Level 5—Short-cycle tertiary; Level 6—Bachelor's or equivalent.
© European Union. Source: Eurostat, 2017, Population and social conditions, table *EDUC_UOE_ENRA01*—Pupils and students enrolled by education level, sex, type of institution and intensity of participation.

Pupils in early childhood education (ISCED level 0)

	2013	2014	2015		2013	2014	2015
Austria	274,060	281,712	289,858	Latvia	79,681	78,732	76,069
Belgium	n.a.	n.a.	n.a.	Lithuania	112,587	118,119	122,333
Bulgaria	235,015	240,622	241,123	Luxembourg	16,488	16,685	16,751
Croatia	128,046	131,037	133,764	Malta	8,901	8,910	9,217
Cyprus	22,783	22,772	29,669	Netherlands	521,306	511,789	511,579
Czech Republic	358,104	367,352	371,690	Poland	1,216,467	1,297,190	1,236,280
Denmark	305,878	300,278	291,683	Portugal	n.a.	n.a.	n.a.
Estonia	67,034	68,684	68,812	Romania	n.a.	n.a.	578,177
Finland	244,601	245,140	245,851	Slovakia	154,680	158,195	161,906
France	2,560,774	2,583,890	2,595,862	Slovenia	83,090	83,090	84,750
Germany	2,884,997	2,970,436	3,014,046	Spain	1,915,000	1,886,886	1,842,383
Greece	216,533	310,118	242,377	Sweden	589,944	599,190	599,719
Hungary	n.a.	n.a.	325,010	United Kingdom	1,516,080	1,596,803	2,035,420
Ireland	n.a.	n.a.	71,098				
Italy	n.a.	n.a.	n.a.	**Total (EU-28)**	n.a.	n.a.	n.a.

© European Union. Source: Eurostat, 2017, Population and social conditions, table *EDUC_UOE_ENRA01*—Pupils and students enrolled by education level, sex, type of institution and intensity of participation.

Pupils in primary education (ISCED level 1)

	2013	2014	2015		2013	2014	2015
Austria	327,187	327,247	327,817	Latvia	114,089	114,660	117,303
Belgium	764,137	773,568	782,606	Lithuania	109,028	108,115	108,038
Bulgaria	253,675	258,840	261,793	Luxembourg	35,250	35,435	35,920
Croatia	160,275	160,819	162,355	Malta	23,655	24,072	24,624
Cyprus	54,069	53,129	53,773	Netherlands	n.a.	1,222,867	1,208,038
Czech Republic	491,828	510,613	534,932	Poland	2,160,861	2,152,655	2,306,102
Denmark	469,568	467,484	468,536	Portugal	693,045	674,038	656,727
Estonia	75,644	77,215	79,594	Romania	931,951	945,742	947,205
Finland	348,432	351,766	355,231	Slovakia	211,407	213,766	216,266
France	4,171,003	4,188,552	4,255,988	Slovenia	109,218	109,218	115,560
Germany	2,890,468	2,862,690	2,879,394	Spain	2,934,648	2,960,626	3,010,404
Greece	633,534	628,753	643,762	Sweden	733,412	757,164	791,893
Hungary	385,466	393,020	395,549	United Kingdom	4,622,158	4,509,479	4,621,192
Ireland	527,768	536,471	544,856				
Italy	2,860,957	2,862,666	2,856,247	**Total (EU-28)**	n.a.	n.a.	n.a.

© European Union. Source: Eurostat, 2017, Population and social conditions, table *EDUC_UOE_ENRA01*—Pupils and students enrolled by education level, sex, type of institution and intensity of participation.

Pupils in lower secondary education (ISCED level 2)

	2013	2014	2015		2013	2014	2015
Austria	336,660	334,201	333,535	Latvia	55,329	54,825	55,331
Belgium	432,877	433,699	444,573	Lithuania	203,027	190,914	182,697
Bulgaria	235,476	232,110	223,664	Luxembourg	21,847	21,969	21,660
Croatia	190,908	184,005	178,650	Malta	13,217	12,812	12,533
Cyprus	28,665	27,837	27,142	Netherlands	n.a.	n.a.	816,476
Czech Republic	365,165	367,021	370,387	Poland	1,188,203	1,149,522	1,116,897
Denmark	244,067	242,432	241,669	Portugal	400,478	383,421	384,971
Estonia	36,946	36,766	37,202	Romania	812,241	806,150	785,100
Finland	181,418	179,375	178,389	Slovakia	259,235	257,407	253,671
France	3,332,338	3,348,855	3,376,340	Slovenia	54,565	54,565	54,595
Germany	4,713,705	4,621,120	4,543,318	Spain	1,663,474	1,625,844	1,624,793
Greece	323,909	314,664	320,754	Sweden	321,148	324,659	333,721
Hungary	390,321	386,602	385,299	United Kingdom	2,379,780	2,361,910	2,334,679
Ireland	189,543	187,826	189,681				
Italy	1,813,862	1,795,246	1,772,841	**Total (EU-28)**	n.a.	n.a.	n.a.

© European Union. Source: Eurostat, 2017, Population and social conditions, table *EDUC_UOE_ENRA01*—Pupils and students enrolled by education level, sex, type of institution and intensity of participation.

STATISTICAL SURVEY — Education

Students in upper secondary education (ISCED level 3)

	2013	2014	2015		2013	2014	2015
Austria	369,842	363,188	357,536	Latvia	71,613	66,755	62,430
Belgium	773,697	776,413	773,339	Lithuania	91,247	86,435	80,545
Bulgaria	284,093	286,804	277,734	Luxembourg	24,409	24,903	25,367
Croatia	188,194	186,351	181,555	Malta	17,772	17,418	16,901
Cyprus	32,128	30,797	30,019	Netherlands	n.a.	n.a.	797,021
Czech Republic	436,149	414,371	400,050	Poland	1,589,524	1,491,765	1,431,508
Denmark	311,211	311,359	311,594	Portugal	398,447	385,210	393,618
Estonia	43,894	41,107	40,708	Romania	851,544	803,109	777,860
Finland	359,603	357,550	361,678	Slovakia	222,339	207,550	200,361
France	2,581,511	2,598,357	2,606,528	Slovenia	92,998	92,998	88,652
Germany	2,575,681	2,579,952	2,569,631	Spain	1,632,885	1,662,580	1,688,334
Greece	371,024	353,054	341,987	Sweden	517,523	502,035	510,391
Hungary	500,438	471,205	441,327	United Kingdom	4,117,193	4,195,081	4,039,996
Ireland	153,401	160,290	164,989				
Italy	2,780,440	2,801,670	2,833,176	**Total (EU-28)**	n.a.	n.a.	n.a.

© European Union. Source: Eurostat, 2017, Population and social conditions, table *EDUC_UOE_ENRA01*—Pupils and students enrolled by education level, sex, type of institution and intensity of participation.

Students in post-secondary non-tertiary education (ISCED level 4)

	2013	2014	2015		2013	2014	2015
Austria	19,827	20,131	20,011	Latvia	3,488	3,945	4,477
Belgium	61,977	70,358	66,118	Lithuania	15,376	17,701	19,903
Bulgaria	2,464	2,166	1,643	Luxembourg	840	702	752
Croatia	n.a.	n.a.	n.a.	Malta	2,366	2,652	3,081
Cyprus	176	372	347	Netherlands	1,571	567	n.a.
Czech Republic	58,513	61,305	65,424	Poland	323,424	273,169	261,921
Denmark	n.a.	n.a.	n.a.	Portugal	10,341	11,544	12,179
Estonia	10,633	11,078	10,248	Romania	92,854	102,677	105,557
Finland	24,188	22,921	23,012	Slovakia	18,384	16,712	15,326
France	34,753	33,167	33,691	Slovenia	n.a.	n.a.	n.a.
Germany	828,667	769,170	764,460	Spain	n.a.*	n.a.*	27,985
Greece	n.a.	n.a.	55,945	Sweden	22,696	23,673	22,468
Hungary	74,261	75,324	75,144	United Kingdom	n.a.	n.a.	n.a.
Ireland	55,594	57,271	81,064				
Italy	8,181	7,493	1,703	**Total (EU-28)**	n.a.	n.a.	n.a.

* Definition differs.
© European Union. Source: Eurostat, 2017, Population and social conditions, table *EDUC_UOE_ENRA01*—Pupils and students enrolled by education level, sex, type of institution and intensity of participation.

Post-secondary non-tertiary students by sex, 2015

	Males	Females	Total		Males	Females	Total
Austria	4,062	15,949	20,011	Latvia	1,772	2,705	4,477
Belgium	32,488	33,630	66,118	Lithuania	9,409	10,494	19,903
Bulgaria	900	743	1,643	Luxembourg	606	146	752
Croatia	n.a.	n.a.	n.a.	Malta	1,743	1,338	3,081
Cyprus	280	67	347	Netherlands	n.a.	n.a.	n.a.
Czech Republic	22,060	43,364	65,424	Poland	77,189	184,732	261,921
Denmark	n.a.	n.a.	n.a.	Portugal	7,906	4,273	12,179
Estonia	3,968	6,280	10,248	Romania	36,001	69,556	105,557
Finland	10,741	12,271	23,012	Slovakia	7,823	7,503	15,326
France	11,836	21,855	33,691	Slovenia	n.a.	n.a.	n.a.
Germany	325,810	438,650	764,460	Spain	11,751	16,234	27,985
Greece	25,374	30,571	55,945	Sweden	10,290	12,178	22,468
Hungary	34,171	40,973	75,144	United Kingdom	n.a.	n.a.	n.a.
Ireland	42,073	38,991	81,064				
Italy	1,036	667	1,703	**Total (EU-28)**	n.a.	n.a.	n.a.

© European Union. Source: Eurostat, 2017, Population and social conditions, table *EDUC_UOE_ENRA01*—Pupils and students enrolled by education level, sex, type of institution and intensity of participation.

Education STATISTICAL SURVEY

Students in bachelor's or equivalent level education (ISCED level 6)

	2013	2014	2015		2013	2014	2015
Austria	180,234	179,406	183,768	Latvia	63,274	57,955	50,634
Belgium	364,202	362,780	365,925	Lithuania	124,519	113,881	108,083
Bulgaria	195,637	191,416	186,702	Luxembourg	n.a.	n.a.	3,231
Croatia	102,795	103,168	100,879	Malta	6,914	6,933	7,026
Cyprus	19,990	19,779	19,994	Netherlands	n.a.	n.a.	646,851
Czech Republic	267,731	256,329	236,887	Poland	1,266,471	1,172,637	1,104,364
Denmark	182,281	187,902	195,054	Portugal	231,528	220,859	203,836
Estonia	44,758	40,539	36,299	Romania	409,606	377,136	354,186
Finland	228,273	223,519	219,370	Slovakia	120,806	113,149	102,434
France	931,748	961,447	991,175	Slovenia	54,865	56,825	48,893
Germany	1,635,907	1,734,827	1,792,434	Spain	1,085,012	1,180,345	1,204,409
Greece	588,201	598,990	598,990	Sweden	252,980	247,169	246,400
Hungary	237,647	228,535	214,737	United Kingdom	1,526,720	1,532,677	1,523,902
Ireland	121,210	154,294	161,302				
Italy	1,108,260	1,090,764	1,076,667	**Total (EU-28)**	n.a.	n.a.	n.a.

© European Union. Source: Eurostat, 2017, Population and social conditions, table *EDUC_UOE_ENRA01*—Pupils and students enrolled by education level, sex, type of institution and intensity of participation.

Bachelor's or equivalent level students by sex, 2015

	Males	Females	Total		Males	Females	Total
Austria	86,998	96,769	183,768	Latvia	21,781	28,853	50,634
Belgium	160,014	205,911	365,925	Lithuania	48,169	59,914	108,083
Bulgaria	88,426	98,276	186,702	Luxembourg	1,588	1,643	3,231
Croatia	47,126	53,753	100,879	Malta	3,049	3,977	7,026
Cyprus	9,514	10,480	19,994	Netherlands	311,049	355,802	646,851
Czech Republic	101,180	135,707	236,887	Poland	483,787	620,577	1,104,364
Denmark	80,224	114,830	195,054	Portugal	94,085	109,751	203,836
Estonia	15,446	20,853	36,299	Romania	172,517	181,669	354,186
Finland	105,154	114,216	219,370	Slovakia	42,152	60,282	102,434
France	412,633	578,542	991,175	Slovenia	20,038	28,855	48,893
Germany	981,474	810,960	1,792,434	Spain	553,642	650,767	1,204,409
Greece*	312,255	286,735	989,990	Sweden	91,195	155,205	246,400
Hungary	100,261	114,476	214,737	United Kingdom	681,722	842,180	1,533,902
Ireland	80,578	80,724	161,302				
Italy	491,350	585,317	1,076,667	**Total (EU-28)**	n.a.	n.a.	n.a.

* Estimates.
© European Union. Source: Eurostat, 2017, Population and social conditions, table *EDUC_UOE_ENRA01*—Pupils and students enrolled by education level, sex, type of institution and intensity of participation.

PERSONNEL

Classroom teachers and academic staff at all levels of education (full-time and part-time)

	2010	2011	2012		2010	2011	2012
Austria	136,201	134,853	139,123	Latvia	34,899	36,018	35,686
Belgium	216,546	216,425	216,250	Lithuania	79,053	77,047	73,772
Bulgaria	91,601	89,731	90,508	Luxembourg	10,553	n.a.	11,673
Croatia	69,040	71,498	72,364	Malta	7,249	7,999	7,558
Cyprus	13,412	13,449	13,357	Netherlands	237,664	249,195	243,750
Czech Republic	140,443	140,188	139,187	Poland	630,301	646,598	642,792
Denmark	n.a.	n.a.	n.a.	Portugal	210,359	206,575	193,804
Estonia	n.a.	n.a.	20,665	Romania	249,402	233,993	227,170
Finland	97,424	101,215	102,227	Slovakia	75,011	74,796	74,760
France	883,057	892,195	882,308	Slovenia	29,158	29,572	30,119
Germany	1,105,045	1,121,464	1,136,008	Spain	756,144	763,755	761,614
Greece	n.a.	n.a.	n.a.	Sweden	207,877	211,033	212,783
Hungary	170,924	169,690	168,758	United Kingdom	777,832	741,401	744,740
Ireland	68,917	72,102	n.a.				
Italy	800,592	779,458	761,035	**Total (EU-28)**	n.a.	n.a.	n.a.

© European Union. Source: Eurostat, 2015, Population and social conditions, table *EDUC_PERSIT*—Teachers (ISCED 0–4) and academic staff (ISCED 5–6) by employment status (full-time, part-time, full-time equivalence) and sex.

STATISTICAL SURVEY — Education

Distribution of teaching staff by level of education,* 2015

	Level 0	Level 1	Level 2	Level 3	Level 4	Levels 5–8
Austria	27,476	30,972	42,227	29,936	1,035	60,894
Belgium	35,254†	69,681	47,829	81,393	5,554	28,623
Bulgaria	18,982	14,769	17,170	21,803	376	23,743
Croatia	10,940	11,849	22,996	19,279†	n.a.	16,121
Cyprus	2,535	4,513	2,580	2,941	63	2,937
Czech Republic	27,624	28,192	31,233	35,622	593	16,515
Denmark	n.a.	n.a.	n.a.	n.a.	n.a.	37,071
Estonia	8,496	7,049	4,686†	4,853†	n.a.	4,836
Finland	n.a.	26,150	19,888	21,954	1,296	14,866
France	127,032	235,659	230,974	231,194	n.a.†	109,154
Germany	469,451	235,571	411,404	174,810	81,042	396,223
Greece	n.a.	n.a.	n.a.	n.a.	n.a.	n.a.
Hungary	26,480	36,029	38,939	41,383	6,265	21,045
Ireland	16,002	33,613	n.a.†	24,455†	n.a.	9,247
Italy	131,922	237,483	165,705	242,161	n.a.	89,972
Latvia	7,532	10,537	7,623	7,038	246	6,837
Lithuania	12,910	8,401	24,365	9,000	1,357	13,075
Luxembourg	1,842	4,247	2,069	2,943	n.a.	773
Malta	732	1,825	1,845	1,930	244	1,634
Netherlands	33,002	103,930	58,900	52,662	n.a.	62,583
Poland	91,024	219,826	127,126	146,355	21,924	97,413
Portugal	n.a.	49,355	39,679	38,739†	n.a.†	32,346†
Romania	35,605	50,098	73,046	56,164	1,866	27,772
Slovakia	13,016	14,182	23,105	17,607	958	12,767
Slovenia	10,782	6,836	7,239	6,797	n.a.	7,116
Spain	152,562	228,299	132,097	144,390	n.a.	157,001
Sweden	110,868	65,459	29,745	35,825	510	34,133
United Kingdom	n.a.	320,014†	312,213†	100,146†	n.a.	148,524
Total (EU-28)‡	n.a.	2,164,823	1,938,802	1,616,839	n.a.	1,448,471

* Definitions: Level 0—Early childhood education; Level 1—Primary education; Level 2—Lower secondary education; Level 3—Upper secondary education; Level 4—Post-secondary non-tertiary education; Levels 5–8—Tertiary education.
† Definition differs. ‡ Estimates.
© European Union. Source: Eurostat, 2017, Population and social conditions, table *EDUC_UOE_PERP01*—Classroom teachers and academic staff by education level, programme orientation, sex and age groups.

Classroom teachers in early childhood education (ISCED level 0)

	2013	2014	2015		2013	2014	2015
Austria	25,189	25,871	27,476	Latvia	5,796	7,252	7,532
Belgium	33,653	34,465	35,254	Lithuania	12,457	12,611	12,910
Bulgaria	18,509	18,769	18,982	Luxembourg	1,690	1,624	1,842
Croatia	10,345	10,614	10,940	Malta	683	676	732
Cyprus	1,409	1,457	2,535	Netherlands	33,768	33,028	33,002
Czech Republic	25,779	26,881	27,624	Poland	81,134	86,968	91,024
Denmark	n.a.	n.a.	n.a.	Portugal	n.a.	n.a.	n.a.
Estonia	7,891	8,271	8,496	Romania	n.a.	n.a.	35,605
Finland	n.a.	n.a.	n.a.	Slovakia	12,250	12,590	13,016
France	125,951	125,976	127,032	Slovenia	10,453	10,558	10,782
Germany	423,536	449,832	469,451	Spain	157,721	153,812	152,562
Greece	n.a.	n.a.	n.a.	Sweden	101,719	113,063	110,868
Hungary	n.a.	n.a.	26,480	United Kingdom	n.a.	83,786	n.a.
Ireland	n.a.	n.a.	16,002	**Total (EU-28)**	n.a.	n.a.	n.a.
Italy	132,718	n.a.	131,922				

© European Union. Source: Eurostat, 2017, Population and social conditions, table *EDUC_UOE_PERP01*—Classroom teachers and academic staff by education level, programme orientation, sex and age groups.

Classroom teachers in primary education (ISCED level 1)

	2013	2014	2015		2013	2014	2015
Austria	30,566	30,533	30,972	Latvia	10,221	10,338	10,537
Belgium	68,576	68,826	69,681	Lithuania	8,642	8,441	8,401
Bulgaria	14,388	14,596	14,769	Luxembourg	4,330	4,338	4,247
Croatia	n.a.	n.a.	11,849	Malta	1,702	1,799	1,825
Cyprus	3,977	3,967	4,513	Netherlands	107,439	104,815	103,930
Czech Republic	25,979	27,339	28,192	Poland	211,238	211,201	219,826
Denmark	n.a.	43,537	n.a.	Portugal	54,222	50,276	49,355
Estonia	6,548	6,771	7,049	Romania	50,626	50,857	50,098
Finland	26,402	26,385	26,150	Slovakia	14,050	14,030	14,182
France	229,471	228,648	235,659	Slovenia	6,468	6,666	6,836
Germany	233,046	232,750	235,571	Spain	220,323	226,066	228,299
Greece	66,735	66,551	n.a.	Sweden	62,105	63,467	65,459
Hungary	37,054	34,955	36,029	United Kingdom	250,693	258,047	320,014
Ireland	32,175	32,828	33,613				
Italy	237,735	237,214	237,483	**Total (EU-28)**	2,015,082	2,065,578	2,164,823

© European Union. Source: Eurostat, 2017, Population and social conditions, table *EDUC_UOE_PERP01*—Classroom teachers and academic staff by education level, programme orientation, sex and age groups.

Classroom teachers in lower secondary education (ISCED level 2)

	2013	2014	2015		2013	2014	2015
Austria	41,256	41,779	42,227	Latvia	7,501	7,602	7,623
Belgium	46,920*	47,390*	47,829	Lithuania	25,978	24,825	24,365
Bulgaria	17,330	17,278	17,170	Luxembourg	2,071	2,100	2,069
Croatia	34,385*	34,470	22,996	Malta	1,797	1,726	1,845
Cyprus	3,031	2,880	2,580	Netherlands	57,637	57,444	58,900
Czech Republic	32,403	30,857	31,233	Poland	131,063	128,508	127,126
Denmark	55,381	23,896	n.a.	Portugal	38,376	39,584	39,679
Estonia	4,615	4,684	4,686	Romania	73,014	74,186	73,046
Finland	20,095	20,074	19,888	Slovakia	23,569	23,527	23,105
France	227,044	228,134	230,974	Slovenia	7,498	7,439	7,239
Germany	417,525	410,255	411,404	Spain	132,206	131,385	132,097
Greece	44,087	40,159	n.a.	Sweden	29,378	29,293	29,745
Hungary	40,318*	37,823	38,939	United Kingdom	146,105	174,092	312,213*
Ireland*	n.a.	n.a.	n.a.				
Italy	167,389	166,192	165,705	**Total (EU-28)**	1,827,913	1,807,708*	1,938,802

* Definition differs.

© European Union. Source: Eurostat, 2017, Population and social conditions, table *EDUC_UOE_PERP01*—Classroom teachers and academic staff by education level, programme orientation, sex and age groups.

Classroom teachers in upper secondary education (ISCED level 3)

	2013	2014	2015		2013	2014	2015
Austria	31,780	30,784	29,936	Latvia	7,741	7,198	7,038
Belgium	80,786*	81,023*	81,393	Lithuania	10,352	9,514	9,000
Bulgaria	22,513	21,946	21,803	Luxembourg	3,744	3,040	2,943
Croatia	18,632	18,830*	19,279*	Malta	2,029	2,115	1,930
Cyprus	3,337	3,152	2,941	Netherlands	48,165	46,342	52,662
Czech Republic	36,984	35,204	35,622	Poland	160,311	150,705	146,355
Denmark	n.a.	25,154	n.a.	Portugal	43,373	38,101*	38,739*
Estonia*	5,240	4,898	4,853	Romania	57,230	56,985	56,164
Finland	22,483	22,011	21,954	Slovakia	19,313	18,312	17,607
France	230,005	227,025	231,194	Slovenia	7,159	6,930	6,797
Germany	179,531	179,775	174,810	Spain	142,187	144,731	144,390
Greece	45,985	40,229	n.a.	Sweden	38,810	36,219	35,825
Hungary	44,676	40,851	41,383	United Kingdom	263,373	275,760	100,146*
Ireland*	n.a.	23,907	24,455				
Italy	236,489	239,908	242,161	**Total (EU-28)**	1,762,101*	1,790,546	1,616,839

* Definition differs.

© European Union. Source: Eurostat, 2017, Population and social conditions, table *EDUC_UOE_PERP01*—Classroom teachers and academic staff by education level, programme orientation, sex and age groups.